Artists in Britain since 1945

Volume 1

A to L

Artists in Britain since 1945

Volume 1
A to L

David Buckman

First published by Art Dictionaries Ltd., in 1998
This new and enlarged edition published in 2006 by Art Dictionaries Ltd, 81g Pembroke Road, Bristol BS8 3EA

info@artdictionaries.com
www.artdictionaries.com

ISBN 10: 0 953260 95 X
ISBN 13: 9780953260959

The publishers gratefully acknowledge the generous sponsorship support which they have received from Bonhams, Christie's, Sansom & Company and Sotheby's, and also the support of the galleries and other organisations which have taken advertising space in the dictionary.

British Library Cataloguing in Publication Data
A catalogue record for this book is available from The British Library.

Typeset by Data Standards, Frome. Printed and bound by Polestar Wheatons, Exeter.

CONTENTS

INDEX OF ADVERTISERS

The advertisements appear in each volume,
on the pages indicated

ACKNOWLEDGEMENTS

In researching and writing this dictionary, I depended on many people. Several have made a major contribution over a long period. Philippa Cooper was early committed to it, bringing her knowledge of painters and the art world, made suggestions towards possible entries, helped with research, filing and proof-reading and put up with the author's obsessions and anxieties over many years. From the outset John Kilgannon has been of enormous help, the backbone of the mailing of several thousand questionnaires, also filing the huge archive of newspaper obituaries. Clara Sansom made a unique contribution towards the volumes' production, the final cutting in of additional entries and new material for existing ones and proof-reading calling for months of meticulous, painstaking work. John Sansom made an invaluable contribution to maintaining textual consistency and accuracy, Charlotte Eager with advertising. A reference work of this type is expensive to produce, and its appearance has been facilitated by the support of our many advertisers and sponsorship by Bonhams, Christie's, Sotheby's and Sansom & Company.

André Dzierzynski has long been an enthusiast for the book, putting me in touch with artists I would not otherwise have discovered. My coverage of the many Polish painters and sculptors who settled in Britain would have been much diminished without his help, and he it was who introduced me to Dr Mirosław Supruniuk and Joanna Krasnodębska who made available invaluable material from The Archives of Polish Emigration at Nicolaus Copernicus University, Toruń.

Other special thanks go to Colin Ashford, for information on transport artists; Pat Bowring, of Woodlands Art Gallery, for background on its many exhibitions; Michael Canney, regarding Cornish artists; Alannah Coleman, for pointers to Australian artists who worked and showed in Britain; John Cranfield; Michael Daykin; Jane England and Peter Gordon-Stable, of England & Co; John Evans; Howard Goodall; Sue Graves, for information on Sheffield artists; Alan Guest, notably for information on artists of the Nottingham area, and for help with proofs; the staff of Islington Libraries, especially the Central Reference Library; Waj and Edna Mirecki, of Chappel Galleries, for information on East Anglian artists; David Mitchell, of the Bankside Gallery archive; Richard Scott, for help with The Suffolk Group; University College, London, notably Joanna Shacklock, Carol Bowen and Wendy Kirkby, for information on Slade School students (in my experience the Slade's ex-student archive is unmatched for comprehensiveness, a model for other such institutions, and unlike some, it sought no charge); Gabriel and Leonie Summers, for help with artists they had researched; the Welsh Arts Council/Arts Council of Wales staff, especially Rhian Basten, Linda Shakespeare and Valmai Ward, for details of Welsh artists; and Grant Waters, who worked with me to gather details on Ruth Doggett.

It would be impracticable to list the many hundreds of artists who have responded to my questionnaires; relations and friends of artists who have provided information; local newspapers, which in printing appeals for information have often proved a last resort in getting what was needed; and others who have put themselves out to assist. I have had endless help from commercial galleries, and have tried to include their names in artist entries, making further reader research possible. Numerous public galleries and museums also helped, and they and members of staff are in this list of organisations and individuals particularly useful to me:

Abbot Hall Art Gallery
Aberdeen Art Gallery
Aberdeen Artists' Society
Margaret Agnew
Ken Aitken
Mairi Allan
Emma Allen
David Alston
Josephine Andersen
Emma Anderson
An Lanntair Arts Centre
Antelope Productions Ltd
Michael Archer
The Argus, Brighton
Arnolfini
Tamar Arnon
Art Gallery of Ontario
Art Gallery of Western Australia
Art Matters
Art Workers' Guild
Artists' General Benevolent Institution
Arts Club
Arts Council of England
Arts Council of Ireland
Arts Council of Northern Ireland
ArtWatch UK Newsletter
Ashmolean Museum
Aspex Gallery
M V Attrill
Auckland City Art Gallery
Patricia Austin
Australian High Commission
The Aviation Bookshop
Charles Baile de Laperriere
Anthony Bailey
Rupert Baker
J Baldry
Joan Banger
Bankfield Museum & Art Gallery
Barbican Centre
Barclays Bank PLC
Francis Bargman

Andrew Barlow
Anne J Barlow
J C S Barnes
Barnet Local History Archive
Bath College of Higher Education
Jeremy Beach
Beecroft Art Gallery
Anthony Beeson
Chris Beetles
Ben Uri Art Society
Jan Benington
Chloë Bennett
Janet Bennett
Susan Bennett
Jon Bennington
Oliver Bernard
Joanne Bernstein
Bethnal Green Museum of Childhood
Jill Betts
Bryan Biggs
Juliet Bingham
Jean Bird
Birmingham Museums & Art Gallery
Birmingham Post
Eileen Black
The Black Watch Archive
Terry Bloxham
Bluecoat Arts Centre
John Blundell
Ronald Blythe
Valerie Boa
Bolton Museums and Art Gallery
Bonhams & Brooks
Book Trust
Bea Bossom
Bournemouth & Poole College of Art & Design
Bournemouth Arts Club
Meirion Bowen
Astrid Bowron
Bradford City Libraries
Fiona Bradley
Laurie Bray
Paul Brazier
Roger Breakwell
Brecknock Museum
Brent Arts Council
D Bridge
Bridport Arts Centre
David Briers
Louisa Briggs
Brighton Area Libraries, Local Studies
Brighton Art Gallery and Museum
Brighton Media Centre
Brighton Polytechnic
Bristol Central Library
The British Antique Dealers' Association
British Film Institute
British Library
British Medical Association
British Museum, Prints and Drawings
British Music Information Centre
British Olympic Association
British Society of Master Glass Painters
The Britten-Pears Library
Anne Britton
Angela Broome
Sarah Brown
Lillian Browse
David C Bryan
Buckinghamshire College
George Bunting
Jane Burkinshaw
The late Hazel Burston
Burstow & Hewitt
Burton Gallery & Museum
Bushey Museum
John Butler
Wendy Butler
Buxton Museum & Art Gallery
Byam Shaw School of Art
Calderdale Central Library
Camberwell College of Arts
Cambridge Society of Painters and Sculptors
Cambridgeshire County Council Arts Department
Camden Arts Centre
Camden Local Studies and Archives Centre
Campbell College
Irene Campbell
Paula Campbell
Vicki Campbell
Campden Hill Club
Jeannette Canavan
Canterbury City Council
Frances Carey
Colin Carlin
Gerry Carr
Kate Rose Carrick
Julie Carrington
Cartwright Hall Art Gallery
Kate Carver
Beverley Casebow
Cathedral and Abbey Church of St Alban
Catholic Enquiry Office
D M Catte
Amanda Catto
Central St Martins College of Art & Design
Stephen Chaplin
Chartered Society of Designers
Michael and Valerie Chase
Chelsea Arts Club
Chelsea College of Art & Design
Chelsea Library
Cheltenham & Gloucester College of Higher Education
Cheltenham Art Gallery and Museum
Cheltenham Ladies' College
Chess Magazine
Tessa Chester
Chevron UK Ltd
Christ's Hospital
Christchurch Mansion
Therese Christie
Christie's South Kensington
Church House Inquiries Centre
Krzysztof Cieszkowski
Mary Clarke
R Aquila Clarke
Angela Clutterbuck
David Cobb
Harry Cobb
David Coke
Colchester Library

Beverley Cole
Collins Gallery
Ian Collins
Kathie Collins
Lisa Collins
Mary Colville
Community Service Volunteers
Bill Connelly
Contemporary Art Society
Peter Cormack
Cornish Studies Library
Lesley Cornish
Country Life
Coventry and Warwickshire Society of Artists
Coventry Art Guild
Coventry University
Alison Cowling
Gina Cox
Treasa Cox
Crafts Council
Crawford Arts Centre
Wendy Crawford
Melva Croal
Crefft incorporating *Artists Notes*
Alan Crookham
Croydon Art Society
Croydon College of Art & Design
Roger Cucksey
Maggie Cullen
Cupar Library
Gillian Currie
Sheila Cutforth
Caroline da Costa
Michael Daley
April Dance
The Dancing Times
Susan Daniel
Tamsin Daniel
Darlington Museum
Gwenlli Davies
Peter Davies
Richard Davies
Judith Davis
Sarah Davy
G M Daw
Ellie Dawkins
Graham Day
De La Warr Pavilion
Raphaël De Smedt
Dean and Chapter of Canterbury
Debrett's Peerage
C Demeulemeester
Denbighshire Art Society
Derby Museum and Art Gallery
Derby Sketching Club
Joanne Déry
Design Museum Library
Designer Trading Cards
De Vere's Art Auctions
Christopher Di Rollo
Hilary Diaper
Catherine Dickinson
Rachel Dickson
Dickson Russell Art Management
Jo Digger
Tamsin Dillon
DLI Museum & Durham Art Gallery
Teresa Docherty
Patricia Dodsworth
Doncaster Museum and Art Gallery
Amanda-Jane Doran
Ivy Dudeney
Meg Duff
Dulwich College
Sophie Duncan
Anne Dunlop
Philip Dunn
Alice Dunne
Roderic Dunnett
Ealing Art Club
East Kent Art Society
East Midlands Arts
Eastbourne Group
Eastern Arts
David Easton
Edinburgh City Art Centre
Mark Ellin
Hilda Elsmere
Janita Elton
Epping Forest District Museum
Eton College
Everard Read Gallery
Frances Everitt
Exeter Art School
Exeter Art Society
Allen Eyles
Falmouth Art Gallery
Family Records Centre
Adrian Farmer
Federation of British Artists
Simon Fenwick
Ferens Art Gallery
Alison Ferguson
Olga Ferguson
James Fergusson
Fermanagh County Museum
Fine Art Catalogues
Sarah Finlay
Fred Fleming
John Fleming
Vernon Fletcher
Focus Gallery
Erica Foden-Lenahan
Ann Forsdyke
Paul Foster
Stephen Foster
Ann Marie Fowles
Roger C C Frame
Jacci Fraser
John Fraser
Free Painters and Sculptors
Tom French
Freud Museum
Jane Furness
Fylingdales Group of Artists
Mireille Galinou
Galleries
Gallery Oldham
Philippe Garner
Gateshead Art Society
Peter Gauld
Rita Gibbs

Margaret Girvan
Christine Gist
Glasgow Art Club
Glasgow Museums & Art Galleries
Glasgow School of Art
Ben Glazebrook
Anne Gleave
Glenrothes Development Corporation
Adrian Glew
Glynn Vivian Art Gallery
Goethe-Institut
Pat Goodall
Anne Goodchild
Elizabeth Goudge
Barbara Graham
Nikki Grange
Graves Art Gallery
Gray's School of Art
Emily Gray
Fleur Gray
Richard Green
Roger Green
Stephanie Green
Linda Greenlick
Greenwich Printmakers' Association
Kevin Grey
Pamela Griffin
Anne Griffiths
Elyn Wyn Griffiths
Gerd Grober
Irving Grose
Grosvenor Art Society
Lavender Groves
The Guardian
Andrew Guest
Debbie Guest
Guild of Aviation Artists
Guild of Motoring Artists
Guild of Railway Artists
Guildford House Gallery
Guildhall Art Gallery
Richard Gundry
Mollie Haig
Ann Hall-Williams
Laura Hamilton
Neil and Christine Hamilton
Catherine Hammond
Hampshire Chronicle
Hampstead Garden Suburb Institute
Marcelle Hanselaar
Rosalind Hardiman
Dorothy Harding
Dennis Hardingham
Harris Museum & Art Gallery
Harrow School
Elaine Hart
Hartlepool Arts & Museum Service
Catherine Harvey
David Harvey
Haslemere Art Society
Hastings Museum and Art Gallery
P Hatfield
Hatton Gallery
Alasdair Hawkyard
Malcolm Hay
Mary Hayes
Sharon Heard
Henry Moore Foundation
Henry Moore Institute
Henry Moore Sculpture Trust
Sarah Hepworth
Herbert Art Gallery and Museums
Hereford Museum & Art Gallery
Nigel Herring
Annabel Hesketh
Alan Hibbs
Hilmarton Manor Press
Simon Hincks
The History of Advertising Trust
Chris Hives
Frank Hodges
Tony Hodges
Sue Holding
Ann Holland
Holloway Art & Materials
James Holloway
Malcolm Holmes
Juliet Hone
Hong Kong Government Office
Hong Kong Museum of Art
Antony Hopkins
Bill Hopkins
Hornsey Library
Hove Museum & Art Gallery
Natasha Howes
Jackie Howson
Bill and Margaret Hume
Christopher Hunt
Peter Hunter
Elizabeth Hutchings
Sarah Hyde
Helen Hyland
Charlotte Ibbotson
Ikon Gallery
Illustrated London News
Imperial War Museum
Independent Art Promotions
The Independent
Institute of Contemporary Arts
Institute of International Visual Arts
Ipswich Art Club
Ipswich Museums & Galleries
Irish Museum of Modern Art
Vicki Irwin
Islington Art Circle
The Israel Museum
Sandra Jackaman
The Jackdaw
Michael Jackson
Valerie Jackson
Zdzislaw Jagodzinski
Helen James
Deborah Jefferis
David Fraser Jenkins
Jerwood Charitable Foundation
Jerwood Gallery
Jewish Chronicle
The Jockey Club
John Hansard Gallery
Penny Johnson
Isobel Johnstone
Barbara Jones

Chris Jones
Paul Joyner
Richard Kay
Valerie Kay
David Kelsall
Ian Kemp
Robert Kennan
Brian Kennedy
Kent Institute of Art & Design
John R Kenyon
Felicity Kerr
Tony Kerr
Leo Kersley
Alex Kidson
King's School, Canterbury
Robin Kingsdown
Kingston-upon-Thames Register Office
Monika Kinley
Charlotte Kirwan
Jemima Kiss
Terry Knight
Vivien Knight
Koninklijke Bibliotheek Albert I
Helena Kovac
I Lackajis
Laing Art Gallery
Lake Artists' Society
Pat Lambert
Ruth Lambert
Lancashire County Museum Service
Langham Sketch Club
Josephine Lanyon
Lawrence Fine Art Auctioneers Ltd
Leamington Spa Museum & Art Gallery
Antonia Lean
Trevor Learmouth
David Lee
Leeds Central Library
Leeds City Art Gallery
Leeds College of Art & Design
Judith LeGrove
Leicester Museum and Art Gallery
Leicester Society of Artists
Leicestershire County Council Information Centre
Leith School of Art
Pauline Lellman
Leo Baeck Institute
Lewes Library
Lianne Jarrett Associates
John Lichfield
Clare Lilley
Ivy Lin
Lindley Library, Royal Horticultural Society
David Linton
Liverpool Daily Post & Echo
Liverpool John Moores University
Liverpool Polytechnic
Livingstone Development Corporation
Karen Livingstone
Lloyd's Register of Shipping
London Group
London Press Club
London Sketch Club
London Transport Museum
London Underground
Grant Longman
Paul Lorimer
Louisiana Museum of Modern Art, Denmark
Rebecca Lowe
The Lowry
Suzanne Lyle
Lyon & Turnbull
Lyttelton Theatre
Caroline McBride
Patrick McCoy
Sarah Macdonald
Vicky Macdonald
Clare McGread
MacRobert Arts Centre
Sarah McCloskey
Patsy Mace
Kay McKelvey
Roderick MacLeod
McLean Museum and Art Gallery
Scott Macrae
Eileen Maitland
Pat Malley
Stephanie Maltman
Malvern Girls' College
Manchester Central Library
Manchester City Art Gallery
Manchester City Council Planning Department
Manchester Metropolitan University
Mander & Mitchenson Theatre Collection
Manor House Museum
Mansfield Society of Artists
Steve Manthorp
Mappin Art Gallery
Rachel Mapplebeck
Peter Marcan
Lorraine Mariner
Catherine Marshall
F Warren Marshall
Lesley Marshall
Sandra Martin
Nicola Mason
Darlene Maxwell
Medici Society
George Melly
Jennifer Melville
Middlesex Polytechnic
Middlesex University
Ariede Migliavacca
Malcolm Miles
Corinne Miller
Dusty Miller
Frances Miller
Ministry of Defence
The Minories
Mary Minshull
Freya Mitton
Alexander Moffat
Mold Library, Museum & Gallery
Michael Molnar
Montreal Museum of Fine Arts
Michael Moody
Alan Moore
Lisa Moran
Patricia Moriarty
Rebecca Morrill
David Morris
Lynda Morris

Fiona Mosley
Mostyn Gallery
Shirley Murdoch
Museum of Childhood, Edinburgh
Museum of London
Museum of Modern Art, New York
Museum of Modern Art, Oxford
Museum of Reading
Pauline Mycock
Constance Nash
National Army Museum
National Art Library
National Gallery of Australia
National Gallery of Canada
National Gallery of Ireland
National Library of Wales
National Maritime Museum
National Museum of Labour History
National Museum of Wales
National Portrait Gallery Heinz Archive and Library
National Railway Museum
National Resource Centre for Dance
National Self-Portrait Collection of Ireland
National Society of Painters, Sculptors and Printmakers
Rosemary Nattrass
Natural History Museum
Naila Nauphal
Hannah-Bar Ner
New York Public Library
New Zealand High Commission
Susan Newell
Newlyn Art Gallery
Newport Museum and Art Gallery
NHS Estates
Catherine Nisbet
Norfolk and Norwich Art Circle
North West Arts Board
Northampton Museum and Art Gallery
Northern Arts
Norwich School of Art & Design
Nottingham Society of Artists
Nuneaton Arts Centre
Nuneaton Museum and Art Gallery
Ella O'Halloran
Sheila O'Hara
Oriel Washington Gallery
Ian O'Riordan
Orleans House Gallery
Österreichische Nationalbibliothek
Outsider Collection and Archive
Betty Owen
Emma Owen
Kath Oxenham
Oxford Art Society
Palace of Westminster
Pallant House
Parker Harris Partnership
Rebecca Parkin
Linda Parry
Godfrey Omar Parsons
Anthony Parton
Janet Partridge
Paul Patterson
Peasenhall Art and Antiques Gallery
B Peckover
Dominic Persad
Helen Pheby
Eric Phillips
Lucy Phillips
Michael Phipps
Lesley Pitman
Inés Plant
Jonathan Platt
N M Plumley
Alison Plumridge
Plymouth City Museums and Gallery
Polish Library
B Pollak
R J I Pollock
Pollock's Toy Museum
Matthew Poole
Elaine Pordes
Robert Porter
Venetia Porter
Portsmouth City Museum and Art Gallery
Post Office Archives and Record Centre
Stephanie Potts
Alan Powers
Susan M Preston
Prontaprint!, Holloway Road, Islington
Public Record Office
Publishers' Association
Punch
Eugene Rae
Denise Raine
Frances Rankine
Roy Rasmussen
Ravensbourne College of Design and Communication
Benedict Read
Mark Read
Reading Guild of Artists
Chris Reeve
H C Reid
Julia Reisz
Paul Rennie
Ross Reyburn
Iris C Rhodes
Derek Rice
Andrew F Richardson
Sarah Richardson
Ridley Art Society
Peter Risdon
Robert Gordon Institute of Technology
The Hon. Mrs Roberts
Fiona Robertson
Rowena Robertson
Judith Robinson
Sonia Robinson
Rochdale Art Gallery
Gavin Roebuck
Royal Academy of Arts
Royal Air Force, Air Historical Branch
Royal Air Force Museum, Hendon
Royal Albert Memorial Museum & Art Gallery
Royal Birmingham Society of Artists
Royal Cambrian Academy
Royal Collection Trust
Royal College of Art
Royal College of Surgeons of England

Royal Cornwall Museum Galleries, Truro
Royal Festival Hall
Royal Geographical Society
Royal Glasgow Institute of the Fine Arts
Royal Hibernian Academy
Royal Institute of British Architects
Royal Institute of Oil Painters
Royal Institution of Cornwall
Royal Marines Museum
Royal Opera House Archives
Royal Photographic Society
Royal Scottish Academy
Royal Scottish Society of Painters in Water-Colours
Royal Society of Arts
Royal Society of British Sculptors
Royal Society of Marine Artists
Royal Society of Miniature Painters, Sculptors and Gravers
Royal Society of Painter-Printmakers
Royal Ulster Academy of Arts
Royal Watercolour Society
Royal West of England Academy
Rugby and District Art Society
Rugby Art Gallery & Museum
Rural History Centre, University of Reading
Lucy Rushin
Russell-Cotes Museum & Art Gallery
Josephine Ryan
Rye Art Gallery
Saatchi Gallery
Sabena
Salford Art Gallery
Alice Wooledge Salmon
Lara Sampson
Marguerite B Sanders
Judith Sandling
Angela Sansom
Fiona Sansom
Jessica Sansom
Gill Saunders
Pat Saunders
Timothy Sayer
Doris Schneider-Wagenbichler
School of Oriental & African Studies
School of Slavonic and East European Studies
Alice Schwab
Walter Schwab
Science Museum
Duncan Scott
Richard Scott
Scottish Arts Club
Scottish Arts Council
Scottish National Gallery of Modern Art
Scottish National Portrait Gallery
Scottish Sculpture Trust
John Seabrook
Victoria Searby
Julie Seddon Jones
Jane Sedge
Bernard Selwyn
Richard Shackle
Margaret Shaw
Irene Shawcock
Jim Shea
Sheeran Lock Fine Art Consultants
John Sheeran
Anna Sheppard
Shirley Sherwood
Shipley Art Gallery
Ann Simpson
Colin Simpson
Sarah Simpson
Tracy Simpson
Neil Sinclair
Victoria Slowe
Charles Smith
Donald Smith
Emma Smith
Gaye Smith
Harold Smith
Gillian Smithson
Thomas B Smyth
Susan Snell
Society of Authors
Society of Equestrian Artists
Society of Graphic Fine Art
Society of Scottish Artists
Society of Staffordshire Artists
Society of Wildlife Artists
Society of Women Artists
Joanna Soden
Ulla Söderbaum
Kathrine Sorley Walker
South African National Gallery
South Australian Birth Register
South Bank Centre
South East Arts
Southampton City Art Gallery
Southbourne Art Society
Gerald Southgate
Spacex Gallery
Margaret Spencer
Michael Spender
Jill Springall
Fay Squire
St Bride Printing Library
St Ives School of Painting
Sonnet Stanfill
Ann Steed
Stenton Gallery
Hugh Stevenson
Ann Stewart
Brian Stewart
Claire H Stewart
Tina Stiles
Stoke-on-Trent Museum and Art Gallery
Isobel Stokes
Philip Stokes
Clare Storey
Strang Print Room, University College London
Judith Stringer
Eumie Imm Stroukoff
Alan Suddes
Siobhán Summerfield
Sunderland Art Gallery
Sunderland University
Swiss Cottage Library
Swiss Embassy
Taliesin Arts Centre
Tameside Museums & Galleries Service
Tate at St Ives

Tate Gallery Library
Tate Gallery, Liverpool
A F Tatham
Alan Taylor
Charlotte Taylor
Pamela Taylor
Ceri Thomas
Charlie Thomas
Christine Thomas
Matt Thomas
Oscar Thompsett
Noel Thompson
Penny Thompson
Betty Thurston
Geoff Tilbrook
The Times
Blair Todd
Cristina Tomas
Mike Tooby
Towneley Hall Art Gallery & Museum
Towner Art Gallery
Rachel Tranter
David Tregunna
Hugo Trotter
Laura Try
Tunbridge Wells Art Club
Dorothy Turner
Sharon Tuttle
Ulster Arts Club
Ulster Museum
United Society of Artists
University of British Columbia
University of Central England in Birmingham
University of Hertfordshire
University of Leeds School of Fine Art
University of Northumbria Gallery
University of Reading
University of Strathclyde
University of Sunderland
University of the West of England
Usher Gallery
Edward Vanderpump
Nino Vella
Jo Velleman
Tony Venison
Victoria & Albert Museum
Victoria Art Gallery, Bath
Carla Vigna
Maija Vilcins
Paul Vining
The Vintners' Company
Eva and Zdenek Voráčkovi
Heather Waddell
Wakefield City Art Gallery
Walker Art Gallery
Rosemary Walker
Catherine Wallace
Olive Waller
Jane Wallis
Walsall Museum & Art Gallery
Jean Walsh
Terry Walsh
Wansbeck District Council
Wapping Group of Artists
Helen Waters
E V Watson
Rebecca Weaver
Jeremy Webster
Ulla B Weinberg
Julia Weiner
Welwyn Garden City Art Club
West Derby Publishing
West Midlands Arts
Westminster Reference Library
Andrew Wheatley
Lucy Whetstone
John Whiddett
Emily White
Whitechapel Art Gallery
Marc Whiteside
Stephen Whittle
Whitworth Art Gallery
Whyte's, Dublin
Michael Wickins
Timothy Wilcox
Sarah J Wilcox-Standring
Alison Wild
Sandy Wilderspin
Stephen Wildman
John Willett
William Morris Gallery
Gower Williams
Williamson Art Gallery & Museum
David Williamson
Margaret Wilson
Carolyn Wingfield
Thelma Winyard
Anne Wishart
Bryen Wood
Helen Lanigan Wood
Mara-Helen Wood
Richard Wood
George A Woods
Margaret Woodward
Robert Woodward
Laura Woolley
Austin Wormleighton
Godfrey Worsdale
Worthing Museum & Art Gallery
Caroline Worthington
Wrexham Arts Centre
Michael Wright
Sir Peter Wright
Wyastone Estate Ltd
Max Wykes-Joyce
Y Tabernacl
York City Art Gallery
Yorkshire Sculpture Park
Pete Zarins
Anja Ziegler

INTRODUCTION

Although some dictionaries of British artists venture beyond 1945, for long there was nothing that attempted a comprehensive survey after that date to the present day. This book concentrates on the period which began with victory in Europe – VE-day was May 8, 1945 – in the belief that what went on before then has been fairly comprehensively covered by other dictionaries, and that the rebirth of the visual and other arts from the war's end demands a new approach. Inevitably, many artists included, as in previous surveys, started their careers before 1945, but thousands of new ones emerge who need recording.

The year 1945 proved an exciting one for a war-fatigued and -ravaged Britain. The Labour Party landslide election victory gave many new hope and shook up government and society. The country's six years of near-isolation culturally soon began to change, and there was a new confidence in the domestic product. In music, Benjamin Britten's opera *Peter Grimes* was a triumph for a British composer in a field where there was no tradition of achievement. Visits by such internationally distinguished performers as the composer Francis Poulenc, the cellist Pablo Casals and the violinist Ginette Neveu enhanced the concert scene. The 1945 drama season was, said *The Annual Register*, "one of the most remarkable in theatrical history ... one of unbroken success", with outstanding performances by Ralph Richardson as Falstaff in Shakespeare's *King Henry IV* and by Laurence Olivier as Oedipus in Sophocles' *Oedipus*. Cinema, still dominated by American imports, saw a new interest in British films, such as *The Way to the Stars*, *Brief Encounter* and *Blithe Spirit*. In literature, George Orwell published *Animal Farm* and Evelyn Waugh *Brideshead Revisited*.

CEMA – the Council for Encouragement of Music and the Arts – was transformed into the Arts Council of Great Britain. It had been an important organiser of exhibitions during a war that had seen restricted showings for artists. Soon after hostilities ended, the dim, deprived art world of London began to come alive again. Just after VE-day, the National Gallery reopened with an exhibition of 50 masterpieces returned from storage in a Welsh slate quarry. The National Portrait Gallery reopened with Sir Godfrey Kneller's Kit-Cat Club portraits. The Royal Academy staged an important exhibition of Soviet graphic art, and one of more than 1,000 works out of the 5,000 commissioned or bought by the War Artists' Advisory Committee since 1940. Particularly enlightening at the end of 1945 were the Victoria & Albert Museum's exhibition of recent paintings by Pablo Picasso and a group of retrospective works by Henri Matisse, and the Tate Gallery's show at the National Gallery – the Tate was still closed for repairs – of pictures by Paul Klee. Such dazzling modern shows were still capable of creating controversy, but they would markedly influence British artists during the ensuing half-century.

This dictionary, which includes such artists, is designed to cover painters, sculptors, draughtsmen, teachers, video, film, installation and performance artists born in the United Kingdom. Foreign artists are included if they have a significant presence. Those who are primarily illustrators or craft workers, such as potters, are usually not included. I have endeavoured to avoid the scant entry often included in dictionaries, going for as reasonably comprehensive a listing as possible. Entries are designed to enlighten anyone spotting an unfamiliar name or canvas in the gallery or auction room, so working name is the principal guide. Therefore, L S Lowry appears as Laurence Stephen Lowry; Ferelyth, who signs thus, appears under that name, but is cross-referenced to Ferelyth Wills. Gilbert and George appear thus, with their full names within that entry. For groups such as the Situationists, Borough Group or New English Art Club there is no separate entry, as members showed under their own names. However, Art & Language and Fine Artz, where participants for a time exhibited jointly, have separate entries, with some individual entries in addition. Chinese names present a problem. The correct Chinese usage is surname first, but some artists adopt the Western practice of surname last, and I have tried to follow what the individual prefers.

Length of entry is not directly related to so-called importance. I hope that the listing for, say, Francis Bacon or Henry Moore supplies the basic facts; the reader can readily find more elsewhere. Entries for lesser-known artists – such as Oswell Blakeston, Louisa Hodgson, Humphrey Slater and William Lyons-Wilson – might be longer, as the published information on them has been hard to assemble, requiring time-consuming primary research. Some entries are not as complete as I would like and a few recommended names, such as Harry Belton, failed to yield essential facts sufficient to compile a satisfactory piece. If anyone can add to what a search of the literature, personal inquiries by phone and letter and letters to newspapers have failed to complete, I would like to hear. In a list of around 14,500 names, mistakes will occur. Any constructive comment on an entry will be welcomed through the publisher (for reply, a stamped addressed envelope is necessary).

An aim has been to assemble entries mainly from primary sources. Even so, I have occasionally found that artists' own memory of the spelling of institutions where they have studied and taught, and the dates when they were there, can be inaccurate and needs correction. Experience shows that dependence on others' research too often leads to repeated mistakes (Mary Kessell is one artist who has suffered badly in this regard), although some use of secondary sources is necessary. I have found that catalogues put out by prestigious galleries and auction houses commonly have wrong years of birth and death

(Ruth Doggett's dates in some published sources appeared to have been assembled by throwing dice). I have tried to update the long-outdated information which often is the only source available for some artists. Francis Butterfield is an example, where in previous sources the artist's entry usually ends in the late 1930s, even though he died in 1968 (the enterprising research of Ron Morley helped me here). Of around 12,000 letters, cards, faxes, e-mails and other communications despatched to gather information, well over 1,500 were to confirm birth and death dates. This research was supplemented by many hours scanning ledgers at the Finsbury Family Records Centre. Experience has shown that even family records may be inaccurate regarding dates, requiring independent checking. Hundreds of sources, ranging from museum and gallery officials in Britain and abroad to artists, their families, newspapers and even vicars checking gravestones have provided invaluable help. Some groups of artists have regularly assisted my researches freely. The insistence by a few on a quite high search fee has made the gathering of some information impracticable.

To give the dictionary a broad base, I have researched regional groups, notably Cornwall, Liverpool, the northeast and East Anglia, and specialists such as motoring, aviation, marine and equestrian artists. Non-inclusion of any artist does not mean he or she has been ignored. Persistent attempts to get some details have met with no response. This includes the artists themselves and those representing them. If some galleries appear to be over-represented in the entries, this is because they have consistently responded to requests for information.

Art galleries listed are in London unless otherwise stated; sometimes location could not readily be determined. Where an autobiography has been published I try to mention this; biographies, because they are constantly appearing, are not usually cited in an entry, although some are listed in the bibliography. Entries adopt the past tense to avoid their being overtaken by events. Quotations are generally from the artists. County of birth is that current at the time, county of current residence usually using the terminology in vogue at time of writing. My use of descriptions such as abstract or Expressionist is a shorthand guide to an artist's style as I know it.

By the time these volumes are published, I will have spent almost 18 years part-time and full-time researching and writing them. Until closure time, artists were being discovered whose work rarely or never gets a mention in national newspapers, the broadcast media or even the specialist press. Too often in covering the visual arts journalistic laziness and sterility of mind have led to a few artists' names being bandied about endlessly to the point of nausea, while fine and original talents continue to be ignored.

David Buckman

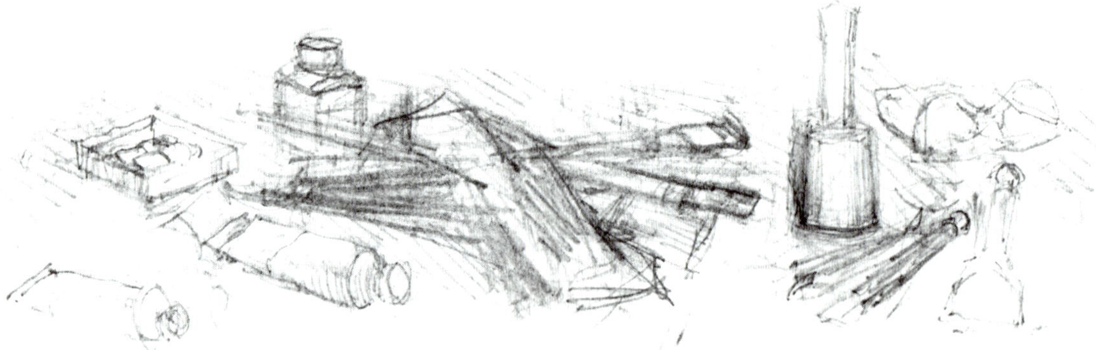

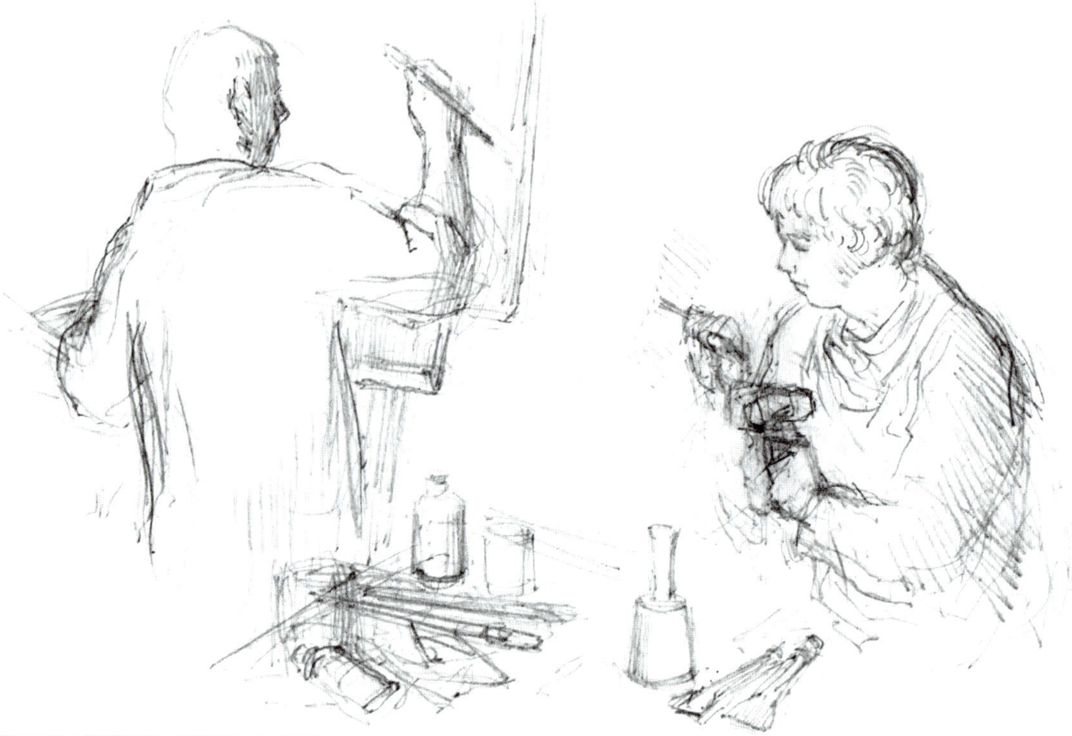

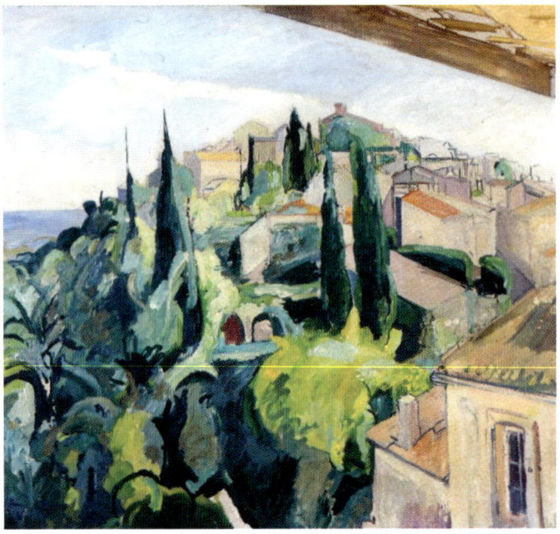

EDWARD WOLFE RA

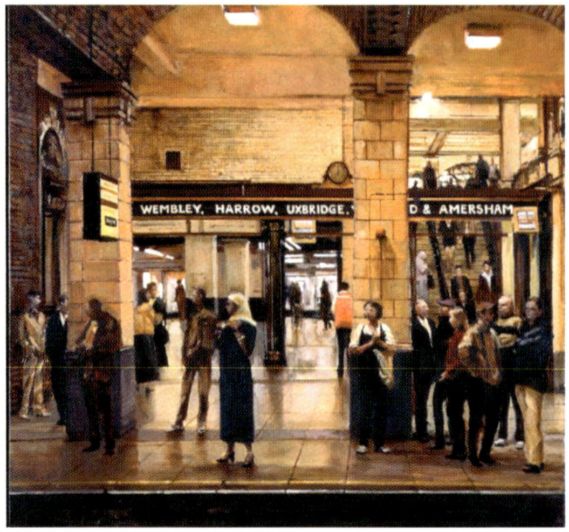

ERIC RIMMINGTON

THE MILLINERY WORKS GALLERY

85/87 SOUTHGATE ROAD, ISLINGTON
LONDON N1 3JS

TEL: 020 7359 2019 FAX: 020 7359 5792
E Mail: antiquetrader@millineryworks.co.uk

Visit us on-line at: **www.millineryworks.co.uk**

JAMES MACKINNON

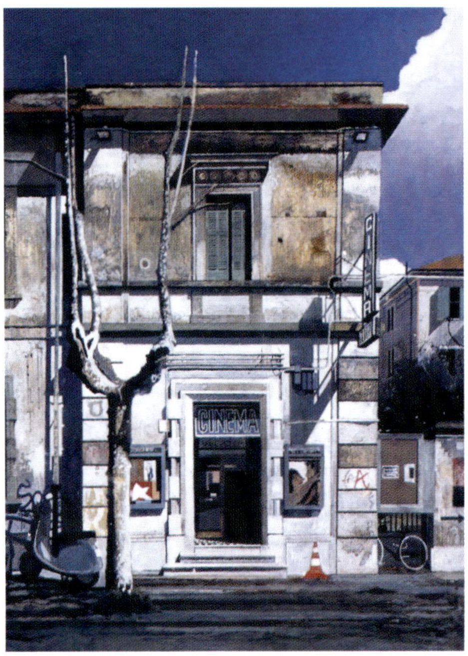

JOHN BRATBY RA

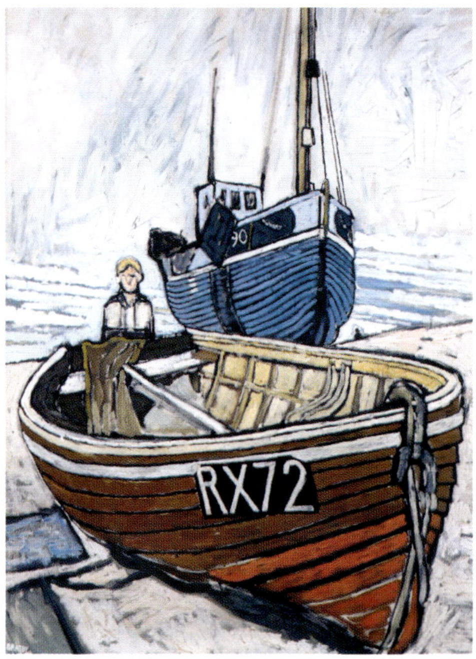

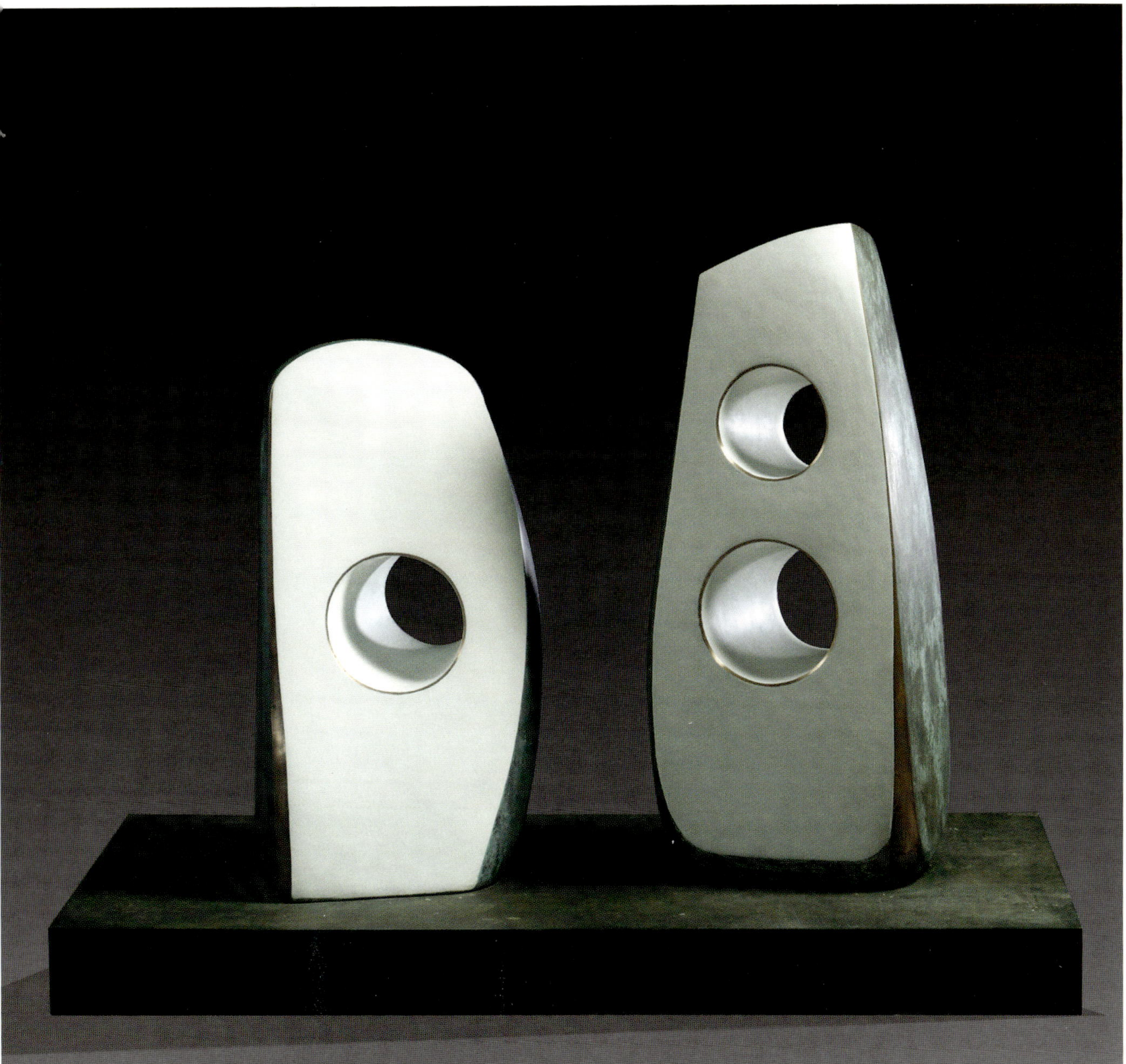

TADEMA GALLERY

20TH CENTURY ABSTRACT ART AND 19TH-20TH CENTURY ARTIST DESIGNED JEWELRY

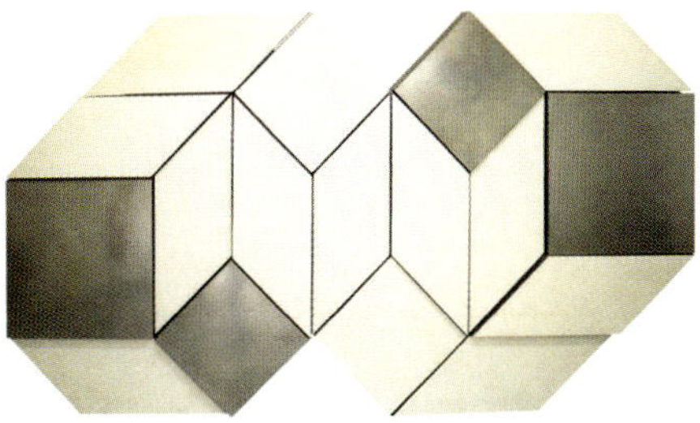

MALCOLM HUGHES 1920-1997
White, Grey & Aluminium Additive-unit Relief 1967

10 Charlton Place London N1 8AJ
Tel/Fax +44(0)2073591055
Mobile +44(0)7710082395
Sonya & David Newell-Smith
info@tademagallery.com
www.tademagallery.com
www.tademagalleryart.com

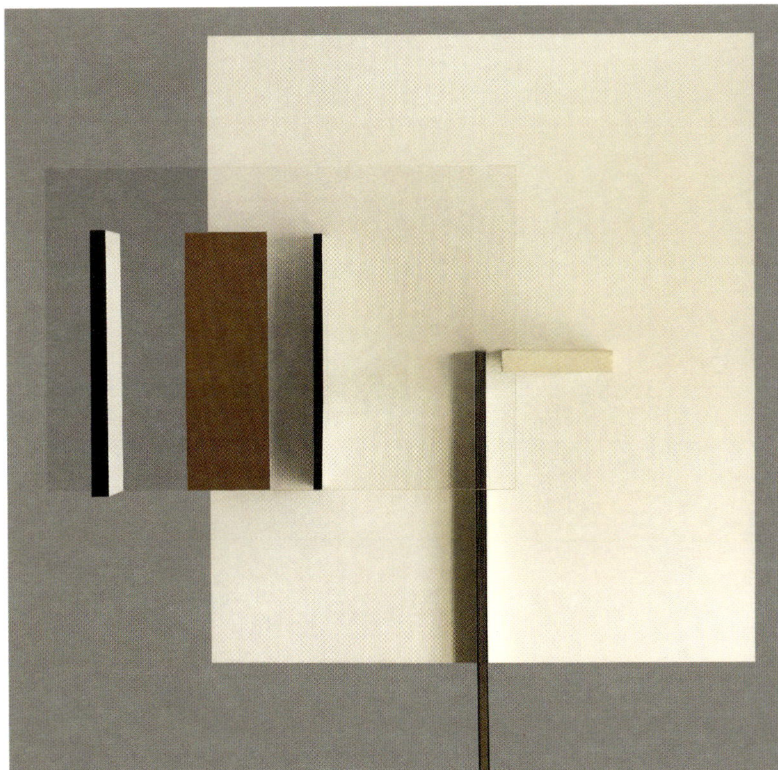

VICTOR PASMORE 1908-1998
Relief Construction in White, Black and Indian Red 1960/61

Benjamin C Hargreaves

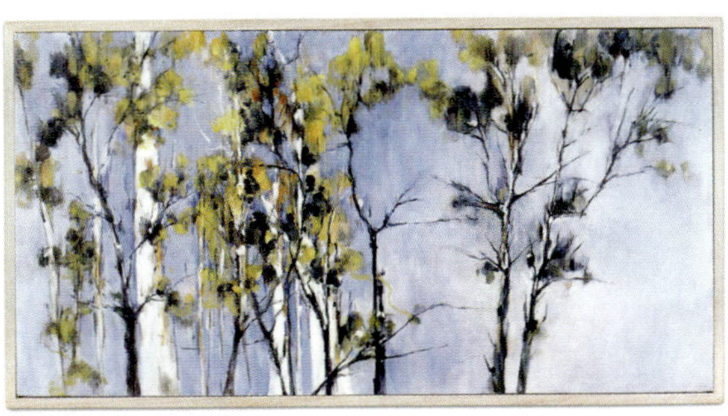

Karyn White: *Gum tree section* – Oil on canvas 20" x 40"

Contemporary Artists
Melissa Alley, Daniel Backhouse, Simon Marsh, Brenda Naylor, Kate Robinson, Nicola Tassie, Janet Q Treloar, Karyn White, Ellie Yannas, Miki van Zwanenberg & others

Enquiries
90 Kenyon Street, London SW6 6LB
020 7385 7757
(visitors welcome by appointment)

Museum standard conservation framing for the ART TRADE
Collection & delivery in central London

TEL. 01233 733353

FAX. 01233 732354

framing@simonbeaugie.com

Manor Farm Workshops
Hamstreet Road
Shadoxhurst
Ashford
Kent TN26 1NW

simon beaugié picture frames ltd

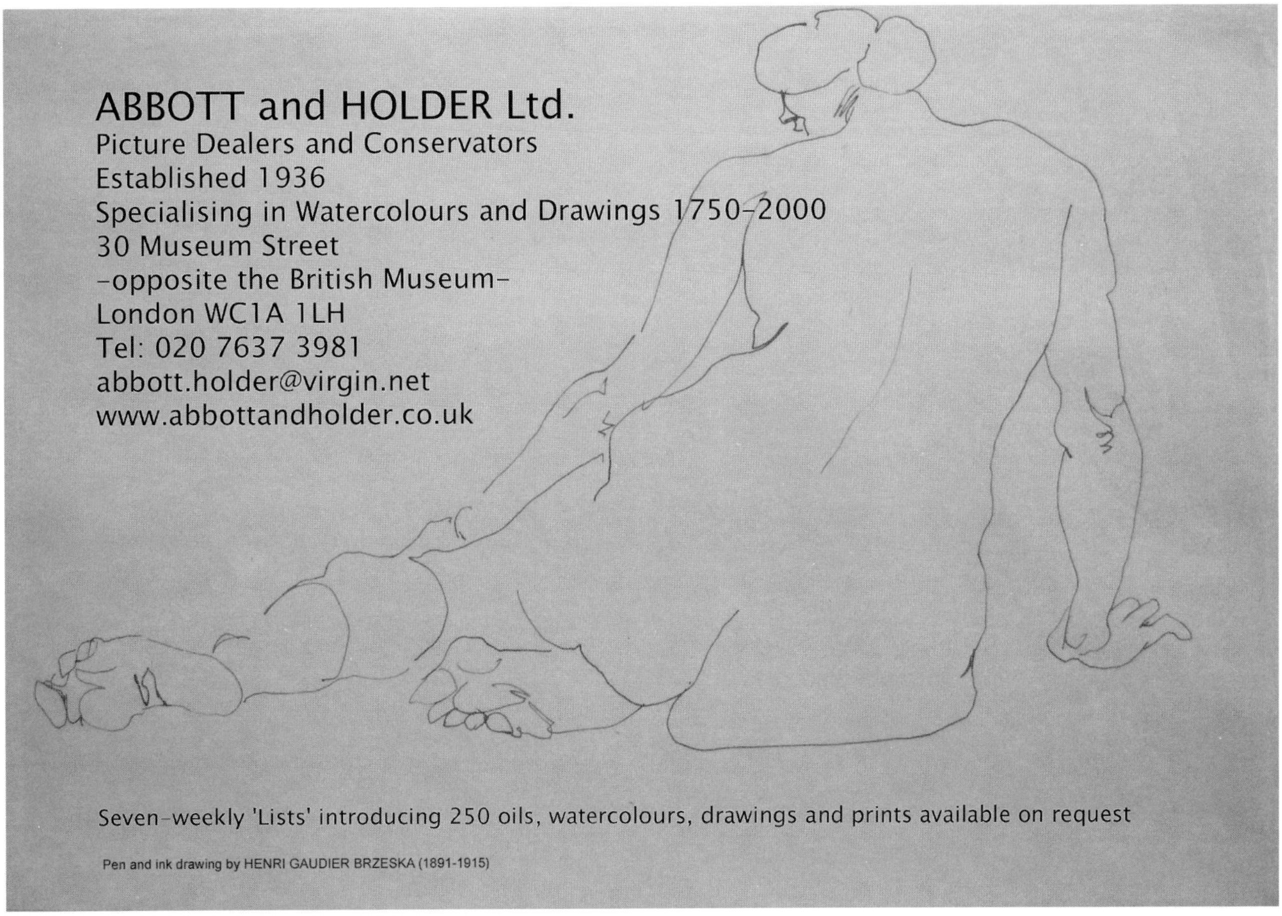

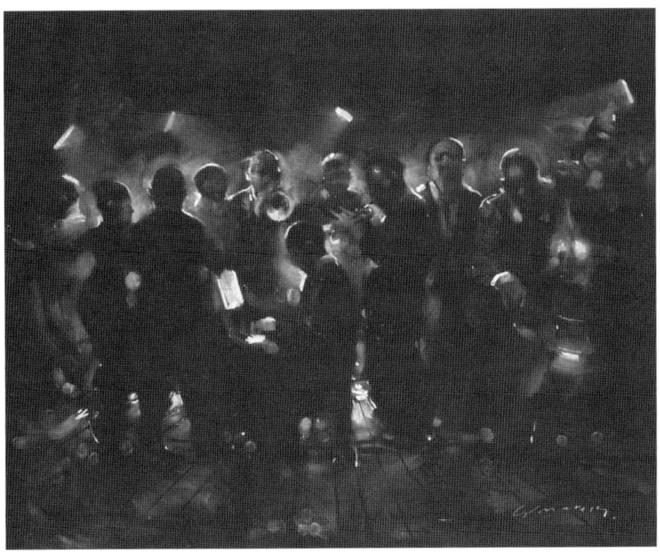

Charlie Mackesy • *New Orleans* • pastel on black paper

BELGRAVIA GALLERY

Belgravia Gallery stocks a large range of works by **Charlie Mackesy**

For a brochure or further details please contact us or visit the website **www.belgraviagallery.com**

Belgravia Gallery:
45 Albemarle Street, London W1S 4JL
T 020 7495 1010
E laura@belgraviagallery.com

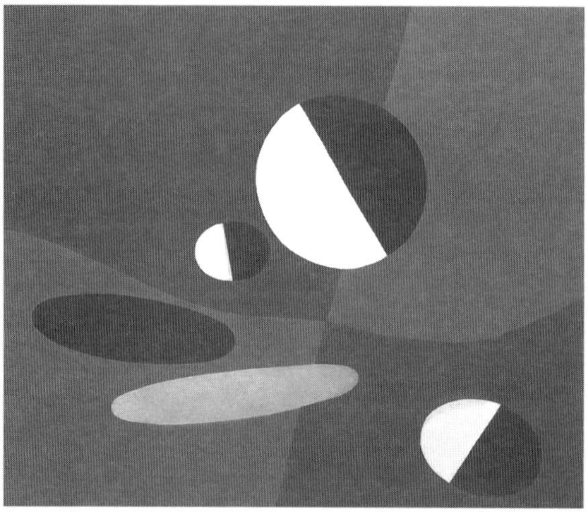

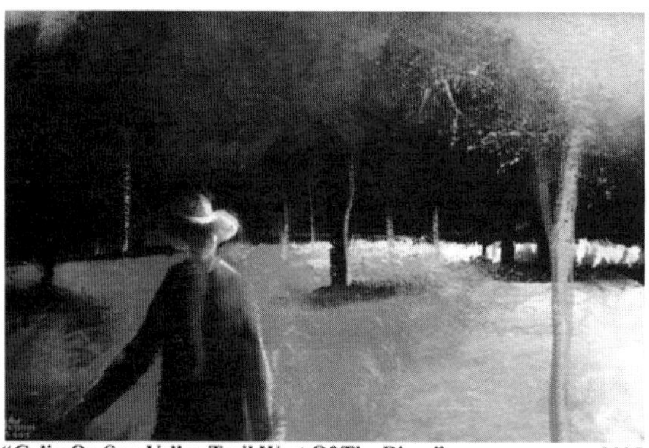

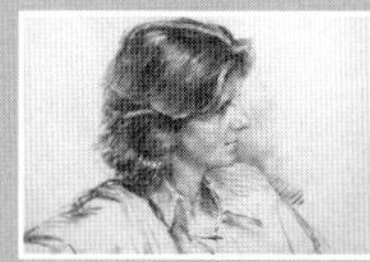

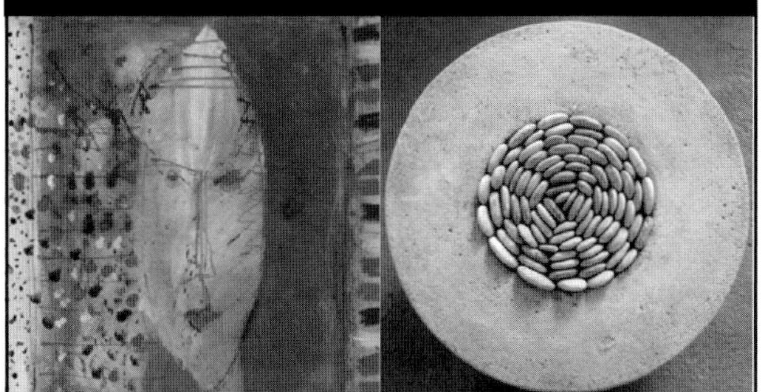

ARTISTS IN BRITAIN SINCE 1945

VOLUME 1
A to L

SYSTEM OF DATING

All reasonable effort has been made to establish correct years of birth and death. Where these are not obtainable, dates when an artist is believed to have flourished are used. The system followed is:

–c.1976	No birth year or time when started exhibiting known; year of death approximate
fl. c.1908–1976	Exhibiting dates both approximate
fl. from c.1908–1976	Death year firm only
1908–c.1976	Birth year firm; death approximate
–1976	No birth year or time when started exhibiting known; death year firm.
1908–	Artist alive at time of compilation; or known/believed to be dead, but year of death not yet available.

ABBREVIATIONS

AAA	Allied Artists' Association
AEB	Art Exhibitions Bureau
AIA	Artists' International Association
BBC	British Broadcasting Corporation
BWS	British Water Colour Society
CASW	Contemporary Art Society for Wales
CEMA	Council for the Encouragement of Music and the Arts
HM	Her Majesty/His Majesty
HMS	Her Majesty's/His Majesty's Ship
HRH	Her/His Royal Highness
ICA	Institute of Contemporary Arts
IS	International Society of Sculptors, Painters and Gravers
LG	London Group
MAFA	Manchester Academy of Fine Arts
MP	Member of Parliament
NEAC	New English Art Club
NG	New Gallery
NPS	National Portrait Society
NS	National Society of Painters, Sculptors and Gravers/ Printmakers
NWG	North Wales Group
OUP	Oxford University Press
PS	Pastel Society
RA	Royal Academy of Arts/Royal Academician
RBA	Royal Society of British Artists
RBC	Royal British Colonial Society of Artists
RBS	Royal Society of British Sculptors
RBSA	Royal Birmingham Society of Artists
RCamA	Royal Cambrian Academy
RE	Royal Society of Painter-Etchers and Engravers/Painter-Printmakers
RHA	Royal Hibernian Academy/Academician
RI	Royal Institute of Painters in Water Colours
RIBA	Royal Institute of British Architects
RMS	Royal Society of Miniature Painters, Sculptors and Gravers/Royal Mail Steamer
ROI	Royal Institute of Oil Painters
RP	Royal Society of Portrait Painters
RPS	Royal Photographic Society
RS	Royal Society
RSA	Royal Scottish Academy
RSMA	Royal Society of Marine Artists/Society of Marine Artists
RSW	Royal Scottish Society of Painters in Water-Colours/Royal Scottish Watercolour Society
RUA	Royal Ulster Academy of Arts/Academician
RWA	Royal West of England Academy/Academician
RWS	Royal Society of Painters in Water-Colours/ Royal Watercolour Society
SBA	Society of British Artists
SEA	Society for Education in Art
SGA	Society of Graphic Art/Society of Graphic Artists/Society of Graphic Fine Art
SM	Society of Miniaturists
SPS	Society of Portrait Sculptors
SS	Screw Steamer/Steamship
SSA	Society of Scottish Artists
SSWA	Scottish Society of Women Artists/Scottish Artists and Artist Craftsmen
SWA	Society of Women Artists
SWAS	South Wales Art Society
SWE	Society of Wood Engravers
SWG	South Wales Group/The Welsh Group
SWLA	Society of Wildlife Artists
TRH	Their Royal Highnesses
UA	United Society of Artists
UNESCO	United Nations Educational, Scientific and Cultural Organization
USA	United States of America
WAC	Welsh Arts Council/The Arts Council of Wales
WIAC	Women's International Art Club
WSW	Watercolour Society of Wales

A

Andrew AARONS 1939– Painter, mostly in oil on canvas, and printmaker, mainly etching, born in London. He studied at Camberwell School of Art junior department, 1952, then between 1955–8 continued at Camberwell to gain his diploma, notable teachers being Gilbert Spencer and Joe Dixon. Aarons was a cricket enthusiast, played for Camberwell School and included sporting pictures in his shows. In 1959 Aarons did a Manchester University postgraduate course in textile design and technology, returning to Camberwell for a postgraduate diploma in printmaking, 1991. Among his awards were the Royal Manchester Institution's Haywood Prize and Silver Medal, both 1959, and several Canadian awards in the 1970s. Took part in many group shows in England and Canada, including South London Art Gallery, 1958; Art Gallery of Ontario, 1974; Castle Museum, Norwich, 1979; Churchill College, Cambridge, 1986; and Yarrow Gallery, Oundle, 1991. Later solo shows included Bodilly Gallery, Cambridge, where he lived, 1994. Canadian Broadcasting Corporation, Toronto; British Rail; and Berlin Museum hold examples.

Mineo AAYAMAGUCHI 1953– Versatile artist, born in Gunma, Japan, who studied at St Martin's School of Art, 1974–8, settling in London. Light was a key factor in Aayamaguchi's art, which early on found expression in performance, drawing, photography and notably video installation. His constant companion was a small, lightweight, hand-held camera, with which he roved through landscape in search of details. His work blended Western and Oriental influences. Latterly, he concentrated on painting highly coloured abstracts. In 1981 he was artist-in-residence, Städtische Galerie Wolfsburg, Germany. Awards included Video Bursary, Arts Council, 1983; Video Bursary, London Video Arts/Arts Council, 1987; and Individual Project Grants, Greater London Arts, 1987 and 1998. In 1992, a public video was commissioned by London Video Arts and the Artangel Trust. Showed widely internationally, later appearances including Kaleidoscope, ICA, 1988; Obelisk, Museum of the Moving Image, 1993; On mouse Up, Sans Walk Gallery, 1996; and The Digital Laboratory, London Electronic Arts, 1998.

Samira ABBASSY 1965– Painter, teacher and film-maker, born in Ahwaz, Iran. She moved to Britain in 1967 and completed a foundation studies diploma at Maidstone College of Art, 1983–4. An honours degree in fine art was achieved with studies at Birmingham Polytechnic, 1984–5, then Canterbury College of Art, 1985–7. From 1987 Abassy (pronounced Ab*bass*y) was busy in group shows, work being included in Coast Lines, at Towner Art Gallery, Eastbourne, and Brilliant New Discoveries, at Drew Gallery, Canterbury, both in 1987; South East Young Painters, at Metropole, Folkestone, 1988, where she gained a first prizewinner purchase award; and at Mercury Gallery, where she had a solo show, 1993. She also gained the M&G Purchase Prize, RA, 1997. Abbassy was an invited lecturer at Kent Institute of Art & Design, 1994; a visiting lecturer, University of East London, 1996; and at the University of the West of England, 1998; and she taught at a printmaking workshop, Hunter College, New York, America, 2001. Was art director for two short films in 1988–9: *Little Lotte* and *Peter and the Wolf*. Her work, often small and rather naïve in appearance, was sometimes based on Iranian folk tales. South Eastern Arts Collection holds her work, as does the Government Art Collection. Abbassy's later solo exhibitions included Skoto Gallery, New York, 2002 and she was one of Two Artists from Iran: Samira Abbassy & Christine Khondji, England & Co, 2004. Her first husband was the artist Len Shelley. After marrying again, she lived for a time in New York.

ABBOTT 1927– Printmaker, painter, designer and teacher, whose correct name was Barry Gordon Cope, born in Birmingham, where he attended art college, then studying at Royal College of Art with Robert Austin and Malcolm Osborne. He held a number of teaching posts, including Carmarthen School of Art and Yeovil School of Art, where he was head for some years. Exhibited widely and prepared official illuminated addresses for local authorities in Lichfield and Carmarthen. Lived in Yeovil, Somerset.

John ABBOTT 1884–1956 Painter in oil from his retirement as a member of the Indian Civil Service in the early 1930s. Studied with Francis Hodge. Exhibited RA, NEAC, ROI, provincial galleries and Paris Salon. Methuen published his book, *The Keys of Power*. Lived at Grasmere, Westmorland.

John ABBOTT 1948– Painter, draughtsman and teacher, born in Manchester, who attended Liverpool College of Art, 1965, West of England College of Art in Bristol, 1966, and Royal College of Art, 1969. From 1974 he taught at the school of art at South Devon Technical College. Abbott's figurative work has a slightly Surrealist quality, as shown in The British Art Show, Arts Council touring show in 1980, chosen by the critic William Packer. Solo shows included Bath Festival Gallery, 1978.

Paul ABBOTT 1960– Painter of portraits and figure studies, born in London. Following an initial solo exhibition at the Civic Centre, Plymouth, in 1979, Abbott had two one-man exhibitions at the School of Architecture there, 1982–3. After appearing in the Hunting/*Observer* Art Prizes at the Mall Galleries in 1992, during the 1990s Abbott had a series of solo and group appearances in Paris, France, including the François-Miron Gallery, 1993; Jean-

Marie Felli Gallery, 1995; Guénégaud Gallery, 1997; and the Théâtre de l'Oeuvre, 1998. In 2000, Abbott showed with RP at Mall Galleries and in the BP Portrait Award, at the National Portrait Gallery, where he gained a commendation and he also had a solo show at Jonathan Cooper. Lived in north Wales.

Wendy ABBOTT 1943– Artist and teacher, born in Leeds, Yorkshire, who graduated with honours in fine art from University of Newcastle upon Tyne, 1962–6; gained a Hatton Scholarship there, 1966–7; and her master's in fine art from University of Reading, 1967–9. Abbott was a fine art lecturer at that University, 1971–4, and a visiting lecturer, University of Leeds, 1974–5. Having moved to Yorkshire in 1975, she settled on the Norfolk coast in 1998. Group exhibitions included London Young Contemporaries, 1964–5; LG, Mall Galleries, 1965; Winter Exhibition, Ferens Art Gallery, Hull, and Print Exhibition, Nahal-oz, Negev, Israel, both 1968; John Moores Liverpool Exhibition, and Open Field Exhibition, Museum of Modern Art, Oxford (purchase prize winner, Southern Arts Collection), both 1972; First British Drawing Biennale, Teesside Museum, Middlesbrough, 1973; with many shows in the north, including Pyramid Gallery, York, and Scarborough City Art Gallery, 1979–98; Eastern Open Exhibition, Fermoy Gallery, King's Lynn, 1999; and Courthouse Arts, Hunstanton, 2001. Among her solo exhibitions were The Playhouse Gallery, Leeds, 1974. The Universities of Leeds and Tasmania, Australia, hold examples.

Faisal ABDU'ALLAH: *see* **FAISAL**

Yuki ABE 1977– Artist, born in Fukuoka, Japan, married to the artist Thomas Lamb. Like him, she graduated in fine art from Wimbledon School of Art, 1997–00, then gained her master's from Chelsea College of Art, 2000–1. In 2003, participated in group exhibitions at The British School at Rome, Italy, and at Eyestorm Gallery, London, in the Lexmark European Art Prize. Lived in Belleau, Lincolnshire.

Roy ABELL 1931– Painter, printmaker and teacher, born in Birmingham, where he attended the College of Art, 1947–52, winning the Jackson Travelling Scholarship. Was then at Royal College of Art, 1954–7, obtaining first-class honours and a Silver Medal (Painting). In 1957 he was included in Jack Beddington's book *Young Artists of Promise*. Taught at Birmingham College of Art (Birmingham Polytechnic) from 1957–82, being made head of the painting school in 1974. Was on the West Midlands Arts fine art panel, 1975–8. His mixed shows included Young Contemporaries, 1956; RA; John Moores Liverpool Exhibition, 1958; Midland Art Now, Ikon Gallery, Birmingham, 1977; Tegfryn Art Gallery, Menai, 1984; and The Birmingham School, City Art Gallery, 1990. Was elected RBSA and had a series of solo shows there from 1961; others included Oriel Gallery, Cardiff, 1983; Keele University, National Museum of Wales, in Cardiff, and Christopher Hull Gallery, all 1985; Birmingham Centenary Exhibition, 1989; and Brian Sinfield Gallery, Burford, 2003. Arts Council, Birmingham City Art Gallery and National Museum of Wales hold his work. Abell was notably a landscape painter, the oils tending more towards abstraction, built up with a heavy layering of paint. Lived at Sutton Coldfield, West Midlands.

Evelyn ABELSON 1886–1967 Painter in oil, born in London, who studied at Campden Hill School and Heatherley's School of Fine Art. Exhibited RA, NEAC, RBA, SWA and elsewhere. Lived in London.

Douglas ABERCROMBIE 1934– Abstract painter, born in Glasgow, where he studied at School of Art, 1952–6, in the latter year winning a RSA Carnegie Travelling Scholarship. In 1957 Abercrombie travelled with the Bertram Mills Circus, then for five years from 1958 was a painter-designer with Glasgow Citizens' Theatre. In 1964 Abercrombie moved to London where he worked at the Royal Opera House, Covent Garden. After living and painting in Barcelona and Minorca for a couple of years from 1965 the artist returned to settle in London. He participated in many group shows and was included in British Painting 1952–1977 at RA in the latter year. His first one-man show was at 57 Gallery in Edinburgh in 1958, others including Citizens Theatre in 1961, Thames Gallery in Windsor in 1963, the Steuer Gallery in Lippstadt, Germany, in 1969 and a studio show at Bombay Wharf, in London, in 1977. Was included in a three-man show with Fred Pollock and Gabriel Flynn at The Living Room, Greenwich, 1995, and in Mainstream Abstract Paintings from the Seventies: Abercrombie, Gouk, Rigden, at Poussin Gallery in 2005.

Anthony ABRAHAMS 1926– Artist who after gaining an arts degree from Cambridge University studied at the Anglo-French Art Centre. After concentrating on painting, he latterly turned to sculpting full-time, producing poised, enigmatic figures. Was included in Sixteen Sculptors at Sladmore Contemporary, 1997. Lived in Gloucestershire, with a studio in Cirencester.

Ivor ABRAHAMS 1935– Sculptor in a variety of materials, and teacher, born in Wigan, Lancashire. He studied at St Martin's School of Art, 1952–3; was in 1954–5 apprenticed to Fiorini Bronze Foundry; in 1954–7 studying with Karl Vogel at Camberwell School of Arts and Crafts. After several years as a display artist, from 1960–70 Abrahams taught sculpture as a visiting lecturer at Birmingham, Coventry, Hull and Goldsmiths' Colleges of Art. Having had a first solo show at Gallery One in 1962, Abrahams launched his international career in 1970 with an exhibition at Richard Feigen Gallery in New York. In London he showed with Felicity Samuel and Mayor Galleries and in 1995 was given a sixtieth birthday retrospective by Bernard Jacobson Gallery. Showed at RA Summer Exhibition and was elected RA in 1991. Working in such materials as flock fibre, latex and bronze, Abrahams focused his work on gardens in a way peculiarly his own, looking at how nature and the artificial coalesced. Arts Council holds his work. Lived in London.

Moich (Martin) ABRAHAMS 1941– Figurative painter and teacher whose work had strong autobiographical and fantasy elements, as illustrated in the ninetieth-anniversary commemorative volume issued by the LG, of which he was a member from 1977. Abrahams was born in Hitchin, Hertfordshire, growing up in Letchworth. He started as a mathematician and teacher, eventually becoming an adviser on special educational needs. Aged 29, he chose to become an artist and trained at Byam Shaw School of Art, 1970–4, where he took a first-class diploma, gaining his master's at Goldsmiths' College, 1980–2. Inspired by an interest in psychology and metaphysics,

Abrahams presented workshops on the art of intuition, which included doodling and drawing to obtain intuitive data. He was based in London.

Peter ABRAHAMS 1958– Abstract artist who worked in a wide range of media, including castings, computers and film. He was born in Liverpool, where he studied architecture at the University for a year before a foundation course at the Polytechnic; Camberwell School of Art, 1978–81; and Royal Academy Schools, 1981–4. Did a postgraduate diploma in advanced printmaking at Central St Martins College of Art & Design, 1989–2. Awards included Aidan Threlfall Trust, travel to Spain, 1981. Richard Ford Award, research in the Prado and other Spanish museums, 1982; British Institution Fund, travel to Rome, 1983; Villiers David Foundation Award, research on pre-Hispanic art in Mexico, 1990; Esmée Fairbairn Charitable Trust, 1995–6; and British Council travel grant for solo show in British Arts Centre, Buenos Aires, 1999. Showed with The New Contemporaries at ICA, 1982; LG, Whitechapel Open and Beardsmore Gallery; and in the 1995–6 John Moores Liverpool Exhibition with a geometric acrylic and oil on canvas Caress of the Engineer. His other numerous mixed exhibitions included Visionfest, Ainscough Gallery, Liverpool, Euclid Prize, 1996; Eagle Gallery, 1999; Beneath the Surface, Sarah Myerscough Fine Art, 2000; and Brussels Contemporary Art Fair, James Colman Fine Art, 2002. Later solo shows included Hanover Gallery, Liverpool, 1987; Creaser Gallery, 1988; Morley Gallery, 1991; and Glimpses East, photographs, Royal London Hospital, 1999. British Museum; Whitworth Art Gallery, Manchester; Walker Art Gallery, Liverpool; London School of Economics; and other public and corporate collections hold examples. Lived in London.

Ruth ABRAHAMS 1931– Painter and teacher, born in London. She studied at St Martin's School of Art, 1951–5, notable teachers being Frederick Gore and Bateson Mason, then did postgraduate fine art at Royal Academy Schools, 1955–9, under Peter Greenham. Among her awards were the Landseer Medal for Drawing, David Murray Landscape Award and Leverhulme Award while at the Schools; in 1960 Abrahams gained the Harrogate Festival Painting Prize to the British School at Rome. In addition to teaching foundation studies at St Martin's, also taught at Trent Polytechnic, Derby Lonsdale College of Art and Loughborough College of Art & Design. Exhibitions included Young Contemporaries, LG and RA, and Singer & Friedlander/*Sunday Times* Watercolour Competition, 1990. In 1985 had a solo show at St Michael's Gallery, Derby. Durham University holds her work. Lived in Sedgebrook, Lincolnshire.

Elda ABRAMSON 1944– Weaver, sometimes of large works, and teacher, born in Croydon, Surrey. Abramson lived in America from 1945–69, graduating with her master's in design from the University of North Carolina. She returned to Britain in 1969, setting up a weaving studio in Manchester, then dividing her time between teaching and commissions. Those included work for the International Centre, Bosenquest Ives Ltd and Hammond Brothers, as well as private homes in England and America. Among her exhibitions were RA and Oldham Art Gallery, 1975; the Textural Art Gallery, 1976–7; and Sanderson, 1977. In 1979, George Melly bought her witty Jumping Jack Flash, of 1975, for the Arts Council.

Philip ABSOLON 1960– Painter and poet, born in Erith, Kent, great-great-grandson of the Victorian watercolourist John Absolon. Absolon was dyslexic. After attending Rede School, Strood, and an educational special unit, Chatham, Absolon studied at Medway College of Art & Design, 1977–9, foundation, and Epsom College of Art, for his diploma, his paintings being thrown into a skip on the principal's orders. After unsuccessful applications to the Slade School and Royal College of Art, in 1993–4 Absolon did a fine art access course at Maidstone College of Art, attending life drawing classes at Rochester Adult Education Centre, 1994. Financial difficulties hindered his taking a degree course at Kent Institute of Art & Design. Absolon was a member of The Stuckists, participating in their many shows, including Artbank Gallery, 2001. His poetry collections *Illicit Meeting* and *Fear of Desire* were published respectively in 1994 and 1999. Lived in Rochester, Kent.

ACANTHUS 1909–1976 Cartoonist, architectural draughtsman, teacher and architect, born in India. His full name was Harold Frank Hoar. He went on a scholarship at 15 from Plymouth College to the Bartlett School of Architecture, London University, where he trained under Sir Albert Richardson. He was a fellow of the RIBA and a doctor of philosophy. He practised for some time as an architect, working on Gatwick Airport, churches in Hythe, Kent, and Woking, Surrey, where he lived, as well as on domestic and industrial buildings. Showed at RA but was mainly known as a cartoonist of architectural subjects with a great sense of fun and clarity of line. His best work was done for *Building* magazine in the 1960s; later he drew political cartoons for *The Sunday Telegraph*.

Victoria ACHACHE 1952– British artist (surname pronounced Ashash) who studied at Byam Shaw School of Art, 1970–4. Mixed exhibitions included RA Summer Exhibition, from 1979; Berkeley Square Gallery Christmas Show, from 1988; Works on Paper, Arts Club, 1989; New Academy and Jill George Galleries, both 1990; and Binder Hamlyn Exhibition, Old Bailey, from 1993. Her solo exhibition with Jonathan Clark Fine Art, in 2002, was her tenth and included loose, colourful, allusive works.

Caroline ACHAINTRE 1969– Artist, born in Toulouse, France, who graduated with a master's degree in fine art from Goldsmiths' College in 2003. Her group exhibitions included Acid Rain, Galerie Michel Rein, Paris, France; Contropop, Vamiali's, Athens, Greece; and The Unhomely, Kettle's Yard, Cambridge. She also made solo shows for spaces including Lawrence O'Hana and Mirko Mayer Galerie, Cologne, Germany. In 2005, she had her first major solo exhibition in a publicly funded gallery with DEEDIE, at The Showroom. Achaintre's work was described as "portraiture of near monsters", as a result of her development of twisted and glamorised imagery from horror films and heavy metal graphics. The Showroom exhibition included two large-scale, hand-tufted rugs, gestural woodcuts and subtle digital and watercolour drawings. Achaintre lived in London.

Anne ACHESON 1882–1962 Sculptor, born in Portadown, Craigavon, Northern Ireland. Attended Belfast School of Art and Royal College of Art, studying with Édouard Lantéri. Exhibited extensively in Britain and abroad, notably at RA, SWA, Paris Salon, in Italy, Belgium, Sweden,

Canada, America and in New Zealand. In 1938 gained an award from the Feodora Gleichen Memorial Fund, administered by the RBS. Lived in London.

Joseph ACHESON 1918–1994 Painter, draughtsman and teacher, born in London. Acheson was educated in North America and England, studying art at Slade School of Fine Art and Courtauld Institute, 1946–50, subsequently in continental Europe and America. He became a member of Society of Industrial Artists. Teaching experience included Wimbledon School of Art; London, Surrey and Open Universities; and Workers' Educational Association. Showed with Leicester Galleries, RA, Arts Council and elsewhere and had work bought by The Football Association and Ministry of Works. Had a retrospective at The New Ashgate Gallery, Farnham, in 1996. Lived in Seale, Surrey.

Gerald ACKERMANN 1876–1960 Watercolourist, born in London, son of the art dealer Arthur Ackermann. After initial education in Eastbourne, he studied art at Heatherley's School of Fine Art, Westminster School of Art and the Royal Academy Schools, where he was a distinguished student. Ackermann painted widely in Britain, having a special affection for Sussex and Norfolk, where he settled at Blakeney. Although he worked on a fairly small scale he favoured big brushes; crisp detail, liquid washes, strong colours and careful delineation of architectural subjects are other features of his work. Exhibited extensively at Fine Art Society and Leicester Galleries, where he had one-man shows, also RA, Walker's Galleries, RI and RBA.

Judith ACKLAND 1892–1971 Watercolourist and artist in mixed media, born in Bideford, Devon. She studied at the Art School there, then at Regent Street Polytechnic School of Art, gaining a bronze medal for figure composition. There she met the artist Mary Stella Edwards, with whom she shared the rest of her life. They exhibited and painted landscapes together throughout Britain and worked jointly on historical models and dioramas, Ackland doing the figures, Edwards the settings. Windsor Guildhall holds examples. Ackland showed at RA, SWA and elsewhere and Victoria & Albert Museum holds her work. Lived in Bucks Mills in Devon and Staines, Middlesex.

Nicola ACKLAND-SNOW 1968– Artist in mixed media who studied at Bournemouth and Poole College of Art and Design and Bath College of Higher Education. Her assemblage Ark was included in Art in Boxes at England & Co, 1991. Ackland-Snow's work was used as a book cover by the publisher Longman Group UK and the artist Peter Blake, himself a box-maker, held an example. Lived in London.

Roger ACKLING 1947– Artist born in Isleworth, Middlesex, who studied at St Martin's School of Art after working as a gardener. He had many solo shows in Britain and abroad including LCF and Lisson Galleries from 1976; Amano Gallery, Osaka, from 1983; Juda Rowan Gallery, 1987; and Annely Juda Fine Art from 1990. His exhibition at Annely Juda in 1994 was largely of driftwood fragments taken from the beaches and foreshores of East Anglia which he then scored by using a burning glass, the ambiguous resulting objects often being quite small. Ingleby Gallery in Edinburgh and Crawford Arts Centre, St Andrews, gave Ackling exhibitions in 2004. Arts Council, British Council, Tate Gallery and many foreign collections hold his work, which was completed in Norfolk and London.

Alfred ACKRILL 1907–1988 Painter and draughtsman for whom art was a vocation, although circumstances prevented his pursuing it as a career. He was rediscovered when Alfred Ackrill: A Manchester Impressionist Rediscovered was put on at Manchester Art Gallery in 2003. The influence of the Impressionists shows in his work and he admired the painters John Singer Sargent and Edward Seago. In 1921, aged 14, Ackrill won a scholarship to Oldham College of Art, but family poverty meant that he had to work, so from then on he spent every spare minute sketching and painting. He attended art classes throughout his life, tutors regarding him as an equal. During World War II, he was a despatch rider with the Army in north Africa. Ackrill painted on board and to save money when his brushes wore out would buy a shaving brush, using the bristles to reconstruct them. His subjects included his work-mates on building sites and the railways, northern industrial back streets and north Wales, where the family would spent their holidays, usually paid for by his winnings as best artist with Oldham Art Society. In 1985, Ackrill entered a competition to paint scenes of the Manchester area, his painting Chester Precinct winning the first prize of a trip to Paris. He and his wife acquired passports, only to be disappointed. The person in second place complained that Ackrill's picture was not of Manchester but Chester, so he was disqualified. It deterred him from showing again. Latterly, motor neurone disease hindered his ability to paint.

Heather ACKROYD and Dan HARVEY: *see* **Daniel HARVEY**

Jane ACKROYD 1957– Sculptor, notably in steel, born and lived in London. She gained a first-class honours degree in sculpture at St Martin's School of Art, 1979, then her master's degree at Royal College of Art, 1983. Among her awards were the Special Melchett Award for work in steel and a travel scholarship to Carrara, Italy. Her commissions included work at the Old Royal Free Hospital, Islington, and The Haymarket, London, wall sculpture. Showed at RA Summer Exhibitions from 1988 and was included in 1st RWA Open Sculpture Exhibition in 1993. Had a series of solo exhibitions at Anderson O'Day from 1988. Arts Council and Contemporary Art Society hold examples.

Norman ACKROYD 1938– Printmaker, painter and teacher, born in Leeds, Yorkshire. He studied at Leeds College of Art and Royal College of Art, 1961–4. Taught at Winchester College of Art and Central School of Art, becoming professor of print at Royal Academy Schools. Won a number of awards at Bradford International Print Biennale, 1972 and 1982; RE in 1984 and 1985; at Frechen Triennale, in Germany, in 1986. Was described by *Financial Times* critic William Packer as "by far our most adventurous and accomplished etcher." Ackroyd had several dozen solo shows, including Anderson O'Day; Aitken Dott, Edinburgh; Jersey Arts Centre, Channel Islands; Compass Gallery, Glasgow, and abroad. Victoria & Albert Museum, British Council and provincial British galleries hold his work. Lived in London and was made RA in 1991, being actively involved in its Summer Exhibition and London Original Print Fair. Ackroyd's Journeys West and East, new etchings and paintings focusing on islands of Connemara and the coast of north Norfolk, was at North House

Gallery, Manningtree, in 2005, as was his show Brancaster Roads, at The School House Gallery, Wighton.

Stewart ACTON 1879–1960 Landscape painter, born in Brighton, Sussex, full name Walter Robert Stewart Acton. After education at the local Grammar School Acton became an antique dealer, like his father. Showed at RA, Brighton Arts Club and elsewhere and had several solo exhibitions in Sussex. In 1990 Canon Gallery, Chichester, held a retrospective. Brighton Museum and Art Gallery holds local views by Acton.

Ken ADAM 1921– London-based designer and painter, born Klaus Adam in Berlin, Germany. Disliking the Nazi regime, his family left for the United Kingdom in 1934, Ken being sent to a boarding school in Edinburgh to learn English, then to a London day preparatory school before attending St Paul's School. Aged 17, he enrolled for evening classes at the Bartlett School of Architecture, by day working with C W Glover and Partners, an architecture and building company. Early in World War II Adam enlisted with the Auxiliary Military Pioneer Corps, transferring to the Royal Air Force in 1941. After training in America, he returned as a fighter pilot, demobilised in 1946 as an acting flight lieutenant. He found employment with Riverside Studios as a draughtsman on the film *This Was a Woman*, 1948; soon became art director, *Around the World in Eight Days*, 1956; then production designer, *Night of the Demon*, 1957. In over 40 years he worked on dozens of notable films, collaborating with such directors as Robert Aldrich, *Ten Seconds to Hell*, 1959; Stanley Kubrick, *Dr Strangelove*, 1963, and *Barry Lyndon*, 1975; Joseph L Mankiewizc, *Sleuth*, 1972; and Robert Siodmak, *The Crimson Pirate*, 1951, and *The Rough and the Smooth*, 1959. Adam created singular designs for seven James Bond films, from the first, *Dr No*, 1961, to *Moonraker*, 1979. He also designed opera sets; worked as an interior designer for private clients and coffee bars; and designed for Seven Hills: Images and Signs of the 21st Century, the Berlin millennium exhibition in the Martin-Gropius-Bau. For best art direction Adam won two Academy Awards as well as British Film Academy Awards and was nominated for many others. The Royal College of Art granted him an hon. doctorate in 1995. In 1994, Adam was the subject of an exhibition at the Forum der Technik of the Deutsches Museum in Munich and in 1999 of Moonraker, Strangelove and other celluloid dreams: the visionary art of Ken Adam, Serpentine Gallery, 1999. He was knighted in 2003.

Zbigniew ADAMOWICZ 1916–1987 Painter, born in Kiev, Ukraine, who then lived in Poland, attending grammar school in Wilno and undertaking military service from 1939. After the war he studied at Cracow Academy of Fine Arts with Professor Z Pronaszkou. He moved to England in 1946, studying at Camberwell School of Arts and Crafts, 1947–50. In 1950, he began exhibiting with Group 49. Solo exhibitions included New Vision Centre, 1957, with a series at Drian Galleries from 1958, and he also took part in mixed shows at those galleries.

Alexander ADAMS 1973– Figurative artist, born in London, who attended Wrexham Art College, 1991–2, and Goldsmiths' College, 1992–5. He sought to make "an image that somehow evokes a range of powerful and deeply felt associations within the viewer." Exhibitions included Cabinet Paintings III, Blue Gallery, 1996–7; Christmas Bazaar, Paton Gallery, 1997–8; The Discerning Eye, Mall Galleries and tour, 1998–9; and group show, British Embassy, Moscow, Russia, 2001. Had a solo exhibition at Wrexham Arts Centre, 2002, and at University of Liverpool, 2006.

Alicia Melamed ADAMS: *see* **Alicia MELAMED**

Bernard ADAMS 1884–1965 Portrait and landscape painter, son of the artist Robert Adams. Studied at Westminster School of Art, in Antwerp and with Philip de Laszlo, George Harcourt and Innes Fripp. Was a member of the Chelsea Arts Club and London Sketch Club. Exhibited RA, especially ROI, Chenil Galleries, Leicester Galleries and Paris Salon, where he won a silver medal in 1957. Lived in London.

Brian Lemesle ADAMS fl. from 1940s– Versatile artist in oil and watercolour, born in Wolverhampton, Staffordshire. After Bryanston School he studied at the Architectural Association, qualifying in 1949 after war service in the Army interrupted his education. Showed with the Soldier Artists' Exhibition in 1944. While working as an architect he continued to show pictures, including RA from 1947, RBA and NEAC. Had a solo show at Everyman Cinema, Hampstead, in 1957, with Sally Hunter Fine Art from 1986, and at Air Gallery, organised by Highgate Fine Art, 2000. Lived in London but painted widely in Britain.

Chris ADAMS 1867– Painter and miniaturist, born in Southampton, who studied at Reading University. Was married to the artist Minnie Walters Anson. Exhibited RA, RMS, in the provinces and abroad. Walker Art Gallery, Liverpool, holds his work. Finally lived at Parkstone, Dorset.

Danton ADAMS 1904– Painter, born in Eastbourne, Sussex. He studied at Putney and Chelsea Schools of Art and was for a time an advertisement manager. Produced the book *Musical Colour*, lectured and founded Wimbledon Art Group, becoming president. Showed with RA, RP, RBA, UA and at Paris Salon. Lived in New Malden, Surrey.

Elinor Proby ADAMS 1885–1945 Painter, teacher and writer, born in Sudbury, Suffolk, who studied at Slade School of Fine Art and won several awards. Showed at NEAC, Goupil Gallery, RA and elsewhere and lived at Sevenoaks, Kent. Miss Adams' ambitious picture Mammon is illustrated in *The Slade*, 1908.

Elizabeth ADAMS fl. from 1950s– Artist born in England who settled in Paris, France, married to painter Pierre Gastaud. She studied architecture and painting at Burslem Art School, Stoke-on-Trent; painting at L'École des Beaux-Arts, Paris; also in Paris being student-in-charge at the workshop of Édouard-Georges Mac-Avoy, Grande Chaumière. Her painting style was described as "solely light – a light that she creates with a limited range of colours but with unlimited tones, which swirl tenderly ...on round or oval surfaces...in stratified layers." Showed at Salon d'Automne et Mai, Paris; Salon International de la Femme, Cannes; Salon de la Création, Bourg-en-Bresse; and Salon de Cernay. As well as group shows had six solo exhibitions in Switzerland and France between 1960 and 1992, the last at Maison des Arts et Loisirs de Sochaux.

Ernest D ADAMS 1884–1963 Painter, printmaker and draughtsman in pen and ink. Born in Margate, Kent, studied at Regent Street Polytechnic School of Art under Harry Watson and Harry Theaker. He did a variety of graphic work, ranging from posters and Christmas cards to illustrations in magazines such as *London Opinion* and *Bystander*. Exhibited RBA, NS, SGA, RA and RI. Lived in Folkestone, Kent.

Gilbert ADAMS 1906–1996 Photographer, painter and teacher, brought up in Oxfordshire, who studied at Reading University's faculty of fine art, 1923–7, with Allen Seaby and Herbert Maryon. He was commissioned in 1945–51 by British Council to make series of photographs publicising Britain. From 1951–2 was technical advisor to Associated British Pathé Film, Coronation of H M Queen Elizabeth II. From 1951–77 Adams was visiting lecturer in photography and fine art at Berkshire and South Oxfordshire Colleges of Art. He showed with RBA, St Ives Society of Artists and Reading Guild of Artists. Was a noted photographer of children, work being published in many magazines. In 1985–6 his work was included in a Brotherhood of Ruralists and Friends show at Piccadilly Gallery. Imperial War Museum holds his work. In 2005, the Museum of Reading acquired a set of 30 photographic prints by both Gilbert and his father Marcus Adams. Ranging from a 1940s image of a Polish airman to a 1960s one of the the pop singer Marianne Faithfull, Gilbert's demonstrated his considerable versatility. Lived in St Ives, Cornwall.

Harry William ADAMS 1868–1947 Landscape painter, born in Worcester, where he was privately educated and made his career. Worked for Royal Worcester Porcelain Factory as decorator for eight years, then studied at Académie Julian, in Paris, 1895–6. Also worked in Switzerland on several occasions and became noted for mountain and winter scenes, such as his Winter's Sleep, owned by Tate Gallery. Showed for about 30 years from 1896 at RA, also extensively at RBA of which he was a member, RCamA and elsewhere.

Hervey ADAMS 1903–1996 Painter, teacher and writer who after Charterhouse School studied painting with Bernard Adams, 1928–30. Taught at Berkhamsted and Tonbridge Schools and wrote several books, including *The Student's Approach to Landscape Painting* and *The Adventure of Looking*. Showed with RBA of which he was a member, RA, Leicester Galleries and elsewhere. Lived at Houndscroft, Gloucestershire, but died at The Priory Nursing Home, Horsley. His wife Iris Adams, also an artist, predeceased him.

James Frederick ADAMS 1914–1984 Watercolour painter, born in Stoke-on-Trent; he studied at the local School of Art, at Burslem, 1930–4, under Harry Tittensor and Gordon Forsyth. Adams spent his career in the printing and advertising industry, working for many years with Purnell & Sons in Bristol. Exhibited widely, including RA, RWS, RI, RWA, in Canada and France. His work was reproduced in *The Studio* and *Staffordshire Life* magazines. Lived in Newcastle-under-Lyme, Staffordshire.

Jonathan ADAMS 1931–2005 Artist, actor and teacher, born in Northampton as John Adams, the change of name to Jonathan in 1959 to distinguish him from another actor, John Adams, who painted and acted from childhood, continuing with both until ill health incapacitated him. He studied at Northampton School of Art, Chelsea School of Art under Ceri Richards and Prunella Clough and at London University Institute of Education. Taught at Brentwood Teacher Training College. Later solo exhibitions included Dixon Gallery, London University, 1985; Barbican Centre, 1986; Harlow Art Gallery, 1987; Central Museum and Art Gallery, Northampton, 1988; Chelmsford Festival, 1996; and The Mill Art Centre, Barnet, 1997. Adams drew inspiration from a vein of Surrealism, which became the vehicle for his own obsessions: "landscapes of the mind which the eye has never seen." During the 1990s, he showed in various mixed exhibitions and had collages accepted for the RA Summer Exhibition, 2002 and 2003. Adams had a wide-ranging acting career. He was with the BBC Drama Repertory Company for periods in 1992–3 and 1996 and performed his own songs on a late-night programme. His many television credits, for the BBC and Granada, included *The Winslow Boy*, *Richard II*, *Antony and Cleopatra*, *The Barchester Chronicles*, *Sherlock Holmes*, and *Howard's Way*, and among his films were *The Rocky Horror Show*, *Squaring the Circle* and *Danny the Champion of the World*. Adams had a character part in the film of *The Rocky Horror Show* and was narrator in the original stage production and revival. His other stage appearances included *Arsenic and Old Lace*, *The Decameron* and *Metropolis* and he toured with his solo show *Jonathan Adams' Happy Hour*. Adams had a successful exhibition, Jonathan Adams in Wonderland, at Riverside Studios just before he died in London.

Joy ADAMS 1921– Painter, notably of flowers, born in Yorkshire, who settled from 1951 in Ealing, west London. Studied art at Ealing Technical College School of Art from 1963. In 1974 Adams won the open painting competition held by *The Artist* magazine; in the same year the Grenfell Silver Medal instituted by the Royal Horticultural Society, then went on to win the Silver-Gilt Medal in 1976 and 1979. Precision of detail and trueness of colour were a notable feature of her studies, shown at Medici Galleries in 1981.

Ken Praveera ADAMS 1933– Painter, sculptor and teacher, born in the Scottish borders area of England, whose father painted and drew. Ken's early interests were philosophy and art, which he studied at Oxford and at the Slade School of Fine Art, 1956–7 and 1961–4, under William Coldstream, Patrick George, Harold Cohen and Frank Auerbach. Sculpture was a subsidiary subject for him at the Slade, where Adams developed a talent for clay modelling and gained a commendation. Taught at the Slade, Central St Martins and Royal College of Art. For a time Adams' work was abstract; when he "returned to figuration in 1968, I was working from dreams, memories and imagination." His solo show at Heifer Gallery, 2000, represented "a return during the last five years to painting directly from the subject in the open air". Earlier solo shows included Grabowski Gallery, 1972; the Alamo, 1977; and the Diorama Gallery, 1986 and 1996. Museum Sztuki, Łódź, Poland, holds his work. Lived in London.

Lindsey ADAMS 1951– Artist and teacher, born in London. Studied at Camberwell School of Arts and Crafts, 1969–74; won a David Murray Travelling Scholarship, 1974; then did postgraduate painting degree course at Royal Academy Schools, 1974–7. Went on to teach at Chelsea and

Westminster, Clapham and Battersea and Southwark Adult Education Institutes and was included in Artists in Adult Education at Woodlands Art Gallery, 1982. Also showed at Stowells Trophy, Mall Galleries, 1971; Seven Dials Gallery and Ellingham Mill, Norfolk, both 1980; and in Three Women Painters at Norwich Castle Museum, 1982. Between 1993–6 Adams completed her master's in design and critical theory at Sheffield Hallam University, and in that period her work "changed considerably and gave me greater freedom to explore new media and ways of working, particularly with sound and installation." In 2000, she began an 18-month residency at Site Gallery, Sheffield, working on a digital arts project, gaining a bursary from the Arts Council. She had a solo show, Watershadows, there in 2001. Adams' later group shows included Lightbox Installation, Fem House, Wirksworth, 2004, and RASA Border Poets, A Brush With Words, Martin's Gallery, Cheltenham, 2005. She was based in Derby.

Mac ADAMS 1943– Versatile artist in a range of media, including sculpture, mosaic and photography, and teacher, born in Brynmawr, Monmouthshire, who became a United States citizen in 1990, based in New York. Adams gained his national diploma at Cardiff College of Art, 1961–6; his art teaching diploma there, 1966–7; then his master's in fine art at Rutgers University, New Jersey, 1967–9. He taught at Rutgers/Douglas College, 1969–70; Nova Scotia College of Art & Design, 1977; Montclair State College; 1975–89; was guest sculptor at Sarah Lawrence College, 1983–4; taught in the environmental design department at Parsons School of Art in New York, 1986, obtaining a chair, 1991–3; and from 1998 was associate professor, State University of New York. Among Adams' awards were National Endowment Fellowship for the Arts, 1976 and 1980; Berlin Deutscher Akademischer Austauschdienst Berliner Kunstlerprogram, 1981; and New York State Fellowship for the Arts, Sculpture, 1982 and 1988. Took part in numerous international group exhibitions, later ones including Eclipses, CEAC, Strasbourg, France, 1999. His many solo shows latterly included The Silence of Shadows, Cardiff Bay Arts United Kingdom tour, 1998; Printemps de Cahors, Cahors, France, 1999; and Galerie Serge Aboukrat, Paris, and The Silence of Shadows, Newport Museum and Art Gallery, both 2000. Later public commissions included, all in 2000: Mustangs at Noon, shadow sculpture, Henry Gonzales Convention Centre, San Antonio, Texas; Wetlands, two glass mosaics of New Jersey wetlands for the concourse, Secausas Transfer Railway Station, New Jersey Transportation; and Wales Millennium Centre, the design team collaborating with Cardiff Bay Arts Trust. Victoria & Albert Museum; WAC; Museum of Modern Art and Guggenheim Museum, both in New York; The Museum of Fine Arts, Houston; and many other international public and corporate collections hold examples.

Marcus ADAMS 1875–1959 Painter and professional photographer, born in Southampton, his father Walton Adams having the same interests. Adams went on to become a member of the London Salon of Photography, specialising in pictures of children. After studying at Reading University and in Paris, Marcus Adams exhibited his oils and watercolours with the St Ives Society of Artists and the Reading Guild of Artists. Adams was best known as a portrait photographer. In 1926 he was asked to photograph the infant Princess Elizabeth, and from then on his portraits of her and her sister, Princess Margaret, were reproduced throughout the world. In 2005, the Museum of Reading acquired 30 photographic prints by him and his son Gilbert Adams. Lived in Wargrave, Berkshire.

Norman ADAMS 1927–2005 Painter, stage and costume designer, mural and ceramics artist and teacher, born in London. He studied at Harrow School of Art, 1940–6, then Royal College of Art, 1948–51. Had first solo show at Gimpel Fils in 1952, later ones including North House Gallery, Manningtree, 2001, and Sailing to Byzantium, works on paper, Fine Art Society, 2004. Adams made an early name as a stage designer, in 1951 handling the Royal Ballet's *A Mirror of Witches* at Covent Garden, in 1953 the Sadler's Wells production *Saudades*. Murals were also a strong theme. In 1969 he gained an Abbey Major Award for the study of mural painting. He won a commission for a ceramic relief of the Stations of the Cross for the Roman Catholic church Our Lady of Lourdes, in Milton Keynes, Buckinghamshire in 1975–6. Stations of the Cross in oils for St Mary's, Manchester, known as "The Hidden Gem", followed in 1994, The Adoration of the Magi for Aylesbury in 1995. From 1962–70 Adams was head of the painting school of Manchester College of Art; he was professor of fine art at Newcastle University, 1981–6; then was professor of painting and keeper at Royal Academy, 1986-95, being elected RA in 1972, Hon. RWS in 1987. Adams said his work was concerned with his religious beliefs or the lack of them. Tate Gallery holds his work. Lived in west London.

Pauline ADAMS 1952– Sculptor using a wide range of materials to produce wall- and floor-mounted work, born and lived in London. She attended Barnet College, 1969–74. Group shows included ICA, 1974; Air Gallery Auction, 1980; and Berry Street Open Studios, 1984.

Richard ADAMS 1960– Painter and illustrator, born in Hampshire, who gained an honours degree in graphic design from Leicester Polytechnic, 1979–81. His extensive client list included Barclays Bank, Penguin Books, Saatchi & Saatchi, Royal Mail, *Cosmopolitan*, *Radio Times*, RA, Tesco and Nationwide Anglia. Adams won a series of awards in open competitions, including several first and second prizes, in the Benson & Hedges Gold and *Reader's Digest* Awards. His own pictures, which could be incident-packed and slightly jokey, were in chalk pastel on paper which was then varnished to give the rich colour and tonal effect of oils. Adams was a prolific artist, keeping copious sketch-books. English vernacular architecture, classic cars, animals and the countryside around Playden, Sussex, where he lived, were inspirations. As well as mixed exhibitions he had solo shows such as One Long Holiday, Hybrid Gallery, 1996; A Day in the Country, Brian Sinfield Gallery, Burford, 2002 and 2004; and Flavours of the Harvest, Hybrid Gallery at Combe House Hotel & Restaurant, Gittisham, and Welcome to Winter, at Hybrid, both 2003. The Inkshed handled his illustration commissions.

Robert ADAMS 1917–1984 Sculptor of abstract and monumental works, designer and lithographer. Born in Northampton, Adams studied at the School of Art there in 1933, although later – 1938–44 – he had to make his living at various jobs while he studied part-time. At first influenced by Henry Moore, he later turned to non-figurative work, notably that of Brancusi and Gonzalez. Taught sculpture at the Central School of Arts and Crafts 1949–60. He exhibited widely internationally, including a number of International Biennales in the 1950s. Work in a series of important collections around the world, including the Tate Gallery, Arts Council, British Council and the Museum of Modern Art, New York. Retrospective Northampton Art Gallery, 1971, another in 2003 at Gimpel Fils, which had represented him from 1947 until his death. Lived at Great Maplestead, Halstead, Essex.

Will ADAMS 1951– Painter and muralist, born in Hunstanton, Norfolk. He studied at Reading University's fine art department, 1969–74. Among group shows he appeared in were a number of Whitechapel Opens; Whitechapel Art Gallery's Art for Society, in 1978; and John Moores Exhibition, Liverpool, 1991–2. Adams held a number of residencies as a community painter in London's East End and he painted a mural Conference of the Birds for a school in Bethnal Green. His solo exhibitions began with one at 57 Gallery, Edinburgh, in 1975, a later being at Camerawork, 1984. Lived in London.

William Dacres ADAMS 1864–1951 Painter who studied at Radley College and Oxford University and art at Sir Hubert Herkomer's Bushey School of Art and in Germany. Adams was a member of NPS and showed extensively at Fine Art Society as well as Leicester Galleries, with Ridley Art Club and RA. Lived in London, then Lewes, Sussex.

Crawfurd ADAMSON 1953– Painter, born in Edinburgh. He studied at Duncan of Jordanstone College of Art, Dundee, 1971–6. Became a full-time painter in 1983. Adamson's pictures explored relationships, real and abstract, through figures posed in interiors or on a seashore. He participated in many group shows and had solo exhibitions including Cylinder Gallery in 1984 and 1985, Thumb Gallery in 1988 and Art First 2000. Adamson's pictures are held by Metropolitan Museum of Art, New York; and Wiltshire Education Department. Lived in St Leonards-on-Sea, Sussex.

Edward ADAMSON 1911–1996 Art therapist and painter who studied at Bromley and Beckenham (later Ravensbourne College of Design and Communication) and took lessons in physiotherapy while working in his father's factory. During World War II he enlisted in the Royal Army Medical Corps, on demobilisation offered to work voluntarily for the Red Cross and for six months taught art to former soldiers suffering from tuberculosis. Was invited to join the staff of Netherne Hospital, a forbidding mental institution in Surrey, where he began innovative art lessons. He said that what he initiated was "less a question of treatment than of developing latent creative possibilities." Adamson's work extended to pottery, woodworking and sculpture and the enhancement of the hospital, as well as the creation of a patients' gallery. After retirement in 1971 Adamson kept in touch with Netherne and when he heard it was to close set up The Adamson Collection, a charity trust, to prevent dispersal of patients' work. Part was housed in a barn on the Rothschild estate at Ashton with a view to a permanent site being obtained. Adamson's own work was exhibited in London and Paris.

George ADAMSON 1913–2005 Humorous illustrator, artist in pen and ink and printmaker and teacher, born New York City. He studied at Wigan and Liverpool Schools of Art under "rigorous teachers" in the 1930s and went on to teach in art schools. During World War II was a Royal Air Force navigator, then was an Official War Artist with Coastal Command. Became a freelance humorist and illustrator, working 30 years for *Punch* and seven for *Private Eye* magazines and was designer and illustrator of 90 books, eight of them his own. Showed at RA, RE and had a solo exhibition in Exeter. Imperial War Museum, British Museum and Exeter and Ulster Museums hold his work. Lived at Countess Wear, Exeter, Devon.

H Leslie ADAMSON 1900– Painter, born in Bilston, Staffordshire. After attending Bishop Vesey's Grammar School in Sutton Coldfield and King Edward's Grammar School, Aston, Adamson served his engineering apprenticeship at Joseph Lucas Ltd and attended Harmondsworth Technical College. For 14 years from 1938 he studied part-time at Birmingham College of Art. Moved to Wales in 1955 and for some years was an evening class lecturer. Adamson was a member of RCamA, having a four-man show with it in 1971 and a solo exhibition in Llandudno the following year. Also showed with RBSA and RI.

Joy ADAMSON 1910–1980 Animal conservationist, painter, writer and lecturer, born Troppau, Austrian Silesia, into a comfortably off family. Her mother painted in oil and watercolour and Joy early developed an artistic talent. Settled in Kenya in 1938, between then and 1946 she became a skilled botanical artist, painting several hundred flower studies, in 1947 gaining the Royal Horticultural Society's Grenfell Gold Medal. For two terms in late-1946/early-1947 Joy attended the Slade School of Fine Art. In 1944 she had married her third husband, the Kenyan game warden George Adamson, and stemming from their life together published the international best-seller *Born Free*, about Elsa their lioness. It was successfully filmed and she wrote other books, including *Living Free*, her sketchbook *Joy Adamson's Africa* and *The Searching Spirit*, an autobiography, which fostered the cause of animal conservation. The Elsa Wild Animal Appeal and four game parks were among her other inspirations. She was a notable painter of African animal, bird and marine life and produced 600 tribal portraits, an invaluable record, now in the National Museums of Kenya. A temperamental, volatile woman, Adamson was murdered while camping.

Michael ADDISON 1957– Artist, notably a printmaker, and teacher, born in York. Studied at local School of Art, 1975–6, Manchester Polytechnic, 1976–9, Chelsea School of Art, 1979–80, and California College of Arts, 1981–2, as a Fulbright Scholar. Taught at Maidstone College of Art and Portsmouth Polytechnic. Addison showed in Britain, continental Europe and America and had work in Manchester Education Committee, Kent County Council and private collections. In 1996 he shared a show called Unreal Cities with Mark Davy at Kent Institute of Art & Design, Maidstone, where he lived.

John ADDYMAN 1929– Painter, ceramist, printmaker and teacher, born in Wallasey, Cheshire, attending the local School of Art, 1945–9. Was then at Royal College of Art, 1949–52, working for the advertising agency Colman, Prentis and Varley the following year. Then began teaching part-time at Swansea School of Art. Also taught

Colchester School of Art, 1956–63; Nottingham College of Art and Design, 1963–7; University of Essex, 1969–70, Trent Polytechnic, 1974–8; and Norwich School of Art, 1978. He moved to Sudbury, Suffolk, in 1967 and was by then closely associated with the area, having a series of solo shows at the Minories, Colchester, starting in 1961; with a major exhibition at Oriel Bangor, 1976; others including Chappel Galleries, Chappel, a retrospective in 2001, with another show in 2005, and Layers of Perception, Llantarnam Grange Arts Centre, Cwmbran, 2004. Also showed with RA, New Grafton Gallery, Christchurch Mansion in Ipswich and was a major prize winner in Singer & Friedlander/*Sunday Times* Watercolour Competition, 1996, a Hunting Group regional prizewinner, 2000, the year after he was elected to WSW. Was included in Artists in Residence Programme at British Embassy, Luxembourg, 1994–7, in 1996 was fellow of Ballinglen Arts Foundation, County Mayo, Irish Republic. WAC, National Museum of Wales in Cardiff, Government Art Collection and other notable collections hold examples. Addyman's wife Madeline was also an artist. They lived in Narberth, Pembrokeshire.

Bernard ADENEY 1878–1966 Painter, mural artist, textile designer and teacher, born in London. He began his art training in St John's Wood when only nine, then studied at the Royal Academy Schools, 1892–7, Académie Julian, in Paris, 1897, Slade School of Fine Art, 1912, and Central School of Arts and Crafts for a year. Took part in the Second Post-Impressionist Exhibition in 1912, becoming a founder-member of LG the following year (he was subsequently president for a time). During World War I served in the Tank Corps painting camouflage, then became an official war artist. Married to the artist Noël Adeney. Founder-member of London Artists' Association, 1925, having three years before held a joint exhibition with Keith Baynes at the Independent Gallery. From 1903 taught at the Central School, where he was head of the textile school, 1930–47. Also taught at Putney School of Art and Blackheath School of Art. Painted murals for Plumstead Library and the Borough Polytechnic. Did textile designs for Allan Walton Textiles, Liberty's and Calico Printers' Association. Work held by Tate Gallery, Imperial War Museum and provincial galleries. Memorial exhibition at Woodlands Art Gallery, Blackheath, 1979. Lived in London.

Noël Gilford ADENEY 1890–1978 Painter, writer and dress designer, married to the painter Bernard Adeney. She studied at the Slade School of Fine Art, 1910–15. During her life she mixed dress designing and painting, one of her dresses being worn by the noted cellist Madame Suggia in Augustus John's portrait. Produced designs for Allan Walton Textiles. Exhibited regularly with LG, also with Cooling and Leicester Galleries and Goupil Gallery, and had memorial show at Woodlands Art Gallery in 1979. In the 1950s began writing and in 1956 published her novel *No Coward Soul*, based on the life of her friend the painter and writer Denton Welch. Lived in London and at Clavering, Essex.

Alex ADGAR 1977– Artist producing paintings based on "patterns of nature, abstractions of molecular structures. The motif of the circle is used to represent universal order." Born in Nottingham, Adgar graduated in 1999 from Bath Spa University College, where he had an honorary fellowship, his tutors being Maria Lalić and Michael Simpson. Solo shows at Mark Wilson Fine Art, 2001 and 2003. Lived in Bath, Somerset.

Hank ADLAM 1922– Self-taught painter whose varied career included Naval fighter pilot, director of Short & Harlands and bursar at Clifton College in Bristol, where he finally lived. Wartime aviation paintings and sail trading ships of the 1840–1920 period were his main themes and in his 2003 solo exhibition at Tollhouse Gallery, Clevedon Pier, Adlam included landscapes and scenes of children at the seaside, based on his own childhood. Adlam also exhibited at RUA and had two one-man shows at Fleet Air Arm Museum Yeovilton, 1997 and 2001. His work is held in the wardroom, Royal Naval Air Service, Yeovilton, and by Tenby Museum.

Louise ADLAM 1972– Artist and teacher who did an access course in art and design at Towbridge College of Further Education, Cardiff, 1993–4; foundation at University of Wales, Cardiff, 1994–6; then graduated in fine art, specialising in film and video, Kingston University, 1996–9. Won a travel scholarship to Milan, Italy, 1998. From 1999–00, produced a video and taught video production and art classes for children and adults, variously with Theatre Venture and Hertfordshire Arts Council and Educational Agency. Solo show, Supermarket Sisters, at Catford Artspace, 2000; group exhibitions included Art from Wales – A New Generation, Open Space, Milan, 2001. National Art Library at Victoria & Albert Museum holds Adlam's book *Noble Offerings*. Lived in Cardiff.

Ivan Walter ADLER 1914–1989 Painter, born in Czechoslovakia, who graduated as a doctor of law at University of Prague, becoming resident in England in 1954. He was reluctant to show or sell his work which had a strong pattern quality with an erotic tinge and recurring themes such as dancing, nudes and cattle. He bred prizewinning pedigree cattle. During his life he had only one solo show, at Drian Galleries, a retrospective occurring at Adam Gallery, Bath, 1993.

Jankel ADLER 1895–1949 Painter, printmaker and teacher, born in Tuszyn, Poland, who attended Düsseldorf Academy, 1911–14. Conscripted into the Russian Army then taken prisoner by the Germans in World War I, he was released and returned to Warsaw, where he began to exhibit. During the 1920s he travelled widely in Europe, settling to teach in Düsseldorf in 1931, but fled to Paris in 1933 where in 1937, after a big retrospective in Warsaw in 1935, he worked with S W Hayter at Atelier 17. After a period in the Polish Army in World War II Adler settled and showed in Glasgow, where he was an influential figure, affecting the work of painters such as Benjamin Creme, then moved to London in 1943, where Robert Colquhoun was a friend. Had a series of shows with Lefevre Gallery, Gimpel Fils Gallery and Knoedler Galleries in New York. Arts Council gave Adler a memorial show in 1953; there was a major show in Düsseldorf, Tel-Aviv and Lodz in 1980; in 1993 his work was included in City Art Centre, Edinburgh, show Polish Roots – British Soil; and John Denham Gallery held a show of work of the 1930s and 1940s in 1996. Tate Gallery and major foreign galleries hold examples.

Valerie ADLER fl. from 1980s– Painter and designer, born in South Africa, who moved to London aged 17, studying at the Inchbald School of Interior Design. In late 1970s moved to Israel where, after studying art history at the Hebrew University, she was taught painting and drawing by Asher Rodnitsky, further studies taking place at Chelsea School of Art from early 1980s. After living in London she returned to Israel in the early 1990s. Exhibitions included Galleria Spania Nuova, Venice, 1986; Solomon Gallery, 1987; and Julius Gottlieb Gallery, Carmel College, Wallingford, 1989. Ben Uri Art Society holds her work.

Mark ADLINGTON 1965– Painter and draughtsman using a range of media and with a special interest in wildlife. He gained his master's degree at the University of Edinburgh, 1984–8; was at Sotheby's, 1989–91; then attended City and Guilds of London Art School, 1991–4. In 1994 he won The David Wolfers and Manya Igel Prizes and the City and Guilds Prize for Drawing. Mixed exhibitions included Tenterden Art Exhibition, from 1994; Highway House, 1995; and Young Masters Exhibition, Battersea Town Hall, 1996. Three-man exhibitions included Heron Pictures, Pangbourne, from 1995, and Arts Club, 1997. In that year he had a solo exhibition at New Grafton Gallery, much of the work inspired by a visit to Velavadar National Park, Gujarat, India. Shorelines followed at JohnMartinChelsea in 2004.

Marion ADNAMS 1898–1995 Versatile artist and teacher, born and lived in Derby, notable for Surrealist works, influenced by René Magritte and Paul Nash. Trained as a teacher of modern languages, gaining an honours degree in 1919. Attended life classes at Derby School of Art; in 1936 began to paint with a view to getting her art teacher's diploma, gained in 1938; was appointed art mistress at Homelands Grammar School for Girls, Derby; in 1946 becoming senior lecturer and head of department in art at Derby Training College. She retired in 1960, then spent much time painting in France. Completed a series of murals for Immanuel Church, Stapenhill, Burton upon Trent, 1964–5, but had to cease painting in 1968 because of failing eyesight. From the end of the 1930s for about 30 years showed continuously in London and the provinces and had a retrospective exhibition at Midland Group Gallery, 1971. Public collections in Manchester, Salford, Nottingham, Leicester, Derby and Wolverhampton hold examples. Adnams was a singular woman, who had lived for years in the same tiny house which, even when she was old and blind, appeared as fresh as a St Ives studio of the 1930s. But she could be difficult to deal with, and among the people she fell out with was her mother, also an artist of talent.

ADRIAN: *see* **Adrian OFFICER**

Said ADRUS 1958– Painter and artist in mixed media, born in Kampala, Uganda. He studied at Stourbridge College of Technology and Art and Trent Polytechnic, Nottingham, where he remained to work. Adrus used self-portraits to discuss his political identity and previous status as a refugee, as shown in his contribution to the Norwich Gallery touring show History and Identity, 1991–2. Adrus took part in many mixed exhibitions in Nottingham and Leicester, in Artists Against Apartheid at Royal Festival Hall, 1985, and Black Art: Plotting the Course, at Oldham Art Gallery in 1988. In 1987 he gained a Gulbenkian Bursary in Community Arts.

Mary ADSHEAD 1904–1995 Artist, decorator, painter of murals and illustrator, born in London, her father an architect and good watercolourist, Stanley Adshead. For several years from 1921 attended Slade School of Fine Art, in 1924 being chosen by Henry Tonks to undertake a mural commission with Rex Whistler, a fellow-student, which led to several more commissions, including murals for Bank underground station, London. In 1929 married the artist and writer Stephen Bone. Following year had a one-man show at Goupil Gallery, also exhibiting at NEAC, RA, SWA and elsewhere. Retrospective at Sally Hunter Fine Art, 1986. Among other work completed by Mary Adshead from the early 1930s was a series of drawings and watercolours of Crystal Palace; London Underground posters; wall panels to decorate the restaurant of the British Pavilion at the 1937 Paris International Exhibition; stamp designs for the General Post Office in 1949; and the decoration of Selfridges' restaurant, in 1950, with jungle murals. In 1962 her growing interest in mosaic led her to study in Ravenna and Sicily and to take a course in Italian techniques at Kingston School of Art. A tireless worker whose illustrations and wall paintings contain much wit and charm. Graves Art Gallery, Sheffield, owns her 1931 self-portrait. That was included in a show of Adshead's work touring from the University of Liverpool Art Gallery in 2005. Lived in London but travelled constantly, even into her eighties.

Idris AERON 1918–1992 Horse artist and photographer, born in Birmingham, where she studied at St Agnes' Convent. Attended Birmingham College of Arts and Crafts, 1939–44, under Bernard Fleetwood-Walker and W F Colley and for some years worked under her actual name of Idris Elgina Williams, signing with initials, until adopting the signature Idris Aeron. Her work was widely used in equine publications and she also exhibited with Society of Equestrian Artists, at Mid-Wales Open and elsewhere and had solo shows backed by WAC. Lived in New Quay, Dyfed.

AERSCHOT: *see* **Peter HATTON 1952–1998**

Maliheh AFNAN 1935– Artist in a range of media, whose work was "rooted in memory, both my own and a more distant, perhaps collective one. I unconsciously but continually refer to places, scripts, faces from the past both real and imagined. I do not plan my work in advance." Afnan absorbed both Middle Eastern and Western influences. She was born in Palestine of Persian parents; moved to Lebanon in 1949, in 1955 graduating from the American University of Beirut; moved to America in 1956, studying at the Corcoran School of Art, Washington, 1957–62, gaining her master's in fine arts from George Washington University, Washington, 1962; lived in Kuwait, 1963–6; Beirut, 1967–73; Paris, 1973–97; then settled in London. Took part in many group shows, and exhibited solo internationally from 1965, having a retrospective in 2000 at England & Co, which produced an accompanying monograph. British Museum and several Paris-based collections hold works.

Eileen AGAR 1899–1991 Surrealist painter in oil and acrylic, collagist and object-maker. Born in Buenos Aires, Argentina, daughter of a businessman, she came to

England in 1911. Studied part-time at the Byam Shaw School with Rex Vicat Cole, then with Leon Underwood at his Brook Green School and at the Slade School of Fine Art with Henry Tonks, Philip Wilson Steer and Walter Westley Russell. Married the artist Robin Bartlett and after divorce the Hungarian writer Joseph Bard. Studied for two years in Paris, where she became familiar with modern movements such as Surrealism. Became friendly with Ezra Pound, Evelyn Waugh, Pablo Picasso, Man Ray, Henry Moore and Paul Nash. Took part in the International Surrealist Exhibition in London, 1936. Began to show widely in London, having a first one-man exhibition at the Redfern Gallery in 1942. Retrospective at Birch and Conran 1988, the year she published her autobiography *A Look at my Life*; there was a centenary show at Scottish National Gallery of Modern Art, Edinburgh, 1999–00, others at the Redfern Gallery, 2000 and 2004–5. The Tate Gallery among others holds her work which has a strong jokey element. Shortly before she died, in London, she was elected RA.

Lionel AGGETT 1938– Landscape painter, muralist, architect and writer, born in Whiddon Down, Devon, and educated at Exeter School. Aggett studied part-time at Kingston School of Art and Architecture; he won two travelling scholarships, spent in Venice and Rome. Aggett was made a member of the RIBA in 1967 and gained six awards for architecture. Exhibited at PS, RWA, RI and South West Arts, where he won five awards. Solo exhibitions included A Spanish Daybook at The John Davies Gallery, Stow-on-the-Wold, 1997. Aggett's commissions included a number of murals and The Presentation of the New Colours by HRH The Duke of Kent to the 4th Battalion of the Devonshire and Dorset Regiment, 1992. His work hangs in public and private collections in Europe, Russia and North America. He published *Pastel Techniques and Acrylic Techniques*, 1992, and *Capturing the Light in Pastel*, 1995. After giving up architecture in 1991 Aggett was able to concentrate on painting, later exhibitions including a shared one at W H Patterson in 2004.

Christopher AGGS 1951– Painter, who studied fine art at the City & Guilds of London Art School, then the Royal Academy Schools. In 1976 he won the David Murray Award for Landscape Painting, in 1977 the Richard Ford Award for travel in Spain. Mixed shows included RA Summer Exhibition and Anna-Mei Chadwick, both 1997. Solo exhibitions included Arun Art Centre, Arundel Festival, 1983; Judd Street Gallery, 1989; Terrace Gallery, Worthing, from 1990; and Worthing Museum and Art Gallery, 2001.

Patrice AGGS 1952– Painter, illustrator and printmaker, born in Detroit, Michigan, America. After studying at St John's College, Maryland, Aggs moved to Britain to attend the City & Guilds of London Art School. Illustration commissions included work on children's books for Methuen, 1979–89; for Simon & Schuster, 1989; Doubleday, 1990; Walker Books and ABC, both from 1991; Penguin Books, Frances Lincoln Publishing and Cambridge University Press, all 1995; and Hodder children's books, Orchard Books and *The Cricket Magazine* Group, all from 1996. Mixed shows included RA Summer Exhibition from 1980, Anna-Mei Chadwick, 1997, and elsewhere in London and Sussex.

Maurice AGIS 1931– Artist and teacher, born and lived in London, who studied painting and sculpture at St Martin's School of Art, 1958–62. He taught at Bath Academy of Art, 1962–4; between 1964–6 at St Martin's, London College of Design and Nottingham and Winchester Colleges of Art; and from 1967–73 at Goldsmiths' College. Agis (pronounced Aygis; hard g) won a series of awards and grants, including the Pratt Bequest for Sculpture, 1960; Sainsbury Award for Sculpture, 1961; a Netherlands Ministry of Education Scholarship, 1967–8; a Scottish Arts Council Award, 1968; and a string of Arts Council Awards, 1968–81. Among commissions received were Glasgow Garden Festival, 1988, and a Bedford Park Sculpture Commission, 1991. He showed at Young Contemporaries, 1960–2; at ICA, 1962; in Blow Up at Arts Council, 1970; and in Encounters at Atrium Gallery, 1994. Among his later solo shows was sculpture at Chelsea Arts Club, 1995. From 1972 evolved Colourspace, following on from Spaceplace. Colourspace was staged at numerous venues, including the 1995 Glasgow Mayfest and Cheltenham International Music Festival. Colourspace was made of many translucent, plastic ovoid units of various colours. A public-participation event, its aim was "to introduce people to their inner resources."

Eric Munro AGNEW 1887–1951 Artist, designer and teacher, born in Kirkcaldy, Fife, son of the Reverend William Agnew. He attended Glasgow School of Art then Slade School of Fine Art for figure drawing and painting, 1919–20. Began showing in mid-1920s, notably at RA, RBA, RP, IS, Goupil and Cooling Galleries. Bonham's sold some work posthumously, notably portraits. Agnew was commissioned and decorated in the Army in World War II. He was married to the dancer, choreographer, actress and teacher Laura Wilson (1901–1999), one of the first local girls to be engaged by Sergei Diaghilev when the Ballets Russes moved to Britain in 1918. Wilson, who took the professional name Olkhina, studied Enrico Cecchetti's method, which formed the basis of the English school of ballet. She received the Cecchetti Society gold medal in 1966. The Agnews lived in London.

Michael AGNEW 1968– Printmaker, painter, draughtsman and teacher, born in Bellshill, Lanarkshire. He studied at Gray's School of Art in Aberdeen, the Royal College of Art and in Delphi, Greece. He was etching printer with Peacock Printers, 1992; lecturer in printmaking at Gray's in 1993; and was a visiting lecturer in printmaking at Duncan of Jordanstone College of Art, Dundee. Awards included George Davidson Scholarship to Ireland, 1990; a Fleur Cowles Award for Excellence and Atlantis Paper Purchase Prize, both 1992; and a Bob Bain Memorial Bursary, 1993. Showed at Aberdeen Artists' Annual Exhibition at Aberdeen Art Gallery from 1988; RSA from 1990; Scottish Prints & Monotypes, Lamont Gallery, 1993; and Royal Over-Seas League Open, 1994. Solo exhibition at Thackeray Gallery, 2001. Gray's School, Royal College of Art and Grampian Hospital Art Project hold examples.

Eleonora AGUIARI 1969– Artist and publisher, born in Genoa, Italy, who was included in the Bowieart inaugural exhibition BLOC at the County Hall Gallery in 2005. She studied philosophy at the University of Statale of Milan, 1987–9, from 1990–7 being founder and director of the publishing house Zanzibar in that city, producing 50 titles and writing two books. She did a foundation course at

Chelsea College of Art and Design, 1998–9; graduated in fine art from Central St Martins College of Art and Design, 1999–02; and gained her master's in sculpture from the Royal College of Art, 2002–4. Her work was covered widely in the international press, including *The Financial Times*, *The Times*, *The Guardian*, *The Independent*, *La Repubblica*, *L'Avvenire* and the *Daily Times*, Pakistan. Among her group exhibitions were Monogatari, Tomato Gallery, 2001; Interim Show, Royal College of Art, 2003; and Art School, Bloomberg Space, 2004. She carried out a number of big installations, including Lamont Road Passage, 2003, and a permanent one in Fontebianca, 2003.

Aine AHERN: *see* **Aine DIVINE**

John AIKEN 1950– Sculptor, installations artist and teacher, born in Belfast, Northern Ireland. He did a foundation course at Chelsea School of Art, 1968, remaining there until 1973 and gaining an honours degree in sculpture. From 1973–5 held a Rome Scholarship in Sculpture at British School, Rome, and while teaching at the University of Ulster returned to the Rome School's faculty, 1977–84. After lecturing part-time at Newport School of Art, 1980–2, Aiken joined the staff of the Slade School of Fine Art, in 1986 being appointed head of the sculpture department, in 2000 Slade Professor. He also taught widely abroad, including Canada, America and China, and in 1983 was artist-in-residence at the Henie Onstad Foundation, Oslo. Commissions included a 40-metre frieze in Purbeck stone for Belfast City Hospital, 1986; a steel sculpture for Arts Council of Northern Ireland headquarters, 1992; and in the same year two monumental sculptures in Portuguese granite, commissioned by the Department of the Environment. Fortifications were a key theme in the work of Aiken, as he explained in a BBC2 television programme on him in 1989, German fortifications in northern France being for him "the most impressive sculpture park in the world." Had a solo show at Arts Council Gallery in Belfast 1978, later ones including Orpheus Gallery, Belfast, 1991, Centre for Contemporary Art, Gulbenkian Foundation, Lisbon, 1995, and Stanley Picker Gallery, Kingston University, in association with The Orchard Gallery, Londonderry, Slade Gallery, and James Hockey Gallery, Surrey Institute of Art and Design, Farnham, all 2003. Arts Council of Ireland, University and Trinity Colleges in Dublin, National Museum of Contemporary Art in Oslo and other public collections hold examples.

John Macdonald AIKEN 1880–1963 Painter, stained glass artist and etcher. Born in Aberdeen, he studied at Gray's School of Art there, at the Royal College of Art under Gerald Moira and in Italy. He was head of Gray's School for three years immediately prior to World War I. Exhibited prolifically at RA, RSA, RE, RI, Royal Glasgow Institute of the Fine Arts and Paris Salon, where he won a silver medal, in 1928. Elected RSA in 1935. Several Scottish collections, including Aberdeen, Glasgow and Dundee, hold his work. Lived in Aberdeen.

John P AIKEN 1920– Painter and teacher, born in Dumbarton, where he lived for much of his life. After education at Dumbarton Academy he studied at Glasgow School of Art under Hugh Adam Crawford and W O Hutchison, then widely in Paris, including Atelier Colarossi. Taught at Glasgow School of Art. Exhibited RSA, SSA, Royal Glasgow Institute of the Fine Arts and on the continent and had several one-man shows in Glasgow and Edinburgh. New Museum and Art Gallery, Newport, holds his work.

Lucy AIKMAN 1889–1955 Artist who was born and lived in Glasgow, where she studied under Robert Greenlees at the School of Art, also in Brussels, Belgium. She was a founder-member of the Glasgow Society of Lady Artists, being made an Hon. Member in 1942. Also showed with Royal Glasgow Institute of the Fine Arts.

David AINLEY 1943– Artist in a range of media and teacher, born in Derby, who settled in Matlock, Derbyshire. He studied at Derby and District College of Art, 1959–63, under Keith Richardson-Jones, then at Manchester College of Art and Design, 1963–4. From 1964 held a number of teaching posts, from 1983–93 being senior lecturer, art and art education, at Derbyshire College of Higher Education/University of Derby, then becoming a freelance artist, lecturer, writer and consultant in art education full-time. In 1995 Ainley said that his work had been concerned "with equivalents of processes of growth and change reflected in the 1960s in biomorphic images and in the 1970s in systems paintings related to the 'life game' of the mathematician John Horton Conway. More recent work has been gestural in character, embracing earlier interests and an exploration of perceptual responses to experience." Was at various times a member of Midland and Derby Groups and of National Society for Education in Art and Design. Had a series of solo shows including Ikon Gallery, Birmingham, 1966; St Michael's Gallery, Derby, 1971; and Derbyshire College of Higher Education, 1991. Among later ones were The Quarrying Series at National Stone Centre, 1997; Landscape Issues and Landscapes: Out of Sight?, Wirksworth Festival, 2002 and 2003; and Paintings from a Cultural Landscape, Banks' Mill Studios, Derby, 2003. Ainley was shortlisted for The Vickers Award in 2001 and his painting Landscape Issues: Dark Prospect won first prize at the Derby City Open Exhibition, 2004. Lincolnshire & Humberside Arts Association; Trent University, Nottingham; and private collections hold examples.

John Anthony AINLEY 1931– Painter and teacher, born in Sheffield, Yorkshire. Educated at Chester College, Ainley went on to specialise in child development and the visual arts, being headmaster of St Philip's Special School, in Chessington, Surrey, for some years. Exhibited RCamA, Graves Art Gallery in Sheffield and elsewhere. Lived in Leatherhead, Surrey, where he was secretary of the Art Club.

George Frederick AINSCOW 1913– Painter and textile designer, born in Manchester, who attended Rochdale College of Art, 1929–33. Went on to show at RA, NEAC, RBA and Paris Salon, gaining gold and silver medals, 1980–1. Had a number of solo shows in Lancashire, including Rochdale Art Gallery and Museum, 1991. Royal Air Force Museum at Hendon holds his work. Lived at Castleton, Lancashire.

Sam AINSLEY 1950– Artist and teacher, born in North Shields, Northumberland. She did an arts foundation course at Jacob Kramer College of Art, Leeds, 1972–3, from 1974–7 studying art at Newcastle upon Tyne Polytechnic. The study of Sukiya architecture in Japan during 1975 proved a key influence. In 1977 she moved to Edinburgh to study tapestry at the College of Art, further influences being the adoption of abstract shapes and brighter colours. Ainsley sought in her wall hangings to create a new image of the female body, using a variety of materials. In 1983 she produced a large tapestry for Perth's General Accident headquarters, the year after making a series of banners for the inauguration of the Scottish National Gallery of Modern Art's new building in Edinburgh. Ainsley's Banner for Greenham, of 1985, indicated a move towards more politically engaged art. She went on to teach at Glasgow School of Art and in 1986 had a show at the city's Third Eye Centre. Her work was included in part of the collection of women's art from New Hall, Cambridge, shown at Agnew in 2004.

Meryl AINSLIE 1960– Sculptor, printmaker, draughtsman and teacher, born in Reading, Berkshire, who gained an honours degree in illustration (printmaking) from Exeter School of Art and Design, 1978–81, followed by a period travelling through Turkey, Greece, the Near East and North Africa, where the sculpture of ancient cultures influenced her. After work in advertising and design, Ainslie opted in 1986 to re-explore printmaking at Bath School of Art, a course which eventually led to her first sculptures. Living in north Wiltshire, she also produced powerful black-and-white landscape drawings on a large scale. Ainslie latterly gained her fine art drawing master's at Wimbledon School of Art. Taught life drawing at Swindon School of Art and Design, other appointments including Chippenham College and Cranfield and Open Universities and in 2004 she founded and co-ordinated the Rabley Drawing Centre. Mixed exhibitions included RWA, 1993; Jonathan Cooper Fine Art, from 1993, with a solo show, 1996; Everard Read, Johannesburg, 1997; and A Sense of Place, Handel House, Devizes, 1998. Among later exhibitions were FOLD, Mount House Gallery, Marlborough, 2001, and Venice Agendas/Venice Revisited/ "Worldly Goods", Tate Britain, 2003.

Sarah AINSLIE 1952– Painter, printmaker and photographer, born in Wiltshire, who studied photography at Derby College of Art, 1969–73. She formed the Printmakers Co-op in 1976–7, in 1980 obtaining a collective bursary from Southern Arts Association for running a workshop at Arnolfini, Bristol; Architects Association; and Museum of Modern Art, Oxford. In 1981, Ainslie was involved in a project at Iffley Mead School, Oxford. Group and mixed exhibitions included Swindon Museum and Oxford Printmakers Co-op, both 1977; Waking Up, collective project at Arnolfini, 1980; and Wapping Artists Open Studios, 1982.

Edgar AINSWORTH 1905–1975 Illustrator, poster designer, painter, printmaker and art editor, who exhibited while a student at the Royal College of Art in the late 1920s. Between the wars he showed at RA Summer Exhibition, Manchester City Art Gallery, NEAC and Goupil Gallery. After painting the friezes at the Imperial Institute in 1929, Ainsworth designed posters for the oil company Shell and the Empire Marketing Board in the 1930s. He illustrated books and was art editor of *Picture Post*, after World War II recording his impressions of Belsen concentration camp for the magazine. In 1948, he wrote and illustrated the story of the final days of the British in Palestine, his pictures being included in Six Artists Abroad, organised by the Association of Industrial Artists in 1949. Ainsworth's death was registered at Cheltenham, Gloucestershire.

Graciela AINSWORTH 1960– Versatile artist, letter-cutter and restorer, who studied at the University of Northumbria in Newcastle upon Tyne, 1979–82, then sculpture restoration and conservation at City and Guilds of London Art School until 1985. Held several residencies and showed widely, with work in public collections. Her 1996 steel and concrete sculpture Circling Partridges, commissioned by Gateshead Metropolitan Borough Council, stands in Hedley Lane, Sunniside. Ainsworth was based in Edinburgh.

Mark AINSWORTH 1954– Painter and teacher who said that "colour and all its magical properties is at the centre of my creative output," and who used a rich palette to create his shapes. He was born in Blackpool, Lancashire, where he attended the College of Art, 1972–3, then Ravensbourne College of Art, 1973–6, and Royal College of Art, 1977–80. His work appeared in John Moores Liverpool Exhibition in 1978 and 1995–6, Arts Council acquiring the acrylic on canvas Crag from the first show. Had solo shows at Moira Kelly Gallery and Grundy Art Gallery in Blackpool, 1980; Kerlin Gallery in Belfast and Dublin from 1986; The Sorcerer and the Apprentice, Belfast and Blackpool, 1993; and Art and Design Matters, Ulster Museum in Belfast, 1994. From 1982 taught at University of Ulster in Belfast, Northern Ireland, where he lived at Holywood.

Reginald AIRD 1890– Portrait and decorative artist and designer, born in London. Studied at Goldsmiths' College and in South Kensington with Arthur Cope and John Watson Nicol, also in France, Spain and Belgium. Aird was at various times consultant to the Calico Printers' Association, Manchester; taught at Salford School of Art, and at the Regional College of Art, Bradford. Exhibited RA, RP, NS, IS and widely in the provinces. Victoria & Albert Museum holds his work. Lived in Bradford.

Anna AIRY 1882–1964 Painter, draughtsman and printmaker, born in London, married to the painter Geoffrey Buckingham Pocock. Studied at Slade School of Fine Art, 1899–1903, under Henry Tonks, Fred Brown and Philip Wilson Steer; she won the Melville Nettleship Prize several times, the Slade Scholarship and all first prizes that could be won. Exhibited for first time at RA in 1905, for the last time in 1956. Also showed at Fine Art Society, RE, ROI, RI and Carfax Gallery extensively, and at many other venues. During World War I completed pictures in munitions factories for Imperial War Museum. In 1930 published *The Art of Pastel*, followed by *London Lyrics* in 1945 and *Making a Start in Art* in 1951. Anna Airy was an artist of great versatility whose work is in Victoria & Albert Museum, many provincial galleries as well as galleries in Australia, Canada and New Zealand. Retrospective at Christchurch Mansion, Ipswich, 1985. Lived at Playford, near Ipswich.

Craigie AITCHISON 1926– Painter, printmaker, brought up in Scotland, full name John Ronald Craigie Aitchison. He adopted his father's name when he became an artist. Studied at Slade School of Fine Art, 1952–4, having rejected law as a career. In 1955 he received a British Council and Italian government scholarship to study in Italy, where the different light and landscape made a marked impression on his work. Aitchison's work took on a strong pastel colouring and he adopted a few simple shapes, such as a figure, a tree or a bird, which were to be his trademarks. His apparently simple pictures can be jokey or sad, but are always original. Had a series of shows at the Beaux Arts Gallery, 1959–64, also showing with LG, Compass Gallery in Glasgow, Knoedler & Co and abroad. Notable exhibitions were held at Kettle's Yard, Cambridge, in 1979, and at the Serpentine Gallery in 1981, with a retrospective at Harewood House, Leeds, 1994, a major show at the Gallery of Modern Art, Glasgow, in 1996, Open Eye Gallery, Edinburgh, 2001, with a further retrospective at RA, Out of the Ordinary, in 2003. Aitchison had been elected RA in 1988. Lived in London and Italy.

Balfour AITKEN: *see* **BALFOUR**

John Ernest AITKEN 1881–1957 Painter in watercolour, mainly of landscapes. Born in Liverpool, son of the artist James Aitken, with whom he studied. Also studied at Manchester, Liverpool and Wallasey Schools of Art. He exhibited widely, in Britain and abroad, river and marine views being favourite subjects, at RA, RWA, RI, RSA, Fine Art Society, Royal Glasgow Institute of the Fine Arts, as well as in Europe, India, Ceylon and North and South America. Wakefield City Art Gallery is one of several holding his work. Lived in Port St Mary, Isle of Man.

Kenneth AITKEN 1929– Artist in watercolour, charcoal, pen and wash and pencil, notable for aircraft and motoring subjects. He was born in Warwickshire and settled at Lillington, Leamington Spa. After leaving Leamington School of Art Aitken worked variously as an advertising agency visualiser; public house sign painter; had six years in the Royal Air Force; was a technical artist with Sir W G Armstrong Whitworth Aircraft; was a Rootes/Chrysler sales training and dealer development artist; then worked freelance. Aitken was chairman of the Guild of Motoring Artists and a member of the Guild of Aviation Artists and of the Coventry Society of Watercolour Artists. Royal Air Force Cosford and the Force's Museum at Hendon hold examples. Signed his cartoons Ken.

Pauline AITKEN 1942– Painter, printmaker and lecturer, born in Bedford, who studied at the Slade School of Fine Art, 1961–6, gaining an Abbey Travelling Scholarship in Painting, British School at Rome, 1965. She lectured in art and design at Lowestoft College of Further Education and held residencies at The Manor House, Bury St Edmunds, and Norwich Castle Museum. Group shows included Heffer Gallery, Cambridge, 1992; Eastern Open, King's Lynn, 1994; and Ipswich Open, Christchurch Mansion, Ipswich, 1995. Among solo exhibitions were Arts Centre Gallery, Lowestoft, and Martha Stevns Gallery, Fressingfield, both 1995. Arts Council, Victoria & Albert Museum, Bradford City Art Gallery, Eastern Arts Board and other public collections in England and Germany held examples. Lived in Eye, Suffolk.

Manuel AJA-HERRERA 1955– Painter and printmaker, born in Spain. He did a foundation course at St Martin's School of Art, 1974–5, graduated with honours in painting, Birmingham Polytechnic, 1975–8, then obtained his master's degree at Manchester Polytechnic, 1978–9. Among his awards were the Sir Wallis Whitworth First Prize, 1977; Midland Open 25 (ATV Network Prize), 1978; and Midland Art 1978 First Prize. Showed in many group exhibitions, including Birmingham Institute, 1977 onwards; Stowells Trophy, 1979; and Air Gallery, 1983. Had a solo show at Midlands Art Centre in 1979, later ones including Woodlands Art Gallery, 1986, when Aja-Herrera's theme was man and the changing urban environment.

AJNA 1954– Artist who drew inspiration from the Aryan, Egyptian and Greek epochs, as in her show at Gallery 27, 2000. She was born in Tangier, north Africa, her actual name being Soni Dalamal Sabnani. After winning an exhibition award at Tangier Gallery, 1964, in 1972–3 she painted at Montreux Atelier, Switzerland; Tagore Techniques, with Dinesh Shah, in Bombay, India, 1973–4; at Byam Shaw School, 1974–5; Southern School Techniques with Chou Shou An, in Hong Kong, 1976; and in 1977–82 anatomy, at Chelsea College of Science and the Royal College of Surgeons, printmaking with John Roberts, sculpture with Mary Gorrara at Camden Arts Centre and drawing and painting with Anthony Dowse. From 1982–3, painted and illustrated on commission in London, works being shown at the bankers Johnson Matthey. From 1984–98 made commissioned paintings in New York, Sri Lanka and Sweden, in 1995 with the sculptor Matt Robinson having an exhibition at Galadari, Sri Lanka, where The Heritage holds her work.

George Dixon AKED 1907–1989 Painter, draughtsman, photographer and traveller, born in Bingley, Yorkshire. After Skipton Grammar School he attended Skipton School of Art, Slade School of Fine Art and Central London Polytechnic, then moved to Paris and studied at Académie Julian. Although in the early 1930s he had begun showing at RA, NEAC and LG, a legacy enabled Aked – always known as Pat – to travel the world until World War II, when he served with ambulance units. Aked eventually settled in Barbados for some years, later sharing his time between England and stays overseas, often at others' expense, part of the time in a converted van. Aked had several solo exhibitions in Britain and abroad, a commemorative exhibition taking place at Sally Hunter Fine Art in 1991 which revealed Aked as a colourful painter. Aked's collection of paintings and photographs form part of the archive at the Pitt-Rivers Museum, Oxford.

Alexander ÅKERBLADH 1886– Painter, initially educated in Uppsala, Sweden. Studied architecture at Glasgow School of Art in 1900, after which he practised for a number of years. Later studied painting at St John's Wood School of Art, 1916, the following year in Munich. His work was featured in *The Studio* and *Colour* magazines and he showed at RA, Fine Art Society, ROI, RBA and in Paris. Huddersfield Art Gallery holds his work. Joined Art Workers' Guild in 1945. Lived in London.

Jeremy AKERMAN 1966– Artist using video, curator and teacher, born in London, who gained a fine art degree at Goldsmiths' College, 1986–9, then did postgraduate studies at Jan van Eyck Academy in Maastricht, Netherlands, 1993–5. He took part in Foto 1 at 152c Brick Lane, 1994; in the Knokke Video Festival, Belgium, 1995; and was in New Contemporaries at Tate Gallery, Liverpool, and Camden Arts Centre, both 1996. Later curatorial projects included: *Artists' Stories*, a compilation of 30 short fiction stories written by leading United Kingdom artists (funded by Arts

Council England) and *Artists Illustrate the Bible*. Projects included: *Life is driven by the desire for pleasure*, the work of Chad McCail (Fruitmarket, Geneva and Luxembourg), plus a publication, *Active Genital*, published by Book Works. Akerman was a postgraduate tutor at Middlesex University; ran courses in curating at Central St Martins; a postgraduate fine art tutor at the Royal Academy; and was an invited public speaker at the Whitechapel Gallery, Tate Modern, South London Gallery and the Royal College of Art. He was a selector for Bloomberg New Contemporaries 2005.

Lizzie ALAGESWARAN 1959– Artist and arts administrator, who studied at Lanchester Polytechnic, 1984–7, and who then was a freelance muralist under her original name Lizzie Murphy. This she used until marriage in 1999. She completed a huge mural in the Museum of British Road Transport, in Coventry, where from 1993–9 she was project manager for Arts Exchange, then was arts development officer for the City Council. She was a participant in the 1995 mosaic Waterwall, commissioned by Groundwork Coventry for Bishopsgate Green, and in the ceramic Snake in the Grass, on Coventry Canal towpath, made for the City Council and unveiled in 1997, both Arts Exchange-related.

Alan ALBINSON 1915– Painter and advertising designer, born in Oldham, Lancashire. Attended Manchester School of Art, exhibiting at the City Art Gallery there, and at galleries in Oldham and Buxton. Completed poster work for Indian government. Lived at West Deeping, Northamptonshire.

Emma ALCOCK 1968– Painter whose work included atmospheric landscapes, as in her solo show at Cadogan Contemporary, 1998. She did an art and design foundation course at Trent Polytechnic, 1986–7; graduated with honours in fine art at Bristol Polytechnic, 1987–90; then studied visual Islamic and traditional arts for her master's at the Royal College of Art, 1990–2. Gained the John Hulla Award and The David Innes Wilkin Art in Architecture Award, Art in Architecture Society, both 1990; and The Kairos Education Trust Award, 1992. Exhibitions included Ibstock Design Centre, Bristol, and RWA, both 1990, and Alan Baxter Gallery and Goldmark Gallery, Uppingham, both 1997. Showed solo at Cadogan Contemporary from 1995, with one at Onereddot in 2004. Alcock was commissioned to paint the 1923 Wembley Stadium for End of an Era and limited-edition prints in 1999, when she was also elected to the Art Workers' Guild.

Eva ALDBROOK 1925– Painter, designer and illustrator, born in Hamburg, Germany, whose family settled in London in 1938. After studying ballet Aldbrook danced until 1943. Following war work she worked for stage and screen and later as a fashion artist, having studied costume design at St Martin's School of Art. Later studied painting at Camden Arts Centre and was for a time vice-chairman of the Hampstead Artists' Council. Travelled widely. Her work was portraits, still life and flower paintings, usually done in Tuscany, Italy, where she settled in Florence. Had a solo show at Camden Arts Centre, 1975, with another in 1985, also Ben Uri Art Society, 1982, which holds her Portrait of Rosemary Friedman. Aldbrook had a solo exhibition in 1995 and joint show in 1999, both at Castellina in Chianti, Siena; a retrospective at the AKAD Art Academy, Stuttgart, 2000; with a solo exhibition at Caffè Storico Letterario Giubbe Rosse, Florence, 2003. Aldbrook's two groups of pastel drawings of Arthur Rubinstein at a master class are in the guest house in Jerusalem where the pianist always stayed and her portrait of Dame Marie Rambert is on permanent loan to the Rambert School of Ballet.

Marc ALDINGER 1968– Artist, born in Göppingen, West Germany, who employed media such as video installation. Studied at Hochschule der Künste, Berlin, and Royal College of Art. Was included in East International at Norwich School of Art & Design, 1999, with Circle Line video – portrait, a man sleeping, 2,4,5,7, portraits of people in the Underground. Lived in London and Berlin.

Eileen ALDRIDGE 1916–1990 Painter and restorer, born in Teddington, Middlesex, wife of the painter William Ware and mother of the artist Martin Ware. She studied at Kingston School of Art, 1933–8, and Regent Street Polytechnic School of Art. Exhibited RA, NEAC, WIAC, RP, Leger and Leicester Galleries and elsewhere. Despite severe arthritis she also wrote and illustrated children's books and published a volume on porcelain; with her husband she gained a high reputation for restoration of porcelain, paintings and frames, work being done for national galleries and museums. Lived in London for many years, then in Burwash, Sussex.

Frederick John ALDRIDGE 1909– Printmaker, born in Barnet, Hertfordshire, who attended Highgate School, followed by years in advertising. After World War II service, including photography in Royal Air Force, Aldridge did more advertising and editorial work, then 20 years in farming, and after retiring in 1974 took a course in decorating textiles, including Batik, lino-cut and screenprinting. He developed a print studio in the one-time farm office. Eventually concentrated on relief printing with lino-cuts. Showed in southern England and London galleries including Zella 9 and Graffiti. Lived at North Waltham, Hampshire.

James ALDRIDGE 1971– Abstract artist, born in Farnborough, Kent, who studied at Manchester Metropolitan University, 1990–3, then Royal College of Art, 1993–5. In 1994 he won a Paris Studio Award, Cité Internationale des Arts, and an IBM Direct Award; in 1995 a J Andrew Lloyd Scholarship. Group shows included Cooltan Arts, and Northern Graduates at New Academy Galleries, both 1993; Summer Profile at Paton Gallery, 1996; and, at that gallery, New Abstraction, 1997; and John Moores Liverpool Exhibition, 1997–8. Lived in London.

John ALDRIDGE 1905–1983 Painter, especially of the landscape of Essex, book illustrator, designer of wallpapers and textiles and enthusiastic gardener and plantsman. Born at Woolwich, Aldridge was a classical scholar at Oxford in the mid-1920s. Had drawn and painted since young, but never had any formal training. In 1933, the year of his first one-man exhibition at the Leicester Galleries, he settled at Great Bardfield, Essex, where he lived until he died. He had first exhibited with the 7 & 5 Society in 1931 at the Leicester Galleries, invited by Ben Nicholson. He became associated with East Anglian painters such as John Nash, Cedric Morris and Edward Bawden, with whom he began designing wallpapers, as Bardfield Wallpapers, in

1938. In 1949 William Coldstream invited him to teach at the Slade School, where he remained until 1970. Elected an RA in 1964. An excellent portrait painter, John Aldridge's portrait of his friend Robert Graves, the poet, is in the National Portrait Gallery, London. Although he began to establish an international reputation by exhibiting at the Venice Biennale in 1934, his work was shown mainly in London, especially at the Leicester Galleries. An exhibition of Aldridge's paintings, 1928–71, was held at the Upper Grosvenor Galleries in 1971 and in 1975 a seventieth birthday retrospective at Miriam and Michael Webber's Radlett Gallery, in Hertfordshire. There were survey exhibitions at the Fry Art Gallery, Saffron Walden, which holds his work, 1999 and 2000. Abbott and Holder showed his wartime pictures in 2001. The Tate Gallery, Victoria & Albert Museum, Contemporary Art Society and many other public collections hold his work. A man of generous nature, Aldridge was a quintessentially English landscape painter, strong in design with often rich colours.

ALEXANDER 1927– Artist in a wide range of media, born in London, who preferred to be known only by his surname. Spent parts of his life in Britain, Australia and America, at Santa Monica, California. He studied at St Martin's School of Art until 1951, then for 20 years painted, for about another 20 was engaged in sculpture and holographic works, then in 1989 returned to painting. Had a first solo show at Artists' House, 1950, after which many one-man and mixed exhibition appearances followed, notably at Holdsworth Galleries, Sydney. In 1979, the year he had a solo show there, Alexander was commissioned to produce a monumental bronze, Jubilee Oracle, for South Bank and The Great Tower for Rutland Water, said to be the largest bronze sculpture of modern times. Some other notable events in Alexander's career were Festival of Perth, Western Australia, exhibition in 1982, including five monumental works mounted around festival theatres; holograms shown at Holdsworth Galleries, in Frankfurt, Tokyo and elsewhere, 1984; holograms chosen shown at Expo '85, Japan, and Pompidou Centre, Paris, 1985; in 1986 commissioned to make big musical sculpture with composer Moya Henderson and developed a new holographic movie process, making the art movie *Masks*, shown for first time at Stella Polaris Gallery, Beverly Hills; in 1987 was commissioned to make eight large holograms for Power House Museum, Sydney; 60 works shown at retrospective at Museum of Contemporary Art in São Paulo, Brazil, 1989; retrospective shown at The Modern Museum of Art, Santa Ana, California. Works by Alexander are held by many important collections around the world.

Catharine ALEXANDER 1904–2004 Painter and draughtsman, married to the publisher and writer Noel Carrington. She was brought up in the village of Walberswick, Suffolk, where her father on retirement from teaching worked as a silversmith, her mother being a musician and painter. At 16 she followed her sister, the letterer Margaret Alexander, to the Slade School of Fine Art, studying under Henry Tonks, Philip Wilson Steer and Walter Russell. When she and Noel Carrington lived in Hampstead until World War II Alexander's circle of friends included the Carline family, the Spencers, Mark Gertler and his wife and Stephen and Mary Bone. After the war Alexander lived and painted at Lambourn, on the Berkshire Downs. She shared a show at New Grafton Gallery in 1976. Lived in Steyning, Sussex.

Christopher ALEXANDER 1926–1982 Artist and teacher, son of a window cleaner, he was born and lived in Margate, Kent. Alexander did military service with 3rd Polish Carpathian Regiment and graduated from Royal College of Art in 1951, his teachers including Robert Sargent Austin. He was described as "a natural and compulsive teacher", from graduation until his death. He served initially on the staff of Thanet School of Art, then at Canterbury College of Art and at other venues. Had a deep love of music. Alexander showed at RA Summer Exhibition. Before his death, with his sons Gregory and Matthew he had two shows in the Margate area, then in 1989 all their work was included in the Kent County Library three-man touring exhibition People and Places, in which Christopher's juicy use of oil paint was seen to good effect.

Elizabeth ALEXANDER 1862–1951 Sculptor, medallist, scholar and musician, born and lived in Glasgow, one of several gifted sisters, among them Ella Alexander, who created something of a salon in the city. Elizabeth attended Glasgow School of Art, 1887–91, and was also a talented cellist. In 1934, she received an honorary degree from Glasgow University, which holds medals by her. She was a member of the Glasgow Society of Lady Artists, also exhibiting at RSA, RSW, Royal Glasgow Institute of the Fine Arts and at Walker Art Gallery, Liverpool.

Elsie ALEXANDER 1912– Painter in oil who was by profession a businesswoman, born in Ware, Hertfordshire. She studied art with Hyman Warsager and Victor Askew, attending Montclair State College, New Jersey, 1958. Showed in the provinces, as a member of Buckingham Art Society, with Wine Trade Art Society and was granted freedom of the Worshipful Company of Painter-Stainers. Had a solo show in Mill Hill in 1971. Lived in Edgware, Middlesex.

Eugenie ALEXANDER 1919–1993 Painter, fabric collagist, teacher and writer, born in Wallasey, Cheshire. She studied at Chelsea School of Art, 1936–9 and 1946–50, teachers including Graham Sutherland and Henry Moore, and Goldsmiths' College of Art, 1950–1. Presented radio and television programmes on her work; fabric collages filmed by Pathé Pictorial; and wrote *Fabric Pictures*. Showed with groups at Victoria & Albert Museum, Portal Gallery and Whitworth Art Gallery in Manchester, solo exhibitions including Arthur Jeffress, William Ware and Medici Galleries. Victoria & Albert Museum, National Museum of Wales in Cardiff and Embroiderers' Guild hold her work. She was married to the artist Bernard Carter and lived in London.

Gregory ALEXANDER 1960– Painter and teacher, born and lived in Ramsgate, Kent, son of the artist Christopher Alexander. He studied at Canterbury School of Art and West Surrey College of Art and Design, Farnham, graduating in 1981. At 23 he became one of the youngest-ever associate members of RWS, becoming a full member in 1987. Also exhibited at Athena Arts Awards, at Barbican Centre; RA Summer Exhibition; NEAC; and in 1989 shared a Kent County Library touring show with his father and brother Matthew. In 1992 shared a show with his brother at Catto Gallery which stemmed from extensive travels through Europe. In 1991 Catto had had an exhibition of Alexander's colourful pictures for an edition of Rudyard Kipling's *The Jungle Book*, one of a continuing series. He was noted for his vibrant, exotic landscapes.

Hazel ALEXANDER 1912– Sculptor in bronze, born in Newcastle upon Tyne, Northumberland. Although she early developed a talent for art and attended Luton Art School, 1936, further studies had to wait until 1970, under Joan Armitage at Camden Institute and privately with Fred Kormis. Showed at Royal Festival Hall, Ben Uri Gallery, Mall Galleries and permanently at Sharon Hotel, Herzliya, Israel. All England Lawn Tennis Club commissioned a sculpture of singles champion Kitty Godfree. The Crouching Child was inspired by the logo of the National Society for the Prevention of Cruelty to Children, and was produced in a limited edition; and Israeli Embassy selected sculpture of politician Golda Meir for the Hisdadrut Building, Tel-Aviv. Work was bought by private collectors around the world. Was the mother of the artist Naomi Alexander. Lived in London.

Herbert ALEXANDER 1874–1946 Painter, born in London, who travelled extensively, notably with the Army in World War I. He studied at Sir Hubert Herkomer's Bushey School of Art and at Slade School of Fine Art. He was a member of RWS and Royal British Colonial Society of Artists, also exhibiting at RA, ROI, Fine Art Society and elsewhere. Lived for a time at Cranbrook, Kent, and was a member of Chelsea Arts and Arts Clubs.

Isabel ALEXANDER 1910–1996 Painter, draughtsman, illustrator, lithographer and teacher, born in Edgbaston, Warwickshire. She studied at Birmingham School of Art, 1929–33, and at Slade School of Fine Art, 1934–5. After teaching, 1936–9, Alexander worked in documentary films (Paul Rotha Productions/Realist Films/Films of Fact), 1939–49, and was a freelance book illustrator during this period; was a lecturer/senior lecturer in art, Saffron Walden College of Education, 1949–70; then in retirement travelled and painted, 1970–95. Alexander illustrated B L Coombes' *Miner's Day* for Penguin, 1945, and wrote and illustrated *The Story of Plant Life*, Puffin, 1946. A number of themes ran through Alexander's work: Social Realism (for example the Rhondda works in Swansea), 1940s and 50s; portraits, 1940s–1960s; landscapes, 1950s; in the 1960s and 70s there was an abstract period grounded in landscape; and during the 1980s there were studies of sea, land and light, dominated by the Hebrides islands. Her many group exhibitions included Linton Festival and Walker's Galleries, both 1957; Saffron Walden Festival, 1958; Colchester Art Society and Phoenix Gallery, Lavenham, both 1960; Pictures for Schools, RA, from 1963; Pictures for Essex Hospitals, from 1968; Crescent Gallery, Scarborough, 1984; and Stonegate Gallery, York, 1989. Her later solo shows included a series there from 1987. Glynn Vivian Art Gallery, Swansea, holds examples. Died in Ilkley, Yorkshire.

James Stuart Carnegie ALEXANDER 1900–1952 Painter of flowers and landscape, his watercolours noted for their simplicity and sense of design. His wife Euphen Alexander was also an artist. He was born near Selkirk, son of a solicitor, and was educated at Haileybury College, spending six months at the Royal Field Artillery cadet school. His artistic career was encouraged by the artists Tom Scott and Robert and Edwin Alexander. From the late 1920s Alexander showed at RSW, RSA, RA, RI, Walker Art Gallery in Liverpool and Royal Glasgow Institute of the Fine Arts. An exhibition at Mainhill Gallery, Ancrum, in 1996 was the first since Alexander's memorial show in 1952.

Jean ALEXANDER 1911–1994 Painter, notably a watercolourist using a loose, deft style, born in Shenfield, Essex, youngest of five children of the amateur artists Robert and Effie Alexander. Effie met her future husband at Hornsey School of Art and was a pupil of H B Brabazon, whose influence is seen in the work of all the Alexander family. Jean studied at Chelmsford Art School, 1928–31, and at the Slade School of Fine Art, 1931–5, where Philip Wilson Steer was another influence, as was Sir George Clausen, with whom she painted in the 1930s. She returned to Essex in 1936 to teach at Brentwood County High School, becoming art department head until her retirement in 1970. Continued to teach art while living in New Zealand, 1970–4, returning to East Anglia in 1974 to live at Thelveton, near Diss, starting an art group there. Showed at RA, NEAC, SWA and was given posthumous solo shows at Brentwood Library, 1997, and Abbott and Holder, 2003.

Lena ALEXANDER 1899–1983 Painter of flowers, portraits and landscapes, including views of Paris and Venice, who studied at Glasgow School of Art. Became a member of the Kirkcudbright School, where she lived from the mid-1930s, and exhibited at RSA, Royal Glasgow Institute of the Fine Arts, RA, SWA and Walker Art Gallery in Liverpool. Was included in Still Life in the Twentieth Century at Bourne Fine Art, Edinburgh, 1999. McLean Museum and Art Gallery, Greenock, owned her work.

Matthew ALEXANDER 1953– Landscape painter, printmaker and teacher, son of the artist Christopher Alexander and older brother of painter Gregory Alexander. He studied at Canterbury College of Art and in the graphic design department of Maidstone College of Art. With his brother also studied at evening classes run by his father at Hilderstone College of Further Education, formerly Thanet School of Art, eventually replacing his father as tutor in figure drawing. Took the post of art teacher at Hartsdown Secondary School in his home town of Margate, Kent, teaching his brother for a time. Matthew Alexander eventually combined travelling for landscape painting with running a business producing limited-edition prints of his watercolours. He was elected an associate of ROI in 1982 and a member of RBA in 1984. Also showed at RA and in 1992 shared a show with Gregory at Catto Gallery which stemmed from extensive travels in Europe. The two sons and the father held three-man exhibitions in the Margate area and in 1989 there was a Kent County Library touring show of all their work. Matthew Alexander's work developed to become cooler, more detached and subtle-toned. Choice of subject was a key feature, as was the relationship of buildings to landscape. Showed annually with Messum's from 1995.

Naomi ALEXANDER 1938– Artist and picture conservator, born in Harpenden, Hertfordshire, daughter of the sculptor Hazel Alexander. She studied at Hornsey College of Art, 1954–9, then Central School of Arts and Crafts, her teachers including Alfred Daniels. She was apprenticed to the chairman of the British Picture Restorers' Association, of which she became a member, for five years, and went on to do work for government and private Old Master galleries. Showed at RA, Mall Galleries, ROI of which she was a member, NEAC, RBA and RP plus provincial municipal galleries. Solo shows included Ben Uri and Seen Galleries and Paintings in Hospitals, The Sheridan Russell Gallery, 1997. There was a retrospective at Buxton Museum and Art Gallery in 2000. In 1997, Alexander had a residency at Chatsworth, her work entering the Duke of Devonshire's collection, and while there painted 40 attic room interiors unseen by the public. She carried out notable commissions, clients including the Victoria & Albert Museum, Sultan of Oman and the Royal Tank Regiment. Alexander held another residency in 2002 at Europos Parkas, Lithuania. Victoria & Albert Museum holds her work. Lived in London.

Robert ALEXANDER 1875–1945 Watercolourist who lived in Brentwood, Essex. The county, especially the barges, windmills and breakwaters around Frinton and Walton-on-the-Naze, featured in much of Alexander's prolific output. His wife was a pupil of Hercules Brabazon Brabazon, whose atmospheric, washy influence can be seen in Robert Alexander's work. Their daughter was the watercolourist Jean Alexander. Although his Presbyterian family urged him to make a career in an export merchant's office in the City, Alexander studied in the evening at Hornsey School of Art and the Slade School of Fine Art and received encouragement from Mark Fisher and George Clausen. Alexander showed his watercolours of England and continental Europe at RA, NEAC and Grosvenor Gallery. Later the Parkin Gallery had several exhibitions of his work, which is held by British Museum, Victoria & Albert and Fitzwilliam Museums.

Louis ALEXANDRE 1867– Painter and sculptor, son of the sculptor F A Alexandre. He was born in Paris, educated in Battersea, then studied art solo in Paris. He exhibited RA, Paris Salon and in the provinces and received a silver medal at the 1900 Paris Exhibition. Collected French and English pictures. Grundy Art Gallery, Blackpool, bought his work. Lived in Woodmansterne, Surrey.

Sara ALEXANDRI 1913– Painter, printmaker and teacher, born in Kherson, Russia. She was educated in Palestine and on the continent, studying art at the Royal Institute d'Arte and the Royal Academy of Fine Arts, Florence, 1936–40 and 1946–7. Showed at RA, RWA, Paris Salon and elsewhere. Lived in Bath, later in St Leonards-on-Sea, Sussex.

John ALFORD 1890– Painter and draughtsman, born Edward John Gregory Alford. He was educated at Tonbridge School and Cambridge University. He did graduate work at University College, University of London, and taught at the Courtauld Institute of Art. Alford became principal of the Ontario Department of Education summer school for teachers of art; special lecturer in art at McMaster University, Hamilton, Ontario; instructor at Queen's University, Kingston, Ontario, in the school of fine arts; then from 1934–45 was professor of fine art and head of the department at the University of Toronto. From 1945–54 he was on the staff of the Rhode Island School of Design as head of the department of art history. Exhibited LG and at several venues in Canada. Lived at East Chatham, NY, in America.

John ALFORD 1929– Painter of landscape, conversation and marine pictures, born in Tunbridge Wells, Kent. Studied at Camberwell School of Arts and Crafts, 1949–53, his teachers including Gilbert Spencer, Richard Eurich and Bernard Dunstan. Went on to become director of art at Shrewsbury School, retiring in 1989, then painting with studios in Shrewsbury, Shropshire, where he lived, and in Cornwall. Elected to NEAC and RBA, also showing at RSMA, RA and RWA. Had solo shows in England, South Africa, France and Canada, later ones including Wenlock Fine Art, Much Wenlock, 2001, and Shrewsbury School, 2004. Reading Borough Council and Shropshire County Council hold his work, which became more complex when retired.

Michael ALFORD 1958– Painter of atmospheric, colourful scenes, as in his exhibition at Duncan Campbell Fine Art in 2004. Alford graduated with honours in Arabic and Spanish from the University of Durham. For three years he lived in Catalonia, northern Spain, and he had a strong liking for the light and landscape of southern Europe. Awards included an Agnes Reeve Memorial Prize, 2000; Primaluce International Mural Festival, Lodi, Italy, 2003; and Green & Stone Prize, 2004. Among Alford's group exhibitions were RFA Gallery, San Francisco, California, America, 1991–00; SF MOMA, Fort Mason, San Francisco, 1992–01; Chelsea Art Society Summer Exhibition, from 1999; El Claustre, Figueres and Girona, and El Quatre Gallery, Barcelona, Spain, 2003; and El Pont Gallery, Besalu, Spain, 2003–4. Corporate collections holding Alford's work included Berkeley Square Gallery; Hill & Knowlton; Sheraton Hotel, Amsterdam; Claridges; and Trust House Forte.

David ALISON 1882–1955 Teacher and painter, born in Dysart, Fifeshire. Studied at Kirkcaldy High School and Glasgow School of Art as well as on the continent. He became head of the drawing and painting school of Edinburgh College of Art, where he was nicknamed Bouff, being a gritty, strict traditionalist, an admirer of Raeburn, Velasquez, Ingres and Goya, but out of sympathy with modern art trends. His portraits of his many distinguished students were fine and he was elected RP and RSA. Showed widely in Scotland and abroad and is represented in many public collections. Lived in Edinburgh.

Hassan ALIYU 1964– Artist, illustrator, teacher and curator, born in Barnet, who continued to live in London. Graduated with honours, fine art, majoring in painting/mosaic and wall decoration, Ahmadu Bello University, Zaria, Nigeria, in 1986, gaining the Nigerian Arts Council Award for Best Final Year Student in Fine Art. Taught and conducted workshops in Britain and abroad, latterly being a tutor with Lewisham Social Services/Community Education. Took part in many group exhibitions, including Spring Salon, 198 Gallery, 1994; Anne Bellion Gallery, 1996; and Transforming the Crown, American tour 1997. Later solo exhibitions included Winds of Change: The Paintings of Hassan Aliyu, Russell-Cotes Art Gallery, Bournemouth, and Bold & Bright: The Work of Hassan Aliyu, Worthing Museum, Sussex, both 1997. Aliyu continued to exhibit in Britain, America and Nigeria. The artist carried out a series of residencies and commissions, including a mural commission residency for the physiotherapy wing of the Maudsley Hospital, a residency at Dulwich High School for

Boys and an outdoor floor mosaic at Grangewood Park, Thornton Heath, for the London Borough of Croydon.

Tony ALLAIN 1949– Painter and teacher, notable for Impressionist pastels full of light and movement, born and raised in the Channel Islands, who settled in the west Cornwall countryside. From 1987, taught in Guernsey, although latterly he concentrated mainly on his own varied-subject work. Took part in many group exhibitions, including The Linda Blackstone Gallery, Pinner, 2002. Later solo shows included Out of the Blue Gallery, Marazion, 2000. Maritime Museum, Castle Cornet, Guernsey, holds his work.

Alexander ALLAN 1914–1972 Painter in gouache and of pastel portraits, pen and ink draughtsman. Born in Dundee, Allan studied art at the College of Art there under the landscape painter James McIntosh Patrick. Allan later taught part-time there. He also studied at Reimann School, in London, and at Westminster School of Art under Mark Gertler. Work in the collections of the Scottish Arts Council, Nuffield Foundation and Dundee Corporation. Lived at Newport-on-Tay, Fifeshire.

Archibald Russell Watson ALLAN 1878–1959 Painter, born in Glasgow where he studied at the School of Art, then in Paris at Atelier Colarossi and Académie Julian. Allan was a member of Glasgow Art Club and showed extensively with Royal Glasgow Institute of the Fine Arts and RSA. Glasgow and Paisley Corporations bought examples. Lived in Stirling.

Eva Dorothy ALLAN: *see* **Julian Phelps ALLAN**

Griselda ALLAN 1905–1987 Painter and lithographer, born into a well-off shipping family in Sunderland, County Durham. She was a student at the local School of Art in the mid-1920s under Richard Ray, contributing three flower panels to the library frieze painted by the students in 1925. Her training was continued at the Royal College of Art and on the continent and she was at the Ruskin School of Drawing, Oxford, under Albert Rutherston, 1935–9. During World War II she taught drawing for several years at the evacuated Slade/Ruskin Schools, continuing after the war at the Ruskin. The 1940s saw her producing some notable pictures, such as New Shipyard at Southwick, 1944, held by Sunderland Museum and Art Gallery. War Artists' Advisory Committee bought Allan's work. Her later pictures, often featuring trees, were not so remarkable. By then she had returned to live in Sunderland.

Jessie ALLAN 1859–1947 Painter and teacher, also known as Janet Russell Allan, sister of the artist Hugh Allan, born in Glasgow. She studied at the School of Art there, 1881–8, also at the Académie run by Eugène Delecluse in Montparnasse, Paris, joining the Glasgow Art School staff, 1900–24. Was a member of the Glasgow Society of Lady Artists, showed extensively with Royal Glasgow Institute of the Fine Arts, also with RSA, RSW and at Walker Art Gallery, Liverpool. Retired to Broughton, Peebles, where she continued to paint and died.

Julian Phelps ALLAN 1892–1996 Sculptor, born in Millbrook, Southampton. Gave up training as a domestic science teacher to study at Westminster School of Art, then from 1922–5 at Royal Academy Schools. Among other awards won RA Gold Medal in 1925, the following year studying with Libero Andreotti in Florence. Three years later changed her name to Julian Phelps from Eva Dorothy. In World War II served in the Auxiliary Territorial Service, becoming a colonel and first president of its War Office Selection Board. Created reliefs at Lambeth and Maudsley Hospitals and elsewhere. Tate Gallery holds her bronze Marjorie and her Mother and Child is illustrated in the volume *RBS: Modern British Sculpture*, published in 1939. She was elected a fellow of the RBS in 1947. Allan was one of a group of eminent sculptors associated with the organisation Sculptures and Memorials, formed in 1934 to promote the commissioning of pieces by British artists in native stones. The third edition of *Sculptured Memorials and Headstones*, 1938, illustrates her work in stone and a rubbing of a brass by her. She was interested in Romanesque and Byzantine sculpture, travelling in France and Yugoslavia to study it, and these styles are apparent in her own output. Showed often at RA Summer Exhibition, 1925–49. For some years lived in Balerno, Midlothian, with a studio in Edinburgh which was taken over by the sculptor Michael Snowden. About 1970 Allan left Scotland, finally living in Henley-on-Thames, Oxfordshire, having for long been blind.

Mary Parsons Reid ALLAN 1917– Painter, draughtsman and teacher, born in Glasgow, who studied at the School of Art there, 1935–9. She retired in 1976 after a long teaching career, briefly in Aberdeen and for a long time at Laurel Bank, Glasgow. Was at various times a member of SSWA, Glasgow Society of Lady Artists and of its Society of Women Artists. Specialised in still life, especially flowers, landscape in Scotland and France and early on some portraits. Also showed with Royal Glasgow Institute of the Fine Arts and RSA. Had solo shows in Edinburgh and at Pitlochry Theatre and in 1983 at Broughton Gallery, by Biggar. Visited and studied pictures in many continental galleries and admired Bonnard, Morisot, early Chagall, Morandi and Cézanne; William and Ben Nicholson, David Donaldson, Duncan Shanks and Elizabeth Blackadder among modern British artists. Won the Lauder Award in 1951 and 1965 for oil paintings. Glasgow Museums & Art Galleries holds Miss Allan's Still Life with fish, 1955. Lived latterly in Helensburgh, Dunbartonshire.

Ronald ALLAN 1900– Painter and draughtsman most noted for portraits and figure studies, born at Cheadle Heath, Cheshire, son of Harry Allan, a shipper. Studied at Manchester School of Art and Slade School of Fine Art. Exhibitions included RSW, RA, RBSA, RCamA, Wertheim Gallery and Senefelder Club in London and Chicago. Solo shows included XXI Gallery, 1928; Salon Club in Manchester, 1930, and at Mid-Day Studios, 1947, where he was a member of the progressive Manchester Group encouraged by Margo Ingham. Salford Art Gallery and Manchester University hold his works as does Manchester City Art Gallery which has his portrait of Kenneth Russell Brady. In 1933, seeking to borrow it in a bid to get RBA membership, Allan wrote that he thought "it would open a new field of attack" as it was "perhaps the best portrait I have done so far." Lived for some years at Heaton Moor, Stockport, Cheshire.

Rosemary ALLAN 1911– Painter and draughtsman, born in Bromley, Kent, wife of the artist Allan Gwynne-Jones and mother of the painter Emily Gwynne-Jones. She studied at Central School of Arts and Crafts, 1928, then the Slade School of Fine Art, 1930–5, under Randolph Schwabe, gaining a Slade Scholarship in 1932. Showed at RA, LG, NEAC and Leicester, Wildenstein and Redfern Galleries. Solo exhibitions included Upper Grosvenor Galleries, 1971. In 1997 she was part of a Gwynne-Jones family exhibition at Sally Hunter Fine Art. Imperial War Museum holds her work. Lived in Eastleach, Gloucestershire.

Gillian ALLARD 1966– Artist and lecturer employing an innovative method using light-sensitive photographic emulsion to print images onto natural surfaces, the result being a lifelike sculpture. Although varnishes were used to slow erosion of the image, eventually the natural surfaces predominated. Allard obtained a London College of Printing diploma in photojournalism, 1987–8, gaining her master's in photography at the Royal College of Art, 1990–2. She taught photography at Suffolk College, Ipswich, 1996–00. In 2000, Allard held a residency at Exmoor, in the same year taking part in Landlines, Torrington. In 2001, she completed a Sculpture in the Park Commission at Christchurch Mansion, Ipswich, in 2002 participating in Making the Connection, firstsite, Colchester/Wolsey Art Gallery, Ipswich.

Reginald Geoffrey ALLARD 1947– Painter, born in Chester, where he attended the School of Art, 1964–6, then studying at Liverpool Regional College of Art, 1966–9. Various shows including solo at Fine Art Society. First National City Bank of New York bought his work. Lived for some time at Upton-by-Chester, Cheshire.

Annette ALLCOCK 1923– Painter in oil or gouache, illustrator and animator, born in Bromley, Kent. In her teens she was a member of Clifton Arts Club, Bristol, where Kit Gunton and Mary Fairclough were influences; studied at West of England College of Art, Bristol, 1941–3, also at other art colleges. Became a greetings card designer, illustrator of children's books and cartoon films animator. Her portraits were mostly of children. Showed at RWA, Beaux Arts Gallery in Bath and extensively around Britain. Admired the work, and was influenced by, Stanley Spencer, who was a distant cousin, visiting him many times at Cookham. Lived latterly in Corsham, Wiltshire.

Walter Herbert ALLCOTT 1880–1951 Painter and teacher, born in Birmingham, who studied at the School of Art there. Early in the 1920s he toured Italy extensively, painting townscapes and landscapes also visiting Spain and Majorca. Exhibited RSBA and Fine Art Society especially, also RA, RI and Walker Art Gallery, Liverpool. He taught in local authority schools and was art instructor, 1945–6, to the Women's Royal Naval Service. Birmingham City Museum and Art Gallery holds his work. Lived at Haslemere, Surrey.

Betty ALLEN fl. from 1970s–2001 Printmaker and sculptor who studied at Centre for Arts and Crafts, Bromley. She showed with South London Artists, at RA and was included in Group '77 Printmakers at Woodlands Art Gallery, 1981. Work held in private collections worldwide and bought by Government of British Columbia, Canada. Died in Bromley, Kent.

Ceri ALLEN 1962– Figurative painter, daughter of the artists Colin and Sadie Allen. She studied fine art, painting, at City & Guilds of London Art School, 1982–5. Produced many commissioned works, including a portrait of the novelist Margaret Forster; a painting for Lord Inglewood, of a Conservative Party rally; and a depiction of Alexander Fleming's laboratory for St Mary's Hospital, Paddington. Mixed shows included Irthing Valley Centre, Brampton; Sark Gallery, Hethersgill (founded by her parents); Contemporary Fine Art, Eton; and Stephen Ferris Gallery, Nashville, Tennessee, in America. Solo shows included Castlegate House Gallery, Cockermouth, 1998. Carlisle City Museum and Art Gallery hold Allen's work. Lived in south London.

Charles John ALLEN 1862–1956 Sculptor and teacher, born in Greenford, Middlesex. Studied at Lambeth School of Art under Edgar Silver Frith, then at Royal Academy Schools, gaining four silver medals. Went on to become vice-principal and teacher of sculpture at Liverpool City School of Art. Was a fellow of RBS and showed extensively at RA, Walker Art Gallery in Liverpool and Royal Glasgow Institute of the Fine Arts, winning a gold medal for sculpture at Paris International Exhibition in 1900. Major works included Florence Nightingale and Queen Victoria Memorials in Liverpool, Glasgow Corporation acquiring his marble The Woman Thou Gavest Me. Was a member of Art Workers' Guild from 1894, retiring in 1936. Lived latterly at Albury, near Guildford, Surrey. The University of Liverpool Art Gallery held a first retrospective of Allen's work, accompanied by an extensive catalogue, in 2003.

Colin ALLEN 1926–1987 Painter, designer, illustrator and teacher, born in Cardiff. His wife Sadie Allen and daughter Ceri Allen were both artists. He studied at the School of Art there, 1942–4, then was in His Majesty's forces until 1948, resuming studies at Royal College of Art, 1949–52, in 1952–3 taking up a Major Travelling Scholarship to Spain, France, Italy, Sicily and North Africa. From the early 1950s taught for many years at Carlisle College of Art and Design. As well as extensive group shows Allen had some solo exhibitions, starting in 1946 at the Chinese Art Gallery, Hong Kong, followed by Howard Roberts Gallery in Cardiff and Border Gallery, Carlisle. With his wife he held nine joint shows in Britain and abroad. He provided illustrations for the publication *The Story of Carlisle*. His Landscape with Snow is in the collection of the Glynn Vivian Art Gallery and Museum, Swansea, other works being held by CASW, Carlisle City Museum and Art Gallery, Reading and Cardiff Universities and numerous education authorities. Lived at Hethersgill, Cumbria.

Daphne ALLEN 1899– Painter and illustrator, born in London. She studied art with her parents, her father being the painter Hugh Allen, and at life classes in Chelsea. As a child she had several shows at the Drummond Gallery, also showing at SWA, Burlington Gallery and in the provinces, notably in the Gloucestershire area, where she lived for many years at Chalford. Her work had a strong religious element and she completed pictures in a series of churches. Her picture The Kingdom was shown at Sir Edward Elgar's centenary exhibition. The Medici Society Ltd and A R Mowbray Ltd, the religious publishers, published her work. Victoria & Albert Museum holds early drawings by her, done about the same time as her two books *The Birth of the Opal* and *A Child's Visions* were published.

Doreen ALLEN 1916–2000 Painter of East Anglian landscapes, married to the artist Ronald Crampton, based in King's Lynn, Norfolk. She preferred to work out of doors, to give her watercolours and pastels spontaneity and freshness. Exhibited with PS, RI, UA and held successful solo shows. Bonhams included a group of Allen's works in The East Anglian View sale at Lynford Hall, Mundford, 2000.

Enid ALLEN 1927– Urban painter in water-based media and teacher, born and lived in north London, who was trained as a scientist, worked as a hospital pharmacist in the managed National Health Service, then took early retirement in 1984. Between 1984–90 was a visiting tutor for the City University. Allen started recreational painting classes at the City Literary Institute from 1955, notable teachers including Rosemary Startrup. She took masterclasses from Margaret Merritt at West Dean College and Chris Gough at Great Missenden College. Allen said that she was influenced in her pictures by "the street scene, modern painters, the Colourists". Group exhibitions included Camden Annual Exhibitions in 1980s, Islington Art Society, Hampstead Artists' Council and Heifer Gallery. Showed solo with Hampstead Artists' Council, 1987, and in 1990 at Rupert Street Junction, Piccadilly; and at Cotton's Café, Chalk Farm Road. Private collections in Britain and abroad hold examples.

Felicity ALLEN 1952– Allen graduated with honours from Exeter University, 1973–7, then attended the Slade School of Fine Art, 1982–4. Her Café Royal installation took place at ICA, 1984–5. Allen was then involved in The Naked City: Durham Effigy, Air Gallery, 1986, and A Spiritual Dimension at Peterborough Museum and in East End Open Studios, at Deborah House, both 1989. In that year, she also had a solo show at Mario Flecha Gallery.

Frank Humphrey ALLEN 1896–1977 Painter in oil and gouache, draughtsman in ink. Born in London, he studied at Chelsea School of Art, 1933–5, under Graham Sutherland and Harold Sandys Williamson. Exhibited at LG, AIA, Leicester Galleries in the provinces and in Paris. The City of Birmingham Museum and Art Gallery holds his work. Lived in Norwich.

George Warner ALLEN 1916–1988 Painter, notably in tempera, and teacher who was born in Paris. He was educated at Lancing College, then studied at Byam Shaw School of Drawing and Painting under Ernest Jackson, eventually returning there to teach. During World War II he was engaged in camouflage work for the Ministry of Home Security. His exhibitions included solo shows at Walker's Galleries and Reading Museum and Art Gallery. That gallery, Tate Gallery and the public gallery in Nottingham hold his work. George Warner Allen was a disciple of the techniques of the Old Masters and regarded modern art as barbaric. In 1973 he was converted to the Roman Catholic faith, thereafter concentrating on religious subjects. Lived at Wallingford, Oxfordshire.

Georgina ALLEN 1954– Painter of abstracts who studied at University of St Andrews, 1973–7, gaining her master's degree with honours in English literature and language, Goldsmiths' College and Chelsea School of Art, 1982–7, obtaining an honours degree in fine art and her master's in painting. Showed at Paton Gallery, Royal Festival Hall and with Contemporary Art Society at Smiths Galleries, all in the 1980s. In 1991–2 was included in the Spanish tour of Six Young British Painters; in 1999 in Pure Paint, at Stephen Lacey Gallery; there again in A Sense of Things: Objects and Paint, 2001; and in New Painters, at Piers Feetham Gallery, 2003. Writing about Allen's solo exhibition there in 2005, the artist Caroline McAdam Clark suspected that the works rarely revealed all their secrets, "even to Georgina, and that this slow release is a vital part of their magic and capacity to haunt the mind". Lived in London.

Harry Epworth ALLEN 1894–1958 Painter, notably in tempera, especially of Derbyshire. Born in Sheffield, Allen attended King Edward VII School for boys, then became a clerk in the steel works of Arthur Balfour, in his spare time attending Sheffield Technical School of Art. Served in the Army in World War I, gaining the Military Medal for conspicuous gallantry. Although badly injured and having an artificial leg Allen continued to paint and became Balfour's confidential secretary until the slump made Allen redundant in 1931. He now painted full-time and joined the new Yorkshire Group of Artists. Began exhibiting RA. Also showed with RSBA and PS. Although Allen's early work is conventionally realistic he soon developed his distinctive style of simplified landscape and figure studies, which eventually were shown abroad in Canada and America. In the early 1940s Allen published a series of articles in *The Artist* on landscape painting in which he expounded his approach. His work is in a number of provincial galleries, notably Sheffield, Wakefield, Newcastle upon Tyne, and Newport, as well as in Australia and New Zealand. Memorial show at Graves Art Gallery, Sheffield, in 1959, which in 1986 held an exhibition of his decorative works, and tour. Lived in Ecclesall, Sheffield.

Heather ALLEN 1952– Sculptor born in Romford, Essex. She studied at University of Reading with Terry Pope. Her sisal and wood entry Plait was included in the 1992 East & South Norwich Gallery/Kent Institute of Art and Design show. Power, repression, containment and enclosure were features of her work. Lived in Norwich, Norfolk.

James ALLEN 1941– Painter, draughtsman, printmaker and teacher, born in Lurgan, Armagh, Northern Ireland, attending Belfast College of Art, 1961–5, then Brighton College of Art, 1965–7. Before returning to Northern Ireland, between 1965–76 he taught for periods at Goldsmiths' College School of Art and Ravensbourne College of Art. Ran a print workshop at Arts Council of Northern Ireland headquarters, Belfast. Exhibitions included Queen's University in Belfast, Serpentine Gallery, Upper Street Gallery, Arnolfini Gallery in Bristol and Tom Caldwell's Galleries in Belfast and Dublin. Queen's University and Ulster Museum hold examples. Lived in Belfast.

Joe ALLEN 1955– Painter and teacher, born in Airdrie, Lanarkshire. He studied at St Martin's School of Art, 1975–6; Camberwell School of Arts and Crafts, 1976–9; and Royal Academy Schools, 1979–82. From 1985 he divided his time between London and Germany, where he was a visiting teacher at the European Academy of Fine Art in

Trier. From 1986–92 showed regularly with Gallery Ariadne, Vienna, later solo exhibitions including Cynthia Bourne Gallery, 1995. In 1995–6 John Moores Liverpool Exhibition Allen showed the oil on canvas Sea Barn.

Judith ALLEN 1964– Sculptor, born in Leicester. She studied in New York, then at Edinburgh University and College of Art, with postgraduate studies at Leicester Polytechnic. She exhibited at RSA; Art into Landscape at Wakefield, where she was a prize winner; also winning an award at Loseby Gallery, Leicester. In 1989 was included in Scottish Connection at Ferringbury Manor, Feering, and Cramond Sculpture Centre, Moray House College, Edinburgh. There, her Looking for a ritual, in wood, willow twigs and cloth, was sited in water.

Julie ALLEN 1960– Artist who attended Hertfordshire College of Art and Design, 1977–9, then gained an honours degree in fine art from North East London Polytechnic, 1979–82. She participated in the Whitechapel Open, at Whitechapel Art Gallery, 1985; Camden Annual, Camden Arts Centre, 1986; Works on Paper, Carlile Gallery, 1986; and East End Open Studios, at Britannia Works, 1989. Solo shows included Carlile Gallery, 1987.

Kate ALLEN 1975– Painter who studied at St Helens College of Art & Design, 1993–4; Bath College of Higher Education, 1994–7; and Slade School of Fine Art, 1998–00. She gained a British Academy Professional Development Award in 1998. Exhibitions included Peter Kinley Prize, Bath, 1997; The Groucho Club, 2000; Bitter Sweet, Danielle Arnaud, and Six abstract painters, Six Chapel Row, Bath, both 2001; and Contemporary Art Society ART*futures*, 2002.

Kathleen ALLEN 1906–1983 Artist, muralist, designer and teacher, born in Acton, west London, known to friends as Kay, who prior to 1938 exhibited as Saywell Allen. She was notable for her views of London, where she lived in Bloomsbury for many years. Educated initially at home because of illness, after Bromley County School for Girls, 1920–4, she studied at the Royal College of Art painting school, 1924–8, then taught in London and the Midlands until 1936, when she set up a studio in the City of London. The late 1930s included studies at the Slade School of Fine Art, 1936–7, painting murals at her old school and elsewhere and more teaching, from 1938 at Henrietta Barnett School. During World War II Allen was seconded by the City one day weekly to record war industries. A bomb in 1941 destroyed her early work. In 1946 Allen was appointed senior lecturer at Goldsmiths' College, from 1960 until retirement in 1966 being principal lecturer and head of art and design. Allen was a member of the central committee of the AIA, 1938–48; was involved in CEMA from 1940; was a member of the Society of Industrial Artists, 1945–9; and was made a member of the Worshipful Company of Painter-Stainers, 1954. A frequent group and solo exhibitor, she had a retrospective at South London Art Gallery, 1983. Tate Gallery archive holds her self-portrait of 1955; Arts Council, Imperial War Museum, Morley College, corporate and local education authority collections also hold examples.

Michael ALLEN 1925– Painter mainly of landscape and marine subjects who was also a commercial designer, Allen was born in Morecambe, Lancashire, and educated at the Friends School, Lancaster. Studied art at Lancaster and Morecambe College of Art 1943–9 with a break in 1944–5 as a prisoner of war. His teachers included Walter Bayes. Exhibited mainly in Lancashire. Lived for a time at Horsforth, Leeds, then later in Welwyn Garden City, Hertfordshire.

Phillip ALLEN 1967– Painter of colourful abstractions that combined imaginary patterns and shapes within spaces that could loosely be described as landscapes. His pictures on board were lined top and bottom with thick, encrusted layers of paint that made the artist's palette part of the painting. His solo exhibitions included Xavier Hufkens Gallery, Brussels, Belgium, and PS.1, New York, America, both 2003, and The Approach, 2004. Allen's work was included in A4 Art Auction, Bonhams, New Bond Street, 2004.

Ralph ALLEN 1926– Painter, sculptor and teacher, educated at Kimbolton School, Huntingdonshire. He attended Sir John Cass College of Art, 1948–50; Slade School of Fine Art, 1950–3, with a postgraduate year there, 1953–4. From 1955–7 Allen assisted Helen Lessore at Beaux Arts Gallery, then moved to Canada. He joined the staff of Queen's University, Kingston, Ontario, in 1958, being full-time professor of fine art from 1972, retiring in 1990. Allen was director of the Agnes Etherington Art Centre, 1963–73, where he had a touring show in 1990 after a long period of non-exhibiting. In 1968–9 Allen had a sabbatical year in England. Showed extensively in Canada, with work in collections of Art Gallery of Ontario, National Gallery of Canada, Art Collection of Kingston, Leeds University and elsewhere. Allen's later work had an icon-like quality, figurative and abstract. Earlier he had produced pictures described as "romantic Impressionism ranging to a modified realism". He lived in Kingston.

Rebecca Boyd ALLEN 1965– Artist who studied at Kansas State University, Manhattan, Kansas, America, 1984–8; New York Studio School, 1988–90; Slade School of Fine Art, on a one-year exchange, 1990–1; then at Parsons School of Design, New York, 1991–3. Using fine oil paints which she ground from pure pigment, Allen worked mainly on boards prepared in the traditional way. The rigid surface allowed her "to rework an image again and again." Her final paintings were "done from memory and usually in one day." In addition to American mixed shows, Allen exhibited at the RA Summer Exhibition and The Discerning Eye, both 2000, and at The Linda Blackstone Gallery, Pinner, 2002. Had solo exhibitions at Letheringham Mill Art Gallery, Suffolk, 1991 and 1998.

Richard ALLEN 1933–1999 Abstract artist, teacher and exhibition consultant, born in Worcester. He attended the School of Art there, 1955–7, after National Service in the Far East, then was at Bath Academy of Art, Corsham, 1957–60. Allen was an Italian Government Scholarship winner, 1960–1, a Commonwealth Scholar, in art and architecture, India, 1966–7, an artist-in-residence with a fellowship at University of Sussex, 1967, then gained a Major Award for Painting from Arts Council, 1973. Allen had begun teaching two days a week at Croydon College of Art, 1962–7, and many appointments to London and provincial colleges followed. From 1973 he was appointed exhibition consultant to the Polytechnic of Central London, also lecturing in visual arts subjects. Allen participated in numerous group shows in Britain and abroad from 1964. His individual shows included University of Sussex, 1966, and Angela Flowers Gallery, 1971, later ones including shows in France, Japan and the Netherlands as well as University of Exeter, 1985, and Printworks Ltd, Chicago, 1987, with a touring retrospective from University of Wales School of Art, Aberystwyth, 1998. Peter Stuyvesant Foundation, Arts Council, Museum of Modern Art in Rome and Chase Manhattan Bank hold his work. Lived in London after periods in Jersey, where he had opened two galleries, promoted establishment of a Jersey Arts Centre and founded the design firm Exart, and Herefordshire.

Sadie ALLEN 1930– Versatile figurative artist, born in Barry, Glamorgan, married to the painter Colin Allen, their daughter being the artist Ceri Allen. Sadie Allen completed her National Diploma in book illustration at Cardiff College of Art, also her art teacher's diploma. Had wide teaching experience, including 10 years as senior lecturer in art and education at Newcastle upon Tyne Polytechnic, with 40 years addressing the Women's Institute, arts and crafts groups, the Workers' Educational Association, Embroiderers' Guild and speaking for Winsor & Newton. Commissions included memorial hanging for Dacre Church, Cumbria; panel for rest room, Carlisle Civic Centre; and Women's Institute jubilee year Cumbria commemorative panel. Published *Creative Embroidery Collage*, 1978. Among her group shows were SEA; Foyles Art Gallery; Whitworth Art Gallery, Manchester; Royal National Eisteddfod, Wales; Embroidery Collage; and Abbot Hall Art Gallery, Kendal. Held joint shows with her husband and daughter, solo exhibitions including Abbot Hall, 1986. Colin and Sadie Allen bought a redundant Methodist chapel in Hethersgill, Cumbria in 1981, which served as a working studio, teaching centre and gallery and which remained her base. Reading University, Abbot Hall, Welsh Schools Museum Service, Bangor Normal College and other public and corporate collections hold examples.

Saywell ALLEN: *see* **Kathleen ALLEN**

Simon ALLEN 1967– Artist who spent a lifetime in the art world, graduating from gallery technician through framer to exquisite skills in metal leafing. After education in Bristol he did a foundation course at the Polytechnic there, 1986–7, gaining an honours degree in fine art from Falmouth School of Art and Design, 1987–9. After working with Waddington Galleries and Stewart Heslop Frames and with the artist R B Kitaj on design and conception of frames for a Tate Gallery retrospective, in 1994 Allen moved back to Cornwall to develop his career. In 1996, he began a picture framing business, with the emphasis on gilding. Gilded wall sculptures developed from this. He was a keen sailor, his work reflecting sense of being at sea. In 1995, Allen showed at Le Chat Noir; in 2001 exhibited paintings and sculptures at Galerie Pelar, Long Island, America, and eight large sculptures at Newlyn Art Gallery, part of the Transitions II series; and from 2002 began showing at Messum's, who included him in Around Two Thousand and Three, in 2003. From 1995, he was a member of the Newlyn Society of Artists.

Thomas ALLEN 1913–1987 Sculptor who studied at Leeds College of Art under Loris Rey. In 1929, Allen's "memory composition" of a young shire colt was singled out by the *Yorkshire Post* reviewer of the annual College exhibition at Leeds City Art Gallery. The writer noted that "The artistic interpretation, the vigour and rhythmic movement are equally remarkable. The whole suggests the work of a student of no little talent." In 1932, John Rothenstein, director of the Leeds City Art Gallery, bought Allen's squat, powerful sculpture The Bull for its collection, the work having been carved directly in Portland stone a year earlier without the aid of drawings or models. Despite his carving skills, Allen's pass in his Board of Education examination in 1933 was for modelling. After these early successes, Allen's life remains obscure. He is recorded as dying in Camden, north London.

Tim ALLEN 1950– Painter and teacher, born in Manchester, who spent his childhood in Durham. Gained a degree at department of fine art in Newcastle upon Tyne, 1968–72, and his master's at Goldsmiths' College, 1978–80. Went on to teach at St Martin's School of Art. Was a prizewinner in the Festival Hall Flag Competition, under auspices of Arts Council, 1977. Mixed exhibitions included Whitechapel Open at Whitechapel Art Gallery, from 1976; Artists for Nuclear Disarmament, Acme Gallery, 1981; Royal Academy Summer Exhibition, 1982; and Paint, Presence, Other Stories, Ikon Gallery, Birmingham, 1983. There his gestural work was described at "improvisatory and accretive". Later group shows included John Moores Liverpool exhibition, 1999. Had a series of solo exhibitions with Rebecca Hossack Gallery from 1989. Lived in London.

John Ivor ALLENBY 1899–1950 Sculptor, born in Breslau, Poland. After studying at Strasbourg University, Allenby studied art at the Bauhaus, Weimar, under Walter Gropius, 1918–21, then in Paris, 1925–33. In England Allenby changed his name from Johannes Ilmari Allerbach; he was a son of the musician Max Allerbach. Exhibited Salon d'Automne and Salon des Tuileries, Paris, Leicester Galleries, AIA, RA, RIBA and elsewhere. Was a member of the AIA. After World War II Allenby taught at the Oxford School of Art. Signed work with monogram. Lived in Oxford.

Renate ALLER 1955– Artist of German nationality whose work could not easily be labelled as she crossed boundaries as painter, printmaker and sculptor. Aller studied ceramics at North London College, 1977–8; at Inchbald School of Art and Design, 1984–5; Chelsea School of Art, 1988–91; and Byam Shaw School of Art, 1991–3. Was included in Global II Collection, Addison Wesley Longman Ltd, Harlow, 1998–9.

Anthea ALLEY 1927–1993 Artist and teacher, whose work developed from figuration to abstraction and who used a variety of materials. She was married, 1955–73, to Ronald Alley, art historian and Tate Gallery curator, their daughters being the artists Melissa and Fiammetta Alley. Born in Seremban, Malaya, she attended Chelsea School of Art, 1948–51, then Royal College of Art, 1951–3, although as a sculptor she was self-taught. For several years she taught at Bath Academy of Art, Corsham. Mixed shows included Young Contemporaries in Manchester in 1954, RA Summer Exhibition and in 1961 she won a painting prize at John Moores Liverpool Exhibition. Her first solo show was at Molton Gallery in 1960. In 1964 solo exhibitions comprised Hamilton Gallery and Arts Council of Northern Ireland Gallery, Belfast; had a solo show at Arnolfini

Gallery, Bristol, and Bradford City Art Gallery and tour, 1969; and shared several shows with Gillian Ayres. In 1990 Alley was Sandra Blow's choice as an Artist of the Day at Flowers East. Arts Council holds her Horse, in welded iron, 1960, and Rock, in steel, 1964. Lived in London.

Melissa ALLEY 1962– Painter and teacher, daughter of the curator and writer Ronald Alley and the artist Anthea Alley. She was married to the artist Paul Tecklenberg and her sister was the artist Fiammetta Alley. She did a foundation course at Wimbledon School of Art, 1982–3; gained an honours degree in painting at Central School of Art, 1983–6; and studied with Cecil Collins, 1985–9. Concentrated on singing and performance, 1987–95. Between 1988–99 worked part-time at the England & Co gallery; she also taught part-time from her studio in Camberwell. Alley described her pictures as "orchestrated through concerns such as colour and line, masculine and feminine, figuration and abstraction, until a harmony is achieved". Mixed shows included Paperworks, Battersea Arts Centre, 1985; England & Co, Christmas Exhibition, 1996–7; and Benjamin Hargreaves, 1997, who gave her a solo exhibition at The Air Gallery, 2000.

Mabel ALLEYNE 1896–1961 Illustrator and printmaker, born in Southampton, Hampshire, who attended Goldsmiths' College School of Art and Royal Academy Schools. Among books illustrated were Shelley's *Adonais* and Emily Brontë's *Wuthering Heights*. She showed at RA, RHA, Redfern Gallery, SWA and NEAC and lived in London.

Nicola ALLFORD 1964– Sculptor in a variety of materials who did a foundation arts diploma at Weston-super-Mare College of Further Education, 1987–8, then an honours degree in ceramics at Bath College of Higher Education, 1988–91. She next spent some time on the continent. Among her exhibitions was 1st RWA Open Sculpture Exhibition, 1993. Lived in Bristol.

John ALLIN 1934–1991 Painter, born in London, who became famous for his simple and direct pictures of East End streets. Many of these depicted scenes he had known as a child. Allin was a fine natural draughtsman who joined prison art classes while serving a sentence for theft, and continued to work in the evenings later when employed as a lorry driver. In the late 1960s began showing at the Portal Gallery and in the 1970s won fame on the continent, in 1979 gaining the Prix Suisse Peinture Naïve award. In 1974 his book *Say Goodbye* was published, with an accompanying text by the playwright Arnold Wesker, who had shared a similar childhood. A second book, *Circus Life*, followed after the artist spent two years with Gerry Cottle's circus.

Edward ALLINGTON 1951– Sculptor, draughtsman, writer and teacher, born in Troutbeck Bridge, Westmorland, who eventually lived in London. For Allington, "drawing is the basis of my practice". He commonly worked in ink and emulsion on used ledger paper from the late 1970s, as in his 2006 show at The Drawing Gallery. "I was looking for a ground strong enough to equal the illusionistic renderings of objects I was drawing. The aim was formal: a very strong 'figure to ground' contrast. The discovery of ledger paper provided this and much more. These pages are fragments of our lives and history". Allington studied at Lancaster School of Art, 1968–71, the Central School of Arts and Crafts, 1971–4, and the Royal College of Art. Had first solo show in 1981 and exhibited regularly at Lisson Gallery. Foreign one-man exhibitions included Diane Brown, New York, 1987, and Fuji TV Tokyo and Gallery Face Tokyo, 1988. Also took part in foreign group shows, including British Sculpture 1960–1988 in Antwerp, in 1988. Participated in John Moores Liverpool Exhibition from 1985, in 1989–90 gaining a prize. Allington was usually identified with British Object Sculptors of the 1980s. His work was said to employ "the assimilation of the abhorrent through the use of contemporary artificial objects and classical imagery." He was Gregory Fellow in Sculpture, 1991–3, and Sargant Fellow at the British School at Rome in 1997, the year his collected essays *A Method for Sorting Cows was* published. He was also a regular contributor to art magazines, such as *Frieze*. Allington became head of graduate sculpture at the Slade School of Fine Art. He completed major public commissions in the United Kingdom, Germany and France. The Arts Council, Tate Gallery, Victoria & Albert Museum, Irish Museum of Modern Art, public holdings France and Japan and numerous private collections hold examples.

Adrian ALLINSON 1890–1959 Painter, sculptor, draughtsman and poster designer. Born in London. He initially studied medicine, but gave this up to study art at the Slade School of Fine Art, 1910–12, where he was a member of a notable group of students working under Henry Tonks, Philip Wilson Steer, Fred Brown and Walter Westley Russell. Won a Slade Scholarship. Allinson was an athletic man, keen on skiing and climbing, a member of the Ski Club. At various times he taught drawing and painting at Westminster School of Art, designed posters for British Railways and was scenic designer for the Beecham Opera Company. Exhibited RA, NEAC, RBA, ROI, Leicester Galleries and Fine Art Society, which put on a retrospective in 1984. Allinson wrote an autobiography, *Painter's Pilgrimage*. Galleries in Manchester, Bradford and Rochdale hold his work. Although he was fond of travelling, Allinson finally lived in London.

Elaine ALLISON 1956– Sculptor who graduated in 1998 in fine art, sculpture, from Duncan of Jordanstone College of Art, Dundee, then taught there part-time. Showed with smaller contemporary galleries in Scotland, widely abroad and at the RSA, which bought her work. There, in 1999, she won The N S Macfarlane Charitable Trust Prize, having the previous year obtained a John Kinross Scholarship which took her to Florence, Italy, for three months, and the Chalmers-Jervis Prize. Completed several public commissions. In 2003, Thompson's Marylebone included Allison's work in The Sculpture Show, her abstracted Turbines being constructed of wood and glass.

Jane ALLISON 1959– Painter, notably of portraits, and designer, educated at Charterhouse, who studied painting at Chelsea School of Art and Slade School of Fine Art until 1982. Held an appointment as artist-in-residence at St Pancras Hospital. Designed book covers for Virago and Women's Press and showed regularly with Contemporary Portrait Society of which she was a member, RP, ROI and The Heifer Gallery.

Maree ALLITT: *see* **Paul ALLITT** and **MAPMAP**

Paul ALLITT 1952– Artist, born in Kingston upon Hull, Yorkshire, who graduated in fine art from Portsmouth Polytechnic, 1978. Produced the video D H Lawrence and the Culture Industry, 1984; video Making Shakespeare, 1989; and showed in Sense & Sensuality, at Kettle's Yard, Cambridge, 1993; Angels and Mechanics, Tullie House Gallery, Carlisle, 1997; and Minus20 @ www.e-2.org Allitt also co-operated with Maree Allitt as mapmap (see separate entry). Lived in Cambridge.

Douglas ALLSOP 1943– Versatile artist and teacher, born in Watford, Hertfordshire, who attended St Albans School of Art, 1960–4. Allsop from 1995 was tutor in painting at the Royal College of Art, also director of studies at Byam Shaw School of Art. His first geometric colour studies/use of the square and its divisions took place in 1965; in 1970 he created his first objects and installations employing electronic and reflective light systems, and in 1974 his first systematic black objects. Allsop participated in many group shows internationally, especially in Germany. These included Kleine Formate, Galerie Wack, Kaiserslautern, Germany, 1985; Kapil Jariwala Gallery, 1987; Minimal Means, The Showroom/John Hansard Gallery, University of Southampton, 1989; Project 30 x 30, Wilhem-Hack-Museum, Ludwigshafen, Germany, 1994; and Repères, Musée des Ursulines, Mâcon, France, 1997. A steady stream of solo shows began with Maynard Gallery, Welwyn Garden City, 1965, later ones including Laure Genillard Gallery, 1994 and 1998, Galerie Victor Sfez, Paris, 2000, Gallery Niklas von Bartha, 2002 and 2003, and Minimalist acrylic plastic wall objects and screens made of video tape at Kettle's Yard, Cambridge, in 2004. In 2001, there was a 30-year simultaneous retrospective at Städtisches Museum, Gelsenkirchen, and Emschertal Museum, Herne, both in Germany. Tate Gallery, Victoria & Albert Museum (National Art Library), The British Library, Museum of Modern Art in New York, City Museum and Art Gallery in Portsmouth and many other British and foreign collections hold examples. Allsop lived and worked in London from 1975.

George ALLSOP 1911– Painter and teacher, born in Hay, Herefordshire. He attended Farnham Grammar School, Surrey, then studied at the School of Art there under Otway McCannell, 1931–3; Malvern School of Art with Victor Moody, 1935–8; and Birmingham School of Art, 1938–9. Showed at RA, RBA, NEAC and elsewhere and lived in Marple Bridge, Cheshire.

Bruce ALLSOPP 1912–2002 Painter, teacher, writer and publisher, born in Oxford. Trained as an architect at Liverpool University's school of architecture, Allsopp went on to write a number of books about art, design and furniture, including *Style in the Visual Arts* and *A General History of Architecture*. He held several teaching posts, for some years lecturing at Durham University. Married to the painter Florence Cyrilla Woodroffe. He was a master of the Art Workers' Guild and was chairman of Oriel Press. Sometimes signed his work B A. Worthing Art Gallery holds his watercolour Bosham Harbour. Lived in Stocksfield, Northumberland.

Darren ALMOND 1971– Artist, born in Wigan, Lancashire, who graduated in fine art from Winchester School of Art, 1993. Group exhibitions included Southampton Quays, Southampton, 1992; Art & Innovation Prize (winner), ICA, and Something Else, Exmouth Market, both 1996; Sensation, RA, 1997; and its successor there, Apocalypse, 2000. Had a solo exhibition at Crawford Art College, Cork, Ireland, 1991; KNI20, at Great Western Studios, 1995; and in 1997 both ICA/Toshiba Art & Innovation Commission, at ICA, and a one-man show at Jay Jopling/White Cube. In Night as Day, at Tate Britain, 2001–2, Almond revisited the locations of famous paintings by J M W Turner and other masters. In 2003, Almond exhibited polar images at White Cube. Saatchi Collection holds his work. Lived in London.

Will ALSOP 1947– Artist, architect and teacher, born in Northampton where he studied at the School of Art, 1967. As well as being a partner for a time in Will Alsop & John Lyall, architects, Alsop taught at the Architectural Association and in the sculpture department of St Martin's School of Art. He had a special interest in photography and video. Showed at Riverside Studios, Fruitmarket Gallery in Edinburgh and abroad. Lived in London.

Rowland Wright ALSTON 1895–1958 Oil and watercolour painter who was for many years curator of The Watts Gallery, established to commemorate the Victorian painter G F Watts, at Compton, Surrey. Alston studied at the Slade School of Fine Art. Showed at the RA and NEAC, sometimes signing work RWA. Lived at Compton.

Ekkehard ALTENBURGER 1966– Versatile artist, born in Waldshut, West Germany, who served a three-year apprenticeship as a stonemason, restoring medieval buildings. Then studied at Edinburgh College of Art, the Hochschule für Künste in Bremen and at Chelsea College of Art, receiving his master's in 1999. After this he moved between stone carving, video, performance photography, but said: "in my heart I'm a sculptor, and interested in the physical world." Altenburger's unusual and unpredictable ventures included, in 1998, incising a stone slab with the words "High Maintenance Life" and lodging it in the pavement in Cambridge, uninterrupted as "they thought I was a council official." Produced several video installations and had a solo show at the Goethe Institute, in Brazil. He was one of eight shortlisted sculptors for the first Jerwood Sculpture Prize, in 2001.

Dora ALTOUNYAN 1886–1964 Painter, born in Windermere, Westmorland, daughter of artist and archaeologist W G Collingwood, her mother being the miniaturist Edith Mary Dorothy Collingwood, her daughter the painter Mavis Altounyan. W G Collingwood was biographer of John Ruskin, a close friend. From 1903, with her sister Barbara, Dora studied at Cope's Drawing School, from 1905–9 at Reading University, where their father had become professor of art. Tutors included Walter Crane and the Arts and Crafts-oriented curriculum included metalwork and art history. During the five years pre-World War I, she attended La Grande Chaumière, L'Académie Nouvelle and L'Académie de la Palette, in Paris, teachers including G D Desvalières, Jean Metzinger and J D Fergusson, and saw Fauve, Cubist and Futurist pictures. Back in England, Dora had limited exhibiting success before marrying the half-Irish, half-Syrian Armenian doctor Ernest Altounyan, settling in Aleppo, Syria 1919–56, where she brought up her family, helped run a hospital and painted. Churches and archaeological sites, her family, the local population and visitors, such as the writers Agatha Christie and Arthur Ransome, were subjects. She also painted colourful images of England on visits, and was elected to the Lake Artists' Society in 1934. After expulsion from Syria Dora returned to Lakeland where at Kendal's Abbot Hall Art Gallery in 1989 she was part of a three-woman show. Two of her pictures are displayed at Clouds Hill, Dorset, the National Trust-run home of T E Lawrence, who was a friend of the Altounyans.

Mavis ALTOUNYAN 1920–1998 Artist producing figurative and abstract work, the third of five Altounyan children made famous by Arthur Ransome as joint dedicatees of his book *Swallows and Amazons*, stemming from 1928 Lake District sailing adventures. She was known in the story and in life as Titty, because of her love of Beatrix Potter's *The Tale of Mrs Tittlemouse*. Her father was an art-loving doctor, Ernest Altounyan, based in Syria, where Mavis was born in Aleppo; her painter mother Dora Collingwood was daughter of John Ruskin's biographer W G Collingwood. After education in England, Mavis was a star pupil under Henry Moore at Chelsea School of Art, studies interrupted by World War II work for a news agency in Jerusalem. While helping to run the hospital founded by her grandfather in Syria, in 1954 Mavis married Melkon Guzelian (pronounced Goozellyan), a refugee from Armenia. When political pressures forced her and her father to leave Syria she settled with her parents at her childhood home at Lanehead, in the Lakes area. Melkon worked as a motor mechanic in Windermere. Family commitments, asthma and her diffidence and self-criticism restricted Mavis' artistic output. The Guzelians latterly lived in Bradford, Yorkshire.

Meyer Daniel ALTSON 1881–1965 Painter, decorative artist and printmaker, born in Middlesbrough, Yorkshire, who studied art at Melbourne National Gallery, gaining a scholarship at 16; and in Paris at Atelier Colarossi and L'École Nationale des Beaux-Arts. Showed a series of portraits at RA between 1925–41, also exhibiting in the provinces. His brother was the artist Abbey Altson. Lived in London.

ALVA 1901–1973 Artist, born in Berlin, Germany, as Siegfried Alweiss, to Austrian parents. At his Jewish school his art master, Otto Geismar, gave encouragement. After a poor academic start, in 1919 he entered Kern's Konservatorium to prepare for the State Academy to become a professional musician, but left the Academy to take over his father's raincoat factory. When it closed, he turned to commercial art for a living and in 1925 went to life classes run by the Freie Secession, signing his work Alva. In Paris in 1928 Alva attended the Atelier Colarossi, sold work and then between 1929–32 travelled through France, Switzerland and Italy. After selling works at Salon d'Automne in Paris in 1933, in 1934 travelled in Palestine, Syria and Greece, having a first solo show at Maskit Gallery, Tel-Aviv. In 1938 Alva settled in England, becoming a naturalised British citizen, but was interned in the Isle of Man in 1940. Had a solo show at Leger Gallery in 1943, after which he had numerous exhibitions internationally, sometimes working from a studio in Paris. In 1973, the year of his solo exhibition at Waddington Galleries, he published his autobiography *With Pen and Brush* which was liberally illustrated. Ben Uri Art Society holds examples of Alva's work, which could be formalised or calligraphic, then from 1969 was strong, based on the nude female figure. Lived in London.

Javiad ALVI 1957– Alvi graduated with honours from Hornsey School of Art, 1983, attending the Royal Academy Schools and winning a Dutch Government Scholarship in 1986. After showing solo at Essex University in 1975 and appearing in New Contemporaries at ICA in 1982, Alvi participated in a group show at The Square Gallery, 1987, and East End Open Studios, based at Vyner Street Arts, in 1989.

Tariq ALVI 1965– Artist, born in Newcastle upon Tyne and raised in Newham, east London. He did an art and design foundation course at the Community College, 1988–9; then studied fine art at University of Brighton, 1989–92; and Jan van Eyck Akademie, Maastricht, Netherlands, where he settled in Rotterdam. In Temporary Accommodation at Whitechapel Art Gallery, 2001, Alvi produced works based on newspapers, magazines, club flyers and hundreds of photographs. Other group appearances included Quarters, Old Bonnefanton Museum, Maastricht, 1995; Pictures of Lily, 30 Underwood Street, 1997; and Black Met White, ANP, Antwerp, Belgium, 1999. Solo exhibitions included Gate Foundation, Amsterdam, 2000.

Siegfried ALWEISS: *see* **ALVA**

William ALWYN 1905–1985 Composer, flautist, teacher, painter and writer, born in Northampton, who from the age of 15 studied flute with Daniel Wood and composition with John McEwen at the Royal Academy of Music. In 1926 he became professor of composition there, in 1927 joining the London Symphony Orchestra as a flautist, combining the two careers for a decade. From 1936 Alwyn was a prolific composer of film scores, by his death having worked on 86 feature films, notably with the director Carol Reed, and 107 documentaries. The former included *The Way Ahead*, 1944, with Reed, and with him also *The Fallen Idol*, 1948, and *The Running Man*, 1963. Among the documentaries were the director and artist Humphrey Jennings' 1942 Crown Film Unit classic *Fires Were Started* and the David MacDonald-directed *Desert Victory*, 1943, which *Variety* called "The greatest battle film of the war". Composing for films honed Alwyn's technique, which was well demonstrated in his five symphonies plus additional instrumental, choral and vocal works. As a composer Alwyn was self-critical, some of the major pre-World War II scores which had been suppressed by him being revived and recorded only after he died. Strength of emotion was a strong characteristic of Alwyn's music, painting and writing. After his death his work was promoted by The William Alwyn Foundation. In 1979 Alwyn showed his paintings with sculpture by Lesley Scott at Halesworth Gallery in Suffolk. In addition, when Chandos issued its long series of compact discs of his music it astutely chose to feature Alwyn's pictures on the cover. Thus in 1993 CHAN 9155, of the first symphony and first piano concerto, featured his painting Dartmoor; CHAN 9187, of the third symphony and violin concerto, his picture Stubble Field; and CHAN 9196, of the fifth symphony and second piano concerto, his painting The Magic Mountain. Alwyn's wife was the composer Doreen Carwithen. CHAN 9524, issued in 1997, featuring her orchestral works, was accompanied by Alwyn's Portrait of my Wife, and CHAN 9596, 1998, of her first and second string quartets and violin sonata, illustrated Alwyn's Portrait of Doreen Carwithen.

Ray AMBROSE 1927–1989 Painter, draughtsman, printmaker and teacher, born in Grays, Essex, married to the artist Moyra Gilchrist. He studied at South-East Essex Technical College and School of Art in Dagenham, 1955, teachers including John Wellings, then at Royal Academy Schools, 1955–6, under Peter Greenham. Taught in London and showed in mixed exhibitions with Young Contemporaries, Upper Street Gallery and Orion Gallery, Penzance, also having many solo shows. Sometimes signed work with initials. Nuffield Foundation and Copenhagen Institute hold examples. Lived in Newlyn, Cornwall, and died at Penzance railway station.

Glenys AMBRUS 1936– Figurative artist, illustrator and teacher who gained her diploma in painting and printmaking at Walthamstow School of Art, studying painting at the Royal College of Art. In 1959, she won the John Murray Award. Like her husband, Victor Ambrus, she was a book illustrator, notably for children, and taught adults part-time. Was a member of PS.

Victor AMBRUS 1935– Book illustrator, graphic designer and teacher, born in Budapest, Hungary, where he studied at the Academy of Fine Art. Arriving in England following the uprising of 1956, Ambrus further studied at Royal College of Art, 1957–60. He taught graphic design at West Surrey College of Art in Farnham. Although he showed at RA and RE, of which he was a fellow, Ambrus was mainly a book illustrator, with several hundred titles to his credit, some of them his own. Military and naval subjects were favoured by him. America's Library of Congress, Washington, holds his work. Lived in Fleet Hampshire, later in Farnham and Runfold, Surrey.

Shenda AMERY fl. from mid-1970s– Figurative sculptor, painter and draughtsman, brought up in Essex, who studied chemistry at college and married an architect who was a pupil of Frank Lloyd Wright in America. Amery studied there with a Japanese artist. Lived in the Middle East for 18 years, returning to London in 1978, sharing her time between a flat in Chelsea and an old mill-house in Cambridgeshire. Originally exhibited as a painter, group shows including Institute of Women Painters, Teheran, Iran, 1975; Loggia Gallery, 1978 (she was a member of the Society of Free Painters and Sculptors); and Trends, Mall Galleries, 1979. Later solo painting shows included Loggia, 1978. Turned to sculpture, mixed exhibitions including Chelsea Art Society, of which she was a member. Had a series of solo sculpture exhibitions at The Orangery, Holland Park. For the Chelsea Conservative Association made a portrait bust of prime minister Margaret Thatcher, presented to her at 10 Downing Street in 1981.

Paul AMEY 1957– Sculptor, born and lived in Oxford, who attended Oxford Polytechnic, 1975, then Hornsey College of Art, 1976–9. He was a founder-member of Oxford Artist Group, 1983–92; Oxford Sculpture Project, 1987; and Chiltern Sculpture Trust, 1990. Took part in many mixed exhibitions, including Camden Annual, 1983; Mappin Art Gallery, Sheffield, 1984; The Day Book Travelling Exhibition, 1988; Museum of Modern Art, Oxford, 1992; and Galerie Horst Dietrich, Berlin, 1995. Had a solo show at Oxford Gallery, Oxford, 1983, later ones including Galerie III, Nijmegen, Netherlands, 1994, and Beaux Arts, Bath, 1995. Installations/Projects included Artweek 83, Oxford, 1983, then subsequent Artweeks; Trustland Sculpture Project II, Oxford, 1989; and Europees Keramisch Werkcentrum, 's Hertogenbosch, Netherlands, artist-in-residence, 1994. Commissions included Wouthill Park Youth Centre, Bracknell, 1984; Basingstoke Hospital, 1988; and House & Smoke multiple for Living Stone Press, The Hague, Netherlands, and Galerie Horst Dietrich, 1994. In his work Amey took objects out of their everyday context: a snake becomes smoke out of a chimney; fish take the place of leaves on a tree; an aeroplane appears to fly out of a wooden head, attached by an umbilical cord. Identity and relationships were questioned.

Maria Ajike AMIDU 1967– Artist, notably in glass and ceramics, born in London, who did a foundation course at St Helens College of Art & Design, Merseyside, 1985–6; gained an honours degree in three-dimensional design at West Surrey College of Art, Farnham, 1986–9; then her master's in glass and ceramics at Royal College of Art, 1990–2. Among awards were the Wingate Scholarship and Eduardo Paolozzi Travel Bursary, both 1991; Prince's Youth Business Trust Award, 1995; and S G Warburg Grant, 1996. Exhibitions included Crafts Council Glass Show, 1993; New Light, Solomon Gallery, Dublin, 1996; Expo Gas International I, Tucson, Arizona, 1997; and 198 Gallery. Victoria & Albert Museum Pilkington Collection holds her work.

Ernest AMOR 1889–1967 Figurative artist producing colourful, naïvely charming scenes of London, where he lived, and the southeast coast. A lifelong bachelor, Amor was a director of a family leather goods manufacturing firm. After being commissioned in the Artists' Rifles and wounded in France in 1917, he studied at Slade School of Fine Art in the mid-1920s, contemporary with Rex Whistler. Between the wars he was a keen territorial in Queen Victoria's Rifles, winning the Territorial Decoration. During World War II, Amor was commandant of a prisoner-of-war camp in England. Exhibited 11 works at RA Summer Exhibition, 1954–64. Sold pictures to many well-known people, including the film actor Cary Grant, who gave some to Prince Rainier of Monaco. Bonhams & Brooks, Lots Road, sold a collection of Amor's works in 2000.

Blair ANDERSON 1967– Painter, born in Glasgow, who studied at Gray's School of Art in Aberdeen and who won an Elizabeth Greenshields Foundation Award, 1993. Group shows included New Generation at Compass Gallery, 1989; Olympia Art Fair, 1990; Trinity Gallery, 1991; and Royal Over-Seas League Open, 1995. Had a solo show at Byzantium Gallery, Edinburgh, 1990, later ones including Rendezvous Gallery, Aberdeen, 1995.

Charles ANDERSON 1936– Painter of landscape and still life in acrylic and watercolour who gained his diploma at Glasgow School of Art, 1959, eventually working as a professional artist on major art and design projects throughout the United Kingdom. Clients included local authorities, property developers, banks and insurance companies. Anderson designed what was at that time claimed to be the tallest sculpture in the United Kingdom, at the headquarters entrance hall of Scottish Amicable Life Assurance, Craigforth. Exhibited at RSW, Royal Glasgow Institute of the Fine Arts, regularly at the annual exhibition of Scottish art at Wren Gallery, Burford, and elsewhere in England and Scotland, as well as having solo shows.

Christopher ANDERSON 1914– Sculptor, painter and teacher, born in Yorkley, Gloucestershire. Studied at Lydney School of Art, at Royal College of Art under Richard Garbe and at Goldsmiths' College School of Art. Taught sculpture at Hornsey School of Art and at Borough Polytechnic. Showed at RA, LG and in the provinces. Lived in London.

Douglas ANDERSON 1934– Portrait painter who studied with Pietro Annigoni in Florence. For a time Anderson lived in London, was a member of Chelsea Arts Club and ran Douglas Anderson Ltd, later moving to Pisa, Italy. Showed at RP and RA, in 1965 Summer Exhibition showing a portrait of HM The Queen.

Gary ANDERSON 1952– After graduating with honours from Manchester Polytechnic, 1976–9, Anderson attended the Slade School of Fine Art, 1979–81. A series of solo exhibitions followed: New Gallery, 1984; Tom Allen Centre, 1985; and Vortex Gallery, 1986. In 1989, he was included in East End Open Studios, based in Robinson Road.

Gary ANDERSON 1960– Painter and draughtsman, born in Baillieston, Glasgow. Anderson studied at Glasgow School of Art, 1980–4, gaining a fine art honours degree. He had early success, winning the John D Kelly Award at the Glasgow School in 1981. Further awards included D W T Cargill Award (under 30), in 1984, and Arthur Young Exhibitionship Prize, 1987, both at Royal Glasgow Institute of the Fine Arts; and in 1989 the Elizabeth Greenshields Foundation Award and the Arts in Fife Purchase Award, Fife House Collection. In 1984 Anderson showed in mixed exhibitions at Compass Gallery in Glasgow and Open Eye Gallery and Mercury, both in Edinburgh, and many other group shows soon followed. His first solo show was at Corners Gallery, Glasgow, 1985, then from the early 1990s Ewan Mundy Fine Art showed Anderson in Glasgow, London and New York. Anderson's work showed fine draughtsmanship, rich colour in the Glasgow tradition and a quirky imaginative streak drawing on such sources as Chinese watercolours and the circus. Lived in Glasgow.

Harry ANDERSON 1923– Artist in various media and teacher, born in Selkirk, Selkirkshire. He studied at Edinburgh College of Art. Gained a post-diploma scholarship and a travelling scholarship to Europe. He taught for London County Council and Harlow Technical College. Showed with AIA Gallery from 1957; Douglas and Foulis Gallery, Edinburgh, 1964; and in 1965 he was included in The Visual Arts, Harlow Arts Festival. Latterly, with his wife, the ceramist Sally Anderson, he was based at Parndon Mill, Harlow, and exhibited at Old Harlow Arts Centre. Glasgow University holds his work.

Janette ANDERSON 1938–1996 Painter of exuberant and colourful still lifes and landscapes in the Scottish Colourist tradition. Studied at Glasgow School of Art under William Drummond, Geoffrey Squire and David Donaldson, graduating with a diploma in drawing and painting, 1956–60, with a post-diploma, 1961. Exhibited at RSA, Royal Glasgow Institute of the Fine Arts, SSWA, and elsewhere in mixed shows. Later solo shows included Lillie Art Gallery, Milngavie, 1992; Torrance Gallery, Edinburgh, 1994; and Duncan Campbell Contemporary Art, 1996, this show finished two days before the artist's death. Many private collections in Britain and abroad hold her work, once described by a critic as "if painted at the wheel of a fast car, the paint flung on with impetuous abandon". She was married to the painter Ralph Anderson.

John ANDERSON 1926– Designer and painter, born in Borrowash, Derbyshire, who studied at Harrow School of Art, his teachers including Maurice de Sausmarez and Christopher Sanders, 1939–43 and 1947–9. Went on to run Anderson Art Studios. He showed at Young Contemporaries, RA and RBA. Lived for a time at Northwood, Middlesex.

Kay ANDERSON 1902– Painter and versatile printmaker who married the artist Thomas Clough. She was a qualified art teacher who studied at Liverpool School of Art and the Royal College of Art under William Rothenstein. Exhibited RA, NEAC, provincial galleries, in France and North America. British Museum holds her work. Lived in London.

Lindsay ANDERSON 1947– Artist, born in Edgbaston, Birmingham, who attended Sutton Coldfield School of Art, 1963–5, then gained a first-class honours degree in sculpture from Leeds College of Art, 1965–8. After a dozen years, Anderson returned to work as an artist in 1980, beginning with drawings and etchings, then in 1988 began to carve and paint simple boxes, which became more narrative and evolved into the panels for which she became known. These were in limewood, painted, and for her were "a kind of drawing with chisels". They expressed a semi-autobiographical narrative, involving mysterious dreaming women, standing winged guardian seraphim and strange, serene faces. Mixed shows included Scottish Gallery, Edinburgh, 1990; The Woodcarver's Art, Crafts Council tour, and Christmas Show, Ruskin Gallery in Sheffield, both 1993; and Fish, Hove Museum and Art Gallery, 1995. Had a solo show at England & Co, 1996. Contemporary Art Society; John Makepeace, at Parnham House and Gallery; and Hampshire Museums Service own examples. From 1995 Anderson lived in London.

Madeleine ANDERSON 1910–1976 Painter and printmaker, born in Belvedere, Kent. She studied at Airdrie Academy, in Lanarkshire, then art at Kingston School of Art, 1931–2, with James Anthony Betts and John Gerald Platt, and Royal College of Art, 1932–4, where her teachers included Gilbert Spencer. Showed at NEAC and elsewhere and had a studio at Lechlade, Gloucestershire. Notable flower painter. Ministry of Works and Cheltenham Art Gallery bought her work.

Margaret ANDERSON 1926–1998 Portrait painter and miniaturist, born in Newport, Monmouthshire, also known as Margaret Anderson-Rees. She studied at Newport Polytechnic, 1944, and went on to exhibit with RMS, PS, RA and elsewhere. Lived in Everton, Hampshire.

Ralph ANDERSON 1927– Painter and teacher, born in Australia, boyhood spent in rural Norfolk, whose pictures reflected his life, work and extensive travels. Completed diploma and post-diploma studies at Glasgow School of Art, 1945–50, teachers including Drummond Bone, Douglas Percy Bliss, Gilbert Spencer and William Armour. After six months' travelling on the continent in 1951, having won an Abbey Minor Travelling Scholarship, Anderson was on the visiting staff of the Glasgow School for eight years and of Carlisle College of Art, 1958–9; then taught at Bearsden Academy, 1960–73, and Whitburn Academy, 1973–92. During summer vacations worked on Scottish lighthouses. Anderson won a RSA Award, 1953, and was Prix de Rome Exhibitor, Imperial Institute, 1955. Showed widely in Scotland and had solo exhibitions at Duncan Campbell Contemporary Art, from 1998. Anderson's picture of the Scottish National Orchestra performing was held at the Henry Wood Hall, Glasgow. Lived in Muirhead, near Glasgow, where he believed in daily drawing and painting. He was married to the artist Janette Anderson.

Sally ANDERSON 1933– Abstract sculptor who studied at Edinburgh College of Art. Her first job was as a technical assistant at Central School of Arts and Crafts. She organised the First Group, five artists who exhibited at municipal galleries in England and gave talks on patronage at the towns visited; also helped to arrange the Resolution 42 exhibition following the Trades Union Congress decision to support the arts; and then Thesis 80, an organisation to promote the visual arts. She showed with 57 Gallery, Edinburgh, in 1959; AIA Gallery from 1961; and in 1965 was included in Harlow Arts Festival's The Visual Arts. Latterly, like her artist husband Harry Anderson, she was based at Parndon Mill, Harlow, and as Sally Anderson Ceramics designed and produced often large murals.

Stanley ANDERSON 1884–1966 Engraver and painter. Born in Bristol, the son of an engraver Alfred E Anderson, Stanley had his initial art education in the city, having been apprenticed to his father's business as an heraldic engraver at 15. He attended the Royal College of Art, 1909–11, and Goldsmiths' College School of Art, but insisted that he was greatly self-educated in art, especially in the British Museum and National Gallery. From the time he won a British Institution Engraving Scholarship in 1909 Anderson marked his course as an outstanding engraver. His delineation of several dozen country craft subjects, which occupied about 20 years from the early 1930s, is a remarkable record, the engravings being meticulously accurate and beautifully composed. Anderson was for many years a member of the engraving faculty at the British School at Rome and in 1938 was chosen by the British Council as the sole British representative of line engraving and drypoint at the Venice Biennale. Elected RA 1941. Anderson won many medals and other awards. His work has been bought widely by British Commonwealth and American galleries and museums. Abbott and Holder had the first show of Anderson's etchings for 60 years in 1995. Lived near Aylesbury, Buckinghamshire.

William ANDERSON 1905–1999 Largely self-taught watercolourist, engineer and soldier, born in Ramsgate, Kent. After attending Rugby School as a scholar, then the Royal Military Academy, Woolwich, where he won the King's Medal for best academic achievement, Anderson gained a first-class honours degree in mechanical sciences at Cambridge. From 1927 was a junior sapper in India's Northwest Frontier area, being made Member of the British Empire, 1937, and winning the Military Cross (MC), 1938. When World War II broke out, Anderson with the Royal Engineers engaged in intensive fighting in France; captured outside Dunkirk, in 1940 winning a bar to his MC, he was eventually sent to Colditz Castle. Painting had fascinated him from childhood, and he now used his artistic talents in two ways: to forge documents and make clothing to aid escapers, make a camera out of old spectacles and repair fighter ace Douglas Bader's artificial legs; and to record the life of the camp, sending work home to his wife, the cellist Kathleen Hunt, to raise awareness of prisoners' needs. A French artist helped him reappraise his style. Shortly before Anderson's death, his son put a selection of his paintings on the Colditz website (www.cimttz.tu-chemnitz.de/colditz). After the war, Anderson served in India and Tanganyika, was appointed chief engineer Malaya Command with the rank of brigadier, being made Commander of the British Empire in 1956, holding a final military appointment as chief engineer, Northern Command, York. As a civilian he worked in surveying and engineering, finally with Costain. After retirement in 1971 Anderson organised volunteers to convert the derelict Farnham Maltings into an arts centre and persuaded the council to abandon a flyover scheme. Continuing to paint, he marked his approaching ninety-second birthday with a retrospective to raise funds for the organ of St Margaret's Lee Church in Blackheath, where he lived.

Margaret ANDERSON-REES: *see* **Margaret ANDERSON**

Eileen ANDERTON 1924– Artist in various media who was born and lived in Bradford, Yorkshire, her father being a teacher of art. Studied at local School of Art, 1939–44, her teachers including Vincent Lines. Showed at SWA, RWS, at City Art Gallery in Bradford and elsewhere in north of England, including Bradford Arts Club of which she was a member.

Michael ANDERTON 1972– Artist employing a wide range of media and materials for whom the imagery of the scooter was important. He studied art and design at Ipswich School of Art, 1990–2, graduated with honours in fine art from the University of Northumbria in Newcastle upon Tyne, 1992–5; then obtained his master's in multidisciplinary printmaking at University of the West of England, Bristol, 1998–01. Exhibitions included RWA Autumn Exhibition, 2000; MA Printmaking, Create Centre, Bristol, 2001; and Over The River, firstsite, Colchester/Wolsey Art Gallery, Ipswich, 2002. Anderton also worked to commission.

Athene ANDRADE 1908–c.1975 Painter, teacher and printmaker who studied at Central School of Arts and Crafts and Bromley and Beckenham School of Art. She showed at RA, SWA, NS and elsewhere. Many of Andrade's subjects had a stage connection, as indicated by a collection of her pictures offered by Rosebery's, the West Norwood auctioneers, in 2002. She taught in the London area, including London County Council schools. Lived in Bromley, Kent.

ANDREA & PHILIPPE: *see* **Philippe BRADSHAW**

Conrad R ANDREAE 1871–1956 Landscape watercolourist, born in London, who was educated at Osborne House in Margate and in Germany. Attended Slade School of Fine

Art, where he won a first-class certificate in figure painting, and at Académie Julian, Paris. Exhibited at RA and Walker Art Gallery in Liverpool, being principally known for his views of England and France. Settled in Brighton, Sussex, where he was a member of the Arts Club and where the Museum and Art Gallery holds watercolours of the beach by him.

Margaret ANDRESEN 1951– Watercolourist and illustrator, born in Dunfermline, Fife. Studied at Duncan of Jordanstone College of Art in Dundee, 1969–75. Had one-man shows in Scotland, including Stirling Gallery. Lived in Glasgow.

Charles Edwin ANDREW 1911–1996 Painter, almost exclusively in oil, and carver of stylised sculptures, born in Bristol, whose natural diffidence probably impeded his establishing a better reputation in his lifetime. Apart from some experiments in abstraction, Andrew took his inspiration from the local scenery of Bristol, Wales, Warwickshire and the Cotswolds, where he finally lived in Chipping Campden, Gloucestershire, from 1990. He was elected RWA and also showed at RA Summer Exhibition. The RWA has works by Andrew in its reserve collection and others were sold at Bristol Auction Rooms in 2001 to support the RWA Appeal.

David ANDREW 1934– Painter, draughtsman and teacher, born in Redruth, Cornwall, living finally in the county at Mousehole. He attended Falmouth School of Art, 1954–8, then the Slade School of Fine Art, 1958–9, but left early, finding his tutor there Claude Rogers unsympathetic. Andrew then did a variety of jobs, including teaching at Bournemouth and Portsmouth Schools of Art, finally becoming associate professor in the art department at Queen's University, Canada, 1971–96. While there he travelled annually to Cornwall and elsewhere and painting assiduously, after retirement using a mobile home to paint around the coasts of North America. Andrew had numerous exhibitions in Canada and America, where his work is in many public and corporate collections. Colour theory and abstraction were interests and his solo show at Messum's in 2006 comprised richly coloured, rather gestural landscapes and was accompanied by a well-illustrated catalogue.

Keith ANDREW 1947– Artist and designer, born in London. He studied at Ravensbourne College of Art & Design, Bromley, his teachers including Michael Tyzack. Worked as a graphic designer for eight years before returning to painting full-time in 1975. This coincided with his move to Holyhead, Anglesey. His exhibitions included RA Summer Exhibition, 1981; Bangor Art Gallery and National Eisteddfod, Swansea, 1982; Mid-Wales Open, 1984, where he won a prize; Prints from Wales, Wenniger Graphics, Boston, 1987; Artists in the National Parks, Victoria & Albert Museum, 1988; The Last Dance, Oriel Theatr Clwyd, 1995; Afon Conwy, National Library of Wales, 1997; National Print Exhibition, Mall Galleries, 2002; and The Chapel Gallery, Llangollen, 2004. Later solo shows included New Directions, an Oriel Mon, Anglesey, tour, 1999–00, and Farmer Street Studio, Anglesey, 2004. In 1981 Andrew was elected a full member of RCamA, from 1993–5 being its vice-president. In 1996, Andrew was shortlisted for the Fine Art Trade Guild Published Artists Award; in 1997, he joined a trade mission to Japan with the Welsh Office and was invited artist at the International Art Symposium, Saalkries, East Germany. CASW, University of Wales in Swansea and University of Wales print collection, Aberystwyth, hold his work.

Neale ANDREW 1958– Notably a portrait sculptor, born in Northampton. He trained at Blackpool College of Art and graduated with an honours degree in fine art from Trent Polytechnic, Nottingham, in 1980. His sporting portraits included the cricketer Geoff Boycott, the golfer Tony Jacklin and footballer Gary Lineker. Major commissions included a bronze for Newark town commemorating the Civil War and the D H Lawrence Memorial for the author's study centre in Nottingham. His work was cast by The Morris Singer Foundry. Among later figures produced were a bronze portrait bust of the cricketer Sir Alec Bedser for Surrey County Cricket Club, and Robin and Marian, two life-size bronze figures of Robin Hood and Maid Marian, Edwinstowe, all 1998; and a life-size bronze of the Olympic oarsman Sir Steven Redgrave, 2002.

Sarah ANDREW 1965– Versatile artist, born in Manchester, who qualified as a lawyer and worked at the BBC. Studied fine art and critical theory at Central St Martins College of Art & Design. Combined printmaking, painting and specific-site installations at Glassworks. Andrew was included in Art on show, The Gallery in Cork Street, 2001.

Arthur Henry ANDREWS 1906–1966 Painter, printmaker and teacher, born in London, married to the artist Sushila Singh. They were fellow students at Hornsey School of Art and Royal College of Art under William Rothenstein, graduating in 1929. He held a number of teaching posts in Sheffield and Derby Colleges of Art and Batley School of Art, eventually being principal of Poole College of Further Education and art adviser to Dorset Education Committee. He showed at Foyles Gallery and at public galleries in Bradford and Leeds one-man, also in group exhibitions at RA, Grabowski and Redfern Galleries. He was made a member of Design and Industries Association in 1934, SWE in 1935. Sir Edward Marsh held his work, as did Victoria & Albert Museum and public galleries in Leeds, Bournemouth and Southport. Lived latterly in Bournemouth, Hampshire.

Christopher ANDREWS 1952– Artist in photography, film and video and teacher, born in Essex. He studied at Sir George Williams University, Montreal, and London College of Printing, going on to teach there and at Southend School of Art and Design. Andrews' exhibitions and screenings included the Arts Council travelling show New British Image; Acme Gallery; Tokyo Video Festival, Japan; Atelier St Anne, Brussels; The Basement, Newcastle; and in 1983 the Goldsmiths' show at Woodlands Art Gallery. ICA Video Library, London Video Arts Library and Sheffield City Polytechnic hold his work.

Edith Alice ANDREWS fl. from c.1900– Painter of portraits, still life, landscape and especially gardens and flowers, illustrator and miniaturist, at first known under her maiden name Edith Alice Cubitt. Studied art at Goldsmiths' College School, winning silver and gold medals, also other prizes. Illustrated children's books for Blackie, Cassell and Oxford University Press and had work used for publicity by Great Western Railway. Exhibited at RA (including several portraits of her son, Edward),

1914–54, also at RI, SWA, Walker Art Gallery in Liverpool and Paris Salon. Queen Mary bought Andrews' picture Old Rose Bush. Was a keen gardener, living from the 1930s at Pembury, Kent.

Edith Lovell ANDREWS 1886–1980 Painter and poster designer, born in Newport, Monmouthshire. She studied at Glasgow School of Art, 1908–10, under Fra Newbery, then with Gerald Massey at Heatherley's School of Fine Art, 1911–14. Miss Lovell Andrews showed extensively abroad as well as in Britain, notably in St Ives, Cornwall, where she lived and was a member of St Ives Arts Club, the Society of Artists and had a solo show in 1957. British Museum holds her work.

Eileen ANDREWS 1897– Painter, craft worker and teacher, notable for her watercolours, born in West Bridgford, Nottinghamshire, as Dorothy Eileen Andrews. She studied at Northampton School of Art, 1916–21, under Oswald Crompton, then with William Rothenstein at Royal College of Art, 1921–3. Then taught at Leyton School of Art and Borough Polytechnic until 1938, when she began 25 years at South-West Essex Technical College School of Art, Walthamstow. Showed at NS, ROI, Russell-Cotes Art Gallery, Bournemouth, and elsewhere. Lived in Woodford Green, Essex, for many years.

Florence Christine ANDREWS 1905– Decorative painter and artist in lacquer, born in Ipswich where she continued to live. She studied at the local Art School with the watercolourist George Rushton and showed in the Ipwich area.

Jane ANDREWS fl. from mid-1990s– Painter, whose figurative pictures could have an amusing-grotesque quality, as in her contribution to Eight by Eight, at Pallant House, Chichester, 1997. She obtained a fine art honours degree at West Surrey College of Art & Design, Farnham, 1991–4. Mixed exhibitions included Fresh Art, Islington, where she was shortlisted for a Space Award, 1994, and No Turkeys, Raw Gallery, 1995. Had solo exhibitions at Sadler's Wells, 1995 and 1996, with one titled Jamboree at Piano Nobile, 1997. Lived in Milford, Surrey.

Kerry John ANDREWS 1956– Artist, composer, designer and freelance lecturer on the history of art and design, who studied at Ruskin School of Drawing, 1976–9, gaining his master's in fine art from Goldsmiths' College, 1981–3. Having originally concentrated on visual art, he later turned to the practice and theory of music, as well as graphic and sound computer programmes. He was interested in work that had no single medium, that transferred ideas across forms and languages, creating pieces that resided outside their physical "forms". An exploration of time and space through stillness and non-linearity as well as a keen interest in contemporary physics were central to these works. From the early 1980s Andrews took part in numerous group shows, later ones including The Contemporary Print Fair at Atlantis Gallery and European Technology Fair, Frankfurt, Germany, both 1999; Digital Expressions, Welsh tour, and Art Innsbruck, 5, Internationale Kunstmesse, Austria, both 2000; Raw Canvas, Aldwych, 2001; and Kunst 2002, Zürich, Switzerland, 2002. He had a series of solo shows at Colville Place Gallery, among later ones there being the Red Earth Series, 2001, also showing at Galerie der Gegenwart, Wiesbaden, Germany, 2002. As a composer, Andrews had a series of works performed, latterly *Piano Field; Lontano*, 2000, Bretton Hall; *Elements*, 2001, IXION Ensemble concert, Bretton Hall, 2001; and *Heidelberg/Ulm Meditation*, 2001, St Cyprian's Church. He performed in concerts, broadcasts and recordings, venues including the ICA, BBC Radio 3, Huddersfield, Spitalfields and Brighton and Hoxton New Music Festivals, Queen Elizabeth Hall and Tate Liverpool. Andrews lived in London.

Lea ANDREWS 1958– Artist born in Sonning Common, Oxfordshire. He studied at Banbury School of Art, 1981–2, Brighton Polytechnic, 1982–5, then Slade School of Fine Art, 1985–7. In 1988 he was artist-in-residence at Tooting Bec Hospital. Also in 1988 he shared a show with Robert Mabb at Riverside Studios; in 1989 he was in Behold the Man, at Stills Gallery, Edinburgh, and tour; and 1990 was in The British Art Show, a South Bank Centre touring exhibition. The year before had had a solo show at Battersea Arts Centre called A Change in Thinking. Later mixed exhibitions included The British Art Show 5, Hayward Gallery tour, 2000–1. Andrews' photographic prints focused on imaginary public sculptures to invent a history of where he had lived. Arts Council holds his work. Lived in London.

Leonard Gordon ANDREWS 1885–1960 Painter and designer, born at Lindfield, Sussex. Studied art at Battersea Polytechnic School of Art, 1900–03, under William Thomas; Clapham School of Art, 1903–4; Regent Street Polytechnic School of Art, 1906, under George Gaskell; Birmingham School of Art, 1908; and West Bromwich School of Art, 1909, under J A Pearce. Andrews held a number of art teaching positions in the West Midlands and London areas, finishing with the South-West Essex Technical College School of Art, 1938–50. He exhibited RA, RBA, ROI, NS and RSMA. Lived at Woodford Green, Essex.

Liam ANDREWS 1913– Painter in oil and watercolour who was brought up in Belfast, where he continued to live. Studied at Belfast College of Art, 1930–6, his teachers including the local artist Seamus Stoupe. Exhibited RUA.

Lilian ANDREWS 1878–c.1975 Watercolourist, notably of birds and animals, daughter of the inventor Stephen Rusbridge, born in Brighton where she studied at the School of Art. She gained a bronze medal and later taught there. Married the artist Douglas Sharpus Andrews, principal of Leeds School of Art, who predeceased her by about 30 years in 1944. She was a member of Leeds Art Club. Exhibited at RA, IS, RSA, Paris Salon and widely in the provinces. Nottingham Art Gallery holds her work and Leeds City Art Gallery holds Douglas' watercolour Ingleton and her Peahen and Chick. She lived latterly in London.

Marcia ANDREWS fl. from mid-1960s– Expressionist painter, born in London, who studied at Medway College of Art, 1960–4, with Eric Frankland. She was on the staff of the British Council. Exhibited abroad and with Free Painters and Sculptors of which she was a member, Medway Little Theatre, Corn Exchange in Chesterfield, Cockpit Theatre and Turret Gallery. University of Surrey holds her work, featured in a series of solo exhibitions. Lived in Chatham, Kent.

Michael ANDREWS 1928–1995 Painter and teacher, born in Norwich, Norfolk, attending City of Norwich School. He studied at Slade School of Fine Art, 1949–53, after part-time study at Norwich Art School. In 1953 won Rome Scholarship in painting and Abbey Scholarship. Showed at Beaux Arts Gallery and at ICA in 1952 and had first one-man show at Beaux Arts in 1958. About this time he decorated the Colony Room Club, and early work was concerned with Soho night-life and party-going, but he tired of these subjects. Taught at Norwich, Chelsea and the Slade Schools, 1959–66. Andrews' later work, mixed realism and fantasy, was often concerned with themes, such as balloons over landscapes, tropical fish and Ayers Rock, in Australia. A cerebral, technically accomplished painter highly regarded by his peers, Andrews latterly showed with Anthony d'Offay and had retrospectives at Hayward Gallery in 1980, organised by Arts Council, and Whitechapel Art Gallery in 1991. Tate Gallery holds his work and held a major exhibition in 2001. Andrews returned to the Norwich area from 1977–92, settling finally in London where he died of cancer.

Sybil ANDREWS 1898–1992 Printmaker, painter and teacher, born in Bury St Edmunds, Suffolk, who began painting as a child. While working as a welder in an aircraft factory in 1918 she took John Hassall's art correspondence course, then went to Heatherley's School of Fine Art, taught by Henry Massey. With Cyril Power, the architect, she formed an artistic partnership which lasted until World War II, while serving as first secretary of Grosvenor School of Modern Art. There she met Claude Flight, pioneer Cubist/Futurist lino-cut artist, by whom she was influenced, and she exhibited reguarly between 1928–37 at Redfern and Ward Galleries. Shared a solo show with Power in 1933 at Redfern. During World War II she worked in boatbuilding at Hythe, near Southampton, and made sketches which formed the basis for seven canvases in collection of Royal Air Force Museum, Hendon. In 1947 she married Walter Morgan and they emigrated to Canada, settling in Campbell River, British Columbia, where Andrews painted and taught. She was a member of the Canadian Painter Etchers and the Print and Drawing Council of Canada. Andrews was included in Parkin Gallery's 1975 exhibition Claude Flight and his Circle and in another in 1978 which also toured Italy. In 1982–3 Glenbow Museum, Alberta, gave Andrews a retrospective which toured. Her work is in several Canadian galleries, Los Angeles Museum, Victoria & Albert Museum and British Museum.

Patricia ANGADI 1914–2001 Painter, notable for her portraits, and writer, born and lived in London. She was married to the Indian writer and teacher Ayana Angadi in 1943. Helped with her money and support Ayana Angadi and friends in Hampstead in 1946 founded the Indian Music Circle, later renamed the Asian Music Circle, a principal promoter of Indian music and culture in the West. Patricia Angadi studied at Heatherley's School of Fine Art, 1933–7, her teachers including Frederic Whiting and Bernard Adams. She became chairman of the Hampstead Artists' Council. Showed at RP, SWA, NEAC, Paris Salon and elsewhere. Birkbeck College holds her portrait of the philosopher C E M Joad and the Maxton Memorial Committee bought that of the Socialist Member of Parliament James Maxton for presentation to the City of Glasgow. Angadi began writing aged 70, publishing her first novel, *The Governess*, in 1985. For the next decade she produced about one novel a year, her own bohemian life an inspiration.

John ANGEL 1881–1960 Sculptor, born at Newton Abbot, Devon. Studied at Exeter College of Art, Lambeth School of Art and the Royal Academy Schools, where he gained several awards, followed by studies in Italy and Greece. Worked in the studio of Sir George Frampton for several years. Exhibited RA, RSA, Royal Glasgow Institute of the Fine Arts and overseas. In the mid-1920s went to live at Sandy Hook, Connecticut. Angel, who was elected a fellow of the RBS, did a volume of work in England and American churches.

Marie ANGEL 1923– Illustrator and calligrapher who studied at Croydon School of Art, 1940–5, then at Royal College of Art design school, 1945–8. Showed at RA, with Society of Designer Craftsmen and widely in America, where she had solo exhibitions. Illustrated a number of books, notably in America. Victoria & Albert Museum and Harvard College Library hold her work. Lived in Warlingham, Surrey.

Cristiana ANGELINI 1937– Painter in oil, draughtsman and teacher, born in Tuscany, Italy. She studied at the Scuola di Belle Arti in Carrara in 1952 and travelled widely through Africa in the late 1950s. Moved to England in 1963, becoming a British citizen. Settled in London. Figure compositions, townscapes and large interiors featured in her work, which had a strong sense of draughtsmanship and mood. From the early 1970s she appeared in many mixed shows, including South London Art Gallery from 1981, Whitechapel Art Gallery Open in 1984, Celebration of London at Smiths Galleries, 1988, and in 1990 she gained first prize for London and South-East Region in Laing Collection Exhibition. Among later mixed exhibitions were Thompson's Gallery, 1992, Southwark Festival, from 1994, RA Summer Exhibition, from 1997, and Valleys of Vision at The Gallery, Southwark Park, 2001. Had solo shows at Woodlands Art Gallery, 1978, Greenwich Theatre Gallery, 1982, Sweet Waters Gallery, 1989, Lyrical Landscapes at Obelisk Gallery, 1991, Timeless Harvest at Heifer Gallery, 1995, Greenwich Visitor Centre, 2001, and Summer Amongst the Reeds, Chapel Gallery, Hall Place and Gardens, Bexley, 2004. Bridgeman Art Library holds her work. From 1985 taught in adult education.

Ethel Elizabeth ANGELL fl. from c.1930– Painter and teacher. Studied at Nuneaton Art School under John Park and Alfred Jones. Exhibited RA, RBSA, ROI and with Warwickshire Society of Artists. Lived at Nuneaton, Warwickshire.

Mea ANGERER 1905– Artist in pen and ink and gouache, but primarily a designer of textiles. Born in Vienna, where she studied at the Academy of Applied Art, Angerer in Britain worked for several bodies connected with textile production, as well as for the 1951 Festival of Britain. Signed work MEA. It is held by the Victoria & Albert Museum. Lived in London.

Christine ANGUS 1953– Sculptor, born in Grimsby, Lincolnshire. She worked for BMW from 1971–3, then in 1974–8 attended Brighton Polytechnic to study sculpture. From 1979 she was self-employed, taking part in a number of group exhibitions. These included Basingstoke Arts Festival, 1982 Serpentine Summer Show and in 1983 she participated in Welsh Sculpture Trust's Margam exhibition, Sculpture in a Country Park. Angus won a Major Bursary from Southern Arts in 1980 and held a solo show at Southampton Civic Centre. She worked in stone, carving objects of a contemplative disposition. Her earliest work was tightly designed geometric forms in which spacing and proportion were key elements; later the forms tended to suggest real objects. Arts Council holds her Bath stone carving Ophidia, of 1982, and in 1984 her Snail Block and Triangle was sited at Milton Keynes General Hospital, commissioned by the Development Corporation there. Lived in Hampshire.

Peggy ANGUS 1904–1993 Painter, draughtsman, designer and teacher, born in Chile, who was brought by her parents to England in 1909. She attended the North London Collegiate School, at 17 a scholarship taking her to the Royal College of Art where she became friends with Eric Ravilious and Edward Bawden. Taught in Nuneaton and Eastbourne, later at the North London Collegiate, after divorce from her husband James Richards, editor of *The Architectural Review*. Angus turned to designing tiles and wall-papers, being retained by Carter's of Poole, in Dorset. For many years Angus lived in a primitive shepherd's cottage in the Sussex Downs near Glynde which became the focus of artistic activity, commemorated in a show at Towner Art Gallery, Eastbourne, 1987. In 1992 she shared an exhibition at Sally Hunter Fine Art which covered her pre-World War II work. Died in London. North London Collegiate held a memorial show in 1994.

Anthony ANKERS 1962– Sculptor who graduated with first-class honours in fine art (sculpture) in 1985 from the Polytechnic in Leicester, which was his base. In 1989, he completed an architectural stonework conservation diploma from Weymouth Technical College. Ankers was for some time resident sculptor at the Sir Henry Doulton School of Sculpture in Stoke-on-Trent. His figurative terracotta Spring and Autumn, 1997, at Leicester University's arboretum used himself and the sculptor Siân Thomas as models. Ankers took part in a three-artist exhibition at Vaughan College, Leicester, in 1998.

Kofi ANKOBRA 1954– Painter, born in Johannesburg, South Africa, who studied at the Ghanatta College of Art in Accra, Ghana, 1975–8. He had a first solo exhibition at Windsor Community Arts Centre in 1985, subsequently showing in London and Santa Fé, in America. He returned to Ghana to paint, one result being his colourful canvas Murokie outside Rasta Bar, shown in 1993–4 John Moores Liverpool Exhibition. Lived in London.

Dorothy ANNAN 1908–1983 Painter, mosaicist, mural artist, potter and teacher, born in Pará, Brazil. Annan's initial education and art tuition were obtained abroad. In 1949 she taught at Bath College of Art and she exhibited at RA, LG, NEAC and elsewhere. Manchester City Art Gallery holds her picture Christmas 1944, and she is also represented in public galleries in Brighton and Stoke-on-Trent. She was a workaholic and completed a great deal of public work in the form of mosaic panels, tiled murals and painted murals in London and the provinces, including Ministry of Education, Durham University Library, Bank of England and 70 Farringdon Road. Known as Dodo or Dolly, Annan lived the artistic life in London with her sculptor husband Trevor Tennant. Died in the Sue Ryder Home, Snettisham, Norfolk.

David ANNAND 1948– Figurative sculptor and teacher who sculpted full-time from 1988, after studying at Duncan of Jordanstone College of Art, in Dundee, and teaching art in a school there. In 1987, he was awarded the Sir Otto Beit Medal for his Deer Leap in the city's Technology Park. Annand went on to complete a number of public sculptures around Britain and is notable for the series of racing drivers Colin Chapman, Jim and Roger Clark and Mike Hailwood, 1997–9, at Mallory Park race track in Leicestershire. In 2003, a public art project, Tumbler Falls, Dundee, was commissioned by Land Securities, managed by Dundee Public Art Programme. Annand's working base was Kilmany, Fife.

ANNE: *see* **Anne ENGDAHL**

Jeremy ANNEAR 1949– Painter and teacher whose work showed Cubist influences. He was born in Exeter and worked in Devon until the late 1980s, after which he was based in Cornwall, with periods working in Germany and Australia. From 1988, showed regularly with Newlyn Art Gallery and the Penwith in St Ives, elsewhere widely and was included in Now and Then, David Messum Fine Art, 1997. He had solo exhibitions in France, Germany and Switzerland as well as Britain, later ones including New Millennium Gallery, St Ives, 2004. As part of the Artsound.co.uk project, Nick Roberts of the Coull Quartet performed *Broken Contour for Unaccompanied Solo Cello* at that gallery, written by James Aitchison and inspired by the paintings. Annear's wife was the painter Judy Buxton.

Richard ANNELY 1962– Sculptor, born in Plymouth, Devon, whose interactive work The Stone Scratcher, made from various materials and emitting a range of ringing tones, was part of the 1997 Lewes Sculpture Trail. After hotel and catering studies Annely worked as a chef and catering manager, and while he was in Germany attended Munich Art Academy, 1990, being a guest student of Tony Cragg at Düsseldorf Art Academy, 1992. Annely gained his master's degree from Chelsea College of Art & Design, 1994, from 1995 working there as masters' technician. Exhibitions included St Wendel, Town Museum, 1992; Neuhauser Strasse Project, Munich, 1993; Galery Annelie Brusten, Wuppertal, with Herbert Willems & five pigs, 1994; and Interface, Sackville Gallery, 1997.

David ANNESLEY 1936– Sculptor, painter and teacher, born and lived in London. From 1947–56 he was educated in England, Australia and Southern Rhodesia, then after two years in the Royal Air Force he was from 1958–61 at St Martin's School of Art. He was to have studied painting, but found sculpture more exciting. For a time Annesley was Anthony Caro's assistant. Spent six months in Majorca in 1962, then in 1963 began teaching at Central School of Art and Croydon College of Art, from 1964 at St Martin's. An important influence on Annesley was the American painter Kenneth Noland, with whom he stayed in 1966. Annesley's sculpture, which could be brightly painted, was abstract, light and lyrical in feeling. In 1969 Annesley resumed painting. Showed with LG from 1989 and RA Summer Exhibition from 1991. In 1993 he was included in 1st RWA Open Sculpture Exhibition. Later solo exhibitions included Anderson O'Day Gallery, 1989, Kingsgate Gallery, 1999. Annesley was a prizewinner in BP Sculpture Competition, 1990, and he did work for Royal Hampshire County Hospital, Winchester, 1992. Tate Gallery in London and Liverpool, Arts and British Council and Museum of Modern Art in New York hold examples.

Lady Mabel ANNESLEY 1881–1959 Printmaker and watercolourist, daughter of the 5th Earl of Annesley, of Castlewellan, County Down, Northern Ireland. She studied in mid-1890s at Frank Calderon's School of Animal Painting and early in 1920s with Noel Rooke at Central School, being elected to SWE in 1924. She was also a member of Belfast Art Society and showed wood engravings at Redfern Gallery, although arthritis later made workingdifficult. During World War II she left Belfast for New Zealand, returning to England in the early 1950s, settling at Clare, Suffolk. Illustrated several books and wrote a part-finished autobiography, *As the Sight is Bent*, published 1964. British Museum and Belfast Museum and Art Gallery hold examples.

Pietro ANNIGONI 1910–1988 Painter of portraits and frescoes, draughtsman and teacher, born in Milan, Italy. He studied at the Accademia delle Belle Arti, Florence. Studying painting with Felice Carena, Annigoni won the Domenico Trentacoste Prize in 1931, being taught sculpture by Giuseppe Graziosi and etching with Celestino Celestini. At the Accademia's Scuola Libera del Nudo he mixed with Renzo Simi and Mario Parri. Painting mainly in oil tempera and travelling widely in Europe, Annigoni produced works signed Canonicus which, like those of the Neue Sachlichkeit movement, assimilated northern Renaissance art. His first solo show in 1932 was acclaimed by Girgio de Chirico and the critic Ugo Ojetti, who included him in an exhibition of Italian art in Paris in 1935. With Gregorio Sciltian and the brothers Anonio and Xavier Bueno, Annigoni founded the Modern Painters of Reality group, 1947–9. For some years from 1950 Annigoni based himself in London for half the year and travelled widely. He acquired new fame in 1955 when his classically styled portrait of the young Queen Elizabeth II, commissioned by the Worshipful Company of Fishmongers, brought instant fame. Crowds went to London to see it and a limited-edition print published by *The Times* was fully subscribed. Former president of the RA, Sir Alfred Munnings, declared Annigoni "the greatest painter of the age". During the 1950s, with a studio in London, Annigoni painted the Duke of Edinburgh and Princess Margaret, other subjects being the ballerina Dame Margot Fonteyn and the Maharanee of Jaipur. A second portrait of the Queen, in 1969, was not so successful, made for the National Portrait Gallery. In 1958 Annigoni returned to Florence, continuing to visit London. In Italy he painted frescoes. In 1976, his wife having died in 1969, Annigoni married his favourite model, Rosa Segreto, and was the subject of a television documentary by HTV (Wales). With the help of Segreto and some pupils he concentrated on religious pictures, notably big fresco cycles, and the paintings of his last decade were of great spiritual expressiveness. Several Italian collections, including Milan's Gallery of Modern Art, hold examples, and the Tate Gallery's archive holds a self-portrait of 1953. *The Memoirs of Annigoni* appeared in 1956, a *Spanish Sketchbook* in 1957 and *An Artist's Life* in 1977. In that year, the National Museum of Wales, Cardiff, gave Annigoni an exhibition, notably of royal portraits, to coincide with Queen Elizabeth's silver jubilee year.

Len ANNOIS 1906–1966 Painter, muralist and graphic artist, born in Malvern, Victoria, Australia, who studied during evening classes at the National Gallery of Victoria art school, 1930–2, and was inspired to concentrate on watercolour by James Flett. He showed with the Victorian Artists' Society, after World War II being on its board and helping to foster public interest in the National Gallery's work. During the war, Annois was production illustrator for the Commonwealth Aircraft Corporation, from 1946–50 serving as advertising manager for the firm G J Coles & Company while painting in his spare time and winning a number of notable watercolour prizes. Soon he could concentrate on painting full-time, and he furthered his education with trips to Europe in 1950–1 and 1952–3. Annois contributed to the first Australian Artists' Association show at the RWS' Conduit Street gallery in 1953; so accomplished was his work that he had been elected an associate of the RWS in 1952, being made full RWS in 1958. A further trip to Europe followed in 1962, the year he showed English watercolours in New York. After a visit to New Guinea in 1965, Annois died the following year in Melbourne. By then he had accomplished a number of murals in fresco and mosaic in public buildings, had achieved 23 solo shows across Australia and in London and had been widely featured in international travelling exhibitions. National Gallery of Victoria has a large collection of Annois' work, which is also held by HM Queen Elizabeth The Queen Mother.

Boris ANREP 1883–1969 Artist in mosaic, born in St Petersburg, Russia, where he first studied law but then Byzantine art. Travelled widely and from 1908 studied in Paris at Académies Julian and La Grande Chaumière and at Atelier La Palette. In 1910–11 he was at Edinburgh College of Art under Frank Morley Fletcher. He was associated with Roger Fry's Second Post-Impressionist Exhibition in 1912 and settled in England after World War I, although he later lived in Paris. Among his mosaics in public buildings are the National Gallery floors, Tate Gallery, Westminster Cathedral and Bank of England. The National Gallery mosaics were installed in four stages, 1929–52, entitled The Labours of Life, The Pleasures of Life, The Awakening of the Muses and Modern Virtues. They feature celebrities from the middle of the twentieth century, including Virginia Woolf, Diana Mitford, Winston Churchill, Margot Fonteyn, Loretta Young, Anna Akhmatova, T S Eliot, Bertrand Russell and Augustus John. In 2004, Lois Oliver's *Boris Anrep – The National Gallery Mosaics*, published by the National Gallery, gave an account of their creation by Anrep, who said: "If there is any feeling of squeamishness in walking over august personages one can easily step around them." Anrep also showed oil paintings at LG in early 1920s. The Anrep family is the subject of a notable painting by Henry Lamb.

ANSCHLEE 1931– Painter and draughtsman, born in Shanghai, China, educated in America, her full name being Anne Schlee. She studied at International School, 1962–5, then Famous Artists' School, 1970–2, gaining her fine art certificate. Teachers included Chow Chian-Chui, Charles Reid and John Pellew. She was a leading member of NS, for a time being its president, also showing with

Chelsea Art Society and elsewhere. Lived in Cranleigh, Surrey.

Norah ANSELL 1906– Sculptor who studied at Birmingham College of Arts and Crafts and part-time with William Bloye. Exhibited RA. Lived at Edgbaston, Birmingham.

William Henry ANSELL 1872–1959 Etcher who was by profession an architect. Born in Nottingham, he studied at the Architectural Association and etching at the Royal College of Art with Sir Frank Short. Became president of the Architectural Association in 1928 and was master of the Art Workers' Guild in 1944. Exhibited RA, RBA and RE. Lived at Sevenoaks, Kent.

Peter Frederick ANSON 1889–1975 Draughtsman, watercolourist and writer, christened Frederick Charles Anson when born in Portsmouth into a naval family. A weak heart prevented his going to Eton College. He studied art at the Architectural Association School, 1908–10, and briefly in 1918 with Frederick L Griggs which was "a turning point in my artistic career". Anson was a Roman Catholic convert and his twin interests were the religious life and maritime subjects. He spent much time in religious communities all over Europe, was an authority on them and eventually became a Cistercian. The name Peter was an adopted one. Anson led a roving life, reflected in such books as *A Pilgrim Artist in Palestine* and *A Roving Recluse*. Was a fine church architectural and marine draughtsman, was a founder member of RSMA and National Maritime Museum has much of his work. Showed with RA, RSA, RHA, Goupil Gallery and elsewhere. Lived much of his life in Scotland (see his book *Harbour Head*), latterly in Montrose, Angus. Died in Edinburgh.

Walters ANSON 1875– Portrait and miniature painter, born in London as Minnie Walters Anson. Studied at Lambeth School of Art, where she won a series of medals. Was married to the miniaturist Arthur Adams. She exhibited RA, Walker Art Gallery, Liverpool, RMS, Paris Salon and in Canada. Lived at Parkstone, Dorset.

Pegaret ANTHONY 1915–2000 London-based lecturer in historical costume and theatre history and painter, until her marriage to John Anthony (Inland Revenue valuer and great-nephew of the Victorian children's book illustrator Randolph Caldecott), known by her maiden name Pegaret Keeling. She was educated at The King Alfred School, Hampstead; King's College of Household and Social Science, University of London; and Central School of Arts and Crafts for four years, the last, 1937–8, as holder of the William Atkinson Scholarship, for theatrical design. As Pegaret Keeling, she was heavily involved in costume, fashion and theatre-related activities in the 1930s, which included a fashion show at Grosvenor House, in 1937, dresses later used at Alexandra Palace for television; décor and scene painting, for part of *St Joan*, the hundredth production of the Play and Pageant Union, 1938; chief designer for the Birmingham Centenary Pageant, 1938, with 5,000 performers; scene painting, for *The Scarlet Pimpernel* at the Embassy Theatre, 1938; and wardrobe mistress, for *Babes in the Wood*, pantomime at Unity Theatre, 1939. Her artistic talent stemmed from her maternal grandfather, the Victorian artist Thomas Howes. She was a prolific artist, including about 100 pictures as a war artist, two being held by the Imperial War Museum. Taught for 40 years at what is now Central St Martins College of Art & Design, then for a further 20 at Motley School of Theatre Design. In the 1960s, Anthony was employed by the American film producer Samuel Bronston to research historical costumes for several films, including *55 Days at Peking*, 1963, and *The Fall of the Roman Empire*, 1964. Anthony amassed a huge archive of source material on costume. *Costume: a general bibliography*, by Anthony and Janet Arnold, was published by the Costume Society in 1974.

ANTI-COOL: *see* **Tomoko TAKAHASHI**

ANTON 1912–70 Artist in pen and ink and wash, real name Antonia Yeoman, she was born in Brisbane, Queensland, Australia, but moved to England as a small girl. After private education she attended the Royal Academy Schools, 1928–30, taught by Steven Spurrier. In the mid-1930s she drew for magazines under her maiden name of Botterill, then from 1937 jointly with her brother Harold Thompson she began submitting humorous drawings under the name of Anton, for which she latterly was mainly responsible. They appeared in magazines such as *Punch* and *Lilliput* and Anton also illustrated a number of books in which her aristocratic, sharply delineated characters were instantly recognisable. Also exhibited at RSA, SGA and in cartoon shows. Lived in London.

Victor ANTON 1909–1980 Sculptor, born in Worthing, Sussex. Anton was a career journalist who worked for almost 30 years on the *Guardian-Gazette* series of newspapers in Chingford and Walthamstow. He took up sculpting untutored in 1949 and had solo shows at Gimpel Fils, 1953; Grabowski Gallery, 1963; Lords Gallery, 1965; and he had a retrospective at University Centre, Birmingham, 1974. In 1992 Belgrave Gallery included his Untitled Sculpture, 1962, in British abstract art of 50s and 60s. Anton worked in a variety of materials and experimented with light in his pursuit of the problems of equilibrium.

Sylvia ANTONSEN 1937– Painter, textile artist and teacher, born in Bournemouth, Hampshire, where she studied painting and textiles at Bournemouth College of Art. Designed at the Royal School of Needlework, lectured in printed textiles at Northampton School of Art, then after raising a family returned to painting full-time from 1991. Her crisply painted, slightly surreal pictures were exhibited at Thompson's Gallery and widely elsewhere.

Myles ANTONY fl. from 1960s– Designer and watercolourist, born in Dublin, Ireland. He studied art under Fergus O'Ryan, then in 1960s was art director for John Stephen when the Carnaby Street craze was going strong. Further work included record covers, television logos and film posters in Britain, continental Europe and North America. Antony began to develop his watercolours in the early 1980s, concentrating on figures and portraits. Mixed shows included RHA, solo exhibitions being at The Other Gallery, in Edinburgh, in 1985; The Cathedral, Bury St Edmunds, Suffolk, in 1988; St Jude's, 1989 and 1991; and Lane Gallery Restaurant, Dublin, 1990–1.

Angela ANTRIM 1911–1984 Book illustrator, cartoonist and sculptor. Born at Sledmere, Malton, Yorkshire, she was educated privately and then studied art in Brussels and at the British School in Rome. One-man exhibitions included the Beaux Arts in 1937 and after World War II the Hamet Gallery and galleries in Belfast. The RA, RHA and RUA had mixed shows including her work. She illustrated several books, including *The Antrim McDonnells* and *Jam Tomorrow*, also magazines such as *Harpers, Queen* and *Vogue*. Signed work A A. She was Countess Antrim, was married to the Earl of Antrim and lived in County Antrim and London. Her son, The Honourable Hector McDonnell, was also an artist.

Enzo APICELLA 1922– Self-taught cartoonist, photographer, illustrator and painter who moved to England in 1954. His great versatility was in evidence soon after arrival, when he began designing posters for Schweppes and sets for ABC Television, as well as working on animated films. It was then that he began collecting art, becoming friends with the British artists Eduardo Paolozzi and Joe Tilson and many Italians such as Paolo Buggiani, Piero Dorazio and Achille Perelli. A selection of their work and his own was included in a sale of part of Apicella's collection at Bonhams, Lots Road, in 2002. At that time, he was still drawing a daily political cartoon for the Italian newspaper *Liberazione*, having cartooned for *The Observer, The Guardian, Punch* and *The Economist*.

Sally APLIN fl. from 1980s– Sculptor, enameller and teacher, who gained a diploma in art education at Bristol Polytechnic, 1984; an honours degree in fine art there, 1992; then her master's degree in fine art at University of Wales, 1995. She was a part-time sculpture and drawing teacher at Filton College, Bristol, 1993, and a visiting lecturer at University of the West of England, 1994–5. In 1989 won a prize at International Enamel Biennale, Laval, Canada, having shown enamels since 1985 in international juried shows. Exhibitions included Senate House at University of Bristol, 1986; Women for Art, Bristol City Museum & Art Gallery, 1990; New Art in the South-West, Spacex Gallery, Exeter, 1995; and 2nd Open Sculpture Exhibition at RWA, 1996. Lived in Bristol.

Leonard APPELBEE 1914–2000 Painter, printmaker, verse writer and teacher, born in London, married to the artist Frances Macdonald. He studied at Goldsmiths' College, 1931–5, under Clive Gardiner, then at Royal College of Art with Barnett Freedman, 1935–8. Taught at Bournemouth College of Art. Appelbee showed at RA, RSA, Arts Council, British Council and in small group shows at Wildenstein, 1947, and Fine Art Society, 1968. His picture One-man Band was one of the 60 Paintings for '51 Festival of Britain show. Had a series of solo shows at Leicester Galleries from 1948 and a notable exhibition at City Museum and Art Gallery, Plymouth, 1977. Appelbee was a distinctive portrait painter, carrying out commissions for Sir Edward Marsh, Eton College, Corpus Christi College in Cambridge and other clients. He won a silver medal at Paris Salon in 1970. Published his book of verse *That Voice* in 1980. Tate Gallery, Arts Council, many provincial and foreign galleries hold his work. Appelbee (pronounced App*el*bee) lived latterly at Kincardine-on-Forth, Fife, then Aberdeen.

Wynne APPERLEY 1884–1960 Painter and draughtsman whose full name was George Owen Wynne Apperley and who was born in Ventnor, Isle of Wight. Although mainly self-taught, he did study with the Herkomer School at Bushey. Lived for much of his life in Spain, where he worked and exhibited, and in Morocco, being honoured by the Spanish government. Exhibited extensively at Leicester and Walker's Galleries, RI and RSA. Apperley was adept in line and wash at catching the sun-filled landscapes of the Mediterranean area. His work is in the Victoria & Albert Museum.

Chris APPLEBY 1951– Painter, born in Birmingham, who studied at Wolverhampton College of Art, 1971–3, then Royal College of Art, 1975–8. Had a studio in east London, showing in East London Open Studios, Whitechapel Open and various gallery mixed exhibitions. His oil on panel Beauty and the Beast was in the 1995–6 John Moores Liverpool Exhibition.

Peter APPLETON 1955– Sculptor, born in Liverpool. He studied at Chester College of Art and Newcastle upon Tyne University, graduating in 1978 and gaining his master's degree in 1982. Appleton won a Yorkshire Arts Bursary in 1985. He took part in A Noise in Your Eye touring international exhibition of sound sculpture in 1985; in 1986 provided the soundtrack for *Children of A Lesser God*, Northcott Theatre, Exeter; and was one of six artists representing Britain at World Expo '88 in Brisbane. Triophonic Water Sculpture and Solar Device for Deep Field Noises were both commissioned by World Expo '88, the second being sponsored by BP Solar Australia.

Richard APPLETON 1909– Painter whose full-time occupation was as chief draughtsman with the Merseyside and North Wales Electricity Board. Born in Norwich, he later studied in the life class at Denbighshire Technical College, going on to exhibit RCamA, at the Atkinson Art Gallery, Southport, NWG, ROI, RWA and elsewhere. Lived in Wrexham, Denbighshire.

Fred APPLEYARD 1874–1963 Painter and mural decorator, born in Middlesbrough, Yorkshire. He studied at Scarborough School of Art, Royal College of Art and Royal Academy Schools, winning the Turner Gold Medal and several scholarships. Was a frequent exhibitor at RA and RWA, of which he was a member. Worked in South Africa, 1910–12. Tate Gallery holds his canvas A Secret and he carried out a number of murals in public places, including Royal Academy Burlington House restaurant and Nottingham General Hospital. Died at Alresford, Hampshire, his home for many years.

Joseph APPLEYARD 1908–1960 Painter and draughtsman specialising in sporting subjects. Studied during evenings, 1925–32, at Leeds College of Art. Exhibited widely in Yorkshire, having one-man shows in Leeds, where he lived at Far Headingley. Appleyard had his work reproduced in Yorkshire newspapers and magazines, gaining a reputation as a horse painter, and he became honorary secretary of the Yorkshire Group of Artists. Newcastle upon Tyne and Wakefield art galleries hold his work.

Vivien AP RHYS PRYCE 1937– Sculptor, medallist and lecturer, born in Woking, Surrey, producing "mainly bronze human figures, also fountains, some based on plant forms." From 1955–7, she attended the City & Guilds of London Art School, studying with David McFall, James Butler and Rodney Burn, also with with Eric Schilsky at Edinburgh College of Art. Won a Beckwith Travelling Scholarship, 1957; Bronze Medal and Certificate of Merit, both 1961; and Feodora Gleichen Award, 1964. Was assistant art mistress at Elmhurst Ballet School, 1961–2; assistant sculpture lecturer at the City & Guilds, 1964–74; and assistant lecturer, art department, Twickenham College of Technology, 1970–2. Elected associate of RBS, 1965, fellow, 1972. Took part in extensive mixed shows, including RA Summer Exhibition, from 1959; SPS, 1960; Royal Glasgow Institute of the Fine Arts, from 1960; RSA, 1963; NEAC, 1965; Marjorie Parr Gallery, from 1968; RWA, from 1969; Wills Lane Gallery, St Ives, Cornwall, 1973; Mignon Gallery, Bath, 1977; Tib Lane Gallery, Manchester, 1979; New Ashgate Gallery, Farnham, from 1986; Armstrong-Davis Gallery, Arundel, from 1992, and elsewhere. Commissions included John Player League Cricket Trophy and Medals, 1969, and Player's No. 6 Trophy (Rugby League) and Medals, 1971. John Pinches Ltd, 1972, and The Tower Mint, 1976, also commissioned medals. National Gallery of New Zealand and other public and private collections in Britain and abroad held work. Lived in Calne, Wiltshire.

Ron ARAD 1951– Designer, sculptor and teacher, born in Tel-Aviv, Israel, who studied at the Jerusalem Academy of Art, 1971–3, moved to London and studied at the Architectural Association, 1974–9. In 1981, with Caroline Thorman, he founded Ron Arad Associates, an architecture and design practice in Chalk Farm, then in 1994 established the Ron Arad Studio, a design and production unit in Como, Italy. Arad increasingly produced pieces of sheet steel, stating that he "always mischievously exploits their formal and functional possibilities to the fullest. The sculptural forms often have an unexpected impact which first emerges during use, and are just as much a result of graphic design as the experimental work that goes on in the workshop." Arad was a guest professor at the Hochschule in Vienna, Austria, 1994–7, later becoming professor of industrial and furniture design at the Royal College of Art, and was guest editor of the 1994 *International Design Yearbook*. Among his major exhibitions were Ron Arad and Ingo Maurer, Spazio Krizia, Milan, 1996–8, and Not Made by Hand, Not Made in China, Galleria Gio Marconi, Milan, and Before and after Now, Victoria & Albert Museum, both 2000. Arad's architectural projects included the Tel-Aviv Opera, Belgo Restaurants in London and development of sport cafés for Adidas and the firm's flagship stadium in Paris. The Victoria & Albert Museum, Centre Georges Pompidou in Paris, the Metropolitan Museum of Art in New York and Vitra Design Museum, Germany, hold examples.

Rasheed ARAEEN 1935– Painter, sculptor, performance artist and polemicist, born in Karachi, Pakistan. After training as a civil engineer at University of Karachi, he travelled to England in 1964 and turned to sculpture full-time, being inspired by Anthony Caro's work at St Martin's School of Art. By this time Araeen had, in Pakistan, produced two seminal works, the painting Ham Raqs and the sculpture Burning Bicycle Tyres. He was concerned to remove gestural and pictorial allusions from his work. "Art should not only be manufactured but mass-produced to make it accessible to everybody." He wanted that "in the end art is no longer a sacred/precious object, but becomes an idea." Won a John Moores Exhibition, Liverpool, prize in 1969 and an Arts Council award, 1978. From 1970 staged a series of performances with public participation; became active in movements such as the Black Panthers and curated The Other Story exhibition at Hayward Gallery, 1989–90, with tour, which included his work; in 1996 had a show of sculpture in grounds of Serpentine Gallery. His autobiography, *Making Myself Visible*, was published in 1984. Arts Council and Walker Art Gallery in Liverpool hold examples.

Alison ARAM 1956– Painter and designer, born in London, who attended Hornsey College of Art, then joined the head-dress and jewellery department of the Royal Opera House, 1976–91. In 1991 moved to Devon to paint full-time, working between figuration and abstraction, using bright colours. Lived near Bideford, where she exhibited at Burton Art Gallery and elsewhere locally, having a first London show at The Heifer Gallery, 1999.

Malcolm ARBUTHNOT 1874–1967 Painter, photographer and sculptor, born in Suffolk, his mother a dedicated amateur artist. Arbuthnot did not take up painting seriously until he was in his late thirties, but as a young man he was a keen photographer. After working as a clerk between 1893–1905 during which time he developed his photographic skills, from around 1906 he was able to set up his own studio. Worked freelance for papers such as *Illustrated London News* and *Sketch* and became a noted portrait photographer. Commissioned by the Goupil Gallery to photograph artists such as Sir Edward Poynter, James Pryde and William Nicholson, Arbuthnot came into contact with Wyndham Lewis and the Vorticists, who influenced his painting style. In 1926 he closed his London studio to concentrate on painting. Earlier he had been taught by C A Brindley, had attended a life class in Liverpool and was later to be instructed by J D Fergusson and W P Robins. While living in France he showed some bronzes at the Paris Salon, and he was also to show at the RA, ROI, Leicester Galleries and extensively elsewhere. One-man shows in London including Fine Art Society, and exhibitions after his death have been held by Grabowski Gallery and David Cross, Bristol. Arbuthnot's work is held by Victoria & Albert Museum and Salford Art Gallery. Finally lived at La Houle, Jersey.

Frank ARCHER 1912–1995 Printmaker, painter and teacher, born in east London, brought up in Eastbourne, Sussex, which remained his home. Archer's chemist father passed on two gifts: knowledge to mix and grind his own pigments, and a profound faith in the Bible, which he read to his family each morning. Studied at Eastbourne School of Art in 1928–32, Royal College of Art, 1932–8, that year winning the Prix de Rome. Was only able to study at British School in Rome for a year due to the war. Later taught at Eastbourne School of Art and became head of fine art at Kingston College of Art. Despite teaching he was a prolific artist. His work, sometimes on themes such as music and musicians, was influenced by his ability as a draughtsman. The earlier work tends to be more architectural in construction, but later it became more personal, and looser. Exhibited at RA, and as a fellow at both RE and RWS. In 1990 he had retrospectives at RWS and Catto Gallery; another at Bankside Gallery, 1992; in 1999 Catto gave him a memorial show; and in 2004 The Studio Art House, Leatherhead, held an Archer show entitled The Colours of Nature and Music. British Council and Walker Art Gallery in Liverpool own examples.

Michael ARCHER 1954– Artist and critic who studied natural sciences and the history of art at Cambridge

University, 1973–6, then aesthetic education at Manchester University, 1980–1. He worked as a freelance critic and with William Furlong ran Audio Arts (see separate entries). Lived in London.

Michael Dan ARCHER 1955– Sculptor, sometimes on a large scale, and teacher, born in Glasgow. Archer studied at Coventry School of Art, 1975–9, then taught English as a foreign language in Japan and Spain for five years and completed sculptures in a number of countries, including Europe and the Far East. A good example is the carved limestone Gateway, 1999–00, created for the Castlemilk Environment Trust in Glasgow, where Archer ran stone-carving workshops for the local Women's Group. His abstract bronze and stone Per Saeculi Quartum (Through a Quarter of a Century) was unveiled in 1991 at Loughborough University. He taught in the art and design school there, with visiting lectureships at Coventry and Derby Colleges of Art, and had a residency at Yorkshire Sculpture Park in 1993. In 1994 Archer was elected RBS and soon after became a council member. Archer showed widely in the United Kingdom and abroad, mixed exhibitions including New Art, Hiroshima City Gallery, Japan, 1984; International Granite Sculpture Symposium, Sardinia, Italy, 1989; and Sculpture in the Close, Jesus College Cambridge, 1992 and 1996. Frequent solo exhibitions included Churchill College, Cambridge, 1998. He was variously based in Leicestershire and Lincolnshire.

Nicholas ARCHER 1963– Artist and lecturer who did foundation studies at Mid-Cheshire College, 1981–2; graduated with honours from Leeds Polytechnic, 1982–5; then, after several abortive applications to the Royal Academy Schools – he continued studying independently, evening classes and life classes in Florence, Italy – was accepted by Leonard McComb, the Royal Academy Schools' keeper, and gained a postgraduate diploma in painting, 1996–9. Archer held residencies at St Paul's Gallery, Leeds, in 1987; Florence Trust, 1991; and the London Business School, 1999–00. Lecturing appointments included Leeds Metropolitan University, 1994; Loughborough University, Winchester School of Art and John Moores University, Liverpool, all 1999; and Heatherley's School of Art, from 2001. Archer was a guest speaker on contemporary portraiture at the National Portrait Gallery in 2005, the year he appeared in the BBC1 television programme *Star Portraits with Rolf Harris*, painting the comedian Adrian Edmondson. Also in 2005 the *Star Portraits* pictures were shown at the County Hall Gallery, plus a tour. Archer won a string of awards, including the Fabriano Prize, National Print Exhibition, 1997; *Galleries* Magazine Award at the National Print Exhibition, the Richard Jack and George Isted prizes for portraiture, Premiums Exhibition, RA Sackler Galleries, the Elizabeth Scott-Moore Watercolour Prize, RWS, Discerning Eye Award for figure painting, and a Commended, BP Portrait Award, National Portrait Gallery, all 1998; London Prize at the Hunting Art Prizes, Haite Travel Scholarship and Cyril Sweet Award, Worshipful Company of Painter-Stainers, for the most outstanding postgraduate show, all 1999; and 1st prize, Hunting Art Prizes, 2002. He gained a Rover Cars Group commission in 1998, another from The Mill film production company, in 2000. Mixed shows included Whitechapel Open, Whitechapel Art Gallery, 1994; RA Summer Exhibition, from 1997; and Singer & Friedlander/*Sunday Times* Watercolour Competition, 1998; Beaux Arts, Bath, from 2001; Jerwood Drawing Prize, Jerwood Space, 2003; and Gibsone Jessop Gallery, Toronto, Canada, 2005. He had a solo exhibition at Long & Ryle, 2000, work stemming from family photographs in which Archer sought for "something that's not quite right" in mundane scenes. Other one-man shows included a series at Sarah Myerscough Fine Art from 2001. Archer lived in Wittersham, Kent.

Peter ARCHER 1946– Artist who studied painting and sculpture at Goldsmiths' College School of Art, 1965–8. Won a Boise Travelling Scholarship, 1968–9, working in Italy and France, eventually settling in Cornwall. Group shows included John Moores Liverpool Exhibition, 1972; Midland Group, Nottingham, 1979; Spirit of London, first prize winner, 1983; Landscappen, Galerie Marie-Puck Brookthaers, Brussels, Belgium, 1990; The Curator's Egg, Anthony Reynolds Gallery, 1994; and Flowers East, 1999. Also showed at RA Summer Exhibition and LG. Later solo exhibitions included Galerie Ferdinand Van Dieten-d'Eendt, Amsterdam, Netherlands, 1997, and Austin/Desmond Fine Art, from 1998. Arts Council and RA hold examples.

Val ARCHER 1946– Painter, notably of meticulous still lifes in oil, and teacher, born in Northampton. She studied at Manchester College of Art and Design, 1964–8, then Royal College of Art, 1968–71, winning the Anstruther Prize for Painting, 1970. She held a number of visiting lectureships, latterly including Crawford School of Art and Cork and Cardiff Colleges of Art. Commissions included a British Rail poster, 1982, and BBC's *Good Food* magazine, 1991–2. Her own books included *A Basket of Berries*, 1992, and *A Basket of Apples*, 1993. Showed solo in Germany and Netherlands, with CCA Galleries from 1993 and with Chris Beetles Ltd, 2001.

William ARCHER 1928– Sculptor, oil painter and draughtsman. Born at Thornley, County Durham, Archer studied art at Sunderland College of Art, 1946, then again from 1949–52, after which he was three years at the Royal College of Art. He began exhibiting at the RA in the mid-1950s, also showing with the RSA and Northern Artists. Northumberland Education Authority owns his work. Lived at Thornley.

Gordon Robert ARCHIBALD 1905–1980 Watercolourist, based for a time in Aberdeen. He showed at Royal Glasgow Institute of the Fine Arts and RSA. McLean Museum and Art Gallery, Greenock, holds his work.

Phyllis ARCHIBALD: *see* **Phyllis Archibald CLAY**

Charlotte ARDIZZONE 1943– Painter and printmaker, born in London, where she lived for some time, later moving to Norfolk. She was the niece of the illustrator Edward Ardizzone. Artist friend Kathleen Allen initially encouraged Charlotte Ardizzone to paint, and she became the youngest ever exhibitor at the RA Summer Exhibition. Studied briefly at St Martin's School of Art, 1960, then at Byam Shaw School of Drawing and Painting, 1961, gaining an Ernest Jackson Scholarship. For periods worked as an art therapist, teacher and illustrator, as well as painting still life and landscape in Britain and on the continent in which a strong sense of light was evident. Showed in mixed exhibitions at NEAC, of which she was a member, RWA and elsewhere. From 1970 had several solo exhibitions at Drian Galleries, later shows including Christopher Hull, 1988, Sally Hunter Fine Art, 1991, Albemarle Gallery, 2001, and Broughton House Gallery, Cambridge, and Louise Kosman, Edinburgh, both 2003. Nuffield Foundation, Dublin University and several overseas galleries hold her work.

Deborah ARDIZZONE 1939– Artist, teacher and gallery owner, born in Rawalpindi, Pakistan, who studied at Guildford School of Art, 1955–8, principal Dudley Holland, then textiles at the Central School of Arts and Crafts, 1958–61, where the head of department was Gordon Crook, "and there was an emphasis on basic design." Among notable teachers were Marianne Straub, Mervyn Peake, Alan Reynolds, Walter Hoyle and Mary Harper. In 1961, she married Nicholas, the younger son of Edward Ardizzone, two children, divorced 1968. With Edward she catalogued a large collection of his sketch-books, presented to the Ashmolean Museum, Oxford. Deborah Ardizzone taught basic design at Delhi Polytechnic for Girls, later teaching from her studio at Yoxford, Suffolk, connected to the Yoxford Gallery, where she showed solo. She was coordinator for Suffolk Open Studios, 1997–01. She exhibited with Suffolk Craft Society, of which she was a full member, other mixed exhibitions including The Grapevine, Norwich; The Black Swan Guild, Frome; and Butley Barns and Halesworth Gallery, both in Suffolk. Ardizzone printed and dyed fabrics for wall-hangings and pictures and worked in watercolour, mixed media, pastel and monoprint. Influences were "colour and light, the brilliance and subtlety of watercolour and fabric dyes."

Edward ARDIZZONE 1900–1979 Book illustrator, lithographer, watercolourist and writer for children. Born in Haiphong, Indo-China, Ardizzone – whose work was sometimes signed DIZ or E A – studied art under Bernard Meninsky and F J Porter at evening classes at Westminster School of Art in 1920–1. After working as a clerk, he decided in 1926 to pursue art full-time; five years later he had his first one-man show at the Leger Galleries. He was an official war artist during World War II, working widely in Europe and North Africa, and his illustrated war diaries are notable records. After the war he established a strong following as a book illustrator, titles ranging from Walter de la Mare's *Peacock Pie* and John Bunyan's *Pilgrim's Progress* to H E Bates' *Uncle Silas* stories and Maurice Gorham's *Back to the Local*. He also wrote and illustrated his own children's books, such as *Little Tim and the Brave Sea Captain*. Ardizzone's intimate scenes of bar-room and back-stage life and street life in London are drawn with a whimsicality and charm that are inimitable and unmistakeable. Retrospective show at the Victoria & Albert Museum, 1974, centenary tour organised in 2000–3 by Wolseley Fine Arts, which also showed original book illustrations, 2004. Lived at Rodmersham Green, Sittingbourne, Kent.

Antonio ARGENIO 1961– Painter, born in Bedford, whose figures had a tortured, Expressionist appearance, as in The Idiot, one of five pictures acquired by New York British art collectors Robert and Susan Summer at Argenio's 1988 sell-out graduation show at Royal College of Art. He had previously studied at Winchester School of Art and was a Delfina Studios Trust resident artist, 1988–90. Argenio also won a Basil H Alkazzi Foundation Award, Aaron Lane Penguin Book Prize and a Slotover Travelling Scholarship, all 1988. Group exhibitions included Mall Galleries, 1986; Paton Gallery, 1988; The Figure Laid Bare, Pomeroy-Purdy Gallery, 1992; and Summer Show at Purdy-Hicks Gallery and Royal Over-Seas League Open, both 1995.

Jeanne ARGENT 1944– Sculptor, painter, printmaker and writer, born in Hastings, Sussex, where she attended the School of Art, 1960–2, for the foundation course. Her career progressed through journalism and freelance writing of books and magazine articles until in the early 1980s, with children at school, she took up art again. She was a member of Surrey Sculpture Society, showing with it at Chilworth Manor Lodge, near Guildford. Shared a show at The Harvey Gallery, Guildford, 1993. As a result of a competition run by Guildford Borough Council Argent was commissioned to produce a sculpture of Alice, erected in 1990 in the Castle Grounds, near Chestnuts, where the author of *Alice Through the Looking-Glass*, Lewis Carroll, stayed just before he died. The sculpture shows Alice making her way through the glass. Argent lived nearby in Merrow, Surrey.

Paul ARGENT 1959– Mixed media/constructions artist and teacher, born in Southern Rhodesia. He studied at Colchester Institute, 1977–8, Chelsea School of Art, 1978–81, then Slade School of Fine Art, 1981–3, where he also taught. His exhibitions included Harrison McCann Show, 1982; City University Gallery, Cockpit Theatre Gallery and 15 British Contemporaries, in California, America, all 1983; Lyric Theatre, 1984; and in 1985 participated in four-man show at Woodlands Art Gallery. Among later appearances were a solo at London College of Furniture, 1987; Open Studios Group Show, The Showroom, 1988; and East End Open studios, based at Robinson Road, 1989.

Margarita ARGÜELLES 1941– Painter, born in Lisbon, Portugal, her parents being Spanish, her father in the diplomatic service. The family moved to London in 1945, Margarita attending the Convent of the Sacred Heart in Tunbridge Wells, Kent, until the age of 11, when her father was posted back to Spain. Although she showed an aptitude for art at school, she studied philosophy at Madrid University, studies interrupted by marriage. After dealing in antiques she returned to art, spending several years drawing before concentrating on oils. Her first solo exhibition was at Galeria Yguanzo in 1986, with a second at Caja de Madrid, 1989. In 1991 Sally Hunter Fine Art gave her a first exhibition outside Spain, showing Spanish and English landscapes and still life.

Saleem ARIF 1949– Painter and sculptor, born in Hyderabad, India, who moved to England aged 17. He studied sculpture and painting, attending Birmingham College of Art, 1969–70, and Royal College of Art, 1972–5. In the early 1980s won Arts Council and British Council awards, and an Italian Government Bursary enabled him to work in Florence, Italy. In a search for a cultural identity Arif travelled widely through India and studied Dante's *Inferno*, both of which experiences influenced his painting. Created his own symbolism, including birds, men and objects, which produced pictures often of great charm and subtlety. Took part in many group exhibitions in Britain and abroad. Solo shows included Art Heritage Gallery, New Delhi, and British Council Gallery, 1984, and Plymouth Arts Centre and Anderson O'Day Gallery, 1988. Participated in The Other Story, Hayward Gallery, 1989–90, and touring. Government Art Collection and Arts Council hold his work.

Ernest ARIS 1882–1963 Black-and-white artist, illustrator and watercolourist. Son of the artist Alfred Aris, Ernest studied at Bradford School of Art under Charles Stephenson, then at the Royal College of Art under Gerald Moira. Exhibited at the RA, RBA, RI, RWS and in the provinces. Aris started as a portrait painter, later taught for a while and was eventually illustrated in publications throughout the world. He illustrated many children's books, including *Tales for Tiny Tots* and *The Brambledown Tales*. Lived in London.

Lesley ARKLESS 1956– Painter, writer and illustrator, born in Northumberland, who after school in Newcastle upon Tyne graduated with honours at West Surrey College of Art and Design, Farnham, 1974–8. Wrote and illustrated *What Stanley Knew*. Showed at Ash Barn Gallery, Petersfield; National Museum of Wales, Cardiff; and at public gallery in Le Havre, Normandy. Lived in Winchester, Hampshire.

Don ARLETT 1937– Watercolourist, notable for his depictions of the Norfolk landscape, born in London. He attended Croydon School of Art, 1952–5, Norwich School of Art, 1955–7, then worked in advertising in London and Vienna from 1958, eventually retiring to concentrate on his own work. He gained many creative awards, from 1982–8 was director of the British Television Advertising Awards and in 1984 was one of the judges at Cannes Film Festival. Had a solo show at Mistral Galleries, 1994.

ARLIE 1914–1994 Painter, full name Arlie Panting, born in Milwaukee, Wisconsin, in America, who married an Englishman and worked for the last 30 years of her life in Somerset, although she had studios in London and New York. Arlie trained at Milwaukee's State Teachers' Training College (later the University of Wisconsin) and the Layton School of Art, also L'Académie de la Grande Chaumière, Paris. Her ethereal figurative paintings were influenced by the Italian Renaissance and School of Paris. Arlie commonly used bright colours and soft, blurred outlines, but she was a constant experimenter with surface techniques. Was a member of the Free Painters and Sculptors and showed in many London galleries, including the Portal and John Whibley, there having a series of solo exhibitions. The Stansell Gallery, Taunton, held a retrospective in 1995.

Frederick Marcus ARMAN 1908–1978 Sculptor in wood and metal, born in Ipswich, Suffolk. He retired in 1970 after a lifetime of work in the Post Office and was the first curator of the National Postal Museum. He wrote authoritatively in the Philatelic Bulletin on Victorian postage stamps and was a member of the Post Office Arts Club. Exhibited at Lincoln Cathedral, New Metropole Arts Centre in Folkestone, elsewhere in the provinces and in America. Lived in Bromley, Kent.

Thomas William ARMES 1894–1963 Artist and teacher, born in St Ives, Huntingdonshire, one of a large family of an innkeeper and farmer. Was encouraged by Walter Dendy Sadler and then studied at Cambridge School of Art, in 1913 being awarded a scholarship to study in The Hague. When World War I broke out Armes joined the Army, served at the front in France and was eventually invalided out. Poor health was to plague his career. Settled in Chelsea in the 1920s and befriended by George Clausen Armes became a prolific artist, showing at RA and RBA and taking private pupils. After a chest operation prior to World War II, during which Armes served in the Home Guard, he chose to settle with his wife Myra in Sheringham, Norfolk, where the climate was more congenial. He completed posters for British Railways and the local council and had three solo shows at Norwich Assembly House, in 1953, 1958 and 1960. In 1975 his widow showed Armes' work at the Little Gallery, which she had opened after his death. It became the Westcliffe Gallery and gave him a retrospective in 1990.

Diana M ARMFIELD 1920– Painter, designer and teacher, born in Ringwood, Hampshire, married to the artist Bernard Dunstan. Her uncle Maxwell Armfield made a notable portrait of her, illustrated in Julian Halsby's book *The Art of Diana Armfield*. She went to school at Bedales, then studied at Slade School of Fine Art and Central School of Arts and Crafts. For several years with Roy Passano ran the Armfield-Passano Partnership as designers. From 1959 she taught at Byam Shaw School of Art. Was included in many mixed shows, including Festival of Britain, and was a member of RWA, RWS, NEAC, RCamA and RA, 1991. After showing solo at Tegfryn Art Gallery, Anglesey, in 1975 and 1978, Armfield began a long association with Browse & Darby, also exhibiting in America and Australia. In 1988 Oriel 31 Gallery in Newtown and Welshpool gave her and Dunstan a combined retrospective. Their work was similarly on a small scale, owing much to the Sickert tradition, Armfield being noted for her sensitive still lifes of flowers. Among her commissions was one from the National Trust in 1988, another from HRH The Prince of Wales in 1989. British Museum, Contemporary Art Society for Wales and Government Picture Collection hold her work, and Victoria & Albert Museum holds textile work. Signed work D M A. Lived in London and Wales.

Maxwell ARMFIELD 1881–1972 Painter and decorative artist, especially in tempera, and writer. Born in Ringwood, Hampshire, Armfield was educated at Birmingham School of Art – there is a Birmingham Arts and Crafts flavour in his pictures – then in Paris and Italy. Exhibited extensively, including RA, Fine Art Society, for long a noted dealer in his work, NEAC, Leicester Galleries and abroad. His work is held by the British Museum, provincial and overseas galleries. He illustrated about 20 books and wrote *A Manual of Tempera Painting*, *Tempera Painting Today*, *An Artist in America* and *An Artist in Italy*. During World War I, with his writer wife Constance Smedley, Armfield attempted to set up a high-flown peoples' Greenleaf Theatre in his studio, an abortive venture amusingly recalled by Margaret Gardiner in her book *A Scatter of Memories*. Armfield was a painter of landscape and still life well crafted and full of detail. Lived in Bath, Somerset.

Stuart ARMFIELD 1916–2000 Painter, notably in tempera, born in Sanderstead, Surrey. He studied at West of England College of Art, Bristol, and was from 1935–40 on the art staff of Ealing Studios. Films worked on included Gracie Fields' *Sing As We Go*, 1934, and George Formby's *I See Ice*, 1938. During a short contract at a Paris film studio, from his cousin Maxwell Armfield he learned the tempera technique. Wrote the manual *Tempera Painting*. Showed at RA, with St Ives Society of Artists of which he was a member, Arthur Jeffress Gallery, RWS and in America. Lived in Looe, Cornwall, later in Plymouth, Devon. After World War II, Armfield produced Symbolist pictures which featured black models, chessboards and keys, sought by collectors such as King Hassan of Morocco, the exiled Prince Chula of Thailand and the actor Eric Portman. Ironically for a Quaker pacifist, who was a conscientious objector in World War II, Armfield's sole work in a British public collection at the time of his death was Anti-Invasion Obstructions, in the Imperial War Museum. James Colman Fine Art held an eightieth-birthday retrospective in 1996, a memorial show in 2000.

ARMFIELD-PASSANO PARTNERSHIP: *see* **Diana M ARMFIELD**

Ann ARMITAGE 1959– Painter, muralist, therapist and teacher, born in Huddersfield, Yorkshire, who studied at Grimsby School of Art & Design and Canterbury College of Art & Design. In 1990 she taught in the London Borough of Hackney, working as an art therapist for Kent County Council, 1990–1. Commissions included a mural for the Barnaby Rudge public house in Broadstairs, and Kent Countryside Productions' *A Midsummer Night's Dream*, both 1989. From 1995–7 Armitage worked with a local artist on an interior mural at the Jamuna Resort Hotel, Rajasthan, India. Group shows included Portraits, Faversham Library, 1989; Pastels Today, Mall Galleries, and Royal Over-Seas League Open, both 1994. Armitage gained an Elizabeth Foundation for the Arts, New York, Award, in 1995, having won *The Art Newspaper* Award the year before, and in 1998 added the Northbrook College Award, RBA, Mall Galleries. Armitage painted her landscapes in the studio from memory. These small pictures were based on the incidental details from scenery – such as farms, tin mines and paths – gleaned during coastal walks on regular visits to West Penwith, in Cornwall. Gordon Hepworth Fine Art, Newton St Cyres, showed her work.

Catharine ARMITAGE 1944– Painter and printmaker, born in Surbiton, Surrey, married to the painter Paul Feiler. She studied at Slade School of Fine Art, 1967–71, then as a postgraduate, 1971–3, under Anthony Gross and Bartolomeu Dos Santos. She showed in groups at Galerie 20, Paris, 1987, and Salthouse Gallery, St Ives, 1988, having solo exhibitions in Wiesbaden, Germany, 1979, and at Chapel Hill and Winston-Salem, North Carolina, 1984. University College London and St Thomas' Hospital hold her work. Lived near Penzance, Cornwall.

David ARMITAGE 1943– Painter, born in Tasmania, Australia. He studied at Royal Melbourne Institute of Technology, 1960–5, lived in New Zealand from 1967–73, then settled in Britain. He had many group shows throughout New Zealand, also appearing at Bonython Gallery, Sydney, in 1972, in Young Artists 75 in New York, 1975, and at Museum of Modern Art in Oxford, 1985, in an exhibition of children's book illustrations. Showed solo with Barry Lett Galleries, Auckland, from 1968, later shows including a shared one at Duncan Campbell Contemporary Art, 1993. All the major public galleries in New Zealand hold his work.

Joshua Charles ARMITAGE: *see* **IONICUS**

Kenneth ARMITAGE 1916–2002 Sculptor and teacher, full name William Kenneth Armitage, born in Leeds, where he studied at the College of Art, 1934–7, then at Slade School of Fine Art, 1937–9. There, the teacher A H Gerrard's enthusiasm for ancient Egyptian sculpture was a strong influence. He served in the Army, 1939–46, then taught sculpture at Bath Academy of Art until 1956, although he was a Gregory Fellow in Sculpture at Leeds University, 1953–5. Armitage had his first solo show at Gimpel Fils in 1952, two years later at Bertha Schaefer Gallery in New York. Was represented in British pavilion at Venice Biennale in 1952, where he showed People in a Wind, of 1950, a characteristic work of this period. Earlier Armitage had been a carver. From the end of the 1960s his technique changed again, figures of plaster, paper and wood being produced. Armitage represented Britain at the 1958 Venice Biennale, winning the David E Bright Sculpture Prize. By then Armitage was launched on an international exhibiting career. Armitage was guest artist in Caracas, Venezuela, in 1964; artist-in-residence at City of Berlin Kunstlerprogram, 1967–9; and guest teacher at centenary year, Boston University, 1970. He had retrospectives at Whitechapel Art Gallery in 1959, the Arts Council in 1972, and an eightieth birthday show at Yorkshire Sculpture Park, Bretton Hall, 1996. Elected RA, 1994. Retrospective at Jonathan Clark Fine Art, 2001. Tate Gallery, Victoria & Albert Museum and many other public collections hold examples. Armitage married the artist Joan Moore in 1940. Lived in London.

George Denholm ARMOUR 1864–1949 Painter and illustrator of sporting and military scenes, born in Waterside, Lanarkshire. He studied at St Andrews University, Edinburgh School of Art and Royal Scottish Academy Schools through much of the 1880s. Armour illustrated for magazines such as *Punch*, *The Tatler* and *The Graphic* and showed at RA, Royal Glasgow Institute of the Fine Arts and RSA. He illustrated many books, including his own *Pastime with Good Company*, 1914, *A Hunting Alphabet*, 1929, and *Bridle and Brush*, 1937. Armour's life was horses and hunting, and he hunted with the Beaufort, Sparkford Vale Harriers and the South Berks. In World War I he joined the Remount Service and ended as director of the Salonica Force. Victoria Art Gallery, Bath, holds his work. Lived for many years in Wiltshire. Calton Gallery, Edinburgh, held a show in 1999.

Hazel ARMOUR 1894–1985 Sculptor and medallist, born in Edinburgh, where she studied at the College of Art, also in Paris, gaining bursaries, an honours diploma and a travelling scholarship. Also worked in southern Africa. Exhibited at RSA, Royal Glasgow Institute of the Fine Arts, RA, SWA and Walker Art Gallery in Liverpool, as well as abroad. For many years she maintained studios in Edinburgh and London. Did work for the Scottish National War Memorial in Edinburgh, Scottish women's hospitals, Edinburgh University and Glasgow School of Architecture. Hunting was a favourite recreation, along with travel and music. Armour's head of the theatrical designer Leslie Hurry is included in Eric Newton's monograph *British Sculpture 1944–1946*, published in 1947. She had work in the collection of the artist Edward Le Bas and was included in the Fine Art Society's Sculpture in Britain Between The Wars, 1986. Died in Aldeburgh, Suffolk.

Heda ARMOUR 1916– Painter and etcher. After private education she attended Guildford School of Art, 1930–3, then for six years was at the Royal Academy Schools under Thomas Monnington and Sir Walter Westley Russell. Exhibited RA and in the provinces. British Museum holds an etching by her, but under her first married name of Heda Napper. Lived at Cranleigh, Surrey.

Keith ARMOUR 1931– Printmaker and teacher who studied at Leeds and Royal Colleges of Art. He was included in the British Printmakers exhibition in 1962–3 and in 1964 in The Teaching Image, work by staff of Leeds College of Art, 1964, at Leeds City Art Gallery. Had solo exhibitions in New York and Hong Kong. After the death of his wife in the early 1980s Armour went to the Far East and subsequently died.

Mary ARMOUR 1902–2000 Painter, notably of flowers and landscapes in oil, using a rich palette, born in Blantyre, Lanarkshire, married to the artist William Armour. Like him she taught at Glasgow School of Art, having studied there, 1920–5, under Maurice Greiffenhagen and David Forrester Wilson. She showed with RSW, RSA and Royal Glasgow Institute of the Fine Arts, being a member of all, as well as SSA and Fine Art Society in Glasgow. She was honorary president of Glasgow School of Art in 1982. There was a tribute exhibition at Lillie Art Gallery, Milngavie, 2001. Collections at public galleries in Glasgow, Paisley, Aberdeen, Perth and Edinburgh hold her work. Lived in Kilbarchan, Renfrewshire.

William ARMOUR 1903–1979 Painter in oil and watercolour, draughtsman in pastel and wood engraver. Born at Paisley, Renfrewshire, Armour studied art at Glasgow School of Art 1918–23 under Maurice Greiffenhagen like his wife Mary Armour, whom he married in 1927. William Armour was for a time head of drawing and painting at the same school. Exhibited RSA, RSW and elsewhere. Painted a notable portrait of his wife as a young woman. Work held widely in public collections in Scotland, and elsewhere. Lived at Kilbarchan, Renfrewshire.

Ian ARMOUR-CHELU 1928–2000 Painter who studied with Vivian Pitchforth at Chelsea School of Art. He was the husband of the artist Angela Burfoot and father of the painter Louise Armour-Chelu. Began painting in 1968 and had the first of a series of solo shows in Britain and abroad in 1972. Showed with Agnew and took part in a family exhibition at Markswood Gallery, Great Bardfield, in 1990. Continental landscapes were a feature of his output. Lived at Wissett, near Halesworth, Suffolk.

Louise ARMOUR-CHELU 1960– Artist in pen and ink and coloured inks, born in London, daughter of the artists Ian Armour-Chelu and Angela Burfoot. She studied at Cambridge College of Arts and Technology under David Baxter, 1978–81, gaining an honours degree in English/History of Art. Worked intermittently as an archaeological illustrator, 1981–7, exhibiting drawings from 1982 and illustrating her first book in 1983. Drew for several publishers and admired the work of children's illustrators Peggy Fortnum, Victor Ambrus and Richard Kennedy. Appeared in mixed shows at Mercury Theatre, Colchester; Markswood Gallery, Great Bardfield; Peter Hedley Gallery, Wareham; and Phoenix Gallery, Lavenham. Had a solo show in 1990 with Max Bally. Lived at Hedenham, Suffolk.

Allison ARMOUR-WILSON 1951– Sculptor, born in Paris, France, who studied at Parson's School of Design. After starting as a garden designer, she soon incorporated her sculptures into her designs. Appeared on television, talking about her dual careers. Designed award-winning gardens for venues such as the Chelsea Flower Show, where she also exhibited her sculptures. Armour-Wilson was included in Art on Show, The Gallery in Cork Street, 2001.

Anthony ARMSTRONG 1935– Versatile artist, teacher and gallery director, born in Ireland, who studied at Glasgow School of Art, 1953–7, attending Jordanhill Training College, with a scholarship to Italy, in 1958. Armstrong taught art, 1958–60; engaged in full-time studio work as artist and designer, 1960–7; was part-time director of various galleries, 1967–79, then became a full-time painter. Armstrong exhibited with NEAC, Paisley Institute, RA, Royal Glasgow Institute of the Fine Arts and Flying Colours Gallery. Studied and worked in the Caribbean, France, Italy, the Sandwich Islands and America, with over a dozen solo shows in Britain and abroad. Portraits included the Earl and Countess of Stormont; ecclesiastical commissions a resurrection mural and Stations of the Cross; and corporate commissions included BBC Television; British Petroleum; Scottish Television; and the Royal Automobile Club. Glasgow Museum & Art Galleries; Hunterian Museum in Glasgow; Paisley Museum; Royal Concert Hall in Glasgow, and several overseas collections hold examples.

Arthur Charlton ARMSTRONG 1924–1996 Artist in oil and mixed media, born in Carrickfergus, County Antrim, self-taught. He lived in London, 1956–61, with frequent periods in Spain, 1960–77. Appeared in travelling Irish Arts Council shows in Europe and America. Had a solo show at Avignon Gallery, 1974, and Kreisler Gallery, 1977, both in Madrid, having an Arts Council retrospective, 1950–80, in Belfast in 1981. Arts Councils in north and south of Ireland hold his work. Was a member of RHA. Lived in Dublin.

Helen ARMSTRONG 1938– Artist and illustrator in a range of media, and teacher, born in Bristol, wife of the artist John Armstrong, their son being the artist Joseph Armstrong. She studied at Chelsea and Brighton Schools of Art, 1954–9, teachers including Elisabeth Frink and George Hooper. Taught art in schools, 1960–2, then worked as a freelance illustrator while raising a family. Armstrong's work was "influenced by Expressionist art, Kathe Köllwitz, Matisse and Georgia O'Keeffe". She was a member of the Society of Sussex Painters, Society of Catholic Artists and the International Society of Christian Artists and her work was included in Gerald Woods' 1996 books *Drawing with Pastels* and *The Artist's Studio*. Armstrong showed regularly in Brighton Festival exhibitions from 1976, and in 1996 at the Identity show at Towner Art Gallery in Eastbourne and the Sussex Open Exhibition at Brighton Art Gallery. The dealer Lucy Wertheim owned her work. Lived in Hove, Sussex.

John ARMSTRONG 1893–1973 Painter of imaginative and classical subjects in oil, tempera and gouache; mural painter; designer of film and stage sets; book illustrator and advertising designer. Born in Hastings, Sussex, after Oxford University Armstrong studied at St John's Wood School of Art, 1913–14, then after service in the Army in

World War I returned to St John's Wood briefly. First one-man show at the Leicester Galleries in 1928, became a member of Unit One in 1933, exhibiting in a group show at the Mayor Gallery, 1934. After Unit One Armstrong's work took on a Surrealist character. In the 1930s Armstrong worked as a designer for the theatre and films, including the first performance of the ballet *Façade* and several films made by Sir Alexander Korda. He also did work for Shell-Mex and ICI. During World War II Armstrong was an official war artist. After it he continued to exhibit widely, including The Storm, for the Festival of Britain in 1951, and at the RA extensively from that year. He painted a ceiling for the Council Chamber, Bristol, in 1955 and a mural for the Royal Marsden Hospital, at Sutton, Surrey, six years later. Armstrong had strong left-wing political convictions and from the time of the Spanish Civil War, when he painted Pro Patria, his pictures occasionally reflected his views. Symbolism is also a feature of his work. Armstrong's pictures are fastidiously painted in muted colours and reflect his own dry wit and gentle nature. Memorial exhibition at RA in 1975, with tour. Lived in London.

John ARMSTRONG 1937– Artist, mainly in oil, and teacher, born in Mitcham, Surrey, husband of the artist Helen Armstrong, their artist son being Joseph Armstrong. John Armstrong studied at Swindon, Walthamstow and Brighton art schools, his teaching including University of Brighton. Armstrong was a painter of Christian and spiritual subjects, a member of the International Society of Christian Artists, Christian Arts UK and the Society of Catholic Artists. The Byzantine and Sienese Schools were an influence. Also showed with the Society of Sussex Painters, at RA and Mall Galleries, and had solo exhibitions at Hove Museum & Art Gallery, 1975, Grange Art Gallery, Rottingdean, 1996, and St Raphael Gallery, 1999. Gerald Woods' books *Art of Landscape and Seascape Painting* and *Practical Oil Painting* included Armstrong's work. Notable work for churches included altarpieces for St Mary's, Bath, and St Peter's, Brighton, 10 paintings for St George's, Hove, and a great crucifix for St Boniface, Tooting. Nuffield Foundation and East Sussex County Council hold examples. Lived in Hove, Sussex.

Joseph ARMSTRONG 1971– Artist and illustrator, using acrylic, gouache and lino-print, born in Brighton, Sussex, son of the artists John and Helen Armstrong. He studied at Norwich Institute of Art and Design, 1990–3, teachers including Robert Mason, then at University of Brighton, 1993–5, under John Lord. Was a member of the Brighton Illustrators Group and showed with the Society of Catholic Artists, 1995. Solo exhibitions included Terre à Terre, Brighton, and the town's Library Gallery, both 1996, and Duke of York's, Brighton, 1998. Lived in Hove, Sussex.

Robin ARMSTRONG 1947– Painter of wildlife and the countryside, commercial artist and teacher, who aged 12 sold his first painting, A Prairie Falcon, to the milkman for £5. In 1966, he joined Phoenix Studios as a trainee illustrator and attended the London School of Printing, the year following sailing around the world as a merchant seaman. On return, Armstrong worked as a commercial artist, had a first solo exhibition in Bromley which sold out at the preview, then in 1970 moved to Devon and began painting full-time. Armstrong taught art at Okehampton Comprehensive, 1971, part-time at Exeter College of Art, 1975, and was artist-in-residence at the National Marine Aquarium, Plymouth, 1998–9. In 1977, Armstrong joined South West Water as a river warden; he also made global field trips and joined an Arctic expedition. Made a number of television documentaries, his books including the best-selling *The Painted Stream*, 1984, *Split Cane & Sable*, 1988, *Under the Bridge*, 1990, and *Riverside Folio*, 1996, with the sculptor and publisher Justin Knowles. Exhibitions included South West Academy of Fine and Applied Arts, Barbican Gallery in Plymouth, Oliver Swann Gallery and abroad. In 2002, he shared a four-man exhibition at The Wykeham Gallery, Stockbridge.

Shearer ARMSTRONG 1894–1983 Painter, printmaker and illuminator, born in Penge, southeast London, as Alixe, also known as Alice, Jean Shearer (her husband was a civil servant, Henry Armstrong). She studied at Slade School of Fine Art, 1912–14, also in Karlsruhe, Germany, and briefly with Stanhope Forbes in Newlyn, having moved to Cornwall in 1921. Armstrong showed with RA, RSA and Penwith Society of Arts of which she was a founder member, with St Ives Society of Arts and Taurus Artists as a member, elsewhere in the provinces and widely abroad. Had solo shows at Chiltern Gallery and Scottish Gallery, Edinburgh. She had a studio in St Ives for many years, living in Carbis Bay. The windswept romanticism of Cornwall was a key element in Armstrong's work. HRH The Duke of Edinburgh, Scottish Education Committee and Cornwall Education Authority hold examples.

Tim ARMSTRONG 1945– Painter, printmaker, artist in opto-kinetic construction and teacher, born in Cambridge. Studied at Cambridgeshire College of Arts and Technology, 1962–4, Nottingham College of Art and Design, 1964–7, where his work was influenced by the tuition of Bridget Riley, and at Slade School of Fine Art, 1967–9, under Robyn Denny. Went on to teach at Glasgow School of Art. Did some scientific book illustration. Showed widely in England and abroad. Work held by Doncaster Museum and Art Gallery, Scottish Arts Council and Cambridge University. Lived for some time at Kirkintilloch, Dunbartonshire.

Valerie ARMSTRONG 1948– Versatile artist, craftsman, art therapist and teacher, born in Stoke-on-Trent, Staffordshire, who made pre-diploma studies at the local College of Art, 1965–6; did a one-year textiles diploma course at Hornsey College of Art, 1967–8; transferred to study printed and woven textiles at Croydon College of Art, 1968–70; and gained a postgraduate diploma in art therapy at St Albans College of Art, 1975–6. Worked as a decorative artist for A/B Gustavsbergs Fabriker, a ceramics firm in Gustavsberg, Sweden, 1970–1, from 1971–5 in Paris as a painter and Batik artist and for Trianon Press, studying mosaics at L'École des Beaux-Arts part-time. The years 1976–86 included periods working as an art therapist in England, travel within Israel and as an English language teacher in Spain. Murals and painted screens were features of Armstrong's artistic work from 1986. Later, it took a semi-abstract turn, which "corresponds to the exciting discovery of the freedom of the monotype and monoprint techniques", producing works which had "an intangible, dream-like quality which radiate colour, warmth and humour." She was elected a member of Suffolk Craft Society, 1992, Norfolk Contemporary Crafts Society, 1994, and of Gainsborough's House Print Workshop, Sudbury. After several years teaching art in Otley

College and to young offenders at Warren Hill Prison, Armstrong became a full-time artist. As well as group shows in East Anglia, Germany and France, had a series of solo exhibitions, later ones including Belstead House, Ipswich, 1998, and 1998 and 2000 at Denis Taplin Gallery, Woodbridge, Suffolk, where she lived. In 2003, she shared a show with Carrie Herries at Aldeburgh Cinema Gallery, Suffolk.

Warwick ARMSTRONG 1919– Painter, designer and teacher, born in Melbourne, Victoria, Australia, a strong draughtsman and Colourist, influenced by Picasso. He attended the Royal Melbourne Institute of Technology, studying interior design, 1937–9, and stage design and painting, 1945–6. For several years he concentrated on theatre design in Melbourne, then moved to Britain, 1949–58, where he worked among others for the Mercury and Mermaid Theatres, Royal Shakespeare Theatre at Stratford-upon-Avon, Glyndebourne Opera, The Old Vic, in films for the J Arthur Rank Organisation, EMI Records and the Royal Opera House. He exhibited with the Australian Artists' Association in its first show at RWS' Conduit Street gallery, 1953. Back in Australia, Armstrong continued with stage work and taught extensively, took part in mixed and solo shows, and had a retrospective at Devise Gallery, Melbourne, 1987, of selected paintings, 1962–86. In 1978–9 he was granted leave by the Chisholm Institute of Technology, where he taught art history, 1961–84, to research the work of several European painters including Picasso, and was for five months at the Michael Karolyi Foundation at Vence, southern France. Melbourne University, other Australian collections and the Royal Shakespeare Theatre Collection, Stratford, hold examples.

Sarah ARMSTRONG-JONES 1964– Painter, draughtsman and designer, born in London, daughter of HRH The Princess Margaret and the photographer the Earl of Snowdon. She did an art foundation course at Camberwell School of Arts and Crafts, 1982–3. Next at Middlesex Polytechnic she studied printed textiles, 1984–5, then at Royal Academy Schools, 1985–8, obtained an undergraduate diploma, in 1988–91 a postgraduate diploma. Gained the Winsor & Newton Drawing Prize in 1988, the Creswick Landscape Prize & Silver Medal in 1990. From 1987 showed at RA Summer Exhibition, taking part in Premium Show, RA, 1988–90. In 2003 had a solo show at Redfern Gallery. After much study of a place it was transformed into space and light in her work, with a strong underlying draughtsmanship and expressive brushstrokes. Like her brother, the furniture designer David Linley, Armstrong-Jones was educated at Bedales School. She was there 1975–82 and like him was included in the 1999 exhibition Bedales Art & Design, organised by William Jackson Gallery at Art99, in the Business Design Centre.

Barbara ARNASON: *see* **Barbara Moray WILLIAMS**

Keith ARNATT 1930– Artist and teacher, born in Oxford. He studied at the School of Art there, 1951–5, then Royal Academy Schools, 1956–8. Arnatt used photographs and text, examples of which are held by Arts Council, parody and irony to comment on the state of art in his time. From the early 1960s he held several teaching posts, including Liverpool, Manchester and Newport Colleges of Art. Arnatt exhibited in a series of British and overseas mixed shows such as Environmental-Reversal, Camden Arts Centre, 1969; Seven Exhibitions at Tate Gallery and The New Art, Hayward Gallery, both in 1972; British Artists of the 60s at Tate Gallery in 1977; and Museum of Drawers at ICA in 1979. His one-man show at Whitechapel Art Gallery in 1977 was called Looking at Me. Arts Council holds works from his 1980s Pictures from a Rubbish Tip and Howlers Hill series. Lived in Llandogo, Gwent.

Raymond ARNATT 1934–2004 Sculptor and teacher, born in Oxfordshire. He studied at Oxford School of Art, 1951–5, and Royal College of Art, 1957–61, in the latter year gaining the Sainsbury Award. During most of the 1960s he taught in art schools, in 1971 becoming senior lecturer in sculpture at Chelsea School of Art. Among Arnatt's commissions were one for Queen's College, Edgbaston, in 1966, and one for Milton Keynes in 1975. He received a prize in the Sir Joseph Swan Memorial Sculpture Competition in 1969 and the Herbert Baker Travelling Award from Royal Academy in 1974. In that year he had a one-man show at Park Square Gallery, Leeds. He also took part in an Arts Council travelling show in 1967 and a group exhibition at the Serpentine Gallery in 1977. Arnatt eventually moved to Canada, living in Cochrane, Alberta, with his sculptor wife JoAnne Schachtel and their daughter Mary. He collaborated with Schachtel on several sculptural projects and multi-media installations. In 1981 he became a member of the faculty of the department of art at the University of Calgary, where he was professor of art (sculpture). He was elected to the Royal Canadian Academy of Art, a founder of the Triangle Gallery of Visual Arts in Calgary and a member of art collectives. Arnatt was well-versed in quantum physics, theoretical mathematics, philosophy and literature and worked in interdisciplinary projects with colleagues, as he "liked to be exposed to different perspectives, genders, approaches and sensibilities." As well as the Triangle Gallery, he showed at Winnipeg Art Gallery, Muttart Public Art Gallery (later known as the Art Gallery of Calgary), Virginia Christopher Gallery, Deacon Ulrich Gallery, Lattice Gallery and Glenbow Museum. There was a major Arnatt retrospective at Triangle Gallery in 2003.

Victoria ARNEY 1965– Abstract painter and teacher, born in Southampton, who studied at Winchester School of Art, 1984–5; gained a first-class honours degree from Wimbledon School of Art, 1985–8; then a higher diploma at Slade School of Fine Art, 1989–91. Among awards were selection from the Slade for the Trinity College Fellowship, 1991; Cheltenham Fellowship in Painting, 1991–2; and in 1992 she gained the Duveen Travel Scholarship to India and won the East & South Open at Norwich Gallery. From 1992 had considerable teaching experience, including Cheltenham & Gloucester College of Art; Nottingham, Northumberland, Staffordshire, Sunderland, Reading and Central England Universities; Wimbledon School of Art; and Birmingham Institute of Art & Design. In 1996 she held a residency at Casa Manilva, Spain. Group shows included Bernard Jacobson and New Academy Galleries, both 1992; Acme Open Studios, 1993; Paintscapes, Harewood House, Leeds, 1995; and Cross Currents, Reed's Wharf Gallery at Barbican Centre, 1996. Solo shows included Isis Gallery, Birmingham, 1993.

Marjorie ARNFIELD 1930–2001 Artist, notably working in acrylic, and teacher, born in Sunderland, County Durham, who was struck by juvenile chronic arthritis aged four, and suffered from arthritis for much of her life. Despite the need for regular hospital treatment, she obtained her design and art teacher's diplomas studying at Sunderland College of Art and at the King Edward VII College of Art, Durham University, tutors including Lawrence Gowing, Harry Thubron, Quentin Bell and Victor Pasmore. She returned to teach at her old school in Sunderland, other experience including adult education departments of Nottingham and Stirling Universities; Cumbria and Nottinghamshire Education Authorities; Workers' Educational Association; King's College in Cambridge; and many painting schools in Britain and abroad. Took part in many mixed exhibitions, including Northern Young Artists Exhibition, touring; Huddersfield Art Gallery; RWS; Lake Artists, Grasmere; Castle Museum in Nottingham; and Laing Art Gallery, Newcastle upon Tyne. In the early 1990s, Arnfield was drawn to record the demise of the coal industry, in 1994 British Coal touring her show: Coal Mining in Nottinghamshire – a Tribute, for which she went underground, in a wheelchair, to see the industry first hand. Exhibitions at Renishaw Hall, seat of the Sitwell family, and at municipal art galleries and museums in Chesterfield, Mansfield and Ilkeston were followed in 1996–9 by a WAC-funded tour through Wales and England. After her death in 2001, a major show of Arnfield's work was held at Djanogly Art Gallery, University of Nottingham Arts Centre. Arnfield had several dozen solo shows. Graves Art Gallery in Sheffield, Sunderland and Middlesbrough galleries and other mining museum and corporate collections hold examples. Lived in Westhorpe, Southwell, Nottinghamshire.

Ann ARNOLD 1936– Painter, born in Newcastle upon Tyne, Northumberland, married to the painter Graham Arnold. She studied at Epsom School of Art, 1956–9, working as an art therapist, 1959–69. Was one of the seven artists who formed The Brotherhood of Ruralists in 1975, which had its first exhibition in 1976. Apart from Ruralist shows she exhibited in mixed shows including Festival Gallery, Bath, 1974; Bristol City Art Gallery, 1975; and RA Summer Exhibition, from 1977. Had her first solo show at Festival Gallery, Bath, 1979, exhibiting with New Grafton Gallery from 1981. She had a strong affinity with the poet John Clare and illustrated *Clares Countryside*, published in 1981.

Charles Geoffrey ARNOLD 1915– Painter, commercial artist and teacher, born in Clayton, Yorkshire, where he finally settled. After a period of initial study at Bradford College of Art, under Henry Butler, 1931–4, Arnold spent five years until early in World War II with the advertising agency Marshall Hardy as a studio artist. After the war he was from 1946–7 at Camberwell School of Arts and Crafts, then at Slade School of Fine Art, 1947–50, his teachers including William Coldstream. Arnold showed with RWA of which he was a member, LG and RA.

Graham ARNOLD 1932– Painter and teacher, born in Beckenham, Kent, married to the artist Ann Arnold. He was one of the seven founders of The Brotherhood of Ruralists, in 1975, which had its first show at RA in 1976. Arnold studied at Beckenham School of Art, 1947–52, and at Royal College of Art, 1955–8. He was awarded a painting scholarship to Italy, 1958–60. For a dozen years from 1961 he taught at Ravensbourne and Kingston Colleges of Art and the Royal Academy Schools. His group contributions included Gimpel Fils, 1955; LG, 1962; Chichester National Art Exhibition, 1975, where he gained major prize for painting; Fischer Fine Art, 1976. Solo shows included Brillig Arts Centre, 1979; David Paul Gallery, Chichester, 1982; Piccadilly Gallery, 1983; and a retrospective at The Tabernacle Cultural Centre, Machynlleth, 1992, with a seventieth birthday show there, 2002. Contemporary Art Society and provincial galleries hold his work.

Liz ARNOLD 1964–2001 Painter, teacher and community worker whose work included brightly coloured, slightly Surrealist pictures such as her Mythic Heaven, 1995, included in New Contempories, 1996, at Tate Gallery in Liverpool and at Camden Arts Centre. She was born in Perth, Scotland, and gained a degree in fine art at Middlesex Polytechnic, 1987–90, and her master's degree at Goldsmiths' College, 1992–4. Other exhibitions included Tinsel Adam Gallery, 1994; and Hard Work Shift One, at London's Exmouth Market, and Cocaine Orgasm, Bank, both 1995. While painting, Arnold pursued a second career in art and community work: at Cambridge House, Camberwell, and at Fast Forward and Only Connect, two clubs in Southwark. In 1999, she was appointed lecturer in painting at Slade School of Fine Art. Had two solo shows at Lotta Hammer; in 1997; and 1999, in which she showed pure landscapes, interiors and still lifes, as well as pictures seemingly influenced by 1950s science fiction films. Lived in London.

Phyllis Anne ARNOLD 1938– Painter and miniaturist, born in Belfast. Her father was an engineer and she worked for a time in the commercial art department of the aircraft makers Short Brothers and Harland, claiming to be self-taught as a painter. She was a Hunting Group competition finalist on several occasions in the early 1980s and showed RA, RMS, SM and widely in Northern Ireland, where she was for a time vice-president of the Ulster Society of Women Artists. Sometimes signed work only with initials. Lived in Bangor, County Down.

William Arthur ARNOLD 1909–1977 Commercial artist in scraperboard and watercolour, born in London. Attended Leyton School of Art. Exhibited at RA and Army Art Society and had a one-man show at the Towner Art Gallery, Eastbourne, in 1947. Sold a watercolour to the Pakistan government. Lived at Chalfont St Giles, Buckinghamshire, and in Bridport, Dorset.

Sally ARNUP 1930– Sculptor and teacher, married to the painter and potter Mick Arnup. From the age of five she wanted to sculpt, attending Kingston School of Art from 1943. Karel Vogel was an influence. From 1950–1 was at Camberwell School of Arts and Crafts, then for several years at Royal College of Art, where Frank Dobson and John Skeaping were important teachers. After marriage settled in Yorkshire and was head of sculpture at York Art School, 1958–72. Showed at RA, RSA, RBA, Paris Salon and John Davies Contemporary, Stow-on-the-Wold. Was made a fellow of RBS. Arnup's speciality was bronzes of animals, created with the live animal in front of her, with great attention to detail. In 1971 she made and cast a silver leopard, presented to HM The Queen by City of York. Arnup had a show of Animal Bronzes at Brian Sinfield Gallery, Burford, in 2003.

Haika AROM 1946– Artist, restorer and teacher working in various media, including textiles and embroidery, born in Israel. Studied art and design at Teachers Training College, Tel-Aviv, 1967–9, gaining an honours degree in fine art from Ravensbourne College of Art, 1969–72. After travel in Europe and America, 1973, returned to Israel and in 1974 taught painting at high school in Beer-Sheva, in 1979 restoring in the archaeology department at Tel-Aviv University. Group exhibitions included Gallery lll, 1986; Linda Blackstone Gallery, Pinner, 1987; British Painters 1988, Mall Galleries; and Ben Uri Gallery and RA Summer Exhibition, both from 1992. There was a solo exhibition in 1999 at St Raphael Gallery of works on hand-made paper. Arom said that all her work was, "really landscape. Some of these landscapes just appear, from within. Others are personal expressions of sights caught by the eye or the edge of the brain.... When it all feels right – I stop." Lived in South Harrow, Middlesex.

Margaret ARRIDGE 1921– Painter and private art tutor, born in Salisbury, Wiltshire. After education in Croydon she attended Chelsea School of Art, where her teachers included Bernard Adams. She eventually settled in Johannesburg, South Africa, where she held a number of solo shows, but also exhibited in England at RA and elsewhere as well as at Paris Salon.

Sydney ARROBUS 1901–1990 Watercolourist, commercial painter and artist in collage, he studied at Heatherley's School of Fine Art. Showed widely, including RI, RWA, SGA and with Hampstead Artists' Council. Also had many one-man shows, including Woodstock Gallery, Cooling Gallery, several times in Everyman Foyer Gallery in Hampstead and Finsbury Library, Islington. Both the London Boroughs of Camden and Islington hold his work, which is notable for its light, often witty touch. Lived in London, where in 2003 Impressions of Arrobus was held at Burgh House.

Sue ARROWSMITH 1950– Artist using photographs and mixed media, born in Lancashire. Symbols were a key element in her work. She studied at University of Nottingham, 1968–71, then Slade School of Fine Art, 1973–5. Was artist-in-residence at Wolfson College, Cambridge, 1986–7. Group shows included John Moores Liverpool Exhibition from 1987; she won a prize in 1989–90. Others were Excavations, Vienna and Southampton, 1988, and Photography Now, Victoria & Albert Museum and Tate Gallery, Liverpool, 1988–9. Her first solo show was at Matt's Gallery, 1982, after which she showed regularly with Anthony Reynolds Gallery. Arts Council holds her work.

Sue ARROWSMITH 1968– Artist producing abstract work, as in her ink and acrylic on fibreboard Forge, made of myriad vertical lines, which won her a prize in the 1997–8 John Moores Liverpool Exhibition. Born in Denton, Manchester, Arrowsmith did a foundation course at Thameside College of Technology, 1984–6, then gained an honours degree in textiles at Goldsmiths' College, 1987–90. Group exhibitions included Woodlands Art Gallery, 1990, and Archbishop Tenison's Grammar School, 1992. Had solo shows at Entwistle, 1994 and 1997; Galerie Frahm, Copenhagen, Denmark, 1999; and Galerie Fahnemann, Berlin, Germany, 2001. In 2004, Arrowsmith was an Artist of the Day at Flowers Central, chosen by Ian Davenport. Arts Council holds her work. Lived in London.

ART & LANGUAGE Group of conceptual artists formed in 1968 by Terry Atkinson, David Bainbridge, Michael Baldwin and Harold Hurrell. Their aim was to produce the magazine *Art-Language*, which first appeared in 1969, and it was to analyse the relationship of the word and the image. Atkinson, Bainbridge and Baldwin were in close contact as they all taught the art theory course at Coventry College of Art from autumn 1969 to mid-1971, when it was terminated. Bainbridge, Baldwin and other staff members were dismissed, Atkinson remaining until the final intake of art theory students graduated in 1973. By then Bainbridge had parted company with Art & Language about two years, and Atkinson, after a period of gradual disenchantment, left in 1975. Eventually, the group would expand to include several dozen people, with an international membership. Their work was to appear under the common Art & Language label, breaking with the tradition of the personality artist. Texts, posters, paintings and other works were given an extensive worldwide showing, Lisson Gallery being a notable venue. Retrospective at Musée d'Art Moderne, Lille, France, 2002. Arts Council holds Art & Language productions. In 2005, Art & Language had a show at the Guildhall Art Gallery, with a linked symposium at London Metropolitan University considering the extent to which the artwork was characterised by complexity. Also in 2005, a Lisson Gallery Art & Language exhibition, Hard to Say When, comprised new work with historic and performance documentation.

THE ARTIST'S PLACEMENT GROUP: *see* **John LATHAM**

ARTLAB: *see* **Charlotte CULLINAN**

ARTO 1940–1987 Painter and writer, full name Arto der Haroutunian, born in the Middle East of Armenian parents. Arrived in Britain in his early teens and qualified as an architect at Manchester University. As well as designing many restaurants, clubs and hotels, he became known as a cookery writer and broadcaster, an authority on the culinary cultures of the Middle East and North Africa, publishing many books. As a painter he was noted for landscapes which drew on Oriental sources and had strong abstract traits. He showed at Central Library, Manchester, 1964; Colin Jellicoe Gallery, Manchester, 1964–86; Manchester University, 1965; Langton Gallery, 1977; Stockport Art Gallery, 1982; and elsewhere. National Art Gallery of Armenia, Sarian Academy of Arts in Syria and several other foreign galleries hold his work.

ARTS EXCHANGE– Coventry-based co-operative involved in communal and community projects. Examples are the ceramic Snake in the Grass, at Trentham Road, Coventry, artists including Jonathan Ford and Lizzie Murphy, commissioned by Coventry City Council, 1997; Ford's metal Schlanke Meth, at Wainbody Wood School, commissioned by Arts Exchange in the same year; and the wooden Mushrooms, for Friends of Canley Ford, sited at Canley, 2000.

James ARUNDEL 1875–1960 Painter, born in Bradford where he died, although he also lived for a time in Lincolnshire. By profession a lighthouse builder and refurbisher, Arundel did not begin painting seriously until shortly before World War II, studying part-time at Bradford Arts Club. Showed at RA, Beaux Arts Gallery, Paris Salon and extensively in the provinces. City Art Gallery, Bradford, holds his work and gave him a retrospective in 1959.

Barby ASANTE 1971– Artist and lecturer, born and lived in London, real name Barbara Asante, whose work offered its audience interactive experiences. For her solo show Journey into the East at The Showroom, in 2002, Asante created the essence of a teashop where people could "gather their thoughts, or meet others over a cup of tea." For periods, it became a salon, "hosting a series of talks to look at colonialism, ethnographic practice and British identity." Asante gained an honours degree in fine art in time-based media at University of East London, 1992–5, additional studies including her master's in visual culture at Middlesex University, 1997–9. Held various residencies, visiting lectureships including University of North London and London Guildhall University. From 1997, was part-time information assistant at The Photographers' Gallery.

Marit Guinness ASCHAN 1919–2004 Painter, enameller and writer who studied in Germany, Italy and France and with Barry Craig. Showed RA, Leicester Galleries, in public galleries in Exeter and Manchester and abroad. Had a solo exhibition at Beaux Arts Gallery in 1948, later ones including Saga Gallery, 1990. She was president of the Artist Enamellers from foundation in 1968 and among her books was *The Art of Jewellery*, published that year. Among her commissions was the focal point for the cross for the high altar in Exeter Cathedral. Victoria & Albert Museum, Royal Norwegian Embassy and Brooklyn Museum in New York hold examples. Chelsea Arts Club member who lived in London.

Pamela ASCHERSON: *see* **Pamela RACHET**

Roy ASCOTT 1934– Artist, theoretician and teacher, born in Bath, Somerset. He studied at department of fine art at King's College, Newcastle upon Tyne, 1955–9, graduating with an honours degree, teachers including Victor Pasmore and Richard Hamilton. From 1960–80 Ascott worked, exhibited and taught as a painter in England and America. From 1980 he worked in cyberspace, mostly with projects involving international telematic networks. He published over 50 theoretic texts. Ascott became director of the Centre for Advanced Inquiry in the Interactive Arts and head of the field of interactive arts at Newport School of Art & Design, Gwent College of Higher Education. He took part in numerous group shows, international and touring exhibitions, 1960–70. Had a solo exhibition at Univision Gallery, Newcastle, 1960, later one-man exhibitions including Dartington Hall, Totnes, 1980. Lived in Bristol.

Barbara ASH 1966– Sculptor in stone who was born and then settled in London. She studied at West Sussex College of Art & Design, 1983–5; Middlesex Polytechnic, 1985–9; and Royal College of Art under Glynn Williams, 1993–5. Group shows included Gloria Gallery in Nicosia, Cyprus; Clevedon Pier Gallery; Bristol Sculpture Shed; and Opus 39 Gallery, Nicosia. Had a solo show at Fallen Angel, Islington, and one in 1993 at Herbert Read Gallery, Kent Institute of Art & Design, Canterbury. She was Henry Moore Fellow, 1992–3. Middlesex Polytechnic, Lemba Pottery in Cyprus, J Sainsbury, and Horice Museum and Rabasova Gallery, both in the Czech Republic, hold her works. Ash latterly had a studio/workshop in Bristol, where she completed Bath stone reliefs at the Sainsbury Winterstoke Road store in 1991.

Bernadette ASH 1934– Painter and draughtsman who was a professional radiographer until 1973. Then studied at Byam Shaw School of Painting, 1973–4, Camberwell School of Arts and Crafts, 1974–7. Showed with NEAC, at RA and RWA. Lived in the Exmoor National Park and featured the countryside in much of her work, which was given a solo show at Woodlands Art Gallery, 1982.

Derek ASHBY 1926– Painter, sculptor in steel and teacher, born in Chadderton, Lancashire. He studied at Edinburgh College of Art, 1948–51, teachers including William Gillies and Robert Henderson Blyth, then at Royal Academy Schools, 1953–6, with Henry Rushbury and Peter Greenham. Lecturer at Gray's School of Art, Aberdeen, 1960–87. Was a member of SSA and Aberdeen Artists' Society, also showing at RA and RSA. Scottish Arts Council, Keston Training College and galleries in Brighton and Dunfermline hold his work. Lived in Banchory, Kincardineshire.

Nigel ASHCROFT 1951– Painter, especially in watercolour, who was born in Heemstede, Holland, living in Sweden and Eire as a child before moving to England in 1965. After education at Berkhamsted School, spent a term at Gloucestershire College of Art & Design, 1969. Exhibited in mixed shows at RA, 1987, RWA 1981–2–4 and abroad, including the Dordogne, France, where he spent many summers painting. Solo shows at Frost & Reed, subject matter "tending towards the familiar", notably buildings, landscapes and everyday objects. Lived near Stroud, Gloucestershire.

Faith ASHE: *see* **Faith WINTER**

Edward James ASHENDEN 1896– Watercolour painter, designer, model-maker and decorative artist. Born at Wandsworth Common, London, he studied at Putney School of Art just prior to World War I, then again 1919–22. Ashenden's designing and model-making skills were employed widely, including the Wellcome Historical Medical Museum and the Century of Progress Exhibition, in Chicago. During World War II he was a camouflage officer with the Air Ministry. Exhibited RA, RI and in the provinces. Lived in London.

Florence May ASHER 1888–1977 Painter and printmaker. She studied at the Royal Academy Schools 1913–18, where she won a silver medal and gained the Landseer Scholarship. She lived in a number of places in southern England and exhibited extensively at RBA, also at Goupil Gallery, RA, SWA and elsewhere. Finally lived in Reigate, Surrey, with the painter Rosalie Emslie.

Colin James ASHFORD 1919– Painter and illustrator in oil and watercolour, born in Ackworth, Yorkshire. He attended Wakefield School of Art, 1933–7, then Glasgow School of Art, 1937–9, under W O Hutchison and Tom Purvis. Ashford worked in advertising studios and magazine publishing before going freelance as a painter and illustrator. He was a founder-member of the Guild of Aviation Artists and a fellow of the Central Institute of Art and Design. Ashford was "influenced by marine artists of the 1920s and 1930s, also poster illustrators of the same period". Took part in group exhibitions at RSMA and RI and had solo shows in Kent galleries. Historical marine and aviation subjects were a speciality. Royal Air Force Museum, Hendon, National Maritime Museum and Ashmolean Museum in Oxford are among collections holding examples. Lived in London.

ASHLEY 1903–1973 Industrial designer, commercial artist, designer and painter, full name Ashley Havinden. He had not received any formal art training when he joined one of London's largest advertising agencies, W S Crawford, in 1922. Influenced by the Bauhaus movement in Germany, he developed a bold, angular style with uncluttered typography. During the 1930s he handled several major advertising campaigns, including Drink Milk Daily. Humorous line drawings were a feature of his work, and he created the Ashley typeface. His skills were also used for the Paris Exhibition of 1937; by the Imperial War Museum for shows; in textile and rug designs, fabrics and posters. After World War II service he resumed his position with Crawford's and made a big contribution to the Britain Can Make It exhibition at the Victoria & Albert Museum in 1946. His paintings, abstract in style, were shown at Marlborough Fine Art, Reid and Lefevre and Leicester Galleries. Official positions included governor, Central School of Arts and Crafts, 1958–67, president of the Society of Industrial Artists, 1953, and president of the Double Crown Club, 1955–6. From 1967–9 Havinden was master of the exclusive Royal Designers of Industry, having been elected in 1947. Lived at Hertingfordbury, Hertfordshire for many years. In 1995 Hertford Museum held an exhibition, in 2003 Dean Gallery, Edinburgh, reviewed his career as painter and designer.

Mike ASHLEY 1937– Painter, born in London, whose recurring interests centred around ancient history; surface qualities such as rust, lichens and water; fighter aircraft; and birds. Ashley studied at Hornsey College of Art, 1958–61. He was included in Young Contemporaries at ICA, 1955, later group shows including Ipswich Open, Christchurch Mansion, 1995, and 49 & Rising, Conservatory Gallery, Cambridge, 2002. Was a member of Suffolk Open Studios and had series of solo exhibitions at John Russell Gallery, Ipswich. Lived at Battisford, Suffolk.

Malcolm ASHMAN 1957– Painter and illustrator, born and lived in Bath, Somerset. He attended Somerset College of Art, 1975–8, studying graphic design, after which he worked on personal projects as a painter. Between 1988–96 completed book commissions for the fantasy publisher Dragon's World, including *Alice's Adventures in Wonderland, Through the Looking Glass, French Fairy Tales* and *Fabulous Beasts*. Was a member of RBA, showed regularly at Mall Galleries, also exhibiting widely in other group and solo shows in London and the west of England, including the South West Academy.

Patricia ASHMORE 1929– Versatile artist in a range of media who studied at Chelsea Polytechnic and portrait painting privately with Sonia Mervyn. Was a member of PS and Association of Sussex Artists, also exhibiting with RP. Lady Ashmore lived in Sundridge, Kent.

ASHTOCK 1932–2002 Interior decorator and painter in oil. His full name was David Ashton-Bostock, which he sometimes used on work. Born in London, he attended Wellington College, then studied at Maidstone College of Art, 1947–50, and Byam Shaw School of Art, 1953–4, under Patrick Phillips. Went on to establish his own interior decorating business in London, where he lived, also near Sittingbourne, Kent. Showed At UA, NEAC, ROI, Ridley Art Club of which he was a member, Paris Salon and elsewhere.

Audrey ASHTON 1892–1985 Painter in oil, born in Ben Rhydding, Yorkshire. She was educated partly in Paris, where she also studied art and at Central School of Arts and Crafts. Showed at RA, RBA, Leicester Galleries, LG and Young Contemporaries. Lived near Ashford, Kent.

Edwina ASHTON 1965– Artist, born in London, who gained an honours degree in philosophy at Gonville and Caius College, Cambridge, 1985–9; made foundation studies at Camberwell College of Art, 1990–1; and graduated with honours in fine art, Goldsmiths' College, 1993–6. In 2003, she had a solo show at Arnolfini, Bristol, part of Recognition: Part Two, for emerging British artists. Ashton's work there was described as "warped and beautiful by turns, brought to life in an energetic combination of fluid watercolour, nervous pen-work, precise pencil studies, and for Arnolfini two specially executed wall drawings. Her world is populated with animals and individuals who, whether noble or eccentric, are equally disconnected from each other and the world around them". By then, Ashton had had two solo exhibitions: We Speak Your Language, Artlab, Imperial College, 2001, and Excusez Moi, hammer sidi, 2002. Later group shows included Videoidyll, Staatesbank, Mitte, Berlin, 2002, and Video Invitational, fa projects, 2003.

Graham ASHTON 1948– Artist in mixed media, born Birkenhead, Cheshire. He studied at Manchester College of Art, 1966–7, Coventry College of Art, 1967–70, and University of Calgary, 1970–1. In 1983–4 Ashton was artist-in-residence at Walker Art Gallery and Bridewell Studios, Liverpool, his Dry Dock being commissioned for International Garden Festival. A dominant theme in his work for many years was the threat of global nuclear annihilation, as in his Is that Death? And are there Two? in John Moores Liverpool Exhibition, 1987. His work appeared in Images of War, at Chapter Art Gallery, Cardiff, 1985. His first solo show was in 1977, later ones including Museum of Modern Art, Oxford, 1985. Arts Council holds his work. Lived in London.

Raymond ASHTON 1929– Painter, poster designer and teacher. Attended Middlesbrough School of Art, 1946–50 then Leeds College of Art, 1950–1. Painted a number of posters and murals, some while serving in Egypt, others in Middlesbrough, where he lived.

Sean ASHTON 1971– Artist producing sculptural and wall-based pieces as in Sonnet, presented by Contemporary Art Society Projects at *The Economist* Tower, 2002. His works there revolved "around the theme of surface. They explore the issues of authorship, originality and authenticity, with a specific focus on the production of *The Economist* newspaper within the building." Ashton was then based in London, studying for his doctorate in fine art at Goldsmiths' College. He gained his master's in sculpture from the Royal College of Art in 1997 and showed extensively in London, notably at Nylon and Modern Art in 1999; Cabinet and Mobile Home in 2000; and at 3 Dingley Place, 2001. He also exhibited internationally at Gavin Brown Enterprises, New York in America, and at KX, Hamburg, in Germany.

Tony ASHTON 1948– Painter of geometrical abstracts who attended Bath Academy of Art, Corsham, Lincoln College of Art and West of England College of Art in Bristol, 1966–71. He took part in Coracle Press Miniatures show which toured Britain. Had solo shows at 5 Dryden Street Gallery and LYC Gallery, Cumbria, and in 1980 at Woodlands Art Gallery. Lived in Plumstead, southeast London.

Will ASHTON 1881–1963 Landscape and seascape painter, born in York, but early on educated in Adelaide, Australia, where he had gone with his family, his father being an artist, James Ashton. Back in Europe John William Ashton, to give him his full name, studied in Paris at the Académie Julian, also under Julius Olsson and Algernon Talmage. Painted widely in Europe and exhibited RA, Goupil Gallery, ROI, RBA and Paris Salon; also established a reputation in Australia, where his work is held in many public collections. He won a number of awards in Australia, such as the Wynne Art Prize, on several occasions, the Godfrey Rivers Prize and the Society of Artists Medal. Served on the Commonwealth Art Advisory Board, of which he was chairman in 1953. Was director of the National Art Gallery of New South Wales, Sydney, 1937–44; was knighted 1960. Lived at Mosman, New South Wales.

Winifred ASHTON: *see* **Clemence DANE**

David ASHTON-BOSTOCK: *see* **ASHTOCK**

Paul ASHURST 1949– Painter and muralist, born in Camberley, Surrey, who studied at Farnham School of Art, 1965–8, then Central School, 1968–71. Murals were completed for Fridge Night Club, 1985 and 1990–1; Southampton General Hospital, 1987; and Fridge Bar and Restaurant, 1996. From around 1995 Ashurst was noted for his British and foreign realistic landscapes in a hard-edged style, often featuring buildings, using either Liquitex on canvas or watercolour/mixed media. Group exhibitions included Low-tech., Coracle, 1984; Icon Show, Mario Flecha, 1987; Fridge Gallery, 1994; and Walcot Square and Sun & Doves Galleries, both 1999. Ashurst had many solo shows in Britain and abroad, later ones including Sun & Doves, London, and Bonnafont Gallery, San Francisco, California, America, both 2001. Lived in south London.

John Atkinson ASHWORTH 1915– Architect and artist, born in Rochdale, Lancashire, who worked in oil and watercolour. He studied at Liverpool University school of architecture, 1932–8, under Charles Reilly, becoming an associate of RIBA. Started in Liverpool Corporation Housing Department, 1938–9; then was with what became Building Design Partnership, Preston, 1939–45; was a principal in Ashworth & Fletcher, Rochdale, 1945–63; being a private consultant architect in Kendal, Cumbria, where he settled, 1963–78. Showed in group exhibitions at Walker Art Gallery in Liverpool and Rochdale Art Gallery, both holding examples.

Walter ASHWORTH 1883–1952 Sculptor, painter and teacher, based in Coventry, Warwickshire, who played a key role in art development there. He was principal of its College of Art, chairman of the Coventry and Warwickshire Society of Artists and was a war artist during World War II. Exhibited at RA and locally. Modernist stone reliefs designed by Ashworth in the mid-1930s adorn the walls of Coventry Technical College.

Elaine ASK 1952– Painter and draughtsman, using a rich palette and with a strong feeling for paint. She worked a lot in Greece, being married to the artist Andreas Kouyioumtzis. She was born in Staffordshire and studied at Padgate College of Education, 1970–2. Group appearances included British Council, Athens, 1978; Batley Art Gallery, 1981; Harris Art Gallery, Preston, from 1982; and Art North Gallery, Huddersfield, 1983. Solo shows included Gallery Arsa from 1972; Citibank, 1975–9; Little Gallery, Diagonios, 1980; and Huddersfield Sports Centre, 1982. Leeds Educational Art Loans Services holds her work. Lived in Liversedge, West Yorkshire.

Victor ASKEW 1909–1974 Artist in various media, born at Rotherham, Yorkshire. Studied part-time at Sheffield School of Art for three years in the mid-1920s. Exhibited RA, PS and ROI and is represented in several public collections including Harris Museum and Art Gallery, Preston, and Canadian galleries. Wrote *Painting for Everyone*. Lived at Bayford, Hertfordshire.

Elizabeth ASLIN 1923–1989 Museum curator, writer and printmaker, the daughter of an architect who pioneered the design of modern local authority schools in Hertfordshire. She entered the Slade School of Fine Art in 1940 and gained her diploma in fine art in 1943. Aslin joined the Victoria & Albert Museum in 1947, one of a fine group of scholars assembled by Peter Floud. She was involved in planning exhibitions to send to museums around the country while undertaking research into more arcane aspects of art history. Aslin was responsible for the furniture segment of the seminal Victorian and Edwardian Exhibition in 1952. She went on to produce a series of important articles and books, notably on E W Godwin, her volume on his furniture and interior decoration appearing in 1986. In 1964 Aslin went to Bethnal Green Museum, which she revitalised as keeper; was assistant director, works, at the Victoria & Albert Museum (V&A), 1968–74; and despite illness remained keen to see scholarly standards there upheld, writing to *The Times* shortly before her death that it had been "taken over by ill-organised and unmotivated administrators". With such strong opinions, Aslin inevitably sparked strong reactions. V&A director Sir Roy Strong found her unco-operative and she was critical of his tenure. In one of his published diary entries at the time he announced he was to retire in 1987, Strong cites her participation in "a fully-fledged half-page of vitriol" in *The Sunday Times*. Aslin's curatorial work reduced the time she could devote to her own artwork. She contributed to the Editions Alecto Public Schools series in the 1960s, the Government Art Collection holding her prints of Oundle School, Northamptonshire; Stowe School, Buckinghamshire; and Chigwell School, Essex.

Ruth ASPDEN 1909– Painter and etcher who studied at Blackburn School of Art, 1927–33, with Arthur Jackson and George Reed, then at the Royal College of Art, 1933–7, under Percy Hague Jowett. During World War II she was employed for several years on camouflage design. Exhibited RA, RE, in the provinces and North America. Blackburn Museum and Art Gallery bought her work. Lived in London.

Sofy ASSCHER 1901– Painter, draughtsman and miniaturist who studied art at Girls' Art School, Amsterdam, where she became a certificated teacher of drawing, at Chelsea Polytechnic and privately. Showed at RA, UA, Leger and Tooth's Galleries and overseas. Solo shows included Foyles Gallery. Lived in London, then Seaford, East Sussex.

Christopher John ASSHETON-STONES 1947–1999 Artist in pastel and writer, born in Ceylon. He did a pre-diploma course at Exeter College of Art, then did his diploma at Bournemouth and Poole College of Art. Was elected to PS aged 21, and became a council member. Signed his work CJA-Stones with year. Also exhibited at RWA, RSMA and Paris Salon and had regular solo shows in Britain and France. Assheton-Stones wrote several books: *Working with Pastel*, 1983; *Buildings and Towns in Pastel* and *Painting with Pastels*, both 1984; and he wrote occasionally for *Leisure Painter* magazine. He described his work as falling into two categories: fairly conventional landscapes and other pictures as an aid to teaching; and semi-figurative serious painting which developed year by year. Lived in Weasdale, Newbiggin on Lune, Kirkby Stephen, Cumbria.

Paul ASTBURY 1945– Ceramic sculptor and teacher, using a variety of materials including found objects. He was born in Cheshire and trained at Stoke-on-Trent College of Art, 1962–8, and Royal College of Art, 1968–71. Awards included Arts Council, 1977. Teaching included Brighton and Middlesex Polytechnics and Central School of Art. Commissions included Liberty's, 1971, and Crafts Advisory Committee, 1974. Mixed exhibitions included Clay Sculpture, Midland Group Gallery, Nottingham, 1972; New Ceramics, Arts Council of Northern Ireland tour, 1974; Clay Sculpture, Yorkshire Sculpture Park, 1980; and The Raw and the Cooked, Museum of Modern Art, Oxford, and tour, 1994. Solo shows included Enhanced Images, Aberystwyth Arts Centre, 1984. Astbury's work was held in many public collections in Britain and abroad, including Crafts Council, Ulster Museum in Belfast, Portsmouth City Museum and Art Gallery and North West Arts in Manchester. Lived in London.

Evelin Winifred ASTON 1891–1975 Sculptor in wood, painter in oil, born in Birmingham. Studied at the local School of Art under Bernard Fleetwood-Walker. Taught at a school for the blind, in Birmingham. Exhibited RSA, RBA, ROI and locally. Lived at Erdington, Birmingham.

Paul ASTON 1948– Sculptor and teacher, born in Awre, Gloucestershire. He studied at Gloucester College of Art, 1964–7, gained a first-class diploma from Leicester College of Art and Design, 1967–70, winning his higher diploma from Chelsea School of Art, 1970–1. In 1971–3 Aston was an Abbey Major Scholar at British School, Rome, then after extensive travel in Italy and the Mediterranean area taught painting at Aegean School of Fine Art, Paros, Greece, 1973–4. He supported his art with a variety of part-time work from then and exhibitions included Ikon Gallery, Birmingham, 1985; Royal Institute, Truro, 1992; and 1st RWA Open Sculpture Exhibition, 1993. In that year he shared a show at Gloucester City Museum and Art Gallery. Lived in Lydney, Gloucestershire.

Sophie ASTON 1970– Painter, born in Kingston upon Thames, Surrey, who studied at Wimbledon School of Art, 1990–1; Glasgow School of Art, 1991–5; and Chelsea College of Art, 1997–8. Among her exhibitions were Hunting Art Prizes, Royal College of Art, 1995; Three Abstract Painters, Duncan R Miller Fine Art, Glasgow, 1997; Contemporary Art from France, Germany & Great Britain, Daimler Chrysler Aerospace, Munich, Germany, 1999; Aspects of Abstraction, Paton Gallery, 2000; and Landscape, Blue Gallery, 2003. In 2004, Aston was included in the John Moores Liverpool Exhibition.

George Thomas ATACK 1886– Watercolourist, born in London, who worked as a stockbroker's clerk. After attending the Borough Polytechnic, he studied art at Camberwell School of Arts and Crafts. Exhibited RI, Stock Exchange Art Society and City of London Art Exhibition, Guildhall, 1954. Lived in West Wickham, Kent.

Kutlug ATAMAN 1961– Artist using film, born in Turkey, who fled the country after the 1980 military coup and attended the film school at University of California Los Angeles. He returned to Turkey to make his first feature film, *Lola and Bilidikid*, described by one critic as "a kind of gay *Streetcar Named Desire*", which was shown at the Berlin Film Festival and toured arthouses. Ataman's second film, *semiha b unplugged*, in which he directed the camera at the Turkish opera singer Semiha Berksoy, lasted almost eight hours and did not appeal to cinemas. After the curator of the 1997 Istanbul Biennale suggested he show it, Ataman made his films for gallery viewings. He claimed his film gave him independence. "No one tells me what to do. Not even collectors, and I feel very free." In 2004 Ataman was on the Turner Prize shortlist and was awarded the Carnegie International Prize for his 40-channel video installation Kuba, which documented the soliloquies of residents of an Istanbul shanty town. The work was shown at the Carnegie Museum of Art, Pittsburgh.

Barry ATHERTON 1944– Artist and lecturer who attended Manchester College of Art and Design, 1961–5, and the Royal Academy Schools, 1966–9, with a Leverhulme Travelling Scholarship studying ancient Egyptian, Greek and Roman art in Europe, north Africa and the Middle East. In 1976, Atherton toured museums and archaeological sites of Central America, gathering information for paintings based on the pre-Columbian period, later, with Scottish Arts Council sponsorship, visiting northern Greece and Turkey to investigate how the ancient Greeks enhanced their sculpture with colour. From 1973, Atherton lectured at Glasgow School of Art, becoming head of fine art. Took part in many mixed shows in Britain and abroad, from 1991 having a series of one-man exhibitions at the New Academy Gallery. Commissions included Julia Somerville for Alexon, 1991; the neo-classical sculptor Alexander Stoddart, 1995–6; and three retiring chairmen of court, University Senate,

Glasgow Caledonian University, 1995–7. Atherton's 2003 solo show at the Art Gallery and Museum, Kelvingrove, Glasgow, included the Stoddart portrait.

John ATHERTON HAWKINS 1918– Painter and constructor in wood who also taught, born in Bristol where he attended the West of England College of Art under Donald Milner, 1936–9, then 1946–8. He held a number of teaching posts in the west of England, then at the County Grammar School for Boys in Barrow-in-Furness, Lancashire, where he lived. Showed with Barnstaple Art Club and elsewhere.

Kevin ATHERTON 1950– Sculptor and teacher, born in the Isle of Man, who attended the College of Art there, 1968–9, then studied fine art at Leeds Polytechnic, 1969–72. His teaching posts part-time included Chelsea and Winchester Schools of Art, Maidstone College of Art and Middlesex Polytechnic. Apart from work in various exhibitions Atherton did commissioned sculptures, such as the ankle and shoe disappearing into a wall at Langdon Park School in Poplar, completed 1983, and A Different Ball Game, at King's Hill business park, West Malling, 1994. In the mid-1990s, Atherton was working at Chelsea College of Art & Design on issues concerning virtual reality.

Peggy ATHERTON 1968– Artist, lecturer and curator, born in Nottingham, who studied at Harrow College of Art & Design, 1990–1 (later working there as a technician), then graduated from Bath College of Higher Education, 1991–4. Mixed shows included Heaven on Earth Gave Me a Migraine, Alternative Space, Bath, 1992; Fresh Art at Islington's Business Design Centre and Start 94, Plymouth Art Centre and tour, both 1994; and Selected Boiled Works, Riding House Street, 1995. Atherton gained national publicity in 1996 with her solo show Road Kills, at The Cut Gallery, in which dead animals scooped up from the road had been dipped in porcelain at her north London studio and fired in a kiln. For several years she had returned each animal so treated to where it was killed as a protest and "to give them their last rites. We are disgusting. I do want to shock people." From 2001, Atherton was curator of The Tablet Gallery, in 2002 receiving an Arts & Heritage commission with Marble Hill House, then launched The Chambers Gallery in 2004. She was senior lecturer in mixed media fine art at the University of Westminster.

Rachel ATHERTON 1969– Painter who was born and lived in Birmingham. She studied at Bournville College of Art and Staffordshire Polytechnic and among her shows was East & South, Norwich Gallery/Kent Institute of Art and Design, 1992.

John ATKIN 1959– Artist working in various media, and teacher. He attended Teesside College of Art, 1977–8, and Leicester Polytechnic, 1978–81, where he graduated with honours in painting. After teaching at Teesside College, 1981–2, Atkin completed his master's degree in sculpture at Royal College of Art, 1982–5, then had a Picker Fellowship at Kingston Polytechnic, 1985–6. He won a string of awards, including a Major Award, Northern Arts, Newcastle, 1981–2, a Henry Moore Foundation Scholarship, 1982, and a drawing prize at Royal College, 1985. He was Grizedale Forest artist-in-residence, 1987, then was for some years in Australia, having residencies at Mildura Arts Centre, Victoria College in Melbourne and at Jam Factory Gallery, Adelaide. Among his group appearances were The Eighties, Juda Rowan Gallery, 1985; National Garden Festival 90, Gateshead; and Sculpture at Canterbury, 1991–2. Had a solo show at Hatton Gallery, Newcastle upon Tyne, 1985, one at Juda Rowan, 1986, later shows including Darlington Arts Centre, 1991–2. His commissions included Head of Mies van der Rohe, KIUK, 1984, and The Watcher, Marina Development, Cleveland, 1988–9. In 2003, Atkin's formidable sculpture Navigator, alluding to Ipswich's maritime history, was unveiled there alongside the River Orwell; the related maquettes and drawings were exhibited at Christchurch Mansion. Atkin, who had a studio in London, had recently shown work at Sculpture at Goodwood, The Kouros Gallery in New York and The Peggy Guggenheim Museum in Venice. In 2004 there was an exhibition at Chappel Galleries, Chappel, including Navigator effigies.

Liz ATKIN 1951– Draughtsman in pencil, born in Stamford, Lincolnshire, daughter of the artist Peter Atkin. She studied at St Martin's School of Art, 1971–4. Solo shows included Laing Art Gallery, and touring, 1990–1. She also participated in mixed shows with Nicholas Treadwell Gallery in England and in continental Europe. *Liz Atkin, Drawings 1987–90* was published by Laing Art Gallery, funded by Northern Arts. Nicholas Treadwell Gallery and Cleveland Gallery, Middlesbrough, hold her work, which is often narrative in nature, on a large scale. Lived at Longbenton, Newcastle upon Tyne.

Peter ATKIN 1926– Watercolourist and teacher, born in Wallasey, Cheshire, father of the artist Liz Atkin. he had no formal training beyond instruction in watercolour by Wilfrid René Wood. Became a part-time art tutor for Northamptonshire County Council Education Department, 1970–91, and ran his own summer classes. Showed at Northampton Central Museum and Art Gallery, RI, RBA, UA of which he became a member in 1968, and NS, his main dealer being Savage Fine Art, Northampton, where he lived at Collingtree. Private collections in Britain and abroad held his work.

Ron ATKIN 1938– Painter and teacher, born in Leicestershire, who studied at Loughborough College of Art, 1954–7, then Royal Academy Schools, 1957–61. He taught at the Beaford Centre in north Devon, living in West Putford. Showed at RA; Plymouth City Museum and Art Gallery; Roland, Browse & Delbanco; and in the West Country. Plymouth City Museum and Dartington Hall hold his work.

David ATKINS 1964– Painter and draughtsman, born in Greenwich, London. He was notable for expressive and richly coloured landscapes, as in his solo shows at Albemarle Gallery, 2002 and 2004. Atkins did a foundation course at St Martin's School of Art, 1982–3; gained a first-class honours degree in fine art, painting, at Winchester School of Art, 1983–6; then obtained his postgraduate certificate, 1993–5. Awards included The Bateson Mason Award for Drawing, 1986; Atlantis Young Artist Award, 1st Prize, 1993; Bideford Open, prize, 1999; The Façade International Prize for Painting at The Discerning Eye and The Chichester Open, prize, both 2000; The Laing Landscape Award, 2001; and The Horan Prize for Painting, NEAC, 2003. Other mixed exhibitions included RA Summer

Exhibition, 1995; Landmark. A Survey of British Landscape Painting, Bournemouth University, 1998; and The Albany Gallery, Cardiff, from 2000. Atkins showed solo with Albemarle Gallery from 2002. Commissions included four murals for the Greater London Council at Eltham Park Swimming Pool, 1986. Atkins was artist-in-residence, North Kingston Centre, Kingston, 1989. Guildhall, Kingston, and Creasey Collection, Salisbury, hold examples.

Ray ATKINS 1937– Painter and teacher, born in Exeter, Devon. He studied at Bromley College of Art, 1954–6, then again, 1958–61, after National Service in the Army. Atkins was much influenced by the work of Frank Auerbach, and while at the Slade School of Fine Art doing postgraduate studies worked in Auerbach's studio. In 1965 Atkins taught at Bournemouth College of Art, from 1965–70 at Reading University's department of fine art under Claude Rogers and in 1971 at Epsom School of Art. After some adult education centre teaching in the early 1970s based in Reading, Atkins went on to teach at Falmouth School of Art. From the early 1970s he showed in many mixed shows, including LG. Had one-man show at Piers Morris Gallery in 1970, then showed regularly solo throughout Britain, with a series at Art Space Gallery from 1989. In 1996 there was a show there to complement Atkins' retrospective at RWA. Arts Council, South West Arts, the British Council and Somerset County Council hold examples. The catalogue for the retrospective traced developments from the dark London period of the 1960s to the mature paintings from Cornwall where Atkins developed "a unique and extraordinary method of working on a large scale from direct observation by erecting structures in the landscape and leaving the work on site until completed".

Anthony ATKINSON 1929– Painter, teacher and exhibition organiser, born in London, who worked in oil and gouache. He studied at Wimbledon School of Art and Royal College of Art, 1951–5, teachers including Rodrigo Moynihan and Carel Weight. He gained a silver medal and edited *Ark* magazine. Became head of Colchester School of Art, 1964–75, faculty head, 1975, and dean of art and music at Colchester Institute, 1986–9. Was organiser for Ernst & Young annual exhibitions from 1986. As a painter of architectural and landscape themes in East Anglia and Provence, Atkinson showed at RA from 1950; Victoria & Albert Museum; NEAC; New Grafton and Leicester Galleries; and elsewhere. His solo shows included Leighton House; Minories, Colchester; Gainsborough's House, Sudbury; Phoenix Gallery, Lavenham; and Coach House Gallery, Guernsey. The John Russell Gallery, Ipswich, showed Atkinson's paintings in gouache and oil in 2003. Work was commissioned by the Post Office, Shell and London Transport. Minories, Essex County Council and Royal London Insurance hold his work. He was an honorary member of Colchester Art Society and a governor of Gainsborough's House Society. Lived in Great Horkesley, Essex.

Charles Gerard ATKINSON 1879–1955 Painter, born at Seaford, Sussex. Studied with Walter Hilton in Liverpool, where he exhibited, also at RWS, RCamA and RBSA. Lived at Grasmere, Westmorland.

Conrad ATKINSON 1940– Artist using variety of media, and teacher, born in Cumbria, whose work frequently had political and social implications and was on occasion controversial. He studied at Carlisle College of Art, 1957–61; Liverpool College of Art, 1961–2; then Royal Academy Schools, 1962–5. In the latter year he gained Leverhulme Award and Abbey Minor Scholarship, then in 1967 won a Granada Fellowship. As well as taking part in a number of important group exhibitions, Atkinson had solo shows; in 1972 his show Strike was held at ICA; the same venue being chosen for Work, Wages and Prices in 1974; then the year following his subject was Northern Ireland at Belfast Arts Council Gallery, this topic being repeated at Art Net in 1976; in 1977 his exhibition Approaching Reality was staged at Northern Arts Gallery, Newcastle upon Tyne. From 1974–6 Atkinson was fellow in fine arts at Northern Arts Association in Newcastle, 1976 onwards joining the staff of Slade School of Fine Art. His installation For Emily: Plus Equals, based on Emily Brontë, was held at Dean Clough, Halifax, 1992, he had a show at Bluecoat Gallery, Liverpool, 1999–00, and in 2002 others at the Courtauld Institute Gallery and Wolverhampton Art Gallery. Arts Council holds his work.

Dale ATKINSON 1962– Painter, born in Sunderland, who did a foundation course at the Art College there, 1981–2. From 1982–6 studied at Newcastle University for an honours degree in painting. In the latter year had a solo exhibition at Anne Berthoud Gallery of paintings, with another of works on paper also in 1986. Additional shows occurred at the same gallery, further showings taking place at Readheads, Newcastle upon Tyne, 1989–90, and at Newcastle Polytechnic Gallery, 1991. In the mid-1980s Atkinson had a studio in Bristol, in 1989 moving to Newcastle, where he exhibited at University of Northumbria on several occasions, including 2002 and 2003. Atkinson was a nonconformist as a student, producing visionary pictures based on stories his father had told him as a child. His later paintings were more pared down, but continued his interest in "the psychology of paint", the way a chance mark or colour change could alter identity and significance.

Eric ATKINSON 1928– Artist in mixed media and teacher, born in Hartlepool, County Durham. He said that his pictures were "records of journeys through the landscape ... and also explorations into the existence of possible bridges between the physical structure of man and his empathy for the environment". Atkinson studied at West Hartlepool College of Art, under Harry Thubron, 1943–7, then Royal Academy Schools, 1950–5, under Henry Rushbury. After teaching at Leeds College of Art, 1964–9, moved to Canada, settling in Ontario, where he was dean in the faculty of applied arts, Fanshawe College, London, 1972–82. Group shows included Tate Gallery, 1954–6; Richard Demarco, Edinburgh, 1967; British Council tour, Tel-Aviv, 1970; Museum of Art, Carnegie Institute, Pittsburgh, 1980; and Art Gallery of Ontario, Toronto, 1984. Had series of solo shows at Redfern Gallery from 1954, later ones including Mendel Art Gallery, retrospective, at Saskatoon, 1980, Concept Gallery, Pittsburgh, 1987, and retrospective, Hartlepool Art Gallery, 2000. Elected to NEAC, 1956, Royal Canadian Academy of Arts, 1978. Many public collections held his work, including Arts Council, Contemporary Art Society and provincial galleries.

Jane ATKINSON fl. from early 1970s– Painter, printmaker and teacher, born in London. She studied at Central

School of Art and Design, 1964–6 and Waltham Forest School of Art, 1966–8, learning printmaking at Morley College from 1978. Became a member of Greenwich Printmakers, 1990. Was an adult education tutor in Kent and for the Inner London Education Authority, 1968–75. Group shows included New Metropole Arts Centre, Folkestone, 1972; Easton Rooms, Rye, 1983; RA Summer Exhibition, from 1990; RWA, from 1991; RE, 1992; and Artmonsky Arts, 1999. Later solo exhibitions included Royal College of Pathologists, 1998, and Stark Gallery, 2002. Lived in southeast London.

Marshall Forster ATKINSON 1913–1990 Artist in various media, born in Gateshead, County Durham, where he continued to live. He studied at King's College, Newcastle. Showed widely, including Royal Glasgow Institute of the Fine Arts of which he was a member, PS, UA, RBA, RWS, RCamA and Paris Salon. Was a member of Univision Group and Gateshead Art Society and was closely associated with Shipley Art Gallery, Gateshead, where he had a solo show in 1952; it holds his work and held a memorial exhibition of his Tyneside shipbuilding and other scenes in 1997.

Shelagh ATKINSON 1959– Figurative artist, born in West Lothian, who gained a higher national diploma in communication studies, 1987–9; did business training, 1990–3, then gained a printmaker award, 1994–5, both in Edinburgh; in 1996 setting up own photographic, printmaking and painting studio in the city. Exhibitions included Lyric Theatre, Hammersmith, 1992; SSWA at RSA, 1993; Black Church Gallery, Dublin, Ireland, and Litografiska '94, Sweden, both 1994; Royal Glasgow Institute of the Fine Arts, 1995; The Scottish Landscape, Firth Gallery, Edinburgh, 1997; and About Face, The Reynolds Gallery, Edinburgh, 1999. Among later solo exhibitions were: Places and Faces, McHardys Art, The Borders, 2002. Between 2003–5, the Scottish National Portrait Gallery bought two prints. Atkinson was based in Dolphinton, Strathclyde.

Ted ATKINSON 1929– Sculptor, etcher and teacher, born in Liverpool. He studied at Liverpool College of Art, 1944–8, under Karel Vogel, then at Slade School of Fine Art, 1950–4, with Reg Butler and Henry Moore. Taught at Exeter and Leeds Colleges of Art, then was head of sculpture at Coventry Polytechnic, 1968–83. Atkinson concentrated on sculpture commissions. His work was "an attempt to crystallise a range of feelings, emotions, undercurrents, facts, conflicts and gestures of the psyche. It asserts that reality simply fails to live up to the demands of art." Major public sculptures were completed in Birmingham, Coventry, Düsseldorf and Hamburg. Atkinson was a member of RE and a fellow of RBS and RE. Group shows included RA, RWA and LG. He was one of six artists representing Britain at World Expo '88 in Brisbane. He was awarded Barcham Prize at RE, 1987, etching prize in RA Summer Exhibition in 1988 and a similar prize at Artists in Essex show, 1990. Later solo exhibitions included Barbican Centre, Keele University and Kunstlerhause, Stuttgart, Germany, and in 1996, *Ted Atkinson Etchings* was published with an introduction by Dr Gottfried Mann in German and English. Ashmolean Museum and Saatchi Collection hold his work. Lived in Wivenhoe, Essex.

Terry ATKINSON 1939– Painter, draughtsman, writer and polemicist, and teacher, born in Thurnscoe, Yorkshire. He attended school in Darlington, meeting Harold Hurrell; was at Barnsley School of Art, 1958–60, getting to know David Bainbridge; and was at Slade School of Fine Art, 1960–4. Atkinson felt that teaching there was not relevant to the society in which he lived. In 1962 he showed Dead Cat on a Runway, at Young Contemporaries, where his Postcard from Ypres won the Arts Council Prize in 1963. World War I was to remain a preoccupation as an artist. Taught part-time at Birmingham College of Art, 1965–7; at Coventry College of Art (later Lanchester Polytechnic), 1966–73, where he met Michael Baldwin; took up a Gulbenkian Foundation Fellowship in 1975, working at Sidney Stringer School, Coventry on the Community Education Video Project; and lectured in fine art at Leeds University from 1977. In 1964 Atkinson helped form the group Fine Artz with John Bowstead, Roger Jeffs and Bernard Jennings, but left it in 1966. In 1967 Atkinson and Baldwin produced a series of prints and texts together, including Notes on Time Show, Declaration Propositions and Types of quasi-intention. The group Art & Language was founded in 1968, the first issue of *Art-Language*, a conceptual art journal, appearing in 1969, edited by Atkinson, Bainbridge, Baldwin and Hurrell. Atkinson left the group in 1975, and the following year a show of his subsequent work was organised for Midland Group, Nottingham, with a tour. Atkinson showed at Sydney and Venice Biennales in 1984 and in 1985 at John Moores Liverpool Exhibition. Had a retrospective at Whitechapel Art Gallery, with tour, 1983–4; another key show, indicating how Atkinson had consistently examined the meaning and purpose of art, was toured from Norwich Gallery, Norwich School of Art and Design, 1996. Arts Council holds his work. Lived for a time in Leamington Spa, Warwickshire, where in 2003 the Art Gallery & Museum showed his 4 Series 1974–92. In 2004 the Jeffrey Charles Gallery exhibited Atkinson's work and the Institute of Contemporary Interdisciplinary Arts at the University of Bath featured the work of Atkinson, Bainbridge and David Rushton.

ATRI: *see* **Atri BROWN**

Mary ATTENBOROUGH: *see* **Mary POTTER**

Jake ATTREE 1950– Painter, notably of landscapes, born in York, who studied at the School of Art there, 1966–8, Liverpool College of Art, 1968–71 and Royal Academy Schools, 1974–7. Two years later Attree began painting full-time, although he did various other jobs such as scene painting at Theatre Royal in Norwich. Exhibitions included RA Summer Exhibition and Serpentine Gallery Summer Show 1 in 1982. Attree was later a resident artist at Dean Clough, Halifax, having a show of his New York drawings in 1996, when he also had an exhibition at Art Space Gallery. In 2003, Hart Gallery exhibited his images of London and New York, part of an ongoing series inspired by various cities. In that year, Bruton Gallery gave him a first New York solo show, other Attree exhibitions including Lea House, New Mill, Holmfirth. There was another Hart Gallery show in 2005. Nuffield Trust holds his work.

Norman Stewart ATTWELL 1921– Painter in oil, born in Hastings, Sussex. Studied at Richmond School of Art, afterwards at Royal College of Art with a break for war service. Exhibited RA, at other London and provincial galleries. Lived at Twickenham, Middlesex.

Clare ATWOOD 1866–1962 Painter, born at Richmond, Surrey, the daughter of an architect. Studied at Westminster School of Art and Slade School of Fine Art under Henry Tonks and Philip Wilson Steer. One-man show at Carfax Gallery, 1911, also showing at NEAC, RA, Ridley Art Club and many other venues. Did World War I paintings for the Canadian government, some of her work also going to Imperial War Museum. Tate Gallery holds her portrait of the actor Sir John Gielgud's room, in 1933. Lived at Smallhythe, Tenterden, Kent, where she was known as Tony, in a group which included Ellen Terry's daughter Edith and the woman writer Christopher St John.

John AUBREY 1939– Painter, sculptor and teacher, born in Pontyberem, Dyfed. After attending grammar school near Llanelli, in 1958 Aubrey studied at the department of fine art at King's College, Newcastle upon Tyne, until 1963 when he began lecturing in fine art at Wolverhampton College of Art, later being on the staff of Wolverhampton Polytechnic. Took part in many group shows including Bear Lane Gallery, Oxford; Howard Roberts Gallery, Cardiff; and John Moores Exhibition, Liverpool, at Walker Art Gallery. WAC holds his work and Royal Academy of Music has his portrait of Sir Thomas Armstrong, a former principal.

Michael AUBREY 1940– Watercolourist, born in Hale, Cheshire, cousin of the artist Arnold Auerbach. Aubrey's work was fluently figurative, in the tradition of John Singer Sargent, Edward Seago and John Yardley. Educated at Clare College, Cambridge, where he was much involved as a stage designer, working closely with Trevor Nunn and George Rylands. Called to the bar by Gray's Inn, practised as a barrister and journalist while painting and exhibiting. Taught at Cambridge University and Oundle School, painting full-time from 1995. Had many group shows and over 20 solo exhibitions, including Newburgh Street Gallery, 1989; Church Hill Gallery, Knutsford, 1995; Walker Gallery, Harrogate, 1996; Art Connoisseur Gallery, 1998; The Gallery in Cork Street, 2000; Wren Gallery, Burford, 2002; with overseas shows in Australia, Malaysia and Sri Lanka under the patronage of the British Council. An interest in ancient buildings and vernacular architecture led to commissions to paint colleges and public buildings, sites including Marlborough, Rugby and Clifton, the Royal Academy of Music, Inner and Middle Temple and King's College. Published *The Magic of Watercolour*, 2000. Lived in a restored sixteenth-century drovers' inn in Oundle, Northamptonshire.

AUDIO ARTS– Organisation run by artists Michael Archer and William Furlong (see separate entries). It participated in the Serpentine Gallery/South Bank Centre's The Sculpture Show, 1983, where it was declared to be "linked with work that is concerned with the urban media environment, with meaning, content and process in relation to electronic media, with the manipulation of such media and the implication of widespread dissemination through magnetic tape, broadcasting and satellite communications". Arts Council holds Audio Arts' Objects and Spaces, 1983, 90-minute sound tapes.

AUDIOVIDEODISCO– This was the name used by David Timmons (see separate entry) and Cathal Connaughton when working jointly.

Mary AUDSLEY 1919– Artist working in a variety of media who entered Westminster School of Art, 1934, her teachers including the sculptor Eric Schilsky and painters Mark Gertler and Bernard Meninsky. She was to have taught at the School, but it closed with the onset of World War II. During the war Audsley served for a short time in the Women's Royal Air Force until she was invalided out. She did teach, but ill-health, family responsibilities and other problems hindered Audsley's artistic career, which she took up seriously again in the early 1970s, producing paintings, ceramics, carvings, prints and collages, her work showing a strong School of Paris influence. Showed RA, LG and in the provinces and in 1990 had solo show at Sally Hunter Fine Art. Audsley's work formed the bulk of Sally Hunter's show Sculptors in Two Dimensions at 9 Clarendon Cross, 2003.

Arnold AUERBACH 1898–1978 Sculptor, painter and etcher, born in Liverpool. He studied at its School of Art, in Paris and Switzerland. Was for a time a lecturer at Regent Street Polytechnic and Chelsea School of Art. Exhibited at RA, Goupil Gallery, Walker Art Gallery in Liverpool and in the provinces. Wrote a number of books on sculpture, such as *Sculpture, a History in Brief*. Work was illustrated in *British Sculpture, 1944–1946*, by Eric Newton, and William Aumonier's *Modern Architectural Sculpture*. Auerbach's work ranged in style from conventional torsos to his heavily stylized Vorticist Head and decorative panels, as at Davis Theatre, Croydon, in the manner of Eric Gill. Lived in London.

Erna AUERBACH 1897–1975 Artist, teacher and writer, born in Frankfurt-am-Main, Germany. She studied at the Art School there, 1917–22, in Paris in 1926, then again in Frankfurt, 1928–30. With the Nazi ascendancy in the early 1930s her ability to work was undermined, and in 1933 Auerbach moved to England, where she settled in London and reassembled her career. Had a first solo show in England at Brook Street Gallery in 1938 and during World War II completed pictures related to the war effort, but destruction of her studio during the Blitz prompted her to do more teaching and writing. Was included in Art in Exile in Great Britain 1933–45 at Camden Arts Centre, 1986.

Frank AUERBACH 1931– Painter, draughtsman, printmaker and teacher, born in Berlin. Settled in England in 1939 and studied at the Borough Polytechnic in 1948, St Martin's School of Art, 1948–52, Royal College of Art, 1952–5, and at evening classes under David Bomberg, 1948–53. Had the first of a series of solo exhibitions at Beaux Arts Gallery in 1956. From that year for about a dozen years he taught, being a visiting teacher for Kent and Middlesex County Councils and including sessions at Camberwell School of Arts and Crafts and Slade School of Fine Art. After an appearance in the Gulbenkian International Exhibition in 1964, in 1965 Auerbach joined Marlborough Fine Art and began to show globally. By 1978 he had a retrospective at Hayward Gallery. Tate Gallery and Saatchi Collection hold his work. From 1954 Auerbach worked in a run-down studio in Camden Town, one of the seedier areas he chose to paint. He also painted certain models obsessively. Their portraits could take 300 sittings and, like the townscapes, were created from a heavily reworked mass of pigment. Auerbach rarely left his studio; he worked from sun-up to sun-down in a race against time every day of the year, the results being shown in a seventieth birthday retrospective at RA, 2001. There was also a show at Marlborough, Some Drawings and Three New Paintings, in 2004. Auerbach married the painter Julia Wolstenholme in 1958, their son being the art documentary film-maker Jake Auerbach, whose film on his father coincided with the RA show.

Lillias AUGUST 1955– Artist, born in Stroud, Gloucestershire, who graduated in fine art from Goldsmiths' College, 1973–7, followed by an undergraduate course in the history of art and design at Birmingham Polytechnic, 1977–8. August exhibited widely in East Anglia, where she lived at Lawshall, Bury St Edmunds, Suffolk, also in London. Among these shows were Laing Exhibition, Mall Galleries (prize winner), 1998; The Old Fire Engine House, Ely, 2000; RI Annual Exhibition, from 2000 (prize winner, 2000 and 2002); Singer & Friedlander/*Sunday Times* Watercolour Competition, 2001; The Hunter Gallery, Long Melford, from 2001; RWS, Bankside Gallery, 2002; Art Works in Mental Health, Royal College of Art and tour, 2003–4; and Arts Council England East grant to tour the Cross Series, Ely, Peterborough and Lincoln Cathedrals, 2005–6. August undertook private and public commissions, including work for St Edmundsbury and Chelmsford Borough Councils, The National Trust and St Bartholomew's Hospital, in London. She was on the management council of the Bury St Edmunds Art Gallery, 2000–4, and was from 2001–5 project artist during the Suffolk Cathedral Millennium Project, which included the completion of the central tower at St Edmundsbury Cathedral. An illustrated book with an essay by Ronald Blythe was produced on her work. Of her manner of working, the artist wrote: "A subject comes to me out of the corner of my eye – often only through a quick glance. I am drawn to places and objects in the landscape that are often taken for granted but retain a strong sense of identity and purpose."

Edward AUGUSTINE: *see* **Edward McGUIRE**

Ian AULD 1926–2000 Ceramist, sculptor and teacher, born in Brighton, Sussex, one of the first important potters to use the slab-building technique. In 2005 he was included in the exhibition Camberwell in the 1970s: Teachers and Students, at Galerie Besson, which highlighted his influence. Auld began painting while in the Navy during World War II, then trained at Brighton College of Art, 1947–8; studied painting and printmaking at the Slade School of Fine Art, 1948–51, in the latter year being taught hand-building by William Newland; and at London University Institute of Education, 1951–2. Auld became a technician at the Central School of Art and Design, 1952–4, after a short period in a commercial pottery. From 1954–7 Auld was based in Baghdad, Iraq, creating a pottery department in the Art School there, travelling widely, Persian ceramics becoming an influence on his work. He then returned to England, based at Wimbish, Essex, 1957–66; shared a studio with Gillian Lowndes in Chippenham, Wiltshire, 1966–76; then gave up potting after a disappointing 1976 show at the British Craft Centre. He interspersed his own work periods as a research fellow at Ife University, Nigeria, 1970–2, an experience which considerably influenced the nature of his potting, and at Camberwell, where he revitalised the staff and teaching in the ceramics department, 1974–9.

Eric AUMONIER 1899–1974 Sculptor, born in Northwood, Middlesex, full name Aubrey Eric Stacy Aumonier, one of a line of artists and writers (the author Stacy Aumonier was his uncle). Eric's grandfather, William, also a sculptor, founded William Aumonier & Son, which specialised in architectural work; William's son William, also a sculptor, was responsible for over 100 war memorials and wrote *Modern Architectural Sculpture*, 1930, in which his son Eric's work is featured. Eric studied at Central School of Arts and Crafts, joining the family business in the early 1920s, eventually working on his own. Notable among Aumonier's achievements were, in the late 1920s, a South Wind figure on the Underground Railway (later London Transport) building in Broadway; in 1930 two terracotta panels on East Sheen cinema; for the 1932 opening of the old *Daily Express* building in Fleet Street, two foyer panels: Industries of the British Isles and British Empire Industries; in 1939 Royal Arms for the British Pavilion at the New York World's Fair, and a striking figure of an archer outside East Finchley underground station; for the 1946 Powell and Pressburger film *A Matter of Life and Death* historical figures up the moving staircase to heaven (*Black Narcissus*, *Ivanhoe*, *Knights of the Round Table*, *Beau Brummell* and *Spring in Park Lane* also used Eric's talents); in 1951 the White Knight statue for the Festival of Britain; in 1960 giant nursery rhyme figures for the Food Fair, Olympia; and in 1964 work on the Fortnum & Mason clock, Piccadilly. In 1968 rheumatoid arthritis forced him to abandon sculpture, so Aumonier and his wife went to live in Ashburton, New Zealand, for his health's sake, and there he died.

David AUSTEN 1960– Artist in oil and mixed media, his pictures frequently containing an assemblage of objects, as in Story, 1996, included in About Vision, at Museum of Modern Art, 1996–7, and tour. Austen was born in Harlow, Essex, and attended Maidstone College of Art, 1978–81, then Royal College of Art, 1982–5. Group shows included Canvass: New British Painters, John Hansard Gallery, Southampton, and tour, 1986; New Editions, Cirrus, Los Angeles, 1991; and Take it From Here, Sunderland Museum and Art Gallery, 1996. In 2001, when he was living in the Blue Mountains, Australia, Austen had a solo exhibition at Christchurch Mansion, Ipswich, linked to its ethnographical and natural sciences collection. Ingleby Gallery, Edinburgh, had an Austen one-man show in 2003. Showed with Anthony Reynolds Gallery solo from 1986. Lived in London.

Winifred AUSTEN 1876–1964 Bird and animal painter and printmaker. Born in Ramsgate, Kent, she studied under Cuthbert Swan and Louise Jopling-Rowe. Made a point of visiting zoos to study animals on site. She was a prolific exhibitor, showing at the RA, Fine Art Society, Leicester Galleries, SWA, RE and elsewhere. Her pictures appeared in a number of books on birds and she is represented in several provincial collections in Britain, in Preston, Bradford and Ipswich, and in America. Lived at Orford, Suffolk.

Frederick AUSTIN 1902–1990 Printmaker and painter, born in Leicester, brother of the artist Robert Sargent

Austin. He studied at Leicester School of Art and at Royal College of Art under Malcolm Osborne, William Rothenstein and Randolph Schwabe, 1924–7. Prix de Rome for engraving won in 1927. Exhibited RA, RE of which he was a member, and extensively abroad. British Museum, Graves Art Gallery in Sheffield and several foreign collections hold his work. Lived in London.

John Anthony AUSTIN 1949– Painter and designer, born in Birmingham, who worked in oil. After 15 years as a creative lighting designer he became a full-time artist, concentrating on trains, planes and automobiles. His main works were "large railway subjects and Severn Valley Railway publicity posters and leaflets". Was a member of the Guild of Railway Artists and showed with Halcyon Gallery, Birmingham, work also appearing in *Railway Magazine*. Lived at Bridgnorth, Shropshire.

Patricia AUSTIN 1954– She graduated with honours from St Martin's School of Art, 1973–7, gaining her master's at Goldsmiths' College, 1979–81. In 1986, Austin was artist in residence at Boston University, in America, having a solo show there. Group exhibitions included Whitechapel Open, at Whitechapel Art Gallery, from 1982: LG, at Royal College of Art, 1984; and East End Open Studios, at Chisenhale Studios, 1989.

Robert Sargent AUSTIN 1895–1973 Printmaker and draughtsman, born in Leicester. He studied at the School of Art there and at Royal College of Art, 1914–16 and 1919–22, winning the Rome Scholarship for engraving in the latter year. Austin married Ada (May) Harrison, with whom he collaborated on *Some Tuscan Cities*, 1924, *Some Umbrian Cities*, 1925, and other books. He taught engraving at Royal College of Art, 1927–44, becoming professor in the department of graphic design, 1948–55. Showed with RWS of which he was a member and president; RE of which he was a member and president; and RA, to which he was elected in 1949. Austin was a meticulous craftsman-engraver and a vigorous draughtsman, as his series of drawings of Women's Auxiliary Air Force and ballooning activities done during World War II shows. In 1956, Austin became adviser to the Bank of England, designing ten-shilling and one-pound notes which went into circulation in 1960. Lived in London and at Burnham Overy Staithe, Norfolk, where he died. An exhibition of Austin's prints and drawings was held at Ashmolean Museum, Oxford, and Leicester Museum and Art Gallery in 1980. A show of prints toured from the Fine Art Society in 2001 and in 2002 it and Paul Liss Fine Art exhibited paintings and drawings including many of Austin's family, a favourite subject. In 2004, Sotheby's at Olympia offered extensive works from the studio. Tate Gallery holds his work.

Trish AUSTIN 1954– Abstract sculptor and teacher, born in Bristol. She studied at St Martin's School of Art, 1973–7, then for her master's degree on the fine art course at Goldsmiths' College School of Art. Did part-time teaching for Inner London Education Authority while maintaining a studio in the capital. Showed in New Contemporaries, 1976; St Martin's South Bank Show, 1977; Waterloo Gallery and New Gallery, Hornsey, both 1980; and in 1982 shared a show at Woodlands Art Gallery.

John AUSTIN-WILLIAMS 1947– Artist in mixed media, oil on canvas/board and charcoal, born in Kew, Surrey, who attended Exeter University, 1966–9. After brief art studies in Dorset, 1970–1, Austin-Williams was trained in the exacting disciplines of the Polish School of Art, 1976–80, under Marian Bohusz-Szyszko, being awarded the diploma of the Stefan Batory University, with distinction. Austin-Williams' work was influenced by music and the output of the Fauves: powerful, colourful landscapes, seascapes and still lifes. He said that one of his pictures was "not necessarily 'about' other things; it is about itself". Was a founder-member of Wessex Contemporary Artists, 1988. Solo exhibitions included POSK Gallery (Polish Cultural Institute), 1983; Alpha House Gallery, Sherborne, 1993; and Dillington House, near Ilminster, 1995. Austin-Williams' main works included the Kerry landscapes series, 1991–5, and Fountain study series, 1995. West Dorset Hospital, Dorchester, holds his work. Lived in Parkstone, Poole, Dorset.

Giles AUTY 1934– Art critic and painter, born in Kent, who studied art privately before National Service. He worked at various jobs before settling in west Cornwall in 1959 to paint full-time. He had a number of solo shows in London and exhibited at Belgrave Gallery in 1970s, when he was starting to write about art, from a conservative standpoint. In 1977–8 had solo show at Belgrave Gallery and in 1992 was included in a show of three critics at Cadogan Contemporary. Was art critic for *The Spectator*, in 1995 moving to Sydney where he wrote criticism for *The Australian*.

Pete AUTY 1954–1999 Sculptor and lecturer who used various, including found, materials. After training at Hull, 1978, Auty gained his master's degree from Newcastle University in 1981. He lectured at Wolverhampton, De Montfort and Northumbria Universities from 1990–5. Auty latterly turned to public sculpture. One ambitious piece was his 1996 copper pipe Water Sculpture, at North Tyneside General Hospital, North Shields.

Josephine AVELINE 1914– Artist, notably in pastel, born in Carshalton, Surrey, who studied at Worthing College of Art under Charles Morris. She became a fellow of the Society of Botanical Artists and a member of PS and SWA. Also showed RP, carrying out a series of commissioned portraits, including work for The Clothworkers' Hall and Royal College of Surgeons of England. Lived in Littlehampton, Sussex.

Simon AVERILL 1961– Painter, printmaker and teacher, born in Brighton, Sussex, where he studied fine art at the Polytechnic, graduating with honours, 1981–5. After running the Balwest printmaking workshop, 1986–90, went on to teach printmaking and drawing part-time at Falmouth School of Art. His work showed essential elements rather than recognizable features in the Cornish landscape. He was included in Artists from Cornwall at RWA in 1992. Among other shows in which he participated were Newlyn Orion Gallery, Penzance, 1990, and Gordon Hepworth Gallery, Exeter, 1991. Solo exhibition at Wilson Stephens Fine Art, 2000, Wilson Stephens giving him a shared show at Archeus in 2002.

Charles AVERY 1973– Largely self-taught artist, born on the Isle of Mull. He was notable for wryly humorous drawings and paintings: Creation of the Omniverse, his solo show in 1998 at Nylon, was a jibe at evolution theory, showing two decrepit old deities knocking over a waitress carrying a glass of rainbow-coloured cosmic fluid. Group exhibitions included Moon, Alternative Arts Space, 1994; Cantaloupe, 1997; Golf Sale, Merc House, 1998; and Flights of Reality, Kettle's Yard, Cambridge, 2002. In 1996 he co-founded, with Peter Harris, Uncle Grey Presents, an artist-run gallery and performance space. Other solo shows were The Underground Exhibition, Aldwych Tube Station, 1997; Charles Avery: Portraits of People Who Never Existed, Entwistle, 1998; and The Life and Lineage of Nancy Haselswon: Charles Avery, at The Tabernacle, Powis Square, 1999; The Ghost of Scirribin, Nylon, 2000; and Percy Miller Gallery, 2001.

Wilfred AVERY 1926– Artist using various media including collage, born in Devon, who trained as an art teacher in Cheltenham in World War II. In 1952 moved to London and showed work during late 1950s at Beaux Arts Gallery and at Gallery One. During 1963–4 worked in France. Returning to England, he settled in Blackheath, southeast London, in 1969. Showed occasionally, then had a major exhibition at Woodlands Art Gallery in 1977 covering 20 years, organised with the assistance of Greater London Arts Association. The work ranged from Cubist-influenced depictions of Devon coast to highly stylised work touching on "the myths, legends and archetypes that are so much part of our inner life".

Michelle AVISON 1965– Printmaker, painter and draughtsman, who gained an honours degree in fine art from Slade School, 1984–8, from 1991–4 obtaining her master's in printmaking from Wimbledon School of Art, with postgraduate certificate of education studies at Greenwich University, 1991–3. Group shows included Portraits North, Harrogate Art Gallery, 1989; LG, selected artist, Barbican Centre, 1993; Prints, Walcot Square Gallery, 1998; and in 1999 Hunting Art Prizes at Royal College of Art, and Artmonsky Arts. Had solo shows at York Royal Theatre, 1991, and Morley Gallery, 1993. Chelsea and Westminster Hospital holds her work.

AVM The co-operative name of the weaver Angie Gilson and artists Vicky Cull and Malcolm Moseley (see their separate entries) to produce textile-based works. There was an AVM exhibition, All Mixed Up, at Christchurch Mansion, Ipswich, in 2003.

Walter AWLSON 1949– Figurative sculptor and teacher who graduated from Edinburgh College of Art in furniture design and sculpture in 1971, in 1972 gaining the certificate in secondary education at Moray House, Edinburgh. He developed an interest in ceramics while teaching in secondary schools and further education, including Falkirk College of Technology, in 1991 resigning from full-time lecturing to develop his own work. Since 1985 he had run a workshop in Alloa, Clackmannanshire, where he produced slip-cast ceramic sculptures in limited editions, specializing in raku firing in two kilns, one gas- and one wood-fired. Awlson was winner of the SPA Alistair Dunn Award, 1990, and became a professional member of SSWA in 1991. Showed at RSA, Open Eye Gallery in Edinburgh, Andrew Usiskin Contemporary Art, Rooksmoor Gallery in Bath and with Royal Glasgow Institute of the Fine Arts and elsewhere. Lidl UK Ltd's supermarket in Alloa has a ceramic mural by Awlson.

AYA: *see* **Aya BROUGHTON**

Raul Ortega AYALA 1973– Artist, born in Mexico City, who was included in the inaugural Bowieart show BLOC at the County Hall Gallery in 2005. In that, he continued "investigation into the principles and world-weariness of office work; the artist creates a fantastical escape out of the materials he finds himself surrounded by during a stint as a jobsworth." Ayala graduated with honours in visual arts, La Esmeralda, National Center for the Arts, Mexico, 1995–00, gaining his fine art master's at Glasgow School of Art in combination with Hunter College, New York, in America, 2001–3. His exhibitions included Altazor, Cloister of Sor Juana, Mexico City, 1996; Designata, Central Gallery of the National Center for the Arts, 1998; Majority Rules, Free Gallery, Glasgow, 2002; Scottish Drawing, Xian and Beijing in China, Catch me if you can, National Gallery in Tirana in Albania, and Rock Candy, Mariakappel, Hoorn, Netherlands, all 2003; and Scope, White House Hotel, 2004.

Alain AYERS 1952– Sculptor, installations artist and lecturer, born in Dartford, Kent, who studied at Hereford College of Art, 1975–6; Exeter College of Art, 1976–9; and Birmingham Polytechnic, 1981–2. He was awarded a South West Arts Bursary, 1980; a Greater London Arts Bursary, 1981; a junior sculpture fellowship at South Glamorgan Institute of Higher Education, Cardiff, 1982–3; and a WAC Young Artist's Grant, 1983. He lectured at Nottingham Trent University, based in the Midlands, and exhibited in Britain and on the continent and showed in group exhibitions. Among Ayers' conceptual and site-specific works are The Kissing Gate, for the Liverpool International Gardens Festival, 1984, and his 1987 stone Hilton Wheel, commissioned by Hilton Parish Council and sited outside the village hall. That is one of several public pieces by Ayers in the northeast of England.

Duffy AYERS fl. from early 1930s– Painter and teacher, who studied at Central School of Arts and Crafts. She was married to the artist Michael Rothenstein, for a time being known as Betty Rothenstein, then to the designer Eric Ayers. The painter Anne Rothenstein was her daughter. Taught painting at the Women's Institute's Denman College for many years. Fry Art Gallery in Saffron Walden holds her portrait of the matron of Dr Barnardo's, Kitty Edwards. As well as being known for her portraits, Ayers produced small, richly coloured and darkish still lifes and genre scenes, a group being included in the Tenth Anniversary show at Cadogan Contemporary, 1996. She also exhibited at RA, SWA and elsewhere and lived in London. Shared an exhibition with Ursula McCannell at Broughton House Gallery, Cambridge, 2003.

Eric AYERS 1921–2001 Designer and teacher, married to the artist Duffy Ayers, born and lived in London. He studied at Beckenham School of Art and Royal College of Art. After freelancing, became a director of the advertising agency C R Casson, working on Belling cookers and Murphy radios; from 1958, was art director for the publisher Weidenfeld and Nicolson, where he designed the jacket for Vladimir Nabokov's novel *Lolita*; was from 1963 a freelance designer for Editions Alecto, later becoming a director; then in 1967 joined Petersburg Press. Taught at London School of Printing and Newcastle University before becoming a senior lecturer in graphic arts at Camberwell School of Arts and Crafts, 1972–83. Became a member of the Society of Industrial Artists/ Chartered Society of Designers. Showed with Council of Industrial Design, at 1951 Festival of Britain and in America.

Stanley AYERS 1915–1996 Painter, born and lived in London, full name Hubert Stanley Ayers. He had a studio in Chelsea, was a Chelsea Arts Club member and produced many scenes of that artistic area. He trained at Kingston School of Art and the Royal College of Art and worked as a painter from 1938. Ayers exhibited 12 times at the RA Summer Exhibition, 1947–63, and elsewhere. Christie's in South Kensington offered a large collection of his townscapes, landscapes and figure pieces in 1996.

Ulmen AYGIN 1959– Sculptor who was born in Limassol, Cyprus. Studied at Istanbul Academy of Fine Art, 1978–9, then St Martin's School of Art, 1980–3. Showed with groups in Kyrenia, Cyprus, in 1978; took part in Kornarija Symposium of Sculpture, Yugoslavia, 1981–3; showed with group at Marusici, Yugoslavia, 1983; and in that year participated in Have You Seen Sculpture from the Body? at Woodlands Art Gallery.

Caroline AYLES 1960– Painter who from 1997 attended courses organised by Wandsworth Adult Education. Ayles' pictures resulted from close scrutiny and craftsmanship, textures carefully replicated with layers of pigment and glazes. Subtle changes of light, temperature and climate were observed on trips to Greece, Italy, Spain and Turkey. Group shows included Chelsea Art Society Annual Exhibition, from 1998 (with its award in that year); Royal Academy Summer Exhibition, 2000; Thompson's Gallery, 2001; and Spring Exhibition, Portland Gallery, 2002. That gallery gave Ayles a solo show in 2004. Palace of Westminster, the writer and lyricist Sir Tim Rice and chef Gary Rhodes owned her work.

Felicity AYLIEFF 1954– Ceramist and teacher, born in Bedfordshire, who attended Bedales School, 1971–2. She studied at Bath Academy of Art, 1972–7, and Goldsmiths' College, 1978. After teaching at Bedales, 1978–82, she taught at Goldsmiths', 1981–93, Bath College of Higher Education, 1982–9, and from 1989 at Bath Spa University. She was postgraduate, Royal College of Art, 1993–6. Aylieff was a member of the Crafts Council Index of Selected Makers. She worked and exhibited all over the world and was included in Bedales Art & Design, the exhibition organised by William Jackson Gallery at Art99 in 1999 at the Business Design Centre. Aylieff's later solo shows including Canary Wharf, 2002. Victoria Art Gallery, Bath, and several foreign collections hold examples.

Maggie AYLIFFE 1968– Artist, born in Birmingham, who studied at Humberside Polytechnic, 1987–90, gaining her master's in fine art, 1992–3, and philosophy master's in painting, gender and abstraction, 1999. Exhibitions included Warped, Painting and the Feminine, Angel Row Gallery, Nottingham, curator and exhibitor, 2001; and in 2003 Sample, Embroiderers' Guild International Open Exhibition, Williamson Art Gallery and Museum, Birkenhead, and Beyond the Endgame: Abstract Painting in Manchester, Manchester Art Gallery, both 2003.

Brian AYLING 1956– Artist who studied at Exeter School of Art and Design, 1975–6, and graduated with honours from Birmingham Polytechnic, 1976–9. Ayling twice won 1st Prize, Sir Whitworth Wallis Trust, 1978 and 1979. Mixed exhibitions included John Moores Liverpool Exhibition, Walker Art Gallery, 1982, and East End Open Studios, at Cable Street Studios, 1989. Ayling had a solo show at Air Gallery, 1985.

George AYLING 1887–1960 Marine and landscape painter and teacher, born in London. The Aylings were associated with sculling and paddlemaking and George pursued the business for some years before studying at Putney School of Art, 1912. He continued to live near the River Thames, was a member of Chelsea Arts Club and the Art Workers' Guild and taught in Middlesex. Exhibited RA, ROI, NEAC, New Grosvenor Gallery and at marine painting shows in France. Lived at Kew, Surrey.

Joan AYLING 1907–1993 Painter in oil and tempera, her married name being Joan Eleanor Rees, who was born in Edinburgh. She studied art at Kilburn Polytechnic, Birmingham School of Arts and Crafts under B J Fletcher and Slade School of Fine Art with Henry Tonks, finally learning etching techniques privately with F L Maur Griggs. She exhibited at RA, RBA, Walker Art Gallery in Liverpool, Birmingham's Arlington Gallery and at Paris Salon, where she gained a Silver Medal, 1952, and Gold Medal, 1957. Was included in the exhibition Sladey Ladies at Michael Parkin Gallery, 1986. Lived in London.

Richard AYLING 1950– Painter, influenced by Cubism, born in Middlesex, who gained a diploma with honours at Twickenham College of Technology, 1967–71. During the period 1971–5 Ayling did a series of art-related jobs, including mural painting and freelance illustration, then he moved to Cornwall in 1977. Exhibited with Camden Arts Centre, RI, Beaux Arts in Bath, Andrew Usiskin, and a number of Cornish galleries including Penwith and Wills Lane Galleries in St Ives and Newlyn Gallery in Newlyn.

AYNSCOMB 1937– Painter, sculptor and teacher, full name Martin Aynscomb-Harris, born in Farnham, Surrey. He attended Folkestone and Dover School of Art, 1953–5, Medway College of Art, 1955–6, Wimbledon College of Art, 1956–8, and Hornsey College of Art, 1958–9. Held several teaching appointments, including Nuneaton School of Art, 1961–3. Mixed show appearances included Phoenix Gallery, Lavenham; Nicholas Treadwell Gallery; Hilton Gallery; and abroad. Solo shows included Heal's Mansard Gallery; Woodstock Gallery; Seen Gallery; and overseas. Royle Publications and Frost & Reed published his work. Oxfordshire Education Committee, Marks & Spencer Ltd and British Airways owned examples. Lived in Sheerness, Kent.

Martin AYNSCOMB-HARRIS: *see* **AYNSCOMB**

Arthur James John AYRES 1902–1985 Sculptor and teacher, noted as a distinguished carver, who was married to the painter Elsa Gronvold who died shortly before him. He studied at the Royal Academy Schools under William McMillan and at the British School in Rome, having won the Prix de Rome in 1931. Ayres was elected a fellow of RBS and showed at RA, RSA, at Royal Glasgow Institute of the Fine Arts, in the provinces and in Rome. Ayres taught carving at the Royal Academy Schools for many years and part-time at City & Guilds of London Art School until he died. He and his wife were active members of the Reynolds Club, for former Royal Academy Schools students, founded in 1951. Bolton Art Gallery holds Ayres' work. His carved brick panel Power is illustrated in Eric Newton's monograph *British Sculpture 1944–1946*. There is a fine relief frieze celebrating the gas industry at 8 The Broadway, Crouch End, in north London. Ayres had a memorial service in Westminster Abbey. Lived in London.

Gillian AYRES 1930– Painter, mural artist and teacher, born in London, where she mainly worked. Was married for a time to the painter Henry Mundy, having shared AIA Gallery administration with him after leaving Camberwell School of Art, where she studied 1946–50. Three years before she left AIA Gallery in 1959 Ayres had first solo show at Gallery One. As well as appearing in many key group shows – such as Tachist and Abstract Art at Redfern Gallery, in 1957; British Painting in the 60s, at the Whitechapel Art Gallery in 1965; and the Royal College of Art show Exhibition Road in 1988 – Ayres had important solo exhibitions at Museum of Modern Art, Oxford, in 1981; Serpentine Gallery, 1983; Gimpel Fils, 1996; and RA, 1997 (she had been made RA in 1991). Later ones included RWA plus a combined show by Neville Keating Tollemache and Alan Cristea Gallery in 2004 and a 25-year career survey at Southampton City Art Gallery in 2005. Awards included an Arts Council Award and Arts Council Bursary. Ayres taught at Bath Academy of Art, St Martin's School of Art, Winchester School of Art and Royal College of Art. Arts Council holds her work, richly coloured pictures in the Abstract Expressionist manner. Ayres said: "Money for me means the time to paint. I get into the studio at about 10.30 every morning and paint into the night. Painting is an act of joy, it is all I want to do. If I'm not working then I feel I am wasting time."

Roy AYRES 1945– Painter, born in Epping, Essex, who studied at South-West Essex Technical College and School of Art, Walthamstow, 1961–5, then at Royal Academy Schools, 1965–8, under Ken Howard, Peter Blake, Derek Hirst and Fred Dubery. Ayres continued painting in London until 1973, worked at other occupations until 1988, then moved from Sussex to Pembrokeshire. Early exhibitions included Young Contemporaries, 1968. Later group shows included Riverside Gallery, Crickhowell, 1992; New Gallery, Swansea, 1993; and in 1995 Mall Galleries for the Laing Competition, National Eisteddfod of Wales and Aberystwyth Art Centre. From 1989 he was gallery artist with West Wales Art Centre, Fishguard, where he had a solo show in 1995 and where he lived. Ayres had found there "an environment providing the impetus and inspiration to restart painting and develop my ideas about landscape". Later he explored the "same elemental forms in the broader landscape of Pembrokeshire's Preseli Hills and coastline".

Tim AYRES 1965– Artist working in variety of media, born in Hastings, Sussex. He studied at Loughborough College of Art, 1985–8, then Chelsea School of Art, 1988–9. Showed at Mall Galleries postgraduate show in 1989, Barclays Young Painters' Award exhibition at Royal College of Art Gallery in the same year and in John Moores Liverpool Exhibition 1989–90. Rocket Gallery included Ayres' work in the Berlin London Minimal, 2002. Lived in London.

Michael AYRTON 1921–1975 Painter and sculptor of imaginative and mythological subjects, theatre designer, illustrator, broadcaster, writer and critic. He was born in London as Michael Ayrton Gould, son of the poet and critic Gerald Gould and Barbara Ayrton, feminist and prominent member of the Labour Party. Eventually Ayrton changed his name by deed poll. He was thus heir to a richly literate, articulate family tradition which became evident in his work. Illness interrupted his education but after wide European travel, where he first became interested in drawing, he attended Heatherley's and St John's Wood Schools of Art. Early influences were Pavel Tchelitchew, Henry Moore and Graham Sutherland, which led to Ayrton's identification with the English Neo-Romantics. He also shared a studio in Paris with John Minton in 1939, studying with the French Neo-Romantic Eugéne Berman. Ayrton taught drawing and theatre design – at 18 he was commissioned to design Gielgud's *Macbeth* – at Camberwell School of Art, 1942–4. His versatility is evident in his acting as art critic for the *Spectator*, 1944–6; serving as a member of the BBC Brains Trust; writing books such as *British Drawings*, 1946, and *Golden Sections*, 1957; and his pursuit of sculpture from the mid-1950s. Ayrton was obsessed by certain themes; the skull, the maze, the minotaur and Daedalus. His work can be disturbing, even sinister, but it has attracted a firm body of admirers. Represented in many public galleries, including the Tate. Retrospective exhibition at Whitechapel Art Gallery, 1955, Agnew 1984, with a show, The Figure Celebrated, at Bruton Gallery, Leeds, 2001. Ayrton's Landscapes: Seen, Imagined and Metaphorical was at Edward Clark Modern British Paintings in 2004. Lived at Toppesfield, Essex.

Millicent AYRTON 1913– Painter whose work in oil was "largely Impressionist, semi-abstract in watercolour". She was born in Hoylake, Cheshire and attended Liverpool College of Art, 1930–5, teachers including Will C Penn. Taught privately and founded Deeside Art Group in 1945, being its chairman for 40 years. Also belonged to Liverpool Academy and RCamA and showed RWA, RA, RI and had a solo show in Hoylake. Williamson Art Gallery, Birkenhead, holds her work. Lived in West Kirby, Wirral, Merseyside.

Mary Anne AYTOUN-ELLIS 1965– Artist, notable as a printmaker, married to the sculptor Marcus Cornish. She did a foundation course at Brighton Polytechnic, 1983–4; studied for first year of a visual arts degree at Lancaster University, 1984–6; gained a fine art degree at Ruskin School of Drawing, Oxford, 1987–90; then her master's in printmaking, Royal College of Art 1990–2. Awards included Geoffrey Rhoades Commemorative Bursary; Egerton Coghill Landscape Prize; Senior Scholarship, St Hugh's College, Oxford; and Beck's Bier Award. In 1992–3 Aytoun-Ellis held an Erna Plachte Fine Art Fellowship at the Ruskin School, specialising in large experimental etching; in 1994–5 she held a residency at Frans Masereel International Printmaking Centre, Belgium; and she won First Prize, The Discerning Eye ABN AMRO Award, 1999. Group shows included Fifth Humberside Print Show, 1991; Flowers East,

1992; BP Portrait Award, National Portrait Gallery, 1994; and RP, Mall Galleries, 1996. Had a solo show at Dolphin Gallery, Oxford, 1990. From 2000, she accompanied HRH The Prince of Wales on several of his tours as official artist. He wrote the foreword to her exhibition Everyman's Journey at Portland Gallery in 2003, the fourth in a series there starting in 1997. Bodleian Library in Oxford and Museum of Modern Art in Wakayama, Japan, hold examples. Lived in Lewes, Sussex.

Nechemia AZAZ 1923– Sculptor in a range of materials, born in Berlin, Germany, who grew up in Palestine and became stonemason in Bologna, Italy. After studying sculpture in the Netherlands and France Azaz eventually moved to England, where he lived in Berkshire. Azaz's 1974 swirling Op. Mobile No. 10, made from painted aluminium tubes, graces the Arts Centre at the University of Warwick, which listed it in its 1997 sculpture trail brochure.

Dia AZZAWI 1939– Artist producing figurative and abstract work in a wide range of media, including large murals and frescoes, born in Baghdad, Iraq. While attending school he discovered modern Arab literature and the theatre, but his interest in painting was stronger, fostered by an art teacher who encouraged Azzawi to paint the real world. Was expelled from school, having supported Abdel Nasser's nationalisation of the Suez Canal, 1956. Readmitted to his studies, one of Azzawi's watercolours was presented to King Faisal II who promised to send Azzawi to study abroad, aborted when the king was assassinated in 1958. Books on art seen at the British Council and America's Information Bureau and the discovery of old copies of *Studio International* expanded Azzawi's knowledge of modern art. In 1962, Azzawi obtained his diploma in archaeological studies from the Faculty of Letters, in 1964 his art studies diploma, having attended evening classes at the Beaux-Arts. Azzawi realised that even in Iraq the rich art heritage of the Arab-Muslim world was being neglected by artists and this, along with popular culture and classical literature, remained key inspirations of his work, injustice and oppression (Azzawi was imprisoned in 1963 during police operations to round up left-wing intellectuals) and the Gulf War being themes explored in the 1980s and 1990s. Azzawi had his first solo show at Galerie A-Wasati, Baghdad, in 1965, the year he was included in the Contemporary Iraqi Art exhibition which toured to Beirut, Rome, Vienna and Madrid. In 1976 he moved to London and worked as a consultant to the Iraqi Cultural Centre, having a solo show at the Patrick Seale Gallery in 1978. Azzawi organised international shows of contemporary Arab art, such as that at the Mall Galleries in 1988, the year Nadine Descendre's documentary on him, *Baghdad Memory*, received a special mention at a UNESCO film festival. In 1994, Azzawi was made artistic consultant to the Arab Museum of Modern Art, Doha, Qatar, where he was given a major show in 2001–2. By then he had had numerous international solo exhibitions and mixed show appearances and had work in many international public collections, including British Museum; Victoria & Albert Museum; Library of Congress, Washington; Gulbenkian Collection, Barcelona; Museum of Modern Art, Baghdad; Museum of the Institute of the Arab World, Paris; plus corporate holdings.

Deborah AZZOPARDI 1958– Self-taught painter who participated in many group shows, solo exhibitions including Henley Festival, 1993, and gallery@oneOtwo, 2003. Bonhams, Knightsbridge, offered examples in Vision 21, 2004. Azzopardi's Pop Art Collection works were "inspired by American lifestyle of the late 1940s...flirtatious and fun, using provocative humour and striking colours to convey energy and vigour...meaning that her paintings don't just hang on a wall – they look back at you!" Private companies and collectors worldwide acquired her pictures. Azzopardi's studio was in north London.

B

Maria Louise BABB 1893–1975 Painter and silversmith, born in Brussels, of Belgian parents. After a convent education she attended finishing school in England, aged 17. In 1914 was in England again as a refugee with her parents. In the 1920s, after a short first marriage, she attended art school in Chelsea and did a course in silverwork. After marrying Captain Babb in 1935 they lived in Cairo, then returned to Godmanstone, Dorset, where she remained, although her husband moved to west Somerset at the end of World War II. Maria Babb travelled abroad during the winter months. She became an accomplished artist in oil, watercolour and pastel, was a keen ornithologist, botanist and herbalist, member of the Buddhist Society and British Society of Dowsers.

Stanley Nicholson BABB 1873–1957 Sculptor, born in Plymouth, where he studied art, also at Royal Academy Schools. Won a gold medal and travelling scholarship, 1901–2, and studied and worked in Italy. Became a member of Art Workers' Guild in 1919, retiring in 1945. Exhibited at RA, RMS, RSA and elsewhere and was a fellow of RBS. Babb's war memorial is outside the civic centre in Tunbridge Wells, Kent. Two examples of his decorative style of sculpture are illustrated in the volume *RBS: Modern British Sculpture*, published in 1939.

Michael BABINGTON SMITH 1901–1984 Self-taught painter who was treasurer of the National Art Collections Fund, 1962–84. Sir Brinsley Ford owned his work.

Irene BACHE 1901–1999 Watercolourist and teacher, born in London. She studied at Croydon College of Art, Central School of Arts and Crafts and Camberwell College of Art. Then taught in a series of schools until she was appointed head of the art department for Swansea College of Education, 1942–66. That College gave her a retrospective show in her final year. She had also had a solo exhibition at the Glynn Vivian Art Gallery, Swansea, in 1954 and showed in group shows with Howard Roberts Gallery, Cardiff; Swansea Art Society, of which she was a leading member; and Dillwyn Gallery, Swansea. On retirement she taught in her own studio, landscape being her speciality. In 1991 had ninetieth birthday shows at Glynn Vivian and Plantasia, Swansea, where she lived at Gower.

David BACHMANN 1964– Artist, born in London, who studied graphic design at Camberwell School of Art, then worked for the National Gallery as an exhibition and publicity designer. In 1989 went to study painting in Florence, Italy, at the Cecil Graves Academy. On his return to London worked for two years as a portrait painter, then settled in Seville, Spain. Exhibitions included ROI and RP, both at Mall Galleries in 1992; Hyde Park Gallery, 1994; and Royal Society of Landscape Painters, Mall Galleries, 1998. Also took part in a shared show with Romanos Moukarzel in 1997 at The Edith Grove Gallery. Bachmann lived in Rome for six months in 2003 for further study. In 2004, exhibitions followed at The Wykeham Gallery in Stockbridge and at Rafael Valls.

Ken BACK 1944–2002 Artist and teacher, born in Guildford, Surrey. He studied at Dover School of Art, 1959–60, Folkestone School of Art, 1960–2, Canterbury College of Art, receiving his diploma in painting and sculpture, 1962–4, then gained a painting certificate with distinction at Royal Academy Schools, 1964–7. He won several prizes at the Schools, including the Eric Kennington Prize for drawing in 1965–6, and Landseer Prize for painting in the same years. From 1963 taught, including Folkestone, Dover and Ipswich Art Schools, Open College of the Arts and Suffolk College of Art & Design, going part-time from 1985 to have more time for painting. Among his group appearances were Metropole Arts Centre, Folkestone, 1966; RA Summer Exhibitions from 1967; Piccadilly Gallery from 1983; and Continuing the Tradition, Chappel Galleries, Chappel, 1993. Nuffield Foundation, St John's College in Cambridge and Sir Brinsley Ford held examples. Lived at Dickleburgh, near Diss, Norfolk, with his wife Corinne, daughter of the sculptor Ivor Roberts-Jones, whose work Back did much to conserve and promote. There was a memorial show, The Ken Back Legacy, at Graham & Oldham Artists' Gallery, Ipswich, in 2004.

Robert BACK 1922–2004 Painter with a strong interest in marine subjects, teacher, born in Adelaide, South Australia. His father, William Edward Back, as a young man sketched regularly in East Anglia with Sir Alfred Munnings, who gave him his first oil paint box, and he had his first solo show in Bond Street aged 18, but family refusal to let him take up art as a career led to his giving it up at 23. Robert himself attended Edinburgh College of Art in 1940 and 1946–9, teachers including William Gillies, Leonard Rosoman and John Maxwell. In World War II Back followed a family tradition and served at sea, participating in Russian and Atlantic convoys and the relief of Malta. He had four years in the merchant navy, taught in various schools and was a noted sailor, being Norfolk Broads dinghy champion three years and an Olympic trialist. A number of Back's works appeared as limited edition prints. Showed at Omell Gallery, RSMA, RSA and David Messum and Malcolm Henderson Galleries. From 1983 had a series of solo shows at The Atlantic Gallery, Washington, America. Campbell College in Belfast, United States Naval Academy in Annapolis and New Orleans Academy hold examples. Back abhorred the sterile approach of many modern marine historical paintings, where "the general effect is brash, the sails too white and transparent." Back's ships inhabit a real time and place. In such pictures as his Georgetown Harbour with Aqueduct Bridge and University 1894, the viewer feels that he is there, participating in a scene that lacks only animation and a sound track. Lived in Seaford, East Sussex.

Daniel BACKHOUSE 1963– Painter and draughtsman in various media, born in Seal, Kent. He did a foundation course at Maidstone College in 1983, teachers including Arthur Neal; in 1984 moved to Norwich, painting at Ethelreda Studios, using the life room at Norwich School of Art, where John Lessore was an influence; then returned to Maidstone College, 1985, for an honours degree course. In 1988 Backhouse travelled in Europe, settling in West Berlin, where he set up a studio for five months; during 1986–7 he worked on various murals in London; then in 1989 moved to Wales, settling at Goodwick, Pembrokeshire. Exhibitions included South East Painters, Maidstone, 1987; Le Weekend Gallery, Berlin, 1988; Mid-Wales Open, at Aberystwyth Arts Centre, 1990; and A Sense of Place, curated by Ian McKay, in association with Rebecca Hossack Gallery, 1985. In 1994 Backhouse shared a show at West Wales Arts Centre, Fishguard. Benjamin C Hargreaves also showed Backhouse's work.

David BACKHOUSE 1941– Sculptor in bronze, born in Corsham, Wiltshire. Studied at West of England College of Art, Bristol, and became a fellow of RBS and member of SPS and RWA. Backhouse taught sculpture in Bristol for a time, then worked extensively abroad: in 1971 in Luxembourg, portrait heads of Prince Charles of Luxembourg and family; in 1972 in Rome and Florence, bronze casting. Among assignments completed were portrait head of the conductor Colin Davis, collection of Royal Opera House, Covent Garden, 1974; sculpture for Mercantile and General Reinsurance Company, Cheltenham, 1977–8; and life-size, three-figure bronze fountain for John Perkins, 1979. Exhibitions included Lad Lane Gallery, Dublin, 1975; Alwin Gallery, 1979; retrospective at Century Galleries, Henley-on-Thames, 1980; and Orangery, Holland Park, 1981. RWA holds his work and included him in its 1st Open Sculpture Exhibition, 1993. In 2002, David Backhouse was chosen as the sculptor of a memorial to animals used by British forces in wartime, a £1 million fund campaign being launched by the novelist Jilly Cooper. Supported by the Animals in War Memorial Fund and sited at Brook Gate, Park Lane, on the edge of Hyde Park, the design featured two heavily laden, lifesize mules struggling towards a Portland stone wall engraved with many other animals. It was unveiled in 2004. There was an exhibition of studies and maquettes for the memorial in 2005 at the Sladmore Gallery. Backhouse lived at Lullington, near Frome, Somerset.

Sonia M BACKHOUSE 1926– Book illustrator, printmaker and watercolourist who studied at Willesden School of Art, 1940–4, and at the Royal College of Art, 1944–7, with Percy Hague Jowett and Ernest Tristram. She exhibited at RA and worked periodically as an illustrator for Folio Society books. Lived in London.

Cecil Walter BACON 1905–1992 Designer and illustrator, born in Battle, Sussex, educated at Sutton Valence School and St Lawrence College in Ramsgate. He attended Hastings School of Art, 1923–5, under Philip Cole, then joined a commercial studio and advertising agency in London in 1926, where he was soon noted for his incisive style. In 1929 Bacon – who signed his work C W B – went freelance, and began to design posters for London Underground and other organisations; these later included British Railways and the Post Office Savings Bank. He began contributing line drawings and scraperboard illustrations for *Radio Times* in 1935, an association which lasted until 1968. He did a number of outstanding covers for the periodical, notably his Festival of Britain, in 1951, and The Queen Returns, in 1953. His work was shown at Folio Society in 1957 and an exhibition was subsequently toured in America by the Arts Council. In 1981 he contributed to the Fifty Years of Design show at London Design Centre and the *Radio Times* show at the Victoria & Albert Museum. In 1984 he had a retrospective exhibition at Hastings Museum and Art Gallery with a memorial show in 1993. Lived at St Leonards-on-Sea, Sussex.

Francis BACON 1909–1992 Painter, by many considered the greatest British artist of his generation. He was born in Dublin of English parents. In the mid-1920s he lived in Berlin and Paris, in London in the 1930s having some success as an interior decorator and designer of rugs and furniture. Self-taught, he began painting in the late 1920s. At first he worked slowly and occasionally, destroying much of his output. In 1934 he had a solo show at Transition Gallery, three years later appearing at Agnew in Young British Painters. With a series of one-man exhibitions at the Hanover Gallery from 1949 – having spent the late 1940s in Monte Carlo – Bacon began to build a London reputation. This was reinforced from 1960 with an impressive series at Marlborough Fine Art. He had a first solo show at Durlacher Bros in New York in 1953 and in Paris at Galerie Rive Droite four years later. His painting was shown in the British pavilion at Venice Biennale in 1954. A series of international one-man shows followed, along with retrospectives. In Britain there was one at the ICA in 1955; one at the Tate Gallery, with a subsequent European and American tour, in 1962–4; another at the Tate in 1985. The Tate Gallery in Liverpool held a show in 1990–1; there was a retrospective at Centre Georges Pompidou, Paris/Haus der Kunst, Munich, 1996; and a reappraisal at the Hayward Gallery, 1998. In 2000 one at the Hugh Lane Municipal Gallery of Modern Art, Dublin, celebrated the gift of Bacon's studio. The Tate Gallery, like other international collections, holds examples of Bacon's work, including one of his long line of triptychs, the key Three Studies for Figures at the Base of a Crucifixion, of 1944, which made Bacon famous in the art world. Bacon's figure studies, such as Two Figures on a Bed; his portraits; and the series based on Velasquez's portrait of Pope Innocent X distort conventional appearances to raw, powerful effect, creating haunting images. He painted a stream of self-portraits plus others of friends such as George Dyer, Muriel Belcher and Isabel Rawsthorne. Bacon lived in London but died in Madrid, Spain, having consistently refused all official honours.

Peter James BACON 1951– Artist and designer creating entirely with materials such as rope and twine, the son of an architect, born in north London. Attended Hornsey School of Art. Showed at Mall Galleries and elsewhere in London and was a member of the Free Painters and Sculptors. Lived in Enfield, Middlesex.

Yehuda BACON 1929– Artist, illustrator and teacher, born in Ostrava, Czechoslovakia, who studied with various Jewish artists in Theresienstadt and Auschwitz camps, 1941–5. In 1945 Bacon (pronounced Bahcon) was a private student of Willi Nowak of the Prague Academy of Art, from 1946–51, with a scholarship, attending Bezalel Academy in Jerusalem under Mordecai Ardon. Further studies followed with work periods abroad; in 1956–7 Bacon studied etching with Merlyn Evans at Central School of Arts and Crafts, with a time on scholarship in Italy in 1956; was at École des Beaux-Arts in Paris, 1957–8; was a private student of Bernard Reder, in Florence in 1958; returned to study etching and lithography at Central School, 1963–4; did advanced studies and experimental work at Pratt Institute Graphics Center, New York, 1971–3; studied teaching methods in various Scandinavian art schools in 1973; then in 1983 had a sabbatical year studying widely on the continent. His own teaching experience began in 1951 in Jerusalem, at Brandeis and other schools; from 1959 he was on the staff of Bezalel Academy; and in 1976–7 lectured at Haifa University. Bacon gained a number of awards and medals and took part in numerous group shows, including RA Summer Exhibition. Several dozen solo exhibitions included University of London Westfield College Library, 1978, and Arts 38 Gallery, 1980. Among many book covers and illustrations completed were Alan Sillitoe's *Out of the Fire*, 1979. Victoria & Albert Museum, British Museum and Ben Uri Art Society hold examples.

Pamela BACZKOWSKA 1938– Sculptor, born in Bradford, Yorkshire, married to the artist Henry Baczkowski. She worked in a variety of materials, figurative and abstract works. Studied at Regional College of Art, Bradford, and trained as a potter for 10 years, in 1963 starting to make ceramic sculpture, then bronzes and carvings, from 1967 working exclusively on sculpture. Travelled in Europe, America and North Africa. Was a member of Free Painters and Sculptors. Exhibitions included Woodstock Gallery; Mall Galleries; Sackville Gallery, East Grinstead; Rudolf Shaeffer Hause, Rotenberg; Riverside Gallery; and Galerie Angle Aigue, Brussels. Deutsche Bank, Heilbronn, Germany, owned her work, one influence on which was the painter Howard Hodgkin. Lived in East Grinstead, Sussex.

John Fanshawe BADELEY 1874–1951 Printmaker, born in Elswick, Lancashire. He was educated at Radley College and Oxford University. Henry John Fanshawe Badeley was in the Judicial Office of the House of Lords and from 1934 was Clerk of the Parliaments, being knighted in 1935. A member of RE, he was noted for his heraldic work, also showing at RA and RMS. Lived in London.

Glenn BADHAM 1972– Began exhibiting from 1994, having graduated in visual arts from De Montfort University, Leicester, also studying with the ceramist Cesare Sartori, in Italy. Venues included Battersea Arts Centre, Numberninethe gallery in Birmingham and in France and Germany.

Stanley Roy BADMIN 1906–1989 Watercolourist, draughtsman and printmaker, born in London. Studied at Camberwell School of Arts and Crafts and Royal College of Art, which he left in 1928. Badmin soon established a reputation for his detailed, affectionate depictions of the English countryside and country life. He illustrated *Shell Guides*, Shell posters, produced over a hundred greetings card designs for Royle's the fine art publishers, produced covers for *Reader's Digest* and illustrated travel and topographical books. Aged 26, he became one of the youngest-ever members of RWS, also becoming a member of RE. Showed Fine Art Society, Leicester Galleries, Arts Council and abroad. In 1985 Chris Beetles Ltd held a major retrospective to coincide with Beetles' biography *S R Badmin and the English Landscape*. Victoria & Albert Museum and British Museum hold his work. Lived for many years in Bignor, Sussex.

Howard BAER 1906– Cartoonist, illustrator, painter and printmaker, born at Finleyville, in the Allegheny Mountain section of Pennsylvania, America, where his father ran a small department store. Settled in New York in 1930 after studying at Carnegie Tech, Pittsburgh. As a young man, apart from his own paintings and prints, Baer was drawing as many as 365 cartoons a year for a newspaper syndicate and magazines, for *Esquire* alone five a month. He became an artist-war correspondent for Abbott Laboratories in 1944 in China, Burma and India, completing paintings of the Medical Corps at the front. This work is now in the Pentagon's Archives of War. Travelled extensively in Europe from 1948, with time in London from 1960. Illustrated many books. He made his debut as an artist in 1941 with an exhibition of paintings at the New York gallery of Associated American Artists. Other shows included Ben Uri Art Society, 1965 and 1972, which holds several examples, as do the Metropolitan Museum in New York and the Butler Art Institute.

Jo BAER 1929– Artist who produced a large body of abstract work, born in Seattle, Washington, America, using oil, various contés, pencils and other media. She trained as a scientist at University of Washington and the graduate facility, New York School for Social Research. Baer's group shows included Kaymar Gallery, New York, 1964; Documenta IV, Museum Friedericianum, Kassel, 1968; Lisson Gallery from 1975; American Painting of the 1970s, Albright-Knox Art Gallery, Buffalo, 1979; and From Minimal to Conceptual Art, National Gallery of Art, Washington, 1994. Had a solo exhibition at Fischbach Gallery, New York, 1966, then showed prolifically, later shows including Rhona Hoffman Gallery, Chicago, 1989; Paul Andriesse Gallery, Amsterdam, 1990; and Paley/Levy Gallery, Moore College, Philadelphia, 1993. Starting in Ireland in 1978 Baer collaborated with Bruce Robbins until 1984, when she moved to the Netherlands, settling in Amsterdam. Their joint appearances included 112 Workshop, New York, 1980; Riverside Studios, 1982; and Oliver Dowling Gallery, Dublin, 1984.

Peter BAER 1924–1996 Printmaker, painter, draughtsman and teacher, born in Berlin, Germany, whose family emigrated to Spain in 1936, then London, where he eventually settled. In 1939 he was interned at Huyton and was a draughtsman in an aircraft factory, 1940–6, from 1947–50 studying at Central School of Arts and Crafts under Anthony Gross and Morris Kestelman. During following years he did many jobs, including printer and photographer. From 1960–5 Baer was a printer of artists' lithographs at Curwen Press, serving an apprenticeship with Stanley Jones which Baer said taught him much. He printed his own etchings in Birgit Skiöld's Print Workshop, 1967–75. Baer was lecturer in printmaking at Hammersmith School of Art, then at Chelsea, from 1970. His work ranged from large, dramatic black-and-white etchings to exuberant, Expressionistic landscapes, employing among other colours vibrant reds and brilliant blues. Mixed shows included RA, Whitechapel Art Gallery, Victoria & Albert Museum and international print exhibitions; he was in the 1986 Berlin show Art in Exile. Solo print exhibitions latterly included Camden Arts Centre, 1981, and University College, 1982; solo shows of paintings Amalgam Arts, 1992, and BBC White City, 1994. Ben Uri Art Society holds his work.

Pier Luigi BAFFONI 1932– Painter and draughtsman, born in Turin, Italy. His uncle, Achille Parachini, was a notable portrait painter. Baffoni studied at College of Art, Turin, 1954–8, with Luigi Guglielmino and privately with Alessandro Pomi, other artists who influenced him being Nino Springolo and Juti Ravenna. In 1963 Baffoni won a prize at an international exhibition in Castelfranco Veneto. After moving to England Baffoni was elected to NS and ROI. He won the Scharf Prize for figure painting at ROI's annual show in 1983, two years later being made a Sociétaire of the Société des Artistes Indépendants after showing at the Grand Palais in Paris. Baffoni held one-man shows in Italy and in the English provinces. Used a rich palette for landscapes, portraits and still lifes. Several of his pictures were bought by the Bedfordshire Education Art Loan Service. Lived in Lower Stondon, Bedfordshire.

Eric BAGGALEY 1935– Painter, printmaker and teacher, born in Manchester, who from 1954–77 was a member of and teacher in the religious order Salesians of Don Bosco, from 1963–77 being a Roman Catholic priest and teacher. From 1977–94, taught as head of modern languages and religious studies. Studied extra-mural at Sheffield Hallam University, 1994–5; at Chesterfield Art College, 1995–7; at Manchester Metropolitan University, 1997–9; and at Mappin Art Gallery, Sheffield, workshops where Peter Gillies and Martin Linsdell were major influences. "Colour of shapes and shapes of colour", also sea, land and city shapes, were themes in Baggaley's work, which was sometimes signed with initials. The artists of St Ives, Mark Rothko, Antoni Tapiès and Joan Miró were other influences. Took part in a mixed printmakers' show at Manchester Metropolitan University, 1999; solo exhibitions included Stair Way there in 1997 and Off the Wall, Salford Museum and Art Gallery, Salford, 2000. Lived in Altrincham, Cheshire.

Alfred Charles BAILEY 1883– Watercolourist, born in Brighton, Sussex, who after private education attended Brighton School of Art under Louis Grier. Exhibited extensively at Goupil Gallery, RBA and Redfern Gallery. In the early part of the century he lived in St Ives, Cornwall, where he was a member of the Society of Artists, later residing in Richmond, Surrey.

Arthur BAILEY 1903– Architect and watercolourist, born in Alsager, Cheshire. Bailey was articled to a firm of architects for several years after World War I, eventually working in a practice known as Ansell and Bailey. He also studied, as an articled pupil, at the Central School of Arts and Crafts. He eventually became a fellow of the RIBA and showed at RA. Reform Club member. Lived in London.

Caroline BAILEY 1953– Painter, born in Chester, Cheshire. She did a foundation course at Mid-Cheshire College of Further Education, 1972, graduating with honours and gaining her master's in printed textiles at Manchester Polytechnic, 1975. Bailey worked mainly in water-based media, often with different types and qualities overlaid. The result produced bright and energetic compositions with a still life or landscape beneath an essentially abstract surface. She was a member of RSW who won the Daler-Rowney Award first prize in 1994 at RWS. Other mixed exhibition appearances included RI, from 1990; RSMA, from 1994; and the Singer & Friedlander/*Sunday Times* Watercolour Competition, 1995. Showed solo at The City Gallery from 1996, also at Thompson's Gallery, 2001. Irish Management Institute holds her work.

Cecil Raymond BAILEY 1907–1973 Artist in charcoal, oil and watercolour, born and lived in London, who won a scholarship to Martin's School of Art, having shown promise as a portrait painter. Family circumstances forced him to leave and take up casual labour. Became a cleaner at Westminster Abbey in 1929, a verger in 1935 and from 1960 was canons verger until he retired in 1972. Art remained a consuming hobby for Bailey, who constantly sketched and studied part-time with David Bomberg at the Borough Polytechnic and also attended Morley College. Bomberg suggested that Bailey join him painting in Spain, but Bailey could not leave his family. He was a founder-member of the Borough Bottega in 1953 and took part in in its exhibitions as well as other mixed shows, and had two solo exhibitions at BH Corner Gallery, 1969 and 1970. Turner, Picasso, Henry Moore, the French Impressionists, the architecture of the Abbey and, latterly, the sombre London skyline were all influences. Bailey's final work was mainly abstract. After retirement Bailey had seven major operations. He was encouraged to jot down his memories which, as *A Verger's Diary*, his wife had published privately in a small edition after his death.

Chris BAILEY 1960– Sculptor using a variety of materials, teacher and curator, born in Oxford, who studied at Cambridge College of Art, 1978–9, gaining an honours degree in fine art from Sheffield City Polytechnic, with four months at San Jose State University, California, America, 1979–82. Bailey worked for the Crucible Theatre in Sheffield, 1982–3; for Yorkshire Sculpture Park, 1983–8, becoming curator in 1985; the Scottish Sculpture Workshop, 1988–93; then as a self-employed artist, handling educational workshops in Aberdeenshire. She said that "An enduring interest in the human condition is the preoccupation of my sculpture." Exhibitions included Aberdeen Art Gallery, 1989; RSA from 1989; Scottish Sculpture Open 6, 1991; Royal Glasgow Institute of the Fine Arts, 1993; and Kingfisher Gallery, Edinburgh, from 1997. The Lost Gallery, Strathdon, permanently showed Bailey's work.

George William BAILEY 1880–1955 Landscape painter in oil and watercolour, born in Spalding, Lincolnshire. Studied at Chelsea School of Art, 1903–4, under Ernest Borough Johnson. Exhibited RWA, RSA, Foyles Gallery and provincial galleries including Usher Gallery, Lincoln, which holds his work. Signed pictures G W B. Was for many years closely associated with Spalding Gentlemen's Society. Lived at Spalding, Lincolnshire.

James BAILEY 1922– Stage designer and painter, born in London. He was initially educated in England and Switzerland, then studied art at the Byam Shaw School and Slade School of Fine Art, 1939–40, where his teachers included Vladimir Polunin. Although he had his first one-man show at Redfern Gallery in 1955, Bailey made his name as a stage designer. He designed for major productions at the Royal Opera House, Covent Garden; the Lyric Theatre, Hammersmith, for *The Way of the World* during a John Gielgud season; for the Old Vic; and for La Scala, Milan. Lived in London.

Julian BAILEY 1963– Painter and draughtsman, born in Cheshire. Bailey studied at Ruskin School of Art in Oxford and was a member of New College there, 1982–5, attending Royal Academy Schools, 1985–8. He was awarded the Egerton Coghill Landscape Prize (Oxford University), in 1984; the David Murray Landscape Award, in same year; the Turner Gold Medal at the Royal Academy Schools in 1986; and Landseer Scholarship in 1988. In 1989 Bailey visited Australia and the Far East, where the strength of light impressed him, as a painter whose debt was to the muted influences of Walter Sickert and the Camden Town Group. Mixed shows included RA, LG, Cadogan Contemporary and New Grafton Gallery, where he had his first solo show in 1991, later ones including more there and Browse & Darby, from 1999. HRH The Prince of Wales, Dorset County Council, The National Trust (Foundation for Art) and several corporate collections held examples.

Keith BAILEY 1929– Sculptor in a variety of materials and teacher, born in St Helens, Lancashire. He attended Liverpool College of Art, 1946–8, Manchester College of Art, 1948–51, then City and Guilds School, 1953–4. Was for some time a visiting teacher at West Dean College, in Sussex. In 1967 had a solo show at Cambridge Building Centre and completed panels for churches and educational institutions in various parts of England. Bailey, who had a studio in Cambridge and who was a member of Letter Exchange, contributed to Stone Words, organised by Wolseley Fine Arts, 2002. Lived for some years at Royston, Hertfordshire.

Liz BAILEY 1951– Artist, born in Broxbourne, Hertfordshire, who worked as a display artist until 1998. She attended Byam Shaw School of Fine Art, her teachers including Elizabeth Magill, Peter Kennard, Sarah Pickstone and Douglas Allsop. Bailey had a residency at Florence Trust Studios in 2003. Her exhibitions included Studio Voltaire, Sarah Myerscough Fine Art and Vertigo Gallery, all 2003; Re-Union at APT Gallery and the RA Summer Exhibition, both 2004; and Absence, Corpus Fine Art at Menier Gallery, 2005. Esmée Fairbairn Foundation and The McGraw-Hill Companies Ltd held her work. Lived and worked in London and Herefordshire.

Neil BAILEY 1958– Figurative painter, notably in acrylic on canvas, whose work drew on a wide range of images, including popular culture, and could have an iconic quality. Studied foundation at Great Yarmouth College of Art, 1977–8, gaining an honours degree in fine art, Loughborough College of Art, 1978–81. Bailey "gave up painting after graduation and moved to London, gave up chess when left out of the Olympic team, took up crosswords, and became a contract cleaner." Between 1982–8, disillusioned with cleaning, Bailey took up signwriting, then started painting again. Between 1988–99 he "averaged two paintings a year during the turmoil of starting the sign company," then "in 1999–2000 ran out of storage space." In 2000, shared a three-man show at The Gallery in Cork Street with Mark Clark and Wayne Robinson. Other exhibitions included Ikon Gallery, Birmingham, 1981; Sadler's Wells Theatre, 1982; People's Gallery, Camden, 1983; and East Cross Centre, Hackney, 1990. Commissions included four pieces for The Hudson Bay free house, Forest Gate, 1999, and 10 for The Briar Rose free house, Bennett's Hill, Birmingham, 2000.

Peter BAILEY 1944–2005 Sculptor and teacher, born near Wrexham, Denbighshire. He studied at University College of Wales, Aberystwyth, then at Bath Academy of Art, from 1969–73 being a part-time tutor in sculpture at the University College. In 1969–70 Bailey was part-time technical assistant to the sculptor and printmaker Michael Pennie, then in the early 1970s he took up a teaching fellowship in sculpture, again at University College of Wales. Bailey participated in many group shows, including Northern Young Contemporaries, Manchester; Laing Art Gallery, in Newcastle upon Tyne; and Arnolfini Gallery, Bristol. WAC and Victoria & Albert Museum hold his work.

Terry BAILEY 1937– Painter and teacher, born in Wolverhampton, Staffordshire. He studied at local Technical High School, then at Wolverhampton College of Art, 1954–8, and Bournemouth College of Art, 1962. Went on to teach at Northumberland College of Higher Education, 1962–79. Showed at RP, at RBSA where he was a prizewinner in the Open exhibition, 1986, and had several solo shows. National Library of Wales, Aberystwyth, holds his work. Lived in Aberdovey, Gwynedd.

William BAILLIE 1905–1999 Painter, photographer and teacher, whose work embraced figurative, Surrealist and latterly entirely abstract pictures. By then, he felt that "the art of painting is not about other things, but has an independent existence of its own." Baillie was born in Larkhall, Lanarkshire, son of a coal miner, and gained his diploma from Glasgow School of Art in 1927, having studied with A E Haswell Miller. He had first exhibited at RSA in 1925 (at this time Baillie's works were mainly in transparent watercolour), and he was to show there regularly, also at the Royal Glasgow Institute of the Fine Arts. Baillie taught from 1928, and for this purpose made an extensive study of modern artistic trends. In 1931, Baillie had works bought to decorate the merchant ship *Monarch of Bermuda*. In the mid-1930s Baillie became interested in photography, in 1936 being elected a member of The Scottish Photographic Circle, at which he lectured and showed, also exhibiting with The Scottish National Salon and in 1938 at the British Empire Exhibition. In 1989 the Fine Art Society, Glasgow, had a show of work by Baillie and his pupil, William J Bunting. Latterly, Baillie lived in Hamilton, Lanarkshire, and was known as William Baillie of Hamilton. The museum there and Perth's art gallery hold examples.

William BAILLIE 1923– Painter and teacher, born in Edinburgh where he continued to live. He studied at Edinburgh College of Art and Moray House College of Education, 1941–51, although from 1942–7 served in Army, mainly in the Far East. In 1955 Baillie became resident tutor at the National Gallery of Canada Summer School, in Ottawa. Then from 1960–88 he taught at Edinburgh College of Art, finally as senior lecturer in the drawing and painting school. In 1980 the English Speaking Union sponsored Baillie to travel to India, Nepal and Sikkim; this resulted in a body of work. Baillie was president of RSW, 1974–88 and was elected RSA in 1979, becoming its president in 1990; he was made Hon. RA and Hon. RWA in 1991. After a one-man show at Saltire Society Festival Exhibition in 1961 Baillie went on to show extensively in Scotland and England, notably at Lower Loomshop Gallery, Lower Largo, Fife; Heal's Gallery; and retrospective at Kirkcaldy Art Gallery in 1977. RSA, Scottish Arts Council and Scottish National Gallery of Modern Art hold his work.

Donald BAIN 1904–1979 Painter, draughtsman and stage designer, born in Kilmacolm, Renfrewshire. After education at Moffat Academy, Bain studied art with W Y MacGregor, one of the Glasgow Boys, who introduced him to the work of S J Peploe and J D Fergusson, whose style is sometimes reflected in Bain's pictures. In the late 1920s Bain went to Paris, where Matisse's work further influenced him. Bain returned to Glasgow in 1940, working in the shipyards and with Fergusson became involved in the New Scottish Group from its formation in 1942. A further stay of several years in France in the period after World War II put him in touch with Cézannesque influences in contemporary French painting before he settled in Glasgow in 1948. There Fergusson's wife Margaret Morris commissioned Bain to design the scenery for a dance version of *A Midsummer Night's Dream*. Bain exhibited widely in France and a touring exhibition in major Scottish cities in 1972–3 revived interest in him, but at time of his death he was suffering neglect. Solo show, curated by William Hardie, at The Collins Gallery, University of Strathclyde, 2000. Scottish Arts Council and Scottish National Gallery of Modern Art hold his work.

Peter BAIN 1927– Painter and draughtsman, born in London, who studied at Bath Academy of Art, Corsham, under William Scott and Bernard Meadows. As well as Army service Bain was a butcher, poultry farmer and a teacher. He showed in London and the provinces. Lived in Old Bosham, Sussex.

David BAINBRIDGE 1941– Conceptual artist and teacher who attended Barnsley Art School in the late 1950s, where he met Terry Atkinson, but left to be a bus conductor. Bainbridge then worked at a Sheffield steelworks, became a shop steward and joined the Communist Party of Great Britain. Bainbridge moved to London in 1963 and enrolled at St Martin's School of Art sculpture department. He began teaching at Coventry College of Art in 1967, the year that he and Harold Hurrell shared the Hardware Exhibition at the Architectural Association. In 1968, Bainbridge, Hurrell, Atkinson and Michael Baldwin formed the influential exhibiting and publishing group Art & Language, but Bainbridge chose to leave it in 1971. This was the year when with Baldwin he was dismissed from Coventry, as the art theory course, on which they and Atkinson had taught, was summarily ended. Settled in Old Swinford, West Midlands. In 2004 the Institute of Contemporary Disciplinary Arts, University of Bath, showed work by Bainbridge, Atkinson and David Rushton.

Eric BAINBRIDGE 1955– Sculptor and draughtsman, born in County Durham, who studied at Newcastle Polytechnic, 1974–7, then Royal College of Art, 1978–81. Bainbridge said that he needed to "play around with the size of objects – increasing them to above human scale – and also to remake them ... into the world of sculpture", as in the giant spoons forming More Blancmange in the South Bank Centre's touring The British Art Show 1990. In 1999 30 huge metal and limestone spheres by Bainbridge, meant to depict heaven, earth and universe, were sited on a roundabout at Marina Way, Hartlepool. Bainbridge participated in many group shows from New Contemporaries, at ICA, in 1981. His solo exhibitions began with Ayton Basement, Newcastle, 1978, later ones including Salvatore Ala Gallery, New York, 1988, Stedelijk Museum, Amsterdam, 1989–90, and Cornerhouse, Manchester, 1997. Arts Council holds his work. Lived in London.

John BAINBRIDGE 1920– Painter, draughtsman and poster artist, born in Sydney, New South Wales. Studied at Swinbourne Technical College, Melbourne, and Melbourne Art Gallery. Exhibited in Australia, where he is represented in National Gallery of South Australia in Adelaide, also at London and Redfern Galleries. Did posters for Ealing Studios, London Underground and British European Airways. Lived for some years in London.

Kenneth BAINBRIDGE 1908– Printmaker, craftsman and teacher, born in Colne, Lancashire. He attended Burnley Municipal School of Art, 1929–34, then Royal College of Art, 1934–8, when Ernest Tristram and the calligrapher Edward Johnston taught him, and simultaneously at Central School of Arts and Crafts. Showed in London and in the Burnley area, where he lived.

Dick BAINES 1940– Painter, printmaker and teacher, born in Hastings, Sussex. He studied at Regent Street Polytechnic School of Art, 1957–61, where his teachers included James Osborne, then at Goldsmiths' College School of Art where Paul Drury taught him. Design lecturer for some years at the London College of Fashion. For a period he was president of the East Sussex Arts Club. Showed NS and ROI of both of which he was a member, and RBA. Had solo show at Hastings Public Museum and Art Gallery; Borough of Hastings holds his work. Lived in London.

Glyn BAINES 1930– Influential teacher and painter in oil whose work included subtle abstracts. Born in Carrog, Merionethshire, Baines studied at Wrexham School of Art and Cardiff Teacher Training College. Until 1961 he worked at home on the farm, then was head of art at Bala Comprehensive School until 1989, latterly working in his own studio. Baines was a member of Gweled, The Welsh Society of Visual Arts. Group shows included numerous appearances at National Eisteddfod of Wales; Broekman Gallery, Chester; Mostyn Open, Llandudno; Y Tabernacl, Machynlleth; and and Invited Artists '96, at RCamA, Conwy. Solo shows included Plas-Glyn-y-Weddw, Llandbedrog; The Gallery at Mold, Clwyd; and Oriel Cantref Bala, Gwynedd, near to where he lived.

Harry BAINES 1910–1995 Realistic figurative painter and draughtsman, full name Frederick Harry Baines, born in Manchester, who attended the School of Art there, 1930–4, gaining a diploma in mural painting. During the next five years Baines completed several murals in the north of England, Timperley Church, Cheshire, and Longford Cinema, Manchester, being represented in the Tate Gallery show Contemporary British Mural Painting, 1938. Service in the Royal Engineers, 1941–6, introduced Baines to India; he was seconded to be design studio director for the Indian government's exhibitions division information department. On later visits Baines recorded impressions of a new steelworks; painted murals for the British pavilion at the Delhi Industrial Fair; with Richard Lannoy prepared the book *The Eye of Love* on temple sculpture, 1976; and produced drawings exhibited as part of the Festival of India, 1983. Baines' interest in Neo-Realism had been stimulated by meeting Italian artists such as Guttuso, Mucchi, Zigaina and Treccani, whose work dominated the Venice Biennale of 1951. Baines' "superb draughtsmanship" was praised by critic John Berger, who noted that "the weight of a stone that a woman carries on her head can be seen in her ankle." Mixed shows included RA, Whitechapel Art Gallery, Leicester Galleries and The Forgotten Fifties, Graves Art Gallery, Sheffield, and tour, 1984. Later solo shows included a series at Camden Arts Centre from 1980; Alpha House Gallery, Sherborne, 1992; and a memorial exhibition at Art Connoisseur Gallery, 1996. Lived in London.

Charlie BAIRD 1955– Painter and printmaker, born in Nairn, who studied lithography and screenprinting at the Instituto Allendes, San Miguel, Mexico; did an art course at Wimbledon; then was in residence at Cité Internationale des Arts, Paris, 1983–5. Mixed shows included Thumb Gallery, 1980; RA Summer Exhibition from 1989; Jonathan Clarke Gallery, 1991; Michael Parkin Gallery, 1994; and Tenth Anniversary show at Cadogan Contemporary Art, 1996. It gave Baird a solo exhibition in 2000, where a subtle colour sense and a wittily idiosyncratic style of landscape were evident.

Edward BAIRD 1904–1949 Painter and teacher, born in Montrose, Angus, where poor health confined him for most of his life. After education at Montrose Academy he attended Glasgow School of Art, 1923–7, winning the Newbery Medal as top student of his year. A travelling scholarship took him to Italy for a year, where the study of early Renaissance pictures influenced his own work. Meticulous detail, Hyper-Realist and Surrealistic elements all had a part in this. From 1938–40 Baird taught at Dundee College of Art. Baird was appointed an Official War Artist in 1943. Much of his output was portraits, examples being in the Scottish Arts Council and Dundee Art Galleries and Museums collections. It was the Council's show of his work in 1968 which revived interest in Baird, then largely forgotten. Scottish National Gallery of Modern Art held a retrospective of Baird's small output – less than three dozen canvases – in 1992. Portrait of a Young Scotsman: Edward Baird 1904–49 was organised by The Fleming Collection in 2004. This included a head of Baird by the sculptor William Lamb and Baird's portrait of the architect George Fairweather, to whose sister Ann the artist was married.

Lucy BAIRD 1959– Sculptor, born in Nyasaland, now Malawi, who graduated with honours in sculpture and a postgraduate diploma from Edinburgh College of Art, 1980–5. In 1984 she won an Andrew Grant Scholarship Award, in 1985 an RSA Travelling Scholarship taking her to Florence, Italy. Baird exhibited in Britain and Germany. While still a student, Baird was commissioned by Irvine Development Corporation to produce her sculpture Mining, 1984, another striking commission being the stainless steel abstract Untitled, mounted on a lift shaft at the University of Glasgow's Rankine Building. That was completed in 1990, the year Baird was appointed artist-in-residence for Irvine New Town, one result being her 1992 piece Birds.

Nancy BAIRSTOW fl. c.1925–55 Miniaturist in watercolour, born in Wolstanton, Staffordshire. She was educated privately, then studied art with the miniaturist Edwin Morgan. Showed extensively at RI, also RA, RMS, Walker Art Gallery, Liverpool, and Paris Salon. Lived at Chorley Wood Common, Hertfordshire.

Farah BAJULL 1964– Artist, born in Iran, who made work "crossing performance and sculpture, using emblematic forms as metaphors for the female body, the notion of the feminine and female survival." Bajull did a foundation course at Camberwell College of Art and Design, 1991–2; diploma in sculpture, Byam Shaw School of Art, 1992–3; gained a first-class honours degree in fine art, sculpture, Chelsea College of Art and Design, 1993–6; and her master's in sculpture from the Royal College of Art, 1996–8. Won the Serenela Ciclitira Award. Exhibitions included If not then, Moravian Burial Ground, 1995; Top Marks, London Institute Gallery, 1996; Handbag, City Gallery, Leicester, 2000; and Fruit-Fall, Vauxhall St Peter's Heritage Centre, 2001. Also in that year, Bajull had a solo show, Foreign Bodies, Stephen Lawrence Gallery at the University of Greenwich, and an exhibition and residency at The Space, Institute of International Visual Arts. Lived in London.

Alexandra BAKER 1947– Watercolourist, born in Southborough, Kent. She came from and was married into a military family and specialised in military subjects. Studied at Sir John Cass School of Arts and Crafts, 1964–5. Was a member of SGA where she showed, also elsewhere in London, and illustrated a number of books with military themes, such as *Gunners at Larkhill*. Was a member of the Society for Army Historical Research and had work in the collections of the National Army Museum as well as various regiments. Lived in Salisbury, Wiltshire.

Anne BAKER 1955– London-based British media artist who between 1982–95 worked in performance and video. With the artist Marty St James she produced a series of artworks called Video Portraits which combined live performance and the electronic image. From 1995 Baker worked in digital media, as shown at Colville Place Gallery, in 1996 starting her website annescafe, showing her own and a variety of alternative interactive work. A year later she joined Flat Earth Communications as designer and co-founder. One of its projects was creating aristsineastlondon.org for Acme Studios, launched in 2001. Three years before Baker had initiated SCARS, a web-based interactive chronicle that gathered and catalogued people's scars and related stories, a project featured as a website in ISEA98, The Revolution, International Technology Biennial Liverpool & Manchester. Her project Container was commissioned and premiered in 2000 at the Montreal Biennale in Canada, a virtual repository for people's memories. In 2001, Baker took part in Silent Motion at the Stanley Picker Gallery, Kingston University.

Bobby BAKER 1950– Artist who was born Lindsey Baker in Sidcup, Kent, married to the photographer Andrew

Whittuck. She employed the media of performance, painting, video and food. Studied painting at St Martin's School of Art, 1968–72, in the latter year starting to perform with food as a medium, venues including galleries, public and domestic spaces. Solo performances from this period included An Edible Family in a Mobile Home, Stepney, 1976; Art Supermarket, ICA, 1978; and Packed Lunch, Hayward Gallery, 1979. After doing no public work for eight years Baker resumed in 1988, selected performances including Drawing on a Mother's Experience, ICA with extensive national and international tour, 1989; Kitchen Show, London, with tour, 1991; How to Shop, London and tour, 1993; and Take a Peek!, South Bank Centre/Arnolfini Gallery, Bristol, 1995. Also took part in group events, including Food Art, Kettle's Yard, Cambridge, 1977; Sucre d'Art, Louvre, Paris, 1978; About Time, ICA/Arnolfini, 1980; and Food as Politics, Camerawork, 1985. Marina Warner, an enthusiast for Baker's work, wrote of her that "she could be called a hunger artist, working with her own cravings and the common needs of people for sustenance, for comfort, for nourishment, of which food is the chief sign ... She is the target of the laughter she provokes, but remains in control." Lived in London, where in 2001 she put on her Box Story performance, the fifth and final piece in the LIFT festival-commissioned Daily Life series. It was performed again at The Pit, Barbican Centre, in 2004.

Catherine BAKER 1959– Artist who graduated with honours from Kingston Polytechnic, 1979–82. Mixed show appearances included Whitechapel Open, Whitechapel Art Gallery, 1983; Pictures from Wapping at Tom Allen Centre and The Moving City at The 39 Steps, both 1987; The South Bank Picture Show, Royal Festival Hall, 1987–8; The Challoner Club, 1988; and East End Open Studios, with Leyton Artists Group, 1989.

Charles Henry Collins BAKER 1880–1959 Painter, art historian and curator, born in Ilminster, Somerset. He was educated at Berkhamsted School and studied art at Royal Academy Schools. Was for a time keeper at the National Gallery, surveyor of the king's pictures and then on the research staff of the Huntingdon Library, California. He was art critic of *Outlook* and of the *Saturday Review* and wrote a series of books, including *Crome*, 1921, and *British Painting to 1900*, 1933. Showed at NEAC, RA, Goupil Gallery and elsewhere. Contemporary Art Society and public galleries in Manchester and Huddersfield bought his work. Lived latterly in London.

Chris BAKER 1944– Painter who was brought up in south London in a tough environment, was a motor mechanic for a decade and did not go to Camberwell School of Arts and Crafts until 1971. After four years there he was at Royal College of Art, 1975–8, in 1977 winning the Lubiam Award in Mantova, Italy. Baker's work reflected his experience of city life transformed on canvas into slowly formed but telling images. Baker had a key solo show at Warwick Arts Trust in 1983, also exhibiting at Paton Gallery. He was included in Exhibition Road in 1988 at Royal College, which holds his work, as does Arts Council.

Christopher BAKER 1956– Painter, printmaker, teacher and writer, born in Essex. He studied at West Surrey College of Art & Design, Farnham, 1974–5, then Gloucester College of Art & Design, 1975–8, under David Carpanini, and at University of Exeter School of Education. He was artist-in-residence at Oundle School, 1981–3, then a full-time art teacher at Kimbolton School, Cambridgeshire, 1983–6. Also taught at West Dean College in Sussex, where he settled at Arundel. From 1987 Baker wrote for *The Artist* magazine, carried out commissioned work and with two other painters ran Herringbroom Studios. Royal Mint commissioned his services. Baker was elected to RBA in 1984, also showing with RWA, Medici Galleries and Portsmouth and Brighton public galleries. Among his solo shows was Pallant House, Chichester, 1993, views of the Portsmouth area.

Darren BAKER 1976– Artist in oil and pastel who graduated from Bradford Art College in 1998 and within a year was invited to exhibit at the United Kingdom Millennium Show in New York. He continued to study the Old Masters and great exponents of still-life painting. Baker's own still lifes were notable for their subtle depiction of light. After his first show in London in 1999 Baker exhibited widely in the United Kingdom and abroad, winning a number of awards, including PS. Aged only 23, Baker was invited to exhibit at the United Kingdom Millennium Show in New York and in the same year was appointed official artist of the Professional Footballers' Association. Many sporting commissions followed, such as the footballer Teddy Sheringham, the boxer Prince Naseem Hamed and the jockey Frankie Dettori. He was included in Old & New, organised by Wolseley Fine Arts at The Gallery in Cork Street, and in The Art of Pastel, W H Patterson, both in 2003. In 2004 Baker painted England's rugby world cup-winning moment, endorsed by the English Rugby Football Union. His attention to detail made him a distinctive portrait painter and some of his portraits were acquired by St James's Palace, the House of Lords and 10 Downing Street. Oakham Galleries Ltd included Baker in its 2005 Spring Exhibition.

Ethelwyn BAKER fl. from c.1930– Sculptor, painter and commercial artist, born in Belfast, daughter of the artist A R Baker. Studied at Slade School of Fine Art and Royal Academy Schools. Exhibited RA, Cooling Galleries, Festival of Britain, AIA and Beaux Arts Gallery. Sometimes signed work E B. Lived in London.

Eve BAKER 1906–1990 Conservator and painter, trained at the Royal College of Art, married to the artist Robert Baker. In 2004, Abbott and Holder offered a study Madonna and Child with Donors by Eve, from the artist's estate, and a strong portrait of her by her husband.

Frederick William BAKER 1916– Stained and painted glass artist, born in London, where he was partly educated, also at technical school in Toronto, Canada. He studied at Blackheath School of Art and Royal College of Art, then went on to carry out many ecclesiastical commissions in England, West Africa, America and Canada. Lived finally in Exeter, Devon.

Geoff BAKER 1950– Architect and artist who gained a Bachelor of Science degree at London University, 1972, then his master's degree at Sheffield University, 1974, and worked as an architect. He exhibited at RA Summer Exhibitions, RCamA and was included in the Walker Art Gallery, Liverpool, 1986–7 touring show Merseyside Artists 3, with two etchings.

Geoffrey Alan BAKER 1881–1959 Painter and teacher, born in Faversham, Kent. He attended Canterbury Art School, 1898–1902, then the Royal College of Art, 1902–07. He became principal of Bournemouth College of Art, 1913–47, and exhibited RA and elsewhere. The Russell-Cotes Art Gallery and Museum, Bournemouth, holds his work. Lived at Christchurch, Hampshire, where he was a member of the Arts Guild.

Gladys BAKER 1889– Painter and draughtsman, notable for her portraits, born and lived in London. She was educated at Queen's College, St John's Wood Art School and Royal Academy Schools, winning a silver medal for composition there. Showed at RBA, RI, NPS, in the provinces and America and frequently at RA, finally in 1947.

Ian BAKER 1923– Painter, draughtsman and architect, who studied at the University of Wales and went on to graduate with honours at the Architectural Association. He was a founding partner of the Leonard Manasseh Partnership, where he designed many important buildings, including the Motor Museum at Beaulieu and the Law Courts, King's Lynn, his perspectives being exhibited almost annually at the RA Summer exhibition. Other shows included RIBA, RWA, Landmark Arts Centre, Battersea Arts Fair, Galerie Colette in Paris and Galerie Montador, Dieppe. Solo exhibitions included The Stables Gallery, Gladstone Park, 2000, and Lauderdale House, 2001, where Baker's elegant and incisive line and often gem-like colours, reminders of the St Ives artists and Italian primitives, were used to depict scenes in England, France and Italy. Lived in south London.

Jo BAKER 1963– Painter, collagist and artist in mixed media, born in London. In 1980–1 she spent a period dancing in south of France and attended evening classes run by Bruce McLean at Croydon College of Art. In 1982 Baker studied at Staffordshire Polytechnic, graduating with an honours degree in fine art in 1985. While there she met Kelvin Bowers, with whom she lived in a converted cowshed in the Staffordshire countryside and collaborated on many projects. In 1985 they showed in Northern Young Contemporaries at Whitworth Art Gallery, Manchester, and two years later they held readings of Christopher Wood's unpublished letters for the Winifred Nicholson touring show Unknown Colour. The mid-1980s saw Baker and Bowers taking part in group shows at the City Museum and Art Gallery, Stoke-on-Trent, and after a trip to New York and New Mexico, in 1989, in 1990 Baker was commissioned to paint a large canvas for St Modwen Developments. In that year they shared a first London exhibition at England & Co. Baker's work mixed Expressionist colour, Primitivism, fantasy and Surrealism.

Joan Elizabeth BAKER 1922– Painter, born in Cardiff. She attended the College of Art there, 1939–44. Then taught briefly at Bath School of Art, taking up a position at Cardiff College of Art in 1945. In 1952 completed a mural in Heol Trelai School in the city. Took part in Six Cardiff Artists shows in Cardiff and at Glynn Vivian Museum and Art Gallery, Swansea, in 1953 and 1955 respectively, as well as in SEA, WAC and SWG shows. WAC and Glynn Vivian hold her work.

John BAKER 1922– Painter, draughtsman, illustrator, writer and lecturer, born in Birmingham, where he attended the School of Art, then Slade School of Fine Art. Worked under the guidance of the prolific newspaper draughtsman Hanslip Fletcher and freelanced for various publications, also lecturing on anatomy at Sir John Cass School. During the 1970s showed at RP, portraying civic dignitaries and show business personalities, then developed towards animal painting, involved in the early days of the Society of Equestrian Artists. Baker from 1966 wrote and illustrated a series of articles in the *Surrey Advertiser* called The Seeing Eye, and gained a local reputation as a controversial critic on architecture. He published *A Picture of Surrey* in 1980. Latterly lived near Salisbury, Wiltshire. Guildford Borough collection holds his works.

Matthew BAKER 1971– Artist, born in Brighton, Sussex, who did a foundation course at Blackpool & Fylde College of Further Education, then obtained an honours degree in fine art at Liverpool Polytechnic and a Bachelor of Science honours degree in architecture in East London University. Exhibitions included Thresher's Open, 1990, Liverpool University; Fresh Art, 1992, Business Design Centre, Islington; BP Portrait Award, 1997; National Portrait Gallery; RP, 1999, Mall Galleries; and The Hunting Art Prizes, 2002, Royal College of Art.

Percy Bryant BAKER 1881–1970 Sculptor in the classical style, born in London, who studied at City and Guilds Technical Institute and graduated from the Royal Academy Schools. Awarded first medal for portraiture, first medal for design in sculpture and other awards. Showed Walker Art Gallery in Liverpool, London and Paris Salons, RA many times and elsewhere. Completed numerous marble busts of notabilities, including King Edward VII, executed for Queen Alexandra, with many replicas made for other members of the royal family; heroic statue of same king, Huddersfield, unveiled by King George V, 1912; Arthur Purey Cust, Dean of York; President Woodrow Wilson, in Boston, America; and General W C Gorgas, bronze bust, Panama City, and replica, Army Medical Museum, Washington. Corcoran Gallery of Art in Washington put on a special exhibition of Baker's works in 1923. Manchester City Art Gallery holds his marble Eros, Hull his marble Memory.

Rebecca BAKER 1972– Painter and teacher, born in Birmingham, who studied at Bournville School of Art and Falmouth College of Art. From 1996 taught art at Bromley College. Group exhibitions included NEAC, Mall Galleries, 1995, and in 1996 the autumn exhibition at Langham Fine Art, Bury St Edmunds, and Royal Over-Seas League Open Exhibition. Baker chose to paint "the ordinary; small, apparently insignificant objects, but obviously selected and very specifically depicted".

Richard BAKER 1948– Versatile painter and draughtsman who studied at Portsmouth and Winchester Art Schools and at Christ's College, Cambridge. Mixed exhibitions included Cambridge Drawing Society, from 1983; RBA at Mall Galleries, 1989; The Hiroko Kato Gallery, Tokyo, Japan, from 1989; NEAC, Mall Galleries, from 1990; RI, Mall Galleries, 1993; CB Academy Gallery, Cambridge, 1996; and The Linda Blackstone Gallery, Pinner, from 2000. Later solo shows included The Whittlesford Gallery,

Cambridge, 1999. Several Cambridge colleges and corporate collections hold examples.

Robert BAKER 1909–1992 Painter, sculptor, potter, conservator and teacher, he was married to Eve Baker, the conservator who died in 1990. Baker trained as painter and sculptor at Royal College of Art. His murals at Coleg Harlech, Gwynedd, and in the village hall at Wood Green, Hampshire, where he finally lived, were notable. During World War II Baker ran the Rural Industries Bureau. He was director of the art college at Stoke-on-Trent, then from 1948–59 was professor of ceramics at Royal College of Art. From late 1950s to 1971 he was chief designer and art director of Royal Worcester, the porcelain company, remaining a consultant until 1982. He was for many years involved in conservation, on which he became a leading authority, at such venues as Winchester, Lincoln and especially Wells Cathedrals. At Wells he was responsible for the saving of almost 200 early sculpted masterpieces as chief conservator of the west front.

Roger BAKER 1935–1989 Sculptor in stone, wood and metals who studied at West of England College of Art, Bristol, and Slade School of Fine Art. Commissioned work included a crucifix for Blackburn Convent, 1958, and a font in Portland stone for Mercers Chapel, in London. Showed at RWA and was included in 19 Young Sculptors at Hillfield Gardens, Gloucester, 1962. Taught at West of England College of Art/Bristol Polytechnic until retirement in 1987. Last solo show was in late 1970s at Gillian Tucker Gallery, Bristol, where he lived.

Sue BAKER 1958– Artist who studied at Harrow School of Art, 1974–9. Group exhibitions included Fertile Eye, Brixton Art Gallery, 1984; Cheek by Jowl, The Showroom, 1985; Icons, Portraits and Colours, Smiths Galleries, 1986; Women Artists Slide Library 1989 Diary Show, 1988; and East End Open Studios, at Carpenter's Road, 1989.

Sadanand BAKRE 1920– Born in Baroda, India, he had early success as a sculptor, winning a number of prizes. He was not recognised as a painter until 1948, when Baroda Museum bought two of his pictures. Bakre was a founder-member of the Progressive Arts Group with Ara, Gade, Hussain, Raza and Souza. Moved to Europe in 1951 and participated in many important group exhibitions there, in America and in the Far East. In Britain showed with Nicholas Treadwell Gallery, his solo exhibitions including Gallery One, 1959, and Centaur Gallery, 1962. Bakre, a Hindu, suffered from tinnitus which undermined his health, and he eventually returned to India.

Marta BAKST 1975– Versatile artist, ranging from photography-based work to sculptural installation, who attended St Bede's College, Manchester, 1986–93. She then did a foundation course in art and design at Manchester Metropolitan University, 1993–4; graduated in fine art from Slade School of Fine Art, 1994–8, with a 1997 Duveen Travel Award for study in Poland; and gained a master's from Chelsea Art College, 1998–00. Exhibitions included Memento, Bury Art Gallery and Museum, 1995; Inaugural group show at Dominic Berning, 1998; and Photopus, Century Gallery, 2000.

Iwan BALA 1956– Painter, born at Sarnau, near Bala, Merionethshire. Studied at University of Wales, Aberystwyth, 1974, Chester College of Art, 1975–6, and Cardiff College of Art, 1976–8. Bala's work could be Expressionist, near-abstract using a rich palette. Mixed exhibitions included National Eisteddfod; Oriel Llangefrai, North Wales; Mid-Wales Open, Aberystwyth Arts Centre; Greenpeace Clean Irish Sea Exhibition; City of Birmingham Museum and Art Gallery; and Café Gallery. Solo shows included Sherman Theatre, Cardiff; Dolman Theatre, Newport; National Gallery of Zimbabwe, Harare; and Glynn Vivian Art Gallery, Swansea, 2000. Bala won the National Eisteddfod of Wales Gold Medal in Fine Art, 1997. Lived in Grangetown, Cardiff.

Suzanne BALCHIN 1963– Painter, born in Woking, Surrey. She studied at Camberwell School of Arts and Crafts, 1983–6, graduating with an honours degree in graphic design. Delicate flower studies were a feature of her work. She shared a first joint exhibition at Hyde Park Gallery in 1991 with George Popesco, another in 1992. Solo show at Pallant House, Chichester, 2001.

Frederick William BALDWIN 1899–1984 Watercolourist and draughtsman who after an elementary school education taught himself to paint. Exhibited RA, RBA and in the Ipswich area. Baldwin was noted for his studies of Suffolk churches and lived in the county at Stoven. The public galleries in Ipswich and Birmingham hold his work.

Gordon BALDWIN 1932– Ceramist and teacher, born in Lincoln, who studied at the College of Art there, 1949–51, then Central School of Art, 1951–4. He taught at Central and Eton College. Took part in numerous group exhibitions, including Primavera Gallery, 1961; New Directions, Oxford Gallery, Oxford, 1972; Clay Sculpture, Yorkshire Sculpture Park, 1980; Artist Potters Now, Museum of Oxford, and tour, 1984; The Raw and the Cooked, Barbican Centre and tour, 1993; and The Jerwood Prize for Applied Arts, Crafts Council, 1996. Later solo shows included Gordon Baldwin Ceramics, Crafts Council Shop at Victoria & Albert Museum, 1995, and Barrett Marsden Gallery, 2001. Many public collections in Britain and abroad hold examples, including Victoria & Albert Museum; Contemporary Art Society; Kettle's Yard, Cambridge; Paisley Museum and Art Gallery; and Usher Gallery, Lincoln. Lived in Market Drayton, Shropshire.

John BALDWIN 1937– Artist noted for his wood carvings, which featured grotesque and amusing characters. He was born in London and studied at Camberwell School of Arts and Crafts, 1962–5, after that working in commercial and visual arts. In 1982 he began carving and was involved in mixed shows including Oxford Gallery, 1985; Primavera, Cambridge, 1986; British Relief Carving, an Arts Council touring exhibition, 1988; and John Hunt Galleries, Brightling, 1992. Had a solo show at Centaur Gallery, Highgate, 1984, later ones including Metropole Arts Centre, Folkestone, 1991, and Sevenoaks Library Gallery, 1992.

Mariella BALDWIN 1958– Freelance botanical painter and teacher, born in Capel, Surrey, who gained her diploma in botanical illustration at The English Gardening School, taught by Anne-Marie Evans, 1988. Her work was reproduced in a promotional card for the School. Baldwin also taught there and at West Dean College, in Sussex, Sarah Raven's Cutting Garden and private classes. She was a fellow of Chelsea Physic Garden Florilegium Society, its archive and the Hunt Institute for Botanical Documentation, Pittsburgh, America, holding her work. Baldwin produced "plant portraits in watercolour, inspired by the masters of botanical painting from the seventeenth and eighteenth centuries, Ehret, Robert and Redouté." Her group exhibitions included Chelsea Botanica, Daphne Johns Contemporary Art, 1999; Watercolours from the Chelsea Physic Garden Florilegium Society at the Hunt Institute, also Bolton Street Gallery and Pupils of Anne-Marie Evans, Ursus Gallery, New York, all 2000; 10th International Exhibition, Hunt Institute, 2001; A View of the Garden, Jointure Studio, Ditchling, 2002; Ebernoe Summer Exhibition, 2003; and Summer Fruits, Jointure Studio, 2004. Her husband, Rodney Baldwin, ran the Chelsea framers and artists' materials shop Green and Stone Ltd. Lived in Lodsworth, Sussex.

Martyn BALDWIN 1959– Artist and teacher, based in Harrow, Middlesex, where he obtained his diploma in illustration at the School of Art, 1980–3, studying etching there, 1983–5. Baldwin taught widely from 1984, including physically handicapped students for the Brent Authority, also at Rooks Heath Adult Education Centre; Harrow Arts Centre; Weald College; University of Westminster; and the Victoria & Albert Museum. His awards included Commended, BP Portrait Award, National Portrait Gallery, and the Michael Harding Award, The Discerning Eye, Mall Galleries, both 1996, and Gilders Workshop Framing Award, PS, Mall Galleries, 2001. Among his many exhibitions were Out, National Theatre, 1983; Alton Gallery, from 1986; RA Summer Exhibition, from 1992; NEAC at the Mall Galleries, from 1993; Exhibitors of the NEAC, Ainscough Contemporary, 1997; Linda Blackstone Gallery, Pinner, 2002; and pictures from the *Star Portraits with Rolf Harris* BBC television programme shown at County Hall Gallery, with tour, in 2005; Baldwin had painted the gardener Charlie Dimmock in the 2004 series. Baldwin also worked to commission. He wrote: "My imagery comes from the structural study of the subject. I use drawing as a means to investigate the motif, searching for the energies and personality which lie within it.... The process, being an empirical one, is reliant on the discoveries made along the way and the energy conveyed by the subject."

Mervyn BALDWIN 1934– Sculptor, draughtsman, restorer and teacher, born in Immingham, Lincolnshire, full name Arthur Mervyn Baldwin. He studied at Grimsby School of Art, 1953–5, and Leicester College of Art, 1953–5. After working as a stonemason and at Leicester College as a caretaker/studio assistant, Baldwin gained the Prix de Rome in sculpture, 1960, then was for two years in Italy. Series of teaching appointments included principal lecturer, Newport College of Art. Was a member of 56 Group, also exhibiting at Ikon Gallery, Birmingham; Grabowski Gallery; Whitechapel Art Gallery; University College of Wales, Aberystwyth; and elsewhere, including abroad. WAC and National Museum of Wales, Cardiff, hold his work. Lived in Cardiff.

Michael BALDWIN 1945– Conceptual artist and teacher, born in Chipping Norton, Oxfordshire, one of several – the others being Terry Atkinson, David Bainbridge and Harold Hurrell – who formed the influential exhibiting and publishing group Art & Language in 1968. Atkinson in 1966 met Baldwin who was in the second year of his three-year course for a diploma in art and design at Coventry College of Art, where Atkinson was to join the staff. Atkinson and Baldwin collaborated for a time on several works, such as Air Show, Air Conditioning Show and Oxfordshire, the Maps. Early in 1967 Baldwin was expelled from Coventry and returned to Oxfordshire, but kept in touch with Atkinson, one outcome being Art & Language's creation. Baldwin returned to Coventry College periodically to teach on the art theory course, but when it was terminated in mid-1971 he, like Bainbridge, was dismissed. Although Atkinson and Bainbridge were to leave Art & Language, Baldwin continued and, with his collaborator Mel Ramsden, settled at Middleton Cheney, Northamptonshire. Art & Language staged numerous exhibitions internationally and published many texts, Lisson Gallery being a notable venue.

Nancy BALDWIN 1935– Painter, born in Sunderland, County Durham, husband of the artist Gordon Baldwin. Attended Lincoln School of Art, 1949–52, then Central School of Arts and Crafts, 1952–4. Showed at Ikon Gallery, Birmingham; Bohun Gallery, Henley-on-Thames; with the Midland Group, and elsewhere in the provinces. Ashmolean Museum in Oxford holds her work. Lived in Eton, Berkshire.

Peter BALDWIN 1941– Artist and teacher, born in Aldeburgh, Suffolk, who studied at Norwich School of Art, 1958–62, with Michael Andrews and Jeffrey Camp. Taught art in various institutions and art schools until 1991, the year he was elected to Norfolk County Council and became lecturer in art history for the University of East Anglia extra-mural board. Baldwin was a member of Norwich Twenty Group from 1962. Showed at Norwich Castle Museum, which holds his work, as does Norwich County Council; also at University of East Anglia; Eastern Open, King's Lynn Arts Centre; and Norfolk and Norwich Festival; in London and abroad. Solo exhibitions included University of East Anglia, 1970, Halesworth Gallery, 1982, and Swan House Gallery, Beccles, 2000. Baldwin described himself as a painter in oil "working within a modernist approach by means of implied narrative and cryptic symbol." Lived in Sheringham, Norfolk.

Rosalind BALDWIN fl. from early 1970s– Painter, draughtsman, teacher and book illustrator, born in Glasgow where she attended the School of Art, 1969–73. After teaching in Scotland she freelanced from 1979. She painted many animal portraits, and her wildlife designs were reproduced as calendars and cards by several publishers and Royal Society for the Protection of Birds. Showed with RSW, Royal Glasgow Institute of the Fine Arts, SSA, SSWA, Society of Equestrian Artists and Patricia Wells Gallery in Thornbury. Held solo shows in Britain and America. Lived for a time in Bourne, Lincolnshire.

Warren BALDWIN 1950– Painter who studied at Wimbledon School of Art and London College of Printing. Showed at RA Summer Exhibition and elsewhere and with the study Wilhelmine II gained a third prize in the 1990 Singer & Friedlander/*Sunday Times* Painting Competition. Was originally a graphic designer. Lived in Bournemouth, Dorset.

BALFOUR 1924–1989 Painter, draughtsman and teacher, full name Andrew Balfour Aitken, born in what is now Uganda. He studied at Edinburgh College of Art under

Leonard Rosoman, 1947–51, in 1951 being awarded a travelling scholarship. Took part in group shows in Edinburgh. Between 1952–9 worked as a sub-editor on *The Sunday Times*, was a studio artist with Everetts Advertising Ltd and was art editor of *Autocourse*, from 1968–82 being head of art at Philip Morant School, Colchester. Balfour's early work was figurative, latterly being influenced by an association with Amnesty International. Had a solo exhibition at Quay Gallery, Sudbury, Suffolk, where he died.

Maria BALFOUR 1934– Painter, born and lived in London, who studied art privately and was married to Lord Balfour of Inchrye. She was a member of Free Painters and Sculptors, also showing with Chelsea Art Society, Kensington and Chelsea Artists and at Paris Salon.

Michael BALFOUR 1918–1997 Character actor, clown, painter and sculptor, who appeared in over 250 films, notable for his good humour, craggy face and stocky figure. Although born in Kent, the son of an Army officer, and a public schoolboy, in 1947 Balfour broke into the professional theatre by assuming a Detroit accent, persuading Laurence Olivier that he was American and should be given a part in Garson Kanin's *Born Yesterday* at the Garrick Theatre. Balfour made his film debut in *Just William's Luck*, 1948; appeared in many British B-movies, commonly in Cockney parts; and went on to act in such notable films as *Reach for the Sky*, *Genevieve*, *Macbeth*, *Farenheit 451* and *The Canterbury Tales*. Balfour overcame many crises, such as a car accident in 1953 which killed his friend Bonar Colleano and left Balfour with almost 100 stitches in his face; a fight against alcoholism; and latterly cancer of the sinus, which necessitated painful, disfiguring operations. Illness at 77 ended his touring as a clown with Gerry Cottle's Circus. Clowns and fantasy were an important part of his prolific output as an artist. He established a gallery near his home in Spain to show his own and others' work. Died at Princess Alice Hospice, Esher, Surrey.

Vincent BALFOUR-BROWNE 1880–1963 Watercolourist who was a keen field sportsman, born and lived in London, although he spent much time in Scotland at Goldielea, by Dumfries, as he was a keen deer-stalker. He was educated at Radley and Oxford University. Showed extensively with the Fine Art Society.

Adam BALL 1977– Artist and teacher, born in Aylesbury, Buckinghamshire, who did a foundation year at Byam Shaw School of Art, 1995–6, gaining an honours degree from Newcastle University fine art department, 1996–00. Taught at Brent Council summer schools, 1995–9. Ball painted "trees and edited versions of the natural world", which were featured on television, radio and in the national press. His huge work The Tree, which took two-and-a-half years to plan, hung on a freestanding frame in Golden Square in September 2002, was claimed to be "the largest outdoor canvas painting in the world." Mixed shows included Air Gallery, from 2001. In 2000, Ball won the Beck's Futures film and video prize at ICA. Lived in London.

Bernard BALL 1921– Sculptor in a wide range of materials, born in Brisbane, Queensland, Australia. Studied sculpture at Sir John Cass College, London, in 1946 with Bainbridge Copnall, then five years later in Paris at Académie Julian. Showed at RA, Loggia Gallery, Birmingham University and elsewhere. Lived in Whitstable, Kent.

Gerry BALL 1948– Painter, notably in tempera, born in Ashton-under-Lyne, Lancashire. He studied art at local College of Further Education. Showed at Agnew, RI, Manchester Academy and with RCamA, of which he was a member. Coleg Harlech, Wales, holds his work. Lived in Ludlow, Shropshire.

Julia BALL 1930– Artist and teacher who studied at Reading University's school of art as a printmaker. She lived in Cambridge from the early 1960s, taught in local schools and from the early 1970s–90 at Anglia University, painting, part-time. Ball's interest was the landscape of East Anglia, especially the Fens. She said that she was "working towards trying to sum up *place*, the place, a particular place, by colour alone ... it should be possible to sum it up with one colour". Her subtly coloured, light-filled pictures had a strong abstract element. Exhibitions included Bluecoat Gallery, Liverpool, 1978; Kettle's Yard, Cambridge, from 1980; University of Nottingham, 1986; Lynne Strover Gallery, Fen Ditton, from 1992. Eastern Arts, Kettle's Yard Loan Collection, Fitzwilliam College in Cambridge and Towner Art Gallery, Eastbourne, hold examples. The North American artist Agnes Martin, given a 20-year retrospective at the Serpentine Gallery in 1993, was an artist admired by Ball.

Martin BALL 1948– Painter and teacher, born in Leicestershire. Studied at Central School, Royal College of Art and Ohio State University, in America. He later taught at Art Institute of Chicago while working in the city. Ball's work, which employed a limited range of primary colours, involved the creation of abstract designs of a gritty nature, reflecting the ambience of the urban areas around him. The artist was included in surveys such as The British Art Show of 1979 and the South Bank Centre's touring exhibition of 1988–9, The Presence of Painting. Ball's early work was shown in solo exhibitions at Ikon Gallery, Birmingham, and Sunderland Arts Centre. He was a member of LG and the Newcastle Group, taking part in its 1990 show The Northern Lights, DLI Museum & Arts Centre, Durham, and tour. Became senior lecturer in painting at Newcastle Polytechnic and visiting lecturer elsewhere. Ashmolean Museum, Oxford, holds his work. Lived in Newcastle.

Peter Eugene BALL 1943– Sculptor and teacher, whose figurative work in found materials, mainly driftwood, drew on ancient and modern mythologies. He was born in Coventry, Warwickshire, where, after comprehensive school, he studied at Coventry College of Art for his design diploma. Rather than sculpt and teach, he opted for labouring and factory jobs. In 1973, began lecturing part-time on sculpture at Lanchester Polytechnic, Coventry, becoming a full-time sculptor in 1975. In 1963, Ball's work had been included in a six-artists show at Herbert Art Gallery, Coventry, and in 1964 he was in mixed exhibitions at Midland Contemporaries, Nottingham, and Marjorie Parr Gallery, where he started to exhibit solo from 1970. His work began to be shown widely internationally. He made sculpture, armour and masks for Christopher Logue's adaptation of Homer, *War Music*, for the Prospect Theatre at the Old Vic, 1977. Ball's first church commission came in 1974, a crucifix for Westminster

Cathedral. Others included a large crucifix and altarpieces at Birmingham Cathedral, 1983, and a crib for Winchester Cathedral, 1991. Later solo shows included Gallery Gilbert, Dorchester, 1997, other major exhibitions being Ely Cathedral 2000, Lichfield Cathedral 2003, and Montpellier Gallery, Stratford-upon-Avon, 2003 and 2005. Latterly lived in Newark, Nottinghamshire, spending summers in the Loire Valley, France.

Robert BALL 1918– Painter, draughtsman, printmaker and teacher, born in Birmingham, son of a silversmith. Attended Moseley Road Junior School of Arts and Crafts there, 1930–3, winning many prizes and a scholarship to Central School of Arts and Crafts/College of Art, 1933–40. Won an exhibition to Royal College of Art, 1941–2, where gained many prizes and scholarships. Held a series of teaching posts, including senior lecturer in drawing and painting at Gloucestershire College of Art, 1954–81. Showed with RA, RE, RBSA, RBA and RWA. Ashmolean Museum in Oxford, a number of other provincial galleries and Victoria & Albert Museum hold his work. Ball's etching Mr Everitt, a Birmingham Tram Conductor, of 1936, is in the collection of the City Museum and Art Gallery, was included in its 1990 show The Birmingham School and was praised by J B Priestley in his book *English Journey*. Cheltenham Art Gallery gave Ball a 60-year print retrospective in 1999. He latterly lived in Painswick, Gloucestershire.

Robin BALL 1910–1979 Painter, draughtsman and teacher, born in Battle, Sussex. He attended Hastings School of Art, then the Royal College of Art, becoming an associate in 1938. Ball won a travelling scholarship to Europe, but this opportunity was cut short by the declaration of war. During 1938–45 Ball served with the Royal Artillery, and while he was never an Official War Artist he did complete many sketches and pictures of service life, with a strong vein of humour which runs through much of his work. From 1946–75 Ball taught at West Surrey College of Art and Design, at Farnham, where he died. Ball's oils and watercolours reflect his interest in the daily life of ordinary people, busy with figures and alive with incident. Some are realistic, some more highly structured, reflecting such developments as Cubism and Futurism. Ball showed in mixed exhibitions at RA, Whitechapel Art Gallery, Ashgate Gallery in Farnham and Roland, Browse & Delbanco, and there was a small retrospective at Connaught Brown in 1987. Imperial War Museum holds his work.

Sarah BALL 1965– Painter, designer and illustrator whose work included simplified images and contours abstracted from landscape. She was born in Rotherham, Yorkshire, gaining her diploma in art and design, 1981–3, with an honours degree in graphic design, 1983–6. Her work was widely illustrated in such publications as *Images* and the *European Illustration Annual* and clients included British Telecom, Morgan Grenfell, *Saturday Times Review*, Clydesdale Bank, Time-Life, Decca, EMI, *New Scientist* and Greenpeace. Co-operative Retail Services' headquarters in Rochdale has a large canvas by her. In 1993 she won W H Smith and Norwegian Gullblyanten awards for illustration. Exhibitions included Gwent Illustrators, AOI Gallery, 1986; Images, The Best of British Illustration, at Smiths Galleries, from 1987; Montpelier Gallery, Bath Contemporary Art Fair, 1993; and New Ashgate Gallery, Farnham, 1995. Solo exhibitions included Contours at Hybrid Gallery, 1996. Lived in South Wales.

Percy des Carrieres BALLANCE 1899–1971 Landscape painter, born in Birmingham, who studied at Slade School of Fine Art. He exhibited RA, Cooling Galleries, RI and Paris Salon, where he gained an Hon. Mention in 1925. Member of Chelsea Arts Club, also of Art Workers' Guild from 1968. Lived in Wells, Somerset.

David BALLANS 1947–2002 Painter, draughtsman and teacher whose early geometric concerns developed into large paintings of organic forms. He was born in Waltham, Lincolnshire, and lived in that county and Manchester. Ballans attended the Royal College of Art, 1966–9, teachers including Peter Blake, Carel Weight and Roger de Grey. For a time Ballans worked as a car sprayer. He also taught drawing and painting at Central Manchester College and City College in the city and at Boston College, Lincolnshire. Was included in joint exhibitions at Axiom Gallery, 1969–70 and Hampstead Gallery, 1971; in Young Generation, Norway and Sweden, 1973; and at RBSA, 2002.

Evelyn BALLANTINE 1931– Painter, draughtsman and teacher, born in London. She attended Beckenham School of Art, 1946–52, and Royal College of Art, 1952–5, her teachers including Carel Weight, Roger de Grey, John Minton, Ruskin Spear and Robert Buhler. She went on to teach part-time at Morley College for many years. Around 1970 Ballantine's work was transformed by the experience of motherhood, and when she had a solo show at Brighton Polytechnic in 1980 Dennis Creffield wrote that Ballantine's painting had "the same vivid physicality as Sylvia Plath's poetry ... Raw, and often awkward, it nevertheless rings with existence". David Bomberg was a strong influence, through Creffield. Christian and pagan subjects were key factors in her pictures. Ballantine was a member of LG, other group appearances including Towner Art Gallery, Eastbourne, and Morley Gallery. Also showed solo there and at Mario Flecha Gallery. Lived in Brighton, Sussex.

Gino BALLANTYNE fl. from early 1980s– Painter and draughtsman who obtained an honours degree from the Glasgow School of Art, 1983–7, specialising in drawing and painting. Soon went on to show in mixed and solo exhibitions in Edinburgh, Glasgow and London, including RSA. One-man show held at Sue Rankin Gallery, 1990.

John BALLANTYNE 1933– Painter and teacher, born in Edinburgh, who studied at the College of Art there, 1952–6; completed his National Service, 1957–9; then taught throughout Scotland, 1959–95. Had solo shows in Edinburgh in 1972 at Great King Street Gallery, in 1974 at Alexander Gallery, in 1990 gaining a commission for a large public office mural in the city. Ballantyne's painting took on a new fervour on his retirement from teaching, as in the visionary oil on board Morning Flight, included in 3 Painters, Roger Billcliffe Gallery, Glasgow, 1999.

Margaret BALLANTYNE fl. from early 1990s– Painter of exuberantly colourful landscapes and still lifes, based in Glasgow, where she attended the School of Art. Worked widely in continental Europe. She was a member of SSWA, Glasgow Society of Women Artists and Paisley Art Institute. Showed with RA Summer Exhibition, RSA, RSW, Royal

Glasgow Institute of the Fine Arts and Laing Art Competition, being included in Laing's 1997 calendar. Exhibited solo with Torrance Gallery, Edinburgh, from 1991, and with The Contemporary Fine Art Gallery, Eton, 1998. Kuwait's royal family and Castle International Asset Management, Edinburgh, held Ballantyne's work.

Arthur BALLARD 1915–1994 Painter and teacher, born in Liverpool, where he spent most of his career. Studied at Liverpool College of Art, 1932–5, then in 1935–6 in Paris at Académie de la Grande Chaumière, and again in Paris in 1957–8 under a Liverpool Corporation release scheme for teachers. Ballard went on to become head of the department of foundation studies at Liverpool Polytechnic. Showed Arts Council, Liverpool Academy, John Moores Exhibition in Liverpool, at Roland, Browse and Delbanco and elsewhere. Ballard painted in a number of styles: abstract, in a Pop Art manner and figurative works recalling the heroes of his youth as a working-class boy in the city. Was president of the Liverpool Academy, 1964–8. Work held by Walker Art Gallery, Liverpool University and Atkinson Art Gallery, Southport. Later lived in Corwen, Clwyd, north Wales. Belgrave Gallery held a show after Ballard's death, in 1996.

Brian BALLARD 1943– Painter, born in Belfast, where he continued to live. He attended the College of Art there, followed by Liverpool College of Art. Ballard was a rich Colourist, in the tradition of the Scottish painters Peploe and Cadell, notable for his still lifes. His exhibitions included Butlin Foundation for Young Irish Artists, Arts Council, Belfast, 1967; Tom Caldwell Gallery, Belfast, from 1972; Main Fine Art, Glasgow, 1986; Mistral Galleries, 1990; Waterman Fine Art Ltd, 1992, and Cadogan Contemporary, 2000. Ballard's work is held by Arts Council of Northern Ireland; Crawford Municipal Gallery, Cork; and Ulster Museum, Belfast.

Morag BALLARD 1961– Producer of abstract reliefs and boxed constructions, born in London. She attended Chelsea School of Art, 1981–2, then Bath Academy of Art, 1982–5. After a period in the southwest of Scotland from late in 1986, in the summer of 1991 Ballard moved to Penzance, Cornwall, important moves as landscape was her principal reference for work in the tradition of Naum Gabo, Peter Lanyon and Ben Nicholson. Group shows participated in included Boxes and Totems and Art in Boxes at England & Co respectively in 1990 and 1991, and in the latter year the gallery gave her the first of several solo shows. Her husband was the painter Alan Kingsbury.

Richard BALLINGER 1957– Artist and teacher producing ingenious constructions from materials including chalk, paper and coloured pencils, as in his solo exhibition Build at Oliver Contemporary in 2005. Ballinger trained as an engineer and draughtsman, studying at Gloucester College, 1974–8, then art access foundation at Stroud Art School, 1988–9. His many exhibitions included The House of James, Cork, Ireland, 1991; Brewery Arts Centre, Cirencester, 1993; 3D Gallery, Bristol, 1996; School House Gallery, Morvah, 2001; RA Summer Exhibition, 2003; and Lynne Strover Gallery, a two-man show, 2004. In 2000 he was made a member of the Newlyn Society of Artists. Ballinger was art project teacher for Artshape Ltd, Gloucester, 1994–5, and was a founder-member of Co-Optic Studios, Cainscross, 1996. Among his commissions were University College, Cork, 1991, and bronzing and patination for Caprisco, 1997–8.

Niel BALLY 1951– Artist and teacher, born in Wantage, Berkshire, who studied at the Ruskin School of Art in Oxford, 1969, and in the fine art department of West Surrey College of Art & Design, Farnham, 1969–74. Went on to teach between 1975–86 at Camden, Central and Putney Inner London Education Authority Institutes, Canterbury, Chelsea, City and Guilds, Kingston and Wimbledon Schools of Art. From 1986–7 lived and worked in Mexico and America; in London, 1987–92; South Africa, 1992–5; then in London and Talgarth, Powys. Exhibited in RA Summer Exhibition from 1975; Whitechapel Open, 1978; Artists in Adult Education, at Woodlands Art Gallery, 1982; England & Co, 1991; and Hunting Prize Awards, from 1996. Later solo exhibitions included Brian Sinfield Gallery, Burford, 1991; Canvas Gallery, 1993; and Great Western Studios, studio shows, from 1995. Bally was fascinated by natural surfaces, and his enigmatic, allusive works, as in his solo exhibition at Brecknock Museum, Brecon, in 2003, left much for the viewer to interpret. Sheffield City Art Galleries, Stellenbosch University Museum and a number of corporate collections hold examples.

Barbara BALMER 1929– Painter and teacher, born in Birmingham, who was married to the artist George Mackie. She studied at Coventry and Edinburgh Colleges of Art, 1946–51, at the latter with an Andrew Grant Scholarship, then in 1951–2 had a travelling scholarship which took her to Spain and France. Was a visiting lecturer at Grays School of Art, Aberdeen. Group showings included John Moores Exhibition, Liverpool, and Richard Demarco Gallery, Edinburgh; Richard Demarco gave her a one-man show in 1970 after one at the Traverse Theatre Gallery 14 years before, after which she had several at the Scottish Gallery in the city as well as an important one at Aberdeen Art Gallery, 1995–6. It holds her work, as do HM The Queen, Scottish Arts Council, Glasgow's Kelvingrove and Lillie Art Gallery, Milngavie. She lived and worked at various times in Aberdeen, Edinburgh and Lincolnshire.

Derek BALMER 1934– Painter and photographer. He was noted for his richly coloured, painterly landscapes of Britain and abroad. Balmer was born and lived in Bristol, where he became a noted photographer, closely associated with the Bristol Old Vic. John Boorman, later a Hollywood director, used Balmer as his photographer during the making of television documentaries. Aged 15 Balmer was accepted at West of England College of Art by Donald Milner, his teachers including Paul Feiler. He was offered a place at the Slade School of Fine Art, but his family could not afford the expense. Group exhibitions included RWA of which he was a member and later president; Fimbarrus and Arnolfini Galleries, in Bath and Bristol; Bear Lane Gallery, Oxford; Louise Hallett Gallery; and New Art Centre. Had a first solo show at Fimbarrus Gallery in 1959, later ones including Gisela van Beers, 1991, and Anthony Hepworth, Bath, 1992. Ancient Places was at Campden Gallery, Chipping Campden, in 2005. Balmer was represented in public and private collections in Britain and abroad.

Mary BALMFORD: *see* **Mary MARTIN 1907–1969**

Thomas BALSTON 1883–1967 Writer and painter in oil, born at Bearsted, Kent. Balston was educated at Eton College and Oxford University. During the 1930s he studied painting for a short period with Mark Gertler and he exhibited extensively at Redfern Gallery. He was a discriminating collector whose own pictures are held by Manchester City Art Gallery and the Ashmolean Museum, Oxford. Balston was a connoisseur who contributed to the specialist periodicals *Image* and *Signature* and who wrote several books on wood engraving, including a study of Robert Gibbings. Savile and Garrick Club member who lived in London.

Ian BAMFORD 1948–1975 Painter, draughtsman, printmaker and teacher, born in Rochdale, Lancashire. Bamford studied at Rochdale College of Art, 1964–6; Coventry College of Art, 1966–9; and Liverpool College of Art, 1969–70. Settled in Leamington Spa and taught art and craft at Beauchamp High School and Myton High School, both in Warwick. Bamford died at 27, a vulnerable, lost figure who left notebooks full of searching introspection. His creativity drew on much lateral thinking and included elegant constructions built up from the simplest shapes, which he cleverly turned and contrasted, heavily shaded pencil drawings and prints. He exhibited at Rochdale Sculpture Gallery and Third International Bradford Print Biennale, both 1972; and Warwick Gallery and Herbert Art Gallery & Museum, Coventry, both 1973. There was a retrospective at Warwick Gallery in 1977 and an exhibition at Herbert Art Gallery & Museum in 2003, drawn from its own and the artist's family's collections.

Kathleen BAMFORD 1879– Oil and watercolour painter, born in Hull. Studied part-time at the School of Art there, in Finland and portrait painting in London with Arthur Hickman-Smith. Exhibited at Hull College of Art, SWA and Islington Art Circle. Lived in Greenford, Middlesex. Diabetes and poor sight prevented Bamford working in her later years.

Oladélé Ajiboyé BAMGBOYÉ 1963– Artist working in a range of modern media, consultant and critic, born in Odo-Eku, Nigeria. He gained a Bachelor of Science degree with honours at Strathclyde University, Glasgow, 1981–5; studied under Peter Ride, Cambridge Darkroom Gallery/Eastern Arts Board, Cambridge Arts Council Exhibition Curatorial Traineeship, 1995–6; then, under Stuart Brisley, gained a distinction in his master's degree in media fine art theory and practice, Slade School of Fine Art, 1996–8. Participated in various international forums. Later residencies included resident research professor, Centre for Contemporary Art, Kitakyushu, Japan, 2000; and Witte de With Centre for Contemporary Art, Rotterdam, Netherlands, 2000–1. Was from 2000 an editorial board member of *FLAG*, a theoretical publication jointly put out by Camouflage Art Culture and Politics. Participated in international group exhibitions, including New British Art 2000: Intelligence, Tate Britain, 2000. Later solo shows included Anne Faggionato, 2000, and Introspect at Spacex Gallery and Studios, Exeter, 2003. Lived in north London.

Dharbinder S BAMRAH 1965– Self-taught painter and draughtsman, born in Kiambu, near Nairobi, Kenya, part of his childhood being spent in India. His early work was portraits and nudes before he concentrated on wildlife. Took part in many international exhibitions and held solo shows, later ones including a series in 2000 at The Gallery in Cork Street; Nature in Art, Twigworth; and The Ringstead Gallery, Ringstead, all in aid of the The Blue Cross animal welfare charity. Art Genesis Ltd published prints of his work, which was in the collections of Sir John Mills, Rula Lenska, Midge Ure and the Earl of Moray.

Christopher BANAHAN 1958– He studied at Liverpool Polytechnic, 1978–9, graduated with honours from Trent Polytechnic, 1979–81, and gained his master's from Goldsmiths' College, 1982–4. Exhibitions included Themeism, Centre Gallery, Liverpool, and Nottingham Castle Local Artists Exhibition, both 1979; Camden Annual, Camden Arts Centre, 1983; and East End Open Studios, at Metropolitan Wharf, 1989.

William BANBURY 1871– Sculptor and craftsman in various materials, born in Leicester, to which he eventually returned, living at Newtown Linford. Studied at Leicester College of Art, the Royal College of Art and in Paris, winning a number of medals. He went on to become head of sculpture at Aberdeen College of Art. Banbury showed at RA, RSA, elsewhere in Scotland and in Leicester. Arbroath Public Library and Forfar Academy obtained his work. Banbury was an honorary member of RBS.

Oliver BANCROFT 1976– Painter and illustrator whose work could be infused by surreal and darkly humorous elements. He was born in Cambridge and made foundation art and design studies at Tresham Institute, Kettering, 1995; graduated in fine art, painting and drawing, with first-class honours, from De Montfort University, Leicester, 1996–00; and gained his master's degree there, with distinction, 2001–3, also studying photography and filmmaking. In 2002, Bancroft won the Stephen George & Partners and Ratcliffe Fowler Design Artists' Awards. He did a variety of jobs, then was artist-in-residence at Marlborough College in 2005, the year of his solo show at the Goldmark Gallery, Uppingham. Other exhibitions included The Showcase, Oundle, from 2000; Open Exhibition, Leicester City Art Gallery, 2002; Drawing and Film on Paper, R K Burt Gallery, 2003; Bloomberg New Contemporaries, The Coach Shed, Liverpool, and at Barbican, 2004; and The World, Abridged, Kettle's Yard, Cambridge, 2005. Among Bancroft's illustrative work was Anthony Ragan's book *Marienburg: Sold Down the River*, 1999. Mike Goldmark collected Bancroft's work.

John BANGS 1949– Artist, teacher and administrator, born in Hendon, north London, who graduated in fine art at Reading University, under Claude Rogers and Terry Frost, 1967–71, with a postgraduate year at Goldsmiths' College, 1971–2. Taught in east London, at Bow Secondary School from 1972–5, at Templars Special School, 1975–90, continuing with own work and showing at Whitechapel Art Gallery Open in 1980s. In 1990, joined staff of National Union of Teachers, from 1993 being education officer. From the early 1990s Bangs participated in Greenwich Open Studios, also showing regularly at Woodlands Art Gallery, Blackheath Concert Halls and Café Gallery, Southwark. Bangs worked mostly in dry pastels, "using colour as a way of recording memories of valued places and people, a visual diary." Edward Hopper and Pierre Bonnard were among influences. Lived in southeast London.

Shirley BANHAM 1942–1991 Draughtsman and painter, notably in egg tempera, born and lived in Chalfont St Peter, Buckinghamshire. Studied at High Wycombe Technical School of Art, 1977–9. Showed with SGA of which she was a member, at Mall Galleries and with local societies.

BANK– Group of artists which emerged in the early 1990s. From summer 1998 it had three members (after Andrew Williamson left): Simon Bedwell, John Russell and Milly Thompson (see separate entries). Although producing individual work, most of their efforts went into Bank. It also ran Gallerie Poo Poo (formerly Dog) until early 1999, when it concentrated on producing shows for other spaces. Bank's co-operative productions "evolved out of a shared interest in the results of group, as opposed to individual, art practice; it also made possible the organising of exhibitions on terms not entirely reliant upon dominant conventions." The group made many appearances, with and without other artists' participation, including Zombie Golf, Bankspace, 1995; The Happy Squirrel Club, De Fabriek, Eindhoven, Netherlands, 1996; Winkle The Pot Bellied Pig and his Woodland Chums, Gallerie Poo Poo and Bricks & Kicks, Vienna, Austria, and Sewage Lust, ICA, both 1997; White3, Gallerie Poo Poo, 1998; Dead Life, The Mayor Gallery, 1999; Protest & Survive, Whitechapel Art Gallery, 2000; and Anthony Wilkinson Gallery, 2002, the year Bank won a prize at the John Moores Liverpool Exhibition.

Brian BANKS 1939– Painter, born and lived in London, who studied at St Martin's School of Art, 1956–7, his teachers including James Dring and Edward Middleditch, and in private studios. Group exhibitions included William Ware, Lower, Ansdell and Obelisk Galleries in London; Colin Jellicoe Gallery, Manchester; Galerie Salammbo, Paris, from 1987; and Austen Hayes Gallery, York. Solo shows were held at Colin Jellicoe, Ansdell and Zaydler Galleries, Trinity Arts Centre in Tunbridge Wells and from 1984 at Leigh Gallery. British and foreign private collections held his work.

Colin BANKS 1932–2002 Graphic designer, prolific lecturer and writer, born in Ruislip, Middlesex, producing work notable for its clarity, simplicity and appropriateness. After polio thwarted his aspirations as a long-distance runner, Banks developed an interest in lettering and calligraphy and studied at art schools in Rochester and Maidstone, although a City and Guilds certificate in typography was his only qualification. After working in a number of prominent London design teams, notably as assistant to Ernest Hoch, he went solo from 1956, then in 1958 formed Banks & Miles with John Miles, whom he had met while studying. The partnership lasted until 1996. Among clients worked for were the Zoological Society of London; the British Council, for whose exhibition Social Communication Banks lectured during its extensive Indian and Far East tour; the Indian Institute of Technolgy, Bombay; *Encounter* magazine; the Consumers' Association; the Post Office; British Telecom; and London Regional Transport. Banks & Miles set up design studies in Amsterdam, Brussels and Hamburg and won many awards. For his 1994 book on the development of Edward Johnston's sans serif type-face for London Underground, *London's Handwriting*, Banks gained the premier award of the Society of Typographic Designers. He was its president, vice-president of the Chartered Society of Designers, chairman of the Double Crown Club and and president of the Wynkyn de Worde Society. Latterly, Banks established a new corporate identity for Oxford University Press and was visiting professor of design at the Danish Royal Academy School of Architecture.

Harry BANKS 1869–1947 Printmaker and painter in watercolour, born in London. He attended Goldsmiths' College, later studying in Antwerp. Designed invitation card for coronation of Edward VII. In 1902 Banks moved to Thorncombe, Dorset, where he was a friend and neighbour of Lucien Pissarro. When the Banks' daughter Audrey was at school in Bristol they would live during term in Clifton, where Banks made prints of the city and docks. He also completed West Country views as well as continental scenes done on holiday. Showed with Bristol Savages, RWA, RI, RA, UA, Paris Salon and Print Makers' Society of California. Banks was unusual in printing his own plates, some in colour. Bristol City Art Gallery has his work. Banks was buried in Salcombe, Devon.

Lesley BANKS 1962– Painter and teacher, born in Oxford, who studied at Glasgow School of Art, 1980–4, gaining an honours degree in drawing and painting. In 1985–6 she won an Elizabeth Greenshields Foundation, allowing European travel, with several months in Amsterdam. After a period working at Compass Gallery, Glasgow, 1987–9, she left to paint full-time, in 1990 being visiting artist on the Castle Toward, Strathclyde Education, art course. Further awards included Royal Glasgow Institute of the Fine Arts David Cargill Award in 1990; and in 1991 the Scottish Artist Prize at Royal Over-Seas League Open and the Scottish Amicable Award at the Royal Glasgow Institute. Banks took part in many group shows from 1984, where she appeared in New Generation Artists at Compass; also Paisley Drawing Competition, Paisley Museum, from 1989; Jobson's Choice, Jill George Gallery, 1992; and Royal Over-Seas League Open, 1995. Was in 1999 artist-in-residence, with a solo show, at Edinburgh Zoo; solo exhibition at Cyril Gerber Fine Art, Glasgow, 2001. Banks' work blended realistic and Surrealist elements. Aberdeen Art Gallery, Lillie Art Gallery in Milngavie, BBC Scotland and Motherwell District Libraries hold examples.

Peter BANKS 1950– Artist and teacher who employed photographs, wooden structures and ceramics to create works for galleries, outdoor walls and hoardings. He was born in Newcastle upon Tyne and studied at Leeds Polytechnic, 1969–72. Was a technician at Lincoln College of Art, 1972–3, teaching appointments including Salford and Southwark Colleges. Showed at ICA, Peterloo Gallery in Manchester and in Summer Show 3 at Serpentine Gallery, 1981. Had a solo show at Monks Hall, Eccles, in 1974, later ones including Whitworth Art Gallery in Manchester, 1980. Lived for a time in London.

Robert BANKS 1911–2000 Watercolourist and architect, born in Cheltenham, Gloucestershire. He was a qualified architect who was professionally engaged in town planning until the late 1950s, when he had more time to paint. Showed at Trafford and Alwin Galleries and lived in London. Banks was a fellow of the RIBA.

Roger BANKS 1929– Artist in watercolour and oil and writer concentrating on botanical subjects. Spent 1952–5 with Falkland Islands Dependencies Survey on Antarctic service, married in 1964 and settled in Crail, Fife. From 1990–4 was chairman of the School of Scottish Artists in Malta. Among his books were *The Unrelenting Ice*, 1962; *Living in a Wild Garden*, 1980; and *Cottage Garden Flowers*, 1983. Showed with the Imperial Institute in 1955, then from 1970 with Oliver Swann Galleries, National Trust, National Trust for Scotland and Scottish Wildlife Trust. Was a member of the Botanical Society of the British Isles who specialised in painting wild flowers on site, especially Scottish arctic and alpine plants. British Museum botanical library and HM Queen Elizabeth The Queen Mother hold his work.

BANKS & MILES: *see* **Colin BANKS**

BANKSY– Cult graffiti artist, associated with protest and rock culture, whose identity was closely guarded but whose simple, graphic images were ubiquitous and seriously collected. Because Bansky did not give interviews, details of his life were imprecise. He originated in Bristol, said to be the "son of a seller of photocopies". When he was 14 street artwork began to appear signed with his name in the city, where he was associated with the music scene including the bands Massive Attack and Portishead. Banksy moved to London, where his stencilled images appeared on buildings. He was fond of plays on words. His website www.banksy.co.uk showed a Dutch boy with a brush and can of paint with the slogan "Banksy The Exterior Paint Specialist Click here for a free quote". Also attributed to Banksy was the inscription "Mind the crap" on the staircase of Tate Britain, a play on the London Underground safety warning "Mind the gap". The mystery of Banksy's identity eventually led to "I am Bansky" teeshirts being worn around the capital. By 2002, the glossy, upmarket *Creative Review* was featuring Banksy in a foldout feature on graffiti artists and offering an original artwork in a reader competition. The artist declined to show through conventional galleries or to sell to collectors, although by 2004, according to an article in the French magazine *Beaux Arts*, the value of his screenprints rose from £50 to £500 in a few months, large works reportedly achieving £3,000. In 2005, Bonhams New Bond Street was offering at auction four of his screenprints (Girl and Balloon, I Fought the Law, Love Bomb, and Rat, a familiar Bansky image) with reserves up to £600. His work was more modestly available direct from www.tomtom.-biz, the Soho outlet, and http://picturesonwalls.com/. Banksy books included *Banging your head against a brick wall*, 2001; *Existencilism*, published under the name Robin Banksy, 2002; and *Cut it out*, 2004. He continued to be associated with the music scene, in 2003 producing the cover for the band Blur's album *Think Tank*, its front man Damon Albarn being one of his fans. New international twists to Banksy's career occurred in 2005. First, he struck for the first time in New York, planting his works in the Museum of Modern Art, the Metropolitan Museum of Art, the Brooklyn Museum and American Museum of Natural History. Later, he created nine stencil spray paintings on the Palestinian side of the Israeli-erected West Bank barrier, one showing children digging what looked like a hole through the wall. Banksy's book *Wall and Piece* was published in 2005.

Delmar BANNER 1896–1983 Oil and watercolour painter specialising in portraits. Born at Freiburg-in-Breisgau, Germany, Banner studied at Cheltenham, Oxford and Regent Street Polytechnic. He married the sculptor Josefina de Vasconcellos, with whom he shared two shows. The Ashmolean, Fitzwilliam and Victoria & Albert Museums hold his work as do many other public galleries throughout Britain. Lived at Little Langdale, Ambleside, Cumbria, Lake District scenes being a feature of his work.

Fiona BANNER 1966– Artist in various media, born Merseyside, who studied at Camberwell School of Arts and Crafts, 1985–6, gained her bachelor's degree at Kingston Polytechnic, 1986–9, and her master's at Goldsmiths' College, 1991–3. Group exhibitions included Artificial Eden, Camerawork Gallery, 1993; Drawings at Laure Genillard Gallery, BT New Contemporaries at Camden Arts Centre with tour, and The Antidote, Centre 181 Gallery, all 1994; 4 Projects, Frith Street Gallery, and Venice Biennale, both 1995. Had a solo show Pushing Back the Edge of the Envelope, at City Racing, 1994; an Art Now exhibition at Tate Gallery, drawing inspiration from popular culture, 1998; and Stop, Frith Street Gallery, 1999–00. In 2001, visitors to the South Bank could pass under Banner's Rainbow, a brilliantly coloured canopy of 2,000 hand-painted flags outside the Hayward Gallery. Banner's 2002 Frith Street exhibition concentrated on recent works by the Turner Prize-shortlisted artist in which she continued to explore that ambiguous area where words and images meet but never quite overlap. Lived and worked in London.

Afrakuma BANNERMAN 1950– Painter in oil and enamel, born in Accra, Gold Coast, who was educated in England, including Malvern Girls' College. Studied art at Kingston Polytechnic, 1969–73, and London University Institute of Education, graduating with honours with an art teacher's certificate. Taught part-time at the Institute in mid-1970s. Showed Mall Galleries, Woodstock and Ibis Galleries and abroad. Lived in London.

Adrian BANNISTER 1975– Artist and teacher, born in Pontefract, Yorkshire. After initial art and design studies at Isle College, Cambridgeshire, 1991–3, Bannister graduated with honours in fine art from University of Northumbria, Newcastle, 1993–6, gaining his master's in fine art from Brighton University, 1998–00. He was an art teacher and art technician at Surbiton High School, 1998–9, from 1999 teaching art as a three-dimension specialist at Hampton School, also a visiting tutor on the foundation course at Isle College, 2001. Bannister produced "contemporary figurative sculpture with a modern vernacular. My early work, such as the installation Swim, explored social space and alienation with sexual undercurrents." By 2003, his work concerned "businessmen and childhood toys. I am exploring the dialogue between work, play, aspirations and life cycles." Group shows included More Upstairs, Brighton University, 2000; Black and White, Karen Taylor's Contemporary Art, St Margaret's, 2001; Bruton Street Gallery, from 2001; and guest artist, Stuckism International Gallery, from 2002. Lived for a time in Ealing, west London.

Geoff BANNISTER 1924– Commercial artist, designer and teacher, born in Birmingham, not far from where he settled in Walsall, West Midlands. During World War II he served in the Royal Navy, in the mid-1940s teaching commercial art while still in uniform. He went on to form his own design consultancy while continuing to paint a variety of subjects.

Adrian BANNON 1959– Artist who studied at University of Reading. He took part in various group exhibitions, including Art in Boxes, England & Co, 1992; The Courtauld Institute, Biennial Exhibition, 1997–8; and La Beauté, The French Government Millennium Exhibition, Avignon, France, 2000. Was artist-in-residence at Goldsmiths' College, 1985–6, in 1987 having a solo show at Oriel Gallery in north Wales. England & Co gave Bannon another one-man exhibition in 1994 of works in the Arte Povera tradition, "using simple or 'poor' materials to create works that are rich in their power to evoke associations or ideas", with further shows from 1996. Manchester Museum of Science and Technology holds a large thistledown coat by Bannon.

John BANTING 1902–1972 Surrealist painter and designer, born in London. Banting studied under Bernard Meninsky at evening classes at Westminster School of Art from 1921, going to Paris the following year for further studies. Returning to London in 1925 he became connected with the Bloomsbury Group painters, joined LG and showed with the 7 & 5 Society. At the beginning of the 1930s he again went to France where he met Breton, Creval, Giacometti, Duchamp and other artists. Further activities included designing for the Carmargo Society ballet *Pomona*; designing book jackets for Hogarth Press; in 1936 contributing pictures to the International Surrealist Exhibition, in London; and travelling to Madrid during the Spanish Civil War, where he met Ernest Hemingway, the writer. During World War II he was involved in Strand Films and was art editor of *Our Time*, a left-wing political monthly. After the war Banting published *A Blue Book of Conversation*. Lived in rural Ireland for a while, then settled near his friend Edward Burra at Hastings, Sussex, where he died. In 1971 had been included in Hamet Gallery's Surrealist show. Since his death Banting has been included in many exhibitions connected with Surrealism, and he was given a retrospective at Oliver Bradbury and James Birch, 1983.

Cuillin BANTOCK 1935– Artist in a range of media, including oil pastel and lino-cut, born in Birmingham. He studied at the School of Art there, 1953–5; Oxford School of Art, 1955–61 (part-time while reading zoology and evolutionary ecology at the University), gaining his bachelor's degree in 1958, then his master's degree and doctorate in 1961; and at Camberwell College of Art, 1961–4. Important teachers were Robert Medley, Henry Inlander, Euan Uglow, Richard Eurich and Anthony Eyton, main influences being Lanyon, de Staël and Hofmann. Bantock spent two decades as a professional environmentalist, with several books and many scientific papers published, then returned to painting full-time in 1989. Bantock regarded himself "as a landscape painter, but I mostly work non-figuratively, as I believe that sensation and metaphor are more important than illusion and narrative ... My background in ecology indirectly informs all my work." Took part in numerous mixed and solo shows, main ones being Clevedon: Sharing a View, APT Gallery and tour, 1997–8; two-man shows at Woodlands Art Gallery in 1995 and Beardsmore Gallery, 1997; with a solo exhibition at Cut Gallery, 1994, The Gestalt Centre, 2001, and a seventieth birthday exhibition at APT Gallery in 2005. Cuillin (pronounced Coolin) Bantock organised a number of exhibitions, such as the inaugural Made in Greenwich 1974–1994, in 1994 at The Living Room. He was also a director of The Art in Perpetuity Trust and helped to run The Bantock Society, the composer Granville Bantock being his grandfather. Lived in London.

Alexandra BARAITSER 1971– Painter and teacher, born in South Africa, who studied at Central St Martins College of Art, 1990–1, Wimbledon School of Art, 1991–4, and Chelsea College of Art, 1994–5. Among her awards, in 1997 she won the Abbey Scholarship in Painting at the British School at Rome, in 1998 a prize in the NatWest Art Prize. She was a visiting lecturer in fine art/painting at Ruskin School, Oxford, at Reading University and Wimbledon School of Art. In the late 1990s, issues of human personality and identity were explored in a series of paintings of football shirts. Exhibitions included Contemporary Artists at Sotheby's, 1993; The John Moores 19, Walker Art Gallery, Liverpool, 1995; London as It is, Alexandra Baraitser and Rebecca Arnold, Barbican Centre, 1996; and Waterstone's Gallery, Cambridge, where she lived, 1998. Commissions included BP Amoco European Lubricants, 2000, and J Sainsbury plc, 2001. In 2002, at Mission Gallery, Swansea, and at Hirschl Contemporary Art, Baraitser showed Mobilia, pictures of furniture.

Stefan BARAN 1922– Versatile artist, born in Lódź, Poland, where he studied drawing and painting in the studio of Wacław Dobrowolski and also in Lvov with Feliks Wygrzewalski. Military service in World War II took him to Glasgow, Scotland, where he concentrated on graphic art at Glasgow School of Art, 1945–9. From 1950 he worked for cartoon film production companies as a designer, animator and model-maker. He exhibited television models in a show organised by the Board of Trade in Chicago, America, and produced theatrical models for the Young Vic and stage designs for the Polish Theatre. Became an associate of RMS in 1955. He also showed with RP, SPS, cartoons in an international exhibition in West Berlin and in an Arts Council exhibition of wood engravings.

Janina BARANOWSKA 1925– Painter, born in Grodno, Poland, where she stayed until World War II, in 1940 being deported to Russia. After leaving there with the Polish Army for the Middle East, she finished her education in Palestine and settled in Britain in 1945. Studied at Borough Polytechnic, 1946–9, Polish University in London, 1951–4, then Putney School of Art, 1955–9. She was a leading member of the Association of Polish Artists in Great Britain, being its chairman, 1980–91. Group shows included New Burlington Galleries, 1955; Grabowski Gallery from 1959; Westminster Cathedral, 1984; and in 1993 she was in Polish Roots – British Soil, at City Art Centre, Edinburgh. As well as a series of solo shows at Drian Gallery from 1958, latterly exhibited at Bloomsbury Gallery, London University, 1988, and Zacheta Gallery, Warsaw, 1991. Public and private collections in Britain and abroad hold her work, including Toruń University, Poland. Lived in London.

Bruno BARBIER 1962– Sculptor and teacher of Swiss origin who completed a foundation course at Watford College of Art, 1980–1, then graduated with honours in sculpture at Canterbury College of Art, 1981–4. He was a part-time lecturer at South Kent College of Technology in Ashford, 1984–5, then had two visiting lectureships in architecture: 1989 at Polytechnic of East London, and 1991 at Oxford Polytechnic. Barbier's mixed shows included St Augustine's Abbey Gardens, Canterbury, 1983; The Festival of London, Alexandra Park, 1988; Swiss Artists in Britain 1991, *The Economist* Building, 1991; and Sculpture at Canterbury, 1992. He had a solo show at Trinity Arts Centre, Tunbridge Wells, 1985; another at Gallery 22, Forest Row, 1986; and Sculpture, Recent Works, at Crypt Gallery, 1991.

Artur Ernesto Teixeira de Verconcelos BARBOSA 1908–1995 Versatile artist, born in Liverpool, son of the Portuguese vice-consul and a half-French mother. Went to school with the flyer Douglas Bader and actors Rex Harrison and Laurence Olivier and while still studying formed the Pandemonium Group with the illustrator Nicolas Bentley, painters Eliot Hodgkin and illustrator and painter Victor Reinganum. From his early twenties, Barbosa designed theatrical costumes; he illustrated for *Harper's Bazaar, Radio Times* and *Vogue*; during World War II worked for the Ministry of Information; and after the war continued with his pre-war work as well as handling commissions for British and American book publishers. Abbott and Holder offered his work.

Claire BARCLAY 1968– Artist creating sculpture and site-specific projects from man-made and natural materials, born in Paisley, Renfrewshire. She graduated in fine art at Glasgow School of Art, 1986–90, gaining her master's there, 1991–3. Won a Sir Harry Barnes Scholarship, 1990, Richard Ellis Scholarship, 1993, and Scottish Arts Council Artists Award, 1997. She held a residency from the Council in Canberra and Hobart, Australia, 1995–6, in 1997 being artist-in-residence, Millennium Park Project, Govanhill, Glasgow, and at 200 Gertrude Street, Melbourne. Took part in group exhibitions in Europe and Australia, later solo shows including Dream Catcher, 200 Gertrude Street, 1998, The Showroom, 2000, and Dundee Contemporary Arts, 2003. In Ideal Pursuits there, she showed unusual hand-made structures created from curious materials, such as fake fur and piano wire, a cluster of aluminium poles like spiders' legs and towering wooden boxes screenprinted with pictures of crystals. She said: "Subversion is something I need to do." Barclay was featured in Art Now at Tate Britain in 2004. That intervention continued her interest in the physical tensions set up between contrasting elements: organic against synthetic, hard against soft, openness against confinement, encouraging an array of associations to be made.

Colville BARCLAY 1913– Painter, born in London, son of Sir Colville Barclay. He was educated at Eton College and Oxford, obtaining a master's degree, studying art at Ruskin School of Art with Albert Rutherston. Showed in mixed exhibitions at RA, RBA, LG and at public galleries in Bradford, Brighton and Sheffield. Arts Council, Bradford City Art Gallery and the London County Council Pictures for Schools scheme held his work. Sir Colville lived near Petworth, Sussex.

James R BARCLAY 1932– Painter and teacher, born in Forfar, Angus, who gained his diploma in drawing and painting from Dundee College of Art, 1953, and a post-diploma scholarship there, 1954. Taught in Fife, latterly at Buckhaven High School, 1957–86, settling in Cellardyke. Was elected a professional member of SSA, 1963, winning a Scottish Arts Council Award, 1970. Took part in group shows at RSA, RWS and SSWA, and Glasgow Group, Douglas & Foulis Gallery, Edinburgh; Dundee and Aberdeen Art Galleries; and The Little Gallery, Pittenweem, also exhibited his work. Solo exhibitions included Loomshop Gallery, Lower Largo; Dunfermline Museum; and Lomond Centre, Glenrothes. Fife and Lanarkshire Councils and IBM hold examples.

John Rankine BARCLAY 1884–1964 Painter and etcher, born in Edinburgh, who studied there and on the continent. He won a Carnegie Travelling Scholarship and the Guthrie Award and showed at RSA Royal Glasgow Institute of the Fine Arts and elsewhere. Barclay was a member of the Edinburgh Group formed just before World War II and was represented in the exhibition covering it at City Art Centre, Edinburgh, and touring, 1983. He went on to paint in an often experimental style and lived for over 30 years in St Ives, Cornwall, where he was associated with such artists as Sven Berlin and Misomé Peile. Stoke-on-Trent City Museum and Art Gallery bought his picture The Pont Neuf.

Stephen BARCLAY 1961– Painter, born in Ayrshire, who did degree and postgraduate studies at Glasgow School of Art, 1980–5. He gained a Hospitalfield Summer Scholarship, 1983, and an Adam Bruce Thomson Award, 1984. His many group appearances included Royal Glasgow Institute of the Fine Arts, 1984; Compass Gallery, Glasgow, from 1984–5; Warwick Arts Trust, 1985; Clare Hall, Cambridge, New Art from Scotland, 1986; and Galerie Bureaux & Magasins, Oostende, 1991. Had a solo show at Paton Gallery, 1987, then a series at Raab Galerie, Berlin and London, from 1989, also Northlands Festival, Caithness, 1994, and Duncan R Miller Fine Arts, 2004. Contemporary Art Society, Metropolitan Museum of Modern Art in New York and provincial galleries hold his work. Lived near Arbroath, Angus.

Dave BARDEN 1943– Painter, draughtsman and teacher, born in Sheffield, Yorkshire, where he studied at the College of Art, 1962–6, winning the Queen's Award travelling scholarship to Italy, 1963, and the Sheffield University Institute art teacher's diploma, 1966–7. Held several teaching posts, latterly principal lecturer in fine art, at University of Northumbria, 1980–95. From Northern Arts won a Printmaking Bursary, 1975, Production Award, 1989, and a Print Award, 1995. Residencies included Wentworth Leisure Centre, Hexham, 1988–9. Commissions included Olympic Games, Barcelona, 1992. Was Sidney Holgate Fellow, Grey College, University of Durham. Later shows included Picturing Sport, retrospective, Customs House Gallery, South Shields, 1998, and Henry Dyson Fine Art at Grey College and the Quaker Gallery, both 2000.

Kenneth BARDEN 1924–1988 Architect, designer, teacher and painter, born in Huddersfield, Yorkshire. He took apprenticeship to a decorator, studying at Huddersfield School of Art, where his father Harry taught, then was at Royal College of Art, 1947, under Gilbert Spencer and Ernest Tristram. Taught at Croydon College of Art, then, although he wanted to paint full-time, joined George Wimpey & Company. As the firm's principal architect he designed several hundred murals worldwide. Was a member of RI and also showed at ROI, RA, at public galleries in Huddersfield and Winchester and in London.

As well as large watercolour landscapes and still lifes, Barden in later years was a witty designer of figure pieces. His murals were in flats in Kingston upon Thames, factories in Sheffield and schools in Croydon. Lived latterly in Chiswick, west London.

Geoffrey BARGERY 1938– Painter and illustrator, born in Cardiff, South Wales. Attended Kingston School of Art, 1953–8, then Royal Academy Schools, 1958–61, when Peter Greenham taught him. Did a considerable amount of mural and other commissioned work for bodies such as the BBC and the Institute of Directors. Nuffield Foundation holds his work. Lived in Surbiton, Surrey.

Jean BARHAM 1924– Painter and printmaker, born and lived in London, whose main interest was depicting the River Thames. She studied at Camberwell School of Art, 1947–50, with Lawrence Gowing, Claude Rogers, Victor Pasmore and William Coldstream. Was a member of Greenwich Printmakers and was an award winner in the Spirit of London Competition at Royal Festival Hall in 1979. Also exhibited at Blackheath Concert Halls and Greenwich Theatre. Had a solo show at World Trade Centre, 1973, another at clipper *Cutty Sark*, Greenwich, 1979. Participated in the annual Greenwich Open Studios.

Daphne BARING: *see* **Daphne POLLEN**

Allen BARKER 1937– Artist who was born in Australia, son of the artist Keith David, who studied at National Art School in Sydney, 1955–60. Showed at Lucy Milton Gallery; Ikon Gallery, Birmingham, ICA; Ferens Art Gallery, Hull; and abroad. British and foreign galleries hold his work. Lived in London.

Audrey BARKER 1932–2002 Versatile and irrepressible artist and teacher, born in London's dockland, who was evacuated in World War II to a farm where she contracted tuberculosis, hospitalisation denying her formal education. Helped by wide reading she won a scholarship to East Ham Grammar School for Girls, attending Walthamstow School of Art, 1950–5, and Leicester College of Art for a year's teacher training. Showed widely at RA Summer Exhibition, Young Contemporaries, NEAC, John Moores Liverpool Exhibition and elsewhere in the provinces. Illness hindered her teaching career and in 1961 she moved to Cumberland to marry the artist and teacher Denis Barker and reappraised her art, taking in environments, performances with artists such as Adrian Henri and assemblages. Had a year at Newcastle University, won an Abbot Hall Art Gallery prize and was fired from Carlisle College of Art, whose conservative atmosphere she disliked. In 1966, a short, inspiring association with Joseph Cornell, in New York, led Barker in the winter of 1967 to show boxes with Dom Sylvester Houédard at the Lisson Gallery; friendships followed with Ken Cox and Li Yuan Chia, who was to open the LYC Museum and Art Gallery near her in 1972. Further illness, including severe arthritis, hindered Audrey's development in the 1970s, although she and Denis started and ran an arts and crafts-related business, Barkers of Lanercost, and developed, in the restored Abbey Mill, an arts centre and sheltered workshop for the disabled until its collapse in 1987, soon followed by divorce. With the slogan "access is a state of mind", Barker's final work phase challenged assumptions about art, disability and access. Notable features were a large piece, Festival of the Five Senses, which in 1989, filled the Wentworth Leisure Centre, Hexham, and Art: An Illusion, at Keswick Art Gallery, 2000. In 1993, at an Arts Council symposium, Barker accepted a Woman of the Decade award.

Cecily Mary BARKER 1895–1973 Painter, illustrator and writer of children's books, born in Croydon. After private education she was largely self-taught as an artist, although she did study part-time at Croydon School of Art and she continued to live in the town for a while, then in Storrington, Sussex. Although she exhibited SWA, RI and elsewhere, she was principally known for her illustrations of fairy children, as in *Flower Fairies of the Spring*, 1923, and *Flower Fairies of the Wayside*, 1948. Also did stained glass windows, her work featuring in St Andrew's Church, Croydon, and St George's Church at Waddon. Signed work CMB.

Clive BARKER 1940– Sculptor in bronze, born in Luton, Bedfordshire. He studied at Luton College of Technology and Art, 1957–9. Mixed exhibitions included Young Contemporaries, RBA Galleries, 1962; New Idioms, Robert Fraser Gallery, 1966; Young British Artists, Museum of Modern Art, New York, 1968; Der Geist des Surrealismus, Baukunst-Galerie, Cologne, 1971; British Artists of the 60s, Tate Gallery, 1977; British Pop Art, Birch and Conran, 1987; and Serpentine Gallery, 1991. After a solo show at Robert Fraser Gallery, 1968, later ones included Boxes, Wolverhampton Art Gallery, 1985, Portraits, National Portrait Gallery, 1987, Whitford Fine Art, 2000, reflecting Barker's interest in popular imagery, such as Mickey Mouse, and Whitford's 2003 show, accompanied by a full catalogue of his works, 1958–2000. Arts Council, British Council, Imperial War Museum and Smithsonian Institute in Washington hold his work. Lived in London.

Dale Devereux BARKER 1962– Versatile artist and lecturer, born in Leicester, who studied at Loughborough College of Art and Design, 1980–1; Leicester Polytechnic (travelling scholarship – award), 1981–4; and Slade School of Fine Art, 1984–6. In 1996 he was elected a fellow of RE. Teaching appointments included visiting lectureships at Leicester Polytechnic, 1986–92, and North Hertfordshire College, 1991–2, from 1991–8 lecturing at University College, Suffolk, then at Harrogate College of Art and Drama, 1997–9, and Leeds Metropolitan University, 1999. Between 1992–6, Barker was workshop co-ordinator at Gainsborough's House, Sudbury. Group shows included The Eagle Gallery; National Print Exhibition, Mall Galleries (Robert Horne Award); 2nd Kochi International Print Biennale, Japan (Commended); 10th and 11th British International Print Biennale, Cartwright Hall, Bradford (Forbo-Nairn Prize for Best Linocut); and Barbican Centre. Had a solo show, Leaves to Find, Galerie Dusseldorf, Perth, Australia, 1989, later ones including a retrospective at The Fermoy Arts Centre, King's Lynn, 1995, Come Upstairs and see my Etchings!, Christchurch Mansion, Ipswich, 1996–7, Excessive Swimming Pleasures, The Gallery, Leisure and Visitor Centre at Stratford-upon-Avon, and Chappel Galleries, Chappel, both 2001, Gainsborough's House, Sudbury, 2003, inspired by its collection, and Jill George Gallery, 2004. That show, Thoughts Made Visible, included enamels, paintings and prints. Commissions included Elton John Aids Foundation; Russell Davies (Container Freight); British Rail Freight; and Lloyds Building. A major commission for the law firm Clifford Chance led to a series of large vitreous enamel panels for Taylor Woodrow Properties and Pool of London Partnership, St Katharine Docks. Victoria & Albert Museum, Ipswich Museums and Galleries, Ashmolean Museum in Oxford, Wakefield Museum, a number of county council and corporate collections hold examples.

David BARKER 1945– A printmaker and teacher, Barker was born in Dorchester, Dorset. He studied at Goldsmiths' College School of Art, 1962–7, where Paul Drury was among his teachers. He was a member of the Printmakers' Council and worked on the printmaking side at the College of Art in Cambridge, where he lived, 1967–8, then moved to Northern Ireland where from 1974 he was senior lecturer at the school of fine art at Ulster College. His many exhibitions included Grabowski Gallery, Octagon Gallery in Belfast, Arts Council of Northern Ireland Gallery and Third Eye Centre in Glasgow. New University of Ulster, Southwark Print Collection and California College of Arts and Crafts in America hold examples.

John Edward BARKER 1889–1953 Painter in oil and watercolour, son of the artist John Joseph Barker. Studied at Bath School of Art, 1905–10, under Nathaniel Heard, and the Camden School of Art, in London, 1910–13. Exhibited at the City Art Gallery, Manchester, and elsewhere in the provinces. Was head of the art department at Bacup and Rawtenstall Grammar School, near where he lived in Rossendale, Lancashire.

John Rowland BARKER 1911–1959 Painter and draughtsman who taught for many years in Sussex and London. Studied at Leicester School of Art until 1932, then moved to London where he began a career as a graphic designer, producing stylised posters and magazine designs for companies such as Shell, Imperial Chemical Industries and British Railways, as well as fabrics for Sanderson. Showed widely in America and his work was reproduced in magazines such as *Graphis* and the *Architectural Review*, sometimes just signed JB. From the 1940s began a series of paintings with nautical links, a group of which was shown at Waterhouse and Dodd in 1991, providing comparisons with Edward Wadsworth or John Tunnard. Lived at Fordingbridge, Hampshire.

Kit BARKER 1916–1988 Painter and teacher, correct name Gordon Barker, he was born in London, the brother of the poet George Barker. He attended Northampton School of Art. In the mid-1940s Barker lived in Cornwall, at Newlyn and near Zennor, before going to America, where from 1949–53 he taught at Skidmore College, New York, and California School of Fine Arts. Many exhibitions included Waddington Galleries and his work is held by extensive collections including Arts Council and public galleries in Aberdeen, Bradford and Eastbourne. Barker's pictures are often of landscape with water in a near-abstract style. Settled in 1953 at Lodsworth, Sussex. Barker's War Composition, of 1944, was included in Messages from Nowhere at Austin/Desmond & Phipps, 1991. Retrospective at Bishop Otter Gallery, University College Chichester, coupled with an exhibition of Barker's watercolours at nearby Pallant House, both 2001.

Margaret BARKER 1907– Figure painter, born in London, who studied at Royal College of Art, 1925–9, under Randolph Schwabe. He pressed her to show her canvas Any Morning at NEAC in 1929, and through the Chantrey Bequest it found its way to Tate Gallery.

Patrick BARKER 1959– Figurative sculptor, creator of free-standing pieces and wall reliefs. He often used a soft limestone to produce amusing, rounded, tactile characters. Born in Shropshire, Barker studied at Bristol Polytechnic, 1978–9, Bath Academy of Art, 1979–82, then did a postgraduate course at Cyprus College of Art, 1984–5. Group shows included RWA, 1986; Millfield Open, Millfield School, 1990; and Ghent International Arts Fair, Belgium, 1992. His solo shows were Andrew Usiskin Contemporary Art, 1991, and Beaux Arts, Bath, 1992. In 1993 Barker shared a show at New Academy Gallery and Business Art Galleries, with another in 2003. Lived in West Harptree, Somerset.

Philip BARKER 1920–2001 Archaeologist, teacher and artist, born in London, who was born to working-class parents, leaving Wembley Grammar School aged 15. Initially shy, he proved himself in World War II as a bomber navigator, winning the Distinguished Flying Cross. In 1949 joined Priory Boys School, Shrewsbury, as art master, but a growing interest in archaeology nudged him into adult education and archaeology full-time. Barker took a part-time degree at Leicester University and joined Birmingham University in 1965, becoming a reader and retiring in 1987. Barker was elected a fellow of the Society of Antiquaries in 1963; he served on the Council for British Archaeology, its regional chairman in the 1970s, and the Clwyd-Powys Archaeological Trust, chairman in the 1980s. In 1971, he helped found Rescue, in 1979 the Institute of Field Archaeologists. As the building's consultant archaeologist, in 1994 he wrote *A Short Architectural History of Worcester Cathedral*. His book *Techniques of Archaeological Excavation*, 1977, and *Understanding Archaeological Excavation*, 1986, were key texts. As well as drawing plans of sites and landscapes, Barker was an accomplished artist, including abstract and three-dimensional works. Exhibiting venues latterly included the Society of Antiquaries of London.

Ruth BARKER 1979– Sculptor and environmental artist, born in Glasgow, who participated in the inaugural Bowieart exhibition BLOC at County Hall Gallery in 2005. There, it was said, "her Dream of the Northern Lights replicates the aurora borealis in miniature, which will be contained in a home-made bell jar." Barker graduated with honours in fine art, environmental art, from Glasgow School of Art, 1998–01, gaining her fine art master's there, 2002–4. In 2004 she also attended Glasgow Sculpture Studios for a wood-carving masterclass, awarded for professional development. Exhibitions included Myth, The White Space, Glasgow, 2000; Mythologies: Domestic Landscape, Transmission Gallery, Glasgow, 2001; Something Haptic: Souter Lighthouse, Project Rooms Gallery, Glasgow, 2002; Looking for Submarines, Scotland 2003, Bezalel Academy, Bezalel, Israel, 2003; and Siege and Counter Siege, Hotel Mariakapel, Hoorn, Netherlands, 2004. She had a public art residency at Kirkstall Abbey, Yorkshire, in 2001, the year she carried out several public art projects, including Considering Distance at the Transport Museum, Glasgow, and North Uist, Outer Hebrides.

Peter BARKER-MILL 1908–1994 Mainly abstract artist in oil, gouache, wood engraving and sculpture, born in Italy. He was married for a time to the artist Elsa Vaudrey, their daughter being the painter Amanda Barker-Mill. Barker-Mill attended Sandhurst, spent several years abroad in the Army, then gave up his commission to attend the Grosvenor School of Modern Art under Iain Macnab for three years, followed by 18 months, from 1932, under André Lhote in Paris. Barker-Mill then showed with LG, NEAC and several London galleries; worked on settings and associated figures for the film *Paper People Land*; was commissioned by Golden Cockerel Press, 1937–55, to make wood engravings for four books; in World War II was in the Civil Defence Camouflage Unit; then in 1944 joined the Ministry of Town and Country Planning Model Unit. Mural materials research occupied him in the 1950s, then from 1961–81 Barker-Mill did commissioned work. He pursued "the communicative power and potential of colour, its organisation upon a surface and in space" in his own abstract pictures. Had an important show at Arnolfini Gallery, Bristol, 1989, another at The Minories, Colchester, in 1991. Lived at Wookey Hole, Somerset, and died from a stroke in hospital in Bristol.

Harold BARKLAM 1912– Painter in oil and watercolour, and teacher, born in Tipton, Staffordshire. He attended Ryland Memorial School of Art, West Bromwich, Royal College of Art under Gilbert Spencer, 1933–6, then Birmingham College of Arts and Crafts, 1936–7. Apart from Army service, 1940–6, taught at schools of art in West Bromwich, Kidderminster, Bilston and Lowestoft, 1937–50, finally at Derby School of Art, 1950–76. Completed a number of mural paintings as well as pictures of stately homes for English Life Publications, Derby. Showed at Derby and Birmingham Art Galleries and elsewhere in Midlands. Lived at Littleover, Derby.

Roy BARLEY 1935– Painter of portraits and meticulous still lifes, the latter included in his shared show with Peter Kelly at Oakham Galleries Ltd in 2006. On leaving school, he trained at the London School of Printing and Graphic Art. During National Service, he designed a number of Royal Air Force badges in co-operation with the Royal College of Heraldry. After resuming his studies, Barley entered advertising; became art director of a leading London agency; and with a colleague began his own agency, counting leading agencies among the clients. He left advertising to paint and was commissioned for a number of portraits, including golfing stars such as Bobby Locke, Gary Player, Sandy Lyle and Tony Jacklin. Through Claus Grimm, met in 1985 when the German professor was compiling his book on Dutch still life painting, Barley became keen to learn their Old Master techniques. In 2001, his show of 21 paintings at the Barry Keene Gallery, Henley, sold out.

Elsie BARLING 1883–1976 Teacher, painter and draughtsman, born in Newnham, Gloucestershire. Little is known of her early life or training, and she appears to have been largely self-taught. Her father died when she was young and, now living in Broadstairs, Kent, she supported the family by teaching in schools. At Queen Bertha's School, Birchington, she and the pupils made a mural of the landing of Queen Bertha. John Craxton, taught by her at Betteshanger School, Eastry, in the early 1930s, called her "an inspired teacher". Pupils' work was shown at Bloomsbury Gallery in 1933 opened by Slade principal Henry Tonks, to national press acclaim. The main influence on Barling was Frances Hodgkins, whom she met at her class at Burford in 1923 and with whom she painted abroad. When World War II broke out Barling moved to Studland, Dorset, teaching at Bryanston School, 1940–3. Barling was a fine draughtsman rather than a notable Colourist, and was fond of working in gouache, as seen in her memorial show at Dorset Country Museum, Dorchester, in 1977.

Alan BARLOW 1926–2005 Theatre designer and director, teacher, painter and muralist, born in Coventry, Warwickshire, who several times won the Gold Medal of the Royal Drawing Society's Red Book scheme for children. He attended Coventry Art School and the Slade School of Fine Art and in 1949 won a European travel scholarship. As a boy Barlow developed a love of Shakespeare, directing his classmates and, aged 17, designed over 200 costumes for the Coventry Cathedral Pageant. After serving as designer at the new Bristol Old Vic, Barlow moved with Hugh Hunt, its director, to the London Old Vic, where his first work was Oliver Goldsmith's *She Stoops to Conquer*. In 1952 he designed the Royal Opera House production of Bellini's opera *Norma*, which introduced Maria Callas to British audiences. After designing the 1953 Robert Helpmann production of T S Eliot's *Murder in the Cathedral* at the Old Vic, starring Robert Donat, Barlow became a Benedictine monk at Prinknash Abbey, where he remained for 11 years, designing a set of Stations of the Cross for the monastery chapel and a tapestry for Glastonbury Church. Soon after leaving the monastery in 1965 he was offered a fellowship in drama at Manchester University, becoming head of design and lecturer in Greek theatre. While there, he designed for the Abbey Theatre, in Dublin. In 1969 Barlow became head of design at the National Theatre School of Canada, in Montreal, moving in 1971 to design for the Shakespeare Festival Theatre in Stratford, Ontario, where he was a success. A return to the Abbey Theatre as head of design and guest director encompassed his 1973 Irish Theatre Critics' Award-winning production of Harold Pinter's play *Old Times*. His next year was particularly outstanding, including his design of Shakespeare's *King Lear* for the Actors' Theatre Company, the New English Opera Company production of Benjamin Britten's comic opera *Albert Herring* at Aldeburgh and Machiavelli's *La Mandragola* in Rotterdam, being based in the Netherlands for most of the next three years. He returned to England to create a characteristically bold and effective set for the world première of John Tavener's opera *Thérèse* at Covent Garden, in 1979, the designs of which were bought by the Victoria & Albert Museum for the British Theatre Museum. Heart problems prompted Barlow's retirement to Norfolk, although in 1995 he did return to Stratford, Ontario, to design a successful production of Euripides' *The Bacchae*. Out of the theatre Barlow established a busy career as a painter, notable for his watercolours and depictions of the figure in movement, portraits and murals. He had solo exhibitions in London, Edinburgh, Lavenham, Ontario and in Norfolk, where in 2000 his design for a stained-glass window of the Annunciation was effected at the Roman Catholic Church of Our Lady of Pity in Swaffham. Barlow's pictures are in many private collections, including that of the Prince of Wales.

Bohuslav BARLOW 1947– Painter, born in Czechoslovakia, who moved to England aged eight. He eventually settled in Todmorden, Yorkshire. Gained honours degree from Central School of Art. Barlow's pictures featured situations such as playing, dreaming or floating, the characters in them being clowns and puppets based on real, life-size figures which he created. The world they inhabit is generally the stony architecture of the Pennines. He began showing with South-East London Art Group and RE in 1970 and went on to appear in numerous group exhibitions, including Hartnoll & Eyre, 1976; MAFA from 1982; Chalk Farm Gallery, 1984; and House of Commons, in a show of Calderdale Artists, 1987. Showed solo at Ginnel Gallery, Manchester, and Grundy Art Gallery, Blackpool, 1989. Rochdale Art Gallery and Museum and Leeds City Council hold his work.

Gillian BARLOW 1944– Watercolourist on paper and vellum, and teacher, noted for her paintings of flowers. She was born in Khartoum, Sudan, and gained a diploma in fine arts at Slade School of Fine Art, 1962–3, before studying with Quentin Bell and Hans Hess at University of Sussex, acquiring a bachelor's and master's degree in the history of art. Her work combined a personal freedom with scientific precision in the tradition of Bauer, Ehret and Redouté, the rose painter. She was sent to India by the British Council as visiting professor at Baroda University, also living in New York producing sets of flower paintings for interior decorators wanting the English look. Showed all over the world, with a solo exhibition, The Botanical Garden, at Spink & Son, 1995. The previous year Barlow had gained the Royal Horticultural Society Gold Medal for painting. British Council; Boscobel Restoration and Vassar College, both in New York; and The Hunt Institute, Carnegie-Mellon University, Pittsburgh, hold examples.

Jeremy BARLOW 1945– Painter, notably of landscapes and townscapes in oil, born in Kettering, Northamptonshire, who studied at Northampton School of Art, 1960. Worked in art studios in London and Midlands, then in 1977 moved to Düsseldorf, Germany, and showed extensively in Germany and Netherlands, returning to live in England in 1983, settling in Norfolk. Mixed exhibitions included RI, RA Summer Exhibition and ROI, of which he was elected a full member in 1993. He served as a council member, 1995–9; won the Stanley Grimm Prize in 1994 and 2000; and the Alan Gourlay Memorial Prize in 1999. Had first solo exhibition at Mistral Galleries in 1994, previous one-mans including Bourne Gallery, Reigate, 1991, and Llewellyn Alexander, 1992. Barlow's exhibition at Bourne Gallery in 2004 was his fourth there and reflected his extensive travels. He spent about three months each year on the continent, in principal cities as well as small towns and villages. Public, corporate and private collections held his work.

Nic BARLOW 1951– Photographer who attended Bath Academy of Art, Corsham, "to study graphic design, already knowing that photography was to be my chosen profession." Finally he spent a year photographing life at Eton College, published as Eton College. *Vogue* in France saw it and ran some of the 200 photographs, prompting a decade of regular commissions to depict English life. Barlow's 20 years as a freelance photographer included work for *Harper's and Queen*, *Tatler*, *The Sunday Times Magazine* and a number of books. The advent of computer digital manipulation returned Barlow "to the ideal of producing images that express both an inner world and a view of the external. The new technology has opened up untold vistas". The result was Dreaming in Digital, a solo show at Rebecca Hossack Gallery, 1999.

Phyllida BARLOW 1944– Sculptor in a variety of media, printmaker and teacher. She was born in Newcastle upon Tyne, Northumberland, and studied at Chelsea School of Art, 1960–3, and Slade School of Fine Art, 1963–6, then returning to Chelsea and the Slade to teach. Early on she participated in group shows such as Young Contemporaries, LG, AIA and at Woodstock Gallery and Camden Arts Centre. In 1976 shared a two-man exhibition with Fabian Peake at St Catherine's College, Oxford. The considerable impression made on Barlow at Chelsea by sculpture tutor George Fullard was outlined by her in an address at the 1998 opening of his exhibition at the Mappin Gallery, Sheffield. Later exhibitions included Furniture, Richard Salmon, 1999 and 2002, and The British Art Show 5, Hayward Gallery tour, 2000–1. Baltic Centre for Contemporary Art, Gateshead, gave Barlow a solo show in 2004–5, Bloomberg Space featuring her Skit in 2005. Lived in London.

Sid BARLOW 1952– Painter, stained glass artist and teacher, born in Chile. He studied at Wolverhampton College of Art, 1972–5, Manchester Polytechnic, 1976–7, and Glasgow School of Art, 1984–5. Went on to teach stained glass at W R Tuson College, Preston. His group shows included Royal Glasgow Institute of the Fine Arts, 1985, MAFA, 1988, and in 1989–90 John Moores Liverpool Exhibition. Had a solo exhibition at Rochdale College of Art in 1987. Lived in Bolton, Lancashire.

Yvonne BARLOW fl. from 1950s– Painter who studied at Central School of Arts and Crafts, Chelsea School of Art and London University. Her work appeared in many mixed shows including RA, Paris Salon, Whitechapel Art Gallery, LG and at Christopher Hull Gallery, where she was given a solo exhibition in 1989. Lived in London.

Gwen BARNARD 1912–1988 Painter and printmaker who studied at Chelsea School of Art. She was for some time chairman of WIAC. As well as group shows she had many solo exhibitions, including AIA, Drian Gallery, Camden Arts Centre, Upper Street Gallery and abroad. Lived for many years in the famous Mall Studios, Hampstead. Her history of them appeared in the *Camden History Review*, in 1980. Barnard's work was originally naturalistic, but under the influence of a Polish painter friend in the 1940s she turned more towards abstraction, being at various times concerned with themes such as river and rock shapes.

Margaret BARNARD 1898–1992 Painter, draughtsman, lino-cut artist and designer, born in India, but moved to Scotland aged seven for schooling. Attended Glasgow School of Art, winnin two travelling scholarships and the Guthrie Award. She journeyed to Italy where she married fellow-student Robert Mackechnie. She loved the light of Italy and they decided that they could live cheaply in a small coastal town not far from Florence. Landscapes, done in Italy and on the Scottish west coast, especially lona, were a key feature of her output, signed MB in monogram form. Her lino-prints typified British graphic work of the 1920s/1930s, with clean lines and subtle colouring. Winter Cavalcade, 1938, and Leisure Days in the

Parks, 1939, were posters commissioned by London Underground. In 1994 there was a memorial show at Rye Art Gallery which holds her work. She lived in the Sussex town from 1934.

Mary B BARNARD fl. from c.1890–1946 Versatile painter, notably of flowers, who trained in Paris. She lived in the London area until a move to Glasgow and then to Oban, Argyll, where she lived for many years with her artist husband Duncan MacGregor Whyte. Barnard's exhibiting venues included Royal Glasgow Institute of the Fine Arts, RSA, RBA, ROI and Walker Art Gallery in Liverpool.

Rebecca BARNARD 1961– Painter, born to farming parents near Saffron Walden, Essex, whose work had nature as a central theme. After completing a foundation art course, she took a gap year that turned into six years' travelling. Returning to England, she studied mixed media at Heatherley's School of Fine Art. Exhibited widely and was included in the Summer Show at Enid Lawson Gallery, 2003.

Roger BARNARD 1951– Artist in variety of media, including set-ups, some including video; mixed-media installations; painting; sculpture; drawing; photography; holography; writing; and teaching, who was born and lived in London. He attended West Sussex College of Design, 1970–1, then graduated in fine art from North Staffordshire Polytechnic, 1971–4. From 1971–2 was engaged in use of holograms; 1976–8 lectured occasionally at Maidstone College of Art and Lanchester Polytechnic and was founder-member and first chairman of London Video Arts (Access); from 1980 being involved in Video Artists on Tour. Took part in mixed shows at Tate Gallery, Serpentine Gallery, Hayward Gallery and in provincial events. Had solo shows at Tate, Air Gallery, Third Eye Centre in Edinburgh, Royal Cornwall Museum in Truro and elsewhere. That museum and Contemporary Art Centre in Osaka, Japan, hold his work.

Thomas Henslow BARNARD 1898– Painter, printmaker and teacher who studied at West of England College of Art, Bristol, having attended Malvern College. He was commissioned as a Sandhurst-trained officer in the Army in both World Wars. Showed at RA, RWA to which he was elected in 1972 and NEAC. Ministry of Works and public galleries in Cheltenham and Gloucester held his work. Was a member of Cheltenham Group of Artists. Lived at Leckhampton, Gloucestershire.

Bruce BARNDEN 1925– Painter and teacher, born H Bruce Barnden, who was for a time head of Chichester School of Art. He exhibited at the RA Summer Exhibition, 1957–67, a picture in 1960 being worthy of reproduction in *The Daily Telegraph*. Barnden's 1961 painting Mill Near Midhurst, depicting Terwick Mill, near Rogate, which closed in 1966, is in the collection of Worthing Museum & Art Gallery. Lived at Cocking, Midhurst, Sussex.

Hugh BARNDEN 1946– Designer and painter, born Oxfordshire, who studied at Royal College of Art, 1968–71. Mixed shows included Crafts Centre from 1964; Eroticism in Fashion at ICA, 1976; London Fashion Designers at Victoria & Albert Museum, which holds his work, 1979; Wapping Artists Open Studios from 1980. Solo exhibitions included Francis Kyle, 1983. Lived for some years in London.

Alfred Richard Innott BARNES: *see* **INNOTT**

Ann BARNES 1951– Botanical artist using airbrush, and teacher, born in London, daughter of the watercolourist William Barnes. Attended Stockwell College of Education, Bromley, and graduated with honours. Showed with Free Painters and Sculptors, to which she was elected in 1974, NS and Society of Botanical Artists. Had a series of solo shows in Home Counties galleries. Lived in Ewell, Surrey.

Desmond BARNES 1921– Painter, commercial artist and printmaker who after several years' initial art training in Birmingham attended the College of Art there, 1936–42, under Bernard Fleetwood-Walker. He went on to show at RA, ROI, RWA, NEAC, in the provinces and at the Paris Salon, where he gained an Hon. Mention and bronze medal in the 1940s. Lived at Handsworth, Birmingham, then in London.

Garlick BARNES 1891–1987 Artist in oil and watercolour, born in London, who showed an early talent but had to defer painting while she brought up four children. She then studied at Sidney Cooper School of Art in Canterbury, Heatherley's School of Fine Art and in 1936 became Walter Sickert's pupil when they were both living in Thanet. She showed a Sickert-influenced picture, La Ballerina, in an exhibition with him at E J Lovely & Sons Art Gallery, Margate. At the outbreak of World War II Barnes moved to Cornwall, where she became a member of the St Ives and Newlyn Societies and a founder-member of the Penwith Society of Arts. She continued to paint, garden and write poetry into her eighties. Barnes' twin sons John and Bill were keen film-makers and students of the cinema, for over 20 years from the mid-1960s running a museum on the subject in St Ives. John Barnes published several volumes on the history of the Victorian cinema.

George William BARNES 1909– Painter, sculptor, printmaker and designer, born in Boothstown, Lancashire. Studied at Huddersfield School of Art, 1925–36. Showed with Huddersfield Art Society, which gave him a one-man show, and with Saddleworth Art Club, being a member of both. Lived in Marsden, West Yorkshire.

Jeannette BARNES 1961– Draughtsman, painter and teacher, born in Great Harwood, Lancashire, and studied at Accrington and Rossendale Foundation College; Liverpool Polytechnic; Royal Academy Schools; and Royal College of Art. She taught at Liverpool Polytechnic, 1984–9; was artist-in-residence at Northampton School for Boys, 1990–1; then became outreach teacher for the RA's education department. Among her awards were a John Moores Scholarship, 1983; Armitage Prize, 1985; Richard Ford Spanish Scholarship, 1987; and she was a Drawings for All prizewinner in 1994. Mixed shows included RA Summer Exhibition from 1986; NEAC, 1991; and Royal Over-Seas League Open from 1992. Had a solo show at Blackburn College of Art, 1984.

Mary BARNES 1923–2001 Artist, poet, writer, nurse and mental health campaigner who for much of her life struggled against mental illness. Born in Portsmouth, Hampshire, Barnes trained as a nurse, joined the Army as a nursing sister and served in Egypt and Palestine before returning to London hospitals. She suffered her first breakdown in 1952, was diagnosed schizophrenic, but was released and worked as a nursing tutor. A devout Catholic, she applied to study for a nursing education master's degree at the National Catholic University, Washington, but the American Embassy in London blocked this, citing her mental condition. When that made it impossible for her to work, she had regression therapy with Joseph Berke and discovered a gift for painting, initially using her own excrement, then oils. Her canvases, vividly colourful, often with religious imagery, were first shown at Camden Arts Centre, 1969. Barnes then assisted Berke and showed her work worldwide, usually with a talk on mental health and her experiences. In 1985, she moved to Scotland, settling in Tomintoul, Grampian; developed spinal arthritis, confining her to a wheelchair; but continued to paint, write and travel. *Mary Barnes: Two Accounts of a Journey Through Madness*, by Barnes and Berke (adapted for the stage by David Edgar) appeared in 1971, her own *Something Sacred* in 1989.

Maurice BARNES 1911–1971 Painter, draughtsman and noted watercolourist, born in Swansea. He was educated in Newport, Monmouthshire, and spent his life there, studying at the local College of Art, Croydon School of Art and with William Watkins. His career was with British Rail, but his two main preoccupations were painting and the Church of Wales. Barnes was a founder-member, chairman and president of Newport Art and Crafts Society, also exhibiting at NEAC, RA, Royal National Eisteddfod, Paris Salon and elsewhere. CASW holds his work, also Newport Museum & Art Gallery, which in 1997 gave Barnes a retrospective, which concentrated on pictures of Newport, St Woolos' Cathedral and Christchurch and St John the Baptist, both severely damaged by fire in 1948.

Melanie BARNES 1966– Artist who worked in mixed media who studied at Leicester and Liverpool Polytechnics. She showed at Fouts and Fowler, Design Association, Association of Illustrators and was included in Art in Boxes at England & Co, 1991.

Pauline Margaret BARNES: *see* **Pauline Margaret BEILBY**

Robert Henry BARNES 1899–1979 Painter who spent much of his life in Surrey after living in London. He showed at Royal Glasgow Institute of the Fine Arts, RBA, Walker Art Gallery in Liverpool and from 1924–53 at RA, latterly having a studio at Bridgnorth, Shropshire. Simon Carter Gallery, Woodbridge, included a typical portrait, Jean, in a mixed show in April 1992.

Ross BARNES 1962– Constructionist/printmaker whose work displayed wit and social comment. He was born at Castallack, Lamorna, Cornwall, eventually having a studio at The Penwith Gallery, St Ives. Barnes began showing at Salthouse Gallery in St Ives from 1990 and joined the Penwith Society of Arts as an associate member. Completed a two-year course in general art and design at Falmouth School of Art, 1991–3, then studied for honours degree in fine art at Canterbury. Further exhibitions included From Cornwall, Art and Inspiration, Anderson Gallery, Broadway, and self-portrait exhibition at Porthmeor Gallery, St Ives, both 1992; New Work, at Rainyday Gallery, Penzance, 1993; and St Ives at David Holmes Contemporary Art, Peterborough, 1996. In 1993 shared an exhibition with David Pearce at Salthouse Gallery.

William BARNES 1916– Watercolour artist and designer, he was born in London and studied art at Camberwell and Wimbledon Schools of Arts and Crafts. He took part in mixed shows at the RI, RWS, RBA, PS and NS and held one-man exhibitions in Croydon, Ealing, Guildford, Leatherhead and Richmond and elsewhere in southeast England. The City of London, Massey Fergusson and the London Goldhawk Building Society own his work and he illustrated *In Britain* for the British Tourist Authority. Lived in London.

Christine BARNETT 1963– Artist in gouache, pen and ink and watercolour. She studied at Gloucestershire College of Arts and Technology, then at West Surrey College of Art and Design where she obtained an honours degree in fine art – painting, 1983–6, being a research fellow, 1987–8. She began to show in mixed exhibitions in 1985 at Whitworth Young Contemporaries, Manchester. After many more appearances she was shown at the Bath Contemporary Art Fair, the Glyndebourne Festival and the 20th Century British Art Fair in 1992, when Marsden Fine Art gave her a solo show at Smith's of Covent Garden. Work included still lifes, often using primary colours and introducing mystical elements, dancing figures and symbolic birds. Lived in Pershore, Worcestershire.

Henry BARNETT 1916– Landscape painter and illustrator who studied at Cheltenham Art School and at the Royal Academy Schools under Thomas Monnington and Walter Westley Russell. Exhibited at RA from mid-1930s. Lived at Isleworth, Middlesex.

John BARNETT 1914– Self-taught painter, born in Manchester, who attended evening classes at Heginbottom School of Art, Ashton-under-Lyne, in textile design. As a painter he was drawn "to the urban landscape of my childhood". Showed at MAFA and elsewhere in north of England. Manchester City Art Gallery holds his oil on canvas Old House, Cheltenham. Lived in Droylsden, Lancashire.

May BARNETT: *see* **Alice May COOK**

Olaf BARNETT 1911– Painter, art dealer and private teacher, born in London. He was educated at Oxford University, studying art at the Ruskin School of Drawing and at the Slade School of Fine Art, his teachers including Randolph Schwabe and Barnett Freedman. He ran the Collectors' Gallery in London and Drusilla's Collectors' Gallery at Alfriston, Sussex. Showed RA, RBA, NS of which he was a member, on the continent and in North America. Towner Art Gallery, Eastbourne, holds his work. Lived in London, then in Seaford, Sussex.

Walter Durac BARNETT 1876– Painter, born in Leeds, where he attended the School of Art, also Wrexham and Lambeth Schools of Art, the latter under Innes Fripp, 1896–1900, where he won a medal and scholarship. During World War I served in Artists' Rifles. Exhibited RA, RP, ROI, NS, Goupil Gallery and in the provinces. Was a member of the Artists of Chelsea, a group living in or connected with that part of London. Cartwright Hall Art Gallery, Bradford, holds his work. Lived in London.

Catherine BARNEZET fl. from 1980s– Painter, printmaker, sculptor, photographer and installations artist, educated in England and France, who during the 1970s trained in beadwork, metalwork and paintwork and black-and-white photography; in 1980 gaining a playleader certificate at the Camden Institute; a certificate in arts, education and artistic therapy at Rudolph Steiner College, Fair Oaks, California, 1989; did an access foundation in art and design at Falmouth School of Art, 1993; then gained an honours degree in fine art at Plymouth University, 1996. Exhibited at Summer Show, Cabrillo Arts Center, Santa Barbara, 1985; Annual Show, Sacramento Fine Art Center Gallery, California, 1989; Aspires, Sherwell Centre, Plymouth, 1995; and Unquiet Voices, Doncaster Museum & Art Gallery, 1997. Lived in Exminster, Devon.

Denis BARNHAM 1920– Painter, draughtsman, writer and teacher, born in Feltham, Middlesex. Studied at Royal Academy Schools with Sir Walter Westley Russell, 1936–9. At end of World War II showed with war artists at National Gallery; also showing at RA, RBA, Leicester Galleries, NEAC and elsewhere. Imperial War Museum holds his work. Taught art for some years at Epsom College, in Surrey, and had strong interest in Oriental art. Lived in Epsom.

Nicholas BARNHAM 1939– Artist in watercolour and relief printing, and teacher, born in Walsingham, Norfolk. He studied painting and stone carving at Norwich School of Art, 1954–60, teachers including Jeffrey Camp and Malcolm Andrews. At various times Barnham lived in Shetland (where he eventually settled at Uyeasound, Unst, from 1984), Essex, Norfolk and north Yorkshire, as he favoured the east coast for his on-the-spot landscapes. In 1967–73 Barnham taught at Cambridge School of Art. Boats and trees were key themes in Barnham's very linear work, with early Mondrian, Edward Bawden, William Blake and Samuel Palmer strong influences. Showed at RA, RE and in Germany and had series of shows at Thackeray Gallery, The Old Fire Engine House, Ely, and at The Shetland Museum Gallery, Lerwick. Collections including his work were those of Cambridgeshire County Council, the musicians Richard Rodney Bennett and Christopher Hogwood, Somerville College, Oxford, and Marks and Spencer.

John BARNICOAT 1924– Painter, administrator and teacher. After World War II service in the Navy, Barnicoat studied history at Oxford University. He was a student at Royal College of Art, 1952–5, then was senior tutor there in the painting school, 1976–80, where he was very influential. He had his first one-man show at Galerie Colette Allendy, in Paris, in 1959. Was included in the Royal College of Art Exhibition Road show in 1988. Lived in London.

Denis BARNS 1946– Mural painter, sculptor, teacher and town art adviser, born in Kirkcaldy, Fife. Studied at Glasgow School of Art for a diploma in mural design, 1964–8, then did a year's post-diploma course. Taught in secondary schools in Dunbartonshire until appointment as town artist to Livingston Development Corporation, 1974. A wide range of artists, including Ian Hamilton Finlay, William Tucker and Andrew Mylius, plus members of the community were engaged by Barns, who in 1979 had received so many offers of work that he resigned his post and set up Town Art & Design Ltd. Barns was then a consultant to many United Kingdom local authorities, also working for Middle Eastern municipalities. Barns' work was collected by Glasgow University, Edinburgh Corporation, Girvan Town Council and private collections, documented work being held in the Tate Gallery and Victoria & Albert Museum.

Wilhelmina BARNS-GRAHAM 1912–2004 Painter and teacher, born in St Andrews, Fife. She attended Edinburgh College of Art, 1932–7, having a studio in the Scottish capital, 1936–40. William Gillies and David Foggie were important teachers. On her quizzing Foggie as to whether or not she would ever be any good as an artist, he replied gruffly: "Come and see me in 20 years and tell me if you're still painting." In 1940 Barns-Graham pursued an Andrew Grant post-graduate travelling scholarship and went to live in St Ives, Cornwall, which with St Andrews remained her base. There she joined the Newlyn Society of Artists, the St Ives Society of Artists and became a founder-member of the Penwith Society in 1949. She had known Margaret Mellis in Edinburgh and now became friends with Ben Nicholson, Barbara Hepworth and Naum Gabo. A key influence was a visit to Switzerland in 1948, where she fell in love with glaciers as a subject, their transparency combined with their roughness. Took up an Italian Government Travelling Scholarship in 1955 which produced another impressive body of work emphasising her incisive draughtsmanship. Taught at Leeds School of Art, 1956–7, then from 1961–3 had studio in London before returning to St Ives. At an early age she had drawn abstracts in coloured chalks, diverse aspects of geometrical and gestural abstraction and landscape were to be explored through constantly inventive career of Barns-Graham, known widely as Willie. She exhibited at Downing's Bookshop, St Ives, in a solo show in 1947 and 1949 and showed steadily after that, selected venues being Roland, Browse and Delbanco; Richard Demarco Gallery, Edinburgh; New Art Centre; and Pier Arts Centre, Stromness. Tate Gallery held three survey exhibitions, in 1977, 1985 and 1986; there were major retrospective shows at Newlyn Art Gallery, 1989–90 and William Jackson Gallery, 1992–3, both touring; in 1999 Tate Gallery St Ives put on an important themed exhibition; and in 2002–3 Crawford Arts Centre, St Andrews, toured the show Painting as Celebration. Art First held a tribute show in 2004, Tate St Ives another covering her life and work, 2005, and Art First in 2006 Important Works from Her Career, selected from The Barns-Graham Charitable Trust. Arts Council and Scottish National Gallery of Modern Art hold her work. In 1949, Barns-Graham married the writer and critic David Lewis, with Peter Lanyon as best man. She and Lewis had an amicable divorce in 1963 and he subsequently moved to America.

Leofric BARON 1957–2000 Self-taught, Outsider artist born in Eastwood, Essex, whose work had a highly individual, cartoonish quality. Baron suffered from epilepsy and schizophrenia. In 1979, he moved to the Barrington Farm and Rookery residential centre for adults with learning and behavioural problems at Walcott, in remote Norfolk, run by Janith Homes, who recognised the value of art therapy. Baron, a reserved man, showed at the Barrington Farm's St Brannocks gallery, in nearby Mundesley, also elsewhere in East Anglia, in London and New York and was represented in America by the Marion Harris Gallery, Connecticut. Although reserved, Baron could be drawn to enthuse about his art, by which he could "make a circle then make it any face you like. With paint I can make a violin into a whale. I can take a trombone and make it into something totally different". St Brannocks held a memorial show in 2000, at which Baron's first artist's book, *A Strong Wind in Broadway Tennessee*, was available. Died in Norwich.

Ian BARR 1946– Painter and administrator, born in Glasgow, where he graduated from the School of Art and where he continued to live. He became director of the Scottish Consultative Council on the Curriculum. Barr showed widely in Scandinavia and Scotland, producing some abstract work. He had solo shows at Compass Gallery in 1973 and 1977 and his work is in Scottish Arts Council and other public and private collections.

Shona BARR 1965– Painter in oil and watercolour who employed brilliant colour and fluent handling of paint. Born in Glasgow, she graduated from the School of Art there, 1984–8; won a postgraduate scholarship, Statens Kunstakademi, Oslo, Norway, 1988–9; and obtained her master's in European fine art from Winchester School of Art (Barcelona) and Southampton University, 1991–2. Awards included Glasgow School Landscape Prize, 1987; Armour Prize for Still Life, 1988; David Cargill Award at Royal Glasgow Institute of the Fine Arts, 1989; and Superior Prize, "Small Paintings, Great Harmony" Exhibition, Nakano, Japan, 1998. Took part in extensive group shows, including Compass Gallery, Glasgow, from 1988; RSW from 1989; RSA from 1990; and RA from 1995. Had a series of solo exhibitions with Flying Colours Gallery from 1989. Lillie Art Gallery in Milngavie and a number of corporate collections hold examples.

Steven Thomas BARRACLOUGH 1953–1987 Printmaker, born in Batley, Yorkshire, where he attended the School of Art, 1969–71; then Camberwell School of Arts and Crafts, 1971–4; and Slade School of Fine Arts, 1974–5. In 1981, Barraclough obtained a one-year fellowship, in etching and lithography, at Manchester Print Workshop, University of Salford; in 1983 was printmaker-in-residence, Arts Council of Northern Ireland; in 1985 being invited for a three-month visit to China by the Minister of Culture, attending Central Academy of Fine Arts Beijing, Hangzhou and Canton Academy. Group exhibitions included RA, from 1974; Leeds City Art Gallery, 1977; Whitworth Art Gallery, Manchester, 1982; Exhibition of Hand Made Paper, Thumb Gallery, 1985; and Dolan Maxwell Gallery, Philadelphia, 1988. Showed with Angela Flowers Gallery from 1979. Victoria & Albert Museum; Museum of Modern Art, New York; Arts Councils of Ireland and Northern Ireland; Leeds Education Authority, and other public and corporate collections hold examples.

Paul BARRAND 1959– Painter who was born in Chesterfield, Derbyshire. He studied at the Polytechnics of Sheffield, 1977–8, Liverpool, 1978–81 and Leicester, 1981–2. He appeared in the Night and Day show in Leicester, 1984, and Metroland, at Loseby Gallery in Leicester, the same year. In 1984–5 Barrand's work was included in Midland View 3, and his landscape canvas Goodbye appeared in the 1987 John Moores Liverpool Exhibition. Lived in Leicester.

Elizabeth BARRATT 1956– Painter and teacher, born in London. She studied at Byam Shaw School of Art, 1974–6, won a David Murray Studentship in 1978, did a postgraduate course at Royal Academy Schools, 1978–81, winning the Henfield Foundation Award in 1980, the Boise Travelling Scholarship, to Italy, in 1981. She taught under a fellowship at Gloucestershire College of Art and Design, 1981–2, then in the latter year the Elizabeth Greenshields Award took her to Italy again. From 1985 taught occasionally at Byam Shaw. Barratt showed in National Portrait Gallery John Player Exhibition in 1984, at the RA from the same year, and a group show at Argile Gallery in 1988, the year she shared an exhibition at Brunel Gallery.

Kenneth BARRATT 1924– Painter, sometimes in semi-abstract style, illustrator, printmaker and teacher. Born in London, he attended East Ham Grammar School, where he initially became interested in painting, then Sir John Cass School of Arts and Crafts under Bainbridge Copnall. Showed at RA, NS, SGA and RI. Lived in London.

Krome BARRATT 1924–1990 Painter, teacher and writer, full name Kenneth Krome Barratt, who signed some work Krome. He studied civil engineering at West Ham College of Technology and art at Sir John Cass College, 1947–51. Was principal lecturer at Polytechnic of North London, lectured on history and technology of painting and was also an engineering designer. Work included abstracts, seascapes and landscapes. Published *Logic and Design* in 1980. Barratt was president of NS and ROI, a member of RBA, showing also at RA and overseas galleries. Had solo shows at Drian Galleries and AIA. Towner Art Gallery, Eastbourne, holds his work. Lived in Hockley, Essex.

Mychael BARRATT 1961– Artist-printmaker and illustrator producing witty, colourful works, born in Toronto, Ontario, Canada, who attended the Symposium School of Art, Winnipeg, then graduated in fine art from Nova Scotia College of Art and Design, Halifax; after he arrived in London in 1984 he worked as a freelance illustrator, studied etching at Central St Martins School of Art and became a full-time printmaker in 1991. As well as working for the department store Liberty, Barratt's work was included in *Images* and the *Encyclopaedia of Printmaking Techniques*. Took part in numerous group exhibitions in Britain and abroad, including National Print Exhibitions at Mall Galleries. Solo exhibitions included Chalk Farm Gallery; Royal Exchange Theatre, Manchester; Dales Gallery, Victoria, Canada; and Cambridge Arts Theatre, Cambridge. Barratt was a member of RE, the Federation of Canadian Artists and the Greenwich and South Bank Printmakers' Associations.

Oliver BARRATT 1962– Sculptor, draughtsman and teacher who obtained his bachelor's degree with honours in sculpture at Falmouth School of Art, 1983–5. He then taught at a Care home for mentally handicapped adults from 1986, at Streete Court School in Surrey, 1988–90, pre-foundation sculpture at Canterbury College, 1991–2, then first-year sculpture at Kent Institute of Art and Design, Canterbury, from 1992. He was Henry Moore Fellow there in 1991–2 and had an exhibition of his work in 1992. Barratt had a two-man show at The Pine Gallery in Tunbridge Wells, 1988; at Winchester Cathedral, 1989, King's Walk Gallery, 1991; *Economist* Building Plaza in 1992, represented by the New Art Centre; and in the same year at Roche Court, Salisbury. Solo exhibition at Beardsmore Gallery, 2000 and 2003. In 2002, the gallery displayed The Everest Memorial, commissioned from Barratt by the Everest Memorial Trust, prior to its unveiling in 2003 in the Himalayas one day's walk from Everest Base Camp. Names of the 150 climbers killed attempting the summit were engraved within the two halves of the stainless steel split cone. His commissions included Fuller's Brewery at Russia Docks, 1988; Eastern Arts, a collaboration project, 1990; and National Power, a Landmark Sculpture Commission, in 1991. The artist wrote that the forms he made had "their origin in experience. They are deeply autobiographical and point to the undefined heart of an experience". Lived in Ightham, Kent.

Guitti BARRATT-DENYER 1942– Painter in oil, also known as Guitti, born in Paris. He studied at University of Western Australia, 1980–4, showed in Western Australia and returned to London in 1985. Also trained under William Ware while living at Burwash Common, East Sussex. Was a member of Ridley and Chelsea Art Societies and showed at Hurlingham, New King's Road and Edith Grove Galleries.

Ronald BARRAUD 1906– Painter and architect who studied at the Welsh School of Architecture, 1925–8. Exhibited RA, NEAC, UA and in the provinces. Lived at Wollaton, Nottinghamshire.

Christopher BARRETT 1954– Artist and teacher using oil for easel pictures, acrylic for murals, specialising in these for hospitals from 1987. He was born in London and graduated in fine art painting from Bath Academy of Art, 1972–5. He taught at Banbury School of Art, 1980–90, then Rycotewood College, Thame, 1986–90. Was artist-in-residence, Chastleton House, Oxfordshire, 1989, and in 1992–3 at Furness General Hospital, Barrow-in-Furness. Was a designer for Dunford Wood hand-painted silk, 1991–2. Group shows included A Century of Art in Oxford, Museum of Modern Art, Oxford, 1993, Christie's, 1994, and Banbury Museum and Woodstock Museum, 1996. Solo exhibitions included Manor House Gallery, Chipping Norton, 1989. Murals included Wokingham Hospital, Berkshire, 1987; John Radcliffe Hospital, Oxford, 1993; Royal Free Hospital, 1995–6; and Leeds General Infirmary, 1997. Institute of Education holds Barrett's work. Lived in Lower Brailes, Banbury, Oxfordshire.

Elsie May BARRETT 1913– Painter, born in Stoke-on-Trent, Staffordshire. After local education she attended St Martin's School of Art under Harold Workman and City & Guilds School of Art, her teachers including Bernard Adams and A R Middleton Todd. Was elected to Royal Glasgow Institute of the Fine Arts and belonged to Free Painters and Sculptors; showed with Harpenden Arts Club, St Albans Art Club; won a number of overseas awards. Lived in Harpenden, Hertfordshire.

Max BARRETT 1937–1997 Sculptor and carver who was born in Penzance, Cornwall. He worked as a steeplejack and as a steel erector, then began sculpting full-time in 1972. His Gentle Wave at Land's End was commissioned by the St Ives Festival Committee in 1982. Barrett's work was included in Artists from Cornwall at RWA in 1992. Later completed a large granite sculpture outside Sainsbury's store in Truro, Cornwall, and lived in the county at Hayle. Had a solo show at The Acorn Theatre, Penzance, 1996. Barrett, who came from old Cornish and gypsy stock, was an uncompromising character, scornful of the orthodox artistic community, its committees and organisations, and this meant his sculpting career was not always smooth. Yet he was a deeply spiritual man who, commonly inspired by music, and using often unpromising materials, strove "to channel the beauty of life through my work".

Oliver O'Connor BARRETT 1908–1987 Sculptor, teacher, poet and composer, born in London, brother of the artist Roderic Barrett. He was educated at the Royal Grammar School, Colchester, and Fircroft College, Birmingham. He showed at RA and had a solo show at Cooling Galleries prior to World War II, then moved to America, 1940–70, where he supported himself and his family as a freelance sculptor and part-time teacher. Teaching positions included Museum of Modern Art, Brooklyn Museum and Cooper Union, in New York, as well as Norton Museum, Palm Beach. He also wrote for and presented a series of programmes on art for the NBC television channel. Additional appearances at RA took place at Summer Exhibitions when he had returned to England from America. Also in his life he showed in Birmingham, Colchester, New Orleans, New York, Palm Beach and Potsdam. Among his notable works are Christ and the Money Changers, 1949; Don Quixote's Deathbed, 1952; and Madonna and Child, 1953. Colchester Public Library and Hudson Walker Gallery hold his work, which is in many private collections in Britain and America. In 1980 the artist published a photographic record of his work with accompanying poems called *Myself Emerging*. Lived for some years in Colchester, Essex, later at Cwm Prysor, Trawsfynydd, Gwynedd.

Roderic BARRETT 1920–2000 Painter, draughtsman and teacher, brother of the sculptor Oliver O'Connor Barrett, born and lived in Colchester, Essex. He studied at Central School of Arts and Crafts, teachers including Bernard Meninsky, John Farleigh and William Roberts, 1936–40. Began teaching in 1947, from 1968 being tutor at Royal Academy Schools. As an artist Barrett strove "to make works which are well made and without false feeling". Barrett's pictures, using a muted palette, were sometimes completed over several years, could be subject to reworking and were notable for the meticulous placing of objects and people within them. Barrett was a member of Colchester Art Society and took part in its Fifty Years Anniversary Exhibition at Chappel Galleries, Chappel, in 1996. Other group shows included LG; Wildenstein; RA; Piccadilly and Mercury Galleries; Roland, Browse & Delbanco and widely overseas. Solo shows included Beaux Arts Gallery from 1954; Minories, Colchester, from 1962; Alwin Gallery from 1966; Oxford Gallery, Oxford, from 1971; Mansion House, Ipswich, 1987; retrospective at Barbican Centre and Minories, 1996; an eightieth birthday show at Chappel Galleries, 2000; and Celebrating Man: Remembering Roderic Barrett, University of Essex, 2002. In 2003, there was an exhibition at Chappel Galleries and launch of David Buckman's profusely illustrated biography of the artist, including a thorough catalogue of pictures. Another followed at The Millinery Works in 2004. Victoria & Albert Museum and many provincial galleries hold Barrett's work.

Sylvia BARRETT: *see* **Sylvia FRANCIS**

Tom BARRETT fl. from mid-1950s– Painter and teacher who studied at Norwich Art School, 1954–5, then at Reading University fine art department, 1955–9. After teaching in various colleges from 1959–62, Barrett was appointed lecturer in fine art at Reading University in 1963. In 1962 he had co-founded Gallery 5 in Reading, which mounted many exhibitions over three years. In 1975 Barrett moved to Dorset, where the area around Lulworth became a central feature of his work, which employed a light palette and often primary colours, while continuing to teach at Reading. Among Barrett's mixed exhibitions were Reading Museum and Art Gallery, AIA Gallery, LG and Graves Art Gallery, Sheffield. One-man shows included Centre for Visual Arts, Cheltenham, in 1981; and Austin/Desmond Fine Art, Sunninghill, 1990.

Alan BARRETT-DANES 1935–2004 Ceramist, whose wife Ruth was also an artist. They created individual pieces hand-modelled and moulded in porcelain, sometimes with the addition of hand-thrown units. Limited editions of work were developed around a central theme. Examples were Cabbage Kingdoms III & IV, shown in Recent Purchases, for CASW, a WAC touring show, 1979. Exhibitions also included New Directions in Ceramics, Oxford Gallery, 1973; Newport Museum & Art Gallery, 1980; Westminster Gallery, Boston, America, 1982. National Museum of Wales, Cardiff; public galleries in Birmingham, Newport, Portsmouth and Southampton; Ulster Museum, Belfast; and Perth and Melbourne public galleries in Australia hold examples. Lived in Abergavenny, Gwent.

Anna BARRIBALL 1972– Artist, born in Plymouth, Devon, who made foundation studies, Falmouth School of Art, 1991–2; graduated with honours in fine art from Winchester School of Art, 1992–5; and gained her master's at Chelsea College of Art, 1999–00. In 2003, she had a solo exhibition at Arnolfini, Bristol, part of Recognition: Part One, for emerging British artists. This featured Barriball's drawings, which arose from interactions with everyday objects and often resulted "in the transformation of the familiar". Her other exhibitions included Works on Paper, The Brooks Centre, Winchester, 1995; New Contemporaries 2000, Milton Keynes Gallery, 2000; Drawings, Frith Street Gallery, and The (Ideal) Home Show, Gimpel Fils, both 2001; and Still Life in Contemporary British Art, British Council tour, 2002–3. In 2004, Frith Street Gallery showed Barriball's new sculpture and drawing and there was a solo exhibition at the Gasworks Gallery in 2005. She was based in Berlin, Germany.

Mardie BARRIE 1931– Painter and teacher, born in Kirkcaldy, Fife. She studied at Edinburgh University and Edinburgh College of Art, 1948–53, and went on to teach at Broughton High School in Edinburgh, where she lived. Barrie, an exuberant painter and Colourist, showed in many group exhibitions in Britain and abroad, notably in the Scottish Arts Council's show Painters in Parallel. In 1963 she had a solo show at Douglas and Foulis Gallery in Edinburgh, with another three years later. She then showed regularly, notably at Scottish Gallery in Edinburgh and Bruton Gallery, Somerset. Many public galleries hold her work, including Glasgow and Laing Art Gallery in Newcastle upon Tyne; a number of Scottish Education authorities; Scottish Arts Council; and HRH The Duke of Edinburgh. Was an RSW member.

Jim BARRINGTON: *see* **Jim GILBERT**

John BARRINGTON 1920–1991 Sculptor, artist, photographer and writer, born as John Engljahringer in London, where he finally lived. Studied at St Martin's School of Art and École des Beaux-Arts, in Paris, where Barrington was friendly with Jean Cocteau. After World War II Barrington engaged in theatre and film journalism; mounted theatrical productions; wrote novels prompted by his friend the theatre critic James Agate; and began taking professional photographs of male nudes, the subjects of many of his sculptures. Barrington's interest in the nude evinced itself in books such as *Art and Anatomy* and *A Camera Life Class* and in contributions to magazines such as *Male Model Monthly*. His autobiography *Inside My Skull* was based on extensive diaries.

June BARRINGTON-WARD 1922–2002 Sculptor and draughtsman, born in London, sister of the painter Susan Barrington-Ward. Their father was the surgeon Sir Lancelot Barrington-Ward whose four brothers all distinguished themselves, R M Barrington-Ward becoming editor of *The Times*. June served as a driver in the Women's Royal Naval Service, 1940–6, and read social sciences at the London School of Economics. Ran a youth club in Bethnal Green for Save the Children Fund to pay her art school fees. Studied sculpture at Regent Street Polytechnic and Chelsea School of Art, teachers including Willi Soukop, Bernard Meadows and Elisabeth Frink, and metalwork with British Oxygen. Figures in welded mild steel, bronzes and pieces which had "a kinship with the Expressionist sculpture of Zadkine and other Eastern Europeans" were among Barrington-Ward's output. Group shows included RA Summer Exhibition, LG, SPS of which she was a member, RSA, Paris Salon and John Moores Liverpool Exhibition. Shared an exhibition with her sister at Gainsborough's House, Sudbury, 1970. Solo shows included Embankment Gallery, 1979. Leicester County Council, Greater London Council and many private collectors in Britain and abroad acquired her work. Signed her drawings JBW, although her sculptures are often unsigned. Had studios at 15 Walpole Gardens in Chiswick and at Castlemawgan, Lanreath, Cornwall.

Susan BARRINGTON-WARD 1919–1995 Painter, draughtsman and teacher, born in London, daughter of the surgeon Sir Lancelot Barrington-Ward and sister of the sculptor June Barrington-Ward. Susan studied at the Regent Street Polytechnic under Norman Blamey and in Munich, Germany. Taught part-time at Colchester County High School, 1966–72, full-time at Hedingham School, Essex, 1972–82, then retired. Showed with NS, NEAC and LG. Exhibited with her sister at Gainsborough's House, Sudbury, 1970. Her solo shows were at The Minories, Colchester, 1961; Gainsborough's House, 1966; The Quay Theatre, Sudbury, 1985; and Century Galleries, Henley-on-Thames, 1987. Signed her work BW. Died at home in Lamarsh, Essex.

David BARRON 1938– Painter and teacher, born in London. After education at Wells House and Oundle Schools Barron attended St Martin's School of Art and Goldsmiths' College School of Art. He took up teaching in 1959 and during the 1960s was at Chester School of Art and Swansea College of Art, from the early 1970s taking over the foundation course at Swansea. Was a member of RCamA and frequent exhibitor there. Lived in Swansea.

Gladys BARRON fl. from c.1905–1967 Sculptor and painter, born in India, who initially showed under her maiden name Gladys Logan. She studied with the sculptor Gertrude Bayes and at St John's Wood Art School and became noted for her portrait busts. Showed at Walker Art Gallery in Liverpool, RSA and RA and lived in Inverness.

Howard BARRON 1900–1991 Painter and draughtsman, born in Sidcup, Kent, who was educated at Christ's Hospital, Horsham. In Sydney, Australia, studied with Will Ashton, 1928–49, and is widely represented in Australian collections, including Imperial War Museum, Canberra. Back in England studied with Robin Guthrie and Ralph Middleton Todd at City and Guilds Art School, 1950–1, and showed at ROI, Fine Art Society and St Ives Society of Artists, of which he was a member. Lived for some years at Copthorne, Sussex.

Jenny BARRON 1951– Painter and illustrator who trained and worked as a textile designer at the Central School, worked in that field, then from 1985 starting to exhibit watercolours, botanical subjects important. Joined the Society of Botanical Artists and won a Royal Horticultural Society Gold Medal. The work of Spanish still-life artists was an inspiration. Barron developed her own technique, similar to the glazing process used in oil by the Old Masters, building up layers of watercolour until a dense effect was achieved. Shadow was a key element, as in Still Life with Artichoke, 1996, shown in Old & New, Wolseley Fine Arts at The Gallery in Cork Street, 2001, and Teacup and Shells, same dealer and venue, 2002.

Julian BARROW 1939– Painter, adept at catching the spirit of a place, who travelled widely. He was born in Longtown, Cumberland, and studied at RWA and Signorina Simi's Academy in Florence, Italy. Was a full member of Chelsea Arts Club, living nearby, and from 1988 was president of Chelsea Art Society. Group shows included RA Summer Exhibition, 1961–99; Paris Salon, 1965; and NEAC, 2002. Had solo exhibitions at Hazlitt, Gooden and Fox 1972–74–77; Morton Morris & Co, 1982–85; Leger Gallery, 1989–92–95; and Fine Art Society 1999–02, plus many others in America and the Middle East. Works held by House of Lords; Honourable Artillery Company; Royal Artillery, Woolwich; the Vintners' and Grocers' Companies; and private collections around the world.

Francis BARRY 1883–1970 Painter and printmaker whose full name was Sir Claude Francis Barry, Bart. Born in London, he was educated at Harrow School, then studied art in Newlyn, Cornwall, with Stanhope Forbes, also being a pupil of Sir Alfred East. Showed at RA, NEAC, RBA of which he was a member, Paris Salon and elsewhere. Sir Francis lived in St Ives, Cornwall, later in Val Plaisant, Jersey, in Channel Islands. There was a retrospective at Collyer-Bristow in 2004.

Jo BARRY 1944– Printmaker, watercolourist, draughtsman and teacher who graduated in fine art from Ravensbourne College of Art and Design. She was a visiting lecturer at Byam Shaw School until 1981, then gave up teaching to concentrate on her own work. Was elected a fellow of RE, of which she was hon. secretary and vice-president. Showed widely in the United Kingdom, including the RA Summer Exhibition, and in America, and solo at New Academy Gallery, 2001, 2003 and 2004. The English countryside, especially the New Forest where she lived, inspired her work.

James BARTHOLOMEW fl. from early 1990s– Painter, son of a Lancashire mining surveyor, a background that prompted an early interest in industrial subjects, for which he won awards. Bartholomew gained an honours degree in graphic design from Leicester Polytechnic in 1992. In 1993, he won prizes in the Laing Art and National Mining Art Competitions, in 1994 a prize in the MAFA Open Exhibition and the Sir Peter Scott Memorial Prize for a Young Artist Under 25, organised by *The Artist* magazine. From that show his gouache Farm Fence and Crows went on display at the Nature in Art Museum in Gloucestershire. Bartholomew was asked to illustrate British marine life for the Chevron UK Ltd 1995 calendar, prompting a second commission to portray the oil company's North Sea Britannia platform and appearance in its 1997 ICA show. Land- and seascapes of Scotland became a feature of Bartholomew's work. He showed at the Mall Galleries in 1996, had several solo shows in and around his home town of Wigan and commissions included one from West Lancashire District Council for large oil paintings for permanent exhibition.

Lindsay BARTHOLOMEW 1944– Watercolourist and teacher, born in Wirral, Cheshire. She studied at Ruskin School of Drawing, Oxford, 1961–4, in the latter year winning the Ruskin Prize for Portraiture. She taught in London for a dozen years, then in 1985 moved to Somerset. After she finished at the Ruskin Bartholomew became especially interested in painting the English landscape in watercolour, developing a technique which employed wet washes and dramatic skies. She took part in many group shows, including New Grafton Gallery, RWA, Maas Gallery and Roland, Browse & Delbanco, and was a frequent solo exhibitor from the mid-1970s. These included several at Austin/Desmond Fine Art, Sunninghill. Stirling University, Trust House Forte and Robert Fleming & Company hold her work.

Stephen BARTHOLOMEW 1941– Artist and versatile teacher, born in Southampton, who studied painting and wood engraving for his National Diploma in Design at Winchester School of Art, 1957–62, main teacher John Elwyn. He then attended the Royal College of Art painting school, 1963–6. Between 1966–7 Bartholomew was assistant lecturer at Folkestone School of Art; from 1966–90 worked with Kent art groups; was unemployed, then a guillotine operator in a greetings card gallery, 1967–70; taught in Borstal and other institutions, with "Koestler Award winners every time, which was most years entered," 1970–91; then at Pent Valley Secondary School in Folkestone, 1974; also with The Gilbert Champernowne Trust, "fostering Jungian psychotherapy and the arts", 1976–7. Between 1990–7, when he moved to Cornwall and shortly after to Long Eaton, Nottingham, Bartholomew was based in west Wales and while there took business courses to help with his future career, with his wife in 1996 setting up Garth Art. Over the years Bartholomew showed with Kent & Folkestone Arts Centre; RE; Wales Open at Aberystwyth Arts Centre; West Wales Arts Centre, Fishguard; Dyfed Art Show Two, Carmarthen, selector

George Melly; and WAC/Glynn Vivian Art Gallery, Swansea. He was a graduate of the Jim Russell International Racing Drivers School (Silverstone), but "gradually lost interest".

Zou-zou Elise BARTHOLOMEW 1911– Miniaturist and watercolourist, who sometimes signed work ZEB, she was born in Hankow, China. Educated in England, she studied art at the Central School of Arts and Crafts, 1928–30, and at the St John's Wood School, 1930–3, where her teachers included Patrick Millard. She became a member of the SM and showed at RI, RA, RMS and in China. Lived in Worcester Park, Surrey.

Jill BARTHORPE 1961– Painter and draughtsman. Studied at Trent Polytechnic, Nottingham, 1980–81. She then completed studies at Slade School of Fine Art, 1981–5, a David Bayley Scholarship taking her to France in 1985–6. She was a busy exhibitor in group shows from mid-1980s, including Martin, Keville, Baily Gallery, in Washington, America, 1986; Six of the Best, at Cadogan Contemporary, 1988; Glittering Prizes, at Alton Gallery, 1989; Kingfisher Fine Art, Edinburgh, 1991; and Spring Show, Francis Iles Gallery, Kent, 1992. She had a solo show of drawings at L'Escargot, 1992, and in that year shared a show at Cadogan Contemporary. Painting in France was a feature of her output, working in the landscape of Quercy, east of Cahors.

Antonin Karel BARTL 1912–1998 Portrait and landscape painter and teacher, born in Francisbad, Austria, who studied at Prague Academy in the 1930s under Oskar Kokoschka, then worked in what is now the Czech capital for the film company Twentieth Century Fox as head of publicity. Because of Communist leanings, in 1940 Bartl was sent by the Nazis to a labour camp, from which late in World War II he escaped, joining the Russians in Vienna. Moved to England on a temporary visa in 1945, stayed on and attended Heatherley's School of Fine Art under Iain Macnab. Became head of the painting department at Lincoln School of Art in 1948 until retirement in 1978. Tony Bartl did much publicity work for the British Welding Institute, designed for it a brass fountain and painted murals for new engineering laboratories in Cambridge. He developed a substantial practice as a portrait painter, showing at the Usher Gallery in Lincoln, with John Moores in Liverpool, also in Cambridge and Nottingham. In 1980, when Lincoln cathedral celebrated its nine-hundredth anniversary, Bartl organised a John Piper exhibition there, which led to Bartl's portrait of Piper for the artist. Bartl died in Lincoln.

Richard BARTLE 1967– Artist who attended Rotherham College of Arts and Technology, 1992–3, then gained a fine art, painting, honours degree at Bretton Hall College, West Bretton, 1993–6. Exhibitions included Red, 1996; Bloc, Yorkshire Art Space, Sheffield, 1997; New Lines, Diorama Gallery, 1998; and Solo, The Forum, Sheffield, 1999. e1 Gallery handled Bartle's work. Was shortlisted for the NatWest Art Prize, Lothbury Gallery, 1998. Represented in One Aldwych Hotel collection.

Adrian BARTLETT 1939– Artist in oil, acrylic, etching and lithography, teacher and writer, married to the artist Victoria Bartlett, born and lived in London. He studied at Camberwell School of Art, 1958–61, under Frank Auerbach and Robert Medley. Went on to become head of printmaking at Morley College and visiting lecturer at Oxford University and Wimbledon School of Art. Bartlett was elected to LG in 1979, and in 1993 became its president and an honorary member of Printmakers' Council. Bartlett contributed to group shows in many countries, including representing Britain at the Florence Biennale, 1976, and RA Summer Exhibitions. Later solo shows included British Council, Athens, 1985; Oxford Gallery, 1987; Blenheim Gallery, 1988; and Tsikalioti Museum, Greece, 1989. Ashmolean Museum in Oxford, British Museum, British Council, provincial and overseas collections hold examples. Bartlett's publications include *Drawing and Painting the Landscape*, 1982, and *British Art in the Eighties*, 1983.

Aelred BARTLETT 1918–2004 Painter, architectural decorator and stage designer, brought up in London, whose family had strong artistic interests. His love of drawing and art developed at Ampleforth College. Bartlett studied for a year at art college on the south coast; visited Jamaica where a brother worked; then returned to study at the Slade School of Fine Art, 1934–7, which he where he met Elizabeth Frere Stephens, whom he married in 1941. With the encouragement of his teacher Vladimir Polunin, in the late 1930s Bartlett designed scenery for the Old Vic. During World War II, as an anti-aircraft gunner in Scotland he brought down a German Ju88 aircraft with a bren gun fired from the hip, afterwards serving in north Africa and Italy. Bartlett re-entered the Slade, 1945–8. His father Henry, a convert to Roman Catholicism, was the owner of the Art and Book Co shop opposite Westminster Cathedral, where Aelred next worked, painting and restoring. This led to his showing at the Leicester Galleries and his principal achievement, completion of marble revetment in Westminster Cathedral to J F Bentley's designs. He also created a mosaic panel of St Nicholas there. In Greece, where he later spent part of the year away from London, Bartlett designed and built a house in the Peloponnese, also painting portraits of the local population.

Charles BARTLETT 1921– Painter and printmaker, born in Grimsby, Lincolnshire. His full name was Henry Charles Bartlett and he was married to the artist Olwen Jones. Studied at Eastbourne School of Art, then Royal College of Art, 1946–50, his teachers including Ruskin Spear and Robert Austin. He was president of RWS and a member of RE, also showing regularly at RA. Had a first solo show in London, 1960, a dozen others following, his work mainly landscape, especially the coast of East Anglia. Victoria & Albert Museum, National Gallery of South Australia, Albertina in Vienna, Department of the Environment and several dozen municipal galleries hold his work. There was a major retrospective at Bankside Gallery, 1997; an eightieth-birthday show at Bohun Gallery, Henley-on-Thames, 2001; and a retrospective of prints and recent watercolours, The John Russell Gallery, Ipswich, 2003. Lived at Fingringhoe, Essex.

John BARTLETT 1960– Figurative painter and teacher, who gained an honours degree in fine art, Maidstone College of Art, 1980–3; a postgraduate higher diploma in fine art, Byam Shaw School of Art, 1990–1; a postgraduate diploma in painting, Royal Academy Schools, 1991–4; then did an Acava digital art computer course, 1995. Bartlett's scholarships included the William Lake Beard Prize, 1979;

Bird's Charity and Bernard Bershinger Bursary, both 1991; Edwin Landseer Scholarship and Eric Kennington Prize for Academic Drawing, both 1992; and in 1994 the Richard Jack Prize and Richard Ford Award. In 1994 he held a residency at Oundle School, including teaching, and in 1995 was commissioned for BAA Art Programme, Art at Heathrow. Exhibitions included Stowells Trophy, RA, 1983; Ways of Seeing, Braintree Arts Centre, Braintree, 1988; RA Summer Exhibition, from 1992; Cocktail, Raw Gallery, 1993; and Out of the Nineties, Mall Galleries, 1994. Bartlett's large History Painting, a depiction of the 1990 Trafalgar Square poll tax riot, sparked controversy and gained national newspaper coverage when shown at the Museum of London in 1997. It had Old Master and Socialist Realist overtones. Lived in London.

June Rosalyn BARTLETT 1947– Painter, notably of portraits, born in Barnet, Hertfordshire. She was educated at Holywell School for Girls, Folkestone. Bartlett earned her living as a portrait painter from 1970. In 1979 she left Britain to live and work in Dubai, having her first exhibition there as part of the British Trade Fair. After that she regularly visited the Middle East, to carry out commissions, and she showed at Mathaf Gallery and had further solo shows in the region. Also showed at UA of which she was a member and ROI. Her portrait of Earl Mountbatten of Burma is in the collection of Fleet Air Arm Museum, Yeovilton. Lived in London.

Nancy BARTLETT: *see* **Margaret Nancy ROBINSON**

Paul BARTLETT 1955– Painter, draughtsman, printmaker, photographer and teacher, born and lived in Birmingham. He studied at Moseley Road Secondary School of Art, Birmingham, 1966–73, under John Swift; Falmouth College of Art, 1973–6, gaining an honours degree in fine art, teachers including Francis Hewlett and Richard Platt; then did a Royal Academy Schools postgraduate course, 1977–80, under Peter Greenham and Margaret Green. From 1986–90 studied at Birmingham Polytechnic for teacher's certificate and further postgraduate work in history of art and design. Among Bartlett's awards were the Turner Gold Medal, 1978; Stowells Trophy overall winner, 1979; Elizabeth Greenshields Foundation Scholarship, 1981–2; Daler-Rowney Prize at RBSA Open, 1996; and pastel and drawing prize at the 2003 open exhibition of the RBSA. In 2004, Bartlett won first prize for a portrait of his grandmother in the *Daily Mail Not* the Turner Prize, at the Mall Galleries. Among his teaching appointments were visiting lectureships at Sutton Coldfield School of Art & Design, 1983–4, and Bournville College of Art, Birmingham, 1984–5. Wrote features for *Leisure Painter*. Group shows included Midland Printmakers, 1972–6; RA Summer Exhibition from 1978; and National Portrait Gallery from 1984. Was a member of RBA from 1981. Solo shows included RA, 1980. Bartlett was well represented in The Human Form, RBSA, 2004.

Robin BARTLETT 1900–1976 Versatile painter, draughtsman, designer and illustrator, born in Brentford, Middlesex, full name Robert Arthur Bartlett, son of Arthur Edward Bartlett, an architect who exhibited at RA before World War I, and Ella Carlin. Robin was educated at Shrewsbury School, entered the Royal Navy as a cadet and was a midshipman from 1918 until late 1919, acting as a French interpreter. After graduating in history from Oxford University, 1921, worked in Paris, attending life classes in the evenings, then studied at the Slade School of Fine Art from 1922 under Henry Tonks (who in 1928 gave him a glowing reference), also history of art. Bartlett won several prizes, including a first for figure drawing and an Orpen Bursary, and did a little teaching. While at the Slade Bartlett began an affair with Eileen Agar, whom he married in 1925, but they divorced in 1929. Bartlett, a member of NS, travelled widely abroad, including California, Florida and New Mexico, where he painted D H Lawrence's widow Frieda, which she said was the "best portrait ever made" of her. Back in England, E McKnight Kauffer offered Bartlett a job with the W S Crawford advertising agency, which led to wide-ranging work and to Bartlett being called "a poster artist of the first rank". He also did freelance work for major railway, oil and telephone companies. In 1939 Bartlett volunteered for the Royal Navy, by 1941 attaining the rank of temporary acting lieutenant-commander, and served in the Intelligence Division. His time included four years at the Admiralty in the key Room 39 and in the underground bunker where he was in contact with Winston Churchill. After hostilities, Bartlett became art director with Erwin, Wasey and Company, where he designed the cupid tailor figure for Kayser Bondor; spent two years visiting America; then had several years as creative director with the Pictorial Publicity Company, while freelancing on book illustrations and covers. He retired in 1963 as a freelance consultant, in 1967 organising the first national anti-litter week. Bartlett's second wife, Peggy Nicoll, encouraged his advertising work and this and his wide range of styles undermined his being taken up by a major gallery. Bartlett's pictures (which included a fine portrait of his third wife, Georgette Holm, and her daughter) were shown at the RA and in a solo exhibition at Selfridges just after the war.

Thomas BARTLETT: *see* **THOMAS**

Victoria BARTLETT 1940– Artist in mixed-media sculpture, wall-hung relief collages, paper, silk and other materials, and teacher, wife of the artist Adrian Bartlett. She studied painting and sculpture at Camberwell School of Art, 1957–61, teachers including Karel Vogel and Frank Auerbach, then was at Reading University, 1961–2. Went on to teach at Morley College, also being a visiting lecturer at Ruskin School of Drawing, Oxford; Goldsmiths' College; and Middlesex Polytechnic. Group exhibitions included Picadilly Gallery, 1976–9; RA Summer Exhibition, from 1979; Edward Totah Gallery, 1984; Ikon Gallery touring show, Birmingham, 1988; and LG Open, Barbican Art Gallery, from 1992. Solo shows included Van Doren Gallery, San Francisco, 1975; Edward Totah and Camden Arts Centre, both 1981; and Benjamin Rhodes Gallery, from 1987. Lived in London.

Anthony BARTLEY 1964– Painter and participant in performance art who graduated from University of Ulster, 1985–9. He was involved in the art therapy movement and was a part-time instructor with the National Schizophrenia Fellowship. Took part in slide shows music and poetry readings in Antwerp in 1992 and Belfast, 1993, and exhibited widely in Irish Republic and Northern Ireland, including Works on Paper, Queen Street Studios, Belfast, 1994.

Glenys BARTON 1944– Sculptor and ceramist, born in Stoke-on-Trent, Staffordshire. She studied at Royal College of Art, 1968–71, winning a Travelling Scholarship in 1970. In 1971 she gained the Ruth Drew Prize for Design, in 1972 being British prizewinner in the International Ceramics Exhibition. Drew served on the Crafts Advisory Council Committee (later the Crafts Council), in 1974–8. The artist's total concern was with the human figure, her heads having a hieratic quality. She took part in many group exhibitions and had a long series of solo shows, from 1974 with the Angela Flowers Gallery. In 1977 Glenys Barton at Wedgwood, at the Crafts Council Gallery, contained 26 pieces of sculpture produced at the Josiah Wedgwood Factory, Barlaston, over 18 months. Later solo shows included Flowers East, 1996, City Museum and Art Gallery in Stoke, 1998, and Flowers West, Santa Monica, California, 2000. Many public collections in Britain and abroad hold examples, including Birmingham, Leeds, Leicester, Manchester, Portsmouth and Southampton, WAC and Scottish National Portrait Gallery, Edinburgh.

Julia BARTON 1959– Sculptor who turned to art after graduating in geography at Portsmouth Polytechnic, 1977–80. She was latterly based in Northumberland and produced a series of landscape sculptures in the north and northeast of England. Her 1995 stone creation Shadow, commissioned by Northumbrian Water, is a good example of Barton's sensitivity to particular environments, in this case the Kielder Forest. In 1989 Barton appeared in East End Open Studios, with the Leyton Artists Group. By then, she had to her credit British Women Artists, Battersea Arts Centre, 1986; Spain 1936 & on..., a touring exhibition; Worker at the Women Artists' Slide Library, 1987–9; and The Demonstration, Transport House, for the Transport and General Workers' Union. In 1988, Barton had a residency at Sir George Monoux Secondary School and was a community artist, 1988–9, including time on the Wandsworth Arts Sculpture Project.

Kate BARTON 1946–1998 Painter of abstracts in oil and watercolour, with many cellular images, her colours often having an alchemical resonance. Mark Rothko, Paul Klee, Prunella Clough, Jennifer Durrant, Thérèse Oulton and Helen Chadwick were influences. She was born and died in Cambridge, although much of her life until she was 40 was spent elsewhere. Despite her early interest in art, instead of art school she trained as a teacher of juniors, specialising in painting, at the Froebel Institute, Roehampton, 1965–8. Did a year's teaching practice in Corby, then worked at several jobs, including university administration, in 1974 marrying lawyer Stephen Barton. As her two daughters grew up she attended classes at The Country Centre, Cambridge; from 1988–90 did a foundation course at Cambridge College of Arts and Technology, teachers including Julia Ball; became a part-time fine art (painting) undergraduate at Central St Martins College of Art and Design, 1990–3; learned she had breast cancer, and while being treated, painted in her Cambridge studio; then resumed her degree full-time, 1995–7. Showed with Cohn & Wolfe, Young Artists Exhibition, and in the finalists' exhibition Art & Music (Mercury Music Prize), Air Gallery, both 1997. Addenbrooke's Hospital, Cambridge, and The London Institute hold her work. A memorial show, with a monograph by her husband, was held at New Hall, Cambridge, 1999.

Leonard BARTON 1893–1971 Painter and teacher, born in Manchester. He studied at Blackburn, Bury and Accrington Schools of Art, 1909–15, then at Royal College of Art, where his teachers included Robert Anning Bell, 1915–21. During World War I he was attached to the Air Ministry as an artist while serving in the Royal Air Force. Held a number of teaching posts, finally as principal of Lancaster and Morecambe College of Arts and Crafts from 1929. He was a member of MAFA, exhibited widely in Lancashire and has work in Lancaster Art Gallery. Lived in Lancaster.

Mary BARTON 1861–1949 Landscape painter, born at Farndreg, County Louth, Ireland. After initial education in England and France she studied art at Westminster School of Art and in Rome. She exhibited extensively at Fine Art Society and SWA, also at RHA, Ridley Art Club, in the provinces and widely abroad. Among her exhibiting venues was Mexico City, and she published *Impressions of Mexico with Brush and Pen*. Lived at Bracknell, Berkshire.

Saxon BARTON 1892–1957 Painter, full name Samuel Saxon Barton, who was by profession a gynaecologist and obstetrician, his wife Dorothy also being a doctor. He was based in Liverpool, having been born in the Toxteth Park area. Was educated at the universities of Edinburgh, Glasgow and Liverpool and studied painting privately with the landscape painter James Thomas Watts. Showed at Liver Sketching Club and with RCamA, of which he was made an honorary academician. The Saxon Barton Prize was awarded annually for the best work by a young artist.

Jordan BASEMAN 1960– Sculptor and teacher who studied at Temple University, Philadelphia, America, at its Tyler School of Art, gaining a bachelor's degree in fine art, 1979–83, obtaining his master's in fine art from Goldsmiths' College, 1986–8. He exhibited in the show East at Norwich Gallery, 1991; in East & South at same gallery in 1992; contributed artwork for Peter Gabriel's album *Us* show at Art 93; and was included in Young Artists VI at Saatchi Gallery, 1996. In 2000 Baseman's shirt Call Me Mister was given to the New Art Gallery, Walsall, by Charles Saatchi. Baseman's 2002 solo exhibition, Circulate, at Royal Pump Rooms Art Gallery and Museum, Leamington Spa, comprised film installations resulting from a collaboration between the artist and a surgeon. Baseman worked with Francis Wells, a leading heart and lung specialist based at Papworth Hospital, to produce semi-narrative poetic films "concerned with questions of truth, beauty and the human condition." Was a visiting teacher at Byam Shaw School of Art and lived in London.

Elton BASH 1950– Painter and printmaker, born in Birmingham, who attended the College of Art there, 1969–72. In 1972 Bash gained the Ethel Isobel Cook Award and travelled in France, 1972–3. He was a postgraduate student at Chelsea School of Art, 1973–4, and a Rome Scholar in Painting, British School at Rome, 1974–6. Group shows included 1st International Miniature Print Exhibition, Graffiti Gallery and foreign tour, 1980, and Wapping Artists Open Studios, 1982. Among his solo exhibitions was Spacex Gallery, Exeter, 1981. Contemporary Art Society holds his work.

Nicholas BASHALL 1956– Painter whose work included military subjects and portraits, born in Chester, Cheshire, whose wide range of influences included many British and overseas artists, ranging from Rembrandt, de Laszlo and Millais to Hals, Hogarth and Sorolla y Bastida. Nick Bashall graduated in law from Cambridge University, 1976–9, then studied at Escuela libre del Metitteraneo, Mallorca, 1991–6, under Joaquim Torrens Llado, having practised as a commercial lawyer in London, Dubai and Pakistan, 1983–90. Bashall took part in a number of London-based fairs with Fine Art Commissions, solo shows including InFinArt, Cape Town, South Africa, 1997; Caelt Gallery, 1998; Majlis Gallery, Dubai, 1999; and Arndean Gallery, 2002. Among portraits in private collections were the Duke of Westminster, Lords Stafford and Daresbury and Anita Rothschild. The Parachute Regiment, Royal Anglians, North Atlantic Treaty Organization Allied Rapid Reaction Force and the 16th Brigade also held Bashall's works. In 2004 Bashall's portrait of the Princess Royal was unveiled, having been commissioned by the Household Cavalry Mounted Regiment of which she was colonel-in-chief. Bashall was a Chelsea Arts Club member with a studio in south London.

Mati BASIS 1932– Printmaker and painter, born in Tel-Aviv, Israel, where he studied art at the Avni Institute, 1956–8, before completing his studies at Hornsey and Chelsea Art Colleges in 1966–9. From 1960–4 he was under contract to the Israel Gallery, Tel-Aviv, but moved to London in 1966. Won several prizes at Tel-Aviv Museum and a scholarship prize at the Israel-America Foundation Competition in 1966. Group shows included Annely Juda Gallery, 1969; 2nd International Print Biennale, Paris and Lister Art Gallery, Johannesburg, both 1970; British International Print Biennale, Bradford, 1974; and Leinster Gallery, 1981. Later solo shows included National Theatre, 1982–3, and Crocodile Gallery, 1993. Israel Museum, Jerusalem; Museum of Modern Art, New York; Utrecht Museum, Netherlands; and Ben Uri Art Society hold examples.

Charles Henry BASKETT 1872–1953 Printmaker, born in Colchester, Essex, son of the artist Charles E Baskett. Studied at Colchester and Lambeth Schools of Art and with Frank Mura. Became principal of the Chelmsford School of Art and exhibited widely, including RE and Walker Art Gallery, Liverpool, especially, as well as Fine Art Society, Cooling Galleries, RA and RSA, signing his work CHB. Work reproduced in *Print Collectors' Quarterly*. Lott and Gerrish Ltd, Marlborough, held an exhibition, The aquatints of C H Baskett, in 1985. Galleries in Liverpool and Manchester hold his work. Finally lived in Southampton.

Leonard BASKIN 1922–2000 Jewish artist, teacher, poet and collector who favoured traditional techniques in drawing, printmaking and sculpture, the figurative and black-and-white. He produced powerful images which took a strong moral line on the harsh and cruel aspects of twentieth-century life, such as the Holocaust. He said that "of overwhelming importance to my art" is "the continuum of human life – that is what makes art sublime." Baskin was born in Brunswick, New Jersey, America, son of an orthodox rabbi. Early in his teens wanted to sculpt, from 1937–9 being apprenticed to Maurice Glickman, holding a first solo show in New York in 1939, his work being given an Hon. Mention for the Prix de Rome. He attended New York University's school of architecture and applied arts, 1939–41, from which he won a scholarship to Yale School of Fine Arts, 1941–3; served in the United States Navy at the end of the war and briefly in the Merchant Marine; was at the New School for Social Research, New York, graduating in 1949 (Tiffany Foundation Fellowship); L'Académie de la Grande Chaumière, Paris, 1950; and Accademia di Belle Arti, Florence, 1951. Early in his studies Baskin had discovered William Blake's illustrated books, prompting him to set up his Gehenna Press, printing his own poems, *On a Pure of Withered Roses*; he went on to publish over 100 other titles. After a New York show and a Guggenheim Fellowship in 1953, Baskin could work much as he wished. From 1953–74 taught at Smith College, then spent a decade living mostly in Devon, near his friend the poet Ted Hughes, with whom he collaborated on several books, moving back to teach at Hampshire College, Amherst, Massachusetts, for a decade from 1984. After a Gehenna Press retrospective was published, a fiftieth-anniversary tour concluded at the Library of Congress in 1994. Baskin was one of five artists who created the Franklin Delano Roosevelt Memorial, Washington, dedicated in 1997. He was widely honoured. Baskin's death coincided with the opening of his exhibition at the Achenbach Foundation, San Francisco.

Frank Greatorex BASS 1915– Painter, draughtsman and teacher, born in Southport, Lancashire. He studied at the School of Art there, 1932–6, his teachers including Ian Grant; at the Slade School of Fine Art, 1936–9, with Randolph Schwabe; then at the Institute of Education, in London, 1939–40. Bass returned to live in Southport in 1949, after a series of teaching posts, to become painting master at his old art school. He showed at RBSA, with Southport Palette Club and widely in north of England.

George BASS 1920– Painter and printmaker, born in London. He studied at Blackheath School of Art, 1935–9, where his teachers included W L Clause and James Woodford, then at Royal College of Art, 1939 and 1946–8 interrupted by World War II, where Edward Bawden and John Nash taught him. He did a substantial amount of publicity and book work for clients such as British European Airways and the General Post Office and London Passenger Transport Board bought his work for its collection. Showed Leicester Galleries, NEAC, RI and with Blackheath Art Society of which he was a member, and had one-man shows at Walker's Galleries. Was latterly at Great Yarmouth College of Art.

Herbert Allen BASS 1897–1967 Painter, notably a watercolourist, born in Beckenham, Kent, who joined the Royal Marines in 1917, serving until 1947, when he requested retirement, as lieutenant-colonel. Took part in the North Russian Campaign, served in H M S *Warspite* and many other ships, was a signals instructor and during World War II spent several years in Colombo. He edited the Marines' *Globe and Laurel* magazine for some years. Bass studied with Percy Bradshaw at the Press Art School and with the marine artist W L Wyllie and exhibited with RI and RWS. He specialised in painting Marine uniforms, and much of his work is held by the Marines' Museum, Southsea, including a composite picture of uniforms from 1664–1964. Bass lived in London.

BASSETT 1888–1972 Painter and draughtsman, married to the artist Muriel Wilson. His full title was Brigadier

Bassett Fitzgerald Wilson. He was a highly decorated soldier who served in the King's Royal Rifle Corps and the 4th American Corps in World War I and on Montgomery's staff and as provost-marshal of the 21st Army Group in World War II. He was educated at Rugby School, read law at Cambridge, was junior diplomat, then practised law in London before war broke out when, severely wounded in France, he was advised to take up art for convalescence. In 1917 had an exhibition of Western Front work at Walker's Galleries. During 1920s with his wife established reputation as a painter, being drawn into modern movement in 1930s after they moved to Paris and made friends with such artists as André Lhote. After successful shows with Knoedler in New York and Chicago at start of decade, Bassett – as he signed his work – showed widely in Paris and elsewhere alongside such artists as Dufy, Friesz, Miró, Kisling and Matisse. The Wilsons travelled extensively in Europe and elsewhere until the war intervened. In 1946 Bassett mounted a large retrospective at Galerie du Bac, Paris, from which the Musée National d'Art Moderne bought one of his chairs series. In 1981 Patrick Seale Gallery held a show of the Wilsons' work.

Vera BASSETT 1922–1997 Painter and draughtsman, full name Elizabeth Vera Bassett-Reynolds, born in Pontardulais, Glamorgan, where she lived until 1972, then moved a few miles to the coastal village of Burry Port. Bedridden while recovering from an accident, Bassett discovered a talent for art. Apart from a short time at Swansea College of Art, she was self-taught. Bassett became a sensitive draughtsman of figure subjects, who from the mid-1950s exhibited extensively, including Beaux Arts, Leicester and Zwemmer Galleries, Pictures from the Margaret Davies Collection at the National Museum of Wales in 1964, SWG, SWAS, Paris Salon, elsewhere on the continent and in America. Had regular solo shows including Howard Roberts Gallery in Cardiff, Stone Gallery in Newcastle upon Tyne, University College in Swansea and Bartley Drey Gallery, 1995, with a retrospective at Carmarthenshire County Museum, Carmarthen, 1998. Her work is held by WAC, British Museum, National Museum of Wales, National Library of Wales in Aberystwyth and Glynn Vivian Museum and Art Gallery, Swansea.

Lewin BASSINGTHWAIGHTE 1928–1983 Painter, relief and printmaker. Born at Southminster, Essex, he studied art at South-West Essex Technical College, St Martin's School of Art and the Royal College of Art. Bassingthwaighte had a one-man show at the Leicester Galleries in 1957, then went on to show widely in London – a series of exhibitions at the Piccadilly Gallery, 1964–72 – as well as Oxford, Los Angeles, Venice and Stuttgart. "My work is about tenderness and humanity," Bassingthwaighte wrote, but an element of the strange is strong in his nudes and figure studies. "There is a sense of isolation, of the wonder of life," critic Terence Mullaly wrote about the 1968 show. Bassingthwaighte's work is in many public collections, including the Arts Council, Victoria & Albert Museum and Chantrey Bequest. Signed work with initials. Lived in London.

Paul BASSINGTHWAIGHTE 1963– Artist, born in London, who gained an honours degree in fine art, 1982–6. Group exhibitions included Spirit of London from 1981; Piccadilly Gallery from 1993; RWS from 1994; and City of London Art Fair with Flying Colours Gallery, 1997. Later solo shows included Bloomsbury Theatre and Mosaic Restaurant, both 1996. Leicester Museums Arts and Records Service holds his work.

Jutta BASTIAN 1967– Painter on a small scale of babies' and children's heads, who had a special interest in their formative weeks and months. Moved to England from Germany, where she was born in Hildesheim and brought up, gained an honours degree and postgraduate diploma in fine art from Bradford University, 1991–4, with additional studies at Chelsea, and a master's under Jon Thompson at Middlesex University, 1999. Showed in Germany, also in the group exhibitions Beginnings, Whitworth Art Gallery, Manchester, 2000, and Over The River, firstsite, Colchester/Wolsey Art Gallery, Ipswich, 2002. Had a solo show at Halesworth Gallery, Halesworth, 2001. Bastian had connections with Worpswede, in north Germany, which had an artists' colony similar to that of Walberswick, Suffolk, where she had a riverside studio.

Stuart BASTICK 1965– Sculptor and painter, born in Beverley, Yorkshire. He studied at Hull College of Art, 1986–7, graduating with first-class honours in fine art (sculpture) from Birmingham Institute of Art and Design, 1987–9, working as assistant to Richard Harris, 1988. Harris was then sculptor-in-residence at Grizedale Forest, Cumbria, and Bastick also had residencies, including Barrow-in-Furness, 1991–2, and Turton Tower, near Bolton, 1993. Bastick was Hull Open Sculpture Competition winner with his Unknown New Cargo, 1991, commissioned for Hull Marina. Also notable is the multi-material abstract Give Us This Day Our Daily Bread, 1994, at Snibston Discovery Park, the former Snibston coal mine in Leicestershire. Solo exhibitions included Dock Museum, Barrow-in-Furness, 1992, and Ludus Gallery, Lancaster, 1995.

Hella BASU 1924–1980 Creative letterer, born at Kassel, Germany, and studied art at the art college there. Exhibited widely, including the Victoria & Albert Museum, Herbert Art Gallery and Museum, Coventry, with one-man shows with the British Council, Berlin, Klingspor Museum, Offenbach, the County Museum, Warwick, and Goethe Institute, Toronto. Was senior lecturer at the Regional College of Art in Hull, where she lived.

Bernard Philip BATCHELOR 1924– Painter, born in Teddington, Middlesex, where he settled at St Margaret's on Thames. Was the son of the artist Roland Batchelor. Studied, 1946–9, at St Martin's School of Art with H Andrew Freeth and Roland Pitchforth, and City and Guilds of London Art School with A R Middleton Todd. Went on to work in publicity department of Iliffe Press, commercial studios and for a construction company. Was elected RWS in 1976, also showing at Business Art Galleries, Wykeham Gallery, Catto Gallery and elsewhere.

David BATCHELOR 1955– Artist and writer, born in Dundee, Angus, who did a foundation course at Watford College of Art, 1973–5; an honours degree in fine art at Trent Polytechnic, Nottingham, 1975–8; and his master's in cultural studies, University of Birmingham, 1978–80. Group exhibitions included Victoria Miro, 1993; Then and Now, Lisson Gallery, 1998; British Art Show 5, various venues, 2000; and Days Like These, Tate Britain, 2003. Solo shows included Apocalypstick, Anthony Wilkinson

Gallery, 2000, "the celebration of dangerous cosmetics", many of the works being made from discarded industrial materials; The Spectrum of Hackney Road, same gallery, 2003; and Ikon Gallery, Birmingham, 2004. Batchelor contributed to *Artscribe*, *Frieze* and *Artforum*, his books including *Minimalism*, 1997, and *Chromophobia*, 2000, on colour and the fear of it. Public commissions included Chapel of Love, Sadler's Wells Theatre, and Chromodesks, Pier Trust, both 2000. Contemporary Art Society holds Batchelor's work.

Robert W BATCHELOR 1929– Painter, printmaker and teacher, born in Georgetown, British Guiana, where he attended Queen's College. Studied painting at Gray's School of Art, Aberdeen, 1946–50, going on to be head of art at various academies in Scotland. Later worked as a painter and printmaker and set up Peacock Printmakers' Workshop in 1974. Was a professional member of Aberdeen Artists' Society and showed with RA, RSA, RSW and SSA. Aberdeen Arts Centre gave him a solo show in 1978. Aberdeen Art Gallery, Grampian Television, Shell UK and Mobil North Sea hold his work.

Roland BATCHELOR 1889–1990 Painter, especially in watercolour, draughtsman and printmaker, born in London, father of the artist Bernard Batchelor. Born Bernard William Roland Batchelor, he started to paint as a child, but his father insisted that he pursue a steady career, so he worked in the Civil Service from 1905–49. In his spare time he studied and painted, learning from George Morrow at Putney School of Art and after World War I service from Harry Watson at Regent Street Polytechnic School of Art. After retirement he had invaluable tuition at the City and Guilds of London School with A R Middleton Todd. Was a regular exhibitor at RA and RWS, member 1966. Centenary show at Catto Gallery in 1989. In 2003, New Academy Gallery showed Roland Batchelor's Etchings, from a series of plates produced in 1936 and published by the Gallery in the 1980s. Batchelor was a fluent French speaker who loved working in France. His watercolours, which commonly include shrewdly drawn figures, have great spontaneity and freedom. Victoria & Albert Museum holds his work. Lived in St Margaret's on Thames, Middlesex.

Valerie BATCHELOR 1932– Painter who studied at Salisbury School of Art. John Singer Sargent and Ken Howard influenced her landscapes, which sought to capture the diversity of light and its reflections, as in her work included in The Christmas Exhibition, The Jerram Gallery, Salisbury, 1997. She regularly showed with PS and RWA.

Francis BATE 1853–1950 Painter, studied at South Kensington Schools, where he won a scholarship, then at Antwerp Academy of Arts. Exhibited NEAC, Goupil Gallery, RBA, Royal Glasgow Institute of the Fine Arts and overseas. In 1887 published a book on *The Naturalistic School of Painting*. For many years he was honorary secretary and honorary treasurer of NEAC. Sometimes signed work with monogram. Lived at Bucklebury, Berkshire.

Howard Edward Davis BATE 1894–1974 Sculptor and teacher, son of the sculptor Adam Bate. Howard Bate studied in Plymouth, 1914, Torquay, 1915, at Regent Street Polytechnic School of Art, 1917, then at the Royal Academy Schools, 1920. Exhibited at RA, which bought his work. Taught at Hampstead Garden Suburb Institute for a time. Lived at Edgware, Middlesex, but retired to Bodmin, Cornwall, where he had originated.

Arthur BATEMAN 1883–1970 Versatile painter and art critic who was ordained in the Methodist ministry. Born in Nottingham, Bateman studied at Leeds University, Nottingham School of Art and in Paris. Held a number of church posts around the country, and while in Birmingham was art critic for the *Birmingham Post*. Lived latterly in the Bedale area of Yorkshire, serving as chaplain to the Royal Air Force Regiment at the nearby Catterick Camp. Showed at RA, RSA, Paris Salon and elsewhere.

Henry Mayo BATEMAN 1887–1970 Illustrator, designer and painter, born in Sutton Forest, New South Wales, Australia. He studied at Westminster School of Art, Goldsmiths' Institute and the studio of Charles van Havermaet for several years. By World War I he was established as a contributor of humorous drawings to magazines, becoming noted in *The Bystander*, *Pearson's Magazine*, *The Tatler* and *Punch*. His The Man who ... social clanger cartoons made him famous and have been much-copied. Book illustrations and advertising added to his considerable income between the wars. *The Man who ... and other drawings by H M Bateman*, 1975, was one of a long line of his books extending over about 60 years. On retirement in 1939 Bateman lived in North Tawton, Devon, spending much time in Malta when he could, dying nearby in Gozo. Latterly he concentrated on more serious painting. After he died the Fine Art Society had a memorial show, and in 1974 the Leicester Galleries held a retrospective. Bateman also exhibited at Brook Street and Chenil Galleries and RA. In 2004, The Cartoon Art Trust Museum organised a Bateman exhibition entitled The Humour of Embarrassment.

James BATEMAN 1893–1959 Painter and wood engraver specialising in rural scenes and farm animals, pictures with a tight composition. Born in Kendal, Westmorland, Bateman came from a farming background. Started to study sculpture at Leeds College of Art, 1910–14, but World War I service injuries forced him to abandon sculpture for painting. Studied at the Slade School of Fine Art, 1919–21, Rome Scholarship finalist 1920. Taught Cheltenham School of Art, 1922–8, then at Hammersmith School of Art. While at Cheltenham exhibited with the Cheltenham Group and Cotswold Group, cycling out to paint the local countryside. Exhibited at the RA from 1924, being elected RA in 1942. Also showed Cooling Galleries, Fine Art Society, NEAC, RHA, RSA and extensively abroad. Many British provincial and Commonwealth galleries hold his work, as do the British Museum and Tate Gallery, which has several examples of cattle auction scenes, for which Bateman is especially noted. Lived in London.

Pete BATEMAN 1968– Artist and illustrator who studied at Staffordshire Polytechnic. He drew for publications such as *The Observer* and *New Statesman* and contributed mixed-media assemblages to Art in Boxes, 1992, at England & Co.

Vic BATEMAN 1950– Artist who was born in London, studying painting at Hornsey and Croydon Colleges of Art, 1968–75. Was visiting artist at Goldsmiths' College School of Art, 1978. His mixed show appearances included

Brixton Art Gallery and Acme Gallery, both 1983; Nettlefold Gallery, 1984; and New Moon Group Show at Woodlands Art Gallery, 1986. Had solo show of paintings and drawings at Greenwich Theatre Gallery, 1982.

Andrea BATES 1943– Versatile artist in pastel and oil, born in Budapest, Hungary. She was educated in Paris and Montreal, studied at the Academy of Fine Arts, Vienna, and eventually settled in north Oxfordshire. Showed with RBA, ROI, PS and The Stour Gallery in Shipston-on-Stour; was a regular participant in Oxford Artweek from 1985; and had many solo exhibitions in London and the provinces.

Denise BATES 1928– Painter, muralist and needlework designer who attended Liverpool College of Art, 1946–8, then Byam Shaw School, 1948–53, gaining Award of Merit, 1952. She showed in mixed exhibitions at RA, RCamA, NEAC, RMS, Patricia Wells Gallery in Thornbury, Paris Salon and elsewhere. Held a number of solo exhibitions in Cheshire, where she lived at Malpas. Carried out mural commissions for the ships *Ivernia*, *Sylvania*, Imperial Institute and elsewhere; tempera commissions for Bunbury Church in Cheshire and Newport Church, Shropshire; and several church needlework designs. Lived at Haughton Thorn, near Tarporley, Cheshire.

Joan Elliott BATES 1930– Painter, born in Sheffield, Yorkshire, who attended the College of Art there, 1947–9, and the Slade School of Fine Art, 1949–52. She showed regularly in the RA Summer Exhibition, also with the RWS, NEAC, ROI, RI, RWA and RE. Bates had work chosen for the finalists' exhibition, Hunting/*Observer* Award; Paris Salon; and The Discerning Eye. She won 2nd and 3rd Prizes at the Laing Painting Competition and a Cornelissen Prize. Commercial galleries shown at included New Grafton Gallery; Cadogan Contemporary; Bohun Gallery, Henley; New Ashgate, Farnham; Alresford Gallery, Hampshire; Albany Gallery, Cardiff; and Beaux Arts, Bath. Bates also had solo exhibitions. In 2005, Messum's included a large selection of her work in Painters and Sculptors of East Anglia, the catalogue illustrating examples of her subtle and atmospheric depictions of coastal Suffolk. Paintings in Hospitals and the Government Art Collection owned her work. She lived in Marlow, Buckinghamshire.

Ken BATES 1927–1985 Portrait and figure painter in oil, pastel, charcoal and graphic media. Born in London, Bates studied at Willesden School of Art in the early 1940s under Maurice de Sausmarez, then for the later 1940s at Guildford College of Art with Maurice Wheatley. Exhibited at SGA, of which he was a council member, NS, RBA and PS. Lived at Earlswood, Redhill, Surrey.

Lynn BATES fl. from late 1970s– Painter and designer who worked in both Britain and South America, producing landscapes and comissioned portraits. Goya, Hogarth and other romantic artists were cited as influences. She studied at Byam Shaw School of Art, 1978–81, and Royal Academy Schools, 1983–6. From 1987–9 she trained as a scenic artist with BBC. Bates showed in mixed exhibitions with Cadogan Contemporary and had a solo show there in 1990.

Marjorie BATES 1883–1962 Painter and draughtsman, born in King's Newton, Derbyshire. Her family moved to Nottingham where she studied at the School of Art, 1902–13. She then travelled on the continent, where she had tuition from J P Laurens, in Paris. Most of her life was spent in Nottingham, although she travelled widely in England, drawing cottages and churches, reproduced as Christmas cards and calendars. Showed at RA, in provinces and at Paris Salon and was a regular exhibitor at Nottingham Castle Museum, which holds her work.

Robert BATES 1943– Artist and teacher, born in Wolverhampton, Staffordshire. He studied at Birmingham College of Art, 1960–5, and Royal College of Art, 1965–8. Taught printmaking at Medway College of Art. From 1970 had many solo shows at Lumley Cazalet as well as one at Hom Gallery, Washington, in 1982. Among the group exhibitions in which he participated was The Broad Horizon, Agnew, 1990. Bates' work was both colourful and precise, small and incorporating distinctive coloured borders. Lived for some years in Shropshire.

Trevor BATES 1921– Sculptor whose grandfather was the sculptor Harry Bates. Born in Eltham, Kent, he was educated at Harrow School, then studied at Slade School of Fine Art, 1947–51, and with Ossip Zadkine in Paris, in 1952, in his private studio at the Académie de la Grande Chaumière. Later taught at Hornsey College of Art. Bates exhibited at RBA and Salon de la Jeune Sculpture in Paris, having one-man show at Waddington Gallery in 1959. In addition to being awarded an Arts Council Prize in The Unknown Political Prisoner competition in 1953, he was granted a prize by the international jury when chosen to represent Great Britain. Bates' work is in the collections of the Arts Council, Victoria & Albert Museum and National Museum of Wales, Cardiff. His sculptures created powerful silhouettes rather than being three-dimensional objects, and Bates commented that it is "the unexpected and apparently illogical form in nature which concerns me". Lived in Sevenoaks, Kent.

BATH, MARQUESS of: *see* **Alexander THYNN**

Judith BATHURST 1931–2001 Judith Countess Bathurst was a watercolourist who also painted in oil. She was born Judith Nelson in London and was married in 1959 to the 8th Earl Bathurst, marriage dissolved 1976. Judith Bathurst was educated in England, America and Switzerland, studied art at Leeds University and attended the life class at Heatherley's Art School. She also had painting tuition from Alison Musker, with whom she painted each year in Venice and with whom she travelled in Rajasthan. Her pictures of Italy, India and Morocco were colourful and full of light. Showed solo in London and Italy; annually with the Chelsea Art Society, 1991–5; and in W H Patterson Fine Arts' annual Venice in Peril Exhibition. Private collections in Britain and abroad hold her work. Lived in London and Italy.

Kevin BATKIN 1949– Painter brought up in East Anglia who, after Royal Air Force service 1965–7, attended North-East London Polytechnic in Dagenham. He had a background in electronics and computer systems and was "particularly interested in computer-aided design and technology". Studied at Norfolk College of Arts and Technology in King's Lynn, 1990–2, then De Montfort University, Leicester, 1992–5. Exhibitions included Lynn Sports Leisure Complex, King's Lynn, 1992; Peterborough

Exhibitions Group, Peterborough Museum and Art Gallery, from 1994; and Towards an Abstraction, David Holmes Contemporary Art, Peterborough, 1995–6. Lived in Eastrea, Cambridgeshire.

Brian BATSFORD: *see* **Brian COOK**

Matthew BATT 1969– Painter, born in Reading, Berkshire, who graduated with honours in fine art, Chelsea College of Art & Design, 1991–4. Everyday scenes and the imaginary inner life were important to Batt, who produced figurative works with a quirky quality. In 1998 and 2002 he was included in the BP-sponsored exhibitions at the National Portrait Gallery, other venues including Red House Museum and Art Gallery, Christchurch; Hampshire Contemporary Artists Gallery; and Oliver Contemporary, 2004.

Mark Wilfred BATTEN 1905–1993 Sculptor, draughtsman and painter, born in Kirkcaldy, Fife. He studied at Beckenham and Chelsea Schools of Art and gained Board of Education drawing and painting certificates. Batten was an advocate of direct carving of stone and published books on the subject: *Stone Sculpture by Direct Carving*, 1957, and *Direct Carving in Stone*, 1966. He gained experience of carving granite in Cornwall in the late 1920s. During World War II Batten served in the Life Guards, training armoured vehicle drivers. Showed with NEAC, Society of Present Day Artists, Royal Glasgow Institute of the Fine Arts and RBA, of which he was made a member in 1962. He was elected a fellow of RBS in 1953 and was its president, 1956–61. Bodleian Library in Oxford contains his work, as do British Museum and a number of provincial galleries. For many years lived a reclusive life at Dallington, Heathfield, Sussex.

Reg BATTERBURY 1928– Painter of landscapes and portraits, designer and teacher, born in east London. Trained locally at West Ham Municipal College of Art, St Martin's School of Art and West of England College of Art, Bristol. Became head of art department of Lockleaze Comprehensive School, retiring in 1978. Batterbury showed at RA from 1951, was a member of RWA and of the Bristol Savages, being president in 1980. American Museum in Bath and Longleat House hold his work. Lived in Bristol.

Elizabeth BATTERSBY 1946– Artist chiefly in oil and charcoal, born in Wiltshire. She did an external diploma London University, in the history of art, 1975–80; gained an honours degree in fine art and critical studies, St Martin's School of Art, 1983–8; and in 1982–4 attended Glamorgan Summer School, tutor Dennis Creffield. Mixed exhibitions included Whitechapel Open, 1983; LG Open, Royal College of Art, 1984; Alton Gallery, 1989; and Galerie Dagmar, 1991. Had a solo show at Morley College, 1987, later ones including The Wine Gallery, 1993. Lived in London.

Martin BATTERSBY 1914–1982 Painter, designer and decorator, printmaker, writer and collector, full name George Martin Battersby, born into a theatre- and cinema-loving family. From childhood, he was fascinated by painting and the decorative arts, spending many hours in museums and galleries. On leaving school, Battersby rejected university and the family law firm, studying architecture at Regent Street Polytechnic, spending five years in the design studio of Gill and Reigate and a year at the Royal Academy of Dramatic Art. After designing and painting scenery in repertory, he was commissioned to design settings for *Hamlet* at the Old Vic under Lilian Bayliss. There followed a string of Shakespeare commissions for Stratford-upon-Avon; modern plays; and operatic productions for Covent Garden and Glyndebourne. As a painter, Battersby specialised in trompe l'oeil, completing many rooms in England, France and America for private and business clients. His lithograph *Archaic Smile* was produced at Curwen Studio in 1981 and published by Ebury Gallery, which held a show of his pictures in 1982. He had first exhibited at Brook Street Gallery, 1948, with other shows at Arthur Jeffress, Redfern and Grosvenor Galleries and in America. Battersby revived interest in the collecting of Art Nouveau and Art Deco works, his books including *Art Nouveau* and *The Decorative Twenties*, both 1969; *The Decorative Thirties*, 1971; and *Trompe l'Oeil or The Eye Deceived*, 1974. Brighton Museum and Art Gallery and Southampton Art Gallery hold his work. Died from cancer in hospital at Lewes, Sussex.

Norman BATTERSHILL 1922– Painter, designer, writer and teacher, born in London, son of the artist Leslie Battershill. He studied at Twickenham College of Art and showed at RBA, ROI and PS of all of which he was a member, RA and NEAC. Was made a fellow of Society of Industrial Artists and Designers/Chartered Society of Designers in 1968 and won ROI's Stanley Grimm Award, 1989. Major companies held his work. Among Battershill's instructional books were *Painting and Drawing Water*, 1984, and *Learn to Paint Trees*, 1990. Lived in Woolland, Dorset.

Dora BATTY 1878–1966 Artist, designer and teacher whose early life and education are obscure. Although she worked in several media, she was particularly known as a prolific designer of London Transport posters and others for the high street shop MacFisheries. As an illustrator, she worked for Curwen Press and contributed to the Britain Can Make It exhibition at the Victoria & Albert Museum in 1946. Batty was a noted textile designer, working for Barlow & Jones and Helios and teaching the subject at the Central School of Arts and Crafts from 1932. She was an innovative and inspiring head of department there, 1950–8, attracting staff including Peter Collingwood, Linda Parry and Marianne Straub. Batty also designed for Poole Pottery.

Christopher BATTYE 1942– Figurative painter, draughtsman and printmaker, from Lancashire, whose work included stylised figurative works which were compared to the work of Vorticists. Battye studied for his Intermediate at Chester College of Art, then illustration and printmaking at Liverpool College of Art, obtaining his Art Teacher's Diploma. Taught for a year in a secondary school in Northolt. Battye settled in London in the 1960s, after parental non-acceptance of his fondness for the Teddy Boy style of dress: drape jacket and duck's arse hairstyle. His subjects, infused with a frenzied, energetic style, included characters encountered in the streets, pubs, clubs and night-life of Soho, such as The French and Colony Room, depicted in his prints in the 1994 RA Summer Exhibition. Battye said: "My working life is extreme. I don't leave the studio for four days of the week. When I do it is to meet friends at these drinking places." Showed widely, at established galleries and drinking dens. Had a solo exhibition in 1994 at Gerry's Club, Dean Street, run by Gerald Campion, the actor famous as television's Billy Bunter. Other exhibiting venues included the Union Club, L'Escargot Restaurant and the Chelsea Arts Club, of which Battye was a member. He was prominent in a group picture in the Club by the artist Howard Morgan. The artists Ivor Abrahams and Barry Flanagan, comedian Robbie Coltrane and actor Peter Bowles owned Battye's work.

Martin BATTYE 1952– Painter, teacher and businessman, born and brought up in Woodbridge, Suffolk, who lived for many years in south Norfolk. After studies at Sunderland School of Art he had various jobs including psychiatric work, teaching and at sea before setting up his own company, Kirton Healthcare, to design and make equipment for the disabled and elderly. This was recognised for its flair and innovation and a range of business awards followed, including the 1986 Marks & Spencer Better Made in Britain. Group shows included Northern Young Contemporaries, Newcastle, 1974; Denis Taplin, Woodbridge, 1988; RA Summer Exhibition, 1998; and Eastern Open, King's Lynn, Harvey & Tollit Watercolour Prize, 2003. Had several solo exhibitions, including Chappel Galleries, Chappel, 2003, where Battye's work saw a shift from landscape painting to pictures more abstract and simple in form and colour range.

John BAUM 1942– Painter and teacher, born in Wales. He studied at Slade School of Fine Art, 1960–4, gaining the first-year drawing prize, 1960 and David Sylvester Prize, 1964; obtained his London University teacher's certificate, 1965; then became a lecturer in foundation studies at the faculty of art and design at Liverpool Polytechnic, becoming head of department, 1989. Took part in a number of group shows, including John Moores Exhibition in Liverpool, Ibis Gallery, WAC and Royal National Eisteddfod, in Wales. In 1999 Ogilvy & Estill, Conway, held a Baum solo exhibition in which the relationship of figures to their environment was examined. In 2002, Bruton Street Gallery gave Baum his first major London showing for nearly 20 years. Both the Arts Council and WAC hold his work.

Lydia BAUMAN 1955– Painter and lecturer, born in Warsaw, Poland, a member of Bigos, the Polish painters' group. She graduated in fine art from the University of Newcastle upon Tyne, 1974–8, then obtained her master's degree in the history of art, graduating first-class with distinction, from the Courtauld Institute of Art, 1978–80, lecturing as a freelance at the National and Tate Galleries. She won the John Christie Scholarship in 1976 and the Hatton Award in 1977. Bauman used a fresco-related technique in which pigments mixed with plaster were layered with resin and wax and then sanded down. After two solo shows at Leigh Gallery, 1985–6, she had many appearances in Britain and Poland, later solo exhibitions including several at Mistral Galleries from 1990 and Catto Gallery, 1993, Moreton Street Gallery, 2001, and From my travels, The Gallery in Cork Street, 2004. Corporate clients included Saatchi and Saatchi, Warner Brothers and Deutsche Bank.

Pauline BAUMANN fl. from late 1920s– Painter, printmaker and teacher, full name Constance Amy Pauline Baumann. She attended St Martin's School of Art, studying under Frank Jones, then Royal College of Art, 1923–7, under William Rothenstein. Exhibited RA, Redfern Gallery, Senefelder Club and elsewhere, being especially noted for her etchings, engravings and lithographs. Lived in London.

Lewis BAUMER 1870–1963 Painter, printmaker and notable illustrator, born in London. He studied at St John's Wood Schools of Art, Royal College of Art and Royal Academy Schools. Exhibited extensively at Fine Art Society and RI, also at Cooling Galleries, ROI and Walker Art Gallery, Liverpool. From the 1920s Baumer concentrated on his illustrative work. He drew for many magazines, including Jerome K Jerome's *The Idler*, *Pick-Me-Up*, *Punch* and *The Strand Magazine*. Authors of books illustrated ranged from Ian Hay to Washington Irving and Mrs Molesworth. He was a light social commentator in his contemporary drawings, which have a fizzy charm. Arts Club member. Lived at Henley-on-Thames, Oxfordshire.

David BAUMFORTH 1942– Self-taught landscape painter whose on-the-spot canvases had a strong sense of light and moved towards abstraction. Baumforth was born in York and had a varied career including marketing sports and racing cars and yachts, as a property developer and the selling and building of swimming pools. Among his group shows were the RA Summer Exhibition and RWS Open. Had solo exhibitions with Scarborough and Scunthorpe Art Galleries; Gascoigne Gallery, Ilkley; Montage Gallery, Castleton; Colin Jellicoe Gallery, Manchester; and at Sewerby Hall, Bridlington. East Yorkshire County Council holds Baumforth's work. Lived in Snainton, Yorkshire.

Charlotte BAWDEN 1902–1969 Painter, potter and teacher. She was born Charlotte Epton and met her future husband, the artist Edward Bawden, at Royal College of Art, marrying him in 1932. After College she studied pottery in St Ives, Cornwall, with Bernard Leach and Michael Cardew, and taught drawing at Cheltenham Ladies' College, Pate's Grammar School and helped found Denman College, the Women's Institute establishment. It and Victoria & Albert Museum hold her work.

Edward BAWDEN 1903–1989 Watercolourist, illustrator, designer, printmaker and teacher, born in Braintree, Essex, the county in which he spent much of his life, finally living in Saffron Walden. Studied at Cambridge School of Art from 1919, then at Royal College of Art, 1922–5, on a scholarship, in the design school being taught by Paul Nash. Soon began on commercial work for Poole Pottery and Curwen Press, then in 1928–9 with Eric Ravilious and Charles Mahoney did decorations for Morley College. Bawden went on studying engraving and bookbinding at Central School Arts and Crafts after leaving the Royal College and himself taught there, the Royal Academy Schools and Goldsmiths' College School of Art. First one-man show at Zwemmer Gallery in 1934, after which he showed extensively including RA, being elected RA in 1956. Work poured from Bawden's studio in the 1930s, for companies such as Shell-Mex; book illustrations such as *Good Food*, 1932, and *The Week-end Book*, 1939; and a mass of often ephemeral work which evinced a wonderful wit, economy and aptness to subject. Official War Artist in World War II, much of his output being in the Imperial War Museum. Tate Gallery and many other public collections hold his work. Bawden did decorations for the ships *Orcades* and *Oronsay* and for the Unicorn Pavilion for the Festival of Britain of 1951. His son was the artist Richard Bawden. Retrospective at Victoria & Albert Museum in 1989, a tribute at Fine Art Society in 1992, a design retrospective at Rye Art Gallery, Rye, 1999, and Fine Art Society and Guildhall Library centenary celebrations in 2003.

Richard BAWDEN 1936– Painter, printmaker, designer and illustrator, son of the artists Edward and Charlotte Bawden, married to the potter Hattie Bawden. He was born at Black Notley, near Braintree, Essex. Bawden attended Chelsea and St Martin's Schools of Art. During National Service he was able to attend Winchester School of Art, then became a student in the school of engraving and etching at Royal College of Art. As well as exhibiting in numerous mixed shows Bawden had several dozen solo exhibitions. He was a member of RE and of the Society of Designer-Craftsmen and was chairman of the Gainsborough's House Print Workshop in Sudbury, a group of printmakers. Bawden completed posters for the London Underground, a large mosaic for a swimming pool in Little Dunmow, murals for restaurants, book illustrations and editions of prints for Christie, Curwen and Editions Alecto, and he also decorated his wife's pottery. Bawden's work combined excellent draughtsmanship, a fine sense of colour and an eye for the unusual. It is in the collections of the Victoria & Albert Museum, the Tate Gallery, Pallant House in Chichester and other public collections. Gainsborough's House gave Bawden a sixtieth-birthday retrospective in 1996. Bawden had a solo show at Chappel Galleries, Chappel, in 2005.

John BAWTREE 1952– Painter who qualified as an architect at Kingston Polytechnic School of Architecture, 1970–3 and 1975–7. He won Elizabeth Greenshields Foundation Awards, 1978–80, and the Foundation holds his work. Was elected RBA in 1984. Also showed in group exhibitions at RA and Richmond Gallery and was included in Summer Exhibition: the Contemporary Orientalists at Mathaf Gallery, 2003. Had several dozen solo shows including Piers Feetham Gallery; British Council, Muscat, Oman; and Caroline Hill Gallery, New York. Bawtree travelled widely. He was the first artist to record the launch of the Social Democratic Party in 1981, between 1983–5 painted scenes from the inquiry into the Sizewell nuclear power station, during the 1990s a set of commemorative paintings of the old British Embassy in Oman for the Foreign Office and he was also commissioned to paint the royal yacht *Britannia* for DML Devonport Dockyard. Chelsea Financial Services holds a large group of his works. Lived in Peasenhall, Suffolk.

Denis BAXTER 1936– Painter in oil, printmaker and lecturer, born in Southsea, Hampshire. After being a tea and rubber plantation manager in India for five years, Baxter was at Bournemouth and Poole College of Art, 1964–5, teachers including Sam Rabin and William Evans, then Stockwell College of Education, Bromley, 1965–6. Taught English in Bournemouth, 1968–87, then became an artist printmaker and lecturer. Was a member of NS and Printmakers' Council, also showing at RA, RWA, RBA, NEAC and RSMA. Had solo shows at Lyric and Mermaid Theatres and in Luxembourg. Baxter's main themes "concentrate around flowers and abandoned railway architectural subjects". Southampton General Hospital holds his work. Lived in Southbourne, Dorset.

Douglas BAXTER 1920– Painter and teacher, born in Kirkcaldy, Fife. Studied at Edinburgh College of Art under William Gillies and others, 1945–50, and at Patrick Allan-Fraser School of Art, Hospitalfield, with Ian Fleming; also won travelling scholarships to Scandinavia and Western Europe. He went on to teach at Loretto School in Musselburgh, Midlothian, where he lived, and was a lecturer at Edinburgh College of Art. Showed SSA of which he was a member, RSA, Royal Glasgow Institute of the Fine Arts, CEMA and elsewhere. Arts Council bought his work.

Glen BAXTER 1944– Artist, author, illustrator and teacher, born in Leeds, Yorkshire, where he studied at the College of Art, 1960–5. He taught at Victoria & Albert Museum, 1967–74, and was part-time lecturer in fine art at Goldsmiths' College School of Art, 1974–86. Was included in The Self-Portrait: a Modern View, an exhibition which toured widely from Artsite Gallery, Bath, 1987. Held a first solo show in New York in 1974 and subsequently had one-man shows in Venice, Cardiff, Bradford, Aberdeen and San Francisco, being represented for a time by Nigel Greenwood, then Richard Dennis Gallery in 1996. Baxter made a name for his artworks published as books, such as *The Billiard Table Murders*, 1990, and *Trundling Grunts*, launched with a show of Baxter's surreal artwork at Chris Beetles Ltd in 2002. Flowers East gave Baxter an exhibition in 2004. Other books included *Atlas, The Impending Gleam, His Life: The Years of Struggle* and *Jodhpurs in the Quantocks*. Arts Council holds Baxter's work, which was figurative and abstract.

Graeme BAXTER 1958– Painter, born in Bridge of Allan, Stirlingshire, who settled at Kippen, Stirling. Studied at Glasgow School of Art, dealt in fine art and established a reputation as a leading realistic golf landscape painter, official artist to the Ryder Cup, European Tour and the Professional Golfers' Association, the Royal and Ancient Golf Club commissioning him to paint the official 2000 Open landscape. His depiction of the view from the Old Course Hotel, alongside the seventeenth fairway, sold for £100,000 in 1995 to the hotel's Japanese owners. It was so lifelike that some golfers had their photographs taken next to it when the course was enveloped in bad weather. Showed solo at St Andrews, Gleneagles, Wentworth, Royal Lytham and elsewhere. Numerous collections worldwide hold examples.

Mark BAXTER 1958– Baxter gained a Bachelor of Science honours degree from North East London Polytechnic, 1977–80, then attended Sir John Cass School of Art, 1980–1. He showed at RA Summer Exhibition, Mall Galleries, Camden Arts Centre and in East End Open Studios, 1989, based at Unit 7, Peckham Road. Among his solo exhibitions were Sue Williams Gallery, 1988, and Vortex Gallery, 1989.

Robert BAXTER 1893– Painter, printmaker and teacher, born in Brighton, Sussex, full name Leslie Robert Baxter. He was apprenticed as an engraver, 1910–15, then studied under Louis Ginnett at Brighton School of Art, 1919–24. Held a series of teaching posts, latterly at Hammersmith College of Art and Building. Showed at RA, AIA, London

Gallery and in Paris and had a one-man show at Mayor Gallery in 1948. Lived in London.

Sandra BAXTER 1968– Prolific printmaker, born in Dunfermline, Fife, settling nearby at Saline. Gained an honours degree in illustration/printmaking, Duncan of Jordanstone College of Art, Dundee, 1986–1990. Awards included St Cuthbert's Mill RWA Printmaking Prize, 1994; Gwen May RE Commemorative Award at National Print Exhibition, Mall Galleries, 1994–5; *Art Review* Prize, The Discerning Eye, 1996; Graffik 97, joint winner, Printmaking Award, 1997; Ian Massie Memorial Quaich, FDPW, 1998; and *Art Review* Purchase Prize, National Print Exhibition, 1999. In 1997 was elected an RE associate. Her numerous exhibitions included Oxford Art Society, from 1993; New Academy Gallery, 1995; Printmakers, Will's Art Warehouse, 1997; SSA at RSA, 1998; and The Stour Gallery, Shipston-on-Stour. Carnegie Trust, Dunfermline, and Ashmolean Museum, Oxford, bought by the Vivien Leigh Fund, hold examples.

Lise Lotte BAYER 1931– Painter and teacher, born in Vienna. After initial education at Bradford Girls' Grammar School she studied art at Reading University with Anthony Betts, 1949–55. She showed at RA, RP, RBA, with the Young Contemporaries, and in the north of England. Member of Bradford Arts Club. Had a one-man show at Galerie Fuchs, in Vienna, 1959, and her work is held in several Austrian public collections. She returned to live in Vienna after a period in Shipley, Yorkshire, where her father, the painter Richard Franz Bayer, also lived. She sometimes signed her work L L B.

Richard Franz BAYER 1901– Painter and teacher at Bradford Grammar School, born in Vienna, Austria. He studied art in Vienna and showed there, in Bradford and elsewhere in the north of England. Member of Bradford Arts Club. Lived for some years in Shipley, Yorkshire, where his daughter the painter Lise Lotte Bayer also lived for a time. Sometimes signed his work R F B.

Gilbert BAYES 1872–1953 Sculptor of figures and monumental designer, born in London, son of the artist Alfred Walter Bayes and brother of the painter Walter Bayes. Studied at City and Guilds, Finsbury, classes and then, 1896–9, at the RA Schools, finally in Paris. He won an Honourable Mention at the Paris International Exhibition in 1900, a gold medal and diploma of honour at the Paris Exhibition of Decorative Art in 1925, as well as several medals at the Paris Salon and RBS. Was master of the Art Workers' Guild, 1925, and RBS president, 1939–44. Among his chief works are Selfridges' great clock, the great seal of HM King George V and the Seagrave Trophy. In 1998 The Fine Art Society held an exhibition to coincide with publication of *Gilbert Bayes: Sculptor*, supported by the Gilbert Bayes Trust. The Tate Gallery holds his work. He was married to the sculptor Gertrude Bayes and lived in London.

Jessie BAYES 1878–1970 Painter, illuminator and muralist who worked in the tradition of Walter Crane and the arts and crafts movement. Her father was the artist Alfred Walter Bayes, her brothers the painter Walter Bayes and the sculptor Gilbert. She was made a member of RMS in 1906, becoming honorary RMS in 1935, also being a member of Arts and Crafts Exhibition Society, Society of Mural Decorators and Church Crafts League. Also showed at RA, Ridley Art Club, Baillie Gallery, Fine Art Society, Walker Art Gallery in Liverpool and elsewhere, including the continent and North America. Detroit Public Gallery had her work, and she completed the roll of honour for the King's Royal Rifles in Winchester Cathedral. Lived in London and Edinburgh.

Walter BAYES 1869–1956 Painter, writer, illustrator and teacher. Born in London, son of the artist Alfred Walter Bayes, brother of the sculptor Gilbert Bayes and of the artist Jessie Bayes. Studied between 1896–1902 variously at evening classes at the City and Guilds, Finsbury, Académie Julian, Paris, and Westminster School of Art, with Fred Brown. From early 1890s began exhibiting at RA and NEAC, his first work for a public collection, Top o' the Tide, being bought by the Walker Art Gallery, Liverpool, in 1900. Bayes was a founder-member of Frank Rutter's AAA in 1908, and thereafter was associated with Walter Sickert and his friends at 19 Fitzroy Street, Camden Town Group and LG. One-man show at Carfax Gallery, 1913. In 1918 Bayes became head of Westminster School of Art, having previously taught at the City and Guilds, Bolt Court and Camberwell School of Arts and Crafts, and he held this post until 1934. From 1934–7 he was a visiting lecturer at Reading University, from 1944–9 being director of painting at Lancaster School of Art. Bayes was a painter of tonal subtlety, an intellectual who excelled at the science of picture-making. Among his grateful pupils was David Jones. At various times Bayes was critic for *Outlook*, *The Athenaeum*, *Saturday Review* and *Weekend Review*. He wrote a number of books, including one on *Turner*, 1931, *The Art of Decorative Painting*, 1927, and a delightful illustrated travel memoir, *A Painter's Baggage*, 1932. Tate Gallery holds his work. Retrospective at Michael Parkin Fine Art, 1978. Lived in London.

Thomas BAYLEY 1893–1966 Sculptor and teacher, also known as C Thomas Bayley, born in Willesden, London. Was educated at Chester School of Art and Royal College of Art, in 1922 gaining his diploma, in 1923 a travelling scholarship. During World War I Bayley had served with the Royal Field Artillery in France, Egypt and Palestine, producing panoramic drawings and maps. For the 1924 British Empire Exhibition Bayley modelled a map of the world. Showed at RA and in the provinces, notably Cheltenham, where he taught at the School of Arts and Crafts. Joined the Art Workers' Guild in 1931. Lived in Cheltenham, Gloucestershire, and in London.

Clifford BAYLY 1927– Painter, illustrator, writer and teacher, who studied at St Martin's and Camberwell Schools of Art, teachers including William Coldstream, Lawrence Gowing and John Minton. He taught at Margate, Canterbury and Maidstone Colleges of Art for 32 years, retiring early to concentrate on painting. Bayly was vice-president of RWS and president of Weald of Kent Art Group and showed at Piccadilly and Mall Galleries. Also showed extensively in Australia. He regarded his series of Alignment paintings as main works, "based on various forms of pathways and ancient sites". Wrote books on painting and drawing and for children. RWS Diploma Collection holds his work. Lived in Staplehurst, Kent.

Gertrude Emily BAYLY 1875– Painter, draughtsman and ivory miniaturist who studied at Margate School of Art, continuing to live in the town. Exhibited SWA, East Kent Art Society, widely in the provinces and in Paris.

Irene BAYMAN fl. from c. 1935– Painter, draughtsman, fabric printer and teacher. Educated in Wigan, Lancashire, she studied art at Wigan Technical College and went on to teach in Lancashire schools, including Eccles Grammar School. Exhibited in Preston and London. Lived in Wigan.

Keith BAYNES 1887–1977 Painter, mainly in oil. Born at Reigate, Surrey, Baynes went to Cambridge and then the Slade School, 1912–15, where he won painting and drawing certificates. After World War I he became a member of the circle around the critic and painter Roger Fry and was strongly influenced by French Post-Impressionist artists. Showed with the London Artists' Association, encouraged and financed by Maynard Keynes and Samuel Courtauld from 1926 to the slump of 1931, which put a stop to the enterprise. Baynes also exhibited with Agnew, Adams Gallery and widely overseas. The British Council, Arts Council, provincial and foreign galleries own his pictures. *The Modern Movement in Art*, by R H Wilenski, features Baynes' work. For a time lived near Rye, Sussex. There was a 50-year retrospective at The Minories, Colchester, in 1969, and a show at The Bloomsbury Workshop in 1994.

Pauline BAYNES 1922– Book illustrator and designer, born in Brighton, Sussex, who studied at Farnham School of Art and Slade School of Fine Art after a childhood partly in India. Early in her career she was a member of WIAC. During World War II she was involved in Army camouflage, then worked for Admiralty Hydrographic Department. Illustrated many books, including *Chronicles of Narnia* and other titles in the series by C S Lewis; Enid Blyton's *The Land of Far Beyond*; and a *Dictionary of Chivalry*, which in 1968 gained her the Kate Greenaway Prize, for which she was runner-up in 1972. Sometimes signed work with a bird. Lived near Farnham, Surrey.

Caroline BAYS 1960– Painter who studied foundation at West Surrey College of Art, 1978–9, then at Epsom School of Art, 1979–82. Exhibitions included The Hogarth Club, 1990; The Surrey Figurative Artists, Fire & Iron Gallery, Leatherhead, 1997; PS and The Gallery, Virginia Water, both from 1997; RP and NEAC both from 1998; Waterman Fine Art, from 1999; and The Bourne Gallery, Reigate, 30th Anniversary Exhibition, 2001, which included Bays' cool, clean-cut still life Composition with Pots.

Jack BAYLISS 1936– Artist who began painting seriously around 1990 "when faced with redundancy after a lifetime in the insurance industry." Did a two-year course in painting and drawing at Sir John Cass, providing a suitable portfolio of work for a part-time course as a mature student at Kent Institute of Art & Design, Canterbury, where he graduated with first-class honours in fine arts, 1997. Elected an associate of NS, 2000. Also showed with NEAC, ROI, Chelsea Art Society, South Eastern Arts Federation, Essex Art Club and at ART*futures*, 2000, organised by Contemporary Art Society at Barbican Centre. Corporate and private collections in Britain and abroad hold examples. Lived in Orpington, Kent.

B B: *see* **Denys James WATKINS-PITCHFORD**

James Prinsep BEADLE 1863–1947 Painter, notably of military subjects, born in Calcutta, India, son of Major General James Beadle. He gained a scholarship to study under Alphonse Legros at Slade School of Fine Art and in Paris at École des Beaux-Arts. Won a bronze medal at Paris Universal Exhibition, 1889. Showed widely at Fine Art Society, RA, RBA, RHA and elsewhere, had much work reproduced and is represented in British and foreign public collections. Lived in London.

John BEAGLES 1970– Artist, born in London, who graduated with honours in fine art from Slade School of Fine Art, 1988–92, gaining his master's at Glasgow School of Art, 1994–6. From 1996 Beagles collaborated with Graham Ramsay as Beagles and Ramsay. Their group shows included Pals and Chums, Camerawork Gallery, 1997; Crash, ICA, 1999; Half The World Away, Hallwalls Art Centre, Buffalo, America, 2002; and 25 Hours, Video Art Foundation, Barcelona, Spain, 2003. Among their solo appearances was Burgerheaven, De Fabriek, Eindhoven, Netherlands, and YYZ Gallery, Toronto, Canada, both 2002. In that, they created a fast food restaurant where the meat tasted like the flesh of dead celebrities. There was a Beagles and Ramsay show entitled Unrealised Dreams at Glasgow School of Art's Mackintosh Gallery in 2004–5, an extension of their project for the Scottish Pavilion at the Venice Biennale in 2003. They described their work as "entertaining yet morally ambiguous in tone."

BEAGLES AND RAMSAY: *see* **John BEAGLES** and **Graham RAMSAY**

Alex BEALE 1941– Artist in a range of media, born in Rustington, Sussex, for whom "man's imprint on the environment is my main interest. I seek to translate the mood and atmosphere of nature and the countryside and highlight the contrast between texture, shape and space." Beale trained as a printer with the General Post Office in London. In 1969, he gained the post of senior technician in the three-dimensional department at Ipswich School of Art, working with Bernard Reynolds and Freda Sage. From 1984, worked in the printing industry until, in 1994, ill-health prompted retirement from full-time employment. Beale studied part-time at Southend School of Art, 1957; painting and drawing under Ralph Nuttall-Smith at Camberwell School of Art, 1959; in 1966, attending Ipswich School of Art to study ceramics and sculpture. He was a founder-member of the Six in Suffolk group, 1976, being elected a full member of Ipswich Art Society, 2001. Shared an exhibition with John Chipperfield at Artists' Gallery, Ipswich, 2001. Ipswich solo shows included Ancient House Gallery, 1997, and Ipswich Hospital Trust, 1999 and 2002. Divided Images was held at Reunion Gallery, Felixstowe, 2004. David Poole Memorial Trust holds Beale's work. Lived in Ipswich, Suffolk.

Edward BEALE 1950– Artist who studied at Camberwell School of Art, initially part-time, then full-time, 1968–72, finally at Royal Academy Schools, 1976–9. Beale showed in RA Summer Exhibition from 1977 and had a solo show in RA downstairs gallery in 1983. Among group exhibitions in which he participated was The Broad Horizon, Agnew, 1990, and Edward Beale's Choice, The Gallery at Architecture Ltd, 1996. Piano Nobile showed Beale's Paintings of the River Thames in 2003.

Helen BEALE 1946– Painter, draughtsman and teacher, born in Keighley, Yorkshire, the county where she made her career, settling in Knaresborough. Early work was signed with her maiden name, Elizabeth Helen Green. She studied at Harrogate School of Art, 1962–3, Brighton College of Art, 1963–4, and Liverpool College of Art, 1964–7. She was interested in decorative and design work and for a time directed a design company. Showed in mixed exhibitions in Yorkshire and London, notably with Free Painters and Sculptors and RA. Had several solo shows including Victoria Art Gallery, Harrogate. York Art Society member. Imperial Chemical Industries, Harrogate, holds her work.

Margaret BEALE 1886–1969 Painter in oil and watercolour, especially of seascapes and yachts, born at Yaldham, Kent. She studied art in London with William Orpen, 1906–8, then for two years in Paris under Percyval Tudor-Hart and with him in London, 1911–12. Exhibited frequently at RSMA of which she was a member, with Chichester Art Society and had a solo show in Chichester. Settled at Chidham, Sussex, had a studio overlooking the harbour and taught adults locally into her seventies until local authority discovered her age and would not let her continue. National Maritime Museum, Greenwich, holds her work.

Philippa BEALE 1946– Sculptor, painter and teacher, born in Winchester, Hampshire, where she attended the School of Art, 1961–5. After Goldsmiths' College, 1965–9, was at University of Reading. Went on to teach at Hornsey College of Art and was first artist-in-residence at City Art Gallery in Southampton, 1983. Among her mixed shows were Woolgate House, 1969; Annely Juda Fine Art and ICA, both 1970; Angela Flowers Gallery, 1972; Woodlands Art Gallery, 1973, in Space from the Quadrangle; and Berry Street Open Studios, 1984 and 1989. Beale was also in Arts Council of Great Britain touring exhibitions. She joined LG in 1977, was its president, 1994–8, and contributed an appreciation of it to its ninetieth-anniversary volume, published in 2003. Solo shows included Angela Flowers, 1982.

Nicola BEALING 1963– Painter, born in Hertford, who completed a foundation course at Herts College of Art and Design, St Albans, 1983, gaining a diploma in fine art from Byam Shaw School of Art from 1984. Group shows included Sue Williams Gallery, 1988; Six Painters from Porthleven, Porthmeor Gallery, St Ives, 1990; South-West Open Exhibition, Plymouth City Museum & Art Gallery and Plymouth Arts Centre, 1992, where she was first prizewinner; Peninsular Journeys, Coventry and Middlesex Universities' Art Galleries, 1993; Royal Over-Seas League Open and Millfield Open, where she won a first prize, both 1995, and Meynell Fenton Prize, Discerning Eye, Mall Galleries, 1999. Had a solo show at St Helier Galleries, Jersey, 1989, later ones including Cadogan Contemporary, 2000 and 2001. Commissioned work included a mural at Quayside Fish Centre, Porthleven, 1988, and Embassy of Sultanate of Oman, 1989. Spanset International in Zürich and Unilever Corporate Collection hold examples.

Frederick Harold BEAMISS 1898–1979 Ink and scraperboard artist, born in Hornsey, Middlesex. Studied art at Cologne School of Art, Tottenham Polytechnic and elsewhere. Sometimes signed work Calbeam. Beamiss specialised in views of Devon and its churches, which he showed with Exeter Art Society. Lived in Exeter.

Anne BEAN 1950– Performance artist and teacher, born in Northern Rhodesia, who studied fine art at University of Cape Town and Reading University, 1968–73. Her first public performance was collaborative in the Piazza del Duomo, Florence, in 1970, after which, apart from many solo works, Bean initiated and participated in numerous joint projects, travelling throughout Britain, the continent, America, Mexico and Japan. The diverse venues included Imports, in the Kitchen Gallery, New York; Hayward Annual, at Hayward Gallery; Punk clubs in Hollywood; a zebra crossing outside Air Gallery; a disused fish factory in Norway; the foreshore on Sado Island, Japan; and the Museum of Modern Art in Oxford, Whitechapel Gallery and Pompidou Centre, Paris. Bean's video collaborations were shown on the BBC and commercial television. In 1983 she co-founded the Bow Gamelan Ensemble with Paul Burwell, the drummer, and sculptor Richard Wilson. In 1991, Bean was awarded, for the second time, the *Time Out* Dance and Performance Award for her long contribution to live arts. With the sculptor Peter Fink, in 1992 Bean realised Light Year, then the largest temporary art project in the United Kingdom, which took Canary Wharf as a canvas for a monumental light sculpture, seen over 40 kilometres by millions of Londoners. In 1993 Bean and Fink won a *Time Out* 25-year anniversary billboard. Later performances included Tribute to Yves Klein at Hayward Gallery, 1995, and Peace in rest, at St Thomas' Hospital, 1996. In 2005, Bean participated in Reap, at Dilston Grove, Southwark Park, with Mark Anderson and Gail Dickerson. Bean taught regularly, especially at Middlesex University. Lived in London.

Frank BEANLAND 1936– Painter and designer in abstract, born in Bridlington, Yorkshire, who married the artist Emily Gwynne-Jones. He attended Hull College of Art, 1952–7, then Slade School of Fine Art, 1959–61, where his teachers included Claude Rogers. From 1961–2 a Boise Travelling Scholarship took him to Stockholm. Beanland began showing in mixed exhibitions in 1960 at Young Contemporaries, also exhibiting at Drian Galleries, LG and Gimpel Fils. Solo exhibitions included Smiths Galleries One, 1990, where the artist showed a series of decorated screens employing oil, aluminium and hardboard, and Belgrave Gallery, 1999. Slade School, Paintings for Hospitals and Leverhulme Trust hold his work. Lived in Frostenden, Suffolk.

George Telfer BEAR 1876–1973 Artist in oil and pastel, born in Greenock, Renfrewshire. He studied at Glasgow School of Art under Fra Newbery and James Dunlop, then lived for a time in Canada. After marrying in 1906, returned to Scotland in the early 1920s, where he was associated with the Colourists. Exhibited extensively at Royal Glasgow Institute of the Fine Arts, also RSA, in London, the provinces and in Paris. Glasgow Museum and Art Galleries, the Scottish National Gallery of Modern Art and other galleries hold his work. Lived at Kilmacolm, Renfrewshire, then in Edinburgh.

John BEARD 1943– Painter of abstract works, designer and teacher, born in Aberdare, Glamorgan. He studied at Swansea College of Art, 1962–5, then University of London, 1965–6. Between 1968–70 Beard taught in various schools and universities in England and was a freelance design consultant, also producing and appearing in BBC television programmes. Was at London University, 1973–6, taught fine art for Milton Keynes College/Open University, 1974–9, then gained his master's degree at Royal College of Art, 1979–81. As well as part-time lecturing at Middlesex Polytechnic/Hornsey College of Art, 1979–83, Beard in 1981–2 co-founded the design-winning firm Artigiani before being appointed to Curtin University, Perth, Australia, in 1983, resigning in 1989 to paint full-time. Beard became a naturalised Australian citizen, although he travelled widely to paint, notably in Europe for a sustained period from 1991. As well as showing widely in group exhibitions in Britain and Australia Beard had many solo shows, starting with WAC in Cardiff, 1966. Later ones included Stephen Lacey Gallery, 2000. National Library of Wales, Royal College of Art, Arts Council and many Australian galleries hold Beard's work.

Leonard BEARD 1942– Largely self-taught painter, apart from studies with a professional artist in Italy, Beard spent his career in the Merchant Navy, then moved to Wales in 1976 and decided to paint full-time. Mixed shows included National Museum of Wales, Cardiff, 1988, and Paris Salon, 1994. Had solo exhibitions at Martin Tinney Gallery, Cardiff, from 1993, that show a sell-out. Beard was included in Contemporary Painters of Landscape, Gallery at St Brides, Saundersfoot, 2002, with his atmospheric Pembrokeshire Coastline. He had a solo show at West Wales Arts Centre, Fishguard, in 2004.

Josias Crocker BEARE 1881–1962 Landscape and architectural painter who practised as an architect. Born in Newton Abbot, Devon, Beare began practising in his home town in 1908 after initial studies in Torquay. Exhibited RA, RWA, RCamA, Walker Art Gallery, Liverpool, and BWS. Lived at Newton Abbot.

Karen L BEARE 1955– Painter and draughtsman who studied at the Art Students' League of New York, 1979–80. Went on to paint portraits, commissions including Anglo-Brazilian Society, 1996. Latterly turned to abstract works. An exhibition at The Gallery in Cork Street, 1997, contained abstracts painted with the left hand, a departure leading to colourful, more spontaneous pictures. Earlier in the year showed at Plazzotta Studio, Cathcart Road. Lived in London.

Cecil BEATON 1904–1980 Photographer, stage and film designer, draughtsman, painter and writer. Born in London, he was educated at Harrow – where he studied art under W Egerton Hine – and at St John's College, Cambridge. From the mid-1920s he fast established a reputation as a society photographer and arbiter of beauty, publishing his *Book of Beauty* and working for *Vogue*. First one-man show at Cooling Galleries in 1927, of photographs, drawings and stage designs. He was to hold a number of exhibitions, in Britain and abroad. Designed for C B Cochran, including Frederick Ashton's ballet *The Last Shoot*. During World War II worked for the Ministry of Information and travelled widely abroad, his *Indian Album* and *Chinese Album* resulting from the trips. Illustrated books such as *The School for Scandal* and *The Importance of Being Earnest*, designed book covers and notable stage and film successes such as *Lady Windermere's Fan* and *My Fair Lady*. Published six volumes of diaries, covering the period 1922–74. Knighted in 1972. Memorial exhibition at the Michael Parkin Gallery in 1983, with a sale at Christie's, London, in 1984. In 2004, the National Portrait Gallery and City Art Centre, Edinburgh, showed Beaton's portraits. Lived at Broadchalke, Wiltshire.

Annette BEATTIE 1957– Artist/embroiderer, married to the etcher David Beattie, she signed her meticulously embroidered pictures of wildflowers and landscapes A L Beattie. She was born in the Vale of Belvoir, Nottinghamshire, and worked as a research technician, during which time she studied for an honours degree in biological sciences. Was taught needlework by her grandmother as a child and began to experiment with machine embroidery after the birth of her daughter in 1985. She prepared her canvas by creating a design in acrylic, then applied free machine stitching to give detail, depth of colour and perspective. Couching and appliqué was also used and some threads were hand-dyed to extend the colour range. Exhibited at studio gallery at Llandygwydd, Cardigan, Dyfed.

Basil BEATTIE 1935– Painter of abstract pictures, printmaker, installations artist and teacher, born in West Hartlepool, County Durham. From 1950–5 he studied at West Hartlepool College of Art, moving to the Royal Academy Schools, 1957–61. The following year Beattie began teaching at Goldsmiths' College School of Art. Beattie showed in groups at John Moores Exhibition in Liverpool, in 1965; in 1971 at Museum of Modern Art, Oxford, in Four Painters; and in 1977 at RA in British Painting 1952–1977. In 1976 he won a Major Arts Council Award. His first one-man show was at Greenwich Theatre Art Gallery in 1968, after which he showed widely, including Minories, Colchester; and Bede Gallery, Jarrow; as well as several galleries in London, including Advanced Graphics London, 2001. Beattie was second prizewinner in the 1989–90 John Moores Liverpool Exhibition. In 2002, Sadler's Wells commissioned Beattie to produce work for its lobby. His response was a sculptural configuration incorporating 40 framed graphite drawings, many suggesting formalised architecture, which were presented in relation to three new oil paintings, one, Beyond Yonder, his largest work to date. Beattie's Stacks Paintings 2000–2004 was at Atkinson Gallery, Millfield, Street, in 2004. Arts Council holds several examples of his work. Lived in London.

David BEATTIE 1955– Etcher principally who also worked in carved wood, welded metal and ceramics, teacher, born in Nottingham. Studied at Loughborough College of Education, 1974–7, as an art and design student to become a teacher, but quit in his final term when early sales of prints made living as an artist seem feasible. Supported himself by working for HM Customs & Excise for several years, but set up his own studio and was able to etch full-time. Beattie was a keen conservationist and horseman whose subjects ranged from his cats to cockerels, farmyard doors, trees and countryside characters. Showed at RA Summer Exhibitions and with Christie's Contemporary Art. Established a studio gallery at Llandygwydd, Cardigan, Dyfed. His wife was the artist/embroiderer Annette Beattie.

John BEATTIE 1980– Painter, born in County Donegal, Ireland, who studied at North West Institute of Further &

Higher Education, Londonderry, 1997–9; National College of Art & Design, Dublin, 1999–03; and the University of Ulster, Belfast, through 2004, when his Connection series 2003/4 was included in the John Moores Liverpool Exhibition. In it he tried, "through recurring symbolical motifs and mark-making, such as the circle, the initial 'E' and dates such as '82', to draw upon memories of specific events and experiences." By then, Beattie had participated in many mixed shows, including Marshal Fields, Thomas Wesley, Chicago, America, 2003, and Panoply, Catalyst, Belfast, and Emerging Artists, RHA, Dublin, both 2004.

Ronn BEATTIE 1943– Sculptor and lecturer in art theory and practice who worked under her maiden name of Ronn Smith until 1971. Beattie gained her National Diploma in fine art, sculpture, from Hammersmith College of Art & Building, 1964; gained a Postgraduate Certificate in Education, with distinction, Garnett College, 1986; graduated in art history from Open University, 1987; obtained her master's in theory of practice from Goldsmiths' College, 1994; and her doctorate from Open University in 2000. Lectured widely, including Epsom, Guildford and Reigate Art Schools, Croydon College of Art and adult classes in Camden, Hertfordshire University, Bretton Hall College, Falmouth College of Arts and Kensington and Chelsea College. Travelled a lot and carried out sculpture commissions for two Surrey schools. Later exhibitions included Maidenhead Sculpture Competition, 1986; Bretton Hall College, from 1995; Lethaby Gallery, 2000; and Heifer Gallery, 2002. Lived in Maidenhead, Berkshire.

Charles BEAUCHAMP 1949– Painter and printmaker, noted for his landscapes and figure subjects, some of whose work had a Surrealist element. He was born in London and attended Chelsea School of Art, 1967, travelled extensively in the Far East, 1968–9, then in 1971–2 studied etching and engraving at S W Hayter's Atelier 17 in Paris. From 1969 took part in many group shows, including Young & Fantastic, ICA and tour, 1969; Third British International Print Biennale, Bradford, 1972; Graves Art Gallery, Sheffield, 1986 in A Show of Hands; and Art into Ambit 2, Smiths Galleries, 1992. Among a series of awards were 1st prize, First Irish Miniprint Exhibition, Hendriks Gallery, Dublin 1986, and Openshaw Printmaking Residency Award, Cumbria, 1994. Had a series of solo shows at Gimpel Fils from 1974. Hirshhorn Museum and Sculpture Garden, Washington; National Gallery of Wales in Cardiff; and Winnipeg Art Gallery, Canada, are among many major collections holding examples. Settled in London with frequent visits to Colombia.

Paul BEAUCHAMP 1948– Artist, designer and teacher, born in Barrow-upon-Soar, Leicestershire. He studied at Loughborough College of Art from 1967, at Hornsey College of Art, 1968–71, then from 1971–3 was a postgraduate student at Slade School of Fine Art. Russian Constructivist art and the work of architects such as Frank Lloyd Wright and Le Corbusier were important influences. After creating a company called Aqua Designs with three other artists, in 1973 Beauchamp lectured part-time at the College of Art in Cardiff, where he settled, and helped turn twilight buildings into artists' studios. The following years saw Beauchamp using glass and silicone constructions, reflecting and refracting light; wall sculpture incorporating wood, paint and glass; cibachrome photographs and drawings; and laser as an art form. In 1983 he was chosen to redesign a room at Chapter Arts, Cardiff, his first commission working directly with an architect. Six years later he worked in Charleston, South Carolina, as an artist and lecturer, having a series of exhibitions. Also showed at Serpentine Gallery, Ian Birksted Gallery in London and New York, Ikon Gallery in Birmingham and National Museum of Wales, Cardiff. Doris and Charles Saatchi bought his work.

Basil BEAUMONT: *see* **Basil RÁKÓCZI**

Frederick Samuel BEAUMONT 1861– Painter and draughtsman in pastel. Studied art at the Royal Academy Schools and at the Académie Julian, Paris. Exhibited widely into his old age, including RA, RI, ROI and Walker's Gallery. Was a member of the Arts Club, London. Lived in London.

Leonard BEAUMONT 1891–1986 Painter, designer and printmaker, born and based in Sheffield, where he was honorary secretary of The Sheffield Print Club. He was associated with the Grosvenor School of Modern Art and his prints show an affinity with the work of Claude Flight. Exhibited at RA, SGA of which he was a member, Redfern Gallery, Walker Art Gallery in Liverpool and elsewhere in the provinces. Victoria & Albert Museum and Scottish National Gallery of Modern Art, Edinburgh, hold examples. Beaumont's work appeared in several art periodicals, including *The Studio* and *Fine Prints of the Year*.

Sharon BEAVAN 1956– Painter and teacher, born and lived in London. She had a great empathy with the city, tirelessly exploring the streets, absorbing and recording what she saw, which emerged in colourful panoramas which could take several years to complete. She studied at Hertfordshire College of Art and Design, 1974–6; Falmouth College of Art, 1976–9; and Royal College of Art, 1981–4. Teaching included Kingston University, Central St Martins School of Art and Hertfordshire College of Art and Design. Group exhibitions included RA Summer Exhibitions from 1985; South Bank Picture Show, Royal Festival Hall from 1987; and The Celebrated City, Barbican Art Gallery, 1992. Had a series of solo shows at Le Chat Noir Gallery from 1991. She was the subject of a London Weekend Television documentary. Guildhall Art Gallery and Museum of London hold examples.

Anton BEAVER 1965– Artist who studied at Liverpool Polytechnic from 1985. He was included in group shows at Acorn Gallery and Playhouse Theatre, Liverpool, in 1986, and in 1986–7 was included in Walker Art Gallery's touring show Merseyside Artists 3, where his acrylic Sunrise over the Mersey was exhibited.

Robert BEAVER 1906–1975 Painter in oil, born in Poole, Dorset, who was by profession a doctor. Educated at Winchester College, Oxford University and St Thomas' Hospital, Beaver studied art privately in Belgium. Exhibited, sometimes as R B, at RA, ROI, NEAC, NS and in Cornwall. Lived in London and then in Cowes, Isle of Wight, where he died.

Tessa BEAVER 1932– Printmaker, painter and teacher, born in London, who gained a fine art diploma from Slade School of Fine Art, 1953, then spent a year etching there under John Buckland-Wright. After six months in Italy and Greece she worked as a freelance illustrator, then as an art editor in publishing. In 1962 Beaver went with her husband to teach in western Kenya, began painting and taught herself woodblock printing, then for 10 years after returning to England showed seriously and in 1972 bought a press and began etching again. By 1977 big editions of her prints were being regularly published by Christie's Contemporary Art and Pallas Gallery. In 1978 she set up her own studio in Leamington Spa, Warwickshire. Took part in many mixed exhibitions in Britain and abroad, including RE, RA, ICA and RWA. Had a series of solo shows at University of Warwick from 1972, later ones including Church Street Gallery, Warwick, 1988. Birmingham City Museum and Art Gallery holds her work.

Ian BECK 1947– Printmaker, illustrator and painter, born in Brighton, Sussex. He studied at the College of Art there until 1968. Went on to work as a freelance illustrator, notably for *Radio Times*, Penguin Books and Conran Associates. His first illustrated children's book was published by Oxford University Press in 1983. Merivale Editions published his four-colour lithograph *Seaside Circus*, 1984. Beck showed paintings with Francis Kyle Gallery.

Paul BECK 1926– Painter, printmaker and teacher, born in Belvedere, Kent, who studied at Gravesend School of Art and Royal College of Art. Went on to teach at Cambridge College of Art. Work appeared in group shows, including RA, Cambridge Print Editions exhibitions, 1964–71, Brooklyn Museum, 1970, and elsewhere. One-man shows included Ludlow Craft Studio and Gallery, 1977, Malvern Festival, 1979, Graffiti Gallery, 1980, and a series at the Old Fire Engine House, Ely. His work is held in collections in continental Europe, Australia and America and in Britain, including Fry Art Gallery, Saffron Walden, which exhibited his posters and prints in 1997.

Stuart BECK 1903–2000 Painter and writer, born in Barnes, southwest London, who began sea painting as a full-time career in 1968. Studied at Rochester School of Art, 1919–21. Was then 15 years a graphic designer with a London colour printing firm; several years head of studio in a publishing company; in World War II did technical illustration for the Admiralty; and after demobilisation in 1946 did a variety of work from technical cut-aways to posters and book jackets as a freelance. Was elected to RSMA in 1980. Also showed with RI, RBA, SGA and elsewhere. Had solo shows at Solent Gallery, Lymington, Hampshire, where he lived; and Skipwith Gallery, Winchester. RSMA holds work in its Diploma Collection as do Royal National Lifeboat Museum, Poole, and National Maritime Museum, Greenwich. Among his books were *How to Draw Fishing Craft* and *The Ship how she Works*.

Haidee BECKER 1950– Figurative painter using a muted palette, born in Los Angeles, California, America, but raised in Rome and Vienna. From 1966 she lived in London, from 1969 studying with Anthony Whishaw, Sophie Wysotsky and Jean Gibson; from 1971–7, with Uli Nimptsch; from 1971–85 with Adrian Ryan; from 1972–85 with Elizabeth Keys; with Fritz Wotruba, at the Vienna Academy; and in 1980 with Herta Koetner and Andrea Moering. Took part in many group exhibitions in Britain and America, later ones including Byard Art, Cambridge, from 2002, and Gallery Timothy Tew, Atlanta, 2003. Showed frequently solo with Timothy Tew from 1991, also with Redfern Gallery, 2002, and Bourne Fine Art, Edinburgh, 2003. National Portrait Gallery and several corporate collections hold Becker's work. The poet Ted Hughes, a collector of her work, wrote that her pictures "became, for me, an ideal.... The painted surface like some kind of precious substance".

Mike BECKET 1946– Designer and artist, several of whose lyrical, circus-oriented acrylic-on-Perspex paintings were included in Vision 21 at Bonhams, Knightsbridge, in 2004. Becket was best known as a set and costume designer for fringe companies and ballet at the Royal Opera House and Birmingham Royal Ballet. In the theatre he worked with leading designers and artists, including John Craxton, David Hockney, Sidney Nolan, Victor Pasmore and John Piper before turning to his own paintings and themes. In these, he cast a wry eye over audiences, figures in the orchestra and backstage events. He had many mixed show appearances, including Elms Lesters Painting Rooms, from 1987; Royal Opera House Foyer, 1994; Heifer Gallery from 1995; Beatrice Royal Gallery, Eastleigh, from 1995, when he was awarded first prize in The Sea Exhibition; Harbour Lights Gallery, Southampton, 1997; and Belgrave Gallery St Ives, from 1999. Beatrice Royal gave him one of his many solo shows in 1998 and there were two at Piers Feetham Gallery and the Royal Opera House in 2002. Langton Street Gallery also showed Becket's work.

Rachel BECKETT 1974– Artist and teacher working in a mix of media, born and lived in Bristol, who did a foundation course at City of Bath College, 1992–3; obtained an honours degree in fine art, sculpture, at Cheltenham and Gloucester College of Higher Education, 1993–6; studied glass techniques/technology at Dudley College, 1996–7; and gained her master's in sculpture at Royal College of Art, 1997–9. Held visiting lectureships at Cheltenham and Gloucester, Kingston University and Kent Institute of Art and Design, all 1999. In 2000, did work for the Euro Disney Parade, London and Paris, and Millennium Dome, then travelled for a year in Malaysia, Australia and New Zealand. Exhibitions included Whitechapel Open, Tannery Gallery, 1998; Pause, *The Economist*, 1999–2000; and Contemporary Art Society's Art2000 in 2000.

Robert BECKETT 1963– Portrait painter and sculptor who graduated in biochemistry and while travelling abroad in 1985 began developing an artistic career. For a time he was a successful wine merchant. He decided to concentrate on art in 1990, after travelling in France to paint from nature, returning to pursue sculpture and portraiture further. Recognition for his bronze, oil and pastel portraits followed and within a few years he was completing over 60 commissions a year in various media. Beckett's group appearances included Cadogan Contemporary and Portraits Inc, New York in America, both from 1995; SPS from 1996; and Yellow Gallery, from 1998. He had solo exhibition with Peter and Georgie Donnelly, London, 1992 and 1995, and at Edith Grove Gallery, 1993. Rob Beckett said: "I like to capture people in their own surroundings. Nearly all of the paintings and drawings of children are done from photographs that I take when they look bright and healthy.... Whenever possible, I like to paint adults from life." Selected commissions included Sir Derek and Lady Bibby, Sir Evelyn Delves-Broughton, Countess Spencer, Mrs Rupert Murdoch and the Countess of Hopetoun. In 2005, Beckett painted the politician Dr Mo Mowlam for the BBC1 television programme *Star Portraits with Rolf Harris*, the resulting pictures being shown at the County Hall Gallery, plus a tour. He lived in Petersfield, Hampshire.

Sarah BECKETT 1946– Painter, notable for rich palette. She studied at Byam Shaw School of Drawing and Painting, 1963–5, then Chelsea College of Art, 1977–80. From the early 1970s she appeared in many mixed exhibitions, including Six British Artists, Trinidad, 1971; San Patricio, Colombia, 1973; People's Gallery, 1982; NEAC, 1983; and Queen Elizabeth Hall, 1986. She had a solo exhibition at Bank of Nova Scotia, Trinidad, in 1971, then at The Gore Hotel, London, 1979. From 1985 showed one-man at Christopher Hull Gallery. National Labour Museum and several foreign public collections hold her work.

Gillian BECKLES 1918– Painter of landscapes who was well featured in international books on naïve artists. Her many group appearances included WIAC, 1948–65; City Art Gallery, Bristol, 1952; AIA, 1957; Basel Gewerbemuseum, Switzerland, 1961; Ben Uri Art Society, 1962–4; Alyce Nash Gallery, New York, 1964; Galerie Creuze, Paris, 1967; Downtown Gallery, Honolulu, 1971 and 1973; Galerie Charlotte, Munich, 1981; and Oliver Contemporary, 2003 and 2004. She won the Prix Suisse de Peinture Naïve, Morges, in 1980 and 1981. Solo exhibitions included Marjorie Parr Gallery, 1973; Galerie Charlotte, 1978; and Grabowski Gallery, 1987.

Janet BECKWITH 1956– Artist in a variety of media, and teacher, who did a foundation art and design course at Wakefield College, Wakefield, 1988–9, gaining an honours degree in fine art at Leeds Metropolitan University, 1989–92, attending a 1992 art therapy summer school at Leeds University. She lectured part-time at Wakefield College, art drama and independent learning skills for students with special needs. In 1997, Beckwith was artist-in-residence for DIVA (Development Initiatives for Voluntary Arts) and Yorkshire Art Circus. Mixed shows included Fresh Art at Business Design Centre, Islington, 1992; Bookies and Boxers, Manor House Gallery, Ilkley, 1993; and Brought to Book, Collins Gallery, Glasgow, and tour, 1996. Her solo show Ties, 1997–8, toured from the Art Gallery in Wakefield, Yorkshire, where she lived, to Hardware Gallery. This explored "ties that bind us together, make us feel safe and protected or tangle us in painful knots".

Roy BEDDINGTON 1910–1995 Painter, with a special interest in watercolours of natural history and the countryside, illustrator and author. Born in London, son of a barrister, he attended Rugby School, where he cultivated his lifelong passion for fishing; was then offered a place at Slade School of Fine Art by Henry Tonks, but spent only a few weeks there; opted instead to read law at Oxford University; then, after private lessons from Bernard Adams, returned to the Slade under Randolph Schwabe, also studying in Florence. His own books included *The Adventures of Thomas Trout*, 1939, and *A Countryman's Verse*, 1981. Among other books illustrated were a series by Stephen Gwynn, including *The Happy Fisherman*, 1936, and J W Walker's *Riverside Reflections*, 1947. Did posters for Shell encouraging travel through Britain. Showed in mixed exhibitions at RA, NEAC, RWS, Whitechapel Art Gallery and Fine Art Society. Ackermann's gave him his first solo pre-war show. He was an Arts Club member and for many years was a leading figure in the Salmon and Trout Association. His daughter Sarah Beddington was also a painter. Lived at Chute Cadley, Hampshire, and died in Salisbury, Wiltshire.

Sarah BEDDINGTON 1964– Painter, born in Wiltshire, who studied at City and Guilds of London Art School and Central St Martins College. Group exhibitions included Concourse Gallery, Barbican Centre, 1992; The Mag Collection, Ferens Art Gallery, Hull, 1997; and Towner Art Gallery, Eastbourne, 1998. In 1999 Beddington was a finalist for The NatWest Art Prize, exhibiting unpopulated scenes based on photographs of the city at night, evoking traces of human presence and with an eerie, dreamlike quality. Also in 1999 exhibited in John Moores Liverpool Exhibition and had a solo exhibition at Hales Gallery.

Sheila BEDELLS 1916– Painter, born in Duston, Northamptonshire, who studied at Epsom School of Art with David Birch, other teachers including Karl Hagedorn and Peter Oliver. Showed variously and did designs for Christmas and greetings cards. Lived in Betchworth, Surrey.

Celia BEDFORD 1904–1959 Portrait and figure painter, printmaker and draughtsman, born in London, daughter of the artist Francis Bedford. Studied at Chelsea School of Art under Percy Hague Jowett and John Revel. Exhibited WIAC, of which she was a member, RA, NEAC, LG and Leicester Galleries. Atkinson Art Gallery, Southport, and Birmingham City Museum and Art Gallery hold her work. Lived in London.

Francis Donkin BEDFORD 1864–1954 Illustrator and painter whose work reflected his architectural training. He was born and lived in London, studied at South Kensington and the Royal Academy architectural schools, then was articled to Sir Arthur Blomfield, the architect, for several years. His wife was the painter Helen Bedford. E V Lucas, W M Thackeray, Charles Dickens and Oliver Goldsmith were among the authors he illustrated. Bedford was a member of the Art Workers' Guild and showed at RA, Ridley Art Club and NEAC.

Helen BEDFORD 1874–1949 Portrait painter, daughter of the artist Hugh Carter and wife of the illustrator Francis Donkin Bedford. The family of the poet Sir Henry Newbolt and the architect Charles Voysey were among her subjects. She was a member of PS, Ridley Art Club and the Women's Guild of Arts, also showing at RA, NEAC and SWA. Lived in London.

Oliver Herbert BEDFORD 1902– Painter, teacher and printmaker, born in Boston Spa, Yorkshire, the son of an architect. Studied at the Royal Institute of Fine Arts in Rome, 1919–23, where he taught for a short time, then at the Courtauld Institute of Art, London, 1935–6. He went on to teach at Truro School of Art and elsewhere in Cornwall, which was the focus of his career, being closely associated with the St Ives Society of Artists and several other such societies within Cornwall. Showed extensively at Fine Art

Society, also RI, SGA of which he was a member and NS. Lived in Truro.

Richard Perry BEDFORD 1883–1967 Sculptor in stone and marble, born in Torquay, Devon. Studied at Central School of Arts and Crafts and Chelsea School of Art. He was keeper at the the Victoria and Albert Museum, 1924–46, first of the Department of Sculpture, then of Circulation, and was then for two years curator of pictures for the Ministry of Works. Exhibited Cooling Galleries, Lefevre Gallery, RA, NS, LG, RWA and elsewhere in the provinces. The Victoria & Albert Museum and Bristol City Art Gallery hold his work. Bedford, who was son of the artist George Bedford, lived finally at West Mersea, Essex, and had a retrospective at The Minories, Colchester, in 1968.

Simon BEDWELL 1963– Artist and lecturer who did foundation studies at St Martin's School of Art, 1982–3, where he gained an honours degree in fine art, painting, 1983–6; a postgraduate diploma in printmaking, Brighton Polytechnic, 1989–91; and his master's in fine art, Goldsmiths' College, 1991–3. From 1998–9 Bedwell did extensive lecturing, including University of Brighton, Leeds University, Chelsea School of Art, Goldsmiths' College and Royal College of Art. Most of Bedwell's energy went into work produced as part of the group Bank (see separate entry). Exhibitions including Bedwell as a named artist included Chlorine, Marshall Street Leisure Centre, 1992; Wish You Were Here, Bankspace, 1994; The Charge of the Light Brigade, Bankspace, 1995; and London Underground's Platform for Art, Piccadilly Circus Station, 2004. Lived in London.

Sara BEE 1951– After education in Gillingham, Dorset, Bee did a foundation course at Bournemouth College of Art, then graduated in graphic design at Maidstone College of Art. She worked in the art department of *Good Housekeeping* magazine, then as a freelance make-up artist and body painter for film and photography. She began painting in 1997, attending Heatherley's School of Fine Art and receiving private tuition, 2000–2, from John Blockley. Bee exhibited from 2000 at the RI and PS, where in 2004 she was a major prize winner. She was elected PS in 2005 and in 2006 won the Linda Blackstone Prize at its annual exhibition. Hicks Gallery, Wimbledon, also showed her work.

Glynis BEECROFT 1945– Sculptor, teacher and writer who was educated at Portsmouth College of Art, 1962–6, then Goldsmiths' College School of Art, 1966–7. Teaching appointments included West Dean College, Sussex, and Southampton College of Art. She was also sculpture assistant to Lynn Chadwick. Exhibitions included Southampton University, David Paul Gallery in Chichester, RBS, Laing Art Gallery in Newcastle upon Tyne and Artmonsky Arts and elsewhere. Her books *Carving Techniques* and *Casting Techniques* were acknowledged primers. Grantham Art Gallery holds her work and her limestone carving Family, 1983, was sited in Stevenage New Town. She was also known as Glynis Owen. Lived in Clanfield, Hampshire.

Lance Antony BEEKE 1939– Representational painter, born in Maidstone, Kent, who attended Gravesend and Maidstone Colleges of Art, 1959–63, graduating after studying fine and graphic art and silversmithing. He served in the Royal Air Force, 1964–6, and painted full-time from 1988. He described himself as an Impressionist plein-air artist, whose influences included Corot, Vuillard, Bonnard and some modern English painters. Living in Cromer, the north Norfolk seaside town, the seascape, fishing boats and towering cliffs provided ready subjects, as well as the Mediterranean island of Gozo, with its rugged rocky landscape and sun-bleached buildings. Beeke's exhibitions included Assembly Rooms, Norwich, 1989; Maddermarket Theatre, Norwich, 1990; Ministry of Culture, Gozo, 1991; Mixed exhibitions, Gozo, 1994–9; RA Summer Exhibition, 1995; winning entry, Laing Art Competition, Mall Galleries, 1997; and Judy Hines of Holt, 2001. Beeke was artist-in-residence, Victoria Citadel, Gozo, in 1992.

Clem BEER 1931– Painter, printmaker, illustrator and teacher, born and lived in London. Studied at Slade School of Fine Art, 1949–52; lived in North Yorkshire for 10 years painting and teaching, having his first solo show at University of York, 1966; returned to Slade as a printmaking postgraduate, 1968–9, under Anthony Gross. In 1979 became chairman of Printmakers' Council. Showed with RWS, RA, Whitechapel Art Gallery, Woodlands Art Gallery and elsewhere, including Spirit of London Exhibition, Royal Festival Hall, 1982, where he was a prizewinner. Work was bought by RA under the Annie Hugill Trust. Beer was "interested in overturning the conventional viewpoint of perspective and allowing my work the freedom to find the new patterns and rhythms of a more personal vision". University College and Guildhall, British Museum and Arts Council plus several foreign collections hold examples.

Richard BEER 1928– Painter, draughtsman and designer, and teacher. He attended the Slade School of Fine Art, 1945–50. Won Robert Ross and Henriques Scholarships. Beer also studied at S W Hayter's Atelier 17, and École des Beaux-Arts, in Paris, under a French Government Scholarship. In 1955 Beer designed sets and costumes for John Cranko's *Lady and the Fool* at Royal Opera House, Covent Garden, later productions including *Change of Tune*, in 1958, at Strand Theatre, and in 1968 *Napoli*, also at Covent Garden. He taught at Slade, 1957–60, and later at Chelsea School of Art, in 1987 being engaged at the British School in Rome. Beer was especially interested in modest, quirky urban architecture, which found its outlet in a variety of printed work including some for Shell, Christie's Contemporary Art and magazine and book illustration. Had many mixed and one-man show appearances, the latter including Parkin Gallery, 1982, and Sally Hunter Fine Art, 1990–2. Tate Gallery, Victoria & Albert Museum and Arts Council hold his work.

Max BEERBOHM 1872–1956 Humorous caricaturist and writer, born in London, his half-brother being the actor-manager Sir Herbert Beerbohm-Tree. Educated at Charterhouse and Oxford University, Max was a leading figure in 1890s literary London. First published drawings appeared in *The Strand Magazine* in 1892 and he contributed to *The Yellow Book*. He succeeded Bernard Shaw as dramatic critic of the *Saturday Review*. First book of caricatures, *Caricatures of Twenty-Five Gentlemen*, was published in 1896 and he had his first one-man show at the Carfax Gallery eight years later. He was associated with the Leicester Galleries, NEAC, National Portrait Society and IS. From 1910, apart from the war years, he lived mainly in Rapallo, Italy. Tate Gallery holds his work. As well as his drawings Max was famous for his novel *Zuleika Dobson*, 1911, a fantastic picture of Oxford life, his essays and his broadcasts, all tinged with a dandyish flair. Tate Gallery holds his work. Knighted, 1939. Memorial exhibition Leicester Galleries, 1957.

Sue BEERE 1944– Artist and teacher who was for a time a research technician in the department of physiology at Oxford University, also working as personal assistant to the lung specialist Professor Ivan de Burgh Daly. Beere studied painting at Walthamstow School of Art, 1966–8, then taught at Royal College of Art, 1968–71. In 1974 she had a painting commissioned for Sir Robert McAlpine & Sons Ltd and taught part-time at the Central School. Was included in the 1978 Hayward Annual at Hayward Gallery, with four items; Installation Piece 1–4, slender geometrical abstracts in wood. Had a solo show at New 57 Gallery, 1973, with a studio exhibition at Butlers Wharf.

Jane BEESON 1930– Painter, born in Weybridge, Surrey, who studied at Kingston School of Art, 1949–51, then at École des Beaux-Arts, Paris, 1951–2, and at Slade School of Fine Art, 1953, with Lucian Freud. After having a family of four she began painting professionally in 1960, showing at John Moores Liverpool Exhibition, 1961, New Art Centre, Rowan Gallery and elsewhere. In 1963 she was a prize-winner at Arnolfini Open Competition, Bristol. Ferens Art Gallery, Hull, holds her work Mauve and Yellow, 1962. Beeson was a member of the St Ives art scene in the 1960s, although living in Devon. "My painting was Abstract Expressionist and was influenced by a period of four years when I was in Canada and America." Lived in Manaton, Devon.

David BEGBIE 1955– Sculptor, draughtsman and print-maker who was born in Edinburgh. He studied at Winchester School of Art, 1975–6, graduated with honours from Gloucestershire College of Art and Design, 1977–80, then was at Slade School of Sculpture, 1980–2. Among his awards was Gane Travel Scholarship, 1979, and Elizabeth Greenshields Award, Canada, 1980. Figurative steelmesh sculpture was a feature of Begbie's output, the results sometimes being hieratic, ambivalent, mysterious. His solo appearances included Brompton Gallery from 1984; Salama-Caro Gallery from 1987; Catto Gallery, 1993; Gallery Differentiate, 2000; and Number Nine The Gallery, Birmingham, 2003. By then, Begbie was an associate of the RBS. Group shows included Open Studios, Wapping, 1982; Young Variety Club of Great Britain, 1987; and International Art Fair, Miami, 1993. Lived in London.

Torie BEGG 1962– Artist, born in London, who studied graphic design at Richmond College, 1980; illustration at City and Guilds of London Art School, 1984; and advanced printmaking at Central School of Art, 1987. Group exhibitions included Benson & Hedges Annual Gold Awards, Hamilton Gallery, 1985; Louise Hallett Gallery, 1987; Sue Williams Gallery, 1988; and Galerie Albrecht, Munich, and Real Art at Southampton City Art Gallery, both 1995. Solo exhibitions included *The Economist* Building, 1992, Art & Public/Pierre Huber, Geneva, 1995; and f a projects, 2002.

Neal BEGGS 1959– Artist, born in Larne, County Antrim, who worked in Glasgow and Nantes, France. Beggs graduated from Sheffield Hallam University, 1992–5, gaining his master's in fine art from Glasgow School of Art, 1996–8. Beggs' residencies included Zoo Galerie, Nantes, 1999; Centre for Contemporary Art, Glasgow, 2000; The Mountaineering Council of Scotland (Scotland's Year of the Artist), 2000–1; and Le Grand Café, Centre d'Art Contemporain, Saint Nazaire, 2003. Took part in numerous group exhibitions in Britain and abroad, later ones including Frozen, 2002, at Site Gallery, Sheffield, a gallery specialising in lens-based and electronic media. Solo exhibitions and projects included The Glasgow Project Room, Le Grand Café in Saint Nazaire, 105A Brixton Hill and Transpalette, Bourges, all in 2003. Among Beggs' commissioned works were Corridor, Centre for Contemporary Art in Glasgow, 1999–2001, and Sparkle, Scottish Cultural Enterprise, Scotland Year of the Artist, 2000.

Reinhard BEHRENS 1951– Artist and teacher, born in Scheeszel, West Germany, who attended Hamburg College of Art, 1971–9. After completing postgraduate studies at Edinburgh College of Art, 1979–80, he gained an Andrew Grant Scholarship (Major Award), 1980–1, from 1982 lecturing part-time there. Was included in Scottish Print Open Three, organised by Dundee Printmakers' Workshop, 1983. Behrens was a member of RSW, at one time president of SSA, also exhibiting at RSA. Solo show at Roger Billcliffe Fine Art, Glasgow, 1999. Lived in Pittenweem, Fife.

Romi BEHRENS 1939– Painter and printmaker, born in London, full name Rosemary Tunstall-Behrens. She had no formal training but was "'discovered' by Michael Canney in 1960". Her work was colourful, figurative but stylized and was shown at Newlyn Society of Artists of which she was a member; Brunswick Gallery; Judd Street Gallery; RA; Salthouse Gallery, St Ives; and in 1993 she was included in Jeremy Le Grice's Cornwall: A Painter's Choice, at Cadogan Contemporary. Portraits of musicians were an important feature of her output. Lived at Rosudgeon, Penzance, Cornwall.

Timothy BEHRENS 1937– Painter, born in London, who studied at the Slade School of Fine Art, 1954–8. Showed at Young Contemporaries, 1955–8, was included in the Café Royal Memorial Exhibition, 1965, and in Helen Lessore and the Beaux Arts Gallery, Marlborough Fine Art, 1967. Behrens was one of a group of painters – including Auerbach, Andrews, Bacon and Freud – who frequented Muriel Belcher's Colony Room drinking club in Soho. He had three solo exhibitions at Beaux Arts from 1960; one at Upper Street Gallery, 1970; another toured from Galleria 88, Rome, 1973; and at William Darby, 1974. He travelled widely in Europe, settling in Italy in 1970. He later lived in Spain, having an exhibition at Casa Charry, Oleiros, A Coruña, in 1998. Arts Council has his oil on board A Lunch Party, 1961.

Pauline Margaret BEILBY 1927– Sculptor and textile designer, born in Bramcote, Nottinghamshire. Portrait busts and equine portraits were an important feature of her output. In 1947–51 studied at Nottingham School of Art. Was a part-time designer for George Pearson & Sons, of Basford, in mid-1950s. Showed at Gerald Anthony Fine Arts and Victoria Gallery, Nottingham. Lived at Woodthorpe, Nottinghamshire. Later showed under her married name Pauline Margaret Barnes.

George BELCHER 1875–1947 Cartoonist, painter and printmaker, born in London. He attended Gloucester School of Art, then gradually became known for his contributions to publications such as *Punch, The Tatler* and *Vanity Fair.* Showed extensively at RA, Fine Art Society and Leicester Galleries, where his shows such as London Types and Characters and London Life and Character before World War I were very successful. Died at Chiddingfold, Surrey, having a retrospective at Cranleigh Hall seven years later, with another at Marc Oxley Fine Art, Uppingham, 1995. Tate Gallery holds his work.

William BELCHER 1923– Painter and creator of boxes and mixed-media constructions. After service in World War II he studied at Worthing School of Art and Royal College of Art, gaining a travel bursary from Royal Society of Arts. He showed at RA Summer Exhibition, AIA and had several mixed-media constructions included in Art in Boxes at England & Co, 1991. Lived at Kew Gardens, Richmond, Surrey.

Anthony BELL 1962– Painter and printmaker who studied at West Sussex College of Design, 1980–1; gained a degree in fine art at Newcastle University, 1981–5; and his master's there, 1985–7. He showed at Cardiff College of Art Inter-college Exhibition, 1984; The Bookhouse, Newcastle, 1985; Worthing Library Art Gallery and in a three-artist exhibition at Linton Court Gallery, Settle, both 1986.

Arthur BELL 1897–1995 Landscape watercolourist, draughtsman, printmaker and teacher who worked in a meticulous style, born in Kettering, Northamptonshire. Showed an early talent for drawing, but poor health restricted him to elementary schooling, then in 1913 he joined the architectural practice of Marriott, Cooper and Williams. During World War I he held an Army commission, being wounded in France. Studied at Bournemouth Municipal School of Art, 1919–21, under Geoffrey Baker, Henry Crocket and Leslie Ward. A fellow-student was Bertha Beal, whom Bell married in 1922, their son being the teacher and artist John Bell. Arthur and Bertha Bell were prolific between the two world wars, having work selected for the RA Summer Exhibition, being members of the Poole and East Dorset Art Society and Bournemouth Arts Club and having joint exhibitions. Bell became Cheltenham College's director of art, was elected RWA in 1947 and showed with Cheltenham Art Society and other local groups in the Cotswolds, living at Brockhampton, Gloucestershire. Retired from teaching in 1957, settling in Stoke Orchard; latterly travelled to Malta, Italy and France; and died in Tewkesbury Hospital. Cheltenham Art Gallery, which held a show of Bell's work in 1987, holds his work, as do the Ashmolean Museum, Oxford, and the Cecil Higgins Museum and Art Gallery, Bedford. There was a commemorative show at the RWA in 1997 with an accompanying booklet detailing Bell's life and output.

Bertha BELL 1898–1955 Multi-talented artist, whose output apart from paintings included pewter and brassware, illuminated texts, textile designs and rugs for Debenhams stores. She was a pupil of Maud Wear, studying at Bournemouth Municipal School of Art after World War I. There she met her future husband, the painter and printmaker Arthur Bell, their son being the artist and teacher John Bell. Showed at RA and in the provinces, several times jointly with her husband, and all three members of the family had works exhibited at RWA in 1955. The booklet accompanying her husband's 1997 memorial show, held at the RWA and which included some of Bertha's work, outlines Bertha's life. She was buried at Leckhampton churchyard, Gloucestershire.

Betsy Tyler BELL fl. from 1980s– Painter, printmaker and teacher, born in Lancashire, who did a foundation course at Oxford Brooks University, then studying at Ruskin School of Art, 1984–8. She graduated in fine art, with her master's from St Edmund Hall. Tutors included Jean Lodge, Stan Smith and David Tindle. Bell was a visiting professor/artist-in-residence at Washington and Lee University, Virginia, also teaching at Sunningwell Art School, Oxford, at Abingdon College and Oxford Printmakers. Landscape, cycles of nature and the elements were key features of Bell's work. Although she might incorporate recognisable images, she preferred "to work in mainly abstract format using the textures of my own handmade paper and the colour of pure pigments together with acrylic", inviting "the viewer to participate in a personal way without preconceptions". Pictures were built up "in layers over many weeks and sometimes months". Group shows included RE Open, Bankside Gallery, 1992; Place Juberon (Festival des Arts), Crest, France, 1994; and Templeton College, Oxford, 1997. Had a solo show at Templeton, 1994, later ones including Linacre College and Whistles Fashions, both in Oxford in 1997. Worked on a mural for children's ward in Westminster and Chelsea Hospital. Washington and Lee University, Southern Arts and Oxfordshire County Council also hold examples. Lived in Oxford, part of the year in Crest.

David BELL 1916–1959 Painter and curator, born in London, son of Sir Harold Bell who was keeper of manuscripts and Egerton librarian at the British Museum. David Bell attended Merchant Taylors' School, then studied art at Chelsea School of Art, 1933, and the Royal College of Art, 1933–7, where his teachers included Gilbert Spencer. Bell then spent two years as a draughtsman with the Egyptian Exploration Society. He was the Arts Council's assistant director for Wales, 1946–51, then until his death curator of the Glynn Vivian Art Gallery, Swansea. That gallery gave him a memorial show in 1960–1, and he had already exhibited widely in Wales. Bell was a prolific writer on art, his books including the notable *The Language of Pictures*, 1953, and *The Artist in Wales*, 1957. Bell died from pneumonia after a successful operation to improve his mobility, having endured multiple sclerosis for many years. He lived in Cardiff and the National Museum of Wales there holds his work.

David C BELL 1950– Artist and writer, born in Lincolnshire, who after attending Trinity House Navigation School joined the Merchant Navy as a navigator. Eight years later, having sailed most of the world's oceans, he gained an honours degree at Hull College of Art. Produced commemorative paintings in the Falklands for the armed forces, but was mainly known as a marine artist, combining imagination and technical accuracy. After writing and illustrating *Britain's Maritime History*, in 1999 Bell produced *A Coastal Passage*, launched with a show at The Tryon & Swann Gallery. HM The Queen owned his painting of Sir Walter Raleigh.

Eileen BELL 1907–2005 Painter of figures, landscape and still life in a vigorous, Expressionist style. She studied at St John's Wood School of Art, 1939, under Patrick Millard, and at Anglo-French Art Centre, 1945. Other teachers included Kenneth Martin, Ernest Perry and Alfred Green. After the war Bell continued to paint but also worked freelance for the Council of Industrial Design on textiles and as an interior designer for exhibitions. She also painted furniture, designed sets and advertisements for magazines and potted. Was a member of AIA, showed by invitation with RBA and LG and exhibited at Leicester Galleries, Young Contemporaries and in the provinces. Later solo shows included Duncalfe Galleries, Harrogate, 1989, and Chappel Galleries, Chappel, 1992. Chappel Galleries gave Bell a retrospective in 2003. The catalogue foreword was by the television gardener and writer Alan Titchmarsh, who included amusing memories of Bell in his 2002 book *Trowel and Error*. She had been his landlady and early cultural mentor when he was a student at the Royal Botanic Gardens, Kew. Bell wrote two children's books, *Tales from End Cottage*, 1970, and *More Tales from End Cottage*, 1972, after she was incapacitated slipping on clay in the potting studio. Christie's in South Kensington had a studio sale of Bell's work shortly after she died in Leiston, Suffolk.

Ellen BELL 1962– Versatile artist using a range of materials, such as paper and feathers, who graduated with honours in both illustration and theatre design. Fairy tales were a strong theme in her work, in which she sought "a tension to exist between the power of the subject matter I am dealing with and the delicacy of the images I make." Bell had a residency, Studio in the City, funded by the North West Arts Board, based at Manchester Craft Centre, and also had a solo show, Telling Tales, there, 1996, with another exhibition at Cambridge Open Studios, 1999. Commissions included Fallen Angel, for Manchester Craft Centre, 1996, and The Holy Spirit in the Image of a Dove, for St Stephen's Roman Catholic Church, Manchester, 1998. Showed with MAFA Open from 1994 and with England & Co.

Gladys Kathleen Madge BELL 1882–1965 Miniaturist, unmarried surname Farrar, married to the stained glass designer Reginald Bell, their son being the artist Michael Charles Farrar Bell. Like her husband, she studied at Cope and Nichols' School of Art. She was elected to full membership of RMS in 1927 and often worked to commission. Exhibited prolifically at RMS, also at RA Summer Exhibition, RI, Walker Art Gallery in Liverpool, SWA and Paris Salon. Died in Haddenham, Buckinghamshire.

Harriet BELL 1976– Painter, a great-granddaughter of the Newlyn School artist Frank Gascoigne Heath. She graduated from the Courtauld Institute in 2000 with a first-class honours degree in the history of art, having specialised in Soviet painting and sculpture. She went on to study fine art at the Surikov Institute, Moscow, in 2002, and the Repin Institute in 2003, both institutions focusing on realistic interpretations of landscape and people. Bell showed regularly at the Century Galleries, Henley-on-Thames and in mixed exhibitions at the New Grafton Gallery, which gave her a show in 2005. The Royal Academician Ken Howard was "impressed by her total commitment to painting" and bought her work.

Harry BELL 1947– Painter, mainly in oil, also acrylic, largely self-taught. He was born and lived in Gateshead, County Durham. Attended local Boys' Grammar School, in 1972 studying art at night classes at Newcastle College of Art and Design. From 1989 he studied painting at Open College of the Arts based on Newcastle Polytechnic, with Liz Rowe and notably William Varley. Bell's interest was "in the forms and colour of the urban landscape, particularly that of Newcastle upon Tyne, and what it can say about its creators. The city is dark, sometimes bleak and unhappy, but it possesses an undercurrent of mystery and allure." He showed at Newcastle Polytechnic, 1991; Federation of Northern Art Societies, 1992; and in 1993 John Laing Exhibition, University of Northumbria and Open Door, at Halton House. University of Northumbria gave him a show in 1995. Bell's work is held by private collections in England and America. In 2004, it was included in L S Lowry and those he inspired, organised by Danny Greening Fine Art at Gallery 27.

Jane BELL: *see* **Jeanne BELL**

Jean BELL 1923–1992 Painter in oil and teacher, born in Cheshire, married to the artist Tom Pemberton. She was the grand-daughter of the Liverpool portrait painter Mona Hopton Bell, 1867–1940. Studied at Liverpool School of Art, then taught at Wirral Grammar School for Girls, 1944–8; lectured at St Helens Municipal School of Art, 1948–50; joining City of Leeds College of Education, 1951–66, finally as senior lecturer. Showed in north of England in group shows, notably with Yorkshire Artists, and in Ashford, Kent, having a solo exhibition of work, 1950–80 at Associate House, Ashford, 1981. Her main works were the garden abstract series. Lived finally in Leeds, Yorkshire.

Jeanne BELL fl. c. 1929–1975 Sculptor, especially in ivory, the sister of the artist Reginald Bell, so brought up in the ecclesiastical Arts and Crafts tradition. She exhibited at RA Summer Exhibition as Jane Bell, 1927–39, then adopted Jeanne Bell, 1940–66, much to the amusement of her nephew Michael Charles Farrar Bell. Other venues included RMS, Walker Art Gallery in Liverpool and at Royal Glasgow Institute of the Fine Arts.

John BELL 1923–1981 Painter and teacher, son of the artists Arthur and Bertha Bell, who attended Cheltenham College, where his father was director of art. During the Burma campaign in World War II John contracted spondylitis, from which he never fully recovered. He had matriculated at Oxford University prior to the war, on demobilisation completing his history degree at Pembroke College, becoming director of art at Manchester Grammar School. Bell took up rock-climbing to relieve the spondylitis, and was attracted to wild, rocky subjects around Britain, his style influenced by the simplified planes of Francis Towne and Oriental artists. With his parents showed at the RWA, 1955; held a joint exhibition with his father at The Old Silk Mill, Blockley, 1979; and there was a memorial exhibition at Manchester Cathedral after his death from a cerebral haemorrhage.

Judson BELL 1877– Watercolourist who was a professional businessman, born in Yeovil, Somerset, but educated in Shropshire. Studied at Welshpool School of Art, then later privately in London. Member of both the Langham Sketch Club and Wapping Group of Artists.

Showed there, SMA and in the provinces. Lived at Pinner, Middlesex.

Julian BELL 1952– Figurative painter, writer, editor and poet whose father was the artist and writer Quentin Bell and who grew up in Newcastle and Leeds. He was early familiarised with Bloomsbury when staying with his grandmother the painter Vanessa Bell and Duncan Grant at Charleston, Firle, Sussex. He read English literature at Magdalen College, Oxford, 1970–3; attended the City and Guilds of London Art School; and from the mid-1970s was a full-time painter working often to commission, his output ranging from group portraits to inn signs. Bell was the author of *Bonnard*, 1994; *What is Painting? Representation and Modern Art*, 1999; and the introduction to *Five Hundred Self-Portraits*, 2000, which included a self-portrait. He also wrote critically for *The Guardian*, *Times Literary Supplement* and *Modern Painters* and published poetry. For three years Bell was an associate editor on *The Dictionary of Art*, published by Macmillan. Exhibited with Francis Kyle from 1993, with a series of solo shows. The Museum of London owns Bell's work.

Laura Anning BELL 1867–1950 Portrait painter, notably in pastel, born in France of English parents. She studied in Paris and at the Slade School of Fine Art with Alphonse Legros. During her first marriage she exhibited under her married name of Laura Richard-Troncy, then after marrying the painter Robert Anning Bell used his surname, sometimes with a hyphen. Showed at RA from 1921, at Paris Salon where her awards included several medals, Fine Art Society, Ridley Art Society and elsewhere. Shared a show with Mary Davis at Fine Art Society in 1919. Tate Gallery has her portrait of Annie Horniman. Died in London.

Lucy BELL 1958– Painter whose output included colourful abstract works, with reference to textiles and collage, as in her solo show at deliART, 2003. There was an earlier one-man exhibition at Logos Gallery, 1997. She trained at the Ruskin School of Fine Art, Oxford, obtaining a postgraduate diploma from the Royal Academy Schools, 1987. Awards included an Egerton Coghill Landscape Prize, David Murray Landscape Scholarship and a British Council Travel Scholarship to Bulgaria, 1988–9. Bell exhibited at Gallery One and Modigliani Centre, Florence Italy, both 2002, and Head Street Gallery, Halstead, 2003. In 2002, she was commissioned to make several paintings for a refurbished 1920s hotel in Chicago's Loop District. Lived in Haverhill, Suffolk.

Malcolm BELL 1963– Artist, born in Rothbury, Northumberland. He attended course at Newcastle, 1981–2, then Birmingham Polytechnic, 1982–3. Moved to Isle of Skye, in 1985 Bell began drawing with Hannah Horsfall, their works being joint efforts in which each had the right to make and obliterate marks. An example of their abstract work was Twentysixth Drawing, in 1992 East & South Norwich Gallery/Kent Institute of Art and Design show. Eventually worked in London.

Martin BELL 1907–1970 Painter and teacher, full name Norman Martin Bell, born in Great Meols, Cheshire. He was brought up in an artistic atmosphere and went on to train at Liverpool College of Art, 1925–30, Royal College of Art, 1931–3. Taught part-time at King's School, Chester, 1933–4, then returned to Liverpool College of Art, becoming head of the school of fine art, 1965–8, before retiring. Early influences on Bell's work were Puvis de Chavannes, the Post-Impressionists and Walter Sickert, but from the late 1950s it became more abstract, Nicolas de Staël's pictures becoming important to him. Recorded war bomb damage in Liverpool. Bell was long a member of the Liverpool Academy, being its president, 1957–60, and showed with Sandon Studios Society. In 1970 the Academy exhibition included a small memorial show of Bell's work, including a contribution from Walker Art Gallery, Liverpool. The rood screen at St Stephen's, Prenton, is a fine example of Bell's figurative work. Lived in Wallasey, Cheshire.

Michael Charles Farrar BELL 1911–1993 Versatile artist, the only child of the stained glass designer Reginald Bell and his artist wife Gladys. Michael was born in London and educated at Harrow School and Edinburgh College of Art and in the 1930s joined Clayton & Bell, noted makers of stained glass and ecclesiastical furnishings, founded in 1856 by Richard Clayton and Alfred Bell. The firm was commemorated in A Century of Stained Glass, held at St Mary's Church, Haddenham, in 1996, organised by Michael's widow Angela Farrar Bell. In 1939, he enlisted in the Army and became a camouflage officer, going to France with the Normandy landings and remaining on the continent until 1945. In 1947 he moved to Haddenham and had a small studio at Townsend Green. He was a practical and inventive man and began designing and painting inn signs, illustrating advertising material, labels and postage stamps for Britain and abroad. When his father died, Michael took over two major jobs, other commissions following. He made all the glass for The Chapel of the Mohawks, in Brantford, Ontario, Canada, many windows for churches all over England, for several livery companies, schools and private houses. A delightful and idiosyncratic example is the memorial window for Betty Dora Leney (1913–81) at Kingston Church, Sussex, incorporating the South Downs with the artist at work accompanied by wildlife. He signed it with the date, 1983, MF and a bell. Bell was the only member of the family who saw his work through from beginning to the end, most often installing the window of the church himself. He showed at the RA and was a fellow and council member of the British Society of Master Glass Painters, a liveryman of the Worshipful Company of Glaziers and Painters of Glass and their master in 1974–5, also an Arts Club member. Among his children was the artist and designer Marilyn Band.

Norman Martin BELL: *see* **Martin BELL**

Ophelia Gordon BELL: *see* **Ophelia GORDON-BELL**

Quentin BELL 1910–1996 Painter, sculptor, potter, writer and teacher, son of the art critic Clive Bell and the artist Vanessa Bell. He went to Leighton School and with some help from Roger Fry studied painting in England and Paris. In World War II Bell was a member of the Political Warfare Executive. Among his teaching positions were Slade professor of fine art, Oxford University, 1964–5, Ferens professor of fine art, Hull University, 1965–6, and professor of history and theory of art, Sussex University, 1967–75, then being made emeritus professor. His books included *Ruskin*, 1963; *Bloomsbury*, 1968; *Virginia Woolf, a Biography*, 1972; a novel, *The Brandon Papers*, 1985; and his memoirs, *Elders and Betters*, 1995. Had a series of solo shows from 1935, with a Crafts Council-funded retrospective tour from 1999. A number of public collections hold his work. With Duncan Grant and Vanessa Bell Quentin Bell painted extensive murals in Berwick Church, Sussex, near where he lived at Firle.

Reginald BELL 1886–1950 Stained glass artist, the only son of John Clement Bell and his wife Mary, his sister being the sculptor Jane/Jeanne Bell. He was born in London and educated at Harrow School and Cope's and Nichols' Art School, Kensington, and joined the family firm of Clayton & Bell, makers of stained glass and ecclesiastical furnishings, in 1907. He served in the Artists' Rifles in World War I and on returning to the studios in 1918 was made a partner. Reginald was keen to abandon the Victorian style and adopt more modern designs. As a member of the Arts Club and Art Workers' Guild he had many artist and architect friends, including S J Lamorna Birch, William Russell Flint and William Orpen. Bell was a founder-member of the British Society of Master Glass Painters and for many years its secretary. His windows in the south transept of Salisbury Cathedral, St Mary's Hall in Coventry and in the chapel of Somerville College, Oxford, are especially distinguished. He received world recognition in 1925 when he was awarded a diploma at the Paris Exhibition and at exhibitions in Brazil and at Wembley. Exhibited frequently at the RA, also at the Walker Art Gallery in Liverpool. After he died at Aylesbury, Buckinghamshire, his son Michael Charles Farrer Bell continued his work.

Richard BELL 1955– Creator of systematic paintings and reliefs, based in London. In 1977 he constructed a series of reliefs funded by Southern Arts Council. Bell was interested in structure, specifically relational qualities of colour, its grammar and figuration expressed within a practice of making paintings and related texts. As well as engaging in group theoretical work, Bell contributed to exhibitions including the 1979 Künstlerbücher show at Galerie Lydia Megert in Switzerland; The House Construction Show at House, 1981; Colour Presentations, Gardner Centre Gallery, Sussex University, and tour, 1986; and Complexions, at Galerie L'Idee, Zoetermeer, Netherlands, and Dean Clough, Halifax, 1989. Arts Council holds Bell's work.

Stan BELL 1928– Mural and relief artist and teacher, born and lived in Glasgow. Studied at local School of Art, 1966–70, where he later taught. His mural work was to be found around the city and he showed with Glasgow League of Artists, Scottish Young Contemporaries and The Clyde Group.

Trevor BELL 1930– Painter and teacher, born in Leeds, Yorkshire, where he attended the College of Art, 1947–52. For several years until mid-1950s he then taught at Harrogate College of Art. On the suggestion of the painter Terry Frost, Bell and his wife sold up their home and motorcycled to Cornwall to work in St Ives. In Yorkshire Bell had painted industrial landscapes, but in Cornwall his work took a new direction, and while still landscape-based he became concerned with land-shape and sea interactions which created abstract pictures. After short periods in Italy Bell took up a Gregory Fellowship at Leeds University in 1960. A number of teaching posts in Britain and America followed until in the mid-1970s he returned to Florida State University, Tallahassee. Bell showed with Penwith Society of Arts from 1956, at Tate Gallery and New Art Centre in group shows. In 1995 a group of his pictures was exhibited at Tate Gallery St Ives and in 1995–6 he was included in the John Moores Liverpool Exhibition. Had a series of solo exhibitions with Waddington Galleries from 1958; Whitechapel Art Gallery; Florida State University; and in 1998 The New Millennium Gallery, St Ives, celebrated Bell's return to Cornwall with his first major show at a private venue since his return to Britain. It gave him further shows in 2003 and 2004–5, Tate St Ives in 2004–5 giving Bell a show entitled Beyond Materiality: Paintings and Drawings 1967–2004. Arts Council holds his work.

Vanessa BELL 1879–1961 Painter, decorator and designer of textiles and ceramics, born in London. She was the daughter of the writer Sir Leslie Stephen, sister of the writer Virginia Woolf and married the art critic Clive Bell, all leading members of what became known as the Bloomsbury Group. She studied with Arthur Cope at the Royal Academy Schools. Worked in the Omega Workshops with Roger Fry and collaborated with Duncan Grant on various decorative projects, eventually living with Grant for many years at Charleston Farmhouse, Firle, Sussex. Was founder of Friday Club in 1910 and two years later participated in the Second Post-Impressionist Exhibition. Showed in groups at Leicester Galleries, NEAC, Lefevre and Redfern Galleries and elsewhere. Had first solo show at Independent Gallery in 1922. Memorial shows held by Adams Gallery in 1961 and Arts Council, with tour, in 1964. In 1996 there was a retrospective as part of Unione Donna's 7th Biennale in Ferrara, Italy, curated with Bloomsbury Gallery, where it was also shown.

Arthur BELL-FOSTER 1900–1978 Versatile painter, designer and illustrator, born in Northallerton, Yorkshire, who attended Sheffield School of Art, 1924–9, under G Vernon Stokes. (His birth was recorded as Arthur Foster; he adopted the name Bell Foster, under both of which he is sometimes listed; is known to have signed work on occasion as Bell-Foster; and at death was recorded as Arthur Bell Foster, surname Foster.) He eventually settled in Birmingham, where he was a member of the RBSA and Birmingham Art Circle, also at various times belonging to the BWS, UA, and Coventry Society of Artists, as well as being a fellow of the Institute of Art and Design. Bell-Foster was a prolific exhibitor, venues including the RA, RSW and RCamA, RBA, RI, various touring exhibitions and abroad. He was a landscape specialist, keen in his on-the-spot pictures to capture mood and atmosphere while exploiting the particular qualities of the medium and support. A good example is his river view of Newcastle upon Tyne included in Percy V Bradshaw's compilation *Water-colour A Truly English Art*. Public galleries in Bilston, Darlington, Dudley and Worcester acquired his work.

David BELLAMY 1943– Self-taught painter, writer, film-maker and teacher, born in Pembroke. He worked in oil and watercolour, specialised in painting mountain and wild coastal scenes and was particularly fascinated by the moods of nature in wild places. He travelled widely, camped in Bedouin tents while seeking subjects to paint and was fascinated by the mountain desert scenery of Wadi Rum and Petra in Jordan, the High Atlas and many of the wild regions of the Middle East. Bellamy sought to promote a greater awareness of threats to the natural environment and was a patron of the Marine Conservation Society's Seas for Life Appeal. His work was included in Summer Exhibition: the Contemporary Orientalists at Mathaf Gallery, 2003, among other venues being Cleveland Gallery, Bath; Lincoln Joyce Fine Art, Great Bookham; and Burford Gallery, Oxfordshire. Among Bellamy's books were *Wilderness Artist*, 1995, which gained an award for excellence from the Outdoor Writers' Guild, and a best-seller on watercolour landscape painting. APV Films produced five films on watercolour painting by Bellamy who ran courses on the medium in Britain and overseas and who had his own series on HTV (Wales).

John BELLANY 1942– Painter, born into a fishing family at Port Seton, East Lothian. He attended Edinburgh College of Art, 1960–5. During his time there, in 1962, he won an Andrew Grant Scholarship, permitting travel to Paris; and for several years with Alexander Moffat he showed his pictures outside RSA, in opposition to the Establishment, work in the Northern European Expressionist-Realist tradition. Studied at Royal College of Art, 1965–8, where he continued to develop his personal symbolism, fed by travels to the Low Countries and Germany and the works and sights he saw there. A large number of watercolour portraits was completed in the 1980s, following a series of serious illnesses. By then Bellany was recognised as an artist of international stature. Had many solo shows, including The Dromidaris Gallery, Netherlands, 1965; a series at Drian Gallery in 1970s; Compass Gallery, Glasgow, 1987 and 1990 Beaux Arts, from 2000; University of Northumbria, Newcastle upon Tyne, 2001; and John Bellany at Sixty, Scottish National Gallery of Modern Art, Edinburgh, 2002; and abroad. His works are in principal public galleries in Britain, including Tate Gallery and Scottish National Gallery of Modern Art. Lived in London and was made RA in 1991.

William de BELLEROCHE 1912–1969 Painter, printmaker, collector and bohemian, born in London, but brought up in Sussex, where he finally lived in Brighton. His father was a painter, Albert, who died in 1944, and William – widely known as Count Willie – inherited the French title. Although he taught himself to paint, William was much influenced by the artist Frank Brangwyn, whom he met in 1934 and befriended for over 25 years. He wrote several books on Brangwyn, who encouraged William to take up printmaking. He was a great collector of objects such as shells, which appear in his paintings, and formed the largest private collection of Brangwyns in the world. Before World War II his initiative led to the foundation of the Brangwyn-de Belleroche Museum in Orange, France. He had a wide circle of friends, including the actresses Hermione Baddeley and Flora Robson, the artists Augustus John and James Fitton and Gwen, Lady Melchett, many of whom he painted. William was very fond of fish, and had a one-man show at Prunier's Restaurant in 1963, another being held in an interior design shop in Brighton the year following. Others followed annually at Upper Grosvenor Galleries. Fine Art Society held a show in 1989 which showed William to have been a witty, amusing Colourist. British Museum and many foreign collections hold his work.

Leslie BELLIN-CARTER 1878– Artist and teacher, born in London. He studied art with F G Stevens and at the Slade School of Fine Art, where he gained the Trevelyan Goodall Art Scholarship, studying with Henry Tonks and Philip Wilson Steer. He published several books on drawing and was for many years a university board adjudicator, having taught at Eton College and while teaching at Wellington College. Exhibited RA, IS, Ridley Art Club and in the provinces. Lived at Woking, Surrey.

David BELLINGHAM 1966– Artist and teacher in various media, born in Thornton Heath, south London, who studied at Glasgow School of Art, 1988–91, teaching there, 1991–9. In 2002 he was an Arts and Humanities Research Board Fellow at Manchester Metropolitan University. A catalogue of works, 1991–00, *All Spare Parts*, was published by the Kunsthaus Nürnberg, Germany, in 2001. Bellingham published books and editions through the imprint WAX366. He was a prolific exhibitor. Mixed shows included Cairn Gallery, Nailsworth, 1997; British Photography, Real, New York, America, 1998; R-cade, Print Studio, Glasgow, 1999; and Evolution Isn't Over Yet, Lugar Comum, Lisbon, Portugal, 2000. Solo exhibitions included Tarnug at Kunsthaus, Nuremburg, Germany, and Measures, Gallery of Modern Art, Glasgow, both 2000. Bellingham lived and worked in Glasgow.

Elinor BELLINGHAM SMITH 1906–1988 Painter and illustrator, born in London, daughter of the surgeon and art collector Guy Bellingham Smith and niece of the painter Hugh Bellingham Smith. Married the painter Rodrigo Moynihan in 1931, separating from him in 1957. Studied piano and dancing to advanced level, but eventually opted for painting, attending Slade School of Fine Art, 1928–31, where Henry Tonks regarded her highly. In 1930s she showed at LG and Leicester Galleries, having her first one-man show there in 1948, and also completed drawings and illustrations for Shell and *Harper's Bazaar*. Her painting The Island, done for the Festival of Britain in 1951, went into the Arts Council collection; the Tate Gallery and provincial collections also hold her work. Finally lived in Boxford, Suffolk, and died in Ipswich. Bellingham Smith was noted for her sensitive pictures of figures in landscape, notably in her later years landscapes of East Anglia and the Fens. Memorial exhibition New Grafton Gallery in 1989, solo show at Chappel Galleries, Chappel, 2001. *Restless Lives: The Bohemian World of Rodrigo and Elinor Moynihan*, by their sports journalist son John, was published by Sansom & Company in 2002.

Alan Waddington BELLIS 1883–1960 All-round architect, modeller, metal worker, painter and teacher, born in Manchester, who studied at Leeds College of Art and at the Royal College of Art, gaining his diploma in 1910. He won an RIBA Travelling Scholarship that took him to Italy, enhancing his architectural knowledge. Exhibited at RA, RWA and in the provinces, from 1921 being a member of Ipswich Art Club. Bellis lived in Ipswich, Suffolk, and taught at its Art School from 1914–48. He designed and made the diocesan crozier for the Bishop of St Edmundsbury and Ipswich when the See was created in 1916. He also carved the head of Sir Thomas Wolsey above the side door to the Wolsey Art Gallery at Christchurch Mansion, Ipswich, where a Bellis show was held in 1997. This included a drawing of Bellis by one of his pupils, Frank Ward, who remembered him as "a beautiful watercolourist who really knew his buildings". Leeds City Art Gallery also holds his work.

THE BELSIZE GROUP: *see* **Adèle REIFENBERG**

Franta BELSKY 1921–2000 Sculptor, born in Brno, Czechoslovakia, who studied at Prague Academy of Fine Arts, Central School of Arts and Crafts, 1939, and Royal College of Art, 1950. After Army service, 1940–5, pursued career making portrait sculptures, figures and monuments. Commissions included Constellation, Colchester, 1953; Joy-Ride, Stevenage New Town, 1958; Fountains, Shell Centre, 1959–61; Mountbatten Memorial in Horse Guards Parade; Winston Churchill statue at Fulton, Missouri; and Lord Cottesloe, at National Theatre. Showed at RA from 1943 and he gained Jean Masson Davidson Award, 1978. Was included in British Sculpture in the Twentieth Century at Whitechapel Art Gallery, 1981–2. Was a fellow of RBS and president of SPS. Lived in Sutton Courtenay, Oxfordshire. In 1997 Belsky married the Czech Sculptor Irena Sedlecká. The Henry Moore Institute, Leeds, holds a huge Belsky archive.

BELT: *see* **Ella GIBBS**

Kate BELTON 1972– Artist working in various media, born in Wrexham, Denbighshire, known for her photographs of purpose-built environments and interiors. She blurred the line between fiction and reality, the handmade and photographic. In 1999, she had a solo exhibition at Nylon, turning her attention to outdoors scenes, mixing watercolour and photographic images. Belton gained an honours degree in painting at Central St Martins College of Art & Design, 1991–4, and her master's in fine art from the Royal College of Art, 1994–6. Took part in many group exhibitions in Britain and abroad, later ones including Hales Gallery and Gimpel Fils, 1999. British Council, British Airways, John Moores and the TI Group held the work of Belton, who lived and worked in London.

Leslie Frederick BELTON 1912– Artist in various media, furniture maker and teacher, born and educated in Birmingham where he attended the College of Arts and Crafts, 1929–34. Showed at RA, PS, NS and widely in the provinces. Royal Air Force College in Cranwell and public galleries in Swindon and Reading hold his work. Lived in Reading, Berkshire, where he was a member of the Guild of Artists.

Peter BELYI 1971– Versatile artist born in what is now St Petersburg, Russia, he was educated in the graphics faculty of the Academy of Arts' secondary school, later in the ceramics department of Mukhinskii Higher College of Art. Moved to the United Kingdom, showing there, in Denmark and in Russia, where he became a member of the Union of Artists and Tirsa Society of Printmakers, both 1994, and Artichoke Print Workshop, 1995. English mixed shows included a print exhibition at Barbican Centre, 1996; Heifer Gallery, 1999; and National Print Exhibition, Mall Galleries, 2003. Belyi had a solo show in 2005 at New Realms Gallery. The specially commissioned installations were photographic, consisting of neon lighting tubes and black-and-white slides and, like his big woodcuts, dealt with urban themes. The focus was on the post-Soviet legacy of redundant industrialism and decaying department blocks. Victoria & Albert Museum holds Belyi's work.

Geoffrey BEMROSE 1896–1974 Watercolour painter, born in Leicester, who studied art under B J Fletcher at the College of Arts and Crafts there. Bemrose, who became director of Stoke-on-Trent City Museum and Art Gallery, was a watercolour and ceramics specialist who wrote on the latter subject. He was finally at the Museum and Art Gallery, Leicester.

Zoë BENBOW 1963– Painter whose work included richly coloured abstract canvases, who studied at Berkshire College, Ravensbourne College and Royal College of Art. She was a British Institute Fund and Barclays Young Painter Finalist award winner. Took part in mixed shows at Long and Ryle, 1989; Sue Williams, 1990; Discerning Eye, at Mall Galleries and Galleria G, Madrid, both 1992; Salama-Caro Gallery, 1993; and Berkeley Square Gallery, 1994, plus regular appearances at LG and Contemporary Art Society Art Market. Later solo exhibitions include Delfina Studios Trust, 1995, and Christopher Hull Gallery, 1996. Shared a show with potter Brian Dewbury at Mall Galleries, 2003. HRH The Prince of Wales, Arthur Andersen & Company and Unilever hold examples.

Claude BENDALL 1891–1970 Painter and musician, who studied the piano under the pianist Jan Paderewski, who became Poland's first prime minister. Although Paderewski declared that Bendall had great musical talent, he opted to become an artist, attending the Sorbonne, Paris. At first he had little success, then his picture South Bank, Paris, was accepted and hung on the line at the RA Summer Exhibition in 1943. Over the next 16 years he showed over 30 works there. Reminiscences was bought for the nation under the Edward Stott Bequest, 1946. Bendall worked in a converted oast house near Wrotham, Kent, helped by his wife Barbara, who was his model. As well as English genre works and portraits Bendall continued to travel to France and Ireland, where he depicted gypsy life. His pictures' detailed, highly worked and intricately coloured surfaces stemmed from his own method of laying down watercolour and gouache on paper with a small metal nail-file. Bonhams, Knightsbridge, offered 22 lots from the artist's estate in 2000.

Mildred BENDALL 1891–1977 Painter of still life and landscape in a rich, Fauve-style manner and palette, born in Bordeaux, France, of Anglo-French parents. Their wealth enabled her to paint for her pleasure. She studied in atelier of Félix Carme, 1910–14, and had early success, the Union Feminine à Bordeaux and Musée des Beaux-Arts both acquiring works, as later did the Musée d'Art Moderne, Paris. In 1927–8 attended Académie de la Grande Chaumière, Paris, and worked closely with Matisse. When the Société des Artistes Indépendants was formed in Bordeaux in 1928 Bendall began a close association with it, holding several positions. She exhibited extensively in ensuing years until she died in Bordeaux, where she was buried in the Protestant cemetery. Large retrospective was held by Société Artistique de Mérignac in 1981. Another notable show was held at Whitford and Hughes, 1987, Whitford Fine Art adding a retrospective in 1996.

Zadok BEN-DAVID 1949– Artist in various materials and teacher, noted for abstract works in wood. Was born in

Yemen, then emigrated to Israel. From 1971–3 studied at Bezalel Academy of Art and Design, Jerusalem. Moved to England as assistant to the sculptor N H Azaz in 1974 and became a student at Reading University fine art department. From 1975–6 studied on the advanced sculpture course at St Martin's School of Art, joining the staff there in 1977. In that year gained a commission for Runcorn Shopping City. Shows included Playhouse Gallery, Harlow, and Air Gallery, 1976; Vehicle Art, Montreal, 1979; and House Gallery, 1981. Had a solo show at Air Gallery, 1980, Woodlands Art Gallery, 1982, and Benjamin Rhodes Gallery, 1992. Cass Sculpture Foundation organised Innerscapes, recent work by Ben-David, in 2004–5. Arts Council holds his work.

Richard BENEDETTI 1925–1992 Painter, draughtsman and sculptor, born in Mulhouse, France, of Italian parents who became an American citizen. Of his disturbing and strange work, Benedetti said: "I wish to show through my paintings the essence of the unfairness of life – and the harshness beneath the beauty of nature." He planned to become an architect, but his father's long illness and World War II, during which he spent time in a forced labour camp outside Berlin, precluded further studies. After the war he worked in a French coal-mine before emigrating to America in 1951. In New York he started sculpting, then studied painting at the Art Students' League, with George Tooker, and National Academy of Design, with Stephen Csoka. Benedetti exhibited with several New York venues, among them the National Art Club, Charles Z Mann and Marisa del Re Galleries, the Bronx Museum of the Arts and at New Jersey Museum. While resident in London, between 1971–4 he produced some of his best work, showing outdoors in Hampstead and Chelsea and having a solo exhibition at the Mountbatten Theatre Gallery, Southampton College of Technology, in 1972. Benedetti died on holiday in Barga, Italy, in 1992. His widow, Elaine, organised a show at the Ashcroft Gallery, Fairfield Halls, Croydon, in 1995. The Modern Art Museum, in the Republic of San Marino, acquired his painting The Puppet.

Leslie Charlotte BENENSON 1941– Sculptor, printmaker, painter, illuminator and calligrapher, born in London, who studied at Regent Street Polytechnic, 1958–63, with Geoffrey Deeley and James Osborne, and manuscript illumination and calligraphy privately with Anthony Wood, 1962–4, during which she moved to Sussex, settling in Bexhill. Became a freelance artist from 1963, "tending to specialise in drawing animals and birds, also some landscape watercolours". Was elected a craft member of Society of Scribes and Illuminators, 1964, a fellow of RE, 1978. Was also a member of Guild of Sussex Craftsmen and the Eastbourne Group. Showed at RA from 1966, at Victoria & Albert Museum from 1971 and had solo shows with Rye Art Gallery, 1971, John Gage Gallery, Eastbourne, 1975, and elsewhere. In 1976 had 23 wood engravings published in *Coursing*. Ashmolean Museum in Oxford, Towner Art Gallery in Eastbourne and some churches hold her work.

Bryan BENGE 1953– Artist, born in London, who did a foundation course at Chelsea School of Art and Design, 1973–4; graduated with honours in fine art from Kingston Polytechnic, 1974–7; gained a Certificate in Education (16+), Garnett College, Thames Polytechnic, 1987–8; and his master's in art and design (applied fine art), Kingston University, 1992–4. Awards included a Stanley Picker Travelling Scholarship, Norway, 1977; Liquitex Excellence in Art Award, America, 1993; and Chartwell Gallery Award for Best Sculpture, 1995. In that year Benge was appointed Hon. Sec., LG, having been made a member in 1994. Benge's many group shows included Young Contemporaries, RA, 1977; St James Gallery, Euston, 1991; Tricycle Gallery, 1992; Barbican, LG 80th Anniversary Show, and American Council for the Arts, International Show, New York, both 1993; Pompidou Centre, Paris, France, and Richard Demarco European Tour, 1993–4; Williamson Art Gallery, Birkenhead, 1999; and The Blackthorpe Barn Art Centre, Bury St Edmunds, 2002. Benge had a solo exhibition at Brighton Marina Gallery, Brighton, 1994. In 1997, the Barbican Centre invited him to show eight works for six months. Lived in Epsom, Surrey.

Aurora BENGOECHEA 1948– After graduating with honours from Chelsea School of Art, 1981–5, Bengoechea studied for a master's degree at the Royal College of Art, 1986–8. Group exhibitions included Camden Annual, Camden Arts Centre, 1986, and East End Open Studios, at Norfolk House Studios, 1989. In that year Bengoechea shared a show at Cadogan Contemporary. There were solo exhibitions at Flaxman Gallery, 1987, and G Comte Gallery, Valencia, in 1988.

Gordon BENINGFIELD 1936–1998 Creator of country books, painter, designer, artist on glass and broadcaster, born in London, his father a Thames lighterman. The family moved to Hertfordshire in the early 1940s, he settled after marriage near Hemel Hempstead and the county's countryside and that of Dorset were favourite subjects. Left school at 15, was apprenticed to Faithcraft, an ecclesiastical art firm in St Albans, then from 1968 freelanced, having had a successful London solo exhibition of wildlife pictures. Beningfield was a knowledgeable entomologist and conservationist. In 1981 the General Post Office commissioned a set of butterfly stamps, in 1985 a set of insects. He was made president of the British Butterfly Conservation Society in 1989, vice-chairman of the Countryside Restoration Trust in 1993 and in 1997 the British Naturalists' Association gave him the Peter Scott Memorial Award. Created a series of memorial windows for the Household Cavalry, Coldstream Guards and Parachute Regiment, in 1995 being elected a freeman of the City of London and a liveryman of the Glass Sellers' Company. He was best known for his many books, which included *Beningfield's Butterflies*, 1978; *Beningfield's Countryside*, 1980; and a pictorial autobiography, *Gordon Beningfield, The Artist and His Work*, 1994. In 2004, Beningfield's Orchards, at Burlington Paintings, featured watercolours and drawings from his new book. Among his enthusiasms were field sports, cricket, steam trains, Spitfires and vintage cars. Died in London.

Ronald BENHAM 1915–1993 Painter, printmaker and teacher, born in London. He studied at Hornsey School of Art, teachers including John Moody, Robert Lyon and Russell Reeve. Became member of NEAC, 1972, and RBA, 1977, also showing at RA, RP, in the provinces and abroad. Taught at Epsom School of Art, lived in Cheam, Surrey, and died after a stroke.

John BENISON 1918– Advertising designer, artist in watercolour, chalk, pastel, pen and ink and pencil, and wood-carver. Born in London, son of the artist Steven Spurrier, Benison went on to hold a number of positions in advertising agencies, with Kemsley Newspapers and as a teacher of advertising design. Studied art at the Central School of Arts and Crafts, teachers including Bernard Meninsky, John Skeaping and John Farleigh, and at the St John's Wood School under Patrick Ferguson Millard and Ernest Perry. Exhibited RA and RBA. Lived at Ashover, Chesterfield, Derbyshire.

Anthony BENJAMIN 1931–2002 Painter, printmaker, sculptor and relief artist and teacher, born in Boarhunt, Hampshire. From 1946–9 Benjamin did a part-time engineering course at Southall Technical College, followed by four years at Regent Street Polytechnic, partly funded by earnings as a professional flyweight boxer, then several months studying drawing in Fernand Léger's Paris studio in 1951. Late in 1955 he moved to St Ives, Cornwall, where he divided his time between flower-growing and the painting of landscape-based abstracts. A French government award enabled him to study with S W Hayter the printmaker at Atelier 17 in Paris, 1958–9; this was followed by another year in Cornwall, 1959–60, then an Italian government award in 1960–1. After six years in London Benjamin taught in Canada and America until 1973, when he returned to London. He had had a solo show at Newlyn Art Gallery in 1958, and by the late 1960s he had embarked on an impressive series of international one-man exhibitions, including Gimpel Fils, 1994. Member of the RE. Benjamin's Hope (Sufferance) Press produced his own and other artists' work. By 2000, almost 60 public collections in Britain and abroad, including Tate Gallery, Arts Council and Museum of Modern Art, New York, as well as numerous international corporate collections held Benjamin's work. There were memorial shows at North House Gallery, Manningtree, and Belgrave Gallery, St Ives, both 2002. Lived at Kelling Village, Holt, Norfolk.

Paul BENJAMINS 1950– Painter, draughtsman and printmaker, born in London, who attended Camberwell School of Art, 1969–73, and the Royal College of Art, 1973–5. His numerous group shows included Hayward Annual, Hayward Gallery, and John Moores Liverpool Exhibition, Walker Art Gallery, both 1982; Art Haus, Dornbirn, Austria, from 1983; Galerie Pascal Gabert, Paris, from 1987; Musée Toulouse-Lautrec, Albi, France, 1992; Print Fair, Barbican Centre, 1994; and Print Studio, Dublin, Ireland, 2000. Among later solo exhibitions were gestural abstract works in Looking for New Horizons, Jill George Gallery, 2000, and in Living in London there, 2004. Benjamins' commissions included 106 drawings, four paintings and a limited-edition lithograph for the P & O liner *Royal Princess*, 1984; Juniper Wool and Thumb Gallery, 1987; Rhomberg, Textil Ges Mbh, Dornbirn, 1988–90; and Edit Works, 1990.

William BENNER 1884–1964 Painter, black-and-white artist and teacher, born in Nottingham, where he settled at Sherwood. After education in Loughborough he studied at Nottingham School of Art, his teachers including Arthur Spooner and Herbert Wilson Foster. At the end of commissioned service with the Sherwood Foresters in World War I, during which he was wounded several times, Benner for four months acted as mayor of the small town Vieux Conde, even though "my knowledge of French comprised three phrases," he recalled in his memoirs. He also painted, selling pictures for 10 francs each. Back in Nottingham, Benner was art master at High Pavement School for 27 years until retirement in 1949 to Blythburgh, Suffolk. Showed at Nottingham Castle Art Gallery and Museum extensively, which acquired his work; also RBA and RI. During World War II Benner, an enthusiast for railway pictures, produced notable work; his painting After The Blitz was reproduced in the 1997 centenary book, *Nottingham – An Illustrated History*.

Alan M BENNETT 1964– Painter, born in Scotland, who studied at Edinburgh College of Art and was represented in The Contemporary Fine Art Gallery, Eton's The Caledonian Show III in 2001. After periods of realist and abstract painting, in 1994 he "came upon a technique of using acrylic translucently with small brushstrokes for modelling. This revolutionised my work". Magritte and Surrealism and American realistic pictures were key influences, particularly Photo-Realism from the 1970s. The work of Charles Bell and Richard Estes, seen in New York in 1994, "crystallized in my mind the direction I wanted to take". SSA, The Scottish and Open Eye Galleries in Edinburgh and Shore Gallery, Leith, showed Bennett's work.

Brian BENNETT 1927– Painter in oil and teacher, who concentrated on the landscape of the Chilterns. He was born in Olney, Buckinghamshire. Bennett became director of art at Berkhamsted School. Obtained master's degree in history, 1954, at Oxford University. Although he had no full-time art tuition, "Peter Greenham taught me English at school" – he attended Magdelen College School – "and encouraged me." In addition, Bennett studied part-time at Ruskin School of Drawing, Oxford, 1950, and Regent Street Polytechnic, 1956. He was made a member of NS, 1985, and president of ROI, 1987–94, also being an honorary member of UA, and showed at RA, RP and NEAC. Bennett was a governor of the Federation of British Artists, 1992–8. His illustrated book *A Painter's Year Twelve Months in the Chilterns* appeared in 2001. Bennett's show The Chilterns was at The Hawker Gallery, Old Amersham, in 2003. Lived in Berkhamsted, Hertfordshire.

Elizabeth BENNETT 1923– Wood-carver, illustrator and mural painter, born in London. She was educated at Cheltenham Ladies' College and studied art at the Slade School of Fine Art, 1940, under Randolph Schwabe, then in 1941 at the Art Students' League of New York. After war service she resumed her studies, 1946–9, at Regent Street Polytechnic School of Art with the sculptor Geoffrey Deeley. Exhibited SGA and was a member of ICA. Signed work E B. Lived in London.

Emma BENNETT 1974– Painter who did a foundation art and design course at Central St Martins College of Art & Design, 1992–3; graduating in fine art from there, 1993–6; with her master's from Chelsea College of Art & Design, 1997–8. Was granted the Thames & Hudson Painting Award and a highly commended in the King Sturge Art Prize, both 1996; an ACAVA First Base Studio Residency, 1996–7; and a British Academy Postgraduate Award, 1997–8. Among exhibitions were Arte Viva, Senigallia, Italy, 1996; Blink, Princelet Street, 1999; Artissima 2000, Turin, Italy, 2000; and A Month in the Garden, The Museum of Garden History, 2001. Her 2002 solo exhibition at Danielle Arnaud Contemporary Art included images of dead animals and spotlit glimpses of a woman in vulnerable situations, images imparting a sense of disquiet, danger and loss.

Evelyn BENNETT 1964– Artist, designer and teacher, born in Gosport, Hampshire, who sometimes worked with Christopher Bennett as Rutter and Bennett (see separate entry). She studied printed textiles, gaining an honours degree from Winchester School of Art, 1984–7, her master's from Royal College of Art, 1987–9. Won a number of awards, including a South East Arts Travel Award, 1995, to study ceramics in Mexico, part of her widespread travels. Teaching experience included Royal College of Art, Norwich School of Art and Kent School of Art and Design. Had extensive experience as a freelance designer from 1989, clients including Esprit, French Connection and Marks and Spencer. Her published work included *Fun with Mosaic*, 1995. Among later shows was Seeing Through Drawing, Kent Institute of Art and Design, Rochester, 1996. Lived in Faversham, Kent.

Frank Moss BENNETT 1874–1953 Painter and designer of costume figures, born in Liverpool, who studied at Clifton College, then Slade School of Fine Art, St John's Wood Art School and Royal Academy Schools where he won a gold medal and travelling scholarship. Showed at Dudley Gallery, RA, RI and Paris Salon and lived in London.

Godwin BENNETT 1888– Painter and draughtsman in pen and ink, born in Brighton, Sussex. By profession an art dealer, he was a self-taught painter who exhibited at RA and elsewhere. Lived finally at Croydon, Surrey.

June BENNETT fl. from 1960s– Painter and artist/jeweller who returned to painting full-time in 1988. She was born in Grange-over-Sands, Lancashire, wife of Michael and mother of Justin Bennett, both artists. She studied at Lancaster and Leicester Colleges of Art. Showed at Goldsmiths' Hall; Midland Group Gallery, Nottingham; Park Square Gallery, Leeds; Mignon Gallery, Bath; and Ashgate Gallery, Farnham. Shared a four-man show at Linton Court, Gallery, Settle, 1992. Had a series of solo exhibitions at Castlegate House, Cockermouth, from 1988, in 2001, showed with her husband at Broughton House Gallery, Cambridge, in 2005, at the Orange Street Gallery, Uppingham. Bennett's jewellery was held by Abbot Hall Art Gallery, Kendal, and Shipley Art Gallery, Gateshead. Her pictures were in the collections of House of Lords, Carlisle Museum and Art Gallery and Copeland Borough Council. The artist lived in Port Carlisle, Cumbria, on the Solway Firth, where the constantly changing light and shifting sands were sources of inspiration.

Justin BENNETT 1964– Artist and teacher, son of the painters Michael and June Bennett. He did a foundation course at Cumbria College of Art and Design, 1982–3; graduated in fine art at Sheffield City Polytechnic, 1983–6, studying sound, performance, sculpture and video; did a sonology course, Institute for Sonology, Koninklijk Conservatorium, Den Haag, 1988–90; then was at Jan van Eyck Akademie, Maastricht, 1991–2. From 1989 he taught there, having in 1987 been a visiting lecturer in the communications arts department, Sheffield City Polytechnic. Collaborative experience included working with a number of performance groups, later work including Frascati, Amsterdam, Action with human pendula, ultrasonics (with BMB con.), 1991, and Maasvlakte, Performance for video, 1992. Solo shows included Galerie Stroom, Den Haag (Dutch Arts Council), 1997. Bennett's illustrated *Noise Map* appeared in 2003. It was made for the "Crashcourse Project" of Meinebank, Berlin, and contained essays on noise, musique concrète, field recording, the correspondences between music and architecture and sound and image. Noise Map, a solo exhibition with new and older soundworks, videos and drawings, was held in Den Haag in 2005 at GEM Museum of Contemporary Art, an extension of the Geementemuseum.

Kiera BENNETT 1971– Artist, born in Oldham, Lancashire, who had a small, untitled paper collage included in John Moores Liverpool Exhibition in 2004. The artist wrote: "These painterly, intricate miniatures are made from thousands of fragments of paper. Every surface is clad; heavy with glue. These gummy, claustrophobic, shadowy worlds choke with fullness." Bennett studied at Mid Cheshire College of Art and Design, Northwich, 1989–90; The Ruskin School, Oxford, 1990–3; and Royal College of Art, 2000–2. Among her exhibitions were Preface, Hatton Gallery, Newcastle upon Tyne, 2000; New Contemporaries, Static, Liverpool, and Barbican Centre, 2002; and Collage, Bloomberg Space, 2004.

Kimberley BENNETT 1954– Artist who graduated with honours from St Martin's School of Art, 1975–7. Took part in The South Bank Picture Show, Royal Festival Hall, 1987; Three Cities, London and tour, and Sun Totem, at Clissold Park, Islington, both 1988; and East End Open Studios, at Martello Street, 1989. Bennett completed a Chartist sculpture for Newport in 1988.

Malcolm BENNETT 1942– Painter and teacher, born in Derby, many of whose canvases were abstracts from the Ulster landscape. After attending the Technical High School in Belfast, 1956–60, Bennett studied at Stranmillis College there. He then spent four years living in parts of Ireland, France and Switzerland before taking up a teaching appointment in County Down in 1970. Exhibitions included Queen's University in Belfast, Ulster Museum and Tom Caldwell Gallery in Belfast both as a member of Group 63 and solo and Barrenhill Gallery in Dublin. Arts Council of Northern Ireland, New University of Ulster and Allied Irish Banks hold examples. The Ards Peninsula, where Bennett lived for a time, was a favourite subject.

Michael BENNETT 1934– Painter and lecturer, born in Windermere, Westmorland, husband of June, father of Justin, both artists. He studied at Lancaster and Leicester Colleges of Art. From 1966–71 lectured in painting at Bretton Hall College of Education. In 1976 gained an Arts Council Grant, then in 1976–7 and 1979–80 Northern Arts Printmaking Bursaries. Bennett eventually settled at Port Carlisle, Cumbria, where he ran a successful specialist dealership in fine art books and catalogues, continuing to paint strongly atmospheric landscapes. Bennett showed in many group exhibitions, including Ulster Museum, Belfast; AIA Gallery; Bradford City Art Gallery; Usher Gallery, Lincoln; Colin Jellicoe Gallery, Manchester; and in America. His many solo shows began at Birmingham University, 1966, later ones including Leeds University, 1969; Gulbenkian Gallery, Newcastle upon Tyne, 1975; Bluecoat Gallery, Liverpool, 1976; Castlegate House, Cockermouth, from 1990, including Recurring Themes, 2004. In 2001, he shared an exhibition with his wife at Broughton House Gallery, Cambridge, in 2005, at the Orange Street Gallery, Uppingham. House of Lords, Lancaster University, Kettle's Yard in Cambridge and Abbot Hall Art Gallery, Kendal, hold Bennett's work.

Michael BENNETT 1948– Painter and teacher, born in Manchester. He studied at Birmingham Polytechnic, 1967–70, Slade School of Fine Art, 1970–2, and had a fellowship at Cheltenham College of Art, 1972–3. He then went on to hold part-time teaching posts from 1974 at St Martin's and Winchester Schools of Art, Kingston Polytechnic and America's Syracuse University. Bennett was interested in "the metaphorical relationship of the materiality of paint to the materiality of earth". He was a rich Colourist, as in his prizewinning canvas Fertile Ground, at John Moores Liverpool Exhibition in 1989–90. Arts Council holds Crimson Lake, 1979, bought from Felicity Samuel Gallery, and Midnight Sonata, 1979–80, obtained by purchase award. Lived in London.

Peter Lloyd BENNETT 1950– After Plymouth College of Art, 1968–70, he studied at Camberwell School of Arts and Crafts, 1970–3. Bennett had solo shows at New Gallery, 1985; University College London, 1986; and Barbican Artworks Space, 1988. Among his group appearances were two in 1989: Air Gallery and East End Open Studios, at Martello Street.

Terence BENNETT 1935– Painter and teacher, born and lived in Doncaster, Yorkshire. He attended the local School of Art, 1951–6, then after National Service taught, giving up teaching to paint full-time in a mining village near Rotherham, 1971. In 1973 gained a Yorkshire Fine Art Fellowship, not long after he had taken up up teaching part-time, eventually becoming head of art department, Thomas Rotherham College, Rotherham. Took part in many mixed exhibitions from series with Yorkshire Artists, Leeds, 1967; others including Park Square Gallery, Leeds from 1968; RA from 1974; Anna-Mei Chadwick, 1987; and Singer & Friedlander/*Sunday Times* Watercolour Competition, from 1991, winning a prize in 1994. Had solo show at Doncaster Museum and Art Gallery, 1967, later ones including Victoria Gallery, Harrogate, 1979, and Quaker Gallery and Grey College, University of Durham, both from from 1998. In 2001, Bennett was Sydney Holgate Fellow at Grey College. The Bank of England, Nuffield Foundation and Yorkshire Arts Association hold his work.

Violet BENNETT 1902– Painter, notably in tempera, born in London. She was privately educated and studied art privately with Otto Flatter, 1946–7, and Ernest Perry, the year following, also receiving tempera instruction from Pietro Annigoni in Italy in the early 1950s. Showed at RA, UA and elsewhere, signing her work V B. Lived in London.

William BENNETT 1917– Painter, notably of miniatures, born in London, who studied art at Sir John Cass College. Showed at RA, Mall Galleries and was a member of RMS. Worked in Britain and Australia, collections there as well as that of HM The Queen holding his pictures. Lived in Sidmouth, Devon.

Ken BENNETTS: *see* **Leonard Kenneth BENNETTS**

Leonard Kenneth BENNETTS 1933–2004 Landscape and figure painter and teacher, born in Dunedin, New Zealand, his maternal grandfather, a creator of ornamental ceilings, being Henry Blanchard Hammond, who encouraged him. Bennetts studied at Canterbury University College, 1948–53, and in Australia at East Sydney Technical College, under Lyndon Dadswell, 1955–6. In Sydney, he showed briefly as Benno. He worked his passage to London as a kitchen porter on a cruise liner. In London he did a number of jobs to survive, at one time being a night-time Post Office telephones supervisor to enable him to paint during the day. Travelled widely in Europe, painting on the spot. Recording the passing buildings of the changing London docklands proved an important theme (Bennetts described himself as "the original retrogressionist (the way forwards is backwards)". Group shows included RA Summer Exhibition, Mall Galleries, Whitechapel Art Gallery and with the Contemporary Art Society. He won a 1st Prize from the Hesketh Hubbard Art Society. Bennetts initiated the first exhibition of New Zealand painters in London in 1965. Also studied at Sir John Cass College under Paul Drury, 1975–82, and with Cecil Collins, 1984–5. An inspirational teacher, Bennetts taught at Hendon College, 1968–92; Barnet College, 1977–82; and the Working Men's College, 1995–6. He was a member of Chelsea Arts Club, 1968–71, the Hampstead Artists' Council, 1962–7, and the Wapping Group, from 1997. He made a return trip to New Zealand in 1987, four years after being included in the Hayward Gallery touring show Landscape Painting in Britain 1850–1950, as Ken Bennetts. Solo exhibitions included Walker's Galleries, 1959 and 1960, and a series at New Zealand House in 1976, 1979, 1981 and 2003. Sydney University, Shell-Mex and BP, Lord Eccles, The High Commissioner of New Zealand and Dean of St Paul's owned examples. Lived in north London.

Ernest Alfred Sallis BENNEY 1894–1966 Painter, designer, teacher and administrator, born in Bradford where he attended the College of Art. Also studied at Royal College of Art. Was the father of the artist Derek Ward Sallis Benney. Sallis Benney went on to hold a series of posts at art schools throughout the country, ending up as principal of Brighton College of Art and director of art education there, 1934–58. Exhibited RA, RBA, Cooling Galleries, NEAC, ROI and provincial galleries. Work held by Victoria & Albert Museum, Towner Art Gallery, Eastbourne and in other provincial galleries. Member of Chelsea Arts Club. Lived in Brighton.

Gerald Sallis BENNEY 1930– Gold- and silversmith, painter and draughtsman, born in Hull, Yorkshire, son of E A Sallis Benney, brother of Derek Benney and father of Paul Benney, all artists. The female nude was a strong feature of Gerald's oils and acrylics, as in his solo exhibition at Century Galleries, Henley-on-Thames, 1998, where works by other members of the family were shown. Gerald was best known for his work in precious metals and jewels and was a Royal Designer for Industry. He held Royal Warrants of Appointment to HM The Queen and other members of the royal family; did commissions for governments and institutions and showed throughout the world; and had work in the collections of The Goldsmiths' Company, The Crafts Council and Victoria & Albert Museum. Richness & Colour was a Benney exhibition at Goldsmiths' Hall in 2005.

Paul BENNEY 1959– Painter, notable for his portraits which while achieving a likeness tended to reveal personality as well. Benney was born and worked in London, but also spent many years in New York. Collaborated with poets and writers. Mixed exhibitions included Slick at Arts Club and Romanticism at New Math Gallery, both New York, 1984; Centre of Contemporary Art in Seattle, 1985; Artisan Space, New York, 1988; and Lamont Gallery, Art92, 1992. Had a series of solo shows at PPOW in New York from 1984, with Nigel Greenwood Gallery, 1992 and Long & Ryle from 1994. In 1994–5 his The Supreme Court, Jerusalem, was shown at National Portrait Gallery prior to display at the Supreme Court Building. It had been commissioned to commemorate its official opening. Portrait retrospective at Mall Galleries, 2001. Sitters for Benney's portraits included Lords Sainsbury, Rothschild and Ashburton and Sir Reresby and Lady Sitwell.

Elspeth BENNIE 1962– Artist in sculpture and metalwork, born in Stirlingshire. She studied at Glasgow School of Art to gain a first-class honours degree in sculpture, 1979–83, then did an advanced sculpture course at St Martin's School of Art, 1983–5, teachers including Alan Gouk, Tim Scott and Katherine Gili. Became a member of British Artist Blacksmiths' Association and the Scottish Society of Artist Craftspeople. In 1985–6 Bennie was resident at the Scottish Sculpture Workshop, travelled in America and Canada, 1986–7, then began full-time as an artist blacksmith/sculptor in 1988. She won the RSA Benno Schotz Prize in 1987. Exhibitions included New Generation Artists at Compass Gallery, Glasgow, 1983; Scottish Drawing Biennial, Paisley Art Gallery, 1985; RSA from 1986; Scottish Sculpture Now, Aberdeen Art Gallery, 1989; Steel and Wood at Royal Exchange Theatre, Manchester, 1991; and The Bonhoga Gallery, Shetland, 1994. Commissions included Centenary Bell Tower, Baillieston Parish Church, in Glasgow where she lived, 1993; Roundabout Sculpture, East Kilbride Development Corporation, and Granite Gate, Fort William High Street, both 1994.

BENNO: *see* **Leonard Kenneth BENNETTS**

Nadia BENOIS 1896–1975 Painter, stage designer and writer, born near St Petersburg, Russia, into a cosmopolitan family that included a number of distinguished artists. Her father was Louis Benois, architect to the Tsar; her uncle, who taught her, was the great stage designer Alexandre Benois. She also studied at St Petersburg Academy. Was married to the journalist Iona Ustinov, their son being the actor-playwright Peter Ustinov. Nadia Benois settled in England with her family and had early successful shows at the Little Gallery, 1924, and with Tooth, 1929. Also showed with the Goupil, Leicester and Matthiesen Galleries and widely abroad. Tate Gallery and Manchester City Art Gallery hold her work, which like the painter was colourful, warm and impulsive. Nadia Benois was for many years an exhibitor and member of NEAC. Her designs for costumes and settings for *The Sleeping Beauty* ballet in London in 1939, at Sadler's Wells and Covent Garden, were a great success. She was included in Three Women Painters, 1975, at Michael Parkin Fine Art Ltd. From early years of World War II lived in Gloucestershire.

Sonja BENSKIN MESHER 1947– Painter, draughtsman and poet whose work, at the time of her solo show at the Museum of Modern Art, Machynlleth, in 2001, was "concerned with combining abstracted sound and landscapes. I use the energetic and expressive marks of drawing to convey mood, emotion, and to fuse the visible and spiritual image." She studied at Bournemouth College of Art, 1964; the College of Further Education there, 1980–2; and Coleg Meirion Dwyfor, Dolgellau, 1998–9. Awards included British Airways, finalist, design prize, 1998; Llanderfel Open Art Exhibition, Bala, prize winner, 1999; Aberystwyth Arts Centre, prize for poetry, and North Wales Wildlife Trust prize for drawing and WAC New Artist Grant, all 2000; Talacre Landscape Competition, purchase prize, painting, 2001; and Meirionydd Perpetual Cup for Art, winner, painting, 2001 and 2002. Took part in many group exhibitions, especially in Wales, where she showed frequently solo, including Theatr Ardudwy, Harlech, 2003. In same year showed at DV8, Penzance. Lived in Llanelltyd, Dolgellau, Gwynedd.

Amanda BENSON 1962– Benson obtained an honours degree from North East London Polytechnic, 1981–4. She then participated in Aspects Gallery, 1985; Camden Annual, Camden Arts Centre, 1986; The Bastille Opens Its Doors to Europe, Paris, 1988; and MM Arts at Skillions Business Centre, Submarine Gallery and East End Open Studios, based at Richmond House Studios, all 1989.

John Miles Bourne BENSON 1889–1950 Figure and flower painter, born in Aberdeen, son of Samuel Benson who founded S H Benson Ltd, later the Benson Advertising Group. It became Britain's largest advertising agency, accounts including Bovril and Guinness; among its employees were the novelist Dorothy L Sayers, whose novel *Murder Must Advertise* was loosely based on her career as a copywriter, and Bobby Bevan, son of the Camden Town Group artist R P Bevan, who became head of the firm. John, known by his family as Jack, came from a family of painters, which included William Gilpin, James Bourne, Frances Benson, his aunt, and his sister, Marguerite. Benson attended Dulwich College, was at the Slade School of Fine Art in 1909 and in 1914 won the Prix de Rome. Volunteered as a private in the Royal Horse Artillery in World War I, in which he fought in Palestine. Afterwards attended the British School at Rome, married an Italian wife – their three sons were bilingual – and remained in Italy until 1937, partly in Anticoli Corrado, partly in Rome, where he ran a business hiring out cars with chauffeurs. In the early 1930s obtained a private pilot's licence, buying a Tiger Moth biplane so that he could fly to London. In 1937, bought a house at Tunbridge Wells, Kent, taking a studio in Chelsea, to which he commuted five days a week and where he painted from the model. In his final years as an invalid was restricted to painting still life at home, also writing much poetry concerned with environmental and wildlife preservation. Private money ensured that Benson did not have to exhibit or sell his pictures, some of which were sold posthumously by Manor House Gallery, Cheltenham, Paul Liss Fine Art and at Bonhams, Knightsbridge, 2002.

Lynn BENSON fl. from 1960s– Painter, printmaker and teacher who attended Wimbledon School of Art, 1963–5, Maidstone College of Art, 1965–8, and Brighton College of Art, gaining a teaching certificate, 1968–9. She taught part-time from 1969–79 at Abbey School, Reading, from 1980 at Caversham Art Centre. Noted for her landscapes, she showed at RA Summer Exhibition, NEAC, ROI, Charles Keyser Gallery, Thackeray Gallery, RBA and Patricia Wells Gallery, Thornbury. Had solo shows at Sadler's Wells Theatre and Century Galleries, Henley-on-Thames. Lived in Burghfield, Berkshire.

Sophie BENSON 1967– Artist and lecturer whose solo show From a Distance, at University of Northumbria Gallery, Newcastle upon Tyne, in 2002, drew on archive photographs found during a residency at Harewood House, 2000. Benson's working methods and materials used were a type of pictorial archaeology, surfaces appearing kneaded or eroded, in a process similar to that of a photographic developing tank, to "imply the passage of time." After obtaining a first-class fine art degree at Canterbury College of Art, 1987–8, Benson gained her fine art master's at University of Newcastle, 1989–91. Awards included Pollock-Krasner Foundation Grant, 1993; Prix Collioure, bursary and invitation to be artist-in-residence and Yorkshire & Humberside Arts Individual Artist Award, both 1995; British Council Exhibition Grant for solo show in Collioure, France, 1996; and Rootstein Hopkins Foundation, Special Project Grant, 2000. Widespread lecturing experience included, from 2000, senior associate lecturer and course leader in painting and printmaking, Sheffield Hallam University. Bernis Foundation, in America; Museum of Modern Art, Collioure; and The MAG Collection hold examples.

Susan BENSON 1931– Painter, illustrator and printmaker, born in Ruislip, Middlesex. Studied at Byam Shaw School of Drawing and Painting, 1947–50, her teachers including Peter Greenham; and at Slade School of Fine Art, 1950–3, with William Coldstream. She showed at Young Contemporaries, WIAC, Beaux Arts Gallery, Leicester Galleries and elsewhere. Her work also appeared in the Journal of the National Book League and in periodicals such as the *Illustrated London News* and *Radio Times*. Lived in London.

John BENSUSAN-BUTT 1911–1997 Artist, notable for landscapes, and writer on painting. He was born in Colchester, where he eventually settled, the family home, 1915–58, being The Minories, later a notable gallery. Bensusan-Butt was an exhibitioner in history at Oxford University, graduating in 1933. Began painting in 1934 and continued, apart from war service, until early 1960s. He studied as a pupil of Lucien Pissarro, 1935–9, his mother's brother-in-law, also etching at Royal College of Art, 1935, and lithography at Central School of Arts and Crafts, 1939. He had shows at French Gallery, 1937, Kensington Art Gallery, 1949, and Leicester Galleries, 1957, being elected RBA in that year; he resigned as inactive in 1975. He also exhibited at Minories Gallery from 1962 and was a member of Colchester Art Society from foundation after the war, usually on the hanging committee. In 1986 had retrospective at Eldon Gallery, Ashmolean Museum, Oxford. His watercolours were shown at The Minories, 2000–1. Bensusan-Butt was art critic to the *Essex County Standard*, 1950–66.

Margaret BENT 1917– Oil painter and teacher, born in London, she was married to the artist John Bent. She studied at Regent Street Polytechnic School of Art, 1936–9, at Bath School of Art, 1942–3, with Clifford Ellis, then in 1948 in Paris. Showed at RA, Victoria & Albert Museum, Tate Gallery and with the Bath Society of Artists. After World War II Margaret Bent taught for a time at Bath Academy of Art, having previously taught at Southlands Training College, London, for two years. Lived in London.

Medora Heather BENT 1901–1992 Painter, notably of furniture, and potter, actual name Alannah Heather Bent. She was much influenced by the places where she lived, including Connemara, Sark and St Ives. Was born in North Kilworth, family home in Connemara, Ireland, being educated in England. Studied at Slade School of Fine Art, 1930–3, with Randolph Schwabe, and Central School of Arts and Crafts, including stained glass. She showed at LG, SGA, SWA and NS. In 1958 her *Paintings of Historical Houses of Purbeck* was published, in 1992 her autobiography. Lived in Wareham, Dorset.

Katy BENTALL 1962– Painter, born in London, who studied at Heatherley's School of Fine Art, 1988–9; Camberwell School of Arts and Crafts, 1989–90; then gained an honours degree at Norwich School of Art, 1990–3. Bentall strove "to explore the relationship between art and life processes." Mixed shows included Nine Elms Group, from 1987; Norwich Castle Museum, 1992; Artworks, Felixstowe, from 1993; and Ipswich Open at Christchurch Mansion, Ipswich, 1995. Lived in Felixstowe, Suffolk.

Philip BENTHAM 1910– Architectural sculptor, son of the sculptor Percy George Bentham (1883–1936), who studied at the Central School of Arts and Crafts, Kennington School of Woodworking and who first worked in his father's London studio. World War II service in the Royal Air Force included several years as a Japanese prisoner of war. After returning and sculpting in London, Philip eventually settled in Worthing, Sussex. Both Benthams have public work in Coventry. Especially notable is Philip's 1965 bronze Coventry Boy, opposite the cathedral. Philip also contributed to the Fortnum & Mason department store clock overlooking Piccadilly, London.

Frank BENTLEY 1941– Untaught painter, particularly of marinescapes, of the naïve school, born in Halifax, West Yorkshire, where he settled at Todmorden. His pictures were worked in acrylic with a mixed medium, giving a matt/chalk-like finish, and were from the imagination. Originally an electrician, then self-employed in the antiques trade, Bentley turned to painting in 1982. Group show appearances included Ferens Art Gallery, Hull, from 1984; RBA Open, 1988; MAFA Open, from 1989; Manchester Art Festival, 1993; and The Northern Art Show, Mall Galleries, 1994. Signed limited-edition prints were published by Portfolio Fine Art, Failsworth, Manchester. Simpson Curtis Permanent Collection, Leeds, holds his work.

Lucy BENTLEY 1968– Figurative painter, born in West Germany, who studied at Salisbury College of Art; Bournemouth & Poole College of Art; and Norwich School of Art. In 1994 she was artist-in-residence, Godolphin School, Salisbury. Group shows included Erasmus Mixed Exhibition, Kunsthalle, Kiel, Germany, 1991; and Small Pictures at Salisbury Playhouse, Salisbury, and Royal Over-Seas League Open, both 1994. Her solo show Vision and Grace took place at Newhouse, Redlynch, Salisbury, 1993.

Nicolas BENTLEY 1907–1978 Illustrator and writer, born in London, son of EC Bentley, who invented the clerihew form of humorous verse and wrote the classic detective novel *Trent's Last Case*. Nicolas Bentley attended Heatherley's School of Fine Art. In World War II he served in Home Intelligence and the Ministry of Information. By then he had begun to establish a solid reputation as a freelance writer and illustrator, consolidated after the war by his work for the *Daily Mail* and *Sunday Times* newspapers. Was also involved in publishing, with André Deutsch and Thomas Nelson. A witty, economical cartoonist and illustrator, his drawings graced many books, including clerihews and biographical writings by his father, Hilaire Belloc's *New Cautionary Tales*, 1930, and *Cautionary Verses*, 1940, and a string of volumes by the humorist George Mikes. Bentley's own book *A Version of the Truth* appeared in 1980. Cartoon Gallery, Chris Beetles and Abbott and Holder showed Bentley's work. Lived in London.

George Bernard BENTON 1872–1959 Painter, illustrator and teacher, born in Birmingham. He attended the College of of Arts and Crafts, later teaching there, and was president of the Art Circle in Birmingham, the city also buying his work. Exhibited RA, RBSA and elsewhere, his pictures often having historical themes. He had a strong interest in the early history of his locality, on which he wrote. Lived finally at Streetly, Warwickshire.

Pip BENVENISTE 1921– Artist, designer, film-maker and teacher, born in Newlyn, Cornwall, studying early with both parents who were artists, later with other Cornish painters. She moved to London in 1946 and from 1948–50 travelled extensively in France and Morocco, painting landscapes. Returned to England where she began exhibiting in many mixed shows in London and the provinces, including Nicholas Treadwell Galleries. In 1957 she spent some time in New York and made first experiments in abstract painting, and after returning to London from 1959 taught, designed fabrics and began working on pictures based on a controlled but intuitive delineation of energy in space. Lao Tzu and contemporary astrophysicists were influences. Benveniste's 1968 film *Eventual*, a rare contemporary glimpse of actions by 1960s artists John Latham, Stuart Brisley and Jeffrey Shaw, was screened by Tate Britain in 2003. From 1990 had a series of solo shows at Primrose Hill Gallery.

Margaret BENYON 1940– Holographic artist, teacher and writer, born in Birmingham, who spent her childhood in Kenya, 1948–58. She studied painting at Birmingham College of Art, 1958–60; then was at Slade School, including a postgraduate year, 1961–6; her doctoral project at Royal College of Art, 1989–94, How is Holography Art, being sponsored by Ilford Ltd. Held a number of fellowships, including Leverhulme Senior Art Fellow, University of Strathclyde, 1971–3, after being Fellow in Fine Art, University of Nottingham, 1968–71, also being Creative Arts Fellow, Australian National University, Canberra, 1978–9. Taught extensively, starting with silkscreen printing at Byam Shaw School, 1965–6, later appointments including visiting tutor to the holography unit, Royal College of Art, 1985–9. Benyon was a professional painter, 1965–70, then pioneered art holography in 1968. Took part in numerous group exhibitions, from Young Contemporaries, 1965, later shows including 4th International Symposium on Display Holography, Lake Forest, America, and Fiat Lux! Holography, at Asturias, Spain, both 1991, and 4 British Holographers, Smiths Galleries, 1992. In 1991 gained commission for Arts Council Award trophy. Had solo show at Nottingham University, 1969, later ones including Conjugal and Cosmetic Series, Interference Hologram Gallery, Toronto, 1987, Cosmetic Series/Conjugal Series, Museum für Holographie & Neue Visuelle Medien, Pulheim, West Germany, 1990, and Gallery 286, 2001. Lived in Broadstone, Dorset.

Helena BEN-ZENOU 1970– Artist in various media, born in Nottingham, who studied at the University of Lancaster. Group shows included The Piece Hall Art Gallery, Halifax (with Liza Dracup), 1997; Scottish Sculpture Workshop, Lumsden, 1998; and The Approach Gallery, 1999. In that year Ben-Zenou was participating in the Acme Fire Station Residency Scheme and was shortlisted for The NatWest Art Prize. There, she exhibited apparently abstract pictures, inspired by cities, aerial views, maps and plans. Solo shows included Brahm Gallery, Leeds, 1993, and Cartwright Hall, Bradford, 1997.

Albert BERBANK 1896–1961 Painter in oil and watercolour, draughtsman in pen and ink and pencil, and wood engraver. Born in Nottingham, Berbank studied at the School of Art there, 1912–16; St Martin's School of Art, 1924–34; and at Westminster School of Art, 1934–6, under Walter Bayes and Bernard Meninsky. He exhibited at RA, NS, RI, SGA and abroad, one-man shows including New Vision Centre and elsewhere. Berbank, who taught and lectured, sold work to Leicestershire Education Committee. President of the London Sketch Club, 1960–1. Lived in London.

Otto BERCHEM 1967– Artist, born in Milford, Connecticut, America, who attended Yale Summer School of Music and Art, 1989; Parsons School of Design, New York, 1990; and the College of Art, Edinburgh, 1994. Exhibitions included several in that city, among them CD Show, Collective Gallery, 1992; Five, Wasps Gallery, 1993; and Aerial '94, 1994. Also in 1994 Berchem was in New Art in Scotland, at the Centre for Contemporary Arts, Glasgow, with installations which "tried to demystify certain notions of the Men's Room."

Philip BERCZUK 1962– Painter who graduated with honours from Duncan of Jordanstone College of Art, Dundee, 1980–4, gaining his master's from Chelsea School of Art, 1985–6. Shows included Prima Materia, Flaxman Gallery, the Royal Over-Seas League Annual Exhibition and A Celebration of the Winter Solstice, Creaser Gallery, all 1988, and East End Open Studios, at Carpenter's Road, 1989.

Alexander BERDYSHEFF 1964– Artist commonly working in mixed media on various supports, based in Tbilisi, Georgia. He graduated from Tbilisi Academy of Fine Arts in 1988 and produced highly personal work. This drew on Georgian and Russian influences, his father having been born in St Petersburg. Berdysheff developed contact with Scotland as a member of a graduate and postgraduate exchange programme permitting him to study at Glasgow School of Art in 1990. Four years later he revisited Scotland for six months, becoming better acquainted with the work of Western artists and taking advantage of materials and techniques unknown or unavailable in Georgia. Group exhibitions included Galeria Brik, Barcelona, Spain, 1990; Artbank Gallery, Glasgow, 1991; Roy Miles Gallery, 1995; Central House of Artists, Moscow, 1996; and in 1997 RSA Summer Exhibition and Midsummer Magic Exhibition at The Scottish Fine Art Group, Inverness. Solo exhibitions included The British Council, Edinburgh, 1994; Royal Concert Hall, Glasgow, 1995; and Edinburgh College of Art (part of the International Festival), 1997.

Jill BERELOWITZ 1955– Artist and designer, notably a sculptor, born in Johannesburg, South Africa, who studied under Karen Jarozynska, Tadeus Jarozynski and Bill Ainslee, 1967–70; majored in sculpture from Johannesburg School of Art, 1970–3; did a diploma course in design, University of Witwatersrand, 1974; and studied clay and glazing techniques with Barry Allison, 1975–8. From 1977–86 had her own sculpture and painting studio in Durban, from 1987 her own sculpture teaching studio in Mill Hill, London, where she lived. Commissions included rowers and tile plaques for Henley-on-Thames housing development, 1989; bronze resin work for Sarum Hall School, Hampstead, 1996; and work in Unilever corporate collection, 1998. Exhibitions included Andrew Usiskin Gallery, 1993; Passion and Sensuality, The Gallery in Cork Street, 1997; and McHardy Sculpture Company, 1998.

BERENICE 1944–1983 Multi-talented, prolific artist, full name Berenice Sydney, born in Esher, Surrey, daughter of the documentary film producer Joseph Sydney Frieze. Showed early talent for art, studied at the Lycée Français in London, then briefly attended Central School of Art before deciding to work independently and dedicatedly. In her Chelsea studio she soon abandoned figuration for abstraction, geometric forms alternating with coloured rhythms. Berenice wrote that she was an artist "for whom colour has been the paramount means of expression.... I feel I could eat bits of one of my paintings." From the mid-1960s developed an interest in many aspects of printmaking, which led her gradually towards a type of representation. Berenice's large oil paintings, with their exuberant colour and sweeping forms, contrast with minutely detailed, chatty, witty pen drawings and prints. Flemish and Egyptian art, classical music, poetry and dancing were some preoccupations of her work. Had numerous group and solo appearances. Groups included Leicester Galleries, from 1968; Demarco Gallery, Edinburgh, 1971; Bibliothèque Nationale, Paris, 1973; represented Britain, Biennale della Grafica m'Arte, Florence, 1974; Exhibition of British Art, Abu Dhabi, 1984; and British Council, Paris, 1985; also with SGA, Hampstead Artists' Council, Free Painters and Sculptors and Chelsea Art Society. Later solo exhibitions included Salute to Berenice, Upstairs Gallery, RA, 1984. There was a posthumous tribute at Edwin Engelberts, Galerie Art Contemporain, Geneva, Switzerland, 1985. Berenice was a woman of striking appearance who died suddenly of an asthma and heart attack in Highgate, north London. Many public collections in Europe and America hold her work, including the British Museum; Victoria & Albert Museum; Tate Gallery; Ashmolean Museum, Oxford; Fitzwilliam Museum, Cambridge; Smithsonian Institution and National Library of Congress, both in Washington; and Fogg Art Museum, Harvard University.

Frank Ernest BERESFORD 1881–1967 Painter, notably of horse subjects, and mural decorator. Born in Derby, he studied at the School of Art there, then St John's Wood School of Art and the Royal Academy Schools, where he finished in 1906. Exhibited RA, ROI, RI, RP and elsewhere. Beresford was a much-honoured painter. He won a British Institution Scholarship which took him on a world tour, as the result of which he gained the first award for art from the Imperial Japanese government, in 1909. For his work with the United States Air Force in World War II he won the Exceptional Service Award, only once before granted to a British subject. Lived at Northiam, Sussex.

Mary BERESFORD-WILLIAMS 1931– Painter, printmaker, draughtsman, photographer and teacher, born in London. She graduated with a class one honours degree at Reading University under J Anthony Betts. Taught mainly in the West Country, including Rolle College, Exmouth. In 1978 won a South West Arts Major Award. Took up photography in 1970, using it in conjunction with screenprinting; between 1985–8 photography became an interest in its own right, then returned to drawing and painting. Was a member of Newlyn Society of Artists and Devon Guild of Craftsmen, also showing at NEAC and RWA. In 1986 was photographer-in-residence for Television South-West. Devon Schools Museums Service holds her work. Lived in Galmpton, Brixham, Devon.

Adrian BERG 1929– Painter and teacher, born and lived in London. From 1949–53 he studied at Cambridge University, switching from medicine to English, and did a higher diploma in education at Trinity College, Dublin. Taught in schools, then studied at St Martin's and Chelsea Schools of Art, then Royal College of Art, 1955–61, his teachers including Ceri Richards. He was senior tutor at Royal College of Art, 1987–8. Showed in London regularly from 1964 as well as on continent and North America. He won a gold medal at Florence Biennale in 1973 and was a John Moores Liverpool Exhibition prizewinner in 1980. Exhibited often at Piccadilly Gallery. Later exhibitions included Serpentine Gallery, 1986, and tour, following a retrospective at Rochdale Art Gallery, 1980. Arts Council, British Museum, British Council and Tokyo Metropolitan Art Museum hold examples. Berg was a compulsive painter of landscape and foliage using a rich palette. He was made RA in 1992.

Kjetil BERGE 1957– Installation artist, who came originally from Sunnhordland, near Bergen, in Norway. She studied at Bergen Kunsthåndverksskole; Escola Superior de Belas Artes, Lisbon; and Slade School of Fine Art, 1989. Exhibited internationally, including shows in Oslo, Bergen Haugesund, Tokyo, Riga, Amman and Sofia. Produced the commission Tärn for Riverside, Norwich School of Art & Design, 1999, which comprised translucent bricks, made of concrete and found objects. In 2003, Berge's piece Lysthus, based on a pavilion commonly found in public spaces in Scandinavia, was shown in the outdoor plaza by *The Economist* building. Lived in London.

George BERGEN 1903–1984 Painter, notably of portraits and interiors, born in Minsk, Russia. The family settled in Brooklyn, in America, in 1909 and they were granted citizenship 10 years later. Bergen studied at various New York art schools, was then taught by George Bellows at the School of Fine Arts, Yale University, and in 1925 crossed the Atlantic on a Yale travelling scholarship, having a first solo show at Goupil Gallery in the late 1920s. He had another in 1932 at Lefevre and also showed at Agnew and Leicester Galleries. Bergen was by then entangled artistically and emotionally with the Bloomsbury Group. In the 1930s Bergen spent part of each year in Spain and he lived for some time in California where he was friendly with stars such as Constance Collier and Charlie Chaplin, whom he painted. In 1939 he settled in New York, but his connections with Bloomsbury painters were renewed in the 1960s. In 1988 Sally Hunter Fine Art held a show, George Bergen and Bloomsbury.

BERGER: *see* **Margarete HAMERSCHLAG**

John BERGER 1926– Author, art critic, painter, film-maker and teacher, born in London. He studied under Robert Kirkland Jamieson at Central School of Arts and Crafts, 1942–3, then at Chelsea School of Art, 1945–7, his teachers including Robert Medley. Exhibited Wildenstein, Lefevre, Leicester and St George's Galleries, Arts Council buying his work. Taught at St Mary's Training College, London, and wrote on art for *New Statesman* and *Tribune*. Berger became a controversial critic, advocating a Marxist approach to art. Later he established an international reputation as a writer of fiction, factual books, works of criticism and as a translator. Also appeared on television. Novels included *A Painter of Our Time*, 1958; *Corker's Freedom*, 1964; *Pig Earth*, 1979; *G*, which won the Booker and James Tait Black Memorial Prizes, 1972; and *King: a Street Story*, 1999. Non-fiction included *Permanent Red*, 1960; *A Fortunate Man: The Story of a Country Doctor* (with Jean Mohr), 1967; *Ways of Seeing*, 1972; *Photocopies*, 1996; and *The Shape of a Pocket*, 2001. In 2005, the National Film Theatre ran an extensive programme of Berger's moving-image works, often in collaboration, including *The Salamander*, 1971; *Ways of Seeing*, 1972; *The Middle of the World*, 1974; *Pig Earth*, 1979; *Another Way of Telling*, 1989; and *The Spectre of Hope*, 2001. Also in 2005, John Berger: A Telling Eye was an exhibition at the Lyttelton Exhibition foyer, Royal National Theatre, on which Berger collaborated with photographer Mohr, director John Christie and artist Maggie Hambling. Lived in Taninges, France.

Joseph BERGER 1898–1989 Architect and watercolourist, born in Vienna, married to the artist Margarete Hamerschlag. Berger was a notable exponent of the Viennese modernist school of architecture who studied at the Technische Hochschule, Vienna, 1917–21, under Adolf Loos and Oskar Strnad. Worked in private practice, then when political situation darkened he lived for a period in the mid-1930s in Haifa, Palestine, moving to England with his wife in 1936. After internment as an enemy alien in the Isle of Man in World War II, Berger eventually joined the London County Council unit concerned with building schools, retiring in 1963. His wife having died in 1959, Berger spent his final years with Regina Gillinson-Schein, the cellist. Lived in London.

Margareta Livia BERGER: *see* **Margarete HAMERSCHLAG**

Sybille BERGER 1962– Artist whose work included brightly coloured geometrical abstracts, such as Without Title, 1994, included in New Contemporaries, 1996, at Tate Gallery in Liverpool and Camden Arts Centre. She was born in Stuttgart, West Germany, and gained both bachelor's and master's degrees in fine art in visual communication at Hochschule der Künste, Berlin, 1985–91, then her master's in fine art at Goldsmiths' College, 1993–5. Other exhibitions included Gallery Lasard, Berlin, 1993; Chisenhale Gallery, 1994; Exmouth Market, 1995; and John Moores Liverpool Exhibition, 1997–8. Lived in London.

Margarete BERGER-HAMERSCHLAG: *see* **Margarete HAMERSCHLAG**

Sylvia BERGIN 1904–1999 Versatile, self-critical artist and commercial designer and teacher working in a wide range of media, born in Pinner, Middlesex, whose father founded the engraving firm J J Bergin. She attended St Martin's School of Art, 1920–3, where she met Owen Rowley, whom she married in 1930. Because of his newspaper commitments they had to move around Britain, as well as travelling privately on the continent. From 1924–30 Bergin was a commercial artist while doing her own work, also attending the Grosvenor and Heatherley's Art Schools under Iain Macnab. In the 1940s she was well known in the Manchester area art world, showing with MAFA and elsewhere, her work being acquired by the Whitworth and Salford Art Galleries. Returning to London in 1947, Sylvia and Owen taught painting for over 25 years in the occupational therapy department for brain-damaged patients of the Atkinson Morley Hospital. They extended their knowledge at the Sir John Cass School of Arts and Crafts and after Owen's death Sylvia instituted the Owen Rowley Prize. Bergin remained prolific, later work tending towards abstraction. Showed at RP, RA Summer Exhibitions, RBA, ROI and elsewhere and with Owen shared three shows, including one at Sadler's Wells, 1976. The Studio Art House, Leatherhead, held a retrospective in 2000, and there were other shows at The Chelsea and Westminster Hospital Mall, 2002, and again in Leatherhead in 2004.

Stephenie BERGMAN 1946– Painter who said that her pictures involved two processes: "The first is preparing material and the second is making something with it." Her entry to John Moores Liverpool Exhibition in 1985, Table, Vase and Fork, employed acrylic paint, canvas and mattress tacking. Bergman was born and lived in London and studied at St Martin's School of Art, 1963–7. After a first show at Garage Art in 1973 exhibited regularly in Britain and abroad. Had a solo show with Crafts Council Gallery in 1984 from which Arts Council bought her creation Thunderthighs.

Xenia BERKELEY 1915– Painter, draughtsman and commercial artist with strong interest in the theatre and ballet, born in London. She drew for magazines with women's interests prominent and illustrated several children's books. Educated in Teignmouth, Devon, she studied at Exeter School of Art. Exhibited NEAC, LG, NS, Arts Council and elsewhere. Sometimes signed work only as Xenia or X B. Lived in London.

Carey BERLIN 1976– Versatile and experimental artist in various media, born in London, who graduated in graphic design from Camberwell School of Art in 1998. She worked as a producer's assistant for Figment and DNA Films. Berlin's own work manipulated flat surfaces to create three-dimensional geometric structures reminiscent of architectural forms. Examples were the tower-like pieces in Perspex boxes, shown at the Albemarle Gallery in 2001, in which precise cuts and folds interacted with the play of light to produce an altering perception of volume as the viewer moved around them.

Greta BERLIN 1942– Sculptor, ceramist, draughtsman and teacher, born in St Ives, Cornwall, daughter of the sculptor Sven Berlin, mother of the artist Zennor Witney. Berlin worked in bronze, plaster, clay, steel and stone. She described her sculptures as "Expressionist, figurative, an exploration of human forms alone and in relationship with each other". Berlin was a lecturer in ceramics at Brockenhurst Tertiary College, 1970–90; in the 1970s she was also engaged in archaeological ceramic research at Butser Hill, Hampshire, in the 1980s working as a copyist at the Victoria & Albert Museum. Carried out many commissions, including a nine-foot bronze of Lord Mountbatten for Timberlaine, Grosvenor Square, Southampton, 1989; the comedian Max Wall, in Theatre Museum collection, 1992; and Birdman, Hampshire County Council, 1993. Group shows included Bristol Cathedral, 1979; RWA and Brighton Polytechnic, both 1985; Eye Gallery, Bristol, 1989; and Gordon Hepworth Gallery, Newton St Cyres, 1993. Had a solo show at Eccleston Square, 1983, later ones including Alton Museum, 1991, and Broomhill Art Hotel, Barnstaple, 2001. Lived in Wootton Fitzpaine, Bridport, Dorset.

Sven BERLIN 1911–1999 Sculptor, painter, draughtsman and writer who led a bohemian, often controversial life. Born in London of an English mother and Swedish father, Berlin was apprenticed as a mechanical engineer, in 1928 enrolled at Beckenham School of Art, but decided instead to pursue a career as an adagio dancer in music-halls. In 1934 and 1938 pursued art studies at Camborne-Redruth Schools of Art in Cornwall as well as other subjects such as poetry, philosophy and comparative religion. Had first one-man show at Camborne Community Centre in 1939, by which time he had begun sculpting. Although a conscientious objector at outset of World War II, he eventually joined the Army. Settled in St Ives, and was co-founder of Crypt Group in 1946 and a founder-member of Penwith Society in 1949, the year his book *Alfred Wallis, Primitive*, was published. Other books included *The Dark Monarch: A Portrait from Within*, about St Ives and its inhabitants; it led to several libel actions. His autobiography *A Coat of Many Colours*, 1994, contains chapters on fellow-artists in St Ives; second volume, *Virgo in Exile*, appeared in 1996. After a few moves, partly by horse and gypsy waggon, Berlin eventually settled at Wimborne, Dorset. He was a regular exhibitor of work sometimes extremely strong, sometimes of variable quality. A notable show was at Belgrave Gallery, 1989. Victoria & Albert Museum, Tate Gallery, National Library of Scotland and other British and foreign collections hold his work. Sven Berlin's daughter Greta Berlin was a sculptor and her daughter the artist Zennor Witney.

Brenda BERMAN 1936– Artist who trained as a painter at Bath Academy of Art, Corsham. She later studied lettering with Berthold Wolpe at City & Guilds of London Art School, where she met Annet Stirling, with whom in 1988 she formed Incisive Lettering (see separate entries).

Mike BERNARD 1957– Painter, born in Dover, Kent, who enjoyed experimenting with media and techniques, exploring textures and light to produce semi-abstract images. He attended West Surrey College of Art and Design followed by postgraduate studies at the Royal Academy Schools. Exhibited at Royal Festival Hall, many London and provincial galleries and was included in a four-artist show at The Linda Blackstone Gallery, Pinner, 2001. He was an Artist of the Month at Rowley Gallery and was included in a three-artist show at The Wykeham Gallery, Stockbridge, both in 2003. Among Bernard's awards were the Stowells Trophy and Elizabeth Greenshields, Silver Longboat and Laing Awards. Elected RI in 1997.

BERNARD-BOWERMAN: *see* **Bernard BOWERMAN**

Lord BERNERS 1883–1950 Composer, painter, writer and eccentric, born at Apley Park, Bridgnorth, Shropshire. He was educated at Eton College and entered the diplomatic service, serving abroad in several posts, then inherited his titles in 1918. He was to become Sir Gerald Hugh Tyrwhitt-Wilson, 5th baronet and 14th Baron Berners. Bought Faringdon House, in Berkshire, where he then lived, although he spent some time in London and in Rome. His main interest was music, which he studied under Stravinsky and Casella. Berners composed orchestral and piano music and opera but was especially noted for his clever scores for Sadler's Wells Ballet and the 1926 success *The Triumph of Neptune* for the Diaghilev Ballet. Berners' playfulness and wit are best shown in his music, less in his landscape paintings, which were in the manner of Corot, whose work he collected along with that of Derain, Matisse, Sisley and Constable. Some of his pictures were in the style of the Douanier Rousseau. He had solo shows at Lefevre Galleries in 1931 and 1936, also exhibiting at Goupil Gallery. As a writer Berners was a satirist of social life, and he also penned two amusing autobiographical volumes, *First Childhood*, 1934, and *A Distant Prospect*, 1945, but failed to finish a third. He was noted for his practical jokes and eccentric behaviour. A centenary exhibition was held at Royal Festival Hall in 1983.

Celia BERRIDGE 1948– Painter, born in Windsor, Berkshire, who studied at the Central School of Art and Design, 1977; Chelsea College of Art, 1993–7; and Central School, 1998–2000. Group exhibitions included The Tannery, 1997; Megalomania, PSI Building, 1999; and John Moores Liverpool Exhibition, 1999. There, Berridge's double-portraits Life/Time examined the effects of age on her mother on her wedding day and aged 80. Lived in Rodmell, Sussex.

John Archibald Alexander BERRIE 1887–1962 Mainly a portrait painter, he was born near Manchester and studied at Bootle and Liverpool Schools of Art, at Hubert Herkomer's School at Bushey, then in Paris. Exhibited at RA, with RCamA of which he became a full member in 1923 and extensively with Walker Art Gallery in Liverpool, which holds portraits of local worthies by him. Had a solo exhibition at Walker's Galleries, 1936. Among his portraits were King George V and Winston Churchill. Lived in London, Harrogate and finally Johannesburg, South Africa.

Peter BERRISFORD 1932– Painter and lecturer, born in Northampton. He studied at Northampton and Chelsea Schools of Art and Bournemouth College of Art, gaining a travelling scholarship in 1953. Went on to lecture for bodies such as National Trust and Arts Council and was head of adult art studies at the College of Arts and Technology in Eastbourne, Sussex, where he lived. In 1957 was selected by Jack Beddington for inclusion in the book *Young Artists of Promise*. Showed RA, John Moores Liverpool Exhibition, Bear Lane Gallery in Oxford, Trafford Gallery, RBA and elsewhere. East Sussex County Council and galleries in Hull, Leicester and Northampton hold his work.

Arthur BERRY 1925–1994 Painter, teacher and writer, born in Smallthorne, Staffordshire, son of a bricklayer. At 13 Berry left council school to attend Junior Art School, at Queen Street, Burslem, in the Potteries. He became a student there in 1940, going to Royal College of Art in 1943. In 1946 Berry began part-time teaching at Manchester College of Art; in 1952 took on same role at Burslem College of Art and Chelsea School of Art, becoming full-time lecturer in Burslem in 1963. He was later principal lecturer in painting at North Staffordshire Polytechnic. In the mid-1940s Berry met Robert Colquhoun and Robert MacBryde, whose work had a great influence on him, and saw L S Lowry's paintings for the first time. In the mid-1970s Berry began writing stage plays, and in 1980 a talk broadcast on Radio Stoke won the Pye Award for the best scripted talk of the year. Berry's work reflects the primitive, gritty world of the pit village where he was born and reared. He was given a retrospective at Stoke-on-Trent City Museum and Art Gallery, 1984, another at The Gallery, Manchester, 1995.

Bill BERRY 1900–1971 Artist and designer, full name Charles William Berry. He trained as an artist at Camden, Bolt Court and at St Martin's School of Art, then was an apprentice at Stone Offset Lithography Works and worked at a process engraver's before joining the Winter Thomas advertising agency. After World War I service in the Royal Flying Corps and a period as art editor for the *Draper's Organiser* Berry between the wars served with various advertising agencies, settling with Lintas in 1933, where he stayed until retirement. He was included in the Lintas Beyond the Horizon exhibition at Agnew, 1988. Had a solo show of watercolours at Batsford Gallery in 1947, was elected RI in 1949 and showed with RSW.

Joanne BERRY 1966– Abstract artist and teacher, born in Bury, Lancashire, whose work explored the inner, subconscious self. She did a foundation diploma at Blackburn College of Art, 1984–5; gained an honours degree in graphic design, Newcastle upon Tyne Polytechnic, 1985–8; a master's in illustration, Royal College of Art, 1988–90; and a master's in fine art printmaking, Camberwell College of Art, 1994–6. In 1993 was artist-in-residence at Lowick House, Cumbria, from 1995 being a part-time art teacher at Loughborough College of Art & Design. Awards included Prince's Trust Business Award, 1990; Yorkshire Printmakers' Prize and Printmakers' Council Student Award, both 1996. Group exhibitions included Camden Arts Centre, 1991; 5 at Roupell Gallery, 1992; in 1996 Redfern Gallery and Royal Over-Seas League Open; and light box drawings, England & Co, 2001. Had a solo exhibition at Gabriele Skelton Ltd, 1992. Berry's show Order, Regimentation, Collision, at Yard Gallery, Nottingham, in 2002, comprised 16 "light drawings" using computer technology and lasers to create abstract geometric shapes. She was then a Loughborough University research fellow. Victoria & Albert Museum holds Berry's work.

June BERRY 1924– Painter and printmaker, born in Melbourne, Derbyshire. She studied at Slade School of Fine Art, 1941–2 and 1946–9. Was elected to RWS and NEAC, also showing at RA, RE and abroad, and had a solo exhibition at Alresford Gallery, Alresford, 2001. National Museum of Wales in Cardiff; Graphotek in Berlin, Germany; and public galleries in Kettering and Oldham hold her work. Lived in Beckenham, Kent.

Peter BERRY 1937– Sculptor and teacher who worked in a commercial art studio in Gloucester before studying at Gloucester College of Art, 1956–60, and Slade School of Fine Art, 1961–3. He taught sculpture at Gloucester, 1964, from 1965 lecturing in pre-diploma studies at Birmingham. Exhibited at John Walter Gallery, Upper Whitechapel Gallery and was included in 19 Young Sculptors at Hillfield Gardens, Gloucester, 1962. In 1966 had a solo show at Ikon Gallery, Birmingham, and was included in The beginning of Ikon there in 2004.

Dave BERRY-HART 1940– Painter, teacher and sculptor using materials such as stone, wood, plastic and hessian. He was born in Trinidad and studied at St Martin's School of Art, 1959–61, his teachers including Frederick Gore, Joe Tilson and Derrick Greaves; then City of Birmingham Polytechnic, 1980–3, his master's degree dissertation being on Gauguin's colour. "Prehistoric and Neolithic art, traditions and folklore" were cited as influences on Berry-Hart's work, which was sometimes signed Jabir. Lectured at North Warwickshire College and elsewhere. Held a number of exhibitions with The Firm, 1983–7, open exhibitions including Liverpool Academy, Walker Art Gallery, 1960; Spectrum Central, 1971; and Mercia Artists, Herbert Art Gallery and Museum, Coventry, 1984. Had a solo show at AIA Gallery, 1969, later ones including Mid-Warwickshire College of Further Education, 1989, Worcester Museum & Art Gallery, 1991, and Brewhouse Theatre and Arts Centre, Taunton, 1999. Imperial College holds his work. Lived in Nuneaton, Warwickshire.

Derek BERRYMAN 1926– Painter, printmaker, sculptor, designer and teacher, born in Chingford, Essex. He studied at Universities of Durham and Bristol, St Martin's School of Art, Sir John Cass College, City of London Polytechnic and in 1960 gained scholarship to Syracuse University, New York State. Held several teaching posts, including head of graphic design at Weston-super-Mare School of Art from 1968. Showed at RA, ROI, RWA and in America. Lived in Hutton, Somerset.

Neville BERTRAM 1908–1999 Sculptor and teacher, born in Cullercoats, Northumberland, full name Charles Neville Bertram. His father was the artist Robert John Scott Bertram, his older brother the painter Robert Bryan Bertram. Based in Newcastle, he studied at Durham University, 1926–9, gaining his diploma in fine art, in 1930 winning his Board of Education drawing and painting certificates, under Robert Lyon. He entered and submitted work for the Rome School, 1931. In 1932 Bertram taught part-time and studied modelling and pottery, also doing some stone carving. He moved to Liverpool in 1933, making commercial sculpture with Herbert Tyson Smith, marrying one of his daughters, in 1936 returning to Tyneside to work on further commercial projects. After six years with the Air Ministry, in 1945 Bertram took on part-time work at Liverpool College of Art, teaching full-time from 1950–73. Bertram joined Liverpool Academy in 1946, becoming honorary treasurer and secretary. About 1950 he was made an associate of RBS. Walker Art Gallery, Liverpool, holds Bertram's Quadripartite Form, of 1959. Lived in West Kirby, Cheshire.

Robert Bryan BERTRAM 1906–1986 Landscape painter and teacher, son of the artist Robert John Scott Bertram, his younger brother the sculptor Neville Bertram. He was born in Newcastle, was a career teacher at the Royal Grammar School and showed at the Laing Art Gallery. After Army service in World War II, he settled in Northumberland at Ponteland.

Robert John Scott BERTRAM 1871–1953 Versatile artist and teacher, father of the painter Robert Bryan Bertram and the sculptor Neville Bertram. Born in Newcastle, son of a ship's chandler, Bertram showed early artistic promise, but had to work for his living after leaving school. While employed as a designer for a furniture shop he joined art evening classes, won a scholarship to the art school of Durham College of Science & Art in Newcastle and in 1895 was made a part-time assistant. By 1920, he had risen to master of design at what was by then Armstrong College, retiring in 1937. His abilities as a draughtsman made him much-used by publishers in the northeast, including the first volume of the *Northumberland County History*. His *Newcastle upon Tyne Sketch Book* appeared in 1914, a *Durham Sketch Book* in 1920. Showed at Laing Art Gallery, Newcastle, where he was one of the artists selected to paint a lunette in 1930, and once at RA Summer Exhibition. Bertram had a strong interest in historical landscapes and building preservation, belonging to the Society of Antiquaries in Newcastle, and its Pen & Palette Club. He retired to Whitby, Yorkshire, where he exhibited at the Pannet Art Gallery.

Don BESSANT 1941–1993 Printmaker and teacher, born in Gillingham, Kent, who attended Rochester School of Art, then gained first-class honours and a gold medal while studying printmaking at Royal College of Art, 1961–4. After lecturing part-time at Maidstone College of Art, moved to Wolverhampton College of Art, 1972–93. Between 1973–5 Bessant printed for Editions Alecto, from 1978–93 for Sky Editions. He was a versatile technician who produced prints for many notable British and foreign artists, including Prunella Clough, Jim Dine, Howard Hodgkin and Dieter Roth. His own work included the landscape around Slad, Gloucestershire, home of his friend the poet and writer Laurie Lee, author of *Cider with Rosie*. Bessant was given a retrospective at Wolverhampton College of Art in 1994.

Anna BEST 1965– Sculptor, born and lived in London, who was involved in installation/environmental/ collaboration/site-specific performance work. Her aim was "to make work, in whatever media are most appropriate, for a specific place and time". She did a Hounslow Borough College foundation course, 1983–4, with Clive Burton and Dave Smith; in 1984 was at Art Students' League of New York; in 1984–7, under Dick Whall, gained a first-class honours degree in fine art (sculpture) at Coventry Polytechnic. In 1991 Best won a British Council travel grant to America and had a Grizedale Forest Sculpture Residency, Cumbria; in 1992 was involved in Le Sens de la Mesure, European competition for residency and exhibition, Melun, France; in 1993 a Sculpture Space Inc., New York, funded residency; and in 1994–5 was a Rijksakademie van beeldende kunsten, Amsterdam, participating artist. She established the Red Cow Studios Co-operative in 1988; was involved in part-time lecturing at Chelsea School of Art and Hounslow Borough College foundation courses from 1989, plus additional teaching at Coventry Polytechnic, 1991. In that year was a participant at Triangle Artists' Workshop in New York, in 1992 being co-ordinator and participant in Shave Artists' Workshop, Somerset. Selected exhibitions included The McGrigor Donald Sculpture Prize Exhibition, with tour, 1990; Lockbund Sculpture Exhibition, Oxford Art Week, and On Site, Bermondsey, 1992; and Burning Toast, a collaborative work with Richard Reynolds, 1993. In 1998, Tate Modern commissioned The Wedding Project, a live art project for Borough Market, in south London. At Tate Modern in 2004 Best led Working Together, which focused on artists who worked collaboratively. Also in 2004, with the composer Paul Whitty, she devised *Vauxhall Pleasure*, described by Richard Morrison in *The Times* as "English eccentricity at its finest", a one-day, 15-hour event during which 38 singers "warbled 18th-century ditties in the centre of Vauxhall Cross Interchange – London's noisiest, nastiest junction", once the site of Vauxhall Pleasure Gardens. Leicestershire Education Authority holds her work.

Eleanor BEST 1875–1957 Oil painter, born at Amport, Hampshire. Studied at the Slade School of Fine Art, 1909–12, with Henry Tonks and Walter Westley Russell. Exhibited RA, RSA, NEAC, NS, in the provinces and in America and Sweden. The Contemporary Art Society and a number of provincial galleries bought her work. Her work was included in Sladey Ladies at Parkin Gallery, 1986. Lived in London.

Gladys BEST 1898– Painter in oil and watercolour of landscapes and architectural subjects. Born in Chiswick, she studied at Exeter School of Art and was for a time on the staff of Cheltenham Ladies' College. She exhibited at the RA, RBA, RSA, RI, in the provinces and at the Paris Salon. The Victoria & Albert Museum and Ministry of Works bought her work and she participated in the Pilgrim Trust *Recording Britain* project. Lived at Topsham, Devon.

Ronald BEST 1957– Painter, printmaker and teacher, born and lived in London, who studied full-time at Byam Shaw School of Art, 1975–6 and 1981–2; Southwark College, 1982–3; Croydon College, 1983–7; and the Royal College of Art, 1988–90; also widely part-time. Assisted the painter Winston Branch; was artist-in-residence, Essendine Centre, 1987–8; and at Chelsea College of Further Education, 1993. Taught at Essendine, 1989–91; Kensington & Chelsea College, 1994; and Heatherley's School of Fine Art, 1997–01. Exhibitions included Young Contemporaries, Whitworth Art Gallery, Manchester, 1987; LG at Royal College of Art, 1989; Portobello Print Open, Metro Gallery, 1990; Acava Open Studios, 1996; and Notting Hill Fine Art, 2001. There was a solo show of prints at W11 Gallery, 1999. Best was a member of the Portobello Group, Portobello

Printmakers and Chelsea Painters and Printmakers. London Art Forms commissioned his work.

Alfred BESTALL 1892–1986 Although he worked as a painter in oil and watercolour, Alfred Bestall is best known as an illustrator whose most notable subject was Rupert Bear in the *Daily Express* newspaper and many annuals. After attending Rydal School, Bestall studied art in Birmingham and in classes run by London County Council and at the Central School. His teachers included A S Hartrick and Noel Rooke. He took part in exhibitions at the RA and RBA. He also worked for *Punch* and *Tatler* and illustrated several dozen books, including *The Spanish Goldfish, Myths and Legends of Many Lands* and *Folk Tales of Wales*. He finally lived at Beddgelert, Gwynedd, in Wales. The Art of Alfred Bestall was held at The Cartoon Art Trust in 2005.

David BETHEL 1923–2006 Painter, printmaker, designer and teacher, born in Bath, Somerset. He studied at Gloucester School of Arts and Crafts, 1946–8, and West of England Art College, Bristol, 1948–51, under Donald Milner. He went on to hold several art teaching appointments, including the directorship of Leicester Polytechnic. Showed at AIA, Kensington Gallery, SGA of which he was a member, and in the provinces, including RWA, which holds his work, as do galleries in Gloucester and Stafford. Lived at Stoneygate, Leicestershire.

Marion Ross BETHEL 1929– Illuminator, born in Wiesbaden, Germany. She studied with Daisy Alcock and Gladys Best. Worked as a map curator at Exeter University, illuminated books and showed at Salon de Société des Artistes Français. Lived in Topsham, Devon.

Peggie A E BETHEL: *see* **Peggie MARKS**

Noel BETOWSKI 1952– Painter and teacher, born in Tilbury, Essex, who gained a degree in fine art at Central School of Arts and Crafts, 1973–6, then his teacher's diploma at London University Institute of Education, 1976–7. For a decade he lived in north London, painting and teaching part-time in adult education, in 1987 moving to Penzance, where he ran The Betowski Gallery. Betowski's work was colourful, figurative-towards-abstract, a notable feature being a motif of tiny ships to form the sea in his seascapes. Group exhibitions included RA Summer Exhibition; Greater London Council's Spirit of London, Royal Festival Hall; New Grafton, Crane Kalman and Mercury Galleries; Camden Arts Centre John Constable Landscape Competition, where he won a third prize in 1987, second prize in 1988; and Islington and Edinburgh Art Fairs, both 1992. Had many solo exhibitions, including Salthouse Gallery, St Ives, from 1982; Porthmeor Gallery there, from 1992; and Highgate Fine Art, 2002.

Desmond BETTANY 1919– Painter, printmaker and teacher, born in Burnley, Lancashire. He studied art at Lancaster School of Art, where his teachers included Walter Bayes, then at Leeds College of Art. He went on to become, from 1950, acting principal of South Shields School of Art, in County Durham, where he finally lived. Bettany showed extensively in the Lancaster and South Shields areas with various clubs and groups.

Peter BETTANY 1945– Artist in a variety of media, born in Colwyn Bay, Denbighshire, who grew up on the coast of north Wales. Studied at Wimbledon Art School, Leicester College of Art and California College of Arts and Crafts, Oakland, America. Showed solo with JPL Fine Arts. Bettany's small sculpture Sinking, of 1974, is held by Arts Council and was included in its 1981–2 tour Fragments Against Ruin. Lived in London.

Anthony BETTS 1897–1980 Painter whose full name was James Anthony Betts, born in Skipton, Yorkshire. Studied at Bradford College of Art, Royal College of Art and overseas. In the 1920s and 1930s he was head of the school of painting at Sheffield College of Art, principal of Kingston School of Art and professor of fine art at Reading University. Exhibited in London, Paris and New York. Lived at Caversham, Berkshire.

Ida BETTS 1871–1951 Watercolour painter, especially of flowers, born in Chipperfield, Hertfordshire. She studied art in Bedford and St Ives and showed at the RA, RI, RBA and Paris Salon. Lived near Newbury, Berkshire.

Simon BETTS 1957– Painter, born in Peterborough, Huntingdonshire. He studied at Cambridge College of Arts and Technology, 1976–7; Sheffield Polytechnic, 1977–80; and Chelsea College of Art, 1991–2. Mixed exhibitions included Arte Viva, Senigaria, Italy, 1992; Post-Decadence at Café Gallery, 1994; and John Moores Liverpool Exhibition, 1995–6. Solo exhibitions included Peterborough City Museum and Art Gallery, 1983; Mappin Art Gallery, Sheffield, 1984; and Café Gallery, 1992. Lived in London.

Tadek BEUTLICH 1922– Printmaker, weaver of tapestries and teacher, born in Lwówek, Poland. He studied in Poland, elsewhere on the continent and in England. Victoria & Albert Museum, British Museum, other museums in Britain and in North America, and Toruń University, Poland, hold his work. Taught for a time at Camberwell School of Arts and Crafts. His work is in the Council for National Academic Awards collection. Beutlich was given a seventy-fifth birthday show at Hove Museum & Art Gallery in 1997, where he held master-classes. Lived nearby at Ditchling, Sussex.

David BEVAN 1915– Painter in oil, who was educated at Eton College. Showed at RA, other London and provincial galleries. Lived in London.

Graham BEVAN 1935– Painter and teacher, born in Pontypridd, Glamorgan. Attended Cardiff College of Art, 1951–3, then after National Service resumed studies at Slade School of Fine Art, 1956–9, followed in 1960 by a London University postgraduate studentship in fine art. Joined Sheffield College of Art Polytechnic as a lecturer in fine art. Participated in many group shows, including Young Contemporaries, 1958–60, LG and the 1964 show of Contemporary British Art in Bradford, having several one-man exhibitions at New Art Centre. Both Arts Council and WAC hold his work.

Oliver BEVAN 1941– Artist who as well as painting was involved in kinetics and light projects, collage and colour photography. He was born in Peterborough, Huntingdonshire, and studied at Royal College of Art, 1960–4. From an early stage he showed in mixed and held solo exhibitions internationally. Regarding group shows, in 1967 he was in Ornamentale Tendenzen, which toured West Germany; in 1971 in Jeux, Lumière et Animation, at Galerie Lacloche, in Paris, and in Play Orbit at ICA; in 1982 at Midland Group, Nottingham, Open Photography show; and in 1982–3 he was in Sainsbury's Images for Today, winning a Commendation Prize. Solo shows included Grabowski Gallery, 1965–7–9; Angela Flowers Gallery, 1981; Rochdale Art Gallery, and tour, 1983; Harlow Playhouse Gallery, Harlow, 1992; and in 1997 his Urban Mirror City Paintings, 1987–1997, was held at Royal National Theatre, revealing Bevan as a portrayer of the London landscape in rich colours. Play, at the same venue in 2002, continued the city theme, with ordinary people doing ordinary things. Bevan was married to the sculptor Pat Thornton. They used part of their west London house as Thornton Bevan Fine Arts to show other artists' works.

Peter BEVAN 1946– Painter, sculptor in various materials and ceramics artist, and teacher, born in the West Midlands. After studying at Gloucestershire College of Art and Royal College of Art, from 1973 Bevan lectured at Glasgow School of Art. He also had an exchange lectureship at Central Michigan University in 1986 and was a visiting artist in India. Among Bevan's mixed show appearances were John Moores Liverpool Exhibition; Smith Art Gallery, Stirling; and Germany. He was prizewinner in Cleveland Drawing Biennale in 1987. Solo exhibitions included Richard Demarco Gallery, Edinburgh, 1981, and Compass Gallery, Glasgow, 1986. Scottish Arts Council holds his work.

Tony BEVAN 1951– Figurative painter, born in Bradford, Yorkshire. He studied at the School of Art there, 1968–71, Goldsmiths' College School of Art, 1971–4, and Slade School of Fine Art, 1974–6. Bevan's work was included in The British Art Show, 1984–5, Human Interest at Cornerhouse in Manchester, 1985, Ikon Gallery in Birmingham, 1986, and John Moores Liverpool Exhibition, 1987, winning a prize there, 1997–8. He exhibited widely abroad. His first solo show was in 1976. There was a retrospective at ICA in 1988 and major ones at Whitechapel Art Gallery in 1993, Michael Hue-Williams Fine Art, 2000 and 2002, and Abbot Hall, Kendal, and Milton Keynes Gallery, both 2003. These revealed Bevan as a singular painter of unsettling male figures and groups. Arts Council holds work. Lived in London.

Maggie BEVERIDGE 1955– Painter of colourful and quirky pictures in which objects and perspectives were restyled to humorous effect. Beveridge was born in Kintyre, Argyll, graduated from Glasgow University with honours in botany in 1976, then spent a year as a graduate student studying lichens in arctic Canada. Worked with fish for 20 years, on a salmon farm in Kintyre and later at Stirling University, before entering publishing, thereafter working part-time as a freelance editor. Began painting around 1990, mainly self-taught apart from summer school attendance. Her many group exhibitions included Cambridge Contemporary Art, Cambridge; Castlegate House Gallery, Cockermouth; Gallery Heinzel, Aberdeen; Leith and Open Eye Galleries, Edinburgh; Queen's Gallery, Dundee; Richard Hagen Gallery, Broadway; and several London galleries, including Ainscough Contemporary Art, in its 2003 Eighth Birthday Show.

Pamela Kathleen BEVES 1920– Illustrator and abstract painter, born in Brighton, Sussex. Studied at Brighton College of Art, 1945–7, her teachers including Dorothy Coke and Leslie Cole. Showed at Redfern, Leicester and Beaux Arts Galleries, NS, Heal's Mansard Gallery, SEA, in Stockholm and widely elsewhere. Had one-man shows at Archer Gallery in 1955 and Woodstock Gallery four years later. Lived in London.

Leslie Cubitt BEVIS 1892–1984 Sculptor and teacher, born in Maidstone, Kent. Bevis joined the Artists' Rifles in World War I, was commissioned as a lieutenant in the Highland Light Infantry in July 1917 and was wounded. He was mainly a teacher, being art master at Bedford School between the wars; was briefly an officer in the Royal Air Force in World War II; then in the Army, specialising in camouflage, working in the Western Desert before the battle of El Alamein. After the war he taught in several art schools in southern England, including Camberwell, Wimbledon and St Martin's, noted for his fastidious approach to sculpting. Bevis' main work was the statue of Sir Thomas More on the embankment at Chelsea, unusual as the face and hands of the statesman and Catholic martyr are gilded. For some years Bevis occupied a studio at The Buddhist Society building at 58 Eccleston Square, although his son reported that "he was not a Buddhist, but straight Church of England." The National Portrait Gallery holds Bevis' sculpture of the Labour Party leader Hugh Gaitskell and associated correspondence. Bevis was a prolific exhibitor at the RA Summer Exhibition from 1946–66. Among the busts and heads he showed there were the violinist Ginette Neveu, 1951; Hugh Gaitskell and the philosopher, physician, musician and missionary Albert Schweitzer, both 1963; and Pope John XXIII, 1964. Bevis died in Croydon, Surrey.

Michael John Vaughan BEVIS 1948– Painter in oil and photographer, his photographic work being signed Vaughan. He was born in London and did a foundation course at Hornsey College of Art, 1966–7, then in 1967–70 Waltham Forest Technical College and School of Art, followed by North-East London Polytechnic, Barking, 1970–2, and London University Institute of Education, 1980–1. His teachers included Stuart Ray and Jack Smith. Went on to head the art and design department of St Peter's High School in Burnham-on-Crouch. Was a member of Free Painters and Sculptors, in 1980 having a solo show at Loggia Gallery, also exhibiting with LG. Bevis' work used bold and highly textured colours, was "preoccupied with structure and relates to a theory of the universe being like a doughnut, layered with endless passages", having "a dream-like quality". Lived in Maldon, Essex.

Pauline BEWICK 1935– Painter, illustrator and set designer, descended from the wood engraver Thomas Bewick. She was born in Corbridge, Northumberland. Had a bohemian, travelling childhood in England and Ireland, as described in her painter mother Harry Bewick's autobiography *A Wild Taste*, published in 1958. Pauline Bewick's prodigious ability as a decorative draughtsman developed in childhood. Aged 15 she was enrolled at the National College of Art, Dublin, but left before taking her teaching certificate examinations. Designed costumes and sets for Pike Theatre, Dublin; drew for Trinity College magazine *Icarus*; in 1954 contributed to the show Irish Living Art; in 1955 illustrated the cover for Thomas

Kinsella's translation of *Thirty Three Triads*, part of *The Dolmen Chapbook*; in 1956 had pictures accepted accepted by the RHA; and in 1957 had a first solo show at Clog Gallery, Dublin. Two followed at Parkway Gallery, 1959–60, and there were many more in London, Dublin, Cork and Belfast. Bewick illustrated many books, notably *The Matchless Mice* series for children, did work for BBC Television and much periodical illustration. Arts Council of Northern Ireland, Arts Council of Ireland and many other public bodies hold her work. Bewick's daughter Poppy Melia was an artist.

Philip BEWS 1951– Figurative sculptor working in various materials who was included in Merseyside Artists 3, a Walker Art Gallery, Liverpool, touring show in 1986–7. Bews gained a diploma in landscape architecture from Manchester Polytechnic, 1970–4, then a first-class degree in fine art from Liverpool Polytechnic, 1983–6, having worked for eight years for Runcorn New Town Development Corporation as an associate landscape architect. Between 1986–8, Bews had a residency at Birchwood education and leisure centre, from 1988–9 being a part-time sculpture and three-dimensional sculpture tutor at Wirral Metropolitan College. Also exhibited at Norton Priory, Runcorn, May Day from 1984, and Bluecoat Gallery, Liverpool, 1986. Bews completed many major sculptural commissions, in Liverpool collaborating with Diane Gorvin. Among his works were Covetina, 1988, Norton Priory Museum, Runcorn; Deal Porters, 1990, Surrey Quays, London Docklands; and Stone Carving, 1994, Grosvenor Park Garden for the Blind, Chester.

Steven BEWSHER 1964– Artist, born in Altrincham, Cheshire, educated at Sale Boys' Grammar School, who studied at Manchester and Wolverhampton, gaining an honours degree in fine art. Landscapes and the canal network in Cheshire were key themes in Bewsher's pictures. Showed at Mall Galleries and widely in the Cheshire and Manchester areas, including Colin Jellicoe Gallery. Lived in Manchester.

Ralph BEYER 1921– Sculptor, letterer, teacher and writer working in a variety of materials, born in Berlin, Germany, who left Nazi Germany as a refugee for England in 1937. He was a pupil of Eric Gill in 1937–8; studied at the Central School of Arts and Crafts, 1938–9; also attending Henry Moore's sculpture classes at Chelsea School of Art. Beyer worked with David Kindersley and the Cambridge firm of Rattee and Kett, from the mid-1950s becoming a freelance architectural and memorial letterer. His major commissions included all the lettering in Coventry Cathedral. Also completed work in several other English cathedrals, churches, public buildings and universities, private gardens and parks. Beyer's largest commission in America was lettering in a park in New Harmony, Indiana, dedicated to Paul Tillich, the German-born, American theologian and philosopher. Beyer taught lettering in various colleges and for 16 years at Reading University. He was a member of Letter Exchange, published articles in numerous books and magazines and was included in the collections of the Methodist Church, Victoria & Albert Museum, Royal College of Art and New Art Centre Sculpture Park at East Winterslow. Was represented in Stone Words at Pentagram, Wolseley Fine Arts and tour, 2002.

Akash BHATT 1972– Artist, born in Leicester, who completed foundation studies at Loughborough College of Art, 1991–2; an illustration honours degree first-class at University of Westminster, 1993–6; and a postgraduate diploma at St Martin's School of Art, 1996–8. He won the BP Travel Award, 1997; was a commended finalist in the BP Portrait Award and gained an Elizabeth Greenshields Foundation Award, both 1999; and won The Villiers David Prize and a prize in The Singer & Friedlander/*Sunday Times* Watercolour Competition, both 2002. Mixed shows included The Hunting Art Prizes, 1995; Map, Rebecca Hossack Gallery, 1999; and RBA, NEAC and The Discerning Eye, all at Mall Galleries, 2001; and RP, Mall Galleries, 2002. Solo exhibitions included Indi-gestion, Rebecca Hossack, 2001, and The Big Payback there, 2003, which resulted from his travels in Papua New Guinea.

Janardan BHATT: *see* **JANARDAN**

Zarina BHIMJI 1963– London-based photography and film-based artist who studied at Goldsmiths' College, 1983–6, then at the Slade School of Fine Art, 1987–9. She began working as an artist from the late 1980s, showing extensively in Britain and abroad. Took part in numerous group exhibitions, including second Johannesburg Biennale and No Place (like home), Walker Arts Centre, Minneapolis, both 1997; East International, Norwich, 2001; and Documenta 11, Kassel, 2002. Later solo shows included Cleaning the Garden, Harewood House, Leeds, 1998, and Talwar Gallery, New York, 2001. In 2002, she received a DAAD fellowship and residency in Berlin. For Documenta 11, Bhimji was commissioned to make *Out of Blue*, her first film, which showed the evocative landscape and architecture of Uganda; it was featured in the series Art Now at Tate Britain in 2003.

Małgorzata BIAŁOKOZ SMITH 1937– Painter, printmaker, textile and photographic artist and teacher, born in Warsaw, Poland. After the German invasion, she remembered "being frightened and hungry and escaping into the unknown with my parents, through vast fields". Her mother's request for her to paint some Christmas cards started her interest in art, and she attended the Technical College of Art and the Academy of Art in Gdansk. Visited England in 1958 and was able to study at St Martin's School of Art, obtaining her further education teacher's certificate from Trent Polytechnic, Nottingham, 1973. Bringing up a family meant shelving her artistic interests, but on returning to them she became a frequent exhibitor. Later group shows included Ebury Gallery, 1982; Galleria el Talla, Lima, Peru, 1984; Pratt Manhattan Center Gallery, New York, and Brixton Art Gallery, both 1985; Open Print Exhibition, Bankside Gallery, 1988; and Oxford Art Society, Museum of Modern Art, Oxford, 1992. She was a member of the Polish group Bigos. Later solo shows included Polish Cultural Institute, 1996, where Bialokoz Smith showed Expressionist works with a predominance of red, and Bartley Drey Gallery, 2000. Ashmolean Museum, Macclesfield House and St Cross College, all in Oxford, hold examples. Taught at various venues, including West of England College of Art, Bristol, 1987, and Bicester Community College, 1988. Lived in London.

Pamela BIANCO 1906–1994 Artist, born in Barnes, who showed precocious drawing talent as a child. Her father was the poet and bibliographer Francesco Bianco, her writer mother Margery Williams penning the famous children's book *The Velveteen Rabbit*. During childhood years in Paris, America and Italy Bianco constantly drew and wrote, attracting the attention of Pablo Picasso and Gabriele d'Annunzio, in 1914 reading Walter de la Mare, a significant influence. In 1914 she had a first solo show, Babes and Fairies, at the Leicester Galleries, contributed to *The Owl* periodical and illustrated de la Mare's poems *Flora*. In 1920, Bianco had a second show at the Leicester Galleries, her patron Gertrude Vanderbilt Whitney buying two works, and visited Richard Hughes, another key influence, going on adventures with William Nicholson, Robert Graves and their families. There was a first American solo show at the Anderson Galleries, New York, in 1921, and in 1922 the Biancos settled in Greenwich Village. In that year there was second American solo exhibition at the Print Rooms, San Francisco, and Bianco's portrait of Hughes was reproduced in his poems *Gipsy Night*. Bianco became a busy solo exhibitor, shows including the Art Institute of Chicago, 1924, and Rehn Gallery, New York, 1926, the year she had a first nervous breakdown, others following in 1939 and 1974. She illustrated her mother's children's book *The Skin Horse*, 1927, William Blake's *The Land of Dreams*, 1928, and Oscar Wilde's *The Birthday of the Infanta*, 1929. In 1930, the year she married the poet Robert Schlick and became an American citizen, Bianco visited Italy under a Guggenheim Foundation Scholarship and wrote and illustrated her first children's book, *The Starlit Journey*. During World War II, she worked for the Office of Censorship's Italian division and renewed contact with de la Mare, in 1950 collaborating with him on a calendar for the children's periodical *The Horn Book*, interviewing him for it in 1952. After marrying the artist Georg Theodor Hartmann in 1955 Bianco was greatly influenced in 1956 by an exhibition of Balthus' work at The Museum of Modern Art, which in 1961 bought an example of her work from her exhibition at the David Herbert Gallery, New York. Other shows included the International Gallery, Baltimore, 1964; Graham Gallery, New York, 1969; Santa Barbara Museum of Art, 1970, and Greenwich Library, Connecticut, 1974. Bianco died in New York. There was a retrospective accompanied by an informative catalogue at England & Co in 2004, following exhaustive research by Leonie Summers.

Judy BIBBY 1947– Painter and teacher, born in Liverpool. She studied at Southport, Liverpool and Royal College of Art 1962–71. Teaching included Lanchester Polytechnic, Coventry, 1971–81; St Martin's School of Art, 1976–96; Kingston Polytechnic, 1987–90; and New Richmond School of Art, Richmond, 1994–7, near where she lived in Twickenham, Middlesex. Prizes and awards included Prize for Europe (Bronze Medal), Ostend, Belgium, 1973; Lina Garnard Memorial Prize, Farnham, 1980; Great London Arts Association Award, 1981; Waterman's Open 85, First Prize Winner, 1985; and Picker Fellow, Kingston Polytechnic, 1987. Group exhibitions included RA Summer Exhibition, and solo shows a retrospective at Hotbath Gallery, City of Bath College, 1999. RA and Atkinson Art Gallery, Southport, hold examples. Bibby's work was "a reflection of how I respond to what is happening in my life."

Nick BIBBY 1960– Wildlife sculptor, born in County Durham, who developed an early interest in natural history exploring the Lake District and Cumbria. Drew and painted from an early age, began sculpting at 16 and attended art school briefly before leaving to work as a freelance designer and illustrator. Became chief design consultant for a French art company and sculptor and modelmaker for London advertising agencies. In 1991 returned to wildlife sculpture, producing detailed bronzes in limited editions. Exhibited with SWLA, 1993; John Davies Gallery, Stow-on-the-Wold, 1994; Gallery Pangolin, Chalford, from 1995; and Jersey Wildlife Preservation Trust, Jersey, 1996. Had a solo exhibition at Wildlife Art Gallery, Lavenham, 1994. In 2004, Bibby's solo exhibition at Gallery Pangolin was Bones to Bronze: Extinct Species of the Mascarene Islands.

André BICÂT 1909–1996 Artist, designer and teacher, working in a variety of media, born in Essex of French and Anglo-Irish parents. From 1947–85 he lived at Crays Pond, near Reading, where he worked in a converted barn, later living in London. Bicât was a Royal College of Art tutor, 1966–74. His varied career included much theatre work in the 1930s before war service, including Mercury Theatre productions from 1932; designing the setting for the New York production of *Murder in the Cathedral*, by T S Eliot, 1938; and designing for Windsor Repertory Theatre, 1939. Showed at RA; Redfern, Wildenstein, Leger and O'Hana Galleries; and with Sally Hunter & Patrick Seale Fine Art; also in Paris at Salon de la Jeune Sculpture and elsewhere widely overseas. Completed a ceramic mural for Hackney Downs School for Inner London Education Authority. Solo shows at Leicester Galleries were extensive, 1949–70, and Bohun Gallery, Henley-on-Thames, 1975–84; he had retrospectives at Reading Museum & Art Gallery, 1966, Attic Gallery, Swansea, 1997, and The Merriscourt Gallery, Sarsden, 1999. In 2002, Christie's, South Kensington, offered works from Bicat's studio. British Museum, Victoria & Albert Museum, Arts Council and provincial galleries hold examples.

Andrew BICK 1963– Artist producing geometrical abstractions, which could take a long time to complete and which might, like his 1997–8 John Moores Liverpool Exhibition entry For the Undecided, in wax and marker pen on wood, "exist as object (sculpture), drawing and painting at the same moment". Bick was born in Coleford, Gloucestershire, and studied at the University of Reading, 1982–6, and Chelsea College of Art, 1987–8. In 1992, he won a prize at the FIAR International Artists Under 30 show, held in several European and American cities. Had initial solo exhibitions at Todd Gallery and Cairn Gallery, Nailsworth, both 1989, later ones including Galerie Louise de Haan, Haarlem, Netherlands, 1996, and Eagle Gallery, 1998. In 2003, shared a show with Patrick Michael Fitzgerald at Rubicon Gallery, Dublin, Ireland. Lived in London.

John BICKERDIKE 1895–1973 Sculptor and wood-carver, born near Bradford, Yorkshire. Apprenticed to a woodcarver when aged 14, Bickerdike attended evening classes at Bradford School of Art. After World War I, during which he served in Mesopotamia, Bickerdike returned to Bradford. He worked mainly for architects and for the brewing firm Watney. For the architect Clough Williams-Ellis he completed sculptures for his village Port Meirion, in Wales, and a large pair of lions at Stowe School. Watney commissions included work on Shakespeare's Head public house in London's Great Marlborough Street. With his wife the artist Rhoda Dawson, whom he married late in life, Bickerdike practised as a puppeteer and made large architectural models, including several for the Museum of Ghana. Was included in the show Sculpture in Britain Between The Wars at Fine Art Society, 1986. Lived in London.

Herbert BICKLE 1911– Painter, draughtsman, printmaker, designer and teacher, born in East Stanley, County Durham. After studying art at Durham University, 1932–6, with Robert Lyon, Bickle worked for much of the 1940s as aircraft design draughtsman, attending Southampton College of Art, 1948–50. Showed at RA, RBA and in the northeast of England. Lived in Southampton.

John BICKNELL 1958– Painter, printmaker and teacher, born in Surrey. He studied at West Surrey College of Art and Design, at Farnham, in 1975–7, at the North-East London Polytechnic, 1977–80, and Slade School of Fine Art, 1981–3. In the latter year he won a Slade Prize and a Boise Travelling Scholarship to Italy. Bicknell won a prize in the 1987 John Moores Exhibition, Liverpool, the same year that he had his first solo show in London at Carlile Gallery, after an earlier one at Eton College. Also showed solo at Pomeroy Purdy Gallery in 1990, and mixed exhibitions included The Last Wapping Show, 1985; Camden Annual, 1986; and XXV Joan Miró Drawing Prize Competition, Barcelona, 1986. In 1989–90 Bicknell was Henry Moore Printmaking Fellow at Leeds Polytechnic, where he went on to teach part-time. The expressive and emotional aspects of colour were important in Bicknell's abstract works. Lived in London.

Les BICKNELL 1943– Creator of bookworks, using a variety of materials ranging from chunks of wood to snail shells. They wittily commented on popular culture and family life, inviting the viewer to "Please touch". Did a foundation course at Lanchester Polytechnic, Coventry, 1981, then obtained an honours degree in graphic design at London College of Printing, 1982–5. Bicknell's residencies included Alnwick Fair, Camden Junior Arts Festival, Morton Hall Prison and Blackburn Museum. He carried out commissions for North Kesteven District Council and Scunthorpe Borough Council. Among positions held were part-time teaching at Lincolnshire College of Art and Humberside Art College. Took part in many group shows, including Arnolfini Gallery, Bristol, 1988, in Rubberstamps and Concrete Verse; and Small Presses, at New York Center for Book Arts, 1989. Had a solo show, from obscurity into oblivion, at London College of Printing, 1986, later ones including travelled books, Scunthorpe Museum & Art Gallery, 1991. Searching – Mapping – Solution, 2002, in the town centre at Louth, works by Bicknell and Laurence Edwards, celebrated the Greenwich Meridian. Victoria & Albert Museum, Rijksmuseum in Amsterdam and New York Public Library hold examples. Lived at Sibton Green, Saxmundham, Suffolk.

Joyce BIDDER 1906–1999 Sculptor in a variety of materials, notably of figures and animals, born in London. She studied at Wimbledon School of Art with Stanley Nicholson Babb, becoming one of his best pupils. In 1933 met Daisy Borne, whom she taught to carve. They worked in a studio in southwest London for many years and shared a liking for elegant, conservative sculpture tinged with modernism. Showed at SWA, RA and RMS and was a fellow of RBS. Her work was included in the Fine Art Society's Sculpture in Britain Between the Wars, 1986, and she shared a show there with Borne in 1987.

Winifred Percy BIDDLE 1878–1968 Watercolourist, born in Kingston upon Thames, who attended Lambeth School of Art, 1899–1910, under Innes Fripp, and Kingston Technical Institute. Exhibited RA, SWA, RI, NS and in the provinces. Lived in East Molesey, Surrey.

Elizabeth BIDDULPH 1927– Painter in oil, born in Port Elizabeth, South Africa. She studied at Wimbledon School of Art, 1944–7, with Gerald Cooper, then Slade School of Fine Art, 1949–51, under William Townsend. She was elected ROI in 1952, and an honorary senior member in 1982. Solo shows included Hornsey Library, 1971, Barclays Bank, Egham, 1973, Egham Library, 1985, then a shared show at Egham Literary Institute, 1991. Wrote for *Leisure Painter* magazine. Lived in Egham, Surrey.

Jon BIDDULPH 1958– Artist, born in Congleton, Cheshire, who was a member of TEA (see separate entry). He studied at Manchester Polytechnic, 1976–7, then three-dimensional design there, 1977–80; from 1980–81 was ceramics fellow at University of Salford. Lived in Manchester.

Rosalind BIEBER 1946– Artist, musician and teacher whose work, serious and humorous, stemmed from constant experimenting with a range of media including the computer and monoprinting as a basis for collage. Bieber took up art fairly late, a promising career as concert pianist and harpsichordist having been cut short by injury. She gained her diploma from the City and Guilds of London Art School, 1974–8, winning a British Council Prize in 1975, later teaching life drawing at her home in Swiss Cottage. Among group exhibitions were Spirit of London, Royal Festival Hall, 1979 and 1980; Contemporary Paintings and Prints, Printmakers' Council, Barbican Centre, 1983; Arcade Digital Creativity, University of Brighton, 1985; National Art Competition, Logos Gallery, 1995; and Symbolist Painters, Talisman Fine Art, 1999. Talisman and Lindsay Wells organised a Bieber solo exhibition at The Sheridan Russell Gallery, 2003.

Peter BIEGEL 1913–1987 Painter of field sports subjects, born in Croxley Green, Hertfordshire. After Downside School and a period in business he studied at the Lucy Kemp-Welch School of Animal Painting, Bushey, at Bournemouth School of Art and worked with the sporting painter Lionel Edwards. The dealer J L W Bird and other galleries in Britain and in North America showed Biegel's work.

John BIGGE 1892–1973 Painter of abstracts who was briefly involved in Surrealism in the 1930s. Although he painted as John Bigge his full name was John Amherst Selby-Bigge (usually hyphenated); he was the son of Sir Amherst Selby-Bigge and was created 2nd Baronet in 1919. Born in Oxford, Bigge was educated at Winchester and Christ Church, Oxford, entered the Slade School of Fine Art briefly in 1914, but had his course "discontinued for military service" in World War I, partly spent with the Macedonian Mule Corps. (Bigge's first wife, Rachel Ruth Humphries, was also at the Slade.) After returning in 1919 Bigge worked as a chicken farmer, then as an estate agent, painting in his spare time. His friendship with Edward

Wadsworth "opened my eyes to the various movements that were evolving in Paris" in the mid-1920s, and they shared an interest in the "aesthetic of machinery", Bigge relishing its forms in the Science Museum. Bigge's first solo show was at the Wertheim Gallery, 1931. Another took place at Galerie Vignon, Paris, 1932, a second London show at Lefevre, 1933. Latterly he was included in Unit I at Portsmouth City Museum and Art Gallery, 1978 (based on the 1934 Mayor Gallery show), and in Leeds City Art Gallery's Surrealist exhibition in 1986. Bigge travelled extensively in Europe from 1936, residing in Austria, France and Spain. During World War II he was a sub-editor with the BBC European News Service and worked with the British Red Cross. Finally lived at Le Bugue, Dordogne, and painted for his own pleasure. He wrote memoirs, unpublished at his death. Public galleries in Leeds and Hull hold Bigge's work.

Clare BIGGER 1967– Sculptor who did a foundation course at Buckinghamshire College of Higher Education, then gained a fine art honours degree from South Glamorgan Institute of Higher Education, Cardiff. Bigger was regional winner, Livewire Award, 1991; regional winner, *Reader's Digest*/Prince's Youth Business Trust Award, 1992; won the Wildlife Art Prize, SWLA, Mall Galleries, 1993; and was a finalist British Airways Award for Young Achievers in Art, 1995. Bigger said that she enjoyed "an active lifestyle which reflects in my work. My main interest outside sculpture is Tae Kwon-do (Korean martial art), which has inspired several works.... My aim is to suggest a gesture, a movement, by utilising the minimum of detail". Took part in many group exhibitions, her solo shows including a series at Bohun Gallery, Henley-on-Thames, from 1992; Guinness Gallery, Dublin, Ireland, from 1994; Milne & Moller Gallery, 1996; and New Academy Gallery, from 1997. Commissions and collections included Taylor Woodrow, Jerwood Foundation, Birmingham Midshires Building Society, Jigsaw and Gazeley Properties.

BIGGLES 1959– Designer, artist, inventor and lecturer, actual name Stephen Riddle, whose nickname – which stemmed from the wearing of his father's flying jacket and a motorcycle helmet – was adopted professionally. He described himself as "a slightly eccentric English gentleman, going on polymorph", a common feature of whose work "has to be flexibility, wit and humour and a belief that all forms of art and design relate". After studying at New School, Kings Langley, founded by Rudolf Steiner, Biggles did a foundation course at Watford School of Art, 1976–7; gained a first-class honours degree in art and graphic design at The London College of Printing, 1977–80; and his master's in graphic design at the Royal College of Art, 1980–3. From mid-1980s was a visiting lecturer in graphic design at a number of colleges and schools of art, including Berkshire, Bath, Camberwell, Watford, Kensington and Chelsea and The London College of Printing. Simultaneously, he was a freelance designer, art director and design consultant. His extensive client list included Bethnal Green Museum of Childhood, British Airports Authority, British Telecom, Cabinet War Rooms, Imperial War Museum, The Open College, Serpentine Gallery, Victoria & Albert Museum and Workers Playtime Records. Events and exhibitions included Typos No 4, National Theatre, 1981; Blue Room Exhibition at Royal College of Art, 1982; Permanent Sand Castle Installations, Margate, 1992; and in 1993 Urban Art Attack I, Epping Forest, and 2, at Brixton. Lived in south London.

John R BIGGS 1909–1988 Painter, printmaker and illustrator born in Derby, where he initially studied art, followed by Central School of Arts and Crafts under John Skeaping, Bernard Meninsky and Noel Rooke. Also studied at London University. He exhibited at RA, RCamA, Redfern Gallery, on the continent and in North America. Biggs, who was a specialist typographical designer, taught for many years, including overseas, being finally at Brighton Polytechnic, 1953–74. It published his *Autobiographica* in his final year there. He also illustrated a number of books; was at various times an art editor and production manager for publishing companies; and for many years ran the Hampden Press privately. Was master of the Art Workers' Guild in 1983 and has work in the British Museum. Lived in Brighton, Sussex.

Jessie P BIGNELL 1896–1992 Watercolourist and teacher, a native of Eltham, in southeast London. She was art and music mistress at the Gordon School, near where she lived. Showed at RI. Miss Bignell was noted for her watercolours of the English countryside, River Thames and old London, influenced by her many teachers. A memorial show was held at Holy Trinity Church, Eltham, in 1992.

Jack BILBO 1907–1967 Painter, sculptor, draughtsman and huger-than-life gallery owner, born in Berlin, Germany, as Hugo Baruch, of German-Jewish and English-Jewish parents. He led a peripatetic life on the continent in his early years and assumed the name Jack Bilbo in the early 1920s when he worked in films and journalism and wrote books, including *Carrying a Gun for Al Capone*. After his family was harried by the Nazis in the early 1930s, Bilbo settled in London in 1936 and began painting and sculpting. Had shows at Arlington and Zwemmer Galleries. After internment on the Isle of Man and brief Army service, Bilbo in 1941 founded the Modern Art Gallery in London and began writing books on art. His solo show at Lefevre in 1943 showed Bilbo as a strident Colourist. Bilbo's work mixed Expressionism, naïvety, humour and the bizarre. In 1949 Bilbo moved the gallery to Weybridge and published his autobiography, *Jack Bilbo by Jack Bilbo*. The following year Bilbo left England on an old barge, settled to work in the south of France, then returned to Berlin in 1956, where he died. In 1988 England & Co held a retrospective, followed by one on his gallery in 1990.

John Gordon BILL 1915–1993 Painter and teacher, born in London, married to the artist Coral Nerelle. After Radley College he studied art at Byam Shaw School with Bernard Dunstan and Charles Mahoney. Was elected RWA in 1978, also showing with RA, NEAC, and Cheltenham Group and had solo shows in Cotswolds area. RWA and Cheltenham Art Gallery hold his work, which went abstract from 1987. Lived in Northleach, Gloucestershire.

Simon BILL 1958– Painter, draughtsman and teacher who was born in Kingston upon Thames in Surrey. He studied at Epsom School of Art, 1976–7, St Martin's School of Art, 1977–80, and Royal College of Art, 1982–5. Went on to teach at St Martin's and Kingston Polytechnic. As well as showing with Anne Berthoud and Philip Solomon Galleries Bill exhibited at John Moores Liverpool Exhibition in 1980, with Still Life, and in 1989–90 with Jesus H Christ, one of a series related to the work of William Hogarth. Showed Bio-Pop: Paintings at Modern Art, 2001, ooo! (oval paintings) at Outport Gallery, Norwich, in 2006, where Bill gave an artist's talk. Lived in London.

Edward S BILLIN 1911–1994 Printmaker and painter who worked as a freelance commercial artist, born and lived in Sheffield, Yorkshire. Studied at Sheffield College of Art with Noel Spencer and Eric Jones. Wrote *Drawing on scraper board*. Showed with RA, SWE, RBA, RSA, BWS and in America, but in later years did not work owing to blindness. Graves Art Gallery, Sheffield, holds his work.

Richard BILLINGHAM 1970– Artist using photography, who grew up in Sunderland, County Durham, where he gained an honours degree in fine art at the University, 1991–4. He won the Prestige Photography Prize at the University, 1994; Felix H Man Memorial Prize, 1995; and The Citibank Private Bank Photography Prize, 1997. Group shows included Who's Looking at the Family?, Barbican Art Gallery, 1994; New Photography 12, Museum of Modern Art, New York, 1996; and the Saatchi Collection-related exhibition Sensation, at the RA, 1997. In that, Billingham recorded the grim squalor of his family's home life in the northeast. "British art has never been as scarily honest," commented critic Waldemar Januszczak. Solo exhibitions included Anthony Reynolds Gallery, the National Museum of Film and Photography, Bradford, and Portfolio Gallery, Edinburgh, all 1996; and a series in America, France and Italy in 1997. Billingham was short-listed for the Turner Prize in 2001 for his solo show at the Ikon Gallery, Birmingham. His Fishtank was displayed at Meeting House Square, Dublin, Ireland, in 2002.

Alfred John BILLINGHURST 1880–1963 Portrait, landscape and genre painter in oil and watercolour. Born at Blackheath, in southeast London, Billinghurst after initial education in England, Germany and Switzerland studied art at the Slade School of Fine Art, 1899–02, with a period at the Goldsmiths' Institute, 1900, then a period in Paris which included time at Académie Julian and Atelier Cormon. Exhibited Paris Salon, ROI, RA, RI and a number of one-man shows. Billinghurst's work, which has about it the flavour of the 1920s and 1930s, is held by Plymouth Museum and Art Gallery. Was a member of the Ridley Art Club and lived at East Sheen, southwest London.

Bill BILLINGS 1938– Artist and teacher, born in London, who trained at the London School of Printing. He settled in Milton Keynes, Buckinghamshire, being involved in community arts there from 1974, was employed as community artist in 1978–80 and undertook two residencies in the city's schools. He was also a published poet, writer and playwright. His Triceratops, in concrete, was sited in 1979 at Peartree Bridge, Milton Keynes. Billings was a part-time lecturer in sculpture at Bletchley College and had an honorary master's degree from the Open University. Billings was included in the 10th Anniversary Exhibition of The Silbury Group of Artists at Milton Keynes Gallery in 2001–2.

Stacy BILLUPS 1965– Painter, born in Surrey, whose work had a strong fantasy element. She studied at Reigate School of Art and Design, 1982–4, Wimbledon School of Art, 1984–7, and Chelsea School of Art, 1987–8. Her work was included in a number of group exhibitions including Young Painters South-East, 1988; Cleveland Drawing Biennale, 1989; Royal Over-Seas League show in 1989 in which she was a prizewinner; and in 1989–90 John Moores Liverpool Exhibition. Had her first London solo show in 1991 at Christopher Hull Gallery. Lived in London.

Kenneth BILLYARD 1943–1976 Painter and teacher of art, born in Sale, Cheshire. He studied art at Newcastle University, 1962–6, under Kenneth Rowntree, Matt Rugg and Richard Hamilton. Showed at Chester Arts and Recreation Trust and at Portico Library, Manchester. His major work was the design for a huge mural on the side of the Museum of Science and Industry in Manchester which had to be executed by another artist as Billyard was killed in a car crash. He taught for several years at college in Salford and his own work, with abstract leanings and influenced by such artists as James Rosenquist, often featured canal boats. Had one-man show at Octagon Theatre, Bolton, in 1975. Lived in Withington, Manchester.

Pearl BINDER 1904–1990 Printmaker, illustrator, painter and writer, born in Fenton, Staffordshire, her father being a Jewish tailor. She arrived in London in 1925 and studied lithography, her favourite medium, at Central School of Arts and Crafts. Became involved in East End life, an active Socialist and member of AIA and freelance artist, writer, lecturer, designer of stained glass and crockery for Wedgwood. Was involved in government information service in World War II and married Elwyn Jones, later Lord Chancellor, when he was reading for the Bar. She was described as "a Bohemian in the heart of the Establishment". Although Lady Elwyn Jones, she remained a propagandist for many causes. Her son, Dan Jones, involved in social and youth work in London's East End, also painted.

Jack Armfield BINDON 1910–1985 Artist in a variety of styles, remembered in Hove, Sussex, where he had a studio, as a character and great self-publicist. Bindon worked variously as an undertaker, as a display artist and graphic designer for commercial enterprises in the Brighton area, as a sometimes cheeky muralist and teacher. He directed The Hove Art Club and conducted lively lecture tours in Europe and the Far East. Painted in Sussex and on the continent and Mediterranean area, in 1949 publishing *Diary of an Artist* about his travels. Showed locally, including Sussex County Arts Club and Hove Museum & Art Gallery, where he had a solo exhibition in 1950. Hove holds his atmospheric acrylic on board St John's Church, Palmeira Square, and an archive of material on Bindon's work and life.

Ginette BINGGUELY-LEJEUNE fl. from 1930s– Sculptor, initially educated in France and Belgium, studied art in Paris then with the sculptor Charles Doman in London. She exhibited RA, Fine Art Society, RBA, Royal Glasgow Institute of the Fine Arts, in the provinces and at Paris Salon. She completed a bust of Lord Nuffield for Nuffield College, Oxford, and her bust of the writer Rudyard Kipling is in the National Portrait Gallery. Lived for a time at Fairlight, Sussex.

Esmond BINGHAM 1948– Sculptor, draughtsman and teacher, born in Belfast, Northern Ireland. He attended Ulster College of Art & Design, 1968–9, Wolverhampton Polytechnic, 1969–72, and Goldsmiths' College School of

Art, 1972–3. Went on to teach at Chelsea School of Art and Middlesex Polytechnic. Showed with Ikon Gallery, Birmingham; Camden Arts Centre; LG; Sir John Cass College; and Woodlands Art Gallery. Bingham shared an exhibition with his wife Lindsay Harris at North House Gallery, Manningtree, in 2004. In that year he also had a show, Presence in Absence, at Christchurch Mansion, Ipswich, and exhibited Installation at The Cut, Halesworth. Bingham's work ranged in scale from the environmental to the miniature and was characterised by lightweight, structural, even skeletal forms in everyday materials.

Dan BINNS 1896–1964 Artist, illustrator, craftsman and teacher, notable for his watercolours, father of the artist David Binns. He was born at Cowling, Yorkshire, and attended Skipton Art School. All his working life he taught at Skipton Secondary School, in the evening teaching bookbinding and lettering. For many years produced the cover for *The Yorkshire Dalesman* (later *The Dalesman*) magazine. Binns was president of Craven Art Club. Showed at RA, RI, RCamA, Royal Glasgow Institute of the Fine Arts and in Yorkshire. Died in the county at Sutton-in-Craven.

David BINNS 1935– Watercolourist, printmaker and teacher, born and lived in Sutton-in-Craven, Yorkshire. Binns worked "to convey the beauty and decorative qualities of wildlife and habitat", leading themes being foxes and ducks. He studied at Skipton Art School under his father Dan Binns, then at Leeds College of Art. Joseph Crawhall and C F Tunnicliffe were influences. Binns became head of art at Ermysted's Grammar School, Skipton, which he had attended, then became a freelance artist, running the Brent Gallery, Cowling. Was from 1968 a member of SWLA, also showing at RI, Manor House Gallery in Ilkley and Patricia Wells Gallery, Thornbury. Was also a member of BWS and Yorkshire Watercolour Society.

Lorna BINNS 1914–2003 Watercolourist, born in Sheffield, Yorkshire, where she attended the College of Art under Maurice Wheatley, 1930–5, then Royal College of Art, 1935–9, under Ernest Tristram. While studying fashion, her great love, Binns entered a watercolour in a competition; it was spotted by Paul Nash, an external assessor, and his dictum that "colour on either side changes the colour in the middle" of a drawing became "the most important thing ever, ever said to me." The outbreak of World War II prevented Lorna achieving her ambition to enter a Paris fashion house. After a short time teaching fashion illustration at Tottenham Technical College, she returned to Yorkshire; married her former industrial design student contemporary at the Royal College John Binns (who became head of the design school at Kingston upon Thames College of Art); and was conscripted for war work. Post-war, they worked as artists for the taxidermist Roland Hill; made a mosaic for Weymouth Theatre, built by Oliver Hill; and designed fabrics. She relearnt watercolour painting fairly late in life; was elected RWS in 1973; and travelled widely in Europe with her friend Joan Vernon-Cryer. After her husband's death in 1980, Binns lived in Surbiton, Surrey, latterly, because of poor health, moving to residential care in Lancing, Sussex. The National Sound Archive at the British Library has archive recordings of her.

Helen BINYON 1904–1979 Watercolourist, illustrator, puppeteer and engraver. Born in London, daughter of the poet and writer on watercolour painting Laurence Binyon. Studied at the Royal College of Art, 1922–6, with Paul Nash, was at the Central School of Arts and Crafts, 1928–30. Exhibited at the Redfern Gallery with Edward Bawden and Eric Ravilious. She created Jiminy Puppets with her twin sister Margaret. Ran a travelling puppet theatre, performances in London including Harold Monro's Poetry Bookshop and the Mercury Theatre. Illustrated several books, including *Pride and Prejudice*, *Brief Candles* and the *Binyon Books*, with words by Margaret. Drew hydrographic charts for the Admiralty in World War II. In 1945–6 taught at Willesden School of Art, then at Bath Academy of Art 1949–65. In 1971 made a survey of professional puppetry in England, commissioned by the Arts Council, having written a standard work, *Puppetry Today*, in 1966. One-man show of watercolours at New Grafton Gallery in 1979. Lived at Chichester, Sussex.

Cyril Walter BION 1889–1976 Landscape painter and draughtsman who moved to Northern Ireland in 1932 to join the mathematics staff of Campbell College. Previous appointments included the University of Hong Kong and Mill Hill School. Bion was a vigorous and upright character, genial and forthright, who encouraged artistic talent at the College. He was an expert architectural and mechanical draughtsman, with a detailed knowledge of ship design. On his retirement, in 1954, *The Campbellian* noted his habit of imparting out-of-the-way facts and "pre-eminently sound, if, occasionally, somewhat caustic advice." The landscape of Ulster, especially its skies and trees, were features of his work, which was exhibited at the Walker Art Gallery in Liverpool, RA Summer Exhibition, RHA Magee Gallery in Belfast. The Frederick Gallery, Dublin, included his drawing Hillside Farm Under Snow in its Important Irish Art Show in 1999. Ulster Museum, Belfast, holds two works and Campbell College his depiction of its grounds in winter. On retirement, Bion and his wife returned to live in Wallington, Surrey.

BIRABONGSE Bhanudej Bhanubandh (Prince Birabongse) 1914–1985 Sculptor, racing driver and glider pilot, born in Burabhabiromse Palace, Bangkok, Thailand, son of HRH Phanurangsri Swangwongse. He was married to Ceril Birabongse, a painter. Educated at Eton College, Prince Bira studied at Byam Shaw School of Drawing and Painting. Wishing to become a sculptor he entered the studio of Charles Wheeler for three years, completing busts and animal sculptures, winning a first prize in a competition with Sealion Swallowing a Fish. Other work by him was bought by the singer Gracie Fields for her garden in Hampstead, made a fountain in Bangkok and a memorial to a car racing rival, Pat Fairfield, was designed by the Prince for Donington Racing Circuit. In his ERA racing car *Romulus* he won many prizes in the 1930s; he was a Grand Prix winner at Monaco. During World War II Prince Bira trained glider pilots for the Royal Air Force. He was known as the Gold Star Prince, whose life was commemorated by an exhibition at the National Gallery in Bangkok in 1989.

Ceril BIRABONGSE 1916– Painter who married Prince Birabongse of Thailand and became Princess Ceril. She studied at Byam Shaw School under Ernest Jackson, 1932–5, and exhibited at RA, ROI and RBA. Latterly lived at Verona, Italy. In 1992 she published *The Prince and I: Life with the Motor Racing Prince of Siam*.

Thomas Towning BIRBECK 1902–1982 Watercolourist, illustrator and writer who was by profession an officer with Chepstow Rural District Council for 40 years from 1927. He was born in Sunderland. In Chepstow he was largely responsible for turning Caldicot village, where he lived, into a Monmouthshire new town and for the purchase and restoration of the castle. He showed with Chepstow Art Society, Wye Valley Art Club and at the Cardiff and Swansea public galleries. He illustrated books, among them his own, published by the Chepstow Society and dealing with local history and issues.

David BIRCH 1895–1968 Landscape painter in oil, portrait painter and illustrator. Studied at Epsom School of Art and Goldsmiths' College School of Art. He became principal of Epsom and Ewell School of Art, 1930–61. He exhibited at the RA, ROI, RBA and Royal Glasgow Institute of the Fine Arts and his work was widely reproduced, notably by Royle Publications. Brighton Museum and Art Gallery and several other provincial galleries hold his work. Lived at Epsom, Surrey.

David BIRCH 1945– Painter and printmaker, born in Birmingham. Although early on interested in painting he went into farming, then for several years in the early 1970s worked in antiques in Broadway, Worcestershire. In 1974 became a full-time artist and five years later took up wood engraving guided by William Rawlinson. Showed at RA, RWA, RI and SWE. Also showed solo with John Noott Twentieth Century, in Broadway. Was commissioned by Confederation Life Insurance Company of Canada to produce views of Bristol.

John Anthony BIRCH 1946– Painter in acrylic with a special interest in audio-visual aids and multi-screen slide projection, born in Clevedon, Somerset. Studied at West of England College of Art, 1964–7. He settled in Bristol and showed at Arnolfini Gallery, Arnolfini Trust holding his work; and Bristol Arts Centre.

Samuel John Lamorna BIRCH 1869–1955 Landscape painter, principally of Cornwall, born in Egremont, Cheshire. Lamorna Birch's early youth was spent working in an office and in cotton mills, sometimes designing, in Lancashire, where he painted part-time. Mainly self-taught, apart from a short period at Atelier Colarossi, Paris, in 1895. From the late 1880s he visited the Penzance region. At this time Stanhope Forbes influenced his work. Eventually settled at Lamorna, adding this to his own name to avoid confusion with the painter Lionel Birch. Exhibited prolifically at Fine Art Society, where he had one-man shows, RWS, Walker's Galleries, RA, Walker Art Gallery, Liverpool, and elsewhere. In 1937 he painted in New Zealand. Elected RA, 1934. Tate Gallery holds his work, which found its way into many collections, and Falmouth Art Gallery gave him a retrospective in 1997, which toured to Plymouth; an exhibition at Penlee House in Penzance in 1995 had marked publication by Sansom & Company of Austin Wormleighton's *A Painter's Laureate: Lamorna Birch and his circle*.

Simon BIRCH 1921–1995 Stockbroker, watercolourist, architect and collector, born in London, who after Stowe School in 1938 enrolled at Westminster School of Art, in 1939 going up to Cambridge to read architecture. In 1941 was commissioned in the Coldstream Guards, on demobilisation in 1946 continuing architectural studies at Regent Street Polytechnic. On family advice, in 1950 became a stockbroker with Rowe Swann, retiring in 1983. Christie's approached him to set up a branch in the City, which closed in the early 1990s, although he remained a consultant. He was a keen clubman, a connoisseur of food and wine, an executive of the council of the City & Guilds of London Art School and was chairman of Minories Gallery, Colchester. Birch was a watercolourist of still life and hunting scenes who early in his career showed with Roland Ward Gallery. Died in Brantham, Suffolk.

Cyril Kenneth BIRD: *see* **FOUGASSE**

Gavin BIRD 1968– Artist, born in Chatham, Kent, who gained an honours degree in fine art at University of Leeds, 1987–91. Until 1992 Bird worked as a partnership with Graham Ramsay as Ramsay Bird. They gained the British Telecom Enabling Award, 1990, and in 1990–1 participated in British Telecom New Contemporaries, tour including Arnolfini Gallery, Bristol. Publications included *BLOC*, 1991. They had a solo show at Church View Gallery, Doncaster, 1989, later ones including Victoria Quarter, Leeds, and Orpheus Gallery, Belfast, both 1991; and Gimpel Fils, 1992, a show laced with humour and titled Post Neo Avant-Garde-ism.

Henry BIRD 1909–2000 Painter, notably of murals and theatre scenery, draughtsman and teacher, born in Northampton, where he lived permanently from early 1950s. Bird did several menial jobs to pay his way through Northampton School of Art, and encouraged by the principal Lewis Duckett won a scholarship to Royal College of Art, gaining a number of awards there, including the Travelling Scholarship. In 1936 Bird was made a lecturer at University College, Aberystwyth, in 1937 marrying the actress Freda Jackson. Her distinguished stage career included major roles in London and the provinces, many film appearances ranging from *Henry V* and *No Room at the Inn* to *The Brides of Dracula* and *Clash of the Titans*. Bird then became head scene-painter at the Old Vic and Sadler's Wells and by the end of World War II theatre designer for Embassy Theatre. He had done some church work in his home area, and now produced a large decoration for its Guildhall concurrently with a decorative scheme for London University Institute of Commonwealth Studies, in 1949. Took up teaching post at Northampton School of Art and continued with decorative schemes in the area, notably murals for Denton Church, 1974, included 35 life-size figures. Also painted safety curtain of Royal Theatre, Northampton. Bird was a brother of Art Workers' Guild and a member of the Tempera Society. His work was shown at Tate Gallery and Victoria & Albert Museum and he had solo shows in London and the provinces. At 73 Bird gained a Civil List pension for services to art. Several provincial collections hold Bird's work, including Northampton, Carlisle and Brighton.

Jim BIRD 1937– Painter, printmaker, muralist and ceramist, born in Bloxwich, Staffordshire, educated at Tettenhall College, Wolverhampton, where the "harsh discipline and cruel punishment left a life-long dislike of all vested authority." Attended Walsall College of Art, 1956, then studied graphic design at Wolverhampton College of Art, 1957–8, passing final examinations with honours. In 1959, was pressed to enter the old family brewing business, becoming director in charge; in 1960 with a partner, Ian Jackson, founded Jackson, Bird and Partners, a graphic design company, painting in his spare time. Showed at RWA in 1962. In 1968, Bird left the family business and with his wife Dorothy and daughter emigrated to Mallorca, Spain. For a time painted in the Op-Art style, but "eventually tired of only using the rational and logical part of his creative possibilities" and "started to paint abstraction closely related to the two landscapes of Mallorca and the Mancha," where he had acquired a summer home. In addition to establishing a close relationship with artists in Spain, Bird became a close friend of leading practitioners of American abstract painting, such as Kenneth Noland, Helen Frankenthaler and Robert Motherwell, while living for long periods in New York City between 1981–97. He also worked closely over years with the Spanish poet Francesc Verdu and held a number of American residencies. In 1997, Bird returned to live permanently in Mallorca, establishing a studio in Santa Maria del Cami. As well as taking part in many group shows, Bird had numerous solo exhibitions in Spain, America and Britain. Two Shoes: A Homage to Dorothy was held at Scolar Fine Art in 2003.

Mary Holden BIRD fl. c.1920–1978 Painter and etcher, mainly of landscapes. Studied at Heatherley's School of Fine Art and went on to show at Fine Art Society, where she had frequent one-man exhibitions, RA, RSW, RBA and Paris Salon. Married to the cartoonist Cyril Kenneth Bird, who drew for *Punch* as Fougasse. Mary Holden Bird's work was widely reproduced by the Medici Society, in Britain and America. She was especially fond of the area around Morar, Scotland, and one of her typical transparent-washed watercolours is illustrated in Percy V Bradshaw's book *Water-Colour: A Truly English Art*. Mary Bird – known to her friends as Molly – lived in London for some time, then finally in Scotland.

Paul BIRD 1923–1993 Painter and teacher, born and lived in London, who studied at Bath School of Art under Clifford Ellis and was influenced by Walter Sickert and the colour theories of Peter Potworowski. After Royal Navy experience in India and the Far East in World War II, Bird studied at Institute of Education under Nikolaus Pevsner, returning to Bath to teach. Following a spell in the early 1950s teaching art at Bretton Hall Training College, in 1953 Bird – always interested in mysticism and religion – joined the Community of the Resurrection at Mirfield, where he stayed for eight years as a lay brother. After teaching at the Royal College of Art, Bird was appointed vice-principal at Central School of Art and Design, 1961–83. His summer school series of lectures The Art of Seeing, 1983–93, was influential.

Philip BIRD 1952– Painter and teacher, born in Bedford. He studied at Berkshire College of Art, 1972–3, and West Surrey College of Art at Farnham, 1975–8. In 1979 he set up a studio at Neatham Mill, near Alton, Hampshire. From 1980 Bird held a number of part-time teaching posts, including West Surrey College and Berkshire College of Art. He also taught mentally handicapped and children's classes. He won a number of Southern Arts Awards, including in 1981 artist-in-residence at Alton 6th Form College. Group shows included Wessex Artists, Southampton Art Gallery, 1980; Platform Four, at Reading Art Gallery and Museum, 1982; and Goldsmiths' show at Woodlands Art Gallery, 1983. Had series of solo shows, including Brillig Gallery, Bath, and Hexagon Art Centre, Reading, both 1979; and Southampton Art Gallery and West End Art Centre, Aldershot, both 1980.

Stephen BIRD 1964– Painter, sculptor and ceramist, born in Stoke-on-Trent, Staffordshire, who gained an honours degree in fine art at Duncan of Jordanstone College of Art, Dundee, 1983–7, with postgraduate studies at Cyprus College of Art, Lemba, Paphos, 1987–8. Awards included Mitchell Painting Prize, travels to Barcelona, Spain, 1984; Ian Eadie Memorial Award, to Netherlands and Spain, 1985; Duncan of Drunfaulk Travel Award, to Italy, 1986; Elizabeth Greenshields Memorial Award, to Cyprus and Spain, 1987; Paper Works, Seagate Gallery, 2nd Prize, to Thailand, 1994; and Eaton Fund for Artists and Mott McDonald Painting Prize, Aberdeen Artists Annual, to New York, both 1997. Was artist-in-residence, Wysing Arts, Cambridge, 1998. Commissions included sculpture for Whitfield, Dundee, from the District Council, a community arts project, 1998; joint work with Neil Irons to make ceramic mural at Charles Square, Old Street, for Hackney Borough Council, 1999; and exterior ceramic sculpture for the Mexican Consulate country residence, Perthshire, 2001. Took part in many group exhibitions, latterly including Continuation, England & Co, 1999, and The Plate Show, Scottish Arts Council tour, 1999–00. Later solo shows included The British Work House Gallery, Dallas Texas, America, 1997; Wysing Arts, Cambridge, 1998; and England & Co, 2000, 2003 and 2004. Bird was associated with the group of artists which met in Dundee at Agacan Restaurant, run by self-taught painter Zeki Agacan. In 2001, Bird visited India and travelled across Asia to Australia before returning to Scotland, his work being acquired by McManus Gallery, Dundee City Art Gallery & Museum; Paisley Art Gallery and Museum, Strathclyde; and National Museum of Scotland, Edinburgh.

Chris BIRD-JONES 1956– Artist specialising in glass constructions and teacher. She studied at Swansea College of Art and Royal College of Art. Went on to teach at schools, polytechnics and universities. As well as doing commissioned and collaborative work in Britain and abroad, she took part in many group shows, including Art in Boxes, 1992, at England & Co, where Nothing's Perfect and Blue were both made of glass. Completed Timepiece for WAC.

Geoffrey BIRKBECK 1875–1954 Watercolourist and muralist in the manner of John Singer Sargent, notable for Norfolk and Italian landscapes, born into a prominent Norfolk family at Stoke Holy Cross, Norwich, and educated at Eton College. His second wife, married in 1930, was Lady Maud Gundreda, daughter of the Earl of Cavan. In 1903 Birkbeck had a solo show at Carfax Gallery, after which he was showing at the New Dudley, Goupil and Walker's Galleries, Fine Art Society and abroad. He was a member of RBA and Norwich Art Circle. At Bracondale Woods he decorated a long room with murals for friend which contained views of lakeland scenery, Venetian lagoons and Italian gardens. Birkbeck is represented in Norwich Castle Museum, where he had exhibitions in 1940 and 1949 and a memorial show in 1954–5. In 1908 he published *Old*

Norfolk Houses, containing 36 colour reproductions, which showed his feeling for the Baroque style.

Paul BIRKBECK 1939– Painter and illustrator who studied at Epsom School of Art. Among his most ambitious book illustration projects was Salman Rushdie's *Haroun and the Sea of Stories*. In his highly detailed pictures, which frequently had a fantastic element, Birkbeck featured such preoccupations as ancient history, Arthurian legend and suburban Raynes Park, in southwest London, where he lived. Shared a show at Gallery 27 in 1997, presented by Keith Chapman.

Edith BIRKIN 1927– Painter in acrylic and teacher, born in Prague, Czechoslovakia. Birkin was deported to Lodz, Poland, in 1941, to Auschwitz in 1944 and then to a labour camp. January 1945 saw her on a death march through snow, then in March she was sent by cattle truck to Belsen. Upon being liberated in 1945 she returned to Prague, but finding no family or friend there joined her older sister in England, where she married and had children. She first studied painting in 1970s at Tetherdown Adult Education Centre, then at Camden Arts Centre. As a schoolteacher she was involved in remedial work. Moved to Hereford in 1980, three years later beginning a long series of works, Memories of the Holocaust. Anton Gill's *Journey Back from Hell*, the front cover of Ronnie Landau's *The Nazi Holocaust* and cover of *Voices from the Holocaust*, a British Library audio set, all featured Birkin's work. Was included in exhibitions at Birmingham and Hereford City Museums and Art Galleries. Solo shows included Coventry Cathedral, Ben Uri Art Society and Hanover Gallery in Liverpool. Ben Uri and Imperial War Museum hold examples.

Tony BIRKS: *see* **Tony BIRKS-HAY**

Tony BIRKS-HAY 1937– Artist in oil and clay (for bronze), graphic designer and teacher, who studied at Slade School of Fine Art under William Coldstream, Reg Butler and Henry Moore. Birks-Hay was an Oxford School of Art lecturer, 1959–63, was head of Art at Radley College, 1961–3, then freelanced. Group shows included RA, RWA and MAFA. Had solo exhibitions at Keble College, Oxford, 1961; Rotunda Gallery, 1970; and Alpha House Gallery, Sherborne, 1991. Portraits in oil or bronze and landscapes in oil were Birks-Hay's main works. St Edmund Hall, Oxford, and many private collections held examples. In 1973 he won the Westward Television Sculpture Award. Arts Club member who lived in Marston Magna, Yeovil, Somerset. Sometimes worked as Tony Birks. He was also a noted writer on ceramics, his book *The Alchemy of Sculpture* appearing in 1998.

Oswald BIRLEY 1880–1952 Portrait painter, born in Auckland, New Zealand, educated at Harrow School and Cambridge University. Also studied art in Dresden, Florence and in Paris at Académie Julian under Marcel Baschet. Birley served with a commission in the Intelligence Corps in France in World War I, gaining the Military Cross. He was a vice-president of RP, also being a member of ROI. Showed also at RA, Walker Art Gallery in Liverpool, RHA, RSA and elsewhere. Birley painted many distinguished figures, including Sir Edward Marsh the collector, the artist Glyn Philpot and the 1st Earl of Birkenhead in the National Portrait Gallery; portraits of King George VI for the Royal Agricultural Society and Royal Naval College, Greenwich; and for that collection a series of portraits of admirals of World War II. He was knighted in 1949. Lived in London and in West Dean, Sussex.

William BIRNIE 1929– Painter in oil and watercolour, and teacher, married to the artist Cynthia Wall. He was born in Bathgate, West Lothian, and studied at Glasgow School of Art, 1946–51, teachers including William and Mary Armour, David Donaldson and Geoffrey Squire, and Hospitalfield House, Arbroath, 1950–1, with Ian Fleming. He painted extensively in Scotland and on the continent, mainly landscape, and preferred "complicated subjects". Birnie taught in west of Scotland schools, 1952–88 and was a principal examiner for the Scottish Examination Board, 1975–9. He was elected a member of RSW in 1964 and of the Royal Glasgow Institute of the Fine Arts, 1993, having been a founder-member of the Glasgow Group, 1958. Had a series of solo exhibitions with Open Eye Gallery, Edinburgh, from 1989. HRH The Duke of Edinburgh, Scottish Arts Council and Glasgow and Paisley Art Galleries hold examples. Lived in Kilbarchan, Renfrewshire.

Val BIRO 1921– Artist in pen and ink, scraperboard, watercolour, printmaker and writer, born in Budapest, Hungary. Aspired early to be an artist, then was sent by father in 1939 to England, where he studied until 1942 at Central School of Arts and Crafts, evacuated to Northampton. His main subject was illustration, his teachers including John Farleigh, Noel Rooke and Bernard Meninsky. In 1942 Biro joined Sylvan Press while working as a part-time fireman, then became art director for John Lehmann, the publisher. Had been freelancing on book jackets and advertising, and in 1953 went freelance full-time. Authors illustrated included C S Forester, Monica Dickens, Evelyn Waugh and Noël Coward. Drew for *Radio Times* for 21 years until 1972. Biro illustrated many children's books, then in 1966 published the first of his many Gumdrop stories, based on his ownership of a vintage car. He also retold traditional tales, with his own illustrations, such as *Hungarian Folk-Tales*, 1981. Also drew for *The Good Food Guide* and was a member of Chartered Society of Designers. Solo exhibition at Pallant House, Chichester, 2001–2. Victoria & Albert Museum holds his work. His name was originally Bálint (translated Val(entine)) Stephen Biro and he settled in Bosham, Sussex.

Bill BIRRELL fl. from mid-1960s– Painter, graphic artist and teacher. After studying at Glasgow School of Art, 1964–6, Birrell worked in Canada and America as a graphic artist for two years, returning to Glasgow where he graduated in drawing and painting in 1970. He went on to teach in a secondary school in the city. Birrell's pictures were figurative, but had a Surrealist tinge. He showed at Royal Glasgow Institute of the Fine Arts, and in group shows in Markham Gallery in Toronto at Galerie d'Art Moderne in Geneva, in 1983, and at International Contemporary Art Fair at Olympia. He showed at Compass Gallery, Glasgow, in the New Generation Show in 1970, then participated in a three-man show there and had solo exhibitions in 1977 and 1988. His work is in extensive private collections in Britain and overseas.

Ronald BIRRELL fl. from 1970s– Artist who was born in Glasgow, where he studied at the School of Art, going on to Royal College of Art and Royal Academy of Fine Arts,

Madrid. He won the Robert Hart Bursary, William Armour Prize and Torrance Award. He became a professional member of SSA, but his career hit a setback with the onset of multiple sclerosis in the late 1980s. A precision of statement marked Birrell's work, which is often tinged with a feeling of solitude. Was included in The Compass Contribution exhibition at Compass Gallery, Glasgow, 1990. Scottish Arts Council and Nuffield Foundation hold his work.

Adam BIRTWISTLE 1959– Painter and draughtsman of portraits, often quirky and witty, with a musical connection, son of the composer Sir Harrison Birtwistle. Studied at Chelsea College of Art. Mixed exhibitions included RA Summer Exhibition, 1984; Salon d'Automne de Notre Dame de Gravenchou Competition, 1st Prize, 1988; and Salon des Indépendants, Paris, 1990. Showed solo frequently in Britain and France, notably at Piano Nobile Fine Paintings, Richmond and Holland Park, from 1986. National Portrait Gallery and Royal Academy of Music hold examples.

Cecil Harry BIRTWHISTLE 1910–1990 Artist in oil, pastel and watercolour, and teacher, son of the painter James Birtwhistle. Brought up in Sheffield, he began showing work as a child. Studied at the local College of Art, 1924–9, under Anthony Betts, then with Barnett Freedman and Gilbert Spencer at Royal College of Art, 1929–32. Birtwhistle later taught at Richmond School of Art. Exhibited RA, Royal Glasgow Institute of the Fine Arts, NEAC and in the north. In later years was a close friend of the artist Ottilie Tolansky, sharing exhibitions with her at Walker's Galleries. After Birtwhistle's death Piano Nobile Fine Paintings, of Richmond, showed fine examples of his Camden Town Group-influenced pictures in its Modern British Masters exhibitions, 1994–5. Lived in London.

John BISCHOFF 1963– Artist producing pictures noted for their radiant and luminous colour. He was born of English-Dutch parents, did a foundation course at Harrow Art School, 1981–2, and graduated with honours in fine art from Middlesex University, 1982–5. Mixed exhibitions included Whittington Hospital; Wimbledon and Goldsmiths' Schools of Art; Forum Hotel; Florence Trust, where he had a residency; Galerie Le Rayon Vert, Nantes, France; and Collectors Choice, Boston, America. Among solo exhibitions were Polish Cultural Centre; 202 Gallery, Kensington Park Road; and Twickenham Festival, All Saints. Bischoff completed commissions for Fat Duck Restaurant, Bray, and Lee Valley Riding Centre. Art for Hospitals; corporate collections; and many private collectors in Britain and abroad held examples.

Edward BISHOP 1902–1997 Painter, printmaker, designer, photographer and teacher who studied and taught at Central School of Arts and Crafts under A S Hartrick and Noel Rooke, 1920–6. In 1929 he joined the advertising agency Lintas, working there as a group art director until 1936, and he was included in Beyond the Horizon: Artists at Lintas 1930–1950 at Agnew, 1988. From Lintas he moved to S H Benson's before joining the Ministry of Information in 1941, where he designed propaganda material for neutral countries. During one night of the Blitz Bishop lost his mother, sister and one of his brothers, and his London flat, with all his completed paintings, was destroyed. In 1945, Bishop became a consultant advertising designer and painter, being particularly noted for his paintings of London. Bishop won the Lord Mayor of London's Art Award in 1975–6, and in 1978 won the first prize in the big Spirit of London competition. Was a member of RBA, 1950, and NEAC, 1960 (he was later appointed its first keeper, a post he held until 1990), was elected to and eventually became president of the London Sketch Club, and as chairman of the Chelsea Arts Club in the mid-1960s lobbied for admission of women. Showed extensively at RA, also at Leicester and Wildenstein Galleries. Nottingham Castle Museum, National Gallery of New South Wales, Sydney, Nottingham Castle Museum, National Gallery of New South Wales, in Sydney, and Department of the Environment hold examples. Bishop was married to the painter Celeste Radloff. Lived in London.

Michael BISHOP 1957– Painter using a rich palette, and illustrator, who took a foundation course at Farnham, then graduated with honours at Brighton Art College. He began work as an illustrator, clients including BMW, British Telecom, London Transport, British Airways, *The Observer*, *Mail on Sunday* and among book publishers Oxford University Press. Early exhibitions, 1983–9, included the Association of Illustrators and a series at Francis Kyle Gallery; from 1989–95, in New York, The Gallery at the Lincoln Center, The Ambassador Gallery and Illustration House; and, latterly, Society of Landscape Painters, Mall Galleries, 2001, Advocate Galleries, 2002, and Highgate Fine Art, 2003. In that show were cityscapes based on memories of New York, semi-abstracted landscapes inspired by cliff walks on the Isle of Wight and in Dorset, and pub interiors with a theatrical quality. In 1996, London Transport commissioned Bishop to design a Soho poster for its series Art on the Underground.

Molly BISHOP 1911–1998 Painter, especially of portraits, and draughtsman, married to Lord George Scott. Her full unmarried name was Mary Wina Mannin Bishop, and she was born in Multan in what is now Pakistan into a military family. As a child she won many Royal Drawing Society awards. She studied at the Royal Academy Schools, 1930–2, under Walter Westley Russell. Worked for *The Bystander*, sketching celebrities of the 1930s. Later, Douglas Fairbanks Junior, Laurence Olivier and Rudolf Nureyev were among her many famous sitters. Exhibited RSA, RBA, Royal Glasgow Institute of the Fine Arts and elsewhere. Lived in Towcester, Northamptonshire, and London.

William Henry BISHOP 1942– Painter, especially of ships and the sea, who raced a Victory class one design yacht, born and brought up in Portsmouth area. As a boy he began drawing and modelling ships. With the help of marine artist W L Wyllie's daughter, who gave Bishop over 50 of her father's brushes, and that of marine artist Richard Joicey, Bishop showed successfully at RSMA. In 1980 the family firm was sold and Bishop began painting full-time, at first in watercolour. Early commissions came from naval officers needing portraits of their ships, and Bishop's pictures proved especially popular in America, where he supplied the Quester Gallery, Stonington, Connecticut. Bishop had a solo show at Royal Exchange Gallery, 1991. The *Mary Rose* Trust asked him to paint several versions of the ship; the Royal Naval Museum a scene from the Battle of Jutland; and he produced company calendars for John Courage Brewery and Chichester Press. Lived at Langstone, Havant, Hampshire.

Osmond Hick BISSELL 1906–1968 Painter, wood engraver and teacher, born at Harborne, Birmingham. Studied at Kidderminster School of Art under William Daly, 1924–8, then at Birmingham College of Art, 1928–9, with Harold Holden. Exhibited RA, NEAC, NS, PS, Paris Salon and elsewhere. He held the post of vice-principal at York School of Arts and Crafts from 1929. York and Kidderminster art galleries hold his work which was included in the *Recording Britain* exhibition at Victoria & Albert Museum in 1990. Lived in Kidderminster, Worcestershire.

Douglas BISSET 1908–2000 Sculptor and teacher, born in Strichen, Aberdeenshire. He served his apprenticeship with an architectural sculptor in the city and then studied at Glasgow School of Art, 1930–3, with Archibald Dawson, winning the Newbery Gold Medal and a John Keppie Scholarship, also serving as an assistant teacher; at the Royal Danish Academy, 1933; then as a Rome Scholar attended the British School in Rome, 1934–5. Was then attached to the British School of Archaeology in Athens for three years. Around the outbreak of World War II he returned to England and began teaching there for a number of years at Leeds College of Art after a short period at Brighton School of Art, also teaching at City and Guilds School of Art. For health reasons, the rarely exhibiting Bisset lived in Mexico, 1980–95, then returned to Glasgow. Exhibited RA, Royal Glasgow Institute of the Fine Arts and elsewhere. Imperial War Museum holds his work.

George BISSILL 1896–1973 Painter, printmaker, draughtsman and furniture designer, born in Fairford, Gloucestershire. He was the son of a coal miner and was a miner himself for several years. Having been gassed during service in France during World War I Bissill studied at Nottingham School of Art, 1920–1. In the early 1920s he moved to London, working for a time as a pavement artist, but was given a solo show at Redfern Gallery in 1924. Also exhibited RA, NEAC, Maltzahn Gallery and Abbott and Holder. Although a landscape painter, Bissill is notable for his powerful images of miners at work. Tate Gallery holds his Landscape, Layton. Lived at Ashmansworth, near Newbury in Berkshire.

Roderick BISSON 1910–1987 Artist and art critic who worked extensively in gouache, born and based in Liverpool, son of a mariner, who was educated at Liverpool Institute. After working in the Picton Library Bisson joined the architectural practice Hinchliffe Davies. An admirer of Wyndham Lewis, Bisson developed an interest in Cubism and Surrealism and as early as 1932 a work of his caused a stir at the Sandon Studios (he became a member and was to publish the definitive account of *The Sandon Studios Society of the Arts* in 1965). Bisson during the 1930s was secretary of the Liverpool Young Communist League, was a conscientious objector early in World War II, but joined up when the Soviet Union was invaded by Germany. He became a cartographer with the 8th Army in the desert and in Italy, where the works of Masaccio and Piero della Francesca moved him. After the war Bisson worked as a design consultant for the local firm Lewis, from the 1950s serving as art critic of the *Liverpool Daily Post*, where he wrote perceptively for 25 years as Z. Unhappy about a possible conflict of interest and with developments in American art, in the late 1950s he gave up painting. Bisson was a reticent man, a rare exhibitor and a fluent French speaker who assembled an impressive library of French art publications. These were sold at Sotheby's shortly before his death, which coincided with a retrospective at Walker Art Gallery, Liverpool, which holds his work.

Bitte B-N 1917– Painter and illustrator, actual name Birgitte Brondum-Nielsen, who was born in Copenhagen, Denmark, where she was educated and studied art at the College of Arts and Crafts. As well as exhibiting in Denmark, showed with RA, RSA, SSA, with RI and SSWA, both of which she was a member, Brighton Art Gallery and Royal Glasgow Institute of the Fine Arts. Also had a series of solo exhibitions in Britain and Denmark. HRH The Duke of Edinburgh and Kelvingrove Art Gallery, Glasgow, hold her work. Illustrated books for children. Lived for some years in Scotland, in Alloa and then Rannoch Station, Perthshire.

Edna BIZON 1929– Painter in oil on canvas, born in London, married to the artist Ken Bizon. She studied at Camberwell School of Arts and Crafts where her teachers included Claude Rogers, John Minton, Lawrence Gowing and Victor Pasmore. Bizon in her still lifes, genre and landscape scenes emulated painters of the Dutch and Norwich schools, believing that "skill in painting is very important to express ideas". She was a member of SWA and showed regularly at RA from 1973. Also exhibited at Thorndike Theatre, Leatherhead, 1971; Hal O'Nians, 1987–90; and she shared a show with Mary Carter at Llewellyn Alexander in 1991. Solo show there, 2001–2. Gulf International holds her work. Lived in North Creake, Norfolk.

Ken BIZON 1927– Painter in oil and watercolour of architectural themes as a background to human activity; teacher. Born in Warham, Norfolk, he studied at Norwich and Camberwell Schools of Art, his teachers including Joseph Dixon and William Townsend. For a time he was involved in exhibition and interior design work; was also senior lecturer in design at South Bank Polytechnic. Member of Royal Society of Arts. Bizon showed at RA; Thorndike Theatre, Leatherhead, 1979; and Llewellyn Alexander. Lived in North Creake, Norfolk, and was married to the painter Edna Bizon.

Anna BJERGER 1973– Painter, born in Sweden, who settled in London, where she graduated with honours in fine art, painting, from Central St Martins School of Art and Design, 1994–7, gaining her master's in painting from the Royal College of Art, 1999–01. Bjerger's work was influenced by that of Edvard Munch, Luc Tuymans and Alex Katz. Her pictures, as in White Paintings, at MW projects, 2002, were sourced from her own and found photographs. Once the image was chosen, Bjerger brought out elements by editing, emphasising or cropping. Group exhibitions included Aldridge Bjerger Joffe, Equilibri Precari, Rome, Italy, 1999; Homage to the Budokan, Foyles Gallery, and Lost in Space, Farg Fabriken, Stockholm, both 2000; and Gallerie RM Art, Essen, Germany, and Neon Shop, both 2001.

Dorothy BLACK 1963– Artist in various media who was particularly noted for her confident ability to make the line; her work had strong decorative and surreal elements and made much use of the human figure. Black was born in Forfar, Angus, and studied at Edinburgh College of Art, 1980–6. She lived and taught in Dunfermline, Fife. Her work was shown in solo and group shows in Britain and America, notably in Edinburgh City Art Centre's exhibition Through Women's Eyes, 1992–3. The Centre, Stirling University and BBC Scotland hold her work.

Dorrit BLACK 1891–1951 Painter and lino-cut artist and teacher, born Dorothea Black in Adelaide, Australia. After initial art education at the Australian School of Arts and Crafts, Adelaide, and at Sydney Art School she moved to London to work under Iain Macnab and Claude Flight at the Grosvenor School of Modern Art, then went to Paris to study with André Lhote and Albert Gleizes. Eventually returned to Australia, where she settled in Magill, South Australia. Black taught at the Modern Art Centre, which she founded. In the mid-1930s she made a return trip to Europe, also visiting North America. Exhibited in Paris, Australia and in Britain at Redfern Gallery and WIAC. Victoria & Albert Museum holds her work.

Hamish BLACK 1948– Sculptor and teacher. Attended Eastbourne School of Art, 1965–7, North-East London Polytechnic, 1967–70, and Slade School of Fine Art, 1970–2. Had extensive teaching experience from 1973, including Workers' Educational Association, Brighton Polytechnic, West Sussex College of Art and Wimbledon School of Art. Took part in extensive group exhibitions, including Brighton Polytechnic Gallery, 1979; as artist-in-residence, Varndean College, Brighton, 1982; Sussex Artists, Brighton Festival, 1991; and Sculpture at Canterbury, 1992. From 1984 Black was in collaboration with the sculptor Anthony Caro. His solo shows included Southover Grange Gardens, Lewes, 1982, and Charleston Farmhouse, Firle, 1989. Black did a substantial amount of public work, including Maygrove Peace Park, Camden Council, 1985; a winning entry for Great Hurricane Sculpture Competition, American Express, Brighton Festival and South East Arts, 1989; and Tree House, Brighton Festival, 1990.

Ian BLACK 1929– Painter, draughtsman and teacher, born in Bury St Edmunds, Suffolk. He studied at Southampton College of Art, 1949, and Bath Academy of Art, Corsham, 1952–6, teachers including Peter Lanyon, William Scott and Martin Froy. Among mixed exhibitions were RWA of which he was a member, 1978, and RA, and he had a series of solo shows. Wadham and St Catherine's Colleges in Oxford as well as the New Zealand government hold his work. Became head of art at Bristol Cathedral School. Lived at Englishcombe, Bath, Somerset.

John Frederick BLACK 1943– Painter, printmaker, textile designer and teacher, born in Appleby Magna, Leicestershire. He studied at Loughborough College of Art, 1960–4, his teachers including Edward Sharp; Brighton College of Art, 1965, under Ronald Horton; then in 1978–9 at Manchester Polytechnic for his master's degree. Went on to become a freelance designer; to operate The Gallery at his home in Wellingborough, Northamptonshire; and to teach at Bedford College of Higher Education. Showed in Britain and abroad.

Maureen BLACK 1926– Painter, printmaker, embroiderer and teacher who studied painting and embroidery at Goldsmiths' College School of Art and etching at Morley College. She was a founder-member of Greenwich Printmakers' Association, showed at RA Summer Exhibition, RE and had a solo show at Woodlands Art Gallery in 1980. Taught at Greenwich Adult Education Institute. In 1977–9 a hanging commissioned by the Ursuline Community to commemorate the centenary of St Ursula's High School, Greenwich, was designed and partly made by Black. Her work is also held by National Maritime Museum, Guildhall Art Gallery and other public collections in Britain and abroad. Lived in London.

Misha BLACK 1910–1977 Architect, industrial designer, academic, writer and lecturer, born in Baku, Russia, taken as an infant by his parents to London. There he was educated at Dame Alice Owen School, Islington, and remained, apart from art studies in Paris. With this modest educational background Black achieved distinction by a crabwise route. Initially, he earned a living from an eyrie in Seven Dials, producing designs for book-plates, book-jackets, posters and exhibition stands. In 1933, Black was a founder-member of the AIA, in which he remained active, and of the British Society of Industrial Artists, later (1954–6) being its president. In 1934, he joined Milner and Thomas Gray and others in the Industrial Design Partnership. He soon achieved eminence for his work as co-ordinating architect at the MARS (Modern Architectural Research Society) exhibition in 1938, and for designing the British Pavilion at the 1939 New York World's Fair. He spearheaded exhibition design at the Ministry of Information, 1940–5; in 1946 with Milner Gray founded the influential Design Research Unit; and was substantially responsible for the Regatta Restaurant at the 1951 Festival of Britain. There were many post-war consultancies with leading British and foreign firms and Black was made a Royal Designer for Industry in 1957. He was president from 1959–61 of the International Council of Societies of Industrial Design, which he had helped form in 1957. Despite his lack of university education, in 1959 Black was appointed professor of industrial design at the Royal College of Art, retiring in 1975. These achievements and his contribution to many public bodies connected with science and the arts prefaced his knighthood in 1972. He had been naturalised in 1950.

Noël BLACK 1931– Sculptor in various materials, ceramist and teacher, born in Prescot, Lancashire. He studied at Loughborough College of Art, 1949–53, then Leicester College of Art, 1953–4. Went on to become senior lecturer in sculpture at Kesteven College of Education and University of Evansville. Showed at Upstairs Gallery, Stamford, and handled public commissions. Lived in Skillington, Lincolnshire.

Roman BLACK 1915–1969 Oil painter, mural and stained glass designer, also known as Roman Black-Blachowski. Born in Poland, he studied at the Central School of Arts and Crafts and Brighton College of Art. Black, who lectured extensively, exhibited at the RA, LG, RBA, Wildenstein and the Paris Salon, where he was awarded a gold medal in 1968. He is represented in public national galleries in Ottawa, Melbourne, Dublin and elsewhere, and Poznan, Poland. Black's book *Old and New Australian Aboriginal Art* was published in Sydney in 1964. Lived in London.

Roman BLACK-BLACHOWSKI: *see* **Roman BLACK**

Sam BLACK 1913– Painter and teacher, born in Ardrossan, Ayrshire, where he attended the Academy. Attended Glasgow School of Art, 1932–6, then studied on the continent. Black was for a time principal lecturer in art at Jordanhill Training College, Glasgow, also an inspector of schools. During World War II his work was bought by the War Artists' Advisory Committee and Glasgow Museum and Art Galleries also hold a watercolour of St Enoch Square, in the city. Exhibited RSA and Royal Glasgow Institute of the Fine Arts. Lived at West Kilbride, Ayrshire.

Simon BLACK 1958– Artist born in Manchester, where he attended the Polytechnic, also Wolverhampton Polytechnic. He travelled on the continent and spent several periods in Israel, returning to England in 1983 and settling in London three years later. Showed with MAFA, where he won a prize in 1985; in 1986 at Ben Uri Art Society, which acquired his work, and at Leo Solomon Gallery in Rochdale; and in 1993 at Five Dryden Street Gallery.

Elizabeth BLACKADDER 1931– Watercolourist and teacher, born in Falkirk, Stirlingshire. She studied at Edinburgh University and Edinburgh College of Art, 1949–54, her teachers including Penelope Beaton, Robert Henderson Blyth and William Gillies. A Carnegie Travelling Scholarship in 1954 allowed her to visit several countries in southern Europe, a postgraduate scholarship in 1954–5 allowing further travels in Italy. In 1956 she married the painter John Houston and began teaching part-time at Edinburgh College of Art. Although she won commissions for stained glass, lithographs and tapestries, Blackadder was best known for her meticulous watercolours in which objects are carefully spaced on her studio table. Elected RSA in 1972 and RA in 1976. Was appointed Her Majesty's Painter and Limner in Scotland, 2001. Showed regularly at Mercury Gallery, elsewhere in Britain and abroad, with a solo exhibition at Browse and Darby, 2002. She was created Dame of the British Empire in 2003. Scottish National Gallery of Modern Art holds her work. Lived in Edinburgh.

Christine BLACKBURN 1963– Artist, notably a printmaker, who studied at Wirral College of Art, 1981, Sheffield Polytechnic, 1982, San Jose State University, 1984, then Sheffield Polytechnic, 1985. She took part in Sheffield Open Art at Mappin Art at Mappin Art Gallery, 1985, Punchlines at Bluecoat Gallery in Liverpool, 1986, and was included in the Walker Art Gallery touring show Merseyside Artists 3, in 1986–7.

Clarence E BLACKBURN 1914–1984 Painter, printmaker, commercial artist and potter, educated in Stoke-on-Trent, then studied at Burslem College of Art. Ran small pottery, 1944–59. Showed RA, RE and abroad. Lived in Hampton Wick, Surrey.

Coral BLACKBURN 1961– Artist who graduated with honours from Manchester Polytechnic, 1980–3. Group shows included Hull Artists Association Exchange Exhibition, 1985; Artworks Space, from 1986; and East End Open Studios, with Barbican Arts Group, 1989. In 1985, Blackburn had a solo show at Wolseys Bar.

David BLACKBURN 1939– Artist in pastel, printmaker and teacher, born in Huddersfield, Yorkshire. His landscapes of England, North America and Australia had strong abstract and visionary qualities. Blackburn studied at Huddersfield School of Art, 1955–9, then Royal College of Art, 1959–62. He became a lecturer in 1966 at University of Manchester's school of architecture, other appointments including visiting lecturer at University of Melbourne, 1969–77; then he was visiting artist at Georgetown University, Washington, 1981, and Yale Center for British Art, 1989. Kenneth Clark and Humphrey Brooke were early supporters of Blackburn, who had his first solo show at Argus Gallery, Melbourne, in 1965. He had a retrospective at Mappin Art Gallery, Sheffield, 1970, others at University of York, 1978, and Huddersfield Art Gallery, 1979 and 1994. Showed at Hart Gallery, Nottingham, from 1989. Yale Center, the Museum of Modern Art in New York, several Australian galleries and Ashmolean Museum, Oxford, hold his work.

Kenneth BLACKBURN 1951– Artist working in a range of media whose starting point was "an underlying faith in the expressive and aesthetic qualities of the materials used." Blackburn's initial aim was "to bring about something that is purely subjective to the medium," paintings then developing "over months with elements being added and sometimes removed." Studied graphic design and foundation art and design at Preston College and Preston Polytechnic, 1990–2, gaining an honours degree in fine art at The University of Central Lancashire, 1992–6. Had a series of solo exhibitions at Curwen Gallery from 1997. Commissions included five themed paintings for BP Amoco's new European headquarters; a 17-foot, integrated fresco for Baxi Partnership's new corporate headquarters; and an integrated triptych for Nova Rehman Associates.

Mavis BLACKBURN 1923– Painter, earlier in oil, later in acrylic; teacher. She was born in Wallasey, Cheshire, and studied at Liverpool College of Art, 1942–8, teachers including Will C Penn, Martin Bell and Alfred Wiffen. Blackburn taught art at Holt Hill School, Birkenhead for two years; freelanced for two more; then taught until retirement in 1984, becoming department head at Upton Hall Convent, Birkenhead. Obtained bachelor's degree in 1980. Although she painted abstracts in 1960s and 1970s, the work of Bridget Riley and the floor of St Mark's in Venice being influences, Blackburn judged abstraction "to be a fascinating blind alley, and I reverted to a naturalistic style". Landscapes and buildings were key subjects. Became a member of RCamA, 1952, also being a member of Liverpool Academy, Wirral Society of Art and Deeside Art Group. Showed at RA, RBA and had a retrospective at Williamson Art Gallery, Birkenhead, which holds her work, in 1992. Lived at West Kirby, Wirral, Merseyside.

BLACK DOG OF WELLS– This was the company name of Kennedy Collings and his wife Philippa Threlfall. It stemmed from the medieval name of their studio site on Wells Cathedral land. They were based in the Somerset city for several decades after the partnership was formed, creating ceramic sculpture for numerous public sites. Bristol is particularly rich in their works, including a dozen reliefs on Broad Quay House, telling the city's history, 1981; Exploration, at Redcliffe Quay Piazza, with James Blunt, 1991; and ceramic tiles on a friendly society building in Colston Street, 1994–5. Collings was born in

1933 in Bristol, where he attended Clifton College, next reading law and history at Cambridge; worked in industry; then formed the partnership. Threlfall, born 1939, studied ceramics and graphic design at Cardiff College of Art and Goldsmiths' College.

David BLACKER 1949– Sculptor of horses and trophy maker, born in Surrey and educated at Milton Abbey, Dorset. Blacker entered racing in 1967 and worked at the stables of trainer Tim Forster, beginning to ride as an amateur, then as a professional, 1969–82. Among his 327 winners were the Whitbread Gold Cup and *Daily Express* Triumph Hurdle and he rode in nine Grand Nationals. Retired from racing to concentrate on sculpture, taken up as a hobby in 1974. His most famous commission was Red Rum, in the grounds of Aintree racecourse. Other important ones included Aldaniti, another Grand National winner, and two Derby winners, Blakeney and Murston. The Hamilton Trophy, Kelso; the Dermot Daly Memorial Trophy, Cheltenham; and John Hughes Memorial Trophy, Liverpool, were made by Blacker, whose work was cast by The Morris Singer Foundry. Among his solo shows was Tryon & Moorland Gallery, 1988.

Doris May BLACKER 1905– Painter, potter and teacher, born in Dewsbury, Yorkshire. Brought up in Morecambe, Lancashire, where she eventually settled, she studied at Lancaster School of Art. For many years she taught at Skerton Girls' Modern School, in Lancaster, showing widely in Lancashire and Yorkshire. She was noted for her watercolours of the Lake District.

Harry BLACKER 1910–1999 Versatile artist and writer, born to Russian immigrant parents into poor circumstances in London's East End. He had to forgo an art scholarship, and at 14 was apprenticed to an engraver, attending Sir John Cass Technical Institute evening classes, taught by Frederick C Herrick and Robert Sargent Austin. During a slump in the printing trade Blacker persuaded the Piccadilly store Simpson's to employ him, where he created eye-turning window displays. In World War II Blacker served in the Royal Artillery, but also drew posters for the War Office. He went on to work in advertising, clients including London Transport, Shell-Mex and BP and the Post Office. As a cartoonist he worked as Nero, in 1962 gaining joint first prize in a competition organised by the *Jewish Chronicle*. A dozen years later he published his illustrated autobiography, *Just Like it Was – Memoirs of the Mittel East*. Other books included *East Endings* and (as Nero), *Some of My Best Jokes are Jewish*, *With Laugh and Affection* and *By My Laugh it's Jewish*. Had a show at Lauderdale House, near where he lived in Highgate, north London, in 1981, another at Ben Uri Art Society, which holds his work, in 1986.

Kate BLACKER 1955– Artist who was born in Petersfield, Hampshire. She was educated nearby at Bedales School, 1970–3, then attended Central School of Art, 1975–6, and Camberwell School of Arts and Crafts, 1976–9. She studied at Royal College of Art, 1979–81. Among her activities was work with performing artists, notably the dancer Gaby Agis. Had a first solo show in 1982 at Coracle Gallery, then widely in Britain and abroad, including Victoria Miro, 1989, Museum of Photography Charleroi, 1992, and in 1993 at John Hansard Gallery, Southampton. In 1993–4 she was included in the Arts Council tour Recent British Sculpture. In 1999, Blacker's large 1988 geometrical abstract Transfer, in corrugated metal and car paint, was illustrated in the publication accompanying the show Bedales & Art Design, organised by William Jackson Gallery at Art99, held at the Business Design Centre. Worked in Britain and France.

Thetis BLACKER 1928– Creator of colourful, visionary pictures who studied at Chelsea School of Art. In 1970, as a Churchill Fellow, she visited Singapore, Malaysia, Thailand, India, Iran and Indonesia, where she worked at the Batik Research Institute of Jogjakarta. Blacker's dyed paintings were commissioned for and exhibited in cathedrals and churches in the United Kingdom, continental Europe and America. Five major series were based on mythical themes: Apocalyse (St Andrew's House); A Bestiary of Mythical Creatures; The Creation (Winchester Cathedral); Search for the Simurgh; and Arbor Cosmica. Later commissions included work for St George's Chapel, Windsor, where a major show of her work was held in 2000; St Alban's Abbey; a phoenix for the dining hall of Grey College, University of Durham, 2000; banners of St Cuthbert and St Oswald, for Durham Cathedral, 2001. Blacker also had three major works in Grey College Chapel: The Creation of Darkness and Light, Imago Lucis and Imago Aquarium, dedicated 2000. Henry Dyson Fine Art put on a show at Grey College, 2001.

Vivien BLACKETT 1955– London-based painter who studied fine art at Goldsmiths' College. She was artist-in-residence at the National Gallery, 1986–7, and Camden Arts Centre, 1992. In that year she was included in Women's Art at New Hall, Cambridge, and in 2003 had a solo show at the London School of Hygiene and Tropical Medicine. Blackett wrote that her work was "concerned with generating new meaning through the juxtaposition of different images, both borrowed and invented. I am interested in our quest for knowledge of the world we inhabit.... The Wellcome Library for the History of Medicine has become one of my most valuable sources.... I borrow images from books on subjects as diverse as chemistry, cooking and witchcraft, which I adapt as I work, often combining them with images of my own invention." She had an "interest in illusion and in the difference between the surface appearance of things, what does or might lie beneath". The London School exhibition included pictures following on from a series of multiple-panel paintings, entitled Above, below, within, which Blackett made for the Adam Gallery in 1997. The British Council and other public collections hold her work.

Dorothy BLACKHAM 1896–1975 Painter, artist in black-and-white and teacher, born in Dublin. Studied at Royal Hibernian Academy School with Dermod O'Brien, 1916–21, and at Goldsmiths' College School of Art, 1921–2, under Edmund J Sullivan and Frederick Marriott. Exhibited extensively in Ireland, including RHA, and LG, Tempera Society and SGA. Was an art teacher attached to the Ministry of Health just after World War II. Lived in London.

George BLACKLOCK 1952– Painter, printmaker, draughtsman and teacher, born in Durham, who studied at Sunderland Polytechnic, 1970–1, Stourbridge College of Art, 1971–4, and Reading University, 1974–6. In 1976–8 he had a junior fellowship in painting at Cardiff College of Art, gained a WAC award and became senior lecturer at

Wimbledon School of Art. Exhibitions included Whitechapel Open, Francis Graham-Dixon Gallery and he won a prize in John Moores Liverpool Exhibition, 1993–4. Had a solo show at Byam Shaw, 1993; later ones including Kapil Jariwala Gallery, 1998; was Artist of the Day at Flowers East, chosen by Carol Robertson, 1999, and shared a show there with Eduardo Paolozzi, 2000; and a first solo exhibition of prints and monoprints, Flowers East, 2001. Arts Council holds his work. Lived in London.

Audrey BLACKMAN 1907–1990 Sculptor, initially in bronze, then in ceramics, of figures; painter. She was born in London into an academic family and married Professor Geoffrey Blackman, who held the Sibthorpian chair in rural economy at Oxford. Having failed to obtain a place to study history at Oxford, Audrey Blackman went to the Kunstgewerbeschule, Graz, in Austria, and contemplated becoming a singer, but returned to her early love of art by studying at Goldsmiths' College School of Art 1926–30, and Reading University, 1931–5. Although her first sculptures were in bronze, she was persuaded by a visit to the Ashmolean Museum to turn to ceramics, learning the techniques at the Oxford School of Art under Gladys Grimshaw. In 1978 she published *Rolled Pottery Figures*. She became strongly involved in such bodies as the International Academy of Ceramics, Crafts Advisory Committee and Federation of British Crafts Societies. Showed RA, elsewhere in Britain and abroad. Work held by Fitzwilliam Museum, Cambridge; Oxfordshire County Museum; and Cecil Higgins Museum, Bedford. Lived at Boar's Hill, Oxford.

Charles BLACKMAN 1928– Versatile and imaginative figurative artist and designer, in whose work themes such as the schoolgirl, family intimacies and blindness (his writer/poet wife until 1980 Barbara (Patterson) early received an invalid/blind pension) were important. He was born and eventually settled in Sydney, Australia, leaving school before his fourteenth birthday after an unsettled childhood. Worked as a copy boy on the *Sun* newspaper, 1942–5, attending evening classes at East Sydney Technical School; then gained a *Sun* art cadetship, 1946–7, having as his only formal painting training a few lessons with Hayward Veal at Meldrum School of Painting. Introduced to modern literature and art by the poet Lois Hunter, he left the *Sun* and began a wandering period of odd jobs, self-education and hard painting, in 1952 attending lithography classes run by technician Ben Crosskell at Melbourne Technical College. Had a first solo show at Peter Bray Gallery, 1953, prompting critical interest. By 1958, Blackman's picture Alice – a Portrait had been accepted by the Musée d'Art Moderne, Paris. In 1959, Blackman became a founder-member of the Antipodean group, work being noticed by Sir Kenneth Clark; in 1960, he had a sell-out show at Johnstone Gallery, Brisbane, and won a Helena Rubinstein Travelling Scholarship; in 1961 sailing with his family to London, where his work was widely praised, helping to represent Australia at the Biennale des Jeunes at Musée d'Art Moderne. A promised retrospective at Whitechapel Gallery had to be replaced by an acclaimed show at Zwemmer Gallery, 1965, Blackman returning to Australia in 1966. London life was finally terminated in 1968 when a Leicester Galleries show disappointed. Back in Australia, with many forays abroad, notably to Paris, Blackman continued to enhance his reputation, notably in the theatre. In 1993, the National Gallery of Victoria held a retrospective. Victoria & Albert Museum and Australian collections hold examples.

Clive BLACKMORE 1940– Painter in oil, watercolour and gouache, born in Kingston upon Thames, Surrey. He attended Twickenham and Kingston Schools of Art, then for many years was involved in pottery, stoneware and porcelain, having moved to Cornwall in 1960. As a full-time painter from 1984 Blackmore "worked mainly in Cornwall and Provence". His group appearances included Newlyn Orion and Penwith Gallery, St Ives; RA Summer Exhibition; NEAC; The Discerning Eye, at Mall Galleries; and in 1992 he was included in Artists from Cornwall at RWA. Had solo shows at Nevill Gallery, Bath, and New Academy Gallery. Of his solo there in 2004, Blackmore said: "The bottles, boxes, tin coffee pots and other objects that I paint are selected for their muted or even lack of colour. It is the light on these objects that interests me." Lived at Rinsey, near Helston, Cornwall.

Katie BLACKMORE fl. c.1910–1955 Painter in oil and watercolour who became an associate of the RBA, 1922, full member, 1925, and an associate of SWA in 1924. She was an extensive RBA exhibitor, also showing at RA, RI, RHA, Ridley Art Club, Carfax Gallery, Royal Glasgow Institute of the Fine Arts and Walker Art Gallery, Liverpool. Travels included Italy. Alfred Bell and Company published her pictures *The Mushroom Dance* and *The Enchanted Pool*. She was a Lyceum Club member who lived latterly in High Wycombe, Buckinghamshire.

Basil BLACKSHAW 1932– Painter, born in Glengormley, County Antrim, Northern Ireland, who was much influenced by Cézanne. His own work was partly autobiographical, much concerned with people, animals, places and experiences. Blackshaw always worked in a free manner, placing emphasis on the act of painting. He studied at Belfast College of Art and in Paris. Among his mixed exhibitions were Belfast Museum and Art Gallery, 1958; Four Ulster Painters, at Arnolfini Gallery, Bristol, 1965; Watergate Gallery, Washington, in America, 1974; Arts Council of Northern Ireland, 1979, Major Award; Rosc '88, Dublin, 1988; and Contemporary Artists from Ireland, at Austin/Desmond Fine Art, 1990. Blackshaw showed solo at CEMA Gallery, Belfast, in 1961. Later shows included Tom Caldwell Gallery, Belfast, from 1973, and in 1974 he had a retrospective in the city at Arts Council of Northern Ireland. Lived in Antrim.

Simon BLACKWOOD 1948– Painter who was born in Colchester, Essex. Studied at Coventry School of Art under Michael Sandle and worked for a time in the restoration department of the Ashmolean Museum. Blackwood painted at Hawick, Roxburghshire, and had a studio on the Bosporus. His great interest in light led to his being termed a Romantic Luminist. Showed in Japan and North America and had a solo show at Michael Parkin Fine Art, 1991.

Alfred BLADEN fl. c.1925–1965 Painter, sculptor and teacher, born in Oldham, Lancashire. He studied at Wolverhampton School of Art and the Royal College of Art. Was for a time attached to Derby School of Art. Showed at RA, RI, Wertheim and Storran Galleries and elsewhere and had solo shows at Wolverhampton Art Gallery and Museum and in Birmingham. The Wolverhampton gallery holds his work. Lived for a time in Derby, then in Shardlow, Derbyshire.

Peter BLAGG 1937– Versatile, innovative artist and teacher, born in Finchley, north London, married to the painter Linda Sutton. Blagg attended St Albans School of Art on a foundation course, 1954; went into the Royal Air Force for National Service in 1955, gaining early release in 1957; then completed his design diploma at St Albans. Teachers included Mary Hoad, Norman Adams, Anthony Blunt, William Scott, Anthony Fry, Carel Weight and Elisabeth Frink. He later obtained his teaching diploma and taught up to graduate level. In 1961 Blagg moved to Cornwall, and had a first solo exhibition at Newlyn Art Gallery in 1963 (a second followed at the Piccadilly Gallery), pictures of the semi-industrial landscape around Redruth. Blagg's writer friend John Branfield based his novel *In The Country* on the painter's experiences. After returning to Hertfordshire in 1964, Blagg's work became more hard-edged, showing Pop influences. Other activities included Jonathan Cape's *Jackdaw* resource series and work on an environmental design programme with Marcello Salvadori. Disenchanted with painting in the early 1970s, Blagg pioneered the application of multi-imaging (electronic media, installations, audio-visuals, live performances, and so on), devised a multimedia imaging course and founded Multivisual. This was a creative consultancy and production centre handling corporate and government presentations and involving work on the world tour of Frankie Goes to Hollywood. Blagg returned to painting in tandem with the multi-media work for rock shows, including Status Quo and Shakin' Stevens. Later exhibitions included a mixed show at Belgrave Gallery, 1996; a retrospective at Boxfield Gallery, Stevenage Arts Centre, and a further show at Stevenage Museum, both 1997.

Ernest BLAIKLEY 1885–1965 Painter in watercolour and etcher of figure studies and portraits. Born in London, he studied art at University College School, London, and the Slade School of Fine Art. He was Keeper of pictures at the Imperial War Museum from 1919 and deputy director, 1950–1. Had articles in *The Times*, *The Studio* and *John O'London's Weekly*. Exhibited RA, RBA, RP, IS and NEAC and his own Museum holds World War I drawings by him. Lived in London.

Iris BLAIN 1918– Artist and teacher, born in London, working in oil, acrylic, ceramic and etching. She studied at Regent Street Polytechnic School of Art, Royal Academy Schools and Anglo-French Art Centre, her teachers including Norman Blamey, Tom Monnington and Ruskin Spear. She practised theatre design with Tavistock Repertory Company, later becoming a professional stage and costume designer. Taught in Cheshire. Had a number of solo shows and group appearances included RA, LG, RBA, RWA, Arnolfini Gallery in Bristol, MAFA, Ben Uri Gallery and elsewhere. Was a member of Hampstead Artists' Council and Ridley Art Society. Hertfordshire County Council holds her work. In 1987 published her autobiographical *Recollections of a Jewish Childhood*. Lived in Kew, Surrey.

Graham BLAINE 1937– Watercolourist, designer and teacher, born in Birmingham, who was by profession a design and development engineer until retirement in 2000. Studied at Moseley Road School of Art, Birmingham, head teacher Harry Adams, 1950–53, and at the city's College of Arts and Crafts, principal Meredith Hawes, head of the department of industrial design Ted Harvey. For 25 years Blaine taught art evening classes. Was a member of RBSA from 1979, also showing from 1977 with RI at Mall Galleries, from 1987–91 with RWA and in the Laing Art Competition, 1992. Had commissions from Allied and Ansell's Breweries and Cadbury's: five local subjects for the firm's staff restaurant. Bristol University also holds Blaine's work. Lived in Solihull, West Midlands.

Bill BLAIR 1953– Artist who for several decades painted works based on the Irish landscape. He had a solo exhibition, Views from a Secret Beach, at Tom Caldwell Gallery, Belfast, pictures deriving from an area of coastline near Ardara in County Donegal. He was better known for his bog-land paintings. Blair had shown previously at Tom Caldwell, including the dealer's 2003 Memorial Exhibition. His other exhibitions included RUA, The Balmoral Gallery, Downpatrick Arts Centre, The Crooked House Gallery in Donegal and Queen's University, Belfast. He was born in the city and there attended Stranmillis College.

Doris V BLAIR: *see* **Doris BOURGUIGNON**

Louise BLAIR 1958– Painter, born in Kent, where she attended Canterbury College of Art, 1975–6; then Hornsey School of Art, 1976–9, and Chelsea School of Art, 1979–80. Her many group shows included Young Contemporaries at ICA, from 1977; RA Summer Exhibition, 1980; Sets for Station House Opera, Waterloo Gallery, 1982; Animals, Edward Totah Gallery, 1985; and Figure II: Naked, Aberystwyth Arts Centre and tour, 1988–9. Had a solo show at Cockpit Theatre, 1981, then a series at Nicola Jacobs Gallery from 1983. Although objects in the natural world might be the starting point for Blair's powerfully emotional works, the final pictures can be ambiguous, ghostly, virtually abstract. Contemporary Art Society holds work by Blair.

Eileen Mary BLAKE 1878– Watercolourist and black-and-white artist, born at Moseley, Birmingham. She studied at Birmingham College of Art and continued to live in Birmingham, where she belonged to leading art groups. Exhibited RBSA, SWA, ROI, RCamA and RI.

Frederick Donald BLAKE 1908–1997 Artist and designer, born in Greenock, Renfrewshire. After two years his parents moved to London, where he continued to live. Aged 13, Blake was funded by his amateur artist father to attend Camberwell School of Arts and Crafts for 18 months. At 15 went into a building trade drawing office, but for 10 years three nights a week attended such schools as Goldsmiths' College and Brixton School of Building. Became head of a drawing office, doing working drawings for swimming baths, pub fronts and cinemas; worked for a luxury bathroom maker; then in World War II drew for Ministry of Information; followed by work for the *Daily Express* and freelancing for 20 years, clients including *Reader's Digest*. Gave up commercial work to paint full-time. Was elected RI, RSMA, was president of the Wapping Group, and a member of London Sketch Club and Chelsea Arts Club. Showed in many London galleries as well as extensively abroad, being noted for his fluid, deft watercolours of ships and the sea and the use of clay-coated paper which allowed novel techniques, especially in the portrayal of textures. Had eightieth birthday show at Linda Blackstone Gallery, Pinner, in 1988.

Martin BLAKE 1955– Painter of abstracts, printmaker and teacher who studied at St Martin's School of Art, 1974–8. Was artist-in-residence at Felsted School, Essex, 1979–81, then went on to teach at Alleyn's School, Dulwich. Blake showed with London Art Schools at Air Gallery, 1978; Minories, Colchester, 1981; Bakehouse Gallery, 1982; and Gainsborough's House, Sudbury, 1983. In 1984 he had a solo show at Woodlands Art Gallery.

Michael BLAKE 1951– Artist in various media and teacher, born in Cheshire. Studied at Jacob Kramer College, Leeds, 1970–1, then Canterbury College of Art, 1971–4, taught by Geoffrey Rigden and Ian Dury, the head of painting, Tom Watt, being an important influence. He taught there, National School of Art in Dublin and on the postgraduate course at Cyprus College of Art. Blake took part in the Cyprus College show at Woodlands Art Gallery in 1983. Other exhibitions included Stockwell Depot, 1979, and Pennies Gallery, Greenwich, 1982. Had a solo show at deliART, 2000. Blake was keen on team sports, reflected in his work, which embraced landscapes and abstracts. Lived in Kent.

Naomi BLAKE 1924– Sculptor, born in Czechoslovakia, a survivor of Auschwitz concentration camp. She trained at Hornsey School of Art, 1955–60, and worked in Milan, Rome and Jerusalem, eventually being based in London. Showed extensively in Britain and abroad, including SPS from 1962; Woodstock Gallery, 1972; Magdalene Street Gallery, 1976; Embankment Gallery, 1980; Norwich Cathedral, 1987; RWA, 1989; and Chelmsford Cathedral Festival, 1991. Was a fellow of RBS. Several dozen works by her were permanently sited in public places, including North London Collegiate School, 1972; Bournemouth Synagogue, 1975; Bristol Cathedral, 1980; St Botolph's Church, Aldgate, 1985; Walsingham Parish Church, 1988; and Hospital for Sick Children, Great Ormond Street, 1990. An exhibition of domestic-scale work by Blake, held at the New Academy, 2002, included typically stylised, smooth, bronze figurative pieces and some abstracts.

Peter BLAKE 1932– Painter, creator of collage and boxes, draughtsman and teacher, born in Dartford, Kent. He attended Gravesend Technical College and School of Art junior department 1946–9, then Gravesend School of Art, 1949–51. After National Service in Royal Air Force went to Royal College of Art, 1953–6, where he won a first-class diploma. A Leverhulme Research Award enabled him to study popular art on the continent in several countries, 1956–7. He taught at St Martin's, Harrow and Walthamstow Schools of Art in the early 1960s, then Royal College of Art, 1964–76. In 1961 he was featured in a BBC Monitor programme *Pop Goes the Easel*. By then he was associated with art concerned with popular images: picture postcards, children's games and magazine covers. A year after he won a junior prize at the John Moores Liverpool Exhibition, in 1961, he had a one-man show at the Portal Gallery. By 1969 he was having a retrospective show at the City Art Gallery, Bristol; others followed in the early 1970s on the continent; his retrospective at the Tate Gallery in 1983, which travelled to Hanover, was the most successful ever there for a living artist; there were more retrospectives at Galerie Claude Bernard, Paris, 1984, and Nishimura Gallery, Tokyo, 1988. In 1996–7 Blake had his Now We Are 64 show at the National Gallery, having in 1994 been appointed its third associate artist. In 2000, Blake selected the exhibition About Collage at Tate Liverpool. His 26 Alphabet screenprints were shown at the Michael Tippett Centre, Bath, 2001–2; in 2002 he had a show at Harley Gallery, Welbeck; and in 2003 The London Institute Gallery displayed 40 years of commissioned work for advertising and design, also his sculpture. In 2002, Blake was knighted in the Queen's Birthday Honours and was also appointed professor of drawing at the Royal Academy Schools. In 2005, Blake resigned as an Academician following Brendan Neiland's expulsion, not wanting, according to *The Times*, "to be part of a group that would do that to someone." Blake also designed record covers and pop concert posters. Strongly associated with the Swinging Sixties, his art mixes fantasy with reality and associative references. Another aspect of his work was his founder-membership of the Brotherhood of Ruralists in 1975. Elected RA in 1981. Tate Gallery, Arts Council, the Victoria & Albert Museum and the Museum of Modern Art, New York, hold his work. Blake was married for a time to the artist Jann Haworth, then to Chrissy Wilson. Lived in London.

Quentin BLAKE 1932– Painter, illustrator and teacher, born in Sidcup, Kent, adept at pen, ink and watercolour work. He was educated at Cambridge University, attending part-time life classes at Chelsea School of Art. From 1957 was a freelance. Was tutor in illustration at Royal College of Art, 1965–78, head of illustration department from 1978, and was made senior fellow, 1988. Exhibitions of his watercolours were held from 1972 at Workshop Gallery, and he had a retrospective at National Theatre, 1983. Blake was noted for his deft, witty book illustrations. Among the many dozens of volumes illustrated were works by Patrick Campbell, Lewis Carroll, Roald Dahl, Michael Rosen and Evelyn Waugh. His own book *Mister Magnolia* won the Kate Greenaway Medal in 1980. He also drew for magazines such as *Punch* and *The Spectator* and for the BBC *Jackanory* television programme. In *Words and Pictures*, 2000, Blake reviewed and illustrated his drawing career. There was a solo show at Chris Beetles Ltd, 2002; a retrospective at Somerset House, 2003–4; and in 2004 Dulwich Picture Gallery held Quentin Blake at Christmas. Lived in London.

Tim BLAKE 1970– Figurative artist who studied at Manchester Metropolitan University and whose awards included commendations from the International Guild of Artists and Lloyds Insurance. Was a member of the National Acrylic Painters Association, National Artists Association and Artist & Designers Network. Clients included Splendid Isolation, Big Fish Recording Studios and Viscount Aldridge. Group shows included *Spectator* Art Award, Fruitmarket Gallery, Edinburgh, and Sotheby's, 1995; Candid Arts, 1997; and Davies & Tooth, Art2000, 2000. Later solo shows included BBC Television Centre, 1999; Grey Space, Great Portland Street, 2000; and Big City Attitude, Catto Contemporary, 2003. There, Blake's interest in street chic and urban glamour was apparent in the often large, richly coloured and hard-edged works.

Gerard BLAKELEY 1922– Painter who gained his diploma from the Camberwell School of Arts and Crafts in 1949, eventually settling in St Ives, Cornwall. He curated the exhibition Camberwell's Evolution & Revolution at Candid Arts Trust in 2005. His oils on canvas board shown there, Guilt, of 1992, and Violence, of 1998–9, were abstracts with strong dynamic and angular elements. Blakeley termed himself an Outsider painter who, in his eighties, was still "seeking to discover a personal language after many career disturbances whose guidelines gradually resolved into a concept of: Freedom within strict boundaries". Blakeley's solo exhibitions were at Dolcoath Gallery, 1964; Orion Gallery, 1978; Theatre Workshop, Edinburgh, 1986; Camborne School of Mines, 1995; Mariner Gallery in St Ives, Gallery 47 and Chessels Gallery, University of Edinburgh, all 1997; The Bakehouse Gallery, Penzance, 1999; and Clapham Arts Centre, 2000.

John BLAKELEY 1946– Sculptor and teacher, born in Blackpool, Lancashire. He studied at the local School of Art, 1962–5, St Martin's School of Art, 1965–6, and City & Guilds of London Art School, 1966–70, with periods in Greece and Italy. Blakeley was a member of SPS and an associate of RBS and was noted for his work in stone and clay. Showed at Guildhall, Royal Exchange, Mall Galleries, and Harris Museum and Art Gallery in Preston. Taught at Sir John Cass College. Lived in Welwyn Garden City, Hertfordshire.

Zelma BLAKELY 1927–1978 Printmaker, illustrator and teacher, born in London, was married to the artist Keith Mackenzie. She studied at Kingston School of Art, 1939–42, her teachers including Wilfred Fairclough, then at Slade School of Fine Art, 1945–8, with William Coldstream, Norman Janes and John Buckland Wright. She went on to teach at Heatherley's School of Fine Art and was elected a member of RE in 1966. Among books illustrated were André Simon's *English Fare and French Wines*, 1958, and the *Reader's Digest Bedside Book of Nature*, 1959. Lived at Pin Mill, Suffolk, where she was a member of the sailing club.

Michael BLAKER 1928– Painter, printmaker and writer on art, born in Hove, Sussex, studying at Brighton School of Art. Was elected RE in 1975 and RWA in 1987, also showing at RA and RP. Contributed to art magazines, edited RE's *Journal* and published several books, including *The Autobiography of a Painter-Etcher*, 1986, the year after he founded Beresford House Press. Victoria & Albert Museum holds his work. Lived in Rochester, Kent.

Oswell BLAKESTON 1907–1985 Painter, draughtsman, writer, lecturer and film maker. (His real name was Henry Hasslacher, the family of Austrian origin, connected with the Deinhard and Company wine importing business. The name Oswell was derived from that of the writer *Os*bert Sit*well*. The mother's surname was Blak*i*ston, which he modified.) Blakeston ran away from a Roman Catholic school and a bourgeois home in 1923. He became conjuror's assistant, a cinema organist and then a clapper boy with David Lean at Gaumont film studios. Began writing film criticism and became associate editor of the influential magazine *Close Up*. With Francis Bruguiere he pioneered abstract films in Britain. Blakeston was also a novelist, poet and writer of film scripts, plays and travel books. His collaborator and companion of many years, Max Chapman, noted Blakeston's "quick eye for the bizarre and the outrageous". A large selection of Blakeston's books was shown at Haringey Central Library, 1980, previous to acquisition by Texas University. Blakeston was a witty artist and illustrator. Almost 100 mixed shows included Leicester and Mercury Galleries, and he had over 40 solo exhibitions, including Drian and Grabowski Galleries, New Vision Centre and Nicholas Treadwell Gallery, Croydon. In 1981 he shared a show with Chapman at Middlesbrough Art Gallery and in 1986 there was a memorial show at Camden Arts Centre. Victoria & Albert Museum, Ulster Museum in Belfast and the national galleries of Finland, Poland and Portugal hold examples. Lived in London.

Norman BLAMEY 1914–2000 Painter, draughtsman, muralist and teacher, born in London, where he continued to work. He studied at Regent Street Polytechnic School of Art, 1931–7, his teachers including Harry Watson and A R Middleton Todd. From 1936–7 did a teacher training course at London University Institute of Education. Taught at Regent Street Polytechnic, 1938–40 and 1946–63, with a break for Army and camouflage service in Middle East and North Africa. From 1963–79 was senior lecturer at Chelsea School of Art, from 1975 onwards teaching at Royal Academy Schools. Was elected RA, 1975, having been elected ROI in 1952 and Hon. ROI in 1974. Also showed with RHA, RBA, NEAC and elsewhere. Among his awards were Roy Miles Award at RA Summer Exhibition, 1978; and Charles Wollaston Award at same venue, 1984. Commissions included 1956 mural for Anglican Church of St Luke, Leagrave. Blamey was a consummate draughtsman whose work had three main themes: family, ecclesiastical pictures and commissioned portraits. He aspired to "stillness and permanence" in his work. Touring retrospective show was based on Norwich Gallery, 1992–3. Tate Gallery holds Blamey's work.

Edmund BLAMPIED 1886–1966 Landscape and figure painter in oil, watercolour and wash; etcher and lithographer. Born in Jersey, he studied art under Philip Connard and at the London County Council Bolt Court Art School, 1905–13. Exhibited at RA, Fine Art Society, RBA, RE, RSW, RHA, Paris Salon and at other venues. Won a gold medal for lithography at the Paris International Exhibition in 1925. Blampied was a noted etcher, with a fine, swirling line. He designed Jersey occupation stamps and a Jersey liberation stamp in connection with World War II. His work is in a number of British and foreign collections. Lived at Beaumont, Jersey.

Emily Beatrice BLAND 1864–1951 Painter, especially of flowers in oil, studied at Lincoln School of Art, then at the Slade School of Fine Art under Henry Tonks and Fred Brown, 1892–4. Exhibited RA, NEAC, Fine Art Society, Goupil Gallery, Ridley Art Club, SWA and elsewhere. Chantrey Bequest bought her Striped Camellias and Yachts at Lymington, both now in the Tate Gallery. Other British and some overseas galleries hold her work. A prolific painter, she had her first one-man show at the Leicester Galleries in 1922. Lived in London.

Sydney Frances Josephine BLAND 1883– Painter in tempera and watercolour, born in York, she studied art at Heatherley's School of Fine Art, 1920–2, under Henry Massey, at Goldsmiths' College School of Art, 1922–3, with Harold Speed, and privately, including time with Bernard Adams. Exhibited SWA, RP, RI and had one-man exhibitions. Produced a number of posters for industry. Lived in

Newlyn, Cornwall, and was a member of both the Newlyn and St Ives Societies of Artists.

Olga BLANDFORD LEWIS 1917–2002 Botanical artist noted for the precision and versatility of her work, much of which was published on greetings cards. She was born in Romford, Essex, as Olga Polychroniadis, daughter of a naval architect who had left Athens to practise in England. Her talent for art became apparent at Romford Grammar School for Girls. In 1938 Olga decided to become a Red Cross nurse, serving during World War II at Harold Wood Hospital. After the war she worked as a medical artist and for the pharmaceutical firm May & Baker, slides of her illustrations being used for medical conferences. In 1951, she married Ronald Blandford Lewis, a shipping agent, becoming a botanical artist when he died in 1978. She exhibited at the Linnaean Society, International Flower Show at Hampton Court, RI and was a founder-member of the Society of Botanical Artists, being its vice-president, 1987–97. Between 1979–00, Blandford Lewis won almost 20 medals at the Royal Horticultural Shows. Its Lindley Library, Royal Botanical Gardens at Kew and Natural History Museum hold examples.

John BLANDY 1951– Painter, draughtsman and performance artist, born in Suffolk, educated at Charterhouse. He attended Norwich School of Art, 1970, gained his fine art diploma at St Martin's School of Art, 1973, and his master's from Royal College of Art, 1976. In 1973, showed at Gallery House with grant from Arts Council; in 1974 at Art Meeting Place, with grants from Arts Council and Greater London Arts Association; in 1979 taking part in group shows with London Calling, again aided by Arts Council. Among his many further group exhibitions were Phoenix Gallery, Lavenham, 1985; Moghul India, 1989, one of many mixed and solo appearances at Francis Kyle Gallery; Mozart, Lincoln Center, New York, America; and Plane Tree, Willesden Gallery, 1996. Among Blandy's extensive solo shows was Following Trees, Elgin, 2002, and one at the Tricycle Gallery, 2003, which comprised a sequence of works from his project Following a Lime Tree, begun in 1997. In 2005, his exhibition Brush with Time, at The Dissenter Gallery, featured paintings of a short section of river near Oxford. Blandy painted extensively on the continent and the Middle East, in 1989 being sponsored by the Government of India Tourist Office to paint Moghul and Rajput sites, and in 1998 was commissioned by the Arab League to record historic sites in the Holy Land. Lived in London.

John Peter BLANDY 1927– Urological surgeon, author and recreational artist, born in Calcutta, India, father of the artist Kitty Blandy. Professor Blandy was professor of urology at The Royal London and St Peter's Hospitals, was at one time vice-president of The Royal College of Surgeons and was the author of many surgical textbooks. He studied with the sculptor Ivan Mitford Barberton in Cape Town, South Africa, in 1943. Blandy was president of the Medical Art Society and a member of the London Sketch Club, with whom he showed. The Royal College of Surgeons and The Royal London Hospital hold his work. Lived in London.

Kitty BLANDY 1966– Artist with no formal accredited training, born in London, whose father, the urological surgeon Professor John Peter Blandy, was a keen amateur artist. Kitty was a board member of the Malaspina Printmakers' Society, 1988–90, and Artropolis 2001, 2000–1, and a member of the Printmakers' Council. In 1990, she was awarded an Elizabeth Greenshields Foundation Grant. Took part in many group exhibitions, including 13th International Print Exhibition, Kanagawa, Japan, 1987; Open Exhibition, RE, Bankside Gallery, 1989; Graffik 97, North Lincolnshire Museum and Art Gallery, Scunthorpe (work commended), 1997; and National Print Exhibition, Mall Galleries, 2002. Solo shows included Anna-Mei Chadwick, from 1993; Lumley Cazalet, 1995; and Elissa Cristall Gallery, Vancouver, Canada, where she lived, from 2001. National Portrait Gallery holds Blandy's bronze of the athlete Sally Gunnell; Chelsea and Westminster Hospital, Royal London Hospital, the Museum of Archaeology, in Valletta, Malta, and the Ukrainian Independent Museum of Contemporary Art, Lviv, also hold her work.

Frances BLANE 1954– Painter and draughtsman, born and lived in London, who studied at the Byam Shaw School of Painting and Drawing, 1988–91, and Slade School of Fine Art, 1991–3. She won the Graham Hamilton Drawing Prize in 1991; a residency at Djerassi Artists' Foundation, Woodside, California, America, 1998; and an award at Cheltenham & Gloucester Open Drawing Show, 1999. Exhibitions included Ben Uri Gallery from 1991; Into the Nineties, Mall Galleries, 1993; Café Gallery, 1994; and In the Looking Glass, Usher Gallery, Lincoln, and tour, from 1996. This included Blane's Expressionistic Self-Portrait, of 1993. Mouths and heads were key features of her work, as "I am a very oral person." Had a solo show at Curwen Gallery, 1995, others in 1997 at 231 St John Street and Shillam and Smith. London School of Economics and Usher Gallery hold examples.

Jeremy Nicholas BLANK 1957– Painter, artist in multimedia, performance, film and video, and teacher, born in Hampton Court, Middlesex. He studied at Colchester School of Art for foundation studies, 1976–8, gaining Prix de Rome/Munnings Award; obtained an honours degree in fine art painting from Chelsea School of Art, 1978–81, teachers including Ken Kiff, Stephen Buckley and Anne Rees-Mogg; and attended Colchester Filmmakers Workshop between 1983–5, teaching life drawing at The Minories, Colchester, 1984–6. Blank was a member of the National Society for Education in Art & Design. He held a number of residencies, including the Eastern Arts Art in School Scheme, 1988. Among Blank's prizes was a first national prize for painting at New Contemporaries, ICA, 1981, and he was a John Moores Liverpool Exhibition prizewinner in 1987. Blank began making experimental work with electronic media in the early 1980s and showed in international film festivals. In Freezeframe at Lamont Gallery, 1996, Blank showed Flare, a collage of film in which he focused on its ephemeral nature by burning and melting it down. Other mixed performances, events and exhibitions included Turin International Film Festival, 1984; Video Danse Internationale, Paris, 1992; and Ritzy Cinema, 1996, paintings and drawings. Had a solo show at Minories, 1983, and at Ganz Gallery, 1991. Blank said that his main works were his neo-classical ones, 1979–84; the Head painting series, 1986–91; and video works, 1991–6. Colchester Institute, Essex University, University of Texas, Waltham Cross Museum, International Video Dance in

Austria and Danse Video, Paris, hold his works. Lived in London.

Slavek BLATTON: *see* **Slavomir Stanislas BLATTON**

Slavomir Stanislas BLATTON 1943– Artist and teacher, born in Limanowa, Poland, also known as Slavek Blatton. His original name was Slawomir Stanislaw Szaybo, and he worked for a time as a graphic designer as Roslaw Szaybo. He was initially educated in Warsaw where he attended the Academy of Fine Arts, 1962–9. Gained a Ministry of Culture Scholarship. In 1970 settled in London, where he taught etching at the Working Men's College. Exhibited in London and the provinces and was included in Berry Street Open Studios Exhibition, 1984. Shared a show with Manka Dowling at Fusion Post-Production, 1999. Lived in London.

Susannah BLAXILL 1954– Botanical watercolourist and draughtsman, born in New South Wales, Australia, who began painting full-time in 1985 after five years' study at University of East Anglia, Norwich. Her draughtsmanship was meticulous, and she used a fine brush and many layers of watercolour to achieve an intense, brilliant image. Exhibition at Royal Horticultural Society, Chelsea Flower Show and Society of Botanical Artists, of which she became a member in 1989. Showed solo at Spink & Son, 1994.

Martin BLAZEY 1975– Versatile artist working in a wide range of media who took part in Art Celebrates Life, Lauderdale House, 2002. The previous year he had moved to Falmouth, Cornwall. While studying for his master's in contemporary visual arts at Falmouth College of Art, in 2002, Blazey was working with digital media, "mostly using film as a means of describing stories of liminal spaces in time and memory." The film preoccupation arose from print works, some of which took a prize at The Apthorp Award for Young Artists in 2001. Among previous mixed shows were Sites, Staffordshire University, 1998. Solo exhibitions included Entropy, The Bull Theatre Gallery, High Barnet, 1999.

Susanna BLECH 1959– Artist and teacher, born in London, who studied at Wimbledon School of Art and at Brighton Polytechnic, gaining an honours degree in painting in 1982. Taught at Blackheath School of Art and Merton Adult College, with a private teaching practice in Wimbledon. Worked both figuratively and abstract, with a special interest in Greek mythology and horses. Showed at Camden Arts Centre and Kingston Hill Art Gallery and was included in People and Places at Gagliardi Gallery, 1993.

Christopher BLEDOV 1957– Painter and teacher, born in Staffordshire, who lived in Nigeria, 1961–3. After attending Hereford College of Art, 1976, taught part-time there, then attended Slade School of Fine Art, 1977–82, with film studies at University College, 1980–1. He won the Sir William Coldstream Prize in 1978, in 1982 gaining the Robert Ross Prize and a Boise Travelling Scholarship. The Slade holds his work. Group exhibitions included Northburgh Gallery, 1981; LG, 1982; Sandford Gallery, 1983; and Berry Street Open Studios, 1984. Elisabeth Gallery gave him a solo show in 1983.

Sarah BLEE 1962– Artist who graduated with honours in fine art from Birmingham Polytechnic, 1983–6, studying for her master's from the Royal College of Art, 1989–91. Mixed shows included Leicester Education Authority Exhibition, 1987, and Art and Nature, Flaxman Gallery, and East End Studios, at Angel Studios, both 1989. She had a solo show at 50-52 Rivington Street in 1988.

Sally BLENKINSOP 1939– Painter and printmaker who began her own work after being a film director for BBC television. She studied at West Surrey College of Art and Design, 1986–7, and the City and Guilds of London School of Art, 1987–90. Group shows included The Discerning Eye, Mall Galleries, from 1991, and NEAC and Orleans House Gallery, Twickenham, both 1996. Had a solo show at Parkshot Centre, Richmond, Surrey, 1993. Sir Brinsley Ford owned her work.

Edith BLENKIRON 1904–1992 Painter, notable as a floral illustrator, born in Northumberland. She studied at Goldsmiths' College School of Art and married the artist Rowland Hilder in 1929. Showed at RA and assisted Hilder with *Wildflowers of the Countryside*, a popular series completed for Shell in the mid-1950s. Their son was the artist Anthony Flemming. Lived in Greenwich, southeast London.

Ernst M BLENSDORF 1896–1976 Sculptor in wood, clay and cement, born in Denmark and studied widely in Europe. Exhibited UA, RBA, RSA, RCamA, Leicester Galleries and Wadham College, Oxford, plus one-man shows at the Cambridge Building Centre and in London. The French publication *La Revue Moderne* featured his work on several occasions. Lived in Bruton, Somerset.

Witold John BLESKY 1934–2000 Sculptor and painter, born in Poland, of American nationality, who was educated in Poland, England and America at San Francisco State College. He showed at Marjorie Parr Gallery, with Free Painters and Sculptors of which he was a member at Loggia Gallery, Round House Gallery, Paris Salon and elsewhere. Private collections in Britain and America held his works. Lived in Walderslade, Kent.

Maurice BLIK 1939– Sculptor and teacher, born in Netherlands. As a Jew he spent three years in Belsen concentration camp, in Germany, in World War II. Moved to Britain with his mother and attended Hornsey College of Art, 1956–60. From 1967–8 was at University of London Institute of Education, gaining a teaching certificate with distinction. Participated in many group exhibitions, including Four Sculptors at Heal's Art Gallery, 1978; Wapping Artists, 1984; RA Summer Exhibition from 1986; Stamford Sculpture Park, Stamford, Connecticut, 1988; RBS at RWA Gallery, Bristol, 1989; and The Sculpture Project, Ardingly, Sussex, 1990. Took part in Sculpture at Canterbury, 1991. Solo exhibitions included Ben Uri Gallery, 1980; Alwin Gallery, 1985; sponsored exhibition with support from Arts Council and Whitechapel Art Gallery, 1989, Blains Fine Art, 1999; and The Chambers Gallery, 2005. Blik produced much commissioned work, including sculptures for East India Dock and London Docklands Development Corporation, 1991. He was principal lecturer in fine art at Middlesex Polytechnic. Lived in London.

Douglas Percy BLISS 1900–1984 Painter, wood engraver, writer and teacher, born in Karachi, who attended Edinburgh University, graduating with a master's degree in 1922. Then studied painting at Royal College of Art under William Rothenstein and wood engraving with Sir Frank Short as a postgraduate during 1922–4. The several strands of Bliss's versatile career then began to unwind. In 1927 he shared a show at the St George's Gallery with Edward Bawden and Eric Ravilious, artists with whom he had a strong affinity. Also showed at RA, SWE and NEAC and had one-man exhibitions with Reid and Lefevre. In the 1930s Bliss taught at Hornsey and Blackheath Schools of Art, just after World War II – during which he served in the Royal Air Force – at Harrow School of Art, then from 1946–64 was the influential director of Glasgow School of Art. In the 1920s Bliss had laid the foundations of his reputation as a writer by acting as London art critic of *The Scotsman* newspaper and publishing, in 1928, his *A History of Wood Engraving*; this was followed over the years by many learned essays and in 1979 his monograph *Edward Bawden*. Bliss, who illustrated many books, was a fine wood engraver; his black-and-white work has tended to overshadow his achievement as a painter. He was married to the portrait painter Phyllis Dodd and lived mainly in Glasgow. There was a watercolour show at Abbott and Holder in 1999.

Gunther BLOCH 1916– Sculptor in various materials and teacher, born in Germany. He studied art there as well as at Leeds College of Art and Regent Street Polytechnic School of Art. His work appeared in the Britain Can Make It exhibition as well as at Cooling, Ben Uri and Berkeley Galleries and in the provinces. Lived in London, where he taught in several schools.

Martin BLOCH 1883–1954 Painter and draughtsman in many media, born in Neisse, Silesia. Initially studied music and architecture. Then opted for art, studying in Munich and Berlin, notably with Lovis Corinth. First one-man show at Paul Cassirer Gallery, Berlin, 1911. Bloch then continued his art education mainly solo for some years in France, Spain and Italy. By 1920 he was able to have a retrospective at the Cassirer Gallery. Until 1933, when he left Germany for England, spending a year on the way in Denmark, Bloch associated with the Expressionists, for 10 years running an art school. Expressionism left an indelible mark on his style and palette even after he settled in Britain, whose citizenship he took in 1947. In Britain Bloch painted mainly in London, Dorset and Wales, although after World War II he was to travel widely in America and Canada, teaching for a time in Minneapolis. For three years before World War II he had run an art school in Britain with Roy de Maistre. Bloch exhibited widely internationally and in Britain, including LG, AIA, Ben Uri Gallery, Leicester Galleries and RA. Memorial exhibitions at Beaux Arts Gallery, 1955, Arts Council, London, and touring, 1957, Kaplan Gallery, 1959, and Ben Uri Gallery, 1963. Work in many galleries, including Tate Gallery. Lived in London.

Gwilym John BLOCKLEY 1921–2002 Painter, teacher and writer, born in Knighton, Radnorshire. Blockley left school at 13 and, at his parents' insistence, served an engineering apprenticeship, after a number of jobs joining the United Kingdom Atomic Engineering Authority in 1952. Spent his spare time painting and, after a successful solo show in 1965, in 1974 began painting full-time, becoming known for rugged landscapes using an ever-developing technique. Was a member of the RI, serving on its council; PS, which he helped to revive, twice serving as its president; NEAC and RWA; also showing at RA and in the provinces. Pitman published his watercolour painting course as well as his book *The Challenge of Watercolour*, and he ran private classes. Among Blockley's several other books was *A Personal Record*, an illustrated acount of a year in his life. His daughter Ann was also an artist. The John Blockley Gallery was at Stow-on-the-Wold, Gloucestershire.

Freda BLOIS 1880–1962 Painter. Lady Blois studied art in Florence. She went on to exhibit with the RA, RBA, NEAC, SWA and the Reading Guild of Artists.

Giles BLOMFIELD 1925– Architect and sculptor, born in Penzance, Cornwall, who settled in Truro. His paternal grandfather was the architect Sir Reginald Blomfield. Studied at Bartlett School of Architecture with Albert Richardson and Hector Corfiato, and at École des Beaux-Arts, Paris, with Eugene Beaudouin. He won the Donaldson Medal, 1954, and RIBA Bronze Medal, 1965. After being attached to a series of architectural practices from 1954, from 1974–87 ran his own, Blomfield Cartlidge, Bayly, in Truro. Blomfield's striking sculpture The Altar of the Sword's Point is in Canterbury Cathedral.

Kathleen BLOMFIELD: *see* **Kathleen HYNDMAN**

Leslie BLOMFIELD 1920– Painter and architect, born in London, from a long line of architects including Sir Reginald Blomfield. Leslie Blomfield worked as an architect for about 30 years, mostly abroad. He settled in the York area in 1984 and practised as a self-taught watercolourist, establishing his reputation by painting a series of cathedrals and churches. His pictures were reproduced as prints by the National Trust and York Civic Trust and in 1990 the Yorkshire Wildlife Trust commissioned him to paint four nature reserves it administered. Blomfield's work was included in Images of the Yorkshire Landscape, organised by Sheeran Lock at Leeds Civic Hall, 1991.

Maxwell BLOND 1943– Painter and printmaker, born in St Annes, Lancashire. He studied at Bath Academy of Art, Corsham, under Howard Hodgkin, and Slade School of Fine Art with Patrick George, leaving in 1965. Blond used a strident, colourful palette, producing pictures with rich imagery. Showed in many mixed exhibitions, including LG, and had solo exhibitions at his brother Jonathan's Allerton Gallery, Liverpool, and in London at Blond Fine Art. Lived in Hoylake, Cheshire.

Paul BLOOMER 1966– Painter and printmaker, born in Dudley, Worcestershire, whose work could have a strong imaginative quality, using an unusual, rich palette, as in his oil Voices, at Royal Over-Seas League Open, 1994. He studied at Stourbridge College of Art, Nottingham Polytechnic and the Royal Academy Schools. Among prizes won were the Arthur Hacker Prize and Hennington Award, both 1992; Dudley Art Gallery Purchase Prize, 1993 (it and Walsall Art Gallery hold Bloomer's work); and the John Purcell Print Prize and Joseph Webb ARE Commemorative Fund Award, both 1994. Had a solo show at The Weathered Wall Gallery, Seattle, America, 1993.

Sandra BLOW 1925–2006 Abstract painter who also used materials such as polyethylene and willow cane to construct pictures. She was born in London, where she continued to live, also having a studio in St Ives, Cornwall. She studied at St Martin's School of Art, 1941–6, under Ruskin Spear, at the Royal Academy Schools, 1946–7, and at the Academy of Fine Arts in Rome, 1947–8. In the late 1940s she travelled in Spain and France. Had first one-man show at Gimpel Fils in 1951, worked in Cornwall, 1957–8, then from 1960 taught at Royal College of Art. Participated in many group exhibitions in Britain and abroad, including John Moores Liverpool Exhibition, 1961, where she won a second prize for painting, as she did in 1965; Camden Arts Centre, 1969, English Landscape in the 20th Century; in 1977 British Painting 1952–1957, at RA, to which she was elected in 1978; in 1994 RA gave her a retrospective; in 2000 Highgate Fine Art showed 30 works from the previous five years; and in 2001–2 Tate St Ives highlighted key moments from her career from the 1950s. Belgrave Gallery, St Ives, showed Paintings & Collages in 2005. Blow has been said to be concerned pre-eminently with the problems of pure painting: balance and proportion, tension and scale. Tate Gallery holds her work.

William James BLOYE 1890–1975 Sculptor and teacher, born in Cornwall, but moved to Birmingham in mid-1890s. Bloye studied at Birmingham School of Art, 1904–9, gaining the William Kenrick Scholarship for 1905–6; from 1910 until World War I began Bloye studied sculpture at Royal Academy Schools. After a couple of years teaching modelling part-time in Birmingham art schools, in 1919 Bloye joined Birmingham School of Art, where he became head of sculpture until his retirement in 1956. Early in 1920s Bloye studied for short periods with Eric Gill, which had a lasting impression on his work. By the mid-1920s Bloye had a busy studio of his own in Birmingham, employing assistants trained by him at the School of Art. He carried out a large amount of civic sculpture in Birmingham and carved the Dudley, Worcestershire, war memorial and reliefs on its town hall buildings. After retirement in Solihull Bloye continued to handle his own commissions. Elected fellow of RBS in 1938. Died in Arezzo, Italy.

Judith BLUCK 1936– Artist, born in London, who progressed through various media to sculpture and who worked on a large scale in a number of materials. She revived the use of pressed brick, her most important work being The Legend of the Iron Gates, an 80-foot relief commissioned by Sainsbury's for a supermarket in Wilmslow. This won the Otto Beit Medal of the RBS, of which she was a fellow. Was also a brother of Art Workers' Guild and a member of SPS. Bluck also held bronze and silver medals from the Société des Artistes Français. Among other works by Bluck are a fountain group of Otters, for Carlisle City Council, at The Lanes, where her Jimmy Dyer mural is sited; a 28-foot Crucible Fountain at Moorfoot, Sheffield; and five new designs of Royal Insignia for Crown Court and prison sites. Bluck's Sheep, in bronze, were sited in Fenny Stratford, funded by the Milton Keynes Foundation. Morris Singer Foundry cast her work. Lived in Hanlith, Skipton, Yorkshire.

Helaine BLUMENFELD 1943– Sculptor who after working in a variety of materials latterly concentrated on marble while living in Tuscany, Italy. As well as drawing on classical mythology for her subjects, she sought "through sculpture to discover a new mythology." Having obtained her philosophy doctorate in 1963, Blumenfeld studied with the Russian-born sculptor Ossip Zadkine in Paris, moving to England in 1969, two years after he died. In 1980, she was made the only American member of the Arts Council's visual arts panel. She was also a member of RBS. Completed a number of public commissions in Britain, a fine example being the stylised bronze Two Sides of a Woman, 1985, commissioned by Coventry City Council and sited outside the Belgrade Theatre in the city centre.

Alfred Richard BLUNDELL 1883–1968 Painter, printmaker and glass engraver, born in Bury St Edmunds, Suffolk. After education there he attended the Slade School of Fine Art, 1913, following a period as a railway clerk. Blundell painted a large number of architectural subjects in Britain and on the continent, showing at RA, NEAC, Alpine Club Gallery and extensively in the provinces. Fitzwilliam Museum in Cambridge, other provincial museums and the Luxembourg, Paris, hold his work. Lived in Icklingham, Suffolk, and for many years at Cavenham Mill, Bury St Edmunds.

Margaret Leah BLUNDELL 1907– Mural painter, commercial artist and printmaker, born at Wallasey, Cheshire. After attending Cheltenham Ladies' College she studied at Liverpool School of Art with Frederick Carter and George Marples, 1925. Exhibited Walker Art Gallery, Liverpool, SWE and RBA. She carried out a number of murals in London and Blackpool in hotels and shops and drew for women's magazines and *Radio Times*. Lived at Rhydwyn, near Holyhead, Anglesey.

Martyn BLUNDELL 1955– Artist and teacher who attended Southport College of Art, 1977–8, and Loughborough College of Art and Design, 1978–81. Taught part-time at Bootle Technical College. Showed in northwest of England, notably in Merseyside Artists 3, Walker Art Gallery and tour, 1986–7.

Ferdinand Victor BLUNDSTONE 1882–1951 Sculptor, born in Switzerland, who studied at the South London Technical Art School and then the Royal Academy Schools, winning a gold medal and travelling studentship and Landseer Scholarship, also studying in Egypt, Greece, Italy and France. In 1925 gained a Silver Medal, Paris Exhibition. Showed extensively at RA, also RSA and Royal Glasgow Institute of the Fine Arts. Among his works is the Plimsoll Memorial on London's Victoria Embankment. Blundstone was notable for a number of memorials after World War I for the Prudential Assurance Company, at Stalybridge, Folkestone and at its Holborn offices. There, after World War II, Blundstone added memorial plaques. He was a fellow of RBS and his works The Elf and Atalanta are illustrated in the volume *RBS: Modern British Sculpture*, published 1939. Lived in London and West Drayton, Middlesex.

James BLUNDUN 1957– Artist who attended Chelsea School of Art, 1976–7, and Canterbury College of Art, 1977–80. Exhibitions included Stowells Trophy, RA, 1980; Festival Theatre, Malvern, 1981; Unit 7, 1984; Diorama, 1987; and East End Open Studios, at Carpenter's Road, 1989.

Peter Alfred BLUNSDEN 1949– Abstract sculptor in steel, born in Norwich, Norfolk, who studied at the School of Art there, 1984–8, graduating with honours in fine art sculpture. His mixed exhibitions included Whitworth Young Contemporaries, Whitworth Art Gallery, Manchester, 1987; L'École Regional des Beaux-Arts, Rouen, 1988; Wingfield College Outdoor Exhibition, Suffolk, and Open Studio Exhibition, Hardingham, Norfolk, both 1992. His workshop involvements included Hardingham Sculpture Workshop, 1990, and Triangle Workshop, New York State, 1992. Philip and Muriel Berman Collection, America, holds his work. Had a studio at Hardingham and lived in Reepham, Norfolk.

Wilfrid BLUNT 1901–1987 Artist, teacher, writer and curator, born in Ham, Surrey. His brother was the art historian and spy Anthony Blunt. Began to paint in childhood. Left Oxford University after two terms and studied in Paris at the Atelier Moderne under Othon Friesz and at the Académie de la Grande Chaumière, Paris, where he had his first one-man show. Entered Royal Academy engraving school in 1922, where his teachers included Frank Short, and worked under Leon Underwood in his studio. Taught at Haileybury for 15 years, interrupted by a period studying singing in Germany and Italy; he sang professionally for a while. Became art master at Eton College, 1938–59, then curator of the Watts Gallery, Compton, Surrey. Showed in England and at Paris Salon. Wrote about two dozen books, including a witty, entertaining autobiography *Married to a Single Life*, 1983, and *Slow on the Feather*, 1986.

Robert Henderson BLYTH 1919–1970 Landscape and figure painter in oil, gouache and watercolour. Born in Glasgow, Blyth studied art under Forrester Wilson at Glasgow School of Art, 1934–9, and under James Cowie at Patrick Allan-Fraser School of Art, Hospitalfield, Arbroath, 1938. He became head of drawing and painting at Gray's School of Art, Aberdeen. Showed widely, including Royal Glasgow Institute of the Fine Arts, RSA, RSW and SSA. The Ministry of Works, Dundee City Art Gallery and Dunbartonshire County Council bought his work, which often has a strongly romantic flavour. Memorial exhibition was held at Aberdeen Art Gallery, 1972. Lived in Aberdeen.

Francis BOAG 1948– Painter and teacher, born in Dundee, Angus, working in a wide range of media, producing colourful landscapes, mostly of northeast Scotland. Boag attended Duncan of Jordanstone College of Art, Dundee, 1965–9, and Gray's School of Art, Aberdeen, 1998–9, obtaining his diploma and master's degree in fine art. He was head of art at Aberdeen Grammar School. Exhibited widely in Scottish and London galleries from 1968, with a solo show entitled joie de vivre at Eduardo Allessandro Studios, Broughty Ferry, Dundee, 2003. Several corporate collections hold examples. His pictures were published as limited-edition prints and silkscreens.

Robert Cresswell BOAK 1875–1949 Painter, printmaker and teacher who was married to the artist Margaret Cooper. Born in Letterkenny, Donegal, he was educated in the north of Ireland and Scotland, then attended Londonderry School of Art, Glasgow School of Art, the Royal College of Art as well as studying in France and Italy. During the period 1900–17 he taught at several art schools in England and Wales. Exhibited RA, RCamA, RHA and provinces, and had several one man shows. Lived in London.

Lynette BOAKYE 1977– London-born painter, sometimes known as Lynette Yiadom-Boakye, who studied at Central St Martins College of Art & Design, 1996–7; Falmouth College of Art, 1997–00; and the Royal Academy Schools, 2000–3. Her oil and acrylic Mature love poetry was included in John Moores Liverpool Exhibition in 2004, one of "a series of portraits. None of them is of existing people, but they are familiar.... I like the decadence of oil paint. I like decadence in general." Boakye's exhibitions included Blackout, Brixton Art Gallery, 2001; Red Mansion Prize, London Institute Gallery, 2002; and 5 Young Painters, Art Space Gallery, 2004, the year she had a solo show at Project Space. In 2005, she was included in the inaugural Bowieart show BLOC at the County Hall Gallery.

Peter BOBBY 1975– Artist and teacher who was "interested in the here and now, the ways in which power is exercised and order supposedly regained....the buildings and spaces that people occupy to escape this chaos." Bobby did art and design foundation studies at Oxford Brookes University, 1994–5; graduated with first-class honours from University of Wales Institute, Cardiff, 1995–8; and gained his master's in fine art there, 1998–00. Bobby's work experience, 2000–1, included teaching at South East Essex College, Southend, and at Swansea Institute and assisting at Stephen Friedman Gallery. Won a Clive Parr Memorial Fund award, 1999; Axis Graduates and Director's Choice Award, West, 1st Ffotobiennial, both 2000; and shortlisting, Purchase Art Prize, University of Wales, Glamorgan, 2001. Bobby's many group shows included Collapse, Chapter Arts Centre, Cardiff, 1997; Matinee, g39, Cardiff, 2000; and Interni, Plastica Gallery, Bologna. Solo exhibitions included Radley College, Oxford, 1999, and Ffotogallery, Cardiff, 2001. Lived in London.

Andrzej Krzysztof BOBROWSKI 1925–2002 Sculptor and medallist born in Warsaw, notable as one of the Polish paper sculptors who flourished in England in post-war years. He studied during World War II at Warsaw Academy of Fine Arts under Franciszka Strynkiewicz and Jerzego Jarnuszkiewicz, participated in the Warsaw Uprising in 1944 and was a prisoner of war in Germany. After hostilities he studied art in Rome, then at Slade School of Fine Art under A H Gerrard, F E McWilliam and Henry Moore. Became a freelance artist and designer for advertising and display, his figures often witty and satirical and capable of movement for animated films. The coronation of Queen Elizabeth II, the London Hilton, Hoover and the electrical firm Philips all absorbed his talents. Worked for both the Diana and De Mayo Studios. Bobrowski created bronze and steel welded sculptures and commemorative medals. Exhibited widely on the continent, in South Africa and in Britain, where he was included in Polish Paper Sculpture at Polish Cultural Institute, 1995. At the Olympiada d'Arte e Cultura, Albano, Italy, he won a gold medal for sculpture. Lived in London. Toruń University, Poland, holds Bobrowski's work.

George Alfred BODEN 1888–1956 Painter, printmaker and black-and-white artist. Born in Lincoln, he studied at the School of Art there, Atelier Colarossi, Paris, Académie des Beaux-Arts, Antwerp, at Camberwell School of Arts and

Crafts and at John Hassall's poster school, in London. Exhibited RA, RBA, RI, in the provinces and at the Paris Salon. Glasgow Museum and Art Galleries hold his work. Lived in Lincoln.

Leonard BODEN 1911–1999 Portrait painter and teacher, born in Greenock, Renfrewshire, married to the artist Margaret Boden, who assisted him in many of his major works. These included 19 royal portraits, including 10 of Queen Elizabeth plus several copies; other subjects as diverse as Pope Pius XII, three lord mayors of London, Field-Marshals Lords Milne and Slim, the singers Boris Christoff and Tito Gobbi, and actors Sir Donald Wolfit, Alistair Sim and Donald Sinden. After Sedbergh School Boden studied at Glasgow School Art, teachers including W O Hutchison, Francis Hodge, John D Revel and Frederic Whiting, and Heatherley's School of Fine Art. As well as showing at RP of which he was a member, exhibited at RSA. Chelsea Arts Club member who lived in London.

Ludovic BODEN 1964– Sculptor, born in London, who studied at the University and College of Art, Edinburgh, with postgraduate studies there. Showed at RSA Student Exhibition; Stirling Bi-annual; Scottish Sculpture Association; LG; and Royal College of Art. In 1989, was included in Scottish Connection at Feeringbury Manor, Feering, and Cramond Sculpture Centre, Moray House College, Edinburgh.

Margaret BODEN 1912–2002 Portrait painter like her husband Leonard Boden, she was born in Ecclesmachen, West Lothian. She studied at Glasgow School of Art and Heatherley's School of Fine Art. Exhibited with UA, SWA and PS all of which she was a member, and RP, ROI and the Royal Glasgow Institute of the Fine Arts. As an artist, Margaret lived a double life. She made a major contribution to her husband's work, to both their regrets not widely recognised, as well as having her own distinguished list of sitters. With Leonard she ran a private school for many years at their studio in Kensington. Their daughter was the notable harpist and teacher Daphne Boden. Lived in London.

Neville BODEN 1929–1996 Abstract sculptor in metal, draughtsman and teacher, born in Albert Town, South Africa, who learned many skills as a boilermaker. From 1958 studied under George Fullard at Chelsea School of Art and was later a Gregory Fellow at Leeds. Taught at London College of Printing, Chelsea, Camden School of Art, Central St Martin's and Kingston. Had a solo show at Whitechapel Art Gallery, 1973, and was president of LG, 1973–8. In later life lived in La Indiana, Andalusia, Spain, but died in London. Arts Council holds his sculpture Red Cross and Tate Gallery Blow in Her Ear.

Richard BODEN 1939– Painter and printmaker, producing landscapes, figure studies and still life, born in London, who studied painting and lithography at Ealing School of Art. He won an RI medal in 1982, became a member in 1983 and was on its council, also being a member of PS. Among several other prizes were the Daler-Rowney Award 2001. The Sheen Gallery also exhibited Boden's work. Many collections in Britain, on the continent and in Europe held examples. Lived in Winchester, Hampshire.

Miles BODIMEADE 1959– Sculptor in stone and wood, and draughtsman, born in Arundel, Sussex. He attended West Sussex College of Art and Design, 1979–80, then Liverpool Polytechnic Department of Sculpture, 1980–3. Among group exhibitions in which he participated were Southern Counties Drawing Competition, 1986; On The Wall Gallery, New York, 1989; and Arundel Gallery Trail, 1989–90. His one-man shows were at Arun Art Centre, 1985; Duff Gallery in Arundel and On The Wall Gallery, 1987; and he shared a show at England & Co, 1991. Bodimeade said that he used the figure "as a springboard for ideas, and abstract it to a greater or lesser degree depending on the theme". NBC Television, New York, holds his work.

Josselin BODLEY 1893–1974 Painter of architectural and landscape subjects, son of the historian J E C Bodley. He studied in Paris, where he died, and was wounded during World War I service in Belgium. Showed at Leicester and Beaux Arts Galleries, at Manchester City Art Gallery and in Paris. Manchester holds his Landscape, oil on canvas, of 1941.

Virginia BODMAN 1954– Painter, draughtsman, printmaker and lecturer, born in Wiltshire, married to the artist Robert Soden. Bodman produced large paintings, drawings and prints with a strong abstract element, colours ranging from sombre to vibrant. Her work combined an interest in painting and feminism. From a farming background, she developed an intimate physical relationship with the land "as a place of the senses", early pictures often holding hidden references to female sexuality. From 1988, when she was expecting her first son, the relationship between landscape and the feminine became more pronounced. Bodman did a foundation course at The College, Swindon, 1973–4; gained first-class honours in fine art, painting, Birmingham Polytechnic, 1974–7, taught by Alan Miller and Roy Abel; and her master's in painting at the Royal College of Art, 1978–81, under Peter de Francia and Jennifer Durrant. Was Abbey Major Scholar in Painting, British School at Rome, 1981–3. Taught extensively, from 1990 being head of painting at the University of Sunderland. Awards included Durham Cathedral Artist's Residency, 1983–4; Leverhulme Fellowship, 1996–7; Berwick Gymnasium Fellowship, 1999–00; and Rootstein Hopkins Sabbatical Award, 2001. Took part in many group shows, her solo exhibitions including Intimacies, Scarborough Museum and Art Gallery, 1999, and Between, Gymnasium Gallery, Berwick-upon-Tweed, plus tour, 2000–1. British School, Rome; Sunderland Polytechnic; Northern Arts; and Durham Cathedral hold her work. Lived in Sunderland.

Francesca BOEHM 1910– Painter in watercolour, born in Germany, who after settling in Britain lived in Cardiff, South Wales. She showed extensively with WAC, WSW of which she was for some time secretary, RWS, SWA and elsewhere and shared two-man shows at Llantarnam Grange, Cwmbran. Oxford Education Authority holds her work.

Janina BOGUCKA-WOLFF 1908–c.1968 Painter, sometimes listed as Janina Bogucka, who graduated from the Academy of Fine Arts in Cracow, Poland. For a time she lived and worked in Paris in a group of Polish artists, during World War II living in the Near East. After the war she lived in England, initially in London, then when seriously ill in the provinces. Her colourful, Expressionist work is held by Toruń University in Poland.

BOHDAN: *see* **Bohdan PARASZCZUK**

Peter BOHN 1930– Sculptor, carving in a variety of materials, born in Coventry, Warwickshire, who studied at Vittoria Street Art School, Birmingham, 1941–4, and part-time at the School of Art there, 1944–56, while working for William Bloye. In 1972, Bohn settled in Malvern, Worcestershire, having freelanced from 1956, apart from the period 1959–71, when he was attached to the Birmingham Guild. In Malvern, he continued to work on his own account, creating new pieces and undertaking restoration, notably in the Midlands area. The Assumption of the Virgin Mary, at Our Lady of the Assumption, Kingstanding, 1957, in Hollington stone, and the relief panel St Augustine's arrival in England, at St Augustine's, Handsworth, Birmingham, 1958, in Portland stone, are early examples of his work.

Marian BOHUSZ-SZYSZKO 1901–1995 Painter and teacher, born in Trokienniki, Poland. He studied at Department of Fine Art at Wilno University, 1921–3, then at the Academies of Fine Arts in Cracow and Warsaw, 1923–7. Bohusz-Szyszko was imprisoned as a Polish soldier by the Germans in World War II, then on liberation became teacher of a group of Polish art students in Rome before settling in Britain in 1946, when he founded the Polish School of Art. His own work drew on religious subject matter and was Expressionist in the Colourist tradition. He showed extensively in Britain and continental Europe, solo exhibitions including a retrospective at Drian Galleries in 1963. In 1981 there was a show at National Museum, Gdansk, and in 1993 he was included in the City Art Centre, Edinburgh, show Polish Roots – British Soil. The Bishop's Palace and Chapel, Winchester, and National Museums of Gdansk, Warsaw and Wroclaw hold his work. More than 60 of his pictures are on permanent display at the St Christopher's Hospice, Sydenham, where he died. He had become artist-in-residence there in 1977 and in 1980 took as his second wife Dame Cicely Saunders, founder of the modern hospice movement. Bohusz-Szyszko was termed "a great artist" by *Guardian* critic Eric Newton on the occasion of the painter's first London show in 1959, at Grabowski Gallery. Toruń University, Poland, holds his work.

Cyril Thompson BOLAM 1908– Painter, self-taught, who was born in Newcastle upon Tyne, Northumberland, where he continued to live. He exhibited at the Laing Art Gallery and Museum, Newcastle, and the Shipley Art Gallery, Gateshead. He held official positions in both the West End Art Club, Newcastle, and Federation of Northern Art Societies.

John BOLAM 1922– Painter, designer and teacher, born in Amersham, Buckinghamshire. The landscape of the Chilterns, English Romantic painters and poets and modern French artists such as Braque and Degas all influenced Bolam's work. He studied furniture design at High Wycombe School of Art and painting at Hornsey School of Art. Went on to become head of the School of Art in Cambridge, 1970–83. Showed at AIA Gallery, Leicester Galleries and one-man exhibitions included New Art Centre. Fry Art Gallery in Saffron Walden holds his work and gave him a 1950–75 retrospective in 1991.

Sean BOLAN 1948– Artist specialising in transport and architecture, using ink and watercolour, born in Rowlands Castle, Hampshire. He was educated in Havant, then studied nearby at Portsmouth College of Art, 1965–8. Showed in mixed exhibitions, work being held by several local authority collections. Was a member of the Great Western Society and lived for some time at Moreton-in-Marsh, Gloucestershire.

Alan BOLD 1943–1998 Prolific poet, writer, critic and painter in watercolour and oil, born in Edinburgh, whose literary hero, Hugh MacDiarmid, provided a foreword to Bold's first collection of poems, *Society Inebrious*, 1965. He was then still a student at Edinburgh University, associated with a remarkable generation of painters, including his friends John Bellany and Alexander Moffat. Bold later wrote a critical study, *MacDiarmid: the terrible crystal*, 1983; edited MacDiarmid's *Selected Letters*, 1984; and his 1988 biography *MacDiarmid* won the McVitie Prize as Scottish Writer of the Year. Bold was also a novelist, short story writer and book reviewer for the *Glasgow Herald*. He was engaged with painting, as practitioner, writer and critic from his student days, arguing for a return to figuration and humanist values. Bold published major texts for the Scottish Arts Council's Scottish Realism, 1971, and for Four Scottish Painters, at Edinburgh's Fruitmarket Gallery, 1975, curating both shows. From the late 1960s until the early 1990s he wrote many catalogue essays, chiefly for Bellany, Moffat and Peter de Francia. He collaborated with Bellany on a series of poems and prints, *A Celtic Quintet*, *Haven* and *Homage to MacDiarmid*, published by Edinburgh's Printmakers' Workshop. Influenced by William Blake, from the late 1960s Bold produced his watercolour and ink "illuminated poems", holding several successful exhibitions. Oil paintings on Robert Burns and his poetry were shown at the Maclaurin Art Gallery, Ayr, 1991, and he had another show at Netherbow Art Centre, Edinburgh, in 1994. Died in Kirkcaldy, Fife.

Gina BOLD 1959– Self-taught artist, born and lived in London, whose career was in fashion production. Bold sought to get on the canvas "the personality of the person I paint. I paint simply and directly, work quickly and believe less is more." Van Gogh, York Minster stained glass, mosaics and other cultures experienced through travel, such as Maori and aboriginal art, were cited as influences. Bold began to paint in the studio at Stuckism International under Charles Thomson's tuition, his work initially influencing her style, and was a guest artist with the Stuckists, participating in the First Stuckist International, 2002, and in 2003 in the Stuckist Summer Show and Art4All, Prince's Trust. She later disassociated herself from the Stuckists, but continued to paint figuratively, with black outlines and flattish areas of colour. Her work gained in strength and inventiveness, moving from observations of people around her to classical mythological subject-matter.

John BOLD 1895–1979 Painter and draughtsman, born in Manchester, where he continued to live. Attended Manchester School of Art and showed regularly at MAFA, serving on the selection committee for its centenary exhibition; also exhibited at Walker Art Gallery, Liverpool, the Mid-Day Studios in Manchester and other northern shows. Manchester City Art Gallery holds his An Aran Village; An Aran Landscape; The Church, Inishmaan; Portrait of a Cat; and A Suburban Landscape, all in Bold's typically precise style.

William BOLGER 1941– Painter in oil on canvas, mainly landscapes of St Ives, Cornwall, where he settled, and symbolic pictures based on Aztec imagery. Bolger was born in Liverpool, where he studied at the College of Art, 1962–5, gaining his master's degree at the Royal College of Art, 1965–7, under Merlyn Evans and Carel Weight. Group exhibitions included Salthouse Gallery, St Ives, 1995, with a solo show at St Ives Public Library, 1994. Casablanca Club, Liverpool, and private collections hold his work.

Elaine BOLTON: *see* **Elaine GILMOUR**

Freda BOLTON 1929– Figurative watercolourist, sometimes of works with a quirky charm, born in Hanmer, Shropshire, her father a Colonial Office water engineer, her mother a teacher. Qualified at Cheshire County Teachers' Training College, her speciality art, then taught in Hull's docklands and in east London. Recommenced teaching as her family grew, becoming a senior supply teacher for Borough of Barnet; attended classes at Camden Arts Centre; and was active in Finchley Art Society. A solo show at Hampstead Garden Suburb Gallery, 1999, prompted commissions. Bolton shared an exhibition with the ceramist Helen Cohen there in 2002. Lived in north London.

Micky BOLTON 1956– Prolific producer of witty sculptures from recycled metal, born in Durban, South Africa, who settled in the United Kingdom in 1974, where his first job was metal picker in a scrap yard. After time panel beating and paint spraying, he ran his own business restoring classic and racing cars. Inspired by metal sculptures from South Africa, Bolton began welding his birds and animals in 1994. Often the parts inspired the final form, the texture, colour and size making each piece unique. Thompson's Gallery, Aldeburgh, showed Bolton's work, Buckenham Galleries, Southwold, giving him a solo exhibition in 2001. Lived in Suffolk.

Richard BOLTON 1950– Watercolourist and writer, born in Aberdeen, who studied at Shrewsbury College of Art, where he developed acute observation and attention to detail. Began his professional career as a technical illustrator with the Royal Air Force. The British landscape, including such features as old farm implements and abandoned cars, was a favourite subject. Wrote a number of books on aspects of watercolour painting. Major awards included the East of England Art Exhibition, lst Prize and special awards, and the New Zealand South Island Art Show, 1st Prize. Exhibitions included The Linda Blackstone Gallery, Pinner, and widely abroad.

Tim Scott BOLTON 1947– Landscape painter and teacher, born in Shropshire, who trained as a land agent, then turned to art as a career. He had been educated at Bromsgrove and the College of Estate Management, London University, painting part-time under Ruskin Spear at Hammersmith College of Art, in 1971–4 working in Kenya valuing farms. In 1984 became a full-time painter, attending Heatherley's School of Fine Art. Visited the Middle East and India, taught watercolour painting twice a year and took groups of artists abroad. Had his own gallery in Wiltshire, The Summerleaze Gallery, at East Knoyle, where he lived and showed other artists. He also showed with the Malcolm Innes Gallery in London and Edinburgh, Tryon & Moorland Gallery in London and Nairobi, Bruton Gallery at Bruton, Somerset, and with Oliver Swann and Mathaf Galleries. H M The Queen; The Dukes of Devonshire, Wellington and Somerset; The National Trust; The Country Landowners' Association; Casimir Prince Wittgenstein and other notable private collectors held examples.

Michael BOLUS 1934– Sculptor and teacher, born in Cape Town, South Africa. Bolus moved to England in 1957 and studied at St Martin's School of Art, 1958–62. For a time he was an assistant to Anthony Caro, who taught there. In 1963–4 Bolus went back to Cape Town on a visit, having a solo show there in the latter year. In 1965 he had a one-man exhibition at Waddington Galleries, the first of a series, then had a solo show at Kornblee Gallery, New York, in 1966. About this time Bolus was teaching at St Martin's, also at Central School of Art and Design. Bolus' work underwent a number of transformations. He was originally a modeller, then a carver rather in the manner of Brancusi, then produced floor-based metal sculptures, abstract and coloured, latterly making grid-style and lattice-form pieces such as he showed in The Condition of Sculpture exhibition at Hayward Gallery in 1975. Bolus' work formed part of The Alistair McAlpine Gift, shown at Tate Gallery in 1971, and the Arts Council also has his work. Among his open-air commissions is Untitled, 1981, in aluminium and steel, at Sutton Manor Arts Centre, Sutton Scotney.

David BOMBERG 1890–1957 Painter and influential teacher, born in Birmingham of Polish Jewish refugee stock. In London from 1905 Bomberg studied with Walter Bayes at City and Guilds evening classes and, having become acquainted with artists such as John Singer Sargent, Ossip Zadkine and Solomon J Solomon, in 1908 broke his indentures while an apprentice to a chromolithographer to study art. For several years studied with W R Lethaby at the Central School of Arts and Crafts and with Walter Sickert at Westminster School, then 1911–13 attended the Slade School of Fine Art full-time, where he won several awards. Prior to World War I designed for Roger Fry's Omega Workshops; travelled to Paris where he met Picasso, Derain and Modigliani; and received acclaim from Wyndham Lewis, being invited to show with the Vorticist Exhibition, in 1915. Exhibited with the Friday Club, NEAC and was a founder-member of the LG. First one-man show at Chenil Galleries, 1914. Travelled extensively in the 1920s and 1930s, notably to Spain and Palestine, which inspired some strongly Expressionist landscape paintings. Began teaching during World War II, forming with his students the Borough Group in 1946. This was followed by the Borough Bottega seven years later with which a retrospective was held in 1954. Bomberg's wife Lilian, whom he often painted, and other members of his family were associated with the Borough Group. Several memorial exhibitions held and a major retrospective at the Tate Gallery, which holds his work, 1988. The London Jewish Cultural Centre held a show of Bomberg's works on paper and paintings, 1914–56, in 2003.

In 2004, Boundary Gallery organised Bomberg and Pupils: The Borough Group 1946–1951. Died in London.

Lilian BOMBERG: *see* **Lilian HOLT**

Arnold BOND 1905– Painter, artist in scraperboard and line, and teacher, born in Bexleyheath, Kent. Studied at Goldsmiths' College School of Art and Bath Academy of Art, Corsham. Showed with RA, Corsham Group and Eastbourne Society of Artists, of which he was a member. Taught art at Eastbourne Technical Institute and lived in St Leonards-on-Sea, Sussex.

Arthur J F BOND 1888–1958 Painter, printmaker and draughtsman, born in Devonport, who after education in Tavistock attended Heatherley's School of Fine Art, Goldsmiths' College School of Art and the Central School of Arts and Crafts. Most of his life was lived in the Thames River area, and he was a member of the Wapping Group of Artists and RSMA. Also exhibited RA, RI and Paris Salon. Lived at Holmbury St Mary, Surrey.

Douglas Cipriani BOND: *see* **Doug CIPRIANI**

Henry BOND 1966– Artist, born in London, who attended West Surrey College of Art, Farnham, 1984–5, graduating with honours from Goldsmiths' College, 1985–8. His group exhibition appearances included East Country Yard Show, Surrey Docks, and The Mulitiple Projects Room, Air de Paris, Nice, both 1990; and Spy-Stories, Sergio Casolini, Milan, Il Compo, Rome, 1991. Solo shows included Documents, with Liam Gillick, at Karsten Schubert Ltd; James Hockey Gallery, Farnham; and Documents, with Liam Gillick, Centre d'Art Contemporain, APAC Nevers, all 1991.

Jane BOND 1939– Painter of portraits who was by profession a costume designer for the stage, television and films, 1960–78. Bond completed a foundation course at St Martin's School of Art, 1956–7. She studied art at City and Guilds of London School of Art, 1978–81, and the Royal Academy Schools, 1981–4. She was included in The Spirit of London, Royal Festival Hall, from 1982; RP from 1983; RA Summer Exhibition from 1984; and The Discerning Eye, Mall Galleries, 1991. She was elected a member of the NEAC in 1989 and RP in 1992. Later exhibitions included Alresford Gallery, Hampshire, 1998; National Portrait Gallery, selection from the RP Annual Exhibition, 1998–9; People's Portraits, a United Kingdom RP tour, and Woodgates Gallery, East Bergholt, both 2000; and Selected Drawings at Glyndebourne Opera House, Glynde, 2001. Bond won several prizes at the Royal Academy Schools, also the Ernest Kleinwort Memorial Prize at the NEAC, 1989, and *House and Garden* Interior Prize, RA Summer Exhibition, 1993. She lived in London. Private collectors including Sir Brinsley Ford owned her work.

John BOND 1945– Painter of landscapes in oil on card using a rich palette, who was obsessed by painting from childhood in Cromer, Norfolk, where he was born and attended school. After studying at Norwich and Central Schools of Art Bond in 1965 became a designer for a book publisher in Guildford, where The Chaucer Studio Gallery gave him a first solo show. A second successful exhibition, at Majorie Parr's gallery in Chelsea, saw Bond established as an independent artist, other exhibitions following at Ralph Lewis Gallery, Brighton; The Upstairs Gallery at RA; and The Westcliffe Gallery, Sheringham. His main outlet was Century Galleries, Henley-on-Thames, where he had an exhibition in 2001.

Marj BOND fl. from mid-1950s– Artist, born in Scotland, who studied at Glasgow School of Art, 1955–60, taught by Alex Dick, David Donaldson, Mary Armour and Benno Schotz. She was a figurative painter, in the Scottish Colourist tradition, with strong poetic and symbolic elements. In 1988 Bond made a trip to India which opened up new visual channels and gave her the opportunity to work on handmade paper. In 1992 she took part in a summer sculpture workshop in Tuscany; 1993 brought journeys to Yucatan, Mexico, and Urbino in Italy; and in 1994 she had a painting residency at Annaghmakerrig, the Tyrone Guthrie Centre, in Ireland. Among her awards was the Anne Redpath Award, 1984; Crawford Arts Centre Special Award, St Andrews, 1987; and an English Speaking Union scholarship, 1994. Was elected a professional member of SSWA in 1975, later a council member; a member of the Dundee Printmakers' Workshop, 1987; and in 1989 member of both RSW and SSA. Showed at RSA regularly from 1983. Showed solo with Open Eye Gallery, Edinburgh, from 1984, Thackeray Gallery from 1992. Edinburgh University, Perth Art Gallery and Art in Hospitals hold examples.

Peter BOND 1961– Artist, designer and lecturer who graduated with honours from Wimbledon School of Art, 1981–3. He was director of Diverse Alternatives Multi Media Workshop, 1985–8; costume and set designer for Alfred Jarry's play *Ubu Roi*, Latchmere Theatre, 1988; and a part-time lecturer at Leicester Polytechnic, 1988–9. Participated in group shows at Kimberlin Hall in Leicester and at Gallery Imago, San Francisco, California, both 1986, and in East End Open Studios, at Cable Street Studios, 1989.

Terance BOND 1946– Self-taught artist, born in Bures, Suffolk, whose career in a drawing office influenced his attention to detail. From an early age he had an interest in wildlife, which developed into an ability to paint from nature. Had a first solo show at Haste Gallery, Ipswich, in 1971, which included him in its fortieth anniversary exhibition in 1998. Bond's work sold widely throughout Britain, continental Europe and America.

Charles BONE 1926– Painter, muralist and ceramist, born in Farnham, Surrey, married to the sculptor Sheila Mitchell. He studied at Farnham School of Art and Royal College of Art. Bone was president of RI for 10 years, a director of the RI Galleries and later the Mall Galleries. Also showed with RA, RBA, NEAC and Federation of Canadian Artists, of which he was an honorary member. He had many solo exhibitions, including Medici Gallery; Gainsborough's House at Sudbury; Canaletto Gallery, Tom Morgan Gallery, Pasadena; New Ashgate Gallery in Farnham; Surrey University; Upper Grosvenor Gallery, and elsewhere. He was an honorary member of the Medical Art Society and of the Society of Botanical Artists. Private collections around the world held his work and he completed murals in Spain, Italy and Malta. In 1989 he gained the Hunting Group Prize for watercolour and in 1991 his book *Charles Bone's Waverley* was published, with a foreword by HRH The Prince of Wales. Lived in Puttenham, Surrey.

Helen BONE fl. from late 1980s– Painter who said that although there was "an obvious gulf between my apparently abstract work and perceptual reality, I am a realist at heart". From 1985–7 studied for a painting diploma at Mid-Warwickshire College; attended Coventry University, 1987–90; from 1990–2 working for a master's degree in fine art at University of Central England, Birmingham. Early exhibitions included Florida and Buenos Aires, then Herbert Art Gallery in Coventry, Bonhams, and Pacesetters at Peterborough Museum and Art Gallery, 1995. Lived in Dunchurch, near Rugby, Warwickshire.

Muirhead BONE 1876–1953 Painter, but mainly printmaker and draughtsman, born in Glasgow, the Bone family producing a number of artists, writers and critics, including Stephen and James Bone. Bone initially trained as an architect, 1890–4, simultaneously attending art classes at Glasgow School of Art under Archibald Kay. Moved to London in 1901 and soon began exhibiting at the RA and NEAC. Had his first one-man show at the Carfax Gallery in 1903, a year later becoming a foundermember of the Society of Twelve. Became the first Official War Artist in 1916, again serving as a war artist to the Admiralty in World War II. His first book was *Glasgow* in 1901, but he went on to illustrate many more by members his family. He was a trustee of the National Gallery, Tate Gallery and Imperial War Museum. Knighted 1937. The Tate Gallery holds his work, which has a strong, linear quality, much of it based on travels on the continent. Died in Oxford, is commemorated with a tablet in the crypt of St Paul's Cathedral, London. Memorial exhibitions in Manchester and at the Arts Council, 1955.

Phyllis Mary BONE 1896–1972 Sculptor of animals in bronze. Born at Hornby, Lancashire, she studied at Edinburgh College of Art and on the continent. She exhibited at the RA, RSA, Royal Glasgow Institute of the Fine Arts, the provinces and abroad. Aberdeen Art Gallery and Dumfries Art Gallery hold her work, which is in the realist tradition. Illustrated in Eric Newton's *British Sculpture 1944–1946*. Lived in Kirkcudbright, Scotland.

Stephen BONE 1904–1958 Painter, wood engraver, illustrator, critic, broadcaster and writer. Born in Chiswick into a family of writers and artists. Stephen's father was the painter Sir Muirhead Bone and Stephen married the artist Mary Adshead. After Bedales School he studied at the Slade School of Fine Art, 1922–4. From 1920 began showing with NEAC; won a gold medal for wood engraving at the 1925 Paris International Exhibition; in 1926 shared a show with Robin Guthrie and Rodney Burn at the Goupil Gallery; and two years later painted a decoration for Piccadilly Circus underground station (eventually replaced by advertisements). Travelled extensively with his wife in the British Isles and on the continent and exhibited widely in the 1930s, including Fine Art Society, Lefevre Gallery and Redfern Gallery. In the late 1930s was active in the AIA, helping German refugees to settle in England and find work. During World War II became an officer in camouflage operations in Leamington Spa, from 1943–5 serving as an Official War Artist attached to the Royal Navy. Bone's speciality was the small oil panel "snapshot". They brilliantly evoke the scenes of his wide travels and illustrate his book *Albion: An Artist's Britain*, published in 1939. After the war his pictures fell out of favour and he concentrated on his ability to communicate with words. Bone could be a spellbinder, with a prodigious memory for facts. He served as art critic for the *Manchester Guardian* in 1948; wrote articles for the *Yorkshire Post* and *Glasgow Herald*; broadcast on radio and television, in such programmes as *The Critics* and *The Brains Trust*; and wrote children's books, sometimes working with his wife. In 1957 was appointed director of Hornsey College of Art. The Tate Gallery holds his work. Retrospective Sally Hunter Fine Art, 1986. Lived in London.

Hein BONGER 1952– Self-taught sculptor, born in Arnhem, Netherlands. Exhibitions included RA Summer Exhibition, 1993; Chappel Galleries, Chappel, from 1994 (in 1996 with Tessa Newcomb); and Ernst & Young, Cambridge, 1995. Bonger was based in Suffolk. He was married for a time to the writer Julia Blackburn, daughter of the artist Rosalie de Meric.

Eliza BONHAM CARTER 1961– Abstract painter who studied at Ravensbourne College of Art, 1982–5, then Royal College of Art, 1986–8, being awarded Abbey Major Scholarship to British School, Rome in the latter year. Group shows included Todd Gallery, 1991, and Aiding and Abetting, at The Gallery at John Jones, 1994. Solo shows included The Berkeley Square Gallery, 1989, and Galleria Sprovieri, Rome, 1992.

Stanley BONNAR 1948– Versatile artist and teacher, born in Leith, Midlothian, whose career was Scotland-oriented after studying sculpture at Duncan of Jordanstone College of Art, Dundee, 1968–72. Bonnar held residencies at Glenrothes New Town, 1973, and at East Kilbride and Stonehaven New Town, 1974–7. After painting scenery for Royal Lyceum Theatre, Edinburgh, he joined the Blackness Public Arts Project, Dundee, 1981–4, taught part-time in the environmental art department of Glasgow School of Art, 1985–92, winning a Scottish Arts Council Award in 1994. Bonnar's sculpture could be tinged with humour, witness his four fibreglass figures, titled The Community, commissioned in 1979 by Reidvale Housing Association for Whitevale Street, Dennistoun.

Mandy BONNELL 1957– She graduated with honours from Gloucestershire College of Arts & Technology, Cheltenham, 1976–9, gaining her master's from Royal College of Art, 1980–3. Took part in the Chicago Art Fair, in America, 1985, other group appearances including 150 Years of Printmaking at the Royal College of Art, 1987, and East End Open Studios, at New Hoxton Workshops, 1989. In 1988, Bonnell showed solo at Anderson O'Day Gallery.

Peter BONNELL 1973– Artist, teacher and illustrator born in Liverpool, where he studied sculpture, completing a master's in fine art at the University of Arkansas, 1999–02. In 2002, he shared an exhibition, Memory & Perception, with Tom Palin at The University of Liverpool. By then he was a full-time artist who had won several awards and residencies, including Young Artist of the Year at the Royal College of Art. For the Liverpool show, Bonnell drew subjects from the glossy clothing catalogues of major North American brands.

George BONNER 1924– Painter, born in Toronto, Canada. Educated at the South-West Essex Technical College, he exhibited at the RA, New Vision Gallery, Towner Art Gallery, Eastbourne – which holds his work – and abroad. Bonner painted in oil and acrylic, his pictures being noted for their texture, as well as in collage. Lived at Bexhill, Sussex.

Lesley BONNER 1954– Artist who was originally trained in sculpture, but more often worked in relief. Her meticulous obsession with and manipulation of materials "related to the natural world as well as the beliefs and iconography of other cultures." Bonner did a foundation course at Harrow School of Art, 1973–4, graduating with honours in fine art from Bristol Polytechnic, 1974–7. She settled in Milton Keynes, where for many years she was employed as a community artist. The Development Corporation commissioned a range of work from her, including Totem Pole, Griffin and Lodge Gates Carving. Bonner was a member of The Silbury Group of Artists and was included in its 10th Anniversary Exhibition at Milton Keynes Gallery in 2001–2. Other later exhibitions included Stantonbury Exhibition Gallery, Milton Keynes, 1999; Garden of Art Ltd, Gestingthorpe, 2000–1; and Memoirs of My Travels, Kauno Galerija Kaunas, Lithuania, and Westbury Gallery, Milton Keynes, both 2001. Milton Keynes Hospital Trust, 1999, and Corporate leasing, Intervet, Milton Keynes, 2001, both hold Bonner's work.

Kirsty BONNING 1974– Painter, daughter of the artist Robin Brooks and sister of the painter Rupert William Brooks, like them based at Black Dog Studios, in Devon. She graduated with honours in textile design at Leeds University, 1995, working mostly to private commission. Painted animal and landscape subjects in oil and watercolour.

Mary BONNING: *see* **Mary JOHNSTONE**

Susan BONVIN 1948– Artist and teacher whose work included abstract sculptures and constructions, with pigment. Was born in London of Anglo-Swiss nationality. Studied at Wimbledon School of Art, 1964–6, then gained an honours degree in fine art painting at Falmouth School of Art, 1966–9, in the latter year winning the Sir Edward Nichol Painting Prize. Was joint editor of the arts anthology *Wallpaper*, also participating in *Wallpaper on Cassette*, Audio Arts. Had an artists in schools residency, Eastern Arts Board, 1989. Between 1970–94 did part-time teaching in schools, further and higher education, from 1994 teaching at Tresham Institute, Kettering. Group shows included On Site, Arnolfini Gallery, Bristol, 1979; *The Economist* Gallery, 1991; and The Table Studio Group, The Living Room, 1996. Had a solo show at Ascham Street Studio, 1986, later ones including Gallery 4, Shad Thames, 1993, and Axis Gallery, Leeds, 2000. In 2002, shared a show with Andrew Eden at Fermyn Woods Contemporary Art, Brigstock. Arts Council holds her work. Lived in Northamptonshire.

Brenda Brin BOOKER 1932– Artist with a strong interest in the romantic, illustrator and teacher, born in Plaistow, east London, who aged 16 gained a scholarship to study at Walthamstow School of Art, attending the Slade School of Fine Art, 1951–4. After graduating, she taught and worked as a freelance artist and illustrator. In the early 1980s began studying social science and psychology, graduating from the Open University in 1985, in 1989 gaining a Bachelor of Science honours degree in psychology at University College. Showed widely in Britain and abroad, including Heifer Gallery.

Sarah BOOKLESS 1950– Glasgow-born artist and teacher who as a child constantly sketched and painted. After graduating from Glasgow School of Art in 1972, she qualified to teach. Bookless used a variety of media, mainly oils, pastels and collage, and was particularly interested in pattern, colour and poetic vision. Her early work was influenced by that of William Blake, her later pictures by early Renaissance painters, the Pre-Raphaelites and the Russian-born abstractionist Wassily Kandinsky. She was included in The Spring Show at The Wykeham Gallery, Stockbridge, in 2005.

Bob BOOTH 1948– Painter and teacher, who grew up in Louth, Lincolnshire. There, "although my aptitude for drawing and interest in art tended towards a naïve preoccupation with realism, my fascination for the painterly style was perhaps the beginning of looking for something more than just a painted illusion of nature." While studying in Yorkshire, an exhibition of Cézanne's watercolours at the Hayward Gallery, although Booth then found them "little to my liking," led to a realisation of "Cézanne's greatness...and apparently his influence can still be detected in my painting." Booth taught art in Lancashire, 1975–82; was ordained for the Anglican priesthood in 1983, during his studies producing a few explicitly religious works, Roualt becoming another influence; then in 1998 he moved to Australia "to take on a parish in the spectacular and, at times, hostile environment of the North West...a passion for the contrast and colour in this area" influencing his landscapes. Booth exhibited solo in Australia and Europe, later one-man shows including Moores Building, Fremantle, 2000; St Michael's Church, Spearwood, and The Gallery in Cork Street, both 2001; St George's Chapel, Windsor Castle, 2003; and The Council of Europe, Strasbourg, France, 2004. Lived in Singleton, Western Australia.

Chris BOOTH 1948– Sculptor, who attended Ilam School of Fine Arts, Canterbury, New Zealand, 1967–8. Between 1968–70 continued specialist sculpture studies, working with prominent British sculptors, including Barbara Hepworth, Denis Mitchell and John Milne; and with Quinto Ghermandi, in Italy. Later awards included Artists in Industry Project, Mildura Arts Centre, Victoria, Australia; Greenham Common Trust Award, Newbury; and 10th Millfield International Sculpture Commission, all 1998. Had extensive group and solo exhibition appearances, one-mans latterly including Meridian Gallery, Melbourne, 1994, Robert McDougal Art Gallery, Christchurch, 1995, and Auckland City Art Gallery, 1997. Carried out numerous public and private commissions from 1976 internationally. Work exhibited by New Art Centre Sculpture Park & Gallery, East Winterslow.

James William BOOTH 1867–1953 Painter in oil and watercolour keen on country subjects, born in Manchester. born in Manchester. Showed extensively at RCamA of which he was a member, RA, Walker Art Gallery in Liverpool and elsewhere. Lived in Scalby, Scarborough, Yorkshire. Manchester City Art Gallery holds examples.

Peter BOOTH 1940– Painter, born in Sheffield, Yorkshire. He attended the College of Art there in 1956–7, emigrated to Australia in 1958, then from 1962–5 studied at National Gallery School in Melbourne, where he continued to live. In the early 1970s worked in framing department of the National Gallery of Victoria, coming into contact with the work of William Blake, which had a profound effect. Booth produced figurative, gestural and semi-abstract works. They were lit by a light that was rarely daylight and while drawing on his experience of the Australian landscape were inspired by dreams and the subconscious. One of the leading Australian painters of his generation, Booth showed widely in mixed exhibitions in that continent. He had his first one-man show at Strines Gallery, Melbourne, in 1967, after that showing often in Melbourne and Sydney; with CDS Gallery, New York, in 1985–7; and had his first European show at Albemarle Gallery in 1988. National Gallery of Victoria and Metropolitan Museum, New York, hold his work.

Raymond BOOTH 1929– Painter of plants and wildlife, based in Leeds, Yorkshire, whose small suburban garden and the county's moors and woods provided subjects for his meticulous pictures. Booth trained at Leeds College of Art in the late 1940s and early 1950s, when he found himself out of sympathy with modern trends in painting. After tuberculosis and an enforced stay in a sanatorium, he found that collectors such as Ernest Thesiger and Lord Fairhaven were acquiring the type of picture he wanted to paint, and he was able to combine his obsessive interests of artist and plantsman. Exhibited solo at The Fine Art Society, his 1982 show providing the means to buy the two things he most needed: another deep-freeze, to keep natural history specimens separate from his food, and a portable spotlight, enabling him during the dull winter months to garden after dark, saving daylight hours for painting. His 2000 exhibition, with an extensive illustrated catalogue, covered a decade's output. Booth was reclusive, never attending his own shows. Leeds City Art Gallery organised a 50-year career survey in 2002.

Roberta BOOTH 1947– Painter and printmaker who studied at Luton School of Art, 1964–6; fine art at Coventry College of Art, 1966–9, gaining her diploma; then obtained her master's degree in printmaking at Royal College of Art, 1969–72. In 1982 obtained an Eastern Arts Association grant. Mixed shows included Hachette Gallery, and British Council Exhibition in Linz, Austria, both 1971; Cracow Print Biennial, Poland, 1972; Five Realists, Minories, Colchester, and Summer Show I, Serpentine Gallery, both 1976; Cambridgeshire Artists, Kettle's Yard, Cambridge, 1983; and Society of Botanical Artists, 1995. Had a solo exhibition at Duncan Campbell Contemporary Art, 1996, of paintings completed 1974–89, in which Booth transformed everyday objects as analogues for humanity, giving them a Surrealistic hint of menace. Booth travelled widely from her tiny studio in Ashwell, Hertfordshire, to explore Buddhism, Hinduism and Sufi mysticism, as evident in her Duncan Campbell show in 2002. Victoria & Albert Museum and University of Waikato, New Zealand, hold examples.

Theo BOOTH 1947– West Country figurative painter whose strongly organised work could have a jokey quality, as in his solo exhibition at Enid Lawson Gallery, 2002. He had shown with Enid Lawson in a two-artist exhibition in 2001 and at Chelsea Art Fair and Affordable Art Fairs in Bath and London. Booth began painting in 1998, having trained as an engineer, also working as a photographer and boat restorer. He cited as influences William Roberts, Tamara de Lempicka, Ernst Ludvig Kirchner, Picasso and Modigliani, his favourite painting being The Geranium, by Max Weber.

Daphne BOOTHBY fl. from late 1950s– Sculptor, painter and draughtsman who studied at West of England College of Art, Bristol, gaining a diploma with first-class honours, and an art teacher's diploma. She travelled in Italy, studying painting and sculpture at Academy of Fine Arts Pietro Vannucci, Perugia. In 1981 was elected a brother of the Art Workers' Guild. Boothby worked in fine hardwoods, direction of the grain relating to carefully developed abstracted forms. Italian historic urban architecture was a constant influence on her paintings and drawings, which were also abstracted. Group shows included Loggia Gallery from 1981. From 1965 held regular open studio exhibitions in west London. Others included William Penn House, 1968; University of Surrey, 1970; Ice House Gallery, 1982; Palazzo del Priori, Perugia, 1989; and Quaker Gallery, 1994. BBC, London College of Furniture and Church of St John the Baptist, Neath Abbey, hold examples.

Toby BOOTHMAN 1973– London-based figurative painter and draughtsman who attended the University of the West of England. He then moved to the thirteenth-century medieval village of Monflanquin, southwest France, studying for three years at Atelier Neo Medici under Patrick Betaudier. There, he learned a modern version of the Renaissance method known as Technique Mixed, combining layers of egg with oil glazes, as used by the Flemish master Jan van Eyck. Boothman used photographs to capture detail and light that characterised his work and latterly employed computer software to juxtapose and manipulate the images to create one image. Took part in a number of group shows, including Lamont Gallery, 1998, and ROI at Mall Galleries, 1999, where he was runner-up for a Winsor & Newton Award. Had a solo exhibition at Albemarle Gallery, 2003, which included works in oil on panel, oil on linen and tempera and oil on linen.

Karolina BORCHARDT 1913– Painter, born in Minsk and educated in Wilno and Cracow, Poland, who later adopted British citizenship. Studied art at University of Stefan Batory in London and in Italy. Was a member of Free Painters and Sculptors, showing at Loggia Gallery, also in mixed exhibitions at Barbican Art Gallery, Centaur Gallery and abroad. Solo shows were held at Richmond and Barrett Galleries and in America. Lived in London.

Dorothy BORDASS 1905–1992 Painter, artist in collage and printmaker, born in London. She studied with several teachers throughout the 1920s, including R T Mumford, at Académie Julian in Paris, and at Heatherley's School of Fine Art under Iain Macnab. Took part in many group shows, including Redfern and Mercury Galleries and extensively abroad; had solo shows at New Vision Centre Gallery, Woodstock Gallery, in the provinces and overseas. South London Art Gallery, other British and Commonwealth galleries hold her work. This sometimes has both a seemingly naïve and jokey quality. A show of her output over the period 1954–90 was held at Chappel Galleries, Chappel, Essex, in 1992. Lived for some years in Cambridge.

Wendela BOREEL 1895–1985 Painter and printmaker, born in Pau, France, she studied at the Slade School of Fine Art, the Westminster Technical Institute under Walter Sickert and the Central School of Arts and Crafts. Boreel became closely associated with the Sickert circle and it was because of her brilliant studies in gouache that he became interested in the medium. She was an especially accomplished printmaker and her subjects, such as the actress Gwen Frangcon-Davies, the Café Royal and London street scenes, owe much to his influence. She exhibited RE, NS, NEAC, Redfern and Walker's Galleries and had a number of one-man shows in London and abroad. Victoria & Albert Museum holds her work. Finally lived in Mougins, France.

Wyn BORGER 1933– Painter and teacher, born in Withington, Manchester, her father a senior London Midland and Scottish Railway freight official. After education at Whalley Range High School for Girls, spent two years at Manchester School of Art, then three at Bath Academy of Art, Corsham, teachers including Colin Thompson, Reg Butler, Peter Potworoski, William Scott, Peter Lanyon, Litz Pisk, Brian Wynter, James Tower and Lyn Chadwick. From 1959–83 was head of art department and exhibitions organiser at Brunel University. In 1957 married the behavioural psychologist Robert Borger (previously exhibited under her maiden name Winifred Frost). Exhibitions included Bath Library, LG, Bedford Park Festival and elsewhere. Lived in London.

Andrzej Maria BORKOWSKI 1949– Versatile artist, teacher and critic, born in Warsaw, Poland, who gained his master's in art history, Warsaw University, 1975, with a similar degree at the Courtauld Institute, University of London, 1988. In Warsaw, he was a founder-member of the theatre co-operative Akademia Ruchu, with whom he performed and created happenings and installations in Poland and abroad, 1973–80. From 1977–82 he lectured in art history at the Academy of Fine Arts, Gdansk, and worked with Hesitate & Demonstrate visual theatre, 1982–4. Based in London, Borkowski from 1984 was as a freelance actor, designer and art critic and a founder-member of Bigos, artists of Polish origin, which had an exhibition at Brixton Gallery and The Crypt, St George's Church, Bloomsbury Way, in 1986. He also participated in Form and Colour, a Congress of Polish Culture Exhibition of Fine Arts by Polish Artists in Britain, POSK Gallery, 1995. His solo shows included Warsaw Musical Society Gallery and Salon Debiutow, Warsaw, both 1971. Toruń University, Poland, holds Borkowski's monoprint The origin of Mermaids (The Comet), 1997.

Chrissie BORLAND: *see* **Bryn HILLIER**

Christine BORLAND 1965– Artist using such media as photography and installations, born in Darvel, Ayrshire. The experience of mortality was a key feature of her work. She gained an honours degree at Glasgow School of Art, 1983–7, then her master's at University of Ulster, Belfast, 1987–8. Group shows included Speed at Transmission Gallery, Glasgow, 1991; Aperto, Venice Biennale, 1993; Institute of Cultural Anxiety, ICA, 1994; and British Art Show, with tour, 1995–6. Solo shows included From Life at Tramway, Glasgow, 1994, Kunstwerke, Berlin, and the British Council Gallery, Prague, both 1995, De Appel, Amsterdam, Netherlands, 1998; and Lisson Gallery, 2001 and 2004. Borland gained a DAAD Scholarship, Berlin, 1996, and was shortlisted for the 1997 Turner Prize. Lived in Glasgow.

Deirdre BORLASE 1925– Painter, printmaker, collagist and teacher, born in London, who from childhood wanted to paint, but received little early encouragement. She studied at Bromley School of Art, 1940–4, then at the Royal College of Art, 1944–6, where teachers included Ruskin Spear and Carel Weight and where she met her future husband Frederick Brill (she was included with him and their children in Relative Values at The Smith Art Gallery & Museum, Stirling, 1993). Lectured at Harrow School of Art, 1946–8, and Kingston School of Art, 1948–50. Bringing up a family curtailed her artistic activity for some years, although she continued to fill sketch-books. After the Brills bought a cottage in Carperby, North Yorkshire, in 1967 she began to paint the landscape, Venice being another favourite subject of her pictures, which often took a witty turn. During 1977 Borlase attended a course in printmaking at Morley College, in 1992 began to decorate furniture and also began experimenting with a computer paintbox. Showed extensively at RA Summer Exhibition from 1946 and elsewhere in mixed shows. Had a solo show at David Thompson Gallery, 1979, later ones including Broughton House Gallery, Cambridge, from 1989. Commissions included six paintings for St Luke's Hospital, Bradford. Graves Art Gallery, Sheffield, holds her work.

Daisy Theresa BORNE 1906–1998 Sculptor in a variety of materials, and teacher, born in London. An interest in religious themes was a feature of her output, which was elegant and conservative while being tinged with modernism. Borne travelled widely with her family, being educated partly in America, then returned to London where she studied sculpture at Regent Street Polytechnic School of Art with Harold Brownsword. Also studied singing, but declined to take up the stage professionally. Learned to carve with Joyce Bidder, with whom she shared a studio in southwest London for many years. Some work was signed TB, joined. Showed at RA, RBS of which she was an associate, and was vice-president of RMS. Her work was included in a two-artist show with Joyce Bidder at Fine Art Society, 1987.

Jacob BORNFRIEND 1904–1976 Painter in oil and tempera, mainly of landscape and still life. Born in Zborov, Czechoslovakia (as Bauernfreund, later Anglicised), he was educated at the Academy of Fine Arts, Prague, 1930–5, under Willi Nowak. All early work lost when he moved to England in 1939. First one-man show at Roland, Browse and Delbanco, London, in 1950. Painted a large mural for the Jews' College, London, in 1957, having done mural work in Czechoslovakia. The Tate Gallery, Southampton City Art Gallery, several colleges at Oxford and many galleries abroad hold his work. Lived in London.

Eleanora Anderson BORRIE: *see* **Eleanora HOPE HENDERSON**

Charles Gordon BORROWMAN 1892–1956 Watercolour, pastel and pencil artist, born in Edinburgh. Having attended Edinburgh University, he studied at the College of Art there on occasions between 1912–20 with David Alison and William Walls. After being commissioned in the Indian Army just before World War I, Borrowman served for over 30 years with the 4th Gurkha Rifles, whose history he wrote. Exhibited RSA, RSW, Royal Glasgow Institute of the Fine Arts and RSMA. The Indian Army Museum, Sandhurst, and the Russell-Cotes Art Gallery and Museum, Bournemouth, hold his work. Lived at Dunkeld, Perthshire.

Jiri BORSKY 1945– Painter and teacher, born in Dobrany, Czechoslovakia. He drew from an early age, then while attending Building College in Prague in 1960 began painting. From 1964 attended Prague University to study architecture, at instigation of father and to avoid military service, and began to exhibit pictures. After first visit to England in 1967 and another in 1968, in 1969 moved permanently, settling in Potteries, working as draughtsman for Wedgwood's, then as architectural assistant with borough of Newcastle-under-Lyme. Became British citizen in 1975, in 1976 enrolled at North Staffordshire Polytechnic to study painting and graduated in fine art in 1979. Took part in mixed shows in Midlands and elsewhere. After a one-man show at Brampton Museum, Newcastle, in 1971, others included Keele University on several occasions from 1977, and City Museum & Art Gallery, Hanley, Stoke-on-Trent, 1980. Wenlock Fine Art, Much Wenlock, gave him a show in 2006. Taught at Keele, which holds his work, as do several provincial galleries including Stoke. Borsky's work was figurative, often autobiographical, influences being Klee, Miró, Chagall, Dubuffet and Dix.

Alfred Edward BORTHWICK 1871–1955 Painter, stained glass artist and printmaker, born in Scarborough, Yorkshire. Studied at Edinburgh College of Art, in Antwerp and at Académie Julian, Paris, under Adolphe Bouguereau. Served in Army in both Boer War and World War I. Prolific exhibitor, especially at RSW and RSA, also at RA, RE, RP and Royal Glasgow Institute of the Fine Arts. Elected RSA, 1938. Lived in Edinburgh.

Mariota BOSANQUET 1923– Painter and draughtsman, in various media and using a sombre palette, born in London. She attended St Martin's School of Art, 1945–9, taught by Russell Hall, Ruskin Spear, Andrew Freeth and Vivian Pitchforth. Bosanquet, who was unmarried and a full-time painter, remained in London until 1977, moving to the Lincolnshire Fenland, living in Boston. She depicted "landscapes, people and other subjects sketched on the spot and worked on for paintings in the studio. Many of my subjects were from Languedoc and Vendée." Mixed exhibitions included Pictures for Schools, Whitechapel Art Gallery, 1954; Artists of Fame and Promise, Leicester Galleries, 1954 and 1955; RA Summer Exhibition, 1983; Lincolnshire and South Humberside Artists Society, Usher Gallery, Lincoln, 1991; Winchester Contemporary Art and Alresford Gallery, both in Hampshire in 1996; and RI, The Mall Galleries, 1997. She had a solo show at home in Islington, north London, 1977. Private collections in several continents hold Bosanquet's work.

Derek BOSHIER 1937– Artist who painted, sculpted and became involved in printmaking, photography and films, writing and books; teacher. He was married to the artist Patricia Gonzalez. Boshier was born in Portsmouth, Hampshire, and attended Yeovil School of Art, 1953–7, and Royal College of Art, 1959–62. After showing with Young Contemporaries in 1959 Boshier was included in several hundred mixed exhibitions internationally. He had a first solo exhibition, Image in Revolt, at Grabowski Gallery, 1962, several dozen following after that, later ones including Texas Gallery, Houston, and Mandeville Gallery, University of California, both 1991, Galerie de Centre, Paris, 1993, and Connaught Brown, 1996. From 1963–73 Boshier was an instructor at Hornsey College of Art, from 1963–79 at Central School and from 1973–9 at Royal College of Art. Many further appointments followed in Britain and abroad, then in 1980 Boshier joined University of Houston, Texas, eventually becoming professor. In the early 1990s he returned to live in England, settling in Kingsbury Episcopi, Somerset. Boshier's art went through various phases, touching on Pop Art, hard-edge Op Abstraction and politically radical conceptual art. Tate Gallery, British Museum, Victoria & Albert Museum and several dozen other notable international collections hold Boshier's work.

Marcus Arthur BOSS 1891– Painter in oil and watercolour, mainly of portraits, Boss was born in London and studied at Birkbeck School of Art, Heatherley's School of Fine Art, 1908–11, and the Royal Academy Schools, 1911–16. Exhibited widely, including the RA, ROI, RP, International Portrait Society and in the provinces. Lived in London and was a member of the Chelsea Arts Club and London Sketch club, where he was a noted character.

Ervin BOSSANYI 1891–1975 Figure painter in oil and tempera, stained glass artist and ceramics maker. Born in Hungary where he initially studied art, then at Académie Julian, in Paris, and Camden School of Art, London. Exhibited RA and Beaux Arts Gallery. One-man shows in London, Edinburgh and Germany. As well as extensive official purchases abroad, Bossanyi's work is held by the Tate Gallery and Victoria & Albert Museum. He lived at Eastcote, Pinner, Middlesex.

James BOSTOCK 1917–2006 Printmaker, painter and illustrator, born in Hanley, Staffordshire. He studied at Medway School of Art, Rochester, 1933–6, and Royal College of Art, 1936–9. Was on staff of Bristol Polytechnic. His book *Roman Lettering for Students* was published in 1959, his wood engravings for *Poems of Edward Thomas* appearing in 1988. Showed at RA, NEAC, Crafts Centre of Great Britain and RBA. There was a solo exhibition of his work from 1938–88 at the 20th Century Gallery in 2002. Victoria & Albert Museum and British Museum hold his work. Was a member of RE, SWE and East Kent Art Society. Lived in Broadstairs, Kent.

Allan BOSTON 1951– Painter, born in Hastings, Sussex. He studied at University of Newcastle, 1973–6, then Chelsea School of Art, 1975–6. Exhibited in groups in Britain and America, and was included in John Moores Liverpool Exhibition from 1976, his oil Car and Hand winning a prize in 1985. Boston was a frequent exhibitor in the Whitechapel Open at Whitechapel Art Gallery from 1978 and in 1989 participated in East End Open Studios, at Carpenter's Road. Had a solo exhibition at Serpentine Gallery in 1975, another at Chisenhale Gallery, 1988. Arts Council holds his work. Lived for a time in London.

James BOSWELL 1906–1971 Painter, illustrator, political cartoonist and printmaker. Born at Westport, New Zealand, Boswell began studying at the Elam School of Art, Auckland, in 1924; after coming to London in 1925 studied at the Royal College of Art, 1925–9. Began showing paintings from 1927 with the London Group and lithographs with the Senefelder Club. Became interested in politics in the late 1920s, in 1932 giving up painting. Joined the Communist Party and took to illustration and graphic design. In 1933 was a founder-member of the AIA, with which he illustrated, at the same time drawing for *Left Review* and contributing anti-Fascist cartoons to the *Daily Worker* under the name Buchan. Boswell combined his position as art director of the publicity department of Asiatic – later Shell – Petroleum with his radical activities. Travelled widely during World War II in the Army, after which he rejoined Shell for two years before joining the staff of *Lilliput* magazine until 1950. He drew for it and was its art editor. Began to exhibit widely, including the RA, Drian Gallery and Paris Salon. Boswell was a persuasive writer, publishing *The Artist's Dilemma* in 1947. While working as editor of the house journal of J Sainsbury Ltd, the retail firm, he wrote its centenary history. The bitingly satirical cartoonist and printmaker, whose work has been compared to that of the German George Grosz, diversified in the 1950s and 1960s. In 1951 he finished a large mural for the Sea and Ships pavilion for the Festival of Britain; he designed the poster Let's Go With Labour and the party's entire publicity campaign for the 1964 general election; film posters included *It Always Rains on Sunday* and *The Blue Lamp*, for Ealing Studios. Having established himself as a fine Colourist, Boswell later worked as an abstract painter. His work is held by many galleries in Britain and New Zealand, including the Tate Gallery. Boswell's work continued to be shown after his death. Sally Hunter & Patrick Seale Fine Art gave it a solo show in 1986 and in 2004 it was included in Pax Britannica A Hellish Peace, at the Aquarium Gallery, curated by Ruth Boswell. Centennial Celebration at Square One Gallery, 2006. Lived in London.

Reginald BOSWELL 1897–1997 Sculptor, who greatly admired Rodin, born in Liverpool. As a boy Reggie had spinal meningitis and at 16 was removed from Harrow School to live at Garsington, Oxfordshire, his intellectual parents, with whom he went on grand tours, being friends of Philip and Lady Ottoline Morrell. He was blissfully happy there, meeting Bertrand Russell, Lytton Strachey, Desmond MacCarthy, Mark Gertler and Stanley and Gilbert Spencer. After several years, Boswell's father bought him a farm near Garsington (he remained a life member of the Farmers' Club). He had a manager to run it, but was lonely, so it was sold and he went to the Slade School of Fine Art, under Henry Tonks. Settled in Chelsea, occupying 3 Rossetti Studios in Flood Street, exhibiting occasionally. His bronze Baby's Head was shown in RA Summer Exhibition, in 1929. Died in London.

William Aubrey BOSWELL 1926–1998 Painter in watercolour and oil and teacher, born in Nottingham. He studied at Nottingham College of Arts and Crafts, 1941–3; was a lithographer in the Royal Engineers, 1944–9; meanwhile attending Kingston School of Art part-time, 1945; Geniefa College, Suez, part-time, 1946; and Royal Air Force School of Art and Architecture, Heliopolis, part-time, 1947. Held a number of teaching posts, eventually becoming principal design officer for county planning for Clwyd, in which he settled at Wrexham. Wrote and illustrated guides to parts of Wales, such as Llangollen, Wrexham, Denbigh and Corwen. He was a member of RCamA and a founder and chairman, 1960–70, of Wrexham Art Group. Also exhibited at Williamson Art Gallery, Birkenhead; Royal Welsh Show; and Manchester City Art Gallery.

Winifred Doris BOSWORTH 1900–1957 Watercolour painter, etcher and embroiderer, born in Bideford, Devon, who signed her work with her maiden name, D Goaman. Studied at Bideford School of Art, 1916–21 under Hugh Heard, and at Bristol College of Art, 1921–3, with Reginald Bush. She held a series of teaching posts, notably at Bideford School of Art and the West of England College of Art in the 1920s and 1930s. Exhibited RWA and elsewhere, Bristol City Art Gallery holding her work. Lived in Carlisle.

Paul BOTHWELL KINCAID 1946– Sculptor and graphic artist, born in Birmingham, Warwickshire, who studied at Stourbridge College of Art and Design, and Dyfed College of Art, 1980–3. Became a member of SGA in 1979, showing with it and around Wales. Bishop Vaughan School in Swansea holds his work. Lived for a time in Newcastle Emlyn, Dyfed.

Dennis Roxby BOTT 1948– Watercolourist, born in London. He studied at Colchester School of Art, 1967–9, then Norwich School of Art, 1969–72, his teachers including Edward Middleditch. He worked full-time as an artist after 1975, claiming "wide-ranging subject matter, including architecture or other man-made influences in landscape". Was elected RWS in 1983, also participating in group shows at Agnew. Had solo exhibitions at Gallery 33 in Billingshurst from 1977; Ogle Gallery, Eastbourne, 1978; and Bourne Gallery, Reigate, from 1986. Towner Art Gallery in Eastbourne and public galleries in Brighton and Hove hold his work. Lived in Milford, Surrey.

BOTTERILL: *see* **ANTON**

Nick BOTTING 1963– Painter who, after studying at Hertfordshire College of Art and Design, graduated with honours from the University of Canterbury in visual and performed arts, 1983–6. He had shown early initiative when he painted pictures of his neighbours' houses during their holidays, selling them to the occupants on return. Botting's style was influenced by Boudin, Corot, de Kooning and Picasso, a sense of place, movement and the physical qualities of paint on canvas being his key concerns. He liked working direct from the motif, and enjoyed "the spontaneity and energy derived from involving myself in the subject." He featured several times in BP Portrait Award at National Portrait Gallery; was 1996 one of Brian Sewell's invited artists following The Discerning Eye show at Mall Galleries; and in 1997 won the Roberson Award at RI show there. Exhibited widely in England and Australia and had solo shows at Catto Gallery, 2000 and 2001; Marylebone Cricket Club, official artist on England tour to Pakistan, 2001; and Portland Gallery, 2003.

Roy Godfrey BOTTING 1909–1999 Painter, printmaker and teacher, born in London, who lived and worked in Chelsea and Kensington for around 60 years. He gained his diploma at the Royal College of Art in the 1920s, winning a painting prize and making a special study of printmaking by nineteenth-century French artists. In 1936,

Botting married the convent-educated Eileen Martin, of an Irish family and with a passion for classic ballet and singing. Their daughter Genia, one of Botting's models, trained at the Royal Ballet School. Botting taught in several London art schools, later holding a lectureship in printmaking at Harrow College of Arts and Technology, retiring in 1974. His townscapes and landscapes included London, Devon and Pembrokeshire. Eileen Botting died in 1988, Roy's death being recorded at Havering, Essex.

Ian BOTTLE 1963– Versatile artist who attended Canterbury College of Art, 1981–2; graduated with first-class honours in fine art, painting, from Newcastle Polytechnic, 1982–5; and gained his master's degree at Chelsea School of Art, 1987–8. Mixed exhibitions included Stowells Trophy, RA, 1984; Jarrow, Impressions of a Town, Bede Gallery, Jarrow, 1986; Young Contemporaries, Whitworth Art Gallery, Manchester, 1988; Cheltenham Drawing Open Exhibition, from 1994; RA Summer Exhibition, 1997; and Selected Works, Arts House, 2001. Solo shows included Jablonski Gallery, 1987. Lived in Woodnesborough, Kent.

Robert BOTTOM 1944– Painter and teacher, born in Cambridge, who studied fine arts at Canterbury College of Art; film-making at Newport; became head of art at Campbell College, Belfast; then painted full-time. He gained an Arts Council Travel Award to New York and was winner of the Laing Painting Competition, Northern Ireland section, both in 1992; was included in the National Self-Portrait Collection of Ireland, Limerick, 1996; was artist-in-residence, Eastern Mediterranean, Baltic and Irish cruises for Voyages of Discovery Cruises, 1997–03; his oil Evening Light (Field of Wild Flowers) was included in Landscapes from North and South, which toured from Glebe House and Gallery, Donegal, 1997–8, in the catalogue of which he was listed as Robert D Bottom; and won an Arts Council Travel Award to Philadelphia in 2002. Bottom took part in many group shows in the United Kingdom and Ireland, his long series of solo exhibitions latterly including Upfront Gallery, Penrith, 2000; Newtown Gallery, Pennsylvania, in America, 2002, the year he had several on board ship, including the *Ocean Majesty* and *Princess Danae*; Cavehill Gallery, Belfast, 2003; and Old Hunts and New Horizons at Tom Caldwell, Belfast, 2005. The Public Records Office, Belfast; Stormont Government Offices; Belfast City Council; and many corporate and private collections held examples. Bottom was a member of the RUA.

Albert Ernest BOTTOMLEY 1873–1950 Painter born in Leeds who studied art with the landscape artist William Edwin Tindall. Exhibited prolifically at RA, RBA, RCamA as well as at many other venues, public galleries in Leeds and Worthing buying his work. Lived at Reigate, Surrey.

Fred BOTTOMLEY 1883–1960 Landscape painter in oil and watercolour. Studied at the Slade School of Fine Art. Exhibited RA, RBA, ROI and with the St Ives Art Club. Lived at Stratford-upon-Avon, Warwickshire.

Peter BOTTOMLEY 1927– Artist in watercolour, gouache and graphic techniques, Bottomley was born at Goole, Yorkshire. He studied at Doncaster School of Art under Thomas Alexander Anderson and at the Royal College of Art under Robert Austin. After studies lasting 1942–52 Bottomley began to exhibit in Britain and America, including the RA and RE. He became principal of Southport College of Art. Lived at Southport, Merseyside.

Pauline BOTY 1938–1966 Painter, who created some of the most memorable images of the 1960s, and actress, born Carshalton, Surrey. She attended Wallington County Girls' School, winning a scholarship to study stained glass at Wimbledon School of Art. From 1959–61 she attended the Royal College of Art. She showed at AIA Gallery in 1961 with notable 1960s artists such as Peter Blake; in 1962 was included in New Approaches to the Figure at Arthur Jeffress Gallery; in 1963 taking part in Pop Art at Midland Group Gallery, Nottingham. In that year she held her first solo exhibition at Grabowski Gallery. As an actress Boty appeared in Frank Hilton's *Day of the Prince* at Royal Court Theatre in 1962, in the same year being featured in Ken Russell's film *Pop Goes the Easel* with Blake, Derek Boshier and Peter Phillips. Boty was married to Clive Goodwin, who was involved in the film business and who died in tragic circumstances in California. Boty died in London after the birth of their daughter. She was featured in The Sixties Art Scene in London, at Barbican Art Gallery, and had a small commemorative show at Mayor Gallery, both in 1993, another at Whitford Fine Art, 1998.

Sava BOTZARIS: *see* **Anastas Botzaritch SAVA**

Sava BOTZARITCH: *see* **Anastas Botzaritch SAVA**

Allan BOULTER 1940– Painter, draughtsman and linocut artist, born in Reading, Berkshire. He attended Willesden Art School, 1953–6, Harrow Art School and gained his Royal Academy Schools certificate, 1961–3, notable teachers including Charles Mahoney. He won three David Murray Scholarships: London, Cornwall and Aix-en-Provence University, France. In 1973 Boulter won the Laing Calendar Prize Competition. Group shows included Penzance Library Art Centre Gallery, 1980–7, and Hampstead Town Hall, 1985–6. Showed solo at Deal Library from 1979, Deal Serendipity Gallery from 1981 and Royal Cinque Ports Yacht Club from 1984. Wandsworth Borough Council holds his work. Lived in Deal, Kent.

Dick BOULTON 1939– Self-taught artist known mostly for his pastels, although also worked for long periods in watercolour. Produced highly stylised landscapes which later tended towards abstraction. Showed with PS, RI, Patricia Wells Gallery in Thornbury and elsewhere and had over a dozen shows in Somerset and Bristol. There was a retrospective at The Strata Gallery, Upper Norwood, 1997. Boulton lived near there, also at Ashcott, near Bridgwater, Somerset.

Doris BOULTON: *see* **Doris BOULTON-MAUDE**

Janet BOULTON 1936– Artist in watercolour, paper relief and pencil, born in Wiltshire, who studied at Swindon School of Art & Design, 1953–5, then Camberwell School of Art, 1955–8, in the latter year winning the David Murray Landscape Painting Scholarship. Began part-time teaching in a Swindon grammar school, 1959, other appointments including Swindon School of Art, 1960–2 and from 1972; Chelsea Westminster Evening Institute, 1962; Hreod Burna School, Swindon, 1970; Pangbourne College, with residency, 1981; residency at Radcliffe Infirmary, 1986; and art teaching at Abingdon School, 1988. Events in Boulton's career were development of an interest in botanical studies, gardens and garden history from 1981, which led to widespread painting of gardens in England, Italy and Scotland; attendance at a papermaking workshop at Oxford Polytechnic, 1987; and the editing of Paul Nash's letters to Mercia Oakley, 1989. Boulton was a member of the Royal Horticultural, Garden History and British Ivy Societies. She admired the work of Juan Gris, Morandi and Lucy Rie. Her still lifes of bottles and jars were notable, and they enabled her "to confront the duality between the vertical and horizontal planes and to exploit their rhythmic potential". Her many mixed shows included Reading Museum & Art Gallery, RA Summer Exhibition, Browse & Darby, LG, Scunthorpe Art Gallery, RWS Open and Flying Colours Gallery in Edinburgh. Solo exhibitions included a series at Mercury Gallery from 1988, and Redfern Gallery, 2001. Southern Arts, Oxford and Isle of Wight Health Authorities and National Gallery of Canada in Ottawa hold examples. Lived in Abingdon, Oxfordshire.

Doris BOULTON-MAUDE 1892–1961 Printmaker (born Doris Boulton, her original exhibiting name) who studied at Burslem School of Art, Stoke-on-Trent, then at Royal College of Art, 1916–21. She showed at RA and was an associate of RE, 1918–21. Went to Egypt, reportedly teaching art in Cairo, and making prints of views there. Back in London in 1930 she attended Slade School of Fine Art for a term and began exhibiting again. Came into contact with modern art movements, was influenced by Franz Marc and the Blaue Reiter style and changed to relief printing methods. Married Lionel Maude, whom she had met at a Fabian summer school (his parents Aylmer and Louise Maude, members of a strongly Socialist family, were Tolstoy's authorised English translators and biographers; they had been part of a late-1890s Tolstoyan community at Purleigh, Essex), and began to exhibit as Doris Boulton-Maude. Showed at NEAC, Redfern Gallery, Walker Art Gallery in Liverpool, SWA and RBA. Lived at Great Baddow, Essex. In 1995–6 a Chelmsford Museums Service show toured the county. Chelmsford and Essex Museum holds her work.

Diana BOURDON SMITH 1933– Painter in oil and watercolour and book illustrator, born in Wallington, Surrey. She studied at Kingston School of Art, 1950–4, under Robin Child and James Anthony Betts. Showed at NEAC, RA, RWA of which she was made an associate in 1984, and elsewhere in south and west of England. RWA holds her work. Lived in Bath, Avon.

Doris BOURGUIGNON fl. from 1940s– Artist whose work fell into two distinct periods, and who worked in a range of media. She studied at Belfast College of Art, then Royal College of Art, initially producing academic work. During World War II she painted American and British personnel and their activities in Northern Ireland and blitzed areas of Belfast. Had two solo exhibitions in Belfast, one in 1948 at the Museum and Art Gallery, which holds her early work (painted under her unmarried name of Doris V Blair) and later contemporary output. Bourguignon studied for that under Wallace Harrison in New York and in Paris with Fernand Léger and André Lhote. In 1975 Bourguignon, living in Belgium, had a solo exhibition at Galerie L'Angle Aigu in Brussels. In mid-1990s settled in London where Bourguignon was painting acrylic works of "Figurative Abstraction". In 1945 she had illustrated *Various Verses* by John o' the North.

Bob BOURNE 1931– Painter, born in Exmouth, Devon. Although mainly self-taught, in the 1950s he attended St Martin's School of Art and West of England Academy in Bristol part-time. Painted abstract and figurative works. Showed with Arthur Tooth, 1973; was included in the Arts Council tour Fragments Against Ruin, 1981–2; and the RWA exhibition Artists from Cornwall, 1992. Arts Council holds his pictures Lover's Leap, 1972, and Self Portrait, 1977. Bourne lived a simple life in a fisherman's cottage at Newlyn, Cornwall.

Christopher BOURNE 1930– Artist and teacher, born in Wolverhampton. After education there and in Newcastle he held a series of teaching posts, including Bath Academy of Art and Chelsea School of Art. A versatile artist, he participated in many group shows, including John Moores Exhibition in Liverpool, SEA, Whitechapel Art Gallery, Piccadilly and Rowan Galleries and New Art Centre. He also did graphic work for Editions Alecto; was commissioned by the BBC to design *Façade*, which was performed at the Barber Institute, Birmingham, and in Cheltenham at the Music Festival; and his sculpture Nativity was completed for Bangor Cathedral. One-man shows included University College of North Wales, Bangor. WAC holds his work.

John BOURNE 1946– Painter and teacher, born in Newcastle, Staffordshire, who specialised in still life and paintings of grouped objects, as in Summer Show Part Two, Highgate Fine Art, 2002. Bourne qualified as an art teacher after three and a half years at St Mary's College, Strawberry Hill.

John Frye BOURNE 1912–1991 Painter in oil and watercolour, who became a popular portraitist. Born in London, he was educated at Bishop's Stortford College, then studied at the Royal Academy Schools, where his teachers included Walter Westley Russell. Bourne claimed to be the youngest student at the Schools since J M W Turner, and was there 1929–34. He showed at RA, RCamA, RP, RWS and elsewhere, his work being published in *Royal Academy Illustrated*. Chelsea Arts Club member who lived in Sidbury, Devon.

John Wilson BOURNE 1943– Painter and teacher, born in Stoke-on-Trent, Staffordshire, mainly self-taught, but who attended a drawing class in Conwy, 1958–60; studied for his art teacher's diploma for one term in 1961; then from 1986 joined life classes at Wrexham Arts Centre. Bourne attended Imperial College of Science and Technology and Ministry of Technology (research, solid-state theory), 1969–72; taught mathematics at Ysgol Dyffryn Conwy (Comprehensive School), 1972–8; lectured in physics at North East Wales Institute of Higher Education, 1978–86; then became a full-time artist. Bourne wrote that he was "a figurative painter inspired by imagination and memories of experiences, drawing on both the modern world and childhood in Northern Ireland. I may have to live with an idea for years before it is ready to be made into a painting. I believe that art is capable of revealing something of a world lying beyond the familiar world of time and space. Initially I was influenced by Stanley Spencer and Surrealism, but am also interested in Godfried

Schalcken, Paul Klee and Outsider Art." Bourne took part in the Mostyn Open at Llandudno from 1989, winning first prize in 1990, also showing with Broekman Gallery, Chester, in 1993, the North Wales Artists' Association, the Wales Open in Aberystwyth and North Wales Open, Mold. He had a solo show at Theatre Clwyd, Mold, in 1991. Having seen a 1999 article in the *Sunday Times* about Stuckism, in 2001 "while feeling disillusioned with the conventional art world" he contacted the group and founded the Wrexham Stuckists. He then appeared in a number of Stuckist exhibitions and set up the Stuckism International Centre (Wales) in 2003. Lived in Wrexham, Clwyd.

Peter BOURNE 1931– Painter in oil and watercolour, and teacher, born in Madras, India, who studied at Glasgow School of Art, 1949–54, with David Donaldson. Went on to combine teaching and painting, being a member of RSW and SSWA. "The Fauves, British colourists and Pop" were among influences on his work, which appeared in group shows in Glasgow and Edinburgh, where he also exhibited solo, also in groups in Kendal, Perth and Newcastle upon Tyne. Paintings in Hospitals, Abbot Hall Art Gallery in Kendal, Edinburgh's city art collection and Mobil Oil have examples. Lived in Aberfeldy, Perthshire.

Bertrand BOUVERIE 1914–1999 Animal artist and sculptor, real name Bertrand Pleydell-Bouverie, born in Wherwell, Hampshire, younger son of the fourth Earl of Radnor. After his parents' death Bertrand went aged eight to Coleshill, Wiltshire, to be brought up by his aunt and two older first cousins. One, Katherine Pleydell-Bouverie, known as Bina, a noted potter and pupil of Bernard Leach, became his artistic mentor. After several years at the Royal Naval College, Dartmouth, Bertrand in 1938 took a degree in medieval and modern languages at Cambridge and got a blue for high-jumping. He then joined the Royal Naval Volunteer Reserve, instead of studying architecture in London, and served in coastal patrols, being mentioned in dispatches; after active service bought his own boat and recuperated for a year on the Isle of Mull; then attended Byam Shaw Art School, in 1950 marrying a fellow-student, Pamela Macdonald. They farmed and painted – she as Pamela Bouverie – in north Essex. He began to show his work, sometimes jointly with his wife, at such galleries as The Minories, Colchester; Gainsborough's House, Sudbury; and the Mall Galleries; and had a solo exhibition at the Theatre Royal, Bury St Edmunds. After giving up the farm and buying a Queen Anne house, open to the public and to the homeless, Bouverie returned for 20 years to Coleshill village. He began sculpting animals after a mid-life car accident and wheelchair confinement, but could not afford to cast his work. Bouts of depression and cancer did little for his career. Died in Fairford, Gloucestershire.

Pamela BOUVERIE 1925– Artist, born as Pamela Macdonald Boyce in India, her father from Galway, Ireland, her mother from Skye. As well as exhibiting as Bouverie, she also showed as Pamela Macdonald and Pamela Pleydell-Bouverie, after in 1950 marrying the artist Bernard (Pleydell-) Bouverie. After being brought to England by her uncle, Colonel R W Macdonald, to be educated, she attended Brighton College of Art under Ernest Sallis Benney, 1942–5; in 1946 was briefly at both Central and Chelsea Schools of Art; in 1947 joined the Auxiliary Territorial Service, attending the Gottingen College of the Rhine Army for a short course in drawing; from 1948–9 studying at Byam Shaw School of Art. She and Bernard Bouverie farmed in Essex, then opened Blue Bridge House, Halstead, to the public, 1969–77, where they sold work to visitors. She also exhibited with him at The Minories, Colchester; Gainsborough's House, Sudbury; the Mall Galleries; and with John Aldridge and the Great Bardfield artists at Coggeshall; and at Ramsbury Gallery, Wiltshire. Lived finally at Coleshill, Highworth, Wiltshire. In 2001, she had a solo show at The Old Carpenters Yard, Coleshill, "to promote awareness of Greyhounds in Need."

Regis de BOUVIER DE CACHARD 1929– Artist in oil, gouache and bronze and printmaker, born in Paris, France, who studied at the École Boule there, then was at the Machasson Textile Studio for Haute Couture, designing for Paris fashion houses. His work comprised stylised landscapes, figure and still life works, using a distinctive palette, with a Surrealist tinge. Group exhibitions included Salon des Indépendants, Paris, 1955; O'Hana Gallery, 1958; and The Guildhall, 1972. Had a series of international solo exhibitions, latterly including Kandinsky Gallery, Madrid, 1976; Sala Giannini, Madrid, 1976; Mall Galleries, 1981; with a retrospective at Tadema Gallery, 1987. Courtauld Institute holds a catalogue raisonné. Public collections include Tate Gallery, Museum of Modern Art in Paris; private collections Duke of Bedford, Alan Ladd, Dean Martin, Frank Sinatra and David Wolfson. Count de Bouvier de Cachard lived latterly at Lyme Regis, Dorset.

BOW GAMELAN ENSEMBLE: *see* **Anne BEAN**

Howard BOWCOTT 1956– Sculptor and artist in other media, born in Manchester. He studied fine art at Newcastle University, 1975–9, from the early 1970s having long stays in area of Blaenau Ffestiniog, Merionethshire, to draw, paint and photograph. Moved to Blaenau Ffestiniog, working as a stone-waller and civil engineer on the railway there, with subsequent years spent working in the landscape. In 1985 Bowcott was assistant to David Nash at Kroller Muller Museum, Arnhem, Netherlands. In 1987 went on cultural exchange visit, part-funded by British Council, to Zimbabwe, with a return visit in 1988. In that year he was also artist-in-residence, National Museum of Wales, Llanberis, and assistant to David Nash at Tournus, France. Took part in extensive group shows, notably in Wales. His solo exhibitions included Bulawayo City Art Gallery and British Council, Harare, Zimbabwe, in 1987, later ones including Glynn Vivian Art Gallery, Swansea, 1993. Bowcott's work is in the collections of Gwynedd County Council and Swansea City Council. From 1991, Bowcott worked mainly on public commissions, such as his Slate Sails at Penarth Marina. His four sculptures of leaves, 2002, are part of the art trail in Louth.

Jonathan BOWDEN 1942– Painter and designer for the stage who studied at Camberwell School of Art, 1965–6, but was mainly self-taught. He showed pictures with George Chapman at Richard Bradley Atelier, Billingford, 1971, also exhibiting at the The Old Fire Engine House, Ely. Private collectors including Sir Brinsley Ford owned his work.

Alice BOWE 1980– Artist and garden designer, born in Redhill, Surrey, a member of the Society of Garden

Designers. She studied at Loughborough High School under Jenny Richardson, 1992–9; the Slade School of Fine Art under Jo Volley, 1999; Kensington and Chelsea School of Further Education under Erica Winstone, 1999–00; and Ruskin School of Drawing and Fine Art, Oxford, where her teachers included Brian Catling, Matt Luck Galpin, Paul Bonaventura, Michael Archer, Sarah Simblet and Richard Wentworth, 2000–3. From 2003–4 Bowe attended the Oxford College of Garden Design, Oxford Brookes University. Colour theory, Josef Albers, Arts and Crafts Movement artists such as William Morris, her teacher Sarah Simblet and Bryan Kneale were cited as influences, and among Bowe's themes were colour and the changing effect of light, the colours and textures of plants, and abstracted drawings of plants, "breaking down the image into pattern so that it is still recognisable as a plant/flower." As an artist Bowe had a studio at Long Eaton, Nottingham, as a garden designer an office in London, with a stand which she took to trade shows. Group exhibitions included The Mine, Birmingham Jewellery Quarter, 2002; Seedy Rushes, Oxford Botanic Garden, 2003; and Artstop, locations around Harrow, 2005. Among her solo shows were Beautiful Things, Magdalen College auditorium, 2001, and Paper Drawing, Ruskin School, 2003. The Magdalen College art collection and private collections around Europe held Bowe's work.

Christine BOWEN 1945– Painter of exuberantly colourful work, born in Cheshire, who was educated there, in Nigeria and Nantes, France. Between 1965–86 she was a colour consultant and designer, completing a one-year certificate in visual education; gained a diploma in fine art with distinction from RTC Sligo, in Ireland; then in 1994 obtained a fine art honours degree, University of Ulster Art & Design, Belfast, Northern Ireland. Group exhibitions included Limerick University Gallery, Limerick; Kenny Gallery, Galway; One Oxford Street, Belfast; and Bank One Gallery, Louisville, Kentuck, America, 2001. Had solo shows at The Vaults Gallery, Theatre Royal, Bath, 1991, The Factory Theatre Gallery, Sligo, 1994, and Tom Caldwell Galleries, Belfast, from 1998. Department of the Environment (Northern Ireland), Northern Ireland Electricity in Belfast and several corporate collections hold examples.

Cliff BOWEN 1942– Sculptor, draughtsman and teacher, born in Ogmore Vale, Glamorgan. He studied at Newport College of Art, then went on to teach at Swansea, Sheffield and Derby Colleges of Art, 1966–72, when he joined Glasgow School of Art's sculpture department. Four years later he was made head of the department. Bowen drew on the countryside and nature for his work, but changed the scale of things to match his own remembered scale of importance. Showed WAC, Axiom Gallery in Exeter and Glasgow School of Art staff show. Had one-man exhibition at Compass Gallery, Glasgow in 1983.

Denis BOWEN 1921–2006 Painter and gallery owner, born in Kimberley, South Africa, but took United Kingdom citizenship in 1962. He was married for a time to the artist Judy Stapleton. Bowen received early education in north of England, and attended Huddersfield Art School on a County Award. He was accepted at Royal College of Art in 1940, but Royal Navy service, which involved extensive travel, put back his studies there to 1946–50, his teachers including Rodrigo Moynihan, John Minton and Carel Weight. Bowen soon began to make a name as a leading experimental painter; he taught at various provincial art colleges as well as Royal College and Central School of Arts and Crafts; in 1952 along with other members of the ICA he founded the Free Painters' Group; and from 1956–66 he founded and directed the New Vision Centre, with Frank Avray Wilson and Halima Nalecz, which became a focal point for the work of advanced artists from Europe and elsewhere. Bowen was appointed associate professor at Victoria University, British Columbia, 1969–72. Contributed to art publications in Britain and abroad and showed extensively internationally. Bowen had a first retrospective show at Bede Gallery, Jarrow, in 1973, and a second at Huddersfield Art Gallery in 1989. A retrospective at Belgrave Gallery in 2001 accompanied publication of Peter Davies' study *Denis Bowen*, there was a show of recent work at Blyth Gallery, Imperial College, in 2002, one at Belgrave Gallery, St Ives, in 2003, and in 2004 Bowen exhibited at Harlequin Gallery. In 1984 Bowen co-founded Celtic Vision, a group representing contemporary art from Europe's main Celtic regions. Bowen's work is in dozens of international public galleries, including Tate Gallery, Victoria & Albert Museum and British Museum. Lived in London.

John BOWEN 1914– Painter, born in Llanelli, Carmarthenshire. After attending Llanelli and Swansea Schools of Art he taught at Llanelli School of Art, 1939–60, also at the Boys' Grammar School there apart from wartime service in the Royal Air Force. He was an artist member of SWG and also showed WAC and at the Royal National Eisteddfod. In 1968 he had a retrospective at Parc Howard Mansion, Llanelli. Painter of landscapes in Britain and abroad and still life, in oil and watercolour whose work is in many public collections, including WAC and Newport Art Gallery and Museum.

Keith BOWEN 1950– Artist who was born in Wrexham, Denbighshire, and trained at Manchester Polytechnic. He was a frequent exhibitor at the Royal National Eisteddfod, gaining first prize in 1983. In 1988 he designed a postage stamp to celebrate publication of William Morgan's *Welsh Bible*, 1588. National Library of Wales in Aberystwyth holds his work.

Owen BOWEN 1873–1967 Painter, born in Leeds, who attended the High School there. He acquired his artistic training studying with Gilbert Foster and also studied printmaking and pottery design. Although Bowen painted on the continent, he was particularly known for his views of Yorkshire, for he settled in Leeds and established his own school of painting there. Also illustrated books. After World War II he was president of RCamA for a number of years, exhibiting with it prolifically, also with Walker Art Gallery, Liverpool, and RA and ROI. Several northern public galleries, including Leeds, Rotherham and Rochdale, hold his work.

Siân BOWEN 1959– Artist and lecturer, born at Birkenhead, Merseyside, who studied at the University of Newcastle upon Tyne, 1977–81; Edinburgh College of Art, 1982–3; then was a Monbusho Scholar, Painting School of Kyoto University of Arts, Japan, 1985–7. She was artist-in-residence, Burford House and John Treasure's Garden, Worcestershire, 1996; had a Grizedale visual arts residency, Grizedale Forest, Cumbria, 1998; an invited artist residency, Villa Romana, Florence, Italy, 2000; was artist-in-residence, Angel Row Gallery, Nottingham, 2003; then held a Time & Space Residency, Metal, 2003–4. From 1998, she was an associate lecturer at the University of Northumbria, based in Haydon Bridge. Bowen won a series of Northern Arts Awards and Grants from 1990, other awards including a Lowick House Printmaking Bursary, 1992; British Council Visitorship to India, 1995; a Northern Print Award, 1996; and second prize, Jerwood Drawing Prize, 2001. Showed widely in group exhibitions in Britain and abroad, later ones including Drawing – The Process, Knights Park Galleries, Kingston University and tour, Jerwood Drawing Prize 2003 at Jerwood Space and Look to This Day, Castlefield Gallery, Manchester, all in 2003–4. Among her later solo exhibitions were Passage, Hart Gallery, 2000; Ream: Aspex Gallery, Portsmouth, and tour (with substantial illustrated catalogue), 2002–3; and Siân Bowen, Galerie am Markt, Kunstverein, Schwäbisch Hall, Germany, 2004. The British Council in India; British Museum; European Patent Office in Munich; Southern Print Studio; and University of Nottingham hold examples.

Thomas BOWEN 1909–1993 Specialist in lithography and fore-edge painting; designer, born in London. Studied at his local School of Art in Clapham, at London School of Printing and at Bolt Court School. Was by profession an industrial and engineering draughtsman. Showed RWS and in the provinces, Warsaw Museum in Poland holding his work.

Nigel BOWEN-MORRIS 1961– Artist producing abstracts who lived in Greece from 1988. He had shows of recent works at 28 Cork Street in 2002 and 2003, another at Y Tabernacl, Machynlleth, 2004. Bowen-Morris wrote that "the curvilinear forms give an organic life to each painting, with each canvas having its own particular rhythm." Recent Work was shown at The Gallery in Cork Street in 2005.

Susan BOWER 1953– Painter, born and lived in Tadcaster, North Yorkshire, who was influenced by Outsider art. She studied at Nottingham University, 1971, University of Sussex, 1974 and Leeds University, 1976. Was a full member of ROI and RBA and took part in numerous other mixed exhibitions in England and Wales. Her work was included in a three-artist show at The Wykeham Gallery, Stockbridge, in 2004. Collections in Britain and abroad hold works.

Bernard BOWERMAN 1911– Painter, technical illustrator and designer, born in London, who attended Leyton School of Art, West Ham School of Art, classes in Walthamstow and privately studied with various artists. Member of the Wapping Group of Artists and showed at RA, RI, RBA and elsewhere, signing his pictures Bernard-Bowerman. Lived at Buckhurst Hill, Essex.

Kelvin BOWERS 1946– Painter, collagist, writer and poet and athlete, born in Stoke-on-Trent, Staffordshire. He was British Junior Indoor mile record holder in 1964, and in 1974–5 travelled to Australia on foot, the longest distance run ever, recorded in his book *Closing the Distance*, published in 1980. Bowers began writing poetry and making collages while training in Australia in 1966–7. In 1983 he enrolled at Staffordshire Polytechnic where he met the artist Jo Baker, with whom he lived in a converted cowshed in the Staffordshire countryside and collaborated on many projects. Bowers graduated with an honours fine art degree in 1986, the year that he published *Fantaisie Valse*, a limited-edition book of collages, with Baker; in that year they shared a show at New Victoria Theatre, Newcastle-under-Lyme. Other shared ventures included two-man exhibitions at Galerie Sud, Galerie Forum and Galeries Kooring-Verwindt, Amsterdam, 1987; in 1989 a photo-montage mural commission for St Edwards Mental Hospital, Cheddleton, and visits to New York and Mexico; and in 1990 a first joint London show at England & Co. They parted in 1991 and from 1992 Bowers lived with the artist Dooze Storey, in France and England. In 1995 had solo shows at Salthouse Gallery, St Ives, and England & Co; and State Gallery of Art, Sopot, Poland, 1996. Bowers was winner of a purchase prize at the Fifth Open Exhibition, Stoke-on-Trent City Museum and Art Gallery, 1991. His work was also owned by the artists Peter Blake, Gordon House and Denis Bowen and is in the permanent exhibition of contemporary British painting assembled in New York by Robert and Susan Summer. Bowers' work mixed Expressionist colour, Primitivism, fantasy and Surrealism. Bowers retold his England-to-Australia run in *Throwing Plates at the Moon*, 2002, with an accompanying exhibition of collages at The Cornerstone Gallery, St Ives.

Leigh BOWERY 1961–1995 Performance artist, costume designer and artist's model, born in the working-class town of Sunshine, Victoria, Australia, where he had a strict upbringing and uneventful, unflamboyant childhood, a contrast to his later life. Attended Melbourne High School, where he showed talent for music and art, then studied fashion at Royal Melbourne Institute of Technology, but became bored in his second year, worked in a department store, saved money and moved to London aged 19. Worked in a burger bar, joined the homosexual club scene, wore cosmetics and made flamboyant clothes, for himself and friends. Bowery worked with the dancer and choreographer Michael Clark, touring with him to Japan; appeared in films made by the artist Cerith Wyn Evans; and developed an outrageous, scatological performance act, with his own deliberately offensive group, Minty. At Taboo club met the artist Lucian Freud, becoming one of his notable models. Lived in a council flat in Stepney, east London, a temple of kitsch. Shortly before he died, of Aids in Middlesex Hospital, Bowery married Nicola Bateman, another Freud model. After his death, Freud paid for Bowery's huge corpse to be flown to Australia, for burial. Early in 1995 the Fine Art Society held a brief show of his costumes and in 2002 the ICA showed previously unpublished portraits of Bowery by the photographer Fergus Greer. Tate Britain holds Freud's 1991 portrait of Bowery.

John BOWES 1899–1974 Painter, pen and ink draughtsman and singer, born in Oldham, Lancashire. He was educated at Manchester Grammar School and attended the Royal Military Academy, Sandhurst, in World War I. Was professional singer, while also painting, for 20 years until 1943, then when became deaf took up full-time painting. Was made member of RCamA in 1965, also joining Manchester and Liverpool Academies, Manchester Society of Modern Painters and Lancashire Group of Artists. Had solo shows starting with 1946 at Salford Art Gallery, including retrospective at Atkinson Art Gallery, Southport, 1971. Public galleries in Derby, Liverpool,

Salford, Southport and Newcastle upon Tyne hold his work. Lived in Southport, Lancashire.

Druie BOWETT 1924–1998 Painter, writer and poet, born in Ripon, Yorkshire. She studied at Harrogate School of Art and later with Jean-Georges Simon, a pupil of Bourdelle. She wrote a memoir of him and her illustrated book of poems *Painter's Poetry* was published in 1986. Parisian influences were apparent in Bowett's pictures, which while showing a strong command of natural form had a notable pattern element. Was a member of Midland Group, Industrial Painters' Group, WIAC and other international bodies, also showing at RA, Paris Salon, LG, RP and RSA. Had many solo exhibitions from 1957 at Midland Group Gallery, Nottingham, later ones including The Pierrepont Gallery, Newark, 1991, and Cartwright Hall, Bradford, 1995. HRH The Duke of Edinburgh holds her work. Died Bassetlaw, Nottinghamshire.

Olwyn BOWEY 1936– Painter and draughtsman, born Stockton-on-Tees, County Durham. Attended West Hartlepool School of Art and the Royal College of Art and was awarded a travelling scholarship. For a time she taught at Waltham Forest School of Art. Showed at New Grafton Gallery and elsewhere, and became RA in 1974, also being a member of RBA. Work held by Tate Gallery, Arts Council, RA, Ministry of Public Building and Works and provincial galleries. Lived in Heyshott, Midhurst, Sussex.

David BOWIE 1947– Musician, actor, painter and sculptor, born in London as David Jones. His first hit single record, in 1969, was *Space Oddity*, after which many followed, including *The Rise and Fall of Ziggy Stardust and the Spiders from Mars*, 1972, *Scary Monsters and Super Creeps* in 1980 and *Never Let me Down*, 1987. In 1989 Bowie was executive producer and wrote the score for *The Delinquents*. Among his films were *The Man Who Fell to Earth*, 1976, and *Absolute Beginners*, 1986, and he appeared in stage and television plays. Before committing himself to performing Bowie had studied art, which he collected, notably works by modern British painters. In 1997, Bowie and others launched the 21 partnership, which sought to open up art writing to a younger audience by publishing more approachable titles. Bowie's own artworks appeared in Bosnia War Child at Flowers East, and in Minotaur Myths & Legends at Berkeley Square Gallery, both in 1994, and in Minky, Manky at Arnolfini Gallery, Bristol, 1995. His solo exhibition New Afro Pagan and Work 1975–95 was held at The Gallery in Cork Street, 1995. In 1995 he was also commissioned to prepare the Montreux Jazz Festival poster. In 1997, with his dealer friend Kate Cheverton, Bowie launched the virtual gallery bowieart.com to promote young artists alongside successful colleagues, taking no commission. A notable later event in Bowie's career was *Meltdown 2002* festival, which opened with the first London performance in five years of the American composer Philip Glass's *Heroes & Low*, from the music of Bowie and the British artist and composer Brian Eno. In 2003, Bowie released his new album *Reality* and began his European Reality Tour, with a highly successful European concert in Manchester. In 2004, the re-release album *Diamond Dogs: 30th Anniversary Edition* appeared, with an informative booklet written by the Bowieologist David Buckley. A series of exhibitions, entitled BLOC, was launched by Bowieart at the County Hall Gallery from 2005. The Bowie-funded foundation set out to give young artists a platform. David Bowie was then living in New York. Whitworth Art Gallery in Manchester, the Jacksonville Museum of Modern Art in Florida and Saatchi Collection hold examples of Bowie's work, which can be highly colourful.

Jonathan BOWKER 1963– Painter of Expressionistic figure groups, born in Huddersfield, Yorkshire. He graduated from Lanchester Polytechnic, Coventry, in 1987 with an honours degree in fine art. He took a studio in the Coventry Canal Basin, was a member of Coventry Artists' Group and showed in the city, in Liverpool and in the Pacesetters 8 exhibition in Peterborough, 1988. Had a solo show at Cotton Art Gallery, Midlands Arts Centre, Birmingham, in 1989, and in 1990 shared a three-man show at Woodlands Art Gallery.

Philippa BOWLEY 1948– Artist who studied at Heatherley's School of Fine Art, Hammersmith College of Art and Building and the London College of Printing. Her solo exhibitions included Holland Park, 1982, and Mompesson House, Salisbury, Wiltshire, 1992. Private collectors including Sir Brinsley Ford owned her work.

Frank BOWLING 1936– Painter and teacher, born in Bartica, Guyana, who completed his schooling in England from the age of 14. Bowling was one of the most prolific Colourist painters of his time, with work in numerous international public and corporate collections, including Tate Gallery; Victoria & Albert Museum; Metropolitan Museum of Art, New York; Museum of Fine Arts, Boston; and National Gallery of Jamaica, Kingston, West Indies. He won many awards, gained enormous press coverage, held several residencies and taught widely, including Camberwell School of Arts and Crafts, 1963–83; Reading University, 1964–6; Columbia University, New York, 1968–9; Douglass College, Rutgers University, New Jersey, 1969–70; Massachusetts College of Art, Boston, 1970–1; School of Visual Arts, New York, 1975–6; and Byam Shaw School of Painting and Sculpture, 1975–86. Originally intended to be a writer, but after travelling on the continent and seeing the work of certain European masters he returned to England, began work as an artists' model and decided to become a painter. Attended City and Guilds School, joined the Royal College of Art in 1959 and after a short time at the Slade School of Fine Art returned to the Royal College to complete his Master of Arts degree in 1962. Bowling had already made his mark with work showing the influence of Francis Bacon, his picture Mirror being made Painting of the Year at 1966 RA Summer Exhibition. Disenchanted with the art scene in London Bowling moved to New York in 1966, receiving Guggenheim Memorial Foundation Fellowships in 1967 and 1973. Returned to London in 1976, but continued to show widely internationally, with several one-man shows at Tibor de Nagy, New York; Serpentine Gallery, 1986; RWA, Bristol, 1989; and City Gallery, Leicester, 1996, entitled Bowling on Through the Century. Others included UFA Gallery, Chelsea, New York, from 1999; Georgetown Gallery of Art, Washington, 2000; G R Namdi, Detroit, and Bowling, Bending the Grid, an ongoing series, aljira, Newark, New Jersey, both 2003; What's Underneath, deliART, 2003–4; and Frank Bowling – A Survey, Broadbent, 2004. The son of Bowling and the writer Paddy Kitchen was Dan Bowling, Punk writer and musician. Bowling was latterly based in London and Brooklyn, New York. He was elected RA in 2005.

BOWMAN: *see* **Malcolm BOWMAN**

Betty BOWMAN 1923– Painter, etcher and teacher, born in Ealing, west London. Her father was head of a glass and pottery firm, Edward Bowman & Son, and for many years Betty Bowman worked in it as a designer, being the first artist since Ravenhead to produce freehand decoration which could be fired into opalescent ware and glass. Studied at Central School of Arts and Crafts, 1944; privately with Mabel B Messer; Regent Street Polytechnic School of Art from 1953, where her teachers included Norman Blamey; and City and Guilds of London Art School, 1967–70, where she studied under Rodney Burn and Robin Guthrie. Moved to Cotswolds where she converted an old mill and ran her own school. As well as many group show participations had regular solo exhibitions, starting with Woodstock Gallery, 1963, others including John Whibley Gallery, Drian Gallery and Mall Galleries. Noted for her portraits and atmospheric landscapes in pastel, many of which were featured on the sets of television programmes. Davy International Corporation holds her work. Lived in Stourton, Warwickshire.

Malcolm BOWMAN 1941– Painter and teacher, born at High Hoyland, near the Yorkshire Pennines, son of a forester on the Bretton Estate of Lord Allendale, and settled at West Bretton. He attended grammar schools in Wakefield and Hexham, a notable cross-country runner. Graduated in fine art at King's College, Durham, University, tutors Victor Pasmore and Richard Hamilton, the only fine art student to complete the gruelling Three Peaks Race. Did wide-ranging teaching, including liberal studies at Wakefield Technical College, 1969–72; travelled on the continent and in Israel; worked as a spray painter, psychiatric nurse, sheep farmer and forester, his father's occupation; and studied Unidentified Flying Objects at Warminster for several years. Was painter for the BBC *Omnibus' Van Gogh*, by Patrick Barlow, and Alan Bennett's *A Question of Attribution*, filmed by John Schlesinger. During the 1990s was a full-time painter, settled at West Bretton, near the Yorkshire Sculpture Park. The Euston Road period Pasmore and Walter Sickert's nudes were early influences on Bowman's work, which from the mid-1950s focused on facets of popular culture, later pictures including abstract elements. His solo show Fin de Siecle, at Wakefield Art Gallery, 1999, contained over 100 pictures, the viewer being allowed to choose his own titles. In 2002, had a show at Millfield Art Projects, Atkinson Gallery, Street, as Bowman.

Michael BOWMAN 1943– Landscape and portrait painter, notably of English, French and Italian scenes, influenced by both the Impressionists and Post-Impressionists. After studying painting and lithography at Bournemouth School of Art and obtaining his postgraduate teaching qualification at the University of Southampton he taught art, latterly being head of art at Hardye's School, Dorchester, then in 1997 retired to become a professional painter. Bowman's work of the 1960s developed along largely abstract lines, drawing inspiration from the relationship between the female human form and organic shapes underlying the Dorset landscape. From 1973, lived in Stratton, near the River Frome, one of his expanding sources of inspiration. Was included in the 1999 Christmas Exhibition at The Jerram Gallery, Salisbury. Had a first solo exhibition at Dorset County Museum, 1971, followed by many others including The Catto Gallery, 2002. Bowman was chosen to exhibit in the Florence Biennale, 2003. Private and public collections in Britain and abroad hold examples.

Pat BOWRING fl. from 1970s– Painter, draughtsman and printmaker whose work contained an element of fantasy. She studied painting with Morris Weidman in Tunbridge Wells in 1970–7, then moved to Greenwich and worked with the painter George Gault and sculptor Gerda Rubinstein. She was a member of NS, chairman of the Blackheath Art Society, 1981–4, a member of Greenwich Arts Council and Woodlands Art Gallery advisory group. Showed with RBA, UA, South London Artists and elsewhere. Shared a show at Tudor Barn Art Gallery in Eltham in 1983, was one of four artists who exhibited at Woodlands in 1988 and also showed solo.

John BOWSTEAD 1940– Artist, born in Northampton, who obtained a national diploma in design, painting, at Coventry College of Art, 1958–62. At Coventry a fellow-student was Roger Jeffs, and together they had a show, A New Kind of Brightness, at the Umbrella Club, Coventry, in 1961. In that year Bowstead took part in Eclectics at Nottingham Art Gallery and exhibited in Midland Young Contemporaries, also in Nottingham. In 1962 Bowstead shared a show at ICA with Maurice Agis, David Hockney and Peter Phillips and was included in an Arts Council tour selected from Young Contemporaries. Arts Council acquired Bowstead's oil on board The Language of Love, of that year. Bowstead attended the Slade School of Fine Art, 1963–4. In the latter year he, Jeffs and two other Slade students, Terry Atkinson and Bernard Jennings, formed Fine Artz, which produced the work Action Chair. They also presented a project and sound show called Miss Misty and the Tri-Cool Data at Birmingham Polytechnic in 1966. After Fine Artz Bowstead continued working with Jeffs until 1968–9 in Light-Sound Workshop, a research unit at Hornsey College of Art. Bowstead settled in east London.

David T BOWYER 1950– Printmaker, born in Coventry, Warwickshire. Attended Bournville School of Arts and Crafts, Birmingham; Ravensbourne College of Art and Design, Bromley; then did postgraduate work at Manchester Polytechnic. Bowyer was trained as an abstract painter, but matured as an etcher with an interest in landscape, wildlife and architecture. In 1980 he was engaged to work on the *Banks Florilegium* project for Editions Alecto and British Museum, in 1982 moving to Clarendon Graphics to work with contemporary artists under Anthony Benjamin. From 1987 worked in own studio at Blackheath, southeast London. Showed with Greenwich Printmakers and was a member of it and Printmakers' Council. Many mixed shows included RA Summer Exhibition and Whitechapel Open, at Whitechapel Art Gallery. Solo shows included Axis Gallery, Brighton, 1977, Woodlands Art Gallery, 1992, and Greenwich Printmakers, 2002.

Francis BOWYER 1952– Artist, and teacher, creating richly colourful works, whose interest was in "the brief moment captured." Bowyer was the son of the artist William Bowyer and the brother of the painter Jason Bowyer. He did a foundation course at St Martin's School of Art, 1971–2; graduated with honours there in art and design, 1972–5; completing a course in etching at Chelsea

School of Art, 1978; and one in painting there, 1978–80. Bowyer was a partner and director, Vera Small Designs, 1976–96; taught part-time at Richmond Art School from 1976; course tutor from 1991 at RWS, from 1994–9 being its education courses chairman; drawing tutor with NEAC from 1993; and from 2000 Royal Academy Schools life drawing tutor. He was elected an associate of RWS in 1986, a full member in 1991, from 1996–9 being its vice-president, in 2000 its president; in 1991 became a member of NEAC. Commissions included National Grid, 1993, and London Federation of Clubs for Young People, 1996. Among awards were the Southwark Theatre Drawing Award, 1975; W H Patterson Fine Art Award, 1993 and 1995; Arts Club Prize at RA Summer Exhibition, 1994; and St Cuthbert's Mill Award, NEAC, 2002. Other mixed shows included Bedford Park Summer Exhibition, from 1988; The Discerning Eye, from 1991; and Woodgates Gallery, East Bergholt, from 1997. Solo show at New Academy Gallery, 2002, The Sheen Gallery, 2003. Work held by Royal Collection and HRH The Prince of Wales. Lived in west London.

Jason Richard BOWYER 1957– Painter and teacher, born London, son of the artist William Bowyer. Jason Bowyer attended Camberwell School of Arts and Crafts, 1975–9, and Royal Academy Schools, 1979–82. Among his many awards were the British Institution Award in 1982; Elizabeth Greenshields Award in 1983; British Council Visit Award to Bulgaria in 1990; and three awards at NEAC Open in 1999. Bowyer was artist to Fulham Football Club, 1985–6. His mixed shows included RA, NEAC and Christie's Post-Graduate Exhibition, 1982. Had a solo show at Lyric Theatre, Hammersmith, with a series at New Grafton Gallery from 1991. He was a part-time lecturer at Sir John Cass College, ran the NEAC school of drawing and offered short courses from his studio, in the Kew Bridge Steam Museum. His work was held by Arts Club, S G Warburg, the Museum of Modern Art at Smolyen, Bulgaria and Museo Taurino, Pamplona, Spain. Lived in Brentford, Middlesex.

William BOWYER 1926– Painter and teacher, father of the artists Jason and Francis Bowyer. He was educated at Burslem School of Art and Royal College of Art. Bowyer won the City of London Art Award in 1963. Went on to become head of fine art at Maidstone College of Art, 1971–82. As well as painting landscapes Bowyer was a noted portrait painter, his portraits of Arthur Scargill, the miners' leader, and Viv Richards, the cricketer, being bought by National Portrait Gallery in 1988. He was commissioned by Marylebone Cricket Club to paint the Bicentenary Game at Lord's in 1988. Bowyer was a member of RWS, RP and RBA and was honorary secretary of NEAC, also showing at RA, to which he was was elected in 1981, New Grafton Gallery and elsewhere. There was a retrospective at Messum's, with an extensive catalogue, 2003, his first London solo show. RA, Chantrey Bequest, Arts Council and other public collections hold his work. Lived in London and at Walberswick, Suffolk.

E BOX 1919–1988 Painter in a poetic, naïve style reminiscent of the work of the Douanier Rousseau, her real name was Eden Fleming. She adopted E Box when she began exhibiting in the late 1940s, having trained for two years at Regent Street Polytechnic School of Art, then being prevented from painting by the war years. Was married to Marston Fleming, senior research fellow at Imperial College, and with him travelled widely in continental Europe, North America, Russia, Africa and Asia, what she saw contributing to her pictures. An admirer of these was the artist Howard Hodgkin, who wrote an appreciation for the catalogue of her retrospective at David Carritt Ltd, 1981. Other retrospectives were held at St George's Hall, King's Lynn, 1956, and Fermoy Art Gallery there, 1979. Tate Gallery, Arts Council, Southampton City Art Gallery and Dunedin Art Gallery in New Zealand hold examples.

John BOX 1920–2005 Art director and draughtsman, described as "Britain's finest film production designer", born in Hampstead, north London. Some early years were spent in Ceylon, where his father worked as an engineer. Box studied at the London School of Architecture, enlisting in the Royal Armoured Corps during World War II, served in France, was mentioned in dispatches, and ended up as acting colonel aged 25. He entered films as a draughtsman, initially for Two Cities Films. He was promoted to art director on *The Million Pound Note*, 1953, then soon established a reputation as principal designer of big-scale productions in Britain and America. Objections by the Nationalist Chinese leader Chiang-Kai-shek to the script of *The Inn of the Sixth Happiness*, 1958, gave Box, its relatively untried art director, his big career opportunity. Box made it possible to replicate the ambitious Chinese scenes in Wales, building a walled Chinese city at Nantmor, in Snowdonia. "It was down to me," he later recalled. "There was a huge amount of money involved with Ingrid Bergman's salary.... I just had a feeling that Wales and Chinese watercolours had an affinity." Box won a string of awards. These included *Our Man in Havana*, 1959; *Lawrence of Arabia*, Academy Award (AA), 1962; *Doctor Zhivago*, AA, 1965; *A Man for All Seasons*, British Academy of Film and Television Arts Award, 1966; *Oliver!*, AA, Moscow Festival Award, 1968; *Nicholas and Alexandria*, AA, 1971; *Rollerball*, 1975; and *A Passage to India*, 1984. His last film was *First Night*, 1995.

Richard BOX 1943– Painter, draughtsman, fabric collagist and teacher who studied fine art at Hastings School of Art, 1960–2, then Goldsmiths' College School of Art, 1962–5. Taught at Eltham Green Comprehensive School for three years, then at Avery Hill College. His exhibitions included a one-man at Woodlands Art Gallery, 1980, where flowers were the main theme. In 2004, the Bristol-based Box won the £20,000 Bombay Sapphire Prize for Field, an installation of over 1,000 fluorescent lights lit by the electromagnetic fields of overhead power cables.

Kate BOXER 1961– Printmaker, who studied at Edinburgh University, producing figurative works with a quirky originality. Mixed exhibitions included Laing Competition and National Print Exhibition, both at Mall Galleries, 1994; Folio Society, from 1995; Christopher Hull Gallery, 1996; Cassian de Vere Cole Fine Art, 1997; and Glasgow Art Fair, 1998. In 1997, Boxer won the National Print Exhibition Arcturus Prize. Had a first solo show at Elsie Duncan Gallery, 1994, later ones including Jonathan Clark, 1998 and 2000, and Oliver Contemporary, 2002. In 2004, she shared a show there with Basia Lutman. Mainhill Gallery, Ancrum, also exhibited her work.

Martin BOYCE 1967– Artist who was born and lived in Glasgow, where he attended the School of Art, 1986–90 and 1995–7, also California Institute for the Arts, 1997. In 1999 exhibited at Fruitmarket Gallery, Edinburgh, in Visions for the Future, Part I, with Ross Sinclair. Had a solo show at The Jerwood Gallery, 2000, Boyce's When Now is Night wallpaper of a diagonal black linear grid pursuing his interest in the relationship between design and everyday life and in the role that design has in public consumption and popular culture.

Sonia BOYCE 1962– Painter, artist in collage and mixed media, born in London of parents from Barbados and Guyana. Studied at Stourbridge College of Art and Technology, 1980–3. Attended first National Conference of Black Artists in Wolverhampton in 1982. Artist-in-residence, Skinners Company's Girls' School, 1985. Using a combination of figurative and decorative images, Boyce was concerned to regenerate her cultural identity in what she considered a racist society. Solo shows included Black-Art Gallery, 1986, and Whitechapel Art Gallery, 1988. In 1998, Boyce had a show at Cornerhouse, Manchester, following a residency at Manchester University, based in the department of art history. A publication documented her time there. Boyce participated in The Other Story, Hayward Gallery and tour, 1989–90. Arts Council and Tate Gallery hold her work. In 2002–3, Tate Online featured Boyce's From Tarzan to Rambo, in which she examined "her own sense of self in relation to media images of blackness and whiteness."

Hugh BOYCOTT BROWN 1909–1990 Painter and teacher, born in Bushey, Hertfordshire, where his father Allan Robert Brown was art master at the Royal Masonic School. Several other members of the family were artists (including Hugh's brothers Michael, whose surname used a hyphen, and Robert Brown). Boycott Brown learned from his father and studied at the Margaret Frobisher School, Bushey. In 1929 he began teaching at Royal Masonic Junior School, but he continued his studies in the evenings at Watford School of Art; during holidays studied at Heatherley's School under Frederic Whiting and Bernard Adams; and during the 1930s was much encouraged by Sir John Arnesby Brown. By then Boycott Brown had begun his association with the East Anglian coast, a major theme in his work, although he also painted a lot abroad. Catching fleeting effects of light and colour, especially sky effects, were the artist's strong point, using small panels and oils. In 1947 Boycott Brown bought a cottage in Blakeney, Norfolk, where he lived permanently after retiring in 1970. Later exhibitions included Southwell Brown Gallery, Richmond, 1985; Belgrave Gallery, 1986; and in 1991 there was a memorial show at Abbott and Holder. Signed work HBB and must not be confused with Hercules Brabazon Brabazon, the much-faked artist who did the same.

Michael BOYCOTT-BROWN 1910– Abstract artist, using collage, watercolour and oil, and teacher, brother of the painters Hugh Boycott Brown (who chose not to hyphenate the surname) and Robert Brown. He was born in Bushey, Hertfordshire, and studied at British Colombia College of Art in Vancouver; at Datillo Rubbo's School of Art, Sydney; at Académie Julian, Paris; and at Westminster School of Art under Mark Gertler and Blair Hughes-Stanton. Worked as an assistant at Zwemmer Gallery, 1938–9, and taught at Paston Grammar School, North Walsham, and at Norwich School of Art. He was an honorary member of Hampstead Artists' Council and a member of National Collage Society. Took part in numerous mixed exhibitions from 1958, with the Cambridge Society of Painters and Sculptors, at Arts Council Gallery, Cambridge, later ones including Eastern Open/93 and 95 Exhibitions at Fermoy Gallery, King's Lynn; Heffer Gallery, Cambridge, Laing Art Competition, 1995; Business Arts Fair, Islington, 1995; and English Artists at the Académie Julian, at Michael Parkin Gallery, 1996. By 1996 Boycott-Brown, who named Kurt Schwitters and Nicolas de Staël among key influences, had had two dozen solo shows, mainly in Cambridge, Heffer Gallery, Clare Hall and Gallery Soleil among the venues. In 1996 Boycott-Brown shared a show at Cambridge Arts, Ely, with his wife Eira John. They lived in Cambridge.

Arthur BOYD 1920–1999 Painter and artist in variety of media such as tapestry, ceramics and sculpture, born in Murrumbeena, then just outside Melbourne, Australia, brother of the artist David Boyd. Boyd's grandfather Arthur Merric Boyd gave him lessons in painting and he had his first show in Melbourne aged 19. He attended evening classes at National Gallery of Victoria School of Art, then after war service founded a pottery with his brother-in-law John Perceval. That lasted until 1958, the following year settled in England, and then he divided his time between the two countries. Boyd was a powerful and mystical landscape and figure painter who drew on his own folklore associated with Aboriginal life. Among other activities he illustrated Pushkin's fairy tales; designed the décor for the ballet *Renard* for the 1961 Edinburgh Festival; and was commissioned to complete a big series of ceramic panels for the 400th Shakespeare Anniversary, also for Edinburgh. His later output included the Half-Caste, Nebuchadnezzar and St Francis series in a variety of media; prints on Lysistra and Narcissus; a tapestry for the Parliament House Authority, Canberra; and 16 canvases for the foyer of the State Theatre at the Victoria Arts Centre, Melbourne. Participated in many group shows and had series of solo exhibitions at Fischer Fine Art, which represented him. Among retrospectives of his work were Whitechapel Gallery, 1962, and Richard Demarco, Edinburgh, 1969, and Art Gallery of New South Wales, Sydney, 1993. Boyd was voted Australian of the Year in 1995. Arts Council, National Gallery of South Australia in Adelaide and many other public galleries hold his work. Died in Melbourne.

Cherith BOYD: *see* **Cherith McKINSTRY**

David BOYD 1924– Ceramic sculptor, painter and potter, grandson of the artist Arthur Merric Boyd and brother of the painter Arthur Boyd. His studies took place within the family and at Melbourne National Gallery School. In the 1950s Boyd became noted for his ceramics. He later became a painter to produce a series of large panels inspired by Arthur's work and influenced by his brother-in-law, John Perceval. Boyd lived in England, France and Spain, 1950–5; was president of the Contemporary Art Society in Melbourne, 1960–1; but resigned to accept an Italian Government Travelling Art Scholarship, which took him to Rome, after which he worked in England. Boyd's painting style was original and figurative with an almost sculptural depth. He showed in the Antipodean exhibition in Melbourne in 1959 and at Whitechapel Art Gallery in 1960. Examples of his pottery are in the National Museum of Modern Art, Tokyo, and other work is in Australian state galleries.

Graham BOYD 1928– Abstract painter and teacher, born in Bristol, who attended Watford School of Art, gaining his diploma in 1951, with a year at Institute of Education at London University until 1952. Was resident in Southern Rhodesia, 1953–5. Boyd was visiting artist at Reading University, 1975–83, having had a similar post at Plymouth State College, in America, 1972–3. Among other positions held was head of painting, Hertfordshire College of Art & Design, 1976–93. Boyd was influenced by American abstract painters, learning there the technique of working with large canvases on the floor, freeing him to apply paint in broad, sweeping bands of colour. Landscape was an inspiration. Mixed shows were participated in at Waddington Galleries from 1957; he also took part in John Moores Liverpool Exhibitions, LG and RA. Had a solo show at AIA in 1962, later ones including Spacex Gallery, Exeter, 1983. In 1994 he shared an exhibition with Katherine Gili at The Charterhouse Gallery. There was a retrospective at University of Hertfordshire Galleries, Hatfield, 2001. Boyd had a show of new paintings, Striking Lights, at deliART, 2004, commenting: "There is no substitute for the physical presence of paint." Walker Art Gallery in Liverpool holds his work. Lived in Chipperfield, Hertfordshire.

James BOYD 1943– Artist, notable as a printmaker, born in Dundee. He studied at Duncan of Jordanstone College of Art there and at Patrick Allan-Fraser School of Art, Hospitalfield, Arbroath. In 1982 was elected RE. Showed at RSA, International Print Biennales in Korea and Republic of China, at Mercury Gallery, International Art Fair in Basle, 1985, and in The Compass Contribution at Compass Gallery, Glasgow, 1990. Had a solo show at that gallery in 1976.

James Davidson BOYD 1917– Artist in oil, watercolour and enamel, and gallery curator, born in Glasgow. He was married to the artist Elizabeth A Ogilvie. Studied at Falkirk High and Technical Schools, then Glasgow School of Art, 1936–40. Was director of Dundee Art Galleries and Museums, 1949–82. Lived in Dundee, Angus.

Jamie BOYD 1948– Painter, printmaker and draughtsman, born in Melbourne, Australia, son of the painter Arthur Boyd. Moved to London with his family in 1959, starting to paint full-time in 1965. In 1968 went to the Michael Karolyi Foundation in south of France on a painting award. Boyd was given technical instruction by his father and attended Central School for two weeks in 1969 on a diploma course, but was essentially self-taught. Turner, the Impressionists and Bonnard were influences. Although he went with his wife and children to live in New South Wales in 1978 Boyd remained based in London, returning to Australia every few years to paint the landscape. He had many solo exhibitions commencing with Bonython Galleries, Adelaide, 1966, later shows including Palazzo Strozzi, Florence, 1989, Boundary Gallery, 1990, and Chappel Galleries, Chappel, 2005. Universities of South Australia and Western Australia are among public collections with his works.

Jane BOYD 1953– Artist and teacher, born in London, who gained a Diplôme Français (Grade 1) from L'Institut Français de la Sorbonne, Paris, 1971; a foundation diploma from Camberwell School of Arts and Crafts, 1971; and an honours degree in fine art there, 1975. Held a wide variety of visiting teaching posts in Britain, India, Australia, America and the Netherlands, being from 1997 on the graduate fine art sculpture course at Tilburg Academie voor Beeldende Vorming, Netherlands, resident in Amsterdam. Undertook a large number of research projects, her interests being "time, memory and consciousness, drawing and communication." Among Boyd's many awards and commissions were Fellow-commoner in Creative Arts, Trinity College, Cambridge, 1981–3; in 1998, Abbey Rome Fellow at the British School at Rome, 1999; Oppenheim-John Downes Memorial Trust Award and London Institute College Research Award, both 1999; AHRB Research Award in Creative Arts, 2000; and Leverhulme Trust Artist-in-Residence, 2001. Took part in numerous group shows, including Seeing Things, Newlyn Art Gallery, 2004, later solo exhibitions including Palindrome, The Warburg Institute, 2001. British Museum, Victoria & Albert Museum and Usher Gallery in Lincoln hold examples.

John BOYD 1957– Painter, who studied at Slade School of Fine Art, 1976–8, after a foundation year at Newcastle College of Arts, then at Newcastle University, 1978–80. Boyd's group appearances included Northern Young Contemporaries, Manchester, in 1980; the Open Eye Gallery, Edinburgh, in 1987–8; and Christopher Hull Gallery, 1988. Boyd had a solo show at Below Stairs Gallery, Newcastle, in 1981, with others following in Newcastle, Antibes and Rotterdam until in 1989 Christopher Hull gave him a first one-man show in London. Later ones included The Rites Of Man? at Archeus Fine Art, 2000, of Boyd's hard-edged, sometimes masked and highly stylised figures. AIB Bank Collection, Ireland; Merrion Group; Christie's, Morgan Grenfell and other corporate collections hold examples. Lived in County Kilkenny, Irish Republic.

John G BOYD 1940– Painter in oil and teacher, born in Stonehaven, Kincardineshire. He studied at Gray's School of Art, Aberdeen, 1958–62, and Patrick Allan-Fraser School of Art, Hospitalfield, Arbroath, 1961, teachers including Robert Henderson Blyth and David Michie. He moved to Glasgow in 1962 and became a part-time lecturer at the School of Art, 1967–88, later in further education. Boyd's main works were portraits, still life and composition. He was a member of RP and Royal Glasgow Institute of the Fine Arts, also showing at RA, RSA, Fine Art Society and Cormund Gallery in Glasgow, Open Eye Gallery and Bourne Fine Art in Edinburgh and Portland Gallery. Lillie Art Gallery, Milngavie; Paisley Museum & Art Gallery; and People's Palace in Glasgow hold his work. William Hardie Gallery, Glasgow, held a retrospective in 1994.

Margaret BOYD 1920– Painter, teacher and artist in ceramics, born in Bristol. She studied at West of England Art College there and went on to exhibit extensively, including LG, SEA, WIAC, of which she was a member, RWA, Redfern and Leicester Galleries. She was included in a group show at the AIA in 1950. Boyd taught during World War II, then travelled, working in France and Persia. She was also employed on several Technicolour cartoons. Coventry Training College holds her work. Lived in Bristol.

Muriel BOYD: *see* **Muriel BOYD SANDEMAN**

Patrick BOYD 1960– Artist in a variety of media who studied at London College of Printing, West Surrey College of Art in Farnham and then holography at Royal College of Art. He went on to make a special study of holography. As well as gaining a Fulbright Arts Fellowship in Light Transmission and a fellowship at the Academy of Media Arts in Cologne, he was artist-in-residence at the Museum of Holography in New York, 1989–90. He took part in many solo and group exhibitions, contributing boxed constructions to Art in Boxes at England & Co, 1992.

Stephen BOYD 1959– Artist and teacher, who gained a first-class honours degree in painting at Glasgow School of Art, 1976–80, and was highly commended, postgraduate studies diploma there, 1980–1; a Gillies Bequest, RSA Travelling Scholarship and Elizabeth Greenshields Foundation Fellowship enabled him to work at San Gimignano, Italy, 1981–3. Among his many awards were first prizes at Castel Vecchio Drawing Competition, San Gimignano, 1982, and 4th Stoke Open, Potteries Museum, Hanley, 1990. Boyd was a senior lecturer in fine art at Staffordshire University. Group exhibitions included John Player Portrait Award at National Portrait Gallery, and RSA Summer Exhibition, both from 1983; Mercury Gallery, 1985; Mappin Open, Mappin Gallery, Sheffield, 1988; Stockport Museum & Art Gallery, 1990; East, Norwich Gallery, 1991; and Far From Perfect Strangers, Real Gallery, New York, America, 1998. Had a solo show, European Rustic, at Real Gallery, 1999, and in 2000, as Proximity, Boyd's works were sited within the permanent collection of the Museum & Art Gallery, Kelvingrove, Glasgow, challenging the viewer to look anew at established pictures. Glasgow School of Architecture, Paisley Art Institute and Hanley City Museum and Art Gallery hold examples. Lived in Newcastle-under-Lyme, Staffordshire.

BOYD and EVANS 1968– This is the year the partnership began of Fionnuala Boyd (born Welwyn Garden City, Hertfordshire, 1944) and Leslie Evans (born St Albans, Hertfordshire, 1945). Boyd studied at Leeds University, 1963–7, Evans at Leeds College of Art, 1967–8. Boyd and Evans used photography and painting to create their representational yet allegorical art, several examples of which are held by Arts Council. Their first solo show was held at Angela Flowers Gallery in 1972, after which many such exhibitions were held there. Boyd and Evans were twice prizewinners in the Bradford Biennale in the 1970s, also participating in Tokyo Biennale and John Moores Exhibition, Liverpool, both in 1974. In 1977–8 they travelled in America as Bicentennial Fellows, did work in that country and showed at Fendrick Gallery, Washington, in 1978. A Decade of Paintings toured from Milton Keynes Exhibition Gallery, 1982–3. In 1991 Boyd and Evans were invited by the Royal Geographical Society to join the Brunei Rainforest Project as artists-in-residence, and resulting paintings toured in England and abroad from Flowers East in 1993. Later exhibitions included Western Photographs, Flowers West, Santa Monica, California, 2000; retrospective, Flowers East, 2002; and photographs inspired by natural and man-made wonders in the American landscape at Milton Keynes Gallery, 2005. Tate Gallery, Arts Council, British Council and many British provincial and foreign collections hold examples.

Glynn BOYD HARTE 1948–2003 Painter in watercolour, draughtsman in coloured pencil and lithographer, and teacher, born in Rochdale, Lancashire, married to the artist Caroline Bullock. He studied at Royal College of Art, 1970–3, teachers including Brian Robb, Edward Bawden and Peter Blake. Taught part-time at Cambridge School of Art, 1973–83. Boyd Harte became a brother of the Art Workers' Guild. He illustrated the literary page of *The Times*, 1986–90, the *Sunday Telegraph* from 1990. Decorated the Dolphin Brasserie, 1986; started the Dolphin studio, for fabrics and wallpapers, 1989; and did murals for Crabtree & Evelyn in Rockefeller Center in New York, 1991. He produced *Venice*, 1988, and *Mr Harte's Holiday*, 1990, as well as publishing several limited-edition books of lithographs, including *Metro-land*, with verse by Sir John Betjeman. Boyd Harte said that he intended to "carry on the English tradition of Bawden and Ravilious, topographical views and applied decorative art". He took part in innumerable group shows, his solo shows including a series at Francis Kyle Gallery from 1978, also at Albemarle Gallery from 1988 and Portland Gallery from 1992. In 2000, the Museum of London, associated with Curwen Gallery, showed Building the Millennium, Boyd Harte's views of spectacular new projects in the capital. His solo still life show, Apples and Artichokes, was at Curwen Gallery in 2003. Victoria & Albert Museum holds his work. Lived in Veules-les-Roses, northern France.

Bertha Stanfield BOYDELL 1899–1978 Sculptor and potter, born in Cobridge, Staffordshire. She attended Hanley School of Art under Ernest W Light, 1916–20, and Goldsmiths' College School of Art, 1920–2, under Frederick Marriott, thereafter for a short period assisting the potter Charles Vyse. She was married to the artist Phillip Boydell and signed her work B S B. Exhibited RA and RMS. Lived in London.

Phillip BOYDELL 1896–1984 As well as being an artist in oil and watercolour, Boydell was a notable designer and typographer whose career included positions as art master at Croydon and Blackheath Schools of art and at the Royal College of Art 1923–6. Born at Tyldesley, Lancashire, he studied art at Manchester School of Art and then at the Royal College of Art under Sir William Rothenstein and Robert Anning Bell. For 35 years from 1926 he was with the London Press Exchange, holding posts as art director and creative director. He designed the typeface known as Festival for the Festival of Britain in 1951. Because of his work on many national press and poster campaigns he was well qualified to write *The Artist in Advertising*. He was also a book illustrator. The Imperial War Museum and Trinity College, Oxford, own examples of his work. Married to the sculptor Bertha Stanfield Boydell. Lived in London.

Alma BOYES fl. from late 1970s– Sculptor, ceramist, designer and teacher who had a special interest in wildlife sculptures, notably of endangered species, developed during a long association with wildlife sculptor William Timym. Graduated as a ceramist from Bath Academy of Art in 1978, in 1980 gaining a British Council Scholarship to work in Mexico. From 1982 she attended North Staffordshire Polytechnic, concentrating on industrial production techniques, gaining her master's degree in 1984. Lectured at several universities and colleges and was included in 1st RWA Open Sculpture Exhibition, 1993. Lived in London.

Alicia BOYLE 1908–1997 Painter, quill pen draughtsman, muralist, printmaker, theatre designer and teacher. A rather solitary figure, her work was influenced by Surrealism and the light, colour and landscapes of Greece, Ireland and Spain. She was born in Bangkok, Thailand, and spent her early years in Limavady, County Londonderry, then London, where she studied at Clapham School of Art for four years, which she regarded as a waste of time. Won a scholarship to Byam Shaw School of Drawing and Painting, under Ernest Jackson. As a student had first picture accepted at RA in 1932; in 1934 gained a commission for a mural of St James's Park for the nurses' home of Great Ormond Street Hospital. After staying in the School for Artists in Mykonos, Greece, in World War II taught in Northampton. Showed with Leicester and Leger Galleries, where her use of light and colour, swirling imagery and allegory were praised. Boyle began to show in Ireland, at CEMA in Belfast and Waddington Gallery, Dublin. In 1971 settled at Reenacapull, County Cork, later living in Dublin. The Sweeny Series of paintings, from 1978, based on the mad, seventh-century northern king, was important. Had many solo shows, from Peter Jones Gallery, 1945, including Crawford Municipal Art Gallery, Cork, 1988, with a catalogue of work, 1932–88. That gallery, Bank of Ireland and Irish Arts Council hold her work.

Jimmy BOYLE 1944– Sculptor in bronze and marble, and writer, born in the Gorbals, Glasgow, notorious for razor gangs and acute poverty. To survive, Boyle embraced this culture and, apart from 12 months, ended up in institutions from the age of 11 to 38. In 1967 he began a 15-year sentence in prison, convicted of a murder he claimed that he did not commit, and led riots against a brutal prison regime. He was kept naked in solitary confinement for almost seven years. When in 1973 he was transferred to an experimental unit in Barlinnie Prison where he learned, with art therapist Joyce Laing, to model in clay, "it was like a dam bursting in me." In prison Boyle also wrote his autobiography, *A Sense of Freedom*, made into a film, and co-wrote the acclaimed play *The Hard Man*, which became a Broadway musical. He later published prison diaries, *The Pain of Confinement*, which spawned the play *The Nutcracker Suite*, performed in Britain and Australia, and an uncompromising novel *Hero of the Underworld*. While in prison Boyle married the psychotherapist Sarah Trevelyan and on his release in 1982 they set up The Gateway Exchange Trust in Edinburgh, to help young people at risk. Boyle's raw, bleak figurative sculptures, dealing with subjects such as dislocated and displaced people, and political events in Bosnia, Rwanda and South Africa, were successful internationally. His exhibition at the 1996 Edinburgh International Festival, In Praise of the Human Spirit, was critically acclaimed. Success enabled him to live in Edinburgh and Cannes, France.

Mark BOYLE 1934–2005 (and family) Artist, born in Glasgow, who worked as one of a team, other members of which were Joan Hills, born in Edinburgh in 1936; and the Boyle children: Sebastian, born 1962, and Georgina, born 1964. Mark Boyle after Army service studied law at Glasgow University, 1955–6, then did a variety of jobs such as clerk and waiter. In addition, he put on exhibitions and took part in performance art. In 1964 he and Hills made a replica of a piece of ground, the beginning of a project called The Journey to the Surface of the Earth. The aim of this was to duplicate meticulously 1,000 portions of land, normally about six feet square, chosen by throwing darts at a map. A cast of the section was exactly painted to reproduce it. Boyle aimed at complete objectivity. He also produced a series of constructions using modern consumer waste. Had numerous solo shows, later ones including Turske & Turske Gallery, Zürich, Switzerland, 1989; Nishimura Gallery, Tokyo, Japan, 1990; and Scottish National Gallery of Modern Art, Edinburgh, 2003. That gallery, the Arts Council, British Council, Scottish Arts Council and many other collections hold examples. In the year of Mark Boyle's death Leeds City Art Gallery acquired Chalk Cliff Study, 1999, related to Journey to the Surface of the Earth. Latterly lived in southeast London.

Vernon Carr BOYLE 1895–1954 Maritime watercolourist who, after Bideford Grammar School, attended University College, Exeter, and London University, graduating in science with honours. He was the son of Vernon Boyle, writer of songs and verses including *The Little White Town* and *The Lads That Are Away*, and like him and his younger brother, Jack, was active in Bideford Amateur Athletic Club, rowing in several successful crews. After World War I service in the 2nd VIth Devons overseas, which made him a pacifist, Boyle taught at Poole Grammar School, 1920–9, at The Perse School, Cambridge, until 1942, then returned to Bideford to run the family business, Buckleigh Laundry. Boyle sketched from an early age, latterly seeking out old sailors to record reminiscences of old Bideford and delineating the changing river and estuary; his archive went to the Appledore Maritime Museum and other local museums. He was active in the Bideford Society and Bideford Labour Party and worked for famine relief in Europe. The local Burton Art Gallery & Museum held a show in 2001.

BOYLE FAMILY: *see* **Mark BOYLE**

Judy BOYT fl. from 1980s– Sculptor and ceramist who trained at Wolverhampton and graduated with a master's degree in industrial ceramics from Stoke-on-Trent. She worked in the design industry for several years, producing figurative work for bone china and porcelain production. Her first freelance commission was a high-bas relief of polo playing for Garrard, the Crown Jewellers. Then in 1991 she won the British Sporting Art Trust Award. As an experienced rider Boyt was well equipped to create the statue of Grand National and Cheltenham Gold Cup winner Golden Miller; she also consulted trainers, jockeys and contemporary newsreels to finish the bronze, at Cheltenham race-course. Boyt handled royal commissions. She showed on the continent, in America and with the Tryon Gallery. The Morris Singer Foundry handled her work.

Rosemary BRABANT 1905–1987 Painter, whose work had both Impressionistic and abstract influences, born in Cottesloe, Western Australia. She studied at Melbourne National Gallery Art School, at Hammersmith College of Art and in Italy. In 1970 was elected to Free Painters and Sculptors, which gave her a memorial show in 1988, and also exhibited at New Vision Centre, Woodstock Gallery, Cockpit Theatre, AIA and abroad in mixed and solo shows. Lived in London.

Dorothea BRABY 1909–1987 Illustrator, printmaker, commercial artist and painter, born and lived in London.

After attending St Felix School in Southwold, between 1926–30 she studied at Central School of Arts and Crafts under John Farleigh, in Italy, at Heatherley's School of Fine Art, and in France. For 30 years she freelanced, Imperial Chemical Industries, *Radio Times* and *The Studio* using her work. Showed with SWA, Hampstead Artists' Council, Arts Council and abroad. Her instructional book *The Way of Wood Engraving* was published in 1953. Among books illustrated by her were John Keats' *Poems*, 1950, and Oscar Wilde's *Lord Arthur Savile's Crime*, 1954.

Andrew BRACEY 1978– Artist, lecturer and curator, born in Bristol, who did a foundation course at Plymouth College of Art, 1996–7; gained an honours degree in fine art, Liverpool John Moores University, 1997–00; and his master's at Manchester Metropolitan University, 2000–01. Bracey was visiting lecturer at both John Moores and Manchester Metropolitan and took part in Vivid children's workshops at Cornerhouse, Manchester. He was also curator and collaborative artist involved in Loose ends, with David Osbaldeston and Magnus Quaife, participating in several exhibitions in Manchester, where he was based at West Didsbury. Bracey's many exhibitions included Mixed Bag, Hope Street Gallery, Liverpool, 1998; Grotto Show, Castlefield Gallery, Manchester, 2000; Rooms With a View, The Mill, Salford, 2002; Beyond the Endgame: Abstract Painting in Manchester, Manchester Art Gallery, 2003; and John Moores Liverpool Exhibition, 2004.

Arthur BRADBURY 1892–1977 Painter, etcher and teacher who before taking up painting was a merchant marine cadet; the sea and ships were fond subjects of his. Studied art at St John's Wood School of Art and Royal Academy Schools. Exhibited RA, RWA, RI, extensively at Walker's Galleries, and elsewhere. Imperial War Museum and Russell-Cotes Art Gallery and Museum, Bournemouth, hold his work. Lived at Sandbanks, Poole, Dorset.

George Eric BRADBURY 1881–1954 Sculptor and designer, born in London, son of the sculptor Frederick Bradbury. Studied at Lambeth School of Art, where he won several medals, after this studying stained glass design. Exhibited RA, Walker Art Gallery, Liverpool, in France and America. He specialised in memorial plaques and tablets. Lived at Ringmer, Sussex.

Helen BRADBURY 1963– Versatile artist and lecturer, educated in England, who attended Mid-Warwickshire College of Further Education and Wolverhampton Polytechnic, gaining a first-class fine arts honours degree in 1986. In 1986–7 worked on a Common Ground project, in 1988 starting an illustration and textiles business. Lectured at University of Ulster, 1990, thereafter for the Workers' Educational Association and Banbridge and Downpatrick Colleges of Further Education. Gained residencies, notably at the City Hospital, Belfast; and awards, including several from the Arts Council of Northern Ireland. Did extensive public mural work connected with community centres, hospitals and schools in Ulster. Mixed shows included Stoke Garden Festival, 1986; Narrow Water Castle Gallery, Newry, from 1988; RUA Annual Exhibition, from 1990; and RHA, 1997. Later solo shows included Tom Caldwell Gallery, Belfast, 1998. Down Museum in Downpatrick, Bank of Ireland and BBC hold examples. Lived in Rathfriland, County Down.

Susan BRADBURY 1949– Stained glass artist and teacher, born in Stoke-on-Trent, Staffordshire, who studied at Swansea College of Art, 1977–80, with Tim Lewis and Majory Walters. She was a fellow of both the British Society of Master Glass Painters and Royal Society of Arts and a member of the Scottish Glass Society. Among teaching posts were lecturing part-time at Sunderland Polytechnic, 1984–6, and in 1982 at the Architects' Institute, Leningrad, and Artists' Union, Moscow, and in 1990–1 to Indonesian art colleges. In 1981 Bradbury with Paul Lucky formed the Stained Glass Design Partnership and in 1981–3 she was town artist for Irvine New Town, completing nine commissions there. Bradbury's work was architectural, and included stained glass windows and screens at Newcastle School of Art; a window at Cockermouth School, Cumbria; and two windows for Laigh Kirk, Kilmarnock. Solo shows included Harbour Arts Centre, Irvine, 1984, and Northern Centre for Contemporary Arts, Sunderland, 1986. Worked at Kilmaurs, Kilmarnock.

Tim BRADEN 1975– Artist, born in Perth, who attended Wimbledon School of Fine Art, 1993–4; St Petersburg Academy of Art, Russia, 1994; studied history and French at Bristol University, 1995–6; and graduated in fine art from Ruskin School of Fine Art, Oxford, 1996–9. He won the Sotheby History of Art Prize, 1993; Spink, Newbury Spring Festival Painting Prize, 1996; Egerton Coghill Landscape Prize, a scholarship from Brasenose College in Oxford and was shortlisted for the RA Richard Ford Award, all 1998; and in 1999 gained the Profumo, McKie Award and Vivien Leigh Drawing Prize. Later group exhibitions included Mostyn Open 11, Oriel Mostyn Gallery, Llandudno, 2000; An Elephant Station, Vilma Gold, 2001; and Wilson Stephens Fine Art, 2002. Among solo shows were Head, Pace Collection, New York, America, 1998; and The Eiger Sanction, Michelin Building, 2000. Ashmolean Museum, Oxford, held Braden's work. Lived in London.

Dorothy BRADFORD 1918– Painter and printmaker, and lecturer, born in Cockermouth, Cumberland. She studied at Liverpool College of Art, Leeds College of Art, Central School of Arts and Crafts and St Martin's School of Art, her teachers including Ruskin Spear and Maurice de Sausmarez. Showed at Bluecoat Gallery in Liverpool, Woodstock Gallery, at Royal Festival Hall and American Embassy in London, as well as abroad. She held a number of versatile roles during her career, such as art adviser to Ilkley Council, in Yorkshire, and official artist to the New Philharmonia Orchestra during its 1971 American tour. Bradford was also official artist to the Leeds International Pianoforte Competition in 1975. She lectured extensively in Yorkshire and Lancashire and interpreted music performances in the United Kingdom and abroad. As a result, an exhibition of her work related to music, Rhythms of Life, was held at The School of Music, Leeds, in 2003, coinciding with the start of that year's Competition. It was accompanied by a similarly titled publication by Mary Sara. Continued to live and work mainly in the Liverpool area.

Geoffrey BRADFORD 1947– Maker of box sculptures from odds and ends of material found on various coasts. He was born in Leytonstone, southeast Essex. Exhibitions included Contemporary Art Fair in Islington, Beside the Seaside at Worcester City Art Gallery and Y Tabernacl International Open (where he was a prize winner),

Machynlleth, all 1994; The Boat Show, Kilvert Gallery, Clyro, 1995; and Gordon Hepworth Fine Art at 23 Smith Street, 1997. Two-man exhibitions included Kilvert Gallery, 1994, and Cleveland Craft Centre, Middlesbrough, 1995. A show of paintings by Sarah Bradford and assemblages by Geoffrey was held at Newport Museum and Art Gallery, Newport, 2003. Geoffrey Bradford's show About My Feet the Sea was at Oriel Canfas Gallery, Cardiff, in 2004.

Robert BRADFORD 1945– Painter in acrylic, film-maker and teacher, born in London. He studied at Beckenham School of Art, 1961–3, Ravensbourne College of Art, 1964–7, and Royal College of Art, 1967–70, his teachers including Brian Fielding and Alan Green. Taught part-time at Maidstone College of Art, but his exhibiting career was established in the west of England, where he showed with Arnolfini Gallery, in Bristol where he lived, Bath Festival Gallery and elsewhere; also showed at ICA. Sometimes signed work R B.

Eric BRADFORTH 1920– Artist born in Sheffield, Yorkshire, where he studied at the College of Art, later at Royal College of Art. Although destined for teaching, instead Bradforth took up an invitation to establish a graphic arts department for the Royal Artillery at Manorbier, Pembrokeshire, described to him as "Paradise". He built up a team of artists, photographers and model-makers which created resources used globally by the Royal Artillery. When the school closed he and his team moved to Larkhill, Wiltshire, but on retirement Bradforth returned to Pembrokeshire, settling in Tenby. Included in his War Office work was the building of a realistic Malaysian jungle; the drawing of a life-sized Russian bomber for a firing range; design of a battle scene in a display window at the main recruiting centre in the Strand so effective that it disrupted traffic; and creation of exhibitions and displays for the Royal Tournament and the Aldershot Tattoo. After retirement Bradforth painted a seagull's eye-view of sixteenth-century Tenby for the town's Museum – which gave him a solo show in 1995–6 – and a large mural depicting Tenby history in its market hall.

Florence BRADLEY 1902– Painter and artist in black-and-white, born at Gledhow, Yorkshire. After education at Leeds Girls' High School and privately in London, she studied art with Albert Ludovici, 1916–32, having settled in Hampstead. Elected UA, 1944, and was a founder-member of the Milldon Art Society. Exhibited SWA, RBA and widely in the provinces.

Frank BRADLEY 1903–1995 Painter, theatrical designer and chartered architect, born in Manchester, where he attended the College of Technology and School of Art, then the Newlyn School of Painting under Stanhope Forbes. He was a member of RCamA, also showing with UA, at Victoria & Albert Museum, at Manchester City Art Gallery, with the Lancashire and Cheshire Artists and abroad. Had a solo show at Salford Art Gallery in 1958. Lived in Chinley, Derbyshire.

Helen BRADLEY 1900–1979 Artist in oil and watercolour, born in Oldham, Lancashire, who attended the local Art School for two terms only in 1914, but did not start painting seriously until 1960. Her pictures reflected her childhood world in a naïve style and were compared with those of L S Lowry, although she insisted they had nothing in common. Her work became very popular in reproduction through her books such as *And Miss Carter Wore Pink*, *The Queen Who Came To Tea* and *Miss Carter Came With Us*. Retrospective at W H Patterson, 2000. Died in Wilmslow, Cheshire.

James Tomlinson BRADLEY 1919– Sculptor, painter and teacher, born in Droylsden, near Manchester. Although he was mainly self-taught, Bradley attended some life classes at Leeds College of Art He went on to teach maladjusted children for a time and also lectured part-time at Somerset College of Art, in Taunton. Bradley showed widely in the north of England, including Manchester Arts Club, MAFA, RWA and elsewhere, and had a one-man show at the New Vision Centre of his sculpture in 1958. Signed his work J B. Finally lived in Winscombe, Somerset, where he taught in a local school.

John BRADLEY 1960– Bradley graduated with honours from Reading University, 1987. His exhibitions included Bedford Hill Gallery tour, 1987; Meta Incognita at Café Gallery, Café Gallery Open and Print Exhibition, Pomeroy Purdy Gallery, all 1988; and What No Words Can Paint: Wonders of the World, at St James's Church, also East End Open Studios, Bradley being then based at Unit 7, Peckham Road, both shows in 1989.

Martin BRADLEY 1931– Painter, draughtsman, muralist and sculptor, born London. He was an illegitimate orphan initially living in deprived circumstances, but eventually enabled through a wealthy father to attend St Paul's School. Ran away to sea at 14 and for several years served as a cabin boy on the Central and South American run, during which he began serious painting, mostly academic portraits of shipmates. Was a dishwasher or waiter in London restaurants and became well known to artistic circles as The Rimbaud of Soho because of his drinking, drug-taking and promiscuous life. A number of prestigious galleries, such as Gallery One, Gimpel Fils and the Redfern Gallery began to show his work. Went to Paris where he was taken up by Rudolphe Augustinci, director of the Rive Gauche Gallery, showing artists such as Max Ernst, Yves Tanguy and René Magritte. Notable British collectors such as Sir Roland Penrose, Sir Herbert Read and Dame Barbara Hepworth acquired Bradley's work. In 1962 Bradley decided to rethink his career, left Paris and travelled for many years in the Far East. Served for a period in the Spanish Foreign Legion, seeing action. This period cultivated Bradley's ability as a linguist; he was able to speak about ten languages, including Chinese, Japanese, Tibetan and Hindi. Became converted to Nichiren Shoshu Buddhism "which changed the whole foundation of my thinking". Bradley's work, largely abstract, is difficult to pigeonhole, having strong calligraphic, symbolic influences. It is in many international collections, including the Museum of Modern Art, New York. England & Co showed Paintings: 1950–1970, in 1988, Crane Kalman, works 1960–06, in 2006. Bradley then lived in Bruges, Belgium.

Sarah BRADPIECE 1954– Artist who studied at Hornsey College of Art, 1976–7, then Chelsea School of Art, 1978–9. Was included in 1981–2 Woodlands Art Gallery touring show of Greater London Arts Association award winners. Also showed in 1980 at ICA, Arnolfini Gallery in Bristol and Third Eye Centre, Glasgow, and in 1981 in Summer

Show 3 at Serpentine Gallery. She worked as an animatronics designer for the *The Muppets* show on television. Lived in London.

Brian BRADSHAW 1923– Printmaker, painter and teacher, born in Bolton. Studied at Bolton and Manchester Schools of Art, at the Royal College of Art through a scholarship, 1948–51, then at the British School in Rome for two years. In the 1950s Bradshaw was appointed to teach etching at the Heginbottom Art School in Ashton-under-Lyne, where his northern directness was said to be appreciated by students, and in 1960 he took up the post of professor of fine art at Rhodes University, Grahamstown, South Africa. Bradshaw exhibited at RA, RE, with Liverpool Academy of Fine Arts and frequently at the Manchester Academy, as well as Crane Gallery, Manchester, and elsewhere. He was one of the painters contributing to a new post-war Lancashire realist school. Lived in Bolton and Fachwen, Caernarvonshire.

Constance BRADSHAW 1872–1961 Painter in oil. Studied Spenlove School of Art. Exhibited RA, RBA, ROI, NEAC, Goupil Gallery, SWA – of which she was acting president for several years prior to World War II – Paris Salon, in the provinces and in New Zealand and Canada. Several of her landscapes, mainly in Wales, were reproduced. Lived at Bickley, Kent.

Dorothy BRADSHAW 1897– Oil and watercolour painter, born in Calcutta, India. She studied art under Jack Merriott in Polperro, Cornwall, and went on to exhibit at the Chelsea Art Society, Leighton House in Kensington, the RI and SWA. Lived at Budleigh Salterton, Devon.

George Fagan BRADSHAW 1887–1960 Marine painter who had a career as a Naval officer. Born in Belfast, he was educated at HMS Britannia, Dartmouth, gaining his artistic education in St Ives and Malta. Exhibited with RSMA, of which he was a founder-member, St Ives Art Society, RA and RSA. Sunderland Art Gallery holds his work. He lived at Ship Studio, St Ives, Cornwall, and was the husband of painter Kathleen Bradshaw.

Kathleen BRADSHAW 1904– Painter who was married to the artist George Fagan Bradshaw. She was closely associated with the artistic life of St Ives, Cornwall, where she studied, exhibited and was a member of the Society of Artists. Also showed at RA, ROI and Paris Salon.

Laurence BRADSHAW 1899–1978 Sculptor, painter and printmaker, born in Cheshire. After attending Liverpool University went to the School of Art there, 1916–7, under William Penn. Also worked in Frank Brangwyn's studio in the 1920s and studied sculpture in London and Paris. Exhibited at the RA, RWS, St George's Gallery, in Budapest, Prague and Moscow; one-man exhibitions at Architectural Association Gallery. His work is held by the Victoria & Albert Museum, Brompton Oratory, Worthing Town Hall and the Marx-Engels Museum, Moscow. He made a number of portrait busts, including the journalist Hannen Swaffer for the London Press Club, Karl Marx, Lenin and the British Communist leader Harry Pollitt, some of these pieces being in the Soviet Union. In 1958 he was master of the Art Workers' Guild. Lived in London.

Mark BRADSHAW 1968– Painter, born in what was Rhodesia, now Zimbabwe, who gained his master's degree in medieval history at Cambridge University. His partner was the Polish sculptor Marta Firlet. Bradshaw's studio and farm were in the Goromonzi area of Zimbabwe, close to Harare, and he exhibited in the country regularly from 1995. Began by painting abstracts in response to the local landscape, using strong colours and textured surfaces, but by the time of his solo show at Stephen Lacey Gallery, 2000, having had to flee to England from his home because of unrest, Bradshaw's work had developed in technique and concept. Landscape was now explored from the perspective of those living there. He was working on objects, such as doors and windows, used to assemble homes in black shanty towns, symbolising the power to invite or shut out. These were wrapped in acetate and were painted in bright cartoon colours – masked but not hidden by an alien Western, plastic culture. Exhibitions included Modern British V, Bloomsbury Workshop, 1996; Another Africa, Colourfield Gallery, Harare, 1997; shared show with the black sculptor Lazarus Takawira, Zimbabwe House, 1998; and Myths and Movements, Alchemy Gallery, 1999. A Rockefeller Collection and *Reader's Digest*, both New York, America, hold examples.

Peter BRADSHAW 1931– Painter, mostly in oil, born in London, who studied at Northampton School of Art, 1945–7. After leaving school he found no artistic employment, doing other jobs for 30 years, taking up painting as a hobby in 1961, then "found that my work was saleable, which eventually enabled me to turn professional". His pictures were "mainly railway subjects, landscapes and old-time gaslit scenes." Showed with UA, ROI and in the area of Northampton, where he lived, and had work published on greetings cards. Private collectors throughout the world held his pictures, which "featured trademarks of a cat and a robin".

Philippe BRADSHAW 1965–2005 Eccentric artist, born in Stamford, Lincolnshire, his father English, his mother French. The bilingual Philippe, after a sordid existence in London, spent his last years in Paris, and aged 39 was found dead in the Seine. Bradshaw studied at Leicester Polytechnic, then from 1985–8 at Goldsmiths' College. He became known as one of the most outlandish Young British Artists, working from an unconverted ladies' lavatory found for him by his close friend, the artist Tracey Emin. From early in his career Bradshaw collaborated with Andrea Mason, by whom he had a daughter, as Andrea & Philippe. In 1989 they curated West Norwood 1, at Arches 7, 8 & 9, East Place, West Norwood, comprising work by Bradshaw, Alan Murray, Ian Davenport, Steve Adamson, Craig Wood and John Franklin. Philippe at the School House, at The Assembly Hall, The School House, Lambeth High Street, followed in 1992. Its catalogue stated that, after West Norwood 1, Bradshaw "has, among other projects, dug a series of small earthworks on (disused) sites around London. He has also worked with glass in various ways." The Vending Machine, by Bradshaw and Mason, was at Centre 181 Gallery, in 1994. The release for Andrea & Philippe presents Philippe Bradshaw, in 1999 at The Showroom, Bethnal Green, recorded that for several months Bradshaw had been a "growling presence" there, "emanating from the depths of his lair created underneath the stage, also built by the artist". His needs and creations included "an Emperor-size bed, a lean-to shed, a collapsible boudoir, a showering area, cooking facilities, a mini-menagerie." On leaving London, Bradshaw piled up everything from his Brixton studio before setting it all on fire and filming the process. In Paris, his dealer and patron was Thaddaeus Ropac, who saw Bradshaw's career flourish as never before. He collaborated with the choreographer Merce Cunningham, had commissions from major collectors, and showed widely in continental Europe and America. Bradshaw is buried in Perpignan, where his parents lived.

Raymond Henry BRADSHAW 1918–1997 Painter, draughtsman and teacher who studied at Bancroft's School, where he eventually taught art. Attended West Ham School of Art, 1935–6, then Westminster School of Art, 1936–8, where his teachers included Bernard Meninsky and Mark Gertler. Showed RA, RBA, RP and elsewhere. Lived in Loughton, Essex.

Philippa BRADSTOCK 1936– Painter who worked for 10 years with Robin Child and Maggi Hambling, who found delight in Bradstock's "personal touch of paint and rich sense of colours." Her sell-out solo show at Gallery 27, 2000, included work done in England, Scotland and France. Bradstock also exhibited at Independent Art Space, 1997; Sotheby's, 1999; and Art Additions, 2000. Lived in Biddesden, Hampshire.

Kenneth Russell BRADY 1884–1953 Businessman, architect, artist, cartoonist and writer, born in Northern Ireland of a Donegal family. Settled in England in 1900, trained as an architect in Newcastle, moved to Manchester in 1909 and in 1910 joined the *Manchester Guardian* as a cartoonist and illustrator. After Army service as an officer in France in World War I, Brady returned to become business editor of the *Manchester Guardian Commercial*. In 1924 he became first director of the Liverpool Organisation, being responsible for the first Liverpool Week. In 1926 Brady joined Manchester Ship Canal Company, retiring in 1949 having held senior positions, remaining an architectural consultant. He had during these years written articles on industrial design, decorative art and architecture and showed at MAFA. Brady was responsible for persuading the editor of the *Manchester Guardian*, C P Scott, to sit for T C Dugdale, and he presented the portrait to Manchester Press Club in 1928. Brady's own portrait, by Ronald Allan, is held by Manchester City Art Gallery.

Stephen James BRAGG 1947– Self-taught painter who was "interested in the luminosity of watercolour and particularly its perverse difficulty.... Collision and contraction coupled with an intense use of full and vibrant colours." Reflections, details, unusual viewing angles, two-dimensional representation of three dimensions and sunlight and shadow were key features of Bragg's pictures. Brian Cook, Kandinsky, Klee, Mackintosh, David Roberts and Walcot were cited as influences. Bragg was born in Bristol, studied at the Oxford School of Architecture and was a partner in and director of the large practice Broadway Malyan Architects from 1985. He was a committee member of the Society of Architect Artists. Exhibited at RA Summer Exhibition, 1992; Alresford Gallery, from 1994; RI from 1995; RWS, 1996; RWA from 1998; and Tig Fili Gallery, Cork, 1999. Had a solo exhibition at Blanc de Bierges Gallery, 1996, and in 2002 shared a show with Rhiannon Howells at The Gallery in Cork Street. Lived in Eversley Cross, Hampshire.

Philip BRAHAM 1959– Painter, born in Glasgow. He studied at Duncan of Jordanstone College of Art, Dundee, 1976–80, then was visiting artist at University of California, Los Angeles, 1981–2. Notable for his Scottish landscapes. Braham took part in Scottish Art Today – Artists At Work, a 1986 Edinburgh Festival exhibition, and the following year in The Vigorous Imagination at Scottish National Gallery of Modern Art, Edinburgh. Solo exhibitions include Glasgow Arts Centre, 1987; Scottish Gallery, Edinburgh, 1988; and BCA Boukamel Contemporary Art, 2000. Lived in Edinburgh.

Victoria BRAILSFORD 1966– Sculptor who attended Humberside College of Higher Education, honing her abilities with wood by learning chainsaw use at Bishop Burton Agricultural College, then working with the noted timber sculptor, David Nash. She held a number of sculpture park residencies in Britain and Canada and completed a series of public commissions. Brailsford's Tugboat, completed in painted wood in the early 1990s, was commissioned by Cleveland Arts and is sited on a riverside path in Middlesbrough.

Ann BRAIN 1944– Artist and teacher, born in Coventry, Warwickshire, who settled in the county at Bilton, Rugby. She graduated in fine art from Coventry University, 1962–6, taught by Terry Frost and Michael Sandle; gained her Art Teacher's Certificate at London University Institute of Education, 1966–7; then pursued a teaching career which included her own adult education art classes, talks and demonstrations. Brain said of her work that it reflected her "affinity with the natural world." Her oil paintings could be "both benign and unsettling", her works on paper setting out to "record the actuality of objects in an acute and penetrating way." Annie Brain was a founder-member and chairman of Rugby Artists' Support Group, chairman of the Association of Midland Artists, a member of the Tantalus Project, Leamington Studio Artists and Rugby and District Art Society. Mixed shows included RA Summer Exhibition, from 1986; Twelve woman artists, Herbert Art Gallery, Coventry, 1989; Maltese Biennale, special Distinction award, 1995; Llewellyn Alexander Gallery, from 1998; and Rugby Open, Rugby Art Gallery & Museum, from 2001. That venue, which acquired her work, gave her a retrospective, Six Decades, in 2004.

Kate BRAINE 1964– Figurative sculptor, who learned marble carving at Carrara, Italy, and attended Heatherley's School of Fine Art followed by City & Guilds of London Art School. Commissions included Ian Board, Saffron Aldridge and David Tang. Braine also took body casts. Showed widely in London, including Birch & Conran and Berkeley Square Gallery, and was included in Sixteen Sculptors at Sladmore Contemporary, 1997.

Percy BRAISBY 1910– Sculptor, potter and teacher who studied at Gloucester and Cheltenham Colleges of Art. He became head of painting at the Gloucestershire College of Art in Cheltenham, where he lived, in 1964 converting Barratts Mill into a studio, helped by his assistant Miss D G Sutton. Braisby showed at Royal Society of Arts, RWA, the 1951 Festival of Britain, was a prizewinner at the

International Eisteddfod in Wales in 1952 and in 1962 was included in 19 Young Sculptors at Hillfield Gardens, Gloucester. Cheltenham Art Gallery & Museums holds Braisby's clay figure of a potter, of about 1950.

Barbara BRAITHWAITE 1930– Artist in variety of media, latterly with an interest in stained glass, born in Sheffield, Yorkshire. She studied with Eric Jones at the College of Art there and at Slade School of Fine Art under William Coldstream, Lucian Freud, Thomas Monnington and Graham Sutherland. Between about 1960 and 1988 Braithwaite stopped painting while raising a family, resuming after her husband's death. Showed at ICA, Beaux Arts Gallery, Zilla Bell in Thirsk and Brantwood Gallery, Coniston, having solo exhibitions at Old School Workshops, Middleham, and at Swaledale Festival, North Yorkshire. Arts Council holds her work. Lived in Horsehouse, Leyburn, North Yorkshire.

Christopher BRAMHAM 1952– Painter and teacher, born in Bradford, Yorkshire. Although his father was a newsagent and his mother a school dinner lady, who split up when Bramham was young, he was enabled to spend some time at a preparatory school, but failed Common Entrance. An old part-work magazine inspired Bramham to be an artist. He attended Bradford College of Art, 1970; his desire for a more traditional teaching and to work from nature took him to Kingston School of Art, 1971–3, after which he was a part-time teacher in schools, 1974–86, by now with a family and hard up. A meeting with Lucian Freud in 1982 led to Bramham showing with Agnew, although he was several times rejected by the RA, so he became disillusioned with the selection procedure. Had a show with Fine Art Society in 1988, then from 1992 had a series of highly successful exhibitions with Marlborough Fine Art, craftsmanlike and intense landscapes, still lifes and interiors. Bramham admired Freud (who owned his work and painted him and his family), Bacon, Andrews, Auerbach and, among foreign artists, Giacometti, Picasso and Matisse. Lived in Richmond, Surrey.

Leonard Griffiths BRAMMER 1906–1994 Painter and printmaker, born in Burslem, Stoke-on-Trent; he eventually became supervisor of art for the local Education Authority, 1951–69. Studied at Burslem School of Art, 1923–6, under Gordon Forsyth, then Royal College of Art, 1926–30, where his teachers included William Rothenstein, Malcolm Osborne and Robert Austin. Was elected RE in 1956, also showing RA. Victoria & Albert Museum, Tate Gallery and Ashmolean Museum, Oxford, hold his work. Brammer was noted for his depictions of the industrial landscape of the Potteries, its ovens, kilns, workshops and canals. Lived finally in Porthmadog, Gwynedd.

Robert BRAMWELL-JONES 1947– Painter, born in Pretoria, South Africa, a graduate in architecture, Johannesburg, 1971, moving to London, 1973, gaining his Byam Shaw School of Art diploma, 1980–4. Participated in East End Open Studios, at Berry Street, 1989. Took part in many group shows, later ones including New Art in Exeter, Spacex Gallery, and RUA Open, both 1991; Ask the Poets, Knapp Gallery, 1994; Fitzrovia Open, 1996; and Angel Blues, Bang the Gallery, Cape Town, 1999. That gallery also gave Bramwell-Jones a solo exhibition in 1999, as did Technikon Gallery, Durban; showed one-man at M&S Corporate Headquarters, 2000. Bramwell-Jones every day made a small painting "as my minimum art practice." These were "celebrations of being alive, reflecting much of the joy, frailty and humour of the human condition." They were assembled in grids and friezes. Bramwell-Jones called them Holons, "a term coined by Arthur Koestler to describe something that is itself a whole but also a part of some other whole".

Joy BRAND 1923– Painter and lithographer of British and continental landscapes, born in Westcott, Surrey, who studied under William Coldstream at Slade School of Fine Art, 1948–52. She was a medical artist with Moorfields Eye Hospital, 1952–74. Mixed appearances included RA Summer Exhibition, RI, RWS and Casa Pupo and Clarges Galleries and Buckinghamshire Art Society, of which she was a member. Solo shows included Lancaster Arts Centre, High Wycombe, and Nicholas Brown and Hawker Galleries, both in Amersham. Produced many lithographs for Christie's Contemporary Art. Lived in Seer Green, Buckinghamshire.

Walter BRAND 1872–1959 Artist in pencil and wash; architect, born in Ipswich, Suffolk. Studied at Ipswich School of Art and Heatherley's School of Fine Art. Exhibited RBSA, RIBA, Leicester Society of Artists and extensively in the Midlands. Lived in Leicester.

Margaret Elizabeth BRANDEBOURG 1926– Sculptor, born in Surbiton, Surrey. She studied at Kingston School of Art and at the Royal Academy Schools under Denis Dunlop. Lived in Kingston upon Thames, Surrey.

Stephen BRANDES 1966– Artist working in mixed media, sometimes on a huge scale, born in Wolverhampton, Staffordshire. He studied at Bournville College of Art and Design, 1984–5, and at Bath Academy and Bath College of Higher Education in 1985–8. Exhibited widely in West Country and gained RWA award in 1988–9. In 1989–90 his picture (The Return of) The Prodigal Farmer appeared in John Moores Liverpool Exhibition. One of Brandes' more remarkable achievements was his Hill Figure for Bath, a 70-foot drawing in 12 tons of Bath stone. Lived in Bath, Somerset.

Marion BRANDIS 1956– Mural and mosaic artist and teacher, born in Hamburg, West Germany, who had a studio in Brighton, Sussex, from 1985. She gained an honours degree at Edinburgh College of Art, 1977–81, with a postgraduate diploma in 1982, then was junior fellow in ceramics at South Glamorgan Institute of Higher Education, Cardiff, 1983–4. Teaching included Loughborough College of Art and Central St Martins School of Art, and she was an external course adviser at Edinburgh College of Art. Among Brandis' awards was a South East Arts Travelling Grant to visit Hispano-Mooresque architecture in Spain, 1993. Exhibitions included Design for Living, Gardner Arts Centre, Brighton, 1987; garden show at Oxford Gallery, 1989; and a similar exhibition at Barbican Centre, 1991. Commissions included mosaic mural for Ashford Library, Kent, with Nicholas Martin, 1990; tiled mural for Northampton Guildhall extension, 1993; and large glass tile mosaics for Govan Housing Association, 1994.

Hugh BRANDON-COX 1917–2003 Painter, illustrator, explorer, film-maker and writer whose father was killed just before Hugh was born, his mother when he was five, so that he was brought up by various relations. This gave him a sense of independence, which helped direct his life. In his teens Brandon-Cox learned Swedish, hoping that it would serve him as an Arctic explorer. When during World War II he was deployed in Norway with special forces, helping Allied escapers from Germany to return to Britain, the impression of bleak grandeur of the northern islands left a lasting impression. After founding a magazine, *The West Countryman*, he moved to Cambridge to work as a journalist and became a self-taught filmer of wildlife at Wicken Fen nature reserve, taking the results to television companies. Backed by The Educational Foundation for Visual Aids, he made two films in Norway: *Arctic Nomads*, 1969, and *Summer of a Million Wings*, 1974. Based in Norfolk, the four-times-married Brandon-Cox concentrated latterly on watercolours of its distinctive landscape, writing a nature column for a regional magazine and books. *Mud on My Boots*, 2002, chronicled his walk along the Norfolk coast, *Softly Wakes the Dawn*, 2003, being a digest of his self-illustrated magazine columns.

Anne BRANDON-JONES 1878–1968 Painter and embroiderer, whose unmarried name was Anne Brandon. She studied painting with her husband, the Slade School of Fine Art-educated Philip Brandon-Jones (1876–1944), their son being the architect Philip Brandon-Jones. Anne showed at RA, RBA, ROI and RP. Lived for a time at Berkhamsted, Hertfordshire.

R A BRANDT: *see* **Rolf BRANDT**

Rolf BRANDT 1906–1986 Painter, designer, illustrator and teacher. Although born in Hamburg, Brandt was British. He was the younger brother of the photographer Bill Brandt, with whom he remained close. Rolf was a professional actor who in the 1920s became interested in Dada and Surrealism, which remained a potent influence on the work of both Brandts. Lived permanently in England from early 1930s and as well as studying art in Paris attended Amédée Ozenfant's London school. Showed at LG, Arts Council, AIA and had several one-man shows in England and Italy, one at Paris Gallery, London, 1961; another at ICA, 1965; and he shared an exhibition with Timothy Driver at Lisson Gallery, 1970. Did some mural work; had illustrations in publications such as *The Listener* and *Radio Times*; and illustrated a number of books, including works by Balzac and Rabelais, his pictures often having a droll but eerie quality. Taught for some years at London College of Printing and Byam Shaw School of Drawing and Painting. Lived in London, where for a time Rolf continued to work as an actor. Both brothers in the 1930s and 1940s were part of Hampstead's intellectual set. At that time Rolf, working as R A Brandt, established a reputation for haunting, eerie illustrations and pencil drawings. This was brought out in the retrospective at England & Co in 2004 which coincided with a major exhibition of Bill Brandt's work, Other Sides of Bill Brandt, at the Victoria & Albert Museum. It included an album of collages and drawings by Rolf from its collection.

Frank BRANGWYN 1867–1956 Decorative painter often on a large scale, creator of murals and printmaker. Born in Bruges, Belgium, where a museum to commemorate him was opened in 1936, Brangwyn had tuition from his architect father, but was mainly self-taught. After working in William Morris' business, 1882–4, Brangwyn went to sea and he retained a love of the sea and travel. As a young man lived in Kent, selling drawings, then from the mid-1880s started to exhibit at the RA and to establish his reputation which soon became international. Won a gold medal at Chicago Exhibition for his picture The Convict Ship. Elected RA in 1919. By then he had painted mural decorations for Skinners' Hall, 1904–9. Other notable such large-scale works were murals commissioned for the House of Lords in 1926, rejected and acquired by Swansea City Centre seven years later; and murals for the Rockefeller Center, New York, 1932, where Brangwyn's collaborators were José Maria Sert and Diego Rivera. A 1924 retrospective in London was extremely successful, being opened by the new Labour prime minister Ramsay MacDonald. Brangwyn exhibited prolifically, notably at Fine Art Society and RA. Received many academic honours. Further retrospectives followed in Worthing, 1951, RA, 1952, and a memorial show was held at the Fine Art Society, 1958. Brangwyn, who died at his Ditchling, Sussex, home, remains famous for his grandiose and colourful pictures of exotic and historical scenes. Tate Gallery holds his work. In *Brangwyn Talks* his friend William de Belleroche records the artist's opinions. In 2006, Liss Fine Art, which claimed to hold the largest stock of works by Brangwyn (www.brangwyn.net), organised a major exhibition at The Fine Art Society.

Leslie Maurice Leopold BRANGWYN 1896– Wood engraver and etcher, born in London. He studied at Goldsmiths' College School of Art with Stanley Anderson and James Bateman. Became a member of the Art Workers' Guild in 1949, retiring in 1966. Exhibited RA, NS, RCamA, RSA and Paris Salon. Lived in Orpington, Kent.

Alison BRANIGAN 1969– Sculptor, medallist, jeweller, photographer and performance artist, sometimes working in mixed media, who was educated in Scarborough, Yorkshire. She completed a foundation year, diploma credit, at Harrogate College of Art and Technology, 1988–9; gained a fine arts honours degree at Birmingham Institute of Art and Design, 1989–92; then from 1995 was on the master's degree applied art and visual culture course at Sir John Cass, London Guildhall University. Her work experience included art classes at Salvation Army hostel, Digbeth; assisting the sculptors Malcolm Poynter and Bo Carter; and working on the restoration of St Paul's statue in St Paul's Cathedral. Awards included Jerwood Allied Craft Award, first prize, 1996, and joint first prize at the Birmingham Assay Office Silver Design Awards, 1997. In 1996 was elected an associate member of the Society of Numismatic Artists and Designers. Took part in many mixed shows, one-mans including Sad Tidings at Simmons Gallery, 1997. Lived in London.

Edward Eaton BRANNAN 1886–1957 Painter, printmaker and potter, studied under Herbert Rollett at Grimsby School of Art. His sons were the artists Noel Brannan and Peter Brannan. Exhibited RA, Walker Art Gallery, Liverpool, RWS, RCamA, UA and Paris Salon. One-man show at Usher Gallery, Lincoln, which holds his work. He was a member of the AIA and Lincolnshire Artists' Society. Lived in Lincoln.

Noel BRANNAN 1921–2001 Artist and teacher, born in Tynemouth, Northumberland, who worked in oil, watercolour and felt pen and wash. He studied at Lincoln School of Art, 1947–51, then Leicester College of Art, 1951–2, although he had begun painting in 1940. Taught art for 28 years, taking up full-time art in 1980. Was one of the painters chosen for Jack Beddington's 1957 book *Young Artists of Promise*. Became member of AIA, also showing with RA, RBA, LG and elsewhere including Lincolnshire and South Humberside Artists' Society. Brannan liked to work on the spot, with an inclination for industrial subjects. Had a solo show at Willoughby Memorial Trust Art Gallery, 1985, in Corby Glen. Usher Gallery, Lincoln, and Nuneaton Art Gallery hold his work. Lived in Burbage, Leicestershire. Goldmark Gallery, Uppingham, held an exhibition of Brannan's late 1940s work in 2004, with a well-illustrated catalogue.

Peter BRANNAN 1926–1994 Painter, draughtsman, printmaker and teacher, born in Cleethorpes, Lincolnshire. He studied at Grimsby School of Art, then Leicester College of Art. He taught mainly in Newark, Nottinghamshire. Brannan was elected RBA in 1960 and was president of Lincolnshire and South Humberside Artists. He showed in mixed exhibitions at RA, NEAC, LG and elsewhere, having a series of solo shows with Trafford Gallery, one at Usher Gallery, Lincoln, 1978, and a retrospective at Goldmark Gallery, Uppingham, in 1995. Usher Gallery, Grundy House Museum in Blackpool and Lincolnshire Education Committee hold his work. Brannan admired the work of French Post-Impressionists, also Cotman and Chardin. Lived in Welbourn, Lincoln.

Allan BRANSBURY 1942– Sculptor and teacher, born in Jersey, Channel Islands. He studied at Bristol's West of England College of Art, then University of London Institute of Education. He next studied in North America for a while. Was especially interested in large-scale sculptures sited in natural settings. After serving as artist-in-residence at the University of Sussex, Brighton, in 1976, Bransbury was from 1977–80 principal of Bromley Centre for Arts and Crafts, then was attached to the Highlands and Islands Development Board, in Scotland, living for some years at North Kessock, Inverness.

Rosa BRANSON 1933– Painter, artist in embroidery and fabric collage, daughter of the artist Clive Branson, and the social campaigner and historian of the British Communist Party Noreen Branson, she married and divorced the painter Alan Hopkins, who was diagnosed a schizophrenic. She had four years at Camberwell School of Arts and Crafts and one at the Slade School of Fine Art, but regarded herself "as a classical painter". Dissatisfied with her art school training Branson came to spend six years in the National Gallery, copying and learning the techniques of the Renaissance. Her early work stemmed from painstaking sketches of London scenes, such as cafés; there was a period of embroidery pictures and fabric collages; many years painting still life, portraits and landscapes; then after the death of her second husband Branson, although an athiest, painted a long series of heavenly scenes and Red Cross panoramas in which friends and neighbours were used as models. These, like her many still lifes of fruit, were on a large scale. By the mid-1990s she had completed almost 500 pictures. Mixed exhibitions included RA, ROI, LG, Young Contemporaries, Royal Festival Hall and Mermaid Theatre. Had a solo show at Woodstock Gallery in 1962, later ones including Lyric Theatre, 1987, Highgate Cemetery Chapel, 1992, and Brontë Restaurant, Oulton Hall, 1993. Branson painted free many large canvases to help charities raise funds. Among such works was a large canvas, donated in 2002 to the Coram Family, formerly the Coram Foundation. Containing 196 portraits, it illustrated the history of the Foundling Hospital set up over 250 years before by Captain Coram. Branson won the Morrison International Decanter Design Competition and was guest at the 1993 Woman of the Year lunch at Savoy Hotel. De Vere Hotel Group, Marquess of Sligo, Lambeth Palace and the Nuffield Foundation hold examples. Lived in London.

John BRASON 1924– Painter, draughtsman and teacher, who was born in South Shields, County Durham. Attended the School of Art there, 1940–4, then the Royal College of Art, 1944–7, under Gilbert Spencer, Percy Horton and Eric Gill. For a time taught at St Martin's School of Art and Camberwell School of Arts and Crafts. Brason also had musical and theatrical interests. Exhibited RA, Arts Council and elsewhere. Lived in London.

David BRASSINGTON 1947– Collagist, painter in oil and screenprinter, born in Coventry, Warwickshire. He studied art in Leamington Spa with Trevor Halliday, also the history of art at Ealing Polytechnic and at Camden Institute. Had solo shows at Square Gallery, 1990, and with David Birkett, 1991. Kurt Schwitters, Robert Rauschenberg, John Walker and Juan Gris were influences. Lived in London.

Jean BRATBY: *see* **Jean COOKE**

John BRATBY 1928–1992 Painter, novelist and teacher, born in London. He studied at Kingston School of Art, 1948–9, then Royal College of Art, 1951–4. Married the painter Jean Cooke, 1953, marriage dissolved in 1977. Through the 1950s Bratby regularly showed at Beaux Arts Gallery in solo exhibitions, the first being in 1954. He won Abbey Minor, Italian Government and Royal College of Art Minor Travelling Scholarships in 1954, the year following receiving a prize in the *Daily Express* Young Artists Competition. Bratby taught at Carlisle College of Art, 1956, then at Royal College of Art, 1957–8. He represented Britain at Venice Biennale in 1956 and gained the Guggenheim Award, and in 1958. In that year he was commissioned to paint the pictures for the film of Joyce Cary's novel *The Horse's Mouth*. He wrote his own first novel, *Breakdown*, 1960. Bratby was a prolific exhibitor, having painted over 1,500 portraits alone by 1991, when a retrospective was held by National Portrait Gallery, which holds his work. In the same year there was a solo show at Albemarle Gallery and the Mayor Gallery included him in The Kitchen Sink Artists Revived, which drew attention to his 1950s pictures. After a retrospective at Catto Gallery, 1997, there were shows at The Millinery Works, 1999 and 2002. Bold images, thick paint and primary colours were Bratby's trademarks. He was elected RA in 1971. Lived in Hastings, Sussex.

Allin BRAUND 1915–2004 Painter, printmaker and teacher, born in Northam, Devon, full name Ralph Allin Braund. Studied at Bideford School of Art, 1932–6, then Hornsey School of Art, 1936–9, Norman Janes his notable printmaking teacher. He went on to teach at Hornsey College of Art and was ultimately a lecturer at Middlesex

Polytechnic, retiring early in 1976 to return to Bideford and painting. Showed widely, including RE, Redfern Gallery, St George's Gallery, Zwemmer Gallery, RA and abroad. In the British section of the 1954 Venice Biennale, Braund was included with illustrious contemporaries, including Francis Bacon, Lucian Freud, Henry Moore, Eduardo Paolozzi, Ceri Richards and William Scott. Was a member of the Society of Industrial Artists. Arts Council, British Council, Victoria & Albert Museum and a number of provincial and foreign galleries bought his work. Lived for many years in London, where his panels, representing abstract motion, on the Harrow Road elevation of Paddington Green police station were a notable feature. Retrospective at Burton Art Gallery & Museum, Bideford, 2002.

Fruin Bruce Charles BRAVINGTON 1910–2000 Representational painter who studied architecture at Trinity College, Cambridge, and who built houses in Tufton Street, Westminster, and several villages outside Henley-on-Thames. He was related to the Bravingtons Ltd wholesale jewellery company. After serving as an ambulance driver in World War II, he devoted himself to painting, showing at Arthur Tooth and Sons. Studied under J B Manson, whose work was in Bravington's notable collection, and Clifford Hall and was a friend of the sculptor John Skeaping. Bravington was also a noted philanthropist and linguist. Lived for a time in Bournemouth, Dorset. Rosebery's Auctioneers and Valuers offered a group of Bravington's pictures in 2001.

Alan BRAY 1920– Architect and artist, born and lived in Hull, Yorkshire, who attended Hull Grammar School and Hull School of Architecture. He had a pupilage with the architect and painter Allanson Hick, by whom he was "strongly influenced". Bray was an associate of RIBA and an architect in private practice, a partner in Gelder & Kitchen, of Hull. He showed locally, at one time being Hon. Sec. of Hull Art Club, also showing at RWS Summer Open in 1992. Ferens Art Gallery, Hull, owns his work.

Charles BRAY 1922– Artist especially notable for cast glass and structures in glass and stone, also some graphic works. Bray was an hon. fellow of the University of Sunderland and a fellow of the Society of Glass Technology. His *A Dictionary of Glass, Materials and Techniques* was published in 1995, *Ceramics and Glass. A Basic Technology* in 2000. Took part in numerous group exhibitions internationally, solo shows including Sunderland University; Invetro Galerie, Hanover, Germany; Galerie HD Nick, Aubais, France; 639 Gallery, Edinburgh; Fountain Fine Arts, Llandeilo; Glass Designs, Bath; Salford Art Gallery; Tullie House, Carlisle; The Customs House Gallery, South Shields; and in The Sculpture Show, Thompson's Marylebone, 2003. His work was in many international collections, including Shipley Art Gallery, Gateshead; Glasmuseum, Ebeltoft, Denmark; Royal Scottish Museum, Edinburgh; Corning Museum of Glass, New York, America; Kelvingrove Museum and Art Gallery, Glasgow; and Ulster Museum, Belfast. Lived in Farlam, Cumbria.

Phyllis BRAY 1911–1991 Painter, illustrator, muralist and collector, born in Norwood, London. She was married for several years to the painter John Cooper, until the marriage was dissolved (early work sometimes signed Phyllis M(ary) Cooper), their daughter being the artist Philippa Cooper, then married Eric Phillips. Her father was William de Bray, who had been attaché to Maria Fyodorovna, mother of the murdered Tsar Nicholas II. As a child she wanted to be an artist and claimed to be the youngest scholarship student at the Slade School of Fine Art when she joined it, was a favourite of Henry Tonks and was a certificate, prize and diploma winner, attending 1927–31. In the mid-1920s Cooper spearheaded formation of the East London Group of painters with which Phyllis Bray was closely involved. Her connection with the East End was strengthened when she completed three large murals for the People's Palace in the Mile End Road. For over 40 years helped the mural painter Hans Feibusch, working in many churches around Britain. Bray joined LG in 1934, showing with it regularly, also at Leicester Galleries, Wildenstein, Drian Gallery and Mignon Gallery, Bath. She also did a large volume of publicity, including work for Shell, the John Lewis Partnership and London Transport; her book illustrations included Alison Uttley's *A Traveller in Time*, 1939, Jo Manton's *The Story of Titania and Oberon*, 1945, and Rhoda Power's *Here and There Stories*, 1953. In the 1950s and 1960s Bray collected medieval and Renaissance jewellery for modest sums; the Phyllis Phillips collection was sold at Christie's in 1989 for £576,000. Parkinson's Disease latterly prevented her from painting, and she died in Hampstead, north London. Memorial show at Collyer-Bristow, 1998, with a successful studio sale at Duncan Campbell Fine Art, 2005. The Walker Art Gallery in Liverpool, Blackpool Art Gallery, Contemporary Art Society and Department of the Environment acquired Bray's work.

Richard BRAY 1951– Sculptor and photographer who graduated in photographic arts from the Polytechnic of Central London, 1973–6, then turned full-time to sculpture and carving wood. Exhibitions included Twenty East Anglian Artists, Kettle's Yard, Cambridge, 1995; Sculpting, Fine Art Society, 1996; Sculpture in the Gardens, Wimpole Hall, Royston, 1997; Houldsworth Fine Art, which represented him, from 1997; and Exterior/Interior, Hammerson plc, 1998. Bray created abstract carvings which explored and exploited the nature of each piece of timber. He used "the way things overlap or combine, the direction of light and the changing angles of perspective. I want movement and joy to be in the work." Was included in a three-man show Reflections at the Babylon Gallery, Ely, in 2001. He lived outside Cambridge.

David BRAYNE 1954– Painter whose work could include a fantasy element, as in Boy Scaring Birds, at a four-man show at The Sheen Gallery, 2001. Brayne studied at Nottingham School of Art, 1973–4; Gloucestershire College of Art, 1974–7; and philosophy at the University of Exeter, 1983–5. Exhibited at RA Summer Exhibition; Bankside and Mall Galleries; RWA; private galleries; in the Millfield, Chichester, Laing and Hunting Opens, winning a number of awards; and was elected a full member of the RWS in 2003. In 2002 he shared a three-man show at The Wykeham Gallery, Stockbridge. Lived in Evercreech, Somerset.

Antanas BRAZDYS 1939– Sculptor in stainless steel, and teacher, born in Lithuania. He studied at Art Institute of Chicago, 1962–4, then Royal College of Art. Went on to become senior sculpture lecturer at Cheltenham College of Art for a time. Brazdys participated in a number of influential group exhibitions, including Towards Art II, Arts Council, 1965; Open-air Sculpture Exhibition, Battersea Park, 1966; and the RA's British Sculptors '72. Solo shows included Hamilton Galleries, 1965; Arnolfini Gallery, Bristol, 1966; and Annely Juda Fine Art, 1971. A tie-up with a New York dealer meant that he did not have solo shows for some time in Britain, although he did show at RA and did commissioned work for Harlow New Town, some on a very large scale. Arts Council and British Steel Corporation hold his work. Lived in Tewkesbury, Gloucestershire, and had a studio in London.

Alfred Keeley BRAZIER 1894–1979 Painter and craftsman who originally began as an apprentice ceramic artist at Coalport China Works, in Ironbridge. Then studied art under William Hentry Gates at Coalbrookdale School of Art, 1911–15, later at Birkenhead and Hammersmith Schools of Art. Early on he favoured still life in oil, but later turned to landscape watercolours. He was a skilled carver. Member of BWS, also showing with UA, RWA, RBSA, RCamA and NWG and was a founder and chairman of Merioneth Artists' Society. Lived in Barmouth, Merionethshire.

Kenneth BRAZIER 1933– Painter, from a working-class background, who studied at the Slade School of Fine Art, 1958–62. He lived temporarily in a house owned by John Minton, was painted by Ben Levene and Lucian Freud and exhibited in Young Contemporaries, 1960 and 1961. His gestural, richly coloured self-portrait, bought by Ruth Borchard, is illustrated in Philip Vann's book *Face To Face*, published by Sansom & Company Ltd/Piano Nobile Fine Paintings in 2004.

Charles BREAKER 1906–1985 Painter and teacher, born in Bowness-on-Windermere, Westmorland. He worked with his father as a boatbuilder, then during the 1930s travelled widely in Europe with his lifelong friend, the painter and illustrator Eric Hiller, who was to show extensively at Goupil Gallery. When World War II broke out Breaker returned to England and worked for Vickers Armstrong in the drawing office. In 1947 he and Hiller moved to Cornwall, settling in Newlyn where they founded the Newlyn Holiday Sketching Club, This they ran for 15 years, and when Hiller died Breaker moved to Penzance. Showed widely in Britain and on the continent, in later years his work being exhibited by Nina Zborowska Fine Paintings, Painswick.

Ian BREAKWELL 1943–2005 Artist using a variety of media; teacher; administrator. Born in Derby, Breakwell studied at the local College of Art, 1961–5, after which he attended the West of England College of Art, Bristol. In 1967 he staged his performance Restaurant Operations at Exeter Festival and Bristol Arts Centre. In 1969 Unword 1 was staged at Compendium Bookshop, Unword 2 following at ICA. By then Breakwell had established his preoccupation with the relationship between word and image, which was to appear in many forms in ensuing years. After being visual arts director at Bristol Arts Centre, 1967–8, Breakwell taught at Somerset College of Art, 1969–73. Other examples of the artist's output were: one-man shows at Angela Flowers Gallery, Arnolfini Gallery and Scottish Arts Council Gallery, Edinburgh; the making of the films *Repertory* and *The Journey* in the 1970s; and his publication of *Diary Extracts, Continuous Diary* and *Fiction Texts*. Anthony Reynolds became Breakwell's dealer in 1983 and he was the first artist to have a solo show at Reynolds' new London gallery two years later. Breakwell's 1989 exhibition National Sport at Reynolds' gallery dealt with the mass hysteria that huge sporting events could provoke. Breakwell's 1994 film *Auditorium*, made with the composer Ron Geesin, was particularly memorable, consisting of an audience facing the viewer, which, after the lights dim, reacts with alarm to an unseen performance and disquieting sound effects. After a residency at the school of anatomy at Cardiff University, Breakwell put on an uncompromising 1998 show at the Ffotogallery, Cardiff, called Death's Dance Floor, filled with skeletal imagery. In 1999 The University Gallery, Loughborough, showed Breakwell's Textworks 1969–1999, and in 2000 the De La Warr Pavilion, Bexhill-on-Sea, screened *Auditorium*. He had a one-year residency there, 2000–1, resulting in a solo show in 2002. *The Other Side*, a De La Warr commission filmed in the Modernist building, was a further disquieting piece: a tranquil dance scene eventually disrupted by the sound of breaking glass, thunder, screaming gulls and darkness. It was acquired by the Tate Gallery. The Arts Council also holds Breakwell's work.

William Ramsden BREALEY 1889–1949 Portrait painter in oil, born in Sheffield where he studied at the School of Art, then Royal College of Art. Exhibited RA, RBA especially, ROI, RSA and Paris Salon, where he gained an Hon. Mention in 1925. The Ministry of Information bought his picture The Gas Mask during World War II. Lived in London.

Antony BREAM 1943– Extensively internationally travelled landscape painter and etcher, born London. He studied with Peter Greenham at Royal Academy Schools, 1964–7. Among Bream's shows were Fine Art Society, 1979; Jonathan Poole Gallery, New York, 1983; Richmond Gallery, 1988; and a solo exhibition at Cadogan Contemporary, 1992. Bream did a lot of commissioned work. In 1981 he travelled to North Yemen on an expedition, preparing work for a book and two exhibitions; in 1985 he painted in Colorado for *Forbes Magazine*; and in 1989–90 he engaged in industrial commissions to paint gold mining in Spain and cable-laying in Bermuda. Exhibited with Messum's from 1994.

Evelyn BREARLEY 1906–1985 Painter and teacher, born in Douglas, Isle of Man. After education in England and Wales she attended Manchester College of Art, teaching part-time while still a student. A number of further school appointments followed in the north of England and finally Wales, where she was also a part-time teacher for the Workers' Educational Association and Gwent County Council. Showed in groups at Bradford City Art Gallery, Paris Salon, SEA, SWG, NEAC and widely in the provinces; one-man shows included Newport Museum and Art Gallery, Exeter University and University College, Cardiff. CASW holds her work. This was representational and abstract, strong in colour and line. Lived in Griffithstown, Pontypool, Gwent.

Alan BREESE 1922– Sculptor. Breese for a while attended the London County Council School of Building in Brixton. His art studies were pursued at Richmond School of Art under the sculptor James Wedgwood; City and Guilds

School, Kennington; London School of Art with the sculptor Edgar Allan Howes; and drawing with Ralph Middleton Todd and with Vivian Pitchforth at Camberwell School of Arts and Crafts. For some time Breese was involved with work on St Paul's Cathedral. Exhibited RA, LG, RBA and elsewhere. Breese's plaster Head of a Painter is illustrated in Eric Newton's monograph *British Sculpture 1944–1946*. Lived in London.

Gary BREEZE 1966– Sculptor and letter-cutter, born in Hockley, Essex. After a foundation course at Suffolk School of Art, 1987, Breeze graduated with honours in graphic design from the Norwich School of Art, 1990, served an apprenticeship with the letter-cutter and carver David Holgate, 1988–92, was assistant to Richard Kindersley, 1992–3, working on numerous large carving projects, including the Prudential building in Holborn, then set up his own workshop. Breeze won a competition for a 115-foot frieze at Glasgow Judiciary Buildings, Saltmarket, 1995, completed 1997, the year of his Stations of the Cross path at Quenington Old Rectory, Gloucestershire. In 1998, he was commission by London Carvers & Sculptors to do an inscription for Princess of Wales Memorial Temple, Althorp. In 1999, Breeze designed a memorial to the writer A L Rowse for the National Trust, Cornwall, in 2000 collaborating with the poet laureate Andrew Motion on a sand-blasted poem at Edward Square. He was elected a full member of Letter Exchange in 2001. Took part in many group shows and in 2002 his Latin Lyrics were shown at New Sculpture Park, Roche Court, East Winterslow. Lived in Kilverstone, Norfolk.

Jane BRENNAN 1966– Producer of site-specific paintings, recalling Renaissance frescoes, as included in New Contemporaries, 1996, at Tate Gallery, Liverpool, and Camden Arts Centre. She was born in Edinburgh, and gained a fine art degree at Central St Martin's School of Art and Design, 1989–92, then a postgraduate higher diploma in sculpture from Slade School of Fine Art, 1993–5. She was included in a number of 1995 exhibitions: Gasworks Group Show at Gasworks Gallery, Cardoso Art 95 in Cardoso, Italy, and White Trash at Lost-in-Space, and in 1998–9 in the ICA's Die Young Stay Pretty.

Robert BRENNAN 1925– Painter, printmaker and illustrator, born in London, who had no formal art training. Brennan began painting seriously in 1950, after wartime Army service in Italy and work as a medical laboratory technician at Hammersmith Hospital. After travelling, including living on a boat, in the early 1950s, moved to Cornwall, settling in Penzance, showing with the Penwith Society in 1953. Was elected a member in 1957. Brennan began making monotypes in 1958, "after watching the poet W S Graham make some during all-night sessions"; in 1962 did illustrations for *Jazz Monthly* and *Audio and Record Review*; and in 1970 spent three months in Amsterdam. Had a first solo show at Objet d'Art in Action, with a catalogue introduction by David Lewis, 1956. Later solo shows included Orion Gallery, Penzance, 1973, and Mill House Gallery, Penzance, 1990.

Sara BRENNAN 1963– Artist who produced woven tapestries, using differently coloured square and rectangular shapes, as in New Art in Scotland, Centre for Contemporary Arts, Glasgow, 1994. She was born and lived in Edinburgh, where she attended the College of Art, 1982–6, after National Arts School, Papua New Guinea, 1981–2. Exhibitions included Artist in Industry, tour including Aberdeen Art Gallery, 1989; Interwoven, Abbot Hall, Kendal, 1990; Fine Art Consultancy, Shad Thames Gallery, 1992; and Artist of the Week, Collective Gallery, Edinburgh, 1994.

Catherine BRENNAND 1961–2006 Painter and graphic artist who studied at Bishop Otter College, Chichester. Work in the construction industry as a technical and graphic artist promoted Brennand's interest in architecture. She employed watercolour with wax resist to create a rich pattern of textures and travelled widely in Britain, on the continent and in America for inspiration. John Piper, Graham Sutherland and Winslow Homer were influences. Won a Winsor & Newton Young Artist's Award at RI in 1991, then a Frank Herring & Sons award for the Best Painting of an Architectural Subject in 1992, after which she was elected RI. Also exhibited at The Linda Blackstone Gallery, Pinner.

Michael BRENNAND-WOOD 1952– Artist, designer and lecturer, born in Bury, Lancashire, who attended Bolton College of Art, 1969–72; gained an honours degree in textiles at Manchester Polytechnic, 1972–5; and his master's degree in textiles at Birmingham Polytechnic, 1975–6. In 1977 he established a studio in Bedfordshire, where he settled at Sandy, and was largely concerned with the construction of individual textiles/mixed-media works. Brennand-Wood was from 1977 associated with Goldsmiths' College as a part-time lecturer, being senior lecturer, 1983–9. Other teaching posts included University of Ulster, Royal College of Art, Glasgow School of Art, Middlesex and Trent Polytechnics and elsewhere, and he lectured extensively overseas. He was on many committees, notably for the Crafts Council and Eastern Arts Board, and held extensive British and overseas residencies. Among awards received were medallist, Munich Exempla Exhibition, 1980; British Council Award and Travel Grant and a Major Award, Visual Arts/Crafts Board of the Australia Council, all 1988; and Distinguished Visiting Fellow, British Council, Kyoto City University, Japan, 1990–1. He was curator for the Japanese Fibre Exhibition Restless Shadows, which toured the United Kingdom, 1991–2. Commissions included Law Courts, Ilkeston Council, 1975–6; Cheshire County Council, 1980–2; LRC International, 1987; and in 1989 Automobile Association, Basingstoke, and Robin Gibson/St Stephen's Cathedral, Brisbane, Australia. Brennand-Wood took part in numerous group shows, solo exhibitions latterly including Galerie RA Amsterdam, Netherlands, and Gallery/Gallery, Kyoto, Japan, both 1990, and Canberra Institute of Arts, Australia, 1991. Retrospective, Piece Hall, Halifax, 1999. Victoria & Albert Museum, Crafts Council, National Museum of Modern Art, Kyoto, and many other local authority, overseas public gallery and corporate collections hold examples, including Conoco in Warwick; its work, Overlays, was made of recycled books and tea tins.

William BRENNEN 1971– Painter, who said that "every day I feel a responsibility to paint." Brennen was born in Westminster, London, studied at St Martin's School of Art, then attended the Royal Academy Schools, 1997–00, participating in the final year show. He won the Royal Academy Gold Medal. Brennen exhibited widely, including BP Portrait Award, National Portrait Gallery, 1996, picture chosen by the artist John Bellany; Risk Annual Business Conference, Geneva, Switzerland, 1997; Risk Annual Business Conference, Brussels, Belgium, 1998; and RA Summer Exhibition, 2000. Lived in Broadoak Brede, near Rye, Sussex.

Angus BRENT 1903– Painter of landscapes and seascapes, whose full name was Ralph Richard Angus Brent. He studied at St Martin's School of Art with Bertram Nicholls. Exhibited widely in New Zealand and in Britain, including RA, RBA, Fine Art Society and in the provinces. Much of his work was done in Hampshire, where he showed in Southampton and Bournemouth and lived at Fordingbridge.

Gillian BRENT 1959– Abstract sculptor, born in Bedfordshire. She attended Wimbledon School of Art, 1978–81, then St Martin's School of Art, 1981–3, for postgraduate studies. In 1984–5 her work appeared in Have You Seen Sculpture From The Body?, Tate Gallery and tour. She shared a four-man show at Woodlands Art Gallery, 1990. Had a solo show at Worcester City Art Gallery, 1988. Worked in Sheffield, Yorkshire.

John BRENTON 1964– Representational painter, born in Plymouth, Devon, who painted his native Cornwall and the surrounding area after graduating from art college in the 1980s. Exhibited locally and was included in Artists of Fame & Promise at Panter & Hall, 2002 and 2003. That gallery gave him his first London show in 2004.

Dorothy BRETT 1883–1977 Painter of figure subjects and latterly of Indian life, born in London, daughter of Reginald Brett, 2nd Viscount Esher. She studied at Slade School of Fine Art, 1910–16. Showed in England at NEAC and elsewhere and in America, having a retrospective at America British Gallery, New York, 1950. She had gone to live in New Mexico in 1924 with the writer D H Lawrence and his wife. She remained there, dying in Taos. In 1933 she published the book *Lawrence and Brett: a Friendship*. Tate Gallery holds her work. Although formally known as The Hon. Dorothy Brett she came to be known to friends just by her surname.

William BRETT 1932– Painter, notably a watercolourist, born in London. Showed throughout his working life, varying from a commercial art studio to Dover Harbour Board. Showed with South London Artists' Group from 1965 and was an active member of the Arts Group in Sandwich, Kent, where he lived, Canterbury Society of Art and East Kent Art Society. Had a solo show at Deal Library Gallery in 1995.

Walter BRETTINGHAM 1924–2002 Painter in oil and teacher, born in London. He studied at Sir John Cass College, 1948–51, when Bainbridge Copnall was principal; St Martin's School of Art, 1951–3, with Frederick Gore as head of painting; and Bournemouth College of Art, 1953–4. Taught at several schools from 1954, finally art and art history at Spelthorne College, Ashford, Middlesex, 1959–81. Was a life member of National Society for Education in Art & Design. Brettingham's mixed shows included Plymouth Artists, 1957; Swindon Artists, 1958; ROI from 1963 – winning a prize in 1987, but being disqualified for being over age; Furneaux Gallery, Wimbledon, 1970; Staines Artists, 1973; and Holkham Gallery, 1982. After a solo show at Berystede Hotel, Ascot, in 1972, later exhibitions included Bloomsbury Gallery, London University, 1984. Lived in Virginia Water, Surrey.

Mo BREUER 1974– Artist and shop-owner, born in North Rhine, Westphalia, Germany, in whose work leading themes were "the human body, the unconscious, meditative landscapes and African symbolism." She was "influenced by Egon Schiele, Frida Kahlo, Max Ernst, Otto Dix and Pablo Picasso." From 1994–6, she studied history of fine art, Technische Universität Berlin; painting, drawing and stage set design, Die Etage, School for the Performing Arts; and traditional painting techniques and life drawing at Hochschule der Künste Berlin. In London, from 1997–00, she studied psychology and fine art, London Guildhall University; and from 2000–2 art psychotherapy at Goldsmiths' College. In 2000, Breuer opened a shop for African art and furniture in Greenwich, where she lived. Group shows included Lewisham Art House, Goldsmiths' College and Framework Gallery, all 2001, with solo open studios, 2001–2.

David BREUER-WEIL 1965– Artist who was born and lived in London, who completed a foundation course at St Martin's School of Art, but opted to read English at Cambridge University. Although working in a responsible job, he was prolific as an artist, as shown in his solo exhibition at Boundary Gallery, 1997. Breuer-Weil produced autobiographical paintings and drawings; landscapes, often tiny, with an abstract, dreamlike quality; and sculptures, based mainly on the male figure, made from smashed rocks which were reassembled. In 2001, Breuer-Weil's The Project, a cycle of large canvases exploring the human condition, was shown at Roundhouse.

Henry Charles BREWER 1866–1950 Painter, especially in watercolour, son of the artist Henry William Brewer. Studied at Westminster School of Art with Fred Brown. Exhibited extensively at Fine Art Society and RA, RI of which he was a member, widely in provinces and abroad. Lived in London, views of which he painted, including views of bomb damage, featuring St James's Piccadilly, the area around St Paul's Cathedral and the City. A studio sale at Christie's, South Kensington, 1989, also included pre- and post-World War I views of Tangiers, Spain, Belgium, France and Gibraltar.

Paul BREWER 1946– Photographer and draughtsman whose methods included photo-mechanical printmaking. He was born and based in Cardiff, from 1972 having a studio there. Studied at Newport College of Art, 1965–9; from 1972–3 was at University of Wales Institute of Science and Technology; from 1973–4 at Cardiff College of Art's art education department. Brewer won a series of WAC Awards and was in its collection, also in National Museum of Wales, Cardiff, and Newport Museum and Art Gallery. Exhibited widely in Wales, including WAC tour of Recent Purchases by CASW in 1979, and had a series of solo shows, including Oriel, Cardiff, 1981.

Martyn BREWSTER 1952– Painter, printmaker and teacher, born in Oxford. He studied, 1970–1, at Hertfordshire College of Art and Design, then from 1971–5 at Brighton Polytechnic. In 1977 he gained Eastern Arts Awards. Brewster went on to teach for a time at East Herts College, being a visiting lecturer at Winchester

School of Art. As well as participating in many group shows, Brewster showed solo frequently. These included Harlow Playhouse Gallery, Essex, 1982; Bury St Edmunds Art Gallery, 1984; Warwick Arts Trust, 1986; and The Winchester Gallery, Winchester, and tour, 1986; and Jill George Gallery, 1994. Using a mainly bright palette, Brewster's work hovered on the edge of figuration and abstraction. Brighton Polytechnic, The Open University and Winchester School of Art own his work. There were retrospectives at Russell-Cotes Art Gallery & Museum Bournemouth and at Coram Gallery, in 1997.

BRIAN: *see* **Brian STONEHOUSE**

Sydney BRIAULT 1887–1955 Painter and illustrator, born in London. Initially studied art at evening classes at the Regent Street Polytechnic School of Art, and at St Martin's School of Art. He did a large amount of commercial work: book jackets and illustrations and drawings for *Strand* and *Windsor* magazines. During World War II he was for several years studio manager with a leading London advertising agency. A member of Croydon Art Society, he lived at Shirley, Surrey.

Michael BRICK 1946– Painter and teacher who studied fine art at Newcastle University where he eventually taught, also being a visiting lecturer elsewhere. Won a Granada Fellowship in Painting at York University. His group exhibitions included John Moores Exhibition, Liverpool, 1978, where he was a prizewinner; Surfaces at Postgraduate Gallery, Hull, 1979; Centrum Beeldende Kunst, Groningen, Netherlands, 1988; and the Newcastle Group show The Northern Lights, DLI Museum & Arts Centre, Durham, and tour, 1990. Solo exhibitions included a series at Anne Berthoud Gallery from 1981. Arts Council, British Council and Contemporary Art Society hold his work. Lived in Newcastle.

Elizabeth BRIDGE 1912–1996 Painter in oil and watercolour of still life, figures and landscapes, sometimes with a pattern element, who aged 17 gained a scholarship to Hornsey School of Art. She began by carrying out small commissions and illustrations for newspapers. Was a member of RI and ROI, also exhibiting at RA, SWA, RSA and with the Industrial Painters Group, and gained an Hon. Mention at the Paris Salon. Many of her flower paintings and some of her portraits were reproduced. In 1997, Christie's South Kensington included a group of Bridge's pictures in a Modern British sale.

Eoghan BRIDGE 1963– Ceramist, born in Edinburgh, who studied at Harrogate College of Art and Leeds Polytechnic. His exhibitions included Duncalf Galleries, Harrogate, 1987; RSA from 1989; Mistral Galleries, from 1991; The Leith Gallery, Edinburgh, from 1996; City Gallery, Leicester, 1998; and Linda Blackstone Gallery, Pinner, from 2000. Eoghan (pronounced Ewan) Bridge's figure works, shown with Graham H D McKean's pictures at The Leith Gallery, 2001, were stylised and figurative.

Millie BRIDGE 1934– Artist in various media, including collage, and teacher, born in Rome, Italy. She studied at St Martin's School of Art, teachers including Ruskin Spear, John Minton and Frederick Gore. Bridge began as a graphic designer in advertising agencies, then taught in Hampshire and Sussex, latterly art at Chichester College of Further Education. She preferred abstract work, with rocks, cliffs and mountains key later themes. Group shows included Redfern Gallery, Mall Galleries, Westminster Gallery and Bishop's Palace, Chichester. Her work is held in many collections in Britain and abroad. Lived in Chichester, Sussex.

Edwina BRIDGEMAN 1959– Versatile artist who tried "to create a feeling of optimism and joy and a sense of moving forward" in works influenced by Peter Blake and Alexander Calder, with journey and voyage as important themes. What she produced could be quirky, using found objects, as in the piece Zarafa, the Giraffe that went up the Nile. Bridgeman was born in Windlesham, Surrey, and studied technical theatre at the Rose Bruford College of Speech & Drama, 1978–80. She worked with Terry Murphy Scenery Ltd, 1980, and between 1981–5 was a scene painter with Bristol Old Vic. Was a full member of Bath Network of Artists, based in the Somerset city. Group shows included Making their Mark, Six Chapel Row, 2000, and Miracles, Victoria Art Gallery, 2003, both in Bath. The solo exhibition The Voyage out, 2001–3, toured from Black Swan Arts, Frome. Whitstable Art Gallery and Museum and Royal United Hospital, Bath, hold examples.

John BRIDGEMAN 1916–2004 Sculptor and teacher, working in fibreglass, plastics, concrete, bronze and ciment fondu. He was born in Felixstowe, Suffolk, studied at Colchester School of Art with Barry Hart and Edward J Morss, later at Royal College of Art, 1947–9, with Frank Dobson. Bridgeman won the Otto Beit sculpture award in 1947. After working as a letter-carver for Misha Black's Design Research Unit in 1951, and contributing big panels to the Dome of Discovery at the Festival of Britain, he was appointed head of sculpture at Carlisle College of Art in 1951. He became head of Birmingham Polytechnic school of sculpture, 1956–81, succeeding William Bloye. Bridgeman's idiosyncratic and democratic method of running a sculpture school inspired loyalty from his students, who refused to join the widespread revolt of the late 1960s at such centres as Hornsey College of Art. His own work, which established a reputation mainly outside the London commercial gallery system, was deeply influenced by his experiences during World War II as a conscientious objector, rescuing bombed civilians. Bridgeman was made a fellow of RBS in 1960 and was a member of RBSA. His commissions included Madonna Dolorosa, for Coventry Cathedral; a Group of Warriors, for St Catherine's College, Cambridge; sculptural decorations for the 1951 Festival of Britain Dome of Discovery; and Cosmic Energy, an abstract panel for Aston University, Birmingham. He showed with RA; Roland, Browse & Delbanco; public galleries in Birmingham and Liverpool; and at Anthony Hepworth Fine Art, Bath. Lived in Leamington, Warwickshire.

Peter BRIDGENS 1947– Sculptor and teacher who studied at Bath Academy of Art, Corsham. Teaching experience included ceramics at Bristol Polytechnic and head of the School of Art and Design in Queen's Road, Clifton. Landscape, architecture and stone structures in the Cotswolds, Pembrokeshire and Umbria were influences on Bridgens' abstract work. He was included in the 2nd Open Sculpture Exhibition at RWA, 1996. Lived in Marshfield, Chippenham, Wiltshire.

Alan BRIDGWATER 1903–1962 Sculptor, painter, printmaker and teacher. Studied at Birmingham College of Art, 1923–33, the staff of which he later joined. Exhibited RA, NEAC, RBA, RSA and RBSA. Bridgwater was made an associate of that body in 1935, an associate of RBS in 1948 and a full member in 1949, also being a council member. Birmingham City Museum and Art Gallery holds his work and he also completed a war memorial for Kings Norton Grammar School. Bridgwater also had strong links with Dudley, teaching at its School of Art, 1948–54. With Charles Upton he formed the sculpture partnership Bridgwater and Upton, and their work included novel sculptural decoration for Dudley police headquarters. Lived in Edgbaston.

Barbara Helen BRIDGWATER 1919– Painter, textile artist, photographer and teacher who was married to the sculptor Alan Bridgwater. She studied at the College of Arts and Crafts in Birmingham, 1936–41. Started teaching at Malvern College of Art in 1941, later appointments including senior lectureship at City of Birmingham College of Education, 1956–75, and Birmingham Polytechnic Centre for Education, 1975–7. Showed at RA, RBA, NEAC and elsewhere. Lived latterly at Hawkhurst, Kent.

Emmy BRIDGWATER 1906–1999 Surrealist painter, draughtsman and, from the 1970s, collagist, born in Edgbaston, Birmingham. She studied art there, in Oxford and London; Bernard Fleetwood-Walker taught her at Birmingham School of Art, Iain Macnab at Grosvenor School of Art. When in 1936 she saw the International Surrealist Exhibition in London this shaped the future course of her work, and soon after this she joined the Birmingham Group of Surrealists and the Surrealist group in England in 1940. Became a member of the LG and lived in London for periods. Held a first solo show at Jack Bilbo's Modern Art Gallery in 1942. During the 1940s she contributed to several international Surrealist publications, then in 1947 was invited by André Breton to the Galerie Maeght international Surrealist show in Paris where she signed the English group's *Declaration*. After some years of neglect, when she was unable to paint because of family responsibilities, interest was revived in Bridgwater's work when she was included in the Hamet Gallery's Surrealist show in 1971, as she was in several further reviews in the 1980s. Blond Fine Art gave her a solo show in 1990. Bridgwater was a notable practitioner of Automatism, designed to liberate the imagination, as theorised by Breton. She left much unpublished poetry which also employed her powerful visionary imagination. Lived just outside Birmingham.

Kathleen BRIDLE 1897–1989 Landscape painter and influential teacher, known informally as Pindi, born in Swalecliffe, Kent. As her father was a coastguard officer there were frequent moves and she was mainly educated by her mother. Her early talent was encouraged and after the final move, to Holyhead, in 1913, and tuition by a local art teacher, John Owen Owen, Bridle enrolled at Dublin Metropolitan School of Art, 1915, under Sean Keating, Oliver Shepherd, James Golden and George Atkinson, who especially influenced her watercolour technique. She completed her certificate course with distinction in 1918; among awards was the Dublin Society Taylor Scholarship, 1919–20, enabling her to attend the Royal College of Art, 1921–5, under William Rothenstein, Thomas Derrick being an important teacher, Cézanne a key influence. In her final year she taught night classes at the Elephant and Castle School of Art. Her close friends included Henry Moore, Raymond Coxon, Edna Ginesi, Robert Lyon and Phyllis Dodd. From the end of 1925 she painted glass in Clarke Studios, Dublin, from 1926 teaching at schools in Enniskillen, which remained her home; was art organiser in Fermanagh, 1945–51; then was appointed full-time at the Collegiate School in 1955. William Scott and T P Flanagan were notable pupils. Throughout her life she travelled abroad extensively. Bridle won prizes at the Royal National Eisteddfod, showed regularly with the RHA, in 1934 was a founder-member of the Ulster Unit, in 1935 was elected an associate of the Ulster Academy, an Hon. RUA in 1962 and took part in the first Contemporary Ulster Group Exhibition, 1951. In 1980 the Northern Ireland Arts Council funded the film *Reminiscence by Kathleen Bridle*. Solo exhibitions included a retrospective at Ardowen Theatre, Enniskillen, 1986; the catalogue for the major show which toured from Fermanagh County Museum, Enniskillen, 1988–9, carried an extensive biographical essay by Carole Froude-Durix. That museum, Ulster Museum in Belfast and other Northern Ireland public collections hold examples.

Edith Elizabeth BRIER: *see* **Elizabeth SCOTT-MOORE**

Argent BRIERLEY 1893–1960 Landscape painter and teacher who after attending George Heriot's School in Edinburgh gained his diploma at the College of Art. After World War I service with the Royal Scots Regiment he taught at Manchester School of Art, L S Lowry being a pupil. Later appointed art master at William Hulme's Grammar School, taking a similar post in 1945 at Lawrence Sheriff School, Rugby, eventually settling in Salisbury, Wiltshire. He died on a business trip to Manchester, where the City Art Gallery holds many examples. Showed at MAFA, RSA, with Wessex Artists and with Civil Defence Artists, having been a warden in World War II.

Louise BRIERLEY 1958– Artist whose oil on panel Naughty puppies no.12 was included in the 2004 John Moores Liverpool Exhibition, one of 13 in a series finished at the end of 2003. "They were inspired by the no-man's land of Hackney Marshes". Brierley was born in Glossop, Derbyshire, and studied at Manchester Polytechnic, 1977–80, and the Royal College of Art, 1980–3. In 1996, she received the *New York Times* award for the best artist's book of that year. A solo exhibition toured four Japanese national museums in 1997. London exhibitions included The Discerning Eye, Mall Galleries, 2002, and East End Academy, Whitechapel Art Gallery, 2004.

David BRIGGS 1956– Versatile artist and lecturer, born in Burnley, Lancashire. Briggs worked as an interior designer, 1972–8. He then did a foundation course at Burnley Art College, 1978–80; obtained a Higher National Certificate in ceramics at Cornwall College; and an honours degree in fine art from the University of Central Lancashire, Preston, 1980–83. Briggs assisted the sculptor in wood David Nash, 1982, learning bronze welding in Anthony Caro's studio, 1983. As well as sculpting commercial figurines, 1983–7, Briggs obtained his teacher's certificate from Burnley College, 1984–5, lecturing in painting at the University of Central Lancashire, 1987–9. From 1989–90, he designed logos for glass makers and was a part-time craft instructor, pottery and weaving, at Padiham Technical College, Lancashire, 1990–3. Briggs moved to St Ives, Cornwall, in 1994, running the Spirit of the North Gallery, 1994–6. After from 1995–7 obtaining a postgraduate diploma in fine art from Falmouth Art College, from 1998–9 Briggs was a part-time sculpture tutor at Cornwall College. Briggs' many group shows included the Lancashire Art Exhibition at Harris Art Gallery, Preston, 1982; Bluecoat Gallery, Liverpool, 1983; Mid-Pennine Art Gallery, Burnley, where he was an award winner, 1984; Bakehouse Gallery, Penzance, 1995; Geevor Tin Mine Art Project, Summer Sculpture Exhibition, 1999; and Lemon Street Gallery, Truro, 2000, which gave him a one-man in 2002. Briggs was a member of the Society of Artists in Newlyn, Vanguard Group of Artists there and the Wimbledon Arts Group. His solo shows included two at the Belgrave Gallery in 2001, in St Ives and London, in which his paintings formed "a visual representation of the ideas, thoughts and imagery that have fascinated and haunted me over the past few years". There was another show, The Bigger Picture, at Badcock's in Newlyn in 2003.

E Irlam BRIGGS fl. early 1890s–1950 Modeller, painter and artist in fresco who studied at Wimbledon College of Art after private education. Also attended St John's Wood School of Art, Royal Academy Schools and Académie Julian, Paris. Miss Briggs was brought up in a religious environment and did work for a number of churches in England and America. Exhibited RA, Walker Art Gallery, Liverpool and elsewhere in the provinces. She was closely associated with the East Dorset Art Society, living at Parkstone.

William BRIGGS 1888–1978 Painter, engraver and photographer, born in London, where he had a studio at 22 Chenies Street. He was educated at the Borough Polytechnic and Bolt Court art school. Was elected a member of The Royal Photographic Society in 1933, being admitted as a full fellow in 1936. Showed at Ridley Art Club, ROI and extensively along the south coast, where he settled at Steyning, Sussex.

Isobel BRIGHAM 1963– Painter, born in Fareham, Hampshire, who studied at Chelsea College of Art, 1988–92, teachers including Helen Chadwick, and Slade School of Fine Art, 1992–4, where "I was unhappy". Her figurative, painterly pictures were usually made over sustained periods, "change the whole time and I do a lot of scraping off". She admired Rembrandt, Van Gogh, Ingres and Goya. Exhibitions included The Discerning Eye, Mall Galleries, 1991; BP Portrait Award at National Portrait Gallery and Royal Over-Seas League Open, both 1992; Fresh Art, Business Design Centre, 1994; and In the Looking Glass, Usher Gallery, Lincoln, and tour, 1996–7. Lived in London.

Kate BRIGHT 1964– Painter, born in Suffolk, who attended Ipswich School of Art, 1979–85, graduated from Camberwell School of Arts and Crafts, 1985–8; with a master's from Goldsmiths' College School of Art, 1994–6. The structure of natural and man-made features in landscape was of key interest to Bright, who took part in group shows at London Institute Gallery, 1987; Homerton College, Cambridge, 1989; South Bank Centre's touring exhibition The British Art Show 1990; and dumbpop, Jerwood Gallery, 1998–9. Had a strong connection with Yugoslavia, having a solo show at Galerija Arts, Llubljana, 1989, later ones including Penton Space, 1993, and landscape paintings at The New Art Gallery Walsall, 2003. Lived in London.

Ken BRIGHT 1939–2005 Sculptor and draughtsman, notable for bird and animal subjects; teacher. He was born on the Isle of Wight and studied at Portsmouth College of Art and Goldsmiths' College School of Art. Became head of ceramics at Goldsmiths' and a member of the Crafts Centre of Great Britain. Had work shown in England abroad and in private collections worldwide. Had solo exhibition at Woodlands Art Gallery, 1978, work being made from studies at Falconry Centre, Gloucestershire, and Police Stables, Dulwich.

Charlotte BRILL 1950– Artist, born in London, daughter of the painters Frederick Brill and Deirdre Borlase, whose activities included set and costume design, performance art and stand-up comedy, storytelling, site-specific sculpture, works on and with paper and arts administration. She was strongly committed to feminism, radicalism and direct verbal address rather than creating the permanent art object. Studied at Wimbledon School of Art and Central School of Art & Design, 1968–72, then worked as a theatre designer, 1972–80; as a performer, 1979–83; then from 1984 as an administrator. She was included in Relative Values, the Brill family exhibition, at The Smith Art Gallery & Museum, Stirling, 1993.

Frederick BRILL 1920–1984 Teacher, painter and writer, born in London. He studied at Hammersmith School of Art, 1934–9, Slade School of Fine Art, 1940–1, and Royal College of Art, 1941–5, where he won a medal for distinction in painting. After six years of part-time teaching Brill in 1951 became a lecturer at Chelsea School of Art, rising to become principal, 1965–79. He wrote a monograph on *Matisse*, 1967, and another short publication on *Turner's Burial at Sea*, 1969, which contained prose compared with John Ruskin's. Showed with LG, RBA, RA and NEAC and had several solo shows. In 1985 Chelsea School of Art staged a memorial exhibition. Lived finally at Carperby, Yorkshire, an area much painted by him. Was survived by his wife, painter Deirdre Borlase, and was included with her in Relative Values, The Smith Art Gallery & Museum, Stirling, 1993.

Patrick BRILL 1963– Performance artist, born in London, married to Jessica Voorsanger, also known as Jessica Voorsanger-Brill. He was the son of the artists Frederick Brill and Deirdre Borlase and was included in the Brill family exhibition Relative Values, The Smith Art Gallery & Museum, Stirling, 1993. He studied at the University of Reading, 1981–5, winning a Rome Prize in the latter year. Gained a Harkness Fellowship with the Cooper Union School of Arts and Sciences, New York, America, 1988–90. After Brill's solo exhibition I want children's TV: I want children's TV banned, at Sue Williams Gallery in 1991, Brill turned from the painted image to satirical performance. He invented Bob Smith and simulated game shows in which members of the audience participated using his Home Sculpture System. An example was Dont Hate Sculpt, at Arnolfini Gallery, Bristol, 1997–8, in which both Bob and Roberta Smith rather than Patrick Brill were billed. In 2000, Turnaround featured installations around the Hayward Gallery. In Nuffin is Reel, at meddievalmodern, in 2003, most of the show centred on a comic persona, The Uncommon King of Leytonstone, a Rabelasian character whose erotic misadventures were charted in a poem. In 2004–5 the Baltic Centre for Contemporary Art, Gateshead, staged a work in progress exhibition: Bob and Roberta Smith help build the ruins of democracy.

Reginald BRILL 1902–1974 Artist in oil and watercolour and fine draughtsman of landscapes, figure studies and portraits. Born in London, Brill studied under Henry Tonks at the Slade School 1921–4 after a period at the St Martin's School of Art. Won the Prix de Rome for painting and was at the British School in Rome 1927–9. Worked in Cairo, 1930. Exhibited at the RA, Leicester Galleries and in East Anglia, where he lived, at Lavenham. Was principal of Kingston School of Art. Wrote *Modern Painting* and *Art as a Career.* Kingston Polytechnic, the Royal Borough and the Phoenix Gallery organised a retrospective in Kingston in 1985, with another at Stanley Picker Gallery, Kingston University, 1999.

Victoria BRILL 1958– Artist, designer and teacher using a wide range of media, born in London daughter of the painters Frederick Brill and Deirdre Borlase and married to the artist Stephen Gavin. Allegory, moral issues, everyday objects and routines and art history references were all found in her work. She studied at Camberwell School of Arts and Crafts, 1976–7, then Kingston Polytechnic, 1979–82, winning a Stanley Picker Travelling Scholarship to Venice, 1981, and the *Guardian* Purchase Prize, New Contemporaries, 1983. Designed *Faust* set and costumes for Mantis Dance Theatres, 1985, designing and painting model theatres for Channel 4 Television's *A Map of Dreams*, 1986. From 1989 taught for North Yorkshire County Council. Was Artist of the Day, Angela Flowers Gallery, 1985; Showed at Linton Court Gallery, Settle, 1987–90; and at Stonegate Gallery, York, 1987–91. In 1993 she was included in the Brill family show Relative Values at The Smith Art Gallery & Museum, Stirling.

Fredda BRILLIANT 1908–1999 Sculptor, born in Łódź, Poland, real name Alfreda Brilliant, married to the British Russophile translator and film producer Herbert Marshall. They were both closely and long associated with the left-wing Unity Theatre, founded in the 1930s, detailed in Colin Chambers' 1989 history, *The Story of Unity Theatre*. She established an international career, although she had no formal art training, gaining her first commissions in Russia in the 1930s. She depicted in bronze politicians, film-makers and writers, such as Molotov, Eisenstein and Chekhov. She had already established a career as an actress in Australia, to which her family had emigrated in 1924, co-founding the Melbourne Theatre; had acted in America after emigrating there in 1930; and was to return to acting and scriptwriting when she and Marshall moved to England in 1937. From the late 1940s she and Marshall spent much time in India. In England she showed at RA, RWS, Leicester Galleries, Whitechapel Art Gallery and elsewhere. Among her public works are the Mahatma Gandhi memorial in Tavistock Square and the portrait of Sir Isaac Hayward for the Royal Festival Hall, while her head of the statesman Krishna Menon is in the National Art Gallery in New Delhi and Southern Illinois University and National Art Gallery in Sydney, New South Wales, also hold her work. Lived for a time in Sussex, also in Carbondale, Illinois, in America. In the 1980s a number of books by her were published in India, including the short story collection *Truth in Fiction*; *Women in Power*; and *The Black Virgin. Biographies in Bronze* covers her work as a sculptor. Brilliant was a member of the SPS.

Max BRIMMELL 1917–1993 Artist, notably of watercolour landscapes, actor and bookseller, born in London. His real name was Ronald Arthur Brimmell, Max stemming from a part played on the stage. During World War II Brimmell was in the Royal Navy, rising from the rank of ordinary seaman to the command of several ships. After the war he studied at Putney School of Art under John Bowyer and Francis Edwin Hodge. Showed at RI, UA, PS, RBA and at the Stables Theatre and Museum in Hastings, where he settled from 1963, being a founder-member of Old Hastings' Town Week, president of its Preservation Society and a founder- and playing member of its Cricket Club. As an actor Brimmell appeared in a film with Boris Karloff, on the West End stage, for 18 years in the radio serial *The Archers* as the vicar and on television as the sidekick of chief superintendent *Fabian of the Yard.* Realising he could make more money from antiquarian bookselling than acting, Brimmell turned to this, becoming an authority on children's literature and publishing two books. Continued to paint at weekends, when he reckoned to complete two pictures. Finally lived at Bexhill-on-Sea, Sussex.

Sharon BRINDLE 1958– Draughtsman and painter working in pastel/conté and oil on canvas, born in Staffordshire. She studied at Camberwell School of Art, 1979–82. Took part in a number of mixed shows, including Art '92 and Art '93, Islington; and at Camden Galleries. The Fine Art Society, Julian Hartnoll, Duncan Miller and Falle Fine Art, in Jersey, exhibited her work, which also appeared at the RA Summer Exhibition, the Whitechapel Open and Royal Festival Hall. Had a solo show at Boundary Gallery in 1992, another at Portland Gallery, 1993, and Stephen Lacey Gallery, 2003. Brindle was notable as a draughtsman of the female nude, believing that "all the universe and its forces are concentrated in the unclothed human body". Her work was included in Ron Bowen's 1992 book *Drawing Masterclass*. Lived in London.

Donald BRINDLEY 1928– Sculptor of horses in various materials, born at Penkull, Stoke-on-Trent, Staffordshire. He studied at Burslem College of Art, then at Royal College of Art until 1951, teachers including John Skeaping and Frank Dobson. He was a consultant to several British and foreign porcelain makers, including Royal Worcester Porcelain and Josiah Wedgwood & Sons. Was elected a fellow of RBS in 1973. HM The Queen holds his work. Lived in Stoke-on-Trent.

John BRINE 1920– Painter and teacher, born in Sydenham, southeast London. He attended Clapham School of Art, 1935–9, teachers including Roland Pitchforth, then Royal College of Art, 1946–9, under Ruskin Spear and Rodrigo Moynihan. Went on to become head of fine art school at Ravensbourne College of Art & Design. Was a member of RBA and showed at RA, LG and SEA. Hertfordshire Education Committee bought his work. Lived in Bromley, Kent.

Mike BRISCOE 1960– Painter and advertising illustrator, born and lived in Colwyn Bay, Clwyd. He studied at Wrexham College of Art under David Cooper, 1978–9, then Sheffield City Polytechnic, 1979–82, where teachers included Terry Lee. Showed at RA Summer Exhibition from 1983, at Piccadilly Gallery from 1984 and in same year at Palais des Nations, Paris. Was a Stowells Trophy prizewinner. Solo show at Martin Tinney Gallery, Cardiff, 2002.

Stuart BRISLEY 1933– Painter, producer of structures in various materials, performance artist and teacher, born in Haslemere, Surrey. He attended Guildford School of Art, 1949–54; Royal College of Art, 1956–9, with an Abbey Minor Scholarship in the latter year; in 1959–60 won Bavarian State Scholarship and studied at Akademie der Bildenden Künste, Munich; then studied at Florida State University, Tallahassee, 1960–2. Brisley gained a Fulbright Travel Award for 1960–4 and the Hille Fellowship, 1970–1. In 1973–4 Brisley won DAAD Berlin Artists' Programme Award. He was town artist at Peterlee, County Durham, 1976–7. Brisley became reader in charge of media-fine art at Slade School of Fine Art in 1985. He followed a period producing fairly formalist structures with the utilisation of movement and light and work as a performance artist. This comprised various rituals which carried social and political messages. With Leslie Haslam, as Brisley/Haslam (see separate entries), he collaborated on a number of performances. They were included in the big British Council exhibition English Art Today 1960–76, at Palazzo Reale, Milan, Italy, in 1976. He had retrospectives at ICA in in 1981 and Serpentine Gallery in 1986, with a show at South London Gallery, 1996. Vardy Gallery, University of Sunderland, held Stuart Brisley: Peterlee Project 1976–2004 in 2004, curated by Tim Brennan. Arts Council holds his work. Lived in London.

BRISLEY/HASLAM– Stuart Brisley and Leslie Haslam (see separate entries) collaborated from the mid-1970s on a series of performances at a time when around 150 artists were involved in such activities in Britain. As Brisley/Haslam they were represented at the big British Council 1976 exhibition English Art Today 1960–76, at the Palazzo Reale, Milan, Italy. Their other collaborations had included Die Hochzeit, video film, and Bath Work – Berlin, both 1974; Aktion Rottweil 12 Days – Kunstforum, Rottweil (Moments of Decision/Indecision), and 6 Days Warsaw Teatra Studio. Palac Kultury I Nauki, Warsaw, both 1975; and Peterlee project, Peterlee, 1 Jan 1936 – 31 Dec 1976, 1976.

Sophy BRISTOL 1973– Realistic and atmospheric painter who graduated from the Surrey Institute of Fine Arts in 1995. Spent part of each year at the family farm in South Africa, part at her south London studio, showing in Cape Town, Chicago and London. There, Panter & Hall included her in Artists of Fame & Promise in 2002. Panter & Hall gave Bristol solo shows from 2001 which reflected her wide travels and interest in the London scene.

Charles Edward BRITTAN Junior 1870–1949 Landscape watercolourist and illustrator who studied with his father, Charles Edward Brittan Senior (1837–1888), with whom he is often confused. Brittan Junior lived at Sheepstor, Devon, on the edge of Dartmoor. The Maas Gallery offered his brooding Dusk over Dartmoor in 2004. Exhibited at RA Summer Exhibition and RI and had a show at St James' Galleries in 1901. He illustrated an edition of R D Blackmore's novel *Lorna Doone*, published in 1930.

Nan BROACKES 1908– Painter and draughtsman who studied at Leeds College of Art under Arthur Pope. Showed her work at RA, SSA and Royal Glasgow Institute of the Fine Arts. Lived for a time at Currie, Midlothian.

Clio BROAD 1934– Artist in watercolour, gouache and pastel, and teacher, born in Aberystwyth, Cardiganshire. She attended Lancaster and Morecambe College of Art, 1951–3, and Swansea College of Art, 1953–5, taught by Howard Martin and William Price. From 1955–6 Broad worked as a stained glass painter for Bell's, of Bristol, then taught art in Maesydderwen Comprehensive School, Ystradgynlais. Mixed show appearances included Attic, Mumbles and Ceri Richards Galleries, Swansea; National Museum of Wales, Oriel Albany and Manor House Fine Arts, in Cardiff; Mold National Eisteddfod; Llewellyn Alexander Gallery; and Coal Industry National Art Competition & Exhibition, Blackpool. Had solo shows at Ystradgynlais Library and Gorseinon Institute. Lived in Ystradgynlais, Swansea.

Arthur BROADBENT 1909–1994 Painter, ceramist and teacher, born in Belfast, Northern Ireland. Studied at Royal College of Art design school, teachers including Henry Moore. Taught at Lincoln College of Art; was a camouflage officer in Royal Air Force, 1939–45; then taught at Shrewsbury School, 1945–70. His main works included murals in St Tim's and St Ambrose, Everton, demolished 1970. Broadbent, who adored the work of Bonnard, showed with Shropshire Art Society, elsewhere in the country and had a solo exhibition at Shrewsbury School in 1980.

John BROADBENT 1926– Artist, teacher and writer, born in London, husband of Caroline Hoskin, daughter of the sculptor John Hoskin. He studied at Edinburgh University and for a year at Norwich School of Art and Design. Served in the Royal Marines, was a fellow of King's College, Cambridge, and professor of English at the University of East Anglia. Broadbent completed numerous academic studies of English literature and produced art history programmes for BBC Television in the 1960s. He was a member of the Norwich Twenty Group and took part in various group and mixed shows, including Norwich Castle. Had solo exhibitions at King of Hearts Gallery, Norwich, 1993 and St Margaret's, Norwich, and Tavistock Centre, both 1998. King of Hearts and Norfolk Contemporary Art Society/University of East Anglia hold examples. Lived in Norwich, Norfolk.

Stephen BROADBENT 1961– Sculptor, born in Wroughton, Wiltshire, who trained with the sculptor Arthur Dooley in Liverpool, 1979–83, having a first solo exhibition at Aberbach Gallery, London, 1982. Among Broadbent's public commissions were the stylised figurative cast-iron Reconciliation, in Concert Street, Liverpool, 1990 (copies stand in Belfast and Glasgow); bronze relief panels The Trades and Professions of Edinburgh, Saltire Court, Edinburgh, 1991; and the bronze Challenge, outside Capital House, Chester, 1993. Broadbent was based for some time in Liverpool.

Robina Margaret BROADFIELD 1906–1993 Painter, born in Hebburn, Country Durham, married to the art teacher Aubrey Broadfield. Apart from six weeks of evening classes at Leicester College of Art she was self-taught. She was a leading member of Leicester Society of Artists and showed at public galleries in Leicester and Nottingham, in Germany and Italy. Her work was "from memory, or imagination" and was signed with initials. Lived in Glenfield, Leicester.

Barry BROADIE 1940– Painter and teacher, born in Manchester. He was educated at George Heriot's School in Edinburgh, where he settled. Taught art at Basil Paterson Tutorial College. Broadie showed widely in Scotland, including RSW, RSA and Scottish Gallery group shows and had a number of solo exhibitions in the city. Royal Edinburgh Hospital owns his work.

Bob BROADLEY 1939– Painter, based in Suffolk, but born in Surrey where he attended Kingston School of Art, 1955–9. His work was figurative with an underlying abstract quality that could intensify the viewer's feelings; imaginative and essentially narrative, its story was secondary to its inherent design. Exhibitions included Brandler Gallery, Brentwood; Duncan R Miller Fine Arts; Mall Galleries; Contemporary Fine Art Gallery, Eton; and RA Summer Exhibition. Broadley had solo shows at The John Russell Gallery, Ipswich, 2002 and 2004. Private collections in Britain and abroad held works.

Denise BROADLEY 1914– Painter, and latterly a collagist, who before World War II started tuition with Cedric Morris, who ran The East Anglian School of Painting and Drawing, staying with it during its various moves. In the 1930s she toured continental Europe with Lucy Harwood, painting in the streets of Dieppe, Bruges, Nantes and Paris. After the war Broadley joined the Anglican religious order Community of the Servants of the Cross, where she was known as Sister Gillian and where for a long time her art was not encouraged. While in Australia this attitude softened and she began painting the streets of Sydney. Exhibited with NEAC and RA Summer Exhibition and in 1999 had a solo show at Graham & Oldham, Ipswich, where Broadley showed collages and paintings using broad brush strokes and vibrant colours.

John Christopher BROBBEL 1950– Painter, teacher and writer, born in Hartlepool, County Durham, where he settled. He studied at the local College of Art, 1969–71, at Byam Shaw School of Drawing and Painting, 1971–4, then at Royal Academy Schools, 1974–7, where his teachers included Peter Greenham and Norman Blamey. Showed RA, NEAC and RBA, of which he was a member, also of the Watercolour Society of Ireland and a freeman of the Worshipful Company of Painter-Stainers and had several solo exhibitions. Sometimes signed work only with initials. Wrote *Pencil Drawing* and *Drawing with Ink* and taught for a time at Hartlepool College of Further Education and Cleveland College of Art. Brobbel was in The Irish Show at The Wykeham Gallery, Stockbridge, in 2005.

Henry Matthew BROCK 1875–1960 Illustrator, designer and watercolourist, born and lived in Cambridge, younger brother of the illustrator Charles Edmund Brock. Studied at local School of Art, worked alongside his brother and by the mid-1990s was a busy illustrator of periodicals. His work appeared in *Boy's Own Paper, The Graphic, Pearson's Magazine* and *The Strand Magazine*, plus many others, and he illustrated many books. He was elected RI in 1906, also showing at RA, RSA and Walker Art Gallery in Liverpool, producing attractive landscapes.

Janice Sylvia BROCK 1950– Self-taught artist, born in Withington, Manchester, who painted exuberant, colourful pictures, including nudes and still life, using an Impressionist style inspired by the Caribbean. When young she was a competitive sportswoman, with medals for swimming and skating, but aged 10 she developed Still's Disease, a virulent form of rheumatoid arthritis. Aged 13, she was given a paint box and brushes, because of pain at first working with brush strapped to her hand. From 1969 she was a professional artist, gaining extensive media coverage. Among her mixed and group shows were Gallery Nouveau, St Tropez, France, 2000; Atlanta Arts Fair, America, 2002; Gallery of Caribbean Art, Barbados, 2003; and Henley Arts Festival, 2003 and 2004. She also had many solo exhibitions, including Villa Espelho, Portugal; British High Commission, Barbados; Will's Art Warehouse; and Sandy Lane Hotel, Barbados. Brock's books were *Poetic Thoughts*, 1983, and *Impressions of the Caribbean*, 2002. Prints of her pictures were published by Rosenstiel's. Brock also engaged in a range of arts-related activities which included art therapy classes for patients at Cheadle Royal Hospital, 1984–8; lecturing to The International School, Algarve, Portugal, 2001; forming the Arts Clubhouse, Barbados, 2002; and being artist-in-residence, Villa Nova Hotel, Barbados 2001–2. She was made Cheshire Woman of the Year, 1985, and was elected to the Chelsea Arts Club, 2002. Among owners of her work were The White House, in America; Villa Nova in Barbados, where she was a member of the Arts Council; Brown Shipley and Company; plus many private collectors, including The Dukes of Devonshire and Westminster, John Madejski, Neil and Christine Hamilton and the comedian Ken Dodd. She lived in Alderley Edge, Cheshire.

Albert Ernest BROCKBANK 1862–1958 Painter who was born and lived in Liverpool, studying at the School of Art there, in London and at Académie Julian in Paris. He was president of both the Liverpool Academy and Liverpool Sketching Club and showed extensively at Walker Art Gallery which holds his work, as does Harris Museum and Art Gallery, Preston. Also showed at RCamA, RBA, RA and RI.

Russell BROCKBANK 1913–1979 Humorous illustrator, born in Niagara Falls, Ontario, Canada. Brockbank was educated at Ridley College, Ontario, studying art at Buffalo New York School of Art in America, then with Harold Sandys Williamson at Chelsea School of Art, 1931–2. Showed at SGA, but was most known for his illustrations in a variety of magazines, notably *Punch*, of which he was art editor for just over a decade from 1949. Also illustrated a number of books, including *The Brockbank Omnibus*. Chris Beetles Ltd held a show in 1999. Lived in Thursley, Surrey.

Gerald Leslie BROCKHURST 1890–1978 Painter, etcher, draughtsman and teacher, born in Edgbaston, Birmingham. So gifted was Brockhurst as a draughtsman that he was admitted to Birmingham School of Art aged 12. He entered the Royal Academy Schools in 1907, in 1913 winning a gold medal and a travelling scholarship. In 1913–14 he visited Paris and in Italy studied the Quattrocento painters, whose style influenced his own portraits. Had a one-man show at Chenil Gallery in 1919, in 1920 deciding to concentrate on etching, which he did lucratively for the next decade. Brockhurst's election to RE in 1921 and RP in 1923 was followed in 1928 by his winning associate status at RA and being elected a visitor to the Royal Academy Schools. He was elected RA in 1937. Two years later Brockhurst left for New York with his model Kathleen – known as Dorette – Woodward, whom he was to marry after divorce from his wife Anaïs, also a notable model for his work. By this time Brockhurst was established as a sought-after portrait painter, able to ask 1,000 guineas a canvas. His models were to include The Duchess of Windsor, Marlene Dietrich and J Paul Getty. For his remaining years Brockhurst undertook many lucrative portrait commissions, exhibiting with Knoedler and Portraits Incorporated, dying at Franklin Lakes, New Jersey, with a reputation which had largely faded in Britain, although collectors remembered him as a masterly etcher. His reputation was revivified by the 1986–7 exhibition of his work which toured from Graves Art Gallery, Sheffield. Public galleries there, in Oxford, Preston, Hull, Glasgow and elsewhere hold his work.

Keith BROCKIE 1955– Wildlife illustrator and artist, born in Haddington, East Lothian, he moved to Strathmiglo, Fife, aged 13, from there going to Bell Baxter High School, which had a good art department. After school spent four years at Duncan of Jordanstone College of Art, Dundee, gaining a diploma in illustration and printmaking. Worked for some months as illustrator for Dundee Museum, but disliked working in an office so went freelance. He believed in constant field work, and was a bird ringer. Showed Brotherton Gallery and elsewhere and had a Scottish Arts Council show in 1981. Lived at Carse of Gowrie, Scotland.

Jo BROCKLEHURST 1935–2006 Artist, born in London, educated at St Martin's School of Art, where she completed four years' study after entering on a scholarship at 14. Following a 1979 solo show in Amsterdam, Netherlands, Brocklehurst became known for her energetic drawings in mixed media, attracting attention with her contribution to the controversial Women's Images of Men show at ICA, 1980. Her first London solo exhibition was The London Drawings, at Francis Kyle Gallery, 1981, followed by London Take Two there in 1982. Brocklehurst explored the American scene with an exhibition of drawings at the Leo Castelli's Green Street Gallery, New York, in 1983, and in 1984 at Connecticut State University Gallery, in that year having another solo show at Wave Gallery, Amsterdam. Returning to America, she was influenced by the new luminous technology being developed there, then by the German avant-garde theatre, which prompted shows of drawings at Oberhessisches Museum, Giessen, 1988, and the University of Giessen, 1989. Among later exhibitions were figure paintings and drawings at Knapp Gallery, 1993; dramatic fluorescent paintings, featuring underground cyber figures at Vic Naylor's, 1994; and in the same year her figure drawings appeared in Street Style, at the Victoria & Albert Museum, which holds her work. Latterly, Brocklehurst concentrated on a collection of cyber-animated computer drawings and studio installations, titles including A Womb of My Own; Punkwall Paper; and Brocklehurst Threw the Looking Glass. John Denham Gallery also showed her work.

Michael BROCKWAY 1919– Painter, son of the musician Sir William Harris, who studied at Stowe School and Cambridge University. Attended Farnham School of Art, 1946–50, Cheltenham School of Art, 1950, and Ruskin School of Drawing in Oxford, 1951–4. He was a member of NEAC, also showing with RA, RBA and RI. His study of the watercolourist Charles Knight was published in 1952. Lived in Burford, Oxfordshire.

Cleo BRODA 1970– Artist noted for her maps and signage for particular locations. Research for her 2000 show Guides to *The Economist* Plaza, the venue for the exhibition, "employed her rigorous, if unorthodox, surveying technique. This entails loitering, chatting to strangers, taking photos, observing and following any line of enquiry which comes to mind or is suggested by others." Before then, she had produced *Local Information Guides* for areas of London and Liverpool as part of New Contemporaries 99 (in Liverpool as part of the Liverpool Biennial and in London at the Milch Gallery). These presented an alternative view of places in a familiar official form, but instead of symbols for roads, churches or tube stations, had ones for sites such as "Rubbish likely to contain hair/cheese" and "Popular place to pee". Broda attended Slade School of Fine Art, 1996–8, to obtain her master's in fine arts. Shortly after the *Economist* exhibition she began a six-month residency at the London School of Economics.

Laurence BRODERICK 1935– Sculptor in various materials of animals, birds and human figures; teacher. After six years in Regent Street Polytechnic School of Art and Hammersmith School of Art until 1961, with a large family to support Broderick for the next 20 years was an historical and educational illustrator and painter and teacher. Began sculpting full-time in 1981. Showed at RWA, RBA and RA. Had one-man show at Belgrave Gallery, 1979; Otter Trust, Bungay, 1982; Manor Gallery, Royston, 1986; Warrington Museum and Art Gallery, 1992; and in the same year at Gallery An Talla Dearg, Isle of Skye, the island which was the source of much of his inspiration. Commissioned work included Madonna and Child, All Saints, Weston-super-Mare; The Swimming Otter, The Otter Trust, Earsham; and Teko – The Swimming Otter, Clan Donald Centre, Armadale. Worked at Waresley, Bedfordshire.

Muriel Alice BRODERICK 1910–1954 Designer, illustrator and teacher, born at Torquay, Devon. Studied at the Southern College of Art, Bournemouth, 1928–34, under Leslie Ward and Harold Williamson, where she later taught. Exhibited RA and elsewhere, often as M A B. Completed a lot of commercial work, illustrated books published in Britain and America, drew for the *Illustrated London News* and *Sketch* and widely for women's magazines, including *Woman's Own* and *Woman's Journal*. Lived in Bournemouth, Hampshire.

Richard BRODERICK 1963– Sculptor and designer who studied at Newcastle Polytechnic, 1982–5, and who early exhibited in London with the Nicholas Treadwell Gallery, being in the first Fresh Art show, 1986. Broderick soon after decided to concentrate on collaborative projects, especially in the northeast of England, based in North Tyneside. He was a leading member of the group Northern Freeform, involved in such ventures as the North Shields

Fish Quay Festivals and playground projects. Broderick's own work Groove, in concrete and copper and commissioned by North Tyneside Council, was installed in 1998 at Buddle Arts Centre, Wallsend. A fine example of his work for Northern Freeform is the polished steel Wave, of the same year, outside North Shields Metro station.

Sally BRODHOLT fl. from 1970s– Printmaker, born in West Indies. She studied at Centre for Arts and Crafts, Bromley. Showed at RA, Mall Galleries and was included in Group '77 Printmakers at Woodlands Art Gallery in 1981. Lived in London.

Carol R BRODY 1943– Sculptor in a variety of materials who was born in New York. She studied at the Art Students' League of New York and at the New York School of Design, then in London, 1973–7, at Camden Arts Centre, Hampstead. Showed with NS of which she was a member, SWA, NEAC and elsewhere. The Israeli Embassy, London, holds her depiction of the Israeli politician Golda Meir. Lived for a time in Gerrards Cross, Buckinghamshire.

Frederick J BRODY 1914– Designer, craftsman, painter in tempera and teacher, born and lived in Sheffield. He studied at the local College of Art, 1929–34, then at Royal College of Art, 1934–7, his teachers including Eric Ravilious, Ernest Tristram, Edward Bawden and Barnett Freedman. Showed at Paris International Exhibition in 1937, Festival of Britain in 1951 and in America.

Horace BRODZKY 1885–1969 Artist, writer, critic and teacher, born in Melbourne, Australia, of Jewish parents. In 1901 he enrolled for drawing tuition at National Gallery of Victoria School of Art, then in 1904 moved to America, where in 1906 he joined the National Academy of Design, in 1908 moving to London. There he enrolled at City and Guilds Art School and had a first solo show. He became friendly with such artists as Henri Gaudier-Brzeska, Jacob Epstein, David Bomberg and Mark Gertler; his biography of Gaudier appeared in 1933. Brodzky's theatrical design work was included in a show which toured the continent. In 1914 he joined the LG and began to be included in modern art shows, in New York, 1915–23, editing several magazines. Taught at London County Council evening classes from 1924–34. Brodzky was included in the first show of British lino-cuts organised by Claude Flight at the Redfern Gallery in 1929. Six years later James Laver's *Forty Drawings by Horace Brodzky* revealed the artist's stature as a fine draughtsman. Among Brodzky's later publications were a biography of Pascin and one of Gaudier-Brzeska's drawings, both in 1946. Eightieth birthday shows took place at the Ben Uri Gallery and Oxford Union Cellars in 1965. Other retrospectives were at the Jewish Museum of Australia, Melbourne, 1988, and Boundary Gallery, 1989.

Michael BROIDO 1927– Artist and teacher, born in London, who lived in South Africa, 1929–49. He was a self-taught artist who worked in the clothing industry for many years and lived in Cornwall, 1956–80. He was a part-time gardener for the artist Patrick Heron, having an attic studio in his Eagles Nest home, 1956–8; moved to St Ives and was a studio assistant to Barbara Hepworth, 1959–62, teaching at Truro Art School, 1960–80. Showed regularly with Penwith Society and then Fore Street Gallery and was included in Belgrave Gallery 1992 show British abstract art of the 50s and 60s. After producing little work for about 20 years from 1965, Broido resumed painting. Pier Gallery Arts Centre, Stromness, holds his work.

John BROKENSHIRE 1958– Painter producing abstract work, born in Lydney, Gloucestershire, who did a foundation course at Waltham Forest College, 1989–90, gaining a fine art degree at Sheffield Hallam University, 1990–5. Group shows included Northern Graduates, Royal College of Art, 1995, and A Sense of Scale, Curwen Gallery, 1996. Showed solo at New Academy Gallery from 1997. Middlesex Hospital holds his work.

William David BROKMAN DAVIS 1892–pre-April 1993 Painter and printmaker, born in Birmingham, who studied at the School of Art there. Exhibited RA, RSA, RCamA and elsewhere and was an associate of RE; its records show that Brokman Davis became an honorary retired associate in 1967 and died "pre-April 1 1993". He was also a member of Chelsea Arts Club. Work is held by British Museum, National Museum of Wales in Cardiff, British Council, British provincial museums and galleries overseas. He lived for a time in Leek, Staffordshire, latterly at West Parley, Dorset.

David BROMLEY 1960– Versatile, self-taught artist working imaginatively in a wide range of media, born in Sheffield, Yorkshire, who arrived in Australia in 1964. Before becoming a fine artist he was a sign-painter and potter. Bromley was a prolific exhibitor, mixed shows including La Trobe Gallery, Brisbane, Gold Coast Invitation Art Prize, 1988; winner, Fishers Ghost Award, New South Wales, finalist Moet & Chandon Award, 1993; Archibald Prize, Art Gallery of New South Wales, Sydney, 1999; and Archibald Sporting Portrait Prize, Art Gallery of New South Wales, 2000. Bromley's solo exhibition Buckets of Fun, at Rebecca Hossack Gallery in 2002, included evocative images of boyhood. By that time he had achieved over 30 one-mans at home and abroad, *Australian Art Collector* magazine having named him as one of the 50 most collectable artists in the continent. He had another Rebecca Hossack Gallery show in 2004, Luck and Pluck, "paintings about childhood adventures and a loss of innocence", his 14 Nudes being shown simultaneously at the Charlotte Street Gallery. Many Australian public galleries, universities and corporate collections hold examples.

Tom BROMLY 1930– Painter, draughtsman, photographer and teacher, born in Los Mochis, Mexico. He studied at Canterbury College of Art, 1946–50, then Leeds College of Art, 1953–4. Began teaching painting, 1955–61, at Newcastle College of Art & Design, eventually becoming dean of the faculty of arts and design at Newcastle Polytechnic, 1987–92. Bromly was closely connected with the development of art and design education throughout Britain. In 1992 he was co-author of *Capability Through Art & Design*. Bromly was a founding member of the Newcastle Group in the 1960s, creating large hard-edge pictures, but the constraints on his time determined a change in scale and subjects over the years. As well as mixed shows in the northeast and elsewhere Bromly had a series of solo exhibitions, with a retrospective at University Gallery, University of Northumbria, 1993–4. Newcastle Polytechnic portrait collection includes his work.

Birgitte BRONDUM-NIELSEN: *see* **Bitte B-N**

Licia BRONZIN 1960– Artist in various media, born in Adelaide, Australia. She studied painting at the Academy of Fine Arts, Venice, 1980–4, then film and video at London College of Printing, 1987–90. Portraits and film work combining animation and live action were special interests. She showed at New Era Gallery, Adelaide, in 1985, her first main exhibition in Britain being John Moores Exhibition, Liverpool, in 1991–2, with Woman with Colours. Lived in London.

Dorothy BROOK 1951– Sculptor, draughtsman, potter and graphic designer, born and lived in London, whose grandfather founded the art publisher Phaidon on the continent, later sold by her parents. She graduated in graphic design at St Martin's School of Art, 1969–73; then studied pottery at Marylebone Institute, 1974–6; life drawing at Camden and Hampstead Schools of Art, from 1986; and at the Jill Berelowitz Sculpture Studio, from 1990. Brook was a graphic designer at Linguaphone Ltd and at Roger Hughes Advertising, 1974–5, then went freelance, 1976–88. Dance, theatre and music triggered ideas for her sculptures, in which she aimed "to present abstracted human forms in the most aesthetically pleasing and harmonious way." Group shows included Ben Uri Gallery, 1969; Summer Exhibition, Andrew Usiskin Gallery, 1992; Eight plus One, The Gallery in Cork Street, 1997; Contemporary Sculpture, Rob Whittle Fine Art, Moseley; 1999; and Autumn Show, McHardy Sculpture Company, 2000. Solo exhibition, The Gallery in Cork Street, 2001. Unilever, Compaq and other corporate collections hold examples.

George BROOK 1898– c.1955 Painter, designer and black-and-white artist, born in Leicester. Studied at the College of Art there. Showed at Leicester Museum and Art Gallery and was a member of Leicester Sketch Club. Illustrated children's and educational books and magazines. Lived in Leicester.

Helen BROOK: *see* **Helen LESSORE**

Ian BROOK 1934– Artist, born in Sheffield, Yorkshire. He began painting in France aged 15, but "my parents denied me any formal art education, so I am a late starter. I have concentrated on watercolour and latterly oil pastel and conté crayon." Brook studied with the Danish watercolourist Agnete Varming in Copenhagen, 1964–6, and Josh Partridge for watercolour and drawing, workshops in London and the provinces, 1978–88. As a businessman from 1957–90 he painted all over the world, exhibiting in Britain and France, then became a professional from 1990. Brook said that he was a "strong believer in painting from nature in the open air". He was taught by Agnete Varming, in Copenhagen, 1964–5, and Josh Partridge in London, 1978–84. Had a solo show of landscapes of Provence at Eygalières, 1990, then one of Thailand landscapes at Joy Thornton, 1992. Later shows included Le Comtat Venaissin, Provence, Mark Senior Gallery, 1995; Gower – Watercolours from Wales, Bartley Drey Gallery, 1997; Images of China and Tibet, Carlyle Gallery, 2002; and Hadrian's Wall, at Gallery, 5 Park Walk, 2004. Logica Ltd holds his work. Lived in London and in Khon Sawan, Chayaphum Province, Thailand.

James BROOK 1959– Painter, born in Huddersfield, Yorkshire. He studied at Exeter College of Art, 1981–4, then Chelsea School of Art, 1989–90. He held a solo show at Red Herring Gallery, Brighton, in 1986. Exhibited with LG, 1989; Riverside One, 1990, winning a prize; New Contemporaries, 1990–1, at Arnolfini Gallery, Bristol, and tour; and in 1991–2 he won a prize at John Moores Exhibition, Liverpool, with his picture Water. For this he used television and magazine photographs as source material. His 1995–6 entry was the ingenious Road (with Raindrops, Eye). Lived in London.

Peter BROOK 1927– Painter and teacher, born in Holmfirth, Yorkshire. After Barnsley Grammar School he attended Huddersfield School of Art and Goldsmiths' College School of Art. Taught at Rastrick Secondary Modern School, 1949–57, and Sowerby Bridge Grammar School, 1957–77. He was one of Jack Beddington's chosen *Young Artists of Promise*, in the 1957 book of that title. Initially Brook painted industrial scenes, then from the 1960s Pennine rural landscapes, especially winter scenes, from 1980 Scottish and Lancashire landscapes. From 1979–83 completed 52 Hannah Hauxwell pictures. Was elected RBA in 1962. In 1960 had a solo show at Wakefield City Art Gallery; from 1968–72 was contracted to Agnew, with seven solo shows, two in Palm Springs and two in Adelaide; in 1990 had retrospective at Brighouse Art Gallery; showed with New Grafton Gallery from 1999, with a retrospective there, 2004. Many notable actors owned Brook's pictures, including James Mason, 30 examples; Tommy Steele; Alan Ladd; and Keith Barron. Lived in Brighouse, West Yorkshire.

Anne BROOKE 1916–2002 Painter and teacher, born at South Crosland, Yorkshire, who worked in oil, the Bible being a key theme of her work. She attended Chelsea School of Art, 1937–9; Huddersfield School of Art, 1939–41; and London University Institute of Education, 1941–2. Was a member of Leeds Fine Art Club. Showed with RA, RSA, RCamA, WIAC, NEAC, RBA, ROI and Paris Salon. Had a solo show at Swarthmore Centre, Leeds, 1962, and Renoir Gallery, Harrogate, 1977. Her work was held by public galleries in Harrogate, Keighley, Wakefield and Southend, and by local education committees in Hertfordshire, Lincolnshire, Northumberland and Bristol. Lived in Harrogate, North Yorkshire.

Eleanor Christina BROOKE fl. c.1955– Painter who studied at Académie Julian, Slade School of Fine Art and Heatherley's School of Fine Art. Showed in London and provinces, sometimes signing work E C B. Lived for a while at Eastcombe, Gloucestershire.

Geoffrey Arthur George BROOKE 1920– Painter in oil, born in Bath, Somerset. He came from a Naval family and served in the Navy after attending Royal Naval College in Dartmouth. In 1949–50 he studied art with the painter Sonia Mervyn and went on to show with the Army Art Society. Lived in Sussex, at Ringmer, then in Balcombe.

Horace BROOKE 1897– Watercolourist and printmaker, mainly doing commercial work. Brought up in Yorkshire, he attended Ossett Municipal Technical School and Royal College of Art, Leeds College of Art and Royal College of Art. Showed RA and elsewhere and lived in St Albans, Hertfordshire.

Iris BROOKE 1908– Portrait painter and draughtsman, book illustrator and writer. Studied at Croydon School of Art, 1923–6, and Royal College of Art, 1926–9. Although Brooke sometimes ventured into humorous books, her reputation is based on volumes concerned with historical costume, launched by the title *English Children's Costume*, 1930. Lived for some time at Widworthy Barton, near Honiton, Devon.

James Leslie BROOKE 1903–1973 Decorative artist in a variety of media, born and lived in Huddersfield, Yorkshire, who studied at the College of Art there with John Gauld. Also studied in Italy, France and North America. Exhibited at RA, RBA and in Yorkshire.

Janet BROOKE 1947– Printmaker and teacher who trained in Birmingham and Brighton and taught printmaking at Newham College of Further Education from 1974–90, then pursued her own work full-time. Was an associate of RE and a founder-member of East London Printmakers. Group shows included Imprint, Sunderland Arts Centre, 1980; Whitechapel Open, Whitechapel Art Gallery, 1986; RA Summer Exhibition, 1991; and National Print Exhibition, Mall Galleries, from 1994. Her later solo exhibitions included City Fragments, prints 1980–2000, at The Spitz Gallery, and Off the Wall, Sutton House, Hackney, both 2000. "I enjoy looking for the strange, slightly surreal juxtapositions that occur in familiar and unfamiliar settings: the odd signs and graffiti, abandoned objects and weird mixture of architectural styles". Commissions included Nicklin Advertising, 1992. The Open University, Ragged School Museum, Museum of London and corporate collections hold examples. Lived in London.

Julia BROOKER 1963– Painter producing non-representational works using acrylic on aluminium. She was "determined to eliminate the superfluous; I want to be sure that my paintings contain only the essentials...to concentrate and hold the viewer's eye." Brooker passed her foundation course with distinction at University of Wales Institute, Cardiff, 1997, gaining a first-class honours degree in fine art (painting) from University of Gloucester, 2000. In 1999, won a Williams Travel Bursary to visit New York, in 2000 a Simon Beswick Travel Award to Tokyo. Shared a show at New Academy Gallery, 2003, with solo exhibitions in 2004 at Llantarnam Grange, with tour, and Oriel 31, Davies Memorial Gallery, Newtown. Among sponsorships were Alcan and Ikea, both 2000; Black Sheep Design, 2001; and Powell Dobson Partnership, 2002.

William BROOKER 1918–1983 Painter in oil, especially of interiors and still life. Born in Croydon, Surrey, Brooker studied at Croydon School of Art 1936–9, Chelsea School of Art 1947–9 and Goldsmiths' College School of Art 1948–9. From 1949–53 he taught at Bath Academy of Art, living for a time with Brian Wynter, then Terry Frost. Howard Hodgkin, a pupil, called him "a great teacher". In 1953 Brooker became head of painting at Willesden School of Art, 1958, senior lecturer in painting at Harrow School of Art and was at Ealing School of Art from 1960. In 1965 became senior lecturer at the Central School, then was principal of Wimbledon School of Art 1969–81. Exhibited from early 1950s with LG, also with Arthur Tooth and Son and Agnew. A retrospective was held at Newcastle Polytechnic in 1987, toured to Agnew. Brooker's work can be reminiscent of pictures by Walter Sickert, palette and subjects being similar, although Brooker remained his own man. His work is held in a large number of public collections in Britain and abroad, including the Tate Gallery, Arts Council, Aberdeen Art Gallery and galleries in Canada, Australia, New Zealand and Brazil. Lived at Carshalton, Surrey.

Daysi May BROOKES 1886–1981 Painter, especially of portraits and miniatures, born in Norwich, Norfolk. After initial education there she studied art with J S Watkins in Sydney, Australia, and at the Julian Ashton school there. Exhibited widely in Australia; was a member of the council of the Australian Art Society for several years after World War II; and had a miniature accepted by the National Gallery of New South Wales, Sydney. In Britain she exhibited RMS, SM, Paris Salon and with the Norfolk and Norwich Art Circle. Lived latterly in Norwich.

Kenneth BROOKES 1897–c.1978 Watercolourist and commercial artist, born in Manchester. Studied at Watford and Harrow Schools of Art, 1913–16. Member of London Sketch Club, of which he was president in the early 1950s, also showing at RA, RBA and RI. Lived in Harrow, Middlesex.

Lionel BROOKES 1915– Painter and teacher, a native of Staffordshire who studied at Royal College of Art under Gilbert Spencer, 1937–40. For a time he was on the staff of Northampton School of Art and had work in the Central Museum and Art Gallery there. Showed at RA and RBA. Lived in Loughborough, Leicestershire.

Malcolm John BROOKES 1943– Artist in oil, gouache and pastel, and teacher, born in Birmingham. He attended the College of Arts and Crafts there, 1959–64, when Gilbert Mason was head of the painting school. Started teaching at local grammar school, then at Droitwich High School, from 1984 being head of design and technology at Stourport-on-Severn High School. In his own work Brookes favoured "a regular change of emphasis which keeps me alert and avoids predictability. I most admire the understatement and contemplative quality of such artists as Morandi and Gwen John." Was a member of RBSA and an associate of RCamA, other group appearances including Ikon Gallery in Birmingham, RWA, Mall Galleries and Dudley Art Gallery. Had a series of solo shows in Midlands, including Worcester Art Gallery; Bulls Eye Gallery, Lichfield; Compendium Gallery and Midlands Art Centre, both in Birmingham. That Centre, RBSA and Worcester College of Higher Education hold examples. Lived in Bromsgrove, Worcestershire.

Alan BROOKS 1965– Artist and teacher, born in Southend, Essex, who studied at Jacob Kramer School of Art, Leeds, Reading University and Slade School of Fine Art. From 1993 he was a visiting lecturer at Reading. He gained an Owen Ridley Drawing Prize, 1990; a Royal Academy Grant, 1991; a Slade Project Grant for study in Berlin, 1992; and a London Arts Board Award, 1996. Group exhibitions included New Art in Yorkshire, University Art Gallery and St Paul's Gallery, Leeds, 1987; Into the Nineties IV, Mall Galleries, 1992; Los Angeles Art Fair, 1993; and in 1996 Whitechapel Open at Whitechapel Art Gallery and Royal Over-Seas League Open, where Brooks won first prize. In 1999 Brooks was a prizewinner at the John Moores Liverpool Exhibition and a finalist for The NatWest Art Prize, showing abstract canvases meticulously worked up over several months from a rapidly scribbled original. Had a solo show at Wet Paint Gallery, 1994; Marlene Eleini Gallery, 1998; Galerie Albrecht, Munich, Germany, 1999; Percy Miller Gallery, 2000; and Mobile Home, 2001. British Museum and Reading University hold his work. Lived in London.

Ern BROOKS 1911–1993 Painter and illustrator, born in Manchester into a large working-class family. Was an apprenticed lithographer with George Faulkner, studying painting and drawing at Manchester School of Art. Worked as a commercial artist, which sapped his strength for other painting, while keeping abreast of European trends in art, being a keen disciple of Picasso. In 1951 Brooks created the mural Public Health for a floating exhibition on HMS *Campania*, part of the Festival of Britain; and in that year his lino-cut Men of Tolpuddle sold to raise funds for the *Daily Worker* newpaper. His lifelong companion, the painter Barbara Niven, also a Communist Party member who died in 1971, ran the *Worker's* Fighting Fund for over 20 years. In the 1930s they had helped found the Manchester Theatre Union, in which the director Joan Littlewood and folk singer Ewan McColl were involved. Brooks showed at AIA, of which he was a member, Gimpel Fils and Arts Council shows of realist work at Whitechapel Art Gallery. A major theme in his later work was the field gate, symbol of an uncertain future.

Jason BROOKS 1969– Figurative painter whose work has been compared in style with that of Hans Bellmer and Francis Bacon. Born in Rotherham, Yorkshire, he studied at the local College of Arts & Technology, 1986–7; Goldsmiths' College, 1987–8; Cheltenham and Gloucester College of Art, 1988–91, with a Rome Travel Bursary, British School at Rome, 1990; and Chelsea College of Art and Design, 1991. Group exhibitions included Remakes, Young Unknowns Gallery, 1990; Gerald Davies Gallery, Dublin, 1992; British Telecom New Contemporaries, Manchester and tour, 1993; and Art94, with Paton Gallery, Business Design Centre, Islington, 1994. In 1996 Brooks shared a show at Paton with Clive Head. Won a purchase prize and portrait commission from Cheltenham & Gloucester Building Society, 1991, another prize at John Moores Liverpool Exhibition, 1997–8. Brooks won the 1999 NatWest Art Prize, showing paintings that looked like huge black-and-white photographs, meticulously recording each pore, wrinkle and hair. Showed solo at Entwistle, 1997–8. Saatchi Collection holds his work. Lived in London.

John Charles Vine BROOKS 1901–1991 Painter of landscapes, mainly in oil in the Post-Impressionist manner, born in Tonbridge, Kent, where he lived, dying nearby in Tunbridge Wells. He was married to the artist Mary Brooks from 1933. Owing to disability, Jack Brooks had no formal schooling, apart from individual music tuition (he composed for the piano) and painting lessons in the 1940s from Hesketh Hubbard. For about 20 years until 1936, Brooks was an employee and director of Chas Baker & Company, the family car distribution firm. During World War II, he was an observer in the Royal Observer Corps, later devoting time to his property interests. From 1930 for about 40 years, Brooks originated and developed a system of Colour Harmony, despite being dyslexic, leaving raw material later put into final form by his son Dominic. Elliott Seabrooke was one artist impressed by the idea. Brooks also designed his own rotating perspective ruler. The innovations were employed in Brooks' own work, hung between 1937–45 at LG, NEAC, RBA, RA, RWS and elsewhere.

Louie BROOKS 1900– Part-time painter, born in Manchester, who studied at the College of Art there, teachers including Albert Dodd. She was a member of MAFA from 1943, showing elsewhere in the Lancashire area, with RBA and RP. Lived latterly in Colwyn Bay, Clwyd.

Marjorie BROOKS 1904–1980 Painter and decorative artist, born and lived in London, married to the architect Lord William Holford, who died in 1975; she was sometimes known as Marjorie Holford. Studied at Central School of Arts and Crafts and Royal Academy Schools, winning its Gold Medal and Edward Stott Travelling Studentship, 1927, and bronze medals for design, decoration and figure painting. Showed at RA, Walker Art Gallery in Liverpool (where she designed costumes for the Liverpool Playhouse) and elsewhere. Worked for the British Council. She bequeathed her picture Tea On the Lawn to Brighton Museum and Art Gallery in 1980.

Mary BROOKS 1897–1991 Artist in oil, watercolour and pastel of landscape and still life, originally known as Edith Mary Brown (a limited amount of work was completed using the name Mary Brown), born in Barnsley, Yorkshire. She studied at Leeds School of Art, 1915–20, teachers including Haywood Rider and Walter Pearson, and Royal College of Art, 1920–4, with William Rothenstein and Gerald Moira. Her contemporaries there included Henry Moore, Barbara Hepworth, Eric Ravilious, Douglas Percy Bliss and Phyllis Dodd (Bliss' wife, who painted a portrait of Mary in 1930). Mary was married to the Royal College-trained artist George Konow Branson until 1933, when after divorce she married the painter J C V Brooks. His Colour Harmony theory was to influence her pictures. She was art mistress at Cambridge County School, 1924–8, and showed at RA, WIAC of which she was a member, RBA and elsewhere. Lived for many years at Tonbridge, Kent, dying near Bath, Somerset.

Mary BROOKS 1906– Self-taught painter who was born and lived in London. She was a member of Free Painters and Sculptors and was closely involved in running the Loggia Gallery. Showed in London, the provinces, America and France.

Robin BROOKS 1943– Self-taught maritime painter whose output was noted for its historical accuracy, born in Warwickshire, father of the artists Rupert William Brooks and Kirsty Bonning and like them working at Black Dog Studios, Devon. Robin painted maritime subjects from 1966, specialising in sailing vessels from the eighteenth and nineteenth centuries. His leading theme was the three voyages of Captain James Cook. He also focused on Brixham trawlers. Among later works was The Defining Moment, Trafalgar 1805, a specially commissioned canvas to which Brooks devoted several years' research and execution. Exhibition venues included RSMA, Guildhall and Mall Galleries; Royal Exchange and Harrods Galleries; E Stacy Marks, Polegate; Alexander Galleries, Bristol; and Kirsten Gallery, Seattle, and Purnell Galleries, Baltimore, both in America. City of Exeter Guildhall and City of Plymouth Council Chambers both hold examples.

Rupert William BROOKS 1976– Figurative painter, working mainly in oil and from life, born in Exeter, Devon, son of the artist Robin Brooks and brother of the painter Kirsty Bonning, all working in the county at Black Dog Studios. He gained an honours degree in art and art history from Aberystwyth University, 1994–7, notable teachers including John Harvey, Alistair Crawford and Simon Pierse. Showed at South West Academy Open, Exeter, from 2001, in 2002 winning the David Messum Award. Brooks' work was "largely based upon the singular figure. I am interested in how a figure reacts to its surroundings within the canvas boundaries and how I can imply narrative and ambiguity through objects, expression, structure, and so on."

Drake BROOKSHAW 1907–1993 Painter in oil, artist in line and wash and lithographer, born in London. He studied at Central School of Arts and Crafts with John Farleigh, Bernard Meninsky and F C Herrick. Brookshaw's career was as an illustrator, designer, painter and teacher of lithography at Goldsmiths' College School of Art. He worked for International Wool Secretariat; *The Times*; London Transport; Shell-Mex and B P; J Arthur Rank; *Radio Times*; British Rail; and completed drawings and book covers for numerous publishers. His work is in the Royal Air Force Museum, Hendon, and in the Fleet Air Arm Museum. From 1964 he lived part-time in Spain, painting portraits and landscapes, and in 1991 Homenaje to Drake Brookshaw was held by Ayuntamiento de Mijas (Town Hall). From 1959 he showed regularly in Cornwall, where he lived finally in a nursing home in Wadebridge. Was a member of the Senefelder Club and Art Workers' Guild.

Marion BROOM fl. c.1920–1960 Painter in oil and watercolour. Born in Norfolk, she studied at the Royal College of Music and sang in opera for a time. Exhibited RA, RI, RWA and RCamA. Leamington Spa Art Gallery and several overseas galleries hold her work. Lived at High Wycombe, Buckinghamshire.

Mollie BROOME 1910–1994 Painter and photographer, notable for portraits, born in the Southsea area, Hampshire, her father a bank cashier. During World War II she served in the Auxiliary Territorial Service, commissioned acting junior commander, involved partly in photography at an anti-aircraft battery. After the war she studied art, industrial design and drawing. Worked at a studio in Ilford for two years, then opened her own photographic studio in Fareham, Hampshire. After marrying Wing-Commander George Potter in 1959 she resigned as a technical illustrator for the civil service and moved to Bushey, Hertfordshire, where she set up studio at home and concentrated on portraits. Bushey Museum Trust holds Broome's work.

Frances BROOMFIELD 1951– Painter in oil and tempera on wood panels with gesso ground, usually on a small scale; also an illustrator. C G Jung's ideas of the collective unconscious were an influence, painting being Broomfield's "way of exploring the world of the imagination". Born in Warrington, Lancashire, she attended the local College of Art and Newport Art School, in 1990 joining Cecil's Collins' life classes at the Central School of Art. Published work included book-jackets for Cape, Bodley Head, Century Hutchinson, Little, Brown & Company and others; the 1995 calendar for Colin Dann's *Farthing Wood* series; and greetings cards for Royle, Santoro Graphics, Pharaoh Fine Arts and others. She was a member of the Women's Art Library and was featured in the International Women Artists' Diary in 1988 and 1996. Awards included North West Arts, 1989; Pollock Krasner Foundation, 1991; Oppenheim-John Downes Trust, 1993; and London Arts Board, 1995. From 1977, Broomfield showed almost exclusively with Portal Gallery. Other shows included Sue Williams Gallery and Art Works for London Lighthouse, both 1988; Birmingham City Art Gallery, 1991; and she shared an exhibition at Bremen Art Gallery, Germany, 1992.

James BROTCHIE 1909–1956 Painter in oil and watercolour and museum curator. Born in Glasgow, Brotchie studied art at the School of Art there, 1928–32, then in several centres on the continent. He was the son of Theodore Brotchie, an artist who was primarily an art administrator, and James spent most of his life on similar work, eventually becoming keeper of prints and drawings at the National Gallery of Scotland, Edinburgh. He also published articles in a number of Scottish publications, including *The Scotsman*, *Scottish Art Review* and *Glasgow Herald*. Exhibited RSA, SSA and the Royal Glasgow Institute of the Fine Arts. Lived in Edinburgh.

William BROTHERSTON 1943– Sculptor and teacher, born in Edinburgh. His usually small pieces, mostly achieved by casting geometrical forms from wax to bronze, were understated and allusive, with careful attention to the surface. He studied at Cambrige University, 1962–5, and from 1965–71 at Edinburgh College of Art, where he then began teaching. He exhibited regularly at RSA, Federation of Scottish Sculptors of which he was a member, as he was of SSA. As well as taking part in a number of group shows of Scottish sculpture, Brotherston showed solo at Pier Arts Centre, Stromness, and elsewhere. Scottish Arts Council holds his work.

Alan BROUGH 1890–1986 Sculptor, born at Morley, near Wilmslow, Cheshire. He studied at Manchester School of Art and was a member of MAFA, where he exhibited. Moved to Prestbury, Cheshire, in 1930, where he established a small shop to exhibit his carvings and to deal in antiques. Brough had a studio in Wilmslow, adjacent to the railway station. He retired in the 1960s, and from then on did little work. As well as doing some traditional carvings of figures including members of his family, Brough did more advanced sculpture in stone and wood. Manchester City Art Gallery holds his sculpture Primavera, of 1927. Although he continued to live in Prestbury, Brough died at his daughter's house in Marchamley, near Shrewsbury.

Robert BROUGH 1916–1984 Painter and draughtsman, born in Cambuslang, Glasgow, who was by profession an electrical engineer. After education at Rutherglen Academy he studied art in Glasgow and London. Exhibited extensively throughout Britain and Ireland in group shows, including PS, UA, Ridley Art Society of which he was vice-chairman, Ealing Arts Society and Bladon Arts Society and had solo shows in London and the southern counties. Barclays Bank Ltd bought his work. Brough was especially known for his marine pictures and landscape and portrait pastels. Lived in Brentford, Middlesex.

Aya BROUGHTON 1912–1997 Painter, muralist and lecturer, born in Kyoto, Japan. After education in Japan she studied at Newton Abbot School of Art and Dartington Adult Centre. She was a member of NS, Free Painters and Sculptors, WIAC, SWA and was an Associate of Société des Artistes Français. Also showed at RA, RI, RBA and elsewhere and in 1972 gained silver medal at Paris Salon. Private collections worldwide hold her work. Also used painting name Aya. Lived in Torquay, Devon.

Michael BROUGHTON 1977– Painter, born in Braintree, Essex, who studied at Falmouth College of Arts, 1996–9, after City of Bath College, 1995–6. He showed in Summer Light at Falmouth Art Gallery, 2000; Summer Show, Lemon Street Gallery, Truro, 2001; and in Four For Fore Street, Belgrave Gallery, St Ives, 2003.

BROUN-MORISON of Finderlie fl. c.1950–1970 Henry de Annand, nineteenth Laird of Finderlie, painted flowers in oil on wooden panels. Exhibited London and the provinces. Signed work with letter F.

Allan Robert BROWN 1890–1947 Landscape watercolourist and teacher, born in Horsham, Sussex, father of the painters Hugh Boycott Brown, Michael Boycott-Brown and Robert Brown. He was senior art master at the Royal Masonic Senior School in Bushey for many years. Was a member of Watford and Bushey Art Society. In 1994 Bushey Museum Trust held a joint exhibition of pictures by Hugh and his father.

Arnesby BROWN 1866–1955 Painter of landscapes, especially with cows. Born in Nottingham, John Arnesby Brown studied art there, with Andrew McCallum and then with Sir Hubert von Herkomer at his Bushey School of Art, 1889–92. Brown's wife Mia was also a painter. Brown's reputation became international, but he concentrated his work on St Ives, in Cornwall, and Norfolk, although for about the last 20 years of his life, after his wife's death, he lived in London for much of the time. Exhibited RA, Leicester Galleries, Goupil Gallery, RSA and at many other venues. In 1934 Brown was represented at the Venice Biennale, having a retrospective at Norwich Castle Museum the following year. Tate Gallery holds three typical scenes: Morning, Silver Morning and The Line of the Plough. Brown was elected RA in 1915 and was knighted in 1938. Died at Haddiscoe, Norfolk, in 1955, with a memorial exhibition in Norwich, 1959.

Atri BROWN 1906– Sculptor and teacher, married to the painter Veronica Pieris. He studied at Wolverhampton School of Art under Robert Emerson and at the Royal College of Art under Ernest Cole. Brown was a Prix de Rome winner in 1928. Taught at Epsom and Ewell School of Art. Exhibited RA, NS and in America and the British Council bought his work, 1939. Taught at Chelsea Polytechnic School of Art, 1934–9. Sometimes signed work Atri. Lived in London.

Bob BROWN 1936– Painter covering "a wide range of subjects...throughout which the unifying theme is light." Born in London, Brown studied at Croydon College of Art under Fred Dubery and Lionel Bulmer. Was elected a member of NEAC, 1964, its assistant keeper, 1994. Won the Barney Wilkins Howard Prize, 1992, and Llewellyn Alexander Prize, 1997. Mixed shows included RA Summer Exhibition, RP, Manya Igel Fine Arts, Llewellyn Alexander and W H Patterson. Later solo exhibitions included Hellenic Cultural Institute, 1996 (Brown was artist-in-residence, Britain in Greece Festival, Athens, 1995); Mall Galleries, based on a trip to China, being artist-in-residence with the Royal Academy of Music Sinfonia, 1998; and Alresford Gallery, Alresford, 1999. CASW and Unilever hold examples.

Bonnie BROWN 1952– Artist in oil, gouache and mixed media and teacher, born Dorking, Surrey, married for a time to the painter Padraig Macmiadhachain. She was "proud to be a self-taught painter", having attended Winchester School of Art to study textile design, graduating with honours in 1981, in 1982 gaining a postgraduate diploma in printmaking. Obtained a travel award to Holland. Began teaching in 1982, appointments including Southampton Institute of Higher Education, Chelsea and Winchester Schools of Art and Maidenhead College of Art and Design. Exhibitions included Picture Post Gallery, 1981; Salisbury Playhouse, Salisbury, 1984; Stephen Bartley Gallery from 1988; RWA from 1990; The Discerning Eye, 1992, where she won a prize; and Laing Competition, Winchester, 1993. Lived at White Yard Studio, Swanage, Dorset. The Purbeck landscape and seascapes were cited as her "biggest influence".

Cecil BROWN 1902– Painter and architect who was educated at St Paul's School and studied art privately. Showed RA, Guildhall Library and Art Gallery, New Zealand House and Grundy House Museum in Blackpool. He illustrated a number of books to do with ecclesiastical architecture. Lived in London.

Cecily BROWN 1969– Painter of raw and hectic, colourful, Expressionistic figure pictures, often on a large scale, born in London. Brown was the daughter of art critic David Sylvester and the novelist Shena MacKay. She obtained a diploma in art and design from Epsom School of Art, 1985–7; attended drawing and printmaking classes at Morley College, 1987–9; and graduated with first-class honours in fine arts from the Slade School of Fine Art, 1989–93, in 1992 having attended New York Studio School in New York, America, where she settled to work after her Slade studies. Had a solo show at Eagle Gallery, 1995. Among later ones were Deitch Projects, Storefront Gallery, New York, 1997; Serenade, Victoria Miro Gallery, 1999; Gagosian Gallery, Beverley Hills, from 1999; Gagosian Gallery, New York, from 2000; Days of Heaven, Contemporary Fine Arts, Berlin, Germany, from 2001; Directions – Cecily Brown, Hirshhorn Museum and Sculpture Garden, Washington, 2002; MACRO, Rome, Italy, 2003; and Galerie Lisa Ruyter, Vienna, Austria, and Museo Reina Sofia, Madrid, both 2004. Was included in the Saatchi Collection. Brown took part in Saatchi Gallery's Neurotic Realism series of exhibitions launched in 1999; the Whitney Biennial 2004, Whitney Museum of American Art, New York, in 2004; and The Triumph of Painting, Saatchi Gallery, 2005. She had her first solo exhibition in a United Kingdom public gallery at Modern Art Oxford in 2005.

Charles William BROWN 1882–1961 Primitive artist, born at Robin Hill, north Staffordshire, son of a miner; he had a hard, poverty-stricken childhood. Left school at 12 and worked on farms and in pits. Eventually became manager at Newbury Collieries, Coleford, in 1923, but this job turned sour and he was employed elsewhere in mining until retirement in 1948. Then concentrated on his painting, showing with Society of Staffordshire Artists. Lived for much of his life in Etruria, Staffordshire, and bequeathed a collection of pictures and autobiographical writings to City Museum and Art Gallery, Stoke-on-Trent. It held a retrospective exhibition in 1993.

Chloë BROWN 1964– Artist and teacher whose work included installations incorporating sound, featuring such objects as stuffed animals and artificial snow. Her work was included in Frozen, Site Gallery, Sheffield, 2002. Brown did a foundation course at Chesterfield College of Art and Design, 1982–3; graduated in fine art from University of Reading, 1983–7; and gained her master's from Chelsea College of Art and Design, 1993–4. She held a number of teaching posts, from 2002 at The University of Derby. Awards included The Ravenscroft Foundation, 1993; Oppenheim-John Downes Memorial Trust, 1994; and a series of Yorkshire and Humberside and Yorkshire Individual Artist's Awards through 2002. Among residencies were Castle Museum, Nottingham, 1992, and three Sheffield schools: Abbeydale Grange, 1997, Dobcroft Junior, 2001, and Springfield Junior, 2002. She shared an exhibition with Duncan Higgins at Blue Gallery, 2002.

Chris BROWN 1949– Artist who trained at Hereford and Hornsey Colleges of Art and sold work through the Treadwell Gallery, based in Aigen, Austria. On its website, Brown described his output as "A Mythology for our present Gold Age. And my own secret amusement."

Christopher BROWN 1953– Printmaker and illustrator, born in London. He left Royal College of Art in 1980, then went on to work as an illustrator for *Radio Times*, *The Observer* and on book covers for Penguin Books and Faber & Faber. Illustrated Somerset Maugham's *Short Stories* for The Folio Society, had his colour linocut *The Sculler*, 1984, issued by Merivale Editions and showed his work at Michael Parkin Gallery.

Christopher BROWN 1973– Versatile artist and administrator, born in Worcester, who did a foundation course in art and design at Hereford College of Art & Design, 1991–2, graduating with honours in fine art at Kent Institute of Art and Design, Canterbury, 1994–7. In 1998, Brown assisted Anthony Shapland, artist-in-residence at Glyn Derw School, Cardiff, with a pinhole camera project for children, after that being development officer at the WAC-funded Contemporary Temporary Artspace, Cardiff, where Brown then lived. Exhibitions included Reframing the Family, Hereford City Art Gallery, 1994; Unbound, Site Gallery, Sheffield, 1996; Ffotogallery Annual, Cardiff, 1999; and Perforated Building, site-specific installation, Cardiff, 2000.

Cleveland BROWN 1943– Painter born in St Katherine, Jamaica, brought up in a strict religious household. He emigrated to Britain as a skilled carpenter and began to paint in 1973 after working at Sotheby's auction house. Brown reckoned that if he could build he could also paint. He produced only a few pictures annually, topical subjects including the Spaghetti House Siege, the Grunwick Picket Line and the Royal Family. In 1978 he was commissioned by a newspaper group to paint the Notting Hill Festival and by the RA's Edwin Abbey Trust. Brown took part in mixed shows of naïve painters in London, including the Olympia Jubilee Exhibition, 1977, the National Theatre, 1978, and the City of London Carnival, 1979. In that year George Melly bought Brown's St James's Park, a work of 1978, for the Arts Council, commenting: "The picture is as well dovetailed as a skilful piece of cabinet-making. It is whole-heartedly devoted to the pleasure principle and reveals a wicked sense of humour."

Colin BROWN 1962– Painter, artist in construction and collage, born in Dundee, Angus, raised in Kingussie, Inverness-shire, who attended Duncan of Jordanstone College of Art, Dundee, 1982–7. After periods in Glasgow and Düsseldorf, Germany, from 1995 settled in Stonehaven, Aberdeenshire. Brown gained a RSA John Kinross Scholarship, 1987, and a Pollock-Krasner Award, 1996. He took part in numerous group exhibitions, including Diadem Centenary, Perth (second prize), 1984; RSA and Compass Gallery, Glasgow, from 1986; Fine Art Society, Glasgow, from 1991; Open Eye Gallery, Edinburgh, 1995; and Roger Billcliffe Gallery, Glasgow, 1997. Had a solo show at Barbizon Gallery, Glasgow, 1989, later ones including Peacock Gallery, Aberdeen, 1997, with frequent solo exhibitions in Germany. Peacock Visual Arts, Aberdeen, showed Brown's Urban Dada in 2004. Highland Regional Council and Norddeutsche Landesbank, Hanover, hold examples.

Deborah BROWN 1927– Sculptor in glass fibre, papier mâché and bronze, born in Belfast, where she settled. Brown developed from being a painter. Her work was figurative and abstract, noted for its delicate colour, serenity and calm. She studied painting at Belfast College of Art, 1946, then National College of Art in Dublin, 1947–50, subsequently in Paris. Her teachers included Maurice McGonigal and Sean Keating. She took part in many mixed exhibitions, including RHA, RUA, WIAC. Had a solo show at CEMA Gallery, Belfast, in 1951, others including New Vision Centre, 1959–64; Arts Council Gallery, Belfast, 1962; David Hendriks Gallery, Dublin, 1966–84; and a mid-career retrospective at Ulster Museum, Belfast, and tour, 1982. In that year she became a member of the Sculpture Society of Ireland. Among her commissions was a Drover and Seven Sheep for Arts Council of Northern Ireland Sculpture Park, installed 1992. The Council, Municipal Gallery of Modern Art in Dublin, Arts Council of Southern Ireland and other collections hold her work.

Denise BROWN 1911–1998 Printmaker and painter, born in London, daughter of artist Frederick Peter Brown. After education in Germany she studied at Royal College of Art, having gained a British Institution Scholarship; her teachers were Malcolm Osborne and Robert Austin; after gaining her diploma, in 1935, in 1936 she won a Rome Scholarship in Engraving and a Travelling Scholarship. Brown was elected RE in 1959 and RWA. Was a regular exhibitor at RA and abroad, as well as illustrating children's and gardening books. Victoria & Albert Museum and Ashmolean Museum in Oxford hold her work. Lived in Church Westcote, Oxfordshire.

Dexter BROWN 1942– Artist in nearly all media, born in Hayes, Middlesex, settling nearby at Pinner. He attended Harrow School of Art, 1956–9. In 1960 Brown, who also worked under the name De Bruyne, became a freelance illustrator, in 1965 taking up automobile art, for which he became noted, having great ability to depict authentic cars at speed. Between 1969–79 Brown had a period of portraiture including pop stars. His work appeared in periodicals such as *Car Collector* and *Ferrari World*. Solo shows included Monte Carlo Galleries, Alexandria, Virginia, and in 2002 The Saab Showroom, Piccadilly. Also showed at Auto Art in Connecticut, and Abarth Galleries and Porsche Museum in Tokyo. Was commissioned by Pininfarina in Turin, Italy. Another of Brown's interests was mechanical transport of the Edwardian period, which he painted as De Bruyne in the Impressionist style, having a solo show at John Noott Galleries, Broadway, 2001.

Diana Elizabeth BROWN 1929– Painter and illustrator who sometimes worked on china, born in Cambridge. She specialised in wildlife subjects and was a member of SWLA. Studied at Tunbridge Wells School of Art, 1947–51. Showed with SWLA and in Scotland and illustrated for periodicals as well as a number of books. Lived in Aboyne, Aberdeenshire.

Don BROWN 1962– Artist whose output included figurative sculptures, life-size and tiny, and computer-enhanced photographs. Born in Norfolk, he attended the Central School of Art, 1983–5, and Royal College of Art, 1985–8. Group exhibitions included LG, Royal College of Art, 1988; Wonderful Life, Lisson Gallery, 1993; B-Movie, Nicole Klagsburn at San Francisco Art Fair, San Francisco, America 1995; A Sense of Scale, Ikon Gallery, Birmingham, and tour, 1997; and Sadie Coles HQ at Contemporary Fine Arts, Berlin, Germany, 1999. Solo exhibitions included Don, Sadie Coles HQ, 1997, and Jerwood Space Inaugural Sculpture Court Installation, 1998.

Elaine BROWN 1961– Painter, born and lived in London, who graduated with honours in fine art, 1980–4, at University of Reading, then gained a postgraduate diploma from Cyprus College of Art, 1985–6. Her pictures, serene and considered, placed objects in a format where they interacted, suggesting metaphysical aspects. Group shows included New Contemporaries 1984 at ICA; Three Women Painters, Rochester Art Centre, 1987; and Espace Vega, Paris, 1994. Among her solo exhibitions was Harriet Green Gallery, 1995.

Frank Percival BROWN 1877–1958 Designer of mosaics and other works. Born in Staffordshire, studied art at the Royal College of Art, 1902–7 under Gerald Moira, W R Lethaby and others. Held a number of teaching positions in London, including visiting art master at Merchant Taylors' School. Was for a time chairman of the South Kensington Sketching Club and began the old students' association at the Royal College of Art just before World War I. Did design work for Josiah Wedgwood and Sons. Lived at Rottingdean, Sussex.

Geoffrey Houghton BROWN 1903–1993 Artist and designer, son of a barrister, Houghton Brown was educated at Rugby School, the Slade School of Fine Art and in Maurice Denis's Paris workshop studio. From 1925 until World War II he was a pioneering designer and interior decorator, notably of the Blue Train restaurant in Stratton Street, completed 1928. This prompted many decorative commissions: the Ice Club, Five Hundred Club, a Pompeian bathroom for the collector Edward James and a dining room for the Marchioness of Dufferin and Ava. Noël Coward, Nigel Playfair and Syrie Maugham were other clients. Brown became a Catholic in 1924, was a founder-member of the Guild of Catholic Artists and produced mostly religious easel pictures, eclectic in influence. His aim was "to restore to Christendom a great deal of the imaginative, intellectual and spiritual expression which were lost to her by the rise of Naturalism." Although he exhibited at the Leicester, Leger and Mayor Galleries, he lamented the Church's poor response to his art. From the 1950s until his death Brown restored and decorated decaying or threatened country houses. James Huntington-Whiteley latterly showed his work.

Glenn BROWN 1966– Painter and sculptor, born in Hexham, Northumberland, who did a foundation course at Norwich School of Art, 1984–5, gained an honours degree in fine art at Bath Academy of Art, 1985–8, then a master's at Goldsmiths' College, 1990–2. Brown was included in Young British Artists V, at Saatchi Gallery, 1995, where he showed a range of paintings which took the works of artists such as Dalí, Auerbach and Appel as their starting point, displaying great technical skill. Brown was shortlisted for the Jerwood Prize, 1996. His solo exhibition at Jerwood Gallery, 1999, included pigment-encrusted sculptures and major canvases, such as The Tragic Conversion of Salvador Dalí (after John Martin) and Böcklin's Tomb (after Chris Foss). There was a survey of his work at the Serpentine Gallery in 2004. Lived in London.

Hannah BROWN 1886– Painter and draughtsman, born in London. She studied singing privately and painting with the watercolourist Myles Birket Foster. However, she was mostly self-taught, studying intensively while living in Italy for about 10 years from the late 1920s. Brought up at the Foundling Hospital in London, she recalled her experiences in *The Child She Lay Bare*, published in 1919 under the pen-name A Foundling. Exhibited RA and in Sussex, where she lived latterly at Rottingdean.

Heather BROWN 1958– Painter and muralist whose work included delicately coloured pictures of animals and birds, as shown by Boundary Gallery at Affordable Art Fair, 2003. She was born in Newcastle upon Tyne, gaining her master's in fine art from the University there, 1982–4, having graduated in fine art from Central School of Art & Design, 1976–9. Won an Oppenheim-John Downes Memorial Trust award, 1993. Mixed shows included 6th International Cleveland Drawing Biennial, 1983; Art for Sale, Whiteley's, 1992–3; and 5th Istanbul Art Fair, Turkey, 1994. Among her solo and two-man shows were the Municipal Art Gallery, Bursa, Turkey, 1993; National Gallery of Albania, Tirana, 1996; and Boundary Gallery, 1999. Commissions included painted decorative murals in a six-storey building in Istanbul, 2001–2. National Gallery of Albania and Spanish Tourist Board acquired examples of her work.

Helen Paxton BROWN 1876–1956 Artist, versatile craftsman and teacher, born and died in Glasgow, where she studied at the School of Art, 1894–01. She joined its staff, 1911–17, also during World War I doing welfare work. She was a prominent member of the Glasgow Society of Lady Artists, winning its Lauder Award in 1923 and being its secretary, 1943–8, in the latter year becoming an Hon. Member. Between the wars she lived for a time at

Kircudbright. Showed extensively at Royal Glasgow Institute of the Fine Arts, RSA and Walker Art Gallery in Liverpool, also at RSW.

Hilary BROWN 1963– Sculptor and teacher working in a variety of materials. Born in Portsmouth, she studied at Ruskin School of Art, Oxford, 1981–4, then Birmingham Polytechnic, 1985–6. She had a sculpture fellowship at Cheltenham College of Art, 1986–7. Went on to become a visiting lecturer at various art schools and colleges, including Birmingham, Cheltenham and Ruskin. Her sculpture The Weak Spot was included in East & South Norwich Gallery/Kent Institute of Art and Design exhibition in 1992. Lived in London.

Irene BROWN 1960– Versatile artist whose output embraced sculpture, installation, theatre, animation and interior design. She studied at Cardiff College of Art and Design, Nottingham Trent Polytechnic and Reading University between 1979–87. Among her public works were the fibreglass Newcastle bull terrier-inspired Caesar's Sofa, for the 1990 Gateshead Garden Festival, and the lively multi-material Racing Ahead sculpture of greyhounds, commissioned by Cleveland Arts and completed in 1995 for Dovecot Street, Stockton-on-Tees.

James C BROWN 1917– Self-taught sculptor and letter-cutter, born in Paris, France, where he studied law at L'École des Sciences Politiques. After working until 1945 in the Finance Ministry he turned to art, gradually developing an interest in materials such as brick and plastics. While employed in Coventry's architecture and planning department in the 1950s Brown produced several works, such as his cartoon-like relief Children Cat and Elephant, at Corley's Residential School.

Jennifer BROWN 1950– Painter in oil, tempera and watercolour and teacher who attended college in Ireland, then taught in Belfast and Pimlico. Originally her work was representational, inspired by urban landscapes and inner-city gardens, but later it moved towards abstraction, drawing on her teaching of textile design. Squares, reminiscent of a patchwork quilt, were a feature of her output in the 1990s, a 1999 visit to the Vasarely Foundation in Aix-en-Provence injecting a new element. Brown won first prize in the 1975 Picture of Camden competition, organised by the London Borough of Camden and Young & Rubicam Ltd, and took part in many mixed exhibitions, including Modern & Contemporary British Art at The Millinery Works, 2000.

John BROWN 1887–1966 Painter who was educated at Cambridge University, then studied at Westminster School of Art, 1926–9, with Walter Bayes. Showed at RBA, RCamA, Paris Salon and Lincolnshire Artists' Society, sometimes just signing work J B. Lincoln's Usher Gallery holds his works: A Break in the Clouds, November Sky and Humberstone Foreshore, all presented by Sir Hickman Bacon in the 1930s. Lived at Grimsby, Lincolnshire.

John BROWN 1931– Sculptor producing stone carvings and bronzes, mainly based on the human form, realistic, simplified or abstracted. He studied at Hornsey School of Art and at Hampstead Garden Suburb Institute with Howard Bate. Was a fellow of RBS. In 1989, he was the first prize winner of a Business Arts Award, and in 1995 Brown's Love of the Family was placed in the children's wing of King's College Hospital. He carried out a number of church commissions. Linda Blackstone Gallery, Pinner, and The John Russell Gallery, Ipswich, were among galleries showing Brown's work.

John Caldwell BROWN 1945– Artist and teacher, born in Scotland, who graduated from Glasgow School of Art, 1963–8, teachers including David Donaldson and Duncan Shanks. Brown won many awards, including latterly Arts Club Award, SSWA, and Scottish Provident Award there, both 1993; and Heinzel Gallery Award, 1994. He taught from 1968, later positions including head of art at The Edinburgh Academy, Edinburgh from 1988; visiting lecturer, Leith School of Art, Edinburgh, 1991–4; and from 1994 visiting lecturer at Edinburgh College of Art and board director at Leith School of Art. Brown regularly exhibited with RSW, RSA, Royal Glasgow Institute of the Fine Arts and SSWA, taking part in many other group exhibitions, especially in Scotland. Had a solo show in 1970 at both Glasgow School of Art and Ayr Gallery, Ayr, later ones including The Open Eye Gallery, Edinburgh, and Duncan R Miller Fine Arts, both 1996. Commissions included Portrait of Hugh McDiarmid, 1968; Portraits of Two Royal Archers, 1970; and Portrait of Viscount Arbuthnot, 1972. Brown constantly experimented with form, expression, colour and texture, employing a rich palette in oils, collage and mixed media, figurative and abstract elements. Lived in Edinburgh.

John Ernest BROWN 1915– Sculptor, painter and teacher, born in Shawforth, Lancashire. Studied at Manchester's Municipal School of Art and after World War II taught at Monmouthshire Training College. He became closely involved with the development of art studies in Wales and was a member of SEA and National Union of Teachers. During World War II War Artists' Advisory Committee had bought his work, as had the War Office; he also showed at public galleries in Southport, Manchester and Belfast and at the National Museum of Wales, Cardiff. Based at the Monmouthshire Training College, Caerleon.

Katy BROWN 1976– Painter producing landscapes and seascapes with a strong abstract element who did a foundation course at Winchester School of Art, 1995–6, then graduated there with an honours degree in fine art, painting, 1996–9. Group exhibitions included Seven of the Best, Jersey Arts Centre, 1997; Perceptions 2 – Art in the Frame, Sanctuary Restaurant, Jersey, 1999; Garden Seascape Series, Mourier House, Jersey, 2000–1; Quintessence, David Hicks Antiques, Jersey, sponsored by Lloyds TSB, and Oliver Contemporary, both 2002; and Sussex Open, Brighton & Hove Museum, 2003. Had a solo exhibition, St Ouen's Bay – The Submerged Forest, Jersey Arts Centre, sponsored by PricewaterhouseCoopers, 2002. Commissions included Jersey Telecoms, cover for telephone directory, 1997; Jersey Telecoms phonecard for the Millennium (winning design), 1999; and chief officer, Policy and Resources Department, paintings for office, 2000.

Keith BROWN 1947– Sculptor and teacher, born in Hexham, Northumberland. He won a scholarship to Michigan University, in America, 1969, studying at Royal College of Art, 1972–5. Taught in early 1980s at Manchester Polytechnic. Solo shows included Serpentine Gallery, 1977, Leeds Polytechnic, 1979. Brown's multi-piece Untitled,

1981, in wood, is held by South Hill Park Arts Centre, Berkshire.

Mary BROWN: *see* **Mary BROOKS**

May Marshall BROWN 1887–1968 Painter and teacher, born in Edinburgh, was married to the artist William Marshall Brown. She studied at Edinburgh College of Art, in Ireland and on the continent. Taught at St Margaret's School, Edinburgh, for many years. She contributed to the Pilgrim Trust *Recording Britain* project and exhibited RSA and RSW extensively, also Royal Glasgow Institute of the Fine Arts and in the English provinces. The art gallery in Auckland, New Zealand, holds her work. Member of SSA. A May Marshall Brown Award is made at the RSW's annual exhibition. Lived in Edinburgh.

Mimi BROWN 1920–1996 Painter of still life and landscape with a careful regard for tonal values, born in Belgium. She married two British bankers, taking her name from the first. Travelled widely abroad. Lived finally in Eastbourne, Sussex, where she died in a nursing home in The Meads. Sometimes signed work M B. Premier Gallery, Eastbourne, showed work after her death.

Mortimer BROWN 1874–1966 Sculptor of religious and classical subjects, born in Stoke-on-Trent, Staffordshire. He studied at Hanley School of Art around 1890, then for several years in the early 1890s at Royal College of Art and at Royal Academy Schools, 1896–1901; his teachers included Richard Ledward, Alfred Gilbert and Éduardo Lantéri and he won a number of medals and awards. Further study followed in Italy and Greece. For some years Brown worked with the sculptor William Hamo Thornycroft. Showed RA, ROI and RI and was made a fellow of RBS. Tate Gallery holds his bronze Shepherd Boy. Lived in Twickenham, Middlesex.

Neil Dallas BROWN 1938–2003 Painter and teacher, born in Elgin, Moray. He studied at Dundee College of Art, and Patrick Allan-Fraser School of Art, Hospitalfield, Arbroath, as well as Royal Academy Schools. Won a travelling scholarship to the continent and a number of notable awards and prizes. In 1967 visited New York with a Scottish Arts Council Award; in 1970 took part in the Arts Council of Northern Ireland Open, winning a major prize; and in 1981 won a bursary to the Scottish Arts Council studio in Amsterdam. From 1968–78 was visiting lecturer at Duncan of Jordanstone College of Art in Dundee, then joining the staff of Glasgow School of Art. Dallas Brown participated in dozens of group shows in Britain and abroad and his one-man schedule was equally hectic. He had a one-man show at Duncan Institute, Cupar in 1959; others followed at Compass Gallery, Glasgow; there was a series at Piccadilly Gallery; a retrospective toured from Stirling University in 1975; and Perth Art Gallery followed in 1987 and Thackeray Gallery in 1989. Birds and humans featured in Dallas Brown's pictures which are tinged with mystery, menace and Surrealism. Walker Art Gallery in Liverpool, Arts Council of Northern Ireland and many Scottish galleries hold his work. Lived in Cellardyke, Fife & Kinross.

Nellie BROWN 1900–1970 Artist in oil, watercolour and black-and-white. Born in Wolverhampton, she studied at the School of Art there. Her father William Brown, who started a printing company in Wolverhampton, W Brown and Sons, was for a time an ecclesiastical carver. Exhibited RA and RBSA, principally rural views. She signed her work NB with the date. Lived in Wolverhampton, Staffordshire.

Nicholas BROWN 1980– Artist whose work was "about the juxtaposition of different visual languages, both to create a specific effect and to allow space for a range of interpretations." He was included in Small is Beautiful XXII at Flowers Central, 2004–5, having recently been "influenced by the current crop of American artists bringing new elements into the realm of painting such as Inka Essenhigh and Laura Owens." Brown studied foundation at Wimbledon School of Art, 1998–9; graduated with honours in fine art from the University of East London, 1999–02; and gained his master's from the Slade School of Fine Art, 2002–4. Other exhibitions included Emu, The East London Gallery, 2001; Jamboree Beside the Sea, University Way, 2002; The Salon Show, Columbia Road, 2003; and Toni Heath Gallery, 2004.

Paul BROWN 1967– Painter of atmospheric landscapes, beach scenes and seascapes, sometimes with figures, born in Surrey. Although while at school he won three prizes, including a 1st in 1986, in the Johnson Wax Art Competition, Brown was denied a place at Farnham College of Art as he "didn't have the right attitude to become a painter". Read economics at Cardiff University, 1986–9, continued to paint while working in the City and had a solo show at St Mary-le-Bow church, 1992. Worked to commission in France, America and Italy and travelled extensively in Venice, Ireland and Istanbul, took part in many mixed exhibitions and had solo shows including Air Gallery, 1999, and Gallery 47, 2001, inspired by trips to Barbados and Greece. Corporate collections hold his work. Lived in Hove, Sussex.

Paul S BROWN 1967– Painter of landscape, still life and portraits, and teacher, whose work was characterised by the use of hand-made oil paints, Old Master techniques and precise draughtsmanship. He was born and raised in North Carolina, in America. Aged 10, he received classical drawing lessons from the painter D Jeffey Mims, to whom he would return years later for a two-year apprenticeship. After university Brown went to Italy for four years, trained at the Studio Cecil-Graves and later taught at the Florence Academy of Art. From 1995 he showed in London with W H Patterson in its Select and Christmas shows. In 2005 he had a solo exhibition there and participated in the BP Portrait Award at the National Portrait Gallery. In 2003, Brown was invited to show a selection of his pictures at the Panorama Museum, Bad Frankenhausen, in Germany, and this was also seen in New York. His work in is public and private collections in the United Kingdom, on the continent and in America.

Percy BROWN 1911–1996 Sculptor and potter. Studied at the Royal College of Art. Then taught sculpture at Leicester College of Art, was head of the school of sculpture and pottery at Leeds College of Art, later head of the department of art and architecture at Hammersmith College of Art. Exhibited RA, Leicester Galleries, Gimpel Fils and at other London galleries. Leicester Museum and Art Gallery and several other public collections hold his work. Brown's work was in two phases as shown in his retrospective at The Canon Gallery, Chichester, in 1991: from 1937–55 he did portraits and sculptures related to buildings, including ceramics and nude studies; from 1963 he started abstract compositions in bronze and wood. Lived at St Margaret's on Thames, Middlesex.

Peter BROWN 1967– Painter and draughtsman, born in Reading, Berkshire, who did a foundation course at Bath College of Higher Education, 1986–7; gained a fine art honours degree, Manchester Polytechnic, 1987–90; and his teaching certificate at University of Greenwich, 1992–3, becoming a full-time artist from 1994. In his open-air street scenes and landscapes Brown was "obsessed with different weather". He was a member of NEAC, RBA, Bath Society of Artists and PS, being featured in its centenary book, *Pastel Painting and Drawing, 1898–2000*, and an associate of ROI. Group shows included Albany Gallery, Cardiff, and Linda Blackstone Gallery, Pinner. Won a string of awards, later ones including W H Patterson Memorial Award, NEAC, 2000, and Arts Club Award, PS, 2001. Brown was represented by W H Patterson, where he had a series of solo shows, with one at Victoria Art Gallery, Bath, 2000. Messum's exhibited his works based on London and the Thames in 2004. Victoria Art Gallery, the National Library of Wales, Aberystwyth, and Holburne Museum, in Bath, Somerset, where he lived, hold examples.

Philip BROWN 1925– Painter and stained glass artist, born in London, who did a lot of work for religious buildings. Was educated at St Paul's School, then Oxford University. Studied art at Slade School of Fine Art, 1945–7, at L'Académie de la Grande Chaumière, 1948, and also in Paris at L'Ateliers d'Art Sacré, 1949–50. There followed a stream of work for churches in Britain and overseas, notably in Liverpool, Scunthorpe, Pershore and Eastbourne. Brown also exhibited in mixed exhibitions and had solo shows at the Galerie St Placide, Paris, and Ashley Gallery in London in the early 1950s. Lived in St Leonards-on-Sea in Sussex, later in Madrid, Spain.

Philip BROWN 1958– Versatile artist, born in Leeds, Yorkshire, where he did a foundation course at Jacob Kramer School of Art, 1977–8; gained an honours degree in fine art at Manchester Polytechnic, 1978–81; and a higher diploma at Slade School of Fine Art, 1981–3. In 1983–4 Brown used a Boise Travelling Scholarship to study Islamic architecture in Morocco and its influence in Spain; in 1984–5 he held a residency at Lady Lodge Arts Centre, Peterborough, working with local industries, and in 1986 a brief residency at Bretton Woods School there, helping with the organisation of three murals. Shows included MAFA from 1979; Beaumanor Hall, Leicestershire, 1983; Werner-Jaeger Halle, Viersen, West Germany, 1986; and Art '87, at Peterborough's Lady Lodge Arts Centre, 1987. Solo shows included one there, 1984–5.

Ralph BROWN 1928– Sculptor and teacher, born in Leeds, where he studied at the College of Art, 1948–51, following encouragement at Leeds Grammar School and Royal Air Force Service from 1946. Early inspirations were Henry Moore and Jacob Epstein. Was then at Hammersmith School of Art, 1951–2, taught drawing by Leon Underwood, followed by tuition from Frank Dobson and John Skeaping at Royal College of Art, 1952–6. Also studied under Zadkine, but was less influenced by him at this time than by the sculpture of Germaine Richier and that of Rodin. Brown was to live in France 1973–76. Held a number of teaching posts in England, including Royal College of Art, 1958–72, being elected RA in latter year. Showed Leicester Galleries and Taranman Gallery and completed many public commissions, including Swimmers for Hatfield New Town and Meat Porters for Harlow New Town. Brown's bronzes were often of figures in motion, and if they sometimes appear awkward they are always infused with a strong sense of passion and humanity. The retrospective at Henry Moore Centre for the Study of Sculpture, Leeds, in 1988, indicated Brown's abilities as a draughtsman. Tate Gallery and Arts Council hold his work. Lived in Amberley, Gloucestershire.

Reginald Victor BROWN 1897– Painter, designer and teacher, born in Brighton, Sussex. He was brought up in Hull where he attended the School of Art, then going to Manchester School of Art and Milan. During World War II he was an official war artist attached to Ford Motor Company, in Trafford Park, Manchester. He earned his living thereafter as a commercial artist. He was a life member of the Manchester Athenaeum Graphic Club and helped to organise exhibitions at the City Art Gallery on Rowley Smart, the Annual Athenaeum Graphic Exhibitions and the Five Manchester Art Clubs Exhibition of 1929 and the Six Manchester Art Clubs Exhibition of 1930, for which he designed the catalogues. Also showed at Walker Art Gallery in Liverpool, RA, RCamA and elsewhere in the north of England, Manchester City Art Gallery buying his picture The Wye River. Lived for 50 years in Manchester, then at Harwood, Bolton, Lancashire.

Richard BROWN 1965– Self-taught sculptor working mainly in sandstone and slate, born in Lanarkshire. He was winner of the 1995 Royal Glasgow Institute of the Fine Arts N S Macfarlane Charitable Trust Award, shared with William Selby. Ewan Mundy Fine Art in Glasgow, where Brown lived, included him in the 1996 exhibition Spring '96. Brown's figurative reliefs, in the manner of Eric Gill whom he much admired, often used the pale red sandstone retrieved from demolished Glasgow buildings.

Robert BROWN 1918– Landscape painter in oil, and teacher, born in Bushey, Hertfordshire, into an artistic family, his brothers being the painters Hugh Boycott Brown and Michael Boycott-Brown. From 1977 he became interested in the Llangollen Canal, near his home at Tetchill, Ellesmere, Shropshire, its history, architecture and boats, several hundred of which he painted. Brown studied at Watford Art School, St John's Wood Art School under P F Millard, Westminster School of Art with Adrian Hill, and Cotswold School of Landscape Painting under Hervey Adams. Served in the Army in World War II, being involved in the D-Day and Normandy landings. Taught art and pottery at Ellesmere College, 1946–77. Brown exhibited widely, including NS, Whitechapel Art Gallery, Mid-Day Studios in Manchester, Royal National Eisteddfod, South Shropshire Arts Festival, with Flintshire and Shropshire Art Societies and at the London Canal Museum. Constable, Boudin, Sisley and the French Impressionists were cited as influences on his breezy, on-the-spot style.

Robin BROWN 1950– Sculptor, painter and teacher. He attended Bromley College of Technology, 1967–8 and University of York, 1969–72. From 1973 at various times he studied part-time at Instituto de Espana, City Literary Institute and painting with Roy Oxlade. Brown was sculptor-in-residence at Kent Institute of Art & Design,

1989–91. His group exhibitions included Galeria Nueva, Banco Central, Bogota, in 1983; Hall Palace, Bexley, 1985–7; and Sculpture at Canterbury from 1990. In 1991 he had a commission from St Paul's Church, Canterbury. Brown was noted for sculpting with a variety of woods.

Rodger BROWN 1961– Sculptor in mixed media and teacher, who gained an honours degree in fine art at Sheffield Polytechnic, 1983–6, then his master's degree at Nottingham Polytechnic, 1988–90. Went on to work in the school of art and design at University of Derby. His sculptures appeared in many mixed shows including Mappin Art Gallery, Sheffield; Whitworth Art Gallery, Manchester; Castle Museum, Nottingham; Bread Street Gallery, Penzance; Smiths Galleries; and in East, in 1991, at Norwich School of Art Gallery. His 1990 work Bookshelf there was made up of shelf brackets, books and nests. Lived in Wirksworth, Derbyshire.

Samuel John Milton BROWN 1873–1963 Watercolourist and draughtsman of marine views. Born at Wavertree, Liverpool. Studied at the Liverpool School of Art, 1888–1900, under John Finnie. Exhibited RI, Walker Art Gallery, Liverpool and RCamA. Liverpool Corporation bought his picture Ploughing Her Way. Published several books on Liverpool, illustrated by him. Was at various times president of the Liver Sketching Club, Liverpool Academy of Arts and Flintshire Art Society. Lived at Upton, Chester.

Simon BROWN 1968– Painter of colourful small pictures, full of whimsical figures, in unusual frames. Born in Kent, Brown did a foundation course at Maidstone College of Art, 1988–9, then studied at Leeds Polytechnic, 1989–92. In 1989 he was runner-up in the Light in Art competition in Leeds. His 1992 appearances included Northern Graduates Exhibition and in 1993 he shared a show at New Academy Gallery and Business Art Galleries.

Stephen BROWN 1947– Painter in oil, mainly of West Country landscapes and seascapes, born and lived in Chard, Somerset, who trained as an engineer. He attended Somerset College of Art, 1966–70, through the 1970s painting with Patrick Larking at his home in Colyton. From 1980 showed at RWA, from 1990 at RA and was elected an associate of the RBA. Thompson's Gallery, The Gallery in Dorchester and other London and provincial galleries showed Brown's work. Ainscough Contemporary Art gave him a solo exhibition in 1997.

Steve BROWN 1956– Artist and lecturer whose output included site-specific work. After a five-year precision engineering apprenticeship in Blackpool, 1972–7, Brown graduated with honours in fine art and education studies at Worcester College of Higher Education, 1993–6, gaining his master's in fine art, University of Wales Institute, Cardiff, 1996–8, where he lived and later taught degree courses. Exhibitions in 1998–9, all in Cardiff, included Riser, Centre for Visual Arts; Ffresh 2, Chapter Arts Centre; and Pistol/Dryll, g39. In 2000, Brown collaborated with Michael Cousin on video projects.

Tina BROWN fl. from early 1980s– Artist in various media who studied at Cyprus College of Art, 1978, then Royal College of Art, 1979–82. She exhibited in Stowells Trophy, 1978; British Council in Nicosia, 1979; Kyklos Gallery, Nicosia, 1981; Hayward Annual, 1982; and in British Artists at Cyprus College of Art at Woodlands Art Gallery, 1983.

Varuni BROWN: *see* **VARUNI**

William BROWN 1953– Painter and printmaker, born in Toronto, Ontario, Canada, of Scottish parents. He trained as a sculptor and went on to travel and read widely, reflected in his work. This used stylized imagery and appeared naïve, his landscapes having an emphasis on the solid structure of objects, rhythm and design being other key features. Brown gained several awards, including a South West Arts Travel Award (Tunisia and Algeria), 1986, and a WAC Award (Orkney), 1992. He was the organiser of several projects including Contemporary Printmaking in Wales, 1993–6, which toured Britain and the continent, and 6 x 6, which toured, 1994. Had a major exhibition at Glynn Vivian Art Gallery, Swansea, 1996. Plymouth City Museum, National Maritime Museum and Peel Heritage Museum in the Isle of Man hold examples. Lived in Bridgend, Mid Glamorgan.

Alan Charlson BROWNE 1903–1970 Painter and photographer who studied at Liverpool School of Art, in Hope Street, and at Christchurch School of Art, in New Zealand. While in New Zealand Browne exhibited widely and was a member of Canterbury Society of Arts, appearing in its *Jubilee Catalogue 1881–1930*. Browne also showed at RCamA, Walker Art Gallery in Liverpool, Royal Geographical Society (of which he was made a fellow in 1933) and at a number of public galleries in the north of England. During World War II he was attached to the Air Ministry as a camouflage officer. Lived near Wigan, Lancashire.

Charles Egerton BROWNE 1910–1996 Artist noted for his animal sculptures, and engineer, whose early education was blighted by dyslexia, so that he resorted to night school and self-education. Trained as a toolmaker, he became a chartered engineer. Was the founder and chairman for over 40 years of the Egerton Group of Companies, which from the early 1940s was involved in the aerospace industry, based in Burnt Oak, Middlesex. Browne studied sculpture in the studios of L Cubitt Bevis and Ernest Shone-Jones; pastels and oil with Helen Wilson at Heatherley's School of Fine Art (he helped save it when it hit hard times in the late 1960s); animal painting with Marguerite Frobisher in Bushey; and bronze casting with Michael Gillespie at Hertfordshire College of Art and Design, St Albans. Browne mainly worked in bronze, also using marble, stone, terracotta, cement and plaster, and engraved glass with an abrasive wheel. Exhibited in many London exhibitions, especially at SWLA, RBA, NEAC and Hesketh Hubbard Society, and had solo shows at Watford and Bushey Museums. He was made an associate member of the Société des Artistes Français in 1984, winning the Salon Gold Medal that year, and in 1995 was made an associate of RBS. Two years before, he had been elected a fellow of the Zoological Society of London, having researched animal subjects extensively at London and Whipsnade Zoos. The French animalier tradition, Édouard Lantéri, Sir Alfred Gilbert, Lucy Kemp-Welch, Sir Alfred Munnings and Frank Calderon were key inspirations. He was a keen medal-winning shot and fisherman. Browne created public works for Whitbread's stable block and the Farmers' Club, both in London; the Shire Horse Society headquarters in Peterborough; and the memorial to Bushey artists in St James' Church there. Bushey Museum, which gave him a memorial exhibition in 1996, holds his work.

Clive Richard BROWNE 1901–1991 Painter, mainly of landscapes in oil, and teacher of art, born in Keelby, Lincolnshire, who attended St John's College, York. He studied at Grimsby Art School and under Herbert Rollett. Was a member of North Lincolnshire Art Society and of Lincolnshire Artists' Society, also exhibiting at RA, RCamA RBA, RHA, RBSA, NS, Walker Art Gallery in Liverpool and at Paris Salon. His main works included On the Cornish Coast, Still Grinding and Near Lizard Point. Usher Gallery, Lincoln, holds his work. For many years lived at Waltham, Lincolnshire, latterly at Horsforth, Yorkshire.

Gilbert BROWNE 1954– Artist, notably a printmaker, born in Girvan, Ayrshire. He studied at Leeds Polytechnic, 1973–6, under Norman Webster, then Chelsea School of Art, 1976–7, with Dick Hart. Went on to establish own studio in London, showing at RA Summer Exhibition, Christie's Contemporary Art, Graffiti Gallery and abroad.

Kathleen BROWNE 1905– Painter, printmaker, teacher and art historian, born in Christchurch, New Zealand. Studied and taught at Canterbury College School of Art, Christchurch, 1920–4, from 1925–31 teaching at various schools. Browne attended Chelsea School of Art, 1932–3, as well as evening classes at Central School, in 1934 Royal College of Art. In 1935 was proposed as a candidate for Prix de Rome, but was too old. Taught at various venues until in 1949 founded own school. In running this she was helped by Marian Kratochwil, whom she married in 1961. Retired in 1979 to concentrate on her own work, notably portraits, which included the pianist Krystian Zimerman, and moved to Hampstead. Browne won a bronze medal at Paris Salon, 1947. She was a member of the Senefelder Club and Graphic Arts Society and showed at RA, RSA, Leicester Galleries and in 1950 shared a three-man exhibition at Prince Galitzine Gallery. Painted on the continent, notably in Portugal. National Portrait Gallery, British Museum and Cambridgeshire Education Authority hold her work. At one time she was art education policy adviser to the colour-makers George Rowney and Company. A perceptive monograph was published privately on her work by her husband, with whom she shared a retrospective at Polish Cultural Institute, 1994.

Matthew BROWNE 1959– Painter, draughtsman and teacher whose output included abstract works such as Home, oil on canvas, shown at Royal Over-Seas League open, 1995. He studied at Camberwell School of Arts and Crafts, then began a series of teaching appointments, including drawing tutor with Hackney Adult Education, 1988; visiting tutor at Chelsea College of Art & Design, 1989–90; visiting tutor at Outreach Community Art Centre, Auckland, 1992; plus several other New Zealand posts. Group shows included Iraqi Prize Exhibition, South London Art Gallery, 1982; RP, Mall Galleries, 1986; The Family in Art, New Zealand Academy of Fine Arts, Wellington, and Wallace Awards, Customs House, Auckland, both 1994. Had a solo show at Sue Rankin Gallery, 1986, later ones including Souvenir, Ferner Gallery, Auckland, 1995.

Michael BROWNE 1930– Artist and teacher, born in Wigan, Lancashire, son of a Lancastrian father and New Zealand mother, both painters. After studying at New Zealand's University of Canterbury School of Fine Art, Browne won a scholarship to the Royal College of Art, graduating in 1958. Spent the next two years travelling in Europe, working in S W Hayter's atelier in Paris and in Amsterdam taking up a Netherlands International Cultural Relations Fellowship. In 1960, returned to Britain, spending the next 20 years in art education, finally as senior lecturer in painting, Chelsea School of Art. In 1986, resumed painting full-time, showing regularly at RA Summer Exhibition and Mall Galleries, including NEAC and RP. From 1989, lived and worked in London and Wellington. Later group shows included Fathers and Sons, Pataka Museum of Arts and Culture, Porirua, with Matthew Browne and six others. Held many solo exhibitions, notably at Argile Gallery, from 1988, and Janne Land Gallery, Wellington, from 1995, with a retrospective at Menier Gallery, 1956–02, in 2002. Museum of New Zealand, Te Papa; Gerneendt Museum, The Hague; Inner London Education Authority and many other public and corporate collections hold examples.

Piers BROWNE 1949– Painter, printmaker and teacher, born in London, who studied at Byam Shaw, 1968–70, with Maurice de Sausmarez and Bernard Dunstan, and at the Royal Academy Schools, 1972–5, with Peter Greenham. Browne went on to lecture and teach occasionally, running an art class locally for 10 years, having settled in Askrigg, north Yorkshire. He showed with Askrigg Artists every year and by 2003 had had 50 solo exhibitions over the previous 25 years. He worked in traditional romantic landscape mode, latterly influenced by Scottish landscape painters. Books illustrated by Browne included A E Housman's *A Shropshire Lad*, 1988; William Wordsworth, *A Lakeland Anthology*, 1991; and *The Glorious Trees of Great Britain*, foreword by HRH The Prince of Wales, with an accompanying show at North Light Gallery, Huddersfield, 2002. Plymouth City Art Gallery, Münster Art Gallery and other collections in the United Kingdom and abroad hold examples.

Richard BROWNE 1921–1990 Sculptor in various materials, born in London. He studied at Wimbledon School of Art, 1948–52, then Slade School of Fine Art, 1953. Browne was made a fellow of RBS and became president of SPS, being noted for his portraits. These included the ballerina Dame Alicia Markova, in 1992 taken into National Portrait Gallery collection. Work by Browne is in Guildford Cathedral, City of London University and Crawley New Town. Lived in Old Heathfield, Sussex.

Rory J BROWNE 1966– Painter, draughtsman and teacher, born in Alton, Hampshire, who graduated from Chelsea School of Art in 1988. He became head of art at St George's, a Hertfordshire comprehensive school, and settled in St Albans. Exhibited in many mixed shows, including regularly in RA Summer Exhibition. Browne was a finalist in several national art competitions and won an Elizabeth Greenshields Award. He sometimes employed collage to give depth to the urban landscapes for which he was noted, being interested in natural and man-made structures such as girders and gasometers. Had a solo show at Edith Grove Gallery, 1997, another at A & K Wilson Gallery, Harpenden, 2001. London Borough of Barnet,

British Gas and Mowlem, the building firm, owned examples.

Raymond BROWNELL 1934– Artist and architect, born in Hobart, Tasmania, Australia, who gained his architecture diploma at Hobart Technical College, 1959; a diploma in town and country planning, Edinburgh College of Art, 1977; and graduated with the Open University, 1989. His main career was architecture in Britain, France, Denmark and Australia. He was latterly project manager for the £60 million major refurbishment of the Foreign & Commonwealth Office's main building in Whitehall, for which he was made Member of the British Empire. Brownell produced "colourful mathematics-based geometrical constructions, acrylic on canvas, influenced by the Swiss Concrete Art movement: Max Bill, R P Lohse and others. Each work has its genesis in a mathematical idea. Then begins the search for a formal structure and colours that will most clearly convey the mathematical principles and relationships involved." Brownell was elected a UA associate in 1999. He took part in group shows in London, the southeast of England, France and Australia from 1996. Among his solo shows were Greenman Gallery, Eastbourne, 2001; Burstow Gallery, Brighton College, 2002, which holds his work and where he gave a lecture on The Marriage of Mathematics and Art; and George Street Gallery, Brighton, and Crypt Gallery, Seaford, both 2003.

Amy Katherine BROWNING 1882–1978 Painter in oil and teacher, follower of the Impressionists, subjects including flowers, children and landscape. She was born at Bramingham Hall, Bedfordshire, one of eight children, was brought up in the country and was encouraged by her parents to paint. After schooling in Ripon and Luton she went, aged 18, to Royal College of Art under Gerald Moira, gaining a scholarship to continue without paying, then studied in Paris, where she worked much in the open air, concentrating on problems of painting sunlight. In 1916 married the painter T C Dugdale. Taught at Camberwell School of Arts and Crafts, then replaced Percy Hague Jowett at Bromley and Beckenham School of Art until end of World War II. During war ran a Red Cross point and took in evacuees. In Paris she had exhibited at the Salon, where she won gold and silver medals; the French government bought two pictures for the Luxembourg collection, including The Red Shawl. Exhibited flower paintings at Fine Art Society in 1925, and also showed RA, NEAC, NS, ROI and extensively abroad. Her work is in many British provincial collections, including Manchester, Southampton and Glasgow, and those abroad. Brownie, as she was known to artist friends, latterly lived in Chelsea, where she had a studio, and Saxmundham, Suffolk, where she painted flowers from her own garden, insisting that "bought flowers have no character". The artist's great-niece, the actress Joanna Dunham, organised a large show of Browning's work at Christchurch Mansion, Ipswich, 1995.

Stephen James BROWNING 1953– Painter who went on to manage Greenwich Theatre and oversee its Art Gallery and who was born and lived in London. He graduated from Oxford University in 1974 with a degree in modern history, after attending Marlborough College. In 1971 he studied at Putney and Byam Shaw Schools of Art. Showed with Free Painters and Sculptors, at Mall Galleries and in the provinces.

Harold BROWNSWORD 1885–1961 Sculptor in bronze, wood and marble. Born in the potteries area of the West Midlands, son of a book-keeper at Wedgwood's, Brownsword studied at Hanley School of Art, then at the Royal College of Art, 1908–13. While at Hanley he won a gold medal for the design of a sundial, at the Royal College winning a travelling scholarship to Rome. He then taught sculpture, 1914–38, and was headmaster of Regent Street Polytechnic, 1938–50, where he executed a bronze relief of Major Robert Mitchell. Brownsword exhibited in London and the provinces and designed and executed war memorials at several locations, including Hanley and Northallerton, Yorkshire. He was a sculptor in the classical tradition, capable of images of great tenderness, as in his The Little Flower, illustrated in *RBS: Modern British Sculpture*, published in 1939. Brownsword was a fellow of the RBS. Lived in London.

Neil BROWNSWORD 1970– Ceramic artist, modeller and teacher, born in Stoke-on-Trent, Staffordshire, who studied at Newcastle-under-Lyme College; Cardiff Institute of Higher Education; and Royal College of Art. Brownsword was winner of the 1995 Royal Over-Seas League Award at the Royal College, providing two trophies for the League's Open in that year. Brownsword held a number of modelling and designing posts in the period 1990–94, including work for Josiah Wedgwood and *Spitting Image* Workshops, the firm that provided satirical puppets for television; then was assistant to Martin Smith at the Royal College and resident artist at Charleston Farmhouse, both 1994; and in 1995 taught at Bath College and Cardiff Institute of Higher Education and was modeller and assistant to Sir Eduardo Paolozzi. Awards included Potclays Award for Ceramics, 1990 and 1994; Cardiff Institute Award, 1992; Examiner's Award at Royal College, and Fletcher Challenge Ceramics Award, Auckland, both 1995. Group shows included Annual Open Art Exhibition, Stoke-on-Trent Museum & Art Gallery, from 1990; Workshop Gallery, Chepstow, 1993; and Museum of Mankind Student Showcase, 1995.

Anne BRUCE 1927– Painter and designer, born in Stoke Poges, Buckinghamshire. She studied theatre design and painting and drawing at Slade School of Fine Art, 1945–53, her teachers including Vladimir Polunin, then went on to Edinburgh College of Art. Was a prizewinner at John Moore's Exhibition, Liverpool, 1962. Showed widely, including New Art Centre, RA, Richard Demarco Gallery in Edinburgh and Galerie Creuze, in Paris. One-man exhibitions included Camden Arts Centre, 1978, and she had a shared exhibition at Austin/Desmond Fine Art, Sunninghill. Bruce was pioneer and director of Burleighfield Art, 1970–6, and was chairman of WIAC, 1973–9. From 1981 she lived in Somerset. She worked in watercolour on a large scale, producing landscapes of England and abroad, describing her pictures as "the summing up of my experience of living". She was included in Women's Art at New Hall, Cambridge, in 1992. Bruce's husband was the stained glass designer Patrick Reyntiens.

George J D BRUCE 1930– Painter in oil, born and lived in London, who attended Westminster School, then Byam Shaw School of Drawing and Painting, his teachers including Peter Greenham and Patrick Phillips. The Hon. George Bruce was elected RP in 1959 and occupied senior positions, being vice-president from 1984.

Margaret BRUCE: *see* **Margaret Bruce WELLS**

Marion BRUCE 1946– Artist in various media who was for some years with Ballet Rambert as a dancer from early 1960s. Began art studies in 1967, later concentrating on printmaking at Wimbledon School of Art. From 1980 she took part in many group exhibitions, including Camden Arts Centre, Arnolfini Gallery in Bristol and England & Co's 1992 Art in Boxes. She designed for Houston Ballet and showed in Houston, Texas.

Matt BRUCE 1915–2000 Artist in various media and charasmatic teacher, born in Shanghai, China. He studied at Edinburgh College of Art, 1932–9, teachers including John Maxwell and William Gillies, whom he revered, along with Monet and the other French Impressionists. Trained as a teacher at Moray House, but his date with the art room was postponed by six years as a gunner with the 79th Highland Division of the Royal Artillery. Went on to teach in several schools, including Varndean School for Boys in Brighton, where he settled, and part-time at College of Art there. Showed at RI of which he was a member, RA and RBA. The focus of Bruce's later years was his annual exhibition at the David Curzon Gallery, Wimbledon. Bank of America, De Beers, Legal & General, Shell, Whitbread and other corporate collections held examples.

John Harold BRUCE-LOCKHART 1889–1956 Watercolour painter, born at Beith, Ayrshire. Was educated at Sedbergh School, of which he was later headmaster, Cambridge and on the continent. Exhibited RA, RI, RSW and with the Lake Artists' Society. Lived at Sedbergh, Yorkshire.

Mabel BRUCE LOW 1883–1972 Watercolourist and printmaker, born in Edinburgh, educated at Dulwich High School and in Germany. Studied art under Walter Sickert at Westminster School of Art and with Robert Burns at Edinburgh College of Art and Richard Jack at London School of Art. Exhibited RA, RSA, IS, NEAC, SWA and especially at RBA. British Museum and several provincial galleries hold her work, which often features flower paintings. Lived in Bournemouth, Hampshire.

Sonia BRUCE 1975– Artist, born and worked in London, who was brought up in Southeast Asia until 1985, then returned to Kent. Did a foundation year at Camberwell Art College, 1994–5, then graduated from Wolverhampton University, 1995–8, studying glassmaking, sculpture and installation. Group shows included one at The Jelly Leg'd Chicken, Reading, 2000, the year of her first solo show in London, at Mellow Birds. This comprised a floor-based light source illuminating a mirror-faceted ball above it which cast flecks of light into numerous hand-made paper receptacles on floor, walls and ceiling.

BRÜER 1939– Artist and teacher, full name Brüer Tidman, under which name he latterly exhibited, who was especially interested in the human figure. Born in Norfolk, he trained at Great Yarmouth College of Art, 1957–61, and at Royal College of Art, 1961–4. Taught at Chesterfield College of Art and then at Lowestoft College School of Art and Design, 1976–84. Awards included 1st Athena International Art Awards, 2nd Prize, Mall Galleries 1985 (Brüer's picture The Rehearsal emerged from about 1,000 drawings made at the Hippodrome Circus, Great Yarmouth, in the summers of 1984–5); East Anglian Artists Open Exhibition, 1st Prize, 1986; Drawings for All, Gainsborough's House, Sudbury, 2nd Prize, 1996, and 1st Prize, 2000. Among later group shows were The Wahrenberger Gallery, Zürich, Switzerland, 1996; Twin Images, Fine Art Society, 1998; and Eastern Open, Fermoy Centre, King's Lynn, 1999. Solo exhibitions included Chappel Galleries, Chappel, from 1990; Michael Richardson Contemporary Art, 1991; Rijkers Art Diffusion, Amsterdam, Netherlands, 1992; John Russell Gallery, Ipswich, from 1998; and Norwich Union House, Manchester, and Frames Gallery, Norwich, both 2000; Works, SeaChange Gallery, Great Yarmouth, 2002; and Waiting for the Miracle to Come, Frames, Norwich, 2003. Works by the artist from his own collection were shown at the Warehouse Arts Collective, Lowestoft, in 2004. Was commissioned by Norwich City Hall, 1991; and in 2002 was featured in *Art in the Home*, co-commissioned by Wingfield Arts and Anglia Television, and *Arty Facts* for Imago Productions. Imperial College, University of Essex, The James Paget Hospital in Great Yarmouth, and Castle Museum and Playhouse Theatre, both in Norwich, hold examples. Lived in Lowestoft, Suffolk.

Tony BRUMMELL SMITH 1949– Artist working in various media including pastel, born in Berkshire. He worked in commercial art and music before settling to painting seriously and professionally in 1970, working from a studio near Harrogate, north Yorkshire. The countryside and gardens featured strongly in his work. Group showings included RWS, PS and Bankside Gallery; in 1989 he was a Royal Horticultural Society Silver Medal Winner, and in the 18th Laing Art Competition, 1990, he was a regional first prize winner. Brummell Smith had a solo show at Century Gallery in Henley-on-Thames in 1975, later ones including Duncalfe Galleries, Harrogate, 1989–90, Bourne Gallery, Reigate, 1993, and Thompson's Gallery, 2002.

Reginald BRUNDRIT 1883–1960 Landscape and figure painter in oil and watercolour. Born in Liverpool, he studied at Bradford School of Art, the Slade School of Fine Art and under the animal painter and sculptor John M Swan. Exhibited RA, ROI, NEAC, RSA, Walker Art Gallery, Liverpool, Paris Salon and elsewhere abroad. Yorkshire was a favourite subject of Brundrit's, and the Tate Gallery holds several examples. Other English provincial and Australian galleries hold his work. Elected RA 1938. Lived at Masham, Yorkshire.

Jacques B BRUNIUS 1906–1967 Versatile Surrealist poet, collagist, film-maker, film actor, writer and broadcaster, born in Paris, France, who died in Exeter, Devon. Brunius (real name Jacques Cottance) was from the 1920s associated with the French avant-garde film, working with the directors René Clair and Jean Renoir. Perhaps his best film was *Violin d'Ingres*, made for the French Pavilion at the 1939 New York World's Fair, about the ways that eccentrics find creative outlets alongside their regular occupations. As an actor he appeared in a variety of movies, including *L'Age d'Or*, 1930, *Partie de Campagne*, 1937, *Sea Devils*, 1953, *To Paris with Love*, 1955, *House of Secrets*, 1956, and *Orders to Kill*, 1958. He moved to London in 1940, where he was a member of the English Surrealist group. Brunius could be a forthright polemicist on the printed page, for example in 1944, with the Surrealist dealer E L T Mesens, publishing

Idolatry & confusion, a reply to an article by Arthur Koestler the year before in *Tribune*. Brunius was also an articulate contributor on many aspects of the arts to the long-running BBC radio programme *The Critics*. In 1967, with John Lyle, Conroy Maddox and Mesens, Brunius helped organise new Surrealist activities within a Festival of Modern Arts in Exeter, a magazine called *TRANSFOR-MAcTION* also being launched. Examples of Brunius's artwork were included in Surrealism in England 1936 and After, at The Herbert Read Gallery, Canterbury College of Art and tour, 1986. Brunius liked humour and was an expert on the writer Lewis Carroll.

Isabel BRUNNER 1969– Painter who attended Camberwell College of Art, 1990–1; Ruskin School of Drawing and Fine Art, Oxford, 1991–4; and the Royal Academy Schools, 1997–00. Her oil on canvas In the Wild Places was included in the final year show there. Lived in west London.

John BRUNSDON 1933– Printmaker, painter and teacher, born in Cheltenham, Gloucestershire, where in 1949–53 he attended the College of Art. Moved to Royal College of Art, 1955–8, under Julian Trevelyan. He became head of printmaking at St Albans School of Art and wrote a standard textbook: *The Technique of Etching and Engraving*, 1965. Among his commissions was one for Houlder Bros, for their Mahe Beach Hotel, Seychelles. Showed widely in mixed exhibitions in Britain and abroad. Solo shows were held in Lund, Sweden, 1965, and Curwen Gallery, 1967, later ones including Alice Simsar Gallery, Ann Arbor, Michigan, John Owen Gallery in Cardiff and Chapman Gallery, Canberra, all in 1984; his Celebration of the Shakespearian Properties, at Shakespeare Centre, Stratford-upon-Avon, 1990; CCA Galleries, 1996; with a retrospective at Bankside Gallery (he was an associate of RE) in 1998, others at The John Russell Gallery, Ipswich, 2002 and 2004. There was a major show of etchings at Rostra & Rooksmoor Gallery, Bath, in 2006. Although Brunsdon's early work was influenced by the American Abstract Expressionists, his mature pictures were representational. He was a full-time artist from 1977, with a studio in Stradbroke, Suffolk. Arts Council, British Council, Tate Gallery Museums of Modern Art in Edinburgh and New York and other public collections hold examples.

Ann BRUNSKILL 1923– Printmaker, draughtsman and painter, born in London. She studied at Central School of Arts and Crafts and Chelsea College of Art, gaining her diploma in 1962. Crafts Advisory Committee Index of Craftsmen awarded her a bursary which enabled her to study art and design in India. Her ideas were mainly about people and their relationships. Showed with RE of which she was for a time a member, RA and Victoria & Albert Museum. Solo shows included Easton Rooms, Rye, from 1983; Drew Gallery, Canterbury, 1991; and Duncan Campbell Contemporary Art, 1994. Victoria & Albert, Library of Congress in Washington, National Library of Australia in Canberra and other notable international collections hold her work. Lived latterly in Egerton, Kent.

Stanislaw BRUNSTEIN 1914–1994 Versatile and durable artist and designer, who created vibrantly colourful paintings, born in Warsaw, Poland. He studied there and in Paris and worked as a cartoonist and scenic designer for the Jewish Theatre, Warsaw. Served in the Polish Army during World War II, in 1940 being imprisoned by the Russians. After the war went to Rome, in 1946 moving to England. In London's East End he established a tailoring business specialising in children's clothing, moved to Ilford in 1956 and resumed painting in 1962, producing over 1,600 paintings, drawings, cartoons and sketches. There were important exhibitions of his work at the Ben Uri Art Society, 1984, and The Sternberg Centre for Judaism, 1997.

Elizabeth York BRUNTON fl. c.1905–1960 Painter and wood engraver in colour who studied at Edinburgh College of Art, then in Paris. She exhibited RSA, RSW, Paris Salon, Royal Glasgow Institute of the Fine Arts and extensively abroad. British Museum holds her work. Lived in Edinburgh.

Violet BRUNTON 1878–1951 Miniature painter and woodcarver, born at Brighouse, Yorkshire, daughter of the artists Arthur and Annie Brunton. She was educated at Southport and Liverpool Schools of Art and the Royal College of Art. Won several medals there and the County Palatine Scholarship in Liverpool. Exhibited RA, RMS, RBA, Walker Art Gallery, Liverpool, and had several one-man shows. Victoria & Albert Museum holds her work. Lived in London.

Winifred Mabel BRUNTON 1880–1959 Watercolourist specialising in miniatures. After early art education in South Africa, studied at the Slade School of Fine Art. Married the Egyptologist Guy Brunton and wrote several books on ancient Egypt. Showed in Egypt and South Africa, where galleries hold her work and in England at the RA, RBA and RMS. Many one-man shows at the Arlington Gallery. Signed work with initials W M N B. Lived at White River, Eastern Transvaal, South Africa.

Lief BRUYLANT 1954– Painter, muralist, photographer, illustrator and lecturer, born in Kinshasa, Zaire, formerly Belgian Congo, of Belgian parentage, who studied at the Académie Royale des Beaux-Arts, Liège, Belgium, 1973–9; L'Institut Communale des Arts Décoratifs, Liège, 1979–90; then gained her master's in photography from the Royal College of Art, 1980–2. She was audio-visual co-ordinator at the Photokina, Cologne, Germany, 1982; a freelance photographer, 1982–5; a visiting lecturer, photography, at St Martin's School of Art, 1983–5, and in painting at South Kent College, Ashford, 1989; from 1985 working as a freelance mural artist, painter and illustrator. Bruylant travelled widely in the early 1980s as a freelance photographer. Her work was shown at many venues in the United Kingdom, Belgium and France, with the Museum of Photography, Charleroi, Belgium holding examples. Among her painting exhibitions were ones in Liège, 1979, and Sandgate, 1999, and at Canterbury, Festival of Art, 2003 and 2004. Bruylant carried out numerous public and private mural and trompe l'oeil commissions in the United Kingdom (including the London Lord Mayor's Show), Ireland, on the continent and in Kenya. Oaten Hill Mews Garage and St George's Brasserie, both in Canterbury; Stone Green Hall hotel, Mersham, near Ashford; Howfield Manor hotel, Chartham; and Paul's restaurant, Folkestone, were among venues where she worked. She explored the use of various media, such as acrylics, ceramics and natural materials, was fascinated by the human figure, but latterly her work was "mostly about the natural world and especially trees. I experiment with colour as an expressive and healing medium and enjoy finding ways to bring humour into the work." She lived near Wye, Kent.

John BRYAN: *see* **Bryan de GRINEAU**

Mary BRYAN 1918– Embroiderer and textile designer, painter and teacher, born in London. Attended Putney High School, then studied at Bromley College of Art, 1936–41, and Royal College of Art. In 1949 she joined Brighton College of Art specialising in dress, following several years at Worthing School of Art, staying at Brighton for many years. She exhibited extensively, including Heal's Mansard Gallery, Crafts Centre of Great Britain, Red Rose Guild, UA, RBA and in industrial design touring shows. Her work was illustrated widely in crafts and design magazines and was bought by Victoria & Albert Museum and London County Council. Lived in Worthing and later in Lower Beeding, Sussex.

Dena BRYANT 1930– Artist, gallery owner and restorer, born in Gloucester, who studied at Royal West of England Academy, Bristol. Went on to run her own gallery for 26 years. Showed at St Albans Museum, 1970; St Albans Gallery, which holds her work, from 1975; at Salon des Nations in Paris, 1983; Royal Horticultural Society International Exhibition, at Mall Galleries, 1984; Galerie Salammbo, Paris, 1988; and had solo show of flower watercolours in St Albans Abbey, 1991. Sometimes signed work Dena, with initials or snail. Lived in St Albans, Hertfordshire, and at East Hyde, Luton, Bedfordshire.

Emma BRYANT fl. from early 1980s– Painter, muralist and teacher who trained from 1978–84 at Camberwell School of Arts and Crafts, Brighton Polytechnic and Central School of Art & Design. She showed regularly from 1982 and was included in a four-man exhibition at Woodlands Art Gallery, 1988. There she showed work which built up a picture of southeast London's river front. Bryant worked on several mural projects at school and hospital locations and taught at Morley College and Goldsmiths' College School of Art.

Gordon BRYCE 1943– Painter and teacher, born in Edinburgh. He studied drawing and painting at Edinburgh College of Art, 1960–5, in 1965 winning an Andrew Grant Travelling Scholarship to Spain. From 1968 he was a lecturer in printmaking at Gray's School of Art, Aberdeen. A painter of still life and landscape, Bryce employed a rich, warm and luscious palette in the Scottish tradition. Elected RSW, 1976. He won many awards, including a Sir William Gillies Travelling Scholarship; Scottish Arts Council Award; and an RSW May Marshall Brown Award. Was elected RSA and showed often at RA and SSA. Had two solo shows at New 57 Gallery, Edinburgh in 1966 and 1968. Later showed at Scottish Gallery, Edinburgh; Yperifanos Gallery, New York; and Sue Rankin Gallery. Numerous public collections hold Bryce's work, including Scottish National Gallery of Modern Art, Scottish Arts Council and National Trust for Scotland. Lived in Aberdeenshire.

Ken BRYCE 1956– Painter, draughtsman, printmaker and lecturer, born in Mancot, Flintshire, who after foundation and degree studies in Wales went to Royal College Art, gaining his master's in printmaking, 1988. Won WAC awards and commissions in 1979 and 1981. Was a visiting lecturer at Chelsea and Falmouth Schools of Art, Manchester and Seychelles Polytechnics and Chesterfield College of Art & Design. Took part in mixed and two-man shows in London, the provinces and Wales and had a solo show at Lamont Gallery before, in 1990–2, living in the Seychelles archipelago. The outcome was a solo exhibition, Reflections from a Small Island, at Oriel Contemporary Art, 1996. Rank Xerox, Penguin Books, Lowick House Print Trust, WAC and Royal College of Art hold Bryce's work. Lived in Hampshire.

Una BRYCE 1964– Painter and teacher, born in Londonderry, Northern Ireland, who did a foundation course in Liverpool, graduated from Coventry Polytechnic, then gained her master's degree in fine art painting, 1988, from Birmingham Polytechnic. She held a fellowship at Limerick College of Art and Design, where she was artist-in-residence, 1991–2, and was a visiting lecturer at Cork and Limerick Colleges of Art. Showed in England, Greece and extensively in Northern Ireland, being based in Queen Street Studios, Belfast.

Dilys BRYON 1930– Painter, printmaker, ceramist and teacher, using a rich palette, who was a purely figurative artist until the early 1970s; then a painting, Trapped Bird, using bright colour constrained by a black grid, led her to move towards abstract, stained glass-like works. She studied at Wimbledon School of Art, obtaining a national diploma in design (painting), gaining her art teachers' diploma at London University. In 1974 began to study etching and mezzotint with Mark Balakjian at Morley College, in 1991 studying the etching techniques of S W Hayter at Atelier Contrepoint, Paris. Taught as head of department in private and state schools at secondary level, in adult education and higher education colleges. Was vice-chairman and chairman of the Printmakers' Council, also a member of NS, and exhibited with North and South Printmakers and Wandsworth Printmakers. Open exhibitions included RE; Curwen Gallery; Barbican Centre; and National Open Print Exhibition, Mall Galleries. Had a solo show at Gallery 20, Brighton, 1978, later ones including Pump House Gallery, 1995. Scarborough Art Gallery, Brunel University and several foreign collections hold examples. Lived in Fetcham, Surrey.

Mary BRYSON 1905–1994 Painter, printmaker and draughtsman of cool, restrained portraits and landscapes, born in Douglastown, growing up in Forfar, the countryside and people of Angus featuring in her early work. From 1921, studied at Edinburgh College of Art with David Foggie, Henry Lintott and D M Sutherland, but when her family moved to London in 1923 she transferred to the Central School of Arts and Crafts, later to Chelsea College of Art where Terence Cuneo was a friend. She was employed at the School of Tropical Medicine and at the Cancer Hospital (later the Royal Marsden) as a medical draughtsman. There she met Charles Bryson, married him just before the outbreak of World War II, changing her name from May Johnston Riach to Mary Bryson, and when he was appointed a consultant pathologist at the Whittington Hospital in north London they settled nearby in Highgate. In the 1950s she attended a portrait class run by Jesse Dale Cast at Hornsey School of Art. After her husband's death, in 1972, she painted little, concentrating on her garden. Early in her career she had shown at the

RSA, Senefelder Club and SWA. In 1997 there was a memorial show at The Highgate Gallery.

Magdalena MARIA-BRZESKA 1976– Artist, born in Warsaw, Poland, who settled in the United Kingdom in 1989, continuing her education. She studied painting at Chelsea College of Art and Design. Her exhibitions included Young Artists, Dartford, 1994, and Congress of Polish Culture Exhibition of Fine Arts by Polish Artists in Britain at POSK Gallery, 1995. In 1997, she was chosen for the Transcription Project at the National Gallery. She lived for a time in Kent.

BUCHAN: *see* **James BOSWELL**

Dennis BUCHAN 1937– Painter and teacher, born in Arbroath, Angus. Buchan studied at Duncan of Jordanstone College of Art in Dundee and continued with postgraduate studies at Patrick Allan-Fraser School of Art, Hospitalfield, Arbroath, 1954–9. He taught part-time at Dundee in 1962–5, then joined the full-time staff. Buchan participated extensively in group shows in Scotland. He won a number of awards, gaining the Keith Prize and Latimer Prize at RSA in the early 1960s, in 1973 winning a Scottish Arts Council Major Award. In 1988 he gained the William J Macaulay Award for the most distinguished work in the RSA, to which he was elected. Buchan's first one-man was at Malcolm's Furnishing Store, Dundee, in 1959. Others included Compass Gallery, Glasgow, in 1994. Scottish Arts Council holds his work.

Anne BUCHANAN 1929– Painter, born in London where she continued to live; she was also known as Anne Buchanan-Crosby, having been the first wife of the sculptor Theo Crosby. Studied at Worthing School of Art and in 1948 at Camberwell School of Arts and Crafts with John Dodgson. She was a member of LG and was included in the Arts Council's British Painting '74, in 1974, where two Scenes from the Myths of Antiquity were shown, accompanied by a lengthy artist's statement. Had solo shows at AIA, 1971, and Meridian House International, Washington, 1979.

David BUCHANAN 1912–1999 Painter and teacher who studied at Hornsey School of Art from 1930 and, after service in north Africa and Italy in World War II, enrolled at Bath Academy of Art, Corsham, in 1946. After obtaining his teaching diploma, he taught at Marlborough School for many years. Exhibited at RA Summer Exhibition, ROI, RP and elsewhere and was a senior member of RWA, where he showed prolifically. His colourful mid-career scene Street Games: November Evening was included in 20th Century British Paintings & Drawings at Katharine House Gallery, Marlborough, in 2002.

Elspeth BUCHANAN 1915– Painter in watercolour and oil, and teacher, born in Bridge of Weir, Renfrewshire. Studied at Edinburgh College of Art, 1933–8, on an Andrew Grant Open Scholarship, her teachers including Hubert Wellington and Robert H Westwater; then gained a Travelling Scholarship, 1938–9. During World War II worked in Naval Intelligence in Oxford, where in 1943 she studied art with Bernard Meninsky. Buchanan was noted for her small watercolour landscapes of Edinburgh, in a representational style. She showed with RSA, RA, NEAC and LG while teaching, 1947–72. Was a member of SSWA and SSA. Had her first solo show at Great King Street Gallery, Edinburgh, 1972, and lived in the city. Her mother was the artist Oughtred Buchanan.

Hugh BUCHANAN 1958– Landscape and still life painter, born in Edinburgh, who studied for a degree in drawing and painting at College of Art there, 1976–80. In the latter year an Andrew Grant Travelling Scholarship took him to the Middle East. After undertaking a postgraduate course back at Edinburgh College with distinction, 1980–1, Buchanan in 1981 gained a Helen Rose Bequest to Northern Italy and Yugoslavia, also undertaking commissions for the National Trust. He went on to travel extensively in Britain and the continent, architecture featuring strongly in the resulting work. In addition to group showings, including Fine Art Society and Francis Kyle Gallery, Buchanan had solo exhibitions which included Scottish Gallery, Edinburgh, and Francis Kyle. In 2002–3, that gallery's show of Buchanan's work included period interiors in England and Scotland, the artist's interpretations of the government buildings of Delhi, India, by Sir Edwin Lutyens and Sir Herbert Baker and his watercolour of the lying-in-state of Queen Elizabeth the Queen Mother. Commissioned by the House of Lords' Advisory Panel on Works of Art, it was added with another Buchanan picture to the Lords' permanent collection. HRH The Prince of Wales and the National Trust hold his work.

June BUCHANAN 1920– Artist mainly in pastel, full name Elizabeth June Buchanan, born in Ashwell, Hertfordshire, into an artistic family (the metalworker Edward Spencer was an uncle, the painter Ethel Spencer, a pupil of Gauguin, an aunt). In 1932 she gained a full certificate from the Royal Drawing Society, under her maiden name June Spencer. Work and bringing up a family prevented her from pursuing art until later in life. During World War II Buchanan was an ambulance driver. Studied at Marlborough Institute, Sloane Avenue, with I Bassingthwaighte. Mainly showed at Hurlingham Club exhibitions. The work of Paul Maze, colour and light inspired her. Lived in London.

Mary BUCHANAN 1876–1958 Sculptor and watercolourist who studied at Paisley School of Design and Glasgow School of Art under the sculptor Johan Keller. She lived for a long time in Paris, working in the studios of Bourdelle and Zadkine, showing at the Salon. Also exhibited at RA, Royal Glasgow Institute of the Fine Arts and at Sculpture in the Open Air, Glasgow, 1949. Notable for figures and heads in wood and marble; she presented her Female Portrait, in oolitic limestone, to Glasgow's Art Gallery and Museum, Kelvingrove, in 1945. Late in life she became an enthusiastic watercolourist.

Oughtred BUCHANAN 1883–1979 Painter, whose full name was Evelyne Oughtred Buchanan, born at Stockton-on-Tees, County Durham. After attending the High School there she studied for a few months with Stanhope Forbes, but mainly taught herself. Showed at RA, RSA, SSA, Royal Glasgow Institute of the Fine Arts, SSWA with which she was closely associated, and extensively in the English provinces. Glasgow Museums and Art Galleries hold her work. Lived in Edinburgh. Her daughter was the painter Elspeth Buchanan.

Roderick BUCHANAN 1965– Versatile artist and lecturer, born and lived in Glasgow, who graduated from the local School of Art, 1984–9, gaining his master's at University of Ulster, Belfast, 1989–90. Buchanan won the inaugural Beck's Futures Award in 2000 with a video of small children sitting in a van trying to hold their breath for the length of the Clyde tunnel. He had a number of visiting lectureships in Britain and abroad and was associate professor, Kunstakademiet I Trondheim, Norway. Awards and commissions included John & Anna Laurie Bequest, 1989; BBC Billboard Commission, 1992; and Scottish Arts Council Award, 1994. Artist's books included *Yankees*, 1997. Among his video programmes were Magnetic North, National Film Theatre, 1999, and Black-Box Recorder, British Council international tour, 2000, the year Buchanan held a Sargant Fellowship, British School at Rome. Took part in numerous group exhibitions in Britain and abroad, solo shows including Turnaround, Hayward Gallery, 1998, and Dundee Contemporary Arts, 2000. In 2004, Buchanan won a Paul Hamlyn Award for the Visual Arts.

Stuart BUCHANAN 1970– Figurative painter and gallery administrator, born and lived in Glasgow, where he attended the School of Art under Jack Knox, 1988–92. Influences included "William McTagggart senior and John Bellany." Had a Hospitalfield House, Arbroath, residency in 1998. Group exhibitions included SSA Annual at RSA, Edinburgh, 1995; BP Portrait Award, National Portrait Gallery, from 1995; and Glasgow Now, Crickethill Gallery, New York, America, and Paint, Will's Art Warehouse, both 2002, where Buchanan said that his works sought "to invoke strangely familiar scenes, like snapshots or memories in a personal history. At the same time they remain ambiguous". Solo exhibitions included Firth Gallery, Edinburgh, 1997, and New Works, Egg Gallery, Glasgow, from 2000. Sheriff's Court, Glasgow, holds Buchanan's work.

Ian BUCHANAN-DUNLOP 1908– Painter and draughtsman in ink, full name Archibald Ian Buchanan-Dunlop, he was born in Whitefield, Lancashire, and became a professional soldier, attaining the rank of brigadier. Was educated at Sandhurst's Royal Military Academy. Showed at RWS of which he was a member, and in military art shows. Until 1975 after retirement from the Army he was principal of the Scottish Office. Mainly known as a watercolourist. Lived in Colinton, Edinburgh.

John Sandford BUCK 1896–1988 Painter, draughtsman and printmaker, born in Minehead, Somerset, but his family soon moved to Monmouth where he attended Monmouth School. In 1914 he joined the Army but contracted rheumatic fever on Salisbury Plain and was ill for three years, being discharged as "unemployable". He went to live with his parents at Brains Green, Blakeney, in Gloucestershire, where he eventually settled. After trying to train for office work at Clark's College in Bristol and having studied etching with Reginald Bush at the Municipal School, Buck decided to make his living as a painter. His pictures were mainly local or holiday scenes, worked up from pastel sketches on the spot. Showed with BWS of which he was a member, RWA, RBSA and RI. Newport New Museum and Art Gallery holds his work. Member of Wye Valley Art Society and Gloucestershire Society of Artists. Retrospective show at Dean Heritage Centre, Soudley, Gloucestershire, in 1988.

Jon BUCK 1951– Figurative sculptor and teacher, born in Bristol. He attended Cardiff College of Art, 1975–6, Trent Polytechnic, where he obtained a bachelor's degree in fine art, 1976–9, and Manchester Polytechnic, 1979–80, for his master's degree. Buck was appointed fellow in sculpture at Cheltenham College of Art, 1980–1, was sculptor-in-residence for Borough of Thamesdown, 1985, and from 1987 lectured at Southampton Institute. His highly stylised work was shown at RWA annual exhibition from 1987; Sculpture in the Garden, Abergavenny, 1990; Gallery Pangolin, Stroud, from 1991; and Bath Art Fair, 1992. Buck's public commissions included Clifton Zoological Society, Bristol, 1986–7, and Old Cattle Market Site, Swindon, 1989–90. His work is in many private collections worldwide. Lived in Bath, Somerset.

Michael BUCK 1954– Painter and teacher who studied at High Wycombe College of Art and Further Education, at Ruskin School of Drawing in Oxford and at Bretton Hall College of Further Education, Yorkshire. Buck was a fine, atmospheric landscape painter who reckoned that his knowledge of the countryside was deepened by an interest in hang-gliding and in garden design. He lectured at the Inchbald School of Garden Design, Banbury College of Art and several schools. Showed in group exhibitions at RA, Dwarves Gallery in Oxford and Sue Rankin Gallery, his solo shows including Sue Rankin, 1987. Lived in Oxford.

Allan BUCKETT 1953– Sculptor and teacher, born and lived in London, who studied at St Martin's School of Art, 1971–5. Worked at Meridian Bronze Foundry, 1976–9, then became a visiting lecturer at Edinburgh College of Art. Group shows included New Contemporaries at Camden Arts Centre, 1975, St Martin's Sculpture at South Bank in 1977 and Summer Show 3 at Serpentine Gallery, 1980. There he showed smallish mild steel works which "would generate some fresh ideas. Using colour was important. I wanted to discover, for myself, if colour could be useful in sculpture."

Jean BUCKLAND 1950– Artist who studied at Chelsea School of Art, 1982–5. She participated in Uses of Drawing, Whitechapel Art Gallery, 1979; Exploring Female Imagery, Battersea Arts Centre, 1985; Group Show, Gallery 111, 1986; and East End Open Studios, at Carpenter's Road, 1989. Among her solo exhibitions was Camden and Westminster Teachers Centre, 1979.

John BUCKLAND WRIGHT 1897–1954 Painter, draughtsman, but primarily an etcher and engraver who was self-taught. Born in Dunedin, New Zealand, Buckland Wright studied history at Oxford and then architecture in London. He soon realised that he wanted to be an artist more than an architect and by 1921 he was living in Belgium and was elected a member of the Gravure Originale Belge in 1925. Was also a member of Xylographes Belges, SWE and LG. During the 1930s Buckland Wright lived and worked in Paris and frequently visited S W Hayter's Atelier 17. He had one-man shows in London and throughout the continent, sometimes signing his work J B W. Work held by Victoria & Albert Museum, British Museum and many galleries and museums in Europe and America. A master printmaker with an assured, swirling line, Buckland Wright passed on his skills after World War II when he taught at Camberwell School of Arts and Crafts, from 1948, and the Slade School of Fine Art, from 1953, the year that his book *Etching and Engraving: Techniques and the Modern Trend* was published. He illustrated over 50 books. Retrospective Blond Fine Art, 1981, Wolseley Fine Arts reviewing his Surrealist work, 1999, and The Golden Cockerel Years, 2001. In 2003, that gallery staged For My Own Pleasure – The Autonomous Prints, 1925–54, with an extensively illustrated catalogue. Lived in London.

Claude BUCKLE 1905– Painter, especially in watercolour, born in London, educated at Wolverhampton Grammar School. He trained as an architect, but gave this up in the late 1920s to become a full-time painter, exhibiting widely in England and America. He was a member of both RSMA and RI. Lived for many years in Andover, Hampshire.

Sydney H BUCKLE 1912– Painter, printmaker, designer and teacher, born in Stockton-on-Tees, County Durham. Attended Darlington School of Art, Northern Polytechnic and Garnet College. He held a number of teaching posts in the Stockton and Darlington areas and was a member of Darlington Society of Artists. Lived in Stockton.

Guy BUCKLES 1964– Artist born in Iowa, America, who studied at Hong Kong University; Hastings College of Art; and the Slade School of Fine Art. Showed at Victory Gallery, Hastings from 1989; Rye Society Summer Show from 1992; and from 1992 at Royal Over-Seas League Open, having a solo exhibition there in 1994.

Howard BUCKLEY 1909– Watercolourist, printmaker and teacher, born in Croydon, Surrey. Studied at Croydon School of Art and Royal College of Art. Buckley went on to teach, eventually becoming principal at Derby School of Art. Exhibited RA, RWA, in the provinces and in Chicago. He completed mural paintings in Worthing pier pavilion, Sussex, and other work held by Southampton and Brighton Art Galleries. Lived in Wheatley, Oxfordshire.

Jim BUCKLEY 1957– Highly versatile artist and teacher, born in Cork, Ireland, who attended Crawford School of Art there, 1975–80. Was joint head of sculpture, Gray's School of Art, Aberdeen, from 1995. Buckley was involved in a series of imaginative creations, ranging across boxes with interiors, video and ambitious installations such as Flood, at Meiho, Japan, 1993, involving concrete tanks, water, paint and lights. Group exhibitions included World in a Box, City Art Centre, Edinburgh, and tour, 1994, preceded by Human Properties, Ikon Gallery, Birmingham, 1992, and Speed at Transmission Gallery, Glasgow, 1991. Solo shows included Illuminations at The Collective Gallery, Edinburgh, 1991; Access, at University of Strathclyde, 1992–3; and Kyoni Gallery, Tokyo, 1994. Lived in Dennistoun, Glasgow.

Stephen BUCKLEY 1944– Artist and teacher working in an often unconventional range of materials. He was influenced by Pop Art and Dada and while his work appears abstract it hints at everyday objects and appearances. Born in Leicester, Buckley studied at University of Newcastle upon Tyne, 1962–7, then Reading University, 1967–9. He taught at Canterbury and Leeds Colleges of Art and Chelsea School of Art, 1969–71; was artist-in-residence at King's College, Cambridge, 1972–4; and was visiting tutor at Royal College of Art, 1976 and 1986. After showing in Six at the Hayward, Hayward Gallery in 1969, Buckley had a one-man show at Nigel Greenwood in 1970. He was a John Moores Exhibition, Liverpool, prizewinner in 1974 and 1979. Collaborated with Rambert Dance Company, 1988–90. Buckley soon built up an impressive list of British and foreign showings and had a retrospective at Museum of Modern Art, Oxford, 1989, with an exhibition at University Gallery, University of Northumbria, 1994, others at Austin/Desmond Fine Art from 1999. Shortlisted for Jerwood Painting Prize, 1995, the year after he was appointed professor of fine art at University of Reading. Arts Council, Tate Gallery, British Council and many other British and foreign collections hold his work. Lived in London.

Sydney BUCKLEY 1899–1982 Painter and printmaker with a strong interest in Lake District and architectural subjects. He was born in Oldham, studied at the School of Art there and between 1927–32 was on its staff. He was an architect by training and during World War II was engaged in war claims work. After the war he went to live in Cartmel, Cumbria, with a sister, unmarried like himself, who was a craftsman and weaver. For some time they had a studio in the Cartmel Priory gatehouse. He showed in his studio and RI, RSA, RSW, Lake Artists' Society and MAFA. Helped to illustrate a Forestry Commission handbook. Oldham Art Gallery holds two pictures by him of local scenes. His sister died a month before him early in 1982.

Christopher BUCKLOW 1957– Self-taught artist in various media, born in Manchester, in whose work aspects of religion and nuclear themes were important, as in his show The Mancunian Heresy at Anthony Wilkinson Gallery, 1999. Group exhibitions included Inside a microcosm, Laure Genillard Gallery, 1992; Wonderful Life, Lisson Gallery, 1993; Silhouettes (with Elliott Puckette and Adam Fuss), Paul Kasmin Gallery, New York, America, 1995; and Object and abstraction, Museum of Modern Art, New York, 1997. That Museum as well as the Metropolitan Museum of Art, New York; Museum of Fine Arts, Houston; British Council; Yale Center for British Art, New Haven, America, and other public collections hold Bucklow's work. Bucklow also wrote catalogue texts on artists including Mark Francis, Susan Derges and Simon Callery. Christopher Bucklow & William Blake: I Will Save Your Life was held at Riflemaker in 2004.

Martin Arnold BUCKMASTER 1862–1960 Painter, teacher and writer, born in London, where he finally lived. Studied at Royal College of Art, where he specialised in architecture, a subject on which he wrote several books and published many articles. Exhibited RA, RI and RBA. Taught art at Tonbridge School. Member of the Arts Club.

George BUDAY 1907–1990 Printmaker, teacher and writer, born in Hungary, where he was educated at Kolozsvar and Szeged University, gaining his doctorate in 1934, also studying art in Italy. He lectured on graphic arts at Franz Joseph University, 1934–41. In England he became a book illustrator, published his own *Little Books* for a number of years and in 1954 *The History of Christmas Cards*. Buday was elected RE in 1953 and a fellow of SWE in 1954. Also showed at RA and elsewhere. Arts Council bought his work. Lived latterly in Coulsdon, Surrey.

Zbigniew BUDAY 1944– After attending Camberwell School of Arts and Crafts, 1963–5, Buday graduated with honours from Hornsey College of Art, 1965–8. He had a solo exhibition at Losin Winn Gallery, Austin, Texas, America, in 1971, participating in Contemporary Southwest Art, Fort Worth Arts Centre, Texas, in 1972, then had another one-man at Souyun Yi Gallery, New York, in 1988. He appeared there in a group show in 1989, the year he was included in London's East End Open Studios, based at Richmond House Studios.

Herbert Ashwin BUDD 1881–1950 Painter and teacher, born at Ford Green, Staffordshire. After private education he attended Hanley School of Art, then the Royal College of Art, 1903–8, under Gerald Moira. Taught at St Martin's School of Art, 1929–49, and Hornsey School of Art, 1930–49. Married to the artist Helen Mackenzie. Exhibited RA, NEAC, RP, ROI and Royal Glasgow Institute of the Fine Arts. Imperial War Museum and galleries in Bradford and Oldham possess his work. Lived in London.

Kenneth George BUDD 1925–1995 Designer of murals, mosaics and windows, born in London, who studied at Beckenham School of Art, 1941–4, then Royal College of Art, 1947–50, his teachers including John Cole, Kenneth Rowntree and Charles Mahoney. He exhibited at RA, Young Contemporaries, AIA and in the Power and Production Pavilion at London's South Bank Festival Site. Budd also did a substantial amount of advertising designing, but was better known for public building designs, including windows in the Church of the Good Shepherd, Brighton; a coat-of-arms in the foyer of Guy's Hospital; and work in the Medical Centre at Westerham, Kent, where he lived. Budd was a member of the Art Workers' Guild. After Budd's death, his son Oliver, with whom he had completed joint commissions, continued the practice.

Rachel BUDD 1960– Painter, born in Norfolk, who graduated from Newcastle University, 1978–82, gained her master's degree at Royal College of Art, 1983–6, then obtained a fellowship at Kingston Polytechnic, 1986–7. Among her awards were the LG Henry Moore Prize, 1987, Mark Rothko Memorial Trust Fund travel grant to America in 1988 and British Council Botswana workshop grant, 1991. Took part in the Three Ways Arts Council/Royal College of Art European tour, 1990–3. Later solo shows included Purdy Hicks Gallery, 2002. Government Art Collection and Contemporary Art Society hold examples.

Graham BUDGETT 1954– Artist and teacher using photography, who graduated in fine art from Trent Polytechnic, 1973–7; did an advanced diploma in sculpture at St Martin's School of Art, 1977–8; and a master's in fine art at Stamford University, California, based in sculpture, 1979–82. From 1977–8 Budgett co-ordinated seminars for advanced students at St Martin's, from 1979–82 taught at Stamford University and from 1982–5 lectured at University of California, Santa Barbara. Exhibited widely, later shows including collaboration with Jane Mulfinger on the work A Grey Area, for the touring exhibition Boxer, 1995, Walsall Museum & Art Gallery. This installation in Plasticine and Astro-turf recorded the names of boxing champions. Victoria & Albert Museum holds Budgett's work in its photographic collection.

Friedel BUECKING 1946– Sculptor who used a variety of materials, such as railway sleepers, carpet, stone and wood. Took up carving and sculpture full-time in 1979, then between 1985–90 took a part-time honours degree in fine art/sculpture in Hertfordshire. Work in public spaces and exhibitions included a nativity set for St Albans Cathedral, comprising chainsaw carvings, 1984; Wharf – carving and construction on Gasriec's Wharf, South Bank, 1989–90; Hull Dock Museum, the installation of wood and stone Atlantis, 1991; and Sculpture at Canterbury, 1992. One-man works included an installation at Tobacco Dock, 1992. Worked in London.

Mirjam BUERGIN 1967– Artist born in Basle, Switzerland, who did a foundation course and textile degree at the School of Art and Design, Zürich, 1987–92; pursued postgraduate studies in fine art at Goldsmiths' College, 1997–8; and obtained a master's at the Slade School of Fine Art, 1998–00. Awards included Symposium des Arts, nord-sud dialogue: Toubad-Dialaw, Senegal/St Anton, 1995; Atelier Neti-Guy Dalar, Senegal, 1996; and Beck's Futures Student Film and Video Prize, 1999. Exhibitions included Sub-Nord, National Gallery, Dakar, and Shedhalle, Zürich, 1995; Videotage, Schlotterbeck, Basle, 1997; Head-cleaners, performance with Tabatha Anders, Bloomsbury Theatre, 1999; Polyvision screen, Sadler's Wells, 2000; and Art2001, represented by Dominic Berning, Business Design Centre, Islington, 2001. Lived in London.

Michael BUHLER 1940– Painter in oil, creator of painted wood boxworks and teacher, born and lived in London, son of the artist Robert Buhler. He studied at Royal College of Art, 1960–3, teachers Carel Weight, Ceri Richards, Ruskin Spear and Colin Hayes. Buhler taught part-time in many art schools, university art departments and at Imperial College. He was a prolific exhibitor, including RA, John Moores Exhibition in Liverpool, Camden Arts Centre, Arts Council of Northern Ireland and elsewhere. Had solo shows at New Arts Centre, 1966–71, Architectural Association, 1968, and Maclean Gallery, 1981–92. Buhler's one-man exhibition Street Life and Beyond, at Chappel Galleries, Chappel, 2002, reflected the artist's strong interest in Unidentified Flying Objects. Arts Council, British Museum, Eastern Arts Association and Liverpool University hold his work.

Robert BUHLER 1916–1989 Painter and teacher, born in London of Swiss parentage, he was early encouraged to paint. In the early 1930s he studied painting initially in Zürich and Basle, and attended Bolt Court, St Martin's School of Art and the Royal College of Art. He left the Royal College after a few months and with the help of a little money left to him took a studio and began to paint professionally, encouraged by the patron Edward Marsh. His mother had a café in Charlotte Street, so he became familiar with Fitzrovia and was friendly with the Euston Road School painters, whose style left an imprint on his work. Around the late 1930s Buhler did work for Shell-Mex and BP; was associated with the AIA; began a notable series of portraits with Dickie Green and Stephen Spender, bought by the Contemporary Art Society in 1938; and contributed to exhibitions at the Leicester Galleries. He exhibited with the NEAC from 1945, showed at the RA from 1946, becoming RA in 1956. Taught at Chelsea School of Art, Central School of Arts and Crafts and from 1948–75 was a tutor at the Royal College of Art. Three of his pictures were bought under the terms of the Chantrey Bequest and there are quite a lot in collections in the provinces and abroad. Buhler preferred to choose the subjects of his portraits, who included the critic John Davenport, the actor Sir Donald Wolfit and the poet Laurie Lee. In later life he concentrated more on landscape. Buhler, whose son was the painter Michael Buhler, lived in London.

Simon BULL 1958– Etcher, teacher and illustrator, born in Bedfordshire. He travelled the world with his parents before settling in Yorkshire in 1977, where he studied fine art at Leeds Polytechnic. He taught etching part-time at Leeds University and Bretton Hall College and illustrated several books. Bull liked to work on location, especially in the Lake District and Yorkshire dales. Mixed exhibitions included RA Summer Exhibition, Leeds Art Fair and 8th British International Print Biennial, Bradford. Had a solo show at Hong Kong Hotel, Hong Kong, 1976, a series at Fairfield Halls, Croydon, from 1978, also Bretton Hall College, 1984. Had studio at Clayton, Bradford, Yorkshire.

Paul BULLARD 1918–1996 Painter mainly in oil, born in London. Studied at Clapham School of Art, 1934–8, then Royal College of Art, 1938–40 – war service in the Royal Artillery intervened – and 1946–7, notable teachers being R V Pitchforth and Charles Mahoney. Bullard taught at various London art schools during 1947–58, from 1958–78 being head of the department of foundation studies at Camberwell School of Arts and Crafts. His exhibitions included Phoenix Gallery, 1947, RA from 1948 onwards, LG, NEAC, the Football Centenary Exhibition in 1953 and Belgrave Gallery, 1988. Collections holding his work include Imperial War Museum, Football Association and Shropshire Education Committee. Lived at Stanstead, Suffolk. Died in St Helena Hospice, Colchester.

Anne BULLEN 1914– Painter, draughtsman and illustrator, born in Norwich, Norfolk. She specialised in animal subjects, especially horses, and came from a military family, a connection strengthened by marriage. After education privately and in Paris, she studied art at Académie Julian there, in 1930, followed by Chelsea School of Art. Showed at UA and in Devon; lived for a time at Charmouth, Dorset. She illustrated a number a books with horse and pony themes, fiction and non-fiction.

Duncan BULLEN 1962– Painter, draughtsman, printmaker and teacher, producing contemplative, Minimalist abstract works, born in Norwich, Norfolk. He studied at Great Yarmouth College of Art and Design, 1983–5; gained a fine art honours degree from Leeds Polytechnic, 1985–8; then his master's in printmaking from the Royal College of Art, 1989–91. Awards included Atlantis Paper Prize, CCA Gallery Prize and Dell' Arte Award, all 1991. Residencies included Cité Internationale des Arts, Paris, 1990; Rome Scholarship, British School at Rome, 1991–2; and artist-in-residence, Eremo di Santa Caterina, Isola d'Elba, Italy, 1992–5–7. In 1998 Bullen was appointed senior lecturer in fine art printmaking at University of Brighton. Took part in numerous group exhibitions, later solo shows including Jill George Gallery from 1993. British School, Rome; Leeds Education Authority; and a number of corporate collections hold examples.

Maud BULLEN 1906–1993 Watercolourist, born and lived in Dorking, Surrey. A physically handicapped, naïve artist, she studied with Ursula Hulme at Rentwood Occupational Therapy Centre at Fetcham. Took part in mixed exhibitions at Mall Galleries, New Metropole Arts Centre in Folkestone and in Best of British Naïve Artists at Lyric Theatre. Had a solo show at Loggia Gallery, being a member of Free Painters and Sculptors.

Stephen BULLER 1958– Artist who graduated with honours from Manchester Polytechnic, 1980–3. He had a series of solo exhibitions, including Sayat Nova Gallery, Actors Institute and Dance Attic Studios, all 1987; and Framers Gallery and Wigmore Hall, both 1988. In 1989, Buller participated in East End Open Studios, at Carpenter's Road.

Molly BULLICK fl. from late 1970s– Artist who gained a diploma in architecture, 1964, then began printmaking in 1978–9. She was awarded a Barcham Green Printmaking Competition Student Prize, 1980; gained two Scottish Arts Council bursaries, 1979 and 1981; and was elected to SSA in 1982. Took part in Scottish Print Open Three, 1983, organised by the Dundee Printmakers' Workshop, also showing with RSA and SSWA.

Angela BULLOCH 1966– Versatile conceptual artist in a variety of media, born in Ontario, Canada. She gained an honours degree in fine art at Goldsmiths' College of Art, 1985–8, won a Whitechapel Artists' Award, 1989, and had a two-month residency, Arcus-project, Moriya, Japan, 1994. Bulloch said that she was "interested in how things evolve, or shift their meaning when you move them into various different contexts ... I like the apparent contradictions of defining something which is always subject to change." She first showed her work in the 1988 exhibition Freeze in the PLA Building, thereafter participating in numerous group exhibitions internationally and getting wide press coverage. In the mid-1990s she was working on a number of public projects, including Belisha Beacon Indicator System, 1996, a permanent work at the Leipziger Messe, Leipzig, and Panorama Island, a project for a disused jetty on the Thames, in front of Bankside Power Station. She was keen on the idea of sculptures as places of social interaction. Video compilations included 240 minuten, 1992, and Unplugged: the Demo Video Tape, 1993. Bulloch's first solo exhibition was at Interim Art, 1990. Many others followed in Europe and America, later ones including, in 1996, Galerie Walcheturm, Zürich, and Robert Prime, and Magnani, 2001. Modern Art Oxford gave her a show in 2005. Lived in London.

Caroline BULLOCK 1947– Naïve painter, born in Cornwall, working in oil and gouache. She was married to the artist Glynn Boyd Harte. Attended Bedales School, taught by Christopher Cash. Mixed appearances included Penwith Society, in St Ives, and she had solo exhibitions at Sheviock Gallery in Cornwall, Michael Parkin Gallery, Rebecca Hossack Gallery, 2001, and Charlotte Street Gallery, 2004. Lived in Veules-les-Roses, Seine-Maritime, France.

Hazel BULLOCK fl. from 1960s– Painter who studied at Sir John Cass School of Art, teachers including David Graham and Roland Pitchforth. In 1970 she was elected to Free Painters and Sculptors, also showing at RBA and Browse & Darby. Had solo show at Loggia Gallery in 1973, later ones including Phoenix Gallery in Lavenham and Highgate, both 1989. Lived in London.

Jean BULLOCK 1923– Sculptor in a variety of materials, designer and printmaker, born in Bristol, married to the artist John Bullock. She studied at Watford School of Art and Camberwell School of Arts and Crafts, her teachers including Karel Vogel. She was elected to SPS in 1964, also showing with RA, in the provinces and abroad. South Norwood School and Ministry of Defence hold her work, and she designed a stained glass window for St Giles, Lockton, not far from her home near Pickering, North Yorkshire.

Stephen BULLOCK 1889–c.1972/3 Painter in oil and watercolour, born in Salisbury, Wiltshire. He studied under Austin Garland at Lincoln School of Art. Showed at Foyles Gallery and in the provinces. From 1927–70 he showed with the Lincolnshire Artists' Society at the Usher Gallery, Lincoln, being the Society's chairman and deputy chairman at times in the late 1940s/early 1950s. Usher Gallery holds two watercolours by him: Romance; and Farmstead, Donington on Bain. He lived in Lincoln.

Clifford Derek BULLOUGH 1917– Painter and teacher, born in Barrow-in-Furness, Lancashire. He studied at Bolton School of Art, 1935–9, and Manchester School of Art, 1939–40. Exhibited PS; Manchester City Art Gallery holds his work. Lived in Isleworth, Middlesex.

Lionel BULMER 1919–1992 Painter and teacher, born in London. Was married to the artist Margaret Green. Bulmer studied at Royal College of Art just after World War II and taught for many years at Kingston College of Art. His special subject was the Suffolk landscape, often small pictures painted with a quiet, sensitive precision and using such colours as lemon, emerald and lilac. As well as showing at Leicester Galleries, RA, NEAC and RWS (of both of which he was a member), Bulmer had solo exhibitions at New Art Centre. Lived at Onehouse, near Stowmarket, Suffolk. Lionel Bulmer: The Walberswick Influence was held at Messum's Fine Art, 2002. In the same year Messum's organised From City to Sea the painterly journey of Lionel Bulmer and Margaret Green.

William Harold S BUNCE 1921– Painter and teacher, who gained art and teaching diplomas at Manchester School of Art, becoming art master at Stretford Grammar School. Stationed in Germany in World War II he attended a painting course at Gottingen University. Showed with MAFA; his Peak Farm, of 1958, bought from its Centenary Exhibition, 1959, was painted in Derbyshire, a favourite subject. Lived in Hale Barns, Cheshire.

Gary BUNT 1957– Painter, born in East Peckham, Kent, whose work, according to Maurice Sheppard, "carries a feeling of freshly dried varnish and barely dry paint – the energy of his former life as a musician runs on into his essential identity as an artist." Nicholas Bowlby, Owl House, Poundgate, showed Bunt's colourful and witty pictures of his family and others.

John BUNTING 1927–2002 Sculptor in wood, stone and bronze, and teacher, born in London. He attended Ampleforth College, 1941–4, and Oriel College, Oxford, 1945, serving in Royal Marines, 1945–7. After Robert Thompson, Kilburn, in 1948, Bunting studied under Walter Marsden at St Martin's School of Art, 1949–51, then with John Skeaping and Leon Underwood at Royal College of Art, 1951–4. Bunting was appointed drawing and art master at Ampleforth in 1955, where he proved an inspiring teacher, pupils including the painter Andrew Festing and sculptor Antony Gormley. He became sculptor-in-residence in 1984, continuing to make new works until 1995. He showed with RA, York Festival, and elsewhere in mixed exhibitions. Had a solo show with Fischbacher, Paris, in 1965, and a retrospective at Billingham Forum in 1972. Bunting did much public work for schools, churches, hospitals, community centres and memorials, the War Memorial Chapel at Hambleton, Yorkshire, being a key work. He was a fellow of RBS, 1972. Lived in Nunnington, York.

Peter BUNTING 1947– Painter whose work included Surrealist-type images, born in Switzerland. He was educated at Cambridge University and Byam Shaw School of Painting. Group exhibitions included Moira Kelly Gallery, 1982; New Grafton Gallery, 1985; Contrariwise (Surrealism and Britain 1930–86), touring show, 1986; Richard Pomeroy Gallery, 1987; Sandra Higgins Fine Arts, 1990; Obsessive Visions, England & Co, 2001; and Paintings from the New World there, 2003. Solo shows included Pomeroy Purdy Gallery 1989. Churchill College in Cambridge and Sheffield City Art Galleries hold examples.

Biddy BUNZL 1952– Painter and sculptor who studied at Vienna Kunst Akademie, 1969–70, then obtained degree in sculpture at Camberwell School of Arts and Crafts. She spent a year at Rietveld Akademie in Amsterdam on a British Council scholarship and undertook postgraduate studies at Reading University. Bunzl turned to painting in 1980 and showed widely, in group shows – including RA Upstairs Gallery, Hayward Annual and Riverside Gallery – and solo at Odette Gilbert Gallery. Shared an exhibition at Framework Gallery, 2002, with a one-man at Cambridge Contemporary Art, Cambridge, in 2003. Bunzl initially made purely abstract, formal colour paintings, then moved on to more figurative work, which employed a rich palette.

James BURBIDGE 1959– Sculptor and creator of mixed-media constructions who studied at West Surrey College of Art and Design, Farnham. Mixed show appearances included LG, Smiths Galleries and England & Co, 1991, in Art in Boxes. Had a solo show called Made for Other Reasons in 1989 at Michaelson and Orient, another at England & Co in 1992. There Burbidge showed small lead foil-covered boxes containing strange and haunting worlds created from materials such as papier mâché, wood and polished brass.

Claire BURBRIDGE 1971– Multi-media artist and teacher whose special interest was the human figure in motion, influenced by her association with dancers of the Royal Ballet and Rambert School. Burbridge gained an honours degree in fine art at Oxford University, then her master's in printmaking at Camberwell College of Arts. In 1991–2 she curated the Magdalen College art collection; in 1992 edited *Isis* magazine and undertook an exchange scholarship at Karl Marx University, Budapest; and in 1993 gained the Vivien Leigh Prize, having work bought by the Ashmolean Museum, Oxford. Exhibited in 2nd Open Sculpture Exhibition at RWA, 1996. Lived in London.

Lawson BURCH 1937–1999 Artist, teacher and writer who worked in various media, notably acrylic, born in Belfast, Northern Ireland. He studied at Stranmillis College with Cyril Mount, and with Belfast College of Art with John Luke. Between 1959–78 taught in various secondary and grammar schools, then became a full-time artist. Burch was an academician of RUA and chairman of Ulster Arts Club, 1986–8. In 1980 he won the George Campbell Award, which enabled him, like Campbell, to live and work in Spain, and to exhibit there. Burch had stories broadcast on BBC radio and presented arts programmes on television. The poet Gerard Manley Hopkins was an inspiration, as was the wild beauty of the Donegal landscape, where he settled in Glenties. Group exhibitions included RHA; Independent Artists, Solomon Gallery and The James Gallery, all in Dublin; and Irish Contemporary Art, Boston. Solo shows included Arts Council and The Bell Galleries and Queen's University, all in Belfast; Image Gallery, Dublin; and The Willow Island Gallery, Enniskillen. Arts Council, Queen's University, Northern Ireland Tourist Board and Department of the Environment and the national self-portrait collection at Limerick University all hold Burch's work.

Gina BURDASS 1953– Painter of abstracts, such as Soliton 3, acrylic with marble dust on canvas, in 1997–8 John Moores Liverpool Exhibition. Born in Shrewsbury, Shropshire, Burdass studied at Hammersmith College of Art, 1972; Central School of Art, 1973–6; and Wimbledon School of Art, 1982–5. From 1986–91 she was a part-time assistant to the the artist Bridget Riley. Burdass taught at Putney School of Art, 1981–5; was a visiting lecturer at Newport, Gwent, 1985; also at Byam Shaw School of Art, 1986; and taught at Wimbledon School of Art, 1987–9. Showed widely internationally in group exhibitions, which included Space Open Studios from 1993 and Salon des Graphiques, Curwen Gallery, from 1995. Later exhibitions included Hunting Art Prizes, Royal College of Art, and Accrochage, Elisabeth Costa Galerie, Pontresina, Switzerland, both 2002; Gina Burdass and Kevin Laycock: New Paintings, Art First, 2004; and a solo show at Archeus, 2005. Archive 90, International Reference Collection; Mondriaanhuis, Amersfoort, Netherlands; several corporate collections; University of London; and Victoria & Albert Museum hold examples. Lived in London.

Alan BURDEN 1938– Artist and teacher, born in Stanmore, Middlesex, originally studied and worked as a metallurgist. At Harrow School of Art, 1962–6, gained a diploma in painting and lithography, a diploma in education at University of Newcastle upon Tyne, 1966–7. Taught at a Newcastle comprehensive, 1967–72, then was head of art departments in Wigan and Essex. Took part in North West One, Chenil Gallery, 1976; Five Painters, at Salford City Art Gallery, 1979; and MAFA, 1980. Shared an exhibition at Scene Gallery, Newcastle, 1969, having a solo exhibition at Colin Jellicoe Gallery, Manchester, 1981. Burden said that his paintings "strive for autonomy, but the emotional drive behind them is, more often than not, some well-loved place, some memory or feeling about that place that I wish to encapsulate within an essentially two-dimensional surface."

Daniel BURDEN 1928– Painter, artist in collage and printmaker, born in Paris. After education at Kilburn Grammar School in northwest London, Burden attended Willesden Art School, 1949–52, where his teachers included James Neal, and the Royal College of Art, 1952–5, where teachers included Ruskin Spear, John Minton and Rodrigo Moynihan. He exhibited with RWA of which he was a member, RA, AIA, LG, elsewhere in England and also in France, where he settled for some years at Miramont de Guyenne in the Lot-et-Garonne region in the southwest. University of Leicester and RWA hold his work.

Ruth BURDEN 1925– Artist and teacher, born and finally settled in Worcester, who studied at Birmingham College of Art, 1945–50, under Bernard Fleetwood-Walker and Katherine Fryer, then at Bath Academy of Art, 1950–1, with William Scott and Peter Potworowski. Was a gallery assistant at Worcester Art Gallery and taught in girls' schools in Birmingham and Abingdon until 1972. Showed WIAC, AIA, RBSA, NEAC and RWA. Katharine House Gallery, Marlborough, latterly exhibited Burden's pictures and Duncan Campbell Contemporary Art gave her a solo show in 2000. Coventry Pictures for Schools holds her work. Burden painted buildings with figures, landscapes and still lifes in a richly individual palette. She named Christopher Wood and L S Lowry as influences on her pictures, which could be endearingly quirky and which were also "influenced by surroundings and memories, subject-matter close at hand – everywhere I look."

Angela BURFOOT 1934–2006 Painter and draughtsman, born in Cookham, Berkshire, who studied at Slade School of Fine Art with William Coldstream, 1952–6, while there gaining the Philip Wilson Steer Prize for Still Life and Landscape and a Henry Tonks Drawing Prize. She was the wife of the artist Ian Armour-Chelu and mother of the painter Louise Armour-Chelu. Commissioned portraits were a feature of her work. She showed at RA Summer Exhibition, had solo shows in London and abroad and in 1990 took part in a family exhibition at Markswood Gallery, Great Bardfield. Lived in Wissett, near Halesworth, Suffolk.

Andrew BURGESS 1969– Artist in a range of media, lecturer, born and lived in north London. He was notable for striking British and foreign cityscapes with unusual perspectives and singular colouring. After gaining an honours degree in politics and parliamentary studies from Leeds University, 1987–91, Burgess did a foundation course in art and design, National Diploma, at Barnet College, 1991–2, then an honours degree in fine art at Byam Shaw School of Art, 1994–6. Won a painting prize, Apthorp Fund for Young Artists, 1994; a Worshipful Company of Painter-Stainers bursary and certificate of excellence, Academy of Young Jewish Artists, both 1995; and a NEAC Drawing Scholarship, 1999. Taught art at the Jewish Association for the Mentally Ill, lectured in art history at The London Jewish Cultural Centre and was a RA part-time tour lecturer. Mixed shows included The City Gallery, from 1997, and Beardsmore Gallery and NEAC, both 1998. Later solo exhibitions included Pryory Art, 1999, and The Gallery in Cork Street, 2000.

Arthur James Wetherall BURGESS 1879–1957 Marine artist and editor, born in Bombala, New South Wales, Australia. He studied art in Sydney and St Ives, Cornwall. As well as being art editor of *Brassey's Naval and Shipping Annual*, Burgess was Australia's official naval artist in 1918. Showed at RI and ROI both of which he was a member, RA,

RHA, RBA and elsewhere. National Art Gallery of New South Wales in Sydney and several British public collections, including Lincoln and Nuneaton, hold examples. Settled in London, where he was a member of Langham Sketch Club. Malcolm Innes Gallery held a show of Burgess' marine, fishing and ski-ing oils and watercolours in 1996.

Cefyn BURGESS 1961– Artist, notable as a textile designer, born at Bethesda, Caernarvonshire, settling nearby at Penmaenmawr, Gwynedd. He did an arts foundation course at Birmingham Polytechnic, 1979–80; gained an honours degree from the fashion/textiles department of Manchester Polytechnic, 1980–3; and obtained a master's degree at Royal College of Art, 1983–5. Was a member of the Craft Council of Wales Committee, National Eisteddfod Craft Committee and North Wales Art Association Committee and showed in the principality. Solo exhibition of chapel illustrations and textiles, Oriel Coliseum Gallery, Aberystwyth, 2001.

Christine BURGESS 1937– Sculptor in weatherproof and low-fired ceramic and other materials, painter and draughtsman in various media, and teacher, born in Manchester, where she attended the Regional College of Art, 1954–9, with a Lady Whitworth Scholarship. Teachers included William Tocher, William Bailey and Harry Sutcliffe. In 1959, she married Peter Burgess, lecturer in ceramics, and from then taught full- or part-time in schools and colleges of art. After raising a family, in the early 1970s resumed personal work mainly in ceramics, in 1984 settling in Oxford and concentrating on sculpture. After remarriage in 1989, in early 1990s diversified materials and started experimenting with surfaces. Became chairman of Oxford Art Society and co-ordinator of the Oxford Confederation of Artists and Makers, a group pressing for a city gallery. Burgess' sculpture stemmed from the human form, although she avoided working direct from the model "because this is found to be inhibiting and sometimes inappropriate to the medium". Institution of Mechanical Engineers gave her a Queen's Silver Jubilee Award design commission. Group exhibitions included Museum & Art Gallery, Swindon; County Museum, Woodstock; Pittville Gallery, Cheltenham; Museum of Modern Art, Oxford; RBSA; RWA and elsewhere. Later solo shows included Bentlies Gallery, Woodstock, 1993. Wiltshire Country Council and Thamesdown Councils hold examples.

Eliza Mary BURGESS 1878– Watercolourist, especially of portraits, born in Walthamstow, where she studied, also at the Royal Female School of Art with the aid of a scholarship. Gained several medals. Exhibited RA, RSA, Cooling Galleries, Walker Art Gallery, Liverpool, Paris Salon and elsewhere abroad. Walker Art Gallery, Liverpool, and Graves Art Gallery, Sheffield, hold her work. Lived in London.

Paul BURGESS 1961– Printmaker, designer, illustrator, artist in mixed media and teacher, he studied printmaking at Camberwell School of Arts and Crafts and textiles at Royal College of Art. He then freelanced in a number of fields. Showed at Whitechapel Open; New British Design, in Tokyo; Royal Festival Hall in South Bank Picture Show, where he was a prizewinner; England & Co Art in Boxes, 1992, and elsewhere.

Peter BURGESS 1952– Painter, born in St Albans, Hertfordshire. He attended Watford School of Art, 1970–1, Wolverhampton Polytechnic, 1971–2, Wimbledon School of Art, 1972–4, and Royal Academy Schools, 1974–7. He won the David Murray Award in 1975–6–7 and the British Institution Award, 1976. Burgess was notable for his depictions of beaches and the seaside in vibrant colours. Showed at RA, Nottingham Castle Museum and Derby City Art Gallery in mixed shows, winning several prizes. Had a solo show at Nottingham Castle Museum in 1982; Blackfriars Arts Centre, Boston, Lincolnshire, 1986; and from that year showed at Thackeray Gallery. Contemporary Art Society, Nottingham City Council and several local authorities hold his work. Lived in Nottingham.

Trevor BURGESS 1963– Painter, draughtsman and teacher, born in Harrogate, North Yorkshire, who graduated in literature at the University of East Anglia, 1982–5, gaining his master's in European fine art, Winchester School of Art, 1997–8. He won Eastern Arts Board Awards, 1996–7, and an Oppenheim-John Downes Memorial Award, 1997. Among Burgess' jobs were life drawing at the University of East Anglia Students' Union, 1987–91; and at Warehouse Artists' Studios (of which he was founder and chairman, 1990–7), 1994–7; visiting lecturer, Universidad Naçional de San Juan, Argentina, 1998; and from 1999, assisting at Paton Gallery and project manager, cultural services, Prevista. Group shows included Constable Landscape Competition, Camden Arts Centre, 1988; Eastern Open, King's Lynn Arts Centre, 1995–8; Kettle's Yard Open, Kettle's Yard, Cambridge, 1996; Galerie Daniel Wahrenburger, Zürich, Switzerland, from 1997; and Noise paintings, The Dockroom, 2001. Later solo exhibitions included Galerie Daniel Wahrenburger, 1999, and Els Castellers, Galerie Groc, Barcelona, Spain and tour, 1999–00. Lived in London.

Victor BURGIN 1941– Artist and teacher, born in Sheffield, Yorkshire. Burgin used text, photographs and prints to create his pedagogically oriented art in which issues such as power in society and sex were examined. Burgin studied at Royal College of Art, 1962–5, then Yale University, 1965–7. He took part in When Attitude Becomes Form at ICA in 1969, then from 1970 soon built up an impressive range of one-man shows, venues including Daniel Templon Gallery, Paris; Protech-Rivkin Gallery, Washington; Lisson Gallery and Nigel Greenwood; and Museum of Modern Art, Oxford, where he had a retrospective in 1978. Later shows included ICA and Kettle's Yard, Cambridge, both 1986; Family Romance at Karl Bornstein Gallery, Los Angeles, and John Weber Gallery, New York, both 1990; and and in 1991–2 Passages, at Musée d'Art Moderne, Villeneuve d'Ascq/Ville de Blois. From 1973 Burgin taught at Central London Polytechnic; from 1976 at Yale, Princeton and elsewhere; he held a DAAD German Government Fellowship in 1978–9; in 1980 became Picker Professor at Colgate University, New York; and Millar Professor of Fine Art, at Goldsmiths' College, from 2001, having moved back to work in London. In 2002, Arnolfini, Bristol, presented an overview of Burgin's output and the film *Listen to Britain*, about his experience of returning, and Matt's Gallery showed *Watergate*. Arts Council and Royal College of Art hold examples.

Greig BURGOYNE 1968– Figurative artist, born in Glasgow, who studied at Cumbria College of Art & Design,

Carlisle, 1987–9, West Surrey College of Art & Design in Farnham, 1989–92, and Royal College of Art, 1992–4. Public commissions included murals for stairwells at West Surrey College, 1991, and in 1992 extensive murals for Old Arcade Shopping Centre in Aldershot. Exhibitions included Ditchling Gallery, Ditchling, 1990–1, LG at Morley Gallery in 1993, Five RCA Painters at Paton Gallery in 1994, The Discerning Eye at Mall Galleries in 1997, Harlech International Printmaking Open in 2000 and Novgorod State Museum, Russia, in 2001. Burgoyne's solo exhibitions included London Calling, a Scottish Arts Council tour, 1995–6; Sadler's Wells, 1995; Still Lives, Folkestone Museum, 2000; Falmouth Art Gallery and Novgorod State Museum, both 2001; and Encounters by the Sea, Art Space Gallery, 2003. In that year, Burgoyne won a Valparaiso Foundation Residency in Spain, one of several awards. Russian State Museums, Royal College of Art and several corporate collections hold examples.

Robert BURKALL MARSH: *see* **Robert MARSH**

Ian BURKE 1955– Painter, draughtsman and teacher. He studied at Newcastle University and Goldsmiths' College ATC Department. Went on to teach at Wandsworth Comprehensive School. Burke's exhibitions included Northern Contemporaries, 1976; Mid-Wales Open and Moira Kelly Summer Show, both 1981; and Goldsmiths' exhibition at Woodlands Art Gallery, 1983.

Patrick BURKE 1932– Painter, printmaker and teacher, born in Shoreham, Sussex. He studied at Brighton College of Art and Royal College of Art and was a Rome Scholar, 1957–9, specialising in etching. Burke taught at Brighton College of Art and became head of painting at Brighton Polytechnic, retiring in 1989. Some of his work was Pop-influenced, as in The Sussex Scene, Towner Art Gallery, Eastbourne, 1993.

Peter BURKE 1944– Artist and lecturer, born in London, who after City of Bath Technical School studied art at Bristol Polytechnic, 1973. Had a solo show with Gilbert Parr Gallery in 1978, later venues including Victoria Art Gallery, Bath, 1986, The New Art Centre, 1992, Roche Court, Salisbury, 1993, and Atrium Gallery, Coopers and Lybrand, 1994. Burke's figurative works from reclaimed metals featured in Gallery Artists 2000, at Stephen Lacey Gallery, 2000. Was elected to RWA in 1985, which holds his work. Lived at Bradford-on-Avon, Wiltshire.

Thomas BURKE 1906–1945 Painter and designer, born and died in Liverpool, who studied at College of Art there and Royal College of Art. He travelled extensively, was a radio officer in the Merchant Navy and during World War II was a prisoner of war during which he designed posters. Showed at RA, RP, RHA and Walker Art Gallery in Liverpool, which holds his canvas The Student.

Norman BURKETT 1942– Painter who studied at the Royal Academy Schools, 1971–4. Sir Brinsley Ford owned his work.

Jude BURKHAUSER 1947–1998 Curator and artist, born in Trenton, New Jersey, America, who studied at Rutgers and New York Universities, moving to Glasgow School of Art in 1987 for postgraduate study on Scottish women artists. Driven by a fierce feminism, Burkhauser researched for three years and in 1990 presented an exhibition at Glasgow's Kelvingrove Art Gallery entitled Glasgow Girls – Women in Art and Design 1880–1920. It was hugely successful and she was bitter that her attempts to tour it to North America were thwarted. She incurred heavy financial and health costs, being financially liable for printing of the American edition of the exhibition book. As an artist Burkhauser produced a vibrant railway history mosaic, commissioned from her by ScotRail in 1990, for Glasgow's Central Station. Translucent window banners by her remained there after her death. Latterly, she was working on drawings on Mexican bark paper entitled The Spirits of the Wood and had plans for a large tapestry.

Averil BURLEIGH 1883–1949 Painter whose husband was the painter C H H Burleigh, her daughter the artist Veronica Burleigh. A versatile painter, she showed at the RA, RI, SWA, Sussex Women's Art Club and RCamA and was elected an associate of the RWS shortly before she died. Brighton Art Gallery held a memorial show in the year of her death. Lived in Hove, Sussex.

C H H BURLEIGH 1869–1956 Painter of landscapes, townscapes, still life and interiors. These sometimes featured his family, his wife being the artist Averil Burleigh, his daughter the painter Veronica Burleigh. He studied at Brighton School of Art and in Paris, where his teachers included Jacques-Emile Blanche. Showed at RA, Fine Art Society, ROI of which he was a member, and RI. Lived in Hove, Sussex.

Veronica BURLEIGH 1909–1999 Painter in oil and watercolour, daughter of the artist C H H Burleigh, born in Hove, Sussex. Studied at Slade School of Fine Art, 1927–30, under Henry Tonks. Exhibited at RA, SWA, Sussex Women's Art Club and with the Sussex Painters, at Worthing, where the public gallery holds her work. Her main works included Little Ballet Dancers, Scene Painters and Calliope. During World War II served in the Women's Auxiliary Air Force. Burleigh's work was mainly portraits until 1970, when she moved into the country, living at Henfield, Sussex. For 20 years she commuted yearly to Rhodesia, where she held 23 one-man shows.

David William BURLEY 1901–1990 Watercolourist, commercial artist, printmaker and teacher, born in Greenwich, southeast London. He studied at Goldsmiths' College School of Art and showed at RA, RBA, RI and in the provinces. Was an adult tutor, conducting painting holidays. Lived in Birchington, Kent.

Barry BURMAN 1943–2001 Mixed-media artist, born in Elstow, Bedfordshire, and teacher. He studied at Coventry College of Art under Michael Sandle, then Royal College of Art with Harry Weinberger. He was a part-time lecturer in painting at Mid-Warwickshire College of Art, 1974–92, then became a full-time artist, being represented by the Goldmark Gallery, Uppingham. Burman was a prizewinner in Mercia Art at Herbert Museum and Art Gallery, Coventry, which holds his work, 1985, and he gained first prize in the 1991 Hunting/*Observer* Awards. His mixed exhibition appearances began with Through Drawing at ICA, 1966; was also in Modern Drawings at Angela Flowers Gallery and in British Figurative Art in Copenhagen, both 1972; also Mayor Gallery, 1988. Had a solo show at

Coventry College of Art, 1969, later ones including Nicholas Treadwell Gallery, 1982, and Goldmark Gallery, three between 1992 and 1999. His work was included in several books on erotic and Superhumanist art. Burman suffered from clinical depression, which he termed "Gloom Alley", reflected in his pictures, the subjects of which ranged over serial killers and rapists to John Bunyan's *The Pilgrim's Progress*. Lived in Leamington Spa, Warwickshire, where the Art Gallery & Museum held a posthumous exhibition in 2004. Burman died in Warwick.

Chila Kumari BURMAN 1957– Artist and teacher, born in Liverpool, who attended Southport College of Art, 1975–6; Leeds Polytechnic, winning a first-class honours degree, 1976–9; and Slade School of Fine Art, 1980–2. Burman worked in a wide range of media, including etchings, cibachrome prints, photo-based works and three-screen video installation with sound track. When her retrospective was held at Bluecoat Gallery, Liverpool, in 1995 she was said to stand "at the vanguard of politically radical art, occupying a position within discourses around black art and issues of cultural identity, representation and gender". From 1984 Burman taught widely on a visiting or part-time basis, including Brighton Polytechnic, Central School of Art, Birmingham Polytechnic, Chelsea School of Art and Middlesex University. She conducted a range of workshops and presentations, holding many residencies. Commissions included the mural Southall Black Resistance, with Keith Piper, for Great London Council, 1985; mural for London Borough of Haringey, 1987; and work Body Weapons for Walsall Art Gallery, 1992. Mixed shows included New Contemporaries, ICA, 1981; Artists Against Apartheid, Royal Festival Hall, 1985; and Contemporary Black Art, Stoke-on-Trent Garden Festival, 1986. She was latterly represented by the Andrew Mummery Gallery. Victoria & Albert Museum and public galleries in Birmingham and Walsall held examples. Lived in London.

John BURMAN 1936– Artist in paint, plastics and clay, and teacher, born in Creeting St Mary, Suffolk, older brother of the painter Peter Burman. He was mainly self-taught, although study periods included a year part-time at Valletta Art College, Malta. He concentrated on exhibiting landscapes, with special interest in East Anglia and its transient weather. Mixed shows included NEAC, RWS, RI, Mandell's Gallery in Norwich and The Frederick Gallery, Raveningham, where in 1993–5 he showed abstracts. Among Burman's many other solo exhibitions was a series of studio shows at Old School, Freston, Suffolk, from 1976. Collections holding work included Barclays Bank, Royal Bank of Scotland and the Museum of Fine Art, Valletta.

Peter BURMAN 1941– Painter and designer, younger brother of the artist John Burman, who was born in Ipswich, Suffolk, which remained his home county. Burman began as a graphic designer, producing posters, becoming a full-time artist in 1964. In 1981 he was encouraged by gallery owner and art historian Stephen Reiss to have a first London solo show in the RA's Upstairs Gallery, with a series until 1990. Later exhibitions included one-mans with John Martin of London, from 1997. Edward Seago was an inspiration for Burman's light-filled, high-skied East Anglian landscapes and seascapes.

Bill BURN 1964– Self-employed watercolour miniaturist and potter/ceramist, born in Guildford, Surrey, nephew of the artist David Maude-Roxby-Montalto di Fragnito. William Burn attended Epsom School of Art and Design, 1982–5, whose varied career included a period on motorway maintenance/litter-picking for Hampshire County Council when "times were hard", 1987. Eventually abandoned pottery to concentrate on miniatures. Was a member of Sherborne Art Club, living nearby at Alweston, Dorset.

Gerald Maurice BURN 1859–1945 Painter and printmaker concerned with marine and architectural subjects. He was born in London, son of the architect and painter George Adam Burn. Studied at South Kensington, later studies taking place in Germany, Belgium and France. Often working on a large scale, Burn showed at RA, RBA, Walker Art Gallery in Liverpool and with Portsmouth and Hampshire Art Society. Travelled widely, eventually settling in 1907 in Amberley, Sussex, to use the studio of the watercolourist Rose Barton. National Maritime Museum, Science Museum and other public venues in Britain and abroad hold his work.

Hilary BURN 1946– Bird artist and illustrator, born in Macclesfield, Cheshire, who graduated in 1967 in zoology from Leeds University. She showed with Wildfowl Trust and Royal Society for the Protection of Birds, illustrating its *Book of British Birds*, 1982. Later books on which Burn worked included *Crows and Jays: An Identification Guide*, 1993, and *The Handbook of Bird Identification*, 1998. Was a member of SWLA from 1983 and lived at Huish Champflower, Somerset.

Rodney Joseph BURN 1899–1984 Figure and landscape painter, mainly in oil, and teacher. Born in London into a wealthy family, Burn went to Harrow School, then after a period in the Army during World War I he attended the Slade School under Henry Tonks, Walter Russell and Philip Wilson Steer. At the Slade he had a brilliant career, winning six major prizes between 1918–22, and he merited an article on him while still a student in the *Burlington Magazine*. Married the sculptor Margaret Sharwood-Smith. Held several teaching posts, at the Royal College of Art before and after World War II, at the City and Guilds School and at Camberwell School of Art. From 1931–4 he and the painter Robin Guthrie were appointed joint directors of painting and drawing at the Boston Museum School of Fine Arts, in America. Served in the Camouflage Directorate at Leamington Spa, 1940–5. Was Hon. Secretary of NEAC, 1946–62 and was elected RA, 1962. The Chantrey Bequest and Contemporary Art Society bought his work, which is in the Tate Gallery, British Museum print room and in galleries in Bristol and Brighton. Independent means enabled Burn to spend his later years sailing, in European travel, staying on the south coast of England near Chichester and working in his final studio, on the banks of the Thames at Chiswick. Retrospective Austin/Desmond Fine Art, 1989.

Geoffrey BURNAND 1912– Painter, theatrical designer and mural artist. After education at Imperial Service College, Windsor, Burnand studied art at Farnham School of Art, with Otway McCannell, 1929–31, and at the Royal Academy Schools, 1931–2, under Thomas Monnington. He was a Prix de Rome winner and attended the British

School in Rome, 1933–5. Exhibited RA, RBA, NEAC and throughout the West Country. Signed work with initials plus date. Completed a number of church commissions in the south of England and East Anglia. Lived at Bordon, Hampshire.

Robert BURNAND 1929– Watercolourist, printmaker, glass engraver and teacher, born in Malacca, Malaya. He studied at High Wycombe, Harrow and Brighton Colleges of Art, his teachers including the painter and illustrator Morgan Rendle. Became an associate of RE in 1968 and was a member of Somerset Society of Artists, living at North Petherton. Among books illustrated was Rider Haggard's novel *She*.

Edith BURNET: *see* **Edith Burnet HUGHES**

Henny BURNETT 1962– Artist who graduated with honours from Edinburgh College of Art, 1982–5, staying on for an extra year there, 1985–6. Exhibitions included The Blenheim Gallery, 1987; Brewhouse Theatre and Arts Centre, Taunton, 1988, the year Burnett gained an Andrew grant Travel Scholarship to New York; and East End Open Studios, at Carpenter's Road, 1989.

James Walton BURNETT 1874– Watercolourist, especially of architectural and marine subjects; he retired as a marine architect shortly before World War II, and worked for some time for the shipbuilders Cammell Laird at Birkenhead, Cheshire. Studied at Birkenhead School of Art, 1889–92, then at Liverpool School of Art in 1900 and again in 1907–8. Liver Sketching Club member. He showed at the public galleries in Liverpool, Manchester and Southport, RCamA and had a one-man show at Williamson Art Gallery and Museum, Birkenhead, which holds his work. Lived in Bebington, Cheshire.

Rosamond BURNETT 1904–1998 Painter, printmaker, teacher, sculptor and potter noted for her striking figurative images in strong colours. She was born in London and from the 1920s attended Heatherley's School of Fine Art, the Slade School of Fine Art for life drawing, studying pottery at Farnham Art School, 1951–60. Until marriage, she used her maiden name Rosamond Selby-Hall. Until that time, 1930, she had a studio in Kensington; she also taught at Brunswick Preparatory School, with Anthony Whishaw one of her pupils; and ran an hotel in Sussex, 1946–51. Burnett was a member of Gainsborough's House Art Society and of the Bucks Pottery and Sculpture Society. She showed at the Redfern Gallery, Gainsborough's House in Sudbury (also exhibiting solo in the town) and in Amersham, latterly living in Buckinghamshire. Turner and Hogarth were favourite artists and travels in Yugoslavia influenced her work. This included portraits, bird sculptures in later years and church commissions for such subjects as Stations of the Cross. Burnett's daughter was the artist Zan Stevenson.

Christopher Anthony BURNHAM 1956– Painter and printmaker, born in London. After East Ham Grammar School he studied at Cardiff College of Art with Ian Grainger. Showed Chapter Arts Centre in Cardiff, where he lived at Roath, and elsewhere.

David BURNHAM 1940– Artist, craftsman and teacher working in a variety of media. Initially Burnham trained as a bookbinder, then studied design under Edgar Mansfield at London School of Printing and Graphic Art. In 1960 he began painting and experimenting with sculpture, in 1968 moving on to pottery and ceramic sculpture. Taught pottery for some time at Eltham Adult Education Institute. His exhibitions included Ewan Phillips Gallery, 1965–7; Tudor Barn Gallery, Eltham, 1974; Blackheath Gallery from 1975; and Woodlands Art Gallery, 1977. In 1964 British Drug Houses commissioned a bronze from Burnham. Lived in London.

Alexander Sillars BURNS 1911–1987 Painter and draughtsman, born in Newmilns, Ayrshire. He did diploma and post-diploma studies at Gray's School of Art, Aberdeen, followed by a travelling scholarship. Additional studies included a short time at Slade School of Fine Art, for drawing, and in France. He won the Keith Prize in the RSA competition in 1934. Showed in a variety of exhibitions and was a member of SSA. Aberdeen Art Gallery and Newport Art Gallery hold his work. Lived in Aberdeen.

Brendan Stuart BURNS 1963– Painter and teacher, born in Nakuru, Kenya, whose output included landscape work with strong abstraction. He studied foundation then gained a first-class degree in fine art from Cardiff Faculty of Art and Design, 1981–5, then did postgraduate painting at Slade School of Fine Art, 1985–7. Awards and prizes included Welsh Arts Council travel scholarships, 1989 and 1992; Gold Medals in Fine Art, National Eisteddfod of Wales, Llanelwedd, 1993, and Bro Ogwr, 1998; and The Friedrich Könekamp Award for Painting, 1997. In 1991, Burns was artist-in-residence, Llanfrechfa Grange Mental Health Unit, Cwmbran, he held several part-time lectureships and was full-time lecturer on the foundation course at Glamorgan Centre of Art and Design Technology from 1994. As well as participating in numerous group shows, solo exhibitions included Y Tabernacl, Machynlleth, and National Museum of Wales, Cardiff, both 1999, and Newport Museum and Art Gallery, 2002. Gordon Hepworth Fine Art, Newton St Cyres, and West Wales Art Centre, Fishguard, which gave him a one-man show in 2003, represented him. Lived in Cardiff.

Charles BURNS 1961– Artist who graduated with honours from Wolverhampton Polytechnic, 1981–4, winning a Tim Turner Travelling Scholarship, 1983–4. Burns took part in The Wolverhampton Artists Group, Wolverhampton Art Gallery, 1985; The Waterfall, Merridale, Wolverhampton, 1986; Two Views, Wapping Sports Centre, 1987; and Easter Exhibition at Blackheath Gallery and East End Open Studios, at Carpenter's Road, both 1989.

Gerard M BURNS 1961– Representational painter, teacher and musician, whose work could have a narrative quality, as in his picture Interior of the Glasgow Art Club at The Caledonian Show III, The Contemporary Fine Art Gallery, Eton, 2001. Burns graduated with honours from Glasgow School of Art in drawing and painting, 1983. Began teaching in 1987, eventually at St Aloysius College, being made principal of art, 1990–9. Showed widely in mixed exhibitions, especially in Scotland, including RSA, Royal Glasgow Institute of the Fine Arts and Compass Gallery in Glasgow, and won a number of prizes. Solo shows included J D Kelly and Art Exposure Galleries, both in Glasgow; Green Gallery, Aberfoyle; and Veem Gallery, Philadelphia, America. Among Burns's many portraits were the Member of Parliament Brian Wilson, Minister for Industry & Education, Scotland, and Jake Scott, director of RSA Films in New York. Burns was a singer-songwriter and guitarist who played with various bands and created film soundtracks, including *Happy the Man* and *I know what you did last summer*.

Glynis R BURNS 1966– Painter, born in Belfast, Northern Ireland, who gained an honours degree in fine art from the University of Ulster, 1989, but who learned much from her father, the artist William Henry Burns. Her work featured people and combined many elements: love of colour and pattern, social interaction, dance, music, nature and the outdoors. Showed with RUA and other Northern Irish groups. With her mother and sister she held a show, Three of a Kind, at Ards Arts Centre, 1990, and they regularly exhibited at her own W H Burns Gallery, Donaghadee, County Down. The Eakin Gallery, Belfast, also showed her work.

Kitty BURNS 1925– Painter, notably of frescoes and murals, born in Edinburgh, whose full name was Katherine Burns McKeon. She studied at Edinburgh College of Art, 1946–50, where her teachers included William Gillies and Leonard Rosoman. She won a number of painting prizes, including a first prize at RSA, also showing in Scotland with SSA and Arts Council. In addition she showed widely internationally, including completing murals for the Hong Kong and Shanghai Bank in Paris and the Queen Elizabeth Stadium in Hong Kong. Lived for some years at Flayosc in the Var region of southern France.

Pamela BURNS 1938– Artist working in a range of media including oil, gouache and charcoal and photography, and teacher, born in London, although she moved to Worcestershire in 1945. Studied painting at Leicestershire College of Art, 1957–60; won a college bursary award and visited Italy, 1960; studied painting at Royal Academy Schools, and visited France, 1960–3. Further European travels were to include the Netherlands. Futher teaching included Ravensbourne College of Art and Design, Southend College of Art, London College of Furniture and St Martin's School of Art. Was a member of AIA. She showed there from 1965; at the Downs Gallery, Manchester, 1967; at Parkway Focus Gallery, 1975; and was in the Hayward Annual, at Hayward Gallery, 1978.

William BURNS 1921–1972 Painter, especially of landscapes, born in Newton Mearns, Renfrewshire. He studied at Glasgow School of Art, 1944–8, his teachers including Ian Fleming and David Donaldson. Showed widely in Scotland, was a member of RSW and had several solo exhibitions with Aitken Dott, Edinburgh. Is in RSA collection and in public collections in Paisley, Dundee and Glasgow. Lectured in art at Aberdeen College of Education and lived in Balmedie, Aberdeenshire. Sea Crane, held by Glasgow's Kelvingrove Art Gallery, is typical of Burns' almost childlike landscape- or seascape-cum-abstracts which have a strong-image quality.

William BURNS 1923– Painter and architect, full name Cecil William Burns, born in Sheffield, Yorkshire. He briefly attended Sheffield College of Art; qualified as an architect in 1956; then from 1962–88 ran his own practice alongside a burgeoning career as a painter. Burns appeared in mixed shows at RA, ROI and at Mall Galleries. He had solo shows at Mayfield Gallery, Sheffield, 1985–6, then began to show solo in London, later exhibitions including Medici Gallery, 1991–2. Burns was a fellow of RIBA and of Society of Architectural Illustrators. Lived in Sheffield.

William Henry BURNS 1924–1996 Self-taught painter, father of the artist Glynis R Burns, born in Belfast, Northern Ireland. Harry Burns developed a traditional landscape style based on fast, on-the-spot brushwork in weather that sometimes necessitated anchoring his easel with stones. He left school at 14, was apprenticed as a fitter with the Ulster Weaving Company and ended employment with Short's, the aircraft firm, in 1965 to fulfill his childhood ambition to be a professional painter. Initially a watercolourist Burns changed mainly to oils, depicting the Lagan Valley, glens near Belfast, Antrim Coast, Mourne Mountains, west of Ireland and especially Donegal. Elected RUA in 1947, and showed widely, being especially collected in America and Australia, sometimes painting to commission. The Eakin Gallery, Belfast, latterly showed his pictures.

Vivien BURNSIDE 1958– Artist in a wide range of media, teacher and administrator who after graduating in fine art at University of Ulster in Belfast, where she was based at the Queen Street Studios, returned for her master's degree, 1993–5. In between studies Burnside was an arts administrator and part-time tutor in Belfast; in 1992, with an Arts Council Bursary and Travel Award, studying Renaissance drawing in Florence. She was later artist-in-residence at Crescent Arts Centre, Belfast. Group shows included Irish Women Artists, Douglas Hyde Gallery, Dublin, 1987, and Relocating History, Fenderesky Gallery, Belfast, and tour, 1993. Solo exhibitions included Bluecoat Gallery, Liverpool, 1985.

James BURR 1926– Relief printer, teacher, writer and critic, born in Bedfordshire, who studied at Bromley School of Art, Slade School of Fine Art, and in Paris at Académie de la Grande Chaumière, Atelier 17 and L'École des Beaux-Arts. He won a Wilson Steer Medal for Painting in 1951 and a State French Scholarship, 1952. Was a founder-member of the Printmakers' Council of Great Britain and a member of the International Association of Art Critics. Became head of the art department at the City Literary Institute, 1961–88, was art critic for *Apollo Magazine*, 1961–91, and also wrote for *Printmaking Today*. Exhibitions included Roland, Browse & Delbanco, 1959; Zwemmer Gallery, 1965; Consort Gallery at Imperial College, 1970; Curwen Gallery, 1976; St John's Smith Square, 1987; and Burgh House, Hampstead, 1991. His work was in many public and corporate collections in Britain and abroad, including Leeds University; Walker Art Gallery in Liverpool; New York Public Library; University College; Cincinnati Museum of Fine Art; and London Business School. Lived in London.

Joan BURR 1934– Sculptor, painter and teacher, born and lived in London, who attended Chelmsford School of Art, 1950–4, and Camberwell School of Arts and Crafts, 1954–60. She taught at Camberwell, 1958-60; Beckenham School of Art, 1962–4; and from 1964 at Beckenham Arts Centre (later Bromley College). After studying Burr produced little work while bringing up her children, but started making constructions in 1968 and began to paint in 1970. She won second prize in the Open Air Sculpture show in Battersea Park, 1953, other mixed shows including Young Contemporaries, RBA Gallery, and Whitworth Art Gallery, Manchester, both 1954; Space from the Quadrangle, Woodlands Art Gallery, 1973; Space Open Studios, 1973-83; Cockpit Theatre Gallery, 1983; Lyric Theatre Gallery, 1984; Gallery 7 Greenwich, 1985–7; and Studio 92 Gallery, 1988–9. There was then another hiatus in her exhibiting. Shared a show at Greenwich Theatre Gallery, 1978, with another at Woodlands Art Gallery, 1983. Burr had works in private collections in Britain and abroad.

Victor BURR 1908–1993 Painter, born in London, who attended West Sussex School of Painting and Drawing under R O Dunlop. Showed at RA, NEAC, RP and in Sussex, where he lived for many years at Crawley.

Edward BURRA 1905–1976 Watercolourist, draughtsman and printmaker, born into prosperous circumstances in London. While still at school he developed anaemia and rheumatic fever which terminated early his formal education, but from 14 he was able to devote his energies to drawing. Studied at Chelsea School of Art, 1921–3, and Royal College of Art, 1923–4. Had his first solo show at Leicester Galleries, 1929. He was a member of Unit One in 1933 and showed with the English Surrealists later in the 1930s. Despite his poor health Burra travelled widely. Influences on his work, usually watercolour on a large scale in strong colour, were many: the negro dives of Harlem; the Spanish Civil War; English horror novels and books by older French and Spanish writers; and the work of artists such as Picasso, Wyndham Lewis and Dalí. They prompted an art concerned with the sinister, bizarre and picaresque. Also designed for the stage, including the Camargo Society's ballet *Rio Grande* and Sadler's Wells' *Miracle in the Gorbals*. Tate Gallery, which holds his work, gave him a retrospective in 1973, and there was a loan exhibition at the Olympia Fine Art and Antiques Fair, 2001. In 2003, James Hyman Fine Art showed Burra's stage and cabaret work. There was another show at Connaught Brown in 2004. Lived near Rye, Sussex.

Lorraine BURRELL 1963– Artist in a wide range of media who graduated from Liverpool Polytechnic in 1989. Her work gained considerable media attention and was included in many group exhibitions, including Old Museum, Belfast, 1991, and One Oxford Street and Flax Studios there, 1992, as well as Head Gallery in Dublin, 1994. Had solo exhibitions in Belfast, where she was based at the Queen Street Studios, at Crescent Arts Centre in 1992 and The Plaza, 1993.

Louie BURRELL 1873–1971 Miniaturist, portrait and landscape painter, born into a family of artists, father William Luker, mother Ada Margetts. They did not wish her to study painting and took her away from the South Kensington Art School, sending her to teach art in a local high school. By 1900 she had earned enough money to attend Herkomer's School, Bushey, where she was a star pupil, showing annually at the RA. Leaving Bushey in 1904 she moved to Cape Town, married Philip Burrell, but returned to England in 1907 for the birth of her daughter Philippa. Her husband having died Burrell resumed her career, becoming a leading miniaturist, painting members of the royal family, showing at Fine Art Society, Walker and other galleries. In 1912 she moved to Ottawa to restore her health from overwork, and embarked on a life of extensive travel, including visits to America, India and Canada again, eventually returning to England again, where she died in Barnet, Hertfordshire. Bushey Museum Trust held a major show in 1989 and acquired a selection of Burrell's work, as did the Victoria & Albert Museum and National Gallery of Canada, Ottawa. Her life is included in her daughter's autobiographical books *The Golden Thread*, *The Horses & the Charioteer* and *The Dance of the Opposites*.

Mark BURRELL 1957– Painter of allegories, fables and fictions fantasies, born and lived in Lowestoft, Suffolk, where in 1975–6 he did a foundation course at Lowestoft College, from 1991–4 engaging in adult education there. He was artist-in-residence, Oriel High School, Gorleston, and worked with children on a mural at the Seagull Theatre, Lowestoft. Took part in numerous mixed exhibitions, including Eastern Open at King's Lynn (Highly Commended, 1994), Norwich Twenty Group and RA Summer Exhibition. In 1991 Burrell was awarded both Anglia TV's Moving Art Prize and the Lucy Morison Memorial Prize in A View of the New at Royal Over-Seas League. Later solo shows included Chappel Galleries, Chappel, 1998–9.

Frederick BURRIDGE 1869–1945 Printmaker and teacher, born in London, studying under Frank Short at Royal College of Art. He was finally, from 1912–30, principal of the Central School of Arts and Crafts. He was elected RE in 1898 and was also a member of Art Workers' Guild, showing at RA, Walker Art Gallery in Liverpool and Royal Glasgow Institute of the Fine Arts. Before Burridge settled in London he taught for 15 years in Liverpool.

Peter BURRIDGE 1960– Jewellery designer, printmaker and teacher, born in Taunton, Somerset. He studied at Solihull College of Art, 1977–9, and Birmingham Polytechnic. Showed at RA Summer Exhibition, Zebra One Gallery, Barbican Centre and abroad. Lived in Solihull, West Midlands.

Helen BURROUGH: *see* **HELEN**

Thomas Hedley Bruce BURROUGH 1910–2000 Watercolourist, draughtsman and architect, who wrote and lectured on architecture at Bristol University. He was born in Newport, Monmouthshire, studied at Clifton College and then Royal West of England Academy school of architecture, 1928–32. Was married to the artist Helen Burrough. He became a member of RWA, which holds his work. Burrough's writings included *An Approach to Planning* and *Bristol Buildings*. Lived for many years at Frenchay, near Bristol.

Dorothy BURROUGHES fl. from c.1920–1963 Poster artist, printmaker and illustrator, born and lived in London. She studied at Slade School of Fine Art, Heatherley's School and in Germany, produced animal posters for London Underground, illustrated for magazines such as *Bystander* and *Illustrated London News* and for a string of her own children's books with animal themes. Was for a time a member of RBA, also showing with Fine Art Society and SWA. Victoria & Albert Museum holds her work.

James BURROUGHS 1961– Sculptor, born and worked in London, who lived in Bedford, 1963–81. Did a foundation course at Mander College there, 1981, then a bachelor's degree in fine art at Wimbledon School of Art, 1982–5, after which he set up a studio in Peckham. Exhibitions included Cannizaro Park, Wimbledon, from 1982; Spirit in the Mass, Wells Arts Centre, Norfolk, 1986; Leighton Buzzard Arts Centre, 1987; and Carving in Christchurch at Christchurch Park, Ipswich, 1988. In that year he had a solo show at 47 Gallery, Great Russell Street. Bedford County Council holds Burroughs' work.

Victor Hugh Seamark BURROUGHS 1900– Painter in oil and watercolour, born in London. Studied art at Camberwell School of Arts and Crafts, Southampton Row School of Design, Goldsmiths' College School of Art and at Reading University. Exhibited RA, RMS, RCamA and Paris Salon, where he won a silver medal in 1973. Lived near Reading, Berkshire.

Carey BURROWS 1968– Artist who trained at Chelsea School of Art, the Slade School of Fine Art, 1987–8, City and Guilds and London College of Printing. Burrows initially concentrated on sculpture, but soon found that she preferred the immediacy of painting. Using mixed media, she developed a fluid, spontaneous and colourful style. She applied silver leaf and paint with her hands and used a variety of pens and markers to create immediacy. Letters, dates, times, figures and text sometimes appeared. Burrows' children would also contribute to pictures which were a continuous narrative of the artist's life, as in her show The Meaning of Life, presented by MacLean Fine Art at Arndean Gallery, 2004.

David BURROWS 1965– Artist, curator and writer on art, born and lived in London, who gained his master's in fine art at Goldsmiths' College, 1992–4. He took part in numerous group exhibitions in Britain and abroad, later ones including It, Sali Gia, curated show, 1998; East Wing Collection Courtauld Institute, 1999; Funny, Andrew Mummery Gallery, 2000; Beck's Futures 2, ICA, 2001; and Nausea: Encounters with Ugliness, Djanogly Art Gallery, Nottingham, 2002. In that year he showed solo at f a projects and at Frederieke Taylor Gallery, New York, America. New Life, a "major new installation relating to growth and chaotic systems", was held at Chisenhale Gallery, 2004. Among publications written and reviewed for were *Art Monthly*, *Variant*, and *New Left Review*. Burrows was editor of *Who's Afraid of Red, White & Blue*, 1999, and was co-editor of *Making a Scene*, 2000. In 2004 Burrows' Snowy Landscape with Wreckage was at Wolverhampton Art Gallery.

Geoffrey BURROWS 1934– Figurative painter in oil and watercolour, born in St Faiths, Norfolk, the county where he settled at Spixworth. Burrows was self-taught and began serious painting in the late-1960s. He was a member of Norfolk and Norwich Art Circle and showed at RA Summer Exhibitions from 1980, also ROI, RBA, RSMA, RI, NEAC and Paris Salon. Atkinson Art Gallery in Southport and Norfolk County Council hold his work.

Kevin BURROWS 1954– Painter who studied at Southend School of Art, 1973–6, and Winchester School of Art, 1976–9. In 1981 gained financial support from Eastern Arts for the making of large works and was on Eastern Artists' Register, in 1983 being on Epping Forest District Museum Artists' Register. Mixed shows included Stowells Trophy at RA, 1979; Trends 80, Mall Galleries, 1980; Artists in Essex, Loughton School of Art, 1984; and in 1985 shared four-man exhibition at Woodlands Art Gallery. Had solo show at Towngate Theatre Gallery, Basildon, 1983.

Matthew BURROWS 1971– Painter and teacher, born in Clatterbridge, Wirral, Cheshire. Gained a first-class honours degree in fine art at University of Central England, Birmingham, 1990–3, then his master's in painting, under Paul Huxley and Peter Doig, Royal College of Art, 1993–5. Was senior lecturer, University of Huddersfield from 1997, having residencies at Gloucester Cathedral, 1999–00, and National Gallery, 2000–1. A solo exhibition based on Dante Alighieri's *The Divine Comedy* toured from Gloucester Cathedral, 2000–1. Other one-man exhibitions included Lamont Gallery, 2000. Group shows included Lannon Gallery, New York, America, 1994; Mona Bismarck Foundation, Paris, France, 1995; Beaux Arts, 1996; and Eagle Gallery, 2000 and 2003. In 2001, Burrows won second prize in The Hunting Art Prizes. Burrows claimed literature, history painting and especially the work of Giotto, Titian, Poussin, Goya, Manet, Jeff Wall and Anselm Kiefer as influences on his work, which "explored ideas of narrative and myth." RA, Gloucester City Art Gallery, Robert and Susan Summer and TI Group owned examples. Lived in east London.

Roy BURROWS 1922– Painter of landscapes and teacher, born in Crewe, Cheshire. He attended Nottingham University and studied art at St Peter's College, Peterborough, 1947–8, and at Nottingham College of Arts and Crafts, 1948–50. He taught at Cartref Melys School, in Conway, also teaching art summer schools at Coleg Harlech. Showed with RCamA and elsewhere in Wales and the provinces and one-man shows included Peterloo Gallery, Manchester. Stoke-on-Trent City Museum and Art Gallery holds his work. Lived in Colwyn Bay, Clwyd.

Donald BURT 1923– Artist in watercolour, gouache and clay, teacher and poet, born in Southampton, Hampshire. He studied at Exeter College of Art, 1940–2 and 1945–7, with William Ruscoe for ceramics, and at London University, 1947–8. Became ceramics senior lecturer at Stourbridge College of Art. "Form and texture in ceramics, composition and vigour in paintings and rhythm and humour in poetry" were criteria. Burt's work was featured in *Ceramic Review* and his poems were published by Arrival Press of Peterborough and the International Society of Poets. Group shows included London Artists at Shrewsbury School, 1968; Nesscliffe Gallery; Sidmouth Visual Arts; and Queen Elizabeth Hospital and the Design Centre in Birmingham. Had one-man shows at Butlin Gallery, Dillington House, Somerset; and Theatre on the Steps, Bridgnorth. Signed work with a D B monogram in a square. Lived at Sidmouth, Devon.

Lawrence BURT 1925– Sculptor and teacher, born in Leeds, Yorkshire. Between 1939–49 Burt worked as an industrial metal worker, apart from service in the Army in World War II, although he did sculpt in his spare time. From 1948–55 he studied part-time at Leeds College of Art, making assemblages, sculptures and reliefs, then he taught at Leeds, 1956–60. This was the first of a series of teaching posts throughout England, including art colleges in Leicester, Cardiff, Wolverhampton and Falmouth. He had his first one-man show at Drian Gallery in 1961, others following at Exe Gallery, Exeter, and Angela Flowers. Oriel Gallery, Cardiff, gave him a retrospective in 1980. Burt had a close connection with Cyprus, living and working there for a time, with two others opening the Pisces Art Gallery in Famagusta in 1972 and teaching at summer school there. Work held by Arts Council, WAC, Tate Gallery, Cyprus Cultural Office and Public Collection and other public galleries.

Robert BURT 1971– Painter, who gained an art and design diploma, with distinction, at Solihull College of Technology, 1988–90; first-class honours in fine art, painting, at Central St Martins College of Art, 1990–3; then a postgraduate higher diploma, with distinction, at Slade School of Fine Art, 1993–5. Showed widely in London, including Out of the Nineties, Mall Galleries, 1995; Studio 3, 1996; 12 Abstract Painters, Tom Blau Gallery, 1997; and Connaught Brown, 1998. E1 Gallery handled his work.

Rupert BURT 1970– Painter who between 1990–5 graduated with first-class honours from Central St Martins College of Art & Design and gained a fine art painting distinction at Slade School of Fine Art. He wrote of his work that it was "made by a complex process that is similar to watching a photograph develop.... The paintings are carefully constructed yet constantly appear to be on the cusp of emergence or dissolution." Group exhibitions included Raw Gallery in New York, Connaught Brown, and Blue Gallery, all 1998. Blue Gallery gave him a solo exhibition in that year. In 2002, Burt exhibited at The Hunting Art Prizes. Lived in London.

George Ray BURTENSHAW 1888– Painter who studied at Reigate Commercial School and Redhill Technical School, Surrey, some time with William Tatton Winter. Exhibited in Birmingham, widely in Surrey and lived in Reigate. Sometimes signed work Geo. Ray.

Alice Mary BURTON 1893– Painter and draughtsman, born in Nogent-sur-Oise, France, but was educated in England. She studied at the Byam Shaw and Vicat Cole School of Art and at the Regent Street Polytechnic School of Art, winning a series of medals. She was noted for her charcoal drawings and pictures of people and flowers and showed frequently at RA, 1929–68, also at RP and Paris Salon, where she gained an Hon. Mention. With the artists Elsie Gledstanes and Agnes Tatham she ran the Unique Studio for Children art school in London for some years. Regent Street Polytechnic bought decorative panels by her. Lived in London and latterly in Silverstone, Towcester, Northamptonshire.

Andrew BURTON 1961– Sculptor and draughtsman, born in Kent. He took a first-class honours degree in fine art at Newcastle University in 1983, gaining his master's degree there in 1986, when a British Academy Travelling Scholarship took him to India. Burton won a prize for sculpture in 1983 at the Tyne Tees Northern Open, in 1991 taking the McGrigor Donald Sculpture Prize. In 1990 he won commissions for three bronzes for Newcastle Business Park and Gateshead Garden Festival, then in 1991 commissions for Stevenage Museum. From the outset he was a busy exhibitor, including RA, the 1988 Manchester City Art Gallery Summer Exhibition and Pelter/Sands, Bristol, which gave him a solo show in 1991. Towers, ziggurats and elephants featured in the Bristol show, which revealed Burton's gift of mischievous wit. Lived in Newcastle upon Tyne, Tyne and Wear.

Charles BURTON 1929– Painter and teacher, born in Treherbert, Mid Glamorgan, Wales. He studied at Cardiff College of Art and the Royal College of Art. Went on to hold a number of teaching posts, including head of the department of art at Liverpool College of Art and head of the department of art and design at Glamorgan College of Education, in Barry. Had one-man shows there and at the Prospect Gallery, in London, group shows including SEA, SWG and WAC. He gained a gold medal at the 1954 Royal National Eisteddfod. Work is held by Cambridge University, WAC and Department of the Environment. Lived for a time at Southport, Lancashire, then retired to Penarth, South Glamorgan. There was a fifty-year retrospective at Brecknock Museum and Art Gallery, Brecon, 2000–1, and Martin Tinney Gallery, Cardiff, showed his paintings in 2005. He was married to the painter Rosemary Burton.

David BURTON 1883–1945 Watercolourist and pavement artist, born and died in London, one of five sons of a soldier, whose mezzotints of the Indian Mutiny inspired David to draw as a child, even though blind in his right eye from birth. After school worked for a printer and in Sheerness shipyards, served in King's Royal Rifles in World War I, joined the Great Western Railway, then while serving on the Underground was badly burned. He was "boiling some wax, when it exploded". This necessitated a long convalescence, when Burton took up painting. After being a gardener for a girls' school in Buckinghamshire, in the early 1920s became a pavement artist in the Hampstead area, based on Rosslyn Hill, although he was to work a number of pitches around London. The Depression reduced his takings to a few shillings a day, so that by the time he was discovered by Lucy Wertheim Burton was physically in poor shape. She gave him a show of 23 watercolours in 1938, believing that his brightly coloured pictures of stories from newspapers, animals and historical events were the best by a self-taught artist shown at the Wertheim Gallery. Unshaven and tieless, Burton had to be lent a suit for the private view. Wertheim showed Burton's work elsewhere, illustrated it in her memoir *Adventure in Art*, corresponded with him during World War II and sent him small gifts of money until his death, when he was living in the down-and-out Rowton House hostel in Camden Town. Burton continued as a pavement artist, lamenting that the best pitches were "going down in value", concrete had replaced Bath stone and "you can't get a good surface to crayon on." Duncan Campbell held an important show of watercolours from the Wertheim Collection in 2005.

Esmond BURTON 1885–1964 Sculptor-carver in wood and stone who, after attending Marlborough College, learned his trade from the decorative carver Laurence Turner. Like Turner, he was, in his case from 1919, elected to the Art Workers' Guild, was a member and president of the Master Carvers' Association and a member of the Vintners' Company, its master in 1948–9. Burton completed substantial works in London and the provinces, working with architects on a number of projects. Two examples in the capital from the 1950s indicate his mature style and versatility: his Africa-oriented stone frieze on the block west of the Shoe Lane underpass near Holborn Viaduct and the more traditional figures on the Broad Street and Cheapside fronts of New Change Buildings. Out of London, Burton's achievements included figures on the screen of Ripon Cathedral and the big stone eagle on the Royal Air Force memorial screen at Brookwood Cemetery.

Helena BURTON 1968– Painter whose work included pictures inspired by underwater photographs taken on holiday in the Caribbean and trips to the London Aquarium. She sought "to discover the essential character of things beneath their superficial appearances". Born in Sweden, she attended St Paul's Girls' School, 1981–7; read history of art at Warwick University, 1987–91; worked in art galleries and television, 1991–5; did a foundation course at Chelsea, 1995–6; then studied fine art at Kensington and Chelsea College, 1996–8. Group shows included The Leighton Open, Leighton House, from 1996; Quantum Contemporary Art, from 1998; and Will's Art Warehouse, from 1999. Solo exhibitions included Space Gallery, 1998. Lived in London.

Kenneth W BURTON 1946– Representational artist, born in Peterborough, whose interest in art began at school, prompting an initial career in design and engraving. After working in public service, in 1985 Burton chose to freelance and set out to record on the spot The Counties of Great Britain in watercolour. He also produced a series of British Motoring Classics, available in limited-edition prints. Amy Vanburgh of Burford, Oxfordshire, was among the dealers in Burton's work that sold widely in Britain and abroad, especially America.

Nancy Jane BURTON 1891–1972 Watercolourist, notably of animals and birds, and teacher, born in Insh, Inverness-shire. She studied at Glasgow School of Art, 1909–15, gaining her diploma in 1914. Taught at Callender and in 1934 visited India. From the mid-1920s she was a member of the Glasgow Society of Lady Artists. Won its Lauder Award, 1924–31–46–53. Burton was a prolific exhibitor at Royal Glasgow Institute of the Fine Arts, RSA and RSW of which she was a member from 1932, also showing at Walker Art Gallery in Liverpool. Lived in Aberfoyle, Perthshire, dying in Stirling.

Philip BURTON 1936– Bird artist, born in London, who graduated from University College, London, as a zoologist in 1958, gaining his doctorate 11 years later. Went on to work in natural history department of British Museum. A keen ornithologist, he showed with SWLA of which he was a member, and his illustrations appeared in a number of bird books. Ulster Museum, Belfast, holds his work. Lived in Berkhamsted, Hertfordshire.

Phyllis Marie BURTON 1913– Painter who studied at Cheltenham School of Art, under Seaton White, 1932–3, then at Reading University, under Anthony Betts, 1933–6. Exhibited SWA, RBA and Association of Sussex Artists. Lived at Hoddesdon, Hertfordshire.

Ralph Molyneux BURTON 1922– Sculptor in a variety of materials and teacher, brought up in Cheshire and educated at King's School, Macclesfield. Studied at Royal College of Art, 1947–50, where his tutors included John Skeaping and Frank Dobson. Taught for some years at the Adult Education Centre in Tunbridge Wells, Kent, and completed public commissioned work, mainly in the south of England. Lived in Ticehurst, Sussex.

Rosemary BURTON 1939– Artist, born in Cardiff, who trained at the Polytechnic of Wales, 1974–8. Over the years, she drew, painted and made collages depicting flowers, which became an important part of her work, her father having been a keen gardener. One result was a solo exhibition in 2003 at Oriel Washington in Penarth, South Glamorgan, where she lived. Mixed exhibitions included Martin Tinney Gallery, Cardiff, from 2001. She shared an exhibition at Y Bont Gallery, Treforest, in 1987, her solo exhibitions including Old Hall, Cowbridge, and Servinis, Cardiff, both 1989; Oriel Ci Melyn, Cardiff, 1999, and Café Bravo, Poncanna, Cardiff, 2000. Works by Burton, who was married to the painter Charles Burton, were included in Welsh Painters Past and Present, organised in 2005 by John Davies Fine Paintings at Upper Swell, Stow-on-the-Wold.

Rosemary BURTON 1951– Painter and draughtsman who studied at Slade School of Fine Art, 1972–8. Mixed exhibitions included Barry Barker Gallery and her Drawing of a Man, of 1976, was included in Arts Council tour Fragments Against Ruin, 1981–2, having been taken into their collection. Lived in London.

William Francis BURTON 1907–1995 Painter in oil, born in North Walsham, Norfolk, whose first wife was the artist Elizabeth Crampton-Gore, their daughter being the painter Georgina Saunders. Burton was mainly self-taught, although he had some lessons in the mid-1940s from his father-in-law William Gore. Travelled extensively through India, Singapore and Australia, where he exhibited as Angelo Perini. Turner, Seago, Montague Dawson and William Russell Flint influenced Burton's style. He was noted for his marine paintings and for views of East Anglia, where he lived much of his life, dying at Ramsey, Essex. Showed with RSMA, at Guildhall and elsewhere and had many paintings reproduced as prints; *Evening Gold* and *Eventide*, scenes at West Mersea, were among the most popular prints of the late 1960s.

Keith BURTONSHAW 1930– Painter of "traditional landscape and marine subjects, especially the Lake District", born and lived in Beckenham, Kent, who was self-taught and retired early after part-time painting to be a full-time artist. His full name was John William Keith Burtonshaw. He was a member of BWS, UA, NS and London Sketch Club and he showed at RSMA and RI, having solo exhibitions in Croydon.

Ernst BURWELL 1911– Painter and stage designer, full name William Ernst Burwell, born in Kingston-upon-Hull, Yorkshire. Studied at Hull and Brighton, Sussex, Colleges of Art. Showed at NEAC, RI, RA, in the northern provinces, including Hull's Ferens Art Gallery, and in Australia. Imperial War Museum holds his work. Lived at Hillingdon, Middlesex, and Eton in Buckinghamshire.

Adrian BURY 1891–1991 Artist and writer, born in London, his father being a sculptor and bronze-caster, his uncle the sculptor Alfred Gilbert. Bury's first job was as an office boy in a tobacco-pipe factory. Learned shorthand in the evenings and joined the Graphic Photo Union, then the *Bystander* where he became familiar with many artists and writers. Attended evening art school, then in 1914 began studies at the Académie Julian, Paris, and Atelier Colarossi. Rejected for Army service, in London began work as freelance writer and cartoonist, then joined the *Sunday Pictorial*. In early 1920s studied art at English School in Rome. Continued to travel widely throughout his life. Chelsea Arts Club stalwart. In 1947 Bury changed his name from Buhrer to Bury, under which he had written for many years. Published his autobiography, *Just a Moment, Time*, in 1967. Other books include volumes on Francis Towne, Reginald Eves and Alfred Gilbert. Exhibited RA, Leger Gallery and RWS, whose Club's annual volume he edited for a time. Lived in London.

Gaynor Elizabeth BURY 1889–1975 Painter of landscapes and interiors, born in London, who after a private education studied at the Royal Academy Schools, winning a Creswick Prize and Silver Medal. Lived for some years in Bournemouth, Dorset, where she was a member of the Arts Club. Exhibited at RA, ROI, RWA and Walker Art Gallery, Liverpool. Abbott and Holder also showed her work, which reflected her love of travel, notably in France and the Channel Islands.

Morley BURY 1919–1999 Painter in oil and teacher, born Bournemouth, Hampshire, and christened John Morley Bury. Grew up in Holdenhurst and "made up my mind to be an artist while I was still at the village school." After Bournemouth School he attended Bournemouth Municipal College Art, 1937–9, where his teacher Johnny Walker was a strong influence, then Reading University, 1939–40. Bury spent six years in the Army, with a tank regiment in the Western Desert, then as a prisoner of war in Italy and Germany, being freed by Russian troops and repatriated. After the war Bury returned to Reading University, where he met his wife, art historian Shirley Bury, also attending Regent Street Polytechnic and Goldsmiths' College. He also attended evening classes in textiles at Central School of Arts and Crafts and a course of lectures at the Courtauld Institute. He taught part-time at Emanuel School, Wandsworth, from 1948–58, then part-time at Hornsey College of Art until retirement in 1984. Mixed shows included NEAC, 1950; LG and *Daily Express* Young Artists, both 1954; Vision and Reality, Wakefield City Art Gallery, 1957; 3 Artists, South London Art Gallery, 1961; Centaur Gallery, 1970; and The Forgotten Fifties, Graves Art Gallery, Sheffield, and tour, 1984. Bury also showed with AIA, Hampstead Artists' Council, Heal's Mansard Gallery and Everyman Foyer, Hampstead, where he had a series of solo exhibitions from 1960. Public collections include Victoria & Albert Museum, Salford Art Gallery, Nuffield Foundation and various education committees, plus Cambridge University and corporate collections including Staveley Industries, Lintas and Rank Xerox. Tate Gallery archive holds Bury's self-portrait. Bury's interest in figure subjects in the 1950s changed to landscape in the 1960s, landscapes "not real but a collection of seen ideas. Gradually texture of the paint became more important." He wrote that "studies in the organisation of colour relationships and the optical qualities which create a sense of space" were important to him. Lived in London.

George BUSBY 1926–2005 Painter and draughtsman, born in Birmingham, full name Cecil George Busby. He attended evening classes at Birmingham College of Art, teachers including Bernard Fleetwood-Walker and William Eggison. Busby worked as a designer/illustrator in the display business for many years, taking up watercolour in 1969 and becoming a freelance artist in 1978. He was a member of the Chartered Society of Designers, RBSA and Guild of Railway Artists. Busby was especially interested in buildings, canals, railways and industrial archaeology in his work, which was shown at Mall Galleries, Ombersley Galleries and Westcliffe Gallery, Norfolk. He shared a show at Edwin Pollard Gallery, Wimbledon, having solo exhibitions at Tegfryn Gallery, Menai; Heathrow Airport; and Solihull Library. National Library of Wales, Aberystwyth, holds his work. Lived in Solihull, West Midlands.

John BUSBY 1928– Painter, sculptor, designer and teacher, born in Bradford. He studied at Leeds and Edinburgh Colleges of Art, being awarded a postgraduate period of study and a Major Travelling Scholarship. From 1956 he was on the staff of Edinburgh College of Art. In 1978 he was artist-in-residence in Orkney. For almost 20 years from 1958 Busby was actively involved in the 57 Gallery in Edinburgh. Busby was a founder-member of the SWLA with a special interest in birds. Ornithology took him on trips to Jordan and the Indian Ocean and he visited Shetland to illustrate Hugh Miles' book *Track of the Wild Otter*. He was the author of *The Living Birds of Eric Ennion* and *Birds in Mallorca*. Busby designed a big tapestry for Edinburgh Tapestry Company and made carvings for St Martin's Church, Bradford. He was president of SSA, 1973–6, and was elected RSW in 1982. Exhibited at Pier Arts Centre, Stromness; Darlington Arts Centre; Peter Potter Gallery, Haddington; Compass Gallery, Glasgow, and abroad. Scottish Arts Council, Oxford University and many provincial galleries hold his work. Lived at Ormiston, East Lothian, Scotland.

G Felicity BUSH 1913– Painter and modeller, born in St Helens, Lancashire. She studied at Liverpool School of Art under Will Penn, 1929–34, then at Royal College of Art, 1934–8, with Gilbert Spencer. Exhibited at RA and in the provinces. Lived in London.

Harry BUSH 1883–1957 Painter of landscapes, figures and townscapes, born in Brighton, Sussex, married to the artist Noel Laura Nisbet. He studied at Regent Street Polytechnic School of Art and elsewhere in London, where he lived. Sometimes signing his work H B, he showed with ROI of which he was a member, RA, RWA, RSA and Paris Salon. Work is held by British and Australian galleries. In 1985 Oscar and Peter Johnson had an exhibition.

Reginald Edgar James BUSH 1869–1956 Painter, draughtsman, printmaker and teacher, born in Cardiff, Wales. He was married to the watercolourist Flora Bush, his father James Bush having been head of Cardiff School of Science and Art. Reginald studied there and at Royal College of Art. He went on to teach, being principal of Bristol Municipal School of Art for about 40 years from 1895. Exhibited RA, RWA, RE extensively, Walker Art Gallery, Liverpool, Paris Salon and elsewhere overseas. Bristol and Cardiff bought prints by him. Lived for many years in Bristol, and in London.

Chris BUSHE 1958– Artist who studied at Gray's School of Art in Aberdeen. His paintings were influenced by the rich colours and light of the Mediterranean, with a strong abstract element, as in Golden Evening, included in Panter & Hall's show Artists of Fame & Promise in 2002. In that year the gallery gave Bushe a solo exhibition, with another, Aegean Journey, in 2003. Was a member of RSW. Murray International Metals, Premier Property Group and Scottish Life held examples.

Fred BUSHE 1931– Sculptor and teacher, born in Coatbridge, Lanarkshire. He studied at Glasgow School of Art, 1949–53, and University of Birmingham's School of Art Education, 1966–7. Fred Bushe lectured in sculpture at Liverpool College of Education, 1962–9, and Aberdeen College of Education, 1969–79, when he became a full-time artist. He played a big part in widening interest in sculpture in Scotland, establishing the Scottish Sculpture Workshop in 1979 and the Scottish Sculpture Biennale Exhibition from the early 1980s, besides promoting several other such gatherings. As well as taking part in important mixed shows in Britain and abroad, Bushe had solo exhibitions: at 57 Gallery, Edinburgh, in 1962; Bluecoat Gallery, Liverpool, 1966; and more recently Talbot Rice Art Centre, Edinburgh, 1982. Elected RSA in 1986. Scottish Arts Council and Aberdeen Art Gallery are among public collections with his work. Lived in Lumsden, Aberdeenshire.

Robbie BUSHE 1964– Artist in mixed media and teacher whose work was tinged with a unique wit. Born in Aberdeen, where he became a lecturer at Gray's School of Art, Bushe completed his degree and postgraduate diploma in painting at Edinburgh College of Art, graduating in 1990. Quickly had a series of solo exhibitions, won two awards in RSA shows and was included in 1993 Thompson's Gallery exhibition Contemporary Art From Scotland. Edinburgh College of Art, Edinburgh City Council and RSA hold examples.

Lynn BUSHELL 1946– Artist whose work included stylised landscapes in a rich palette, born in Kent. Studied at Edinburgh University and Edinburgh College of Art. Mixed exhibitions included Roland, Browse & Delbanco; Scottish Gallery and Richard Demarco Gallery, Edinburgh; and a four-man show at Thackeray Gallery, 1977.

Sarah BUSHMAN 1961– Painter whose pictures mingled colourful shapes and symbols redolent of Australian aboriginal paintings, and who studied at Central School of Art. Group shows included Eye Gallery, Bristol, and Rooksmoor Gallery, Bath, from 1984; Galerie Sparts, Paris, France, and Mercury Gallery, from 1990; Rebecca Hossack Gallery, from 1991; and Wilson Stephens Fine Art, 1996. Had a series of solo shows, including Smiths Galleries, from 1991; Rebecca Hossack, from 1992; and Mary Kleinman Gallery, 1997.

Jane-Simone BUSSY 1906–1960 Painter whose work included delicate still lifes, daughter of the artist Simon Bussy and his wife Dorothy Strachey. She remained with her parents, spending the winter months in France at Roquebrune within sight of the Mediterranean, returning with them to England in the spring. Her work was included in the show Sixty Years On, at The Bloomsbury Workshop, in 1998. For this Angelica Garnett wrote a memoir of Janie Bussy, recalling her Anglo-French cultivation, slim and slightly curved figure, fragile health and croaky voice caused by chronic bronchitis, unerring taste in clothes and "lively and life enhancing nature."

Simon BUSSY 1870–1954 Painter and draughtsman, notably in pastel, who used a bright palette, had a strong decorative sense and completed many small pictures of animals and birds from observation in London Zoo. Bussy was born in Dôle, France, into a peasant family. A scholarship took him to Paris where in 1886 he entered École des Arts Décoratifs. Four years later moved to École des Beaux-Arts where he studied under Delaunay and Moreau. Whistler and Japanese prints were key influences. Had his first solo show at Galerie Durand-Ruel, Paris, in 1897, then went on to show widely in England and France. He married Dorothy Strachey in 1903 and settled in Roquebrune, in the south of France, spending frequent summers in Britain. Their daughter Jane-Simone Bussy also painted. Among his portraits were Lady Ottoline Morrell, in Tate Gallery collection. Died in London. In 1964 Sotheby's held two important sales of Bussy's pictures from the John Strachey collection. Dorothy Strachey was for many years a friend of the French writer André Gide, translating all his major works into English. *Selected Letters of André Gide and Dorothy Bussy*, edited by Richard Tedeschi, appeared in 1983, containing references to Simon and Jane-Simone.

Jane BUSTIN 1964– Artist noted for Minimalist, monochromatic panels with delicate surfaces which revealed nuances and changes when viewed over sustained periods and in altered atmospheric conditions. Bustin attended Hertfordshire College of Art, 1982–3; gained an honours degree at Portsmouth Polytechnic, 1983–6; attending Labotatorio per Affresco, Prato, Italy, 1990. She won a Pollock-Krasner Foundation Award, 1993, and a London Arts Board Award, 1996. Her many group shows included Aspex Gallery, 1986; Modern and Contemporary Painters, Christie's, 1991; Art Cologne, International Art Fair, 1993; The Abstract Landscape, Milton Gallery, 1995; ART*futures*, Contemporary Art Society, Royal Festival Hall, 1999; and New Prints, Flowers Graphics, 2000. Among her solo exhibitions were Atemwende (Breathturn), Eagle Gallery, 2000. Bustin's books included *Correspondences*, 1999, also *And a year ago, I commemorated a missed encounter*... in 2000. Victoria & Albert Museum's National Art Library, Chelsea College of Art & Design and several corporate collections hold examples.

Alice Caroline BUTLER 1909– Watercolour miniaturist, born in Kent, who studied at St Albans School of Art. Before she was married, in 1938, ran a studio-shop in Malmesbury, Wiltshire. She illustrated her husband Maurice H Bizley's book *Friendly Retreat*. Was a member of RMS and St Ives Society of Artists, specialising in wild flowers and cats. Lived in Perranporth, Cornwall.

Anthony BUTLER 1927– Painter and teacher, born in Liverpool, who studied at the local School of Art, 1944–5 and 1948–50, interrupted by Royal Air Force service. His teachers included Martin Bell, Alfred Wiffen and Allan Tankard. He taught at St Helens Art School, then, until retirement, as head of art at Birkenhead School. Showed at RA, Crane Gallery in Manchester and at the City Art Gallery there, at Agnew and in Northern Young Contemporaries. Butler's output was not large but of high quality, with a leaning towards nostalgic subjects and abstraction.

Walker Art Gallery in Liverpool and several other leading northern galleries hold his work. Was elected RCamA in 1960. Lived at West Kirby, Wirral, Merseyside.

Arthur Stanley George BUTLER 1888–1965 Architect, painter and writer who, after attending St Andrews University, studied at the Architectural Association. Keen European traveller, whose books included *The Substance of Architecture* and *Plain Impressions*. Was a member of Chelsea Arts Club. Exhibited RA and RI and lived in London. Manchester City Art Gallery holds his work.

Auriol BUTLER fl. from 1930s– Artist in oil, watercolour and pastel, notably of landscapes and portraits. These included HRH The Princess Royal. Butler started at Exeter School of Art as a child, then was at Byam Shaw School with Ernest Jackson, at Slade School of Fine Art with Randolph Schwabe and in Paris at Académie Julian, L'Académie de la Grande Chaumière and elsewhere. Was a member of Tavistock Group of Artists and Devon Art Society, also showing with LG, RBA and elsewhere. Lived in Cornwood, Devon.

G A BUTLER 1927– Painter who studied at Liverpool College of Art during late 1940s. In 1959 he was appointed head of art at Birkenhead School. From the early 1950s showed RA and with Crane Kalman Gallery in London, but was mainly represented in the north of England, showing at Liverpool Academy and with local societies. Was also a member of RCamA. Birkenhead, Liverpool and Manchester Corporations hold his work. Butler's tiled mosaic for the Churchill shopping precinct at Dudley, Worcestershire, was of a striking Cubist design.

George BUTLER 1904–1999 Watercolourist, noted for sensitive portrayals of young girls, often ballerinas, and the English and French landscape, born in Sheffield, Yorkshire, who attended the College of Art there, 1922–3, then Central School of Arts and Crafts, 1923–6. Joined the advertising agency J Walter Thompson in 1925, soon becoming head of art and a director, holding both posts until 1960. Butler married Kcenia Kotliaresvskaya in 1933 and they had two children. After living in London and Hertfordshire, after World War II they moved to Bakewell, Derbyshire. From 1960–80 lived partly in Provence, France, building a house there. For J Walter Thompson Butler carried out commissions in Berlin and New York; he pioneered new techniques such as overhead photography and prepared the agency for commercial television; and among talents chosen by him were David Hicks the interior designer, Alexander Mackendrick the film director and artist Bridget Riley. In World War II he helped equip and run a propaganda unit at Woburn Abbey. For Butler, good drawing and the right materials were of key importance. Butler became a member of NEAC, RBA and RWS. The Graves and Mappin Art Galleries in Sheffield hold examples. Arts Coritani, Swineshead, Lincolnshire, held a Butler retrospective in 2002 and continued to show his work. Butler's grandfather had acquired a farm at nearby Bicker Fen many years before which the artist continued to visit.

Henry BUTLER 1882–1967 Painter, muralist, printmaker, sculptor and teacher who studied at Liverpool School of Art, silver medallist for drawing, design and painting and King's Prizeman; and in Paris under Amédée Ozenfant. Having been head of the department of pictorial design at Derby School of Art and second master at Bristol School of Art, Butler – also known as Harry – was for many years on the staff of Bradford College of Art; in the 1938–9 prospectus, shortly before retirement, was listed as deputy and acting principal. After retirement to Bournemouth, Hampshire, Butler travelled to Australia, which proved an artistic stimulant. Several years before his death he married Nance, the widow of the artist Jasper Salwey, who was involved with Edward Maufe on the design of Guildford Cathedral. Butler was a prolific exhibitor at RBA of which he was a member, also showing in Liverpool, Bristol and Leeds. The British Museum owns two small abstract woodcuts by Butler and Bradford City Art Gallery some prints.

James BUTLER 1931– Sculptor and teacher, born in London, who studied at Maidstone School of Art, 1948–50, then St Martin's School of Art, 1950–2, followed by National Service, 1953–5, in Royal Corps of Signals. Taught for many years at City & Guilds of London Art School after working as a stone-carver for 10 years. Butler's work was figurative, especially the female figure. As a contrast, his first major commission was a twice-life-size portrait statue of President Jomo Kenyatta of Kenya, for Nairobi. Other commissions included more African statues; one from the Richard III Society for a memorial statue of the king at Castle Gardens, Leicester; portrait statue of Sir John Moore, at the barracks of that name, Winchester; John Wilkes, the political figure, in New Fetter Lane; and Skipping Girl, Harrow. Was elected RA in 1972, RWA in 1980 and a fellow of RBS in 1981, also a member of SPS. Lived at Radway, Warwickshire.

Jonathan BUTLER 1960– Stained glass artist, born in Surrey, who attended Reigate School of Art and Design for four years studying architectural decoration. After graduating in 1981 he worked independently as a designer/maker, believing that contemporary designs could be used in any context depending on the sensitivity of the designer. He was awarded the Worshipful Company of Glaziers Stevens Competition first prize in 1980, third prize in 1981 and the Sir Arthur Evans Travelling Scholarship in 1981. His commissions for stained glass include Our Lady's Church, Battersea, 1985; six windows for a Saudi Arabian palace, 1986; Fulham United Reformed Church, 1987; Lambeth Community Care Centre, 1988, and many other works in private homes and commercial properties. Worked in London.

Liz BUTLER 1948– Watercolourist, illustrator and teacher, born in Brampton, Cumberland, who attended Liverpool College of Art, 1966–70, gaining her master's degree from Royal College of Art, 1970–3. She later studied the history of garden design at Birkbeck College, and took part in The Art of the Garden exhibitions at venues throughout England. Teaching included Colchester School of Art, 1973–82, Camberwell College of Arts and Crafts, 1982–92, and elsewhere. In 1996, Butler was made an associate of RWS. From 1979 showed solo with Francis Kyle Gallery. Her clients included British Gas, *Times* Newspapers, Usborne Publishing, Penguin Books and The National Trust; The Earl of Harewood commissioned a series of paintings; and in 1983 the General Post Office sought designs for stamps commemorating British gardens. Butler's publications included *The Herb and Spice*

Book, 1979, and *The Seasons*, an exploration of twelve country walks, 1982. Government Art Collection and Abbot Hall Art Gallery, Kendal, hold examples. Lived in London.

Margaret BUTLER 1932– Painter and printmaker, born in Cleckheaton, Yorkshire. Studied at Dewsbury and Batley Technical and Art School and at Royal College of Art, where her teachers included Edward Ardizzone and Edwin La Dell. Showed Victoria & Albert Museum, Batley Art Gallery, elsewhere in north of England and at Yale University in America. Lived in Cleckheaton.

Paul BUTLER 1947– Painter, muralist and draughtsman, and teacher, born in Bristol. Butler studied there at the West of England College of Art, 1965–6, and at Kingston upon Thames College of Art, 1966–9. In the 1980s he worked on a number of London murals, including the Shepherd's Bush Peace Mural, near where he lived, and the Labour History Mural at the Trades Union Congress National Education Centre. Mixed exhibitions included Hunting/*Observer* Awards, 1992, and John Moores Liverpool Exhibition, 1995–6. Had a first solo show at Air Gallery, 1980, one at Montpelier Sandelson in 1996 indicating Butler's affinity with Frank Auerbach, Leon Kossoff and Jack Yeats in his handling of paint. The anonymous dramas of city life were featured. Arts Council, Harris Museum and Art Gallery in Preston, Rochdale Art Gallery, Museum of London, National Museum of Mineworkers and Edinburgh City Council hold examples. From 1988 Butler was head of painting at Surrey Institute of Art & Design, Farnham.

Perryn BUTLER 1953– Sculptor and teacher, born in Malta, whose output included stylised, figurative carvings notable for their tenderness and emotion in the handling of materials. She studied at Carmarthenshire College of Technology & Art. Butler's work was influenced by primitive and Celtic art and "the touch and sensuality of the stone". She taught at Stockpole Trust, near Pembroke; Noel Lavin Resource Centre at Farnham Road Hospital, Guildford; and privately. Group shows included Tregaron Sculpture Exhibition, Fishguard Arts Guild Exhibition and Workshop Wales Gallery, near Fishguard. Had a solo exhibition at Pembroke Library, 1992. The Dockside Gallery at Milford Haven and private collections hold examples. Lived at Haverfordwest, Pembrokeshire.

Reg BUTLER 1913–1981 Sculptor and teacher who trained as an architect. Born at Buntingford, Hertfordshire, Butler became an associate of RIBA in 1937, practising between 1936–50 as Cottrell Butler. Lectured for a time at the Architectural Association School, then worked as technical editor of *The Architect's Journal* in the late 1940s. In 1941–5 Butler had worked as a blacksmith in Sussex. He started to become a sculptor in 1947, in that year joining Henry Moore as an assistant. His first one-man show was at the Hanover Gallery, London, two years later. The early 1950s were years of sharp advance in Butler's career. In 1950 he began teaching at the Slade School and became Gregory Fellow at Leeds University, two years later being represented at the Venice Biennale. He became famous in 1953 when he won the grand prize in The Unknown Political Prisoner sculpture competition. Finished teaching at Slade 1980. Towards the end of his life he produced a series of drawings and sculptures concentrating on nude female figures, featured in his Tate Gallery retrospective 1983–4. There was a retrospective at Gimpel Fils, 2003. Butler's work is in numerous international public collections including Tate Gallery; British Museum; Hakone Open Air Museum, Japan; Peggy Guggenheim Collection; Museum of Modern Art New York; and the Smithsonian Institution, Washington. Lived in Berkhamsted, Hertfordshire.

Richard BUTLER 1921– Painter and designer, born in Essex, who studied at Salisbury School of Art. Showed RA, Arts Council, Walker's Galleries and elsewhere and lived for many years in Horsham, Sussex.

Stephen BUTLER 1954– Painter and collagist, born and lived in Nottingham, who gave up working as a computer programmer in 1978 to attend West Surrey College of Art and Design, Farnham, graduating with honours in fine art, 1979–82. He wrote that his paintings were "heavily influenced by Surrealism, while my collages bring together found objects both natural and man-made in a variety of configurations". Butler was a founder-member of Can Studios in Nottingham, 1988. Group shows included 12 Notts Artists, Palace of Culture, Poznan, Poland, 1992; Innovart, Leicester Museum and Gallery, 1993; and Fragments, Ikon Gallery, Birmingham, and tour, 1994. Had a solo show at Castle Museum and Gallery, 1991, and Yard Gallery, Wollaton Park, 1998, both in Nottingham. Butler's main works were the Earth Table series of collages, 1992; Lost Haven, painting, 1995; and Talisman, collage, 1997. His work appeared in A Pearce's *The Art and Craft of Collage*, 1997, and Nottingham Trent University and the Boots company hold examples. In 2004, Butler won 1st Prize in the Nottingham City Open, £1,000.

Vincent BUTLER 1933– Sculptor of figurative-naturalistic work, mainly in bronze, and teacher, born in Manchester. He studied at the Accademia di Belle Arti, Milan, with Marino Marini, and went on to be head of the sculpture school at University of Northern Nigeria, 1960–3, then lectured at Edinburgh College of Art, 1963–90. Was a member of RSA and Royal Glasgow Institute of the Fine Arts. Had solo shows at New Grafton Gallery; Birley Gallery in Manchester; Goosewell Gallery, Menston; the City Art Centre, Open Eye Gallery and Kingfisher Gallery, all in Edinburgh; plus Finkbeiner Galerie, Wolfsburg. Also participated in numerous group exhibitions. Scottish National Portrait Gallery, Edinburgh, holds his work. Lived in Edinburgh.

Louise BUTLER ADAMS 1970– Painter, born in Surrey, who studied foundation at Camberwell School of Arts and Crafts, 1989–90; gained an honours degree, Kent Institute of Art & Design, 1990–3; studying postgraduate at Royal Academy Schools, 1993–6. Awards included RTZ Scholarhip, 1993–6; Royal Academy Schools Prize, 1995 and 1996; and in 1996 the Cromwell Hospital Award. Group shows included RA Summer Exhibition from 1994, solo exhibitions Jill George Gallery, 2000. Unilever, Robert Hiscox Holdings, Gartmore Investment Management and Mezzanine Management hold examples.

Ann-Marie BUTLIN 1965– Painter using a rich palette who studied at Harrow College of Art and Loughborough College of Art & Design. She was a prizewinner at Loseby Gallery, Leicester, and won a 1st Prize, Nottingham Castle Museum, both Open Exhibitions in 1988. Also showed at

RA and SWA and at The Linda Blackstone Gallery, Pinner, where she had a solo exhibition in 1988. Leicester Education Authority bought her work in 1989.

Hamad BUTT 1962–1990 Installations artist, born in Lahore, Pakistan, who graduated from Goldsmiths' College in 1990. He made three installations: Transmission, at Milch Gallery, 1990; Familiars, at John Hansard Gallery, Southampton, 1992, which was remade two years later at Milch; and he exhibited in 1995 at Tate Gallery as part of the show Rites of Passage. Before he died he began to plan a publication about his work, which formed part of a posthumous book, with contributions by others, issued in 1996 – as *Familiars – Hamad Butt* – by the Institute of International Visual Arts with John Hansard Gallery.

Victorine BUTTBERG 1904– Painter, teacher and designer, born in Edinburgh, where she continued to live and show oils and watercolours. Aquatic scenes and harbours and flowers were favourite themes. For a number of years after leaving school Miss Buttberg drew for fashion advertising in the studio of the Edinburgh department store Jenner's, prompted by economic need. She then obtained a diploma in drawing and painting from Edinburgh College of Art and from 1934, having gained her art teacher's certificate at Moray House College of Education, Edinburgh, taught art in several schools until retirement. Was a member of SSA, with which she showed regularly, also with RSA.

Francis BUTTERFIELD 1905–1968 Mainly abstract painter and draughtsman, born in Bradford, Yorkshire, who attended evening classes with Henry Butler at the local School of Art while working in woolstapling. From 1929 he rebelled against this and began painting in earnest under considerable difficulty, but encouraged by collectors such as Sir Michael Sadler. Butterfield became a member of the Seven and Five Society and had solo shows with Zwemmer Gallery in 1934 and Leicester Galleries in 1937. He settled in London about 1937, spending some time in a studio on the Left Bank in Paris, then his career faded, and he was latterly art editor and wrote for a glossy magazine. Having suffered from heart trouble and cancer he died in Greenwich Hospital. Some of Butterfield's work had landscape allusions; sometimes he painted in hot glue, sprinkling this with sand or brickdust; cement and a flashlamp were also used. Public galleries in Leeds, Sheffield and Wakefield acquired Butterfield's pictures, as did the museum of the Raja of Aundh, India.

Lindsay P BUTTERFIELD 1869–1948 Notable designer of floral textiles, wallpapers and prints, and teacher, born in Lambeth, south London. After evening classes at Lambeth School of Art, 1887–8, Butterfield briefly studied architecture under his cousin Philip Johnstone, then was for three years at the National Art Training School in South Kensington. By the age of 25 he had established a career as a freelance designer and began teaching at several art schools. In 1916 Butterfield joined the design staff of the Central School of Arts and Crafts, remaining until 1934 and teaching in both the costume and textiles schools. His long-established reputation as a textile designer for major companies, such as Liberty, was enhanced when in 1922 he published *Floral Forms in Historic Design*. In 1930, Butterfield was a founder-member of what is now The Chartered Society of Designers, the world's first society of industrial designers. Butterfield died in Islington, north London.

Ron BUTTERFIELD 1920– Sculptor and designer in various materials, born and lived in Sheffield, who studied at the local College of Art full- or part-time, 1934–40. He was a member of Guild of Yorkshire Craftsmen and Society of Church Craftsmen and completed much ecclesiastic work. This included pieces in churches in Sheffield, Nuneaton, Melksham, Bradwell and abroad.

Sarah BUTTERFIELD 1953– Artist in oil and watercolour, born and lived in London. Her husband was the leading Conservative Member of Parliament, David Willetts. The Hon. Sarah Willetts studied painting at Ruskin School, Oxford, 1975–8, where her teachers included Jane Dowling. Also studied architecture at Edinburgh and Bristol Universities, qualified as an architect and practised until the mid-1980s, then chose to paint full-time. Beach, garden and sporting pictures were a strong feature of her work, often rich in sunlight. She was a member of NS and showed in groups at Agnew, Mall Galleries and Richmond Gallery. Solo shows included Judd Street Gallery, 1987, and Cadogan Contemporary, 1991. In 2004, Butterfield was included in Albemarle Gallery's big international Summer Show. By then she had completed numerous corporate and private commissions, including 12 large views of England for the British Airways pavilion departure lounge at Heathrow Airport and seven more for the same client at Gatwick Airport. Bank of America, Wimbledon Lawn Tennis Museum, Prudential Assurance and other corporate collections held examples. Her Albemarle Gallery solo exhibition Memory and Desire in 2005, with its nudes and Mediterranean scenes, emphasised her love of gestural brushstrokes and varied palette.

Elizabeth BUTTERWORTH 1949– Painter, draughtsman and printmaker, with a strong interest in natural history subjects depicted with delicacy and precision, born in Rochdale, Lancashire, and attended the School of Art there, 1966–8; Maidstone College of Art, 1968–71; and Royal College of Art, 1971–4. Group shows included British Drawing 1952–1972, Angela Flowers Gallery, 1973; English Realists – The Figurative Approach, Fischer Fine Art, 1976–83; 8 British Realists, Louis K Meisel, New York, 1981; and The Rainforest Art Exhibition, Natural History Museum, 1990. Had a solo show at Angela Flowers Gallery, 1975, later ones including Redfern Gallery, 1997. Butterworth's work is held in many international collections, including British Government Art Collection, Museum of Modern Art in New York and Victoria & Albert Museum.

John Malcolm BUTTERWORTH 1945– Painter, printmaker and teacher, born in Lancashire, who studied at Rochdale College of Art, 1961–3, Newport College of Art, 1965–6, then Cardiff College of Art, 1965–6, gaining a Royal Academy David Murray Scholarship in 1965. Went on to teach art at Southampton Institute of Higher Education. Showed at National Museum of Wales in Cardiff, Cleveland Drawing Biennale and abroad in mixed exhibitions; solo shows included University of Surrey and Southampton City Art Gallery. Surrey University and several education authorities hold his work. Lived in Winchester, Hampshire.

Jon BUTTERWORTH 1968– Painter whose work "reaches out to the ambitions of the later Abstract Expressionists", born in Oldham, Lancashire. He studied at Loughborough College of Art and Design in Leicestershire, where he lived, 1987–90. Contributed to East at Norwich Gallery, 1991.

Alfred BUXTON 1883–1963 Sculptor, born in London. Studied at City and Guilds of London Art School, Finsbury School of Art and Royal Academy Schools, under Hamo Thornycroft and Thomas Brock. Buxton won a gold medal and Travelling Scholarship for sculpture, which enabled him to study widely on the continent. Exhibited RA, Paris Salon, where he gained an Hon. Mention in 1924 for his statue Isabella, based on Keats' poem, and other venues. He completed a large volume of church and memorial carving. Lived in London.

Jennifer BUXTON 1937– Artist in various media, notably a miniaturist, born in London. She studied at Frobisher School of Animal Painting, 1948–53, then Byam Shaw School of Drawing and Painting, 1954–7, her teachers including Lucy Marguerite Frobisher and Bernard Dunstan. Was made a member of RMS in 1970, also showing widely in provinces and at Paris Salon. Lived in Ulverston, Cumbria.

Judy BUXTON 1961– Painter, draughtsman and teacher, born in Sydney, New South Wales, Australia, who moved to England in the early 1980s, where she eventually settled on the Lizard peninsula, Cornwall. "To create grandeur and evocation of space rather than figurative representation" was a key aim. Studied at Falmouth College of Art and Royal Academy Schools, 1987–90 and 1990–93, later teaching at Falmouth. Awards included the Richard Jack Interior and Portrait Awards and Henfield Drawing Award, all 1992; in 1993 the Creswick Landscape Prize, David Murray Travel Scholarship, RWS Award and the Painter-Stainers' postgraduate Cyril Sweet Award; winning the Painter-Stainers' 1st Prize, 1996. Buxton was a NatWest Art Prize finalist and prize winner, 1997. Group exhibitions included New Generation at Newlyn Orion, Cornwall, 1990; Salthouse Gallery, St Ives, 1994; and Royal Over-Seas League Open, 1996. Solo shows included The Oxford Gallery, Oxford, 1996, Messum's, 2000, and New Millennium Gallery, 2004. Buxton's husband was the artist Jeremy Annear, with whom she shared an exhibition at the Lynne Strover Gallery, Fen Ditton, in 2002. Cornwall County Council and several corporate collections hold examples.

Sophie BUXTON 1972– Artist who attended Gray's School of Art, Aberdeen, 1991–5, and the Royal Academy Schools, 1997–00. She appeared in the final year exhibition there, showing the etching Nightpiece No. 2. Buxton won an Artescape Fellowship, Lincoln, 1995–7, and the Worshipful Company of Painter-Stainers' Award, 1999. Exhibitions included Umbrellasquash: Bend in the river, Gainsborough, and Art at 100 Park Lane, both 1998. Lived in east London.

Donald BUYERS 1930– Painter and teacher who was born and lived in Aberdeen. He studied at Gray's School of Art there, 1948–51. Was a member of RSW, mixed exhibition appearances including Young Scottish Contemporaries, Arts Council, 1963–4; Glasgow Group Exhibition, 1975–80; BWS, 1987; and Open Eye Gallery, Edinburgh, Six East Coast Artists, 1990. Had a solo show at Gaumont Gallery, Aberdeen, 1954, later ones including University of Aberdeen, from 1970, and Torrance Gallery, Edinburgh, 1991. HRH The Duke of Edinburgh, Scottish Arts Council and many other Scottish public and private collections hold his work.

Edwin BYATT 1888–1948 Landscape and flower painter, especially in watercolour. His early career was spent working as a lithographer, then as a commercial artist with a printing company. Medici Society reproduced his work, and he exhibited RA, RI, ROI, Walker Art Gallery, Liverpool, and Paris Salon. Russell-Cotes Art Gallery and Museum in Bournemouth holds his work. Lived in Ewell, Surrey.

Gordon BYATT 1907– Painter and decorative artist, born in Cleethorpes, Lincolnshire. Exhibited at Foyles Gallery, Usher Art Gallery in Lincoln and elsewhere in provinces. Lived in Cleethorpes.

Leonard BYNG 1920–1974 Sculptor, born in London. After attending Harrow School and Oxford University Byng studied at the Ruskin School of Drawing and Fine Art, Oxford, 1939, under Albert Rutherston, and in 1944 at the Slade School of Fine Art with Randolph Schwabe. His sculpture has a classical simplicity, as shown in Eric Newton's monograph *British Sculpture 1944–1946*. Exhibited RA and was an associate RBS. Lived at various times in Sandwich, Kent, Paris and London.

Mark BYNON 1971– Artist, based in London, who graduated from Byam Shaw School of Art, gaining his master's degree at University of Northumbria. His exhibitions included Fresh Art at Business Design Centre, Islington; Located, The Globe Gallery, North Shields; and Sweetie, at The Levi Gallery. In 2001, he presented a new work, De-Sign, conceived especially for *The Economist* Building plaza, which consisted of two shimmering cubes.

Charles BYRD 1916– Painter, sculptor and kinetic artist working in a variety of materials, born in Pontypridd, Glamorgan. After an elementary education Byrd did a variety of jobs, ranging from photographer to aircraft fitter, becoming a full-time artist in 1950. From the early 1950s he participated in a wide range of group shows, including WAC, Compendium Gallery in Birmingham and Howard Roberts and Arlington Galleries, Cardiff. In the early 1970s he participated in Kinetic Art, in Glynn Vivian Art Gallery in Swansea, and in Edinburgh; and Wales and the Modern Movements, at University College of Wales, Aberystwyth. One-man shows included Chapter Arts Centre, Cardiff. Glamorgan, Merthyr and Gwent Education Authorities hold his work.

Andrea BYRNE 1962– Painter, fashion illustrator and lecturer who was born in Islington, north London, moving aged seven to Lancashire. After an art foundation course she gained a degree in fashion/textiles from John Moores University, Liverpool, 1981–4. While studying, she was a *19* magazine Young Designer of the Year finalist and was chosen for the Olympia Student Fashion stand. Byrne moved to London in 1986 and had an internationally successful career in fashion illustration, working for leading advertising agencies, magazines and design groups, clients including the Natural History Museum.

In 1988 she won *The Guardian* Illustration Award, representing the publication and illustrating for it during Japanese Fashion Week in Tokyo; in April 2000 her large nudes were featured in *Vogue*; and she completed commissions for Aquascutum's Spring 2003 press campaign, on view at the Regent Street store. Byrne also lectured in life drawing, fashion and printed textiles in London art schools. Latterly, she concentrated on painting, initially large nudes, then flowers. In 2004 she started studying for her master's degree at St Martin's while continuing with commissioned work. Byrne began exhibiting with Hicks Gallery, Wimbledon, in 2001, "our best-selling artist", having a large sell-out show there in 2002, another in 2003 and at the Affordable Art Fair in 2006. She also exhibited in New York.

John BYRNE 1940– Painter, designer and writer, born in Glasgow. He attended the School of Art there, 1958–61; Edinburgh College of Art, 1961–2; Glasgow School of Art, 1962–3; then a travelling scholarship took him to Italy in 1963–4. Among his many pursuits Byrne worked as a graphic artist for Scottish Television; did carpet design; and designed record sleeves and book-jackets. He had his first one-man show at Glasgow's Third Eye Centre in 1975, having become a full-time painter in 1968, signing his work Patrick. This early work was frequently of a whimsical Scottish nature, work under his own name being more mainstream. Byrne was strongly associated with Portal Gallery. Developed another career as a scriptwriter and playwright, writing the successful television series *Tutti Frutti* and *The Slab Boys Trilogy*. John Byrne @ 60 was held at Paisley Museum and Art Galleries, 2000, and New Works were shown at the Fine Art Society in 2004. Byrne was married to the actress Tilda Swinton and lived in a seaside town near Inverness, Scotland.

Nicholas BYRNE 1979– Painter, born in Oldham, Lancashire, who in 1998 was an Under 25 Winner & Choice Award, Laing Painting Prize, in that year starting studies at Manchester Metropolitan University, gaining the Manchester Foundation Drawing Prize, his work being collected by the University in 1999. In the same year, Byrne started studies at Slade School of Fine Art, until 2003. He showed with MAFA, winning the Edward C Oldham Trust Award, in 2000, being elected a MAFA member and a member of Saddleworth Group of Artists in 2001. Other group shows included All Night & All of the Day, The Cooper Union, New York, America, 2001, and The Singer & Friedlander/*Sunday Times* Watercolour Competition, 2002, where he won The Young Artist Award of £5,000. Had a solo exhibition at Saddleworth Art Gallery, 2000.

Alfons BYTAUTUS 1955– Artist and teacher, who gained his diploma at Edinburgh College of Art (drawing and painting), 1972–7, lecturing in printmaking there, 1978. From 1979 he was employed as a printmaking technician in the Edinburgh Printmakers' Workshop, studying at Atelier 17, Paris, 1983. He showed at Printmakers' Workshop Gallery, Edinburgh, 1981; Peacock Printmakers' Gallery and Forebank Gallery, in Dundee, both 1982; and was included in Scottish Print Open Three, 1983, organised by Dundee Printmakers' Workshop. Was made an associate of RSA and lived in Edinburgh.

Marjorie BYWATER 1905– Painter and teacher, born in Ealing, where she studied at the local School of Art, at the Royal College of Art, 1927–30, under Ernest Tristram and Reco Capey, then from 1935–6 at the Slade School of Fine Art with Vladimir Polunin. Exhibited RA, RWS, WIAC and Paris Salon. Active member of Questors Theatre Club, Ealing. Lived in London.

C

C: *see* **Christopher Herbert Henry CATLIN**

Anthea C: *see* **Anthea CHAPMAN**

Leonard CACKETT 1896–1963 Painter of landscapes and seascapes, in London. Studied Bolt Court School of Art and Hackney Institute. Exhibited RA, RWA, RSMA, PS, RWS and widely in the provinces. Was a member of St Ives Society of Artists, the Society of Sussex Painters and the West Sussex Arts Club. Folkestone Museum and Art Gallery holds his work. Lived at Ferring, Sussex.

Panayotis CACOYANNIS 1955– Artist whose work included mixed media constructions. Studied at Oxford University, Central School of Art and Design, Middlesex Polytechnic and Royal College of Art. Showed in mixed exhibitions at LG, Royal Over-Seas League and in 1991 Art in Boxes, at England & Co. In 1993 was a finalist in Bank of Cyprus Art Award, work shown at Gallery K. Had solo shows at Angela Flowers, Todd Gallery and Alexander Roussos Gallery.

Kathleen CADDICK 1937– Painter, designer and printmaker who studied at High Wycombe College of Art. She worked for several years as a graphic designer before starting to paint full-time in 1968. Began etching in 1976, combining a strong line with delicate colouring. Weathered buildings, bleached grasses, winter trees and snow were recurrent themes. Caddick showed extensively in the Britain, where Belgravia Contemporary Arts sold her work, in the Middle East and gained a large following in Germany. In 1977 a major show of her pictures toured Europe.

Stefhan CADDICK 1969– Photography-oriented artist and teacher who attended Cambridge College of Art and Design, 1988–9; University College of Wales, Aberystwyth, 1989–92; and University of Wales College, Newport, 1996–8, mastering in documentary photography. Caddick had wide work experience, including conservation contract worker for Countryside Council for Wales, 1992–3; hospital arts therapies assistant, 1993–5; Artists in Schools Project, Cardiff, 1996–7; and Mosaic Mural Project, Pontypridd, 1997. As a freelance, latterly his work included tutor and co-ordinator at the Video Workshop, Cardiff; visiting lecturer at University College of Wales, Newport; and director, Banquet Films. In 1998, Caddick produced cover images for Struan Sinclair's book *Strange Comforts*. Exhibitions included video installation Pleasure City, Chapter Arts Centre, Cardiff, 1998; Eat Me, Oriel Myrddin, Carmarthen, 1999; and Terra Infirma, site-specific exhibition, Hurst Castle, Hampshire, 2000. Lived in Cardiff.

Florence St John CADELL fl. from c.1900–1960 Landscape and figure painter who spent much time in Scotland, sister of the artist Agnes Morison Cadell. She travelled widely and showed at Alpine Club Gallery, RSA, Royal Glasgow Institute of the Fine Arts and elsewhere.

William CADENHEAD 1934– Painter, draughtsman and teacher, born in Aberdeen. He studied at Duncan of Jordanstone College of Art, Dundee, under Alberto Morrocco, 1951–5, later teaching there; in Italy and France, 1956; at Patrick Allan-Fraser School of Art, Hospitalfield, Arbroath; and under Peter Greenham at Royal Academy Schools, 1957–61, gaining the David Murray Scholarship in 1957. In 1969 was elected a professional member of SSA, also showing at RSA, RSW and Compass Gallery, Glasgow. Showed solo at Scottish Gallery, Edinburgh, from 1981, and Woodstock Gallery. Scottish Arts Council and members of the royal family owned his work. Lived at Muir of Lownie, Forfar, Angus.

Michael CADMAN 1920– Painter and teacher, born in Epsom, Surrey. Studied at Wimbledon School of Art, 1937 and 1940–1, under Gerald Cooper and Robert Buhler, then Royal College of Art, 1941–4, with Gilbert Spencer, Percy Horton and Robert Austin. He taught at Epsom School of Art from 1947–68/9. Cadman said that design, colour and atmosphere were most important in his work, notable features being architectural and hedgerow themes, water reflections and cattle compositions. Was a member of RI, 1970, also St Ives Society of Artists and some minor societies. Showed at ROI, RWS, RA, RBA and in many other group shows. His solo exhibitions included Canaletto Gallery, 1963–4, Whitehall Galleries, Cheam, 1967, and Southampton, 1982. Work also appeared in Royle's *Artists' Britain* calendars. Lived in Sherborne, Dorset.

John CAHILL 1954– Painter and gallery owner, born in Golborn, Lancashire. He studied at Wigan Technical College for foundation work, 1971–3, gained his honours degree in fine art at Portsmouth Polytechnic, 1973–6, then his master's degree in painting, 1977–80, at Royal College of Art. Among his awards were Jeffrey Archer Prize for best painting by an artist under 30, 1980; two Elizabeth Greenshields Foundation Sponsorships, 1980–2; and first prize at Royal Bath & West Show, 1987. In 1988 he opened The Harbour Gallery, Tenby, Dyfed. Mixed exhibitions included RA Summer Exhibition from 1982 and Wales Art Fair, Cardiff, 1993. Had a one-man show at Harris Museum & Art Gallery, Preston, 1978, and at Wyeside Arts Centre, Builth Wells, 1986. Cahill painted minutely detailed landscapes.

CAI XIAOLI 1956– Painter and teacher, born in Xian, central China, married to the artist Wang Jianan. She graduated in 1982 from the Chinese Painting Department of the Central Academy of Fine Art of China and went on to teach in the Academy. Became director of the Contemporary Fine Brush Painting Association. The artists worked individually and jointly and won prizes in the 6th National Art Exhibition of China and the Beijing Artists' Association in 1986. In 1988 they moved to Britain. They evolved a unique technique of watercolour painting based on traditional methods from the Shong dynasty for painting on silk. The two artists outside China showed widely, including Eastern Art Gallery, 1988; OneOneNine Gallery, 1989; RA and Royal Festival Hall on several occasions; in Hamburg, Tokyo and Hong Kong; and in 1992 they shared an exhibition at Gruzelier Modern and Contemporary Art. Collections include Central Academy of Fine Art, China; British Museum; and Victoria and Albert Museum.

CAI YUAN 1956– Painter, born in China, who took images from printed sources "to express my mixed feelings towards the contemporary art scene". After Nanjing Academy of Arts studied at Chelsea College of Art and Royal College of Art. Group shows including his work were: 2nd Biennale of European Art Schools, Antwerp, 1989; LG, Royal College of Art, 1990; Beardsmore Gallery, 1993; and Journeys West, University of Essex touring exhibition, 1995. Awards included J Andrew Lloyd Scholarship, 1991.

Judith CAIN 1944– Painter and teacher, born in York, who earned her national diploma in painting at Leeds College of Art, 1960–4, teachers including Harry Thubron and Tommy Watt, then gained her teacher's certificate at Goldsmiths' College of Art, 1965. For some years after leaving college Cain taught textile design and printmaking, lecturing part-time at many colleges including Canterbury, Colchester Technical, Jacob Kramer in Leeds and at the Polytechnic there. From 1985 was full-time painting co-ordinator at Leeds Metropolitan University's department of fine art. In 1995 she was Laing Regional Exhibition 1st Prize Winner; its National Exhibition major prizewinner; and was a prizewinner, Harewood Award, at Harewood Landscape Open. Later solo exhibitions included Thackeray Gallery and Dean Clough Galleries, Halifax, both 1996, and Adam Gallery, London and Bath, 2001. Leeds University and Leeds Metropolitan University both hold examples. Cain only rarely used brushes, her fluid, translucent pictures resulting from the use of devices such as rags and sponges. Images which nourished her work included early Roman glass, Middle Eastern carpets, Indian miniatures and flower and tree forms in early Italian pictures.

Osmund CAINE 1914–2004 Artist in oil, watercolour and stained glass and teacher, born Manchester, full name George Osmund Caine. Studied at Birmingham College of Art, 1930–7, and in Italy, 1938. Served in the Military Police during World War II. Gained an honours degree in medieval and modern history and studied singing at Guildhall School once he had begun teaching, singing lieder and choral works on the radio and in concerts. He taught, 1945-76, including principal lectureship in graphic design at Twickenham College of Technology. Caine was a forceful, unconventional teacher who developed a successful, broad-based vocational course embracing illustration, exhibition and graphic design, typography and photography. In 1966 he made two films: *The Ruskin Country*, and, with his wife Mary, *The Glastonbury Giants*. Her associated book, *The Glastonbury Zodiac: key to the mysteries of Britain*, appeared in 1978. Took part in numerous mixed exhibitions, including NEAC, RBSA and RA, and had many solo shows in Britain and France, later ones including Duncan Campbell Fine Art, 1986, Galerie Salammbo, Paris, 1987, and retrospective at Orleans House Gallery, Twickenham, 1998. English hill figures, British castles, monumental effigies, Kew Gardens and France were notable themes in his work. Caine completed 15 stained glass windows in Britain and abroad, including St Gabriel's Church, Cricklewood, and St Cuthbert's Church, Copnor. In the mid-1980s Caine gained a Durham University honours degree in medieval and modern history. Ministry of Transport and London University, City of Birmingham Art Gallery and Victoria & Albert Museum hold his work. Lived in Kingston upon Thames, Surrey.

Florence Blanche CAINS 1905– Painter and artist in patchwork and knitwear; teacher. She was born and lived in Bristol, studying at the School of Art there, 1922–7. For her art teacher's diploma she specialised in calligraphy and embroidery. Became head of art department at St George Grammar School, Bristol. Was a member of SWA and showed at RA, RI and RWA. From around 1960 her works "assumed abstract forms, influenced by wood grains and bones".

Gerald Albert CAINS 1932– Painter and teacher, born in Stubbington, Hampshire. He attended Southern College of Art, Portsmouth, 1949–53. After National Service in Egypt, gained art teacher's diploma, at Bournemouth, then an advanced diploma in art education at Cardiff, 1977. Notable among his teachers was John Elwyn. Taught art, 1957–85, mainly in Bristol, then painted full-time. Cains was early influenced by the social realism of Camden Town and LG painters, and was notable for subdued-colour townscapes. He was elected RWA in 1978, also being a member of Bath Society of Artists. His work was included in Football and the Fine Arts, Football Association show in 1953; also RA from 1964; ROI from 1983; and Brewhouse Open Art, Taunton, 1986. Had a solo show at Patricia Wells Gallery, Thornbury, 1976, also Harlequin Gallery, Bath, 1982, and Toll House Gallery, Clevedon, 2002. RWA holds his work; Walsall Education Authority holds Towards Temple Meads; and Longleat House's Wessex Collection The Miner in his Garden. Lived in Clandown, near Bath, Somerset.

Joyce W CAIRNS 1947– Painter and teacher, born at Haddington, East Lothian. She graduated at Gray's School of Art, Aberdeen, followed by a postgraduate year. Further studies at Royal College of Art earned her a master's degree and a fellowship course at Gloucester College of Art and Design, Cheltenham, followed. Joyce Cairns won a large number of prizes and awards, including the Hospitalfield Prize, 1969; RSA Student Prize, 1970; Carnegie Travelling Scholarship to America, 1971, and the English Speaking Union Scholarship there in 1972; and the RSA's Latimer Award in 1978 and the first prize in its Morrison Portrait Competition in 1989. She was elected RSW in 1979. From 1977 Cairns was a lecturer at Gray's School of Art while also teaching at Dundee and Glasgow Art Schools. In 1985 she was the first woman president of Aberdeen Artists. She took part in many group exhibitions, including RA and SSA, and after a solo show at Compass Gallery in 1980 others were at Perth Museum and Art Gallery in 1986, the 369 Gallery in Edinburgh in the same year and the Third Eye Centre, Glasgow, 1987. Her pictures drew on partly fictional and partly biographical material to create densely packed and compelling images.

Paul J CAIRNS 1971– Artist who worked in oils on shaped canvas and freestanding forms. He was born in Londonderry, Northern Ireland, did his foundation at Camberwell College of Art, 1995–6; graduated with honours in fine art, University of East London, 1996–9; and gained his master's there, 2000–2. Group shows included A Fresher View, The Millinery Works, 1997; Togetherness, artists-in-residence, St Christopher School Halls, Silversands, Barbados, 1999; Friday 13th, Beaconsfield, 2001; and Mythic Mushroom, Sheridan Russell Gallery, 2003. Among his solo exhibitions were Celt-O-Maniac, Platform Gallery, 2002, and Overwhelming Minority, Seven Seven Gallery, 2003. Lloyds TSB and Paintings in Hospitals hold examples. Lived in London.

CALBEAM: *see* **Frederick Harold BEAMISS**

Richard CALDICOTT 1962– Photography-based artist who graduated at Royal College of Art, 1981–4, then gained his master's and undertook research there, 1984–7 and 1988–92 respectively. Group exhibitions included Project Title, Chrome Factory, 1988; Nomadic Wall, video project, 45th Venice Biennale, 1993; A Glass of Water, Chelsea Arts Center, New York, America, 1996; and in 1999 he was one of three artists in Still, Houldsworth Fine Art, 1999–00, works based on plastic storage containers. Solo exhibitions included Hamiltons Gallery, 1999. Miller et Bertaux, in Paris, and Kunstmuseum, Bonn, hold examples.

Alexandra CALINESCU 1967– Artist whose work included abstract paintings such as At the Still Point of the Turning World, in Royal Over-Seas League Open, 1994. She was born in Cambridge, studying there at the Cambridgeshire College of Arts & Technology; City and Guilds of London Art School; and Royal Academy Schools. Won a series of awards, including Philip Connard Travel Award, 1988; Richard Ford Award for Travel, 1989; Landseer Scholarship, 1991; David Murray Travel Scholarship, 1991–2; and Vincent Harris Award. Took part in many group shows, including Janus Avivson Gallery, 1990; Bankside Gallery Open, 1991; LG Open, Barbican, 1993; and ASC Studios, 1994. Had a first solo exhibition, from Three Lines, at Stephen Lacey Gallery in 2003, a British Council-sponsored show which toured to Romania in 2004, starting at the National Museum of Modern Art, Bucharest. Calinescu was of Romanian descent, her grandfather, Armand Calinescu, being the country's prime minister until 1939.

Edward CALLAM 1904–1980 Painter in oil and watercolour of landscapes and architecture, black-and-white artist, designer and typographer. Born at Great Kimble, Buckinghamshire, he studied art under F F May. Exhibitions included the RA, Société des Artistes Français, RBA, ROI, the Russell-Cotes Art Gallery and Museum, Bournemouth, Foyles Gallery and the Brighton and Worthing Art Galleries, in Sussex. Was a member of the Society of Sussex Painters. Official purchases include Maidstone Corporation, Luton Art Gallery and Luton Corporation. *Sphere, Tatler, The Christian Science Monitor* and Penguin Books used his work. Lived at Bexhill, Sussex.

Jonathan CALLAN 1961– Artist, born in Manchester, who graduating with first-class honours from Goldsmiths' College, 1980–4, obtaining a higher diploma in fine art, sculpture, from Slade School of Fine Art, 1988–90. He was awarded a Boise Scholarship, 1990, and was Henry Moore Fellow in Sculpture at Winchester School of Art, 1993. Took part in group shows internationally and shared an exhibition with Georgie Hopton at firstsite, Colchester, 2003. Using seemingly destructive techniques, Callan transformed found objects. Obsessive cutting, scratching, folding and hole-punching of books and photographs were key elements of his method. Later solo exhibitions included Hales Gallery and Nicole Klagsbrun Gallery, New York, both 2000. Leeds Museums and Galleries hold works on paper by Callan. Lived in London.

Ruth CALLAND 1963– Artist and teacher, born in Scunthorpe, Lincolnshire, who attended Lincolnshire College of Art, 1981–2; gained a first-class degree in fine art from Coventry (Lanchester) Polytechnic, Coventry, 1982–5; then her master's in painting, Chelsea School of Art, 1986–7, with a Boise Travelling Scholarship in 1987. From 1987–8 was fellow in painting at Gloucestershire College of Art & Technology (Gloscat), Cheltenham, founding the Gloscat Women's Group, 1987. Held a number of visiting lectureships, including Wimbledon School of Art, Croydon and Barnet Colleges and Nene College in Northampton. Other features of her career included membership of Coventry Artists Group, 1985–6; freelance art consultancy, 1989–90; being a counsellor for Relate from 1992; and between 1994–6 being a member of the Stoke Newington Arts Project and the Newham Counselling Forum. Mixed shows included New Contemporaries, ICA and tour, 1986; Three Figurative Painters, Paton Gallery, 1987; New Art, Atrium Gallery, 1991; An English April, Lamont Gallery, 1992; and Unquiet Voices, which she also curated, at Doncaster Museum & Art Gallery, 1997. She had a solo exhibition there, 1998, having had one at Atlantis European, called Mother's Suite, 1995–6. Leicestershire Collection, Coventry (Lanchester) Polytechnic, British Gas and Slade School of Fine Art hold examples. Lived in London.

Elaine CALLEN fl. from early 1980s– Artist notable for depictions of natural forms in pastel, who lived and worked in Belfast, Northern Ireland, and was a founder-member of Queen Street Studios there. She graduated from the University of Ulster in 1981 and took part in many group shows in England, Scotland and Ireland including Works on Paper at Queen Street Studios, 1994. Her many solo shows included Lyric Theatre, 1989, and Harmony Hill Arts Centre, 1990, both Belfast.

Robert CALLENDER 1932– Artist working in a variety of materials to make realistic objects; painter, teacher and curator. He was born in Mottingham, Kent. Studied at South Shields Art School, 1948–9. After attending Edinburgh University, 1951–4, and the College of Art, 1954–9, he gained an Andrew Grant Scholarship which took him to the British School in Rome. First solo show at 57 Gallery, in Edinburgh, in 1963, becoming its director, 1966–9. By this time Callender was well established as a constructor of objects. They could be boats or part of boats, made from paper, card or balsa-wood and realistically painted.

Callender had a number of solo shows, later ones including Kirkcaldy Museum and Art Gallery, 1994, and Northlands Festival, invited artist, Helmsdale and Thurso, 1997. Was president, SSA, 1969–73, re-elected in 1976. Scottish Arts Council, Scottish National Gallery of Modern Art, Edinburgh, and many other collections hold examples. Lived in Kinghorn, Fife.

Simon CALLERY 1960– Painter, photographer and sculptor, born and lived in London, who studied at Berkshire College of Art and Design, 1979–80, and South Glamorgan Institute of Higher Education, 1980–3. He won Arts Council Young Artists Awards in 1983 and 1986, gained a Gold Medal at Welsh National Eisteddfod, 1986, and won a prize at John Moores Liverpool Exhibition, 1993–4. Solo exhibitions included Anderson O'Day, 1993, Christian Stein, Turin, 1995, Anthony Wilkinson Gallery, 1996, and Art Now 19, Tate Gallery, 1999, in which a group of large works developed the artist's awareness of luminosity, line, rhythm and scale. As part of his interest in other disciplines, in 1997 Callery worked alongside archaeologists from The Institute of Archaeology, Oxford, during excavation of an Iron Age hill fort, which resulted in his photographic survey The Segsbury Project. An associated exhibition was shown at The Officers' Mess, Dover Castle, in 2003. Saatchi Collection holds his work.

Roy CALNE 1930– Painter in all media whose works depicted transplant surgery, patients, nurses and medical colleagues "from the human point of view". Calne was born in Richmond, Surrey, was a medical graduate of Guy's Hospital, 1952; served as medical officer to a Gurkha Regiment in Hong Kong and Malaya, 1954–6; taught anatomy at Oxford University, 1957–8; trained in surgery at the Royal Free Hospital and started research on organ transplantation in 1959; lectured in surgery at St Mary's and Westminster Hospitals, 1961–5; in 1965 taking up the appointment as professor of surgery at Cambridge University. He became one of the most distinguished surgeons in the transplant field and was knighted in 1986. Calne was a Sunday painter, encouraged in art at school, whose later teachers included Francis Russell Flint and Ron Ranson. A decisive turn came with the arrival of the painter John Bellany at Addenbrooke's Hospital in 1988; this third teacher of Calne's convinced the surgeon of the therapeutic effect of art. Calne's exhibition The Gift of Life toured from the Barbican Centre in 1991, sales of pictures and catalogues supporting The University of Cambridge Children's Liver Fund. Calne also showed in Germany, Singapore and in Japan's Kyoto Museum in group exhibitions. Other solo shows included Richmond Gallery and Science Museum which holds his work, as do Wellcome Museum and Royal College of Surgeons. Lived in Cambridge.

Michael CALVER 1942– Painter, born in Farnborough, Kent, who did a pre-diploma course at St Martin's School of Art, 1958–9; foundation at East Ham College, 1967–8; graduated in fine art with honours from Winchester School of Art, 1968–71, winning the Tom Phillips Painting Prize, 1970; and obtained his teaching certificate at Brighton Polytechnic, 1971–2. In 1968, Calver was studio assistant to the artist David Leverett. Calver was a member of the Newlyn Society of Artists and a committee member of Art Haven, an artist-led initiative supported by Exeter City Council. Among solo shows were Black Swan Guild, Frome, 1999. Later group exhibitions included RWA, 1999; Beatrice Royal Contemporary Art, Eastleigh, and Affordable Art Fair, Battersea, both 2000; and Will's Art Warehouse Spring Show, 2001. At that time Calver's paintings had "evolved from a concern with the urban landscape and the dominant format of the screen image...with some of the abstract but immediately felt qualities of music." Lived in Tiverton, Devon.

Diana CALVERT 1941– Painter in oil of landscapes, interiors, still life and flowers who from 1959–62 studied at Byam Shaw School of Drawing and Painting under Charles Mahoney and Bernard Dunstan, in 1959 winning the Ablett Scholarship. Calvert first showed at the RA in 1963 and after that at various London and provincial galleries, the RP, RBA and NEAC, of which she became a member in 1979. She served on its committee, 1988–96, and again from 1999. Calvert won the John Brandler Prize at the NEAC in 1987 and 1991 and the Llewellyn Alexander Award at the 2001 Open Exhibition. She was represented in numerous private collections in Britain and abroad and lived in Walsham le Willows, Suffolk.

Gwendoline May CALVERT 1908– Sculptor in terracotta and painter, born in Swansea, who was a nurse by profession. She studied art at the Bolt Court School, Fleet Street, and showed at Guildhall in London and widely in the provinces, from 1978–88 being a member of Hesketh Hubbard Art Society. Burnley Hospital holds her work. Lived for some years at Brierfield, Lancashire.

Rosemary CAMDEN 1921–2004 Painter, notably of portraits, daughter of Brigadier Hanbury Pawle, a director of the Hertford brewery McMullen & Sons and a deputy lieutenant for Hertfordshire. She was educated at a private school in Hampshire and a finishing school in Switzerland. In 1941 she married Peter Townsend, a Royal Air Force flying ace who in 1944 was asked to become equerry to King George VI. This drew him and Rosie into court circles and led to a much-publicised romance between him and Princess Margaret which became public after several years. Townsend became equerry to Queen Elizabeth when in 1952 her father George VI died, by which time the group captain's marriage to Rosie had ended in the divorce courts. The ground was her adultery with John de Laszlo, son of the society portrait painter Philip de Laszlo. During her marriage to John, who worked in export and then as a stockbroker, Rosie developed as a painter, from which she made an income. Her second marriage was dissolved in 1977 and in the following year she married, as his third wife, the 5th Marquess Camden, becoming Rosemary Marchioness Camden. Townsend had been unable to marry Princess Margaret. He remarried, settled in France, lived by writing and in 1978 published his autobiography, *Time and Chance*.

David Young CAMERON 1865–1945 Painter, notably of rather dour Scottish mountain subjects, and printmaker, born in Glasgow. Studied at evening classes in the early 1880s at Glasgow School of Art, in 1885 joining Royal Institution, Edinburgh, as a full-time student. Cameron soon built up an impressive exhibiting record. He was made a member of RWS in 1906, RSA in 1918 and RA in 1920. In 1924 he was knighted and was made King's Painter and Limner in Scotland, 1933. During World War I the Canadian government commissioned him to paint war pictures in France. Cameron was a trustee of the Scottish National Galleries and of the Tate Gallery, which holds his work, 1921–7. He was a noted etcher, examples being featured in a number of books, including Sir Herbert Maxwell's *Story of the Tweed*, 1905. From 1898 Cameron lived in Kippen, Stirlingshire, whose church includes his work and that of other notable Scottish artists. His sister was the artist Katherine Cameron. He died in Perth. There were shows of Cameron's work at Ewan Mundy Fine Art, Glasgow, 2002 and 2004; at The Fleming Collection, 2003; and the National Gallery of Scotland, Edinburgh, 2004.

Emma CAMERON 1964– Painter and printmaker, born in Ross-shire, who attended Fortrose Academy, 1975–81. Did a foundation course in art and design at Camberwell School of Arts and Crafts, 1981–2; an honours degree in fine art (painting), at Central School of Art and Design, 1982–5; and a diploma in advanced printmaking at the Central, 1985–7; with a postgraduate certificate in education, University of East Anglia, 1990–1. Mixed shows included RA; RSA; Artefact, Bankside, Stephen Bartley, Boundary and October Galleries; Alba Fine Art; and Phoenix Gallery, Lavenham. In 1996 had a solo show at Chappel Galleries, Chappel. Her solo exhibition at North House Gallery, Manningtree, in 2003 revealed a substantial body of work subsequently produced. Cameron chose to "start a painting very impulsively, with sweeping areas of saturated colour. Later there is a still, reflective phase of contemplation as I try to allow the colours and brushstrokes to suggest the way ahead." Her paintings were about "fundamental, deeply human qualities such as vulnerability, beauty, ambivalence, awkwardness, grace, innocence, mischief."

Eric CAMERON 1935– Artist and teacher, born in Leicester, who eventually claimed dual British and Canadian citizenship. He studied painting at King's College, Newcastle upon Tyne, 1953–7, under Lawrence Gowing, Victor Pasmore and Richard Hamilton, gaining first-class honours; then the history of art at the Courtauld Institute, 1957–9, under Anthony Blunt. Cameron lectured at the University of Leeds, 1959–69. He moved to Canada in 1969 to become associate professor, department of fine art, University of Guelph, in Ontario; was from 1976 associate professor, from 1981 full professor, at Nova Scotia College of Art and Design, Halifax, until 1987; then was full professor, head of the art department, University of Calgary. Cameron gave many public lectures on his own work and that of other artists and was on numerous critical, curating, art gallery and academic committees, boards and juries. Among his awards was the prestigious Governor General's Award in the Visual and Media Arts, 2004. Cameron took part in many mixed exhibitions, especially in Britain and Canada, and held a series of one-man shows, later ones including the National Gallery, Ottawa, 1990, and in 1993 the Southern Alberta Art Gallery, Lethbridge, and the École Nationale de la Photographie, Arles, France. Although Cameron's work over the years employed a range of media, from drawing and painting to installation and video, he became known, from 1979, for his Thick Paintings, in which everyday objects were transformed with thousands of thin coats of gesso. He said that "they take their own form so completely that they take me by surprise continually."

Gordon Stewart CAMERON 1916–1994 Painter and teacher, born in Aberdeen. He was married to the painter Ellen Malcolm. After education at Robert Gordon's College in Aberdeen Cameron attended Gray's School of Art there, 1935–40, his teachers including D M Sutherland. He went on to teach at Duncan of Jordanstone College of Art, in Dundee. His work, which shows a fine knowledge of anatomy, is in several Scottish collections, including Aberdeen Art Gallery. Lived in Invergowrie, Perthshire.

Katherine CAMERON 1874–1965 Painter, printmaker and book illustrator. Born in Glasgow, sister of the artist D Y Cameron. Studied at Glasgow School of Art, 1898, under Fra Newbery, then at Atelier Colarossi, Paris. Exhibited flower paintings and landscapes prolifically in Britain and abroad, including RA, Royal Glasgow Institute of the Fine Arts, RSW, Walker's Galleries. The Tate Gallery, Victoria & Albert Museum, British Museum and Library of Congress, Washington, in America, hold her work. Contributed to *The Yellow Book* and illustrated a number of other titles, including James Aitken's *In a City Garden*, 1913, and Iolo Williams' *Where the Bee Sucks*, 1929; her husband, Arthur Kay, was more enthusiastic about this work than she was, for she preferred painting. Had a one-man show at the Annan Gallery, Glasgow, 1959. Lived in Edinburgh.

Moira CAMERON 1962– Artist born and lived in London who spent some time working in New York. She attended Ravensbourne College of Art, 1980–4, gaining a first-class honours degree, then won her master's degree at Chelsea College of Art, 1984–5. Group shows included Mall Galleries, 1984; Lisson Gallery, 1985; Patricia Knight Gallery, from 1987; LG from 1989; and Twining Gallery, New York, 1992. Solo exhibitions included Twining Gallery, 1991. Curwen Gallery also stocked her work.

Shirley CAMERON 1944– Sculptor, lecturer and events artist, born in Oxford. She studied at Sutton School of Art, 1959–62, then in the sculpture department of St Martin's School of Art, 1960–6. Had a period as a youth leader in the late 1960s. Lectured 1969–72 at Dyfed College of Art, then received an Arts Council grant for work with Roland Miller. In the early 1970s she took part in a variety of events in Britain and on the continent, including Railway Images, at Leicester Arts Festival; Swansea Valley (Land Art); Coventry Arts Festival; and Fanfare for Europe, Hull and Cardiff. One-man shows included University College, Swansea. Miller & Cameron were included in the big British Council 1976 exhibition English Art Today 1960–76, at Palazzo Reale, Milan Italy. There were then around 150 performance artists active in Britain.

Zoe CAMERON 1959– Painter, draughtsman and teacher who studied at Maidenhead College of Art & Design, 1975–7, then Gloucestershire College of Art & Design, Cheltenham, 1977–80, where she graduated with honours. From 1990 lectured part-time at Falmouth School of Art. From 1980 showed with Cheltenham Group at Cheltenham Art Gallery & Museum; Rooksmoor Gallery from 1981; Delahaye Gallery, Cirencester, 1985; and Stephen Bartley Gallery, 1991. Solo show at Rooksmoor Gallery, 1984, later one-man exhibitions including Salthouse Gallery, St Ives, Cornwall, 1990. In 1993 shared a show at Cadogan Contemporary. Her pictures attempted "to express a recognition of the human condition in all its extremes". Lived in Cornwall.

Florence CAMM 1874–1960 Stained glass artist who studied at Birmingham School of Art. She was in business under her father's name, Thomas William Camm, with her brothers Robert and Walter Herbert Camm. Exhibited extensively RA, Walker Art Gallery, Liverpool, RSA and abroad. Lived at Smethwick, Birmingham, and continued to work into her eighties, being referred to by her brother Walter as "our best man".

Robert CAMM 1878–1954 Stained glass artist who studied at Birmingham School of Art. He was in business under his father's name, Thomas William Camm, with his brother Walter Herbert and sister Florence. Exhibited RA and in Turin, Italy, where at the International Exhibition he won the only prize for stained glass. Lived at Smethwick, Birmingham.

Walter Herbert CAMM 1881–1967 Stained glass artist who studied at Birmingham and West Bromwich Schools of Art. His father had founded the family stained glass business about 1850, selling it later and starting afresh in 1885 not far away in Smethwick, Birmingham, where it remained. When Thomas William Camm died the business was taken over by Walter Herbert Camm, his brother Robert and sister Florence, who all worked in it to an advanced age. Camm exhibited extensively at RA, RSA, Walker Art Gallery in Liverpool and elsewhere. In 1911 the Camms won a medal in Turin for a window called Dante and Beatrice and their last big window was a Warwickshire Regiment memorial in Warwick Parish Church. Other work was done for Christchurch in New Zealand, for the collector J Pierpont Morgan in America, for a children's hospital in Kimberley, South Africa, as well as extensive windows in England. A room devoted to the family's works was created in the Staffordshire industrial museum at Shugborough Hall. Camm lived at Warley Woods, Oldbury.

Donald CAMMELL 1934–1996 Film director, screenwriter and portrait painter, son of the writer and poet Charles Richard Cammell. He began to paint when aged three, being judged a prodigy. Left Westminster School at 16, attended Byam Shaw School of Art, gained a scholarship to the Royal Academy Schools, then studied in Florence with Pietro Annigoni (his father's *Memoirs of Annigoni* appeared in 1956). Became a full-time portrait painter in the early 1950s, with a studio in Chelsea. Although he had success, including a society portrait of the year (the subject was Sheridan, Marquis of Dufferin and Ava, a page boy at the coronation of Queen Elizabeth II), Cammell decided to change course, in 1961 moving to Paris, but he failed to find a satisfactory new style. Exhibitions included a solo show at Gallery One, with another at Bertha Schaefer Gallery, New York, 1961. In Chelsea Cammell had met the Greek film actress Maria Andipa, whom he married, and in the 1960s films displaced art as his main preoccupation. His first screenplay, *Duffy*, was produced in England in 1968. In 1970, *Performance*, which Cammell wrote and co-directed with Nicholas Roeg, caused a stir, with its atmosphere of surreal decadence, the cast including James Fox and Mick Jagger. Cammell's first Hollywood film was *Demon Seed*, 1977, starring Julie Christie. *White of the Eye*, 1987, and *Wild Side*, 1995, were also directed by Cammell, who was latterly based in Los Angeles. His second wife, China Kong, who worked with Cammell on many of his screenplays, was introduced to the former painter by his friend Marlon Brando. Cammell killed himself with a shot in the head.

Jane CAMP 1932– Self-taught painter in oil and gouache, born in Clapham, south London. She began painting in 1981 and took her subjects from her immediate environment, people in their daily occupations, her garden, animals and children; she also enjoyed creating dramatic sporting pictures. Lived near Dorking, Surrey, being a member of its Group of Artists, other mixed shows including RI and SWA, and Medici Society published cards of her pictures. Had a series of solo shows at The Westcott Gallery, Westcott.

Jeffery CAMP 1923– Artist and teacher, born in Oulton Broad, Suffolk. He studied first at Lowestoft and then at Ipswich School of Art, then from 1941–4 was at Edinburgh College of Art under William Gillies and John Maxwell. He returned to Suffolk at the end of 1944 and won an Andrew Grant Travelling Scholarship in 1945 and a David Murray Bursary for landscape painting in 1946. His first solo show was with Beaux Arts Gallery in 1959. He was married to the painter Laetitia Yhap for a while from 1964, living in Hastings, although he later moved to London. Camp taught at Slade School Fine Art, 1963–88, and was elected RA in 1984. In addition to several shows at Beaux Arts he had major solo exhibitions at New Art Centre, 1968; a retrospective at South London Art Gallery in 1973; Serpentine Gallery, 1978; several at Nigel Greenwood Gallery from 1986; RA, 1988; Browse & Darby Gallery, 2001; and a small retrospective of paintings, 1970–02, at Art Space Gallery, 2002. Camp's pictures were included in several major international touring exhibitions in the 1980s. In 1981 he published the book *Draw*, which was frequently reprinted. Art Council holds several examples of Camp's work, which was full of movement and colour and often featured south of England coastal scenes, as well as landscapes with figures.

Sokari CAMP: *see* **Sokari DOUGLAS CAMP**

Estella CAMPAVIAS 1918–1990 Self-taught British artist of Spanish extraction, brought up in Turkey. She began her career in 1955 as a ceramist, aiming to produce works of art rather than craft pieces. After a period of reflection and experiment she turned to sculpture, producing flowing, smooth figurative sculptures with strong abstract tendencies that sought to reveal the subject's inner character. Showed in France, Italy and the United Kingdom, notably with Wolseley Fine Arts, which included her in Modern and Contemporary Sculpture, 2004.

Alex CAMPBELL 1932– Artist in acrylic and gouache, and teacher, born in Edinburgh, where he lived. He studied at Edinburgh College of Art, where he was on the staff from 1960, studying under William Gillies and Robin Philipson, and obtaining his master's degree with honours, 1951–8; gained an Andrew Grant Travelling Scholarship to France, did a postgraduate scholarship and then obtained an Andrew Grant Travelling Scholarship to Spain, Morocco and Italy. Among a series of awards was the RSA Guthrie Award, 1963; May Marshall Brown Awards, 1979 and 1986; Grampian Region Award, 1980; and Alexander Graham Munro Award, 1991. Campbell became a member of SSA, 1966; SWLA, 1967; RSW, 1976; and RSA, 1981, being its librarian in 1982. Campbell took part in many group shows, especially in Scotland, from 1962. Had a string of one-man exhibitions, later ones including Kingfisher Gallery, Edinburgh, 1990; Lamp of Lothian Collegiate Trust, Haddington, 1991; and Loomshop Gallery, Lower Largo, 1993. Among many public collections holding examples were Edinburgh City Art Centre, Government Art Collection, Keighley Art Gallery, RSA and Scottish Arts Council.

Andrew CAMPBELL 1969– Trained as a sculptor, Campbell's "approach to images and materials was very much a making process. Objects are selected rather than found, the choice being made by association with its history or a personal response." He did a foundation course at Cambridge College of Arts and Technology, 1987–8; attended Falmouth School of Art for fine art honours degree studies, in 1988; transferred, graduating at Norwich School of Art, 1989–91; then did a postgraduate diploma in sculpture at Edinburgh College of Art, 1991–2. From 1993–4, Campbell was part-time studio assistant to the sculptor Richard Wentworth; in 1995 had a residency in the studio of Guiseppe Penone, in Turin, Italy; in 1997 being involved in Iron Pour, UK, Suffolk. Campbell gained the SSA's Munro Award for Sculpture at RSA, 1992. Mixed shows included Ten Graduates, King of Hearts Gallery, Norwich, 1991; Kettle's Yard Open, Kettle's Yard Gallery, Cambridge, 1995; and Elm Hill Contemporary Art, Norwich, 1998. In 1996 he shared a sculpture show with Louise Richardson, his wife, at Aldeburgh Cinema Gallery. Solo exhibitions included Constellation, Robert Sandelson, 1999.

Catriona CAMPBELL 1940– Painter, mainly in oil of figurative work, born in Dollar, Clackmannan, whose sister was the illustrator Jennifer Campbell and whose daughter was the artist Gwen Jones. Campbell was early taught by her portrait painter father Ian Campbell, then she attended Glasgow School of Art, 1957–61, under David Donaldson and Mary Armour. After marriage and a family and some teaching, she from 1981 painted full-time, "for my enjoyment and that of the viewer. Arrangement of shapes in a space and the play of light upon them seems enough to strive for". Velázquez, Van Dyck, Uccello, Degas and Picasso were mentioned as influences. Campbell was a member of SSWA, also exhibiting in open exhibitions with RSA, RP, SSA, Royal Glasgow Institute of the Fine Arts, and in group exhibitions at Stirling Gallery, Stirling, 1981; Peter Potter Gallery, Haddington, 1982; Gatehouse Gallery, Glasgow, from 1992; Gallery 41 and Firth Gallery, both Edinburgh in 1994; and Catto Gallery, 1996. Later solo shows included Dundee Repertory Theatre, 1985, and Gallery Quinn, St Andrews, 1986. Shared an exhibition at Flying Colours Gallery, 1999, with a solo show there in 2004. BBC Scotland held her work. Lived in Letham, Cupar, Fife.

Christopher CAMPBELL 1956– Sculptor, born in Blackpool, Lancashire, who studied at the local College of Technology and Trent Polytechnic in Nottingham, where he settled. His large wooden sculpture Camel was sited in 1984 at Milton Keynes General Hospital, commissioned by the Development Corporation. Leicestershire Education Authority and Sheffield City Art Galleries also hold examples.

David CAMPBELL 1957– Artist, born in Corbridge, Northumberland, who studied in Liverpool and Leeds. He was a contributor to the group Common Culture (see separate entry). Lived in Crewe, Cheshire.

Felicity CAMPBELL 1909– Painter, illustrator and commercial artist, brought up in Sussex. Studied art widely on the continent and in London with the illustrator Edmund J Sullivan. Exhibited Walker's Galleries, IS and elsewhere. She illustrated a number of books, including *The Pond*, by Marjorie Bowen. Lived for some time at Guestling, Sussex.

George E CAMPBELL 1899–1976 Portrait, figure and religious sculptor, born in Liverpool, who worked mainly in bronze, wood and terracotta, some stone. After Royal Navy service, 1916–18, Campbell studied for five years at Royal College of Art, winning the Whitechapel 1st Prize, then continued his studies in France, Italy, Switzerland and America. Lived in several places in France, 1930–9, followed by World War II service with Royal Air Force and Royal Navy, then reopened his studio in London. Was elected a fellow of RBS in 1951. Showed at RA, RSA and Royal Glasgow Institute of the Fine Arts. Glasgow's Art Gallery and Museum, Kelvingrove, has Campbell's Torso, in wood, of 1944.

Ian CAMPBELL 1902–1984 Painter, notably of portraits, also landscapes, and teacher, father of the artist Catriona and the illustrator Jennifer Campbell. He was born in Oban, Argyll, and studied at Glasgow School of Art, 1921–6, under Maurice Greiffenhagen, who remained an influence. Campbell taught art for 40 years, at first in Glasgow schools, from 1937 until he retired in 1968 as head of department at Dollar Academy, Clackmannanshire, where he died. Continued to paint until the day of his death. Showed widely, including RSA (won the Guthrie Award, 1931), Royal Glasgow Institute of the Fine Arts, RI, RA, RWS, SSA and elsewhere. His drawing of Cosmo Lang, Archbishop of Canterbury, completed in 1936, is held by National Portrait Gallery.

Irene CAMPBELL 1914– Painter in oil, gouache and acrylic, and teacher, born London. Studied in 1930–5 at Chelsea and Hornsey Schools of Art, teachers including Henry Moore and Graham Sutherland. She taught in London and worked at Harefield Hospital, 1940–6, then married and raised a family in Newlyn, Cornwall, where she settled. After these responsibilities returned to painting pictures that were "exciting with colour and composition that warrant further study". Her abstracts were based on windows and doors in her house and abroad, as well as old family photographs, work with a strong sense of pattern with a felicitous line. Showed at Chenil Gallery in the 1970s and Newlyn Orion Gallery in 1980s and in 1985 had a solo show at Penzance Arts Centre.

James CAMPBELL 1942– Ceramist/potter and draughtsman, whose work had a strong Neo-Romantic flavour. The Hon. James Campbell was born at Cawdor, Nairnshire, second son of the 6th Earl of Cawdor, brought up there and in south-west Pembrokeshire, "two landscapes of great lyrical beauty which are decisive influences on my work." He was educated at Eton College and was introduced to ceramics by Gordon Baldwin. Campbell trained at the Royal College of Art, 1960–4, "where I was taught to draw by Dicky Chopping." Over the years, Campbell was variously involved in sculptural ceramics, drawing, then "pots and drawings, sometimes combined, sometimes not." The imagery was "still informed by the landscapes of my childhood, remembered and observed." He returned to Pembrokeshire in 1995. Campbell was on the Crafts Council list of selected makers and the WAC visual arts and craft panel. Group shows included 24 And Out, Amalgam, 1997; Three handbuilders, Alpha House Gallery, Sherborne, 1999; and Get Real, Aberdeen Art Gallery, 2000. In that year, had a solo exhibition at West Wales Arts Centre, Fishguard, where at a mixed show private view, including Campbell's work, in December 2002 The James Campbell Jazz Quartet performed. Campbell played cornet and flugelhorn.

Joan Betty CAMPBELL 1923– Watercolourist, miniaturist and teacher, born in London. Apart from some lessons at evening school in Ilford, was mainly self-taught. Became a member of SWA in 1975, RMS in 1980. Sometimes signed her work with initials only. Showed at Bankside and Mall Galleries, at Paris Salon and in America. Lived in Ickenham, Middlesex.

Oona CAMPBELL 1967– Painter who gained an honours degree in visual and performing arts, Brighton University, 1986–9. Group shows included 22 Chiltern Street, 1995; Artpool, Budapest, Hungary, 1997; ROI, Mall Galleries, 1999; and Well Oiled, MacLean Fine Art Christmas Show, Arndean Gallery, and Hunting Art Prizes, Royal College of Art, both 2001. MacLean gave her solo exhibitions in 2000 and 2004, the latter including painterly, atmospheric landscapes featuring wild, open spaces. Wilfred Sirrell Memorial Collection (City of Westminster Permanent Exhibition) and several corporate collections hold examples.

Peter CAMPBELL 1931–1989 Versatile artist and lecturer, born in London, who studied graphic design at the London School of Printing and Graphic Arts and painting and drawing as a part-time student at Goldsmiths' College. He was a graphic designer until 1965, then concentrated on his own work. Campbell was a visiting lecturer in enamelling at London University's Institute of Education, his own ambitious, multi-fired enamels being notable for their rich, lustrous finish. In 1971 he moved to Eye, Suffolk, with his wife and son, remaining until his death. Campbell's work had many inspirations: the seasons of the Suffolk countryside, which he walked with his dogs, and its past; areas such as Ireland, France and Wales; a considerable library; the country writer George Ewart Evans, "whose books have taught me that history is not only made of great events but also of the life and work of ordinary men and women"; mythology, old age and youth; and the output of artists such as Piero della Francesca, Pierre Bonnard, Ivon Hitchens and his friend, David Jones. Campbell wrote: "My intention is not to reproduce the apparent physical appearance of the natural world, but rather to choose and reshape the essence, as I see it, of the thing seen. I try not to allow the 'subject' to get in the way of making the painting." In 1973, Campbell illustrated *The Death of Hector*, René Hague's translation of Virgil, and in 1985 *Alexander's Feast*. Campbell participated in numerous exhibitions, his later solo shows including Peinture Fraiche, Paris, 1986; Phoenix Gallery, Lavenham, 1987; In Celebration of T S Eliot, Bury St Edmunds Cathedral, and The Quay Gallery, Sudbury, both 1988; Bircham Gallery, Holt; 1990; and Chappel Galleries, Chappel, 2005. Leicestershire and Suffolk Education Committees; the Schools Museum Service; Christchurch Mansion, Ipswich; St Edmundsbury Borough Council, Cambridge Libraries Association; St Brendan's Church, Clonfert, Ireland; and Vancouver City Art Gallery, Canada, hold examples.

Raymond CAMPBELL 1956– Painter of meticulous still lifes, born in Surrey, who determined from childhood that he would make painting his life. His career began to form in the late 1970s after studying and travelling through Europe, where Campbell was impressed by the Dutch Old Masters. Over many years he assembled interesting items, sometimes included in his compositions. Exhibited in Britain and abroad, including at RA Summer Exhibition; in The Bourne Gallery, Reigate, 30th Anniversary Exhibition, 2001; and by Tallantyre Gallery, Morpeth, at Affordable Art Fair, 2002. In that year, Bourne Gallery gave Campbell a solo show.

Rosalie Delaquis CAMPBELL: *see* **Rosalie Delaquis GRAY**

Rosi CAMPBELL 1944– Painter, muralist, teacher and gallery owner, born in Morden, Surrey. She studied at St Albans School of Art, 1960–5, where her "wonderful tutors included John Mills, Euan Uglow, Timothy Gibbs, John Brunsdon and Marc Vaux." She taught art in the United Kingdom and Bolivia, with other teaching in Nigeria, Malawi and Ecuador. She was involved in The Stencil Factory, 1989–01, then was director of the Arts Coritani, gallery at Swineshead, Lincolnshire, from 2002. An admirer of Brueghel and Schiele, Campbell produced "figurative, richly coloured paintings, warped by personal experience." She completed murals for the Students' Union, Dundee University, 1964; John o' Gaunt Hotel, Daventry, 1984; Holmes Place Health Clubs in Chelsea, 1997, 1999 and Crouch End, 2000; for Henley Festival, 1986, 1988, 1990 and 1997; and for private homes and garden walls. Campbell took part in mixed shows in Malawi and Bolivia in the 1970s and 1980s; then Annual Art Exhibition, Louth, 1991–02; Foresters Court Galleries, Swineshead, 1996–04; Eastern Open, 1998; and at Arts Coritani from 2003. She had a solo show in Louth, 1990, then The Warp of Memory at Arts Coritani, 2004. Holmes Place Health Club in Lisbon, Portugal, Bloomsbury Hotel and private collections hold examples.

Scott CAMPBELL 1924– Painter, maker of reliefs and teacher, born in Buxton, Derbyshire. After attending Bradford Grammar School he studied art at King's College, Newcastle upon Tyne, 1948–53. He worked for the North East Regional Office of the Arts Council, 1953–5, and taught art at King's College. Had several solo shows, including Drian Gallery, 1960–3, and Hatton Gallery, Newcastle, 1962. Was included in the Arts Council show Construction England in 1963 and in Belgrave Gallery's 1992 exhibition British abstract art of the 50s and 60s. Lived in Newcastle.

Steven CAMPBELL 1953– Painter, born in Glasgow where he spent seven years in a steelworks as an engineer after leaving school. Studied at Glasgow School of Art, 1978–82, winning the J D Kelly Award, Bram Stoker Gold Medal and a Fulbright Scholarship which took him to New York. There he held two one-man shows in 1983, at Barbara Toll Fine Arts and at the John Weber Gallery, and other exhibitions in America, Germany and London soon followed. In 1987 he had a major show at Marlborough Fine Art and another three years later at Third Eye Centre, Glasgow. New work by Campbell was the Edinburgh Festival Exhibition at Talbot Rice Gallery, 2002. Also took part in extensive group shows in Britain and abroad. Campbell's pictures, often with complex titles, owe much to Dada and Surrealism in the way that they question traditional logic and ways of looking at things in a satirical way. Scottish National Gallery of Modern Art holds his work.

J CAMPBELL-BRADY 1943– Artist, born in Glasgow, who said that "the potent exile of the mind, which is well known to many Scots, is vital for my work". He studied at Camberwell School of Arts and Crafts and in 1980 had a first solo show at Bristol Arts Centre. Also had a shared exhibition with Richard Kennedy at Neville Gallery, Bath; showed at first International Arts Fair at Barbican, London, where work was bought by the committee; and showed with the Open Circle, Glasgow, at the Growth Festival. William Hardie Ltd, of Glasgow, represented Campbell-Brady at the London Contemporary Art Fair, Art 92.

Eleanor CAMPBELL-ORDE 1908–1996 Painter, charity worker and lifelong Christian Scientist, born Eleanor Watts in Cheadle Hulme, Cheshire, her father's warehouse business in Manchester funding a private education. Studied history at Lady Margaret Hall, Oxford, where her friends included John Betjeman, Osbert Lancaster and Stephen Spender, but left the University early to join the Central School of Arts and Crafts. A long engagement to the actor Valentine Dyall (later famous as the radio storyteller The Man in Black) ended when she left to study in Florence. During the 1930s she was a pupil of the Georgian artist Prince Aleksandr Konstantinovich Schervashidze and the Russian painter Mikhail Larionov, helping them to produce backcloths for the Ballets Russes in Britain and Spain. In 1938 she married Sir Simon Campbell-Orde, banker and Scottish landowner. After World War II the Campbell-Ordes set up a market garden at Bishop's Stortford. They continued to support educational and artistic projects: the Arts Educational Schools, Tring; Yehudi Menuhin's music school; and the Harlequin Ballet Trust, for which she designed and painted more attractive sets. She was a considerable world traveller who eventually settled in Dedham, Essex, where she showed her work locally and died. Her husband had predeceased her in 1969.

Oliver CAMPION 1928–2000 Painter and teacher, born in Brasted, Kent, his family being distantly related to the Elizabethan poet, Thomas Campion. Campion painted still life and landscape. His scenes in the south of France and still life studies were in colour and construction in the Cézanne tradition. He studied at Central School of Arts and Crafts and Slade School of Fine Art. Campion taught at Oxford School of Art, Morley College and at Camberwell. After solo shows at Mayor Gallery in 1968 and 1971 he had a succession of exhibitions from 1975 at New Grafton Gallery, which gave him a memorial show in 2001, another in 2004. The Arts Club, *Financial Times* and Magdalen College, Oxford, are among the owners of his work. Died in London.

Sue CAMPION 1944– Colourist with strong sense of design, who trained and worked as a display artist, 1960–9, studying at Nottingham Polytechnic, 1986–90. Mixed exhibitions included Barnes Gallery from 1991; Wykeham Galleries, Stockbridge, from 1992; and Alresford Gallery, Alresford, 1997. She was a Patchings Award prize winner, Patchings Gallery, Nottingham, 1991. Had solo exhibitions with Artz Gallery Bors, Belgium, and Rowleys House Museum, Shrewsbury, both 1984, later ones including New Grafton Gallery, 2001. Rowleys House and Swedish Airlines Arts Club, Stockholm, hold examples.

Chan CANASTA: *see* **Chananel MIFELEW**

Neil CANAVAN 1948– Sculptor using mainly found materials who studied at Hull and the University in Newcastle upon Tyne, where he was based. Among commissions in his region is the 1996 steel Viewpoint Marker, at Hebburn Riverside Park, completed with Matthew Jarratt and commissioned by the Tyne and Wear Development Corporation.

Leslie CANDAPPA 1927– Painter and sculptor, brought up in Ceylon. He showed paintings, gouaches and collages at New Vision Centre Gallery in 1958. Lived for a time in London.

Eric CANEY 1908–1979 Illustrator in watercolour, ink and pencil. Born in London Caney, an architect, showed at the RA, RI, RBA and NS as well as locally in Chelsea. Lived in Guildford, Surrey.

Ashton CANNELL 1927–1994 Mainly a watercolourist, teacher, born Edward Ashton Cannell in the Isle of Man. He attended the School of Art there, then Liverpool College of Art. He taught at Isle of Man School of Art and became head of art for various London schools as well a senior assessor for examinations. Became a full-time painter in 1973. Carried out commissions for British Petroleum, Bass International. Foyles and Cassells. Was a member of RSMA, London Sketch Club, BWS and Wapping Group, also exhibiting at RA, Linda Blackstone Gallery in Pinner, Archer Gallery and Paris Salon, where he won a silver medal in 1973, a gold in 1975. Department of the Environment holds his work. Lived in London.

Michael CANNEY 1923–1999 Painter, relief maker, writer, broadcaster and teacher, born in Falmouth, where he was early on taken to art shows. His teacher at school in Taunton, W Lyons-Wilson, encouraged Canney, who at start of 1940s joined full-time classes at Redruth and Penzance Schools of Art and St Ives School of Painting, under Leonard Fuller. After Army service, 1942–7, which included travel to Italy, where he continued to draw, Canney studied at Goldsmiths' College School of Art, 1947–51, and after a bout of pulmonary tuberculosis spent six months in postgraduate study at Patrick Allan-Fraser School of Art, Hospitalfield, Arbroath. Around the time that he was teaching in London, 1952–7, Canney started making reliefs and pursued neo-Cubist work. In 1956 he was appointed curator of Newlyn Art Gallery, supplementing a meagre stipend with freelance broadcasting, contributing about 200 documentary programmes to radio and television. In 1964–5 Canney taught part-time at Plymouth College of Art; was in 1965–6 appointed visiting gallery director and lecturer at University of

California, Santa Barbara; then joined the staff of West of England College of Art (subsequently Bristol Polytechnic), 1966–83. In 1984 Canney chose to live in Italy, in a village between San Gimignano and Siena, continuing to paint, but in 1985 scripted a documentary film for television on painting in Newlyn which won an award in New York. Canney exhibited regularly at group exhibitions in Britain and abroad. His later one-man shows included Newlyn Art Gallery, 1983; Prescote Art and Design, Edinburgh, 1984; and Belgrave Gallery from 1990. In 2003, the Paris-based dealer Martin du Louvre held an exhibition of Canney's late works, 1973–93, and began to promote him internationally. Katharine House Gallery, Marlborough, gave Canney a 1940s–1990s retrospective in 2005. Mondriaanhuis, in Amsterdam, Netherlands, Plymouth City Art Gallery and several other public collections hold his work. Lived in Devizes, Wiltshire.

Neil CANNING 1960– Painter and illustrator, born in Enstone, Oxfordshire. Rather than attend an art school he chose to study in the studio of a professional artist. Canning had his first solo show at Bodkin Gallery, Chipping Norton, 1979, and he soon exhibited at RA and RI, in 1983 becoming the youngest artist ever to be elected an associate member of the RBA. Later solo shows included The Book Gallery, 1997, and The New Millennium Gallery, 2000 and 2004, both in St Ives, Cornwall. In 2002, Canning shared an exhibition with David Holmes at Fermynwoods Contemporary Art, Brigstock. In 1982 Canning's work was bought for the Nuffield Fund Paintings in Hospitals scheme, the University of Wales and many corporate collections holding examples. He illustrated Graeme Garden's *The Skylighters*, published in 1988. Canning shared his time between Wales, the south of France and St Ives.

Mark CANNON 1972– Artist who studied at Wigan College of Technology, 1988–90; gained an honours degree in fine art at Winchester School of Art, 1990–3; and a postgraduate diploma at Slade School of Fine Art, 1993–5. Group shows included The Gasworks and Lisson Galleries, both 1995; Car II, Hales Gallery, 1996; and in 1999 Formerly at Jerwood Gallery, where Cannon showed works based on Formica recalling Barnett Newman's abstractions "reinvented through the aesthetics of 1950s décor and South London grunge." Solo exhibitions included Duncan Cargill Gallery, 1998. The Department of Trade and Industry holds Cannon's work.

CANONICUS: *see* **Pietro ANNIGONI**

James CANT 1911–1982 Versatile artist, born in Melbourne, Victoria, Australia, married from 1945 to the artist Dora Chapman. He studied in Sydney with Dattilo Rubbo and Julian Ashton, at the East Sydney Technical College and at the Central School of Arts and Crafts in London, having moved there in the early 1930s. Cant experimented with several styles, became associated with the Surrealists and showed with the new modern generation of British painters such as Victor Pasmore, John Piper, Graham Sutherland and Francis Bacon. Cant returned to Melbourne in 1939, by which time he had embraced Social Realism, evidenced in a number of powerful anti-war pictures such as The Merchants of Death and The Bomb, in the collection of the Art Gallery of South Australia, Adelaide. He enlisted in World War II and after it helped to found SORA (Studio of Realist Art). For about five years to 1955 Cant lived in England, where he was included in the first exhibition of the Australian Artists' Association, at the RWS' Conduit Street gallery, 1953. He exhibited widely internationally. Settled in Adelaide, where his wife came from, Cant became famous for hyper-realistic studies of nature which had an abstract, patterned quality. During his final years multiple sclerosis confined Cant to a wheelchair and prevented him painting pictures, but he was able to decorate pots produced by his wife. There were retrospectives at the South Australian Art Gallery, 1984, and Niagara Galleries, Melbourne, 1993.

Jean CANTER 1943– Artist in various media and teacher, born and lived in Epsom, Surrey. She studied at the local School of Art, 1956–61, then Wimbledon School of Art, 1961–3. Taught part-time for Mid-Surrey Adult Institute. Canter became a member of SGA in 1977, later vice-president and in 1984 was its Rexel Prizewinner. Also showed with RI and RWS. Ewell Museum holds her work.

Davide CANTONI 1965– Artist born in Milan, Italy, who studied at Kingston Polytechnic, 1983; Slade School of Fine Art, 1985–9, with a period at the Hochschule der Kunst, Berlin, 1988; and in 1991–3 at Royal College of Art. His exhibitions included an installation for Negative Image in Art of Photography at Royal College in 1989. His work Bend in the Nile was included in East & South at Norwich Art Gallery/Kent Institute of Art and Design, 1992, and in 1993–4 two panels, computer spray on canvas, entitled Sat F, were included in John Moores Liverpool Exhibition. Lived in London.

Estella CANZIANI 1887–1964 Painter, decorator and artist in black-and-white, writer and muralist. Born in London, the daughter of the painter Louisa Starr, Canziani studied at Arthur Cope and Erskine Nicol's School, in London, and the Royal Academy Schools early in the century. Exhibited prolifically and widely, including RA, Walker's Galleries especially, SWA, RMS, RI, RBA and on the continent; held a number of one-man shows. A multi-talented woman, she did medical illustration during World War I; collected peasant dress and handicrafts and wrote about them in such books as *Costumes, Traditions and Songs of Savoy*, 1911, and *Through the Appenines and the Lands of the Abruzzi*, 1928; was a member of the National Art Collections Fund and a fellow of the Royal Geographical Society; and wrote about the house where she was born and continued to live in *Round about Three Palace Green*, 1939.

Nuria CAPDEVILA 1963– Painter, printmaker and teacher, born in Barcelona, Spain, to which she returned to live after three years in Britain from late 1980s. She gained a degree in fine arts at University of Barcelona, 1981–6, followed by a postgraduate printmaking year, 1987, also studying at Academia Ramon Sanvicens Barcelona, 1982–4. In 1992 she participated in the international symposium Behind the 7 Seas at Stadt Wernigerode, Germany. Capdevila's awards included an East Midlands Arts Starter Grant, 1990, and Project Grant, 1991. Among her prizes were first prizes at Banco de Vizcaya and first prize Club Turo Blanc, both Barcelona, 1987, and a third prize, Silver Palette, Derby Museum, 1990. Capdevila undertook extensive teaching plus artist-in-residencies, including Highland Printmakers, Inverness, Leicester Print

Workshop and Nottingham Castle Museum. Group shows included Open Exhibition, Castle Museum, Nottingham, and Prisoners Abroad, Blackbull Gallery, both 1990; and The Discerning Eye, Mall Galleries, 1992. Solo shows included Vases in the Sky, Castle Museum, Nottingham, 1991.

Reco CAPEY 1895–1961 Designer for industry in many materials, but also showed paintings and sculpture. Born at Burslem, Staffordshire, he studied art at the Royal College of Art, 1919–22, and widely on the continent. He held several positions at the Royal College for 30 years from 1924 and was chief examiner in industrial design for the Board of Education, 1937–40. Exhibited RA and widely overseas. Lived at Alfriston, Sussex.

John CAPLE 1966– Self-taught painter, and illustrator, who began painting in the mid-1980s, attracted by the independent style of primitive painters like Alfred Wallis and the folk art of the West Country. For generations Caple's family had been farmers and land workers in the Mendips, and much of his art was concerned with the light, scenery, inhabitants and mythology of that part of Somerset. Caple's illustrations appeared on many of Penguin Books' covers, notably an edition of Roald Dahl's novels. Showed paintings with John Martin of London.

John CAPSTACK 1957– Painter, born in Halifax, West Yorkshire. He studied at Percival Whitley College, Halifax, 1975–7, and at Manchester Polytechnic, 1977–80. He was a figurative painter concerned with man, his environment and symbols, as shown in his entry for East, Norwich Gallery, 1991; also in East & South, at same gallery and tour, 1992; and in his prizewinning Expulsion No II at John Moores Exhibition, 1991–2. Lived in Leeds, Yorkshire.

George T CAPSTICK 1895–1964 Architectural sculptor, born in Stapleford, Nottinghamshire. He was based in Liverpool, where he died in the suburb of Broad Green. In 1911, Capstick exhibited at the Walker Art Gallery, Liverpool. Between the wars Capstick set up in business with Edmund C Thompson as Thompson & Capstick, completing public projects in the city. Capstick helped carry out Thompson's designs for the entrance to the Mersey Tunnel and they worked together on the Exchange Buildings and George's Dock Building. Capstick was married to the sculptor Edward Carter Preston's sister Winifred and was remembered by Edward's daughter Julia as "rather a quiet man."

Malcolm CARDER 1936– Artist and teacher who studied architecture, sculpture and painting at Kingston College of Art, 1955–9, then worked as a freelance graphic designer, 1959–61. From 1961–4 lectured at Plymouth College of Art; from 1964–6 taught constructional sculpture at Farnham School of Art; then in 1967 took up a research fellowship in visual communications (media) at Portsmouth School of Architecture. Carder received a commission for the British Pavilion, Expo '67, in Montreal. Between 1969–71 Carder worked on exhibitions with Nigel Greenwood, London; Hans Meyer, Krefeld; Hayward Gallery; and Wilfried Reckermann, Koln. Carder then worked for Theo Crosby at Pentagram on the Arts Council exhibition and book *The Environment Game*, where his assistant again was the artist Judy Clark. Carder's own mixed shows included Constructions at Axiom Gallery, 1966; Unit-Series-Progression, Arts Council, Cambridge, 1967; L'Art Vivant, Fondation Maeght, France, and Prospect '68, Düsseldorf, both 1968; and Plans & Projects as Art, Kunsthalle, Berne and Munich, 1969. There was a solo exhibition at Axiom, 1968. In 1974 Carder went with Judy Clark to India and he became involved with the teacher Baghwan Shree Rajneesh and lived at the ashram at Poona, Maharashtra, until about 1981. When the ashram moved to Oregon in that year Carder, then called Swami Anand Yatri, went briefly to London before going on to Oregon. He was involved in the production of books documenting lectures by Rajneesh published by Osho International (Rajneesh was latterly known as Osho by his followers), which had offices in London. In 1996 Yatri declared that "Malcolm Carder no longer exists. He is no longer a sculptor." Carder's work, latterly sold by Nigel Greenwood, is held by Arts Council, Tate Gallery, Contemporary Art Society, Kelvingrove Art Gallery in Glasgow, Middlesbrough's public gallery and several American collections.

Margaret CARDEW 1899–1961 Painter, born in Wolverhampton, Staffordshire, as Margaret Stokes, being related to an eminent local family. She studied at Slade School of Fine Art and Académie Julian, in Paris. She showed at Paris Salon and elsewhere, living in Paris and London. Her small, subtle oil Normandy Village is in the Garman-Ryan Collection at Walsall Museum & Art Gallery.

Seth CARDEW 1934– Artist in ceramics, sculptor and teacher, son of the potter Michael Cardew, born in Winchcombe, Gloucestershire. He studied under Karel Vogel at Camberwell School of Arts and Crafts, 1955–9. Sculpted and taught at Twickenham College of Technology for 10 years, in 1975 starting to work at Wenford Bridge Pottery, St Breward, Bodmin, Cornwall. He was a member of the Craftsmen Potters' Association and Cornwall Craft Association. In 1968 was included in From Life at Camden Arts Centre. His solo shows included Craftsmen Potters' Gallery, 1984. Cardew's main works were large dishes with characteristic painting. He said that Vogel was "a strong influence on the visual side. Later an ethic of tactile quality became added". Victoria & Albert Museum holds his work, which he expounded at workshops abroad.

Conrad H R CARELLI 1869– Watercolourist who, after private education in England, attended Académie Julian, Paris. Son of the artist Gabriel Carelli. Exhibited RA, RI, Walker Art Gallery, Liverpool, and had one-man show at Walker's Galleries. Queen Mary bought his work. Was a member of Langham Sketch Club and lived in London.

June CAREY 1942– Painter, draughtsman and printmaker who studied at Glasgow School of Art, 1960–2, and Edinburgh College of Art, 1978–82. Carey produced richly coloured works with a dream-like quality, as in her solo exhibition at Castle Gallery, Inverness, in 2002. This was inspired by the poetry of Jamie Ingles, the text of which was engraved into the frames or drawn onto the angels depicted. The art critic Clare Henry wrote about Carey's "journeys of imaginative splendour releasing a torrent of dark riders, moon creatures, eagle-headed figures, androgynous guitarists, tattooed musicians – all night hawks captured in rich dark tones". Carey won many awards, including the European City of Culture "Woman 2000" first prize, 1990; British Council Grant for research in Mexico, 1992; and an Anne Redpath Award, 1996. She was a member of, and held senior positions in, Edinburgh Printmakers' Workshop, SSWA and SSA, served on the selection committees for major Scottish societies showing at RSA and lectured in Scotland and abroad. Took part in numerous mixed shows. Among later solo exhibitions were Glasgow Print Studio, 1993; Scottish Arts Club, Edinburgh, 1994; and Roger Billcliffe Fine Art, Glasgow, 1996. BBC Television, Royal Bank of Scotland, Dundee District Council, Scottish Arts Council and Oxford University are among collections holding her work.

Margaret CAREY 1961– Artist in various media who gained an honours degree in fine art at Liverpool Polytechnic, 1981–4. She completed 16 glass panels for International Garden Festival in Liverpool, 1984; was included in Artists under 30 at Royal Liverpool Hospital, 1985; and was in Walker Art Gallery, Liverpool, touring Merseyside Artists 3, 1986–7. Had a solo show at Bridewell Gallery in the city, 1986.

Penny CAREY 1939– Landscape painter, designer, teacher and illustrator, born in east Yorkshire. She trained at Académie Julian, Paris, Kingston School of Art and Brighton College of Art. She taught in Battersea, then worked as a freelance illustrator and book-jacket designer, later returning to teaching in Plumstead, southeast London. Among her exhibitions was a four-man show at Woodlands Art Gallery in 1981.

Peter Leonard CAREY 1931– Painter, sculptor and administrator, born in Manchester, who sometimes signed his work P L C. Studied at Oldham School of Art, 1946–51, then trained as a teacher at Manchester College of Art, 1951–2. Exhibited Northern Young Artists of which he was a member, Archer Gallery, Crane Gallery in Manchester and in public galleries in Oldham, Salford and Wakefield. He completed a mural for Park Mill Spinning Company, in Dukinfield, Cheshire. Lived in Oldham, later in Worcester, where he had a show of paintings and collage at the City Museum and Art Gallery, 2000–1.

Anne CARLINE 1862–1945 Naïve painter, wife of the artist George Carline, and mother of the painters Richard, Sydney and Hilda. She started painting in watercolour, in the hope that she could illustrate stories she wrote for children, in 1928. She had an exhibition at French Gallery in 1934, around then beginning to paint in oil. In 1939, on the initiative of the artist André Lhote, she held an exhibition at Galerie Pittoresque, in Paris, where Soutine was among her admirers. Also exhibited at LG and AIA and was included in the 1971 Leicester Galleries show The Carline Family.

Hilda CARLINE 1889–1950 Painter, born in London, whose family were artists, notably her brothers Richard and Sydney. She studied at Percyval Tudor-Hart's Académie de Peinture in Hampstead in 1913, then during World War I worked in the Women's Land Army in Suffolk. Studied at Slade School of Fine Art from 1918, taking several prizes, and through Gilbert Spencer got to know his brother Stanley, the painter, whom she married in 1925, eventually settling in Cookham. There were two daughters, Shirin, and Unity who also studied at the Slade. She showed at RA, Goupil Gallery and NEAC, but the breakup of her marriage was followed by a decline in health in 1942. Although she resumed painting, another breakdown followed. Was included in The Carline Family exhibition at Leicester Galleries, 1971. A retrospective toured from Usher Gallery, Lincoln, 1999. In 2003, Christie's in South Kensington offered works from her studio. Harris Museum and Art Gallery, Preston, holds her work.

Nancy CARLINE 1909–2004 Artist notable for landscapes and townscapes and deft portraits, born and lived in London. Married the artist Richard Carline. She studied at Slade School of Fine Art under Henry Tonks and Allan Gwynne-Jones, 1928–31. From 1933–5 worked at Sadler's Wells Ballet, in 1933–4 attending Vladimir Polunin's class for stage design at Slade, then late in 1930s Euston Road School. Was for many years an art examiner for Cambridge Local Examinations Syndicate. Joined Hampstead Artists' Council, also showing with AIA, LG, NEAC and RA. Was represented in The Carline Family, Leicester Galleries, 1971, and Spencers and Carlines, Morley Gallery, 1980, and tour. Had a retrospective at Camden Arts Centre, 1985. Latterly lived in Oxford, to which she had moved after her husband's death, nearer her son Francis and his family at Wallingford, where she died in a nursing home. Between 1987-01 she holidayed with them on the Isle of Portland, Dorset, painting "luminous scenes of the seascape of Chesil Cove", reminiscent of her earlier pictures of Venice. In 1997, her work was included in a show of Carline-circle artists organised by Michael Dickens at the National Theatre.

Richard CARLINE 1896–1980 Painter, writer and administrator, born in Oxford. His father, George Carline, his mother Anne and brother Sydney, his sister Hilda (Mrs Stanley Spencer) and his wife Nancy were all painters. Carline in 1913–15 attended Percyval Tudor-Hart's Académie de Peinture, in Paris, then London. After a short period teaching Carline served in World War I in the Army, in the Royal Flying Corps, then as a war artist. With his brother he became noted for war pictures from the air. Elected LG in 1920 and at this time the Carlines' Downshire Hill house became a centre for artists such as Henry Lamb, John Nash and Mark Gertler. Between 1924–9 Carline taught at Ruskin School of Drawing, Oxford, in 1928 making an extensive lecture tour of North America. He had his first solo show at Goupil Gallery, 1931. The mid-1930s saw Carline involved in negro art, organising a show at Adams Gallery in 1935, and contributing the main text to *Arts of West Africa*, edited by Michael Sadler. During World War II Carline supervised camouflage of factories and airfields. He was involved in AIA, helping to found the Hampstead Artists' Council in 1944; in 1946–7 was first art counsellor of UNESCO; and from 1955–74 was chief examiner in art for the Cambridge Local Examinations Syndicate. His books included *Pictures in the Post, the story of the Picture Postcard*, 1959: *Draw They Must*, 1968; and *Stanley Spencer at War*, 1978. Carline died in Hampstead and in 1983 Camden Arts Centre there organised a memorial show, and tour. Imperial War Museum holds his work.

Anne CARLISLE 1901– Painter, born in London into a military family. After private education she attended Byam Shaw School of Art, also studying in Romania and France. She showed at Redfern, Mayor and Lefevre Galleries, also showing in Paris and New York; her first one-man show was in the late 1920s at Marcel Bernheim's Paris gallery. She wrote a book on *English Drawings of the 19th Century*. She held a number of art administrative posts, including two regional directorships, of CEMA and then the Arts Council; and partly concurrently, in the 1940s and 1950s, the post of art adviser to the United States Information Service, in London. Lived latterly for some years at Chateauneuf-de-Grasse, in France.

Fiona CARLISLE 1954– Painter, born in Wick, Caithness. After studying at Edinburgh College of Art, 1972–6, she was granted an Andrew Grant Postgraduate Scholarship, 1976–7. From 1978 she had a series of solo shows at 369 Gallery, Edinburgh, and she showed in many exhibitions of mixed work in Scotland and London. In the 1980s she tended to abandon her earlier style employing flat areas of colour and black lines for more vigorous brushwork, her palette gaining strength. From 1984, Carlisle lived in Crete and Scotland. Later group exhibitions included Lord Provost's Prize Exhibition, Gallery of Modern Art, Glasgow, 1998; and Expressions: Scottish Art, Aberdeen Art Gallery and Contemporary Arts Gallery, Dundee, both 2000. Later solo exhibitions included Archeus Fine Art, 2001, sponsored by Caledonian Brewery, Edinburgh, where Carlisle had been artist-in-residence from 1999. Scottish Arts Council; Scottish National Gallery and Scottish National Portrait Gallery, both in Edinburgh; Glasgow Museum and Art Galleries; Highland Regional Council; Contemporary Art Society; and many other public and corporate collections held examples.

Michael CARLO 1945– Versatile artist using all print processes, draughtsman, watercolourist and teacher, born in Glemsford, Suffolk, later settling in Boxford. He attended Colchester School of Art, 1961–4, notable teachers including Edward Bawden, Peter Coker, John Nash and Edward Middleditch. Then was at Royal College of Art, 1964–7. He taught part-time in art schools, then set up own studio. Landscape was the theme of Carlo's work, documenting a small area around his studio, a mile from his birthplace. The Set Aside farm scheme was a feature of his exhibition Changing Suffolk at Christchurch Mansion, Ipswich, in 1992. Carlo was a member of RE, also showing at RA Summer Exhibition, Serpentine Gallery and elsewhere. Solo exhibitions included Bolton Museum, Usher Gallery in Lincoln, Southampton City Art Gallery and John Russell Gallery in Ipswich from 1985. Tate Gallery, Laing Art Gallery in Newcastle and London Transport hold his work, which is also in American collections.

Ron CARLSON 1936–2002 Sculptor, ceramics artist and teacher, born in Newport, Monmouthshire. He studied at Newport College of Art, 1952–6, and the Royal College of Art, 1956–9, then aided by two government scholarships worked in Belgium and Sweden. Went on to become senior lecturer at Newport College. Participated in group shows at Piccadilly Gallery, Demarco Gallery in Edinburgh and widely in Wales, including Royal National Eisteddfod, Howard Roberts Gallery in Cardiff, and WAC, which holds his work. One-man shows included Howard Roberts and Keele University, Staffordshire. Included in WAC touring exhibition of drawings The Probity of Art in 1980.

John CARLYON 1917–1982 Sculptor in stone, born in Cornwall. Exhibitions included RSMA, SWLA and Mall Galleries. Had a one-man show at the Moorland Gallery, which specialised in the wildlife subjects Carlyon favoured. His work is in the RSMA's Diploma Collection. Lived at the Lizard, Cornwall.

Linda CARMEN 1910-1991 Surrealist artist and writer, born in north London, who studied under Henry Tonks at the Slade School of Fine Art, 1928–32, holding the Slade Scholarship, 1930 and 1931. In 1940 Carmen married John Parry, who after World War II was appointed chief psychologist to the Royal Air Force. Marriage, friendship with Ithell Colquhoun and association with the Hampstead Artists' Council, which she helped found in 1944, all contributed to Carmen's move from academic pictures towards a personal Surrealism in which she explored private dream images and visions of voluptuous and exotic nature using an iconography of flowers, water and elemental forms. After the war she used themes of resurrection and rebirth, allegories of a post-apocalyptic renaissance. Trips to India with Parry were an influence. By this time she was a key member of the WIAC. Between 1957–61 Carmen published three novels under the name of Leo Townsend: *The Young Life*, *The Peacock Trees* and *The Law Shop*. In 1971 she moved to Woodgreen, Hampshire. There was a retrospective at Salisbury Library, 1980, another at England & Co, 1998.

Andrew CARMICHAEL fl. from 1970s– Conceptual sculptor and installations artist, born in Hull, Yorkshire, who trained at Goldsmiths' College, Royal College of Art and the British School at Rome. Mixed shows included Woodlands Art Gallery, 1985, and Made in Greenwich, at The Living Room, 1994. Had solo shows at Mario Flecha Gallery. In 1993 he completed an artist placement for the Greenwich Waterfront Development Partnership. Was based in London.

Rodick CARMICHAEL 1931– Painter, born in Edinburgh. He studied at the College of Art there, 1948–53, then at British School in Rome, 1957. Among group exhibitions participated in were Young British Artists, Museum of Modern Art, New York, 1953; the Arts Council 4 Scottish Painters, 1959–60, Edinburgh and tour; UNESCO's 25 Years of British Painting, 1972; and University of New South Wales Invitation, 1984–6. Among prizes won were the Georges Invitation Prize in 1976; the Capital Permanent Prize in 1978–80; and the Gold Coast Prize, 1983. After a solo show at the 57 Gallery, Edinburgh, in 1959, others were held at the Scottish Gallery there; Gallery West, Los Angeles, 1969; Bartoni Gallery, Melbourne, 1975; Melbourne University Art Gallery in 1983; a Perth Festival retrospective at University of Western Australia in 1984; and in 1989 Scottish Gallery in London held An Antipodean Decade 1979–1989, to coincide with a major show at Macquarie Galleries, Sydney. Among Carmichael's publications was *The Iconic Language of Painting*, in 1981, and *Artisan and High Technology*, 1985.

Stewart CARMICHAEL 1867–1950 Painter, decorator and architect, born in Dundee, Angus, where he spent much of his life. He was educated at the High School and studied art in Dundee, Antwerp, Brussels and Paris. Exhibited extensively at RSA, also at Royal Glasgow Institute of the Fine Arts, Walker Art Gallery in Liverpool and on the continent, Bourne Fine Art, Edinburgh, posthumously showing his work. London County Council and in Dundee the Morris Trust and Liberal Association bought examples.

Carmichael signed with his initials, the S enclosed by the C.

Gillian CARNEGIE 1971– Painter, born in Suffolk, who studied at Camberwell School of Art, then gained her master's degree at the Royal College of Art in 1988. An intensely private person, she declined interviews and was reported to have hesitated before agreeing to a nomination for the Turner Prize shortlist in 2005. Her work included small still life, landscape and portrait paintings, in which quite a lot of impasto could be used. In 2003 several of her pictures, including views of her own backside, appeared in the group show Days Like These at Tate Britain. Carnegie was represented by Cabinet and lived in north London.

Alberto CARNEIRO 1937– Sculptor and teacher, born in Portugal, who as a child learned the basics of his craft in religious sculptural workshops. He further studied in Oporto, then at St Martin's School of Art, in London, until 1958, where Anthony Caro had revitalised the sculpture department. Carneiro returned to Portugal where he often exhibited, won prizes and taught sculpture at the University of Oporto's architecture faculty. He returned to England to create Stones Garden, on open ground at Blaydon, a commission from Gateshead Metropolitan Borough Council stemming from the 1996 Year of Visual Arts, part of the several-years-old Marking the Ways project. Carneiro was aided in the 1997 Zen-inspired piece by a recent graduate from the University of Northumbria, Tom Scicluna.

Andrew CARNIE 1957– Versatile artist in a range of media and teacher, born in London, where he continued to live. He studied chemistry and painting at Warren Wilson College, North Carolina in America, zoology and psychology at Durham University, then graduated in fine art and gained his master's in painting successively at Goldsmiths' College School of Art, 1979–82, and at Royal College of Art, 1983–6. Took part in group exhibitions at Bluecoat Gallery, Liverpool, 1984, Whitechapel Open from 1987 and in 1989–90 John Moores Liverpool Exhibition showed the canvas Swing. Exhibited solo with Angela Flowers in 1987 and Giray Gallery, 1988. Carnie ran such ventures as the Carnie Chaple Gallery from 1986-8 and the Tram Depot Gallery, from 1994-6, working as a consultant for Greater London Arts. He collaborated with the group No Limits on art-based projects. He taught regularly at Winchester School of Art from 1991. Among later exhibitions were Betwixt and Between, Tram Depot, 1995; Return Journey, Columbus University Gallery, Georgia, 1997; and Travelogue, Flemming Gallery, Thorpe, Surrey, 1999. He was then engaged on Head On for the Science Museum in 2002, produced in collaboration with The Wellcome Trust, also taking part in Silent Motion at the Stanley Picker Gallery, Kingston University. As Stanley Picker Fellow in Fine Art Carnie had a solo show there in 2004. Entitled Slices and Snapshots, it related to his collaboration with developmental neurologists "to explore the human self as a physical and psychological construct." Informed by contemporary scientific imaging, the show paid homage to the pioneering work of Kingston-born photographer Eadward Muybridge on the centenary of his death.

Anthony CARO 1924– Sculptor and teacher, born in London, married to the painter Sheila Girling, their son being the artist Paul Caro. After studying engineering at Cambridge University, 1942–5, Caro studied sculpture at Regent Street Polytechnic, 1946, then at the Royal Academy Schools, 1947–52. He worked as a part-time assistant to Henry Moore, 1951–3. From 1952–79 Caro taught at St Martin's School of Art, a dynamic period in which it was said that his students learned "not a style, not a dogma, but a discipline of doubt and enquiry". Also taught at Bennington College, Vermont, in mid-1960s. Caro's first one-man show was at Galleria del Naviglio in Milan in 1956. Then showed at Venice and Paris Biennales and elsewhere worldwide. A retrospective was held at Museum of Modern Art, New York in 1975 with tour; there was a large Tate Gallery exhibition in 1991–2 which showed that although Caro had become famous for bolted and welded steel and aluminium sculptures which were light and graceful he was later capable of monumental works such as After Olympia; in 1994 a seventieth birthday retrospective was held at Annely Juda Fine Art; in 1995 a major show being held at Tokyo's new Museum of Contemporary Art; in 2001, a retrospective and workshops at the Town Hall, Lewes, Sussex. Caro's initial work was figurative in lead and bronze, but 1959 saw a change to non-figurative pieces, his 2003 show at Annely Juda, The Barbarians, being a return to figuration, comprising six warriors as an anti-war protest. In 2004 there were Caro displays at Kenwood House and The Orangery Gallery in Holland Park and in 2005 Tate Britain held a major Caro retrospective, coinciding with the artist's eightieth birthday. He was knighted in 1987, Order of Merit, 2000. In 1996 Caro was part of a team, that included the architects Sir Norman Foster and Partners and the engineers Ove Arup and Partners, which won an international design competition for a new pedestrian bridge to link St Paul's Cathedral to the new Tate Gallery of Modern Art at Bankside and the Globe Theatre. The Tate, the Arts Council and other major collections hold Caro's work.

Paul CARO 1958– Versatile artist, fond of bright colours, born and based in London, who attended Oxford University to study zoology and the Slade School of Fine Art. While in Oxford he organised a Kenneth Noland retrospective show, then in 1987 he worked at the André Emmerich Gallery in New York. Caro attended Emma Lake and Triangle Artists Workshops; took part in group exhibitions, including Whitechapel Open from 1988, and Made in Greenwich at The Living Room, 1994; and had solo shows, including The Pike Gallery and deliART, 2002. His mother and father, Anthony Caro and Sheila Girling, were artists, and he was married to the painter and sculptor Jill Pollard.

David Lawrence CARPANINI 1946– Painter, draughtsman, printmaker and teacher, born in Abergwynfi, West Glamorgan, married to the artist Jane Carpanini. He studied at Gloucestershire College of Art, 1964–8, Royal College of Art, 1968–71, and University of Reading, 1971–2. Taught at Oundle School, later becoming head of art and design in faculty of education at Wolverhampton Polytechnic. Carpanini was a member of RBA, 1976, being awarded its de Laszlo Medal in 1980; fellow of RE, 1981; and in 1983 a member of RWA and NEAC. Also showed at Piccadilly Gallery, New Art Centre, Agnew and Business Art Galleries. Later solo exhibitions included Attic Gallery,

Swansea, 2002. Carpanini's work was largely devoted to the industrial scene in South Wales. National Museum of Wales in Cardiff, National Library of Wales in Aberystwyth, Contemporary Art Society for Wales and other public collections hold examples. Lived in Leamington Spa, Warwickshire.

Jane CARPANINI 1949– Watercolourist, born in Bedfordshire, married to the artist David Carpanini. She was a regular tutor on weekend courses and contributed to the instructional magazines *The Artist* and *Leisure Painter*. Studied at Luton College of Technology, 1967–8, Brighton College of Art, 1968–71, and Reading University, 1971–2. She was elected to RWA in 1977, and in 1978 to RBA and RWS, eventually serving as its honorary treasurer. Much of Carpanini's work was inspired by Snowdonia; she lived at Caernarfon, Gwynedd. Her pictures were tinged with an intense, almost severe realism. She showed at many private galleries, including Patricia Wells Gallery, Thornbury; Fosse Gallery in Stow-on-the-Wold; and Albany Gallery, and her pictures were reproduced in limited edition prints, as postcards and Christmas cards. Solo shows were organised by WAC and National Museum of Wales, Cardiff. The Museum and National Library of Wales, Aberystwyth, hold her work.

Anne CARPENTER: *see* **Anne ENGDAHL**

Benedict CARPENTER 1975– Artist and lecturer, born in Ascot, Berkshire, whose three-dimensional forms, derived from Rorschach blots, lushly flocked in monochromatic colours, were included in Natural Dependency at The Jerwood Gallery, 1999. Carpenter gained a distinction, sculpture, in his foundation course at Cheltenham and Gloucester College of Higher Education, 1993–4; an honours degree in fine art, sculpture, at Chelsea College of Art, 1994–7, with a three-month Erasmus Exchange at Vestlandets Kunst Akademi, Bergen, Norway, 1996; and his master's in sculpture at Royal College of Art, 1997–9. He won The Cass Centenary Scholarship, 1998, the Dussek-Campbell-Yeats Award, 1999. From 1998, was a casual lecturer at Kingston University's sculpture and intermedia departments. Group shows included Creatures in Clay, Red Gallery, Southsea, and Ida Branson Bequest Exhibition, Millfield, Somerset, both 1998. Had a solo exhibition at Mellow Birds, 1999, sharing one at Henry Peacock Gallery, 2000, with another one-man show there, 2001. In that year he won the first Jerwood Sculpture Prize. Lived in London and in Malvern, Worcestershire.

Sue CARPENTER 1957– Performance artist who made sculptures to wear, working with children and women, and on large-scale public art events; teacher. She studied fine art at Newcastle University, 1975–81, starting her teaching and performing in 1979. Her appearances included Pompidou Centre, Paris, and with New Moon Group, including its show at Woodlands Art Gallery, 1987.

Allan CARR 1914– Painter, draughtsman and teacher, born in London. Studied at Thanet School of Art, 1933–5, then at the Slade School of Fine Art, 1935–8, with Randolph Schwabe. Taught for a while at Edinburgh College of Art. Exhibited NEAC, SSA and RSA. Lived in Edinburgh.

Andrea CARR 1962– Theatre designer and artist who graduated with honours from Trent Polytechnic, 1981–4, attending the Slade School of Fine Art, 1984–6, for her master's in theatre design. By the time that she was included in East End Open Studios, based at Red Cow Studios, 1989, Carr listed among her credits set designs for *What is Seized*, Drill Hall; *Through a Glass Onion*, Duke of Cambridge; and *Christie in Love*, Open Plan Theatre, all 1988–9. She was then set designer at ALRA College.

Barbara CARR: *see* **Barbara GILLIGAN**

Claudia CARR 1965– Painter, restorer and teacher, related to the painter and collector David Carr, who graduated in painting from the Slade School of Fine Art, where she also obtained her postgraduate higher diploma in painting. Notable teachers were Euan Uglow, who became a friend and was an important stylistic influence, and Norman Norris. She lived in Italy, 1984–5 and 1991–3, painting and restoring frescoes. Taught at the Slade, Royal College of Art and Heatherley's School of Fine Art. Mixed shows included A Second Perspective, Leighton House, 1991; Christmas Exhibition, New Academy Gallery, 1993; RP, 1995; Four Man Painting Show, Slade, 1997; The Importance of Drawing, Royal Museum & Art Gallery, Canterbury, 1999; and Fresh Paint 2, MacLean Fine Art, 2002. Carr won the Rodney Burn Prize for best figurative work, 1989; a Boise Travel Scholarship, 1991; Italian Government Scholarship, 1991–2; Winsor & Newton Young Artist 1994 Award, 1st Prize, 1994; and was a finalist in the NatWest 90s Prize for Art, 1995. Between Territories, a solo show at 5 Blenheim Crescent in 2005, included works painted in southern India. University College London, Cable & Wireless, NatWest Bank and Paul Smith owned examples. Lived in London.

David CARR 1915–1968 Painter and collector, born in London into wealthy family. Attended Uppingham School and left to join the family biscuit-making business, but left because he hated it and went to read history at Oxford University. On holiday in Italy he determined to become an artist against his father's wishes, studied briefly at Byam Shaw School in the late 1930s, then for several years at Cedric Morris's East Anglian School of Painting and Drawing where his future wife, Barbara Gilligan was also a student. Bought Starston Hall, Harleston, Norfolk, and began to paint there and in London, where he became a discerning collector and the friend of painters such as the Roberts Colquhoun and MacBryde and other Soho-based artists. Although Carr was prominent in the Norfolk Contemporary Art Society and was included by Bryan Robertson in a survey of British painting at Whitechapel Art Gallery in 1953 and in a show at Southampton City Art Gallery a few years later, it was not until the Mayor Gallery show of 1987 that his true stature was appreciated in London (he had died just before a show at the Bertha Schaefer Gallery in New York). Carr completed a remarkable series of oils in a post-Cubist style on the theme of man and the machine and a series of inventive late watercolours described by Robertson as "of special importance in British art of this period". In 1997, his work was shown alongside that of his friend Prunella Clough at Austin/Desmond Fine Art.

David CARR 1944– Painter, draughtsman and teacher, born in Middlesbrough, Yorkshire. He studied at Slade School of Fine Art, 1962–6, where he won the Tonks Drawing Prize, prizes for landscape drawing and first prize in the Summer Composition. On leaving, a David Murray Landscape Scholarship awarded by RA and a Boise Travelling Scholarship from University College permitted Carr to spend time at British School in Rome. In 1965 he was president of Young Contemporaries. Carr was head of pre-foundation studies at Camden Arts Centre, 1969–82, eventually returning there as tutor. Other teaching was done at Goldsmiths' College School of Art, Birmingham School of Art's postgraduate department and Kingston School of Art. Carr showed with RA and LG, being elected to LG in 1987. His prizes included the Cleveland Drawing Biennale and South Bank Picture Show. Carr had solo shows at Camden Arts Centre in 1987, Cadogan Contemporary in 1989 and The Walk, 1997, in which his interest in landscape in Britain and abroad were exemplified. In 2003 at The Walk Carr shared a show with three Slade contemporaries, John Arnold, Mike Knowles and Peter Prendergast. Inner London Education Authority and University College London held his work.

Edith CARR 1875–1949 Portrait and miniature painter, born in Croydon, Surrey. After private education she studed at Croydon School of Art and in Paris. Member SWA. Exhibited RA, RMS, SWA and Paris Salon. Lived in South Croydon.

Eric CARR 1916–1991 Painter and sculptor, born in Liverpool, where he died. After attending primary school in Everton Carr left aged 14 to work as a signwriter, then in the 1930s joined the Bertram Mills Circus, for which he was a scene designer. After World War II Royal Air Force service he returned to Merseyside and with his brother Leslie set up signwriting in Birkdale. From then he became a prolific sculptor and painter. He was noted for his ecclesiastical work, including carved Stations of the Cross for the Roman Catholic Cathedral in Salford and a large statue of Christ for the Liverpool International Garden Festival, in 1984. He also did work for public houses and restaurants and was a member of Liverpool Academy. A large exhibition of his work was held by Liverpool's Central Library in 1991.

Francis CARR 1919– Artist in many media, teacher, administrator and writer who moved to England from Hungary in 1938, settling in London. Carr, who was originally Francis Peters, was called "a maverick, a citizen of the world" and "a socially motivated artist". He studied at Central School of Arts and Crafts, 1938–41, then after five years' war service, from 1948 for many years held a series of teaching appointments including London College of Printing, Croydon College of Art and Open University. He was a pioneer in exploiting the creative potential of silkscreen printing. His achievement, working with one of his students, Sarah Firmin, whom he married, was celebrated with an exhibition in the Eckersley Gallery, London College of Printing, in 2002. From 1965–8 Carr was design consultant to the Greater London Council Housing Division, in 1967 devising the Artists & Architecture show at The Building Centre, which gave him a retrospective in 1993. From 1968–74 Carr was chairman of The New Organisation, concerned with the visual quality of the urban environment. In 1972 Carr organised the Urban Cinema Festival at the National Film Theatre. As well as participating in many group shows in Britain and abroad, Carr had solo exhibitions, his Woodstock Gallery show in 1959 marking a turning point towards a monumental, three-dimensional approach and polychrome sculpture. Carried out many commissions, including a mixed-media relief mosaic at Holman Hunt Infant School, 1961; commemorative area and sundial, Port Talbot Tidal Harbour, 1970; and in 1990 his The Tree of Life stone maze, in Kazakhstan. Arts Council and British Museum hold his work.

Henry CARR 1894–1970 Landscape and portrait painter in oil and watercolour, and teacher. Born in Leeds, Carr studied at Leeds College of Art and the Royal College of Art. He exhibited at the RA – he was elected RA eventually – as well as the NEAC, RBA, RP, provincial galleries and the Paris Salon, where he won a gold medal in 1956. Taught at Beckenham School of Art. His work was widely reproduced, in *The Artist*, *The Studio*, *Time* and *Life* and in the book *War Pictures by British Artists: Air Raids*. Carr was an official war artist with the First Army in North Africa and Italy for some years in World War II. The Imperial War Museum holds his work. Carr wrote the book *Portrait Painting*, 1952, and lived in London.

James (originally Joseph) Lloyd CARR 1912–1994 Novelist, publisher, artist and teacher, born in the North Riding of Yorkshire. He trained to be a teacher at Goldsmiths' College; taught in Birmingham before and after World War II, in which he was commissioned in the Royal Air Force; became headmaster of Highfields Primary School, Kettering, in Northamptonshire, where he settled; then retired at 55 to become a writer. The relationship of J L Carr, as he is generally known, and the local authority was often uneasy, as he ran the school, just as he conducted his subsequent career as a writer and publisher, on eccentric lines. He self-published much of his work under the imprint Quince Tree Press, including his unique maps and little books, the classic being *Carr's Dictionary of extra-ordinary English Cricketers*, 1977. Two of Carr's novels, *A Month in the Country*, 1980, and *The Battle of Pollocks Crossing*, 1985, were shortlisted for the Booker Prize, the former winning the *Guardian* Prize and being filmed with Kenneth Branagh, 1987. Carr was also a talented painter, draughtsman and sculptor, often in a Neo-Romantic vein. He compiled his Northamptonshire Record over 40 years in a range of media and in 1984 replaced the statues of St Peter and St Paul on Kettering Parish Church. Kettering Library holds a substantial Carr archive.

Julian CARR 1943– Painter, draughtsman and designer, born in Reading, Berkshire, who as a boy lived on the edge of Romney Marsh where he developed a love of wildlife and became adept at drawing. Entered Hastings School of Art in 1958, but, disliking urban life, left in 1959; went to work with stock on a mixed farm and read agriculture; but from 1966–8 returned to his studies at Hastings, where the principal, Vincent Lines, was an influence. Carr developed a passion for Rodin's life drawings, one of many influences over the years, including Turner, Palmer and other English Romantics, the Impressionists, Fauves, Italian Futurists, De Kooning and Pollock, the Bauhaus and especially Graham Sutherland, many of whose inspirational sites Carr visited. From 1970–89 Carr was a commercial artist contracted to West End stores, including Liberty, Harvey Nichols, Russell & Bromley and Habitat, but remained interested in landscape painting. In 1989, with his wife he moved to a remote farmhouse on the north side of the Aveyron Valley, south of the Lot, France, where they were largely self-sufficient in food and educated their children. Carr painted full-time from 1997 and in 2000 began a series of Bournazel and Anglarès lake paintings. These were shown in the luminous Images du lac d'Anglarès at The John Davies Gallery, Stow-on-the-Wold, 2003.

Matthew CARR 1953– Figurative draughtsman who attended Camberwell School of Art, 1970–1, and Cheltenham School of Art, 1972–4. He exhibited at Robert Fraser Gallery, 1983; at Wildenstein and Co, 1993; and Marlborough Fine Art, 2003. There, whether he was depicting the human face, male genitalia or monkey heads, Carr scrutinised his subject with meticulous concentration. Reviewing the exhibition, the *Daily Telegraph* critic recalled being drawn by Carr as "not an experience I would choose to repeat. Hunched over a stool about 18 inches from my face and turning a harsh electric light towards me, he asked me not to move a muscle for an hour and a half or more. During each of our three sittings there was no conversation, just tedious hours sitting in frozen-faced silence".

Tom CARR 1909–1999 Painter, born in Belfast. From Oundle School he went to Slade School of Fine Art, 1927–9, studying under Henry Tonks. He then spent six months at Settignano, near Florence. In the 1930s he was associated with the Objective Abstractionists and the Euston Road group of painters, but his naturally lyrical manner, best shown in his landscape pictures, did not make him a satisfactory theory painter. Returned to Ireland in 1939, having established himself in mixed shows such as LG and NEAC, and he had shown with Victor Pasmore and Ceri Richards at Zwemmer Gallery, 1933. First solo show was at Wildenstein, in 1940. Although in the next decade he had shows with Redfern Gallery, Leicester Galleries, Wildenstein again and Agnew, apart from a retrospective at Ulster Office in 1980 Carr showed mainly in Ireland. He had a big retrospective in Belfast and Dublin in 1985 and in 1989 three eightieth birthday shows were held: at Eakin Brothers, Belfast; Tom Caldwell Gallery, Belfast; and National Gallery of Ireland, Dublin. Tate Gallery, Ulster Museum in Belfast and other public collections hold Carr's work. Died in Norwich, Norfolk.

Tom Dickens CARR 1912–1977 Sporting painter, illustrator and printmaker with a special interest in hunting. Carr began as a colliery blacksmith, working for the Royal Navy in World War I. Industrial injury money enabled him to attend King's College at Newcastle upon Tyne and to study under George Vernon Stokes. The Midlands and north of England became his favourite painting spots. Although passionately keen on fox-, otter- and stag-hunting and other field sports, as well as golf and racing, Carr was eventually prevented from riding by spinal problems, so he moved around by car. He spent his last years at Southdean, Roxburghshire, where he continued to work. Carr showed in the northeast of England, including Laing Art Gallery, Newcastle, and in 1987 the Bondgate Gallery, Alnwick, held a major show of his pictures. Durham Cathedral and private collections in the north of England hold examples.

Alexander CARRICK 1882–1966 Sculptor and notable teacher, born in Musselburgh, Midlothian. Carrick originally trained as a stone carver in the studio of Birnie Rhind, Edinburgh, then studied sculpture at the College of Art there and Royal College of Art. He joined the staff of Edinburgh College of Art in 1914, and apart from a break for military service, 1916–18, he was to continue his teaching career at the College until around 1942, for the last 14 years being head of sculpture. Carrick showed at RSA, RA and Royal Glasgow Institute of the Fine Arts, but he is especially remembered for his sculptures related to architecture. Between the wars he carried out many commissions on a large scale, including the Animal Wall extensions at Cardiff Castle, 1923; the exterior figures of Justice and Courage and the interior bronze reliefs for the Scottish War Memorial, 1924–7; and the carving of William Reid Dick's designs for St Andrew's House, Edinburgh, 1936. RSA holds his figure Felicity.

Edward CARRICK 1905–1998 Printmaker, painter, film art director and designer, and writer, born in London. His real name was Edward Anthony Craig, he was the son of the artist Edward Gordon Craig and grandson of the actress Ellen Terry. For many of his early years he lived with his father and studied in Italy, returning to England soon after the mid-1920s. Exhibited at St George's and Redfern Galleries, at Art Institute of Chicago and with the Grubb Group, of which he was founder and president; his illustrations appeared in such publications as *Artwork*, *Architect's Review* and *Bookman's Journal* as well as in several books, including Edmund Blunden's *In Summer* and Edith Sitwell's *In Spring*, both 1931; and he painted murals in a number of theatres, including Cambridge Theatre, the Victoria News Theatre and at Easton Manor, near Dunmow, Essex. He was art director for Ealing Studios, 1936–8, then the Crown Film Unit and Army Film Unit, 1939–47. He founded the first school in England specialising in the study of cinema, in 1937. Carrick was the author of *Designing for Moving Pictures*, *Art & Design in the British Film* and *Designing for Films*. His many film credits included *Western Approaches*, 1944; *Tiger Bay*, 1959; *Macbeth*, 1960; and *Nanny*, 1965. In 1968, Carrick published *Gordon Craig: the story of his life*, and he was responsible for establishing collections about his father throughout the world (there is a notable archive at Eton College). British Museum, Victoria & Albert Museum and Metropolitan Museum of Art in New York hold examples of Carrick's work. Died at Thame, Oxfordshire.

Elsie CARRICK 1894– Painter and draughtsman, mainly working in watercolour with some oil, born in Middlesbrough, Yorkshire. Miss Carrick attended Sunderland High School, then the Slade School of Fine Art, 1915–17, gaining first-class certificates in drawing, painting, design and perspective and a first prize in artistic anatomy. She went on to teach and joined the Norfolk and Norwich Art Circle in 1946 after she had moved to Norwich to teach at the Blyth School, serving on the Circle's council and as its secretary. After over 30 years she left Norwich and the Circle.

Ian CARRICK 1939– Sculptor and teacher, born in Rugby, Warwickshire, who gained his National Diploma in sculpture, 1962, and Slade Diploma in 1964. He lectured at Wrexham School of Art, 1964–6, was head of fine art at University of Nigeria, 1966–8, was senior lecturer in sculpture at at Liverpool Polytechnic, 1968–76, then was head of sculpture and of fine art and vice-principal at Falmouth School of Art and Design, 1976–91, continuing to live in the Cornish town. Showed at Herbert Art Gallery in

Coventry, Penwith Gallery in St Ives, Bluecoat Gallery in Liverpool and elsewhere, and was in Falmouth Connections at Falmouth Art Gallery in 1994. Australian and New Zealand High Commissions and Ford Motor Company commissioned him.

Gisel CARRICONDE-AZEVEDO 1960– Artist born in Brazil who attended University of Brasilia, 1984 and 1992; the University of Brighton, 1997; and University of Sussex, 1998. Exhibitions included Sussex Open 98, Brighton Museum & Art Gallery and Jheglejland, Decima Gallery, both 1998; and The Flower Show, Phoenix Gallery, Brighton, in 1999, the year she was Artist of the day at Flowers East, chosen by Laurence Preece.

Donald P CARRINGTON 1907– Painter and teacher, born at Outwood, near Wakefield, Yorkshire, where he attended the Grammar School, the School of Art, 1924–6, then the Royal College of Art, 1926–30. He taught at the Huddersfield, Sheffield and Leicester Schools/Colleges of Art. Exhibited RA and extensively in northern municipal galleries including Graves Art Gallery, Sheffield, which holds his work. Lived in Leicester.

Jennifer CARRINGTON 1946– Painter who studied at Camberwell School of Art, 1962–7, and the Royal Academy Schools, 1969–71. In 1973 with Peter Jamieson, Martin Rose and John Whittall she formed The Lane Studio, and exhibited with it at Roehampton in 1974. An exhibition of the Studio's work was held at the RA in 1975. Like the other three members, Carrington had work in Sir Brinsley Ford's collection.

Joanna CARRINGTON 1931–2003 Painter and teacher, daughter of the publisher Noel Carrington and niece of the artist Dora Carrington. She studied with Cedric Morris at the East Anglian School of Painting and Drawing, in Suffolk, with Fernand Léger in Paris and at Central School of Arts and Crafts. She went on to teach at Hornsey College of Art, Regent Street Polytechnic School of Art and at Byam Shaw School of Art. Her book *Landscape Painting for Beginners* was published in 1979. Among her many solo shows was one at New Grafton Gallery in 1982, where in 1991 she shared one with her husband Christopher Mason, later ones including Thackeray Gallery, 1997. Lived mostly in France, in the early 1990s settling in St Savin, Vienne. Gauguin, the Nabis, Bonnard and Matisse were important influences, as was a film made by her husband about Alfred Wallis in 1973. Carrington's wit was evident in her many caricatures and in her invention of Reginald Pepper, a primitive like Wallis. As Pepper she exhibited a number of naïve pictures at the Portal Gallery. She painted landscape, still life and kitchen interiors in oil, using a rich palette, notable for strong design, mixed perspectives, non-naturalistic colour and deliberate imbalance. Good examples of pictures were illustrated in *Joanna Carrington*, the memoir by her husband that appeared at the time of her Thackeray Gallery memorial show in 2005.

Leonora CARRINGTON 1917– Surrealist artist and writer, born at Crookhey Hall, Cockerham, Lancashire, daughter of a cotton magnate. She began writing and illustrating stories as a small child, her birthplace being frequently featured in her art. After a convent education Carrington went to Miss Penrose's finishing school in Florence and was presented at court. In 1936 joined Amédée Ozenfant's private art school in north London, met the Surrealist Max Ernst and returned with him to France to live together, settling in the south in 1937. But it was a difficult relationship, as Ernst was married, and in 1940 Carrington had a breakdown, described in her autobiographical writing *Down Below*. By this time she was a member of the Surrealist circle, having shown her work for the first time in Paris in 1937. By the time of her breakdown Carrington was living in Spain, where in Picasso's studio she met a diplomat, Renato Leduc, whom she married and accompanied to New York. In 1942 they went to live in Mexico, where she remained until her move back to New York in 1985. She eventually settled near Chicago, still working. Carrington wrote in French and English, her stories including *The House of Fear*, 1938, her first book, as well as *The Oval Lady*, 1939, and *Little Francis*, 1986. A retrospective of her paintings, drawings and sculpture was held at Serpentine Gallery, 1991–2.

Sarah CARRINGTON 1977– Painter, born in Edinburgh, who graduated from the University there in 2000 with a sell-out degree show. Her work, often large, concentrated on the Scottish coastline, capturing moods of sea and sky. Paintings were frequently executed in the studio from on-the-spot sketches of areas known from sailing holidays in childhood. Carrington was included in the trio show Art in the Abstract, Catto Gallery, 2001. Her solo exhibition, Iona: Time and Tide, was held at Catto Contemporary, 2002.

Neil CARROLL 1958– Painter employing a rich palette, born in Rhymney, Monmouth, who settled in Monmouth. After Bedwelty Grammar School, 1969–76, Carroll completed an art foundation course and gained a first-class honours degree in graphic design (illustration), Newport College of Art & Design, 1976–80; obtaining his University of Wales postgraduate art teacher's certificate, UWIC Cyncoed, 1983–4. Carroll wrote that his work evolved "out of many starting points, and it could be seen as autobiographical.... I want to make paintings which relate to a sense of place, my home and family, and the music and films I enjoy." The poet Idris Davies was a "primary influence". "Cézanne, Bonnard, Monet, Hopper, Wyeth, Matisse, Constable and many more" painters helped in "crafting my own language in paint." Exhibited with the Welsh Group from 1980; *Reader's Digest*/Association of Illustrators Exhibition, Covent Garden, 1985; South Glamorgan Young Artists (work bought by County Council), 1986; Summer Exhibition, Albany Gallery, Cardiff, 1996; and National Eisteddfod of Wales, Denbigh, 2001, the year Carroll was featured in *First Hand*, on BBC Radio Wales. Had a solo exhibition at Newport Museum & Art Gallery, Newport, 2004.

Derek CARRUTHERS 1935– Artist in various media and teacher, born in Penrith, Cumberland. Studied art at King's College, Newcastle University, 1953–7, teachers including Victor Pasmore and Lawrence Gowing. Taught at Sunderland College of Art, 1957–64, and eventually retired as professor of fine art at Trent Polytechnic, Nottingham. Carruthers was early influenced by Pasmore, but eventually went through what he called a "post-Modernist rethink" and produced metaphysical landscapes. He had solo shows at Univision Gallery, Newcastle, in 1957 and at Drian Galleries, 1963–5. Was included in the Arts Council show Construction England, 1963, and in Belgrave Gallery's 1992 exhibition British abstract art of the 50s and 60s. Carruthers' work was part of L.S. Lowry and those he inspired, an exhibition organised by Danny Greening Fine Art at Gallery 27 in 2004. Leicester University and public galleries in Bradford and Kendal hold his work. Lived in Nottingham.

Mary CARRUTHERS 1878–1962 Painter and modeller, born in London, sixth daughter of the 1st Baron Trevor. The Hon. Mrs Carruthers' second husband was Douglas Carruthers, the explorer. She studied at Norwich School of Art, 1928–30, then at the Grosvenor School of Modern Art, 1929–30, with Iain Macnab. For a time she was chairman of the Norfolk and Norwich Art Circle. Exhibited with RBSA, RSA, SWA, RI, Paris Salon and prolifically with the Art Circle, especially portraits and flower pictures. Late in life, when settled in Burnham Market, she again studied at Norwich School of Art.

Robert CARRUTHERS 1925– Sculptor and teacher who studied at Cheltenham College of Art and the Royal College of Art, winning a Major Travelling Scholarship, 1953–4. Taught at the Royal College under Robin Darwin, obtaining a French Scholarship, 1958, then at Swindon College of Art. Showed work in the RA Summer Exhibition, at AIA Gallery, Museum of Modern Art in Oxford and other mixed shows. In 1972 the Peter Stuyvesant Foundation with the Arts Council commissioned Carruthers' huge mixed-media, Japanese-influenced Gate Construction, initially located at Colmore Circus in Birmingham, moved soon after to its Bell Barn Road site.

Rose CARRUTHERS: *see* **Rose ELLENBY**

Evelyn CARSLAW 1881–1968 Artist and illustrator who early in her career showed under her maiden name of Evelyn J L Workman. She studied at Glasgow School of Art, 1897–1907, also in Paris and travelled on the continent. Was a member of the Glasgow Society of Lady Artists from 1905, also exhibiting with the Royal Glasgow Institute of the Fine Arts. In 1907, Evelyn married Dr R B Carslaw and they had four sons and a daughter. Living in Rhu enabled her husband to sail extensively off the west coast of Scotland. She illustrated his book *Leaves from* Rowan's *Logs*, published during World War II. Evelyn Carslaw died in Helensburgh, Dunbartonshre.

Fiona CARSON 1947– Sculptor, draughtsman and teacher, born in Edinburgh. She gained an honours degree in art history at Courtauld Institute, London University, 1965–8, then travelled in India, drawing, 1969–71. After lecturing in art history at West Surrey College of Art, Farnham, 1972–5, Carson completed a degree in fine art (sculpture) at St Martin's School of Art, 1976–80, after a period of "dawning feminism". From 1976 she also taught part-time at various centres including Goldsmiths' College. Her abstract sculptures featured found objects. Showed in groups at Clare College, Cambridge, 1967; Lauderdale House, 1978; LG, 1982; and Woodlands Art Gallery, 1983. Later appearances included New Contemporaries, ICA, 1984; Dialogues, Art Research Group, Haworth Gallery, 1986; and A Clue of Thread, Dixon Gallery, and East End Open Studios, based at Robinson Road, both 1989.

John Paddy CARSTAIRS 1916–1970 Painter in oil, gouache and watercolour, writer and film-maker, real surname Keys. Studied art at the Slade School of Fine Art, exhibited at Leicester Galleries, RBA, RA and Paris Salon. Extensive one-man shows, including Redfern Gallery, Leger Galleries and Walker's Galleries. Wrote a book: *Watercolour is Fun*. Is in the collections of Trinity College, Oxford, City Art Gallery, Manchester, and Kirkcaldy Museum and Art Gallery, Fifeshire. Carstairs began his film career as a camera assistant and went on to direct 45 feature films. The first was *Holiday's End*, 1937, and among his versatile output was a series with the comedian Norman Wisdom, starting with *Trouble in Store*, 1953. He wrote over 30 books. Lived at Kingston Hill, Surrey.

Thelma CARSTENSEN 1906–1992 Artist, mainly watercolour and etching, born in London. She studied at Hornsey School of Art, 1924–7, then Slade School of Fine Art, 1927–30, her teachers including Allan Gwynne-Jones, Randolph Schwabe and Norman Janes. Was a member of WIAC, also showing at Goupil Gallery, Walker's Galleries, RA, NEAC and in the provinces. Lived in Moulsford, Oxfordshire.

Robert CARSWELL 1969– Abstract artist whose work employed grids. He was born in Edinburgh, where he attended the College of Art, 1986–91, then Chelsea College of Art & Design, 1991–2. In 1992 Carswell gained a Repton College painting residency. Group shows included Bruntsfield Gallery, Edinburgh, 1989; Malvern Open Drawing Competition in Great Malvern, 1992; LG at Morley Gallery, 1993; and Aspects of Abstraction at Paton Gallery, 1995.

Albert Clarence CARTER 1894–1958 Sculptor and goldsmith, born in London, who was a goldsmith's apprentice and studied art at Lambeth and Central Schools. Carter was made a fellow of RBS, showing at RA. His marble figure Primavera is illustrated in Eric Newton's 1947 monograph *British Sculpture 1944–1946*. In later years he was based in Reading, Berkshire.

Albert Henry CARTER 1928– Painter and teacher who graduated with honours from St Paul's College, Cheltenham, 1973–7. Taught art at Oundle School. He showed at RBA, of which he became a member in 1983, then honorary treasurer, also at RWA and in the provinces. American Embassy holds his work. Lived in Oundle, Northamptonshire.

Bernard CARTER 1920– Painter and curator, born in London where he continued to live, married to the artist Eugenie Alexander. Carter was educated at Haberdashers' Aske's School, then Goldsmiths' College School of Art. He went on to be keeper in charge of pictures and conservation at National Maritime Museum, Greenwich, retiring in 1977. With his wife he published *Art for Young People*. Had a solo show with Arthur Jeffress in 1955, then a long series with Portal Gallery. Also appeared at RA, British Council, Arts Council and abroad. Carter's Abstract Composition, completed in the mid-1950s, was included in Paule Vézelay's Groupe Espace exhibition at Royal Festival Hall in 1955.

Bernard Arthur Ruston (Sam) CARTER 1909–2006 Painter in oil, teacher and writer, born in Kenilworth, Warwickshire. He was married to the artist Jane Tresidder. Sam Carter gained his master's degree in the modern languages tripos at Cambridge, 1930–2. He also attended Grenoble and Innsbruck Universities, and the Central

School of Arts and Crafts part-time, his teachers including John Cooper, John Farleigh, Fred Porter and Bernard Meninsky, as well as the Euston Road School. He was on the staff of Camberwell School of Art, 1945–9, and of the Slade School of Fine Art, 1949–78, becoming professor of perspective at Royal Academy Schools, 1975–83. Contributed to a number of learned journals on perspective, as well as *Oxford Companion to Art*, 1970. Showed with East London Group, LG, Arts Council Euston Road touring exhibition, 1948–9, and RA Summer Exhibitions. Arts Council, London Museum, Contemporary Art Society and other collections hold his work. Lived in London, finally in Mousehole, Cornwall.

Frederick CARTER 1883–1967 Painter, printmaker and writer, born in Bradford, he studied art in France, Belgium and London. Exhibited extensively at RE and Baillie Gallery, also RA, NEAC and ROI. Among his books were *The Dragon of the Alchemists* and *Florentine Nights*. He was a member of the Chelsea Arts Club. Lived in London. Richard Grenville Clark's 1998 publication *Frederick Carter A.R.E. 1883-1967. A Study of his Etchings* catalogues the artist's output and examines each period of his career and techniques.

Jack CARTER 1905–1992 Painter in watercolour, who died in about his eightieth year. Was a greengrocer and self-taught flower painter of professional standard who showed locally in the Horsham, Sussex, area where he lived, his work always being in demand. He was said to have declined a contract with the dealer Frost & Reed, which could have given him a national name.

John CARTER 1908–1983 Painter and designer, born in London where he lived for many years, eventually settling in Hastings, Sussex. He studied at Regent Street Polytechnic School of Art, Central School of Arts and Crafts and St Martin's School of Art, 1925–30. Worked for Heal's in London from 1963–74, and managed their design studio. Showed with RI and RBA, both of which he was a member. Carter won the Philip de Laszlo Medal and was a runner-up for the Hunting Group's watercolour of the year award.

John CARTER 1927– Painter and sculptor, born in east London, whose work was characterised by vigorous drawing and luminous colour. He studied at St Martin's School of Art and Sir John Cass College. Latterly lived in Spain, where he held shows in Figueras and Crespia, also exhibiting at RBA, ROI. Was included in Spring Show, The Barnsdale Gallery, Yoxford, 2001.

John CARTER 1942– Painter and teacher, born Middlesex. Was at Twickenham School of Art, 1958–9, and Kingston College of Art, 1959–63. In 1963–4 he won a Leverhulme Travelling Scholarship, enabling him to work on the continent including a period at British School in Rome. In 1966 he was assistant to Bryan Kneale and began teaching at London College of Printing. After travelling to America on a Peter Stuyvesant Foundation Travel Bursary, 1966–7, Carter taught widely, including Royal College of Art and University of Reading. From 1968 had a series of solo shows at Redfern Gallery, later showing with Nicola Jacobs Gallery. Was a Tolly Cobbold Exhibition prizewinner in 1981. Carter's work was enigmatic, abstract, graceful and still, with a painter's interest in colour and space. Arts Council holds examples. There was a show of Carter's recent work at The Blue Gallery in 2004 and in 2005 he shared an exhibition with Julia Farrer and Noel Forster at The Eagle Gallery.

John Sydney CARTER 1936– Sculptor who contributed to Thompson's Marylebone's The Sculpture Show, 2003, with works in plaster for bronze and aluminium. Carter was an industrial designer when he began to draw and paint, continuing during two years' National Service when he painted from life in Leicester and Portsmouth. During the 1960s he became creative director of a design company while privately pursuing his painting and experimental sculpture, showing with RBA. Travelled extensively in the Americas, Australia and Europe through the 1970s and 1980s and during frequent visits to Lanzarote began working on a series of metal sculptures called The Edge, inspired by the local landscape and the sea. After becoming a full-time painter and sculptor in 1995 Carter began a year's study in 1998 at The Frink School of Sculpture, becoming a fellow and trustee of it in 1999. He was made an associate of RBS in 2001. Exhibited in the provinces and carried out many commissions, clients including the shipping company P & O and car firm Porsche.

Justin CARTER 1973– Sculptor and teacher, born in Nairobi, Kenya, who graduated with first-class honours in sculpture at Glasgow School of Art, 1991–5, obtaining his master's in fine art there, 1998–00, with an exchange studentship at The School of The Art Institute, Chicago. Carter was based in Glasgow, much of his work referring to the city and surrounding countryside. Teaching included periods at Glasgow School of Art, Glasgow Academy and Barrow College, in the Lake District. Residencies included Grizedale and he was Momart Fellow at Tate Liverpool, both 2001. Among group shows were Call Of The Wild, Transmission Gallery, Glasgow, 1996; and Perspectives 2000, in that year at Ormeau Baths Gallery, Belfast. Commissions included The Prince's Trust, Diorama Building, Regent's Park, 1995; Glasgow Museums, 1998; and University of Plymouth, project for East of Eden, Spacex Galllery, Exeter, 2001.

Kenneth CARTER 1928– Yorkshire-born sculptor in stone and metal and teacher for a time at Exeter College of Art. He won the Leeds Gold Medal for sculpture in 1973 and was a fellow of RBS. Exhibited in RA Summer Exhibition. Public work includes carvings on Exeter Cathedral and stone reliefs at Queen's Gardens in Kingston-upon-Hull. Lived for a time in Lympstone, Devon.

Mary CARTER 1909– Painter in oil who was educated at Bury Grammar School and Queen Elizabeth College in London. Mrs Carter studied at Heatherley's School of Fine Art and Sir John Cass School of Arts and Crafts. Showed and lived in London. Member of Free Painters and Sculptors and ICA.

Mary Elizabeth CARTER 1947– Painter, born in London, was married to the artist J B Hiscock. She studied at Kingston School of Art, then Royal College of Art. There her teachers included Carel Weight and Roger de Grey. She won the Princess of Wales Scholarship and British Institution Award and in 1985 was winner of the Three Friends Prize at RA, at which she showed from 1968. Showed at New Grafton Gallery, RMS, RWA and elsewhere and in 1991 shared an exhibition at Llewellyn Alexander. Mary Carter's work was on a small scale and dealt with daily life in the home and country and portraits. RA holds her work. Lived in Hemyock, Devon.

Pam CARTER 1952– Painter and teacher, born in east Africa, who studied at Glasgow School of Art. Teaching posts included two years at Seychelles Polytechnic and later Falkirk College. Although a sense of place was important in Carter's work, she was not concerned with complete accuracy. "I often interpret the scene with abstract elements allowing the paint to work for me." Worked widely in Scotland, the effect of the elements and its special quality of light being of key importance. Skye, Lewis, Harris and the Uists, Tiree and Coll were favourite subjects. Held many solo exhibitions in Britain and abroad, later ones including Lloyd Jerome, Glasgow, 1997, and Richmond Hill Gallery and Ainscough Contemporary Art, both 1999.

Rob and Nick CARTER– This was the joint exhibiting name of a husband and wife team based in London: Rob Carter born 1968, and Nicky Carter, born 1969, who graduated with honours and art history at Goldsmiths' College in 1991. They claimed a unique working method, each artwork being original. "As opposed to canvas and paint, light and light-sensitive paper are used. In complete darkness the image is gradually built up through added increments of light." The Carters had several solo shows in Britain and abroad, including The Museum of Neon Art, in Los Angeles, California, 2002; Leeds City Art Gallery, with *Colour Changing Spiral*, a short film made in collaboration with The Music, 2004; What Was and What Will Never Be, Said Business School, in collaboration with the British Arts Council, and Painting Photographs, at The Fine Art Society, both in 2005. Among their group shows were Making a Move, Nottingham Museum, and Index of Colour, at Leeds City Art Gallery, both 2003; and Some Versions of Light, North Yorkshire, and The Liverpool Biennial, both 2004. Corporate collections included J Sainsbury's; Seagram; Reuters; The Virgin Group, EMI; 19 Management; and The Royal Bank of Scotland. Sir Elton John and David and Victoria Beckham were among private collectors.

Sam CARTER: *see* **Bernard Arthur Ruston (Sam) CARTER**

Sheila CARTER 1928– With her blacksmith husband Ron and sons at Trapp Forge, near Burnley, Lancashire, Carter created widely commissioned decorative ironwork, for private and public clients. A good example of the latter is the sign for Birmingham Nature Centre, completed in 1990, the delicacy of which indicated her textile industry experience. Born in Bolton, Carter attended the local Art School, winning a scholarship to the Royal College of Art, 1949–51, under Robin Darwin. H M The Queen, The Hon. Artillery Company, Manhattan Brewing Company in New York and Crown Prince Khalid of Saudi Arabia were among Trapp Forge's clients.

Simon CARTER 1961– Painter, brought up in East Anglia, whose work stemmed from its landscape although veering towards abstraction. He completed a foundation course at Colchester Institute, 1980–1, then in 1981–4 an honours degree at North-East London Polytechnic. Appeared in many group shows, especially in East Anglia, including Colchester Arts Centre, 1981–4; the 1987 East Anglian Artists' Open, in King's Lynn, where he was specially commended; The Glory of the Garden at Brett Gallery, Hadleigh, 1991; and Ipswich Open at Christchurch Mansion, Ipswich, 1995. Had a one-man show at Stamford Arts Centre, 1988; Chappel Galleries, Chappel, from 1991; Gainsborough's House, Sudbury, 1993; Bury St Edmunds Art Gallery, 1994; Trinity Studios Gallery, Colchester, 1995; North House Gallery, Manningtree, 2001; and firstsite, Colchester, 2003–4, gestural paintings fed by daily drawing at the beach near where he lived, in Frinton-on-Sea, Essex. In 2000, Carter was artist-in-residence at firstsite. Suffolk County Libraries loan collections hold his work.

Tony CARTER 1943– Sculptor and teacher who used mainly found objects which acquired a new meaning when assembled by him. He studied at University of Newcastle upon Tyne, graduating in fine art, 1962–6, obtaining his master's degree at University of Reading, 1966–8. Carter became principal of the City and Guilds of London Art School. He was Henry Moore Foundation artists fellow at Christ's College and Kettle's Yard, Cambridge, 1990. Among Carter's awards were Peter Stuyvesant Foundation Prize, Young Contemporaries, 1967, with a similar prize at Northern Young Contemporaries, 1968. He also gained an Arts Council Major Award, 1975–80. Carter was a prizewinner at Tolly Cobbold Open Exhibitions in 1977–85, and in 1988 gained Unilever Award in Whitechapel Open Exhibition. Carter took part in numerous group exhibitions from Young Contemporaries, 1967, in Britain and abroad. He had a solo show at Garage Ltd in 1975, later ones including Imperial War Museum, 1992, the year he also showed at Anthony Reynolds Gallery. Arts Council and Contemporary Art Society hold his work.

Walter Dyke CARTER 1894–1966 Painter and etcher. Studied at Royal College of Art and Manchester University and Bolton Schools of Art. After World War II he was art master at Prince Henry's Grammar School, Otley, in Yorkshire, becoming a member of both the Otley Arts Club and Bolton Art Circle. Exhibited RA, RCA and in public galleries in Liverpool, Manchester, Preston and Bradford. Died in the Walsall area of Staffordshire.

Edward CARTER PRESTON 1885–1965 Sculptor, designer, painter and printmaker, father of the artist Julia Carter Preston, born in Walton, Lancashire. He received his early training at the University Art Sheds, Liverpool, one of the tutors being Augustus John. Although early in his career Carter Preston worked in many two-dimensional media, later he developed an interest in three-dimensional ones, producing sculptures in stone and wood. He became proficient in designing and producing medals, largely encouraged by his success in winning the open competition for the next of kin plaque at the end of World War I – under assumed names he won first and second prizes, the same design being used for World War II. Commissions for many medals followed, including the Distinguished Flying Cross, Coronation Medal and Queen's Seal for the County Palatine of Lancashire. In 1930 a major commission came in the form of sculpture for the Anglican cathedral, Liverpool, work that continued for almost 35 years; it was to involve aspects such as processional silver, robes and service sheets. Other ecclesiastical commissions followed, notably for buildings by Giles Gilbert Scott. Carter Preston was a founder-member of the Bluecoat Society of Arts and a member of the Sandon Club. Showed with Fine Art

Society, RMS of which he became a member in 1929, Walker Art Gallery in Liverpool which holds his work and elsewhere. Died in Liverpool, where the University's art gallery held an exhibition in 1999.

Julia CARTER PRESTON fl. from 1960s– Ceramist and teacher, for long based in Liverpool, daughter of the sculptor Edward Carter Preston. She studied at the local College of Art, combined studio work with teaching in Lancashire art colleges, ran the ceramics section of Liverpool Polytechnic, then worked full-time at a studio in Bluecoat Chambers. Her work unusually combined earthenware with sgraffito decoration. Had major shows at Bluecoat Display Centre from 1966, exhibited in Merseyside Artists' exhibitions from 1983, also at Walker Art Gallery, Liverpool; Williamson Art Gallery in Birkenhead; Atkinson Art Gallery, Southport, and elsewhere. Liverpool's Anglican Cathedral, Town Hall and University hold examples. Carter Preston produced many commemorative and presentation items and ecclesiastical ceramics, usually font bowls, including St Nicholas and Our Lady, Liverpool; St Columba's Church, Anfield; and The Church of the Holy Family, Southport. In 1988 was artist-in-residence at Walker Art Gallery.

Doris H de CARTERET 1897–1956 Landscape painter in oil. Studed at Byam Shaw and Vicat Cole School of Art, 1915–19. Exhibited RA, RBA, ROI, RSA, Ridley Art Club and widely in the provinces. Lived in Arundel, Sussex.

Mary CARTLEDGE 1923-2000 Painter of mainly abstract works, born in Manchester, married to Donald Cartledge, godson of the artist William Cartledge. Mary graduated in medicine in 1947 and worked as a psychiatrist and school doctor. She joined Prestwich Hospital, 1948, and was involved in child welfare for Stockport Corporation, was doctor at Withington Girls' Schools and a lecturer and examiner for the British Red Cross until her death. She studied at Manchester Regional College of Art with Ian Grant, Frederick Deane and Terry McGlynn and became a member of the Society of Modern Painters and MAFA. Group shows included Manchester Business School. Had solo exhibitions with Christie's Art Gallery, Withington; Withington Hospital; and at Margo Ingham's Mid-Day Studios, Manchester. She retired to Dent, Cumbria, in 1983, rearing Swaledale sheep for five years. Died in Morecambe Hospital.

William CARTLEDGE 1891–1976 Painter and teacher, born in Manchester where he studied at the School of Art, then Slade School of Fine Art where his teachers included Henry Tonks, Fred Brown and Tancred Borenius. He held a number of teaching positions in Liverpool, Shipley and Pudsey, finally – from 1932–51 – being principal of Staffordshire County School of Art and Crafts as well as art adviser to the county. Exhibited RA, Alpine Club Gallery, RCamA, extensively at Arlington Gallery, and RBA. Manchester City Art Gallery and several other northern galleries hold his work. Finally lived at Birdham, Sussex.

Hilary CARTMEL 1958– Sculptor, notably in wood, born in Wendover, Buckinghamshire, who studied at Exeter College of Art, 1976–7, then Trent Polytechnic, 1977–80. Held a number of residencies, including Carlton Hayes Hospital, Leicestershire, 1982–3. Solo exhibitions included Centre Gallery in Cheltenham, 1982, and Loughborough Art Centre, 1983. Arts Council holds Sprawling Red Woman, 1984, in stained wood, bought from Bluecoat Gallery, Liverpool, and Rufford Country Park, Ollerton, has several examples.

John CARTMEL-CROSSLEY 1933– Painter and teacher, born Southport, Lancashire, who studied at local Art College and Liverpool College of Art, 1949–54. For 15 years from 1954 worked as a non-figurative painter in and around Merseyside, then taught in London, 1969–72, and Norfolk, 1972–4. Then moved to Orkney Isles to work as a full-time artist, concentrating on watercolours. After 10 years moved to Northumberland to set up Rock South Studio and Gallery. Showed at Patricia Wells Gallery, Thornbury, and held many solo exhibitions from 1955. Work held in public and private collections throughout the world. Lived at Alnwick, Northumberland.

Caitriona CARTWRIGHT 1964– Stone-carver and letterer who in 1986 graduated with honours from Manchester University in art history, concentrating on medieval art, then completed a City and Guilds stonemasonry course at Weymouth Technical College, 1987. From 1987–91 she worked on the restoration of Salisbury Cathedral with other masons, one of whom she married, and on the restoration of Wilton House. While at Salisbury she gained a Travelling Fellowship with the Society for the Protection of Ancient Buildings, 1989, as part of this studying letter-cutting with John Green. Cartwright moved to Herefordshire when expecting her first child and from 1992 freelanced. Traditional English lettering, eighteenth-century headstones and the work of Eric Gill were influences on her very varied output. As well as obtaining many commissions, she showed with the Hay Makers Gallery in Hay-on-Wye, at Parnham House and the Hereford Contemporary Craft Fair and in 2005 at Abbott and Holder, which represented her.

Peter CARTWRIGHT 1939– Abstract painter and teacher, born in Derby, attending its College of Art, 1956–8, then Royal College of Art, 1958–61. Then lived in Nottingham and taught at its College of Art. Showed with Young Contemporaries, AIA Gallery and was included in 1965 John Moores Liverpool Exhibition. In 1967 Cartwright's oil on canvas Three was included in Survey '67 Abstract Painters at Camden Arts Centre and it was taken into the Arts Council collection.

Reg CARTWRIGHT 1938– Artist and illustrator, born in Leicester, who settled in Leicestershire at Kibworth Beauchamp, 1970. Cartwright did his National Service as a musician in the Leicester Regiment, 1957–60, then worked in studios as a commercial artist and art director for 13 years, becoming a full-time painter and illustrator in 1974. Mixed shows included Portal Gallery, 1972; Piccadilly Gallery, 1979; 16th Exhibition of Original Pictures of International Children's Books, Japan, 1981; and Royal Festival Hall Books of the Year Exhibition, 1986. Solo shows included Portal from 1974; Leicester Museum and Art Gallery, which holds his work, 1980–1; Woods Gallery, Leicester, 1990; Goldmark Gallery, Uppingham, 1995; and Cambridge Contemporary Art, Cambridge, 2001.

Richard CARTWRIGHT 1951– Painter of imaginative, dreamlike landscapes, he studied at Goldsmiths' College

School of Art and drew inspiration from sources as diverse as the early Sienese School, Alfred Wallis, Samuel Palmer, Morandi and Corot. In 1990 he was elected a member of RWA. Group shows included Campbell and Franks, 1976–7; Jablonski Gallery, 1987; and Waterman Fine Art, 1990. Cartwright had a solo show at Marches Gallery, Hereford, 1977, later ones including Rooksmoor Gallery, Bath, from 1987; Adam Gallery, from 1993; Fosse Gallery, Stow-on-the-Wold, 1998; and John Martin of London, 1999. His exhibition Sanctuary was at JohnMartinGallery in 2005.

Simon CARTWRIGHT fl. from mid-1980s– Painter who studied at University College of Wales, 1980–4; University of California, San Diego, Santa Cruz, 1982–3; and London University, 1988–9. Group shows included Fosse Gallery, Stow-on-the-Wold, and Selective Eye Gallery, Jersey, both 1991. Had a solo exhibition at Frost & Reed, 1990. This featured a number of themes common to Cartwright's work: still life, effect on landscape of the post-war agricultural revolution, architecture and political assassinations.

Caroline CARY 1940– Painter in acrylic and watercolour. She studied at Camberwell and Chelsea Schools of Art in the late 1950s, her teachers including Lawrence Gowing. She ceased painting professionally while bringing up her family, but then resumed, much of her work stemming from travels in Africa, India and the Far East. Although tending towards the abstract, she said that her works revealed "a strong physical presence". Mixed shows included Mall Galleries, Guildford University, Clarges and Jonathan Poole Galleries. From the mid-1970s was a frequent solo exhibitor, notably at Loggia and Langton Galleries, later shows taking place at Leighton House, 1983, Sue Rankin Gallery, 1990, Z Gallery in Soho, New York, 1993, The Millinery Works, 1999, The Carlyle Gallery, 2002, and New Grafton Gallery, 2004. Worked in London and Devon.

Ateo J CASADIO 1905–1987 Painter of Italian descent, who spent most of his life in England, noted for still life. In 1969 showed Adam and Eve in RA Summer Exhibition and work also handled by Phipps & Company and The Wykeham Gallery, Stockbridge. Lived in Nazeing, Essex.

Wyn CASBOLT 1914– Painter, draughtsman and printmaker, she was born in London. Studied at Slade School of Fine Art with Norman Janes and Randolph Schwabe. Exhibited WIAC, Redfern Gallery, with Newbury Art Society and abroad. For much of her life Casbolt suffered poor health, but this did not prevent her producing fine landscapes and abstracts in the late 1950s and early 1960s. Lived in Newbury, Berkshire, later in southwest London.

Tony CASEMENT 1949– Abstract artist, noted for paintings on canvas and paper with an emphasis on the use of colour, direct mark and surface, and teacher, born in St Eval, Cornwall. He studied at the fine art department at the University of Newcastle upon Tyne, 1967–71, then was one of a specialist printmaking group at Brighton Polytechnic, 1971–2, returning to Newcastle as research assistant fine art, printmaking, media, 1972–4. His teachers included Ian Stephenson. After being a part-time lecturer at Hertfordshire College of Art, St Albans, 1976–8, from 1978 Casement was a visiting lecturer at venues including Hull and Canterbury Colleges of Art; Portsmouth Polytechnic; Sir John Cass; Southend and Suffolk Colleges; and Norwich School of Art. Between 1990–4, he was a founder-member and co-ordinator for Open Studios and Workshops in northeast Suffolk, where lived at Wangford; joined Health Images, 1991; spent some time in Dhaka, Bangladesh, and was a member of Halesworth Gallery committee, both 1992; and joined Bearing 090° (European artists exchange), 1993. Mixed shows included Young Generation, Norrköping Museum, Sweden, and International Drawing Biennale, Teesside, from 1973; Eastern Open, Fermoy Centre, King's Lynn, from 1987, being a prizewinner in 1992; and Kettle's Yard Gallery Open, Cambridge, 1995. Had a solo show at Calouste Gulbenkian Gallery, Newcastle Polytechnic, 1973, later ones including Martha Stevns Gallery, Fressingfield, 1995.

Comhghall CASEY 1976– Painter of small still lifes, portraits and landscapes, born in Letterkenny, County Donegal, Ireland, who moved to Omagh, County Tyrone, in 1979, then to Belfast in 1994 to study for an art and design foundation at University of Ulster. In 1998, graduated with an honours degree in fine arts, specialising in painting. After two years in Belfast, moved to live and work in Dublin, where in 2002 he was one of Two Northern Contemporaries shown by Gorry Gallery. Casey's awards included Anderson Auctioneers and Valuers Prize, Best Self-Portrait, RUA, 1996 and 1999, also in 1999 the Young Artist of the Year + Regional Prize (Belfast), Hunting Art Prizes, Royal College of Art and Association of Art Historians Thesis Prize. In 1998, Casey was commissioned to produce drawings for the Ulster-American Folk Park, Omagh, and in 1999 he had a fellowship at Ballinglen Arts Foundation, Ballycastle, County Mayo. Took part in many mixed shows in Ireland, solo shows including Murneen Gallery in Antrim Town, Omagh Arts Festival at The Gallery, Omagh, and The Emer Gallery, Belfast, all 1999, also at Emer Gallery in 2001. Ulster Museum, Department of Education and Ballinglen Arts Foundation Archive hold examples.

Christopher CASH 1919–1982 Painter, draughtsman and teacher, educated at Stowe School, who attended Hertford College, Oxford, 1937–8. After service during World War II, 1939–46, Cash attended Camberwell School of Arts and Crafts, 1946–8. Cash was an inspiring head of art at Bedales School, 1950–78, where he encouraged, among other pupils, the artist Sarah Raphael, also William Jackson, who later ran the William Jackson Gallery and who organised the exhibition Bedales Art & Design at Art 99, Business Design Centre, 1999, including Cash's work. Little of this is extant, as Cash destroyed pictures which did not meet his exacting standards. Died in London.

Francis Milton CASHMORE 1892–1971 Architect and painter whose buildings and watercolours were marked by an urbane style. He was born in London and attended University College School, where he developed as a fine pianist, noted mathematician and perspective draughtsman. Studied architecture at Regent Street Polytechnic and at Royal Academy Schools, where Edwin Lutyens was his mentor. After World War I service with the Aircraft Manufacturing Company as a design engineer, in 1920 Cashmore qualified at RIBA, of which he was made a fellow in 1932. In 1921 joined Dunbar Smith and Cecil Brewer, who were involved with National Museum of

Wales in Cardiff and Heal's department store, London. Aged 35 Cashmore joined Messrs Joseph as design architect, becoming a partner in 1932; in 1960 he became senior partner and the firm was renamed Messrs Joseph, F Milton Cashmore and Partners. Among notable buildings he worked on were Shell-Mex House, on the Embankment; Melbury Court, Kensington High Street; Springbok House, Leatherhead Court, Surrey; and Britannic House, Moorfields. Many watercolours of buildings made by Cashmore in the post-war period have become valuable records. A successful show was held at Comedy Gallery, 1963, with another at The Medici Gallery, 1992, to celebrate his centenary.

Ann CASIMIR 1935– Sculptor and printmaker, born in Montreal, Canada, where she studied at McGill University. Studied art at Montreal Museum of Fine Arts, in Italy and at Sir John Cass School of Art. Showed at Free Painters and Sculptors, of which she was a fellow, and elsewhere in London, where she had several solo exhibitions and lived.

Nigel CASSELDINE 1947– Painter, notable for richly coloured, painterly landscapes of Ireland and East Anglia, as in his solo show at The Medici Galleries, 1996. He initially worked as a studio assistant to F V Magrath, studying part-time at the Sir John Cass and Camberwell Schools of Art, 1967–72. After this, he formed the Romney Studio Workshop. Casseldine won The Brandler Painting Prize in 1988 and in 1991 was elected a full academician at RWA, having been an associate from 1985. Also exhibited at Nina Zborowska Fine Paintings in Painswick, RA, Rooksmoor and Adam Galleries in Bath, Wykeham Gallery and Penwith, St Ives. Lived in Chalford, Stroud, Gloucestershire.

Julia CASSELS fl. from 1980s– Painter who after a couple of years in advertising and design went to live in Africa for a time in the Rift Valley, Kenya. On her return to England, not wishing a routine job she pursued her enthusiasm for painting by producing watercolours for exhibition and commission. Travelled in Italy and Britain. Exhibitions included Guildhall Gallery, Winchester; Mall Galleries, Art for Youth Exhibition, 1990; Hurlingham Gallery; Percy Bass Ltd; and in 1991 she had a solo show at Charlotte Lampard Gallery.

Hugh CASSON 1910–1999 Architect, watercolourist and illustrator, author and teacher, born and lived in London. He studied architecture at Cambridge University; Craven Scholar, British School at Athens, 1933; and at Bartlett School, University of London. He was in private practice as an architect from 1937. During World War II was camouflage officer with the Air Ministry. Neville Conder joined Casson's practice after the war and as Casson, Conder & Partners they produced buildings sensitive to their surroundings, examples being the arts faculty site at Cambridge and the Ismaili Centre near the Victoria & Albert Museum. From 1948–51 was director of architecture for the Festival of Britain. He held many official appointments. From 1953–75 was in charge of the new school of interior (later environmental) design, at the Royal College of Art, with his wife Margaret as senior tutor; effectively, it was a school of architecture. Casson was knighted in 1952; was elected RA in 1970; was president of the RA, 1976–84; and was made a Companion of Honour, 1985. His publications included *New Sights of London*, 1937; *Bombed Churches*, 1946; *Diary*, 1981; *Hugh Casson's Oxford*, 1988; and *Hugh Casson's Cambridge*, 1992. Casson's wife's photographs were shown at the Fine Art Society, 2000, under her maiden name, Margaret MacDonald.

Lucy CASSON 1960– Creator of small sculptures, born in Prestwood, Buckinghamshire, who graduated from Camberwell School of Arts and Crafts in 1981. Went on to show her witty, colourful works in Britain and abroad, in 1996 being given a small show at Hove Museum & Art Gallery in its First Sight showcase, others at Ruthin Crafts Centre, Ruthin, 2001, Burton Art Gallery & Museum, Bideford, 2002, and Rebecca Hossack Gallery, 2003. Casson said that her work was "made of recycled tin, wire, twigs, cloth, rubber, gloves and found objects, soldered, rivetted or stuck together. I gather my inspiration from observation of people and animals, instances, stories, moments and moods."

Simon John CASSON 1965– Artist and teacher, born in York, who lived in Zambia, until 1982. Gained a first-class honours degree in fine art painting at Exeter College of Art and Design, 1985–8, in 1987 studying in Rotterdam; attended Central St Martins College of Art and Design, part-time, for a postgraduate diploma in printmaking, 1988–90; then gained his master's degree at the Royal Academy Schools, 1991–4. Among many awards and prizes won were the Cecil Collins Memorial Prize for Fine Art, 1990; David Murray Studentships, Travel Scholarships to Spain and Italy, 1993 and 1994; and in 1994 the Royal Academy Gold Medal for Painting. Teaching included Bournemouth and Poole College of Art and Design. Mixed exhibitions included RA Summer Exhibition and RE, both from 1989 (he was made an associate of RE in 1992); National Printmaking Exhibition, Mall Galleries, 1994; and Ainscough Contemporary Art, 1996. In 2000 he had solo shows at The Gallery, Poole, and Long & Ryle, where in his exhibition Tantalus, said *The Independent*, "turbulent canvases wrench Old-Master classicism into the graffiti-gun chaos of the 21st century."

Jesse Dale CAST 1900–1976 Painter, draughtsman and teacher, born in London. From 1914–17 Cast studied at School of Building, Brixton, intending to become an interior decorator, then for three years was employed successively in design studios of Maples, Harrods and H & C Davis (Radiation Ltd). He attended life classes at St Martin's School of Art in the afternoons, and in the evenings at Camberwell School of Arts and Crafts. In 1919 a large watercolour was hung in the architectural room of the RA. Awarded a scholarship by London County Council, Cast studied at Camberwell 1920–2, under Albert Rutherston, then from 1922–6 under Henry Tonks at Slade School of Fine Art, winning first prize in painting from life and first prize in decorative design, 1924–5; first prize in drawing heads from life, 1925–6; and, on leaving, the Robert Ross Scholarship in Fine Art. Cast showed at NEAC for first time in 1926 at the start of a period when he lived abroad, in Bruges, Belgium; then Soller, Majorca. From 1930–9 Cast showed at RP, to which he was elected in 1957, and annually at RA from 1934, but he later declined offers of nomination for election. During the war Cast worked in the Ministry of Aircraft production, then afterwards taught at Harrow School of Art, Central School of Art and Design and Hornsey College of Art, where he accepted a permanent appointment. Because he was so self-critical and because a large number of paintings was destroyed during the war, Cast's extant output is small. He was highly regarded by his peers as a meticulous draughtsman and craftsman. A memorial show was held at South London Art Gallery, 1980, another at University College, 1994. Tate Gallery, National Maritime Museum and British Museum hold examples. Lived in Tunbridge Wells, Kent.

Elinor Beryl Morley CASTLE 1912–1998 Artist, notably a watercolourist and draughtsman, born in London, one of two daughters of the artist Harry Morley (1881–1943) whose work she promoted from the early 1970s. Her mother was the embroiderer and calligrapher Lilias Helen Swain (1880–1973). Beryl trained at the Royal Academy Schools in the 1920s, originally exhibiting under her maiden name, notably with RP, in 1939 marrying Captain John Castle, who after World War II service represented a paint manufacturer. Castle was a colourful character, who did his job using a 1920s Rolls-Royce open tourer, one of several that he owned, and he and his vivacious wife were prominent at 20 Ghost Club rallies. From the early 1950s the Castles became enthusiasts to preserve declining inland waterways and made ambitious trips using the *Maybug*, a novel pontoon houseboat with rear-mounted paddles which Castle designed. Beryl filled many sketchbooks with the vanishing life of Britain's working canals, made a careful study of traditional canal-ware decoration, exhibitions including RA Summer Exhibition. Died in Kings Langley, Hertfordshire.

Eva CASTLE 1922– Sculptor, potter and designer, born in Aarhus, Denmark. She studied at Royal Academy in Copenhagen, 1944–7, then at Slade School of Fine Art, 1948–50, with A H Gerrard and F E McWilliam. Produced textile designs and ceramics in Britain and on the continent. Was a founder-member of SPS in 1953 and was a fellow of RBS. Her sculpture Clearance was in the Football Association's show Football and the Fine Arts, 1953, and in 1956–7 she was guest artist at Chelsea Pottery. Showed at RA from 1951 as well as in leading London and provincial galleries. Her Madonna is in St John's Church, Newbury. Castle was married to the actor Tony Britton and lived in London.

Florence E CASTLE 1867– Painter and illustrator, brought up in Croydon, Surrey. Studied at Lambeth School of Art with Sir William Llewellyn, then in Paris. Showed RA, ROI, SWA and NEAC. Lived in London.

Frances CASTLE 1966– Computer animator, reflected in her own work as a painter, and musician, born in Kingston upon Thames, Surrey. Did a foundation course at Richmond College, 1983–5; a Higher National Diploma in illustration at Lincoln College, 1985–7; a wide range of jobs in Britain and abroad, 1987–95; and in 1995–6 a postgraduate diploma in computer imaging and animation at Guildhall School of Music & Drama. Created music on a computer and four-track machine, released two singles and had her own music and art websites. Exhibitions included Maze Gallery, Brighton; Smiths Galleries; Chamber of Pop Culture; and with the Stuckists, of which she was a member, at Artbank Gallery, 2001. Lived in London.

Patricia CASTLE fl. from 1940s– Artist, born and eventually returned to London, who studied for a short time at Camberwell School of Arts and Crafts, also in evenings at St Martin's School of Art. In early 1970s she moved to Ramsgate, became involved in town conservation and converted a disused hardware shop into a gallery. Castle later showed and travelled in America. Mixed exhibitions included Datchet Gallery in Datchet, 1978; Flint House Gallery, Broadstairs, 1982; Plaza Gallery, Houston, 1985; New Academy Gallery, 1987; The Heifer Gallery, from 1990; and Platform Gallery, Folkestone, 1991. Had a first solo show in early 1960s, later ones including Canterbury Festival, 1988, and Burgh House, Hampstead, 1990–1.

Shelley CASTLE 1967– Artist working in mixed media, born and lived in London, who obtained a first-class honours degree from Central St Martin's College of Art & Design, 1989–92. Showed at Cromwell and Ward and Fresh Art, 1992 and in Biennale in Naples, Madrid and Brussels, 1993, sharing an exhibition at Morley College in the same year. Chelsea Arts Club holds work.

Edmund CASWELL 1938–1996 Artist, notably a muralist, born in Bangalore, India, remaining there seven years before his family returned to England, where Edmund grew up in Coventry. Although at 13 he won a scholarship to the local School of Art, a love of horses prompted him to study at agricultural college in Oxford, after which his varied career including being a coal miner, soldier, decorator and stage designer. Aged 38, Caswell decided to be a full-time artist, attending life classes at Heatherley and St Martin's Schools of Art and a part-time foundation course at Sir John Cass. At 40, Caswell was accepted for the fine arts degree course at Middlesex Polytechnic, and in his first year completed a mural in the geriatric ward of Colindale Hospital. In his final year, 1980, Caswell began his huge mural based on J M Barrie's *Peter Pan* at the Hospital for Sick Children, Great Ormond Street, a vivid depiction of 450 figures drawing on his Indian memories. It was finished in 1988, and thereafter Caswell was involved with a number of *Peter Pan* ventures for Barrie's birthplace at Kirriemuir. Further projects included 10 large paintings linked to Mussorgsky's *Pictures from an Exhibition* music; it developed into a live multi-media production which had a Scottish première at Dundee University and an exhibition there, both in 1993. Caswell also produced a painting for Dundee developer Michael Johnston's new headquarters in 1994, and soon after he painted Robert Burns' *Tam O'Shanter* for the same building. Caswell did illustrations for Jane Austen's *Pride and Prejudice*, for Black Swan Press, 1985–6, and in 1994–5 painted portraits for Dundee University, including one of Barrie. Caswell's last painting was for St Mary Magdelene Church in Dundee, where his funeral service was held after his death from cancer. Ninewells Hospital in the city, where he had lived from 1990, held a memorial exhibition, 1996–7.

Bob CATCHPOLE 1949– Sculptor, born in Norwich, who studied at the Slade School of Fine Art, 1973–5, where he was awarded a Higher Diploma in Fine Art. Became head of sculpture at Eton College. Showed widely in southern England, including the RA Summer Exhibition. Art on show at The Gallery in Cork Street, 2001, included Catchpole's witty Dancing Ladder, one of the surreal works, using found objects, with which he recalled his childhood in Norfolk, where maintained a studio.

Heather O CATCHPOLE 1942– Miniaturist, notable for her portraits, born in Winnipeg, Canada. She studied at Natal School of Arts and Craft, South Africa. Became a member of RMS, also exhibiting at RA, Hilliard Society and elsewhere. Lived at Fitzhead, Somerset.

Annalisa CATELLI 1969– Painter, born in Turin, Italy, who, after graduating in French literature at the University of Bologna, moved to New York in 1992 and worked for the Morgan Library Museum. In 1997, she enrolled at the City and Guilds of London Art School, graduating in fine arts, painting, in 2001. Based in London, Catelli participated in group shows at Birmingham University, Air Gallery and Walton Gallery, all 2001, and The Bettie Morton Gallery, 2002. Walton Gallery gave Catelli a solo exhibition in 2002. It featured apparently abstract pictures in reds and blues, but in the catalogue Julian Bell noted that the artist's work "abstracts – 'draws away' – from familiar images of the figure, but only to draw closer to the mystery of what a human being is." Catelli's work was acquired by public and private collections.

Paul CATHERALL 1967– Artist whose main theme was architectural lino-cuts but who also illustrated newspaper articles and book-jackets. He was born in Lichfield, Staffordshire, attended Leicester Polytechnic, 1986–9, and became a full member of the Association of Illustrators. Group shows included Affordable Art Fairs in Bristol, London and New York, 2002, and National Print Collection, Mall Galleries, 2002 and 2003. Had solo exhibitions at Clapham Art Gallery from 1999. Catherall was also featured in Platform for Art, on the London Underground, in 2002. Lived in London.

John Denis Harwood CATLEUGH 1920– Painter, designer, architect, theatre designer and collagist, born in King's Lynn, Norfolk. He was also a noted collector of British ceramics, especially William De Morgan. Catleugh attended Oundle School and London University, qualifying as an architect in 1949 after World War II service. Apart from this, Catleugh did not have a formal art training and his career was multi-faceted. Early on he made a series of Perspex and wood reliefs and did furniture designs, as well as creating collages and relief paintings in plaster. In 1953 he was a prizewinner in the Furniture Makers' Guild Coronation Design Competition. In 1951 Catleugh designed sets for Picasso's play *Desire Caught by the Tail*, at the Watergate Theatre. A significant development was seeing in 1949 a Jackson Pollock exhibition in Venice, which launched the artist on an exploration of the drip-and-pour technique; it led to a series of space-time pictures. Among the important group shows in which he participated were British Abstract Art at Gimpel Fils, in 1951 and This is Tomorrow, at the Whitechapel Art Gallery, 1956. AIA and Redfern Gallery also exhibited the work of Catleugh and England & Co gave him a shared show with John Milnes-Smith in 1988. Lived in London.

Christopher CATLIN 1902–1977 Self-taught artist, born and lived in London, who commonly signed his work C. After attending elementary school he eventually became a taxi-cab driver. Painted from early in life, favouring pastel and tempera, his subjects market scenes and people, with a special interest in people and their faces. His work brought him a circle of friends including notabilities such as Sir Charles Tennyson and C V Wedgwood, and artists Polly Hill Clark and Helen Stuart Weir. Catlin's wife cleaned for the artist Orovida Pissarro and, in gratitude for the Catlins' help and friendship, Orovida bought them a house in Fulham after selling one of her grand-father, Camille's, pictures. Catlin was a member of RBA, showed at RA and in local independent exhibitions and had a solo show in Kensington Church Street shortly before he died.

Brian CATLING 1948– Artist and teacher working in a wide variety of media, including abstract sculpture in steel, born in London. He studied at North-East London Polytechnic and Royal College of Art and in 1982–5 was the first Henry Moore Fellow at Norwich. Became head of sculpture at the Ruskin School of Drawing and Fine Art, Oxford. Exhibited at Air Gallery, 1977, Camden Arts Centre, 1979, Arnolfini Gallery, Bristol, in 1980, and Ikon Gallery, Birmingham, 1981. In 1983 was included in British Artists at Cyprus College of Art at Woodlands Art Gallery. Later works included The Blindings, Serpentine Gallery, 1994; an eight-hour video Cyclops, South London Gallery, 1996; and, with Tony Grisoni, the film *Vanished!*, in E S P – Contemporary Artists Investigate the Paranormal, Ikon Gallery, 1999. Arts Council holds several examples.

Lance CATTERMOLE 1898–1992 Painter who studied at Central School of Arts and Crafts, 1922–3, teachers including Bernard Meninsky and James Grant, then Slade School of Fine Art, 1923–6, under Henry Tonks and Philip Wilson Steer. Showed with RA, ROI of which he was made a member in 1938, RBA and widely in the provinces. National Army Museum holds his work. Lived for many years at High Salvington, Sussex. Cattermole came from a line of artists: his father was Sydney, a painter who followed on from George, illustrator of Charles Dickens' *The Old Curiosity Shop* and other works.

Fred CATTON 1889– Self-taught watercolourist, brought up in London. Exhibited RWS, RBA, UA and with Civil Defence Artists. Lived in London and later at Welling, Kent.

Annie CATTRELL 1962– Artist and teacher, notably in glass, born in Glasgow, who gained a fine art honours degree at the School of Art there, 1980–4; her master's at University of Ulster, Belfast, 1984–5; studied at International Glass Centre, Birmingham, 1995–6; and her master's in glass, Royal College of Art, 1996–9. Awards included Solar Glass Scholarship, 1996–9, and Pilkington Scholarship, 1998–9; residencies Royal Edinburgh Hospital, 1990–1, and Millay Colony for the Arts, New York State, America, 1994. Lectured at Cheltenham and Gloucester College of Higher Education, 1992–9, then Edinburgh College of Art, and held a number of visiting lectureships. Exhibitions included Fruitmarket Open, Edinburgh, 1989; 21 Prints, Crawford Arts Centre, St Andrews, and tour, 1993; Detectable, Real Gallery, New York, 1998; and Pause, *The Economist*, 1999–00. Aberdeen Art Gallery, Glasgow Museums and Art Galleries and Scottish Arts Council hold examples. Lived in London.

Louise CATTRELL 1957– Painter, notably of landscape, born in Glasgow. She studied at Duncan of Jordanstone College of Art, Dundee, 1975–80, then at Royal College of Art, 1980–3. Among her awards were the Duncan of Drumfork Travelling Scholarship, in 1978; an Adam Bruce Thomson Award from RSA and a Scottish Education Travelling Scholarship, in 1979; the Farquahar Reid Award, in 1980; and the John Minton Award, in 1983. Cattrell took part in a number of group shows, including SSA, RA and the Whitechapel Open. Had a solo exhibition at Beaux Arts, Bath, 1992, her Northern Arts-supported touring show Coast including Towner Art Gallery, Eastbourne, 1999.

Ian CAUGHLIN 1948– Painter and teacher, born in Lancaster, who studied painting at St Martin's School of Art, 1966–71. He then settled in London, teaching English part-time to foreign students. His group exhibitions included Young Contemporaries, Burlington House, 1970; Martello Street, 1973; and House at Home: A Birthday Celebration, House, 1979. In that year he shared a show at House, 62 Regent's Park Road, with Caroline Putt and George Melly bought his 1976–8 oil on canvas View from a Roof, Rostrevor Road, Fulham, for the Arts Council. He called it "a remarkable accomplishment for so young a man".

Luke CAULFIELD 1969– Figurative painter, born and with a studio in London, who was son of the artist Patrick Caulfield. Luke studied at Kensington and Chelsea College, 1995-6, then Slade School of Fine Art from 1996. He won a prize in the NatWest Art Prize, 1998, and had a picture, Missing Person, in John Moores Liverpool Exhibition, 1999. There was a solo exhibition at The Place, 1998, and one of large portraits at Dazed and Confused Gallery, 2001.

Patrick CAULFIELD 1936–2005 Painter, printmaker and teacher, born in London, where he continued to live. He was the father of the artist Luke Caulfield. Patrick studied at Chelsea School of Art, 1956–9, and Royal College of Art, 1960–3. In the latter year he taught at Chelsea School of Art. By then Caulfield had shown several times with Young Contemporaries and in 1964 was in The New Generation at Whitechapel Art Gallery. Caulfield's first one-man show was at Robert Fraser Gallery in 1965, and he soon made an impression in mixed and solo international shows. A print retrospective toured California in 1977; in 1981 there was a retrospective at Walker Art Gallery, Liverpool, and Tate Gallery; Serpentine Gallery in 1992–3; and Hayward Gallery, 1999, plus foreign tour. Caulfield's illustrations for the poems of Jules Laforgue were shown at MAC, Birmingham, 2001. Later exhibitions included Waddington Galleries, 2002. The artist's early mature works were black-and-white, depicting familiar objects, and he was seen as one of the later generation of Pop painters. When he worked in colour this was black-outlined and without modulation, although later works depended more on painterly illusion, such as in the 1984 acrylic on canvas Fish and Sandwich, in the Saatchi Collection. From the 1980s Caulfield extended his range in response to many commissions. These included a huge painting for the headquarters of the London Life Association, in Bristol; designs for Michael Corder's 1984 ballet *Party Game*, at the Royal Opera House, Covent Garden; in 1990 a stained glass window for the Ivy Restaurant; a big carpet for the atrium of the British Council headquarters in Manchester in the early 1990s; followed in 1994 by a ceramic mosaic for the National Museums and Galleries of Wales; a maquette-sized design tapestry for the new British Library, inspired by Laurence Sterne's novel *Tristram Shandy*, unrealised at the artist's death; and in 2001 mosaics for the Arco di Travertino station, part of the Rome metro and big paintings for the Portsmouth Cathedral organ. In the following year Caulfield was diagnosed suffering from mouth and tongue cancer, although he continued to produce impressive work. Arts Council and many other public collections hold his work. Elected RA, 1993.

Ian CAUNCE 1947– Sculptor who studied at Liverpool Polytechnic, 1982–5. His exhibitions included Riverside, Widnes, 1981; Beaumanor Hall, Leicestershire, 1985–6; and the Walker Art Gallery touring Merseyside Artists 3, 1986–7.

William Sidney CAUSER 1876–1958 Painter in various media, born in Wolverhampton, Staffordshire. Studied at Wolverhampton School of Art, in London and in several countries on the continent. Exhibited RA, NEAC, Leicester Galleries, RI and Royal Glasgow Institute of the Fine Arts; one-man shows Fine Art Society and Leger Gallery. Work held widely in provincial collections. His books include *An Artist in Spain*. Lived in London.

Peter CAVACIUTI 1952– Painter whose work reflected an interest in classical Chinese art and Japanese poetics. He used handmade paper from China, Korea, Japan and Nepal; Chinese ink and traditional pigments; and developed methods of mixing colours from seventeenth-century Chinese recipes. Cavaciuti spent seven years studying with the foremost Chinese artist Fei Cheng Wu; continued with Professor Bao, the noted flower and bird painter; and attended the Central School of Art, Beijing. Exhibitions included RA Summer Exhibition, RWS, Sebastian Pearson Gallery, Broughton House Gallery in Cambridge, Benjamin Hargreaves and Belgium and Japan.

John CAVANAGH 1931–c.1995 Artist, born in Manchester, who studied there at the College of art and Design. Had a solo exhibition at City Art Gallery, Salford, 1961, then a series in the north of England, also at Drian Galleries from 1974, including figurative-towards-abstract pictures, and Compendium Galleries, Birmingham, 1975.

Sue CAVE 1949– Painter and muralist, born in Grimsby, Lincolnshire. She studied at the local School of Art, 1965–8, then Kingston College of Art from 1968, in 1971 gaining a scholarship to study in Egypt. Was commissioned to paint a mural for Grimsby Parish Church and painted harpsichords created by the musical instrument maker Robert Goble. These were exhibited at music festivals in Britain and on the continent. Had a first solo exhibition at Oxfordshire County Museum in 1981 and in 1985–6 was included in the Piccadilly Gallery's show The Brotherhood of Ruralists and Friends.

Lucy CAVENDISH 1973– Painter who graduated in fine art from the City and Guilds School, 1991–4. In 2002 she attended Prince Charles's painting academy in Normandy. She received awards from the Goldsmiths' Company; the RA's David Murray Award; and a David Twendle Award. Cavendish had artist residencies at Marrakesh in Morocco, 1997, and Delfina Studios in Spain, 1998. Among her mixed shows were Bartley Drey Gallery, 1996; xxx Gallery, 1997; and Accademia Italiana, London, 1998. Cavendish's first solo show at Thomas Williams Fine Art in 2002 was almost a sell-out. Her second, in 2004, was a collection of romantically textured and often darkly moody paintings in oil, mostly of England and Italy, with a particular focus on the sea and motion of the water.

Sarah CAWKWELL 1950– Artist producing drawings, monoprints, reliefs and sculpture, born in Oxford, who in her work was "interested in the repetitive minutiae of life." Influences were "The history of art, Western and African." After working in the Arts Council's art department, 1969–71, and the Whitechapel Art Gallery, 1971–4, Cawkwell graduated in fine art at the Central School of Art, 1980–3, taught by Cecil Collins, David Haughton, Marc Vaux, William Turnbull and Patrick Reyntiens. Group exhibitions included Stowells Trophy, RA, and Hunting Group Exhibition, Mall Galleries, both 1983; Young Blood, Barbican, and Leicestershire Collection Exhibition, both 1984; Camden Annual, Camden Arts Centre, 1985; Feminist Update, The People's Gallery, 1988; Vision and Practice – Seven Women Artists, St George's Crypt, Bloomsbury, 1989; Threadlines, Harriet Green Gallery, which Cawkwell curated and showed in, 1995; Marking Presence, Artsway, Sway, Meeting in Art 1, in Istanbul, Turkey, and Unfolding, St George's Hospital, southwest London, all 1997; and Sartorial, England & Co, 2003. Drawing Threads, Jacqueline Morreau and Sarah Cawkwell, was a touring show, including Babylon Gallery, Ely, 2004–5. It was accompanied by a catalogue featuring Cawkwell's work, as was her solo exhibition Large Drawings and Reliefs, Fermoy Gallery, King's Lynn, 1998. Among her other one-man shows were Work, The 39 Steps, Whitechapel, 1987; Drawn Threads, New Hall, Cambridge, and Large Charcoal Works, Standpoint Gallery, both 1995; Large Charcoal Images, The King of Hearts, Norwich, 1996; and Drawings and Reliefs, Christ Church Picture Gallery, Oxford, 2001. The Arts Council, New Hall, Wolfson College in Oxford and Detroit Receiving Hospital, in America, hold examples. Lived in north London.

Herbert Harry CAWOOD 1890–1957 Sculptor, notably of portraits, and founder, born in Sheffield. He studied at the Technical School of Art there, winning several medals subsequently at the Royal Academy Schools. He exhibited at RA and in the provinces. Cawood was a fellow of the RBS, becoming honorary treasurer for a time just after World War II. Lived in London.

Alfred CAWS 1912– Painter, draughtsman, designer and teacher, born in Bembridge, Isle of Wight. He studied at Heatherley's School of Fine Art under Patrick Larking and Frederic Whiting and went on to teach in further education classes. Caws said that his main objectives were "relationship of shapes and unity of colour". He was a member of NS, also showing with ROI, Artists of Chelsea, AEB, Wessex Artists and elsewhere. His work was reproduced in commercial publications. Lived in Shanklin, Isle of Wight.

Hermon CAWTHRA 1886–1971 Monumental sculptor, draughtsman and teacher, born Joseph Hermon Cawthra in Baildon, Yorkshire. From the ages of 14–21 he was apprenticed to a monumental mason, but studied in the evenings from 1904 at Saltaire Art School and in 1907–9 at Leeds School of Art. Then studied full-time at Royal College of Art, 1909–11, and Royal Academy Schools, 1912–16, when he was found unfit for Army service so carved propellors for the Royal Flying Corps. Worked for a short time for the sculptor Paul Montford after the war, then was on his own until 1939, when World War II forced him to close his studio. He had been elected a fellow of the RBS in 1937. When war broke out Cawthra joined Brighton College of Art, in 1941 going to Hull as head of sculpture, where he stayed until war's end. After reopening his London studio Cawthra taught part-time, until he had to retire, at 70, at Bournemouth Municipal College of Art. Cawthra, who intensely disliked the modern movement in sculpture, had made his name with the Bootle War Memorial in 1922. Other notable works included the Burns statue in Dumfries; The Orator, drawn from life at Hyde Park Corner; Britannia and the Lion, on the County Fire Office, in Piccadilly; and the memorial to the Earl of Meath at Lancaster Gate. Cawthra worked for the leading architects of his day and much of his sculpture went overseas, having a strong Empire theme. After Sir William Reid Dick he was one of the leading classical sculptors of his time. He showed at RA extensively as well as in Bradford, Liverpool and Glasgow. Cawthra was a brilliant portrait draughtsman and a sculptor of great range, examples being included in the volume *R B S: Modern British Sculpture*, published in 1939; and in Eric Newton's monograph *British Sculpture 1944–1946*. Latterly lived in Sheen in southwest London, but died on a visit to Cottingley, Yorkshire. His daughter was the architectural and costume historian Doreen Yarwood.

Mark CAZALET 1964– Painter, draughtsman and printmaker notable for fantastic landscapes, born in London. He studied at Chelsea and Falmouth Schools of Art, 1982–6. Won many awards, including a French Consul National Studentship at L'École Nationale Supérieure des Beaux-Arts, in Paris; a residency at the Cité-Internationale des Arts, also in Paris; and a Commonwealth University Scholarship to Baroda University, India. As well as being included in many group shows, Cazalet showed solo at Arts Centre Group, Waterloo, and at Gallery 7 in Bombay, but his first major exhibition in London was at Christopher Hull Gallery, 1992. Later solo exhibitions included Six Chapel Row, Bath, 2001.

CAZIEL 1906–1988 Painter whose work was strongly influenced by Cézanne and Cubism, born in Sosnowiec, Poland. His real name was Kazimierz Zielenkiewicz, with which he signed his work until in 1940s the name Caziel was adopted as more easily memorable. He studied at Warsaw Academy of Fine Arts, 1931–6, showed in Poland and then gained a state scholarship to Italy and Paris, 1937. In 1939 he volunteered for the Polish Army in France, settled in the country in 1946 in Aix-en-Provence, then in Paris, and designed Poland's pavilion for the Unesco International Exhibition of Modern Art. In 1947 had a solo show at Galerie Allard, Paris, shortly after which he began a long friendship with Picasso. In 1951 the Musée National d'Art Moderne bought a big canvas by Caziel, and two years later the Vatican commissioned four large pictures for its Museum of Religious Art. In 1957 Caziel married the Scottish painter Catherine Sinclair. He had the first of several one-man shows at Grabowski Gallery in 1966, three years before setting in Somerset, where he died. He bequeathed 10 paintings to the National Museum of Modern Art in Warsaw, Toruń University also holding his work. In 1990 the Polish Cultural Institute in London held a memorial exhibition, another show being organised by Whitford Fine Art in 1995. Whitford showed works on paper from 1965 in 2001 with another show of Abstraction 1963–7 in 2004, the Polish Cultural Institute holding an exhibition, 2004–5. Tollemache House at Thurso, Caithness, contains a fresco designed by Caziel in 1963.

Janina CEBERTOWICZ 1953– Painter, draughtsman and teacher, born in Manchester, with a special interest in art and musical education. She studied at Bath Academy of Art, 1972–5, and Manchester Polytechnic, 1977–8, gaining an honours degree in fine art, her teachers including Donald McKinlay, Peter Kinley, Michael Kidner, William Scott, David Pearson and Adrian Heath. Held a number of teaching posts in Lancashire, where she lived at Cloughfold, Rossendale, from 1989 being head of art at Bury Grammar School for Girls. Residencies included Royal Northern College of Music from 1991. Cebertowicz was elected to MAFA from 1984 and was active in its running. Group shows included Portraits North at Salford Art Gallery, 1988; Bede Gallery, Jarrow, Van Gogh Centenary Exhibition, 1990. Had a solo show at Bluecoat Gallery in Liverpool, 1981, later ones including Tib Lane Gallery, Manchester, from 1989, and Royal Northern College of Music there from 1992.

Karol CEBULA 1946– Painter and artist in mixed media who also employed means such as tape recordings; teacher. He was born in Pittenweem, Fife. Studied at Edinburgh College of Art, 1964–9, gaining the Andrew Grant Travelling Scholarship, 1969–70. He attended Moray House College of Further Education in 1972. Two years later Cebula won a Scottish Arts Council Award. He was for a time an art teacher in Dunfermline. Cebula participated in group shows held by Young Scottish Contemporaries in the late 1960s, was included in Seven Scottish Artists at ICA in 1969, the Arts Council Travelling Exhibition Art Spectrum Scotland in 1971 and in A Choice Selection at Fruit Market Gallery, Edinburgh, 1975. In 1974 he had a solo show at Kynd Kyttock's Gallery, Falkland. Fife Education Committee and Scottish Arts Council hold his work.

Roger CECIL 1942– Painter, draughtsman and teacher who lived in the house in Abertillery, Monmouthshire, where he was born and brought up. He produced work rich in imagery, poetry and colour which drew on his environment, the industrial valley towns and mountains. Prolific and obsessive, he was a solitary artist, with affiliations to no group. Cecil joined Newport College of Art in 1959, teachers including John Wright and Thomas Rathmell; in 1963 he gained the highest award that year in the national diploma in design. Won the David Murray Landscape Award from the RA. Cecil was offered a place at Royal College of Art, but after a few weeks was unsatisfied and took up manual work in opencast mines and on building sites. The BBC made a television documentary on Cecil's work called *The Gentle Rebel*. Taught in Ebbw Vale. In 1995–7 he gained his master's with distinction in communication design from Central St Martins College of Art & Design. For a long time Cecil did not exhibit, through choice, and it was friends who helped to promote him. Had a series of exhibitions at Business Art Galleries from 1987 and in 1995 the Hill Court Gallery, Abergavenny, held a retrospective of work special to the artist. Gordon Hepworth and Y Tabernacl both showed Cecil's pictures.

Rose CECIL 1956– Painter and draughtsman who studied at Byam Shaw School of Art and City and Guilds of London Art School. Had a show of docklands pictures at Michael Parkin Gallery, 1988; travelled in Tibet, China, Nepal, Guatemala and Belize; and had a show in 1996 at Parkin of Galapagos Islands paintings.

Séan CÉITINN: *see* **John KEATING**

Morris CHACKAS 1916–2000 Painter, notably of portraits and still life using a light palette and careful disposition of forms, born in London. Chackas, known as Charlie, reckoned that his painting developed in earnest only after he left the Army in 1945, including service in Burma, settling in Oxford. There he began an intensive study of portraiture which lasted six years. For several decades Chackas lived in a wooden garden hut, hot in summer and cold in winter, within which he built a more congenial closet containing his bed, television, radio, phone gas heater and other essentials to cope with the bleakest conditions. Despite having damaged the sight of one eye, Chackas painted incessantly and obsessively. For him, portraits were "terribly exacting and tedious, but the best kind of education in the feel of paint". Among his subjects was Sir Reader Bullard, retired British ambassador to Persia. This period ended in a "spontaneous sort of branching out". Having been tremendously struck by an ancient cave painting, "I saw something special about the way an object sits in space, a kind of reality different from an imitation of reality, and I've been working toward it ever since." African art, Japanese flower arrangements, Cézanne, Matisse, de Staël and William Scott were apparent influences. Among Chackas's mixed appearances were Grosvenor Gallery, 1966, and Marjorie Parr, 1968–72. Shared a show with Sandra Blow at Bear Lane Gallery, Oxford, 1968. Outside Oxford, his solo exhibitions included Ikon Gallery, Birmingham, 1969. Many American academics visiting Oxford became keen collectors of works by Chackas, a man of dry wit and a keen Marxist. Duncan Campbell Fine Art held a studio sale in 2002. Pembroke, Keble and St Hugh's Colleges, Oxford, hold examples.

Ashton CHADWICK 1944– Artist and teacher, born in Cornwall. Studied at Falmouth School of Art, 1961–5, Brighton College of Art, 1965–6, and Royal Academy Schools, 1966–9. Teaching appointments included Basingstoke Technical College and widely in adult education, being an exhibitor at Artists in Adult Education at Woodlands Art Gallery, 1982. Other exhibitions included Oxford Press Gallery, 1969, Heal's Mansard Gallery, 1969–71, and Camden Arts Centre, 1981, where Chadwick was senior lecturer and Centre head.

Daniel CHADWICK 1965– Artist, born in Gloucester, who worked with Zaha Hadid Architects, 1987–91, then with the artist David Medalla, 1994. Among his many commissions were Heineken, Amsterdam, Netherlands, and Boots Group, Nottingham, both 1996; Sheppard Robson & Partners, for No 1 London Wall, 1997; and Greycoat, for 99 Gresham Street, and Tetra Pak Ltd, both 1998. Group shows included Blains Fine Art and solo shows Lefevre Contemporary Art, both 2000, with a solo exhibition at Beaux Arts in 2005.

Enid Mary CHADWICK 1902–1987 Church decorator, book illustrator and calligrapher, born in Basingstoke, Hampshire. Studied art with W B Morrell in Exeter and in Brighton at the College of Art with Lawrence Preston and with Louis Ginnett. Reflecting her religious upbringing Chadwick concentrated on children's book illustration with a Christian theme and she decorated a number of churches mainly in Britain but also in America and South

Africa. The Shrine of Our Lady of Walsingham contains her work. She was artist at the Shrine, near where she lived, from 1934–87. Signed work E M C.

Ernest Albert CHADWICK 1876–1956 Watercolourist, wood engraver and draughtsman, son of the artist John Chadwick, born in Marston Green, Warwickshire. He was one of the most prolific exhibitors at RBSA, of which he became a member in 1912. Was also a member of New Society of Artists, 1924, RCamA, 1929, and RI, 1939. Chadwick was noted for his pictures of English rural life, especially Cornish fishing villages, and used a bicycle to carry his painting equipment. Birmingham City Museum and Art Gallery holds his work. Lived in Henley-in-Arden, Warwickshire.

Helen CHADWICK 1953–1996 Artist in various media, born in Croydon, Surrey. She studied at Brighton Polytechnic, 1973–6, gaining an honours degree, obtaining her master's at Chelsea School of Art, 1976–7. Twice nominated for the Turner Prize, Chadwick unsettled many with her concentration on subjects such as defecation and decay. Piss Flowers, 1994, was a series of 12 bronzes cast from holes in the snow where she and her partner had urinated. She was in the group shows Long Live the New Flesh, Kettle's Yard, Cambridge, and Postmodern Prints, at Victoria & Albert Museum, both 1991; and in Twelve Stars, Belfast Arts Council Gallery and tour, 1992–3, which showed her Self Portrait, 1991, in ciba transparency, aluminium on glass, electrics, acquired for the European Parliament Collection. Tate Gallery and British Council also hold examples. Began showing solo soon after graduation, including Aspex Gallery, Portsmouth; Museum of Modern Art, Oxford; Museum of Modern Art in New York; and in 1996 the exhibition she was working on at the time of her death was held at Portfolio Gallery as part of the Edinburgh International Festival. There were retrospectives at Ferens Art Gallery, Hull, 1998–9, and Barbican Gallery, 2004, with a show at Zelda Cheatle, 2003. Henry Moore Institute, Leeds, organised My Personal Museum, from Chadwick's collection of material used to create her work, donated by Cheatle and the artist's estate, and Barbican Art Gallery held a retrospective, both 2004.

Lynn CHADWICK 1914–2003 Sculptor in metal, born in London. He is noted for his mobiles and for abstract shapes, dancing children and waiting and watching figures. After education at Merchant Taylors' School, although Chadwick wanted to become a sculptor, his family persuaded him to enter an architect's office, and he stayed an architectural draughtsman until World War II, when he became a Fleet Air Arm pilot. Working with the architect Rodney Thomas after the war Chadwick began experimenting with mobiles, partly inspired by the work of Alexander Calder. First showed at LG in 1950, in that year having initial one-man show at Gimpel Fils. Gained a national prize in The Unknown Political Prisoner competition in 1953; won International Sculpture Prize at Venice Biennale, 1956; and first prize at Concorso Internazionale del Bronzetto, in Padua, 1959. Showed regularly with Marlborough Gallery since 1961. Exhibited extensively around the world, being represented in many major collections, including Tate Gallery and Museum of Modern Art, New York. Retrospective at Yorkshire Sculpture Park, 1991–2; there was a solo show in 2001 at Beaux Arts, which, with Tate Britain, gave him a retrospective in 2003, and another exhibition in that year, Coming from the Dark, at Gallery Pangolin, Chalford. Lived at Stroud, Gloucestershire.

Paxton CHADWICK 1903–1961 Illustrator and designer with a strong interest in natural history. Born in Fallowfield, Lancashire, he attended Manchester School of Art. Exhibited in London, Manchester, in France and North America. He illustrated a large number of books on plants, birds and animals for leading publishers, such as the Educational Supply Association and Penguin Books Ltd. Lived at Leiston, Suffolk.

Sam CHADWICK 1902–1992 Watercolourist and printmaker, notable for his pictures of the Yorkshire dales. He was born in Leeds and, with the exception of 18 months spent in York in the early days of his training and two years in a London studio, lived and worked there. Upon retirement after 50 years as a commercial artist he devoted the last 15 years to landscape painting, employing a soft and fluid palette with refined tonal qualities. Chadwick was also an accomplished photographer.

Simon CHADWICK 1943– Sculptor whose works stemmed from observation of the structures, contours and growth of nature; the human body; and the movements, systems and repetitions of musical form, reflecting early years as a musician and musical instrument maker. Graduated from Bath Academy of Art in fine art, gaining his master's at Wimbledon School of Art. Exhibitions included Diorama Gallery, 1998; and Vital Art, The Gallery in Cowcross Street, and e1 Gallery at artLondon, both 1999. Solo shows included Jonathan Poole Gallery, Compton Cassey, 1997. Among Chadwick's commissions were: One Aldwych Hotel; Lynn Chadwick; in Newcastle upon Tyne the Sculpture Park and St Catherine's Hospital Trust; a temporary exhibition at Yorkshire Sculpture Park, Bretton Hall; and Next Retail corporate headquarters.

Myung Sook CHAE 1958– Artist, born in South Korea, who gained an honours degree at Seo Won University there, 1976–80; her master's at Seong Shin University, 1981–3; and a master's in printmaking at Royal College of Art, 1997–9. Chae became known for monochrome white embossed prints and minimal abstractions from nature. Her discreet, delicate watercolours had some affinity with the subtle grids of Agnes Martin, but Chae worked direct from landscape, making marks that enigmatically described empty fields after harvest, the calm surface of a lake or a bridge mirrored in water. Awards included Dong-A Art Festival, National Museum of At, Kwa-Chun, Seoul, 1990; Dong-Kyung Art Festival Award, Veno Art Centre, Tokyo, Japan, 1993; Tim Mara Award, Royal College of Art, 1998; and Alistair Grant Award, 1999. Showed widely in South Korean group exhibitions, also in the Japan-Korea Interchange Exhibition, Chi-Va Art Centre, Japan, 1993, and in England with Aylesford-Newsprint, 1998, and England & Co at ART2000, 2000. Had three solo exhibitions in Seoul: Grorich Gallery, 1982; Yoon Gallery, 1990; and To Art Space, 1994.

Douglas H CHAFFEY 1924– Artist born and lived in Poole, Dorset, who ran the Trinity Art Gallery in Wareham. He was self-taught and had exhibitions widely in the provinces.

Hayman CHAFFEY: *see* **HAYMAN**

Marc Camille CHAIMOWICZ 1946– Artist, born in Paris. He studied at Camberwell School of Arts and Crafts, 1964–8, then Slade School of Fine Art, 1968–70. In 1971 had a solo show at Sigi Krauss Gallery, others following in 1972 at Gallery House and Serpentine Gallery. Chaimowicz went on to exhibit internationally, taking part in a number of performances. In 1977 Doubts, a sketch for video camera and audience, was presented at several venues on the continent and in London; in the same year he published *Dream*, an anecdote, through his dealer Nigel Greenwood. Arts Council holds several examples of his work, using objects such as adapted photographs, glass, gloss paint and wood, as in (For Mantelpiece) Interval No. 3, 1979. 4 Rooms: Anthony Caro, Chaimowicz, Richard Hamilton and Howard Hodgkin, was curated by Michael Regan for the Arts Council in 1984 at Liberty's, Regent Street. In 2003, Jean Cocteau, a project by Chaimowicz, was held at Norwich Gallery, Norwich School of Art and Design. Chaimowicz's experience of life in France and England was reflected in his show at Angel Row Gallery, Nottingham, 2004.

Martyn CHALK 1945– Creator of reliefs and floor sculptures and draughtsman, born in Trowbridge, Wiltshire, who lived and worked in Hull from 1967. Chalk graduated from Portsmouth College of Art and went on to teach at the school of fine art at Humberside College of Higher Education. He reconstructed reliefs by the Russian artist Tatlin which were widely shown in museum exhibitions and were held by many public and private collections. Exhibited his own work widely, including Ferens Art Gallery, Hull, having a solo show in 1992. Of those works he said: "Apparent references to objects or to direct visual experience have no more (and no less) significance in the final form of each construction than geometric and non-objective shape, or than details produced by structural necessity." Also showed solo at Juda Rowan Gallery on a number of occasions and abroad. Chalk was included in Masterpieces of the Avantgarde at Annely Juda Fine Art/ Juda Rowan Gallery, 1985. Contemporary Art Society, Ferens Art Gallery and University of Hull hold his work.

Michael CHALK 1933– Painter who studied at Royal College of Art, winning an Abbey Major Scholarship in 1958. Showed at Gimpel Fils and in the provinces and lived in South Croydon, Surrey. Was included in The 1960's at England & Co, 1993.

Jack CHALKER 1918– Artist, illustrator and teacher, born in Croydon, Surrey, who studied graphics and painting at London University, 1936–9, served in the Royal Artillery during World War II, was captured by Japanese at the fall of Singapore, in 1945 being attached to Australian Army Headquarters as a war artist and illustrator. Studied at Royal College of Art, 1946–9, having in 1939 had to decline a scholarship due to the war. In 1950 moved to Falmouth as principal of Falmouth School of Art, which he helped establish, also being county art adviser for Cornwall. From 1958–84 was principal of West of England College of Art in Bristol with a concurrent lectureship at local University. Exhibited widely throughout world, including Falmouth Connections at Falmouth Art Gallery, 1994, shortly after he had published a book of his Japanese prisoner of war drawings. He also illustrated children's books and medical and surgical books and in 1991 was elected fellow of the Medical Artists' Association. Solo shows were held at RWA, Cheltenham Art Gallery, Cardiff and Bridgwater Arts Centre. Lived near Wells, Somerset.

Brian CHALKLEY 1948– Painter and teacher, who studied at Chelsea School of Art, 1970–3, and Slade School of Fine Art, 1973–5. He taught at Norwich School of Art, 1975–84, in 1983–4 holding a six-month placement with British Steel Corporation as Artist in Industry on Teesside. Went on to be a part-time teacher at Chelsea School of Art, in 1989 gaining a six-month Rome Award in Painting spent at British School in Rome. Chalkley made frequent appearances at John Moores Liverpool Exhibition from 1980 and was included in Artists in Industry at Hatton Gallery, Newcastle, with tour, in 1984. Had several solo shows in northeast of England, others including Howard Gardens Gallery, Cardiff, 1985, and Lanchester Gallery, Coventry Polytechnic, 1988. Arts Council holds his work. Lived in London.

Rosemary Ann CHALKLEY 1931– Painter and designer for television, born in Hull, Yorkshire. Studied at Central School of Arts and Crafts, 1950–51, her teachers including Keith Vaughan and Victor Pasmore; Byam Shaw School of Art with Peter Greenham and Patrick Phillips, 1952–3; in 1952 with Ernest Jackson; and in 1953 with David Murray. Showed at RA and NEAC and lived in Richmond, Surrey.

Mike CHALLENGER 1942– Painter, sculptor and printmaker who studied at Goldsmiths' College School of Art and Slade School of Fine Art in the early 1960s. His highly coloured, hard-edged and forceful screenprint Red Snort, of 1971, was included in Mods and Shockers at Cheltenham Museum & Art Gallery, 1996. Lived in London.

Sarah CHALMERS 1957– Painter in oil and watercolour of landscape in Britain and abroad. She did a foundation course at Chelsea School of Art, then gained her bachelor's degree in fine art at Hornsey College of Art. Six months were spent at L'École des Beaux-Arts, Aix-en-Provence, in France, plus City and Guilds teaching certification. Showed at King Street Gallery, Bristol, Maas and Cadogan Galleries. After organising several one-man shows in and around London, Chalmers had a solo exhibition in 1992 at New Grafton Gallery, others including Art First, 1998, and another at New Grafton Gallery in 2004. By then, Chalmers had work in several notable collections, including Burmah Castrol, Fountain Court Chambers, A T Kearney and Arco British.

Victoria CHALMERS 1970– Figurative painter, born and lived in London, who graduated in fine art from Falmouth School of Art and Design, 1990–3, from 1994–6 gaining a postgraduate higher diploma in fine art from Slade School of Fine Art. Chalmers was included in the Neurotic Realism series of exhibitions launched at Saatchi Gallery from 1999, and is in the Saatchi Collection.

Michael CHALWIN 1943– Artist in a variety of materials and teacher, brought up in Oxfordshire, who attended Oxford School of Art, 1959–63. After a period teaching, two years on the Isle of Skye, an education course in Oxford and more teaching, Chalwin settled in Newlyn, Cornwall, in 1978. He became a member of the Society of Artists there. His work was included in the 1989 Newlyn Orion

Galleries exhibition A Century of Art in Cornwall 1889–1989. Images, icons and the topography of Cornwall were important features.

Brenda CHAMBERLAIN 1912–1971 Painter and poet, born in Bangor, where she died. First wife of the artist John Petts, with whom she founded the Caseg Press. After a visit to Copenhagen in 1930, where she was much impressed by Gauguin's early work, Chamberlain in 1931–6 studied at Royal Academy Schools, Ernest Jackson and Walter Westley Russell being among her teachers. She also studied at University College of North Wales, Bangor. Chamberlain participated in many group shows, including Heal's Mansard Gallery, 1948; The Influence of Wales in Painting, Brighton, 1957; and Eisteddfod Gold Medallists, WAC, 1967. One-man shows included Gimpel Fils on several occasions in the 1950s; Zwemmer Gallery, 1962; and a memorial exhibition at National Museum of Wales, Cardiff, 1973. Her books included *The Green Heart*, 1958; *The Water Castle*, 1963; and *The Protagonist*, a play performed in Bangor in 1970. Her work is widely held in Welsh collections, including National Museum of Wales.

Christopher CHAMBERLAIN 1918–1984 Painter, draughtsman and teacher, born in Worthing, Sussex, as George Christopher Chamberlain. He was married to the artist Heather Copley. After private education Chamberlain studied at Clapham School of Art, 1934–8, in 1935 being awarded a London County Council three-year intermediate scholarship. In 1938 he accepted a Royal Exhibition and studied at Royal College of Art, 1938–9 and 1946–8, interrupted by war service, his final year being for postgraduate studies. Chamberlain taught at Camberwell School of Arts and Crafts and Bromley College of Art, ending as principal lecturer at Camberwell, his visiting lectureships including Sheffield, Colchester, Bournemouth and Ravensbourne. In 1984 he was selected to get a Civil List Pension. Chamberlain carried out a substantial volume of graphic work for such clients as Phoenix House, The Bodley Head, National Savings and Jonathan Cape. Commissioned works included British Rail and British Electricity Authority. He contributed to the Football Association show Football and the Fine Arts, 1953, was a regular exhibitor at RA Summer Exhibitions and had a solo show at Trafford Gallery, 1953. As a landscape painter Chamberlain believed in knowing his location meticulously, as shown in The Dangerous Corner, owned by Tate Gallery and painted near where he lived in Chelsea.

Edmund CHAMBERLAIN 1968– Artist, born in Beverley, Yorkshire, who studied at Newcastle University, 1986–90 and in 1994 won an Elizabeth Greenshields Foundation Award. Shared a show with his brother Lewis Chamberlain at The Guillaume Gallozi Gallery, New York, in 1993, when he made his first appearance in BP Portrait Award at National Portrait Gallery. In 1996 was included in a three-man exhibition, Drawing, at Fine Art Society. Browse and Darby gave him a solo exhibition in 2003.

Lewis CHAMBERLAIN 1966– Artist born in Hull, Yorkshire, who studied at Slade School of Fine Art, 1984–8. In 1994 he won the Pollock-Krasner Foundation Award. Shared a show with his brother Edmund Chamberlain at The Guillaume Gallozi Gallery, New York, in 1993, having had a solo exhibition there is 1991. In 1994 took part in BP Portrait Award, National Portrait Gallery, in 1996 taking part in three-man show, Drawing, at Fine Art Society. In 2002, Chamberlain won the ING first prize in The Discerning Eye, Mall Galleries, with his subtle study Brixton Academy – Mid Afternoon.

Trevor CHAMBERLAIN 1933– Painter, born in Hertford, who was self-taught. Apart from National Service in the Army, 1953–5, until 1964 Chamberlain worked as an architectural assistant, then painted full-time. He liked to paint his pictures of the sea, townscapes and landscapes in one session on the spot, which gave them great spontaneity. Chamberlain was elected a member of NS in 1968, RSMA in 1970 and ROI in 1972, also being a member of Chelsea Art Society and Wapping Group of Artists. Among awards won were Lord Mayor of London's Art Award, 1976; James Bourlet Prize at ROI, 1980; Chris Beetles Watercolour Award at RWS Open, 1987; and Llewellyn Alexander Award at ROI, 1991. Solo shows included Ash Barn Gallery, Petersfield, 1971–83, and Inspirations of Armenia and Persia, Piano Nobile Fine Paintings, 2002. Guildhall Art Gallery and National Maritime Museum, Greenwich, hold his work. Lived in Hertford, Hertfordshire.

Derek CHAMBERS 1937– Artist, born in Ilford, Essex, who had no formal art training apart from a few months at St Martin's School of Art. He spent 40 years in London working as a graphic designer, illustrator and photographer, which helped cultivate a natural gift for drawing, his first discipline. He moved to Aldeburgh, Suffolk, in 1993 to concentrate on painting. Charcoal and watercolour were his favoured media, to which he added etching and printmaking. Showed at RA Summer Exhibition, with RWS, NEAC and in other exhibitions at Mall Galleries and also in shows around East Anglia, where he was a member of The Suffolk Group.

Eddie CHAMBERS 1960– Artist in collage, born in Wolverhampton, who attended Lanchester Polytechnic, Coventry, 1980, and Sunderland Polytechnic, 1983. While still doing his foundation course he became noted for his work Destruction of the National Front. With other artists, notably Keith Piper, he established The Pan-Afrikan Connection. A show was held at Wolverhampton Art Gallery in 1981, Chambers claiming that the black artist's work should be "a tool to assist us in our struggle for liberation." Exhibited widely in London and the provinces and participated in The Other Story, Hayward Gallery and touring, 1989–90. Arts Council and Sheffield City Art Galleries hold his work. He was based in Bristol.

Mic CHAMBERS 1965– Self-taught painter and sculptor, born in Nuneaton, Warwickshire. He originally worked as an underwoodsman, later making wood sculptures with a chainsaw. As a painter he produced portraits and "an autobiographical accounts of modern man." Numberninethegallery, Birmingham, showed Chambers' work.

Stephen CHAMBERS 1960– Painter and printmaker, born in Montevideo, Uruguay, who studied at Winchester School of Art, 1978–9; St Martin's School of Art, 1979–82; and gained his master's degree at Chelsea School of Art, 1982–3. Gained a Rome Scholarship, 1983–4; in 1985 was artist-in-residence at Portsmouth Polytechnic; was painting fellow at Winchester School of Art, 1986–7; in 1987 won Greater London Arts Association and Oppenheim-John

Downes Trust Award; with a Mark Rothko Memorial Trust Travelling Award in 1989; and an Elephant Trust Award, 1995. Collaborated on two dance works for Royal Ballet with choreographer Ashley Page. Books included *Long Pig* and *Four Heads*, both published by Imprints. Chambers took part in numerous group shows, including Warwick Arts Trust, 1983; Nigel Greenwood Gallery, 1988; Artists' Books at Eagle Gallery, 1993; and The Hare, City Gallery, Leicester, 1996. Had a solo show, Strange Smoke, Winchester Gallery, 1987, then a series at Flowers East from 1989. Retrospective at Kettle's Yard, Cambridge, 1999, connected with an artist-fellow residency there and at Downing College. Solo show, Flowers Central, 2002, and Flowers East, 2003. Arts Council, Manchester University, Victoria & Albert Museum and Metropolitan Museum of Art, New York, hold examples.

James CHAMBURY 1927–1994 Artist, designer and illustrator, brought up in London where he cultivated an interest in drawing. Studied at the Central School of Arts and Crafts and Sir John Cass College and developed a career as a commercial artist, concentrating on magazine design and illustration. Left London for East Anglia to be a full-time artist, becoming a member of the East Anglian Group of Marine Artists and Suffolk Art Society. Was a frequent exhibitor with RSMA, PS and BWS and had several solo shows with a first with Haste Gallery, Ipswich, which included him in its fortieth anniversary exhibition in 1998.

Barbara CHAMIER 1885– Miniaturist and painter in oil, born in Faizabad, Uttar Pradesh, India. She studied at King's College Art School; in London her teachers included Rex Vicat Cole and Byam Shaw. Exhibited RMS, of which she was an associate, RA, SWA, Royal Glasgow Institute of the Fine Arts and in Paris. Lived latterly at Warsash, near Southampton.

Catherine CHAMNEY 1894– Watercolourist whose early life was spent in India and South Africa, her father being a civil servant. Studied art with L Burleigh Bruhl. Showed at RI, RCamA, Walker Art Gallery, Liverpool, SWA and elsewhere. She was a noted painter of the British landscape and is represented in Northampton Central Museum and Art Gallery. Lived in Bushey, Hertfordshire.

Walpole CHAMPNEYS 1879–1961 Painter, designer and teacher, born in Woking, Surrey. After part-education in France, he attended Teddington School of Art, and, after marriage in 1907, continued studies at South Kensington School of Design, winning first-class honours in design. In 1910–11 Champneys studied anatomy at King's College Hospital and attended life classes at Bolt Court. During World War I Champneys' career as a designer gained momentum, with jobs as varied as book covers for the *Tarzan* series, posters for London Underground and war posters. His circle of friends included the artists Robert Bevan, Walter Bayes and Walter Sickert. Although Champneys was appointed to the demanding post of master of the decoration course at the Architectural Association, 1923–7, he undertook many major public commissions during the 1920s and 1930s, including murals for the British pavilion at the big international decorative arts exhibition in Paris in 1925; designs for the Savile Theatre and Savoy Hotel; a mural for the Wembley Exhibition; and he was appointed colour consultant for the Shakespeare Memorial Theatre, Stratford-upon-Avon. Champneys retired in 1939 and died in Brightlingsea in Essex. A major retrospective was held at The Minories, Colchester, 1977. In addition to his public work Champneys made tiny pictures for his own pleasure, landscapes and visionary studies which owe much to William Blake, Paul Nash and the marshland of East Anglia. Gothick Dream Fine Art promoted their cause. Victoria & Albert Museum holds Champneys' work.

Veronique CHANCE 1967– Artist who gained an honours degree in fine art, Manchester Polytechnic, 1987–90; a postgraduate diploma in fine art from Glasgow School of Art, 1990–1; and her master's in printmaking from the Royal College of Art, 1994–6. Much of Chance's work reflected "on ideas surrounding self-identity and self-image." Exhibitions included Leicester Museum, 1995, and The Large Print Show, Christchurch Mansion, Ipswich, 1997. Lived in London.

John CHANCELLOR 1925–1984 Painter of sailing ships over the period 1780–1970 in oil and watercolour, marine draughtsman and writer, who was obsessed by drawing and the sea as a small boy in Portugal. After his family had returned to England, aged 11 Chancellor was granted a reprieve from school to attend Vita Art Studio, Bexhill, winning Royal Drawing Society medals. Boarded at Wycliffe College until in 1942 he signed as an apprentice officer in the merchant marine. During World War II was sunk twice by enemy action. Bought and renovated his own sailing barge; did illustrating work for nautical journals such as *Yachting Monthly*; drew a strip-cartoon, Captain Crest, for the comic *Eagle*; and illustrated Fred Cooper's *Sailing Barge Handbook*. Chancellor worked for Lapthorns, a barge and tug operator, in 1963 settling in Brixham, Devon, where he fished and then did hydrographic surveys with his own vessel, *Exact*. By the early 1970s Chancellor was turning more to painting, in 1973 having a sell-out exhibition – one of several – organised by Triton Gallery, Torquay. Chancellor's pictures could take up to six months to paint and are notable for their exact detail combined with superb sea and atmospheric effects. A few of Chancellor's pictures appeared as signed limited editions. A selection of his work, *The Maritime Paintings of John Chancellor*, was published in 1984, including accompanying text by the artist; in 1989 *John Chancellor's Classic Maritime Paintings* appeared, introduced by his widow, Rita.

Alec CHANDA 1962– Painter and teacher who studied at Camberwell School of Arts and Crafts, 1979–83. For two years he then travelled through Indonesia, Australia and India, returning in 1985 to paint in London, teaching art part-time in Richmond. He showed at the Whitechapel Open in 1985; the John Player Portrait Award at the National Portrait Gallery, 1988; at Cadogan Contemporary, with Simon Barry, in 1989; and in 1990 he won second prize, Hunting Group Art Prizes, at Mall Galleries. In 1991 he shared a show with two painters at Cadogan Contemporary.

Colin CHANDLER 1955– Artist in mixed media producing non-figurative, decorative works, born in Luton, Bedfordshire. He showed exclusively with the John Russell Gallery, Ipswich, which gave him solo shows from 1986.

Public and corporate collections held his work. Lived in Suffolk.

Cynthia CHANDLER 1937– Painter and illustrator, born in Isleworth, Middlesex. She studied at Twickenham School of Art. Showed at PS, UA and in the Midlands, being a member of Rugby and District Art Society and Coventry and Warwickshire Society of Artists. Lived in Rugby, Warwickshire.

Eileen CHANDLER 1904–1993 Painter and draughtsman, born in London where she died, was married to the illustrator Roland Chandler from 1930 until he died in World War II. Studied at Hornsey School of Art, gaining a scholarship to Royal Academy Schools. She was a noted portrayer of children, and an article in *Illustrated London News* launched her on a successful career making watercolour portraits of film stars in Hollywood. Liza Minnelli the singer and actress, Sheridan Morley the writer and Bamber Gascoigne, the television personality and author, were among her subjects. Chandler became better known in America and Sweden than in Britain, her many Swedish commissions including the royal family. On her wide travels she completed effective watercolour landscapes.

Robert CHANDLER 1952– Artist, art dealer (he ran the Mowbray Gallery, Hampstead, where he settled) and picture framer, born in London. He was self-taught, having studied with Anthony Green at Highgate School, and later was notable for abstract works. Mixed shows included Andrew Usiskin Contemporary Art and 33 Mossop Street both from 1993; RA Summer Exhibition, from 1993; Llewellyn Alexander Gallery and Beatrice Royal Gallery, Eastleigh, both 1994; and Contemporary Art Society, from 1995; Belgrave and Blue Galleries, from 1997; England & Co and Cross Street Gallery, 1998; Artmonsky Art, from 1998; Catto Contemporary, 2001; and Adam and Cork Street Galleries, 2002. Solo shows included Andrew Usiskin, 1992, and Courcoux & Courcoux, Salisbury, 1993. Chandler's early works were "clamped and tight," his later ones "loose and free" after he had discovered his own pictorial language although these did not show "the long physical and emotional labour involved.... I start with a blank canvas and find it exciting to see what evolves." Instead of using a brush, Chandler's technique involved "layering, scraping and even pouring directly on to canvases." Several corporate and three major London galleries held examples.

Avinash CHANDRA 1931–1991 Painter, born in Simla, India, who studied at Delhi Polytechnic, 1947–52, and won first prize at the First National Exhibition of Art in New Delhi in 1954. Had several one-man shows there in the early 1950s before moving to London in 1956, the following year having his first British solo show at Commonwealth Institute. Won a gold medal at the Prix Européene in Ostend in 1962, three years later moving to New York. Won several fellowships in America before returning to live in London in 1971. Showed extensively in Britain, on the continent and in America, notably at Bear Lane Gallery in Oxford, 1961; Patricia Judith Gallery, Miami, 1984 and 1985; and Horizon Gallery, London, 1987. Participated in The Other Story, Hayward Gallery and touring, 1989–90. His work, influenced by that of Van Gogh and Soutine, was noted for its strongly erotic element, although the later paintings were more poetic, turning less to the human figure, rather to birds and flowers. Tate Gallery, Victoria & Albert Museum and Arts Council hold his work.

Chien-Ying CHANG 1915–2003 Watercolourist, born in Kiangsu, China, married to the artist Cheng-Wu Fei. She graduated from National Central University, Nanking, 1931–5, then studied at Slade School of Fine Art, 1947–50, under Randolph Schwabe and William Coldstream. Was a member of RI, RWA and SWA, also showing at RA and RBA. Had a series of solo exhibitions at Leicester Galleries from 1951. Graves Art Gallery, Sheffield, and St John's College, Oxford, hold her work, which was signed in Chinese characters. Lived for many years in north London.

Belinda CHANNER 1961– Painter, printmaker, draughtsman and lecturer, born in Twyford, Berkshire, married to the artist William Latham. She graduated with honours from Newcastle upon Tyne Polytechnic, 1981–4, and gained her master's from the Royal College of Art, 1984–7, with a five-month award to Rijksakademie, Amsterdam, 1985. In 1988, Channer gained a Polish government and British Council Award for a 10-month fellowship in Poland, based in Cracow. She lectured at Central School of Art & Design, London College of Printing, Winchester School of Art and Canterbury College of Art. Group exhibitions included Stowells Trophy, RA, 1984; Rijksakademie, 1986; LG tour, 1987; and Eight British Artists, Galleria M, Warsaw, 1989. Had solo shows at Playhouse Gallery, Newcastle, 1985, and Galleria Forum, Cracow, 1989. Museum of London, British Museum, London Lighthouse, English Heritage and corporate collections hold examples. Lived in Brighton, Sussex.

Leslie Thomas CHANNING 1916– Landscape watercolourist who was by profession an architect, born in Weymouth, Dorset. He studied at Regent Street Polytechnic School of Architecture, 1934–9. During World War II he was involved in Royal Air Force camouflage, then worked as an architectural assistant to London County Council and Middlesex County Council, finally with the Church Commissioners, 1956–78. Became a member of UA, 1973, also being vice-president of Thames Valley Arts Club, a member of Richmond Art Society and associate member of NS. Showed at RI and had solo exhibitions at Fairfield Halls, Croydon, and St George's Church, Hanworth. Lived at Hampton Wick, Middlesex.

Marie F CHANT 1917– Painter in oil, gouache and watercolour, lithographer and textile designer. Born in Rugby, Warwickshire, she studied at Rugby School of Art, the Slade School of Fine Art and the Central School of Arts and Crafts. Work reproduced in a number of magazines, including *Vogue*, *House and Garden* and *Homes and Gardens*. Exhibited RBA, Walker's Galleries and the provinces. Lived at Tilehurst, Reading, Berkshire.

Tom CHANTRELL 1916–2001 Commercial artist who showed early ability, aged 13 winning a national competition for a League of Nations disarmament poster. Attended Manchester School of Art, then headed by Robert Dawson, until he was 15; joined a local advertising agency; then in 1933 moved to London where, after five years, he began to specialise in film posters. His first was for the star-studded *The Amazing Dr Clitterhouse*, 1938, by Barré Lyndon. After Army war service and demobilisation in 1946, Chantrell returned to his old agency where, into the 1970s, he produced several thousand posters, ranging from *Brighton Rock*, 1947, and *Carry on Cleo*, 1964, to *Dracula Has Risen from the Grave*, 1968. Chantrell needed only a plot and some stills to produce a poster, for which friends and family sometimes posed. These might be designed before the film was shot, with the artwork helping to sell the idea to distributors to raise money for production. When original artwork for such posters became unfashionable, Chantrell designed video covers. In old age, he saw his work attaining cult status.

Bob CHAPLIN 1947– Printmaker, artist in film and photography and teacher, born in Hastings, Sussex. He studied at Ravensbourne and Brighton Colleges of Art, 1965–73. Mixed shows included Tate Gallery and Victoria & Albert Museum, which hold his work, and International Print Biennales in Cracow, Llubljana, Biella, Florence, Wakayama, Kanagawa and Fredrikstad, where he was a prizewinner. Chaplin also won prizes at 5th, 6th and 9th British Print Biennales. His solo shows included Riverside Studios, Arnolfini Gallery in Bristol and Gardner Arts Centre, Brighton, as well as abroad. Chaplin's work is represented in over 90 collections in Europe. His teaching experience included West Sussex College of Design in Horsham as well as visiting lectureships at Chelsea, Brighton, Ravensbourne and Maidstone Colleges of Art. Lived latterly in New York.

Charles Herbert Arthur CHAPLIN 1907–1987 Printmaker, born and lived in Watford, Hertfordshire, whose loss of a right eye in an accident aged 12 did not deter his artistic ambitions. Studied art alongside an apprenticeship at Sun Printers of Watford and produced etchings and drypoints. By the early 1940s his prints had been accepted for the RA Summer Exhibition and RE, of which Chaplin was made an associate in 1950 and a fellow in 1961. Malcolm Osborne admired Chaplin's early work and he was invited to study as a part-time external student at the Royal College of Art under Osborne and Robert Austin, although he continued as an engraver and printing manager at Sun Printers until retirement. Chaplin also exhibited in Canada and Sweden, and several prints were bought for public collections in Britain, Canada and New Zealand. The landscape around Rickmansworth and its animal and bird life were favourite subjects. Hilary Chapman Fine Prints held a show at the 20th Century Gallery, 2003. There was another at Abbott and Holder in 2005, to celebrate publication of *Charles Chaplin 1907-1987 – Artist, Engraver, Printmaker*, by Jon Chaplin.

Michael CHAPLIN 1943– Printmaker and teacher, born in St Neots, Huntingdonshire, who went on to study at Watford College of Art, 1961–4, and Brighton College of Art, 1967–8, for postgraduate work. Taught at Maidstone School of Art and Kingston Polytechnic. Showed at RA Summer Exhibition and elsewhere. Lived in Maidstone, Kent.

Stephen CHAPLIN 1934– Painter, muralist, draughtsman, lecturer and archivist, born and eventually settled in London. After gaining his fine art diploma from the Slade School of Fine Art, 1952–5 Chaplin graduated with honours in art history, 1955–8, at the Courtauld Institute of Art, working in the library there, 1958–9. After assisting Lawrence Gowing, head of Chelsea Art School, 1959–61, Chaplin lectured in art history and complementary studies at Leeds College of Art, 1961–6, then in the fine art department at University of Leeds, 1966–91, finally as department head, 1982–5, becoming senior fellow after early retirement, 1990–1. From 1968 he was an external examiner in art and art history widely throughout Britain. During 1990–7, Chaplin was Slade School archivist, Hon. Research Fellow and afterwards Leverhulme Research Fellow at University College London, creating A Slade Archive Reader 1986–1975, an invaluable source compiled from documents as well as diaries and interviews. Chaplin completed murals at University of Leeds, 1981; Cookridge Hospital, 1983; and Ida Hospital National Rehabilitation Centre, 1984–7. He had many solo and shared shows, having established the habit of drawing and note-taking as a child. By the time of his exhibition Narrative Objects, at Leeds University Gallery, 2002, he had assembled over 21,000 drawings in 300 books, providing what he called a "life-trace", resultant paintings of places being images of abstract simplicity. In the same year he had a show, Wandsworth Observed, at Wandsworth Museum, the result of a two-year project during which Chaplin helped children at nearby West Hill School create two large paintings. The Arts Council, Leeds City Art Gallery, several universities and other public collections hold examples.

Anthea CHAPMAN 1933– Painter and teacher, brought up in Sussex, living for a time at Herstmonceux. She was married to the painter David Chapman. Educated in Hove, she studied art at Brighton College of Art and Crafts, 1949–55, with Raymond Cowern and Charles Knight. Taught at Eastbourne School of Art, was a member of the Eastbourne Group. Her work, signed Anthea C, is in the collections of the Tel-Aviv Museum, Israel, and Stoke-on-Trent City Museum and Art Gallery.

David CHAPMAN 1933– Painter, draughtsman and teacher who was educated at Brighton Grammar School and the local College of Art, 1949–54. After teaching in a number of schools for 12 years, Chapman worked with dancers in a specialist college of physical education. He joined the faculty of art and design at Brighton Polytechnic in 1972, teaching drawing, and also worked as an external examiner, eventually becoming head of foundation at Brighton. In 1986 he had a six-month sabbatical to develop his own work which culminated with a show at Wren Gallery, Piccadilly. In addition to mixed shows in London and the provinces Chapman shared an exhibition at Brighton Polytechnic Gallery in 1988. Latterly lived in Brighton and in France.

Della CHAPMAN 1931– Etcher, christened Adella, born in Bolton, Lancashire, and married to the artist Martin Chapman. She did not study etching at Goldsmiths' College School of Art, which she attended 1949–53, as it was "very rarely done by anyone at that time"; instead, her teachers were Adrian Ryan and Kenneth Martin, painters, and the sculptor Robert Jones. Settled at Hitcham, Suffolk, where close-up study of nature was of key importance. Group shows included Greenwich Printmakers, RA Summer Exhibition, Gainsborough's House Print Workshop in Sudbury and Suffolk Craft Society. Solo exhibitions included Luton Museum, Gainsborough's House and elsewhere in East Anglia.

Dinos and Jake CHAPMAN Creators of sculptures and dioramas, the brothers worked jointly. Dinos was born in

1962 and gained his bachelor's degree at Ravensbourne College of Art, 1979–81, his master's at Royal College of Art, 1988–90. His brother, born in 1966, gained his master's there at the same time, having obtained an honours degree at North-East London Polytechnic, 1985–8. Examples of the brothers' work were their life-size version of the castration of Spanish prisoners, using shop dummies, based on Goya's Disasters of War series of etchings, smaller versions of the etchings being made painstakingly from tiny model soldiers. Group shows included Matter & Fact, Katherine Hamnett Building, 1993; Liar, Hoxton Square, 1994; and General Release: Young British Artists, Venice Biennale, Scuola di San Pasquale, 1995. We Are Artists was a solo installation at Hales Gallery, 1992, others including Great Deeds Against the Dead, Victoria Miro Gallery, 1994, and Bring me the head of Franco Toselli!, Ridinghouse Editions, 1995. The Chapmans were in the RA's Sensation show in 1997 and in its successor, Apocalypse, in 2000. In that, their work Hell included a death camp, Holocaust recreation and featured many tiny and mutilated plastic bodies in the shape of a reverse swastika. The Rape of Creativity, at Modern Art, Oxford, in 2003, comprised the Chapmans' reworkings of a set of prints of Goya's Disasters of war, replacing faces with clown faces or animal masks. In the same year, they won the £25,000 Charles Wollaston Award at the RA Summer Exhibition and had a retrospective at Saatchi Gallery. A comprehensive review of the Chapmans' output, with a major new project, was arranged by Tate Liverpool, 2003–4, and there was an exhibition at the Contemporary Art Centre, Malaga, Spain, in 2004. A Tate Liverpool show of their work in 2006–7 would further survey their career. Saatchi Collection holds their work.

George CHAPMAN 1908–1993 Painter and printmaker, born London. Studied at Gravesend School of Art, Royal College of Art and Slade School of Fine Art, having worked in advertising to save money to study. Earliest influences were Walter Sickert and the Euston Road School painters. Early in World War II he visited the Rhondda Valley, Wales, which gave his work new direction, leading to a prolific period. Lived in Great Bardfield, Essex, 1948–60, then moved to Aberaeron, Wales, in 1960. He was the subject of a BBC *Monitor* television programme in 1961, the Chapman script appearing in Sir Huw Wheldon's book *Monitor* in 1962. Chapman took part in many mixed shows, one-man exhibitions including Piccadilly Gallery, Zwemmer Gallery and Howard Roberts Gallery, Cardiff. His work is in a number of public collections, including Victoria & Albert Museum, Whitworth Art Gallery, Manchester, and Glynn Vivian Art Gallery, Swansea. Chapman withdrew from exhibiting for much of the 1970s, but this period of reinterpretation led to a new spate of work in the 1980s. Retrospective Aberystwyth Arts Centre 1989 and touring, another at Goldmark Gallery, Uppingham, 1992. Chapman, who in 1957 won the Gold Medal for Fine Art at Royal National Eisteddfod, described his association with the mining communities of south Wales as "a love affair". He died at Aberaeron.

Jake CHAPMAN: *see* **Dinos and Jake CHAPMAN**

Joanna CHAPMAN 1965– Versatile artist and teacher in a range of media, born in London, who gained a diploma in art and design, Hounslow Borough College, 1981–3, and an honours degree in embroidery, City of Birmingham Polytechnic, 1983–6. From 1991–6 she was employed as embroidery/textiles technician at Goldsmiths' College, also as a part-time tutor on various courses, Access, City & Guilds adult education. Commissions included Sheard & Hudson, 1994; a large wallpiece for Wolff Olins, client The Co-operative Bank, Rochdale, 1996; and two wallpieces for Workplace Art Consultancy, client King of Saudi Arabia, 1998. She took part in trio show, Constructions, England & Co, 2000, one of a number of mixed exhibitions. Solo shows included Pallant House, Chichester, 1997. Royal Brompton Hospital, Hertfordshire Education Authority and several corporate collections hold examples.

John Lewis CHAPMAN 1946– Painter noted for meticulous pictures of transport and machinery subjects, sometimes in rural and period settings. He was born in Blackburn, Lancashire, and left school in 1961 to work as a layout artist for the local evening newspaper. Studied at Blackburn Art College, 1963–4, then in 1965–8 worked as a technical illustrator for a local engineering company. Chapman was a member of Blackburn Artists' Society and showed at the local public gallery as well as RA Summer Exhibition, W H Patterson, Warrington Art Gallery and elsewhere. A number of signed limited-edition prints were produced of his scenes. Blackburn Art Gallery holds his work. Lived in Bolton, Lancashire.

June CHAPMAN 1939– Painter in oil, born in Ruislip, Middlesex. She studied at Camberwell School of Arts and Crafts, 1955–6, and went on to paint professionally, specialising in interiors, domestic scenes and still life. Showed at RA, ROI, RBA, UA, Edwin Pollard Gallery and Blackheath Gallery. In 1982 she was awarded the Diploma of Merit at University of Arts, Parma, Italy.

June Crisfield CHAPMAN 1934– Prolific figurative printmaker, painter, lecturer and writer, born in Kent but educated in Scotland. Living in Dunlop, Ayrshire, she developed an interest in wild plants. Graduated in wood engraving at Glasgow School of Art, where theatre became an enthusiasm. These twin interests were reflected in her work. Mixed exhibitions included SWE Open, from 1976; RE Open, from 1978; Printmakers' Open, from 1987; Edinburgh International Festival, from 1988; Chaucer Society, from 1989; RSA Open, from 1992; National Print Open, from 1995; and The Garrick/Milne Prize, Christie's, shortlisted, 2003, where she won a Commissioning Prize. Among her many solo exhibitions were latterly Kelvingrove Art Gallery, Glasgow, 1993; Upper Waiting Hall, House of Commons, 1997; County Hall Gallery, Chelmsford Cathedral Festival, 1998; and Dorset County Gallery, Dorchester, 1999. During the Glasgow City of Culture Year, 1990, Chapman painted a series of gouaches called Tribute to Scottish Theatre. Her work appeared in several publications, including *Radio Times* and The Folio Society Shakespeare. She gave demonstration talks on printmaking and wood engraving for The British Library and Victoria & Albert Museum, judged, and made an educational film about her work. Among the subjects of her portraits were the musicians Lord Menuhin and Julian Bream, the actress Beryl Reid, mime artist Marcel Marceau and singer Willard White. Ashmolean Museum, Kelvingrove Art Gallery, Edinburgh Art Centre, Aberdeen Hospital Board and Essex Education Authority are among collections holding her work. Lived in Billericay, Essex.

Martin CHAPMAN 1930– Artist and teacher, married to the etcher Della Chapman, who studied at Goldsmiths' College School of Art, 1946–9, then Royal College of Art, 1951–4. Chapman, who painted in oil and had an extensive knowledge of the history of art, lectured part-time at Morley College from 1969. Had work in a number of private collections including that of Gustav Delbanco, one of the partners in Roland, Browse & Delbanco. Worked in Suffolk, where he lived at Hitcham, and in Cornwall and Dorset.

Max CHAPMAN 1911–1999 Versatile artist, critic, illustrator and poet, born and lived in London. Chapman's mother, Bertha Cregeen, and her two sisters were artists. He attended Dulwich College and Byam Shaw School, 1927–30, where he was taught and befriended by the artist Charles Ricketts, who funded a scholarship to Italy, 1934, and "the European Grand Tour". This disturbed Chapman, who felt that instead he must adjust his art to modern trends. Although Chapman was a figurative artist who later returned to figuration, much of his work was abstract. Zdzislaw Ruszkowski, John Coplans and Jackson Pollock were influences. Collage noyé was one of Chaman's innovations while experimenting with new media. He showed at RA, LG, RBA and elsewhere and had solo exhibitions at Storran, Leger, Molton and Leicester Galleries, Camden Arts Centre, New Vision Centre Gallery and in Paris and Zurich. In 1981 there was a selective retrospective at Middlesbrough Art Gallery when Oswell Blakeston also showed. They were companions for decades and collaborated on projects. Chapman was art critic for *What's On in London* for about 25 years.

Robin CHAPMAN 1944– Printmaker and photographer, born in Essex. Studied, 1961–4, at London College of Printing where he gained a first-class diploma. In the mid-1960s emigrated to America and joined big photographic studio in New York, returning to England soon after to avoid the Vietnam draft. In London opened a freelance studio specialising in still life and worked for most of top advertising agencies. Tired of commercial photography he moved to Spain and for a decade worked in film production of television commercials. Again in London, Chapman divided his time between painting and managing an art gallery. His screenprints were sold by Belgravia Contemporary Arts.

Dick CHAPPELL 1954– Painter and teacher, born in Chesterfield, Derbyshire, who studied at local College of Art, 1972, then at Goldsmiths' College School of Art, 1973–6. After working at British Museum, 1977–85, taught art at Lincoln, Portsmouth and Hereford. Regularly showed at RA Summer Exhibition from 1980s; with Islington Group, 1983–4; Hill Court Gallery, Abergavenny, 1992; Keith Chapman Gallery, 1993; and shared a show with Dewi Tudur at Martin Tinney Gallery, Cardiff, 1994.

Valentinos CHARALAMBOUS: *see* **VALENTINOS**

Agnes CHARLES fl. from early 1930s– Designer and maker of stained glass windows and painter in oil. She studied at Royal Academy Schools, 1930, and Central London Polytechnic, 1952. Her business St Crispin's Glass was based at her home in Codicote, Hertfordshire. Her work can be seen in churches in Codicote, Knebworth and Houghton Regis and in Brentwood Cathedral. She exhibited at RA, Leicester, Leger and Alpine Galleries and elsewhere in London.

Eleanor CHARLESWORTH 1891– Painter, notably of flowers, who was born and lived in London. After education at Northlands, Englefield Green, in 1925–6 she studied at the Slade School of Fine Art. Exhibited widely, especially at ROI and SWA, also at RA, RI, NEAC, RSA and Paris Salon.

John CHARLESWORTH 1947– Painter, born in Manchester, whose detailed, subtly coloured pictures were Surrealist in manner and packed with personal iconography. Studied fine art at Reading in the late 1960s and early 1970s. Never painted more than 10 pictures in a year and for a long time suffered ill-health. Although he exhibited in many regional shows and in London, Tokyo and Vancouver, Charlesworth was neglected until he had a solo exhibition at Courcoux & Courcoux, Stockbridge, 1999, others following in 2001 and 2003. Lived in Cumbria.

Kristin CHARLESWORTH 1955– Painter who studied at Camberwell School of Arts and Crafts, 1973–4; Bath Academy of Art, 1974–6; and Hornsey College of Art, 1976–8. Among the mixed exhibitions she took part in were Haringey Arts Centre, 1979, gaining the award for the best overall exhibit; Foyles Gallery, 1979; RA and NEAC. In 1990 had a solo show at New Grafton Gallery.

Nicole CHARLETT 1957– Artist who studied fine art at Portsmouth Polytechnic, where she began a systematic and constructive approach to her work. From 1978, she inquired into quantitative and qualitative colour relations in paintings, drawings and prints. Charlett's work was included in The House Construction Show, 1981; in Colour Presentations, Gardner Centre Gallery, Sussex University, and tour, 1986; and Complexions, at Galerie L'Idee, Zoetermeer, Netherlands, and Dean Clough, Halifax, 1989. Arts Council holds her work. From 1979 she lived in London.

Alan CHARLTON 1948– Painter, born in Sheffield. He attended Camberwell School of Art and the Royal Academy Schools. In reaction against the traditional figurative and landscape work being taught Charlton began to create simple, grey abstracts based on rectangular shapes. Usually they have a planned location, where they take on the light and space of the space occupied, and they call for a measured response by the viewer. After 1972 Charlton showed frequently, especially on the continent. He was in The New Spirit in Painting in 1981 and Documenta 7, Kassel, 1982, and was included in the South Bank Centre's touring exhibition of 1988–9, The Presence of Painting. After 1979 he had frequent solo shows, including Amsterdam, Eindhoven, Brussels, Edinburgh and London, where Annely Juda exhibited 10 paintings in 1996, more in 2001. In 2002, a panel of judges awarded Charlton the Charles Wollaston Award for the "most distinguished work" at the RA Summer Exhibition. Arts Council holds his work.

Alan Bengall CHARLTON 1913– Watercolourist and draughtsman, born in North Shields, Northumberland. Studied art at the King Edward VII School of Art, Durham University, and under Percy Bradshaw at the Press Art School. Exhibited RI, Manchester City Art Gallery and at

Laing Art Gallery, Newcastle. Lived at Corbridge, Northumberland.

Daphne CHARLTON 1909–1991 Painter and draughtsman, born near York as Daphne Gribble, the daughter of a civil engineer. She studied at the Slade School of Fine Art from 1927, among her teachers George Charlton, whom she married in 1929. They spent their honeymoon at the Mill House, Tidmarsh, home of the writer Lytton Strachey, the artist Dora Carrington and her husband Ralph Partridge. The Charltons settled in Hampstead, north London, but the quiet and gentle romantic Charlton was unequal to the sexual demands of the vibrant, attractive Daphne. Her conquests included Stanley Spencer, whose fine portrait of her is in the Tate Gallery collection. There is an illuminating account of Daphne in the catalogue of the exhibition of George Charlton's work at The Chambers Gallery in 2005. It is by Ian Kellam, who knew Daphne for many years. The exhibition included some of her work.

Evan CHARLTON 1904–1984 Painter, teacher and administrator, born in London, husband of the artist Felicity Charlton and brother of George. He studied at London University, 1923–7, then at the Slade School of Fine Art, 1930–3. Began teaching in Bristol in 1935 and became head of Cardiff School of Art, 1938–45, being a war artist during World War II. From 1945–66 he was an Her Majesty's Inspector for art in Wales. Charlton took part in a number of group exhibitions, mainly in Wales, including SWG, Royal National Eisteddfod, WAC and National Library of Wales, Aberystwyth. He had a series of solo shows, including Welsh Gallery, Abergavenny, 1973. Charlton's work can have a slightly Surrealist quality, as in Promenade Restaurant, held by Glynn Vivian Art Gallery, Swansea. National Museum of Wales, Cardiff, which gave him a memorial show in 1985, also holds his work. Died at Porthkerry, South Glamorgan.

Felicity CHARLTON 1913– Painter in oil and watercolour, born in Clifton, Bristol. She studied 1932–7 West of England College of Art, Bristol, where her teachers included the painter Evan Charlton, whom she married. Her work consisted of "scenes of interiors and gardens, with imaginary figures and other details", and was widely exhibited in group shows including RWA, WAC, Royal National Eisteddfod and Howard Roberts Gallery, in Cardiff. WAC, Newport and Swansea art galleries hold her work. Had a number of shows with husband including a major retrospective at Newport Museum and Art Gallery in 1981. The gallery gave her another retrospective in 1993. Other solo shows included Andrew Knight Gallery in Cardiff, 1985; Underground Gallery, Bath, 1989; and Rooksmoor Gallery, Bath, 1991. Lived at Porthkerry, near Barry, South Glamorgan.

George CHARLTON 1899–1979 Painter and teacher, born in London. He studied at the Slade School of Fine Art from 1914, joining the staff in 1919. Taught at Willesden School of Art, 1949–59, and was an examiner in art for the University of London school examinations for many years. Was a governor of several schools of art. Showed widely in London, having first one-man show at Redfern Gallery in 1924, also showing solo at Beaux Arts Gallery. Tate Gallery has his picture Elephants and the Arts Council his watercolour of Brighton. His wife, Daphne Charlton, who survived him until 1991, was for many years a close associate of the painter Stanley Spencer. Charlton's house in Hampstead, north London, was described as "an Aladdin's cave of pictures". The artist Evan Charlton was George's brother. There was a George and Daphne Charlton show at The Chambers Gallery in 2005. It was accompanied by a well-illustrated catalogue in which Ian Kellam provided enlightening information about the Charltons and memories of their singular marriage.

Mervyn CHARLTON 1945– Painter, born in Woodford, Essex. He attended Nottingham Art College, 1974–7. Was artist-in-residence at Guildford House, Guildford, in 1983, the year he won Gulbenkian Printmaker Award. Charlton participated in many group exhibitions, including Whitechapel Art Gallery, RA, Bath Festival Show and Thumb Gallery. He had two solo exhibitions at Moira Kelly Fine Art in the early 1980s and later two with Sally Hunter Fine Art, 1985–9. Charlton used a sophisticated technique to create a fantasy world in which archetypal and everyday images coalesced. British Petroleum Ltd, Achim Moeller Ltd and Unilever Ltd own his work.

Clifford CHARMAN 1910–1993 Painter who was born and worked in Bexleyheath, Kent. He studied at Regent Street Polytechnic School of Art, 1936–9 and 1948–50. Showed at RA, NS, RBA, Chelsea Art Society, Bristol City Art Gallery, New Metropole Arts Centre in Folkestone and abroad. He was elected ROI in 1954 and won the James Bourlet Prize at the 1982 centenary exhibition. Charman was also a prizewinner in the 1977 Greater London Council Spirit of London show. City of London Guildhall holds his work.

Dorothea CHAROL 1895–1963 Sculptor and painter, born in Germany, who studied art in Dresden, became a member of Die Abstrakten group in Berlin and made porcelain figures for the Rudolstadt-Volkstedt factory. She married the artist Adolf Kiglsperger, whom she divorced in 1930, the year she moved to Paris, later settling in west London. Exhibited as a sculptor at RA Summer Exhibition in 1937 and 1950, when her entry was a head of the former High Commissioner for Canada, Vincent Massey.

Siegfried CHAROUX 1896–1967 Sculptor of figures and draughtsman, born in Vienna where he studied at the School of Arts and Crafts, then at the Vienna Academy of Fine Arts. Was a political cartoonist until 1933, when he began a series of monuments in Vienna. Moved to England in 1935 and was naturalised 11 years later. Charoux was interested in sculptural techniques employed in classical times, as evident in his terracotta Youth, in the Tate Gallery. Exhibited RA, LG, Royal Glasgow Institute of the Fine Arts, Piccadilly Gallery and widely in America. Elected RA in 1956. Among his public works are a memorial to the flyer Amy Johnson in Hull and his huge group The Islanders for the South Bank Exhibition, 1951, as well as carvings for the School of Anatomy and the Engineering Laboratory at Cambridge. His figure Motor Cyclist stands outside Shell Centre, on London's South Bank. There was a retrospective at Ashgate Gallery, Farnham, 1975. Lived in London.

Lord CHARTERIS OF AMISFIELD 1913–1999 Sculptor, educated at Eton College and Sandhurst, who served in the Army in World War II in Palestine, attaining the rank of lieutenant-colonel. Then became private secretary to HM The Queen, 1952–72; was keeper of HM Archives,

1972–7; and was a permanent Lord in Waiting from 1978. He was provost of Eton, 1978–91, was a trustee of the British Museum and chairman of the trustees of the National Heritage Memorial Fund. Was created Baron (life peer, United Kingdom), 1977. Lord Charteris' sculpture was inspired by the work of Oscar Nemon, with whom he studied and shared a studio in St James' Palace for many years. In addition to many private commissions, including a fountain in the shape of a lion's mask for the Marquess of Anglesey at Plas Newydd, north Wales, his work was included in Sixteen Sculptors at Sladmore Contemporary, 1997. Lived at Wood Stanway, Cheltenham, Gloucestershire.

Michael CHASE 1915–2001 Painter in watercolour and designer, gallery director and lecturer, born in London. He was the son of the painter William Chase and his second wife was the artist Valerie Thornton, with whom he often showed. They formed a distinguished art collection, part of which was shown at The Minories, Colchester, in 1994. Chase attended evening classes at Hornsey, Central and Chelsea Schools of Art. After war service he became a trainee in a firm of interior decorators, then ran the Kensington Art Gallery; Zwemmer Gallery, 1954–65; and The Minories, 1966–74. His technical mentors were John Nash and Edward Bawden, and Paul Nash, Arthur Boyd and Paul Klee were a constant source of inspiration. He was "not concerned with actual places as with the visual ingredients they portray". Took part in many mixed shows, including RA Summer Exhibitions and Colchester Art Society, and won the Barcham Green Company award at open exhibition at Bankside Gallery in 1986. Solo exhibitions included a tour based on The Minories, 1981, later shows including Clare Hall, Cambridge, 1992; Printworks, Colchester, and John Russell Gallery, Ipswich, both 1994; and Chappel Galleries, Chappel, 1996. Chappel Galleries held a Chase family show in 2000 including work by Val Maskell Chase, third wife of Michael, and there was a memorial exhibition at The Minories, 2002. Department of the Environment, International Chemical Industries and public galleries in Bolton, Leicester and Sheffield hold his work. Died in Hadleigh, Suffolk.

Peter CHASE 1921– Printmaker, photographer and teacher who took an honours degree in fine art at school of fine art, Newcastle upon Tyne University. Later spent four years as a studio assistant at Slade School of Fine Art, then taught printmaking at Burslem School of Fine Art and Bournemouth College of Art. Pathé made a film of Chase's work, *Lithography on Stone*, 1966. He became a member of Printmakers' Council. The big city, with its heavy industry, dockland, slums and bars was Chase's subject. Exhibited widely including RA Summer Exhibition, 1984, AIA, Senefelder Club, Hiscock Gallery in Portsmouth, Lamont Gallery, Zella Nine and elsewhere. Solo exhibitions included Chiltern and Woodstock Galleries, Univision Gallery in Newcastle upon Tyne and Southampton Art Gallery. Lived in Shirley, Southampton, Hampshire.

Daniel CHASIN 1967– Painter and photographer, born in New York. He studied at King's Lynn College of Arts and Technology. His work was included in Young Painters Exhibition at Blenheim Gallery in 1989; showed photographs at East West Gallery; and had exhibits in England & Co's 1990 show Art in Boxes. Victoria & Albert Museum holds his work.

Philip CHATFIELD 1958– Sculptor in stone, born in Southsea, Hampshire. After education at Monmouth School Chatfield declined a sponsored commission in the Royal Artillery in favour of a place at Newcastle University fine art department, where learned stonemasonry and lettering under Roy Kitchin and Jonah Jones. After this Chatfield was a stonemason in Somerset and Dorset; becoming self-employed, he interspersed masonry and lettering with making sculpture in his Taunton studio. After a solo show at Swansea Arts Workshop in 1983 he became employed by Swansea City Council on its maritime development scheme. Was included in Seven Sculptors Working in Wales at Glynn Vivian Art Gallery & Museum, Swansea, in 1986.

William Henry CHATTAWAY 1927– Sculptor and draughtsman, born in Coventry, Warwickshire. After King Henry VIII School went to Art School in Coventry, 1943–5, then Slade School of Fine Art, 1945–8. Two years later he settled in Paris. He showed in inaugural ICA show in 1950 and John Moores Exhibition, Liverpool, 1956. On the occasion of the dedication of Coventry Cathedral in 1961 he took part in exhibition at Herbert Art Gallery, which holds examples of his sculptures and drawings. Chattaway also showed at Hanover and Leicester Galleries, having solo shows at that gallery and Herbert Art Gallery in 1969. Also exhibited extensively in Paris, New York and Belgrade. Commissions executed included ones for Sir Basil Spence, the architect, Hutchinson Press and Midland Bank, overseas branch, London.

Geoffrey CHATTEN 1936– Self-taught artist noted for his depiction of the East Anglian coast, especially the skies and landscape of Norfolk. He was an associate of the RBA, also exhibiting at the RA Summer Exhibition, ROI, with Judy Hines of Holt and at other galleries in East Anglia. Commissioned work included The Maritime Trust. Collectors in Britain and abroad owned his pictures.

Daniel CHATTO 1957– Painter and draughtsman who was educated at Westminster School. He started painting in his early thirties after an acting career, working on a modest scale. He did a foundation course at City and Guilds of London Art School, and he also attended New College, Oxford. Chatto travelled widely in Britain, northern Spain and the Western Himalayas. He had a show at Cadogan Contemporary in 1992.

Enid CHAUVIN 1910– Artist and teacher, born in Blackheath, southeast London, where she attended the School of Art under John Platt, also going to Goldsmiths' College School of Art. Prior to World War II she taught in Hong Kong, then held a series of appointments in the southeast of England. Exhibited RA, AIA, ROI, UA, SWA, NS, Redfern Gallery and elsewhere. Lived in Weybridge, Surrey, later in Corsica.

Shiavax CHAVDA 1914– Artist, born in India, who studied at Slade School of Fine Art and in Paris. He showed paintings and drawings of India at AIA Gallery in 1955. Tate Gallery archive holds his Self-Portrait, scraperboard and Indian ink.

Michael CHECKETTS 1960– Painter and draughtsman who sometimes used collage to create his pictures. He studied at Norwich School of Art, 1981–4, and the Royal Academy Schools, 1984–7. Among Checketts' widespread exhibitions were BP Portrait Award, National Portrait Gallery, 1990; *Spectator* Art Competition, first prize winner, 1994; and Eastern Open, King's Lynn, first prize winner, 1997. He participated in Making the Connection, firstsite, Colchester/Wolsey Art Gallery, Ipswich, 2002, having had a one-man exhibition at The Room Upstairs, Wolsey Art Gallery, in 1998. Paintings 1994–2004 was a solo show at The Warehouse, Lowestoft, in 2004. Manchester City Art Gallery, University of East Anglia Library and Adam and Company, Edinburgh, held examples.

Carl CHEEK 1927– Painter and teacher, educated in England and Sweden, who studied at Chelsea School of Art, 1944–7, under Raymond Coxon, Robert Medley and Ceri Richards, then at the Royal College of Art, 1948–51, teachers including Ruskin Spear, Carel Weight, Robert Buhler, John Minton and Francis Bacon. Taught at Berkshire College of Art. Showed widely, including RA Summer Exhibition, NEAC, Redfern Gallery and elsewhere. Offer Waterman & Co latterly sold his work, which is in the Government Art Collection.

Malvina CHEEK 1916– Painter, studied at Wimbledon School of Art and Royal College of Art. She took part in the Pilgrim Trust *Recording Britain* project and exhibited with war artists at the National Gallery. Exhibited at RA, RBA, NEAC and elsewhere. Victoria & Albert Museum holds her work. Lived in London.

Bernard CHEESE 1925– Printmaker, watercolourist and teacher, born in Sydenham, southeast London. He was the husband of the artist Sheila Robinson, their daughter being the artist Chloë Cheese. Studied at Royal College of Art, 1947–50, where Edwin La Dell persuaded Cheese to make lithographs. Taught printmaking at St Martin's School of Art, Goldsmiths' College and Central School of Art and Design. Was elected RE in 1988. Exhibitions included Senefelder Club, Beaux Arts and St George's Galleries, Heffer Gallery in Cambridge, John Russell Gallery in Ipswich, which gave Cheese a seventy-fifth birthday show in 2000, and RA. HM The Queen, Arts Council, Victoria & Albert Museum, Fry Art Gallery in Saffron Walden and several major American collections hold examples. Cheese went to live in Thaxted, Essex, in the 1950s and remained for many years in the county. The Fry Art Gallery at Saffron Walden showed his work in 2005.

Chloë CHEESE 1952– Illustrator, painter and printmaker, born and lived in London, daughter of artists Bernard Cheese and Sheila Robinson. She attended Cambridge School of Art, 1970–3, Royal College of Art, 1973–6, winning a drawing prize in 1972, then worked in Paris in 1974. Began drawing for *Sunday Times Colour Magazine* and also worked for *The Observer*. Her prints were sold through Curwen Gallery and Christie's Contemporary Art. Cheese's first solo exhibition was at Curwen Gallery in 1979, others taking place at Thumb Gallery; in Japan, with which she had a strong working connection; and at Curwen put on a retrospective to 1973 in 1996. In 1985 a British Council touring exhibition was entitled British Illustration from Caxton to Chloë, acknowledging her contribution. Images of her new house, explorations of the shape and colour of domestic artefacts and memories of a trip to Dieppe were featured in Cheese's paintings and prints at The John Russell Gallery, Ipswich, in 2005. Work is held by Fry Gallery, Saffron Walden, and Arts Council.

Mark CHEESEMAN 1959– Painter who studied at the Royal Academy Schools, 1979–82. His work was owned by Sir Brinsley Ford.

Doreen CHEESMAN 1915– Artist in oil, watercolour and chalk, wife of the painter Harold Cheesman. She studied at Plymouth School of Art and the Royal College of Art and went on to teach at Parsloe's School in Dagenham and Onslow School, Guildford, later teaching adults and children in Farnham, Surrey, where she settled. Marriage interrupted her painting, but she showed at Rye Art Gallery and with Farnham Art Society.

Harold CHEESMAN 1915–1982 Painter, mainly of landscapes, in oil, watercolour and gouache, and teacher, born in Rye, Sussex. He married the artist Doreen Cheesman. After study at Hastings School of Art, 1932–5, he attended the Royal College of Art, finishing with a postgraduate year and the award of the J Andrew Lloyd Scholarship for Landscape Painting in 1939. Showed at RA, NEAC, RWS, and in the provinces, having a series of exhibitions at the Ashgate Gallery, Farnham, between 1963–80. He was elected a fellow of the RWS in 1974. Cheesman taught part-time at Farnham School of Art from 1946; was full-time from 1948; retired in 1971; and had a retrospective there, 1980. The Imperial War Museum, Towner Art Gallery in Eastbourne, Melbourne City Art Gallery and other provincial galleries hold his work. Lived in Farnham, Surrey.

Henry CHEETHAM 1877– Watercolourist who was a professional commissioned soldier in the Indian Army, born in London. He studied part-time by post with Sam Spencer. Showed at Fine Art Society, at the public gallery and Little Gallery in Worthing, and with the West Sussex Art Club and Lancing Art Club, in Sussex, which he founded in 1953. Lived in Worthing, Sussex.

Edward CHELL 1958– Painter and teacher, born in Huddersfield, Yorkshire, who studied at University of Newcastle upon Tyne, 1977–81, and at Royal College of Art, 1987–9. Took part in Hunting Group Awards, 1988, winning first prize; Snapshots, Eagle Gallery, 1993; and John Moores Liverpool Exhibition, from 1995–6. Had a solo show at Dove Arts Centre, Stockton, 1985, later ones including Anthony Wilkinson Fine Art, 1995. Arts Council holds his work. Lectured at Canterbury College of Art. Lived in London.

Gang CHEN 1961– Painter, born in Nanjing, China. He attended the Art Academy there, 1983–4, after Jiangxi Art College, 1972–81. Studied at Chelsea College of Art, 1990–1. Awards included Delfina Studios Trust and BT New Contemporaries, both 1992; and Arthur Andersen Prize, 1993. Group exhibitions included Bernard Jacobson Gallery, 1992; and John Moores Liverpool Exhibition and Paton Gallery, both 1993. In that year had a solo show at 63 Union Street Gallery in London, where he lived, with others at Aspex Gallery, Portsmouth, 1994, and Cubitt Gallery, 1999. In 1995 gained an Abbey Award in Painting at the British School at Rome, in 1999 a prize at John Moores Liverpool Exhibition.

Jonathan CHEQUERS 1954– Sculptor in stone, wood and plaster, born in Croydon, Surrey. His work was mainly abstract, related to organic forms. He studied with Open College of the Arts, on short courses and privately and showed with Sussex Sculptors and at Star Gallery, Lewes. Lived in West Hoathly, Sussex.

Peggy CHERNIAVSKY 1923– Modeller, strongly influenced by the idea of the clown and the Italian comedy tradition, born in Bristol. Studied at Camberwell School of Arts and Crafts, 1951–2, then concentrated on sculpture at Chelsea School of Art, 1957–60, with Willi Soukop and Bernard Meadows, and was at Royal College of Art, 1960. Showed RA, RMS, Whitechapel Art Gallery and elsewhere. Sometimes signed work PCC. Imperial Arts League member who lived in London.

Arthur William CHESHER 1895–1972 Primitive painter born in Bedfordshire. He remained a countryman, having worked originally on his father's farm and become enthusiastic about traction engines and steam lorries as a young man. Accidents forced him to retire in his mid-40s, so he turned to painting, rural life and old farm machinery forming the core of his subject-matter in brightly-coloured pictures. In a quarter of a century he produced about 300 of these. Showed at Arthur Jeffress Gallery, then when that closed at the Portal Gallery. Was the subject of a Ken Russell *Monitor* BBC television documentary in the mid-1960s.

Sheila CHESSER 1915– Painter, born in Cheshire, married to Dr Eustace Chesser, the noted medical practitioner and writer. A self-taught artist, she belonged to WIAC and Free Painters and Sculptors, and showed at Redfern and Leicester Galleries, Whitechapel Art Gallery, Bradford City Art Gallery and in Ireland in mixed exhibitions. Solo shows included Midland Group Gallery in Nottingham and Greenwich Theatre Gallery. Leicester University holds her work. Lived in London.

Elwyn Charles CHESTERFIELD 1913–1991 He was an independent Glamorgan-based miner-artist, nephew of the miner-photographer Morgan Charles Chesterfield, who worked at Rock Colliery, Glyn Neath. He was then employed for several years by George Wimpey and Company, operator of a site depicted in Chesterfield's mid-1950s picture Wimpeyland. This scene of devastation caused by opencast mining at Aberpergwm, Glyn Neath, was shown in Miner-Artists: The Art of Welsh Coal Workers, at National Museum & Gallery, Cardiff, 2000.

Charles Sidney CHESTON 1882–1960 Painter and etcher. Born in London, he studied at the Slade School of Fine Art, 1899–1902. Exhibited widely, including RA, RHA, Goupil Gallery, RWS, Fine Art Society and NEAC. First one-man show at Colnaghi's in 1929, the year his artist wife Evelyn Cheston died. He published a monograph *Evelyn Cheston: Member of the New English Art Club 1908–1929*, in 1931. Cheston, made a vice-president of the RWS in 1950, was son of the architect and estate agent to Lord Amhurst, Chester Cheston. Charles' sister was the actress Dorothy Cheston who met the writer Arnold Benett in 1922, had his daughter Virginia in 1926 and became known as Dorothy Cheston Bennett, Bennett's wife Marguerite having refused a divorce. Lived at Polstead, near Colchester, Essex.

Manuel CHETCUTI 1939– Sculptor and teacher, born in Cardiff, where he attended the College of Art, 1959–63. After a period lecturing at Newport College of Art and Chelsea College of Art he joined the staff of the department of art at Sheffield Polytechnic in 1974. Welsh Theatre Company and Llandaff Cathedral commissioned work by him, which was also shown in group shows at Camden Arts Centre, Demarco Gallery in Edinburgh and by WAC, which holds his work.

Annette CHEVALLIER 1944– Artist in mixed media and teacher, born in West Sussex. She attended West Sussex College of Art, 1961–3, and Chelsea College of Art, 1963–6. After working in London, 1966–78, she moved to the northeast of England and settled in Tynemouth, teaching part-time at Cleveland College of Art. She gained Northern Arts Awards in 1980–1, a Charlotte Press Printmaking Bursary in 1981 and a Northern Arts Purchase Award, 1982. Chevallier's work was abstract, sometimes using repeated notations. She took part in many group shows: RA and LG from 1966; Whitechapel Art Gallery from 1968; Art and the Sea, at Ceolfrith Gallery, Sunderland, 1981; Engelsk Grafikk Gallery F15, Moss, Norway, 1982; and Six Artists from the Coast, Laing Art Gallery in Newcastle and Scandinavian tour, 1983. After 1971 solo show at Richmond College, later one-man exhibitions included Camden Arts Centre, 1980, and Hatton Gallery, Newcastle, 1982. Sussex University and Northern Arts hold her work.

Charlotte CHEVERTON 1960–1991 Artist and teacher, born Charlotte Ramsden and known as Lottie. She was born in Sleningford, Yorkshire, and attended the Slade School of Fine Art, 1978–81. She married the artist Mark Cheverton and after teaching at Fettes College she in 1988 with her husband founded the Leith School of Art in Edinburgh in a building which had housed the Mission for Norwegian Seamen. Like Mark she was a committed Christian, which expressed itself in her painting. With him she was killed in a road accident at Wooler, Northumberland. Memorial show at Leith School of Art, 1992.

Mark CHEVERTON 1952–1991 Artist and teacher, born in London. He became art teacher at Marlborough College, 1974–80, then travelling secretary in art for the University and Colleges Christian Fellowship, 1980–2, then in 1982–88 was head of art at Edinburgh Academy. In 1988 with his wife, Charlotte, he founded the Leith School of Art. As a painter and printmaker Cheverton expressed his deep religious faith. He was killed with his wife in a car accident at Wooler, Northumberland. Memorial show at Leith School Art, 1992.

Hugh CHEVINS 1931–2003 Painter, mural artist, designer and illustrator, born in Retford, Nottinghamshire. Studied at Twickenham School of Art, in Paris and at the Royal Academy Schools, winning a bronze medal in 1953. Showed UA, Piccadilly Gallery, in the provinces and at Paris Salon, where he won two silver medals in the 1950s. Did a variety of work for firms such as Imperial Chemical Industries and Shell Petroleum. Science Museum holds his work. Lived in Shepperton, Middlesex.

Maria CHEVSKA 1948– Painter, draughtsman, printmaker and teacher, based in London, who attended Byam Shaw School of Art, 1970–4, including postgraduate studies. Awards included Arts Council, 1977; Greater London Arts Association, 1979–84; Gulbenkian Foundation Printmakers Award, 1982; and Austin Abbey Award, British School at Rome, 1994. Chevska became head of painting at Ruskin School of Drawing and Fine Art, Oxford. She was a prolific exhibitor, who was included in Sister Wendy Beckett's 1988 survey *Contemporary women artists*. Group shows included Art and Sea, John Hansard Gallery, Southampton, and ICA, both 1981; Whitechapel Open, from 1983; Crossover, Anderson O'Day Gallery, 1991; and White Out, Curwen Gallery, 1995. Had a solo show at Air Gallery, 1982, later ones including Weight, Andrew Mummery, 1996 and 2001; and Spoken Image, Kunstmuseum Heldenheim and Museum Goch, Germany, and BWA Gallery, Wrocław, Poland, all 1997; with a tour, Vera's Room, of paintings and a new installation of objects, Maison de la Culture d'Amiens, France, 2002. Can't Wait (Letters R.L.) was at Andrew Mummery Gallery in 2004. Arts Council, Gulbenkian Foundation, Bolton City and Oldham Art Galleries and corporate collections hold examples. Lived in London.

Albert Ranney CHEWETT 1877–1965 Artist and photographer, born in Toronto, Canada, who travelled to England with his family in the late 1890s, attending Herkomer's School at Bushey, Hertfordshire, for several years before studying at Académie Julian, Paris. After time in Canada, where hedecorated the Rotunda of the Prince George Hotel, Toronto, with scenes of pioneering life and showed at the Ontario Society of Artists show in 1905, Chewett had a studio in Florence, Italy, then returned to Bushey, where he settled. Latterly became more interested in photography and radio than art. Showed at RA and Walker Art Gallery in Liverpool and was included in A R Chewett and Friends, mounted by Bushey Museum Trust, 1986.

Anna CHEYNE 1926–2002 Sculptor and Batik artist. She attended Kingston School of Art, then Slade School of Fine Art, studying painting and sculpture. In 1982 gave up a job as a supplier of pottery materials to concentrate on own sculpture. Showed extensively in Ireland and England from mid-1970s, including Lisnagarvey Art Society annual shows, RUA, Oireachtas in Dublin and Cork and Guinness Hop Store, Dublin. Had a solo show at Peacock Gallery, Craigavon, 1984, later exhibitions including Rooksmoor Gallery, Bath, 1988, and Cavehill Gallery, Belfast, 1991. Took part in a number of workshops, including a ceramic workshop with Eduardo Paolozzi, Dublin, 1988. Commissions included ornamental plasterwork for ceiling of Old Town Hall, Belfast, 1982, and a coat of arms for the headquarters of the Northern Ireland Fire Authority, Lisburn, 1987. She was a member of the Society of Sculptors, Ireland, and Association of Artists of Ireland. Lived in Lisburn, County Down.

Ian CHEYNE 1895–1955 Colour woodcut artist and painter, born in Broughty Ferry, Angus. After education at Glasgow Academy, Cheyne studied at Glasgow School of Art under Maurice Greiffenhagen. Originally Cheyne concentrated on painting, but increasingly his time was devoted to colour woodcuts, notably Scottish and continental landscapes. He showed at SSA, RSA, Redfern and Cooling Galleries and was treasurer for the Society of Artist-Printmakers. His work had a marked Art Deco quality. Scottish National Gallery of Modern Art holds. Lived in Bearsden, Glasgow.

Sandro CHIA 1946– Conceptual artist, born in Florence, Italy, who studied at the Istituto d'Arte, then enrolled at the Accademia di Belle Arti in Florence, gaining his diploma in 1969. He travelled extensively in India, Turkey and throughout Europe before settling in Rome in 1970. Throughout the 1970s he exhibited often in Rome and elsewhere in Europe. Having obtained a scholarship from the German city of Mönchengladbach, Chia worked there for a year, 1980–1, then moved to New York, 1981–2, working between there and Ronciglione. In the 1990s he bought Castello Romitorio in Montalcino, working between there, New York City and Rome. The British collector Charles Saatchi bought Chia's work, which he later sold.

Angela Verren CHICK: *see* **Angela VERREN**

Edward T CHICKEN 1940– Painter of wildlife, capable of producing minutely detailed, realistic work. Chicken spent most of his early years in the northeast of England, with frequent visits to the Lake District, which fostered his interest in wildlife, which he began drawing and painting. Began exhibiting in the early 1970s, his contributions to an SWLA show at Mall Galleries, in 1974, and the RA Summer Exhibition, 1975, selling on the first day. A BBC2 television feature on the 1976 Summer Exhibition included Chicken's work. He also appeared in a number of other BBC television programmes: *The Queen's Garden*, *Blue Peter* and *Pebble Mill* and had wide press coverage.

Heather CHILD 1911–1997 Painter, calligrapher and writer, born in Winchester, full name Josephine Heather Child. She studied at Chelsea School of Art and gained an exhibition to Royal College of Art where the noted calligrapher Edward Johnstone taught. Among Child's books were a number dealing with Johnstone's methods; a collection of these books and manuscripts is held by Victoria & Albert Museum. Other books included *Decorative Maps*, 1956; *Heraldic Designs: A Handbook for Students*, 1965; and *The Calligrapher's Handbook*, 1985. Child showed with RMS, was a member of Art Workers' Guild and several other crafts-oriented societies. Lived in Petersfield, Hampshire, for many years with the portrait painter Dorothy Colles, who survived her. Together, they wrote *Christian Symbols Ancient & Modern*, 1971.

St John CHILD fl. from 1960s– Artist in various media who studied at Hornsey College of Art and Royal College of Art, specialising in fine art. Showed at Redfern, Brook Street, Molton and Woodstock Galleries, New Art Centre, Sussex University, Brighton College and in 1993 had solo show at Hove Museum & Art Gallery. That was Windmill Paintings, completed by the artist during cycle rides through Suffolk and Sussex.

Billy CHILDISH 1960– Painter of grittily realistic pictures, musician and dyslexic writer and poet, original name Steven Hamper, born and lived in Chatham, Kent. His older brother was the artist Nichollas Hamper. By the age of 40 this cult figure had painted more than 2,000 pictures, recorded 80 albums of his own music and had published several dozen volumes of poetry and written two novels. His work's strong autobiographical content covered an abused childhood, encounters with alcohol and his long, tempestuous and eventually sour, relationship with the artist Tracey Emin; Childish was the largest of the many names listed in her 1997 Sensation show tent exhibit, Everybody I've Ever Slept With: 1963–1995. Childish, whose father was a commercial artist, left secondary modern school with a single Certificate in Secondary Education in art; was turned down by the local art college; worked as an apprentice stonemason for a year, 1976; was accepted by Medway College of Art, for foundation, 1977–8, where he met and was a strong influence on Emin, until they separated in 1986; then St Martin's School of Art, 1978, to study for a painting degree, but left after half a term; after working as a mental hospital ward porter he returned to St Martin's, 1980–1, but was expelled. Became a member of the Medway Poets. Ran a series of bands, including Thee Headcoats, its style described as "rewriting the same three chords 500 times over", with a following in Europe, America and Japan, and refused offers from big record companies and to stage proper tours. His records and poetry were self-published, his novels produced by a small, independent firm. Was co-founder of the Stuckists (from a comment allegedly made by Emin that Childish was stuck in Chatham), opposing the commodification of art, and the tyranny of the market-place. The first Stuckist show was held at Gallery 108, 1999, with another at Red Dot Gallery, Ipswich, 2000. Childish had a retrospective at Metropole Arts Centre, Folkestone, 1999–00, and was included in British Art Show 5, Talbot Rice Gallery, Edinburgh, and tour, 2000. After he had left the Stuckists to concentrate on his own work, in 2001, his book *Chatham Town Welcomes Desperate Men* was published. In 2002, 25 Years of Being Childish, at Kent Institute of Art & Design, Maidstone, celebrated all aspects of his output; Channel 4 featured Childish in *The Art Show*; and new work, The Idiocy of Ideas, opened at the Covent Garden Gallery. Billy Childish: We are all Phonies was at The Aquarium, 2003, and Billy Childish: Sex Crimes of the Futcher, paintings, books and records, at Simon Finch Fine Art, 2004.

Alan CHILDS 1919-2002 Art teacher, administrator and artist, son of a teacher at Barrow-in-Furness Grammar School. Childs rejected reading mathematics and economics at Cambridge to attend Liverpool College of Art, where his studies were interrupted by World War II. After capture in north Africa, he spent the duration as a prisoner of war. By then, Childs was married to Diana, daughter of the artist Edward Carter Preston, who encouraged Alan's proficiency in a wide range of media. Childs was appointed vice-principal of Bury School of Arts and Crafts in 1949. He also took the initiative in setting up an adult literacy scheme in 1951. Like many other small art schools, Bury closed to full-time students in 1957. When Childs became principal in 1959 he encouraged diversification into adult, non-vocational education, life-painting weekends being especially popular.

Elizabeth CHILTON 1945– Artist in oil, watercolour and bronze, born in Darlington, County Durham. She studied at Ruskin School of Drawing in Oxford where her teachers included Richard Naish and Geoffrey Rhoades. Showed at RA, NEAC, ROI and Paris Salon, work including landscapes, portraits and abstractions. Some Oxford University colleges hold her work. Lived in Toot Baldon, Oxfordshire.

Michael CHILTON 1934– Painter, draughtsman, creator of constructions in a variety of materials, and teacher, born in Leeds, Yorkshire. Chilton's output embraced a wide span in the belief that "a person has many facets, and you would be extremely dull if you only ever saw the world in one way". However, a selection of elements from nature was a key feature of his output, drawing on the landscape. He studied at Leeds College of Art, 1952–6, under Harry Thubron, gained a travel scholarship to Spain in 1956, from 1956–9 studied painting and lithography at Slade School of Fine Art, in 1959 gaining an Abbey Minor Travel Scholarship. Chilton joined Leicester College of Art, 1960–4, being a visiting lecturer at Nottingham and Coventry Colleges of Art in 1963–4, then was a senior lecturer at Hull College of Art, 1965–73. During the 1960s he showed at Grabowski Gallery and in other mixed exhibitions. Had a solo show at Ferens Art Gallery, Hull, and at Suzanne Fischer Gallery, Baden-Baden, 1975. Later solo exhibitions included a major retrospective at Usher Gallery, Lincoln, 1991, and work from 1960–92 at Ferens in 1992. Lived in Hull.

John CHILVER 1964– Artist, born and lived in London, who graduated in philosophy from Reading University, 1983–6, and in fine art from Wimbledon School of Art, 1987–90, gaining his master's at Goldsmiths' College, 1995–7. Group shows included House Party, Harakawa House, Yokohama, Japan, 1993; World of Painting, Unit, 1997; and Printemps, Surfacing ICA, 1998. Solo shows included Morrison Judd in collaboration with Asprey Jacques, 1999, and Asprey Jacques, 2000.

Vasant Narayan CHINCHWADKAR: *see* **VASANT**

James CHINNECK 1973– Artist whose work included his four glass and metal Suitcases, 1996, shown in New Contemporaries that year at Tate Gallery, Liverpool, and Camden Arts Centre. Chinneck was born in Hertford, Hertfordshire, and gained a fine art degree at Leeds Metropolitan University, 1993–6. Other exhibitions included the MISC Group Show at the University's gallery, 1995, and before that Diverse 13, Granary Wharf, Leeds, 1994.

Clare CHINNERY 1973– Painter producing gestural work with evocative handling of vibrant colours. After a foundation course in fine art at Wirral Metropolitan College, 1992–4, Chinnery gained an honours degree from Liverpool John Moores University in fine art painting, 1994–7. Group shows included Unity Theatre, Liverpool, 1995; Northern Graduates, New Academy Gallery, 1997; Sefton Open Exhibition 1999, Atkinson Art Gallery, Southport; and Soup, Hanover Gallery, Liverpool, 2001. New Academy gave her solo exhibitions in 1999, 2001 and 2003. In that year, Chinnery was shortlisted for the Villiers David Travel Prize.

Domenico CHIOCCHETTI 1910–1999 Painter, born and died in Moena, Italy. While serving in the Italian Army in North Africa in World War II, he was taken prisoner and sent to the Orkney island of Lamb Holm to help erect the Churchill Barriers, sealing the eastern approaches to Scapa Flow. When two Nissen huts were made available to the Italian prisoners of Camp 60 in late 1943, Chiocchetti and craftsmen created what became known as the Italian Chapel. The sanctuary vault was frescoed by Chiocchetti, his masterpiece being a painting of the Madonna and Child, behind the altar, based on Nicolo Barabina's Madonna of the Olives, a battered postcard of which Chiocchetti carried. When Camp 60 was disbanded in 1945, he stayed on for a time to complete his work. After the formation of a preservation committee in 1958 Chiocchetti was traced to Moena, where he worked as a painter and decorator, and in 1960 with BBC assistance he returned to Lamb Holm to restore his work. He visited again in 1964, bringing a personal gift of 14 Stations of the Cross, hand-carved in wood, and, from Moena, a standing crucifix and altar cruets in Venetian glass. In 1996 Chiocchetti was granted Moena's freedom, witnessed by three Orcadians. Bishop Mario Conti flew to Orkney in June 1999 to celebrate a memorial service for Chiocchetti.

James CHISHOLM 1917– Painter who was born in Edinburgh, where he continued to live. Studied at Edinburgh College of Art under Francis M'Cracken and at Edinburgh and Glasgow Universities. Showed at RSA and other Scottish galleries. The Reverend Chisholm was for a time director of arts and crafts for the Church of Scotland, later lecturing at Edinburgh University.

Ross CHISHOLM 1977– Painter, born in Redhill, Surrey, who studied at Brighton University, 1997–00, and Goldsmiths' College, 2003–4. He was included in The Valley at Bloomberg SPACE in 2005, the catalogue noting that: "The presiding mood in Ross Chisholm's paintings is one of fracture, their elements brought together rather than belonging together. The imagery, derived from found slide sets, botanical reference books and art history, sit together uncomfortably, never quite forming a whole." Other Chisholm exhibitions included Painting, The Coachhouse, Brighton, 2000; Crystal Peaks, S1 Artspace, Sheffield, 2004; and Sixteen, Royal Brompton Hospital, 2005. The artist lived and worked in London.

Christine CHITTOCK 1952– She gained her diploma in fine art from North East London Polytechnic, 1975–8. From 1984–5 Chittock was involved in art skills sessions in Suffolk, from 1987-9 working as a visiting artist in the county's schools. She was art activities organiser at Sebert Road After School Club in London, 1988. Group appearances included Sixth Annual Artists in Essex, 1988, and Seventh Annual Artists in Essex in 1989, the year she was included in East End Open Studios, with the Leyton Artists Group.

Derek CHITTOCK 1922–1986 Painter, notably of portraits, whose work contained a strong element of Socialist Realism, art critic and historian, who studied at the Slade School of Fine Art, 1942–7, under Randolph Schwabe, and at the Royal Academy Schools under Philip Connard. Exhibited at RA, RP, RBA and NEAC. At the end of World War II Chittock did portrait work for the War Artists' Advisory Committee. In the early 1950s he was one of the artists recruited from the AIA to form a selection committee for the Artists for Peace Exhibitions. Chittock was a paid-up member of the British Communist Party until the Hungarian uprising in 1956 prompted his resignation, and he also was art critic of the *Daily Worker*. He completed covers for the magazine *John Bull*, ranging from the Test Match to London buses, and sometimes used the name James Dudley. His daughter was the actress Emily Morgan, his brother the film critic John Chittock. Lived in Hertford, London and the Sevenoaks area of Kent.

Tim CHITTY 1956– Artist who studied at Burslem School of Art. He drew on Victorian and Edwardian images to inspire boxes, collages and mechanical creations. Among his appearances was Art in Boxes at England & Co, 1991, where his Untitled mixed media assemblage was shown.

Lechosława CHMIELOWSAK-AMIT fl. from early 1950s– Artist, born in Warsaw, Poland, who studied from 1949–55 at the Cracow Academy of Fine Arts under Professor Zbigniew Pronaszko. She lived in London from 1981 and was a member of the Association of Polish Artists in Great Britain. Solo exhibitions included Marina Hotels; Sabra Gallery, New York, America; Ipanema Gallery, Tel-Aviv, Israel; and Corman Gallery. In 1995 she was included in Form and Colour, Congress of Polish Culture Exhibition of Fine Arts by Polish Artists in Great Britain, at POSK.

Herbert William CHOAT 1912– Painter and commercial artist, born in Southsea, Hampshire. After initial education in Portsmouth he studied at the School of Art there, 1928–33. Showed at RA, elsewhere in London and in the provinces. Lived for many years at South Ruislip, Middlesex.

Adam CHODZKO 1965– Artist using various materials, born and lived in London, latterly in Whitstable, Kent. His father was the actor and writer Joseph Chodzko, who described himself as a "Jersey-born, Anglo-Lithuanianised Pole." Adam gained his bachelor's degree at University of Manchester, 1985–8, and master's at Goldsmiths' College, 1992–4. Group exhibitions included Malania Basarab Gallery, 1992; Making People Disappear, Cubitt Street Gallery, and Mandy Loves Declan 100%, at Mark Boote Gallery, New York, both 1993; Galleri Nicolai Wallner, Copenhagen, 1994; and Brilliant! New Art from London at Walker Arts Center, Minneapolis, and tour, and Venice Biennale, both 1995. Had a solo show at Bipasha Ghosh, 1992, with New Commissions at Ikon Gallery, Birmingham, 1999. In 2002, the year Chodzko won a Hamlyn Award at Fabrica, Brighton, his Plan for a Spell employed a wide screen showing looped snippets of film exploring British pagan folk traditions. In 2002–3, he exhibited new comissioned works at Cubitt Gallery and Studios. Arts Council holds his work.

Elzbieta CHOJAK-MYŚKO 1939– Artist and designer, born in Sarny, Poland, who in 1965 finished studying stage design under A Stopka and J Szajna at the Academy of Fine Arts, Cracow. From 1966 she created many stage designs for theatre, opera and television. Settled in London and from 1992 participated in group exhibitions, such as Form and Colour, Congress of Polish Culture Exhibition of Fine Arts by Polish Artists in Britain, POSK, 1995. She also had solo shows. Private collections in France, Germany, Italy, Japan and Poland held examples.

Heather CHONTOS 1978– Painter whose pictures had a spontaneous, intuitive character, the overall Expressionist ground being overlaid by strong calligraphic marks, as in her first major solo exhibition in London, Broken Places, at Stephen Lacey Gallery, 2001. Born in Tarrytown, New York, America, Chontos studied fine art at Barcelona University, in Spain, graduating in the history of art at

University College, London. Although she spent a year as studio assistant with the Catalonian painter Roca Sastre, she regarded herself as self-taught. In London, she worked on illustration, styling and production for a number of publications, including *World of Interiors, Nova, Sunday Telegraph Magazine, Tank* and *Spoon*. Other exhibitions included Linda Kirkland Gallery, New York, 2000.

Henri CHOPIN 1922– Poet, painter, graphic artist and designer, typographer, publisher film-maker, broadcaster and advocate of the international avant-grade, born in Paris, France. Chopin was subjected to forced labour in Germany during World War II from 1943, serving in the French Army in Vietnam, 1948–9. From 1955, Chopin was acquainted with the poet and champion of Surrealism André Breton, writer on art Michel Seuphor and the Lettristes. During the late 1950s and 1960s his activities included radio work in France, Sweden and Czechoslovakia; shows with Jiri Kolar, John Furnival and others; and his classic audio-visual magazines *Cinquième Saison* and *Ou*, each issue containing recordings and texts. Chopin continued publishing *Ou*, his activities as a concrete and sound poet, international performances and recordings while exiled in England, at Ingatestone, Essex, from 1968 into the 1980s. Returned to Paris, 1985. Exhibitions of his work included Queensland College of Art Gallery, Australia, 1992, and Norwich Gallery, Norwich School of Art and Design, 1998.

Richard CHOPPING 1917– Artist, illustrator, writer and teacher, noted for his depiction of natural objects such as butterflies, flowers, insects and fruit, meticulously accurate and showing a delicate sense of colour and texture. He was born and lived most of his life in or near Colchester, latterly long-term at Wivenhoe with the painter Denis Wirth-Miller. Dickie Chopping was part of what was described as The East Anglian Mafia, including the painter Francis Bacon and writer Angus Wilson. Chopping began painting as a small boy, much encouraged by his art master at Gresham's School, Holt, Norfolk; attended the London Theatre Studio and learned stage design under Michel St Denis; and was for a short time student, cook and housekeeper at the East Anglian School of Painting and Drawing run by Cedric Morris and Lett Haines. Morris's portrait of Chopping was included in the Tate Gallery's 1984 Cedric Morris exhibition, illustrated in the catalogue. Until his retirement Chopping was a part-time tutor of plant drawing at the Royal College of Art, where he was a feature of the end-of-term Christmas shows. Among Chopping's mixed exhibitions were Goupil Gallery, 1939; Arthur Jeffress Gallery, 1956, with Robin Ironside and Kenneth Rowell; and The Minories, Colchester, 1959, with Wirth-Miller. He also had solo shows, including watercolours, trompe l'oeils and flowers at The Hanover Gallery, 1953; New Art Centre, 1977; and paintings and graphic work, Aldeburgh Festival Gallery, 1979. Chopping was author and illustrator of natural history and children's books, such as the Picture Puffin *Butterflies in Britain*, 1943; *A Book of Birds, The Old Woman and the Pedlar, The Tailor and the Mouse*, and *Wild Flowers*, all 1944; and *Mr Postlethwaite's Reindeer*, 1945. He designed the dust-jackets for Jonathan Cape's editions of Ian Fleming's James Bond novels. Chopping also wrote two notable novels, *The Fly*, 1965, and *The Ring*, 1967. The gestation of these books and an amusing pen-portrait of their author are included in his 1993 memoir *Aren't We Due a Royalty Statement?* by the writer and editor Giles Gordon, who considered *The Fly* "sufficiently sordid to appeal to voyeurs".

Adrian CHORLEY 1906– Painter, draughtsman and printmaker, especially of landscapes, born in East Bergholt in Suffolk, Constable country. After attending St Paul's School Chorley went to Byam Shaw School of Drawing and Painting, 1924–7, and Royal College of Art. Showed RA, ROI, RBA, NEAC and elsewhere. Lived in Edenbridge, Kent.

Graham CHORLTON 1953– Painter and teacher, born in Leicester. After studying at University of Leeds, 1972–6, he was at Birmingham Polytechnic, 1977–8. He taught there and elsewhere in the West Midlands and was commissioned by Birmingham City Council. Chorlton's group shows included Facade: The City's Face, at Ikon Gallery, Birmingham, with tour, 1987–8; Unfinished Business, Lanchester Gallery, Coventry Polytechnic, 1990; and the 1991–2 John Moores Exhibition, Liverpool. The urban landscape and experience were features of his work, as in the John Moores picture Apartment. Showed solo at Wolverhampton Art Gallery, 1983, and Midlands Arts Centre, 1989. Lived in Stirchley, Birmingham.

Yolanda CHRISTIAN 1957– Artist and lecturer who gained a first-class fine art degree from Wolverhampton Polytechnic, 1977–80, including a student exchange, École des Beaux-Arts, Marseilles, France, 1978; with a master's in printmaking, Slade School of Fine Art, 1980–2. Lectured at art colleges, including Cardiff, Newport and Wolverhampton. Contributed to *Impress, Artists Newsletter* and *Printmaking Today*. Among Christian's travels were a journey through China to research her family roots, which stemmed from Macau. She also visited Clayoquot Sound, Vancouver Island, British Columbia, to study Indian culture. Took part in numerous group shows, later ones including River Deep, Mountain High, touring Scottish galleries and museums, 1997; Cheltenham Open Drawing, tour including Germany, 1998; and National Print Competition, Mall Galleries, 1999. Solo exhibitions included Taking Root, Midlands Arts Centre, 1990. A later work theme was In Between Two Worlds, 10-foot images, financially aided by the Oppenheim Trust. Victoria & Albert Museum; Guildhall Art Gallery & Library; Beijing Academy of Arts, China; South London Art Gallery; Birmingham City Art Gallery & Museum; hospital and corporate collections hold examples. Lived in London.

Cedric CHRISTIE 1962– Self-taught, versatile artist with an imaginative approach, as seen in his first show at Rocket in 2001, which comprised six snooker ball sculptures, four monochrome portraits on solid aluminium and a boxed "doormat" poem. The snooker ball pieces, suspended in stainless steel channels, were inspired by the American artist Ellsworth Kelly's curve paintings. Christie's previous solo shows included Commercial Gallery, 1995 and 1997, and group exhibitions Fun de Siècle at Walsall Museum & Art Gallery, 1999, and Het Voetbal in de Beeldende Kunst 1900-2000, at Kunsthal, Rotterdam, Netherlands, 2000. There was another Rocket exhibition in 2003. Lived in London.

Eleanor CHRISTIE: *see* **Eleanor CHRISTIE-CHATTERLEY**

Fyffe CHRISTIE 1918–1979 Painter, draughtsman, muralist and teacher, born in Bushey, Hertfordshire, son of a commercial artist and illustrator, George Christie. From the age of 12 Christie lived in Glasgow, from 1934 working in a solicitor's office, then became an apprentice lithographic draughtsman and during World War II served in the Scottish Rifles, resulting work finding its way into the Imperial War Museum. Christie studied at Glasgow School of Art, 1946–50, mural painting under Walter Pritchard. He gained the Newbery Medal in 1950 and a post-diploma year's study. After a period teaching and a six-month travelling scholarship taken on the continent Christie resumed teaching and completed many murals, including Glasgow University and the Iona Community House. With his wife Eleanor, a sculptor, he moved to London in 1957 and again taught, while completing murals and much other work. Christie and his wife held a show at Woodlands Gallery in 1979, shortly before he died. This showed him to be a painter with a rich palette, notable for his female nude studies, as well as a consummate draughtsman. His widow did much to promote Christie's work after his death. There were exhibitions at Cyril Gerber Fine Art, Glasgow, and Fairhurst Gallery in 1988, preceded by a show of his drawings at Glasgow School of Art. He was included in Children & Childhood at the City Art Centre, Edinburgh, in 1989; there was a large show of his schoolchildren drawings at the Bethnal Green Museum of Childhood, 1991; and further small exhibitions at Blackheath Concert Halls and in Norwich. In 2004, there was an exhibition at Wimpole Hall, Cambridgeshire, accompanied by a monograph, *Nature and Humanity, The Work of Fyffe Christie 1918-1979*, published by Sansom & Company Ltd.

Stella CHRISTIE fl. from early 1990s– Artist and teacher who gained a first-class honours degree in textiles at Glasgow School of Art, 1983–7, then in 1988–9 was a master of fine art candidate on a Fulbright Scholarship at Tyler School of Art, Philadelphia, America, 1988–9. While in America she taught at Tyler; under the Hope Scott Trust Fund had a studio in New York; and travelled from there to Los Angeles. Further experience included teaching at Elmvale Centre and Easterhouse School, Glasgow, 1990; being a design consultant for the plays *Mourning Becomes Electra* and *Man and Superman* at Citizen's Theatre, Glasgow, 1991; having a studio at British School, Rome, 1992; another six months painting in New York, 1994–5; and voluntary work in the Victoria & Albert Museum prints and drawings department, 1996. Group shows included RSA, 1992; Laing Exhibition at Mall Galleries and Atholl Gallery, Dunkeld, both 1993; and Long & Ryle Art International, 1994. Had a solo shows at Whitechapel Open Studios and Tricycle Gallery, both 1994, and in 1996 shared a three-artist exhibition at Harriet Green Gallery.

Talbot Patterson CHRISTIE 1946– Painter and draughtsman, born in Montreal, Canada. He studied at Byam Shaw School of Art, 1966–70, teachers including Maurice de Sausmarez, then Royal Academy Schools, 1970–3. Exhibitions included Heim Gallery, National Museum of Wales in Cardiff, the provinces and Paris. Lived for a time in Oxford.

Eleanor CHRISTIE-CHATTERLEY 1929– Sculptor and teacher, born and educated in Scotland, whose first husband was the artist Fyffe Christie and who until remarriage showed as Eleanor Christie. She studied sculpture at Glasgow School of Art and Camberwell School of Art. From 1970–84, she was sculpture teacher at London Marylebone Institute (St John's Wood Sculpture School), from 1987–93 at Blackheath School of Art. She was one of four artists exhibiting at Woodlands Art Gallery, 1979, also showing in mixed exhibitions at Blackheath Gallery. Later exhibitions included South Ayrshire Open Art Exhibition and Norwich Warehouse Artists, both 2000; Norwich Open Studios, three painters and one sculptor at Buckenham Galleries, Southwold, and Great Walsingham Gallery Gardens Exhibition, all 2001; and Berghapton Sculpture Trail and a solo show at King of Hearts Gallery, Norwich, both 2002. Christie-Chatterley sold from private commission and from galleries in London, Glasgow, Southwold and Norwich, where she lived. She edited the monograph *Nature and Humanity, The Work of Fyffe Christie 1918–1979*, published by Sansom & Company Ltd in 2004, and oversaw the exhibition of his work at Wimpole Hall, Cambridgeshire, in that year.

John CHRISTOFOROU 1921– Powerfully gestural abstract and figurative artist using a brilliant palette, born in London to parents of Greek origin. Christoforou's mother died when he was a baby, his father in 1932, two years after he and John had moved to Athens. Before returning to England in 1938 Christoforou studied at L'École des Beaux-Arts in Athens, where Byzantine art impressed him. After serving in the Royal Air Force, 1941–6, Christoforou studied modern art by visiting the National and Tate Galleries, in 1949 having a first solo show at 20 Brook Street Gallery. During a stay in Paris, 1951–2, where he continued to visit major galleries, Christoforou destroyed all his prentice works. Returned to London, 1953, Christoforou showed with Gimpel Fils and at Victor Musgrave's gallery and made the acquaintance of writers including Maurice Collis, Colin MacInnes and Denis Silk. He married in 1956 and decided to settle in Paris. In 1965 Christoforou received the prize of the International Association of Art Critics in London. Went on to exhibit extensively, retrospectives including Randers Kunstmuseum, Denmark, 1974; L'École Regionale des Beaux-Arts d'Angers, and tour, 1985; and Fondation d'Art Moderne en Picardie, Amiens, 1988. He took French nationality in 1990. Tate Gallery archive holds Christoforou's self-portrait.

Ann CHRISTOPHER 1947– Non-figurative sculptor in bronze, born Watford, Hertfordshire. Inspiration ranged from the cycladic pieces of ancient Greece to modern buildings such as skyscrapers, lending them a contemplative presence. She studied at Harrow School of Art, 1965–6, then West of England College of Art, Bristol, 1966–9, her teachers being Ralph Brown and Robert Clatworthy. After graduating she worked as a freelance sculptor. Among her main works was a bronze in Tower Bridge Road, London, completed in 1990, and another, Lines from Within, for Castle Park, Bristol, 1993. She was elected RWA, 1983, RA in 1989. Among Christopher's awards were first prize in the Harrison-Cowley Sculpture Competition, 1968; the Peter Stuyvesant Award, 1971; Birds Charity Award, 1973; and South-West Arts Award in 1976. Began showing in mixed exhibitions at Mignon Gallery, Bath, and RWA, 1969; RA Summer Exhibition from 1971; Marjorie Parr Gallery; LG and JPL Fine Arts, 1975; New Art Centre, 1987; and Lynne Stern Associates, 1988. Showed solo at City of Bristol Museum & Art Gallery and Mignon Gallery, 1972, later shows including New Ashgate Gallery in Farnham, 1987, and Dorset County Museum & Art Gallery, Dorchester, 1989. There was an exhibition at Jubilee Park, Canary Wharf, in 2004. Bristol University, RWA, Contemporary Art Society and Glynn Vivian Art Gallery, Swansea, hold her work. Lived in Marshfield, near Chippenham, Wiltshire.

Anne CHRISTOPHERSON 1921– Painter in oil and teacher, born in Simla, India, married to artist John Christopherson. Although between 1958–67 she moved from the figurative to the abstract, her work was mainly figurative, notably maritime industrial scenes based on the Thames. Christopherson studied at Bournemouth College of Art, 1946–8, Goldsmiths' College School of Art, 1948–50, and Hornsey School of Art, 1950–1, her teachers including Leslie Ward and Kenneth Martin. From 1951–62 she taught art at Blackheath High School. Was a member of Blackheath Art Society, Hampstead Artists' Council, WIAC and Greenwich Open Studios, and in addition had a series of solo shows, starting with Siri Colvin Gallery, 1967. Later ones included Higherwater Gallery, 1990. A well-illustrated collection of Christopherson's work, *Greenwich – Times and Tides*, appeared in 2001. National Maritime Museum, Greenwich, holds her work. Lived in London.

John CHRISTOPHERSON 1921–1996 Painter and artist in collage, born in Blackheath, southeast London, where he mostly lived. After a series of administrative jobs in 1959 resigned from the Civil Service to paint full-time, although he had only studied for a short period in the evenings from 1955 at Chelsea School of Art. Christopherson became attracted to the art world at the time of the 1951 Festival of Britain, when he began collecting modern paintings and sculpture. His influences were many: pictorial, literary and musical, especially the music of Debussy and Ravel. Encouraged by Jean Dubuffet, Victor Pasmore and Anthony Caro he began showing at mixed exhibitions at the Leicester, Redfern and Mercury galleries. He had a one-man exhibition at the Hyde Park Gallery in 1961, followed a string of solo shows at such galleries as ICA, Marjorie Parr and England & Co, which gave him a memorial exhibition in 1997. There were retrospectives at Woodlands Art Gallery, 1972 and 1995. Arts Council holds Christopherson's work, which range from a private-image world of abstraction to haunting, unpeopled townscapes of deceptive simplicity. Was married to the painter Anne Christopherson.

José CHRISTOPHERSON 1914– Painter and artist in mixed media, born in Manchester, who was married to the artist Richard Weisbrod. She studied in London for five years, notably with Iain Macnab at Grosvenor School of Modern Art. She exhibited in London and Manchester, then her career was interrupted by World War II forces service. Appeared in group exhibitions put on by Lucy Wertheim and was influenced by the work of Chagall and Christopher Wood; showed at Mid-Day Studios and with Manchester Group and at Great House Gallery near Bolton. Had solo shows in London, Manchester and Winnipeg in Canada. The circus and landscape were leading features of her pictures, which are held by Blackburn and Salford Art Galleries. Lived latterly in Vaud, Switzerland.

Andreas CHRISTOU 1953– Sculptor, born in Cyprus, who attended Goldsmiths' College, 1971–2, Sunderland College of Art, 1972–3, and Central School of Art & Design, 1973–5. Exhibitions included 55 Wapping Artists, 1979; Wapping Artists, 1981; and Wapping Artists Open Studios, 1982, in which Christou showed the plywood abstract Cutis Clock.

Frank Harcourt CHUBB 1894– Painter and teacher who specialised in watercolours, born in Plymouth, Devon. He was largely self-taught. Showed at RI, RBA and at Paignton Art and Crafts Society, of which he was a prominent member. Lived in Paignton, Devon.

Ralph Nicholas CHUBB 1892–1960 Imaginative watercolourist, illustrator and teacher. Born in Harpenden, Hertfordshire, he was educated at Cambridge University and the Slade School of Fine Art, where he gained the life painting prize. Went on to become art master at Bradfield College and tutor of life drawing at St Martin's School of Art. Exhibited RA, Goupil Gallery, NEAC, Alpine Gallery and in the provinces. Notable titles were The Sacrifice and The Torture of Creation. Manchester City Art Gallery holds his oil on canvas Berkshire Farm, 1926. Chubb described his work as having a "visionary" quality, evident in his 1925 picture The Enchanted Valley, in the Ferens Art Gallery, Hull, collection. He lived in the county near Newbury.

Brian CHUGG 1926–2003 Artist, author and lecturer, born and lived in Braunton, then latterly at Bishops Tawnton, Devon. He studied at Bideford School of Art, 1946–9, then Camberwell School of Arts and Crafts, 1949–50. After architectural experience, 1944–6, Chugg lectured in art at North Devon College, 1953–79. From 1980 he was a freelance author and artist. Group show appearances included RBA, Woodstock and Piccadilly Galleries. He had a retrospective in Barnstaple in 1953, showing rock paintings in 1958, with a solo exhibition at The Burton Art Gallery & Museum, Bideford, 2001. Between 1964–87 Chugg was a contributor to Country Diary in *The Guardian*. His publications include *Victorian & Edwardian Devon*, 1975, and *Devon: A Thematic Study*, 1980.

Jagjit CHUHAN 1955– Painter, draughtsman and teacher, born in India, who studied at Slade School of Fine Art, 1973–7, where her teachers included William Coldstream, Lawrence Gowing and Jeffery Camp. On leaving the Slade Chuhan's work was Expressionistic; then experimented with various ways of working, including semi-abstracts based on nature, which later incorporated figures from Indian classical dance; and in mid-1990s was painting series of self-portraits. In 1992, Chuhan was granted a Fellowship in Sculpture, funded by The Henry Moore Foundation, established at Liverpool John Moores University, where she was a part-time lecturer, visiting lectureships including Royal College of Art. Mixed exhibitions included In the Looking Glass, Usher Gallery, Lincoln, and tour, from 1996. Had a solo show at Oldham Art Gallery, Oldham, 1984, later ones including Drumcroon Arts Centre, Wigan, 1992. Arts Council holds her work. Lived in Chorlton, Manchester.

Katherine CHURCH 1910–1999 Painter, born in London, married for a time to the writer Anthony West, son of the writers H G Wells and Rebecca West. Church's father was a barrister, her mother a socialite and her younger sister

Margaret, the first woman to be elected to RIBA, was married to the Modernist architect Berthold Lubetkin. She attended Brighton Art School, 1928–30; Royal Academy Schools, 1930–3; then the Slade School of Fine Art, 1933–4. The free landscape style of her friend Ivon Hitchens was a strong influence. Church's friends included John Piper, his wife Myfanwy Evans and the painter Frances Hodgkins, whose portrait of Church was bequeathed to the Tate Gallery. Took part in mixed shows including RA, NEAC, AIA, National Museum of Wales in Cardiff and Tate Gallery. Had a show at Wertheim Gallery in 1933, others including Sally Hunter & Patrick Seale Fine Art, 1984, and a retrospective at Duncalfe Galleries, Harrogate, 1988. Contemporary Art Society and National Museum of Wales, Cardiff, hold her work. Lived in Wimborne, Dorset.

John Spencer CHURCHILL 1909–1992 Painter, especially of murals, sculptor, writer and flamboyant character, the nephew of Sir Winston Churchill. He was the son of Major John Churchill, grandson of Lord Randolph Churchill. He was educated at Harrow School and Oxford University where he was a distinguished gymnast. After briefly working on the Stock Exchange he studied at Royal College of Art, Central School of Arts and Crafts, Westminster School of Art and Ruskin School of Drawing. He also received private tuition from several artists including Bernard Meninsky and William Nicholson. His first commission was a mural for Lady Islington, followed by one to decorate the Renaissance palace in India of the Maharanee of Cooch Behar. Many others followed, for or featuring Spencer Churchill's society friends. Spencer Churchill also successfully sculpted a figure of his uncle. After a period in Spain at the time of the civil war, he opened a shop in front of his studio in Chelsea, then during World War II worked in camouflage and was claimed to have been the only artist present to make sketches of the Dunkirk evacuation. A prodigious drinker, Spencer Churchill was arrested with his wife in 1955 for being drunk and disorderly. He was accused of howling like a dog, but claimed to have been singing opera. Published his autobiography, *Crowded Canvas*, in 1961.

Martin CHURCHILL 1954– Painter, born in Glasgow. He lived in Edinburgh and studied at the College of Art, 1972–76, being awarded a postgraduate year in 1976–7 and the Adam Bruce Thomson Prize. In 1980 he won a Latimer Award and in 1981 a Guthrie Award. Churchill appeared in group exhibitions at the Stirling Gallery, the 369 Gallery in Edinburgh, and the Roseangle Art Centre in Dundee; in 1981 he participated in Scottish Gallery, Edinburgh, show Contemporary Art from Scotland. Churchill had solo exhibitions at 369 Gallery and Chenil Gallery. Hove Museum and Art Gallery holds his work. He was an exhibitor in The Garrick/Milne Prize, 2003.

Vernita CHURCHILL 1882– Painter, born in London. She studied art privately and at Heatherley's School of Fine Art. Showed at ROI, RI and NEAC. Lived in London.

Winston Spencer CHURCHILL 1874–1965 Statesman, politician, soldier, writer and artist. Born at Blenheim Palace, elder son of the Right Hon. Lord Randolph Churchill, he was educated at Sandhurst, thereafter serving abroad as a soldier and war correspondent. Entered parliament as a Conservative in 1900, later being successively a Liberal and a Conservative. Became a minister in 1905, over the next 35 years at various times being given a series of senior positions such as First Lord of the Admiralty and Chancellor of the Exchequer under various governments. Prime minister 1940–5 and 1951–5. Awarded Nobel Prize for Literature, 1953. Among his books are *Marlborough*, *World Crisis* and *History of World War II*. Made Companion of Honour, 1922, awarded Order of Merit, 1946, and knighted, 1953. Although Churchill only painted part-time, he produced over 500 pictures. He describes in his book *Painting as a Pastime*, 1948, how he began. Exhibited at the RA from 1947 and was elected Hon. RA in 1948. The Tate Gallery and RA Diploma Gallery hold his work. Churchill had a retrospective exhibition at the RA, 1959, with an American and Commonwealth tour, and there was an exhibition at Sotheby's in 1998. Although he attempted portraits and interiors, Churchill is best known for his landscapes, of Kent where he lived and abroad. Died in London.

Colin CINA 1943– Painter and teacher, born in Glasgow. He attended the School of Art there, 1961–3, then moved to London to take up a postgraduate course at Central School of Art, 1963–6. He went on to become head of fine art at Chelsea School of Art. A Peter Stuyvesant Foundation Bursary awarded in 1966 enabled Cina to travel in America for several months, where the work of artists such as Barnett Newman and Frank Stella made a major impression. Over the following years his work was to pass through a series of phases, with influences from Surrealism and Pop Art. A notable series was the MH paintings of the 1970s where a unified surface is crossed by thin vertical and angled lines. The careful arrangement of colours and forms in a Cina picture can give it a lively surface, similar to the work of the Russian artists Kandinsky and Malevich. Cina had many one-man shows, including Serpentine Gallery, 1970 and 1980. Scottish National Gallery of Modern Art holds his work.

Ricardo CINALLI 1948– Figurative artist who employed gouache, and pastel on tissue paper layers, to create works with mythological themes, sometimes with a teasing quality. He was born in Argentina, where he obtained a degree in psychology/philosophy at the University of Rosario, 1966–72. Moved to England in 1973, studied at Harrow School of Art, 1977, and Hornsey College of Art, 1978–80. Among his public commissions were King's Observatory, Kew Gardens, 1984; Londesborough Room, Alexandra Palace, and Embassy of Argentina, both 1987; British Petroleum, Hemel Hempstead, 1989; and a front-drop design for National Theatre's production of Jean Cocteau's *Les Parents Terribles*, 1994. Group exhibitions included Five Drawings, Classon House, 1981; Homage to the Square, Flaxman Gallery, 1989; and Galleria Futura, Stockholm, 1994. Had many solo shows, including Galerie de l'Université, Montreal, 1979; Museum of Modern Art, Rio de Janeiro, 1984; Jill George Gallery, 1988; James Hockey Gallery, Farnham, 1992; Beaux Arts, 1994–5, and Atlas Space Southbank and Long & Ryle, both 2003. Lived in London.

Philip CIOLINA 1948– Painter and draughtsman, born in England into a Swiss-Italian family originally from Toceno, in northern Italy. He studied painting at the Royal College of Art, where he gained his master's degree, and had a residency at Cité Internationale des Arts, Paris. He wrote that his pictures "incorporating drawing, refer directly to the European tradition of collage. The images, often of landscape, are concerned with memory. Travelling from an early age between two cultures, England and Switzerland, left deep and lasting impressions." Ciolina's first group show was The Square & The Circle, in 1981 at Jenny Stein's House Gallery alongside work by Ben Nicholson, Victor Pasmore and Robert Mangold. Subsequently, his many mixed exhibition appearances included collages and drawings at the Hayward Gallery Annual and Gallery d'Or, Hamburg, Germany, both, 1982; Barbican Centre, 1992; Earth, Fire, Air & Water at Courtauld Institute of Art, 1996; Model, Centre Cultural Borges, Buenos Aires, Argentina, 1999; Art First and Vessel, Studio d'Arte Contemporanea Valentina Zatta, Brescia, Italy, both 2000; The Discerning Eye, Mall Galleries, and The Fine Art Society, both 2003; and The Millinery Works and The Hunting Art Prizes at Royal College of Art, both 2004. Among Ciolina's solo exhibitions were Parkway Focus Gallery, 1982 and 1984, and Burgh House Trust, 1997–04. Private collections in the United Kingdom, France, Denmark and Switzerland held Ciolina's work, among them that of the painter Derek Hill. Other collections included that of the Royal College of Art and the The Young-Mallin Archive, New York: The Swiss Series and Palm for Paul Valery, alongside works by Joseph Cornell, Marcel Duchamp, Gordon Matta-Clark and Man Ray. Ciolina had studios in London, Deal in Kent and in the south of France.

Doug CIPRIANI 1928–1999 Artist and designer, full name Douglas Cipriani Bond, born in London. He studied at Twickenham College of Art, 1942–6, and privately. He was a member of Free Painters and Sculptors, also showing at Victoria Art Gallery in Bath, Towner Art Gallery in Eastbourne and elsewhere. Solo exhibitions included Worthing Museum and Art Gallery and Sussex University. Lived in Hove, Sussex.

Vittorio CIRAFACE 1949– Painter who studied at Manchester School of Art and Design, 1967–8, Chelsea School of Art, 1968–71, and the Royal Academy Schools, 1971–4. Sir Brinsley Ford owned his work.

Ferdinand CIREL 1884–1968 Cirel was by profession a transport driver for Cardiff Corporation, self-taught as an artist. Around 1920 he began showing his work locally, then showed with SWG, Royal National Eisteddfod, SEA, in the English provinces and RA. WAC gave him a retrospective in 1953. It holds his work, as does the Glynn Vivian Art Gallery, in Swansea, and the National Museum of Wales, Cardiff. Cirel died in Cardiff.

CJA-STONES: *see* **Christopher John ASSHETON-STONES**

George CLAESSEN 1909–1999 Self-taught artist and poet with a mystical outlook, born in Colombo, Ceylon. Began to draw and paint aged 29 after joining the Colombo Port Commission as a draughtsman, continuing in that occupation until retirement. He moved into pure abstraction about 1947. Claessen was a founder-member of the '43 Group in Ceylon, also belonging to Victorian Artists' Society in Melbourne and in London Free Painters and Sculptors, Hampstead Artists' Council and Islington Art Circle. Showed at Venice Biennale in 1956 and at its equivalent in São Paulo, Brazil, in 1959, where he won an award. Solo shows included Velasquez Gallery, Melbourne, 1947; Archer Gallery, 1949; and New Vision Centre, 1962. In 1945 War Artists' Advisory Committee bought a work by Claessen, who sometimes signed with initials only. Published *Poems of a Painter*, 1967, *Poems about Nothing*, 1981, and *Collected Poems*, 1995. There was a retrospective at Frank T Sabin Ltd, 2000.

CLAIRE 1907– Painter, born in Glasgow, full name Claire Ritson. She studied at Edinburgh College of Art, at Frobisher School of Painting, with Hayward Veal and Arthur Segal. Member of WIAC; also showed RBA and ROI and with Hampstead Artists. Lived in London.

Christopher CLAIRMONTE 1932– Painter, draughtsman and teacher, producer of decorative views notable for a felicitous line, who studied at Wimbledon School of Art and the Royal College of Art, teachers including John Minton. Became a full-time lecturer at Epsom School of Art. Lived in Hove, Sussex, where the Museum and Art Gallery holds his ink and gouache The Natural History Museum, London. Had a solo exhibition with Patrick Seale Gallery, 1981, sharing one with Roy Spencer at Sally Hunter Fine Art in 1987. Terrace Gallery in Worthing and Cowfold Gallery, Cowfold, also showed Clairmonte, who later lived in Cyprus. Christopher's brother Hugh founded the Clairmonte Galleries in Brighton.

Catherine CLANCY 1955– Sculptor, born in Wilmslow, Cheshire, who in 1993 obtained a place at Central St Martins School of Art. In 1994 Clancy met the French sculptor Jean Touret, who had worked with Pablo Picasso and had works displayed at Notre Dame, Paris. He invited Clancy there to study with him. She had several solo exhibitions and was included in Art on Show, The Gallery in Cork Street, 2001.

Helen CLAPCOTT 1952– Painter, notably of landscape, and teacher, born in Blackpool, Lancashire, who gained an honours degree in fine art from Liverpool School of Art, 1971–5, then did postgraduate studies at Royal Academy Schools, 1978–9. In Liverpool she won the David Murray Travelling Scholarship, painting in Morocco, and in 1975 had a solo show at the Liverpool Academy, which invited her to join. She won the David Murray prize three years in succession at the Academy Schools, and in her final year show the RA bought her picture Life Room. On leaving the Academy she won the Elizabeth Greenshields Foundation scholarship which enabled her to paint for a year, when she began to paint pictures of her home town, Stockport. Teaching included Northwich School of Art and Southampton College. Clapcott soon gained a flurry of solo exhibitions, in 1984 alone showing at Salford City Art Gallery, Stockport War Memorial Gallery and The Ginnel Gallery, Manchester. Mixed shows included long associations with RA Summer Exhibition and New Ashgate Gallery, Farnham. There was a solo exhibition at Scolar Fine Art, 2003, by which time Clapcott had work in the collections of the RA, Graves Art Gallery in Sheffield and Hayworth Art Gallery, Hyndburn.

Molly CLAPHAM: *see* **Molly FIELD**

Peter CLAPHAM 1924– Creator of constructions in various materials, space light structures, painter and draughtsman, born in London, who studied at the Architectural Association, 1947–52. Group exhibitions included AIA from 1962; Richard Demarco Gallery, Edinburgh, from

1966; Marlborough New London Gallery, Marlborough-Gerson Gallery in New York and Marlborough Graphics, all from 1967; The Jewish Museum, New York, 1969; and Galerie Contemporaine, Geneva, 1971; and Hampstead Artists' Council, 1974. Solo shows included Battelle Gallery in Geneva and Kenwood, both 1971. Arts Council holds his work.

Thomas John CLAPPERTON 1879–1962 Figure and memorial sculptor, born in Galashiels, Selkirkshire, who studied at Glasgow School of Art and Royal Academy Schools, winning a Gold Medal and travelling scholarship. He was elected a fellow of RBS and his figure of King Robert the Bruce, at gateway of Edinburgh Castle, and his Galashiels war memorial, Border Chivalry, are illustrated in *R B S: Modern British Sculpture*, published in 1939. Showed at RA, RSA and Royal Glasgow Institute of the Fine Arts. Lived in London.

John CLARE 1911–1983 Painter, draughtsman and teacher, born in Manchester. Apart from five years' World War II service in the Middle East, he lived and worked there all his life. He began painting in middle age and attended part-time classes at Manchester Regional College, Withington College of Further Education and Manchester Polytechnic. For the last seven years of his life he conducted weekend courses in life drawing and painting at North Hulme Centre, Manchester. For a time Clare was chairman of Salford Art Club, which inaugurated a John Clare Award annually when he died. A memorial show was held at City of Salford Art Gallery, 1984.

Peter CLARE 1935– Painter of pictures with Christian themes, born in London. Raised as a Quaker, he converted to Catholicism in 1958. Clare was brought up and educated in Sheffield and at Southampton University, graduating in mathematics in 1963, for many years teaching this subject in secondary schools and colleges. Clare exhibited widely from 1959, with over 20 solo shows, many in central galleries in London, Birmingham, Manchester, Portsmouth and abroad. His main cycle of pictures was The Journey, worked on from 1979, first shown at St George's Church, Bloomsbury, during Lent, 1993, then toured. It provided a platform to raise funds for projects including street children in Latin America. Clare's other themes included The Earth Mother, The Cana Cycle and The Little Flowers of St Francis. Lived in Cleobury Mortimer, Shropshire.

Stephen CLARE 1958– Painter with a special interest in the British tradition of landscape painting from Constable through to Bomberg. He was born in Walsall, Staffordshire, and studied at the School of Art there, 1975–6, then Sir John Cass College of Art, 1977–80. His exhibitions included Poole Fine Art, London and New York, 1983 (a two-man show with Michael Ayrton); 20th Century Gallery, 1984; Adam Gallery, 1985; Jablonski Gallery, 1986; and John Moores Liverpool Exhibition, 1987, where he showed Beachy Head after a Storm, one of a series, and a departure from earlier imagined landscapes. Lived in London.

Alan CLARK 1926– Watercolourist, born at Campsall, near Doncaster, Yorkshire, son of the artist Edwin Clark. He studied design at Leeds School of Art, from the early 1950s worked in the printing industry and was a founder-member of Scolar Press, which specialised in the production of facsimile publications of rare books from the Bodleian Library, in Oxford, and the British Museum. Clark began painting in 1980, as a landscape watercolourist becoming noted for his Dales pictures, reproductions of which he supervised. Showed with British Society of Painters in Ilkley and was included in Images of the Yorkshire Landscape, organised by Sheeran Lock at Leeds Civic Hall, 1991. Lived at Askwith, Wharfedale, Yorkshire.

Alan Nicholas CLARK 1939– Painter and teacher, born in Leeds where he also lived. After Worksop College Clark studied at Ruskin School of Drawing, Oxford, his teachers including Geoffrey Rhoades and Percy Horton. Among Clark's exhibiting venues was 65 Group, of which he was secretary, a public schools masters' group. He was married to the artist Sherras Clark.

Anthony CLARK 1942– Painter and teacher who studied at Sunderland College of Art, then from 1963–6 at Royal College of Art, his teachers being Carel Weight, Peter Blake and Roger de Grey. Became head of fine art at Monkwearmouth College, Sunderland. Showed in RA Summer Exhibitions, at Hyde Park and Edith Grove Galleries and in 1993 was included in People and Places at Gagliardi Gallery. Exhibited widely. Shortly before his third show at Piers Feetham Gallery, 2001, Clark retired to paint full-time. At Piers Feetham he exhibited mystical paintings, principally watercolours of cathedrals in France and churches in Italy and Russia. Clark's paintings formed civic gifts to President Jimmy Carter and Cardinal Basil Hume. The Universities of Durham and Surrey and other public collections hold Clark's work.

Bruce CLARK 1937– Artist in oil and multi-media and teacher, born in Bedfont, Middlesex. He studied at Bath Academy of Art, Corsham, 1958–60, teachers including Howard Hodgkin, Gwyther Irwin and William Crozier. Clark held a number of posts teaching full- and part-time in Surrey, Worcestershire and Kent, latterly part-time lecturing in adult education. He obtained his master's degree in art and design education in 1985 and was a member of the National Society for Education in Art & Design. Clark's own work was "mainly abstract, with strong landscape influence". His numerous group show appearances included France and North America. Had solo shows at Chiltern Gallery, 1961–2; Worcester City Art Gallery, 1968; University of Kent, 1985; and One Off Gallery, Dover, 1990. Surrey County Council holds his work. Lived in Bossingham, Canterbury, Kent.

Caroline McAdam CLARK: *see* **McADAM CLARK**

Cosmo CLARK 1897–1967 Painter and teacher, born in London. His father was the artist James Clark, his wife the painter Jean Clark. Studied at Goldsmiths' College School of Art, 1912–14 and 1918, Académie Julian, Paris, 1918–19, and Royal Academy Schools, 1919–21, there winning a gold medal and Travelling Scholarship. Taught at Camberwell School of Arts and Crafts, then was head of Hackney Art School. At one time directed the Rural Industries Bureau and was a trustee of the Imperial War Museum. Was elected NEAC, 1946, RWS, 1952, and RA, 1958. Clark, whose work is sometimes similar to that of Edward Wadsworth, exhibited at the RA, NEAC, Leicester Galleries, RI and ROI as well as on the continent and in North America. Huddersfield Art Gallery and the Graves Art Gallery,

Sheffield, hold his work. Lived in London. Chappel Galleries, Chappel, held a joint Jean and Cosmo Clark show in 2002.

Donald CLARK 1965– Painter, born in Irvine, Ayrshire, who produced highly detailed work, as in his solo show at Cyril Gerber Fine Art, 2002. Those pictures were "made during a prolonged stay in Holland... I have a strong interest in the 17th-century Dutch school, particularly the still-life genre." Clark graduated in drawing and painting from Edinburgh College of Art, 1983–7, in 1986 winning an Andrew Grant Travel Scholarship, and obtained his post-graduate diploma in 1987–8. Clark also gained Elizabeth Greenshields Foundation Awards, 1989 and 1993; IBM Prize, SSA, 1990; N S Macfarlane Charitable Trust Award, Royal Glasgow Institute of the Fine Arts, 1993; Cuthbert "New Young Artist" award at the Royal Glasgow Institute, 1994; Howie Purchase Prize, SSA, 1998; Arts Trust of Scotland and Hope Scott Trust Awards, 1999; and in 2000 the Abacus Prize, SSA, and Arts Trust of Scotland Award. Took part in numerous mixed shows in Scotland and abroad. Solo exhibitions included Galerie Pieter Van Ulden, Leiden, Netherlands, 2002. Highland Regional Council, Edinburgh Eastern General Hospital and various corporate collections hold examples.

Edwin CLARK 1897–2003 Landscape painter using a variety of media, born in Adwick-le-Street, near Doncaster, Yorkshire, where he eventually settled in Harrogate. He was a self-taught painter, father of the artist Alan Clark, who oversaw the printing of reproductions of Edwin's work. For many years Edwin Clark was a technical adviser to the National Coal Board. He began painting in middle age, took it up seriously on retirement in the early 1960s and continued into his nineties. His Dales watercolours were based on sketches and memory and were shown at local arts club shows, notably Otley, of which he was long a member. His work was included in Images of the Yorkshire Landscape, organised by Sheeran Lock at Leeds Civic Hall, 1991.

Jake CLARK 1966– Painter, born and lived in London, who studied at Falmouth School of Art, 1985–6, Derbyshire College, 1986–8, Brighton Polytechnic, 1989–91, and Royal College of Art, 1991–3. His awards included Mario Dubsky Travel Award and Christie's Fine Art Prize, both 1992, and Atlantis European Studio Prize, 1993. Christie's Corporate Collection holds Clark's work. Mixed exhibitions included Maze Gallery, Brighton, 1989, Royal Over-Seas League Annual Open, 1992, and John Moores Liverpool Exhibition, 1993–4 and 2002. In 1994 shared a three-man exhibition at Paton Gallery, sun-filled pool scenes incorporating collage elements.

Jean CLARK 1902–1999 Painter, born in Sidcup, Kent, who was married to the artist Cosmo Clark. She studied at Sidcup School of Art, 1913-19, and Royal Academy Schools, 1920, in 1937 at Richard Sickert School of Painting, Broadstairs. Was made a member of RWS in 1972, and she had a retrospective at Bankside Gallery in 1983; also an honorary member of NEAC, 1981. Additionally exhibited at RBA and NEAC. Completed murals for Corpus Christi Church in Weston-super-Mare and ceiling painting for Woodford Green United Free Church. Lived in London, later in Shottisham, but dying in Saxtead, Suffolk. Chappel Galleries, Chappel, held a joint Jean and Cosmo Clark show in 2002.

John CLARK 1943–1989 Painter and teacher, born in Yorkshire. After studying at Hull College of Art, 1961–5, gained a Fulbright Scholarship to study at Indiana University, in America. He lectured in colleges in Britain, America and Canada and from 1978–83 lived and worked in Canada, where he was co-ordinator of painting and drawing at Nova Scotia College of Art and Design. He returned to Britain in 1983, becoming head of painting at Hull College of Further Education. Clark's paintings were seen in many group shows, and he had solo shows at Ian Birksted Gallery; 49th Parallel Gallery, New York; and Wynick/Tuck Gallery, Toronto; and shared a show with David Sweet at Castlefield Gallery, Manchester. Arts Council of Northern Ireland and several important foreign collections hold his work. Died in Alberta, Canada.

John M'Kenzie CLARK 1928– Painter and draughtsman, born in Dundee, Angus, where he continued to live. He studied at the local College of Art, 1945–50, and Norwich College of Art, 1950–1, as well as Patrick Allan-Fraser School of Art, Hospitalfield, Arbroath, 1953, and St Martin's School of Art, 1955–6. Was a member of Royal Glasgow Institute of the Fine Arts and showed at RA, RSW, SSA and RSA. Dundee City holds his work.

Judy CLARK 1949– Artist in a range of media, designer, teacher and administrator, born in Portsmouth, Hampshire. She did a foundation course at Portsmouth Polytechnic fine art department, 1967–8, then gained her diploma with grade one honours (painting/sculpture), 1968–71, teachers including Jeffrey Steele, David Saunders and Noel Forster. Clark obtained her higher diploma in fine art (painting/experimental) from Slade School of Fine Art, 1971–3, taught by William Townsend and Bernard Cohen. Between 1969–71 she was assistant to Malcolm Carder during work for major galleries in Britain and abroad, and she also helped him when he worked for Theo Crosby at Pentagram on the Arts Council exhibition and book *The Environment Game*, 1972–3. Between 1973–4 Clark was a visiting and part-time lecturer at Bath Academy of Art, Hornsey, Winchester, Wolverhampton, the London College of Furniture and elsewhere, in 1974 gaining a Boise Travel Scholarship. Between 1974–80 Clark undertook a period of travel and personal study, including a trip to India with Carder. On returning, Clark resumed teaching and in 1981–2, during Pentagram's refurbishment of Unilever House, she was responsible for design of carpets and other decorative architectural details. After working 1985–9 as a freelance designer for the fashion textile industry – Clear Cut Design, Today Interiors and Sanderson were among her clients – Clark helped run the Sandra Higgins Fine Arts and Nigel Greenwood Galleries, 1989–91. She moved to West Dean College in 1991 as assistant short-course organiser, becoming head of department in 1994. Clark had had a solo show, Issues, at Garage Art, 1973. Later exhibitions included Badge Art, Angela Flowers Gallery, 1982; Whitechapel Open, Whitechapel Art Gallery, 1984; and Open Studios, Carpenters Road, 1989–90. Her initial interest was in mixed-media "issue-based" art, involving "an investigation into the nature of taboo, particularly in relation to women". Later work was "based around ideas concerning consumption". Mary Douglas' book *Purity and*

Danger was important. Arts Council and Tate Gallery hold examples.

Kenneth CLARK 1922– Ceramist who studied at Slade School of Fine Art, 1945–8, then Central School of Arts and Crafts, 1949. With his wife Ann Clark he ran Kenneth Clark Pottery based at Lewes, near his home in Ringmer, Sussex. Exhibited in many group shows and had solo exhibitions at Piccadilly and Zwemmer Galleries.

Laurie CLARK 1949– Artist notable for work in pen and ink, influenced by artists such as F L Griggs and T J Cooper, and interested in dark, shadowy aspects of nature. She was educated in Cheltenham, settled in Nailsworth, Gloucestershire, and ran a contemporary art gallery. Her picture Swan Bank, Nailsworth, of 1994, was included in Mods and Shockers, at Cheltenham Art Gallery & Museum, 1996.

Liz CLARK 1952– Artist and teacher using a range of techniques, such as textile processes, printmaking, collage and stitching, who originally trained as a textile designer, working for many years in the fashion industry. Following foundation studies at Stourbridge College of Art, 1970–1, Clark gained an honours degree in constructed textiles at Winchester School of Art, 1971–4. After obtaining a postgraduate diploma at Goldsmiths' College, 1987–9, she studied for a printmaking certificate at London College of Printing, 1995–7, gaining her master's in the same subject at Camberwell College of Arts, 1999-01. Clark taught at Lowestoft College, Norwich School of Art and the Royal College of Art, completed hospital arts projects and worked to commission. Later exhibitions included Cutting Threads, Rural Arts East tour, 2000; Printmakers' Council at Studio Voltaire and R K Burt Gallery, both 2001; and Over The River, firstsite, Colchester/Wolsey Art Gallery, Ipswich, 2002. Lived in Beccles, Suffolk.

Mark CLARK 1959– Figurative painter, draughtsman and printmaker who studied foundation at St Albans College of Art and Design, 1976-8; graduated with honours, Loughborough College of Art and Design, 1978–81; then did a postgraduate diploma at Royal Academy Schools, 1983–6. Group shows included People's Gallery, Camden, 1983; Morley Gallery, 1984; and RA Summer Exhibition, from 1985. Took part in three-man exhibitions at The Gallery, South Audley Street, 1994, and The Gallery in Cork Street, 2000, with Neil Bailey and Wayne Robinson. Had solo exhibitions at Herstmere Town Hall, Borehamwood, 1982, Gallery 47, 1997, and Frank T Sabin Gallery, 2000. Clark's work was held in private and public collections, including the Canadian National Print Archive. Lived in London.

Michael CLARK 1918–1991 Sculptor, son of the sculptor Philip Lindsey Clark, born in Cheltenham, Gloucestershire. Studied at Chelsea School of Art, 1935–7, then at City and Guilds of London Art School, Kennington, 1947–50. Showed at RA and carried out a great deal of commissioned work, notably at Carmelite Friary at Aylesford, Kent. He gained the Otto Beit Medal for Sculpture for his statue of the Virgin of the Glorious Assumption there, illustrated in the Friars' publication *Image of Carmel*, 1974. Was president of RBS, 1971–6. Had a studio at Churt, Surrey.

Michael CLARK 1954– Artist in oil on canvas, pencil on paper and mixed media, born in Manchester. Intensive study of paintings by such artists as Rembrandt, Titian, Holbein and Chardin in the National Gallery was important to his work. Clark was noted for his realistic portraits, including the artist Francis Bacon, Sickert's model Marguerite Kelsey and Muriel Belcher, proprietor of Soho's Colony Room drinking club. This was commended in the BP Portrait Award 1992 at National Portrait Gallery and Clark contributed to the tribute to Belcher at Michael Parkin Fine Art, 1982. Mixed shows also included 75 Years of the London Group, Royal College of Art, 1988; Acquisitions 1986–1990, British Museum, 1990; and The Portrait Now, National Portrait Gallery, 1993–4. Had a solo exhibition at Birch & Conran Fine Art, 1988; Graves Art Gallery, Sheffield, 1989; City Art Gallery, York, 1990; Pallant House, Chichester, 1993; and Wounds – New Work, at Rebecca Hossack at St James', 1994. This was an intensive study of the human condition through a series of small paintings of wounded flesh. British Museum, Pallant House and Chichester Cathedral hold examples of Clark's work.

Michael CLARK 1959– Painter and designer notable for pleasing, summery watercolours, born in Ayr. After two years as a golf professional Clark went to Edinburgh College of Art where he was taught by Elizabeth Blackadder, John Houston and Robin Philipson, and specialized in illustration, graphics and photography. Worked with the BBC, 1983–9, concentrating on design and animation, then moved to London, freelancing as a visualizer for a golf magazine. Had a first solo show at Sally Hunter Fine Art in 1996, of watercolours which formed the basis of a range of greetings cards published by Woodmansterne.

Norman CLARK 1913–1992 Painter and teacher, born in Ilford, Essex. He studied at Central School of Arts and Crafts, 1929–30, with John Farleigh and Bernard Meninsky, then was at the Royal Academy Schools, 1930–5, under Tom Monnington, Ernest Jackson and Walter Russell. Among a number of awards was the gold medal for historical painting. Clark taught at Brighton College of Art and Brighton Polytechnic, 1947–77. Was elected RWS in 1960. Clark showed at RA between 1933–74, also exhibiting at Brighton Art Gallery, Sussex Watercolour Society, Worthing Art Gallery and elsewhere. Imperial War Museum and Harris Museum and Art Gallery in Preston hold watercolours by Clark, who lived in Hurstpierpoint, Sussex, and drew on idiosyncratic local characters for the subjects of many watercolours. Clark's daughter was the artist Penny Hopkins.

Peter Christian CLARK 1950– Painter and printmaker, born in Bingley, Yorkshire, son of the artist and teacher the Clark. He attended Ruskin School of Drawing in Oxford under Richard Naish. Exhibited in London, where he lived, and elsewhere.

Philip Lindsey CLARK 1889–1977 Sculptor in various materials, born in London, son of the sculptor Robert Lindsey Clark. Educated in Cheltenham, where he initially studied sculpture from 1905–10, his father being a major influence. Then studied at City and Guilds Art School, 1910–14, and Royal Academy Schools, 1919–21. Won the Distinguished Service Order during World War I. Exhibited RA, RBA, RSA and Royal Glasgow Institute of the Fine Arts. Clark completed a number of war memorials, notably the

Belgian soldiers' memorial at Kensal Green, London; he was a fellow of the RBS, and his relief of St Thomas More is illustrated in the volume *RBS: Modern British Sculpture*, published in 1939. Signed work P L C. Like his son Michael he contributed to the restoration of the Carmelite Friary at Aylesford, Kent, being a Carmelite tertiary, featured in the Priory's publication *Image of Carmel*, 1974. Lived in London, finally in the West Country.

Rachel CLARK fl. from mid-1970s– Painter who gained a first-class degree in fine art at West Surrey College of Art and Design, Farnham, 1976, in that year showing in New Contemporaries at RA and with LG at Camden Arts Centre. Other shows included John Moores Liverpool Exhibition, 1978; 4 Elements at Towner Art Gallery, Eastbourne, 1991; BP Portrait Awards, National Portrait Gallery, 1993; RP, Mall Galleries, 1994; and Pacesetters at Peterborough Museum and Art Gallery, 1995. Mrs Clark lived in London.

Robert D CLARK 1951– Painter, teacher and writer, born in Blackburn, Lancashire. He studied at Leeds Polytechnic, graduating with honours in fine art. Went on to teach at Chesterfield College of Art and to write often for *The Guardian*. Solo shows included Leeds Polytechnic Gallery, 1975; Bede Gallery, Jarrow, 1982; Mappin Art Gallery, Sheffield, 1987; and Chesterfield Arts Centre, 1990. Clark's abstract work was shown in mixed exhibitions in Spain, Poland and Britain, and in 1991 he shared a three-man show at Woodlands Art Gallery. Lived in Sheffield, Yorkshire.

Sheila CLARK 1960– Artist, born and lived in London, whose many interests including writing, painting, photography and limited-edition publications which included hand-made elements. Clark worked in the school of fashion and textiles at the Royal College of Art and was an authority on yarn trends and directions. Did a foundation course at Medway College of Art, 1979–80; an honours degree in textiles/fashion at Middlesex Polytechnic, 1980–3; and her master's at Royal College of Art, 1984–6. Was a member of Group Hangman, with Billy Childish and Tracey Emin, 1983–4; was artist-in-residence at Durham School, 1987, having a show there; took part Spirit of London, Royal Festival Hall, 1988; in Two Artists, Endell Street Gallery and in East End Open Studios, with Barbican Arts Group, 1989; and won a Pollock-Krasner Foundation award in 1992. Clark was a member of the Stuckists and was included in their exhibition at Artbank Gallery, 2001. Tate Britain holds her work.

Sherras CLARK 1936– Painter and teacher, full name Elisabeth Sherras Clark, married to the artist Alan Nicholas Clark. She was born in Surbiton, Surrey, and after the Arts Educational Trust studied at Ruskin School of Drawing, Oxford, teachers including Richard Naish and Percy Horton, from 1961–4. As well as exhibiting did illustrative work for British Museum fossil catalogue. Lived for a time in Leeds, Yorkshire.

Thomas Humphrey CLARK 1921– Watercolourist, black-and-white artist and teacher, born in Manchester, father of the artist Peter Christian Clark. He studied at Bradford Regional College of Art, teachers including Fred Cecil Jones. Taught at St Aldate's College, Oxford, and was a member of National Society for Art Education. Exhibited in the provinces, living in Oxford, later in Beemire, Cumbria.

Ann CLARKE 1940–2005 Painter and freelance photojournalist, born in Wolverhampton, Staffordshire, who studied at Bournville Birmingham School of Art. Married with three children, she found it impossible at first to give painting her full attention, so began writing for magazines. This developed to photography, handled by a top London agency, her work illustrating many books and newspaper articles. When her youngest daughter left for university Clarke returned to painting, being noted for strong figurative work: oil paintings of life in the Middle East and watercolour landscapes of Cyprus. She "developed an innovative Pointillism technique, resulting in extremely fine watercolour detail," very time-intensive, using a tiny brush. Cézanne, Lucian Freud, Andrew Wyeth and Paula Rego were influences. Took part in group shows in the Midlands, exhibiting solo at Kyklos Gallery, Paphos, Cyprus. Latterly, Clarke divided her time between Cyprus and Dartmouth, Devon.

Anne CLARKE 1944– Artist and teacher, born in Londonderry, Northern Ireland. She graduated from the University of Ulster in Belfast, 1985. Held residency at the Tyrone Guthrie Arts Centre, Annamakerrig, 1993, having held one at Sculpture Symposium, Waterford, 1990. Lectured at the University of Ulster, at College of Technology in Londonderry and elsewhere. She was a leading member of Queen Street Studios, Belfast, and took part in Works on Paper there, 1994. Solo exhibitions included Temple Court, Belfast, 1993.

Anne CLARKE 1947– Painter, born in Sydney, New South Wales, Australia, who after studying at the National Art School worked as a graphic artist in publishing. In the late 1980s she returned to painting, beach scenes, portraits and still life, as in Apricots and Bridgewater Bowl, 2000, in Old & New, Wolseley Fine Arts at The Gallery in Cork Street, 2001. Clarke had work in many public and private collections in Australia.

Audrey M CLARKE 1926– Artist and designer in various media, born and lived in Huncote, Leicestershire. She studied at Leicester College of Art, 1943–8, and showed at City Art Gallery and elsewhere in the provinces.

Bethia CLARKE 1874–1958 Interior and landscape painter in various media. Born in Blackheath, she studied art in London and Paris. Exhibited widely, including RA, RBA, ROI, SWA and Ridley Art Club. Lived in London.

Brian CLARKE 1953– Prolific stained glass and set designer, using a rich palette to produce abstract and figurative works, born in Oldham, Lancashire. His childhood, the son of a miner and mill worker, was hard. From 1965 began full-time art education at Oldham School of Arts and Crafts under a junior scholarship, involved in such aspects as heraldry, gilding and pigment-making. An interest in art and architecture was inspired by trips to York Minster, Lancashire Priory and Fountains Abbey and by the mid-1960s film of Michelangelo's life *The Agony and the Ecstasy*, starring Charlton Heston. Attended Burnley School of Art, 1968; won a first-class distinction in his diploma at North Devon College of Art & Design, attended from 1970; gaining the Winston Churchill

Memorial Travelling Fellowship to study art and architecture in Rome, Paris and Germany, 1974, with a second part in 1975 which covered contemporary painting in New York and Los Angeles. In 1975 Mid-Pennine Arts Association put on an exhibition of Clarke's glass works, the first of many in British and foreign galleries, later ones including Oldham and Mayor Galleries, 1993. Clarke's glass commissions were also international, including King Khaled International Airport, Riyadh, 1982; Government Building, Doha, Qatar, 1984; Cavendish Arcade, Derbyshire, 1987; Stansted Airport, 1991; EAM Building, Kassel, 1993. Was awarded honorary fellowship of RIBA, 1993. Devised sets for several Paul McCartney World Tours and for a ballet by Wayne Eagling in tribute to Rudolph Nureyev, The National Ballet, 1993. Gagosian Gallery showed Clarke's work in 2005. Clarke lived in London (the spectacular studio of the artist William Russell Flint) and Hastings, Sussex.

Denis CLARKE 1952– Painter, theatrical designer and teacher, born in Sydney, Australia, whose figure and landscape pictures were gestural, using a rich palette. Clarke studied at the National Art School and Alexander Mackie School of Art, Sydney, 1972–5. He won several awards, including an Australian Arts Council Travel Grant, 1975–6, with postgraduate studies at St Martin's School of Art, 1975–6; time at Cité Internationale des Arts, Paris, 1976–7; then life drawing at Morley College, Chelsea and Byam Shaw Schools of Art, 1977–9. In 1982 he designed for Opera Factory London production of Harrison Birtwistle's *Punch and Judy*, then Opera Factory Zürich's staging of Howard Goodall's *Der Glöckner von Notre Dame*, 1983-4. Taught part-time at Camden School of Art, 1992–7. Showed on the continent and Australia and in London was latterly represented by James Colman Fine Art, which gave him a solo show at Montpelier Sandelson, 2000. Fitzwilliam College in Cambridge and several British corporate and Australian collections hold examples. Lived in London.

Derek CLARKE 1912– Painter and teacher. Clarke studied at Slade School of Fine Art, then from 1947–79 lectured at Edinburgh College of Art. Shortly after World War II he and his wife visited Connemara, where he completed a remarkable series of pictures featuring local people in their houses. After retirement Clarke painted portraits and landscapes and did work for churches, including a set of windows in engraved glass. He was a member of RSW and RP and had solo shows with Scottish Gallery, Edinburgh, where he lived. Scottish Arts Council, University of Edinburgh and Dunfermline Art Gallery hold his work.

Dora CLARKE 1895– Sculptor in various materials, but notably a direct carver, born in Harrow, Middlesex. Gained a scholarship to Slade School of Fine Art, where she studied under Henry Tonks and J Havard Thomas, 1910–11 fine art three days a week, 1915–16 sculpture full-time. She was made a member of RBA, also showing at RA, NEAC, Royal Glasgow Institute of the Fine Arts and elsewhere. Was a fine figure sculptor and draughtsman with work held by Ministry of Information and Ashmolean Museum, Oxford. Lived in London for many years.

Edward CLARKE 1962– Painter who studied at Hartlepool College of Art, 1981–2, Sheffield Polytechnic, 1982–5, and Royal Academy Schools, 1985–8. He showed at RA Summer Exhibition from 1986, in the John Player Portrait Exhibition at the National Portrait Gallery in 1988, at WB Gallery in Sheffield in 1989 and in The Broad Horizon, Agnew, 1990.

Eularia CLARKE 1914–1970 Artist in oil, watercolour and pastel, born in London, mother of the artist Rachael Sherlaw-Johnson. She produced mainly landscapes and portraits until 1960, then a series of religious paintings until her death. She studied at the Ruskin School of Drawing, Oxford, under Gilbert Spencer. Group shows including Wessex Artists, Southampton Art Gallery, 1968. Participated in The Church & the Artist (the Methodist Church's collection) at venues including Walker Art Gallery in Liverpool and Manchester City Art Gallery, 1963–5. Had numerous solo shows, later ones including Imperial College, 1968, Winchester Cathedral and Lymington Community Centre, both 1969, and Yoxford Gallery in Yoxford, 1970. As well as the Methodist Church's collection of twentieth-century Christian Art, Clarke is represented in the National Museum of Wales in Cardiff, with slides and archives in the Women's Art Library. Died in Southampton.

Geoffrey CLARKE 1924– Sculptor and artist in stained glass and mosaic, and teacher. He was born in Darley Dale, Derbyshire. Studied at Preston and Manchester Schools of Art, then served in Royal Air Force, 1943–7. Studied Royal College of Art, 1948–52. Went on to teach in Colchester and became head of the department of light transmission and projection at Royal College of Art, 1968–73. Had first solo show at Gimpel Fils, 1952, but worked substantially on commissions. Coventry, Chichester and Lincoln cathedrals all have work by Clarke, who also worked on *Time-Life* Building, 1952, and Thorn Electric Building, St Martin's Lane, 1958. Clarke completed forged and welded sculptures, acquiring knowledge on a course at British Oxygen Company. Having heard about the discovery of casting from expanded-polystyrene models, Clarke produced the first free-standing aluminium scupture for the architect Sir Basil Spence's house at Beaulieu; his technique was described in a pamphlet published by Shell Chemicals; and he went on to develop it in subsequent works. There was a touring retrospective of sculpture and graphic works organised by Ipswich Museums and Galleries, 1994–5, with a 50-year retrospective at The Fine Art Society, 2000, and another show there, 2003. Bury St Edmunds Art Gallery also held a 2003 exhibition. Tate Gallery, Arts Council and Victoria & Albert Museum hold Clarke's work. His son was the sculptor Jonathan Clarke. Lived in Hartest, Suffolk, where he cast works in his own studio. He was elected RA in 1976.

Graham CLARKE 1941– Printmaker, author and humorist who was educated at Beckenham School of Art and Royal College of Art under Edward Bawden. He went on to become one of Britain's most popular image-makers, creating hundreds of pictures of English rural life and history and of the Englishman's view of Europe. He considered himself a Man of Kent, living in the village of Boughton Monchelsea, with a strong sense of tradition and of religious, social and historical continuities. His incident-packed prints were sold in numerous galleries. Clarke's books included *Balyn and Balan* and *Vision of Wat Tyler*, which was praised by Kenneth Clark. Wildenstein held a series of exhibitions of his watercolours, starting in 1990. There was a sixtieth-birthday retrospective at Royal

Museum and Gallery, Canterbury, 2001. Examples of Clarke's output are held in royal and public collections, including Victoria & Albert Museum, Tate Gallery, New York Public Library and Hiroshima Peace Museum.

Helen CLARKE 1966– Sculptor who studied at Suffolk College and Canterbury College of Art. Her work was included in a three-man show of sculptures and drawings at High Street Exhibition Galley, Ipswich, 1992, in which an interest in the living image was the common factor. She set up a studio at Polstead, Suffolk.

Hilda Margery CLARKE 1926– Artist in oil and other media, born in Monton, Eccles, Manchester. She studied privately with L S Lowry; in Hamburg, 1946; at Southampton College of Art, 1960–8; Ruskin School, Oxford, print workshop, 1975; gaining her bachelor's degree, Southampton, 1982. The University there holds her work. Mixed exhibitions included Southampton City Art Gallery, 1963–76; Free Painters and Sculptors, 1974–6; Tib Lane Gallery, Manchester, 1978; and Chalk Farm Gallery, 1981–2. Had a solo show at Hamwic Gallery, Southampton, 1970, later ones including Hiscock Gallery, Southsea, 1977, and The First Gallery, Bitterne, which she ran, 1989. Lived in Bitterne, Southampton.

Jeff CLARKE 1935– Printmaker, born in Brighton, Sussex, who studied at the College of Art there, 1952-6, under Raymond Cowern, Alan Sorrell and George Hooper. He received a British Institute Scholarship and the Rome Scholarship in Engraving, 1956–8. Was archaeological draughtsman for the British School at Athens from the mid-1960s, based at Knossos. Clarke taught part-time at Oxford School of Art, University of Reading, North Staffordshire Polytechnic and the Royal Academy Schools. He was an RE associate, also showing in RA Summer Exhibition, National Print Exhibition at Mall Galleries and Elizabeth Harvey-Lee, at North Aston, showed his etchings. Clarke was long resident in Oxford and had solo exhibitions there at Bear Lane Gallery, Oxford Gallery, the Museum of Modern Art and Christchurch Picture Gallery and in Cambridge at Kettle's Yard. Chiaroscuro was an important element in his landscapes and still lifes. Ashmolean Museum in Oxford and university collections there and in Cambridge and Reading hold examples.

Jocelyn CLARKE 1958– Painter and lecturer, born in Birmingham, who studied at the Slade School of Fine Art, 1976–80, at Goldsmiths' College, 1981–2. After a period in primary education, she lived and worked as an artist in London where she was also a freelance lecturer at the National Gallery, Tate Britain and other public art venues. In 1992 Clarke was artist-in-residence at Camden Arts Centre. Group exhibitions included Whitechapel Open at Whitechapel Art Gallery, from 1984; Anderson O'Day Gallery, from 1989; East, at Norwich Gallery and Norfolk Institute of Art and Design, Norwich, 1994; Nikola Marinov Exhibition, Targovishte Art Gallery, Targovishte, Bulgaria, 2000; and 3 x 2, The Nunnery, 2002. Among solo exhibitions were Adam Gallery, 1994, and Jerwood Artists Platform, Jerwood Space, 2003. There she showed intensive, restrained small paintings in muted acrylic colours on coarse canvas, enigmatic, with allusive titles. Clarke was represented in public and private collections in the United Kingdom and America.

Johnnie CLARKE 1940– Sculptor and painter, born in Iringa, Tanzania, who then lived in Kenya and in Paris. There he studied sculpture under Ossip Zadkine, also painting at Académie Julian, as well as in London at Camberwell School of Art and at Bideford Art School, all in the 1960s. He was a landowner until the age of about 50, from then a full-time artist. Icons of the 1960s, especially the film actress Jeanne Morreau, influenced Clarke's work, others being anthropology and travel. He regularly painted in Kerala, India, using pigment and linseed oil on raw canvas. His group exhibitions included The Brewhouse, Taunton, 2000; The Nude, Goldmark Gallery in Uppingham, Andipa Gallery, The Appledore Art Festival Mixed Exhibition and Art on Paper Fair with RM Fine Art at the Royal College of Art, all 2002; London Fields Exhibition and Christie's War Child Auction, both 2003; and The Affordable Art Fair with RM Fine Art and The Art on Paper Fair with Eyestorm Britart, 2004. Among Clarke's solo exhibitions were Kerala Paintings and other New Works, at Yunomi, Dunster, in Somerset, where after a period in Devon he lived, 1997; New Paintings, 11 Eccleston Street, 2000; and The Apprentice, Cockpit Arts, 2005.

Jonathan CLARKE 1961– Sculptor born in Bury St Edmunds, Suffolk, son of the sculptor Geoffrey Clarke, under whom he served an apprenticeship from 16. He went on to work mainly in sandcast aluminium from his own studio and foundry in Hartest. He was elected RBS in 1994. Shows included Phoenix Gallery in Lavenham; Moya Bucknall, Solihull; Galerie Am Plats Eglisau, Zürich; Coach House Gallery, Guernsey; and RA Summer Exhibition from 1989. In 1993 had a shared show at Chappel Galleries, Chappel, with a solo exhibition there, 1996, and a series at John Russell Gallery, Ipswich, from 1995. Clarke's second solo show at Chappel, in 2000, coincided with publication by the gallery of a monograph on his work, *Head On*, by David Buckman. He had another exhibition there in 2005. Gainsborough's House, Sudbury, celebrated his 21 years of sculpture in 2001. Clarke's commissions included Royal Caribbean Cruise Lines, Tesco, Asda, The Orchard Medical Centre in Ipswich, Southwell Minster and Ely Cathedral.

Joseph William CLARKE 1898– Watercolour painter, industrial designer and teacher. Studied at Chester School of Art under Walter Schroder, 1915–17, then went on to teach art in Chester, where he lived and exhibited. Also exhibited RCamA and with Flintshire Artists.

Katherine CLARKE 1960– Artist and teacher involved in muf (see separate entry). Clarke studied fine art and film at Goldsmiths' College and Bristol, teaching at Chelsea College of Art and the Architectural Association, 1991–5. Exhibitions included Tate St Ives, Southampton and Eastbourne Art Galleries.

Leslie CLARKE 1907–2000 Painter, based in Bakersfield, Nottinghamshire, who was a professional teacher. Studied at Nottingham and Hull Schools of Art and showed with Ilkeston Art Club from 1930–92.

Pat CLARKE fl. from late 1960s– Painter, draughtsman, printmaker and teacher who studied at Reigate Art School, 1966–9. She taught part-time in adult education and various community-based projects. Clarke moved to Cwm Prysor, North Wales, in 1981, in 1984 opening Oriel y Ddraig art gallery with her husband in Blaenau Ffestiniog,

Gwynedd, where they then lived. The Welsh landscape became an important feature in Clarke's work. She was a member of NS, Free Painters and Sculptors, Printmakers' Council and Association of Artists and Designers in Wales. Took part in many group and joint shows. Had a solo show at Fairfield Halls, Croydon, in 1978, later ones among several dozen that followed including Hereford City Art Gallery, 1992. The City Museum there holds her work.

Paul Montem CLARKE 1915– Painter, lithographer and teacher, born in Nova Scotia, Canada, who studied art at Croydon School of Art under Ruskin Spear, 1935–9, then with Spear, Robert Buhler and Rodrigo Moynihan, 1946–9, at Royal College of Art where he gained a silver medal for painting. Exhibited UA, NEAC and elsewhere. Lived in East Croydon, Surrey.

Peter John CLARKE 1927–1997 Watercolourist and printmaker who studied at Northampton School of Art, his teachers including Henry Bird. He showed at RI, UA and elsewhere and lived in Moulton, Northamptonshire.

Richard CLARKE 1955– Painter born in Newcastle upon Tyne who studied at Slade School of Fine Art, 1973–7, a Robert Ross Travelling Scholarship taking him to Rome, 1977–9. In 1989 gained a New York Foundation for the Arts Fellowship. Early in the 1980s he showed with Brooklyn Waterfront Artists in New York, later with The Rotunda Gallery and at the Metropolitan Museum of Art there. The Museum holds his work, which was notable for being oil and tempera on linen. As well as landscapes and portraits Clarke made subject pictures such as New World Order and his Fledgling Democracy, shown in his solo exhibition at Browse & Darby in 1992, which make points about the modern world. Earlier, Clarke had had one-man shows with Drian Gallery, 1980, and John Figura Gallery, Washington.

Richard Cambridge CLARKE 1909–1998 Watercolourist, printmaker and teacher, born in Ilford, Essex, who attended Regent Street Polytechnic School of Art, 1937–8, having attended Bishop's Stortford College, 1921–6, later training as an engineering draughtsman. Between 1957–79 was self-employed as an illustrator and Workers' Educational Association lecturer. In 1981 gained an honours degree through the Open University. Took part in mixed exhibitions at RI, Piccadilly Gallery, elsewhere in London and the provinces, and had solo shows in Bishop's Stortford area every two years from the late 1960s. Letchworth Museum and Art Gallery holds his work. Lived in Saffron Walden, Essex.

Robert CLARKE 1947– Abstract painter, born and lived in London, who attended Ravensbourne College of Art, 1969–73, then Chelsea School of Art, 1973–5. In 1977 he was elected a member of LG, with which he had shown from 1974. Other mixed exhibitions included RA Summer Exhibition and Wapping Artists Open Studios, both from 1979; John Moores Exhibition in Liverpool, 1980; and 16 Artists at Battersea Arts Centre, 1982. Unilever and several other corporate collections hold Clarke's work, which was illustrated in the LG's 2003 ninetieth anniversary commemorative volume.

Roger CLARKE 1966– Artist whose work included floor-based abstract works in steel, born in Buckinghamshire. He studied sculpture at Slade School of Fine Art, 1985–9, and was Henry Moore Sculpture Fellow at Winchester School of Art, 1991, The Winchester Gallery giving him a solo exhibition in 1992. In 1987 he had had a solo exhibition of monoprints at Café Casbar. Also exhibited at Whitechapel Open; was involved in the site-specific exhibition Windfall in Hyde Park, 1988; and showed in Bremen, 1989.

Terence CLARKE 1953– Representational artist, born in Manchester, who said that he "endeavoured to make simple pictures with uncomplicated intentions". He gained his bachelor's degree in fine art at Lanchester Polytechnic's department of art and design, 1972–5; in 1975 won a David Murray Landscape Scholarship; in 1976–9 attending Royal College of Art, while there editing and producing the College magazine *1132*. Took part in Stowells Trophy, 1973; showed drawings at 5 Dryden Street, 1978; and had a series of solo exhibitions at Edward Totah Gallery.

Thomas Flowerday CLARKE fl. c.1930–1960 Painter who studied at Heatherley's School of Fine Art and Central School of Arts and Crafts. Exhibited RA, ROI, Cooling Galleries and in the provinces. Bank of England bought his work. Member Langham Sketch Club and Wapping Group of Artists. Lived at South Croydon, Surrey.

Tim CLARKE fl. from 1970s– Painter and draughtsman who studied at Stourbridge and Cheltenham Colleges of Art, then at Trent Polytechnic. He began exhibiting in 1979, taking part in many group exhibitions in the Midlands and north of England. He also had a number of solo shows, including Sue Rankin Gallery, 1990. Clarke's childhood attachment to Yorkshire led to his frequently painting in that county and the north.

Edna CLARKE HALL 1879–1979 Draughtsman, watercolourist and printmaker, born in Shipbourne, Kent. Her maiden name was Edna Waugh, under which she originally worked. She married William Clarke Hall in 1899, a barrister who was in 1932 knighted for his penal reform work. He encouraged her parents to let her study at Slade School of Fine Art, which she entered in 1894. She was a star pupil of Henry Tonks, winning a Slade Scholarship in 1897. She showed at NEAC, Friday Club and AAA, and had a solo show at Chenil Gallery in 1914. A much larger show followed at Redfern Gallery in 1924, after which she often showed there. Clarke Hall was noted for her lively draughtsmanship, notably in a series of illustrations which she did for Emily Brontë's novel *Wuthering Heights*, but they were not completed or published. She also wrote poetry. Although she was plagued by ill-health, when her husband died in 1932 she took up farming to overcome financial difficulties. There was a retrospective at Manchester City Art Gallery in 1939; New Grafton Gallery held a small hundredth birthday show in 1979, and another in 1982; and Graves Art Gallery, Sheffield, held a major show in 1985. Summer at Gillan Creak: Edna Clarke Hall in Cornwall, 1915–1928 was held at Abbott and Holder in 2005. Tate Gallery, British Museum and Victoria & Albert Museum hold her work. Lived in Upminster Common, Essex, for many years.

Andrew CLARKIN 1975– Painter whose colourful oil on canvas The Great Escape was included in the final year show, Royal Academy Schools, 2002. Clarkin attended the Schools, 1997–00, having previously studied at Scarborough School of Art, 1992–4, and De Montford University, 1994–7. Lived in London.

Jack CLARKSON 1906–1986 Sculptor in various materials, but wood-carving was his favourite method of work. Also painted in oils. Born in Silsden, Yorkshire and studied at Keighley School of Art and Royal College of Art, among his teachers being Henry Moore. He was the head of the sculpture department at Sheffield College of Art, 1930–44, then was for over 20 years principal of the Newcastle, Staffordshire, School of Art. Exhibited RA, in Glasgow and Sheffield and has work in Hanley and Newcastle Art Galleries. In his retirement he devoted his time to wood-carvings of birds in foliage and of the human form. Lived in Newcastle.

Pamela CLARKSON 1946– Printmaker, painter and teacher, born in Lancashire, who studied at Manchester College of Art, 1963–4; Central School of Art and Design, 1964–7; Royal College of Art, 1967–70; University of Chile, Santiago, 1973; and the Catholic University there, 1974. Awards included David Murray Landscape Scholarship, 1967; John Minton Travelling Scholarship, 1970; and President of Chile Scholarship, 1973. While in Chile, Clarkson was artist-in-residence and English teacher at the Grange School, Santiago. Teaching in England included printmaking appointments at Winchester School of Art, Ulster Polytechnic in Belfast, Loughborough College of Art and Design and Wolverhampton Polytechnic. Took part in many group shows including John Moores Liverpool Exhibition, 1976. Solo exhibitions included Penwith Galleries, St Ives, 1978, and Harris Museum and Art Gallery, Preston, 1982. Clarkson admired the work of Peter Lanyon and Roger Hilton and her output included strongly abstracted landscapes.

Shaun K CLARKSON 1961– Sculptor and creator of mixed-media assemblages who studied at West Sussex College of Art and Design and Kingston Polytechnic. His work, which had an ornate quality, was shown at Black Bull Gallery, Crucial Gallery and England & Co, where his two 1991 creations Knife and Fork were shown in Art in Boxes, 1991.

Robert CLATWORTHY 1928– Sculptor, draughtsman and teacher, born in Bridgwater, Somerset. He studied at West of England College of Art, 1944–6, Chelsea School of Art, 1949–51 and Slade School of Fine Art, 1951–4. Clatworthy's mother-in-law was the stage star Gertrude Lawrence, his wife, Pamela, also being an actress. Went on to teach at Royal College of Art and West of England College of Art. He was also governor of St Martin's School of Art and head of department at Central School of Art and Design. Had first exhibition at Hanover Gallery in 1955 with Rosemary Young, and also showed at Basil Jacobs Gallery, RA and Austin/Desmond Fine Art. Thompson's Marylebone specially featured Bob Clatworthy's work in The Sculpture Show, 2003. Major works in London are in Finsbury Avenue and in Alton Housing Estate, Roehampton. Clatworthy's early work involved Expressionistic portrayal of bulls and horses; later he moved further towards abstraction in his human heads, which can be uncompromisingly, almost brutally powerful. Tate Gallery and Victoria & Albert Museum hold his work. Elected RA, 1973. Lived near Llandovery, Dyfed.

Richard CLAUGHTON 1917–1997 Sculptor in a variety of materials, and teacher, born in London. He studied at Slade School of Fine Art, 1946–9, with Randolph Schwabe, later becoming senior lecturer in sculpture there. Exhibited NEAC, RBA, LG, in the provinces and the Netherlands. His work is to be found decorating a number of British buildings as well as in Lagos Cathedral, Nigeria. He was a fellow of the RBS and lived in Battle, Sussex.

William Lionel CLAUSE 1887–1946 Painter in oil and watercolour, born in Middleton, Lancashire, who studied at Slade School of Fine Art. He was a notable painter of rural figure subjects and landscapes whose work became freer in style later in his career. Began showing with NEAC in 1914, later becoming honorary secretary and treasurer. Also exhibited at RA, Cooling and Goupil Galleries, Fine Art Society and elsewhere and, after his death, his work was revived by Gallery Edward Harvane. Bradford's Cartwright Hall Art Gallery holds his picture Marguerite, lent to the 1986 Christie's NEAC centenary show. Lived in London.

Rupert CLAUSEN 1960– Painter, born in Copenhagen, Denmark. He studied at South Glamorgan Institute of Higher Education, 1978–9, then Birmingham Polytechnic, 1979–82. He showed in John Moores Exhibition, Liverpool, in 1989–90 and in 1991–2, his pictures depicting biomorphic forms. Clausen also showed in The Discerning Eye, at Mall Galleries, 1991. Lived in London.

Suzanne CLAUSEN: *see* **SZUPER GALLERY**

A Bourne CLAVERDON: *see* **Alice Buxton WINNICOTT**

Beryl CLAY 1889– Painter, draughtsman, printmaker and teacher, born in London. Educated at Clifton High School, Bristol, where she eventually taught art. Then studied at the Grosvenor School of Modern Art, 1929–31, under Iain Macnab, and in 1936 at the Central School of Arts and Crafts. London Passenger Transport Board reproduced her work. Exhibited LG, Senefelder Club, NEAC and WIAC. Lived in London.

Monica Mary CLAY 1912– Painter, designer and teacher, born in Halifax, where she studied initially at the School of Art, 1929–35. Then studied at Leeds College of Art, her teachers including John Frederic Greenwood, and Bradford Regional College of Art under Reginald Aird, where she specialised in textile design, 1938–41. She held a number of teaching positions including Tiverton School of Art and Poole College for Further Education. Exhibited at public galleries in Leeds, Manchester, Wakefield and elsewhere. Lived in Halifax and latterly in Parkstone, Dorset.

Phyllis Archibald CLAY 1880-1947 Sculptor born in Tunbridge Wells, Kent, early in her career known by her maiden name Phyllis Archibald. She studied at the Glasgow School of Art, 1903-6, following that for several years in Paris. Returning to London before World War I, she lived between the wars in Bletchingley, Surrey. She was a member of the Glasgow Society of Lady Artists and a prolific exhibitor at the Royal Glasgow Institute of the Fine Arts, RSA, Walker Art Gallery in Liverpool and elsewhere. There are four allegorical female figures by her on the front of the Royal Bank of Scotland, in St Enoch Square, Glasgow. Died in Grasmere, Westmorland.

Phillippa CLAYDEN 1955– Artist in oil, collage, inks and pastel, and teacher, born and worked in London. She created a haunting, dreamlike world in her pictures, which were populated by bizarre, memorable figures. After initial ceramic work in Italy in 1972, Clayden was at Central School of Art and Design, 1973–7, graduating with honours. Was a freelance painter and teacher, commencing several years' study of drawing with Cecil Collins, an important influence. Studied stained glass at Central School, 1979–81, doing a postgraduate diploma course at Royal Academy Schools, 1979–82, followed by more teaching. She participated in many mixed exhibitions, starting with New Contemporaries and Whitechapel Open in 1977. Had a solo show at Camden Arts Centre in 1978, with others at Boundary Gallery latterly, starting in 1991. In 1991 was nominated as one of four most promising young artists of that year. Was latterly associated with the Islington Arts Factory.

Harold CLAYTON 1896–1979 Painter of flower pictures in the style of the Dutch Old Masters, such as The White Fluted Vase, Morning Glory, Birth of Spring and Floral Palette, and published by Venture Prints. Although Clayton's pictures commonly fetched good sums in the auctions rooms and were handled by Richard Green, W H Patterson and Frost & Reed Ltd, the artist remained a shadowy figure. Born in the city of London, Clayton studied at Hackney, Harrow, Hornsey and St Martin's Schools of Art, notably under Norman Janes the printmaker. Early in the 1930s Clayton lived in Harrow, showing several times at RA, including a wood engraving. Also worked in Hampstead in north London and in Suffolk, then in a remote old farmhouse in Devon.

Inge CLAYTON fl. from 1970s– Artist working in oil, watercolour, collage and as a printmaker, brought up in Salzburg, Austria. Her work, centred on the human figure, was termed "sensuous, sometimes erotic", owing something to the Vienna Secessionists and Jugendstijl. Clayton came to England in the 1960s, initially working as an interior architect and jewellery designer. From 1976–84 she studied collage with Jack Yates and life drawing with John Nicholl at Camden Arts Centre, also printmaking at St Albans School of Art with Peter Jacques. As well as showing in group exhibitions at RA, in America and widely in Europe, Clayton had a number of solo shows, including Margaret Fisher Gallery, 1979; Chalk Farm Gallery, 1985; Boundary Gallery, 1988; St Jude's, 1990; Enid Lawson Gallery, 2001; The Catto Gallery, 2002; and The Metal Gallery, 2004. Lived in London.

Peter CLAYTON 1959– Artist and teacher, born in Wigan, Lancashire, who did a foundation course at Preston Polytechnic, 1977–8; gained an honours degree in fine art there, 1978–81, tutors Bill Sharp and Alan Powell; and in 1983–4 completed a postgraduate certificate in education at Leicester Polytechnic, and settled there. Clayton had periods as a community arts worker in Lancashire and Leicester; he co-ordinated public art events; was art tutor at Fosse Arts Centre, Sir Jonathan North Community College and Fullhurst Community College in Leicester; and carried out numerous mural commissions for restaurants, leisure centres and schools. He was artist-in-residence, Grizedale Forest, Cumbria, in 1995. Clayton said that his paintings were "concerned with conveying a sense of place and are based on sketches, photographs and memories of my local environment and places I visit... By integrating bold brushwork, rough textures, random scratches and subtle glazes, I want to create images of the landscape that combine strength and beauty with a feeling of being eroded and weather-beaten." Exhibitions included Leicester City Art Gallery Open Exhibition from 1986 (Prizewinner, 1989 and 1991); Present Prints, Royal Festival Hall, 1989; Art for Conservation, Chelsea College of Art, 1991; Wild West, Woods Gallery, Leicester, 1994. He had a solo show at Abbot Hall Art Gallery, Kendal, 1997, another at Tib Lane Gallery, Manchester, 2002. The Grizedale Society and Peterborough Arts Council hold examples.

John CLEAL 1929– Artist, craftsman and teacher, born in South Africa. He trained four years as a signwriter, then worked as a layout artist and illustrator. In London in the 1950s he was an illustrator for a newspaper with his own weekly column as well as being cartoonist for a Norwegian sports paper. Returning to South Africa, Cleal established a design studio for 10 years, then returned to England in 1960 where he became a partner in Henrion Design Associates. In 1962 Cleal moved to Fishguard, Wales, farmed for eight years and then set up the craft complex Workshop Wales, also an art gallery. Clwyd Exhibition Services toured a show of Cleal's work in 1985 called Leather, Wood and Stone. Later exhibitions included Taliesin Arts Centre, Swansea, 2000.

James CLEAVER 1911– Painter, illustrator, printmaker and writer, educated in London. He studied at Camberwell School of Art, 1930–4, then Royal College of Art, 1934–8. His books included *The Theatre Through the Ages*, 1946; *The Theatre at Work*, 1947; and *A History of Graphic Art*, 1963. He was a member of the Authors' Club and of the Society of Industrial Artists. Showed at RA, other London galleries and in the provinces. Later solo shows included one of landscape and theatrical subjects at Arts Club, 1982, and a retrospective at Southend Central Library, 1988. In his eighties he was working on theatrical subjects, portrait heads of literary figures and writing his memoirs. Lived latterly at Westcliff-on-Sea, Essex.

Margrit CLEGG 1941– Artist in mixed media, born in Bremen, Germany, permanently resident in the United Kingdom from 1965. "My work is inspired by archaeology, ancient architecture and the signs and symbols carved in rocks, temples and city walls.... I love the power and simplicity of rock, stone, sand and earth". Clegg followed an honours degree in fine art at Wimbledon School of Art, 1980–3, with a postgraduate printmaking diploma there, 1988–90. She lived in St Ives, Cornwall, from 1994, in 1995 was elected a member of the Newlyn Society of Artists, in 1996 of Porthmeor Printmakers. Her many mixed exhibitions included, RA Summer Exhibition, 1983; French Institute, 1986; Falmouth Arts Centre, 1995; Tate St Ives Café Gallery, 1997; and Newlyn Art Gallery, curated by William Packer, 1999. She had solo shows at New Millennium Gallery, St Ives, 2000 and 2003.

Richard CLEGG 1966– Artist who employed techniques such as hologram, paint and neon and strikingly shaped canvas on panels. He was born in Blackpool, Lancashire, studying at Blackpool and Fylde College, 1985–6, Canterbury College of Art, 1986–9, and Royal College of Art, 1990–3. Group shows included On Sight at Tower Bridge Piazza, 1991, Cooling Gallery in 1992 and Robert & Susan Summer Residency Exhibition, Connecticut, America, 1994. In that year he shared a three-man show at Paton Gallery. Awards included Pemberton Travel Award and John Minton Travel Award to Barcelona, both 1991; Henry Moore Foundation Scholarship, 1992; and Susan Kasen Summer Study Award to Cologne and Summer Fellowship to America, both 1993. British Rail holds his work.

Benjamin CLEMENS fl. from c.1905–1957 Sculptor. Studied at Royal College of Art and afterwards worked as assistant to Édouard Lantéri. Exhibited RA especially, 1906–44, also RSA and Royal Glasgow Institute of the Fine Arts. Among Clemens' public sculpture was work on Africa House in London's Kingsway and a concrete lion for the government building at the 1924 Wembley British Empire Exhibition, illustrated in the volume *RBS: Modern British Sculpture*, published in 1929. Clemens was elected a fellow of the RBS. Lived in London.

Winifred CLEMENT SMITH 1904–2000 Painter and embroiderer, born, educated and lived in Tunbridge Wells. Studied at its School of Art, also at Regent Street Polytechnic School of Art. Showed at ROI PS, RI, SWA, elsewhere in London and in the provinces. Mrs Clement Smith was a member of Tunbridge Wells Art Club. Her husband was an architect, Clement Smith, and Winifred adopted Clement as part of her surname.

Joy CLEMENTS 1921– Artist in wide range of media, notably pastel, born in Burwell, Suffolk, whose paternal grandmother, Alice Munnings, was a cousin of Sir Alfred Munnings. Serious application to painting began in the 1970s, and she was taught at Ulster Polytechnic by John Turner. Dreams were an important influence on "a personal kind of Expressionism ... using rich colours, particularly blues". Main works were figure paintings, still life and portraits, including two of the Duchess of Abercorn. Clements was made an associate of RUA in 1983, was president of the Ulster Society of Women Artists and vice-president and chairman of the Ulster Watercolour Society. Group shows included Eakin Gallery, Belfast, and Jonathan Swift Gallery, Kilroot, and in 1979 she had a solo exhibition with Malone Gallery, Belfast. Ulster Television and the National Self-Portrait Collection of Ireland, University of Limerick, hold her work. Lived in Newtownabbey, County Antrim, Northern Ireland.

Keith CLEMENTS 1931–2003 Painter, draughtsman, teacher and writer, born in Brighton, Sussex. He attended the local College of Art, 1947–53. After National Service he was a visiting teacher of art in Orkney, 1955–8. Following several years teaching in Sussex he did an advanced diploma in art education at Birmingham University and College of Art, 1964–5, becoming senior lecturer in art at Eastbourne College of Education, 1965–76, principal lecturer in art at East Sussex College of Higher Education, 1976–8, then senior lecturer in art history at Brighton Polytechnic, 1978–88. He wrote for *The Artist* magazine and published *Henry Lamb: the Artist and His Friends*, 1985, having completed his doctoral thesis on Lamb. Among Clements' solo shows were Orkney County Library, 1956–8, National Film Theatre, 1972, Castle Rushen in the Isle of Man, 1978, in 1988 he shared a show with David Chapman at Brighton Polytechnic Gallery, further solo exhibitions including Bloomsbury Revisited at the Bloomsbury Workshop in 1992, New Vistas: Sussex from the Bypass, Pallant House, Chichester, 1996, and Thebes Gallery, Lewes, 2002. Lived in Newhaven, Sussex.

Raymon CLEMENTS 1927–1997 Painter, sculptor and teacher, born in Dudley, Worcester. Studied at Birmingham School of Arts and Crafts, teachers including Bernard Fleetwood-Walker. Taught for many years at Rowley Regis Grammar School and Rowley Regis College, also lecturing at Leamington School of Art and Birmingham College of Technology. Showed widely in the provinces, continental Europe and South America. Lived at Penn, Wolverhampton, Staffordshire.

William Charles CLEMENTS 1903–1983 Painter and tutor to adult classes, born in London. He studied under Norman Janes at Hackney Technical College, at South-West Essex Technical College, then with Andrew Gordon at Walthamstow. Showed UA, RBA and East End Academy in Whitechapel. Was president of London Sketch Club and chairman of Essex Art Club. Lived in Chingford, Essex, for many years but moved to Northampton in 1981.

Katie CLEMSON 1951– Printmaker, teacher and writer, born in Temora, New South Wales, Australia. She studied at Croydon College of Art and Central School of Art and Design. Clemson lectured extensively on printmaking, also writing several books on the subject. Was a prize-winner for relief prints at International Print Biennal at Bradford, exhibiting widely elsewhere in England, including RA, RE, Redfern Gallery, where she had a solo show in 1997, and abroad. Was based at White Gum Press, Minstead, Hampshire.

Nola CLENDINNING 1943– Painter who was educated in South Africa and moved to England in 1965. She started painting soon after, self-taught, using watercolour and gouache. Figures, animals and landscapes were copied freely from medieval drawings, bestiaries, church carvings and sketchbooks. Exhibitions included a solo show at University of Southampton Gallery.

Ian CLENTON 1969– Artist, born in Woking, Surrey, who attended Northwich College of Art and Design, 1988–90, then graduated from Goldsmiths' College in fine art and art history, 1990–3. Clenton's early works were made of found objects, to which colour was applied. Later works were on deep, square canvases, with monochrome but textured grounds, as in his solo show at The Blue Gallery, 1996.

Henry CLIFFE 1919–1983 Painter, printmaker and teacher, born in Scarborough, Yorkshire. When he was in Army in World War II met the painter William Scott in Wales, then in 1946 enrolled as student at Bath Academy of Art. He was invited to join the staff and became an influential teacher. Married colleague, Valerie May. The work of Cliffe and his students was shown in a number of international exhibitions, such as Cincinnati International Lithography Exhibitions, 1954 and 1960, and at two Venice Biennales. Cliffe had first solo show of paintings at Redfern Gallery in 1956, and three years later his first one-man print show at St George's Gallery. In 1960 Cliffe won first purchase prize at Philadelphia Print Club and in the following year gained a Ford Foundation Scholarship, Pratt Institute of Art, New York. In 1965 his book *Lithography: A Studio Handbook* appeared. Cliffe had a retrospective show of prints, 1970, at Arnolfini Gallery, Bristol, and in 1977 and 1980 one-man shows of paintings and drawings at Festival Gallery, Bath. In 1996 Phillips auctioned Works from the Studio of Henry Cliffe, revealing four decades of constant inventiveness and experiment, from figurative to abstract and finally back to figurative.

James CLIFFE 1906–1994 Painter and draughtsman, notably of accomplished portraits, born in Liverpool, where he lived at Wavertree. Cliffe was a mainly self-educated artist who attended evening classes for life drawing. He began painting scenery for theatres; did publicity for local picture houses; and worked in the display studio of a city centre store before becoming a self-employed book illustrator, then a portrait painter. For many years Cliffe was a familiar sight at Bluecoat Chambers, in his small black beret, smock and corduroy trousers, having a studio there for over 25 years. His speciality was Liverpool characters such as the sculptor Arthur Dooley; also lord mayors and mayoresses and Queen Elizabeth II. Cliffe's portrait of barrow girl Lizzie Christian is in the Maritime Museum, Liverpool. Showed at RCamA and the Liverpool Academy, where he also exhibited solo. He retired in 1986, the year after he was mugged, and gave a portrait to the Victims of Violence Group to auction for its funds.

Clare M CLIFFORD 1894–1975 Miniaturist and watercolour painter, born in Hythe, Kent. She studied under the miniaturist S Arthur Lindsay. Went on to show with RMS and Exeter Art Society. Her early work carried the signature Clare M Ogilvie (the surname of her first husband; later she was Clare Lady Clifford of Chudleigh). Lived at Newnham, Hampshire.

John Grant CLIFFORD 1944– Painter and teacher, born in Perth, Scotland. He attended Duncan of Jordanstone College of Art in Dundee, 1962–7, then Royal College of Art, 1966–7. He gained a British Institute Award in 1973 and a Latimer Award. For a time he lectured at Duncan of Jordanstone. Among group exhibitions in which he was included were RSA Summer Exhibitions from the early 1970s, Six Dundee Painters at the local art gallery in 1974 and A Choice Selection at Fruitmarket Gallery, Edinburgh, 1975. Scottish Arts Council and Scottish Television hold his work, which included figurative, highly decorative canvases.

Liz CLIFFORD 1961– Artist who studied fine art and education at Homerton College, Cambridge, 1981–5. She took part in Mount San Jacinto Open, in California, 1987; Blast R-101 and Diorama, both 1988; and in East End Open Studios, with Barbican Arts Group, 1989. Clare College, Cambridge, and St Thomas' Hospital owned her work.

Robin CLIFFORD 1907– Painter, born in Gillingham, Kent. Clifford gained a master's degree at Cambridge University. He studied at Maidstone and St Martin's Schools of Art. Exhibited RA, ROI, NEAC. Clifford was a connoisseur, with a collection of pictures featuring leading modern British artists. Lived at Rochester, Kent.

Frank CLIFFORD-SMITH 1906–1968 Self-taught painter, born in Cheshire the son of a photographer, who aged five moved with his family to Paris where he became fascinated with its vigorous artistic scene. Clifford-Smith's earliest works, mainly religious portraits influenced by the work of Georges Rouault, date from the 1940s. He became a professional painter after World War II and with his wife, the artist and designer Joan Glass, moved to Bucks House, Great Bardfield, once home to Eric Ravilious. There, Clifford-Smith produced monumental landscapes of Britain, Ireland and Italy while organising nationally acclaimed exhibitions in artists' homes, avoiding involvement with commercial galleries, of which he was suspicious. Edward Bawden, George Chapman, Audrey Cruddas, Walter Hoyle, Sheila Robinson, Michael Rothenstein and Kenneth Rowntree were closely involved. By 1960 the Great Bardfield artistic community had begun to disperse. After a brief time in London, Clifford-Smith settled with his family at Little Baddow Hall, near Chelmsford, where a dreamlike Lunar Suite was painted. Thick texturing, later achieved by mixing oils with sand or plaster, were features of Clifford-Smith's output. The Fry Art Gallery, Saffron Walden, held a show in 1998.

John CLINCH 1934–2001 Sculptor of large works in metal and fibreglass of a populist nature, and teacher, born in Folkestone, Kent. While training as an accountant, attended evening classes art classes in Richmond, Surrey, then studied at Kingston School of Art, 1951–5, under Reginald Brill, being taught sculpture by Charles Lewis and Douglas Wain-Hobson. Following National Service in the Military Police, 1955–7, Clinch entered the Royal College of Art sculpture school, 1957–61, initially under John Skeaping, then with Bernard Meadows, who gained him a fourth study year. After winning a Silver Medal and a drawing prize, a travel award took Clinch to France and Italy. From 1962, worked part-time at Colchester, Hammersmith and Camberwell Art Schools; in 1964 moved full-time to Nottingham, eventually becoming head of the sculpture department; in 1969 taught at Calgary University, Canada; then took early retirement from Nottingham in 1987 to spend more time exhibiting and on regular commissions. Moved to Tregaron, Dyfed, in 1988, the year before he gained a summer residency at the British School at Rome. In 1992, Clinch was made an associate and then, in 1994, a fellow of the RBS. Tin toys found on holiday in Spain were one source of Clinch's inspiration for pieces such as Wish You Were Here, 1983, Merseyside Development Corporation. Among other public works were The Great Blondinis, 1985, for Thamesdown Borough Council; People Like Us, 1993, Cardiff Bay Development Corporation; and Basketball Players, 1999, Royal Caribbean Cruise Line, Walker Art Gallery, Liverpool, and many other public, corporate and private collections hold Clinch's work.

Margery CLINTON 1931–2005 Potter, ceramic sculptor and lecturer, born in Glasgow, who gained a diploma in drawing and painting at the School of Art there, then studied to teach at Jordanhill College of Education. She was notable as a lustre specialist, inspired by Tiffany glass. In 1973 Clinton took her master's degree at the Royal College of Art, specialising in the then-neglected skill of reduction lustre glazes, which had developed several centuries before in the Middle East, then had declined. Her book *The Complete Potter Lustres*, 1991, is definitive. Clinton returned to Scotland in 1978, establishing a studio at Newton Port, East Lothian, until 1981 with Jan Williamson, continuing herself until 1995, then moving her operation to Dunbar. Clinton completed some important commissions, including reproduction medieval tiles for the Burrell Collection, Glasgow; tiles for several Middle East locations, among them Salalah Palace in Oman and for a new royal palace in Hummar, Jordan; and a ceramic mural of herbs for the tercentenary of Mary Erskine School, Edinburgh.

Joyce CLISSOLD 1905-1982 Textile designer, businesswoman and teacher, who studied under Bernard Adeney and Noel Rooke at the Central School of Arts and Crafts, 1924–7. Clissold was one of the most distinguished woodblock textile designers to emerge from the Central and while there worked at Footprints, a workshop founded in 1925 by another Central student, Elspeth Little, and others. Footprints supplied textiles for Modern Textiles, the shop set up by Little in 1926 and taken over by Clissold in 1929. The business exploited her designs at several fashionable outlets through the 1930s from a base in Brentford, Middlesex. Clissold taught textile design from 1936–40 at the Central and its successor, Central St Martins College of Art & Design, retains copyright to her designs and a large collection of her work. In modest form, Footprints continued until Clissold died.

Gordon CLOSE 1958– Artist in various media and lecturer, trained as a sculptor, and born in Sunderland, County Durham. He attended the local College of Art, 1979–82, at that time producing often large sculptures with a heavy use of classical imagery. He had early success, pursuing public and private commissions and exhibiting at such venues as Aspex Gallery in Portsmouth, Yorkshire Sculpture Park and Wordsworth Museum in Grasmere. From the early 1990s Close concentrated on two-dimensional works (by this time his sculpture was more limited and on a smaller scale), with classical, mythological and domestic themes, their much-refined surfaces having a glowing, luminous quality, as in a shared show at Sally Hunter Fine Art, 1997. He was then a visiting lecturer in sculpture and drawing at Sunderland University, living in Hexham, Northumberland.

Peter CLOSE 1959– Sculptor, born in Somerset where he settled near Long Sutton. Ernst Blensdorf, Umberto Boccioni, Bob Scrivens and Alberto Giacometti influenced Close, who was included in 1st RWA Open Sculpture Exhibition, 1993. Close's early work specialised in whale sculpture carved in local limestone, which brought commissions from Greenpeace and The Whale and Dolphin Conservation Society, which sold his work worldwide. Music and sculpture was a later preoccupation.

Val CLOSE 1949– Abstract painter and teacher, born in Sunderland. She studied at Sunderland Polytechnic and Syracuse University in America. Her awards included the Backhouse Drawing Prize, Syracuse University Scholarship and a Northern Arts Major Bursary and a Travel Award. Close was artist-in-residence with Northumbria Police, 1984–5. She taught in Britain and America, including Newcastle and Sunderland Polytechnics. Group appearances included New Contemporaries, at ICA, 1980; Spacex Gallery, Exeter, 1983; and the Newcastle Group show The Northern Lights, at DLI Museum & Arts Centre and tour, 1990. Later solo exhibitions included Laing Art Gallery, Newcastle, 1988. Contemporary Art Society holds her work. Lived in Newcastle.

Peter CLOSSICK 1948– Painter and art lecturer in adult education, born in London, where he settled. He studied at Leicester Polytechnic, 1966–9, Camberwell School of Art, 1974–8, and Goldsmiths' College School of Art, 1978–9. His group show exhibitions included LG (elected 1999, president 2000), ROI, Whitechapel Open, RA Summer Exhibition and John Moores Exhibition, Liverpool, 1991–2. Had solo exhibitions at Sweet Waters Gallery, 1989, as well as Phoenix Gallery, 1991, the year that *Painting Without a Brush* appeared, and in the provinces. In 2003, Clossick shared a show with Anthony Eyton at Woodlands Art Gallery and participated in LG's ninetieth-birthday celebrations at The Gallery in Cork Street and Gallery 27, writing an introduction to the commemorative volume. He was in 6 Artists, all LG members, at Stables Theatre Gallery, Hastings, in 2004. Clossick lectured at Oxford Brookes University, Open College of the Arts and further education colleges. He was art consultant to Blackheath Conservatoire of Museum and Art and A2 Arts College and was exhibitions adviser, Woodlands Art Gallery. Clossick's subject was "the single figure and occasional still life or landscape, worked from direct observation." He said that he needed "to understand the limits, find means of expression and methods of construction. Not always conceptualising the implications, but working it out in the painting itself, wanting an art of lasting quality."

Anne CLOUDSLEY 1915– Artist in a wide range of media, teacher and writer, born in Reigate, Surrey, who studied at the City Literary Institute, 1971; Byam Shaw School, 1972–6; and Goldsmiths' College, 1976–7. Teachers included John Flavin, Bill Jacklin, Euan Uglow, Bernard Dunstan, Diana Armfield and Peter Gerrard. From 1978–81, Cloudsley was founder and honorary gallery manager at the Africa Centre, from 1982–5 chairman of Westminster City Council's visual arts committee. She was a visiting lecturer at the fine art department at University of Nigeria, Nsukka, 1981, and lecturer in lithography for the Working Men's College, 1982–90. Cloudsley wrote and broadcast on remote peoples and their environments, publications including *Women of Omdurman: life, love and the cult of virginity*, 1983. The culture and life of the Sudanese and other Arab societies as well as abstract works were among her output. Group shows included Air Gallery, 1976; Berry Street Annual Open Studios, 1979–90; RA Summer Exhibition, from 1992; New Burlington Gallery, 1994; and Atrium Gallery, 1997. She completed a design for the Biological Council Medal and had work in the collection of Statoil (UK). Lived in London, where she was a member of LG.

Colin CLOUGH 1903–c.1980 Painter whose correct name was Thomas Collingwood Clough. Born in Glen Conway, Denbighshire, Wales, he was the son of the painter Tom Clough. He studied at the Slade School of Fine Art under Henry Tonks in 1925–7, then at the Royal College of Art from 1928–30 under William Rothenstein. He exhibited at RA, LG and elsewhere. Went on to work widely in Wales, France and Canada. During World War II was a camouflage officer in the Middle East. Lectured at Sir John Cass School of Art and lived in London.

Pauline Susan CLOUGH 1943– She studied at Bournville School of Art, Birmingham, and later became an heraldic embroidery designer before taking up art full-time. Favoured watercolour and pastel, although she was fond of experiment, "so variable, and for me so exciting". Showed at PS of which she was made a member in 1982, RA, RBSA and elsewhere in the provinces and abroad. She won the Daler-Rowney Award, PS, 1982 and 1985; Everyman Award, RBSA, 1986; Daler-Rowney Major Pastel Award, PS, 1987. Lived in Newick, Sussex.

Prunella CLOUGH 1919–1999 Painter and printmaker, full name Cara Prunella Clough-Taylor, born in London, where she continued to work with forays into the provinces. Her father, Eric, was a Board of Trade official who wrote poetry; her mother, Thora, was sister of the noted designer Eileen Gray (as trustee of Gray's estate, Clough was later able to extend her prodigious anonymous philanthropy, from which many artists benefited). Studied at Chelsea School of Art, 1938–9, then during World War II did various jobs, including a stint as a draughtsman. Had a first solo show at Leger Gallery, 1947, later exhibitions following at Roland, Browse and Delbanco; Leicester and Grosvenor Galleries; New Art Centre, and elsewhere. She had a retrospective at Whitechapel Art Gallery in 1960; another at Graves Art Gallery in Sheffield a dozen years later; Warwick Arts Trust, 1982; Annely Juda Fine Art, 1989; in 1996 there was a toured show of work from 1970 which included Oriel 31, Newtown, and Camden Arts Centre; Kettle's Yard Gallery, Cambridge, showed early paintings to recent work, 1999, the year she won the Jerwood Painting Prize; in 2000 Annely Juda Fine Art held a memorial exhibition; in 2001 the Hayward Gallery organised a tour which included Gainsborough's House, Sudbury; unseen reliefs, drawings and prints were shown by Annely Juda and The Fine Art Society held a show of works from the collection of Dr Thomas Sutherland, both 2003; and Andrew Stewart curated the Clough exhibition Seeing The World Sideways at Olympia, 2004. Clough's early work was concerned with industrial subjects which leaned towards abstraction, which later became the dominant mode, with a surprising range of colours and motifs. Tate Gallery and Arts Council hold examples.

Chris CLOVER 1948– Self-taught artist, born in Manchester, who left school at 15. Manchester City Art Gallery holds Clover's Your Memory is Your Bible, Your Imagination Your Future, acrylic on hardboard. Clover claimed to have developed his own form of art, Symbolic Perspective, explained in the artist's privately produced publication *Before the Parable: A Fordigraph Sketch (with poems)*, a copy of which is held by the Gallery's archive.

Harry CLOW 1940– Painter, born in London, who entered world of commercial art aged 16 and two years later become a freelance artist. He specialised in military history, sea battles from Roman times through to Vietnam and other marine work. Many of his pictures were commissioned for the walls of major shipping firms. Clow's range was wide, from yachts to commercial vessels to warships, and he also completed some aviation paintings. With the publisher and former captain Colin Squire, Clow teamed up in the early 1990s to work on what they called the Ultimate Collection, paintings of some of the world's most beautiful yachts and power boats, limited-edition prints being produced. The Collection was launched at Superyacht '91 held at the Barbican, London, in 1991. Strict accuracy was a criterion.

Joy CLUCAS 1931– Textile and embroidery artist and teacher who attended Southampton School of Art, 1950; obtained a National Diploma in fabric printing by hand and machine embroidery, 1952; then qualified to teach at Brighton College of Art, 1953. From 1953–5 taught, then combined part-time teaching with freelance work. Began to exhibit in the 1960s in touring shows organised by Vera Sherman, joined craft societies in East Anglia and the Embroiderers' Guild. Taught at Digby Stuart College, 1970–2, and London College of Fashion, 1971–2. In 1973, had an important show at the Textile Museum, Washington, in America. Continued to teach, completing round-the-world tours in 1984 and 1990. Later exhibitions included Wonders of my Life, Digby Gallery, Mercury Theatre in Colchester, Essex, where she lived, and Over The River, firstsite, Colchester/Wolsey Art Gallery, Ipswich, 2002. National Museum of Scotland, Edinburgh, holds Clucas's work Moonscape.

Shelagh CLUETT 1947– Sculptor and teacher, born in Dorset. She studied at St Martin's School of Art, 1966–7, Hammersmith College of Art, 1967–8, Hornsey College of Art, 1968–71, and Chelsea School of Art, 1971–2, where she later taught. Gained the Sainsbury Award in 1972 and Greater London Arts Association Major Award in 1979. Went on to show on many group exhibitions from 1972 at Museum of Modern Art, Oxford, including New Sculpture at Ikon Gallery, Birmingham, 1979; Acme Gallery, 1980; Paris Biennale, 1982; and Kruithuis, S'-Hertogenbosch, Netherlands, 1983. Was included in 9 Artists from Wapping British tour, based at DLI Museum & Arts Centre, Durham, 1983. Showed solo at Nicola Jacobs Gallery from 1982. An abstract sculptor who was based in London.

Jan CLUTTERBUCK 1919– Artist in watercolour and pastel and teacher, born in Newton, Massachusetts, America. She studied printmaking with Michael Carlo at Harrow School of Art and with Michael Rothenstein, but was largely self-taught. Among her teaching experiences were work at Cassio College, Watford, and summer courses for Cambridge Drawing Society, as well as watercolour workshops in Sarratt, Hertfordshire, where she lived. She was chairman of WIAC, 1965–75. Also exhibited at RA Summer Exhibitions, American Embassy, Hurlingham Gallery and elsewhere. Had a solo show at Forge House Gallery, 1973. Coventry and Gloucester Education Committees hold her work. She said that her pictures were "tranquil studies of isolated places in which there is a quality of timelessness ... I like wide, open spaces with solitary buildings, sheep or cows."

Alan CLUTTON-BROCK 1904–1976 Painter who was better known as art critic of *The Times* and writer of books on painting. He was educated at Eton College and Cambridge University, also studying at Westminster School of Art. Showed at RA, LG and elsewhere. His books include *Italian Painting* and *An Introduction to French Painting*. Sometimes signed work only with initials. Was for a time after World War II a National Gallery trustee and from 1955–8 Slade professor of fine art at Cambridge. Lived in Hadleigh, Suffolk, and finally at Moreton-in-Marsh, Gloucestershire.

Maggi CLYDE 1952– Painter and printmaker, born in Glasgow. She studied at Edinburgh College of Art, 1970–5, and Royal College of Art until 1979. Showed in Norway and elsewhere and had a group of etchings included in Arts Council tour Fragments Against Ruin, 1981–2. Scottish Arts Council also holds her work. Lived for a time in London.

Henry Horne CLYNE 1930– Sculptor in various materials and teacher, born in Wick, Caithness. He produced individually handmade ceramic sheep, dated, stamped and signed by the artist, under the name Sheepshapes. Studied at Edinburgh College of Art, 1948–54, then at Moray House Teachers' Training College, 1954–5. Gained a Harkness Fellowship in America in 1959–61, attending a ceramics course in Tokoname, Japan, 1986. From 1962–73 taught at art schools in Norwich and Cheltenham, being principal lecturer in sculpture at Winchester, 1973–86. Took part in many group shows, from Sculpture Centre, New York, 1961, having solo exhibitions at Arlington Mill, Gloucestershire, 1967, and Eastleigh Museum, Hampshire, 1992. Among larger works completed was a painted wooden structure titled Opening Bend, bought by Scottish Arts Council, 1966, in collection of Stirling University. Lived in King's Somborne, Hampshire.

Thora CLYNE 1937– Artist and teacher, born in Wick, Caithness. She gained her master's degree with honours in fine art at Edinburgh University and College of Art in 1960, teachers including William Gillies and Derek Clarke, then was awarded a year's postgraduate scholarship and travelling fellowship, Andrew Grant Bequest. Was principal assistant at Aberdeen Art Gallery, 1960–1, in 1963 studying printmaking at University of Colorado in America. From 1963 lectured part-time at Edinburgh College of Art. Prizes included the Anne Redpath Award, 1979, and special prize, 1984, both SSWA of which she was a member. Clyne regularly exhibited at RSA, RSW and at RA. Also exhibited in group shows in France and America. Had a solo show at Torrance Gallery, Edinburgh, 1991. Parisian street scenes, wild gardens, cats and unspoilt agrarian landscapes were among key themes. Gillies Bequest at RSA holds her work. Lived at Milnathort, Kinross-shire.

William Daniel CLYNE 1922– Painter, draughtsman, illustrator and teacher, born at Stirkoke Mains, Caithness, in which county he eventually settled at Lybster. Studied at Edinburgh College of Art from 1940–2 and 1946–8, his teachers including John Maxwell and William Gillies; also at the School of Art in Hospitalfield, Arbroath, under Ian Fleming, 1949. Showed at SSA, Society of Caithness Artists, RSA, RSW and in Canada. Edinburgh College of Art holds his work.

Peter COATE 1926– Painter in oil and watercolour and teacher, born in Nailsea, Somerset. He studied at Chelsea School of Art under Ceri Richards and Robert Medley until 1950. Went on to teach in various colleges and schools; from 1972–87 ran The Mendip Painting Centre. Coate painted in Somerset, Suffolk and Wales, churches and country houses and landscape, "the wilder and rockier the better". Was a member of RWA, also showing at RA and ROI. Solo shows included Mignon Gallery in Bath and Mall Gallery, Clifton. Lived in Stone Allerton, Somerset.

Andrew COATES 1939– Artist working in construction, printmaking and drawing media, and teacher, born in Leeds, Yorkshire. He studied at Batley School of Art, 1959–64, under Robert Lee, and at Birmingham Polytechnic, 1975–6. His work was "based on collections of natural and man-made objects which have achieved a richness of colour and texture through exposure to the elements". After lecturing at Shenstone College, Bromsgrove, 1964–8, Coates became senior lecturer at Westhill College, Birmingham, 1969–89, from then being principal lecturer at Newman and Westhill Colleges. He was a member of the National Society for Education in Art and Design. Group appearances included Cleveland International Drawing Biennale, 1979; Midland View IV, at Herbert Art Gallery, Coventry, 1987; The Experience of Touch, at Walsall Art Gallery, 1989; and Ikon Gallery tours, 1989–90 and 1992. Had a solo show at Midlands Arts Centre, 1984, later ones including Bretton Hall, 1991. Lived in Birmingham.

Andrew COATES 1955– Painter, born in Surrey, who began painting professionally after leaving school aged 17 while living in New Zealand, where his family had emigrated when he was four. Without any training he became the Canterbury Society of Arts' youngest merit member and after three solo shows moved to England at 20. With his family he settled in Beer, Devon. Took part in many group shows, including RA Summer Exhibition, A Select Seven, W H Patterson Fine Arts Ltd, 2001, and Seven Selected Artists, same gallery, 2004. Coates had a distinctive ability in his landscapes to capture the effects of light, sun and water.

Joe COATES 1948– Artist in mixed media and teacher, born in Liverpool. He attended the College of Art there, St Martin's School of Art and Reading University between 1967–75. From 1979 taught at the School of Art, Falmouth. He was a member of Newlyn Society of Artists and his work was included in the 1989 Newlyn Orion Galleries exhibition A Century of Art in Cornwall 1889–1989. Coates lived with the artist Mary Mabbutt.

Richard Wallington COATES 1904–1993 Coates was a quiet, unassuming perfectionist in all media who rarely chose to exhibit in London galleries, although urged to by his peers. He was born in London, attended a state school until the age of 15, then gained a scholarship to Leyton Art School for two years. From 1922 he served a five-year apprenticeship with Cash & Clune, printers, gilders and bookbiders, in 1927 entering a commercial studio and making part-time studies at Westminster School of Art. During World War II Coates worked as a fitter of torpedo tubes in Portsmouth Dockyard. Afterwards, because advertising offered little work, he became a freelance artist and set up Studio Griffin off Chancery Lane next to a house in which the writer Charles Dickens had lived. Coates' attention to detail and promptness ensured commercial work until he retired towards the end of 1972. Coates was married for 63 years from 1929, with one daughter. He lived for over 60 years in Chipstead, Kent, and was a long-time member of Sevenoaks Art Club. He moved to Invergarry, Inverness-shire, in 1989, where he continued to paint despite failing health. Coates' pictures are in many collections around the world, but much work remained within the family.

Tom COATES 1941– Artist in oil, watercolour and pastel in the spontaneous, English tradition. He studied at Bournville College of Art, 1956–9, Birmingham College of Art, 1959–61, and Royal Academy Schools, 1961–4, his teachers including Peter Greenham. Won several prizes and scholarships during his studies and many after. As well as showing widely in mixed shows in London and the provinces, Coates was past-president of RBA and PS and a member of NEAC, RP and RWS. His one-man shows included a number at New Grafton Gallery. Coates carried out a series of prestigious commissions, including one for the RWS in 1990 to paint the ceremonial procession celebrating HRH The Queen Mother's ninetieth birthday. Wrote *Creating a Self-Portrait*, 1990. In the winter of 2000 was the commissioned artist with the England cricket team touring South Africa. He shared an exhibition with Donald Hamilton Fraser at W H Patterson in 2003, having a solo show at Archeus Fine Art in 2004. Lived in Hurstbourne Tarrant, Hampshire.

Maureen Margaret COATMAN 1919– Sculptor in various materials, born in Woking, Surrey. She attended Sherborne School for Girls and gained her art tuition privately, watercolour painting with William T Wood and sculpture with Enid Fenton Smith. Went on to complete a number of publicly sited works: in churches and schools in the Home Counties. Examples are to be found in churches at Monks Risborough, Buckinghamshire, and Sonning Common, Berkshire. Sometimes signed work M M C. Lived at Askett, Buckinghamshire.

Helen COATON fl. from late 1930s– Sculptor who after Bristol University studied art at Leicester College of Art with Percy Brown, 1937–42. Exhibited Leicester Museum and Art Gallery and with Leicester Society of Artists, of which she was a member. Also a member of AIA. Lived at Chelmsford, Essex.

Alice Margaret COATS 1905–1978 Wood engraver and painter, born in Birmingham. She studied at the School of Art there, 1922–8, specialising in illustration and lettering and was attracted to the Japanese method of colour printing. Pattern-making is a strong element in her work. She also studied at Slade School of Fine Art, took lessons from the wood engraver Clifford Webb and in Paris in 1930s attended André Lhote's school. Coats showed at WIAC, Redfern Gallery, Ruskin Galleries, Central Club of Colour Woodblock Engravers of which she was a founder-member in 1927, RBSA and with Birmingham Group, of which she was honorary secretary in 1938. Her books on botanical illustration were notable: *Flowers and their Histories*, 1956; *The Quest for Plants*, 1969; and *The Book of Flowers*, 1973. Birmingham City Museum and Art Gallery holds her work. Lived in Birmingham.

Charlie COBB 1977– Artist, born in London, who shared an exhibition with Hiromi Watanabe at the Albemarle Gallery in 2006. There, he showed expressive paintings in a variety of media concerned with London at night, the capital a favourite theme of his. Cobb studied theatre design at Nottingham Trent University before tackling various jobs in the art departments of feature films. He continued painting, in 2003 studying at the Prince's Drawing School, winning a prize that year. The Royal Collection holds Cobb's work.

David COBB 1921– Painter and draughtsman of marine scenes, born in Bromley, Kent, married to the painter Jean Main. After education at the Nautical College, Pangbourne, he studied with the Cornwall-based painter Borlase Smart. Exhibited RBA, SMA and ROI. Charles David Cobb lived in Brockenhurst, Hampshire.

John COBB 1946– Sculptor in wood, and draughtsman, born in Suffolk. He studied for a short time at Great Yarmouth College of Art, at Coventry College of Art and then the Royal College of Art. His sculptures are beautifully constructed and take several forms: some have head themes, as in the Arts Council's Head Case IV, of 1978; the chair was another theme. Among Cobb's showings was the 8th Paris Biennale, of 1973; the 1977 Silver Jubilee Exhibition in Battersea Park; in 1979–80 in Wood at the Yorkshire Sculpture Park; and he participated in the Welsh Sculpture Trust's 1983 Margam exhibition Sculpture in a Country Park. Cobb won the Walter Neurath Award for Sculpture in 1971 and the Sainsbury Award in 1974. In 1980–1 he was the resident fellow-in-sculpture at Yorkshire Sculpture Park and in 1985–8 held a Henry Moore Fellowship in Sculpture at Norwich School of Art. Later group exhibitions included 1st RWA Sculpture Exhibition, 1993, and later solo shows Anne Berthoud Gallery, 1991. In 2005, Cobb was included in the exhibition 1979 at Bloomberg SPACE. Lived in Woodbridge, Suffolk.

Alec COBBE 1945– Painter, draughtsman, designer, restorer, teacher and collector, born in Dublin, Ireland, as Richard Alexander Charles Cobbe. He studied human anatomy at Oxford University, 1963–7, winning a prize for anatomical drawing, from 1969–72 studying painting restoration at Tate Gallery. He became senior restorer at Birmingham Art Gallery, 1972–6, teaching restoration at Hamilton Kerr Institute, Cambridge University, 1976–81. Cobbe had a series of solo exhibitions: at Maclean Gallery, 1983; Bury Street Gallery, 1985–9; Galerie de Staël, Paris, 1990; Ib Jorgensen Fine Art, Dublin, 1992; Royal Danish Embassy, 1995; The Prince of Wales' Institute of Architecture, 1996 (accompanied by *Creations and Recreations, Alec Cobbe: Thirty Years of Design and Painting*, edited by Richard John); and Rafael Valls Ltd, 1999 and 2002. These shows included pictures relating to Ireland, France, Denmark and Spain. Interior views and still lifes were an important feature of Cobbe's work as an artist. That as a designer included museum installations, historic interiors, hanging of pictures collections and graphic design. Cobbe was an associate of The Royal Academy of Music. He founded the Cobbe Collection of composer-associated keyboard instruments, including examples owned or played by Purcell, J C Bach, Mozart, Beethoven, Cramer, Chopin, Liszt, Mahler and Elgar, claimed to be "the largest group of such relics in the world." Monsu Desiderio, James Pryde and Domenico Scarlatti were cited as influences. Victoria & Albert Museum; Royal Collection, Windsor Castle; National Trust; British Embassy, Paris; and Royal Danish Embassy were among collections holding examples of his work. Lived in Surrey and Ireland.

Hilary COBBETT 1885– Painter and teacher, born in Richmond, Surrey, daughter of the artist William Cobbett. She studied at Richmond School of Art 1903–5, then again 1924–7. Exhibited RA, SWA, SMA and elsewhere. Lived in Richmond.

Anne COBHAM: *see* **Anne SAÏD**

David COBLEY 1954– Figurative painter and teacher whose work was "about the way we interact with one another and the world we each inhabit, using light and colour to highlight the drama, mystery and fragility of that interaction." Cobley was born in Northampton, where he did a foundation course in art and design at the School of Art, 1971–2, studying for his diploma (incomplete) at Liverpool College of Art, 1972–3, with Peter Prendergast. Cobley was a teacher of art and drama at the International School of the Sacred Heart, Tokyo, 1981–2, having graduated in comparative culture at Sophia University there, 1979–81. Was elected to RP in 1997, Bath Society of Artists, 2000, RWA, 2001, and NEAC, 2003, exhibiting widely in mixed shows elsewhere. Cobley was shortlisted for the John Player Portrait Award, 1989; gained the John Brandler Prize, 1993; and in 1999 won an award at Tom Rice Gallery in Dublin, Ireland, and a Public Prize and Daler-Rowney Prize, both at RWA. Further awards included the Andrew Brownsword Prize, 2001, and Prosigns and Graphics Prize, 2002. He had solo exhibitions at Beaux Arts, Bath, in 2002 and 2004, one at Messum's in 2005 having an extensively illustrated catalogue. His many commissions included the actor Steven Berkoff; the ballerina Dame Alicia Markova; The National Society for Epilepsy; Royal Horse Artillery; Royal Engineers; Royal Marines, Royal Navy; and corporate collections. Lived in Bradford-on-Avon, Wiltshire.

Jason COBURN 1969– Artist, born in Manchester, whose contribution to New Contemporaries in 1996, at Tate Gallery, Liverpool, and Camden Arts Centre, included the New Contemporaries compliments slip signed with his first name. Coburn gained a degree in fine art at Middlesex University, 1991–4, then a master's in curating and commissioning contemporary art at Royal College of Art, 1994–6. Other exhibitions included Quirk, at The Chocolate Factory, 1994; Deep End, at The Tannery, 1995; and Annexed, 1 Hoxton Street, 1996. In 1999, Coburn's installation Pointless, at Jerwood Gallery's external sculpture space, comprised a five-metre artificial tree and 100 yellow digital watches programmed to activate periodically to "simulate the ambiguous atonal sounds of birdsong marshalled to the rhythm of the life of the building".

Elizabeth COCHRANE 1966– Artist in watercolour and charcoal, and teacher, born in Manchester. She studied at the Polytechnic there, 1984–5, under Norman Adams, then in 1985–9 at Newcastle upon Tyne where she gained the John Christie Prize for Painting and Oliver Hicks Memorial Prize. Went on to run painting courses in Cortona, Tuscany, and in England. Her main works were landscape watercolours, using a rich palette. Group exhibitions included RSW Open Exhibition and Beatrice Royal Art Gallery, Eastleigh. Had a solo show at Galleria d'Arte G Severini, Cortona. Lived in Hale, Cheshire.

Helen Lavinia COCHRANE 1868–1946 Painter, born in Bath, Somerset, who studied at Liverpool School of Art, in Munich and London. From 1915–18 she directed military hospitals in France and Italy, where she painted extensively. She was a member of RI and SWA and showed at RA, Walker Art Gallery in Liverpool and RBA. Had solo exhibitions at Fine Art Society. Lived in Italy and then in London.

Jeannetta COCHRANE 1882–1957 Theatre and costume designer, businesswoman, witty and much-loved teacher who developed an interest in historic dress when a student at the Polytechnic School of Art. In 1914, she joined the staff of the Central School of Arts and Crafts, remaining until 1940, having become head of the theatre design department. In addition, she designed for Heal's and Liberty; founded and ran her own costume business, Sheridan House, which supplied events such as the Lord Mayor's Show; designed for major productions in London and Dublin theatres and the masques in Regent's Park; and was associated with the couture house, Lachasse. Seven years after she died the distinctive Jeannetta Cochrane Theatre, opened near the Central in Southampton Row, realising her long ambition that the School had its own theatre.

Nicholas COCHRANE 1949– Draughtsman, painter and teacher, born in Bath, Somerset, educated at Downside School. He studied at the Ruskin School of Drawing and Fine Art, Oxford, before working for several years in the Old Master department at the auctioneers Christie's. In 1978, he founded Fine Arts College, Hampstead, where he was principal and taught portraiture and drawing and painting from life. Showed with RP from 1997, at Mall Galleries and National Portrait Gallery, in 1999 winning the inaugural Prince of Wales' Award for Portrait Drawing. Also exhibited with NEAC, The Discerning Eye, ROI, RBA, RWS and RI. Held four solo exhibitions at Burgh House, Hampstead. Lived in London.

Rosemarie COCKAYNE fl. from 1960s– Painter and draughtsman whose work had an Expressionist colour and strength. She was born in Montreal, Canada, moving to England when young. She trained at Royal Ballet School under such dancers as Tamara Karsavina and appeared at Covent Garden, dancing leading roles in London and on the continent and became prima ballerina at Basle State Ballet. Her study of painting began at Irene Ironside's school in Kensington under her nephew Christopher Ironside; went on to study art at Kunstmuseum in Basle, influenced by the work of Emil Nolde and Edvard Munch; she later studied at St Martin's School of Art. Cockayne did stage designs for *Nutcracker*, *Coppelia* and *Jazz Ballet*, Dublin. Exhibitions included a series of solo shows at Clarges Gallery and a shared one at Primrose Hill Gallery in 1990. University College Hospital, Clydesdale Bank and Christ's Hospital Art Centre own examples. Lived in London.

Gordon COCKBURN 1944– Painter and draughtsman, born in Maybole, Ayrshire, educated at Carrick Academy. Had a first solo show at Maclauren Art Gallery in Ayr in 1977, then went on to exhibit at John Moores Exhibition in Liverpool and at Walker Art Gallery there. This was followed by a Scottish Arts Council touring exhibition. Around that time Cockburn began writing poetry and painting the area where he had lived as a young boy, the old mining village of Kerse, near Patna, trying to recapture what life was like when the Houldsworth Mine was operating. He began showing at the New Solen Gallery with John Bratby and Shore Gallery, Edinburgh, the Dick Institute in Kilmarnock and McKechnie Institute, Girvan, and by 1991 regularly in top Glasgow galleries, such as Cyril Gerber Fine Art, the Compass and Cormund Galleries and T & R Annan and Sons. A visit to Poland in 1994 prompted his Auschwitz The Visit show at Rozelle House Galleries, Ayr, in 1998. The pictures were shown at the POSK Gallery in 1999. In that year, Cockburn was commissioned by Tony Matteo, proprietor of the City Merchant Restaurant, Glasgow, to paint 14 pictures of Robert Burns' Tam O'Shanter. In 2000, Cockburn's Spooncreel exhibition was at Rozelle House and Auschwitz pictures were shown at the Yom Ha Shoah Commemoration. The Cockburn Gallery, Maybole, opened in 2004 to show the artist's and other painters' work. Maclauren Gallery; Glasgow's Jewish Council and City Merchants; Marcel Marceau, the mime artist, drawn by Cockburn; the actor Fulton McKay; and corporate collections hold Cockburn's work.

James Mitchell COCKELL 1893– Watercolourist and photographer, born in Swindon, Wiltshire, where he continued to live. Studied by post with Percy Bradshaw's Press Art School. Showed at RI, elsewhere in London and extensively in Swindon area.

Douglas COCKER 1945– Sculptor and teacher, born in Alyth, Perthshire. He studied at Duncan of Jordanstone College of Art, Dundee, 1963–8, and won many awards, which enabled him to travel, including extensive trips through Greece, study in Italy and America. From 1972–81 he lived in Northampton, returning to Scotland to Gray's School of Art, Aberdeen, where he became a senior sculpture lecturer. Later visiting lectureships included Edinburgh University, Glasgow School of Art and Duncan of Jordanstone College of Art, Dundee. Cocker was a frequent exhibitor, including Glasgow Garden Festival, New Sculpture in Scotland at Crammond Sculpture Centre and abroad. Had many solo shows, including a key one at Third Eye Centre, Glasgow, 1985. Among later exhibitions were Joan Hughson Gallery, Glasgow, 1996. Arts Council, Scottish Arts Council and several education authorities and universities hold his work. Until the early 1970s this was mainly metal-based, but Cocker then moved towards box constructions including wood and collage elements; from 1985 larger works employing rough logs were assembled, similar to classical architecture. Comments on the current social scene were a feature of the later work. Lived in Aboyne, Aberdeenshire.

Christabel Annie COCKERELL 1863–1951 Painter of children and landscapes. She was a first cousin of Sir Sydney Cockerell, who was director of the Fizwilliam Museum, Cambridge, 1908–37; the wife of the sculptor Sir George Frampton, who like her enrolled at the Royal Academy Schools in 1882; and the mother of the painter Meredith Frampton, who painted a fine portrait of her. She exhibited at RA, New Gallery, ROI, RBA and elsewhere and lived for many years in London.

George COCKRAM 1861–1950 Landscape painter in watercolour, born at Birkenhead, Cheshire. Studied at Liverpool of Art, 1884, then in Paris, 1889. Exhibited RCamA, of which he was a member, especially; also prolifically at RI and Walker Art Gallery, Liverpool, and at RBA and RA. His work is held by public galleries in Oldham, Hull and Birkenhead and the Tate Gallery's example, Solitude – a wide stretch of sand washed by the tide under a grey sky – is typical of this single-minded watercolourist. Lived at Anglesey, North Wales.

Maurice COCKRILL 1936– Painter and teacher, born in Hartlepool, County Durham. He had a peripatetic childhood and after leaving school did a variety of jobs. In the late 1950s he studied painting at evening classes, then in 1960 was accepted by Denbigh Technical College to study painting full-time, attending University of Reading, 1963–4. Taught, including Liverpool College of Art and Liverpool Polytechnic. Took part in group shows including Neptune and Everyman Theatres in Liverpool, Bluecoat Gallery there, Liverpool Academy, Portal Gallery and RCamA. Also showed one-man in Liverpool and in the early 1980s moved to the metropolis, showing at Bernard Jacobson Gallery. Cockrill's Liverpool work was in line with that of such artists as Sam Walsh and Adrian Henri, employing Pop and Photo-Realist styles. Later, he moved towards Romantic Expressionism, as shown in his retrospective at Walker Art Gallery, Liverpool, 1995. Cockrill also published poetry in magazines such as *Ambit* and *Poetry Review*. Elected RA, 1999. In 2002, Belgrave Gallery held a retrospective of Cockrill's paintings from 1978–98, Archeus showing En Plein Air Paintings, 2004.

Bertram H COCKS 1883– Painter, draughtsman and miniaturist on ivory, born in Goring-on-Thames, Oxfordshire. He lived in Reading, Berkshire, and studied at Reading University, 1905–10, with W G Collingwood. Showed at Foyles Gallery, RMS, Mid-Day Studios in Manchester, in the Reading area and in Christchurch, New Zealand.

John Whitlock CODNER 1913– Painter and teacher, born in Beaconsfield, Buckinghamshire, son of the artist Maurice Codner, father of the painter Stephen Codner. He studied at Regent Street Polytechnic School of Art under Harry Watson, 1930–2. Taught at Sir John Cass School of Art, 1947–51. Codner showed at RWA of which he was a member from 1947, also at RA and RP. Had solo shows in London and the west of England, RWA holding his work. Until the death of his father in 1958 Codner signed pictures John Whitlock, thereafter John Codner. Lived in Stokenham, Devon.

Maurice CODNER 1888–1958 Portrait painter, educated at Stationers' Company School. He showed RP, of which he was for a time a member and honorary secretary, RA, RI, NEAC and Paris Salon, where he gained an Honourable Mention in 1938. Imperial War Museum holds his work. Arts Club member who lived in London and was the father of the painter John Codner.

Stephen Milton CODNER 1952– Painter and printmaker, born in Clevedon, Somerset, son of the artist John Codner. He studied at Camberwell School of Arts and Crafts and the City and Guilds of London Art School and showed at RA, RWA and elsewhere. Lived in London.

John CODRINGTON 1898–1991 Watercolourist who was a professional soldier, being a lieutenant-colonel in the Coldstream Guards. The watercolours he did reflected his extensive, compulsive travels as well as battle scenes ranging from the Somme, in 1916, to the Falklands War, in 1981. The enormous output of Coddy, as he was known to fellow-members of the Beefsteak Club, also embraced his love of gardens and garden design. Although he had no solo exhibition when alive, Michael Parkin Gallery staged a memorial show of watercolours 1916–90 in 1992. Lived in London.

John COFFEY 1965– Artist who employed video, born in Belfast, Northern Ireland, who obtained a degree in fine art at Wimbledon School of Art, 1993–6. Exhibitions included Bandits-Mages, Video Festival, Bourges, 1995, and New Contemporaries, at Tate Gallery in Liverpool and Camden Arts Centre, 1996.

Sarah COGHILL 1948– Painter and draughtsman, born in London, who attended Byam Shaw School of Drawing and Painting, 1964–8, then Royal Academy Schools, 1968–71, where in 1969 she won a Special Landseer Prize for four life drawings. Group shows included Frame, Set and Match Gallery, from 1989, The Wingfield Sporting Gallery, from 1991 and Lena Boyle Fine Art from 1992. Among Coghill's two-artist exhibitions were The Knapp Gallery, Regent's College, 1987, and Oriel 31, Davies Memorial Gallery, Newtown, 1989. Later solo shows included The Hoste Arms Gallery, Burnham Market, 1998. Unilever and British and foreign private collections hold examples.

Henry COGLE 1875–1957 Painter, printmaker and teacher, born in Plymouth, Devon. His initial education was at the Devonport Dockyard School, after which he attended Plymouth School of Art. He went on to hold several teaching appointments, being an assistant at Belfast School of Art, then headmaster of Battersea Polytechnic. School of Art until 1936. Showed at RA, LG, Leicester and Redfern Galleries, RHA and elsewhere; had a one-man show at Plymouth Museum and Art Gallery in 1948. That gallery and British Museum hold his work. Lived in Torquay, Devon.

Alfred COHEN 1920–2001 Painter and printmaker, born in America, who studied at the Art Institute of Chicago. In 1929 was awarded a foreign travel scholarship which took him to Europe. He continued studying in Paris at L'Académie de la Grande Chaumière, showing his work in France and Germany. In Paris, Cohen's artistic horizons were widened by friendships such as the American Abstract Expressionist painter Sam Francis, the poet and translator Carlyle F MacIntyre and the actor Anthony Quinn; Cohen knew many famous film and stage actors, directors and producers who bought his work, such as Stanley Baker, James Mason, Sam Wanamaker and Carl Foreman. In 1960 Cohen settled in England and had a long series of shows with Roland, Browse & Delbanco. With his second wife, Diana Snow, Cohen engaged in property development, which led to the creation of The Wighton Schoolhouse Gallery, Norfolk, where Cohen had a studio and where a memorial retrospective was held, with another at London Jewish Cultural Centre, both in 2001, the year The Alfred Cohen Foundation was established. His interiors, still lifes and seascapes had a chunky, richly coloured style. Cohen's work is in many public collections including Contemporary Art Society, Nuffield Foundation, Pembroke College in Oxford and galleries in Rye and Hull, as well as widely abroad.

Bernard COHEN 1933– Painter of abstracts and influential teacher, born in London, where he eventually settled. Brother of the painter Harold Cohen. Studied at South-West Essex Technical College and School of Art, 1949–50, St Martin's School of Art, 1950–1, and Slade School of Fine Art, 1951–4. Awarded a French government scholarship in 1954 and a Boise Travelling Scholarship in 1956 and worked in France, Spain and Italy. Had first solo show at Midland Group Gallery, Nottingham, in 1958, in the same year showing one-man at Gimpel Fils. Contributed to the Situation exhibitions, 1960–1. From the 1960s Cohen began to build up an impressive list of British and foreign exhibition appearances, showing at the Venice Biennale in 1966; having a retrospective at Hayward Gallery in 1972; followed by key appearances in Milan and Paris in the 1970s. For 30 years from 1968 regularly visited New Mexico. In London he showed with Waddington Galleries. Cohen taught for periods at Ealing School of Art, Chelsea and Wimbledon and was Slade professor and chair of fine art, London University, 1988–00. The Tate Gallery and other public collections hold his work which was early on influenced by Abstract Expressionism and later was very colourful and detailed, full of imagery and a variety of texture, as shown in the special 1995 Tate display. There were solo exhibitions at Flowers East from 1998; Flowers West in Santa Monica, California, 1999; and Flowers Central, 2000.

Dave COHEN 1932– Sculptor, ceramics artist and teacher, born in Milwaukee, Wisconsin. He became head of ceramics at Glasgow School of Art after holding a similar position at Edinburgh College of Art. Was active in promoting the Scottish Craft Centre. As early as 1963 Cohen showed at Sacramento Museum Craft Exhibition in America. Arrived in Scotland he showed at 57 Gallery, Edinburgh, British Craft Centre and Carnegie Trust Sculpture Exhibition. Also showed, solo or in groups, at Compass Gallery, Glasgow; Boundary Gallery; and widely overseas.

Harold COHEN 1928– Abstract painter and designer of textiles and furniture, born in London, elder brother of the painter Bernard Cohen. He studied at Slade School of Fine Art, 1948–52, where he also taught, in the latter year winning an Abbey Travelling Scholarship which took him to Italy. He had his first solo show at Ashmolean Museum in Oxford in 1951, followed by a series at Gimpel Fils, the first in 1954. While in America on a Harkness Commonwealth Fellowship, 1959–61, he had a show at Allan Stone Gallery in New York, about the time he was contributing to the Situation exhibitions. There was an important Whitechapel Art Gallery exhibition in 1965. Cohen represented Great Britain in the Venice Biennale, Documenta 3, the Paris Biennale, the Carnegie International and many other important international shows in the 1960s. His interest in computer-created drawings and paintings prompted him to produce a computer-controlled machine. He was author of the AARON program, an ongoing research effort in autonomous machine (art making) intelligence which began when he was a visiting scholar at Stanford University's Artificial Intelligence Lab in 1973. Cohen and AARON showed at Tate, the Brooklyn Museum, the San Francisco Museum of Modern Art, Amsterdam's Stedelijk Museum and more of the world's major art venues. He gave a talk about this work at Tate Modern in 2004. Cohen had a Tate Gallery show in 1983. Arts Council and Tate hold his work.

Isaac Michael COHEN 1884–1951 Portrait painter, born in Ballarat, Victoria, Australia. Studied in Melbourne at National Gallery of Victoria, in 1905 winning a travelling scholarship that took him to further studies in Paris. Exhibited RP, RA, ROI and Walker Art Gallery, Liverpool, exentensively and in Paris at the Salon, where he won gold and silver medals. Williamson Art Gallery and Museum, Birkenhead, and galleries in South Africa and Victoria hold his work. Lived latterly in London.

Mary COHEN 1910– Painter and draughtsman who was born and lived in London. She attended St Felix School, Southwold, and studied in Italy, then went to Slade School of Fine Art, 1928–31, under Henry Tonks and Randolph Schwabe, and several years later the Euston Road School under the direction of Claude Rogers, Victor Pasmore and William Coldstream. Showed at RA, LG, New Grafton Gallery and elsewhere. Whitworth Art Gallery, Manchester, holds her work.

Nathan COHEN 1962– Artist producing deceptively simple paintings and drawings employing lively, hard-edged geometrical shapes in monochrome and a range of colours. Cohen was born and lived in London. He graduated from the Slade School of Fine Art, 1980–4, gaining his master's at Chelsea School of Art, 1984–5. From 1985–92, he was publisher and co-editor of *Constructivist Forum* magazine, being United Kingdom director, Archive 90, International Archive of Abstract & Constructive Art, 1990. Cohen won the Vordemberge-Gildewart Foundation prize, Rapperswil, Switzerland, in 1993; was guest curator, Translations exhibition at Norwich and Reed's Wharf Galleries, 1996; and curator, The Mondriaanhuis/Archive 90 International Reference Collection, in Amersfoort, Netherlands, 2000. Took part in numerous international group exhibitions, showing solo with Annely Juda Fine Art from 1988 and elsewhere abroad. Cardinal Wiseman City Art and Technology College, Leicestershire Education Authority, British and foreign corporate collections and Tokyo Gallery, Tokyo, Japan, hold examples.

Wolfe COHEN: *see* **Wolfe KASSEMOFF**

Ola COHN 1892–1964 Sculptor, teacher and writer, born Carola Cohn in Bendigo, Victoria, Australia. Studied at Bendigo School of Mines, 1909–19, Swinburne Technical College, 1920–5, and in London at the Royal College of Art, 1926–30, where she received much tuition from Henry Moore. Also studied bronze-casting and wood-carving and travelled extensively in Europe. In 1931 she returned to Australia to spread the word about modern sculpture such as that of Moore and Jacob Epstein, but her own work is said to have later become sentimental and folksy. She taught, including the Kindergarten Training College, Melbourne, and her books included *Fairies Tree* and *More about Fairies Tree*. She was in Europe again, 1949–51. In London exhibited RBA, SWA, Leicester Galleries, Redfern Gallery and LG, as well as at Paris Salon and widely in Australia. She won a number of prizes for her work, which is held by public galleries including the National Gallery of South Australia, Adelaide, and the National Gallery of Victoria, Melbourne. Was president of the Melbourne Society of Women Painters and Sculptors, 1948–64, to which she left her Melbourne home as a memorial centre.

Stephen COHN 1931– Sculptor, painter, printmaker, writer and teacher, born in Frankfurt-am-Main, Germany, moving to England with his parents in 1933. Studied at Hammersmith School of Art and the Royal College of Art, after graduating gaining a continuation scholarship to edit the College magazine *Ark*. Worked as a lecturer in art colleges and was acclaimed for his translations of the German poet Rainer Maria Rilke. Exhibitions included Piccadilly Gallery; New Art Centre; Architectural Association; Leicester Art Gallery; Derwent College, York University; Anderson Gallery, Broadway; and The Stour Gallery, Shipston-upon-Stour. Many public and private collections, including the Victoria and Albert Museum, hold examples.

Dorothy COKE 1897–1979 Painter and teacher, born at Southend, who was noted especially for her watercolours. Studied at Slade School of Fine Art under Fred Brown and Henry Tonks, 1914–18. She painted troop scenes during World War I and during World War II was an Official War Artist. Began to teach at Brighton College of Art and settled nearby at Rottingdean, retiring in 1963. Exhibited RA, RWS, NEAC, SWA and elsewhere. Imperial War Museum holds her work which in watercolour has a free, washy, open-air quality.

Peter COKER 1926–2004 Painter, draughtsman, writer, printmaker and teacher, born in London. It was while working at Odhams Press that Coker handled artists' drawings and began studying initially part-time at St Martin's School of Art, full-time, 1947–50, then Royal College of Art, 1950–4, winning a Royal Scholarship in 1951. A British Institution Scholarship followed three years later. From 1954–73 Coker taught at St Martin's School of Art. When he left college Coker became associated with the Kitchen Sink realist painters and had the first of a string of shows at Zwemmer Gallery in 1956. In 1962 he participated in the Arts Council touring exhibition British Painting 1950–7, in 1966 in another Arts Council show, Painters in East Anglia. By then his attention had been diverted from the early butcher's shop subject, which shocked many people, to landscape, which remained his preoccupation. Structure, texture and movement were key features of Coker's analysis of the world around him. He showed regularly with Thackeray Gallery for many years. In 1972 he was elected RA, the year of his retrospective at The Minories, Colchester; a further followed at Chelmsford and Essex Museum in 1978; in 1979 the butcher's shop series was featured in a retrospective in Liverpool plus tour; and in 1992 a retrospective of landscapes toured from Abbot Hall, Kendal. Coker had suffered two heart attacks and a serious stroke in 1990, tried for a couple of years to continue painting, but eventually had to give up both art and the travel he loved. In 2001, in a wheelchair, he visited Paris and began working seriously again. The outcome was exhilarating, energetic and often abstracted oils, drawings, etchings and lithographs stemming from "an explosion of pent-up creativity that, since my stroke in 1990, I had not thought would be possible." His career was further revived with a major retrospective at Chris Beetles Ltd in 2002. In 2003, the privately printed *Peter Coker RA New Work 2002* appeared, accompanying an exhibition at Gainsborough's House, Sudbury. Recent works were shown at RA Friends Room, 2004, when there was another Beetles show of 2002–3 pictures. Peter Coker RA: A Juxtaposition 2004 was at Graves Art Gallery, Sheffield, in 2004–5, and in 2005 Piano Nobile Fine Paintings held a retrospective. In 1976 Coker published *Etching Techniques*. Sheffield City Art Galleries is one of several provincial galleries holding his work. Lived in Mistley, Essex.

Colin COLAHAN 1897–1987 Painter, noted for his portraits, latterly also a sculptor, born into well-to-do family in Woodend, Victoria, Australia. He studied medicine at the University in Melbourne, 1915–16, then art at Max Meldrum School there, 1916–19 (in 1917 publishing *Max Meldrum, His Art and Views*), also in London and Paris. Colahan was a founder-member of the Australian Academy of Art. Moved to London between the wars and was an Official War Artist with the Australian forces from 1942. As well as exhibiting at the RA, ROI, elsewhere in England and at the Paris Salon, Colahan also showed with the Australian Artists' Association, of which he was president, formed in London in 1951. He lived in Whistler's house in Tite Street, where the Association met. By this time the monocled Colahan was well established in England, but in the mid-1960s with his wife Ursula Marks (of the Marks & Spencer chain store family), he moved to the Riviera and died in Menton. He is well represented in Australian public collections.

Anthony COLBERT 1934– Versatile artist, illustrator and teacher, working in oil, acrylic and watercolour, born in Newport, Isle of Wight. Attended West Sussex College of Arts and Crafts, Worthing, 1949; while doing National Service in the Army studied at Farnham Art School. After three years' agency and studio work Colbert was staff artist on *The Observer* for eight years. In 1967 he went to South Vietnam for the Save the Children Fund, resulting works being shown at AIA Gallery that year. In 1968 Colbert became a freelance illustrator. Work included illustrations for the national press, advertising, magazines and billboard hoardings, clients including Penguin Books, *The Times Educational Supplement*, *Nova*, BBC and The Folio Society. He wrote and illustrated two children's books: *Amanda Has a Surprise*, 1971, and *Amanda Goes Dancing*, 1972. For 20 years Colbert lectured part-time at Camberwell, Brighton, Exeter and other art colleges/polytechnics, and was an external assessor at Goldsmiths' for three years. Was a member of the Association of Illustrators. Took up landscape painting in 1986 and held solo shows annually at The Little Gallery, Arundel; the Old Chapel Gallery, Pembridge; and Penrhos Court, Kington. From 1988 lived at Staunton-on-Arrow, Herefordshire.

Lilian Victoria Epworth COLBOURN 1897–1967 Figurative painter, using a rich palette to produce strong and gestural works. She was born Victoria Proctor in Epworth, Lincolnshire, into a nonconformist background, marrying Richard Colbourn, an engineer, in 1922. From then for some years lived at Radcliffe, Manchester. Studied painting and drawing under Joseph Knight at Bury School of Art and had lessons from Emmanuel Levy. Began to exhibit widely at group shows in Preston, Manchester and Liverpool and with BWS, of which she was elected an associate in 1923. For a time she wrote reviews of local and national exhibitions for the *Bury Times*. When her marriage to Colbourn broke down she married Joseph Wilson and lived for a time in Guildford, early in the 1940s settling with him and their daughters in Staithes, Yorkshire, a popular venue for artists. Her oil Fisherwomen, Staithes, was shown at the Paris Salon, 1947. In the 1940s and 1950s Colbourn was critically acclaimed, Eric Newton in *The Listener* in 1953 terming her "passionate, lyrical, utterly sincere – determined to express her turbulent vision with the utmost directness – she has the promise of greatness". Colbourn's work would be exhibited alongside that of Gillian Ayres, Terry Frost, Barbara Hepworth and Henry Moore; the Mayor and Hanover Galleries showed her pictures; she had had a one-man show at Wertheim Gallery in 1937, adding four solo exhibitions at Berkeley Galleries, 1951–66, and one at Stone Gallery, Newcastle upon Tyne, 1960. After her death in Staithes there were memorial shows at Austen Hayes Gallery, York, 1968, and Billingham Art Gallery, 1969. In 1998, Lilian Colbourn, A Turbulent Vision, toured from Myles Meehan Gallery, Darlington Arts Centre. Messum's held an exhibition in 2004 with a comprehensive catalogue.

William COLDSTREAM 1908–1987 Painter of portraits, landscape and still life and influential teacher. He was born at Belford, Northumberland, then studied at the Slade School 1926–9, being awarded Slade Scholarship in 1927. In the 1920s and 1930s he became friendly with the poet W H Auden and the painters Victor Pasmore, Claude Rogers and Walter Sickert. He worked on documentary films with the GPO Film Unit 1934–7, collaborating on one with Auden. In 1938 he participated briefly with the painter Graham Bell in Mass Observation. Was a founder with Rogers and Pasmore of the Euston Road School of Drawing and Painting, later becoming an Official War Artist in the Middle East and Italy. From 1945–9 he was a visiting teacher at Camberwell School of Art, becoming Slade Professor of Fine Art 1949–75. *The Coldstream Report*, which stemmed from his chairmanship of the National Advisory Council on Art Education 1959–60, was of key importance. Among his official positions were those of trustee of both the Tate and National Galleries. Work in many public collections, including the Tate Gallery which gave him a retrospective show in 1990–1. Coldstream's work was based on a system of painstaking measurement, which meant that a portrait could take 60 sittings, with small, red registration marks often left visible on the finished picture. Was knighted in 1956. Lived in London. Coldstream's first wife was the painter Nancy Sharp.

Andy COLE 1960– Cole attended the Slade School of Fine Art, 1982–4, in the latter year gaining a Boise Award and Scholarship and taking part in Pick of the Graduates, Christie's Inaugural Show. Other group appearances included Universiade, Kobe, Japan, 1985; Quadroons Wraith: Vanitas Series, Sherkat Gallery, New York, America, 1987; and East End Open Studios, at Deborah House, 1989. In 1988, Cole had a solo show at Bloomsbury Theatre Gallery.

Elsie Vera COLE 1885–1968 Painter, printmaker and teacher, born in Braintree, Essex. Educated in Gravesend, Kent, she studied art at Norwich School of Art, 1908–10, then at Chelmsford School of Art, 1911–19, under Charles Baskett. For roughly 20 years she taught at Norwich School of Art, starting just after World War I. Showed at RI, SWA and with the Norfolk and Norwich Art Circle, to which she belonged, being noted for her drawings of Norwich, where she lived.

Ernest COLE 1890–1980 Sculptor, draughtsman and teacher. Born at Greenwich, Cole studied at Goldsmiths' College School of Art and went on to become professor of sculpture at Royal College of Art in 1924–6. He was discovered at the age of sixteen and a half by Charles Ricketts and Selwyn Image when examining at the Royal College of Art. He had a prodigious talent, being compared to Alfred Stevens. Ricketts bought drawings which later went to Fitzwilliam Museum, Cambridge. Cole was commissioned to sculpt two large groups for the London County Council building; many other drawings were bought by collectors for high prices. Commissioned during World War I in the Army, Cole was sent on a mission to America where he met his artist wife, Laurie, who predeceased him by about 10 years. His career did not live up to its early promise. When after the war he was converted, as Ricketts said, to "modern art nonsense" Cole lost contact with the collector, who had hoped he would acquire an international reputation as an apostle of classical art. Lived at Kingston, near Canterbury, Kent.

Joe COLE 1920–1984 Teacher and painter who was especially interested in depicting people engaged in a particular activity, the images being simplified into angular shapes. Cole studied at Scarborough School of Art, volunteered for the Royal Air Force at the start of World War II and served in camouflage. During the second wave of the D-Day landings he made vigorous sketches in pen and watercolour, and these with extracts from his diaries formed the basis of his posthumously published book *Road to the Front: Joe Cole's Experience of War*, 1994. After the war, Cole finished his studies at Scarborough, became a lecturer at Middlesbrough College of Art and inspired Peter Sarginson, Len Tabner, William Tillyer and Peter Hicks. His work was included with theirs in Messum's 2005 exhibition The Elemental North. Although Cole participated in Young Contemporaries and Yorkshire shows, he was a diffident exhibitor, terming himself "a background man".

John COLE 1903–1975 Painter in oil and stained glass artist. Born in London, Cole was the son of the artist Rex Vicat Cole. John Cole is most noted for his unsentimental depictions of London shop fronts, often quaint and old-fashioned. He exhibited widely, including the RA, NEAC, RBA, in the provinces and at the Paris Salon, where he won a silver medal in 1952 and a gold medal two years later. His work was widely reproduced, by the Medici Society and others. He held official positions with a number of artistic bodies, such as the Campden Hill Club and the St James' Art Society, of both of which he was chairman. Pictures in public galleries in Britain and abroad, including Hastings Public Museum and Art Gallery, Sussex. Lived in London.

Jonathan COLE 1962– Painter whose output included abstracts such as Untitled, in Royal Over-Seas League Open, 1994. Born in Fareham, Hampshire, he studied at Bristol Polytechnic; École des Beaux-Arts, Marseilles; and Royal Academy Schools. Group shows included Ten Young Artists, Mall Galleries, 1988, and Camden Film Co-operative, 1993. Had a solo exhibition at Earl's Court Gallery, 1991, and Riviera Art Gallery, Hastings, 1994.

Laurie COLE 1890–c.1970 Sculptor, painter, printmaker and artist in black-and-white. Born in New York, she had a distinguished academic career before settling in England, having studied at Columbia University and become a doctor of jurisprudence. Studied art in France and Germany, then with her husband, the sculptor Ernest Cole, with whom she settled near Canterbury, Kent. Exhibited RA, Royal Glasgow Institute of the Fine Arts, Paris Salon and at Columbia University in 1947.

Leslie COLE 1910–1976 Painter and teacher, studied at Swindon School of Art with Harold Dearden, 1927–32; at Birmingham College of Art, 1932–3, with Harold Holden; then Royal College of Art, 1934–7, with Malcolm Osborne and Ernest Tristram. Exhibited RA, RP and widely abroad. Cole was a notable war artist, working for the Ministry of Information in Malta, then for the Admiralty and War Office. For some time he taught at the Central School of Arts and Crafts. Imperial War Museum and Ferens Art Gallery, Hull, hold his work, which is reproduced widely in anthologies of pictures by war artists. In 1985–6 the War Museum staged an exhibition of Cole's World War II pictures called To the Front Line. Lived in London.

Philip William COLE 1884–1964 Painter, stained glass artist and metalworker, born at St Leonards-on-Sea, Sussex. After attending King's College, London, Cole went to Hastings School of Art and the Royal College of Art, 1909–13. He exhibited RA, RBA, Paris Salon and provincial galleries. Was a member of the Art Workers' Guild. Viscount Montgomery and Sir Winston Churchill were among recipients of silver presentation caskets made by Cole, who also completed a number of memorials and stained glass windows in East Sussex churches, notably at East Dean and Bexhill. Lived at Fairlight, Sussex.

Richard COLE 1942– Versatile cartoonist, caricaturist, illustrator and artist in various media, born in Wimbledon, Surrey, son of an ecclesiastical wood-carver. After training at Wimbledon School of Art and Brighton College of Art, Cole established a reputation over several decades with his work for *The Daily* and *Sunday Telegraph* and *The Guardian* in which "there is always an element of exaggeration and distortion". Meanwhile, he continued to produce paintings, wood sculptures and prints, notably inspired by his love of the village and characters of St Geoire-en-Valdaine, in the Chartreuse region of France. Mixed shows included Chris Beetles Ltd and Anna-Mei Chadwick. Cole had solo shows at Heffer Gallery, Cambridge, 1981 and 1982, and Edwin Pollard Gallery, 1989. British Museum; Karikatur Cartoon Museum, Basel, Switzerland; and corporate collections hold examples.

Richard COLE 1952– Sculptor and teacher whose work was inspired by the English northern landscape. He was born in Kent and studied at Newcastle University. He was a visiting lecturer at various places including the Royal College of Art, eventually lecturing in sculpture at Humberside College of Higher Education. Participated in many group shows, including Northern Young Contemporaries at Whitworth Art Gallery Manchester, 1975–7; Moira Kelly Gallery, 1982; Open Air Sculpture Exhibition, Hull and Lincoln Castle, 1986; and the Newcastle Group show The Northern Lights at DLI Museum & Arts Centre, Durham, and tour, 1990. Later solo shows included Bondgate Gallery, Alnwick, 1986. Completed big outdoor sculpture commissions including Windy Nook, Gateshead, Wakefield District Council, 1989, and National Garden Festival, Gateshead, 1990. Lived in Gateshead, Tyne and Wear.

Robert COLE 1964– Sculptor who studied at Thurrock Technical College, 1981–3, then Wimbledon School of Art, 1983–6. From 1986 participated in various group exhibitions. In 1992 took part in British Contemporary Drawing & Print at Isis Gallery, Leigh-on-Sea, and in 1993 in Drawing Towards Sculpture at same venue.

Wally COLE 1913–1999 Potter, sculptor and teacher, born in London, full name Walter Vivian Cole. He obtained one of the few Special Talent Scholarships at 16, studying initially at Woolwich Polytechnic, moving to Central School of Arts and Crafts in 1931 where the sculptor John Skeaping was an influence. In the 1930s he showed sculpture, stoneware pots and drawings, becoming a member of the Arts and Crafts Exhibition Society and of NS and worked on commissions for major clients such as the London Zoo and on big architectural carvings for Eric Kennington. After World War II service, commissioned in the Royal Engineers and specialising in camouflage, from 1946–7 Cole was on the staff of the Council for Industrial Design; he worked on the 1946 Victoria & Albert Museum show Britain Can Make It; and taught on the first industrial design course at Central School. With his brother John he had set up a kiln in the 1930s and in 1947 they reopened the Bellue Vue Pottery in Rye, Sussex, as Rye Pottery. In the late 1950s Wally helped set up the potters' co-operative the Craftsmen Potters' Association, with a shop and gallery in London. Cole handed over Rye Pottery to his son Tarquin in 1978, then concentrated more on sculpture, showing classical and abstract influences. There was an eightieth-birthday retrospective at Rye Art Gallery and in London in 1993. Died in St Leonards-on-Sea, Sussex.

Yvonne COLE 1953– Artist, born in Surrey, who attended Kingston College of Art, 1971–5. Had a first solo exhibition with Thumb Gallery in 1980. Other solo and group shows included Open Eye Gallery, Edinburgh; King Street Gallery, Bristol; Collins Gallery, Glasgow; Andrew Knight and Albany Galleries, Cardiff; Gordon Hepworth Fine Art, Newton St Cyres; and America and Sweden. Cole completed a limited-edition print for the television company ITV. She latterly worked in Devon, where her work was based on the field paths and gateways around the coastal area of Ladram Bay, between Exmouth and Sidmouth. Graves Art Gallery, Sheffield; Chelsea and Westminster, Hammersmith and Dorset Hospitals; *The Economist*; and several corporate collections hold works.

Deanne COLEBORN 1931– Painter and etcher, born in Stourbridge, where she attended the School of Art, later the Royal College of Art. She was the second wife of the painter Keith Coleborn. Originally a glass designer, she then moved to etching and painting, showing at RA, RWA and RE in group exhibitions, one-man shows including Greenwich and Lyric Theatre Galleries and Woodlands Gallery. Member of the Greenwich Printmakers, which gave her solo exhibitions in 1999 and 2002, RE and Printmakers' Guild. Lived at Downe, Kent.

Freda M COLEBORN 1911–1965 Painter, designer, embroiderer and teacher. Born in India, she was married to the artist Keith Coleborn. Studied at Royal College of Art. Signing her work F M C, she exhibited at the RA and in many international shows, being noted for her glass designs. Lived at Downe, Kent.

Keith COLEBORN 1909– Painter, printmaker, stained and engraved glass-maker and teacher, born in Portsmouth, Hampshire. Was married to two artists: Freda Coleborn, then Deanne Coleborn. Studied at Royal College of Art, his teachers including Edward Bawden, Eric Ravilious and Reco Capey. Held a number of teaching posts from 1935 at Stourbridge and Wallasey, finally being principal of Bromley/Ravensbourne College of Art, 1946–75. Was involved in work for university-level recognition of art training. Showed widely, including RA, and internationally. Lived in Downe, Kent.

Alan COLEMAN 1920–1998 Sculptor and teacher, born in Croydon, Surrey, who studied at Goldsmiths' College School of Art and Royal College of Art, where he passed first-class in 1951. In 1952 he was elected to RBA, in 1961 a fellow of RBS. Died after a brief illness. Lived for many years at Wonersh, Surrey.

Alannah COLEMAN 1918–1998 Gallery director, critic, collector and painter, born in Melbourne, Australia, who attended National Gallery of Victoria School for five years in the 1930s, then worked as an artist through the 1940s. She played an energetic role in founding the Contemporary Art Society in Melbourne and promoting art generally. In 1950 she settled in London, painting for a while but becoming increasingly a dealer for fellow artists. This was an intensive period for her, helping to promote such painters as Charles Blackman, Arthur Boyd, Lawrence Daws, Russell Drysdale, Sydney Nolan and Brett Whiteley. The Australian government asked her to act as commissioner-general to the Paris Biennale for Young Painters, 1963. In 1964, she reactivated Heal's Mansard Gallery, with shows of Australian and British artists, from 1970–1 returning to Australia to present distinguished shows at the Bonython Gallery, Sydney. Back in London, she organised exhibitions at the Qantas and New South Wales House galleries. Coleman wrote occasional articles on contemporary art and artists for London publications and was invited to become a member of the International Association of Art Critics. She was an indefatigable attender of private views and such events as the Venice Biennale. Coleman's advice and opinions were sought by museums in Britain and Australia and her easy friendliness and unstuffiness made her many friends in the art trade. She bred Cornish Rex cats, on which she was an expert of show-judge calibre.

Katarzyna COLEMAN 1954– Painter, draughtsman, printmaker and teacher, born in the East End of London, who did foundation studies at Wimbledon College of Art, 1978–9; graduated in fine art, Hornsey College of Art (Middlesex University), 1979–82; gained her master's in printmaking in Manchester, 1982–3; and her teacher's certificate for further and adult education, City & Guilds, 1988–9. She was a part-time lecturer in art and design at Great Yarmouth College, 1991–5; full-time lecturer and course leader there, Edexcel Diploma, Foundation art and design, 1995–02; and from 2003 part-time project co-ordinator for the SeaChange Trust arts orgnisation in Great Yarmouth. Coleman was artist-in residence, Ferry House, Great Yarmouth harbour, 2003; for the Port Authority there, from 2004; and in that year in Gorlice, Poland. Participated in group shows in Britain and on the continent, including Factory Fringe, Bally Shoe Factory, Norwich, 2003, and Warehouse Gallery, Lowestoft, 2004.

Solo exhibitions included Sentinels, SeaChange Gallery, Great Yarmouth, 2003; and in 2004 Wembley Point Foyer in Wembley, and New Cut, Halesworth. Coleman said of her work that it was "predominantly made in response to industrial and urban landscape. Although the source is always observational, these landscapes are a personal meditation, bound up with memories, hopes and fears." Lived in Gorleston-on-Sea, Norfolk.

Trevor COLEMAN 1936– Artist in a wide range of styles and media, photographer, potter, teacher and editor, born in Johannesburg, South Africa. His early studies included chemistry and geology. Attended Witwatersrand Technical College, 1958–60. Decided to concentrate on art as a career and when in London, 1961–5, attended Central School of Arts and Crafts part-time. On returning to Johannesburg taught at the Visual Arts Research Centre, 1966, and privately. He also ran the Trevor Coleman Gallery, 1977–85, and edited *Gallery* magazine, 1981–3. Was a leading member of the South African Association of Arts. Coleman was keenly interested in archaeology, geology, anthropology and African art. He travelled extensively in Africa and abroad, reflected in colourful, hard-edge pictures. Showed widely in group and solo exhibitions in South Africa. In England Coleman was a member of Hampstead Artists' Council, showed in mixed exhibitions at Grosvenor and Whitechapel Arts Galleries, 1964, and with Nicholas Treadwell Gallery, 1965. Had a series of solo shows, including Morocco, The Gallery in Cork Street, 2000, which followed a decade of working with a palette knife. Victoria & Albert Museum print room, Johannesburg Art Gallery, University of the Witwatersrand and other South African collections hold examples. Lived in Johannesburg.

Nathan COLEY 1967– Artist using photography and wall pieces, as in New Art in Scotland, at Centre for Contemporary Arts, Glasgow, 1994. For these, he said that "the reality of images, their authenticity and the cultural trust we place in them, is a point of entry". Coley was born and lived in Glasgow, where he gained a fine art honours degree, 1985–9. Other mixed shows included Festival of Plagiarism, Transmission Gallery, Glasgow, 1989; Love at First Sight, The Showroom, 1992; Swarm, Scottish Arts Council Travelling Gallery, 1995; A Scottish Collection, Berwick Gymnasium Gallery, Berwick, 1997; Correspondences, Scottish National Gallery of Modern Art, Edinburgh, 1997–8; and Days Like These, Tate Britain, 2003. Coley was commissioned to work on the refurbishment of Stills Gallery's Edinburgh premises, 1996–7, from which stemmed *Urban Sanctuary*, a book and solo exhibition at IPA, Edinburgh. Religious architecture was an obsession of Coley's. He produced pieces in response to everywhere from Portugal's Torre de Belém to the 161 places of worship listed in Birmingham's *Yellow Pages*. In 2003 he showed a first site-specific work for consecrated ground: Black Tent, made of coloured panels, strung together to resemble the *Old Testament*, displayed in Portsmouth Cathedral. A career survey with new work was held at Fruitmarket Gallery, Edinburgh, in 2004, Haunch of Venison holding a show in 2005.

Grace Marion COLLCUTT 1875–1954 Landscape painter, daughter of the architect Thomas Edward Collcutt, among whose buildings were London's Savoy Hotel and the Imperial Institute. She studied at Richmond School of Art and the Slade School of Fine Art, and exhibited at the RA, Abbey, Baillie and Goupil Galleries, Walker Art Gallery in Liverpool, SWA and elsewhere. Settled in Brighton, Sussex, where the Museum and Art Gallery holds local views in watercolour by her.

Henry COLLER 1886–1958 Magazine illustrator in line and wash. Born in Wood Green, London, he studied art at Manchester School of Art. Went on to work prolifically for many publications, including *Wide World*, *John Bull* and *My Home*, as well as drawing for advertisements. Lived in London.

Dorothy COLLES 1917–2003 Artist in oil, pastel and pencil, notable for portraits, mainly of children. She was born in Cairo, Egypt, and studied at the Westminster School of Art before World War II with John Farleigh, Bernard Meninsky and Mark Gertler. Between 1940–5 served in the Women's Auxiliary Air Force in the United Kingdom and the Middle East. After hostilities, she worked in Egypt for the Egypt Exploration Society and for the Jordanian government before returning to London, after which she freelanced. She said that pastelists such as Chardin, Degas, La Tour and Angelica Kaufmann and the draughtsmen Augustus John, Rubens and Ingres were influences. Colles was a member of PS, also exhibiting at RP and RA. In 1962 she had a solo show at Leighton House. She wrote *Portraying Children*, 1953, and in 1971 published *Christian Symbols Ancient & Modern* with Heather Child, the artist and calligrapher, who was a lifelong companion. They lived at Petersfield, Hampshire.

Ruth COLLET 1909–2001 Painter, printmaker and illustrator, born in Barley, Hertfordshire. After Bedales School she studied at Slade School of Fine Art, where her teachers included Philip Wilson Steer, Henry Tonks and Franklin White. Collet also studied with S W Hayter, in Paris, and in London with Kathleen Browne and Marian Kratochwil. Her husband was the musician and musical historian Robert Collet and before marriage, when associated with the East London Group, she exhibited under her maiden name, Ruth Salaman, one of a talented family of artists. She showed extensively at Goupil Gallery, RA, WIAC, NEAC, LG, Leicester Galleries and Gainsborough's House, Sudbury, and was a member of Hesketh Hubbard Art Society. Did a number of book-jacket illustrations and hundreds of lino-cuts for Westminster Synagogue. Israeli Embassy and Ben Uri Art Society hold her work, "which was influenced by Dürer, Van Gogh and Rembrandt." Later solo exhibitions included Sue Rankin Gallery, Sternberg Centre for Judaism and Moss Galleries, 1991. There was a memorial show at Broughton House Gallery, Cambridge, 2003. Lived for many years at Northwood, Middlesex.

Reuben COLLEY 1976– Atmospheric landscape painter, born in Sutton Coldfield, Warwickshire. He showed outstanding ability at school before studying for his fine art diploma at Bournville Art College, 1994–5, gaining an honours degree at University of Wolverhampton, 1998. Worked as a framer for Halcyon Gallery, Birmingham, and was featured in its 1999 Art In Miniature exhibition, having earlier that year had a solo exhibition at Circo, Birmingham. Also in 1999 had three pictures produced as silkscreen prints by Washington Green. In 2000 exhibited in a Smirnoff-sponsored exhibition in Manchester.

William Frederick COLLEY 1907–1957 Birmingham-based painter, printmaker and teacher who taught art and design at the city's College of Art. He came into prominence in the 1930s and 1940s, undertaking murals (including a commission for the Federation of British Industrialists in Birmingham) and exhibiting his watercolours and lithographs at the RBSA of which he was a member, RA, NEAC and Redfern Gallery. The discovery of a body of Colley's work prompted an exhibition of his lithographs at the 20th Century Gallery, 1997. The prints, often large, occasionally in colour, indicated his strong interest in the decorative and bizarre and the industrial and leisure activities of Midlands people.

Duda COLLIE-KOLIBABKA fl. from 1960s– Artist who studied painting in London under Professor Marian Bohusz-Szyskzko, at St Martin's School of Art and at Sir John Cass School of Art. Group exhibitions included NS; Hesketh Hubbard Art Society; Hampstead Artists' Council; Trends, Free Painters and Sculptors, of which Collie-Kolibabka was a member; Polish Painters' Association, at POSK; Alpine Gallery; and elsewhere. Among solo shows were Polish Young Men's Christian Association, Royal Free Hospital, 1970; City of Bydgoszcz Modern Art Gallery, Poland, 1973; Loggia Gallery, 1977; and Polish Young Men's Christian Association, Edinburgh, 1978. Collie-Kolibabka's work was held in many European private collections.

Brian COLLIER 1945– Painter and draughtsman, born in Bolton, Lancashire. He studied at the College of Art and Design there, 1960–5, teachers including Tony Bates; at Brighton College of Art, 1965–6, with Jennifer Dickson; Atelier 17 in Paris, 1967, with Stanley William Hayter; then as a Rome Scholar at British School in Rome, 1966–8. Showed at RA, Hayward Gallery, Air Gallery, Serpentine Gallery and elsewhere. Victoria & Albert Museum holds his work. Lived for some time in Hove, Sussex.

Graham COLLIER 1923– Painter, full name Alan Graham Collier, and teacher; born in Manchester. Initially educated in Lancashire and Yorkshire, he studied art at Lincoln School of Art, 1940–2, Newark School of Art, 1942–4, and the Slade School of Fine Art, 1944, with Randolph Schwabe. He went on to hold a number of teaching posts in Yorkshire, then in 1954 became art director at Lancing College, Sussex. Showed LG, at the Leeds and Bradford public galleries and elsewhere. In the late 1940s he was art correspondent for the *Yorkshire Evening Press*. Painted a number of musicians' portraits, including the official Hallé portrait of Sir John Barbirolli, the orchestra's conductor. Chelsea Arts Club member.

June COLLIER 1943– Painter and teacher who studied at the Slade School of Fine Art, 1961–5, gaining a French government scholarship in painting in the latter year. From 1965–79 taught at Byam Shaw, Camberwell, Canterbury, Falmouth, Gloucestershire, Liverpool, St Martin's and Wimbledon Schools of Art. In 1979–80 she spent nine months at the Shree Rajneesh Ashram, India. Was included in Contemporary Artists in Camden at Camden Arts Centre, 1981.

Niki COLLIER 1963– Artist who graduated with honours from Camberwell School of Arts and Crafts, 1984–7. She took part in the Thames & Hudson Book Prize Exhibition at South London Art Gallery, 1985; Leicestershire County Education Authority Painting Exhibition, 1988; and Women's Eye at Lauderdale House, Highgate, and East End Open Studios, at Carpenter's Road, both 1989. In that year, Collier also had a solo exhibition at Everyman Cinema, Hampstead.

Stephen COLLINGBOURNE 1943– Sculptor and teacher, born in Dartington, Devon, where he attended Dartington Hall School, 1948–60, and Dartington College of Art, 1960–1. Was at Bath Academy of Art, Corsham, 1961–4. After teaching at a comprehensive school in Oxford, lectured from 1965–70 at Dartington College of Art. Then did a foundry course at Royal College of Art, 1970; worked at the Serpentine Gallery, 1971; was assistant to the sculptor Robert Adams, 1972; lived and worked in Malaysia, 1972–3; was fellow in sculpture at University College of Wales, 1974; then was appointed lecturer in sculpture at Edinburgh College of Art, 1976. As well as extensive mixed show appearances, Collingbourne had a series of solo shows, starting with Dartington Hall, 1968, later ones including MacRobert Arts Centre, Stirling University, 1979. Commissions included Leicester University Library, 1974, and Royal Mile, Edinburgh, 1983. Scottish and Welsh Arts Councils hold his work. Although early on a painter, Collingbourne said that from 1988 "I have spent most of my time working in two dimensions on paper." He was "not interested in instant impact, but in making sculpture which is capable of changing visual experience and has a timeless quality." Lived in West Linton, Peebleshire.

Anthony COLLINGE 1934– Painter of abstracts and lecturer, born in Cheshire, who studied at Liverpool College of Art under Arthur Ballard and George Mayer-Marton, and at the Slade School of Fine Art under Claude Rogers, Anthony Gross, Ceri Richards and Robert Medley. While at Liverpool was awarded the Blond Travelling Scholarship, visiting Italy, staying at the British School at Rome. Taught at Canterbury College of Art and London College of Printing, then from 1963–96 at Goldsmiths' College School of Art, being head of art education, 1976–85, colleagues including Anton Ehrenzweig and Harry and Elma Thubron. Tony Collinge's exhibitions included LG 75th Anniversary, RCA, 1988; joint show with Elma Thubron, Storey Institute Gallery, Lancaster, 1994; solo exhibition at Woodlands Art Gallery, 1995; and Museum of Installation, 1997. That museum, Arts Council and Goldsmiths' hold examples. Lived in London and Benhall, Saxmundham, Suffolk.

Albert Henry COLLINGS 1867–1947 Prolific and versatile painter, born and lived in London, where he studied. He was a member of RI and RBA, also exhibiting at RA, Fine Art Society and ROI. Won a Gold Medal at Paris Salon, 1907. He did commissioned work for Portsmouth Town Hall and completed portraits of HRH The Prince of Wales. His death was recorded in the Chapel-en-le-Frith area of Derbyshire.

Dahl COLLINGS 1909–1988 Versatile artist, designer, film director and illustrator, born in Adelaide, South Australia, who studied for six years at East Sydney Technical College art school with Raynor Hoff; won two annual drawing scholarships; then spent two years painting at Watkins Studio. In 1933 the year she married Geoffrey Collings the documentary film-maker and designer, she worked as an illustrator and designed covers for Sidney Ure Smith's *Home* magazine. From 1935–8 Collings was based in London, on the continent and in Tahiti, engaged in painting, graphics, constructions, photography and film; working with Modernist artists including László Moholy-Nagy; absorbing the influences of movements such as Surrealism and Constructivism; completing murals at trade fairs in London and Milan; and drawing for *Vogue* and *Harper's Bazaar*. From 1938–50, in Sydney, she was a foundation member of the Contemporary Art Society in New South Wales, the MARS Group and of the Design Centre (with her husband and Haughton James); designed costumes for the Ealing Studios films *The Overlanders*, 1946, and *Eureka Stockade*, 1948; and painted for the London magazine *Lilliput*. In 1950–3, based in New York, Collings was consultant designer for the Australian Trade Commission and the Rockefeller Center and drew for *Harper's Magazine*. Back in Sydney, 1954–71, Collings' output included mural work for the Accountants' Club and direction of Qantas Art Films. From 1971, she painted full-time. As well was taking part in group shows internationally, her solo exhibitions included Bonython Galleries, Sydney, 1976; Holdsworth Galleries, Sydney, 1977; and City of Hamilton Art Gallery, Hamilton, Victoria, 1982. Corporate, institutional and private collections in Australia, Britain, America and Canada hold examples.

David COLLINGS 1949– Painter and teacher who studied at Redruth School of Art, 1965–9, then Berkshire College of Education, 1969–72. He lived in Newlyn, Cornwall, and showed with Newlyn Society of Artists of which he was a member, in southwest of England and abroad. Contemporary Art Society holds his work.

Denis COLLINGS 1934–2000 Heraldic artist, calligrapher and illuminator whose death ended a century-long family tradition in royal palaces, notably with St George's Hall, Windsor, and the Palace of Westminster. Ernest Charles Collings, Herald Painter by Royal Appointment, was succeeded by his son Percy, then in 1968 by his son, Denis. The disastrous fire at St George's Hall in 1992 destroyed the trio's work, although the extensive scheme of armorial decorations in the Dean's Library, Windsor, completed by the Collings family remained intact. Born at New Barnet, north London, Denis served a 12-year apprenticeship under his father. He was responsible for a number of Order of the Garter banners and was appointed Calligrapher to the Queen in 1986. Much of Collings' spare time was given to the Order of St John, of which he became a Knight of Grace in 1994. He had been heraldic artist to the Order since 1968, also holding the office of Great Banner Bearer.

Kennedy COLLINGS: *see* **BLACK DOG OF WELLS**

Dora COLLINGWOOD: *see* **Dora ALTOUNYAN**

Anthony COLLINS 1944– Painter, born in Dublin, Ireland, where he eventually returned to work. Participated in many group shows and early had two solo exhibitions. From 1980–90 he helped establish Austin/Desmond Fine Art. In 1991 studied at Cyprus College of Art in Paphos, showing resulting work at Jonathan Cooper, 1993. Collins said of his method: "I like to use photographs instead of preliminary drawings ... The scene shot in an instant faster than the eye can recall."

Cecil COLLINS 1908–1989 Figure, landscape but essentially visionary painter in oil, pastel, watercolour and gouache, printmaker and draughtsman, Collins is one of the notable individual figures not uncommon in British art. Born in Plymouth, Devon, Collins won a scholarship while at the Plymouth School of Art which took him to the Royal College of Art in 1927–31. Shortly after leaving the College Collins married Elisabeth Ramsden, also an artist, an important influence on his work. She appeared in his pictures throughout his career. Collins had his first one-man show at the Bloomsbury Gallery in 1935 and in the following year took part in the International Surrealist Exhibition. At Dartington Hall he met the American artist Mark Tobey who fostered his interest in Far Eastern art and philosophy. From 1951 taught at the Central School of Arts and Crafts for many years, where his influence was outstanding. In 1947 Collins published *The Vision of the Fool*, the Fool being a recurrent image in his pictures. Designed tapestries and the Icon of Divine Light, for Chichester Cathedral. Many one-man exhibitions, including a major retrospective at the Tate Gallery in 1989 and a commemorative exhibition in 1995. Aberdeen Art Gallery showed selection of Collins' work allocated to it in 2001–2. Tate and other important collections hold examples. Lived in London.

Elisabeth COLLINS 1904–2000 Painter and sculptor, brought up in Yorkshire. Her family owned the *Halifax Courier and Guardian* of which her father was editor. She studied sculpture at Leeds School of Art, then with Henry Moore at Royal College of Art. There she met her husband the artist Cecil Collins, and they were married shortly after leaving, in 1931. She originally exhibited at SWA under her maiden name of Ramsden. After marriage the opportunity to pursue her own work was curtailed, as she helped foster her husband's gift. Her work was not unlike his, with its fokloric, fantastic elements, and it was one of her early drawings, The First Fool, that released in him the inspiration for his long series of works on the theme of the Fool. Her most prolific period was when they were living at Dartington Hall from 1937 until the end of World War II. A retrospective was held at Albemarle Gallery in 1989, another at England & Co, 1996, and it showed Works from the Studio, 2001–2. Lived in London.

George Edward COLLINS 1880–1968 Painter, printmaker and teacher with a strong interest in natural history subjects, son of the artist Charles Collins, who studied at Epsom and Lambeth Schools of Art. His appointments included art master at Guildford Royal Grammar School. Collins' pictures illustrated a number of books, such as Gilbert White's *The Natural History and Antiquities of Selborne*. Showed extensively at RCamA, RBA, Brook Street Art Gallery, RA and elsewhere. Lived in Gomshall, Surrey.

Hannah COLLINS 1956– Artist in various media, born in London. She studied at Slade School of Fine Art, 1974–8, then gained a Fulbright Scholarship to America, 1978–9. Her group shows included Antidotes to Madness, Riverside Studios, 1986; L'Invention d'un Art, Pompidou Centre, Paris, 1989; and The Last Days, Arenal Gallery, Seville, 1992. Solo shows included Film Stills at Matt's Gallery, 1986, later ones including Museum of Modern Art, San Francisco, 1992. Her Nomad II, of 1991, was included in Twelve Stars, Belfast Arts Council Gallery and tour, 1992–3, which was acquired for European Parliament Collection. Arts Council and British Council also hold her work.

Helen COLLINS 1921–1990 Artist and teacher, born in Dorking, Surrey, daughter of the watercolourist George Edward Collins and flower painter Clare Perrin and granddaughter of Charles Collins. She studied at Guildford School of Art and Royal College of Art after World War II. Among her output were drawings of heavy horses in the *Surrey Advertiser*. She taught at Englefield Green School. Guildford Borough collection includes her view of North Street, Guildford.

Henry COLLINS 1910–1994 Painter, designer and teacher, born in Colchester, Essex, who continued to work in that area. He was married to the artist Joyce Pallot. Collins studied at Colchester School of Art and the Central School of Arts and Crafts. After World War II service with the Army he worked as a freelance designer, establishing himself through commissions for Central Office of Information at the 1951 Festival of Britain. He taught for many years in the graphic design department of St Martin's School of Art, at Colchester School of Art and in adult education classes. With his wife he worked on many exhibition designs and murals, including Shell Centre, General Post Office Tower and Grosvenor House; Essex County Council; and Jamestown Festival in America. The two artists shared a retrospective show at The Minories, Colchester, 1984 and 1995, and in 1995–6 Essex County Libraries toured a Collins memorial show.

Jamie COLLINS 1959– Artist, designer and teacher, born in London, who graduated from Falmouth School of Art in 1982. In 1984 he joined Sculptors in Greater Manchester Association, having his studio there for some years. Collins subsequently turned to painting and poetry as a means of expression. An exhibition at Manto's, Manchester, in the mid-1990s won critical acclaim. Collins designed sets and costumers for Duchy Opera's production of Mozart's *The Magic Flute* and carried out a number of large-scale commissions in Manchester. He held the post of lecturer in sculpture at Bolton Institute of Higher Education, 1987–93. In 1996 Collins was included in North by North West, at Bolton Museum and Art Gallery, paintings which flowed "from an eight-and-a-half years' relationship lived under the shadow of Aids".

John COLLINS 1918–1999 Scenic artist, painter, muralist, teacher and writer, born in London, his Irish Catholic father a stagehand at the Old Vic, his mother's family being French-Jewish carpet weavers. John ran errands for a sword and buckle merchant; became a graphic artist with a corset manufacturer; did Army service in World War II; then joined the Old Vic paint shop, briefly teaching at Glyn Byam Shaw's Old Vic school. In 1955, Collins joined Tyrone Guthrie in Canada to work at his Stratford, Ontario, Shakespeare Festival. Guthrie called Collins' sets for *Tamburlaine* "elaborate, but barbaric, a visual complement to the splendour of Marlowe's verse." Collins' definitive book *The Art of Scenic Painting* spells out his approach. After returning to London Collins freelanced at Sadler's Wells; painted for himself, showing at the RA and having several exhibitions, including an Arts Council tour; then joined the Slade School of Fine Art as lecturer in scenic art, staying until his seventies; and handled scenery for a stream of notable productions for the Royal Shakespeare Company, in Stratford-upon-Avon and London, notably Peter Brook's version of Shakespeare's *A Midsummer Night's Dream*. Among Collins' theatre portraits were Ann Todd and Tanya Moiseiwitsch. He also created murals for the Pitlochry Theatre; Stations of the Cross for St Lawrence's Church, Catford; and from his hospital bed was commissioned to do murals for Birmingham University Medical School.

John Walter COLLINS: *see* **Sky COLLINS**

Marjorie COLLINS 1941– Painter in acrylic and watercolour, born in Chicago, Illinois, America, who graduated in fine art, University of Michigan, Ann Arbor, 1958–62, also studying part-time at school of the Art Institute of Chicago, moving to England in 1975, where she settled in Oxford. Initially, Collins' work was people and places, mainly buildings, but from 1990 she focused on still lifes and floral pictures. Although her work was representational, "the actual subject I choose to paint ... is less important than the resulting abstract patterns of light, shape and colour that they create." Joined Oxford Art Society, 1983, SWA, 1994. Group shows included RA Summer Exhibition, Hunting/*Observer* Art Prize, ROI, RWS and Museum of Modern Art in Oxford. Solo shows included Green College in Oxford, Joy Horwich Gallery in Chicago, Barbican Centre, Shire Hall Gallery in Stafford, and Stables and Sunshine Galleries. Oxford City Council, Cole Taylor Bank in Chicago, Cabinet Office and Daler-Rowney hold examples.

Michael COLLINS 1936– Artist in graphic media and teacher, born in New Malden, Surrey. After five years in the management of Clan Line Steamers, Collins studied at Wimbledon School of Art, 1962–5, then Swansea College of Art, 1965–6, his teachers including Lionel Ellis and E M Scales. He eventually became head of the art department at Emanuel School, London. Collins was a topographical draughtsman who showed with SGA and Society of Architectural and Industrial Illustrators, of both of which he was a member. Sometimes signed work with initials only. Lived in Petersham, Surrey.

Michael COLLINS 1963– Painter and draughtsman, born in Chester and brought up in Runcorn, who gained a diploma in general art and design at Halton College of Further Education, Widnes, 1992–4. He graduated with first-class honours in fine art from John Moores University, Liverpool, 1994–7; gained a postgraduate diploma in painting at the Royal Academy Schools, 1997–00, teachers including Leonard McComb, Norman Blamey and Jane Dowling, who wrote of his "lyrical spirit"; and his further education teaching certificate at University of Wales College, Newport, 2002–3. Collins was awarded a David Murray Studentship to study landscape, 1996; in 1998 a Royal Bank of Scotland Drawing Prize at the RA, was joint winner of the Elizabeth Scott Watercolour Prize, obtained another David Murray Studentship, a Sir Brinsley Ford Travel Scholarship and a Rover Commission Exhibition; in 1999 was joint winner of the Cromwell Hospital Joint Prize and solo a Chevron Watercolour, *Nature as Art Calendar 2000* award; and in 2003 an Elizabeth Greenshields Foundation Award. He was a visiting lecturer at Moray College, Elgin, 2000; gave voluntary tutoring in adult education, Prince's Trust, 2001; was artist-in-residence, London Business School, 2000–1; and did part-time teaching, Hastings College of Arts & Technology, 2003–4. Mixed exhibitions included RA Summer Exhibition, from 1999; Blake's Heaven, Scolar Fine Art, 2000; RBA, Mall Galleries, 2001; NEAC, same venue, 2002; and Christmas Exhibition, Russell Gallery, 2003–4. Figures on the English Coast was a solo show at Chappel Galleries, Chappel, 2004.

Peter COLLINS 1935– Painter and teacher, born in Inverness, whose work could have a Surrealist quality. He studied at Edinburgh College of Art, 1952–6, and gained a Post-Diploma Scholarship and an Andrew Grant Major Travelling Scholarship in 1957, studying in Italy, 1957–8. Lectured at Duncan of Jordanstone College of Art, Dundee. He was a professional member of SSA. Group shows included Arts Council of Northern Ireland, New Charing Cross Gallery in Glasgow and in 1970 he was included in Scottish Arts Council show Seven Painters in Dundee, where he lived. Had a solo show at Scottish Gallery, Edinburgh, 1968. Aberdeen Art Gallery, Scottish Arts Council and Edinburgh Education Authority hold examples.

Peter Gerald COLLINS 1923–2001 Painter and draughtsman, born and lived in London, who studied for several years at Royal College of Art from 1946, teachers including Rodrigo Moynihan, Ruskin Spear, John Minton and Robert Buhler. He worked in advertising, ran an antique shop and gallery in Sussex and completed posters for organisations such as British Rail, British European Airways and J Lyons & Company. Showed at RA, Balcombe Galleries, in open studio and at Zella Nine Gallery. Leicester Education Authority holds his work. Chelsea Arts Club member.

Rebecca COLLINS 1970– Painter who trained in Spain before graduating from Brighton College of Art. She was included in Artists of Fame & Promise at Panter & Hall, 2004. Collins latterly worked near the Sound of Sleat, in northwest Scotland.

Roland COLLINS 1918– Painter, designer, photographer, printmaker and writer, born and lived in London, who studied at St Martin's School of Art, teachers including Leon Underwood and Vivian Pitchforth. Collins early began recording the London scene, showing at RA, while working for London Press Exchange advertising agency. After World War II, during which he did agricultural work as a conscientious objector, Collins studied in 1947 in Morris Kestelman's life class at Central School and exhibited at most of London's societies, including LG, PS, RBA, ROI, RSMA, RWS, and in the provinces. In 1945 Collins designed the sleeve for Britain's first long-playing record, issued by Decca; in 1951 wrote a children's book, *The Flying Poodle*; in 1952 edited and illustrated *The Young Ballet Dancer* magazine; and in 1954 illustrated with colour lithographs Noel Carrington's *Colour and Pattern in the Home*. Had a first solo show in 1966 at Fitzroy Tavern, being long active in the association to preserve the Fitzrovia area; had another show at Illustrators' Gallery, 1987; and one at Michael Parkin Gallery, 1994. Shared an exhibition with Richard Slater at Duncan Campbell Fine Art, 2001. London Borough of Camden owns his oil of Bankside.

Sky COLLINS 1965–2004 Painter, born near Troon, Ayrshire, real name John Walter (also known as Wattie) Collins, linked to the Collins publishing dynasty. After education at Glenalmond School Collins did a foundation year at John Moores University, Liverpool; graduated at Nottingham Trent University; then moved to London, where he supported himself in studios by casual work, including washing glasses at the jazz club run by Ronnie Scott. During a visit to Vietnam in 1997 Collins declined the offer of a job at the Institute of Arts in Ho Chi Minh City. Instead, he aspired to a postgraduate place at the Royal Academy Schools; failed the interview in 1997; but was accepted under Brendan Neiland's keepership in 1999, producing exceptional work by the time he completed the course. In 2003 Collins' picture Wolves, bought by the Sheikh of Sharjah, won the British Institution Award in the RA Summer Exhibition. Its cartoon-like savagery stemmed from Collins' memories of school bullying. It followed earlier colour-band pictures, which he called "the stripeys". Alcohol, drugs and periods of isolation that helped undermine a fragile self-confidence all plagued Collins, who was found dead after checking into an hotel and leaving farewell notes. Several months later, the Royal Academy Keeper's Garden was dedicated to Collins' memory.

Susan COLLINS 1964– Artist and lecturer who from 1993 worked extensively with site-specific installations, often as interventions in public spaces. She was born and lived in London and did a foundation course at Chelsea School of Art, 1982-3; gained a fine art honours degree at the Slade School of Fine Art, 1983–7; attended The School of the Art Institute of Chicago, in America, 1990–1; and gained her doctorate in the fine art department at the University of Reading, 2001. Among her many awards, fellowships and grants were an American Association of University Women Rose Sidgwick Memorial Fellowship and Fulbright Travel Award, both 1990; an Arts Council of Great Britain New Technologies Training Grant, 1994; a European Artists Pepinière residency in Cologne, Germany, 1996; Royal Society of Arts Art for Architecture Award, 1998; and Tate in Space nomination for a 2004 interactive BAFTA (British Academy of Film and Television Awards), 2003. Collins held many animation, lecturing, freelance critic, research fellow, arts panel and curating positions, being purchaser for the Arts Council collection, 2002–4, and from 1995 senior lecturer, head of electronic media at the Slade School of Fine Art. Among her numerous exhibitions and installations were latterly the solo shows In Conversation, 1997–01, Brighton and European tour, linking viewers on the internet with pedestrians; and Transporting Skies, 2002, a networked exhibition shown simultaneously at Site Gallery, Sheffield, and Newlyn Gallery, Penzance. Online work included Cruisin', 1999, Inhabited Text, 2000 onwards, and Tate in Space, 2002. She was latterly involved in "exploring the processes of observation, recording and transmission over time and distance, connecting the British landscape tradition with the contemporary world of digital media, networks and connectivity. Fenlandia, a distributable networked live landscape work commissioned by Film and Video Umbrella, was launched in May 2004." She also worked as Susan Alexis Collins.

Susan Alexis COLLINS: *see* **Susan COLLINS**

William Wiehe COLLINS 1862–1951 Watercolour painter, born in London, who studied at Lambeth School of Art, 1884–5, and Académie Julian, Paris, 1886–7. Exhibited prolifically, notably at Walker's Galleries, RI, ROI and at Fine Art Society, as well as abroad. He painted widely in England and on the continent, publishing several books on the cathedral cities of England, Italy and Spain. Manchester City Art Gallery holds his work. Lived at Bridgwater, Somerset.

Hugh COLLINSON 1909– Painter and illustrator, especially of townscapes, and teacher, born in Ipswich, Suffolk. Studied at the School of Art there, 1926–9, under Leonard Squirrell, then at Royal College of Art, 1929–32. Showed RA and extensively in the provinces, Ipswich Art Gallery holding his work. Lived in Leicester, where he taught for a time at the College of Art.

Maurice COLLIS 1889–1973 Writer and critic, administrator and painter, born in Ireland, who after a career as an Indian Civil Servant in Burma, 1912–34, returned to London to pursue a literary life. His daughter was the art critic and writer Louise Collis. He published 35 books, including a biography of Stanley Spencer; was art critic for *The Observer* and *Time & Tide*; and numbered among his many artist friends Henry Moore, L S Lowry, Cecil Collins and Barbara Hepworth. Collis began painting in 1956 and intuitively and spontaneously created his own brightly coloured, phantasmagorically figured and almost surreal world. Although his first solo show, when he was 71, achieved some favourable critical reaction, it was left to England & Co to revive interest in the work with an exhibition in 1998.

Peter COLLIS 1929– Painter, notably of landscapes in a rather sombre palette. He was born in London and studied at Epsom College of Art. Settled in Ireland, where he concentrated on depicting the County Wicklow region near his home. Awards included Royal Trust Company Ltd Award, 1975; Olreachtas Maurice MacGonigal Landscape Prize, 1981; Claremorris Open Exhibition Prizes, 1982, 1990 and 1992; Oireachtas Irish Pensions Landscape Prize, 1983; and James Adams Award, RHA, 2000. Collis was a member of RHA. Showed extensively in group exhibitions, including RA, RP, UA, Austin/Desmond Fine Art and elsewhere. Showed solo at Emmet Gallery, Dublin, 1975–7, later one-mans including John Martin of London, from 1996. Limerick University, National Self Portrait Collection in Ireland and many corporate collections hold examples.

Mat COLLISHAW 1966– Artist who was born in Nottingham. Studied at Trent Polytechnic, 1985–6, then graduated with honours from Goldsmiths' College, 1986–9. Group exhibitions included Ghost Photography, The Illusion of the Visible, Italian tour, 1989, and Modern Medicine, Building One, and A Group Show, Karsten Schubert Ltd, both 1990. Solo shows included Riverside Studios in 1990 and Karsten Schubert, 1991, with a shared exhibition following a residency at Camden Arts Centre, 1995–6. Modern Art Inc showed vivid mosaic works by this London-based artist in 2003 and in 2004–5 there was an exhibition at Inverleith House, Edinburgh.

Alfred James COLLISTER 1869–1964 Painter, mainly of watercolours, brought up in Isle of Man. Studied at Royal College of Art and showed extensively at RBA of which he was a member, RI, Walker Art Gallery in Liverpool and elsewhere. Lived in London for a time but settled finally at Clymping, Sussex.

James COLLYER 1948– Painter, printmaker and lecturer, born and lived in London, who studied at Bournemouth and Poole College of Art, 1964–8, then Kingston College of Art, 1968–9. Having studied the intaglio process with Peter Olley, Collyer was etcher at Editions Alecto, 1969–71. Then founded J C Editions with John Crossley, continuing to do occasional work for Editions Alecto as well as etching for Henry Moore. He also travelled widely abroad and held a number of lecturing posts. With the closure of J C Editions in the late 1980s, Collyer focused on his own printmaking, from the mid-1990s producing mixed-media works on paper.

Nina COLMORE 1889–1973 Painter of equestrian subjects, specialising in Lipizzaner stallions and Egyptian racing ponies. Also painted inn signs. Born in Hounslow, Middlesex, her father was Colonel Gostling Murray, her mother an amateur artist. Colmore studied at Heatherley's School of Fine Art with Henry Massey, in Paris at the Académie Julian and in several studios. She showed at the NEAC and at the Paris Salon, where she won a diploma. Among her patrons were HRH The Maharajah of Jaipur, HRH The Prince Ali Khan and the Duchess of Westminster. During World War I Colmore, who enjoyed travel, drove a mobile canteen in the Middle East. Late in life she drove a car across Africa. Lived near Andover, Hampshire.

Russell COLOMBO 1947– Artist, born in London, who studied drawing and painting at Edinburgh College of Art, 1969–73, completing postgraduate studies in art therapy at Hertfordshire College of Art, St Albans, 1980–1. Then worked as a freelance art therapist. Was included in Scottish Print Open Three, 1983, organised by Dundee Printmakers' Workshop.

Marzia COLONNA 1951– Sculptor and painter, born in Pisa, Italy, who settled in Portesham, Dorset. Studied in Pisa at the Instituto Statale d'Arte, 1963–8, then in Florence at the Accademia, 1968–70, the year she moved to England with her husband. Among her mixed exhibtions were Upper Grosvenor Gallery, 1972; Christopher Hull, 1984; Glydebourne Festival Gallery, Glynde, from 1990; Hannah Peschar Sculpture Garden, Ockley, from 1995; Sausmarez Manor, Guernsey, from 1999; Bournemouth University Gallery, 2001; and Stephen Lacey Gallery, 2002. Solo shows included Campbell & Franks from 1979, and Gillian Jason Gallery from 1987. Among later one-artist exhibitions were the Grosvenor Gallery, 1999, which included figurative and abstract works; for this, Colonna wrote that she had "tried to convey the metamorphosis created by human passions and emotions." She also showed at Six Chapel Row, Bath, 2002; Summerleaze Gallery, East Knoyle, 2003; and in 2004 at both Alpha House, Sherborne, and the Hart Gallery. Colonna was an associate of the RBS. Commissioned work included portraits of Princess Helietta Caracciolo and a small memorial sculpture of the two Vasconsuellos brothers who died in the *Marchioness* boat disaster on the Thames. The writer David Garnett, who owned her small bronze head Emmanuel, said that it was "a precious possession with which I have lived for some years. It is a creation; not a portrait but an imaginary head full of individuality." In 2001, a major sculpture was bought by the Jerwood Foundation; another in 2002 by Newby Hall for its collection; Salisbury Cathedral bought a three-dimensional crucifix in paper and wood by Colonna in 2003;

and Sherborne Abbey commissioned a five-foot bronze sculpture of its founder St Aldhelm for a niche above the entrance, to be sited in 2005.

Ithell COLQUHOUN 1906–1988 Painter, draughtsman, writer, poet and lecturer, born in Shillong, Assam, India. Studied at Slade School of Fine Art, 1927–31, where her teachers included Henry Tonks and Vladimir Polunin, then privately in Paris and Athens. Showed extensively, including LG, Contemporary Art Society, Tate Gallery and abroad, and had solo shows at Fine Art Society, Mayor Gallery and elsewhere. Michael Parkin Fine Art held a show of her early paintings and drawings in 1977, in the same year the Newlyn Orion Gallery organising Surrealism: Ithell Colquhoun. Paintings, Drawings and Collages 1936–1976. She had met Surrealists such as André Breton in Paris and connected with the movement back in London, eventually marrying the artist and writer Toni del Renzio. Bradford and Cheltenham public galleries hold her work, which is often of an exotic nature, revealing fine draughtsmanship. She was interested in such things as natural health cures, psychodynamics and Celtic prehistory. Lived for many years in Paul, Cornwall. Her topographical books include *The Living Stones, Cornwall*, 1957, and she also published articles and poems in such periodicals as the *London Bulletin*, *Enquiry* and *Athene*.

Robert COLQUHOUN 1914–1962 Painter, printmaker and theatre designer, born in Kilmarnock, Ayrshire. He won a scholarship to Glasgow School of Art in 1933 where he met the painter Robert MacBryde. "The Roberts" remained together for life, which was often temperamentally turbulent. Gauguin and Percy Wyndham Lewis were early influences on Colquhoun, who in 1937–9 was enabled to travel in France and Italy with MacBryde. After a brief period in the Army he was invalided out and lived in London with MacBryde and John Minton and associated with other Neo-Romantic artists and Jankel Adler, who encouraged Colquhoun to concentrate on lone figure studies rather than landscapes. Hieratic individuals and abstract forms now became a hallmark of Colquhoun's art. In 1946 the artist visited Ireland, from which monotypes of Irish women emerged; in 1947–8 he worked for the Miller's Press in Lewes; further visits to the continent followed. Colquhoun with MacBryde designed for the ballet *Donald of the Burthens* at Covent Garden in 1951 and for *King Lear* at Stratford two years later. In 1958 a retrospective show was held at Whitechapel Art Gallery. There was a joint show of The Roberts at the Mayor Gallery, 1977, and a retrospective at Glasgow Print Gallery, Glasgow, 1990. Arts Council, Tate Gallery and Scottish National Portrait Gallery hold his work. Died in London.

Peter COLQUITT 1936– Artist and teacher who studied at Nuneaton School of Art and Birmingham College of Art. Went on to teach at Bishop Milner School, Dudley, Worcestershire, where he lived. He exhibited at the RBSA Open, Midland Art Medical Society, Wolverhampton Art Gallery and with the General Post Office, Dudley. Solo exhibitions included Cannon Hill and Compendium Galleries, Birmingham, and at Midland Arts Centre, 1970. Vaughan College holds his work.

Richard COLSON 1955– Painter and draughtsman, born in Edinburgh, who attended Goldsmiths' College, 1973–7, and Garnett College, 1984–6. He was notable for his impastoed landscapes, figure paintings and interiors. Group shows included Art and Computers, Cleveland Gallery, 1988; New Grafton Gallery, 1989; Francis Kyle Gallery, 1990; and Jonathan Clark Fine Art, 1993. In 1996 he had a solo exhibition at Theo Waddington Fine Art. Colson shared an exhibition with Jonathan Tetley at the New Grafton Gallery in 2005. Pearson Holdings and Thomas Agnew and Sons hold examples.

Adam COLTON 1957– Sculptor and draughtsman using a variety of materials, born in Manchester. He studied at Camberwell School of Arts and Crafts, 1975–80, then Ateliers 63, Haarlem, Netherlands, 1981–83. He remained in the Netherlands, where his work attracted immediate attention. In 1987, he was the subject of an extensive feature article in *Metropolis M* magazine. In addition to his formal sculptural training, which emphasised craftsmanship and figurative work, Colton had long sessions in the British Museum, learning how to look and draw. Contributing to his way of seeing things were the weekends with his father and four brothers climbing in the Derbyshire hills and peaks, which gave him an appreciation of structures and surfaces. His first sculptures produced in the Netherlands stemmed from the connection between classical sculpture and the human body. Pieces of bone, which could be scaled up a hundredfold, were an important contributor to Colton's later works, as he explored their inner and outer surfaces. Took part in many group shows in the Netherlands, Germany and England. Among solo shows were Stedelijk Museum, Amsterdam, 2001. Leeds Museums and Galleries hold Colton material.

Brendan COLVERT 1961– Painter, born in Dorset, who studied at Bristol Polytechnic, 1984–7. He showed in a range of mixed exhibitions, including Northlands, Cheltenham, 1987; the Bristol/Hannover Exhibition, Bristol, in the same year; in collaborations at The Cottages and at the St John's Road Site, Bristol, both 1989; and in 1991–2 John Moores Exhibition, Liverpool, where his picture Untitled was a powerful image subtitled The Problem of Pain. Lived in Kingsdown, Wiltshire.

Henry (or Harry) Morton COLVILE 1905– Painter of portraits and landscapes who in 1925 studied in Paris with André Lhote. In 1932 he settled in Aix-en-Provence, three years later exhibiting in Paris at Galerie Zak. Exhibited at RA Summer Exhibition in 1944, when he was living in London, in 1945 sharing an exhibition at Berkeley Galleries with Henry Moore and Matthew Smith, with whose work Colvile's had much in common. Exhibited at Salon d'Automne, Paris, in 1953, three years later being included in Wildenstein's Some Contemporary British Painters show. Colvile's paintings were acquired for Renand Collection, Paris, and for other collections in England, France and America.

Calum COLVIN 1961– Painter, sculptor and photographer, born in Glasgow. He studied at Duncan of Jordanstone College of Art, Dundee, 1979–83, at first concentrating on painting, then sculpture, then photography. His photographic studies were continued at Royal College of Art, 1983–5. Colvin began constructing installations made from found junk objects; onto these he would paint the outlines of figures which would be coloured in sophisticated and complex ways; photographs were then taken and the installation destroyed. The Constructed

Narratives focused on hero-worship, fantasies and desires. The Photographer's Gallery held a show in 1986, and Scottish National Gallery of Modern Art holds Colvin's work, which was featured in the Scottish Art since 1900 show, 1989–1990, at the Gallery and touring. Colvin's 2002 show Fragments of Ancient Poetry, at the Scottish National Portrait Gallery, Edinburgh, used painted photographs to explore Scottish identity, forgery and fact, inspired by the ancient poet Ossian.

Melanie COMBER 1970– Abstract artist and teacher, who did a foundation course at Kent Institute of Art & Design/ Maidstone College of Art, 1989–90; gained an honours degree in fine art painting from Wimbledon School of Art, 1990–3; and her master's in the same subject at Chelsea College of Art, 1993–4. She was a nominee for the David Murray Scholarship, RA, 1992–3; a finalist in the New Art Award, Cubitt Street, 1993; a finalist in the Swiss Bank Corporation European Art Competition, 1994; won a shortlisting, British Council, Brits in Brandenburg, and a prize, NatWest Art Prize, both 1997; and a Blue Gallery sponsorship to Iceland, 1999. Comber worked at the Victoria & Albert Museum, 1994–5; The Icelandic School of Arts and Crafts, Reykjavik, 1999; and from 2000–4 was a part-time lecturer at Wimbledon School of Art. Group shows included Cooltan Arts and Galerie Dagmar, both 1993; No Turkeys at Raw Gallery, 1994; and Jinan Gallery, 1995. Solo shows at The Blue Gallery began with Elemental, 1995. Comber's work included evocations of natural organic structures, as in her Blue Gallery show of 1996, where she built up ribbed, even scarred surfaces with lavish quantities of chalk, sand, oil paint and natural pigments, so that the pictures teetered on the brink between two and three dimensions. Her many later exhibitions included Voyager, New Paintings by Melanie Comber, Fosterart Arts in Hospitals, Fosterart; and Small is Beautiful XXII, Flowers Central, both 2004. In 2005, the Fine Art Society held a sell-out show. Scottish Widows, Caviar House, Deutschebank, RGB Underwriting and other corporate and private collections in Britain and abroad held examples. Comber lived in Rochester, Kent.

Simon COMBES 1940–2004 Wildlife painter and conservationist, born in Shaftesbury, Dorset, whose family when he was very young moved to Kenya, where his father was farm manager on the Lord Delamere estate in the Great Rift Valley. At 18, after attending the Duke of York School in Nairobi, Simon joined the King's African Rifles, at 24 being promoted major, leading the newly established Airborne Division of the Kenyan Army. During his free time from fighting Somali guerrillas instead of drinking and playing cards Combes began painting, "to save my liver and my pocketbook." A solo show in Nairobi in 1969 sold out. On leaving the Army in 1974, Combes set up a studio outside Nairobi. By travelling Africa extensively and working from photographs, observation and knowledge of anatomy gained during hunting, he produced pictures of photographic immediacy. In 1978 he moved to Worcestershire then to Bushley in Gloucestershire so that his children could be educated in England, but usually returned each year to Kenya, supplementing his income by taking clients on Safari. He supported the creation of the Nakuru Park nature reserve, donated pictures to charity, contributed to Rhino Ark and Rhino Rescue Trust, the David Shepherd Conservation Foundation and Daphne Sheldrick's work to save orphaned elephants. Combes's first published book was the autobiographical *An African Experience*, 1989. *Great Cats*, 1998, was commissioned by his printing company Greenwich Workshop, 1998. Among his awards were the Society of Animal Artists' Award of Excellence and Artist of the year in the Pacific Rim Wildlife Art Show. Combes's taste for close encounters with wildlife cost him his life when he was gored to death by a bull buffalo.

Diane COMLEY 1957– Artist and teacher, British with Canadian citizenship, who was awarded a diploma in commercial photography from Dawson College, Montreal, 1990, in 1995 graduating with distinction in fine arts, major photography, from Concordia University, Montreal. From 1993 she taught photography and contextual studies, in Canada, then at South Kent College. Was a member and co-ordinator of Projet Mouvement Synergie, Montreal, 1994–5, and a committee member of Whitstable Contemporary Arts Group from January 1996. Awards included South East Arts, for Reference Points Project, 1999. Later group shows included Private View, Dover Museum, 1998, and Look Left, Phoenix Gallery, Brighton, 1999. Had a photographic and three-dimensional Artist's Project at Tate St Ives, 2000. Lived in Kent.

COMMON CULTURE– Group founded in 1996 by David Campbell, Mark Durden and Paul Rooney (see separate entries). In 1999 Common Culture contributed the 1997 plastic and fluorescent light box Menu 5 to East International, at Norwich School of Art & Design. The work was originally commissioned by Cornerhouse for Common Culture Counter Culture.

William Edmund Hunt CONDON 1886– Watercolour painter and illustrator. Born in Cawnpore, India, Condon pursued a military career, attaining the rank of brigadier. Condon studied art under George W C Hutchinson, in Clifton, Bristol, then in Montreux, Switzerland. Prior to World War II his work appeared for several years in the *Illustrated London News* and elsewhere. While in India he exhibited widely. In 1952 he was made life president of the Exeter Art Society. Lived at Newton Abbot, Devon.

Bert CONN 1897–1973 Painter and docker, brought up in Millwall in London's dockland, where he began painting and drawing as a boy. Enlisted in 1914, advancing his age by a year, serving in the Devon Regiment on the Somme, at Ypres and Passchendale, being severely wounded in the right arm, only just saved from amputation. In 1920 he married a girl met in Plymouth during his basic training and settled in Blackheath, although he retained a love of the West Country. Joined the Port of London Authority's permanent labouring staff, retiring 1962, and was a regular exhibitor to its Staff Arts and Crafts Exhibition; in the 1930s received London press publicity; and in 1974 was given a memorial show at London Dock House. Conn used the family's crowded living room as his studio, with a canvas usually on the piano music rack. His pictures covered a range of subjects and styles, from Cornish village to dock scenes, from photographic representation to Impressionism, media from pencil to oils. A photograph of Conn at work was used in the Island History Trust calendar for 2000. His war diary features in Eve Hostettler's *The Isle of Dogs A Brief History, Volume l, 1066-1918*, 2000.

Roy CONN 1931– Painter, born in London. Trained as a structural engineer, he was mainly self-taught as an artist. In 1958 he moved to St Ives, Cornwall, and became a member of the Penwith Society. He had solo shows at Rowan Gallery, 1966, and Arnolfini Gallery, Bristol, 1969, and in 1992 was included in Belgrave Gallery's British abstract art of the 50s and 60s. Victoria & Albert Museum, Contemporary Art Society and Arts Council of Northern Ireland hold his work.

Betty CONNAL –1999 Printmaker and painter, also known as Betty Peebles, who studied with Stanley Hayter at Atelier 17 in Paris, where she lived for many years. She was in an exhibition of paintings by three artists at the Woodstock Gallery, 1965; in Presents from Paris, prints at Printfolio, 1978; and in a French exhibition organised by Anthony Dawson, the Barnes-based dealer, at St John's, Smith Square, 1986. Connal had a solo exhibition of paintings at Woodstock Gallery, 1960; another there in 1962; and one of aquatints in 1965. A memorial service with burial of her ashes took place at Brockenhurst Church, Hampshire, in December 1999.

Philip CONNARD 1875–1958 Painter and teacher, born in Southport, Lancashire. At first he worked as a house painter and studied art part-time until he won a scholarship to the Royal College of Art and in 1898 a British Institution Prize which took him to Paris. Returning to London he illustrated and taught at Lambeth School of Art. Showed widely, including RA, Leicester Galleries, RWS and NEAC as a member of both, Fine Art Society and elsewhere. Also showed solo at Leicester Galleries, and at Barbizon House. In World War I was an Official War Artist; painted murals for Queen Mary's Dolls' House, Windsor; also did decorations for the liner *Queen Mary*. Was elected RA in 1925 and Keeper, 1945–9. Connard was a painter of many facets, as his holding in the Tate Gallery shows. Died at Twickenham, Middlesex.

Wendy CONNELLY 1969– Painter and teacher who was born in Liverpool. After summer school art courses at the Menia and Nelson Centre, North Wales, 1986–8, did a foundation course at Cheshire College of Further Education, 1987–8; an art history course in northern Italy, 1987, with further tuition there in 1988; and gained an honours degree in painting at Central St Martins School of Art and Design, 1988–91. In 1989 she taught at Menia and Nelson Centre summer school. Among her awards was the Boise Scholarship for travelling in Spain in 1992. Group exhibitions included Winsford Lodge, Cheshire, 1987; RCamA Summer Exhibition from 1990; Mostyn Art Gallery, Llandudno, 1991; and Bath and Islington Art Fairs, 1992. Her first solo show, at Bernard Jacobson Gallery in 1993, sold out. TSB Group holds her work. Lived in Cheshire.

Angela CONNER 1935– Sculptor and painter, born in London, self-taught although she was apprenticed to Barbara Hepworth. Conner was married to the documentary film-maker and photographer John Bulmer. Her sister was the writer and critic Penelope Gilliatt, third wife of the playwright John Osborne. Conner's portrait subjects included Sir John Betjeman, Sir Noël Coward, Lucian Freud, Charles de Gaulle, Lord Goodman, Harold Macmillan, HM The Queen, Sir John Tavener, Lord Rothschild, Lord Sainsbury, The Duke of Devonshire, and HRH The Prince of Wales. Also known for a series of abstract works in a range of materials, Conner claimed that she was "basically a landscape sculptor using natural forces such as wind, water, gravity, sun and shadow." These included the 20-tonne Irish Wave, 129 feet high, of stainless steel and carbon fibre. At the time of its construction it was believed to be the world's highest mobile, and is located in Parkwest business park, Dublin, Ireland. Conner's solo exhibitions including Hirschl Fine Art, London 2001, with others at Browse & Darby, Gimpel Fils, Pittsburgh Museum of Modern Art in America and elsewhere. She won a number of competitions and awards and was a fellow of the RBS. The Arts Council, National Portrait Gallery, Jewish Museum in New York and many other notable public and private collections hold examples. Lived in London.

Joan CONNEW fl. from 1940s– Painter, calligrapher and illuminator, born in Sydenham, Kent. She studied at Brighton School of Art, Beckenham School of Art and Central School of Arts and Crafts, her teachers including the painter Henry Carr. Showed with RA, SWA, RSMA, RBA and Arts and Crafts Exhibition Society. Ministry of Information bought her work. Lived for many years at Shortlands, Kent.

Brian CONNOLLY 1961– Multi-media artist, teacher and events organiser who graduated from the University of Ulster in Belfast, 1984, gaining his master's degree in 1985. He instigated a number of significant arts events including Available Resources, Londonderry, 1991, and was on the editorial board of *Circa*. Won many Arts Council awards. Taught at Nova Scotia College of Art, Sheffield Polytechnic, University of Ulster, Queen's University and Colleges of Art in Cork and Limerick. His commissioned sculpture Turning Point was sited in St Anne's Square, Belfast, where he was a member of Queen Street Studios. Showed there in Works on Paper, 1994, also internationally.

William John CONNON 1929– Painter, draughtsman and teacher, born in Turriff, Aberdeenshire. He studied at Gray's school of Art in Aberdeen, his teachers including Ian Fleming and Robert Henderson Blyth. He later taught at that school and lived in Aberdeen. Was a member of SSA, also showing with Aberdeen Art Society and RSA. Scottish Arts Council holds his work.

Liam CONOR: *see* **William CONOR**

William CONOR 1881–1968 Painter and illustrator, born in Belfast, where he was especially known for his pictures of the city's shipyards and working-class street life. Was born William Connor and sometimes signed work Liam, Liam Conor or Liam O'Conocohair. Began studies at Belfast Government School of Art in 1894. Became an assistant teacher in antique at the Municipal Technical Institute in 1903, leaving the following year to join the lithographic firm David Allen and Sons. Left there after about 10 years to become a full-time painter. Was an Official War Artist in both World Wars. Works first hung at Belfast Art Society in 1910, and from then on showed extensively in the city, at RHA, Royal Glasgow Institute of the Fine Arts, RA and elsewhere. Founder-member of NS and member ROI. Elected RHA in 1946. Illustrated a number of books, including his friend Lynn Doyle's *Ballygullion* and *The Ballygunnion Bus*. Retrospective held by Arts Council of

Northern Ireland at Ulster Museum, 1968. Arts Council of Northern Ireland, Ulster Folk Museum and Manchester City Art Gallery hold his work.

Alfred Charles CONRADE 1863–1955 Painter and modeller who studied art in Germany, France and Spain. Exhibited RA, RIBA and Paris Salon. He was principal artist at the White City, 1911–14, and his work had a strong architectural bias. Lived at Kingston upon Thames, Surrey.

Stephen CONROY 1964– Painter and printmaker, born in Helensburgh, Dunbartonshire. He studied painting at Glasgow School of Art, 1982–7. In 1986, just before he began his postgraduate year, Conroy won first prize for painting at the RA's British Institute Fund Awards, the year that he also had a solo commissioned exhibition at Dumbarton District Council. Group shows included Royal Glasgow Institute of the Fine Arts, 1986; The New British Painting, Cincinnati Contemporary Arts Center and tour, 1988; and Scottish Art since 1900, 1989–90, at Scottish National Gallery of Modern Art, and touring. Conroy had a one-man show at Marlborough Fine Art, 1989. In 2003, Marlborough Gallery in New York showed recent paintings and there was a retrospective in Germany at Schloss Gottorf, Schleswig. Conroy was not a prolific artist, with a queue of ready buyers, which meant that exhibitions were limited. The artist was an admirer of the Scottish painter James Cowie, and in the older artist's manner Conroy's work is exact, tighter and more studied in its brushwork than much modern Glasgow painting. Conroy's reality is mysterious, with a tinge of Surrealism. Scottish National Gallery of Modern Art holds his work. He lived and worked near Glasgow.

Blanche CONSTABLE 1882–1956 Watercolour painter and designer, born in Malton, Yorkshire. Studied at Bradford School of Art under Charles Stephenson, then held a series of teaching posts, notably at Varndean Grammar School, Brighton. Exhibited IS and in the provinces. Member of the Sussex Women's Art Club. Lived in Brighton.

John CONSTABLE 1928–2002 Painter, teacher and conservation campaigner, brother of the artist Richard Constable, and great-great grandson of John Constable of Constable Country fame. John was born in Sandridge, Hertfordshire, and while still small could produce powerful drawings. Aged 11 he won an art scholarship to Marlborough College, then went to Chelsea School of Art, where Robert Medley was an influential teacher. Left mysteriously before completing the course and worked as a lumberjack and on building sites in Canada, also teaching at McGill University, hired by Arthur Lismer of the Group of Seven. Unable to rejoin Chelsea on his return to England because of lack of a grant, he did a variety of jobs to enable him to paint. In 1963 he married Freda Keable, an art historian. After completing his National Diploma at Ipswich Art School he began teaching in 1964 at Leiston School, from 1966 at Claydon Modern School, also teaching adults in Ipswich, drawing at Ipswich School of Art and at Belstead House summer schools. Showed with his brother at Halesworth Gallery, at Aldeburgh Cinema Gallery and at Gainsborough's House, Sudbury, and in 1993 at Salander-O'Reilly Gallery, New York. He was also president of the River Stour Trust and of the Felixstowe Art Group. Lived at Great Glemham, Suffolk.

Martin CONSTABLE 1961– Painter and teacher, born in Toronto, Canada. He studied at Richmond-upon-Thames Polytechnic, 1978–9; St Martin's School of Art, 1979–80; Coleg Elidyr, Camphill, in south Wales, 1980–1; then graduated with first-class degree from Camberwell School of Art, 1983–6; gaining his master's at Goldsmiths' College School of Art, 1988–90. He was a part-time tutor at Central St Martins School from 1994, becoming co-ordinator and drawing course tutor from 1995. Among mixed exhibitions were South London Art Gallery, Thames & Hudson Prize Show, 1986; RA Summer Exhibition and John Moores Liverpool Exhibition, from 1987; The Discerning Eye, Mall Galleries and tour, 1991, where Constable was a first prize winner; Eagle Gallery, 1993; and Royal Over-Seas League Open, 1995. Had solo shows at Long & Ryle Art International, 1992–4. Arts Council, The London Institute and several corporate collections hold examples. Lived in London.

Richard CONSTABLE 1932– Artist in gouache and teacher, born in Lewes, Sussex, brother of the painter John Constable. He gained an art scholarship to Marlborough College, 1945–50, later attending Trent Park Training College and becoming an art teacher in various schools, 1959–67. Participated in group exhibitions with Bath Society of Artists of which he was a member, Ipswich Art Club and SGA. From 1967 had over 40 solo exhibitions, including Heal's Gallery, Cooling Galleries, Radlett Gallery, Mignon Gallery in Bath and extensively abroad. Constable produced "Surrealist landscapes influenced by oriental art". Lived in Norton sub Hamdon, Stoke sub Hamdon, Somerset.

Lyn CONSTABLE MAXWELL 1944– Figurative sculptor, born in London, who was educated at St Mary's, Wantage. She studied fine art at Byam Shaw School and sculpture at Heatherley's School of Fine Art with Cubitt Bevis. An overland trip to India in 1970 led to a first bronze Nepalese Mother and Child. In 1977 Constable Maxwell won a diploma at the Venice Concourso Internationale di Pittura. Became artist-in-residence at Winchester Cathedral in 1991. Among her commissions was the Fourteen Stations of the Cross for St Gregory's Church, Alresford, known as the Patrick O'Donovan Memorial. Had solo shows at Bury Street Gallery in 1981–5, another in 1988 sponsored by Martini Rossi at The Newbury Festival. Work was cast by The Morris Singer Foundry.

Diana CONSTANCE fl. from 1950s– Artist, born in New York City, America, where she gained a scholarship to the Arts Students' League. She was assistant art director for Reporter Publications; did graduate work at the University of New Mexico; then during a five-year residence in Rome developed an interest in photography. Exhibitions included Albuquerque, New Mexico, 1960; at Camden Arts Centre: in 1970, Life Photographs, and in 1973, shared show with the sculptor John Farnham; Space Open Studios, from 1974; LG at Royal College of Art, 1978; and Contemporary Artists in Camden, Camden Arts Centre, 1981. Camden Borough Council, Leicester Education Authority and Mobil Oil Group hold her work. In 1988 her solo exhibition Aids (and nobody wants to know) was held at the Peoples Gallery. Lived in north London.

Denis CONSTANDUROS 1910–1978 Versatile writer and artist born in Sutton, Surrey, who, aged 15, produced caricatures of Wimbledon tennis players for a tournament publication. Attended Chelsea School of Art, where he wrote songs and sketches for end-of-the-year shows, in the late 1930s teaching there half a day a week when Graham Sutherland was too busy. He also did poster work for Shell when the poet John Betjeman was working with the oil company, Constanduros's *Llanthony Abbey* being a fine Neo-Romantic example. Was included in an exhibition of advertising material at Shell-Mex House in 1938, his work being part of the Shell archive. Denis was the nephew of Mabel Constanduros who, as Grandma Buggins, became a broadcasting celebrity providing World War II austerity recipes for housewives. He illustrated some of her books and drew illustrations for his own broadcast plays for *Radio Times*. Denis's first radio play was broadcast in 1936. He went on to write many television plays and adaptations, including the works of Jane Austen and Henry James. His much-loved serial *At the Luscombes* ran on the BBC West of England Home Service for 17 years. Constanduros's first London play, *Acacia Avenue*, appeared in 1943, written with Mabel; Muriel and Sydney Box's film, *29 Acacia Avenue*, based on it, was released in 1945. From 1946 Denis had a long association with the Salisbury Playhouse, not far from his home at Coombe Bissett, Wiltshire. The British Library catalogue lists 18 titles by Constanduros, including the autobiographical *My Grandfather*, 1948, illustrated by him. This was re-published by BBC Publications in 1989 plus an audio-tape in the BBC Radio Collection, read by Benjamin Whitrow. For his own enjoyment, Constanduros painted landscapes, mainly in oil, latterly in gouache, showing occasionally with other artists in Salisbury.

Hervé CONSTANT 1951– Painter, inspired by the poet Arthur Rimbaud, who explored the visual connection between what people see and say and employed a number of treasured forms: the triangle the symbol of the soul, windows of perception and the Christian cross. He was born in Casablanca of a Moroccan Jewish mother and French father and suffered a dislocated childhood. Initially determined to be an actor, but turned to painting. Studied at Conservatoire National de Musique de Toulon, 1967–70; École Nationale Superieure des Arts et Techniques du Theatre, Paris, 1971–3; and Beaux-Arts de Toulon, for printmaking, 1980–3. Group shows included Fischer Fine Art, 1978; Stamford Arts Centre, 1985; Air Gallery, 1989; and Tricycle Gallery, 1993. Also had many mixed exhibitions in France and solo shows from late 1960s; British one-mans included in 1995 Ben Uri Art Gallery, Tricycle Gallery and The Living Room. Commissions/collections included St Martin's Church, Gospel Oak, 1987; Arthur Andersen, 1991; Lynam Richard Partnership, 1994; and Earl Estates Ltd, 1995. Lived in London.

Frank CONSTANTINE 1919– Painter, restorer and curator, born Harry Frank Constantine in Sheffield, where he settled. Studied at Sheffield and Southampton Colleges of Art and at the Courtauld Institute. While in the Army in 1939 began work for Sheffield City Art Galleries, becoming director in 1964 and retiring in 1982. Showed RA, with Sheffield Society of Artists of which he was president, at Graves Art Gallery in Sheffield and elsewhere in the provinces. The Sheffield collection holds a number of landscapes by him.

Costantine CONSTANTINIDES 1950– Ceramist and potter, born in Cyprus, who moved to the United Kingdom in 1972, qualified in computer science at Mander College, Bedford, then worked in the City of London, attending evening classes in ceramics. Later undertook foundation course in art and design at Waltham Forest College and Guildhall University. Exhibitions included Heifer Gallery.

Ellen CONTI 1884– Painter and draughtsman, born in London, of English origin but who married the actor, singer and artist Guiseppe Conti, of Italian background. Educated in south London and in Surrey, she studied art at West Croydon Art School, where she excelled as a pencil draughtsman, later attending Chelsea Art School under Ernest Borough Johnson, Clapham Art School, Heatherley's School of Fine Art and St Martin's School of Art, where her teachers included Conrad Lomax. Showed principally in the Ipswich and Norwich areas and lived at Cavendish, Suffolk.

Dorab Dadiba CONTRACTOR 1929– Artist, notably a sculptor, born in Bombay, India, who became a naturalised British citizen. He studied at Sir J J School of Art, Bombay, qualifying in 1929. Showed in mixed exhibitions with NS of which he was a member, Romford Central Library and Mall Galleries. Had a solo show at India House, 1972, and Woodstock Gallery, 1975, later ones including Kenneth More Theatre, Ilford, 1988. HM The Queen and other members of the royal family hold his work, sometimes signed Dorab. Lived in Gidea Park, Essex.

Francis CONVERY 1956– Painter, draughtsman and teacher, born in Paisley, Renfrewshire. After working as a mechanical engineer, 1972–6, and travel to Europe, 1978, Convery attended Edinburgh College of Art, 1979–83, during which he travelled to Turkey, in 1984 gaining his diploma in postgraduate studies. After part-time lecturing at the College, 1984–6, during which time he visited New York, Convery was appointed lecturer in drawing and painting at Gray's School of Art, Aberdeen, in 1987. His awards included first prize in the Rowney Competition for painting, 1982; Carnegie and John Kinross travelling scholarships in 1983; and a series of RSA awards, including the Latimer in 1984, Scottish Post Office Board, 1992, and Highland Society of London, 1994; and the Shell Expro Award, 1995. Convery was elected an associate of RSA in 1994. Took part in many mixed shows including Scottish Gallery in Edinburgh; Fosse Gallery, Stow-on-the-Wold; and Mercury Gallery. Solo exhibitions included Scottish Gallery from 1991. Edinburgh's University, College of Art, Council and City Arts Centre hold his work.

Dianne CONWAY fl. from late 1960s– Painter and teacher who started on her art training at Aberdeen College of Education, 1968–71, where she worked under James Hardie. After bringing up her family, in 1985 she began a course in fine art at Plymouth, then moved to Exeter for another three years to obtain a degree and professional teaching qualification. Went on to teach in a comprehensive school. Style of painting changed radically over the years, from vigorous representational pictures to more contemplative abstracts. Had a first comprehensive show at Cleveland Bridge Gallery, Bath, in 1991, with a second there in 1992 based on a journey the year before across China.

Edward CONWAY 1872– Flower painter in oil and watercolour, who studied under Henry Tonks at the Slade School of Fine Art, then at Académie Julian, Paris. Exhibited RA, RWA and elsewhere. Lived at Burford, Oxfordshire.

Jennifer CONWAY 1935– Miniaturist and painter in various media, born in Brecon, Wales, who attended Bedford College of Physical Education, 1954–7. She became a member of RMS in 1979 and SM in 1981, also exhibiting at RA, SWA and in America. Brecknock Museum holds her work. Lived in Maescelyn, Powys.

Ben COODE-ADAMS 1964– Sculptor noted for wrought-iron work. He took a first-class honours degree in sculpture at Camberwell School of Arts & Crafts, 1982–6, doing a postgraduate certificate of education at Middlesex Polytechnic, 1986–7. Then did a postgraduate course in bronze casting at Royal College of Art, 1987–8, and his master's degree in sculpture there, 1989–92. He received a number of awards, scholarships, sponsorships and residencies. Exhibited at South London Art Gallery in the Sogat 82 Sculpture Show from 1985; Hannah Peschar Gallery from 1986; Arts Club, Bryan Kneale's Choice, 1990; Geffrye Museum, 1992; and in Drawing Towards Sculpture, 1993, at Isis Gallery, Leigh-on-Sea, in which he showed witty, slightly Surrealist drawings.

Alice May COOK 1876–1960 Book illustrator, especially children's books, sometimes under her maiden name of May Barnett; miniature painter. Studied at St John's Wood School of Art and the Royal Academy Schools. Exhibited RA, RMS, SWA, RSA and RHA, in Canada and South Africa. Lived at Spixworth, Norwich, Norfolk.

Barrie COOK 1929– Abstract painter and teacher, born in Birmingham, where he studied at the College of Arts and Crafts under Bernard Fleetwood-Walker, 1949–54. Taught in secondary schools, then taught at Coventry College of Art, 1961–9; was head of the fine art department at Stourbridge College of Art, 1969–74; senior fellow in fine art, painting, at Cardiff College of Art, 1974–7; Gregynog Fellow, University of Wales, 1977–8; then head of fine art at Birmingham Polytechnic, 1979–83. Was artist-in-residence, Fishguard Arts Festival, 1984, then at the National Museum & Art Gallery, Cardiff, 1987–8, having a studio base in the city until 1992, when he moved to Helston, Cornwall. Cook took part in numerous mixed shows, including Marjorie Parr Gallery, 1963; John Moores Liverpool Exhibition, from 1967; the Arts Council's British Painting '74, 1974; The Presence of Painting, the South Bank Centre's 1988–9 tour; and Cross Currents, Reed's Wharf Gallery at the Barbican Centre, 1996. His work could be both monumental, as at Camden Arts Centre in 1971, and delicate and discreet. Had a long series of solo shows, starting with Herbert Art Gallery, Coventry, 1966, later ones including Spray Paintings, Barbican Centre, 1995. Arts Council, Tate Gallery, WAC and many other public collections hold examples.

Ben COOK 1967– Artist, born in Thornbury, Gloucestershire, who studied at Sunderland Polytechnic, 1986–9. In 1991 he took part in Granada Celebration, Albert Dock, Liverpool, and in 6 Manchester Artists at Castlefield Gallery, Manchester, in 1993–4 being included in John Moores Liverpool Exhibition. Had a first solo show at Chapman Gallery, Salford, in 1993, large abstracts at Mappin Art Gallery, Sheffield, 2000, and Found Paintings at Pump House Gallery, 2003. In that year he curated Beyond the Endgame: Abstract Painting in Manchester at the city's Art Gallery. Lived in Manchester.

Beryl COOK 1926– Popular painter in oil of daily life with a ribald tinge, born in Egham, Surrey. Left Kendrick School at 14 to work in an insurance office. In 1943 began short career as a showgirl, became a model and worked for several dress firms. In 1946 with her mother bought a riverside tea-garden at Hampton and married Merchant Navy officer John Cook. After running a public house in Essex they moved to Southern Rhodesia where Beryl did several jobs and began painting. After a period in Zambia settled in Cornwall, where she started painting on her favourite support, wood. Beryl ran a boarding-house at Plymouth Hoe, Devon, where she settled, and which was the inspiration for many pictures. In the mid-1970s Plymouth Arts Centre put on a show, after which her fame grew fast, with exhibitions at Whitechapel and Portal Galleries. Her first book of paintings, *The Works*, was published in 1978, a second, *Private View*, in 1980. *Beryl Cook's London* followed in 1988. Had a retrospective in that year at Plymouth City Museum, with tour, with another in 1995. In 1998 she moved to Bristol. Later exhibitions included The Collection of Beryl Cook, McNeill Fine Art Gallery, Radlett, 2004. Also in that year BBC One televised *Bosom Pals*, an animated series based on Cook's pictures.

Brian COOK 1910–1991 Painter, designer, writer, publisher and politician, educated at Repton School. In 1928 he joined the family publishing firm B T Batsford in the production department, but attended part-time classes at Central School of Arts and Crafts. His bright, wrap-around cover for *The Villages of England* led to his being used as sole illustrator for the British Heritage series and over 100 distinctive covers in an Art Deco style. He also designed railway, holiday and travel agency posters and showed in Paris. After World War II service in the Royal Air Force he rejoined the firm and took the surname Batsford (his mother's maiden name); his painting career dwindled as he moved to become chairman. He became a Conservative member of parliament in 1958 and held a number of important government and party positions. Sir Brian, knighted in 1974, was chairman of the Royal Society of Arts, 1973–5. The Hayward Gallery show Landscape in Britain in 1983 led to a revival of interest in his work; in 1987 he published *The Britain of Brian Cook* and had a retrospective at the Parkin Gallery. Died in Winchelsea, Sussex.

Christopher COOK 1959– Painter, poet and teacher, born in North Yorkshire. He attended Exeter College of Art & Design, 1978–81, gaining the Gladys Hunkin Poetry Prize, then obtained master's degree in painting, Royal College of Art, 1983–6. Also studied at Rietveld Akademie, Amsterdam, 1985; gained an Italian Scholarship, 1986; and in 1987–8 attended Accademia di Belle Arti, Bologna. Won a number of prizes, including first prize at Camden Annual, 1984, with a prize at John Moores Liverpool Exhibition, 1999. Cook was fellow in painting at Exeter College of Art, 1989; guest artist, Stadelschule Frankfurt-am-Main, Germany, 1991, the year he was head of painting, Exeter Faculty of Art, University of Plymouth, 1991;

visiting artist, Akademie van beeldende Kunsten, Rotterdam, Holland, 1992; visiting fellow at Oxford University, 1993; and reader in painting at University of Plymouth from 1997. In addition to many mixed shows in Britain and abroad, had solo show at Camden Arts Centre, 1985, later ones including a series at Benjamin Rhodes Gallery from 1987–8, Graphites, at Hirschl Contemporary Art, 2000 (from which the Metropolitan Museum of Art, New York, bought three paintings), and Plymouth Arts Centre, 2001. Cook's sixth book of poetry, *For and Against Nature*, appeared in 2000. British Museum and other public collections hold his work. Lived in Exeter, Devon.

Daisy COOK 1965– Largely self-taught painter, daughter of the comedian and satirist Peter Cook. Her only training was a foundation year at Hastings College of Art and Technology, 1984. She travelled extensively, taking photographs which, when left lying around in her studio, nurtured recollections of landscape to be recreated in oil on canvas. The pictures had strong abstract elements, as in her solo show Cuba, at Stephen Lacey Gallery, 1999. Previous one-man exhibitions included The Northcote Gallery, from 1997. Stephen Lacey in 2001 showed Cook's paintings from a journey to the Australian outback, in 2003 pictures based on Hampstead Heath, which had provided her with a first experience of landscape. Cook's mixed show appearances included La Caixa, Casa del Cultura, Majorca, 1990; Open Windows Gallery, 1994; New Grafton Gallery, 1997; and Hunting Art Prizes, Royal College of Art, 1998. Sir Terence Conran commissioned three works by Cook for the Great Eastern Hotel. La Caixa Bank, Majorca; One Aldwych; and Manhattan Loft Corporation hold her work.

David COOK 1940– Wildlife artist notable for his birds, photographer, paper sculptor and lecturer, born in Rochester, Kent. He attended Medway College of Art, 1956–9, under Stanley Hayes, then Regent Street Polytechnic School of Art, 1962. Cook was a photographer with *Country Life* magazine, then a research photographer with Bowater, followed by a career in law, becoming a freelance wildlife artist and paper sculptor. He formed the Cookco Press "to promote not only my own work but that of artists I admire". He gave workshops around the world and demonstrated, mainly for Rexel Ltd with Derwent pencils. Showed with UA, RA, SWA and RSMA and had solo exhibitions widely in Britain. His work is held by a number of civil, corporate, educational and private collections. Lived in Carlisle, Cumbria.

David COOK 1944– Painter and printmaker, whose work included landscapes and surreal compositions. He was born in Bingley, Yorkshire, in the mid-1970s settling in Malham. Studied at Bradford College of Art and Royal College of Art. Exhibited widely abroad and was included in Images of the Yorkshire Landscape, organised by Sheeran Lock at Leeds Civic Hall in 1991. Majestic landscapes of Malham and Gordale Scar were an important feature of Cook's output. Cook was a friend of author Bill Bryson, one of his paintings providing the cover of Bryson's 1995 book *Notes from a Small Island*.

David COOK 1957– Artist, born in Dunfermline, Fife. He studied at Duncan of Jordanstone College of Art, Dundee, 1979–84, and won a travel fellowship that took him to Paris, Amsterdam, Belgium and Cyprus. Cook garnered a number of awards, including first prize at the RSA annual student show, 1983; RSA Guthrie Award, 1985; Scottish Arts Council Awards, 1985–8–9; and McGregor Donald Sculpture Award second prize, 1990. Cook had extensive group showings, including RSA, Mercury Gallery in Edinburgh, Warwick Arts Trust, and Scottish Gallery in Edinburgh and London. A solo show at Traverse Theatre in Edinburgh in 1982 was followed by a series which included 369 Gallery, Edinburgh, 1987–9, and Gruzelier Modern and Contemporary Art, 1991.

Francis Ferdinand Maurice COOK 1907–1978 Painter, born in London, son of Sir Herbert Frederick Cook, Bart. Sir Francis studied art under Harold Speed, John Arnesby Brown and S J Lamorna Birch over a decade from 1926. He then exhibited widely, including RA, RBA, LG and Walker Art Gallery, Liverpool, one of several provincial collection holding his work, which is sometimes of an allegorical-cum-religious nature. Sometimes signed work with initials F M C plus date. Had a special interest in the techniques of the Old Masters and connections with St Ives and Jersey artists' colonies and lived in St Aubin, Jersey.

Frederick T W COOK 1907–1982 Painter in oil and gouache of landscapes, marine scenes and flowers. Born in London, Cook studied at the Hampstead School of Art and during World War II was an official fireman-artist. He exhibited widely, at the RA, RSA, RWA and the Leicester, Redfern and Trafford Galleries. The Imperial War Museum and Plymouth City Museum and Art Gallery, Devon, hold his work. *Studio*, *Sphere* and *Tatler* used his pictures. Lived in Polperro, Cornwall.

G Lewis COOK 1913– Painter and designer who was self-taught, born in London where he continued to live. Showed at UA, RBA and RI.

Hubert COOK 1901–1966 Painter, printmaker and teacher, born in Wroughton, Wiltshire. He studied with Harold Dearden at Swindon School of Art, 1926–34, then at the Central School of Arts and Crafts, 1935–38, with Noel Rooke and Percy Hague Jowett. Taught at Portsmouth Technical College. Exhibited RA, UA, RWA, Senefelder Club, Leicester Galleries and overseas. Swindon Museum and Art Gallery is among several holding his work. Lived in Swindon.

Ian David COOK 1950– Artist and teacher, born and lived in Paisley, Renfrewshire. He studied at Glasgow School of Art, 1969–72, teachers including David Donaldson, with a postgraduate diploma, 1972–3. Gained the Hutcheson Drawing Prize, 1972; Cargill Travelling Scholarship to Spain and North Africa, 1974; and a Scottish Arts Council Travelling Bursary to Central Africa, 1984. He was a member of RI and RSW, 1978, also exhibiting with Royal Glasgow Institute of the Fine Arts and extensively elsewhere. Showed solo with Kelly Gallery, Glasgow, from 1979, later exhibitions including Flying Colours Gallery in Edinburgh, 1989, and African Images at Scottish Gallery there, 1990. BBC and Trustee Savings Bank hold examples.

Jenny COOK 1942– Artist born in Preston, Lancashire, who studied at Harris College locally, 1960–5, then Leicester College of Art, 1965–6. She showed in mixed exhibitions at RA from 1975 and Medici Society reproduced her work. Showed solo at Mercury Gallery from

1976 and Leicester Museum and Art Gallery, 1982. Lived in Leicester.

John Kingsley COOK 1911–1994 Painter, muralist, wood engraver and teacher, born in Winchcombe, Gloucestershire. He studied at Royal Academy Schools under Thomas Monnington and Walter Westley Russell, gaining the Gold Medal and Travelling Scholarship; then at Central School of Arts and Crafts, for wood engraving under Noel Rooke. Cook served as a Merchant Navy radio officer in World War II, making an extensive record of his experiences at sea and in an Algerian prison camp. Imperial War Museum as well as London's Guildhall Library, the Library of Congress in Washington and Bristol Museum and Art Gallery hold his work. Cook went on to become head of the design school at Edinburgh College of Art. He also produced a book of poems and wood engravings called *Aftermath* and toured a moving image show called *Microcosm*. Was a member of SWE and SSA, also showing in mixed exhibitions at RA Summer Exhibitions, RSA and elsewhere. Solo exhibitions included Demarco Gallery and Open Eye Gallery, both in Edinburgh; and at the Gallery Upstairs, at RA. In 1995 there was a memorial show at Edinburgh College of Art, a retrospective at Open Eye, 1999. John Sell Cotman and Samuel Palmer were influences cited by Cook, who also had an abstract phase and produced large pictures on ecological themes. Lived finally in London.

Martin COOK 1958– Having come from an unbroken line of stone carvers dating back to 1630, Cook from 1979–82 trained as an apprentice stonemason. He then began work for the Department of the Environment carving studio in south London; in 1984 assisted the artist and letter-carver Alec Peever; and in 1990 helped the designer Michael Harvey, carving inscriptions on the new Sainsbury Wing of the National Gallery. Cook opened his own workshop, at Loudwater, Buckinghamshire, in 1994, which led to royal commissions, London embassy projects and collaborations in the late 1990s with the Scottish artist Ian Hamilton Finlay. The architect Sir Norman Foster awarded Cook his most prestigious commission: to carve all inscriptions and an inlaid floor inscription for the British Museum Great Court project. Cook was included in Stone Words at Pentagram and Wolseley Fine Arts and tour, 2002.

Olive COOK 1912–2002 Writer, painter and teacher, born in Cambridge, who was married to the artist Edwin Smith. After reading modern languages at Cambridge University, Cook worked as a typographer for the publisher Chatto and Windus, then joined the staff of the National Gallery. Although not professionally trained as a painter, she gained help from her husband and Thomas Hennell, and spent a short time at Cedric Morris' East Anglian School of Painting and Drawing. Early watercolour landscapes were acquired for the Pilgrim Trust's *Recording Britain* project. In 1954 Cook was second prizewinner in an Italian government painting competition, she showed at Leicester Galleries, LG and WIAC and she had solo exhibitions at Arcade Gallery and at the Old Fire Engine House, Ely, 1979–84. Ferens Art Gallery, Hull, and Nuffield Foundation hold her work. Lived for many years in Saffron Walden. She wrote the guide to the Fry Art Gallery's collection there, having a solo show in 1996, gave it a substantial bequest and is represented in it. Contributed to *The Saturday Book*, texts for a number of her husband's books and with him produced the ambitious *The English House through Seven Centuries*, 1968. Cook edited *Edwin Smith: photographs 1935–1971*, 1984. For many years she taught at the Women's Institute's Denman College and she was a fierce campaigner for Saffron Walden's architecture and against Stansted Airport.

Richard COOK 1947– Painter, draughtsman and teacher, born in Cheltenham, Gloucestershire. Having begun to paint in his early teens Cook left boarding school as soon as he could and went to St Martin's School of Art, 1966–70, where he became impressed by the work of David Bomberg and Leon Kossoff, influences seen in his own figure paintings and landscapes. After the Royal College of Art he eventually moved from London to Cornwall in 1985, settling in Newlyn, from 1990 teaching part-time at Falmouth School of Art and Design. Among the group exhibitions he appeared in were The Human Clay, an Arts Council show at Hayward Gallery, 1976; British Art 1940–1980, in 1980, with a similar sponsor and venue; Serpentine Gallery Summer Show in 1982; A Century of Art in Cornwall, at County Hall, Truro, in 1989; and Stephen Bartley Gallery, 1991. After a solo show at House Gallery in 1981 he had others with Odette Gilbert Gallery, 1989, Newlyn Art Gallery, 1992, Austin/Desmond Fine Art, 2000 and 2003, and Tate St Ives, 2001. Arts Council and British Museum hold his work.

Richard COOK 1949– Painter of portraits and landscapes, born in Grimsby, Lincolnshire. He studied at the College of Art there, Maidstone College of Art, 1968–71, and Royal Academy Schools, 1972–5. While there he won the E T Greenshields Award for Study Abroad and the David Murray Landscape Award. In 1980 he held a one-man show at Royal Academy Schools' Gallery and gained a Richard Ford Travelling Scholarship to Spain to study at the Prado. Ford showed often at RA, was a member of RBA and also took part in mixed exhibitions at NEAC, RP, RI and widely in the provinces. Lived in Brighton, Sussex.

Rosemary COOK 1952– Sculptor who made figure and animal pieces in bronze or bronze resin. She worked from life in clay, using drawings and photographs for reference. After studying at Chichester College, 1970–2, Cook was a conservator and restorer. Frank T Sabin sold her sculptures.

T R COOK 1964– Painter, creator of collage boxes and painter who studied at Harlow Technical College and Birmingham Polytechnic. Cook's work had a witty quality, as seen in several examples at England & Co in the 1991 show Art in Boxes. Had one-man exhibitions at Swiss Cottage Library and Playhouse Gallery, Harlow, and at England & Co in 1994.

Anthony R COOKE 1933– Artist and teacher, born in London. He studied at Worthing School of Arts and Crafts, then at Royal Academy Schools, his teachers including Peter Greenham, Carel Weight and Ruskin Spear. Exhibited widely, and was chosen by Jack Beddington for his 1957 volume *Young Artists of Promise*. Public galleries in Batley, Leicester, Nottingham, Preston and Worthing hold his work. Taught at West Sussex College of Art and Design. Signed work with initials. Lived at Shoreham-by-Sea, Sussex.

Arthur Claude COOKE 1867–1951 Painter especially of figures, born in Luton, Bedfordshire, who studied at the Royal Academy Schools. He won silver and bronze medals at the 1895 Crystal Palace Exhibition. Showed at RA Summer Exhibition, Walker Art Gallery in Liverpool, RBSA and ROI. His work was widely illustrated. Durban Municipal Art Gallery in South Africa holds his work. Lived in Radlett, Hertfordshire.

Barrie COOKE 1931– Painter and draughtsman, born in Knutsford, Cheshire, to an English father and American mother, the family moving to the United States in 1947. In 1953 Cooke graduated in art history from Harvard University, Boston, attending summer schools in painting at Skowhegan College, Maine; in 1955 went to Salzburg, Germany, studying at Oskar Kokoschaka's School of Seeing. Moved to the Irish Republic in 1954, settling at Boyle, County Sligo. Cooke liked spontaneity, rarely making preliminary drawings. He was "a Romantic in the real sense, an empathist. The less there is of me in the painting the better. Empathy is when you've lost yourself." His canvases drew on landscapes around the world and interrelated themes such as nude, knot and water. Cooke held many solo shows in Ireland and abroad. In 1992 Rudi Fuchs, curator of the Gemeentemuseum, organised a solo show of paintings in The Hague, Netherlands; later ones included works on paper, Fenderesky Gallery, Belfast, and tour, 1955–94, in 1994; Fenderesky showed paintings of the 1990s in 1999; Kerlin Gallery, Dublin, 2001 and 2003; and in 2002 Fenton Gallery, Cork, exhibited works including New Zealand landscapes and fish imagery. Irish Arts Council; Ulster Museum, Belfast; Hugh Lane Municipal Gallery of Modern Art and Trinity College, both in Dublin; Crawford Municipal Art Gallery, Cork; and The National Self-Portrait Collection, Limerick, hold examples.

Beth COOKE 1920– Landscape and plant painter and draughtsman, born in East Dulwich, southeast London, full name Elizabeth Hannah, her father the ecclesiastical and heraldic designer Percy John Hill. Graduated in horticulture at Studley hoping to make a career in plant-hunting, but war diverted her into agricultural research at Rothamsted, where she met her husband-to-be, the notable soil scientist George William Cooke, whom she married in 1944. Having illustrated a Pitman manual *Botany for Gardeners*, Cooke began studying with Gerhart Frankl from 1950–1, but the use of colour and the inspiration of Emil Nolde and German Expressionism turned her towards painting. Had work accepted for Redfern Gallery Summer Exhibition in 1951; by Derbyshire Education Department, 1953; WIAC and LG in 1955; then concentrated on her family until after her husband's death in 1992. Later solo shows included Royal Agricultural Show, Stoneleigh, from 1993; CRA Gallery, St Albans, 1994; Atrium, from 1995; Burgh House, Hampstead, and The Gallery, Carnegie Library, Herne Hill, both 2003; and Points of Departure, New Hall, Cambridge, 2004. She had work held there in National Women's Collection. Cooke's landscapes, real and imaginary, had as their main literary influence writings by the Westmorland novelist Constance Holme. The artist lived in Harpenden, Hertfordshire.

E F COOKE 1905–1963 Painter in oil, born at Stone, Staffordshire. After education at Stafford Girls' High School, Mrs Cooke studied art at the Kitchener Institute, in Stone, then at Carlisle School of Art. She continued to live in Stone, exhibited widely in the north of England and was associated with the Whitehaven Art Club.

Ida COOKE fl. from late 1930s– Artist in various media, born in New Plymouth, New Zealand. She studied at Slade School of Fine Art where she won a prize for life painting; also attended Oskar Kokoschka's School, Salzburg, Austria. Exhibited extensively in mixed exhibitions, including RA, RP, John Whibley Gallery and elsewhere. Gained gold medal, Accademia Italia. Had solo shows at Woodstock Gallery, 1966, and Clarges Gallery, 1973, later ones including Centaur Gallery, 1980. Lived in Windsor, Berkshire.

Jean COOKE 1927– Artist in oil, watercolour, pastel and clay, and teacher, born and lived in London, married to the painter John Bratby. Some of her work, such as the Tate Gallery's Self-Portrait, of 1959, was inscribed Jean Bratby. She painted Bratby and appeared in many of his works. She studied at Central School of Arts and Crafts, 1943–5; Camberwell School of Arts and Crafts and Goldsmiths' College School of Art, 1945–9, and at City and Guilds School of Art; and at Royal College of Art, 1953–5, under Carel Weight and Ruskin Spear, having run a pottery workshop in Sussex, 1950–3. Was a lecturer at Royal College, 1965–74. In 1972 was elected RA, was also a member of RBA. In addition to mixed show appearances had many solo exhibitions, early ones including Establishment Club, 1963, and Leicester Galleries, 1964, later ones including Agnew and Ansdell Galleries, 1974. Cooke was noted as a realistic painter of everyday life, citing "figures in light and space" as an important theme.

John COOKE 1929– Versatile and prize-winning artist and illustrator, using a variety of media, born in Sheffield, Yorkshire, who studied at Stoke-on-Trent College of Art. He was best known for his landscapes, especially of the Lake District, where he lived, also for his portrayal of the desert, in the Middle East, where his work sold well. Completed many calendars, cards, posters and book-jackets, notably the cover of E Nesbit's *The Railway Children*, Penguin Popular Classics, the only contemporary artist featured in the series. HRH The Duke of Kent was among famous collectors of Cooke's work.

Liadin COOKE 1958– Artist, born in Ireland, who attended the National College of Art & Design, Dublin, then Goldsmiths' College, 1994-6. Group exhibitions included Dublin Film and Video Festival, 1984; Metafurniture, Sculptors' Society of Ireland Exhibition, Limerick and tour, 1987–8; Irish Artists in New York, tour, 1990; and 0044, PS1 Contemporary Art Centre, New York, and American and Irish tour, 1999–00. Later solo shows included Sliced, City Arts Centre, Dublin, and Two Worlds, Green on Red Gallery, 1994, both in Dublin. Among Cooke's commissions were Irish National Insurance, Dublin, 1987; Office of Public Works, Dublin, 1993; Camden Town Hall, 1997; and Ballroom (ornament), for Henry Moore Institute, Leeds, 2003. That was one of a series of works in which Cooke was inspired by the lost or the forgotten, which she interleaved with her own recollections.

Madeleine COOKE 1975– Artist and lecturer whose work mainly comprised photography, performance, projection and print. Cooke set out to "question photographic images in fashion and advertising which tend to reduce the body to a superficial 'surface'." She studied at Surrey Institute of Art and Design and the Royal College of Art, graduating in 2000 and lectured in the school of fine art at Kingston University and at the Surrey Institute. Exhibitions included Absolute Vodka, Gulbenkian Gallery, Royal College of Art, 1999 and 2000. Cooke was a Picker Fellow in print-based media at Kingston University, 2000–1, and was included in Picker Fellows 2001 at Stanley Picker Gallery there, 2001.

Randal COOKE 1946– Painter, printmaker and teacher, born in southeast London. He studied painting at Camberwell School of Arts and Crafts and Chelsea School of Art. Went on to become a tutor in lithography at Camberwell and Cambridgeshire College of Art and Technology. Among his many exhibitions was a four-man show at Woodlands Art Gallery, 1988. Had a solo show at Kent Institute of Art & Design, Maidstone, 1993. Lived in east London.

Stanley COOKE 1913– Painter in oil and watercolour and freelance commercial artist, He was born in Mansfield, Nottinghamshire, between 1924–32 studying at the local School of Art, then illustration through Percy Bradshaw's correspondence Press Art School. Cooke's work was reproduced on greetings cards and he showed in mixed exhibitions at RA, ROI and UA. Drian and Mansfield Art Galleries gave him solo shows. Lived for many years in Guildford, Surrey.

William Cubitt COOKE 1866–1951 Watercolourist, draughtsman, printmaker and teacher, born and lived in London. He was apprenticed to a chromo-lithographer and did a lot of commercial work, studying at Heatherley's and Westminster Schools of Art, also at Cook's, but was mainly self-taught. He was a member of Langham Sketch Club and walked constantly with a sketch-book. His work appeared in magazines such as *Illustrated London News* and *Harmsworth's* and in books published by Blackie, Dent, Methuen and others. Showed at RA, RI and RBA.

Julian COOKSEY 1960– Figurative and non-figurative sculptor, and teacher, employing a range of natural and man-made materials. He gained a degree in English literature from Magdelen College, Oxford, 1979–82; was a management trainee with Trafalgar House, 1982–5; regional administrator, Association for Business Sponsorship of the Arts, 1985–8; did a foundation course at Chelsea School of Art, 1988–9; then graduated in sculpture from Central St Martins College of Art & Design, 1989–92. During that time he was a part-time foundry worker at Arch Bronze, Putney, from 1993–5 undertaking technician work and part-time teaching at Brunel University Arts Centre and Kingston University, from 1994 also teaching sculpture part-time at Kensington & Chelsea College. Exhibitions included 1st RWA Open Sculpture Exhibition, 1993, and a shared show with Barbara Delaney at Brunel University, 1997. Had a London studio.

Simon COOLEY 1955– Sculptor in various materials and teacher, born in London, who eventually settled to work at Govilon, Abergavenny, Monmouthshire. He was apprenticed to the sculptor Bernard Saunders at Augustine Studios in London, 1970–2; to the sculptors Edwin Russell and Lorne McKean, 1972–4; then graduated with honours in sculpture from Central St Martin's School of Art, 1994–7. Cooley worked extensively as a sculptor in film, television and theatre and taught in many schools, colleges and community venues, as well as running regular private workshops in life drawing and portrait modelling. His work followed three directions: site-specific sculpture; the head and portrait; and work originating through specific pieces of music. Public sculptures included Hornsey School; St Edward's School, Romford; Shaftesbury Centre, Hammersmith; Institution of Highways and Transportation, Hammersmith; and Chisenhale School, Bethnal Green. He had a solo show of sculpture influenced by music at Nine Clarendon Cross Gallery in 2004.

Charles John Franklin COOMBS 1907–1989 Painter, illustrator, naturalist and medical practitioner, born in Bristol. He was self-taught as an artist, although he was much-influenced and helped by the artist Robert Gillmor. Coombs studied at Clifton College and Cambridge University and was a Bachelor of Civil Law. While in general practice in the area of Truro, Cornwall, for 40 years Coombs was heavily involved in ornithological research, belonging to a number of related organisations. Was a member of SWLA, showing elsewhere in Britain and abroad. Among books illustrated were his own *The Crows*, 1978. Ulster Museum in Belfast holds his work.

Daniel COOMBS 1971– Artist who was born and lived in London. He gained an honours degree at Ruskin School of Art, Oxford, 1989–92; obtained his master's degree in painting from Royal College of Art, 1992–4; then won a Scholarship to the British School at Rome, 1994–5. Exhibitions included Young British Artists VI, Saatchi Gallery, 1996, and Saatchi Collection holds his work. Had solo exhibitions at The Approach, 1997, Zwemmer Gallery, 2000, and at Habitat Café, 2001, where he showed paintings made from assembled objects representing the city and urban parks. Coombs said that his work was "about the blandness that comes from not having a voice beyond the common, anonymous popular one".

Caroline COON fl. from 1960s– Figurative painter who as a child boarded at Legat Russian Ballet School, later at Royal Ballet School, appearing at Covent Garden. Attended Central School of Art and in 1965, while working as a model, appeared in Ken Russell's television film *Rossetti*. In 1967 she co-founded the drugs advisory group Release, in the 1980s managed the Punk group the Clash, in 1988 publishing *The Punk Rock Explosion*. Coon's exhibition No Future?, photographs of the Punk era, was held at Light House Media and Conference Centre, Wolverhampton, 2001. Coon was included in The Sixties Art Scene in London, at Barbican Art Gallery, 1993, in the same year in People and Places at Gagliardi Gallery. The poet Christopher Logue, the actress Julie Christie and other notable collectors acquired Coon's work.

Hubert COOP 1872–1953 Painter notable for his landscapes and seascapes of England, which he travelled widely. He was born in Olney, Buckinghamshire, and worked as a draughtsman in industry, being elected to RBA aged 22. Ebb Tide, Whitby and Chalk Cliffs at Dover are among his main works. Showed at Walker Art Gallery in Liverpool, RA, RCamA and RI and had work bought by Oldham Corporation. In 1999, The Burton Art Gallery & Museum, Bideford, put on a Coop show: The Complete

Collection. The co-founder's bequest to the Gallery. Lived latterly in Northam, Devon.

Alfred Egerton COOPER 1883–1974 Portrait and landscape painter, born in Tettenhall, Staffordshire, who studied at Bilston School of Art and Royal College of Art, graduating in 1911. Served in Artists' Rifles in World War I. He was elected RBA in 1914. In 1921 Cooper's picture London from an Airship was a notable feature of the RA Summer Exhibition and three years later he won an Hon. Mention at Paris Salon. Also showed Walker Art Gallery in Liverpool, ROI, RI and Goupil Gallery. King George VI and Sir Winston Churchill were among Cooper's portrait subjects. Lived in London and was a member of Chelsea Arts Club.

Austin COOPER 1890–1964 Maker of abstract collages, watercolourist, poster designer and teacher, born in Souris, Manitoba, Canada. The family moved to Cardiff, Wales, when Cooper was six years old. He studied at the School of Art there, winning a scholarship to the Patrick Allan-Fraser School of Art, Arbroath, where he studied 1905–9. In London, in 1910, he attended evening classes under Innes Fripp at the City and Guilds School. After a period in Canada as a commercial artist and interior designer Fripp served in the Army during World War I, had another spell in Canada, returning to England in the early 1920s where he designed posters and began to paint seriously in the early 1940s. First one-man show at London Gallery in 1948; showed at Gimpel Fils from 1955; also exhibited at Galerie Craven, Paris. Tate Gallery holds several examples. Lived in London.

Constance COOPER 1905–1998 Painter, born in Shoreham, Kent, who studied at Croydon College of Art. She was vice-president of SWA and president of Croydon Art Society and showed in London, the provinces and abroad. Lived in Croydon, Surrey.

David COOPER 1952– Painter and draughtsman, born in London. Cooper was a mature student at Goldsmiths' College School of Art under Leonard McComb, having worked for a decade from 1968 as a mason pavior for the London Borough of Southwark. After four years at Goldsmiths', from 1978, Cooper began to show in mixed exhibitions, notably New Contemporaries. In 1985 he shared a show at Goldsmiths', exhibiting large figurative paintings. The following year he participated in Cityscape: The changing face of London, an Arthur Andersen and Company exhibition, then in 1986–7 he was included in A Reputation Amongst Artists, a Norwich School of Art Gallery touring exhibition. Cooper was a meticulous artist who drew on his experiences in London's East End and its street life, notably the theme of children playing. Arthur Andersen and Leicestershire Education Authority hold his work.

Eileen COOPER 1953– Painter, draughtsman, printmaker and teacher, born in Glossop, Derbyshire. Aged 17 she did a foundation course in Ashton-under-Lyne, then was at Goldsmiths' College School of Art, 1971–4, then Royal College of Art, 1974–7. Later she was a visiting lecturer at Central St Martins. Cooper was noted for her studies of the human figure, often large and of a Chagall-like intensity. From the mid-1980s she participated in numerous mixed exhibitions in Britain. After a solo exhibition at Air Gallery in 1979 others included House Gallery in 1981; Blond Fine Art, 1982–3–5; Artsite Gallery, Bath, 1987; a series at Benjamin Rhodes Gallery from 1988; and in 2000, after being artist-in-residence at Dulwich Picture Gallery, a show there and at Art First, which gave her another in 2003. Among her commissioned work was a Staircase Project at ICA, 1982, and a series of book covers and frontispieces. Elected RA, 2001. Arts Council, British Council and Victoria & Albert Museum hold her work.

Francis Glanville COOPER 1918– Watercolourist, potter and teacher, born in Portsmouth, Hampshire. Studied at Kingston School of Art with Henry Hammond, 1945, then the Burslem School of Art in 1947 and Woolwich Polytechnic. Younger brother of the potter Ronald Glanville Cooper. Like his brother he went on to teach, for periods at Sheffield and Maidstone Colleges of Art and Southend School of Art. Cooper showed at Design Centre, Red Rose Guild of Craftsmen and elsewhere. Wakefield City Art Gallery holds his work. Signed his work in monogram form. Lived in Sheffield for some years.

George Ralph COOPER 1909– Painter and businessman, born in Aylmerton, Norfolk. Initially educated in Norwich, he later attended the University of Wales and obtained a doctorate of philosophy. He studied art in the 1920s and 1930s in Wales, America and Scotland. Showed at RA, ROI, AIA and with Hertford Art Society, which he founded in 1953. Official collections in Bedford and Letchworth hold his work. Lived in St Albans, Hertfordshire.

Gerald COOPER 1898–1975 Painter, sculptor and teacher whose works included children's portraits, landscapes and horses, but who was noted for his meticulous flowers in the manner of the Dutch Old Masters. He was married to Muriel Minter, their daughter being Jenifer Cooper; John Denham Gallery held a family show in 1984. Cooper was born in West Bromwich, Staffordshire. During World War I he served in the Observer Corps and Royal Flying Corps, afterwards attending West Bromwich Art School. From 1921 Cooper studied at Royal College of Art, where in 1925 he shared the Drawing Prize of the school of painting with Phyllis Dodd. Cooper became principal of Wimbledon School of Art, 1929 until retirement, and was keenly interested in art education. He was a member of the Bray and National Committees on Art Education and was an examiner for the Ministry of Education. Was also a member of NS, and showed at NEAC, E Stacy-Marks in Eastbourne, RA extensively until the year of his death and elsewhere in Britain. Lived in London.

Isolde Frances COOPER 1903–1953 Painter in oil, born in London, she was the daughter of Lord Borthwick and married Sir George Cooper. Lady Cooper studied at Heatherley's School of Fine Art under Iain Macnab. Exhibited RBA and ROI. Lived at Hursley, Winchester, Hampshire.

Ivor COOPER 1899–1987 Advertising executive and part-time artist who studied architecture in England and America. He took a first job in advertising with Wilson's agency in 1919, then eventually joined Lever House Advertising House Advertising Service aged 26. After the formation of the Lintas agency in 1928 his charismatic personality helped give it an international thrust. He retired from Unilever in 1964 to give himself time for interests including painting and his work was included in the Lintas Beyond the Horizon show at Agnew in 1988.

Jenifer COOPER 1935–1969 Picture restorer and artist, who showed early promise as a painter, daughter of the artists Gerald Cooper and Muriel Minter (in 1984, John Denham Gallery held a family show). She studied at Wimbledon School of Art, 1952–6, then graduated from the Courtauld Institute in 1960, marrying fellow-student Paul Hetherington. The small body of Cooper's work was interesting, the pictures generating a psychological tension absent from those of her parents. She chose to concentrate on picture restoration, active from 1962 until her death, being principal restorer for Castle Museum, Norwich. She made a particular study of the technique of John Crome, many of whose pictures she restored, plus other painters of the Norwich School.

Jessica COOPER 1967– Painter and draughtsman, born in Bristol, who did a foundation course at Falmouth School of Art, 1985–6, then graduated with honours in fine art/textiles at Goldsmiths' College, 1986–9. Co-ordinated the education programme for Newlyn Art Gallery, St Ives International, 1997, in 1999 organisation and leading a course, The Representational to the Abstract, at Dartington Hall. Was elected a member of the Newlyn Society of Artists, 1995 (committee member, 1999), and an associate member of Penwith Society, 1996. Mixed shows included Salthouse Gallery, St Ives, 1989; Rainyday Gallery, Penzance, from 1993; Great Atlantic Gallery, St Just, from 1996; and White Gallery, Hove, 1999. Had a solo exhibition at Newlyn Gallery, 2001. The Jamieson Library, Newmill, and Slaughter and May held examples.

John F COOPER 1929– Artist, teacher and educationist, born in Merthyr Tydfil, Glamorgan. He studied painting and stained glass from 1949–56 at Swansea College of Art and was technical assistant at Glynn Vivian Art Gallery for two years. Held a number of teaching posts in the Midlands and South Wales, then did a diploma in art education at Cardiff College of Education in the late 1960s. Took part in a number of group shows including Young Contemporaries at Chenil Galleries, 1953, then in Wales at Royal National Eisteddfod, SWG, WAC and elsewhere.

John Hubert COOPER 1912– Artist and teacher, born in Pemberton, Lancashire. Cooper studied at Wigan School of Art, 1930–5; at Liverpool University Department of Education; taught at Gosport Country Grammer School and Bay House School, Gosport, 1936–75, also being an adult education tutor; in the 1970s graduating through the Open University. Was a member of BWS and Royal Drawing Society, also showing in Hampshire and Wessex Artists Exhibitions and at Paris Salon. Designed and etched windows for Gosport Town Hall. Lived latterly in Banstead, Surrey.

Josephine Mary COOPER 1932– Miniaturist, painter and printmaker, born in Brighton, Sussex. She studied at St Albans School of Art, Mid-Hertfordshire College of Further Education and privately. Had a number of solo shows; was a member of SM from 1974; UA from 1975; RMS from 1983; and SWA from 1988, also exhibiting at RSMA and at Paris Salon, where she gained a Silver Medal, 1974. Lived in Welwyn Garden City, Hertfordshire.

Julian COOPER 1947– Painter and teacher, born in Grasmere, Westmorland, who lived for a time at Ambleside, Cumbria. He studied at Lancaster School of Art, 1964–5, and Goldsmiths' College of Art, 1965–9, winning a Boise Travelling Scholarship, 1969–70. He held a Karolyi Foundation in France in 1976, followed by a fellowship at VCCA in Virginia, 1981, won a Northern Art Bursary in 1982 and was visiting lecturer at Sunderland Polytechnic the same year. Cooper's series of pictures Under the Volcano, based on the novel by Malcolm Lowry, was important and was featured in Summer Show 2 at Serpentine Gallery, 1983. Other group exhibitions included RA Summer Exhibition, 1972; Deck of Cards, JPL Fine Art, 1976; and Northern Open at Ceolfrith Gallery, Sunderland, 1982. Cooper was a frequent exhibitor with LG annual shows from 1967. Solo shows latterly included The Alpine Club and Cliffs of Fall at Art Space Gallery, both 2004, and Museo della Montagna, Turin, Italy, 2005. Arts Council, University College in London and galleries in Bolton, Lancaster and Newcastle hold examples.

Lilian COOPER 1965– Artist, born in Paris, France, of British and Dutch nationality, who was educated at St Mary's Hall, Brighton, 1978–81, then The British School in The Netherlands, Voorschoten, 1981–3. Gained an honours degree at the School of Architecture, University of Portsmouth, 1983–6; did a foundation course at Vrije Academie, The Hague, 1986; then graduated and obtained her master's degree in fine art at Rietveld Academie, Amsterdam, 1987–92. Landscape was an important feature of Cooper's work and from 1988–99 trips included Italy, Australia, Scotland, Ireland and South Africa. As well as mixed shows she had solo exhibitions at An Lanntair Museum and Art Gallery, Stornoway, 1996, and Barbican House Museum, Lewes, 1999. Commissions included Archaeological Museum, Utrecht, 1991. Lived in Amsterdam, Netherlands.

Margaret COOPER 1893– Painter and writer who was married to the artist Robert Cresswell Boak. After studying at Queen's University, Belfast, she attended the Slade School of Fine Art, then studied in Paris. Lived in London.

Mary COOPER 1911– Collagist and artist in various materials who studied at Central School of Arts and Crafts with Bernard Adeney. She showed at RA, Leighton House and was a member of Free Painters and Sculptors. Signed work with initials. Lived for a time at Richmond, Surrey.

Michael COOPER 1943– Painter in oil, born in Birmingham, self-taught and by profession a picture restorer. Music "played an important part" in creating his small, subtle, understated pictures which were exhibited at RA Summer Exhibition, Bruton Street Gallery, Phoenix Gallery at Lavenham and Towner Art Gallery, Eastbourne. Showed solo with Star Gallery, Lewes. Cooper sometimes signed pictures with initials only.

Michael COOPER 1944– Sculptor, often on a monumental scale in stone and marble, born in Dublin, Ireland. He studied in England under Anthony Gray, showing widely in England, Ireland and America. As well as a nine-foot Sailfish sited in Florida, and a Troubador figure in the Mandarin Hotel, Hong Kong, Gray completed large pieces for public and private sites in England. Was included in Sixteen Sculptors at Sladmore Contemporary, 1997.

Paul COOPER 1923– Sculptor in many materials, born and lived in Wool, Dorset, married to the artist Audrey Carnaby. He studied at Poole College of Art, 1939–41, at Goldsmiths' College School of Art, 1948–51, then at Lincoln College in 1958. Showed at RA, with RBS of which he was a fellow and elsewhere in London and the provinces. Did widespread church work in Britain and abroad. Oxford and Lincoln Education Authorities hold examples.

Paul COOPER 1949– Sculptor and teacher, born in Manchester. He studied sculpture at Newcastle University and went on to lecture at University of Lancaster. In 1981 he was in Baltimore as a visiting artist at the Maryland Institute of Art. Cooper worked at various times in wood, mild steel and hollow cast concrete, in the last case usually in limited editions which could be placed at various locations. He was interested in patterns to be found in both man-made and natural forms and pursued a special study of mathematical systems and series. Showed in the Welsh Sculpture Trust Margam Park Sculpture in a Country Park exhibition in 1983; solo exhibitions included Leeds Polytechnic, 1980; and commissioned works included Quincunx, 1983, five concrete spheres, at Rufford Country Park, Ollerton.

Philippa COOPER 1934– Representational painter in watercolour and pen and ink, printmaker and teacher, born and lived in London, daughter of the artists John Cooper, (1894–1943), founder of the East London Group, and Phyllis Bray. She admired the work of William and Ben Nicholson, John Sell Cotman, Eric Ravilious and Edward Bawden. After South Hampstead High School, she was granted a major scholarship to Slade School of Fine Art, 1950, gained her diploma in 1954, and was awarded postgraduate study year, 1954–5. Teachers included William Coldstream, Lucian Freud, B A R Carter, John Piper, Edward Ardizzone, Robert Medley and John Buckland Wright. She had a strong interest in architecture, her first husband being Geoffry Powell, winner of the Golden Lane housing scheme and founder of Chamberlin, Powell & Bon, architects of the Barbican scheme for the City of London. She was for 26 years planning adviser to the Borough of Ealing for the conservation of Bedford Park. Teaching included London County Council and Inner London Education Authority schools, Wormwood Scrubs Prison and Chiswick Polytechnic. Mixed shows included Young Contemporaries; A Family of Painters – 3 Generations, Queen Mary College, 1978 (which she organised); Sally Hunter Fine Art and Collyer-Bristow Gallery, both 1997; Currells, Islington, 1999; The Millinery Works, from 1999; and St Raphael Gallery, 2000. Had solo exhibitions at Judd Street Gallery, 1987 and 1990, in 2001 sharing a show with Noriaki Maeda at Grosvenor House, in 2005 another with Peter Kelly at Chappel Galleries, Chappel. Sometimes signed work P C.

Phyllis COOPER 1895– Miniaturist and heraldic artist, born in London. She studied at Frank Calderon's School of Animal Painting, with the miniaturist Norah Bourne and elsewhere in London. Showed at RA, RMS, SWA, RI and Walker Art Gallery in Liverpool. Much of her work was done for Debrett's Peerage Ltd. Member of SM, and lived in Worthing, Sussex.

Phyllis Mary COOPER: *see* **Phyllis BRAY**

Robert COOPER 1949– Ceramist and lecturer who referred to his work as collages of cultural experience, being influenced by visits to America in the 1980s. Studied interior design at Kingston College of Art, gaining his master's at the Royal College of Art. Taught at Chelsea College of Art and City Literary Institute. Designed station identities for London Underground, including Northern and Piccadilly Line platforms at Leicester Square. Shipley Art Gallery, Gateshead, and Glasgow Gallery of Modern Art hold his work. Was included in Atlantic Crossings at Barbican Centre, 1998.

Rosamund COOPER fl. from early 1930s– Painter, commercial artist and teacher, educated in Hampstead, north London. Studied at Heatherley's School of Fine Art, her teachers including R O Dunlop, Frederic Whiting and Bernard Adams. She was there 1938–40 and again in 1947, early in World War II having a spell in an advertising agency. Later taught art in Norfolk, settling there at Sheringham. Exhibited at Heal's Mansard Gallery, RBA, ROI, Cooling Galleries and in Norwich.

Simon COOPER 1960– Artist, born in Newcastle upon Tyne, who graduated from Duncan of Jordanstone College of Art, Dundee, 1979–83, with an honours degree in illustration and printmaking. In 1983 was included in Scottish Print Open Three, organised by Dundee Printmakers' Workshop.

Stephen COOPER 1951– Painter and creator of wall-mounted, abstract, totem-like objects from such objects as cistern ballcocks, paint and refuse bags. He was born and based in London and attended St Martin's School of Art, 1971–5, then Royal College of Art, 1976–9. Awards included Pratt Award at St Martin's, 1974; John Minton Travel Award, 1976; Anstruther Drawing Prize, 1977; Berger Award (major), Royal College, 1979; and a painting fellowship at Ulster University, Belfast, 1980. Took part in many group shows including Young Contemporaries at ICA, 1975; John Moores Liverpool Exhibition, 1976; Winchester Gallery, Winchester, 1984; On a Plate, Serpentine Gallery, 1987; and Made in Greenwich, The Living Room, 1994. Had a solo show at Hull School of Art, 1979, from 1989 having a series at Smith Jariwala/Kapil Jariwala Galleries.

Thomas Joshua COOPER 1946– Artist using framed photographs and brief texts who, according to the catalogue of New North (Tate Gallery Liverpool, 1990), was "not concerned to document facts. Instead he employs the camera in search of a greater sense of meaning ... The significance of the work resides in our own imaginative response to all that the artist has embraced in his involvement with the places he depicts." Born in San Francisco, California, America, Cooper became founding head of the Glasgow School of Art's fine art school, in 1982. After leaving America, Cooper lived in Derbyshire, then the west of Scotland. Later solo shows included Where the Rivers Flow, Fruitmarket Gallery, Edinburgh, 1997–8, Blains Fine Art, 2002, and Mount Stuart, Isle of Bute, 2002. Arts Council holds examples.

Waistel COOPER 1921–2003 Potter and painter who signed his work with his Christian name, of Yorkshire origin. He was born in Ayr where he attended the Academy and showed such promise that, aged only 15, he was encouraged to attend Hospitalfield School of Art, later Edinburgh College of Art. Although he was initially a painter, it was the work of the sculptors Barbara Hepworth and Henry Moore that cultivated Cooper's lifelong interest in sculpture through ceramics, producing a number of solid sculpted, abstract forms. Invalided out of the Army in World War II he returned to Edinburgh College of Art, worked for a few years as a freelance artist, then received a life-changing commission to paint portraits in Iceland. After a solo show of paintings in Reykjavik, Cooper was invited by the sculptor Gestur Thorgrimsson to set up a pottery locally and "from the first moment I put my hands in clay I was hooked." Returned to Britain in 1950 and set up a studio in Somerset, experimenting with materials for two years. After showing as one of six British potters at the Stedelijk Museum, Amsterdam, in 1954, in 1955 had a first solo show of pots at Primavera Gallery. Moved to Penzance, Cornwall, in the early 1980s, establishing the Barbican pottery. Cooper showed regularly with the Penwith Society, St Ives. His last solo exhibition locally was at the Out of the Blue Gallery, Marazion, in 1998, having had a retrospective at Manchester City Art Galleries, 1994. Royal Museum of Scotland in Edinburgh and Victoria & Albert Museum hold examples.

William COOPER 1923– Self-taught artist who was born in Merthyr Tydfil, Glamorgan. He attended Westminster School and Cambridge University. Cooper was for many years on the staff of Sherborne School, also lecturing independently and for Bristol University extra-mural department. Cooper began specialising in collage and mixed media in 1963, later adding oil, acrylic and watercolour. He was elected RWA in 1973, joining its council in 1991. His many mixed exhibition appearances included RA, NEAC, Swansea University and Newlyn Orion Gallery. Solo shows included Drian Gallery, 1971, and Albany Gallery in Cardiff, 1972, later ones Rona Gallery, 1988. Cooper was winner of a first prize at International Exhibition of Artists, 1964; prizewinner Westward Television Open, 1973; also at Wessex Artist, 1977; and South West Open, Plymouth, 1992. Cooper had a New Gallery, RWA, retrospective in 2005 accompanied by the monograph *Why Collage*. Welsh Development Corporation, Staffordshire Education Authority, Bryanston and Sherborne Schools hold his work. Lived in Sherborne, Dorset.

William Heaton COOPER 1903–1995 Landscape painter, writer and lecturer, born in Coniston, Lancashire. Studied partly with his father, Alfred Heaton Cooper, and at Royal Academy Schools, 1922–5. His many depictions of the Lake District were based on years of experience as a fell walker and climber. Cooper was an honorary life-member of the Lake Artists' Society. His book *Illustrated Hills of Lakeland* appeared in 1938, later ones including *Lakeland Portraits*, 1954, and *Mountain Painter*, 1984. Alpine Club and Abbot Hall Art Gallery, Kendal, hold his work. He was elected RI in 1953, also showing at RA and RBA and having several solo exhibitions. Was married to the sculptor Ophelia Gordon-Bell. Lived in Grasmere, Cumbria.

Yvonne COOPER 1951– Painter who attended Wimbledon School of Art, 1969–70; Chelsea School of Art, 1991–2, Byam Shaw School of Art, 1992–5, and the Royal Academy Schools, 1995–8, being included in the Final Year Show there. Cooper's scholarships included Byam Shaw, 1992–5, Pitchforth Royal Academy, 1995–8 and Leverhulme Royal Academy, 1996-8. Among her awards were a Painters and Stainers painting bursary, 1994, Richard and Landseer Prizes, both 1997, and the Geoffrey Ball Memorial Prize, 1998. Other exhibitions included Mall Galleries and Marks & Spencer Show, both 1998. Lived in High Wycombe, Buckinghamshire.

Mira COOPMAN 1924– Painter and draughtsman in pen and ink, born in Łódź, Poland. She was educated in Poland, Israel and Beirut and studied art in Jerusalem in the mid-1940s, then attended Slade School of Fine Art, 1946–8. Exhibited in Middle East, with British Council and in London with Ben Uri Art Gallery. Lived in London.

Mark COOTE 1932– Painter, draughtsman and teacher, born in London. Coote was given a mural commission for Festival of Britain in 1951, then attended Royal College of Art, 1954–7. He soon established a following, appearing through the 1950s in Young Contemporaries, in a 1955 Arts Council travelling show and at Leicester and Redfern Galleries. In 1957 he was one of six young painters chosen for a Critics' Choice exhibition at Gimpel Fils. But Coote wanted to avoid being manipulated and sought time to work out his own ideas. Eventually moved north and became senior lecturer in art at Warrington College of Education, giving up teaching in 1983 for a period of self-imposed isolation and intense work. By this time his pictures had attracted the attention of Kenneth Clark and Graham Sutherland, who noted Coote's special abilities as a landscape painter. From the early 1970s Coote had a series of one-man exhibitions, notably at Didsbury, 1972; Portland Gallery, Manchester, 1974; then a series with Tom Caldwell Galleries in Belfast, Dublin and London, having an Irish retrospective in 1988. Manchester City Art Gallery, Bolton Museum and Art Gallery and North West Arts Collection hold his work.

Ronnie COPAS 1936– Versatile artist, designer and teacher, born in London and sometimes known as Ronald Copas, his brothers, Eric and Roy Holt, also being painters. Ronnie studied drawing at Epsom School of Art and etching at Royal West of England Academy. He progressed from his first solo London show in the 1950s through teaching, scene painting and graphic design back to fine art. Copas took part in group exhibitions in Newlyn and St Ives, Cornwall. Among his most notable works was the early 1970s triptych Robert Aitken preaching at Pendeen, for the Church of St Andrew, Pencoy, illustrated in Michael Day's *Modern Art in English Churches*, 1984. Copas's work was also featured in several books on naïve and primitive artists, including Eric Lister's *Portal Painters*, 1982. Copas had a number of solo shows in London at the Portal Gallery, mainly culled from his experiences as a boatman and guide at St Michael's Mount, some included in his 2002 Portal one-man exhibition. Sir Peter Scott and the Wildfowl Trust commissioned Copas to paint a large canvas, St Francis and the Wildfowl, as a result of which the artist was given honorary life membership. Later, Robert Pennant Jones commissioned a major piece incorporating a definitive scene from 37 of William Shakespeare's plays; this was unveiled at the Swan Theatre, Stratford-upon-Avon, toured the country with the Royal Shakespeare Company art collection and was installed in the patron's London home. Copas lived in Crewkerne, Somerset.

Barry Gordon COPE: *see* **ABBOTT**

Elizabeth COPE 1952– Painter of bold, colourful still lifes and landscapes, born in County Kildare, Ireland, setting in County Kilkenny. She attended the National College of Art and Design, Dublin, 1970; Sir John Cass School of Art, 1972–4; and Chelsea School of Art, studying fine art, 1974–7. Among many awards were a Spanish Government Grant to Segovia and Madrid, 1974; a French Government Grant to Aix-en-Provence, 1982; a Travel Award to Zurich, 1992–3; and an Arts Council Travel Bursary to Somalia, 1994. Group shows included Odette Gilbert Gallery, 1987; Claremorris Open from 1989; Brontë Contemporary Art, Boston and Florida, 1993; and John Martin of London, 1995. Had a solo exhibition at Peacock Theatre, Dublin, 1979, then showed frequently, later ones including Solomon Gallery, Dublin, and Park Walk Gallery, both 1995.

Jill COPE 1944– Painter, draughtsman, printmaker and teacher, born in Shrewsbury, Shropshire, where she attended the College of Art and Leeds College of Art in the 1960s. Taught in Manchester, in 1974 moving to Dorset where she was head of art at Gillingham Comprehensive School. Left full-time teaching in 1988, moved back to Shropshire, settling at Woolston, Craven Arms, in a converted cowshed with a garden studio, and began painting seriously in 1990. Mixed exhibitions included Hereford Museum and Art Gallery and Millfield Open Art Exhibition, both from 1991; West Midlands Open, Dudley, and Davies Memorial Gallery, Newtown, both 1992, and in both a prizewinner; and Millfield Open, Machynlleth Tabernacle Open and Newtown Open in Powys, all three in 1993, a prizewinner in each case. Had a solo show at Museum of Modern Art, Machynlleth, 1994. It, Millfield School and Dudley Museum and Art Gallery hold examples. Cope wrote that she loved "making marks, laying on paint or scratching a line ... I suppose I should be an Abstract Expressionist" but "the figure, whether human or animal has been the primary basis for representational art and I find myself bound to that tradition."

Constance Gertrude COPEMAN 1864–1953 Painter, printmaker, poster designer and teacher. Was born in Liverpool, where she studied under John Finnie at the School of Art, 1891–1900, then in St Ives, Cornwall, with Julius Olsson. Sometimes signed work C G C. Exhibited extensively at RCamA, RE and especially Walker Art Gallery Liverpool, which holds her work; also at RA and Royal Glasgow Institute of the Fine Arts. Lived in Liverpool where records show her to have died "very poor".

John COPLANS 1920–2003 Artist, teacher, art magazine founder and editor, curator and photographer, born in London into a household with a passion for art. Coplans' parents moved to South Africa after his father's World War I service, where they became prosperous. John moved to join them there; they returned to London where John attended Marylebone Grammar School and began painting and drawing; then back to Johannesburg. With World War II looming, Coplans worked his way to England, to fulfill an ambition to become a Royal Air Force pilot, but was barred from serving because of an old rugby injury; and transferred to the Scottish Rifles in Africa, eventually joining the Burma campaign. Back in London, he began to show as a self-taught painter, supporting himself by painting and decorating, refurbishing and renting out flats. Showed abstracts with RBA, 1950; LG, 1954; New Vision Centre, 1957, and elsewhere. Inspired by the new American painting seen at ICA and Tate Gallery, Coplans moved to California. He taught design; exhibited at John Bolles Gallery, San Francisco; with Bolles' director, Philip Leider, he founded the controversial magazine *Artforum*; and curated his first exhibition, Pop Art USA, at Oakland Art Museum. Coplans became curator at the University of California and then Pasadena Art Museum, where he showed such key artists as Roy Lichtenstein, Andy Warhol and Donald Judd. In 1971 Coplans joined *Artforum* in New York as editor-in-chief. He developed an enthusiasm for photography, with which his father had experimented, and wrote books covering a wide field of interests. Having in 1978 changed direction again, becoming director of the Akron Art Institute and setting up a new art magazine, *Dialogue*, Coplans soon wearied of an art world that he felt had become money-obsessed and settled in New York to concentrate on his series of unsparing body self-portrait photographs resembling landscapes and sculptures. His first show was at Pace/MacGill Gallery, 1986, later ones including The Dean Gallery, Edinburgh, 1999. In 1997, he married Amanda Means, also a photographer. Coplans' work is in dozens of public collections worldwide, including the Museum of Modern Art, New York, and in England at the Tate, Plymouth and Hull.

Heather COPLEY 1918–2001 Painter, graphic artist and teacher, full name Diana Heather Pickering Copley, born in Brewood, Staffordshire. She was married to the artist Christopher Chamberlain. Studied at Clapham School of Art, 1933–9, and Royal College of Art, 1940; after part-time teaching she returned to Royal College, 1945–7, in 1948 having a postgraduate year. Among her notable teachers were Vivian Pitchforth, W A Wildman and Carel Weight. From 1948–83 taught mainly part-time at St Martin's School of Art, drawing and painting. Between 1955–68 did graphic work for various outlets including Phoenix House, Bodley Head, Law Society and John Lehmann. Showed at RA Summer Exhibitions from 1950; Arts Council travelling exhibitions from 1960; Seven Dials Gallery, 1982; and Richard Allan Gallery, 1988. RA holds her work Lake Trasimeno, bought in 1978. Lived in London.

John COPLEY 1875–1950 Painter and printmaker, born in Manchester. Studied at the University there, then at the School of Art; at the Cope and Nicol School of Art; then at the RA Schools. Married to the artist Ethel Gabain. Travelled extensively in Italy. Exhibited extensively at Cooling Galleries, Goupil Gallery and RBA, also with NS, NEAC and abroad. Became honorary secretary of the Senefelder Club, 1910–16, only three years after taking up lithography, for which he won principal awards at an international exhibition at Chicago Art Institute in 1930. Was an honorary foreign member of Pulchri Studio, in The Hague. British Museum, Victoria & Albert Museum, provincial and foreign galleries hold his work. In 1985 Garton & Cooke put on a show of prints by Copley and his wife; in 1990 the Yale Center for British Art, in America, and Agnew both staged exhibitions by Copley. Semi-reclusive and a semi-invalid, Copley lived in London.

Edward Bainbridge COPNALL 1903–1973 Sculptor, teacher, and painter. Born in Cape Town, South Africa, Copnall – father of the painter John Copnall – studied at Goldsmiths' College School of Art and at the Royal Academy Schools. He turned to sculpture in the late 1920s. He exhibited widely, including RA, LG, NEAC, RP, RSA, NS, ROI and at the

Paris Salon. His commissions included figures on the RIBA building, Portland Place; St Columba's, in Pont Street; and several dozen carvings for the liners *Queen Mary* and *Queen Elizabeth*. Copnall was head of Sir John Cass College, 1945–53, and president of the RBS, 1961–6. His work is in a number of British and foreign collections. Lived at Littlebourne, Canterbury, Kent. The Henry Moore Institute in Leeds holds a Copnall archive.

Frank Thomas COPNALL 1870–1949 Portrait painter, born in Ryde, Isle of Wight, married to the artist Teresa Copnall. He studied at Finsbury College and began a business career in Liverpool, painting in his spare time, then a commission enabled him to become a professional portrait painter from 1897. He was a member of NPS, Liverpool Academy and Liver Sketching Club, also showing at Liverpool Autumn Exhibition, RA, RP, RSA and abroad. Williamson Art Gallery & Museum, Birkenhead, has several portraits of local dignitaries by Copnall.

Hugh COPNALL 1918–1998 Farmer and artist, born at Horsham, Sussex, real name Hubert Copnall. He was the younger brother of the sculptor Edward Bainbridge Copnall, with whom he worked on heads decorating Broadcasting House; carved designs for the liner *Queen Mary*'s dining and state rooms; London fountains and other commissions. Studied at the Central School of Arts and Crafts under Bernard Meninsky and William Roberts, abandoning art for the land, to Roberts' regret. Hugh was early influenced as an artist by his uncle Frank Copnall, the portrait painter, observing his techniques, which he was quick to absorb. Modigliani, Cézanne and Rembrandt were key influences on his work. Showed in Dunwich, Suffolk, where he lived and painted local landscape and sea-related scenes, although he was primarily a portrait painter. Among his portraits was one of Roderic Barrett, with whom he shared a room as a student. Copnall combined acute artistic abilities with the many practical ones that sustained him as a farmer.

John COPNALL 1928– Painter and teacher, born in Slinfold, Sussex, son of the sculptor Bainbridge Copnall. He studied at the Architectural Association, 1945–6; did his National Service in the Army; from 1949–50 studied with his father at Sir John Cass College; then under Henry Rushbury at the Royal Academy Schools until 1954, the year he won the Turner Gold Medal for landscape painting. Went to Spain to live until 1958, initially being a figurative painter, but by the time he returned he was committed to abstraction. Gesture and colour are distinguishing features of Copnall's work, themes derived from sources such as jazz, window-bars in a studio or landscape. Copnall taught for many years from 1973 at Central School and was a visiting teacher at Canterbury College of Art for a time. He won an E A Abbey Scholarship in 1970; Arts Council Awards, 1972–3; a British Council Award, 1979; and in 1989 was elected a LG member. Group shows included Wildenstein, 1958; Annely Juda Fine Art, from 1969; John Moores Liverpool Exhibition, from 1972; RA Summer Exhibition, from 1980; British and Irish Modernist Art, Christie's, 1986–9; and Cross Currents, Reed's Wharf Gallery at Barbican Centre, 1996. Had a solo exhibition at Piccadilly Gallery, 1955, later ones including Reed's Wharf and De La Warr Pavilion, Bexhill-on-Sea, both 1996. In 2005, Modern British Artists showed Landscape Forms, Copnall's early works. Arts Council, Aberdeen and Bristol public galleries and other notable collections hold examples. Lived in London.

Teresa COPNALL 1882–1972 Painter, notably of flowers. She was born Theresa Norah Butchart in Haughton le Skerne, Darlington, County Durham, her father a company director; was educated in Brussels, Belgium; and by the time that she entered the Slade School of Fine Art to study painting and drawing 1903–5, under Frederick Brown, Henry Tonks and Philip Wilson Steer, had her home at Barrow in Furness, Cumbria, where she had attended the local art school. She was also a pupil at the school founded by Sir Hubert von Herkomer in Bushey. After marrying the artist Frank T Copnall they settled at Hoylake, Cheshire. At various times she was a member of UA, Royal Glasgow Institute of the Fine Arts and the Deeside Art Group. She showed over many years at the RA Summer Exhibition, also at ROI, RCamA, RSA, SWA, at Paris Salon and in Canada, work being signed with a TNC monogram or Teresa Copnall. Work was reproduced by the Medici Society and Raphael Tuck and is held by the Walker Art Gallery, Liverpool.

Tim COPPARD 1957– Versatile artist, born and lived in London, who studied at Byam Shaw School of Art, 1976–7, and Bristol Polytechnic, 1977–80. Exhibitions and commissions included LAF studio shows, from 1996; Rope (bronze), East London Landmarks, 1996; Hotlink (sound, light and video installation), 1997; Hackney Clocktower, 1998; and John Moores Liverpool Exhibition, 1999, where Coppard's arresting oil on panel Film Fiction recalled a moment captured on film.

James COPPER 1967– Sculptor in stone, and lecturer, who had an early introduction to sculpture through his godfather the sculptor John Farnham, who worked with Henry Moore and took James many times, as a child, to visit Moore. James studied at Ware College, 1984–6; St Albans College, 1986–7; and Canterbury College of Art, 1987–90. Although he spent most of his foundation course drawing and painting, at Canterbury he concentrated on sculpture for his degree thesis and to further his carving skill worked as a mason on the Cathedral. In 1990, the year he won a Tom Pemberton Travel Award, Copper became a visiting lecturer, South Kent College of Technology, Canterbury Technical College, and took part in international carving workshops. From 1990–6, was a fine-art technician with Momart, from then on being a sculpture consultant with The Henry Moore Foundation. Took part in many group exhibitions, a solo show of his fine figurative work at Chappel Galleries, Chappel, 2001, indicating Copper's strong underlying interest in ancient Egyptian, Latin American and Chinese carvings and artefacts.

Robert COPPILLIE 1951– Painter and teacher, working in watercolour and gouache, born in London. He moved to Suffolk in 1976 and produced meticulously detailed pictures of its flowers and wildlife. Taught courses at the Snape Maltings, where he showed, also at SWLA and Haste Gallery, Ipswich. Held solo exhibitions at Harrods and at several galleries in East Anglia.

Sioban COPPINGER 1955– Sculptor and teacher, born in Canada, whose childhood was spent abroad. She gained an honours degree at Bath Academy of Art, 1974–7. Taught at

Downe House School, Hermitage, Berkshire, 1991–2. Coppinger worked extensively in the field of public sculpture. In 1982 won competition and was commissioned by Nottinghamshire County Council to create sculpture for Rufford Country Park; in 1991 completed work for Donnington Valley Hotel; in 1992 Elephant Waterworks for Basingstoke District Hospital. She was made an associate of RBS in 1991, later being elected to council. In 1993 was included in 1st RWA Open Sculpture Exhibition and showed at Chelsea Harbour Yacht Club Gallery. A sense of fun was a strong feature of Coppinger's work. Lived in Newbury, Berkshire.

Trewin COPPLESTONE 1921– Artist, publisher, lecturer, broadcaster and writer, born in Dartmouth, Devon, who studied at Nottingham College of Arts and Crafts and Goldsmiths' College School of Art. In a diverse career, he taught mural painting at Hammersmith College of Art; was a visiting art history lecturer; editorial director, later director of publishing for the Hamlyn Group; ran his own publishing company; broadcast on television, including the London Weekend Television series *Art for All*; and wrote and edited art books, among them *Architecture, an introduction for children*, 1969. Copplestone also designed theatre sets and costumes for Bernard Miles' Mermaid Theatre and the Margate Stage Theatre. Public works included the fibreglass Bull Forms for the Bull Ring Shopping Centre, Birmingham, 1963, and a mural for Carlisle Civic Centre, 1965. Took part in London mixed exhibitions, having a solo exhibition at the Matthiesen Gallery, 1957.

Helen Dorothy COPSEY 1888– Painter, notably in tempera, and teacher. She was born in London, her father being an art dealer. Attended Regent Street Polytechnic School of Art, 1905–10, then Royal College of Art, 1910–12. She exhibited NEAC, RA, RBA, WIAC of which she was a member, and SWA. Her work is illustrated in George Orwell's monograph on *The English People* and she has pictures in the collections of Derby Museum and Art Gallery and Russell-Cotes Art Gallery and Museum in Bournemouth. Lived in London.

Rick COPSEY 1964– Artist, born in Bishop Auckland, County Durham, who graduated with honours in fine art, Falmouth School of Art & Design, 1985–8, gaining his master's from Manchester Metropolitan University, 1993–4. Exhibitions included New Art North West, Cornerhouse, Manchester, 1991; Material World, Bury Art Gallery & Museum, 1993; Cool Britannia, British Lime Gallery, Santa Ana, California, America, 1998; Imagination for Cancer, Imagination Gallery, 2000; and Beyond the Endgame: Abstract Painting in Manchester, Manchester Art Gallery, 2003.

Horace COPSON 1903– Watercolourist and designer, born in Bedford. He studied at Northampton Art and Technical School, then privately. Exhibited with ROI, RBSA and with NS, of which he became a full member in 1968, showing annually until 1979, also at Paris Salon. Later solo shows included Alfred East Gallery, in Kettering, 1974, and Woburn Abbey, 1975. Lived in Northampton.

Michael COPUS 1936–2000 Muralist and teacher who initially worked in oil and later in acrylic, using several layers of colour. He produced realistic pictures, often landscapes, with a strong sense of design. Copus was a star pupil at Kingston Art School, then the Royal Academy Schools, where he won a bronze medal. Before leaving he was commissioned to produce his first mural, of Mount Kenya for the Commonwealth Institute, done in 1962, later used on Kenyan postage stamps. Copus worked from photographs in that case, otherwise archaelogical plans and a written brief were adequate. His largest work, completed in 1963, was a 150-foot mural for the Nature Conservancy, of Britain from Scotland to the South Downs. For a short time after leaving the Royal Academy Copus taught still life and life painting at Kingston and Harrow Art Schools. Other notable murals were for the Geological Museum; Lawn Tennis Museum; Princess Diana Conservatory, Kew Gardens; National Motor Museum, Beaulieu; Dover Museum; Guinness, Dublin; Saratoga Horse Museum, New York; and the National Museum of Natural Science, Taiwan, the designer, James Gardner, being a close friend and advocate. Copus also lucratively sold holiday paintings to Arabs through an agency in Paris.

Steven COPUS 1956– He graduated with honours from Camberwell School of Art and Crafts, 1980–3. Copus was featured in New Contemporaries, ICA, and New Graduates, Christie's, both 1983; South London Open, at South London Art Gallery, and Drawing Open, Café Gallery, both 1986; and Critics Space 5, at Air Gallery, and East End Open Studios, based at Richmond House Studios, both 1989.

Lydia CORBETT 1934– Watercolourist, born in Paris into an artistic environment, her father being a dealer, her mother a painter. Corbett was self-taught, her pictures having a springy line and gay washes, featuring still lifes and figure studies with witty additions. During the 1950s Corbett met Picasso at Vallauris on the French Riviera. In 1993, to accompany the Tate Gallery exhibition of Picasso's sculpture and painting, BBC2 television showed a documentary about Corbett with Picasso. She became the model for a sustained cycle of works, known as the Sylvette paintings. Moved to England in 1968, settling in Devon. She was represented by Francis Kyle Gallery from 1989, when she appeared in the theme show Blue and White. From 1989 held solo shows with the gallery. Corbett had a solo exhibition at Fosse Gallery, Stow-on-the-Wold, 2004.

Peter CORBETT 1952– Painter and teacher, born in Rossett, Denbighshire, who studied foundation under Maurice Cockrill at Liverpool College of Art and Design, 1970–1, gaining an honours degree with tutor Brendan Neiland at Manchester Regional College of Art and Design, 1971–4. He was a speaker at the Workers' Educational Association, 1995, and life drawing tutor, Bluecoat Chambers, 1996, both in Liverpool where he lived. Corbett's prizes and awards included a Merseyside Contemporary Artists Exhibition Purchase Prize, 1988; International German Art Prize, St Lukas Academy, Memmelsdorf, 1998; and a Vincent van Gogh Award there, 2000; and an International Peace Prize, United Cultural Convention, America, 2002. In 1996–7, Corbett was the originator of Liverpool European Capital of Culture 2008. As well as participating in many group shows, by the time of his 1987–02 retrospective at the Senate House Gallery, University of Liverpool in 2004, he had achieved a dozen solo exhibitions. The work that he showed at the retrospective consisted of a technique he had discovered in August 1987, termed Double-Edging. The pictures stemmed from earlier studies of cell, water and organic forms and the philosophy of Taoism, Zen Buddhism and Theosophy in the 1970s; in addition, the New Science, such as Chaos Theory, Fractal Geometry, Zero Point Energy and Quantum Physics, among other things, in the 1980s and 1990s. Liverpool University, the Atkinson Gallery in Southport and private collections in Europe, America and Australia held examples.

Thomas James CORBIN 1906– Painter, printmaker and teacher, born in London. Studied at Croydon School of Art, 1922–7, with Oswald Crompton, then at Royal College of Art, 1927–30, with Reco Capey. Corbin held several teaching appointments for almost 20 years from 1930, including Edinburgh and Leicester Colleges of Art, eventually becoming a schools inspector specialising in art. He showed at RA, in the provinces and in Sweden and wrote several books on fabric printing and design. Lived in Elsworth, near Cambridge.

Tim CORBY 1966– Artist who graduated with honours in fine art, Middlesex Polytechnic, 1984–7, in 1984 winning the Munnings Award, British School at Rome. He showed there, Whittington School of Art, Wimbledon School of Art and Goldsmiths' College. Corby was included in East End Open Studios, at Angel Studios, 1989.

Roger CORCORAN 1943– Artist whose work included collage, born in Liverpool. He attended the College of Art there and Royal College of Art. Group exhibitions included Liverpool Academy; London Artists at Shrewsbury School, 1968; BBC Television and elsewhere. Lived for a time in Streatham, south London.

Mario CORDEIRO 1975– Artist, designer and performance artist, born in Lisbon, Portugal, who lived and worked there and in London. In 1998 in Lisbon, Cordeiro graduated with honours in set design from the College of Theatre and Cinema (ESTC), in 2004 graduating with honours in fine arts, painting, from the University of Lisbon (FBAUL). In 1998 Labirintico, Machine of Peregination, was a performance at Mundial Exhibition Expo '98, in Lisbon; then in 1999 Cordeiro won drawing honours at both Cena D'Arte 99, Lisbon, and Jov' Arte 99, in Loures, also a first prize at Jov' Arte 99. Other appearances included Gasthof, Frankfurt, Germany, 2003; Winner Best Overall Entry, Margaret Harvey Gallery, St Albans, 2004; and Young Artists 2005, at the Portuguese Centre of Art and Ideas, Lisbon, in 2005. In that year Cordeiro also had his first United Kingdom solo show, The Presence, at the Margaret Harvey Gallery. It comprised two installations. His work was said to "begin with an exhaustive reading and analysis of 'fine art' language, science and aerospace technology, confronting its concepts, conventions and methodologies."

Magda CORDELL: *see* **Magda Cordell McHALE**

Donald CORDERY 1942– Watercolourist and teacher, born in Hampshire, who studied at Winchester School of Art and the Royal Academy Schools, later working as assistant to Edward Bawden. Was a visiting lecturer at Manchester College of Art, later lecturing part-time at Berkshire College of Art. Much of Cordery's career was spent on very concentrated pictures of birds and animals, commissioned works for large companies and publishers. Later figure pictures and landscapes were in a looser style, India being a subject that fascinated him. Exhibitions included Brian Sinfield Gallery, Burford. In 1998, Cordery was a runner-up in the Singer & Friedlander/*Sunday Times* Watercolour Competition. Lived in rural Gloucestershire.

Denise de CORDOVA: *see* **de CORDOVA**

Paul CORDWELL 1963– Artist who studied for his higher education diploma in fine art and the philosophy of twentieth-century art from Manchester Polytechnic, 1984–6; graduated with honours in fine art from Staffordshire Polytechnic, 1986–9; and gained his master's from Manchester Metropolitan University, 2002–4. Group shows included Young Contemporaries, Whitworth Art Gallery, Manchester, 1987; Plato's A Dog, performance, Green Room, Manchester, 1993; Local 02 – Banal Ground, Parkhaus Gallery, Berlin, 1999; and Beyond the Endgame: Abstract Painting in Manchester, Manchester City Art Gallery, 2003. Later solo exhibitions included Images for Aliens, Crescent Art Centre, Scarborough, 2002; and in 2003 Ugly Little Ornaments (sound work with Loopaznavour), KFAI radio station, Minneapolis, and KKUP, Cupertino, and Paintings That Changed The World (ongoing project), at American, Scottish and Spanish venues. Cordwell lived in Prestwich, Manchester.

Philip CORE 1951–1989 Figure painter and draughtsman, also well known as a broadcaster on arts and as a photographic critic in British national press. He was born in Dallas, Texas, spent the first few years of his life in India, then returned to New Orleans. Aged six he entered military academy, and aged seven won first prize in the Vieux Carré Artists Open Competition. While at Middlesex School at Concord, Core won every possible prize for art and literature during the period 1963–9, when he entered Harvard on a scholarship. After a short period he obtained leave to go to Paris, where he helped research a book on the Symbolists, returning to graduate in 1973. Later that year he attended Ruskin School of Drawing, Oxford, then in 1974 Accademia di Belle Arti, Florence, moving permanently to London in 1975. Core's work appeared in *Vogue, Vanity Fair, New Society, Illustrated London News* and elsewhere. Core carried out a number of commissions, including a mural for the Ritz Hotel in 1980; Cyclorama, commissioned by BBC Television in 1984; and Joy, a sculpture for The London Lighthouse Project, in 1987. His publications included *Camp: the Lie that Tells the Truth*, 1984. Took part in mixed shows in London and abroad and was given a memorial exhibition at St Jude's, 1990. Arts Council holds his work.

Mark CORETH 1958– Self-taught sculptor who, after spending his childhood on the family farm in Kenya until 1971, served from 1979–93 in the Blues and Royals. During Army service he began to sculpt and in 1986 was commissioned to create and cast in silver the regiment's drum horse Belisarius for the warrant officers' mess. A second cast, in bronze, was the Household Cavalry's wedding gift to the Duke and Duchess of York. Animals continued a strong theme in his work, which was exhibited internationally. Coreth had a first solo show at the Sladmore Gallery in 1986; took part in Zoo Sculpt 93, an exhibition of life-size animal sculpture at the London Zoo; and in 2005 was included in The Spring Show at The Wykeham Gallery, Stockbridge. In January that year Coreth travelled to Ladakh to study snow leopards in the wild, was fortunate to see one and fulfilled his ambition to make a maquette in the field.

Alfred James CORFIELD 1904– Painter, designer and teacher, born in Portsmouth, Hampshire. Although mainly self-taught, he studied for short periods in the 1920s and 1930s with private teachers. He lived in Newton Heath, Manchester, and exhibited widely in that area, including Stockport and Oldham art galleries, Stockport Art Guild and Oldham Society of Artists.

Colin CORFIELD 1910–1991 Painter of portraits, full name Thomas Charles Collingwood Corfield, who specialised in boardroom commissions. He studied at Leeds College of Art, Royal College of Art, gained a travelling scholarship in 1934, and attended Académie des Beaux-Arts in Paris. A Chelsea Arts Club member, he showed at RP and elsewhere. Lived in Chelsea, later in Selling, Kent.

Colin M CORKEY 1947– Painter, sculptor and teacher, born in Belfast, Northern Ireland, who was educated at Belfast Royal Academy, Stranmillis College and Queen's University. From 1970–97 taught at secondary schools, also at Lisburn Institute and School of Adult and Community Education. Exhibited in group shows, from 1974 at RUA, where in 1988 he was runner-up for the Wellington Park Hotel Award; also at Orchard Gallery, Londonderry, 1996; and 1997 Summer Exhibition at Tom Caldwell Gallery, Belfast, which gave Corkey solo exhibitions in 1998, 2000 and 2003. Northern Ireland's Department of the Environment and Ulster Arts Club hold examples.

Michael CORKREY 1962– Painter who was educated at Bedford College of Higher Education, 1981–2. Then studied at Leeds Polytechnic, 1982–5, and Royal Academy Schools, 1986–9. In 1987 Corkrey won the Henfield Award, followed by Worshipful Company of Painter-Stainers' Prize in 1988 and the De Segonzac Travelling Scholarship in 1989. Among mixed exhibitions Corkrey in the second half of the 1980s appeared at John Player Portrait Award Exhibition at National Portrait Gallery; he was a Winsor & Newton Finalist, ROI, at the Mall Galleries; and was in the Cadogan Contemporary Christmas Show, 1989. In 1990 he shared a show with two other painters at New Grafton Gallery.

John Elmer CORLEY 1950– Painter, printmaker and stained glass artist, born in Peterborough, Huntingdonshire. He studied at Northampton School of Art, 1968–70, teachers including Henry Bird, then at Canterbury College of Art, under Geoffrey Rigden and Stass Paraskos. Showed at New Metropole Arts Centre, Folkestone, 1973, Northampton Art Gallery, 1974, and elsewhere. Lived in Tilmanstone, Kent.

Ruth CORMAN 1939– Artist, photographer and consultant, born in Manchester, who studied at the University of Durham. She worked as a public relations consultant for arts organisations and was a director of the British Israel Arts Foundation and of the consultancy Thomas Corman Arts. She was a founder of the Designer Crafts Foundation and of the Israel Crafts Foundation. In middle age, Corman took up photography "initially inspired by the work of the great European and American photographers, in particular the London-based photographer Dorothy Bohm." She travelled extensively, producing abstract and painterly images notable for a strong use of colour, light and shadow. She then moved on to mixed-media works stemming from photography, creating "ambiguous and abstract images by the use of paint, pastel, textured gels and collage to alter and extend the form." Mixed shows included Keith Chapman & Ardent Art at 28 Cork Street, 2002. Corman also had solo exhibitions: at the Opera House, Tel-Aviv, 1998, part of the fiftieth anniversary celebrations of Israel's founding; Figuratively Speaking, at the Royal Opera House, Covent Garden, 2004; with another there in 2005. Logica UK Ltd, Reuters Ltd, Haymarket Group and other corporate and private collections hold examples. Lived in north London.

David CORNELL 1935– Sculptor and painter, born in London. From 1952–62 he attended the Central School of Arts and Crafts and Harrow School of Art, teachers including Roger Hilton and Philip Turner; was then at Academy of Fine Art, University of Pennsylvania, in America, studying anatomy under Robert Beverley Hale, 1968–70; and worked in collaboration with Marc Chagall in France. Gained five Arts Council Awards. In 1965 Cornell won a Royal Mint national selection and was appointed coin and medal engraver/sculptor, a position held until 1969. He was elected a fellow of RBS in 1971, becoming vice-president of SPS in 1977. In 1982 Cornell was awarded the Diploma di Merito Universita delle Arti, in Italy. Cornell took part in many exhibitions in Britain and abroad, including RA, 1967; 14th International Medaille, Koln, 1971; Plazzotta Studio, 1984; Cadogan Gallery, and Armstrong-Davis Gallery, Arundel, both 1985; and Henry-Brett Galleries, Stow-on-the-Wold, 1991. Among Cornell's commissions was one by jockey Lester Piggott to sculpt his retirement bronze riding Nijinsky; also completed a life-size unicorn in bronze for The Welcome Foundation building in Euston Road, London. Lived in Tunbridge Wells, Kent.

May CORNET 1975– Cornet studied textiles at Goldsmiths' College, was the founder of Dyson Art Studios, worked as project assistant to the artist Mona Hatoum and was involved in many exhibitions and residencies in Britain and on the continent. She was the daughter of the embroiderer Annie Freud, herself the daughter of the painters Kitty Garman and Lucian Freud, May thus being the great-granddaughter of the sculptor Jacob Epstein. She participated in Kitty Garman and Co at New Art Gallery Walsall in 2003–4, for which she created many new works, for which she sought "the inherent qualities of a landscape. I want them to have the famliarity of a vision from a dream, something we have experienced but is not tangible. That's why I work with small, dot-like forms: they have the ability to suggest anything – humidity, pollen, holes, swarms of insects, a crowd." Cornet's output often crossed the boundaries of fine art and craft, integrating embroidery, photography, stencilling, painting and sculptural construction. She was the photographer of the work of her mother, with whom there was an interaction of ideas and influences.

Christopher CORNFORD 1917–1993 Artist, cartoonist, writer and teacher who was born and died in Cambridge.

His great-grandfather was Charles Darwin and his mother Frances and brother John were both poets. After education at Stowe School and Leys School, Cambridge, attended Chelsea and Slade Schools of Art. Cornford was in the 1930s politically active as a member of the Communist Party and remained a rebel in spirit. His first important post was in 1947 at Newcastle and finally he was head of humanities at Royal College of Art, 1962–79. From 1984 taught in Cambridge for University of the Third Age. Cornford's book of cartoons *Drawn to Protest* was published by Cambridge Campaign for Nuclear Disarmament shortly before his death. Work by Cornford and his aunt Gwen Raverat was shown at Broughton House Gallery, Cambridge, in 2004.

Matthew CORNFORD 1964– Sculptor born in Watford, Hertfordshire, who studied at St Martin's School of Art in 1987, where he met David Cross, graduating from the Royal College of Art in 1991. He worked with David Cross as Cornford & Cross (see separate entries). Lived in London.

CORNFORD & CROSS– Matthew Cornford and David Cross (see separate entries) produced a commission for Riverside, Norwich School of Art & Design, 1999. The sculpture, placed on the playing fields of Norwich School, consisted of a life-sized figure of a military cadet standing to attention, bearing a rifle. By casting it in lead, like a toy soldier, they aimed "to connect 'base metal' with the ideals of duty, courage and self sacrifice." It was displayed on a stone plinth inscribed "Jerusalem". Cornford & Cross exhibited extensively in the United Kingdom and abroad. Earlier work included New Holland, for East International, in Norwich, 1997. In 2000, the artists' video installation Childhood's End was shown at Norwich School's Norwich Gallery, with an accompanying publication. For this project, Cornford & Cross chartered a privately owned ex-Red Arrows display team military jet and commissioned a pilot to sky-draw an Anarchy symbol with smoke. Later shows included Childhood's End at University of Hertfordshire Galleries, St Albans, and one at Nylon Gallery, both 2002.

Amanda CORNISH 1966– Figurative painter, trained at Chelsea School of Art, 1985–7. Exhibitions included ROI and Frank T Sabin; in 1995 Cornish won the Chelsea Art Society Award for Painting and RSMA's Charles Pears Award for the best work by a non-member.

Charlotte CORNISH 1967– Printmaker, painter and teacher, born and educated in Cambridge, who gained an honours degree in fine art (printmaking) at University of Brighton, 1987–90; a postgraduate diploma, Slade School of Fine Art, 1990–2; did an advanced printmaking course part-time at Central St Martins College of Art & Design, 1992–4; and was honorary research assistant in printmaking at the Slade, 1993–6. She lectured part-time in printmaking at De Montfort University, Lincoln, 1994–6; then became a full-time artist. Cornish's vibrant, sunnily coloured, gesturally abstract pictures captured the essence of exotic locations such as Macau and Mexico. She won commissions and awards, working with Bartolomeu Dos Santos on panels for Lisbon Underground and The Macau Museum, herself handling painting commissions for Cambridge University Department of Chemistry, British Telecom and TSB. Other corporate and university collections, such as University College and University of Brighton, held examples. Among her solo shows was Colouring Experience, Cambridge Contemporary Art, Cambridge, 1999.

Marcus CORNISH 1964– Sculptor and teacher who studied at Camberwell School of Arts and Crafts, 1982–6; Middlesex Polytechnic, to gain a Certificate in Education, 1986–7; Royal College of Art, 1987–8, for postgraduate studies in bronze casting; then obtained his master's degree there, 1989–92. From 1985 he exhibited widely, initially in the South London Art Gallery Sogat 82 Sculpture Show; Hannah Peschar Gallery from 1986; Arts Club, Bryan Kneale's Choice, 1990; The Discerning Eye, Mall Galleries, 1992; and in 1993 at Isis Gallery, Leigh-on-Sea, in Drawing Towards Sculpture. Cornish gained a large number of residencies and awards, notably Henry Moore Foundation Scholarship, 1989–91, and Elizabeth Greenshields Foundation Award, 1992. He was sculptor-in-residence at the Museum of London in 2005. Solo shows included Artist of the Day at Angela Flowers, 1994. Held a number of residencies, including Ravensbourne School, 1990, and Ibstock, West Hoathly, 1993, the year he was elected an associate of RBS. Commissions included Reading Town Council, Reading Civic Society sculpture of Francis Kendrick, 1991, and Head of Alberti, sponsored by Olivetti, 1992. Later teaching posts included De Montfort University, 1994, and Royal Academy Schools postgraduate school, 1995. Cornish was one of many young artists who benefited from the Prince of Wales' patronage, accompanying him on official foreign visits as artist-in-residence. Work done in Kosovo, where Cornish became involved in depicting the effects of modern warfare on a civilian population, was included in the group show About Face at Croydon Clocktower Gallery, 2002. Cornish's father was the artist and teacher Peter Cornish and his wife Mary Anne Aytoun-Ellis. He lived in Lewes, Sussex.

Norman CORNISH 1906– Sculptor and modeller in various materials, son of the architect Stephen Cornish. Educated at the Grammar School in Eastbourne, Sussex, he attended the School of Art there, 1922–9, studying under Arthur Reeve-Fowkes and Oliver Senior. Later was employed by the British film production company Gainsborough Pictures in their studios. Exhibited at RA and lived in London.

Norman CORNISH 1919– Painter, draughtsman and teacher whose work concentrated on the mining world of the northeast of England. Born in Spennymoor, County Durham, aged 14 he became a miner, like his father, retiring from the National Coal Board after 30 years. Then taught at Sunderland Art College. Showed at Northern Academy and with the Stone Gallery, Newcastle upon Tyne, later exhibitions including Nicholas Bowlby, Tunbridge Wells, 1995. In 1962 Cornish was commissioned by Durham County Council to paint a big canvas for the new County Hall. He appeared in a number of television films, including the BBC's *Two Border Painters* (the other was Sheila Fell) in 1963 and Tyne Tees Television's *Shapes of Cornish*, 1976. The library of the University of Northumbria, in Newcastle upon Tyne, has a unique collection of pictures by Cornish on permanent display, including the major paintings Pit Road near a Colliery, Winter, and Pit Road with Telegraph Pole and Lights. In 1999, the University of Northumbria published *Cornish and Spen-*

nymoor, a selection of his drawings, sketches and reminiscences, and gave him a solo show in 2003. A previous autobiographical volume, *A Slice of Life*, had accompanied his seventieth-birthday show at the University, in 1989. Cornish was self-taught, apart from attendance at the Spennymoor Sketching Club.

Stroud CORNOCK 1938– Artist in sculpture and print, interactive systems. draughtsman and curator, born John Stroud Cornock in Epsom, Surrey. He attended Kingston and Royal Colleges of Art, teachers including Hubert Dalwood and Peter Atkinson. In the late 1950s Cornock was engaged in sculpture restoration; in Minimal sculpture to 1968, his main work being Labyrinth; then was involved in interactive art systems, 1968–72. Eventually became curator of the collection of the Council for National and Academic Awards, preparing its catalogue in 1992, when it was shown at John Jones Gallery. Cornock's own exhibition appearances were Sculpture Annual, AIA Gallery, from 1962; Young Contemporaries, FBA Galleries, from 1963; Survey '68: Abstract Sculpture, Camden Arts Centre, 1968, and elsewhere. He was involved in the organisation of a number of exhibition and interdisciplinary group projects and participated in many conferences, regularly at conferences of the Society for General Systems Research, Design Research Society and Brain Research Association, 1970–82. He was co-author of *A Sculptor's Manual*, 1968, and contributed frequently to scholarly publications. Lived in London.

Arthur CORNWELL 1920– Artist, notably an illustrator interested in marine subjects, born in Vancouver, British Columbia, Canada. His education included Page Military Academy, California. Attended Art Centre School in Los Angeles; Regent Street Polytechnic School of Art; Heatherley's School of Fine Art; and Académie Julian, Paris. Showed at RA, which holds his work, also SGA, RSMA, and in the provinces. Lived in Ruislip, Middlesex.

Ken CORNWELL 1955– Artist and teacher who studied at Liverpool Polytechnic, 1972–7, gaining an art honours degree, also a teacher's diploma. Went on to lecture at Mabel Fletcher College in Liverpool. He showed at Sculpture in the Garden at Bluecoat Gallery, Liverpool, 1984, and from 1985 was included in Walker Art Gallery's touring Merseyside Artists shows. In 1986–7 he showed the collage Tua Poh, produced in response to a trip to Southeast Asia in 1985.

Christopher CORR 1955– Artist and teacher, born in London, who gained an honours degree in graphic design from Manchester Polytechnic, 1974–7, with his master's in illustration from Royal College of Art, 1977–80. Corr won a Leverhulme Travelling Scholarship to America in 1979; Royal College of Art Drawing Prize, 1980; Lloyds Bank Printmaking Scholarship, 1983; and Chelsea Arts Club Graphics Prize, 1984. He taught drawing and printmaking at Central St Martins College from 1982 and held a wide range of visiting lectureships. Driven by an "endless curiosity", Corr travelled and painted the world from the age of 18, and his work appeared on book-jackets, posters and stamps as well in galleries. Appealing colours, witty subjects and odd perspectives were characteristics. Mixed shows included Hayward Annual Drawing Exibition, Hayward Gallery, 1982; RA Summer Exhibition, 1983; Made in China, Curwen Gallery, 1987; Tuscany and Provence, Cadogan Gallery, 1992, and In-Flight, Berkeley Square Gallery, 1997. One-man exhibitions included Berkeley Square Gallery and Greene Gallery, Connecticut, both 1990, and Berkeley Square again in 2002, paintings from Madagascar, Miami, London, Los Angeles, New York, Peru and Tahiti.

Elizabeth CORSELLIS 1907–2005 Painter and etcher who studied art under Graham Sutherland at Chelsea School of Art. Exhibited RA and NEAC. She was married to the designer Richard Guyatt and the aunt by marriage of the painter Jane Corsellis. Lived at Ham, Marlborough, Wiltshire.

Jane CORSELLIS 1940– Painter, draughtsman and printmaker, writer and teacher, born in Oxford. She termed herself a "member of the modern figurative movement, continuing a great tradition that began with Sickert and his early followers". She studied at Byam Shaw School of Art, 1960–4, gaining the Leverhulme Scholarship and final year painting prize. While still a student showed with Young Contemporaries and at RA Summer Exhibition. After college she painted in Spain before teaching for two years. From early 1970s she travelled extensively, including Canada, Malaysia, India, Thailand, Indonesia and Australia. As well as showing abroad she continued to exhibit with NEAC and RBA, RWS and RCamA, all of which she was a member, and RWA, of which she was an associate. Exhibited solo abroad, and from 1985 at New Academy Gallery, including 2004. Awards included De Laszlo Medal and the NEAC Critics', Hallam Purchase, Warburg, Richard Hagen and W H Patterson Prizes. Carried out major commissions for the Foreign & Commonwealth Office, London Capital Club and corporate clients. General Medical Council, REME, Arborfield, Industrial Bank of Japan and other corporate clients owned examples. Corsellis's books included *Painting Figures in Light*, 1981; *Oil Painting Techniques*, 1983; and *Atelier Series: A Personal View*, 2000. In that year, APV Films produced *Jane Corsellis: Landscapes in Oils*. Lived in London.

Georges CORWIN: *see* **Jerzy MŁODNICKI**

Sophie CORYNDON 1975– Versatile artist, born in Taunton, Somerset, who studied at Swindon College of Art, 1993–4, graduating with honours in fine art from Cardiff Art College, 1994–7. After a six-month apprenticeship in the family furniture design, reproduction and restoration business she was a specialist artist in Wiltshire, working to commission, then settled in Brighton, Sussex. There, she concentrated on a series of decorative, richly coloured and dramatic flower paintings. Commissions included six painted coats of arms for the singer Joe Cocker, 1995; working on the film *Milk*, recreating interiors of the Bloomsbury Group house Charleston near Firle, Sussex, 1997; six paintings for Luton Airport, 1998; and two commissioned by Nina Campbell Ltd for Villa Nova Hotel, Barbados, 2000. Coryndon was a member of Drawings '96, Cardiff, 1996; had an exhibition at the Elaine Somers Gallery, Holywood, Northern Ireland, 1999; and in 2000 joined the Lucy B Campbell Gallery, which showed her work at The Spring Fair, Olympia, 2002.

COSEY FANNI TUTTI 1951– Performance artist, born in Hull, who worked as COUM with Genesis P-Orridge from 1969–79 and co-founded Throbbing Gristle in 1976. She was based in England and performed internationally. Her career included: Prostitution magazine action, Curious, London, 1974; Omissions, a series of actions over 10 days, Kulturamt, Kiel, Germany, 1975; Life Forms, 1973–9, Cosey in Masculine & Feminine exhibition, Graz, Austria, 1979; Action, three-day action by Cosey, Hayward Annual, Hayward Gallery, 1980; Popocultural, South London Gallery, 1997; Out of Actions: Performance and the Object 1949–1979, touring exhibition, Museum of Contemporary Art, Los Angeles, California, America, 1998; and DiRT Gallery, new art works in group show, Santa Monica, Village Disco, Cabinet Gallery, 1999. In 2000, Cosey was included in Protest & Survive, Whitechapel Art Gallery.

James COSGROVE 1939– Printmaker, painter, sculptor, artist in ceramics and teacher, born in Glasgow. After joining the Army in 1955 as a cartographic draughtsman, Cosgrove was a telecommunications officer for a decade, then studied in prints and textile department of Glasgow School of Art, 1967–71. He concentrated on screenprints. After graduation Cosgrove worked in the department, becoming its head a few years later. In 1982 he took over as head of first-year studies. Cosgrove was mainly a painter, although in 1980 he had an exhibition of drawings at Glasgow Print Studio, followed six years later by a paintings show at Corners Gallery, Glasgow. In 1989 Cosgrove took part in the show Crossing Boundaries at Compass Gallery, Glasgow.

Milein COSMAN 1922– Draughtsman, printmaker and painter in oil, born in Gotha, Germany. She was married to the musician and broadcaster Hans Keller and was noted for her portraits of musicians, dancers and figures in movement. After education in Germany and Switzerland she studied at Slade School of Fine Art, 1939–42, notable teachers including Harold Jones for lithography. Her work appeared in a number of musical books, and in periodicals such as *Radio Times*, *Ballet* and *Opera*. In 1958 she prepared a schools drawing course for Independent Television. Mixed shows included RA, Mercury and Roland, Browse & Delbanco Galleries, RE and abroad. Had many solo exhibitions including Berkeley Galleries, 1949; Camden Arts Centre, 1969; British Council, Paris, 1970; Ryder Gallery, Los Angeles, 1974; Menuhin School and Dartington Hall, both 1982; Clare Hall, Cambridge, 1990; and Belgrave Gallery, 1996. Victoria & Albert Museum, *Financial Times*, University College in Cardiff, National Portrait Gallery and several overseas collections hold her work. Lived in London.

Frank Montague COSSELL 1930–2000 Sculptor, born in Hampton, Middlesex, who after Hampton Grammar School attended Ealing Art School, 1948–50. Rodin and Epstein were the idols of the perfectionist Cossell, who declined to exploit his talent by taking up many gallery offers. Instead he worked to commission for private studios in London, among them McCutcheon Studios, Kensington, and Thurlow Models, with much prop work for Teddington Studios; then for the architects' department of British Rail, London Midland Region; finally freelance as F C A Associates, working from a studio at Charing, Kent. A Labour government initiative that a tiny percentage of nationalised industry's budget should be spent on the arts led to Cossell's British Rail appointment as token artist/model-maker; thus, he referred to himself as "Mr 1%". Cossell's first large commission was St Christopher for Northampton station, 1966. He also completed a boot and shoe industry bas-relief for the Tannery Buildings, Northampton. In 1967, working in the Euston Road at West Lodge, one of two flanking the removed Doric Arch, Cossell sculpted the figure Locomotion, for British Rail, Glasgow. Asked by an official delegation from that city what he intended to do about the eight-foot naked man's genitalia, Cossell jokingly suggested "a jock-strap". Advised that while "that may be funny down here, it certainly wouldn't be up there," Cossell devised a fudged alternative. According to Sue Cossell, who assisted him: "It was the only time that my husband made the *News of the World*, which pleased him enormously." The Cossells had to postpone their wedding and be married by special licence to accommodate the mould drying, which Cossell hastened with an internal string of light bulbs. Cossell also completed a memorial plaque for York station and murals for other stations, Underground stations and restaurants. In the early 1970s he was privately commissioned to make a sculpture, Water Skiers, for the powerboat engine manufacturer Evinrude at the entrance hall of a new factory at Fond du Lac, Belgium. At Charing he modelled a mural for the paint maker Humbrol Ltd's new Hull area offices, Yorkshire. There were also private commissions, such as trophies for the powerboat industry, golf and othe sports. Latterly, Cossell collaborated with the architect Neil Thomas, of Atelier One Ltd, on various projects: lightweight structures, futuristic designs for Expo, the central feature of the Millennium Dome and the pontoon and legs of the London Eye. He died in Herne Bay, Kent.

Mary COSSEY fl. from 1970s– Painter, printmaker and draughtsman who studied fine art at Bromley College of Art. In 1970 she gave up work in advertising to paint full-time, in 1979 returning to part-time work. Showed at RA Summer Exhibitions; Spirit of London at Royal Festival Hall; ROI; NEAC; South London Art Gallery and elsewhere. Had solo shows at Woodlands Art Gallery, 1983, Greenwich Printmakers Gallery, 1999. The artist favoured still lifes of plants.

Brian S COSTALL 1943– Painter, printmaker and teacher, born in London. He attended Harrow School of Art, 1959–64, then Royal College of Art, 1964–7, where his teachers included Carel Weight and Peter Blake. Showed at Trafford Gallery and elsewhere.

Jensine COSTELLO 1886– Painter born in Norway, where she was brought up, also in America. Then studied at Heatherley's School of Fine Art under Bernard Adams and Frederic Whiting. Exhibited ROI, SWA, NS, RP and Paris Salon. Lived in Exmouth, Devon.

Simon COSTIN 1962– Artist in various materials who studied biology and taxidermy at Natural History Museum and theatre design at Wimbledon School of Art. Among his exhibitions were Aspects Gallery; Bergdorf Goodman, in New York; Rebbeca Hossack Gallery; and in 1990 he was included in England & Co's Art in Boxes. Costin made jewellery for Derek Jarman's film *Caravaggio*.

Mabel Winifred COTTEE 1905–1991 Watercolourist who was by profession a civil servant. She attended Nottingham College of Art part-time, 1924–34, belonged to Nottingham Society of Artists and exhibited at the

Nottingham Castle Art Gallery, as well as elsewhere in the provinces. Lived in Nottingham.

Fran COTTELL 1954– Abstract sculptor and teacher, born in Bexley, Kent. She studied at Reading University department of fine art, 1973–7, then worked for her master's degree in fine art at Goldsmiths' College School of Art, 1979–81. Taught part-time in adult education while maintaining a studio in London. Exhibitions included John Moores Liverpool Exhibition, 1978, Waterloo Gallery from 1980 and in 1982 shared an exhibition at Woodlands Art Gallery.

Maud COTTER 1954– Artist employing a wide range of materials, including wax, steel, cardboard, concrete and La Farge model plaster. Rubicon Gallery, Dublin, which showed her work, described it as "a group of related concepts focusing on the theme of the reciprocal relationship between the human body, the structures that we build around it and the presence of one within the other." Born in Wexford, Ireland, Cotter graduated from Crawford College of Art, Cork, in 1978. She was co-founder of the National Sculpture Factory and a member of Aosdana. Was based in London at Delfina Trust, 1992–7, and completed a residency at the British Embassy, Luxemburg. In 2000, she was shortlisted for the Glen Dimplex Award. Her work featured in group shows and solo projects in Europe and America from the early 1980s. The Parish Church of St Pancras, Kingston, Sussex, has a window by Cotter in memory of Michael Scott, one of its vicars, who "spoke for the oppressed." It was dedicated by Desmond Tutu, Archbishop of Cape Town, 1992.

Arthur COTTERELL 1917–1994 Artist in oil and watercolour, noted for his landscapes, born in London. He attended Regent Street Polytechnic School of Art, 1937–9, notable teachers including Norman Blamey, then during World War II studied at Leicester, Hereford and Hamburg Art Schools. After 20 years of self-employment and a period on the staff of London University, Cotterell retired early to paint full-time. He was a member of UA from 1979, and was president of Cantium Group, also belonging to South-East London Art Group and London Sketch Club. Showed at ROI, Guildhall and Mall and Westminster Galleries in mixed exhibitions. Solo shows included Fairfield Halls in Croydon and Woodlands Art Gallery, 1980. Whitbread held his work. Lived in Orpington, Kent.

Allan COTTERILL 1913– Painter, sculptor and teacher, born in Southport, Lancashire. Attended the School of Art there, Liverpool School of Art and Central School of Arts and Crafts. He held a series of teaching posts, including Carmarthen School of Art and Cardiff College of Art. Showed in public galleries in Preston, Southport and Liverpool. Lived in Winchester, Hampshire.

Reginald Thomas COTTERILL 1885–1966 Sculptor, painter and teacher, born in Hanley, Stoke-on-Trent, who married Ethel Goldberg. She was taught by him and in November 1924, aged 22, won the British Institute's Scholarship in Sculpture, worth £150. After education at Chester City and County School he became an associate of the Royal College of Art, 1914, sculpture, 1915, and was a Royal Exhibitioner. Cotterill was appointed to re-establish the sculpture department at Leeds College of Art in 1919, apparently in response to Henry Moore's wish to take the Board of Education examination. Moore later said that "For a whole year, I was Cotterill's only full-time student, and he looked after me like a child." From 1927, replaced at Leeds by Loris Rey, Cotterill was finally principal of the York School of Arts and Crafts, remaining in the city until he died. He exhibited at Walker Art Gallery in Liverpool and at Leeds City Art Gallery. His wife showed at Manchester City Art Gallery in 1928 and at SWA in 1929.

Alan COTTON 1938– Painter, teacher and writer, born in Redditch, Worcestershire. Studied at Ruskin Hall, Bournville School of Art, Birmingham College of Art and, after three years in the painting school there, completed his training at Birmingham University. In late-1970s he became a research fellow at University of Exeter, and for some years was senior lecturer in charge of painting and art history at Rolle College, Exmouth, resigning in 1982 to paint full-time. Did work for Open University, wrote articles for art magazines and was co-author of a book on child art: *Learning and Teaching through Art and Crafts.* Showed with RBA, RWA, at Stroud and Sidmouth Festivals and had several dozen exhibitions, including City of Plymouth Art Gallery, City of Exeter Art Gallery and elsewhere throughout the west of England. Cotton was elected the first president of the new South West Academy of Fine and Applied Arts, launched in 2000. In 2001, David Messum exhibited French, Irish and Italian pictures by Cotton, in which thick impasto and a rich palette featured. It was followed in 2004 by As I See it, views of Provence, Ireland, Sicily, Venice, Piemonte and Hartland. Had a studio at Colaton Raleigh, Devon.

Christopher COUCH 1946– Realistic painter, born in Hemel Hempstead, Hertfordshire, who studied at the Art School at Leamington Spa, Warwickshire, 1963, where he eventually settled, attending Slade School of Fine Art for a term in 1964. He then worked on his own, exploring various styles including abstraction, but on seeing a Rembrandt exhibition in the Netherlands in 1968 decided to abandon painting, entering an Anglican order as a novice, remaining for five years. In 1978 Couch, supported by a small legacy, took a house in Brighton and set himself to work out a style under the influence of Pablo Picasso and Francis Bacon. Regulation of the quality of light was of key importance in Couch's pictures: still lifes, figure studies and self-portraits. He believed that "painting should look ordinary, part of everyday experience," defining a good work of art as a "perfect balance of intellect, spirit, emotion and body." In 1982 Couch was artist-in-residence at Birmingham Museums and Art Gallery, which acquired Afternoon, 1982, for the permanent collection. From 1986 had a series of solo shows at Marlborough Fine Art.

Francis COUDRILL 1914–1989 Enterprising painter, puppeteer, ventriloquist, designer and inventor, born in Warwick, father of the artist and musician Jonathon Coudrille. Coudrill was originally a science teacher, then a self-taught artist, holding a successful first solo show at Warwick Galleries, Birmingham. In the 1930s Coudrill did extensive publicity work for British film companies, including a life-size model of the actress Anna Neagle for Herbert Wilcox and Seven Dwarfs masks for the film *Snow White.* Painted inn signs for Ind Coope. Coudrill had taught himself ventriloquism, making his own puppet, William Casanova, including hair from his mother's head.

To support his art, Coudrill toured the variety halls, signing for his first professional engagement in 1947; he entertained troops in the Middle East; then appeared on television with Hank the Cowboy, who became a star on BBC Television's *Whirligig*. When commercial television came, Coudrill wrote, animated and filmed Hank cartoons, creating his own superbly crafted alternative animation machine. Through the 1950s fan mail arrived by the sackful, and no home was complete without Hank glove puppets, guns, jigsaws and tea towels. Determined to be a serious painter, Coudrill settled in Cornwall and opened the Mermaid Art Centre in St Ives, later moving to Studio Golva, Cadgwith. Showed in St Ives and Newlyn. In 1991 David Lay's Penzance auction house sold Coudrill's studio contents, including figurative and abstract art.

Jonathon COUDRILLE 1945– Surrealist painter, writer, composer and guitar virtuoso, born in Warwickshire, son of the artist and performer Francis Coudrill and married to the South African poet M J (Gretl) van der Merwe. He was taught silversmithing by Art Nouveau jeweller Poppy Quelch; studied at High Wycombe School of Art; sculpture under Denis Mitchell at Redruth Art School; then painting with John Tunnard. Parallel with art, Coudrille was a musician. He was musical director on his father's *Hank Rides Again* cowboy cartoon series; had his own programme, *Young Tomorrow*, on Westward Television; in the late 1960s performed with experimental and fringe bands; was topical singer-songwriter on the radio programme *Day By Day*; and toured with the World Famous Kazatka Cossacks. His children's books included *Farmer Fisher*, the first picture book on the British market to incorporate a record. Mixed shows included Penwith Society and The Cadgwith Society of Painters, of which he was a member. Solo exhibitions included The Picture House Gallery, St Ives, 1995. Produced a series of pictures: Laying the Ghost of my Father's muse. Bank of Nova Scotia, Canada, holds his work. Lived at Studio Golva, Cadgwith, Cornwall.

Mary Louise COULOURIS 1939– Painter, printmaker and teacher, born in New York, daughter of the actor George Coulouris. Educated in London, she studied at Slade School of Fine Art, 1958–62, where her teachers included Anthony Gross; the École des Beaux-Arts, in Paris, 1963–4, in the former year gaining a French government scholarship; and for the same period at Stanley William Hayter's Atelier 17. As well as eight years' part-time lecturing in London art schools, was a tutor with the Open College of the Arts and in Greece and led workshops in Scotland. Became a noted professional printmaker and member of the Printmakers' Council, showing extensively at RA and having one-man shows in London, the provinces and abroad, Club of Greek Artists, Athens, 1998, and Hellenic Centre, 1999. Carried out extensive public art comissions, including Scottish Poetry Library, 1999, and Millennium Award Mosaic, 2000. New York Public Library and Bibliothèque Nationale, Paris, hold her work. Lived for periods in London and in Linlithgow, West Lothian.

Michael COULTER 1937– Figurative watercolourist and teacher, born in Ellesmere, Shropshire, who studied at Hereford, Stafford and Leeds Colleges of Art. He was head of art at Woolverstone School, Ipswich, 1966–87, then painted full-time. Coulter depicted everyday life in a colourful, lighthearted way, mixing movement, pattern and gentle humour. Exhibitions included RWS, 1983–5; RA Summer Exhibition, 1983–6; Peter Hedley Gallery, Wareham, from 1989; and The Cosmos, Washington, America, 1993. Coulter was closely associated with the John Russell Gallery, Ipswich, where he had a first solo show in 1985, others including Now and Then, 2004, which incorporated early work. For many years Coulter and the gallery donated a watercolour to reproduce as a Christmas card in support of SCOPE (formerly The Ipswich and East Suffolk Spastics Society). To mark the Millennium several watercolours were used to produce the SCOPE 2000 calendar, in association with *The East Anglian Daily Times*. From 2002, a Coulter Christmas card was sold to aid Victim Support.

COUM– In 1976, when the number of performance artists in Britain was put at 150, Coum was one of the most prominent, being chosen for the big British Council exhibition English Art Today 1960–76 at the Palazzo Reale, Milan, Italy. Featured were Genesis P-Orridge and Cosey Fanni Tutti (see separate entries), although it was stated that "The personnel of Coum is not fixed. Coum is the sum total of the right people at the right time... Next time it could be you." Actions by Coum were listed as 145 in six countries since 1968; exhibitions over 30 static in 13 countries; publications by Coum, 85; publications on Coum, 64; and collections, 17.

Melanie COUNSELL 1964– Artist involved in site-specific installations, born in Cardiff. She studied at South Glamorgan Institute, 1982–6, gaining a bachelor's degree in fine art, and was at Slade School of Fine Art, 1986–8. Gained a Boise Travel Scholarship in 1988 and a Whitechapel Artists' Award in 1989. Her group shows included Anthony Reynolds Gallery, 1988, and she was in South Bank Centre's touring exhibition The British Art Show 1990. Had a solo show at Matt's Gallery, 1989. Lived in London.

Graham COUPE 1950– Painter and teacher born in Accrington, Lancashire. He studied at Rochdale College of Art, 1969–70, Ravensbourne College of Art, 1970–3, then Goldsmiths' College School of Art, 1974–5. Went on to teach part-time in east London. His work was included in a Goldsmiths' show at Woodlands Art Gallery, 1983.

Glenys COUR 1924– Painter, artist in collage and teacher, born in Fishguard, Pembrokeshire. Studied at Cardiff College of Art, then went on to lecture in painting at Swansea College of Art. Took part in a number of group shows, including stained glass at Victoria & Albert Museum in 1957, SWG of which a member, and CASW; had shared shows with her husband Ronald Cour, Victor Neep and Ray Howard-Jones in Wales. Completed commissions for murals for Trustee Savings Bank in Swansea area. Was a member of WAC art committee for a time. Had a solo show at Swansea University in 1974, others including Universities of Exeter and Swansea in 1982 and Glynn Vivian Art Gallery, Swansea, 1986. That gallery, WAC and CASW hold her work.

Ronald COUR 1914–1978 Sculptor and teacher, born in Swansea, South Wales, where he attended the College of Art and then Royal College of Art. In 1947 joined the staff of Swansea College, to which he was attached for many years. He completed a number of commissions, including a head of the Member of Parliament Percy Morris for

Swansea Guildhall and work for the Foreign Office. Participated in many group shows including SWG of which he was for a time chairman, Glynn Vivian Art Gallery in Swansea and New Vision Centre. Also had one-man exhibition at University College, Swansea. In 1936 Cour won the Royal National Eisteddfod Sculpture Prize. WAC and many other institutions hold his work.

Tim COURAGE 1967– Abstract artist, born and lived in Poole, Dorset. He studied at Wimbledon School of Art, 1987–90, and exhibited at East & South, Norwich Gallery/ Kent Institute of Art and Design, 1992. His work Untitled was one of a series which he said were "parodies of formalist abstraction".

Emily COURT fl. from 1905–1957 Painter in oil, especially of flowers, born in Newport, Essex. She studied at the Slade School of Fine Art under Henry Tonks and Walter Westley Russell. Court exhibited RA, NEAC, ROI and SWA extensively, and abroad. Lived in London.

Ethol COURT 1898– Portrait miniaturist in oil and watercolour. Born in Preston, Lancashire, she studied with Harold Charles Bartlett and Margaret Oldbridge. Exhibited at RA, RMS, Paris Salon and in Brussels. She was a member of Ealing Art Club and lived at Southall, Middlesex, where she taught miniature painting.

Inga COURTAULD 1911–1971 Figurative painter, mainly in oil, born in Stockholm, Sweden, as Inga Holm, her father Oscar a successful architect. He collected art and was a friend of the playwright August Strindberg. Inga's early summers were spent on the island of Arholma, which inspired her later work, children being another favoured subject. After school she attended Stockholm Academy of Art; in 1930 joined Munich Academy, Germany, where she met her future husband; moved to England, enrolled at the Slade School of Fine Art, where she reacquainted him; in 1933 they married while he was still a student at Cambridge University, and she had her first solo show at the old Festival Theatre in Newmarket Road; and in 1934 the couple took a studio in Park Walk, Chelsea. A visit in 1935 to Spain, with its bright colours, fostered her mature style: fast painting with a palette knife using pure paint on canvas. Later that year she had a solo show at Wertheim Gallery. After periods in Nailsea and Chelsea again and the dissolution of her marriage in 1951, in 1955 she returned to Sweden where she continued to paint, dying in Stockholm. There was a retrospective show at London University's Institute of Education Arts Centre in 1977.

Jeffery COURTNEY 1947– Painter, notably of portraits. These included Lord Amory, four portraits of former Lord Mayors of London and Masters for the Worshipful Company of Haberdashers, the Earl of Cranbrook and Viscount Runciman. He studied at Hornsey College of Art and Royal Academy Schools until 1972, in that year winning the Elizabeth T Greenshields Scholarship. Showed at RA, RP, New Grafton Gallery and elsewhere and had several solo exhibitions. Had a studio in London.

Ruth Margaret COUSENS 1930– Watercolourist and teacher, born in London. She studied at Rolle College, Exeter, 1948–50, then went on to teach, including Maidstone Technical High School and Sittingbourne Girls' Grammar School. Showed at RA, RI and Paris Salon, gaining a gold medal there in 1973. Solo shows included Townley House, Ramsgate, 1973, and Royal Museum, Canterbury, 1978. Thanet Council holds her work. She was founder and project director of the Castle Trust Arts Centre in Ramsgate, Kent, where she lived.

Michael COUSIN 1965– Artist using modern media who gained a first-class fine art honours degree at Southampton Institute of Art and Technology, 1993–6, and his master's at University of Wales Institute, Cardiff, where he settled, 1996–8. Exhibitions included Cardiff Art in Time, Howard Gardens, Cardiff, 1996; Pistol/Dryll, g39, Cardiff, and Rant from Another Realm, Abraza Interno Gallery, New York, America, both 1998; Dialogues, Manege Exhibition Hall, St Petersburg, Russia, 1999; Half A Tick, g39, first major solo show, 2000; and Young Gallesi Artists, Arengario, Milan, Italy, 2001. From 2000, Cousin collaborated with Steven Brown on video projects.

Timothy COUSINS 1952– Gestural, Expressionistic artist and teacher, especially in acrylic and gouache, whose work was "rooted in an attempt to assert an identity on a surface". Cousins was born in Weston-super-Mare, Somerset, and studied at Exeter College of Art and Design, 1976–7; Ravensbourne College of Art and Design, 1977–81; and Roehampton Institute, 1982–3, Brian Fielding being an important teacher. Taught in London, where he was based at The Art in Perpetuity Trust Studios. Exhibitions included Citizens' Gallery in Woolwich and Harlech Biennale, both 1996, and Clevedon: Sharing a View, APT Gallery and tour, 1997–8, with a solo show at Colston Hall, Bristol, 1977.

Graça COUTINHO 1949– Painter, born in Lisbon, Portugal, where she studied at School of Fine Art, 1969–71, then St Martin's School of Art, 1974–7. Group appearances included John Moores Liverpool Exhibition from 1987, other provincial shows in England and Wales, on the continent and in South America. Showed solo in Portugal from mid-1970s including Calouste Gulbenkian Foundation, Lisbon, 1989, as well as Todd Gallery. Lived in London.

Marion COUTTS 1964– Sculptor, draughtsman, performance artist, musician and teacher whose recurring theme using a range of media was the communal existence of people and animals. She was born in Nigeria and gained an honours degree in drawing and painting at Edinburgh College of Art, 1982–6. Based in the Netherlands, 1986–94 and living there, 1990–4, she was a performance artist and musician, touring Europe, Canada and America. Awards and scholarships included a silver medal, 4th International Triennial of Drawing, Wrocław, Poland, 1988; British Council Scholarship to the Wrocław State School for the Arts, 1989–90; Pollock-Krasner Foundation Award, 1993–4; Rome Scholarship, British School at Rome, 1999; and a Momart Fellowship, Tate Liverpool, 2000–1, with an accompanying exhibition. From 1996 was a part-time tutor at The City Literary Institute; from 1997 a freelance artist in gallery education at several London venues including RA, Serpentine and Whitechapel Galleries; and from 2000 was part of the education network team at Tate Modern. Took part in many group exhibitions internationally, later solo shows including Yorkshire Sculpture Park, 2000, Chisenhale Gallery, 2002, and firstsite, Colchester, 2003. In that year she shared a show at Kettle's Yard, Cambridge, with Claude Heath, where she was the incoming artist fellow, he the outgoing. Coutts' Everglade was at 2 Princelet Street in 2004. Lived in London.

Kenneth COUTTS-SMITH 1929– Painter and art critic. Studied at Heatherley's School of Fine Art. Among his books was *The Dream of Icarus*. Took part in group exhibitions in Britain, on the continent and in North America and had a string of one-man shows, including New Vision Centre Gallery, 1963. Towner Art Gallery, Eastbourne, is one of several British collections holding his work, which is also in galleries in Yugoslavia and America. Lived in London.

Jack COUTU 1924– Printmaker, watercolourist, sculptor and teacher, full name Raymond John Coutu, born and lived in Farnham, Surrey, area. He studied at local School of Art, 1947–51, sculpture; Royal College of Art, 1951–4, stained glass; and Central School of Art, 1951–5, where Merlyn Evans was a notable influence on Coutu's printmaking. Coutu taught printmaking at Central School, 1957–65, then at Farnham, West Surrey College of Art & Design, 1965–85. His career as a notable carver of netsuke began in 1968, and he became a member of the America-based Netsuke Kenkyukai Society. Was also a member of RE and Printmakers' Council. The Japanese influence on Coutu's work was "due to a stay during my Army career with the occupation forces". Showed in groups at RA, at Bradford Print Biennale and elsewhere in the provinces; in leading netsuke conventions; had a two-man show with Michael Rothenstein at Alecto Gallery, 1965; and a solo exhibition at Graphic Arts Gallery, 1968. Arts Council and Victoria & Albert Museum hold his work.

Lucie-Renée COUVE DE MURVILLE 1920–1995 Painter in oil, ink wash using Chinese brushes and pastel, born in Majunga, Madagascar, of Anglo-French nationality. She spent all her early life in France, was in Mauritius, 1935–9, returning to Paris just before the war. Studied by correspondence with ABC School of Art, 1937–9, then under Emma Ruff in Paris for five years while her father, who was British, hid in the family flat. She moved to England in 1945 and contributed to mixed shows in London, Wakefield, Bradford and Bristol. In 1975 had a solo show at RWA covering her career to date. In 1957 she was chosen by Jack Beddington for inclusion in his book *Young Artists of Promise*. She was made Chevalier de l'Ordre des Palmes Académiques in 1967 and in 1982 Chevalier de l'Ordre National du Mérite. Couve de Murville specialised in portraits, flower studies, landscapes and seascapes, signing her work C de M. Young Women's Christian Association holds an example. Lived for many years in Clifton, Bristol.

Ethel Louise COVE 1916–1978 Artist, calligrapher, designer and teacher, born in Sidmouth, Devon, married to the artist and teacher Harold Cove. She attended Leeds School of Art, 1935–7, then the design school of Royal College of Art, 1937–40, teachers including Ernest Tristram and Edward Johnston. Among her commissions was *Book of the Dead and the Living*, Earls Barton, 1946, her last being *The Family Tree of Sir John Barton Townley, Bilsborough Hall, Lancaster*, 1978. Was a member of the Scribes Society. In 1964 she showed an abstract fabric collage in The Teaching Image, work by staff of Leeds College of Art at the City Art Gallery. Died at Horsforth, near Leeds, Yorkshire.

Frederick Halford COVENTRY 1905–1997 Artist in various media, born in New Zealand. Studied at Elam School of Art in Auckland, Julian Ashton Art School in Sydney and in London at Grosvenor School of Modern Art. Was made a member of the Society of Industrial Artists in 1946, next year joining the Society of Mural Painters. Showed widely, including RA, Council of Industrial Design, Imperial Institute as well as in Australia and New Zealand. British Museum, Imperial War Museum and overseas collections hold his work. Lived in London for many years.

Gertrude Mary COVENTRY 1885–1964 Painter, notably of portraits, landscapes and coastal scenes, born in Glasgow, daughter of the artist Robert McGown Coventry. She studied at Glasgow School of Art, 1902–11, and painted with her father in the Netherlands, Belgium and at Pittenweem, Fife, where she met her future husband, Edward Robertson. She married him in 1915, the year after her father died. After her husband had relinquished the chair in semitic languages at Bangor, north Wales, 1921–34, she moved to Didsbury, near Manchester, then in 1962 to Canada, where she died in Hudson, Ontario. Coventry joined the Glasgow Society of Lady Artists in 1905, also exhibiting extensively with the Royal Glasgow Institute of the Fine Arts, RSA, RCamA, RA and elsewhere.

Keith COVENTRY 1958– Painter and sculptor, born in Burnley, Lancashire, who graduated from Brighton Polytechnic, 1978–81, gaining his master's degree at Chelsea School of Art, 1981–2. Coventry was included in Young British Artists V, at Saatchi Gallery, 1995, where he exhibited apparently white abstracts which had an underlying reference to the royal family and establishment, the privileged and ceremonial. Was also included in Sensation, at RA, 1997, the year of his solo exhibition at The Showroom. He was a founder of the gallery City Racing, celebrated at ICA in 2001 with City Racing 1988–1998: A Partial Account. In 2004, Coventry had a solo show at Rove. Coventry has works in the collections of the Arts Council; British Council; Contemporary Art Society; and in America at the Museum of Modern Art, New York; Walker Art Center, Minneapolis; and Museum of Modern Art, San Diego. Lived in London.

Terence COVENTRY 1938– Sculptor who gained his National Design Diploma at Stourbridge School of Art, 1954; exhibited with Young Contemporaries, 1956–8; completed National Service, 1959–61; then attended the Royal College of Art, 1961. In 1962 Coventry started farming in west Cornwall, returning to sculpture in 1985. The land and its occupants, human, bird and animal, their ruggedness and gentleness, movement and behaviour, were central to his output. His many exhibitions included Beaux Arts, Bath; New Craftsman Gallery, St Ives; Henry Brett Gallery, Stow-on-the-Wold; Gallery Pangolin, Chalford; Lineart, Ghent, Belgium; and Berkeley Square Gallery. Commissions included Predator, Nature in Art Museum, Gloucestershire, 1992; Spiralling Rooks, Health Centre, St Keverne, 1995; and An Gof, St Keverne, commemorating 1497 Cornish rebellion, 1997.

COVENTRY ARTS EXCHANGE: *see* **ARTS EXCHANGE**

Victor COVERLEY-PRICE 1901–1988 Painter and writer who was for about 20 years from 1925 a professional diplomat. Was born in Winchester, Hampshire, and obtained his Master of Arts degree from Oxford University. He published *An Artist Among Mountains*, illustrated books for children and showed widely abroad as well as at RA, RI, UA and in the provinces. Lived in Cirencester, Gloucestershire.

Peter COVIELLO 1930– Painter, potter and teacher, born in Harrow, Middlesex. He studied at Willesden and Guildford Schools of Art, gaining his diploma in painting in 1951, and went on to teach at Maidstone College of Art and Central School of Arts and Crafts, 1957–68. His first solo show was in 1957 and he represented Britain in abstract painting exhibitions in Scandinavia and Australia, 1960–1. Coviello moved to Canada in 1968 and became co-ordinator of creative art, Sheridan College, Oakville. From 1969 he was involved with pottery after meeting Glasgow-born Liz Brown, whom he married. In both pottery and painting Coviello worked on a big scale. Arts Council holds Coviello's abstract Hanuman, of the mid-1960s. Lived for some years at Plainfield, Ontario, often showing with his wife. Later returned to London and was a resident artist at Florence Studios, showing with England & Co in 1993. During 1998, Coviello moved to Wales, where he continued to paint. His first major exhibition in London for 15 years, colourful abstract works, was at Woolff Gallery in 2003, shared with Barbara Delaney, Anne Podbielski and Denise Stonebridge.

James COWAN 1948– Painter and draughtsman, born in Glasgow in 1948. His awards included Morland Lewis Travelling Scholarship, 1981, and Tower Hamlets Arts Award, 1984. Among his many exhibition appearances were New Contemporaries at ICA, 1979; Stowells Trophy at RA and LG at Morley Gallery, 1981; Cockpit Theatre Gallery and City University, 1983; Aspex Gallery, Portsmouth, 1984; and in 1985 participated in four-man exhibition at Woodlands Art Gallery. Later appearances included Camden Annual, Camden Arts Centre, 1986; The Warehouse Exhibition, 1988; and East End Open Studios, based at Robinson Road, 1989. Peterborough City Art Gallery holds his work.

Jean Hunter COWAN fl. c.1935–1965 Sculptor and painter, educated at St Leonard's School, St Andrews, Fife. She showed at RSW, RSA, SSA, Royal Glasgow Institute of the Fine Arts and SSWA, of which she was president for most of the 1950s. She had a number of other careers, winning international golf and tennis titles; performing as a notable amateur violinist; travelling extensively, especially in Africa; and being claimed as the first woman to fly, in 1911 (a record disputed by the Royal Aeronautical Society). Lived in Edinburgh.

Judith COWAN 1954– Artist in various media, and teacher, born in London. She did a foundation course at Bristol College of Art, 1973–4, followed by Sheffield College of Art, 1974–7, then Chelsea School of Art, 1977–8. She was a Gulbenkian Rome Scholar, attending British School there in 1978–9. From 1979 taught at various art schools and was a sessional lecturer at Reading University. Her exhibitions included Northern Young Contemporaries, at Whitworth Art Gallery, Manchester, from 1975, being a prizewinner in 1977; Rassegna Internazionale di Scultura Contemporanea, San Marino, Italy, 1979, where she was a prizewinner; and Woodlands Art Gallery touring show, 1981–2, of Greater London Arts Association award winners. Had a solo show at Kettle's Yard, Cambridge, 1996, of sculpture and photosculpture. Arts Council holds her work.

Noël COWARD 1899–1973 The author of over 50 plays; 25 films as writer, director or star; hundreds of songs; a ballet and two autobiographies, he began sketching during his childhood in south London. He resumed watercolour painting in the early 1930s, usually at home in Kent. He was encouraged by Sir Winston Churchill to take up oils, which Coward employed to create colourful, stylish, a little naïve and sometimes theatrical views around his English, Swiss and above all Jamaican homes. Artists such as Derek Hill, who painted his portrait, also advised him. Coward had an allergy to turpentine, so he wore gloves when painting and used casein as a medium. Although Coward, knighted in 1969, did not design for his own shows, he completed a poster for his musical *Sail Away*. He gave a few pictures away, but they did not reach public notice until an auction of 34 at Christie's in 1988 fetched £786,000. In that year Sheridan Morley's *Out in the Midday Sun: The Paintings of Noël Coward* told their story. Died in Jamaica.

Kate COWDEROY 1875–1972 Painter and miniaturist who studied at Herkomer Art School at Bushey, Hertfordshire, from 1899. The Cowderoy family eventually settled there, and Kate became one of a circle of artists celebrated with an exhibition by the Bushey Museum Trust in 1988. From 1904 for a time Cowderoy lived in Karlsruhe, Germany, looking after two girls, through a Herkomer family connection. In the summer of 1914 Cowderoy visited Paris for a few months, later showing at the Salon, and she painted landscapes in northern France and Belgium. As well as landscapes, portraits and genre pictures, she gained many commissions for miniatures, latterly favouring flowers, gardens and cats as subjects. Exhibitions also included RA and Walker Art Gallery, Liverpool.

Ian COWELL 1964– Painter who studied at Manchester Polytechnic, 1983–4, and Leicester Polytechnic, 1984–7. Showed widely, including Smiths Galleries; Cleveland College of Art and Design; MAFA; RP from 1989; and at Agnew in The Broad Horizon, 1990.

Jenny COWERN 1943– Prolific and versatile artist and teacher, born in Worcester, daughter of the etcher R T Cowern and partner of the artist Raymond Higgs. She studied painting at Brighton College of Art, 1959–63, under Bevil Roberts, Norman Clark and Ian Potts, then at Royal College of Art, 1963–6, with Carel Weight, Colin Hayes, Jean Bratby and Leonard Rosoman. Taught at Sheffield College of Art, 1966–8, also holding visiting lectureships in English art schools and residencies in Cumbrian schools, having settled in Langrigg, Wigton. In 1979, Cowern began feltmaking, self-taught after seeing the exhibition The Art of the Feltmaker. She became a member of New Fibre Art and the International Felt Association. Took part in numerous mixed shows and had many solo exhibitions, later ones including Felts & Paintings, Keswick Theatre, 1999, and Time and Place, felts and drawings, Pendle Arts Centre, Lancashire. Commissions included enamel mural for Heworth Metro Station, Newcastle upon Tyne, 1990; felt triptych wall hanging for Hastings Hospital, 1990–1;

and two enamel murals for Queen Elizabeth Hospital, Gateshead, 1996. Shared a show with Rosemary Gascoyne at Linton Court Gallery, Settle, 2003. Victoria & Albert Museum; Whitworth Art Gallery, Manchester; Abbot Hall Art Gallery, Kendal; Carlisle Art Gallery; Paintings in Hospitals; and other public collections hold examples.

Raymond Teague COWERN 1913–1986 Although he was a versatile painter and illustrator, Cowern is noted especially for his fine work as an etcher. Educated in Birmingham, he went on to study at the Central School of Art there and at the Royal College of Art and just before World War II at the British School, Rome. The British Museum as well as galleries in Glasgow, Birmingham, Liverpool, Oxford and abroad own his work. He exhibited at the RA – of which he became an associate in 1957 and a full academician in 1968 – as well as the RWS, RE and other leading London and provincial galleries. There was a large show at Stables Gallery, Oxford, in 1996, organised by Elizabeth Harvey-Lee, North Aston. Lived in Whitehaven, Cumbria.

Hilda COWHAM 1873–1964 Illustrator of children's books and painter, born in London, who married the artist Edgar Lander. Studied at Wimbledon and Lambeth Schools of Art and Royal College of Art. After winning a prize in a competition run by the magazine *Studio* she quickly built a reputation as a magazine illustrator, noted for her facility in drawing with the brush in the Chinese and Japanese manner. One of the earliest women illustrators to work for *Punch*, she also drew for *The Graphic*, *Little Folks*, *Pearson's Magazine*, *The Sketch*, *The Sphere* and many others and illustrated a number of books. James Thorpe cites her "fantastic impressions of children" in the magazine *Moonshine*. Exhibited RA, RWS, in the provinces, Paris Salon and in North America. Wrote a number of children's stories and like her husband did some etched work. Lived in Guildford, Surrey.

Bel COWIE 1943–1983 Printmaker, watercolourist, teacher and theatre designer, born in Dundee. She studied at Gray's School of Art, Aberdeen, 1960–64, and in Berne, Switzerland. She taught at Gray's School of Art and at Aberdeen College of Education; was involved in theatre design; and between 1975–8 was director of Aberdeen's Peacock Print Workshop. Took part in many Scottish group shows including SSA of which she was a member, RSA, RSW and Compass Gallery, Glasgow. Public collections include Scottish Arts Council. Lived in Aberdeen.

James COWIE 1886–1956 Painter, draughtsman and teacher, born in Cuminestown, Aberdeenshire. In 1906 he started studying for an English degree at Aberdeen University, but association with the art teacher James Hector deflected Cowie's enthusiasm to art, and he eventually passed teacher-training examinations in drawing. From 1909 Cowie was art master at Fraserburgh Academy, then from 1912–14 he studied at Glasgow School of Art and was appointed art master at Bellshill Academy, in the Glasgow area. War cut this appointment short, but Cowie was able to resume at Bellshill, 1918–35, after a time in the Pioneer Corps as a conscientious objector. The pupils at Bellshill inspired his own painting which was meticulous in its draughtsmanship and preparation and which from the 1940s took on a Surrealist tinge. Cowie was one of the great individualists of modern Scottish painting. In 1935 he was appointed head of painting at Gray's School of Art, Aberdeen, two years later becoming warden of the Patrick Allan-Fraser School of Art, Hospitalfield, Arbroath. In 1943 he was elected RSA. Scottish Arts Council, Aberdeen Art Gallery and Museum and other Scottish galleries hold his work, of which there was a memorial show organised by Scottish Arts Council in 1957. Died in Edinburgh.

Barbara COWLES 1898– Oil painter, born in Melksham, Wiltshire. After education at Trinity Hall, Southport, she exhibited at the RA. Lived in London.

Allan Rees COWNIE 1927– Artist in oil and watercolour, pastel and black-and-white, born in Cardiff, south Wales. From 1970 he was a freelance portrait painter. Cownie studied at Kingston School of Art and Manchester Regional College of Art. His group shows included Alderley Gallery; Royal Exchange and Colin Jellicoe Galleries, Manchester; and Weaver Gallery, Weaverham. His series of solo exhibitions included Salford Art Gallery; Pitcairn Gallery, Knutsford; Howarth Gallery, Accrington; and University of Manchester. His portraits included the singer Sir Geraint Evans and the astronomer Sir Bernard Lovell. Reynards Ltd and Barr's Soft Drinks Ltd hold his work. Lived in Pwllheli, Gwynedd.

Frank Cadogan COWPER 1877–1958 Painter of historical subjects in the manner of the Pre-Raphaelites; portrait painter. Born at Wickham, Northamptonshire, he studied art at the St John's Wood School of Art, 1896, at the Royal Academy Schools, 1897–1902, and with the American-born historical painter E A Abbey, followed by studies in Italy. Exhibited prolifically at the RA; also showed at ROI, Fine Art Society, Walker Art Gallery, Liverpool, RP and elsewhere. Elected RA in 1934. He completed mural paintings in the Houses of Parliament, London, and the Tate Gallery and Leeds City Art Gallery hold his work. Lived in Cirencester, Gloucestershire.

Geoffrey COWTON fl. from 1950s– Watercolourist, printmaker, teacher and gallery proprietor, born and educated in Bradford, Yorkshire. Trained as a teacher of art at St John's College, York, later studying printmaking at Leeds College of Art. For some years he was head of art and design in a Halifax school, later working as a freelance artist and proprietor of Glendale Studio in Halifax, West Yorkshire. Cowton was a noted Dales landscape painter, his love of the area beginning with a school geography excursion to Grassington and Malham. His son Martin was an artist.

David COX 1914–1979 Painter in oil, and teacher, born in Falmouth, Cornwall, who studied art in London, France and Italy. He was closely associated with the St Ives Society of Artists and the Penwith Society of Arts in Cornwall, being honorary secretary of both. He showed at many venues, including RA, ROI, NEAC, RWA, NS, Leicester Galleries, Leger Gallery, Marlborough Gallery and widely overseas. Had one-man shows in London. Living at Stoke-by-Nayland, near Colchester, he ran his own art school for several decades.

David COX 1947– Artist in various media who began to create sculpture, toys and furniture in early 1970s, within a few years being granted a bursary by Southern Arts to work full-time. It eventually organised a touring show of Cox's creations. He also showed solo at Bath Festival, Winchester Gallery and Victoria Art Gallery in Bath and in 1992 his mixed-media constructions were included in Art in Boxes at England & Co. Cox held a series of artist-in-residencies.

Dorothy COX 1882–1947 Landscape artist and portrait miniaturist whose early years were spent in London and its southern suburbs. In 1901 she was elected RMS, also showing widely at Walker Art Gallery in Liverpool, RA, RHA, RI, Fine Art Society and elsewhere. In 1925 she settled in Shoreham-on-Sea, Sussex, where the Brighton Art Gallery holds her watercolour The Abandoned Quarry.

Elijah Albert COX 1876–1955 Painter, poster and mural artist and book illustrator, born in London. He studied at the People's Palace Technical School, Whitechapel, then at Bolt Court School. Worked as a designer in industry, which later proved useful in his public poster and mural work. Also assisted Frank Brangwyn. Exhibited RA, RI, SGA, Whitechapel Art Gallery and elsewhere. Illustrated several books. Public galleries, including Preston, Bristol and Canterbury, hold his work. Lived at Woolage Green, near Canterbury, Kent.

Ernest Moses COX 1885– Painter, born in Kettering, Northamptonshire. Studied at Bradford College of Art and exhibited extensively in Yorkshire. He was a leading member of Bradford Arts Club, with which he exhibited at Cartwright Hall for the last time in 1958. Lived in Shipley, Yorkshire.

Gertrude Florence Mary COX fl. c.1930–1980 Painter in oil and watercolour and etcher. Studied art under R Kirkland Jamieson, she went on to exhibit widely, including ROI, RBA, Paris Salon, RWA and RI. The Royal Albert Memorial Museum and Art Gallery, Exeter, holds her work. Lived in Exeter.

Ian COX 1951– Representational painter and teacher, with a crisp, fresh style, who attended Southend College of Art, 1970–2, received the Lord Leverhulme Scholarship to attend the Byam Shaw School of Drawing and Painting and in 1975 won the David Murray Landscape Prize. Taught at Southend College of Art. From the mid-1990s showed in the Essex Open Exhibition at Beecroft Art Gallery, Westcliff-on-Sea, Essex, where he lived. In 1997 was included in Four British Artists at Grosvenor Gallery.

John COX fl. from late 1980s– Wildlife painter and illustrator with a special interest in birds who in 1989 won the Bird Illustrator of the Year award presented by *British Birds* magazine, when living in Romford, Essex, and working in a London office. The year before, he had won its Richard Richardson Award for Bird Artists under 21. His painting career was launched when Chevron UK Ltd, the oil company, asked Cox to illustrate its 1990 calendar. Many commissions for books and magazines followed, Cox began to exhibit and was elected a member of SWLA, joining its council and showing with it at the Mall Galleries. In 1997 he exhibited in Chevron's calendar artists show at the ICA.

Mary COX 1938– Figure and portrait sculptor using resin bronze, born in Guildford, Surrey. She studied at Chelsea School of Art, 1959–61, under Willi Soukop, Bernard Meadows and Elisabeth Frink. Cox showed widely in London, including RBS of which she was an associate, SPS and SWA. Also worked to commission. Among her portraits were the writers and journalists Malcolm Muggeridge and William Deedes, Lord Justice Lloyd, Lord Mackay of Clashfern and Lord Glynn of Hadley. Lived at Brightling, Sussex.

Morris COX 1903–1998 Printer, writer, poet, printmaker, painter and puppeteer, born and lived in London, he won a scholarship to West Ham School of Art aged 13 and joined an advertising agency in the late 1920s. Cox found the job unattractive so turned to printmaking and writing, drawing cartoons for children's annuals, designing book-jackets, writing unpublishable novels and briefly running a bookshop in Sicilian Arcade selling only his own work. In 1940 he married Winifred Cresswell, her modest earnings enabling Cox to continue his chosen career. Although short stories appeared in *World Review* in the 1950s and Routledge published *The Whirligig and Other Poems* in 1954, Cox in 1957 set up Gogmagog Press to publish his work, and 35 highly original books followed (in 1991 the Private Libraries Association produced *Gogmagog*, a bibliography and appreciation by David Chambers, Colin Franklin and Alan Tucker), a further 38 volumes appeared in what Cox called the Gogmagog Photocopy Library, ending 1989. *War in a Cock's Egg*, 1960, recalled World War II privations, when Cox was leader of a light rescue squad. Cox also produced painted and produced lino-cuts: spirited abstracted figures, contorted portraits and subjects from nature. In 1994 a show of Cox's work was held at the Victoria & Albert Museum, after the gift of his own collection to the National Art Library. Katharine House Gallery, Marlborough, and James McWhirter, organised a substantial show of Cox's paintings and prints in 2005 accompanied by an informative and well-illustrated catalogue.

Neil COX 1955– Wildlife artist in watercolour and oil, born near Watford, Hertfordshire. He was interested in wildlife from an early age and began drawing it while studying law at Southampton University. After graduating and encouraged by the interest of many galleries, started painting full-time. Showed at Tryon, Burlington and Malcolm Innes galleries, at annual exhibition of SWLA at Mall Galleries and regularly at Wren Gallery, Burford. In 1992, was a finalist in the European Bird Artist of the Year competition. Cox's work sold extensively abroad, especially in America, Germany, Switzerland and Sweden. Lived in Devon.

Paul COX 1975– Sculptor and printmaker, born in Shoreham-by-Sea, Sussex, producing work "influenced by domestic and industrial life." He studied at Northbrook College of Art and Design, Worthing, gaining a distinction in his National Diploma, 1991–3 (and was artist-in-residence there, 1998); graduated with first-class honours, in fine art, sculpture, Winchester School of Art, under John Gibbons, 1993–6; then obtained his master's in sculpture, Royal Academy Schools, under Phillip King, 1996–9. Cox won many awards, including a Henry Moore Scholarship and R K Burt Prize, both 1996; Landseer Scholarship and British Institute Sculpture and Printmaking Awards, both 1998; and a Landseer Scholarship, Dunoyer de Segonzac Travelling Scholarship and RBS/Bronze Art Foundry

Bronze Casting Award, all 1999. Was shortlisted for several public sculpture projects, in 2000 installing a piece for Marylebone Warwick Balfour, Riverside, Norwich. Mixed exhibitions included In The Mind's Eye, Mall Galleries, 1994; Doubled Up, Union Place Gallery, Worthing, 1997; RA Summer Exhibition, from 1999; and Recent Graduates, Cranleigh Arts Centre, Cranleigh, 2000. Solo shows included Boy Wonder, Atrium Gallery, Pricewaterhouse-Coopers, 1999, and RBS Gallery, 2001. Metlife Investments and Connex South Central hold Cox's work. Lived in London.

Philip COX 1945– Self-taught artist using cardboard and salvaged paper papier mâché, born and lived in the Nottingham area. Until 1986 Cox worked in industry and local government, after which he was a full-time artist, working to commission, creating exhibitions and undertaking residencies. He made life-size figures, wryly observed, in everyday situations. Cox participated in the Open Show at Nottingham Castle Museum and Art Gallery from 1982, other mixed show appearances including The Crescent Gallery, Scarborough, 1987, and Whitworth Art Gallery, Manchester, 1989. His solo exhibition Scrap People toured from Midland Group Arts Centre, Nottingham, 1986; later tours included People in Place, nationally, based on The Turnpike Gallery, 1990–3. Cox created 60 figures for the permanent exhibition The Tales of Robin Hood. In 2001 Dudley Museums Service organised Cox's tour exhibition Strangely Familiar, featuring life-size figures of famous artists. Bedfordshire and Somerset County Councils and Epping Forest District Museum hold Cox's work.

Richard COX 1946– Artist, teacher and administrator, born in Aylesbury, Buckinghamshire, who did a foundation course at Southend School of Art; graduated from Newport College of Art; gained his master's degree at Birmingham College of Art; and his teacher's certificate at London University. Cox held full- and part-time teaching posts in the 1970s and early 1980s; moved to live in Cardiff in 1975; from 1983–94 worked at South East Wales Arts; and WAC, 1994–8. Visiting lectureships included British, American, Norwegian and Indian appointments. Foreign residencies included School of Fine Art, Kunstakademiet i Trondheim, Norway, 1987; School of Painting, Montmiral, France, 1991; and Bemis Centre for Contemporary Arts, Omaha, Nebraska, 1999. Although Cox did some figurative work, including Photo-Realist drawings of American cars, his work was mainly non-figurative, as in the three-man touring exhibition Analogue, originated at Newport Museum and Art Gallery, Wales, 1999. Later solo shows included Art Heritage Gallery, New Delhi, India, 1999, and a retrospective at Newport, 2005. WAC, CASW, Newport and Dudley Art Galleries and other public, university and foreign collections hold examples.

Sally COX 1955– Sculptor, born in London, who worked as a gardener and dress designer before moving to Yorkshire in 1990 "to enable me to concentrate on art". An exhibition of Zimbabwean sculpture at the Yorkshire Sculpture Park persuaded Cox to focus on local stone. After gaining an honours degree in history at University of York, 1974–7, she trained as a teacher at the Froebel Institute, 1977–8. Took part in sculpture and life drawing classes at Camden and Islington Adult Education, 1988–90, at periods between 1989–92 continuing her studies at Open College of the Arts and Rochdale College. Her work was included in Islington Arts Group at Hardware Gallery, 1989; Turret Studio Group, The Turret, Hebden Bridge, 1992; Yorkshire Women Artists, Elizabethan Gallery, Wakefield, 1993; and it was also shown by The Gallery, Manchester.

Stephen COX 1946– Sculptor, born in Bristol. He studied there, at Loughborough and at Central School of Art, 1964–8. He first showed in London in 1976, after which he exhibited widely elsewhere in Britain and on the continent, notably at the Lisson Gallery. In 1985 had a major exhibition at Arnolfini Gallery, Bristol, which reviewed his work from 1977–85. He usually worked in stone, but also employed materials such as sand and lime on plasterboard and wood. Cox was preoccupied with architectural shapes and the Italian Renaissance tradition of stone carving and chose to spend much of his time in Italy. The marble Tondo 1981 in Tate Gallery collection employed red marble from Verona, carved under his supervision by local craftsmen. In 1995 Cox had a show at The Henry Moore Institute, Leeds, called Surfaces and Stones of Egypt. Arts Council holds several of his works.

Sue COX 1933– Artist in ceramics and porcelain, born in Singapore, who studied with Lucie Rie and Hans Coper at Camberwell School of Arts and Crafts, 1960. Her early work was architectural ceramics and studio pottery, sculptural work starting in 1990, "influenced by colour and simple form and calligraphy". Was a member of the Society of Sussex Sculptors, Society of Scribes and Illuminators and North Downs Calligraphers. Showed at Brighton Pavilion, Worthing Art Gallery and Museum and at East Grinstead Autumn Art Show. Allied Dunbar and CP Carpets hold her work. Lived in Oxted, Surrey.

Trena Mary COX: *see* **Trina Mary COX**

Trina Mary COX 1895–1980 Stained-glass artist who had a studio in Birkenhead during World War I and in the early 1920s, but by 1924 had moved to Chester, where she died. She was a fellow of the British Society of Master Glass Painters. Cox exhibited at RA and Walker Art Gallery in Liverpool. Among her output was a lancet for St Bartholomew, Thurstaston, Cheshire, included in the exhibition Stained Glass Designs, organised by Rachel Moss at Maas Gallery, 1998. There and elsewhere she was listed as Trena Mary Cox, although birth and death records give Trina.

Bernadette COXON 1958– Painter and draughtsman who studied at Newport School of Art, 1977–80, teachers including David Dobson, then Royal Academy Schools under Peter Greenham. She graduated with honours in 1980, four years later gaining a Sir James Knott Scholarship. Showed at RA, National Portrait Gallery and in the provinces, signing work with initials. Lived for a time in London.

Raymond COXON 1896–1997 Painter, mural artist, printmaker and teacher, born in Hanley, Stoke-on-Trent, Staffordshire. After serving in Cavalry in Palestine in World War I he studied at Leeds College of Art, 1919–21, and Royal College of Art, 1925. At Leeds he knew Henry Moore, of whom he painted a notable portrait, as he did of the sculptor Jacob Epstein. With Moore, Leon Underwood and others he formed the British Independent Society in 1927. Taught at Richmond School of Art. Was associated with the Chiswick Group and also showed with LG of which he was a member, and the Redfern, Leicester and Cooling Galleries. Had first solo show with London Artists' Association at Cooling in 1928. Official War Artist in World War II. Married the artist Edna Ginesi, with whom he had a joint show at Parkin Gallery in 1985. There was a retrospective at Stoke-on-Trent City Museum and Art Gallery in 1987, a memorial show at The Walton Gallery, 2001. Tate Gallery and Manchester City Art Gallery hold examples. Lived in London.

Damien COYLE 1957– Artist, born in Dungannon, County Tyrone, Northern Ireland, who gained his bachelor's degree in fine art from University of Ulster, 1981, his master's in 1982. He was a founder-member of Queen Street Studios, Belfast, and in 1993 was invited to join the editorial board of *Circa*, to which he regularly contributed. Exhibited in Independent Artists at Douglas Hyde Gallery, Dublin, in 1984; in a three-man show at Arts Council Gallery, Belfast, 1993; in two shows associated with the Queen Street Studios in 1994, Works on Paper and Beyond the Partitions; and in the Netherlands and America. Art for Dyslexics, recent paintings, was held at The Old Museum Arts Centre, North Belfast, in 2003.

John COYLE 1928– Representative painter and teacher, based in Ireland. After initial studies at the National College of Art and Design, Dublin, Coyle attended L'Académie de la Grande Chaumière, Paris, and Glasgow School of Art. He also worked in artists' studios in Spain and Italy. He was elected to RHA in 1981, becoming Keeper in 1992 and in 1996 Professor of Painting. Exhibited in Ireland and London and was included in The Irish Show, The Wykeham Gallery, Stockbridge, in 2003. Coyle's work was held by many public collections, including those of the Irish government and the European Parliament.

Moya COZENS 1920–1990 Painter, printmaker and teacher, born in Forest Hill, London, who spent some of her early life in Australia. She studied at Slade School of Fine Art, 1938–41, winning prizes. Exhibited RA, Ashgate Gallery in Farnham, Herbert Art Gallery in Coventry, Heal's Mansard Gallery, Zwemmer's Gallery and in America and South America.

Mary COZENS-WALKER 1938– Artist in cloth, stitch, paint and mixed media, born in London. Cozens-Walker studied at the Slade School of Fine Art, 1957–61, and Goldsmiths' College, 1981–3. Her extensive travels included America, where she also lived and worked, 1967–9, and subsequently Japan, Russia and India. Took part in many group shows, including RA Summer Exhibition from 1982; RIBA, 1986; Commonwealth Institute and Piccadilly Gallery, both from 1990; Flowers East, from 1992; and Alles Theater, Galerie Rose, Hamburg, Germany, 1999. Two-man shows included several with her husband, Anthony Green, including Obsessions, King's Lynn Festival, 1996, and Brewery Arts Centre, Cirencester, 2003. Awards included joint winner, Open Towner Art Gallery, Eastbourne, 1993, and *Eastbourne Herald*, Readers' Prize, 1993. Among later solo shows were Bankfield Museum, Halifax, and Boundary Gallery, both 2001. That included typically quirky, humorous works based on affecting memories and trivial incidents, "capsules of my life, like grains of dust in the sunshine." Arts Council and Setagaya Art Museum, Tokyo, Japan, hold examples.

Richard CRABBE 1927– Artist in oil, acrylic, watercolour, chalk and collage, and teacher, born in Horley, Surrey. He was at Croydon School of Art, 1941–5; did National Service in coal mines, 1945–8; then was at Royal College of Art, 1948–51, under Ruskin Spear, John Minton and Carel Weight. Taught full-time at Derby and Manchester Colleges of Art and Portsmouth Polytechnic, 1951–87. Was exchange professor, Eastern Illinois University, 1975; gained an Arts Council bursary, 1976; founder-member and director of Art Space, Portsmouth, from 1980; and for two months in 1984 was resident artist for city of Düsseldorf. Was a member of International Association of Artists. Crabbe's work "passed through three main periods, in all of which colour played a major role: 1943–65 figuration; 1965–87 Geometric Abstraction; from 1987 returned to figuration." Took part in four-man show at Galleri 17, Stockholm, 1984. Had a solo exhibition at Peterloo Gallery, Manchester, 1976, later ones including Havant Arts Centre, 1990. Portsmouth City Museum, Wigan Education Committee and overseas collections hold Crabbe's work. Lived in Southsea, Hampshire.

Jack CRABTREE 1938– Painter and teacher, born in Rochdale, Lancashire. He attended the local College of Art, 1955–7, St Martin's School of Art, 1957–9, and Royal Academy Schools, 1959–61. Teaching positions included Colleges of Art in Salford, at Royal College, Newport and Belfast. He was Professor and Head of Fine Arts at the University of Ulster, 1984–6. Crabtree participated in many group shows, including membership of 56 Group, SWG and Royal National Eisteddfod. In the 1970s Crabtree was known as a Social Realist, being commissioned by National Coal Board to paint the working lives of miners in south Wales. Other commissions included British Petroleum, Rochdale Education Authority and a mural for the Diocese of Monmouth. Solo shows included the Howard Roberts Gallery in Cardiff, Trafford Gallery and Kerlin Gallery, Dublin, 1990, where he showed several dozen studies of the Irish writer Francis Stuart, some paying homage to the painter Francis Bacon, whose work Crabtree revered. National Museum of Wales in Cardiff and many provincial collections hold Crabtree's work. The Glynn Vivian Art Gallery, Swansea, has Save This Pit, a fine example of his hard-hitting style. By the late 1990s Crabtree had had over 50 solo shows. Later ones included Y Tabernacl, Machynlleth, 2004.

Peter CRABTREE 1930– Painter and teacher, born in Morecambe, Lancashire, but brought up in industrial West Riding of Yorkshire. At Leeds College of Art, 1947–51, Crabtree was impressed by the teaching of Tom Watt. He then studied at Royal College of Art, where the teachers included John Minton, Ruskin Spear and Carel Weight, 1953–6, in the latter year winning an Abbey Minor Scholarship, enabling him to study in Italy. Crabtree taught at Yeovil School of Art, 1957–8, Batley College of Art, 1958–62, then for many years at Liverpool College of Art. Crabtree was notable as a landscape painter whose big canvases were brought to fruition over a long period and which had a singular quality of light and atmosphere. Among group shows he participated in was Norwich School of Art Gallery's 1986–7 touring exhibition A Reputation Among Artists. Early in 1960s showed solo with Crane Gallery in Manchester and at Crane Kalman Gallery, later exhibitions including Bluecoat Gallery in Liverpool in 1975 and the city's Royal Hospital, 1986. Lived in Southport, Lancashire.

Trevor CRABTREE 1945–2005 Sculptor and teacher, born in Bradford, Yorkshire, who studied at the local College of Art, then Hornsey and Royal Colleges of Art, in 1970–2 being a Rome Scholar. Held a number of teaching posts, from 1975 being senior lecturer at Manchester Polytechnic/Manchester Metropolitan University. Exhibited widely from 1965, when appeared in Young Contemporaries, later appearances including RA Summer Exhibitions from 1987; Grundy Art Gallery, Blackpool, 1989; Storey Institute, Lancaster, 1992; and 1st RWA Open Sculpture Exhibition, 1993. Lived in Rusholme, Manchester.

Adrienne CRADDOCK 1964– Artist and teacher, a printmaker creating hand-coloured drypoints and collographs, born at Lower Eaton, Herefordshire. Her father was Kenneth Craddock, principal of Herefordshire College of Art. Adrienne grew up in a farming area on the Welsh border, and her interest in rural life and the relationship of man and animals was reflected in her bold, imaginative work. She did a foundation course at Hereford College of Art, 1982–3; gained a first-class honours degree, specialising in printmaking, from North Staffordshire Polytechnic, 1983–6; then studied fine art printmaking at Manchester Polytechnic for her master's degree, 1987–9. From 1989 lectured in printmaking at the Polytechnic and taught in art centres, schools and colleges around Britain. In 1989 was included in Whitworth Young Contemporaries at Whitworth Art Gallery, Manchester; in 1990 in Open British Printmaking at Bankside Gallery; in 1993 was elected a member of MAFA; participated in 1994 in BBC Television's *The Art* educational series, and was shown at Benjamin Rhodes Gallery, also being included in Short Stories – Tall Tales, a tour organised by City Art Gallery, Leicester. In 1995–8 Chanticleer: Prints and Sculpture by Adrienne Craddock and Marjan Wouda toured the United Kingdom, organised by Sheeran Lock. Craddock lived in Brockhall Village, near Whalley, Lancashire.

Vivian Claud CRADDOCK WILLIAMS 1936– Artist in oil, pen and wash and ceramics, born in London, who signed his work V C C W. He was educated at Repton School under Arthur Norris and Denis Hawkins, then at Ruskin School of Drawing in Oxford under Percy Horton. Craddock Williams worked in London at studios in the World's End and Parsons Green and with the Chelsea Pottery. From 1971 he worked in Africa. He was a member of Wye Valley Art Society, Art Centre Foundation of Zambia and National Arts and Crafts Committee, Uganda. Showed with the Wye Valley Art Society, 1950–60, and with Chelsea & Kensington Art Society Exhibition, 1960–70. Kensington Borough Council and Zambia National Gallery, Lusaka, hold examples. Craddock Williams cited the sculptor Jacob Epstein and his son the painter Theo Garman as influences. Lived in Kampala, Uganda.

Tony CRAGG 1949– Sculptor and teacher, born in Liverpool. he studied at Gloucester, Wimbledon and the Royal College of Art, 1969–77. In that year he moved to Wuppertal, Germany, teaching at Düsseldorf Kunstakademie. Within a decade he had several dozen solo shows, including London, Berlin, Hamburg, Paris, Naples, Genoa, Tokyo, New York, Toronto and Middleburg. In the late 1980s Cragg represented Britain at the Venice Biennale and won the Turner Prize, 1988. From the outset Cragg used found objects to create his sculptures, as diverse as seashore objects or plastic debris. Cragg was also interested in the creation of monolothic forms, from metal, stone and glass, as in Subcommittee, shown in his 1991 Lisson Gallery exhibition. Much of Cragg's work with everyday objects started with the idea that it was the artist's duty to discover the poetry, pathos and hidden values in them to transform our way of looking at them. Retrospectives in 1992 at Tramway and Centre for Contemporary Art, Glasgow, with one at Whitechapel Art Gallery, 1996. Cass Sculpture Foundation organised "the largest exhibition of Tony Cragg's outdoor sculptures in Britain to date" in 2005–6. Cragg was elected RA in 1994. Arts Council and Tate Gallery hold his work.

Adam CRAIG 1946–2002 Artist producing kinetic works and installations in a variety of materials. His output was rooted in the landscape tradition, his father and grandfather having both been established artists, but he eschewed image-making. Craig gained a diploma in art and design at Camberwell School of Arts and Crafts, 1967–70, obtaining a fine art fellowship at Southampton University, 1970–1. Commissions included installations for a new Banque Paribas building in Marylebone and for the boardroom of design group Coley Porter Bell, another for GlaxoSmithKline plc, 2001. Showed at RA Summer Exhibition, 1996, 1998, and 2002, and Conversation Pieces, Hammerson plc, 1999. Craig was art editor for *Reader's Digest*, 1979–00. Lived in London.

Ailsa CRAIG 1895–1967 Illuminator, letterer and teacher, born in Dumfries, Dumfriesshire, who gained her diploma from Glasgow School of Art in 1916. She attended the School 1912–18 and was on its staff, 1931–4. In 1948, her manual *Design and Spacing of Lettering* appeared. Craig was a member of the Glasgow Society of Lady Artists from around 1929, the year she won its Lauder Award. She concentrated on illuminated addresses and rolls of honour, but also exhibited at the Walker Art Gallery, Liverpool. Lived latterly at Bridge of Allan, Stirlingshire, but died in Edinburgh.

Barry CRAIG 1902–1951 Landscape and portrait painter, draughtsman and teacher, full name Frank Barrington Craig, whose son was the artist Adam Craig. Barry's father was the painter Frank Craig, the artist Leonard Campbell Taylor shared the family home and painting was a lifelong obsession. After studying at the Slade School of Fine Art, 1919–24, where his friends included Tom Monnington, Rodney Burn and Mary Potter, Barry Craig went to South Africa, becoming professor of painting at the Michaelis School, 1926–33, returning to London where he was a highly regarded teacher at St Martin's School of Art until 1950. During the war he was involved in camouflage and received commissions from the War Artists' Advisory Committee. Craig lived in London and exhibited at the RA Summer Exhibition, as a member of the NEAC from 1946 and RP from 1949, at the Goupil and Cooling Galleries, RI and elsewhere. Bradford's Cartwright Hall Art Gallery holds his Concarneau Harbour, a bold design in the Fauve manner lent to Christie's NEAC centenary show in 1986. A First Retrospective Exhibition in 1987 at the New Art Centre included sensitive portraits, one of his wife Dosia, and landscapes of Brittany and Provence, with appreciations by Hugh Casson and the late Robin Darwin.

Edward Gordon CRAIG 1872–1966 Theatrical designer, printmaker, actor and writer. Craig was the son of the architect E W Godwin and the great actress Ellen Terry, and the father of Edward Anthony Craig (who worked as Edward Carrick), artist, theatre and film designer. A flamboyant polemicist, Craig told of his early life in *Index to the Story of my Days*, 1957. He was for a time an actor, but gradually turned to the theory and practice of scene design and direction, his extremely simple sets having a big influence on the theatre in America and in continental Europe, rather less in England. Early on he became interested in wood engraving, in which he was substantially self-taught and prolific, although he learned simplification of design from William Nicholson and James Pryde, working as the Beggarstaff Brothers. Was an original member of the SWE. Among books illustrated by him are his own *Book of Penny Toys* and *The Art of the Theatre*, 1905, and W B Yeats' *Plays for an Irish Theatre*, 1913. He also contributed to periodicals such as *The Dome* and *The Mask*, which he founded while living in Italy.

Henry Robertson CRAIG 1916–1984 Realistic painter in oil, commonly of figures in landscape and flower studies in a pleasantly muted palette. Born of Scottish-Irish parentage, Craig trained at Dundee College of Art where he met his lifelong friend, the artist Patrick Hennessy. In 1938 he won the Travelling Scholarship, the year after Hennessy won it, but was unable to travel due to the outbreak of World War II, during which Craig worked in espionage, including maps and camouflage. After demobilisation in 1946 he moved to Ireland, re-met Hennessy and they set up a joint studio, in Cork, then Dublin. Craig received important commissions and began his long association with the RHA, being made a full academician in 1956. In that year, with Hennessy, he helped David Hendriks set up the Ritchie Hendriks Gallery on St Stephen's Green. The Guildhall Gallery, Chicago, and then the Conacher Galleries, San Francisco, helped make Craig's reputation in America, and in 2000 Gorry Gallery, Dublin, sold a rare batch of works from an American collection. National Gallery of Ireland holds Craig's work.

Michael CRAIG-MARTIN 1941– Sculptor, painter and teacher, born in Dublin. He made works which brought together a number of materials and objects – such as milk bottles, metal brackets and water – his earlier productions employing texts, his later ones large wall projections. Craig-Martin went to America in 1946 and studied at Yale University, 1961–3, and Yale School of Arts and Architecture, 1964–6. From 1966 he was resident in Britain, his teaching appointments including Bath Academy of Art and Canterbury College of Art, then Goldsmiths' College School of Art, 1973–88, where he nurtured talents at the forefront of British art in the 1990s. He was later Goldsmiths' Millar Professor of Fine Art, retiring in 2000. Craig-Martin's belief that "a thing was not a work of art because it was made of bronze or paint, but defined by something else," giving the artist "the opportunity to use all the materials in the world" led to attacks by more conservative critics. After a first solo show at Rowan Gallery in 1966 he exhibited there frequently, also taking part in important international mixed shows. He had a retrospective at Whitechapel Art Gallery in 1989 and an exhibition at Waddington Gallery in 2000, which displayed his Works 1984–1989 in 2002. He was a trustee of the Tate Gallery; with the architects Herzog & de Meuron, Craig-Martin designed The Swiss Light which illuminates the top of Tate Modern's chimney. Arts Council holds his work. The photographer Jessica Craig-Martin was his daughter.

Heather CRAIGMILE 1925– Painter and draughtsman, born in Birkenhead, Cheshire. She was educated at Downe House, Newbury. Studied at Chester School of Art and privately with Harold Workman and Arnold Mason. Was a member of UA and Chelsea Art Society, also exhibiting with RCamA and RBA. Had solo exhibitions in Wales, where she lived at Conway, Gwynedd.

Anthea CRAIGMYLE 1933– Painter, whose colourful work mixed fantasy and reality, brought up by the River Thames on Chiswick Mall, where she later had a studio. She studied at Chelsea School of Art, 1950–2. Took part in mixed shows at RA, Toswitta Haftmann Gallery, Zürich, and New Grafton Gallery. It gave her one-man exhibitions, including 2000, previous solo shows having taken place at Clytie Jessop Gallery, 1970, and Yehudi Menuhin School, 1973. Lady Craigmyle lived in London.

Michael CRAIK 1972– Artist, born in Scotland, who was based in Edinburgh. He studied at Telford College there, for a National Diploma in Art and Design, 1990–2; gained a fine art honours degree at Gray's School of Art, Aberdeen, 1992–6; then his master's at Winchester School of Art, 1999–00. Won a Coopers & Lybrand Art Award, 1995; a John Lewis Partnership commission, 1999; and The Cross Trust Award for Postgraduate Studies, 2000. Group shows included RSA Student Exhibition and New Scottish Graduates, Art Exposure Gallery, Glasgow, both 1996; SSA at RSA, 1998; and in 2000 both Rates of Change, Diorama Gallery, and Big Small New, Houldsworth Fine Art. At Houldsworth, Craik presented work from his Constructional Elements series; using photographs of the fronts and features of skyscrapers, he cropped images and remade them into new structures. Solo shows included Gap, Panorama Gallery, Barcelona, Spain, 2000. John Lewis Partnership, Grampian Hospital Art Trust, Coopers & Lybrand and Boland Holdings owned Craik's work.

Elizabeth CRAMP 1929– Painter, born near Rye, Sussex, wife of the artist Jonathan Cramp. She studied at Hastings School of Art and Royal Academy Schools until 1953, in 1954 settling in Wales. Was a member of WSW and RWS and showed with NEAC, at RA and elsewhere, including own home in Fishguard, Pembrokeshire. In 1987, Cramp gained a WAC Travel Grant to draw in Japan, work shown in 1989 at the West Wales Arts Centre, Fishguard; a tour with the BBC Welsh Orchestra in Japan in 1991 led to an exhibition that year at St David's Hall, Cardiff; and in 1994 she was artist-in-residence at Fishguard Music Festival's silver anniversary. HRH The Prince of Wales and WAC hold her work.

Jonathan CRAMP 1930– Painter and teacher, born in Ninfield, Sussex, married to the artist Elizabeth Cramp. He studied at Hastings School of Art and Bournemouth College of Art into early 1950s, his teachers including Vincent Lines. He was a teacher and head of art at Fishguard County Secondary School, 1954–81. Showed with

NEAC and RWS of which he was a member, LG, New Art Centre, RWA and elsewhere, as well as at home in Fishguard, Pembrokeshire. WAC and National Museum of Wales, Cardiff, hold his work.

Leigh CRAMPTON 1937– Artist working in a variety of media, born in Surrey, who studied at Finnish Academy of Fine Art, 1962–4, then Camberwell School of Arts and Crafts, 1966–70. Went on to teach part-time in London, where he lived. Showed at Air Gallery, 1975, and in Summer Show 2, at Serpentine Gallery, 1980. Solo exhibitions included Gardner Centre for the Arts, University of Sussex, and University of Essex, 1977.

Ronald CRAMPTON 1905–1985 Painter, notably of landscapes made on the spot in watercolour, born in Nottingham, where he studied privately with Arthur Spooner and was a member of the Society of Artists. During Royal Air Force service in World War II Crampton discovered East Anglia and eventually settled in King's Lynn, Norfolk, the area's flat landscape and wide skies suiting his style, which included a deft use of the paper for highlighting. Crampton was a member of the Norfolk and Norwich Art Circle, other group exhibitions including RWS, RBA, RI, RSMA, provincial galleries and Paris Salon (gaining an Hon. Mention, 1966, and Silver Medal, 1976). Also held a series of solo shows, the last at Fermoy Centre, King's Lynn, two months before he died. Abbott and Holder latterly sold his work and Bonhams included a group in The East Anglian View sale at Lynford Hall, Mundford, 2000. Crampton's wife was the painter Doreen Allen.

Seán CRAMPTON 1918–1999 Sculptor, painter and printmaker, born in Manchester, who also created some silverwork and mosaics; full name was Arthur Edward Seán Crampton. Son of the architect Joshua Crampton. Studied at Vittoria School of Art, Birmingham, 1930–3, then Central School of Art there, and in Paris in Fernand Léger's studio. Commissioned in the 1st Battalion of the London Irish Rifles (London Division) in World War II Crampton saw action in the Western Desert and Italy, winning the Military Cross and George Medal, and had to have a leg amputated. Showed RA, Leicester Gallery, RSA and Alwin Gallery. Taught sculpture for several years in late 1940s at Anglo-French Art Centre, London. Sometimes signed work with his initial only, encircled. Had many solo shows in London and was included in 1st RWA Open Sculpture Exhibition, 1993. Figure groups, nude male and female figures, birds and animals were favourite subjects. Was a member of RBS from 1953, its president, 1966–71; was from 1971 a member of the Art Workers' Guild, in 1978 its master. Several of his most notable works earned RBS and Civic Trust awards and he was asked to create the war memorial for his own regiment. Lived in Calne, Wiltshire.

Elizabeth CRAMPTON-GORE 1925– Painter in various media, born in London, but brought up in France among professional artists. She was taught from early childhood by her artist father William Gore, also attending Folkestone Art School for seven years part-time. She taught art, music and languages. Showed with Folkestone Art Society, of which for a time she was a member, and elsewhere. Her work included flower studies, sea and landscapes, religious, Symbolist and abstract pictures. Crampton-Gore (later Mrs Elizabeth Parry-Crooke) was the first wife of the artist William Francis Burton, their daughter Georgina Saunders also being a painter. Crampton-Gore lived in Folkestone, Kent.

William CRAMPTON GORE: *see* **William GORE**

Doris CRANE 1911– Sculptor, born in London, studied with William Everatt Gray, who like her worked in wood and ivory. Showed with RMS of which she became a member in 1958, RA, RSA and Paris Salon. Was a member of Deben Art Club. Lived for many years at Old Felixstowe, Suffolk.

Andrew CRANSTON 1969– Painter, born in Hawick, Roxburghshire, who studied at Manchester Polytechnic, Gray's School of Art in Aberdeen and Royal College of Art. He gained the NatWest Prize for Art and John Kinross Travelling Scholarship, both in 1993, and Alistair Gilchrist Fisher Memorial Awards, 1996. Group shows included Project Perec at French Institute, Edinburgh, 1993; Aberdeen Artists' Society, Aberdeen Art Gallery, 1994; and Royal Over-Seas League Open, 1996. In 2000 Cranston showed work at the RSA inspired by a visit to Scandinavia, after he won an Alastair Salvesen Scholarship. Mappin Art Gallery gave him a solo exhibition in 2002.

David CRANSWICK 1954– Of Australian nationality, Cranswick graduated from Camberwell School of Arts and Crafts; gained his master's from the Royal Academy Schools; was apprenticed to the artist Cecil Collins, 1986–90; and obtained his doctorate from the Prince of Wales Institute for research into, and demonstrations of, materials and techniques used by European Old Masters. His aim was "to create paintings whose colours will last through the centuries, retaining their luminosity and brilliance, by incorporating methods that have proven themselves down the ages." Cranswick painted still lifes, portraits and landscapes, his work being included by Wolseley Fine Arts in Old & New at The Gallery in Cork Street in 2003.

Alistair CRAWFORD 1945– Painter, printmaker, photographer, art historian and teacher, born in Fraserburgh, Aberdeenshire. He attended Glasgow School of Art, 1962–6, under Robert Stewart, and began teaching in 1966. His appointments included professor of art at University College of Wales, Aberystwyth, the first in its history, from 1990. Crawford travelled in Norway, Italy, Holland, France, Greece and America. Among his many activities he gained a commission for the mural The Palio at Siena, University of Leeds, 1971; in 1978 he made Vedute di Roma prints at the British School at Rome; gained a British Council Artists Award, 1981; won the Gold Medal in Fine Art at Royal National Eisteddfod of Wales, 1985; and in 1988 founded Aberystwyth Printmakers with Robert Meyrick. Crawford took part in over 100 exhibitions in Britain and abroad, having over two dozen solo shows. His work was held by many collections, including WAC, Hunterian Museum and Art Gallery in Glasgow, British Council and Imperial College. He was co-author of *John Thomas 1838–1905: Photographer*, 1977, and author of *Mario Giacomelli*, 1983, and several other books. He was the younger brother of the artist John Crawford and lived in Comins Coch, near Aberystwyth, Dyfed.

Cara Mckinnon CRAWFORD 1962– Landscape painter and teacher using a rich palette, in the Scottish Colourist tradition, born in Campbeltown, Argyll. She studied at Glasgow School of Art, 1980–4, the second generation of her family to be an artist, her father being the painter John Mckinnon Crawford. Taught in Highland Region secondary schools, 1985–97, and was an art and design examiner, Scottish Qualifications Authority, 1991–9. She was a regular exhibitor, RSA and Royal Glasgow Institute of the Fine Arts. Had a series of solo exhibitions in Scotland and England, later ones including Images of a Nation at Royal Glasgow Institute's Kelly Gallery, 2002, and New Grafton Gallery, 2003. Her 2002 solo show at Conoco Gallery, Aberdeen, featured paintings of the fishing villages Gardenstown, Pennan (made famous by the 1983 film *Local Hero*) and Crovie (pronounced Crivvy), to which she was introduced when a second-year art student. Some of the profits from this show were donated to the restoration fund for Crovie's vital pier. Lived in Glasgow.

Heather CRAWFORD 1926– Painter, notably of posters, artist in various materials and teacher, born in East Boldon, County Durham. Studied art at Lincoln Training College, 1944–6, College of Arts and Crafts in Hull, 1951–2, Sunderland College of Art and in Glasgow. Exhibited with Federation of Northern Art Societies and at Shipley Art Gallery, Gateshead. Also showed with Sunderland Art Club of which she was a member, living at Roker, Sunderland.

Hugh Adam CRAWFORD 1898–1982 Painter, mural artist, designer and teacher, born in Busby, Lanarkshire. Was married to the artist Kathleen Mann. Crawford studied at Glasgow School of Art under Maurice Greiffenhagen, 1919–23; at Central School of Arts and Crafts, 1924–5; and at St Martin's School of Art. He joined the staff of Glasgow School of Art in 1925, where he was an influential teacher, and was head of painting until 1948 when he became head of Gray's School of Art, Aberdeen. He was there until 1954, then was principal of Duncan of Jordanstone College of Art, Dundee, 1954–64. Crawford painted a strong series of portraits in the 1930s. Among his murals were some for the Roman Catholic chapel at Bellahouston and others for John Brown's shipyard and Scottish Brewers, Glasgow. Glasgow Art Club gave him a retrospective in 1971, the Third Eye Centre in Glasgow showing selected works from 1928–78 in 1978. His work is in Scottish collections.

John Gardiner CRAWFORD 1941– Painter and teacher, born in Broadsea by Fraserburgh, Aberdeenshire, older brother of the artist Alistair Crawford. After Fraserburgh Academy he studied at Gray's School of Art, 1959–64, including a postgraduate year, and at Patrick Allan-Fraser School of Art, Hospitalfield, Arbroath. He was made a member of RSW in 1974, RBA in 1983 and RI in 1984. Among his awards was first prize for painting at Gray's in 1962; first prize in Scottish Arts Council Open Exhibition in 1969; and Hunting Award, first prize for watercolour, 1982. Having come from a long line of fishermen, Crawford painted boats and the sea in great detail. His teaching appointments included Dundee College of Education until 1980, when he left to concentrate on painting, although he was artist-tutor at Newbattle Abbey College, Midlothian, 1980–85. His solo exhibitions included William Hardie Ltd, Glasgow, 1993. Scottish Arts Council and Robert Fleming Holdings hold his work. Lived in Arbroath, Angus.

Nellie CRAWFORD 1949– Largely self-taught painter, notable for detailed still lifes, born in Lavenham, Suffolk, who grew up in the Jarrah and Karri Forest country of southwest Australia. Graduating from Edith Cowan University in 1978, she taught for 19 years in schools and technical colleges throughout Western Australia and on Christmas Island, also travelling and working in Europe. In 1999, after some years painting part-time and working with recognised Australian artists, including Murray Gill and Graeme Wild, she started painting full-time. Worked from a studio in the harbour town of Fremantle, Western Australia, returning to painting in England and continental Europe for several months each year. Showed in England at Angel Gallery, Lavenham; Broad Curve Gallery, Chipping Campden; Fosse Gallery, Stow-on-the-Wold; and Priory Gallery, Broadway; and in Western Australia at Monsoon Gallery, Broome, and Yallingup Galleries, Yallingup, in 2001 her Still Life with Figs and Still Life with Lemons both winning first prize for small paintings in the Beverley Art Exhibition.

Richard CRAWFORD 1945– Artist who studied at Hornsey College of Art, 1963–7, and Goldsmiths' College, 1979–80. He participated in the Whitechapel Open, Whitechapel Art Gallery, 1984; Art Now: Surreal Tendency, SPACE Studios, 1987; and Critics Space 5, at Air Gallery, RA Summer Exhibition and East End Open Studios, based at Richmond House Studios, all 1989.

Sarah CRAWFORD 1970– Artist and teacher employing a wide range of materials in sculpture and jewellery, born in Oxford. She studied at Middlesex Polytechnic/University, 1989–95, finally gaining her master's in design (jewellery), tutors including Pierre Degen and Caroline Broadhead. Was then self-employed as a designer-maker, lecturing part-time at Central St Martins and London Guildhall University, with visiting lectureships at Middlesex and Edinburgh Universities and London College of Fashion. Awards included an International Prize for Design, Talente Handwerkskammer, Munich, Germany, 1996. Later group shows included Branching Out, Galerie V&V, Vienna Austria, 1998; Book Art, Mobilia Gallery, Cambridge, America, and tour, 1999; and Kunst Hautnah, Kunstlerhaus, Vianna, 2000. Among her later solo works were Plasticity, An Tuireann, Portree, Isle of Skye, and tour, 1999–00, and a window installation piece, Angel Row Gallery, Nottingham, 2000. Crafts Council and Bankfield Museum, Halifax, hold examples. Lived in London.

Thomas Hamilton CRAWFORD fl. from c.1890–1948 Artist in watercolour and mezzotint, son of the sculptor John Crawford. He studied in Glasgow and Edinburgh and showed at RA, RSW, RSA, Fine Art Society and Paris Salon. He was a Savage Club member who lived at Berkhamsted, Hertfordshire.

Eileen CRAWFURD 1916–2006 Painter born in Haywards Heath, Sussex, who attended Roedean School, then studied at Slade School of Fine Art with Randolph Schwabe, 1934–5, as well as the Sir John Cass School of Arts and Crafts. She showed at SWA of which she was a member, RWA, RI, in the provinces and on the continent. Lived in Salcombe, Devon.

Tim CRAWLEY 1955– Architectural sculptor and stone carver, a designer of original work for new and period buildings and restorer, who "often looked to the past, especially to medieval work from the Romanesque and Gothic periods." He attended Manchester University, 1974–7, graduating with honours in art history, specialising in medieval architecture; did foundation studies at Sir John Cass School of Art, 1979; then gained his diploma from the City & Guilds of London Art School, 1979–82, taught by Arthur Ayres. Crawley became an associate of the RBS, a full member of the Art Workers' Guild, a committee member of the Association of Master Carvers and was chairman of the National Guild of Stonemasonry and Carving, 1996–7. He was a freelance stone carver in London, 1981–9; was head carver, Rattee and Kett, Cambridge, 1989–99; from 1999 being art director of Fairhaven of Anglesey Abbey Ltd. Crawley worked to commission and won a string of awards. In 2000 alone, these included three Stone Federation Awards, two for craftsmanship: Senate House, Cambridge, and Guildhall (he did the busts of Samuel Pepys, Oliver Cromwell, William Shakespeare and Sir Christopher Wren); and one for restoration, Westminster Abbey (10 Modern Martyrs). Lived in Cambridge.

Alwyn CRAWSHAW 1934– Popular painter, lecturer and demonstrator, born in Mirfield, Yorkshire, who studied under Vincent Lines at Hastings School of Art, 1949–51. From 1957–80 directed Russell Artists Merchandising in Kingston upon Thames, and also demonstrated for Daler-Rowney & Company. Crawshaw was a member of SEA and BWS, also president of the National Acrylic Painters' Association. His solo exhibitions included Harrods, Barclay Art Gallery in Chester and Guildford Galleries in Surrey. As well as radio and television appearances Crawshaw was author of many instructional books, such as *Learn to Paint Boats and Harbours* and *Sketching with Alwyn Crawshaw*. *The Artist at Work* was tutorial with an autobiographical strand. Felix Rosenstiel's produced his first print. Lived in Dawlish, Devon.

E Burnett CRAWSHAW fl. c.1930–1950 Painter who was by profession a barrister and medical practitioner. Exhibited RA, RMS and Paris Salon. Lived in Epsom, Surrey.

Frances CRAWSHAW 1876– Painter who was married to the artist Lionel Crawshaw. She attended Scarborough and Westminster Schools of Art, as well as studying in Italy. Exhibited RA, WIAC, RSA, NEAC and elsewhere. Lived in Droitwich, Worcestershire.

Lionel CRAWSHAW 1864–1949 Painter and printmaker who was born near Doncaster, Yorkshire, and married the artist Frances Crawshaw. He attended Cambridge University, qualified as a solicitor, then studied art in Germany and Paris. Early in the century he worked in Yorkshire, based at Whitby. Exhibited RA, Walker's Galleries, RSW, ROI and at many other galleries. Signed work L C in the form of of a monogram. Towards the end of his life lived at Newton Abbot, Devon.

John CRAXTON 1922– Painter and designer, born in London, son of the pianist Harold Craxton. When only 10, he had paintings exhibited in schools group at Bloomsbury Gallery. In 1939 studied life drawing at L'Académie de la Grande Chaumière, Paris, returning to study in 1940 at Westminster School of Art and Central School of Art with P F Millard and Eric Schilsky. The following year he studied drawing at Goldsmiths' College School of Art with Clive Gardiner. About this time Craxton was friendly with Graham Sutherland and Lucian Freud and became recognised as a member of the Neo-Romantic group of painters. He had his first solo show at Leicester Galleries, 1944. In 1946 Craxton visited Greece for first time, whose landscape was eventually to leave its mark on his work. After a joint show with Freud at London Gallery in 1947, with whom he had worked in Greece, in 1948 Craxton visited Crete for the first time; in 1960 he rented a house in Hania there which subsequently became his home, although Craxton was an indefatigable traveller in several continents. In 1951 Craxton designed sets and costumes for *Daphnis and Chloe* at Covent Garden; in 1966 he helped restage it for Athens Festival and completed designs for the ballet *Apollo* at Covent Garden. Between 1971–4 worked on Landscape with the Elements as the Cottrell Memorial Tapestry for the McRobert Centre, Stirling University. Craxton had a retrospective show at Whitechapel Art Gallery in 1967 and in 1985 a show of paintings and drawings appeared at the Chrysostomos Gallery, Hania; British Council, Athens; and Christopher Hull Gallery. John Craxton: From the Artist's Collection was at Pallant House, Chichester, 1998–9, Works on Paper, 1942–2001, was at Art First, 2001. Tate Gallery and other major collections hold his work. Elected RA, 1993.

Fred CRAYK 1952– Painter who said that his work exploited "the tension between abstraction and representation". The decaying mining landscapes and communities of West Lothian were among his subjects. Born in Portsmouth, Hampshire, Crayk studied in Paris, 1971–2, Duncan of Jordanstone College of Art, Dundee, 1972–6, then Edinburgh College of Art, 1976–7. He was awarded a Scottish Education Department Minor Travelling Scholarship to France; won the Greenshields Foundation Scholarship (Canada) in 1978; in 1980 won Scottish Arts Council Amsterdam Studio Bursary. As well as participating in many group shows, Crayk had one-man exhibitions at Torrance Gallery in Edinburgh and Compass Gallery, Glasgow, and at Lamont Gallery, 1997. In 2003, he shared a show, Flesh, at Pilgrim Gallery. Scottish Arts Council and City Art Centre, Edinburgh, hold his work.

John CREALOCK 1871–1959 Painter in oil of portraits and landscapes. Born in Manchester, after education at Sandhurst Royal Military Academy and service in the Boer War, Crealock studied art at the Académie Julian, Paris, 1901–4. Exhibited RA, RP, Goupil Gallery, NEAC and elsewhere. Williamson Art Gallery & Museum, Birkenhead, and several other galleries in England and France hold his work. Lived in Hove, Sussex.

Anne-Marie CREAMER 1966– Artist, born and lived in London, whose work drew on photographic and cinematic sources, as in her canvas Chimera (Dynamite Lady), shown in 1992 at East & South, Norwich Gallery/Kent Institute of Art and Design. She studied at Middlesex Polytechnic, 1986–8, then Royal College of Art, 1988–90.

Frank CREBER 1959– Figurative painter and etcher who graduated in painting from the University of Newcastle upon Tyne, 1981, gaining his master's at Chelsea College of Art, 1987. Awards included a Herbert Read Fellowship at

Chelsea, 1986; Barclays Bank Young Painters Award, 1987; and Picker Fellowship, Kingston University, 1988. Later group shows included Large Drawing – The Great Banquet, Banqueting House, 1995; Rare Devices, Homerton Hospital, 1996; and CAN, Haymarket, 2000. Had a series of solo exhibitions at Sue Williams Gallery from 1989, later shows including Stanton Guildhouse, Stanton, 1999 and 2001; Art House, Peterborough, and Turtle Arts, Nottingham, both 2002; New Greenham Arts, Newbury, 2003; and Art Space Gallery, 2004. His work there included the richly coloured and vibrant oil on canvas Community Picnic, 2002. Art for Hospitals, Mildmay Mission Hospital and several corporate collections hold examples.

Alexander CREE 1929– Artist in pastel, oil watercolour and teacher, born in Dunfermline, Fife. Cree studied at Edinburgh College of Art, 1946–52, his teachers including William Gillies, Robin Philipson, William MacTaggart and Leonard Rosoman. He won an Andrew Grant Postgraduate Scholarship, 1950–1, and Travel Scholarship, 1951–2. Taught in state schools, from 1963–87 being principal teacher of art at Dunbar Grammar School. Showed with RSA, SSA, RSW and Royal Glasgow Institute of the Fine Arts. His solo shows included Lyceum Gallery, Edinburgh, 1957, Demarco Gallery, Edinburgh, 1968; and Macaulay Gallery, East Lothian, 1990. Cree said of his subjects that these were "mainly the landscape of lowland Scotland, but I am also interested in the people". Scottish Arts Council, Nuffield Foundation and British Transport Hotels hold his work. Lived in East Linton, East Lothian.

Janet CREE 1910–1992 Painter, notably of portraits in tempera with an early-Italian feel, born in London. She was married to the barrister John Platts-Mills and was the mother of the film-maker Barney Platts-Mills, notable for the 1970 film *Bronco Bullfrog*. She studied with Ernest Jackson at Byam Shaw School of Drawing and Painting. Showed at RA, Phoenix Gallery in Lavenham and elsewhere. Tate Gallery holds her early Oriental Portrait. Lived in London and near Uckfield, Sussex. Died in London.

John CREED 1938– Sculptor in metal, blacksmith and teacher, born in Heswall, Cheshire, who studied at Liverpool College of Art, 1955–9, gaining his art teacher's diploma at Liverpool University. From 1971–95, he taught in Glasgow School of Art's silversmithing and jewellery department. Having established a forge at Milton of Campsie, Dunbartonshire, in 1988, Creed carried out a series of notable commissions. These included entrance gates for the Borders Regional Council, Newton St Boswells, 1990; internal doors for the Royal Museum of Scotland, Edinburgh, 1995; Roof Sculpture and Entrance Gate for the Royal Glasgow Institute of the Fine Arts, 1996–7; and the Benchmark seats for Norrie Miller Park, Perth, 1998. Public collections hold work by Creed.

Martin CREED 1968– Artist born in Wakefield, Yorkshire, who studied at the Slade School of Fine Art, 1986–90. He worked as a sculptor, including sound sculptures, and wrote and performed music with his systems- or sequence-based three-piece band Owada. Creed was influenced by the 1960s Fluxus movement's low regard for institutionalised art, his output including a sheet of paper crumpled into a ball. His many group shows included The Black Bull, curated by Tess Jaray, 1989; Zombie Golf, Bank, 1995; transistors, Hashimoto Museum of Art, Morioka, Japan, and Royal Museum of Scotland, Edinburgh, 1998–9; and Protest & Survive, Whitechapel Art Gallery, 2000. Solo exhibitions included Victoria Miro Gallery and The British School at Rome, both 1997, and Southampton City Art Gallery and Art Now, Tate Britain, both 2000. In 2001, Creed won the Turner Prize for The lights going on and off. His first one-man exhibition after that, in 2004 at Hauser & Wirth, included Work No.370: Balls, a room filled with 750 multi-coloured balls that could be kicked across the floor. Creed lived in London.

Dennis CREFFIELD 1931– Painter and draughtsman, born in London. From 1948–51 he studied with David Bomberg at Borough Polytechnic and from 1957–61 at Slade School of Fine Art. Creffield became Gregory Fellow in Painting at University of Leeds, 1964–7. By then he had taken part in many mixed exhibitions, including John Moores Exhibition, Liverpool, 1961, where he was a prizewinner, and with LG, of which he was elected a member in 1962. He had a solo show at Leeds City Art Gallery in 1966, others including Queen's Square Gallery, Leeds; Brighton Polytechnic Gallery; and Serpentine Gallery, 1980. He won a Major Arts Council Award in 1977. Creffield had an ambition to draw every cathedral and abbey church in England, and from this stemmed the South Bank touring exhibition of 1988–90 and *English Cathedrals*, with a text by Creffield, published in 1987. He won a series of National Trust Foundation for Art commissions from 1990. His first one-man show at a private venue in London was at Albemarle Gallery in 1991. Paintings and Drawings of London, 1960–90, was held at Barbican Gallery in 1992 and his Paintings of Petworth toured from Gillian Jason Gallery, 1993–5. Impressions of Castles was held at the globegallery, Hay-on-Wye, in 2002 and there was a retrospective at Flowers East in 2005. Creffield was a powerful artist in the Bomberg Expressionist tradition. His work is held by Arts Council, Tate Gallery and many other public gallery and university collections. Lived in Brighton, Sussex.

Benjamin CREME 1922– Painter, designer and illustrator, born in Glasgow. He began painting aged 14, left school at 16 to paint but was too young to enter local School of Art, although he attended life classes there. Feeling he had become a modern painter and that the School of Art was too academic Creme declined to pursue studies. In 1940 held a joint show with Douglas Campbell at a trade union club, where Josef Herman and Jankel Adler gave encouragement. Studied for several years with Adler. In 1942 Creme and Robert Frame illustrated W S Graham's poems *Cage Without Grievance*. Moved to London in 1946 when Creme met up with John Minton, Prunella Clough and Keith Vaughan and his pictures had a marked Neo-Romantic tinge. In the mid-1940s Tyrone Guthrie commissioned Creme to do sets for his production of *Carmen* and Creme began to show widely, at AIA, LG, Gimpel Fils, Redfern and Leger Galleries. A visit to south of France in 1950 prompted Creme to adopt a lighter palette and to move towards abstraction. Had one-man show at Gallery Apollinaire in 1952 and exhibited in America, other solo shows including St George's Gallery, 1955; Bryant M Hale Gallery, Los Angeles, 1964; and Dartington New Gallery, 1977. After Jane England organised a retrospective at Themes and Variations Gallery in 1985 England & Co gave Creme several partial retrospectives. Victoria & Albert Museum and British Museum hold his work. In addition to his painting Creme was a frequent lecturer, advocating the mission of Maitreya the Christ.

Fred CRESS 1938– Painter and teacher, born in Poona, India, who studied at Birmingham College of Art, 1954–9, moving to Australia in 1962. From 1964–76 he worked in Melbourne, later living in Sydney, New South Wales, and France, seeking the summer in each. He was artist-in-residence, SUNY Purchase, New York, America, 1979–80; Australian representative at the 5th India Triennial, New Delhi, India, 1982; artist-in-residence, Curtin University, Perth, 1986; gained the Archibald Prize for Portraiture and People's Prize, Art Gallery of New South Wales, both 1988; had a studio, Cité Internationale des Arts, Paris, 1992; and was judge for the Sulman Prize, Art Gallery of New South Wales, 1995. Cress completed a number of portraits, including the artists Colin Madigan, Sandra Leveson and John Beard. As a painter he straddled the European and Australian traditions, creating a unique style belonging to neither continent. Having been an ardent abstractionist, he returned to figuration in the 1980s. He was latterly known as a maker of big works, sometimes harsh, often bold and biting allegories of modern life and manners, and of small, dark, moody Goya-esque drawings. By the time of his first London solo exhibition, at East West, 2000, Cress had logged almost 50 solo shows, numerous group appearances plus a huge volume of reviews, catalogues, books and television programmes. There was another East West exhibition in 2004. In Australia, Annandale Galleries, Sydney, latterly exhibited Cress's work, which was held by many public galleries and corporate collections.

Alexander CRESWELL 1957– Watercolourist and teacher, who studied history of art at Winchester College. Then went on to West Surrey College of Art and Design and Byam Shaw School of Drawing and Painting. Creswell began painting professionally in 1981 and participated in many group shows as well as holding numerous solo exhibitions in Britain and abroad. Later ones included Spink & Son, The Atlantic Hotel, in Jersey, and Save Britain's Heritage, at Mappin & Webb site, all in 1991, Cadogan Gallery in 1992, New Academy Gallery, 1999, and John Martin of London, 2002. Creswell's fine technique as a watercolourist was employed for the Spink show, called The Silent Houses of Britain, in which over five years he recorded 45 grand country houses, since abandoned. This coincided with the publication of his book of the same title. Creswell was a tutor at The Prince of Wales' Summer School in Civil Architecture, in Rome, in 1991. Creswell's commissioned work included Wiggins Teape plc, Burmah Castrol plc and the Parliamentary Art Collection in the Palace of Westminster. Lived at Ewhurst, Surrey.

Emily Grace CRESWELL 1889– Miniaturist and portrait painter, born in Ravenstone, Leicestershire. She studied art, after attending University College, Reading, at Leicester School of Art. This was followed by periods at Harrogate and Leamington Schools of Art plus some time with the miniaturist S. Arthur Lindsay in Chelsea. She sometimes signed her work E G C or G C and exhibited RMS, RI, SWA and elsewhere. Lived in Harrogate, Yorkshire.

Benjamin CRESWICK 1853–1946 Versatile figurative sculptor, architectural decorator and teacher, born in Sheffield, Yorkshire, who died in Sutton Coldfield, Warwickshire, having established his reputation in nearby Birmingham. Creswick was apprenticed as a knife grinder, began modelling in clay and was encouraged and supported by the writer and artist John Ruskin, opening a London studio in 1884. Through Ruskin Creswick was introduced to the Art Nouveau pioneer Arthur H Mackmurdo, producing work for his Century Guild. After periods in Liverpool and Manchester Creswick moved to Birmingham where he taught at the School of Art, 1889–1918. He showed with RA, Walker Art Gallery in Liverpool, Sheffield Society of Artists, RBSA and elsewhere in Birmingham and produced a variety of work around the city. His stone panels Scenes from Birmingham's Industrial Past for Handsworth Library, 1891, are good examples.

Joseph CRIBB 1892–1967 Sculptor, draughtsman and letter-cutter, son of Herbert William Cribb and brother of Lawrence Cribb, both artists. From 1906–13 was apprenticed to Eric Gill, settling in Ditchling, Sussex. After World War I service became almost a founder-member of the Guild of St Joseph and St Dominic and for many years was in charge of the stonemason's shop. Cribb did a lot of work for the Brighton architectural practice of John Denman and worked on the tabernacle of the London church of St Simon Stock. Cheltenham and Hove Museums and Art Galleries hold his work.

Kevin CRIBB 1928– Sculptor and letter-cutter, son of Lawrence Cribb and nephew of Joseph Cribb, both artists. He was born in Abergavenny, Monmouthshire. He was apprenticed to his father and David Kindersley in the Eric Gill workshop and worked for many years with Kindersley before going independent. Cribb exhibited in Bath, many times in Cambridge and in Bruges, Belgium. He worked in wood and stone, completed a headstone commemorating the inventor Barnes Wallis and has works in Winchester Cathedral and Wye College, Kent. Lived in Haslingfield, Cambridgeshire.

Lawrence Walter CRIBB 1898–1979 Sculptor, born in Twickenham, Middlesex, father of Kevin Cribb, son of Herbert William Cribb and younger brother of Joseph Cribb, all artists. He studied under his brother and Eric Gill, working with Gill from 1921. After the death of Gill in 1940 Cribb carried on in the workshop with Denis Tegetmeier, moving to north Wales late in the 1950s. From 1925 Cribb had many exhibitions. He worked with Gill on the League of Nations mural and St James' Park Underground Station as well as other commissions. Died in Barrington, Cambridgeshire.

Frances CRICHTON STUART 1951– Artist in oil, tapestry and pencil, muralist and illustrator, born in Dublin, Ireland, adopted and brought up in Scotland, educated at a Catholic convent. In 1972 enrolled at St Martin's School of Art, taught by Gillian Ayres, John Hoyland, Frederick Gore and Jennifer Durrant. Crichton Stuart was early influenced by Seurat, the Symbolists and Jung; also interested in travelling, "the different values of Man and Man's search for enlightenment" and the Painting and Prayer Movement, serving it as a tutor. Activities included murals at St Bartholomew's Hospital radiotherapy unit and Laycock School, Islington, 1973; in 1976–7, after leaving St Martin's, a mural at Charing Cross Hospital, aided by an Arts Council grant; in 1977–8 was assistant to artist Gary

Stephan, in New York; lived in Greece, 1981; helped organise Matthew Smith show at Barbican Gallery, 1983; travelled in Australia, Colombia, Yugoslavia and Italy, 1986–7; began designing and making tapestries, 1988; and illustrated *Alex*, by Peter Ryde, 1994. Later exhibitions included RSA, 1996, and solo shows at Kirkcaldy Museum and Art Gallery, 1998, and icons at Galerie art témoin, St Tropez, France, 2002. Lived in London.

Stephen CRIPPS 1952–1982 Pyrotechnic sculptor and performance artist, who was early encouraged at Cranleigh School by his art master Howard Pickersgill. Attended Bath Academy of Art, Corsham, 1970–4, where he reconstituted salvage and explored the possibilities of automatism. Then took a studio in east London, 1975–9. Economic pressures made Cripps take on a series of temporary jobs, such as scene shifting at Raymond's Revue Bar and photographing for a detective agency, then in 1979 he joined the London Fire Brigade, where as a nonconformist in a regulated atmosphere he found life tough going on occasions. Striving to break free of alcohol and heroin dependency Cripps misjudged a dose of methadone and died the following morning. Cripps had three shows at Acme Gallery, between 1978–81. Among the many multi-media performances he took part in were those with Paul Burwell and Anne Bean, whose Bow Gamelan Orchestra worked with the sculptor Richard Wilson. Bean and Burwell helped form The Stephen Cripps Trust, to prevent dispersal of his work. An installation and a performance to mark the tenth anniversary of Cripps' death took place at Serpentine Gallery in 1992, along with publication of an extensive monograph, supported by Acme Housing Association.

CRISPIN: *see* **Geoffrey WHEELER**

Keith CRITCHLOW 1933– Figurative and abstract artist, architect, teacher and writer. He studied at St Martin's School of Art and Royal College of Art, 1954–7, teaching at the Royal College from 1973. He was an early disciple of the American architect Richard Buckminster Fuller, whose first London exhibition he organised, and he ran his own architectural consultancy, Keith Critchlow Associates. Critchlow was interested in a variety of subjects related to art and architecture: geometry, mathematics, pattern and order in space. He was an expert on sacred architecture. Was represented in the 1988 Royal College of Art show Exhibition Road. Lived in London.

Michael Bernard CRITCHLOW 1904– Painter and illustrator, brought up in Wolverhampton, where he attended the School of Art under Robert Emerson. Did a considerable amount of illustrative work for magazines such as *Strand Magazine*, *Britannia and Eve* and *Nash's Magazine*. Exhibited RA, NEAC, ROI and elsewhere. Chelsea Arts Club member who lived in London.

Ariel CRITTALL 1914– Painter and draughtsman, born in Essex where she settled at Great Bardfield. Studied in Munich, Germany, 1934, then courses in life drawing and sculpture at St Martin's School of Art, 1935, and Slade School of Fine Art, 1935–6, her teachers including Vivian Pitchforth and A H Gerrard. Crittall's painting and drawing was confined to her spare time until 1980, when her husband died, then she concentrated on it seriously. Mixed shows included Bury St Edmunds Art Gallery, 1983; work accepted for RA Summer Exhibition, 1985; and in 1994 both Braintree Town Hall and Fry Art Gallery, Saffron Walden. Had a solo show at Quay Gallery, Sudbury, 1986, later ones including University of Essex, 1992; Braintree Town Hall, 1994; and Guild Hall, Thaxted, 1996. Crittall was a member of Colchester Art Society and was included in its Fiftieth Anniversary Exhibition at Chappel Galleries, Chappel, 1996. Gwen John, Winifred Nicholson and Matisse were cited as influences and Crittall aimed at "a palimpsest: richness and depth of tone, one thing half seen through another". Essex University Library, Braintree Library and Sir Stephen and Lady Tumim held examples.

James CRITTENDEN 1947– Artist and teacher who studied at Walthamstow School of Art, 1963–6, and Royal Academy Schools, 1966–9. He won the David Murray Landscape Scholarship, 1965, and Frank Herring Award, 1990. Taught from the early 1970s. Showed at RA Summer Exhibition and with PS, which he joined in 1991. Lived for a time at Alnwick Moor, Northumberland.

Manja CRNKOVIC: *see* **Manja SCOTT**

Andrew CROCKER 1962– Artist, born in North Yorkshire, who studied at Cleveland College of Art, 1981–2, then graduated from Goldsmiths' College with a degree in fine art, 1982–5, with postgraduate studies there, 1987–9. Exhibitions included Cleveland International Drawing Biennale 1989; Cricket Hill Gallery, New York, USA, 1993; Lamont Gallery, 1995; and Paul Smith, New York, 1996. Commissions and collections include London Underground, Ladbroke Group and Ernst & Young.

Barbara CROCKER 1910– Painter of pictures and murals, printmaker and illustrator and art lecturer, born in London, married to the writer Eric Whelpton. She studied at Slade School of Fine Art, 1927–30, under Henry Tonks, Philip Wilson Steer and Tancred Borenius, continuing her studies in France and Italy. Worked as a professional painter backed up by lecturing, notably to troops in World War II. Travelled throughout Europe, the Middle East and Russia. Showed with LG, RSW, Alpine Gallery and WIAC. From 1960 held studio shows about once a year. Completed murals in offices and restaurants in London, also in Natural History Museum. Art gallery in Rye, Canada House in London and New York Museum hold her work. Among her publications was *Art Appreciation Made Simple*. Lived in Rye, Sussex.

Jeremy CROCKER fl. from early 1980s– Painter, printmaker, muralist and teacher, who did a foundation course at Somerset College of Arts and Technology, 1977–8; gained a first-class honours degree in painting from Wolverhampton Polytechnic, 1978–81 (including a term at Orleans, France); then did postgraduate studies in printmaking at Central School of Art and Design, 1983–5. Crocker gained a Tim Turner Travelling Scholarship, 1981; Prix de Rome (Printmaking), British School at Rome, 1986–7; and an Italian Government Bursary to study in Rome, 1990. Crocker's work included figure groups, including nude and clothed figures, giving them a slightly stagey quality, as in A Clear Picture at Collyer-Bristow Gallery, 1997. Other mixed shows included Stowells Trophy from 1980; The Brewhouse Open, Taunton, from 1981; Open Print Exhibition, Bankside Gallery, from 1988; and LG, from 1992. Later solo shows included 30 Brook

Street, 1994. Crocker held a teaching fellowship at Christ's Hospital, Horsham, 1985–6; was a visiting lecturer at the Central School (The London Institute), 1987; he taught at St Paul's School from 1988; and also gave adult classes. Commissions included four mural paintings at the Royal Surrey Hospital, Redhill, commissioned by the Public Art Development Trust, 1985.

John CROFT 1923– Artist in oil and collage, born in London, full name Ivor John Croft. He was by profession a civil servant who after Westminster School studied at Oxford University, London University's Institute of Education and the London School of Economics, obtaining his master's degree. Had no formal art training and produced "non-figurative, Minimalist, work derived from landscape". Participated in group shows at Piccadilly and John Whibley Galleries, at Camden Arts Centre in its survey of abstract artists in 1967, Bear Lane Gallery in Oxford in 1968, Covent Garden Gallery, 1973, Artspace Gallery in Isle of Man, 1990, and Newport Art Gallery, Isle of Wight, 1993. Had a solo exhibition at University of Sussex's Gardner Centre in 1970, a year later at Warwick University. London Borough of Camden and London School of Economics hold his work. Lived in Bath, Somerset, where Anthony Hepworth Fine Art represented him.

Marjorie CROFT 1889– Painter and printmaker. She showed NEAC, SWA, RA, RBA and elsewhere and lived in London for many years after an early period in Penshurst, Kent.

Paul John CROFT 1963– Printmaker, draughtsman and lecturer, born in Belfast, Northern Ireland, who graduated with honours in fine art, Edinburgh College of Art, 1981–5, completing his postgraduate diploma there in fine art printmaking, 1985–6, principal teacher Elspeth Lamb; was printmaking assistant, Dundee Printmakers' Workshop, 1986–8; then gained his Certificate in Education, University of Ulster, 1989–90. At that University Croft was associate lecturer in printmaking, 1990–4 and 1996–9, from 1994–6 pursuing the master printer training programme at Tamarind Institute, Albuquerque, New Mexico, in America, where his principal teachers were Jeffery Sipple, Bill Lagattuta, Marjorie Devon and Clinton Adams; then was lecturer in printmaking, Aberystwyth School of Art, from 1999. Grants in 1992 and 1994 from the Elizabeth Greenshields Foundation permitted Croft to travel to Japan and to take up the place at Albuquerque, which led to the show From Tokyo to Tamarind at the University of Wales, Aberystwyth, 2000. Was commissioned by A&C Black to write books on stone and plate lithography, for publication in 2001–2. Croft was a versatile printmaker, latterly "mainly a lithographer", for whom "the communal aspect of printmaking is in itself an attractive quality." Croft's "work of the early 1990s was heavily influenced by images of Japan and Japanese calligraphy, more recent works have been concerned with rock carvings and Petroglyphs found in the deserts of New Mexico and Arizona." Arts Council of Northern Ireland and The Ulster New Zealand trust hold his work. Lived in Aberystwyth, Cardigan.

Richard John CROFT 1935– Artist in a wide range of media, and teacher, born in London, who studied at Bromley College of Art, 1951–5, then Brighton College of Art, 1957–8. Between 1958–86 he taught, for a time being head of the art department at Annadale Grammar School, Belfast; in 1984 he moved from Belfast to Dundrum, County Down; and in 1986 began to paint full-time. Croft began as a realistic painter but quickly became influenced by Geometric Formalisation and later by Geometric Abstraction, leading to constructions in wood and Perspex. In the 1960s he produced several kinetic works; in the 1970s slowly returned to realism, but still with a bias towards Geometric Cubism and a simplification of statement, using very thin paint and pale colour; with the move to Dundrum the move to realism continued, but his palette brightened. From 1962 Croft regularly showed work at the Irish Exhibition of Living Art in Dublin and Belfast, RHA and RUA; he became an Ulster Academician in 1967, eventually RUA president, and won the Conor Prize in 1970. In 1963 Croft was a founder-member of Group '63 and in 1973 with his artist wife Helen Kerr he helped found the Octagon Gallery. After a solo show at Piccolo Gallery, Belfast, in 1960 Croft regularly had one-man exhibitions, a retrospective at Flowerfield Arts Centre, Portstewart, going to several venues in 1993–4. Ulster Museum, Oxford and London Universities, Northern Ireland Arts Council and many other public and corporate collections hold examples.

Stuart CROFT 1970– Artist who painted and used adhesive tape, who said that his work had "always formed an exploration into the possibilities and history of abstractions". Studied in 1989 at Harrogate College of Arts and Technology, in 1990–2 at Newcastle upon Tyne Polytechnic, in the latter year having an Erasmus EC placement at the National College of Art and Design, Dublin. From 1992–3 lived in Berlin, in 1993–4 attending Wimbledon School of Art. Exhibitions included Squires Gallery, Newcastle, 1991; Zwemmer Gallery, Courtauld Institute, 1993; three-man show at University of Surrey, Guildford, 1994; and Pacesetters, Peterborough Museum and Art Gallery, 1995. Lived in London.

Michael John CROFTON 1961– Sculptor, restorer and teacher who obtained first-class diploma in sculpture from City and Guilds of London Art School, 1980–4. Crofton engaged in a wide variety of work, including wax and rubber moulding, freelance casting for sculptors and part-time teaching at Fulham and Chelsea Adult Education Institute, 1987–9. Showed at RSA and RA from 1988; Keith Chapman Gallery, 1989; West Wales Art Centre, Fishguard, 1992; and 1st RWA Open Sculpture Exhibition, 1993. Lived in Hebron Whitland, Dyfed.

Stella Rebecca CROFTS 1898–1964 Painter, sculptor and potter of portraits and animals, born in Nottingham. Studied at Central School of Arts and Crafts, 1916–22, and Royal College of Art, 1922–3. Exhibited RA, RMS, SWA, Crafts Centre of Great Britain and widely abroad. Nottingham Castle Museum, Hanley Museum in Stoke-on-Trent and Manchester City Art Gallery hold her work, as does Victoria & Albert Museum. Lived at Billericay, Essex.

Sally CROMBIE 1964– Artist, theatre tour administrator and teacher, born in Cambridge, who worked for a time as Sally Crumbie Ekpenyong. She graduated in fine art with first-class honours from Manchester Polytechnic in 1987, completing a postgraduate course in printmaking at the Slade School of Fine Art, 1989. After two years as technical adviser and part-time teacher in the printmaking department of East London Polytechnic, she moved to Nigeria in 1991 and co-established the Lagos arts company Iwana Arts. Several productions toured the region, including *The Courageous Cry*, Nigeria's largest ever theatre tour. The British Council supported Crombie's exhibitions and theatre tours, also funded by British Airways, the Netherlands Ministry of Foreign Affairs and the Ford Foundation. Chevron, Anadrill and the Hilton in Abuja, Nigeria, commissioned Crombie. On returning to the United Kingdom in 1997 she taught fine art at Middlesex University, working on art projects and residencies in Newham schools. Celia Purcell Contemporary showed Crombie's work.

Gertrude CROMPTON 1874– Watercolour and oil painter and teacher, born in West Tanfield, Yorkshire. After initial education in London she studied at the Westminster School of Art under William Mouat Loudan, then in Paris. She exhibited SWA, Goupil Gallery, with the St Ives Society of Artists and at the Paris Salon. While living in Cornwall was a justice of the peace, retiring just after World War II. Then lived at Nailsworth, near Stroud, in Gloucestershire.

David CRONE 1937– Painter and teacher, born in Belfast, Northern Ireland, who attended Belfast College of Art from 1956, then taught art at Larkfield Secondary School in the city, 1961–3, next at his old grammar school, Annadale, 1963–75, then went on to teach at Ulster College. He gained a number of awards, including an Arts Council of Northern Ireland travel scholarship to the continent, 1964, commissions including a mural for Ulster '71. As well as painting portraits Crone was a significant landscape artist whose pictures variously showed Expressionist and Cubist influences. Exhibitions included CEMA, Magee Gallery in Belfast, Arts Council of Northern Ireland which holds his work and Tom Caldwell Gallery, Belfast. There was a retrospective at Ulster Museum, Belfast, in 1995. Later shows included Fenderesky Gallery, Belfast, and Hillsboro Fine Art, Dublin, both 2004, and JohnMartinChelsea in 2005. The British and Irish Arts Councils, Irish Museum of Modern Art, Ulster Museum, Contemporary Arts Society in Dublin, Ulster University as well as corporate and many private collections hold Crone's work.

Edward CRONSHAW 1961– Sculptor who worked from a studio and foundry in Halifax, Yorkshire, and showed internationally, outlets including 108 Fine Art, Harrogate. Ed Cronshaw studied at St Martin's and the Royal College of Art. Among his commissions were a four-metre-high horse for Liverpool and a seven-metre-high figure for Nottingham, both in bronze. Many public and private collections held his work.

Hugh CRONYN 1905–1996 Painter in oil, watercolour and mixed media, and teacher, born in Vancouver, British Columbia, Canada. He was educated at Ridley College and after a brief period in business studied with the landscape painter Frank Johnston, one of the Group of Seven, then at the Art Students' League of New York, 1929; in 1930 at the American School of Fine Arts, Fontainebleau; then for several years in Paris including time with André Lhote, 1932. After settling in London, with the outbreak of World War II Cronyn was commissioned in the Royal Naval Volunteer Reserve, 1940, serving in several ships, his final posting being to Saigon. Early in the war Cronyn had volunteered for bomb disposal; he was awarded the George Medal for defusing a bomb in the volatile tanker *Chesapeake*. After demobilisation, Cronyn became director of art at the Architectural Association's school of architecture, 1946–9, then taught painting at Colchester School of Art, 1949–69. He showed at The Minories, Colchester; Canada House; Nancy Poole's Studio, Toronto; Phoenix Gallery in London and Lavenham (with a retrospective there in 1990); RA; and LG. In 1989, by which time Cronyn's eyesight was failing, he published a memoir, *Steady As You Go; A Canadian At Sea*. Finally lived in London, spending part of the year at a house in the southwest of France. Highgate Fine Art showed his Thames pictures in 2001.

Eleanor CROOK 1966– Sculptor, installations artist and lecturer who gained an honours degree at Oxford University, 1985–9; another in fine art, sculpture, from Central St Martins, 1990–3; and a postgraduate diploma in sculpture, Royal Academy Schools, 1993–6. Won a de Segonzac Travel Award, 1996. Lectured in anatomy, Byam Shaw School of Art, where she held a Henry Moore Fellowship, 1997–8. Mixed shows included RA Summer Exhibition, 1995; Mercury Gallery, 1996; and British Figurative Art II, Flowers East, 1998. Commissions included a portrait, Southall & Company, Birmingham, 1993; installation, collection N & B Kamerer, New York, 1996–7, and sculpture, Vanderbilt University, 1997–8, both in America; and an installation, The Gallery of the Future, Loughborough, 1998. Had a solo exhibition at Gallery M, 2001, including anatomically uncompromising works such as flayed and opened-up torsos.

Gordon CROOK 1921– Painter, tapestry designer and teacher, born in Richmond, Surrey. After initial education in Chichester, Sussex, Crook attended St Martin's School of Art and the Central School of Art & Design. He showed at Redfern and O'Hana Galleries, at the Bear Lane Gallery in Oxford, in Scotland and in America. Lived in Great Yeldham, Essex.

Linda CROOK 1946– Stone sculptor and medallist who studied at Camberwell School of Arts and Crafts, 1979–83, and Goldsmiths' College, 1984–6, where she gained her master's degree. Her Big Cat, in alabaster, and Sea Horse medal, bronze, were included in Animal Kingdoms at Simmons Gallery, 1998.

P J CROOK 1945– Pam Crook was born in Cheltenham, and was married to another painter, Richard Parker. She studied at the Gloucestershire College of Art, 1960–5. Showed at RA Summer Exhibition from 1978, RWA and John Player Portrait Award Exhibition at National Portrait Gallery, 1986. Had a series of solo shows at Portal Gallery from 1980, in 1986 and 1995 at Cheltenham Art Gallery & Museum, which holds her work, and from where a retrospective toured in 1996. Westminster Cathedral, Tewkesbury Abbey and the parish church in Bishop's Cleeve, Gloucestershire, where she lived, also hold examples. Crook's figurative works had a slightly Surrealist, haunting quality and were unusual in that the image spilled from the canvas on to the wooden frame.

Thomas Mewburn CROOK 1869–1949 Sculptor and teacher, born at Tonge Moor, Bolton, Lancashire. After a religious schooling he attended Manchester Technical

School and then the Royal College of Art, gaining three silver and five bronze medals and his diploma in 1902, followed by extensive studies on the continent. He was elected RBA in 1910 and a fellow of RBS in 1923. Crook's Mysteries and his Pieta, erected in St Katherine's, Rotherhithe, are illustrated in *RBS: Modern British Sculpture*, published in 1939. Showed at RA, Royal Glasgow Institute of the Fine Arts, RBA, ROI and RI. Between 1894–5 Crook taught modelling at the Royal College, then from 1896–1905 modelling and anatomy at Manchester School of Art. He was an Arts and Savage Club member who lived in London.

Irene M CROOKENDEN 1880–1957 Flower painter in oil, pastel and watercolour. Born in Camberley, Surrey, into a military family, she studied art at the Slade School of Fine Art and the British School at Rome, where she won the Calderon Prize for portraiture. Exhibited RA, Goupil Gallery, SWA, RBA and widely in the provinces. Lived in London.

Barbara CROOKS 1904– Painter in oil, born in London. She was educated at Southend High School, The Froebel Institute at Roehampton and London Academy of Music & Dramatic Art, becoming a kindergarten teacher. From the 1960s "to prove that I can paint and as a prophylactic against family tragedy" Crooks took up painting in oil, attending evening classes at Southend-on-Sea Art School and adult leisure classes, mainly producing landscapes. Was a member of NS and Southend Art Club and also showed at ROI, NEAC, Paris Salon and elsewhere. Sometimes signed work B G A, her full name being Barbara Gwendolen Anne Crooks. Lived in Thorpe Bay, Essex.

John CROPTON: *see* **David STAINER**

William CROSBIE 1915–1999 Painter, draughtsman and mural artist, born in Hankow, China, of Scottish parents. The family stayed in China until 1926; Crosbie had a Chinese tutor, and Oriental philosophy remained a potent force in his life and work. After toying with the idea of a commercial career back in Glasgow, Crosbie decided instead to be a painter and studied at the School of Art, 1932–5. A Haldane Travelling Scholarship took him to Paris, where he studied history of art at the Sorbonne and worked under Fernand Léger and Aristide Maillol. He then joined an archaeological expedition to Egypt, where he copied friezes on temple walls, but was back in Britain to serve in the Merchant Navy and Civil Defence during World War II. Crosbie now made a name as a mural painter through his association with architects such as Basil Spence; the Victoria & Albert Museum's Britain Can Make It show in 1946 and the Festival of Britain, in 1951, were examples. He did some book illustration, designed the sets of Eric Chisholm's ballet *The Earth Shapers* and produced wood and stone carvings for churches. Crosbie showed regularly in mixed Scottish exhibitions, having many solo shows. There were retrospectives at Scottish Gallery, Edinburgh, in 1980, and at Ewan Mundy & Celia Philo, Glasgow and London, 1990. Ewan Mundy put on an eightieth birthday exhibition in Glasgow in 1995, a memorial show in 2000. Crosbie was made an associate of RSA in 1953, a full RSA 20 years later. His work is hard to classify, as he was extremely versatile, a fine draughtsman and brilliant Colourist. Scottish Arts Council and Scottish National Gallery of Modern Art hold his work. Latterly Crosbie worked mainly at Petersfield, Hampshire.

Clem CROSBY 1958– Painter of monochrome and Minimalist works, born in Aldershot, Hampshire, who studied at Trent Polytechnic, Nottingham, 1979–82. Group exhibitions included Wonderful Life, 1993; Six Painters, Lisson Gallery, 1994; Real Art, Southampton City Art Gallery, 1995; Jerwood Prize Shortlist, 1996; British Painting, Galerie Hollenbach, Stuttgart, Germany, 1998; Howard Yezerski Gallery, Boston, Massachusetts, America, 2000; and Minimalism: Then and Now, Berkeley Museum, San Francisco, California, America, 2001. Clem Crosby New Paintings was at program in 2005. Released to coincide with this, his first solo show, were four songs from *Kunstick*: Crosby, music and guitars, David Stephenson, words and vocals. Crosby lived in London.

Dido CROSBY 1961– Sculptor and teacher, born in London, daughter of the architect and artist Theo Crosby and the painter Anne Buchanan. Dido attended Bedales School, 1973–80; had a year out in Paris, France, assisting Sheila Hicks, then Rhodes, Greece, with Polly Hope, 1980–1; gained an honours degree in zoology, St Hilda's College, Oxford, 1981–4; was secretary to Pentagram Design, 1984–5; while working in Brighton attended courses at the Polytechnic there, 1985–6; in London took classes at Chelsea Schol of Art and Morley College, 1986; helped the actress Sarah Miles and the playwright Robert Bolt and widened her studies at Hackney College and Sir John Cass School, 1987–91; then graduated in fine art, sculpture, from Central St Martin's College of Art and Design, 1991–6. Teaching included Sir John Cass and London College of Fashion. Exhibitions included Portsmouth "See" Group, Mountbatten Centre, Portsmouth, 1989; Sculpture in the Park, St Mary's Park, Whitechapel, 1991; Open Studios, Spitalfields Market Artists, 1997; and with Csáky Art at The Arndean Gallery, 2002. Among later commissions were Athene Owls, two pairs in brass in hand-rails on internal bridge, Barbican Centre, 1994; Dragon Head and Tail, reclaimed teak and marbles, garden for visually impaired children, Woodside Family Centre, Kingswood, Bristol, also Four Falcon Finials and pair of Acanthus Leaf Balls, restaurant building, Shakespeare's Globe, Southwark, both 1996; and a life-size The Ram for Csáky Art, exhibited at Palm Beach, Miami, America, 2001.

Theo CROSBY 1925–1994 Architect, sculptor and writer, born in Mafeking, South Africa. He studied at University of Witwatersrand, Johannesburg, moved to London in 1947 and that year studied part-time at Sir John Cass School of Art, then Central School of Arts and Crafts, 1950–4, and St Martin's School of Art, 1956–8. Crosby was a fellow of RIBA and of the Chartered Society of Designers and was made RA in 1990. He became a partner in Pentagram Design Partnership. As a sculptor he made large terracottas and stone carvings, in later years moving towards a more classical imagery and technique. He was commissioned to make a drinking fountain in Hyde Park for the Great Children's Party, 1979, also working on the Shakespeare Globe Centre and National Police Memorial in The Mall. His publications included *Le Corbusier*, 1959, and *Let's Build a Monument*, 1987. Crosby was professor of architecture and design at Royal College of Art, 1990–3. His first wife was the artist Anne Buchanan, his second Polly Hope. Lived in London.

David CROSS 1964– Sculptor, born in Canterbury, Kent, who studied at St Martin's School of Art in 1987, where he met Matthew Cornford, graduating from the Royal College of Art in 1991. He worked with Matthew Cornford as Cornford & Cross (see separate entries). Lived in London.

Dorothy CROSS 1956– Artist, designer and teacher, born in Cork, Ireland, who employed unorthodox materials such as cows' udders and snakes in silver cases. She gained a bachelor's degree at Leicester Polytechnic and her master's degree in fine art from San Francisco Art Institute, California. Teaching and lecturing experience included Crawford School of Art, Cork; National College of Art and Design, Dublin; Waterford and Belfast Colleges of Art; Williams College, Massachusetts; Oberlin College, Ohio; and School of the Museum of Fine Arts, Boston. In 1992 and 1994 handled set and costume designs for Opera Theatre Company for various Irish venues. From 1985–8 Cross was a committee member for the Irish Exhibition of Living Art, from 1992 a member of Aosdana. Group shows included Strongholds, Tate Gallery in Liverpool and Hilden Museum, Tampere, Finland, 1991; Welcome Europe, Holsterbro Kunstmuseum, Jutland, Denmark, 1992; and Fetishism, South Bank Centre tour, 1995. Later solo shows included Frith Street Gallery, 1994; Kerlin Gallery, Dublin, 1995; and Arnolfini Gallery, Bristol, 1996. Irish Museum of Modern Art, Dublin; Arts Councils of Ireland and Northern Ireland; and Tate Gallery hold examples.

Gwen CROSS 1900–1966 Painter, printmaker, jeweller, cutler, sculptor, illustrator and teacher, born in Bristol, married to the artist Fred Whicker. Despite family opposition she studied at Bristol Municipal School of Art under Reginald Bush, returning to teach there until towards the end of World War II. In 1934 she was a founding member of New Bristol Arts Club, serving as its first president, its aim being to enliven the city's art scene. Cross made etchings of Bristol, in its City Art Gallery collection. Soon after the war the Whickers moved to Falmouth and became members of the St Ives Society of Artists. Gwen became a noted flower painter, a leading figure at Falmouth School of Art as a teacher and governor. She showed at RA, SWA, RWA, ROI and extensively overseas. The Whickers' lives in Cornwall, as representational artists overtaken by the modern movement, were lived in straitened circumstances. There was a joint retrospective at Falmouth Art Gallery and RWA in 1994.

Julian CROSS 1952– Painter who studied at Hornsey College of Art, 1967–70, Walthamstow College of Art, 1970–3, and the Royal Academy Schools, 1973–6. He exhibited at the RA Summer Exhibition from 1974 and won the Richard Ford Award, 1979. Had a solo exhibition at RA, 1980. Sir Brinsley Ford owned his 1976 self-portrait.

Nicolette CROSS 1930– Painter in variety of media, born in London, who studied at Byam Shaw School of Drawing and Painting, 1947–52, with Peter Greenham and Patrick Phillips. She eventually moved to Canada, settling latterly in Bowen Island, British Columbia, after some years in Vancouver. She was a member of UA and Federation of Canadian Artists, also exhibiting with NS, NEAC, RWA and elsewhere.

Roy CROSS 1924– Painter of historical ships and aircraft, born in London. His work was widely available in limited-edition prints. Became a member of Society of Aviation Artists in 1952 and 25 years later the RSMA. Showed at Börjessons Gallery, Gothenburg, Sweden, from 1975 and Marine Arts Gallery, Salem, Massachusetts, from 1976. Lived in Langton Green, Tunbridge Wells, Kent.

Roy CROSS 1927–1987 Painter and teacher, born in Liverpool, producing strongly stylised and abstracted oils, including figures and Essex landscapes. He studied at Liverpool School of Art and became head of art at St Helena School, Colchester, Essex, where he settled. Cross was a member of Wivenhoe Arts Club. In 1958 he was a prize winner at the John Moores Exhibition in Liverpool and he exhibited at the Walker Art Galllery there. He also showed with LG, at RWS Gallery, Cartwright Art Gallery in Bradford, in an Arts Council Travelling Exhibition and in Amsterdam, Paris and Washington, his solo exhibitions including Drian Galleries, 1961 and 1963.

Tom CROSS 1931– Painter, printmaker, constructions maker, teacher and writer, born in Manchester. He attended the College of Art there and Slade School of Fine Art. In 1956–8 travelled and painted in Italy and France on Rome and French Government Scholarships. From 1959–63 was assistant director of the WAC. He then held several teaching posts in Britain and abroad, being from 1976–87 principal of Falmouth School of Art. He was a member of LG and chairman of Penwith Society of Arts, 1982–4. In the latter year he published *Painting the Warmth of the Sun, St Ives Artists, 1935–75*. Wrote *Artists and Bohemians: 100 years with the Chelsea Arts Club*, 1992, and *The Shining Sands, Artists in Newlyn and St Ives 1880–1930*, 1994. Cross was a prolific exhibitor, group exhibitions including John Moores Exhibition in Liverpool, Reading Museum, SWG, SEA and elsewhere. His many solo shows included Paintings of Cornwall and Wales, University of Wales, Aberystwyth, and tour, 1995. Lived in Constantine, Cornwall.

Will CROSS 1888–1971 Painter in oil of portraits and landscapes, born in London. After education at King's College, he studied with W R Lethaby at the Central School of Arts and Crafts, at the Slade School of Fine Art under Randolph Schwabe and with Albert Rutherston in Oxford at the Ruskin School of Drawing. Exhibited at UA, RBA, RI, with Artists of Chelsea and the Chelsea Art Society, in the provinces and America. Lived in Sutton Courtenay, Berkshire.

Bob CROSSLEY 1912– Painter and printmaker, born in Northwich, Cheshire, who attended Heybrook School, Rochdale. Crossley was always an experimental artist, who had a deep interest in form and colour tensions and whose pictures, abstract and figurative, had great verve and energy. His early career was in the north of England. After military service in the Royal Air Force, 1941–5, Crossley showed in various exhibitions such as RA, SGA, Paris Salon and Manchester Academy, being elected a member in 1950. In 1959 he moved to St Ives, Cornwall, and London, showing with Penwith Society of Arts, Newlyn Society of Artists, AIA, Piccadilly and Redfern Galleries and elsewhere. Had a solo show at Crane Kalman Gallery, Manchester, 1959, later ones including a retrospective at Penwith Galleries, St Ives, 1992, a post-retrospective there, 1999, and a retrospective at Rochdale Art Gallery, 2004. Contemporary Art Society, Winnipeg Art

Gallery in Canada and Museum and Art Gallery in Durban, South Africa, hold Crossley's work. Lived in Porthgwidden, Cornwall.

Clare CROSSLEY fl. from 1920s– Painter and draughtsman, notable for small, delicate landscapes of scenery around her home Combermere Abbey, Shropshire. Her father was Brigadier Alan Thomson, her sister Baroness Tweedsmuir, her husband the politician Anthony Crossley and her daughter Taisa Camu, an artist. She had early encouragement in sketching from Robert Morley, then from Augustus John, a neighbour in Chelsea in the 1920s. She attended Académie Julian, Paris, in 1925; Slade School of Fine Art under Henry Tonks; in the 1930s was with Vladimir Polunin as a private pupil and at the Slade again, in 1936; also making abstract colour prints at S W Hayter's Atelier 17, in Paris. Showed at NEAC, LG, Leicester Galleries and Trafford Gallery. Had a solo show at Storran Gallery in 1931, another at Chenil Galleries, 1969, and in 1975 was one of Three Women Painters at Michael Parkin Fine Art.

Cuthbert CROSSLEY 1883–1960 Painter, printmaker and designer, notable for landscapes and architectural subjects, sometimes employing unusual means. He was born in Halifax, Yorkshire, where he early showed artistic gifts. Studied advanced applied design at the local School of Art, winning a King's Prize. Crossley was a member of the School of Art Sketching Society and a founder-member, around 1907, of Halifax Arts and Crafts Society. Soon after World War I Crossley became a designer for John Crossley & Sons, carpet makers, at the Dean Clough works, but by the early 1920s had become a full-time artist. He drew for the *Halifax Courier*; in 1928 completed etchings of old Halifax, including the three gates of the Piece Hall; and in 1933 illustrated T W Hanson's *Old Inns of Halifax*. Showed in Yorkshire and at RA, RI, RSA, RBA, Walker Art Gallery in Liverpool and at the Paris Salon. Bankfield Museum in Halifax and public galleries in Leeds and Newcastle upon Tyne hold Crossley's work, which could sometimes show a Cubist influence. Moved from Halifax soon after World War II to St Ives, Cornwall, where his wife shortly, and he later, died. In 1962 there was a Crossley Memorial Exhibition at Bankfield, with a further show there in 1973.

Gordon CROSSLEY 1929– Painter and teacher, born in Surrey, who studied at Wimbledon School of Art. He became senior lecturer in art and design at Barking College of Technology. Showed with NS of which he became a member in 1983, RA and NEAC, and had a series of solo exhibitions in East Anglia. Lived at Sheering, Hertfordshire.

Harold CROSSLEY 1900–1993 Sculptor, painter and printmaker, born in Thornton, Yorkshire, attending the nearby Bradford Art School, 1915–19. He showed at public art galleries in Bradford, Liverpool, Preston and Manchester but latterly did not contribute to exhibitions. Was for some years a member of Bradford Art Club. Lived in Knott End-on-Sea, Blackpool, Lancashire.

John CROSSLEY 1946– Printmaker, born in Bradford, Yorkshire, where he studied fine art at the local College of Art, 1963–4. After attending Hornsey College of Art, 1964–8, was master etcher at Editions Alecto, 1969–71. With James Collyer, he then established J C Editions, which existed until the late 1980s. For several years continued to work for Editions Alecto, then for for Henry Moore. From 1988 worked as Crossley Intaglio, based in Islington, north London.

John CROSSLEY 1952– Artist, lecturer and gallery manager, born in Dagenham, Essex, who did a foundation course at East Ham College of Technology, 1969–70, then graduated with honours in sculpture, 1970–3, from St Martin's School of Art, taking postgraduate sculpture there, 1973–4. Teachers included William Tucker, Phillip King and Anthony Caro. From 1974–5, Crossley assisted Caro; from 1975–85 he managed Camden Arts Centre; in 1985 attending Triangle workshop, Pine Plains, New York, America. He won Sainsbury and Arts Council Awards. Was a LG member from 1978. Taught widely, latterly being senior lecturer at Chelsea College of Art & Design. Crossley said that his painting "evolves through a state of addition and subtraction, enabling an orchestration of movements and bands to occupy an area, and emerge or recede to form an elusive arena, where absence and memory negotiate their boundaries." Received commissions from Unilever House, 1982, and Hillingdon Hospital, Uxbridge, 1985. Participated in numerous group shows, later solo exhibitions including Oriel Gallery, Mold, 1990, and The Milton Gallery, 1996. In 1999 shared a show with Steven Foy at The Start Gallery. Among collections were London Borough of Camden, Leicestershire Education Authority, Sunderland Arts Centre and Rochdale Art Gallery.

Brian CROUCH 1929– Painter and draughtsman who gained his Intermediate Diploma in Design, Brighton College of Art, 1948, his National Diploma there, 1950, and his Art Teacher's Diploma, 1951, then studied as a postgraduate at the Royal Academy Schools, 1956. He had two pictures selected for Jack Beddington's 1957 book *Young Artists of Promise*. Crouch was a part-time lecturer at Battersea Institute, 1955–62; Brighton College of Art and Design, 1962–5; Kingston Polytechnic/University, 1963–88; West Surrey College of Art and Design, 1965–76; and Epsom School of Art and Design, 1982–5. His early work was shown in many group exhibitions, including the LG, Wildenstein, Young Contemporaries, Grabowski Gallery, the AIA and elsewhere, later appearances including Vital Art, Atlantis Gallery, 1998. He had two retrospectives at Johnson Wax Kiln Gallery, Farnham Maltings, in 1981, with a further exhibition there in 1987. Then, Crouch explained how he had over the years experimented with more abstract and self-contained pictures, colour-field paintings and smaller reliefs before in 1980 again making works which were freer in execution, often in construction form, which referred to events, moods and places important to him. After a solo show of Recent Work at the Pike Gallery in 1992, Llantarnam Grange Arts Centre, Cwmbran, toured his show Gardens And Landscapes through Wales in 1992–4. There was a one-man of Recent Work at Gallery 7, Hong Kong, in 1994; Works on Paper, Pallant House Gallery, Chichester, 1995, and Kingston University, 1996; and another Llantarnam Grange show, Brian Crouch, Home and Away, Recent paintings, toured Wales from 2000. British Rail, *Financial Times*, Cambridge City Education Committee and other public collections held works.

Patrick CROUCH 1954– Sculptor and teacher who was an assistant to Edward Bainbridge Copnall, 1970–3, studying sculpture and anatomy with Tony Gray, 1970–2, and attending Sir John Cass School of Art, 1970–3. Between

1973–5 Crouch studied construction with Vincent Arnall and church organ restoration with Tom Robbins. From 1974–5 he was again at Sir John Cass, in 1976–9 graduating with an honours degree in sculpture from St Martin's College of Art. Crouch had substantial teaching experience in the mid-1980s in adult education in the southeast of England, and at Canterbury College, the John Makepeace School of Craftsmen in Wood, Central St Martins College of Art and Kent Institute of Art & Design, Canterbury, where in 1992 he took part in Sculpture at Canterbury. His residencies included Tunbridge Wells, Sevenoaks Festival and Harlow Carr Gardens in Harrogate, 1983–6. Crouch showed in numerous mixed exhibitions, including RA, New Metropole in Folkestone, Christopher Hull Gallery, Roy Miles Gallery and LG 92 at Morley Gallery.

Barbara CROW 1942– Printmaker, illustrator and teacher, born in Liverpool. She studied at Slade School of Fine Art, 1959–62, under William Coldstream, then did a postgraduate course in printmaking at Bristol Polytechnic, 1982–4. Was a member of RCamA, Association of Illustrators and the Association of Artists/Designers in Wales. Also exhibited at Arnolfini Gallery and RWA, both in Bristol. Lived in Llangattock-vibon-Avel, Gwent.

Derek Walter CROW 1928– Painter, draughtsman, printmaker and potter, born in Strood, Kent. He was brought up in Rochester, then studied at Medway School of Art, 1945–7, and at Royal College of Art, 1949–52, where his teachers included Rodrigo Moynihan, John Minton and Robert Buhler. Went on to teach in Jersey, Channel Islands, where he settled in St Helier. Showed Young Contemporaries, RI, RBA, SGA, in the provinces and elsewhere. National Film Theatre, London, holds his work.

Kathleen Mary CROW 1920– Painter in mixed media, mainly oil and watercolour, born and lived in Oxton, Nottinghamshire. Studied at Nottingham Polytechnic, 1964–76, with Ronald Thursby, then at Leicester, 1976–82, with Leslie Goodwin, both part-time. Became member of NS in 1983 and ROI in 1988, also showing with RA Summer Exhibition, RI, Nottingham Society of Artists and Rufford Craft Centre. She had a joint exhibition with Leslie Goodwin at RWA. Crow was a landscape painter who signed work with a monogram of her three initials.

Ron CROWCROFT 1953– Painter and writer, born in Hastings, Sussex. He was educated partly in Cyprus, partly in Chichester, Sussex. Attended West Sussex College of Design, Worthing, and Leeds Polytechnic in the early 1970s, his teachers including Jeff Nuttall and Glynn Williams. Showed at Sheffield College of Art and Leeds University Gallery, Leeds City Art Gallery holding his work in its collection. Lived for a time in Leeds, Yorkshire.

Barbara CROWE fl. from 1950s– Painter in oil and watercolour of English landscape and flowers. She taught painting widely in England and Wales and wrote and illustrated verses and stories for children. Born in the northwest of England, Crowe studied at Croydon and Bolt Court Schools of Art. She was a member of RI, SWA and Society of Botanical Artists, also exhibiting with Westminster and Chenil Galleries. Had a series of solo shows in Surrey, where she lived in Hammerfield, Abinger Hammer.

Maida CROWE: *see* **MAIDA**

Nick CROWE 1965– Artist, born in Macclesfield, Cheshire, who studied at the University of Hull. From the mid-1990s he worked collaboratively with Graham Parker and Ian Rawlinson on performances and art multiples. Their work related to the geographical location of their projects, as in Project for the River Medlock, Manchester, part of artranspennine98, in 1998. They also exhibited together at Kingsgate Gallery, Bluecoat Gallery in Liverpool and City Racing. Crowe was included in In Memoriam, New Art Gallery Walsall, 2000–1. His installation Getting On, concerned with age, youth and contemporary Britain, was at Chisenhale Gallery, 2003. Lived in Manchester.

Victoria CROWE 1945– Painter, printmaker and teacher, born in Kingston upon Thames, Surrey. She studied at Kingston School of Art, 1961–5, and Royal College of Art, 1965–8. From 1968 she became a part-time lecturer at Edinburgh College of Art. Crowe won the David Murray Landscape Scholarship in 1968, the Anne Redpath Award in 1973, Scottish Arts Council Bursaries in 1969 and 1975 and the *Glasgow Herald* Art Exhibition Award in 1981. The following year she was elected RSW, since when she won a number of awards and prizes. Crowe showed extensively in mixed shows in Scotland and England. She had solo exhibitions at Waterhouse Gallery in 1969 and 1971, a series at Scottish Gallery, Edinburgh, in the 1970s, then at Thackeray Gallery, Mercury Gallery in Edinburgh, Fine Art Society in Edinburgh and Glasgow and Bruton Gallery, Somerset, in 1989. In 2000, Crowe's A Shepherd's Life: Jenny Armstrong, at the Scottish National Portrait Gallery, Edinburgh, caught the atmosphere of the bleak Pentland Hills. This was a rare distinction for a living artist. Further solo shows included On Reflection at the Thackeray Gallery in 2005, celebrating the artist's sixtieth birthday, her twenty-fifth year of association with the gallery and her tenth solo exhibition there. Thackeray was involved in the book *Victoria Crowe Painted Insights*, which appeared in 2001, including texts by the artist and her husband, the artist and lecturer Michael Walton. The profusely illustrated volume included fine examples of Crowe's richly imaginative work as well as her many distinguished portraits, among her subjects the composer Ronald Stevenson, the poet Kathleen Raine and actor Graham Crowden. Scottish Arts Council, Scottish National Gallery of Modern Art and many other public collections hold her work. Lived at West Linton, Borders.

Graham CROWLEY 1950– Artist and teacher whose work could include bizarre and fantastic elements. He was born in Romford, Essex, and studied at St Martin's School of Art, 1968–72, and Royal College of Art, 1972–5. Gained Arts Council awards in 1976–8. Crowley was artist-in-residence at St Edmund Hall, Oxford, 1982–3; was senior fellow in painting, South Glamorgan Institute of Higher Education, 1986–9; and in 1991–2 held the Riverscape International Drawing Residency, Cleveland. Became professor of painting at the Royal College of Art, 1998, having been head of fine art at City and Guilds of London Art School. Group shows included RA; John Moores Liverpool Exhibition on several occasions including 1987 when he was joint second prizewinner; Peter Moores Liverpool Project 7 As of Now, 1983–4; and Twinings Gallery, New York, 1985. His one-man show Home Comforts toured in 1983 and other major solo exhibitions included Totah Gallery New York, 1986, and London from 1984, including Lamont Gallery, 1995 and 1997, and Beaux Arts, 2001 and 2005. There was a retrospective in 2002–3 at Christchurch Mansion, Ipswich. It and the Arts Council hold the work of Crowley, who latterly lived in west Cork, Ireland. There he completed a series of joyful landscapes, following a period of preoccupation with visions of a failing society.

Hugh Melvill CROWTHER 1914–2003 Artist in oil and pastel, born at Newby, near Scarborough, Yorkshire. He studied at Newport College of Art, becoming a freelance painter and teacher at further education classes in Chepstow for 21 years. Crowther was a member of West Gloucestershire Art Society, Wye Valley Art Society and Gloucestershire Society of Artists. His portraits and landscapes were also shown at Royal Glasgow Institute of the Fine Arts, elsewhere in the provinces and in London. Newport Museum holds his work. Lived in Tidenham, Gwent.

Michael CROWTHER 1946– Painter and teacher, born in County Durham. He studied at Leeds College of Art, 1964–8, and from 1970 taught at South Glamorgan Institute of Higher Education. He was included in WAC show The Probity of Art and the Paris Biennale in 1980, and was included in John Moores Liverpool Exhibitions starting in 1982. Had solo shows in London, Aberdeen, Exeter and Newcastle. Arts Council holds his acrylic on cotton duck Salvo II, of 1981. Lived in Cardiff.

Stephen CROWTHER 1922– Artist in oil, pastel, charcoal and conté, and teacher, full name Deryck Stephen Crowther. He was born in Sheffield, Yorkshire. Studied at the College of Art there, winning a Royal College of Art scholarship, 1941. After war service, 1941–6, was at the Royal College, 1946–9, teachers including Gilbert Spencer, Rodrigo Moynihan, Carel Weight and Ruskin Spear. From 1950–87 was a lecturer in drawing and painting at Cleveland College of Art & Design, Hartlepool. Crowther was included in Jack Beddington's 1957 volume *Young Artists of Promise*. He was made a member of RBA in 1958 and became president of Hartlepool Art Club. Crowther said that he owed a debt to the Old Masters and tried "to apply the lessons learnt to my own work, which reflects my life and environment". In 1989 Crowther won a Higgs & Hill Bursary, being commissioned to paint Port Solent Marina, Portsmouth, for the company. In 1992 two oils were commissioned by the Sultan of Oman. Showed at RA, RP, Leicester Galleries and elsewhere in mixed exhibitions. Showed solo at Gray Art Gallery & Museum, Hartlepool, from 1967; Billingham Art Gallery, 1970, later shows including Middlesbrough Art Gallery, 1984. Lived in Seaton Carew, Hartlepool, Cleveland.

Kathleen CROZIER fl. from 1970s– Artist in various media, and teacher. She studied at Fishponds College of Education, Hastings; Birmingham Central and Goldsmiths' College Schools of Art; and at Morley College. Taught art, notably ceramics, in schools and at adult institute level. Upon retirement concentrated on printmaking, mainly etching, and was a founder-member of Greenwich Printmakers' Association. Was elected to NS in 1976. Showed widely in group exhibitions in London and Sussex and took part in four-man show at Woodlands Art Gallery, 1988. Solo shows included Stables Gallery, Hastings, from 1976; Conway Hall, 1983; and Tudor Barn Art Gallery, Eltham, 1985.

Philip CROZIER 1947– Painter and teacher, born and lived in London. He trained at Bath Academy of Art, Corsham, 1966–70, and Goldsmiths' College, 1978–80. Crozier was visiting tutor at Greenwich College and Central St Martins College of Art. He was elected to the LG in 2001. Group exhibitions also included Kettle's Yard, Cambridge; City University; South Bank Picture Show, prize winner, 1991; RA Summer Exhibition; and Blackheath Halls. Among solo shows were Caius College, Cambridge, 1970; Gardner Centre Gallery, Brighton, 1974; Woodlands Art Gallery, 1979; Old Mill Studios, 1986; Raven Studio, 1996; and Royal Teas, 2002. East Sussex County Council, Goldsmiths', Lambeth Health Trust and private collections in the United Kingdom and America hold Crozier's work, which could have a strong pattern element. Of his Woodlands show he said the works contained "many direct and indirect borrowings from forms and processes of painting outside the Fine Art sphere, as well as non-Western art".

William CROZIER 1930– Painter and teacher, born at Yoker, Glasgow, who studied at the School of Art there, 1949–53. Having worked for two years as a theatre decorator, Crozier from the mid-1950s travelled widely in Europe. He then taught at Bath Academy of Art, the Central School of Arts and Crafts and Winchester School of Art. He retired as head of fine art there in 1987 to devote all his time to painting. From 1957 Crozier had a series of solo exhibitions at Drian Galleries, abstracts with landscape references. He was influenced at this time by American Abstract Expressionism. His later work employed more obvious landscape references, but vibrant colour and vitality continued to be key elements. Crozier exhibited at Arthur Tooth and Sons, Compass Gallery in Glasgow, Serpentine Gallery, Scottish Gallery and abroad. Scottish National Gallery of Modern Art gave him an important show in 1995, with another at Fenton Gallery, Cork, Ireland, 2002. Collections in Glasgow, Aberdeen, Birmingham and overseas hold examples.

Audrey CRUDDAS 1912–1979 Stage designer and painter, born in Johannesburg, South Africa. She was educated in England and attended St John's Wood School of Art, Royal Academy Schools and Byam Shaw School of Drawing and Painting. After painting for a year in Europe and North Africa, during World War II Cruddas was in the Women's Land Army, strenuous work which made her ill, and during convalescence she began stage design. This led to Robert Helpmann asking her to create the costumes for his production of *The White Devil*, by John Webster. Cruddas became a noted stage designer, working for Covent Garden, The Old Vic, the York Mystery Plays and the Edinburgh Festival, producing both costume and set designs. She retired to Great Bardfield, Essex, in the late 1950s to concentrate on watercolour painting and showed locally, with Augustin Gallery and with Leigh Underhill Gallery. Victoria & Albert Museum, British Museum and Fry Art Gallery, Saffron Walden, hold her work.

William CRUICKSHANK 1974– Painter and sculptor who attended Manchester Metropolitan University, 1994. Exhibitions included Fuel Dry 201 Gallery, Manchester, 1996; Just, Soap Gallery, Kokura, Kitakyushu-shi (solo show of five sculptures made while working in Japanese studio for six months), 1998; and Fairlands Valley Farmhouse, Stevenage, 2001 (after a year's work there, Digswell

Arts Trust Fellowship Award, 2000). Also in 2001 Cruickshank took part in a three-man show Food Hall at Houldsworth, a departure from his earlier works, exhibiting pictures of supermarket shelves and off-licences which were more suggestive and representational than his minimal paintings. Commissions included stairway and wall sculptures, both at Afflecks Palace, Manchester, 1996 and 1997; Arawak Walton Park Development Competition, first prize winner and commission of design, Muscari Walk, Manchester, 1997; and installations, Grinch Wine Bar, Manchester, 1998 and 1999. Rosy Wilde gave Cruickshank a solo exhibition, Projects, in 2004.

Sally CRUMBIE EKPENYONG: *see* **Sally CROMBIE**

Colin CRUMPLIN 1946– Painter and teacher, born in Hertfordshire. He attended Leicester School of Art, 1964–5, then Chelsea School of Art, 1965–8, and Slade School of Fine Art, 1968–70, having from 1967 begun showing at LG and at Young Contemporaries. Group show appearances included John Moores Liverpool Exhibition from 1987 and Corsham A Celebration, Victoria Art Gallery, Bath, 1988–9, and tour. His solo exhibitions included Garage Art Ltd in 1975; 1985 Salisbury Festival; 1986 Axiom Gallery, Cheltenham; and in 1997 both Todd Gallery and John Hansard Gallery at University of Southampton. Taught at various art colleges, eventually becoming head of fine art at Bath College of Higher Education. In 2005 Crumplin's Paintings 1995–05 were shown at Six Chapel Row Contemporary Art, Bath, by which time he was reader in fine art at Bath Spa University. Arts Council holds his work. Lived in Bath, Somerset.

Robert H CRUTCHLEY 1943– Sculptor and teacher who studied at Birmingham College of Art, then became senior lecturer at Bournville College of Art. Exhibitions included Portfolio, RBSA, 1988; Ikon Gallery, Birmingham, 1991; and 1st RWA Open Sculpture Exhibition, 1993. In 1990 he created statue of St Michael for St Michael's Church, Manor Park. Lived in Hockley, Birmingham.

Michael CRYER 1940– Printmaker, painter and teacher, born in Blackburn, Lancashire, son of the painter and engraver Wilfred Fairclough, husband of the artist Mary Malenoir. He studied at Kingston College of Art, 1957–61, was a Rome Scholar in Engraving, 1964–6, attending the British School in Rome, 1964–7, and Stanley Hayter's Atelier 17 in Paris, 1967. Taught for a time at Farnham School of Art. Lived in Kingston upon Thames, Surrey.

Michael CUBEY 1964– Painter whose output included abstract pictures, born in Wellington, New Zealand, where he studied at Elam School of Fine Arts and Auckland University. Group shows included Bowen Galleries, Wellington, from 1985; South Bank Picture Show, Royal Festival Hall, 1991; Beardsmore Gallery, from 1992; Cable Street Open Studios and Wellington City Art Gallery, Wellington, both 1994; and Royal Over-Seas League Open, 1995. Had solo shows at Bowen Galleries from 1986, later ones including Islington Arts Factory, 1993, and Beatty Gallery, Sydney, Australia, 1994–5. University of Wellington holds his work.

Edith Alice CUBITT: *see* **Edith Alice ANDREWS**

Mikey CUDDIHY 1952– Abstract artist and teacher, born in New York, America, who studied at Edinburgh College of Art, 1969–71, Central School of Art and Design, 1971–4, then Chelsea School of Art, 1974–5. As well as doing a range of jobs, from working in an art gallery to time as a waitress, she taught part-time, including Newcastle Polytechnic and St Martin's School of Art. Showed with LG, Angela Flowers and Air Galleries and in Summer Show 2 at Serpentine Gallery, 1981. Solo shows included The Gallery, Acre Lane, 1980, later ones Aimee in Galashiels and other paintings, Flowers East, 1995, and James in Limbo, Peer, 2003.

Jack CUDWORTH 1930– Artist and career jazz musician who was born in Leeds, Yorkshire, where he attended the College of Art, 1947–53. He lived in Dublin, Ireland, 1953–75, painted in Suffolk, 1975–84, then moved to Harrogate, north Yorkshire, where he continued to paint full-time. Cudworth's prizes included Bilan de l'art contemporain and Paris, Laing and Barnsley Art Gallery Competitions. Mixed shows included RA Summer Exhibition; Ferens Art Gallery, Hull; RHA, RSA; and RWS. Among other one-man and group shows were Belgrave and Medici Galleries; Seen Galleries in London and Seattle, America; Tom Caldwell Galleries, Belfast and Dublin; Harrison Galleries, Vancouver, Canada; Town Hall, Paris; Polder Gallery, Netherlands; and Cottage Gallery, California, in America. Works were held by the Arts Councils of Ireland and Northern Ireland, Bank of Ireland, Bord Fáilte and The Haverty Trust, as well as private collections in Europe and America.

Nick CUDWORTH 1947– Draughtsman, illustrator and teacher with a special interest in anatomical art, born in Derby. He attended the College of Art there, 1964–6, then did graphic design at Chelsea School of Art, 1966–9, his teachers including Brian Mills and Edward Wright. During the ensuing years Cudworth, as well as being a freelance artist, did a variety of jobs, ranging from recording musician, ward orderly in a geriatric hospital and postman to lecturer in graphic design at Trent Polytechnic, Nottingham, and lecturer in drawing at Winchester School of Art. He took part in numerous group exhibitions, including Mall Galleries, Arnolfini Gallery in Bristol, La Scala opera house in Milan and the New York Art Fair. He had a solo show at Newcastle University in 1969, others including Thumb Gallery, ICA, Battersea Arts Centre and Nicholas Treadwell Gallery, with which he was long associated, and Portal Gallery, 2002. Arnolfini and Nicholas Treadwell Galleries hold his work. Lived in Stroud, Gloucestershire.

Richard CUERDEN 1963– Artist who graduated with honours in fine art, painting, Winchester School of Art, 1996–9, gaining his master's in painting, Royal College of Art, 1999–01. He won the Equity Trust Fund Award, 1999, and in 2000 the Henderson Parkinson Travel Award to Italy and the TI Group Travel Award to Budapest, Hungary. Group exhibitions included New Artists, John Martin of London, 1999; Beck's Futures, ICA and tour, 2000; and ART 2001 with Wilson Stephens Fine Art, 2001. Had solo shows at Sutton House, 1997, and Vertigo, 2003. Several corporate collections in London and Switzerland hold examples.

Bill CULBERT 1935– Painter and artist using a range of freestanding objects and light installations. He attended Canterbury University School of Art, in New Zealand,

1953–6. Won a travelling scholarship in 1957, and attended the Royal College of Art, 1957–60, where he gained a silver medal for painting. He won first prize in the Open Painting Competition, Arts Council of Northern Ireland, in 1964, four years later gaining another prize. Was artist-in-residence at Museum of Holography, New York, in 1985. The year after, Culbert had a retrospective at ICA. In 1997, there was an exhibition at Serpentine Gallery Lawn. His dealer in London, where he lived, was Victoria Miro. Culbert's work took a profound shift in the mid-1960s, when he changed from painting to using such items as a light bulb-holder, a light bulb and a jug to create his work. Royal College of Art and Arts Council hold examples.

Vicky CULL 1967– Versatile artist who graduated with honours in textiles at Huddersfield Polytechnic, then gained a master's in fine art textiles at Central St Martins College of Art & Design. Exhibitions included Pitti Fillatti, Florence, Italy, 1993; Indigo, Paris, France, and Congress House (Trades Union Congress headquarters), 1994; Juice 1/2, Forefront Gallery, Ipswich, 1996 and 1998; Viscera, installation exhibition, Red Dot Gallery, Ipswich, 1999; Suffolk Printmakers, Pond Gallery, Snape Maltings, 2001; and Over The River, firstsite, Colchester/Wolsey Art Gallery, Ipswich, 2002. In 1996, shared a two-man show, Above and Below the line, Forefront Gallery, Ipswich. Cull also collaborated with the weaver Angie Gilson and painter Malcolm Moseley as AVM, to produce textile-based works, shown in All Mixed Up at Christchurch Mansion, Ipswich, in 2003.

Gordon CULLEN 1914–1994 Architect, artist and writer, full name Thomas Gordon Cullen, he was educated at Prince Henry's Grammar School in Otley and then trained as an architect at Regent Street Polytechnic. Cullen was assistant to the Russian architect Berthold Lubetkin and worked on major buildings such as the Finsbury Health Centre, for which he supplied an entrance mural, and Highpoint apartment block, Highgate. For most of World War II Cullen was in Barbados with the Colonial Office planning team, in 1946 becoming deputy editor of the *Architectural Review*, which developed his interest in urban renewal. His ignored proposals for the redevelopment of Westminster, *Westminster Regained*, were regarded by many as visionary. He became a cult figure, and his style of drawing was much-copied. Cullen's book *Townscape* appeared in 1964 and there were exhibitions of his work all round Europe. By then he had become townscape consultant to the Ford Foundation in New Delhi and Calcutta, other consultancies following for Liverpool, Llantrisant, Tenterden, Peterborough, Ware, London Docklands and Glasgow. With David Price he founded his own architectural practice. Cullen won the American Institute of Architects Gold Medal in 1976 plus many honorary doctorates.

Mick CULLEN 1946– Painter, born in Kilcool, County Dublin, Ireland, studying in Dublin and at the Central School of Art and Design, London. Travelled within continental Europe, Africa and America, sometimes staying for long periods. He frequently included himself in a work, often in a humorous or self-mocking pose. National Self-Portrait Collection of Ireland, University of Limerick, holds his work.

Patrick CULLEN 1949– Painter who studied at St Martin's and Camberwell Schools of Art from 1972–6. He won a number of prizes, including Spirit of London Competition, Royal Festival Hall, 1984–5; Watercolour Prize, RA, 1989; Daler-Rowney Prize, PS Annual Exhibition, 1990 and 1995; and Abbott and Holder Travel Award, RWS Open Exhibition, 1991. In 1991 Cullen was elected PS. Notable for his landscapes of Italy. Cullen's solo shows included Ogle Gallery, Eastbourne, 1978; several at the Amalgam Art Ltd; and Thackeray Gallery, from 1992. RA, Sheffield City Art Galleries and Paintings in Hospitals hold examples. Lived in London.

Matthew CULLERNE-BOWN 1956– Artist in mixed media, and writer, born and lived in London. Attended Camberwell School of Art, 1975–9, Slade School of Fine Art, 1979–81, Stroganov Institute in Moscow, and the Moscow University. Showed with Northern Young Contemporaries, Whitworth Museum and Art Gallery, Manchester, 1979; New Contemporaries, ICA, 1980–1; Whitechapel Open, 1983; Warwick Arts Trust and Air Gallery, 1984; and in 1986 The Wissarth Gallery, Berlin, and The Minories, Colchester, where he was one of 4 London Artists. Also showed in four-man exhibition at Woodlands Art Gallery, 1989. His book *Art Under Stalin* appeared in 1991.

Derek CULLEY 1952– Self-taught artist, born and educated in Dublin, Ireland, with an Irish father and English mother. Culley did his master's degree in marketing at Brunel University, 1992–4, his dissertation subject being "Marketing of the visual artist in Britain – are there lessons to be learned from Europe?" Culley was a founder and chairman of Celtic Vision with the painters John Bellany and Denis Bowen, and participated in the group's exhibition tour in 1986–7. He took part in many other group shows, including LG tour, 1987; Knapp Gallery, from 1988; 2000 Years Celebration, Customs House, Dublin, 1991; Modern Irish Painting, Dillon Gallery, 1995; and Skopje Museum of Contemporary Art, Republic of Macedonia, 1996. Solo shows included Five Years of Culley, Royal Hospital Kilmainham, Ireland, 1989, and The Irish Club, 1996. Strong chiaroscuro, heavy impasto, vigorous brushwork and direct, expressive handling were characteristics of Culley's work, in which Celtic imagery and associations were important. Lived in Windsor, Berkshire.

Michael CULLIMORE 1936– Painter and teacher, born in Bradford-on-Avon, Wiltshire, who studied at Swindon College of Art and Goldsmiths' College School of Art. Early in the 1960s he moved to north Wales and taught and from the early 1970s was curator of the University College of North Wales, Bangor, Art Gallery. Retired in 1983 because of ill-health and returned to Wiltshire to live in Hindon. Participated in a number of touring exhibitions and had one-man shows including Bangor Art Gallery and Austin/Desmond Fine Art. Gavin Graham Gallery showed Works on Paper in 2003. WAC, National Museum of Wales in Cardiff and Swansea's Glynn Vivian Art Gallery hold Cullimore's work, which is in the English romantic landscape tradition.

Charlotte CULLINAN 1959– Artist who studied at Canterbury, Ravensbourne and Royal Colleges of Art, also with George Baselitz. Showed at RA, Smith's and New Academy Galleries, at Sainsbury Centre in Norwich and Camden Arts Centre. Was included in Six Young British Painters, toured Spain, 1991–2. In 2002, for the International Institute of Visual Arts, Cullinan and Jeanine Richards in east London "drew together elements of cinema, sculpture, painting and video to provide a supportive environment in which the artists and their collaborators can show work." Part of the scheme involved constructing outdoor cinemas at two sites. As ARTLAB, Cullinan and Richards collaborated from 1998, including Cowboy Cinema at Mobile Home, 2001.

Bernard CULSHAW 1944– Painter who was educated at the Oxford School of Art, Goldsmiths' College and the Royal Academy Schools. In 2005 he was included in Artist of the Day at Flowers Central, chosen by John Lessore.

Stuart CUMBERLAND 1970– London-based artist who studied at Bath Academy of Art and the Royal College of Art and who won the Saatchi Fellowship, 2001–2. The most notable motif in his work, featured in the A4 Art Auction at Bonhams in 2004, was a solitary arm that appeared alone or buried among abstract shapes. Cumberland's work was included in Dirty Pictures, The Approach, 2003, and Works on Paper, at Sprüth Magers Lee, Munich, Germany, 2004. In 2003 he had a solo show at the Kate MacGarry Gallery.

Janet Agnes CUMBRAE STEWART 1883–1960 Artist in watercolour and pastel, born in Brighton, Victoria, Australia, youngest of 10 children of Francis Stewart and his wife Agnes. Like her brother Francis, Janet adopted the surname Cumbrae Stewart, but omitted the hyphen. (She is sometimes listed as Cumbrae Stewart, also as Agnes Cumbrae Stewart or Janet Cumbrae Stewart.) After working with John Mather she studied at the National Gallery School, Melbourne, 1904–7, under Bernard Hall and Frederick McCubbin. While a student, she won second place in the National Gallery's Travelling Scholarship competition. She became a leading member of the Victorian Artists' Society, showed with Queensland Art Society and in 1914 gained a silver medal at the Panama-Pacific Exposition in San Francisco, California. With a sister in 1922 she travelled to London, remaining in Europe until her 1939 return to Australia, where she had continued to exhibit, settling in South Yarra. While in Europe, where she travelled extensively, also to Canada, she lived for periods in France (where she exhibited at the Salon, gaining an Hon. Mention), and Italy. She was a prolific exhibitor in England, notable venues being Beaux Arts and Walker's Galleries, also at RA, ROI, SWA, and Royal Glasgow Institute of the Fine Arts and Walker Art Gallery, Liverpool. Cumbrae Stewart is listed in the PS 1898–2000 memorial volume, published in 2000. Chris Beetles Ltd in 2002 offered The Blue Bathroom, typical of the artist's series of female nudes.

Frederick George Rees CUMING 1930– Painter, born in London, of English, Scottish and Irish descent. A subtle Colourist who specialised in landscapes in Britain and on the continent. He trained at Sidcup School of Art, 1945–9, and after National Service attended Royal College of Art, 1951–5, winning an Abbey Minor Travelling Scholarship which took him to Italy. Was elected RA in 1974. He took part in many mixed shows and had a string of one-man exhibitions, including New Metropole Gallery, Folkestone; Leonie Jonleigh, Guildford; Little Studio, New York; and from the early 1980s a number at New Grafton Gallery. He was joint winner of the Grand Prix Contemporary Art Award, Monte Carlo, 1977; and the Sir Brinsley Ford Award, NEAC, of which he was a member, 1986; and *House & Garden* Award, 1994. His work is in a number of British public galleries, including National Museum of Wales, Cardiff; Towner Art Gallery, Eastbourne; and Monte Carlo Museum. Lived for some years at Ashford, Kent.

Belle Skeoch CUMMING 1884–1964 Watercolourist, studied at Liverpool School of Art, Byam Shaw School of Art and Edinburgh College of Art. Was married to the artist William Skeoch Cumming. Exhibited RSA, RSW, SSWA, Royal Glasgow Institute of the Fine Arts and Paris Salon. Was a member of Glasgow Lady Artists' Club. Lived in Edinburgh.

Diana CUMMING 1929– Painter, draughtsman and printmaker, born in Hereford. Cumming said: "I draw when I paint," drawing being "not easy, but essential." Her pictures could be witty or apparently naïve with elements of fantasy, and sometimes employed a Pointillist style. She studied at Slade School of Fine Art, 1950–4, teachers including William Coldstream, B A R Carter and F E McWilliam. Won several awards, including Rome Scholarship, 1954–6. Took part in many group exhibitions, including Young Contemporaries, 1952; Walker Art Gallery, Liverpool, 1957–63; LG, 1958–9; and RA Slade centenary exhibition, 1971. Had a solo show at Beaux Arts Gallery, 1964, later ones including Cooling Gallery and Hereford Museum and Art Gallery, both 1990. After an exhibition at Chateau de Montmarin Gallery in Brittany in 1999, Paintings from 1953–2005 in 2005 at Thompson's Marylebone explored the full range of Cumming's unpredictable output. Arts Council, Contemporary Art Society and Ministry of Works hold examples. Lived in London.

James CUMMING 1922–1991 Painter and teacher, born in Dunfermline, Fife. He studied at Edinburgh College of Art, 1939–41, then after five years with the Royal Air Force Volunteer Reserve returned to the College, 1946–50, for postgraduate work and travelling scholarships. He was in many mixed exhibitions in Britain and abroad. In 1955 he had a solo show at Gallery One in London, others following steadily, especially at the Loomshop Gallery in Lower Largo, Fife, and there was a series of retrospectives, including Lothian Region Gallery, Edinburgh, in 1981. Collections include HRH The Duke of Edinburgh, Arts Council and Scottish National Gallery of Modern Art. Cumming was a member of SSA, being its president for a time, and was treasurer and secretary of the RSA and a member of RSW. From 1950 for many years he taught at Edinburgh College of Art. Cumming's work for long drew its inspiration from life on the Isle of Lewis, but in the early 1960s it changed course and examined abstract themes, such as cellular structure, while retaining his unique colouring. Scottish Gallery in Edinburgh, where Cumming lived, held a memorial show in 1995.

Peter CUMMING 1916– Painter and teacher, born in London, who was educated at St Paul's School. Studied art at Royal Academy Schools, 1936–40, under Sir Walter Westley Russell after a period at Hammersmith Art School. Exhibited RA and RBA, of which he was a member. Lived Lancing, Sussex, where he joined Brighton Arts Club, later living in Old Woodstock, Oxfordshire.

Albert Runciman CUMMINGS: *see* **Albert RUNCIMAN-CUMMINGS**

Jane CUMMINGS 1917– Painter, printmaker, illustrator and teacher, born in Richmond, Surrey. Studied at Harrow School of Art, Chelsea School of Art under Graham Sutherland and Harold Williamson and Central School of Arts and Crafts with Clarke Hutton. She exhibited in south of England and had work purchased by the London County Council and Hertfordshire Education Committees. Published a title in the Penguin Books Limited Puffin series: *Theatre You Can Make*. Lived in Northwood, Middlesex.

Gus CUMMINS 1943– Painter, sculptor and teacher who studied at Sutton and Wimbledon Schools of Art and Royal College of Art. He taught at Hammersmith, Sutton and Croydon Schools of Art and part-time posts included Ravensbourne, Chelsea, Hastings, City & Guilds of London and Royal Academy Schools. Cummins was noted for his industrial scenes. Among awards won were Henry Moore Prize (LG), 1982; First Prize, Hunting Group, 1990 and 1999; and Blackstone Award, 1992. Showed annually at RA Summer Exhibition from 1982, in 1992 being elected RA; Rye Society of Artists, Rye, from 1983; and New Grafton Gallery from 1991, having a solo show there in 1993. At the 2005 RA Summer Exhibition Cummins revealed a new twist to his career when he won The Jack Goldhill Award for Sculpture, worth £10,000, with his piece Off The Wall. Lived in Hastings, Sussex.

Charles CUNDALL 1890–1971 Painter, pottery and stained glass artist, born in Stratford, Lancashire. After working as a designer for Pilkington's Pottery Company under Gordon Forsyth, Cundall studied at Manchester School of Art, obtaining a scholarship to Royal College of Art, 1912. After World War I Army service he returned to Royal College in 1918, then was at Slade School of Fine Art, 1919–20, and in Paris. Cundall travelled widely in several continents and became noted for his panoramic pictures, such as Bank Holiday, Brighton, in Tate Gallery's collection. He was a member of NEAC, RP, RWS and other bodies and was a prolific RA exhibitor. Had first solo show at Colnaghi, 1927. Official War Artist in World War II, during which he was elected RA, 1944. His wife was the painter Jacqueline Pietersen. Lived in London.

Nora Lucy Mowbray CUNDELL 1889–1948 Painter and writer, born in London, granddaughter of the artist Henry Cundell. She studied art at Blackheath School of Art, Westminster Technical Institute with Walter Sickert and part-time, 1911–14 and 1919, at the Slade School of Fine Art. Cundell was noted for her figure compositions, having won the Melvill Nettleship Prize for Figure Composition in 1914. Cundell exhibited at RA, NEAC, Goupil Gallery, SWA, NS and elsewhere, and her picture Smiling Woman is in the Tate Gallery. She was one of the founder-members of the NS in 1930, five years after her first one-man show, at Redfern Gallery. Travelled widely in America. Wrote and illustrated *Unsentimental Journey*, 1940. Lived at Dorney, near Windsor, died in London, and had a memorial show at RBA.

Clifford Benjamin CUNDY 1925–1992 Sculptor and painter, born in Wallasey, Cheshire. Awarded a scholarship to Oxford University to study engineering in 1944, Cundy was rusticated two years later for being unable to pay his wine bill. By then he had attended part-time classes under Albert Rutherston in drawing at Ruskin School of Drawing and life classes with Peter Greenham. Did several jobs to earn a living; was in Iran for a period; and returned in 1948 with the object of becoming a monk; but marriage to his muse Hazel Hazlewood determined Cundy to become a full-time painter, which he did in 1964. His portraits and still lifes in oil owed much to the inspiration of Van Gogh. From early 1970s Cundy mastered sculptural techniques, creating free-standing figures and bas-reliefs; he used the lost-wax method and eventually built his own foundry in his Richmond, Surrey, garden. A prolific worker, he showed at NS of which he was a member, as he was of the Sketch Club, also exhibiting at RP, RA, Alwin Gallery and Upper Street Gallery in Islington.

John CUNDY 1937– Painter, professionally involved in printing, based in Ilkeston, Derbyshire. He was painting secretary jointly of its Arts Club, 1973-80, and its archivist. He wrote the Club's centenary publication in 2002. Exhibitions included Derby Open, where he was a prizewinner, and Nottingham Castle.

Nell Tenison CUNEO 1867–1953 Illustrator and painter, especially of portraits, born in London. Her original name was Nell Marion Tenison. After working as an illustrator, she met her future husband, the American-born artist Cyrus Cuneo, at the Atelier Colarossi, Paris, having previously studied in London at Cope and Nicol's School of Art. Her son was the artist Terence Cuneo. She exhibited RA, SWA, Goupil Gallery and elsewhere and illustrated especially girls' and women's magazines and a number of girls' books, such as Angela Brazil's *A Terrible Tomboy*, 1915. When her husband died in 1916 she travelled widely in England, latterly living at Shamley Green, Surrey.

Terence CUNEO 1907–1996 Painter in oil, noted for his realistic, atmospheric pictures of railway engines. He was born in London, son of the artist Nell Tenison Cuneo. He studied at Chelsea School of Art and Slade School of Fine Art. Became a member of War Artists' Advisory Committee, a member of Royal Glasgow Institute of the Fine Arts, vice-president of the Guild of Aviation Artists and president of the Society of Equestrian Artists. Showed at RA, ROI and RP. Exhibited one-man at RWS Galleries from 1941, Sladmore Gallery from 1971 and in 1988 had major exhibition at Mall Galleries. Cuneo painted a number of portraits of HM The Queen, notably on the occasion of her coronation, as well as portraits of Field-Marshal Bernard Montgomery and the one-time prime minister Sir Edward Heath. Cuneo's pictorial trademark was a tiny mouse, and in 1977 he published his autobiography *The Mouse and His Master*. Lived in East Molesey, Surrey.

Vera CUNINGHAM 1897–1955 Painter, draughtsman and theatre designer. After brief study at the Central School of Arts and Crafts, she began exhibiting with the LG in 1922. In the same year she became friendly with Matthew Smith, who frequently painted her, and with him exhibited in Paris, at the Amis de Montparnasse and the Salon des Indépendants. She had her first one-man show at the Bloomsbury Gallery in 1929. Towards the end of the 1930s did a series of theatre designs, but although the stage world appealed to her extravert, bohemian personality, she opted to return to easel painting to avoid having her independence threatened. Helped to organise the Civil Defence Artists shows at Cooling Galleries during World War II; also exhibited with the Storran Gallery and Redfern Gallery. Support for her work after World War II came mainly from the Paris dealer Raymond Creuze, who put on three shows, in 1948, 1951 and 1954, and who assembled an important collection of her pictures, publishing a lavish monograph on her in 1984. Although Vera Cuningham's figure paintings of the 1920s and 1930s are of their period, in her later work she developed a singular style, using a curving line and sombre palette: an English original, as she was as a character. Lived in London. A retrospective show was held at the Barbican Art Gallery in 1985.

Mitzi Solomon CUNLIFFE 1918– Sculptor in many materials, and designer, born in New York. She was educated in America, Sweden and France, her art tuition including Art Students' League of New York, 1930–3, and Columbia University, 1935–40. Exhibited widely in several continents, especially in North America, including Festival of Britain in 1951. Solo exhibitions included Exeter University, 1969. Work widely reproduced, especially in architectural journals, and is held by Leeds and Liverpool Universities. Lived for periods in Manchester, Brighton and London.

Chris CUNNINGHAM 1970– Versatile artist in modern media, born in Reading, Berkshire, whose success in the field of commercials and music videos followed an accomplished career in feature films. In 1987, aged just 17, Cunningham led the Creature FX team on *Alien 3*, nominated for a special effects Oscar. His work as a print cartoonist led to *Judge Dredd Magazine* and the UK Comic Art Awards judges to name him Best British Newcomer of 1992–3. Cunningham's talent for making special effects models prompted the film-maker Stanley Kubrick to hire him. In 1995, Cunningham joined the production company Black Dog, and its sister company for commercials, Ridley Scott Associates. He started his second career by directing videos for music artists. In 1996, he began making commercials, Mary-Sue Lawrence and Rosie Elston, at Mustoe Merriman, calling him "the best talent in Soho". The Sony PlayStation commercial *Mental Wealth* won a Silver Award, one of a string of D&AD Awards and other industry trophies lavished on Cunningham. They were also gained by his music videos in the late 1990s, notable among which were *Only You* (Portishead), *Come to Daddy* and *Windowlicker* (both Aphex Twin), *Frozen* (Madonna) and *All is Love* (Bjork). Cunningham's videos were shown in several exhibitions, venues including The British School at Rome; Apocalypse, at the RA; and a retrospective, ICA, all 2000. In that year Cunningham launched his career as an independent artist with a first show at the Anthony d'Offay Gallery. Lived in London.

Jane CUNNINGHAM 1958– Ceramic sculptor who attended North Staffordshire Polytechnic, 1976–7; gained an honours degree in ceramics, Loughborough College of Art and Design, 1977–80; then her fine art master's from Texas Christian University, 1982–4. She showed with Hull Artists Association Exchange Exhibition, 1985; Inside/Outside, Artworks Space, 1987; Penny Bank Gallery, 1988; and East End Open Studios, with Barbican Arts Group, 1989.

John CUNNINGHAM 1926–1998 Painter, born in Lanarkshire. He studied at Glasgow School of Art, 1943–50, excluding war service, 1944–8, then was a senior lecturer there, 1967–85, retiring to paint full-time. Cunningham was elected to Royal Glasgow Institute of the Fine Arts in 1980 and won the Torrance Award as well as the MacFarlane, Cargill and Scottish Amicable Awards. He showed in group exhibitions at RSA, Flying Colours Gallery and Portland Gallery. Glasgow Art Club gave Cunningham a seventieth-birthday retrospective in 1996. Glasgow's Kelvingrove Art Gallery, Hunterian Gallery and University of Glasgow hold his work, which was in the Scottish Colourist tradition. Died in Glasgow.

Keith CUNNINGHAM 1929– Painter who studied at Central School of Arts and Crafts, 1949–52, then the Royal College of Art, 1952–5. In the 1950s he showed at RA, Beaux Arts Gallery, with LG and elsewhere in London, where he lived.

Owen CUNNINGHAM 1954– Sculptor and teacher, born in Birmingham, who studied at Manchester Polytechnic, 1975–8. After St Martin's School of Art, 1978–80, Cunningham was assistant to Anthony Smart, 1980–1. Then went on to teach at St Martin's and in north of England. Gained The Sykes Prize (1st) in 1980. Showed with Northern Young Contemporaries and MAFA in 1977; Liverpool University Senate House Gallery, 1978; and in Have You Seen Sculpture from the Body? at Woodlands Art Gallery, 1983. Tyne and Wear Museums Service holds his work.

William CUNNINGHAM 1946– Largely self-taught painter of strongly coloured landscapes, who grew up near Crossgar, County Down, Northern Ireland, and began painting from an early age. He went to university at Queen's in Belfast, York and London. Until 1978 lectured for several years, then decided to go professional after a successful first exhibition. Tom Carr, J Humbert Craig and Frank McKelvey influenced Cunningham's style. Showed at Tom Cromie Gallery and The Eakin Gallery, Belfast, and in Dublin at Oriel Gallery and Combridge Fine Arts. In 1996 Felix Rosenstiel's published four Cunningham paintings as prints, which were also released as cards and calendars.

Elizabeth B CUNNINGTON 1914– Sculptor and watercolourist who was born in London and studied at Oxford University. Studied at Slade School of Fine Art under Randolph Schwabe and George Meldrum, 1936–9. Showed at NS, RWS, RA and elsewhere and lived near Oxford.

Peter CURL 1921–1959 Painter, printmaker and designer. Born at Southsea, Hampshire, Curl studied at the Southern College of Art in Portsmouth and at Brighton College of Art. Taught at Mansfield School of Art in the late 1940s, then from 1950 at Tunbridge Wells School of Art. He did a wide range of commercial design work, clients including the Council of Industrial Design, book publishers and the BBC. Lived in Cranbrook, Kent.

Peter CURLING 1955– Painter whose speciality was the racehorse in action and the atmosphere of the racecourse. He was born in Waterford, Ireland, studying in England at Stonyhurst College and then Millfield, where he won an art scholarship. From 1971–3 he studied under Signorina Simi in Florence, in 1974 briefly with John Skeaping. His first solo show was with Tryon Gallery in 1976, which continued to exhibit his work. Curling was closely involved in racing: he rode on the Berkshire Downs and at Newmarket; rode his own horse Caddy, trained by Edward O'Grady, to victory in a bumper race in Ireland; and he hunted regularly with the Tipperary, where he settled. Curling completed many commissioned pictures of well-known horses; he also painted landscapes; and his largest assignment was a huge mural for John Mangier at Coolmore. Later solo exhibitions included The Gallery in Cork Street, 2003.

Terry CURLING 1958– Figurative painter and muralist, born in London, who was married to the artist Paul Rumsey. Completed a foundation course at Chelsea School of Art, 1975–8, gaining her degree there, 1978–81, then did a history of modern art course in 1982. Painted a big landscape mural, on canvas, for Charing Cross Hospital, Hammersmith, 1984, then a series for St Stephen's Hospital, Kensington and Chelsea, 1985. Took part in the John Player Portrait Award Exhibition, National Portrait Gallery, 1988, and appeared in mixed shows at East West Gallery, 1995–7. Had a solo exhibition at Trinity Street Studios, Colchester, 1998, another at Chappel Galleries, Chappel, 1999. Lived in Essex.

Muriel CURR fl. from 1940s–1993 Painter and teacher, daughter of the artist Tom Curr, she was born in Edinburgh, which she continued to use as her base although she held a number of posts in England. Studied at Edinburgh College of Art, 1938–43. She taught in Hertfordshire and in London and was attached to Pinewood Studios, the film studio, for a time. Showed with SSA and SSWA, both of which she was a member, as well as RA and elsewhere.

Tom CURR 1887–1958 Artist and cartoonist, born in Edinburgh, where he continued to live. He was educated at Daniel Stewart's College, the old Life School at the Mound and at Edinburgh University. From the life class he went to Edinburgh College of Art when it opened in 1909, where he met his wife, who taught drawing. After commissioned Army service in World War I Curr returned to the printing firm McLagan and Cumming, which he had entered as an apprentice artist, eventually becoming managing director. Much of his early work was black-and-white, but later he showed annually in RSA and other exhibitions, finding many subjects in the countryside. Work bought by Scottish Office, London. Curr was a staunch Baptist, active in the life of Edinburgh, of which he was a bailie.

Alan CURRALL 1964– Artist using video, born in Stoke-on-Trent, Staffordshire, who gained a degree in fine art at the county University, 1989–92, with a master's at Glasgow School of Art, 1993–5. Exhibitions included Videos aus Glasgow Un-Fair, Cologne, and Five British Artists at Kunstalle, Mannheim, both 1995; and Pandaemonium, ICA, and New Contemporaries, at Tate Gallery, Liverpool, and Camden Arts Centre, all 1996, the year that Currall was artist-in-residence, Fringe Gallery, Glasgow. In 1997, Currall participated in Video Positive 97: Escaping Gravity, organised by Fact, Bluecoat Arts Centre, Liverpool.

Peter CURRAN 1949– Artist and teacher, born and lived in Bristol who began painting at 17 inspired by the English landscape school, especially Turner, Palmer and Constable, and who favoured on-site drawing. Studied graphics at West of England Academy, 1965–7; did a foundation course at Filton Technical College, 1969–70; studied fine art and printmaking at Central School of Art and Design, 1970–3, under Cecil Collins, Adrian Berg and Paul Huxley; then did a postgraduate certificate in education at Bristol University, 1974–5. From 1989 attended a life drawing class, with a renewed interest in the human figure. Early work was signed Peter Curran Murphy (Murphy was his stepfather's name). Curran wrote that he was "much disappointed with modern art since 1945, and find much abstraction decorative." Over the 30 years from the mid-1960s Curran found inspiration in many sources, including Poussin, Piero della Francesca and de Chirico; the Italian Futurists; Sickert, Auerbach and Bacon; cricket; the Severn Estuary; and the decommissioning of Berkeley nuclear power station. Group shows included Arnolfini Gallery, Bristol, 1979; RA Summer Exhibition, 1983; Summer Show at England & Co., 1989; and The Horse in the Environment, 1993. Later solo exhibitions included First Barcelona Works, Eye Gallery, Bristol, 1989. Nuffield Foundation, Imperial Chemical Industries and British Institute in Florence, Italy, hold examples.

Anthony CURRELL 1942– Artist and teacher, born in London, who studied at Bideford School of Art and then Central School of Arts and Crafts, 1960–3, attending Atelier 17 for further printmaking studies, 1963–4. After teaching at Preston College of Art, 1964–5, he was at Plymouth College of Art, 1966–80, then as head of printmaking from 1980 at Chesterfield College of Art. While he was still a student Currell was chosen by Robert Erskine for The Graven Image at St George's Gallery. Currell was around this time involved in a series of prints based on Rhondda Valley coal miners, issued by Editions Alecto. His later exhibitions included Rotherham Art Gallery, 2000, and Derby Museum and Art Gallery, 2002. Victoria & Albert Museum, Government Art Collection, Arts Council and other public collections hold examples.

Esmé CURREY fl. from c.1905–1973 Artist in tempera and pencil; printmaker. Born in London, Miss Currey studied at the Slade School of Fine Art, in Melbourne, Australia, under Max Meldrum, and at Goldsmiths' College School of Art under the engraver Stanley Anderson. She is noted for her precision of line, like Anderson. She exhibited at many venues, including RA, RBA, RE, UA and Paris Salon. Lived in London.

Joe CURRIE 1970– Painter, sculptor and photographer who gained his master's degree in fine arts/sculpture at the Royal College of Art, 1997–9. Exhibitions included a solo show at James Colman, 2002. In that he evoked "some of the escapist tendencies found within the American Dream". Another Currie exhibition with Colman in 2004 was entitled Escape to Nowhere.

Ken CURRIE 1960– Painter, printmaker, mural artist and film-maker, born in North Shields to Scottish parents who moved with him to Glasgow when he was a baby. Currie studied social science at Paisley College of Technology, 1977–8, then attended Glasgow School of Art, 1978–83, his teachers including Alexander Moffat. He won several awards. Currie's intention was to pursue film production as a career, and from 1983–5 he directed and produced films at Cranhill Community Arts Project. But in 1985 the problems and expense involved in film-making turned Currie back to painting. A committed Socialist, he projected a series of pictures devoted to labour history in Scotland. A key work was the Glasgow Triptych, of 1986, now in Scottish National Gallery of Modern Art. Murals for The People's Palace followed. By 1988 Currie had a solo show at the Third Eye Centre, Glasgow, and the Raab Gallery, Berlin, later ones including BCA Boukamel Contemporary Art, 2001, Tullie House, Carlisle, 2002, and Flowers East, 2003.

Denis CURRY 1918– Sculptor, painter, draughtsman and teacher who combined a profound knowledge of nature's engineering structure with a poetic vision. He was born in Newcastle upon Tyne and drawing was central to his life from the age of about three, "even on my mother's black skirt with white chalk". After studying architecture at Durham Curry graduated in painting and sculpture from the Slade School of Fine Art, 1945–50, where he won numerous prizes. Slade teachers included William Coldstream, A H Gerrard, Henry Moore, Stanley Spencer and Reg Butler. Gerrard, who called Curry "one of the most outstanding thinkers since Leonardo", used him as his assistant on large commissions including Hemel Hempstead town centre. Curry's first full-time teaching post was as head of sculpture at Exeter College of Art. Moved to Bristol in 1961 and was head of the department of foundation studies at a critical time in its history, 1962–76, when Curry left to pursue his own work on a remote hill farm at Llanycefn, Clynderwen, Dyfed. In 1976 Pelter/Sands Gallery, Bristol, held a comprehensive show of Curry's work called Shapes of Flight. Curry had long been interested in animal flight. In 1967 he was granted the first patent for a variable-geometry ornithopter (in 1978 being invited by the Historic Aircraft Museum to place it there). A paper was published by the Royal Aeronautical Society in 1975. The wild life of Pembrokeshire inspired much of Curry's later work, and in the mid-1990s he worked on a series of earth paintings involving tractor wheel patterns. Elected RCamA 1992; also showed at RA, LG, RWA, WSW, West Wales Arts Centre in Fishguard and National Eisteddfod of Wales. In 1999 and 2002 he shared exhibitions with Elizabeth Haines at Heifer Gallery. Taking Wing, images from Curry's research into the form and movement of wings in nature, was at Fishguard Library, 2004. National Museum of Wales in Cardiff, Pembrokeshire Museum and Bristol Schools Art Service hold examples.

Stanley CURSITER 1887–1976 Painter, printmaker, writer and curator, born in Kirkwall, Orkney. Cursiter originally served apprenticeship as a chromolithographic designer before studying at Edinburgh College of Art. He was a keen follower of Post-Impressionism and of the Futurists, which he saw in London and Scotland just before World War I. His seven Futurist works, all painted in 1913, are superbly composed and very elegant. He also painted fine interiors, landscapes and portraits in a more conventional manner, as in his paintings of Orkney and France at Bourne Fine Art, Edinburgh, 2000. Exhibited RA, RSA, Royal Glasgow Institute of the Fine Arts and elsewhere. His work is in a number of Scottish and English galleries. For a time Cursiter was keeper of the Scottish National Portrait Gallery, was responsible for pioneering work in art education and picture restoration while director of the National Gallery of Scotland, 1930–48, and in 1948 he was appointed King's Painter and Limner in Scotland, after which he retired to Orkney. Among his books is one on the artist S J Peploe, 1947, also *Looking Back: A Book of Reminiscences*, 1974. Centenary exhibition held at Pier Arts Centre, Stromness, 1987.

Anthony CURTIS 1928– Painter, and in 1960s–70s ceramist, born in Wakefield, Yorkshire. He studied at Loughborough College, 1948–50, at Bath Academy of Art, Corsham, 1950–1, and did postgraduate diploma at London University, 1974–6, his teachers including William Scott, Peter Potworowski, Bryan Wynter, Peter Lanyon and Kenneth Armitage. In 1955, Curtis was among those in the big *Daily Express* Young Artists' Exhibition at The New Burlington Galleries and in 1957 he was included in Jack Beddington's book *Young Artists of Promise*. Was a member of Free Painters and Sculptors, also showing at RWA, of which he was a member, also LG, RSW, Redfern and Zwemmer Galleries. In 1960–1 was included in Arts Council tour Modern Stained Glass. Solo shows began with Bear Lane Gallery, Oxford, 1959, later ones including a part-retrospective at Bloomsbury Gallery, London University, which led to a self-financed working visit to Australia in 1988–9, Management College, Henley, 1991, and Woburn Festival, 1992. In 1995 Curtis's Australian paintings, including the Aboriginal Echoes series, were among works by Seven Academicians at RWA; from 2000 he showed at London art fairs at Royal College of Art/with Julian Lax; and in 2002 at RWA he won the Mail Marketing International Prize. He showed with Bucks21, 2001–3, later resigning. RWA and Bristol Education Committee hold his work. Lived at Flackwell Heath, High Wycombe, Buckinghamshire.

David Jan CURTIS 1948– Self-taught artist, designer and teacher, born and in lived in Doncaster, Yorkshire. He served an apprenticeship in industry, then headed an engineering design team with Hawker Siddeley, commencing full-time painting in 1988. Curtis painted in many parts of Britain. He was a commission painter for Federation of British Artists, lectured to art groups and taught part-time at Doncaster Faculty of Art and Design. He was elected a member of RSMA in 1983 and of ROI in 1988. Took part in many mixed exhibitions, including RA Summer Exhibition, RWS Open and elsewhere. He was a Stanley Grimm Memorial Prizewinner at ROI in 1991. Had series of solo shows with Richard Hagen Ltd, Broadway, from 1990. The Sultanate of Oman, HM Crown Commissioners and British Gas hold his work.

Gertrude M CURTIS: *see* **Gertrude M KNOPP**

Mark CURTIS 1964– Painter who studied at City & Guilds School of Art, 1988–92. He won the Chadwick Healey Painting Prize in 1991 and 1992 and the Villiers David Travel Prize in 1992. Exhibitions included Fresh Art at Business Design Centre and Art Parcels at Frost & Reed, both 1992; Arcana Open Studios, 1993; and Tradition and Consequence at Hyde Park Gallery, 1994. Curtis had a solo exhibition at The Blue Gallery, 1995, when his work was described as "figurative, abstract, Constructivist and conceptual all at the same time". In 1997 Blue Gallery published *The geometry of DNA: a structural revision*, in which Curtis suggested "a modification to the structure for the salt of deoxyribose nucleic acid (DNA), proposed by

Crick and Watson in April 1953", illustrated with drawings and paintings by the artist. There was another Blue Gallery exhibition in 2003.

Simon CURWEN 1977– Painter, born in Derby, notable for atmospheric paintings of wildlife, as shown on the Colourbox stand at The Affordable Art Fair, 2003. Curwen completed foundation diploma studies at Loughborough College of Art & Design, 1966, graduating with honours in fine art from Leeds Metropolitan University, 1999. Mixed shows included Leeds City Open, Leeds City Art Gallery, and Sefton Open, Atkinson Gallery, Southport, both 1999 and 2002; and Santa at Snow Gallery, Leeds, Jacksons Nine at Brahms Gallery, Leeds, and Graduate Works at Aartvark Gallery, Dewsbury, all 2000. Lived in Doveridge, Derbyshire.

Noel William CUSA 1909–1990 Wildlife artist in watercolour and pen and ink, born in Hull, Yorkshire, who was self-taught. He graduated with a Bachelor of Science degree from University College, Nottingham, 1930, obtaining his doctorate, 1933. He was a patents and research chemist with Imperial Chemical Industries until 1966, then a full-time artist. Was a member of SWLA from 1965, becoming its chairman, also a member of MAFA, showing regularly at both venues, in the provinces and abroad. British Museum and Natural History Museum hold his work, which also appeared in a number of books on birds. Lived in Topsham, Devon.

Eugene CUSACK 1940– Painter, draughtsman and printmaker, noted for his portrait studies and Rembrandt-like etchings, born in New York, America. From 1963–5 he attended the Art Students' League of New York as a Ford Foundation Scholar; studied in Mexico, 1965–8; and won a series of John and Anna Lee Stacy Scholarship Fund Awards between 1968–72. Cusack won the Jane Peterson Prize for Oils, 1968, and the Salmagundi Club Prize for Oils, 1971, both at the Allied Artists Exhibition. He also showed at the Audubon Exhibition in 1971 and at the Nineteenth Annual Print Exhibition at Brooklyn Museum, 1974. His solo exhibitions in America included a series from 1969 at the Harbor Gallery, New York; one at Court Galleries, Cincinnati, Ohio, 1971, and Capricorn Gallery, Bathesda, Maryland, 1973. In 1971, Cusack moved to Clifton, Bristol, in England, and in 1972 had a solo exhibition at David Cross Fine Art. Eventually returned to New York. Smithsonian Institution, Washington, bought Cusack's etching Father.

Alan CUTHBERT 1931–1995 Painter in oil and teacher, born in Southend-on-Sea, Essex. After studying geology, working for a surveying firm, serving in Royal Air Force signals and working for John Taylor & Sons, mining engineers throughout the period 1948–57, Cuthbert in 1957–61 studied at Goldsmiths' College School of Art, 1957–61, under Sam Rabin and Kenneth and Mary Martin. After teaching part-time at Wimbledon School of Art, 1961–3, between 1963–79 Cuthbert was head of foundation and vice-principal at Wimbledon, from 1979 until retirement in 1991 being vice-principal. Cuthbert was a member of the Colour Group of Great Britain, long interested in colour research and its application. In this connection he was in 1969 involved in colour related to the Calder motorway bridge; in 1979 designed the ballet *Counterpoint*, to music by Benjamin Britten, at Adeline Genée Theatre, East Grinstead; in 1981, devised an interior for Holy Trinity Church, Forest Row, Sussex; and in 1990 was consultant for the BBC television series *The Colour Eye*. Mixed shows included Structural Growth in Natural Form, Whitechapel Art Gallery, 1967; The Painting School at Montmiral, Camden Arts Centre, 1989; and Diagonale des Arts, Cahors, France, 1995. In 1991 there was a selective retrospective at Wimbledon Library Gallery and the artist's studio. Graves Art Gallery in Sheffield; Towner Art Gallery in Eastbourne; Bedales School; New Metropole Arts Centre, Folkestone; and Universities of Surrey, Kent and Sussex hold examples. Retired to Puylaroque, France, 1992, where he died.

Alfred CUTHBERT 1898–1966 Watercolourist, born in South Shields, County Durham, who went into business as a broker. Studied at South Shields School of Art and continued to live in the area, being a member of the Art Club there. Exhibited RI and elsewhere. Sunderland Art Gallery holds his work.

David CUTHBERT 1951– Versatile artist and teacher, born in Norwich, Norfolk, married to the artist Ros Cuthbert. He attended Somerset College of Art, Taunton, 1969–70; gained his painting diploma at Central School of Art & Design, 1970–3; then was at Institute of Education, London University, 1973–4. Taught at Working Men's College, 1973–6; then did extensive teaching, part-time and summer courses in France and Italy, with periods at Wimbledon College, Loughton College of Further Education and St Martin's School of Art. Was a member of Artists 303. In 1983 gained an artist's placement from South West Arts at Kings of Wessex School, Cheddar. From 1984–90 edited *The Looker*, an art and ideas magazine. Mixed shows included Swiss Cottage Library and Burgh House Contemporary Artists in Camden, both 1981; Off Centre Gallery, Bristol, 1990; and Brought to Book, Flowers East, 1994. Solo exhibitions included Parkway Focus, 1976–84; Consort Gallery, Imperial College, 1981; and his Winscombe Farm Studio, Avon, 1995. In 2003, shared a show with his wife at Six Chapel Row Contemporary Art, Bath. Tate Gallery library, Kings of Wessex School and Electrografia Museo International, Cuenca, Spain, hold examples.

Gwen CUTHBERT: *see* **WENDY WOOD**

Ken CUTHBERT 1929– Painter, notably a watercolourist, who combined a sense of place with inherent abstract design and an interest in man's effect upon wild landscape. Cuthbert was born in Ipswich, Suffolk, his art training beginning in 1950 when he met the locally based Dutch artist and tutor Cor Visser. The Dock End area was an early influence, as were visits to Rye and Dartmoor and visiting artists including David Hockney and especially John Loker. In 1985, Cuthbert visited France for the first time and was so impressed by the colour and landscape of the Dordogne that he bought a cottage there, from then on using it as a base for part of the year. Returned to live in Suffolk permanently from 2000. Mixed shows included RI, 1957. Among later solo exhibitions were the John Russell Gallery, Ipswich, from 2001. In 2002, Cuthbert became president of Ipswich Art Society.

Ros CUTHBERT 1951– Painter, draughtsman, printmaker and teacher, full name Rosalind Cuthbert, born in Somerset, settling in Winscombe, Avon. She was married to the artist David Cuthbert. She studied at Somerset College of Art, Taunton, 1969–71; Central School of Art & Design, 1971–4, teachers including Blair Hughes-Stanton and Cecil Collins; gaining her master's degree in painting at Royal College of Art, 1974–7, under Keith Critchlow and Peter de Francia. Among awards were RWA first prize, 1982. Was tutor in charge of relief printing at Central School, 1978–92, and directed and taught Mendip Painting Centre from 1985. Group exhibitions included Arnolfini Gallery, Bristol, Avon Open Exhibition, 1983; Portrait 1980s, Fermoy Centre, King's Lynn, and tour, 1985–7; and Self-Portraits, Plymouth City Art Gallery, 1992. Solo shows included Camden Galleries, 1989, and Anthony Hepworth Fine Art, Bath, 1995. Published a number of instructional books, and illustrated with wood engravings Yellow Fox Press publications. Contemporary Art Society, National Portrait Gallery, Sheffield City Art Gallery and Eton College hold examples. Was a member of Artists 303 and RWA from 1998. In 2003, she shared a show with her husband at Six Chapel Row Contemporary Art, Bath.

E CUTNER: *see* **Effie SPRING-SMITH**

Herbert CUTNER 1881–1969 Graphic artist and printmaker. Born in Hull, Cutner studied at the London County Council-run Bolt Court School of Art and at the Central School of Arts and Crafts, his teachers including Walter Bayes and Frank Emanuel. Married the artist Effie Spring-Smith. Cutner, who sometimes signed his work H C, mainly showed at the SGA. He was a journalist who wrote on diverse subjects, from articles in the rationalist publication *The Freethinker* to *Teach Yourself Commercial Art* and *Teach Yourself Etching*. Lived in London.

Christiana CUTTER 1893–1969 Painter and draughtsman, born in Wisbech, Cambridgeshire. In 1910 moved to London and attended Slade School of Fine Art prior to World War I under Henry Tonks. There she met the artist Marjorie Lilly, whose brother George she married in 1919. Showed at LG, NEAC and Walker's Galleries and in 1974 was included in Parkin Gallery exhibition The Sickert Women and The Sickert Girls. Died in Chichester, Sussex.

George CUTTS 1938– Sculptor in stone and steel, maker of mobiles and teacher, born in Rugby, Warwickshire. While working at Goole Shipyard he obtained a place at Doncaster School of Art, 1956–8, then the Royal College of Art, 1958–60, teachers including John Skeaping. He later taught there, at Royal Academy Schools, Chelsea School of Art and elsewhere. Exhibited widely in Britain, on the continent and in America, as well as carrying out public commissions. Landscape and the sea were key inspirations. His The Kiss, of 1991, and Sea Change, 1996, were moving sculptures included in the Sculpture at Goodwood displays.

Michael CUTTS 1937– Painter and teacher, born in London, who in 1953 had a trial for Chelsea Football Club, then attended Regent Street Polytechnic School of Art, 1954–8, and London University Institute of Education, 1958–9. For some years worked as a full-time teacher in the Forest of Dean, Newcastle upon Tyne and London, teaching part-time at Camden Institute. In 1967 a series of abstract paintings by Cutts was included in Camden Arts Centre's Survey '67 Abstract Painters. By that time he had had two solo shows: in 1963 at People's Theatre, Newcastle, and in 1966 at Gordon Gallery, Wimbledon. Also exhibited with Young Contemporaries and at Grabowski Gallery. Cubism and the ideas of Marshall McLuhan, on whom Cutts lectured, were important to the artist, who reckoned that he "could make a reality quite apart from the seen world if one regarded paints and brushes as the first stage in a making process, rather than the last act of expressing oneself."

Tadeusz CZERWINKE 1936– Sculptor in various materials, potter and teacher, born in Poland, noted for extensive work in churches in Britain and on the continent. He studied at Winchester School of Art, 1957, teachers including Norman Pierce, and went on to teach at Shoeburyness Comprehensive School. From 1976 was a member of SPS, also showing with Association of Polish Artists and abroad. St Peter's, Hinckley; St Sebastian and St John the Baptist, Preston; and General Sikorski Museum in Prince's Gate, London, hold his work. Lived in London.

Marta CZOK 1947– Painter, of Polish origin, born in Beirut, Lebanon, whose family moved in 1948 to London, where she was educated. Studied at St Martin's School of Art, became a regular exhibitor at RA Summer Exhibition, then in 1974 moved to Rome, where she married and began to establish a career as a professional artist. She showed widely through Europe and America and through her regular collaboration with the Italian national airline in its Alitalia per l'Arte programme was appreciated worldwide. Czok was commissioned by Alitalia to paint a triptych, presented to Pope John Paul II when he reached 80; also by Royal Caribbean Cruise Line to produce works for its ship *Navigator of the Seas*. Czok's painting themes, in an almost naïve style reminiscent of Polish folk art, mixing narrative, symbolism and irony, were underlain by the artist's keen sense of humour, witness the catalogue of her solo show at Albemarle Gallery, 2003.

Andrzej CZYŻOWSKI 1919– Artist, designer and editor, one of the Polish paper sculptors who flourished in England after World War II. Fought in the Polish Campaign and in France, was interned Switzerland studying at Fribourg University, then served in the Polish Army press unit in Italy. After arriving in Britain in 1946, Czyżowski worked until 1964 as a freelance designer, producing paper and metal sculptures for a range of clients including Diana Studio. Humour and satire marked his output. For almost 20 years from 1966 worked for Radio Free Europe in Munich. Returned to London and held a post in the Polish Government in Exile and then, until 1991, was editor-in-chief of *The Polish Daily*. His work was included in Polish Paper Sculpture at the Polish Cultural Institute, 1995.

D

Richard D: *see* **Richard DENT**

Charles DABORN 1920–1968 Painter in oil, born at Woking, Surrey, who attended Kingston School of Art, 1936–9, under Reginald Brill and the Royal College of Art, 1939–40 and then 1946–8, under Percy Jowett. Taught at Winchester School of Art. Completed a mural in the town's council offices. Exhibited RA, at the Bladon Gallery at Hurstbourne Tarrant and at the public galleries in Mansfield and Birkenhead. Lived at Winchester, Hampshire, where colleagues knew him as Stuart, his middle name. His daughter was the painter Erica Daborn.

Erica DABORN 1951– Painter, draughtsman and teacher, born in Winchester, Hampshire, daughter of the artist Charles Stuart Daborn. From 1976–85 she was married to the printmaker Anthony Davies, from 1985 to the American film maker Dennis Lanson. She studied at Winchester School of Art, 1968–72, with John Bellany and William Crozier, and at the Royal College of Art, 1973–4, and 1975–7, with Peter Blake, David Tindle and Leonard Rosoman. Daborn took up a teaching fellowship at Cardiff College of Art, 1977, having a studio at Chapter Art Centre until 1983. Had a residency at the MacDowell Colony, New Hampshire, 1984, moving to America to live in 1985, in California until 1996, then taking a teaching post at Boston Museum of Fine Arts. Daborn created her own world of bizarre people and animals. From 1985–9 her work was "based on social critique. From 1989 to the present the dominant theme is motherhood, images evolving through a painting process that accesses the unconscious." Was a member of 56 Group Wales, 1980–6. Group exhibitions included many in Britain and America; solo exhibitions began with Air Gallery, 1981, later ones including Sherry Frumkin Gallery, Santa Monica, 1993, and Phyllis Kind Gallery, Chicago, 1995. Awards included a number from WAC. It, Contemporary Art Society for Wales, Welsh Development Agency, Newport Museum and Art Gallery and other British and American collections hold examples. Lived in Winchester, Massachusetts.

Leszek DABROWSKI 1942– Painter in oil, born in Sandomierz, Poland, married to the artist Wendy Jones-Dabrowska. He was brought up in Liverpool, attending the College of Art there, 1961–7, gaining a fine art (painting) honours degree in 1966. Teachers included Heinz Koppel, Keith Arnatt, Arthur Ballard, John Edkins and Nicholas Horsfield. As part of his postgraduate year he travelled to the Netherlands, Germany, Czechoslavakia and Poland, visits to his homeland continuing to inform his work. From 1986 he was a member of the Bigos group Polish artists, which in that year had a show Brixton Art Gallery and The Crypt, St George's Church, Bloomsbury. Also exhibited Centaur Gallery, from 1990, and Covent Garden Festival, 1997–8. Had a number of two- and three-man shows including POSK Gallery, 1993, a solo exhibition at Blackfriars Arts Centre, Boston, 1985, another at Heifer Gallery, 2002, and one shared there in 2003 with the potter Jane Bridger. In 1989–90, Dabrowski co-ordinated a major tour of Bigos artists to Poland; in 1997–8, a tour of 12 Kielce, Poland, artists through England. Lived in Fishtoft, Boston, Lincolnshire.

Hugo (Puck) DACHINGER 1908–1995 Painter, designer and draughtsman, born in Gmunden, Austria, who from 1943 was married to the artist Meta Dachinger Gutman. Dachinger studied art in Leipzig, 1929–32, then from the latter year worked in Vienna as a freelance artist and designer. He invented and patented a lettering method that was used principally in window displays. In 1938 when German troops entered Austria Dachinger decided to leave Leipzig, making his way to Denmark, then England. In 1940 he was interned at Huyton, then in the Isle of Man for several months, but on release settled in London to work as an artist. Dachinger was notable for his witty studies of figures and groups of people, which were tinged with a strong humanity. He had an appearance in the Leipzig Kunstalle in a mixed show in 1932; held exhibitions in the Ramsey, Isle of Man, camp in 1940; then soon began to appear at Redfern and Leger Galleries. In the 1950s he also showed with Ben Uri Gallery and Jack Bilbo's Modern Art Gallery. Dachinger showed with his wife in Gmunden in 1980, then six years later appeared in the Art in Exile show; Berlin, Oberhausen, Camden Arts Centre and John Denham Gallery. That gallery gave him a solo show in 1989, a memorial in 1997. His wife Meta (1916–1983) was also an artist. In 2004, Walker Art Gallery in Liverpool held an exhibition of its pictures by Dachinger and others by Walter Nessler, Art Behind Barbed Wire, relating to their internment at Huyton.

Tom DACK 1933– Painter and artist in pen and ink, born in Newcastle upon Tyne, where he attended the College of Art & Design. Most of his working life was spent in advertising agencies and commercial art studios as an illustrator and designer. His own work was concerned with marine, aircraft and landscape subjects. Showed at Darlington Art Gallery; Bede Museum in Jarrow; Sally Port Gallery, Berwick-upon-Tweed; Patricia Wells Gallery, Thornbury, and elsewhere. Lived in Whitley Bay, Tyne and Wear. A major show of Dack's work was held at the Earl of Zetland floating public house and restaurant in North Shields in 2002.

Winifred DACRE: *see* **Winifred NICHOLSON**

William St Alban Rae DADY 1938–1989 Painter, sculptor and teacher, born in Delhi, India. He studied at Goldsmiths' College School of Art, 1956–61, teachers including Sam Rabin, Kenneth Martin and Ivor Roberts-Jones, and became head of art at Stowe School, 1965–87. Joined SPS in 1979, also showing with Federation of British Artists and RA. Lived in Buckingham, Buckinghamshire.

Judith DA FANO 1919–2000 Versatile painter, draughtsman and sculptor, mother of the artist Simon Manby. Da Fano's father was a research doctor, Carrado Da Fano, her mother Dorothea Landau, a painter in the late Pre-Raphaelite manner. Judith was born in Great Missenden, Buckinghamshire, and studied at the Byam Shaw School of Art, 1938–9, with Ernest Jackson, having exhibited at Lucy Wertheim Gallery in 1936, work influenced by a love of ballet. She also studied with the sculptor Judith Wrightson. World War II stalled her decorative studies at the Central School. Had paintings accepted at RA Summer Exhibition from 1945; other mixed venues were to include RP, ROI and NEAC. Moved to the Lake District to farm and run an open studio in 1953. Won a Silver Medal at Paris Salon in 1958, a Gold in 1961; in 1962, HRH Prince Philip bought Farm Scene from RSA; and she had a solo exhibition at Tib Lane Gallery, Manchester, in 1963. After 1963–5 in London, using The Old Courthouse, Hawkshead to sell work, in 1971 Poolgarth Porcelain began, made by Roy Manby whom she had married in 1940, decorated by Da Fano. She continued to exhibit in mixed and solo exhibitions, including America, and in 1987 there was a Manby family exhibition at Brantwood, Coniston, John Ruskin's former house. Da Fano shared a show at the Sheridan Russell Gallery in 1999 and there was a solo exhibition at Lichfield International Arts Festival, 2000. All Saints Church, Gosforth, has Da Fano's carved limewood Christ, completed in 1951.

Arnold DAGHANI 1909–1985 Versatile artist, notable as a draughtsman, and writer, who produced over 4,000 works. He was born in Suceava, then in the Austro-Hungarian Empire, now part of Romania, and showed artistic promise at school. Although he attended art school in Munich, Daghani obtained no formal qualification. Aged 23 he was conscripted into the Army, then after early discharge in the early 1930s he worked for a publisher, doing clerical work, in Bucharest. With his wife Daghani was placed in a forced labour camp by the Nazis, but they escaped and were repatriated. After World War II Daghani lived as an English translator and tutor while practising his art, but, at odds with the regime, in 1959 he took an exit visa to Israel – forfeiting over 900 works on leaving Romania, then settled in Vence, France, 1961–70, and Iona, Switzerland, 1970–7. Among his French achievements was decorating the Anglican chapel of St Hugh, Vence, using an original means of painting on glass. His final move, in 1977, was to Hove, Sussex, where he died. Wartime privations and an unsettled existence had for years undermined his health, and he felt an isolated figure artistically. Arnold Daghani, A relentless spirit in art, was held at Brighton Polytechnic, 1984, and in 1992 Barbican Centre and Ben Uri Art Society, which holds his work, put on shows.

Eric DAGLISH 1894–1966 Wood engraver, watercolour painter and illustrator who was notably an artist depicting birds and country life. Born in London, Daglish attended university there and in Bonn, Germany. Although he exhibited at Redfern Gallery, SWE of which he was a member, and NEAC, Dr Daglish was most known for his illustrative work in which attention to detail was paramount. Paul Nash taught him engraving just after World War I and was friendly with him and Alice Daglish when living at Dymchurch, Kent. Among books illustrated by this naturalist artist were *Woodcuts of British Birds*, 1925; Henry David Thoreau's *Walden*, 1927; and Gilbert White's *The Natural History of Selborne*, 1929. Lived at Speen, near Aylesbury, Buckinghamshire.

Peter DAGLISH 1930– Printmaker, painter and teacher who studied at École des Beaux-Arts in Montreal, Canada, 1956–60, then did postgraduate studies at Slade School of Fine Art, 1963–5. From 1973 taught printmaking on the master of arts course at Chelsea School of Art and painting and printmaking at the Slade, postgraduate students. Daglish's pictures, featuring real and unreal women, had a Pop Art-like directness, and were both jazzily coloured and monochrome. He was a member of RE and showed widely nationally and abroad. Tate Gallery, Victoria & Albert Museum, major Canadian collections and public galleries in Bradford and Hull hold examples. Lived in London.

Michael D'AGUILAR 1924– Painter in oil and printmaker, born and lived in London, brother of the artist Paul D'Aguilar, educated privately in France, Italy and Spain. D'Aguilar studied at Royal Academy Schools, 1948–53, teachers including Bernard Fleetwood-Walker and William Dring. There he won the Armitage and silver medal, 1949, as well as several Royal Drawing Society medals. He showed in mixed exhibitions at RA, NEAC, Young Contemporaries and Leicester Galleries, work distinguished by a rich palette, also having solo exhibitions at New Grafton Gallery, Gimpel Fils and Bruton Street Gallery, 2001.

Paul D'AGUILAR 1927– Painter and draughtsman, born and lived in London, brother of the artist Michael D'Aguilar. He was privately educated in France, Italy and Spain and studied at Royal Academy Schools, 1948–53, under Henry Rushbury. In 1949 D'Aguilar gained first prize for drawing at RA, also winning several Royal Drawing Society medals. Also studied in Italy. Showed in mixed exhibitions at RA, RBA, NEAC and the New Grafton, Leicester and Redfern Galleries, as well as abroad. Retrospective of oil paintings at Carlyle Gallery, 2003.

Saied DAI 1958– Painter, draughtsman and teacher, born in Tehran, Persia (his second name is an abbreviation of the full Persian version). He described himself as "wilfully independent", and was a serious artist who tackled a wide range of subjects without regard to fashion. Dai was brought to England aged six and was largely abandoned by his parents, being sent to boarding schools and uncongenial foster parents. He described his secondary school as "a hermetically sealed society based on physical and psychological violence." Dai studied at Bournemouth School of Art and Design, graduating to the Royal Academy Schools where his teachers included Peter Greenham, Norman Blamey, Roderic Barrett, Lawrence Gowing, Victor Pasmore, William Scott and Leonard Rosoman. He was invited back to teach drawing under Leonard McComb and insisted that "Drawing reveals the way an artist thinks. It is the means by which one makes visual relationships." Dai's solo show at Petley Fine Art in 2005 was accompanied by a well-illustrated catalogue with a perceptive introduction by Roger Berthoud. Dai lived near Bath, Somerset.

Deirdre DAINES 1950– Painter and teacher who studied at Walthamstow School of Art and Royal Academy Schools. She won the Eric Kennington Prize for Drawing, David Murray Prize for Landscape as well as silver and bronze medals. Showed in mixed exhibitions at RA, Langton Gallery, Agnew and New Grafton Gallery. Her solo shows included RA Common Room, 1981, and Cale Art Gallery, 1982. Daines was a sensitive portrait painter. She taught at Harrow and Croydon Colleges of Art as well as adult education classes for the Inner London Education Authority. Lived in London.

Adrian DAINTREY 1902–1988 Painter, illustrator and writer, born in London and educated at Charterhouse, where he early showed a talent for drawing. Studied at Slade School of Fine Art, 1920–4, but found its regime unsympathetic. Instead preferred the company of Augustus John and his circle, sometimes assisting in John's studio. A congenial man, Daintrey gathered a wide circle of friends, who included the artists Nina Hamnett and Rex Whistler, Matthew Smith and Alvaro Guevara and the writer Anthony Powell. After the Slade he continued his studies in the Louvre and L'Académie de la Grande Chaumière, Paris, then became art master at Dean Close School, Cheltenham. First exhibition shared with Paul Nash at Dorothy Warren's gallery in 1928, and as a result Daintrey gained aristocratic patrons who helped ease his money worries. During World War II served widely abroad and was involved in camouflage work. Finding himself unfashionable as an artist after the war he held shows in his studio. He also served as the magazine *Punch*'s art critic, 1953–61; published a pleasant volume of reminiscences, *I Must Say*, in 1963; and from the late 1960s taught part-time at the City and Guilds Art School, eventually becoming its librarian. Latterly Daintrey had successful exhibitions of his witty and attractive paintings and drawings, often featuring the area around his studio in Little Venice, London, at South London Art Gallery, Michael Parkin Fine Art and Sally Hunter Fine Art. British Museum and Imperial War Museum hold his work.

Gabriel DAKEYNE 1916– Artist in collage, watercolour and acrylic, born in Marske-by-the-Sea, Yorkshire. She studied at Swindon School of Art, 1934, under Harold Dearden; in the Netherlands; and in 1953 through Percy Bradshaw's Press Art School. Exhibited at RA, SWA, RWA and at Paris Salon. Had a solo show at St Aldate's in Oxford, 1978. Lived in Winnersh, Berkshire.

Arthur D'ALBERTSON 1964– Painter, black-and-white and commercial artist. Studied at Putney School of Art under R O Dunlop and John Bowyer. Later worked for Henry Squire & Company, advertising agents, and was director and associate editor of *Art Quarterly*. Was chief cartoonist for *Seven Seas Magazine* for several years in the 1930s and also drew for *Punch*. Exhibited RA, ROI, RWA and Paris Salon and had one-man shows in London and the provinces. Lived at Binstead, Sussex.

Arthur DALBY 1900–1961 Printmaker, studied at Liverpool School of Art and the Royal College of Art. By profession he was a government-appointed inspector of art schools. He exhibited RA and Walker Art Gallery, Liverpool. Lived in Camberley, Surrey.

Claire DALBY 1944– Artist in watercolour, gouache and wood engraving, daughter of the watercolourist Charles Longbotham, born in St Andrews, Fife. She studied at City and Guilds of London Art School, 1964–7. Dalby said that in her landscapes and still lifes she was "interested in light falling on objects and in the relationships of objects in the space they occupy". In botanical illustration she strove "to convey the structure of plants as well as appearance". Became a member of RWS in 1973, RE in 1978 and was also a member of SWE. She was elected a vice-president of RWS in 1991. Also exhibited with Clarges Gallery from 1968 and at Halifax House, Oxford, 1987. Had a solo exhibition in Camberley, Surrey, where she lived, in 1975, later ones including Imperial College from 1981 and Shetland Museum, Lerwick, from 1988. Natural History Museum published two wall charts by her on lichens and in 1989 *Claire Dalby's Picture Book* appeared. Science Museum, Natural History Museum, Victoria & Albert Museum and Ashmolean Museum, Oxford, hold her work.

Susan DALE 1953– Sculptor employing mixed media, as in her Wapping Artists Open Studios Exhibition piece Ideogram for the Eighties 1981, shown in 1982. Dale was born in Tyne and Wear and studied at Goldsmiths' College, 1976–80. Lived for a time in Blackheath, southeast London.

Tom DALE 1935– Artist in various media and teacher, born in Greenock, Renfrewshire. He attended the local High School, then Glasgow School of Art, 1953–7. Went on to become art master of Selwood School, Frome, Somerset, not far from his home at West Horrington. Showed at Burwood Gallery, Wells, and elsewhere in West Country and became a member of RMS in 1982.

Anthony DALEY 1960– Painter, born in Jamaica. He studied at Leeds College of Art, 1978–9, graduating at Wimbledon College of Art, 1979–82, gaining his master's degree at Chelsea School of Art, 1982–3. Among his group shows were Christie's Inaugural, 1983; Turnpike Gallery, Leigh, Greater Manchester, 1987; Basel and London Art Fairs, 1986; and Smiths Galleries, 1988. Showed solo with Angela Flowers Gallery from 1986, with a one-man at Woodlands Art Gallery, 1990. Worked in Greenwich Artists' Studios. Daley worked on a large scale, figurative pictures tending towards abstraction.

Angela DALLAS 1946– Painter, printmaker and designer, born in Bradford, Yorkshire. Attended Harrogate School of Art, 1963–4, then Cardiff College of Art, 1964–7. In 1965–6 she attended a fine art summer course at the Academy of Fine Art in Perugia, Italy, and a summer course in photography at Barry Summer School. During 1967 she participated in WAC's poster project, in which a screen print was chosen for enlargement to poster size for use in public throughout Wales. Dallas in 1969 set up as a freelance designer with a special interest in fashion in London, but in 1971 moved to Cyprus. There she continued to paint, with a particular interest in murals. Exhibited widely in Cyprus and in Britain in group shows in Whitechapel Art Gallery; Albany Gallery, in Cardiff; and with WAC, which holds her work.

John E S DALLAS 1883– Watercolour painter of landscapes and townscapes. After education at Alleyn's School, Dulwich, Dallas was at St Martin's School of Art. Showed at RCamA. Lived in Leatherhead, Surrey.

Terence Henry DALLEY 1935– Artist and illustrator, born in Kusumu, Kenya, who worked mainly in watercolour or drawings in pencil or charcoal pencil. He attended St Martin's School of Art, 1954–7, and Royal College of Art, 1957–60, then was at Hochschule für Gestaltung, Ulm, West Germany, 1960–1. Taught at Wimbledon School of Art from 1967. Showed with RWS at Bankside Gallery and in several shows at Mall Galleries. Had a solo exhibition at Upper Grosvenor Galleries, 1971, and elsewhere. Worked as a freelance illustrator for a number of firms and publishers, views of London a common feature, as shown in Peter Marcan's book *Artists and the East End*, 1986. Museum of London and The Fishmongers' Company hold Dalley's work. Lived in London.

Derek DALTON 1929– Painter and teacher, born in Lancashire. He studied at Blackpool and Hornsey Colleges of Art and was for some years head of painting at Newcastle Polytechnic. Dalton was a painter of the northern landscape. Although he did some abstract work, his later pictures were distinguished by a vertical grid-type motif, tending to divide the scene into strips. He showed extensively in group exhibitions, including John Moores Exhibition, Liverpool, 1972; Tom Caldwell Gallery, Belfast, 1978; Ukrainian Institute of Modern Art, Chicago, 1986; Washington Arts Centre, 1989; and the Newcastle Group's The Northern Lights show at DLI Museum & Arts Centre, Durham, 1990, and tour. Awards included a purchase prize at Northern Art Exhibition, 1978, and first prize at Tyne Tees Northern Open, 1985. Later solo shows included Sunderland Arts Centre, 1983, Grey's Gallery, Newcastle, 1985–6, and Galerie La Charbonnière, St Laurent en Grandvaux, France, 1996. Lived in Corbridge, Northumberland, where he participated in the Tynedale Artists' Network annual open studios. In 2001, he showed work there from 1969–99, also having a solo exhibition at Shire Pottery Gallery & Studios, Alnwick. Corporate collections hold examples.

Elisabeth DALTON 1940–2004 Meticulous stage designer and teacher, notable for colourful and authentic ballet and operatic productions, whose work was mostly seen outside Britain. Dalton studied theatre design at Wimbledon School of Art, then from 1962–3 on a non-diploma course in fine art stage design at the Slade School of Fine Art under Nicholas Georgiadis, whose assistant she was at the Royal Opera House in the late 1960s. Her first great success was designing for John Cranko's Stuttgart Ballet production of *The Taming of the Shrew* in 1969. The company performed it at Covent Garden five years later, the Royal Ballet adopted it and Dalton's designs were later used widely abroad. After Cranko died in 1973 she designed new productions of his earlier ballets, notably *Onegin*, in 1991, praised for capturing the essence of Pushkin's Russia. That was a year after her last Stuttgart production, with Marcia Haydée, of Rodgers and Hart's musical *On Your Toes*. Her first opera designs, for Mozart's *Il re pastore*, at Wexford, Ireland, in 1971, were part of a long association with the director John Cox. Their other joint productions included Lehar's *The Merry Widow*, for English National Opera at The Coliseum, 1972, and Strauss's *Der Rosenkavalier*, at Houston in 1975, later seen elsewhere in America and in a Netherlands Opera production. Dalton taught at the Central School and in other art schools in the south of England.

Lesley DALTON 1957– Artist who studied at Loughborough College of Art and Design, 1976–7, then gained an honours degree in painting at Leicester Polytechnic, 1977–80. Her solo exhibitions included St Martin's Gallery, Leicester, 1982; Magazine Workspace and Loseby Gallery, both Leicester in 1984; then in London at Artworks Space, 1986. In 1989, she showed with Barbican Arts Group in East End Open Studios.

Lisa DALTON 1954– Painter and teacher, born in London. She studied at Chelsea School of Art, 1974–7, gaining a first-class honours degree in fine art, then her master's degree after study there, 1977–8. From 1980 was for some years a visiting lecturer at University of Reading fine art department. Completed a number of commissioned works, notably portraits. In 1978 her paintings were used in Arnold Wesker's *Love Letters on Blue Paper*, at National Theatre, and in 1988 a painting appeared in John Schlesinger's film *Madame Sousatzka*. Dalton appeared in many group shows from late 1970s, including Whitworth Art Gallery, Manchester, Young Contemporaries, 1977; Washington, Chicago and Basle Arts Fairs, 1980; Jonathan Poole Gallery, New York, 1983; and Bury St Edmunds Art Gallery, 1988. After a solo show at Robin Gibson Gallery, Sydney, 1979, others included Thackeray Gallery, 1989.

Dexter DALWOOD 1960– Figurative painter and teacher, born in Bristol, who studied at St Martin's School of Art, 1980–5, and Royal College of Art, 1988–90. Went on to be associate lecturer at University of Northumbria, in Newcastle upon Tyne. Mixed shows included Whitechapel Open from 1992; Base/Salama-Caro Gallery, 1994; John Moores Liverpool Exhibition, 1995–6, Die Young Stay Pretty, ICA, 1998–9; and Days Like These, Tate Britain, 2003. Solo shows included Paton Gallery, 1987; Smith Jariwala Gallery, 1992; Galerie Unwahr, Berlin, 1995; and Gagosian Gallery, New York, 2000 and 2004. Arts Council holds his oil The Room, 1984–5. A strong feature of Dalwood's output was paintings of interiors unknown to him. After initial sketches, he used collages of objects, colours and materials from magazines. Based in London.

Hubert DALWOOD 1924–1976 Sculptor and influential teacher, born in Bristol. He worked in a variety of materials, sometimes moulding and sometimes casting his forms, which were abstract and resembled primitive art. For much of World War II Dalwood was apprenticed to the British Aeroplane Company, then after a period in the Royal Navy he attended Bath Academy of Art, Corsham, 1946–9. He held a number of teaching posts at schools of art in England, latterly head of the sculpture department at Hornsey College of Art, 1963–73, holding the same position at the Central School of Arts and Crafts from 1974–6. He showed for many years at Gimpel Fils; won first prize for sculpture at the Venice Biennale in 1962; and was given a retrospective memorial show at the Hayward Gallery in 1979. Other retrospectives at Hebden Bridge Arts Festival, 1996, Gimpel Fils, 1999. Leeds Museums and Galleries hold examples of Dalwood's work. Lived in London.

Jehan DALY 1918–2001 Painter, draughtsman and teacher, notably in pastel, born in Llanelli, Carmarthenshire. His father was the painter William Daly, principal of Kidderminster School of Art, which Jehan attended. Studied at Royal College of Art, 1937–9, where he met his lifelong friend John Ward, returning there after World War II Army service, he and Ward sharing accommodation and a studio in Fulham, 1946–50. Taught at Wimbledon and St Martin's Schools of Art and exhibited RA, NEAC, Agnew and in Canterbury area, where he latterly lived a simple, reclusive life. Was reluctant to exhibit, although his drawings were prized by other artists. Daly had solo shows at Martyn Gregory, 1993 and 1997, and in 1994 shared an exhibition at Hazlitt, Gooden & Fox with John Sergeant and John Ward. Daly is prominent in Ward's picture The East Kent Art Club, owned by the Royal Museum and Art Gallery, Canterbury. Daly was of French and Irish extraction the name Jehan – pronounced John – being of medieval French origin.

William Edward DALY 1879–1962 Painter and artist in glass, born in Manchester. He attended the School of Art there, Royal College of Art and studied in Paris. He was principal of Kidderminster School of Art after Llanelli School of Art, Carmarthenshire. Completed windows in several churches. Showed RA, Manchester City Art Gallery and elsewhere in the provinces. After his retirement from the Kidderminster School about the end of World War II Daly took up portraiture, examples of which were shown at the local Art Gallery in 1950 in a one-man exhibition. It holds two landscapes by him: The Pool, Boncourt; and The Valley of the Loire. Lived in Kidderminster, Worcestershire, and died in Worcester. The artist Jehan Daly was his son.

Matthew DALZIEL 1957– Artist using sculpture, photography and installations, born in Irvine, Ayrshire, who as well as showing individually worked jointly with Louise Scullion as Dalziel & Scullion. He gained an honours degree in fine art (sculpture) from Duncan of Jordanstone College of Art, Dundee, 1981–5, winning the Dalgetty Dunn Scholarship. Won a higher national diploma in documentary photography from Gwent College of Higher Education, 1985–7, then was awarded a postgraduate diploma in sculpture and fine art photography from Glasgow School of Art, 1987–8. He was artist-in-residence for Shell UK Exploration and Production at the St Fergus gas plant, 1988–9; won a Scottish Arts Council Major Bursary, moving to St Combs, 1990–1; gained a short artist's residency at Addenbrooke's Hospital in Cambridge, 1992; then in 1994–5 was artist-in-residence for Banff & Buchan District. Exhibitions and commissions included Forces, Gwent College of Art, 1987; Artists in Industry, Aberdeen Art Gallery, 1990; and Satellites & Monuments, a large light work, commissioned by Lux Europae, Edinburgh, 1992.

DALZIEL & SCULLION– The name under which Matthew Dalziel and Louise Scullion collaborated from early 1990s, working in a range of media. Commissions included 4 Minutes, Science Museum, 1994; and in 1995 The Most Beautiful Thing, for the Scottish Arts Council, and The Gifted Child, outdoor installation for Eastwood Arts Festival, Glasgow. Dalziel & Scullion were artists-in-residence for Banff & Buchan District, 1994–5. They had an exhibition at Arnolfini Gallery, Bristol, 1996. This included impressions of the flat, minimal landscape of northeast Scotland where they lived, unsettling video images of 80,000 battery hens and large photographs accompanied by a scented text. In 1997 Scottish National Gallery of Modern Art, Edinburgh, exhibited their video Endlessly, in 2000 Oriel 31, Newtown, showed the installation Rain; Aberdeen Art Gallery exhibited the recently acquired DVD installation Another Place, celebrating non-urban life, in 2001; in that year there was a sound, light, multiples, sculpture exhibition at Yorkshire Sculpture Park, West Bretton; and there were shows for the pair at Houldsworth, 2002, Manchester Art Gallery, 2002–3, and Aberystwyth Arts Centre, 2004. Arts Council, Science Museum and Victoria & Albert Museum hold their work.

Pam DAN 1938– Painter, draughtsman and teacher, born in Harrow, Middlesex, who studied at Colchester School of Art, 1955–9, and the Royal College of Art, 1959–61, teachers including John O'Connor, Carel Weight and Ruskin Spear. She taught at Colchester School of Art, Greyfriars Adult Education Centre and privately. Dan ran the gallery at Wivenhoe Arts Club for some years, also showing there, other exhibitors including Ted Atkinson; Richard Chopping; Jack and Roy Cross; John Dan; George Miller; Christopher Pask; and Denis Wirth-Miller. Took part in many group shows, especially in Essex, including The Minories, Colchester; Colchester Castle; and Essex University. Among solo exhibitions were Wivenhoe Arts Club and The Minories. Dan was notably a landscape painter, themes including Essex reed beds, Spanish olive and orange trees and sea movements. University of East Anglia and other collections in England and Canada hold examples.

Nikki DANBY 1957– Painter and draughtsman, born in Victoria, British Columbia, who began drawing and painting from an early age. From 1980–3 she studied at Byam Shaw School of Art. Then went on to contribute pictures to mixed shows, including Charlotte Lampard Gallery, Cadogan Contemporary and Zella Nine. In 1992 had first solo show at Cadogan Gallery, of works done between 1987–91, during which time she had received several portrait commissions in Europe and Australia. Her images were described as "sensual and rich in colour and tonal variety".

Clemence DANE 1888–1965 Playwright, novelist, artist and actress, born in Greenwich, southeast London. She was educated in England, Germany and Switzerland and studied at the Slade School of Fine Art, 1905–7, under her real name, Winifred Ashton. Although she intended to make painting her profession, by 1913 the theatre had become her abiding interest and she went on the stage as Diana Cortis. The outbreak of World War I and health problems intervened, and, after teaching in a girls' school, she began writing novels as Clemence Dane. The pseudonym was adapted from the name of St Clement Danes church, in the Strand, and symbolised her love of the Covent Garden area, with which she was to become identified and of which she wrote in her 1964 book *London Has a Garden*. When *Regiment of Women* appeared in 1917 Dane was termed a new novelist of distinction and her reputation grew with the success of her first play *A Bill of Divorcement*, produced at the St Martin's Theatre in 1921. None of Dane's further plays achieved this success, although *The Happy Hypocrite*, 1936, an adaptation of

Max Beerbohm's story, starring Ivor Novello and Vivien Leigh, was notable. A tireless worker, Dane also wrote many radio plays and more novels, particularly *Broome Stages*, 1931. She was advised on this by her old friend Richard Addinsell, composer of the popular *Warsaw Concerto*. Dane made a striking 1935 alabaster bust of him, offered by Bonhams Knightsbridge in 2003, for she continued to paint and sculpt all her life. She was a noted eccentric, the original of the medium Madame Arcati in her friend Noël Coward's play *Blithe Spirit*; she was asked to play Arcati but declined, Margaret Rutherford memorably replacing her. A pastel of Dane by the artist Fred Yates is in the National Portrait Gallery.

John Alexander DANFORD 1913–1970 Sculptor, mural painter and watercolourist. Born in Dublin, he studied at Wimbledon School of Art, 1929–34, under S Nicholson Babb, and at the Royal Academy Schools, 1934–9, where he won a gold medal in 1935. He was granted the Landseer Scholarship in 1934 and a British Institution Scholarship three years later. Exhibited RA, RHA and in Nigeria. Danford was British Council representative for a time in Sierra Leone and his work is in permanent collections in West Africa and Ireland. Finally was known as a colourful character in Kinsale, County Cork, Ireland, walking around the town with a male companion both dressed in African finery. He also completed African murals in Ballinacurra House, where he lived.

Amanda DANICIC 1957– Painter, printmaker and teacher, based in north London. She did a foundation course at Carmarthen College of Art, 1975; graduated in fine art (painting) from St Martin's School of Art, 1989; studied postgraduate printmaking at the Central School of Art, 1994; and for a postgraduate certificate in education at Greenwich University, 2002. Danicic cited as influential teachers Cecil Collins, Jack Piesse and the etcher Norman Ackroyd. She taught extensively, venues including Holloway Prison, Islington adult education classes and the University of East London, there from 2003 as course leader of the design foundation course. Group shows included Ben Uri Gallery, 1992; Amy Friedlander Prize, first prize winner, Camden Central Library, 1998; and The Discerning Eye, Mall Galleries, 2003. Among Danicic's solo exhibitions were The Lyric Gallery, Hammersmith, 1993, and Huntingdon Gallery, 2003. In 2004 Danicic's work was chosen by the television personality Michael Parkinson on the BBC programme *Star Portraits with Rolf Harris*, pictures from which toured from the County Hall Gallery in 2005.

Alice Laura DANIEL 1892– Painter and draughtsman. She studied art privately with the watercolourist J Paul Brinson. Exhibited BWS. Lived near Stockport, Cheshire.

David DANIELLS 1949– Realistic painter, born in Stony Stratford, Buckinghamshire. He worked in varied media and was committed to producing work based on direct observation. Daniells showed at many venues in Britain and abroad and from 1999 with W H Patterson, being included in the gallery's 2004 show Six Selected Artists. Daniells contributed to several magazines and books on painting, being featured in *International Artist*.

Alfred DANIELS 1924– Painter, teacher and writer of books on art, born in London, where he continued to live. Daniels studied at Woolwich Polytechnic, 1943–4, then service in the Royal Air Force, resuming his studies at Royal College of Art, 1947–50, undertaking postgraduate studies in mural design, 1950–2. Daniels was to hold a number of teaching posts: from 1951–76 at Hornsey College of Art; from 1964–9 part-time at Royal College of Art; from 1973–88 part-time at Sir John Cass, City of London Polytechnic; 1976–80 part-time at Middlesex Polytechnic; then again at the Royal College, 1984–7. Daniels showed widely in mixed shows from the early 1950s. He was one of Jack Beddington's *Young Artists of Promise*, in the 1957 book of that title, and his stylised depiction of people and places remained remarkably consistent. He handled a number of commissions, including murals for Hammersmith Town Hall. His books included *Painting and Drawing*, 1961; *Drawing Made Simple*, 1962; and *Landscape Painting in Watercolour and Oil*, 1980. His many solo shows included Zwemmer Gallery from mid-1950s, later ones including Belgrave Gallery, 1989: Alfred Daniels in Israel. Daniels was a member of RWS and RBA. Leeds University and Greater London Council held his work.

Beverley DANIELS 1959– Painter who did a pre-degree access course at Portsmouth College of Art and Design, 1988–9; completed three years of a five-year course for a fine art diploma, Southampton Institute of Higher Education, 1989–92; and gained an honours degree in fine art, painting, at Winchester School of Art, 1992–5. Mixed shows included Guildhall Gallery, Winchester, 1994; Beatrice Royal Gallery, Eastleigh, 1995; New Academy Gallery, 1997; Nature in Art, *The Artist* tour, 1998; and Flowers East, 1999. Later solo exhibitions included Bracknell Gallery, South Hill Park, Bracknell, 1999. Thamesdown Borough Council and Bupa House hold her work. Lived in Fareham, Hampshire.

Harvey DANIELS 1936– Printmaker, painter and teacher, born in London, was married to the artist Judy Stapleton. He studied at Willesden College of Art, 1951–6, Slade School of Fine Art with Lynton Lamb and Ceri Richards, 1956–8, and at Brighton College of Art, 1958–9. Was a member of the Printmakers' Council of Great Britain, taught at Brighton College and at London University. Victoria & Albert Museum, Towner Art Gallery in Eastbourne and several American museums hold his work. Solo shows included Pallant House, Chichester, 1995, with a painting retrospective at White Gallery, Hove, 2001. Lived in Brighton, Sussex.

Leonard DANIELS 1909–1998 Influential administrator, teacher and painter, with a special interest in portraiture, born in London, who studied at Regent Street Polytechnic and Royal College of Art, 1929–32, gaining the portrait prize in his final year. He early on showed sporting prowess, notably as a runner and long-distance cyclist. Exhibited at Goupil and Redfern Galleries in the 1930s. After teaching in several schools, including Taunton's in Southampton, Daniels was on the staff of Southampton and Portsmouth Schools of Art; during World War II, as well as being head of painting at Leeds College of Art, he did commissioned work for the War Artists' Advisory Committee; then in 1947 was appointed principal of Camberwell School of Art retiring in 1974. His predecessor William Johnstone had laid the foundations of an impressive staff, to which Daniels added, teachers during his time there, as its longest serving principal, including Edward Ardizzone, Martin Bloch, William Coldstream, Richard Eurich, Robert Medley, Victor Pasmore, Claude Rogers, Michael Rothenstein and Karel Vogel. Under Daniels' civilised, calm direction, Camberwell was steered through major changes. He was elected president of the National Society for Art Education in 1965. After retirement, Daniels taught adult education classes in Kingston, before moving to Midhurst, Sussex. Died in Winchester, Hampshire, where there was an exhibition of work by him and his wife soon after in the cathedral. Imperial War Museum and Southampton City Art Gallery hold examples.

Peter DANIELS 1937–1998 Landscape painter using a rich palette, born in Salford, Lancashire. He trained at Manchester College of Art, worked in London in advertising and marketing, then in 1975 began painting full-time. In 1984 he moved to Pembrokeshire, in 1987 opening the Pink House Gallery, Nine Wells, Solva, Haverfordwest. Exhibitions included Adams Fine Art, Albany Gallery in Cardiff and Dessin Gallery, in Los Angeles, all 1991; and Cleveland Bridge Gallery, Bath, and International Art Expo, New York, both 1992. In 1993, Daniels was commissioned by the Nimbus Foundation to paint six huge murals for the interior of Wyastone Concert Hall, near Monmouth. After months of detailed research and preparation and the purchase of a larger studio to allow him to work on the canvases, he was found to have inoperable spinal cancer. Lacking the strength to tackle the project, he produced smaller paintings to be digitally enlarged. His widow Elizabeth and Nimbus trustees carried out Daniels' project after his death, the paintings being unveiled in 2003. Later that year, HTV filmed them for a documentary.

Stephen DANIELS 1955– Sculptor who did a part-time course at Bath Academy of Art, 1973–80. Took part in group exhibition at Mignon Gallery, Bath, 1977, from same year showing at RWA Autumn Open; with Bath Society of Artists from 1978; and in 1st RWA Open Sculpture Exhibition, 1993. Had solo show at Alwin Gallery, 1984, which continuously exhibited his work. Horse and Rider, Dark Crusaders and Seafarers were leading themes of his sculptures. Lived in Colerne, Wiltshire.

George DANNATT 1915– Artist in all media, photographer and writer on music who from 1940–70, apart from Army service, 1941–4, was a chartered surveyor in the family business, qualifying in 1940. He was born in Blackheath, London, and attended Colfe's Grammar School and the College of Estate Management. From 1944–56 was a regular *News Chronicle* music critic, being an authority on Sir Arthur Bliss. In 1948 Dannatt began his association with the Dorset area, photographing it and taking up part-time residence in 1958, two years after reviving his interest in painting. In this he was self-taught. From 1963 Dannatt began an association with the Cornish painters. He was influenced by Penwith artists and especially John Wells through Ben Nicholson. Became an associate of Penwith Society of Art and a member of Newlyn Society of Artists. Dannatt had a three-man show with Wells and Alexander Mackenzie at Orion Gallery, Penzance, in 1975 (the same artists shared the exhibition Newlyn Revisited at Broad Street Gallery, Lyme Regis, in 1999), having a solo show at Newlyn Art Gallery, 1976. Other solo exhibitions included Galerie Schreiner, Basel, Switzerland, in 1980–1; Galerie Artica, Cuxhaven, Germany, from 1984; New Ashgate Gallery, Farnham, 1992; Dorset County Museum, Dorchester, 1993; Book Gallery, St Ives, 1995 and 1997; and Russell-Cotes Art Gallery, Bournemouth, 1997, accompanied by the publication of *George Dannatt: Three Essays*. In that year also Quest & Bequest at Dorset County Museum included work by Dannatt and St Ives area artists from The George Dannatt Trust Collection. There were further shows at Maltby Contemporary Art, Winchester, in 2000 and 2003. In 2004 The Winchester Gallery at Winchester School of Art showed works by Dannatt, with others from the collection formed by him and his wife Ann. George Dannatt: Four Decades was at the Osborne Samuel Gallery in 2005. There was a retrospective at Newlyn Art Gallery in 1981. Royal Air Force Museum, Hendon, holds his work, which employed geometric forms with lyricism and which used a warm and economic palette. The monograph *George Dannatt One Way of Seeing*, 1990, in English and German, illuminates the artist's work. Lived in Tisbury, Wiltshire.

Adam DANT 1967– Inventive, idiosyncratic artist involved in printmaking, drawing and installation, also a curator, born in Cambridge. He graduated with first-class honours in graphic design at Liverpool School of Art, 1985–9, under Peter Bailey, with a period under Rini Dhumal at MS University's faculty of fine arts, Baroda, India, gaining his master's degree in fine art printmaking at Royal College of Art, 1989–91, taught by Tim Mara. Awards included Hochschule die Künste, Berlin, Germany, with an Erasmus Scholarship, under Dieter Hacker, and Cité Internationale des Arts, Paris, France, studio award, both 1991, and British School at Rome, Scholar in Printmaking, 1992–3. Among residencies were Eremo di Santa Catarina, Elba, Italy, 1993–4. Later curatorial work included Upset, New approaches to Print, James Colman Fine Arts, 1996. Many group shows included Out of the Wood, Tate Gallery Liverpool, 1992; Whitechapel Open, Whitechapel Art Gallery, 1994; Sex, Flowers East, 1996; Picture Stories, Victoria Miro Gallery; and Host, Tramway, Glasgow, 1998. Later solo shows included Total Liquidation, Galerie Brighi, Paris, 1998, and The Institute of Coincidence, Hayward Gallery, 1999. In 1995 Dant started a five-year project *Donald Parsnips' Daily Journal*, a small comic-type publication which he drew, funded and distributed in his local Shoreditch area. The Donald Parsnips Reality Orchestra, a collection of buskers, performed some of his 1,000 Sung Artworks for World Peace at the ICA in 1998. The Arts Council, Museum of Modern Art in New York and several French public collections hold Dant's work. In 2002, Dant's An Anecdotal Plan of Tate Britain won 1st Prize in The Jerwood Drawing Prize.

Itzhak (sometimes Yitzhak) DANZIGER 1916–1979 Sculptor, painter and teacher, born in Berlin, Germany, who emigrated to Palestine in 1923. He studied with the sculptor Zeev Ben Zvi; at the Slade School of Fine Art with the carver A H Gerrard, 1934–7; then landscape and garden design at London University, 1946–54. From 1955, Danziger taught at the Technion, Haifa, Israel. His most famous sculpture was Nimrod, created in 1939, which became an ideal of the "Canaanites". Danziger was killed in a traffic accident in 1979. A catalogue of his works, *Itzhak Danziger Makom*, was published by Hakibbutz Hameuchad Publishing House in 1982. His son was the sculptor Jeremy Danziger.

Jeremy DANZIGER 1949– Sculptor, draughtsman and printmaker, son of the sculptor Itzhak Danziger, whose mother was also a sculptor. Jeremy gained an honours degree from Camberwell School of Arts and Crafts, followed by a postgraduate degree from Goldsmiths' College School of Art. Exhibited in a number of international drawing biennales and at Mall, Morley and Curwen Galleries. His powerful abstract sculpture Contained was included in Art on Show, The Gallery in Cork Street, 2001.

Peter DARACH 1940– Artist working in a range of media, born in Spondon, Derbyshire. He studied at Royal College of Art, 1962–5, and was an "? [sic] outsider painter since 1968, living in Scotland, Italy and France", later in London. His large oil on board ... Rolled into One won a prize in the 1995–6 John Moores Liverpool Exhibition. Arts Council acquired a series of pencil drawings, Sue in Love, from the artist in 1985.

Stephen John DARBISHIRE 1940– Painter, musician and teacher, born in Greenodd, Lancashire. He won a scholarship to Byam Shaw School of Drawing and Painting, 1957–9, teachers including Peter Greenham, Peter Garrard and Bernard Dunstan. In 1960–1 Darbishire was a lay missionary to West Africa with the Irish Missionary Fathers, teaching art and English, then between 1962–7 was a musician and singer with a band. He then studied at Charlotte Mason, Ambleside, teachers' training college, spending a year at St Martin's in Lancaster, obtaining an honours degree, followed by teaching, 1972–83, then full-time painting. Darbishire was made a member of RBA in 1983, also belonging to Lake Artists' Society, and he showed at RA, RP and NEAC. From 1989 he had annual shows at Richard Hagen Gallery, Broadway. Henry Ling & Sons published greetings cards of Darbishire's work.

Phil DARBY 1938– Self-taught artist in oil and oil pastel, born in Birmingham. Left school at 15 and worked in the printing trade. After finishing his National Service in 1960 Darby began seriously to study painting, taking many jobs to finance it. In 1979 moved to Sennen, Cornwall, where he built his own studio and painted full-time. Became a member of Newlyn Society of Artists in 1974. Showed with RWA, Newlyn Orion Galleries in Penzance, Wills Lane Gallery in St Ives and elsewhere. Had solo shows in 1987 at Galerie Artica, Cuxhaven, Germany, at Queen's Elm Gallery and at Brown's Gallery, Penzance. Open University holds his work. Darby's pictures were mostly small, "both abstract and what I call my Voyages of the Red Ship (a series of highly stylised seascapes suggesting dreamlike voyages)."

John DARGAN 1963– Painter of Hyper-Realist works, such as his oil on panel Caravan (Four), in John Moores Liverpool Exhibition, 1999. His solo exhibition Nothing Much, at Gainsborough's House, Sudbury in 2000, examined anodyne corners of the urban landscape, including paintings, drawings, colour photographs and a video. Born in Margate, Kent, Dargan studied at Canterbury College of Art, 1983–6, gaining his master's at Chelsea School of Art, 1987–8. He was artist-in-residence, Ipswich Town Football Club, 1989–90. Other group shows included Whitechapel Open and Royal Over-Seas League, both 1998. Other solo exhibitions included Estuary English, South Hill Park Arts Centre, Bracknell, and Deadpan, Seven Interactive, both 1999. Lived in London.

Andrew DARKE 1948– Creator of constructions from wood, born in Preston, Lancashire, who began sculpting in mid-1960s. Although he obtained some support from Yorkshire Arts, Darke did a number of part-time jobs. Showed at Huddersfield Piazza, Yorkshire Sculpture Park, and Kenwood House in Hampstead, 1983. Among Darke's publicly sited sculptures are Oak Log Fall, 1981, at Oakwell Country Park, near Leeds, and Sliced Log 4, 1983, overlooking Chesil Beach, Dorset. Darke was a self-taught artist who lived in Holmfirth, West Yorkshire.

Michael DARLING 1923– Painter, born in London, who studied at Harrow School of Art and at the Royal Academy Schools with Henry Rushbury. Showed at NEAC, RA and RBA and London County Council bought his work, which he signed M D. Lived in London.

John Leonard DARLISON 1931– Artist in watercolour, pastel and oil, and teacher, born in Leyton, Essex. He was mainly self-taught, but did have lessons from Angus Rand, John Blockley and Edward Wesson, 1980–3. Darlison became a full-time artist in 1982, ran courses in France until 1986, then from his home address in Glasbury, Herefordshire. Using an Impressionistic technique Darlison aimed "to produce a sense of place and atmosphere in landscape painting". Group exhibitions included Albany Gallery in Cardiff, New Gallery in Swansea and David Curzon Gallery. Had a series of solo exhibitions, including Arts Club, Fairfield Halls in Croydon, St David's Hall in Cardiff, Riverside Gallery in Crickhowell and Island Gallery in Victoria, British Columbia. Government Art Collection (Queen's Jubilee Purchase) holds Darlison's work, as do many private collections in Britain and abroad.

Fred DARRINGTON 1910–2002 Sand sculptor whose creations on the beach at Weymouth entertained visitors for almost 70 years. He was born in Andover, Hampshire. As a child he began building realistic models on the sand, encouraging visitors to throw loose coins into a bucket. Left school at 14 and during the summer months turned his childtime hobby into a business. From an early age Darrington was an accomplished driver and motorcyclist, and although in 1936 he was offered engineering work with Rolls-Royce in London, sand-sculpting continued during frequent trips to Weymouth. During World War II Darrington was employed by the Americans at Bushey Park, afterwards settling at Esher, Surrey, working in electrical engineering until, in retirement, he was able to sand-sculpt for months at a time, staying with his daughter. As well as sand castles, he created human and animal forms, fruit and depictions of Last Supper, models made more realistic with the addition of poster paints. The family tradition was continued after his death by his grandson Mark Anderson. Darrington kept a photographic record of his transitory works. Died in Esher.

John DARWELL 1955– Versatile artist who did a foundation course at Bolton College of Art and Design, 1974–6, graduating with honours from Manchester Polytechnic, 1976–80, from 1999 researching at Sunderland University for his doctorate into the photographic depiction of mental health. Darwell gained many awards, including North West Arts, Arts Council and a series of travel, training and production awards from Northern Arts. He had wide part-time, visiting lecturer and workshop experience in Britain and abroad, also as an external examiner. Among residencies were Bolton College of Education, 1985; Stockport Art Gallery, 1986; Manchester City Art Gallery, 1988; Manor Gallery, Carlisle, 1989; and Durham Art Gallery, 1995–6. His work was widely published in the photographic and other media. Later group exhibitions included The Shed, Collins Gallery, Glasgow, 1999; and Disaster Areas, ArtConnexion, Amsterdam, Netherlands, and A Different World, part of River Journeys, The Lowry, Salford, both 2003. His numerous solo shows latterly included By Association, Tom Blau Gallery, 1998; Legacy, Tullie House Museum & Art Gallery, Carlisle, 2001; Consequences, inaugural exhibition, Gallery Oldham in Oldham, 2002; and *(h)arris* Images from the Western Isles, installed at stations along the Cumbrian Coastal Rail Line in 2004. These works formed one segment of Darwell's ongoing exploration of the line between land and sea. He lived in Carlisle, Cumbria.

Robin DARWIN 1910–1974 Painter and principal of the Royal College of Art. Born in London, Darwin after Eton College and Cambridge University attended the Slade School of Fine Art. He exhibited at the RA and other main London galleries. After World War II service in the Ministry of Home Security, Darwin was in 1945–6 at the Council of Industrial Design. While there he wrote a report titled *The Training of the Industrial Designer*, which led to his appointment as head of the Royal College, where he stayed from 1948–71. Darwin's reforms were considerable. Although he advocated initially that the training of the industrial designer – seen to be essential by the Ministry of Education – meant that easel painting was not a priority, in practice he became an adept promoter of the College's special contribution to the fine arts. The College assumed independent university status under his direction. Darwin's administrative abilities – he was knighted in 1964 – overshadowed his very real talent as a painter. Landscape was his main interest, although he was a good portrait painter, and he produced highly professional and atmospheric examples in oil and watercolour in Britain and abroad. Lived near Marlborough, Wiltshire.

Geoffrey DASHWOOD 1947– Sculptor and draughtsman, most noted for his sculptures of wildlife; a keen naturalist from his early years. For some years Dashwood worked for the Forestry Commission, then for about a decade sold drawings to local collectors, illustrating official wildlife literature. In the early 1960s spent a few weeks at Southampton College of Art, but the environment did not suit him. In 1986–7 Dashwood won Best Sculpture Award for exhibits at SWLA. Showed at Sladmore Gallery; Courcoux and Courcoux, Salisbury; Wildfowl and Wetlands Trust, Slimbridge; and John Davies Contemporary, Stow-on-the-Wold. Solo exhibition of his bronzes at Gallery Pangolin, Chalford, 2002.

May Lilian DAUBAN 1907–1989 Watercolourist, born in Worthing, Sussex, daughter of Sir Claude Ricketts. She was educated at St Michael's, Guildford, also studying art in Paris. Her husband was in the Army and she exhibited widely in India and Pakistan before World War II, winning a gold medal in Calcutta. In Britain was a member of RWS and showed at RBA Galleries and in the provinces, although she withdrew from exhibiting in later years. Lived in Selsdon, Surrey.

Pamela DAUKES 1930– Painter in oil who studied at Bromley College of Art, latterly with Tom Coates and Roy Freer. Was a member of the Reigate Society of Artists; won a drawing award with UA, 1995; other group shows including Cider House Gallery, Bletchingley, Bank Street Gallery in Sevenoaks and Century Gallery, Datchet. Had a solo exhibition at Talent Store. Lived in Oxted, Surrey.

Frank William Leslie DAVENPORT 1905–1973 Painter, born in Harrow, Middlesex, who studied at Harrow Technical School, then Royal College of Art, gaining his painting diploma in 1927. Showed at RA, LG and at *Daily Express* Young British Artists. Among his main works were Pinner View Lane and Crown Street, Harrow on the Hill. Lived at Hillingdon Heath, near where he was born, for many years, later in Norwich, Norfolk. Sometimes exhibited as Davenport or as Leslie Davenport, his singular townscapes being offered by Bonhams in The East Anglian View sales, Lynford Hall, Mundford, 1999 and 2001.

Ian DAVENPORT 1966– Abstract painter, born in Sidcup, Kent. He studied at Northwich College of Art and Design, 1984–5, and Goldsmiths' College School of Art, 1985–8. His group exhibitions included Young Contemporaries, at Whitworth Art Gallery, Manchester, 1985; Karsten Schubert Gallery, 1988; the South Bank Centre's touring exhibition The British Art Show 1990; John Moores Liverpool Exhibition, 2002; and Days Like These, Tate Britain, 2003. Was nominated for the Turner Prize in 1991. Davenport's method of working, as exemplified by his Waddington Galleries show in 1993, was to pour paint from a small scaffold using a vessel with an adjustable head to regulate the breadth of each pour. In 1999 he had solo shows at Dundee Contemporary Arts, Dundee, Whitechapel Art Gallery and Museum of Contemporary Art, Chicago, in America, and won a prize at John Moores Liverpool Exhibition. In 2000–1 he showed work at Tate Liverpool. Waddington Galleries showed his New Paintings in 2003. Davenport was at the John Moores again in 2004. Lived in London.

Leslie DAVENPORT: *see* **Frank William Leslie DAVENPORT**

Edith DAVEY fl. c.1915–1950 Portrait painter, black-and-white artist and miniaturist, brought up in Lincolnshire, who studied at Lincoln School of Art, then Royal College of Art, where she won a silver medal. Exhibited RA, RI, RMS, WIAC, SWA, Walker Art Gallery, Liverpool, and Paris Salon. Davey did a number of book illustrations and had work purchased by Huddersfield Art Gallery. Lived in London.

Grenville DAVEY 1961– Abstract sculptor, born in Launceston, Cornwall. He studied 1981–5 at Exeter College of Art and Design and Goldsmiths' College School of Art, gaining a bachelor's degree in fine art. Took part in many mixed shows internationally and in Britain, including Venice Biennale, 1988; National Museum of Modern Art, Tokyo, 1989; in 1990 Newport Harbor Museum in California and South Bank Centre's touring exhibition The British Art Show 1990. From 1987 had solo shows at Lisson Gallery, others including Primo Piano, Rome, 1989; Stichting De

Appel Foundation, Amsterdam, 1990; Galerie Crousel-Robelin Bama, Paris, and Kunsthalle, Berne, 1991; and Kunstverein für die Rheinlande und Westfalen, Düsseldorf, Galleria Franz Paludetto, Turin, and Chisenhale Gallery, all in 1992. In that year won Turner Prize Award, at Tate Gallery. Leeds Museums and Galleries hold sculpture and works on paper by Davey. Lived in London.

Leonard John DAVEY 1913– Ceramic sculptor and potter, born in Nottingham. He studied at Leicester College of Art, 1926–8, and Edinburgh College of Art, 1945–9. Ran the Davey Pottery at Bridge of Dee, Kirkcudbrightshire, and showed in crafts exhibitions throughout Scotland. Leicester Museum and Shipley Art Gallery in Gateshead hold examples.

Peter DAVEY 1946– Painter in oil, tempera and watercolour, performance artist and teacher, born in Teignmouth, Devon. He studied at Reading University under Claude Rogers and Terry Frost, 1967–8; at Chelsea School of Art under Myles Murphy and Brian Young, 1968–71; and there again with Ian Stephenson, 1975–6. Between 1972–5 Davey was a member of Bernsteins, founders of Obstacle Art; he did occasional performances with The Kipper Kids, and solo; and was a furniture painter, teacher and painter and decorator. Lived in Munich, Germany, 1977–9, and 1992–3. Group shows included Garage, 1975; ICA, Northern Young Contemporaries and Stowells Trophy, all 1976; Hayward Annual at Hayward Gallery and Galerie Defet, Nuremberg, both 1979; and in the 1990s especially in Nuremberg, including Art 5, 1990, and in America. Solo shows included Garage, 1975; Felicity Samuels, 1977; and in 1988 at Kunstfocus, Munich. Davey's main works comprised trompe l'oeil wood and marble grain, 1973–6; large figurative works, 1988–92; large abstract works, 1992–3; and from 1994 watercolours, on-the-spot landscapes. Soutine, John Marin and William Gillies' watercolours were admired by him. Lived in Ashurst Wood, Sussex.

Allen DAVID 1926– Painter, sculptor in glass, photographer, gallery administrator and teacher, born in Bombay, India, who moved to Melbourne, Australia, in 1948. Studied drawing and architecture at the University of Melbourne; had a solo show at Melbourne Tourist Bureau in 1955; and ran the Gallery of Contemporary Art at St Kilda, 1958–60. In 1962, David provided photographs for the painter Russell Drysdale's book *Form, Colour, Grandeur.* By the late 1960s David was working in London, showing at Camden Arts Centre and at All Hallows, London Wall. At both venues, David, who had already been commissioned to provide a large glass screen for Melbourne University, showed a Perspex model of his Glass Fountain, which was eventually erected at Guildhall Piazza, 1969. The story of how it came to be placed there and a photograph of it are in Philip Ward-Jackson's *Public Sculpture of the City of London.* David later lived in Israel, producing public sculpture in Tel-Aviv, and was latterly the staff of the New School in New York, America.

Enrico DAVID 1966– Artist and teacher working in a range of styles and media, born in Ancona, Italy, who settled in London. He was first attracted to the city in 1986, but after seven months, and hating it, he went to New York, in America, and Brussels, Belgium, before returning to London in the early 1990s to study. From 1990–1 he did a Lina Garnade Foundation Course, then graduated in fine art from Central St Martins. After various subsistence jobs, such as market research and translation, he stopped working in sculpture and began cutting out photographs from fashion magazines as a start for paintings. Having built up a coherent body of work, showing in smaller, offbeat galleries, he was spotted by the collector Charles Saatchi, among others, who acquired examples. David's residencies included Camden Arts Centre, 1999, and The British Council, Delhi, India, 2001. He was a visiting fine art lecturer at Central St Martins, 1999; in painting at the Slade School of Fine Art, 2000; and became a full-time lecturer there from 2001. His performances that year included Documentation of a Ceremony, Craft Museum, Delhi, and A Public Appearance, The Russian Bar, London (with Donateller). Took part in many group shows in Britain and abroad and had a series of solo exhibitions from 1999, later ones including Madreperlage, Cabinet, and David, Project Art Centre, Dublin, Ireland, both 2003, and Douche That Dwarf, Transmission, Glasgow, 2004.

Illtyd DAVID 1906–1992 Self-taught painter and sculptor, born at Abertridwr, near Caerphilly, South Wales. He was brought up on a farm, left school at 13 to work on a farm and became a ploughing and hedging champion. After five years in Canada, 1927–32, was an agricultural engineer, 1933–57, then a colliery engineer. Began painting in 1964, inspired by the biography of Sir John Millais by his son. David was a member of RCamA, also showing with NEAC, RA, SEA, at Royal National Eisteddfod and at Paris Salon, where he won gold and silver medals in the mid-1970s. WAC and National Museum of Wales hold his work, which was included in Miner-Artists: The Art of Welsh Coal Workers, National Museum & Gallery, Cardiff, 2000. This demonstrated David's antiquarian's curiosity about the agricultural and industrial life of his valley, preserved in writing and a number of ambitious narrative pictures, such as his Grosfaen and Rhymney Valley Sagas. Lived at Deri, Mid-Glamorgan.

Michele DAVID 1968– Painter who gained an honours degree in fine art, painting, at Glasgow School of Art, 1986–90, where she won the John and Mabel Craig Bequest in the latter year. Among other awards were a Scottish Arts Council Grant in 1993 and the Villiers David Travel Prize, 1996. She won an Alastair Salvesen Trust Art Scholarship, RSA, west and southwest states of America, and a Winsor and Newton Award, Art in Nature Competition, Gloucester, both 1998. She was a member of the Glasgow Society of Women Artists. She was artist-in-residence, Shetland Isles, appointed by the Scottish Arts Council and Shetland Arts Trust, in 1992, in 1994–5 holding a residency at Drumcroon Education Centre, Wigan. Others included James Cook University, Queensland, Australia, 1996, and School of Art, Hobart, Tasmania, 1997. In 1995 The Archer Group Commissioned her, and in 1996 both Victoria Hospice, Kirkcaldy, and *Shetland Isles Calendar* (for 1997). Group shows included Berkeley Square Gallery, 1990; Ben Uri Gallery, 1991; Worcester Art Gallery & Museum, Worcester, 1994; Christopher Hull Gallery, 1996; and Young Contemporaries, Albemarle Gallery, 2002. In 1997 she shared a show at Cadogan Contemporary, later solo shows including Shetland Museum (which holds her work), 1996, and Berkeley Square Gallery and RSA, both 1998. David said that her work offered "a close up and intimate view of the environment in which we live, emphasising different aspects of the natural world, free from human existence...focusing on the landscape's delicate and vulnerable fragments."

Nathan DAVID 1930– Figurative sculptor and teacher, born and lived in London, who was in advertising until 1960, teaching graphic design part-time at Watford College of Art. Studied sculpture at City & Guilds of London Art School, teaching it part-time at Sir John Cass College. Showed at RA Summer Exhibition. Commissions included Ondine, Dame Margot Fonteyn, 1975, near Reigate railway station, and fountains, 1982, at Sutton Court, Surrey, all works in bronze.

Yael DAVID-COHEN 1942– Artist whose output included coloured abstract etchings and paintings on textiles, born in Jerusalem in what is now Israel. She graduated from the Art School and University in Tel-Aviv, with postgraduate studies at St Martin's School of Art. Took part in numerous mixed exhibitions internationally, including Triennale of Israeli Graphic Art, Haifa, 1983; Three-artist show, The Craft Centre, Royal Exchange Theatre, Manchester, 1991; Printmakers' Council, Making a Print tour, 1992–3; prize winner, Contemporary Prints, Hatton Gallery, Newcastle upon Tyne, 1994; Textiles Exhibition, Drumcroon Education Art Centre, Wigan, 1996; International Biennial of Drawing and Graphic Art, Gyor, Hungary, 1999; and American Craft Museum Collection UBS PaineWebber Art Gallery, New York, 2002. Later solo exhibitions included The Coningsby Gallery, from 2000. British Museum, Victoria & Albert Museum, The Philadelphia Museum of Art and The American Craft Museum are among public collections holding examples. Lived in London.

Colin DAVIDSON 1968– Painter, illustrator and designer, born in Belfast, Northern Ireland, where he was educated at the Methodist College, 1980–7, gaining a first-class honours degree in illustration and design at University of Ulster, Belfast, 1987–91. He formed Colin Davidson Design in Hollywood in 1994. In that year Davidson won the Creative Review Award; Winsor & Newton Gold; Association of Illustrators Award; ICAD Craft Award, Dublin; and in California, America, the Communication Arts Award; in 1997 the RUA Silver Medal. Painting commissions included the Coal Advisory Service, 1990; Shell UK, 1992; and for Cobra Golf USA portraits of Greg Norman, Hale Irwin, Ben Crenshaw and Seve Ballesteros, 1995–6. Group shows included RUA, Mall Galleries and BBC. In 1997 Davidson had a first solo show at Tom Caldwell Galleries, in Belfast, having painted a portrait of Caldwell in 1996, with others in 2002 and 2004. Other one-man exhibitions included Solomon Gallery, Dublin, 1999. Davidson's landscape and figurative work was characterised by strong, Expressionist brushstrokes. The BBC, Queen's University, Belfast, and corporate collections hold examples.

Ian Stuart DAVIDSON 1936– Sculptor and teacher, son of an artist, born in Sheffield, Yorkshire. He was educated in South Africa, studying art at Camberwell School, 1960–1, Chelsea College of Art, 1962–3, and did a postgraduate certificate under Bernard Meadows at Royal College of Art. Lectured at Rochdale College of Art and at other schools in the provinces, showing in London and elsewhere. Manchester Loan Collection holds his work. Lived for a time in Brixham, Devon.

Lindsay DAVIDSON 1948–1986 Artist, born in Yorkshire, who studied at Exeter Art School, 1966–9. She was a founder-member of the Black Box Theatre, an experimental visual theatre company formed by John Epstein in 1969, which until 1972 gave performances throughout the country. These included Museum of Modern Art, Oxford, and the Round House. Davidson's group shows included LG, Whitechapel Art Gallery, 1972; The Nude, Morley Gallery, 1976; and Award Winners, Thorndike Gallery, Leatherhead, 1979. In 1982 she shared a show, Figurative Art Today, with John Epstein and Dennis Creffield, at 7 Dials Gallery. Later solo shows included Morley Gallery and Southover Gallery, Lewes, both 1979, the year Davidson won a major award from South East Arts Association.

Majel DAVIDSON 1885–1969 Artist, born in Aberdeen where she was educated at the High School, then graduated in 1907 from Gray's School of Art, having specialised in painting and pottery. In 1908 Davidson moved to Paris, studying with Charles Guérin and starting a life's friendship with the artist Edward Overton-Jones who was through his family strongly connected with the pottery industry. Although Davidson exhibited at the Salon d'Automne in 1912, World War I interrupted; she earned the Military Medal as a volunteer ambulance driver. Prompted by the Canadian artist Katrina Buell, Davidson moved to Toronto in the mid-1920s where she associated with Group of Seven artists. Back in Europe, she concentrated on pottery and her work for the International Council of Women, only returning seriously to painting in her mid-sixties while living near Stirling. Her work shared a show with that of Alexander Graham Munro which was put on in 1989 at Portland Gallery, in association with William Hardie.

Rowland DAVIDSON 1942– Painter and teacher, born in Belfast, Northern Ireland, who graduated in fine art from the local College of Art, teachers including Tom Carr and John Luke. Became head of department at a Belfast boys' school, in 1981 began to paint seriously again and in 1987 gave up teaching. Davidson's painting, inspired by Rembrandt, Degas, Van Gogh, Auerbach and Kokoschka, was figurative, often of domestic interiors, always demonstrating an interest in light. His work was used on book-jackets, calendars and prints. Showed widely in galleries throughout Ireland, including The Eakin Gallery, Belfast, and had several one-man exhibitions.

Aubrey Claud DAVIDSON-HOUSTON 1906–1995 Painter and draughtsman, born in Dublin, Ireland, into a military family. He attended Royal Military College, Sandhurst, and was a regular soldier for 23 years, always interested in art. While a prisoner of war in Germany for five years made drawings of 600 fellow-prisoners. Upon retirement in 1949 Davidson-Houston studied at Slade School of Fine Art with William Coldstream for three years. Attended St Martin's School of Art part-time and worked for a time with Sir Gerald Kelly. Davidson-Houston was noted as a portrait painter, exhibiting at RP, NS, RCamA, RSA and at Paris Salon. Had a solo show at Walker's Galleries. HRH The Duke of Edinburgh was among his subjects and his works are held by several members of the royal family. Lived in Esher, Surrey, with a studio in London. Died at Allington Court, St Albans, Hertfordshire.

Alan DAVIE 1920– Painter, born in Grangemouth, Stirlingshire, whose father was a painter and printmaker. Studied at Edinburgh College of Art, 1937–40, where he was influenced by John Maxwell. Won several scholarships. After serving in Army in World War II Davie worked for a time as a professional jazz musician. He was also interested in writing poetry, designed textiles and pottery and worked as a jeweller. By the time of his first solo show, at Grant's Bookshop, Edinburgh, in 1946, Davie's interest in the work of Paul Klee and primitive artists was evident. Over the years there were a number of such influences on his work: the American Abstract Expressionists such as Pollock and Gorky, Oriental mysticism including Zen Buddhism, gliding and swimming and Indian mythology. Davie viewed art as a way of gaining spiritual enlightenment. His later work was less expressionistic, more full of symbolism. In 1947 Davie married the artist and potter Janet Gaul, travelled in Europe and met Peggy Guggenheim, the collector, which expanded his horizons. From 1950 he was having solo shows with Gimpel Fils and had his first New York exhibition at the Catherine Viviano Gallery in New York in 1956. Was Gregory Fellow at Leeds University, 1957–9. In 1962 Davie had retrospective at Stedelijk Museum, Amsterdam, which toured, and from then he consolidated his international reputation with a number of overseas retrospectives. Fifty-year retrospective at McLellan Galleries, Glasgow, 1992, also at Barbican Art Gallery, 1993. Later shows included Scottish National Gallery of Modern Art, Edinburgh, 2000–1; Adam Gallery, Bath, 2001, an eightieth-birthday show toured by the University of Brighton; Gimpel Fils, 2001–2, small paintings from 1949–2001; and paintings and screenprints at Mercer Art Gallery and Godfrey & Watt, both in Harrogate, 2002. Jingling Space, at Tate St Ives in 2003–4, highlighted the evolution of Davie's work from the 1930s, particularly relating to his interest in Surrealism. Open Eye Gallery, Edinburgh, held an exhibition in 2004 in which recent paintings by Davie revealed that his capacity to create rich imagery was not diminished by age. Tate Gallery holds his work. Lived in Hertfordshire, St Lucia and Cornwall.

Joseph DAVIE 1965– Artist, notable as a printmaker, who was born in Glasgow and studied at its School of Art, 1983–7. He won the Guthrie Award at RSA in 1990. His exhibition A Journal of the Blackout was shown at Glasgow Print Studio in 1991, the year when he participated in Danger Artists at Work, a City Art Centre, Edinburgh, touring show. The city's collection holds his work.

Alex DAVIES 1970– Sculptor, born in Surrey, whose career included work as a blacksmith and bronze founder. Davies did a general art and design course at West Surrey College of Art and Design, Farnham, 1990–2; gained his Higher National Diploma in metal crafts, with distinction, Plymouth College of Arts, 1992–4; and attended the Frink School of Figurative Sculpture, 2000–1. He worked predominantly in steel and bronze. Exhibited in the Corpus Fine Art exhibition Hard Bodies at Arndean Gallery in 2005 and had work in the permanent collection of the McHardy Sculpture Company. Lived in Leytonstone, east London.

Alexander William DAVIES: *see* **J A D**

Allan DAVIES 1954– Artist and teacher, born in Aberdare, Glamorgan, who studied fine art at Bath Academy of Art, 1974–7. From 1978 taught art at City of Portsmouth Boys' School. His Chichester Cathedral is in the collection of the local Pallant House Gallery, which gave Davies a solo show of landscapes in 1994.

Anne DAVIES 1966– Painter, output including geometrically precise abstract work, who studied at Chesterfield College of Art, 1985–6, gaining a fine art honours degree at University of Newcastle upon Tyne, 1986–90. Exhibitions included Stonegate Gallery, York; Chalk Farm Gallery, 1994; Galerie Michel Bigue, Quebec, Canada, 1996; Byard Art, Cambridge, 1998; and Whale Contemporary Art, Exeter, 1999; Gordon Hepworth Fine Art, Newton St Cyres, 2000; Charleston Farmhouse, Firle, 2001; and New Ashgate Gallery, Farnham, and People & Places at Oliver Contemporary, both 2002. Solo exhibitions included Stables Gallery, 1997, and The Jelly Leg'd Chicken Gallery, Reading, 2003. Davies was artist-in-residence, Aycliffe Centre for Children, County Durham, 1990.

Anthony DAVIES 1947– Printmaker, born in Andover, Hampshire. He studied at Manchester School of Art and Royal College of Art, winning the Prix de Rome, British School in Rome. In 1985 Davies established his own printmaking workshop in Belfast, the year following gaining a printmaking fellowship at the Royal College of Art. Participated in many group shows in Britain and abroad and had many solo exhibitions, including Birmingham Polytechnic; Compass Gallery in Glasgow; Bluecoat Gallery, Liverpool; Hendricks Gallery, Dublin; and Limerick Gallery. In 1988 and 1989 he was resident artist in Northern Ireland and in 1990 in Hungary. Several dozen public collections in Britain, on the continent and elsewhere abroad hold work by Davies, which is infused with a strong sense of social conscience. Was married for a time to the artist Erica Daborn. Eventually moved to Grey Lynn, Auckland, New Zealand.

Arthur Edward DAVIES 1893–1989 Painter and draughtsman born in Pontrhydygroes Ystrad Meurig, Cardiganshire. He studied at Metropolitan School of Art in Dublin. Showed RA for many years, RWA, in the provinces and abroad. National Library of Wales in Aberystwyth holds his work. Lived in Norwich, Norfolk. Bonhams East Anglia included Davies's light, breezy oil on canvas The Seine at Les Andelys in its sale The East Anglian View, at Lynford Hall, Mundford, 2000.

Austin DAVIES 1926– Painter and teacher, born in Liverpool, which was the focus of his career. Studied at Liverpool School of Art, 1946–51, with Arthur Ballard and Martin Bell. Davies was a prominent exhibitor in the Liverpool Academy in the 1950s, often showing taut, gritty pictures of the city. He painted a notable portrait of the local Member of Parliament Mrs Bessie Braddock, and Davies' portrait of his first wife, the novelist Beryl Bainbridge, is in the collection of Manchester City Art Gallery. Davies also showed Arts Council, AIA, public galleries in Salford and Newcastle upon Tyne and had several one-man shows including Piccadilly Gallery, and Coombs Contemporary, 1997. Davies remarried and settled in Australia.

Benedict DAVIES 1913–1995 Painter and teacher who sometimes worked under the name Turkletob, her father's original name, and whose real name was Beatrice Rozenberg (Davies being her maiden name). She was born and educated in London and studied at Royal Academy Schools, 1934–9, under Sir Walter Russell and Thomas Monnington, winning the Arthur Hacker Silver Medal for portraiture in 1937. During World War II taught for a short time at Bideford School of Art. Trained to be a draughtsman, during World War II working for Miles Aircraft near Reading, after the war in London working in advertising for Colman, Prentis and other companies. Showed at RA and had one-man exhibitions, in 1962 and 1976, at Ben Uri Art Society. As well as still-lifes, portraits and genre scenes, in latter years she painted a major series of compositions on Jewish holocaust, having researched vanished Jewish communities in Eastern Europe. John Lewis Partnership holds her work. Her two sons from her marriage to Zigmund Rozenberg, in 1949, were Asher, also a painter, and Joshua, broadcaster and legal editor for *The Daily Telegraph*, and they helped organise a show of her work at the John Denham Gallery in 2002. Lived in Bushey Heath, Hertfordshire.

Brian DAVIES 1942– Painter, born in Isleworth, Middlesex, who pursued a banking career in London and Sydney, Australia, until 1967. From that year he was a self-taught artist whose meticulously studied work, still life and occasional Surrealism, reflected an interest in seventeenth-century Dutch and Flemish painting. Davies showed at the Paris Salon, 1974; RA Summer Exhibition from 1974; Harrods; Whitgift Galleries, Croydon; in the provinces; with Steiger in Düsseldorf, Germany; and in Hamilton, Bermuda. He had solo shows at Nishiki Gallery, Hong Kong, 1991; Granby Gallery, Derbyshire, from 1992; Unicorn Gallery, Cheshire, and Tallantyre Gallery, Morpeth, both 1993; and John Adams Fine Art, at Ebury Galleries, from 1997. Many British and foreign private collections hold examples. Lived in Twickenham, Middlesex.

Charles Richard Anthony DAVIES 1930– Painter, potter and teacher, born in Broadstairs, Kent. Studied at Southport School of Art, 1945–53, and Manchester Regional College of Art. He held a number of teaching appointments, including his old college in Manchester and Durham Technical College. Showed RCamA, at public galleries in Salford, Southport and Preston and in Belgium. Lived for some time in Durham.

Claire DAVIES 1973– Artist, born in Warrington, Cheshire, who gained her National Diploma in Design from West Surrey College of Art & Design, 1989–91; graduated with honours from Bath College of Higher Education, in fine art, painting, 1991–4; obtained an interior design certificate from Trowbridge College, 1994; attended Cyprus College of Art, Lemba, 1995; then became a Fine Art Trade Guild-commended framer, 1998. Inspired by the writing of the American nineteenth-century naturalist and philosopher Henry David Thoreau, Davies produced flower pictures in vibrant colours, as in her shared show at Pilgrim Gallery, 2002. Solo exhibitions included Source, Bath, 2000; Shannon, Bath, 2001; and Gina Conway Salon Gallery, 2002. In 1995, Davies devised an Art Trail for the City of Bath Fringe Festival, then in 1998 completed interior mural paintings for the restaurant Cubana, Lambeth. Lived at Herriard, Basingstoke, Hampshire.

Douglas DAVIES 1946– Painter, potter and teacher, educated in Edinburgh, where he studied ceramics and glass design, 1966–70, at the College of Art, with a postgraduate scholarship in ceramics and a travelling scholarship to Italy, 1970–71. Davies taught part-time at Moray House College of Education, 1971–2 and lectured in ceramics at Glasgow School of Art, 1973–86, then becoming a full-time potter and painter. His pots, stoneware and porcelain, were functional, decorative and exuberant in style; his gouache and acrylic paintings used the shape, pattern and colour of landscape almost to abstraction. Davies was a regular solo exhibitor, later shows including Macaulay Gallery in Stenton and Castlegate House, Cockermouth, both 1994, and The Scottish Gallery, Edinburgh, 1996. Douglas Davies RSW: New Works was held at Stenton Gallery in 2002. He had a studio gallery at Skirling, Biggar, Lanarkshire.

Elwyn DAVIES: *see* **John ELWYN**

Emrys DAVIES fl. from 1920s– Self-taught artist, born in Pont-rhyd-y-groes, Cardiganshire. He was by profession a retail chemist. He was made a member of PS in 1928, also exhibiting at NS and in France. Lived for many years in Maidenhead, Berkshire.

Geoff DAVIES 1944– Printmaker, painter and teacher, born in St Albans, Hertfordshire. He attended Goldsmiths' College School of Art, 1960–3 and the Royal College of Art, 1963–6. Then went to Cardiff College of Art to lecture. Took part in a number of group shows in Wales, including WAC and 56 Group, of which he was a member; as well as group exhibitions in London, including RWS show Graven Image, in 1963. Designed several theatrical sets for the Welsh Theatre Company. National Museum of Wales, Cardiff, holds his work.

Gerald DAVIES 1957– Artist and teacher born in South Wales who gained an honours degree in fine art at Wolverhampton Polytechnic, 1977–80, and his master's degree at Royal College of Art in painting, 1981–4. His teaching experience included both Wolverhampton and the Royal College as well as Bournemouth and Poole College of Art, Sunderland Polytechnic and Lancaster University, where he taught drawing full-time, becoming head of art. He was also a visiting professor at Purdue University in America, to which he gained a Fulbright Scholarship, 1990–1. Davies was the winner of a scholarship at Cité Internationale des Arts, Paris, 1983; was artist-in-residence at Durham Cathedral, 1988–9; was commissioned by the Fawe Street Press to produce work for a limited edition book *More songs from the recent wars* in 1989; and in 1993 was visiting artist in Norfolk schools. Group shows included Printmakers' Council, 1986; Artists who studied with Peter de Francia, Camden Arts Centre, 1987; and Cheltenham National Drawing Competition, 1994. He shared a show with Paul Gladwyn at East West, 1995. Later solo shows included Recent Drawings at Contact Gallery, Norwich, 1993.

Gordon DAVIES 1926– Painter, muralist, worker in many other media, designer and teacher, born in London. After Army sevice in World War II Davies studied at Camberwell

School of Arts and Crafts, 1948, and Royal College of Art, 1950–3. Taught drawing part-time at Canterbury College of Art. In 1962 assisted his friend John Ward with murals at Challock Church, Kent, and went on to complete others for Braxted Park, Essex, the Chateau Segonne in Bordeaux, the Chandos Memorial Chapel, Whitchurch, and elsewhere. Work regularly appeared at RA Summer Exhibition from early 1950s. Had solo shows at Wye College, 1967, Waterhouse Gallery, 1973, from 1977 at King Street Gallery and in 1993 at Sally Hunter Fine Art. Had a retrospective at Royal Museum and Art Gallery, Canterbury, in 1990. Extensive work for *House and Garden*, wallpaper designs for Shand-Kydd and Sanderson, shell-work panels and carpet designs were other aspects of Davies' output. Lived in Hastingleigh, Kent.

Hanlyn DAVIES 1942– Painter, printmaker and teacher, born in Dunvant, Swansea. From 1960–3 was at Swansea College of Art and from 1963–4 there and at University College, Swansea. From 1964 Davies' career was America-oriented. After two years as an assistant at Yale School of Art and Architecture and assisting Joseph Albers, held posts at Universities of Vermont and Massachusetts. Having exhibited in Britain at WAC, Royal National Eisteddfod and Glynn Vivian Art Gallery in Swansea, Davies had many solo shows in America, winning a large number of prizes. WAC and a series of American public collections hold work.

Hugh DAVIES 1949– Painter and teacher, born in Germany. He studied at Brighton College of Art, 1964–8, then Chelsea School of Art, 1968–9, eventually becoming senior lecturer at Chelsea. He exhibited at John Moores Liverpool Exhibition, 1987, having solo shows at Redfern Gallery from 1984 and at Cartwright Hall, Bradford, 1986. Artificial light and space and theatricality were features of Davies' work, which was "more concerned with the metaphor than the simile". Lived in London.

Ivor DAVIES 1935– Painter, printmaker, performance artist, writer and teacher, born in Treharris, Glamorgan, where he settled at Penarth. From 1952–6 Davies studied at Cardiff College of Art; 1956–7 at Swansea College of Art; then was at University of Lausanne, 1959–61, as an assistant teacher of English. A series of university teaching posts followed; Davies was from 1971–8 curator of Talbot Rice Art Centre, University of Edinburgh; and from 1978–88 was principal lecturer in history of art and head of the school of cultural studies, Gwent College of Higher Education, Newport. Exhibited widely in mixed shows, including Royal National Eisteddfod, SWG and SEA and was a member of RCamA, The Welsh Group, WSW and Beca, as well as the Association of Art Historians and International Association of Art Critics. Had a solo show at Traverse Theatre, Edinburgh, 1968, later ones including touring exhibition from Wrexham Arts Centre, 1992–3; Bruton Gallery, Bath, 1993; Martin Tinney, Cardiff, 1994; and Brecknock Museum, Brecon, 1995. Davies won The Gold Medal in Fine Art at the 2002 National Eisteddfod, at St David's. WAC, Edinburgh and Stirling Universities hold examples. Among Davies' interests were the organisation of multi-media and experimental theatrical performances, participation in seminars on such topics as Kinetic Art and Space Art, and languages: he was fluent in, or had a working knowledge of, Welsh, English, French, Spanish, Italian, German and Russian.

Jacqueline DAVIES 1968– Artist whose work drew on a wide variety of sources, including contemporary popular culture and ephemera. Graduated with honours in printed textile design at Liverpool John Moores University, 1992, and went on to handle a variety of workshops for children, adults and the disabled. She also worked to commission, including a series of paintings for J D Wetherspoon's Matchmaker public house in the Roman Road. Exhibitions included Kar Krafts, Studio Voltaire, 2001. Participated in Making the Connection, Colchester Railway Station, firstsite, Colchester/Wolsey Art Gallery, Ipswich, 2002. Lived in Colchester, Essex.

John DAVIES 1946– Sculptor, painter and teacher, born in Cheshire, whose art education covered 1963–7. He studied painting at Hull and Manchester Colleges of Art, then after two years at Slade School of Fine Art he won a sculpture fellowship at Gloucester College of Art. Sainsbury Award, 1970. Arts Council and Tate Gallery hold Davies' work, the Tate's Young Man, of 1969–70, stemming from the period when Davies was teaching at Cheltenham Art College. His first sculptures were shown at Whitechapel Art Gallery in 1972 and prompted attention because of their disturbing realism. Davies' young men had parts, such as heads and hands, cast from life, lifelike wigs and items of clothing worn by the artist or bought at jumble sales. During the 1970s Davies produced groups of figures. Later he made small, acrobatic figures and a series of huge heads. Numerous group exhibitions included 8e Biennale de Paris, France, 1973; Documenta VI, Kassel, Germany, 1977; 3rd Biennale of Sydney, Art Gallery of New South Wales, Australia, 1979; British Sculpture in the Twentieth Century, Whitechapel Art Gallery, 1981–2; The Hard-Won Image, Tate Gallery, 1984; 100 Years of Art in Brain, Leeds City Art Gallery, 1988–9; Surrealism and After, Scottish National Gallery of Modern Art, Edinburgh, 1997; and Elogio de lo Visible, International Figuration Exhibition, Galeria Marlborough, Madrid, Spain, and tour, 2000. Davies' many solo exhibitions latterly included Marlborough Fine Art (where he had frequently shown from 1980); Purdy Hicks Gallery, 1998; in 1999 University Gallery in Newcastle upon Tyne and Plymouth Arts Centre; and One Canada Square, 2001–2. Lived in London.

John A DAVIES 1901– Painter in oil and watercolour with a strong interest in maritime subjects, born in Ware, Hertfordshire, not far from where be finally settled at Therfield. After education at Clifton College and the Royal Military Academy at Woolwich, he studied painting at Heatherley's School of Fine Art, with additional tuition from Jack Merriott and other painters. Was a keen member of the Wapping Group, for a time being its chairman. Showed there, RWS and RSMA and also as a member and elsewhere. National Maritime Museum, Greenwich, holds his work.

John Elwyn DAVIES: *see* **John ELWYN**

John R DAVIES 1899–1985 Painter and draughtsman, born in Wolverhampton, Staffordshire, who on leaving school at 14 attended evening classes at Manchester School of Art. After serving in Lancashire Fusiliers from 1917, Davies studied full-time at the School under Adolphe Valette with whom, after he joined the family business, Davies continued to study as well as at the studio of MAFA, of which he became a member. He was also a member of Stockport Art Guild, becoming its president in 1959, was elected RI and on retiring became a member of Haslemere Art Society and was a founder-member of the Art Society in Midhurst, Sussex, where he lived. Showed at RA and had several solo shows in Buxton and Manchester, where Tib Lane Gallery exhibited a selection of his work in 1994. Oldham, Buxton and Stockport public galleries hold examples.

Kate DAVIES 1954– Figurative painter and draughtsman, and teacher, born in Cheshire, who described her pictures as "landscapes of emotion". She obtained a first-class honours degree at Brighton Polytechnic, 1972–5, with a postgraduate vocational year there, 1975–6, in 1979–82 gaining a postgraduate diploma in painting from the Royal Academy Schools. Was awarded a David Murray Studentship for landscape painting, 1982, and was a prize winner, Manchester Artists' Studio Association Friends Exhibition, Cavendish Gallery, 1988. For many years conducted part-time courses at University College, Salford. Mixed exhibitions included The Importance of Drawing, South East Arts tour, 1976; National Portrait Gallery, Imperial Tobacco Portrait Exhibition, 1982; Castlefield Gallery, Manchester, 1988; and Mostyn Open, Oriel Mostyn, Llandudno, 1995. Solo shows included Aytoun Gallery, Manchester, 1995, Turnpike Gallery, Leigh, 1997, and University of Liverpool Art Collections, 2001. Nuffield Hospitals holds Davies's work.

Marcus DAVIES 1965– Interpretative photographer, son of the artist and teacher Nathaniel Davies, their work being shown at the Royal Albert Memorial Museum, Exeter, in 1995. Marcus was born in Newton Abbot, Devon, and studied fine art at Falmouth School of Art. After graduating, he rejected documentary photography in favour of a more subjective and oblique interpretation of what he saw. The farming community of his home town was the subject of an ongoing series of images examining the relationship between man and animal. This work was furthered in 1992 with a Project Award from South West Arts to photograph bullfighting in Spain. In 1993 Davies began experimental photography of butterflies and fish in close-up and in sections with high-contrast film, images which launched a larger body of work about animals, some specimens from Exeter City Museums' natural history collection. Davies participated in the South West Open, Exeter, and Brewhouse Open, Taunton, both from 1990, also showing at Photographers' Gallery. Solo exhibitions included Plymouth Arts Centre, 1992 and 1994.

Michael DAVIES 1947– Painter and teacher who was born in Tonbridge, Kent. He studied at Hastings College of Art and Technology, 1976–81, gained an honours degree in fine art at Canterbury College of Art, 1981–4, then his master's degree at Manchester Polytechnic, 1984–5. Among his teachers were Dennis Creffield, Fabian Peake and Stass Paraskos. Davies was a part-time lecturer at Hastings College of Art, 1986–9, also teaching at Cyprus College of Art, Paphos, 1987–91. Group shows included Olympia Contemporary Art Fair, 1986, and The Big Fight, Vanessa Devereux Gallery, 1987. He had solo exhibitions at Wedges Bistro, Hastings, 1988, and Music Room Concerts, St Leonards-on-Sea, 1993. Towner Art Gallery, Eastbourne, holds his work. Was a member of the Society of Sussex Downsmen. Lived in Bexhill-on-Sea, Sussex.

Miles DAVIES 1959– Sculptor, born in Leigh, Lancashire, who studied at Leamington Spa School of Art and fine art at Brighton Polytechnic, 1978–81. Group shows included Birmingham Museums and Art Gallery, 1991, and Bilston Art Gallery, 1994. Among solo exhibitions were Arnolfini, Bristol, 1990, and Yorkshire Sculpture Park, West Bretton, 1991. Davies's public commissions included Open Door, Ashton Court, Bristol, 1989, and the bronze and phosphor Aqueduct and Gates, Brindleyplace Plaza, Birmingham, 1995, resulting from a competition held by Brindleyplace Plc and the RBS.

Nathaniel DAVIES 1922–1996 Painter, draughtsman, printmaker and teacher, full name Thomas Nathaniel Davies, who sometimes signed his early works Thomas N Davies, for example his Portrait of Alan Shipton, used in Jack Beddington's 1957 volume *Young Artists of Promise*. Davies was born in Dowlais, Glamorgan, where his stonemason father worked intermittently in the local steelworks. When the works closed the family moved to Cardiff, where Davies excelled at art and football. Cardiff city scouts expressed interest, but art won and Davies became the first member of his family to pursue higher education when he entered Cardiff College of Art in 1939, Ceri Richards teaching and befriending him. After World War II service in the Royal Corps of Signals in North Africa Davies returned to Cardiff, completed his teaching diploma and in 1947 joined the staff of Newton Abbot Art School, later amalgamated with South Devon College. Briefly in the 1950s he was also a visiting lecturer at the Royal College of Art. Around this time produced a fine group of self-portraits, an example included in Philip Vann's book *Face to Face*, published by Sansom & Company/Piano Nobile Fine Paintings in 2004. There were also portraits as well as paintings reflecting his childhood in south Wales and Devon. Post-Impressionism and the work of Picasso influenced him. Through the 1960s Davies's work moved towards abstraction, using simple, spare geometric forms; followed in the early 1970s by large abstracts which eschewed figuration but retained a strong underlying linearity; and he also made constructions from coloured Perspex and wood. Davies retired in 1984 as head of the school of art and design in Torquay, to which it had moved in the early 1970s. He latterly concentrated on drawing and woodcuts with Welsh mining landscape, mythological and Biblical themes. Royal Albert Memorial Museum, Exeter, showed his work and that of his photographer son Marcus Davies in 1995. Davies took part in group exhibitions, including Leicester, St George's and Whitechapel Galleries, showing solo with Howard Roberts Gallery, Cardiff. The National Library of Wales, Aberystwyth, holds Davies's work.

Ogwyn DAVIES 1925– Painter, ceramist and teacher, born in Trebanos, near Swansea. After Royal Air Force service, 1943–7, Davies attended Swansea College of Art, 1947–52, then taught in several schools in England and Wales, at Tregaron Secondary School, 1955–85. Group exhibitions included Leicester Galleries, CASW, Royal National Eisteddfod, SWG and Howard Roberts Gallery, Cardiff. Showed solo at University College, Wales, Aberystwyth, where the National Library holds several pictures, with religious themes. It gave Davies a retrospective in 1994. This revealed Davies's long preoccupation with Welsh landscape and its buildings; his love of calligraphy; of the mysterious and the spiritual in pictures tinged with a

Celtic melancholy; and his indebtedness to the Catalan painter Antoni Tàpies, whose work prompted Davies's own materials paintings from 1974. WAC also holds Davies' work. Lived at Tregaron, Dyfed.

Paul DAVIES 1947–1993 Sculptor, performance artist, art historian and teacher, born in Mumbles, Swansea, went to school in Wales, West Germany and Devon. He was at Northampton School of Art, 1965–6, studied sculpture at St Martin's, 1966–9, sociology at University of Essex, 1969–72, and did postgraduate design at University of Liverpool. After temporary posts he became head of art at Plymouth and Mannamead College, 1973–4; lecturer at Cheshire School of Art and Design, 1974–80, and held various visiting lectureships; then was lecturer in art and design at Coleg Gwynedd, Bangor. He was involved in many Welsh groups, including 56 Group, and showed widely in Wales. Inspired by the Rebecca Riots of 1843, he and his brother Peter launched the Beca Group in 1983. By then Davies was known as a radical figure, having as a student burned oil-painted surfaces to blistering finishes; been involved in the International Destruction in Art Symposium in Better Books' basement, 1966–7; also the occupation of Hornsey College of Art, 1968. The National Eisteddfod was a notable venue where in 1974 Davies dressed as a type of red dragon with a concealed flame-thrower. He helped establish art classes for the unemployed and a community arts centre. Died of a heart attack in Bangor during the organisation of the show Official Status – Beca at the Gate, Colwyn Bay Library, 1993–4, plus tour. Wrexham Arts Centre organised a retrospective, 1998.

Paul DAVIES 1947– Painter, born and lived in Swansea, who worked as a Corgi-registered heating engineer. As an artist, he referred to himself as "a kind of semi-abstract symbolist". Davies trained with Michael Freeman at Port Talbot Arts Centre from 1993 and was a member of Freeman's Friday Group from 2000. He exhibited with it regularly, also showing at summer open shows at the Glynn Vivian Art Gallery in Swansea, and at other venues in south Wales. Private collections held examples.

Peter DAVIES 1937– Artist in a variety of media, born in Liverpool, who studied at Swindon School of Art until 1961. He was dissatisfied with "the then accepted concept of painting", and with the encouragement of the sculptor John Hoskin and the painter Patrick Caulfield set out to develop his "own completely personal means of expression", living in London. In 1965 Davies returned to Swindon and set up a workshop with other artists, helping to promote local craftsmen. By 1966 it had begun to claim too much of his time, so he moved to Oxford. After a year of painting had a show at Mansfield College there in 1968.

Peter DAVIES 1944– Administrator and artist, born in Swansea, where he studied at the School of Art, then Goldsmiths' College, University of Wales Cardiff and the Royal College of Art. Like his brother, Paul Davies, Peter was a founder-member of the Beca group of Welsh artists and exhibited regularly. He was head of visual arts at Northern Arts, 1973–92; for five years was a freelance visual arts consultant with several public and private organisations in the United Kingdom, including, in Wales, Butetown Artists, Cardiff Bay Arts Trust and Cywaith Cymru. Artworks Wales; from 1998-9 was senior visual arts and craft development officer in the artform development division for WAC, leaving to resume freelance work.

Peter DAVIES 1953– Writer on art and painter, born in Pontypool, Monmouthshire, whose pictures were mainly plein-air landscapes, especially of Cornwall and France. Davies studied art history at the University of East Anglia, 1972–6, then life drawing under Joe McGill at Chelsea School of Art evening classes, 1985–90. Davies wrote a string of books on modern British art, including the pioneering *A Northern School*, 1989, *Liverpool Seen*, 1992, also *St Ives Revisited*, 1994, *After Trewyn: St Ives Sculptors since Hepworth*, 2001, and a monograph, *Bratby*, in 2002. Group shows included A Northern School, Grundy Art Gallery, Blackpool, 1990; Domino Gallery, Liverpool, 1992; Harlech Biennale and Graham Gallery, Tunbridge Wells, both 1996; and Clevedon: Sharing a View, APT Gallery and tour, 1997–8. Had solo exhibitions at Bridewell Studios, Liverpool, 1992; Porthmeor Gallery, St Ives, 1994; and in 1995 shared an exhibition at The Living Room with Charmian Leonard. Private collections holding his work include Jilly and Leo Cooper, George Melly, Bob Simm, Michael Kenny and Denis Bowen. Lived in Bristol.

Peter DAVIES 1970– Painter, born in Edinburgh, who graduated from Goldsmiths' College in 1996. His work appeared in Die Yuppie Scum, at Karsten Schubert, 1996; in 1997 in Artists and their Spread, 53 Exmouth Market, and in the Saatchi Collection-related show Sensation, at the RA; in 1998–9 in Die Young Stay Pretty, at ICA. In Sensation he was described as making "obsessional paintings about the medium of painting itself ... The work is at once fastidious and awkward, painted in a faux-naïf style". In 1997, Davies was commissioned by Habitat to create a work entitled Small Circle Painting. Solo shows at The Approach, 1998, and Gagosian Gallery, 2001. Davies won first prize in the 2002 John Moores Liverpool Exhibition with Super Star Fucker – Andy Warhol Text Painting. He commented that "for some years I have been making text paintings alongside abstract paintings. Both types feed off and inform one another.... I want to make paintings that combine the sensuality and beauty of formalism with the humour and toughness of conceptualism." Had a studio in east London.

Philip DAVIES 1953– Painter and teacher, born in Pudsey, Yorkshire. He attended Loughborough College of Art, 1972–5, then Royal College of Art, 1978–81. He went on to teach at Brighton Polytechnic and Ulster University. From the mid-1970s Davies was a prolific exhibitor, making several appearances at John Moores Exhibition in Liverpool, at LG, Christopher Hull and Cooling Galleries and Royal Over-Seas League. In 1986 he was winner of the League's first prize. Had a solo show at Polytechnic Gallery, Stoke, in 1987, others including Christopher Hull Gallery 1988–90–92, and Six Chapel Row Contemporary Art, Bath, 2002, entitled Enigma and Myth. Lived in London.

Raymond Edgar Monson DAVIES 1924–1995 Artist in watercolour and mixed media whose chief interests were landscape and the buildings in it. By profession he was a pharmaceutical journalist, being a Master of Pharmacy of the University of Wales. He was largely self-taught, but did a correspondence course tutored by G John Blockley.

Davies began painting in 1974. He belonged to NS, 1983, also showing with RI, RBA and RMS and in Surrey, where he lived at Woodham.

Roger DAVIES 1938– Painter, born in Neath, Glamorgan. After attending Lancing College, Sussex, 1951–6, Davies went to Swansea College of Art, 1956–7, and then Chelsea College of Art, 1957–61, Bernard Meadows and Prunella Clough being among his teachers. For a time he then worked in the family steel company while continuing to paint. In 1963 he won a WAC Prize at SWG exhibition, and he also showed at SEA and with Howard Roberts Gallery, Cardiff. WAC holds his work.

Roland DAVIES 1904–1993 Cartoonist, commercial artist and painter, born in Stourport, Worcestershire. Aged 13 he attended evening classes at Ipswich School of Art for two years, then full-time for two more. Left home and became apprenticed to a litho-printing firm in West Drayton, designing cinema and other posters. Began to offer cartoons as a freelance to *Motor Cycle News* and *Autocar* magazines. Davies created his genial, plodding carthorse cartoon strip Come On, Steve!, which appeared in the *Sunday Express* from 1932–9, then in the *Sunday Dispatch*. The character also featured in animated films, and Davies developed a career drawing for other papers and children's comics. In World War II Davies worked for the Ministry of Information. By 1972, under the guidance of art dealer Alan Class, Davies had turned to painting in oils, creating nostalgic London street scenes, marine and cowboy pictures. Showed at RBA, RSMA and elsewhere.

Ron DAVIES 1921– Creative photographer and teacher whose exhibition Up Close and Personal, at Aberystwyth Arts Centre in 2004, was notable for a series of flowers enclosed in ice. Davies was born and lived in Aberaeron, Cardigan. From 1946–7, he was an Official War Photographer with the Royal Air Force, attached to the staff of Lord Mountbatten of Burma, working in India and the Far East, from 1947–50 becoming a freelance photographer mainly in west Wales. A motorcycling accident in 1950 meant that Davies was officially unable to work, being confined to a wheelchair, paralysed from then on from the chest down. From 1954–85 he resumed his career, freelancing for publications including *Y Cymro, Western Mail, Barn, Daily Express* and *Y Drych*, and as a cameraman for television with the BBC, TWW and HTV. His photography was remarkable in that many of his well-known scenes were taken from the front seat of a car. Davies also taught widely, including Further Education College, Aberystwyth, 1979–81; Carmarthen College of Technology and Art, 1982–98; and Aberystwyth Arts Centre, from 2000. His books included *Images of Wales*, 1989, *The Seven Wonders of Wales*, 1993, and *Ron's World – Byd Ron*, published in 2001 by the National Library of Wales, which gave him a touring show, 2002, one of his numerous exhibitions. Davies gained membership of the Kinemagraphic Society, 1978; the Master Photographers' Association, 1980; fellowship of the Disabled Photographers' Society, 1992; associateship of the Royal Photographic Society, 1993; and credit, Photographic Alliance of Great Britain, 1998. In 2002 he was awarded the Gorsedd of Bards' highest accolade (white robes) for services to the Gorsedd and the arts in Wales and in 2004 the Order of the British Empire for services to photography.

Rosemary DAVIES fl. from 1970s– Painter and muralist who trained at Harrow School of Art and Mid Warwickshire College of Art. Showed in many mixed exhibitions, including four-man show at Woodlands Art Gallery, 1988. Painted two murals for East Birmingham Hospital, 1985, and Warwick Central Hospital, 1987, pictures by her being bought by the Paintings in Hospital committee. From 1979 had a series of solo shows.

Ruth Llynfi DAVIES fl. c.1940– Miniaturist and portrait painter, often working on ivory, born in Llansamlet, near Swansea, South Wales. Studied mainly at Swansea School of Art and showed at RA, in Wales and Scotland. Lived at Mumbles, Glamorgan.

Siobhan DAVIES 1966– Artist who through the medium of installations worked "to capture things intangible and transitory." An example was her neon lights piece Window (proposition for gaining time) in the show East, Norwich Gallery, 1991. Davies studied at Newcastle Polytechnic, 1986–9, then Birmingham Institute of Art and Design, 1990–1. Showed in BT New Contemporaries, ICA, 1993. Lived in Moseley, Birmingham.

Stephanie DAVIES 1910–1990 Artist, designer and costume historian, born in Bristol where she attended the West of England College of Art, also the University, 1927–32. At various times she was head of painting at the Ladies' College, Cheltenham; director of the Channel Islands School of Painting; and taught at Schools in Chester and Malvern. As well as showing extensively on the continent Davies exhibited at RBA, SWA, UA, NS and in the provinces. Solo shows included Bristol Old Vic and University College, Exeter. Lived in Malvern Link, Worcestershire, then Upper Breinton, Herefordshire.

Thomas DAVIES 1899– Painter in oil and watercolour. Born at Colwyn Bay, Denbighshire, North Wales, Davies studied art privately under Robert Evans Hughes. He went on to exhibit with the Flintshire Art Society, North Wales Group and Denbighshire Art Society; had a one-man show at Gwrych Castle. Lived at Abergele, Clwyd, Wales.

Thomas N DAVIES: *see* **Nathaniel DAVIES**

Tim DAVIES 1960– Artist and teacher, born in Haverfordwest, Pembrokeshire, who, after several years engaged in music, did a foundation course at Ravensbourne College of Art & Design, 1986–7; gained an honours degree in fine art at Norwich School of Art, 1987–90; then his master's, on issues of art and architecture, at Kent Institute of Art & Design, Canterbury, 1991–2. After an unsatisfactory experiment with painting, Davies made the site-specific installation Flags over Solva, 1992, which pointed the way to the creation of others as well as performance works which explored dispossession and disempowerment. These were painstakingly crafted using a multiplicity of materials, and included Paran Chapel, 1993; Solfach, Burnt Wall, 1993–4; Alphabeca, 1995; and Tatters, 1996. Davies' work experience included a residency at Bedford Modern School, 1990–1, and part-time teaching at Carmarthen College of Technology & Art and at HM Prison, Swansea, 1995. Davies was a member of the Beca Group and of Artists' Project. Showed widely in Britain and abroad, with solo exhibitions at Spacex Gallery, Exeter, and at Glynn Vivian Art Gallery, Swansea, where he lived, in 1997. His exhibition in 2003 at Wrexham Arts Centre coincided with the publication of *Process: Explorations of the Work of Tim Davies.*

William DAVIES 1928– Painter in oil, born in South Wales, who served in the Royal Navy until 1962. He was noted for his fluent, on-the-spot pictures of Venice and London, where he also painted from the life over several years at the Royal Academy of Music. Was a member of the Wapping Group, also showing at ROI and RSMA. Lloyd's of London used one of Davies' Thames scenes on its calendar. Solo shows included Omell Galleries, Windsor, 1990, and Century Galleries, Henley-on-Thames, 1998. Lived in West Hyde, Rickmansworth, Hertfordshire.

W Mitford DAVIES 1895– Illustrator and painter who studied at Liverpool School of Art, 1920–4. Exhibited RCamA. He was principally known as an illustrator of books in Welsh who was closely associated with the Welsh League of Youth. Lived at Gaerwen, Anglesey.

Arna DAVIS fl. from c.1990– Sculptor and Jungian analyst, born in Finland, who settled in Britain as a young adult, eventually at Watford, Hertfordshire. In 1973, she qualified as a social worker while training to become a psychotherapist, becoming a member of the British Association of Psychotherapists and a member of the International Association for Analytical Psychology. Long interested in art, Davis started art training at St Albans School of Art and Design, 1989, obtaining her honours degree in fine art from University of Hertfordshire in 1995. Group shows included Hertfordshire Visual Arts Forum, CRA Gallery, St Albans, 1992; Take 16, Margaret Harvey Gallery, St Albans, 1993; Sculpture Exhibition, Watford Area Arts Forum, Royal Caledonian Schools, Bushey, 1996; and Unquiet Voices, Doncaster Museum & Art Gallery, 1997. Had a solo show, Screen 24 x 24 = 576, sculpture, University of Hertfordshire, 1995–6.

Arthur Joseph DAVIS 1878–1951 Watercolourist who was an architect by profession. Studied at L'École des Beaux-Arts, Paris, 1896–1900 and in several artists' studios there, having been born in London and educated in Brussels, Belgium. In 1900, he took a junior partnership with Charles Mewés. They moved to London and produced buildings in the French classical style, notably the Ritz Hotel, Piccadilly, 1906–9; Inveresk House, Aldwych, 1907; and the Royal Automobile Club, Pall Mall, 1908–11, of which Davis was a member, along with the Garrick Club. After Mewés death and his own World War I service, Davis teamed up with C H Gage. He was elected a fellow of RIBA in 1914 and became a member of the Royal Fine Art Commission. Davis was a consultant on the Cunard Building at Pier Head, Liverpool, 1913–18; designed the war memorial outside; and for Cunard White Star worked on decorations for liners such as the *Aquitainia, Laconia, Franconia* and *Queen Mary*. He remained a prolific architect between the wars, designing what became the National Westminster Bank in Threadneedle Street, 1922–31, which gained him the London Street Architecture Medal, 1930. Exhibited RA, being elected a full Academician in 1942. Was an Officer of the Legion of Honour. Lived in London.

Bernard J DAVIS 1932– Artist, notably a sculptor and mosaicist, born in the Farnham area of Surrey, married to the painter Diana Hammond. He studied at Winchester School of Art, 1949–53, and Royal Academy Schools, 1953–5, Maurice Lambert among his teachers. At RA Summer Exhibition in 1955 showed two heads, one of an Eastern girl, also exhibiting at Herbert Art Gallery, Coventry, and Towner Art Gallery, Eastbourne, which holds a bronze cast, Pandora. Davis' body of ecclesiastical and school commissions included work for St Philip's Cathedral in Birmingham, Holy Family Church in Dagenham, the Augustinian Priory, Hammersmith, and Imberhorne School, East Grinstead. Was based for periods at Debenham, Suffolk, and Haywards Heath, Sussex.

Derek DAVIS 1926– Ceramist, born in London, who studied painting at Central School of Arts and Crafts with Robert Buhler and Keith Vaughan, 1946–50. He gained a fellowship as artist-in-residence, University of Sussex, 1967, and a Southern Arts Association Bursary, 1978. He was a member of Contemporary Applied Arts and of International Academy of Ceramics and a fellow of the Craft Potters' Association. His exhibitions included Primavera, Cambridge, 1965; University of Sheffield, 1971; Blond Fine Art, 1985; and Sheila Harrison from 1986; also showed extensively abroad. Davis was "influenced by painters, Picasso among others", in his work, which was held by Victoria & Albert Museum, Southampton City Art Gallery, Westerwald Keramic Museum, Germany, and elsewhere. Lived in Arundel, Sussex.

Elizabeth DAVIS 1921– Painter, constructions artist and restorer, born in Johannesburg, South Africa, where she was educated. In the late 1960s-early 1970s she showed extensively in Italy, winning the Viscontea Prize, Milan, in 1970. Solo shows included Galleria Pater, Milan, 1969, and Woodside Gallery, 1972. She directed that gallery for some years in Epsom Downs, Surrey, where she lived.

George DAVIS 1930– Painter, draughtsman, muralist and teacher, born in Hobart, Tasmania, where he continued to live, making regular visits to Tasmania's islands. Davis studied painting at Hobart Technical College, 1949–51, under Jack Carrington Smith and Dorothy Stoner. After being awarded a Tasmanian Government Travelling Arts Scholarship in 1951, from 1952–4 he studied at the Royal Academy Schools in London under Bernard Fleetwood-Walker, travelling around Great Britain, Ireland and continental Europe. From 1958–9 Davis taught painting part-time at Hobart Technical College, for the Adult Education Board in Hobart and privately. In 1961, he won a design competition for the external wall mural on the ABC Television Studio Building, Hobart; in 1976 a commission from the Tasmanian Arts Advisory Board for drawings and paintings of Tasmania's islands; in 1981 with Stephen Walker he restored Lyndon Dadswell's wall sculptures at the Commonwealth Bank, Hobart; and in 1984 was commissioned to paint replacements for 10 portraits of composers in the renovated dome of the Theatre Royal, Hobart. Davis contributed to many group shows in Australia and had a series of solo exhibitions there, notably one of Portraits, People and the Figure at the Tasmanian Museum and Art Gallery, Hobart, in 1988, which holds his work.

George Horace DAVIS 1881–1963 Artist, born in London, who studied at Ealing School of Art. He was for a time staff artist on the publications *Graphic* and *Sphere* and in 1923 became chief staff artist on the *Illustrated London News*. During World War I he was head of aerial diagrams for the Royal Flying Corps and an Official War Artist. Davis wrote many articles connected with marine illustration and was very prolific as an illustrator, famous for his diagrammatic drawings and cross-sections of ships. He was a member of RSMA and a founder-member of the Society of Aviation Artists. Showed at RA, Imperial War Museum which holds his work and elsewhere. Lived in Ewell, Surrey, then latterly in Brighton, Sussex.

Heather St Clair DAVIS 1937–1999 Equestrian artist, born in Cheltenham, who grew up on a farm in the Cotswolds hunting country. She had a passion for horses from an early age, hunting, competing in point-to-points and helping to train steeplechasers over the hills above Cheltenham racecourse. Studied at Cheltenham College of Art & Design and Birmingham College of Art, graduating in life drawing, sculpture and three-dimensional design. Married Captain Bill Davis, retired from the American special forces. After hair-raising trip across Altantic in a converted cutter, including a shipwreck after which she swam to shore with a baby tied to her chest, eventually settled with young family in Vermont, America, in the early 1960s, where she farmed, bred and trained event horses, was an International Dressage judge, painted and taught art in local schools. Encouraged by art dealers Frost & Reed, she returned to Gloucestershire to paint seriously in 1988, thereafter showing with that gallery. Continued to live in Vermont, and was a member of the American Academy of Equine Art. Memorial show, Frost & Reed, 2000.

Hilda DAVIS fl. c.1935–1960 Painter who was married to the artist Cyril Davis. She studied at the Grosvenor School of Modern Art, with Iain Macnab, 1935–9. Exhibited NEAC, RBA, ROI, AEB and widely in the provinces. NS member. Lived in London.

James DAVIS 1926– Sculptor and restorer in stone, born in London, who studied at Sir John Cass School of Art, 1949–53, under Edward Bainbridge Copnall. He became a freeman of the Worshipful Company of Painter-Stainers in 1972. Showed at Guildhall, Leighton House and Mall Galleries. Chelsea and Kensington Town Hall and St Nicholas' Church in Elm Park, Essex, hold examples. Had a studio and lived in Shoeburyness, Essex.

James Spence DAVIS 1944– Painter of landscape, born in Glasgow, where he studied at the School of Art with William Armour and David Donaldson, graduating in 1967. He was a member of The Scottish Ruralists who worked on-the-spot regardless of climate. Was an exhibiting member of Glasgow Art Club, Royal Glasgow Institute of the Fine Arts and Paisley Institute of Fine Arts, also showing regularly with RSA and RSW. In 1993 was included in Contemporary Art From Scotland at Thompson's Gallery. HRH The Duke of Edinburgh holds his work.

John DAVIS 1956– Wildlife painter, mainly in watercolour, and illustrator, who studied wildlife illustration at Dyfed College of Art in the mid-1970s. In 1987 elected to SWLA. Won the Royal Society for the Protection of Birds' Fine Art Award twice, in 1987 and 1991, in 1991 also winning *British Birds'* Bird Illustrator of the Year Award. Extensive magazine work included *Birds*, *British Birds* and *BBC Wildlife*, book illustration John Burton's *Downland Wildlife* and Ernest Neal's *Badgers*. Frank T Sabin sold Davis's work.

John Pyper DAVIS 1973– Figurative painter and sculptor, born in Paisley, Renfrewshire, who graduated from Glasgow School of Art in 1996. He early on exhibited widely, venues including RSA; Royal Glasgow Institute of the Fine Arts, where he won an award; Compass Gallery, Glasgow; on the continent, including Kumulus Gallery, Maastricht, and World Trade Fair, Amsterdam, both in the Netherlands; and Thompson's Gallery. Won the Mayfest Painting Prize. Davis's Seven Deadly Sins, seven sculpted heads for Precious Records, received wide media attention. He was a member of Glasgow Art Club.

John Warren DAVIS: *see* **John WARREN DAVIS**

Judith DAVIS 1933– Artist in oil, acrylic, watercolour, pastel and Batik, born in Dewsbury, Yorkshire. She studied at Wimbledon School of Art, 1951–4, then Royal College of Art, 1954–5, notable teachers including Gerald Cooper. Married straight from College and after her children were in their teens began teaching: Bury's Court Preparatory School and adult education classes. Joined the Reigate Society of Artists in 1973, becoming honorary secretary. Group shows also included *Daily Express* Young Artists Exhibition at New Burlington Galleries, 1955; RA, 1980; SWA, 1982 and 1989 at Mall and Westminster Galleries; Fairfield Halls, Croydon, 1987 and 1995; and Guildford Gallery, 1991. Lived in South Nutfield, Surrey. Early work was signed with her maiden name, Judith Fitton.

Kate DAVIS 1960– Mixed-media and performance artist who studied at Hertfordshire College of Art and Design, 1978–9, then Falmouth School of Art, 1979–82, and Slade School of Fine Art, 1983-6. Group shows included Ox-Skull/Pterodactyl, an installation with Graham Hubbard at Falmouth School Gallery, 1981; New Contemporaries at ICA, 1982; and Wapping Artists Open Studios, from 1983. In that year took part in Fairies and Water Maidens are the only other Alternatives (The myth of Housework being a Creative Activity), Loughborough Polytechnic and Central Art School. Solo exhibitions included Whitechapel Art Gallery as Young Artist of the Year, 1989; Milch and tour, 1997; Newlyn Art Gallery, Leipzig Kunstverein in Germany, and Erfrischungsraum in Luzern, Switzerland, 1998; New Burlington Street Gallery, 1999; and in 2000 she shared a show at Rhodes + Mann. Lived in London.

Marie Thérèse DAVIS 1964– Artist employing strong figurative images, and teacher. She graduated from Queen's University, Belfast, in social anthropology in 1986, then, having completed her postgraduate certificate in education there in 1987, Davis gained a certificate in art and design from Oxford Polytechnic, 1990. In that year she worked as a visiting artist in a young offenders institution in Oxfordshire, and was a visiting lecturer in Oxford Polytechnic's printmaking department, also teaching music. She was associated with Queen Street Studios in Belfast, taking part in the 1994 shows Works on Paper and Beyond the Partitions. In the same year she had a solo exhibition at Harmony Hill Arts Centre.

Michael DAVIS 1943– Artist and teacher, notable as a draughtsman preoccupied with still life and landscape, conveying a strong sense of place, haunting and pensive. Studied at Birmingham and Royal College of Art, winning a Silver Medal for painting. Became principal lecturer in painting at Kent Institute of Art and Design. Showed at Young Contemporaries and RA Summer Exhibition, from 1966; Lisson Gallery, 1968; 3me Biennale Internationale de l'Image, Epinal, France, 1975; Hayward Drawing Annual, Arts Council Purchase, 1982; 15 British Painters, British Council, Barcelona, Spain, 1988; South Bank Show, Royal Festival Hall, 1992; and RA Summer Exhibition, *House & Garden* Prize, 1996. Later solo exhibitions included Cassian de Vere Cole Fine Art, 1996.

Mike DAVIS 1946– Stained glass artist and conservator, and teacher, born in London, who did a foundation course at St Martin's School of Art, 1965–6, then his diploma at Hornsey College of Art, 1967–70, tutor Jack Smith. A course at Patrick Reyntiens' studio in 1968 prompted an interest in architectural glass. He held a fellowship in stained glass at Digswell Arts Trust, Welwyn Garden City, 1970–4, and worked there until 1981, when he set up a studio in Durham. Became senior lecturer in architectural glass at University of Sunderland from 1994, having taught part-time at Sunderland Polytechnic from 1982. Davis was an associate of The British Society of Master Glass Painters and of Art and Architecture. Exhibitions included RIBA Gallery, The Design Centre, Southwark Cathedral and Victoria & Albert Museum, which holds his work. Davis carried out many commissions, churches including St John's Church, Digswell; St Nicholas' Hospital Chapel, Gosforth; and St Elizabeth of Hungary, Aycliffe. Secular commissions included Monkseaton Metro Station, Tyne and Wear; Guildhall, Durham; and entrance screen for Greatham Hospital. His main concern was "to render the image by the texture of light". Lived in Brandon, County Durham.

Myra DAVIS 1915–1994 Artist using charcoal, oil, pencil and collage, born in London, who attended Heatherley's School of Fine Art in the mid-1930s (Michael Ayrton was a contemporary), with Paul Drury as one teacher, also studying with André Lhote in Paris prior to World War II. Although her work attained a high standard, Davis was shy of exhibiting. Her first public show was in John Minton and Friends, at Michael Parkin Gallery, 1997. Minton was a friend, and they produced portraits of each other. Died in Sussex.

Noel Denholm DAVIS 1876–1950 Primarily a portrait painter, Davis was born in Nottingham, where he studied at the School of Art for five years in the 1890s and was then at the Royal Academy Schools. Worked for a decade in London as a portrait painter, but continued to show in Nottingham. Among his portraits were General William Booth of the Salvation Army and the Victoria Cross-holder Captain Albert Ball. He eventually returned to live in Nottingham and in 1929 his frescoes in the Council House Arcade were unveiled, showing scenes from city history. Died on a visit at Goring-on-Thames, Oxfordshire.

Pamela DAVIS fl. from 1970s– Painter of botanical subjects in a realistic style who studied at Twickenham College of Art. She was a founder-member of the Society of Botanical Artists, a vice-president of SWA, a member of RMS and Hilliard Society. In 1987 she won the Suzanne Lucas Award, in 1991 winning RMS Gold Memorial Bowl. Mixed exhibitions included Medici Gallery and Linda Blackstone Gallery, Pinner.

Percy Charles Clement DAVIS 1867– Watercolourist who served lifelong with the Great Western Railway. Exhibited BWS, of which he was a member, and widely in the Midlands and south Wales. Lived in Cambridge.

Peter DAVIS 1926–2000 Painter, draughtsman and teacher, born in Brentford, Middlesex. He attended Ealing School of Art, 1941–5; Central School of Art (John Cass Institute), 1946–8, under Nicholas Egon and Stanley Spencer; then as a Royal Scholar was at Royal College of Art, 1948–51, teachers including John Nash, Ruskin Spear and John Minton. He lectured at Hammersmith School of Art, 1955–75, then at Chelsea School of Art, 1975–80, retiring to paint full-time. Davis' main works were Eros and Agape, Don Quixote and Gethsemane. Exhibitions included Piccadilly Gallery and Miami Beach, Florida. Solo shows included Felix Gallery, 1957; Pantiles, Tunbridge Wells, 1962; Framlingham Castle Gallery, 1965; Aldeburgh, Suffolk, 1970; Halesworth Gallery, 1976; and Barn Gallery, Butley, 1999. Lived in Metfield, Suffolk. He was sometimes known as Peter Frazer Davis.

Peter DAVIS 1972– Painter, born in Sutton, Surrey, who studied at Goldsmiths' College, 1990–3. Group exhibitions included Six Painters at Karsten Schubert, 1994, and Real Art at City Art Gallery in Southampton, 1995. Had a solo show at Karsten Schubert in 1994, Asprey Jacques, 1999.

Peter Frazer DAVIS: *see* **Peter DAVIS 1926–2000**

Philomena DAVIS 1949– Sculptor of works of a populist nature, born in London, who trained at City and Guilds of London Art School and Royal Academy Schools, winning the Gold Medal in 1973. She lived in Japan for over two years, studying Japanese art and architecture. Moved to Milton Keynes, Buckinghamshire, in 1980, opening a bronze foundry in New Bradwell. Milton Keynes Development Corporation commissioned her bronzes Dream Flight, Flying Carpet and High Flyer, sited in 1989 in the Shopping Building, Queens Court. In 1990 Davis was elected president of RBS.

Robin DAVIS 1925–1999 Self-taught artist who was educated at Bournemouth Grammar School and St Catherine's College, Oxford, who began painting in 1956. Had solo exhibitions at Woodstock Gallery, 1960, St Martin's Gallery, 1962, New Vision Centre, 1964, and Aston University, Birmingham, 1965, showing Abstract Expressionist work. From 1966–79 Davis did little painting, training as a psychologist, psychotherapist and group analyst, restarting with wood collages and then paintings again, in an abstract style. His work was "full of skeletal forms, fractured images and eroded earth qualities which lead to an impression of continued disintegration and re-integration", as shown at Belgrave Gallery, 1995, to mark Davis' 70th birthday. Cornwall was for many years an important influence on Davis' output, "its rocky coastline, and the way in which the light plays on the sea", and he finally settled there, in Penzance.

Roger C DAVIS 1942– Sculptor, draughtsman, jeweller and teacher, born in Weymouth, Dorset. Became seriously interested in art aged 16, then from 1961–2 studied with the artist Sven Berlin at his New Forest studio. Spent three years on Isle of Portland familiarising himself with stone, then a decade involved in jewellery, abandoning this in 1979 to teach art at Weymouth Grammar School. Wales, Celtic cultures, mythology and poetry influenced his work. Exhibitions included solo show, Drunk on the Moon, Dorset County Museum, Dorchester, 1988.

Rosemary DAVIS fl. from late 1940s– Painter, draughtsman, illustrator and teacher, she won scholarships to Wallasey and Chelsea Schools of Art, 1945–7. As a freelance she concentrated on fashion illustration for magazines and newspapers and taught art to children before turning to fine art in 1981. Showed at Knapp and Heifer Galleries, with British Council in Cyprus and elsewhere.

Francis DAVISON 1919–1984 Painter and collagist, born in London. He was married to the artist Margaret Mellis. Davison was brought up by adoptive parents in France and England. After reading English and anthropology at Cambridge University he wrote poetry, then began to draw in 1946. Two years after he married Margaret Mellis, in 1948, they moved to Suffolk, running a smallholding at Syleham for much of the time, in 1976 settling in Southwold, where Davison died. By the early 1950s his paintings became simplified shapes, then in 1952 he became a collagist. Over the next 20 years reference to landscape disappeared and the colour range was extended. Davison said that he was the only true collagist, as he relied entirely on found, used and not painted papers, which were cut and fitted with great exactness. When he was half-paralysed Mellis would hold the papers while he tore them. Davison was included in the South Bank Centre touring show The Experience of Painting, in 1989. He had solo shows at Graves Art Gallery, Sheffield, 1981; Museum of Modern Art, Oxford, 1982; Hayward Gallery, 1983; and Austin/Desmond Fine Art, 2003. Redfern Gallery has mounted several posthumous exhibitions. Arts Council holds his work.

Philippa DAVISON 1972– Painter and printmaker who attended Mid-Cheshire College of Further Education, 1990–1; Falmouth School of Art, 1991–4; and the Royal Academy Schools, her colourful oil on gesso board Eryngium being included in the final year show. Among Davison's awards and scholarships were Rinto Tinto Scholarship, Royal Academy Schools; Winsor & Newton Young Artists Award, finalist, 1996; and Tesco's "A bag for life", to celebrate education into the Millennium, 1998. Davison's exhibitions included Floor to Ceiling, Swanston Street Gallery, Melbourne, Australia, 1993; Fresh Art, Business Design Centre, Islington, 1994; ROI, Mall Galleries, 1996; National Print Exhibition, 1998; and RP, Mall Galleries, 1999. Lived in Ollerton, Knutsford, Cheshire.

George Mark Oswald DAVY 1898–1983 Painter and sculptor, born in Doncaster, Yorkshire, who was by profession a soldier, his military training including Royal Military Academy. He had private teaching as an artist, 1904–15, attending Byam Shaw School, 1959–62, under Peter Garrard. Exhibitions included RBA, NS, RWS, RSA and Paris Salon, and he was vice-president of Chelsea Art Society. Imperial War Museum holds four works by Brigadier Davy, including a painting of the sinking of HMS *Eclipse* and two sculptures of Admiral of the Fleet Sir Algernon Willis, a former chairman of the museum's trustees. Davy lived latterly at Alyth, Perthshire.

Leo DAVY 1924–1987 Figure and landscape painter, born in Shipley Moor, Yorkshire, who refused to exploit his art to live, shunning dealers and critics, believing that his pictures were sufficient without their promotion and interpretation. Davy studied at the Slade School of Fine Art, 1943–5, during its wartime relocation to Oxford, also taking lectures in philosophy. It remained his life's preoccupation. His father Hubert, who taught art, and his mother Dorothy, daughter of the artist Henry Thurlow Hunt, were Theosophists. Apart from John Latham and Kyffin Williams, Leo's close friends were philosophers rather than artists: John Tucker, who became professor of philosophy at Waterloo University in Canada and R D Laing, author of *Self and Other* and *Knots*. Davy taught art for a few years at St Aloysius Boys' School, Highgate, but found this interfered with his painting. When he met Antonia Davy in 1955 he was a part-time packer in a health food store, paying £2 a week for bed and breakfast and a bare room, painting in his overcoat to save fuel. In 1959, Davy learned frame-making and after that earned what he needed by gilding, carving and restoring. The Davys moved to north Cornwall in 1968 and in 1969 he had a first show at the Beaford Centre, north Devon. There was a posthumous show at Arnolfini Gallery, Bristol, in 1990. Piano Nobile Fine Paintings latterly represented his estate. Davy's work defies easy interpretation, although Antonia Davy believed that "he was looking for a way to express the relationships that preoccupied him: between inner and outer, self and not-self, experience and reality." Davy's early self-portrait is included in Philip Vann's book *Face to Face*, published by Sansom & Company/ Piano Nobile in 2004.

Lesley DAVY 1953– Versatile artist who gained an honours degree in the history of art and architecture from University of East Anglia, 1974–7; a fine art diploma in printmaking from London Guildhall University, 1989–93; and studied postgraduate printmaking at Central St Martins School of Art, 1993–5. From 1979–83 Davy set up and ran a picture library at The Photographers' Gallery, from 1983–93 being a freelance picture researcher in publishing and television with Channel 4. At National Print Open in 1995 won the Zenith Gallery Prize, in 1997 the Falkiner Fine Papers Prize. Carried out installation commissions for University of Salford's Chapman Gallery and Pitshanger Museum. Exhibitions included Impressive Woman, London Print Workshop, 1992; Curwen Gallery, Salon des Graphiques, 1994; Innovations & Transformations, Mappin Art Gallery, Sheffield, 1997; and Artmonsky Arts.

Cedric DAWE 1906– Artist in conté crayon, born in London, who studied at Royal College of Art and elsewhere in London. He was by profession a film art director. Belonged to UA, also showing with RA, RI, ROI and RWS. Lived in Chartridge, Buckinghamshire.

Andrzej DAWIDOWSKI 1933– Artist who was born in Wilno, Poland. After being deported to Siberia, 1940–2, he went with Polish children to Iran, then to New Zealand, where he attended Wellington Art College, 1956–9. After arriving in England, he studied in the studios of Professor Marian Bohusz-Szyszko from 1962–4. Took part in group shows in New Zealand and England, including Form and Colour, Congress of Polish Culture Exhibition of Fine Arts by Polish Artists in Britain, POSK Gallery, 1995.

Kathleen DAWKIN: *see* **Kathleen PAENSON**

Sidney DAWLSON 1917–1990 Artist in various media, born and lived in London, who worked for the daily parliamentary record *Hansard*. He studied at Central School of Arts and Crafts, 1937–8. Was a member of Free Painters and Sculptors, also exhibiting with RSMA, ROI, RBA and in the provinces. Solo shows included Loggia Gallery, 1975.

Denys DAWNAY 1921–1983 Versatile artist, educated at Westminster School, who attended the Euston Road School and who showed in its exhibitions and at RA. Developing diabetes as a child and tuberculosis as a young man hindered his pursuing a full artistic career. Dawnay was a close friend of King George VI and other members of the royal family. He suggested to the Duke of Edinburgh that he take up painting shortly after his marriage in 1947, giving him his first paintbox and easel, long in use; he subsequently helped Princess Margaret design a tea service, made by Spode in 1956, later in regular use at Kensington Palace; and he also gave painting instruction to the Prince of Wales. The Queen asked Dawnay to paint a game book, which was not finished, and he produced a book of dog caricatures for Lord Lambton, the dogs dressed as famous artists. Later in life, living in Scotland, Dawnay became an accomplished photographer and created a sensational garden. Dawnay's work was in the collections of Humphrey Brooke and Sir Houston Shaw-Stewart, Dawnay's step-brother and first cousin, Lord Salisbury, Lady Harrod, Lady Mersey and the royal family. He died in hospital at Greenock, Renfrewshire. He is sometimes referred to as Denis or Dennis Dawnay.

Lawrence DAWS 1927– Landscape painter and printmaker, born in Adelaide, South Australia, who studied engineering and architecture at the South Australian School of Mines and while painting at Hahndorf in his spare time met the artist Hans Heysen. After commercial surveying in New Guinea, in 1949 he began a four-year full-time painting course at the National Gallery School, Melbourne, winning among other awards the Hugh Ramsay Portrait Prize. After exhibiting in Australia and in the Pacific Loan Exhibition, in San Francisco, America, in 1956, in 1957 Daws won an Italian Government-Flotto Lauro-Dante Alighieri Scholarship, enabling him to work in Italy, leaving for London in 1959 after European travels and a show at the Macquarie Galleries, Sydney. The 1960s onwards saw Daws travelling extensively worldwide, with periods in London, among early highlights being his inclusion in Recent Australian Painting at the Whitechapel Art Gallery, 1961; a first solo show in London at the Matthieson Gallery in 1962; an Hon. Mention in the São Paulo Bienal, Brazil, in 1963; inclusion in Young Australian Painters, in Kyoto and Tokyo, Japan, in 1964; and a major retrospective at the Adelaide Festival of Arts in 1966. By the mid-1970s Daws had established a relationship with the Philip Bacon Galleries, Brisbane, which would give him many solo shows over the next 30 years, his 2005 exhibition there being preceded by one in London at Nevill Keating Pictures Ltd in 2003, and there was a series with Robin Gibson, Sydney, including one in 1997. Work on etchings and screenprints were other features of Daws's career, as were a number of murals, including one for the Supreme Court, Brisbane, in 1981, and a large one for the Performing Arts Complex in the city in 1984–5. Many Australian collections hold Daws's work, as do the Auckland Art Gallery, New Zealand; National Gallery of Beijing, China; Tate Gallery and Victoria & Albert Museum, in London; and the Scottish National Gallery of Modern Art, Edinburgh.

Alan DAWSON 1947– Versatile artist, craftsman and teacher, born in Whitehaven, Cumberland, who studied woodwork at Loughborough College of Art; taught for several years; became a candlemaker at Cape Wrath; then after attending the first meeting of the British Artist Blacksmiths' Association in 1978, turned to hand-forged production, establishing Alan Dawson Associates Ltd in Workington, Cumbria. His varied output included decorative ironwork, including an exotic peacock, for Princes Square, Glasgow, from 1985; a typewriter-based piece for the *Daily Express* headquarters, 1990; and Tree of Life for Hill Samuel Life Assurance, St Vincent Street, Glasgow, 1997. Overseas clients included the Sultan of Brunei and Disneyworld, Paris.

Alva DAWSON 1915– Artist and teacher, born in Leicester, who studied at Nottingham School of Art and part-time at Goldsmiths' College School of Art, 1933–8. She was head of art at Rock Hills Girls' School, Bromley, to 1975 and from 1947 was an art tutor in adult education in Nottingham, Bromley and Sevenoaks. Buildings, demolition, docks with shipping and roof tops were her principal subjects. She was president of Bromley Art Society and a member of Sevenoaks Art Club. Also exhibited at Keele University in Staffordshire, Sevenoaks Library and The Old Bakehouse Gallery, Sevenoaks. Lived in Sevenoaks, then in Chipstead, Kent.

Anthony DAWSON 1947– Largely self-taught artist, producing meticulous "prints and drawings of the English coast and countryside." He was born in Scarborough, Yorkshire, and was "for some years a civil engineer before I became a full-time printmaker." Dawson was a fellow of the RE, showing at Bankside Gallery, RWA, RA Summer Exhibition, John Davies Gallery in Stow-on-the-Wold, Thompson's Gallery in Aldeburgh, The City Gallery and at Barbican Concourse. The Ashmolean Museum in Oxford and Hereford City Museum hold examples. Lived in Eckington, Pershore, Worcestershire.

Byron DAWSON 1896–1968 Artist, illustrator and teacher, born in Banbury, Oxfordshire, with a special interest in architectural subjects. As an engineering apprentice in Newcastle upon Tyne, where he settled, he was encouraged to study art at Armstrong College, teaching there until 1927. Success at the RA in 1928 launched his professional painting career, which soon was concentrated in the northeast of England, although Dawson did show briefly at RSA. Drew for the *Newcastle Journal*. Dawson contributed nine Lancashire scenes to the Pilgrim Trust *Recording Britain* project and was included in the 1990 show at the Victoria & Albert Museum, which holds his work, as do Laing Art Gallery in Newcastle and Shipley Art Gallery, Gateshead. His latter years until a final illness were marked by financial hardship. In 1993 Dean

Gallery in Newcastle held a major show of Dawson's work to mark the twenty-fifth anniversary of his death.

Chris DAWSON 1942– Abstract sculptor in various materials and teacher, born in Liverpool. He studied at the School of Art there and Royal College of Art. Making forms that allowed people to become part of them, Dawson showed at AIA Gallery and Camden Arts Centre. He was eventually appointed to the staff of the University of East London.

David DAWSON 1960– Painter of abstracts on a large scale, born in north Wales. He did a foundation course at Cardiff College of Art, 1980–1, then an honours degree in fine art, painting, at Chelsea School of Art, 1984–7, completing his master's degree in painting at Royal College of Art, 1987–9. Dawson won a David Murray Studentship in 1988. He exhibited in group shows from the mid-1980s, including Young Masters at Solomon Gallery, 1987; The Abstract Connection at Flowers East, 1989; and at Cooling Gallery, 1991. In 1989 he was given an Artist of the Day solo show at Flowers East, chosen by Joe Tilson.

Edward DAWSON 1941–1999 Painter and teacher who was born in Northumberland, where he was educated at Alnwick. He graduated from King's College, Durham University, 1960–4, teachers including Victor Pasmore. Dawson initially taught at the College of Art & Industrial Design, Newcastle, shortly after taking up a post at Epsom and Ewell School of Art. During that time he started to review an early interest in abstract painting, becoming increasingly influenced by Impressionism. In 1971, he began an association with the Furneaux Gallery, with mixed and solo exhibitions; in 1977, he was elected a member of NEAC; and shortly after that he gave up teaching, moving to Wiltshire to spent more time painting. Further solo shows included Edwin Pollard Gallery from 1983 and The Guggleton Farm Arts Project, Stalbridge, Dorset, 1998, where he did some part-time teaching. After Wiltshire, Dawson lived for a few years in France, then at Buckhorn Weston, Dorset. A memorial show of his work was held at Lincoln Joyce Gallery, Great Bookham, Surrey, in 2000, showing work loaned by his artist widow Gillian.

Eric DAWSON 1918– Watercolourist and commercial artist, born in east London, who began drawing when very young. He was encouraged at his secondary school by his art master Rupert Shephard and gained a scholarship to West Ham Art School. During war service in North Africa and the Middle East Dawson drew for forces' publications, worked in camouflage and taught drawing in the Army School of Education at Beirut University. On demobilisation he chose commercial art as a career, for many years working as a freelance art director. After a first one-man show at Sally Hunter Fine Art in 1987 Dawson gave up all commercial work to concentrate on exhibiting. His series of solo shows included a second with Sally Hunter in 1991. Dawson's watercolours take a wry look at everyday life, contemporary and of his childhood.

Gladys DAWSON 1909–1993 Artist in watercolour, line and wash, born in Rochdale, Lancashire, who sometimes exhibited under her married name Gladys Woodruff. She studied at Heatherley's School of Fine Art, 1936–9, teachers including R O Dunlop, Paul Drury and Frederic Whiting. She was successful in a number of commercial fields, such as textile designs for Liberty and Courtauld, greeting cards for Raphael Tuck and Valentine and book jackets. She was a member of RCamA from 1946, SWA from 1953, becoming its vice-president and president. Also exhibited with RI, RWA, Walker Art Gallery in Liverpool and elsewhere. She had a number of solo shows including several in Colwyn Bay, 1947–54; Trinidad, 1954; Kenya, 1963; and Bourne Hall, Epsom, 1974. Williamson Art Gallery in Birkenhead holds her work. She specialised in making watercolour records of windmills, castles and old buildings plus birds and the small animals of Britain. Lived in Banstead, Surrey.

Janet DAWSON 1935– Artist, teacher and gallery director, born in Sydney, Australia, who studied at the National Gallery of Victoria School, 1951–6, then in London at the Slade School of Fine Art, 1957–8, on a National Gallery of Victoria Travelling Scholarship, 1956. She also won a Boise Scholarship, 1959; Archibald Prize, 1973, for a portrait of her husband, Michael Boddy; Gold Coast Purchase Prize, 1975; Trustees (Purchase) prize, 1975; and Mosman and University of New South Wales Prizes, Sydney, 1979. After periods studying and working on lithography and etching in Paris, and printing at Anticoli Corrado, Italy, Dawson returned to Australia in 1961, where her career showed impressive versatility. She directed Gallery A in Melbourne, where in the early 1960s she ran a print workshop and held classes, then oversaw Gallery A in Sydney. She was also engaged over the years on work at the Australian Museum, set and costume design for theatrical productions and poster design. In addition, she produced her own pictures, ranging from portraits to abstraction, notable for the use of a subtle palette. Dawson's work was exhibited in group and solo shows, the Australian National University, Canberra, giving her a big exhibition in 1994. She is represented in many Australian public collections.

Mabel DAWSON 1887–1965 Painter, decorator and embroiderer, born in Edinburgh, where she studied at the College of Art under William Walls and Frank Calderon. Exhibited her work, which regularly featured animals and birds, at RA, RSW and RSA especially, Royal Glasgow Institute of the Fine Arts and abroad. She did work for the Scottish Society for the Protection of Wild Birds in the 1930s. Newport Museum and Art Gallery holds her work. Lived in Edinburgh.

Montague DAWSON 1895–1973 Painter of ships and the sea in oil and watercolour. Born in London, Dawson studied under the noted marine painter Charles Napier Hemy. Contributing to Dawson's background were the fact that his grandfather had been the painter Henry Dawson, his father was a sea captain and Dawson himself served at sea during World War I and afterwards. After Royal Navy service he began painting full-time, contributing pictures to the RA, leading London and provincial galleries as well as showing overseas. His work is owned by the National Maritime Museum, provincial and foreign galleries. Dawson's clipper ships are distinctive, and he retains his position as a premier marine painter in the realist tradition regardless of changes in artistic fashion. Lived at Milford-on-Sea, Hampshire.

Patricia Vaughan DAWSON 1925– Printmaker, watercolourist and artist in papier mâché, and teacher, born in Liverpool. Until marriage in 1948 she showed under the name Patricia Wright. She studied at Croydon School of Art, 1941–5, under Reginald Marlow and Ruskin Spear. Some of her work was inspired by the writings of the novelist John Cowper Powys and was illustrated in *The Powys Review*. From 1945–6 Dawson worked in the studio of Raoh Schorr, a Swiss sculptor based in Chelsea; from 1946–8 taught art at Ashfold, a preparatory school; then in 1963–6 she lectured at the Tate Gallery. She produced a series of slide strips and booklets introducing art to children. Showed with LG, Bear Lane Gallery in Oxford, London Building Centre and elsewhere. Had a solo show at St John's, Smith Square. British Museum, Victoria Art Gallery in Bath and other provincial collections hold her work. Lived in Ludlow, Shropshire.

Peter DAWSON 1947– Artist in oil, watercolour and mixed media and teacher, born in Leeds, Yorkshire. He studied at Bingley College of Education, 1967–71, teachers including Robert Lee. Until 1979 Dawson painted almost entirely in oils, mainly the human figure; there followed several years' experiment with watercolours; some years of exploration, involving buildings and things seen during extensive travels; then work affirming past interests and using objects such as Egyptian wall paintings, icons and Islamic miniatures. Was elected RI in 1982. Solo shows began with Anthony Parton Gallery, Bradford, 1972, later ones including Luton Art Gallery, 1982. In 1989 Dawson was co-author and co-illustrator with his wife Andrea of *Albania – a Guide and Illustrated Journal*. Many of Dawson's pictures were in public and private collections, some being published as limited editions, posters and reproduction prints. Lived in Little Hadham, Hertfordshire.

Phyllis DAWSON 1903– Illustrator and wood engraver, born in London. She studied at Clapham School of Art with William Washington, then at Canterbury School of Art under John Austen. Drew for magazines and showed at RBA and in the Kent area. Work in Canterbury Royal Museum. Lived in Canterbury.

P Norman DAWSON 1902– Painter and teacher, born in Chadderton, Lancashire. He had a widespread education, including Glasgow University, universities in Canada, Royal College of Art, 1921–7, where his teachers included Frank Short, the British School in Rome and elsewhere abroad. He held a number of teaching appointments, including Camberwell and Winchester Schools of Arts and Crafts and the principalship of the Southern College of Art. Exhibited LG, Leicester Galleries, Cooling Galleries, London Gallery and at the Museum of Modern Art, New York, which holds his work. Lived in Winchester, Hampshire.

Rhoda DAWSON 1897–1992 Artist and craftsman, born in London where she died, daughter of the artists Nelson and Edith Dawson. She married the sculptor John Bickerdike. After St Paul's School Dawson attended Hammersmith School of Art and then the Royal Academy Schools, where her teachers included Walter Sickert. She then worked for Heal's Art Gallery until 1930, when she went for some years to Newfoundland and Labrador to join the Grenfell Medical Mission. There she taught crafts and rug design, examples including her own work being shown at Canada House in 1991. After returning to England Dawson studied anthropology briefly at London School of Economics, aided Bickerdike with models for the Museum of Ghana and worked in Gunnersbury Museum. She had a show of her Canadian watercolours at Fine Art Society in 1989, and a large group was bought by the Memorial University Art Gallery in St John's.

Robert DAWSON fl. from c.1900–1948 Decorative designer, painter, craftsman and teacher, born in Bingley, Yorkshire, where he eventually returned. After studying at Royal College of Art Dawson was assistant master there for two years, was headmaster of Belfast Municipal School of Art for 18 years, then became principal of Manchester's equivalent School, 1919–39, where he greatly expanded its role in the region. He showed at RHA, RA and Walker Art Gallery in Liverpool.

Robert DAWSON 1926–1997 Prolific, auto-didactic landscape painter and teacher, son of a Staffordshire postman, Dawson early aspired to be an artist. Left Leek High School at 17; was offered a scholarship to Stoke-on-Trent College of Art, but his mother persuaded him not take it up; joined a solicitor's office; then aged 22 successfully joined a dance band, playing the alto-saxophone, and touring United States Army Air Force bases in Germany. After studying English and art at Clarendon College, Nottingham, in 1965, in 1966 began a two-year teacher training course at Sidney Webb College, to become a primary school teacher, teaching in London, then from 1971 until retirement 20 years later at Trent Bridge Junior School, Nottingham. Was a member of RCamA, the Society of Staffordshire Artists and had several solo exhibitions. In 1973 and 1974 won the Holbrook Prize at Nottingham Castle Museum. Dawson collected pictures, influences on his rather dour landscapes being John Elwyn, Sheila Fell, Josef Herman and Joan Eardley. There was a retrospective show, Mainly Wales, at Goldmark Gallery, Uppingham, in 2000; in 2002, Goldmark released its film on Dawson, *Just Being An Artist*. There was a Dawson show at De Lacey Fine Art, Liverpool, in 2002, another at The Albany Gallery, Cardiff, 2003. Lived in West Bridgford, Nottinghamshire.

Elsa DAX 1972– Versatile artist, whose major work themes as a painter were "myth, legends and fairytales. The reason for this is because I find reality terribly sad and cruel. I need to escape to another dimension.... People think that my style is like Chagall's." Dax gained her master's in cinema, Russian art studies, Constructivism and Suprematism at the Sorbonne, in Paris, where she was born. In 1996, she was both a multi-media assistant, Pompidou Centre, and television production assistant at the Musée d'Orsay for *Whistler, an American in Paris*, directed by Edwige Kertes; in 1997, was a production cinema assistant, Ciné Lumière, South Kensington; and from 1998 worked as a television encoder and editor for Xtreme Information Ltd; in 1999 working as an editor at the Cannes Advertisement Festival. Dax was founder of the Paris Stuckists and from 2001 took part in many international Stuckist shows. Her solo exhibitions latterly included Westminster Gym, Houses of Parliament, and Lourdes Museum, Pau, France, both 2002. Lived in north London.

Anthony DAY 1922– Painter, born and lived in Wicken, Cambridgeshire, who "concentrated solely on the towns and landscapes of the fen country, poetic in spirit, updating the English watercolour tradition." Day studied under John Hookham at Cambridge School of Art and with J Anthony Betts at Reading University. Group shows included RA Summer Exhibition, RBA, NEAC and Laing Art Competitions. By 2000 Day had had more than 80 solo exhibitions, among them five in London, mainly in East Anglia, including Castle Museum, Norwich, and Old Fire Engine House Ely, 2000. Herbert Art Gallery, Coventry; Nuffield Foundation; Oxford and Cambridge colleges; and several education committees held Day's work.

Harold Armstrong Edward DAY 1924– Painter of landscape in a rather naïve style, born in Crewe, Cheshire, who obtained a Ford Scholarship and qualified as a mechanical engineer. Went on to deal in pictures in Eastbourne, Sussex, as Eastbourne Fine Art, his son John taking over the business in the early 1970s. Wrote a number of books on Constable, Stannard and the East Anglian painters. *Day's Diary* described a year's dealing and *I Harold* was his diary as an artist after moving to Nedlands, Perth, Australia. Day built up a collection of Australian artists.

Pamela DAY 1953– Painter and teacher, born in Halifax, Yorkshire. She studied at Percival Whitley College of Further Education there, 1971–2, then Byam Shaw School of Art, 1972–5. After Royal Academy Schools, 1975–8, Day was at University of London Goldsmiths' College ATC Department, 1979–80. Taught in London for a year, then from 1982 at Stourbridge College of Technology and Art. Among Day's Awards were Eric Kennington Prize, Armitage Prize and Landseer Prize at Royal Academy Schools. Shows included RA Summer Exhibition from 1977; Pictures for Schools at National Museum of Wales, Cardiff, 1978; Two Young Painters at Chalmers Art Gallery, 1980; and Woodlands Art Gallery Goldsmiths' show, 1983.

Paul DAY 1967– Sculptor of reliefs, notably in terracotta, and draughtsman, who did a foundation course at Colchester Institute, 1987–8; attended Dartington College of Arts, 1988–9; and gained an honours degree in fine art at Cheltenham School of Art, 1989–91. Although featuring modern people and settings, Day's reliefs had a magical, poetic quality and included recurring images such as sleepers and staircases. Awards included The Sir Alfred Munnings Prize, 1988; Prince's Trust Award, 1991; and The Taylor Foundation Prize, Salon des Artistes Français, 1993. Among commissions was the Conversation Triptych, for Hilton International's headquarters at Watford, 1996. Group shows included Fresh Art, Business Design Centre, Islington, 1991, and Unicorn Pictures Ltd, Palace of Westminster, 1997. Had a solo show at Cheltenham Museum and Art Gallery, 1992; a series in France; then Duncan Campbell Contemporary Art, 1997; and Sculpture at Goodwood, 2001. In that year Day's huge terracotta frieze Bruxelles – La Comédie Urbaine was unveiled at the Galerie Royale St Hubert, Brussels, depicting daily life in the Belgian capital. In 2003, it was announced that Day's monument depicting Royal Air Force Battle of Britain pilots scrambling, and inscribed with the names of every one of The Few – almost 3,000 airmen – would be placed on the Embankment near the London Eye. Two sculpted reliefs on the bronze and granite memorial would show the battle being fought in the air and on the ground. The London Battle of Britain Monument was unveiled in 2005, with an accompanying exhibition at the Cass Sculpture Foundation. Day lived in France. Houses of Parliament and Lord Archer hold examples.

Michael DAYKIN 1947– Artist, teacher, exhibition organiser, studio manager and editor, who studied at Watford School of Art, 1970–1, St Martin's School of Art, 1971–4, and Royal College of Art, 1974–7, there gaining his master's degree. He won the Oppenheim-John Downes Memorial Award. After teaching at Havering Technical College, 1978–84, Daykin taught extensively in England and America, latterly at Barnfield College, Luton, and Middlesex Polytechnic from 1991. Organised extensive exhibitions, notably at Black Bull and St James' Galleries, 1989–92. Between 1980–93 was founder and partner, Metropolitan Wharf and Cable Street Studios. For periods in the 1980s he was listings editor for *Art Line Magazine*. Mixed exhibitions included Stowells Invitation, Mall Galleries, 1972; San Mateo University, California, 1976; Air Gallery, 1984; XO Gallery, 1992; and Gallery K, 1995. Later solo and two-man exhibitions included Studio Gallery, 1984, and XO, 1991. Benchmark Holdings; Musée d'Art Contemporaire, in Skopje; Northern Arts; and Quaglino's hold examples. Lived in London.

Charles Ernest DEACON fl. c.1934–1965 Watercolourist who studied at Richmond School of Art. Exhibited RA, RBA, RI, RWS, of which he was an honorary member, RCamA, SMA, Paris Salon and widely in the provinces. Lived at High Wycombe, Buckinghamshire.

Richard DEACON 1949– Sculptor and teacher, born in Bangor, Caernarvonshire. He studied at Somerset College of Art, St Martin's School of Art and Royal College of Art, 1968–77. Went on to teach at Central School of Art and Bath Academy of Art. The artist became caught up in the movement to redefine the ways of making sculpture and its purpose. He worked in a variety of materials, ranging from metal and wood to linoleum, and was especially interested in day-to-day objects such as pots and chairs. The German poet Rainer Maria Rilke and the philosopher Martin Heidegger aided Deacon's studies of language and meaning. As well as taking part in key group shows Deacon had many one-man exhibitions, including Lisson Gallery, Serpentine Gallery, 1997; and Tate Liverpool, 1999, where his show New World Order displayed inventive industrial-cum-organic pieces, sculpture on the edge of architecture; Glynn Vivian Art Gallery, Swansea, 2002; L A Louver, Venice, California, America, 2004; and Tate St Ives, 2005. Won the Turner Prize, 1987. He was included in the Arts Council's 1993–4 tour Recent British Sculpture and Days Like These, Tate Britain, 2003. Public commissions include University of Warwick and Bank Centre in Auckland, both in 1991, and Musée d'Art Moderne, Villeneuve d'Ascq, France, 1992. In 2000, Deacon broke new ground for a British sculptor when his We Are Not Alone was unveiled in Beijing, China, for COSCO Corporation. Tate Gallery, Arts Council and Saatchi Collection hold his work. Elected RA, 1998.

Liz DEAKIN 1929– Artist in various media and teacher. She studied at Poole School of Art, 1948. Showed with SWA of which she was a member and elsewhere. Lived in Butts Knapp, Shaftesbury, Dorset.

Cyril DEAKINS 1916–2002 Painter, draughtsman, printmaker and teacher, born in Bearwood, near Birmingham. He studied at Hornsey College of Art, 1934–40 and 1946–7, teachers including J C Moody, Norman Janes and Douglas Percy Bliss, his studies interrupted by Army service. During this, which involved postings in England and north Africa, while stationed at Waddon Deakins was able to attend art classes run by Ruskin Spear at Croydon and John Farleigh at the Central School of Art. He taught at Edmonton County School, 1947–8; lectured in illustration at Willesden School of Art, 1949–52; was art editor for Iliffe & Sons, 1953–7; was a freelance illustrator, 1957–71; then from 1971–81 was head of art at St John Payne School, Chelmsford. Deakins showed with RA, NEAC, RBA, RI and RE. His solo shows included Reade Gallery, Aldeburgh, 1973, and a retrospective at Thaxted Guildhall, 1986. With his artist son Tom and Sylvia Deakins, Cyril shared shows at Gallery 44, in Aldeburgh, 1990 and 1999; Hylands House, Chelmsford, 1996; and Lindsell Gallery, Dunmow, 1998. Chappel Galleries, Chappel, gave Cyril a memorial show in 2004. For the 2000 Millennium celebrations Deakins designed a stained-glass window for the parish church at Great Dunmow, Essex, where he lived and a sports hall mural for Dunmow's twin town in France. Victoria & Albert Museum and South London Art Gallery hold his work. Deakins wrote widely on art, including articles for *Leisure Painter* and *The Artist*.

George DEAKINS 1911–c.1982 Painter in oil, self-taught, born in Gosport of a naval family. Deakins served with the Royal Navy for 22 years from 1927. During this time he exhibited throughout the world, with over 60 one-man shows. When he retired he opened a studio at Dunster, Somerset, where he lived.

Tom DEAKINS 1957– Painter, especially of the East Anglian landscape, and teacher, born in Essex, son of the artist Cyril Deakins, growing up at Duton Hill, near Dunmow. Gained a fine art honours degree at Newcastle Polytechnic, 1980, then an art teacher's certificate, Leeds Polytechnic, 1982. Taught full-time from 1982–4, then part-time 1984–91, at Felstead, Essex. Mixed exhibitions included RA Summer Exhibitions from 1983; from 1984 at ROI, where he was several times a finalist in the Winsor and Newton Young Artists Award; 1988 onwards at Fry Gallery in Saffron Walden; and in 1992 at Khoetsu Fine Art, Tokyo. Had a solo exhibition at Medici Gallery, 1989; William Hardie, Glasgow, 1991; and Chappel Galleries, Chappel, 2000. Year before was elected chairman of Dunmow Art Group. Newcastle University, Beecroft Art Gallery in Southend and Epping Forest District Museum hold examples.

Joxé de ALBERDI 1922– Sculptor and teacher, born in Azcoitia, Spain, where he was initially educated. Studied art in San Sebastian and London. For a time he lectured at St Martin's School of Art and at Sir John Cass School of Arts and Crafts. Showed RA, LG, NS and in the provinces. Lived in London but returned to Spain in the early 1970s, where he also exhibited. His aluminium Abstract Form, 1972, was sited in Stevenage New Town.

William DEALTRY 1915– Painter of atmospheric subjects, and teacher, born in York, where he studied at the School of Art. Taught for many years at Pickering, north Yorkshire and the northwest coast of Scotland featuring strongly in his work, plus other parts of Britain, New Zealand and the continent. Showed at RA, ROI and RWS. Had a solo exhibition at Brian Sinfield, Burford, 1999.

Beryl DEAN 1911–2001 Radical, innovative embroiderer, designer, teacher and writer, brought up in Bromley, Kent, who from 1929 trained at the Royal School of Needlework with Rebecca Crompton; studied millinery and dress design under Elizabeth Grace Thomson at Bromley School of Art for 18 months; then won a Royal Exhibition to the Royal College of Art, 1935–8, studying embroidery while teaching at Bromley School of Art. Taught at Eastbourne School of Art during World War II and, having a love of ballet, designed and made costumes and sets for Arts Theatre Ballet, based at the town's Winter Gardens Theatre. Her designs were included in *British Stage Design*, published in 1950 by the Victoria & Albert Museum, which holds her first important religious embroidery panel, Madonna, of 1934. In 1946, Dean began lecturing at King's College, Newcastle upon Tyne. From 1947 returned south to nurse her parents, from 1953 completing five exemplary pieces for the Needlework Development Scheme, set up to raise standards. Having from 1952 begun teaching part-time at Hammersmith College of Art and Building, in 1958 Dean began an ecclesiastical embroidery class there, in the same year having a solo show at the Colour Council and publishing the first of many books, *Ecclesiastical Embroidery*. She involved her students in five notable copes for Canterbury Cathedral. She also made a cope and mitre for Edward Maufe's Guildford Cathedral; a Madonna for All Saints, East Finchley; and five big neo-Byzantine panels for St George's Chapel, Windsor. In 1990, she organised British Ecclesiastical Embroidery Today at St Paul's Cathedral. Died in London.

Catherine DEAN 1905–1983 Painter and teacher, married to the artist Albert Houthuesen. She was born in Liverpool where she attended the School of Art, then Royal College of Art. She lectured in art at St Gabriel's Training College in London, where she lived. Late in life she showed with Mercury Gallery. Tate Gallery holds her picture Sheep's Skull and Ferns.

Frank DEAN 1865–1947 Painter, born in Headingley, Leeds, Yorkshire, who studied at Slade School of Fine Art and in Paris. He travelled widely in North Africa, the Middle East and India and lived in various parts of England. Was a prolific exhibitor, showing Fine Art Society, RSA, ROI, Walker Art Gallery in Liverpool, NEAC and elsewhere. For a time Dean was a member of RBA.

Graham DEAN 1951– Watercolourist who worked on a large scale, concerned with the human figure and using a bright palette. Dean was born at Birkenhead, Merseyside. He attended Laird School of Art there, 1968–70, was at Bristol Polytechnic faculty of art and design for three years, was a full-time painter from 1974, then in 1991 was awarded a Senior Abbey Award in Painting at British School in Rome for 1992. Dean was also involved in a number of films and collaborated with Darshan Singh Bhuller of London Contemporary Dance on several productions. Dean participated in many mixed shows after appearing with British Realists at Ikon Gallery, Birmingham, in 1976, both in Britain and abroad. He had a solo show at Bristol Arts Centre in 1973, others including several exhibitions with Nicholas Treadwell Gallery from

1974, Roundhouse in 1982, Austin/Desmond Fine Art from 1988, Nerlino Gallery in New York from 1989, and Stephen Lacey Gallery, 2001 and 2004. Arts Council, Contemporary Art Society and Victoria & Albert Museum plus several foreign collections hold his work. Lived in Brighton, Sussex.

John DEAN 1930– Self-taught artist, born and lived in Grassington, North Yorkshire. He was a notable painter of his home area, producing large oils as well as piano key ivory miniatures. He trained as a master butcher, worked in farming and the building trade and was an experienced dry stone waller. Took up painting after leaving the Army in 1950. Dean was a fellow of the British Society of Painters and a member of RMS and SM. Shell Oil and John Ward Textiles hold his work.

Judith DEAN 1965– Sculptor who in 2005 won the £25,000 commissioning Jerwood Sculpture Prize with a proposal to cast a small rectangular section of ploughed field in bronze among the lawns at the Jerwood Sculpture Park, Ragley Hall. Dean graduated with honours in fine art painting from Wimbledon School of Art in 1988, continuing her studies at the Rijksakademie van Beeldende Kunsten, Amsterdam, 1991–3. She exhibited throughout Europe, group appearances including La Malterie, France, De Praktijik, Amsterdam, and Galerie Voss, Germany, with two solo shows at Hales Gallery.

Margaret DEAN fl. from 1960s– Painter, muralist and teacher, born in Lancashire, married to the sculptor Roger Dean. She trained at Liverpool College of Art and obtained a European travelling scholarship in 1963. From then she taught in a number of art colleges in Britain; at the Red Deer College of Arts in Alberta, Canada; and from 1990 at Exeter Community Centre, for Devon County Council. Showed widely in mixed exhibitions in London, the provinces and North America, solo exhibitions including Kayler and Spacex Galleries in Exeter, Bluecoat Gallery in Liverpool, Compendium Gallery in Birmingham and Bowes Museum, County Durham. She completed site-specific works for Oxford Architects' Partnership, 1983–6, and a large mural for Exeter City Swimming Pool, 1984. City councils in Exeter, Liverpool, Manchester and Plymouth hold examples. Lived at Pennsylvania, Exeter, Devon.

Mark DEAN 1958– Versatile artist, born in Stockport, Cheshire, who gained a fine art honours degree in painting from Brighton Polytechnic, 1977–80, his master's from Goldsmiths' College, 1992–4. His first video was shown in 1992, venues that year including Riverside Studios and City Racing; he often used material appropriated from film and music, as well as working with self-made texts, animations and audio. In the 1993 tour BT New Contemporaries 93 Dean won an award. Later group shows included Host, Tramway, Glasgow, 1998; Imaginaria, ICA, 1999, a disturbing and evocative tribute to the computing pioneer Alan Turing; City Racing 1988-1998: A Partial Account, ICA, 2001; and Geometers, Nylon, 2002. Solo shows included Ikon Gallery, Birmingham, and Leeds City Art Gallery, both 2001; Laurent Delaye Gallery, 2002; and Sketch, 2004.

Roger DEAN 1937– Sculptor and teacher, born in Warrington, Lancashire, who modelled in clay, cast into a variety of materials. He studied at Liverpool College of Art, 1953–9, under Philip Hartas and George Yoonson, then spent several months at Brera Academy in Milan under Marino Marini. Teaching experience included Bradford and Liverpool Colleges of Art, Red Deer College in Canada and eventually Exeter College of Art, where Dean was head of sculpture. He was also external examiner to many colleges. Dean said that the main influences at the start of his career were Rodin and Germaine Richier, "work concerned with the structure and mechanics of organic forms within a literal framework, dealing with the cycle from birth to death and the regeneration thereafter". Main works were Armillary Sphere, Customs House, Exeter, 1991; Market Arch Relief Sculptures, Ilfracombe, 1992; and Memorial Fountain, fiftieth anniversary of the Exeter Blitz, 1993. Mixed shows included John Moores Liverpool Exhibition, where he was a prize winner, 1964; Millfield Open Exhibition, and Peri-Renneth Gallery, New York. Had a series of solo shows including Bluecoat Gallery in Liverpool; Compendium Gallery, Birmingham; Lane Gallery, Bradford; Exe Gallery, Exeter; and the University there and at Keele. Walker Art Gallery, Liverpool; Atkinson Art Gallery, Southport; Keele University, Crewe & Alsager College in Staffordshire and Gulbenkian Foundation hold examples. Lived in Pennsylvania, Exeter, Devon. His wife Margaret was also an artist.

Ronald DEAN 1929– Self-taught artist who was by profession an insurance broker. Born in Farnborough, Hampshire, he attended the local Grammar School. Became a member of RSMA in 1970, also showing at RBA, National Maritime Museum in Greenwich, with Tonbridge Art Group of which he was a member, and abroad. Lived in Bidborough, Kent.

Tacita DEAN 1965– Artist who employed film and installation, studied at Slade School of Fine Art, 1990–2. Among her awards were BT New Contemporaries Award Winner, 1992; Arts Council of Great Britain Film and Video Award and Barclays Young Artist Award, runner-up, both 1993; London Arts Board, 1994; and FRAC Award in Bourges, France, 1995. Group shows included Six Slade Students, Rijksakademie, Amsterdam, 1992; Peripheral States at Benjamin Rhodes Gallery, 1993; Dew of Gold, Frith Street Gallery, 1995; and British Art Show 4, with tour, 1995–6. Her Foley Artists solo show was at the Tate Gallery, 1996, and Recent films and other works at Tate Britain in 2001. In 2003, Dean had an exhibition at Musée d'Art Moderne de la Ville de Paris, France. This comprised two new works, Boots and Pie, shown with earlier creations. Others followed at De Pont, Stichting voor Hedendaagse Kunst, Tilburg, Netherlands, and Frith Street Gallery, both 2004, and there was one at Tate St Ives, 2005–6. Dean constantly travelled abroad with her film camera, seeking evocative scenes. An interesting development in the artist's career took place in 2005 when An Aside, at Camden Arts Centre, comprised Dean's choice of other artists, including Rodney Graham and Sharon Lockhart.

Angela DEANE: *see* **Angela THORNE**

Caroline DEANE 1961– Painter and draughtsman with a strong interest in the human form. From 1981–2 she studied fine art at Plymouth College, from 1982–5 at Cheltenham College of Art, with a postgraduate course at

Byam Shaw School. In 1983 Deane won a scholarship to the British School, Rome, to study Italian Renaissance painting; in 1989 the British Council funded a year in China to research its traditional painting and calligraphy, which influenced her own work. Won first prize at Winsor & Newton Award Exhibition Britain's Painters 1988, at Mall Galleries. Thompson's Gallery showed her work.

Frederick DEANE 1924– Portrait painter, born in Manchester, where he studied at the Junior School of Art, Manchester College of Art, 1940–2, then the Royal Academy Schools, 1946–51, taught by Philip Connard. Had several one-man shows. He did a number of portraits in a formal style of notable people and dignitaries, including the writer Lord David Cecil. Manchester City Art Gallery holds his portrait of Edward John Stanley, Earl of Derby. Chelsea Arts Club member who lived at Llan Festioniog, Gwynned.

Chris DEARDEN 1941– Painter in watercolour and oil and teacher, born in Halifax, Yorkshire, who studied at Huddersfield School of Art. He was a textile designer in Bradford and Belfast for 18 years, from 1982 teaching landscape painting. Settled in Ireland from 1973, living at Greenisland, County Antrim. Dearden was an associate of RUA and a member of Ulster Watercolour Society. Also showed with RHA; Narrow Water Gallery, Warrenpoint; Kelly Hotel, Wexford, annual show from 1988; and at Dublin Castle, 1995. Among awards was the Queen's Award for Export, 1978. Had many solo shows, including a series at Queen's University, Belfast, also Ulster Arts Club, Newry Art Centre, Seymour Gallery in Lisburn, Trooperslane Gallery, Carrick, and Cavehill Gallery, Belfast. HRH The Prince of Wales, BBC, Albert Reynolds the former Irish prime minister and many private collections in Britain and abroad hold examples.

Harold DEARDEN 1888–1962 Painter in oil and watercolour, draughtsman in ink and wash. Dearden studied at Rochdale School of Art under H Barrett Carpenter, 1905–10, then at the Royal College of Art for five years under Gerald Moira. Dearden, a strong draughtsman, went on to become head of Swindon Art School for 30 years from 1920 and was president for a time of Swindon Artists' Society. He exhibited in London and provincial galleries and Swindon Museum and Art Gallery holds his work. Lived in Swindon.

Alison DEBENHAM 1903–1967 Painter, whose work was closely concerned with her family, London house and the south of France. Family money – her father, Sir Ernest Debenham, ran the store business – enabled her to choose her life. After a finishing school in Paris she entered Slade School of Fine Art for several years in 1921, in 1928 moving to Paris, in 1929 to south of France where she studied with Simon Bussy and met painters and writers such as Matisse and André Gide. Married the artist René Leplat in 1930. They showed at Galerie Vignon, Paris, Alison in 1932. In 1935 had a show at Zwemmer Gallery, London, and was associated with the Euston Road painters. There was a memorial show at Richmond Hill Gallery, 1968, another show at Belgrave Gallery in 1976.

Charles DEBENHAM 1933– Painter and designer, born in Colchester, Essex, settling nearby at Great Horkesley. Aged 14, began evening classes at Colchester School of Art, training there as an illustrator full-time from 1948–53, teachers including John O'Connor, Blair Hughes-Stanton, Hugh Cronyn and Carel Weight. Aged 21, Debenham joined an advertising firm, eventually setting up his own design business, where he "moved into public information, selling ideas rather than things." His client list ranged from America's Department of Agriculture, Anglian Water, British Telecom and the National Grid to Bowater, St Paul's Cathedral and London International Boat Show. For these, he travelled extensively, designing exhibitions. Simultaneously, Debenham gained a reputation as a painter, mixed shows including RA, RWA, South West Academy and Colchester Art Society, of which he was a senior member. One-man exhibitions included The Minories and Digby Gallery, both in Colchester; Gainsborough's House and Quay Theatre, both in Sudbury; and Chappel Galleries, Chappel. His show there in 2000 coincided with the publication of *Charles Debenham's East Anglia*, by David Buckman, published by Sansom & Company. It included a profile of the artist, anecdotes and extensive illustrations of lesser-known corners of the region which Debenham had painted since he was a student. Colchester Museums Service and Sir David Frost held examples.

De BRUYNE: *see* **Dexter BROWN**

Coralie de BURGH: *see* **Coralie KINAHAN**

Lydia de BURGH 1923– Painter in oil and watercolour, notable for her portraits, born in London. As a child she was taught by Ruth Stalder, of Switzerland. Later in London she studied privately with Sonia Mervyn the portrait painter, 1948–51, more teaching coming from Byam Shaw School of Art, 1952, and Edward Wesson. She was elected Hon. RUA, 1984, being a member of Chelsea Art Society, SWLA, Ulster Watercolour Society and the Ulster Society of Women Artists. Also exhibited at RP, RBA and Royal Glasgow Institute of the Fine Arts. Solo shows included Ulster Office, London, 1956. Most of de Burgh's work was commissioned. She had a contract with Rowland Ward Gallery in London and Nairobi from 1960–9 to paint African wildlife. Painted HM The Queen and other members of the royal family from personal sittings. Her autobiography, *Lydia's Story*, was published in 1991. Lived in Clough, County Down, Northern Ireland. Her sister was the artist Coralie Kinahan.

ALEXANDER de CADENET 1974– Versatile artist and lecturer who won a Harrow Lincoln-Seligmann Art Prize in 1992, graduating from the Courtauld Institute of Art, 1993–6. Short films included *Energy Sources on Bayswater Road*, 1997; *Erection of Masai Golgotha*, 1999; and *The Scream*, 2000. He gave lectures on the Masai Golgotha in 1999 at the Courtauld Institute and the Royal Geographical Society. Curatorial projects included 23 Smith Street, Liberty, a selection of artwork by people in special hospitals and prisons in the United Kingdom, 1995, and The Polstar Art Programme @ Home on the digital billboard in Leicester Square, 2000. Among his group shows were VTO Gallery, 2000; Between Heaven & Earth, Museum of Modern Art, Ostend, Belgium, 2001; and Pax Britannica, Aquarium Gallery, 2004. Included in de Cadenet's solo exhibitions were Cadogan Gallery, 1993; The Mark, King's Road, 1996; Notting Hill Arts Club, 1997; Victoria & Albert Museum, 1998; Erection of the Masai Golgotha, Kenya, 1999; 30 Underwood Street, 2000; and

British Spies, Courtauld Institute, 2003. De Cadenet's work was in many international collections and he was represented by Briggs Robinson Gallery, New York.

Andy DeCOMYN 1966– Sculptor, born in Hollywood, Worcestershire, who gained a diploma in three-dimensional design at Bournville College of Art, 1984–6; was a self-employed sculptor and designer, 1986–7; studied life sculpture under Stuart Osborne, 1987; graduated with honours in art and design from Birmingham Institute of Art and Design, 1997–00; then was a self-employed public artist. Collaborated with the Essex School of Woodcarving on the Berlin Airlift Memorial, at National Memorial Arboretum, near Lichfield, 2001. In that year, DeComyn's own Shot at Dawn Memorial, also at the Arboretum, commemorated the 306 British soldiers shot by their own side during World War I. His Piper's Memorial was completed for Longueval, on the Somme battlefield, in northern France, 2002. DeComyn "developed a self-hardening clay mixture which the sculptures are finished in." Lived at Northfield, Birmingham.

Denise de CORDOVA 1957– Sculptor, sometimes listed alphabetically under Cordova, who graduated with honours from Brighton Polytechnic, 1977–80, gaining her master's from the Royal College of Art, 1980–3. She took part in Sculpture in the Cloister, Jesus College, Cambridge, and Contemporary Portraits, Flowers East, both 1988, and East End Open Studios, at Carpenter's Road, 1989. In 1988, de Cordova had a solo exhibition at The Showroom, in 1988–89 completing public sculpture for council buildings in Bury St Edmunds.

Hilda E DEE fl. c. 1930-1980 Painter and potter, based in Woodbridge, Suffolk, where she exhibited. The pots Dee produced on occasion became subjects for still life paintings, and she tackled other subjects. Her work was offered by the Woodbridge auctioneers Neal, Sons & Fletcher and by the Peasenhall Art and Antiques Gallery, Peasenhall.

John DEE 1938– Sculptor, born in Northampton, who studied at Reading University and Slade School of Fine Art. He was included in the Arts Council's touring Contemporary British Sculpture of 1966, by which time his work was "a synthesis of the forms of art known as 'painting' and 'sculpture', 'costructivism and 'surrealism'", he said. The Arts Council acquired Dee's 1966 abstract work Revelation, in fibreglass and plywood. Also took part in mixed shows at AIA Gallery and Leeds (Merrion Centre) National Sculpture Competition, in which he won a prize. Solo shows included Hull University, 1966.

Heather DEEDMAN 1960– Artist who graduated with honours from Stourbridge College of Art, 1981–4, then the Slade School of Fine Art, 1984–6. She participated in New Contemporaries, ICA and tour, 1986; Death, Cambridge Darkroom/Kettle's Yard, Cambridge, 1988; and East End Open Studios, at Carpenter's Road, 1989. There, she showed The Death of Albert, an installation with cloth, clay and paint. Deedman was artist-in-residence, Ravenor School, 1986–7. In 1988, she shared an exhibition at Towner Art Gallery, Eastbourne.

Geoffrey DEELEY 1911– Sculptor and teacher, born in Netherton, Worcestershire. He studied sculpture at Wolverhampton School of Art and Royal College of Art, winning Prix de Rome which enabled him to study in Rome in 1935. The relief with which he won the prize was bought by Dudley Art Gallery and is called The Conquest of Air by Man. Deeley went on to become head of sculpture at Goldsmiths' College School of Art, retiring in 1975. Deeley's Staindrop Sandstone sculpture Christ and Mary Magdalene, in Gornal Wood Crematorium Garden of Remembrance in Dudley, completed in 1962, has slightly Primitivist tendencies, in the manner of Epstein.

Stephanie DEES 1974– Atmospheric painter and draughtsman, born in Hexham, Northumberland, who graduated with honours from Edinburgh College of Art, 1992-6, gaining her master's in painting there, 1996–8. Awards included Scottish Gallery Prize for Drawing, Eastern General Hospital, 1996; Highly Commended, D M Hall Centenary Exhibtion, and Andrew Grant Bequest Prize for Drawing, both 1997; and Scottish International Educational Trust Award, 1998. Was a prolific mixed-show exhibitor throughout Britain, solo exhibitions including Scottish Gallery, 2001. The urban landscape of Edinburgh was important in Dees' work. Chartered Surveyors of Scotland, Eastern General and Princess Margaret Rose Hospitals, Caledonian Hotel and several corporate collections hold examples.

Polly de FALBE 1961– Painter, notable for still life, who studied at Slade School of Fine Art, gaining a bachelor's degree, 1979–83. Mixed shows included Christie's Pick of Graduate Art, Wigmore Hall Foyer, 1983; Kingsgate Workshop Gallery, from 1985; and Blenheim Gallery, 1988. Shared a show with David Drey at Bartley Drey Gallery, 1995.

Georges F M de FOSSARD 1898– Painter, miniaturist, illustrator and mural artist. He studied under the portrait painter Robin Watt, 1924–6, then at St Martin's School of Art, 1927–8. Exhibited SGA, PS, RMS, NS and elsewhere. Lived for a time in London.

Robert de FRESNES 1908–1995 Painter in oil and watercolour, subjects including portraits, thoroughbred racehorses, still life and flowers. He was a member of the Interior Decorators and Designers' Association and acted as a consultant designer. Born in Glasgow, de Fresnes' original name was Conroy-Robertson; he assumed the title of Baron de Fresnes by deed poll in 1944. He studied art in France, Italy and America from 1934–9, having been at Glasgow School of Art, 1930, under W O Hutchison. His work was held by many private collections in Britain and abroad. Lived in Galston, near Kilmarnock, Ayrshire.

Liam Breandán de FRINSE 1949– Widely travelled multimedia artist, poet and writer, born in Belfast, Northern Ireland. Although known most widely for his painting, he was also an installation artist, involved in art film and video, who represented Ireland at the International Celtic Festival in Lorient, France, in 1997. Showed regularly at Tom Caldwell, Belfast, from 1989, having solo exhibitions in 2000, 2002 and My Secret Garden, 2004. Marx Memorial Library, Gulbenkian Foundation, Northern Bank and other corporate collections hold examples.

Paul DEGGAN 1932– Painter who attended Chichester High School in Sussex. Studied at Kingston School of Art,

1945, under Reginald Brill, then at Chichester School of Art, 1952–3. Showed at RA, LG, Young Contemporaries, Piccadilly Gallery and David Paul Gallery, Chichester.

Jane de GLEHN 1873–1961 Painter, born in New Rochelle, New Jersey, America, as Jane Erin Emmet, a cousin of the novelist Henry James. She married the painter Wilfrid de Glehn, then still known as Wilfrid von Glehn, in 1904. The couple had become engaged the previous year when Wilfrid was visiting America with his friend the painter John Singer Sargent and exhibiting there. The de Glehns were to travel extensively, including Italy with Sargent, who immortalised them in his watercolour Sketching on the Giudecca. Jane was also the subject of work by her husband. The de Glehns' London home at Cheyne Walk, Chelsea, became a gathering place for England's leading artists, as well as actors and musicians. As a portrait and landscape painter Jane showed extensively at the RA, RP, RHA, Walter Art Gallery in Liverpool, NEAC, London Salon and elsewhere. Latterly, the de Glehns lived at Stratford Tony, near Salisbury, Wiltshire.

Wilfrid Gabriel de GLEHN 1870–1951 Painter, born in London, studied at the South Kensington Schools and École des Beaux-Arts, Paris. The family name was originally von Glehn, but was changed in 1917 by deed poll. Married to the painter Jane de Glehn. Early on in his career de Glehn began exhibiting at the Paris Salon, RA and NEAC, as well as Fine Art Society, Leicester Galleries RP, RA, RHA and at many other venues. First one-man show at Carfax Gallery, 1908. De Glehn travelled widely, which provided many of his subjects and additional exhibition venues. He was a painter of beautiful people and places, rather in the manner of John Singer Sargent, whose friend and painting companion he was. Elected RA, 1932, having been elected NEAC in 1900 and RP in 1904. David Messum held an exhibition in 1989; in 1994 a show of both de Glehns entitled The American Connection; and a major exhibition in 2003, to coincide with the publication of Laura Wortley's biography *Wilfrid de Glehn RA A Painter's Journey*. Lived at Stratford Tony, near Salisbury, Wiltshire.

Jules de GOEDE 1937– Abstract painter and sculptor and teacher, born in Rotterdam, Netherlands. He studied at Academie voor Beeldende Kunsten en Kunstnieverheid, Arnhem, 1953–5; Eindhoven School of Art, 1955–61; Orban School of Art, Sydney, Australia, 1957–9, then Canberra School of Art, 1959–61. He went on to be associate senior lecturer at Middlesex Polytechnic, later University, from 1972–03, Anish Kapoor and Langlands & Bell among his students, also visiting other colleges. De Goede showed with Young Contemporaries in Sydney, 1966, followed by extensive mixed exhibitions in Britain and abroad, including Five Dutch Artists, Serpentine Gallery, 1974; Arts Council Collection, Design Centre, 1989; and Unilever Collection, International Art Fair, Olympia, 1991. Showed at Studio Nundah, Canberra, solo from 1963, with a series at Grabowski Gallery from 1967, and House Gallery from 1979, later one-mans including XO Gallery, 1992, and Greenwich University, 2005. Arts Council, Contemporary Art Society and provincial galleries in Newcastle and Bristol hold his work. This was spare and elegant, as illustrated in the ninetieth-anniversary commemorative volume issued by the LG, of which de Goede was a member. The artist said that: "A reflection of the world like it visually appears is not quite enough. It is what things could be that matters." Lived in London.

Roger de GREY 1918–1995 Landscape painter and teacher, born in Penn, Buckinghamshire, nephew of the painter Spencer Gore and married to artist Flavia Irwin. Was at Chelsea School of Art, 1936–9 and again 1946–7, his teachers including Ceri Richards, Robert Medley and Raymond Coxon. His time at Chelsea was divided with Army service in World War II. Taught at King's College, Newcastle upon Tyne, 1947–54, then until 1973 at Royal College of Art, when he became principal of City and Guilds of London Art School. From 1984–93 he was president of the RA, having been elected in 1969 and treasurer for a time. He showed at RA and New Art Centre, having had his first one-man exhibition at Agnew, 1954. De Grey's landscapes, near his studio in Kent or house in the Charente Maritime, France, were quiet in colour and orderly in construction and were given a memorial show at RA in 1996. Tate Gallery and Arts Council hold de Grey's work. He was knighted in 1991.

Bryan de GRINEAU 1883–1957 Draughtsman, illustrator, painter and printmaker, born and lived in London. He was christened Charles William de Grineau and published early work as John Bryan. His father was the artist Alfred Bryan and the son drew from an early age in his studio. During World War I de Grineau served as captain and adjutant in the 41st Brigade, Royal Field Artillery, and sent home vivid sketches from the front for *Illustrated London News* and *Illustrated War News*. For some years after 1919 he lived abroad because of shell-shock, studying with Maurice Denis in Paris and Joseph Pennell in New York. In 1939 de Grineau had a solo show of Caribbean drawings at Walker's Galleries. He became noted for his motor racing pictures, early achievements in aviation and architecture, having a special ability to depict cars at speed. Fine examples were included in the Royal Automobile Club's Diamond Jubilee Exhibition which toured Britain in 1957. The artist also drew for the *Sporting and Dramatic News*, covered events such as the Queen's wedding and coronation and was *Illustrated London News* special correspondent in World War II. Some 237 drawings by him from the magazine's archive are held by the Imperial War Museum at Duxford Airfield.

Anthony DEIGAN 1945– Painter, printmaker, collagist, draughtsman and teacher, born in Ireland. Moved to Essex as a boy and studied at Walthamstow, then at Maidstone College of Art, 1964–7. In 1968 won an Anglo-French Scholarship to study printmaking in Paris. From that year he taught at St Martin's School of Art. Deigan travelled widely in Australia and Indonesia, where he also taught. Had a first solo show at Editions Alecto in 1969, otherwise appearing at Bradford International Print Biennale, RA, Kettle's Yard in Cambridge and abroad. Deigan painted several murals in Saffron Walden, Essex, where the Fry Art Gallery holds his work. It is also in the collections of Fitzwilliam Museum in Cambridge, British Council and Sheffield University. Lived in Saffron Walden for some years. After a decade of annual visits to Australia, Deigan moved there in 1991. He continued to work as an artist, teaching etching at Berrima District Art Society, Bowral, New South Wales.

Peter DEIGHAN 1941– Prolific painter, and teacher, born in County Monaghan, Ireland, who spent his first 14 years on a farm, which gave him a special understanding of animals. Deighan (pronounced Dee-han) worked for a furniture-making firm Kerr Brothers, then was a welder at Vauxhall's Luton plant, where his winning submission in a factory art competition led to the offer of a scholarship to study art. He attended Luton College of Art and taught 10 years part-time. When the young Deighan requested of the butler at Woburn Abbey that he be allowed to paint the Duke of Bedford, the subject was so pleased by the outcome that he commissioned further works for the family, among whom his daughter-in-law, the Marchioness of Tavistock, opted for a portrait of her mare Golden Plate. There followed the first major exhibition of Deighan's work at the Abbey. Legendary racehorses such as Arkle, Desert Orchid and Mill House; jockeys including Lester Piggott and Willie Carson; other sportsmen including the boxers Lennox Lewis, Frank Bruno and Mike Tyson; Diana, Princess of Wales; and entertainers including Elvis Presley and The Beatles were painted by him and issued as limited-edition prints by Deighan Prints. Deighan had acquired a considerable reputation as a portrait painter before being introduced to the equestrian world. His work hung regularly in the annual shows of RP and The Society of Equestrian Artists, The Solomon Gallery, Dublin, also showing his pictures. By 2004, he had had 20 exhibitions in England, Ireland and Spain. Other portrait commissions included Cardinal Basil Hume; the British prime minister John Major; Irish politician Charles Haughey; and the writer Frederick Forsyth. The Vatican is among collections holding his work. Lived in Luton, Bedfordshire.

Brian DEIGHTON 1950– Painter and teacher, born in Harrogate, Yorkshire. He attended Byam Shaw School of Art as a mature student as well as Goldsmiths' College School of Art, his teachers including Robin Klassnik and Wynn Jones. The work of Joel Fisher and Tony Bevan were influences. After gaining his master's degree Deighton went on to teach part-time. He was a founder-member of the Riverside Artists Group, 1986, showing in Soviet Union in 1988–9. Public art projects participated in were Shepherd's Bush and Shaftesbury Mosaics, 1989–91. His work was included in East & South Norwich Gallery/Kent Institute of Art and Design show, 1992. Lived in London.

Martine DEJEANS 1952– Painter, born in France, whose geometrical abstract All the lies (5) was included in the John Moores Liverpool Exhibition in 2004. She said that "The underlying concern of my work is the changing relationship between the individual as a living organism and the technological, consumer environment in which we live.... In this painting the different colours represent various systems or entities, each at a certain degree of completion or visibility, but all competing for space and attention". Dejeans studied at Kingston University, 1998–02, and Wimbledon School of Art, 2002–3. Her exhibitions included Real Site, Fake Site, Old Truman Brewery, Brick Lane, 2000; Pick and Mix, Knight's Park Gallery, Kingston, 2001; Digi-Monde: Painters of Modern Life, Orleans House Gallery, Twickenham, 2002; Diverse, Hansbury Gallery, 2003; and Living for the City, Blue Wing Gallery, Kew, 2004.

Dorrit DEKK 1917– Painter, printmaker and designer, born in Brno, Czechoslovakia. She studied at Kunstgewerbe Schule, Vienna, 1936–8, then Reimann School, London, 1938–9. After working as a radio intelligence officer in the Women's Royal Naval Service in World War II Dekk began a career in graphic design. She worked for Central Office of Information, 1946–8; was a stage designer and illustrator in Cape Town, 1949; then between 1950–79 was in private practice in London, where she continued to live, clients including Air France, British Rail and London Transport. She illustrated several books. Was elected a fellow of the Society of Industrial Artists in 1956. Dekk returned to painting after a design career, having a fascination with back streets and their inhabitants, markets and ruins in Britain and abroad. Mixed shows included Barbican Centre, The Best of British Naïve Artists, 1984; Sue Rankin Gallery, 1987; and Edith Grove Gallery, 1988. Solo shows included Clarendon Gallery, 1984–86 and Maltings Gallery, Farnham, 1985.

Brian De La COUR 1946– Versatile artist and teacher who wrote that his work was "image-derived abstraction, as opposed to gestural Abstract Expressionism and the subconscious manifestations of Automatism. My aim is to transmogrify perceived images, forms and sensations, imbuing them with emotional abstract content. I work from photographic sources". De La Cour was born in Hertfordshire; trained at Harrow School of Art and the Royal College of Art, where he gained his master's in 1968; and was assistant to Eduardo Paolozzi, 1969–71. From 1971 he taught part-time at Croydon College. Group exhibitions included Gold Medal, International Ceramics, Biennale, Florence, Italy, joint project with Paolozzi, 1970; Jewellery, Three Aspects, Wakefield Art Gallery, 1984; Contemporary Artists, Small Works, Mark Senior Gallery, 1995; and The Art on Paper Fair, Royal College of Art, represented by Benjamin Hargreaves. One Aldwych Hotel; the jewellery collection, Shipley Art Gallery and Museum; and in Germany Kunstgwebe Museum in Berlin and Stadt Museum, Munich, hold his work.

Angela De La CRUZ 1965– Painter, born in La Coruña, Spain, who, after studying philosophy at Santiago de Compostela, 1985–9, and moving to England, studied at Chelsea College of Art, 1989–90, Goldsmiths' College, 1991–4, and Slade School of Fine Art, 1994–6. Took part in group and solo shows from 1993, in 1999 being a prizewinner at John Moores Liverpool Exhibition. Later solo exhibitions included Everyday Painting: Anthony Wilkinson Fine Art and John Weber Gallery, New York, America, both 1998; Galerie Krinziger, Vienna, Austria 1999; and Lisson Gallery and Museo de Arte Contemporánea, Vigo, Spain, both 2004. In Everyday Painting, De La Cruz wanted her pictures to be ordinary, like people, with the autonomous personalities that they have.

Jonathan DELAFIELD COOK 1966– Notably a draughtsman with a strong interest in natural history subjects, who cited as "influences: Dürer, Stubbs, Hurst, Mark Dion, Richard Long." He spent "a lot of time in natural history museums" and "bird watching" and tried "to find form and order within chaos – there is a fair amount of editing and simplification in each drawing." Delafield Cook spent two years working with Riken Yamamoto in Tokyo, Japan, then studied at the Royal College of Art, with a Darwin Scholarship, 1994-5. Awards included first prize, Tohoku

Architectural Competition, Japan, with Yamamoto, 1993; The Folio Society Awards, commendation, 1994, with a second prize, 1995; in that year he also won *The Art Newspaper* Award. Group shows included GA Galleries, Tokyo, 1990; The Discerning Eye, Mall Galleries, selected by Bryan Kneale, 1995; and Mercury Gallery Summer Exhibition, 1998. Solo shows included Abitareitalia, Tokyo, with Yamamoto, 1992; Rex Irwin Art Gallery, Sydney, Australia, 1997; and Houldsworth Fine Art, 2002 and 2004. Chelsea and Westminster Hospital commissioned life-size rhinoceros drawing, 1996, and several corporate collections hold his work.

Lucette de la FOUGÈRE fl. from 1950s– Painter and ceramist, born in London where she continued to live. She was educated there and in France, studying art with Léopold Pascal, her husband. She was a member at various times of Free Painters and Sculptors, ROI, RBA and NS, also exhibiting at RA Summer Exhibitions. Had a solo show at Mall Galleries. National Museum of Wales, Cardiff, holds her work.

Muriel de la HAYE 1937– Painter in oil and teacher, born in Oldham, Lancashire, who studied in the early 1950s at Manchester Regional College of Art under L S Lowry. She taught art for five years, spent eight years with Jersey Potteries in the Channel Islands, then lived and worked in Wales at Borth, Dyfed. Her work was "mainly figurative, colour and composition almost as important as Expressionistic approach to figures in landscape". From 1970 took part in many exhibitions in Wales and in 1994 won first prize in an open competition, The Sea, The Sea, at Y Tabernacl, Museum of Modern Art, Machynlleth. She showed solo there, also at Oldham Library Art Gallery and in Aberystwyth at the Museum and the Arts Centre. Y Tabernacl holds her work.

Louise de la HEY 1959– Painter, born in London where she continued to work. She attended Byam Shaw School of Drawing and Painting, 1977–81, then in 1982 worked in Italy. She was a resonant Colourist, fond of still life and interiors. Her work appeared in RBA, RA, Newburgh Street Gallery, Charlotte Lampard Gallery and other mixed shows. In 1990 she shared an exhibition at Cadogan Contemporary.

Serena de la HEY 1967– Artist and lecturer, born in Eldoret, Kenya, who completed foundation studies at Yeovil College, graduating with an honours degree in fine art from Falmouth School of Art, 1986–9. From 1992 she taught extensively across the United Kingdom at schools and other institutions, including the Edinburgh International Music Festival, in Somerset, 2001, and Giants Project, Boscastle, Cornwall, 2004, and was a part-time lecturer at Bicton College, near Exeter, teaching as part of a foundation in environmental art and rural crafts. She gained a Jerwood Foundation Award in 1994; Lowick House Printmaking Residency, Ulverton, 1996; Arts Council South West Annual Award, 1998; and Arts Council South West Year of the Artist Awards, 2000 and 2001. De la Hey contributed to group exhibitions in Britain and America, later ones including Canvas and Camera 3, Photographers' Gallery, 1998; Tooth and Claw, RWA, 2003; and Somerset Man, Messum's, Marlow and London, 2004. Among her solo exhibitions were Ilsington House, Dorset, 1992-3, and Chateau Crosville-sur-Douve, Normandy, France, 1995. De la Hey's work gained widespread broadcast and printed media coverage. A prominent piece was the United Kingdom's largest-known willow figure, The Willow Man, 2000 (rebuilt after vandalism, 2001), sited between junctions 24 and 23 on the M5 motorway at Bridgwater, commissioned as part of the Year of the Artist. This was "created to make a positive statement about regional creativity. It has become a regional icon." Among her many other commissions were Burning Man, Nevada Desert, in America, 1992; Musgrove Park Hospital, Taunton, 1995; Interactive Sculpture, The Lost Gardens of Heligan, Cornwall, 1997; Willow Festival, Rockefeller Center, New York, 1998; and Vessels, Eden Project, Cornwall, 2003. She was based in Stoke St Gregory, Somerset.

Giles DELAMERE 1973– Artist, born and lived in London, who studied at Croydon School of Art and University of Plymouth. Took part in many group exhibitions, including Art on Show, The Gallery in Cork Street, 2001, which included his abstract, Untitled.

Arthur DELANEY 1927–1987 Painter of nostalgic scenes of the industrial Manchester of his childhood, where he was born in the All Saints area. Delaney had a stage background. His mother was a dancer. His father was the zany, anarchic comedian Frank Randle (Arthur McEvoy), who entered the music-hall aged 15 as one of The Three Ernestos, a slapstick act, later making a series of popular, low-budget films (Gracie Fields thought him "The greatest character comedian that ever lived"). Delaney joined a textile design studio aged 13 and stayed with it for 32 years. He married his childhood sweetheart, had four children and began painting as a hobby, the work of L S Lowry being an influence. Limited-edition prints were made of his pictures, which were shown in a solo sell-out exhibition at the Tib Lane Gallery, Manchester, in 1974, and were accepted for the RA Summer Exhibition. Grove Fine Art latterly stocked his work; Louise Kosman in Edinburgh offered it; and there was a good example, New Cross, Manchester, in a Sotheby's, Olympia, sale in 2005.

Barbara DELANEY 1941– Painter, draughtsman and teacher, born in Osnabrueck, Germany, who was married to Patrick Delaney, a student of Peter Lanyon. She studied at Central School of Art and Design, 1968. Gained an Arts Council Award, 1972; a Greater London Arts Award, 1976; and was a finalist for a Gregory Fellowship, Leeds University, 1978. From 1979–85 was a part-time lecturer in fine art (painting) at de Montfort University, Leicester; Kingston University; and Camberwell College of Art. Group shows included Kansas City Art Institute, America, 1975; Anne Berthoud and Redfern Galleries, both 1980; New York Contemporary Art Fair, 1992; Hong Kong Contemporary Art Fair, 1995; Art96, 1996; Drawing Parallels, Birmingham Museum & Art Gallery, 2002–3 (with a solo exhibition there, with chosen pieces from its ethnographic collections, 2004); and Woolff Gallery, 2003. Solo exhibitions included Air Gallery/Surrey University, Guildford, 1978; Atkinson Art Gallery and Museum, Southport, 1979; Sally East Gallery, 1981; Bassetlaw Museum, Retford, 1996; Wolverhampton Art Gallery and Friends Room, Victoria & Albert Museum, both 2002; Tale of Two Cities, Derby Museum and Art Gallery, 2003; and Selective Affinities, Southampton City Art Gallery, 2005. That was Delaney's twenty-eighth one-man exhibition, from which the City Art Gallery acquired her 2003 painting The Meeting of the

Dragon, the Bull and the Anteater. Of her abstract works Delaney said: "After-images interest me, also double images: a thing being more than itself – reflections in water, on glass", or "music like Satie's piano works, or jazz". Public collections holding examples include British Museum; Birmingham and Leicester Museums & Art Galleries; Government Art Collection; Contemporary Art Society; Brunel, Open, Southampton and Surrey Universities; and Nuffield Foundation. Lived in London.

Diarmuid DELARGY 1958– Artist, notable as a draughtsman and printmaker, born in Belfast, who studied there at the Ulster Polytechnic, and at the Slade School of Fine Art. From 1980 he took part in solo and group shows in Ireland, continental Europe and America. The National Self-Portrait Collection of Ireland, University of Limerick, holds his work. Lived in County Down, Northern Ireland.

Lisa de LARNY 1965– Sculptor, painter and draughtsman, born in Hertfordshire and educated in Essex, who graduated in sculpture from Canterbury College of Art, 1983–6. Her work had strong fluid and expressive qualities and was compared to that of Auguste Rodin and Egon Schiele. De Larny was based in the northeast of England, from where she exhibited widely, also completing public commissions. Group shows included Roy Miles Gallery, Blackheath Gallery, The Bruton Gallery in Leeds and Tallentyre Gallery, Morpeth. Had solo exhibitions at Caedmon Gallery, Gateshead, and The Upfront Gallery, Penrith. In 2003, de Larny showed a range of work in a shared exhibition with Sandra Riley at Park Hotel, Tynemouth.

Elise D'ELBOUX 1870– Painter, draughtsman and teacher, born in Southampton, daughter of the artist Walter D'Elboux. She studied at Hartley Institute School of Art, Royal College of Art, Académie Julian in Paris, Camden School of Art and Chelsea School of Art with Ernest Borough Johnson. Signing her work E D' E, she exhibited at RA, Walker Art Gallery in Liverpool, RSA and elsewhere. She held a number of teaching positions, including Royal College of Art, 1897–1901. Lived in London.

Lillian DELEVORYAS 1932– Artist and designer, born in Chicopee Falls, Massachusetts, America. She studied at Pratt Institute in Brooklyn, graduating from Cooper Union for the Advancement of Science and Art. She exhibited in mixed and solo shows in Britain, America and Germany, one-mans including Medici Galleries. Temple Newsam, Leeds, holds her work. Lived in Stroud, Gloucestershire.

Vera DELF 1904–1999 Artist, gallery owner and protester, dubbed the "authoritarian anarchist", born in Cawnpore, India, into a fourth-generation colonial family, whose early rejection of feudal attitudes towards the local population coloured the course of her life. As Vera Hart she attended Glasgow School of Art for a year in 1924, but had little patience with academic teaching, instead favouring the direct approach, her portraits, especially of children, being much in demand. Returned from India with her husband, Brigadier Charles Delf, after World War II and settled in Yoxford, Suffolk. Disliking "swamp Tory tendencies" in local politics, Delf espoused single-issue causes including the Campaign for Nuclear Disarmament, the release of Nelson Mandela and opposition to nuclear power and American bases. Wrote prolifically to newspapers and lectured widely abroad to publicise her opinions. With the help of her painter friends Julian Trevelyan and Mary Fedden, in the early 1960s in the grounds of her home she set up the Yoxford Gallery and showed notable artists. A small memorial show was held there shortly after she died.

Denys DELHANTY 1925– Artist and teacher, full name Harold Denys William Delhanty, married to the painter Kate Delhanty. Born in Cardiff, he studied at the College of Art there, 1942–4, under Ceri Richards and Evan Charlton; served in the Army, 1944–7; then returned to Cardiff, 1948–50, under Eric Malthouse. Became head of art, Cheltenham Ladies' College, 1951–64; lecturer in art, Rolle College, Exmouth, 1964–6; then senior lecturer, Gloucestershire College of Education, 1966–80. Was a member of the RWA, Cheltenham Group and Fosseway Artists. Mixed exhibitions included Royal National Eisteddfod, SWG, SEA, a six-member show at RWA, 1976, and Six Academicians there, 2001. An article in *Leisure Painter*, July, 1988, described Delhanty's working method. His early output was lyrically and romantically centred on landscape, but in the late 1970s he introduced torn and cut paper, "and gradually this technique gave both discipline and freedom to explore new avenues." National Museum and Gallery, Cardiff; WAC; Cheltenham Museum and Art Gallery; and RWA hold examples. Lived in Sheepscombe, Gloucestershire.

Kate DELHANTY 1928– Painter and teacher, born in London, married to the artist Denys Delhanty. She was the daughter of Frank Ormrod, painter, textile designer and Slade teacher. She studied at Reading University fine art department, 1946–50, under Anthony Betts, then at the Slade School of Fine Art, 1950–3, under William Coldstream. Taught art at Cheltenham Ladies' College, 1953–61, and local art school evening classes. Delhanty was a member of the RWA, Cheltenham Group and Fosseway Artists. She participated in a six-member show at the RWA, 1976, and in Six Academicians there, 2001. In the 1980s and 1990s she published articles in *Leisure Painter*. Cheltenham Museum and Art Gallery and RWA hold her work. Lived in Sheepscombe, Gloucestershire.

Joseph DELISS 1917–1969 Painter in oil and watercolour, born in Vienna, Austria, who studied at the Academy there, moving to England in 1938. He served as a glider pilot in World War II. Deliss worked in England, France and the Ticino and was included in a group show at the AIA in 1950. Died in Chelsea, southwest London.

Mickey DELL 1943– Painter and printmaker, born in Penang, Malaya, who graduated from Rachel McMillan College, 1972–6; gained an honours degree in painting, Wimbledon School of Art, 1987–90; with a master's in fine art, printmaking, from Chelsea College of Art & Design, 1990–1. Dell made images by mechanical means using photographs as a starting point. Mixed exhibitions included The Contemporary Print Show, Barbican Centre, 1996; National Print Exhibition, RE, Mall Galleries, 1994; and The Large Print Show, Christchurch Mansion, Ipswich, 1997. Had a solo exhibition, Alternative Arts, 1996. Lived in London.

DELLA: *see* **Della HOLLOW**

Roger DELLAR 1949– Self-taught professional figurative artist and teacher, born in St Albans, Hertfordshire, working in oils, pastel, mixed media, acrylics and water-based media. His interest was in observing people in their environment and capturing light effects. Dellar was elected a member of The Wapping Group of Artists, 1996, the Chelsea Art Society, 1997; The Langham Sketching Club, 2000; RI, 2001; and PS, 2003. He also exhibited at many other venues including RA, RSMA, NEAC, RBA, RWA and in the Singer & Friedlander/*Sunday Times* Watercolour Competition. Dellar had several solo shows and was represented in America by the Peninsula Gallery, Lewes, Delaware. He held a City & Guilds Teaching Certificate, demonstrated to art societies, taught at his Nutcombe Hill Studio, in Hindhead, Surrey, and widely elsewhere, including Dedham Hall, Dedham; The Earnley Concourse, Chichester; Phillips House, Dinton; West Dean College, West Dean; and The Old Rectory, Fittleworth; and in France and America. Dellar was artist-in-residence, Petworth House, 1996–8, and at The Petersfield Music Festival, 1997. Among his many awards were ROI as a non-member, 1999; PS Annie Longley Award and RWS Abbott and Holder Travel Award, both 2000; ROI Stanley Grimm Award, 2002; PS Unison Pastel Award and RI Llewellyn Alexander Award, both 2003; and PS Daler-Rowney Award of Excellence, 2004. He contributed to *The Artist* magazine.

Ron DELLAR 1930– Self-taught artist in watercolour and oil, born in London. He worked "in solitude and without any external connections". Dellar showed at RP, New Art Centre, Leicester Galleries, *Daily Express* Young Contemporaries and elsewhere in mixed exhibitions. Showed solo at Archer Gallery and several times in Germany. He did a quantity of magazine and other commercial work. The Rother levels in Romney Marsh were a feature of his later pictures. Lived in Rye, Sussex.

Jeremy DELLER 1966– Artist born and based in London who sometimes collaborated with others, including social groups and artists such as Alan Kane and Karl Holmqvist. The ambiguities of language and communication were a feature of his work, which included printmaking, garnering artefacts and events, text-based works, curating and performance. Among Deller's group shows were Protest & Survive, Whitechapel Art Gallery, 2000, and the Hayward Gallery tour The British Art Show 5, 2000–1. Solo exhibitions included Galleri Larsen, Stockholm, Sweden, 1998. Arts Council holds Deller's screenprint The History of the World, 1998, bought from the dealer Paul E Stolper. In 2002, Deller was event creator for the Channel 4's *Artangel: The Battle of Orgreave*, a recreation of the violent confrontation of police and striking miners in 1984. In 2004 he won the Turner Prize.

Jeff DELLOW 1949– Painter and teacher, born in Newcastle upon Tyne. He studied at St Martin's School of Art, 1968–9, Maidstone College of Art, 1969–71 and Slade School of Fine Art, 1972–4, followed by a Cheltenham Fellowship, 1974–5. He then went on to appear nationally in group shows, including John Moores Exhibition, Liverpool, in 1976, 1989 and 1991–2, when he was a prizewinner. He had solo shows at Castlefield Gallery, Manchester, 1988, Todd Gallery, 1989, and deliART, 2001, abstract works showing the influence of his stay in Zimbabwe, 1990. Dellow was also an Athena Awards prizewinner in 1988. Was head of painting at Kingston Polytechnic. Public and private collections hold examples. Lived in London.

Koert DELMONTE 1913– Painter and black-and-white artist, born in Amsterdam, Netherlands. Studied there and in Brussels. As well as showing on the continent, in England he exhibited with Wildenstein, Redfern Gallery and RA. British Transport used his posters. Lived in Purley, Surrey.

Toni del RENZIO 1915– Artist, poet, editor, writer and theorist, born in Tsarskoe Selo, later Pushkino, Russia, who played a key role in maintaining British Surrealism during World War II. He said that he was a "Surrealist in spite of himself", although "never a formal member of any Surrealist group". Del Renzio spent his youth in Italy. Under threat of being sent by the Fascists to Abyssinia to fight, he escaped through north Africa to Spain. Having fought with the left-wing POUM during the Civil War, when the republic fell del Renzio had to flee across the Pyrenees to Paris, where he became acquainted with the Surrealists, notably Matta, but when World War II broke out he was forced to move to England. Del Renzio worked briefly with the Free French. In London he linked up with Surrealists around the dealer E L T Mesens, attended some of the Barcelona restaurant meetings in Soho and when the group was dispersed addressed the role of Surrealism in wartime. He was editor of the Surrealist publication *Arson*, 1942. As a militant Trotskyist del Renzio intended that *Arson* should make a durable political contribution, but lack of funds curbed his publishing ambitions. He also edited a Surrealist section in *New Roads*, 1943. About this time del Renzio encountered the work of Ithell Colquhoun, whom he married. After a long-running confrontation with Mesens and other Surrealists, the isolated del Renzio came to feel "unable to practise as a Surrealist and turned to other spheres, including the mid-fifties Independent Group at the ICA." Eventually, "the quarrel with Mesens and Penrose was forgotten and friendship resumed with the one and cordial relations with the other." Del Renzio was in Italy from 1961–74, working on *Vogue*, and he also he worked on *Harper's and Queen* in London. Richard Lannoy, who knew him through the Independent Group, named del Renzio as "a mine of information on art and design from the 1930s until the 1980s." He also contributed to exhibition catalogues on Surrealism, the Damiano collection, Francis Bacon and Ralph Rumney. In 1986, del Renzio and Duncan Scott were involved in organising the important exhibition Surrealism in England 1936 and After, at The Herbert Read Gallery, Canterbury College of Art and tour. Del Renzio latterly lived in Ramsgate, Kent, where he began to work again on paper and collage.

George Frederick DEMAINE 1892–1966 Architectural sculptor and landscape painter, notably in watercolour, born in Keighley, Yorkshire. Studied at the local School of Art, then gained a West Riding County School Scholarship to Royal College of Art, winning his diploma in 1921, and an exhibition. Showed at RA, RWA, Alpine Club Gallery and Cartwright Hall, Bradford, main works including Westminster Embankment, Hampstead Heath and Poole Harbour. Joined Art Workers' Guild in 1950. Lived in London and in Bushey Heath, Hertfordshire.

Richard DEMARCO 1930– Artist, illustrator, gallery director and teacher, born in Edinburgh, where he continued to live. He studied at the College of Art there, 1949–53, then after Army service in 1954–6 was art master at Duns Scotus Academy, 1956–7. In 1963 Demarco was a founder-member of Traverse Theatre. The 1960s also saw him launch the Richard Demarco Gallery and become elected to SSA and RSW. The gallery became a focal point for innovative art and theatre, and in 1975 Demarco gained a Scottish Arts Council Award for services to the contemporary Scottish art world. Demarco was closely involved in promoting eastern European events in Britain, in 1976 gaining the Gold Award of the Polish People's Republic. He directed the Edinburgh Arts Summer School, was closely involved in the Edinburgh Festival and was a visiting lecturer at over 50 educational institutions in Europe and North America. Red tape and reliable funding were problems Demarco enterprises commonly encountered. Demarco's publications included *The Artist as Explorer*, 1978, and *The Road to Meikle Seggie*, 1979. He published a number of suites of prints, including *The Malta Suite* for Editions Alecto, 1970. In 2000, Stanley Picker Gallery, Kingston University, held the exhibition On the Road to Meikle Seggie, and a symposium celebrating the seventieth birthday of Demarco, who was Professor of European Cultural Studies there. Demarco Focus 1, 2 and 3, at the Dean Gallery, Edinburgh, 2003–5, provided a comprehensive survey of the artist's life and work. Victoria & Albert Museum, Scottish Arts Council and Philadelphia Museum of Art hold his work.

Adrien de MENASCE: *see* **MENASCE**

Rosalie de MERIC 1916–1999 Painter in oil and acrylic, draughtsman and teacher, born in Weymouth, Dorset. Her earliest training was with the Vorticist artist Claude Flight in France and Dorset. Then studied with Mark Gertler and Bernard Meninsky at Westminster School of Art, 1936–9; at St Martin's and Central Schools, 1939–45; at Medway School of Art, Rochester, 1945–8; then obtained an honours degree in fine art from Norwich School of Art, 1984–7. Her early work was landscape, followed by a series of imaginative allegorical pictures, a period of Abstract Expressionism, hard-edge geometric acrylic pictures, then a return to landscape from 1983. De Meric was a fellow of Free Painters and Sculptors. She showed at Leeds, Bradford and Wakefield public galleries, Grabowski and Drian Galleries as well as abroad. Later solo exhibitions included Halesworth Gallery, Halesworth, 1989. Between 1963–77 de Meric was a lecturer at Sir John Cass School of Art, London College of Printing and Croydon College of Art. De Meric was married to the poet Thomas Blackburn, separating from him when their only child, Julia, was 12. Julia Blackburn, a writer, edited her father's volume *For a Child*, published in 1999, shortly before her mother's memorial retrospective at Gissing Arts, Gissing. There was a retrospective at Halesworth Gallery, Halesworth, 2002. Lived for many years at Westleton, Suffolk.

Andrew DEMETRIUS 1971– Painter who completed a foundation diploma at Wimbledon School of Art, 1989–90; graduated with honours in fine art, University of Brighton, 1990–3; gaining his master's at Wimbledon, 1999–00. There, in 2000, he won the Burt's Paper and BHF Bank Awards. Group exhibitions included Spirit of June, Henry Peacock Gallery, 1999; Scrounge, Lexington Street, 2001; and Irregular ArtBeat, 2002. In 1999 he had a solo show, Welcome, at Orleans House Gallery, Twickenham, and in 2003 shared an exhibition, Paintings on Aluminium, with Julia Brooker at New Academy Gallery. His pictures there drew on architecture from various sources and ranged over several centuries. BP Corporate Collection held Demetrius's work.

Cathy de MONCHAUX 1962– Sculptor of enigmatically titled, often richly ornamented works, created from a variety of materials who was born and continued to live in London. She studied at Camberwell School of Arts and Crafts, 1980–3, and Goldsmiths' College School of Art, 1985–7. She gained a Steinberger Group Award in 1988, in 1989 the Greater London Arts Individual Artist's Award. From 1986 showed at Whitechapel Open; had a two-man show at Goldsmiths' Gallery in 1989, the year she was in Barcelona Biennial, in Spain; and then was in The British Art Show 1990, toured by South Bank Centre. Had solo shows at Winchester Gallery in 1985; Mario Flecha Gallery, 1988, the year when she was an Artist of the Day at Angela Flowers Gallery; Laure Genillard Gallery, 1990; and Whitechapel Art Gallery, 1997. Arts Council holds her work. Her father was the sculptor Paul de Monchaux.

Elizabeth de MONCHAUX 1965– London-born and -based sculptor, daughter of the sculptor Paul de Monchaux. She studied at Chelsea School of Art, 1984–5, graduated with honours in fine art (sculpture) from Central St Martins School of Art, 1985-8, and gained her master's in fine art there, 1996–8. Later group exhibitions included Process-Space Festival, Balchick, Bulgaria, 1999, and Glas Gallery, 2002. Among her solo shows were Commercial Gallery, 1997, and Cable Street Galleries, 1999. De Monchaux was shortlisted for many commissions and among those carried out were banisters and gate for 190 Alexandra Park Road, 1996, for Susan and Adrian Corbett, and sculpture for the garden of Andrew and Leonie Wilson, 1997. She said that "Through creating sculptural installations using light and illusory mass, which require the audience to pass around and through them to fully experience each piece, I am aiming to make visual events."

Paul de MONCHAUX 1934– Sculptor in stone and metal, draughtsman and teacher, born in Montreal, Canada, father of the sculptors Cathy de Monchaux and Elizabeth de Monchaux. His wife Ruth de Monchaux was also an artist, sharing studio shows with him. He studied at the Art Students' League of New York, 1952–4, and the Slade School of Fine Art, 1955–8, teachers including Reg Butler, F E McWilliam and A H Gerrard. After teaching at the Nigerian College of Technology, 1958–60 and Goldsmiths' College, 1960–5, de Monchaux was at Camberwell School of Arts and Crafts as head of sculpture, 1965–83, then head of fine art, 1984–6, after which he mainly concentrated on commissioned sculpture. He gained an Arts Council Major Award, 1980, and a Northern Electric Environment Award, 1990. Was a member of LG, mixed show appearances including John Moores Liverpool Exhibition, 1961; Notices, Camden Arts Centre, 1979; the Serpentine Gallery/South Bank Centre's Sculpture Show, 1983, for which he was a selector; and Whitechapel Open, 1994. Had a solo exhibition (artist-in-residence), Chesil Gallery, Portland, 1991. Commissioned work included Bench Sculptures for British Rail, 1990; Basilica for Coventry Crown Court, 1991; and

Wilfred Owen Memorial, Shrewsbury Abbey, 1993. In 2004, de Monchaux achieved extensive press coverage for his BBC commission Song, a memorial to Sir Winston Churchill after he had been voted the greatest Briton by television viewers. The de Monchaux abstract tower of 20 interlocking units of sawn green English heart oakwood was for siting in a BBC London building, after an unveiling in Westminster Great Hall and a tour of other venues. Contemporary Art Society and Colchester District Health Authority also hold examples. Lived in London.

Lisa de MONTFORT 1906–1990 Portrait painter and miniaturist, born in Pietermaritzburg, Natal, South Africa. She was educated in South Africa and England, then studied art with Henry Tonks and Philip Wilson Steer at the Slade School of Fine Art, finally in Italy. Exhibited RMS, of which she was a member, RA, NEAC, LG, RP and elsewhere. She was a member of the group of artists in the 1950s living around Charlotte Street, London (including Harry Jonas, who drew her), written about in Clifford Bax's book *Rosemary for Remembrance*.

Miles Fletcher de MONTMORENCY 1893–1963 Painter, baronet, son of Hervey Lodge de Montmorency and husband of the artist Rachel de Montmorency. He studied at Dover School of Art, the Byam Shaw and Vicat Cole School of Art and Royal Academy Schools. Exhibited RA, RBA, Walker's and Cooling Galleries, ROI and at the National Gallery, London, with war artists. Elected RBA, 1935, of which he was in the mid-1940s honorary librarian. Wrote *A Short History of Painting in England*. Lived in London.

Mark DEMSTEADER 1963– Painter, draughtsman and printmaker, born and based in Manchester, who studied at Rochdale College, Oldham College and as a postgraduate at the Slade School of Fine Art. His awards included The Lyceum Prize and The Sidney Andrews Scholarship. Demsteader's work developed from a fascination with the human form and an obsession with classical themes. Texture and compositional balance were important. Demsteader was a frequent exhibitor, his exhibitions in 2002 including Blackheath Gallery; Karen Taylor Contemporary Art, Twickenham; Grey McGear Modern Inc, Santa Monica, California, America; Affordable Art Fair, Battersea; Chelsea Art Fair, Mosaic Gallery, Buxton; The Art Store, Dublin; and Tallentyre Gallery, Morpeth. Later solo shows included Panter & Hall, 2004. Many collections held his work.

DENA: *see* **Dena BRYANT**

John DENAHY 1922–1999 Painter and draughtsman, born in London, who studied art at Eltham Art Centre. He was elected to NEAC in 1980, also showing with RA, RWE and with Eltham Group. Won Daler-Rowney first prize at RBA in 1987. Had solo shows with Anna-Mei Chadwick gallery from 1989. Bank of England holds his work. Lived in Sidcup, Kent.

Melita DENARO 1950– Painter, born in the Irish Republic, notable for gestural, atmospheric landscapes, inspired by countryside around her house in County Donegal. She painted in the open air, producing small panels plus sketches for bigger oils on canvas developed in her London studio. Did a ceramics degree at Central School of Art & Design in the 1970s and completed a three-year postgraduate painting course at Royal Academy Schools, 1995. Awards included Armitage Prize and David Murray Scholarship, 1994, and Creswick Prize and RA Silver Medal, 1995. Mixed shows included RA Summer Exhibition, from 1990; Hunting Art Prizes, from 1993; The Discerning Eye, Mall Galleries, from 1995; Whitechapel Open, 1996; and Solomon Gallery, Dublin, 1997. Solo exhibitions included Adam Gallery, Bath, 1999, and A Field We Knew Together, at JohnMartinLondon, 2004. The Irish State Collection, Guinness, Hambro and Allied Irish Bank hold her work.

David DENBY 1946– Artist, notable for his sensitive portrait drawings and imaginative still lifes, who attended St Albans Art School, 1965–6, Walthamstow Art School, 1966–8, then Royal Academy Schools, 1968–71. Among his awards were the David Murray Landscape Scholarship and Leverhulme Scholarship, 1968–9, and Royal Academy Schools Portrait Silver Medal, 1969–70. His work was included in exhibitions at RA from 1969; at Mall Galleries, 1988; in Continuing the Tradition, Chappel Galleries, Chappel, 1993; and he also exhibited regularly in Sweden and Denmark. Solo show at Chappel Galleries, 1994, with another, called Everything As It Is, at Archeus, with an illustrated catalogue, in 2005.

Jacquie DENBY 1939– Painter, mainly in acrylic, producing figurative work with abstract qualities, notable for its lightness of touch and palette. She was inspired by St Ives artists, Scottish Colourists and the landscapes of Joan Eardley. Studied at Harrogate School of Art. By the time of her inclusion in Showcase, organised by Bruton Gallery, Holmfirth, in 2003, Denby had taken part in more than a dozen shows, including four solo exhibitions.

Helen DENERLEY 1956– Sculptor, born in Roslin, Midlothian, who attended Gray's School of Art, Aberdeen, 1973–7, and who in 1999 produced Milly – The Millennium Horse in scrap metal. Group exhibitions included from 1991 SSA, of which she was elected a professional member in 1995; RUA, 1993; The Scottish Gallery, 1994; Mayfest, Glasgow, 1996; and Art97, Business Design Centre, Islington, 1997. Later solo shows included Heinzel Gallery, Aberdeen, 1995; The Kenny Gallery, Galway, 1996; The Kilmorack Gallery, By Beauly, 1998; and Phillips, 2000. Rhue Art, Ullapool, also handled Denerley's work, which was widely commissioned in Scotland, including Aberdeen District and Clackmannanshire Councils and corporate clients. Lived in Strathdon, Aberdeenshire.

Henry DENHAM 1893–1961 Painter, draughtsman, commercial artist and teacher. Born in Bristol, he studied at Bristol School of Art, 1906–13, under Reginald Bush and John Fisher, after which he was painting and life master there for a decade. Member of Langham Sketch Club and of the Wapping Group. Exhibited at RA, Cooling Galleries, RI, RWA, RSMA and many public galleries in the provinces. Lived at West Wickham, Kent.

DENIS 1913–1997 Painter, printmaker, draughtsman and critic, full name Denis Mathews. He was born in London, son of the Canadian artist Richard George Mathews. Attended Highgate School and was at the Slade School of Fine Art, 1930–3 and 1935–6. Worked as a medical artist and during World War II showed in war artist exhibitions organised by Vera Cuningham. From 1945–56 Mathews was secretary of the Contemporary Art Society. He also appeared on the BBC's radio programme *The Critics*. His work reflected wide travels in several continents. Mathews was a francophile, who illustrated Pierre Poupon's and Pierre Forgeot's *A Book of Burgundy*, published in 1958. Showed with LG, Agnew, Redfern Gallery and had a first solo exhibition at Leicester Galleries, 1947. There was a retrospective of work done 1940–75 at Bartley Drey Gallery in 1994, another at Y Tabernacl, Machynlleth, 1997. Lived for many years at Felin Fach, Brecon.

Dominic DENIS 1963– Artist, born in London, studied at Chelsea School of Art, 1984–6, graduating with honours from Goldsmiths College, 1986–9. Group shows included Freeze, PLA Building, 1988; and Modern Medicine, Building One, and British Art, Basel, both 1990. Had a solo show with Harry Zellweger, Lugano, 1990.

David DENISON 1939– Surrealist artist and teacher, born in Wakefield, Yorkshire, who studied at Doncaster College of Art, 1972. Showed with Camden Arts Centre and widely in north of England in mixed exhibitions. Had solo exhibitions at Manor House Museum and Art Gallery, Ilkley, from 1970, later ones including Cartwright Hall, Bradford, 1980. Brighton Museum and Art Gallery holds his work. Lived in Burley-in-Wharfedale, Yorkshire.

Stephen DENISON 1909– Landscape painter in oil, born in Leeds, he was self-taught. Was educated at Oundle School and Oxford University. A member of the Arts Club, he contributed to *Isis* magazine while at Oxford, 1929–31, and later exhibited at the RA. Lived at Ramsgill, near Harrogate, Yorkshire.

Gladys DENMAN 1900–1999 Painter and miniaturist, born in London as Gladys Denman-Jones, a name that sometimes appeared on her earlier work. Studied with Henry Tonks and Walter Westley Russell at the Slade School of Fine Art, 1919–23, exhibiting at RMS, of which she became a member in 1960, RP, ROI and elsewhere. Lived in Chagford, Devon, later in London.

Gladys DENMAN-JONES: *see* **Gladys DENMAN**

Noel DENNES 1908–1988 Painter, notably in tempera, and printmaker, born in Lowestoft, Suffolk. He studied at Norwich School of Art under Ernest Whydale. From 1961–2 was chairman of Norfolk and Norwich Art Circle and showed at NS, RE and RA. His solo shows included Assembly House, Norwich. Lived at Costessey and died at St David's Nursing Home, Sheringham, Norfolk.

Trevor DENNING 1923– Artist, teacher and writer, born in Moseley, Birmingham, studying painting and graphics at the College of Art there and continuing to live in the city. Denning became senior lecturer in the faculty of art and design at Birmingham Polytechnic (now University of Central England) school of foundation studies/art education until 1985. He was co-organiser of the Birmingham Artists' Committee, 1948–52; in the 1950s was hon. secretary of the RBSA; became a member of the Society of Industrial Artists and Designers, 1956 (worked in book design and film); and in 1965 was a founder-member of the Ikon Gallery, Birmingham. Denning completed several mural decorations, including mosaic, and had a solo show at Ikon, 1966. He was in 1972 a founder-member of the International Playing-Card Society and become a world authority on Spanish playing-cards. In 1989 Denning was made the first Member of Honour of the Asociación Española de Coleccionismo e Investigación del Naipe, Madrid, and in 1993 won the (International) Modiano Prize for the best work of research into the history of playing-cards. Publications included *The Playing-Cards of Spain*, 1997. In 2004, Denning was included in The beginning of Ikon, at the Ikon Gallery.

F Madeline DENNIS fl. from c.1925– Miniaturist and landscape painter who studied at the Slade School of Fine Art with Henry Tonks and Walter Westley Russell, then in Italy. Sometimes signed work F M D. Exhibited RA, RI, SWA and SM, of which she was a member. Lived in London, then at Angmering-on-Sea, Sussex.

Jeffrey DENNIS 1958– Painter and teacher, born in Colchester, Essex, who said that he wanted "to make a new kind of Pre-Raphaelite painting; but not in a revivalist or nostalgic sense". Studied at Slade School of Fine Art, 1976–80. From the late 1970s Dennis took part in many group exhibitions, including Whitechapel Open, 1980; Castello Colonna, Genazzano, Italy, 1985; Comic Iconoclasm, at ICA, 1987; South Bank Centre tour The British Art Show, 1990; and John Moores Liverpool Exhibition, from 1997–8. One-man shows began with 5 Dryden Street Gallery and University of Essex, both 1979; a series with Salvatore Ala Gallery, New York, Milan and London, from 1985; Anderson O'Day Gallery, 1994, Chelsea College of Art and Design, 1999, and Art Space Gallery, 2003. He was tutor in fine art at Ruskin School of Drawing, Oxford, from 1991–7. Dennis was senior lecturer in painting at Chelsea College of Art from 2000. His work was held by many public collections, including Arts Council; British Council; Leeds City Art Gallery; Saatchi Collection; Stedelijk Museum, Amsterdam; and Tate Gallery. Lived in London.

Michael DENNIS 1941– Sculptor in wood, iron and stone, born in Los Angeles, California, America, who studied at Reed College, Portland, Oregon, 1963, and Stanford University, Stanford, California, 1967, where he gained his doctorate. Was involved in teaching and research in neurobiology at Harvard Medical School, Boston, 1967–70; at University College London, 1970–2; and at University California Medical Centre, San Francisco, from 1972, becoming professor, 1978–80. Decided to abandon this career, moving to Denman Island, British Columbia, where he had bought land in the late 1960s and where until 1984 he was self-employed in residential design and construction. During a period at University of Nicaragua in 1984 Dennis took up sculpting, and on return to Denman concentrated on this. He won the Design Vancouver Sculpture Competition, 1992, and in 1993 the Sculpture Margam International Competition with a year's residency at Margam Park, Port Talbot, Wales. On Denman Island, Dennis followed loggers, "retrieving large hunks of cedar trees and sculpting from them archetypal forms which allude to the human figure," sometimes draping "these minimal forms with rent auto body metal." Later, he "became interested in creating outsized archetypal tools ... monuments to the first utensils of our forebears." Exhibitions included Emily Carr College, Vancouver, 1986; Surrey Art Gallery, Surrey, British Columbia, 1989; Diane Farris Gallery, Vancouver, 1993; American Visionary Art Museum, Baltimore, Inaugural

Show, 1995; and Outsider Art Fair, New York, 1996. A number of public collections in British Columbia and Washington state; University of California, San Francisco; and Volary, Czech Republic, hold examples. Two sculptures completed for Margam were sold at Phillips, London, 1997.

Lynn DENNISON 1958– Artist, born in Penrith, Cumberland, who studied at Norwich School of Art, 1981–2, then Slade School of Fine Art, 1987. She was included in the Arts Council touring show The Tree of Life, 1989–90, Reclaiming the Madonna at Usher Gallery, 1993–4, and was an Artist of the Day at Angela Flowers Gallery, 1994, chosen by Tai-Shan Schierenberg. Solo and group exhibitions were held at Diorama Gallery from 1987, solo at Gallery M, 2001.

Robyn DENNY 1930– Painter and teacher, born in Abinger, Surrey. He studied at St Martin's School of Art, 1951–4, then Royal College of Art, 1954–7, and was exhibiting with Young Contemporaries in 1953. In 1958 he had his first solo show at Gallery One. Denny was influenced by American colour-field painters and produced rectilinear abstracts. He wrote on art for *Das Kunstwerk* and *Art International*. Teaching posts included Bath Academy of Art, Slade School of Fine Art and visiting professorship at Minneapolis School of Art. Denny participated in many international group shows and had solo exhibitions widely abroad. He represented Britain at Venice Biennale in 1966 and seven years later had a retrospective at Tate Gallery. Showed with Waddington Galleries and Bernard Jacobson in New York, recent works being exhibited at Hirschl Contemporary Art, 2001, 2002 and 2004. Arts Council holds his work.

Thomas DENNY 1956– Painter and stained glass artist, born in London, who studied at Edinburgh College of Art, 1974–9. As a painter, he had solo shows at Bernard Jacobson Gallery, New York, 1984; Frith Street Gallery, 1989; and Six Chapel Row Contemporary Art, Bath, 1999. Stained glass commissions included three windows at Gloucester Cathedral, 1992; a west window for St Peter's Church, Martley, 1999; a window for All Saints Church, Bolton Percy, 2000; and two windows for Tewkesbury Abbey, 2002. Writing in *The Times*, Sue Corbett described Tom Denny's Tewkesbury windows, in the Chapels of St Catharine and St John the Baptist, as "vibrant", adding that his style was "undeniably modern but it also has links to the breathtakingly beautiful 14th-century glass for which the abbey is already famous." After a year's work there, Denny prepared to create two new windows for Malvern Priory. He was based in Hinton St Mary, Dorset.

Joyce DENNYS 1893–1991 Illustrator, painter and writer, born in Simla, East Punjab State, India. Soon after studying at art school in London she completed World War I propaganda posters. She also made her name as a writer of the *Doctor Dose* books in the 1930s and in World War II wrote humorous articles for *The Sketch* magazine, reprinted in book form in the 1980s as *Henrietta's War* and *Henrietta Sees it Through*, followed by plays and a West End musical, *Kookaburra*. She took up oil painting at 70, initially flowers and later pictures of Budleigh Salterton, Devon. Imperial War Museum holds her work. Lived in London.

Ann Langford DENT 1924– Painter and teacher, born and lived in London. Because of her Quaker origins Ann Dent did not attend any school. She studied at Coventry School of Art, 1940–2; St Martin's School of Art, 1942–3; Central School of Arts and Crafts, 1946–7; and École des Beaux-Arts, 1948–9, in Paris, her teachers in London including Rodrigo Moynihan, Ruskin Spear and Robert Buhler. From 1943–6 during World War II she worked in the government codes and ciphers section at Bletchley. She went on to teach at Colet Court Boys' School and Kensington High School for Girls. Exhibited RA, LG and Chelsea Art Society, of which she was a council member, also being arts adviser to Chelsea Festival. Studies of people made in Calcutta, India, and of cherry blossom in Japan were important. Degas and Rowlandson were key influences. Shared a show with Trevor Chamberlain at Newbury Festival, 1982; was artist-in-residence at Aldeburgh Festival, with a resulting show at Marland Gallery, Snape Maltings, 1998. National Portrait Gallery holds her portrait of the writer Sir Angus Wilson; Hinckley Borough Council, Leicestershire, and several notable corporate and private collections also hold examples.

Richard DENT 1902–1981 Self-taught artist who also did repoussé work in copper and enamel. Born in Hereford he exhibited with the Loggia Gallery, Free Painters and Sculptors and elsewhere. Sometimes signed work Richard D. Lived in London.

Robert Stanley Gorrell DENT 1909–1991 Watercolourist, etcher and teacher, born in Newport, Monmouthshire. In late 1920s he entered an engineering course at Newport Technical College, but later moved to Art School. From there he gained a place at Royal College of Art in the engraving school, 1931. In 1933 he gained his diploma and the British Institution Scholarship and was runner-up in Prix de Rome Scholarship, 1935, when he joined staff of Cheltenham School of Art. Served in Army, 1942–4, and resumed teaching at Cheltenham when invalided out, becoming principal in 1950 until 1974. Was appointed RE, RWS and RWA, also showing at RA, RSA, NEAC, RBA, Art Institute of Chicago and elsewhere. A memorial exhibition of his etchings was held at Cheltenham Art Gallery in 1991. It, Newport Art Gallery and Museum, RWS, RWA and National Library Wales, Aberystwyth, hold his work. Lived in Charlton Kings, Cheltenham, Gloucestershire.

Kate DENTON 1954– Sculptor and teacher, whose bronzes were notable for capturing animal movement. She was born in Sheffield, Yorkshire, where her family ran a steel foundry for several generations. In 1966 they moved to Jersey, where Kate was greatly influenced by wild life in Gerald Durrell's zoo. Gained an honours degree in fine art at Goldsmiths' College, 1976, completing a postgraduate course in bronze casting there, 1980. Was employed by A&A Fine Art Foundry, 1982; lectured at Bromley Adult Education Institute, 1983; and Sir John Cass School of Fine Art, 1988. Mixed shows included RBS Annual Exhibition, 1981, and RA Summer Exhibition, from 1982 and Bloxham Gallery. Later solo exhibitions included Piano Nobile Gallery, Richmond upon Thames, 1995. She showed at Chappel Galleries, Chappel, in 2002. Denton was elected an associate of the RBS, 1993. Commissions included Lord Coutanche, Royal Square, Jersey; Conder Group, Winchester; The Jersey Hospice; and a War Memorial of Running Pilot, West Malling Airfield, 2001. Lived and had a studio in south London.

Kenneth DENTON 1932– Painter in oil of traditional landscape and marine pictures, and teacher, born Chatham, Kent. He won a scholarship to Rochester School of Art in 1944, in 1946 becoming an apprentice to decorative artist Arthus Charles Gull. Also studied at night classes and was encouraged by the painter and musician David Mead. After National Service in the Army, in 1954 Denton set up as a freelance decorative artist while gaining fellowship of the British Institute of Interior Designers and The Chartered Society of Designers. Had several teaching posts, including Maidstone College of Art and Royal School of Military Engineering. Became a member of RSMA and International Society of Marine Painters. In 1983 Denton won the Hunting Group Art Award. He held several dozen solo shows in Britain and abroad. National Maritime Museum, Greenwich, holds his work. Lived in Sporle, King's Lynn, Norfolk.

Jenifer de PASS fl. from early 1970s– Painter, designer and printmaker, forbidden at the age of 17 by her parents to attend art school. While bringing up a family, she attended the City Literary Institute one day a week, studying the designing and screenprinting of fabric. Moved to Suffolk in 1973, taking over the house and studio of Josef Herman, and began self-taught painting, initially of landscape, later concentrating on still life, deriving "my inspiration from the intrinsic quality and beauty of individual objects grouped together". Shortly after starting to paint had a solo show at Minories, Colchester, later ones including Chestenet European Arts Centre, 1980, Digby Gallery in Colchester, 1987, and Chappel Galleries, Chappel, 1997.

Matthew De PULFORD 1980– Painter, born in Oxford, who studied at Kent Institute of Art and Design, 1999–00, and the University of the West of England, Bristol, 2001–4. In that city he took part in several group shows at Spike Island, 2003–4, and other venues. In 2004, De Pulford participated in Encore at RWA, Lux in The Crypt at St Paul's Church and in the John Moores Liverpool Exhibition, where he showed his oil on hardboard Keep it real America.

Robert de QUIN 1927– Sculptural artist in a variety of materials; teacher. He was born in Namur, Belgium, and studied at Hornsey College of Art, 1945–50. Member of NS and Free Painters and Sculptors, of which for a time he was vice-chairman. Took part in many group exhibitions in Britain and abroad and had solo shows at Mall Galleries and elsewhere. Lived for some time in London.

Susan DERGES 1955– Artist and lecturer working in a variety of media, including etching, photography, acrylic, card on wood and enamel on Perspex. Born in London, she studied at Winchester School of Art, 1972–3; gained a first-class honours degree in painting at Chelsea School of Art, 1973–6, while there helping in the workshop of John Ernest with experiments in sound vibration; then in 1977–9 made postgraduate studies at the Slade School of Fine Art in painting and computer graphics, with DAAD and Boise travelling scholarships to Germany and Japan, the former involving metamorphosis and periodic transformation of visual elements. Derges continued to have close connections with Japan: in 1981–2 she won a Rotary Foundation Scholarship there, in 1982–3 doing research into audio-visual media at Tsukuba University, later organising workshops in Tokyo. From 1978 held a series of visiting lectureships in London and the provinces, and became department of media lecturer at University of Plymouth, Exeter, in 1994. Group exhibitions included Hayward Annual, at Hayward Gallery, 1978; Presence 2, Gallery On, Poznan, 1988; New Acquisitions, Arts Council Collection, South Bank, 1993; and Cameraless Photography, Yokohama Museum of Art, Japan, 1994. Showed solo with Gallerie im Zentrum, West Berlin, from 1978, later exhibitions including James Danziger Gallery, New York, and Arnolfini Gallery, Bristol, both 1995, Art Centre Sculpture Park and Gallery, East Winterslow, 2000–1, and Michael Hue-Williams Fine Art, 2002. Victoria & Albert Museum, Metropolitan Museum of Modern Art in New York and several Japanese public gallery and corporate collections, hold examples. Lived in Okehampton, Devon.

Brigid DERHAM 1943–1980 Artist and teacher, born and died in London. Derham was a prolific painter of large, colourful and vibrant pictures, such as circus scenes, figurative but tending towards abstraction. She studied at Slade School of Fine Art, 1961–6, gained her diploma with distinction in painting in 1965, then a postgraduate diploma in 1966. Her teacher Frank Auerbach remembered her as a "rather beautiful and brilliant" student, and Michael Andrews and Bert Irvin also admired her work. Derham won the Walter Neurath Prize for Drawing and Painting, 1962; an Italian Government Scholarship for study in Italy and an Ian Stevenson Travelling Scholarship, both 1965; Boise Travelling Scholarship, 1966; and an Arts Council Grant, 1972. She taught part-time at Byam Shaw School of Art and occasionally at the Slade. Group exhibitions included New Art Centre, where she had a solo show in 1974, and RA Summer Exhibition; she was included in British Painting '74 by the Arts Council in 1974.

Jupp DERNBACH: *see* **Jupp DERNBACH-MAYEN**

Jupp DERNBACH-MAYEN 1908–1990 Versatile artist in many media, although he was mainly interested in painting in oil and watercolour and printmaking. He was born Appollonia Herman Joseph Dernbach in Mayen, Germany (he later added Mayen to his surname and styled himself Jupp Dernbach-Mayen; there was a monogram of the three initials in a box, which was sometimes used). Jupp, whose father was a stonemason, was when aged 12 apprenticed to a house painter, acquiring skills later useful in supplementing income from such jobs as scene painting at the Berlin State Theatre. His employer paid for him to attend Cologne Art School in the mid-1920s, from which he won a scholarship to study under Max Kaus and Hans Orlowski at the Berlin Academy. In the early 1930s Jupp met his wife-to-be, Miette. Although a Roman Catholic he helped Jewish friends flee Nazi Germany, but found it prudent to move abroad; after living in Ibiza and France he closed his Berlin studio in 1938 and settled in England. After internment at Huyton, service in the Pioneer Corps and a nervous breakdown, Jupp shortly after World War II became assistant to the potter Lucie Rie for about four years. Began working on his own account, an early commission being a big mosaic for the 1951 Festival of Britain Dome of Discovery. Other commissions included mosaics and fountains for Sanderson's, 1960; a welded sculpture for the Westminster Bank, New Oxford Street, 1962; a fountain for Centrepoint, St Giles Circus, and a font and cross for the Church Missionary Society, Waterloo Road, both 1966. Mixed shows included Society of Mural Painters, first exhibition, 1950, and Smithsonian Institution, Washington, and tour, 1962. There was a memorial show at Belgrave Gallery, 1996. Victoria & Albert Museum holds ceramic work by Dernbach-Mayen, who lived in London.

Sophie de ROMER: *see* **Zofia ROMER**

Gerard de ROSE 1918–1987 Portrait painter and teacher, born in Accrington, Lancashire, his father a surgeon and professor of music of Russian descent. Attended Accrington School of Art, then won a Royal Exhibition in textile design to Royal College of Art. He studied there in 1939 and returned to the painting school, 1946–50; during World War II served in the Royal Engineers, taking part in the Dunkirk evacuation. From 1950–8 de Rose taught at various art colleges, including London College of Printing, then was head of the faculty of fine art, Maidstone College of Art, 1958–67. He was elected RBA in 1961, also showing at RA, RP, Zaydler Gallery, Bradford and Manchester Art Galleries, Paris Salon and other venues. Solo shows included Trafford, Alwin and William Ware Galleries, Haworth Art Gallery in Accrington which holds his work and widely in America. In the 1960s de Rose developed a reputation as a painter of the famous, subjects including the Duke of Bedford, Julie Christie, Vita Sackville-West, Rod Steiger, Sammy Davis Junior, Claire Bloom and Vladimir Nabokov, this portrait appearing on the cover of *Time* magazine. The portraits are notable for their astute placing of the subject against a plain background. By his peers de Rose was remembered as a flamboyant character. A small man with red hair and a stutter, he was a convivial member of the Chelsea Arts Club, a skilled amateur magician and in his youth a formidable boxer. Died in Hammersmith Hospital.

Freda DERRICK 1892–1969 Artist in pen and ink and watercolour, and writer, born in Cheltenham, Gloucestershire, where she eventually settled, although from youth until 1950, her most prolific period, she worked occasionally from a hut at East Brent, Somerset. She was the daughter of the Reverend J G Derrick, chaplain to the Cheltenham Workhouse and a keen amateur photographer, and was educated at Pate's Grammar School for Girls, Cheltenham School of Art and at London art schools. From 1920 travelled extensively by bicycle, mainly in Gloucestershire and Somerset, putting up at farms where they would take her in. She made meticulous drawings of churches, farm buildings, village scenes, country crafts and working life, inspired by William Morris and the Arts and Crafts Movement. Most were for magazine articles or her own books; she also produced animal books and alphabets for children. Her first publication was *The Ark Book*, 1921. Others included *Gothic Wanderings in Somerset*, 1930; *Tales Told in Church Stones*, 1935; *A Traveller Among The Farms*, 1936; *Country Craftsmen*, 1945; *Cotswold Stone*, 1948; and *A Trinity of Craftsmen*, 1950. In 1995 Cheltenham Art Gallery and Museums, which holds her work, put on an exhibition.

Thomas DERRICK 1885–1954 Painter of pictures and murals; book illustrator. Born in Bristol, studied at the Royal College of Art, where he later taught decorative painting. Sometimes signing his work T D, he exhibited at the RA, NEAC, Fine Art Society, IS and overseas. Derrick was employed by Hilary Pepler as an illustrator for St Dominic's Press, based at Ditchling, Sussex. Lived in Newbury, Berkshire, later in Canada.

Kenneth DERRINGER 1925– Painter and teacher, born and lived in Liverpool. He studied at Liverpool University School of Architecture and Liverpool College of Art and eventually became principal of Warrington School of Art. Derringer was a Sandon Studios, Liverpool Academy and Wirral Art Society member who also showed with RCamA, and public galleries in Birkenhead, Preston, Manchester and Liverpool, where the Walker Art Gallery holds his gouache April Showers, bought from the artist in 1951.

Pamela DERRY 1932–2003 Artist in oil, born in Welwyn Garden City, Hertfordshire. A painter of atmospheric landscapes, she was self-taught. She was a member of NS and showed at ROI, SWA, RBA, NEAC, Century Galleries in Henley-on-Thames and widely in south of England and at Paris Salon. Russell-Cotes Art Gallery and Museum, Bournemouth, holds her work. Lived in Holt, Wimborne, Dorset.

Jane de SAUSMAREZ 1938– Painter, printmaker, textile designer and teacher. She studied at Farnham School of Art, 1955–7; Central School of Art and Design, 1957–60; and Royal College of Art, 1988–9. Taught at Byam Shaw School of Art, showing with its staff. Exhibited at RA Summer Exhibition from 1980. Among her commissions were banners for Phoenix Gallery and the Worshipful Company of Goldsmiths. Private collectors including Sir Brinsley Ford owned her work.

Maurice de SAUSMAREZ 1915–1969 Painter, teacher and writer on art education who after Christ's Hospital studied at Royal College of Art. Among his teaching positions were the principalship of Byam Shaw School of Drawing and Painting and a period as head of the department of fine art at Leeds University. He participated in the Pilgrim Trust *Recording Britain* project. Among his writings was the book *Basic Design*, which had a revolutionary effect on art education in many parts of the world. Showed at RA, LG, NEAC and Leicester Galleries. In 1971 Homage to Maurice de Sausmarez at Upper Grosvenor Galleries included work by him and his friends. Works are held by Victoria & Albert Museum and several northern galleries. He was a Chelsea Arts Club member who lived finally in London.

Alice Des CLAYES 1891– Painter and illustrator, born in Aberdeen, Scotland, sister of Berthe Des Clayes and Gertrude Des Clayes, both painters. Studied at Bushey School of Art with Lucy Kemp-Welch and Rowland Wheelwright, at the Newlyn School of Art, then with Dudley Hardy at Ambleteuse, in France. Like her sisters, Alice Des Clayes spent some time in Canada and like them exhibited there, but whereas Alice and Gertrude ultimately settled in Britain, Berthe opted for Lunenburg, Nova Scotia, and died in 1968. Alice, like her sisters, painted pastoral scenes, all having a fondness for horses. She exhibited in England at RA, in the provinces and at Paris Salon and has work in the collection of the National Gallery of Canada, Ottawa. Finally lived in Newton Abbot, Devon.

Gertrude Des CLAYES 1879–1949 Painter, born in Aberdeen, Scotland, sister of the artists Alice Des Clayes and Berthe Des Clayes. She studied with Bertha Herkomer at Bushey School of Art, then with Tony Robert-Fleury and Jules Lefebvre at Académie Julian, Paris, but was substantially self-taught. She painted a large number of portraits and genre scenes, such as The Pearly King, exhibited in 1934 in Winnipeg. Spent many years in Canada, like her sisters, but returned to London where she died. She exhibited RA, Paris Salon and widely in Canada, and National Gallery of Canada, in Ottawa, holds her picture Young Canadian Girl, of about 1920.

Steven des LANDES 1962– Painter, graphic artist and teacher, born in Preston, Lancashire, where he gained his honours degree in fine art, 1980–3. He then worked as a full-time painter and community artist, teaching painting in workshops and being closely associated with Liverpool Education Authority. He was also a part-time lecturer at Southport College of Art and Arts Centre, 1989. Mixed shows included Acorn Gallery in Liverpool from 1987 and Broekman Gallery in Chester from 1992. Had a solo exhibition at Bridewell Gallery, Liverpool, where he lived, 1987. Others included Skillion Business Centre Liverpool Visionfest, 1992.

Anne DESMET 1964– Painter, printmaker and teacher, born in Liverpool. Graduated from the Ruskin School, Oxford, 1986, with a master's degree in 1991, gaining a postgraduate diploma in printmaking at Central School in 1988. Went on to lecture at Royal Academy Schools, Ruskin School, Middlesex University and Leeds Polytechnic. She was elected a fellow of the RE in 1991, being its honorary curator of prints. As well as regularly showing with the RE, in 1991 Desmet was elected a member and exhibited with SWE, and she showed with Printmakers' Council and at RA Summer Exhibitions. Awards and prizes included Elizabeth Greenshields Foundation Award, 1989 (and 1996); British School at Rome Scholarship in Printmaking, 1989–90; artist-in-residence, Oriel 31, Newtown, 1990; Gordon Tuffrey Memorial Award, RWA Open Print Exhibition, Bristol, 1995; Exhibition Medal, Ex Libris Museum, Moscow, Russia, 1995; and Pollock-Krasner Foundation Award, 1998. Completed commissions for Oxford University Press and *The Times*. She showed solo with Ruskin School in 1990, with Duncan Campbell Gallery from 1991 and Royal Over-Seas League, 1992. Ashmolean Museum, from which her retrospective Towers and Transformations toured, 1998–9, holds her work. Desmet was editor of *Printmaking Today* and was co-author, with Jim Anderson, of *Handmade Prints*, 2000. Lived in London.

Pascoal de SOUZA 1928– Painter in oil, born in Goa, Portuguese India, who studied at Sir John Cass and St Martin's Schools of Art, gaining the de Laszlo Award in 1959. Was a member of RBA and ROI, showing at RA and Paris Salon, and having a series of solo exhibitions at Trafford and Alwin Galleries. Lived for many years at St Margaret's, Twickenham, Middlesex.

Paul DESSAU 1909–1999 Painter in oil who was born in London, was apprenticed to a commercial studio, then set up his own with his brother Bernard, studying art part-time at Hornsey, Central and St Martin's Schools of Art. Dessau's reputation rests on pictures as a fireman artist in World War II: his painting And So To Bed, held by the Imperial War Museum, is sombre and elegiac; four canvases generally titled Menace, in the London Fire Brigade Museum, reflect Dessau's first-hand knowledge of conflagrations during the Blitz; and there are works in several public galleries in the Midlands, including Worcester Art Gallery. After the war Dessau moved to the country to be a portrait painter; he was also an accomplished self-taught pianist and inventor. As a child he tried to fly by fitting wings to his bicycle, later notions including a bedside tea-making machine too large for the bedroom. Exhibitions included RA, RP, Cooling Galleries, the provinces and North America. Died in Bedford.

Gerard de THAME 1958– Painter and sculptor, born and lived in London. He studied at Brighton Polytechnic, 1978–81, Chelsea School of Art, 1981–2, in 1982 won a one-year Rome Scholarship in sculpture and in 1984 a Mark Rothko Travel Award to America. Arts Council holds his acrylic on paper Tall and Old, bought from Air Gallery, 1983. Also in 1983 de Thame showed at Hayward Gallery; in 1984 at Riverside Studios; and in 1985 at Nicola Jacobs Gallery and John Moores Liverpool Exhibition, where he was a prizewinner.

Edward Julius DETMOLD 1883–1957 Watercolourist, illustrator and printmaker specialising in natural history subjects and the creation of his own fantastic worlds. Like his twin brother Charles Maurice he was educated privately and studied creatures in the zoo, and he worked with him until Charles Maurice's death in 1908. Edward Julius settled in Montgomeryshire, by which time he had established a reputation as a book illustrator, working with great exactitude. *The Fables of Aesop*, 1909, and Maurice Maeterlinck's *The Life of the Bee*, 1911, were notable examples. For a few months in 1905 the brothers were associates of RE, but resigned. Edward Julius was a prolific exhibitor at Fine Art Society, Brook Street Art Gallery, Arlington and Baillie Galleries, NEAC, RA, RI and elsewhere. Committed suicide.

Anthony DEVAS 1911–1958 Painter, principally of portraits. Born in Bromley, Kent, he studied at the Slade School of Fine Art, 1927–30, where he was friendly with William Townsend, Geoffrey Tibble and others associated with the Euston Road School in the late 1930s. Married Nicolette Macnamara, the writer and painter. In the 1930s began to establish a reputation as a portrait painter, painting HM The Queen in 1957. First exhibited at Cooling Galleries in 1936, from 1940 at the RA. Also showed at Agnew, NEAC, RP and the Leicester Galleries. Devas' work is in several public collections, including the Tate Gallery, which has his portrait of the poet Dylan Thomas' wife Caitlin, sister of Nicolette Macnamara. Devas' portraits of women and children can be very sensitive as his memorial show at Agnew in 1959 showed. Exhibitions at Graves Art Gallery, Sheffield, in 1991, and Tenby Museum and Picture Gallery, 1992, concentrated on the Devas family circle pictures. Lived in London.

Nicolette DEVAS 1911–1987 Painter and writer, daughter of the Irish wit and landowner Francis Macnamara, of Ennistymon, County Clare. Her sister Caitlin married the poet Dylan Thomas. The story of her unusual bohemian childhood is told in her book *Two Flamboyant Fathers*, 1966, in which Augustus John's family features strongly. Aged 16 she entered the Slade School of Fine Art, studying under Henry Tonks. There she met the painter Anthony Devas, whom she married in 1931. Seven years after he died, in 1958, she married the artist Rupert Shephard. Birds were a favourite theme in Devas's paintings. She showed at NEAC, RA and LG and had a solo show at Storran Gallery, her painting name sometimes being Macnamara. Bringing up a family restricted her painting and she developed her writing, in 1958 publishing her first novel *Bonfire*; several other books followed. In 1987 her work was included in a show of Slade Contemporaries at Sally Hunter Fine Art.

Josefina de VASCONCELLOS: *see* **VASCONCELLOS**

Bob DEVEREUX 1940– Painter, performance poet, librettist, gallery proprietor and festival organiser, born in Dorking, Surrey, who trained as a graphic artist at Kingston School of Art, 1957–61, moving to Cornwall in 1965, based in St Ives. Founded the Salthouse Gallery in 1979, having previously run Sloop Gallery, to show his own pictures, 1973. Devereux exhibited widely, including Newlyn Orion Gallery in Penzance on various occasions; Manchester City Art Gallery, 1983; Black Horse, Frome, 1991; in 1992 was included in Artists from Cornwall, RWA; and Showcase, Truro Museum, 1994–5. Later solo shows included Salthouse Gallery, 1996. Devereux began work as a performance poet with the group Mask, 1970; among his many other activities in subsequent years were the pamphlet *Be Green*'s publication in 1973; first performance with Clive Palmer, founder-member of The Incredible String Band, 1974; a first collaboration with the composer Christopher Brown, on *Seascapes*, 1979; libretto for the children's opera *The Ram King*, with Brown, 1982; in 1985–6 librettos for Rudi Van Dijk for the opera *Kalma Loka* and Jonathan Lloyd for the chamber opera *The Uncertainty Factor*; in 1988 presentation of a programme about St Ives artists for BBC World Service; publication of six poems in Martin Leman's *Just Bears*, 1992; and the cantata *Fluid Form*, with composer Stephen McNeff, 1994. Devereux was closely associated with the St Ives Festival from 1970. His work was widely distributed throughout Europe.

Hilary Joy DEVEREUX 1959– Painter who studied at Loughborough College of Art and Design, 1979–82, and the Royal Academy Schools, 1983–6. She was in a group show at Ikon Gallery, Birmingham, 1982. In 1986 others included the Bankside Gallery Open, Camden Arts Centre in Hampstead Then and Now and a mixed exhibition at Morley Gallery. Sir Brinsley Ford and other private collectors held her work.

Richard DEVEREUX 1956– Sculptor, born in Lincolnshire, who studied at Portsmouth College of Art, where he won a scholarship. He had a first solo show in 1979 at Axis Gallery, Brighton, after which he was involved in many mixed exhibitions, showing regularly at the New Art Centre and Sculpture Garden, Roche Court, Wiltshire. In Stillness and in Silence, "a collection of works reflecting on the sacredness of the earth", toured from Usher Gallery, Lincoln, in 1994. There was a solo show at Yorkshire Sculpture Park, West Bretton, 2002. Tate Gallery, Bodleian Library in Oxford and several other libraries hold his work, which ranged over a wide variety of media.

Phyllis DEVEY 1907– Portrait painter in oil and teacher, born in Birmingham. She studied at the College of Arts and Crafts there, her teachers including Bernard Fleetwood-Walker. Went on to hold a number of teaching posts in the Midlands, notably at Windylow School in Solihull and at the Bournville School of Art. She showed at NS, SWA, ROI, Paris Salon and extensively in the provinces. Lived Wootton Wawen, Warwickshire.

Pamela de VILLE 1923– Sculptor in bronze and ciment fondu, born in Saxilby, Lincolnshire. She studied and worked under T B Huxley-Jones, Anthony Gray and Nathan David. Lady de Ville was a member of RMS. She showed with SPS, MAFA, Lake Artists' Society, SWA, Phoenix Gallery at Lavenham and Pitcairn Gallery, Knutsford, and cast bronzes in her own foundry. Private collections in Britain and abroad hold her work. Lived in Sonning, Berkshire.

Jephan de VILLIERS 1940– Unique sculptor, set designer and painter, born in Le Chesnay, near Versailles, France, who had a lonely childhood, confined by illness. Aged about 12, he produced his first pictures and sculptures, eventually building vast villages from twigs and pieces of bark and paintings using eggs. Shortly before moving to London in 1967, he started a series of slender white sculptures that would occupy him for a decade. Began to exhibit, while living in comparative poverty, in 1968 becoming the first artist to show in Coventry Cathedral. Exhibited at David Hicks Gallery and André Pacitti Gallery, Paris, in 1969, and in 1972 at Sphinx Gallery, Amsterdam. In 1977, resettled in Brussels, Belgium; began a new period of work using paper, wood, earth, leaves and feathers, which was progressively shown internationally. Between 1982–92 de Villiers participated in more than 100 group exhibitions and had over 40 solo shows. In 1986 he designed sets for Paul Claudel's *Cantate à trois voix* for the New Theatre of Belgium, and had a successful show at the Patras Festival, in Greece; in 1987, a space devoted to his work was installed for two years at L'Autre Musée, Brussels; in 1988–9 he designed sets for the choreographer Michèle Swennen; in 1989 had a work placed in the Museum of Modern Art, Brussels, and settled at Jolymont, on the edge of Soignes Forest, for long an inspiration. Among later solo shows was Roseline Koener Art Gallery New York, 1999, including the hybrid creatures with tiny, mask-like faces for which he had become noted.

Nick DEVISON 1966– Artist and teacher, born in Wolverhampton, Staffordshire, who earned a foundation diploma at the Polytechnic there, 1984–5, graduated with honours in fine art, painting, at Wimbledon School of Art, 1985–8; and gained his master's in fine art printmaking from Camberwell College of Arts, 1999–00. Devison became subject leader for printmaking degree courses at Cambridge School of Art, having previously taught at Cavendish College, on the Lewisham Foundation course and extra-mural programme at Goldsmiths' College. Among his awards were an Intaglio Print Prize, 1999 and the Edward Ardizzone Print Prize, 2000. In 2003 Flowers East nominated him for the Jerwood Platform Prize. His exhibitions included Flowers East; Curwen Gallery; London Print Studio; Harrow Museum and Art Gallery; New Ashgate Gallery, Farnham; Inside Space; Harley Gallery, Welbeck; Morley Gallery; St Monde Arts Centre, Paris; Shipley Art Gallery, Newcastle; and King's College, Cambridge. Cable and Wireless and British Airports Authority were among corporate collections owning his work. Lived in east London.

George DEVLIN 1937– Painter, printmaker, artist in ceramics and teacher, born in Glasgow. He attended Glasgow School of Art, 1955–60. Was awarded numerous prizes, including the Robert Harr, Chalmers, Haldane and Carnegie Travelling Scholarships. In 1968 he was awarded a Major Arts Council Award, in 1971 the Cargill Award and seven years later the Exhibit of the Year Award at Royal Glasgow Institute of the Fine Arts. He was elected RSW in 1964, chairman of the Glasgow League of Artists in 1977 and a member of the Royal Glasgow Institute in 1989. He was made president of Glasgow Arts Club, 1997. In the late 1960s he set up his own painting school in France, re-establishing it in 1989. For some years he taught in design department of Glasgow College of Building and Printing. Travelled extensively in Europe and Africa. Devlin designed and illustrated books and in 1973 designed the set and costumes for Scottish Ballet. Had many solo shows, later ones including Portland Gallery, 2000 and 2002, and Scottish Gallery, Edinburgh, 2001. Scottish National Gallery of Modern Art holds his work, one of many acquisitions by public, local authority, corporate and private collections. Lived in Glasgow.

Gerry DEVLIN fl. from mid-1970s– Painter and teacher who won his bachelor's degree and an advanced diploma in painting from University of Ulster, Belfast, 1977–8, then gained a Ford Foundation Grant to study at Syracuse University, New York, where he won his master's degree in 1981. As well as being artist-in-residence for the Artists in Prison Scheme, Dublin, Devlin taught widely in Ireland, including Dublin, Cork, Waterford and Belfast Colleges of Art and the Workers' Educational Association. He was invited to contribute to the *Great Book of Ireland*, shown at Ulster Museum, Belfast, 1991. He was a prizewinner in 1987 and 1994 at the Claremorris Open Exhibition, also at Works on Paper at the Fenderesky Gallery, Belfast, 1988. In 1994 he was included in Beyond the Partitions, put on by Queen Street Studios, Belfast, with which he was associated. Solo shows included Crawford Municipal Art Gallery, Cork, 1990.

Andy DEWAR 1944– Artist and teacher, born in Dundee, Angus, who studied graphics and silversmithing at Gray's School of Art, Aberdeen, 1962–6, lecturing for a period at Aberdeen College of Commerce from 1969. He was a member of the management committee of Peacock Printmakers, Aberdeen, where he exhibited, other group shows including RSA, Aberdeen Artists' Society, Aberdeen Arts Centre and Scottish Print Open, at Artspace in Aberdeen and tour. Had solo shows at Peacock Gallery and elsewhere. Public, private and local authority collections hold Dewar's work.

Margaret de Courcy Lewthwaite DEWAR 1878–1959 Metalworker, enameller, painter, black-and-white artist and teacher, born in Kandy, Ceylon. She attended Glasgow School of Art, 1892–99, absorbing its style, and the Central School of Arts and Crafts, in London, teaching enamelling at the Glasgow School, 1898–1928. She joined the Glasgow Society of Lady Artists in 1905; won its Lauder Award in 1936; was its president, 1934–7 and 1952–5; and wrote its history in 1950. Miss Dewar's presentation casket with the arms of Glasgow, which gained her the Lauder Award, is reproduced in both P Wylie Davidson's *Applied Design in the Precious Metals*, 1929, and Gerald and Celia Larner's *The Glasgow Style*, 1980. Dewar travelled widely. Her work was exhibited in Turin, Italy, in 1902, and she completed a panel for the Forestry Hall at the 1924 Wembley British Empire Exhibition. Also showed Royal Glasgow Institute of the Fine Arts, RSA, RSW and Walker Art Gallery in Liverpool. Died in Glasgow.

John DEWE MATHEWS 1946– Painter, teacher, photographer and architect, born in London, who attended Ampleforth College, 1959–63; gained an architecture diploma, Central London Polytechnic, 1964–70; then practised architecture in London, New York and Oaxaca, Mexico, 1970–3. Dewe Mathews conducted studio workshops, 1993–7; taught at Byam Shaw School of Art, 1995; ran Princeton University art workshops, 1996; and taught art for the unemployed, Dulwich Picture Gallery, 1997–9. His many mixed and solo exhibitions included exuberant watercolours, Alegria – Brazil, Rebecca Hossack Gallery, 2001. Fitzwilliam Museum, Cambridge, holds his work.

Hugh de WET 1931–1998 Painter of landscape and still life in oil, born in South Africa, who was a reporter there and then on *The Times* in London. Trained as an artist at City and Guilds of London Art School. Showed at RA Summer Exhibition, NEAC, various commercial galleries and had a solo show at 20 Fournier Street, Spitalfields, in 1996.

Louis de WET 1930– Painter using an Old Master mixed technique, egg emulsion and oil glazes combined, born in Durban, Natal, South Africa, which he left permanently at the end of 1952. Studied in Paris at L'Académie de la Grande Chaumière, 1953–6, and in the meisterklasse, Academy of Art in Vienna, 1969–71, under Rudolf Hausner. Had a studio in London, then in 1983 bought Wenlock Abbey, Much Wenlock, Shropshire, which he and his actress wife restored. Was a member of the Historic Houses Association. De Wet was "much influenced by continental Old Masters, but [I] paint as a twentieth century painter." He believed that originality was not merely innovation, but that it and real value were "new links in a very old chain. I see my roots as Flemish, English, French and German." In later years sold only to private clients direct from his studio, although he had solo shows in Paris, Milan, Brussels and Venice in 1994.

Antonia DEWHURST 1953– Dewhurst studied at West Surrey College of Art & Design, Farnham. She participated in a group show at The Showroom, 1985; Music Sketches, Whitechapel Library, 1986; Colour, Rhythm and Sound, Spitalfields Workspace, 1987; and Woodlands Art Gallery and East End Open Studios, based at Robinson Road, both 1989. She had work in private collections in Britain, on the continent and in America.

Paul Edward DEWS 1961– Artist and musician, born in Hitchin, Hertfordshire, working in a range of media. After leaving school Dews became a landscape gardener, a silkscreen printer for eight years, then studied Art and Social Context at Dartington College of Art, graduating with an honours degree in 1989. From then he worked in Huddersfield, Yorkshire. His work was strongly figurative, often incorporating a narrative text. Mixed exhibitions included The Northern Art Show, Mall Galleries, 1994. Had a series of solo shows including Fairbairn House, Leeds; Bradford Community Arts Centre; Walton Gallery, Guisborough; Marsden Mechanics, Huddersfield; and Gallery on the Street, Cambridge.

Sheila DEWSBURY 1939– Painter in oil and teacher who studied at Sedgley Park College. She taught in comprehensive and further education painting semi-professionally until 1989, then painted full-time. Her main theme was "elemental aspects of nature, spending most time painting the wilder parts of Britain and the west of Ireland". Dewsbury was a member of MAFA. She exhibited with ROI, RCamA, and at the Edinburgh Festival and Bath Contemporary Arts Festival. Showed solo at Saddleworth Festival regularly from 1984. Lived in Greenfield, Oldham, Lancashire.

James DEXTER 1912– Artist and designer who studied at Leicester College of Art. He lived in Leicester for many years and the local corporation owned his work. Showed at RA, LG, NEAC and in the provinces.

Katy DEXTER 1972– Sculptor, draughtsman and teacher, brought up on a farm in Cheshire and who, by the time she was shortlisted for the first Jerwood Sculpture Prize, 2001, was strongly exploring animal images. Dexter studied fine art at Falmouth College of Art, completing her master's at the Royal College of Art. She had numerous exhibitions around Britain, was a visiting tutor at Falmouth College of Art and Kent Institute of Art & Design, Canterbury, and worked as a part-time studio assistant to Rachel Whiteread and Kerry Stewart.

Walter DEXTER 1876–1958 Painter in oil and watercolour and illustrator. Born in Wellingborough, Northamptonshire, he studied at Birmingham School of Art, 1892–1900, at the Birmingham Royal Society of Artists and on the continent. Exhibited RA, RBSA, RI, ROI, RBA and elsewhere. Castle Museum, Norwich, holds his work. Dexter was a prolific writer on art and illustrated a number of books, including E V Lucas' *A Wanderer in Paris*. Lived at King's Lynn, Norfolk.

Henry Cotterill DEYKIN 1905–1989 Painter in oil, sculptor, furniture maker and teacher, born in Edgbaston, Birmingham. He studied at the College of Arts and Crafts there and at Slade School of Fine Art. Deykin taught at Warwick School, 1936–65, except for a period in camouflage work in World War II. In 1950–1 Deykin was commissioned by Geoffrey Pugh, head of Atco Ltd, the lawnmower company, to complete 23 paintings showing the progress of grass sports in the twentieth century. They were given a countrywide tour. The collection was sold at Sotheby's in 1982. Some are illustrated in M A Wingfield's *Sport and the Artist*, volume one on ball games, published in 1988. Showed RA, Whitechapel Art Gallery and elsewhere in mixed shows. Sponsored solo shows included Eton, Harrow and Cambridge and Norwich Art Schools. Latterly Deykin concentrated on furniture, until arthritis made it difficult for him to stand. Lived at Leamington Spa, Warwickshire.

Avtarjeet DHANJAL 1939– Sculptor, born in Dalla, Punjab, into a crafts-oriented peasant family. After working as a carpenter and at other jobs, he studied at Government College of Arts, Chandigarh, 1965–70, then went to East Africa, where he taught sculpture at Kenyatta University College, in Nairobi, Kenya, for two years. After arriving in Britain in 1974 he did the advanced sculpture course at St Martin's School of Art, but left after a short time. As artist-in-residence at Alcan Aluminium at Tipton, in the Midlands, he was sponsored to complete a number of sculptures, having a show at Dudley Castle in 1975. Travelled widely, including a return to Punjab, to take part in sculpture seminars. Much of Dhanjal's work was for public commissions, using man-made and natural features, abstract and often untitled. Had a solo show at Horizon Gallery, 1987; participated in The Other Story, Hayward Gallery and tour, 1989–90; and was given a major exhibition at Pitshanger Manor and Gallery, Ealing, 1997, in which Dhanjal's concern to explore and resolve opposing elements and polarities, his striving for formal simplicity and clarity of purpose and his range of work from kinetic aluminium sculptures to slate pieces were explored.

Pierre DIAMANTOPOULO 1952– Self-taught figurative sculptor, born in Cairo, Egypt, of a Greek father and French mother, moving to England during the Suez Crisis of 1956. He obtained an honours degree in literature from University of Essex, 1973, and was an advertising copywriter for the agency Foote, Cone & Belding, 1974–89. In the latter year he took his first studio as a professional sculptor in Brighton, Sussex, where he continued to live. Exhibitions included Tryon Gallery from 1990; Garrard, 1991; Harrods, 1991–2; South Bank Centre National Touring Exhibition, 1995; and in 1996 Beaux Arts in Bath and 2nd RWA Open Sculpture Exhibition.

Anne DIAMOND 1908–1985 Painter, embroiderer and designer who, as Anne Hauser, studied costume design at Willesden Art School aged 15-17. Worked for a gown maker in London's West End until her marriage in 1930 to Claude Diamond, after which they settled in Leamington Spa. She then tried wallpaper design and oils at Leamington College of Further Education, also studying in St Ives. Showed at Paris Salon, 1965. After turning to embroidery, she shared a show of fabric pictures and collages at Herbert Art Gallery and Museum, Coventry, 1970, also taking part in an Embroiderers' Guild show at Foyles Art Gallery, 1973, the year Diamond's painting of Lansdowne Circus, Leamington, was bought by the town's art gallery. With her husband she moved to South Kensington, where Diamond at the nearby Royal School of Needlework produced many fabric collages and embroideries and studied the history of tapestry. After her death, Claude endowed an apprenticeship at the School. Some of Diamond's oils, as exhibited at the Graham Gallery, Tunbridge Wells, indicated a strong interest in abstraction.

Colin DICK 1929– Painter. Studied painting for four years full time at St Martin's School of Art under Frederick Gore, R V Pitchforth and James Stroudley. He was closely associated with the Thames, living for six years in the Thames Valley as a child, at Henley and later on at Chiswick Mall. Showed at RA from early 1960s. Herbert Art Gallery and Museum, Coventry, has many paintings of local interest in its collection.

J Alix DICK 1896–1976 This was the working name, in block letters, of Jessie Alexandra Dick, painter and teacher. She studied and taught at Glasgow School of Art. Miss Dick was a member of Glasgow Society of Lady Artists, also exhibiting at RSA, Royal Glasgow Institute of the Fine Arts and Walker Art Gallery in Liverpool, RSW and RE. McLean Museum and Art Gallery, Greenock, holds her work.

Jessie Alexandra DICK: *see* **J Alix DICK**

William DICK 1950– Painter whose works "through their repainting portray a powerful sense of illumination, both light and dark, thereby generating a spiritual atmosphere." He drew "on ancient symbols from my own Scottish background and elsewhere". Born in Glasgow, Dick attended Glasgow School of Art, 1971–2, studying fine art at Duncan of Jordanstone College of Art, Dundee, 1972–6, with postgraduate studies there, 1976–7, also attending St Martin's School of Art, 1977–8. Among Dick's many awards were First Prize, Grampian Television Award, 1974; Carnegie Scholar, RSA, 1975; Elizabeth T Greenshields Scholarship, 1977; Pollock-Krasner Foundation Award, 1989; British Council Awards, 1990, 1992 and 2001; and an Adolph and Esther Gottlieb Foundation Award, 2001. Later residencies included Crawford Arts Centre, St Andrews, 1991, and Darat al-Funan Art Center, Amman, Jordan, 2001. Dick participated in numerous group shows from 1974, later ones including Resonant Colours, Coningsby Gallery, 1998; Reflections, Southside Arts, Southampton, 2000; and Dean Clough Galleries, Halifax, 2001. By the time of his solo exhibition Trace, at Pilgrim Gallery, 2002, Dick had had almost 30 one-man shows. Dick shared an exhibition with Janet Patterson at Pilgrim Gallery in 2003. Aberdeen Art Gallery, Scottish Arts Council, Russia's Moscow Union of Artists and many other public and corporate collections held examples.

William Reid DICK 1879–1961 Sculptor in the classical tradition of portraits, figure studies and public monuments. Born in Glasgow, he studied at the School of Art there until 1907, then at the City and Guilds School, Kennington. Showed at the RA from 1912, and was elected RA, 1928. He was president of the RBS, 1915. Knighted in 1935. Was King's Sculptor in Ordinary for Scotland, 1938–52, and Queen's Sculptor from 1952. Also exhibited Royal Glasgow Institute of the Fine Arts, IS, RSA, RSW, RI and Paris Salon. Reid Dick was an astute businessman who fulfilled many public commissions, whose work can achieve technical excellence with dignity and sensitivity. Among his notable works are heads of Sir Winston Churchill and King George VI; Dawn, in the Tate Gallery; the equestrian group Controlled Energy on Unilever House, London; Godiva, for the City of Coventry; the Kitchener Memorial Chapel, in St Paul's Cathedral; and the statue of David Livingstone at Victoria Falls, in Africa. Lived in London. Reid Dick's daughter Mary Hart was an artist.

Lucy DICKENS 1958– Painter, photographer, illustrator, writer and teacher, whose great- great-grandfather was the novelist Charles Dickens, her father being a journalist. She graduated in photography from the University of Westminster. Dickens gained The Fuji Student Award, Home Truths, 1995, and in 1996 and 1997 The John Kobal Photographic Portrait Award. She worked in Ethiopia and taught photography part-time at Huntercombe Young Offenders Institution. Dickens illustrated for newspapers and magazines, wrote and illustrated a series of children's books – she was married with four children – then turned to painting in oils. From 1995 she had a series of exhibitions at the Belgrave Gallery and later ones included Mood Swings at the Osborne Studio Gallery in 2005: paintings including jazz players, restaurant interiors, seascapes and still life. Dickens also showed at the RA Summer Exhibition and undertook portrait commissions. Dickens lived at Frieth, Henley-on-Thames, Oxfordshire.

Pip DICKENS 1962– Painter who graduated from Slade School of Fine Art in 2000, when she had a first London solo show at Elgin. She showed large, predominantly black abstract paintings, absorbing and contemplative.

Sophie DICKENS 1966– Sculptor in a variety of materials interested in the dynamism and rhythm of the human form, for which she made special anatomical studies at London University, 1991. She was educated at Charterhouse, Godalming, 1982–4; gained an honours degree in art history at the Courtauld Institute, 1984–7; trained at Sir John Cass School of Art, 1988–92, in the latter year winning the sculpture prize; in 1991 also studying ceramic shell bronze casting at Central St Martins School of Art. Exhibitions included Fresh Art, Business Design Centre, 1992; Albion Fine Art, 1994; and Usiskin Gallery and The McHardy Sculpture Company, both from 1995. Had a solo exhibition at Andy Elton Studios, 1994.

Charles George Hamilton DICKER 1896–1977 Painter and Church of England priest, born in Ouse, Tasmania, his father also an ordained minister. After his mother's early death, was taken to England by his father and was brought up by two maiden aunts. Studied at Oxford University and in late 1920s at Slade School of Fine Art, where William Coldstream was a close friend. Supported by a small private income, Dicker continued to paint until World War II, showing at East London Group Lefevre exhibitions, NEAC and elsewhere. Had long been interested in religion and in 1942 was ordained in Leicester. Eventually became vicar of South Stoke, near Bath, in 1948, where he remained for 18 years, then retiring to Wells. Is buried at South Stoke, Somerset.

Kate DICKER 1953– Artist and lecturer to whom the interpretation of place and environment were important. She was born in Hampshire, sister of the artist Tim Dicker and daughter of Molly Dicker. She did a foundation course at West Sussex College of Design, 1979–80; graduated with honours in graphic arts at Camberwell College of Arts, 1980–3; and gained a modern art history postgraduate diploma from the School of Art in Winchester, where she lived, 1992–4, and her master's in fine art printmaking there, 2003–4. After prison teaching in 1989 Dicker taught at Camberwell College, 1990; Bournemouth & Poole College of Art, 1994; Winchester School of Art, 1995; and from 1995–00 was a part-time lecturer at Southampton Institute, from 2002 at Portsmouth University. In 2001, she had a Southern Arts "Colle Verde" residency near Lucca, Italy. As well as varied commissions for commercial clients, Dicker completed military paintings for Winchester's City Council and four murals for its Health Authority. She was a committee member of SWE, other group shows including British Month, Roy Miles Gallery, 1991; Zella 9 Gallery, 1995; RWS Open, Bankside Gallery, from 1997; RA Summer Exhibition, 1998; and NEAC, from 1998. Among solo exhibitions were Working Horses of London,

The Guildhall, Winchester, and Stephen Bartley Gallery, both 1991.

Molly DICKER 1924–2000 Painter notable for portraits, draughtsman, etcher and teacher, born in Kent, who studied stage and costume design in the early 1940s at Gravesend School of Art. After serving as a nurse in World War II, marriage and children (Tim and Kate, both artists), she resumed painting in the 1950s. Dicker also organised painting weekends for the Carnegie Trust and was involved in art groups around Hampshire, where she settled in East Meon. In the 1960s and 1970s studied part-time at Southampton Art College with Peter Folkes and James Sellars. In the 1980s began to concentrate on drawing, which led to etching. The Hampshire countryside and travels to India, Italy and the Bernese Oberland provided subjects. She was elected SWA, 1987, serving as a council member. Exhibitions included RBA, from 1972; RA Summer Exhibition, from 1983; RWA from 1992; and PS, 1996. Alresford Gallery held a solo show of etchings in 2001.

John DICKERSON 1939– Ceramist, draughtsman, mixed media sculptor and teacher, born in Swaffham, Norfolk. He studied at Goldsmiths' College School of Art, Art Students' League of New York and Pratt Institute there, gaining his master's degree in 1968, then doctorate from Royal College of Art, 1971–4. He wrote extensively on raku ware. His own work was shown and held widely in Britain and abroad. Lived in London where he was in the fine arts division of Richmond College, The American International College.

Robert DICKERSON 1924– Australian painter and draughtsman and printmaker, born in Sydney. He was self-taught from an early age, left school at 14, became a professional boxer two years later and at 18 joined the Royal Australian Air Force, serving in Borneo in World War II. After the war Dickerson worked for a decade as a labourer, continuing to paint, selling a picture to the National Gallery of Victoria in 1956 and three years later becoming a full-time painter. In 1959 he was the only Sydney representative in the Antipodeans, a group set up in support of figurative art. Recent Australian Paintings, at the Whitechapel Art Gallery, in 1961, and the 1963 show Australian Painting at the Tate Gallery were dominated by the Antipodean style. Dickerson made the loneliness of city life his special theme. He went on to show widely in Australia, and is represented in all state and provincial galleries. In 1989 he travelled in Britain, Germany and Netherlands and in 1991 England & Co gave him a solo show.

Edward Montgomery O'Rorke DICKEY 1894–1977 Painter, printmaker, teacher, administrator and curator, born in Belfast. He obtained his master's degree from Cambridge University and studied painting under Harold Gilman at the Westminster School of Art. From 1926–31 Dickey was professor of fine art and director of King Edward VII School of Art, Armstrong College, Newcastle upon Tyne. He was then staff inspector of art, Ministry of Education, 1931–57, but from 1939–42 was secretary of the War Artists' Advisory Committee, in 1942, on the recommendation of Kenneth Clark, joining the committee, while returning to the Ministry, until the war's end. Eventually Dickey became first curator of The Minories, Colchester. The Imperial War Museum holds extensive wartime correspondence involving Dickey and a copy of a television documentary on war art in which he appeared. The Minories' collection of Dickey's work includes a self-portrait. Dickey painted extensively on the continent, public galleries in Manchester, Belfast and Cork holding examples. He showed at RA, NEAC and LG. An upright, gentlemanly figure, Dickey was notable for always carrying a sketch-book in his pocket. Lived latterly at Turvey, Bedfordshire.

Jeremy DICKINSON 1963– Painter of Hyper-Realist work, such as his oil and acrylic on canvas Buses, in the John Moores Liverpool Exhibition, 1999. Born in Halifax, Yorkshire, Dickinson studied at York College of Arts and Technology, 1982–3, and Goldsmiths' College, 1983–6. Group shows included Wonderful Life, Lisson Gallery, 1993; Obsession, The Tannery, 1995; Empty Container, Refusalon, San Francisco, America, 1998; and John Moores Liverpool Exhibition, 1999. Later solo shows included Lotta Hammer Gallery and Galerie Axel Thieme, Darmstadt, Germany, both 1999. Lived in London.

Mary DICKINSON fl. from c. 1935– Painter and draughtsman in black-and-white, born in Liverpool. She was initially educated in England, France and Germany, then studied at Liverpool School of Art and in London at Frank Spenlove-Spenlove's Yellow Door School of Art. Exhibited widely, including ROI, RA, PS and SWA both of which she was a member, NEAC, NS and Paris Salon, where she gained an Honourable Mention. RSA, where she also exhibited, bought her work. Lived in London.

Peter DICKINSON 1961– Artist producing colourful, gestural abstract works, as in Six abstract painters, at Six Chapel Row, Bath, 2001. Dickinson attended Buckinghamshire College of Higher Education, 1980–1, and Chelsea School of Art, 1981–4. Exhibitions included Hampstead New End Theatre, 1984; Alpha House Gallery, Sherborne, 1997; Cheltenham & Gloucester Open Drawing Competition, 1998; and Glowing Hands Clapping, The Tobacco Factory, Bristol, 1999.

Roger DICKINSON 1960– Sculptor and arts administrator who studied at Sunderland Polytechnic, 1979–82, and Newcastle Polytechnic, 1989–91. Between 1983–8, Dickinson assisted the artists Raf Fulcher and George Carter. Dickinson was involved in organising exhibitions and public art projects in the north of England as well as creating his own works. His enigmatic, multi-material 1998 Mars Garden, commissioned by Chester-le-Street District Council, stands in the town's Riverside Gardens, near the Root House and Sun Temple, also designed by Dickinson.

Adam DICKS 1967– Freelance illustrator and painter, born and lived in London, who chose to create "paintings about people, their characters and how they behave (to each other) or react to their environments". He studied at Richmond-upon-Thames College, 1985–7, and Middlesex Polytechnic, 1987–90, gaining an honours degree in illustration and graphics. Commissions included cover illustrations for publishers including Macmillan Publishers and HarperCollins. Group shows included Chartwell House, 1992; Summer Show at Burlington New Gallery, 1994; Royal Over-Seas League Open, 1996; The Top 20, The

Osbourne Studio Gallery, 2002; and with Purcell Contemporary at The Art on paper Fair, Royal College of Art, 2003. Exhibited solo at Artomatic +, 2000; Arrival & Departure at Attendi Art Gallery, 2003; and Urban Nature at the Royal Over-Seas League, 2004. He latterly worked as Adam Dix. His father was the artist Edward Dicks.

Edward DICKS 1928– Painter, teacher and musician, father of the artist Adam Dicks (Dix), born in London. He studied painting at Hornsey School of Art, the Royal College of Art and in Venice. After a short period teaching art and English, abandoned teaching to pursue a career in music. This resulted in two West End shows: *Look Who's Here* and *And Another Thing*; film scores; and several popular songs, performed by artists such as Petula Clark, Bernard Cribbins, Topol and Matt Monro, including *Hole in the Ground, Right Said Fred* and *Mouse in the Windmill*. Throughout this period he continued to paint and exhibit, at RA, several London galleries and with Celia Purcell Contemporary. His pictures included landscapes, portraits and club and jazz scenes.

Evangeline Mary Lambart DICKSON 1922–2004 Artist mainly in watercolour, mixed media and pastel, born in Sheffield, Yorkshire, studied under Violet Garrod and Anna Airy. The British landscape and its history were key themes in her work, as in her show Ancient Places, at Salisbury & South Wiltshire Museum in 1992. Commissioned work included illustrations for *In Search of Heathland*, by Lee Chadwick, 1982. She was a member of BWS and exhibited in many shows in London and East Anglia, notably RI, RWS, and at Paris Salon. Solo shows include Clarges Gallery and Christchurch Mansion, Ipswich. Graves Art Gallery, Sheffield, and Ipswich hold her work. Lived in Westerfield, Ipswich, Suffolk.

James Marshall DICKSON 1942– Painter and draughtsman, born in Kirkcaldy, Fife, where he settled at Lochgelly. Studied at Edinburgh College of Art, 1960–4, teachers including Stuart Barrie. Was made a member of RSW in 1972, also showing with public galleries in Kirkcaldy and Perth and at Royal Glasgow Institute of the Fine Arts. Angus and Banff County collections hold his work. Dickson was in charge of art at Lochgelly Centre.

Jennifer DICKSON 1936– Painter, printmaker and teacher, born in Piet Retief, South Africa. She studied at Goldsmiths' College School of Art, 1954–9, then at S W Hayter's Atelier 17 in Paris, and is mainly noted for her prints. She exhibited internationally and work is held by the British Museum, Victoria & Albert Museum, Metropolitan Museum in New York and other collections. RE member, elected RA, 1976. Was in charge of printmaking at Brighton College of Art, then taught at the Faculty of Fine Arts at Concordia University, Montreal, Canada. Latterly lived in Ottawa, Ontario. The City Gallery showed new works in 1997.

Joan DICKSON 1913– Painter and teacher, born in Southampton, where she studied at the School of Art, 1929–35, and Royal College of Art, 1935–8. She later taught for some years at the Southampton School. Showed at RA, LG and NEAC. Married to the artist Michael Platt and lived for a time at Brockenhurst, Hampshire.

Mora DICKSON 1918–2001 Painter, draughtsman, writer and organiser, born in Glasgow, who spent her early years in Moffat, Dumfriesshire, to avoid air pollution, then became head girl of St Felix's School, Southwold. Her studies at Edinburgh School of Art were halted by World War II, by the end of which she was in charge of a large canteen at Nijmegen, on the Dutch-German border. During studies at Byam Shaw School of Drawing and Painting she met her future husband Alec Dickson, with whom she founded the Man O'War training centre in Nigeria, followed in England by Voluntary Service Overseas and Community Service Volunteers. To mark VSO's fortieth anniversary she produced and donated a collage with gouache depicting its early years, hung in its Putney offices. Dickson wrote over 20 books, including war poems; *A Chance to Serve*, 1976, about VSO's beginnings; and *Nannie: A Lifetime Of Devotion, 1988*. After Alec's death in 1994 Mora settled in Edinburgh.

Nell Gwenllian DICKSON 1891–1967 Watercolour landscape painter, born in Reading, Berkshire. She studied art prior to World War I under W G Collingwood, at Reading University with Alan Seaby, then at Heatherley's School of Fine Art with Herbert Maryon; from 1935–38 she studied with Leonard Richmond, later working under Hervey Adams and David Cox. Exhibited RA, SWA, RBA, RSA and with the Norwich Art Circle. Had several one-man shows in Norwich, where she lived, in the 1950s and 1960s. Was chairman of the Norfolk and Norwich Art Circle in 1951.

Rodney DICKSON 1956– Painter, sculptor in wax and teacher, born in Bangor, County Down. Studied at Liverpool College of Art, 1979–83, graduating with grade 1 honours. From 1983–4 lived in Amsterdam with his partner the designer Judith Hone, then returned to live in Devon for five years, followed by Liverpool. Dickson went to New York in 1992 under an Ireland/America Arts Exchange. Among his other awards were a David Murray Travelling Scholarship, 1983. He was a John Moores Liverpool Exhibition prizewinner, 1987, and won several South West Arts and Northern Ireland Arts Council Awards. Dickson taught part-time at Southport and Liverpool Art Colleges, and was artist-in-residence at Walker Art Gallery, Liverpool, 1990. Had a solo show there, 1990, others including Cartwright Hall, Bradford, 1992–3. Dickson painted on a large scale in oil, the paint often thick and dark, the images sometimes disturbing. Walker Art Gallery, University of Liverpool and Arts Council of Northern Ireland hold his work.

Thomas Elder DICKSON 1899–1978 Painter, teacher and writer, born in Barrhead, Renfrewshire. He studied at Glasgow School of Art, 1920–4, under Maurice Greiffenhagen, then went on to hold a number of teaching posts, latterly as vice-principal of Edinburgh College of Art, where he lectured on the history of art. He wrote several books on painting and design and wrote for art magazines. Exhibited SSA, of which for a time he was president after World War II, RSA, RSW and Royal Glasgow Institute of the Fine Arts. Dr Dickson lived in Edinburgh.

Wesley DICKSON 1925– Painter and draughtsman, by profession a civil servant, born in Belfast where he continued to live. Studied art at Belfast Academy with John Turner and exhibited RUA.

Xenia K DIEROFF 1965– Artist using video, born in Hamburg, West Germany, who gained a degree in fine art at University of Brighton, 1990–3, and her master's at Goldsmiths' College, 1994–6. Exhibitions included BT New Contemporaries 92, tour, 1992; Nobby Stiles, Vandy Street, 1995; and New Contemporaries, Tate Gallery in Liverpool and Camden Arts Centre, 1996.

Grace DIGBY 1895– Landscape painter, jewellery designer and musician, born in Scarborough, Yorkshire. Studied art in Brussels. Exhibited RA, Walker Art Gallery, Liverpool, RCamA, on the continent, in Australia and America. Lived at Edgbaston, Birmingham.

Violet M DIGBY fl. from 1930s–1960 Artist in oil and pastel who was born in Plymouth, Devon. Studied at Hastings School of Art under Philip Cole and Leslie Badham, at the Slade School of Fine Art, 1938, and the following year in Paris. She exhibited ROI, RCamA, UA, at the Paris Salon and in India. Lived at St Ives, Cornwall, where she was a member of the St Ives Society of Artists.

Jane Chadderton DIGGLE 1882– Painter and poster artist, born in London, who after education there and in Paris studied at Heatherley's School of Fine Art, the Central School of Arts and Crafts and privately. Exhibited RA, RI, WIAC, NS and elsewhere. Lived in Tenterden, Kent.

Philip DIGGLE 1956– Painter and teacher, born in Manchester, where he attended the Grammar School, then Chelsea School of Art, gaining his master's degree in art history. He taught in a tough secondary school in London, where he lived. Mixed shows included Pure Paint, Stephen Lacey Gallery, 1999, the year he had a solo exhibition at Highgate Literary Scientific Institution, with another at Highgate Gallery in 2003. Works there were described as "rippling with bright colours and dancing with Pollock drips and smears...the sum of a multitude of split-second decisions interspersed with contemplation over weeks and months." Rockefeller Center, New York, in America; Chase Manhattan Bank; and the television company Granada owned his work.

Stanley Victor DIGGLE 1919– Painter, draughtsman and teacher, born in Leicester, where he settled. His father's job as a landscape gardener probably contributed to his interest in depicting the countryside, which features in much of his work. Studied at Leicester College of Art, 1947–9, then in 1949–51 at Camberwell School of Arts and Crafts, where his teachers included Claude Rogers and Richard Eurich. Showed Young Contemporaries, AIA, NEAC and South London Art Gallery. Held several art teaching posts, latterly in Coventry.

Megan Ann di GIROLAMO 1942– Ceramist, teacher and illustrator, born in New Delhi, India, married to the artist Romeo di Girolamo. She studied at High Wycombe College of Further Education, Hornsey School of Art and South Glamorgan Institute of Higher Education, gaining her master's degree in ceramics in 1987. She illustrated several books, including *The Crab and its Relatives*. Exhibited in London and Ireland, sharing a show with her husband at Thomas Plunkett Fine Art, St Albans, 2001. Was a member of RBA and SPS and an associate of RBS. Lived in Wendover, Buckinghamshire.

Romeo di GIROLAMO 1939– Painter and teacher, born in Civitella, Italy. He was educated in England and studied art at High Wycombe School of Art, 1954–9, on a county scholarship. He won the Granada Theatres National Painting Prize in 1957, the RA's David Murray Travelling Scholarship in 1959. Eventually became head of painting at Amersham College of Further Education. Was president of RBA and Hon. RBSA; shared a show with his wife at Thomas Plunkett Fine Art, St Albans, 2001; also exhibiting at RA and elsewhere in mixed shows as well as solo shows. Lived in Wendover, Buckinghamshire, married to the ceramist Megan Ann di Girolamo.

Paul DIGNAN 1962– Abstract painter employing bright, narrow bands of vertical and horizontal colour. He was born in Dundee, Angus, and attended Gray's School of Art, Aberdeen, 1981–5, and Slade School of Fine Art, 1985–7. In 1993 Dignan was awarded a residency by the Reykjavik Municipal Art Museum in Iceland, in 1995 gaining a Rome Scholarship, British School at Rome. Group exhibitions included RSA Student Exhibition, Edinburgh, 1985; Vik Gallery, Edmonton, Alberta, 1988; Abstract Art – The Next Generation, Mall Galleries, 1994; and Aspects of Abstraction at Paton Gallery, 1995.

Beatrice DILLISTONE 1899– Painter, illuminator, black-and-white artist and teacher, born in Brighton, Sussex, where she continued to live. Attended Brighton School of Art, 1917–21, then the Royal College of Art, 1921–3. Taught art at Wakefield School of Art and Crafts and Thornes House School, 1923–59. Among illuminated work commissioned was a roll for York Minster.

Angela DILLON 1955– Abstract artist whose works reflected her Spanish/Mexican antecedents and who was born in Campeche, Mexico. She was educated at Robert Gordon University and Gray's School of Art, Aberdeen, 1992, then Royal College of Art. In 1992 gained the RSA's Thompson Award. Exhibitions included Aberdeen Artists' Exhibition and RSA, 1991–2, Atlantis Galleries, 1993, and in 1994 Battam Studio in Connecticut, America, and Five RCA Painters, at Paton Gallery.

Gerard DILLON 1916–1971 Versatile artist, born in Belfast, Northern Ireland, full name Francis Gerard Dillon, the son of a postman, Gerard was "always trying to see with a child's innocence and sincerity." He left school at 14 to work as a painter and decorator and, apart from a fleeting attendance at Belfast Art School in his early twenties and a life class in London in 1967, was self-taught, determined to preserve an individual style. Dillon existed by doing odd jobs in London for several years in the 1930s, returning there for a sustained period after World War II. During the war he lived in southern Ireland, discovering the landscape of Connemara, a major influence. Dillon did some teaching in London and in Dublin, where at The Country Shop he had his first solo exhibition in 1942. Wartime bombing destroyed much of his early output. Other solo shows included CEMA in Belfast, Victor Waddington and Dawson Galleries in Dublin, Arts Council of Northern Ireland Gallery in 1966 and in 1972 a retrospective there and at Ulster Museum in Belfast which toured to Dublin. Dillon was elected RHA; showed in group exhibitions for many years with the Irish Exhibition of Living Art; at Leicester Galleries; and in 1958 represented Ireland at the Guggenheim International and Great Britain at the

Pittsburgh International Exhibition. Other aspects of Dillon's output are his contributions to the magazine *Ireland of the Welcomes*, creation of a wall hanging for Dublin Tourism, the use of his painting Black Lake on an Irish postage stamp and his designs for Sean O'Casey's play *Juno and the Paycock* at Dublin's Abbey Theatre. His late emergence as an etcher was impressive. Dillon's work is in the principal Irish public collections. Died in Dublin, where he shared a house with Arthur Armstrong.

Norman DILWORTH 1931– Sculptor, draughtsman, painter and teacher, born in Wigan, Lancashire, attending its School of Art, 1949–52. Then studied at Slade School of Fine Art, under William Coldstream, 1952–6, winning the Tonks Prize, and the *Sunday Times* Drawing Prize, 1956. Gained a French Government Scholarship to study in Paris, 1956–7. Dilworth participated in many group shows from Young Contemporaries in 1953, John Moores Liverpool Exhibition, 1959, LG for some years, and progressively abroad. After a solo show at Redmark Gallery, 1968, in 1970 he began to exhibit on the continent, especially in the Netherlands. Later shows included Galerie Elke Dröscher, Hamburg, and Art Affairs, Amsterdam, both 1993, with a residency exhibition at The Gallery, St Peter Port, Guernsey, 1999. From the mid-1970s Dilworth had a base in Amsterdam, settling there in 1982. His major commissions included a fountain for the Crown Offices, Cardiff, first prizewinner in Arts Council competition; relief for Stadsdeel Zeeburg, Amsterdam, 1990; and tower for Rijkerswoerd, Arnhem, 1991. Arts Council, Tate Gallery, British Council and many continental collections hold Dilworth's work. He became progressively a sculptor, completing wooden abstract floor and wall pieces, saying of his work: "It is the parallel to nature which fascinates me ... I am not attempting to make an illusion of something else."

Steve DILWORTH 1949– Sculptor using a wide range of found and other objects, and teacher, born in Kingston-upon-Hull, Yorkshire. He studied at Maidstone College of Art, 1967–71, and won a series of awards from Arts Council, Scottish Arts Council and Henry Moore Foundation. Was a visiting lecturer at Winchester, Cheltenham, Wolverhampton, Dundee and Glasgow Colleges of Art; Royal Academy Schools; and Ruskin School of Drawing, Oxford. Exhibitions included Upper Street Gallery, 1975–6; Ikon Gallery, Birmingham, 1980; Goldmark Gallery, Uppingham, 1991; Paper Works IV, Dundee, where he was first prize winner, 1993; and The Gallery in Cork Street, 1994. Was included in In Praise of Trees, Stephen Lacey Gallery in 2002.

Bruno Di MARIO 1957– Painter, printmaker, photographer and teacher, born in Rome, Italy, who produced geometrical abstracts, although he did "not relate to art in terms of whether it is abstract or not." Di Mario graduated from Chelsea School of Art, 1983–6, and gained his master's there, 1986–7, obtaining an Italian Scholarship, Urbino, 1987–8. He taught art/design and photography in a Surrey secondary school, living in the county at Ashtead. Exhibitions included Hammersmith and Fulham Summer Exhibitions; The London Institute; Cadogan Contemporary; Globe and Acava Studios; and The New Constructivists, Cotton's Atrium, 2002. St Thomas's Hospital held Di Mario's work.

Phyllis DIMOND 1911– Watercolourist, born and lived in London, whose work was "mostly topographical, mainly local, commissioned and sold privately". She attended Hammersmith School of Arts and Crafts, 1926–9, and Royal College of Art design school, 1931–4, for her diploma, tutors Edward Bawden and Eric Ravilious. From 1934–9 she gave part-time tuition at Bolt Court School of Photo-Engraving and Lithography; was also a freelance designer; and did some animated cartoon drawing. Her career "took off after 1942". She contributed 12 London pictures to the *Recording Britain* project, and was included in the associated National Gallery show, 1942–3, and Victoria & Albert Museum's 1990 exhibition. Also showed at RA, 1958; Lord Mayor's Award Shows, 1963–5–6; and Westminster Artists, 1966. Latterly contributed watercolour still lifes to St John's Wood Church Christian Aid Exhibitions. Victoria & Albert Museum and St Marylebone Library local history collection hold examples of Dimond's work, which also appears in the volume *Londoner's England*, 1947.

Jim DINE 1935– Prolific American artist, illustrator, stage designer and poet, born in Cincinnati, Ohio, where he studied at the Arts Academy, 1951–3, then at the Boston Museum School and Ohio University, 1954–7. Having married and moved to New York, Dine became involved in Happenings, 1959–60, and began making his first assemblages and producing the paintings, sculptures and prints related to everyday objects for which he became famous, as well as art focusing on the materials of the artist and tools. Repetition of a theme in various mediums was a characteristic of Dine's output. His work was widely exhibited in America, where he set up numerous temporary studios, but from the mid-1980s he was based in New York and Washington. His work was also exhibited widely internationally, later British shows including Tools and Plants, Alan Cristea Gallery, 2005. Dine had had a first painting show at the Robert Fraser Gallery in London 1965 and in 1966 a big section of the exhibition entitled London there, in which he collaborated with Eduardo Paolozzi, was seized by the police under the Obscene Publications Act. From 1967–71 Dine lived and worked in London, where he was involved in producing prints with Editions Alecto and the Petersburg Press. Victoria & Albert Museum; Museum of Modern Art in New York; National Museum of American Art in Washington; Bibliothèque Nationale in Paris; National Gallery of Canada, Ottawa; and National Gallery of Australia, Canberra, hold Dine's prints.

Maria DINELEY 1971– Painter of landscape with a bravura style in oil and colourful palette, born in Dorset, where she established a strong local following for her views around Berwick St John. In the early 1990s attended the Charles Cecil Studios in Florence. Had a solo show at Christopher Wood Contemporary Art, 1995.

Naomi DINES 1968– Sculptor and artist in various media, born in Fareham, Hampshire. She gained a first-class honours degree in fine art, sculpture, at Chelsea School of Art, 1988–91, then her master's degree at Royal College of Art, 1991–3. Dines won an Alfred Munnings Award in 1988, Paul Dowson Memorial Trophy, 1989, and in 1992 was a prizewinner at East & South, at Norwich Gallery/Kent Institute of Art and Design. Other exhibitions included Osborne Gallery, 1989; in 1990 Art '90, at Business Design Centre; and Under Sail at 1991 Chichester Festival. Lived in Maldon, Essex.

Jan DINGLE fl. from 1970s– Printmaker and designer who originally studied graphic design at Hornsey College of Art, taking up etching some years later. Subsequently worked in studios and ateliers developing the varied techniques used in her coloured etchings. The Norfolk Broads, where she cruised for much of the year, featured strongly in her pictures. Showed at RA Summer Exhibition, with other major societies and had a series of solo shows. These included Trumpington Gallery, Cambridge, 1984; Medici Gallery and Casson Gallery, Eastbourne, both 1986; and Stevenage Leisure Centre, 1990. Lived in Waltham Abbey, Essex.

Kenneth DINGWALL 1938– Painter, constructions artist and teacher, born at Devonside, Clackmannanshire. Dingwall studied at Edinburgh College of Art, 1955–9. After being an Andrew Grant Postgraduate Scholar, 1959–60 and living in Greece, 1961–2, Dingwall began teaching at Edinburgh College of Art in 1963. From 1973–4 he was visiting professor at Minneapolis College of Art and Design in America. In 1988 he was appointed professor at the Cleveland Institute of Art, Ohio. It was from around 1973 that Dingwall developed his abstract paintings and constructions, influenced through work seen in America by Mark Rothko and Robert Ryman. Dingwall's method of painting was laborious and careful, usually in sombre colours, his aim being to reveal shifts between what we feel and what we reveal. Dingwall had solo shows at Scottish Gallery, Graeme Murray and Scottish Arts Council Galleries, all in Edinburgh, in the 1960s and 1970s. A more recent solo show was at the Peter Noser Galerie, Zurich, 1987. Scottish National Gallery of Modern Art holds his work.

Phoebe DINGWALL 1965– Painter and draughtsman, born in Edinburgh, who graduated in fine arts, Ruskin School of Drawing, Oxford, 1983–6; gained a postgraduate diploma from Royal Academy Schools, 1986–9; then attended L'École Nationale Supérieure des Beaux-Arts, Paris, 1989–92, where she won a painting prize. Other awards included a Royal Academy travelling scholarship, 1986; Celia Walker Prize, 1987; French government grant, 1989; and travelling scholarships to Finland and Italy in 1993 and 1994. Among group shows were Chicago Art Fair, America, from 1990; RA Summer Exhibition, 1992; Salon de la Jeune Peinture, Paris, 1996; and The Reynolds Gallery, Edinburgh, 2000. Later solo exhibitions included Curwen Gallery, 2001, where Dingwall showed paintings using subtle bands of colour, uprights and grids inspired by Scottish and French landscapes.

Ernest Michael DINKEL 1894–1983 Painter of landscapes, Biblical subjects, flowers and portraits who practised in oil, tempera, watercolour and pencil, and who also worked in stained glass, engraved glass and made sculpture. Born in Huddersfield, of German descent, Dinkel was a man in the arts and crafts tradition. He studied at Huddersfield School of Art and at the Royal College of Art 1921–5. Dinkel won the Owen Jones Travelling Scholarship to study art and architecture in France and Italy. Married the artist Emmy Dinkel-Keet. Assistant to Ernest William Tristram at the Royal College 1925–40, was principal of the School of Art, Stourbridge in 1940–47, from 1947–61 being head of the school of design at Edinburgh College of Art. Designed inn signs and posters, for London Transport. Exhibitions include RA, NEAC and RWS, with a major exhibition at the Art Gallery, Cheltenham, 1980. Official purchases include the Tate Gallery. Lived at Bussage, near Stroud, Gloucestershire.

Emmy Gerarda Mary DINKEL-KEET 1908–2003 Painter noted for exquisite fine brush drawings and watercolours, and teacher, married to the artist Michael Dinkel. During World War I Dinkel-Keet left her native Holland to join her father in England. She won the Essex County Art Scholarship in 1927 to attend Southend College of Art, 1927–30, then was at Royal College of Art, 1930–3, teachers including William Rothenstein, Ernest Tristram, Malcolm Osborne, Edward Johnstone, Edward Bawden and Eric Ravilious. Studied peasant embroidery and design in Hungary, teaching these subjects at London County Council Institutes and arts and crafts at Sherborne School for Girls. After freelancing, 1937–9, she taught at Malvern College of Art, married, then taught part-time in Scottish schools. She was made RWA in 1987, also showing at RSA and RA and sharing a show with her husband at Stroud Festival, 1984. *Dream Children: collected works of Emmy Dinkel-Keet* was published privately in 1991. Lived at Bussage and then Cirencester, Gloucestershire.

Mary DINSDALE fl. from 1960s– Painter and illustrator who trained at Guildford and Harrow Schools of Art. She began painting in 1980, having previously worked as a freelance illustrator, including a long spell with *Radio Times*, latterly illustrating for *Punch*. Worked in a variety of media, notably gouache. Drawing was a strong element in her work, which had a Neo-Romantic flavour. Dinsdale showed widely in the south of England. She was a member of Rye Society of Artists and Hastings Arts, showing regularly at Easton Rooms, Rye. Work also appeared at Hastings Museum and Art Gallery, Wedges Gallery in Hastings and Dandelion Gallery, Tunbridge Wells. Work held in public collections.

Eve DISHER 1894–1991 Painter, born in London, who studied at Hornsey School of Art. During World War I she worked for the London Fire Service. After leaving home to marry the theatre critic Willson Disher she became friendly with members of the Bloomsbury Group. When her marriage broke up in the late 1920s she began a relationship with a member of John Grierson's General Post Office film unit and became involved in its work. After the war she travelled widely, living in South Africa and Jamaica, paying her way by painting portraits. For many years shared a studio with Vera Cuningham, whose work influenced her style. Disliking the smell of oil paint Eve Disher opted for gouache, and as well as portraits – which included Professor J B S Haldane, now in the National Portrait Gallery – she sometimes painted flower pictures and urban scenes. Showed with London Artists' Association, SWA, WIAC and Mattheisen Gallery. Died in London.

Michael DISLEY 1962– Sculptor in stone who worked in Britain and Japan, but principally held residencies and completed commissions in the north of England. He studied at Sunderland and Trent Polytechnics, 1981–6. Some of Disley's figurative public works had historical allusions. Thus his Meeting Point, of 1992, in High Street, Spennymoor, relates to the town's past.

Arturo Di STEFANO 1955– Artist working in various media who was born in Liverpool, where he completed a foundation year at the Polytechnic, 1973–4. He then studied at Goldsmiths' College School of Art, 1974–7, and Royal College of Art, 1978–81. His first solo show in 1985 was followed by a year at Accademia Albertina, Turin, backed by an Italian Government Scholarship. He was a prizewinner at John Moores Exhibition, Liverpool, 1991–2. His solo show appearances included Pomeroy Purdy Gallery, 1989–91, several abroad, Walker Art Gallery, Liverpool, 1993, Museum of London, 2000; and Purdy Hicks Gallery, 2001.

Aine DIVINE 1970– Painter and teacher, born in Cork, Ireland, originally working under her maiden name Aine Ahern. She studied at Crawford College of Art and Design in Cork, in 1987 for a certificate in visual education, in 1991 gaining an honours degree in fine art, painting, in 1995 a higher diploma in the principles of teaching art. From 1991 Divine worked as a commissioned portrait artist, from 1995–6 teaching full-time at St Aloysius Secondary School, Cork, from 2000 part-time at Penicuik High School, Midlothian. She was an associate member of Visual Arts Scotland and a full member of Penicuik Community Arts Association. After being shortlisted for two years, Divine was in 1993 an award winner at Arnotts Irish National Portrait Competition and Exhibition; was shortlisted at the Miniature Painters' exhibition at the Mall Galleries, 2004; and in 2005 painted the chosen portrait of the politician Dr Mo Mowlam in the BBC television series *Star Portraits with Rolf Harris*, an accompanying exhibition taking place that year at the County Hall Gallery with tour. Divine had a solo exhibition with Penicuik Community Arts Association in 1999, at Silkart Gallery, Penicuik, 2001, and Outrageous Art, Bruntsfield, Edinburgh, in 2005. She was long interested in depicting the human face and figure, was drawn to similar art by Michelangelo, Rembrandt, Vuillard and Van Gogh "and more recently Andrew Wyeth and Lucian Freud," admiring variously "contorted positions", "sensitivity", and "free and loose brushstrokes", and "the intricacy and detail of the skin in Wyeth's work and in some of Lucian Freud's descriptions of flesh. Skin fascinates me and I love to describe the play of light on the skin in an analytical way, in portraiture I try to describe every subtle variation of tone on a person's face". Her commissions included the barrister Ralph Sutton, concert pianist Charles Lynch, His Honour Judge Harvey Kenny and John Gleeson, the Irish Attorney General's father. Divine lived in Roslin, Edinburgh.

Adam DIX: *see* **Adam DICKS**

Alan DIXON 1936– Artist, poet and teacher who began making sculpture from scrap metal during National Service in the Royal Air Force, 1954–6, work that has not survived. Studied at Goldsmiths' College, 1956–63, where he was unsympathetic to the "subdued, laborious naturalism of a Euston Road kind" then prevailing "and was fascinated by Dada, particularly the earliest brief outbreak in Zürich," had "Robert Motherwell's pioneering book on more-or-less permanent loan from the library" and "found out about Schwitters' works at Lords Gallery." Dixon went on to teach art in schools in London and Peterborough, 1959–87. He published several collections of poems, some decorated with his own woodcuts; some were produced by Poet & Printer, a press which used Dixon's woodcuts in other publications. His poems were also published in *The Listener, The Observer, London Review of Books, The Times Literary Supplement* and elsewhere. Dixon published translations of Hungarian poems and poems by Max Jacob. In the early 1960s Dixon showed woodcuts, paintings and drawings at the AIA Gallery. In 1990 an exhibition of his drawings and watercolours of cats was held at David Holmes Contemporary Art, Peterborough, and constructions from scrap materials in 1995–6. He also made stone carvings.

Anna DIXON 1873–1959 Painter who was born in Edinburgh. Studied at the Royal Scottish Academy Schools under Charles Mackie and E A Walton. Exhibited RA, Royal Glasgow Institute of the Fine Arts, RSA, RSW of which she was a member and in the Scottish and English provinces. President of the SSWA, 1930–42. Lived in Edinburgh. Pictures by Dixon, from the Fleming-Wyfold Art Foundation collection, were offered by Christie's, South Kensington, in 2002.

Jane DIXON 1963– Painter, printmaker, draughtsman and teacher, born in Bolton, Lancashire, who studied at the College of Higher Education there. Also attended West Surrey College of Art & Design, Farnham; and Royal College of Art. She was course tutor at Goldsmiths' College, 1991–3; and in 1994 visiting tutor at the Royal College of Art and Gray's School of Art, Aberdeen, also working on Macmillan's *Dictionary of Art*. Dixon gained a Rome Scholarship in printmaking, 1989; a British Council Travel Grant for Czechoslovakia, 1992; a Purchase Prize, Oriel Mostyn Open, Llandudno, 1993; and was artist-in-residence, Lowick House, Cumbria, 1994. Took part in numerous group shows, including Fresh Art, Barbican Centre, 1986; Work in Progress, Anderson O'Day, 1988; Editions 1/90, International Art Fair, Basel, 1990; and Royal Over-Seas League Open, 1994. Solo exhibitions included Kettle's Yard, Cambridge, in 2000. Oriel Mostyn, Sussex County Council and Leeds Borough Council hold examples.

Jo DIXON 1950– Figurative artist, born in Willingham, Lincolnshire, who believed strongly in good drawing. She studied at Hammersmith College of Art, 1969–72, later at Whitelands College, then taught art in several London schools. After bringing up her children she returned to exhibiting after a dealer had noticed her work, initially in Devon where she lived with her general practitioner husband. Countryside Gallery, Tiverton, gave her a show, and she sold regularly from Drewe Arms, Broad Hembury. In 1996 had a successful exhibition at St John's Smith Square.

Joe DIXON 1915– Painter and teacher who studied at Royal College of Art, being awarded a postgraduate year and a Travelling Scholarship. He went on to teach at Camberwell School of Arts and Crafts and was senior fellow at British School in Rome, 1980. He showed at Opix Gallery, Woodlands Art Gallery, in other mixed exhibitions and in Italy in Rome and Assisi. A figurative artist, notable for his landscapes.

Mark DIXON 1957– Versatile artist, businessman and teacher. He worked full-time in archaeology, 1975–8, around England; set up and ran a screenprinting company, Squeegee Printers, in Stowmarket, Suffolk, 1979–96; and was a part-time tutor in screenprinting and graphic design, degree course, at Colchester Institute, 1982–3. He studied general art and design at Ipswich Art College, 1990–2, graduating with honours in fine art from Norwich Art School, 1992–5, with a dissertation on figures in landscape. From 1990, Dixon was engaged on diverse projects, including, between 1990–5, land art at Old Newton, sponsored by several firms; 1996, an ice sculpture performance in Lowestoft and a kiln building project in Cumbria; 1997, setting up and running St Margaret's Printmakers Experimental Printmaking Workshop and Exhibition, Norwich; 2000, experimenting with electrochemistry as a new form of expression; and 2001, working with microscopic imagery using high voltage. Dixon won a number of prizes and took part in many group exhibitions, his residencies including in 2001 Kansas State University, in America, where he was a visiting artist in 2002. Making the Invisible Visible was in 2004 a solo show at Christchurch Mansion, in Ipswich, Suffolk, where he lived.

Rex DIXON 1939– Artist, born in London, and teacher. He studied at Newton Abbot School of Art, 1966–8, then Stourbridge College of Art, 1968–71, where he later taught part-time. Was also visual arts officer for Midlands Arts Centre. He showed solo there from 1973, also exhibiting at Ikon Gallery, Birmingham, 1971, and Dudley Art Gallery, 1976. Lived for a time at Stourbridge, Worcester.

Stephen DIXON 1957– Ceramic sculptor and teacher whose satirical works dealt with political and social issues. Studied at University of Newcastle upon Tyne and gained his master's in ceramics from the Royal College of Art in 1986. Taught at various colleges and in 1998, when he was featured in Atlantic Crossings at Barbican Centre, was research fellow in ceramics at Manchester Metropolitan University. Solo shows included Scottish Gallery, Edinburgh, 1996, and Webster University, St Louis, 1998. Manchester City Art Gallery and Ulster Museum, Belfast, hold examples.

Sylvia Mary DIXON-WARD 1931–2001 Painter of portraits, landscapes, still life and fantasy pictures. Her work, usually on a modest scale, was signed variously with initials and as Dixon Ward, from about 1990 Dixon-Ward being her preferred surname. Sylvia was born in Leeds, Yorkshire; during World War II the family lived in south Wales, at the end of hostilities moving to London, where Sylvia lived from 1962 in East Dulwich, for many years with her mother (who as Wilhelmina Margaret Hull trained at Sunderland School of Art in the early 1920s). After studying art at Goldsmiths' College from the late 1940s, Sylvia attended secretarial college and worked. After her father died, in 1959, she developed an allergic condition, by 1964 could not work and retired to paint. Between then until cancer intervened shortly before her death she is known to have produced at least 276 works, selling about 10%, giving away more. Her records show that between 1992–7 Miss Dixon-Ward showed with the SWA, RSMA, Society of London Artists and RBA; venues included the Mall, Westminster and South London Art Galleries, although she persistently failed to enter the RA Summer Exhibition.

DIZ: *see* **Edward ARDIZZONE**

Jovan DJORDJEVIC 1957– Versatile artist and illustrator, born in Rochdale, Lancashire, who did a foundation course at the College of Art there, under Alan Green, 1975–6, graduating with first-class honours in fine art, Lanchester Polytechnic, Coventry, under Dick Whall, 1976–80. Between 1981–9 Djordjevic was employed on diverse contracts, including marcher and official photographer, People's March for Jobs, Liverpool to London, 1981; graphic designer, 2D Design and ICA, between 1982–3; graphic designer, Lambeth Inner City Consultative Group, 1984; graphic designer and illustrator, Information Design, 1985; photographic technician, London College of Printing, 1985–6; and crew member, Edwin Shirley Staging, Britain and abroad, 1986–9. Among residencies held was Camp 84, Cleobury Mortimer, Coventry Education Department, 1984. By 2004, Djordjevic's client list approached 100 publications and organisations, including *The Economist*, *Fortune Magazine*, *New Statesman*, *Reader's Digest*, British daily and Sunday broadsheeets, plus major firms such as BOC, British Telecom, Harrods and Oxford University Press. Montage, collage, steel engraving and gravure during the nineteenth and twentieth centuries and more recent digital developments were among Djordjevic's interests. He was a member of the Association of Illustrators and DACS. Took part in many group shows, later ones including Artists in Industry, West Midlands tour, 1984. In that year he had a solo exhibition, With These Hands, at Oxford Polytechnic. Lived in east London.

Zoran DJORDJEVIC 1952– Painter of abstract work, and teacher, who studied at Hornsey College of Art, 1972, Chelsea School of Art in 1973 and gained a French government scholarship in 1976, the following year setting up a studio in Rotherhithe. In 1979 he taught at Barnfield College school of art and design and was manager of Round House Gallery. Exhibitions included Westminster Artists at Alpine Gallery, 1978; 5 Dryden Street and Moira Kelly Fine Art, both 1980; and LG at Morley Gallery and Contemporary Artists in Camden, at Camden Arts Centre, both 1981.

M Wilson DOAR 1898– Painter, draughtsman and wood carver specialising in depictions of dogs. Miss Doar studied at Heatherley's School of Fine Art, 1936, with Frederic Whiting and Bernard Adams, then went on to show with RSA, RCamA, RBA and elsewhere. Lived in London.

Stanley DOBBIN 1929– Printmaker, draughtsman and mixed media artist, and teacher, born in Birmingham. He studied at the College of Art there, 1947–52. Taught at Newton Abbot Grammar School, 1954–9, then Manchester College of Art/Polytechnic, 1959–84. German Expressionism, the British Neo-Romantics and Edward Wadsworth were influences. Was a member of MAFA. Also showed at Bluecoat Gallery, Liverpool, in mixed exhibitions in 1970s; 1983 in Woodworks at Plymouth Art Centre; 1987–93 at Acorn Gallery, Liverpool; in 1990 in Vincent at Bede Gallery, Jarrow, and elsewhere. Had solo shows in 1970s at Bluecoat and in 1980s at Acorn. Figure and landscape woodcuts done in Scotland, Cornwall and North Devon were cited by Dobbin as his main works. Provided illustrations for Jack Clemo's *Clay Cuts* poems, 1991, and Fiona Pitt-Kethley's poems *A School for Life*, 1993. Lived in Cheadle Hulme, Cheshire.

Honor DOBBS 1902–1987 Printmaker and painter who studied Beckenham School of Art. She took part in mixed shows at RA from 1964, others being at Free Painters and Sculptors of which she was a member, Bankside Gallery, Fairfield Halls in Croydon and Ripley Arts Centre. In 1985 she shared a four-man exhibition at Woodlands Art Gallery. Solo exhibitions included Woodlands and the Churchill Library, Bromley. Lived in Chislehurst, Kent, and Cushendall, County Antrim.

Frank Sellar DOBLE 1898– Painter who was by profession a photographer. He was brought up in the Liverpool area and went to the School of Art there and continued to live at Crosby. Doble was a member of the Liverpool Academy of Arts and Liver Sketching Club and exhibited there and at the Walker Art Gallery. Was president of Liver Sketching Club in 1934.

Valentine DOBRÉE 1894–1974 Artist, writer and poet who described herself as "one who regards the arts as a many-faceted crystal rather than as personified by separate Muses". She was married to the writer and critic Bonamy Dobrée, professor of English literature at the University of Leeds, 1936–55. The Dobrées' archive is held by the University, which put on a show of Valentine's paintings and collages in 2000. She exhibited with the LG and Salon des Indépendants, Paris, in the early 1920s, when her friends included the artists Dora Carrington and Mark Gertler. Her early figure paintings diversified into analytical Cubism and Surrealism. From the early 1930s she experimented with collage, a show being held at the ICA, 1963. Dobrée published two novels, *Your Cuckoo Sings by Kind*, 1927, and *The Emperor's Tigers*, 1929, and a book of short stories, *To Blush Unseen*, 1935. A selection of her verse appeared as *This Green Tide*, 1965.

Antoni DOBROWOLSKI 1919–1987 Painter, designer and sculptor, one of the Polish paper sculptors who flourished in Britain after World War II. He was born in Pinsk, was commissioned in the Polish Army and granted leave to study art at the Polish School of Painting in Rome and England, where his strongly individual style developed. Intricate detail, charm and accuracy and imaginative use of materials characterised his output. Moved to England in 1947 where he enrolled at the Sir John Cass School of Arts and Crafts. Worked for Diana Studio. During the coronation of Queen Elizabeth II, despite being confined to bed with illness, Dobrowolski was heavily involved in decorative work for the celebrations in Regent and Oxford Streets. Industrial clients included Vat 69 Whisky, British Railways and KLM, work being done for the Brussels World Exhibition. Decorations for the grand ballroom of the Dorchester Hotel, Hoover and the White Eagle, Knightsbridge, were notable successes. His work was included in Polish Paper Sculpture at the Polish Cultural Institute, 1995.

Chris DOBROWOLSKI 1968– Creator of sculptures and installations, who attended Braintree College of Further Education, 1987–8; Humberside University, Hull, 1988–91; and Royal College of Art, 1994–6. Exhibitions included Vehicular Excess, Trinity Street Gallery, Colchester, 1993; Essex Open, The Minories, Colchester (awarded Education Commission), 1994; Atrium Gallery, Coopers and Lybrand, 1996; 64AE, Trinity Street Studios, Colchester (Lottery Award Gallery Project), 1997; Ferens Art Gallery, Hull (permanent collection), 1998; Aerial: Wind, Sun and Radio, Sculpture in Christchurch Park, Ipswich, 1999; and Big Country, firstsite, Colchester, 2004. Dobrowolski complemented the park's undulations with a wind-powered moving cable, from which were suspended solar-powered radios; as a windmill caught the breeze the cable rotated, enabling radios to traverse the landscape.

Cowan DOBSON 1893–1980 Portrait painter, born in Bradford, Yorkshire, son of the artist Henry John Dobson. He was educated at George Watson's College, Edinburgh, studying art in the Scottish capital, London and Paris. Showed at RA from 1913–59, including portraits of notable sitters including Admiral of the Fleet the Earl Beatty, 1934, and The Earl Attlee, 1956. Was elected RBA in 1922, also exhibiting at Fine Art Society, Royal Glasgow Institute of the Fine Arts, RSA, Walker Art Gallery in Liverpool and elsewhere. Glasgow Corporation bought his work. Lived finally in London and was an Arts Club member.

Eric DOBSON 1923–1992 Artist and influential teacher, born in County Durham, who gained a scholarship to Dame Allen's School, Newcastle, 1934–41, then received a first-class honours degree at King's College 1942–3 and 1946–50, studies interrupted by Royal Navy service. Dobson stayed on to work as a tutorial student under Lawrence Gowing, Roger de Grey and Christopher Cornford, later becoming a full-time member of staff at Newcastle University. An accidental head injury led to his retirement in 1989. Dobson was a representational and abstract painter, the Euston Road School and especially Victor Pasmore being influences. He showed in London and Paris and had a memorial exhibition at University of Northumbria, Newcastle, in 1994.

Frank DOBSON 1886–1963 Sculptor, draughtsman and painter in oil and watercolour. Born in London, the son of an artist with whom he initially studied, Dobson first attended Leyton School of Art, 1900–2, was an apprentice studio boy with the sculptor Sir William Reynolds-Stephens, 1902–4. After a time in Cornwall was, 1906–10, at Hospitalfield Art Institute, Arbroath, finally attending the City and Guilds School, Kennington, 1910–12. Although he made his first wood-carving just before World War I, Dobson's first one-man show, at the Chenil Galleries, 1914, was of paintings and drawings. During World War I enlisted in Artists' Rifles and continued working, Imperial War Museum acquiring his large oil The Balloon Apron. After the war Dobson met Wyndham Lewis and exhibited with Group X in 1920; had a first one-man show as a sculptor at Leicester Galleries, 1921. First sculptures were very stylised, but later work influenced by the work of Aristide Maillol. During the inter-war years Dobson consolidated his reputation – with Epstein he was called "a keeper of tradition", bridging classical and modern sculpture – by making the backdrop for the first performance of William Walton's *Façade*; showing internationally; designing glazed pottery reliefs for Hay's Wharf, London; completing his large carving Pax and notable portraits. Official War Artist in World War II. Professor of sculpture at the Royal College of Art, 1946–53. Elected RA, 1953. Dobson is represented in many public galleries, including the Tate Gallery. Arts Council memorial exhibition 1966, and touring; retrospective Kettle's Yard, Cambridge, 1981–2, toured; major reappraisal at Henry Moore Institute, Leeds, 1994. The Fine Art Society exhibited The Trask

Bequest, works by Paul Nash and Dobson, in 2004. Died in London.

Martin John DOBSON 1947– Artist in oil, chalk pastel and photography, born in Manchester. He was self-taught and began painting seriously and exhibiting in the early 1970s while employed in commercial photography, later dividing interest between the two. Dobson's main theme was steam railways in landscape. He chiefly worked "in monochrome or muted colour to evoke the atmosphere of the steam railway in its declining years". Was a member of Guild of Railway Artists. Showed extensively in group and open exhibitions, including Colin Jellicoe Gallery, Manchester; Manchester Academy; Astley Cheetham Gallery, Stalybridge; Bath and Edinburgh Festivals; Torr Top Gallery, New Mills; and Lyric Theatre. Solo shows included Past Trains, Manchester and Salford University Library, 1979; and Fire and Water, Colin Jellicoe, and Charlotte Mason College, Ambleside, both 1988. Greater London Council bought two works. Lived in Hyde, Cheshire.

Mary E DOBSON 1912– Painter, draughtsman, mural artist and illustrator, born in London. Studied at Bournemouth Municipal School of Art, 1930–4, Chelsea Polytechnic, 1936–7, then in 1938 at Central School of Arts and Crafts. During World War II she served in the Women's Royal Naval Service. She drew for a wide range of publications, including *Strand Magazine*, the *Daily Mail* and *Daily Herald* and *Nursery World*. Exhibited RA, SWA and NEAC. Lived in London and in Shipbourne, Kent.

Scott DOBSON 1918–1986 Painter, designer, art critic and teacher whose full name was Edward Scott Dobson and who was born in Blyth, Northumberland. Studied art at King Edward VII College, Newcastle; at Freckleton, in Lancashire; and Leeds College of Art. Sometimes signing work only S D, showed New Vision Centre, Redfern Gallery, RSA and in his home area of Newcastle upon Tyne. For a time he was art critic of the *Evening Chronicle* newspaper there and he also taught art for several years at Manchester Grammar School, as well as running the Westgate Gallery in Newcastle. Shipley Art Gallery in Gateshead and Laing Art Gallery and Museum in Newcastle hold his work.

Michael DOCHERTY 1947– Painter and creator of artworks using found objects, born in Alloa, Clackmannanshire. He studied at Edinburgh College of Art, 1964–8, an Andrew Grant Scholarship permitting him to travel in France and Spain. Docherty gathers found objects, which he paints and which together chronicle his travels. Scottish National Gallery of Modern Art holds an example: An Object Fixed in Time, constructed in 1977. He was in the Gallery's exhibition Scottish Art since 1900, 1989–90, which toured; Docherty's first solo show was in 1970 at Richard Demarco Gallery, Edinburgh.

Alan DODD 1942– Painter, muralist and designer, born in Kennington, Ashford, Kent. He studied at Maidstone College of Art, 1958–63, teachers including Christopher Ironside, Robin Ironside, Gerard de Rose, Margery Gill and David Hockney; then at Royal Academy Schools, 1963–6, under Peter Greenham, Charles Mahoney, Fred Dubery, Graham Arnold, Edward Bawden, Richard Eurich and Gertrude Hermes. Until 1975 Dodd concentrated on easel pictures, then he added mural works, small architectural details and became an adviser on historic colour detail. Dodd was a member of the Art Workers' Guild from 1982. He took part in the RA Bicentary Exhibition, 1967–8, and had a series of solo shows at New Grafton Gallery, 1969–72. He completed five capriccio panels for the Painted Room, Victoria & Albert Museum, 1986; work in the Painted Hall, Great Fosters, Egham, 1989; and in New Picture Room, Sir John Soane's Museum, 1992. Lived in London.

Francis DODD 1874–1949 Draughtsman, painter and printmaker, especially of portraits, born at Holyhead, Anglesey. Studied at Glasgow School of Art under Fra Newbery and Archibald Kay, winning the Haldane Scholarship in 1893, travelling to France, Italy and later to Spain. For about 10 years from 1895 lived in Manchester, then settled in Blackheath in southeast London, which he often painted and drew. Dodd was an Official War Artist during World War I and was a trustee of the Tate Gallery, 1928–35, being elected RA in 1935. Dodd exhibited extensively at NEAC, RA and RWS and at many other venues and his work is in a number of British public collections, including Tate Gallery, in South Africa and Australia. His work is comparable to that of his brother-in-law, Muirhead Bone, although Dodd can be a lively and perceptive portrait painter: witness his portraits of the critic Edward Garnett in the Tate Gallery and the painter Henry Lamb in Manchester's City Art Gallery. A retrospective of Dodd's work was held at Cheltenham in 1944. Memorial shows took place at Bluecoat School, Liverpool, 1949, and South London Art Gallery, 1950.

Phyllis DODD 1899–1995 Painter, notably of portraits, born in Chester. Her parents encouraged her early interest in art. She won a Royal Drawing Society prize in 1909 and her mother took in paying guests to send her to Liverpool School of Art, 1917–21, where Will Penn taught her the use of a limited palette; by the 1950s she developed an interest in more positive colour. In 1921 won a Royal Exhibition, one of many awards, to Royal College of Art, 1921–5. While teaching at Walthamstow Technical College, 1925–30, obtained portrait commissions through William Rothenstein, in 1928 marrying the artist Douglas Percy Bliss. She being a perfectionist in all things, domestic life eroded Dodd's time for painting. Although when a student she had painted so concentratedly that she forgot to eat and became ill, as a housewife she said that "when there is dust on the stairs, I cannot settle down to painting." Showed at RA, with a notable success in 1939; had a joint exhibition with her husband at Derby Museum & Art Gallery, 1947; another joint show at St Michael's Gallery, Derby, 1983; a ninetieth-birthday show at Hatton Gallery, Newcastle, 1989; and a retrospective at the public gallery, Derby, again in 1995. Glaucoma was diagnosed in 1976; she suffered a major stroke which badly damaged her sight in 1986, a year after she painted her last major portrait; and in 1992 she became totally blind. Lived for many years in Glasgow.

Robert William DODD 1934–1997 Painter, textile designer and lecturer, born in Lowestoft, Suffolk, but essentially a Northumbrian. He was noted for his images of Northumberland and Surrey, West Country and Venetian landscapes. Dodd attended Sunderland College of Art, 1952–4, under Harry Thubron; completed two years' National Service in the Royal Air Force; then attended Royal College of Art, 1957–9, teachers including Humphrey

Spender, Wyndham Goodden, John Drummond and John Minton; and Konstfackskolan, Stockholm, 1959–60, under Viola Gråsten. Dodd was a freelance textile designer, occasional lecturer and painter and a fellow of the Society of Industrial Artists and Designers. He took part in group shows at RA and Whitworth Art Gallery, Manchester, having a solo exhibition at Guildford House Gallery, in Guildford, where he lived. Victoria & Albert Museum and Whitworth Art Gallery hold examples.

William DODD 1908– Watercolourist who studied at Kendal School of Art, 1926–33. He was a member of Lancaster Art Group and the Lake Artists' Society. Showed NEAC, RWA, RCamA and elsewhere. Lived at Arnside, Westmorland.

Andrew DODDS 1927–2004 Watercolourist, illustrator and teacher, born in Gullane, East Lothian. His son was the artist James Dodds, with whom he collaborated on books. He studied at Colchester School of Art, 1942–5, then Central School of Arts and Crafts, 1947–50, teachers including John Minton, Keith Vaughan, Bernard Meninsky, Ruskin Spear, R S Badmin and John Farleigh. He was a part-time tutor at St Martin's School of Art, 1952–75, then principal lecturer in the art and design department of Suffolk College, Ipswich, 1975–89. Dodds illustrated several dozen books, including *East Anglia Drawn*, 1987, *London Then*, 1994, *East Anglian Sketchbook*, 1999, and *Here & There*, 2003, with an accompanying show at Christchurch Mansion, Ipswich. He drew for the *Eastern Daily Press* for 47 years. Dodds was elected a member of the Society of Industrial Artists in 1951 and a fellow of the Chartered Society of Designers in 1983. He was a member of Colchester Art Society, which held his work, and exhibited at RA. Had a solo exhibition at Studio Club, 1961, others including Minories, Colchester, from 1970; Mermaid Theatre, 1975; Digby Gallery, Colchester, 1991, and Chappel Galleries, Chappel, 1999. In 2002, Dodds was included in the Ashmolean Museum, Oxford, exhibition *Artists of Radio Times*. He was from early in his career a prolific illustrator for the magazine, creating the original drawings for the serial *The Archers*, Dan Archer modelled on a local farmer, Doris on Dodds' mother, Margaret. Dodds produced advertising material for the Royal Air Force, British Railways, Shell, Decca, National Westminster Bank and other corporate collections. Lived in Lower Raydon, Ipswich, Suffolk.

Andrew DODDS 1969– Artist from Northern Ireland who settled in London. Dodds used a range of modern media. He gained a master's degree in fine art from Slade School of Fine Art, 1998–00. Exhibitions included Puppylove, Barbican Centre and Ikon Gallery, Birmingham, tour, 1999; New Horizons at The Lux, 2000; East of Eden, Spacex Gallery, Exeter, 2001; and in 2002 at *The Economist* Tower he presented What can be imagined, can be created. This comprised three new video works for which the audience donned headphones and became "immersed in the mesmerising and seductive audio-visual experience." It followed the award of the Dolby Travel Prize 2001, which funded a study trip to Las Vegas in America and the Galapagos Islands.

James DODDS 1957– Artist born and settled in Brightlingsea, Essex, who was an apprentice shipwright, 1972–6, then attended Colchester School of Art, 1976–7, Chelsea School of Art, 1977–80, and Royal College of Art, 1981–4. From 1980 was a prolific exhibitor, including The Minories, Colchester, 1983, Hatton Gallery at Newcastle upon Tyne, 1985, Camden Arts Centre, 1987, Gallery 44 at Aldeburgh Festival, 1990, and Sue Rankin Gallery, 1992. Solo exhibition of recent paintings was held at Chappel Galleries, Chappel, 1994, also Shipshape at firstsite, The Minories, Colchester, and tour, 2001–2, at National Maritime Museum, 2003, Messum's in 2004, with another at Chappel in 2005. Ipswich and Horniman Museums and the Britten-Pears Library hold examples. Commissions included two big paintings for Clacton and Rochford Hospitals, The National Trust and Kent Opera and Tollesbury stained glass window working with Stourside Glassworks. Dodds' paintings and prints displayed an intimate knowledge of ships and how they were built. He collaborated on books with his painter and illustrator father Andrew Dodds. In 1984 James founded the Jardine Press, which produced fine books using texts by himself and other authors, illustrated with his own woodcuts and linocuts.

Joan Kathleen DODDS 1918– Artist and illuminator, born and lived in York and studied at the School of Art there. She was by profession a bank clerk but also did part-time art teaching. Dodds joined the PS in 1967, belonged to York Art Society and showed with RI and Paris Salon. York Minster holds illuminated work by her. Latterly she retired from exhibiting.

Eveline DODGSON 1901–1995 Artist who was born at Long Marston, Yorkshire, first cousin of the artist John Dodgson. After her parents died when she was young she was brought up by her uncle Campbell Dodgson, keeper of prints and drawings at the British Museum. She studied at Edinburgh College of Art and Slade School of Fine Art, in Paris and Italy. She was married to James Byam Shaw, second son of the artist Byam Shaw, then to William Winkworth, an authority on Oriental ceramics. Exhibited NEAC and elsewhere and decorated All Hallows Church, Poplar, in 1924. After her husband's death Eveline converted to Roman Catholicism and liked to be called Margaret. Lived latterly in the Isle of Wight.

John DODGSON 1890–1969 Painter, printmaker, teacher and collector, born in Murree, Punjab, India. His mother was a keen amateur painter, his uncle Campbell Dodgson, of the British Museum, and early on he gained a love of Renaissance Italy. After attending Oxford University, 1909–13, Dodgson studied at Slade School of Fine Art, 1913–15, with Henry Tonks. Served with Army during World War I, carried out a commission for Imperial War Museum and in 1919 was for a short time assistant director at National Gallery under Sir Charles Holmes. Showed with NEAC, LG of which he was president in 1950–2 and with London Artists' Association, of which he was also a member. After World War II Army Service Dodgson taught at Camberwell School of Arts and Crafts, 1946–50, then at Chelsea School of Art, 1950–8. His first one-man show was at Claridge Gallery, 1928; he had another, in 1959, at Beaux Arts Gallery. Dodgson's work owes something to the Camden Town and Euston Road traditions, but there is a strong Symbolist strain, as in the Tate Gallery's Giant Snail. Dodgson was a keen collector, having private means, and owned pictures by Bonnard, Pasmore, Steer, Claude Rogers and Duncan Grant, as well as by his students. His own studio was burned to the ground in 1964, so remaining work is limited. Memorial show at South London Art Gallery, 1971. Major show at Fine Art Society and tour, 1995. Lived at Chelsworth, Suffolk.

Tom DODSON 1910–1991 Self-taught painter, born in and lived in the Salford area of Lancashire, the eldest of a poor family of five children. Although keen on art as a child – top of the class for drawing, he chalked the local pavements with his depictions of local characters – he had to leave council school at 14 and join the grocery trade, during his life doing a number of jobs in industry to support his family. Shortly before retiring as a caretaker he took up art again, painting scenes of his youth with sincerity and warmth, having a first solo show at Bell Galleries, Sale, in 1974. This sold out, and soon over 30,000 prints from 36 of his original paintings were sold (usually the signed, limited editions were 850). By 1985, some paintings were selling at almost £2,000. Tom and his wife Lily toured Lancashire in their Reliant Robin three-wheeler to find new subjects. In 1998, Salford Quays Heritage Centre, helped by Studio Arts, Lancaster, put on a commemorative exhibition.

Samuel DODWELL 1909–1990 Painter, draughtsman, teacher and broadcaster, born in London, who attended Regent Street Polytechnic School of Art and began painting seriously after World War II. He was by profession a banker with an American bank, retiring at 59 to concentrate on art and teaching. Impressionism, sound draughtsmanship and a tendency towards abstraction all played a part in his diverse output, which included portraiture. Dodwell was elected RI in 1965, also taking part in mixed shows such as RA Summer Exhibition, RP and RBA. Held solo exhibitions in London, the provinces and abroad, including Athens and Amsterdam. Among Dodwell's commissions was a large mural of sunflowers for the Imperial Hotel, Torquay, one for the American Chamber of Commerce, London, and portraits in Beirut, Lebanon, where he appeared on television. He also featured in *Portrait in Oils*, a Westward Television programme. The Nuffield Foundation bought three works. Lived in Reigate, Surrey, later in Lostwithiel, Cornwall.

Ruth DOGGETT 1881–1974 Painter, printmaker and teacher in the Camden Town Group tradition, second eldest of 10 children, born in Cambridge, of George Doggett. He was a director of Robert Sayle, a local general store, and a strong nonconformist. Miss Doggett studied for several years at Westminster School of Art, teachers including Walter Sickert, gaining a medal in 1913. Because she became a teacher Doggett's own painting was restricted to holidays, so her output was small. East Anglia, the West Country and Cornwall were favourite painting spots. Doggett lived in London until 1939, when she returned to Cambridge, and about this time seems to have stopped painting. She was a member of the LG, showed at ROI and at Walker Art Gallery in Liverpool and had a solo show at Fine Art Society in 1934, where a few pictures sold. Although Doggett's work is not often shown Sickert, Harold Gilman – who painted a notable portrait of her – and the critic Frank Rutter all thought highly of her abilities. In 1946 she settled in St Leonards-on-Sea, Sussex, with several sisters, devoting much time to botany and gardening.

Maggie DOHERTY 1957– Versatile artist working in a range of media, particularly interested in sculptural and organically inspired forms. Doherty studied English literature and fine art at Liverpool University; took a studio in the city; joined Artfeste, working there for two years; was for two years studio assistant with the sculptor Arthur Dooley; and studied blacksmithing and welding. Showed extensively in the northwest of England and in the south after moving in 1995, settling in East Anglia. Worked to commission and was included in Making the Connection, firstsite, Colchester/Wolsey Art Gallery, Ipswich, 2002.

Mary Jo DOHERTY 1971– Ceramic artist, born in Londonderry, Northern Ireland, who studied at University of Ulster and Royal College of Art. She gained a Northern Ireland Education Board Scholarship, 1994–6, and a Wedgwood Scholar Prize, Royal College of Art, 1996. Won the Royal Over-Seas League Trophy Commission in 1996, the resulting work being inspired by seventeenth-century Meissen figurines.

Moira DOHERTY fl. from mid-1980s– Figurative artist, muralist and teacher who graduated from the University of Ulster, Belfast, with a fine art degree in 1985. She was involved in the education of the young disabled and the supervision of drama workshops and murals. The resulting work won many awards, including the first prize, Barclays Young Artist Award, and was performed and shown throughout Northern Ireland. Showed with the Claremorris Open Exhibition, in the annual Independent Artists Exhibition at Arts Council in Belfast and in Beyond the Partitions, put on by Queen Street Studios, Belfast, with which Doherty was associated.

Willie DOHERTY 1959– Artist employing photographs and text, born in Londonderry, where he continued to live. Studied at Ulster Polytechnic, Belfast, 1977–81. From early-1980s took part in many mixed shows, including Performance, Live Work, at Crescent Arts Centre, Belfast, 1982; Oliver Dowling Gallery, Dublin, 1987; Three Artists, Battersea Arts Centre, 1988; and South Bank Centre's The British Art Show 1990. Had solo shows at Orchard Gallery, Londonderry, from 1980, and elsewhere, including video and photography at Matt's Gallery, 2002. There was a retrospective, False Memory, at the Irish Museum of Modern Art, Kilmainham, 2002–3. Was included in Twelve Stars, Belfast Arts Council Gallery and tour, 1992–3, showing work chosen for the European Parliament Collection.

Maxwell DOIG 1966– Painter, draughtsman, teacher and printmaker who abandoned a graphics course in the early 1980s because it restricted his vivid imagination. Encouraged by the artist David Blackburn he was accepted for Manchester School of Art in 1985. The following year he had a two-man show at Manchester University, had work accepted for Manchester Academy Summer Exhibition and won a prize for the best print shown. By the time Doig graduated in 1988 he had shown at Whitworth Art Gallery, Manchester, in the Young Contemporaries exhibition and at Bankside Gallery, in 1990 winning the Joseph Webb Scholarship for the best draughtsman under 35. He won the Villiers David Prize in 1997, having been shortlisted in 1995. Doig took up a postgraduate scholarship to Slade School of Fine Art 1988–90, where he won a Laura Ashley

Scholarship. He was awarded a place as artist-in-residence at Hochschule der Kunst, Berlin, 1991–2. Doig travelled extensively through America, Mexico and Australia, 1997, and was a part-time lecturer at Leeds Metropolitan University, 1999–01. His first show after finishing at the Slade was at Hart Gallery, Linby, Nottingham, in 1990, which continued to show him, also Albemarle Gallery, 2002 and 2004. Universities of Manchester and London hold examples.

Peter DOIG 1959– Painter, born in Edinburgh, who attended Wimbledon School of Art, 1979–80, St Martin's School of Art, graduating 1980–3, then gained his master's degree at Chelsea School of Art, 1989–90. Mixed exhibitions included New Contemporaries at ICA, 1983, Barclays Young Artist Award, Serpentine Gallery, 1991, and Days Like These, Tate Britain, 2003. Showed solo at Articule, Montreal, Canada, 1990, and Whitechapel Artist Award, Whitechapel Art Gallery, 1991, with another exhibition in 1998. Doig's landscape Stealth House, 1992, was included in Twelve Stars, Belfast Arts Council Gallery and tour, 1992–3, being acquired for European Parliament Collection. Doig won first prize in John Moores Liverpool Exhibition, 1993–4, and in 1994 won the Eliette von Karajan prize in Salzburg, Austria, and had a solo exhibition at Victoria Miro Gallery, one of several there. Tate Gallery, Contemporary Art Society, Arts Council and European Parliament hold examples. Lived in London.

Eric DOITCH 1923–2000 Printmaker, draughtsman, painter and teacher, born illegitimate in Vienna, Austria, as Siegfried Steiner. He was adopted by the orthodox Jewish family of his father, Edmund Deutsch. While Edmund was in England Doitch was permitted to move there with his stepmother to avoid Nazi persecution, and his name was anglicized. After farm work and a period at St Martin's School of Art Doitch was interned as an alien, worked in a munitions factory, then entered Camberwell School of Art, 1946–9, where Victor Pasmore and Claude Rogers were influences. After Camberwell, he studied printmaking part-time at the Central School of Arts and Crafts, where he was taught by Andrew Freeth and William Palmer Robins and met Alice FitzPayne, whom he married. He attended the Royal College of Art, 1951–4, initially in the painting school, then studied engraving under Edward Ardizzone and Robert Sargent Austin. Doitch taught at Camberwell, Guildhall, City and Guilds and Chelsea School of Art, in the 1970s settling in Lincolnshire, where the fenland landscape was an inspiration. From a show at Staatsdurckerie Gallery, Vienna, in 1962, the Albertina Museum bought several etchings. Latterly, Doitch and his wife showed together, notably at the Usher Gallery, Lincoln, 1983, and Robert Christian Gallery, 1995, in Boston, where Doitch died. In 2001, his Freiston Shore paintings were shown in the Guildhall Museum there.

Miriam DOKOTLIVER 1954– Painter using mixed media, born in Ukraine, who studied for an honours degree in fine art at Glasgow School of Art, 1987–91, gaining her master's in fine art and design, Gray's Art School/Robert Gordon University, Aberdeen, where she lived, 1993–4. Mixed shows included Ben Uri Gallery, 1990; RSA from 1991; Roger Billcliffe, Compass Gallery and Royal Glasgow Institute of the Fine Arts, all Glasgow in 1994; and Rendezvous, Candlewick and the City Art Gallery, all in Aberdeen in 1996. Later solo exhibitions included The Lemon Tree, Aberdeen, 1995, and The Gallery at Heatherslaw Mill, Northumberland, 1996.

Germaine DOLAN 1945– Artist and teacher in acrylic and watercolour, born in Cambridge of Irish parents. She travelled extensively with her Royal Air Force family and subsequently. Studied at Ealing School of Art, 1969–70, and Canterbury College of Art, 1970–3, notable teachers including Geoffrey Rigden and Mali Morris, with Matisse a key influence. Dolan said that "I draw fast – gathering information – and paint slow, synthesising and considering. Attention must be rigorously drilled by hand and eye to be limber. New signs must be found, the briefest possible indication." Took part in many mixed shows in Canterbury and in Clevedon: Sharing a View, APT Gallery and tour, 1997–8. Solo exhibitions included The Grange Museum, Neasden, 1985; Darwen College, University of Kent, 1992; and in 1996 at The Friars Gallery, Canterbury, where she lived. The Sinai Desert was her second home, where she ran occasional art courses. Latterly had a series of solo shows at deliART, including Still, paintings and prints, 2002.

Patrick DOLAN 1926–1980 Painter of abstracts in oil, and teacher, born in Ireland. He studied at Architectural Association in 1950s, was an associate of Francis Bacon and, largely due to Adrian Heath, in 1960s moved to St Ives, Cornwall, in 1965 becoming a member of Penwith Society of Arts. From 1969 until his death he was a senior lecturer at Cardiff School of Art. In 1962 Dolan shared a show with Anthony Shiels and Alan Wood at Gallery 60 in Chichester, organised by Rawlinsky Gallery; in 1965 he shared an exhibition with Wood at Queen Square Gallery in Leeds, also showing with Midland Group in Nottingham; and in 1995 a group of Dolan's works was shown by Belgrave Gallery. He remains a rather mysterious figure, who died of cancer.

James DOLBY 1909–1975 Painter, printmaker and draughtsman, born at Oxenhope, near Haworth, Yorkshire. Studied at Keighley School of Art and at the Royal College of Art under Robert Austin and Malcolm Osborne. Exhibited RA, SWE, RBA, in the provinces and widely abroad. The Victoria & Albert Museum and Whitworth Art Gallery, Manchester, among a number of provincial galleries, hold his work. Dolby was on the staff of Bournemouth College of Art in the 1930s, then was head of Blackburn School of Art, 1947–69. He served in the Royal Navy during World War II and wrote a book called *The Steel Navy*. His work ranged over a variety of subjects, including industrial scenes, interiors and abstract paintings of the sea. Lived at Southampton.

Katherine DOLMAN 1978– Artist born in London, who moved to Newcastle upon Tyne in 1981. She did a foundation course at North Tyneside College, graduating with honours in fine art at Manchester Metropolitan University in 2000. In that year Dolman was tipped by *Art Review* as one of 20 artists to look out for in 2000, *The Independent on Sunday* naming her as a young British artist "heading for the top". Dolman initially exhibited in Manchester, including Contact Theatre, 1998, and smaller venues, being included in Cherubim and Seraphim at east73rdgallery, 2000. Her work there represented "the ambivalence between innocence and desire, between childhood and adulthood, and the anxiety experienced in having to conform to adult expectation."

Anne Katrine DOLVEN 1953– Artist using painting, film and video, born in Oslo, Norway, who lived in London from 1987. She studied at L'École des Beaux-Arts, Aix-en-Provence, 1972–3; L'École Nationale Supérieure des Beaux-Arts, Paris, sculpture, 1973–8; Statens Kunstakademi Oslo, painting, mixed media, 1982–6; and gained a DAAD/ Norwegian Ministry of Foreign Affairs grant, Kunstlerhaus Bethanien, Berlin, 1987–8. Dolven took part in numerous group shows internationally and had many solo shows, for which she often made cards and posters. She saw painting and film as integral to each other. Her large, minimal, abstract paintings exploited the subtle effects of light on surface, questioning the viewer's perception, as at Sadler's Wells in 2001. Later solo exhibitions also included Anthony Wilkinson Gallery and Caisse des Depots, Paris, both 2000, and Northern Gallery of Contemporary Art, Sunderland, and Kunstalle Bern, Bern, both 2001. The many public collections holding Dolven's work included Philadelphia Museum of Art; Berlinische Galerie, Museum for Modern Art and Photography, Berlin; and National Gallery, Oslo.

Ian DOLWIN 1968– Figurative painter and printmaker who gained a diploma in exhibition design from Hastings College of Art, fine art honours degree from Kent Institute of Art & Design and a postgraduate diploma from Royal Academy Schools. In 1995 won a Cyprus Travel Award, in 1998 the Aeneas Travel Scholarship to Italy and Armitage Prize for figurative painting. Exhibitions included Hastings Marina, 1993; National Print Exhibition, Mall Galleries, 1998; and Artmonsky Arts, 1999. Lived in London.

Krystyna DOMAŃSKA-HERLING: *see* **Krystyna HERLING-GRUDZIŃSKA**

M F DOMMEN: *see* **Marguerite France DOUGLAS**

Jacqueline DONACHIE 1969– Artist using sound installations and photographs, born and lived in Glasgow, who studied at the School of Art there, 1986–91. In 1995–6 she gained a Fulbright Fellowship to New York. Group exhibitions included Information, Paisley Museum and Art Galleries, 1989; New Art in Scotland, Centre for Contemporary Arts, Glasgow, 1994; Make Believe, Royal College of Art, 1995; and Correspondences, Scottish National Gallery of Modern Art, 1997–8. Had a solo show, Part Edit, at Tramway, Glasgow, 1994, later ones including Home Taping, Marian Goodman Gallery, New York, 1996. In 2004, Leeds City Art Gallery displayed Donachie's sound installation In the Arms of Strangers, commissioned by Leeds Museums & Galleries in 2001.

Kaye DONACHIE 1970– Painter, born in Glasgow, who studied at the University of Central England, Birmingham, 1989–92, and Royal College of Art, 1995–7. She won the Christie's and Deloitte and Touche Awards in 1997. Her 1998 picture Mobile Home was included in East International at Norwich School of Art & Design, 1999, the year she won a prize at John Moores Liverpool Exhibition. In 2003 Donachie was included in Prague Biennale 1, Peripheries Become the Center, Veletrzni Palac, Prague, Czech Republic. Maureen Paley/Interim Art and Artist Space, New York, America, both gave Donachie solo shows. Lived in London.

Ernest DONAGH 1941– Artist and teacher, born in Wednesbury, Staffordshire, who studied lithography and painting at Stafford Art School, 1958–62, gaining his art teacher's certificate at Goldsmiths' College, 1962–3. For several years he undertook commercial and exhibition projects. Joined Ian Lawson, whom he had met at Stafford, at Editions Alecto, 1968–9, then was with Petersburg Press, 1969–77. After teaching life drawing part-time at Putney College of Art, 1977–86, Ernie Donagh continued to teach, produce and show his own work.

Rita DONAGH 1939– Draughtsman, painter, collagist and teacher, born in Wednesbury, Staffordshire. After studying at University of Durham, 1956–62, she taught at Reading University's School of Fine Art, 1964–72. Further teaching followed at Slade School of Fine Art and Goldsmiths' College School of Art. Donagh participated in a number of influential group shows and had a first solo exhibition at Nigel Greenwood in 1972, showing thereafter. In 1977 had retrospective at Whitworth Art Gallery, Manchester, and tour. Arts Council holds her work, which was often of a highly experimental nature, drawing on inspirations as diverse as police photographs of nightlife in New York; an Irishman killed in Dublin by a car bomb; and the American writer of *Walden*, H D Thoreau. Her working method was painstaking, with precise draughtsmanship. Later exhibitions from the culturally observant artist included Ikon Gallery, Birmingham, 2005.

Anne DONALD 1941– Painter, printmaker and museum keeper, born and lived in Glasgow, who studied at the School of Art there, 1959–63, under David Donaldson, William Armour and W Drummond Bone. She worked at Glasgow Art Gallery and Museum, 1959–63, latterly as keeper of fine art; was a part-time artist until 1993, then full-time. Was a member of Royal Glasgow Institute of the Fine Arts, Glasgow Society of Women Artists and SSWA, also showing at RSA and RSW and with several Glasgow dealers in mixed exhibitions. Had a two-man show at Lillie Art Gallery, Milngavie, 1977; a four-man there in 1994; with a solo exhibition at Greenock Arts Guild, 1978. Glasgow Art Gallery and Museum, Strathclyde University, Lillie Art Gallery and Tayside Regional Council hold Donald's work, which was still life and landscape "influenced by Scottish art from the Glasgow Boys and Scottish Colourists onwards".

George DONALD 1943– Painter and teacher, born in Ootacamund, southern India. He was awarded an Andrew Grant Scholarship in the mid-1960s, attending Edinburgh College of Art, 1966, winning a postgraduate scholarship in 1967 and a Helen A Rose Travelling Scholarship, 1967–8. Donald was a visiting scholar at Benares University in 1967, then was at Hornsey College of Art, 1969. In the 1970s he won a series of awards and bursaries followed by more in the 1980s, including the RSA Gillies Prize and RSW May Marshall Brown Award. Donald was a member of RSA, RSW and SSA. He worked as a visiting artist in China and Thailand, lectured at Edinburgh College of Art and was director of Edinburgh Festival Summer School in the Visual Arts. Donald showed widely in Britain and abroad in mixed exhibitions. Main solo exhibitions ranged from 57 Gallery, Edinburgh, in 1971, through Scottish Gallery and Open Eye Gallery there to Christopher Hull Gallery in 1992. Donald did commissioned portraits for Scottish Arts Council and Glasgow University and a window design for the Scottish National Library. Victoria & Albert Museum, Scottish Arts Council and Glasgow University hold his work.

Antony DONALDSON 1939– Painter, sculptor and teacher, born in Godalming, Surrey. His work often reflected ephemeral events and personalities and the media. Studied at Regent Street Polytechnic School of Art, 1957–8, and Slade School of Fine Art, 1958–62, obtaining a London University postgraduateship of fine art in 1962–3. He showed with Young Contemporaries and LG and had first one-man show at Rowan Gallery in 1963. Joined teaching staff of Chelsea School of Art in 1962, the year before he won a second prize in John Moores Liverpool Exhibition. Between 1966–8 Donaldson worked in California, America, on return to London producing sculptures based on his paintings of Los Angeles cinemas. Beach and nocturnal Parisian scenes followed, as well as girl and hanging trapeze sculptures. Donaldson was interested in unusual pigments such as metal-flake car paint and iridescent fish-scale paint, sculpture materials including fibreglass, stone and metals. Completed commissions for Hong Kong, Singapore and Tokyo; a fountain at Tower Bridge Piazza and large torso in Anchor Court were tourist attractions; later works including Master of Suspense, a hugh sculpture of the film director Alfred Hitchcock for the site of the old Gainsborough Studios, Islington. Exhibited extensively in Europe. There was a retrospective of Donaldson's highly coloured sixties' pictures, based on girlie magazines and pin-ups, at The Mayor Gallery in 1999, with an exhibition entitled Hollywood 1968 Remade, Paintings and other works, in 2004. Donaldson lived in London and southwest France. Tate Gallery and Arts Council hold his work.

David DONALDSON 1916–1996 Painter and teacher, born in Chryston, Lanarkshire. He was married to the artist Marysia Donaldson. He studied at Glasgow School of Art, 1932–7. In 1936 Donaldson won the Directors Prize and a year later the Haldane Travelling Scholarship, visiting Italy and France. After additional tuition at Glasgow School of Art he took up part-time teaching there, becoming a full-time teacher and eventually head of the department of drawing and painting. Was elected RSA and won its Guthrie Award. In 1977 he was appointed Painter and Limner to HM The Queen in Scotland. Although versatile, Donaldson became known as one of Scotland's leading portrait painters. He participated in many group shows in Britain and abroad. Had a one-man exhibition at Henry Hillier's Studio, Glasgow, in 1961, others including the French Institute, Glasgow, and Mall Galleries, 1980. Donaldson's work is held by HM The Queen, Scottish Arts Council and many Scottish galleries. Lived in Glasgow, but had a house in France.

John DONALDSON 1945– Landscape painter, born in Sussex, who received much of his early training from his grandfather, an English Impressionist artist. In 1975, he settled with his family in a rural valley near Dartmouth, Devon, and began to paint full time. From the late 1980s he shared his time between studios in Devon and the south of France, painting subjects drawn from rural and Mediterranean France and Italy. His watercolours were shown at the Simon Drew, John Gillo and Andras Kaldor Galleries in Dartmouth, his oil paintings at Omell Galleries and he participated in Artists in Dartmouth.

Kim DONALDSON 1952– Painter and sculptor, born in Rhodesia. He grew up on his grandfather's ranch, where he began to sketch while still at school. After experimenting in various styles and media, in 1972 he became a full-time artist, wildlife his subject. Donaldson developed an encyclopaedic knowledge of the flora and fauna of southern Africa and was noted for his subjects' anatomical accuracy, based on living rough close to them in the wilderness. Donaldson's work, which was included in several books on wildlife art and was reproduced in limited edition plates, had many solo showings. His exhibition Safari was held by The Halcyon Gallery, Birmingham, 1994. Donaldson latterly settled in Florida, America.

Marysia DONALDSON fl. from 1950s– Painter, sculptor and designer, born in Warsaw, Poland. She moved to Scotland at an early age, where she was educated. Studied at Glasgow School of Art under her husband-to-be, the painter David Donaldson, and afterwards with Hugh Adam Crawford. On leaving art school she took up sculpture and fashion design, later returning to painting, in which she was a rich Colourist. Showed at RSA, RA, Royal Glasgow Institute of the Fine Arts and Fosse Gallery, Stow-on-the-Wold, in mixed exhibitions. She had solo shows at Macauley Gallery, Stenton, in 1985; at Washington Gallery, Glasgow, 1986; and in 1987 at Ancrum Gallery, Roxborough. Her work is in collection of HRH The Duke of Edinburgh and in many private holdings throughout the world. Had a studio in London.

Rory DONALDSON 1965– Artist in mixed media, notable for photomontage work, born in Aberdeen, Scotland. Studied at Gray's School of Art, Aberdeen, and after graduating with honours studied at University of Ulster to gain master's degree, over period 1982–7. In 1986 gained Shell UK Prize, also Rank Xerox, Marlow, award. Group exhibitions included Time at Museum of Modern Art in Oxford, 1988; the Fruitmarket Open, at Fruitmarket Gallery, Edinburgh, 1990; and Gruzelier Modern Art, 1992. Solo exhibitions included Physical Manners at Project Gallery, Dublin, and Interference, Art Advice, Belfast, both 1989. In 1992–3 Donaldson was included in the Arts Council Gallery, Belfast, show Twelve Stars, the work State 13, of 1991, being acquired for European Parliament Collection.

Thea DONIACH 1907–1986 Artist in oil, watercolour and ink, she was born into an artistic family at Chevreuse, France, her father being the Polish Jewish painter Leopold Pilichowski. In 1932 she married the distinguished scholar of Judaic and Semitic languages, lexicographer, linguist and civil servant Nakdimon Doniach, who died in 1994. After education at the Lycée Français de Londres Doniach in the early 1950s studied art in London, first under Frederick Gore at St Martin's School of Art, then at Goldsmiths' College. She acted as a part-time tutor in Oxford, where she lived. Work is in the collections of RWA and City of Oxford Education Committee and the junior common rooms of Corpus Christi and University Colleges, Oxford.

Mary DONINGTON 1909– Sculptor and musician, born in London, who studied at Royal Academy of Music. She was mainly self-taught in art, but had a year under the sculptor Frank Dobson, 1945–6. Showed at RA, WIAC, NS and elsewhere. Lived for many years at Headley Down, Hampshire.

Godfried DONKOR 1964– Artist, curator and teacher, who graduated in fine art painting at Central St Martins College of Art, 1984–9; studied painting under a UNESCO grant in Barcelona, Spain, 1991–2; then gained his master's degree studying African art history at the School of Oriental and African Studies, 1994–5 (he had a solo show there, 1995). In 1995, he lectured on African art at the Royal Academy. Donkor worked as a curator at 198 Gallery, 1995–8, where he also exhibited. He gained a *Daily Mail* Best Newcomer Exhibition award at Olympia, 1991. Group shows included Thapong International Artist Exhibition, Botswana, 1994, and Transforming the Crown, American tour, 1997. Installations included The Seven Lives of Picasso, 1994, and Glamour, 1995, both Harvey Nichols. Smithsonian Institution, Washington, America; Paintings for Hospitals; University of Helsinki, Finland; and Unilever collections hold examples. Lived in London.

Leonard David DONNE 1926– Painter, printmaker and teacher, born in Leicester. He studied at the College of Art there under the portrait painter Donald Carrington, eventually becoming head of art at Cheshunt School. Donne, who signed his work D D, was a member of Free Painters and Sculptors, having a series of solo shows at Loggia Gallery from 1973. Others included Hitchin Museum, 1977. Lived for many years at Ware, Hertfordshire, latterly at Leintwardine, Herefordshire.

Frances DONNELLY 1970– Painter, born in Lurgan, Northern Ireland, who studied at Kingston University, 1988–9; University of Ulster, 1991–3 (which owns her work); and Royal College of Art, 1993–5. In 1992, she gained a placement at Bazalel Academy of Art and Design, Jerusalem, in 1994 a travel award to Asilah Studio, Morocco. After leaving the Royal College, Donnelly began establishing a name as an abstract painter, but by the time of her solo exhibition at Paton Gallery, 1997, her work was figurative, with a forceful style, a tendency to pattern making and elements of Symbolism. She was "interested in the collective memory of enchanted places". Group shows included Belfast Young Contemporaries, Oxford Street Gallery, Belfast, 1992, and Stratocruising at Raw Gallery, 1996.

Helen DONNELLY 1974– Painter for whom "the spatial atmospheric qualities in the shifting movements of light, colour and shape" were important in highly structured landscapes. She gained a design diploma from Scarborough Technical College, 1990–3, completing a foundation art and design course with merit, 1992–3, then graduated with honours in fine art from Loughborough College of Art & Design, 1995–8. Among various projects undertaken were workshop artist at Scarborough Art Gallery and completion of a mural of Scarborough Castle and bay for Edgehill Youth Club, Scarborough, both in 2000. In that year she had a residency at Pindar School, Eastfield. Exhibitions included Scarborough Art Gallery and Scarborough Library, both 2001; The Land, Oliver Contemporary, 2002 (where she shared an exhibition with Philip Turner in 2004); and Oriel Plas Glyn-y-Weddw, Pwllheli, 2003.

Micky DONNELLY 1952– Artist, teacher and writer in whose work enigmatic images and symbols were featured. Was born in Belfast, where he gained his bachelor's degree at University of Ulster in 1979, his master's two years later, then in 1985 won the Arts Council of Northern Ireland Scholarship at the British School at Rome. He wrote and lectured extensively on art, and was for a time on the editorial board of *Circa*. He was chosen for many key Irish art exhibitions which toured abroad, including On the Balcony of the Nation, America, 1990–2, and The Fifth Province, Canada, 1991–3. In 1994 he was included in the shows Works on Paper and Beyond the Partitions, put on by Queen Street Studios, Belfast, with which Donnelly was associated. Had numerous solo shows in Ireland and abroad, including Taylor Galleries, Dublin, 1988 and 1992, and Anderson O'Day, 1991. Ulster Museum in Belfast; Arts Councils of Great Britain, Northern Ireland and the Republic of Ireland; British Council; and the European Parliament hold his works.

Mike DONNELLY 1957– Prolific and popular wildlife and landscape painter who graduated in graphics and illustration from Liverpool College of Art in 1979, becoming a commercial illustrator. Donnelly's pictures combined the tight control and realism of the trained illustrator with the enthusiasm of a naturalist with a sure understanding of anatomy and form. He was a practising falconer and was well known for his depictions of birds of prey and hunting scenes. Exhibited solo and in mixed exhibitions in Britain and abroad, Mathaf Gallery showing his work. Donnelly's paintings were published as cards, prints and in books and magazines.

James DONOVAN 1974– Artist, born in Aberdare, Glamorgan, whose pictures could contain humour and fantasy. He attended the Mid Glamorgan Centre for Art and Design, 1992–4, and Swansea Institute of Higher Education, 1994–7, being artist-in-residence, Swansea College of Further Education, 1997–8. In 1998 Donovan won the Glynn Vivian/Sir Leslie Joseph Young Artist of the Year Award. Group shows included Attic Gallery, 35th Anniversary Show, Swansea, 1997; Highgate Fine Art, from 1998; and Ten Welsh Painters, University of Surrey at Guildford, 1999. Among his solo exhibitions were Martin Tinney Gallery, Cardiff, 2001, Procession, Newport Museum and Art Gallery, 2002, and in 2004 he shared an exhibition with Kathy Ramsay Carr at Hutson Gallery. Donovan said: "My work revolves around the history of my family and the legacy they have left for me.... The stories told to me by my father and grandfather, both of whom worked underground, have proved to be a rich source of information, with historical, mythical and actual characters interacting to form a collection of images which investigate the ethos of the past, present and future Welsh mining community." CASW, Glynn Vivian Art Gallery in Swansea and other Welsh public collections hold examples.

Arthur DOOLEY 1929–1994 Self-taught sculptor in metal who scorned art schools, born and worked in Liverpool. Big Arthur, as he was known, was a Liverpudlian character who applied to be town planner because he was against a tower block city, helped reform the Liverpool Academy, being its chairman, and campaigned to revive the South Docks. After leaving school at 14 Dooley served on Mersey tugboats and was also to work on the *Ark Royal* in Cammell Laird's shipyard, important to his development as a sculptor. He joined the Irish Guards playing as a bagpiper; went absent without leave and served as a colonel with the Palestine Liberation Organization; and was jailed for his absence, in prison experimenting with sculpture. Back in London he joined a drawing class at Whitechapel Art Gallery, worked as a janitor and part-time model at St Martin's School of Art and eventually returned to Liverpool where a time working for Dunlop's at Speke helped him refine his sculptural technique. An important breakthrough was getting a commission to work on the Stations of the Cross for St Mary's Church at Leyland, near Preston. Other work included The Risen Christ for Our Lady of the Wayside in Solihull and the statue of St Mary in the Mariners' Chapel of the Quay in the Liverpool parish church of St Nicholas. Dooley, a Communist and a Catholic, spurned London art galleries, although his shows included the dungeons of Windsor Castle in 1990. Latterly his son Paul, a trained stonemason, helped him. Walker Art Gallery, Liverpool, holds The Soldier.

DORAB: *see* **Dorab Dadiba CONTRACTOR**

Barbara DORF 1933– Artist in oil, watercolour and charcoal pencil, and art history teacher, born and lived in London. Dorf favoured architectural subjects in a distinctive style characterised by delicate tonal watercolour washes against clear, simple forms. She attended Central School of Arts and Crafts, teachers including Keith Vaughan, and Slade School of Fine Art, leaving in 1962, under Tom Monnington, E H Gombrich and Francis Haskell. Dorf's teaching appointments included Ruskin School of Drawing, Oxford, and Brookes University there. Among her mixed shows were RA Summer Exhibition and NEAC. Solo shows included Michael Parkin Gallery from 1978, Montpelier Sandelson, 1981, and Maas Gallery from 1986. In 1993 she was in a three-artist exhibition at Jerram Gallery, Salisbury. British Museum; Lady Margaret Hall and St Edmund Hall, Oxford; Sir Ernst Gombrich; the actress Dame Judi Dench; and actor Alec McCowen held examples.

Simon DORRELL 1961– Painter and illustrator, born in Worcestershire. After an arts foundation course in Hereford, in 1984 Dorrell gained an honours degree from Maidstone College of Art. Then moved to Camberley, Surrey, to pursue career as a freelance illustrator. After a period in Herefordshire from the mid-1980s, where he returned to an earlier interest in landscape painting, in 1989 set up a studio in Elan Valley, mid-Wales, where he restored and developed an Edwardian garden as well as painting. Showed widely, including Five Dials Gallery, 1984; Silk Top Hat Gallery, Ludlow, 1988; Upton Lodge Galleries, Tetbury, 1991; and Sue Rankin Gallery, 1992, where he also in same year shared a show.

Bartolomeu Dos SANTOS 1931– Printmaker and teacher, born in Lisbon, Portugal. He studied at Escola Superior de Belas Artes in 1950–6, then studied at Slade School of Fine Art until 1958. Returned to Portugal while retaining connections with London. After Anthony Gross's retirement, in 1961 took over as professor of printmaking at Slade. Showed in Britain, Portugal and elsewhere, his prints sometimes incorporating photographic imagery. Retrospective was held at Centro de Arte Moderna of the Gulbenkian Foundation in Lisbon in 1989; in 1990–1 was included in British Museum show Avant-Garde British Printmaking 1914–1960; and in 1996 his exhibition Reminiscences on Fernando Pessoa was held at Strang Print Room, University College, following his retirement from the Slade. In 2002, the Strang Print Room had a show entitled Printmaking at the Slade 1960–94: The Gift of Bartolomeu dos Santos. There were also one-man exhibitions at London Institute Gallery, 2001, and Slade Gallery, 2003. Lived in London.

Robert DOSWELL 1960– Artist who attended the Slade School of Fine Art, 1979–85, winning the Sir William Coldstream Prize, 1980, and the Maria Reischitz Award, 1982. He took part in The Icon Show, Mario Flecha Gallery, 1987; Group Shows, Hampstead Theatre and Diorama, both 1988; and East End Open Studios, at Carpenter's Road, 1989.

John DOUBLEDAY 1947– Sculptor, born in Maldon, Essex, where he continued to live. Doubleday studied in Paris and at Goldsmiths' College School of Art, 1965–8. Had a solo show at Waterhouse Gallery, 1968, followed by several dozen others, latterly Beecroft Art Gallery, Southend-on-Sea, 1985; Boundary Gallery, 1989; and Oriel Gallery, 1990. Among his many public works were Dr Michael Ramsay, Archbishop of Canterbury, Lambeth Palace, 1974; Earl Mountbatten of Burma, Broadlands, 1976; Charlie Chaplin, Leicester Square, 1981; The Beatles, Liverpool, 1984; and The Cricketer, County Square, Chelmsford, 1992. Doubleday's sculpture of the fictional detective Sherlock Holmes was erected outside Baker Street tube station in 1999. Ashmolean Museum in Oxford, Tate Gallery, Victoria & Albert Museum and National Museum of Wales, Cardiff, hold his work. Lived in Great Totham, Maldon, Essex.

Eric John DOUDNEY 1905–1986 Industrial designer, sculptor in many materials and teacher, born in Watford, Hertfordshire, as Henry Eric John Doudney; he signed work E J D. After Acton and Chiswick Polytechnic Doudney studied at Richmond School of Art, then Royal Academy Schools sculpture department and Kennington School of Art, his teachers including Charles Wheeler, William McMillan and E S Frith. Taught before World War II at Twickenham Technical College, then designed for Hawker Aircraft and Halex Ltd before joining the staff of the University of Canterbury in Christchurch, New Zealand, in 1950. Showed in England at RA, RBA and elsewhere, his work being sited on various public buildings in London and the north of England. Was elected a fellow of the RBS, his Slate Carving, in the manner of Eric Gill, being illustrated in the book *R B S: Modern British Sculpture*, published in 1939.

John DOUGILL 1934– Painter, artist in variety of graphic and photographic media, and teacher, born in Liverpool. He attended West Sussex College of Art, 1950–5, then Royal College of Art, 1957–60, becoming a tutor at Royal College in 1977. In the early 1970s Dougill, a committed teacher, gravitated to the organisation of students in photographic, film and poster work, becoming interested in community and environmental affairs. Participated in RA exhibition Thirty London Painters in 1985; was included in

Royal College of Art's show Exhibition Road in 1988; and was Artist of the Day at Flowers East, 1999, chosen by Norman Ackroyd. Later solo shows included Winchester Gallery, 1998, and studio 1.1 in 2004. Lived in London.

Anna DOUGLAS 1963– Photographer and curator, born in Leeds, Yorkshire. With Janet Hodgson she contributed The Text Garden: A Composition in Time to artranspennine98, in 1998, for a location in Liverpool, where she lived. Douglas worked extensively as a curator and contributed to many publications. Her photographs were included in shows at Leeds City Art Gallery, Impressions Gallery in York and Mappin, Gallery, Sheffield. *Artists' stories*, edited by Anna Douglas and Nicholas Wegner, appeared in 1996.

Anne DOUGLAS 1948– Sculptor, draughtsman and teacher. After studying anthropology at Durham University Douglas studied sculpture at Camberwell School of Arts and Crafts. She was Rome Scholar in Sculpture, 1976–8, and artist-in-residence at the British School in 1984. In 1987 she gained a travel grant to New York. Douglas' teaching venues included Slade School of Fine Art and Royal College of Art. She took part in many group shows including British School, 1977–8; Newcastle Polytechnic Gallery, 1978–9; Artsite Gallery, Bath, 1986; and the Newcastle Group's 1990 show The Northern Lights at DLI Museum & Arts Centre, Durham, and tour. Her later solo shows included Bondgate Gallery, Northumberland, 1986, and St Martin's Gallery, 1989. Arts Council holds examples. Douglas said that she was "concerned with constructing a plastic equivalent for experience," not just imitating reality. Lived in Gateshead, Tyne and Wear.

Brian DOUGLAS 1948– Painter who studied at York School of Art, 1963–7, Manchester College of Art, 1967–70, and the Royal Academy Schools, 1970–3. Participated in the NEAC Open at Mall Galleries from 1971 and RA Summer Exhibition from 1972. Private collectors including Sir Brinsley Ford owned his work.

David DOUGLAS 1965– Artist in various media, born in Daventry, Northamptonshire. He studied art at foundation school, Nene College, Northampton, 1981–3, and Maidstone College of Art, 1983–5. Showed at RA and elsewhere. Paintings in Hospitals bought his work. Lived in Weedon, Northamptonshire.

Emma Cathleen DOUGLAS fl. from 1970s– Printmaker who did a foundation course at Central School, 1975–6, graduating in fine art from Middlesex Polytechnic, 1976–9. Was affiliated to the École des Arts Decoratifs, Paris, 1979–80, gaining a master's degree in printmaking at Royal College of Art, 1980–3. Shows included Stowells Trophy at RA from 1979; Hayward Annual, 1982; Battersea Arts Centre, 1985; Angela Flowers Gallery, 1986; and Royal Over-Seas League, 1988. She was Lowick House artist-in-residence, 1984, and a junior fellow in the Royal College of Art's department of printmaking, 1988. Lived in London.

Jane DOUGLAS 1918– Painter, stage designer and teacher. She studied at the Slade School of Fine Art, at St Martin's School of Art and at Goldsmiths' College School of Art. Showed RA, LG, SWA and in the provinces. Lived in London.

Liz DOUGLAS 1945– Painter, born in Forfar, who studied at Edinburgh College of Art, 1975–7, and 1989–91, gaining an honours degree in drawing and painting; did postgraduate studies, 1991–2; then her Master of Fine Art Painting degree, 1992–3. In 1991 she won the Angus Award for Landscape and was commended in the Borders Biennial and in 1993 gained the John Florent Stone Scholarship. Was granted an Ettrick & Lauderdale Museum Service commission, Written on the Rock, 1995, and was elected professional member of SSA, 1997. Showed with Flying Colours Gallery from 1989. Standard Life, The National Trust for Scotland, Paintings in Hospitals Scotland and East and Midlothian Art Fund hold examples.

Marguerite France DOUGLAS 1918– Painter and printmaker and farmer, born in Derbyshire of Swiss parents. She sometimes signed work M F Dommen, her unmarried name, also M F D. Studied with Ernest Townsend in Derby, followed by a year in 1935 at Lausanne École des Beaux-Arts, then painting, 1936–9, at Royal Academy Schools with Walter Westley Russell, Tom Monnington and Ernest Jackson. Between 1939–45 Douglas was in the Women's Land Army, mostly as a timber measurer in the New Forest which inspired an interest in trees. Showed landscape and portraits with SSA and with SWA. In 1959 Douglas became a corresponding member of the International Institute of Arts and Letters and in 1968 showed in Ancona, being awarded a Diploma of Merit. William Johnstone much influenced her work in the 1970s. Lived in Earlston, Berwickshire.

Phoebe Sholto DOUGLAS 1906– Portrait miniaturist, painter, enameller and teacher, born in London. She studied at Eastbourne College of Art under Arthur Reeve-Fowkes and Oliver Senior. Was a member of RMS from 1972, exhibiting at RI, RA and in the Kent area, where she lived at Goudhurst, teaching art at Bethany School. Sunderland Museum & Art Gallery holds her portrait of the artist Lawson Wood.

Sholto Johnstone DOUGLAS 1871–1958 Painter and draughtsman, notably of portraits, eldest son of a Scottish laird, Arthur Henry Johnstone Douglas, of Lockerbie, Dumfriesshire. This large, talented family had wide sporting and artistic interests and Sholto was encouraged to study painting in Dresden, Germany. There he contracted pleurisy and recovered by sailing around the world in the three-masted schooner *Macquarie*. Returned to Paris, Douglas attended Académie Julian, teachers including William Bouguereau; moved to Antwerp, taught by Jean Guillaume Rosier; then joined the Slade School of Fine Art for tuition during 1895 under Henry Tonks, Fred Brown and Philip Wilson Steer, who was a particular influence. Prior to World War I Douglas acquired a strong reputation as a portrait painter, his eight auburn-haired sisters and the Scottish gentry and aristocracy proving ready models. He exhibited at NEAC, RP and RA, from 1905–20, where his huge figure studies in the manner of John Singer Sargent received much attention, and with Scott and Fowles, New York, in America. Had a successful solo show at the Alpine Club Gallery, 1907. During World War I he joined the Royal Naval Reserve and, as an Official War Artist, painted the fleet for the Imperial War Museum. SS *Cedric*, White Star Liner, lying in the Mersey, is a fine and atmospheric example of Douglas's work there. After resuming portrait painting in London, in 1926 he settled at

Vallescure, near St Raphael on the French Riviera, where he turned to landscapes. Douglas had to vacate a studio full of pictures on the outbreak of World War II, escaping on a coal boat and American troop carrier. After living in London during the Blitz and several moves around Scotland and England, he settled in Beccles, Suffolk. A stroke hampered his sight, resulting in a series of blurred, Monet-like canvases. Latterly, Katharine House Gallery, Marlborough, sold Douglas's work.

Sokari DOUGLAS CAMP 1958– Sculptor in welded steel, often of everyday people and events, born in Nigeria, sometimes refered to as Sokari Camp. She graduated from Central School of Art and Design, 1983, gaining her master's degree at Royal College of Art, 1986. Among awards was the Saatchi and Saatchi Award in 1982 and the Prince of Wales Scholarship and Henry Moore Bursary, both in 1983. Took part in many group shows from New Contemporaries, 1983; From Two Worlds, Whitechapel Art Gallery and tour, 1986–7; and Africa Explores, at New Museum for Contemporary Art, New York, and tour, 1991–3. Had solo show at Bluecoat Gallery, with tour, 1988, later ones including Redfern Gallery, 1993, Morley Gallery, 2000, and The Lowry, Salford, 2002. In that year, Douglas Camp's sculpture Man on Man was unveiled at the forecourt of The Commonwealth Institute following an award from the Jerwood Art Commissions Scheme. Then, her work was said to "refer largely to the masquerade tradition of the Kalabari, challenging a Eurocentric understanding of African culture by bringing performance, West Africa's highest form of art, to a Western tradition of sculpture." Arts Council holds her work. Lived in London.

Pat DOUTHWAITE 1939–2002 Painter and printer, born in Glasgow. As a small girl she studied movement and mime with Margaret Morris, wife of the painter J D Fergusson; he encouraged her to paint, but otherwise she was self-taught. In 1958 she lived in Suffolk with a group of artists, including Robert Colquhoun, Robert MacBryde and William Crozier. In 1960, Douthwaite married the artist and illustrator Paul Hogarth and with him lived at Deya, Majorca, where she entered the circle of the writer Robert Graves. The marriage was competitive and stormy and was eventually dissolved. From 1959 for some years she travelled worldwide, then settling to work in Britain. Had first solo show at 57 Gallery, Edinburgh, 1958. Participated in many group shows in Britain and abroad and had regular one-man exhibitions, including a retrospective at Third Eye Centre, Glasgow, in 1988–9, and tour; and exhibitions at the William Jackson Gallery and The Scottish Gallery, which held a memorial show in 2005 with an extensive catalogue. Douthwaite's pictures, often tinged with sadness or anguish, pursued a variety of themes, such as the Manson Trial, American Women Bandits and Amy Johnson, Aviator. Aberdeen Art Gallery, Ferens Art Gallery in Hull and Scottish Arts Council hold her work. Died in Dundee, Tayside, where Douthwaite had moved latterly to hone her skills in a printmaking workshop.

Margaret DOVASTON 1884–1954 Painter of costume pieces, such as Searching the Deed, included in Gladwell & Company's 2005 Autumn Exhibition. Dovaston was born in Wandsworth, lived in Ealing and attended at the School of Art there, South Kensington under Charles West Cope and John Watson Nicol and then for five years the Royal Academy Schools. She studied there under various teachers, winning a British Institution Scholarship and several Silver Medals. Dovaston was elected RBA in 1910, also exhibiting at the RA Summer Exhibition and Walker's Galleries. Her highly detailed pictures endeavour to represent life in bygone, especially eighteenth-century, England. Although Dovaston depicts imaginary scenes she said that "They tell a story in which the spectator is invited to fill in the details at will". Their historical authenticity was supported by her collection of costumes, furniture and antiques. Her death was recorded in Lambeth.

Stephen DOVE 1949– Prolific artist and teacher, born in Leicester, a notable Colourist as a painter. Dove said that his paintings "lie in that area that exists between abstraction and figuration ... The human form and the landscape are frequent sources that are referred to directly or else merely hinted at." He gained his art and design diploma, attending Lanchester Polytechnic in Coventry and Hull College of Art, obtaining his art teacher's diploma at Birmingham Polytechnic. In 1976 Dove moved to Zennor, Cornwall, from 1980 settling in St Ives. He gained South West Arts Minor Awards, 1980 and 1981. Taught part-time at Falmouth School of Art, Falmouth School and Richard Lander School in Truro. Dove was a member of the Penwith Society and Porthmeor Printmakers, both in St Ives, and Newlyn Society of Artists. He had many mixed exhibition appearances, including Cannon Hill Arts Centre, Birmingham, 1974; Salthouse Gallery, St Ives, from 1980; New Street Gallery, Plymouth, 1987; Demarco's Choice, Newlyn Gallery, 1993; and Eight Painters, Rainyday Gallery, Penzance, 1994. Had a solo show at Plymouth Arts Centre, 1980; at Salthouse, from 1981; and Beaux Arts, Bath, 1984. St Thomas' Hospital, Royal Cornwall Museum in Truro and Cornwall School Collection hold examples.

Peter DOVER 1954– Painter, relief printmaker and teacher, born in Merseyside, who gained a first-class honours degree at Leeds Polytechnic, 1981–4, and his master's in fine art, with Alistair Grant, at Royal College of Art, 1986–8. Won many awards, including *Galleries Magazine* award (Open to Print), 1988; London Contemporary Arts and Friends of Bradford Art Galleries awards, 11th British International Print Biennale, 1990; *Printmaking Today* award, Federation of British Artists Print Exhibition, 1994; and Stinger Purchase Prize and Estonia National Art Museum Purchase Prize, Tallinn International Print Triennale, 1995. Held many residencies and lectureships, later visiting posts including Leeds Metropolitan University and Kent Institute of Art and Design. Among Dover's commissions was a silkscreen mural project for Great Ormond Street Hospital, 1990–1. He was made an associate of RE in 1995 and took part in many group exhibitions, including Marlborough Graphics, 1991; British Art Fair, Royal College of Art, 1993; Salon des Graphiques at Curwen Gallery, 1995; and Bracknell Gallery, South Hill Park, 1996. Showed solo with New Academy Gallery from 1991. Tate Gallery, Ashmolean Museum in Oxford, Estonia National Art Museum and public galleries in Dudley and Plymouth hold examples. Lived in London.

Alexander Warren DOW 1873–1948 Painter, printmaker and writer, born in London. Studied at Cambridge University in the 1890s, then studied art with Norman Garstin in Penzance, with Frank Brangwyn in London, at Heatherley's School of Fine Art and in Paris. Exhibited RBA extensively, also at RI, ROI, Walker Art Gallery, Liverpool and Paris Salon. Wrote on painting for such publications as *John O'London's Weekly, Daily News, The Tablet* and *Colour*, to whose staff he was attached. Lived in London.

Harold James DOW 1902–1967 Sculptor, born in north London, educated on a London County Council (LCC) Scholarship at Walter St John's School. After taking instruction from Ferdinand Victor Blundstone and working for three years as Paul Mountford's assistant, Dow won an LCC Scholarship to the Royal College of Art, studying for a term at the Central School of Arts and Crafts. Dow was elected an associate of the RBS in 1951, a fellow in 1961. In 1960, his 1958 stone and fondu cement Bergamasque was included in the LCC Sculpture in the Open Air show at Battersea Park. By then, Dow's stone Owl, of about 1920, was in the Leeds City Art Gallery, other public works being at Bassingbourn Village College, his Juggler at a Camberwell housing estate, a bronze memorial fountain was in Nairobi, Kenya, and there were carved stone panels on the corner of Half Moon Street and Piccadilly as well as sculptures in private collections. Dow showed at the RA Summer Exhibition and at the RMS.

James H DOWD 1884–1956 Painter, draughtsman and printmaker who spent part of his early life in Sheffield but later settled in London. He contributed to publications including *Punch* and produced a popular book, *Important People*. Exhibited RA, RP, Cooling Galleries and elsewhere in London.

Natalie DOWER 1931– Painter and sculptor in various media, born in London, where she eventually settled to work part of the year, also in Portugal. She was also a teacher, including St Albans, Camberwell and Byam Shaw Schools of Art; Bath Academy of Art in Corsham; and at the American School of Tangier, Morocco, where she lived from 1966, moving to Portugal in 1973, returning to Britain in 1982. Dower said that her style moved from that of the Euston Road School to Constructivism. She attended St Martin's School of Art, 1948–9; Camberwell School of Art, 1949–52; and Slade School of Fine Art, 1952–4. Group shows included Fox Fine Art, 1977; Hayward Annual, 1982; Systematic Constructive Drawings at Wentworth Gallery, University of York, 1986; Chicago International Art Exposition from 1988; and First International Female Artists' Art Biennial, Stockholm, 1995. Among later group exhibitions were Mondiale Echos, Mondriaanhuis, Amsterdam, Netherlands, 2000, and Camberwell's Evolution & Revolution, Candid Arts Trust, 2005. Had a solo show at Polytechnic of Central London, 1979, later ones including Out of the Arc, Curwen Gallery, 1995, Mathematics – The Visual Arts, Rowley House, Oxford, 1996, and Within Measure, at Francis Graham-Dixon Gallery, 1997. Arts Council, Government Art Collection and Arthur Andersen & Company hold her works.

Sean DOWER 1965– Artist educated at Camberwell School of Art and Rijksakademie van Beeldende Kunsten, Amsterdam, Netherlands. He was included in prominent group exhibitions: Lost Property, W139, Amsterdam, and Great Western Studios, 1995; and Against, Anthony d'Offay Gallery, Pandemonium at ICA and Rational Behaviour, The Tannery, all 1996. In 1997, Dower completed his first major commission for a public gallery, No Room in Hell (Absent Qualia), for Matt's Gallery, a three-dimensional video installation mixing the visual conventions of low-budget 1970s horror films with contemporary street culture and the mythology of the undead found in voodoo.

Ann DOWKER fl. from 1970s– Painter, draughtsman, printmaker and teacher, born in Sheffield, Yorkshire. After studying at Bath Academy of Art, Corsham, she taught in East End of London, attending evening classes in life drawing at St Martin's School of Art. In 1978 she began etching one day a week at Camden Institute, in 1981 taking part-time course in lithography at Central School of Art. She taught part-time at adult education classes and at Byam Shaw School of Art. Dowker was a prolific artist, interested in the human figure, who viewed her work "as a form of research, a process of discovery, invention and constant optimism". Showed in group exhibitions at House Gallery, 1981, and Moira Kelly Gallery, 1982, and was included in the Norwich School of Art Gallery 1986–7 touring show A Reputation Amongst Artists. Had a solo exhibition at Christchurch Mansion, Ipswich, 1994, another at Theo Waddington Fine Art, 2000–1. Government Art Collection holds her work.

Daniel DOWLING 1954– Painter, born and lived in Belfast, Northern Ireland, where his works were based on ordinary people's lives, observed with wit and humanity. On leaving school Dowling became a banker, but reserved time to study, paint and exhibit. In 1997 he left the bank to paint full time. The National Self-Portrait Collection of Ireland, University of Limerick, holds his work.

Jane DOWLING 1925– Painter and teacher, born in London, who was married to the artist Peter Greenham. She took a degree at Oxford University, 1943–6. Studied at Slade School of Fine Art and Ruskin School of Drawing, Oxford, Byam Shaw School of Art and Central School of Art, concluding her studies in the early 1960s. She went on to teach at Byam Shaw, Maidstone College of Art and Royal Academy Schools. Showed at RA from 1961. She had a series of solo shows at New Grafton Gallery from 1974. Had a joint Arts Council and Norwich School of Art touring show in 1984–5 with her husband. Her work was bought by Farringdon Trust, more being in John Radcliffe Hospital, Oxford. Had a 20-year retrospective at Mompesson House, Salisbury, 1992, with a solo show at Chappel Galleries, Chappel, in 2002. Dowling was elected a member of Art Workers' Guild in 1980, Hon. RBA, 1997, and a member of the Society of Tempera Painters, 1999. Carried out commissions, including the Edwin Abbey Mural Fund at Oxford Oratory Church, houses and gardens for The National Trust and other owners and portraits. HRH The Prince of Wales, the Ashmolean Museum in Oxford and Southampton City Art Gallery owned examples. Lived at Otmoor, Oxfordshire.

Mańka DOWLING 1937– Painter, designer, printmaker, muralist and teacher for whom "theatre has been my great passion since childhood". She was born Maria Skibińska, graduating with a master's honours degree under that name from the Academy of Fine Arts, Warsaw, Poland, supporting herself by creating textiles for Wzor

Arts and Crafts Co-operative. After working for the Foreign Trade Fairs & Exhibitions Company in Warsaw, 1967–70, she moved to England, entered advertising as a graphic designer, and had first solo exhibition of "post-Fauvist erotic paintings" at Woodstock Gallery, 1972. After a 1973 visit to Greece, she began creating three-dimensional pictures, "unanimously rejected by gallery owners until 1980," when they were well received at a New Talent Store solo show. In 1979, Dowling had joined the graphic arts studio at Hounslow College of Art, making many silk-screens and etchings with theatrical themes. In 1984 she developed an interest in holograms, exhibiting at Boulevard Jardin Exotic Gallery, Monte Carlo. Travels in the 1980s in Europe and to the Museum of Modern Art and Guggenheim Museum, New York, influenced Dowling's work. From 1983 she ran courses, including Spring Grove Adult Education Centre; Middlesex Hospital, where she created murals; and Watermans Art Centre, Brentford. Other murals included Bertolucci's Restaurant, Covent Garden, 1984, and the Ministry of Agriculture, Fisheries & Food centenary, Tolworth, 1989. Took part in many mixed shows, later solo exhibitions included Watermans, 1994; and Elia Hushka Gallery, 1995; and The Grove Gallery, 65 The Grove, Ealing, in 2005. Lived in Isleworth, Middlesex.

Jan DOWMAN 1942– Sculptor who studied at the University of New Brunswick in Canada, 1975–6, gaining an honours degree at Hertfordshire College of Art and Design, 1979–86. Group shows included LG, Camden Arts Centre and tour, 1982; Six Sculptors, Great Linford Arts Centre, Milton Keynes, 1983; In the Making, Hertfordshire Open Exhibition, Watford Museum, 1986–7; Exhibition One, University of London Institute of Education, 1987; and East End Open Studios, at Chisenhale Studios, 1989.

Avril DOWN 1900– Painter and teacher, born in Penang Island, Malaya. Educated in England, she attended Slade School of Fine Art, where her teachers included Henry Tonks and Walter Russell. She went on to teach in the Bishop's Stortford area, where she belonged to the local Art Society, living at Elsenham, Hertfordshire. She showed with UA, RI, in the Bishop's Stortford and Sutton Coldfield areas and in India. Completed a number of murals in public buildings in England and India. Sometimes signed work with initials only.

Vera DOWN 1888– Painter and printmaker, born in London. She studied at Walter Donne's Grosvenor Life School, the Central School of Arts and Crafts and in Paris. Taught for a time. Showed at RA, Walker's Galleries, Ridley Art Club, SWA and elsewhere. Lived in Woldingham, Surrey.

Caroline Antoinette DOWNEY 1958– Artist, born in Harmondsworth, Middlesex, who was "mostly self-taught." A wide-ranging certificate in fine art course at Herefordshire College of Art & Design, 1993–5, "introduced me to new ideas and the opportunity to practise new skills." Downey had moved to the Golden Valley, Herefordshire, in 1974 and from 1980–95 ran her own business and, using scraperboard artwork, produced prints, stationery and calendars, mostly of local scenes. She eventually settled at Cwmyoy, Llanthony Valley, Monmouthshire, where she sold her work from the Downey Barn Gallery, a member, with Christine Hunt, of Galleries in the Black Mountains. In 1997 Downey developed the sculptured board painting, when her blacksmith husband Peter gave her a panel that he had grooved and scuffed using carpentry tools. Downey showed at the Hay-on-Wye literature festival from 1999 and from 2001 at both the Abergavenny Food Festival and Soil Association Exhibition, Harrogate. In 2002 she was winner of the Daler-Rowney Worldwide Golden Jubilee Painting & Story Competition with her sculptured board picture Millennium at the Crooked Church of Cwmyoy. Signed her work Caroline Goodman until 1995, then as Caroline Downey or with initials CAD.

Kate DOWNIE 1958– Artist employing a variety of media, including film and performance, who was born in America. Studied at Gray's School of Art in Aberdeen, 1975–80. Downie made a number of residencies, including Scottish Arts Council residency in Amsterdam and at Total's North Alwyn oilfield in the North Sea. Solo shows included Amsterdam and Denmark and one at Collins Gallery, Glasgow, in 1990 after a year's residency in Paris. She showed frenetic images evoking the speed and bustle of the city. Downie's work was in Through Women's Eyes, at City Art Centre, Edinburgh, 1992–3. Is represented in collections throughout Europe and America.

Linda DOWNIE 1964– Artist born in Dunfermline, Fife, who gained a fine art honours degree at Duncan of Jordanstone College of Art, Dundee, 1982–6, with post-graduate studies at Nova Scotia College of Art, Halifax, Canada, 1984; then attended Royal College of Art, 1987–9, for her master's in fine art, with an exchange scholarship in Vienna, 1988. Among awards were an Elizabeth Greenshields Memorial Award, 1987, and a London Institute Purchase Award, 1996. Participated in group exhibitions in Britain and Switzerland, solo shows including Category & Allegory, Lamont Gallery, 1998, where fantastic images mingled human, animal, bird and vegetable elements and drew on ancient myth. Publications included *Le Bain* and *The Bad Book Suit*.

Nigel DOWNING 1964– Painter, draughtsman and teacher, born Middlesbrough, Yorkshire. He did a foundation course at Cleveland College of Art and Design, 1984–5, an honours degree in fine art at Canterbury College of Art, 1985–8, and his master's degree in fine art (painting) at University of Newcastle, 1988–90. In 1988 won a Chatham College of Further Education mural award. Held a residency at Sir William Turner 6th Form College, Redcar, in 1991, the year he was also artist-in-residence at Pilkington Glass International Ladies' Tennis Championships at Eastbourne. Downing taught part-time at University of Newcastle. In 1990 he had a solo show at Picture Gallery, Newcastle, the year after at Cleveland College of Art. In 1992 Downing was artist-in-residence at Towner Art Gallery, Eastbourne, which gave him a one-man show of his Pilkington tennis pictures. These showed Downing's fluid use of paint, bright palette and studies of figures in action to good effect.

Peter DOWNING fl. from 1950s– Artist and teacher who lived near the edge of Morecambe Bay, Lancashire. His work celebrated its peculiar qualities and light as well as being, in his words, "landscapes of an interior space that mirrors and reflects the external flow and change". Downing studied at Leeds and Royal Colleges of Art. Was a teacher of fine art, 1954–84, when he took early retirement from his post of principal lecturer at Preston (later Lancashire) Polytechnic. Then painted full-time. From 1952 Downing's work was seen throughout the country in many solo and mixed exhibitions. These included an Arts Council tour, Bradford Print Biennale, the International Drawing Biennale in Cleveland and Lancashire South of the Sands, which toured from the County and Regimental Museum, Preston, 1988.

Edgar DOWNS 1876–1963 Painter, especially of animals, born at Claughton, Birkenhead, Cheshire. After education in Birkenhead he studied at Munich Academy of Arts, winning a silver medal. Exhibited extensively at ROI, also at RCamA, RA and Walker Art Gallery, Liverpool. Latterly lived at Mudeford, Hampshire.

John DOWNTON 1906–1991 Painter and draughtsman, born in Erith, Kent. He read art history at Cambridge, 1925, gaining a first-class honours degree. Then entered Slade School of Fine Art, 1928, under Henry Tonks and Philip Wilson Steer. A private income enabled Downton to travel widely in Western Europe in the period before World War II. What he saw in museums, his reading and understanding of the Italian Quattrocento encouraged him to develop a style of portraiture, mainly in tempera, of meticulous heightened realism. The artist was a keen Morrisian Socialist and pacifist and a conscientious objector. His pictures were shown to acclaim at RA Summer Exhibitions in late 1930s and his portrait of Joan Harris was included in Prominent Living Artists at Russell-Cotes Art Gallery, Bournemouth, in 1937. Otherwise his work remained unseen until a retrospective at Fine Art Society in 1993; followed by a major tour from Graves Art Gallery, Sheffield, during 1996. Downton lived variously in Cambridge, London and Florence, settling finally at the family home near Sevenoaks, Kent.

Katharine DOWSON 1962– Sculptor, born in London, daughter of the president of the RA, Sir Philip Dowson. She studied at Heatherley School of Art, 1984–5; gained her degree at Camberwell School of Arts and Crafts, 1985–8; then studied for her master's degree in sculpture at Royal College of Art, 1989–92. Among awards were the Princess of Wales Scholarship, 1989–92, and 1st Prize for Egg Loo at Royal College, 1991, the year she won a Granada Foundation Prize. Took part in many group shows, including On Site, Tower Bridge Piazza, 1991; BT New Contemporaries tour, 1992–3; Art in Boxes, England & Co, 1993; and Growth, Norfolk & Norwich Hospital, Norwich, 1994. Had a solo show at 181 Gallery, 1993, in 1995 Mayor Gallery staging her exhibition Growth, in which such topics as "the physical interiors of man and nature" and "human mortality in relation to the universal" were explored. The Saatchi Collection held her work. Lived in London and Norfolk.

James DOXFORD 1899–1978 Painter and teacher, born in North Shields, Northumberland. After education locally he studied at department of fine art, Durham University, under E M O'Rorke Dickey and Richard Hatton, 1922–6. He was principal of Bridgwater Art and Technical School, 1932–8, its equivalent at Barnstaple, 1938–44, then for many years from 1945 was head of the art department at Gateshead Grammar School. Showed with RWA, of which he was a member, RA and elsewhere in the provinces. RWA, Laing Art Gallery in Newcastle and Shipley Art Gallery, Gateshead, hold his work. Lived in Gateshead for many years, latterly in Canterbury, Kent.

Rem DOXFORD: *see* **Anthony HILL**

John DOYLE 1928– Artist in watercolour, pastel and oil, born in London. He grew up near Chevening and, touring Kent in his grandfather's open-topped Buick, learned his love of landscape. After starting an iron foundry Doyle put in a manager, enabling him to attend evening classes under Gerry de Rose and Paul Wyeth in the early 1960s at Maidstone School of Art. Doyle believed that painting could not be taught formally, one could learn most "just from being with other painters and observing." John Ward was "a good friend who has given much help and advice." Mixed shows included RA Summer Exhibition. Had a series of solo shows at Spink and Sons from 1981. Exhibitions at Canterbury Cathedral led to a commission for a painting of it from the Archibishop of Canterbury, later Lord Coggan, to present to Pope Paul VI when Coggan visited the Vatican. In 1989 Doyle's book *An Artist's Journey down the Thames* appeared, the pictures being exhibited at Catto Gallery. Doyle won a runner-up prize in the Singer & Friedlander/*Sunday Times* Watercolour Competition, 1994. In 1993, Doyle had been asked by the Dean of Canterbury to mount an exhibition to celebrate the fourteenth centenary of its foundation by St Augustine in 597; Doyle suggested walking from Canterbury to Rome, painting as he went, resulting in 300 pictures; a selection was shown at Spink, then all were exhibited at the Chapter House, Canterbury, in 1997. Later solo shows included Sanders of Oxford, 1999, and Chris Beetles Ltd, 2002. Doyle was president of the RWS, 1997–00. Lived in Warehorne, Ashford, Kent.

Cecil Rochfort D'OYLY-JOHN 1906–1993 Painter, brought up in Durban, South Africa, who claimed relationship to the artist Augustus John. D'Oyly-John (sometimes unhyphenated) became a widely recognised painter for several decades after World War II with his idealised sun-drenched views of a never-never south of France and the Mediterranean, a few reproduced as prints, often high in the Printsellers' Association's popularity poll. He eventually settled in Rottingdean and was known as the Van Gogh of Sussex after a colourful past which included working on a Japanese tramp steamer, life-saving in Colombo and pearl-fishing in Manila and "a bit of hush-hush gun-running". He also served for eight years with the police in Tanganyika, rising to district commissioner. When war broke out he returned to England, joined the Military Police, and served in Africa and the Middle East, later with Civil Affairs on the continent. "Mentally badly blitzed" by a V2 rocket D'Oyly-John recuperated with his friend the artist and teacher Edmund Fearnley-Whittingstall, who encouraged him to paint. He adopted a palette knife technique gleaned from a Belgian artist seen on holiday, later picking up tips from the Nice artist Paul Negeli. When KLG, the sparking plug firm he worked for, was taken over, D'Oyly-John and and his wife moved to South Africa, where he began painting seriously, with interest from the English dealer Frost and Reed. The D'Oyly-Johns lived in Cannes for some years before settling in England, but he continued to tour the continent as Gough's Gallery, Bognor Regis, where he had a solo show in 1965, Stacy-Marks in Eastbourne and dealers around the world took up his work. Queen Elizabeth, visiting Africa as Princess Elizabeth, found her Treetops hotel decorated with several D'Oyly-Johns and acquired his work for the Royal Collection. A stroke in 1987 incapacitated the artist, partially paralysing him and blinding him in one eye.

Milena DRAGICEVIC 1965– Artist who produced paint-based work with references to architecture and film. She was born in Krajina, Serbia, but was brought up in Canada, where she gained a fine arts honours degree from York University, Toronto, 1984–8. She was artist-in-residence, advanced studies programme, Dundas Valley School of Art, Dundas, Ontario, 1988–90, then obtained a master's in painting, Royal College of Art, 1990–2. Was resident in Britain from 1998, after several years in San Francisco. She won a series of awards, including a Stanley Picker Fellowship, Kingston University, 1992–4. Dragicevic took part in extensive group exhibitions internationally, including Blind Date, Clove Two Gallery, 1993; Whitechapel Open, Whitechapel Art Gallery, 1994; East Coast West Coast, 168 Haight, San Francisco, America, 1996; Cheltenham Drawing Open 1998, Cheltenham & Gloucester College, Cheltenham, 1998; The Chinese Room, Void Gallery, 1999; and Doubles II – with Artlab, Jeffrey Charles Gallery, 2002. Solo shows included Watermans Arts Centre, Brentford, 1994, and Damtsahaberz, 2000. Her works were held by Royal College of Art, Kingston University, Morley Gallery and other public, corporate and private collections. Lived in London.

Elizabeth DRAKE 1866–1954 Painter, printmaker, miniaturist and teacher, born at Chatham, Kent. After studying at Rochester and Westminster Schools of Art she lived in Paris, working at Atelier Colarossi. Exhibited RA, RWS, RI and elsewhere. Painted widely throughout England, France and South Africa, where her work is in public collections. Lived at Wokingham, Berkshire.

Chris DRAPER 1965– Artist in various media who studied at St Martin's School of Art and Royal College of Art. He was notable for his mixed-media boxes, displayed at England & Co's Art in Boxes in 1992 and incorporated in moving form in a video made for the band Miro. Other group appearances took place in England, France, Japan and Netherlands and in 1990 he had a solo show at Wave Gallery, Tokyo.

Kenneth DRAPER 1944– Sculptor, draughtsman and painter, and teacher, born in Sheffield, Yorkshire. He studied at Chesterfield College of Art, 1959–62, at Kingston School of Art, 1962–5, then Royal College of Art, 1965–8. Draper won the sculpture prize at Young Contemporaries in 1965, then four years later had a one-man show at Redfern Gallery The 1970s saw him taking part in important foreign shows and in British Sculptors '72 at RA, the year he gained a commission for John Dalton Building, Manchester Polytechnic. An important commission, in 1977–8, was his Oriental Gateway for Bradford University. In 1977 Draper took part in the Silver Jubilee Contemporary British Sculpture Exhibition in Battersea Park, the year he won a Major Arts Council Award. Arts Council holds several examples of his work, which was abstract. From mid-1970s taught at Goldsmiths' College School of Art and Camberwell School of Arts and Crafts. Had retrospective at Warwick Arts Trust, 1981. Later solo shows included Austin/Desmond Fine Art and Glen Green Gallery, Santa Fe, 1991, the year Draper was elected RA, and Hart Gallery, 1996. Draper latterly lived on the island of Menorca.

Matthew DRAPER 1973– Artist who graduated from Falmouth College of Art, 1995. He settled in Edinburgh, a prime subject for his atmospheric pastels. He was included in Artists of Fame & Promise at Panter & Hall, 2003. Glasgow Museums and Art Gallery holds his work.

Joshua DRAPKIN 1959– Painter, born and lived in London, who was educated at Whitgift School, Liverpool University and Università degli Studi, Venice (graduating in Italian and French), 1978–82, Courtauld Institute, London University and Fondazione Giorgio Cini, Venice, on an Italian government scholarship (Master of Philosophy, eighteenth-century art history), 1983–7. He completed 12 articles for the 1996 Macmillan *Dictionary of Art*. Drapkin trained as a solicitor and qualified through Denton Hall, 1987–91, and from then practised. He was a member of the Institute of Trade Mark Attorneys, 1994–8; Law Society Equal Opportunities Committee & Group for Solicitors with Disabilities, from 1997; and British-Italian Lawyers Association. Exhibitions included Watercolour C21, Bankside Gallery, 1999 and 2001, and RI, 2001. Baroque and twentieth-century art history and architecture, painting and drawing were among his interests. His strongest pictorial influences were "Klimt, Kandinsky and the German Expressionists, although, according to my children, I probably know more than anyone needs to know about the French and Venetian painters of the *Ancien Régime*."

Jasmina DRAŠKOVIĆ-JOHNSON 1943– Icon painter and restorer, born in Kruvsevac, Yugoslavia, brought up and educated in Belgrade. Studied prehistoric and classical archaeology and art history at Universities of Belgrade and Michigan, in America, gaining a master's degree. Went on to work as an archaeologist, conservator and illustrator, participating in field expeditions and museum work in Europe, Africa, the Middle East and North America. Worked on restoring the monastery church of St Peter in Ras, Yugoslavia; excavating a medieval church near Siena, Italy; on classical Greek vase painting in the British Museum; and as an artist-conservator at American Museum of Natural History, New York. Icons mainly in the Serbian Byzantine style were shown at four-man exhibition in Woodlands Art Gallery in 1981.

John DRAWBRIDGE 1930–2005 Versatile and adventurous artist and teacher born in Wellington, New Zealand. From 1947 he studied at Wellington Technical College of Art, where Fred Ellis was head of school; at Wellington Teachers' Training College, 1948–9; and in 1950 completed his third year of training at Dunedin Teachers' Training College, teachers including Fred Shewell and William Reed. By then he had exhibited at Helen Hitchings Gallery, Wellington, and had produced watercolours for the National Film Unit production *The Ascent of Mount Aspiring*. After being art adviser to Wellington Education Board and lecturing at Wellington Teachers' Training College, in 1957 Drawbridge won a National Art Gallery Travelling Scholarship to study in London, extended for a year, which enabled him to attend the Central School of Arts and Crafts, winning a Diploma of Distinction, and tour Europe. In 1960, he married the sculptor Tanya

Ashken, exhibited at the RA Summer Exhibition and was elected an associate of RE, also showing at Zwemmer and Piccadilly Galleries. From 1960–1 Drawbridge studied with S W Hayter and Johnny Friedlander in Paris, showed with the LG, was commissioned to paint a mural for New Zealand House in London and had another bought by Leicestershire Education Committee. Drawbridge taught at Isleworth Polytechnic, 1962–3, and in 1963 had a solo show at Redfern Gallery and four large paintings in the First Commonwealth Biennale of Abstract Art. After returning to New Zealand, in 1964 Drawbridge began teaching at Wellington Polytechnic School of Design. Drawbridge's career continued to develop, with important mural and stained glass window commissions, exhibitions at home and abroad and international recognition such as his major prize at the 10th International Exhibition Bianco e Nero, Lugano, Switzerland, 1968, previous winners including David Hockney, Pablo Picasso and Jacques Villon. Wellington's City Gallery gave him a retrospective in 2001–2.

Shmuel DRESNER 1928– Artist in a range of media, including printmaking and collage, born in Warsaw, Poland. With the help of the Central British Fund charity organisation Dresner arrived in England in 1945, starting to paint during a four-year stay in sanatoriums. He then studied at Heatherley School of Fine Art, 1949, and at Central School of Arts and Crafts, 1953. St Martin's Gallery gave him shows in 1962 and 1966; Ben Uri Art Society, which holds a range of examples, in 1975; Galerie Roche, Henstedt, 1980; and Galerie Slavia, Bremen, 1981. Lived latterly in Middlesex.

George Cuthbert DRESSER 1872–1951 Landscape watercolourist, younger brother of the artist Alfred Dresser, who was born and lived in Darlington, County Durham. By profession he was a draughtsman, showing for many years with Darlington Society of Arts of which was a member and RI. The local art gallery holds his work.

Timothy DREVER 1935– Artist who shared an exhibition of new paintings with Rolf Brandt at Lisson Gallery in 1969, in the catalogue of which he explored the implications of hanging a canvas diamond-wise instead of in conventional rectangular mode. Drever said that his preferred territory lay "between aesthetics and logic." He had a solo show at Galerie Fuchs, Vienna, Austria, in 1963. Other exhibitions included John Moores Liverpool Exhibition, 1965; Soundings 3, Signals, 1966; Edinburgh Open 100, 1967; 25 Camden Artists, Camden Festival, and a solo show, The Dreams of Euclid, Lisson Gallery, 1968; and Four-colour theorem, environmental project at Kenwood, 1969. The Arts Council acquired Drever's abstract oil on canvas Negatron, 1968, other public collections holding his work including Albertina Vienna, Kulturamt der Stadt Wein and Victoria & Albert Museum.

Jacob DREW 1909– Painter, decorative artist and teacher, born in Stoke-on-Trent, Staffordshire, where he attended the School of Art, 1926–9, then the Royal College of Art under Ernest Tristram and William Rothenstein, 1929–33. After World War II Drew was head of painting for several years at Camberwell School of Arts and Crafts, then became principal of Willesden and Ealing Schools of Art. He was honorary secretary of the Arts and Crafts Exhibition Society and a council member of the Craft Centre of Great Britain. Showed at RA, and Victoria & Albert Museum holds decorated glass by him. Lived for many years in London, in 1993 moving to France. He was married to the artist Jean Drew.

Jean DREW 1904–1994 Painter, weaver and teacher who studied textiles and weaving at the Royal College of Art and had a studio in Chelsea. She taught in London art schools and ran the textile department at Guildford College of Art. Her rugs were sold under the name Jean Finn at Heal's store and she received many commissions, including the Festival of Britain, 1951. Victoria & Albert Museum hold examples. An exhibition emphasising Drew's flower painting, which flourished with the making of two gardens following her move to Llangorse, 1964, and then Brecon, Powys, in 1988, was held at Brecknock Museum, Brecon, in 1995. Strong design and a feeling for colour were enhanced by her world travels in later years. Her husband was the artist Jacob Drew.

Pamela DREW 1910–1989 Artist in various media, born in Burnley, Lancashire, who studied with Dorothy Baker, with Iain Macnab at the Grosvenor School of Modern Art and in Paris. For five years during the 1950s Drew was an Air Ministry accredited war artist, during which time she handled the Royal Air Force Coronation Review. Had many solo shows in Britain and overseas, work being held by Imperial War Museum, Port of London Authority and Royal Air Force Museum, Hendon. Lived in Milnthorpe, Cumbria.

Knowles DREWE 1878– Painter and teacher who was born Reginald Frank Knowles Drewe. He studied art with Audley Mackworth and showed at RA and Paris Salon. Medici Society reproduced his work. Lived at Berkhamsted, Hertfordshire.

Eva DREWETT 1957– Sculptor in metal and ceramic, born in Warsaw, Poland, who moved to England in the late 1970s, studying at Chelsea School of Art, 1982–3; Central School of Art and Design, 1983–7; and Royal College of Art, 1987–9. She drew on the human form to produce powerful, abstracted works, often on a big scale, as in The Human Side of Being II, of 1991, displayed in Sculpture at Goodwood, 1996–7. Royal Hong Kong Jockey Club, at Kowloon Sculpture Park, holds Drewett's sculpture.

Geoffrey Crellin DREWITT 1921– Painter, muralist and teacher, born in Little Gaddesden, Hertfordshire, whose school has murals by him. After Berkhamsted School he studied at Westminster School of Art and Central School of Arts and Crafts, 1938–40, then in 1946–7 at University of London Institute of Education. Began teaching at Pinner County School, 1947, and after appointments in Norwich and Liverpool was art adviser to Northumberland from 1967, living in Newcastle upon Tyne. Showed at RA, NS, RBA and ROI.

Yvonne DREWRY 1918– Painter, printmaker, typographer and teacher, born in Chiswick, west London, who studied at Liverpool College of Art, 1934–6, then at Edinburgh College of Art, with a Senior Andrew Grant Scholarship, where teachers included William Gillies, Joan Hassall and John Maxwell. She lived in Suffolk for 50 years, finally based at Hollesley, Woodbridge, teaching "students from 8–80 years to see and to paint, print, engrave" (including Maggi Hambling, at Amberfield School, Nacton). Drewry ran a private press, Centaury Press, producing small books, and claimed to be "a lone worker". Was a member of Ipswich Art Society, mixed shows including Laing Art Competition at Mall Galleries, 1991, highly commended 1994; Drawings for All, Gainsborough's House, Sudbury; and Ipswich Open at Wolsey Art Gallery, Ipswich, 1995. Had solo exhibitions at Ipswich, Woodbridge, Colchester, Aldeburgh and Sudbury. Work in many private collections in Europe and Australia.

Agnes DREY c.1890–1957 Painter in oil, born in Withington, Manchester, sister of the art and theatre critic Oscar Raymond Drey who was husband of the artist Anne Estelle Rice. She studied with Frances Hodgkins, who painted her portrait, in the Drey family collection. In the early 1930s Drey moved to St Ives, Cornwall, where she died. She exhibited with WIAC, the Newlyn and St Ives Societies, Lanham's Gallery and Castle Inn in St Ives and was a founder-member of the Penwith Society, which holds her work and gave her a memorial show. Designs by Drey and others were screenprinted onto table mats by the local firm Porthia Prints.

David DREY 1962– Painter who gained a diploma in acting at Drama Centre, Chalk Farm, 1981–4. He then attended John Cass, 1986–7, winning his diploma from Byam Shaw School of Art, 1987–90. Took part in Summer Show, Chenil Galleries, 1990; Florence Trust Open Studio, 1993; and Digswell Trust Group Exhibition at Whiteley's, 1994. In 1995 shared a show with Polly de Falbe at Bartley Drey Gallery. David Drey came from an artistic background. His father was the antique dealer David Drey, his mother the dealer Gill Drey, his grandfather the art critic O Raymond Drey, whose wife was the painter Anne Estelle Rice.

James DRING 1905–1985 Painter in oil and watercolour. Born in London he studied at Clapham School of Art from 1920–7, then at the RCA under Sir William Rothenstein. Exhibited at the RA, RBA, ROI, Wertheim Gallery, in provincial galleries as well as abroad in Paris, Brussels, Sweden and the USA. The Contemporary Art Society purchased his work and the Medici Society, London, reproduced it. The Victoria and Albert Museum, Southampton Art Gallery and Brussels and Mons Museums hold examples. Between 1943–72 he taught at the St Martin's School of Art. Younger brother of the painter William Dring. Lived in London.

Melissa DRING 1944– Artist in pastel and oil, born in Hampshire, daughter of the artist William Dring. She studied at Winchester School of Art and Royal Academy Schools and worked as a portrait painter, police forensic and television courtroom artist. In addition to her art training, Dring honed her skills on the Federal Bureau of Investigation's intensive course for police artists and also had a Bachelor of Science degree in the psychology of facial identification. In 2002 the Jane Austen Centre, Bath, displayed a much-praised portrait of the novelist created by Dring 185 years after Austen's death, based on contemporary evidence. She had earlier produced a portrait of the eighteenth-century Italian composer Antonio Vivaldi for a film biography, having been recommended to its producer by Scotland Yard. Showed at RA, RP, RBA and PS of which she was a member. Lived in Northampton, where the Central Museum & Art Gallery holds her work, as do Trades Union Congress headquarters and Wellington Park Hotel, Belfast.

Susan DRING 1952– Bristol-born figurative sculptor who benefited from a long family tradition of stone-carving. After her children left school, Dring began sculpting, enhancing her knowledge when she joined her brother, Trevor Dring, of Phidias Neoclassical, Bristol. Mary with Christ Crucified for the Belgian war memorial, Kensal Green, is by Susan Dring, although most of her work was commissioned for churches, stately homes and public buildings in the west of England. Examples are the crest on Bristol Crown Courts and the restored Arnos Court Triumphal Arch in the city.

William DRING 1904–1990 Painter, draughtsman and teacher, born Dennis William Dring in London, known colloquially as John; brother of the artist James Dring; married the painter Grace Elizabeth Rothwell; his daughter Melissa Dring was also an artist. Studied under Henry Tonks at Slade School of Fine Art, 1922–5, and emerged as a fine draughtsman, a sympathetic portrait painter, fond of using his family as subjects, and deft watercolourist. Won several prizes and scholarships at the Slade. Taught until 1940 at Southampton School of Art, then became an official war artist, whose work is well represented in the Imperial War Museum. After the war he became a noted RA exhibitor, being elected RA in 1955, producing a stream of boardroom and official portraits and depicting a number of royal occasions. Lived at Compton, near Winchester, Hampshire.

Barry DRISCOLL 1926–2006 Wildlife sculptor, painter, illustrator and muralist, real name Barrington Driscoll. Driscoll was highly regarded by both his artistic peers and naturalists for his realistic, anatomically accurate depiction of wildlife. Although born in London, Driscoll spent part of his youth in Shropshire where he developed a love of nature, sketching and reading, Gilbert White's classic *The Natural History and Antiquities of Selborne* a favourite book. Following commissioned service in the Army in India, Palestine, Egypt and Northern Ireland, he studied from 1948 at St Martin's School of Art, teachers including Archibald Ziegler, James Stroudley, Jehan Daly and Nigel Lambourne. After gaining his diploma, he went to the Royal College of Art under Robin Darwin, studying in Professor Richard Guyatt's illustration and graphic design department. Among his teachers were John Nash, Edward Bawden, Abram Games and Basil Taylor, the expert on George Stubbs, who was a special influence. Driscoll became a freelance illustrator, early completing drawings for several books by René Guillot, Henry Williamson seeking him out to illustrate a new edition of his 1927 classic *Tarka the Otter* and its 1935 sequel *Salar the Salmon*. They became friends, Driscoll and his wife Kiffy staying for a time in a caravan on Williamson's land at Georgeham, Devon, the crabby, right-wing Williamson a contrast to the gregarious anarchist-socialist Driscoll. Driscoll also illustrated books by Desmond Morris and Gavin Maxwell. In 1960, Driscoll painted three big murals for London Zoo; he also wrote and illustrated a column for several years for the *Sunday Express*; in 1970 was commissioned by *Time-Life* to paint Arizona fauna; and in 1990 created a series of stamps for the Post Office of cattle, having earlier handled this subject for a Moscow

Trade Fair, the Irish Post Office also commissioning his work. By the early 1980s Driscoll was sculpting wildlife, modelling in wax, the resulting bronzes being cast at the Mariani foundry near Pietrasanta, Italy, and The Arch Bronze foundry in London. Driscoll showed as a member with the SWLA, with the Phoenix Gallery in Lavenham and was included in the big 2002 international wildlife exhibition originated at the Accademia Nazionale d'Arte Antica e Moderna in Turin, Italy, which toured to Barcelona, Spain, then the SWLA. Died in London.

Zorica DRLJACHA 1942– Sculptor and draughtsman, brought up initially in Yugoslavia. Was educated partly there, partly at Luton College of Technology before studying at Goldsmiths' College School of Art, then Royal Academy Schools. Her teachers included Charles Mahoney and Sir Henry Rushbury. Won several prizes and Landseer Scholarship. Showed RA, RBS and elsewhere and did commissioned work for Expo '67, held in Montreal, Canada. Lived for some years in London.

George DROUGHT 1940– Artist and teacher who studied at St Helens School of Art, Liverpool College of Art and Central School of Arts and Crafts. Drought won a John Moores Scholarship, taught etching at Bluecoat Chambers in Liverpool and showed widely in mixed exhibitions in the northwest as well as having many solo shows. Two drawings by him were included in the Walker Art Gallery, Liverpool, 1986–7 touring Merseyside Artists 3.

Elsie DRUCE fl. from c.1905–1965 Painter and printmaker, born at Weybridge, Surrey. After education at Roedean School, studied art under William Rothenstein. Exhibited RA, SWA, Goupil Gallery, RP and at many other venues. Member of East Kent Art Society and lived at Rye, Sussex.

Amy Julia DRUCKER 1873–1951 Painter, miniaturist, printmaker and teacher. After initial education in London she studied at St John's Wood and Lambeth Schools of Art and Atelier Colarossi, Paris. She was a versatile, prolific and much-travelled artist who as well as exhibiting at London venues such as RA, RMS, Goupil Gallery, RI and ROI showed abroad, where her work is widely distributed. Was commissioned to paint a portrait of the Emperor of Abyssinia, Haile Selassie. Ben Uri Art Society holds examples. Lived in London.

Michael DRUKS 1940– Artist who used "a variety of techniques ... My work is mainly concerned with group and individual behaviour in the environment. I focus on the conflict between the individual and the crowd." Born in Jerusalem, Druks from 1966–7 studied at the Bat-Yam Institute of Art and the Art High School in Tel-Aviv. He began showing in the early 1960s, participating in the 10+ group. Having in 1970 gained the Working Award for the Creative Artist from the American-Israeli Cultural Foundation, he spent three months in America. In 1971 he taught at Jerusalem's Bezalel Academy of Art, also organising his first street event, the peeling of a public noticeboard, aided by the Tel-Aviv city authorities and the Israeli Broadcasting Association. After visiting Amsterdam in 1972 Druks moved to London, where he settled, helping to found the Art Meeting Place in Covent Garden in 1974. Photography, video tapes and sound were features of his work, which was shown in Contemporary Art in Camden, in 1981, at Camden Arts Centre. Solo exhibitions included Whitechapel Art Gallery, 1976, and later ones Julie M Gallery, Tel-Aviv, from 1990, and Beardsmore Gallery, from 1994. In 1973 Druks received the W Sandberg Prize from the Israeli Museum, which holds his work, as do the Tel-Aviv Museum, Museum of Modern Art in Haifa and Jan van Eyck Academie, Maastricht.

Blaise DRUMMOND 1967– Painter, born in Liverpool, who contributed "an epic painting, at least for me", entitled Little Western World, oil on canvas on board, to the 1997–8 John Moores Liverpool Exhibition. Drummond studied at Edinburgh University, 1985–9, then at the National College of Art and Design, Dublin, 1990–4, and for his master's degree at Chelsea College of Art, 1997–8. Later solo exhibitions included The Natural Order of Things, Rubicon Gallery, Dublin, 1997.

Gordon DRUMMOND 1921– Watercolourist, scale modeller and miniaturist, born in Sale, Cheshire. Immediately prior to World War II, during which he served in the Royal Engineers, L T Gordon Drummond was apprenticed as an architect in Manchester. After Army service he was a freelance artist for a while, his art training being undertaken at Manchester College of Art. Showed there, also RWS, but was mainly known as a commercial artist employed by fine art publishers such as Kardonia Ltd, of which he was for a time senior artist. Lived in Potters Bar, Middlesex.

Violet Hilda DRUMMOND 1911–2000 Illustrator and writer of children's books, watercolourist and printmaker, born and lived in London. She studied at the Links School, Eastbourne, finishing school in Paris and St Martin's School of Art. During World War II served in the First Aid Nursing Yeomanry. Her book *Mrs Easter and the Storks*, 1957, won her the Kate Greenaway Award. The *Little Laura* series of books by her resulted in cartoon films which she produced for BBC Television. Showed at Oliver Swann, Chenil and Upper Grosvenor Galleries. Lived in London.

Chris DRURY 1948– Sculptor, born in Colombo, Ceylon, who gained his sculpture diploma at Camberwell School of Art, 1966–70. He won a South East Arts Award, 1976, and a British Council Northern Norway Exchange, 1988. Group shows included The Unpainted Landscape, a Scottish Arts Council tour, 1987; Woodlands, Angel Row Gallery, Nottingham, 1990; Art in Nature, Arte Sella, Sella Valley, Italy, 1994, and Pure Paint, Stephen Lacey Gallery, 1999. Had a solo show, Medicine Wheel, Coracle, 1983, later ones including Rebecca Hossack Gallery, 1993, Vessel, Towner Art Gallery, Eastbourne, and tour, 1995, Silent Spaces, Janus Avivson Gallery, New York, America, 1999; De La Warr Pavilion, Bexhill-on-Sea, 2002; and Heart of stone, Stephen Lacey, 2004, which toured from Wales. Later public commissions included Covered Cairn, Tickon Sculpture Park, Langeland, Denmark, 1993, Vortex, Lewes Castle, Sussex, 1994, Grizedale Sculpture Forest, Cumbria, 1999; and Cloud Chambers, Eden Project, Cornwall, 2002. Drury travelled extensively and used various, including found, materials to create baskets, cairns and shelter forms. Arts Council, Contemporary Art Society, Royal Botanic Garden in Edinburgh and galleries in Leeds and Cheltenham hold examples.

Henry Myles Reilly DRURY 1904– Watercolourist, printmaker and architect, born in Marlborough, Wiltshire. A qualified architect and fellow of the RIBA, Drury was by profession surveyor to the Dean and Chapter of Exeter Cathedral, having studied at the Architectural Association, 1922–7. He exhibited in the Exeter area, mainly with Exeter Art Society, and lived at Ebford, Devon.

Paul DRURY 1903–1987 Printmaker, painter and teacher, born in London, son of the sculptor Alfred Drury, his mother was also an artist. Studied at Goldsmiths' College School of Art under Edmund Sullivan, Malcolm Osborne, Clive Gardiner and Stanley Anderson, becoming one of the finest exponents of the Goldsmiths' school of printmaking, his work being influenced by the pastoral tradition of Samuel Palmer. Drury went on to teach at Goldsmiths', also at Sir John Cass School of Art. Although he left Goldsmiths' for a time in the late 1930s he returned after World War II part-time and retired in 1969, having been principal of the School of Art for two years. During the war Drury worked in the plaster department at Queen Mary's Hospital, Roehampton, putting to use skills learned working in his father's studio. He also did work for the War Artists' Advisory Committee. Exhibited widely in Britain, continental Europe, in North and South America. British Museum, provincial and foreign galleries holding his work. Retrospective at Goldsmiths' College Gallery, 1984. Lived at Nutley, Sussex.

Alexandra DRYSDALE 1962– Abstract artist, born in London, who studied fine art at Chelsea School of Art, 1980–4. She exhibited in London, Stockholm and Amsterdam and in 1996 had a solo show at Gainsborough's House, Sudbury, having moved to East Anglia two years before. Drysdale's works were grids of repeated relief forms combining delicate pencil draughtsmanship with paper cubes, sewing thread, feathers and other materials. Intricately made and largely monochromatic, they were intended "to emphasise the impermanence of physical forms by drawing attention to shadows and using simple materials and motifs".

Russell DRYSDALE 1912–1981 Painter of landscapes and figures, mainly of Australian subjects, whose full name was George Russell Drysdale. Born in Bognor Regis, Sussex, he went as a child to Australia where his family had interests in farming. Drysdale first visited Europe early in the 1930s, one of a series of visits, after which he decided to relinquish farming and to study art with George Bell in Melbourne for three years from 1935. He was again to study with Bell in 1939–40, but meanwhile he studied in Paris at L'Académie de la Grande Chaumière and Atelier Colarossi, then in London with Iain Macnab at the Grosvenor School of Modern Art. Back in Australia his reputation steadily grew after his first one-man show at the Macquarie Galleries, Sydney, 1942. Had a first London one-man show at Leicester Galleries in 1950, other following in 1958, 1965 and 1972. Represented in many Australian Galleries and in Tate Gallery. Retrospective at National Gallery of Victoria, Melbourne, in 1960. Died at Hardy's Bay, New South Wales.

Jaroslav DUB 1878– Painter, born in Veltrusy, Bohemia, who attended Prague School of Art. Initially exhibited in that city, then after settling in Rhyl, Flintshire, about start of World War II began exhibiting RCamA.

Fred DUBERY 1926– Painter and teacher, a native of Suffolk, where much of his work – intimate, in the manner of Bonnard and Vuillard – was painted. He studied at Croydon School of Art, 1949–50 and at Royal College of Art, 1950–3. From 1964 he taught for many years at Royal Academy Schools, being appointed professor of perspective in 1984. From 1950 was a regular RA exhibitor, also showing at NEAC, Leicester Galleries and Roland, Browse & Delbanco. He had solo shows at Trafford Gallery, 1957 and 1963, and New Grafton Gallery, 1974 onwards. Wrote several books on drawing and perspective. The Arts Club and public galleries in Brighton and Huddersfield hold his work. Lived at Great Finborough, Suffolk.

Du BROUILLARD: *see* **Neil FOGGIE**

Stanisław DUBIEL 1913– Artist and medical practitioner, born in Przemysl, Poland, who studied there in the studio of Joseph Wilk and continued in Lvov. During World War II he served in the Parachute Brigade and the First Polish Army Division. On demobilisation he graduated from the medical faculty of Edinburgh University, eventually settling in London as a general practitioner. He continued his art studies until 1964 in the private school run by Professor Marian Bohusz-Szyszko. Dubiel was an active member of the Association of Polish Artists in Great Britain where his works were in private collections, also being widely held abroad.

Henrietta DUBREY 1966– Painter, born in Cuckfield, Sussex, who attended West Sussex College of Art & Design, 1984–5; Byam Shaw School of Art, 1985–6; graduated with honours, Wimbledon School of Art, 1986–9; and gained her diploma, Royal Academy Schools, 1989–92. Group shows included RA Summer Exhibition, from 1991; Contemporary Art Society Market, from 1992; New Collectables, Rye Art Gallery, 1994; Gallery 7, Hong Kong, 1996; and Five Painters from Cornwall, Belgrave Gallery, St Ives, 2001. That gallery showed her solo in 2002, as had Star Gallery, Lewes, from 1990, with another at Belgrave, 2004. Dubrey's pictures indicated a familiarity with the work of notable Cornish painters such as Peter Lanyon and Terry Frost and the landscape which inspired them. This stemmed from her childhood, in which she had painted with her father, visited galleries and met local artists. She then determined to become a professional artist, her love of Cornwall drawing her back to settle at west Penwith.

Mario DUBSKY 1939–1985 Painter and teacher, born in London. He studied at Slade School of Fine Art, 1956–61, the final year doing postgraduate work. Between 1962–3 Dubsky undertook part-time painting, including Morley College. An Abbey Major Scholarship took him to the British School in Rome, 1963–5. During rest of the 1960s and early 1970s Dubsky taught at various art schools and colleges, including Camberwell, Wimbledon, Brighton, and Central, while a Harkness Fellowship was granted him in 1969–71 for travel to America. Dubsky lived in New York, 1973–4, and he was artist-in-residence at British School, Rome, 1982. He was a tutor at the Royal College of Art, 1981–5, having a retrospective at South London Art Gallery in 1984, 15 years after his first one-man, at Grosvenor Gallery. Boundary Gallery held a two-part retrospective, in 1990 and 1999. Dubsky was a powerful painter, whose work featured harrowing subjects such as the Holocaust. Arts Council holds. Lived in London.

Catherine DUCKER 1973– Artist and teacher, whose output included colourful representational as well as abstract works, born and lived in Wallingford, Oxfordshire. She gained a foundation diploma at Central St Martins College of Art & Design, 1990–1, and a fine art honours degree there, 1992–6. Travelled extensively, 1992–5. In 1996 Ducker won the Sainsbury's Wine Label Award. Teaching included part-time screenprinting, Reading Technical College of Art & Design. In 1997 she was elected an associate of the RWS. Exhibitions included Bankside Gallery, student prize, 1995; Candid Arts Trust and Beetle and Wedge Hotel, Moulsford, both 1997; Royal Over-Seas League, 1998; and Art on Paper, Royal College of Art, 1999.

Richard DUCKER 1959– Ducker graduated with honours from the University of Reading, 1977–82. In 1987 he was shortlisted for a British Rail sculpture commission. Exhibitions included The Showroom, 1985; Brixton Art Gallery and Coracle, both 1986; and East End Open Studios, based at Robinson Road, 1989.

Ernest John DUCKETT 1916–1997 Painter, notably of portraits, born at Much Wenlock, Shropshire. He studied at art schools in Shrewsbury and Stoke-on-Trent. Was elected PS in 1951 and showed at RA, NS, in the provinces and at Paris Salon. Lived for many years in Kent, at Sevenoaks and later at Southborough.

Aidron DUCKWORTH 1920– Sculptor, painter and teacher, born in Lincoln. He was married to the sculptor and potter Ruth Duckworth. After initial education in Spalding, Duckworth in 1949 studied with Seán Crampton at the Anglo-French Art Centre; also at Chelsea School of Art, 1949–51, where his teachers included the sculptor Willi Soukop, and at the Royal College of Art, 1951–4. Showed widely in England and America, including Woodstock Gallery, New Art Centre and Arnolfini Gallery, Bristol. Was for some time professor of sculpture at Syracuse University, New York, and lived for a while in Kew, Surrey.

Barbara DUCKWORTH 1913– Artist in various media, professionally engaged in medical work, born in Wallasey, Cheshire, settling eventually nearby in Heswall, Wirral. She was a State Registered Nurse and studied at Liverpool College of Art, 1934–8. As well as illustrations for medical books and periodicals, showed with Liver Sketching Club and Walker Art Gallery, Liverpool. She was a fellow of the Medical Artists' Association.

Philip DUCKWORTH 1976– Artist, born in Iselohn, West Germany, who graduated with honours in fine art from Coventry University, 1996–9. Exhibitions included SUS69, Coventry University, 1998; Big Warm Open, Cambridge Darkroom Gallery, 1999; Boring, Works Gallery, Birmingham, 2000; Nothing Happens, The Gallery, Stratford-upon-Avon, 2002; and Joanne Jones & Philip Duckworth, Rockface, Birmingham, 2003. From 1999 Duckworth worked jointly with Ben Sadler as juneau/projects/ (see separate entry).

Ruth DUCKWORTH 1919– Sculptor and potter, born in Hamburg, Germany. Studied art in Liverpool, 1936–40 and Kennington School of Art, 1942–3; studied pottery at Hammersmith School of Art and Central School of Arts and Crafts. Showed at RA, elsewhere in London and in North America, including several solo shows. Worked for some time in Chicago, notably on the design for a huge mural on University of Chicago's geophysical building. Lived for some years in Kew, Surrey, and was married to the sculptor Aidron Duckworth.

Wilfred DUDENEY 1911–1996 Sculptor and teacher, born in Leicester. He was educated at St Paul's School, then Central School of Arts and Crafts, 1928–33, with Alfred Turner. Held a number of teaching posts, latterly at Isleworth Polytechnic, Middlesex. Showed, sometimes only signing with initials, at RA, NEAC, RHA and elsewhere. Dudeney's carved elm Falcon is illustrated in Eric Newton's monograph *British Sculpture 1944–1946*. Elected a fellow of RBS in 1952, of which he became vice-president, 1971-5. Dudeney was the son of Leonard Dudeney, a journalist. Wilfred completed some striking sculptures in New Street Square, near Fleet Street, in the mid-1950s: a relief panel with a printer; a figure, Youth; and a Group of Newspapermen. Lived in London for many years, but died in Blackpool.

Gerry DUDGEON 1952– Artist and teacher, born in Darjeeling, India. He gained an honours degree in modern languages at Cambridge University, 1970–4, studying German art history at Freiburg University, Germany, 1972–3, then worked for Museum of London on excavations, 1974–5. Gained an honours degree in fine art, 1975–9, then his master's degree at Reading University, 1979–81. Won a Boise Travelling Scholarship to New York, 1981, then was a visiting lecturer at art colleges and polytechnics in England from that year. Showed with New Contemporaries from 1977; RA Summer Exhibition from 1983; Riverside Open in 1986; and Change of Seen Gallery, Dorchester, 1988. Solo exhibitions included Derby Hall, Bury, 1982, Vortex Gallery from 1986, Indian landscape-inspired paintings at Exeter Phoenix, Exeter, 1999. Lived in Beaminster, Dorset.

Anna DUDLEY: *see* **Anna Dudley NEILL**

Colin DUDLEY 1923– Painter, sculptor and teacher, born in Greenwich, southeast London. After initial education at Eltham College he studied art at Sidcup School of Art and Goldsmiths' College School of Art. He held a number of teaching positions in schools and training colleges, including Christ Church College, Canterbury, Kent. Showed at RA, NEAC, SEA, LG and elsewhere, London County Council and Derbyshire Education Committee buying his work.

Geoffrey DUDLEY 1918–1986 Sculptor and teacher, born in Wednesfield, Staffordshire, who studied at Wolverhampton School of Art, 1936–9, and Royal College of Art, 1939 and 1945–6, being a Travelling Scholar in 1946. Dudley had worked as an engineer, 1940–5, and his sculpture, in metal, blending realism and abstraction, was preoccupied with themes such as trains and railways. He lectured in sculpture at Newcastle upon Tyne University, 1946–63, being an extra-mural lecturer at Durham University, 1949–58. Between 1963–84 he held several posts at Chelsea School of Art, being head of the department of sculpture from 1974. Did extensive commissioned work. Showed at AIA Galleries, RA, RSA, Stone Gallery in Newcastle and elsewhere and had memorial exhibitions at Chelsea School of Art, 1986, and Hatton Gallery, Newcastle, 1987. The lost wax method of casting was used by Dudley, who had work acquired by West Midlands Arts, RA (Chantrey Bequest) and Inner London Education Authority.

James DUDLEY: *see* **Derek CHITTOCK**

John DUDLEY 1915– Painter and miniaturist, born in Eton, Buckinghamshire, taught art at home by his mother, the artist Ada Dudley. He retired from the Army and began painting seriously in 1967. Joined PS, 1972, RMS, 1984, and SM in 1985. Dudley painted over 400 portraits and was accredited portraitist to the Army Air Corps and Parachute Regiment. Lord Aberdare, the Bishop of Credition, Admiral of the Fleet Sir Henry Leach and General Sir Frank King were among his subjects. He also painted landscapes, horses and dogs. In 1984 he won the Bill Mundy Gold Sovereign Award. Lived at Chilmark, Salisbury, Wiltshire.

Graham Seaton DUDLEY-PAGE: *see* **Graham Seaton Dudley PAGE**

Debbie DUFFIN 1953– Versatile artist and teacher who studied at Coventry University, taking part in degree show at Herbert Art Gallery there, 1976, in the same year being a prizewinner at Winsor & Newton Exhibition at Mall Galleries. Other mixed show appearances included Masks, Café Gallery, 1984; London Pride at Lamont Gallery, 1986; A Drawing Show, Waterman's Art Centre, 1990; and John Jones Open, The Gallery at John Jones, 1994. Awards included Oppenheim-John Downes Memorial Award to Artists, 1985; Publication Grants from Arts Council, 1987 and 1992; and London Arts Board Award, Research and Development, 1994. Had a solo show at The University, Keele, 1975, later ones including Trespass, at Adam Gallery, 1991, and Barbican Centre, 1996. In that, Duffin showed fragile and elegant linear constructions which stemmed from intensive drawing. In 1995 Duffin was commissioned by British Telecom to create a sculpture out of the relics of old telephone exchange equipment. Duffin had extensive teaching experience, including workshops on professional practice. Latterly this included course co-ordinator and tutor for Open College of the Arts, 1990–2; from 1994 co-ordinator, professional practice, Wimbledon School of Art; and from 1995 visiting lecturer at Central St Martin's School of Art. Coventry University and Women's Art at New Hall College, Cambridge, hold examples.

John DUFFIN 1965– Painter, draughtsman and printmaker, born in Barrow-in-Furness, Lancashire, where took an apprenticeship at Vickers Shipbuilding & Engineering and qualified as a draughtsman, 1981–5. Attended Goldsmiths' College, 1985–8, graduating in fine art, completing a postgraduate diploma in advanced printmaking at Central St Martins College of Art, 1988–90. Based in London, between 1989–91 Duffin worked with Tom Phillips, including all the etchings in Dante's *Inferno*; also with Norman Ackroyd on a mural for Lloyds Bank, 10 feet by 150 feet, in etched stainless steel. Mixed shows included Lake Artists' Exhibition, Grasmere, 1986; Whitechapel Open, at Whitechapel Art Gallery, 1988; RA Summer Exhibition, from 1990; Bankside Gallery, Members' Show, 1992; and Kerb Scrawlers, The Living Room, Greenwich, 1994. Solo exhibitions included Coachhouse Gallery, Grasmere, 1992, Lamont and Kaleidoscope Galleries, 2001, and Vertigo, 2002.

Robbie DUFF SCOTT 1959– Self-taught figurative painter, born in Bristol, where he was educated at Clifton College, who then read English, American and French literature at York University. From the early 1980s he lived mostly in Umbria, Italy. For 17 years he was married to the novelist Lisa St Aubin de Terán, author of *The Slow Train to Milan* and *The Hacienda*, who had commissioned him to paint her portrait. Duff Scott established a strong following on the continent, with solo exhibitions in Rome, Milan, Cologne and Amsterdam. In 1982 he was chosen for the National Portrait Gallery John Player Exhibition. Duff Scott was represented by the Francis Kyle Gallery from 1997; was a major participant in The Art of Memory: contemporary painters in search of Marcel Proust, a 2000 exhibition which travelled to the National Theatre in 2001; and had his first solo show with Francis Kyle in 2000. Reviewing it in *The Independent*, the critic John Walsh found the artist's figures "racked with ambiguity. Sexy and traumatised, they seem trapped between dereliction and desire." Caravaggio was an artist Duff Scott greatly admired.

Damien DUFFY 1967– Artist, born in Londonderry, Northern Ireland, who graduated with honours from Goldsmiths' College. He gained a Rachel Whiteread "K Foundation" Award in 1994 and was a Beck's Futures 1, 2000, nominated artist in 2000. Group exhibitions included A4 Favours, 3 Month Gallery, Liverpool, 1996; Mutoidi, Naples, Italy, 1997; Group Show, Jan Wagner Gallery, Berlin, Germany, 1998; Poster Show, Cabinet Gallery, 2000; and Art2001, represented by Dominic Berning, Business Design Centre, Islington, 2001. Had a solo show with Dominic Berning in 1996, then a series in London, Belgium, Italy and Spain, latterly at 30 Underwood Street, 2000. In 1997–8 Duffy carried out the Villiers Square Project – 20k commission, panels for Villiers redevelopment, for Haworth Tompkins Architects.

Daniel J DUFFY 1878–c.1955 Painter in oil, born at Coatbridge, Lanarkshire. Studied at Glasgow School of Art under Fra Newbery and widely on the continent. Exhibited RA, RSA, ROI, RHA, Royal Glasgow Institute of the Fine Arts and Paris Salon, where he gained Honourable Mentions in 1936 and 1938. Member of Glasgow Art Club. Lived in Coatbridge.

Emlyn DUFFY 1916– Artist in coloured inks with a science fiction bias. Born in Croydon, Surrey, Duffy, who signed his work Dy, held a number of one-man shows in the 1970s at galleries including the Loggia, Woodstock Gallery and the Paris Salon. Regency Press published two volumes of poetry written and illustrated by Duffy. He also had work reproduced by *Science Fiction Monthly* as well as German and Dutch periodicals. By profession a biologist, he worked in London's Natural History Museum.

Manny DUFFY 1954– Artist and illustrator who attended Harrow College of Art from 1971, then Norwich School of Fine Art from 1973. During the 1970s she worked as an artist for a publishing house, was a natural history illustrator for an educational design group and began working as a freelance artist in advertising and publishing. Belgravia Contemporary Arts showed her work.

Paul DUFFY 1968– Painter, born in Paisley, Renfrewshire, who after a foundation course at City & Islington College studied fine art at University of East London. Group shows included New Art, New Danger, The Millinery Works, 1997; Hidden Art of Hackney, The Rosemary Branch, from 1998; Highgate Church Mixed, 1999; and Modern & Contemporary British Art, The Millinery Works, 2000.

Rita DUFFY 1959– She was mainly a figurative and narrative artist, whose pictures were often autobiographical, including themes and images of Irish identity, history and politics. Duffy was born in Belfast, Northern Ireland, and graduated at the Art and Design Centre, obtaining her master's from the University of Ulster. In 2002 she showed at Lead White Gallery, Dublin, the series House to House: eight large female portraits from the Quaker Cottage cross-community centre for families which had experienced violence. The exhibition toured to Northern Ireland and New York. Lead White featured Duffy's work at ART2003, Business Design Centre, Islington, in 2003. In 2004 the Art and Design Gallery, University of Hertfordshire, Hatfield, organised Duffy's show Contemplating an Iceberg in which she used "the *Titanic* as a metaphor for Northern Ireland's struggle in the 20th Century." It included a video of icebergs filmed during a residency in Newfoundland. In 2005 Tom Elkin, mayor of Belfast, backed Duffy's proposal that an iceberg be towed to the Belfast shipyard where the *Titanic* was built, drawing attention to a quarter of the city that had been redeveloped. Jacqueline Stanley chose Duffy as an Artist of the Day at Flowers Central in 2004.

Terry DUFFY 1948– Painter, born in Liverpool, who studied at the College of Art there, 1973–6. He was Liverpool chairman of the British Art and Design Association. Duffy's mixed show appearances included Contemporary Art Society art market; the Francis Graham-Dixon and Benjamin Rhodes Galleries; and in 1991–2 John Moores Exhibition, Liverpool, where he showed the abstract: The Miraculous Draught of Fishes. He showed solo at Air Gallery, 1981, Harris Museum and Art Gallery, Preston, where he had a North West Arts Major Fellowship, 1984; Laing Art Gallery in Newcastle upon Tyne, 1989; and The New Millennium Gallery, St Ives, 1997. Lived in the Wirral Peninsula, also having a studio in east London.

Dinah DUFTON 1967– Painter whose facial images were "inspired by notions of identity and perceptions of the visual ideal," as at her first major solo show at Mark Jason Fine Art, 2002. Dufton studied at St Martin's/Central School in 1983. Exhibitions included Vanessa Suchar, Le Salon, from 2000 and Roman Black Gallery and Apart, both 2001. Among commissioning clients were Credit Suisse, Deutsche Bank, Bank of America and Apollo Records.

Alexandra du GARD 1974– Versatile artist who did a foundation diploma at Central St Martin's College of Art & Design, 1993–4, graduating with honours in fine art, painting, Winchester School of Art, 1994–7. In her work she tried to draw attention to the distinctions between painting, installation and domestic design. Her pictures thus shifted between consumer object and painting, as in the mixed show Exterior/Interior, Hammerson plc, 1998.

Thomas Cantrell DUGDALE 1880–1952 Painter mainly of portraits in oil; textile designer. Born in Blackburn, Lancashire, T C Dugdale studied at Manchester School of Art, Royal College of Art, the City and Guilds School in Kennington, then at the Académie Julian and Atelier Colarossi, Paris. From early in the century he showed with the NEAC and RA, being elected RA in 1943. Having served in the Army during World War I, he held an exhibition in 1919 at the Leicester Galleries of pictures of the Middle East. Married to the painter Amy Katherine Browning. During the inter-war period Dugdale consolidated his position as a leading portrait painter and was for 20 years from 1919 art adviser to Tootal Broadhurst Lee, the textile company. Exhibited widely in Britain and overseas, the Tate Gallery and many provincial galleries acquiring his work. Lived in London.

Arthur Radclyffe DUGMORE 1870–1955 Painter and printmaker of landscapes, animals and birds. Born in Betws-y-coed, Wales, after an international schooling Dugmore studied art in Italy and America. He went on to travel widely to study wild life in Europe, America, Africa and Asia, sometimes lecturing. He also wrote magazine articles and published many books, including *Nature and the Camera* and *African Jungle Life*. Lived in Christchurch, Hampshire, and was president of the Southbourne Art Society, 1947–50.

John DUGUID 1906–1961 Painter, teacher and traveller, associated with the Downshire Hill group of artists in London's Hampstead. His brother was the writer Julian Duguid, author of *Green Hell*. After Harrow School and New College, Oxford, Duguid (pronounced Doogid) studied there with Sydney Carline at Ruskin School of Drawing in the late 1920s, then at Bauhaus in Germany with Josef Albers and Wassily Kandinsky, 1931–2. Duguid's letters to the painter Richard Carline graphically illustrate the tense atmosphere at the Bauhaus between Nazis and Communists. In 1930 Duguid had sailed with Carline to Venezuela on one of the last square-rigged ships, *Grace Harwar*. Duguid worked and taught in Chile from 1936–48. He showed at Goupil Gallery, RA, LG and contributed to an exhibition of Negro Art at Adams Gallery in 1935. Had a solo show at Grabowski Gallery, 1960. Died in Aberystwyth General Hospital. A memorial show was organised by Anglo-Chilean Society at Canning House, Belgrave Square, in 1962. The catalogue is an excellent review of his life and work. Abbot Hall Art Gallery, Kendal, holds Duguid's pictures.

Ken DUKES 1943– Artist in mixed media, acrylic and wood, stage designer and teacher, brother of the artist Ashley Dukes. He studied at Swansea College of Art, Brighton Polytechnic, then taught in schools with all age groups, eventually in a sixth-form college. Work in the theatre included repertory and small touring opera companies. Exhibited with SWG of which he was a member, having solo shows at Blue Room in Weymouth, and in Worcester at the City Art Gallery, Arts Workshop and Swan Theatre. Influences cited were Josef Albers, William Coldstream, Euan Uglow, Carl André and Henri Edmond Cross. Lived in Worcester.

Robert DUKES 1965– Painter, mainly of still life, born in Hull, Yorkshire, who attended Grimsby School of Art, 1981–4, then the Slade School of Fine Art under Lawrence Gowing, Euan Uglow and Patrick George, 1984–8. Group exhibitions included Cheltenham Drawing, from 1998, and The Discerning Eye, Mall Galleries, and RA Summer Exhibition, both from 2000. Lived in London.

Edmund DULAC 1882–1953 Leading book illustrator, decorative artist and painter. Born in Toulouse, France, he initially studied law at Toulouse University, then attended the Art School for three years, followed by brief studies at Académie Julian, Paris. Although he had shown portraits at the Paris Salon early in the century, Dulac was especially attracted by British book illustration, so he moved to England to work on periodicals such as *The Pall Mall Magazine* and in 1912 took British naturalisation. Dulac proved a versatile artist, designing theatrical costumes and scenery, producing designs for medals, banknotes and stamps, as well as designing furniture. He was a fastidious draughtsman, whose most notable achievement was his illustrations for fine books, including Edgar Allan Poe's *The Bells and Other Poems*, 1912, Robert Louis Stevenson's *Treasure Island*, 1927, and Alexander Pushkin's *The Golden Cockerel*, 1950. Represented in a number of public collections. A centenary exhibition toured from Mappin Art Gallery, Sheffield, 1982–3. Dulac's death was probably brought about by a heart attack, prompted by his late enthusiasm for flamenco dancing. Lived in London.

David DULY 1946– Artist, designer and teacher, born in Hastings, Sussex. He studied physiology and pathology in Oxford, and art at the Ruskin School there, at the Brassey Institute and at Brighton College of Art. Work experience included theatre design and direction and teaching anatomy and drawing, including classes in Winchester. Duly's group shows included St Edmunds Gallery, Salisbury, 1977, and in 1979 Centra, Reading, and Hayward Annual. Solo exhibitions/performances included Boldrewood Gallery, Southampton, 1975.

Elizabeth Althea du MANOIR 1910– Portrait artist, born in Bushey, Hertfordshire, daughter of the Royal Academician figure and portrait painter George Harcourt. She studied at Slade School of Fine Art, was a member of SWA and showed in England, America and South Africa, signing work with initials. Settled finally in Charmouth, Dorset.

Royston du MAURIER-LEBEK: *see* **ROYSTON**

Ted DUMMETT 1906–1989 Self-taught painter in oil, acrylic and watercolour, sometimes known by his full name, Edwin James Dummett. He was born at Castle Cary, Somerset. Worked in the building trade until 1939, was then in HM Forces until 1945, was a civil engineer, 1945–71, retiring to Trefriw, Gwynedd. He was elected RCamA in 1977, in 1978 to its governing council. Dummett won a number of Italian awards, including Accademico d'Italia con Medaglia d'Oro, Salsomaggiore; Premio Il Centauro d'Oro, Accademia Italia, Salsomaggiore, 1982; Diploma di Maestro di Pittura Honoris Causa, Seminario Internazionale d'Arte Moderna e Contemporanea, Salsomaggiore, 1983. His work appeared in 1972 show An Alternative Tradition, WAC and Scottish Arts Council tours. Also showed at Williamson Art Gallery, Birkenhead; Victoria Art Gallery, Conway; Mostyn Art Gallery, Llandudno; and Salon des Nations, Paris.

Elizabeth DUN 1923–1995 Artist in various media, excluding oil, using figurative and abstract modes. She was born in Rawalpindi, India, where her father was British Army medical officer. Began school in Heliopolis, Egypt, being sent aged eight to board at Wycombe Abbey preparatory school, then went to Sherborne and read social studies at Edinburgh University. Studied art in Italy in the studio of Renato Guttuso and first exhibited. Then worked part-time in London hospitals to enable her to study at Central School of Arts and Crafts. Went to Hong Kong where she was director of the Save the Children Fund, creating day and residential centres for poor street children. Studied art with Lui Shou Kwan, her paintings then reflecting a mix of Chinese and Western styles. Returned to England, she spent 17 years at Westminster Hospital, caring for neurological patients and their families. Created paintings, embroideries and stained glass in studios in Islington and Spitalfields. Travelled repeatedly to Italy, perfecting her Italian. Became the first woman to qualify as a London Guide, guiding on the continent, too, in Italian. Exhibitions included Comedy Gallery, 1961; Ashmolean Museum, Oxford, 1969; Warwick Gallery, Warwick, 1972; Pinacoteca Civica, Macerata, Italy, 1981; and Sackhouse Gallery, Wells-next-the-Sea, 1985.

Emma DUNBAR 1961– Artist using variety of techniques, with a strong sense of colour and decoration, whose prolific output reflected her fondness for travel. She gained an honours degree in fine art, printmaking, from West Surrey College of Art and Design, Farnham, 1981–4, and then exhibited widely. Group exhibitions included Sue Williams Gallery, 1988; CCA Galleries, Farnham, from 1990; Turtle Fine Art, Cheltenham, 1992; Ansty House, Alton, 1996; and Artists of Fame & Promise, Panter & Hall, 2002. Had a solo show at Wandle Gallery, Sutton, 1985, later ones including New Ashgate Gallery, Farnham, 1998.

Evelyn DUNBAR 1906–1960 Painter, mural artist, illustrator and teacher, born in Reading, Berkshire. She studied at Rochester and Chelsea Schools of Art and Royal College of Art, 1929–33. A member of the Society of Mural Painters, she painted murals at Brockley County School, Kent, 1933–6, and at the Training College, Bletchley, in Buckinghamshire, 1958–60. During World War II she was an Official War Artist, being especially known for her paintings of the Women's Land Army. Was a visiting teacher at Ruskin School of Drawing, Oxford, from 1950. Latterly she concentrated on portraits. There was a strong pastoral theme in Dunbar's work, and she was an apt choice, with Cyril Mahoney, to illustrate *Gardener's Choice*, in 1937. Showed with NEAC and Goupil Gallery. In 2006, an exhibition at the St Barbe Art Gallery, Lymington, included many of her major works. It was curated by Gill Clarke, whose biography of Dunbar was published that year by Sansom & Company. Imperial War Museum, Tate Gallery and Manchester City Art Gallery hold her work. Died near Ashford, Kent.

Lennox DUNBAR 1952– Painter, printmaker and teacher, born in Aberdeen, where he attended Gray's School of Art, 1969–74, eventually returning there as printmaking subject leader. After studying at Gray's, Dunbar was etching technician at Peacock Printmakers, 1978–86; visiting artist-tutor at Louisiana State University, America, 1986; also a visiting lecturer at various art schools. Awards included a series of travel awards across Europe and to America; the RSA's Meyer Oppenheim Award, 1976 (he was made an RSA associate in 1990); its Latimer Award in 1978, the year he set up the Amsterdam Studio for the Scottish Arts Council; the RSA Guthrie Award, 1984; and Shell Expro and the RSA Highland Society of London Awards in the early 1990s. In 1987 Dunbar won 1st Prize in the Paisley Art Institute Drawing Competion, two years after winning the 2nd Prize. He was a Major Prizewinner, Cleveland Drawing Biennale, 1989. Selected exhibitions included Double Elephant, British Prints, Barbican Centre, 1985; Printmakers' Drawings, Mercury Gallery, Edinburgh, 1987; and Paperworks IV, Seagate Gallery, Dundee, 1993. There was an important solo show at Hatton Gallery, Newcastle, and Peacock Printmakers, Aberdeen, 1995. The strongly patterned pictures in this exhibition drew on implements and materials used to shape the traditional landscape around Dunbar's studio at Auchnagatt, as well as new images such as kit house building and plantation trees. Collections holding his work include Scottish Arts Council, RSA, and Aberdeen, Paisley and Middlesbrough public galleries.

Peter DUNBAR 1929–1983 Painter, illustrator, graphic designer and art editor, working in oil and pen and ink, born and died in London. He attended Woolwich Polytechnic art school, 1944–46; Camberwell School of Art, 1946–7, where John Minton and Lawrence Gowing were influences; and the Anglo-French Art Centre, 1948–9. Dunbar was an illustrator on the *Financial Times*; art director of *The Economist*, 1959–68, then a consultant; director of PD Associates; Matthews, Miller, Dunbar; and art director, Ballantine Books. Group shows included St George's Gallery, 1953; 4 Young Painters, Blackheath, 1955 (the others were Robert Hunt, Gordon Richards and Owen Wood); and Camberwell School of Art, 1964–5.

DUNBAR-MARSHALL-MALAGOLA: *see* **MARSHALL-MALAGOLA**

Amanda DUNCAN 1963– She graduated with honours from Ravensbourne College of Art & Design, 1983–7. Duncan won The Prince's Youth Business Trust Award in 1989, the year she appeared in East End Open Studios while based at Red Cow Studios. She was a member of the Society of Designer-Craftsmen, The London Potters Association and The Kent Potters Association.

Ana DUNCAN 1960– Self-taught sculptor, born in Dublin, Ireland, who studied bronze casting at the National College of Art & Design, 1990, for three years. Exhibitions included Solomon Gallery, Dublin, from 1996; John Martin of London, 1997; Lavitt Gallery, Cork; and The Lost Gallery, Strathdon, 2003.

Clare DUNCAN 1956– Artist in various and mixed media, including performance work, and poet, born Anne Clare Cardew Duncan, who also worked under her married name Clare Turner. She was born in Arusha, Tanganyika, and was educated in Edinburgh, attending Telford College, 1975–6, and from 1979–81 Portsmouth and Canterbury Colleges of Art, then Lanchester Polytechnic. Was elected UA in 1979, also exhibiting at SWA and RSA, having a solo show at Hiscock Gallery, Portsmouth. Lived for a time in Cranfield, Bedfordshire.

Clive DUNCAN 1944– Sculptor and teacher, born in London, married to the painter Janet McQueen. Studied at High Wycombe College of Art, 1961–4; Camberwell School of Arts and Crafts, 1964–6, under Sydney Sheppard and Giacomo Baragli; and City and Guilds of London Art School, 1966–8, under James Butler and David McFall. Taught sculpture at Heatherley School of Art (head of School); was principal lecturer in charge of sculpture at Sir John Cass School of Art, London Guildhall University (head of School, 1972–1993), and was a visiting teacher at Slade Summer School and City and Guilds Sculpture School. Was elected a fellow of RBS in 1983, a member of RBA in 1984 and was president of the Thomas Heatherley Trust, 1973–94. Apart from portrait sculptures, Duncan's work, in a variety of materials, was dominated by serious political, social and sexual themes. He developed ideas in the early 1970s for sculpture, dance and music. Among his portraits is Myfanwy Piper, wife of John Piper. His nine-foot-high Rose Images are also notable. Exhibited frequently at RA fom 1968, also RP, Royal Glasgow Institute of the Fine Arts, Portland Sculpture Park, Nicholas Treadwell Gallery and elsewhere. He was an exhibition consultant for Sotheby's and produced a booklet for Victoria & Albert Museum: *From Lost Wax to Found Bronze*. Solo shows included London Guildhall and Playhouse Gallery, Harlow. Lived in Shiplake, Oxfordshire.

Colin DUNCAN 1966– Painter and designer, born in Floriana, Malta, who studied at Cumbria and Canterbury Colleges of Art & Design. He was stage set designer for Blur, world tour, 1993, and construction assistant for the Agongo Exhibition, Edinburgh International Festival, 1994. Group shows included Herbert Read Gallery, Canterbury, from 1986; CD Show, Collective Gallery, Edinburgh, 1992; Demarco European Art Foundation, Edinburgh, 1994; and Royal Over-Seas League Open, 1995. Had a solo show at Fruitmarket Gallery, Edinburgh, 1991, later ones including Chessel's Gallery, Edinburgh, 1994. In 2003 Duncan had an exhibition of new work at Scotch Malt Whisky Society, 19 Greville Street, following four months in Australia, Cambodia and Thailand, also showing paintings based on the female nude done in Spain, where he was based in Barcelona.

James DUNCAN 1946– Painter who specialised in stylised landscapes and figurative work influenced by the Scottish landscape where he lived in Aberdeenshire. For some years he restored a castle there, making a gallery to show work by himself and other artists with local connections. Duncan studied at Edinburgh College of Art. Awards included the Andrew Carnegie Award and a bronze medal, Salon des Nations. Shows included RSA Summer Exhibition, 1983; Greenwich Gallery and Museum Gallery in Elgin, both 1986; Talent Store, 1987; and in 1997 he shared an exhibition, Land & Sea, with Christopher Stiling at Gallery Forty Seven.

Janet McQueen DUNCAN 1944– Painter, designer and teacher, born in Marlow, Buckinghamshire, wife of the sculptor Clive Duncan. She worked in watercolour, drawing media and oil, landscape and studies of light on water being notable themes. Studied at High Wycombe School of Art. She was a theatre set designer, was involved in theatre wardrobe, and taught art to advanced level and privately. Showed with RBA, at Castle Hill Gallery in High Wycombe and at Henley's Arts and Music Festival. Had many solo exhibitions including Century Galleries in Henley and Hartley Wintney and in Windsor, and also worked to commission. Lived in Shiplake, Oxfordshire.

Jean DUNCAN 1933– Painter, printmaker and video artist, originally known as Jean Fraser, whose son Alastair Duncan was a tapestry artist. She was born in Edinburgh, where she obtained her diploma at the College of Art, 1951–5, under William Gillies, Robin Philipson and Leonard Rosoman, gaining a postgraduate diploma in printmaking, 1980–1, under David Barker at University of Ulster. Became co-director of Seacourt Print Workshop at Bangor, County Down, Northern Ireland, having settled in Belfast. She was an academician of RUA and a member of the Artists' Association of Ireland. Interested "in the power of repetitive shapes and rhythms in visual art", in 1993 Duncan began a series of etchings prompted by composer John Tavener's *The Protecting Veil*, shown at Royal Northern College of Music, Manchester, in 1994. Later solo shows included One Oxford Street, Belfast, 1995. Awards included Mini Print International, Cadaqués, Spain, 1988, and Arts Council of Northern Ireland, 1990. It holds her work, as do University College in Dublin, Dundee City Art Gallery and other public collections. Duncan held a residency at Tyrone Guthrie Centre, Annaghmakerrig.

John DUNCAN 1866–1945 Painter, illustrator, mural artist, stained glass designer and teacher, born in Dundee, Angus. As a schoolboy he began evening classes at the local School of Art and for some years became a newspaper illustrator in Dundee and London. Further studies followed in Antwerp and Düsseldorf, in Dundee with George Dutch Davidson and in Rome, where the early Italian artists made a lasting impression. In Edinburgh Duncan became involved with the Celtic Revival leader Patrick Geddes, for whose home he painted murals. After a visit to America with Geddes in 1899, Duncan taught at Chicago University, 1902–4, before settling back in Edinburgh. He was made RSA in 1923 and RSW in 1930. Scottish National Gallery of Modern Art holds his work.

McG DUNCAN: *see* **T G McGILL DUNCAN**

Marjorie DUNCAN 1905– Painter, born in London, who studied at Froebel Educational Institute and art with Bernard Adams. She was a member of The Eastbourne Group and exhibited with NS, RP, Royal Glasgow Institute of the Fine Arts and elsewhere. Lived for many years in Alfriston, Sussex.

Mary DUNCAN 1885–1964 Painter and etcher, born in Bromley, Kent, where she attended the School of Art. Later went to the Slade School of Fine Art and studied in Paris. Exhibited extensively at RHA, RA, NEAC, RSA, ROI and Goupil Gallery. Leamington Art Gallery and Plymouth City Museum and Art Gallery among others hold her work. Lived at Mousehole, Cornwall.

Stephen DUNCAN 1952– Sculptor, born and worked in London, who did a foundation course in art and design at Watford School of Art, 1970–1; graduated with a first-class honours degree in sculpture and printmaking from Wimbledon School of Art, 1971–4; gained a postgraduate certificate in sculpture and printmaking, with a Silver Medal, Royal Academy of Art, 1974–7; with further postgraduate studies, under a British School Scholarship, at Accademia di Belle Arti, Rome, 1978–9; and was at British School at Rome, Rome Award in Sculpture, 1992–3. Teachers included Peter Startup at Wimbledon and Willi Soukop at Royal Academy Schools. Worked in Britain, widely on the continent and in America, and obtained a South East Arts Travel Award, from 1973. As well as sculpting, Duncan practised as a poet, lectured in fine art in universities and colleges and wrote for journals including *Artscribe*. Duncan's work also appeared in the Bridport Prize, Hutchinson and Quartet anthologies, the *TLS*, *Poetry Review*, *New Welsh Review*, *Daily Telegraph* and *Poetry Matters*. The use of mythology, metaphor and narrative were important. He was an associate of RBS and took part in group shows including Artspace, Oxford, and Philippe Daverio Gallery, both 1994, and Ben Uri Gallery from 1994. Had a solo exhibition at St Albans Cathedral in 1979, later ones including Lanchester Gallery, Coventry University, 1995, and Woodlands Art Gallery, 1997. Commissions included River God relief at Elm Quay, Nine Elms Lane, 1988, and Lotus, bronze sculpture at Nottingham Trent University, 1994. Wandsworth Council and National Hospitals Collection also hold works.

Terence Edward DUNCAN: *see* **TERRY**

Brian Redvers DUNCE 1937– Artist in all two-dimensional media, and teacher, born in Surrey, where he had a studio at Wonersh. In the late 1950s he studied at Guildford and Salisbury Schools of Art and at Reading University, teachers including Jack Rodway and Peter Startup. From 1960 Dunce worked in art and design practice and was involved in the curating and design of Arts Council exhibitions. British romantic art, mythology, folk culture, Celtic imagery and the work of Paul Nash and Ivon Hitchens were influences on Dunce's work, which included autobiographical, moon and ambiguous landscape series as well as a modern crucifixion, sponsored by Winsor & Newton. Dunce was a member of PS and took part in numerous mixed shows, including Bankside Gallery, RI, NEAC, London Contemporary Art Fair, Kettle's Yard in Cambridge and Mall Galleries. By the mid-1990s he had had 14 solo shows including Chelsea School of Art, University of Surrey, Yehudi Menuhin School, Cobham, and St Martin's Gallery. Taught at Chelsea School of Art, Bath Academy of Art in Corsham, Middlesex University, Heatherley's School of Fine Art and Yehudi Menuhin School. Victoria & Albert Museum, Price Waterhouse & Company and English Trust Company hold examples.

Mark DUNFORD 1964– Painter, draughtsman and teacher, born in Poole, Dorset, married to the artist Kay Vinson. He did foundation studies at Bournemouth & Poole College of Art & Design, 1980–2, gaining an honours degree in fine art from Slade School of Fine Art, 1982–7, teachers including Lawrence Gowing, Patrick George, Euan Uglow, Norman Norris, Patrick Symons and Stuart Brisley. Won The Robert Ross Scholarship, from the Slade, and the Royal Academy Richard Ford Award (enabling him to study at the Prado Museum, Madrid, Spain), both 1987; and Young Artists' Award, RI and Winsor & Newton, 1993. After part-time teaching at Bournemouth & Poole College and Symondsbury School of Art in the late 1980s Dunford taught painting and drawing full-time at James Allen's

Girls School from 1987, becoming head of art, 1994, in 1998 organising To See is to Understand, a show of pupils' work at the Mall Galleries. Dunford was elected a LG member, 2001, having shown with it from 1993. His work was illustrated in its 2003 ninetieth-anniversary commemorative volume. Other group shows included Churzee Gallery, 1989; A New Perspective, Leighton House, 1990; May Exhibition, Vaughan/Luyten Gallery, 1993; Thirteen Contemporary Artists, Dulwich Picture Gallery, 1996; and Christie's, in aid of Paintings in Hospitals, 2001. He shared an exhibition with Robert Brooks at Sheridan Russell Gallery, 1998. For Dunford, "drawing is all.... Painting is very difficult and exciting." Lived in London.

Mike DUNFORD 1946– Film-oriented artist, born in Oxford, who studied sculpture and film at Goldsmiths' College. He was involved with the London Filmmakers' Co-op, 1968–70, and started work in 16-millimetre film. The period 1973–4 saw the culmination of materialist work in film with *Logical Proposition* and in 1975, Dunford became engaged in political films. He was included in the big British Council exhibition English Art Today 1960–76, at Palazzo Reale, Milan, Italy, in 1976. By then, his films included *Angie*, 1968; *Wave Manipulations*, 1971; *Logical Propositions*, 1973; and *Still Image*, 1975.

Joanna Elizabeth DUNHAM 1936– Actress and artist, born in Luton, Bedfordshire, daughter of the architect and artist Peter Browning Dunham. She was educated at Bedales, the Slade School of Fine Art, 1954–6, and the Royal Academy of Dramatic Art, afterwards working as a professional actress on the stage, screen and television. Her first professional appearance was at the Royal Court, Liverpool, in 1958, in *The Deserters*, with a London début at the Westminster in *Visit to a Small Planet*, 1960. Dunham joined the Old Vic company in 1961 and made her New York début in 1962 as Juliet in *Romeo and Juliet*, which she had played at the Old Vic, touring America and Europe in this role. Other parts were Vera in *A Month in the Country*, Cambridge Theatre, 1965; Desdemona in *Othello*, Oxford Playhouse, 1970; and, at the Hong Kong Theatre Festival, Vera West in *Rosmersholm*, 1978. Dunham first appeared in films as Mary Magdalen in *The Greatest Story Ever Told*, 1965. Television appearances included *The Passenger*, in the BBC1 series *Francis Durbridge Presents...*, 1971; Granada Television's *Love Among the Artists*, 1979; and the BBC1 thriller *Moondial*, 1988. As an artist she exhibited with the RP and Ipswich Art Society, showed solo with Piers Feetham Gallery and had work produced in greetings card form. Her book about her great aunt, *Amy K Browning – an Impressionist in the Women's Movement*, was published to coincide with the Browning exhibition at Christchurch Mansion, Ipswich, in 1995, which she organised. Dunham signed her work Joanna Dunham, Joanna Elizabeth Dunham and J E D. Lived in Sternfield, Suffolk.

Peter DUNHAM 1911–1997 Painter in oil and watercolour and architect, born in Luton, Bedfordshire, father of the actress and artist Joanna Elizabeth Dunham. From 1928, he studied at the Bartlett School of Architecture and part-time at Slade School of Fine Art. Dunham was a fellow of RIBA and was a practising architect from 1933, when he was a Donaldson medallist. He always painted, mostly landscapes in East Anglia, Italy and Austria, and was influenced by his uncle and aunt, the painters T C Dugdale and A K Browning. Was a member of Architect Artists of RIBA and showed at RA Summer Exhibitions, in East Anglia and in Austria. Lived at Sternfield, Saxmundham, Suffolk.

James DUNKLEY 1944– Dunkley studied at Birmingham College of Art, 1960–4. Group appearances included Athena Art Awards, at Barbican Centre, and MM Arts Inaugural Exhibition, Butler's Wharf, both 1987; Heads & Figures, Anderson O'Day Gallery, 1988; and Critics Choice 5, Air Gallery, and East End Open Studios, based at Richmond House Studios, both 1989. In that year Dunkley also had a solo exhibition at Albemarle Gallery.

Keith DUNKLEY 1942– Painter and teacher, born in Corbridge, Northumberland. He studied at Kingston School of Art, 1960–4, then Royal Academy Schools, 1964–7. Dunkley taught at Sheridan College, Toronto, in Canada, 1969–73. He showed with RWS, of which he was a member, RA and elsewhere, and from 1978 had a series of one-man exhibitions with John Davies in Stow-on-the-Wold. Dunkley painted in the Scottish borders country, in France and elsewhere on the continent and lived near Edinburgh.

Sue DUNKLEY 1942– Painter, printmaker, teacher and writer. She studied at Bath Academy in Corsham, 1959–61, Chelsea School of Art, 1961–3, and Slade School of Fine Art, 1963–5. Among her awards were a Morland Lewis Travelling Scholarship to Australia, 1963, and a Boise Travelling Scholarship to Italy, 1965. In 1967 she was art correspondent for the magazine *Nova*. From about this time she began a series of teaching appointments, which included Chelsea School of Art, St Martin's School of Art, Goldsmiths' College and Slade School of Fine Art. Undertook a number of grant-sponsored work trips and was artist and technical advisor on location for filming in Donegal in 1991. Unpeopled landscapes and small-scale, intimate studies of women were aspects of Dunkley's art, shown in mixed exhibitions at LG, Nicholas Treadwell Gallery and abroad; and in solo shows at Bolsover Street Gallery, 1973, Thumb Gallery from 1979 and Curwen Gallery, 1986. Dunkley's show Journey, at Curwen in 2003, continued the artist's walking theme, this time along the Pacific shore of Australia, "a strange place, yet it held me." Borough of Camden and Unilever hold her work.

Alison DUNLOP 1958– Painter of still lifes, born in Canada, who completed postgraduate studies at Edinburgh College of Art in the 1980s, settling in Scotland. Showed widely there, winning frequent prizes. Elected RSW and was for several years president of Visual Arts Scotland. Work included in Panter & Hall's Artists of Fame and Promise in 2002. That gallery's 2003 exhibition 200 Years of Scottish Painting included Dunlop's oil still life Quill, typical of her meticulously detailed, slightly surreal and witty output.

Hazel Bruce DUNLOP 1911– Painter, mainly of portraits, born into a military family in British North Borneo and studied at Slade School of Fine Art with Henry Tonks, Philip Wilson Steer and Randolph Schwabe. She was married to the artist Francis Edwin Hodge. Member of the UA, with which she showed, also with SWA, ROI, RA and Paris Salon. Lived in London.

Ronald Ossory DUNLOP 1894–1973 Painter in oil of landscapes, seascapes, figure studies, portraits and still life. Born in Dublin, Dunlop studied at Manchester School of Art, then Wimbledon School of Art and in Paris. Had spent some time working in an advertising agency. He became a prolific exhibitor, venues including the RA, NEAC, Leicester and Redfern Galleries, RSA, RHA and the Royal Glasgow Institute of the Fine Arts. His first one-man show was at the Redfern Gallery, 1928. In 1923 Dunlop founded the Emotionist Group of writers and artists, and his own work is characterised by a painterly exuberance. Dunlop's work is in a number of public galleries, including the Tate. He wrote *Understanding Pictures* and his autobiography, *Struggling with Paint*, 1956. Lived at Barnham, Sussex.

Albert DUNN 1908– Landscape painter, born in Farnborough, Hampshire. He was educated in Newcastle upon Tyne, studying art there, 1925–30, with William Fenton. He settled in Powick, Worcestershire, belonged to Worcester Art Society and Malvern Art Club, showed in RA Summer Exhibitions and had several solo exhibitions at Malvern Art Gallery.

Alfred DUNN 1937– Artist and teacher, born in Wombwell, Yorkshire. He studied at Royal College of Art, 1959–61, eventually becoming senior tutor there. Showed at Redfern Gallery from 1965 and extensively in Germany and Italy. Arts Council holds his work. Lived at Trawden, Lancashire. Sometimes signed work E(rnest) A(lfred) Dunn.

Anne DUNN 1929– Painter, born in London. She was married first to the artist Michael Wishart, in whose autobiography *High Diver* she appears, then Rodrigo Moynihan. She attended Chelsea School of Art, 1947–50, the Anglo-French Art Centre, 1951, then in 1952 Académie Julian, Paris. From the mid-1950s she was a regular exhibitor for many years at Leicester Galleries, also participating in mixed shows at NEAC, RA and abroad. From 1964–8 was editor of *Art and Literature*. Had many solo exhibitions, starting with a series from 1957 at Leicester Galleries, then an extended series from 1967 at Fischbach Gallery, New York, later shows including Maison des Jeunes et de la Culture, Paris, in 1988, and Christopher Hull Gallery in 1990. Arts Council, CAS and other public collections hold her work. Lived in Lambesc, France.

Ernest Alfred DUNN: *see* **Alfred DUNN**

George DUNN 1914– Sculptor who was educated at Bemrose School, Derby, 1926–32, where he proved a distinguished academic and sports all-rounder. Gained a scholarship to Derby School of Arts and Crafts, 1932–7, where he won a string of first prizes for landscape and still life, designed and painted scenery for Derby's Centenary of Local Government Exhibition in 1935, exhibited at Winsor & Newton's Exhibition of Contemporary Art in Birmingham in 1936 and was secretary of Derby Graphic Club, 1935–7. Studied at Slade School of Fine Art, 1937–40, on a number of Derby Borough Major Scholarships, winning a series of prizes, with a refresher course in sculpture and drawing, 1946–7. Eventually joined staff of Leeds College of Art, in charge of photographic records, and was included in The Teaching Image, College staff show in 1964 at Leeds City Art Gallery. Showed elsewhere in Yorkshire.

Michael DUNN 1968– Painter of detailed pictures, who was educated at the Royal Belfast Academical Institution; gained a foundation diploma at Liverpool Polytechnic, 1990–1; and an honours degree in design for communication media (illustration), Manchester Metropolitan University, 1991–4. Mixed shows included Night and Day Café, Manchester, 1994; Laing Landscape Competition, Salford Art Gallery, 1995; Magpie Studios, Belfast, 1996; and Glimpse, Belfast Studios, 1999. Solo shows included Tom Caldwell Gallery, Belfast, 1998. Lived in Newtownabbey, County Antrim.

Reginald George DUNN 1907– Painter, born in Windsor, Berkshire. The Reverend Dunn studied at the All Nations Missionary College, in London, privately in Greece during World War II and then at Torquay School of Art, 1949–50. Showed RCamA and elsewhere and lived in Paignton, Devon, for some years.

Joe DUNNE 1957– Painter, born and lived in Dublin, Ireland, who obtained his diploma in design at the capital's National College of Art & Design, 1978, with studies at the Charles H Cecil Studios, Florence, in 1994. Dunne's exhibitions and awards included Oireachtas, 1987–8 (Life & Pensions Award for landscape, 1987); National Portrait Awards, Arnotts, Dublin (Under 35s Award, 1990); National Portrait Awards, Arnotts, (Anniversary Award, 1993); and RHA Annual Exhibition (Silver Medal, 1986, Niccolo Caracciolo RHA Awards 1993 and 2001). Among other group exhibitions were Tom Caldwell Gallery, Belfast, 1994; BP Portrait Award, National Portrait Gallery, London, 1997; Watercolour C21, RWS, 1999; Jorgensen Fine Art, Dublin, from 2001; and Boyle Arts Festival, County Roscommon, 2004. Later solo shows included RHA, 2001, and Jorgensen Fine Art, 2004. He gained a fellowship at Ballinglen Arts Foundation, Ballycastle, County Mayo, 2002, and a residency, Scoil Naithí, Ballinteer, 2004. The Royal Dublin Society, The Adelaide Hospital in Dublin, Office of Public Works, Dublin Dental School and Hospital and other public and private collections hold examples.

Dorothy DUNNETT 1923–2001 Author and painter, born in Dunfermline, Fife, as Dorothy Halliday, under which name she published thrillers. Dunnett's cult status as a writer stemmed from her intricate, carefully researched, multi-volume historical novels. As a painter, her love of landscape is evident in the six-volume *Lymond Chronicles*, which covered 15 years in the life of a sixteenth-century figure, Francis Crawford of Lymond. The first book, *The Game of Kings*, appeared in the early 1960s in America, then in Britain. Her background as an painter also emerges from references to Renaissance painting in her eight-volume saga *The House of Niccolo*, set in the previous century. Dunnett was educated at James Gillespie's High School for Girls, Edinburgh, where she was partly contemporary with the novelist Muriel Spark, who transformed it into the Marcia Blaine School in *The Prime of Miss Jean Brodie*. After Edinburgh College of Art, Dorothy attended Glasgow School of Art. Dunnett worked as a civil servant until 1955, from 1950 also being a professional portrait painter. She showed at the RSA and she was commissioned by prominent Scottish public figures. Dunnett was encouraged in her twin careers by her husband Sir Alastair Dunnett, editor of *The Scotsman* newspaper. She died in Edinburgh.

Isabel (Isabella) McGregor DUNNETT 1876–1965 Watercolourist, printmaker and teacher, born in Montrose, Angus. She studied at the National Art Training School, 1893–6, and from 1896 at the Royal College of Art, winning the Queen's Prize for Drawing. Dunnett's watercolours included floral studies, herbaceous borders, seascapes and a few exceptional portraits, mostly of her family, in watercolour and charcoal. Several black-and-white engravings, in limited series, are among her finest works. In 1900 she married Harding William Dunnett (1868–1949), later secretary to the Manila Railroad in the Philippines, and was the mother of twin sons, the artist Valentine and the architectural writer and designer Harding McGregor Dunnett. The family lived initially at Ashtead, Surrey, where she taught art locally, for a time in Hereford and Montrose and latterly in Blackheath, southeast London.

Valentine (Val) McGregor DUNNETT 1909–1985 Enterprising and versatile artist and teacher, born in Ashtead, Surrey, son of Harding William Dunnett and the artist Isabel McGregor Dunnett. He was educated at Montrose Academy, Hereford Cathedral School and Dulwich College, where in 1923–5 he won the Melton Fisher, Founder's and Yates Thompson Prizes for Art (with the last, £25, he bought a BSA motor-cycle). Dunnett studied at Goldsmiths' College and taught at Beckenham, Sidcup and St Martin's Schools of Art, drawing and painting, 1945–71, and at Goldsmiths', from 1959 perspective, life drawing and sculptural welding. Dunnett painted many characterful portraits in oils. Some of his most original work was watercolours of steam trains and traction engines, for which he was especially noted, also Kentish landscapes and London scenes. Showed in Blackheath and at Dulwich. With Stanley Paine he illustrated G J Romanes' *Traction Engines in Retirement*, 1961. Fleeing from St Martin's Dunnett would take his students, including the designer Mary Quant, sketching by the Thames or at King's Cross Station, where he would convey his passion for steam. Unconventional and unmarried, Dunnett lived with his mother Val at Shooter's Hill, keeping a traction engine and three vintage Alvis cars in the front garden.

Chris DUNSEATH 1949– Sculpture and lecturer, who gained an honours degree at Gloucestershire College of Art and Design, Cheltenham, 1968–71; did postgraduate diploma studies at Slade School of Fine Art, 1971–3; and held a sculpture fellowship at Cardiff College of Art and Design, 1973–4. From 1986 Dunseath was associate senior lecturer head of sculpture, at Coventry School of Art and Design, Coventry University, his visiting lectureships including Cheltenham, Birmingham, Manchester, Falmouth and Portsmouth Colleges of Art, the John Makepeace School for Craftsmen, Royal Academy Sculpture School, University of Wales Institute in Cardiff and the Universities of Warwick and the West of England. His many group shows included New Sculpture, Ikon Gallery, Birmingham, 1978; Yorkshire Sculpture Park, 1980; Alwin Gallery, 1988; Portrait: An Exploration, The Coventry Gallery, 1994; and 2nd RWA Open Sculpture Exhibition, 1996. Had a solo show at Oriel Gallery, Cardiff, 1974, later ones including Department of National Heritage and Civic Trust, 1994. Dunseath won a major commission for West Bromwich High Street, Sandwell, 1989; another for The Waterfront, Dudley, for Richardson Developments, 1992. Arts Council, WAC, South West Arts, Henry Moore Institute in Leeds and other collections hold examples. Lived in Hinton St George, Somerset.

Jenny DUNSEATH 1978– Artist who studied at the Royal Academy Schools. In 2005 her Etching of an Egg Timer – Plan 2 was in the RA Summer Exhibition, and in the same year Allsopp Contemporary included her work in Next Step: Selected 2005 Graduates. Her large, abstract pâpier maché casts there were described as "spontaneous, experimental and hugely bold." Dunseath was at that time based in London.

Bernard DUNSTAN 1920– Painter, draughtsman and teacher, born in Teddington, Middlesex. He was married to the painter Diana Armfield. Dunstan was a painter on a small scale brought up in the Sickert-Degas-Vuillard tradition, who developed a keen following for his intimate interiors with nude and semi-draped figures and views of Venice. He studied at Byam Shaw School of Art, 1939, then Slade School of Fine Art, 1939–41. From 1946–9 taught at West of England School of Art in Bristol, Camberwell School of Art, 1950–64, Byam Shaw 1953–74, Ravensbourne Art College, 1959–64, and City and Guilds of London Art School, 1964–9. His reputation was established with a series of solo shows at Roland, Browse and Delbanco, then Agnew. He was a member of NEAC, RWA (being its president in 1979) and was elected RA in 1968. Among his several books were *Learning to Paint*, 1970, and *Painting Methods of the Impressionists*, 1976. Arts Council holds his work. Lived in Kew, Surrey.

Thea DUPAYS fl. from early 1950s– Painter, draughtsman and teacher who studied painting at Goldsmiths' College School of Art for four years in early 1950s. She then went to West Africa where she held her first solo show and illustrated books for Oxford University Press and Longmans. On returning to England in 1960 she settled in Bath and continued to illustrate, teach and paint, but family concerns reduced her painting time until in 1984 she returned seriously to work. Showed RWA, RP and Bath Art Society and in 1992 had solo show at Hill Gallery, Bradford-on-Avon. Dupays was notable as a landscape painter, with an ability to match her style to the place depicted.

H Enslin du PLESSIS 1894–1978 Painter and journalist, born in Standerton, Transvaal, South Africa. Was educated in Cape Town, but had no formal art training. During World War I saw service in wide area of Middle East and acted as a correspondent for newspapers in South Africa. Took up painting seriously in his thirties and showed in England from the late 1920s. Exhibited extensively with Goupil and Arlington Galleries; also Leicester Galleries; Roland, Browse and Delbanco; LG and elsewhere. Contemporary Art Society and Arts Council bought his work, which is in a number of South African galleries. Manchester City Art Gallery's Boats, La Rochelle, is typical of the artist's delicate, Impressionist manner. Press Club member who lived in London.

Jack DUPLOCK 1975– Painter, born in Bridport, Dorset, who attended Yeovil College of Art, 1993–4; Southampton Institute of Higher Education, 1994–7; and the Royal Academy Schools, 1997–00, appearing in the final year show. It included his atmospheric oil on canvas Flooded Forest. Duplock gained an Erasmus Travel Scholarship,

Greece, in 1996, a Vincent Harris Mural Prize, 1998, and a David Murray Landscape Travel Scholarship, Spain, 1999. Among Duplock's exhibitions were Delfos, Delphi Annexe, Athens School of Art, Greece, 1996; Night Display, Entwistle Gallery, 1997; Well, Foxley Studios, Charmouth, 1998; New Paintings, The Town Mill, Lyme Regis, 1999; Louder than Bombs, Millais Gallery, Southampton, 2000; John Moores Liverpool Exhibition, 2002; and The Valley, at Bloomberg SPACE, 2005. The catalogue of that show said: "The collaged pictures that Jack Duplock makes are somewhere between posters, film stills and images dredged from paperback horror." He had a solo exhibition at the Keith Talent Gallery in 2003. He lived in north London.

Charles DURANTY 1918–2006 Watercolourist, born in Romford, Essex, who was self-taught. He worked in journalism, agriculture and for most of his life in book publishing, finally with Gerald Duckworth & Company. He published a small collection of his verse, *Audition*. Duranty said that his pictures were "a personal interpretation of rural life in Essex and Suffolk in the past half century". He took part in many group shows, including Thackeray, New Grafton and Leicester Galleries; Roland, Browse & Delbanco; Mercury and Zwemmer Galleries and abroad. Solo exhibitions included Thackeray and New Grafton Galleries. Paintings in Hospitals, the Wentworth Hotel in Aldeburgh and private collections hold Duranty's works. Lived in Merrow, Guildford, Surrey.

Leslie DURBIN 1913–2005 Silversmith and designer, born the son of a railway clerk in Fulham, southwest London, who became one of the most notable British silversmiths of the twentieth century. Aged 13, he won a London County Council scholarship to study at the Central School of Arts and Crafts after normal schooling in the morning. Three years later, his department head at the Central recommended him as an apprentice to the leading silversmith of the day, Omar Ramsden, Durbin continuing with Central School classes in his spare time. In 1939 he won the second of two awards from the Worshipful Company of Goldsmiths, a travelling scholarship, enabling him to explore European art prior to World War II. While serving in the Royal Air Force Durbin was called on to decorate the Sword of Honour, designed by Professor R M Y Gleadowe, which was presented to the Soviet leader Joseph Stalin at the 1943 Tehran conference. Commissioned by King George VI, it honoured the defence of Stalingrad. After the war Durbin entered into partnership with Leonard Moss and he also collaborated with the glass engraver Laurence Whistler on prestigious commissions. Many ceremonial pieces followed. In 1982, the Goldsmiths' Company staged the exhibition Leslie Durbin: Fifty Years of Silversmithing. Durbin forged a second career latterly designing coins for the Royal Mint. In 1997, aged 84, he produced the reverse-side design for a gold £5 proof coin commemorating the golden wedding of Queen Elizabeth and Prince Philip. From 1940, Durbin was married to the painter Phyllis Ginger.

Sarah DURCAN 1969– Painter, born in London, who studied at National College of Art & Design, Dublin, and Winchester School of Art. She won an Arts Council materials grant, 1991; Arts Flight, 1994; and EVA Open Award, 1995. Group shows included Triskel Arts Centre, Cork, 1988; Iontas, Sligo Art Gallery, Sligo, 1993–4; Delfina Studios Gallery, Byam Shaw School and Royal Over-Seas League Open, all 1995. Had a solo show at Arts Council, Dublin, 1992.

James DURDEN 1878–1964 Painter born in Manchester, where he studied at the School of Art, then Royal College of Art. Exhibited RA, ROI, RP, Royal Glasgow Institute of the Fine Arts and Paris Salon, where he gained a silver medal in 1927. Also showed in the provinces, South Africa, New Zealand and Australia. Manchester City Art Gallery and several foreign galleries hold his work, which was reproduced by the Medici Society. Lived near Keswick, Cumberland.

Mark DURDEN 1964– Artist, born in Stourbridge, Worcestershire, who studied at Exeter, Glasgow and the University of Kent. He was a contributor to the group Common Culture (see separate entry). Lived in Stoke-on-Trent, Staffordshire.

Nommie DURELL 1905–1989 Painter and teacher, born and died in London, christened Mary Louise Lasenby. She was related to the Liberty family and was brought up in the libertarian arts and crafts tradition. After Roedean School she attended Slade School of Fine Art, married Harry Durell the architect and pioneered art teaching methods which gained the approval of Herbert Read and other educational progressives. Her exhibition of child art at Zwemmer Gallery in 1938 gained much attention. During World War II she and her husband, as conscientious objectors, moved to Dartington Hall and worked on the land. She resumed her teaching, including a spell at Bedales, then when divorced after the war set up a boarding-house in Hampstead. Journeyed annually to a cottage at Menton, on the French Riviera, to paint, later working each year in Greece. She had shown in mixed exhibitions such as NEAC before World War II, but much of her output remained unshown until Sally Hunter Fine Art exhibited some in 1992. Sally Hunter held further shows in 1994 and 2005 and there was one at Lauderdale House, Highgate, in 2000.

Terry DURHAM 1936– Versatile artist, born in East Ardsley, Yorkshire, father a steel worker, his mother employed in a mill. Worked as a painter and decorator, attending Batley College of Art part-time, then studied for a year at Leeds College of Art, working mornings in a Wakefield mill to pay for the course. After National Service washed dishes and painted in the Isles of Scilly for two years, then spent about 10 years in London, returning to Yorkshire in the early 1970s. Mixed shows in London included Nicholas Treadwell Gallery, and had a series of solo exhibitions including New Vision Centre Gallery, 1963, and Queen Square Gallery, Leeds, 1965. Durham's other works included a huge abstract mural for Morley Corporation swimming baths, early 1970s; publication of the book *Angus Pangus* and the *One Jump Giant*, 1973; from the late 1970s creation of pictures based on real-life Yorkshire characters; and in 1992 production of forest folk sculptures at his studio in the Walkley Clogs complex, Mytholmroyd. Muriel Spark and Olivia Manning, the novelists, Pop music star Bill Wyman and scientist Dr Jacob Bronowski all owned Durham's pictures.

Alan DURMAN 1905–1963 Verstile artist and photographer, born in Weymouth, Dorset, who trained there with a photographer, then moved to London, where he made window displays. He next worked as an artist and photographer with Imperial Tobacco Company, then with the printer Mardon, Son and Hall, and in World War II was commissioned in the Royal Army Service Corps. Durman moved to Bristol about 1950. He was elected an artist member of Bristol Savages in 1946, was made its president in 1952 and exhibited prolifically, 1946–63, portraits and landscapes, and with RWA occasionally, 1934–49. The Savages held work by, and a caricature of, Durman, who was remembered as "small in stature with a twinkle in his eye ... When he joined the club he was clean shaven, but in the late 1950s he grew a moustache and beard." Durman also produced posters and murals, venues including the Berkeley Café, Saltford Community Hall and the Cabot Grill. A copy of Ernest Board's famous picture of Cabot leaving Bristol was another of Durman's notable pictures.

Michael DURNING 1970– Artist whose subjects stemmed "from concerns over the destruction of Scottish architecture, industry and sites of historic importance.... I find a stark and strange beauty in the monuments of our past". Durning gained a fine art honours degree from Duncan of Jordanstone College of Art, Dundee, 1988–92, his master's in fine art and design, Gray's School of Fine Art, Aberdeen, 1994–5, and won a number of awards, including a RSA John Kinross Scholarship, 1992; Royal Glasgow Institute of the Fine Arts Exhibition Award, 1994; and a Talented Individuals Award, North Ayrshire Council, 1997. As well as mixed shows and participation in 3 Painters at Roger Billcliffe Gallery, Glasgow, 1999, Durning's solo exhibitions included J D Kelly, Glasgow, 1995, and Glasgow Vennel Museum, Irvine, 1997. RSA, Dundee Port Authority and North Ayrshire Council hold examples.

Jennifer DURRANT 1942– Painter and teacher, born in Brighton, Sussex, where she studied at College of Art, 1959–63, then Slade School of Fine Art, 1963–6. In 1964 she received an Abbey Minor Scholarship and two years later was a Young Contemporaries prizewinner. After participating in several important group exhibitions, such as John Moores in Liverpool in 1970, Durrant had a one-man show at Serpentine Gallery in 1974. Others included Arnolfini Gallery in Bristol, 1979; retrospective at Serpentine Gallery, 1987; and Barbican Concourse Gallery, 1992. Taught at various colleges including Royal College of Art and Chelsea School of Art. She was an Arts Council award winner in 1976, and has work in its collection, and won the Athena Prize, 1988. Elected RA, 1994. Was included in 5x20, "five abstract painters twenty years on", at Galerie Kegelbahn, Carl von Ossietzky University, Oldenburg, Germany, 2001. Durrant painted abstract pictures on a large scale which can be complex, ambiguous and lyrical. Lived in London.

Roy Turner DURRANT 1925–1998 Painter and poet, born in Lavenham, Suffolk. After a childhood addiction to drawing aeroplanes, he did war service in the Army, then attended Camberwell School of Arts and Crafts, 1948–52, being influenced by Keith Vaughan and John Minton. In 1950s developed from figuration to abstraction. He said that any titles on his pictures were "meant to be interpreted as poetry, to engender a state of mind rather than describe exactly what the particular picture is". Was influenced by European abstractionists and by English poetry, such as that of Gerard Manley Hopkins and Thomas Hardy, also by the work of James Joyce, Samuel Beckett and Dylan Thomas. As well as painting, Durrant was employed in administrative work at Vickers from 1956–63 and was a director of the Heffer Gallery, Cambridge, 1963–76. Showed with Free Painters and Sculptors, of which he was a fellow, and with NEAC, of which he was a member, and quite often with RA from 1950. In 1960 his poetry *A Rag Book of Love* was published. After a solo show at Guildhall, Lavenham, in 1948, he showed regularly, later exhibitions including Loggia Gallery, Gallery of Britsh Art in Lausanne and Belgrave Gallery, 1991. Roy Turner Durrant, Painter and Poet, was held at Chappel Galleries, Chappel, in 2003. Modern British Artists also sold his work. Several dozen public collections hold his work, including Imperial War Museum, Bradford City Art Gallery and Balliol College, Oxford. Lived in Cambridge.

Alan Lydiat DURST 1883–1970 Sculptor in wood, stone and ivory of figures, religious subjects and animals. Born at Alverstoke, Hampshire, Durst studied at the Central School of Arts and Crafts under Richard Garbe before and after World War I, during which he served with the Royal Marines (he had been in the Marines for some years prior to his Central School entry in 1913). Durst also studied in Chartres, France. After several years working as a sculptor, he taught wood-carving at the Royal College of Art 1925–48, with the exception of the war years, when he again served in the Marines and was at the Admiralty. Durst had his first one-man show at the Leicester Galleries in 1930 and was a member of the LG for about 25 years from the late 1920s. Wrote *Wood Carving* in 1938. Durst carved figures for the Royal Academy of Dramatic Art in 1931, did a quantity of ecclesiastical carving, including the west front of Peterborough Cathedral, and a memorial to the artist Randolph Schwabe in Hampstead Parish Church graveyard. The Tate Gallery holds his work, which is also illustrated in Arthur T Broadbent's monograph *Sculpture Today in Great Britain 1940–1943*. Durst, who sometimes signed his work A L D plus the date, lived in London.

Graham DURWARD 1956– Painter, born in Aberdeen, who studied at Edinburgh College of Art, 1973–7, with a postgraduate year in 1977–8. In 1982 he won a Scottish Arts Council Young Artists Bursary. Among group shows Durward participated in the Scottish Arts Council's Scottish Art Now show in 1982, and his one-man exhibitions included 369 Gallery, Edinburgh, 1979 and 1981. He also did some film work. Durward's work pursued an Expressionistic form, at the same time adopting a strong vein of Post-Cubism. Lived in Edinburgh.

Ian DURY 1942–2000 Cult singer and lyricist with a fruity, barrow-boy voice, artist and teacher, born in Upminster, Essex. Aged seven he contracted polio, leaving him with a bad limp and a caliper. Dury attended grammar school in High Wycombe and the painting school at the Royal College of Art, 1963–6. A close friend was the painter Geoff Rigden, mutual interests including jazz, button-down collar shirts, gangster movies and pinball. Whereas Rigden became a colourful abstractionist, Dury adhered to objective figuration. In 1967, Dury had a solo show at the ICA, featuring pin-ups and gangsters. After Rigden took a part-time teaching job at Canterbury College of Art in 1970 he recommended Dury to the head, Thomas Watt. When Dury began teaching there he was starting to collaborate with the pianist Russell Hardy, composing songs eventually performed under the band name Kilburn and the High Roads. Dury's concentration on gigs and failing to turn up for teaching led to his sacking from Canterbury. When his original band broke up the remnants formed a new line-up, the Blockheads, and in 1975 they were signed up by Stiff Records. The group's debut *New Boots and Panties* received superlative reviews and spent over a year in the United Kingdom albums chart. In 1979, Dury's number *Hit Me With Your Rhythm Stick* topped the charts. Dury continued to make thoughtful, witty and polemic records in the 1980s; in 1989 had success with the musical *Apples*, with another former Blockheads member, Mickey Gallagher; in the 1990s hosted the late-night television programme *Metro*; and continued to tour. After being diagnosed with terminal cancer, in 1998 Dury reunited with the Blockheads for the well-received *Mr Love Pants*. He latterly lived in Hampstead, north London. The earliest manifestation of the Kilburns included the artists Chris and Keith Lucas, Paul Tonkin and Humphrey Ocean. They were included in the homage exhibition Canterbury Kilburns, "friends from Ian Dury's days at Canterbury College of Art", held at deliArt in 2003.

Philip G DUTHIE 1957– Painter and draughtsman, born in Aberdeen, where he studied at Gray's School of Art, 1957–9. He then painted full-time, based in Belmont and Wasps Studios in Aberdeen, eventually settling in Edinburgh, where he exhibited at RSA from 1981. Also showed in Members' Drawings, at Peacock Printmakers, and Inaugural Exhibition, Artspace Galleries, both Aberdeen in 1980; and Cleveland 5th International Drawing Biennale, 1981. Gray's and private collections in Britain and America hold Duthie's works.

Monika DUTTA 1967– Artist employing modern media such as video, as in her exhibition at the Institute of International Visual Arts in 1998. That resulted from a residency which led "to an exploration of the fragmented nature of the female body which results from the sophisticated techniques used in imaging the body under biomedical gaze." Dutta's previous residencies were at North Tyneside Arts, as digital artist in residence, Isis Arts, Tyne and Wear, 1998–9, and European Studio Programme, ACC Gallery, Weimar, Germany, 1999. Dutta gained an art and design foundation diploma at Kingston Polytechnic, 1985–6; an honours degree in fine art sculpture, Winchester School of Art, 1987–90; and a postgraduate diploma in fine art media from the Slade School of Fine Art, 1991–3. As well as group, solo and collaboration exhibitions, she undertook public sector, community and commissioned work, latterly including Digital Co-ordinator, Peacock, Aberdeen, 1999–01, and *Four Walks Around Cartmel*, a short film for permanent installation, Cartmel Gatehouse Heritage Centre, South Lakes.

Harold John DUTTON 1889–1971 Painter, draughtsman, scraperboard artist and teacher, born in Birmingham. Studied at the School of Arts and Crafts there with Arthur J Gaskin. He was a leading figure in the Nottingham Society of Artists and showed extensively in Nottingham, Birmingham and other Midlands and northern towns. Nottingham Castle Art Gallery and Museum holds his work. Dutton moved to Nottingham aged 20 and taught at Claremont Secondary School. He was noted for landscape pencil drawing of great charm and delicacy and encouraged many pupils to take up art as a career. Lived in Sherwood, Nottingham.

Orlando DUTTON 1894–1962 Sculptor and portrait painter whose career was mainly in Australia. Born in Walsall, Staffordshire, Dutton initially studied art locally, then in 1909 was apprenticed to the Lichfield-based sculptor Robert Bridgeman. From the 1920s he built a reputation for himself in Australia, where he exhibited widely and worked extensively on public buildings. The National Gallery of South Australia, Adelaide, holds his work, as do Melbourne University, Anzac House, St John's Church and St Patrick's Cathedral, all in Melbourne. Lived at Wayville, near Melbourne.

Ron DUTTON 1935– Medallist, sculptor and teacher, born in Nantwich, Cheshire. He studied in the department of fine art at the University of Newcastle upon Tyne and was for some years head of sculpture at Wolverhampton College of Art from 1964. Showed at RA; in London Artists at Shrewbury School, 1968; Crane Kalman, 1977; The Medal, Mirror of History, at British Museum, 1979; and at Ina Broerse Gallery, Amsterdam, 1982. Had a solo show at Laing Art Gallery, Newcastle, 1964, later exhibitions including Tettenhall Gallery, Wolverhampton, where he lived, 1982 and 1984. Retrospective Simmons Gallery, 1999. Gained a number of awards and has work in public and private collections in Britain and abroad. Carried out many medal commissions, including Victorian Society, 25th anniversary, 1983; and in 1984 Fabian Society and Wolverhampton Art Gallery centenaries.

Dorothy Zinaida DUVAL 1917– Painter in oil and teacher, born in Ipplepen, Devon. She studied under Anthony Devas and attended Slade School of Fine Art, 1949–55. As an artist Duval had an aptitude and liking for capturing subjects on the spot, and admired Manet and Corot. She taught at Felixstowe College, girls' public schools and at adult classes. Showed at UA of which she was a member; was also a fellow of British Academy and a lay member exhibitor at RSMA shows. Also exhibited at RBA, ROI, RP and Ashmolean Museum in Oxford. Gained silver medal at Paris Salon in 1959, an Accademia Italia gold medal in 1980. Solo shows included Saffron Gallery, Saffron Walden, 1973; Broadstairs Library Gallery, 1978; and Margate Library, 1989. Grenadier Guards holds her portrait of the Victoria Cross winner Harry Nicholls. Lived in Kingsgate, Broadstairs, Kent.

Leslie DUXBURY 1921–2001 Painter, teacher and writer who in the 1950s produced pictures of the type popularly known as Kitchen Sink School. He was born in Accrington, Lancashire, attending the local Art School, then was briefly at Royal College of Art in 1941, returning to it, after Army service, in 1944–6. Settled in London and showed with LG; Roland, Browse & Delbanco; and AEB, from which his oil on canvas Tenement Dwellers was acquired in 1956 by Arts Council. In 1984 he was included in the Graves Art Gallery, Sheffield, touring show The Forgotten Fifties. Taught for many years at Kingston-upon-Thames School of Art, in charge of printmaking. Teaching curtailed Duxbury's painting time, so that he turned to etching, after retirement frequently sketching concert musicians for his prints. Duxbury wrote and broadcast stories for the BBC, *Armistice Day* having several November repeats. There was a memorial exhibition at Haworth Art Gallery, Accrington, 2003.

Timur D'VATZ 1968– Painter, born in Moscow, Russia, who attended the Republican College of Art, Tashkent, 1983–7, then, under a Jack Goldhill Scholarship, studied postgraduate at Royal Academy Schools, 1993–6. Mixed shows included Cricket Hill Associates, New York, America, 1994; RA Summer Exhibition, from 1994, when awarded Guinness Prize for First Time Exhibitor; Mistral Galleries, 1995; Degree Show, RA, 1996, A T Kearney Prize; and Castlegate House Gallery, Cockermouth, and Centro Camuno di Studi Preistorici, Capo di Ponte, Italy, both 2000. Showed solo with Cadogan Contemporary from 1996.

Lucille DWECK 1963– Artist who attended St Martin's School of Art, 1981–2, then Byam Shaw School of Art, 1982–5, with a 1983–5 scholarship place. Group shows included The Crypt Gallery, London, 1986; Mario Flecha Gallery, 1986 and 1987; The Immaculate Conception, The Young Unknowns Gallery, 1988; and East End Open Studios, at Cable Street Studios, 1989.

Andrew DWYER 1967– Artist and designer who studied three-dimensional design at Carlisle and Exeter Colleges of Art, after which his output included writing, furniture-making and exhibition work. About the time that he was studying public art with the Freeform Arts Trust, which added a new twist to his career, Dwyer was engaged on designing the striking steel spiral Coventry Blue Ribbon Sculpture. This was completed in 1998, artists Carl Fleischer and Tanya Matthews, commissioned by Groundwork Coventry, and sited at Foleshill Road, Coventry.

DY: *see* **Emlyn DUFFY**

David DYE 1945– Film-oriented artist, sculptor, photographer and teacher, born in Ryde, Isle of Wight. Between 1964–7 Dye did a variety of office, shop and manual jobs, then studied sculpture at St Martin's School of Art, 1967–71. From 1972–6 he taught at Brighton Polytechnic, moving to Newcastle Polytechnic in 1979. He won an Eastern Arts Grant in 1978. Dye showed with Young Contemporaries in 1970 and in the following year in the English avant-garde at New York Cultural Centre and Art Systems at the Museum of Modern Art, Buenos Aires. Dye's solo shows included a first at the ICA, 1972 and Lisson Gallery, 1975, with further exhibitions there and at the Robert Self Gallery, London and Newcastle. He was included in the big British Council exhibition English Art Today 1960–76, held in 1976 at the Palazzo Reale, Milan, Italy. For that he wrote: "A series of works using mirrors led, in 1970, to film. Since then all my work has used film as its medium; it has been primarily about film – about the process of filming and the projection of film. I have done nothing to exploit the possibilities of the 'image'". Dye broke down his output into four categories: films plus performance pieces, installation pieces and still pieces. The Arts Council holds his work. For a time he lived in Saffron Walden, Essex.

Alan DYER 1944– Painter, born in Nelson, Lancashire. He took a business training for six years before attending art school in Bristol and studying for a Master of Philosophy degree at Reading University. Showed in RA Summer Exhibition and had solo show at Sandford Gallery, 1981. His multi-image Desert Painting No 3, of 1979, was included in Arts Council tour Fragments Against Ruin, 1981–2, and is now in the collection. Lived for a time in Coventry, Warwickshire, and was also known for a series of family portraits.

John DYER 1968– Painter of exuberantly coloured landscapes with figures, and designer, son of the artist Ted Dyer and married to the painter Joanne Short. The three occasionally worked on collaborative projects, such as Italy, Luce e Colore, arranged by the Falmouth Gallery Beside The Wave at Gallery 27, Cork Street, in 2003. John was painter-in-residence at The Eden Project, Cornwall, 2000–1. He had many group exhibitions, one-mans latterly including A Piece of Eden, Beside The Wave, 2001. His work was frequently published, including an Art Group poster distributed through Habitat, 1996; the official limited-edition print for the *Cutty Sark* Tall Ships' Race, 1998, and Roaming around the Rainforest, for The Eden Project, 2001.

Ted DYER 1940– Painter of richly coloured landscapes and coastal scenes, father of the artist John Dyer, his daughter-in-law being the painter Joanne Short. He collaborated with them in several projects, such as the exhibition Paintings of Provence, organised by the Falmouth gallery Beside The Wave at Gallery 27, Cork Street, 1999. Ted was born in Bristol, where his grandfather, Edward Dyer, was at one time both lord mayor and chairman of the docks. After the Blitz and a series of business ventures the family settled in Taunton where Ted's father ran an hotel. Although early on Ted's ability to draw and paint was encouraged, circumstances prevented his attending art school and he eventually became a radiographer and spare-time painter. Treasure Trove Gallery, Newquay, began selling his work, and by 1973 Dyer was able to move to Holywell, near Newquay, to paint full time. Showed in many galleries and solo regularly with Beside The Wave, including the exhibition Clear Light, Tresco, 2002. The gallery also issued limited-edition prints of Dyer's work, as did The Medici Society, Felix Rosentiel's Widow and Son, Michael Stewart Fine Art and others. The National Trust reproduced his painting Nocturne: Proms in the Park, Lanhydrock, in 1995, on its centenary year brochures.

Dorothy DYMOCK 1881–1984 Painter in oil, aunt of the artist Rachel Windham, born in Bedford. Dymock was a hospital cook with the Red Cross during World War I. Then received a grant from WTE – Central Committee on Women's Training to study full-time at the Slade School of Fine Art, 1921–2, under Henry Tonks, on whom she made a good impression. Dymock considered continuing for the 1922–3 session, then cancelled. She also attended Westminster School of Art. Showed at RA, SWA, Ridley Art Club, ROI and elsewhere. Miss Dymock produced her strong, Colourist work until she was 91 and even during her later blindness maintained a keen interest in painting.

Lucy DYNEVOR 1934– Painter, printmaker and restorer, born Sheffield, daughter of art expert Sir John Rothenstein and niece of the artist Michael Rothenstein. She studied painting under Percy Horton at Ruskin School of Drawing, Oxford, and restoration with Helmuth Ruhemann. For some years she combined painting with freelance restoration. She was noted for her paintings of trees. Was a member of Oxford Printmakers' Co-operative. Had first solo show in London at New Grafton Gallery in 1991. Dynevor's oil painting Dynevor Park, Wales, was included in the large Rothenstein family collection sale at Sotheby's in 2003, which she consigned. Lived at Shotover, Oxford.

Noel DYRENFORTH 1936– Batik artist, born in London and continued to live there. After education at St Clement Danes, London, went on study and travel tours throughout Asia, Far East and America. Extensive international exhibitions, including many one-man shows which included Heal's Mansard Gallery, Oxford Gallery, Lincoln Craft Centre. Wrote several books on the technique of Batik. Work held by Victoria & Albert Museum.

Dierdre DYSON 1943– Painter, notably of large, colourful still lifes, born in London, who trained for two years at Byam Shaw School of Painting and Drawing and for three years as an illustrator/graphic designer at Wimbledon College of Art. She began work as a graphic artist in the 1970s and gained early recognition for her *Vogue* magazine illustrations, later working as an independent artist with a West Country studio. She reached an international audience when her paintings were reproduced in a series of cards published and distributed globally by Prime Arts. Showed throughout Britain in group exhibitions. Her 1997 sell-out solo show at Simon Capstick-Dale Fine Art in London was followed by an exhibition with the same dealer in New York in 1998, then others at Grosvenor Gallery, 2000, and Albemarle Gallery, 2003.

Douglas DYSON 1918–2003 Artist in oil, pastel, pen and pencil and teacher, born in Halifax, Yorkshire, married to the painter Sylvia Dyson. He studied at Huddersfield School of Art, 1935–9, then Royal College of Art, 1946–9, teachers including Gilbert Spencer, Rodrigo Moynihan, John Minton, Ruskin Spear and Carel Weight. He joined the Manchester Muncipal School of Art staff in 1949, which became the faculty of art and design, Manchester Polytechnic, retiring in 1981. Dyson said that "my first priority has always been as a teacher." He was a member of MAFA. Also showed at RA, Manchester City Art Gallery which holds his work, Manchester Polytechnic and Atkinson Art Gallery, Southport. Baptism of Christ, an oil in St John's Church, Newton Heath, Manchester, was a principal work. Lived in Hale, Altrincham, Cheshire.

Julian DYSON 1936–2003 Draughtsman and painter who qualified as a dental surgeon in 1959, but 10 years later reduced his surgery hours to concentrate on painting. Took part in numerous mixed exhibitions, including Ashbarn Gallery, Petersfield; Aberystwyth University; Cleveland Bridge Gallery, Bath; Newlyn Orion Gallery, Newlyn; and Gordon Hepworth Gallery, Newton St Cyres. When The Group of Twelve was formed in 1992, Dyson was elected president. Solo exhibitions included Falmouth Art Gallery, Falmouth, 2001. In 1996 the book *36 Drawings by Julian Dyson* was published. Although he worked in many parts of the country Dyson, a self-taught artist born in Cornwall, returned there in the early 1980s, its landscape being a key element in his work. Lived at St Mawes. There was a retrospective at Archeus Fine Art, 2004–5.

Sylvia DYSON 1917–1987 Watercolourist and illustrator who was brought up in Lancashire. She attended Huddersfield School of Art, 1935–40, then Royal College of Art, 1940–3, under Ernest Tristram. Married the artist Douglas Dyson and lived at Hale, Cheshire. She illustrated for Penguin Books and showed with LG, NEAC and elsewhere.

André DZIERZYNSKI 1936– Painter and critic, born in Warsaw, Poland, as Andrzej-Leszek Dzierzynski, who was brought up in the country near the Kazimierz-on-Vistula art colony. His father was in the Polish Army under British command in World War II, his mother becoming a naturalised British citizen. He studied history of art at Warsaw University, 1953–7, then moved to London, where he was encouraged by the sculptor Irena Kunicka to take up painting in 1958. Travelled widely on the continent. Mixed shows included Upper Grosvenor Gallery, The Sail Loft Gallery in St Ives and Crane Kalman Gallery. In 1963 he shared a show at the Centre Charles Peguy with Elena Gaputyte and had over a dozen solo exhibitions, including Upper Grosvenor and Hamet Galleries and abroad. Dzierzynski said that he worked "outside main streams and fashions" and "as a policy does not want to be included in any public collection". Until the late 1970s he worked in oil and in acrylics; then began using both egg and beeswax tempera, encouraged by the American painter Philip Tarlow; and from the mid-1980s worked only in egg tempera. From 1970 he shared his time between San Gimignano, Italy, and London, latterly spending periods in Provence. Dzierzynski was a member of The International Association of Art Critics' British section and of UNESCO's International Association of Art. He contributed to the BBC's Polish language service.

Krystyna Shackleton DZIESZKO fl. from 1970s– Versatile artist and teacher, born in London of Anglo-Polish origin, who explored ideas about crossing boundaries, location and dislocation, cultural identity and diversity. Completed a foundation course at St Martin's School of Art, 1965–7; gained an art and design diploma at Manchester School of Art, 1967–70; then a postgraduate certificate in education at Manchester Polytechnic, 1970–1. Taught art at Marylebone Paddington Institute, 1973–6, other appointments including Camden Arts Centre, 1978–92. Commissions included panels for Churchill Hotel, 1968, and constructions for Holloway Community Centre, 1973. Group exhibitions included BP Arts Festival, Barbican, 1985; Hampstead Artists, Camden Arts Centre, 1986; On Uncommon Ground, Arts Council exhibition at Cartwright Hall, Bradford, 1991; and Instituto Nacional de Bellas Artes, Mexico City, 1994. Held a number of solo shows at POSK Gallery and East End Open Studios in Milborne Street, both from 1989. In 1990, Stanisław Pater made a film, *The Evolving Image*, about her for Polish Television.

Kazimierz Tadeusz DŹWIG 1923–1994 Artist, born in Cracow, Poland, in 1923, who after the outbreak of World War II was sent by the Germans to a labour camp from which he escaped to Italy in 1943, joining the Italian partisans and Polish Second Corps. Studied painting at the Polish School of Painting in Rome and later in England, where he moved late in 1946, and soon joined the Sir John Cass School. Also took lessons with Henryk Gotlib in 1948–9 and with Camberwell School of Arts and Crafts. In 1952 he began work in Thomas De La Rue's banknote design department, retiring from it in 1988. Continued to paint in his spare time and showed widely in Britain, Poland and elsewhere. In 1995 the Polish Cultural Institute held a retrospective show. National Museums in Warsaw and Gdańsk hold examples.

E

Paul EACHUS 1944– Artist in various media, born in Liverpool, where he attended the College of Art, 1961–6, then Royal College of Art, 1967–70. Exhibitions included Liverpool University, Reeves Bi-centenary Pictures for Schools, London Artists at Shrewsbury School, 1968, and later exhibitions East at Norwich Gallery, Norfolk Institute of Art & Design, 1991. Nuffield Foundation and Gloucester Education Committee hold examples. Lived in London.

Edward EADE 1911–1984 Versatile artist and teacher, born in Tottenham, north London, his father a railway ticket collector. Edward early showed artistic talent and was encouraged by his domineering mother, who inadvisedly termed him "the boy genius", to pursue it as a career. He attended the Slade School of Fine Art, 1929–30, with a Slade Scholarship, where he gained his teaching diploma with honours and a first-class prize for drawing plus awards for history of art. At the Royal Academy Schools, 1930–2, he won the Landseer Scholarship and was a first-class silver medallist for life painting. He also studied art history under Roger Fry, Cambridge University, and sculpture with Henry Moore. Taught widely from 1933, including Beckenham, Wimbledon and Sidcup Schools of Art and Medway and Rochester, Maidstone and Hornsey Art Colleges. Eade liked teaching art history to adults, notably HM Forces (chief lecturer, Aldershot Command), Red Cross, Young Men's Christian Association and elsewhere. Although he showed widely in London, including the LG and NEAC, his lack of self-promotion prevented his name becoming known, he sold little and in later life became over-protective of his work, which fell into neglect. A retrospective organised in 2000 at Lauderdale House, Highgate, near where he lived, helped rescue his reputation. There were other shows at Art Edinburgh, 2001, and Louise Kosman, Edinburgh, 2003. *The Gentle Artist: The Life and Work of Edward Eade (1911–1984)* was published in 2004, a well-illustrated appreciation by his son, Oliver Eade.

Russell EADE 1969– Versatile painter, born in Epsom, Surrey, who studied at Camberwell School of Art. He was resident artist, Paynes Poppets Chocolate Factory, 1987; Heathrow Airport, 1989–90; and London Transport, 1993–4. Was a foundryman at Meridian Fine Art Bronze Foundry, 1995, the year his oil on cotton duck Immortally Yours was shown at Royal Over-Seas League Open. Other group shows included Young Unknowns Gallery, from 1988; Limboland, Imperial College, 1989; The Discerning Eye, Mall Galleries, 1992; and Pulse, at Minet Road Gallery, 1993.

Ian EADIE 1913–1973 Painter, muralist and teacher, born and died in Dundee, who showed an early talent for drawing, leaving Harris Academy as Dux Medallist in Art. From 1931 studied under J Milne Purvis at Dundee College of Art, gaining his diploma after three years, then a postgraduate year. He won the first travelling scholarship awarded by the College, which enabled him to study under Ferdinand Sabatté in Paris at the École des Beaux-Arts and to travel in Italy, a tour cut short by the death of his father. Aged 22, Eadie had shown at the RSA, to which he was soon to add RP and RWS. Eadie was commissioned to paint murals for the 1938 British Empire Exhibition in Glasgow. In 1939 he studied for four months at Westminster School of Art under Mark Gertler, then began teaching at Dundee College of Art until World War II interrupted. Joined the Gordon Highlanders and, taking a commission, served with the 51st Highland Division widely abroad as divisional war artist, his work eventually being taken by the Imperial War Museum and public galleries in Aberdeen, Dundee and Glasgow. There was an exhibition of the war pictures at the Scottish Gallery, with tour, in 1944. Demobilised in 1946 Eadie soon returned to Dundee College of Art to teach, part-time until the end of his life as he wished to freelance. This involved periodic economic hardship, disappointments and bouts of hard work. He had solo exhibitions at Panmure Art Salon, Dundee, 1947, and Blyth Hall, Newport, 1953. Eadie's heavy workload as a mural painter from the 1950s eroded time for easel painting. There were many commissions for ships, others including Shoppers, for the Overgate Shopping Centre, Dundee, and one for the Aviemore Holiday Centre. Travels on the continent saw him latterly returning to easel painting, but heavy smoking and a dependence on alcohol undermined Eadie's health and cut short his working life. Dundee College of Art awards an Ian Eadie Prize.

Robert EADIE 1877–1954 Painter, printmaker and poster designer who was educated in Glasgow, studied at School of Art there and in Munich and Paris. In World War I served in the Royal Engineers. He was a member of Glasgow Art Club, living in Cambuslang, and the city's Art Gallery holds his watercolour Stirling Bridge. Other main examples of Eadie's work include St Monans; Snow on the Roofs; Old Bridge, Stratheven; and Dinan Market. He was elected RSW in 1916, also showing at RSA, Royal Glasgow Institute of the Fine Arts, RA and Walker Art Gallery in Liverpool.

Aileen EAGLETON 1902–1984 Wood engraver, painter in oil and watercolour. Born in Bexley, Kent, studied art under Louis (Louisa) Thomson. A member of the SGA, she exhibited with the RA, SWA, RI and ROI, Walker Art Gallery, Liverpool, and Paris Salon. Lived at East Molesey, Surrey.

Godfrey EAGLETON 1935– Painter, draughtsman and teacher, full name Godfrey Paul Eagleton (sometimes painted as Paul). Studied for national diploma in painting and textiles at Camberwell School of Arts and Crafts, 1955, teachers including Gilbert Spencer and Martin Bloch; did National Service in Army as a photoprinter artist, 1955–7; obtained diploma in painting and etching, with first-class honours in art history, at Slade School of Fine Art, 1957–9, teachers including Claude Rogers; and gained art teacher's certificate at University College, 1959–60. Extensive teaching included Camberwell School of Art and Putney Art Centre, both 1962–7; Regent Street Polytechnic, 1963; London College of Fashion, 1967; Henry Thornton Youth Centre, 1972–6; Lewisham Inner London Education Authority Art Centre, 1976–87; and Summer Craft Centres in Westminster and Lambeth, 1989–90. Was a member of South London and South-East London Groups. Had a series of solo exhibitions including Battersea Art Centre and Opus Gallery, showing figurative and non-figurative work. Lived in London.

Paul EAGLETON: *see* **Godfrey EAGLETON**

Angela EAMES 1951– Abstract artist in various media, born in Malmesbury, Wiltshire, who taught part-time and lived in London. She studied at Bath Academy of Art and Slade School of Fine Art. Among her exhibitions was Five at Woodlands Art Gallery, 1982.

Enid EARDLEY 1916–1999 Painter, notable for portraits, who studied at Central School of Arts and Crafts in 1939, then in mid-1960s with Stanley Grimm and Steven Spurrier. She was a member of SWA and had a series of solo exhibitions including Alpine Gallery, 1981. Lived in Old Amersham, Buckinghamshire.

Joan EARDLEY 1921–1963 Painter and draughtsman, born in Warnham, Sussex. In 1938 she enrolled at Goldsmiths' College School of Art, staying for several months, then was at Glasgow School of Art, 1940–3, under Hugh Adam Crawford, graduating with several prizes. After a brief period at Jordanhill College of Education and a period as a joiner's labourer, in 1947 Eardley spent six months under James Cowie at the Patrick Allen-Fraser School of Art, Hospitalfield, before in 1948 taking up her post-diploma scholarship at Glasgow School of Art. A travelling scholarship took her to France and Italy in 1948–9, the resulting work being shown at her first solo exhibition at Glasgow Art School in 1949. Eardley now embarked on her two main themes as a painter: Glasgow tenement life, with its studies of children; and from 1951 pictures of the sea and coast at Catterline, on the northeast coast, where she latterly spent much time, these works having an Abstract Expressionist force. In 1960 she was a guest teacher at Hospitalfield. Eardley was elected SSA in 1948 and RSA in 1963 not long before dying of cancer in hospital near Glasgow. Scottish National Gallery of Modern Art has an extensive collection of her work. In 1988 a major retrospective was held at Talbot Rice Centre and RSA, Edinburgh, where the City Art Centre held a paintings and drawings show in 2002, The Scottish Gallery another in 2003.

Paul EAREE 1888–1968 Artist who was professionally trained as an ecclesiastical architect, art teacher and illustrator, but poured his spare-time creative energies into paintings, etchings and drawings with a strong regional content. Although he showed locally, Earee was rarely persuaded to part with his work for money, and only gave it away if he was sure the recipient's feelings for it matched his own. As an architect Earee designed council houses and the pulpit of St Gregory's Church, Sudbury, Suffolk, where he was a notable personality. Earee was a friend of the artists Rowland Suddaby and John Rimmer, their ideas strongly interacting. In 1920 Earee was a founder of the Sudbury Dramatic Society. He collaborated with his architectural business partner H A F Haslewood to paint scenery for the original, locally famous production of *Brer Rabbit and Mr Fox* at the Victoria Hall in 1921 and for *La Poupée* in 1923. There was a retrospective show, Landscapes and Dreams, at The Quay Theatre in 1983 and in 1996 Chappel Galleries, Chappel, included Earee in its Colchester Art Society Fifty Years Anniversary Exhibition.

Honor EARL 1901–1996 Portrait painter and draughtsman, whose natural talent for art (what she called her ability "to do certain tricks") helped her overcome the demoralizing effects of dyslexia and to support charities. Edith Honor Betty Earl was the second daughter of the 1st Viscount Maugham, Chancellor of the Exchequer under Neville Chamberlain and brother of writer W Somerset Maugham. Although the Hon. Honor Earl's subjects were often drawn from the top rank of society, including four generations of the British royal family and stars of stage and screen, she chose to mix with the under-privileged. In 1937 Earl became a prison visitor; during World War II she worked to employ refugee talent; she raised funds for the All-Nations Voluntary Service League; and donated the proceeds of exhibitions to such causes as the National Council for the Unmarried Mother and Child, the Actors' Orphanage and The National Society for Prevention of Cruelty to Children. She founded, and acted as chairman of, the Young Musicians' Fund. Earl was especially good at portraying children, holding their attention while sketching with one hand and operating a glove puppet with the other, or playing tunes with a comb and paper. Lived in London and at Martyr Worthy, Hampshire.

Donald Maurice EARLE 1928– Artist in various media and teacher, born in Melksham, Wiltshire. He attended West of England College of Art, Bristol, 1944–7, and 1949–51. Dr Earle was head of art department in various schools in Britain, latterly Great Baddow School in Chelmsford, Essex, where he lived. He showed with RWS, NEAC, RWA, RBSA and Colchester Art Society. Solo exhibitions included Mercury Theatre, Colchester, 1983; Barbican Centre, 1986; and Norwich, 1988.

Kim EARLEY 1952– Sculptor of abstracts in metal, born in Christchurch, New Zealand, who studied at St Martin's School of Art, 1973–5. Earley's work was included in St Martin's and South Bank shows in 1977 and Serpentine Summer Show 2 at Serpentine Gallery, 1979. The artist was then living in northwest London.

Chloe EARLY 1980– Artist and designer, born and lived in London, who graduated with first-class honours in textile design from the National College of Art and Design, Dublin, Ireland, 1999–03. Early said of her work that its "key themes include the female presence in the urban landscape and the relationship between this individual and the exterior environment. Ideas of scale, position and the significance of the figure in the landscape are alternated to create a reflective disposition and a quality of space in this turbulent environment." Group shows included RDS Travelling Exhibition, exhibited in Dublin, 2003–4; Apple Loft Gallery, Easkey, Sligo, 2004; and Hard Bodies, Corpus Fine Art at the Arndean Gallery, 2005. In 2004 she shared a show with Clive Bright at Gallery 9, Cork. Jannsen Pharmaceuticals, Little Island, Cork, and City Manager, Cork City, hold examples.

Tom EARLY 1914–1967 Painter with a naturally primitive style and rich palette, by profession a doctor, whose talent was spotted by Ben Nicholson when Early was convalescing in Carbis Bay, Cornwall, 1946. He was befriended by the sculptor Denis Mitchell, with whom he had three shows in St Ives: two at Castle Inn, 1947–8, and one at Downing's Bookshop, 1949. Returned to medicine in 1952 after marrying Eunice Campbell, who published a memoir of him (*The Magic Shuttle – The Story of Tom Early: St Ives and After*), 1994, which coincided with a memorial show at Belgrave Gallery and later at The Book Gallery, St Ives. Early became registrar at the county mental hospital, Derby, and was a founder-member of the Derby Group, which held its first show at Derby Art Gallery, 1961. Early's last show in his lifetime was at Midland Group Gallery 1965. In 2005 Sansom & Company published a well-illustrated catalogue raisonné, which the Belgrave Gallery, St Ives, marked with a small exhibition.

Anthony EARNSHAW 1924–2001 Painter, creator of cartoon strips, prints, boxed assemblages and "books of a sort" and teacher, who was born in Ilkley, Yorkshire. Left school at 14 and worked for a time as an apprentice fitter, lathe turner and crane driver. He was an auto-didact who "through an enthusiasm for poetry discovered Surrealism in the mid-40s 'which changed my life'". This started him on making his various artefacts and "all in all making a general nuisance of myself". His assemblages sometimes used found objects and were noted for their biting wit and singular vision. Tony Earnshaw was the subject of several television films. Published a number of shrewd, witty and aphoristic books, titles including *Wintersol* (with Eric Thacker), 1971; *Flick Knives and Forks*, 1981; and *Carping and Kicking*, 1987. His exhibitions included a retrospective at Leeds Institute, 1966; Angela Flowers, 1972; Dean Clough Contemporary Art Gallery, Halifax, 1986–8–92; retrospective at Leeds City Art Gallery, 1987; Graves Art Gallery, Sheffield, 1988; and Flowers East, 2000. After his 1966 show Earnshaw was offered a day's teaching weekly at Harrogate School of Art, which led to other teaching; in 1972, he was granted a fellowhip at Leeds Polytechnic; then from 1985 concentrated on his own work full-time. Arts Council and Leeds City Art Gallery hold his work. Lived at Saltburn-by-the-Sea, Cleveland.

Taylor EARNSHAW 1931– Painter and sculptor, studied at the College of Art, Liverpool, where he lived, under George Mayer-Marton and Arthur Ballard. Group shows included Frost & Reed, Bristol; ROI; RSMA; International Exhibition, Sculpture, Museo d'Arte, Castellanza, Milan, Italy (Museo d'Arte Moderna there holds his work); and Windsor & Eton Fine Arts, Windsor. Among solo exhibitions was a retrospective at Hanover Galleries, Liverpool, 2000.

Eliab George EARTHROWL 1878–1965 Versatile artist and teacher, notably an etcher, born and lived in London, who studied at Goldsmiths' College School of Art, becoming a tutor at Hammersmith School of Art. He won a number of prizes, became an associate of RE in 1924, was an associate of SGA and a member of the Print Makers Society of California. Exhibited at RA, Royal Glasgow Institute of the Fine Arts, Walker Art Gallery in Liverpool and abroad. Contemporary Art Society, British Museum and North American collections hold examples. The name Earthrowl (pronounced Earthrole) is believed to be of East Anglian and Huguenot origin.

Steve EASBY 1958– Painter and illustrator, producing exquisite, minutely detailed pictures strongly influenced by music. He was born in Derby, the son of a commercial artist, and was encouraged to paint; his mother, a pianist, played Steve Chopin preludes. After St Helens College of Art and Design, graduated in Coventry. Mixed exhibitions included RWA, from 1978, and RA Summer Exhibition, 1980. From 1988, he also exhibited with the U S Open Pro. Indoor Tennis Art Exhibition, Philadelphia, Pennsylvania. Having visited the Portal Gallery as a student, Easby began showing there in 1986, having a series of solo exhibitions from 1991. Monet, Seurat, the Pre-Raphaelites, Klimt, O'Keefe and Turner were all cited as influences, "because they pierce the usual barriers of human consciousness while still maintaining an empathy for humanity and nature." Easby's published work included the cover for the *Illustrated London News*'s Christmas 1990 edition.

Thomas EASLEY 1949– Portrait painter and miniaturist working on various supports, self-taught, born in Oroville, California. Showed in America, in Venice and in London with RMS of which he was a member, Medici Society Ltd, ROI and elsewhere. London Sketch Club member. Work in many private collections including that of TRH The Prince and Princess of Wales. Lived for some years in Venice, Italy.

Mary Alexandra EASTLAKE 1864–1951 Versatile painter who was born in Douglas, Ontario, Canada. After studying in Paris she moved to England, in the late 1890s became associated with the St Ives, Cornwall, artists' colony and married the landscape painter Charles Herbert Eastlake. She was a prominent member of PS and showed widely in England, on the continent and in North America. Venues included Baillie Gallery, RA, SWA and Walker Art Gallery in Liverpool.

Max EASTLEY 1944– Artist, musician and teacher, born in Torquay, Devon. He studied sculpture at Middlesex Polytechnic (Hornsey College of Art), 1969–72. Eastley was fellow/lecturer in audio/visual art at Exeter College of Art, 1972–3, and in sculpture at North-East London Polytechnic, 1974–5, also being a visiting lecturer at Slade School of Fine Art and Falmouth School of Art. He taught musical instrument construction at Morley College and at Science Technology & Craft Centre, 1974–8. Eastley won an Arts Council Bursary, 1977. Group exhibitions included 6 Times, Serpentine Gallery, 1976; he shared a show with David Toop at Chapter, Cardiff, 1978; and had solo shows at Exe Gallery in Exeter, 1973, and Spectro Gallery, Newcastle upon Tyne, 1977. As a sculpture student Eastley began to investigate the relationship of chance to music, using shadow projections, graphic scores and kinetic sound machines. As an instrument builder he worked in performances ranging from his own installations and machines to musical compositions, recording and improvisation. In 1990 the range of Eastley's work in sound and vision was documented in a television film, *The Clocks Of The Midnight Hours*, shown on Channel 4. Later examples of his works included a Concert tour of Japan with Toop, 1993; *Buried Dreams*, with Toop, Beyond Records, 1994; Installation and concert, Purcell Room, South Bank, 1995; and another at Cannon Hill Park, Birmingham, 1996. Lived in London.

Arthur EASTON 1939– Painter, printmaker and teacher, born in Salfords, Surrey. He attended Reigate School of Art, 1963–6. Went on to teach part-time at Reigate and Bletchingley Adult Education Centres and ran his own art classes, having previously taught at Reigate School of Art. Also worked as an art therapist in psychiatric hospitals. Easton gained a diploma of merit, University of Arts, Italy, in 1982 and the Stanley Grimm Prize at ROI annual show in 1991. He was a member of ROI and NS. Easton was a still life painter of meticulous exactness, in the northern European tradition. One-man shows were frequent, including Phoenix Gallery in Lavenham, 1991, and he shared an exhibition with three painters at Mistral Gallery, 1992. HRH The Princess Michael of Kent and the Museum of British Labour hold his work. Lived in Reigate, Surrey.

Bella EASTON: *see* **Isabella EASTON**

David EASTON 1935– Painter, graphic designer, teacher and writer on art, born and lived in Leicester, where he attended the College of Art for his National Diploma, 1952–6, graduating Bachelor of Education at Leicester University, 1973–6. From 1959, his wife was the painter Shirley Easton. David was a graphic designer, 1958–72; part-time adult tutor from 1962; and taught art in schools, 1976–82. Easton's work was mainly still life and flower motifs until 1998, then he concentrated on landscape, Cézanne, Paul Nash, Samuel Palmer and Graham Sutherland being influences. His book *Watercolour Flowers* appeared in 1993, *Watercolour Inspirations*, 1997, and both were reissued as paperbacks, 2001. Group shows included RI, of which he was a full member, from 1983; RA Summer Exhibition, 1986; Singer & Friedlander/*Sunday Times* Watercolour Competition, 1991; and provincial galleries in England and Wales. Had two solo exhibitions in Leicester, 1984 and 1995.

Hugh EASTON 1906–1965 Artist in stained glass, born in London, who studied art in France and Italy. Completed many windows, including examples at St Andrew and St Patrick, Elveden, Suffolk; and Brechin, Durham and Winchester Cathedrals. Easton's upper lights pencil study for the Battle of Britain memorial in Westminster Abbey was included in a 1999 auction room sale at Phillips. Lived in London.

Isabella EASTON 1971– Painter, printmaker and collagist, born in Epsom, Surrey, daughter of the artist Timothy Easton and restorer Christine Easton. Studied at Suffolk College of Further and Higher Education for a national diploma in art and design, 1988–90, then gained an honours degree in fine art, painting at Winchester School of Art, under Vanessa Jackson, 1990–3. Undertook a number of study visits in France, Germany, Spain and Italy; in 1992 went on a three-month exchange to Hochschule der Kunst, Berlin; Royal Academy Schools postgraduate diploma, painting, 1997–00. She said that, "using architecture as the main reference, my geometric compositions are constructed by superimposing one image over the other by the multi-layering of glazes in the watercolours and oil paintings. The etchings consist of two and three plates separating the various colours which, when overlaid, are intended to give the illusion of the interaction of space and solid." Awards included R K Burt Award for imaginative use of paper, 1993, and Eaton Fund for Artists, 1995. In 1995 Easton was elected a member of United Abstract Artists. Exhibitions included County Architect's Office, Winchester, 1992; Winchester Gallery, Winchester, and Slaughterhouse Gallery, both 1993; Tabernacle and Ben Uri Galleries, both 1995; Battersea Arts Fair, 1996; and RA Summer Exhibition, 1999, where Easton showed prints from her book *Alf 'n' Betty*, GEN foundation, Osaka, Japan, bought a set and she won the M&G Purchase Prize. Also in 1999, she won second prize in Sotheby's Chichester Open, at Pallant House, in 2000 the David Murray Landscape Prize. In that year, as a consequence of her book project, Easton was awarded a two-year fellowship at the City and Guilds of London. In 2001, she was selected as the UK Travel Scholar of the Royal Over-Seas League, which enabled her to work in India on the second book in her series *English Fish in Foreign Lands*. She participated in the League's Travel Scholars Exhibition in 2002. There were solo shows at New Academy Gallery, 2002, Curwen Gallery, 2003, Royal Over-Seas League and British Council, Delhi, both 2004, and Delhi to Kerala – A Monsoon Journey, New Ashgate Gallery, Farnham, 2005. Lived in London.

Shirley EASTON 1935– Artist and teacher, born and lived in Leicester, who gained her National and Teaching Diplomas at the School of Art there, 1952–7. She married the painter David Easton in 1959, her work appearing in his watercolour instructional books and as prints issued by Felix Rosenstiel's Widow & Son Ltd. Easton was a part-time tutor in adult education, 1962–97. She was a member of SWA, 1987-92 and showed at RI from 1984 concentrating on landscape, gardens and still life. Had a solo exhibition at Bottle Kiln Gallery, Ilkeston, 1989.

Timothy EASTON 1943– Painter and sculptor, born in Tadworth, Surrey. From 1960–4 Easton attended Kingston College of Art and Heatherley's School of Fine Art, studying painting. He began making his living as a mural and portrait painter and soon had offers to exhibit in Chicago and Kansas, where his work proved a success. In 1966–7 he travelled in Italy and northern Europe on scholarship. In 1969 he had a solo show at Woodside Gallery, Ewell, with many exhibitions – mixed and group – following in Britain and abroad. Easton's sculptures dated from about 1970. They were strongly influenced by classical themes, were produced in the lost wax way and were in bronze overlaid in silver and gold. Many of Easton's paintings were associated with the restoration of his fifteenth-century house near Woodbridge, Suffolk, on which he wrote for learned journals. Easton was also a student of the idea of The Fool, which has appeared for centuries in art and literature. In 1989 Easton painted Restoration to commemorate 50 years of the unit at the Queen Victoria Hospital, East Grinstead, set up to deal with treatment and rehabilitation of injured airmen by the plastic surgeon Sir Archibald McIndoe and the oral surgeon Sir William Kelsey-Fry. A 1996 Winston Churchill

Travelling Fellowship enabled Easton to work in Italy and Spain. Later solo exhibitions included Chris Beetles Ltd, 1990; Cadogan Gallery from 1991 (part of his Henley series in 1996); Bourne Gallery, Reigate, 1997 (coinciding with the publication of his book *Oil Painting Techniques*); and Museum of Garden History, 1999. One daughter, Isabella, was a painter, with whom he shared a show at the John Russell Gallery, Ipswich, in 2002, his daughter Lucy a jeweller. Easton had a solo exhibition of oils at Chappel Galleries, Chappel, in 2006.

William George EASTON 1879– Scraperboard artist, draughtsman and watercolour painter, born in London, who studied at Bolt Court School with Cecil Rea, then at Lambeth School of Art with Innes Fripp. Signed work W G E. Illustrated for national press and did book illustration. Exhibited RA and lived in London.

Nicholas EASTWOOD 1942– Artist and lecturer, who said that his paintings were "like visual records of an idea". Born in Winchester, Hampshire, Eastwood studied at Exeter College of Art, 1959–62, and from 1972 was on the staff of University of Exeter New Library, where he was deputy head and co-founder of the audio-visual section. Eastwood was a busy lecturer in Britain and abroad, modern and contemporary art being key subjects. Mixed shows included Harry J Lunn Gallery, New York, 1960; Whitechapel Art Gallery, 1976; Spacex Gallery, Exeter, from 1982; and Gordon Hepworth Gallery, Newton St Cyres, 1991, in Devon Artists. Had a solo exhibition at Galerie Jean Camion, Paris, 1960, later ones including Falmouth Art Gallery, 1997. Lived at Pinhoe, Exeter, Devon.

Roger EASTWOOD 1942– Artist mainly in oil and pastel, born in Ashton-under-Lyne, Lancashire. He was mainly self-taught, subjects being the street scenes of Oldham, Rochdale and Manchester and female nude studies. Eastwood was elected to MAFA in 1979, also showing with Oldham Society of Artists, Oldham Group of Artists and Colin Jellicoe Gallery, Manchester. Lived in Delph, Oldham, Lancashire.

Edwin EASYDORCHIK 1949– Artist producing abstract work in mixed media and teacher, born in Northumberland, who settled to work in Tynemouth, Tyne and Wear. He studied at Central School of Art 1968–71, in 1971 travelling to Italy with a Sir James Knott Travelling Scholarship. In 1973–5 he was a postgraduate painter at Newcastle University. From 1974 held several part-time lectureships, from 1982–5 lecturing in painting at Newcastle University, from 1985–7 being fellow in painting at University of Lancaster. In 1979 gained an Arts Council Purchase Award, and won several Northern Arts Grants. Took part in many group shows, from Young Contemporaries, 1970, others including Sunderland Arts Centre and tour, 1975; XI Paris Biennale, 1980; and Six Artists from the Coast, Laing Art Gallery in Newcastle and Scandinavian tour, 1983. One-man exhibitions began with Sunderland Arts Centre, 1975, later ones including the same venue, 1983, and Atlantis Gallery, also 1983. Easydorchik latterly lived in Australia. He was senior lecturer in painting and drawing, University of Western Sydney, Macarthur, New South Wales, 1991–6, then joined the staff of University of Newcastle in that state. Australian solo shows included Pendulum Gallery, Sydney, 1997. Arts Council holds several drawings.

Belinda EATON 1960– Versatile artist, born in Mombasa, Kenya, and schooled in Spain, who led a nomadic existence, eventually settling in Barcelona. Her art studies comprised a foundation course at St Martin's School of Art, 1979; graduation in fine art there, 1983; and a postgraduate etching programme at Central School of Art in 1984. She wrote: "My paintings are my world, my fascination for people, plants, animals and colour. They are how I perceive things with all their energy. I was influenced by early Renaissance art and illuminations along with Primitive art where the rules had not yet arrived and a naïvety still existed, then the beauty of form in artists like Piero della Francesca and Mantegna inspired me." Vuillard, "for his colour and use of paint"; Rothko, "for his magic"; Paula Rego, "for her strength of imagery and the worlds she creates"; and Ron Mueck, "for his incredible sculptures which have souls of their own", were also cited, along with "graffiti; music videos, a major influence when I lived in New York in the eighties; film; video; and photography." Eaton's chequered career included managing the etching department at St Martin's in 1983; writing and illustrating a children's book, *Seaweed the Dog*, 1984; between 1991–7 designing hand-painted silk scarves for Harvey Nichols, also a menswear collection for Fortnum and Mason, submitted to the collection of the Victoria & Albert Museum; in 1997 body painting on the title sequence of the James Bond film *Tomorrow Never Dies*; in 1998, at Pinewood Studios, body painting for a Dow Jones American commercial and launching a new silk collection, The House of The Pomegranate, in London and Milan; 2000, producing paintings for the film set of *102 Dalmatians*; and 2005, appearance on BBC television programme *Star Portraits with Rolf Harris*, painting the television performer and singer Cilla Black, work exhibited that year at the County Hall Gallery with tour. Group shows included Zanzibar Gallery, London, 1983; Urban Voices, Karachi, 1998; and RP, Mall Galleries, from 2003. Among later solo exhibitions were Ziggurat II, Karachi, 1997, and The A N Gallery, Karachi, 1998.

Bertram EATON 1912–1977 Northampton-born, self-taught sculptor in wood who, after several office jobs, from age 21 was employed by a leather manufacturer near the town until retirement in 1977. By the late 1930s Eaton had become fascinated by modern sculpture and while a conscientious objector during World War II carved a wooden figure based on his wife. She in 1948 took examples of his work to the Leicester Galleries in London, two being accepted. Friendship with the sculptor Robert Adams proved a spur and by the time of Eaton's only London solo show, at the Galerie Apollinaire in 1950, his output was almost entirely abstract. He also exhibited with the LG, Groupe Espace at the Royal Festival Hall, other London galleries, RSA and annually at Northampton Town and County Art Society, of which he was president, 1968–9. By the time of Eaton's second one-man exhibition at Central Art Gallery, Northampton, 1975, his sculptures were severely geometrical, such as his Single Form, of that year, in University of Leicester library. East Midlands Arts toured a show of Eaton's work, with an informative catalogue, in 1980.

David EATWELL 1960– Self-taught artist, born in Oxford, who left school at 16 and began painting aged 25. His early work was concerned with the effects of nature on man-made and natural surfaces; later pictures were abstract:

referential, geometric and organic. Eatwell showed in small-scale exhibitions in London and the provinces, later at The Lower Nupend Gallery, Cradley.

John EATWELL 1923– Painter and creator of mixed-media constructions. Studied painting at Chelsea School of Art. He showed widely in Britain, Germany and America, mixed exhibition appearances including LG, Warwick Arts Trust, Portsmouth City Art Gallery and England & Co. Had a solo show at The Minories, Colchester, 1989. Surface tones and textures were key features of his abstract studies.

John EAVES 1929– Painter, ceramist and teacher, born in Bristol. He studied at Bath Academy of Art in 1949–52, then began teaching pottery there, remaining on staff until 1979. In 1963 he had a solo ceramics exhibition at Forum Galleries in Bristol, the year later at New Vision Centre Gallery. In 1966 Eaves had a solo show of paintings at Arnolfini Gallery in Bristol, and he won a Winston Churchill Memorial Trust Fellowship to work as a painter in New Mexico. In 1986–7 he gained a Leverhulme Emeritus Fellowship to study Emile Nolde and paint in Germany. Eaves continued to exhibit widely, having a retrospective at Victoria Art Gallery, Bath, in 1987. Arts Council holds his work. Lived in Bath.

ECCLES 1920– Painter, designer and illustrator, full name Ferelith Eccles Williams, born in Oxford. She was initially educated in Wantage, then studied at Oxford Technical School, 1937–9, the Slade School of Fine Art, 1939–40, and Central School of Arts and Crafts, 1945–6. Her work was widely illustrated on the printed page, including *London Opinion*, *Sunday Times*, *Designers in Britain* and *Lilliput*. Showed at Heal's Mansard Gallery, LG, AIA and elsewhere. Lived for many years in London.

Harry Norman ECCLESTON 1923– Painter in watercolour, printmaker and teacher, born in Bilston, Staffordshire. He studied at the College of Art in Birmingham under Richard Stubbington, 1939–42, then at Royal College of Art under Robert Austin, 1947–51. From 1952–8, lectured in printmaking and illustration at South-East Essex Technical College. From 1958–83 he was artist designer at Bank of England Printing Works, where he was designer of the Series D notes: £1, Newton; £5, Wellington; £10, Nightingale; £20, Shakespeare; and £50, Wren. He was elected RE in 1961, being its president in 1975, the year he was elected a fellow of RWS. Was also a member of RWA and honorary member of RBSA, also a member of Art Workers' Guild. Eccleston's watercolours were much concerned with subjects on the water's edge and his prints, mainly of industrial subjects, included a water-edge suite, 1987. Also showed at RA from 1949, at NEAC and at Art Fairs in London and Bath. Bank of England Museum, British Museum and Ashmolean Museum in Oxford hold his work. Lived in Harold Hill, Romford, Essex.

Myles Richard ECKERSLEY 1923– Painter in oils, acrylic and other media, and teacher, the son of Captain Peter Pendleton Eckersley, pioneer of wireless, a founder-member of the BBC who in 1923 made its first live outside broadcast from the top of Nelson's Column in Trafalgar Square. Myles's mother was Stella, granddaughter of Sir George Grove, musicologist and first author of *Grove's Dictionary of Music*. Eckersley was with the Royal Air Force, 1943-6, training in Canada, serving in the Far East. In 1946 he joined Tunbridge Wells School of Art, in 1949 Sir John Cass School of Arts and Crafts and in 1951 West of England College of Art, Bristol, under Donald Milner. He was art master at Embley Park School, 1952–86. On retiring, he spent four years at Southampton College of Art on an experimental art course. Eckersley wrote: "I think that my dispersal of style is because I developed an inability to settle into a mould; but I am obstinate in believing that I am free to experiment, and I cannot help being inconsistent." Notable in his output were realistic London street scenes painted in the 1950s, a political-prisoner series and another entitled Yup's Progress, inspired by William Hogarth's Rake's Progress. Eckersley travelled extensively, reflected in his subjects. Although the demands of teaching eventually encroached on his painting time, Eckersley early in his career showed locally and sent work to major exhibitions. These included Young Contemporaries, 1951, and Various Wessex Artists, 1955–65. He had solo shows at Hamwick Gallery, 1969, Elm View Studio, 1988, Southampton Library Civic Centre, 1999, and one at Duncan Campbell Fine Art which sold well in 2004. Lived in Lockerley, Hampshire. Among Eckersley's portraits was the playwright Peter Terson.

Tom ECKERSLEY 1914–1997 Designer, muralist, illustrator and teacher, born in Newton-le-Willows, Lancashire. He studied at Salford College of Art, 1930–4, under Martin Tyas. Moved to London in 1934, where with a fellow-student, Eric Lombers, he established Eckersley Lombers, with a reputation for fine poster design. Eventually Eckersley counted among his clients London Transport, Shell-Mex, the Post Office, Gillette and the Royal Society for the Prevention of Accidents. His posters got their message over simply in two-dimensional form, with a strong idea, taste and good humour, with words well matched to the graphics. Eckersley Lombers was forced to close during World War II. Eckersley served as a cartographer in the Royal Air Force, eventually moving to the Air Ministry's publicity office. After the war Eckersley Lombers was briefly revived, then Eckersley built up a successful freelance practice. Before the war Eckersley had taught at the Westminster School of Art and Borough Polytechnic. For 20 years from 1957 he was head of graphic design at the London College of Printing, which gave him a retrospective in 1975. He published *Poster Design* in 1954. Among several books illustrated was his first wife, Daphne's, *Cat o'Nine Lives*, in 1947 (his second wife was the artist Mary Kessell). Among Eckersley's murals is that at Heathrow Airport underground station. Eckersley's work was shown at many international exhibitions and is included in the collections of the Victoria & Albert Museum, Imperial War Museum, London Transport Museum and in overseas holdings. Among honours received was his appointment as a Royal Designer for Industry, 1963, and Chartered Society of Designers' medal, 1990. Eckersley's sons Richard, Paul and Anthony and Richard's son Sam all became graphic designers. Lived in London.

Robin ECKARDT 1980– Painter, born and who spent the first 10 years of his childhood on the Caribbean island of Puerto Rico, graduating with a fine art honours degree from Bath Spa University College in 2003. This background "strongly influenced my outlook on the world, particularly my depiction of colour and texture". In 2005

The Lennox Gallery gave Eckardt a show of large, vividly hued and dynamic pictures covering subjects as diverse as the Thames at Dusk, Eiffel Tower and Times Square Reflections to Shores of Lombok and Spitfire. Previous solo exhibitions included The Red Gallery, Thame, in 2004 and 2005. Eckardt also exhibited widely at art fairs in London, the provinces and Glasgow.

Royston ECROYD 1938– Artist noted for his watercolours and pen-and-wash drawings based on scenes from everyday life, often tinged with pathos. He was born in Accrington, Lancashire, studying in Burnley and at the Slade School of Fine Art under Claude Rogers. Ecroyd lived in France for 40 years, first in Paris, later in Normandy. Had numerous exhibitions in Britain, France, Luxembourg and Germany. The New Academy Gallery held a series of solo shows from 1997.

Jane EDDEN 1966– Versatile sculptor and artist whose creations included articulated boxes and machines. She did a preliminary course and a foundation diploma at West Sussex College of Art & Design, 1982–4, completing an honours degree in engineering industrial design at Manchester Polytechnic, 1984–8, deferred one year in 1986–7 for travel in China and Southeast Asia. During 1984–8 was assistant to Lincoln Seligman, mural and trompe l'oeil painter, a period spent researching perspective and architectural framework calculations and drawings through finished paintings, working on a number of projects including The Brushstrokes Mobile at 100 New Bridge Street for Rosehaugh Stanhope Developments; in 1988–9 was self-employed, projects including painting/furniture restoration; in 1989 worked on voluntary projects in Nicaragua and for Banner Arts, San Francisco: pattern cutting and construction of large-scale fabric artworks for architectural applications; and from 1989–96 worked for Dick Stringer Associates Ltd, designers and makers of retail and office systems. Mixed exhibitions included Summer Exhibition, Cadogan Contemporary, from 1995; Still Life, Collyer-Bristow, 1998; and Galerie Vieille du Temple, Paris, France, 2000. Later solo exhibitions included Fly on the Wall, Idee Gallery, Tokyo, Japan, 1999; Solar Labels, Blumenthal & Lynne, New York, America, 2000 (in that year created an installation, Solar Insects, for New York-based Richard Blumenthal); and England & Co, 2001.

Maurice EDELMAN 1911–1975 Politician, writer and recreational painter who was educated at Cardiff High School, was an exhibitioner in modern languages at Trinity College, Cambridge, 1929, graduated in 1932 and gained his master's in 1941. From 1932–41 was involved in the application of plastics to aircraft building, then was a journalist and war correspondent in North Africa and France. After World War II held various appointments in international bodies, notably with a French connection, and was vice-chairman of the British Council, 1951–67. He was Labour Member of Parliament for Coventry constituencies between 1945–74. Books included *The Birth of the Fourth Republic*, 1945; political novels, including *Who Goes Home*, 1953; and television plays. There was a memorial show at Herbert Art Gallery, Coventry, 1977.

Andrew EDEN 1946– Artist and teacher, born in Hemel Hempstead, Hertfordshire, whose work included abstract sculptures in various materials, including pigment. He attended Byam Shaw School of Art, 1963–4, then gained a first-class honours degree in fine art painting at Wimbledon School of Art, 1964–9. He was joint editor/contributor, *Wallpaper* arts magazine, also participating in *Wallpaper on Cassette*, Audio Arts, Whitechapel Art Gallery, Gallery. From 1983 was associate lecturer in painting and history of art, Tresham Institute of Further and Higher Education, Kettering. Group shows included Young Contempories, 1968; On Site, Arnolfini Gallery, Bristol, 1979; Six Attitudes, Peterborough Museum and Art Gallery, 1983; and The Table Studio Group, The Living Room, 1996. Had a solo show at Daniel Shackleton Gallery, Edinburgh, 1971, later ones including Tower Bridge Piazza Gallery from 1991, and Streitenfeld Gallery, Oberursel, Frankfurt, 1995. In 2002, shared a show with Susan Bonvin at Fermyn Woods Contemporary Art, Brigstock, and was featured in John Moores Liverpool Exhibition, in 2003 having another one-man at New Gallery, Northampton. Lived at Southwick, Peterborough, Cambridgeshire.

Denis EDEN 1878–1949 Painter, son of the watercolourist William Eden, born in Liverpool. He was educated at University College School, studying under F G Stephens; at the St John's Wood School of Art; and at Royal Academy Schools. Historical subjects were a feature of his work, which was shown at RA, Royal Glasgow Institute of the Fine Arts, Fine Art Society and RSA. Lived at Woodstock, Oxfordshire.

Margaret Ann EDEN 1939– Lady Eden, painter and school director, was born and lived in London. She studied at Byam Shaw School of Art with Bernard Adams for portrait painting, also botanical illustration with Anne Marie Evans. Eden was a member of the American Society of Botanical Artists, NEAC and Chelsea Physic Garden Florilegium Society. Group and mixed shows included Tryon and Horsus Galleries and Ursus Gallery in New York. Heralding a comeback of botanical art in the *Financial Times* in 1999, John Windsor referred to Eden as a "star pupil" of Evans, "whose opening night at the Spink Gallery three years ago was a sell-out." The Hunt Institute for Botanical Illustration and the collections of Shirley Sherwood and the Earl of Mansfield held examples.

Max EDEN 1923– Artist in various media, teacher, born in St Helens, Lancashire. He attended Liverpool College of Art, 1948–51, at École des Beaux-Arts in Paris, 1951–2, and at Royal Academy in Copenhagen, 1954. A landscape painter in a rich palette, Eden claimed as his chief influences Cézanne and the School of Paris; Spain, the Lake District and Scotland were favoured subjects. Eden showed in France and Denmark in the 1950s. In Britain showed at Redfern Gallery and in many group shows in the north-west. Had a solo show at Acorn Gallery in Liverpool, 1985; Atkinson Art Gallery, Southport, 1988; and with his son John Eden at Orsini Gallery, 1991. There was a retrospective at the University of Liverpool Art Gallery in 2005 which included hard-edge abstracts, a series inspired by the BBC television series *Come Dancing* and Spanish landscapes. Atkinson Art Gallery holds his work. Eden lived in Southport, Merseyside, and was a lecturer at College of Art there, 1960–85.

Annette EDGAR 1943– Artist and teacher who was born and lived in Glasgow, as an adult graduating from the School of Art there, 1976–80, under David Donaldson,

Barbara Rae, Duncan Shanks and Sandy Moffat. For a while she taught art in London and Glasgow, but from 1990 painted full-time. Edgar won or was shortlisted for several awards. She was a member of the RGI, a professional member of the SWA and SSA. Group exhibitions included Painting in Scotland, Glasgow Print Studio; Art Expo, New York; RSW; RSA; Vigorous Scots, Los Angeles; Cheltenham Drawing Open; and CCA, Glasgow. She had many solo exhibitions, including Schomburg Gallery, Los Angeles; Compass Gallery, Glasgow; Bohun Gallery, Henley-on-Thames; and 369 Gallery, Edinburgh. Edgar claimed to be "equally at home with large vibrant abstract paintings or lyrical colourful landscapes"; London and St Ives Schools and the Expressionists were cited as influences. "Previous themes were isolation, fear, bereavement, journey and the environment, latterly evolving into relationships – human/human, human/land." Many public, corporate and private collections held Edgar's work, including the Scottish National Portrait Gallery; Prior's Court School, Oxfordshire; Arthur Andersen, Edinburgh; Heriot-Watt University, Edinburgh; East Lothian District Council; Royal Bank of Scotland, Edinburgh.

Norman EDGAR 1948– Painter in the Scottish Colourist tradition of landscape and still life, and teacher, born in Paisley, Renfrewshire. He studied painting at Glasgow School of Art, 1966–70, then taught until 1990, when he resigned to paint full-time. In 1991 Edgar was elected a member of the Royal Glasgow Institute of the Fine Arts, also showing at RP, RSA, Fosse Gallery in Stow-on-the-Wold, Richard Hagen Gallery in Broadway and elsewhere. Edgar received many portrait commissions, from bodies such as the University of Glasgow, The Archdiocese of Glasgow and the Royal College of Obstetricians. Had a solo show at Glasgow Art Club in 1977, later ones including Roger Billcliffe Fine Art, Glasgow, in 1996. Paisley Art Gallery and HRH The Duke of Edinburgh hold Edgar's work. In 1993 he was made president of Glasgow Art Club. Lived in Gourock, Renfrewshire.

Ursula EDGCUMBE 1900–1985 Sculptor in bronze, stone and wood, and painter, of figure groups and birds. Born at Sandy, Bedfordshire, Edgcumbe worked in the studio of the sculptor Havard Thomas, then studied under him at the Slade School where she won the scholarship for sculpture in 1918. When she left in 1921 she turned from modelling to direct carving for architectural projects, especially for George Kennedy. Lack of commissions and of sympathy with current trends prompted Edgcumbe in 1940 to turn from sculpture to painting. She had had a one-man sculpture show at the Leger Galleries in 1935; several painting shows followed after World War II. Commissioned work includes the large granite war memorial at Zennor, Cornwall. Work reproduced in William Aumonier's *Modern Architectural Sculpture*, Kineton Parkes' *The Art of Carved Sculpture* and the Fine Art Society catalogue *Sculpture in Britain Between the Wars*, 1986. Signed work with her initials. Lived at Ballingham; Hereford.

Reginald Edward EDGECOMBE 1885–1966 Painter, draughtsman, printmaker and designer-craftsman in glass and metal, born in Birmingham, where he finally lived. Studied at Birmingham School of Art, where he won the Messenger Prize for metalwork. Around this time he was a keen athlete, competing as a gymnast with the British team at the Antwerp Olympic Games in 1920. Member of Birmingham Art Circle. Exhibited RBSA on many occasions, also in Royal Society of Arts competitions.

Henry EDION 1905–1987 Artist on paper, born Heinrich Edelstein in Vienna, Austria. While in a Nazi concentration camp was encouraged to paint by the German Expressionist Gert Wollheim, also a prisoner, then after World War II attended L'Académie de la Grande Chaumière, in Paris. Lived and worked in Indo-China, Australia, Italy, France, Canada and America, eventually moving to England for his wife to be treated for cancer. The threat of nuclear war and rockets was a recurrent theme in Edion's work, which employed humour, strong colours and thick black lines, as in his exhibits in Fragments Against Ruin, the Arts Council touring show of 1981–2. Edion also exhibited in North America, with Crane Kalman Gallery in 1962, and after his death was shown at that gallery in 1993 and at Ben Uri Art Society, 1994, which holds examples. Lived finally in west London.

John EDKINS 1931–1966 Figurative and hard-edge abstract painter, photographer, draughtsman and teacher, born in Bromley, Kent. Attended Ealing Junior School of Art, 1942–5, then the senior school, 1945–8. Between 1945–8 Edkins painted, gardened and taught part-time, then entered the school of painting at Royal College of Art, 1954–7. After a travelling scholarship to Greece, from 1958–61 taught at Bideford School of Art, lecturing in painting at Liverpool College of Art, 1961–6. Exhibited at Liverpool Academy and was a prizewinner at John Moores Liverpool Exhibition in 1965. Although Edkins was absorbed in his work, three major heart operations undermined his strength. He was a dedicated teacher, a man with wide, lively and quirky enthusiasms, ranging from music, personal products of the industrial age and motor racing to the making and launching of fire balloons. Had a solo show, organised by the Liverpool Academy, at Bluecoat Chambers, 1966, shortly after he married and went to live in the Formby, Lancashire, area. Died in Guy's Hospital. Walker Art Gallery, Liverpool, which owns his work, organised a retrospective in 1967, toured to the Royal College of Art.

Angela EDMONDS 1946– Versatile artist and teacher, born in Hendon, north London. She did a foundation course at Watford College of Art and Design, 1983–4; graduated with honours in fine art, University of Hertfordshire, 1985–90; did an introductory course, on a bursary, at the British Institute of Psychoanalysis, 1990–1; then gained her master's in visual culture, Middlesex University/Royal College of Art joint course, 1995–7. A series of awards included The Hunting Art Prizes, Mall Galleries and tour, 1988; first prize, Hertfordshire Open, Watford Museum and tour, 1989; first prize, Drawings for All, Gainsborough's House, Sudbury, and tour, 1992; Paul Hamlyn Foundation bursary, 1996; and nomination for The Margaret James Award for Women's Education, 1998. Taught part-time at Aldenham School, Radlett, and West Herts College. In later years Edmonds' output spanned figurative drawing and conceptual art. A series of assemblages and photoworks, informed by Surrealism and psychoanalytic theory, combined everyday objects in unusual ways. Exhibited widely, later shows including Landmarks, CyberAxis, and Galerie Am Fischtor, Mainze, Germany, both 2000; Bushey and Hertford Museums, both 2001; and One Heart One World, The Atrium, Cotton's Centre, and international tour, 2001–2. Watford and Bushey Museums and other public and corporate collections hold examples. Lived in Oxhey, Hertfordshire.

Edith EDMONDS fl. c.1920–1955 Watercolourist who studied at Liverpool School of Art, 1921–2 and in Paris at Atelier Delbos, 1923–4. Showed at RA, SWA, RCamA, in the provinces and at Paris Salon. Lived in Conway, Carnarvonshire.

Michael EDMONDS 1926– Sculptor, watercolourist and draughtsman. After education in the south of England he served in south Wales coal mines, 1944–7, then qualified as an architect in 1953. First one-man show at Cooling Galleries, 1943. Was a founder-member of the 56 Group and joined the Society of Christian Artists. Had a retrospective toured by Oriel 31, Newtown, 2001 and took part in group shows including RCamA, WAC, SWG and *Daily Express* Young Artists Exhibition in 1955. Commissioned work included National Union of Mine Workers and Medical Research Council, for which he completed a tile mural. Contemporary Art Society and Pembroke College, Oxford, bought his work.

Simon EDMONDSON 1955– Artist who was born and lived in London. He studied at City & Guilds School of Art, 1973–4; Kingston Polytechnic, 1974–7; and at Syracuse University, New York, 1978–80. He held a first solo exhibition at Syracuse in 1979, after which he had one-man shows in Berlin, Zürich, New York and London, where Nicola Jacobs Gallery exhibited him for a time. Later solo shows included Jason & Rhodes Gallery, 1995. In 1987 Edmondson was included in The Self Portrait: A Modern View tour, originating at Artsite Gallery, Bath.

Nathan EDMUNDS 1974– Painter, born in Nuneaton, Warwickshire, who studied at Kent Institute of Art and Design, 1992–3, and University of the West of England, Bristol, 1993–6. Exhibitions included West by South West, The Tannery, 1996; Michael Wright Fine Art, Bristol, 1998; and John Moores Liverpool Exhibition, 1999.

Nellie Mary Hepburn EDMUNDS fl. from 1895–1953 Miniature and portrait painter who studied at Slade School of Fine Art under Fred Brown and at Westminster School of Art. She was a prolific exhibitor at RMS, in which she held a number of senior positions. Also showed at RA, SWA and RI. Lived in Bexhill, Sussex.

Stuart EDMUNDSON 1976– Artist and lecturer, who graduated in fine art from the University of Central Lancashire and Queensland University of Technology, Brisbane, Australia, 1996–9, gaining his master's at Manchester Metropolitan University, 1999–00. He was student mentor on the graduate course at that University during his time there, then taught fine art at University of Central Lancashire, 2000–02. Among his residencies was Spot Light programme, The Lowry Centre, Salford, commissioned new work for Shine, 2002, and Manchester Art Gallery, 2003. Group shows included Possibly 20, The H Gallery, Brisbane, 1998; Seven7, Cornerhouse, Manchester, 2000; In Residence, The Zion Centre, Manchester, 2001; and Beyond the Endgame: Abstract Painting in Manchester, Manchester Art Gallery, 2003. Among his solo exhibitions was In Progress, Glass Box Gallery, Salford University, 2002.

May de Montravel EDWARDES 1887– Painter and miniaturist who studied at the Cope and Nicol School, in South Kensington, then at the Royal Academy Schools, 1907–12, where she was a bronze and silver medallist. Exhibited RA, RI, SM, of which she was a member, Brook Street Gallery and Paris Salon. She was fond of historical subjects and her picture of General Wolfe on the Heights of Abraham before the Battle of Quebec was one notable example. Lived in London.

Adrian EDWARDS 1947– Painter who graduated in fine art from College of Art, Exeter; gaining a postgraduate education certificate from Manchester Polytechnic; then his master's in the history of modern art and design. Went on to work "as a leader in the education sector". Shape, form and colour of objects and their specific arrangement and setting were important in Edwards' work. Group exhibitions included Dartington Hall, Devon, 1965; National Museum of Wales, Cardiff, 1970; RWA, from 1993; and County Hall, Truro, 1995. Among solo exhibitions were Falmouth Art Gallery, 2001.

Alan EDWARDS 1947– Artist and teacher who gained an honours degree at Liverpool Polytechnic, 1979–82, and who taught at Plessington High School. He showed at Five Artists, Liverpool's Unity Theatre, 1980; Stowells Trophy at RA, 1982; and was included in Walker Art Gallery, Liverpool, touring exhibition Merseyside Artists 3, 1986–7, showing the wood/collage Door II.

Arthur Sherwood EDWARDS 1887–1960 Architect and sculptor who spent much of his spare time painting. He was born in Leicester and studied in Grimsby and Newcastle, where he gained a bronze medal. Notable among his public works are his mosaic of the Battle of Waterloo for Manchester's Free Trade Hall; Sculptures at the back of that building; and his prizewinning war memorial at Sale, Cheshire, to the 10th Battalion Lincolns, a marble statue of St George. Few of his paintings were commissioned and most remained unframed until the death of his wife, after which there was a studio sale at the Manchester Auction Mart in 1980. Manchester City Art Gallery holds his work, which was also exhibited at RA, RI, RCamA, Walker Art Gallery in Liverpool and at Royal Glasgow Institute of the Fine Arts. Lived for some years in Ashton-on-Mersey, Cheshire.

Barry EDWARDS 1952– Artist who graduated with honours in fine art from Middlesex Polytechnic, 1972–5, gaining his master's from the Royal College of Art, 1975–8. In 1983, Edwards showed at Cheltenham Park Gallery, in the *Evening Standard* Awards and at the South Bank Exhibition at the Royal Festival Hall; at Penny Bank Gallery, 1988; and in East End Open Studios with Barbican Arts Group, 1989.

Benjamin Ralph EDWARDS 1950– Painter, printmaker, draughtsman and teacher, born in London, where he lived. He studied art privately, at City and Guilds of London Art School, 1968–72, then with S W Hayter at Atelier 17 in Paris, 1972–3, and Roderic Barrett at Royal Academy Schools, 1973–7. Taught part-time at City and Guilds. Showed from 1977 at RA Summer Exhibitions, RE and abroad and illustrated several books. Victoria & Albert Museum holds his work.

Brigid EDWARDS 1940– Botanical artist and illustrator, born in London, who studied illustration and graphic design at the Central School of Art, 1960–3. She worked first as a researcher, then as a producer/director on television current affairs and documentary programmes, 1966–76. Her group exhibitions included RA Summer Exhibition, 1990; The Linnaean Society, 1991; Seventh International Exhibition of Botanical Art and Illustration, The Hunt Institute, Pittsburgh, America, 1992; Kew Gardens Gallery, 1994; Contemporary Botanical Paintings from the Shirley Sherwood Collection, Scottish National Gallery of Modern Art, Edinburgh, and New Orleans Museum of Art, both 1997; S H Ervin Gallery, Sydney, Australia, and The Yasuda Kasai Museum of Art, Tokyo, Japan, both 1998; Millesgarden Museum, Stockholm, Sweden, 1999; Smithsonian Institution National Museum of Natural History, Washington, 2003; and A New Flowering: 1,000 Years of Botanical Art, Ashmolean Museum, Oxford, 2005. Edwards had solo exhibitions at Thomas Gibson Fine Art in 1995 and 1997 and at Beadleston Gallery, New York, in 2000. Her work was included in J Richards's 1993 book *Primula*. The Hunt Institute and Royal Botanic Gardens, Kew, hold examples. Lived at Nancherrow, St Just, Penzance, Cornwall.

Cyril Walduck EDWARDS 1902– Painter in oil and watercolour, mainly of landscapes. Studies pursued at Regent Street Polytechnic School of Art. Exhibited at RA, RBA, RI, ROI and Paris Salon, Laing Art Gallery in Newcastle buying his work. Lived at Upper Wyche, near Malvern, Worcestershire.

Gareth EDWARDS 1960– Artist and teacher whose work included Minimalist landscapes and abstract work in a muted palette, born in Berkshire. He gained a Bachelor of Science honours degree from Goldsmiths' College, 1976–7; an honours degree in art history from London University, 1981–4; with a postgraduate art teacher's certificate from Goldsmiths' in 1988. Held extensive lecturing posts from 1984, latterly including Swindon and Chelsea Colleges of Art and Coventry University. Group shows included Whitechapel Open, 1989, and POSK Gallery, 1992. Among his later solo shows were Bird & Davis, 1995, Original Gallery, 1998, and Hart Gallery, 2000–1. In 1998 he founded Conductor, a co-operative group of painters and composers.

Griff EDWARDS 1920– Painter and teacher, born in Port Talbot, Glamorgan. After attending Swansea College of Art Edwards did military service 1940–7, but managed to study part-time at Bournemouth College of Art, completing his formal studies at Paignton School of Art, 1947–9. From 1949 was on staff of Swansea College Art, latterly as the head of technical graphics department. Showed RCamA, SEA, Royal National Eisteddfod and elsewhere in Wales, where his drawings of chapels were a notable feature done in connection with WAC.

Helen EDWARDS 1882– Landscape painter and writer on art who also worked under her maiden name Helen Sutton. She studied at Algernon Talmage's school in St Ives, Cornwall, and with A Moulton Foweraker, 1906–8, and H Dawson Barkas in Reading, 1909. Showed at SWA, PS, UA and in the provinces, notably with art societies in Hampshire and Dorset, where she lived at Parkstone. Medici Society reproduced several pastels, including *After the Shower* and *Untrodden Snow*.

Jeffery EDWARDS 1945– Painter and printmaker, born in London, who attended Leeds College of Art, 1964–7, then the Royal College of Art, 1967–70, winning the Printmaking Prize. His many group shows included Young Contemporaries, 1970; Venice Biennale and Bradford Print Biennale, where he was a prize winner, both 1972; British Printmakers, Brooklyn Museum, New York, 1974; Thumb Gallery, 1984; Chelsea Arts Club Centenary Portfolio, 1992; and The Large Print Show, Christchurch Mansion, Ipswich, 1997. Had a solo exhibition at Serpentine Gallery, 1972, later ones including On Reflection, Flowers East, 1995. His 1999 Flowers East show, The Whole Truth, depicted three geometrically shaped characters painted with carefully wrought tones in primary colours. Arts Council, Bradford City Art Gallery, British Council, Brooklyn Museum in New York, Tate Gallery and Whitworth Art Gallery, Manchester, hold Edwards' work.

John EDWARDS 1938– Painter and teacher, born in London, where he continued to live. Edwards studied at Hornsey College of Art, 1953–60, with a spell in Royal Air Force, 1956–8. In the early 1960s Edwards taught at Brighton College of Art and Leeds University Institute. After a British Council Scholarship took him to Belgium in 1963–4, Edwards embarked on a busy teaching career which included periods at Chelsea and Brighton and St Martin's School of Art, where he was senior lecturer in painting. In the mid-1970s he taught at a number of American colleges and universities and was artist-in-residence at Syracuse University, New York. Edwards took part in many group exhibitions and from 1967 had extensive solo shows at Rowan Gallery. In 1979 a Newcastle upon Tyne Polytechnic Art Gallery show toured England. Edwards' abstract pictures had many influences over the years, including Rothko, Noland, David Smith and Anthony Caro. The surfaces could be highly charged and sometimes he used basic configurations in series, such as X's, T's, crosses and arcs. Arts Council holds his work.

John EDWARDS 1940– Portrait, wildlife and sporting artist who aimed to "continue the traditional methods of naturalistic painting, drawing and sculpture" in his work. He was born in Kidderminster, Worcestershire. Was at Stourbridge Art School, 1953–5, then was a carpet designer, 1955–62. From 1962–3 studied art with Pietro Annigoni in Florence, then was at Royal Academy Schools. Gained four silver and bronze medals and the Elizabeth Greenshields Memorial Foundation Award, 1965–6 and 1968–9. Edwards was made a member of RP in 1970. In 1986 won the World Wildlife Fund Art Award. Among Edwards' subjects were the politician Margaret Thatcher and the actress Helen Mirren. He showed with Moorland and Malcolm Innes Galleries; Solent Gallery, Lymington; Chesterville Gallery, Kidderminster; RA Summer Exhibitions; SWA; Ashmolean Museum in Oxford, and elsewhere. Gordonstoun School, The Kennel Club and Oxford and Cambridge University colleges hold his work. Lived in Kidderminster.

John D EDWARDS 1952– Painter, sculptor, printmaker and teacher, born in London. He studied, 1971–4, at Harrow School of Art and Central School of Art and Design, his teachers including Adrian Berg, John Hoyland and Paul Huxley. In 1973 Edwards was the first president of New Contemporaries, was an assistant to both Hoyland and Berg and began a working relationship with Waddington Galleries interspersed with teaching. In late 1970s travelled extensively through Europe and America. The early 1980s saw Edwards working as the sculptor Barry Flanagan's assistant, also with Allen Jones and Ivor Abrahams. Edwards had his first solo show with Odette Gilbert Gallery in 1985, several more following. In 1991, Edwards began work on major outdoor sculptures privately commissioned and had his first solo show with Mayor Gallery, having had his first solo exhibition in America, at Carone Gallery, Florida, in 1990. Later solo exhibitions included an eight-city tour of America and exhibition of monoprints and sculpture at CCA, London, 1994, and Lefevre Contemporary Art, 2001. From the mid-1990s, Edwards worked in various American studios, in 1996 starting a collaboration with John Battenberg on a European tour of Battenberg's work. Group shows included Lefevre, 2000–1. The Government Art Collection and a number of corporate collections hold examples. Edwards latterly lived in London; San Francisco, California; and Phoenix, Arizona.

Joseph B EDWARDS 1933– Painter of landscapes, portraits and self-portraits, muralist and art teacher, born in Aberdeen. Joe Edwards studied locally under Robert Sivell at Gray's School of Art, 1950–4; completed his National Service, 1954–6; and on demobilisation went with his wife Betty to live in the bothy at Home Farm, Kingswells, a village just east of Aberdeen. Three years later they settled at nearby Speedwell Cottage. Kingswells gradually became a suburb and Edwards devoted much of his time as a painter to depicting changing country life and farming personalities, his enthusiasm triggered by his 1958 portrait of farmer George Findlay. Edwards completed a cycle of notable murals held by Aberdeen University. These were based on the seasons, including Harvesters, 1966, and Plough: song of the earth, 1967. Edwards' humanist philosophy was shared by his contemporaries in the Aberdeen Adelphi Group, 1959, who believed that artists had to "make some positive attempt to relate in some way to the rest of the world." He also showed with Aberdeen Artists' Society and in 1995 had an exhibition at the Scottish Agricultural Museum, Ingliston. Aberdeen Art Gallery holds Edwards' 1985 oil on canvas Lord Provost Alec Collie, a City Council commission.

Kevin EDWARDS 1962– Artist who after a foundation year at Bangor, 1981–2, studied at Liverpool Polytechnic, 1982–5. Showed with Liverpool Four at Theatre Gwynedd, 1984; Bluecoat Gallery BA Graduates, 1985; and with Walker Art Gallery, Liverpool, 1986–7 touring exhibition Merseyside Artists 3. In 1986 shared a show at Theatre Gwynedd.

Laurence EDWARDS 1967– Sculptor, draughtsman and teacher, born in Suffolk, where he set up a foundry at Laxfield and ran classes. Did a foundation course at Lowestoft College, 1983–4; gained his degree from Canterbury College of Art, 1985–88; and made postgraduate studies in bronze casting and sculpture at Royal College of Art, 1988–90. There he was awarded a Henry Moore Bursary, the Angelani Prize for Bronze Casting and an Intach Travelling Scholarship, enabling him to study in India traditional casting methods. Had solo shows at Chappel Galleries, Chappel, 1998, and John Russell Gallery, Ipswich, 2000. Lived in Yoxford, Suffolk, where in 2004 he showed Festival Sculptures, during Yoxford Arts Festival, at Gallery-26.

Lionel EDWARDS 1878–1966 Painter and draughtsman, magazine and book illustrator and writer, famous for his sporting, particularly fox- and stag-hunting, and military subjects. Edwards studied with the painter Arthur Cope and at Frank Calderon's School of Animal Painting. Edwards reported in Spain for *The Graphic* in 1910, then served with the Army Remount Service during World War I. Thereafter he became a favourite contributor to sporting and other magazines, such as *Punch*, and began to be known for his illustrations to several dozen books with horsing and country themes. He was the author, mostly on hunting subjects, of more than a dozen books. His *Reminiscences of a Sporting Artist* appeared in 1948. For a time he was a member of the London Sketch Club. Edwards knew his subjects at first hand, as he hunted with 91 packs of foxhounds and at the age of 80 was still jumping gates. A quiet, gentle man who looked like an old soldier, he earned a reputation as a first-class sporting artist, exemplary at representing the English landscape during the seasons. Exhibited RCamA and RI especially, also RA and Walker Art Gallery, Liverpool. British Sporting Art Trust held his work. Lived at Buckholt, Wiltshire.

Malcolm EDWARDS 1935– After retiring as an architect, Edwards devoted many years to depicting the dramatic landscape of north Wales, based in a former lead mining village in Flintshire. Good examples were included in the 2005 exhibition Welsh Painters Past and Present at John Davies Fine Paintings at Upper Swell, Stow-on-the-Wold. Edwards was by then a former president of the RCamA; winner of the People's Favourite Prize at Welsh Artists of the Year, at St David's Hall, Cardiff, 2002 and 2003, and of the Sponsors Patrons Prize in 2003; and winner of the Ailsa Owen Memorial Prize at The Museum of Modern Art Wales Competitions in Machynlleth in 2002 and 2003. CASW, The National Museum and Gallery of Wales in Cardiff and the National Library of Wales in Aberystwyth hold examples of his watercolours. Experiment with media was a feature of Edwards's work.

Mary Stella EDWARDS 1898–1989 Mystic poet, painter and model-maker, born in London. Studied at Battersea and Regent Street Polytechnic Schools of Art. There she met Judith Ackland, with whom she spent the rest of her life, painting around Britain and exhibiting together and jointly making models and dioramas, Edwards painting the settings. Windsor Guildhall holds examples. She illustrated for publishers such as Chapman and Hall; showed at SWA, RBA and elsewhere; and published several volumes of poetry. The first book, *Time and Chance*, was published by Leonard and Virginia Woolf at Hogarth Press, 1926. London Museum holds her work. Lived in Staines, Middlesex.

Peter EDWARDS 1955– Figurative painter in oil, born in Chirk, Denbighshire, who studied at Shrewsbury, 1974–5, and Cheltenham, 1975–8, after which he was based in Shropshire, settling in Oswestry. Showed at RA Summer Exhibition and regularly in portrait exhibitions at National Portrait Gallery, which toured his Contemporary

Poets show, 1990–3. The Liverpool poets, also Seamus Heaney, John Heath-Stubbs, Michael Longley, Douglas Dunn and Bobby Charlton were among Edwards' main works. National Portrait Gallery, Ulster Museum in Belfast, Ferens Art Gallery in Hull, National Library of Wales in Aberystwyth, Williamson Art Gallery in Birkenhead and a number of university colleges hold examples. Chelsea Arts Club member.

David EDWICK 1954– Stone-carver, letter-cutter and conservator, based in Hexham, Northumberland. Edwick was a stonemason at St Paul's Cathedral, 1975–9, then worked at English Heritage Sculpture Studio in Vauxhall, 1979–87. Thereafter he freelanced, completing a number of commissions in the northeast of England. Later works included the panel Seven Ages of Man, on Alnwick Playhouse, 1997; and Pigeon Race, 1998 (the first of three big related sculptures by Edwick), marking Sunderland's boundary at Easington Lane, both in sandstone.

EFF: *see* **Roy FERGUSON**

Felim EGAN 1952– Painter and sculptor, born in Strabane, County Tyrone. Studied at Northern Ireland Polytechnic, then 1975–7 did Slade School of Fine Art postgraduate study. Mixed shows included Third Eye Centre, Glasgow; Graeme Murray Gallery, Edinburgh; Art Cologne '88 and '89; and Fruitmarket Gallery, Edinburgh. From 1979 had a series of solo shows at Oliver Dowling Gallery, Dublin. Others included Purdy Hicks Gallery, 2004. Two major commissions carried out by Egan were a neon construction for Ardhowen Theatre, Northern Ireland, 1986, and a wall construction for the conference hall in Dublin Castle, 1989. Ulster Museum, Belfast; Arts Council of Northern Ireland; and Contemporary Irish Arts Society hold Egan's work, which included Minimalist paintings and bronzes, abstract with landscape references. Worked in Dublin and Edinburgh.

Shan EGERTON 1948– Landscape artist in pastel and oil, born in London but brought up on the Welsh border, her mother a painter from an artistic family. From 1966–70, Shan studied at Byam Shaw School of Art, teachers including Bernard Dunstan and Diana Armfield. After art school she divided her time between her home near Hay-on-Wye and London, which she eventually gave up. Travelled in India, China, Nepal, Mongolia and Tibet, making sketches later worked up in the studio. Mixed appearances included RA Summer Exhibitions, PS, NEAC and Kilvert Gallery in Clyro. Had several solo exhibitions at Oliver Swann Galleries from 1980, later ones including Sally Hunter Fine Art, 1997.

Anne EGGEBERT 1958– Artist, and teacher, using media such as video and site-specific live art and installation, individually and collaborating with Polly Gould as Eggebert & Gould (see separate entries). Eggebert gained a first-class honours degree in critical fine art practice, Central St Martins College of Art & Design, 1990–3, then her master's in media fine art, Slade School of Fine Art, 1993–6. Central to Eggebert's work was "the deconstruction of the notion of Englishness and its related ideological fictions." Between 1996–9 she held several posts as project artist at Towner Art Gallery in Eastbourne, Kettle's Yard in Cambridge and the British Library. Her many teaching appointments included senior lecturer at Central St Martins from 2000. Individual exhibitions and commissions included The Visit of a Stranger, Imperial College, 1994; Beside, Towner Art Gallery and tour, 1996–7; and That's nice dear, the sink overlooks the garden, Standpoint Gallery, 1999. Lived in London.

EGGEBERT & GOULD– The collaborative name used by Anne Eggebert and Polly Gould (see separate entries). They made site-specific installations using photography, video, sound, assemblages and drawing, "exploring the history and architecture of a site to engage the audience in a critical appreciation of what may be forgotten stories." Eggebert & Gould started in 1999 at the British Library with a sound work around the King's Library. In 2000, they made a performance installation at Bury Museum & Art Gallery using found objects from its archive. During their 2001 residency at Cambridge University Botanic Garden they created video works installed among the glass-houses plant collection. Television and Aeroplane was held at Hastings Museum & Art Gallery in 2003.

Frank EGGINTON 1908–1990 Watercolour painter of landscapes, born in Wallasey, Cheshire, son of the artist Wycliffe Egginton and brother of Lucy Egginton. Studied with his father, at Newton Abbot and Exeter Schools of Art. Showed extensively at Fine Art Society, RCamA of which he was a member, RHA, Annan and Sons in Glasgow and elsewhere. Queen's University, Belfast, and the City Hall, Waterford, hold examples. Lived in Donegal, in the west of Ireland, for some years, having married a local woman, and died at Dunfanaghy.

Wycliffe EGGINTON 1875–1951 Landscape painter, born in Birmingham. Educated there and at Liscard Art School, Wallasey. Exhibited prolifically at Fine Art Society and Walker's Galleries, at both having one-man shows, also at RA, RCamA, RI and RHA. Father of the artists Frank and Lucy Egginton. Victoria & Albert Museum, Walker Art Gallery, Liverpool, several other English provincial galleries and the public gallery in Auckland, New Zealand, hold his work. Lived in Teignmouth, Devon.

William Stanley EGGISON fl. from c.1910–1956 Portrait painter and teacher who studied at Birmingham Municipal School of Art and won a scholarship which he chose to take in Paris at Académie Julian just before World War I. Although Eggison had been the most brilliant student of his period in Birmingham, problems in leaving France and the loss of all his work done there exacerbated health problems and and his promise faded. He painted and showed little on return to England, but was elected a member of RBSA in 1930 and was recognised as a fine teacher in the life class at Birmingham School of Arts and Crafts.

Philip EGLIN 1959– Ceramic figure sculptor, born in Gibraltar, who studied at Harlow Technical College, 1977–9; Staffordshire Polytechnic, 1979–83; and Royal College of Art, 1983–6. He showed with Contemporary Applied Arts from 1986; Garden Show, Gainsborough's House, Sudbury, 1989; The Decade Ahead, Scottish Gallery, Edinburgh, 1990; Colours of the Earth, British Council show touring India, 1991; and The Raw and the Cooked, Barbican Art Gallery and tour, 1993–4. Solo shows at Barrett Marsden Gallery and Victoria & Albert Museum, both 2001, and Barrett Marsden, 2003–4. Victoria & Albert

Museum, Fitzwilliam Museum in Cambridge, Contemporary Art Society and public galleries in Brighton and Hove, Gateshead and Portsmouth hold examples. Eglin won the Jerwood Prize for Ceramics in 1996.

Nicholas EGON 1921– Painter, draughtsman and lecturer, born in Brno, Czechoslovakia, who was a Czech war artist during World War II, 1939–44, then served with the British Army in the Middle East, 1944–6. Egon studied with private tutors, Birkbeck College, Oxford; at the British Museum reading room and print room; at the Ashmolean Museum print room, in Oxford; and in the library of Mirza Mohammed Khan Bahadur in Basra, Iraq. Between 1939–44 Egon was a member of the Surrealist group, taking part in mixed shows at Zwemmer Gallery, occasionally exhibiting with the RWS, RP and at Wildenstein and the Fine Art Society. From 1946-50 he was senior lecturer in fine art at Sir John Cass College, with other lectures at the National Gallery on art and evolution and occasional ones in Oxford and Cambridge. In 1950, Egon's Tribute to Greece: Drawings & Paintings for a Greek War Memorial was held, with a catalogue by William Gibson, keeper, the National Gallery; 10 solo exhibitions were arranged at West End galleries, 1950–84; in 1982, Landscapes of Jordan, at the National Gallery, Amman; and in 1984, Landscapes of Jordan at the Aga Khan's Zamana Gallery, in London. Books included *Some Beautiful Women*, introduction by Maurice Collis, 1952, and *Paintings of Jordan*, introduced by Edward Lucie-Smith, 1984. In 1989, Egon was chairman of Patrons of The Centre for Hellenic Studies, at King's College, establishing the annual Runciman Lecture there. Egon's work is held by the National Portrait Gallery; Casa Toscanini, Parma, Italy; and the National Gallery of Jordan, which has 57 portraits and 128 landscapes by him. He is represented in the Royal Collection at Windsor Castle; similar collections in Greece, Spain, Saudi Arabia, Morocco and Oman; and in those of the Dukes of Bedford and Devonshire and the Marquess of Bath. Egon was based in London, Corinth and Athens.

Uzo EGONU 1928–1996 Painter, designer and typographer, born in Onitsha, Nigeria. In his early teens he won a national school art competition in Nigeria, then came to England, finishing his initial education in Norfolk. Studied at Camberwell School of Arts and Crafts, 1949–52, having been encouraged to seek London art education in Nigeria by the sculptor Ben Enwonwu. Egonu travelled widely in Europe, supporting himself by lecturing and selling his work. Back in London in 1954 he was lucky to find a private patron for several years. Egonu began as a naturalistic painter, but his painted world became more stylized as he parted company with straight realism "to explore all the possibilities to use form". Took part widely in group shows in Europe. One-man exhibitions included Commonwealth Institute, 1973 and 1982; Black-Art Gallery and Royal Festival Hall, 1986. Participated in The Other Story, Hayward Gallery and tour, 1989–90, and the Institute of International Visual Arts toured a solo show by him in 1997, venues including Oldham Art Gallery. Victoria & Albert Museum, provincial and overseas galleries hold his work.

Georg EHRLICH 1897–1966 Sculptor of animals, draughtsman and etcher. He was educated and studied art in Vienna at the Kunstgewerbeschule, 1912–15, and began to exhibit widely on the continent. Settled in England and showed at the RA, RSA, with the Arts Council of Great Britain and elsewhere, as well as continuing to show widely on the continent and in North America. He completed public sculpture in Britain and abroad. Extensive one-man shows, including Venice Biennale, 1958, a series in London from 1938–60, and in Columbus, Ohio, 1948. His work was widely reproduced and is in many public collections, including Tate Gallery, British Museum and Victoria & Albert Museum. Lived in London.

Cae EINION: *see* **Raymond George PERRY**

Susan EINZIG 1922– Illustrator, printmaker, painter and teacher, born in Berlin, Germany, who studied at the Breuer School of Design there before settling in London, where she attended the Central School of Arts and Crafts, 1939–42, followed by World War II factory work. Was a part-time lecturer at Camberwell School of Arts and Crafts, 1946–50, with John Minton and Keith Vaughan, other teaching posts including St Martin's School of Art, 1959–60; and Chelsea School of Art, 1959–65, latterly becoming senior lecturer in drawing and illustration. By then, she was known as a sensitive book illustrator, her drawings for Philippa Pearce's *Tom's Midnight Garden*, 1958, winning a Carnegie Medal. She illustrated for major publishers such as Oxford University Press, The Folio Society and The Bodley Head; periodicals, including *Good Housekeeping*, *Lilliput*, *Radio Times* and *Reader's Digest*; and for firms such as British Petroleum and Imperial Chemical Industries. As a printmaker, she showed with Artichoke Print Workshop. Paintings were exhibited at RA, Victoria & Albert Museum, Camden Arts Centre, Barbican Art Gallery, Michael Parkin, Austin/Desmond and abroad. In 2001, she was one of five artists in Valleys of Vision at The Gallery, Southwark Park.

Ernst EISENMAYER 1920– Sculptor in various materials and painter, born in Vienna, Austria. After secondary education there he moved to London in 1939 and studied at Camberwell School of Arts and Crafts, 1947, teachers including Victor Pasmore. Showed at Leicester Galleries and Marjorie Parr Gallery and had a series of solo shows at Mercury Gallery between 1964–72. Among his international commissions was metal sculpture for British pavilion at Expo '70, in Japan. His Family Group, stylised figures in bronze presented in 1970, stands at Carlton Forum Estate in Nottingham. Eisenmayer later moved to Italy.

George EISLER 1928–1998 Expressionist painter, draughtsman, printmaker, illustrator and teacher, born in Vienna, Austria, son of the composer Hanns Eisler, his mother the singer Charlotte Eisler. From 1936 Eisler spent 20 months with his mother in Moscow, but during the return to Vienna they learned that Hitler had arrived there, so they stayed in Prague, having to move to England in 1939. Settled in Manchester, Eisler attended the Central High School for Boys and was encouraged in his painting by art historian Margaret H Bulley, who acted as a patron. Eisler attended the Stockport, Manchester and Salford Schools of Art, in 1944 showing at Foyles Gallery in an exhibition of Austrian artists in England including Oskar Kokoschka, who taught him. Eisler had his first solo show in Manchester in 1946, the year he returned to Vienna, where he studied life drawing in the evenings at the Academy. From the late 1940s Eisler travelled and showed extensively across Europe. Notable events included Otto Klemperer's request for set and costume designs for Mozart's *The Magic Flute* at Covent Garden's Royal Opera House, 1962; award of the Austrian Staatspreis for painting and major shows at the Vienna Secession and at Weinmüller's, Munich, 1965; election as president of the Secession in 1968 (until 1972); publication in 1970 of a monograph by Otto Breicha on Eisler's works, with a solo show at the Secession; award of the Prize of the City of Vienna, 1971; of the Cross of Honour for Science and Art, 1974; and the Klimt Award of the Vienna Secession in 1976; followed by a retrospective in Graz in 1977. In 1979 Edition Tusch published a portfolio of Eisler's etchings, entitled *Imaginary Portraits – 14 Poets*, the year he illustrated Dashiell Hammett's detective stories. Eisler participated in the Venice Biennale in 1982. Eisler's teaching included International Summer Academy in Salzburg, 1981–2–4, and the University of New Mexico, 1983–5. His later exhibitions included Landscape of Exile, 1988, at Manchester City Art Gallery, evocative views of the city.

Andrew EKINS 1961– Artist and lecturer, born in Preston, Lancashire, who studied at Medway College of Art, 1979–80; Canterbury College of Art, 1980–3; with a postgraduate in printmaking at Camberwell School of Art, 1984–5, becoming a Printmakers' Council member; and his master's in painting, Royal College of Art, 1999. He was artist-in-residence at the Chisenhale Gallery, 1995, having lectured part-time at Kensington & Chelsea College from 1991 and Epping Forest College from 1992. Won a City of Westminster/Arts Council Award, 1992, and a South East Arts Travel Award, 1995–6. In 1986 gained work commission for Collins/Granada Publishers. Group shows included Barbican Centre, 1985; A Simple Twist of Fate, Riverside Studios, 1992; and Royal Over-Seas League Open, 1996. Had a series of solo shows, including South Hill Park Arts Centre, Bracknell, 1995. Riverside Health Authority held Ekins' work which was non-descriptive but made "oblique references to elements from my experience and habitat".

Sarah ELDER 1966– Painter and illustrator, born in Cyprus and brought up in Fiji, whose extensive travels were reflected in her colourful pictures. She exhibited extensively from the early 1990s, group shows including the Anderson Gallery, Burford; Chelsea Art Society; Collins and Hastie; Foss Fine Art; Lennox, Mall and Osborne Studio Galleries; and Thompson's Gallery, Aldeburgh. Her solo exhibitions included the King's Road Gallery, 1991; House of Commons, 1996; South African Embassy, 1997 and 2002; Zimbabwean High Commission, 2000; Osborne Studio Gallery, 2001; and Gallery 27, 2005. In the four years before that show Elder had travelled through India, Sri Lanka and Vietnam, providing work for the exhibition, the nude and still life also featuring in her output. She also illustrated several books on Africa. Elder was based in south London.

John ELDERFIELD 1943– Curator, historian, teacher, writer and painter, born in Yorkshire, a co-curator of the major Matisse Picasso exhibition at Tate Modern in 2002. He studied at University of Manchester school of architecture, 1961–2; University of Leeds department of fine art, 1962–6; taught at Winchester School of Art, 1966–70; was awarded a Harkness Fellowship, research in history of art, at Yale University, 1970–1; researched at Museum of Modern Art, New York, 1971–2; and from 1972 studied at Courtauld Institute, gaining his doctorate. Taught art at University of Leeds, 1973–5. From 1975 was on the staff of the Museum of Modern Art in New York. In 2003, Elderfield was appointed chief curator of the department of painting and sculpture, the Museum's most senior position. Among his published works was *Henri Matisse: A Retrospective*, to coincide with the exhibition at the Museum in 1992. Producing abstract works, Elderfield took part in a number of mixed shows, including Cunningham Ward Gallery, New York, and British Painting '74, organised by the Arts Council, both 1974. Solo shows included University of Guelph, Canada, 1971, and Park Square Gallery, Leeds, 1974. Was a contributing editor to *Artforum*, 1972–4, and *Studio International*, 1973–5. Lived in New York.

Harold ELDRIDGE 1923–2001 Painter, muralist and teacher, born in London. He attended Camberwell School of Arts and Crafts, Royal College of Art and went on to teach at art school in Coventry, Warwickshire, where he settled. Showed at RA, LG and elsewhere. One of his murals is in Mortlake Primary School, Surrey. His portrait of John Minton was included in John Minton and Friends, Michael Parkin Gallery, 1997.

Mildred E ELDRIDGE 1909–1991 Painter, muralist and book illustrator, born in Wimbledon, Surrey. She studied at the School of Art there, Royal College of Art and at British School in Rome. She was involved in *Recording Wales* for the Pilgrim Trust, 1944–6. Completed a 120-foot mural for the nurses' home at Robert Jones and Agnes Hunt Orthopaedic Hospital, Oswestry. Showed with SEA, WAC, RCamA, RSA, RWS and elsewhere. She had a show at National Library of Wales, Aberystwyth, in 1959, and at Powys Fine Art Room, Welshpool, in 1961. In 1993 there was a tribute show at Abbott and Holder. Victoria & Albert Museum; National Museum of Wales in Cardiff; and Oldham and Sheffield Councils hold her work. Lived at Rhiw, Pwllheli, Gwynedd, wife of the poet R S Thomas. Thomas was ordained in the Church of England and Eldridge brought an artist's eye to the decoration of the austere poet-priest's churches.

Pennie ELFICK 1948– Artist whose work was "an investigation into the formal aspects of abstract relationships and the way in which they can allude to meaning and metaphor." Elfick was born in Carshalton, Surrey. She studied theatre costume design at Croydon College of Art, 1965–8; graduated with honours in fine art from Sir John Cass Faculty of Fine Art, London Guildhall University, 1993–6; gaining her master's in painting at Wimbledon School of Art, 1999–00. She was a finalist in the Mercury Music Art Prize '97 and gained 2nd Prize, the City Airport Art Awards, both 1997. Mixed exhibitions included Morley Gallery, 1992; Queen's Hall, Edinburgh, from 1993; Quantum Contemporary Art, 1998; and Will's Art Warehouse, Art on Paper, Royal College of Art, 2002. Had a solo exhibition, Gallery for Life, Torbay Hospital, 1998. Bromley Hospital Trust and several corporate collections hold examples.

Victor ELFORD 1911–2003 Artist and furniture designer, born in Plymouth, Devon, who moved to Buckinghamshire at the age of two. He spent most of his life in the county, at Hughenden, then Speen, eventually returning to Devon, where he died. Elford attended the Royal Grammar School in High Wycombe, before studying at the local Art College. He spent nine years at Waring & Gillow, working on the interior of ships, including the liner *Queen Mary*. During World War II, Elford's ship was torpedoed and he and comrades were forced to abandon her. While stranded in west Africa he used campfire charred wood to draw. Returned to England, Elford became a popular and prolific artist. Members of the Fine Art Trade Guild voted him the most popular artist of the year; in 1969 he gained an award for one of his most famous works, Burnished Gold, a painting of anchored boats at sunset; and his picture of the Olympic oarsman Jack Beresford at 1925 Henley Regatta later fetched a high price at Sotheby's. Wycombe Museum holds Elford's work.

Gertrude ELIAS 1913– Artist producing cartoons, graphic art and posters, by profession an illustrator, born in Vienna, Austria, studying at the State School of Applied Art. She won the Werkbund Prize for a poster, aged 19. She did extensive commissioned work for Bodley Head, Constable, Collins, Frederick Muller, Duckworth and Contemporary Films. Exhibitions included Women's Images of Men, ICA, 1980; Art & Society, Whitechapel Gallery, and Contemporary Artists in Camden, Burgh House, both 1981; and Midland Group, Nottingham, and Intergrafik, Berlin, both 1984. Had a retrospective at Margaret Fisher, 1984. In 1993–4 her autobiography appeared: *The Suspect Generation*, extensively illustrated, mainly with political cartoons from British and foreign journals for which she had written articles. Victoria & Albert Museum and The Museum of Labour History, Manchester, hold examples. Lived in London.

Ken ELIAS 1944– Painter and teacher, born and lived in Glynneath, West Glamorgan, who originally studied medical laboratory technology at Neath General Hospital/ Neath Technical College, 1961–5, before taking a foundation course at Cardiff College of Art, 1965–6. Gained an honours degree from Newport College of Art and Design, 1966–9, did a postgraduate teaching certificate at University College Cardiff, 1969–70, gaining his master's in fine art at South Glamorgan Institute of Higher Education, 1985–7. After a series of teaching posts from 1970, from 1980 Elias was head of the art department at Aberdare Girls' Comprehensive, being a visiting lecturer at South Glamorgan Institute, 1988. He won several WAC awards and is represented in its collection as well as those of West Wales Arts Association and Bangor Normal College. National Museum of Wales and Brecknock Museum and Art Gallery also hold examples. Elias was a member of The Welsh Group and of RCamA, sharing a show there in 2002. His later solo exhibitions included Brecknock Museum and Art Gallery, 1997, Wrexham Arts Centre, 1999, National Museum of Wales, 2000, and National Library of Wales and University of Glamorgan, both 2001. *Ken Elias: The Pictures*, which accompanied that show, included an appreciation of Elias's often enigmatic pictures by the artist Ceri Thomas, who quoted Elias's remark: "I appear to be attempting to create something solid and substantial out of memory, creating a kind of geometry of my earlier life."

Jago ELIOT 1966–2006 Multi-faceted artist, described in a *Guardian* obituary as "a large, bear-like man with enormous blue eyes, and a shock of golden hair". He was the eldest of three sons of Peregrine Eliot, 10th Earl of St Germans, and was raised on the Port Eliot family estate in Cornwall, where he died after an epileptic fit. Lord Eliot was educated at Millfield School. While a schoolboy he became a surfer of great daring, in 1992 Spanish national body-board champion, finishing 17th in the Hawaii world championships. In the 1980s and 1990s, as a Covent Garden street performer, he hammered long nails up his nostrils, blew fire and performed other tricks, entertaining also at British and European festivals. From 1987–93, he promoted performance art at the Zap Club in Brighton, in the early 1990s driving a Sussex University-Save the Children lorry to aid refugees in northern Bosnia and southern Croatia. Around this time Eliot was working with computers, demonstrating his sound-sculptures in Plymouth in 2002 and in 2003 staging performances in Holland Park, also graduating in medialab arts at Plymouth University. In 2004, he co-founded Liberarti at the Liverpool Biennial; set up Invisible Sculptures in London for Ars Electronica; and promoted in Liverpool a mobile phone-based, interactive performance, Karaoke, Talkaoke. After in 2005 taking his master's in digital futures at Plymouth, he continued with his innovative artistic and digital schemes, notably at the Port Eliot Literary Festival. Shortly before his death he was awarded a creative technology fellowship by the computer firm Hewlett Packard.

Benno ELKAN 1877–1960 Sculptor, printmaker and draughtsman, born in Dortmund, Germany. Studied painting in Germany, Switzerland and then took up sculpture privately in Paris. Exhibited widely on continent and in London and the provinces, having settled in England in the early 1930s. Elkan's work was purchased widely for European collections and is in the House of Lords, bust of Marquess of Salibury and King's College, Cambridge, Lord Keynes. Sometimes signed work B E. Among his books was *Spain Seen by an Artist*, which he illustrated. Lived in London.

Maggie ELLENBY 1954– Artist, born in Newcastle upon Tyne, who graduated in economics and international relations at University College, 1972–5; gained her master's in that subject at University of Yale, in America, 1975–7; then her master's in fine art at Goldsmiths' College, 1988–90. Took part in many group exhibitions, galleries including Camerawork, Angela Flowers, Maureen Paley/ Interim Art, Royal College of Art and Whitechapel. Had numerous solo shows, principally at her 108 Rosebery Avenue base, including window installations and paintings and interval pieces. Public art projects in which she took part included All that Glisters is not Gold, installation in Jewellery Quarter, Birmingham, 1999. Grants included Arts Council research grant with Kay Roberts, to research new technology and art, 1997; Oppenheim-John Downes Memorial Trust Award, 1999; London Institute research grant, 1999–00; and RSA Art for Architecture Award with Ash Sakula, 2001. This was followed in 2003 by three Roofrite linked text pieces on the roof of Hothouse, Free Form Arts Trust's new building in Hackney.

Rose ELLENBY fl. from 1940s– Painter and illustrator, born and lived in London. Sometimes she exhibited under her married name Rose Carruthers. She studied at Central School of Arts and Crafts, 1939–43, with Bernard Meninsky and Noel Rooke. Among her book illustrations were two

King Penguins: *Edible Fungi* and *Poisonous Fungi*. Showed at New Burlington Galleries and Victoria & Albert Museum, which owns her work.

Jenny ELLERT 1945– Artist, of South African/British nationality, who practised as a radiologist for several years before attending art school. She gained an honours degree from Hertfordshire College of Art & Design, St Albans, 1987–91; her master's in fine art, sculpture, from the Royal College of Art, 1993–5; then studied computers for fine art at Tower Hamlets College, 1997. Ellert was interested in the interaction between art and science, the computer for her becoming a new type of sketch-book. Was included in Global II Collection show at Addison Wesley Longman Ltd, Harlow, 1998–9.

Brian ELLERY 1943– Artist, known especially as a portrait sculptor, designer and teacher, who attended Wells Cathedral School, then graduated in English at Exeter University and sculpture at Exeter College of Art. Influenced by Eduardo Paolozzi, Allen Jones and George Fullard and the 1960s art scene, Ellery initially produced brightly coloured mixed-media work, which he described as Surrealist Pop. Set up a studio near Urbino, Italy, where he taught at the University, in 1970 having a first solo show at Galleria Segnapassi, Pesaro. Returned to England, Ellery directed his own building and design company, 1975–95. Several high-profile commissions, including the actress Julie Christie, Arts Council chairman Lord Gowrie and the playwright John Mortimer, prompted Ellery in 1995 to concentrate on sculpted portraiture, travelling extensively abroad. Former *Private Eye* editor Richard Ingrams was another subject. Group exhibitions included RA Summer Exhibition and Mall Galleries. Solo shows included several at the Rocket Gallery and in 1999 Lasalle Gallery, Singapore, and Barbican Library. Blenheim Palace, Royal Academy of Music, Eton College Library and St Petersburg Conservatoire hold his work. Ellery was a SPS member, based in London, whose impressions in clay were "a synthesis of feelings and observation."

Paul ELLIKER 1979– Birmingham-born painter who studied at Liverpool John Moores University, 1998–01. In 2004 his acrylic on canvas Mambo nomads was included in the John Moores Liverpool Exhibition. "Mambo nomads is part of a series of works focusing on illustrations of geological phenomena." Other group shows in which Elliker participated included The small work show, View Two Gallery, Liverpool, 2001, and Plastic Journeys, Hub Café, Liverpool, and Liverpool 8, Senate House, University of Liverpool, both 2002. His solo exhibition Belle Vue took place in 2003 at Philips Contemporary Art, Manchester, where he often showed.

Ashley ELLIOTT 1974– Painter of abstracts, born in Bristol, who gained a fine art degree at Slade School of Fine Art, 1992–6. Exhibitions included Detour, Disused Bus Depot, King's Cross, 1994, and in 1996 New Contemporaries at Tate Gallery, Liverpool, and Camden Arts Centre. Rhodes + Mann solo show, 2000, documented the impact of bullets on rifle range targets. Arts Council and British Land hold his works. Lived in London.

David Raymond ELLIOTT 1942– Watercolourist, born and lived in Stockport, Cheshire. He was mainly self-taught apart from studies with Francis Pratt at Montmiral, France. Elliott left the printing trade in 1988 to become a freelance artist. Limited-edition prints from watercolours of the Lake District were sold in the northwest of England. Elliott's interest was mainly landscape, influences being the work of William Russell Flint and John McCombs. He was a member of Stockport Art Guild and showed with BWS and Ginnel and Colin Jellicoe Galleries in Manchester.

Geoffrey ELLIOTT 1935– Painter, muralist, draughtsman, printmaker and teacher, born in Tideswell, Derbyshire. He studied at Derby and Brighton Colleges of Art, 1952–7. After lecturing at Brighton and Wolverhampton Colleges of Art and winning an Italian Government Travelling Scholarship, 1969, in 1983 Elliott emigrated to Australia, establishing a studio in Brisbane. Travelled and worked in Australia, Britain, America, Bali, on the continent and in Cyprus. Exhibited widely in solo and group shows in England and Australia. There his main works included pictures for Jupiter's Casino, Ramada, and Sea World, Nara, on the Gold Coast; Daydream Island Hotel in the Whitsundays and Kooralbyn Valley Heart Resort in the Gold Coast hinterland. Completed large murals for Dockside Restaurant, Kangaroo Point, Brisbane, and Kooralbyn Valley Conference Centre, a triptych for Albert Park Motor Inn, four big still lifes for the Brisbane Hilton, two large landscapes for Brisbane City Travelodge and large works for the members' stand at Rosehill Racecourse, Sydney. Tate Gallery, British Council, Australian and many corporate collections hold examples. Lived in Indooroopilly, Queensland.

Lee ELLIOTT: *see* **Theyre LEE-ELLIOTT**

Margaret ELLIOTT 1922–2002 Artist and businesswoman, born in Budapest, whose family left Hungary when Margaret was tiny to avoid anti-Semitism. After periods in France, Spain – where her father, Nicholas Kove, started a successful plastics factory – and Italy, the Koves moved to England. There Nicholas made and sold air-filled mattresses, in 1939 setting up Airfix, which became heavily involved in World War II contracts and which then diversified into plastic models. Margaret helped her father until the birth of her first child in 1944, then on the collapse of her first marriage in 1951 opened a London beauty salon which served famous, society and minor royal clients. After the 1957 death of her father and the 1960 closure of the clinic Margaret sold her Airfix holding and moved to Majorca, where she took up painting and became a well-known hostess. When she lost money heavily in the Cadco Pig Scheme, she rethought her life: concentrated efforts to have shows in London, Paris and other European cities; opened the Nauti Club in Majorca; and in 1968 founded the Majorca Cultural Centre, bringing ballet and classic music to Palma. By the early 1980s she had returned to her London apartment. Although there were second and third marriages and a much-publicised 1975 engagement to the much younger artist Geoffrey Stuart-Daniels, she died unmarried.

Marguerite ELLIOTT 1943– Artist and teacher who studied at Brighton College of Arts & Crafts, 1959–63, Royal Academy Schools, 1964–7, then British School in Rome, 1967–8. She went on to become a part-time teacher at Chester College of Further Education. Took part in mixed shows at Mercury and Odette Gilbert Galleries, RA Summer Exhibition from 1985 and at Ash Barn Gallery in

Petersfield. In 1986–7 she had a number of still lifes, a key interest, in Merseyside Artists 3, toured by Walker Art Gallery in Liverpool. Had a solo show at Duncan Campbell Contemporary Art, 1997. Hove Museum and Art Gallery, BBC and Lever Bros hold her work.

Marion ELLIOT 1964– Artist with a special interest in ceramic figures. She studied for a bachelor's degree in fine art at Liverpool Polytechnic, 1982–5, then worked for a diploma in ceramics at Sir John Cass, City of London Polytechnic. She was included in Artists under 30, Royal Liverpool Hospital, and Graduates '85, at Liverpool's Bluecoat Gallery, both 1985. In same year began showing with Walker Art Gallery's touring shows Merseyside Artists.

Mike ELLIOTT 1933–1999 Artist and lecturer, full name Michael James Elliott, born into a working-class background in London. At 16, he decided to paint, and with London County Council funding attended Camberwell School of Art, then for three years the Slade School of Fine Art, including a postgraduate year. After graduating in 1957 he married fellow-student Robina Evans and with a French government grant they lived in Paris, Elliott exhibiting with various galleries, including Gimpel Fils, London. From 1959 until his death Elliott returned to teach at Camberwell. In the early 1960s with Brian Elliott he established a studio and silkscreen workshop, around which the Constructivist group Ko5 was formed. It led to exhibitions and contacts abroad, such as the revolutionary South American Group Mardi. Latterly, German Expressionism influenced Elliott's output. Died in London.

Richard ELLIOT 1960– Painter, born in London. He attended Ravensbourne College of Art, 1982–3, then did an honours degree in painting at Duncan of Jordanstone College of Art, Dundee. Showed at RSA, the 1988 South Bank Show, Art Miami '92 at the Miami Beach Convention Centre and at Art92, Islington Business Design Centre, represented by Contemporary Artists' Forum. In 1990 had a solo show at Boland's Gallery. Of his large, colourful townscapes in thick impasto Elliot commented that his ambition was "to produce paintings with figurative and abstract elements supported by a loose, almost coincidental, narrative". Lived in London.

Richard ELLIOT 1964– Atmospheric landscape painter in oil and watercolour who studied at Chester School of Art, 1983–4, Manchester Polytechnic, 1984–7, then did postgraduate painting at Royal Academy Schools, 1987–90. Among his awards were 1987 David Murray Landscape Studentship; 1988 Singer & Friedlander/*Sunday Times* Watercolour Competition Student Prize; and 1990 *Antique Dealers' and Collectors' Guide* Prize. Elliott was commissioned to produce pictures for the oil company Chevron's 1991 calendar. Shows included Manchester Polytechnic, 1986; Mall Galleries and Lynne Stern Associates, both 1988; and solo exhibitions Gallery North, Cumbria, and Art Directions, both 1989.

Tom ELLIOTT 1965– Painter of still life in the manner of the Dutch Old Masters, born in London. He moved to Bath, Somerset, where he was educated and attended the School of Art, later Bower Ashton College, Bristol. Early in his career he visited Italy to study Renaissance painting, followed by frequent trips to Amsterdam and Rotterdam to learn about local seventeenth-century pictures. Showed at the RWA, in the Bath area, including the Contemporary Art Fair (with Boundary Gallery) and Anthony Hepworth Fine Art, and shared an exhibition at the Bishopsgate Institute. The Landmark Trust commissioned a Bath scene and Chelsea & Westminster Hospital holds his work.

Walter Albert ELLIOT 1936– Artist in various media, born in Wembley, Middlesex. He studied at de Havilland Aero College, became a design and development engineer with de Havilland Engine Company and was elected a fellow of the British Interplanetary Society for his contribution to rocket design. Studied art at Harrow College of Art and Hammersmith Polytechnic. Was a member of PS and UA and of the Torbay Guild of Artists and was president of Ilfracombe Art Society. Also showed with RI and in Paris and in 1981 won gold medal and membership of Accademia Italia. Lived in Ilfracombe, Devon.

Belinda ELLIS 1949– Abstract painter, born and lived in London, also pursued landscape, life drawing and photography. She studied at Sir John Cass School of Art, 1967–9, and North-East London Polytechnic, 1969–72, with a postgraduate fine art course in painting and printmaking at St Martin's School of Art, 1972–3. In 1974, Ellis was commissioned to complete murals at the Polytechnic of Central London. Mixed shows included Space Open Studios, 1975; 55 Wapping Artists, 1979; from 1980 Wapping Artists Open Studios; Whitechapel Open, 1985; Starting a Collection, Warwick Arts Trust, 1988; Blue, Beatrice Royal Gallery, Eastleigh, 1995; Art and Jazz, Mill Arts Centre, Banbury, 1998; and Idlicote Manor, Warwickshire, 2002. Ellis led and participated in a number of workshops. In 1997, with other north Oxfordshire artists, she founded Earth and Fire to promote abstract art, an Arts Council grant aiding an exhibition in Oxford. Her later solo exhibitions included deliART, 2003. Ellis said that she was "interested in the tension or effect created by the use of differing or opposing elements.... The work is a synthesis of the internal and external, colour, light and form seen and imagined." Lived in Bloxham, Oxfordshire.

Bill ELLIS 1944– Painter in oil and watercolour, born in Rhyl, Flintshire, where he continued to live. He was "self-taught, but had good advice from Welsh artist Robert Evans Hughes, who lived in Rhyl". Ellis was an insurance agent before taking up art full-time. He painted many portraits, including the acting partnership Richard Burton and Elizabeth Taylor; landscapes; and abstracts, where the "main influence was Salvador Dali". Ellis was a member of the Prestatyn 57 Group, Clwydian Art Society and Flint and Deeside Art Society and exhibited in many libraries, including Rhyl, and in Rhyl Town Hall. He had a great interest in music-hall and published *Seaside Entertainment: 100 Years of Nostalgia*, and *Rhyl in Old Photos*.

Brendan ELLIS 1951– Versatile artist and teacher, based in Belfast, Northern Ireland, who studied at Ulster College Northern Ireland Polytechnic for diploma (first-class honours) and post-diploma work until 1974, having left St Mary's Grammar School in 1969; in 1977 he gained his master's degree at Royal College of Art, also winning the John Minton Drawing Prize. Between 1974–9, Ellis held a number of positions, including teacher, mural painter for Belfast City Council and clerical officer with the Water Service, from 1979 being a medical artist at Royal Victoria

Hospital in Belfast. From 1987 he was shop steward for the Confederation of Health Service Employees at the Hospital. His output was varied, including Stations of the Cross for St Columba's Roman Catholic Church, Annan, Dumfriesshire, 1984; commissions for churches in England, from 1990; and a commissioned self-portrait for the National Collection, Limerick, 1992. Solo shows included Kerlin Gallery, Belfast, 1990. Arts Council of Northern Ireland holds Ellis' work.

Clifford ELLIS 1907–1985 Printmaker, designer, painter and teacher, married to the artist Rosemary Ellis. He was born in Bognor Regis, Sussex. He spent a year at St Martin's School of Art before studying illustration at Regent Street Polytechnic School of Art, 1924–7; Ellis then did a year's postgraduate teacher-training course and in 1929 gained a diploma in art history at London University. It was while teaching at Regent Street Poly from 1928–36 that Ellis married his wife, with whom he was to collaborate on so much work. During the early 1930s they did many notable book-jacket, mosaic and poster designs, patrons including London Transport and the Post Office. In 1936 Clifford Ellis joined the staff of Bath Technical College, in 1938 was appointed head of the School of Art, eventually Bath Academy of Art, where he devised a pioneering syllabus and assembled a notable staff. Although Ellis was always busy with his own work, designing book-jackets for the Collins *New Naturalist* series, working for the Pilgrim Trust *Recording Britain* project and being active in Bath Art Club, the Academy was his main achievement, as the exhibition at Michael Parkin Gallery in 1989 and its catalogue showed.

Cuthbert Hamilton ELLIS 1909–1987 Historian and self-taught artist of railways, born in Petersfield, Hampshire, whose memories of steam pre-dated World War I. Ellis was educated at Westminster School, in Munich and at Exeter College, Oxford. He began his writing career in 1922 on the staff of *Country Life*, also working for *Modern Transport* and *Railway Magazine*. Ellis wrote over 40 books and was notable for his histories of several major British lines, such as the London and South Western and the North British Railway, was a pioneer student of carriages and charted the early history of model railways. *The Trains We Loved*, 1947, was typical of his slightly patrician, aesthetic approach, *Rapidly Round the Bend*, 1959, employing a dry sense of humour. Ellis was a prolific painter and illustrator. His pictures often show railways bathed in a warm Edwardian sunshine. *The Splendour of Steam*, 1965, is illustrated with his own sketches. *The Sunday Times* issued a set of reproductions of his works which was popular, as were paintings commissioned to decorate British Rail carriage compartments, the originals being held by the National Railway Museum, York. Ellis's other books included *Modern Railways*, 1962, *The Pictorial Encyclopedia of Railways*, 1968, and *The Love of the Train*, 1971.

Edwina ELLIS (E N ELLIS) 1946– Engraver and printmaker, born in Sydney, Australia. She studied painting at National Art School there and at John Ogburn Studio, 1963–9. Moved to London, 1972, studying metal engraving at Sir John Cass College, then wood engraving with Simon Brett Summer School, 1981 and 1983. Ellis was elected to SWE membership in 1984 and fellowship of RE in 1987. Showed with RA Summer Exhibition from 1984, at Lumley Cazalet group shows and at Bradford Print Biennale in 1990. Had a solo exhibition at Oxford Gallery, Oxford, 1984, later ones including Godfrey and Twatt, Harrogate, 1991. Her main works included The Maxims of the Duc de la Rochefoucauld, 1986; Seven Products of Virtue as Garden Prigs, 1987; and Three Locks, 1990. Victoria & Albert Museum, Ashmolean Museum in Oxford and Fitzwilliam Museum Cambridge as well as American and Australian collections hold her work. Ellis moved to Wales in 1991, living at Tyn-y-Graig, Ystrad Meurig, Dyfed, although travel in Africa, Arabia and Australia remained an inspiration to her work, which showed a preoccupation with warm light and colour engraving. In 2003, the Royal Mint published four new designs for pound coins to be released one at a time from 2004 until 2007, designed by Ellis and celebrating British bridge engineering achievement.

Eleanor Joan ELLIS 1904–1989 Wood engraver and painter, born in southwest London, known to friends as Joan Ellis. She was educated in Malvern Wells, then attended Leon Underwood's Brook Green School of Art, 1923–5. Ellis exhibited with Underwood's English Wood Engraving Society, with SWE, NEAC, RBA, RHA – her travels included Ireland in 1931 and Southeast Asia in the late 1940s – and Redfern Gallery. In 1927 she had an exhibition at Gieves Art Gallery, along with work by her friend Marjorie H Ballance. After her mid-1930s marriage to an Army officer, Peter White, Ellis completed little artistic work.

Harold ELLIS 1917– Painter, draughtsman and commercial artist, born and lived in Baildon, Yorkshire. He attended Bradford Grammar School, then entered the commercial art studio of Field, Sons & Company, Bradford, 1933–9. Was a Bradford Arts Club member who also exhibited at Cartwright Hall in the city.

Joan ELLIS: *see* **Eleanor Joan ELLIS**

Lionel ELLIS 1903– Painter, wood engraver, modeller and teacher, specialising in portraits, flowers and horses. Born in Plymouth, Devon, Ellis studied at Plymouth School of Art, 1918–22, Royal College of Art, 1922–4, where he obtained a Travelling Scholarship, Atelier Colarossi in Paris, and in Italy. Ellis' liking for the Old Masters of painting influenced his illustrations, in the 1920s, of Robert Herrick, Theocritus and Catullus for the Fanfrolico Press. He exhibited at RA, NS, of which he was a member, NEAC and extensively at Redfern Gallery. Victoria & Albert Museum, British Museum and several provincial galleries, including Plymouth, hold his work. Lectured on painting at Wimbledon School of Art, 1937–68, although in his later years led a reclusive, back-to-the-land type of existence at Headley, Surrey.

Liz ELLIS 1960– Ellis gained an honours degree from St Martin's School of Art, 1983–8. She was visual arts workshop leader with SHAPE, the studios group, from 1983 and an Inner London Education Authority arts tutor at East London Day Centre from 1986. She was also a member of the editorial collective of *Feminist Art News* in 1988. Participated in Workshops on Demand, Whitechapel Art Gallery, 1988, and in a group show at the Tom Allen Centre and East End Open Studios, based at Pixley Street Studios, both 1989.

Nigel ELLIS 1960– Sculptor, draughtsman and teacher who attended St Albans College of Art and Design, 1978–9; gained a first-class honours degree in sculpture, Canterbury, College of Art, 1979–82; then his master's, Chelsea School of Art, 1983–4. Among his awards were Eirlys Tynan Travel Award, to Italy, 1991, and Elephant Trust, 1995. Ellis was studio manager and joint artistic director of The Florence Trust Studios, 1991–7; attended the Braziers International Workshop, at Braziers College, Oxfordshire, 1998; and took part in the Artists' Access to Art Colleges Scheme, Central St Martins, 2000. He was fellow in sculpture at Exeter College of Art & Design, 1984–5, and was a visiting teacher, Central and Cheltenham Schools of Art and Camden Institute, and undertook private teaching, 1985–00. Mixed exhibitions included West Soho Gallery and Sculpture in the East End at Lamont Gallery, both 1993; 9+1, Florence Trust Studios, 1997; and Sculpture at Goodwood, Goodwood, 1998. Among later solo shows were e 1 Gallery, 2000, which included abstract works with enigmatic and humorous titles. London Art House also showed Ellis's work. Collections and commissions included British Standards Institution, Sculpture at Goodwood and several corporate collections. Lived in London.

Noel ELLIS 1917– Painter and printmaker, born in Plymouth, Devon. He studied at the School of Art there and then at Royal College of Art until 1948. Showed at RA, LG, NEAC, ROI and in the provinces. Lived in London for many years.

Norman ELLIS 1913–1971 Painter who was by profession a builder, born and lived in Leicester. He studied at the College of Art there and Lincoln College of Art and was a member of Leicester Society of Artists and Leicester Sketch Club. He also showed with ROI, RBA and widely in the Midlands. Leicester Museum and Art Gallery holds his work.

Penelope ELLIS 1935– Sculptor and teacher, born in London, who attended the Slade School of Fine Art, under William Coldstream and F E McWilliam, 1953–6; won a British Institute in Paris Scholarship, 1956–7; and gained her teaching qualification at London University Institute of Education, 1957–8. Taught art and design in Bristol, 1958–97. Exhibited at Young Contemporaries; WIAC; ICA; Bristol Building and Design Centre; and Graves Art Gallery, Sheffield. Her 1958 multi-material relief Badger adorns a wall of Brockington College, Enderby, Leicestershire.

Peter ELLIS 1955– Painter, born in Manchester. He attended Camberwell School of Arts and Crafts, 1979–83, then Royal College of Art, 1984–7. Ellis often painted in acrylic, abstracts employing circles and elliptical themes. Won the Mario Dubsky Travel Award in 1987 and gained a Rothko Fellowship in 1990. Appeared in group exhibitions at Pomeroy Purdy Gallery, Camden Arts Centre, Nigel Greenwood Gallery, Fischer Fine Art and Cooling Gallery. In 1989 he was an Artist of the Day at Flowers East; he was in American Passion: The Collection of Susan Kasen Summers and Robert Summers, McLellan Galleries in Glasgow and Royal College of Art, both 1995; and in the 1997–8 and 1999–00 John Moores Liverpool Exhibitions. Exhibited solo with Anthony Wilkinson Fine Art, from 1994.

Ray ELLIS 1921– Painter who was born in America into an artistic family. He studied from 1939–41 at Philadelphia Museum School of Art and graduated from Pennsylvania Academy of Fine Arts. After four years in the Navy he resumed painting, had a successful solo show at Pennsylvania Academy of Arts, but on marrying he moved professionally into advertising until 1969, when he set up a studio at Chatham and became involved in New York's art scene. He had been made a member of New Jersey Watercolour Society in 1960, in 1964 became a member of Salmagundi Club and in 1967 had work accepted by the American Watercolour Society, also becoming a member. His book of watercolours *South by South-East*, text by Walter Cronkite, recording a voyage from Chesapeake Bay to Key West, was published in 1983; it sold over 150,000 copies and led to more such volumes. Chris Beetles Ltd gave solo shows to Ellis in 1987 and 1989, the latter comprising pictures of a journey along the Thames. Lived latterly in Savannah, Georgia.

Richard H ELLIS 1905– Sculptor and painter. He exhibited at Lucy Wertheim's Gallery in 1931 and at the Storran Gallery and lived in London.

Robert ELLIS 1928– Painter, illustrator, designer and teacher, born in Northampton. Studied at the School of Art there, 1942–7, where his teachers included Frederick Courtney, and then at Royal College of Art, 1949–52, under Rodrigo Moynihan, Ruskin Spear, John Minton and others. He exhibited RA, RWS, AIA, SEA, in New Zealand and America. Had a series of one-man shows in Auckland. Derbyshire Education Committee and galleries in Invercargill and Hamilton, New Zealand, hold his work. For four years from 1953 Ellis taught at Yeovil School of Art, then took a post in 1957 lecturing at Auckland University, where he eventually held a senior post in the fine arts department.

Rosemary ELLIS 1910–1998 Artist and teacher, born in London, wife of the artist Clifford Ellis, with whom she closely collaborated. She studied at Regent Street Polytechnic School of Art, from about 1927–31, marrying her husband while there, and with him worked in the early 1930s on poster designs, mosaics and book-jackets, clients including London Transport, Jonathan Cape and Shell-Mex and BP. Living in Bath, in 1938 Rosemary Ellis began to teach art at the Royal School for Daughters of the British Army and became closely associated with local art life. With her husband she designed many book-jackets for Collins from 1945 and in 1946 a mural for the Britain Can Make It exhibition at Victoria & Albert Museum. At Bath Academy of Art with her husband Rosemary Ellis taught many subjects as the need arose, creating one of Britain's key art learning centres after World War II. Latterly lived in Devizes, Wiltshire.

Susan ELLIS 1930– Representational artist who showed widely in Britain and Ireland, including the RWA and PS, of which she was a member. Lived in Fifehead St Quinton, Dorset.

Zavier ELLIS 1973– Artist and gallery proprietor who graduated with honours in the history of modern art at the University of Manchester, 1993–6. From 1998 he co-founded and ran Clapham Art Gallery, to "show fresh and modern painting in an approachable environment." His own work, produced at a studio in Brixton, "used mixed media on canvas with a heavy reliance on house paint and DIY materials". He created "a combination of busy, textured surfaces and lesser worked more evanescent canvases. The heavier of these relate directly to urban surfaces that we see around us." Showed at Affordable Art Fair, Battersea, and One Foot Two, Mafuji Gallery, both 2000, having a solo exhibition at Clapham Art Gallery, 2001.

Roy ELLSWORTH 1940– Versatile, self-taught artist, illustrator and teacher, born in Australia, who moved to London in 1964, working as an advertising studio illustrator. Went freelance in 1969, travelled in Greece to paint landscapes and spent some time in Amsterdam, Netherlands. Settled in London in 1974 where he continued to illustrate book covers and do work for magazines and newspapers, especially *The Times*, and his own work. Ellsworth taught at summer school in California in 1984. Exhibited in Dutch, German, British and Belgian art directors' exhibitions, receiving awards, also one from The American Institute of Graphic Arts. Had a solo show at Artistic Licence in 2002.

George Montague ELLWOOD 1875–1955 Decorator and designer, born in London. Studied art at Camden School of Art, Royal College of Art, where he won medals, and on the continent. Exhibited RA, RI, Paris Salon, where he won a silver medal in 1900, in the provinces and elsewhere in Europe. Signed work G M E. Was married to the painter Ida Ellwood. Ellwood completed a large volume of commercial work, such as theatre and railway posters; painted some murals; and wrote books on architecture, furniture and anatomy, notably *Studies of the Human Figure* and *Human Sculpture*. During World War II he was for a time design master at Camden School of Art. Lived at Boscombe, Hampshire.

Sheila ELMHIRST 1920– Painter and illustrator, born in Eastbourne, Sussex. Studied at the Slade School of Fine Art, 1936–9, under Randolph Schwabe and at the London Polytechnic. Exhibited RA, SWA and ROI. Was a keen collector of early English portraits. Lived in London, later in Ipswich, Suffolk.

Pat ELMORE 1937– Sculptor, notably of portraits, born in Rugby, Warwickshire. She attended Wellingborough High School and Dame Alice Harpur School. Showed at RBA, RWA and elsewhere in west of England in group exhibitions. Solo shows included Bedford Library, Wantage Museum and Central Library in Oxford. Thamesdown Arts holds her stone sculpture Heidi and the Duck. Lived in Faringdon, Oxfordshire.

Essil R ELMSLIE 1880–1952 Figure and portrait painter, wife of Charles Rutherston, brother of the artists William Rothenstein and Albert Rutherston. Charles Rutherston was a noted collector, who made a bequest of works to Manchester City Art Gallery in 1925; it holds Elmslie's oil on canvas Emma, Covent Garden, of 1909. She exhibited at NEAC, London Salon, Goupil Gallery and Walker Art Gallery, Liverpool.

Sharon ELPHICK 1968– Versatile producer of ubiquitous images with an urban flavour who said that she had "created my own market. I'm not an artist, textile designer or graphic designer, but I encompass all those things." Born in Leeds, Yorkshire, Elphick gained a diploma in printed textiles from Northbrook College of Design and Technology, 1986–8, and an honours degree in printed textiles at John Moores University, Liverpool, 1988–91. After college she was granted a Prince's Trust Award to produce teeshirts. Exhibitions included Alternative Arts and Paul Smith, both 1996; Mission Gallery, 1998; and Museum of London, 1999. There, in a show examining high-rise living, Elphick showed dazzling photomontages stemming from three years of photographing tower blocks in London, Paris, Berlin and São Paulo, Brazil. Creation Records, Jigsaw Menswear and Derwent Valley Holdings commissioned work from Elphick, who liked "straight lines, concrete, repetition, height and scale."

William Graham ELPHINSTON fl. from 1930s–1952 Watercolour painter, born in Winchester, who served in the Indian Army, 1905–38. Studied at Regent Street Polytechnic School of Art under Giffard Lenfestey, then at the Slade School of Fine Art, 1938–9, under Randolph Schwabe, also privately with William Wood. Exhibited RA, RI, NS and RBA. Lived in London.

Shona ELRICK 1964– Painter, draughtsman and ceramist, born and brought up in rural Aberdeenshire, where the open, ever-changing landscape was a powerful influence on her richly coloured and gestural pictures. Graduated from Gray's School of Art, Aberdeen, in 1986, showing in same year at the RSA. She moved to London in 1987, undertaking a part-time degree in ceramics at Middlesex University, 1990–5, but completed this "a very frustrated painter, and immediately set up studio in Finsbury Park" with the porcelain maker Sue Paraskeva, with whom she shared a show at Heifer Gallery in 2002. Returned to painting in 1995, a family cottage in Suffolk and the west coast of Scotland providing some of the non-Aberdeenshire subjects for the Heifer exhibition. Elrick also showed with the UA, at the Westminster Open, had two solo shows in the Stoke Newington Festival and in 1998 was part of Deep Frieze, a travelling exhibition to Greenland which later toured to Scotland.

Joseph ELSE 1874–1955 Sculptor and teacher, born in Nottingham, who studied at Royal College of Art, taught at Belfast School of Art and then became principal of the School of Art in Nottingham. Later lived in Newnham-on-Severn, Gloucestershire. Showed at RA and at public gallery in Nottingham. He was a fellow of RBS and his Bronze Mask and powerful Zeus, The Philanderer, are illustrated in the 1939 volume *RBS: Modern British Sculpture*.

Stephen ELSON 1963– Sculptor who spent his youth in Hatfield, Hertfordshire, where he attended Hatfield School, then did a foundation course at Hertfordshire College of Art and Design, St Albans, later the faculty of art and design at the University of Hertfordshire. He won an Elizabeth Greenshields Foundation Award, 1985. In 1986–8 he was a Rome Scholar in Sculpture, in the latter year taking part in a group show there. In 1989, Elson was included in East End Open Studios at Angel Studios. Elson was fascinated by the methods of industrial production, admiring the skills, knowledge, casting techniques and processes used in the manufacture of common objects.

This was reflected in his solo show Hatfield and The North at the faculty in 2002.

Cecile ELSTEIN 1938– Artist and teacher who was born in Cape Town, South Africa. She worked as a laboratory technician, studying sculpture at Michaelis School of Art and with Nel Kaye. Always an extensive traveller, Elstein settled in England in 1960. She studied ceramics with Catherine Yarrow, 1965–9, setting up a studio in Southampton, 1969–70, where she extended the range of her work. After studying sculpture and printmaking at West Surrey College of Art and Design, Farnham, 1975–7, in 1978 set up Spath Road Workshop where she lived in Didsbury, Manchester, teaching "awareness through art". Showed in many group exhibitions including MAFA, Hampstead Artists' Council, with Chilford Hall Press and abroad. In 1983 she gained a North West Bursary Award concerned with designs for inflatable spaces, 1986 bringing a colour prize at British International Print Biennale, Bradford. Had a series of solo shows including Boldrewood Gallery, Southampton, 1974, later ones featuring Clare Hall, Cambridge, and Casabella Gallery, Manchester, both 1988.

Ray ELTON 1914– Self-taught painter in oil, born in Cardiff, south Wales, father of the sculptor Andrew Elton. Elton lived in London for many years and was a member of Hampstead Artists' Council, exhibiting in mixed shows around Britain. Landscapes and abstracts featured in his output, sometimes geometrical and brightly coloured. Elton had a solo exhibition at Wilson Gallery in 1945. Others included Nicholas Treadwell Gallery, 1970; Camden Arts Centre, 1987; and Camden Art Gallery, 1990. Works were signed with a monogram.

Robin ELVIN 1957– Painter, born in Birmingham but brought up in rural west Norfolk, who as a child prodigy taught himself to paint in oils and was soon selling pictures. Attendance at art college proved abortive, and he was "asked to leave when it became apparent that he was more accomplished than his tutors". While he was working as a builder's labourer, a businessman offered Elvin a studio and paid him to produce enough pictures for an exhibition, the artist meanwhile having to relinquish his career as a promising boxer because he might harm his hands. The sell-out exhibition gained media exposure and Elvin had another at the Fortnum & Mason department store in Piccadilly. He painted Lady Diana Spencer and Prince Charles before their wedding, three Elvin pictures being held by the Royal Collection, also the world heavyweight champion boxer Muhammad Ali. In 1995 Elvin was approached by the Louisiana State Musical Heritage Commission to depict legendary blues performers, a three-year project resulting in an acclaimed American exhibition tour. Following this, Elvin designed and produced all the artwork for the guitarist Walter Trout's first live album *Face the Music*; a Jimi Hendrix memorial album cover *Blue Haze*; and a cover for guitar virtuoso Danny Bryant's album *Shadows Passed*. In 2002, Elvin was approached by the BBC to participate in a pilot programme for a series called *Painting Stars*, in which he and other artists painted the singer Lesley Garrett. Although that was shelved, Elvin did appear in the 2004 BBC1 series *Star Portraits with Rolf Harris*, painting the television chat show host Michael Parkinson, the pictures being exhibited in 2005 at the County Hall Gallery with a tour. Elvin's appearance prompted many further commissions. Elvin was based in King's Lynn, Norfolk.

Brian ELWELL 1938– Painter, printmaker, mural designer and lecturer, born in St Helier, Jersey. He studied at Chelsea School of Art, Birmingham Polytechnic and Wimbledon School of Art. He was a Leverhulme Scholar and gained the Falkiner Award. Elwell was senior lecturer in fine art at Southampton Institute of Higher Education and was a visiting lecturer at Tower Hamlets College. He was interested "in light, movement and change in nature, subjects mainly landscape and water reflections". Major exhibitions were at the Ikon Gallery in Birmingham; John Hansard Gallery, Southampton; Southampton City Art Gallery; and Victoria Art Gallery, Bath, 2000. Also sold work through Berkeley Square Gallery. Southern Arts Association, Southampton University, Salisbury General Hospital and Falkiner Fine Papers hold examples. Lived in New Forest at Nomansland, near Salisbury, Wiltshire.

Frederick William ELWELL 1870–1958 Versatile painter, notably of genre scenes, born in Beverley, Yorkshire, son of the wood-carver James Elwell. Studied at Lincoln School of Art, winning the Gibney Scholarship in 1887. Next studied at Academy Schools, Antwerp, worked for a while in London and Beverley, then continued his education at Académie Julian, Paris. From mid-1890s exhibited at RA and Paris Salon, also showing at ROI, RSA, Walker Art Gallery, Liverpool, and in Scotland. Elwell's career became based in Beverley from the early years of the century. His picture of the Beverley Arms kitchen is held by the Tate Gallery and the town's gallery has a collection of pictures by Elwell and his wife Mary Dawson Elwell (Holmes). He was elected RA in 1938. A large retrospective was held at Laing Art Gallery, Newcastle upon Tyne, 1993–4. Elwell was a perfectionist, who "once took three hours to get a thumb just right," according to a video on his life shown at Ferens Art Gallery, Hull. It holds several fine pictures by him, including a 1911 self-portrait.

Mary Dawson ELWELL 1874–1952 Painter, notably of interiors, also landscapes, born in Liverpool, daughter of a shipping merchant. She married Hull oil broker George Holmes who died in 1913, then the painter Fred Elwell, with whom she studied, in 1914. His portrait of his wife is held by the Borough Council in Beverley, Yorkshire, where they settled. Her money enabled the Elwells to travel extensively on the continent. She exhibited often at RA, also at SWA, RSA, Walker Art Gallery in Liverpool and elsewhere, although a stroke in 1945 incapacitated her. There was a retrospective of the work of the two Elwells in 1953 at Beverley Art Gallery and Ferens Art Gallery, Hull.

Cecilia ELWES 1874–1952 Flower painter. Studied in Cornwall with Stanhope Forbes and S J Lamorna Birch, then in Switzerland. Exhibited ROI, SWA, RI, SWA, in the provinces and Montreux. Wrote *Flower Painting in Watercolour*, 1932. Lived in Oxford.

Gervase ELWES 1956– Artist whose family included a number of painters, his namesake being an early-twentieth-century distinguished singer. Elwes graduated from the Slade School of Fine Art, 1981, also studying at Edinburgh College of Art, in Italy and at La Grande Chaumière, Paris. His work included depictions of comedians and large religious drawings for churches. In 1999,

Elwes had a show, Pastiche for Comic Relief, at Crane Kalman Gallery, 50% of the sale price of paintings going to the charity for which he had been official artist for the previous year. Lenny Henry, Joanna Lumley and Ruby Wax were among the personalities portrayed. Elwes also showed at the RA Summer Exhibition. Lived in Stigg, Lincolnshire.

Helen ELWES 1958– Painter, born in London. She attended Ruskin School of Art, 1979–82, after West Surrey College of Art and Design, 1976–7. Then was taught by Peter Greenham at Royal Academy Schools, 1983–6. Among awards won were Worcester College Travel Award, 1981, Landseer Scholarship and Arthur Hacker Portrait Prize in 1984, Fred Elwell Prize and Humphrey Brooke Award, 1985, and Richard Ford Award, 1986. In 1987 gained a setting-up grant from WAC. Showed at RA Summer Exhibitions from 1984, New Grafton Gallery, RP, NEAC and elsewhere and in 1982 had solo exhibition Oxford Arts Centre. Her portrait of Frank O'Donnell, head boatman of St Michael's Mount, Cornwall, was commissioned by the National Trust. Lived in Mells, Somerset.

Luke ELWES 1961– Painter who studied at Bristol University and RWA, 1980–3, then at Camberwell School of Art, 1983–4. From mid-1980s quickly had several solo exhibitions, including Rebecca Hossack Gallery, 1990. Later solo shows included Art First, 2000, paintings inspired by a visit to Cappadocia, in central Anatolia, responding to the spirit of the place without being specific to it, with another exhibition there in 2002, also one at Art First, New York. Among mixed exhibitions he took part in The Broad Horizon, Agnew, 1990.

Simon ELWES 1902–1975 Portrait painter in oil, born at Theddingworth, near Rugby. He studied at the Slade School of Fine Art under Henry Tonks, 1918–21, and in Paris, some time with André Lhote. Exhibited at RA from 1927 and was elected RA 40 years later. Also showed Arts Council, RP of which for a time he was a council member, Royal Glasgow Institute of the Fine Arts, Walker Art Gallery, Liverpool, and Paris Salon, where he gained a silver medal in 1948. During World War II he was an Official War Artist in India and Southeast Asia and painted leading military figures, such as Field-Marshal Sir William Slim and Field-Marshal Jan Smuts. Imperial War Museum holds his work. Lived for a time in London and died in Amberley, Sussex. His son Dominic was also an artist, his father the singer Gervase Elwes.

John ELWYN 1916–1997 Painter, printmaker, book illustrator and teacher, born in Newcastle Emlyn, South Cardiganshire, his real name being William John Elwyn Davies (early work could be signed Elwyn Davies or J E D). He studied at Carmarthen Art School, 1933–7, Bristol College of Art, 1937–8, Royal College of Art, 1938–9 and 1946–7. Elwyn taught at Portsmouth College of Art, 1948–53, then for many years at Winchester College of Art. Elwyn was closely identified with the landscape of Cardiganshire and its people, notably groups emerging from chapel on a Sunday morning in Sunday-best and dark suits and bowler hats. He wrote that he "continued using figures until about 1962, then for about 10 years worked in a semi-abstract manner with subjects taken from my garden. Eventually I returned to the landscapes of West Wales, without figures." Elwyn took part in numerous mixed shows in Britain and abroad from 1942. One-man exhibitions included Leicester Galleries, Howard Roberts Gallery in Cardiff, National Library of Wales, Tegfryn Gallery in Anglesey and in 1988 he shared a show with Thomas Rathmell at Ceri Richards Gallery, Swansea. National Library of Wales, Aberystwyth, put on an eightieth birthday retrospective in 1996, touring a memorial show from 1999. Commissioned work was done for Barclays Bank, Shell, *Radio Times*, Harlech Television and the General Post Office. Originally a Welsh speaker, Elwyn was made an honorary member of the Gorsedd of Bards and of RCamA. In 1956 he won the Royal National Eisteddfod gold medal. Elwyn's work is held by many public collections, including National Library of Wales, Aberystwyth; National Museum of Wales, Cardiff; Welsh Arts Council; and Leeds University. Lived in Winchester, Hampshire.

Charles Herbert Lewis EMANUEL 1868–1962 Painter and craftsman in various materials, such as silver and ivory. He was educated at Harrow School and Oxford University, graduating with a master's degree, and became a solicitor by profession. A keen photographer, he exhibited with the London Salon of Photography, also SGA, with the Goldsmiths' Company and in Italy. Was a member of Art Workers' Guild from 1933, its honorary librarian, 1938–62. Lived in London.

Frank Lewis EMANUEL 1865–1948 Painter, printmaker, draughtsman and writer, born in London. After the Slade School of Fine Art under Alphonse Legros, Emanuel worked under W A Bouguereau at the Académie Julian, Paris. From the late 1880s he began to show at the RA and Paris Salon, also exhibiting NEAC, ROI, RI and many other galleries. Emanuel had a varied career, travelling widely in Europe, Africa and Ceylon; being chief examiner for the Royal Drawing Society; publishing art criticism and topographical drawings in the *Manchester Guardian* and *Architectural Review*; and teaching etching at the Central School of Arts and Crafts, 1918–30. Was a keen collector of watercolours. Wrote a number of books, including *Etching and Etchings*, 1930. In his writings Emanuel opposed new trends in art. The Tate Gallery holds his picture Kensington Interior. Lived in London.

John EMANUEL 1930– Painter in oils and mixed media, born in Bury, Lancashire. Emanuel served an apprenticeship in decorating, signwriting and graining and did his National Service with the Army in Hong Kong. Did not begin painting until in his thirties and then did not show any work for a decade. Lived in St Ives, Cornwall, from the mid-1960s where, although he had no formal art training, he was helped by Denis Mitchell, John Wells and Alexander Mackenzie. Emanuel was noted for nude studies which he said were "also about Penwith, its standing stones, cliff faces and countryside, about living here". He was a member of Penwith Society of Arts and of Newlyn Society of Artists, of which he was chairman, 1977–8. Took part in numerous mixed shows in Britain and abroad. Had two solo shows at Wills Lane Gallery, St Ives, 1975–6, others including Montpelier Studio from 1979 and Beaux Arts Gallery, Bath, from 1988, also Maltby Gallery, Winchester, in 2004. Cornwall County Council Schools Library Service and Parnham House, Beaminster, hold his work.

Jane EMBLETON 1964– Versatile artist and designer who graduated with honours from St Martin's School of Art, 1983–6. Embleton in 1987 was involved in creative therapy sessions at Castledean Special School in Brighton and an environmental gardening project with Queens School further education group. She designed for the 1988 performance of Peter Maxwell Davies's *Miss Donnithorne's Maggot* at the Almeida Theatre, in Islington. Exhibitions included A Room of One's Own at William Morris Gallery and East End Open Studios, with Leyton Artists Group, both 1989.

Ronald EMBLETON 1930– Painter and illustrator, born in London. Studied art with David Bomberg at South-East Essex Technical College and showed in London, the English provinces and in America. Some of his work was of an experimental nature. Wrote and illustrated for children. London Sketch Club member who lived for some years in Bournemouth, Hampshire.

Keyna EMERSON 1922– Painter, born in Southampton, who sometimes worked as K R Emerson. She abstracted and interpreted what she saw from a variety of subjects, working mainly in gouache and acrylic. As Keyna Parson, she studied at the Slade School of Fine Art, 1945–7, taking theatre design as an extra with Vladimir Polunin. She returned to painting in 1977 after her family had grown up and other commitments had precluded it. Exhibited regularly at RWA from 1978, and at the Mall Galleries with RI, from 1977; RBA, Britain in Watercolours, 1979; and NEAC, from 1982. In 1984, she won first prize in the Wessex Open Exhibition, at Southampton City Art Gallery. Also showed at Salisbury Playhouse, Russell-Cotes Art Gallery and Museum in Bournemouth, St Barbe Museum in Lymington, The Gallery in Dorchester and elsewhere in the provinces. Lived at Milford-on-Sea, Hampshire.

K R EMERSON: *see* **Keyna EMERSON**

Arthur EMERY 1896–1980 Painter and draughtsman, born in Penmaen, Glamorganshire, he spent much of his life as a merchant navy officer. Studied at the Slade School of Fine Art, in Oxford then in London, for two periods: 1939–40, then 1946–8, his teachers including Randolph Schwabe and Allan Gwynne-Jones. He did a variety of ephemeral illustrative work, but also showed at RA and RCamA. A slow worker, Emery painted mainly landscapes in watercolour, with a few portraits. Lived in Bodfean, Caernarvonshire.

Terence EMERY 1933–2003 Artist, theatre designer and teacher, born into a theatrical family in Windsor, Berkshire, who aged one year was carried on stage in the arms of the music-hall star Nellie Wallace. He performed in plays as a schoolboy, developed an interest in puppetry at grammar school and studied theatre design at Wimbledon and the Slade School of Fine Art under William Coldstream, Robert Medley, John Piper and Nicholas Georgiadis. From 1958–62 Emery was in the production department of the Royal Opera House, then moved to Western Theatre Ballet, designing *Coppelia* in Norway and Japan and *Le Renard* in Liverpool and at the Promenade Concerts. His work for opera included *Don Pasquale* at Sadler's Wells, *Let's Make an Opera* with Benjamin Britten at Aldeburgh and *Orfeo* in Florence and London. Emery was involved with the Consort of Musicke and designed many productions for Lina Lalandi and the English Bach Festival. In the 1980s he worked at the Royal Exchange Theatre, Manchester, in 1987 creating costumes for a Broadway production of *Pygmalion*. He was also a member of the Equity theatre designers committee. Emery taught at Wimbledon, Birmingham and Central Schools of Art; at what became Nottingham Trent University from the 1960s to 1980s; and was at the Guildhall School of Music and Drama for 17 years, becoming Professor of Design and a fellow in 1993. Abbott and Holder gave him an exhibition in 2003.

Rowland EMETT 1906–1990 Humorous illustrator and inventor of eccentric machines, born in London, son of a journalist and amateur inventor. Emett studied at Birmingham School of Arts and Crafts, then worked in a commercial studio in that city. After war work as a draughtsman concerned with jet engine design Emett's reputation as a cartoonist and illustrator gained momementum. His second contribution to *Punch* about the time World War II was getting under way began a strong association with the magazine, where his endearing steam engines and the Far Twittering and Oyster Creek Railway attracted a keen following. The Railway was given tangible life during the 1951 Festival of Britain, which led to a new career as a creator of comical working machines. They were commissioned by industry and others and have been shown in places such as Ontario's Science Museum and Washington's National Museum of Air and Space. He worked on the 1968 film *Chitty Chitty Bang Bang* and in 1974 unveiled his large Rhythmical Time Fountain in the Victoria Centre, Nottingham. Emett was also a noted book illustrator, particularly for Walter de la Mare. In 1988 he had a show at Chris Beetles Ltd, which travelled to America. Lived in Ditchling, Sussex, and died nearby at Hassocks.

Tracey EMIN 1963– Artist using a variety of materials, born and worked in London, was raped at 13, had an abortion and suffered depression and suicide attempts. Emin, nevertheless, gained a bachelor's degree in fine art from Maidstone College of Art, 1986, then attended the Royal College of Art, graduating in 1989. Mixed shows included Hotel Carlton Palace Chambre 763, at Hotel Carlton Palace in Paris, 1993; Karaoke & Football, Portikus, Frankfurt, 1994; Brilliant! New Art from London, Walker Art Center, Minneapolis, 1995 (in which Emin exhibited a tent inside which she had sewn the names of everyone she had slept with including the artist Billy Childish. Her work was sometimes similar to his in its confessional subject-matter, language and ideas; her photograph I've Got It All, showing her with coins and banknotes, reminiscent of his much earlier photo I've Got Everything Indeed, depicting Childish with coins and banknotes); and A Grapefruit in the World of Park, Transmission Gallery, Glasgow, and Sad, at Gasworks, both 1996. In 1993 Emin with the artist Sarah Lucas for several months ran The Shop, at 103 Bethnal Green Road. In 1995 the artist set up the Tracey Emin Museum at 221 Waterloo Road. In 1994 Emin conducted Exploration of the Soul – Journey across America, in which readings were staged at venues including the Museum of Contemporary Art in San Diego, and My Major Retrospective was held by Jay Jopling at White Cube. Other solo shows included Exorcism of the Last Painting I ever Made, Galleri Andreas Brandstrom, Stockholm, 1995, in 1996 Full House at Wolfsburg Museum, Wolfsburg, Germany, in

2001 You Forgot to Kiss My Soul at White Cube², and Tracey Emin, Counter Gallery, 2003–4, sculptures made from the artist's memorabilia. British Museum and South London Gallery, where in 1997 Emin appeared in I Need Art Like I Need God, hold the artist's works, as do several American collections. Charles Saaatchi bought Emin's creased and stained My Bed, which was exhibited at the Tate Gallery when she was shortlisted for the 1999 Turner Prize. This Is Another Place, in 2002 at the Museum of Modern Art in Oxford, Emin's first solo exhibition in a public gallery for five years, contained her rickety reconstruction of a Margate pier. In that year, the BBC commissioned a £500,000 autobiographical film from the artist. Her film *Top Spot* was released in 2004, the year that Tate Britain dedicated a whole room to her works and bought nine of them. Emin represented Britain at the 2007 Venice Biennale.

Lohan EMMANUEL 1971– Painter, born in Sri Lanka, who spent most of his life in England and who graduated from St Martin's School of Art, 1994. From 1995 had a series of solo shows with Cassian de Vere Cole Fine Art. Emmanuel's canvases were in the style of the Old Masters, with figures whose heads faded into the landscape, giving them a slightly Surrealist quality.

John Victor EMMS 1912–1993 Painter and teacher, born in Bordon, Hampshire. He studied at Woolwich Polytechnic Art School, 1930–4, where his teachers included Louis Prince; Hornsey School of Art, 1946–8, with Frederick Mitchell and Arthur Mills; then Goldsmiths' College School of Art, 1948–9. Emms held several teaching posts, including latterly Woolwich Polytechnic Secondary Art School. He exhibited with RA, East End Academy, Liberty the London store and in provincial galleries. Lived in Leatherhead, Surrey.

EMMWOOD 1915–1999 Cartoonist, painter and teacher, real name John Bertram Musgrave-Wood, son of the painter Gerald Musgrave-Wood, born in Leeds, Yorkshire. He was one of the last of a great generation of political cartoonists whose names became well known during World War II and the succeeding years. Early becoming disenchanted with work in an advertising agency, Musgrave-Wood began studies at Leeds College of Art, but after 18 months signed to serve on a cruise liner. He supplemented his salary as chief fruit steward by selling passengers their likenesses for 30 shillings each. Returning to England in the late 1930s he taught with a brother in Jewish youth clubs in Whitechapel, joining the Army when war broke out. He was commissioned with the Sherwood Foresters, was sent to India and served with General Orde Wingate's guerrilla force, the Chindits, in Burma. With another Chindit, Patrick Boyle, who became the 13th Earl of Cork and Orrery, in 1944 he produced a humorous, illustrated account of their experiences, *Jungle, Jungle, Little Chindit*. His drawings were signed Jon but, to avoid confusion with another cartoonist using that signature, Musgrave-Wood changed his to Emmwood. In 1948, he began studying painting at Goldsmiths' College while contributing caricatures to *Tatler & Bystander* and other drawings to *Punch* and the *Sunday Express*. He became political cartoonist on the London *Evening Standard* in 1955; was then editor of the *Junior Express*; in 1957 becoming deputy political cartoonist at the *Daily Mail*. He retired in 1975 and moved to France. He was a founder-member of the British Cartoonists' Association in 1966 and had work in major exhibitions, at the National Portrait Gallery, 1970, and Press Club, 1977. In retirement he concentrated on painting landscapes at Vallabrix, Provence.

Kenneth EMSLEY 1921– Watercolourist, pen and ink draughtsman and teacher, born and lived in Shipley, Yorkshire. He was educated at Loughborough College and Cambridge University, obtaining his master's degree. His studies at various art schools included tuition by Arnold Dransfield and Edward Wesson. Emsley was a member of Leeds Fine Art Club, chairman of Bradford Arts Club and president of both SM and BWS. He showed at Mall and Bankside Galleries, in the provinces and in America.

Paul EMSLEY 1947– Draughtsman, painter, designer and teacher, born in Scotland. His family went to South Africa in 1949 and he obtained his national diploma in graphic design at Cape Technical College, 1969. Worked in advertising, 1970–6, latterly beginning to draw and paint, being self-taught as a painter. From 1976–7 Emsley lived in England, and on returning to South Africa taught design and drawing, from 1983 at Department of Creative Arts, University of Stellenbosch. Emsley said that constant drawing had taught him "the deep significance of even the most ordinary forms ... I try to draw not only what I see, but also what I wish I had seen." He took part in South African Art, 1978–9, touring America, which went to São Paulo, Brazil; and in Cape Town Biennial and Triennials from 1979. Later solo shows included Redfern Gallery, 1994. Johannesburg Art Gallery and other notable collections hold his work. In 2002, Emsley won the £15,000 first prize in the Singer & Friedlander/*Sunday Times* Watercolour Competition for his picture Rhinoceros.

Rosalie EMSLIE 1891–1977 Painter, draughtsman and artist in black-and-white, born in London. She was the daughter of the artist Alfred Edward Emslie and daughter of the miniaturist Rosalie M Emslie. After private education she attended the Royal Academy Schools, 1913–18, then studied in France, Italy and Spain. Exhibited extensively at RBA, also at RA, Goupil Gallery, SWA, NEAC, in Italy and America. Canadian government bought her work. Lived in Petersfield, Hampshire, and in Reigate, Surrey, with the painter Florence May Asher.

Ruth END 1959– Versatile artist and teacher, born in London, who worked especially in acrylic and oil on canvas. Her paintings depicted "single figures or groups and their relationships with each other, or with themselves. I choose the setting and objects to enhance or question the nature of these." End studied from 1977–8 at Jacob Kramer, College, Leeds, graduating in fine art from South Glamorgan Institute of Higher Education, 1978–81. In 1980 held a solo show of sculpture, prints and performance at Kingsgate Gallery, exhibiting in Stowells Trophy at RA in 1981. In 1982 End moved to Cheltenham, Gloucestershire. There she held workshops for children at Bournside School, 1988–90. In 1992 was commissioned to design and make a donation box for Pittville Pump Room Museum and held a show at Turtle Gallery of bowls, boxes and wall reliefs. Held a workshop for mentally ill adults in 1993, in 1994 being commissioned to design and make a donation box for Holst Birthplace Museum Trust, Cheltenham. In 1995 held a solo exhibition at Veale Wasbrough, solicitors, Bristol, in which three-dimensional wooden cartoons, made to commission, were featured. In 2004, at the Café, Cheltenham Art Gallery & Museum, End had a solo show of landscapes and seascapes.

Eden ENDFIELD 1960– Painter, notably of portraits, born in London, who studied at Camberwell, Chelsea and Slade Schools of Art. Won a Wyndham Lewis Scholarship and an Elizabeth Greenshields Foundation Award. Group shows included A New Perspective, Leighton House Gallery, 1990; BP Portrait Award, National Portrait Gallery, 1994; and Royal Over-Seas League Open, 1995. National Westminster Bank and Lord Irvine of Lairg hold examples.

Anne ENGDAHL 1940– Versatile artist, photographer, teacher and broadcaster, born at The Lizard, Cornwall, who studied at Portsmouth Training College, art teaching with Derek Riley and primary method, 1958–61; Epsom Art School, sculpture, modelling and casting, 1962–3; after a move to Australia, ceramics in Sydney with the Danish potter Jan Gluck, 1965–6; Royal College of Art, London, life drawing and painting, 1968–9; Sydney, printmaking with Una Foster, 1970; Sydney Potters' Society, ceramics and design with Peter Travis, 1971–3, and again in 1974 with Ian Curry. In 1990 she wrote a study of the life and work of the film-maker and designer Geoffrey Collings, husband of the artist Dahl Collings, and in 1999 a thesis for the degree of Bachelor of Education with honours on the history of art schools in Sydney and Canberra. Engdahl taught at Great Bookham Primary School, 1962–4, where she wrote, designed and produced a version of Shakespeare's *A Midsummer's Night's Dream* for primary children. From 1965–7 she taught art in New South Wales High Schools; returned to Surrey, she taught primary, 1967–9, and again in New South Wales, 1970; from 1974–02 being senior art teacher in a high school there. From 1982 Engdahl was a music programmer, broadcaster, concert organiser and board member of Radio 2MBS FM in Sydney. Group and mixed exhibitions included Leatherhead Theatre, oil paintings of local landscapes, 1964; Argyle Arts Centre, Sydney, large fibre weavings, 1970; S H Ervin Gallery, New South Wales, On the Other Hand, watercolour illustrations, 1992; and Macrossin Gallery, Port Douglas, Queensland, Photographs, 1997. Engdahl had a solo exhibition of large colour-field paintings, serigraphs and figure drawings at Bondi Pavilion Gallery, Bondi, New South Wales, 1982. Her later output included large oil portraits and book illustrations. In 2005 Engdahl was artist-in-residence at Kemptville College, Guelph University, in Ontario, Canada. Lived in Newcastle, New South Wales.

Florence ENGELBACH 1872–1951 Painter, principally of flowers, born in Jerez de la Frontera, Spain, of English parents. Studied at Westminster School of Art, at the Slade School of Fine Art, in the mid-1890s, with Fred Brown, then in Paris. Began exhibiting under her unmarried name of Neumegen, but after marriage early in the century ceased painting, resuming about 1930. Exhibited RA, ROI, NS, Lefevre and Goupil Galleries and elsewhere. First one-man show at Beaux Arts Gallery, 1931, and memorial show at Leicester Galleries, 1951. Tate Gallery holds her work. Engelbach's interest in flower painting was inspired by her Warwickshire garden after she had returned to the easel having brought up her family. She also painted good landscapes and delicate, atmospheric nudes. Lived latterly in London.

Frederick ENGLAND 1939– Artist, designer, teacher and gallery proprietor, born in London. He studied at Brighton College of Art, 1956, teachers including Raymond Cowern, Charles Knight and Ernest Sallis Benney, in Norway, 1960, and in 1961 at London University with Ronald Horton. Went on to teach at Leek School of Art. England was president of the Society of Staffordshire Artists and a member of the Free Painters and Sculptors. Showed at RI, RBA, widely in the provinces and at Paris Salon, where he won silver and gold medals. Solo shows included Octagon Gallery in Bolton, University of Keele and abroad. Stoke-on-Trent City Museum and Art Gallery holds England's work. Lived in Leek, Staffordshire, where he ran his own gallery.

Nora ENGLAND 1890– Painter and versatile designer for interiors and the performing arts, born in London, daughter of the artist Edwin Ward. She studied art at Royal College of Art and Westminster School of Art and with the figure and portrait painter Sir James Shannon. She exhibited RA, SWA, RI, IS, RP and elsewhere. Lived in London.

Robert ENGLAND 1949– Artist whose work employed everyday objects in unfamiliar settings. He studied at Thurrock Technical College, 1973–5, Maidstone College of Art, 1975–8, and was included in 1983 in a second year master's show, Goldsmiths' College School of Art, at Woodlands Art Gallery. Other exhibitions included Rye Art Gallery, 1979, and The Hall, Stanford, Essex, 1980.

Grace ENGLISH 1891–1956 Painter and etcher, born in London. Studied at the Slade School of Fine Art, 1912–14, where she won a painting prize, then learned etching under Sir Frank Short at the Royal College Art, 1921. Exhibited RA, RP, NEAC, RBA and in the provinces. Leeds City Art Gallery holds her work. Lived in London.

James ENGLISH 1916–1988 Painter, collagist and teacher, born and lived in Bristol. He studied at West of England College of Art there, his teachers including Evan Charlton, Reginald Bush and Donald Milner. English held several teaching appointments in Bristol, including latterly Clifton High School, and until 1952 assisted at evening classes at West of England College of Art. Was from 1949–53 a member of SGA and was for many years an associate of RWA, which holds his work. Also exhibited at Arts and Crafts Exhibition Society.

James ENGLISH 1946– Painter who was mainly known for his still lifes, such as Mango, Herbs and Wallet, in September Show, 2003, at The Wykeham Gallery, Stockbridge, but who also painted landscapes. English was a National Hunt jockey before studying painting at the National College of Art and Design, Dublin, Ireland. First exhibited in 1974, after which he showed extensively in Europe and America. Venues included RHA and Jorgensen Fine Art, both in Dublin.

Michael ENGLISH 1941– Multi-faceted artist, born in Bicester, Oxfordshire, who attended Ealing School of Art, studying under a number of avant-garde teachers and participating in The Ground Course, "a revolutionary method of art teaching" which "released a great wealth of creative talent". In 1967 English became involved in the hippie movement in England and America, producing large volumes of psychedelic posters and painting fashionable shopfronts. Was involved in forming the Rock group Hapshash & the Coloured Coat in 1968, named after the design partnership that he formed with Nigel Waymouth. An album was released on the Liberty label. With the decline in hippiedom English in 1969 – the year of his first solo show, at Motif Gallery – shifted towards a personal style of Super-Realism, which manifested itself in limited-edition prints entitled *Food Synaesthetics and Rubbish*, as the result of which his work gained global exposure. In 1973 began to paint canvases, abandoning the more Pop-oriented work of the prints, man-made objects taking the role of pollutants, as in his painting No Deposit No Return. From 1975 there was a shift in content, monumental works of great detail featuring transport machinery. From 1986 English became dissatisfied with Hyper-Realism, seeking a new personal style. English's books include *3-D Eye*, 1979, and *The Anatomy of an Illusion*, 1989. He showed at galleries in London, New York, Tokyo, Paris and the south of France and was featured in the Barbican's The Sixties Art Scene in London, 1993. Museum of Modern Art in New York, Arts Council and British Council and Victoria & Albert Museum hold examples. Much of English's later work was sold direct to the buyer instead of through galleries plus some advertising commissions "which I enjoy". English wrote: "I have attempted to convey the feel and smell of objects, to cross the boundaries of the senses, to evoke by painting alone the sense of smell, sound and touch. The by-product of this technique has been a certain sexuality...eroticism." Lived in London.

Simon ENGLISH 1959– Figurative painter on a grand scale but with a restricted palette, English was concerned with the contemporary world while harking back to the Old Masters and traditional icons, as in his works at The Saatchi Gallery Young British Artists III show, 1994. He was born in Berlin, Germany, and did a foundation course at Bournemouth College of Art, 1977–8, then an honours degree in fine art painting at Central School of Art & Design, 1978–81. Solo exhibitions included Laurent Delaye, 1992, and Rhodes + Mann, 2004. Saatchi Collection holds his work.

Stanley Sydney ENGLISH 1908– Sculptor and artist in ceramics, born in Romford, Essex. Studied at City and Guilds of London Art School under a scholarship, then at Royal Academy Schools with William McMillan. He went on to spend much of his career in the Liverpool area, where he lectured at the College of Art from 1946. Member of Sandon Studios Society Club. Showed at RA and elsewhere. Work also done for Bank of England, South Africa House and a number of churches in the Liverpool locality, where he lived, having a studio in Bluecoat Chambers. Married to the artist Rachel Russell.

Augustus William ENNESS 1876–1948 Landscape painter, born in Bocking, Essex. Studied at Slade School of Fine Art and at Académie Julian in Paris, and was elected RBA in 1925. He was a prolific exhibitor there and at ROI and Fine Art Society, also showing at RA, Ridley Art Club, RSA and Walker Art Gallery in Liverpool. Lived in London.

Eric Arnold Robert ENNION 1900–1981 Bird artist, naturalist and teacher, born in Kettering, Northamptonshire. He was educated at Epsom, Cambridge University, St Mary's Hospital and worked as a general practitioner, 1926–46. Dr Ennion was next to be warden of Flatford Mill Field Centre, Suffolk, 1946–51; ran Monks House Bird Observatory and Field Research Centre, Northumberland, 1951–61; then retired to Shalbourne, Marlborough, Wiltshire, but remained active painting and conducting courses. Ennion was a self-taught artist, his son being the wild life painter Hugh Ennion. Dr Ennion was founder-chairman of SWLA. He carried out many commissions, notable illustrations appearing in the *Shell Bird Book*, 1966. Among other volumes including his work was the posthumous *The Living Birds of Eric Ennion*. He had four solo shows at Ackerman's, 1937–9, then every year he participated in many solo and shared exhibitions, including Sladmore Gallery, Henley Galleries and William Marler Gallery.

Hugh ENNION 1932– Watercolourist and teacher, born in Burwell, Cambridgeshire, son of the bird painter E A R Ennion. Hugh Ennion was "self-taught under the wing of my father, starting in 1966". Ennion used broad, graduated and superimposed washes to convey atmosphere and place, later defining small areas of detail. Edward Seago and Edward Wesson were influences. Latterly he began drawing and painting birds, having established a reputation as a landscape and estuarial artist. Ennion was an Army officer from 1952–63; was a watercress farmer from 1963–72; then taught from 1973, latterly part-time. He shared shows at Croft Gallery, Bristol; Bernard Rose Gallery, Newbury; RI; and Manor House Gallery, Chipping Norton. Solo exhibitions included Patricia Wells Gallery, Thornbury. HRH The Duke of Gloucester bought his work. Lived in Shalbourne, Wiltshire.

Richard ENNIS 1958– Painter, draughtsman and teacher producing highly stylised figure paintings, with claustrophobic, disturbing and humorous elements, which drew on his imagination, dreams and life events. As a child he was fascinated by his nurse mother's anatomy and physiology books from which he would copy, and Ennis remained a compulsive sketcher. Born in Clitheroe, Lancashire, he did a foundation art course at Burnley College of Art and Technology, 1977; graduated with honours from Bristol Polytechnic, 1978–81; then completed a postgraduate teaching certificate at Reading University, 1982–3, after which he taught, from 1991 at Reading Blue Coat School, Sonning-on-Thames. Mixed shows included Stowells Trophy Competition, RA, 1981; RWA from 1981; Summer Exhibition at Anthony Hepworth, Bath, 1991; and The Jelly Leg'd Chicken, Reading, from 1994–5. He had a solo exhibition at Karen Hamilton, 2000.

Brian ENO 1948– Rock musician, artist and teacher, born in Woodbridge, Suffolk, who from the mid- to late-1960s attended Ipswich and Winchester Schools of Art. He was a founder-member of Roxy Music, then left it in 1973 and began his solo career with the album *Here Come the Warm Jets* and released a number of critically acclaimed records. He also collaborated with such artists as John Cale, Nico, Robert Fripp and the band James. As a record producer, Eno was noted for his ability to steer artists into radical new areas; he was a pioneer in tape-looping and other versions of sound manipulation. Eno continued to work in the visual medium, his video installations being shown around the world, including the Stedelijk Museum in

Amsterdam; at the Venice Biennale; the Pompidou Centre in Paris; as well as a permanent exhibition opened in 1995 at Austria's Swarovski Museum. As a visiting professor at the Royal College of Art, in 1995 Eno collaborated with Laurie Anderson and some of his students on the Self-Storage installation in Wembley. Eno's diary for 1995, *A Year with Swollen Appendices*, documents hectic activity, including his association with the performers David Bowie and Bono. In 1996 Eno's work was included in Freezeframe at Lamont Gallery. His ambitious installation Lightness – described by him as "something between cinema, firework display, environmental music and installation" – was staged at the Russian Museum's Marble Palace, in St Petersburg in 1997. In 2003, Eno created a sound installation for the Science Museum's new exhibition Treat Yourself, which explored changing attitudes to healthy living.

Madeleine ENRIGHT 1920– Painter, collagist and draughtsman, born in Paris, France, her mother French, her Dutch father a Batik artist who supplied major Paris and New York fashion houses in the late 1920s. Enright lived in Egypt, Thailand and Japan before taking up painting seriously in the 1960s in Singapore, where she began exhibiting. Her teacher and mentor was the Chinese artist Cheong Soo Pieng; an Oriental influence was apparent in her work, which could display dreamlike and visionary elements. Settled in England, Enright was given a solo show at Drian Gallery in 1979; she continued to exhibit there, work being acquired by Gdansk National Museum, Poland. She also showed at Ashgate Gallery, in Farnham, and at POSK Gallery. She was married to the writer and poet D J Enright, and her work was on the cover of his book of essays *Signs & Wonders*, 2001. In that year, Harlequin Gallery gave her a post-1978 retrospective. Lived in London.

Kathryn ENSALL 1956– Artist, notably in pastel, and teacher. She studied from 1975–86 at University of Lancaster, Leeds Polytechnic and Newcastle Polytechnic. Went on to teach at Huddersfield Polytechnic and at Huddersfield College. Held a number of residencies and awards, including artist-in-residence, Yorkshire and Humberside Museums Council. Worked for a time in the artists' workshops at Tate Gallery, Liverpool. Among her frequent exhibitions was a three-man shared show at Woodlands Art Gallery, 1991, where her work explored "the themes of image-making between the sexes". Solo shows of paintings and drawings at Jill George Gallery, 2001 and 2003. Lived near Huddersfield, Yorkshire.

John ENSOR 1905– Industrial designer and painter, born in Cardiff. Studied art in Italy and at Royal College of Art. Worked for Imperial Chemical Industries as a designer in 1930s and in World War II was a war artist. Showed RA, NEAC, Leicester Galleries and widely in North America, Imperial War Museum holding his work. For many years Arthur John Ensor worked in Canada, establishing Ensor Industrial Design Associates in Toronto, where he also lived.

Matt ENSOR 1954– Artist who was awarded a print school diploma from Birmingham College of Art and Design, 1969–70; an art and design foundation diploma from Solihull College, 1975–6; graduated with first-class honours from Leeds Polytechnic, 1976–9; and gained his higher diploma in fine art from the Slade School, 1979–81. Ensor's work was offered by the Treadwell Gallery, based at Aigen, Austria. On its website he explained that: "To me there is nothing more interesting than observing people. So I have to describe myself as a humanist. Through my work I try to give an insight into human behaviour.... I am keen to produce art that is accessible, non-elitist and enjoyable."

Mark ENTWISLE 1961– Painter and illustrator who studied at Cambridge College of Arts & Technology, 1980–1, and Brighton Art College, 1981–4. Then worked extensively as an illustrator in Britain, on the continent and in America, including a Penguin edition of Gabriel Garcia Marquez's books, the Vintage edition of P G Wodehouse and covers for Somerset Maugham, Aldous Huxley and Colin Thubron. Other commissions included *Time*, *Der Spiegel*, leading British broadsheet newspapers, the London Underground and the National Theatre. In the late 1990s Entwisle gained a number of awards, including Regional Prize Winner, Hunting Art Prizes, 1998. Had a series of solo exhibitions with Beaux Arts, Bath, 1990-8, then Long & Ryle, 2000.

Ben ENWONWU 1921–1994 Painter, sculptor and teacher, born in Onitsha, Nigeria, where he died in Lagos. His gifts were noted when he was at primary school and flourished at Government College, Umuahia, between 1934–9. Taught from 1940–4, then a Shell Mexico scholarship took him to Britain after an early work, Making Man, in woodbrush and leaves, gained attention. Enwonwu studied at Goldsmiths' College School of Art, 1944; Ruskin School of Drawing, Oxford, 1944–6; then achieved a first-class honours degree at Slade School of Fine Art, 1946–8. HM The Queen sat for him for a statue which was placed at entrance of Parliament Buildings, Lagos. In 1959 Enwonwu rejoined Nigerian public service as art supervisor, giving up this job nine years later to concentrate on his own work, holding exhibitions in Europe, North America and elsewhere. In 1971 went as visiting professor in African studies to Howard University, Washington, in America, in the same year being appointed professor of fine arts at University of Ife, Illife, Nigeria, retiring in 1975. Died at his home in Ikoyi, Lagos.

Jacob EPSTEIN 1880–1959 Sculptor of monumental works and portraits, watercolourist and draughtsman. Born in New York of Polish Jewish parents, he was interested in art from childhood. Aged about 16 attended classes at the Art Students' League and at night school. Money earned by illustration paid for him to travel to Paris, where he studied the work of Rodin and other sculptors, also attending the École des Beaux-Arts and Académie Julian. Moved to London in 1905, becoming a British citizen two years later. He became a controversial figure as the result of several commissions: figures on the British Medical Association building in the Strand, London, 1907–8; the Oscar Wilde Memorial, Paris, 1910–11; and the W H Hudson Rima memorial in Hyde Park, 1925. After meeting advanced artists such as Picasso and Brancusi in France just before World War I Epstein became associated with the Vorticist movement in England, producing his Rock Drill construction in 1913–14. Successful both as a modeller and a carver, Epstein continued for several decades to produce busts of notable people, such as Joseph Conrad, Albert Einstein and Somerset Maugham; to create religious and other public sculptures; and to produce controversial images such as Genesis and Adam. Founder-member of the LG, exhibited many times at the Leicester Galleries and had first one-man show at the Twenty-One Gallery, in 1913. Published his autobiography *Let There Be Sculpture*, 1940. Knighted 1954. Many galleries, including the Tate, which held a retrospective in 1980, have his work. Lived in London. His son was the painter Theo Garman, his daughter the artist Kitty Garman.

John EPSTEIN 1937–1997 Artist and teacher, born in Sutton, Surrey, who studied painting at Central School of Arts and Crafts, 1957–61. Epstein was a member of Situation, taking part in the RBA Gallery show in 1960 and Situation's Arts Council tour, 1962–3; also showed with LG, 1977–8. His solo exhibitions included University of Essex, 1979. Theatre productions were an important part of Epstein's career. In 1969 he founded the Black Box Theatre, an experimental visual theatre company, which until 1972 performed throughout Britain, including Museum of Modern Art, Oxford, 1970, and Round House, 1970–1. Had extensive teaching experience, including Exeter College of Art, Bristol and Belfast Polytechnics as well as Morley College and Sir John Cass School of Art part-time. Latterly Epstein suffered from Alzheimer's Disease and lived in London.

Kate ERIC– This was the working name of two artists: Kate Tedman, born in Cumbria in 1979, and Eric Siemens, in Oregon, America, in 1974. Their rather surreal pictures were inhabited by a number of recurring characters delineated by fragmentary line-work and injected with vibrant colour. Kate Eric's work was included in the Albemarle Gallery's Summer Show 2004, the catalogue noting that their recent pictures had "centred around modern society's abandonment of traditional moral and sociological structures in pursuit of the enticing concept of personal freedom and the individuality it implies." There was a Kate Eric Albemarle exhibition in 2005 with a profusely illustrated catalogue. In the introduction the critic Edward Lucie-Smith compared the artists' work with that of the illustrator Arthur Rackham, also late-nineteenth and early-twentieth century Symbolists and Secessionists.

Benjamin ERLAND 1964– Painter and draughtsman, born in London, both parents involved in art education, in whose classes he early on worked as a technician. Attended Camberwell College of Art, 1985–6, worked regularly with a life model concentrating on drawing, 1987-90, then developed his oil painting technique. Painted both still life and atmospheric, crepuscular views, exhibitions including Savile Row Galleries, from 1987; L'Escargot, from 1990; Attendi Gallery, 1997; and Anna-Mei Chadwick at Gallery 27, 1999. In 1994 had solo show at Pump House Gallery. In 2004, had a joint exhibition with his sculptor mother Sukey Erland at the Glastonbury Rural Life Museum. His brother was the artist Simon Erland.

Simon ERLAND 1961– Sculptor in bronze, born and based in London, both parents involved in art education, his mother the sculptor Sukey Erland, his brother the painter Benjamin Erland. It was an environment where Erland associated with his parents' sculptor friends such as Henry Moore, Elisabeth Frink and Anthony Caro. Erland learned "mostly from my parents", also studying at Sir John Cass School of Fine Art with Clive Duncan as a postgraduate after degree studies in mechanical engineering at King's College, London. Manzù, Rodin and Marini were influences on Erland's work, informed by conceptualist ideas and employing "figurative forms, often men in relation to animals to carry metaphor." From an early age Erland was taught to ride by his mother, graduating to show jumping, cross-country events and dressage. Aged 20 he went to be trained in haute-école dressage by Hans Riegler at the Spanish Riding School in Vienna, from 1980 riding almost every year in the Austrian city. Erland showed with the Sladmore Gallery and SPS from 1982, other galleries exhibiting his sculptures including Arthur Ackermann, Frank T Sabin, RA Summer Exhibition and widely in America. In the mid-1990s Erland made many portraits of racehorses prior to his portrayal of the 1991 Derby winner Generous, spending time at the Banstead Manor Stud, Newmarket. From a first visit to Spain in 1996 Erland became preoccupied with the matador and bull theme, as in his solo show at the Cuatro Diecisiete Galeria, Madrid, in 2000. The Mellon and Packer collections, respectively in America and Australia, were among notable international owners of Erland's work.

Sukey ERLAND 1927– Sculptor, full name Susan Antoinette Erland, mother of the artists Simon and Benjamin Erland. She was born in Pilton, Shepton Mallet, Somerset, where she was latterly based. Studied at Farnham School of Art and then Chelsea School of Art under Willi Soukop. She was director of Ceramics London Ltd and lectured in three-dimensional studies at Chelsea and Westminster Institute. Erland was a member of SPS and the 303 Art Society. Other group shows included RA Summer Exhibition, RWA, artLONDON and several sculpture parks. Exhibited solo at studio during Somerset Art Week and at Otterton Mill. In 2004, she shared a show with her son Benjamin at Glastonbury Rural Life Museum. Collectors in Australia, Japan and America held her work, which comprised "figurative portraits of people and animals and mythological subjects."

John ERNEST 1922–1994 Sculptor and maker of reliefs, born in Philadelphia, America. He studied at its Settlement School of Music and Art with Antonio Cortizas, 1939–41. Lived and worked in Sweden, 1946–9, and in Paris, 1949–51, settling in London in 1951. Studied sculpture at St Martin's School of Art, 1952–6. During the latter part of the 1950s Ernest began making geometric constructions and scientific models. He taught at Bath Academy of Art, Corsham, Regent Street Polytechnic School of Art and Chelsea School of Art. Showed in Britain and abroad. Commissions included a relief mural and tower, International Union of Architects Congress, 1961. Arts Council holds his work, which was produced slowly and little of which survives. Died in Exeter, Devon.

Arthur Frederick ERRIDGE 1899–1961 Versatile artist, noted for his stained glass and ecclesiastical designs. He was born in London and studied at the Central School of Arts and Crafts. Erridge signed his work Arthur F Erridge, V in a circle or as Virge, having served as a verger for some years at St Paul's Cathedral. He worked for James Powell & Sons of the Whitefriars Glass Works, then with Wippells & Company, of Exeter. He was a member of the British Society of Master Glass Painters and is in the permanent collection of English, American and other overseas churches. As well as his ecclesiastical work Erridge was an artist in oil, tempera and watercolour. He lived latterly at Little Cornard, near Sudbury, Suffolk. There is a memorial window to him in St Andrew's Church, Marks Tey, Essex, erected by his wife, children and colleagues in 1968. It shows Christ as an artist, with palette and brushes.

Ilene ERSKINE 1933– Printmaker, notable for etchings in colour using a rich and distinctive palette and strong images, and teacher, born in Stirlingshire. She said that "like Matisse, I want my work to be colourful and cheerful." Graduated with a master's honours degree from University of Edinburgh, 1955, gaining her master's in education, 1964, adding an honours degree in sculpture, 1991, from Edinburgh College of Art. For most of her life she worked as a teacher and psychologist, then as a printmaker, taking part in many group exhibitions. Was a professional member of SSWA. Lived in Edinburgh.

Ken ERSSER 1940– Painter who studied at Camberwell School of Arts and Crafts and Royal Academy Schools. In 1965 he won the David Murray Scholarship, in 1966 the Leverhulme Award. Mixed shows included Young Contemporaries, Ikon Gallery in Birmingham, Opix Gallery and Figurative Painters at Woodlands Art Gallery, 1980. Had a solo show at Arnheim Centre in 1969; later ones including British Council in Athens, where he completed a mural, 1971; and Petit Gallery, Chicago, 1978.

Edward Frederick ERTZ 1862–1954 Painter and printmaker, born in Chicago, where he began as an illustrator and engraver, becoming involved in artists' organisations in the city. After working on a publication *The Century* in New York in the mid-1880s, Ertz travelled to Paris to continue his artistic education, where he taught for most of the 1890s. Eventually he settled in England, exhibiting at RBA extensively, as well as RA, ROI, Royal Glasgow Institute of the Fine Arts and Paris Salon. Was married to the miniature painter Ethel Horsfall Ertz. His work is in a number of public collections. Lived at Pulborough, Sussex.

Miriam ESCOFET 1967– Versatile artist, born in Barcelona, Spain, who moved to England in 1979, graduating with an honours degree in three-dimensional design, and majoring in ceramics, in 1990, from Brighton College of Art. She was fond of depicting architecture, architectural instruments and old objects such as drawing instruments. Her pictures were meticulously arranged and rendered in fine detail with almost tactile qualities. Was included in Millennium 2000 at Albemarle Gallery, 1999–00.

Gloria ESCOFFERY 1923–2002 Artist, teacher, poet, writer and gallery administrator, born in Gayle but brought up in Brown's Town, Jamaica, her father a doctor descended from white Haitians, her mother's family being English and Jewish-Jamaican. After high school education, Gloria went on scholarship to McGill University, Montreal, Canada, then returned to Jamaica, becoming literary editor of the People's National Party weekly *Public Opinion* and designing sets for the Little Theatre. Studied at Slade School of Fine Art, 1950–2, taught by Lucian Freud, her early works, such as Banana Plantation Workers, 1953, identifying with Jamaica's early nationalist realists. Her acrylic The Old Woman, 1955, was included in Jamaican Art 1922–82, at the Smithsonian Institution, Washington, America. Later, Escoffery's work became more experimental, dreamlike and surreal, full of literary allusion and often employing decorative friezes. From the late 1950s Escoffery moved from Kingston to Rio Bueno where she painted, ran an art gallery and taught in local schools, before returning to Brown's Town, where she spent the rest of her life in the grounds of her old family home with a huge library of art books. From 1975–85, having gained a teaching diploma at the University of the West Indies, she taught English literature at the local community college. Wrote for the *Jamaica Journal* and had a weekly column in the *Gleaner*. Latterly drew on a computer and created layouts for her poems, of which there were two published collections: *Loggerhead*, 1988, and *Mother Jackson Murders the Moon*, 1998.

Amy ESHOO 1961– Artist and lecturer, born in America, who studied at Wellesley College, 1979–83; Art Institute of Chicago School, 1986–7; then Goldsmiths' College School of Art, 1988–90. Lectured at National and Hayward Galleries. Her An Open Book was included in East & South at Norwich Gallery/Kent Institute of Art and Design, 1992. Danielle Arnaud showed her work, 1999. Lived in London.

Patricia ESPIR 1934– Artist in a variety of media, in oils and pastel using a rich and colourful palette, notable for portraits of children. She was born in London and spent her childhood in Egypt, returning for school and college to London, where she settled. Studied at RA Schools under Mike Biddulph. Showed at RA Summer Exhibition and Chelsea Art Show and solo in Britain and abroad, including Ben Uri Art Society at The Sheridan Russell Gallery, 1999.

Tom ESPLEY 1931– Artist in oil, tempera and watercolour and teacher, born in Aberdeen. He studied at Camberwell School of Arts and Crafts, then Slade School of Fine Art. His teachers included William Coldstream, Claude Rogers, B A R Carter, Robert Medley, Patrick George, Andrew Forge and Victor Pasmore. After National Service in the Royal Air Force as a photographer Espley worked in special effects with the film company Metro-Goldwyn-Mayer at Borehamwood, 1957–63, then taught part-time painting, drawing and photography at Camberwell, Hornsey and Central Schools of Art. Espley painted still life, nudes, landscapes and portraits, appearing regularly at RA Summer Exhibitions; Browse & Darby; Camden Arts Centre; South London Art Gallery and elsewhere. Solo shows included Green and Abbott, Belgrave and Amwell Galleries, Menuhin School and Alliance Building Society. British Rail, Chase Manhattan Bank and several other firms hold Espley's work. Lived in London.

Melanie ESSEX 1959– Painter of spare urban landscapes using a distinctive palette. She was brought up among notable painters in eastern Long Island and Maine in America, her studies at the New York Studio School, 1990–4, emphasising drawing and painting from perception. She gained a Merit Award for Excellence in Painting and Drawing there in her final year, in 1992–3 having won a Milton Avery Scholarship, in 1993 a Venice Travel Fellowship. Previously she had graduated from Harvard University in 1981, in 1981–2 attending the Institut National Supérieur des Arts de Spectacle (Film) under a Rotary Scholarship in Brussels, Belgium. Essex showed widely in group exhibitions in America and Britain and had a series of solo shows in both countries. These latterly included The Groucho Club, 1997; Caldbeck Gallery, Rockland, Maine, 1998; Cassian de Vere Cole Fine Art, 2001 and 2002; Icehouse Gallery, Greeenport, New York, 2004; and New Grafton Gallery, 2005.

EST: *see* **Elizabeth SCOTT-TAGGART**

Jack ESTERHUISEN 1949– Artist and teacher who studied at Canterbury College of Art, 1969–70, Brighton Polytechnic, 1970–3, and Royal Academy of Arts and Liu Academy of Taoist and Ch'an Buddhist Arts, 1974–7. From 1978 Esterhuisen held a number of part-time teaching posts, including Winchester and Canterbury Colleges of Art, North-East London Polytechnic and Cyprus College of Art. In 1983 he was included in British Artists at Cyprus College, at Woodlands Art Gallery. From 1982 he taught full-time at Newcastle Polytechnic.

Frederick ETCHELLS 1886–1973 Painter, draughtsman, architect and translator, born in Newcastle upon Tyne. Etchells studied for several years at Royal College of Art and for an equal period in Paris up to World War I, where he became interested in Fauve and Cubist painting. He showed with Roger Fry's Post-Impressionist exhibitions in London in 1912–13, by which time he was practising as an architect; became involved in the Omega Workshops; then accompanied Wyndham Lewis when he left to found the Rebel Art Centre. Participated in the Vorticist movement and contributed drawings to *Blast*. Also showed with Group X and LG, of which he was a founder-member. As a war artist he was notable for his painting of Armistice Day for the Canadian War Memorial. He then abandoned painting for architecture, becoming a fellow of RIBA in 1931. Among his notable buildings are the new library at Godolphin and Latymer School, Hammersmith, and the Crawford Building, Holborn. Did much church work and wrote on architecture and Anglican worship. Also translated Le Corbusier's *Towards a New Architecture*. Tate Gallery holds his work. Died in Folkestone, Kent. Etchells' second wife was the artist Hester Sainsbury.

Ian ETHERIDGE 1962– Sculptor and teacher using traditional materials who studied foundation at Maidstone College of Art and sculpture at Wimbledon School of Art. After opening a studio in Kent worked as a commercial wood-carver, also producing sculptures to commission and ran adult wood-carving classes in Canterbury. Etheridge was also an experienced children's teacher. In 1996 moved to Suffolk, based in Ipswich, spending more time on sculpture, church carvings and large plaster-works being strong features of his output. Was included in Making the Connection, firstsite, Colchester/Wolsey Art Gallery, Ipswich, 2002.

Ken ETHERIDGE 1911– Writer, painter and teacher, born in Ammanford, Carmarthenshire. He attended Swansea School of Art and studied English at University College, Cardiff, for three years from 1933. After various teaching jobs he was from 1947–71 head of the art department at Queen Elizabeth Boys' Grammar School, Carmarthen. Showed Paris Salon, Piccadilly Gallery, Woodstock Gallery and for many years at Royal National Eisteddfod where he won a number of awards. Had several solo shows, including Woodstock Gallery. Among his writings were books on scenic design and stage costume; a number of radio plays in English and Welsh; and *Collecting Drawings*. WAC holds his work.

Margaret EULER fl. from c.1925– Painter and teacher, born in London. Studied at Goldsmiths' College School of Art and at the Royal Academy Schools under various teachers, including Sir George Clausen and Sir Walter Westley Russell. Showed at RA, AIA of which she was a member, at Paris Salon and in the provinces. Lived in Bromley, Kent.

Richard EURICH 1903–1992 Painter and draughtsman, born in Bradford, Yorkshire, who settled for many years at Dibden Purlieu, near Southampton, and who had as a principal theme the sea, ships, ports and beach life. Father of the photographer Crispin Eurich. Richard Eurich's interest in painting was encouraged at Bradford Grammar School, then he went on to study at Bradford School of Art, 1920–4, and at the Slade School of Fine Art, 1924–6. There he concentrated on drawing, having his first one-man show of drawings, at the Goupil Gallery, in 1929, work of impressive quality. First one-man show of paintings at the Redfern Gallery four years later. He was aptly made an Official War Artist attached to the Admiralty during World War II, during which he completed his notable picture Survivors from a Torpedoed Ship, in the collection of the Tate Gallery. Imperial War Museum, National Maritime Museum at Greenwich and many provincial galleries hold his work. From 1949 taught for a period at Camberwell School of Arts and Crafts. Elected RA in 1953. Retrospective exhibition Bradford Art Galleries and Museums, 1979–80, and tour, and there was a memorial touring show based on Southampton City Art Gallery, 1994. In 2003, Eurich's centenary was commemorated with a touring show of his paintings that visited Yorkshire venues including Wakefield Art Gallery, organised by Helen Robinson of Bruton Gallery. In the same year, there was also a show at the Millais Gallery, Southampton Institute, and one at Southampton Art Gallery which toured to The Fine Art Society. Eurich's work depicted everyday events but sometimes had an English element of oddness, as in his picture The Mummers, in Hove Museum of Art. Other national and regional collections hold examples.

David EUSTACE 1950– Painter, muralist and jazzman, born in Birmingham, who produced detailed and quirkily imaginative and enigmatic landscapes with figures, animals and fish. Although Eustace was early encouraged to attend art school a lack of money prevented this, so he completed a carpenter's apprenticeship. He eventually attended Sutton School of Art for a two-year course, aged 21, then Exeter College of Art until 1976, but insisted that "I really taught myself the craft of painting." After gaining a teaching qualification at Leicester Polytechnic, Eustace spent some time in America, painting murals. Eustace liked working in series. After laying out his picture in acrylic he overpainted in oil using brushes, palette knife and kitchen scourers, which gave a soft finish. Group shows included the RA; RBSA; Royal Albert Museum, Exeter, where he lived; Camden Arts Centre; and Beaux Arts, Bath. Eustace was elected a member of the RBA in 2002 and was awarded the David Wolfers Memorial Prize, Mall Gall Galleries, and The Marine House at Beer Prize, South West Academy, both 2003. Solo exhibitions included Highgate Fine Art, from 2001, and Hutson Gallery, 2004. For many years Eustace played with the

Junk Yard Angels band, latterly with a four-man group called Shufflebones.

e-2: *see* **SIMON FAITHFULL**

Alun EVANS 1945– Artist, teacher and designer, born Haverfordwest, living in Narberth, Pembrokeshire. He studied fine art at Newport College of Art & Design, 1963–7, teachers including Lil and Tom Rathmell, Ernest Zobole and John Selway; completed the postgraduate teacher's certificate at Hornsey College of Art, 1967–8; worked as art master at Somerset High School, Tottenham, 1968; was product designer with SDC Products Ltd, 1969–70; then lectured in fine art at Cheshire School of Art and Halton College, Cheshire, 1970–96. Showed widely solo and in two-man and group exhibitions. From 1964 Evans was associated with the Rhymney Valley, south Wales, marrying a fellow art student, Elizabeth Beaton-Jones, who had been born and grew up there. Although the Bargoed coal mine was the third largest in Europe, it closed and in 1995 Evans learned that its massive waste tip was to be removed and the area landscaped, which inspired his show Black Wound, Newport Museum and Art Gallery and tour, 2000. National Museum and Gallery of Wales, Cardiff; National Library of Wales, Aberystwyth; Atkinson Art Gallery, Southport; and other public collections hold examples.

Ann Catrin EVANS 1967– Versatile artist, and teacher, working in a wide range of materials, born in Bangor, Caernarvonshire. She did a foundation course at Gwynedd Technical College, 1985–6, graduating with honours at Brighton Polytechnic, 1986–9, specialising in three-dimensional design in wood, metal, ceramics and plastics. In 1989, she joined the graduate enterprise business programme and went on to travel extensively connected with her work. Awards included 1st Prize National Eisteddfod of Wales, Builth Wells, Gold Medal Winner and £1,000 for Craft Masterpiece, and 1st Prize, Women in Enterprise, sponsored by Targed and Midland Bank, both 1993; 1st Prize, National Eisteddfod, Bala, £1,000 for Craft Masterpiece, 1997; and WAC £5,000 bursary to develop new work, 2000. Held a number of residencies and participated widely in group shows in Britain and abroad, later ones including New Ashgate Gallery, Farnham, and Scottish Gallery, Edinburgh, both 2000. Among solo tours was Llantarnam Grange Arts Centre, Cwmbran, 1995. Taught widely, including Coleg Menai and University of Wales, 2000–1, both in Bangor. Later large commissions included Museum of Modern Art, Machynlleth, 1997; BBC Radio Cymru, 2000; and Wolverhampton Borough Council, 2000–1.

Barry EVANS 1923– Mural painter and illustrator, born in London, married to the artist Mary Evans. Studied at Kingston School of Art, 1937–41, then at Royal College of Art, 1941–4, under Ernest Tristram. Work on paper included illustrations in publications and magazines such as *Lilliput* and *Picture Post*, covers for *The Economist*, posters for the British Tourist Authority and record sleeves. Extensive mural commissions from 1947, including a series for Central Office of Information; Festival of Britain Farming Pavilion and Dome of Discovery, 1951; Bruxelles Exposition, Belgium 1958; Jamaica, glass mural, Commonwealth Institute, 1972; Alexandria mural, Museum of the Diaspora, Tel-Aviv, Israel, 1978; Garden of Eden, Evoluon Museum, Eindhoven, Netherlands, 1980; and Concentration Camp mural, Detroit Holocaust Center, America, 1984. Latterly concentrated on oil, tempera and acrylic paintings, living in London.

Bernard EVANS 1929– Painter, draughtsman and teacher, born in Liverpool where he studied at the College of Art. Also studied at Camberwell School of Arts and Crafts, teachers including Richard Eurich and Martin Bloch. Taught art in the north of England for 20 years. He went on to direct the Mounts Bay Art Centre in Newlyn, Cornwall, where he settled, in 1976, in the 1990s being chairman of Newlyn Society of Artists. While running the residential art school Evans continued to paint, showing widely in the west of England and the east coast of America. The closure of the school enabled Evans to tackle a bold, three-year project: panoramic views of London, some from elevated vantage points, an idea nurtured by a visit to his son's high-rise office in the capital. The result was Evans' show Views of London, his first in one of its galleries, at Connaught Brown in 2003. He sometimes signed work only with initials.

Bob EVANS 1947– Painter, artist in ceramics and lecturer, born in Cardiff where he attended the College of Art, 1964–8. Was next at Chelsea College of Art, 1968–9, and Hornsey College of Art, 1970–1. Did a variety of jobs then, while continuing to paint. Showed Young Contemporaries, 5 Artists at University College in Cardiff, Royal National Eisteddfod, SEA and SWG and had a one-man exhibition at Serpentine Gallery, 1972. WAC holds his work and he was included in its 1980 touring show of drawings The Probity of Art. Lived in London for a time.

Carole EVANS 1944– Painter of atmospheric figurative and landscape work, born and lived in Neath, West Glamorgan, who, after early promise, resumed painting in 1991, having met her husband, Peter. Attended Swansea University extra-mural department classes run by Michael Freeman. She showed with the Theodore Group; with Neath Arts Society, including Neath Museum & Art Gallery, 2001; and was a founder-member of the Friday Group in Swansea. In 2001, was accepted for open show at Museum of Modern Art, Machynlleth. Joint shows with her husband included Neath Museum & Art Gallery, 1999, and Fane Arts Centre, Glynneath, 2000. Many private collections held her work.

Cerith Wyn EVANS 1959– Tape, slide, video and film, sculpture and installation artist, born in Llanelli, Carmarthenshire. Did a foundation course at Dyfed College of Art, 1976–7; obtained a first-class honours degree in fine art at St Martin's School of Art, 1977–80; and a master's honours degree in film and television, Royal College of Art, 1981–4. Awards included The Worldwide Video Festival, The Hague, first prize, with a similar prize at 3e Semaine Internationale de Video, Geneva, both 1989. Evans' prize-winning film *Degrees of Blindness* included, as did many others, the performance artist Leigh Bowery, who named this as his favourite film of 1989. Participated in extensive exhibitions and screenings, including solo show at London Filmmakers' Co-op, 1981; another at B2 Gallery, 1982; The New Art, Tate Gallery, 1983; Cinema as Art, National Film Theatre, 1986; retrospective screenings at London Filmmakers' Co-op and masterclass lecture at Riverside Studios, both 1988; and Signs of the Times,

Museum of Modern Art, Oxford, and Video sculpture, installation commissioned by Kijkhuis in Den Haag, part of a retrospective, both 1990. Was included in Sensation, at RA, 1997. Evans' Cleave 00, in the Art Now series at Tate Britain, 2000-1, reflected the artist's later concentration on sculptures and installations using combinations of materials such as neon lighting, mirrors, fireworks and plants. Had a solo exhibition at White Cube, 2003.

David EVANS 1893–1959 Sculptor and carver in various materials, painter and teacher, born in Manchester, where he attended the School of Art, gaining a Senior Scholarship. He won a National Scholarship, Royal College of Art, where he was taught by Francis Derwent Wood, being awarded his diploma in 1920; saw active service in World War I; and attended the Royal Academy Schools, winning a British Institution Scholarship, 1921, Landseer Prize, 1922, and Prix de Rome, 1923, enabling him to work at the British School at Rome. Held a number of teaching appointments, including Hammersmith, Central and Bromley Schools of Art and New York University. He was sculptor-in-residence at the Cranbrook Foundation, Bloomfield Hills, Michigan, in 1929. While in America, Evans did some important work on New York's public buildings. Exhibited extensively at RA Summer Exhibition; also at Walker Art Gallery, Liverpool; Royal Glasgow Institute of the Fine Arts; Manchester City Art Gallery; Metropolitan Museum of Art, New York; and elsewhere in Europe. Evans was a fine craftsman, producing decorative and realistic work, a fellow of the RBS whose work merited serious coverage in the art press. His bust of Sir Arthur Evans is illustrated in the 1939 volume *RBS: Modern British Sculpture*; his Panel in Arthur T Broadbent's 1944 book *Sculpture Today in Great Britain 1940–1943*; and his Gog and Magog, of 1950–3, for Guildhall, and later work on New Change Buildings are both covered in Philip Ward-Jackson's *Public Sculpture of the City of London*. Collections holding Evans' work include public galleries in Cardiff, Manchester and Newport; the Dick Institute, Kilmarnock; Cranbrook Art Academy, Michigan; and Philadelphia Art Museum. Evans latterly lived in Welwyn Garden City, Hertfordshire.

David EVANS 1929–1988 Painter of landscape, still life, fantasies and murals, born in London. Studied at Central School of Arts and Crafts with Keith Vaughan. Early in his career he showed photomontages at Gallery One and gained several commissions; these included a design for the Hollywood Room in the *Observer* Film Exhibition, 1956, and a mural for the Soup Kitchen, Knightsbridge. He began painting watercolours and gouaches in 1967, two years before he settled in Suffolk. They were not shown until 1973, when his work was included in a mixed show at Deben Gallery, Woodbridge. In 1975 his work was included in summer show at Redfern Gallery, where he held solo exhibitions from 1979, after showing one-man at McMurray Gallery for three years, 1976–7–8. After his death in a road accident, Redfern gave him a small memorial show in 1988.

David EVANS 1942– Painter and teacher, born in Abercarn, Monmouthshire. He studied at Newport College of Art, 1959–62, then at Royal College of Art, 1962–5; in 1965 he won the College's Silver Medal for Painting. Travelled in Spain and Morocco before becoming a lecturer at Edinburgh College of Art, being based in the city. Evans was Granada Arts Fellow at University of York, 1968–9, and travelled through America in 1975–6. He was a member of RSW and was elected RSA in 1989. Evans was noted for his Hyper-Realist interiors which often have a tinge of suspense or mystery about them. He had a one-man show at New 57 Gallery in Edinburgh in 1966, others following at Marjorie Parr and Gilbert Parr in London. Lived in Edinburgh.

David EVANS 1950– Artist, especially in pastel, who did much landscape work in Kent and Surrey. He studied at Croydon College of Art, 1973–7. After that he had many exhibitions including Green Party Fayre, 1988; Holland Gallery, 1989; Laing Collection Art Show, 1990; London Ecology Centre, 1990; and in 1992 he shared a show with three other artists at Anna-Mei Chadwick.

David Lloyd EVANS 1916– Painter and teacher who married the book illustrator Grace Gabler. He studied at Wimbledon School School of Art with Gerald Cooper, 1935–8 and at the Royal College of Art with Gilbert Spencer, 1938–40. For two years from 1943 was art master at Sedbergh School, Yorkshire, then instructed at Stoke-on-Trent Art Schools. Exhibited RA. Lived near Stone, Staffordshire.

Evelyn EVANS 1915– Painter, designer, printmaker and teacher who was born in Burford, Oxfordshire. She studied at Cheltenham School of Art, 1932–5, with Gerald Gardiner, then at the Royal College of Art, 1935–9, with John and Paul Nash and Edward Bawden. Exhibited RA, RBA, and NEAC. Victoria & Albert Museum holds her work. She taught at Blackpool School of Art, then Epsom and Ewell School of Art. Lived in Puttenham, Surrey, for some time.

Garth EVANS 1934– Sculptor, draughtsman and teacher, born in Cheadle, Cheshire. From 1955–7 studied at Manchester School of Art, 1949–57, then at Slade School of Fine Art, 1957–60. Evans showed at John Moores Exhibition, Liverpool, in the 1960s, and had his first solo exhibition at Rowan Gallery in 1962, the first of many there. In 1964 he gained a Gulbenkian Purchase Award, in 1966 an Arts Council Sabbatical Award. In 1966 Evans began teaching at St Martin's School of Art, gained a British Steel Corporation Fellowship in 1969 and the year following became a visiting lecturer at Slade School of Fine Art. Other teaching posts were at Royal College of Art, Camberwell School of Arts and Crafts and Minneapolis College of Art and Design. Further selected awards included: Arts Council Major Award, 1975; British Council Exhibitions Abroad Grant, 1979; John Simon Guggenheim Memorial Foundation Fellowship, 1986; Pollock-Krasner Foundation Award, 1996; and Artists Fellowship Award, 1999. Evans took part in many influential mixed shows in Britain and abroad. Commissions included Ebbw Vale Urban District Council and Peter Stuyvesant Sculpture Project, Cardiff, 1972. Tate Gallery, Museum of Modern Art in New York and Victoria & Albert Museum hold his work, the Arts Council holding his abstract works Relief in White No. 7 and Blue No. 30, of 1962 and 1964. Later shows included Mayor Gallery, 1991; Sculptures & Works on Paper, Korn Gallery, Drew University, New Jersey, 1996; and The 1982 "Yaddo" Drawings, Halsey Gallery, The College of Charleston, Charleston, South Carolina, 1998. From late 1970s lived in New York.

George Brinley EVANS 1925– Miner-artist, working independently, who originally drew political cartoons while living in Banwen, Glamorgan, employed at Onllwyn Colliery. The earliest examples, in the early 1950s, demonstrated outrage at the conversion of the Tir John Power Station, Swansea, from anthracite to oil. Another early work was his tender, Neo-Romantic painting Peggy the Papers, a portrait of his wife, with whom he ran a newsagent's while working as a miner. Other pictures reflect pit life, using household emulsion and artists' watercolour on cheap paper. After losing an eye in a mining accident in 1961 Evans began modelling figurines of national heroes and workmates, using basic materials to produce figures misshapen from a life of tough, cramped graft. Pieces by Brinley Evans were included in Miner-Artists: The Art of Welsh Coal Workers, National Museum & Gallery, Cardiff, 2000. Evans also gave a talk about the show.

Georgina EVANS fl. from early 1990s– Mixed-media and performance artist, born in Lagos, Nigeria, who did foundation studies at Camberwell School of Art, 1989–90; gained an honours degree in fine art from Goldsmiths' College, 1990–3; and studied multi-media authoring at Lambeth College, 1995–6. From 1996 in London and Amsterdam pursued studies in movement, dance, theatre and voice. Awards included two from London Arts Board, 1996 and 1998. Among her group shows were Moot Lenses, with Jon Rowe, ICA, 1995; Case Study Home, Skuc Gallery, Ljubljana, Slovenia, 1998; and Tolv Netter, with Jon Rowe, United Sardine Factory, Bergen, Norway. Had a solo show at 198 Gallery, 1993. In 1998–9 Evans was artist-in-residence at Union Dance Company, appointed by the Institute of International Visual Arts. Lived in London.

Geraint EVANS 1968– Painter and draughtsman, born in Swansea, south Wales, where he studied at the Institute of Higher Education, 1986–7, then at Manchester Polytechnic, 1987–90, and Royal Academy Schools, 1990–3. Evans drew on images from books, magazines and catalogues for his tidy suburban interiors, with sometimes an autobiographical or bizarre element. Exhibitions included Into the Nineties, Mall Galleries, 1993; Whitechapel Open and Mostyn Open, Llandudno, both 1994; and John Moores Liverpool Exhibition, 1995–6. Had solo exhibitions at Gallery 1010, University of Tennessee, America, 1994, and Anthony Wilkinson Gallery, 2000. Lived in London.

Gwendoline Edith Marion EVANS: *see* **Gwen TAYLOUR**

Gwyn EVANS 1931– Painter, born Tonypandy, Glamorgan, who attended Cardiff College of Art, 1948–54. After a period teaching in Coventry in the late 1950s he returned to Tonypandy to teach at the Grammar School. Showed with Young Contemporaries in London in 1950, then with Royal National Eisteddfod, SEA and SWG. Solo shows included Rhondda Heritage Park, Trehafod, 2001.

Handel EVANS 1932–1999 Painter, draughtsman and printmaker, born in Pontypridd, Glamorgan. He studied at Cardiff College of Art, 1949–54, teachers including David Tinker and Eric Malthouse. From 1947–58 Evans made studies in the Alexander Technique and music, attending the Clifford H Lewis School of Music, receiving the Licentiate of the Royal Academy of Music diploma in 1958. After painting in the Caribbean (where he taught briefly), Germany and Italy, 1959–62, in 1962–3 Evans was at the British School at Rome. In 1975–6 he studied with Stanley William Hayter at Atelier 17, Paris, other teachers including the etcher Anthony Gross. Otherwise, Evans lived by painting in the Caribbean, notably the Bahamas, the Americas and many European countries. Music remained a key influence on pictures which had man and technology as a theme and which indicated an acquaintance with Futurism, Surrealism and Cubism, using a distinctive palette. Had extensive exhibitions in Germany, including Deutscher Beamtenbund Berlin, 1992, and Preussen Elektra, Kassel, 1995, with a memorial show at the Museum, Korbach, 1999. British shows included Mario Flecha Gallery, 1982, and Clare Hall, Cambridge, 1987. Ashmolean Museum in Oxford, Clare Hall and National Gallery of Jamaica hold examples. Died in Thanet, Kent.

Hugh EVANS 1946– Printmaker and designer, born in Cardiff. After studying at Newport College of Art, where in the early 1970s he worked for a few years as a technician, Evans studied textile design in Denmark and Finland. From 1973 he worked as a printmaker in his own studio. Showed at Glynn Vivian Art Gallery in a show called Welsh Artists One and at Royal National Eisteddfod. Did some work on sets for the television station HTV.

James EVANS 1964– Sculptor, born in Romford, Essex. He studied at Central School of Art and Design, 1984–7, then University of Colorado, 1987–90. He went on to teach part-time at several colleges of art. A leading interest of Evans' work was opulent domestic interiors, especially of the Victorian era, as in his clay Thigh Grasp Comforter, shown in the 1992 East & South Norwich Gallery/Kent Institute of Art and Design show. Was included in Atlantic Crossings, Barbican Centre, 1998, among solo exhibitions Tram Depot Gallery and Pegasus Studio, 1996. Lived in London.

Margaret Fleming EVANS 1952– Painter and teacher, born in Glasgow where she studied at the School of Art, 1970–4, teachers including David Donaldson, Leon Morrocco and James Robertson. She taught in adult education, was a member of UA and showed in London and the provinces. Lived in High Halden, Kent.

Merlyn EVANS 1910–1973 Painter, printmaker, sculptor and teacher, born in Cardiff, noted for his Surrealist and abstract works which often have an overtone of menace. He studied at Glasgow School of Art, 1927–30, a travelling scholarship enabling him to work extensively on the continent until he resumed studies at the Royal College of Art, 1931–3. His full name was Merlyn Oliver Evans and the second name was sometimes indicated when he signed. Further studied under Stanley William Hayter in Paris, 1934–6. Was influenced by Surrealism and the Vorticists, exhibiting at the International Surrealist Exhibition in London in 1936. Began teaching in London, then lived and taught in South Africa, 1938–42, having his first one-man show at Durban's City Art Gallery in 1939. After widespread World War II Army service Evans settled in London, where he became a member of LG. With his ex-Army grant took a refresher course at Central School of Arts and Crafts. From 1965–73 taught at Royal College of Art. Tate Gallery and other major galleries hold his work. Retrospective at Whitechapel Art Gallery, 1956, another at Art Institute of Chicago, in America, 1967, and memorial show at National Museum of Wales, Cardiff, 1974. Later exhibitions included Tate Gallery, 1985, and retrospectives at Mayor/Redfern Galleries, 1988. Evans was married to the pianist Margerie Few, sister of Elsie Few, Claude Rogers' wife. Lived in London.

Michael EVANS 1934– Artist and lecturer who studied at Leeds College of Art, 1952; attended the Slade School of Fine Art, for printing and sculpture 1953; and won a Robert Ross Scholarship for study abroad, in Italy, 1957. He showed at the New Art Centre, 1958; Finchley Public Library, 1964; and The Gordon Maynard Gallery, Welwyn Garden City, 1966. In 1968 there he shared a show with Mary Hoad and Leslie Summers. By that time he had held various part-time teaching posts, had been a lecturer for the department of extra-mural studies at the University of London and was currently in charge of painting and cine photography at All Saints College of Education, Tottenham. Hertfordshire County Council and private collections bought Evans' work.

Nicholas EVANS: *see* **Nick EVANS 1907–2004**

Nick EVANS 1907–2004 Painter, sculptor and teacher, born and lived in Aberdare, Mid Glamorgan, sometimes exhibited as Nicholas Evans. Evans was self-taught as an artist and began painting at the age of 70, using his fingers and rags. His father was a miner and mining was a leading feature of his work, along with the Jewish Holocaust, of which he produced a record. Evans' grim, large monochrome pictures of mining life in the 1920s and 1930s were featured in a solo show at St David's Hall, Cardiff, in 1993. Evans was a Christian and Pentecostal lay preacher. He was aware of the link between scripture and the colliery, "the horrible pit", as in his work included in Miner-Artists: The Art of Welsh Coal Workers, at National Museum and Art Gallery, Cardiff, 2000. His Oils: Nicholas Evans, paintings using finger and rag technique, was held at the Heritage Park, Rhondda, 2001. He was elected RCamA in 1981, also showing with RA, Turner Gallery in Penarth, Browse & Darby, RWA, Swansea University and abroad, winning many prizes. Tate Gallery, National Museum in Cardiff, Arts Council and WAC hold his work. Evans published a book on his work, *Symphonies in Black*, in 1987.

Nick EVANS 1976– Sculptor, mixed-media artist and teacher, born in Mufulira, Zambia, who did foundation studies in art and design at Yeovil College, Somerset, 1997; attended the Royal College of Fine Arts, Stockholm, Sweden, 1999; and gained first-class honours in fine art, sculpture and environmental art from Glasgow School of Art, 2000. Significant teachers were Derek Boshier, David Harding, Ross Sinclair, Christine Borland and Claire Barclay. Evans settled in Glasgow and there won a School of Art Travel Scholarship in 2000 and Scottish Arts Council individual artist's assistance grants in 2001, 2002, 2003 and 2004. He had a South West Arts Regional Arts Lottery Programme residency at The Town Mill, Lyme Regis, 2001, other residencies including Grizedale Arts, Cumbria, 2002, and Cove Park, Helensburgh, 2003. Evans was a visiting lecturer, master of fine art department at Glasgow School of Art in 2003, and in 2004–5 at the School's painting and historical and critical studies departments. He was a committee member of Transmission Gallery in Glasgow, 2002–4, and from 2005 one of the board of directors of Glasgow Sculpture Studios. As well as taking part in group exhibitions, Evans was a regular solo and shared show exhibitor, later ones including Lumumba is Dead, Transmission Gallery, and Remember Old Pineapple Face, Glasgow Project Room, both 2002; Red Bus Go (with Laurence Figgis), 273 High Street, Glasgow, 2004; and Nick Evans/Tobias Buche, Mary Mary, Glasgow, 2005. In 2006–7 Evans would be the fourth Tate St Ives artist-in-residence and exhibited there. In his work he employed a range of media, from resin to hand-built ceramic sections, according to the Tate: "his eclectic practice probing the history of sculpture while decoding contemporary social, political and cultural representations."

Peter EVANS 1943– Painter, designer and businessman, born in Handsworth, Birmingham. From 1960 attended Birmingham College of Arts and Crafts to study exhibition design. While employed as a designer produced in his own time abstract constructions and paintings which were included in shows at Compendium Galleries, Birmingham; Pentagon Gallery, Stoke-on-Trent; Bear Lane Gallery, Oxford; and Compendium II, London. From 1966–84 took over Warwick Fine Arts, dealer and picture framer, in Edgbaston. In 1978 Evans abandoned abstraction and became interested in what was termed Romantic Realism. By 1984 and retirement to paint full-time, Evans was established as an exhibitor at RA. He went on to have solo shows at Seen Gallery, 1986; and from 1987 several with John Davies Contemporary Painters, Stow-on-the-Wold. Evans, whose later exhibitions included The Catto Gallery, 2001, was noted for his pictures of town and countryside in France. Lived in Solihull, Warwickshire.

Peter EVANS 1950– Painter of atmospheric figurative and landscape works, born and lived in Neath, West Glamorgan, married to the artist Carole Evans. Peter in 1966 undertook a four-year apprenticeship as a painter and decorator, from 1978 for two years attending Swansea University art classes run by Mike Freeman, with whom he founded the Friday Group. From 1984, for two years taught art for the Workers' Educational Association. Exhibitions included Afan Arts Centre; Neath Gwyn Hall; Glynn Vivian Art Gallery, Swansea; Fane Arts Centre, Glynneath; and Museum of Modern Art, Machynlleth. In 1989, had three pictures chosen for the Best in the West Artists and Designers in Wales Exhibition at Swansea Workshops, in 1992 being chosen to represent Neath Town Council in its twin town show in Vienne, France.

Powys EVANS 1899–1981 Caricaturist and painter, also known as Quiz, born in London, son of a county court judge, William Evans, and brother of the artist Gwen Evans. He studied with Spencer Gore and Robert Bevan, the Camden Town Group painters; under Henry Tonks at Slade School of Fine Art, 1915–17; and with Walter Sickert and Sylvia Gosse with a period at Westminster School of Art. Served with Welsh Guards on the Western Front in France, 1918. Visited Sickert in Dieppe, 1920. Evans' early aspirations as a painter of London scenes were cut short when he began drawing for publications which included *The London Mercury* and *The Saturday Review*. His caricatures could be cruelly grotesque, as work in his two Leicester Galleries exhibitions in the mid-1920s and one at Colnaghi, in 1932, the latter two sell-outs, showed. He drew five prime ministers, four chancellors of the exchequer and 30 judges. His books included *The Beggars' Opera*, 1922; *Eighty-Eight Cartoons*, 1926; and *Fifty Heads drawn by Powys Evans*, 1928. An enigmatic figure, he retired when still at the height of his powers to Dolgellau, Merioneth, where he lived as a semi-recluse. In 1975 there was a retrospective at Langton Gallery, which gave him and Edmond Xavier Kapp a show in 1985. National Portrait Gallery holds many sketch-books and studies by Evans, including Sir Arnold Bax the composer, Sir Jacob Epstein the sculptor and writers A A Milne and J B Priestley.

Ray EVANS 1920– Painter, illustrator, writer and teacher, born in Hale, Cheshire. He studied at Instituto di Belle Arti, Florence, 1945–6; Manchester College of Art, 1946–8; and Heatherley's School of Fine Art, 1948–50, under Iain Macnab, termed "a great influence". Evans worked for six months with the advertising agents Colman, Prentis & Varley, 1950–1, then as a freelance. Among various teaching appointments was Southampton College of Art, 1956–66. Did commissioned work for major companies such as British Petroleum, Eagle Star, banks and government. Many solo exhibitions included Thackeray, Furneaux and Canaletto Galleries; Winchester city art gallery; and Ashbarn Gallery in Petersfield. RA and RI, of which he was a member, RBA and RWA were among group show appearances. Shared a three-man exhibition at The Wykeham Gallery, Stockbridge, 2002, another at The Albany Gallery, Cardiff, in 2003. Among Evans' books were *Travelling with a Sketchbook*, 1980, and *How to be a Successful Illustrator*, 1993. National Library of Wales in Aberystwyth, Southampton Education Authority and Winchester gallery hold his work. Lived in Salisbury, Wiltshire.

Simon EVANS 1963– Sculptor in steel who studied at Blackburn School of Art and Design and Coventry Polytechnic. While at Coventry he created the scrap metal Steel Horse for Coventry City Council, part of a competition to mark Industry Year 1986. The rampant horse was sited at Warwick Road in Coventry's city centre. Other wildlife sculpture by Evans included a Minotaur, displayed near Coventry's Cathedral in 1988, and a horse, shown at Earls Court, 2000. Evans was based in Trawden, Lancashire.

Sybil EVANS fl. from 1950s– Painter who studied at The College in Pontypool, Monmouthshire; in the same county at Newport College of Art; and at Hornsey College of Art. Showed at RA, NEAC and elsewhere. Lived for some time in Torquay, Devon.

Tom EVANS 1948– Photographer, painter, lecturer and writer, born and lived in London. Evans attended University of Bristol department of architecture, 1966–9. From 1972, he was a visiting lecturer at London College of Printing, from 1979 photography correspondent of *Art and Artists*. His group exhibitions included Design Centre, 1971; Dramatic Focus, Shaw Theatre, 1976; and Whitechapel Open and Wapping Artists Open Studios, both 1982. Among his solo exhibitions were Autour de St Didier d'Allier, fnac, Paris, and tour, 1981–2, and Photographs of Wapping, London Borough of Tower Hamlets tour, 1982. That borough, Bibliothèque Nationale in Paris, Chicago Beach Hotel in Dubai and many private collections in Britain and abroad hold his work.

Vincent EVANS 1896–1976 Painter, printmaker and teacher, born in Ystalyfera, Glamorgan, South Wales. Worked for a time in coal mining. Studied at Swansea School of Art and at Royal College of Art until 1924 under William Rothenstein and Frank Short. He went on to become art master at Slough Grammar School, 1940–61, after a period in New Zealand, then taught at Slough College until 1968. Exhibited RA, NEAC, RWS, Leicester Galleries and Paris Salon. National Museum of Wales, Cardiff, and Glynn Vivian Art Gallery, Swansea, bought his work. Lived in Slough, Buckinghamshire.

Will EVANS 1888–1957 Painter, designer and printmaker, born and died in Swansea, south Wales. After leaving school at 14 Evans became an apprentice tinplate printer at South Wales Canister's works, eventually becoming their chief designer after attending lessons part-time from 1910 at Swansea School of Art. Showed RCamA, SWG, SWAS and elsewhere and was given a memorial show at Glynn Vivian Art Gallery, Swansea in 1958, a dozen years after his one-man exhibition there. That gallery and National Museum of Wales, Cardiff, hold his work which was frequently landscapes of the Swansea area in watercolour.

William EVANS 1911– Painter, born in London, studied at Hammersmith School of Art and Royal Academy Schools. Showed at RA, LG, RBA and RP, his work being held by public collections in Oxford, Cambridge and Reading. Lived at Abinger Hammer, Surrey.

Esmé EVE 1920– Painter in gouache, teacher, book illustrator and designer, born in London. She studied at Croydon School of Art and Royal College of Art. Miss Eve taught graphics at various art colleges and embroidery design at Royal School of Needlework. Book illustrations were completed for Blackie, Odhams, Longman's, Macdonald's, Hamlyn and other publishers, and she contributed designs for charity greetings cards, as well as Medici. She wrote and illustrated *The Christmas Book* under the name Eve, which she sometimes used for pictures. Lived in Seaford, Sussex.

Eamon EVERALL 1948– Painter and teacher, born to an Army family in Aldershot, Hampshire, so he attended a dozen schools, including abroad. Did a foundation course at Folkestone School of Art, 1967–8; fine art painting diploma at Waltham Forest School of Art, 1968–72; a postgraduate printmaking course at Wimbledon School of Art, 1972; a variety of jobs, 1973–4; won a scholarship for Architectural Association School of Architecture, 1974–6; and gained his master's in visual theory, University of East London, 1996. From 1988 he was head of art and design at Redbridge Institute. Everall gained a commission for a Millennium sculpture in east London, where he lived. Buddhism, meditation, Tai-chi and Cajun dancing were interests. Everall's paintings were from life and took a long time. He was a member of the Stuckists and was in their show at Artbank Gallery, 2001.

Roberta G EVERETT 1906– Sculptor and teacher, born in Surrey, who attended Goldsmiths' College School of Art and City and Guilds of London Art School. She taught at Brentwood College of Education, Essex. Exhibited RA, Royal Glasgow Institute of the Fine Arts and at Paris Salon. Lancashire Education Committee holds her work. Lived in Hornchurch, Essex, then Harrow, Middlesex.

Graham EVERNDEN 1947– Printmaker and designer, married to the painter Sue Evernden. He was born in Kent and studied at Maidstone College of Art, graduating with a first-class honours degree in 1970. Worked in London as a graphic designer and illustrator for four years, going freelance in 1974. In 1975 was elected to Printmakers' Council. Set up own printmaking studio in Sussex, running a separate studio for editioning etchings for other artists. Dorset and Sussex were key elements in his work, which was shown at RA Summer Exhibition from 1977, Mall Galleries from 1978 and widely abroad. Gillridge Gallery, Crowborough, gave him a solo show.

Leonard Charles EVETTS 1909–1997 Stained glass artist, teacher, watercolourist and, like his father, a skilled letterer. He was born in Newport, Monmouthshire. Aged 18, he won a short scholarship to the Royal College of Art, with a three-year one covering the years 1930–3. His teachers included Edward Johnston for calligraphy, for whom he served as a demonstrator, and Martin Travers for stained glass. Evetts taught at Edinburgh College of Art from 1933–7, in 1938 publishing his book *Roman Lettering*, which establish him as an authority on ancient calligraphy. From 1937 Evetts taught for about 40 years in the department of fine art at King's College, Newcastle, eventually becoming department head. During World War II he was engaged by the government for camouflage work. Newcastle's Cathedral Church of St Nicholas has a fine east window, of 1962, by Evetts, one of over 300 completed in Britain and abroad. He favoured traditional architecture as a setting. In 1995, the Church of England acknowledged Evetts' achievement with a Lambeth doctorate. Showed at RA. Laing Art Gallery, Newcastle, holds his watercolour Bamburgh Castle. Died at Woolsington, Tyne and Wear. Hatton Gallery, Newcastle, held a large exhibition of Evetts' output in 2001. His wife was the artist Phyl Dobson, with whom he occasionally showed.

David EVISON 1944– Abstract sculptor in metal and wood, sometimes painted, and teacher, born in China. He studied at Leeds College of Art, 1963–7, then St Martin's School of Art, 1967–8, where he taught part-time. Group shows included Stockwell Depot I and Prospect '69, Düsseldorf, Germany, both 1969; Sculpture in Holland Park, 1972; and The Condition of Sculpture, Hayward Gallery, 1975. Had solo shows at Kasmin Gallery, 1971–2, and at Museum of Modern Art in Oxford, 1976. His Untitled sculpture, of 1979, was sited in Grizedale Forest Sculpture Park. Arts Council and Whitworth Art Gallery in Manchester hold examples. Lived in southeast London.

David Shanks EWART 1901–1965 Painter, born in Glasgow, who spent most of his life there. After a short period in business after leaving school, Ewart attended Glasgow School of Art, his teachers including Maurice Greiffenhagen and Fra Newbery. On graduating in 1924, he used a scholarship to take him to Italy and France. On his return, in 1926 his picture The Emigrants was a great success at Royal Glasgow Institute of the Fine Arts show, a companion picture, The Return (now in the collection of Scottish National Gallery of Modern Art), appearing the following year. Ewart showed also at RA and RSA, where he won the Guthrie Award in 1926 and the Lauder Award in 1927. His work is notable for its hard-edged, ultra-realistic quality, very suited to the pictures of American tycoons and their wives which he painted during prolonged visits from the mid-1940s.

Michael EXALL 1950– Painter, printmaker, draughtsman and teacher, born in Norwich, Norfolk. Attended Hornsey College of Art, 1968–72, under Norman Stevens, and Royal Academy Schools for postgraduate studies, 1972–5. Anthony Gross and Giorgio Morandi were influences. From 1976 Exall taught part-time at Manchester Polytechnic and University, providing him time and money for his own work. Group exhibitions included Bradford International Print Biennale from 1976, the year he showed in British Realists at Ikon Gallery, Birmingham; Hull Print Exhibitions from 1984; and RA Summer Exhibitions. Had a solo show at Trinity College, Oxford, 1974; Angela Flowers Gallery and City Art Gallery in Barnsley, both 1986; Dean Clough, Halifax, 1990; and Salford Art Gallery, 1991. Public galleries in Leeds, Norwich, Sheffield and Wakefield hold examples, as does Skopje Museum in former Yugoslavia. Lived in Todmorden, Lancashire.

Neil EXETER 1975– Painter who gained a first-class honours degree in visual arts at Lancaster University, 1994–7, and his master's in fine art at Central St Martins College of Art & Design, 1999–00. Exhibitions included Wimbledon Studios Open, 1998–9; Open Studios, Limehouse Arts Foundation, and ART*futures*, organised by the Contemporary Art Society at Barbican Centre (where Exeter showed abstracts in pastel colours), both 2000; and Ida Branson Memorial Bequest Exhibition, Millfield, 2001. Lived in south London.

Till EXIT 1962– Artist working in a mix of media who completed a DAAD postgraduate scholarship at Chelsea College of Art and Design in 1996. Exhibitions included Kunstverein Elsterpark-Projectgalerie in Leipzig, Germany, and Milch Gallery, both 1997; Leonhardi-Museum in Dresden, 1998; and Loop-Raum für aktuelle Kunst, Berlin, 1999. In 2000, he shared a show at Rhodes + Mann. Exit was commissioned to make a work for the courtyard of the new German Bundestag, Berlin.

James Robert Granville EXLEY 1878–1967 Painter, printmaker and teacher, born at Great Horton, Bradford, Yorkshire. He studied at Skipton Art School and Royal College of Art, graduating in 1907. Among his appointments was headmaster of Hull Municipal Art School, 1912–19. Natural history and the countryside were key subjects. Exley was elected RE in 1923, also showing at RA, Redfern Gallery and Royal Glasgow Institute of the Fine Arts. British Museum, Victoria & Albert Museum and Fitzwilliam Museum in Cambridge hold examples. Lived in London, then at Grassington, Yorkshire.

Ray EXWORTH 1930– Sculptor, draughtsman and teacher, born in Ipswich, Suffolk. He attended the local School of Art, 1951–5, then Royal College of Art, 1955–9. He had a solo show at Whitechapel Art Gallery, 1975, Felixstowe Remembered, 1970–4, as well as other sculptures and drawings; was also shown at Chappel Galleries, 1992, and in same year was included in Artists from Cornwall at RWA. Awards included Arts Council, 1975–7–84, and a South West Arts Fellowship, 1985. Taught at Falmouth School of Art and lived in Praze, Camborne, Cornwall. Arts Council holds several examples.

Sophie EYNON 1967– Artist born in Swansea, Glamorgan, latterly based in London. In 1985 she studied sculpture and life drawing at Centro Verrochio, Tuscany, Italy, also art history and drawing in Florence and Venice, 1985–6. After teaching art at St Lawrence School Sinar, Himachel Pradesh, in India, 1986, Eynon did a foundation course at the London College of Printing; gained a fine art degree at Byam Shaw School of Art, 1987–90; studied at the fine art faculty of Universidad Catolica de Santiago, Chile, 1990–1; and obtained her master's in fine art at the University of East London, 2000. Eynon began exhibiting in 1985 in a group show at Canterbury Arts Festival, and had a solo exhibition, The Culture of Representation, at Bucci Gallery, Santiago de Chile, 1990. Fifty illustrations of Amazonian flora in 1992–4 were "used medicinally by the Huaoroni people, for the Rainforest Information Centre, Ecuador." Secrets of the Shaman was a solo exhibition, at the Chelsea Physic Garden, 1994, and in 1995 Burchell's Zebra was another at Diaz y Larrouy, Madrid, Spain. Other one-mans included Arca de Noe, Casa de la Cultura de Noia, Santiago de Compostela, Spain, 1996; Lepidoptera, Centro Cultural Puerta de Toledo, Spain, 1997; Pure Image, International House, Danan Gallery, 1999; and Recent Paintings, England & Co, 2003. In that exhibition were atmospheric, uncannily calm paintings of places Eynon knew well and which she felt moved by and connected to in some way. Among later group events for Eynon was International Young Art, a curated auction at Sotheby's New York and Tel-Aviv, Israel.

Frank EYRE 1953– Painter and draughtsman who graduated from University of Belfast, 1989, later studying there for his master's degree. Showed in mixed exhibitions throughout Ireland, including Works on Paper and Beyond the Partitions, put on in 1994 by Queen Street Studios, Belfast, with which Eyre was associated. His work sometimes used unconventional media, such as charcoal and car spray. Solo exhibitions included Rubicon Gallery in Dublin, 1990, and One Oxford Street, Belfast, 1992.

Erica EYRES 1980– Versatile artist, born in Canada, who was included in the inaugural Bowieart show BLOC at the County Hall Gallery in 2005. Eyres graduated with a fine art degree, sculpture, from the University of Manitoba, 1998–01, and gained her master's in fine art from Glasgow School of Art, 2001–4, in 2003 attending Skowhegan School of Painting and Sculpture. Exhibitions included Don't Look a Dead Horse in the Mouth, with Chris Cooper, University of Manitoba Architecture Gallery, 2002; International Contemporary Drawing, Gallery of the Academy of Fine Arts, Guangzhou, with China tour, 2003; and in 2004 the Portobello Film Festival and International Exchange Exhibition, Hunter College Gallery, New York, America. Among her solo exhibitions were two in 2004: 'neath the green green grass of home, Mary Mary, Glasgow, and Gallerie Dwarf, Reykjavik, Iceland.

Bernard EYRE-WALKER: *see* **Bernard Eyre WALKER**

Anthony EYTON 1923– Painter and teacher, born in London, where he continued to live. He was educated at Canford School, Dorset, then studied fine art for a term at Reading University in 1941, serving in the Army, 1942–7, painting occasionally. From 1947–50 studied at Camberwell School of Arts and Crafts, in 1951–2 gaining an Abbey Major Scholarship to work in Italy. Began to show with LG and RA and in 1955 had first one-man exhibition at St George's Gallery. From 1957 Eyton taught at Camberwell School of Art, other teaching following at Royal Academy Schools from 1965 and in 1969 at St Lawrence College, Kingston, Ontario. Among other notable events in Eyton's career were winning a prize at John Moores Exhibition, Liverpool, in 1972; travels in Italy and India in the 1970s; membership of LG, RWA, RWS and NEAC and election to RA in 1987. Eyton showed with Browse & Darby and had a retrospective South London Art Gallery and tour in 1980. In 2000, a show in the Friends' Room at the RA linked Eyton's work with that of his mother, Phyllis, who died in a hunting accident in 1929, when he was six. There was a 10-year retrospective at King's Road Gallery in 2002. He was a landscape and still life painter in the tradition of Euston Road School and Camberwell School of Art who believed that art stemmed from a regard for nature, balancing fact and abstract. Arts Council, Tate Gallery and Imperial War Museum hold his work.

F

F: *see* **BROUN-MORISON of Finderlie**

Miche FABRE-LEWIN 1956– Artist and art therapist, born in what is now Zimbabwe, who moved to England in 1980, settling in Oxford. She gained an honours degree in comparative literature/art history at East Anglia University, Norwich, 1975–80; studied stained glass at École des Beaux-Arts, Aix-en-Provence, 1978–9; and was apprenticed to the Patrick Reyntiens Stained Glass Studio, Beaconsfield, 1980–1; gained an art therapy diploma, Hertfordshire College of Art and Design, St Albans, 1988–9; then obtained her master's in art therapy at Hertfordshire University's school of art, 1992–4. Group shows included Three Women, at The Studio, Oxford, 1986; Diorama Arts Centre, 1990; Wolfson and Stables Galleries in Oxford, both 1992; Ben Uri Gallery, Annual Open, 1995; and Unquiet Voices, Doncaster Museum & Art Gallery, 1997.

William Bateman FAGAN 1860–1948 Sculptor, born and lived in London, educated at Dulwich College and married to the painter Betty Fagan. He was elected a fellow of RBS in 1938 and showed at RA, Royal Glasgow Institute of the Fine Arts, Walker Art Gallery in Liverpool, ROI and elsewhere. Was a Chelsea Arts Club member.

Graham FAGEN 1966– Installations artist, born and lived in Glasgow, who gained a fine art, sculpture, honours degree at the School of Art there, 1984–8, then his interdisciplinary master's in art and architecture at Kent Institute of Art & Design, Canterbury, 1989–90. Mixed shows included Wonderful Life, Lisson Gallery, 1993; Fall Out, Wacker Kunst, Darmstadt, Germany, 1996; and Backspace, Matt's Gallery, 1998–9. In 1999 Fagen (with Johnny Spencer and Neo Rauch) was in The Golden Age, at ICA; there his installation involved a television documentary about a Scottish housing estate in which he explored themes of social control, paternalism and isolation. Solo exhibitions included Henry Moore Institute, Leeds, 1999, and Yorkshire Sculpture Park, West Bretton, 2000; a stint as a war artist in Kosovo also led to a show in 2000 at Imperial War Museum. Fagen curated several exhibitions, including No Tell Hotel, Tramway, Glasgow, 1996.

Mateusz FAHRENHOLZ 1963– Creator of boxed constructions, printmaker, born in St Andrews, Fife, his parents Polish exiles. He explored suffering and exile in his work, which used photographs of unknown people and places and a range of domestic items which he specially aged. In 1984–5 did summer studies at Academy of Fine Arts in Cracow, Poland, then in 1984–8 gained an honours degree in fine art, printmaking, from Gray's School of Art in Aberdeen, doing his postgraduate diploma there, 1988–9. Gained a Go and See grant from the Prince's Trust, 1990, and a Go Ahead grant to work with the Polish sculptor Piotr Bies in 1992. In 1991 was artist-in-residence at Aberdeen Art Gallery. Group shows included Polonia Society, Cracow, 1984; Open Prints Exhibition, Bankside Gallery and New Generation Artists at Compass Gallery, Glasgow, both 1988; and CD3, Collective Gallery, Edinburgh, 1994. Had a solo show at Aberdeen Art Gallery in 1991, later ones including England & Co, 2002. Aberdeen Art Gallery, National Library of Scotland and the libraries at St Andrews and Dundee Universities hold his work.

Jonathan FAIRBAIRN 1961– Ceramist and teacher who studied at Laird School of Art, 1977–8, next Wallasey School of Art, 1978–81, then becoming a ceramics technician and lecturer at Wirral Metropolitan College. Fairbairn said that his work was designed "with the mystical lost rituals and ceremonies of ancient cultures in mind", such as Ceremonial Jug, shown in the 1986–7 Walker Art Gallery, Liverpool, Merseyside Artists 3 touring exhibition. Also exhibited at Wirral Spring Exhibition, Williamson Art Gallery, Birkenhead, 1986, and in same year Fourplay at Acorn Gallery, Liverpool.

Bernard FAIRCLOUGH 1915– Painter and teacher, born in Glossop, Derbyshire. He studied at Manchester School of Art, teachers including Leslie Baxter, going on to teach for many years until 1975 at Darlington School of Art, of which he became head. Showed with RSA, Arts Council, Whitechapel Art Gallery and widely in the provinces. Manchester Education Committee holds his work. Lived in Newbiggin, Barnard Castle, County Durham.

Mary FAIRCLOUGH 1913– Painter, printmaker, illustrator, potter and writer, born in Keynsham, near Bristol, Somerset, where she continued to live, was a councillor and was active in Keynsham Local History Society (later Keynsham Civic Society). She studied at home with Kit Gunton, 1926–30, then part-time at West of England Art College, Bristol, until 1939. Served in Women's Voluntary Service in World War II, but her mother's illness and failing sight and her own asthma restricted her activities. Through Gunton Miss Fairclough showed with Clifton Arts Club and had her work seen by Claude Flight, participating in his lino-cut exhibitions ("as a group we exhibited at the Ward Gallery, London and Brighton"); also showed with RWA; and locally in Keynsham. Fairclough illustrated, mostly books and magazines for children, for publishers including Macmillan, Evans Brothers, George Newnes and Pearson's. She published *Miskoo The Lucky, a tale for children with illustrations*, 1947; *Little Dog and The Rainmakers*, 1949; *The Blue Tree*, 1960; and *John Barleycorn*, 1962. Her ballad opera *John Barleycorn*, for which she wrote the libretto and designed the costumes, was performed at Wellsway School, Keynsham, in 1968, music by Bruce Montgomery and published by Novello.

Fairclough's smaller art works and crafts were signed M F in monogram form, with the date.

Michael FAIRCLOUGH 1940– Printmaker, painter, muralist and teacher, born in Blackburn, Lancashire, son of the artist Wilfred Fairclough, married to the painter Mary Malenoir. He studied at Kingston School of Art, 1957–61; was a Rome Scholar in Engraving, 1964–6, at British School in Rome, 1964–7; then was at S W Hayter's Atelier 17, Paris, 1967. After teaching at Belfast College of Art, 1962–4, was at West Surrey College of Art, Farnham, 1967–79. He completed the National Trust commemorative stamps for the Post Office in 1981. Among his solo exhibitions was Bohun Gallery, Henley-on-Thames, 1981. Ashmolean Museum in Oxford and Victoria & Albert Museum hold his work. Was made a fellow of RE, 1973, and a member of Printmakers' Council, 1981. Lived in Farnham, Surrey.

Wilfred FAIRCLOUGH 1907–1996 Etcher, watercolourist and teacher, born in Blackburn, Lancashire, husband of the painter Joan Vernon-Cryer and father of the artist Michael Fairclough. Left school at 14 to work in a mill, then trained as an audit clerk while attending evening classes at Blackburn School of Arts and Crafts, passing the Board of Education's drawing examination in 1930, the year he was appointed a part-time teacher at Blackburn. Determination gained him entry to the Royal College of Art's engraving school, where he excelled, 1931–4, under teachers Malcolm Osborne and Robert Austin. He was a Rome Scholar in Engraving, 1934, attending the British School in Rome, 1934–7. Rome was a favourite subject, later replaced by Venice. Lived in Kingston upon Thames, Surrey, and was principal of the School of Art there, 1962–70, assistant director of Kingston Polytechnic, 1970–2. Fairclough had joined the staff at Kingston in 1938, then spent his wartime service in the Royal Air Force; he worked on models employed in planning the bouncing bomb attack on the Mohne dam; and was latterly in India. Fairclough was elected RE, 1946, and RWS, 1968, also showing at RA, RSA, Royal Glasgow Institute of the Fine Arts and at the Redfern Gallery, as well as widely overseas. Contemporary Art Society bought his work, also held by Ashmolean Museum in Oxford and Victoria & Albert Museum, which has the almost 60 watercolours which Fairclough completed during World War II for the Pilgrim Trust's *Recording Britain* project.

Frederick Park FAIRER 1910– Portrait painter, born in Hull, Yorkshire. He studied art at the Borough Polytechnic with David Bomberg in 1948, City and Guilds of London Art School in Kennington in 1950 and the Central School of Arts and Crafts in 1951–3. Showed at RA, NEAC and RP. Lived in London.

Hugh FAIRFAX 1958– Artist whose work commonly featured wildlife found by the sea, where he lived. Fairfax trained at Cambridge College of Art. His pictures appeared in *The Times* and *Harpers & Queen*. Showed regularly in London and was included in Autumn Exhibition, The Wykeham Gallery, Stockbridge, 2001.

Michael FAIRFAX 1953– Sculpture and lecturer, born in Windsor, Berkshire. He attended Portsmouth College of Art for foundation studies, 1976–7, then graduated with honours from Gwent College of Higher Education, 1977–80. Gained several Southern Arts and WAC grants and was an Eisteddfod prizewinner, 1992. Did an extensive amount of educational and lecturing work in Britain and abroad; residencies included Margam Sculpture Park, 1991, and Forestry Commission, Garw Valley, 1992. Between 1986–91 travelled in Italy, Egypt, Spain and America. His work in public places included Margam Sculpture Park and Ebbw Vale, for Garden Festival. Had a solo show at Newbury Spring Festival, 1983, another at St David's Hall, Cardiff, 1991. Lived in Canton, Cardiff, south Wales.

Edmund FAIRFAX-LUCY 1945– Painter who studied at City and Guilds of London Art School, 1963–6, then Royal Academy Schools under Peter Greenham, 1967–70. He won the David Murray Travelling Scholarship, 1966, 1967 and 1969. From 1967 he was a regular exhibitor at RA, and was also a member of NEAC. Showed in group exhibitions at New Grafton Gallery, which gave him a first solo show in 1971. Sir Edmund Fairfax-Lucy was noted for his sensitive landscapes and interiors in which the play of light was a special feature. Lived at Charlecote Park, Warwick. He became 6th Baronet in 1993.

James FAIRGRIEVE 1944– Painter and teacher, born in Prestonpans, East Lothian. He studied at Edinburgh College of Art, 1962–8, and was awarded an Andrew Grant Scholarship and one-year postgraduate study, David Murray Landscape Award and Travelling Scholarship to Italy. He went on to teach painting and drawing at Edinburgh College of Art. Fairgrieve was a member of RSW and was president of SSA in 1978. Birds, animals and the natural world featured strongly in his pictures, which were shown widely in Scottish group exhibitions. One-man shows included New 57 Gallery and Scottish Gallery, in Edinburgh, and Mercury Gallery in London and Edinburgh. Scottish Arts Council and many other Scottish collections hold his work. Lived in Gordon, Berwickshire.

Angus FAIRHURST 1962– Artist in mixed media, born in Kent, where he studied at Canterbury College of Art, 1985–6, completing an honours degree at Goldsmiths' College School of Art, 1986–9. Among his group shows was Modern Medicine, Building One, 1990, and Summer Group Show, Karsten Schubert Ltd, 1992. The year before had a solo show at Karsten Schubert. Fairhurst's Scuba Blue Attachment, of 1992, was acquired for the European Parliament Collection and was shown in the Arts Council, Belfast, touring show Twelve Stars, 1992–3. In 1998 he shared an exhibition, Odd-Bod Photography, with Sarah Lucas at Sadie Coles HQ.

Enoch FAIRHURST 1874–1945 Painter, miniaturist, designer and illustrator, born and lived in Bolton, Lancashire, father of artist Jack Fairhurst. He was elected a member of Manchester Academy, 1932, and of RMS in 1943, having earlier been an associate for a time. Showed also at Walker Art Gallery in Liverpool, RA, RSA and RCamA.

Jack FAIRHURST 1905–1989 Painter, draughtsman and teacher, son of the miniaturist Enoch Fairhurst, born in London. He studied at Camberwell School of Art, 1919–23, under Albert Rutherston, then Royal College of Art, 1923–7, with William Rothenstein and Randolph Schwabe. Held several teaching appointments in the London area, between 1941–57 acting as head of Richmond School of Art. Was a member of Ridley Art Club, South London

Group, Richmond Art Group and the Society of Fulham Artists, also showing RA, RP and in the provinces, having several solo shows in and out of London. Lived latterly in Dallinghoo, Suffolk.

Miles Christopher FAIRHURST 1955– Painter, born in Norwich, son of the landscape artist Joseph Fairhurst. He studied art with his father and at University of Aix-en-Provence, France. Showed his work in his own gallery in New King's Road, London, and in various mixed exhibitions, having a first substantial showing at Park Grosvenor Galleries in 1992. In late-1980s returned to East Anglia to breed waterfowl and paint landscape, which he did rather in the manner of Edward Seago.

Dorothy M FAIRLEY 1894– Etcher, wood engraver, painter and stone carver. Studied at Richmond Art School and Regent Street Polytechnic. One-man show in 1946 at Walker Galleries, also showed in mixed exhibitions at many venues, including RA, NEAC, SWA, Paris Salon and Chicago Institute of Fine Art. Lived at Robertsbridge, Sussex.

George FAIRLEY 1920–2003 Painter, sculptor and teacher, born in Dunfermline, Fife. After studying at Edinburgh College of Art Fairley, who had been taught by David Alison, William Gillies and Adam Bruce Thomson, learned in the studios of several Paris artists, including Fernand Léger, returning to England when World War II started. He served as a radar technician in the Royal Air Force, was involved in the D-Day landings and Allied push through France, the Low Countries and into Germany. Demobilised, he was for 15 years from 1947 lecturer in fine art at Swansea College of Art, then moving to head the foundation studies department at Croydon College of Art. Showed with 56 Group of which he was a member, Leicester Galleries, SEA, WAC and in other group shows, having several solo exhibitions with Gimpel Fils, at Bear Lane Gallery in Oxford and at the Universities of Southampton and Surrey. Among his commissions were stainless steel murals for National Westminster Bank in the Home Counties area. WAC and Worcester College, Oxford, hold his work. In 1981, Fairley and his wife moved to a converted windmill at Wisborough Green, Sussex, where he ran hugely successful art classes.

Rob FAIRLEY 1953– Artist, lecturer, inspirational teacher and author, born in Edinburgh, who attended the College of Art there under Robin Philipson, 1970–4. He was artist-in-residence, Acharacle Primary School, 1985–96; a lecturer at Aberdeen University's department of continuing education, from 1988; Room 13 artist-in-residence, Caol Primary School, Fort William, where he lived, from 1994; conducted the Kinlochleven Century to Century project with Age Concern Scotland, 1998–9; and was fine art consultant to Kathmandu University, Nepal, from 1999. In 2003 Caol Primary won the £20,000 Barbie Prize, offered by Ivan Massow. Robert Fairley's approach was to allow children to explore their own responses to situations in their own ways. Over the years Fairley's work prompted substantial press coverage. He and Room 13 were the subjects of *The Art Show* on Channel 4 television in 2004. Fairley took part in many group shows in Britain and abroad, later ones including Five Scottish Painters, Artifex Gallery, Sutton Coldfield, 2001, and Indo/British Group, Indian tour, 2002–3. Solo exhibitions included Inverness Museum and Art Gallery, from 1981; Open Eye Gallery, Edinburgh, from 1982; West Highland Museum, Fort William, 1995; and Meghraj Gallery, 1998. Fairley believed that painting and all the arts "should not be competitive", so for many years did "not enter competitions and turned down awards made through 'open' exhibitions." Inverness Museum and Art Gallery, West Highland Museum, Highland and Strathclyde Regional Councils, Glasgow Chamber of Commerce and other public and private collections in Britain and abroad held examples. His books included *Jemima, the paintings and memoirs of Jemima Blackburn*, 1988; *Blackburn's Birds*, 1991; and *Drawing Hands and Feet*, 2001. He was a member of the Alpine Club and a fellow of both the Society of Antiquaries of Scotland and the Royal Society of Arts Manufacturers and Commerce.

Churton FAIRMAN 1924–1997 Sculptor in wood and stone, broadcaster, actor, photographer and musician, born in London, full name Austin Churton Fairman, son of the actress Hilda Moore, leading lady for Gerald du Maurier. Attended Aldenham School and Oxford University, but left early to joint the Ballet Rambert. After World War II service in the Ulster Rifles, Fairman became a ballet photographer. His first wife was Spanish; with her he returned to Spain and wrote *Another Spain*, 1952, about its countryside. Through the director Peter Brook, he became involved in the theatre; then Independent Television religious programmes; and, as Mike Raven, as a disc jockey for pirate radio and BBC Radio 1, eventually with the *Mike Raven Blues Show*. Appeared as Mike Raven in several horror films, including *Crucible of Terror*, 1971. Early in the 1970s Fairman and his second wife, Mandy, moved to Cornwall to live in a converted pigsty, from 1980 running a dilapidated farm near Blisland, by which time Fairman had been carving about six years. A first show in Cornwall ran into difficulties because of the controversial nature of Fairman's work, but he was to have two exhibitions at St George's Church, Bloomsbury, in 1990 and 1992, and in 1993 his The Deposition from the Cross was exhibited in the Images of Christ touring show in Northampton and at St Paul's Cathedral.

Sean FAIRMAN 1965– Artist creating mixed-media abstract pictures and site-specific installations. He often used a muted palette to make works which had a strong archaeological element, as in his solo show Foraminifera, Blue Gallery, 2000. Fairman studied printmaking at Camberwell School of Art, 1985, then attended Sir John Cass School of Art and Design, 1990–2, and Guildhall University, 1992–3. Commissions included Lambeth Council site-specific mural, Effra Nursery, Brixton, 1995; Breathe, installation and performance, Naoko Kawase, Tokyo, Japan, 1997; and *Tomb Raider*, Paramount Pictures, 2000.

Sheila FAIRMAN 1924– Artist in oil and miniaturist, born in South Benfleet, Essex. She attended Southend College of Art, 1938–40. Fairman's main works were still life, her Shells and Feathers series being shown at various venues. In 1967 with a revived interest in painting she returned to Southend College of Art to study portrait and life drawing at evening classes and she began painting miniatures in 1979. She was a member of RMS from 1981; was a member of Hilliard Society of Miniaturists; in 1985 was elected to SWA; and in 1986 was a founder-member of Society of Botanical Artists. Also exhibited at RSMA, ROI, RI and in the provinces. She gained several placings in the Hunting Group Art Prizes and won the RSM Gold Bowl in 1989. Beecroft Art Gallery, Southend, holds her work. Lived in Leigh-on-Sea, Essex.

Mark FAIRNINGTON 1957– Painter, born in Gateshead, County Durham, who studied at Goldsmiths' College School of Art. In 1993, he gained the Arthur Andersen Award for Figurative Painting, in 1999 The Sargent Fellowship, British School at Rome. Group shows included Death, Kettle's Yard, Cambridge, 1988; Picturing People – British Figurative Painting 1945–1988, British Council international tour, 1989; Whitechapel Open, Whitechapel Art Gallery, from 1992; Postcards on Photography, Cambridge Darkroom Gallery and tour, 1998; and Saatchi in Sheffield, Mappin Art Gallery, Sheffield, 1999. Fairnington's solo show Staying Alive at Mobile Home in 2001 transported subjects from seventeenth-century still-life paintings into a Disneyesque vision of life, all in meticulous detail. He had another exhibition there, 2003. Arts Council, British Council, Imperial War Museum, Saatchi and corporate collections hold his work.

Tom FAIRS 1925– Artist in mixed media, stained glass designer and teacher, born and lived in London. He studied at Hornsey College of Art, 1948–50, and Royal College of Art, 1950–4. Became senior lecturer in theatre design at Central School of Art & Design. Fairs after a period of abstract work painted landscape, interiors and still life. He showed at RA Summer Exhibitions, Rooksmoor, Covent Garden and Thackeray Galleries. Was a member of the Society of Landscape Painters and the Society of Small Paintings. Stained glass was prepared for baptistry and day chapel lights for Our Lady of the Wayside, Shirley, Birmingham; Holborn College of Law, Languages and Commerce; and Officers' Club, Bahrain.

Dorothy FAIRWEATHER 1915– Artist in various media, born in Folkestone, Kent. She attended the local School of Art, Liverpool University and Richmond Art School. At times was engaged in photography and running an art gallery. Exhibited solo at Turnpike Gallery at Leigh; Stables Gallery in Hastings; The Old Bakehouse, Sevenoaks; Woodlands Art Gallery; and Mount Street Post Office. Mixed exhibitions included RA, the provinces and abroad. Lived in Sevenoaks, Kent.

Ian FAIRWEATHER 1891–1974 Painter, born at Bridge of Allan, Stirlingshire. He is believed to have studied forestry and botany as a young man before serving in World War I, during which he was a prisoner of war in Germany. Then studied art in Netherlands and was at Slade, 1920–3. Although he had shows at Redfern Gallery in 1930s, Fairweather's life for much of the inter-war years was that of a traveller, especially in the Far East and Australia, which became his home. During World War II he served in British Army. In 1952 he tried to sail to Timor on a home-made raft, was reported missing but turned up shortly after in Timor, was sent to Britain and then back to Australia, where he lived at Bribie Island, Queensland. His work is original, brilliant and sensuous and often employs unconventional materials. It is in Tate Gallery and all Australian state galleries. Died in Brisbane.

FAISAL 1969– Artist, notably a printmaker, and teacher, full name Faisal Abdu'allah, who did a foundation course at Harrow School of Art, 1987-8; gained a first-class honours degree in fine art printmaking at Central St Martins School of Art, 1989–91, in 1989 attending the Massachusetts College of Art in Boston, in America; then gained his master's degree in fine art printmaking at the Royal College of Art, 1991–3. He had a residency at Furness School, 1993, and gained the Art in the City Award, 1995–6. Teaching included Falmouth School of Art, Middlesex and East London Universities, Royal College of Art and Wolverhampton University. Faisal's work appeared in many magazines and newspapers. Exhibitions included Brent Arts Festival, 1987; Photographers' Gallery, from 1993; and University of East London, 1996. Had a solo show at 198 Gallery, 1993, others at The Agency, 2001, and Harrowed, prints on themes on cultural sterotyping and the urban environment, London Print Studio, 2003. Victoria & Albert Museum holds his work. Lived in London.

Kay FAITHFUL 1930–1999 Painter, born in Greenock, Renfrewshire, who after a traumatic World War II trained as a nurse and midwife, then married Will Faithful, a Cornish civil engineer. They lived in Bermuda, the Middle East, Cyprus and Jamaica before moving to Canberra, Australia, in 1972, where she was able to concentrate on painting. In 1987, she held her first major exhibition of 30 large works, The Barrier Reef Series, at Holdsworth Contemporary Galleries, Sydney, followed by others at the Eltham and Rathdowne Street Galleries, Melbourne. In 1991 Faithful visited the United Kingdom and the continent for her first overseas exhibitions. Australian Landscapes – Visual Reflections, 29 paintings, was shown in Glasgow, Greenock and at the Australian Embassy, Paris. A second show, of 30 smaller works, Gardens & Flowers, was exhibited at Edith Grove Gallery, Chelsea. In 1992 Faithful completed a series on the Brindabella Ranges and showed again at Holdsworth: 20 large canvases, Recent Landscapes, depicting Australian bush and beach scenes. Faithful had a major show of 35 paintings at Daimaru Gallery, Tokyo, in 1993, part of Celebrate Australia, a government initiative to demonstrate the country's achievements to an important trading partner. There were further shows at Edith Grove Gallery and at Lillie Regional Art Gallery, Glasgow, in 1994, part of the Mayfest. Faithful continued to show in Australia, in 1996 returning to the United Kingdom with 35 large acrylic canvases and 30 watercolours for a combined series called Diversity Exploration of Landscape. Her last exhibition was of the Brindabellas in 1998 at Strathairn Gallery, Canberra. McLean Museum and Art Gallery, Greenock, holds her work.

Leila FAITHFULL 1896–1994 Artist in a variety of media, born in Walton, Lancashire, daughter of Sir James Reynolds, Bart, but brought up in Liverpool. She married George Faithfull in 1917 and after he died in early 1940s took as her second husband in 1943 the writer and critic Cuthbert Worsley. After the war while they were on a trip through France he left her, in Marseilles, and she stayed on to work. She frequently painted alone abroad. Faithfull studied at Slade School of Fine Art, 1923–4, later at L'Académie de la Grande Chaumière, Paris. For a time Faithfull was surgical artist to Sir Archibald McIndoe, the pioneer plastic surgeon, at Queen Victoria Hospital in East Grinstead. Leila (pronounced Lyla) Faithfull was noted for her portraits, shown extensively at Leicester Galleries,

NEAC, RBA, RA, ROI and elsewhere. She was in the private collections of Lord Clark and Sir Edward Marsh and had works accepted by War Artists' Advisory Committee and Contemporary Art Society and public galleries in Aberdeen, Birmingham and Manchester. In later years she created heads, figures on horses and the occasional dancer in metal: cut-outs from sheets or as wire shapes and outlines, but these were not commercially successful. Died in St Angela's Convent, Bristol, where she had lived for several years.

Simon FAITHFULL 1966– Artist and teacher who used rudimentary and sophisticated technical devices to create simple installations with strong metaphorical qualities. For Temporary Accommodation, at Whitechapel Art Gallery in 2001, he transformed half the upper gallery into his workshop, centred on a home-made hot air balloon that rose and fell as its temperature changed. Born in Ipsden, Oxfordshire, Faithfull graduated first-class in theatre design at Central St Martins School of Art, 1986–9, in 1994–6 gaining his master's in fine art from Reading University. From 2000 he was a visiting lecturer at Goldsmiths' University, fine art/history of art, in 2001 being a visiting lecturer in the University of London's architecture department. Residencies included Triangle, New York, America, 2000. As well as participating in group shows, Faithfull was co-writer and director of films and videos, including *Isle of Dogs*, 1996, televised by BBC2, and Faithfull publications was active from 1996. In 1998, Faithfull was involved in founding the digital arts organisation e-2, its collaborations being viewable at www.e-2.org. Solo exhibitions included Moth Island, Lotts Island and Watermans Arts Centre, Brentford, 2000, and Pump House Gallery and Aspex Gallery, Portsmouth, both 2004.

Bushra FAKHOURY 1942– Sculptor, born in Beirut, Lebanon. Dr Fakhoury attended St Paul's, Wimbledon School of Art, Beirut University College, American University of Beirut and London University. Exhibitions included Bloomsbury and Mall Galleries, 1986; Jablonski Gallery, 1987; Kufa Gallery, 1989; and 2nd Open Sculpture Exhibition at RWA, 1996. Her themes and subjects included human and animal, some merging into surreal figures of myth and fantasy. Lived in London.

Roland FALCON 1914– Sculptor in various materials and photographer, educated in Copenhagen, Berlin and London. He was official sculpture photographer for the Tate Gallery and exhibited his photographs in London. Also showed RMS, RSA, Russell-Cotes Art Gallery and Museum in Bournemouth and Foyles Gallery. Lived in Edgware, Middlesex.

Brian FALCONBRIDGE 1950– Sculptor, draughtsman and teacher, born in Norfolk. He studied at Canterbury College of Art, 1968–9, Goldsmiths' College School of Art, 1970–3, and Slade School of Fine Art, 1973–5. Gained the Walter Neurath Art History Award in 1972, Arts Council Minor Award, 1976, the Eastern Arts Association Award in 1977, and four years later the Tolly Cobbold/Eastern Arts Regional Prize. In 1984 won the E Vincent Harris Award for Mural Decoration at RA, in 1988 was a prize winner at the 3rd International Exhibition of Miniature Art, Del Bello Gallery, Toronto, Canada, then in 1991 Falconbridge won the Blackstone Prize at RA. Went on to teach extensively throughout Britain, notably various posts at Goldsmiths' College from 1976; Eton College, 1977–81; Slade School of Fine Art, 1979–86; Blackheath School of Art, 1985–9; and in 2001 was promoted to personal chair of visual arts at Goldsmiths'. Falconbridge took part in Goldsmiths at South London Art Gallery in 1972; showed with LG and New Contemporaries; RA; and in 1983 was Artist of the Day at Angela Flowers Gallery. Numerous other group shows followed, latterly including Absolut Secret, Royal College of Art, 2000; London Underground, Sungkok Art Museum, Seoul, South Korea, 2001; and Blue, Place Arte Contemporanea, Cavagnolo, Italy, 2002. In 1984 The Minories put on a show of his work which toured England. Among later one-man exhibitions were Jill George Gallery, 1990; Masterpiece Art Centre, Taipei International Convention Centre at the World Trade Centre, Taipei, Taiwan, 1996; Chappel Galleries, Chappel, 2002; and Fermoy Gallery, King's Lynn Arts Centre, Norfolk, 2003. Falconbridge was elected a fellow of RBS in 1997 and served on its council. Falconbridge's coloured, abstract sculptures were on a small scale, in wood and other materials, and employed geometrical shapes. Arts Council, Contemporary Art Society and University of East Anglia hold his work. Lived in London.

David FALCONER 1967– Sculptor, born in Newcastle upon Tyne, Northumberland, who obtained his master's degree in art theory from Goldsmiths' College School of Art, 1994. For a time Falconer was studio assistant to Jake and Dinos Chapman. Falconer's work was included in the Saatchi Collection and was part of the Neurotic Realism series of exhibitions which Saatchi Gallery launched in 1999. His striking, eerie cast-resin and enamel-paint sculpture Vermin Death Stack was depicted in the book *The New Neurotic Realism*, which preceded the exhibitions, published in 1998. That year Falconer had a solo show, Stacked, at Chapman Fine Arts, with another at Asprey Jacques, 1999. In 2002 Falconer's exhibition at Modern Art, comprising a big ball of rats made out of resin, was accompanied by a film which used a night vision camera to record the antics of the rodents that lived in his London studio.

Wojciech FALKOWSKI 1930– Artist, born in Poland, who studied medicine in Dublin, Ireland, and obtained postgraduate qualifications in London (Master of Philosophy, Psychology and Philosophy). He was a fellow of the Royal College of Psychiatrists. Falkowski was awarded a diploma by Marian Bohusz-Szyszko Painting School in 1988. He took part in group shows, including Form and Colour, Congress of Polish Culture Exhibition of Fine Arts by Polish Artists in Britain, POSK Gallery, 1995. In 1991, he received a first prize for oil painting from the Arts Council of the Royal Borough of Kensington and Chelsea. Among solo exhibitions were Polish Young Men's Christian Association, POSK and Questors Galleries and St George's Medical School.

Conor FALLON 1939– Self-taught sculptor, born in Dublin, Ireland, where he latterly settled in Kinsale, County Cork, with his painter wife Nancy Wynne-Jones. Between 1966–72 Fallon lived in Cornwall. Group shows included Newlyn Orion Gallery from 1966; RHA from 1977; and Contemporary Artists from Ireland, Austin/Desmond Fine Art, 1990. Had a solo show at Newlyn Orion, 1972, later ones including Arts Council tour, 1983.

Keith FALLSHAW 1946– Commercial artist, painter and sculptor, born in London. He studied typographical design at London College of Printing; was also a pupil of the portrait painters Leonard and Margaret Boden. Showed at NS, UA, elsewhere in London and at Deben Gallery, Woodbridge. Lived in Bishop's Stortford, Hertfordshire.

Joe FAN 1962– Painter, draughtsman, teacher and designer, born in Hong Kong. He studied graphic design at Aberdeen College of Commerce, then at Gray's Art School, Aberdeen, under Alexander Fraser and Gordon Bryce, where he later taught. Fan obtained a first-class honours degree in drawing and painting. His pictures mixed Eastern figures, over-ripe fruit, pigs and carved grotesques and were painterly with a pleasingly muted palette. In the mid-1980s Fan acquired a batch of awards, including first prize in the Commonwealth Section of the 1985 Rank Xerox Selected National Competition 86; a first prize in the 1987 Wood Group Young Artists' Award; and in 1988 a Carnegie Travelling Scholarship, RSA. Further awards included first prizes, Royal Over-Seas League, 1993, and The Morrison Portrait Award, 1995. Group shows included RSW. Solo exhibitions at Compass Gallery, Glasgow, and Sue Rankin Gallery, both 1991, later ones including Rendezvous Gallery, Aberdeen, from 1995, and Thackeray Gallery, 2000 and 2002. Scottish Arts Council, Gray's School of Art and Aberdeen Royal Infirmary hold his work.

Barry FANTONI 1940– Cartoonist, designer, writer and broadcaster who studied at Camberwell School of Arts and Crafts as a Wedgwood Scholar. He was a member of the satirical magazine *Private Eye*'s staff from 1963; was cartoonist for *The Listener*, 1968–88; wrote art criticism for *The Times*, 1973–7; and was its diary cartoonist from 1983. Fantoni also designed film and television posters and painted a mural at the Queen Elizabeth Conference Centre, 1985. In that year Fantoni published *Barry Fantoni's Chinese Horoscopes*, followed by *The Royal Family's Chinese Horoscopes*, 1988, and he broadcast on the subject for the London radio station LBC. Among his books was *The Best of Barry Fantoni Cartoons*, 1990. Was chairman of Chelsea Arts Club, 1978–80. His solo shows included Woodstock Gallery, 1963; Brunel University, 1974; and he had a retrospective at Cadogan Contemporary, 1991. Fantoni makes an appearance in the literary agent Giles Gordon's 1993 memoir *Aren't we due a Royalty Statement?*

Cyril Arthur FAREY 1888–1954 Architect and watercolourist, born and lived in London, father of the architect and painter Michael A J Farey. He was educated at Tonbridge School, won a Gold Medal at Royal Academy Schools and a Sloane Medallion from RIBA. Exhibited extensively at RA, also at RSA and Royal Glasgow Institute of the Fine Arts. In 1996 Gallery Lingard held a show of Farey's architectural sketches and watercolours, Thumbnotes & Masterpieces.

Tim FARGHER 1952– Painter, and sculptor, born in Lincolnshire, who graduated from St Martin's School of Art, 1979. His exhibitions included Camden Arts Festival, 1978; RP; Fraser Gallery, Woodbridge; Long & Ryle Art International; and Portland Gallery, 1992. He was guest artist at Glyndebourne Festival Opera in 1991. Fargher's commissions included 14 big oils on a theme of mythological and extinct creatures for Tim Walker, late chairman of the World Wildlife Fund, in 1985; and 85 paintings for HM The Sultan of Oman, 1985–8. Portrait commissions included Sir Peter Pears, 1980; Sir Kenneth Berrill, 1988; and The Reverend Dr Edward Carpenter, 1989. Later solo shows included Partridge, New Bond Street, 2002.

Elsie FARLEIGH: *see* **Anne NEVILLE**

John FARLEIGH 1900–1965 Oil and watercolour painter, wood engraver and printmaker. Studied at the Central School of Arts and Crafts, 1917–21, under James Grant, Bernard Meninsky and Noel Rooke. Married to the artist Elsie Farleigh. Exhibited LG, Leicester and Redfern Galleries, RE, RSA and in the provinces. He taught at Rugby School, 1922–4, then joining the Central School staff as head of the book production department. Published several books, including his autobiography *Graven Image*, 1940. 20th Century Gallery showed Farleigh's wood engravings in 1997. Lived in London.

Charles William FARLEY 1893–1982 Portrait and genre painter in oil and watercolour who served in the Queen's Westminsters in World War I and was a captain/adjutant in the Army in World War II, having seen service in India and the North-West Frontier. Prior to the second war Farley was living at Richmond, Surrey, showing at RA Summer Exhibition and elsewhere, later at East Molesey. After demobilisation in 1945 he moved to Cheltenham, Gloucestershire, where he was a member of the Cotswold Art Club and a founder-member of Cheltenham Art Club. He also exhibited with RI, 1940, RWA from 1956, and RP from 1957. Cheltenham Art Gallery holds his picture The Woodyard.

Francis FARMAR 1948– Painter, draughtsman and art consultant, born in Surrey and educated at Eton College, winning the School Drawing Prize. He spent every spare moment in the drawing schools there before continuing his studies at the Simi Academy, Florence, Italy, 1967, St Martin's School of Art and West of England College of Art, Bristol, 1967–68 and 1968–71. He joined the auctioneers Christie's in 1971, remaining until 1986 by when he had become director of their modern British picture department. Farmar then took the radical step of moving to the Morayshire coastal village of Findhorn to concentrate on his own painting while continuing as a consultant for Christie's and for private clients. He was responsible for the Painters of Camden Town exhibition and catalogue at Christie's in 1988. Farmar's work, influenced by the St Ives and Neo-Romantic painters, included landscapes around his Scottish home and in the south of France. William Hardie Gallery gave him a solo show in Glasgow in 1991, Duncan Campbell Fine Art a series from 1997, and he took part in many mixed shows. Farmar specialised in house portraits. His quirky panoramic aerial views, revealing his love of buildings, gardens, people, birds and beasts, aimed to "encapsulate as much as possible of the life, spirit and form of each place." Lived latterly in Sedgehill, Dorset, and London.

Bernard FARMER 1919–2002 Painter and maker of abstract constructions, born and lived in London. He studied at Chelsea Polytechnic School of Art and showed with LG, New Vision Centre, St Martin's Gallery and AIA. Solo exhibitions included Heal's Art Gallery, 1964, and Angela Flowers Gallery, 1982. Farmer said that "the more simple I can make an image the better I like it ... The less can always expand in the mind, whereas more either constricts or becomes too much." Farmer was co-organiser with Malcolm Hughes of Directions-Connections at AIA Gallery, 1961, and had work reproduced in Frank Avray Wilson's *Art as Understanding*, 1963. The painter Adrian Heath was a strong advocate of his work. Arts Council and Contemporary Art Society hold examples. John Davies Fine Paintings helped reawaken interest in Farmer's neglected work by showing examples in a mixed exhibition at The Gallery in Cork Street in 2005.

James C FARMER 1925–1970 Watercolourist who in the early 1960s ran a bookshop in Westbury Park, Bristol. He exhibited two pictures at the RWA in 1966.

John FARNHAM 1942– Sculptor and draughtsman, born in Perry Green, Hertfordshire. In 1958 he joined his father's building business, in 1965 becoming a full-time assistant to Henry Moore, having previously worked part-time. At first Farnham's sculptures were fairly conventional, but in the mid-1970s they began to get more personal and complex, with a greater exploration of the abstract. In 1969 Farnham showed at Pace Gallery, then after further showings had a solo exhibition in 1973 at Old Bakehouse Gallery, Sevenoaks, the year he carried out his first major commission: Winged Figure, commissioned by Department of the Environment for Royal Air Force, Naphill. In 1973 also gained an Arts Council grant. Further commissions included Life Form, of 1980, commissioned by Institute of Biology. Other exhibitions included a one-man show at New Art Centre, 1976, a shared exhibition at Leeds City Art Gallery, 1984, and tour, and University of Hertfordshire Galleries, St Albans, 2002.

Emma FARQUHARSON: *see* **Roy HOBDELL**

Giles FARQUHARSON: *see* **Roy HOBDELL**

Linda M FARQUHARSON 1963– Printmaker, illustrator and lecturer, born in Aberdeen, who gained an honours degree, specialising in illustration and printmaking, from Duncan of Jordanstone College of Art, Dundee, in 1985, winning the Sekalski Prize for printmaking. Stayed on for a year under a postgraduate scholarship in design specialising in printmaking, from 1993 lecturing there part-time. In 1990 Farquharson bought and restored a Columbian printing press. Showed at Compass Gallery, Glasgow, 1986; Printmakers' Workshop, Edinburgh, 1990; Barbican Centre and SSA, both 1993; RSA, 1995; and Roger Billcliffe Fine Art, Glasgow, 1996. Bank of Scotland, The Royal Bank of Scotland, The Scottish Office and other collections hold her work.

Mo FARQUHARSON 1953– Sculptor and draughtsman, born in Aberdeenshire, to which she frequently returned from London. She trained as a sculptor in Edinburgh under Edward Gage; for three years at the Ruskin School of Drawing, Oxford, where Chris Dorset was influential; and for a year at Massachusetts College of Art, Boston, in America. Became a member of RBS. Exhibited widely in Britain, including a solo show at The Gallery in Cork Street, 1997. This included expressive sculptures and drawings of animals, birds, fish and people, including figures exploring urban relationships. These were inspired by her London Bridge sculpture, acquired by Paribas Ltd. Other commissions included Edinburgh Zoo, bust of its president, Viscount Arbuthnott; two life-size coal miners for Hamilton, Lanarkshire, for Akeler (Scotland) Ltd; and a figure of John Lennon, commissioned by record company HMV for charity auction at the Silver Clef Awards. HRH The Duke of Edinburgh holds Farquharson's work.

Heather FARR 1912– Painter, especially of landscapes, born in Nottingham, initially educated in Scarborough, Yorkshire. She studied art at Nottingham School of Art and the Slade School of Fine Art, exhibiting at NEAC, WIAC and Nottingham Museum and Art Gallery. For a time she taught art at Geffrye Museum and lived in London.

Simeon FARRAR 1975– Artist who graduated from Surrey Institute of Art and Design. He took part in many exhibitions, especially in London's East End. He was involved in the Uncut show of urban art at ICA, 1997, and in The New Urbanites, at Catto Contemporary, 2002.

Anthony FARRELL 1945– Painter, draughtsman and teacher, born in Epsom, Surrey. He studied at Southend School of Art, 1961–3, Camberwell School of Arts and Crafts, 1963–5, and Royal Academy Schools, 1965–8. From 1976 he taught part-time at various art schools and centres, in 1981–2 winning an Eastern Arts Association Fellowship and the Association's Exhibition Award. Farrell took part in many group exhibitions, notably RA, Serpentine Gallery mixed shows and the Norwich School of Art Gallery's 1986–7 touring exhibition A Reputation Among Artists. His first solo show was at Brunel University in 1972, later ones including The Minories, Colchester, 1983, and Art Space Gallery, 1992, and Gainsborough's House, Sudbury, 1998. Farrell lived at Leigh-on-Sea, Essex, and was notable for his lively, figure-packed seaside scenes. Arts Council, Minories and Epping Forest Museum hold his work.

Christopher FARRELL 1971– Painter who did a foundation course at Berkshire College of Art and Design, Maidenhead, 1989–90; then graduated with first-class honours, specialising in painting, from De Montfort University, Leicester, 1990–3; with a postgraduate diploma in painting from Royal Academy Schools, 1994–7. Awards included the David Murray Studentship Award for Landscape Painting, 1992 and 1996; Jack Goldhill Scholarship for painting, Royal Academy Schools, 1994–7; and Young Artist of the Year, Hunting Art Prizes, Royal College of Art and Hunterian Museum, Glasgow, Turner Gold Medal for painting, Premiums Exhibition at RA, and Cromwell Hospital Award, all 1997. Chris Farrell had a varied career, including a commission to produce a watercolour based on a sea theme for Chevron's 1997 calendar; being artist-in-residence, London Business School Regent's Park, and producing a painting for Ove Arup/Contemporary Art Society Projects, both 1997–8; as well as private commissions and extensive website designing, from 1999. Showed widely, latterly including Urban Heights, Vertigo Gallery, 2000; Sarah Myerscough Fine Art, 2001; and Hunting Art Prizes, 2002, at Royal College of Art. Lived in London.

Micheál FARRELL 1940– Versatile artist and teacher, born in Kells, County Meath, Ireland, who studied at St Martin's School of Art, 1957–61. His teaching included East Ham College of Art, Norwich School of Art, Brighton College of Art, and Pratt Institute, New York, America.

Farrell soon won a series of awards, including an Abbey Travelling Scholarship to Italy, 1964; Laureat, Paris Biennale, 1967; and Prix de la ville de Liége, 1969. In the 1960s Farrell was a scenic artist on the films *The Lion in Winter, Dracula Rises from the Grave* and *The Country Dance*. While early and later producing figurative work, Farrell was in the 1960s one of the first artists of his generation to adopt rigorous abstraction. Other pictures from the 1970s made "every possible statement on the Irish situation, religion, cultural, political, the cruelty, the horror, every aspect of it." Works from the 1980s were light and rich in colour, drawing on his experience of Paris to which he had moved in 1971, later settling in Provence. From his base, Farrell travelled Europe to exhibit, "taking a train to wherever it is. I work like a gypsy." Later exhibitions included Images and Insights at the Hugh Lane Municipal Gallery of Modern Art, Dublin, 1993. It, the Arts Council of Ireland, Manchester City Art Gallery, Ulster Museum in Belfast and other public and corporate collections hold Carroll's work, which was included in A Land of Heart's Desire: 300 Years of Irish Art, Ulster Museum, 1999. He is in the National Self-Portrait Collection of Ireland, University of Limerick.

Michael FARRELL 1964– Artist born in Paisley, Renfrewshire, who studied at St Helens College of Art and Design, then graduated in fine art from Birmingham Polytechnic. Farrell's stone Flywheel, opposite the Council House in Coventry's city centre, was installed in 1987 as part of the On the Town Midlands View 4 Sculpture Show. Farrell contributed to group exhibitions in the Midlands area. His solo shows included Highcroft Hospital, 1986, and Midland Arts Centre, 1987, both in Birmingham.

James FARRELLY 1959– Artist and teacher, one of the sons of the poet George Barker, born and lived in New York City but brought up in Rome, Italy. He studied with Gretna Campbell at Yale University. An early influence on his work was fresco wall paintings in Renaissance buildings. Farrelly was a painter of everyday things such as the pleasures of the beach, the leisure of the breakfast table, a figure reading in a chair. He had a sell-out exhibition at Rebecca Hossack Gallery in 1994, the first in a series there. Among group and mixed shows were Presenze, Comune di Perugia, 1991; University of North Carolina, 1999; and Rhythm and Light, The Painting Center, New York City, 2000. Farrelly taught drawing at Trinity University for five years and sculpture at St Stephen's School for a year, both in Rome.

David FARRER 1968– Artist, born in Leeds, Yorkshire, where he trained in printmaking at the Metropolitan University. He exhibited internationally and worked to commission, most notably for the Public Record Office. In 2005 Farrer had a solo show, Zebra, at the Rebecca Hossack Gallery, where he showed recycled animal heads made from old magazines. He had had the idea several years before while working in South Africa, travelled extensively in that part of the world and was interested in ecology and green matters. Afterwards he diversified into European and North American beasts, such as deer, bears, moose and bulls.

Julia FARRER 1950– Artist whose work included geometrical abstractions, and teacher, born and lived in London. She studied at Slade School of Fine Art, 1968–72, then taught there for two years. A Harkness Scholarship took her to America, 1974–6, and she worked in Paris, 1978–9. Also taught at Wimbledon and Byam Shaw Schools of Art. Group exhibitions included First Nuremberg Drawing Biennial, 1979; British Artists' Books, Atlantis Gallery, 1984; Harkness Artists 58–85 at Air Gallery, 1985; and in 1988 Composition/Structure at Galerie Lüpke, Frankfurt. Had a solo show at JPL Gallery, 1980; Air and Huddersfield City Art Galleries, both 1983; Curwen Art Gallery and Imprints, both 1986; Francis Graham-Dixon Gallery, 1995; and @Backroom, 2000. In 2005 she shared an exhibition with John Carter and Noel Forster at The Eagle Gallery. Ashmolean Museum in Oxford, University of Austin in Texas and University College, London, hold examples.

John FARRINGTON fl. from 1950s– Painter and teacher whose work has a gritty realism. He attended School of Art in Dudley, Worcestershire, influenced by the principal, Joe Jago, and Ivo Shaw, who encouraged Farrington to study illustration and printmaking. In 1957 did teacher training year at Leicester College of Art. Christopher Wood, Edward Bawden, John Minton, Jack Smith, Edward Middleditch, Alan Reynolds and Oskar Kokoschka were influences. Farrington painted the Black Country and also worked in series, such as bird men, flying men, Icarus, fairgrounds and circuses. He depicted the grimmer aspects of farming, having worked as a cowman. In 1984 Farrington produced the paintings for Granada Television's *The Ebony Tower*, based on John Fowles' novel. Solo shows included Goldmark Gallery, Uppingham, 1993.

Richard FARRINGTON 1956– Versatile artist who studied sculpture and printmaking at Bath Academy of Arts, 1975–9. Children's drawings sometimes inspired his commissions. Farrington often worked in metal, as for his three steel sculptures Trawl Door, Pillar and The Circle, sited in 1990 on a cliff top on the Cleveland Way, at Skelton. They stemmed from a New Milestones residency organised by Cleveland Arts working with Common Ground.

Andrew FARROW 1966– Versatile artist who studied at Chesterfield College of Technology and Arts, 1984–5, then graduated with honours from Norwich School of Art, 1985–8. Farrow was artist-in-residence, Fakenham Festival of Music & Arts, 1987; in 1987–8 had work reproduced in *The Rialto* poetry magazine and did location work in Amsterdam, Edinburgh and St Ives; in 1988 created a stage environment for the Design Market fashion show in Norwich; and in 1989 was included in East End Open Studios, based at Vyner Street Arts.

Anne C FARROW 1928– Painter and draughtsman, born in Great Yarmouth, Norfolk. She was initially convent-educated in Reading, attended the University there, joined the town's Guild of Artists and showed elsewhere in the area, where she settled.

Kieron FARROW 1949– Versatile artist and teacher, using a bright palette, who did a painting foundation course at Barnsley School of Art, 1964–7; was at Leeds Polytechnic, part-time photography, 1973–6; Middlesex Polytechnic/Hornsey College of Art, 1979–82; then made an extended study of printmaking at Camberwell School of Art, 1982–3. Worked for a time as a screenprinter and as a professional photographer; taught widely; and was an artist and art consultant from 1990. From 1989–92 he was chairman of the Printmakers' Council. Had numerous group shows, later solo exhibitions including Curwen Gallery, 1999, based on a trip to Polynesia. The Museum of Archaeology in Valletta, Malta, and Royal Borough of Kensington and Chelsea hold examples. Lived in Hornchurch, Essex.

Stephen FARTHING 1950– Painter, printmaker and teacher, born in London. He attended St Martin's School of Art, 1968–73; Royal College of Art, 1973–6; was an Abbey Major Scholar at British School, Rome, 1976–7; lectured in painting at Canterbury College of Art, 1977–9; taught painting at the Royal College, 1980–5; was head of department of fine art, West Surrey College of Art & Design, Farnham, 1985–89; was artist-in-residence at the Hayward Gallery, 1989; then in 1990 was elected Ruskin Master at Ruskin School of Fine Art & Drawing and professorial fellow of St Edmund's Hall, Oxford. Farthing's early work showed some reference to Pop Art, drawing on diverse images. He was a figurative painter who responded in different ways to the environment in which he was placed, his work sometimes having a sinister edge. Took part in numerous group shows, including New Contemporaries, 1975; John Moores Liverpool Exhibition from 1976 at Walker Art Gallery, Liverpool, being several times a prize winner; New Art Centre, 1979; Edward Totah Gallery, from 1985; Heritage Exhibition at Cornerhouse Gallery, and tour, 1990; 20th Century Drawings, Ashmolean Museum, Oxford, 1994; and Collecting the Contemporary, University of Essex, 1995. Had a solo show at Royal College of Art, 1977, later ones including Tales of Topophilia, at Coram Gallery, 1994, resulting from a series of visits overseas as guest of the British Council; The Knowledge: SE1/South, at The Cut Gallery, 1995 (the previous year it had held SE1/North); and Absolute Monarchy, Anne Berthoud, 1996. Ashmolean Museum, Arts Council, British Council, National Museum of Wales in Cardiff and many other public collections hold examples. Elected RA, 1998. Prize winner, John Moores Liverpool Exhibition, 1999. Farthing's Trees in Snow series was at The Drawing Gallery in 2005. Lived in Oxford.

Suzy FASHT 1964– Painter, born and lived in London, who began her studies with a foundation course at Sir John Cass School of Art, 1991–2; gained a fine art honours degree, painting, at Wimbledon School of Art, 1992–5; then did a postgraduate fine art diploma at the Royal Academy Schools, 1995–8. In 1997 she won the M&G RA Summer Exhibition prize for an artist under 35, the Creswick Prize for landscape and the RA Silver Medal. She was commissioned by Chevron UK Ltd to provide watercolours of Lewis and Harris, Outer Hebrides, for its 1998 calendar, and was featured in the oil company's show in 1997 at the ICA. Mixed shows included Cut Gallery, 1994; Wimbledon Library Gallery, 1995; Attendi and Ben Uri Galleries, both 1996; and Beatrice Royal Gallery, Eastleigh, 1997. Had a solo show in that year at The Cromwell Hospital.

Kaffe FASSETT 1937– Self-educated textile and knitwear designer, painter and writer, brought up in California, America, where his parents ran a restaurant. There he met people from Britain, became interested in its culture and moved there in the mid-1960s. After a time in Bath, he settled in London to paint seriously and became inspired by the street markets and the Victoria & Albert Museum (it was to give him the first major exhibition for a contemporary textile artist in 1988). Friendship with the designer Bill Gibb and a trip to Scotland inspired Kaffe (pronounced Kayf) to start serious knitting. He held successful exhibitions around the world and produced books such as *Glorious Knitting*, 1985; *Family Album*, 1989; and *Glorious Interiors*, 1995. In 1997 there was a sixtieth birthday show at The Catto Gallery of his colourful still life paintings.

George R FATHERS 1898–1968 Painter and teacher, born in Derby, son of sculptor Caleb Fathers. Studied at Ipswich School of Art, 1918–22, under George Rushton, then at the Royal College of Art, 1922–6, under William Rothenstein. Fathers made a career on the art side of publishing and in process engraving. He exhibited RA, NEAC and in the provinces and was notable for his landscapes. Fathers was a member of both Bradford and Ipswich Art Clubs. At various times he was a visiting teacher at Borough Polytechnic, Leeds and Hull Colleges of Art. Lived in Bradford.

James Alexander FAULDS 1949– Painter and teacher, born and lived in Glasgow. He attended Duncan of Jordanstone College of Art, Dundee, 1968–72. Exhibited at RSA, SSA, Group 81 in Glasgow of which he was a founder-member, RSW and in Germany. Was a Glasgow Art Club member.

Amanda FAULKNER 1953– Painter, draughtsman and printmaker, born in Dorset. She attended Bournemouth College of Art, 1978–9; studied printmaking at Ravensbourne College of Art, 1979–82; then worked for her master's at Chelsea School of Art, 1982–3. She spent two years in South America, part of a two-man team making anthropological films of the Canai Indians of Ecuador, and also worked there as an illustrator of short books on the mythology of an Amazonian group. Among Faulkner's group appearances were Young Contemporaries, ICA, 1981. In 1983 she had a solo show at Woodlands Art Gallery. Her work there and works held by Arts Council, bought from Angela Flowers, 1983, were much concerned with women. Plymouth Arts Centre included Faulkner in a three-artist exhibition in 1996. By then Faulkner had participated in numerous group exhibitions internationally. Her later solo exhibitions included Small Mysteries, Flowers East, 1999, and New Drawings, 2002. For a time she lived in Chatham, Kent.

Howard FAULKNER 1894–1979 Watercolourist, designer and teacher, born in Birmingham, where he was at school. Attended Dudley School of Art. 1910–14, then Royal College of Art, 1919–22, where his teachers included Ernest Tristram. He went on to hold a number of art teaching posts, in Cornwall, Wiltshire and finally in Eastbourne, Sussex, where he settled and where he was a member of the Society of Artists. Showed PS, NEAC and elsewhere. Victoria & Albert Museum and Towner Art Gallery, Eastbourne, hold his work.

Iain FAULKNER 1973– Figurative painter born in Glasgow where he graduated with honours in fine art from the School of Art in 1996. During 1997–8 he showed three times in mixed exhibitions at Albemarle Gallery, which gave him his first London solo exhibition in 1999; there was an initial New York show, in America, that year at the

Eleanor Ettinger Gallery; another Albemarle exhibition in 2003. Bathers, dancers, musicians, board games and the icon were features of Faulkner's pictures, often large and with a narrative element, painterly in the Glasgow tradition.

Neil FAULKNER 1952– Artist in watercolour and oil producing highly detailed work, as in the show he shared with James Longueville at Oakham Galleries in 2005. He was early inspired by Andrew Wyeth after seeing an exhibition of his paintings at the RA, as an adult travelling to America to see more of them. After college Faulkner worked with the china manufacturer Wedgwood for several years, then with Royal Doulton, where he soon became a senior designer. He was responsible for many commemorative projects, including the Silver and Golden Jubilees of Queen Elizabeth II, the weddings of Prince Charles and Lady Diana Spencer as well as other royal occasions. Faulkner eventually became a prolific and well-selling full-time artist, the light and colour of Venice and Spain being particular inspirations.

Richard FAULKNER 1917–1988 Painter, born in Belfast, where he studied at the College of Art. Showed at RHA, RUA of which he was a member, and Belfast Museum and Art Gallery. Lived for many years in Ballycastle, County Antrim.

Trevor FAULKNER 1929– Sculptor and teacher, born Robert Trevor Faulkner in Sheffield, Yorkshire. He worked in most three-dimensional media, with a special interest in metal. Faulkner claimed to "have developed hand-wrought and welded sculpture to a uniquely high level, with a technique impossible to duplicate." He studied at Sheffield School of Art, 1946–50, and with Frank Dobson and John Skeaping at Royal College of Art, 1952–5, after holding a commission in the Army, 1950–2. In 1955 he was a vehicle designer, then went into teaching, becoming principal lecturer at Sheffield City Polytechnic. From 1988 sculpted and worked as a consultant full-time, being a fellow of RBS. He showed with Young Contemporaries, RA and Moorland Gallery. Had solo shows with John Hutton Gallery, Peterborough, 1968; Alwin Gallery, 1980; then became gallery artist with John Noott, Broadway. He carried out work for a number of firms, including British Steel, Expamet and BOC. Cartier, Bond Street, holds his work. In 1978 Faulkner published *Direct Metal Sculpture*. Lived in Bradway, Sheffield.

Emma FAULL 1956– Painter, draughtsman and writer, notable for her studies of birds. She was described by the naturalist and bird painter Sir Peter Scott as "an artist of great distinction. Her bird paintings are large, scientifically accurate and enormously decorative." Born in England, she graduated in geography from Oxford University, then in 1979 travelled to Athens as a draughtsman with the British School of Archaeology. In 1980 she gained a scholarship from the Greek government to write *The Imagery of the Bird in Ancient Greece*. Her book *Endangered Birds* was published in 1992. Among Faull's exhibiting venues were Cadogan Gallery, Addison Ross Gallery, Spink & Son, National Museum of Greece, Wildlife Art Gallery in Lavenham and elsewhere. HM The Queen and HRH The Duke of Edinburgh hold her work. Lived in Jersey.

James FAURE WALKER 1948– Artist, born and based in London, who studied at St Martin's School of Art, 1966–70, and at Royal College of Art, 1970–2. Was editor of *Artscribe* magazine and occasionally taught. Group exhibitions included Stowells Trophy Exhibition, Chenil Gallery, 1969, in which he won a prize; Space Open Studios, 10 Martello Street, from 1973; Style in the Seventies, at Arnolfini Gallery, Bristol, and tour, 1979; John Moores Liverpool Exhibition, 1982; Summer Show 2, Serpentine Gallery, 1983; Gallery North, Air Gallery and East End Open Studios, at Martello Street, all 1989; and John Moores, 2002. Solo shows included Whitworth Art Gallery, Manchester, 1985; Vortex Gallery, 1987, and Colville Place Gallery, 2000, The Colour & Motion Series. Although he came from a traditional painting background, by then he was drawing in "digital paint" with vivid freedom. Faure Walker's pictures celebrated the new technique of digital photography, image processing and layering used with a painter's touch. He incorporated everyday themes, such as shopping, a cup of coffee or pigeons on the pavement. "I like the idea of capturing inconsequential slices of life and weaving them into the fabric of a picture." Faure Walker's paintings were also shown at the Hayward and Whitechapel Galleries and widely abroad. The Victoria & Albert Museum and Leicester Education Authority hold Faure Walker's work.

Shelley FAUSSET 1920–1994 Sculptor in various materials, especially stone, and teacher, full name Philip Shelley I Fausset, born in Newbury, Berkshire. In 1930s studied under Eric Gill. Fausset later started his own press, Linden Press, which published fine illustrated broadsheets on handmade paper. Fausset had attended Friends' School in Saffron Walden and during World War II did farm work and was with a Friends' Ambulance Unit in northern Europe. From 1946–8 was assistant to Henry Moore, then was at Chelsea School of Art, 1948–52, and Slade School of Fine Art, 1952–4. Was a part-time teacher in Cambridge area, 1948–54; was full-time, 1958–81, being head of foundation studies at Central School of Art & Design from 1963; then taught part-time, 1981–7, at Central School and Architectural Association. Fausset took part in many mixed shows from 1955, including Leicester, Obelisk and Brook Street Galleries, RA, LG and New Art Centre. From 1960–70 did not show, working to establish a basis in elemental forms. Had a solo show at Mercury Gallery in 1973. In 1979 organised the Amnesty sculpture exhibition in St Paul's Cathedral; in 1983 was commissioned by Harlow Art Trust; at LG Royal College of Art show in 1984 was nominated for Henry Moore prize; gained Nina Hosali Award for Sculpture, 1989; in same year was commissioned as sculptor for Magna Park development, Leicestershire, completing the 36-piece task in 1991. Elected member of RBS in 1979. WAC holds his work. Lived at Pirton, Hertfordshire.

Pat FAUST fl. from 1950s– Painter, theatrical designer and muralist, born in Lancashire, who studied at Manchester Regional College of Art and Birmingham's Crescent Theatre. Miss Faust was a member of Leeds Fine Art Club and the Arts Society in Scarborough, Yorkshire, not far from where she lived for many years at Filey. Showed with MAFA, RA, RCamA, Royal Glasgow Institute of the Fine Arts and at Paris Salon. Solo shows included University of Hull. Scarborough Corporation owns her work.

Stephanie FAWBERT 1964– Versatile artist and teacher who studied foundation at West Surrey College of Art and Design, Farnham, 1984, gaining an honours degree at Newcastle upon Tyne Polytechnic, 1984–7. Residencies included West Middlesex University Hospital, 1990–2, and Ladevie School of Music, France, experimenting with visual languages to express music, 1993–5. She also lectured in art and graphic design at West Thames College, Isleworth; worked on production at the *Daily Mirror* and *Sunday Mirror*; at a village silkscreen workshop in Botswana; and co-ordinated development projects in a Gambia fishing village. Exhibitions included Glancing, at Kent Institute of Art and Design's Zandra Rhodes Gallery, Rochester, 1998, an installation of nearly 450 portraits in black, white and sepia ink and watercolour washes. Lived in Leeds.

Charlotte FAWCETT: *see* **Charlotte JOHNSON WAHL**

Robert FAWCETT 1966– Figurative painter, born in Cambridge. He studied at Huntingdon Technical College, 1982–4; Cambridge College of Art and Technology, 1984–5; Byam Shaw School of Art, 1986–9; and Royal College of Art, 1990–2. Awards included Burston Print Prize; Daler-Rowney Prize; Elizabeth Greenshields Award; and L'Escargot Restaurant Prize. Mixed, two- and three-man exhibitions included Figure Show, Jill George Gallery, extensively from 1998; Galerie Vielle du Temple, Paris, France, 2000; and LA International, Terence Rogers Gallery, California, America, 2001. In 2004, Jill George gave Fawcett and Daniel Hughes a two-man show.

Charlotte FAWCETT JOHNSON WAHL: *see* **Charlotte JOHNSON WAHL**

Charlotte FAWLEY 1934– Painter, draughtsman and designer, born in Blackpool, notable for her ability to capture energy, fleeting movement as well as a particular light and colour. She studied at Blackpool School of Art, 1953–7, then with Aubrey Williams at Camden Arts Centre, 1964–6. Fawley was a versatile artist whose work ranged from graphics for Falklands War coverage by the BBC 2 television programme *Newsnight*, 1982, to the design of backcloth and costumes for the ballet *Serpentine*, toured by the Royal Ballet in Kenya, 1996. She drew extensively at The Royal Ballet for two decades, which gave her the opportunity to depict in action some of the world's most famous dancers, also at The Royal Opera House. The resulting work was exhibited in her solo show Illuminations at The Gallery, 54 Shepherd Market, 2002, along with landscapes of southwest France. She also exhibited at Royal National Theatre, the Primrose Hill and Soar Galleries and elsewhere. Fawley's work is held in international collections. She lived in London.

Randa FAWZI fl. from 1970s– Painter of strong, colourful images in acrylic which used the triangle as a building block, born in New York, America, educated in England and Switzerland. Seeking her cultural roots she studied at the College of Fine Art, Cairo; did a postgraduate course at Goldsmiths' College; then trained in tempera techniques with Theodor Zeller in Germany. Exhibitions included John Sears Gallery, 1976; Regent Gallery, 1982; Jablonski Gallery, 1987; and Duncan Campbell Contemporary Art, 1997, as well as widely abroad. The Campbell show was based on work done during a decade-long stay in Scotland; latterly, Fawzi lived in England and Germany.

Alan Hardy FAYERS 1926– Painter and teacher, born in Accrington, Lancashire. He studied at Accrington Regional College of Art from 1943–4, then after a wartime break from 1947–51, completing his studies during 1951–2 at Bretton Hall, Wakefield. Held a number of teaching positions, including Malton Grammar School. Exhibited widely in Lancashire, notably with the Lancashire Artists and West Riding Artists. Lived in Ilkley, Yorkshire.

Gordon FAZAKERLEY 1937– Gestural abstract painter, born in Widnes, near Liverpool, his family including a line of grocers. He studied at Liverpool College of Art from 1952, teachers including George Mayer-Marton and Arthur Ballard, then Central School of Arts and Crafts, 1956–7, where he studied painting and stained glass, teachers including William Turnbull. While doing his National Service in the Army Lawrence Alloway showed Fazakerley's work to Herbert Read, which led to a first solo exhibition at ICA, 1959. After the Army Fazakerley did a number of jobs. Having won a small sum of money he went over to Hardy Strid, in Sweden, later to Jørgen Nash and took part in building up the Bauhaus Situationist at Drakabygget, although he later rejected Situationist ideas. In 1962 he met his Danish wife-to-be and settled in Denmark. Exhibited widely in Europe.

Pauline FAZAKERLEY fl. from 1970s– Painter of atmospheric scenes, who studied at Croydon and Camberwell Schools of Art, gaining first-class honours and a Silver Medal in her finals. After graduating she worked as a professional designer for six years, followed by 12 years as head of art at a private school. Exhibited at RA Summer Exhibition, RI of which she was a member, NEAC, RWS and elsewhere in London, including Curzon Gallery, 1999. Among her awards were two from the NEAC and one from RWS, all 1996, and two from the RI in 1997, including its Silver Medal, another in 1998.

Helen FAY 1968– Natural history artist and illustrator and teacher, born in South Shields, County Durham, who did a foundation course at Newcastle College of Art and Design, 1986–7; an honours degree in fine art printmaking, Sunderland University, 1987–90; then her master's degree in natural history illustration, Royal College of Art, 1990–2, in 1992 winning the Sheila Robinson Memorial Prize for Drawing. In 1993 she supplied illustrations and the front cover of *New Scientist* magazine, also teaching part-time at Sunderland University. She was later technician and manager at Oxford Printmakers' Co-operative. Took part in many group shows, including Washington Arts Centre, Tyne & Wear, 1989; Cupola Gallery, Sheffield and Beatrice Royal Gallery, Eastleigh, both from 1995; National Print Exhibition, Mall Galleries, 1997; Jonathan Poole Gallery, Chelsea Art Fair, 1999; and Will's Art Warehouse, 2002.

Moira FEARBY 1969– Artist whose work included abstract pictures, born in Sydney, New South Wales, Australia, and studied at Curtin University of Technology, Western Australia. Group exhibitions included An Aspect, Art Rage Festival, Fremantle, 1991; Young Emerging Artists Exhibition, Crafts Council, Perth, 1992; Moira Fearby & Helore Roberts, Alternative Arts, 1994; and Royal Over-

Seas League Open, 1995. The Bar Chambers Collection, Perth; Highlands Sculpture Gallery, California; and 4011/2 Workshop Collection hold examples.

Ian FEARN 1934– Artist and teacher, born in Newport-on-Tay, Fife. He studied at Duncan of Jordanstone College of Art in Dundee, 1950–6. A Travelling Scholarship took him to the continent and Cyprus in 1956–7. He taught art in Fife for three years from 1959 and in 1962 began to lecture at Duncan of Jordanstone. Among group shows in which Fearn participated were Dundee City Art Gallery; Scottish Arts Council; Compass Gallery; and Dundee Print Workshop. SAC holds his work. Lived in Dundee.

Charmian FEARNLEY 1932– Sculptor in all three-dimensional materials who studied at Gloucestershire College of Art, 1955–7, and Royal College of Art, where she won the Feodora Gleichen Award. Showed at RA, AIA, RWA and Royal Glasgow Institute of the Fine Arts and in 1962 was included in 19 Young Sculptors at Hillfield Gardens, Gloucester, when she was living at Rodborough Manor, Stroud. Fearnley was commissioned to complete a number of portraits and sculpture for BBC Television and the *Daily Mirror* (design for 26 trophies).

Edmund Owen FEARNLEY-WHITTINGSTALL 1901–1972 Painter, draughtsman and teacher, born in Marlow, Buckinghamshire. He was educated at Haileybury College and studied art at Regent Street Polytechnic School of Art, 1922–5, his teachers including Harry Watson, and the Royal Academy Schools, 1925–8, under Charles Sims and George Clausen. For five years shortly after World War II he taught painting and drawing at Sir John Cass School of Arts and Crafts. Showed at RA, RP, NS and elsewhere. He shared his time between London and Ickford, Buckinghamshire.

Ian FEARNSIDE 1948– Painter, lecturer, designer and gallery owner, born in Worcester, who grew up above an artists' materials shop and gallery. Left school at 16 to attend art college, then worked in graphic design, advertising, architecture and the family shop learning the art trade. After successful exhibitions he set up his own art shop in Malvern, Worcestershire, which he ran for 25 years, also designing leaflets for Oxfam, the Campaign for Nuclear Disarmament and the United Nations Children's Emergency Fund (UNICEF), for which he gained an award. From 1995 Fearnside ran a gallery to show his own traditional landscapes and other artists' work.

James FEARON fl. from mid-1980s– Figurative artist who graduated in fine art from University of Ulster, Belfast, 1984. In 1989 he was invited to take up a residency at Banff Arts Centre in Canada and in 1992 he took part in a Belfast/Berlin Exchange, funded by Aer Lingus and Arts Council of Northern Ireland. Showed at Mall Galleries and in 1994 was included in Works on Paper and Beyond the Partitions, put on by Queen Street Studios, Belfast, with which Fearon was associated. Solo shows in Belfast included Kerlin Gallery, 1988, and Orpheus Building, 1990.

Judith FEASEY 1945– Painter, etcher and teacher, born and lived in London. She studied at Guildford School of Art, 1965–9; Royal Academy Schools, 1973–6; and Goldsmiths' College, 1976–7, for a teacher's certificate. While studying she gained the David Murray Landscape Scholarship, 1975–6, the Turner Gold Medal for landscape painting, 1976, and in the same year the Arthur Hacker Silver Medal for portrait painting, among other awards. Many exhibitions included RP, RA Summer Exhibitions, Greater London Council Spirit of London Competitions, Greenwich Printmakers, RWS and Bermondsey Artists' Group Exhibitions. Feasey taught at Brixton College.

Yan Kel FEATHER 1920– Painter of strong figurative pictures, born in Liverpool, son of the Austrian artist Wilhelm Feder. He began painting in 1939 and had a first solo show at Gibbs Gallery, Manchester in 1940. During World War II Feather studied alone at the National and Tate Galleries. He cited Velasquez, Fuseli, Ivon Hitchens, Roger Hilton, Francis Bacon and L S Lowry as influences. After a visit to Cornwall in 1947 Feather returned to Liverpool, for some years running a night club and an antique shop, eventually returning to settle in St Ives in 1977 to paint full-time. Meanwhile, he had continued to paint, solo shows including Archer Gallery, 1950, and Hanover Gallery, 1951; he won The Wolfson Memorial Prize in 1957; was a member of Liverpool Academy, 1960–70; having a solo show at Bluecoat Society, 1972. Became a member of Newlyn Society of Artists, 1980–90, and showed widely in the West Country/Cornwall. Had a retrospective at The New Millennium Gallery, St Ives, 1996. Later exhibitions included Yan Kel Feather: The Post-War Modernist, Great Expectations Gallery, 2003.

William FEATHERSTON 1927– Sculptor and teacher, born in Toronto, Canada, who lived and worked in Britain 1957–71. The latter 10 years of this time was spent teaching at Cardiff College of Art, after which Featherston taught in California and worked as a freelance artist in Vancouver. Featherston showed internationally and while in Britain exhibited with the 56 Group and SEA, having solo exhibitions at Woodstock, New Vision and Grabowski Galleries in London. WAC, Glasgow University and many overseas public collections hold his work.

William FEAVER 1942– Writer on art, broadcaster, teacher and painter. He read history at Oxford as an Open Scholar, 1961–4; taught at Royal Grammar School, Newcastle upon Tyne, 1965–71; then was a James Knott Research Fellow at Newcastle University, 1971–3. Contributed to many national publications on art; was art critic of *Vogue* and *Artnews New York* from 1973; art critic of *Financial Times*, 1973–5; art adviser to *Sunday Times Magazine*, 1973–5; and art critic of *The Observer*, 1975–1998. In the British Press Awards Feaver was voted Critic of the Year, 1983, Commended, 1986. Was a member of Arts Council's art panel, 1974–9; chairman of Serpentine Gallery, 1975–6; and member of art advisory committee for National Museum of Wales from 1991. He taught at many art schools; was an external assessor at Royal College of Art and University of Ulster; and organised a number of exhibitions. These latterly included Lucian Freud, Abbot Hall Art Gallery, Kendal, 1996, and Tate Britain, 2002; Michael Andrews, Thyssen-Bornemisza Museum, Madrid, 2000 and Tate Britain, 2001; and, with Lucian Freud, John Constable, Grand Palais, Paris, 2002. From 1994, Feaver was visiting professor at Nottingham Trent University. Among his books were *Pitmen Painters*, 1988, and *Van Gogh*, 1990. Northumberland was a favourite painting subject. Among exhibitions shown in were A Personal View at Nigel Greenwood Gallery, 1988, and a three-critic show at Cadogan Contemporary, 1992. Feaver shared a show with the critic William Packer at Piers Feetham Gallery in 2005. Lived in London.

Hermann FECHENBACH 1897–1986 Printmaker and painter, born in Wurttemberg, Germany, into a Jewish family. From an early age drawing became a passion and refuge for his shy nature, but his parents wanted a commercial career for him, so he became a window dresser in Dortmund. Conscripted in 1916, in 1917 Fechenbach was badly injured, having a leg amputated. In 1918 he began training at a Stuttgart handicraft school for invalids, graduating to studies of painting and restoration at the Stuttgart and Munich Academies, 1919–22, Max Liebermann being an influence. A year studying classical artists in Florence from 1923 was followed by travels through Pisa, Venice, Vienna and Amsterdam. Returned to Stuttgart in 1924, Fechenbach worked and showed in the contemporary style. In 1930 he married the photographer Greta Batze and they taught students in their studio until Nazi pressure led them to England in 1939. Fechenbach was interned in the Isle of Man, where he produced a powerful series of anti-Nazi lino-cuts. Settled in Oxford in 1941 Fechenbach began to exhibit to critical acclaim, then he had a first London show at the Anglo-Palestinian Club in 1944, the year he moved to the capital. In the mid-1940s he showed at Ben Uri Gallery, which holds examples in its collection. Although Movietone produced a news feature on Fechenbach about 1951, the artist increasingly retired from exposure, settling in Denham, Buckinghamshire, from 1962. In 1969 he published *Genesis*, illustrated with enlarged prints from many small wood engravings, and in 1972 the partly autobiographical *The Last Jews of Mergentheim*, appeared. A show at Blond Fine Art in 1985 revived interest in Fechenbach.

Daphne FEDARB 1912–1992 Painter, born in London, who married the artist Ernest Fedarb, and whose daughter Paulette was also a painter. She studied at Beckenham School of Art, 1928–30, Slade School of Fine Art, 1931–4, then at Westminster School of Art, 1936–9, where Mark Gertler taught her painting and Bernard Meninsky drawing. She married Ernest Fedarb in 1932 and in 1935 they had a joint show at Fine Art Society. Daphne Fedarb became a member of NS, 1940–55, of the RBA in 1948 and WIAC, 1955–68. Between 1961–73 she showed work at RA, NEAC and LG, in America and on the continent. Had a solo exhibition at Gallery 34, Shaftesbury, in 1968, another at Chilham Gallery, Kent, 1972, and shared a second show with Ernest at Sally Hunter & Patrick Seale Fine Art, 1986. Daphne Fedarb won first prize in the Laing Landscape Competition, 1981, and a second prize in 1983, and gained the RBA De Laszlo Medal in 1982. Lived in Nackington, Kent.

Ernest FEDARB 1905– Watercolourist and teacher, born in Canterbury, Kent, married to the artist Daphne Fedarb, their daughter Paulette also being a painter. In 1918 Fedarb attended first art classes at Sidney Cooper School of Art (later Canterbury School of Art), then was at Beckenham School of Art, where his teachers included Percy Jowett, Vivian Pitchforth and Henry Carr. In 1924 he became art master at Kent College, Canterbury, a year later at King's School Canterbury, in 1935 joining the staff of Westminster School of Art, then in 1939 becoming art master at Merchant Taylors' School. In 1940 his Hampstead home was destroyed by a bomb, which cost all his painting equipment and much of his early work. When the Hammersmith School of Art returned from evacuation in 1944 Fedarb joined its staff, then from 1947–65 was a Ministry of Education inspector for art. Fedarb had first showed with RBA in 1926. From the mid-1930s he showed regularly in London and provincial galleries and for many years from 1960 was honorary secretary to the United Kingdom Committee of the International Association of Art, delegate to International Art Congresses in New York, Amsterdam and London. In 1985 he was made president of NS. He had a joint show with his wife at Fine Art Society in 1932 and a second at Sally Hunter & Patrick Seale Fine Art in 1986. The Fedarbs were regular painters in France, Ernest's speciality being delicately coloured still lifes of flowers. Lived in Nackington, Kent.

Paulette FEDARB 1934– Artist in oil, watercolour, pen and ink and teacher, born in Canterbury, Kent, mother of the artist Roger Kelly and daughter of the artists Ernest and Daphne Fedarb. She studied at Chelsea School of Art, 1951–5, Bromley College of Art, 1955–6, then Hornsey College of Art, 1956–7, after which she taught full-time and continued to paint. Family commitments gave little time for painting after marriage in 1964, but from 1968–87 she taught part-time in adult evening classes, including Workers' Educational Association courses for Nottingham University, 1977–9. In 1981 returned to painting, in 1987 giving up all teaching to paint full-time. Her book *Pen and Ink Techniques* was published in 1992. Fedarb said that "my work is figurative, mainly of landscape and plant-derived forms. Textures of surface and pattern are important." Mixed shows included WIAC, NS and Midland Group. Had a solo show at Basement Gallery, Midland Group, 1964, also The Garden, Loughborough, Leicestershire, where she lived, 1985.

Bryant FEDDEN 1930– Glass engraver, letter-cutter and sculptor, born in Esher, Surrey, who was educated at Bryanston School and Cambridge University, where he read history and English, 1950–3. He taught in Britain and Pakistan, 1953–60, turning to letter-cutting and sculpture as a livelihood in 1960. Exhibited in London and the provinces, being included in 19 Young Sculptors at Hillfield Gardens, Gloucester, 1962. Victoria & Albert Museum, Cheltenham Art Gallery & Museums and several cathedrals hold examples. Was a member of the Gloucestershire Guild of Craftsmen and lived in the county at Littledean.

Mary FEDDEN 1915– Painter, notably of murals, and teacher, born in Bristol, married to the artist Julian Trevelyan. She studied at Slade School of Fine Art, as a scholar, 1932–6. She taught painting – the first woman tutor – at Royal College of Art, 1958–64, from 1965–70 at Yehudi Menuhin School. Was a member of LG, 1962–4, and participated in many other mixed shows. Solo shows included Redfern Gallery from 1953, Hamet Gallery from 1970, Heal's Mansard Gallery, Arnolfini Gallery in Bristol and elsewhere in the provinces. Major exhibition at RWA in 1988, by which time she had been its president for several years, with another in 1996. Mural commissions included Festival of Britain in 1951, the P & O liner *Canberra* in 1961, one with Julian Trevelyan at Charing Cross Hospital in 1980, and one for Colindale Hospital, 1985. Fedden was noted for her domestic, modest-sized still lifes, rich in colour and with an immaculate pattern element, as seen in another joint show with Trevelyan's work at Bohun Gallery, Henley-on-Thames, in 2003. Fedden shared an exhibition with Edmund Fairfax-Lucy at the New Grafton Gallery in 2005. HM The Queen, Chantrey Bequest for Tate Gallery and Contemporary Art Society bought her work. Lived in London. Was elected RA, 1992.

Henry FEDERER 1918– Versatile artist and designer, born in Vienna, Austria, who graduated in medicine at Vienna University in 1937. After moving to England in 1938, he was interned in Australia for part of World War II, on return attending St Martin's and Central Schools of Art. Federer became a scenic artist in theatre and film at The Harkers and Pinewood Studios, worked in television design with the BBC for five years and commercial television for 16, also as a European guide and lecturer. Aged 70 he returned to art, specialising in figurative drawings, paintings and sculpture. He had a solo show at The Studio Art House, Leatherhead, 2001.

Jacinta FEENEY 1954– Artist born in Donegal, Ireland, who continued to live there and in London. She graduated with first-class honours from the University of Central Lancashire, 1977–80; gained a master's from the Royal College of Art, 1981–4; and in 20th Century Art and Theory from Goldsmiths' College, 1992–4. Her awards included a Princess of Wales Scholarship from the Royal College of Art, 1981, also a Venice Scholarship, 1985; an Irish Arts Council Award to travel to Spain, 1984; and an Irish Arts Council Bursary, 1987. Took part in numerous group shows, latterly including Art of the State, Office of Public Works, touring northern and southern Ireland and Louvain, Belgium, 1996; Dublin Airport, 1997; and NOW, Whiteley's, 1998. In 2000 she had a two-artist show at Pyms Gallery. Solo exhibitions included Riverrun Gallery, Dublin, 1988 and 1992, and Hammersmith Irish Centre, 1995. Irish Arts Council; Contemporary Arts Council, Ireland; Office of Public Works, Ireland; and Arts Council of Great Britain hold examples.

Cheng-Wu FEI 1914– Painter and teacher, married to the artist Chien-Ying Chang. Studied at China's National Central University, 1930–4, teaching at the Fine Art College there, 1941–6, further studying at Slade School of Fine Art, 1947–50. Published *Brush Drawing in the Chinese Manner*. Showed at RA, NEAC, RWS and elsewhere, having solo exhibitions at Leicester Galleries. Public galleries in Derby and Sheffield hold his work and Tate Gallery archive holds his Self-Portrait, 1953. Lived for many years in north London.

Chien-Ying FEI: *see* **Chien-Ying CHANG**

Hans FEIBUSCH 1898–1998 Mural painter, draughtsman and printmaker, born in Frankfurt-am-Main, Germany. After education in Frankfurt, he studied art in Germany, France and Italy for six years from 1919, exhibiting widely on the continent. In England Feibusch showed at Lefevre Gallery extensively from the late 1930s, also RA, RHA, Cooling Galleries, Leicester and Redfern Galleries, but he was mainly known as a mural painter, a strong draughtsman and Colourist with an interest in religious themes. Victoria & Albert Museum and Leeds City Art Gallery hold his work, but it is predominantly in churches and on public buildings, examples being Chichester Cathedral, which has his Baptism of Christ; a number of parish churches in London and the provinces; Dudley Town Hall, in Worcestershire; and the Civil Centre in Newport, Monmouthshire. Was author of the book *Mural Painting*, 1946. Feibusch continued working to an advanced age and lived in London, to which he had moved in the 1930s when the Nazis condemned and destroyed his work in Germany. Retrospective at Pallant House Gallery, Chichester, and tour, 1995–6. In 1999, Feibusch's studio was moved to Chichester for display at St Martin's Hall.

Frederick FEIGL 1884–1965 Painter, born in Prague in what is now the Czech Republic, who was originally known as Friedrich Feigl. He studied at Prague's Academy of Arts, then at Antwerp Academy in 1904–5, and in Paris. Settled in Germany, where he had a show in Berlin at J B Neumann Graphisches Kabinett in 1912, returned to Czechoslovakia, after a year in Palestine, in 1933, but six years later left for England, where he died in London. In 1940 he had a show with Lucy Wertheim's Gallery, others including one at Ben Uri Art Society, which holds several examples, in 1964.

Maurice FEILD 1905–1988 Painter, printmaker, and teacher. He studied at Slade School of Fine Art in 1920s, then after three years went to teach art at The Downs, a Quaker preparatory school at Colwall, near Great Malvern, where he remained until after World War II. He inspired several dozen notable painters by his direct, open-air teaching methods, including Kenneth Rowntree, Lawrence Gowing, Patrick George and Francis Hoyland. After World War II Feild taught for a time at Camberwell School of Arts and Crafts and he was invited by William Coldstream to teach at the Slade. Feild was a keen painter of landscape who showed at Cooling's and Walker's Galleries and latterly at Austin/Desmond Fine Art. In 1970 Coldstream organised a Grosvenor Gallery retrospective. Lived in London.

Basil FEILDING 1907–1986 Painter who studied at Goldsmiths' College and Ruskin School of Drawing and Fine Art, Oxford, and the Slade School of Fine Art, 1929–37, including a brief period at the Slade, 1936–7. He had a solo exhibition at the Pigeonhole Gallery in 1976. Feilding died in Oxford. Sir Brinsley Ford owned his work.

June FEILER: *see* **June MILES**

Paul FEILER 1918– Painter, originally of representational, but later of abstract work; teacher. He was born in Frankfurt-am-Main, Germany, arriving in England in 1933. Feiler attended Slade School of Fine Art, 1936–39, then during World War II was interned and sent to Canada. Returning to England, he taught at combined colleges of Radley and Eastbourne until the end of the war, then at West of England College of Art from 1946, being head of painting, 1963–75. His first wife was the painter June Miles. He later married the artist Catharine Armitage. Feiler became associated with the St Ives painters after his first visit in 1949, the year before his work moved towards abstraction, and in 1953 he settled in Stanhope Forbes' old studio at Kerris, near Newlyn. Had first solo show at Redfern Gallery in that year, followed by several others. Additional individual exhibitions included Crawford Arts Centre, St Andrews, 1981, which toured; Austin/Desmond Fine Art, 1990; and retrospective Tate Gallery, St Ives,

1996. Tate St Ives gave him a show in 2005. Carried out several architectural commissions for Yorke, Rosenberg & Mardell. Work held by Aberdeen Art Gallery and Museums, Arts Council, many British provincial and overseas galleries.

Eleanor FEIN 1940– Painter, illustrator and writer, born in Oxted, Surrey, who studied drawing, architectural studio, Madrid, Spain, 1960–1, and worked as a children's book illustrator, 1973–90. Her awards included a Nuffield Foundation Award to illustrate science textbooks. She wrote and illustrated *Oscar and his Mouse*, 1990. In 2004 she was Mary Fedden's choice for Artist of the Day at Flowers Central.

Florence Isabel FEIST 1878– Watercolourist and miniaturist, born in London. Studied at Crystal Palace School of Art under Matthew Webb and Herbert Bone. Exhibited RMS and in the provinces. Lived at Henfield, Sussex.

Trevor FELCEY 1945– Painter of figures and landscape and teacher, born in Ferring, Sussex. He studied at Camberwell School of Art, 1963–6, then Royal College of Art, 1966–9. He won Andrew Lloyd and David Murray Scholarships. Went on to teach part-time at Wimbledon and Byam Shaw Schools of Art. Felcey's work appeared in RA, at British Drawing at Hayward Gallery in 1982, in the Norwich School of Art Gallery touring show A Reputation Among Artists, in 1986–7, and in Pure Paint, Stephen Lacey Gallery, 1999. Later solo shows included Plough Arts Centre, Torrington, 1999, and Royal Albert Memorial Museum, Exeter, in 2005. Chantrey Bequest, Nuffield Foundation, Franklyn Memorial Collection at South Humberside and Leicestershire Education Authority hold Felcey's work. Lived in London.

Carl FELKEL 1896–1980 Landscape, figure and portrait painter, studied in Vienna and Munich. In addition to exhibiting widely on the continent, Felkel showed in Britain at the Goupil Gallery and the RA. He travelled extensively in Europe and America. The Vienna Albertina as well as public galleries in Manchester and Derby hold his work. Lived in London.

Brian FELL 1952– Sculptor, born in Liverpool. He studied at Manchester Polytechnic, 1975–9, then spent a year as Fellow in Sculpture at Cheltenham College of Art. He went on to lecture part-time at Blackpool and Rochdale Colleges of Art. Fell was awarded a Major Award by North West Arts and in 1981 the Yorkshire Arts Association Artists in Industry Fellowship. He used pre-formed steel for his sculpture, and this was an opportunity for him to work in a steelworks, surrounded by his material at all its stages of formation. Although Fell's sculptures were abstract, they made allusions to human or machine counterparts, dynamic while being quite compact. Fell took part in a number of group shows, including New Contemporaries at ICA in 1978, the Manchester Academy exhibitions and he was included in the Welsh Sculpture Trust's 1983 Margam event, Sculpture in a Country Park.

Eleanor FELL fl. from c.1900–1946 Painter and printmaker, born in Thetford, Norfolk, and educated in Tewkesbury. She studied at Westminster School of Art, where she won several prizes, and in Paris. Her practice of landscape painting was facilitated by a keen interest in caravanning. She was elected an associated of RE in 1908, also exhibiting at RA, NEAC, SWA, Royal Glasgow Institute of the Fine Arts and at Walker Art Gallery in Liverpool. Lived in Worthing, Sussex.

Michael FELL 1939– Artist and teacher, notable as a printmaker, born in London. After a foundation course at St Martin's School of Art he attended the City & Guilds School of Art, also studying painting and printmaking under a travelling scholarship on the continent. Fell taught at City & Guilds School, finally as head of foundation studies, 1985–96. He was a fellow of the Society of Designer Craftsmen and organised the show Vision and Innovation in St Paul's Cathedral, part of the Society's centenary celebrations, in 1998 being elected an honorary fellow of RE. Group shows included Galleria Renata, Chicago, 1988; Allan Art Galleries, Singapore; Belanthi Gallery, New York; and in 1993 the Chappel Galleries, Chappel, show Continuing the Tradition. British Museum, Arts Council and Royal Academy hold his work. Had a solo exhibition at Grosvenor Gallery, 1996, richly coloured landscapes of the Armagnac region; another at Chappel, 1999; and in 2001 a show at Christchurch Mansion, Ipswich, views of Christchurch Park from his studio. Fell lived in Suffolk and Gascony, France.

Phyllis FELL 1901– Painter and miniaturist, born in Plymouth, Devon. She was of a military family, was educated in Bexhill, Sussex, and studied at Blackheath School of Art, but returned to Plymouth to live. Signing her work P F, she showed at RA, RMS of which she was a member, and elsewhere.

Sheila FELL 1931–1979 Painter, draughtsman and teacher, born in Aspatria, Cumberland, her father a miner. Attended Carlisle School of Art, 1947–9, encouraged to take up textile design; then St Martin's School of Art, 1949–51, with R V Pitchforth and John Napper. Although she left Cumbria at 18 and thereafter only returned on visits, its landscape predominated in her work, her depictions of it being painterly but generally dour. Had a daughter by the Greek sculptor Takis Vassilakis in 1957, the year following winning a Boise Scholarship to Greece. First solo show at Beaux Arts Gallery in 1955, one of a series in the 1950s and 1960s. Joined teaching staff of Chelsea School of Art in 1958, the year after she won a prize in John Moores Liverpool Exhibition. Exhibited also at RA, being elected RA in 1974; Ashgate Gallery, Farnham; and New Grafton Gallery. There was a small memorial show at Abbot Hall Art Gallery, Kendal, in 1981, and a larger one organised by South Bank Centre, commenced Salford Art Gallery, with tour, 1990–1. Tate Gallery and Arts Council hold her work. Lived in London.

Michael FELMINGHAM 1935– Painter, muralist, printmaker, watercolourist and teacher, born in Worcestershire. His first artistic work was published in 1956, and from then on he exhibited in leading galleries in Britain, accepting commissions from major companies including Allied Lyons and Texaco. Between 1968–89 he was lecturer in design history at Coventry College of Art (later Lanchester Polytechnic). He made prints for Royal Academy Graphics Collection at Curwen Studio, was a Saunders Waterford prizewinner in 1981, winning an award in the Laing Competition in 1992. In 1977 he had a retrospective at Herbert Art Gallery and Museum, Coventry. Later solo shows included Midlands Contemporary Art in 1990 and in 1992 Venice Observed at Waterman Fine Art Ltd. A series of watercolours of local views were commissioned by Herbert Art Gallery and are in its permanent collection. Felmingham's *The Illustrated Gift Book 1880–1930* was published in 1990. Felmingham had the fourth of his varied exhibitions at W H Patterson in 2004.

Shirley FELTS fl. from 1950s– Artist in various media who was born in West Virginia, America. She graduated from University of Texas with fine art degree in 1958, then did postgraduate work in graphics at San Francisco Institute of Art. After working in the city as a graphic artist she travelled through Asia and the Far East, 1962–4, eventually settling in southeast London. Showed in mixed exhibitions in America and Europe and had two solo shows in Corpus Christi, Texas, in 1959. Others included The Old Fire Engine House, Ely, from 1970, Gallery 27 in Tonbridge from 1975, Washington Arts Centre in Cumbria, 1983, and Woodlands Art Gallery, 1984. In that show Felts showed landscapes bordering on abstraction. In 1979 Felts was profiled on BBC Anglia Television. Clare College in Cambridge and King's School in Ely hold her work.

Julia FENBY 1968– Painter and draughtsman with a strong interest in human responses to, and relationships with, animals. She studied on a preparatory art course at Herts Regional College; foundation at St Albans College of Art & Design; art access at University of Hertfordshire; and gained an honours degree in fine art, painting, at Wimbledon School of Art. Exhibitions included Not, Wimbledon Library, 1997, and Class of 98, Hanging Space, 1998.

Constance FENN 1933–2001 Painter, freelance illustrator, muralist, portrait copier, restorer and teacher, born and mainly lived in London, who, after a difficult childhood, studied at Camberwell School of Arts and Crafts, 1948–50, teaching there, 1959–60. She won a scholarship to the Royal College of Art, 1950, graduating from the painting school with first-class honours, 1954, and in that year an Edward Austen Abbey Scholarship to Rome. Carel Weight, who taught at the Royal College during her time there, eventually becoming professor of painting, remained an admirer of Connie Fenn's work. Their paintings share a taste for eccentric figures. In 1953 Fenn participated in a large international exhibition in Milan. She showed with the NEAC, 1958–74, of which she was a member, 1969–74, also exhibiting at RA Summer Exhibition from 1956–72; Wildenstein, 1961; and widely elsewhere, having solo shows at Zaydler Gallery, 1973, and Imperial College, 1975. Fenn visited France, Germany and America to paint and eventually to exhibit. As a painter she was influenced by Christopher Chamberlain and William Coldstream, as an illustrator by Edward Ardizzone and Susan Einzig. Her pictures included a series of London river scenes with Chagall-like couples floating in the clouds. Fenn's paintings use a rich, highly personal palette, perspective and iconography. As a draughtsman she was capable of exquisite and assured drawings in ink using distinctive hatching. Periods of mental instability undermined Fenn's career, during which she had to be hospitalised, and she depended heavily on the support of Chamberlain, his wife the painter Heather Copley, Weight and his wife the artist Helen Roeder. Apart from odd exhibitions at such places as the South Place Ethical Society, in her final years Fenn had no regular dealer. She died unremarked in Clapton, east London. Duncan Campbell Fine Art in collaboration with Gabriel Summers showed a fine, revelatory collection of Fenn's oils on board and works on paper in 2005.

Lesley FENNELL 1943– Painter, mainly in oil with a subdued palette, subjects drawn from her life and surroundings. She studied at the National College of Art and Design in Dublin, Ireland, and in London at the Byam Shaw School. Fennell exhibited widely, work in public and private collections, and was included in The Irish Show at The Wykeham Gallery, Stockbridge, in 2005. She lived in Ireland near Althy, County Kildare.

Rachel FENNER 1939– Sculptor, painter and teacher, born in Scarborough, Yorkshire. She studied at Wimbledon School of Art, 1958–62, then sculpture at Royal College of Art, 1962–6. Won a Sainsbury Award Grant in 1966. From 1966 taught sculpture at Winchester and West Surrey Colleges of Art and Wimbledon School of Art and was a visitor to Royal Academy Schools, 1974–6. Arts Council Major Award in 1976 was among several won. Solo shows included House, 1976; Taranman and DLI Museum and Arts Centre, Durham, both 1978; Aspex Gallery, Portsmouth, and Abbot Hall Art Gallery, Kendal, both 1981; and Duncan Campbell Contemporary Art, from 1993. Among many commissions were Saxon Column for Hamwick, Southampton, 1989–90, and Earthworks for Castle Park, Bristol, 1991. In 1994, Fenner was sculptor-in-residence at the Bishop's Palace, St Davids. Arts Council holds her work.

Barbara FENNICK 1957– Artist educated in America who graduated in biology from Lafayette College in Easton, 1975–9, attending Rhode Island School of Design, 1976, then gained her master's at the School of the Museum of Fine Arts, Boston, 1980–3. She studied art history at Heidelberg University, West Germany, 1987–9. Group shows included EMBL, Heidelberg, 1985, and East End Open Studios, with Barbican Arts Group, 1989. In 1986 she had a solo exhibition, Keramic und Kunst, in Heidelberg.

Greta FENTON 1932– Landscape and figure painter, teacher, born London, who studied at Wimbledon College of Arts and Crafts and Central St Martin's College of Art & Design. She worked in the art department of Condé Nast Publications on *Vogue* and *House and Garden* and was an art director for two London advertising agencies. Taught art at Brighton College of Technology. She was an award winner of the International Federation of Art Societies at City of London Guildhall. Showed at Brighton Festival, Guild of Sussex Artists, Hove Museum & Art Gallery and The Grange, Rottingdean. Shared an exhibition at Duncan Campbell Contemporary Art, 1995. Lived in Hove, Sussex.

Max FENTON 1956– Oil on canvas and installations artist; exhibitions organiser, born in Dundee, Angus. He attended Duncan of Jordanstone College of Art there, 1975–9. Among shows participated in were Interference, Riverside Studios, 1986; Riverside Open, 1987; Anomie, Patent House, and Brick Lane Open, both 1992; and Itself, Transmission Gallery, Glasgow, 1993. Lived in London.

Samuel FENTON 1923– Painter and draughtsman who was by profession a commercial traveller, born in London. He studied art at Regent Street Polytechnic School of Art under Harold Brownsword and at Harrow Technical

School. Showed RA, NS, RBA and Sussex County Arts Club. Lived in Brighton, Sussex.

Simon FENTON 1970– Artist in various media, born in Hertfordshire. He studied at Harlow College, 1987–9, obtained an honours degree at Norfolk School of Art & Design, 1989–92, then attended Brighton University for his master's degree, 1992–4. Group exhibitions included Harlow Playhouse, 1989; Black Sheep Gallery, Brighton, 1992; then he in 1993 took part in In Piper's Footsteps at New Academy Gallery. Among Fenton's commissioned work was a mural for Harlow College Sports Hall; another for the College Library; and a set and costume design for *Mask of the Red Death* at Harlow Playhouse.

Cathy FENWICK 1955– Painter and draughtsman who graduated with first-class honours in sculpture from Gloucestershire College of Art & Design, 1977–80, gaining her master's degree from Royal Academy School, 1982–5. She won a Henry Moore Fellowship in 1982 and the Landseer Prize, 1983. Fenwick's work included an unpredictable sense of colour and uncompromising images. Group exhibitions included Ikon Gallery, Birmingham, 1980; Arts Council touring show of drawings, 1980–1; Birch and Conran from 1987; and BP Portrait Award at National Portrait Gallery, 1994. In 1980 had solo show at Jordan Gallery, with a sculpture show at Ikon. From 1992 showed solo at East West, 10-year retrospective, 2002. Arts Council holds her work.

Cyril Lawrence FEREDAY: *see* **Joseph FEREDAY**

Joseph FEREDAY 1917–2001 Artist in oil and acrylic, beyond 1976 mainly an etcher and engraver, teacher, born in Dudley, Worcestershire. He studied at Wolverhampton and Birmingham Colleges of Art and the Slade School of Fine Art, 1946–8, in the evenings pursuing wood engraving at the Central School of Art. Was elected a fellow of RE in 1986, having been made an associate in 1979. Lectured at Portsmouth College of Art and Design, 1948–80. In 1976–8 Fereday conducted two summer schools in printmaking at Hope College, Holland, Michigan. He took part in several shows in Michigan, at Hope College and at Pravna Gallery, Saugatuck; also at RA; Redfern, Piccadilly and Leicester Galleries; and at galleries in the English provinces. Solo shows included Dudley Art Gallery, Wolverhampton Art Gallery, Boldrewood Gallery at Southampton University, Woodstock Gallery and abroad. Plymouth, Bilston and Portsmouth public galleries hold his work. His full name was Cyril Lawrence Joseph Fereday and until election to the RE he was known as Cyril Lawrence Fereday. Lived in Brading, Isle of Wight.

FERELYTH 1916–2005 Sculptor in wood, stone, plastics, bronze and resin bronze, and lecturer, born in London, full name Ferelyth Alison Wills. Studied with John Skeaping at Central School of Arts and Crafts, 1935–9, then did war service, 1941–5. Was a member of Society of Designer-Craftsmen and Petersfield Arts and Crafts Society. She gave illustrated talks and demonstrations on sculpture, animal movement in art and choice of materials. With Bill Wills she wrote *Sculpture in Wood*, 1975. Showed at RA, Crafts Centre of Great Britain of which she was a member until 1970, Wildlife Society exhibitions and elsewhere. Ferelyth retired as a sculptor in 1990, after leaving her Petersfield studio to move to Emsworth. Despite failing eyesight, she wrote *The Antelope Book*, privately published in 1997. This is an entertaining account of her time at the Central School and of how she had become a glider pilot in the late 1950s as well as detailing her life's work. She died in Chichester, Sussex, where Pallant House holds her sculpture Fox and a drawing, Male Dancer, bequeathed in 1989 as part of his collection by Charles Kearley.

Dan FERGUSON 1910– Painter and printmaker, brother of the artist Roy Ferguson, born and lived in Motherwell, Lanarkshire. He studied at Glasgow School of Art after Motherwell's Dalziel High School. Became ROI in 1958. Ferguson also showed at RSW, Royal Glasgow Institute of the Fine Arts, gained a silver medal at Paris Salon in 1961 and a gold medal at Italian Academy in 1980. Public galleries in Glasgow and Paisley hold his work.

John David FERGUSON 1932– Painter in all media, born in Buxton, Derbyshire, who studied at the West of England College of Art, Bristol, and at the Slade School of Fine Art under William Coldstream and William Townsend. Exhibited with LG; *Sunday Times* Exhibition, first prize, 1957; Leicester Galleries; Singer & Friedlander/*Sunday Times* Watercolour Competition, 1994; and in South Africa. Arts Council (he took part in its travelling exhibitions), Derbyshire Education Committee, University College London, University College of St Mark and St John in Plymouth, and Bristol City Art Gallery hold examples. Lived at Pendeen, Penzance, Cornwall.

Malcolm Alastair Percy FERGUSON 1913– Painter, born in Blackwater, Hampshire. He attended Portsmouth and Croydon Schools of Art, 1935–8, and Slade School of Fine Art, 1939 and 1948–51. Was a member of RWA, also exhibiting at RA, RP, Paris Salon and in the provinces and having solo shows in Britain and abroad. Completed a number of paintings in churches in South Africa and Zimbabwe. Plymouth City Museum and Art Gallery holds his work. Lived in North Petherton, Somerset.

Nancy FERGUSON fl. c.1950–1970 Painter and silversmith, born in Belfast, where she continued to live. Studied at Belfast College of Art and showed at RHA and RUA.

Neil FERGUSON 1955– Painter born in Dunfermline, Fife, who studied at Edinburgh College of Art, 1973–7, then Goldsmiths' College School of Art, 1978–9. His many group shows included Seven Young Artists at Talbot Rice Art Centre, Edinburgh, 1977; LG from 1980; Whitechapel Open, 1985; Celtic Vision, 1986–7, Madrid and European tour, where Ferguson shared the Scottish representation; and Tom Allen Centre retrospective and New Moon Group Show, Woodlands Art Gallery, both 1987. Had a solo show at Sir John Cass School of Art, 1985, others including Windsor and Jersey Arts Centres, 1987.

Roy FERGUSON 1907–1981 Watercolourist, caricaturist, teacher and writer, born in Motherwell, Lanarkshire, where he settled. He was the brother of the painter Dan Ferguson. Studied at Glasgow School of Art and taught at Dalziel High School for over 25 years. Showed at RA, NEAC, RBA, RSW of which he was a member, RSA, on the continent – including Paris Salon, where he gained a silver medal – and in Canada. Glasgow Museums and Art Galleries and the corporation in Newport, Wales, hold his work. Ferguson was a caricaturist for the *Scottish Sunday Express*, contributed nature notes to *The Scotsman* and wrote poetry, a collection being published by *The Motherwell Times* in 1972. His caricatures were signed eff.

William FERGUSON 1913–1999 Painter, born in Paisley, Renfrewshire, where at school he came under the influence of Alex MacPherson, eventually notable as a watercolourist. During World War II, as a staff captain with Southern Command, Bill Ferguson wrote and designed tank training manuals. After teaching at Dufftown, Blairgowrie, Perth Academy and as rector of Knox Academy, Haddington, Ferguson developed his own painting style, his favourite painting haunts being the Isle of Coll, East Lothian, Northumberland and Venice. Ferguson had a string of solo shows, The Torrance Gallery, Edinburgh, giving him a memorial exhibition in 2002. He bequeathed some of the proceeds of that show to St Mary's, Haddington, where he was a kirk elder for 45 years and a member of the restoration committee. Ferguson was also an art correspondent for *The Times Educational Supplement*.

Christian Jane FERGUSSON 1876–1957 Landscape painter and teacher, born in Dumfries, Dumfriesshire, who attended the Crystal Palace School of Art, and Glasgow School of Art, 1901–8, gaining two travelling scholarships. Taught at the School of Art and was art mistress at Glasgow High School for Girls and at the Benedictine Convent School, Dumfries. Chris Fergusson, whose husband David was a Dumfries solicitor, joined the Glasgow Society of Lady Artists in 1925 and won its Lauder Award 1933–38–54. She became a member of the SSA in 1928 and joined the SSWA. Was a prolific exhibitor at Royal Glasgow Institute of the Fine Arts, also showing at RSA, RSW, Walker Art Gallery in Liverpool, RA and elsewhere.

John Duncan FERGUSSON 1874–1961 Painter, draughtsman, sculptor and writer, born in Leith, Midlothian. Although he matriculated in medicine at Edinburgh University, Fergusson opted to become an artist, inspired by Glasgow painters. From the mid-1890s Fergusson began to travel on the continent, studying at Atelier Colarossi, in Paris. From 1907 until World War II Fergusson settled in the French capital, began to paint in the Fauve manner, was befriended by the painter Dunoyer de Segonzac and began to sculpt in a Cubist style. In 1911 he was appointed visual arts editor of *Rhythm* magazine, a time when his own work was inspired by vital contemporary dance music. He had had a first one-man show at the Baillie Gallery in London in 1905, and as well as showing in France he had four works in the Post-Impressionist and Futurist Exhibition at the Doré Galleries in London in 1913. In that year he met his wife, the dancer Margaret Morris, who was in 1974 to publish *The Art of J D Fergusson*. After they settled in Scotland in 1939 Fergusson was a founder-member of the New Art Club a year later. From this emerged the New Scottish Group in 1942 and a revitalisation of the Scottish art scene. He was art editor of *Scottish Art and Letters* and author of *Modern Scottish Painting* in 1943, his first retrospective show opening in Glasgow in 1948. Fergusson died in Glasgow. Shortly after, a memorial exhibition was held, Arts Council, RSA and touring. Fergusson will always be remembered as a vibrant Colourist and incisive draughtsman whose luscious depiction of French countryside, life and character and whose sensuous nudes are unmistakable. The Fergusson Gallery, Perth, was set up to honour his work. Its touring exhibition of Fergusson's work, Living Paint: A Scottish Colourist, was shown by The Fleming Collection in 2005. In 2004, the Fine Art Society organised J D Fergusson in France, paintings from private collections, and Abbot Hall Art Gallery, Kendal, showed his work.

Georgina FERMER 1943– Painter and teacher, born in London, whose abstract oils on canvas and paper collages developed ideas from her student years at Hornsey College of Art before London University Institute of Education, 1960–5. Hornsey's notable staff and visiting artists from whose teaching she benefited included Jesse Cast, John Flavin, Richard Fozard, Alan Green, Bridget Riley, Richard Robbins, David Tindle, John Titchell and Marc Vaux. Fermer taught school, adult education and HM Prison classes. She participated in Dorset Open Studios and in group exhibitions, later ones including Dorset Museum, Dorchester, 1997; White Gallery in Brighton and in the Women's International Exchange Exhibition North-current in London, Sweden and Germany, both 1998; Metamorphosis, European Contemporary Art, Highcliffe Castle, Dorset, 2000; Maltby Gallery, Winchester, 2001; and in 2002–3 at venues including Sherborne Contemporary Art and Bettles Gallery, Ringwood. Among her solo exhibitions were Gallery Mascotte, Basel, Switzerland, 1970; Century Gallery, Henley-on-Thames, 1982; Design Centre, Haymarket, 1984; Trinity Arts Festival, Cookham, 1992; Heifer Gallery, 1995 and 2003; Cranbourne Gallery, Dorset, 1996; Red House Museum, Christchurch, 1997; and Arts Institute, Bournemouth University, 1999. Lived in Piddletrenthide, Dorset.

Maria-Theresa FERNANDES fl. from 1970s– Artist in various media, noted for textural reliefs, and teacher, born in Nairobi, Kenya. She studied at Sir John Cass College, 1967–8, then Manchester College of Art and Design, 1968–71 and 1975–6. Gained a number of awards, including British Council, 1981, and Embroiderers' Association of Canada, Toronto, 1982. Held many teaching posts, including Ulster Polytechnic; HM Styal Prison, Cheshire; School for the Mentally Handicapped, Northwich; Manchester Polytechnic; and Belfast School of Fashion and Textiles. Took part in many group shows in Britain and America, including Commonwealth Institute, 1972; RA, 1978; MAFA 1981; and Tennessee State Museum, 1982. Had a solo show at Covent Garden Gallery, 1973, others including Bretton Hall, Yorkshire, 1978, and Woodlands Art Gallery, 1983. Lived in America.

Roberto Gonzalez FERNANDEZ 1948– Artist, born in Monforte de Lemos, Spain, who studied fine arts at Escuela Superior de Bellas Artes de San Fernando, Madrid, 1969–74, living in Edinburgh from 1977. In 1983 he was included in Scottish Print Open Three, organised by Dundee Printmakers' Workshop. Pallant House Gallery, Chichester, holds a collection of his work.

Kenneth FERNÉE 1926–1983 Landscape painter and teacher, born in London, who painted oils of Dartmoor, the rocky drops to the sea of the southwest coastline, beaches and the Welsh hills. Ken Fernée was especially fond of landscape where its basic structure appears through the delicate and vulnerable surface. He took part in a mixed show with Anthony Barson and Jack Wright at the AIA in 1956; in mixed shows at John Whibley Gallery, its Three Painters Group in 1969 and had a solo show there in 1971, when he was head of art in a Devon comprehensive school; also having a one-man at The Hambledon Gallery, Blandford, in 1980. The painter Alan Cotton, an admirer of Fernée's work, helped organise a memorial show at the University of Exeter in 1984, the year that the University acquired an oil on board, entitled Dartmoor, Stone Row.

Martin FERRABEE 1957– Sculptor, born in Nottinghamshire, who attended Jacob Kramer College of Art, Leeds, in 1980–1, then St Martin's School of Art, 1981–3. Took part in Kornarija Symposium of Sculpture, Yugoslavia, 1982, and in Have You Seen Sculpture from the Body? at Woodlands Art Gallery, 1983.

Brian FERRAN 1940– Painter, administrator and teacher, born in Londonderry, Northern Ireland. He studied at St Joseph's College of Education, 1959–62, then St Mary's College of Education, 1962–3, both in Belfast, then taught art, 1963–6. Obtained an honours degree in art history from Courtauld Institute and a postgraduate diploma in business administration from Queen's University, Belfast. In 1970–1 Ferran spent a year at Brera Academy of Fine Art, Milan, Italy. From 1966 he was on the staff of the Arts Council of Northern Ireland, becoming director. He served on many committees and boards and was a member of RUA. Posters, murals and films were among his special interests. The *Irish Times* critic Brian Fallon described his work as "often poetically suggestive rather than explicit". Took part in many group shows in Ireland and abroad, solo exhibitions including David Hendriks Gallery, Dublin; New and Tom Caldwell Galleries, Belfast; Queen's University, Belfast; University of Durham; and a series in America, including University of Wisconsin, Milwaukee, 1992. In 1989 Ferran completed three large stained glass windows for a church at St Patrick's College, Maghera, and in 1990 a mural at the entrance of St Columb's College, Londonderry. Arts Council of Northern Ireland, Ulster Museum, Gordon Lambert Collection, Queen's University and many other Irish collections hold examples. Lived in Belfast.

Denise FERRAN 1942– Art educationist, historian, writer and painter of landscapes, born in Northern Ireland. She studied in Belfast at St Mary's College of Education and at Queen's University, then at the Courtauld Institute, London, and at Trinity College, Dublin. Ferran combined educational and cultural institution work in Belfast and abroad with her own private artistic output. Became art and design education officer at the Ulster Museum, Belfast. Had many solo and group exhibitions including RUA, Society of Ulster Women Artists, the Oireachtas at Trinity College, RHA and the Municipal Gallery of Modern Art, Dublin. Her 1999 self-portrait, in the collection of the National Self-Portrait Collection of Ireland, University of Limerick, alludes to her researches on the painter William Leech; National Gallery of Ireland published Ferran's book *William John Leech: An Irish Painter Abroad* in 1996. Ferran's acrylic Towards Carndonagh was included in Landscapes North and South, Glebe House and Gallery, Donegal, and tour, 1997–8.

Ginger FERRELL 1944– Stained glass artist and teacher, born in Cleveland, Ohio, America, moved to St Petersburg, Florida, from 1951. From 1965–81 Ferrell was engaged in visual merchandising. She studied fine art photography at Florida State University, 1970–3; graduated from the University of South Florida in mass communication, 1976; was engaged in a workshop with Ludwig Schaffrath, at Deland, 1980; and involved in Illuminations, a stained glass co-operative, at Tampa, 1981–3. After moving to London in 1983 Ferrell worked with Stained Glass Supplies, 1983–5; Goddard & Gibbs Stained Glass Studio, 1985–7; The London Door Company, 1988–92; and took part in a design seminar with Johannes Schreiter at Swansea Institute, 1993. In 1992 she became self-employed, latterly with a studio at Deptford in southeast London. From 1987 she also taught a range of courses around Britain, among them drawing at the City Lit, Blackheath School of Art and the Prince's Drawing School. Ferrell was a member of the Women's International Stained Glass Workshop (WISGW) from 1993 and an associate of the British Society of Master Glass Painters (BSMGP) from 1997. She won an Artists in Schools Award, Central St Martin's School of Design, in 2001. Ferrell's work was influence by "The Japanese feeling towards nature. The underlying symbolism of their decorative work." Group shows (among them WISGW and BSMGP) included Layers of Experience, Park Gallery, Tokyo, Japan, 1995; Clerkenwell Green Association, from 1995; Traces of Travel, Crawford Municipal Art Gallery, and London Glass Art Gallery, both 1997; Exhibition, Golden, Colorado, 2000; Glass with Altitude, Auckland, New Zealand, 2002; Spirit of Place, Toronto, Canada, 2004; and 30cm2, Cochrane Gallery and tour, 2004–5. Northlands Creative Glass, Lybster, Caithness, holds Ferrell's work.

Moira FERRIER 1939– Watercolourist who was born in Glen Lethnot, Angus, into a farming family. After Brechin High School she attended Gray's School of Art, Aberdeen, her teachers including David Michie, Ian Fleming and Robert Henderson Blyth, gaining her diploma in 1961. Ferrier was a regular exhibitor at RSW, of which she became a member in 1979, and she had a series of solo exhibitions, including Ancrum Gallery, Ancrum, 1991. Lived for a time at Strathdon, Aberdeenshire.

David Dawson FERRY 1957– Painter, printmaker, artist in mixed media and teacher, born in Blackpool, Lancashire. Ferry did foundation studies in fine art at Blackpool College of Higher and Further Education, 1974–6; he gained a first-class honours degree at Camberwell School of Arts and Crafts, 1976–9, with a commendation in printmaking, Agathe Sorel being a notable teacher; then did postgraduate studies in printmaking at Slade School of Fine Art, 1979–81, notably under Mario Dubsky. In 1981–2 did extended studies certificate in printmaking at Camberwell. Ferry held a number of teaching posts. In 1991 he was appointed senior lecturer in fine art at Kent Institute of Art & Design, Canterbury, also visiting lecturer at Fachhochschule Design, Düsseldorf. His *Painting Without A Brush* was published in 1991, the year he was commissioned by British Nuclear Electric to produce a picture of Sizewell B Power Station. Group exhibitions included 2nd National Exhibition of Modern British Prints, Grundy Art Gallery, Blackpool, 1981; RA Summer Exhibitions, from 1985; Five Contemporary Printmakers, National Museum of Wales, Cardiff, and tour, 1987; and Volcanic Landscapes,

Boundary Gallery, 1991. Later solo shows included Roe and Moore Rare Books, 2003. At that, Ferry showed new prints and artist's books "from an ongoing defilement of popular tourist literature, entitled *Some Aspects of Our National Heritage...a small library*, and a new suite of lithographs depicting early English historical sites including Stonehenge, Corfe Castle and The Long Man of Wilmington." At that time Ferry was artistic director of the Curwen Print Study Centre, Cambridge; head of fine art at Winchester School of Art; and a visiting professor at Long Island University, New York. He received Arts and Humanities Research Board funding in 2000–01 and was a Pollock-Krasner grant winner in 2002. The Art Insitute of Chicago, the Polish Book Museum in Łódź and public galleries in Blackpool and Maidstone hold Ferry's work.

Edori FERTIG 1957– Painter, printmaker and teacher, born in New York City. Studied at Massachusetts College of Art, Boston, 1980–2, after a design course at Rhode Island School of Design, Providence, 1975–9. Showed widely in group shows on America's east coast, then in London at Diorama Arts Centre, 1986, and Morley Printmakers at Morley Gallery, 1989. In 1990 she shared a three-man exhibition at Woodlands Art Gallery. Taught at American Community School in Surrey.

Andrew FESTING 1941– Self-taught portrait painter, born in Chalford, Gloucestershire, who lived in London and Northumberland for many years. He attended Ampleforth College, where his art teacher was the sculptor John Bunting. His father was Field-Marshal Sir Francis Festing and he was also a soldier, 1960–8. He worked at Sotheby's, 1968–81, being director of the English picture department, 1971–81, then took up painting full-time. Showed annually with RP from 1981, becoming a member in 1989, in 2000 being appointed vice-president, in 2002 president. Painted portraits of many well-known people, including HM Queen Elizabeth II and other members of the royal family. The Royal Collection, National Portrait Gallery, House of Lords, House of Commons, Marylebone Cricket Club at Lord's and National Gallery of Ireland, Dublin, hold examples. Festing's recreations were hunting, shooting, fishing and gardening; his portrait of the Northumbrian huntsman Owen Balding was included in the RP exhibitions People's Portraits, which toured in 2000–1, including DLI Museum & Art Gallery, Durham. As well as maintaining a studio in London, Festing lived at Colwell, near Hexham, Northumberland, for many years.

Elsie FEW 1909–1980 Painter in oil, artist in collage and teacher, brought up in Jamaica. She studied at the Slade School of Fine Art, in Paris and at the Bartlett School of Architecture. Married the artist Claude Rogers in 1937 and became associated with the Euston Road School, participating in the Euston Road exhibition at Wakefield City Art Gallery in 1948. She exhibited in London, later shows including Whitechapel Art Gallery, 1973, and Christopher Hull's Annexe Gallery, Wimbledon, in 1979. In 1981, there was a memorial exhibition at Bury St Edmunds Art Gallery, which included sensitive landscapes from the Euston Road period and abstract collages, which she had begun to create in 1968 shortly before a stroke and partial paralysis. For a time she was a member of LG and RWA and was senior lecturer and head of the art department at Gipsy Hill Training College. Victoria & Albert Museum and Arts Council bought her work. Lived for some years at Somerton, Suffolk. In 2002, the Belgrave Gallery held a joint Rogers and Few show.

Michael FFOLKES 1925–1988 Cartoonist, illustrator and writer, born and lived in London, his real name was Brian Davis and he was the son of commercial artist Walter Davis. He chose his pseudonym out of *Burke's Peerage*, and it suited his quirky, flamboyant, irreverent personality. ffolkes was educated at Leigh Hall College, Essex, then St Martin's School of Art, 1943, under John Farleigh. After Royal Naval service he was at Chelsea School of Art, 1946–9, with Ceri Richards and Robert Medley. After graduation for seven years ffolkes freelanced; his work was to appear in *Punch*, *Playboy*, *Reader's Digest*, *Private Eye* and the *New Yorker*. He created characters in the *Daily Telegraph's* Peter Simple satirical column and illustrated over 50 books, including Claud Cockburn's *Aspects of English History* and the Folio Society edition of Anita Loos' *Gentlemen Prefer Blondes*. His own publications included *How to Draw Cartoons*, 1963; *ffolkes' Companion to the Pop Scene*, 1977; and his picture autobiography *ffundamental ffolkes*, 1985. Balliol College, Oxford, contains a set of commissioned caricatures of eminent dons by him. Retrospective at The Cartoon Art Museum, 2003.

Charles FFOULKES 1868–1947 Museum curator, writer and painter, born in London, who studied at Oxford University, and in Paris including lessons from Carolus Duran. He became an expert on armoury, for many years curator of armouries at the Tower of London, from 1917–33 curator at Imperial War Museum. He lectured at Oxford University and wrote a series of books, including *The Armourer and his Craft*. Showed at RA, RBA, Walker Art Gallery in Liverpool and at Paris Salon. Lived finally in Oxford.

Terry FFYFFE 1957– Figurative artist, born in Melbourne, who studied there at Praluan College of Art, 1975–7, then travelled extensively through Australia, in 1979 spending time painting with the Aborigines of Millingimbi Island, Darwin. Won a first prize, Discerning Eye, 1995, and a Lady Cholmondeley Prize, Eastern Open, 1997. Mixed shows included Christian Art, Crypt Gallery, 1994, and Erotica, The Erotica Gallery, Olympia, 1997. There were solo exhibitions at Alternative Arts, 1993, and Studio Secrets, Lamont Gallery, 1998, with further shows including 2004.

Elizabeth FIDDAMAN 1911– Painter, mural artist, printmaker and teacher; her father was an architect, William Fiddaman. She was educated in Coulsdon, Surrey, and continued to live in that locality, latterly at Sanderstead. She studied at Croydon Art School, her teachers including Kenneth Holmes and Maurice Wheatley, 1930–4, then at the Royal College of Art, 1934–7. During the war she was engaged in camouflage work for Ministry of Home Security for five years, then taught part-time at Croydon and Sutton Schools of Art. Exhibited RA.

Nic FIDDIAN-GREEN 1963– Sculptor and draughtsman, notable for his studies of horses' heads, heads of Christ and romantic landscapes in charcoal. Fiddian-Green gained a foundation diploma at Chelsea College of Art; an honours degree in sculpture at Wimbledon College of Art; then a diploma in lost-wax bronze casting at Central St Martins College of Art. He was married to the potter Henrietta Hutley. For the first two years they lived on the island of Gozo, where he established the first foundry, and from the early 1990s he worked on commissions for the cathedral and Capuchin monastery there. Fiddian-Green showed widely in Malta and London, where in 1997 he participated in a mixed show at the Sladmore Gallery and had a solo exhibition at Air Gallery. Walton Contemporary Art, Melitensia Gallery near Valletta, Glyndebourne Opera House and the Hannah Peschar Gallery & Sculpture Garden at Ockley had work on permanent exhibition. Fiddian-Green cast pieces at his foundry in a barn adjoining his cottage at Bramley, Surrey; he worked mainly in bronze, also in lead, marble, copper and clay.

Constance Louise FIDLER 1904– Portrait painter and teacher. She was educated at Wigan Girls' High School, then attended Liverpool City School of Art, under George Marples, and Royal College of Art under William Rothenstein. After studying to teach she held a series of art teaching posts, latterly in the Southport and Liverpool area, where she was associated with the Boys' Clubs movement. Exhibited NEAC, RBA and had one-man shows in Birmingham and Liverpool, where the City Libraries bought her work. Member of Sandon Studios Society and Liverpool Academy. Lived at Freshfield, near Liverpool.

Frank FIDLER 1910–1995 Self-taught artist, born into a family of flower growers in north London at Edmonton. He showed an early talent for drawing, but was given no encouragement. Fidler was involved in the business after school and during holidays from early childhood, an experience which he said gave him his first sense of colour values. After becoming a nurseryman at Hoddesdon, he started a successful greengrocery at Waltham Cross, taking up painting, mainly flower studies, in 1947, working well into the night. Having sold his pictures and had encouragement from other painters, in 1954 he disposed of his two shops and became a full-time artist, experimenting with various styles and other media such as abstraction and sculpture. From the late 1950s he showed at the Drian Gallery and with the Free Painters and Sculptors, of which he was a fellow, being in its First Two Decades 1952–72 show in 1989. Solo exhibitions also included Lundsbjerg Art Gallery, Denmark, 1961. The landscape around Barkway, Hertfordshire, where he settled in the 1960s, converting three cottages into a single, thatched, sixteenth-century house, was an important influence on Fidler's work. He completed commissions for public buildings in Hertfordshire, including two ceramic murals for the Civic Centre in St Albans. He was an active member of Harlow Playhouse Gallery, where he became friendly with Henry Moore. Leicestershire Education Authority and the Art Gallery of New South Wales, Sydney, Australia, hold his work, which was shown by The Harlequin Gallery in 2004.

Dick FIELD 1912– Painter, draughtsman and teacher, born in Winson, Gloucestershire, who was married to the artist Molly Field. Studied at Cheltenham School of Art under Gerald Gardiner and the Royal College of Art with Gilbert Spencer. Taught at Dewsbury School of Art, Yorkshire. He exhibited RA and widely in the provinces. Lived in Wakefield, Yorkshire.

Dorothie FIELD 1915–1994 Painter, draughtsman, art promoter and teacher, born in London, who sometimes signed work Dorothie Langridge. She studied at Highbury Hill School (with Nan Youngman), 1927–31; Chelsea School of Art (teachers including Henry Moore), 1931–2; Nottingham School of Art, 1933–6; and Birmingham University, for a social services diploma, 1941–2. Despite two marriages and having children, she continued to paint, in a variety of styles. Field was a full-time artists' consultant and freelance exhibitions organiser from 1964, founding the Gallery 359 and Field Galleries. Coal mining, war and peace, the origins of life and death and environmental problems were key themes, pursued over long periods. She was represented in group shows organised by the Arts Council, SEA, AIA and Pictures for Schools. Had numerous solo shows, starting with Wertheim Gallery, 1937, with a retrospective at Nottingham University, 1990; and exhibitions at Manor House, Ilkley, 1992; Usher Gallery, Lincoln, 1994; and Rufford Craft Centre, 1995. Bradford University and other public collections hold examples.

Jonathan FIELD 1963– Artist and teacher, born in Ipswich, Suffolk, who gained his master's in visual art at Lancaster University, 1981–4, then a doctorate there, 1991–8, his thesis being on the late abstraction of Gerhard Richter. During that time he lectured at Suffolk College, later moving to America to teach at Savannah College of Art and Design, Georgia. Exhibited in France, Germany, Italy, Belgium and Canada and regularly in East Anglia. In 2000, his solo exhibition Maxwell's Demon at Christchurch Mansion, Ipswich, which used black rubber and pins to form images of his lover Yuka Hasegawa, suggested constellations of stars or molecules in flux.

Molly FIELD 1912– Painter, born in Keighley, Yorkshire, who originally worked under the name of Molly Clapham. Married the artist and teacher Dick Field. After Keighley Girls' Grammar School attended Leeds College of Art, 1932–3, then Royal College of Art, 1934–8, with Ernest Tristram. Showed at RA, WIAC and the Art Gallery, Wakefield, the Yorkshire town where she lived.

Natalie FIELD 1898–1977 Painter and miniaturist, born in London, but resident in South Africa from the year of her birth. She studied at Slade School of Fine Art, 1916–22, where her teachers included Henry Tonks, Frederick Brown and Philip Wilson Steer, and at the Westminster School of Art under Walter Sickert. Returning to South Africa, she lived at Umkomaas, Natal, and took part in group exhibitions and had many solo shows. She was a member of the South African Society of Artists and just before World War II helped found the Transvaal Art Society, of which early on she was president. South African National Gallery, Cape Town, holds her work.

Patricia FIELD 1926– Mural painter and illustrator, born in Hull, Yorkshire. Attended Malvern College for Girls, then Manchester School of Art, 1945–8, under Ian Grant. Exhibited Festival of Britain and in Yorkshire, where she lived at Hessle.

Peter L FIELD 1920– Painter, modeller, printmaker and teacher, born in Winson, Gloucestershire. He studied at Cheltenham School of Art, 1937–9, with A Seaton-White, then at Goldsmiths' College School of Art, 1946–9, under Clive Gardiner. After teaching in Paignton and Swindon he went to Birmingham, retiring in 1982 as head of the art and design faculty at City of Birmingham Polytechnic. Showed at RA and in the provinces and Swindon Museum

& Art Gallery holds his work. Lived in Bournville, Birmingham.

Stanley FIELD 1908– Watercolourist and teacher, born in London. He studied at St Martin's School of Art and at the Royal College of Art, his teachers including Gilbert Spencer and William Rothenstein. Taught for London County Council from 1934, until World War II followed by periods at Reimann and Bath Schools of Art. After wartime service lecturing on art to servicemen and as an official war artist Field taught at Gravesend School of Art and Borough Polytechnic before moving to South Africa until 1958 where he lectured at Witwatersrand Technical College and was from 1954–8 a senior lecturer and then head of the Port Elizabeth Technical College. While there he had several solo shows. In 1958 Field emigrated to Australia.

Steve FIELD 1954– Artist in acrylic, true fresco, mixed media and sculpture, including bronze, steel and concrete. He was born in Saltash, Cornwall, graduating from Sheffield University and gaining his master's degree in fine art from Wolverhampton Polytechnic, 1981–4, teachers including Malcolm Hughes, Knighton Hosking and Graham Cooper. Field was a joint research fellow at Wolverhampton Polytechnic, 1981–4; was a member of the West Midlands Public Art Collective, 1985–8; from 1989 being artist-in-residence for Dudley. In 1992 he won a Royal Society of Arts Art for Architecture Award. Was a member of LG, Midlands Group, Art and Architecture and the Birmingham Art Trust. Field's murals were influenced by the artists Edward Wadsworth and Percy Wyndham Lewis, his sculptural works by organic, especially spiral, forms, as in his Thomas Attwood memorial at Halesowen. He shared a show at Wolverhampton Polytechnic, 1984, also being featured at Ikon Gallery, Birmingham. Lived in Leamington Spa, Warwickshire.

Brian FIELDING 1933–1987 Painter and teacher, born in Sheffield, Yorkshire, where he attended the local College of Art, 1950–4, then Royal College of Art, 1954–7. He gained an Abbey Minor Travelling Scholarship in 1958. Although he had a one-man show at Rowan Gallery in 1962 and again in 1964, Fielding's work was rather neglected by the dealers. His works, influenced by Zen Buddhism, were highly regarded by his peers. Fielding was an influential teacher at Ravensbourne College of Art and Design from 1962. He was included in the Survey of Abstract Painters at Camden Arts Centre in 1967 and had several more solo exhibitions before gaining a retrospective at Mappin Art Gallery, Sheffield, and tour, 1986. In 1995 David Holmes Contemporary Art, Peterborough, reviewed Fielding's output. Arts Council and Royal College of Art hold examples. Lived in London.

Jim FIELDING 1962– Painter, illustrator and maker of mixed-media constructions. He studied at Camberwell School of Arts and Crafts and Royal College of Art. Showed at Royal College as well as Cartoonists Gallery, Coliseum Theatre, Royal Festival Hall, Gardner Arts Centre in Brighton and England & Co, where his Locomotive was included in the 1991 show Art in Boxes.

Duggie FIELDS 1945– Painter in acrylic on canvas, born in Salisbury, Wiltshire, brought up in Tidworth, who attended Chelsea School of Art, 1964–8, after briefly studying architecture at Regent Street Polytechnic. Teachers included John Hoyland, Ian Stephenson, Lawrence Gowing, Allen Jones, Patrick Caulfield and Bernard Cohen. As a student his work moved from Minimal, Conceptual and Constructivist phases to a more hard-edge, post-Pop figuration. After he had visited America for the first time in 1968, Fields said that "my perspective on life was never the same." By the mid-1970s his work included many elements that were later defined as Post-Modernism. In 1983 in Tokyo, sponsored by the Shiseido Corporation, a gallery was created especially for his show, and the artist and his work were simultaneously featured in a television, billboard and subway advertising campaign throughout the country. In London Fields lived in a flat that reflected the 1950s–1960s, wore makeup and a Teddy Boy haircut. Mixed shows included Fashion and Surrealism, Victoria & Albert Museum, 1988. Had a solo show at Hamet Gallery, 1971, later ones including Albermarle Gallery, 1987, and Rempire Gallery, New York, 1990. Shared an exhibition with Andrew Logan at A&D Gallery, 2002; had a solo exhibition at Zimmer Stewart Gallery, Arundel, 2003; another, Digital Age, at A&D Gallery, 2004. Arts Council holds his work, which had wide international press and television documentary coverage.

Lis FIELDS 1963– Painter, born in Annapolis, Maryland, America, married to the artist Mark Hutchinson. She grew up in Cambridge, England, doing a foundation course in art and design at the College of Art & Technology there, 1982–3; graduated with honours from Camberwell School of Arts, 1983–6; studying drawing and painting with Maggi Hambling at Morley College, 1986. Fields lived in New York, 1987–91, and in Los Angeles from 1991–8, from 1992–6. She was personal assistant to the film director John Dahl, then returned to England, based in London. Notable exhibitions included solo show, Source, The Wellcome Trust Genome Campus, Hinxton, Cambridge, 2000; Space SE1 Gallery, 2001; Fusion, Spring Break and Stars of the East, Britart, and solo show, Saatchi & Saatchi, both 2002; and Selfridges, window installation, and solo show, Michael Naimski Gallery, both 2003. Bank of New York, London; Nanoscience Centre, Cambridge; Mackenzie Editorial, New York; Smith & Nephew, Huntingdon; and Instant Genetics, Paolo Alto, were among many corporate collections holding works.

Ray FIELDS 1930– Graphic designer and film-maker who from 1960 was employed as a full-time teacher of graphic design after studying in various schools. He went on to become senior lecturer in the faculty of art and design at Liverpool Polytechnic. Fields' films were shown at ICA in London and widely in the north of England. Showed from 1954 with Liverpool Academy, with RCamA of which he was president and elsewhere. Solo exhibitions included Rushworth Gallery, Liverpool.

Celia FIENNES 1902–1998 Wood engraver and painter, a direct descendant of Celia Fiennes the seventeenth-century traveller. She was the last survivor of the group of engravers chosen by Robert Gibbings to illustrated Golden Cockerel Press books between the wars. For him she illustrated *Aesop's Fables*, 1926, and would have added Nicholas Breton's *Twelve Months* but meningitis meant that Eric Ravilious had to do it. Celia, also known as Molly, Fiennes studied with Noel Rooke at the Central School of Arts and Crafts from 1924; he found her work with the Arts and Crafts Exhibition Society, organising exhibitions; and she married him in 1932. Rooke produced some sensitive studies of his much younger wife. Her absorption into the Arts and Crafts movement was deepened when she moved into the Rooke family home in Bedford Park, for several years living with her father-in-law Thomas Matthews Rooke, who had been associated with Edward Burne-Jones, William Morris and John Ruskin. In 1960 Celia moved to Culworth, Oxfordshire, where she resumed her own work, occasionally acting as a guide for the family seat, Broughton Castle, Banbury.

Jini FIENNES 1938–1993 Writer and painter, born in Chichester, Sussex (her unmarried name was Jennifer Lash, which she used for some of her books), her father Brigadier Hal Lash, of the Indian Army. She married farmer-turned-photographer Mark Fiennes, with whom she led a nomadic life in England and Ireland, renovating many properties. They raised seven children, including a foster-child, among them the actors Ralph and Joseph Fiennes. An unhappy childhood spurred Jini to give out to people, her intense spirituality evident in her books and pictures. After an unhappy convent schooling she left home, worked as under-matron in a preparatory school and at 23 published her first novel, *The Burial*, to critical acclaim. Her last novel, *Blood Ties*, published posthumously in 1997, was featured in a BBC2 Television programme, in *The Works* series, that year. Jini, who worked in gouache, charcoal and oil, attended Farnham Art School, 1954, and Byam Shaw School of Art, 1982. Took part in a group show at Penwith Gallery, St Ives, in 1985; also had solo exhibitions in Suffolk at Halesworth and Westleton Chapel Galleries, both 1987, and in London's Holland Gallery, 1988. In 1986, she developed cancer and embarked on a tour, on foot and with a backpack, of the holy sites of France and Spain, the book *On Pilgrimage* appearing in 1991. Died in Odstock, Wiltshire.

Susannah FIENNES 1961– Painter and teacher who was born and continued to work in London. She attended Slade School of Fine Art, 1979–83, obtaining a first-class honours degree. In 1983 she won a Boise Travel Scholarship to Italy, the year following gaining an RA British Institution Fund Award. Taught art and history of art at Dulwich College part-time, 1985–7, then conducted a private drawing class. Fiennes showed in Christie's Pick of Graduate Art in 1983, two years later appearing in a watercolour show at Alpine Gallery. Other mixed exhibitions included Agnew Young Contemporaries in 1988 and John Player Portrait Award in 1989. In 1990 Fiennes shared a show at Cadogan Contemporary, having a solo exhibition there in 1992 and one of Oman and Uzbekistan pictures at Grosvenor Gallery, 1999.

FIENNES-FOSTER 1918– Painter whose married name was Barbara Otley. She studied painting in early 1960s with Kristin Berge, a student of Oskar Kokoschka. Became a member of Free Painters and Sculptors in 1964, also belonging to Chichester and Downland Art Societies and other Sussex groups. Showed also at Chenil and Mall Galleries. Lived in Rustington, Sussex.

Denis FILDES 1889–1974 Painter, born in London, son of the Victorian narrative artist Sir Luke Fildes. He was educated at Stone House, Broadstairs, and at HMS *Britannia* and became a professional sailor, attaining the rank of commander. He was badly injured and burned when the HMS *Natal* was blown up at Cromarty in 1915. Invalided out, he turned to painting for a living. Early on he produced flower pictures and seascapes but, failing to find a market, concentrated on portraits. Fildes considered his finest examples were HM Queen Elizabeth II at the Royal Air Force Club; Field-Marshal Lord Montgomery, at St Paul's School, Barnes; and Sir Edmund Hillary, conqueror of Everest. The large double portrait of The Queen and Duke of Edinburgh at the Royal Naval College, Greenwich, is stiffer and less successful; Fildes was an uneven painter. He was a member of the United Services Club and exhibited at Walker's Galleries, RA, Walker Art Gallery in Liverpool and elsewhere. For many years he was curator of the Antrobus family museum at Amesbury, Wiltshire, but health in 1973 forced him to give up residency there, and he had a bungalow built nearby. The Imperial War Museum has Fildes' archive.

Michael FINCH 1957– Artist and teacher, born in London, who graduated in fine art from Ravensbourne College of Art, 1976–80, obtaining his master's at Royal College of Art, 1982–6. Won the Wiggins Teape Award, 1976; Milner Kite Award, 1982; Burston and Unilever Awards and Unilever Purchase Prize, all 1985. As well as a number of visiting lectureships, including Ravensbourne, Wimbledon and St Albans Schools of Art and Kent Institute of Art & Design, Finch taught at Richmond College, London, 1988–91, and from 1994 at Parsons School of Art, in Paris. Showed at Northern Young Contemporaries, Manchester, 1978; Peter de Francia and Artists Who Studied Under Him, Camden Arts Centre, 1987; *Economist* Building Gallery, 1993; Credo, 1994, at Purdy Hicks (he had been co-ordinator and curator for its predecessor, Pomeroy Purdy Gallery, 1989–92); and Towards An Abstraction, David Holmes Contemporary Art, Peterborough, 1995–6. Had a solo show at City Museum, Peterborough, 1983, later ones including Purdy Hicks, 1994, and David Holmes, 1995. Lived in Senlis, France.

Patricia FINCH 1921–2001 Sculptor of figurative works in clay, teacher, born and lived in London. She was the daughter of a doctor and studied medicine, including two years' anatomy at King's College and West London Hospital, her ambition "to be a plastic surgeon or a sculptor". Studied art at the Hampstead Institute, 1953–7, and taught dancing part-time. Finch received her first portrait commission in 1958. Was elected to SWA, SPS, Society of Numismatic Artists and Designers, Art Workers' Guild and Contemporary Portrait Society and became a fellow of RBS in 1990. She was a demonstrator to the Tate Gallery Summer Course in Sculpture, 1983, and tutor to the Hulton Studio for the Visually Handicapped, 1986–90. Showed at RA and had exhibitions in London and widely abroad, including a solo show with the Foreign Press Association, 1999. Royal Academy of Dancing holds her commemorative medal of Dame Margot Fonteyn, and Bank of England Museum, Royal Academy of Music and Poetry Society also hold her work. One of Finch's daughters was the musician and broadcaster Lucie Skeaping.

Richard Henry Carew FINCH 1908–1985 Landscape painter in oil. Born in London, Finch studied at the Bartlett School of Architecture, 1928–33, and for a time practised as an architect. He then studied art at the Grosvenor School of Modern Art. Exhibited at the RHA and elsewhere in Dublin, where he lived, signing his work C F or Carew Finch. Finch wrote a number of pamphlets on aspects of architecture and is remembered as "a quiet, unassuming gentleman of a very charitable disposition".

Roger FINCH 1924–1989 Painter, teacher and illustrator, notable for seascapes of English east-coast barges, born in Harrow, Middlesex. After service in the Fleet Air Arm and qualification as an art teacher, Finch moved to Ipswich, Suffolk, in 1948, teaching in several local schools. His detailed knowledge of boats and the sea enabled him to illustrate marine books as well as make accurate portraits of Thames spritsail barges. Shared a show with Roger Hollis at Haste Gallery, Ipswich, in 1959, and was included in its fortieth anniversary show in 1998.

William Robert FINCH 1905–2003 Self-taught artist in various media, journalist and teacher, born in Lowestoft, Suffolk. He trained to teach at College of St Mark and St John. Showed at RA, East End Academy and widely in the provinces. He was head of the art department at Beal Grammar School, Ilford, and Chigwell School. While still at Beal's, Finch developed a successful sideline as lecturer to adult groups, rural architecture a particular subject, writing on it for Essex and Kent newspapers. A significant spin-off was his authoritative book *Country Buildings: how to appreciate them and how to sketch them*, 1951. Having come from a sea-going family, he wrote and illustrated an account of the East Anglian fishing industry, *The Sea in My Blood*, 1992, which sold out and was reprinted. Finch donated over 100 works, his own pictorial record of Lowestoft and its fishermen, to Lowestoft Library. Lived at Weybread, Diss, Norfolk.

Anna R FINDLAY 1885–1968 Colour woodcut and linocut artist producing work in the manner of the Grosvenor School of Art, simplified and lyrical designs. Lived in Glasgow, where she studied at the School of Art, 1912–14, exhibition venues including RSA, Royal Glasgow Institute of the Fine Arts, Manchester City Art Gallery and Redfern Gallery. From 1925 she was a member of the Glasgow Society of Lady Artists.

Denise FINDLAY 1973– Figurative painter and draughtsman who gained an honours degree in fine art from Glasgow School of Art, 1996. She was elected a member of Glasgow Art Club, 1997, and received the Elizabeth Greenshields Foundation Awards, 1998 and 2001. Findlay believed "that painting is a purely visual experience...and should speak for itself.... Artists that have influenced me are Vermeer, Andrew Wyeth, the Glasgow Boys, the drawings of Claudio Bravo, Velázquez, Alison Watt and Rembrandt." Exhibitions included SSA, 1995; New Generation Show, Compass Gallery, Glasgow, 1996; Kumulus Gallery, Maastricht, Netherlands, 1997; The Academy for Fine Arts, Bilzen, Belgium, 1998; Royal Glasgow Institute, McLellan Galleries, 2000; and Spring Exhibition, Portland Gallery, 2002. Among her solo shows were the Scottish Gallery, Edinburgh, from 1999. HRH The Prince of Wales and Picardy Television hold Findlay's work.

Margaret Cross Primrose FINDLAY 1902–1968 Sculptor and teacher, born in Glenlivet, Banffshire, who attended Glasgow School of Art, 1920–5, under Archibald Dawson. She taught at Beacon School, Bridge of Allan, and Hillhead High School in Glasgow. Among her public works were a sculpture for the Mercat Cross there, 1930, and a frieze of figures for the Glasgow Empire Exhibition, 1938. Findlay joined the Glasgow Society of Lady Artists in 1926. She also exhibited at the Royal Glasgow Institute of the Fine Arts; RSA, winning its Guthrie Award in 1928, enabling her to study in Italy; Walker Art Gallery, Liverpool; and RA. Died in Bearsden, Dunbartonshire.

Peter Gillanders FINDLAY 1917– Painter and teacher, born in Madras, India. He was educated in Suva, Fiji, then in Yorkshire. He studied art at Leeds College of Art, 1935–9, under Douglas Sharpus Andrews, then at the Slade School of Fine Art, with Randolph Schwabe, from 1939–40, then after a war interval from 1944–5. Taught for a period at Accrington School of Art, Lancashire. He did some technical book illustration and showed widely in Yorkshire. Lived in Accrington.

Sheila FINDLAY 1928– Painter, designer and illustrator, born in Auchlishie, Kirriemuir, Angus. She was noted for her richly coloured, decorative domestic scenes and still lifes. Studied at Edinburgh College of Art, specialising in stained glass and mural painting and working in the department of design, 1945–51, her teachers included John Maxwell and Leonard Rosoman. In 1949 gained a postgraduate studentship, followed by a year's senior travelling scholarship, spent in France, Italy and Sweden. In 1950s worked in London as a freelance designer and illustrator, working for major publishing houses while showing at RA, LG and elsewhere, being elected RWS in 1968. Had solo show at Catto Gallery, 1990. Later appearances included The Autumn Show, The Wykeham Gallery, Stockbridge, 2004. By then Findlay's work was in the collections of the Cambridge Education Authority, the Government Art Collection and Edinburgh College of Art. Was married to the artist Alfred Hackney and lived in Cobham, Kent, with another studio in Edinburgh.

FINE ARTZ 1964– A group formed in this year by Slade School of Fine Art students Terry Atkinson, John Bowstead, Roger Jeffs and Bernard Jennings which collaborated on a work called Action Chair. In 1966 Fine Artz presented a projection and sound show entitled *Miss Misty and the Tri-Cool Data* at Birmingham Polytechnic. Jeffs later wrote that although Fine Artz was shortlived it "served its purpose (thorn in the side of the Slade and we had fun!). Apart from the Chair, etc, we wrote essays which appeared in *Ark*, journal of the Royal College of Art, circa 1964–5, the nearest we got to a Fine Artz manifesto."

Stephen FINER 1949– Painter, mainly of the human head on a small scale, born and based in London. Mixed shows included Small Work, Nicola Jacobs Gallery, 1981–2; Berkeley Square Gallery, from 1988; Basle Art Fair, 1991; The Portrait Now, National Portrait Gallery, 1993–4; The Discerning Eye, Mall Galleries (invited by Martin Gayford), 1996; and About the Figure, Six Chapel Row, Bath, 1999. Had a series of solo exhibitions at Four Vine Lane from 1981, later ones including Bernard Jacobson Gallery from 1992, Heads, Agnew, 1998, Paintings, Pallant House, Chichester, 2001, People. Charleston Gallery, Firle, 2002, and Paintings, Art Space Gallery, 2004. In 1999 Agnew showed his portrait of the judge Sir Morris Finer. Arts Council, British Council and Contemporary Art Society hold examples.

Peter FINK 1948– Sculptor and teacher, born in London, graduated as an engineer from University of Prague,

Czechoslovakia, 1969; studied sculpture at St Martin's, 1969–72; taught there for three years; then graduated in philosophy at University College, 1978. He was sculpture consultant to Newport, Gwent, where he was based, 1988, gaining a research fellowship at Cardiff Art School, 1989. Fink said that he was "interested in working with architects and others who are committed to the built environment," which stemmed from "my belief that artists should work openly in the public domain." Commissions included Shiva, Punjabi University, India, 1980; Castle Cross, Banbury, Oxfordshire, 1981; Ark, Jerusalem, Israel, 1986; and Riverfront Promenade, Newport, 1989. Fink latterly worked extensively with the performance artist Anne Bean. In 1992 they realised Light Year, then the largest temporary public art project in the United Kingdom, which took Canary Wharf as a canvas for a huge light sculpture, seen from over 40 kilometres and by millions of Londoners.

Ian Hamilton FINLAY 1925–2006 Writer and artist in many media, born in Nassau, Bahamas, of Scottish parents; brought to Scotland as a child. After a short period at Glasgow School of Art Finlay saw military service in Germany, then did a variety of agricultural jobs including shepherding in the Orkneys. Began to write fiction, drama and poetry, some single-word poems presaging concrete poetry. In 1961 Finlay with Jessie McGuffie started the Wild Hawthorn Press to publish contemporary work, for most of the 1960s publishing the magazine *Poor. Old. Tired. Horse.* In 1966 Finlay and his wife Sue moved to an isolated farmhouse near Dunsyre, Lanarkshire, transformed the garden into a sculpture park as an antidote to the modern movement and sought to promote an art which pays homage to a lean, classical tradition. Aptly he changed the name of his home to Little Sparta. Finlay had many solo shows, including Deichtorhallen, Hamburg, and Buro Sophia Ungers, Cologne, both in Germany, respectively 1995 and 1997, Aberdeen Art Gallery, 2001, Tate St Ives, Ingleby Gallery, Edinburgh, and 100 Postcards at Milton Keyes Gallery, all 2002; Victoria Miro, 2003; and prints at UBS Painewebber Art Gallery, New York, 2004. His later installations included Serpentine Gallery, The Ark and Den Haag, Netherlands, all 1998. In addition to Little Sparta, Finlay created another equally poetic garden in France, unknown to anyone except his closest associates. It was celebrated in his book *Fleur de L'Air: A Garden in Provence*, published by Wild Hawthorn Press in 2004. There was an eightieth-birthday show at Inverleith House, Royal Botanic Gardens, Edinburgh, in 2005. He was shortlisted for the Turner Prize in 1985. The Scottish National Gallery of Modern Art holds a body of work by him.

Ann FINLAYSON 1943–1999 Painter, draughtsman and teacher, born in Glasgow, daughter of the artist Helen Hay. Annie Finlayson studied at Glasgow School of Art, 1960; gained her National Diploma, Kingston School of Art, 1960–4; and her master's, first class, Royal College of Art, 1965–8. At the Royal College she won the Henriques Gift, 1968. Finlayson was assistant to Bridget Riley and Peter Sedgley at St Katherine's Dock Scheme for Artists' Studios, 1969–71; to Alistair Grant, 1971; to Leonard Rosoman, for large murals, 1972–4; and to Ken Baynes, design consultant, during preparation of WAC exhibitions, 1972–6. Finlayson's teaching experience comprised visiting lecturer, Exeter College of Art, 1970–1; Vauxhall Manor Secondary School, 1971–2; part-time lecturing at City and Guilds School of Art, 1976–8; Kingston Polytechnic, 1976–90; Berkshire College of Art, 1978–84; and London Guildhall University (Sir John Cass), 1984–5. She travelled extensively in Europe and North America. Finlayson participated in numerous group exhibitions, in 1984 winning the RA Daler-Rowney Watercolour Award. Solo and two-artist exhibitions included New Art Centre, 1969; Triad Gallery, 1975; Oxford Gallery, at invitation of Carel Weight, 1976; Stirling Gallery, also at his suggestion, 1982; Adam Gallery, 1985; and Thornton Bevan Arts, 1997. In 1995, Finlayson married the ceramist and designer John Barham Adams, also Royal College of Art-trained, whose father John Adams was founder, managing director and designer of Poole Pottery and whose daughter, Louise Adams, was art director at Royal Crown Derby China. Bolton Museum and Art Gallery, the Bank of Boston and Glyndebourne Opera House are among collections holding the work of Finlayson, who latterly contracted and died from multiple system atrophy.

Donald FINLEY 1902–1981 Artist and writer, born in Australia at Victoria, studying art in Melbourne at its National Gallery. He moved to England and became films and exhibitions officer at Australia House, 1945–67. An industrious man, Finley helped found the Australian Artists' Association in London. He had an interest in amateur theatricals, and in the Association's first exhibition at the RWS Conduit Street gallery in 1953 showed two stage designs. In 1963 his book *Modern Australian Painting* was published, an excellent, well-illustrated account. The National Library of Australia, Canberra, holds Finley's archive, and typescript of *John Peter Russell: the lost impressionist 1858–1930*, compiled between 1963 and 1981.

Jean FINN: *see* **Jean DREW**

Michael FINN 1921–2002 Painter, sculptor, administrator and teacher, who grew up near Brooklands, Surrey. His father was an architect. After serving in World War II in the Royal Air Force, training as a pilot in Canada, Finn taught in Somerset, then became head of Falmouth School of Art, 1958–72, and Bath Academy of Art, Corsham, 1972–82, starting to paint full time in the latter year. Earthy, luminous colours were a characteristic of his work, which was shown in Artists from Cornwall, RWA, 1992. He also took part in mixed shows at Newlyn Orion Gallery, Penzance, at the Wolf at the Door gallery there and at Penwith Society of Arts. Solo shows were held at Festival Gallery, Bath, 1978; Newlyn Orion, 1989; and Newlyn and Falmouth Art Galleries, both 2001. Lived in St Just, Cornwall.

Paul FINNEGAN fl. from early 1980s– Figurative artist whose work had a strong decorative element, he graduated from University of Ulster in Belfast, Northern Ireland, 1981, where he remained. Showed widely through Ireland and had work chosen for shows in England, France and Scotland. Took part in RUA Exhibition, Ulster Museum, and in Oireachtas, both 1986; in 1994 participated in Works on Paper and Beyond the Partitions, put on by Queen Street Studios, Belfast, with which he was associated. Solo shows included several in Belfast: Crescent Arts Centre, 1983, Fenderesky Gallery, 1984, and Art Advice Gallery, 1989, and his Head to Head was shown at Zakks Barbers Shop, 1990.

Peter FINNEMORE 1963– Artist, and teacher in a range of modern media, including installation and performance, schooled at Pontyberem, studying foundation nearby at Dyfed College of Art, Carmarthen, 1981–2. Then gained an honours degree in fine art, photography, at Glasgow School of Art, 1984–7; his postgraduate diploma there, 1987–8; and a fine art master's in photography at University of Michigan, Ann Arbor, America, 1992–4. Awards included 1st and 2nd Prizes for colour photography, National Eisteddfod of Wales, 1990; Thomas and Elizabeth Williams Scholarship, 1992–4; fellowship, American Photography Institute, 1995; and joint winner, Eighth Oriel Mostyn Open Exhibition, 1996. Later residencies included Light Work Visual Studies, Syracuse, New York, 1999. Had considerable teaching experience in Britain and America, including assistant professorship in photography, University of Michigan, 1995. From 1996, Finnemore was a self-employed photographic artist and teacher, including Bournemouth & Poole College of Art & Design; Swansea Institute of Higher Education, University of Wales Institute, Cardiff; and University of Wales College, Newport. His work was widely published and featured in group exhibitions. Later solo shows included Oriel 31, Newtown, 2001. English and Scottish Arts Councils; Oriel Mostyn, Llandudno; and several American public collections hold examples. Lived in Pontiets, Carmarthenshire.

Hubert Arthur FINNEY 1905–1991 Painter, draughtsman and teacher who in 1915 was invited to attend evening classes at Bromley School of Art, in 1918 winning a trade scholarship to Beckenham School of Art. Finney studied painting with Amy Katherine Browning and etching with Eric Gill. Around 1927 he won a scholarship to the Royal College of Art, where he studied under William Rothenstein, who befriended and drew him, other artists encountered there including Barnett Freedman, Percy Horton, Albert Houthuesen, Morris Kestelman and Gerald Ososki. In 1929 after graduation he took up a travelling scholarship, returning to teach part-time at Chelsea School of Art under Percy Hague Jowett, then Harold Sandys Williamson. In the period 1927–34 Finney exhibited several times at the NEAC and in 1935, after the birth of his first son, Brian, his painting Mother and Child was sold to Carlisle Art Gallery. Finney joined the light rescue service of Civil Defence in 1939 and lost touch with the Royal College, which was evacuated. After teaching for a time at Sutton School of Art until illness intervened, he then taught part-time under Anthony Betts at Reading University and was in charge of life drawing there when he retired in 1970. Although he was reclusive and hated showing his work, Finney did exhibit at the RA Summer Exhibition, with the PS, RP and at the Paris Salon. A large solo exhibition took place at the University of Oxford's Institute of Education in 1964.

Rose FINN-KELCEY 1945– Sculptor, performance and installations artist, teacher, born Northampton. She studied at the School of Art there, at Ravensbourne College of Art and Chelsea School of Art for postgraduate work. Finn-Kelcey usually created for a particular space, such as Steam Installation, 1992, for Chisenhale Gallery, likened to a huge steam press. Group exhibitions included the Arts Council's The British Art Show, 1984; Shocks to the System, Royal Festival Hall and tour, 1991; and Young British Artists II, Saatchi Gallery, 1993, which, like Arts Council, holds her work. Solo shows included Bureau de Change at Matt's Gallery, 1988, Camden Arts Centre, 1997, and The Irish Museum of Modern Art, Kilmainham, 2003. Teaching included Byam Shaw School of Art. Lived in London.

Richard FINNY 1909–1987 Painter, draughtsman and teacher, born in London. After Dulwich College Finny attended Byam Shaw School of Drawing and Painting. He won the Rome Scholarship for mural painting in 1929, the youngest winner at the time and the first from Byam Shaw. His two years in Rome, however, were overcast by the depression which was to plague the rest of his life. In 1934 he began teaching art in schools, including Oundle. During World War II he was in Royal Engineers' camouflage section, seeing service in India and Burma. Unable to paint on demobilisation, he joined the Old Bleach Linen Company in Northern Ireland as assistant to director of design and publicity, but after two years returned to London to paint, then teaching, which he did until 1966. Alcoholics Anonymous helped him overcome a drink problem, but depression continued. Retrospective at Byam Shaw in 1988, proceeds to Medical Research Council. Finny's output was small, as he was so self-critical, but he did show at RA and Nineteen Thirties Society. Lived in Camberley, Surrey.

Joy FINZI 1907–1991 Portrait draughtsman of great sensitivity, musician and writer, born as Joyce Black in London where she studied at Central School of Arts and Crafts with John Skeaping. She married the composer Gerald Finzi in 1933 and they built their home at Ashmansworth, near Newbury in Berkshire, just before World War II, where she died. When early in the war Finzi founded the Newbury String Players she was administrator and played in the violins. She was careful in nurturing Finzi's work even after his terminal illness was diagnosed in 1951 and after his death founded the Finzi Trust. Many of her drawings were of musicians and writers, including Ralph Vaughan Williams, Howard Ferguson, Helen Thomas and David Jones. Her *Portrait Drawings* were published in 1987 and several volumes of poetry. Work held by National Portrait Gallery.

Sylvia FINZI 1948– Painter, draughtsman, printmaker and teacher who studied at Slade School of Fine Art. In 1983 she was visiting artist at Westfield College and she taught as visiting lecturer at Heatherley's School of Fine Art and at Munich's Volkshochschule. She was commissioned to make a mural for a new wing of Lewisham Hospital in the late 1980s. Finzi took part in many group exhibitions, including 1982 Hayward Annual and Woodlands Art Gallery in 1988. Also had a series of shows in England and abroad, including Swiss Cottage Gallery, Central Library, 2006. Victoria & Albert Museum and Bibliothèque Nationale, Paris, hold examples. Lived in London.

Liza FIOR 1962– Architect and teacher who was involved in muf (see separate entry). Fior studied at the Polytechnic of Central London and Canterbury College of Art and taught at the Architectural Association, 1989–95, and Royal College of Art, 1998–00.

Salvatore FIORELLO 1976– Painter, born in Wales, who gained a diploma in art and design at Hull College, 1993–5; a fine art honours degree, painting, University of Central England, Birmingham, 1995–8; and his master's in painting at Royal College of Art, 1998–00. He won the George Jackson Educational Award, 1995–6; Laing Painting Prize, 1998; T I Group Scholarship, 1998–00; Henderson Parkinson Travel Award (Italy) and John Crane New York Travel Award, both 1999; and Stephenson Harwood Prize, 2000. Group shows included Winter Exhibition, Ferens Art Gallery, Hull, from 1995–6; De Fine Art, Custard Factory, Birmingham, 1998; and On Swedish Ground: Young European Contemporary Art, Kristinehamns Konstmuseum, Sweden, 2000. Among solo exhibitions were Laurent Delaye Gallery, 2001. There, Fiorello showed emptied urban environments, uninhabited but "giving the impression of a space being watched."

Sarah FIRMIN 1933– Versatile artist, designer and teacher, born and lived in London, who gained her painting diploma at St Martin's School of Art, 1950–5, and her master's in contemporary art practice from Kingston University, 1996–8. Working at the London College of Printing as a student of Francis Carr, whom she married, Firmin helped pioneer the use of screen-printing as a fine art medium, as shown in an exhibition at the College's Eckersley Gallery in 2002. Firmin taught at Croydon College of Art and St Martin's and was a freelance textile and wallpaper designer. Sea, sky and land were themes in her work which included installation, mixed media and book art. She was involved in forming The Paper Group from 1995, during which time it went on tour, and later combined digital art with conventional media and investigated art for healing. Firmin was a member of the Landscape & Arts Network and the Women's Art Library. Group shows included International Book Art, New York Public Library, 1984; Pitshanger Museum and Gallery/ Chapman Gallery, Salford University, 1997–8; and Ikon Gallery, Birmingham, tour, 1999–00. Among solo exhibitions were ICA, 1970; Gardner Art Centre, Sussex University, 1982; Barbican Centre, 1991; and First Edition, Canary Wharf, 2002. British Museum and Victoria & Albert Museum hold examples.

Christopher FIRMSTONE 1937– Originally trained as an architect, by the time he was included in Contemporary British Art at The Millinery Works, 2003, Firmstone was mainly a painter. During his architectural career he specialised in art gallery and museum work, being responsible for major shows at the RA, Birmingham Museum and Art Gallery, Victoria & Albert and London Museums and the Tate and National Portrait Galleries. Firmstone designed the Victoria & Albert Museum's twentieth-century British art and design gallery and helped restore and adapt the Strand block of Somerset House for the Courtauld Gallery. His many mixed exhibitions as a painter and draughtsman included RIBA; Singer & Friedlander/*Sunday Times* Watercolour Competition, at Mall Galleries; and RBSA, where he was awarded the Caran D'Ache Prize in 1998. His first solo show was at Dudley Museum & Art Gallery, 2002.

David FIRMSTONE 1943– Painter who worked initially as an art adviser before becoming a full-time artist in 1998. During his career he travelled widely, painting in oil, tempera and watercolour. His pictures, sometimes on a vast scale, explored the effects of man and nature on changing landscapes. These included Crete, Italy and around Bembridge, in the Isle of Wight, where Island Fine Arts showed his work. Firmstone was an associate of RWS, showed elsewhere in London, won a number of awards and had work in corporate and private collections.

Margaret FIRTH 1898–1991 Painter, especially of still life which latterly moved towards abstraction, born in Saltaire, Yorkshire. She rarely left the West Riding. Firth was born into prosperous circumstances, her father a Bradford textile manufacturer, surrounded by paintings and art books. Studied at Bradford School of Art from 1914–21, although her mother's health prevented regular attendance. Teachers were Fred Stead and Harry Butler. Eventually set up her own studio and additionally studied with Bertram Priestman and Arthur Reginald Smith, although for 20 years Firth found little time to paint, showing occasionally at RA, LG and in Yorkshire. After the death of her parents and brother, in 1948 Firth settled in Ilkley and began painting seriously again, attending Maurice de Sausmarez's art history lectures, travelling extensively in Italy and establishing a keen local following for her work. This included textile collage flowerpieces and Tulips, sold to Wakefield Art Gallery in 1950. Had three solo shows at Hawksworth Gallery, Ilkley, between 1984–7, then in 1988 Bradford Art Galleries and Museums, which holds her work, organised a touring exhibition.

Mark FIRTH 1952– Sculptor, installations artist and teacher, whose work reflected his family's background – Thomas Firth & Sons of Sheffield, later Firth Brown, world-famous specialist steel forgers and precision-machiners – and his own as a mathematician and engineer. Firth was drawing resident at Glyptoteket Museum, Copenhagen, 1970–1; studied mechanical engineering at Birmingham University, 1971–2; attended Camberwell School of Art, 1972–6; then Slade School of Fine Art, 1976–8. He won a travel scholarship to Japan, 1979; research grant into lasers/holograms as sculptural media, 1980; and taught in British art schools, 1980–90. Commissions included White Noise, Greater London Council, 1983; Goodyear Tire and Rubber Company, America, 1992–3; and 150th Anniversary Sculpture, Institute of Actuaries, 1998. British Airports Authority, Scottish Equitable and Derek Stow and Partners hold examples. The show Mass and Symphony, at Jill George Gallery, 1998, demonstrated Firth's fascination with the infinite number of ways aluminium cubes and bars could be reshaped and toned by milling, boring, cutting and turning and then finished. There was another Jill George exhibition in 2001.

FISH fl. from c.1913–1964 Painter, illustrator and textile designer, born in Bristol, Anne Harriet Fish in 1918 married Walter Sefton. She studied under Charles Orchardson, John Hassall, at the London School of Art and in Paris. She exhibited at RA and Fine Art Society, which gave her a solo show. Did extensive work for *Punch, Tatler, Vanity Fair, Vogue* and *Cosmopolitan* and illustrated a number of books including her own *Awful Weekends and Guests*, 1938. Her work was stylish and Beardsleyesque with a satirical tinge. Tall and and rather grand in manner, she lived in St Ives, Cornwall, where she collected some good local paintings and was a member of the Penwith Society of Arts and St Ives Society of Artists.

Doug FISHBONE 1969– Artist, born in New York, who participated in the inaugural Bowieart exhibition BLOC at the County Hall Gallery in 2005. He was described as "the artist who recently brought 30,000 bananas to Trafalgar

Square who is transporting soil from Israel onto the gallery floor of County Hall, a minimal gesture with massive geo-political clout." Fishbone graduated in music from Amherst College, Massachusetts, 1988–91, gaining his fine art master's in London at Goldsmiths' College, 2001–3. He took part in numerous mixed shows internationally, among them AQA, New York, 1997; Counting Coup, Theater for the New City, New York, 2001; Arch Gallery, 2003; Portobello Film Festival, Bowieart Screening, 2004; and London>Vienna, Kunsburo, Vienna, Austria, 2005. Doug Fishbone/Cathie Pilkington was at Program in 2005.

Alfred Hugh FISHER 1867–1945 Painter, printmaker and writer, born in London. After working in a city office he gained a scholarship to Royal College of Art, then studied in Paris. For three years he travelled the British Empire as artist attached to the Visual Instruction Committee of the Colonial Office, writing books including *Through India and Burmah with Pen and Brush*. He was a prolific exhibitor at RE of which he was an associate, RA, NEAC and elsewhere. Lived in Princes Risborough, Buckinghamshire.

Andrea FISHER 1955–1997 Artist and lecturer whose education included London School of Economics, visitor by special permission, 1972–3; honours degree in history, University of Sussex, 1973–4; seminars in phenomenology and psychoanalytic theory, Philadelphia Association, London, 1974–5; sculpture, Sir John Cass School of Art, 1977; advanced course diploma in sculpture, St Martin's School of Art, 1978; honours degree in fine art (sculpture), St Martin's, 1980; and her master's degree, with distinction, social history of art, University of Leeds, 1982. Fisher gained many awards and residencies, in Britain and America, lectureships from 1983–96 including St Martin's, South Glamorgan Institute for Higher Education, Goldsmiths' College and Jan Van Eyck Academie, Maastricht, Netherlands. Her publications included *Let Us Now Praise Famous Women: Women Photographers for the US Government, 1935–1944*, which appeared in 1987, on which she curated an exhibition at the National Museum of Photography, Film and Television, Bradford. Took part in numerous group shows in Britain and abroad. Had solo shows at DIY Gallery and The Drawing Room, both 1986, later ones including Museum voor Modern Kunst, Arnhem, Netherlands, 1997. In 1999, Gimpel Fils held a show to celebrate Andrea Fisher – installations photographs, a full catalogue of her work, the first book published by the Andrea Fisher Memorial Trust, which also organised an annual lecture.

Chris FISHER 1950– Artist and teacher, born in London. He studied at Winchester School of Art, 1967; St Martin's School of Art, 1967–70; and Royal College of Art, 1970–3. He won an Abbey Major Travelling Scholarship, the John Minton Award and the Anstruther Award, 1973. From 1974–94 Fisher taught at Royal College of Art, from 1993 being fine art course director at Goldsmiths' College. Fisher was keen that an artist should not repeat himself, his own work employing mixed media and an interest in unconventional tapestry. Royal College holds his Mixed Media Composition, 1974, the Arts Council his tapestry Blindfolded, 1977. From 1989 Fisher translated and illustrated a series of European poets for Cahill Press. Fisher showed regularly in London. He was a prizewinner in the 1976 John Moores Liverpool Exhibition, also showing in the 1995–6 show. Lived at Weston, Newark, Nottinghamshire.

Craig FISHER 1976– Artist who gained his art and design foundation diploma from Wigan and Leigh College, 1995–6; graduated with honours in fine art from the University of Northumbria, Newcastle upon Tyne, 1996–9; and was awarded his master's degree in fine art from Goldsmiths' College, University of London, 1999–00. He was Saatchi fellow at Goldsmiths', 2000–1; fine art fellow at Cheltenham, University of Gloucestershire, 2001–2; and similarly a fellow at ECAV, École Cantonale D'Art du Valais, Sierre, Switzerland, 2002–4. Fisher's work was covered extensively in the art and consumer press and he took part in many group shows in Britain and abroad. Latterly these included Stranger than Fiction, Nylon, 2002; Ex Voto Schloss Leuk, Leuk, Switzerland, 2003; and Boys Who Sew, Crafts Council and tour and But not as we know it, Kontainer Gallery, Los Angeles, California, America, both 2004. Among his solo exhibitions were Recent Work, Cinch, 2000; Break Glass in the Event of an Emergency, solo window installation, Bowieart at the Tardis, 2001; Clear and Presentable Danger, Hall Palermo, Appartment D'Art Contemporain, Geneva, 2003; and Aftermath, Studio Voltaire, 2004. Fisher was latterly a signed artist with Rokeby Gallery.

Don Mulready FISHER 1923– Painter and designer for films and the theatre, born in London. Studied art in Hampstead, 1940–1, then at St Martin's School of Art with Ruskin Spear, 1943–6. Was a member of the Society of Industrial Artists and Free Painters and Sculptors, also exhibiting at NS, ROI, LG and Piccadilly Gallery. Solo exhibitions included Loggia Gallery, Barbican Centre and Salon des Nations in Paris. Lived in Paris, France.

Felicity FISHER 1922– Painter and printmaker, born in Chelsea, who as Felicity Sutton attended Chelsea Art School, in 1939, under its principal Harold Williamson, tutors including Henry Moore, Ceri Richards, Geoffrey Monk and George Day for wood engraving. During World War II she was attached to the Directorate of Camouflage, 1941–4, returning to study at Chelsea, 1945–7. She was a member of the AIA and took part in group shows at the RA, SWA and RP. In 1948 she married the classical scholar Henry Fisher (1918–2005), eldest son of Archbishop Lord Fisher of Lambeth, who became a distinguished lawyer, banker and president of Wolfson College, Oxford, 1975–85, knighted in 1968. Her sensitive 1949 study of him accompanied his obituary in *The Times*. Felicity Fisher listed the "French Impressionists, Vuillard. Portraits, people and places at home and abroad" among her influences and work themes. She studied at the Royal College of Art as a mature student and at Goldsmiths' College after having a family, etching under Paul Drury and lithography with Edwin La Dell, "making etchings at home with a small press from T N Lawrence as well as wood engravings." Lady Fisher had two exhibitions in Haslemere, one shared with Kate Ponsonby; two at The Diamond Gallery, Londonderry; and two in Marlborough, Wiltshire, to which the Fishers moved in 1985. The Ashmolean Museum in Oxford holds prints by her.

Gareth FISHER 1951– Versatile sculptor and teacher, born in Keswick, Cumberland, who from early on was influenced by the American sculptor Donald Judd. Fisher's mature work reflected contemporary issues, was built in plaster and used found material and could take some time to complete. He attended Edinburgh College of Art, 1969–76. Went on to live in Dundee, Angus, where he lectured in sculpture at Duncan of Jordanstone College of Art. From 1978 Fisher showed at New 57 Gallery, of which he was chairman, 1979–80, and Talbot Rice Gallery, both in Edinburgh; Artists' Space Gallery in New York; Art Gallery of Nova Scotia, Halifax; Hatton Gallery in Newcastle upon Tyne; Camden Arts Centre; and Third Eye Centre, Glasgow. A 1986 solo exhibition at The Fruitmarket Gallery, Edinburgh, toured Scotland; later one-man shows included Galleria Antonia Jannone, Milan, Italy, 1998. From 1984–6, Fisher was chairman of the Blackness Public Arts Programme, Dundee, where the Museum and Art Gallery holds his work.

Geoffrey FISHER 1953– Constructions artist, most of whose works were "conceived as belonging to a series of inter-related pieces that can exist independently but have different meanings when viewed in series. Their structure is based upon a concern with repetition, grids and scale". Fisher obtained an honours degree in fine art from Hornsey College of Art, 1973–6; assisted various artists living abroad, 1977–87; and worked in art education from 1989. In 1999, he obtained regional Arts Council funds to join a tour of contemporary art. Showed in group exhibitions at England & Co from 1997, in 2000 sharing a trio exhibition, Constructions, there.

Janice FISHER 1971– Artist who graduated in printmaking from the Royal College of Art in 2000. Shortly after, she shared a show with Elizabeth Haven at Elgin, work referring to the past.

Joel FISHER 1947– Sculptor, draughtsman and teacher, born in Salem, Ohio, America, who lived in Britain periodically from 1970, mainly between 1976–83. He graduated from Ken on College, 1969, Magna Cum Laude, Phi Beta Kappa. Gained a number of awards, prizes and fellowships, including Thomas J Watson Traveling Fellowship, 1969; Gast der Berliner Kunstlerprogram des DAAD, 1973–4, 1994; Pollock-Krasner Foundation, 1993; and John Simon Guggenheim Fellowship, 1993–4. Had extensive teaching experience, including Goldsmiths' College, 1978–9, and Bath Academy of Art, 1980–2, mainly in America. Fisher said that his lineage was "directly from the teaching of Josef Albers"; he later spent some time with Albers and at Goldsmiths' "once taught a variation on Albers' excellent colour course". Participated in numerous group shows internationally, British ones including the Arts Council's British Art Show with tour, 1984; Vessel, at Serpentine Gallery, 1987; and Todd Gallery, from 1994. Showed solo extensively with Nigel Greenwood Gallery until 1989; later solo shows included Lawrence Markey Gallery, New York, 1994, and Galerie Rochefort, Montreal, 1995. Fisher's work was included in several dozen international public collections, Arts Council, Leeds City Art Gallery and Victoria & Albert Museum having examples.

Myrta FISHER 1917– Painter, initially in oil, later in acrylic, and teacher, born in Wimbledon, Surrey. She attended Huddersfield Art School, 1935–7, then Slade School of Fine Art, 1937–40, being a Henriques Scholar. She had periods of full-time and part-time teaching after World War II and had a year in Greece, 1954–5, a student of the British School at Athens. Showed with AIA and Eastbourne Group, of which she was a member, for many years, solo exhibitions including AIA, Ansdell Gallery, The Grange in Rottingdean, and two private shows in Newhaven. Harold Mockford, Braque and other early twentieth-century painters were influences. Towner Art Gallery, Eastbourne, holds her work. Lived in Newhaven, Sussex.

Norman FISHER 1958– Painter of landscapes, usually small and in oil on board, which had a luminous quality. He was born in Darlington, County Durham, and studied at Humberside College of Higher Education. Concentrated on painting the Humberside estuary and Wolds region. Fisher set up and administered the Unit 50 Studios on the River Hull in 1983 and was a leading member of Hull Artists' Group. There was a major show of his landscapes at Scarborough Art Gallery in 1990 and in 1991 he was included in Images of the Yorkshire Landscape, organised by Sheeran Lock at Leeds Civic Hall.

Roger FISHER 1919–1993 Marine painter, born in Dover, Kent. After Clifton College he was 37 years in the Royal Navy, which gave his pictures great authenticity. Was elected to RSMA in 1983, also showing with Wapping Group of Artists and Armed Forces' Art Society. Royal Naval Lifeboat Institution and Yarrow Shipbuilders hold examples. Lived in Snape, Suffolk.

Rowland FISHER 1885–1969 Marine and landscape painter in oil and watercolour and ship modeller, born in Gorleston, Norfolk, son of a master mariner. Originally he wanted to go to sea but instead worked at Jewson & Sons timber yard, Great Yarmouth, for 50 years, becoming president of the local Society of Artists. In addition to Norfolk scenes he painted landscapes after trips to France, the Netherlands and Italy. Fisher was a member of the RSMA from 1938, later joined the ROI and St Ives Society of Artists, in Cornwall, and exhibited at RA, RBA, RI and RWS as well as on the continent. His work reflected the tranquillity and hostility of the sea, as in examples offered by Bonhams in The East Anglian View, Lynford Hall, Mundford, 2000. A large collection of his more vigorous pictures hangs in the James Paget Hospital at Gorleston.

Sandra FISHER 1947–1994 Figurative painter and printmaker, born in New York, her mother an artist. In 1968 graduated from California Institute of the Arts. After working for a year at Gemini print studio in Los Angeles moved to London, becoming studio assistant to R B Kitaj, whom she married in 1983. Her fluent, colourful work became popular through the 1989 picture Boating at Regent's Park, commissioned by London Underground and used for the poster *Days on the water*. Had solo show at Lefevre Gallery, 1993. Fisher's pictures were commonly modest in scale. She admired the work of Delacroix, Monet and Matisse, from the Israeli painter Avigdor Arikha absorbed the rule that a picture should be finished in one session and chose to paint in front of the subject. The male nude was a favourite. She collaborated several times with the poet Thomas Meyer on fine, limited edition books. Died in London where British Museum holds her work.

Stefani Melton FISHER 1894–1963 Painter, notably of portraits, printmaker and teacher, son of the artist Melton Fisher, born and lived in London. He was educated at Westminster School, studying then at Byam Shaw and Vicat Cole School of Art and Royal Academy Schools. Became art master at Dulwich College. Was a member of ROI and PS, also showing at RA, RI and elsewhere.

Tyson FISHER fl. from c.1920–1962 Painter of murals and stage sets as well as pictures, born in Waterloo, Lancashire. Studied art in the south of France. Lectured on art and was a member of the Liver Sketching Club. Exhibited RCamA, Walker Art Gallery, Liverpool and RWS. Lived at Crosby, Lancashire.

Gerald FISHON fl. from mid-1950s– Painter whose work showed the influence of such artists as Beckmann, Nolde and Soutine, born in London. In 1955 he studied at St Martin's School of Art with James Dring. Subsequently he attended City & Guilds of London Art School, Sir John Cass College and Morley College, teachers including Maggi Hambling, John Bowles and David Graham. Fishon worked as a commercial artist, helping to prepare major exhibitions on the history of the Crusades and French Revolution. In 1976 he showed a self-portrait in the Whitechapel Art Gallery exhibition of East End artists. Fishon also participated in two two-man shows at Primrose Hill Gallery, 1989–93.

Clifford FISHWICK 1923–1997 Painter and teacher, born near Accrington, Lancashire, married to the painter Patricia Fishwick. He attended Liverpool School of Art, 1940–2, then after Naval service returned to complete his studies, 1946–7, including art teacher's diploma. Fishwick combined a busy painting career with teaching at Exeter College of Art, becoming principal, 1958–84. He was a member of the Newlyn Society from 1952–83 and exhibited at the Penwith Society in 1950s–1960s and had a solo show in 1983. Fishwick showed solo at St George's Gallery, in 1957, others including Dartington Hall, 1959; Exeter University, 1961; Plymouth City Art Gallery, 1966; Essex University, 1976; Spacex Gallery, Exeter, 1982; and works of the 1950s at Austin/Desmond Fine Art, 1989, with other works, 1990. Also showed with Bruton Street Gallery. The Universities of Exeter and Plymouth jointly supported memorial exhibitions in 1998. Over the years Fishwick's style changed as certain influences took effect, the Neo-Romantics, the Cornish painters and the second School of Paris painters such as Nicolas de Staël. His later work was darker, more loosely put together and more abstract. Public galleries in Exeter, Plymouth and Bradford hold examples. Lived in Topsham, Devon.

Patricia FISHWICK 1929– Artist in oil, pen and watercolour and teacher, born in Liverpool, where she attended the College of Art, 1947–9, then Exeter College of Art, 1949–52, where she was taught by Clifford Fishwick, whom she married. She taught history of art at Exeter College, 1972–84. Patricia Fishwick was a member of Newlyn Society of Artists, 1952–83. also a member of the Kenn Group of Artists and Exeter Society of Artists. She took part in RWA shows, John Moores Liverpool Exhibition and Westward Television Open Art. Solo shows included Exeter University. Plymouth City Art Gallery holds her work. Lived in Topsham, Devon.

Anoushka FISZ 1969– Photography-based artist, born and lived in London, who in 1988–90 served an apprenticeship with Plichta, Hollywood portrait photographer of the post-World War II years. Fisz worked in Paris, 1990–2. Group exhibitions included Air de Paris "La Table", Paris, 1998. Solo exhibitions included Galerie Pierre Nouvion, Monaco, 1997; Jason McCoy inc, New York, 1998; and Alien Sex Mother, The Mayor Gallery, 1999.

Ben FITTON 1972– Artist and lecturer who created silhouettes of historically significant images from wooden garden trellis-work, as with his La Barricade de la Rue Basfroi, based on a photograph of the insurrection that led to the Paris Commune of 1871, shown at *The Economist*, 2002. Fitton did a foundation art and design course at Norton College, Sheffield, 1991–2; graduated with honours in fine art, Nottingham Trent University, 1994–7; gained his master's in fine art at Chelsea College of Art & Design, 2000–1; with a teaching fellowship there, 2001–2. Lectured at Nottingham and Chelsea and at De Montfort University, Leicester. He curated several shows, at Nottingham Trent, Zwemmer Gallery and VTO, and took part in group exhibitions, including Nerve, ICA, 1999; and Museum Magogo, Glasgow Project Space in 1999 and PB Gallery, Melbourne, Australia, 2000.

James FITTON 1899–1982 Painter, advertising and poster designer, draughtsman and printmaker, born in Oldham, Lancashire, where he was educated at a board school. Was apprenticed as a calico designer in Manchester where for some years he attended the School of Art part-time, getting to know the painter L S Lowry. In London attended evening classes under A S Hartrick at Central School of Arts and Crafts from 1925, in 1928 marrying the artist Margaret Cook and settling in Dulwich, where he continued to live. The 1930s were very active for Fitton, who exhibited at such venues as RA and NEAC; was appointed art director for the C Vernon and Sons advertising agency; had his first one-man show, in 1933, at Arthur Tooth and Sons; and began to teach in that year at Central School. Fitton's father had been a trade union leader, active in the Labour movement, attitudes which left their mark on Fitton. He became active in AIA, drew cartoons for the *Daily Worker* and *Left Review* and became known for his brilliantly witty and adroit caricatures of political leaders such as Mosley, Churchill and Mussolini. Other work over the years included posters for London Transport; illustrations for *Lilliput* and other magazines; wartime work for the Ministry of Food, Ministry of Information and Ministry of Education; and a number of notable film posters. Elected RA in 1954. In his pictures Fitton was a shrewd and perceptive observer of London low life, of its cafés, markets and characters. A Very English Painter was a Fitton show at Crane Kalman Gallery, 2004–5.

Judith FITTON: *see* **Judith DAVIS**

Margaret FITTON 1902–1988 Painter, illustrator and sculptor, born in London, married to the artist James Fitton. Her mother had studied at Royal Academy Schools and her uncle had founded the Cook School of Art. She studied at Central School of Arts and Crafts under Bernard Meninsky and met her husband in a lithography class there in the 1920s. Renoiresque in appearance, she modelled for a number of artists including Barnett Freedman. First job was illustrating books for Warne &

Company and also illustrated for *Lilliput* and *The Listener*. Sculpted a head of her husband, who frequently used her as a model. Exhibited RA, AIA, LG, Arts Council and Storran Gallery. In 1937 the critic Anthony Blunt wrote that Margaret Fitton's Ironing and Airing was the one submission worth noting in an RA spring exhibition. She was an AIA and Arts Club member and lived in London.

Patrick Michael FITZGERALD 1965– Artist, born in Cork, Ireland, who graduated with first-class honours and his master's in fine art from Chelsea School of Art in 1988. He moved to Bilbao, Spain, where he settled. Fitzgerald won many awards, including the Purchase Prize, VIII Biennial of Pamplona, and artist-in-residence, Sirius Arts Centre, Cobh. In 2003, Fitzgerald shared an exhibition at Rubicon Gallery, Dublin, with Andrew Bick. By that time, his paintings had become quite sculptural, as the gallery described them, "with slight openings and incisions, awkwardly projecting from the wall as much as 15 or 20 centimetres, so that the whole painting as an object becomes evident. The 'figure' elements are always off-centre, creeping in from the edge or edge off it, trapping the paintings and the gaze in a moment of tension."

Peggy FITZGERALD 1923– Painter and draughtsman, born in Hastings, Sussex, where she attended the High School, then the School of Art, 1944–6. Free Painters and Sculptors member who also showed with UA, at Loggia Gallery and widely in the provinces, especially Home Counties. Farnham Art Society member who lived in Aldershot, Hampshire.

Pete FITZGERALD fl. from late 1960s– Painter, sculptor, draughtsman, printmaker and teacher, born in Woolwich, southeast London. He studied at Central and Camberwell Schools of Art. Went on to teach in London social priority schools, in 1978–9 painting on secondment at Goldsmiths' College School of Art. Had a solo show at Woodlands Art Gallery, 1981. The works on show, heads and figures, were, according to Fitzgerald, "not arrived at by abstracting down from a human starting point, but rather in a building up of shapes until a human presence is suggested".

Sue FITZGERALD 1946– Painter, whose work included landscapes and richly coloured still life, who initially studied at York Art College, 1963–5, then Sunderland Art College, 1965–7. While living abroad she graduated in 1978 from the Open University, gaining her master's degree in 1988 from the University of Kent. Had a studio at Montpellier, in the south of France, also having lived in the Middle and Far East. Showed at Catto and Medici Galleries, Nevill Gallery in Canterbury, Adam Gallery in Bath and Bourne Gallery, Reigate, where she had solo exhibitions in 2001 and 2003. The second show followed a visit to the Hawaiian islands. Fitzgerald's work was featured at length in Simon Jennings' 2003 volume *The Artist's Colour Manual*. Lived in Kent.

Elizabeth FITZHERBERT: *see* **Elizabeth MACFADGEN**

David FITZJOHN 1963– Painter, born in Wembley, Middlesex. He studied at High Wycombe College of Higher Education, 1981–2, then Canterbury College of Art, 1983–6. Took part in group exhibitions in Aylesbury and Canterbury in mid-1980s and participated in John Moores Liverpool Exhibition, 1987. Lived in Aylesbury, Buckinghamshire.

Leo FITZMAURICE 1963– Artist who did a foundation art and design course at Leicester Polytechnic, 1988–9; gained a first-class fine art honours degree from Liverpool Polytechnic, 1989–92; his master's at Manchester Metropolitan University, 1992–3; and a postgraduate certificate in education at Bolton Institute, 1995–6. Group shows included Northern Young Contemporaries, Whitworth Art Gallery, Manchester (prize winner), 1993; Select, Bluecoat Gallery, Liverpool, 1996; 9th Oriel Mostyn Open, Llandudno, 1997–8; and in 1998, mounted by the group Core, All in the Mind, at West Cheshire Hospital, Chester, a former mental institution, and Turnpike Gallery, Leigh. There, Fitzmaurice played on the notion of the patients' childlike dependence on the institution and its staff by making deliberately confusing collages of words and pictures from children's books, displaying them behind the glass of fire alarms. Fitzmaurice was artist-in-residence at Walker Art Gallery, Liverpool, 1996, with a solo show, later ones including Bond Gallery, Birmingham, 1997. He was included in the 2004 John Moores Liverpool Exhibition. Arts Council holds his work. Lived in Heswall, Wirral.

Andrew FITZPATRICK 1966– Stylish painter whose work had a narrative element, as in his canvas Before the Opera, in The Caledonian Show III, The Contemporary Fine Art Gallery, Eton, 2001. Fitzpatrick studied drawing and painting at Glasgow School of Art under Geoffrey Squire. Other exhibitions included a retrospective at Meddeus Kunst, Amsterdam, Netherlands, 1993, and Emotion Recollected at The Edinburgh Gallery, Edinburgh, 1998.

Mary FITZPAYNE 1928– Figurative painter and draughtsman, born in Catterick, Yorkshire, full name Alice Mary FitzPayne, who married the artist Eric Doitch. Obtained her diploma from Leeds College of Art, 1941–7; studied etching, lithography and painting at Central School of Art, 1948–9; then was in the painting school at Royal College of Art, 1949–52, teachers including Carel Weight, Rodrigo Moynihan and Ruskin Spear. Taught art to adults part-time. FitzPayne created imaginative compositions in oil, her charcoal and pen-and-ink drawings focusing on the circus and down-and-outs in London. Group shows included South London Art Gallery, 1971; Lufthansa Gallery, 1973; Leighton House, 1975; 1917 Gallery, Spilsby, 1981; Pfalzgalerie, Kaiserslautern, West Germany, 1985; and Galerie Hüsstage, Hertogenbosch, Netherlands, 1987. Had solo exhibitions at Usher Gallery, Lincoln, 1983; Blackfriars Art Gallery, 1988; Usher Gallery, Lincoln, 1989, and Guildhall Museum, Boston, 2000. Westminster and Swindon Education Authorities hold examples. Lived in New Bolingbroke, Lincolnshire.

Joyce FITZWILLIAMS 1912–1969 Prolific artist whose life in parts remains a mystery. Her father was in the Army, so her childhood was unsettled, and she was educated by a governess. She attended Royal Academy Schools, 1933–8, winning the Landseer Prize and a Silver Medal for a painting of two figures from life. After teaching art for a time Fitzwilliams went into a convent, but near to taking her final vows she became ill and left. She then taught at Llandysul County School, for girls, near Newcastle Emlyn, Cardiganshire, location of her family home Cilgwyn. Joyce was to live in its dower house for a time with her mother.

Eventually she went to America and taught art at the Annie Wright Seminary, Tacoma, Washington state, run by a cousin. She was there, 1960–8, was known as Miss Joyce and in 1967 gained her master's degree from the University of Puget Sound. Fitzwilliams' output moved from straight figuration towards Surrealism, and in America she took up screenprinting. Learning that she had cancer, Fitzwilliams went to the Philippines hoping for a faith healing cure. This did not happen and she died in Honolulu, Hawaii. An endowment fund was donated to the Seminary (now the Annie Wright School) in her memory. National Library of Wales, Aberystwyth, holds her picture Hafod.

Barry FLANAGAN 1941– Sculptor in a variety of materials, draughtsman, film and furniture maker and teacher, born in Prestatyn, Flintshire. He studied at St Martin's School of Art, 1964–6, receiving the ICA Dover Street Materials Award in 1965. In 1972 he won the Gulbenkian Foundation Grant to work with the dance company Strider, three years later gaining an Arts Council Award, which allowed him to undertake kiln work. Flanagan's teaching included St Martin's School of Art, 1967–71, with further sessions at Newport School of Art and Omaha Municipal University, Nebraska. After a first solo show at Rowan Gallery in 1966, Flanagan showed there many times, and also exhibited solo at Hester van Royen Gallery and Waddington Galleries as well as widely overseas. In 1978 had one-man show at Serpentine Gallery, later ones including Tate Liverpool, 2000. Among his commissions were Peter Stuyvesant Sculpture Project, Cambridge, 1972, and City Square, Ghent, 1980. Exhibition at Yorkshire Sculpture Park, 1992. Arts Council holds a wide selection of Flanagan's work. He was elected RA in 1991.

John FLANAGAN 1889–1976 Irish painter and film-maker who in 1928 at the Café Royal was introduced by Augustus John to the singer Gracie Fields. The "every-scatty" Flanagan, who rented a studio from John in St John's Wood and made a modest living as an artist, painted Fields' portrait. Although she was still married to her first husband, the impresario Archie Pitt, she moved in with Flanagan who accompanied her on her first trip to America in 1930, where she was booked for two weeks at the Palace Theatre, New York. They also visited Dublin and Donegal Bay after her big 1931 film hit *Looking on the Bright Side*. In 1933, the contents of Flanagan's studio were moved to Capri, for which Fields had formed her long-standing attachment. Two years later, the much-praised film *Riders to the Sea* was released, based on J M Synge's play, which Flanagan had travelled to the west of Ireland to shoot. The director was Brian Desmond Hurst, the production/releasing company Flanagan-Hurst, MGM, leading players including Sara Allgood, Denis Johnstone, Kevin Guthrie and Rita Mooney. Fields funded the film, according to David Bret in his 1995 *Gracie Fields The Authorized Biography*, which details Flanagan's relationship with her. He says that Fields hoped to have a child by Flanagan but failed, after which the relationship began to disintegrate. During their last trip to Capri, Flanagan told Fields that "he did not want to be a kept man, and though they remained close friends until his death in 1976, what little was left of their love affair ended abruptly." Bret recounts that later Fields gave Flanagan "a large sum of money which enabled him and [his writer friend] Henry Savage to open a club-restaurant in Knightsbridge – it became a popular retreat for painters and actors." Among Flanagan's exhibits was the landscape Cagnes, France, at the RA Summer Exhibition in 1939.

Terence P FLANAGAN 1929– Painter, draughtsman and teacher, born in Enniskillen, County Fermanagh, Northern Ireland. He studied at Belfast College of Art, 1949–53, in 1954 starting to teach at St Mary's College of Education. Flanagan was a notable landscape watercolourist. He participated in many mixed exhibitions, including Four Ulster Painters, at Arnolfini Gallery, Bristol, 1965; Two Irish Painters, with Colin Middleton, Herbert Art Gallery and Museum, Coventry, 1968; The Gordon Lambert Collection, at Hugh Lane Municipal Gallery of Modern Art, Dublin, 1972; Armstrong Gallery, New York, and Smithsonian Institution, Washington, and tour, 1986; and Contemporary Artists from Ireland, Austin/Desmond Fine Art, 1990. Flanagan had a solo show at CEMA, Belfast, 1961, later exhibitions including an Arts Council of Northern Ireland 1967–77 retrospective in 1977 and Places, 1960–85, Fermanagh County Museum, 1986. Lived in Belfast.

Dennis FLANDERS 1915–1994 Artist in watercolour, carbon pencil and black and brown ink, born in Walthamstow, Essex. He attended Merchant Taylors' School, worked for periods in chartered accountancy, interior decorating, then printing, then became a freelance artist. "The beauty of Britain and its architecture and landscape" were leading themes in Flanders' work; as well as the early English watercolourists he cited Piranesi, Meryon, Muirhead Bone, F L Griggs and Henry Rushbury as influences. Flanders' art education was evening classes at Regent Street Polytechnic School of Art. By the early 1990s he had completed over 3,000 drawings, mainly of Britain, also of Venice and Rome. Flanders was a member of RWS and RBA and an honorary freeman of the Painter-Stainers' Company. Flanders' books, such as *Dennis Flanders' Britannia*, 1984, and *Dennis Flanders' London*, 1986, were celebrated with shows at Fine Art Society and Guildhall Library. The Library and Guildhall Art Gallery hold an extensive collection of his work. Lived in London.

Moyna FLANNIGAN 1963– Painter, born in Scotland, who gained an honours degree at Edinburgh College of Art, 1985, then her master's degree from Yale University School of Art in America, 1987. She had obtained a Yale University Scholarship in 1985, other awards including Scottish Arts Council Artists Award in 1994, and Scholar, British School at Rome, 1997. In 1999, Flannigan was a finalist for The NatWest Prize, showing figurative pictures that were "less about the individual but rather are representative of social and psychological ideas...a gallery of human types". Flannigan was artist-in-residence at Aberdeen Art Gallery, 1990. Showed widely in Scotland and had a solo exhibition at 369 Gallery Edinburgh, 1990, later ones including William Jackson Gallery, 1994, Lotta Hammer, 1998. Aberdeen Art Gallery, City Art Centre in Edinburgh and Scottish Arts Council hold examples.

Alastair FLATTELY 1922– Painter and teacher, born in Inverness, who was educated at Maiden Erlegh School, Reading, and Glasgow University, gaining a postgraduate scholarship, Edinburgh College of Art, 1949–50. He obtained an Andrew Grant Travelling Scholarship to Spain, 1950–1 and Fellowship in Painting, 1953–5. Flattely won a Charles Jervase Prize, 1950, and Stewart Prize, 1952, both RSA. He lectured at Edinburgh College of Art, 1952–3; Gray's School of Art, Aberdeen, 1955–9; and was principal there, 1972–87, having been vice-principal and then principal of Gloucester College of Art, Cheltenham, 1960–72. Flattely was a member of RWA. His exhibitions, restricted by teaching commitments, included Wildenstein; Roland, Browse & Delbanco; Scottish National Gallery of Modern Art, Edinburgh; Upper Grosvenor Gallery; and Aitken Dott, Edinburgh. Lyon & Turnbull, Edinburgh, held a show of Flattely's work over 50 years in 2003. Aberdeen, Cheltenham, Dundee, Glasgow and Hull public galleries hold Flattely's pictures, as do RSA, RWA and The Nuffield Foundation, private collections including HRH The Duke of Edinburgh. Lived in Beaminster, Dorset.

Joseph Otto FLATTER 1894–1988 Versatile artist, born in Vienna, Austria, where he enrolled at the Academy of Fine Arts in 1914. Had to serve as an infantry officer for over three years before he could resume his Academy studies, supported by work as an itinerant portrait painter. In 1934 Flatter married the concert pianist Hilda Loewe, settling with her in England in 1935. Shortly before World War II Flatter produced a series of cartoons warning of the Nazi threat. Nevertheless, when war began he was interned on the Isle of Man, although he was soon released to do extensive propaganda work for the Ministry of Information and the exiled Belgian government. Flatter was commissioned as an Army captain and made an Official War Artist at the Nuremberg Trials. After the war Flatter found it hard to resume his career as a portrait painter, in which Rembrandt was always his main inspiration. Instead he bought and restored Old Masters. His own final series of pictures was in tempera, many influenced by the death of his wife in 1976; much of the work was satirical, drawing on literature and personal experience, and it also emphasised essential human values. Imperial War Museum holds a large collection of Flatter's war illustrations. Some were included in Art in Exile in Great Britain 1933–45, Camden Arts Centre, 1986. Lived and worked in London.

Zena FLAX 1930– Artist and designer, born and lived in London. She attended Chelsea School of Art, 1949–53, focusing on illustration, then became interested in etching, which she pursued at Central School of Arts and Crafts, 1953–5. Worked as a graphic designer. Showed etchings at Whitechapel Art Gallery, RA Diploma Gallery, elsewhere in London and in the provinces. Was a member of Printers Inc. Workshop. Exhibited with it at Ben Uri Art Society, which holds her work, in 1990, and in 1991 had a solo exhibition at Sternberg Centre for Judaism. In 2004, she participated in a four-artist show at The Stables Gallery, Dollis Hill.

Hugh FLEETWOOD 1944– Writer and painter, born in Chichester, Sussex, who on leaving school at 17 went to live in Paris, later Rome, eventually being based in England. His second novel, *The Girl Who Passed For Normal*, won the John Llewellyn Rhys Memorial Prize; his sixth, *The Order of Death*, was made into a film starring Harvey Keitel and John Lydon (Johnny Rotten). Fleetwood also wrote film scripts in Italy and designed the jackets for several of his books. Alongside writing Fleetwood was a self-taught painter using a dark palette, his figurative pictures reflecting his love of early Italian painting. Initially he showed in Rome and Spoleto. To coincide with publication of his novel *Brothers*, in 1999 the St Raphael Gallery in London gave him a first exhibition in Britain.

Neville FLEETWOOD 1932– Painter, born in Huddersfield, where he studied at the School of Art, 1947–53. On graduating he began work in a graphic studio, started up his own business, then retired early to return to full-time painting. Showed with RBSA, NEAC and ROI, where in 1997 he won the president's prize and was elected a full member. Fleetwood produced richly coloured and textured acrylic landscapes and coastal scenes of his native Yorkshire, also still lifes with a distinctive flattened perspective. His sell-out solo show at Panter & Hall in 2001 was the first of a series.

Bernard FLEETWOOD-WALKER 1893–1965 Painter and draughtsman mainly of figures and portraits. Born in Birmingham, where he lived most of his life. Initially was a modeller and metalworker, then studied painting at Birmingham School of Arts and Crafts, followed by London and Paris. Wounded and gassed during World War I service in Artists' Rifles, but continued to paint and draw. After war taught for about 10 years at King Edward's Grammar School, Aston, in 1929 leaving to teach at Birmingham School of Arts and Crafts. Exhibited extensively at RA from 1925 – he was elected RA 1956 – and otherwise showed mainly at RWS, NEAC, RBSA and RP. Also had a one-man show at Ruskin Gallery, Birmingham, 1925, and won a silver medal at Paris Salon. Moved to London after retirement from teaching in Birmingham in 1951 to give more time to students at Royal Academy Schools, where he had been appointed assistant keeper. RA, Leeds City Art Gallery, other provincial and foreign galleries hold his work. Memorial exhibition in Birmingham, 1965; retrospective John Lindsay Fine Art, Solihull/Belgrave Gallery, 1981.

Carl FLEISCHER 1968– Artist who gained his master's in fine art from the University of Sussex. His video installations were shown widely in Britain and on the continent. Took part in the Brighton International Arts Festival. Public commissions in which Fleischer was involved included the Coventry Blue Ribbon Sculpture, 1998, and Watford Memory Wall, 2000.

Arthur FLEISCHMANN 1896–1990 Sculptor in various materials, notably a pioneer in the use of carved Perspex and water, and teacher, born in Bratislava, Slovakia, then part of Hungary. He studied medicine and art at the Prague Academy, winning a scholarship to the Master School of Sculpture in Vienna, also studying in France and Italy. Fleischmann taught art in Vienna, 1935–7, and also held classes for the Czech Army. After periods in South Africa, Bali and Australia, where he lived from 1939, he settled in London from 1948, there exhibiting at RA, NS and RBA. Public galleries in Bratislava, Sydney and Blackburn, Lancashire, hold his work, which is contained in buildings and churches in Britain and abroad. Fleischmann was a devoted Roman Catholic. He was the only artist to sculpt four Popes from life. Among his many other portrait sitters were the industrialist Lord Robens, the singer Kathleen Ferrier and the actor Trevor Howard, in National Portrait Gallery. Fleischmann's work was originally figurative, becoming more abstract from the 1960s. He was a fellow of the RBS. Died in Tenerife, Spain.

Joanna Barnes Fine Arts held a centennial celebration show in 1996, which toured to the Mestke Múzeum, Bratislava, Slovak Republic, and the Slovak Institute, Vienna, Austria, both in 1997. In 2002, the Museum Arthur Fleischmann opened in Bratislava. The Arthur Fleischmann Foundation Ltd was established as a registered charity, website www.fleischmann.org.uk.

George FLEMING 1941– Painter and lecturer, his figurative work related to public concerns and social issues. After some years in the Royal Navy and British Merchant Navy, Fleming graduated from University of Ulster, Belfast, 1987–91, completing a postgraduate diploma in applied arts in 1992. Ran workshops at Ulster Folk and Transport Museum, Harmony Hill Arts Centre and the Slane Arts and Crafts Gallery. Also lectured to such bodies as the Northern Ireland Patchwork Guild and Quilt Art Workshops as well as his old university. Took part in many group shows in Belfast, including Arts Council Gallery, 1988, and in 1994 Works on Paper and Beyond the Partitions, organised by Queen Street Studios, Belfast, with which he was associated. His solo show Echoes toured Northern Ireland, 1993–4.

Ian FLEMING 1906–1994 Painter, printmaker and teacher, born in Glasgow where he attended the School of Art, 1924–9. Chika Macnab and Charles Murray were his initial printmaking teachers, then he worked with Robert Sargent Austin and Malcolm Osborne for several months of a travelling scholarship at Royal College of Art, additional studies being made in France and Spain. Fleming taught at Glasgow School of Art, 1931–48, at Hospitalfield from 1948–54, then he was principal of Gray's School of Art, Aberdeen, 1954–72, where he developed printmaking. Fleming was elected RSA in 1956. Having been a permanent member of the council of the Society of Artist Printmakers, he was in 1974 appointed chairman of Peacock Printmakers. Fleming scored an early success in 1931 when he engraved Gethsemane, bought by the French government and also in the collection of Scottish National Gallery of Modern Art. His later work was notable for experiment both in printmaking and in watercolour. Glasgow School of Art holds Fleming's fine picture The Painters Robert Colquhoun and Robert MacBryde, who were his pupils. Died in Aberdeen.

Jean FLEMING 1937– Painter and draughtsman, born in Glasgow. She studied at the School of Art there, 1953–8, and at Patrick Allan-Fraser School of Art, Hospitalfield, Arbroath. Showed Royal Glasgow Institute of the Fine Arts, RSW of which she was a member and elsewhere. Paisley Art Gallery and the Nuffield Foundation hold her work. Lived in Crail, Fife.

John B FLEMING 1912–1991 Watercolourist, draughtsman and academic registrar at Glasgow School of Art. He was born in Dumbarton, Dunbartonshire, and studied at the Academy there. Went to Glasgow School of Art, 1930–5, his teachers including W O Hutchison, then in 1943 to Art Students' League of New York. Fleming was made a member of Society of Industrial Artists and Designers, 1956, RSW, 1960, and an honorary member of Royal Glasgow Institute of the Fine Arts, 1985. Also showed at RSA and in private galleries. Public galleries in Glasgow and Paisley hold examples. Lived finally in Crail, Fife.

Ken FLEMING 1944– Printmaker, designer and illustrator who showed in range of exhibitions. He was born in Middlesbrough, Yorkshire, and grew up in London. Leaving school in 1963 he rejected formal art training, instead working in an advertising agency. While serving in several agencies he began to make prints, initially lithographs, in 1968 moving back to Yorkshire where he ran his own design business from 1972–6. After a return to London and becoming a freelance illustrator Fleming gradually concentrated on printmaking. Meticulously detailed areas of printing in otherwise simple images often produced an ethereal, dreamlike result.

Peter FLEMING 1949– Painter and teacher, born in London, who studied at Hammersmith College of Art and Building, was married to the Austrian artist Irmgard Parth and lived in Austria during the summer. He taught part-time for many years and often worked to commission. Fleming exhibited widely in Europe and America, venues including the RA, London, and Galerie Hilger, Vienna. He said that in his pictures he was trying to share "small moments of vision." Fleming was shortlisted in the 2003 Singer & Friedlander/*Sunday Times* Watercolour Competition.

Anthony FLEMMING 1936– Versatile, prolific painter and designer, son of the artists Rowland Hilder and Edith Blenkiron. He graduated with first-class honours from Goldsmiths' College School of Art, 1961, having studied painting, lithography, etching and design under his father, Sam Rabin and Ivor Roberts-Jones. Flemming then produced racing car designs for clients including Jack Brabham and Bruce McLaren, in 1970 returning to full-time painting. He was a keen yachtsman, manned many vessels and maintained his own yacht on the Medway. Travelled extensively in Europe, often working on the spot, using traditional techniques and a modern palette. Took part in many mixed shows, including RA, RI, RSMA, Wapping Group of Artists, at Cowes Gallery in the Isle of Wight and widely elsewhere in London and the provinces. Solo exhibitions included Duncan Campbell Fine Art, 2001 and 2003. Lived in London.

John FLEMONS 1934– Abstract painter and teacher who studied at Chelsea School of Art, 1951–3, then 1955–8. Then went on to University of London Institute of Education, 1958–9, and Birmingham School of Art Education, 1970–1. Flemons won the Morland Lewis Travelling Scholarship (second prize), 1956, (first prize), 1958. He taught at Morley College as head of art and design. Was included in Woodlands Art Gallery 1982 show Artists in Adult Education. Other exhibitions included John Moores Liverpool Exhibition, 1961, Gallery 273 at Queen Mary College, 1975, and Brunel University, 1977. Had a solo exhibition at Morley Gallery in 1993. Lived in London.

Alan FLETCHER 1931– Designer and writer, born in Nairobi, Kenya, who fast rose to fame in the 1960s as one of the first generation of Royal College of Art graduates to call themselves graphic designers. He also studied at the Central School of Arts and Crafts and Yale University School of Art. Fletcher began his career in New York, where he worked for the Container Corporation, *Fortune* magazine and IBM. After returning to London in 1962 he co-founded Fletcher/Forbes/Gill, which served such clients as Pirelli, Cunard, Penguin Books, British

Petroleum and Olivetti. He co-founded Pentagram in 1972 and created design programmes for Reuter, Lucas Industries, The Mandarin Oriental Hotel Group, Victoria & Albert Museum, Lloyd's of London, Daimler Benz, Arthur Andersen and ABB. In 1992 he left Pentagram to work alone, among his clients Dentsu, London Transport, Shell and Toyota; he was design consultant to Phaidon Press and Novartis Campus. By this time Fletcher had established an international reputation. He gained gold and silver awards from the British Designers & Art Directors' Association (D&AD), of which he was president in 1973, and from the New York "One Show". In 1977 he shared the D&AD President's Award for outstanding contributions to design with Pentagram partner Colin Forbes. The Society of Industrial Artists and Designers in 1982 awarded Fletcher its Annual Medal for outstanding achievement in design; in 1993 he gained The Prince Philip Prize for the Designer of the Year; and in 1994 he was inducted to the "Hall of Fame" of the American Art Directors' Club. Among Fletcher's books was *Beware Wet Paint*, 1996, and *The Art of Looking Sideways*, 2001. His exhibition Thoughts On A Wall was held at England & Co in 2002.

Alan FLETCHER 1936–1958 Painter, draughtsman and printmaker, born in Glasgow. He studied at the School of Art there, 1952–5, and was awarded a travelling scholarship to Italy in 1957, where he died in an accident the following year. Consequently Fletcher's exhibiting career was short, although his work was shown in London and New York in the late 1950s and he was included in Painters in Parallel at Edinburgh College of Art in 1978. Scottish Arts Council, Dundee and Aberdeen Art Galleries and Glasgow University hold his work.

Amanda FLETCHER 1960– Painter of still life in the Old Master tradition with a warm, individual style, as in her contribution to Old & New at Wolseley Fine Arts, at The Gallery in Cork Street, 2002 and 2003. Born in London, Fletcher was educated in England and the studio of Cecil Graves, Florence, Italy. Lived in Sweden from the late 1980s, travelling widely elsewhere in Europe and in America.

Benjamin FLETCHER 1868–1951 Artist-craftsman and teacher who worked for the Coalbrookdale Company, Shropshire, as a boy, from 1885–8 studying part-time at the local School of Art. He was a disciple of the art-into-manufacture-inspired principal Augustus Spencer who, upon becoming head of Leicester School of Art in 1888, took Fletcher onto his staff. When Fletcher succeeded him, 1900–20, he and his students produced many pieces for the Dryad Metal Works, influenced by the Arts and Crafts movement. Fletcher was subsequently principal of Birmingham School of Art, 1920–7. He contributed to The Ethelfloeda Fountain, part of which was subsequently moved to the City Rooms, Leicester.

Doreen FLETCHER 1952– Painter and teacher, born in Stoke-on-Trent, Staffordshire, who depicted urban landscapes, which included London's East End where she lived, and latterly views of southern France eastern Europe. Did a foundation course at Newcastle School of Art, 1972–3, then gained distinctions at Croydon College of Art and Design, 1973–6. From 1982 was a visiting lecturer at Croydon College and elsewhere in London. Later awards included a prize in the Art of Housing Competition, 1997–8. She took part in extensive group shows. Exhibited solo at City Museum & Art Gallery, Stoke, 1980, later ones including Wigmore Hall and Ogilvy & Estill, Conway, both 1999. Public galleries in Stoke and Newcastle, Foreign Office, Corporation of London and several London boroughs hold examples.

Eileen FLETCHER 1948– Self-taught painter who began painting in 1970, influenced by medieval, Oriental and primitive art and who admired artists such as Rousseau, Chagall and Richard Dadd, whose apparently naïve images found a reflection in her own acrylics and gouaches on board. Born in Liverpool, after a period in London she moved to the Isle of Man in the mid-1970s, settling in Laxey and bringing up a family. Group shows included RA Summer Exhibition from 1972; 7 Dials Gallery, 1981; and Summer Show 2 at Serpentine Gallery, 1983.

Frank Morley FLETCHER 1866–1949 Noted colour woodblock printer, painter and teacher, born in Whiston, Lancashire. He studied at Atelier Cormon, in Paris. Fletcher was head of the art department at University College, Reading, 1898–1906, from 1908 being director of Edinburgh College of Art. In 1923 he left Edinburgh for California, three years later being naturalised an American citizen. Fletcher showed paintings and prints at RA, ROI, RSA, Paris Salon and especially at IS, of whose council he was a member, 1903–9. He was responsible for promoting the colour woodcut in the Japanese style and in 1916 published *Wood-block Printing*. Scottish National Gallery of Modern Art holds his colour woodcut Girl Reading.

Geoffrey FLETCHER 1923–2004 Draughtsman in pen, ink and wash, painter in oils, illustrator and writer, born in Bolton, Lancashire, to which he finally returned. After studying at the Bolton School of Art, in 1945 Fletcher attended the Slade School of Fine Art under Randolph Schwabe. London became Fletcher's enduring interest and during these early years he relaxed in the capital's remaining music-halls which, with the songs he learnt in them and offbeat aspects of the city, remained a passion. While still at University College he studied with Sir Albert Richardson at the Bartlett School of Architecture. In 1950 Fletcher's drawings began to appear in *The Manchester Guardian* and he contributed to *Sphere*, recording old and changing London, in 1958 being taken on by *The Daily Telegraph*. During the next 30 years hundreds of his drawings accompanied its diary column. Fletcher's first book was *The London Nobody Knows*, 1962, and a documentary film with that title, directed by Norman Cohen, scripted by Fletcher, with James Mason as the guide, was produced by British Lion Films in 1967. Another 17 London-oriented titles appeared, the last being *London a Private View*, 1990. Fletcher also produced *The Elements of Sketching*, in 1966, one of several such manuals. He campaigned for the preservation of the best of historic London, being aggrieved at such wanton destruction as the demolition of The Coal Exchange. His work became so well known that on one occasion, as he was sketching, a passer-by tapped him on the shoulder and said: "You must change your style. You are too much like Geoffrey Fletcher." Fletcher also travelled in France, the Netherlands and Italy, the last documented in his book *Italian Impressions*, 1974, also drawing the figure and still life. He exhibited at the RA, RBA, NEAC and in the north of England. The Guildhall Library print room and Guildhall

Art Gallery hold large collections of his work, the latter organising the exhibition Geoffrey Fletcher's City Sights in 2005.

Hanslip FLETCHER 1874–1955 Watercolour painter and printmaker with a special interest in London's architecture. Born in London, he was educated at Merchant Taylors' School. Became a member of the Art Workers' Guild. Fletcher's work featured regularly in London's serious daily and Sunday newspapers, and he exhibited RA, Goupil Gallery, NEAC, RI and in other London galleries. The Guildhall Library and Southampton Art Gallery hold his pictures. Lived in London.

Henry FLETCHER 1901– Painter and teacher, born in Bradford, Yorkshire, where he studied and taught at College of Art. His teachers there, 1915–18, included Fred Stead. Was then at St Martin's School of Art under John Allen, 1921–2, after spending 1920 in Paris at Atelier Colarossi. Showed at RA, Goupil Salon RBA and widely in the provinces. Lived for some years in Earley, Berkshire.

Michael FLETCHER 1944– Painter and teacher, born in Gloucestershire, who studied at Chelsea School of Art, 1962–6. He went on to teach at Putney School of Art and was included in 1982 Woodlands Art Gallery show Artists in Adult Education. Other exhibitions included Young Contemporaries and Arts Council's Young Contemporaries Travelling Exhibition, 1965, LG from 1973 and South London Art Gallery, 1980.

Paul Wilfred FLETCHER 1928– Sculptor and teacher, born in Harold Wood, Essex, who studied at Goldsmiths' College School of Art under Sam Rabin and Ivor Roberts-Jones, 1949–52, then at the Royal College of Art, 1952–6, with John Skeaping and Leon Underwood. He taught at Hammersmith and Ravensbourne Schools of Art and Bournemouth & Poole College of Art. Fletcher joined the RBS in 1958, resigning in 1992, by which time he was a fellow, from 1997 being a member of the SPS. Group exhibitions included RA Summer Exhibition; Summerleaze and Bruton Galleries; and The Gallery in Cork Street. Fletcher carried out many public commissions for banks, schools, churches, building societies and development schemes, private commissions coming from Sir Hugh Casson, Gordon Maynard, Henry Morris, Hugh Harrison and others. Lived at Brinecombe, Templecombe, Somerset.

Rosamund M B FLETCHER 1914–1993 Sculptor and letterer, daughter of the artist William Blandford Fletcher, born in Dorking, Surrey. She studied at Ruskin School of Drawing in Oxford and Slade School of Fine Art. Was a member of the Guild of Lettering Craftsmen and a fellow of RBS. Fletcher's work was heavily biased towards religious subjects. She showed at RA and RBA, but much of her output is in churches, schools and religious houses in Britain and abroad, as in St Mary's Convent, Ascot; St Mary's Roman Catholic Primary School in Wimbledon; and Richmond Roman Catholic Secondary School. In 1948 Fletcher gained both the RBS's Feodora Gleichen Memorial Fund award and Olympic Bronze Medal. She lived in Oxford, later at St Francis Convent, Braintree, Essex.

Saul FLETCHER 1967– Artist employing photography, born in Barton, Yorkshire, who worked as a stevedore in Hull, 1983–9. Took part in group shows at Photographers' Gallery from 1995; in Photography, Drawing at Anton Kern Gallery, New York, America, 1997; and View One, Mary Boone Gallery, New York, 1998. Anton Kern gave Fletcher solo exhibitions from 1997; Sadie Coles HQ in 1998; and Kolnischer Kunstverein, Cologne, Germany, 1999. Lived in London.

James FLETCHER-WATSON 1913–2004 Watercolourist, mainly of landscape, and teacher, born in Coulsdon, Surrey. He was a student at Royal Academy School of Architecture, gaining a silver medal for design, 1936, but as a watercolourist was essentially self-taught, between 1930–4, concentrating on Cotman and the Norwich School. During World War II he was in the Army as a major, working in camouflage and runway construction in India and Burma. He taught at summer schools and wrote several instructional books. Fletcher-Watson was elected RI in 1952, RBA in 1957. He showed at RA and at Paris Salon in mixed exhibitions and had solo shows in own gallery at Windrush, Oxfordshire, where he lived, in Australia and America and at Chris Beetles Ltd, 1989. Fletcher-Watson said that he was "a *strong* believer that we should maintain the traditional thread from the early watercolourists right through to the future and let the modern ideas come and go as they please on the way."

Alex FLETT 1914– Painter, born in Findochty, Banffshire. Studied at Gray's School of Art, Aberdeen, under D M Sutherland. Showed RA, RSA, SSA, Leicester and Redfern Galleries and NEAC. Lived for many years in London.

Sonya Dawn FLEWITT 1967– Sculptor-artist who wrote that her work "develops primarily through body casting and expressive painting. Working between the figurative and expressive forms, I use plaster, aluminium, canvas and wet mediums to explore relationships made on a personal, cultural and international level." Flewitt did a fine art foundation course at Wirral Metropolitan College, Birkenhead, 1999, then was a graduate student at North West Wales Institute, Wrexham, until 2002. From 1998, she carried out a series of commissions, including Groundwork Wirral, Ellesmere Port, chainsaw sculpting project, 2001; Artswave, Kisses Across the Irish Sea, Wales and Ireland, from 2003; and Artscare, Building Blocks, Carmarthen, from 2004. Among her group exhibitions were Black Sheep Gallery, Hawarden, 2001; Sam Slone Gallery, Edinburgh, 2002; West Wales Arts Centre, Fishguard, from 2003; and Sculpture Cymru Group, Terrasa, Barcelona, Spain, 2004. She lived in Little Newcastle, Haverfordwest, Pembrokeshire.

Charles W FLIESS 1899–1956 Painter and draughtsman, born in Germany, who moved to England in 1939. In 1954–5 he was included in an exhibition called Four Palettes at Derby Museum and Art Gallery. The year after he died Derby was given three pictures by Fliess' brother, Dr Robert Fleiss of New York, through the artist Clifford Hall. Ben Uri Art Society also holds examples.

Claude FLIGHT 1881–1955 Painter, printmaker, interior designer and sculptor. Born in London, Flight trained as an engineer, then became a librarian, in 1906 beginning seven years of beekeeping and farming in Sussex. Began to study at Heatherley's School of Fine Art, resuming his studies in 1918 after Army service, with a special interest in lino-cutting, of which he was to become a master. In the

1920s began to exhibit on the continent, in 1925 having lino-cuts bought by the Contemporary Art Society and the British Museum. Two years later formed interior decorating business with the artist Edith Lawrence, experimenting with lino-cutting, textiles, picture panels and wall hangings. In 1931 had one-man show at Redfern Gallery, in 1935 a joint exhibition with Edith Lawrence at the French Gallery. They were responsible for the First Exhibition of British Lino-Cuts at the Redfern in 1929, an annual event until 1937. During World War II many of Flight's paintings and colour blocks were destroyed by enemy action. For a time Flight was editor of *Arts and Crafts Quarterly*, and he also published a number of books, including *Lino-Cuts*. S C Kaines-Smith called Flight "the only true futurist that this country has produced". His vital, dynamic prints were early recognised as masterpieces in a neglected medium. In later life lived with Edith Lawrence at Donhead St Andrew, Wiltshire. Memorial show at Parkin Gallery, 1973.

Alex Russell FLINT 1974– Representational painter included in Artists of Fame & Promise at Panter & Hall, 2003, by which time Flint had shown nationally. Studied with Ted Seth Jacobs at L'École Albert Defois, in the Loire Valley, France, and at Studio Charles H Cecil, Florence, Italy.

E M FLINT 1883–1968 Painter and teacher, born in Loughborough, Leicestershire. She attended Birmingham School of Art. From 1914 she was principal of Lichfield School of Art and from 1915–49 art director of Queen Mary's Grammar School for Boys, Walsall, where she originally went temporarily and made a lasting impression. Known as Emma, she was acknowledged to be a strict disciplinarian who did not suffer fools gladly; she was also a character, who prior to World War I was riding a motorcycle with her mother in the sidecar. Shortly before her death she was made mayor and when she successfully fought to get an art gallery in Walsall it was named after her. Miss Flint set up Queen Mary Grammar School's art sixth form and in the year after her death 32 old boys were attending Birmingham School of Art. Showed at RA, RBSA and RWA and lived in Walsall, Staffordshire.

Francis Russell FLINT 1915–1977 Oil and watercolour painter. Studied at the Grosvenor School of Modern Art, Royal Academy Schools and in Paris. Son of Sir William Russell Flint, RA, Francis was an official Admiralty artist who exhibited at the RA, RSA, elsewhere in Britain, Africa, Canada and the USA. His pictures were mainly of marine subjects and they were reproduced in many publications, including *Royal Academy Illustrated, Illustrated London News, Sketch* and *Tatler*. He wrote for *The Artist* and *The Studio* and several books on watercolour painting. Lived at Burgess Hill, Sussex.

Geoffrey FLINT 1919– Painter and teacher, born in Woking, Surrey. Studied at Kingston School of Art and Royal College of Art and eventually became principal of Eastbourne School of Art, latterly the College of Art and Design. The local Towner Art Gallery holds his work. Lived in Eastbourne, Sussex.

Purves FLINT 1883–1947 Landscape artist and printmaker, born in Edinburgh, son of the artist Francis Wighton Flint and younger brother of the painter William Russell Flint. His full name was Robert Purves Flint. He was educated at Daniel Stewart's College in Edinburgh and served in the Army in France in World War I. He was a member of RSW and an associate of RWS and was a prolific exhibitor, also showing at Leicester Galleries, Fine Art Society, Royal Glasgow Institute of the Fine Arts and elsewhere. Lived for many years in Whitstable, Kent.

Robert FLINT 1880– Sculptor in wood and stone, born at Shoreham-on-Sea, Sussex. Studied at Putney School of Art under Charles Doman, 1929–39, then City and Guilds, London, 1939–41. He exhibited at the RA and in the provinces and his work is held by Russell-Cotes Art Gallery and Museum, Bournemouth. Was elected RMS in 1948. Lived at Southwick, Sussex, and was a member of the Society of Sussex Artists.

William Russell FLINT 1880–1969 Watercolourist, printmaker and illustrator, born in Edinburgh. He was the son of the artist Francis Wighton Flint, elder brother of the landscape painter Purves Flint and father of the artist Francis Russell Flint. Apprenticed when he left school to a firm of lithographers, Flint attended art classes, and after moving to London at the turn of the century worked as a medical illustrator before joining *The Illustrated London News'* staff. In his spare time he studied at Heatherley's School of Fine Art. His first book illustration success was H Rider Haggard's *King Solomon's Mines*, 1905, to be followed by many titles including *The Song of Songs*, 1909, Charles Kingsley's *The Heroes*, 1912, and Homer's *The Odyssey*, 1924. Took up etching, which he studied at Hammersmith School of Art, 1914. After service in the Royal Naval Volunteer Reserve and Royal Air Force in World War I Flint continued to establish his reputation as a technically superb watercolourist and skilled etcher. His books, such as *Models of Propriety*, 1951, and *Minxes Admonished or Beauty Reproved*, 1955, gained him great popularity, along with prints produced for wide distribution, but his concentration on semi-draped pin-ups in continental settings took him out of critical favour. He was a prolific exhibitor, especially at Fine Art Society, RWS, RSW and RWA, and his work is in many public collections around the world. Elected RA, 1933, and knighted, 1947. Lived in London.

Helen FLOCKHART 1963– Painter, born in Hamilton, Lanarkshire. She studied at Glasgow School of Art, 1980–5, then in following year at State Higher School of Fine Art in Poznan, Poland. Flockhart's work was reminiscent of primitive paintings and was influenced by naïve, folk art pictures and icons. Woman's role as Maiden, Madonna and Mother were features of her meticulously painted canvases. She showed solo in Poznan in 1986 and at Fruitmarket Gallery, Edinburgh, 1990. In 1992–3 she appeared in Through Women's Eyes at Edinburgh City Art Centre. Won the Noble Grossart Painting Prize, 2000, in 2001 having a solo exhibition, The Verdant Maze, at Rebecca Hossack Gallery, with another there, Dryland, Wetlands, in 2003. Scottish Arts Council holds her work.

Alan FLOOD 1951– Painter and etcher, born in Lancashire, who attended Blackburn School of Art and Leeds School of Fine Art. He began his career as a freelance illustrator, but after six years resumed painting. Flood's subjects included portraits, cityscapes, interiors and still life. Exhibitions included Blackburn and Manchester City Art Galleries, National Portrait Gallery, Leeds University

Gallery and Opera North Grand Theatre, Leeds, 1996. In 1993 Flood completed a series of etchings of the playwright Samuel Beckett, *A Beckett Metamorphosis*, and *The Leeds Centenary Print Edition*, both published by Sheeran Lock Fine Art. Two years later, Flood finished a residency with Opera North; in 1996 was commissioned by the Christian charity Caring for Life to produce drypoint etchings; and in 1996–7 Opera North commissioned Flood for portrait work. Commissioned portraits included Geoffrey Lehmann, R A Clegg, Charles and Elizabeth Noble and the Solabarrieta family. National Library of Ireland, West Yorkshire Playhouse, Leeds City Art Gallery and Leeds General Infirmary and Thomas Danby College hold examples. Flood was based in Leeds.

Mary Sargant FLORENCE 1857–1954 Painter of pictures and murals working in tempera and watercolour. Born in London, sister of the sculptor Francis W Sargant, she studied at the Slade School of Fine Art under Alphonse Legros and in Paris, partly at Atelier Colarossi. Exhibited RA, NEAC, SWA and elsewhere. She was interested in the theory of colour, on which she wrote. The Tate Gallery owns her work. She designed her own house at Marlow, Buckinghamshire, but died at Twickenham, Middlesex.

Ron FLORENCE 1935– Sculptor, conservator and restorer, originally known as Ron Florenz, a South African who moved to Nottingham in the late 1960s, who for a time ran a gallery there at Canning Circus. He came of a talented family, his brother being the London impresario Norman Florenz, his nephew Trevor Jones, who wrote acclaimed music for the 1981 John Boorman-directed Arthurian film *Excalibur*. Florence went on to run Florence Conservation and Restoration in Long Eaton, Nottingham. Among his portrait sculptures was a joint one in bronze of HRH The Prince of Wales and Lady Diana Spencer, shown at Mall Galleries in 1981. He also sculpted Dame Joan Sutherland, the opera singer, and Dr George Birkbeck, founder of the Mechanics' Institute. Desford County Primary School has Florence's stylised cold-cast bronze and steel Child and Bird, presented in 1983.

Ron FLORENZ: *see* **Ron FLORENCE**

Cedric FLOWER 1920–2000 Painter, draughtsman, stage designer, illustrator and writer, born in Sydney, New South Wales, Australia, eventually settling in the state at Werri Beach. Flower left school to work as a commercial artist, attending evening classes at the Dattilo Rubbo Studio. From 1950–5 he was overseas, in Britain "making a living in the more mundane branches of advertising" and taking part in the first Australian Artists' Association exhibition at the RWS Conduit Street gallery, 1953. Back in Australia, he had many solo shows in Sydney, Melbourne and Adelaide, becoming known for pictures with a strong decorative quality. His books include *Duck and Cabbage Tree*, 1968; *The Antipodes Observed*, 1974; and *Illustrated History of New South Wales*, 1981. National Gallery of Australia, Canberra, and other Australian public collections hold examples.

Nigel A FLOWER 1931–1985 Painter, designer and teacher, born in Ashbourne, Derbyshire. Flower attended Cardiff College of Art, 1947–53, then held a number of teaching posts, returning to Cardiff College, 1964, to study graphics and photography. He then joined Rhondda Borough Council, in Wales, as a graphic designer and photographer. Showed Royal National Eisteddfod, SWG and WAC, which holds his work.

Terry FLOWER 1953– Sculptor, photographer and teacher who graduated with honours in fine art, sculpture, at Goldsmiths' College, gaining a master's in sequential illustration and photography at the University of Brighton. Taught the art foundation course at Braintree College, 1992–5 (also having a residency there), then was senior lecturer, University of Brighton, from 1995. Other residencies included schools for the visually impaired, dockyards and salerooms. Won a photography commission, Beaford Photographic Archive, north Devon, and a sculpture commission, Stitching Promoties, Hook of Holland, Netherlands, both 2000, and a photography bursary, Focal Point Gallery, Southend/Norwich Arts Centre, 2001. Exhibitions included This Flat Earth, University of Essex Gallery, Colchester, 2000; Migration, Focal Point and Norwich Arts Centre, 2001 and 2002 respectively; and Over The River, firstsite, Colchester/Wolsey Art Gallery, Ipswich, 2002. Lived in Gestingthorpe, Essex.

Peter FLOWERS 1916–1950 Landscape painter. Initially educated in Switzerland, he studied art under Bertram Nicholls, then went on to show at the RA, RBA and ROI, also becoming a member of the Society of Sussex Painters. His work was reproduced by the art dealer Frost and Reed and the greetings card firm Raphael Tuck. Lived at Steyning, Sussex.

Christina FLOYD 1949– Artist and teacher, born in London, who studied at Central School of Art, 1968–9, Hornsey College of Art, 1969–72, then Royal College of Art, 1972–5. She taught at University of Pittsburgh, in America, 1975–8, later teaching part-time at Stourbridge College of Art and Hull College of Higher Education. Group shows included Northern Young Contemporaries, at Whitworth Art Gallery in Manchester, 1974; Museum of Art, Carnegie Institute, Pittsburgh, 1976; and Summer Show 3 at Serpentine Gallery, 1980. There she exhibited work in a variety of media. Solo exhibitions included, 1977, University of Pittsburgh, which holds her work, as does Leicester Education Authority. Lived in Ilford, Essex.

Donald Henry FLOYD 1892–1965 Painter of the Monmouthshire landscape, born in Plymouth, Devon, where he studied at Plymouth College, 1908–12, with the Cornish artist John Barlow. During World War I served with the Devon Regiment in India and Egypt, painting while off-duty. In 1920 married a Newport, Monmouthshire, teacher Annie Rogers, moving to Chepstow to live. Became a regular exhibitor at RA, 1920–1950. In 1948, was commissioned by Ceylon government to produce a suite of 68 pictures to celebrate independence. Many public and private collections hold Floyd's work, shown in A Feeling for Landscape by Newport Museum and Art Gallery in 1998.

Joan FLOYD: *see* **Joan MANNING-SANDERS**

Ceal FLOYER 1968– Artist employing slide projection and such objects as bulb and flex, and film, who was born in Karachi, Pakistan. Obtained a degree in theatre studies at Dartington College of Arts, 1989–90; did an art and design foundation course at Sir John Cass School of Art and Design, 1990–1; obtaining a degree in fine art at Goldsmiths' College, 1991–4. Group shows included Hit & Run, Tufton Street, 1992; Fast Surface, Chisenhale Gallery, 1993; General Release, Scuola di San Pasquale, Venice, 1995; British Art Show 4, with tour, 1995–6; and Days Like These, Tate Britain, 2003. She had solo shows at Ikon Gallery, Birmingham, 2001, and Lisson Gallery, 2002 and 2006. Humour was a defining factor in Floyer's work, her dry wit often depending on double meanings and careful timing.

Peter FLUCK 1941– Versatile artist and illustrator who studied at Cambridge High School for Boys and School of Art and who became famous when the Luck and Flaw partnership, formed with Roger Law, 1974–82, spawned the hugely successful 18-series television satire *Spitting Image*, which ran from 1982–94. Prior to that, Fluck had worked as an artist-reporter and illustrator, 1961–70, then as cartoonist and caricaturist, 1970–82. From 1994, he was a freelance artist and sculptor of abstract kinetics, with interests in ceramics, printmaking and electronic music working with the University of York. Fluck's exhibitions included Chaotic Constructions (with Tony Myatt), Tate Gallery St Ives and Edinburgh International Festival, both 1997; RIBA, 1999; and in 2004 the Study Gallery in Poole and Yew Tree Gallery in Cornwall, where he lived at Cadgwith.

Herbert FLUGELMAN 1923– Sculptor, painter, printmaker and teacher, Bert Flugelman was born in Vienna, Austria, settling in Australia in 1938. He attended the National Art School and East Sydney Technical College, both in Sydney, 1947–50, then travelled and worked in Britain, continental Europe and America, 1951–6. Support from the RA enabled Flugelman to work on the island of Ibiza, 1951. In 1953 he took part in the first Australian Artists' Association exhibition at the RWS Conduit Street gallery and had a solo show of paintings at the Piccadilly Gallery. Flugelman held a number of teaching posts in Australia, notably at the University of Wollongong, where he was made a professional fellow from 1991. After early developing as a painter, despite the crippling limitations of polio he became noted as a sculptor, winning many awards and competitions, his metal sculptures being well suited to public places. Commissions included University of New South Wales, 1964; Festival Hall, Adelaide, 1973; and Lawrence Hargrave Memorial, Wollongong, 1988. Later solo exhibitions included Irving Sculpture Gallery, Sydney, 1988. National Gallery of Australia, Canberra, Wollongong University and other Australian public galleries hold examples.

Brian FLYNN 1964– Artist, born in Toronto, Ontario, Canada, who did a foundation year at Dundas Valley School of Art there, 1985–6; gained an honours diploma in painting at Alberta College of Art, 1988–92; then his master's in fine art at University of Ulster, from 2001. Showed widely in Canada, including The Object Singular: The paintings of Brian Flynn and Mary Lottridge, Art Gallery of Peel, Brampton, 1999. He was also included in Small Islands, Big Ideas: New work by artists based at the Queen Street Studio, Belfast, at Irish Art Centre, New York, America, in 2001; and in 2002 was in Souvenirs, DeLeon White Gallery, Toronto, and in The Hunting Art Prizes, at Royal College of Art. There, Flynn showed The Power Dot Series, "a very important departure". In these, he "contrasted imagery and icons from various art historical periods with more contemporary references," being interested in "the difference between past and present aesthetics." Lived in Belfast.

Michael FLYNN 1947– Painter, sculptor in ceramic and metal, printmaker and teacher, born in Ireland. Over many years of exhibiting in mixed and solo shows Flynn built a name primarily as a sculptor whose work had a notable animal energy, its own symbolism, humour and a special concern with organs of touch. His reputation was especially strong on the continent, where he worked and taught, as he did in colleges of art in Britain. Group shows included International Print Biennale, Epinal, France, 1977; Fire and Smoke, Midland Group, Nottingham, and touring, 1983–4; Sculpture from Wales, Oxford Gallery, 1987; and Gainsborough's House, Sudbury, 1991. Selected one-man exhibitions included painting, Ikon Gallery, Birmingham, 1975; Sculpture in Ceramic and Bronze, 3D Gallery, Bristol, 1986; Goya Gallery, Antwerp, 1991; and Martin Tinney Gallery, Cardiff, 1993. Flynn's ceramics were included in A Serious Magic at Newport Museum & Art Gallery, 2004–5. Crawford Municipal Art Gallery, Cork; Crafts Council; and Victoria & Albert Museum hold his work. Lived in Cardiff.

Trevor FLYNN 1955– Artist who gained a Leicester Polytechnic graduation travel award, 1975–8. Group appearances included Whitechapel Open, Whitechapel Art Gallery, 1984; A London Reflected, Artworks Space, 1985; The South Bank Picture Show, Royal Festival Hall, 1987; and MA Degree Show, at Goldsmiths' College, and East End Open Studios, with Barbican Arts Group, both 1989. In 1986 Flynn had a solo show with the Mario Flecha Gallery.

Florian FOERSTER 1968– Printmaker, painter, draughtsman and teacher, born in Oldenburg, West Germany, who moved to England in 1989. He did a foundation course at Manchester Polytechnic, 1989–90, from 1990–3 obtaining a fine art degree, art and design, at Liverpool and Manchester Polytechnics, specialising in printmaking (in 1991 spending several months travelling in Brazil, studying printmaking at the Museu Lasar Segall, São Paulo). From 1993–4, taught printmaking part-time at Salford University College. Between 1994–7, Foerster obtained a structural engineering degree at Manchester Victoria University. Group exhibitions included Skelmersdale Arts Centre, 1993; MAFA Open, 1994 (awarded a print prize, another in 1996); Tib Lane Gallery, Manchester, from 1994. Had a solo exhibition at Liverpool University School of Architecture, 1995, with two others in 1996 at Royal Northern College of Music, Manchester, and Galerie Zunge, Berlin, Germany, another at Tib Lane Gallery, Manchester, 2004.

Pat FOGARTY 1940–1999 Illustrator, painter of portraits and abstracts, photographer and teacher, born in Cradock, Cape Province, South Africa, full name Patricia Marion Fogarty, who retained her childhood nickname Piffy. She was a charismatic figure, small and combative, a natural entertainer and mimic who was obsessed by Hollywood movies and who became a skilled punter on the horses. Lived for a time with her farming family in Grootfontein in what was to become Namibia. Graduated in art from Port Elizabeth Technical College, 1959–62, but disliked Apartheid and in 1965 moved to England where she taught art. She also painted on the Greek island Skiathos;

designed film posters in Paris; then returned to England in 1975, settling in north London. There she took up freelance commercial illustration, noted for her working speed. Clients included *The Daily Telegraph*, *Reader's Digest*, Tesco and Penguin Books, for which she completed a classic book-jacket portrait of the writer John Mortimer. As computer-generated images eroded the need for her type of work, Fogarty, who had been for several years a volunteer for the Lesbian and Gay Switchboard, began studying therapy and counselling and helped out at an HIV/Aids centre. Died of cancer.

Mary FOGG 1918– Painter, ceramic sculptor and teacher, born in Poulton-le-Fylde, Lancashire. From 1942–4 she studied at Preston and Liverpool Arts Schools part-time, then worked widely in England and Wales as a radiographer during the rest of the war. In 1945 settled in North Wales and studied etching and sculpture, in 1964–7 studying painting and ceramics at Bath Academy of Art, Corsham. Did a variety of teaching in the Oswestry, Shropshire, area where she lived. Fogg was a member of WIAC, The Welsh Group and Free Painters and Sculptors. Showed at Royal National Eisteddfod, RCamA, WAC and elsewhere and had a series of solo shows. Among her commissions was a Mother and Child for St John's Church, Stoke-on-Trent. University College of Wales, Aberystwyth, holds her work.

David FOGGIE 1878–1948 Painter, draughtsman and teacher, born in Dundee, where he studied at the High School. Encouraged by the local Art Society and with £30, Foggie went to Antwerp to study art, remaining ten months on that sum. After further studies there Foggie established himself as an artist in Dundee. In 1919 he moved to Edinburgh, where he obtained a part-time teaching post at the College of Art, held until 1939. Foggie was elected RSA in 1930, six years after being made RSW, then in 1932 he was made secretary of the Academy, a post he held until his unexpected death during an attack of asthma, which had plagued him since his early thirties. Foggie's abilities as a fine painter and superlative draughtsman have been for many years underrated. He was a master of the human figure, but he never became a society portraitist and lack of commissions forced him to select models from manual workers, professional models, members of his own family or friends – especially people of character. He painted at every opportunity. Examples of his work are in galleries in Dundee, Paisley, Edinburgh, Aberdeen, Glasgow and elsewhere. The National Portrait Gallery has a series of Edinburgh portraits. Centenary show 1978 at Dundee Museums and Art Galleries. His son was the painter Neil Foggie. Lived in Edinburgh.

Neil FOGGIE 1912–1995 Artist and teacher, born in Balmullow, Fife, son of the artist David Foggie and married to the painter Margaret Hendry. Foggie was predominantly a landscape painter, mostly in oil, who drew cartoons as Du Brouillard. He attended Edinburgh College of Art, 1930–4. Was art master at Dollar Academy, 1934–48 (interrupted by war service with the Argyll & Sutherland Highlanders, where he rose to major), then was principal art teacher at Galashiels Academy, 1948–72. In 1955–6 Foggie made a teaching exchange to Toronto, Canada, where modern Canadian painting, especially the work of the Group of Seven, impressed him, and where he showed and sold well. Years later, Canadians would seek out Foggie's Scottish works. Showed at Royal Glasgow Institute of the Fine Arts, RSA, SSA, Aberdeen Artists' Society, RSW and elsewhere. Solo shows included Old Gala House, Galashiels, 1952, and Galashiels Public Library, 1972. Lived partly in Edinburgh, partly in Mull, where he died.

Brian FOJCIK 1960– Figurative painter and draughtsman, born in Kirkcaldy, Fife, who studied at Duncan of Jordanstone College of Art, Dundee, 1979–83, with a postgraduate year, 1983–4. Prizes included John Milne Prize in Painting; George Duncan of Drumfork Travelling Scholarship, both at Duncan of Jordanstone; Elizabeth Greenshields Award, 1988; and Maude Gemmell Hutchison Prize, RSA Summer Exhibition. Fojcik was elected to SSA in 1992 and to SSWA in 1993. Group shows included Gallery 22 and Compass Gallery, both in Glasgow, and RSA, all 1988; RA Summer Exhibition, 1989; and Roots, Kirkcaldy Museum and Art Gallery, 1993. Had a solo show at Gallery 22, Cupar, 1984, later ones including The Scottish Gallery in Edinburgh, from 1993, and Thackeray Gallery, 1996.

Peter FOLDES 1924–1977 Artist and film director, animator and scriptwriter, born in Budapest, Hungary. He studied at Courtauld Institute from 1946, also at Slade School of Fine Art and had an exhibition at Hanover Gallery, 1953. At the Courtauld, Foldes met his future wife, Joan, also born in 1924. They were encouraged to make films by John Halas (who with Joy Batchelor made the pioneering 1955 British cartoon film *Animal Farm*, based on George Orwell's novel). Peter and Joan made two together, the latter, *A Short Vision*, being screened at Tate Britain in 2003, an animated painting preoccupied with the threat of nuclear war. In the year that film appeared, Foldes returned to painting, moving to Paris, then resumed filming, having his greatest success in France from the mid-1960s. Among his titles was *Bilitis*, 1968, and a Canadian film, *La Faim*, about world famine, 1973. In the year of his death a documentary about Foldes, *Image de Peter Foldes*, drew attention to his contribution as an early computer-animation man. Tate Gallery archive has his striking Self-Portrait, 1953. After Peter Foldes died in Paris, his wife continued to live there. She made other animated and live action films and wrote poetry.

Sydney FOLEY 1916–2001 Representational painter, especially of scenes with a watery theme. These included the Rivers Thames and Medway, East Anglia and on the continent, especially Venice. Born in London, Foley attended Tottenham County School, winning a Saturday morning scholarship to Hornsey School of Art until World War II interrupted. He joined the Royal Artillery, 1939–46, after D-Day serving in France and northwest Europe, on demobilisation returning to a career in education administration with Surrey County Council. From 1963 was able to devote more time to painting, showing with the ROI (winning its Stanley Grimm Prize) and RSMA, of both of which he was a member, the London Sketch Club and the Wapping Group of Artists of which he was president, 1992–7. Had several solo shows with The Century Gallery, Datchet, which held one in his memory, 2001. Lived at Laleham, Surrey.

Charles FOLKARD 1878–1963 Illustrator and painter, born in London, father of the sculptor Edward Folkard. He attended Goldsmiths' College School of Art, Blackheath, Sidcup and St John's Wood Schools of Art and is most famous for creating the comic strip for children *Teddy Tail* in the *Daily Mail* in 1915, which lasted for 45 years. Also drew for other newspapers, for magazines and illustrated several dozen books. These include *Aesop's Fables*, 1912; *Mother Goose's Nursery Rhymes*, 1919; and George Macdonald's *The Princess and the Goblin*, 1949. Lived in London for some years, finally in Heathfield, Sussex.

Edward FOLKARD 1911– Sculptor, of figurative work and teacher, son of the illustrator Charles Folkard, born in London. He studied at Goldsmiths' College School of Art and the Royal Academy Schools and was elected a fellow of the RBS in 1955. His teachers included Clive Gardiner, Walter Russell and John Skeaping. Taught at Royal College of Art. Showed at RA, RBA, LG and Royal Glasgow Institute of the Fine Arts and was a member of Chelsea Arts Club. Sometimes signed work E F. Ted Folkard lived latterly in Builth Wells, Powys, having moved to Wales in 1972, and solo exhibitions in the principality, where he became recognised for wood-carvings in churches. Other materials employed included ciment fondu and clay. Aged 91, Folkard wrote: "I truly believe that my work is improving. I have been called a 'liberated academic'. I like to have adventures with clay." Folkard's later output included a six-foot figure of Gaia, the earth goddess, commemorating the 1993 National Eisteddfod and sited at the entry to County Hall, Powys, and a life-size figure of Henry VII, centrally placed in Hay-on-Wye. Museum of Modern Art, New York, America, and National Museum, Tokyo, Japan, hold examples.

Peter FOLKES 1923– Painter in oil, watercolour and acrylic, and teacher, born in Beaminster, Dorset. Studied at West of England College of Art, Bristol, 1941–50, his studies being interrupted by Army service, 1942–7, abroad. He went on to become head of the department of fine art, Southampton Institute of Higher Education, retiring in 1989. Became a tutor for Artscape Painting Holidays and a consultant and demonstrator for Winsor & Newton. In 1963 Folkes won a Goldsmiths' Travelling Scholarship which enabled him to travel widely in America. In 1959 he was elected RWA, in 1969 RI, holding senior positions with both bodies. Had a series of solo shows, beginning with Rumbold Gallery, Midhurst, 1962, later ones including RWA, 1986, and St Paul's School Gallery, 1992. Arts Council and RWA hold his work. Lived in Swaythling, Southampton.

Ron FOLLAND 1932–1999 Largely self-taught artist in oil, acrylic and watercolour, who studied for a time in Paris having been born in Portsmouth, Hampshire. He was noted for his landscapes, especially of English villages. Folland twice achieved the number one position in the Fine Art Trade Guild nationwide poll and was for many years from 1965 rated in the Top Ten Artists Poll more times than any artist. His solo shows included Frost & Reed, Bristol, from 1976; *To-Day*, Southern Television, from same year; Frost & Reed, Worthing, 1978; and St Helier, Jersey, 1980. His limited-edition prints sold widely and included *Spires of Paris, Springtime in London* and *Dimanche*. Collectors around the world hold examples. Lived in Ickenham, Middlesex.

Ursula FOOKES 1906–1991 Lino-cutter and painter in oil and watercolour, whose early life is a mystery. She studied at the Grosvenor School of Modern Art, 1929–30. Her highly stylized work showed the influence of one of its founders, Claude Flight, who included it in exhibitions at the Ward Gallery in the 1930s, a period when Fookes travelled and painted abroad with her artist friend Pauline Logan, with whom she shared a studio in Pimlico, and produced more conventional Post-Impressionist works. These were exhibited at NEAC, and she also showed at Redfern Gallery and SWA. In 1939 Fookes, her mother and an aunt moved to Lymington, Hampshire, where she did war work, then she travelled to the continent in 1945, running a mobile canteen for the troops. Later settled in Norfolk and bird watching became a keen interest, while the art work had diminished. It was only after her death that a body of pictures was found, reviving interest in her earlier output, and dealers began to show them. Fookes' diary of her time in Germany, 1945–6, was edited for private circulation by Alan Guest, a copy being placed in the Imperial War Museum.

Susan FOORD 1945– Painter, born in London, who studied at Jacob Kramer College and at Leeds Polytechnic faculty of art and design. She created small, delicate pictures which tended "to be evocative of landscape or seascape and sometimes still life". Showed at RA, RWA (elected in 1997), Dean Clough, Halifax, Manchester Academy of Fine Arts, Waterman Fine Art, in Hong Kong at Gallery 7 and in Eight by Eight at Pallant House, Chichester, in 1997, the year she had a solo exhibition with Offer Waterman & Co Fine Art. Other solo shows followed, at RWA in 1999, Adam Gallery, London 2000-1-3 and Bath 2005. Work held in Provident Financial Collection, RWA Permanent Collection and Arts Club, Royal Academy. Lived in Bristol.

Victorine FOOT 1920–2000 Artist in oil, watercolour and pastel and teacher, born in Pembury, Kent, from 1946 married to the sculptor Eric Schilsky. She studied at Central School of Arts and Crafts, Chelsea School of Art and Edinburgh College of Art, teachers including Morris Kestelman, Ceri Richards, Leonard Rosoman and William Gillies. After settling in Edinburgh she taught at the College. Foot was one of Jack Beddington's *Young Artists of Promise* in the 1957 book of that title. Painting "moments that surprise me", she exhibited at LG, NEAC, RA, RSA and SSA in mixed shows, having several solo exhibitions at Scottish Gallery, Edinburgh, from 1969. Scottish Arts Council and War Artists' Advisory Committee acquired her work, Foot having worked under the Directorate of Camouflage during World War II.

Winslow FOOT 1939– Sculptor, painter and teacher who studied at Philadelphia Museum College of Art in America, 1956–9, concentrating on sculpture and three-dimensional design. He returned to England, instructed in sculpture and photography at Plymouth College of Art, then from 1963–8 taught at Leeds College of Art and was included in its staff exhibition The Teaching Image at Leeds City Art Gallery, 1964. Was later on the staff of Wolverhampton Polytechic in the product design department, then lived in London. In the 1980s, Foot turned from sculpture to boatbuilding, although he eventually returned to it, from the early 1990s with the sculptor Marigold Hodgkinson tackling large site-specific and kinetic works. Leeds Museums and Galleries hold sculptures by Foot.

Enid FOOTE WATTS 1924–2003 Artist working in mixed media who studied at Glasgow School of Art and Washington Art Centre. She was a member of Glasgow Women's Art Society and the Paisley Art Institute, where she won the William Bowie Award in 2001. For many years she showed with the RSA, Royal Glasgow Institute of the Fine Arts, also with the Wren Gallery, Burford, and held regular exhibitions at Torrance Gallery, Edinburgh. Her work was held by private collections in Scotland, England and America. Critics referred to Foote Watts as a Romantic Colourist. She enjoyed painting the Clyde valley, also the Scottish islands and on the continent. Wren Gallery gave her a memorial show in 2003.

Arthur FORBES: *see* **Arthur FORBES-DALRYMPLE**

Donald FORBES 1952– Painter in oil, by profession a restorer with National Gallery in Edinburgh, where he lived. He was born in Glasgow, studying at its School of Art, 1970–4, teachers including David Donaldson. Showed with RSA and Royal Glasgow Institute of the Fine Arts, solo exhibitions including Lillie Art Gallery, Milngavie.

Harry FORBES 1949– Self-taught draughtsman and maker of assemblage sculptures using found objects and pigment. A group was offered at Bonhams, Knightsbridge, in 2002. Had solo exhibitions in London, Paris and West Germany. Forbes originally lived in London, later Leicestershire.

Michael FORBES 1968– Artist, born in Dingwall, Ross and Cromarty, where he attended the Academy, 1979–85, starting to paint full-time in 1989. In 1997, Forbes was a finalist in the J D Fergusson Arts Award for the most promising young Scottish artist. Group exhibitions included Myth and Symbol, Inverness Art Gallery, 1993; Compass Gallery, Glasgow, 1995; and RSA, 1996. Solo exhibitions included Eden Court Theatre, Inverness, 1989; Flying Colours Gallery, Edinburgh, 1991; and Chalk Farm Galleries, from 1996. United Distillers holds his work.

Richard FORBES 1953– Painter, born and based in London, who trained at Wimbledon School of Art, 1973–7, and the Slade School of Fine Art, 1977–9. He went on to work in the technical services department of the Tate Gallery. Forbes produced paintings concerned with theories of colour and language in the manner of the Systems Group: groups of multi-coloured squares and rectangles. His work was included in A Disquieting Suggestion, John Hansard Gallery at the University of Southampton, 1988. Arts Council and Conoco Centre, Warwick, hold examples.

Ronald FORBES 1947– Painter and teacher, born Braco, Perthshire. He studied at Edinburgh College of Art, 1964–9, with Robin Philipson, and at Jordanhill College of Education in Glasgow. Forbes taught at Bell College, Hamilton, then was appointed Leverhulme Senior Art Fellow at Strathclyde University, Glasgow. He next moved to Cork where he was head of painting at Crawford School of Art, returning to Scotland in 1978 to be artist-in-residence Livingstone, West Lothian. He then lectured at Glasgow School of Art for four years, from 1983 being on the staff of Dundee College of Art. In the early 1970s Forbes was founder-chairman of the Glasgow League of Artists and when in Livingstone was chairman of the Art Foundation there. He won a number of awards for films. Forbes had solo shows at Compass Gallery in Glasgow, Drian Galleries, Third Eye Centre in Glasgow and at Seagate Gallery, Dundee, 1990. Arts Council of Northern Ireland, Cork Art Gallery and SAC hold his work. Lived in Livingston, West Lothian.

Stanhope Alexander FORBES 1857–1947 Painter and teacher, born in Dublin, who was married to the artist Elizabeth Armstrong. Forbes studied at Lambeth School of Art, Royal Academy Schools, 1874–8, then for two years in Paris. He was influenced by Jules Bastien-Lepage. Settled in Cornwall in 1884, became a leading member of the Newlyn School of open air painters specialising in local landscapes and the lives of fishermen and their families. The Tate Gallery's picture The Health of the Bride is a good example. Forbes was a founder-member of NEAC in 1886 and two years later began showing with RA, being elected RA in 1910. Also travelled extensively on the continent. With his wife he founded the Newlyn School of Art in 1899, and he remained an influential teacher for many years. Died in Newlyn.

Stephen FORBES 1973– Painter and lecturer, born in Newry, County Down, Northern Ireland, who gained a distinction on his foundation course at John Moores University, Liverpool, 1991–2, graduating with honours from there, 1992–6. From 1996–7, Forbes held painting and research scholarships and lectured at St Helens College, from 1998–01 gaining a postgraduate diploma in fine art from the Royal Academy Schools. He was a visiting lecturer at St Helens College and Liverpool University's department of fine art. Forbes's group exhibitions included St Helens Open, Merseyside, 1998; RA Summer Exhibition, from 2000; Flash, Adelaide Street, Belfast, 2002; and Living for the City, Waterfront Hall, Belfast, and RUA, Ulster Museum, Mills Selig Prize, outstanding work by a young artist, both 2004. Among his solo shows were Pierre Victoire Buildings, Liverpool, 1996; Leisure, Elaine Somers Gallery, Belfast, 2003; and Activity, Tom Caldwell, Belfast, 2005.

Arthur FORBES-DALRYMPLE 1912– Painter in oil, gouache, pastel and watercolour. Born in Edinburgh, he studied under Henry Massey at Heatherley's School of Fine Art, 1930–2, and at Goldsmiths' College School of Art under Clive Gardiner, 1932–4. Exhibited RA, NS, ROI, NEAC, RBA and extensively in Paris, including the Salon. Sometimes signed work Forbes. Lived in London.

Deborah FORD 1968– London-based graphic designer who studied at Coventry Polytechnic, 1987–90. In her final year she completed the bronze relief Cofa's Tree, said to be the origin of the name Coventry. It was placed in the foyer of Friars House in the city's centre.

George Henry FORD 1912–1977 Sculptor, studied at Hornsey School of Art under Harold Youngman. Exhibited RA, Royal Glasgow Institute of the Fine Arts, Walker Art Gallery, Liverpool, and elsewhere in the provinces. His teak figure Eve is in the collection of Bradford City Art Gallery. Work also featured in Arthur T Broadbent's monograph *Sculpture Today in Great Britain 1940–1943*. He was a fellow of the RBS and lived in London.

Jane FORD: *see* **Jane TRESIDDER**

Jenifer FORD 1934– Painter, born in Cape Town, South Africa. She studied at Michaelis School of Fine Art, University of Cape Town, 1951–3, then 10 years later with Bernard Adams in London. Showed NS of which she was a member, ROI, RP and elsewhere and had a number of solo shows including British Council, Munich, West Germany, where she lived for some years.

Jonathan FORD 1971– Sculptor making publicly commissioned works in metal who graduated from Coventry University in 1995. Ford was a member of Coventry Arts Exchange, with that organisation working on the ceramic Snake in the Grass, at Trentham Road, in the city, 1997, commissioned by Coventry City Council. Other notable pieces by Ford are the painted metal Giant Vacuum Cleaner, Chainset and Handlebars, 1998, behind a community centre, made for Groundwork Coventry; and his scrap-metal, child-oriented construction Schlanke Meth, at Wainbody School, Coventry, commissioned by Arts Exchange. Ford also completed sculptures for other sites in England and Wales including the kinetic piece Rotor-Relief, 1998, for Wysing Arts, Cambridge.

Ken FORD 1930– Sculptor, draughtsman and teacher, born in Birstall, Leicestershire, whose interest in the countryside was fostered by visits to his grandparents. Although as an artist Ford's main interest became landscape and the human being within it, he had "no desire to be descriptive; I consider myself to be a mystical artist, that is to say, I wish to indicate the cause behind the effect." Ford attended Gateway School, Leicester, 1943–6, winning the Sir Jonathon North Gold Medal, 1944. Studied at Leicester College of Art and Design, 1947–9, winning The Clephan Prize, 1947; Royal College of Art, 1950–4, winning The Continuation Scholarship, 1953; and won Prix de Rome for Sculpture, 1955, attending the British School, Rome, 1955–7. In 1961 Ford won the National Sculpture Competition, Newcastle upon Tyne. Became head of sculpture at Leicester Polytechnic, 1967–8, from 1998 being a visiting lecturer at the Elisabeth Frink School of Sculpture, Stoke-on-Trent. Took part in many group exhibitions, solo shows including Goldmark Gallery, Uppingham, 2002. Public sculpture commissions included Charles Keene College Courtyard, Leicester, 1960; Sir Frank Whittle Commemorative Sculpture, Lutterworth, 1987; and Surrey Heath House, Camberley, 1993.

Laura FORD 1961– Artist in various media and teacher, born in Cardiff, who studied at Bath Academy of Art, 1978–82, with an exchange term at Cooper Union, New York, then Chelsea School of Art, 1985. Her group shows included Whitworth Art Gallery, Manchester, 1982; Serpentine Gallery, 1983; Sculpture in the City, Bath, 1986; Mappin Art Gallery, Sheffield, 1988; and Six of the Best at Christopher Hull Gallery, 1989. Had a solo show at Nicola Jacobs Gallery, 1987; Benjamin Rhodes, Gallery, 1991; and Spacex Gallery, Exeter, 1996. In Ford's sculpture exhibition Desperados, at Houldsworth Fine Art, 2001, the gallery was cluttered with soft, benign, childlike figures, dressed as for a playground, yet the patterns and textiles of their skin disguised their faces. Violence lurked within calm, horror within charm. At De La Warr Pavilion, Bexhill-on-Sea, 2003, Ford showed animal figures, which she called "sculptures dressed up as animals which are dressed up as people." In that year, Ford also exhibited a major installation at the Dick Institute, Kilmarnock, and had a solo show, The Great Indoors, at Harris Museum and Art Gallery, Preston. Arts Council, Contemporary Art Society and Unilever plc hold examples.

Leslie FORD 1885–1959 Pastel and watercolour artist, born in Bow, London. Studied at West Ham School of Art under Mervyn Lawrence and Arthur Legge. Exhibited PS, RI and elsewhere in London. Was an active member of the Wapping Group of artists, of which he was secretary for a time after World War II, and the Langham Sketch Club. Sunderland Museum and Art Gallery holds his work. Lived at Gidea Park, Essex.

Malcolm Stephen FORD 1914– Painter, printmaker and teacher, born in Newport, Monmouthshire. He studied at Newport School of Art and Royal College of Art. Did work as a book illustrator and jacket designer and held a number of teaching posts, being vice-principal of Birmingham College of Art for some years, then dean of art and design at Birmingham Polytechnic. Lived at Sutton Coldfield, Warwickshire.

Mary FORD 1944– Painter of figurative pictures, of restricted palette and simplified form to emphasize their abstract qualities, born in London. She was brought up in Cornwall from the age of six, having "an idyllic childhood" on the family ketch moored at St Mawes. From 1970–6 attended Byam Shaw and Royal Academy Schools, where William Scott taught her. The work of the St Ives painters Alfred Wallis ("painted purely from the heart") and Ben Nicholson ("I admire the sophistication") was a strong influence. Group exhibitions included New Contemporaries, 1972; Wills Lane Gallery, St Ives, from 1975; Eastgate Gallery, Chichester, 1987; and Roy Miles Gallery, 1994. Had solo exhibitions at Sadler's Wells Theatre, 1975, and Eastgate Gallery, 1986. There was a further solo exhibition, Horizons, at Oliver Contemporary in 2003, coinciding with publication of the Tate's 2004 diary series, for which Ford's work Boats – Antibes, 1979, was chosen from its collection to illustrate the front cover. Truro Crown Courts and Slaughter & May held Ford's work.

Michael FORD 1920– Painter and black-and-white draughtsman who handled a wide variety of subjects, including portrait commissions. He studied at Goldsmiths' College School of Art, 1937–40, teachers including Clive Gardiner. Went on to do war artist work, several pictures being held by Imperial War Museum. Ford's War Weapons Week in a Country Town is illustrated in Eric Newton's 1945 book *War Through Artists' Eyes*. Ford showed RA, RBA, NEAC, Towner Art Gallery in Eastbourne and at Paris Salon and continued painting at an advanced age despite being profoundly deaf. Lived in Winsor, Southampton.

Peter FORD 1937– Artist and printmaker, born in Hereford, where he attended the College of Art, 1955–6. Was then at St Mary's College for teacher training, at Strawberry Hill in Twickenham, 1957–60; Brighton College of Art, 1960–1; and London University Institute of Education to gain diploma in education of maladjusted children. Among Ford's awards were a bursary from Scottish Arts Council, 1976, and a South West Arts Minor Award, 1980, the year he took part in its touring show Seven Print

Makers. In 1977 Ford was elected a member of the Printmakers' Council, in 1979 a participating member of World Print Council. He was also an associate of the RWA, a senior fellow of the RE and a member of the International Association of Papermaking Artists. Residencies included Openshaw Print Residency, Cumbria, 1994; Boise State University, Idaho, America, 1996; Art in Action, Oxford, 1999 and 2000; and Nature in Art Museum, Gloucester, 1999. Among his mixed exhibitions were the RA Summer Exhibition from 1975, and among later ones the 12th Norwegian Print Triennale, Fedrikstad, 1999; International Print Triennale, Cracow, Poland, 2000; and In Praise of Trees at Salisbury Arts Festival and Stephen Lacey Gallery, both 2002. Later solo shows included Printspace, 2002. From 1987, Ford ran the Off-Centre Gallery, in Bristol, where he lived. Many international public and corporate collections held Ford's work, including Tate Gallery, Ashmolean Museum in Oxford, Unilever and Prudential Insurance.

Reginald William FORD 1909–c.1973 Designer, calligrapher, illustrator and artist, born in Reading, Berkshire, where he settled at Earley. Studied part-time at the local university. Worked for Oxford University Press, Macmillan and others. His book *Record of a Pilgrimage* was published in 1936. Showed with Reading Guild of Artists and had work bought by the Corporation and Art Gallery.

Chris FORDHAM 1949– Abstracted landscape painter working in mixed media, born in London. Fordham studied for an interior design diploma in London, 1967–71, obtained a diploma in art, Alexander Mackie, Sydney, Australia, 1976–9, postgraduate work at Alexander Mackie, 1981. In 1984 gained a Bachelor of Arts degree at City Art Institute, Sydney. Lived in Sydney, 1974–87, showing regularly in mixed exhibitions and competitions in New South Wales from 1976. Had solo exhibition at Arcana Gallery, Kelso, 1977, and Montmartre Gallery, Canberra, 1982. In 1982 gained Warringah Contemporary Art Prize, in 1983 Blackheath Art Prize. After returning to Britain Fordham showed in mixed exhibitions in south of England and had a one-man show at Albion Gallery, Lewes, 1990. Several public collections in Australia and Bank of Ireland hold work.

Mollie FORESTIER-WALKER 1912–1990 Painter and draughtsman. Brought up in Devon, she studied at the West of England School of Art, in Bristol, and privately with T P Anderson. During World War II the War Artists' Advisory Committee bought her portrait of Wing-Commander Guy Gibson for the Imperial War Museum. Exhibited RP, NS, PS and Paris Salon, where she gained an Hon. Mention in 1949. Lived in London and at St Mawes, Cornwall.

Andrew FORGE 1923–2002 Art critic and writer, teacher and painter, born in Hastingleigh, Kent. He studied at Camberwell School of Arts and Crafts, 1947–9, under William Coldstream and Victor Pasmore. Was senior lecturer at the Slade School of Fine Art, 1950–64; head of the department of fine art at Goldsmiths' College, 1964–70; lecturer in the department of art at Reading University, 1971–2; visiting professor, Cooper Union, New York, 1973–4; associate dean, New York Studio School, 1974–5, visiting professor, 1975–02; professor of painting, Yale University, 1975–91, dean of the school of art, 1975–83, and William Leffingwell Professor of Painting, 1991–4 (emeritus). He held a number of official appointments, including trustee of the Tate Gallery, 1964–71 and 1972–4 and of the National Gallery, 1966–72. Was president of LG, 1964–71. Wrote books on a series of artists, including Klee, Vermeer, Soutine and Manet. Tate Gallery holds his work. Lived at Elmsted, Kent, and New Milford, Connecticut, where he died. Forge was originally a figurative artist, with a deep attachment to the Kent landscape. His last show of figurative work was at the AIA Gallery in 1963, immediately after which he flew to America, where a meeting with the artist Robert Rauschenberg opened up his vision. This was the beginning of a 40-year exploration in which dots and dashes, which Forge termed "sticks" dominated his output. Later exhibitions included a retrospective at Yale Center for British Art, 1996, and Watercolours, with Garth Evans, Kendall Art & Design, Hudson, New York, 1998.

Charlotte FORMAN fl. from 1950s– Painter, illustrator and teacher who trained at the Central School of Arts and Crafts, 1940–3 and 1946–8, then Bath Academy of Art, Corsham, 1957–9. She taught at Southwark College, in London schools and adult education. Did book illustrations and jacket designs for such publishers as Michael Joseph, Victor Gollancz and Bodley Head. Her pictures, in a detailed style, were shown at LG, Pictures for Schools, AIA, Hampstead Artists' Council, South London Artists and in a four-man show at Woodlands Art Gallery, 1981.

Robert FORMAN 1912– Interior decorator and artist in wash and pen and ink, born in Berwick-upon-Tweed, Northumberland. He was self-taught. Wrote a number of books, including *The Art of Scraperboard* and *Design for Commercial Artists*. Lived in Redland, Bristol.

Archie FORREST 1950– Artist and teacher, born in Glasgow where he studied at the School of Art, 1969–73. He was then a teacher at Dunbartonshire schools, 1974–85, and a tutor at Glasgow School of Art, 1978–85, in the latter year becoming a full-time artist. Forrest was a prolific exhibitor in group shows, including Kelly Gallery in Glasgow, Lillie Gallery in Milngavie, Fine Art Society in Glasgow and Royal Glasgow Institute of the Fine Arts, to which he was elected in 1988. He was a winner of its Torrance Award and of the Benno Schotz Sculpture Award, Scottish Amicable Painting Prize and Arthur Andersen Award. Forrest painted a lot in France and Italy, his one-man shows including a series of own-studio exhibitions and Portland Gallery, 2003. The Duchess of York, Scottish National Portrait Gallery and Glasgow Art Club hold his work.

Edwin FORREST 1918–2002 Painter in oil, born in Birkenhead, Cheshire, self-taught apart from criticism from his friend and noted local teacher Will Penn. Became a freelance decorative artist and signwriter and was curator of the Williamson Art Gallery and Museum. Two key influences on Forrest's pictures were "the story of landscape and transient effects of sunlight and shadow across sea and land". Forrest was a member of RCamA. Exhibited in groups including Festival of Britain and Merseyside Artists, both at Walker Art Gallery, Liverpool; Atkinson Art Gallery, Southport; Grosvenor Museum, Chester; MAFA; and Williamson Art Gallery. Had solo shows with RCamA, Conway; Rushworth's Gallery, Liverpool; and Lady Lever Art Gallery, Port Sunlight. There was a retrospective at RCamA, 2003. Lived in Trefriw, Gwynedd.

Norman John FORREST 1898–1972 Sculptor in wood. He studied under Thomas Good at Edinburgh College of Art. Went on to exhibit at RSA, SSA, Royal Glasgow Institute of Fine Arts as well as in London and the provinces. Forrest did a lot of ecclesiastical work as well as sculptures for the liners *Queen Mary* and *Queen Elizabeth.* His work often has a strong, elemental, primitive quality in the manner of Epstein. Illustrated in Eric Newton's monograph *British Sculpture 1944–1946*. Lived in Edinburgh.

Denzil FORRESTER 1956– Painter, and teacher, brought up in Grenada until in the late 1960s he moved to London. He attended Central School of Art and Design, 1975–9, and Royal College of Art, 1980–3, a Rome Scholarship in the latter year taking him to the British School in Rome, 1983–5. A Harkness Fellowship took him to live in New York, 1986–8. Forrester's pictures were commonly on a large scale, mixing West Indian and European culture, Rastafarianism and traits to be found in German Expressionism and Italian Futurism, with bold, radiating lines of brilliant colour. He had his first solo show at Riverside Studios in 1983; another at Commonwealth Institute in 1986; was included in Exhibition Road show in 1988 at Royal College of Art which, like the Arts Council, holds his work; and had a further solo exhibition at 198 Gallery in 1995. Taught at Morley College and was involved in the Islington Arts Factory.

John FORRESTER 1922– Painter, born in Wellington, New Zealand. Forrester began painting in the late 1930s, soon after going overseas where he associated with modern art groups. He was in South Africa, 1939–45. After war service he lived in St Ives, Cornwall, 1953–8, from 1958–60 in Italy, then from 1960 in Paris. Among his solo shows in England were Gimpel Fils, 1955, and McRoberts and Tunnard, 1962, and he also exhibited in France, including Galerie du Fleuve, 1965, and New Zealand. Forrester was interested in the relationship between pictures and architecture and in the 1950s was appointed design consultant to the Sheffield, north Yorkshire, Park Hill high-rise housing development. He was included in Belgrave Gallery's 1992 shows British abstract art of the 50s and 60s. Arts Council holds his canvas Two of a Kind, 1962. Julian Hartnoll and Paisnel Gallery also handled Forrester's work.

Anthony Gordon FORSEY 1926– Painter and printmaker, born in Birmingham, where he studied at the College of Arts and Crafts. He also studied etching and engraving with Robert Austin at the Royal College of Art. Exhibited RA. Lived for some time in London.

Catherine FORSHALL 1958– Painter and draughtsman with a special interest in the landscape of the Lot region, France, where she settled in 1985. She was born in Scotland, studied art in Florence, with Signorina Simi, moved to London to begin a career in ceramic restoration, then returned to Scotland to paint. As a developing painter, apart from self-tuition she learned a lot from her friend and mentor Professor George Harris, an American, who had taught in Alcatraz prison. Had a first solo show in 1988 in Cahors, began to exhibit regularly at Salon d'Automne, Paris, other shows taking place elsewhere in France and New York. Had a first solo show in London in 1996 at Portland Gallery, others including Elgin Gallery, 2001, and a shared exhibition with Julian Meredith, River & Sea, at Oliver Contemporary, 2004. Oliver Contemporary gave Forshall a solo show in 2005, the year after she returned to England after two years living in Spain.

Cyril FORSSANDER 1913– Medical practitioner and artist, born in London, educated at Highgate School, who studied medicine at the Middlesex Hospital Medical School. After war service in the Royal Air Force and a period in general practice, he went to North America where he took up a research fellowship in applied physiology at the University of Pennsylvania, then joined the Department of Tuberculosis Control in British Columbia, Canada, where he urged patients to use art therapy; latterly he was with the Canadian Foreign Service as a consultant and medical attaché overseas. Forrsander wrote extensively on the relationship between the body and its environment, an offshoot of which was his booklet *The Meaning of Imagination*, Hanover Press, 1995, dealing with such topics as language and its restrictions on creativity. Forssander was a pupil of the artist R O Dunlop and studied life drawing at the Philadelphia School of Fine Art. Exhibited widely with the Federation of British Artists, Federation of Canadian Artists and American Physicians' Art Association and held many solo shows in England, North America and France, where he settled in Brittany at Perros-Guirec. An exhibition there in 2005–6 covered work from 1950.

David FORSTER 1962– Self-taught painter who gained a Bachelor of Science degree in biochemistry from York University, 1981–4. Group appearances included Summer and Winter Exhibitions, St James' Gallery, Bath, 1987–92; Singer & Friedlander/*Sunday Times* Watercolour Competition, from 1991 (second prize, 2005); Compass Gallery, Glasgow, from 1998; SSA and Aberdeen Artists' Society, both 2000; and RSW, 2001, winning the John Grey Award. Held a series of solo exhibitions in France and Scotland from 1994, later ones including Collective Gallery, 2002, where Forster's The Personville Animation consisted of panels, or stills, with text taken from the 1929 Dashiell Hammett novel *Red Harvest* and the thematically linked 1965 Jean-Luc Godard film *Alphaville*. Theatre Royal in Bath, the Abbey dean and chapter there and corporate collections in England and France hold examples.

Juliana FORSTER 1943– Sculptor, born in Dorchester, Dorset, who studied with Willi Soukop and Elisabeth Frink at Chelsea School of Art, 1962. She became an associate of RBS in 1970. Exhibitions included Ewan Phillips Gallery and David Paul Gallery, Chichester. Lived in West Lavington, Sussex.

Michael FORSTER 1907–2002 Painter, draughtsman, muralist, art critic and writer, born of British parents in Calcutta, India, educated there at La Martinniere College and in England at Lancing College. Forster studied art at the Central School of Arts and Crafts under Bernard Meninsky and William Roberts, then in Paris at Atelier Colarossi. In 1928, he began travels which would take in Canada, America, Mexico and the Caribbean. In Canada he did commercial work and mingled with the Group of Seven, A Y Jackson a friend and mentor. In America he was a set designer for Selznick International Pictures and launched his exhibiting career with the CSGA at the New York World's Fair, 1939, organised by the National Gallery of Canada. He then had his first solo show in 1941 at the Picture Loan Society, Toronto. As an Official War Artist for the Canadian Navy in World War II, Forster broke with convention and produced realist, abstract and surreal works; contributed to the 1946 War Art Show in Toronto; and had 27 pieces acquired by the Ottawa War Museum. He became a Canadian citizen and married Adele Davis. Settled in Montreal in the 1950s, Forster painted, exhibited and was art critic for *The Standard* before, in 1952, moving with his wife to Mexico, where they stayed 11 years. Forster worked on murals, taught stained glass design at the Universidad Ibero-Americano; was befriended by the artists Diego Rivera and Rufino Tamayo; painted, in 1960 having a big solo exhibition at the Museo Nationale de Arte Moderno, a rare honour for a foreigner; and, when money was short, wrote fiction as Michael Forrestier. His stories appeared in magazines such as *The Saturday Evening Post* (*Gem Thief* was used as an episode in the television series *77 Sunset Strip*, winning an Emmy Award in 1959), *Ellery Queen Mystery Magazine* (winning a best first story award) and *Argosy*. After returning to Canada and the death of his wife in 1974, in 1975 Forster moved to England to care for his widowed sister and thereafter lived at Treen, Cornwall, with his second wife, Gloria Ochitwa, whom he had met earlier in Canada. Forster's art evolved into luminous colourism, the Canadian art historian Paul Duval writing: "As a colorist, Forster must be considered among the pre-eminent of the twentieth century." Although he showed with the Newlyn Society of Artists for some years, the rather reclusive Forster was largely unknown in Britain. However, he had many exhibitions around the world at important venues, including retrospectives at The Robert McLaughlin Gallery, Oshawa, Canada, 1993, and Galerie d'Art Déclic, Luxembourg, 2002. Other shows included one in 2002 at the MacLaren Art Centre, Barrie, Canada, which holds over 2,000 of his drawings. After his death, Messum's handled his work.

Noel FORSTER 1932– Abstract painter and teacher, born in Seaton Delaval, Northumberland. He studied at University of Newcastle upon Tyne from 1950–3 and 1955–7. During the 1960s had solo shows at Ikon Gallery, Birmingham, and University of Sussex, while taking part in group exhibitions, including John Moores Exhibition, Liverpool; there he gained a third prize in 1972 and a first prize in 1978. From 1970–1 Forster taught at Minneapolis College of Art and Design, teaching at Slade School of Fine Art from 1971. In 1975–6 Forster won an Arts Council Major Bursary, became artist-in-residence at Balliol College, Oxford, and showed at Museum of Modern Art there. In 1975–6 won an Arts Council Major Bursary, in 1976–8 the Gulbenkian Award. Was principal lecturer in painting at Camberwell College of Art, 1983–90, then at Chelsea College of Art and Design, 1990–7. From 1987 Forster showed solo regularly with Anne Berthoud Gallery, among his many other one-man exhibitions being a series at Flowers East from 1999. In 2005, Forster shared an exhibition with Julia Farrer and John Carter at The Eagle Gallery. Lived in London and France.

Rebecca FORSTER 1960– Artist, born in St Albans, Hertfordshire, whose output ranged from zinc sculptures to three-dimensional, paper-based works. She completed a foundation course at Hertfordshire College of Art and Design, 1978–9; fine art, sculpture, honours degree, Norwich School of Art, 1979–82; postgraduate course, Cyprus School of Art, 1987–8; and a diploma in the conservation of architectural stonework, Weymouth College, 1990–1. Numerous group shows included Life's Too Short, Eridanus Gallery, Nicosia, Cyprus, 1988; Disordine, Galleria Spaziotemporaneo, Milan, Italy, 1993; Sentimento della Citta, Fondazione Corrente, Milan, 1995; Isole Felici, Palazzo Verbania, Luino, Italy, 1997; and Out of the Blue, Mashrabia Gallery, Cairo, Egypt, 1999. Later solo exhibitions included England & Co, 2000. Forster lived and worked in the United Kingdom and in Milan.

Richard FORSTER 1970– Artist, born in Saltburn-by-the-Sea, Yorkshire, who studied at Manchester Polytechnic, then the University of East London. His work Plug in Painting No. 2: Office in a Big Town was shown at Andrew Mummery Gallery, 1999, and in 2001 Mummery gave him his first London solo show. This stemmed from five years' work in which Forster was "developing a project which attempts to define his painting in the faces of processes which exist outside the two-dimensional frame." Other group shows included Sub-Lima, Conductor's Hallway, 1997; Roomworks, Sali Gia Gallery, 1998; and Paint Too, Northern Gallery for Contemporary Art, Sunderland, 2000. Lived in County Durham.

Gordon Mitchell FORSYTH 1879–1952 Painter, stained glass artist and potter, born at Fraserburgh, Aberdeenshire. He studied at Gray's School of Art, Aberdeen, and at the Royal College of Art, completing his studies in 1903. He worked as a designer at Pilkington Tile and Pottery Company as well as serving as art director at Stoke-on-Trent School of Art. Signing his work G M F, he exhibited mainly landscapes and townscapes at RA, RI, Fine Art Society and the Royal Glasgow Institute of the Fine Arts. Eton College as well as galleries in Leeds, Stoke-on-Trent and Newcastle upon Tyne hold his work. He wrote several books on the art and craft of pottery. Lived at Woore, near Crewe, Cheshire.

James FORSYTH 1910– Painter in oil who studied at Cambridge University. Studied art at the Slade School of Fine Art, 1932–3, with Randolph Schwabe, then two years later in Florence. Showed RA, Leicester Galleries, NEAC and in the provinces. Lived in London.

Moira FORSYTH 1905–1991 Stained glass and pottery designer and watercolourist, born in Cresswell, Staffordshire, daughter of the ceramic designer Gordon Forsyth. She was encouraged to work in clay from an early age and trained in ceramics at Burslem School of Art. Lack of work prompted her to enter the Royal College of Art with a national scholarship to study pottery, but having seen the glass in Chartres Cathedral she instead studied glass design with Martin Travers. Exhibited at RA and at public galleries in Bristol and Stoke-on-Trent. During World War II attached to the research department of the Ministry of Town and Country Planning she worked on two major surveys, on Oxford and Canterbury, then returned to glass work. An ardent Catholic, she especially liked making windows for Catholic churches, and among her major commissions are a transept window at the Benedictine Abbey in Fort Augustus. Her most significant works are in two cathedrals, Guildford and Norwich, and in St Columba's Church in Pont Street, London, where she lived.

Philip FORTIN 1901–1985 Painter, printmaker, sculptor, draughtsman and teacher, born in London. He was a talented violinist who early had to choose between a career in music and art. Attended St Martin's School of Art, 1917–20, under the sculptor Harry Parr, then the Royal College of Art, 1920–3, teachers including Gerald Moira and William Rothenstein. Showed at Zwemmer Gallery, New Burlington Galleries and elsewhere. Did some advertising work, occasionally condensing his name as a signature to Pif, by which he was generally known to his students and family. Fortin held several teaching posts, including Ipswich School of Art. On retirement in 1962 he moved from the Suffolk town to Cassis, in the south of France. Exhibited abstract paintings and drawings there and in Marseilles, jointly with his wife Yetta. After her death Fortin became reclusive, describing himself as an "aggressive eccentric", but he remained a great communicator on art, history and music and an enthusiastic advocate of the twentieth century. He returned to live with his daughter in St Osyth, Essex, where he died.

Peggy FORTNUM 1919– Artist in various media, designer, book illustrator and teacher, born in Harrow on the Hill, Middlesex. She was married to the artist Ralph Nuttall-Smith. She studied at Tunbridge Wells School of Art with E Owen Jennings and then at Central School of Arts and Crafts with John Farleigh and Bernard Meninsky. She was an arts and crafts teacher, 1940–1; an Auxiliary Territorial Service signals operator, 1942–3, being discharged with a pension and war grant after injury; an illustrator of children's books, 1944–89; and a textile designer, 1947–50. Fortnum was noted for her sprightly line as a book illustrator, notably accompanying Michael Bond's many Paddington Bear books; in 1975 her own *Running Wild* appeared. Fortnum also did work for Imperial Chemical Industries and for BBC Television programmes, *Playschool* and *Jackanory*. Exhibited at The Minories, Colchester, British Museum, Victoria & Albert Museum and in regional books shows, as well as abroad. Lived in West Mersea, Essex.

Rebecca FORTNUM 1963– Painter who was born and continued to work in London. She attended Oxford University to read English, 1983–6, before gaining a Master of Fine Arts degree from Newcastle University, 1986–8. Travelled to New York on a Northern Arts Travel Award in 1989, then held the 1989–90 fellowship in painting at Exeter College of Art. She exhibited widely, including solo shows at the Collective Gallery in Edinburgh and Southwark College Gallery and group exhibitions at Spacex Gallery, Sheffield, Pomeroy Purdy and Herbert Art Gallery, Coventry. In 1991 she took up a fellowship at Skowhegan School of Painting and Sculpture in America, then in 1992–3 was the visiting fellow in painting at Winchester School of Art.

Frank FORTY 1902–1996 Painter and draughtsman, by profession a surgeon, who during his student days lived in Edgbaston, showing with the RBSA, 1932–40, living at the same address as artist Gerald C Forty and influenced by his painter friend Bernard Munns. After marrying an anaesthetist, Irene Maude, Forty moved to Mill Hill, northwest London, joining the Mildon Art Society; then Edgware, joining the Edgware General Hospital; and finally Stanmore, Middlesex, where he joined Stanmore Society of Artists. In 1969 began showing with RBA, RSMA and Paris Salon; in 1970, when he was also accepted by the PS, the Salon gave him an Hon. Mention. In addition to his many views of the countryside north of London, Forty worked in Ireland, France, Spain, Portugal and Italy. His early style was formal but in later years it became freer with vibrant colour, under the influence of the French Impressionists. Geoffrey Norman – Affordable Collectables, Hitchin, posthumously showed Forty's work.

Hubert FORWARD 1927–1998 Painter, ceramist, printmaker and calligrapher and teacher, born in north London. He studied at Hornsey School of Art, 1945–52, teachers including Russell Reeve, Allin Braund and Henry Holzer. Held several teaching posts, eventually becoming head of ceramics at Norwich School of Art, 1953–82. Was a member of Federation of British Artists, Norwich Twenty Group and SGA and showed with RI and East Anglian Artists. University of East Anglia holds his work. In 1957 Forward was chosen for inclusion in Jack Beddington's *Young Artists of Promise*, his picture Hayfever, 1954, being illustrated. Signed some work with initials only. Lived in Norwich, Norfolk.

Anthony FOSTER 1909–1957 Sculptor in stone and wood and teacher, born in India, father of the sculptors Peter and Stephen Foster. He was a pupil of Eric Gill, 1930–8. Worked as a sculptor, 1939–57, farming as a conscientious objector from 1941–5. Taught at Camberwell School of Arts and Crafts, 1953–7. Foster's work was figurative with a strong Christian content. He showed at RA and Ashley Gallery. Died in London.

Arthur Bell FOSTER: *see* **Arthur BELL-FOSTER**

David FOSTER 1961– Having studied at Goldsmiths' College, 1981–4, Foster was included in Pick of the Graduates, Christie's, in the latter year. Other appearances included New Contemporaries, ICA, 1986; Camden Arts Centre, 1987; and Six British Artists, Selected Work, Rijksakademie Gallery, Amsterdam, Netherlands, 1989. In that year Foster obtained his master's degree from Goldsmiths' and took part in East End Open Studios, based at Unit 7, Peckham Road.

Deryck FOSTER 1924– Marine artist with a strong interest in sailing, born in Bournemouth, Hampshire. After King's School, Canterbury, he studied at Southern School of Art, 1939–42, teachers including Leslie Ward and Geoffrey Baker, then Central School of Arts and Crafts, 1946, where John Farleigh, Laurence Scarfe and Jesse Collins were on the staff. In 1957 Foster was included in Jack Beddington's book *Young Artists of Promise*, his Lady Francesca Entering St Vaast illustrated. Was a member of RSMA and has work in National Maritime Museum, Greenwich. Lived in Yarmouth, Isle of Wight, later in Bailey's Bay, Bermuda.

Fiona FOSTER 1961– Sculptor, lecturer and art therapist whose mesmeric works were created from found objects. There were strong organic references in her pieces, which were influenced by the Scottish countryside of her childhood; the work of Kurt Schwitters, notably Ambleside Merz, at Hatton Gallery, Newcastle University; and Indonesia, especially Bali. Foster did a foundation course at Newcastle College of Arts and Technology, 1978–9; graduated with honours, Edinburgh College of Art, 1979–82; gained a postgraduate diploma in sculpture, Edinburgh College of Art, 1982–3; a diploma in art therapy, Hertfordshire College of Art and Design, 1983–4; and her master's there, 1988–90. She won an Andrew Grant Travelling Scholarship, 1982. Foster was an art therapist in mental health services, 1984–92; visiting lecturer, Newcastle College of Art and Camberwell College of Arts, 1985 and 1992 respectively; full-time sculptor, 1992; lived with Balinese family of artists, 1993–4; and was a visiting lecturer, Kent Institute of Art and Design, 2000, where she had solo shows in Maidstone and Rochester. Later group exhibitions included England & Co, 2000.

Graham FOSTER 1950– Painter and sculptor, born in Halifax, Yorkshire, who settled nearby at Skipton. He studied at Bradford College of Art, 1968–70, Leeds Polytechnic, 1970–3 and Royal College of Art, 1973–6. His work could be fetishistic, with overt sexual imagery, sculptures using a range of materials. Showed in north of England, solo exhibitions including Cartwright Hall, Bradford, 1978. His large Untitled, of 1976–9, in oil, acrylic and industrial paint, was included in Arts Council's 1981–2 tour Fragments Against Ruin, being taken into the collection.

John FOSTER 1951– Sculptor, born in London. He studied at Epsom School of Art with Peter Hide, 1969–73. Foster was then at Stockwell Depot, 1973–5; Triangle Workshops, New York State, with Anthony Caro, 1982 and 1985; and in 1986–8–90 organised Hardingham Sculpture Workshops. His Lazy E, made in steel painted and waxed, an abstract piece, was shown in the show East at Norwich Gallery, 1991. Foster's publicly sited sculpture includes Untitled, 1980, in metal, commissioned by Peterborough Development Corporation for Herlington Township Centre. Lived in Hardingham, Norfolk.

John Ernest FOSTER 1877–1968 Painter, born in Hull, Yorkshire, son of a nurseryman which encouraged him to garden and paint flowers. Landscapes and nudes were other subjects. Foster studied at the Royal College of Art. As a young man he spent some time in Cork, Ireland, before returning to Yorkshire, then settled for many years at Dedham, Essex. Showed at RA Summer Exhibition, Walker Art Gallery in Liverpool, RI, London Salon and elsewhere. Ferens Art Gallery, Hull, has Foster's oil on canvas Delphiniums and Roses, 1928, presented by the artist in 1954 in memory of his wife.

Judith FOSTER 1937– Artist and teacher who, according to the artist and critic Colin Moss, had "the unique ability to see her subject as a collection of impersonal, abstract shapes, which she rearranges on her own terms." She was born in London and after studies at Ipswich School of Art attended the Royal College of Art, with an Abbey Scholarship in 1962. Taught in further and adult education. Mixed shows included Young Contemporaries; Arnolfini, Bristol; Drawings for All, Gainsborough's House, Sudbury; and Suffolk Group, of which she was a member. Manor School of Ballet, Edinburgh; Cleveland Bridge Gallery, Bath; and John Russell Gallery, Ipswich, gave her solo exhibitions. In 2000–1 Drawing in the Dark, at and about Christchurch Mansion, Ipswich, stemmed from 18 months working there. Bedford Education Authority and Ipswich Borough Council hold examples. Lived at Bramford, Suffolk.

Lilian Lee FOSTER 1897– Painter, born in Boston, Lincolnshire. She was educated in Boston, then studied at Leeds College of Art, 1928, with the watercolourist and etcher Harold Holden. She showed widely at public galleries in Leeds, Bradford, Hull and Lincoln and at RWA. Was a member of Lincolnshire Artists' Society.

Marcia Lane FOSTER 1897–1983 Her favourite medium was wood engraving, and she also painted portraits in oil and watercolour, did pen and ink book illustration, silkscreen printing and extensive publicity work for firms such as Kodak, Cadbury and Nestlé. Born in Seaton, Devon, Foster – who married the artist and writer Dudley Jarrett – began studies at St John's Wood School of Art during World War I, where she was influenced by the teaching of Leonard Walker. Was then at Royal Academy Schools and Central School of Arts and Crafts, where she learned wood engraving under Noel Rooke. She illustrated several dozen books, notably titles by Viola Bayley and Pamela Brown. Never had a solo show, but was a prolific exhibitor with RA, RE, SWE, NEAC, at the Paris Salon and the Art Institute of Chicago. Her sketches of children, called *Let's Do It*, was published in 1938. Died in Wincanton, Somerset.

Peter FOSTER 1943– Sculptor in stone and wood and letter-cutter, son of the sculptor Anthony Foster and older brother of the sculptor Stephen. He attended High Wycombe College of Art under Darsie Rawlins, then City and Guilds of London School of Art, 1964. Worked as a sculptor and letter-cutter, 1965–72, emigrated to Australia, 1972–6, then from 1976 worked in Britain. Church work was especially important in Foster's output and he acknowledged his father, Eric Gill and David Jones as "exerting a strong influence". His Saint Martin and Beggar is in St Martin's Church precinct, Basildon, Essex. Lived at Watlington, Oxfordshire.

Richard FOSTER 1945– Painter and printmaker of landscapes and portraits, who favoured what he called "runny" paint, his work reminiscent of the grand manner, fluidity and light of John Singer Sargent. The artist John Ward was a hero and mentor. Foster was born in London, where later mainly lived and worked, but was brought up in Norfolk. He was educated at Harrow School and Trinity College, Oxford, where he read history, studying art at Studio Simi in Florence, Italy, 1963–6, and at the City and Guilds of London Art School, 1967–70, where "etching was the thing that interested me most and I did almost no painting." He was a frequent exhibitor at RA Summer Exhibition, became a member of the RP in 1976 and was its vice-president, 1991–4, also belonging to the Art Workers' Guild. He showed regularly at the RA and in 1972 won a Lord Mayor's Award. Had solo shows at Jocelyn Fielding Fine Art, 1974; Spink & Son, from 1978; a retrospective at Rafael Valls Ltd, 1999; and Partridge Fine Arts, 2003. Foster's portraits included HRH The Princess of Wales; Lord Mexborough; Lord Trend; and Lady Fulford. Eton College; Lincoln College, Oxford; The Royal College of Pathologists; and the Royal College of Physicians and Surgeons of Glasgow owned examples.

Tony FOSTER 1946– Artist, administrator and teacher, born Lincolnshire, who studied at Birmingham College of Arts and Crafts, 1972–4, and at Cardiff School of Art, 1976–8, with an interval teaching in the Cayman Islands. Began work as an arts organiser, notably with South West Arts, Exeter. Then in 1986 he returned to painting full-time, having established a studio at Tywardreath, near Par, Cornwall. He became a renowned traveller who walked hundreds of miles in wild places to paint "a celebration of the wilderness and the idea of a journey or series of journeys". His Thoreau's Country was featured at Yale Center for British Art, New Haven, Connecticut, 1985; John Muir's High Sierra at Smithsonian Institution, Washington, 1989; and Rainforest Diaries at Royal Albert Memorial Museum and Art Gallery in 1993. Foster's work was included in the Newlyn Orion Galleries 1989 exhibition A Century of Art in Cornwall 1889–1989. In 1988 Foster was awarded the Yosemite Renaissance Prize and his work is in the collection of Yosemite National Park. Denver Art Museum holds a major series. In 2001, Frye Art Museum, Seattle, organised a retrospective which toured America. Lived in Tywardreath, Cornwall.

Simon FOSTER-OGG 1960– Sculptor and teacher. He studied at Maidstone College of Art, 1982–3, and Goldsmiths' College School of Art, 1983–6. For three years, 1978–81, he had been a stonemason working on Canterbury Cathedral. He went on to teach at Kent Institute of Art & Design, South Kent College and Portland Sculpture Park, where he had a residency, from the early 1990s. Public commissions were carried out for Whitstable Sea Front in 1990 and Portland Sculpture Park in 1991. Among Foster-Ogg's group appearances were Light Waves Dark Tidings at Herbert Read Gallery, Canterbury, in 1991; in the following year he was in Sculpture at Canterbury.

Lesley FOTHERBY 1946– Painter and teacher, born in London. Studied at Bath Academy of Art, Ravensbourne College of Art and Leicester Polytechnic. She left teaching in 1984 to become a professional watercolourist. Exhibited regularly at Royal Horticultural Society, winning two of its silver medals. She had a first solo show at Chris Beetles Ltd in 1985, others following.

Clare FOTHERINGHAM 1890– Painter in oil and watercolour. Born at Ovenden, Halifax, she studied at Goldsmiths' College School of Art, 1909–14, under Frederick Marriott and Percy Buckman. She went on to teach art and exhibited widely, including RA, RI, SWA, RSA and RBA. Lived at Hollingbourne, Kent.

James FOTHERINGHAME 1970– Painter interested in depicting wildlife who studied at Mid-Warwickshire College, 1989–90; Nottingham Trent University, 1990–3; and Royal Academy Schools, 1993–6. Group exhibitions included RA Summer Exhibition from 1994, the year he was awarded the British Institution Fund, W H Patterson Prize and gained third prize, Singer & Friedlander/*Sunday Times* Watercolour Competition. Had a solo show at Cadogan Contemporary, 1995, another at New Grafton Gallery, 1997.

FOUGASSE 1887–1965 Cartoonist, illustrator and designer, real name Cyril Kenneth Bird. After Cheltenham College, Bird studied engineering at King's College, London, but also attended classes at Regent Street Polytechnic School of Art and Bolt Court, Fleet Street. World War I injuries prevented his practising as an engineer, so took course with Percy V Bradshaw's Press Art School, and his work soon appeared in *Punch*. He became art editor of the magazine in 1937, then was editor four years from 1949. Bird's sparse, graphic style became famous during World War II when he designed posters for the government, notably *Careless Talk Costs Lives*. He also exhibited extensively at the Fine Art Society and at RSA. Illustrated a number of books, including *A Gallery of Games*, 1921, *The Changing Face of Britain*, 1940, and A P Herbert's *A School of Purposes*, 1946. Was master of the Art Workers' Guild for a time and on the council of both the Imperial Arts League and the SGA. Married to the artist Mary Holden Bird. Lived at Laughton, Sussex.

Helen FOULDS 1902– Painter and teacher, born in Romiley, Cheshire. She obtained a Froebel diploma, studying art at Camden Art Centre, Hampstead, where she also exhibited. Showed at SWA, RWS and had solo exhibitions in post offices in London, where she lived.

Mark FOULDS 1963– Painter, born in Leeds, Yorkshire, who attended Jacob Kramer College, Leeds, 1981–2; graduated from Trent Polytechnic, Nottingham, 1982–5; and studied for his master's at Chelsea School of Art, under Jennifer Durrant, 1987–8. Foulds was Barclays Bank Young Painter of the Year, 1988. Group shows included East End Open Studios, at Metropolitan Wharf, 1989, Beautiful, Oxo Tower, 2000, and John Moores Liverpool Exhibition, 2002. Showed solo in Germany and new abstract work in gloss paint, Broadbent, 2004. Lived in London.

Cherryl FOUNTAIN 1950– Painter and teacher. She studied at Reading University, 1968–72, and Royal Academy Schools, 1974–7. From 1973 she taught in Kent schools and education centres. Fountain won a number of prizes and awards, which included a bursary from the Worshipful Company of Painter-Stainers, in 1975, also the David Murray Studentship for Landscape Painting. She won the Studentship again in 1976, the year she won the Richard Jack Award for Portraiture. In 1977 she gained the British Institution's First Prize for Drawing and a first prize in the *Observer* Jubilee Print Competition. The Italian Government bursary for landcape painting and study of art history, which took her to Perugia, was won in 1978, three years before winning the Richard Ford Award to study in the Prado Museum, Madrid. As well as exhibiting at RA from 1975 and in other mixed shows including Maas Gallery and Piccadilly Gallery, Fountain had a solo show at Royal Museum, Canterbury, in 1983, shared a show at New Grafton Gallery in 1981 and had a solo exhibition there in 1986. Fountain's pictures frequently featured gardens and plants, painted with great intensity.

Marian FOUNTAIN 1960– Sculptor and medallist, born in New Zealand, who lived and worked in Auckland, London, Rome and Paris. She graduated in sculpture and design at Elam School of Fine Arts, University of Auckland, 1979–82, studying at Scuola della Medaglia, Rome Mint, Italy, 1985–6. Awards and residencies included Queen Elizabeth II Arts Council Major Travel Grant, 1984; residency at National Gallery of Modern Art, Edinburgh, and Prix de Sculpture, first prize, French Mint, both 1990; and Lipworth Foundation Sculpture Prize, 1993. She won a number of commissions from the British Art Medal

Society, 1985–90. Group shows included National Exhibition, Crafts Council, Wellington, 1981; MAFA Open, 1988; and Press Museum, Istanbul, 1996. Was a frequent solo exhibitor from 1983, later shows including Simmons Gallery, 1997.

Christian FOURNIER 1962– Abstract painter, born in Livry-Gargan, near Paris, France, mainly working in oil but also mixed media. From 1979–82 studied graphic design at Lycée Corvisart in Paris, then attended L'École des Beaux-Arts there, 1982–5, gaining a part-time diploma at City of London Polytechnic, 1987–91. To support his studies and painting Fournier did a number of jobs: in Paris, 1984–5, working as a lay-out artist, other positions including sales assistant in a London card shop. Exhibitions included Southwark Open, 1995, and 1995–6 his Untitled canvas appeared in John Moores Liverpool Exhibition.

Nancy FOUTS fl. from late 1960s– Artist and gallery owner, born in America, who studied at Chelsea School of Art, 1964–8, then Royal College of Art, 1968. She established the Shirt Sleeve Studio, then in 1987 the Fouts and Fowler Gallery. She had a first solo show at Angela Flowers Gallery in 1974 and in 1994 was an Artist of the Day there, chosen by Les Coleman.

David FOWKES 1919– Painter in oil and teacher, born in Eastbourne, Sussex, son of the artist Arthur Reeve-Fowkes. He studied at Reading University, 1938–40 and 1946–8, under Anthony Betts. Fowkes first taught at Winchester School of Art, then for 30 years at Gray's Art School in Aberdeen, resigning as senior lecturer in the painting school in 1980, moving to live in York. He was a figurative artist, working from drawings made in and about York and in and around Italy, which he visited annually. Piero della Francesca, Seurat and Balthus were influences. Group exhibitions included NEAC, Michael Parkin Gallery and Scottish Arts Council tours. Had a solo show at Douglas and Foulis, Edinburgh, 1970, later ones including Abbot Hall, Kendal, and Charlotte Lampard, both 1989. Scottish Arts Council, Aberdeen Art Gallery and HM The Queen and HRH The Duke of Edinburgh hold examples.

Bertha FOWLE 1894–1964 Painter of miniatures, flowers and landscapes, born at Gravesend, Kent. Studied and taught at the School of Art there. Exhibited RA, RMS and RI especially, SWA and Walker Art Gallery, Liverpool. HM Queen Mary bought her work. Lived at Gravesend.

LeClerc FOWLE fl. from 1950s–1992 Painter and draughtsman, born in Haslar, Hampshire. She studied privately and at Slade School of Fine Art. Was a member of RWA and ROI. Exhibited in mixed shows at RA, NEAC, RSA and in the provinces, won first prize in Laing Competition in 1979 and gained gold and silver medals at Paris Salon. Had a series of solo shows. Lived in London.

Alex FOWLER 1975– Painter of portraits, landscape and still life, born in London, who did a foundation course at Chelsea College of Art and Design, 1994–5; gained his master's with honours in the history of art from Edinburgh University, 1995–9; then completed a two-year portrait painting diploma at Heatherley's School of Art, 1999–01. He painted portraits to commission and became a member of the RP and NEAC. Group exhibitions included Works on Paper, Cedar House Gallery, Ripley, and Carlyle Gallery, Chelsea, both 2003; and Yvonne Arnaud Art Annual Exhibition, Guildford, from 2003. Fowler had a solo show at Carlyle Gallery in 2003.

Kenneth FOWLER 1955– Painter, born in Hull, who over the years worked as a window-cleaner and as a lifeboatman based at Withernsea. His witty, mannered, figurative picture The Exhibition, 1983, was shown in the 1984 Winter Exhibition at Ferens Art Gallery, Hull, which acquired it for its collection.

Richard FOWLER 1921– Sculptor in all three-dimensional materials and teacher who studied at West of England College of Art in Bristol and at the Royal College of Art. He was a member of Cheltenham Art Group and showed at RA and RWA and in 19 Young Sculptors at Hillfield Gardens, Gloucester, 1962. Fowler became head of sculpture at Gloucestershire College of Art and Design, Cheltenham. After retirement, Dick Fowler lived in France.

Ron FOWLER 1916– Versatile printmaker, born in London. He studied at Glasgow School of Art, 1941, Warrington School of Art, 1955, and Chester College of Adult Education, 1979–80. Began printmaking in 1978 after retiring from a career in chemical engineering, having attended Birkbeck College at London University. Fowler joined SGA in 1982, becoming a member of its council in 1985. Showed with Society of Botanical Artists, NS and Mall Prints. Buxton Museum and Art Gallery holds his work. Lived in Lower Whitley, Cheshire.

FOWOKAN 1943– Sculptor, full name Kenness George Kelly, born in Kingston, Jamaica, mainly self taught and practising from 1980. Fowokan was involved in promoting African history and art to schools and other educational institutions around Britain. Commissions included three pieces for Greater London Council South Bank Spring Festival, 1983; two for Borough of Hammersmith and Fulham Marcus Garvey centenary, 1987; and one for African Peoples' Historical Foundation building, Brixton, 1988. Exhibitions included Brixton Art Gallery opening show, 1983; 198 Gallery, from 1988; RA Summer Exhibition, 1991; and Transforming the Crown, Harlem Studio Museum, New York, America, 1997.

Christine FOX 1922– Sculptor and teacher, born in Bridlington, Yorkshire, who specialised in sculpture at Bath Academy of Art in Corsham, 1956–9. She was a part-time lecturer in sculpture at Cambridgeshire College of Arts & Technology, 1964–88. Took part in many sculpture park shows, including Sculpture in a Garden, Tatton Park, Cheshire, 1982; Yorkshire Sculpture Park, Bretton Hall College, Wakefield, 1986; and Art of Sculpture, Broxbourne Civil Hall, Hertfordshire, 1993. Showed annually with Cambridge Society of Painters & Sculptors from 1970 and in the Studios & Sculpture Gardens Open, triennially during the Cambridge Festival, from 1975. Solo exhibitions included Richard Bradley Atelier, Norfolk, 1972; Marjorie Parr Gallery from 1976; Gilbert Parr Gallery, 1980; and latterly Sculpture into Landscape at Peterborough Arts Centre, 1990, and Landscape of Trees, Broughton House Gallery, Cambridge, 1995. Sculpture bought for public places included Axe Carrier, Clare Hall Garden Court, Cambridge University, 1975; Batrachian Cascade, Stony Stratford, Milton Keynes, 1981; Gathering of Owls, Darwin's Aviary, New Hall, Cambridge University, 1992; and Sentinel, Girton College, Cambridge, 1993. Worked in Coton, Cambridge.

Kathleen FOX 1948– Artist employing oil on board, oil on gesso and collage and three-dimensional work in bone and wax, born in Durban, South Africa, her son being the painter Nicholas Fox. She studied in Durban, 1966–70, and in Cape Town with Michael Pettit, 1980–1. She was a member of the Women's Art Library, South East Arts and Hourglass. Fox defined her artistic interests as "mystery, ambiguity, dreams and childhood memories, subconcious levels of thought, mythology, forces that move beneath the observable surface of reality". Group exhibitions included Forum Gallery, Cape Town, 1981; UVA, Paris, 1991; England & Co, 1992; Rye Art Gallery, Rye, 1994; and Mall Galleries, 1995. Had a solo exhibition with South African Association of Arts, Cape Town, 1986, later ones including Trinity Arts Centre, Tunbridge Wells, and St Martin-in-the-Fields, both 1990; and Trinity Arts Centre, 1996. Ernst & Young and PPP Ltd hold examples. Lived in Cranbrook, Kent.

Mary FOX 1922– Painter and printmaker, born in Atherstone, Warwickshire, who studied at Leicester School of Art, 1939, then lithography at the Central School of Arts and Crafts. She was very influenced by the work of Polish and German painters, including several who moved to England, particularly Zdzislaw Ruszkowski, Walter Nessler and Jan Wieliczko. Group shows included RA, NEAC, WIAC, Christopher Hull Gallery and the Camden Annual. Had a series of shows at John Whibley Gallery from 1960, later ones including Sue Rankin Gallery, 1986, and Stables, Birmingham, from 1993. Her work was included in Ian Simpson's 1990 book *The Challenge of Landscape Painting*. Arts Council; Victoria & Albert Museum; Nuneaton, Beecroft in Southend and Portsmouth Art Galleries; and many education committees held Fox's work. Lived in London.

Peter FOX 1952– Artist notable for mixed-media assemblages. He studied at Kettering Technical College and Falmouth School of Art. Fox envisaged Art as having power to counter potentially technologically harmful forces. He showed in groups at Newlyn Orion Gallery, Penwith Gallery and in Art in Boxes, England & Co, 1991. His solo exhibitions included Falmouth School of Art, Yeovil Museum and Salthouse Gallery, St Ives, Cornwall.

Lesley FOXCROFT 1949– Abstract sculptor, born in Sheffield, Yorkshire. She studied at Camberwell School of Arts and Crafts, 1970–4. Her group shows included Fruitmarket Gallery, Edinburgh, 1981, Victoria Miro, 1991, and in 1993–4 she was in the Arts Council's touring Recent British Sculpture. Her solo shows included Konrad Fischer Gallery, Düsseldorf, 1974, Museum of Modern Art, Oxford, 1975, Laure Genillard Gallery, 1988, and Cairn Gallery, Nailsworth, 1993. Foxcroft's exhibition Combination was at Annely Juda Fine Art in 2004. Lived in London.

Maurice FOXELL 1888–1981 Watercolour painter, artist in pastel, lino-cutter and wood engraver. From an ecclesiastical family, Maurice Foxell, who took holy orders, was educated at Christ's Hospital and Queen's College Oxford. Exhibited at the Abbey Gallery and Walker's Galleries in the inter-war years. Was a Knight Commander of the Royal Victorian Order and lived in retirement in Lingfield, Surrey.

Nigel FOXELL 1931– Draughtsman and watercolourist, and versatile writer, born in London where he continued to live. He studied at various evening classes in London, notably at Central School of Arts and Crafts under Merlyn Evans. Had an especial interest in depicting aspects of London before demolition and lectured on architecture for Workers' Educational Association. Ran the private Earl's Court Gallery at his home in Earl's Court. Showed at RBA, East Kent Art Society and elsewhere.

Marianne FOX OCKINGA 1943– Printmaker, draughtsman and painter, born in Baarn, Netherlands, who initially worked under her maiden name Marianne Ockinga. She studied at Bath Academy of Art, Corsham, 1960–3, then Rijksakademie, Amsterdam, 1963–6. Took part in mixed shows in Netherlands, having a solo exhibition at Galerie Merlo, Amsterdam, 1984. English mixed exhibitions included the RA Summer Exhibitions, RE, Printmakers' Council and The Square Gallery. Among her solo exhibitions were the Upper Street Gallery, 1976; White Space Gallery, 1985; and a series at Mary Kleinman Gallery. AMRO Bank in Netherlands holds her work. She lived in north London.

Steven FOY 1961– Painter, draughtsman and musician, born in Manchester, who was indebted to the Abstract Expressionists and Mark Rothko. Childhood convalescence from eye operations, including periods of blindness, "heightened his sensitivity to his surroundings," compelling him "to look at things properly for the first time," as the collector Tim Sayer wrote when Foy showed solo with Beardsmore Gallery in 2001. There was a further exhibition there, Isolation, in 2003. After school Foy was initially a Punk musician, playing in four bands, then he attended Rochdale College of Art & Design, 1981–3, and Ravensbourne College of Art & Design, 1983–6. Afterwards he worked continuously as an artist, apart from two more years in a band. In 1996–8 he attended Goldsmiths' College for history of art/theory and was a LG member, 1996–9. Other shows included LG 80th Anniversary Open, Barbican Centre, Daler-Rowney Prize winner, 1993; The 2nd Christmas Cabinet Art Show, Blue Gallery, 1995; Inside Out, Start Gallery, with John Crossley, 1999; and Karl Hofer Gesellschaft, Berlin (Cheltenham Open Drawing Tour), 2000.

Richard FOZARD 1925–2000 Printmaker, painter and teacher, born in Leeds, Yorkshire, who, according to his obituarist Richard Robbins, "seemed to step straight out of the Old Testament", preaching "morality based on 'the conscience of humanity, the underlying forces of nature' and the ability of art to express them." He began work at 14 for Gilchrist Bros, process engravers, who paid for evening studies in design and life drawing. Early in World War II Fozard returned to Yorkshire, working on country estates, which he enjoyed, then served widely abroad in the Royal Navy, honing his technique by taking an art correspondence course. Demobilised in 1946 Fozard studied painting and illustration full-time at Leeds College of Art, then engraving at the Royal College of Art with Robert Austin. After freelance work on fashion and children's books for Odhams Press, in 1951 Fozard won the print Prix de Rome, spending three years exploring southern Europe.

He was appointed to the printmaking staff of Royal College of Art in 1956 under Julian Trevelyan; collaborated with S W Hayter and others in Paris editioning for many artists and galleries; in 1961 moved to Hornsey College of Art, later merged with Middlesex Polytechnic, teaching part-time. After retirement he continued to promote printmaking, demonstrating at craft festivals. There was a memorial exhibition at Middlesex University in 2002. Died at Minety, Wiltshire.

Rose FRAIN 1939– Artist and lecturer using a range of media, born in County Durham. She graduated with fine art honours from the University of Durham, King's College, Newcastle, 1958–62, taught by Victor Pasmore, Richard Hamilton, Lawrence Gowing and Ralph Holland. Frain taught in the extra-mural department at King's College and at Newcastle College of Art and Industrial Design. In 1971 she moved to Edinburgh, where in 1973 at the University's Moray House Institute she gained her teaching certificate. In 1989 Frain had a solo show at 369 Gallery, Edinburgh. Projects from 1986–96 explored A Feminine Symbolic and installations including Towards an Archaeology of the Unconscious, 1994, and Love, Work and Knowledge, 1996, in an art train moving across Europe (Zij Sporen), were realised. From 1992–4 she undertook higher research with Griselda Pollock at Leeds University. From 1998 Frain's project was This Time in History, citing critical moments. Examples included Radio Vaticana, an installation realised during her Scottish Arts Council residency in Rome, 2000, and What I brought with me, 2003. Frain was a frequently invited guest artist at institutions across the United Kingdom and abroad. Examples of her work are held by the Scottish National Gallery of Modern Art in Edinburgh, the Victoria & Albert Museum, and New Hall at Cambridge University.

Meredith FRAMPTON 1894–1984 Painter and etcher, born in London, full name George Vernon Meredith Frampton. He was the son of Sir George Frampton, sculptor of Peter Pan, his mother being the artist Christabel Cockerell. Meredith Frampton attended Westminster School, had additional art tuition, then after some months in Geneva learning French enrolled at St John's Wood Art School. From 1912–15 and in later years during some evenings he studied at Royal Academy Schools, winning a first prize and a silver medal. After World War I Army service Frampton began his professional career. He was already a member of the Art Workers' Guild. From 1920–45 he showed at RA, being elected RA in 1942 but retiring in 1953. By the end of World War II he had found that his eyesight was insufficient for the type of detailed work he did. Frampton was a slow worker, producing meticulous portraits of singular realism which nevertheless often give a sense of unease, of the slightly sinister. After years of obscurity a retrospective at the Tate Gallery in 1982 revived his reputation. His subjects included King George VI, Sir Johnston Forbes-Robertson the actor and the architect Sir Edwin Lutyens. Tate Gallery and Imperial War Museum hold his work. Died in Wiltshire.

Russell FRAMPTON 1961– Painter, designer and jazz guitarist producing landscapes with a strong abstract element. He was born in Warsash, Hampshire, and attended Portsmouth Art College, 1978–9; graduated with honours in fine art from Exeter College of Art and Design, 1979–83; gained his teaching certificate at Exeter University, 1993–4; and his master's in fine art postgraduate diploma from Plymouth University, 1998–01. As a digital set designer at the University Frampton used computers to manipulate scanned images of the early stages of his paintings to achieve the final canvas, on which he built up complex surface levels using layering techniques. He lived in the West Country, where the coastal and moorland environment of Devon and Cornwall were important inspirations. Music often set the mood for his pictures. Participated in many British and Japanese group exhibitions and showed solo at Highgate Fine Art from 2000.

Peter de FRANCIA 1921– Painter, draughtsman, teacher and writer, born in Beaulieu, France. He studied at Academy of Brussels and Slade School of Fine Art, 1938–40. In the late 1940s and early 1950s de Francia worked in Canada, was at the American Museum in New York and for several years was in British television, responsible for arts programmes. From 1954–61 he taught at Morley College and St Martin's School of Art; was at Royal College of Art from 1961–9; then after a few years at Goldsmiths' College School of Art in 1972 de Francia joined Royal College of Art as professor of painting, a position he held until 1986. He was held in high regard as a teacher. He was an acknowledged and published expert on Fernand Léger, his important study appearing under the Yale University Press imprint in 1983. De Francia was a fine draughtsman who worked in series, his figurative pictures often having a political or social message. Retrospectives at Camden Arts Centre, 1977 and 1987. After the Bombing was at James Hyman Fine Art in 2005. Arts Council holds his work. Lived in London.

Angela FRANCIS 1960– Figure painter and musician, born in Jamaica, who lived in London. She graduated from Birmingham Conservatoire in 1985 with a degree in piano and composition, taught piano and composed for string quartet, piano, voice and choir. Art education included part-time course at Bournville and Chelsea Schools of Art and Richmond College. The female figure, often solitary, was the subject of Francis' oils. Later solo shows included Duncan Campbell Contemporary Art from 1996.

Brian Jabez FRANCIS 1927– Glass engraver, born in Dersingham, Norfolk. Attended London and Nottingham Universities and studied art at Canterbury and Exeter Colleges of Art. Showed RMS and SGA, of which he was a member, and overseas. Paris Salon medallist. Lived in Thorney, Cambridgeshire.

Eric Carwardine FRANCIS 1887– Architect, born at St Tewdric, near Chepstow, Monmouthshire. Francis studied with the Royal Academician and architect Sir Edward Guy Dawber. Francis' work was shown at the RA and RWA, which holds it in the permanent collection. *The Architectural Review* and *Country Life* printed examples. Lived at West Monkton, Taunton, Somerset.

Iris FRANCIS 1925– Painter and printmaker, born in Dereham, Norfolk. Studied at Slade School of Fine Art, 1942–3 and 1945–6, with the intervening two years at Norwich School of Art; then at Manchester School of Art, 1947–8, with Harold Williamson, Swindon School of Art, 1948–50 with Harold Dearden, and the East Anglian School of Painting and Drawing with Cedric Morris. Exhibited SWA and widely in East Anglia including Norfolk and

Norwich Art Circle, of which she was a member and which holds her work. Lived in Norwich.

Mark FRANCIS 1962– Abstract artist, born in Newtownards, County Down, Northern Ireland. He studied at St Martin's School of Art, 1981–5, then Chelsea School of Art, 1985–6. Was included in New Contemporaries at ICA, 1983; Whitechapel Open, 1990; Twelve Stars, Arts Council Gallery, Belfast, and tour, 1992–3 (Francis' work Union 2, of 1992, was shown there, being acquired for European Parliament Collection); in 1993 won the Grand Prize at Tokyo International Print Exhibition; and was in the 1995–6, 1997–8 and 2002 John Moores Liverpool Exhibitions. Later solo shows included Harewood House, Leeds, 1996, Mary Boone Gallery, New York, 1997; and Milton Keynes Gallery, 2000; there, Francis worked from the body's microbiology plus his antiquarian prints of dissections, diseases, flora and fauna. There were also exhibitions at Michael Kohn Gallery, Los Angeles, California, in 2003, and Maureen Paley/Interim Art in 2004. His work was collected widely in the United Kingdom and abroad.

Mike FRANCIS 1938– He was born in Tooting, south London, lived for a while in Sidcup and settled in Eltham. While training to become an illustrator, Francis studied at St Martin's and Central School of Art. Joined the Furneaux Gallery in 1960, where he had his first solo show; in 1972 won the National Gallery's 150th anniversary poster award; also exhibited with Nicholas Treadwell in Britain and widely abroad. Had a solo show at Whitford Fine Art, 1998, which comprised Super-Realist pictures strong in sexual allusion and innuendo. Jamaican Embassy and a number of corporate collections, including Pears and Shell UK, hold examples. There were five further shows at Whitford, 1999–04.

Sylvia FRANCIS 1910–1996 Versatile artist, designer and teacher in various media, born Sylvia Barrett in Plumstead, Kent. After training at Blackheath School of Art, 1925–8, she worked in London commercial studios including Raphael Tuck, continuing her art studies part-time. During World War II, Sylvia served in drawing offices for the War Department and married Alphons Kowalewski, but when the marriage failed she changed her name by deed poll to Sylvia Francis. After the war she taught painting while still studying, showing regularly at the RA Summer Exhibition, RP, PS, RI and elsewhere. For the last 25 years, Francis spent much of each year painting in East Anglia from her family base near Huntingdon. Bonhams offered her pictures, designs and sculptures in The East Anglian View sale, Lynford Hall, Mundford, in 2000, with ceramics by her cousin Kay Hill.

FRANCYN fl. c.1940–1970 Painter, born in Portsmouth, Hampshire, whose real name was Cynthia Dehn Fuller. She showed with WIAC and NS both of which she was a member, Hampstead Artists' Council and Free Painters and Sculptors and abroad and had several one-man shows. Lived in London.

Eva FRANKFURTHER 1930–1959 Artist, born in Berlin, Germany, who was brought to England by her family in 1939, settling in London's East End. Attended St Martin's School of Art, 1947–52, but taught social work at the London School of Economics. Her book *People* had an introduction by the artist and critic Mervyn Levy. Ben Uri Art Society, which has her Portrait of a Woman, gave her a show in 1962, three years after she committed suicide. Memorial show, Boundary Gallery, 2001.

Gerhart FRANKL 1901–1965 Artist in various media who developed his own techniques and who late in life pursued religious themes. He was born in Vienna, Austria, the only son of cultured parents, and briefly studied chemistry before concentrating on art. Although he studied for several months in 1920–1 with Anton Kolig in Noetsch, Frankl was mostly self-taught, not wishing to join any art movement. From 1922 he travelled in North Africa and widely in Europe and held several exhibitions; in 1930 the Munich Pinakothek bought a landscape and the art historian Hans Tietz wrote a monograph cataloguing Frankl's etchings. Emigrated to England in 1938. Participated in the Venice and São Paulo Biennales and the Pittsburgh Triennale and in 1961 the president of Austria, which he occasionally visited, bestowed the title professor on Frankl. After his death in Vienna there was a memorial show at Hayward Gallery in 1970 organised by the Arts Council which, like Pallant House Gallery Trust in Chichester, holds Frankl's work, with another exhibition at Fitzwilliam Museum, Cambridge, in 1997. There is a Gerhart Frankl Memorial Trust, based in London.

John FRANKLAND 1961– Artist working in a wide range of materials, born in Rochdale, Lancashire. He did a foundation course at the College of Art there, 1979–80, then an honours degree in fine art at Goldsmiths' College, 1980–3. After leaving college Frankland supported himself as a carpenter and decorator, refurbishing old houses. Was included in Young British Artists IV at Saatchi Gallery, 1995. The work Ohne Titel employed part of a tree trunk and paint; Untitled was a garden shed in reflective silver polythene over wood. Was also included in British Art Show 4, and tour, 1995–6. Had solo exhibitions with Hales Gallery fom 1993 and one at Matt's Gallery, 1996: What you lookin' at? Lived in London.

Trevor FRANKLAND 1931– Artist and lecturer, born in Middlesbrough, Yorkshire, who studied at Laird School of Art, Birkenhead, and Royal Academy Schools. He lectured part-time at Medway and Hornsey Colleges of Art and at Middlesex University. Frankland was elected a fellow of the RE, 1993; member LG, 1996; and full member RBA and RWS, of which he was hon. curator, in 1998. Won a large number of awards, later ones including John Purcell Paper Award, 1992, Wandsworth Arts Grant Aid, 1994, and the St Cuthbert's Mill and RBA de Laszlo Medal, both 2001. Took part in numerous group shows in Europe, Australia, North America and India. including Singer & Friedlander/*Sunday Times* Watercolour Competition and Exhibition, 1994; Images from Shakespeare, National Theatre, 1995; and National Print Exhibition, Mall Galleries, 1996. Later solo shows included Middlesbrough Art Gallery, 1988, and Chelsea Arts Club, 1999. He served on British committee of the International Association of Art Critics. His piece of garden art: Summer River Bed, Winter Flood Plain, was featured in several television programmes, 1988–92. Middlesbrough Art Gallery; Shipley Art Gallery, Gateshead; Williamson Art Gallery, Birkenhead; and other public and corporate collections hold examples. Lived in London.

Alan FRANKLIN 1954– Sculptor in a variety of materials, born in Oxford. He studied at Banbury School of Art, 1972–3, St Martin's School of Art, 1973–4, worked as a landscape gardener in southern Spain, then studied at West Surrey College of Art & Design, Farnham, 1975–7. His exhibitions included South Hill Park Arts Centre, Bracknell, from 1979; Johnson Wax Kiln Gallery, Farnham, 1981; Aspex Gallery, Portsmouth, and Reading Museum and Art Gallery, 1982; and in 1983 a Goldsmiths' show at Woodlands Art Gallery.

Ben FRANKLIN 1918–1986 Sculptor and teacher, born in Petworth, Sussex. From 1933–9 he worked as a lithographic artist, for the last three years studying part-time at Croydon School of Art. He resumed his studies there after Army service in World War II, resolving to be a sculptor. From 1947–50 studied at Goldsmiths' College School of Art under H Wilson Parker, in 1950 being assistant to Frank Dobson for Festival of Britain work. Started showing at RA. From 1949 Franklin began a series of teaching posts, culminating in his appointment as head of sculpture at the West Surrey College of Art and Design, in Farnham, Surrey, 1969–81. Showed widely in Britain and abroad and carried out many private and public commissions, figurative and abstract. Franklin's involvement in Buddhism, Indian and Chinese art and philosophy gave his work qualities of tranquillity and harmony. Retrospective at West Surrey College of Art and Design, 1988, and touring. Lived in Farnham, Surrey.

Jenny FRANKLIN 1949– Painter and teacher, born in Durban, South Africa. She studied at University of Natal, 1967–72, gaining a postgraduate honours degree; gained an education diploma at University of Cape Town, 1975; settled in London in 1979, obtaining a postgraduate diploma in art and design from Goldsmiths' College, 1979–80; her master's degree in painting, Royal College of Art, 1986–8; then was at British School at Rome, 1988–9. For many years she undertook part-time teaching and she travelled widely. Took part in many group shows, solo exhibitions including Artist of the Day, selected by Jennifer Durrant, Flowers East, 1989; and Crane Kalman Gallery from 1991. Graves Art Gallery in Sheffield holds her work which used a rich and vibrant palette and imagery derived from such subjects as graffiti, textile decorations, mythical birds or fish.

Kim Hunsdon Eastwood FRANKLIN 1955– Painter, notably in tempera, born in Natal, South Africa. He studied at Michaelis School of Fine Art, Cape Town, graduating in 1977. Was a member of SWLA, showing elsewhere in Britain and abroad. National Gallery of Botswana holds his work. Lived in Teddington, Middlesex.

L Michèle FRANKLIN 1958– Painter, printmaker, sculptor and teacher, born in Vermont State in America, of American/British nationality. Attended Camberwell School of Arts and Crafts, gaining an honours degree in fine art with a commendation for sculpture. In 1984 studied etching there, also at International School of Graphics, Venice. In 1981 did part-time teaching including art therapy, women's art classes, in 1988 taking up post of associate lecturer at Camden Adult Education Institute. Mixed exhibitions included RA, 1982; Wapping Wall Studios, 1984; Ben Uri Art Society, 1987; and Whitechapel Open Studios – At Home, 1992. Shared a show at Sue Rankin Gallery, 1992, solo exhibition at The Sternberg Centre for Judaism, 1999. Ben Uri holds her work. Lived in London.

Kristian FRANKS 1976– Artist, born in Birmingham, who graduated in fine art from Ruskin School of Drawing and Fine Art, Oxford, 1995–8, gaining a master's degree at Chelsea College of Art and Design, 1998–9. Was included in group show at Museum of Modern Art, Wales, Machynlleth, 2000. In same year had solo shows Space is for Free, Colombia University, New York, in America, and The Language for the Kiss, Cannes, France. Lived in Borth, Cardiganshire.

Matt FRANKS 1970– Sculptor, born in Yorkshire, who graduated from Goldsmiths' College School of Art in 2000 with the sculpture Foooooom!, acquired by the British Council. He then participated in several London exhibitions (VTO, Cell Project Space and Hallucinating Love at Asprey Jacques) and in two British Council shows: London Orphan Asylum, 2000, and Tailsliding, which toured Scandinavia in 2002. In that year Franks had a first solo exhibition at Asprey Jacques, introducing a mythological theme with three new pastel-shaded Styrofoam, steel and epoxy resin sculptures; also, his work transcendent plastic infinite, which referred to and parodied the new, large, colourful abstract sculpture that appeared in Britain in the 1960s, was included in the Art Now programme at Tate Britain.

Alexander FRASER 1940– Painter and teacher, born in Aberdeen. He studied at Gray's School of Art there, 1958–62, completing a postgraduate year. A Travelling Scholarship took him to France and Italy. Fraser won a number of awards including the RSA Guthrie Award, the Sir William Gillies Bequest allowing him to travel in Egypt. Fraser joined the staff of Gray's School and became senior lecturer in charge of painting. From the mid-1960s he had a steady stream of solo exhibitions, figurative and abstract work, including 57 Gallery, Edinburgh; Sheffield University; Compass Gallery, Glasgow; Aberdeen Art Gallery; Talbot Rice Art Centre, Glasgow, 1987; and Cyril Gerber Fine Art, Glasgow, 1995. In that exhibition Fraser showed small paintings and drawings intended to engage the viewer's imagination and which were "open to interpretation", tinged with a Surrealist oddness. Among Fraser's administrative roles were serving on Grampian Hospitals and Health Care Art Project Committee, and on the councils of the SSA, Aberdeen Arts Society, RSA and RSW. He won the inaugural Noble Grossart Prize in 1996.

Cameron FRASER 1968– Artist, born on Vanuatu, who graduated at La Trobe University, in Australia, 1987–9; gained a postgraduate diploma in fine art from Victorian College of the Arts, Melbourne University, 1992–3; and his master's in fine art, Barcelona, Spain, and Winchester, 1995–6. He had a series of solo exhibitions at Darren Knight Gallery, Melbourne, from 1997, also in that year at Panorama Gallery, Barcelona. In 1997 Fraser participated in The Large Print Show, Christchurch Mansion, Ipswich, commenting about his Dry Shave print of a razor: "Contemporary objects imbued with a quiet force and beauty are the essence of my work." He was then based in Sheerness, Kent, with an address in Sale, Victoria, Australia.

Colin FRASER 1956– Teacher and painter of still life and interiors whose work included a strong autobiographical symbolism, born in Glasgow. He gained an honours degree at Brighton and had a first solo show there in 1978. Many others followed, including Catto Gallery from 1994 and The Gatehouse Gallery, Giffnock, Glasgow, 2004. Also exhibited in RA Summer Exhibitions and with NEAC and RWS. Spent many years perfecting the egg tempera process. Moved to Sweden in 1985, where he lived in Lund and taught at its School of Art.

Donald Hamilton FRASER 1929– Painter, printmaker, writer and teacher, born in London. He studied at St Martin's School of Art, 1949–52, having his first solo show at Gimpel Fils in 1953. Showed frequently there and at Paul Rosenberg & Co in New York and elsewhere abroad in mixed exhibitions. The ballet and landscape were common themes in his work, which was largely figurative and influenced by the School of Paris, where he studied under a French Government Scholarship, 1953–4. Taught at Royal College of Art, 1957–83. Was elected RA in 1985 and was a member of Royal Fine Art Commission in 1986. There was a print retrospective at CCA Galleries, 2000. He shared an exhibition with Tom Coates at W H Patterson, 2003, having had a 50-year retrospective there in 2002. His wife Judy was also an artist. Arts Council holds his work. Lived in London.

Elizabeth FRASER 1914– Sculptor in various materials and painter, born in Teddington, Middlesex. She studied at Birmingham, Central and Westminster Schools of Art and at Edinburgh College of Art under the sculptor Eric Schilsky. Showed with SPS of which she was a member, RA and in the provinces, having a series of solo exhibitions. Lived in London.

Eric FRASER 1902–1984 Painter in oil and watercolour, stained glass designer but especially an outstanding pen and ink draughtsman. Fraser studied at Goldsmiths' College School of Art under Frederick Marriott, Edmund J Sullivan and Clive Gardiner, all strong black-and-white men. He exhibited at the RA and SSA, but it is on the printed page that he established his reputation. He worked for the Folio Society, Golden Cockerel Press, *Radio Times*, *The Studio* and *Punch*, among many others. Murals were done for the navigators memorial in Westminster Abbey and Babcock House, and a huge one in connection with the Festival of Britain in 1951. Latterly Fraser said that he preferred commissions which meant he could use his imagination and did not have to represent reality. A wide-ranging exhibition of Fraser's work was held at the Royal College of Art in 1991, sponsored by British Gas, Fraser having invented Mr Therm, the gas symbol. The firm was one of Fraser's many industrial clients. Lived at Hampton, Middlesex.

Ian FRASER 1933–1987 Painter, printmaker and teacher, born in Newcastle upon Tyne, Northumberland. Fraser studied at Leeds College of Art, 1949–53, then at Royal College of Art, 1955–8. He taught at Hornsey College of Art and was head of the BA Hons Fine Art course at Middlesex Polytechnic. Lived in Shepperton, Middlesex.

Jean FRASER: *see* **Jean DUNCAN**

Jeremy FRASER 1941– Painter of landscapes, who attended Ipswich School of Art, 1988–90. As well as Spain, France and Ireland, Fraser especially depicted the river, marshland and beach at Shingle Street, Suffolk, "making discoveries that are increasingly lyrical and mysterious," according to painter Maggi Hambling. Mixed shows included New Grafton Gallery, from 1990; Cinema Gallery, Aldeburgh, 1991; Haste Gallery, Ipswich, 1993; RA Summer Exhibition, 1996; and from 1994 the John Russell Gallery, Ipswich, which gave him a solo exhibition in 2000.

Neil FRASER 1955– Versatile artist, maker of boxed sculptures which he called 3D collages, inspired by a single object for which he created a life history. Born in Ealing, Middlesex, Fraser early wanted to be an artist, from 12 inspired by Surrealism, notably Magritte, Ernst and de Chirico and the wonders of the Science Museum. He graduated from the Central School of Art and Design, 1973–7, where he was interested in performance art, particularly lighting and building, while carrying on his own sculpture. Fraser used objects from the Greenwich foreshore near his home, or, in the case of his show Gas Pie, at The Mayor Gallery, 1998, ideas gleaned on a trip to eastern Europe. Work themes included "disasters, airships, evolution".

Norman FRASER 1943– Artist, notably a draughtsman, and teacher, whose work was influenced by Op Art, Celtic designs and the computer at various stages. He was born in Belfast, Northern Ireland, and studied at the College of Art there, 1960–5, and Hornsey College of Art, 1965–8. Returned to Belfast to teach, appointments including a lectureship at Ulster College. In 1974 he gained a travel bursary from Arts Council of Northern Ireland, which holds his work, to research computer art in North America. Exhibitions included the Arts Council of Northern Ireland's Gallery in Belfast, Octagon Gallery in the city and Third Eye Centre, Glasgow.

Simon FRASER 1950– Artist, born in Inverness, who studied at the Ruskin School of Drawing, Oxford, and Gray's School of Art, Aberdeen, 1968–72. Whether he worked in oil on canvas or in colour or black-and-white etchings, Fraser's art was permeated by poetry and mythology, especially Celtic myth. He illustrated the poetry of George Mackay Brown, Aonghas MacNeacail and T S Eliot. Group shows included Contemporary Landscape, Edinburgh City Art Centre, 1985, and Newcastle Maritime Festival, Laing Art Gallery, Newcastle, and The Human Touch, Fischer Fine Art, both 1986. He had a series of solo shows throughout Britain, starting with Bristol Arts Centre and Plymouth Hoe Theatre, both 1979, later ones including An Lanntair, Stornoway, and Peacock Printmakers, Aberdeen, both 1985, and Artspace Galleries, Aberdeen, 1986.

William Miller FRAZER 1864–1961 Landscape painter, born at Scone, Perthshire, who attended Perth Academy, then studied at Royal Scottish Academy Schools, winning the Keith Prize, then in Paris. Elected RSA in 1924. Exhibited there and prolifically at Royal Glasgow Institute of the Fine Arts, and at RA, RBA, RHA and ROI. Closely involved with Scottish Arts Club, of which he was for a time president. Lived in Edinburgh.

Nigel FREAKE 1959– Painter, born in London, who studied at Exeter University/College of Art & Design, 1978–81, then Goldsmiths' College, 1991–3. He was finalist, New Art Award for Postgraduates, in the latter year. Group exhibitions included Library Gallery, Exeter University, 1982; Spacex Gallery, Exeter, 1983; Cable Street Studios Open Studios, 1990; Into the Nineties 5, Mall Galleries, 1993; and Cable and Wireless, 1995. In Blush, shared with Julie Major at Paton Gallery, 1996, Freake showed work indicating Carl André's Minimalist influence. Painted in acrylic and synthetic resin on linen, the paintings had as their origin dresses, patterned fabrics on a moving female body. The Courtauld Institute East Wing Collection holds Freake's work.

Naomi FREARS 1963– Artist and teacher, born in Leicestershire, who did a foundation course at Loughborough College of Art; in 1986 gained an honours degree and printmaking prize from Sunderland College of Art and Design; and also attended Cyprus College of Art. After a 25,000-mile motorcycle journey through Asia and Australia in 1989 she settled in St Ives, Cornwall, starting to paint and make prints. In 1990 Frears was one of 10 invited artists in a portfolio of etchings to raise money towards building Tate in St Ives. In 1992 she took an exhibition of her own and other St Ives' artists work to Bangkok, Thailand, the profits building a school for Karen tribe children; and as a Porthmeor Printmaker made a lino-cut for a portfolio to help fund renovation of Porthmeor Print Workshop. Taught widely in Cornwall. Exhibition venues included Marsden Contemporary Art; Adam Gallery, Bath; and in St Ives at the New Craftsman, Penwith Gallery and New Millennium Gallery, where she had solo shows in 2003 and 2005. Falmouth College of Art, Sunderland University, Cornwall County Council and Royal Cornwall Museum hold examples.

Harry FRECKLETON 1890–1979 Painter in oil, born in Nottingham, where he continued to live. He was the husband of the artist Vera Freckleton. He attended Nottingham School of Art, 1904–12, his teachers including Wilson Foster, and was influenced by the local painter Arthur Spooner. Freckleton worked as a lithographic artist, served in the Army during World War I, worked as an artist for New Zealand Ciné Studios and then ran his own photographic business, 1924–65. He showed at RA, RP, RBA and with the Nottingham Society of Artists of which he was a member. Represented in public collections in Nottingham, Blackpool, Huddersfield and elsewhere.

Vera FRECKLETON 1899–1989 Painter and miniaturist, noted for her work on ivory, born in Nottingham, where she continued to live. She was the wife of the painter Harry Freckleton, and her uncle Arthur Redgate and grandfather Sylvanus Redgate were both Nottingham artists. Studied at local College of Art, 1917–20. She showed her work at RMS, 1955–74, of which she became a full member in 1971. Also exhibited at Paris Salon where she gained an Hon. Mention in 1955, a silver medal in 1965 and a gold medal in 1972.

Jane FREDERICK 1969– Painter, lecturer and muralist, born in Lincoln, who gained a general art and design diploma at Lincolnshire College of Art and Design (where she later taught), 1985–7; a fine art honours degree at Nottingham Polytechnic, 1987–90; and her teacher's certificate at University of Central England, Birmingham, 1992–3. Other teaching venues included Bournville College of Art, Birmingham; North East Worcestershire College; and Colchester Institute. Was artist-in-residence, Barr-Beacon School, Birmingham, 1993. She was shortlisted for the NatWest Art Prize, 1995 and 1998. In 1997 she gained a Lottery-funded commission for Brookside Primary School, Telford, and a murals commission for J Sainsbury, Stamford House. Mixed shows included Singer & Friedlander/*Sunday Times* Watercolour Competition, Mall Galleries, 1989; Ipswich Open, Christchurch Mansion, Ipswich, 1995; and the BP Portrait Award, National Portrait Gallery, from 1998. Among her later solo shows were The Green Room, at Minories Art Gallery, in Colchester, Essex, where she lived, 1999, in which Frederick explored the "many similarities between the language of garden design and that of painting"; and Artist Space there in 2005, in which she turned the downstairs area "into a temporary studio to create her large-scale snapshot paintings."

Waveney FREDRICK 1911–1999 Artist in various media, notably pastel and charcoal, born in Luton, Bedfordshire. Until she married a schoolteacher, John Fredrick, in 1969, she was known by her maiden name, Waveney Payne. Under this name, as a keen viola player she helped found the Midland String Quartet, her playing career being cut short by tuberculosis and the loss of a lung; made an impressive career as a librarian, expanding the Shakespeare Library and its seven-volume *Shakespeare Bibliography* catalogue, published in 1969; and established her early career as an artist, in 1950 founding the Harborne Group, which aimed at jettisoning academic restraints. In 1984 with Gordon Yapp and Alex Jackson she went on to co-found the Birmingham Pastel Society, holding a first show. She studied at King Edward VI School, Birmingham, where she lived, and art at East Anglian School of Painting with Cedric Morris. Became a member of RBSA in 1978 and PS in 1983. She won the Feeney Award, Birmingham, 1977, PS' Herring Award, 1983, and Pastel Society of Canada Award, 1989. Took part in Five Artists at RBSA Galleries, Birmingham, 1990. Solo shows included Birmingham University; Oxford University; Keele University; Walsall Art Gallery; Royal Shakespeare Theatre, Stratford-upon-Avon; and in America.

Katerina FREDYNA 1906– Painter and draughtsman, notably in gouache, born in Kharkov, Russia. After education there she studied at St Martin's School of Art from the mid-1950s under Muriel Pemberton. Was a member of WIAC, Free Painters and Sculptors and Campden Hill Club, also exhibiting at Whitechapel Art Gallery, Camden Arts Centre and at Paris Salon. Bibliothèque Nationale, Paris, holds her work. Lived in London.

Susan FREEBOROUGH 1941– Figurative sculptor who gained a first-class honours degree at Chichester College of Higher Education, 1986, then an honours degree in fine art at Cheltenham College of Art, 1991. Between 1991–2 she was employed by Pangolin Editions sculpture foundry at Chalford, Gloucestershire. Showed in degree exhibition at Cheltenham College and in Fresh Art at Business Design Centre, Islington, both 1991, and in 1st RWA Open Sculpture Exhibition, 1993. Lived in Sheepscombe, Stroud, Gloucestershire.

Colin FREEBURY 1946– Painter producing large gestural abstracts in which pastel colours were predominant, born in London. Studied for his art and design diploma at Falmouth School of Art, gaining a teaching qualification from Cardiff University. In 1979 became a member of Penwith Society of Arts and worked in a studio in Penwith Gallery, St Ives, Cornwall. Exhibitions included Rainyday Gallery, Penzance, 1994, and The Edge of Beyond, Belgrave Gallery, 1995.

David FREED 1936– Artist and teacher, born in Toledo, Ohio, America, who graduated with a fine arts degree from Miami University of Ohio, earning a master's (cum laude) from the University of Iowa in 1962, studying under the noted printmaker Mauricio Lasansky. Freed also studied at the Royal College of Art, London. His awards included a Fulbright Grant, 1963–4; World Print Competition, 1977; Nattie Marie Jones Fellowship, 1983; Virginia Museum of Fine Art, 1983–4; Faculty Grant-in-Aid, Virginia Commonwealth University, 1983–4 and 1989–90; and Theresa Pollak Prize for Excellence in the Arts, Richmond, Virginia, 2001. After Fulbright, Freed returned to America to teach sculpture, design and children's classes at the Toledo Museum of Art School. He moved to Richmond in 1966 to start a printmaking programme at Richmond Professional Institute, which later became Virginia Commonwealth University, eventually becoming professor of printmaking with his own studio in Richmond. As well as working in Paris for four months after being granted a studio apartment and a Virginia Museum of Fine Arts Fellowship, Freed held a number of visiting lectureships, including Central School of Art, 1969, 1976, 1977, 1986 and 1989; Ruskin School of Drawing, Oxford, 1970 and 1972; University of Virginia, Charlottesville, 1974 and 1997; Loughborough School of Art, 1976 and 1986; Is Bisonte, Florence, Italy, and Brighton School of Art, both 1989; and Reading University, 1992. Freed took part in many international mixed shows, later solo exhibitions including a retrospective at Anderson Gallery, Virginia Commonwealth University, 2001. Among the large number of notable public collections holding his work are the Art Institute of Chicago; Fitzwilliam Museum, Cambridge; Library of Congress, Washington; Museum of Modern Art, New York; Victoria & Albert Museum; and Yale University, New Haven, Connecticut.

Barnett FREEDMAN 1901–1958 Painter, printmaker, draughtsman and teacher, born in east London to a poor Jewish family recently arrived from Russia. He was bedridden for several years as a child and largely taught himself basic education, music and to draw. By 1916 he was able to earn his living as a draughtsman to a monumental mason. For five years he studied part-time at St Martin's School of Art. The personal influence of William Rothenstein enabled him to study full-time at the Royal College of Art, 1922–5. Then he went through a lean period as a freelance. After two years he was commissioned to illustrate Laurence Binyon's poem *The Wonder Night*, he began to exhibit at the NEAC and became a pioneer in reviving colour lithography. At various times taught at the Working Men's College, Crowndale Road, Ruskin School of Art, Oxford, and the Royal College of Art. Official war artist in World War II. By his death Freedman had established an enviable reputation as an illustrator and designer of posters, stamps, books and book-jackets. He believed there was no such thing as commercial art, "only good art and bad art". First exhibition at the Literary Bookshop, Bloomsbury, 1929; memorial exhibition Arts Council, 1958, and tour; Manchester Polytechnic, which holds the Freedman archive, held a major show in 1990. Freedman lived in London, married to the artist Beatrice Claudia Freedman. Tate Gallery holds his work.

Beatrice Claudia FREEDMAN 1904–1981 Artist, illustrator and teacher, born in Formby, Lancashire, of Sicilian ancestry. She worked as Beatrice Claudia Guercio, her maiden name; Claudia Freedman; or just C F. Was married to the artist Barnett Freedman. She studied at Liverpool School of Art under Frederick Carter, then at the Royal College of Art with Malcolm Osborne. Exhibited at RA and Walker Art Gallery, Liverpool. In addition she did a wide variety of graphic work, designing an alphabet for the Baynard Press; producing designs for advertising; as well as drawings for the General Post Office, Fortnum and Mason, Medici Society and Curwen Press. Among books illustrated were her own *My Toy Cupboard*; the *Little Book of Parables*, 1944, perhaps her most important work in this field, for which her husband did the page lay-outs; and Eleanor Graham's editing of *The Puffin Book of Verse*, 1953. Victoria & Albert Museum holds her work. Lived in London for many years, but died in Sussex.

Claudia FREEDMAN: *see* **Beatrice Claudia FREEDMAN**

Constance FREEDMAN 1927–1982 Sculptor in a variety of materials and painter, wife of a furniture manufacturer, Joseph Freedman. She studied at Sir John Cass School of Art, 1963–8. In 1979 she was awarded a Church Fellowship for environmental and functional sculpture. For most of her life Freedman lived in Hackney, east London. The Chalmers Art Gallery there holds her portrait bust of Big Dave, a market character, and in 1980 Prince Philip unveiled her powerful Javelin Thrower, in welded copper, which stands outside the Britannia Leisure Centre, Shoreditch. Generals Eisenhower and Montgomery were portrayed by her and her head of the ballet dancer Anton Dolin is on permanent view at Sadler's Wells Theatre. Showed at RA, Whitechapel and Ben Uri Galleries, Paris Salon and elsewhere abroad and had a series of solo exhibitions, including Chalmers, 1969–72, and Brunswick Gallery, 1977. She was a member of SPS and was made a fellow of RBS in 1978. Freedman died in the Royal Marsden Hospital, Fulham.

Anthony FREEMAN 1939– Painter, born in Surrey, who attended Kingston School of Art. While a student there, in 1960 he sold a sombre self-portrait to the collector Ruth Borchard and it is included in Philip Vann's book *Face to Face*, published in 2004 by Sansom & Company Ltd/Piano Nobile Fine Paintings. Freeman exhibited with Young Contemporaries and at the RA Summer Exhibition.

Arthur FREEMAN 1927– Painter, born in Maidstone, Kent, where he studied at the College of Art. He was an experienced watercolourist, from the early 1970s developing a new interest in seascapes, given a solo show at Thackeray Gallery, 1978. Mixed exhibitions included Roland, Browse and Delbanco; Campbell and Franks; Mercury and Belgrave Galleries. City of Glasgow, Government Art Collection and the county collections of Essex, Kent, Norfolk, Somerset and Wiltshire hold examples.

Barbara FREEMAN 1937– Painter, printmaker, sculptor and installations artist, and teacher, born in London. She studied at St Martin's, Camberwell and Hammersmith Colleges of Art, gaining her diploma in 1962, doing a postgraduate diploma at University of Leeds, 1972. Taught part-time in several colleges. Freeman made sculpture until 1982, when she changed to painting and printmaking, including mixed media pieces. She travelled widely, which was reflected in the subjects of her work, both figurative and abstract, often using a rich palette. She was a member of the Association of Irish Artists. Group exhibitions included Magnetic North, Orchard Gallery, Londonderry, 1987; Art London 89, Art Fair, 1989; and Abstract Representation, Triskel Arts Centre, Cork, 1991. Was later represented by Hart Gallery, Nottingham. West Yorkshire County Council, Leeds City Council and University of Bradford are among British and foreign collections holding examples. Lived in Belfast, Northern Ireland.

Barry FREEMAN 1947– Artist and teacher who was largely self-taught, although he did study part-time at St Martin's School of Art and Morley College. Landscapes, coastal and figure pictures in oil and pastel were a strong feature of his output. Freeman worked as a demonstrator for the artists' materials firm Daler-Rowney and taught at Earnley Concourse, Chichester. He was a member of PS, other venues including Fairfield Halls, Croydon, 1985–9; Edwin Pollard Gallery, 1987; RBA, 1990; Bourne Gallery, Reigate, 1990–1; and in 1992 he shared a three-man exhibition at Anna-Mei Chadwick. Freeman won the Willi Hoffmann-Güth Award, PS, 1995; Highly Commended Award, Daler-Rowney, PS, 1995; and George Barnes Award for pastels. His work was featured in many books.

Esther J FREEMAN 1939– Sculptor who worked in a variety of traditional and modern materials. She studied at West of England College of Art in Bristol and at the Slade School of Fine Art. Her plaster Sculpture of Haptikos, of 1962, was included in that year in 19 Young Sculptors at Hillfield Gardens, Gloucester, at which time she was living in London.

Janet FREEMAN 1933– Painter, notably of meticulously placed and richly coloured still lifes in which the frames enhanced and complemented the work. She studied at Goldsmiths' College School of Art in the 1950s, tutors including Adrian Ryan, Sam Rabin and Kenneth Martin. In the 1970s she returned to study at Bath Academy of Art and Bath College of Higher Education, from then on continuing to work in life classes. She showed at the RWA, Bath Society of Artists, NEAC Laing Landscape Exhibition, South West Academy and RA, having a solo exhibition at Duncan Campbell Fine Art in 2003. Freeman lived in Bath, Somerset.

John Tatchell FREEMAN 1958– Painter, printmaker and illustrator, born in London, who studied at Bath Academy of Art, 1976–7, and Chelsea School of Art, 1977–80. His Arts Council residencies included the Royal Surrey County Hospital, 1986; Park Barn School, Guildford, and Epsom Hospital, both 1990; and Folly Hill School, Farnham, and Winston Churchill School, Woking, both 1991. Among Freeman's group exhibitions were National Portrait Gallery, John Player Portrait Award, 1984 and 1989; Bluecoat Gallery, Liverpool, 1985; Association of Illustrators Gallery, 1986; New Ashgate Gallery, Farnham, 1989; Collins Gallery, University of Strathclyde, 1994; and The Folio Society Jubilee Exhibition, British Museum, 1997. Freeman's drawings and prints illustrated a series of books, including *The Graphic Guide to Thatcher*, Ed Harriman, 1986; *Eight Scandinavian Poets*, 1992; and *A Life Going On*, poems by David Allison, 1993. Regular solo shows included Camden Arts Centre, 1988; Royal Festival Hall, 1991; Balliol College, Oxford, 1994; Helsinki City Library Gallery, Finland, 1995; Southampton City Art Centre, 1996; and Descent to Byworth at Abbott and Holder, 2002. He lived in Guildford, Surrey.

Lily FREEMAN 1920– Painter and lecturer, born in Vienna, Austria. She studied art there and with Arthur Segal in London. Exhibitions included Loggia Gallery, Cockpit Theatre, Ben Uri Gallery, Hampstead Town Hall and Royal Over-Seas League. Lived in London.

Mary FREEMAN 1888–1974 Watercolourist, born on St Patrick's Day and known as Pat. She trained at Kingston School of Art, having been born in Surbiton, Surrey, then lived for 40 years in Shere, only moving to an old people's home in Woking in her seventies when she became ill. She was then still painting and was known for her watercolours of local woods and the market and cafés of Guildford. A group of her paintings was donated to Guildford House Gallery, and there are works by her in other galleries in the southeast of England.

Michael FREEMAN 1936– Visionary painter, draughtsman, printmaker and adult educationist, born in Swansea. Having always lived near the sea, except for London in the 1960s where a post on a Fleet Street newspaper "nearly stifled creative work," he "found that the rhythm of the tides deeply influenced his work and outlook," and returned to Swansea. Among Mike Freeman's series of paintings were Shipwrecks, from the early 1970s; the Book of the Crab, begun in the early 1980s; and Canute, exhibited at The Bar Covent Museum, York, 1993. Other solo shows included a 1964–84 retrospective at Glynn Vivian Art Gallery & Museum, Swansea, 1985, and Queen's Hall, Narberth, 2001. A seventieth-birthday retrospective was at Neath Museum & Art Gallery in 2006. Freeman was an erudite musician and musicologist and the relationship between art and music was important to him. He was an expert on the life and music of the composer Joseph Holbrooke, on whom he wrote. Freeman produced witty, figurative programme illustrations for concerts by the PM Music Ensemble at the Norwegian Church Arts Centre, Cardiff Bay, and Marco Polo and Naxos used his pictures on their compact discs. For several decades Freeman's students showed annually as The Theodore Painters at the Port Talbot Art Centre. In 2000, he formed the Friday Group there; it saw "the handling of paint, and other traditional two-dimensional media as still sufficient for the presentation of vital artistic ideas." WAC, Glynn Vivian and many private collections in Britain and abroad hold Freeman's work.

Ralph FREEMAN 1945– Painter of abstract pictures in oil and watercolour, collagist, relief-maker, designer and teacher, born in London. He studied at St Martin's and Harrow Schools of Art, 1961–5, then worked as a jazz pianist, artist and designer in London, Hamburg and Frankfurt. Commissions included murals and social, film and exhibition posters, 1965–74. He also lectured at

Bournemouth College of Art. Later commissions included the stage set for *Nevermore* at Half Moon Theatre, 1985, and a series of works on Man, Spirit and Energy, 1990. Freeman was a member of Newlyn Society of Artists and Penwith Society of Arts. Mixed show appearances included Boundary and Ben Uri Galleries, Camden Arts Centre and Anderson O'Day. He had a solo show at Camden Arts Centre in 1983, later ones including several in Milan and Hamburg, Royal Cornwall Museum Galleries, Truro, 1992, and The New Millennium Gallery, St Ives, 1999 and 2003. Lived in St Ives, Cornwall.

Richard FREEMAN 1932– Versatile artist and teacher whose work included painting, ceramics and sculpture, married to the painter Janet Freeman. Between 1950–6, Freeman studied at Goldsmiths' College and Chelsea School of Art and taught in London schools. Between 1956–72, he was self-employed with his own studio-workshops, was a founder-member of the Craftsmen Potters Association and exhibited in Britain and abroad, through the Design Council, Heal's, Liberty, Primavera and other outlets. During 1972–82, Freeman lectured part-time in ceramics and sculpture at Bath Academy of Art and Bath College of Higher education, part-time study at Bristol University achieving a Master of Education degree, while continuing to exhibit in London and the provinces. Between 1982–97, Freeman became a full-time senior lecturer at Bath College of Higher Education, incorporating Bath Academy of Art, exhibiting at the RWA from 1992, winning a prize at its Open Sculpture Exhibition in 1996. He was elected RWA in 1998 and sculpted and painted full-time. Freeman shared a show with his wife at Duncan Campbell Fine Art in 2006. Lived in Bath, Somerset.

Allen FREER 1926– Painter, miniaturist and illustrator, he was a frequent solo exhibitor at Tib Lane Gallery, Manchester, from 1970. Later solo shows included Linton Court Gallery, Settle; Oriel 31, Welshpool; and Austin/Desmond Fine Art. Freer also appeared in mixed shows at Agnew, Hamet Gallery and New Grafton Gallery. He illustrated books for Cambridge University Press and T R Henn's autobiography *Five Arches*. Freer was noted for his landscapes, notably those of the English countryside, which had a fine sense of atmosphere.

Mavis FREER 1927– Landscape painter and teacher who was born in Chesterfield, Derbyshire. From 1943–9 she studied at the School of Art there and Goldsmiths' College School of Art. Taught part-time at Grinling Gibbons School, Deptford. Showed frequently in mixed shows and had a solo exhibition in Canterbury in 1976, another at Woodlands Art Gallery in 1977.

Roy FREER 1938– Painter using a rich palette, and teacher, born in Birmingham. He trained at Bournville School of Art and Birmingham College of Arts and Crafts between 1956–8. He was a member of ROI, PS and RI whose later work became looser and broader, more about the substance of colour, brushmark and paint. Freer took part in many mixed shows, including RA Summer Exhibition, NEAC (of which he also became a member), Linda Blackstone Gallery in Pinner and Adam Gallery in Bath. A large number of solo exhibitions included Anna-Mei Chadwick, 1993, Catto Gallery, 2002, and Chappel Galleries, Chappel, 2005. Among his awards were the RI bronze medal in 1986; ROI Cornelissen Prize same year; PSCD Soar Prize, 1990; and ROI Catto Gallery Prize, 1992. Open University holds his work. Lived in London.

Hubert Andrew FREETH 1912–1986 Etcher and painter, especially of portraits and figure subjects. Born in Birmingham, he attended the School of Art there, then won an engraving Rome Scholarship in 1936, subsequently spending three years at the British School in Rome. During World War II he was an Official War Artist in the Middle East, his drawings and prints being bought by the War Artists' Advisory Committee. Work also owned by British Museum and many other public collections. Freeth contributed to the Pilgrim Trust *Recording Britain* project and was widely anthologised in collections of war artists' work. Exhibited RA, and was elected RA 1965, also RE, RWS, RP and elsewhere. Freeth was noted for his superbly accomplished etchings. Taught at St Martin's School of Art and Central School of Arts and Crafts. Lived at Northwood, Middlesex.

Peter FREETH 1938– Printmaker and teacher, born in Birmingham, who studied at Slade School of Fine Art, 1956–60, gaining the Prix de Rome for engraving, 1960. He taught at Royal Academy Schools and Camden Institute. From 1973 showed at RA, elsewhere in mixed shows in London, as well as extensively abroad. Elected RA and RE, 1991. Elected RA and RE, 1991. From 1987 had solo shows at Christopher Mendez, 1987–9, others including Friends Room at the RA, 1991; Santa Maria a Gradillo, Ravello, Italy, 1997; Word Play, RA, 2001; and Christ Church Picture Gallery, Oxford, in 2005. He shared an exhibition with Marianne Kreeger at Beardsmore Gallery, 2002. British Museum, Victoria & Albert Museum, Arts Council and Metropolitan Museum hold his work. Lived in London.

Thomas FREETH 1912–1994 Painter, draughtsman and teacher who worked for a time as a designer/painter on porcelain, studied at Royal College of Art for four years, then travelled in France and Spain. He joined the Army in April 1941, from September that year serving as a sapper with Headquarters, 9th Armoured Division. War Artists' Advisory Committee bought several works by Freeth, in collections of Imperial War Museum and Royal Pavilion Art Gallery and Museums, Brighton. At that time he was based in Halifax, Yorkshire, but by late 1940s, when he showed at RA Summer Exhibitions, Freeth was living in Bromley, then Beckenham, Kent, where he taught at the Art School. He retired as head of painting at Ravensbourne College of Art (formerly Bromley) in 1977. He was remembered by a former colleague as "a sound man, rather retiring, a loner".

Chloe FREMANTLE 1950– Painter, born in London, output including abstract work, who studied at Byam Shaw School of Art, 1968–72. She then lived in Italy, Scotland and France, 1972–82; in London and New York, 1982–7; then settled in London. Held many solo exhibitions from 1973, later ones including Jernigan Wicker Gallery, San Francisco, California, 1996; Chelsea & Westminster Hospital and Eagle Gallery at Sheridan Russell Gallery, both 1999; and Curwen Gallery, 2002. J Walter Thompson, De Beers, Mobil and other corporate collections held work in Britain and abroad.

Annie FRENCH 1872–1965 Watercolourist, illustrator, designer and teacher, born in Glasgow and married to the artist George Wooliscroft Rhead, who predeceased her by 45 years. French studied at Glasgow School of Art under Fra Newbery and taught in the department of design there from 1909, but after marrying Rhead she settled in London in 1915. She was a prolific exhibitor at RSA and Royal Glasgow Institute of the Fine Arts, also showing at RHA, RA and elsewhere. Her work was highly detailed, mixing Art Nouveau, the style of Jessie M King and a touch of Aubrey Beardsley. Scottish National Gallery of Modern Art holds several works by her.

Dick FRENCH 1946– Painter, born in South Shields, County Durham. He studied at Sheffield College of Art, 1962–7, his teachers including Robin Plummer and Kevin Farrell, then at Royal College of Art, 1967–70, under Carel Weight and Peter Blake. For a time he was resident artist at Lanchester Polytechnic, Coventry. He won the Harmstone Bequest, 1967, and Burston Award in 1970. Among mixed exhibitions were John Moores Liverpool Exhibitions, 1976 and '87, in both of which he won prizes, as well as City Artists, 1985–6. Had solo shows at South Hill Park in 1985 and City Artists Gallery, 1986. Public galleries in Wolverhampton and Sheffield hold his work. Lived in London.

Stanisław FRENKIEL 1918–2001 Painter, writer and teacher, born in Cracow, Poland, where he attended the Academy of Fine Arts, 1937–9. During the Nazi occupation he escaped to Lvov, was arrested by the Russians and deported, in 1942 joined the Polish Army in Russia and travelled to the Middle East, moving to London in 1947. His *Beirut Drawings 1944–7* was published in 1986. Frenkiel was eventually emeritus reader at London University and head of the Institute of Education, 1973–83. He was a member of LG and the Association of Polish Artists in Great Britain and RWA. His colourful figurative paintings were shown in Britain and continental Europe, and he was included in City Art Centre, Edinburgh, 1993 show Polish Roots – British Soil. His solo exhibitions included Grabowski Gallery from 1960; Tamara Pfeiffer Gallery, Brussels, from 1973; Newman Galleries, Philadelphia, from 1976; a Polish retrospective tour, 1981–3; and retrospectives at Bloomsbury Gallery, London University, 1983–7. That university, the University of Pennsylvania and several Polish collections, including University of Toruń, hold his work. Lived in London, where Frenkiel attended an exhibition at POSK Gallery days before his death. There was a small retrospective at RWA, 2003.

M Hanbury FRERE 1866–1956 Watercolour and pastel artist, born at Horham, Suffolk. Studied at Wimbledon with Leonard Pocock and Alfred Drury, then exhibited in London and in East Anglia. HM Queen Mary bought her work. Lived in Norwich.

Matthew FRERE-SMITH 1923–1999 Sculptor in various materials and teacher, son of barrister Percival Frere-Smith, born in London, whose initial education at a small Quaker school excited an interest in painting and drawing. After Sutton Valence School he joined the Royal Navy, 1941–7, training at Dartmouth Naval College and holding commissioned rank. Frere-Smith studied at Wimbledon College of Art, 1947, then sculpture at Royal College of Art, 1949–52, graduating top of his year. In 1950 he married Patricia Ryall, a dress design student at Wimbledon; although they separated in 1972 and eventually divorced, they had 12 children, several pursuing artistic careers. He started teaching at Burslem College of Art, 1952, other posts including part-time at Norwich School of Art, Yarmouth College of Art and finally full-time at Lowestoft College. Having worked with a stonemason on church restoration in the 1950s, in the 1960s Frere-Smith's sculpture developed into abstract and geometric forms using metal and wire. In 1959, he started making drawings based on impossible geometry "as part of research into the creation of lightweight, mobile, airborne, multi-dimensional expressive forms." Worked with the architect Ernö Goldfinger on the 1960s Elephant and Castle redevelopment. He won an international sculpture competition in Milan, Italy, 1974. Latterly, after ill-health had hindered hand-eye co-ordination, Frere-Smith's work became more figurative and he turned to ceramics and mosaics. Transcendental meditation, mysticism and the cultures and beliefs of primitive societies were important to him. He showed internationally, solo exhibitions including King's Lynn Festival, 1962; Drian Galleries, from 1965; Maddermarket Theatre, Norwich, 1987; Burnham Overy, 1997; and a retrospective at Buckenham Galleries, Southwold, 2003. Frere-Smith completed sculptures for many public buildings, churches and shopping centres and has work in the Sainsbury Centre at University of East Anglia. He lived in Briston, Norfolk.

Annabel FREUD 1952– She was the youngest daughter of the painters Lucian Freud and Kitty Garman and with her sister Annie spent a number of her early years at their grandfather Jacob Epstein's house. His sculptures and magnificent collection of African carvings made a strong impression and from childhood Annabel demonstrated a precocious talent for the visual arts. After studying English at university, she achieved a diploma from Kensington School of Art and studied printmaking at Camberwell School of Art. Annabel's work employed diverse techniques and styles. Like that of her mother, it often had personal and familial origins, as in her double portrait of herself and Lucian in his studio at Glen Artney. Her pictures were included in Kitty Garman and Co at New Art Gallery Walsall, in 2003–4.

Lucian FREUD 1922– Painter and teacher, born in Berlin, son of Ernst Freud, architect, and grandson of the analyst Sigmund Freud. Arrived in England in 1932 and became British subject seven years later. During the next few years studied at Central School of Art, East Anglian School of Painting and Drawing and Goldsmiths' College School of Art, having first one-man show in 1944 at Lefevre Gallery. In 1946–8 visited France and Greece and in 1951 won Arts Council Prize at Festival of Britain Exhibition. Three years later a group of his works was shown at British Pavilion at Venice Biennale. Taught at Norwich School of Art and Slade School of Fine Art. A series of solo shows in 1970s at Anthony d'Offay Gallery and a one-man exhibition at Davis & Long Company, in New York, consolidated Freud's position as a leading British realist painter, notable for his almost clinically raw portraits and nude studies. There was a retrospective at Hayward Gallery in 1988 and in 1993 a major show at Whitechapel Art Gallery was toured to Metropolitan Museum, New York, and Reina Sofia, Madrid. Several critics termed Freud Britain's greatest living painter. Tate Britain's 2002–3 retrospective spanned more than 60 years of Freud's output. Timothy Taylor Gallery's 2003 show covered 1940 drawings, then Lucian Freud: Etchings 1946–2004 was at the Scottish National

Gallery of Modern Art, Edinburgh, there was an exhibition of recent paintings at the Wallace Collection and Acquarella, New York, organised a show. In 2005 there was a survey show of his etchings at Marlborough Fine Art and a major retrospective at Correr Museum in Venice during the Biennale, including work featuring the sculptor Alexandra Williams-Wynn. Tate Gallery, Arts Council and other major collections hold his work. Freud was granted the Order of Merit in 1993. Until 1953 he was married to the painter Kitty Garman, their daughters Annabel and Annie Freud also being artists.

Jacqueline FREWING 1937– Sculptor in a variety of materials, painter in oil mainly of portraits and teacher, born in West Wickham, Kent. She studied at St Martin's School of Art, 1955–8, with Vivian Pitchforth, Frederick Gore, Anthony Caro and Elisabeth Frink. After a short period as a freelance illustrator, Frewing was involved in advertising, 1960–5, then had family commitments for almost 20 years; from 1985 returned to Brighton University to retrain, diversifying into oil painting, sculpture and teaching, teachers including Helen Collis and Robert Ellis. As a sculptor Frewing said that her "working approach is to build with clay, rather than to scrape away, which accounts for the textured surface typical of my work". Was a member of the Society of Sussex Sculptors and Three Counties Sculpture Society. Showed widely in Sussex and at Westminster Gallery, SWA. Had a solo show at Kilvert Gallery, East Grinstead. Lived in Copthorne, West Sussex.

David FRIED 1958– Artist who worked in a wide range of media, including three-dimensional, born and based in London. He did a foundation course at East Ham Technical College, 1975–6; gained an honours degree in fine art at Middlesex Polytechnic, 1976–9; obtained a master's in painting, Royal College of Art, 1980–3; then studied for a postgraduate diploma in art therapy at Hertfordshire College of Art, 1990–1. Notable teachers included the sculptor Paul Neagu and the painter John Loker. From 1992 was a member of the British Association of Art Therapists, from 1993 the Japanese Vintage Motorcycle Club. Illustrated many German publications, notably books by Erich Fried and Geoffrey Trease, and was included in Peter Marcan's 1992 publications *An East London Album* and *A Bermondsey and Rotherhithe Album*. Fried tended to show at publicly funded venues and public spaces temporarily converted for exhibitions rather than commercial galleries, and had no dealer.

Klaus FRIEDEBERGER 1922– Artist mainly in oil paint, born in Berlin, Germany. He arrived in England in 1939, Australia in 1940, and studied painting as an ex-service student at East Sydney Technical College, 1947–50, returning to London in 1950, settling in Blackheath. Friedeberger won the Mosman Art Prize, 1949, the Europe Prize, Ostende, 1964 gold medal. An important series of Friedeberger's pictures was about children. From the 1970s his paintings were not about something outside themselves. "I want them to have a presence with a convincing reality of their own." As well as many group shows in Europe and Australia from 1944 Friedeberger had solo exhibitions at Hamilton Galleries and New Gallery, Belfast, 1963; Warwick Arts Trust, 1986; Eva Jekel Gallery 202, 1990; and a retrospective at Woodlands Art Gallery, 1992.

Arthur FRIEDENSON 1872–1955 Painter of landscapes and coastal scenes, born in Leeds, Yorkshire. After apprenticeship to a sign painter, from late-1880s he studied at Académie Julian, Paris, and at Académie Royale des Beaux-Arts, in Antwerp. Worked in Netherlands, where he was influenced by local landscape painters. From about 1910 he worked at various locations in Dorset, dying at Parkstone after prolonged ill-health. Friedenson showed prolifically at RA, Fine Art Society, Goupil Gallery and elsewhere, and Tate Gallery holds his work.

Alexander FRIEDMAN 1972– Painter and printmaker who graduated with honours from the University of the West of England, 1992–5, gaining his postgraduate diploma in fine art from the Royal Academy Schools, 1995–8, appearing in the final year show there. Friedman won a Vincent Harris Mural Prize, 1996, and in 1997 a Minigowa Scholarship to Japan and Landseer Scholarship. Exhibitions included Making a Mark, Mall Galleries, 1996; Premiums, RA, 1997; and National Print Show, Mall Galleries, and RA Summer Exhibition, both 1998. He lived in east London.

Donald FRIEND 1915–1989 Versatile artist and writer, born in Cremorne, Sydney, Australia, as Donald Moses, son of a grazier Leslie Moses, who adopted his mother's surname around 1920. Donald claimed paternal descent from Oscar Wilde's foe the Marquis of Queensberry, through the maternal line from John Wilmot, 2nd Earl of Rochester, reputed author of the Restoration farce *Sodom*, of which Friend in 1980 produced an illustrated edition; this aristocratic pedigree determined many of his adult attitudes. While still at school he began art lessons with Sydney Long, leaving home after his father opposed an artistic career, in 1934 joining Anthony Dattilo Rubbo's classes. Friend moved to England in 1936, studying at Westminster Art School under Mark Gertler and Bernard Meninsky, experiencing bohemian penury, homosexual adventures and designing costumes for Sadler's Wells Ballet. He shared his first group show with Augustus John, Walter Sickert, Stanley Spencer and Tiepolo at R E A Wilson's Gallery and helped paint a mural for the Australian Wool Corporation at the British Empire Exhibition, Glasgow, both in 1937, having his first solo show at Wilson's, 1938. In 1942, after extensive travels, back in Sydney he had a first Australian one-man exhibition at Macquarie Galleries; had a work acquired by the National Gallery of New South Wales; joined the Army; and developed a strong friendship with Russell Drysdale. In 1945, Friend was commissioned as an Official War Artist, accompanying an invasion force into Borneo. After demobilisation in 1946 he resumed a busy exhibiting career. Friend returned to Europe and London in 1949, in 1950 having a successful drawings show at the Redfern Gallery. Several visits to England followed, part of extensive foreign travels, especially to Bali, Indonesia, among his English showings being a solo exhibition at Heffer Gallery, Cambridge, 1953, and inclusion in Recent Australian Painting, Whitechapel Gallery, 1961. Illness plagued his final years. Friend was a prolific writer, whose diaries are held by the National Library of Australia. He died at Woollahra, New South Wales. The Art Gallery of New South Wales, which holds Drysdale's portrait of the artist, gave him a retrospective in 1990.

Ian FRIEND 1951– Sculptor, born in Eastbourne, Sussex. He studied at Exeter College of Art, 1969–70, Birmingham College of Art, 1970–3, and Slade School of Fine Art, 1973–5. In latter year gained Boise Travelling Fellowship. Group exhibitions included Third British International Drawing Biennale, Dorman Museum, Cleveland, 1977; House Gallery, 1979; and Serpentine Summer Show 1, 1980. Also had a solo exhibition at House Gallery, 1978. Lived in London.

Ian FRIERS 1910–1975 Sculptor who was by profession a civil servant, brother of the artist Rowel Friers. After initial education at the Model School and College of Technology in Belfast, where he was born, Friers was a self-taught artist who held senior positions in the RUA. He exhibited there, RHA and in Bradford, CEMA in Northern Ireland buying his work. Lived in Dundonald, County Down.

Rowel FRIERS 1920–1998 Painter, cartoonist, book illustrator, stage designer and muralist, born in Belfast, Northern Ireland, brother of the artist Ian Friers. He attended Belfast College of Art on a scholarship, having trained in lithography with S C Allen, Belfast. Most Irish newspapers went on to use Friers' work, plus periodicals such as *Radio Times* and *Dublin Opinion*. He was noted for his amusing caricatures of notabilities, such as the politicians Enoch Powell and Ian Paisley, in the National Portrait Gallery. Ulster Museum and Art Gallery and Arts Council of Northern Ireland also hold his work. He was a member of RUA and Ulster Watercolour Society. Friers was granted an honorary master's degree by the Open University for contributions to art. He showed with CEMA, RHA, Arts Council of Northern Ireland and in the American tour of Contemporary Ulster Artists. His books included *Wholly Friers* and *The Revolting Irish*. Lived in Holywood, County Down.

Elisabeth FRINK 1930–1993 Sculptor, draughtsman, printmaker and teacher, born Thurlow, Suffolk. Studied at Guildford School of Art, 1947–9, and Chelsea School of Art, 1949–53, under Willi Soukop and Bernard Meadows. She taught at Chelsea School of Art, 1951–61, St Martin's School of Art, 1954–62, and at Royal College of Art, 1965–7. After early exhibiting with LG, Frink had a one-man show at St George's Gallery in 1955 and four years later at Bertha Schaefer Gallery, New York. Over the years she established herself as a sculptor concerned with themes, such as goggle men, running men and horses with and without riders. She worked on many major public commissions, such as Wild Boar for Harlow New Town; Blind Beggar and Dog, at Bethnal Green; and a noble horse and rider, Piccadilly, London. The predatory and the vulnerable are both important aspects of Frink's work. She was elected RA in 1977 and five years later became Dame Elisabeth Frink. Made a Companion of Honour, 1992. Exhibited extensively internationally, with work in major collections including Tate Gallery and Arts Council. While fighting cancer Frink struggled to complete her last commission, a monumental but unusual figure of Christ for the front of the Anglican cathedral in Liverpool, unveiled a week before her death in Woolland, Dorset. There was a memorial show at Yorkshire Sculpture Park, Bretton Hall, 1994, an extensive survey of work, 1963–89, at Jerwood Sculpture Park, Great Witley, 2000, and a show at Djanogly Art Gallery, Nottingham, 2001. Frink's son was the painter Lin Jammet.

Paul FRIPP 1890–1945 Painter, draughtsman, photographer and teacher, born in Mansfield, Nottinghamshire, into a family which on both sides included artists. He attended Bristol and Leicester Schools of Art, then in 1909 won the Bennet Scholarship and a free studentship to the Royal College of Art; returned to Leicester for two years to train for his painting diploma; and postponed return to the Royal College when World War I began. He was commissioned in the Army and served in Gallipoli, Egypt and Palestine, was mentioned in dispatches and was twice wounded. With a miniature camera in his tobacco pouch he took hundreds of films (in 1931 Fripp was elected a fellow of the Royal Photographic Society and he won several medals). Returned to Royal College in 1919, graduating in 1921. Taught at Cheltenham Ladies' College, becoming a member of Cheltenham Camera Club and then its president and showing with Cheltenham Group of Artists, 1921–32. Also showed at RA and NEAC. After heading the Art Schools at Bideford and Bath Fripp was appointed principal at Carmarthen, where he died. He was a big, humorous, enthusiastic man, always preoccupied by some invention or idea. Fripp was celebrated with a show at Cheltenham Museum and Art Gallery, 1986. Carmarthen Museum holds examples.

Clifford FRITH 1924– Painter, draughtsman and teacher, born in London. He studied at Camberwell School of Arts and Crafts, where he later taught, and at St Martin's School of Art. His teachers included Victor Pasmore and R V Pitchforth. Frith also taught at Goldsmiths' College School of Art. Exhibited RA, Wildenstein and Redfern Galleries and elsewhere. Did lithographic work for the catering firm J Lyons & Co and had work bought by Contemporary Art Society. Lived in London.

Edgar Silver FRITH 1890–1974 Sculptor and teacher, born and lived in London, son of the sculptor William Silver Frith. Studied at Kennington and Lambeth Schools of Art and Royal Academy Schools and went on to become head of the sculpture section at City and Guilds of London Institute, Kennington and Lambeth Art School. Joined Art Workers' Guild in 1923 and was made an associate of RBS in 1932. Showed at RA, Walker Art Gallery in Liverpool and elsewhere.

Michael FRITH 1951– Painter and illustrator, born in Kingston upon Thames, Surrey, who studied graphic arts at Canterbury College of Art. Among his many illustrative jobs was sketching the trial of the politician Jeremy Thorpe at the Old Bailey and, for Independent Television News, that of the Yorkshire Ripper murderer, Peter Sutcliffe. He also painted the portrait of the publisher Robert Maxwell for the National Portrait Gallery. Exhibited at Smiths Galleries, the Illustrators' Gallery and National Portrait Gallery and in 1993 had a solo show at John Adams Fine Art Ltd with Canon Gallery of restaurant watercolours done while illustrating the Craig Brown Table Talk column in the *Sunday Times*. In 2000, Frith's Pallant House, Chichester, show East Head, West Wittering provided a visual record of a disappearing coastline near where he lived at Earnley, Sussex. His Marine Watercolours were exhibited at Canon Gallery, Petworth, 2003.

Lucy FROBISHER: *see* **Marguerite FROBISHER**

Marguerite FROBISHER 1891–1974 Painter and teacher, born Lucy Marguerite Frobisher in Leeds, Yorkshire. She studied at the Kemp-Welch School of Painting from about 1911, and like her teacher specialised in animal subjects. Between 1916–21 Frobisher returned to Leeds, then went back to Bushey, lived with Kemp-Welch and became secretary of her school. Two years after it was closed, in 1928 Frobisher opened her own, as The Frobisher School of Art. Although she continued to teach until her death, from the early 1940s until Kemp-Welch died in 1958 Frobisher again lived with her as friend and companion. Kemp-Welch left Frobisher her property and pictures and for some years from 1967 a Lucy Kemp-Welch Memorial Art Gallery existed, until the pictures had to be put into store. Frobisher exhibited widely, including RCamA and SWA both of which she was a member, also RBSA, Paris Salon, RSA and other venues. Bushey Museum has shown her work.

Fanchon FRÖHLICH fl. from 1960s– Printmaker, philosopher and painter, born in Iowa, America, as Fanchon Angst. She studied philosophy at University of Chicago, continuing her studies with Rudolph Carnap and doing postgraduate work in Oxford with Sir Peter Strawson. A section of her thesis on The Logical Qualities of Material Objects was published in *Mind*. Married the theoretical physicist Herbert Fröhlich. Began painting under her married name, studying at Liverpool College of Art under a postgraduate scholarship; with Peter Lanyon in Cornwall; Japanese ink painting with Goto San in Kyoto; and etching with S W Hayter, of Atelier 17, in Paris. Hayter's ideas were important to Fröhlich, who wrote papers for conferences and contributed to books on such subjects as aesthetics and the relation of physics to biology. Formed a group of artists known as Collective Phenomena in Liverpool, where she lived, in 1990. In the group, "two or more painters intertwine their strokes and areas of colour on the same canvas according to visual counterpoint." Exhibited at Picton Library, Liverpool, in 1992, and in Paris in 1994 "where several people painted before the audience accompanied by music by a composer improvising according to our movements" and had work exhibited. Exhibited her own work in Atelier 17 shows internationally, also in Japan and at Liverpool Academy. Walker Art Gallery, Liverpool, and Bowes Museum, Newcastle, hold Fröhlich's work.

Hester FROOD 1882–1971 Painter, draughtsman and printmaker, notably of architectural subjects, born in New Zealand. She was educated at Exeter High School and studied art in the city and at Atelier Colarossi, Paris, for six months. In 1906 on a visit to Scotland she met the artist David Young Cameron who said that he would teach her to etch. She early on showed at RA and RSA with success and had a first solo show at Colnaghi's in 1925, followed by another at Dunthorne's in 1927. Towards the end of World War II Frood had the first of two shows in Glasgow, and in 1946–9 final exhibitions with Colnaghi's. By then she was long settled in Topsham, Devon. Fry Gallery put on a show of her work in 1990. British Museum, Victoria & Albert Museum and Scottish National Gallery of Modern Art hold examples.

Millie FROOD 1900–1988 Painter, draughtsman and teacher, born in Motherwell, Lanarkshire. She studied at Glasgow School of Art and taught at Bellshill Academy. Early on she showed with RSA and RSW and with the arrival of the painter J D Fergusson and his dancer wife Margaret Morris from France in 1939, and the influx of foreign painters such as Josef Herman and Jankel Adler, Frood became part of a movement which revitalised the arts in the city after World War II. She showed with the New Scottish Group and designed the costumes and set for the ballet *The Harvesters*, put on in 1961, dance in Scotland having been given new life with Margaret Morris' Celtic Ballet Club, the Celtic Ballet of Scotland and the resulting Scottish National Ballet. Frood had a number of solo shows in Lanarkshire and Glasgow, latterly her work was exhibited in America and Japan and in 1989 Cyril Gerber Fine Art, Glasgow, held a show linking her with the New Scottish Group.

Michala FROOM 1925– Landscape painter, born in Denmark, who spent her adult life in England. She began to paint in 1960 and gained her master's degree in art therapy. The coasts of Denmark and Suffolk and landscape of the Lot Valley, in France, were Froom's inspiration. She was included in a three-artist exhibition at The Halesworth Gallery, Halesworth, in 1999.

Alistair FROST 1981– Painter, born in Cheltenham, Gloucestershire, who lived and worked in Glasgow. He studied at the School of Art there, 2000–4. Frost's atmospheric Et Nunc et Semper, of 2004, and The Fallen, of 2005, were included in the exhibition The Valley at Bloomberg SPACE, in 2005. Of his work, the catalogue said: "Frost's landscapes typically have a low horizon line, with the features looming over us. They give the impression that the viewer is standing at the bottom of a hill or in a valley, looking up at the land rising away from them. The world they portray is decrepit, abandoned, forlorn." Frost's other shows included Voodoo Shit, Hales Gallery, and New Generation, Compass Gallery, Glasgow, both 2004.

Andy FROST 1957– Sculptor and draughtsman, born in Bedford. Andrew Frost studied at Lanchester Polytechnic, Coventry and Reading University. In 1979–80 Frost was in Rotterdam on a Royal Netherlands Scholarship, then in 1982 visited America on a Boise Travel Scholarship. He then became Henry Moore Foundation Fellow in Sculpture at Camberwell School of Arts and Crafts. His sculptures utilised a range of materials, from wood and steel to plastic and fibreglass. Although they had titles such as Batmobile (1983, Arts Council collection) and El Cid Chancing his Arm and could be entertaining and amusing, Frost's creations were often quite frightening and dynamic depictions of energy and power. He showed in a number of British galleries, was included in New Contemporaries at ICA, was in the 1983 Whitechapel Open Exhibition and in the Welsh Sculpture Trust's Margam event Sculpture in a Country Park in the same year.

Anthony FROST 1951– Painter in acrylic and teacher, born in St Ives, Cornwall. His family moved to Banbury when he was young and he went to the Art School there, 1967–70, then Cardiff College of Art, 1970–3. Returned to live in Cornwall in 1974, at Morvah, with a studio in Penzance. He commonly worked to a background of Rock music and designed an album cover and backdrop in 1990 for the world tour of a favourite group, The Fall. Frost was much in demand as a teacher of colour to children. He said he wanted his own pictures "not to be influenced. I want them to be colour and shape. I don't want people to see things in them ... It's like creating your own language." Took part in many mixed exhibitions, solo shows including Newlyn Art Gallery, 1979, later ones Gordon Hepworth Gallery, Newton St Cyres, and Royal Cornwall Museum Galleries, Truro, both 1991. Contemporary Art Society, Nuffield Trust and John Moores hold examples. His father was the artist Terry Frost.

C J Fenton FROST: *see* **Cyril James FROST**

Cyril James FROST 1885– Portrait painter and printmaker, born in Croydon, Surrey, who studied at the School of Art there under Francis Jackson. Exhibited RA, RP, UA and RBA, sometimes signing his work C J Fenton Frost. Lived at Banbury, Oxfordshire.

Dennis FROST 1925– Portrait painter in oil and pastel. Born in London, Frost studied art at St Martin's School of Art and Putney School of Art. Exhibited RP. He illustrated Ernest Savage's book *Painting in Pastel* and Joe Singer's *Figures in Pastel* and it is in this medium that many think Frost's best work was done. Lived at Eastergate, near Chichester, Sussex.

Jill FROST 1964– Painter of detailed landscapes which can have a surreal element, born in Auckland, New Zealand, who did a foundation course at Central St Martins School of Art, 1989–90, graduating with honours from London Guildhall University, 1992–7. Mixed shows included Art Aid, Cornhill, 1995, and Whitechapel Open, Whitechapel Gallery, from 1996. Had solo shows with Ellipse Gallery, Brussels, Belgium, 1997, and Jill George Gallery, 2001 and 2003. The Saatchi Collection holds her work.

Shirley Jane FROST 1935– Painter, craftsman, jeweller and teacher, born in London. She was educated partly in England at Roedean School, partly in South Africa and attended Worthing and Wimbledon Schools of Art and the Royal College of Art, 1957–60. Went on to teach at Birmingham Polytechnic. Showed at London Design Centre, elsewhere in Britain and on the continent and in America.

Stuart FROST 1960– Sculptor, born in Bath, Somerset, using a variety of materials, whose output was characterised by an interest in natural objects, their place within an environment and their relationship to culture, myth and history. Frost drew inspiration from wide travels, including the Central Americas and Scandinavia, where he was based in Bergen, Norway. Frost attended Bristol Polytechnic, 1979–80; gained a fine art honours degree from Wolverhampton Polytechnic, 1980–3; and obtained his master's in sculpture from the Royal College of Art, 1983–6. From 1984 held many residencies, later ones including Dumfries and Galloway, 1997. Group shows included Mikkeli Taide Museo, Finland, 1988; Nordnorsk Samtidskunst, Norway, 1991–6; and Høstutstillingen, Oslo, 1994–6. Had a solo exhibition at Oulu Taide Museo, Finland, 1988, later ones including Victoria Art Gallery, Bath, 1997. Several Norwegian collections, including its Arts Council, hold examples.

Terry FROST 1915–2003 Painter, printmaker and teacher, born in Leamington Spa, Warwickshire. Did a variety of jobs after leaving school, then served in the Army and was held as a prisoner of war. Imprisoned in Bavaria he met the painter Adrian Heath who encouraged Frost to paint in oil. After the war Frost studied in the evenings at Birmingham College of Art, then at St Ives School of Painting and at Camberwell School of Art in the late 1940s. Frost later went on to teach at a number of art schools, including periods at Reading and Newcastle Universities and at Banff Summer School, Canada. Frost began abstract painting in 1949, shortly before returning to St Ives where he worked, 1950–2, as assistant to the sculptor Barbara Hepworth. Frost is notable for his use of primary colours and of shapes reflecting Cornish marine life, its bobbing boats and heaving water. Completed much work in paint and collage, which has a spare, taut quality. He exhibited widely internationally and in England, notably at Redfern Gallery, New Art Centre, Austin/Desmond Fine Art, and Belgrave Gallery, with a retrospective at RA, 2000. Tate St Ives and Belgrave Gallery both gave Frost shows in 2003, Belgrave Gallery St Ives showing works on paper from the artist's studio in 2004 and 50 Years of Prints in 2006. Frost, whose son was the artist Anthony Frost, was elected RA in 1992 and was knighted in 1998. Tate Gallery holds his work. Had a studio at Newlyn, Cornwall.

Winifred FROST: *see* **Wyn BORGER**

Jonathan FROUD 1958– Sculptor, whose output included installations and performance pieces, and teacher, born in Hengistbury Head, Dorset. Direct contact with the public was important to Froud when creating works, which included materials such as plastic waste pipes and computer printouts. Froud studied at Bournemouth and Poole College of Art, 1975–6; Brighton Polytechnic, 1976–9; and Royal College of Art, 1979–82 (he later taught there part-time). In 1982–3 he worked and travelled in South America. Awards included Cox Award; Royal College Award to work in Carrara, Italy; British Council Royal Wedding Award; Royal College Major Travelling Scholarship; a Henry Moore Foundation Award; Greater London Arts Association Award; and Chelsea Arts Club/Guinness Award for Most Promising Young Sculptor. In 1984–5, Froud was Fourth Merseyside Artist in Residence at the Bridewell Studios and Walker Art Gallery, having a solo show at the Walker in 1985. Other exhibitions included New Contemporaries, ICA, 1979 (where he was a prize winner); Quarries, Camden Arts Centre, 1983; and Drawings, Chelsea School of Art, 1985.

Martin FROY 1926– Painter, mural artist and teacher, born in London. After studying history at Cambridge University and service in the Royal Air Force, Froy was at Slade School of Fine Art, 1949–51, being Gregory Fellow in Painting at University of Leeds, 1951–4. From 1953–8 Froy was artist-consultant to Coventry's city architect. He also designed murals for the Belgrade Theatre there. From 1953–5 Froy taught engraving at Slade School of Fine Art; taught at Bath Academy of Art, 1954–65; was head of painting at Chelsea School of Art, 1966–72; being professor of fine art at University of Reading, 1972–91, then emeritus. Froy had a solo show at Leicester Galleries in 1961, others following at University of Sussex, Arnolfini Gallery in Bristol, Park Square Gallery in Leeds, and Reading University in 1979. His paintings, constructions and drawings,

1968–82, were shown at Serpentine Gallery, 1983. Arts Council holds several examples of his work.

Anthony FRY 1927– Painter and teacher, born in Theydon Bois, Essex. Studied under Maurice Feild at the Downs School, Colwall, and attended Bryanston, where he continued to paint. Was at Edinburgh College of Art, 1946–7, then Camberwell School of Art, 1948–50, and was Rome Prize winner 1950. Having been taught by Victor Pasmore and Claude Rogers at Camberwell, Fry was a natural participant in the 1948 Wakefield City Art Gallery Euston Road Group show. He became member of teaching staff at Bath Academy of Art in 1954, joining Camberwell two years later. Had first one-man show at St George's Gallery in 1954 and in New York at Durlacher Bros in 1961, later ones including Browse & Darby Gallery, 1999 and 2002. Also showed at LG of which he was a member, ICA, RWA and elsewhere. Arts Council and Tate Gallery bought his work. Lived in Box, Wiltshire.

Gladys Windsor FRY 1890– Artist in various media and teacher, married to the painter Windsor Fry. She met him in 1906 when he was teaching and she was a student at Hammersmith School of Art, marrying him 16 years later. She also studied with the Horsham-based artist Florence Davey and with G H Catt, in Chichester. Fry was a King's Prize winner for design and gained City and Guilds embroidery honours. Her publications included *Working Drawings for Embroidery* and *Embroidery and Needlework*. Showed at RBA, Walker Art Gallery in Liverpool, at the Festival of Britain in 1951 and in the provinces. Lived for many years at Hove, Sussex, later in Brighton.

James FRY 1911–1985 Artist in watercolour, pastel and oil, photographer and designer, born in London, who studied at Watford School of Art under Arthur Scott. During World War II Fry was a committed conscientious objector who worked in forestry alongside German and Italian prisoners. Fry was employed as a colour retoucher on the magazine *Picture Post* and designed neck-ties for Liberty. In 1954, disenchanted with commercial life in London, he moved to Corfe Castle, in Dorset, where he set up his studio. Fry was with his wife Ivy a committed environmentalist, teetotal, living frugally eating a vegetarian diet, who shunned television, the telephone and newspapers and never learned to drive. He cycled around the county carrying a camera loaded with colour transparency film, which he would later project to complete a painting on canvas. Friends called Fry "the last of the English Impressionists", because of his fascination with the play of sunshine and reflections on water. When they complained that he charged too little for his pictures, he replied: "I charge what I think is right. I couldn't live with myself if I charged more." When Ivy died seven years after him, a collection of nearly 7,400 slides taken in and around the Purbecks was found, 295 being donated to The Dorset County Museum by a family member. It holds several of his paintings and in 1999 included him in the published series *Dorset Worthies*.

Lawrence FRY 1948– Artist, composer and musician, born in London, who lived in Wales from 1967. He studied biochemistry and African history at University College of North Wales, Bangor. Fry began painting in oil in the late 1960s, inspired by the abstracts and landscapes of L S Bangdel, from 1990 working mainly in pastel and watercolour. He said that his paintings paid "close attention to visual detail in order to explore the emotional impact of significant places, objects and memories." Exhibitions included a one-man, Gardens, Ferns and Waterfalls, at Taliesin Arts Centre, University of Wales Swansea, 2001.

Malcolm FRY 1909–2000 Arts administrator and artist, born in London, full name Arthur Malcolm Fry, son of a bricklayer who became a clerk of works. After Latymer Upper School, Hammersmith, in Bournemouth – where the family had moved Fry worked for an estate agent, attending spare-time classes at Bournemouth College of Art, teachers including Leslie Ward; worked as an engineering draughtsman for the Post Office until World War II; was sent to France as a member of the supplementary reserve of officers, at Dunkirk being taken prisoner-of-war in Germany, where he painted scenery for theatricals; and retired as a major two years after hostilities, having been an art instructor. After briefly being director of the Central Institute for Art and Design, he was for three years registrar of the RI, then for 26 years secretary of the RWS, simultaneously secretary of the RE, Imperial Arts League, London Salon of Photography, SM and the SPS, which he helped to found. Fry oversaw the move of the RWS and RE to the South Bank, inaugurated 1980, three years after he was made a member of RWS and prior to his retirement in 1983. He then concentrated on his own watercolours, mainly of English and French landscapes. Fry showed in the main London galleries, in the provinces and abroad and had a series of one-man exhibitions. Bournemouth Corporation holds his work. Died in Orpington, Kent.

Mark FRY 1952– Painter who grew up in England and Italy, studying under Prima Conti at the Accademia delle Belle Arti, Florence, in the 1970s. He then collaborated with other artists and musicians in Italy and travelled extensively in Europe and West Africa. From 1990 he had a studio near Dieppe, France. Fry's work was shown in nine group and three solo exhibitions, in 1993, 1995 and 1998, at Christopher Hull Gallery, with a one-man at The Charleston Gallery, near Firle, in 1996. In 2001 and 2003 Archeus Fine Art gave him solo exhibitions of abstract work.

Maxwell FRY 1899–1987 Architect, teacher, painter and collector, born in Wallasey, Cheshire, full name Edwin Maxwell Fry, educated at the Liverpool Institute and Liverpool University School of Architecture, graduating in 1923. With several other forward-looking architects in 1931 he established the Modern Architectural Research (MARS) group, which was influential in Britain and abroad. In 1943 with his second wife Jane Drew he was appointed town planning adviser in West Africa and in 1951 he went to India as senior architect with Le Corbusier for Chandigarh, the new capital city of Punjab. Fry's books included *Autobiographical Sketches* and *Art in the Machine Age*. In his later years he became the RA's professor of architecture and turned to painting. He had been elected a fellow of RIBA in 1930, winning its Gold Medal in 1964. Fry was elected RA in 1972 and showed with Drian and Fieldborne Galleries. He was a noted patron of young artists. Lived finally at Cotherstone, County Durham.

Windsor FRY 1862–1947 Painter and teacher, full name Harry Windsor Fry, born in Torquay, Devon, married to the artist Gladys Windsor Fry, whom he met while he was teaching at Hammersmith School of Art. He was educated privately in Torquay, studying at St John's Wood School of Art and Royal Academy Schools, where he was a medal winner. During World War I he served with the Royal Fusiliers, 1914–19, and was renowned for his physical fitness and brilliance as a swordfighter. Fry was a prolific exhibitor, showing many times with RBA of which he was a member, RA, RHA, RI, ROI and elsewhere. Liverpool Corporation bought his picture Youth and Age. Lived in London.

Katherine Mary FRYER 1910– Painter, wood engraver and teacher, born in Leeds, Yorkshire, where she studied at the College of Art, 1926–31. Went on to teach at Bath School of Art for a period, living in Bath, Somerset. She exhibited Redfern Gallery and in north of England galleries, Wakefield and Harrogate Art Galleries buying her work. Ninetieth birthday exhibition, One Point of View, RBSA, 2000, coincided with the publication of *Before the war...and long ago*, Fryer's reminiscences and prints. Later lived at Harborne, Birmingham.

Stan FRYER 1906– Painter and draughtsman, born and lived in Manchester, who studied at the local School of Art, in Italy and Africa. He did a considerable amount of illustrative work for national and provincial press. Showed at RI, RCamA, with Army Art Society, UA and widely in the provinces.

Wilfred Moody FRYER 1891–1967 Painter, commercial draughtsman and teacher, born in London. Studied at Bradford School of Art. Exhibited RA, RBA, RI and widely in the provinces. Was a member of Croydon Art Society; Langham Sketch Club, of which for a time he was chairman; and the Wapping Group of Artists, of which he was president. Lived at Addiscombe, Surrey.

Akiko FUJIKAWA 1948– Printmaker, born in Kyoto, Japan, married to the artist Geoffrey Earle Wickham. She gained her bachelor's degree at Kohka College, Kyoto, 1970, then studied traditional Japanese woodblock printing, moku hanga, at Asahi School of Art, 1977–81, with Takeji Asano. From 1980 showed with Shinanokai Group in Kyoto, in 1985 taking further courses with Japanese masters. In 1986 set up Chapel Studio, Burnham-on-Crouch, Essex, with Wickham. Took part in open exhibitions at Beecroft Gallery, Southend-on-Sea, from 1990. Solo shows included Mildmay House, Burnham, 1993. British Museum holds her work.

Raf FULCHER 1948– Sculptor and teacher, born in Essex, who studied at University of Newcastle upon Tyne, 1966–72. Went on to teach at Sunderland Polytechnic, settling at Ramshaw, Bishop Auckland, County Durham. Fulcher worked in a variety of materials and was included in the Serpentine Gallery/South Bank Centre's The Sculpture Show, 1983, at that time contending that British art was "characterised by a peculiar reserve or reticence when dealing with the intensely subjective". His Garden Front, of 1981, was sited at Jesmond Metro Station, Newcastle. Later works included The Swirle Pavilion, 1998, at Quayside, Newcastle. This ambitious construction is both sculpture and architecture: a big gilded orb within a spherical metal frame set upon a stone and concrete pavilion opening towards the River Tyne and sited beside the Gateshead Millennium Bridge.

George FULLARD 1923–1973 Sculptor in metals, wood, rubbish and objects from toy shops. Was also an outstanding draughtsman and teacher. Born in Sheffield, Yorkshire, the son of a miner, he studied art at the College of Art there, 1938–42. After war service in the Army, during which he was badly injured at the battle for Cassino, Fullard studied at Royal College of Art, 1945–7 under the sculptors Frank Dobson and Richard Garbe, then lived in Paris. From 1963 he was in charge of the sculpture department at Chelsea School of Art. Militarism and ships and the sea were leading themes in Fullard's work, which was always an exploration into unknown possibilities. He said that "the artist works towards the miracle of making visible that which apparently did not exist." He showed in John Moores Liverpool Exhibitions from 1957; Contemporary British Sculpture, the Arts Council touring show, from 1958; Gimpel-Hanover Gallery, Zürich, 1963; British Sculpture at Redfern Gallery in 1972, and elsewhere. Had a solo show at Woodstock Gallery in 1958; Gallery One, 1961; Marlborough New London Gallery, 1964; Park Square Gallery, Leeds, 1972; there was a major retrospective at Serpentine Gallery, 1974; a selective one at Yorkshire Sculpture Park, 1997; another key show at Mappin Art Gallery, Sheffield, 1998. Arts Council, West Riding Education Authority, Ferens Art Gallery in Hull and Australian and American collections hold examples. Lived in London.

James FULLARTON 1946– Painter and lecturer, born in Glasgow, where he studied at the School of Art under David Donaldson, gaining his diploma in 1969. From that time he painted full-time while lecturing for Scottish Arts Council. He won the David Cargill Award, 1976, the Britoil Award, 1986. Fullarton used a broad palette, with colour the dominant feature, for portraits, landscape and still life in oil and acrylic. Showed with RSA and Royal Glasgow Institute of the Fine Arts. Solo exhibitions included Lillie Art Gallery, Milngavie; John D Kelly Gallery and Ewan Mundy Fine Art, both Glasgow; Macaulay Gallery, Stenton; new paintings at Roger Billcliffe Gallery, Glasgow, 2001; and Thompson's Gallery, 2004. Lillie Art Gallery, Robert Fleming Holdings and Royal College of Physicians and Surgeons, Glasgow, hold examples. Lived in Straiton, Ayrshire.

Cynthia Dehn FULLER: *see* **FRANCYN**

Dorothy FULLER 1904– Painter and teacher who was born and lived in Brighton, Sussex, for many years. Her earlier work was signed with her unmarried name Dorothy Sawyers. She studied at Brighton College of Art, 1919–26, with Louis Ginnett; gained the Turner Gold Medal and British Institutional Scholarship in 1927, then the Edward Stott Travelling Scholarship and Gold Medal in 1929, while studying at Royal Academy Schools under Walter Westley Russell; then travelled abroad, 1929–30. Taught at Worthing College of Art, 1931–42. She was a member of Sussex Women's Art Club and Reynolds Club and showed at RA and public galleries in Brighton and Hove.

John FULLER 1954– He attended St Albans School of Art, 1972–3, graduating with honours from Goldsmiths' College, 1973–6. Mixed exhibitions included Sculpture '75 ILEA, Whitechapel Art Gallery, 1975; Paul-Louis Weiller Sculpture Competition, Académie des Beaux-Arts, Paris, 1976; Contemporary Printmakers' Council Print Fair,

Arnolfini, Bristol, 1988; and East End Open Studios, at Chisenhale Studios, 1989. In 1979, Fuller had a solo show at Hertfordshire College of Art and Design, St Albans.

Leonard John FULLER 1891–1973 Portrait, figure, still life and landscape painter in oil. Fuller studied art at Clapham School of Art and the Royal Academy Schools, then began his notable career as a teacher of painting and drawing at St John's Wood Art Schools 1922–32. From 1927–37 was assistant art master at Dulwich College, where he had been educated. In 1938 Fuller moved to St Ives, Cornwall, where he founded the St Ives School of Painting, which he ran until he died. Although Fuller was a painter of a traditional kind, he was open to new ideas, advocating a more tolerant approach to modern art in 1953 in St Ives, four years after the founding of the Penwith Society of Arts, of which he was elected chairman. Advanced artists such as Terry Frost and Bob Law were to study with Fuller. Fuller exhibited widely, including RA, RSA, RP and Paris Salon, where in 1927 he gained a silver medal. Newport City Museum and Art Gallery and Plymouth City Museum and Art Gallery hold his work. Lived in St Ives.

Martin FULLER 1943– Painter and draughtsman, born in Leamington Spa, Warwickshire. He attended Mid-Warwickshire College of Art, 1960–2, then Hornsey College of Art, 1962–4, in the latter year being awarded a Guggenheim-Mckinley Scholarship, American Workshop, Italy. Fuller's work was abstract with references to landscape and figurative allusions and was described as having "painterly elegance and wit". Among Fuller's group appearances were Richard Demarco Gallery, Edinburgh Festival; Arnolfini Gallery in Bristol; Angela Flowers and Redfern Galleries and Barbican Centre. After a solo show at Arnolfini in 1968, many others followed including Camden Arts Centre, 1971; RZA Galerie, Düsseldorf, Germany, 1983; with a retrospective at Warwickshire Art Gallery & Museum, Leamington Spa, 2001. In 2003, Two Queer Fellows was a shared exhibition with Edward Burra at Jonathan Clark. Fuller's prizes included Discerning Eye, *Modern Painters* Prize, Mall Galleries, 1996, and first prize, Hunting Art Prizes, Royal College of Art and Hunterian Museum, Glasgow, 1997. Bristol City Art Gallery holds his work. Lived in London, but for a time was artist-in-residence in Santa Fe, America.

Moss FULLER 1937– Versatile artist and teacher, born in Suffolk, originally known as Rosamund Steed. She studied at St Martin's School of Art and printmaking at the Royal College of Art. Returned to Suffolk in 1972, after living in Bristol and at Sevenoaks, Kent. Fuller ran courses in printmaking at her home in Laxfield and also taught at The Print Workshop, Gainsborough's House, Sudbury. Exhibited widely in the provinces, solo exhibitions including outdoor sculptures at Gainsborough's House in 2001. She had begun making these in 1988. Although ephemeral, Fuller liked "to change the landscape briefly and then return it to its original state. The pieces live on in the memory of the viewer and the artist uses them as inspiration for prints and drawings developed in the studio." She took part in Landscapes & Figures at North House Gallery, Manningtree, in 2004.

Overton FULLER fl. c.1940–1960 Painter whose full name was Violet Overton Fuller. After education in Belgium and Wales she attended Beckenham School of Art, under Percy Hague Jowett, the Central School of Arts and Crafts with Robert Kirkland Jamieson and St Martin's School of Art. She was especially fond of painting flowers. Her husband was an Indian Army officer, so that she exhibited partly in India, but also widely at RWS, UA, BWS, SWA, PS, WIAC.

Richard Lee FULLER 1944– Figurative painter employing a rich and vibrant palette, born in Ashtead, Surrey. He studied at Epsom and Guildford Schools of Art, gaining his master's in fine art from the Royal College of Art. Fuller painted full-time from the late 1980s, having several successful exhibitions at the Hyde Park Gallery and Claremont Fine Art. In 2002, there was a solo show at Gallery 27. He had then "recently completed a 12-month private commission for a mural depicting scenes from his client's life, including 64 individual portraits of family and friends." Lived in Putney, southwest London.

Ron FULLER 1936– Maker of witty animated models and toys, printmaker and teacher, born in Cornwall. He studied fine art at Plymouth, Falmouth and the Royal College of Art, then taught printmaking in Bristol and in London colleges. In 1972, Fuller moved to Laxfield, Sussex and reduced his teaching commitments to concentrate on toys and models, gaining international recognition. He used largely traditional techniques in painted wood and sheet metal and was influenced by folk art. His masterwork was his contribution to The Ride of Life, an extraordinary fairground-style ride made in sections by over 20 artists, commissioned for a shopping centre in Sheffield, but not installed. It was resurrected for Fuller's solo show at Gainsborough's House, Sudbury, 1996.

Violet FULLER 1920– Artist in watercolour and oil, born in north London, who studied at Hornsey School of Art, 1937–40, with Russell Reeve, then at Stroud School of Art, 1942–4. She "concentrated mainly landscape, the elements and the quality of light" in her work. Fuller, who did graphic work, was a prolific exhibitor. She was a fellow and founder-member of the Free Painters and Sculptors, having solo shows including the Loggia Gallery, Woodstock Gallery and Old Bakehouse Gallery, Sevenoaks. Mixed shows included RA, RBA, RI, and NEAC. London Boroughs of Enfield and Haringey hold her pictures. Lived in Woodingdean, Sussex.

Michael FULLERTON 1971– Artist, born in Bellshill, Strathclyde, who studied at Glasgow School of Art. He took part in many group shows in Britain and abroad, later ones including Transmission Gallery in Glasgow, Project Space in Athens, Greece, and Gwangju Biennal, Gwangju, South Korea, all 2001; Felixleiter Raum für Kunst, Berlin, Germany, 2002; Collective Gallery in Edinburgh and Bloomberg New Contemporaries, Cornerhouse in Manchester and 14 Wharf Road, London, all 2003; and Wider Than The Sky, Neon Gallery, and Quodlibet, Galerie Daniel Buchholz, Cologne, Germany, both 2004. Fullerton had solo exhibitions at Art in the Square, Glasgow, 2001; Andrew Mummery Gallery and Tramway, Glasgow, both 2002; Generator Projects in Dundee, and Are You Hung Up? at Transmission Gallery and Counter Gallery, all 2003; and Suck on Science, at CCA, Glasgow, and Art Now, Tate Britain, both 2005. Suck on Science, an installation of works incorporating painting, sculpture and film, the Tate explained, explored "the transmission and reception of information. Fullerton's work, consists of two apparently distinct strands which appear to share little aesthetic common ground: portrait paintings skilfully executed in the tradition of eighteenth-century English painters such as Gainsborough, and more conceptual works that span screenprints and film." Fullerton lived and worked in Glasgow.

Hamish FULTON 1946– Artist, born in London, who created "art resulting from the experience of individual walks". Between 1964–9 Fulton studied at Hammersmith College of Art, St Martin's School of Art and the Royal College of Art. From 1969 he made walks through several continents, adhering to strict, self-imposed programmes, such as "a continuous 106-mile walk without sleep", featured in Into the Night at Annely Juda Fine Art, 1993. Showed frequently and widely in Britain and abroad, and numerous public collections, including Tate Gallery; Bibliothèque Nationale in Paris; Metropolitan Museum, Tokyo; and The Brooklyn Museum, New York, hold examples. There were solo exhibitions at the Sainsbury Centre for Visual Arts, University of East Anglia, Norwich, 2001; and Tate Britain, 2002; and Maureen Paley/Interim Art, 2005. That show, entitled To Worcester 8 Miles, covered a walk from Saltwood, near Dover, to the Stiperstones in Shropshire by the Welsh border, 320 miles in 14 days in the spring of 1972.

Gillian FURLONG 1948– Figurative painter, born in Kingston upon Thames, Surrey, who attended Epsom School of Art, 1965–7, then Camberwell School of Arts and Crafts, 1967–70. She was awarded the David Murray Landscape Prize by RA, 1968, and showed often at its Summer Exhibition. Her many other shows included John Davies, Stow-on-the-Wold, from 1979; Fenny Lodge Gallery, Bletchley, from 1985; John Noott, Broadway, from 1991; The Discerning Eye, Mall Galleries, from 1997; Thompson's Gallery, from 1999; and 30th Anniversary Exhibition, The Bourne Gallery, Reigate, 2001. Lived in Leatherhead, Surrey.

William FURLONG 1944– Artist and teacher, born in Surrey, who attended Guildford School of Arts and Crafts, 1960–5, then the Royal Academy Schools, 1965–8. Went on to be head of the foundation department at Wimbledon School of Art. With Michael Archer he ran Audio Arts (see separate entries). Furlong's solo audio installation Sound Garden was staged at Serpentine Gallery, 1998, another at South London Gallery, 2002–3. Lived in London.

Stephen FURLONGER 1939– Sculptor in all media and teacher, born in Hindhead, Surrey. He studied at Christchurch University, New Zealand, and Royal College of Art under Bernard Meadows. Furlonger was a Gulbenkian Rome Scholar who did part-time teaching at various colleges. Then taught full-time at Lanchester Polytechnic and became head of sculpture at Central School of Art & Design and Central St Martins College of Art & Design. Furlonger wrote that most of his work "has involved the use of water as a medium." Collective exhibitions included Towards Art II; Survey '68: Abstract Sculpture, at Camden Arts Centre, 1968; Jubilee Show of British Sculpture, Battersea; and Hayward Annual, 1978. Solo exhibitions included Galerie Swart, Amsterdam, and a number of studio shows. Arts Council and public galleries in Auckland and Wellington, New Zealand, hold examples.

Alan FURNEAUX 1953– Musician-turned-painter whose work included colourful Mediterranean and north African scenes, inspired by the work of Patrick Heron and Terry Frost. Furneaux was born in London and from 16 did a two-year foundation course at Reigate School of Art. Then, after 20 years in a rhythm and blues band, in 1990 he moved to the southeast of England where his grandfather artist George Hann revived Furneaux's interest in painting. Furneaux completed a series of pictures for Royal Caribbean Cruise Line. He showed in the south of England, venues including The Arundel Furniture Company, Arundel; The David Curzon Gallery; and a studio show, Brighton, Sussex, all 1999. There was a solo exhibition at The City Gallery, 2001.

James FURNEAUX 1935– Watercolourist, printmaker and teacher who gained his diploma from Gray's School of Art in Aberdeen, where he continued to live, in 1958, the year he won the RSA Chalmers-Jervis Prize. Exhibited for many years with RSA, SSA and Peacock Printmakers in Aberdeen. Was included in Six Members of Staff, Aberdeen College of Commerce, at Artspace, 1981; 10 North-East Artists, Artspace Aberdeen Edinburgh Festival show and tour, 1981–2; and Scottish Print Open Three, organised by Dundee Printmakers' Workshop, 1983. Solo shows included Aberdeen Arts Centre, 1978, and restaurant at Aberdeen Art Gallery, 1997.

Paul FURNEAUX 1962– Painter and printmaker, born in Aberdeen. He studied at Edinburgh College of Art and won a postgraduate diploma with distinction. Furneaux's pictures are singular, being inhabited by mystical figures. The painter won many awards. These included the RSA's Keith Award for Best Student in 1986; Young Scottish Artist of the Year, sponsored by Miller Homes, which provided him with a studio in Paris for a year; and the *Sunday Times Scotland* Mayfest Award in 1989. After working in Paris he had a solo show at Todd Gallery and at Compass Gallery, Glasgow, with one of wood block prints at The Firth Gallery, Edinburgh, 2001. Aberdeen Art Gallery is among several public collections holding his work.

Bettina FURNEE 1963– Sculptor in a variety of materials, and letter-cutter, born in the Netherlands. After studying art history at Leiden she trained with the noted Cambridge-based letter-carver, sculptor and typographer David Kindersley. The result is evident in her 1995 work Moon Pool, carved in Stancliffe stone, and sited at University of Warwick Business School. Furnee was shortlisted for a water feature in the Royal Pump Rooms, Leamington Spa, 1999.

Jane FURNESS 1931– Painter, artist in collage and mixed media, draughtsman and teacher, full name Valerie Jane Furness, who was born in South Molton, Devon. She studied at Wimbledon School of Art with John Ward and Gerald Cooper, also at University of London Institute of Education. Landscape, the human figure and a series based on families in part of Bristol were among her subjects. From 1957–63 worked in Cornwall, showing regularly at Newlyn Gallery and Penwith Society of Arts, joining it in early 1960s. She later lived and taught in London, Bristol and Cornwall, was head of art at Red Maids' School, Bristol, 1979–86, and taught in illustration department of Falmouth College of Art, 1986–95. Returned to Clifton,

Bristol, Furness travelled extensively abroad, returning regularly to work in her Penzance studio. Furness had numerous solo exhibitions, including Oxford Gallery, Oxford, 1963; Humanist Association, 1970; Penwith Gallery, St Ives, 1980; retrospective of figurative and abstract work, Penlee House Museum, Penzance, 1989; Wills Lane Gallery, St Ives, 1990–03; Nina Zborowska, Painswick, 1991–5; Lauderdale House, Highgate, 1995; and Wilton's Music Hall, 1998, where Furness's work was linked to the launch of an opera by Alwynne Pritchard. Furness had a show at the RWA's Mary Fedden Gallery in 2005 accompanied by *Morocco: Paintings and Poems*, a book of her paintings with poems by Denay Howard. Queen's Hotel in Penzance, Nina Zborowska, Wills Lane and many private collections hold works.

John FURNIVAL 1933– Artist in pen and ink, mixed media, printmaker and teacher, born in London. He attended Wimbledon College of Art, 1951–5 and Royal College of Art, 1957–60. In 1960 he moved to Gloucestershire, settling in Woodchester. He taught at Stroud and Cheltenham Art Colleges until 1966, when he taught initially at Bath Academy of Art and then at Bath College of Higher Education. With Dom Sylvester Houédard set up Openings Press in 1964 and with him staged many shows of concrete poetry stemming from schemes worked on at Bath Academy with students. Took part in international shows and had retrospective at Laing Art Gallery in Newcastle upon Tyne in 1971. The following year he won Arts Council Prize at International Print Biennale, Bradford. Arts Council holds his work.

Christian FURR 1966– Painter whose "main aim is to contemporise the classical figurative genre." He was born in Heswall, Wirral, Cheshire, studied foundation at Wirral Metropolitan College, Wallasey, and graduated with first-class honours in fine art from De Montfort University, Leicestershire. Furr was a prolific mixed-show exhibitor, including National Portrait, Francis Kyle and Mall Galleries. He won an Elizabeth Greenshields Foundation Scholarship, 1991, and Winsor & Newton Young Artist's Award, ROI, 1993, and his work received considerable national and specialist press coverage. Had a joint exhibition at Tricycle Gallery, 1993. Solo exhibitions included Duffer of St George, 1993, and Royal Over-Seas League, 1993 and 2001. Aged 28, Furr became the youngest artist to officially paint Queen Elizabeth II, for the Royal Over-Seas League headquarters, after the Queen chose him from a shortlist. There were many other British and overseas private and official commissions, including Cardinal Cormac Murphy O'Connor and portraits of two bishops for Westminster Cathedral. Furr was a member of the Chelsea Arts Club. He lived in Richmond-upon-Thames, Surrey.

Patrick FURSE 1918–2005 Artist and teacher, born in London, son of Sir Ralph Furse, for a time Winston Churchill's private secretary. Patrick's sisters Jill, the actress, and Theresa were successively married to the glass engraver Laurence Whistler. Having entered Eton College on a scholarship, Furse was encouraged to paint and etch by Robin Darwin. He abandoned reading classics at Balliol College, Oxford, and enrolled in London at Byam Shaw School of Drawing and Painting. Through Jill, he was able to draw backstage at the Royal Opera House and Sadler's Wells. During World War II Furse served in the Rifle Brigade, was involved in air reconnaissance and Army-Royal Air Force liaison and work with the Polish Air Force, was mentioned in dispatches and left with the rank of major. He then worked as a storyboard artist in films; with his wife Elisabeth Haden-Guest opened a prints and antiques shop near Sloane Square; while continuing to paint, sculpt and deal in pictures ran a restaurant and club called Bistro; worked as darkroom assistant to the fashion photographer Claude Virgin; and in the late 1950s concentrated on enamelling. In 1959 he took on the enamelling department at the Central School of Arts and Crafts, running it for 24 years with distinction, experimenting with new mixes of metal and glass oxides to create rich colours and tackling large works. He collaborated with the noted enameller Stefan Knapp on installations at Terminal 2 at Heathrow Airport and Sidney Nolan's Eureka Stockade mural for the Reserve Bank of Australia, Melbourne. After retirement, Furse continued to paint, also studying Arabic calligraphy and Chinese.

Roger FURSE 1903–1972 Artist in various media, film and stage designer. Born at Ightham, Kent, he studied under Henry Tonks at the Slade School of Fine Art, 1920–4, after education at Eton College. Exhibited at the Leicester and Berkeley Galleries and the Salon d'Automne, Paris. The Imperial War Museum holds his work. Furse was principally known as a theatrical designer, of settings and costumes. He had to his credit dozens of productions at major London theatres, such as the Old Vic, Lyric and Haymarket, plus provincial and foreign venues. He also designed costumes and armour for Laurence Olivier's film *Henry V*, in 1944, plus other notable films such as *Odd Man Out*, *Spartacus* and *The Roman Spring of Mrs Stone*. Lived in London.

Hideo FURUTA 1949– Artist and teacher, notable as a sculptor, born in Hiroshima, Japan. From 1969–71, Furuta attended Tokyo Visual Art College, Tokyo, for foundation and sculpture; for five years, after involvement in the student movement, studied art, mathematics and physics; concentrated on etching and engraving at Hijiyama Art College, Hiroshima, 1977–8; then comparative philosophy and aesthetics at Hiroshima University, 1978–80. He worked as a quarry man at Ishizaki Quarry, Kurahashi Island, 1982–3. After a period teaching in Chile in 1984, Furuta in 1985 began teaching and sculpting in Wales, and went on to hold a large number of posts and residencies in Britain; was a visiting lecturer at Trondheim Art College, Norway, in 1991; and was Henry Moore Fellow in Sculpture at Northumbria University, Newcastle, 1992–4. His sound works and public performances included an African Drum Performance there, 1993. Furuta took part in many group shows in Britain and abroad. He had a solo exhibition of silkscreen prints at Saeki Gallery, Hiroshima, 1977, later ones including sculptures, drawings, photos and video works at University Gallery of Newcastle, 1997. This featured granite and basalt spheres and cones, carved at a quarry on the Solway Firth, when Furuta was described as "an artist who powerfully embodied a synthesis of conceptual and physical concerns". By that time, Furuta's public commissions numbered almost a score, later ones including a monumental outdoor sculpture for Gateshead Sculpture Park, Gateshead: Axiom, in white granite and black basalt, 1993–6. In 2000–1, Furuta's sculpture Juxtapositions was shown in Regent's Park under the auspices of Daiwa Foundation Japan House. Collections holding his work included Margam Sculpture Park, Port Talbot;

Edinburgh Printmakers' Workshop, Edinburgh; Gallery Oriel 31, Newtown; and Glynn Vivian Art Gallery and Museum, Swansea.

Anne FURZER: *see* **Anne ENGDAHL**

Anne FURZER-ENGDAHL: *see* **Anne ENGDAHL**

Irena FUSEK-FOROSIEWICZ fl. from 1950s–2002 Painter, born in Charewicz, Poland, where she studied at the High School of Agriculture in Warsaw and during the World War II German occupation took part in that city's uprising. After the war she was one of the organisers of opera in Silesia, working there from 1945–58. She then settled in London and studied with the School of the Academic Community of Wilno University and Marian Bohusz-Szysko. Working in the Post-Impressionist tradition of colour and light, she made the landscapes of the Sussex Downs, Italy and Spain her main themes. Was active in the Association of Polish Artists in Britain. Took part in group exhibitions at POSK Gallery, in 1982 having a solo shows there and at Christ's Hospital Arts Centre, Horsham. In 1996, she had another at the Polish Cultural Centre. Toruń University, Poland, holds her work, as do many private collections in Britain and abroad.

Władisław FUSEK-FOROSIEWICZ 1907–1983 Painter, born in Poland, who at the Cracow Academy of Fine Arts in 1931 gained his painting and teaching diploma. Before World War II he took part in the Annual Exhibition of Painting in Cracow and won a Ministry of Communications Award, 1938. In 1939, he joined the Polish Army, in 1940 the Polish Underground Army, in 1945 leaving the country to join the 2nd Polish Corps in Italy. At the British 8th Army Art Festival in Rome, 1946, he was awarded 1st Prize in the figurative section. Fusek-Forosiewicz then moved to England and settled in Sussex, although he continued to travel occasionally to Africa, Italy, France and especially Spain. Group exhibitions included Contemporary Art by Polish Artists abroad at Imperial College, 1970, and annual shows of the Association of Polish Artists in Great Britain, of which he was a member. In 1974, he was awarded the Garby Prize. Among his one-man exhibitions were Edinburgh, 1955; Ipswich, 1959; Accra, Ghana, 1960; and POSK Gallery, 1975, 1979 and 1981. Fusek-Forosiewicz's painted landscapes, still lifes and portraits, showing a Post-Impressionist influence and vibrant use of colour. His painter contemporary Stanisław Frenkiel said of his work that it was "pervaded by unabashed thirst for sensuous textures brought out by light." The Cracow National Museum in Poland and many private collections around the world hold examples.

Michael FUSSELL 1927–1974 Painter, collagist and teacher who did figurative and abstract work, with a special interest in weather and the sea. He was born in Southampton and educated in Bournemouth, Hampshire. Studied at City & Guilds Art School, St Martin's School of Art, 1946–9, and Royal College of Art, 1949–52, under Rodrigo Moynihan. Taught at St Martin's and from 1964 was head of fine art at Wimbledon School of Art. Showed at RA, Young Contemporaries and in the provinces and had a first solo exhibition at Beaux Arts Gallery in 1956. Tate Gallery and Arts Council, which in 1976 staged a retrospective, hold examples. Lived for many years in London and was married to the artist Evelyn Williams.

G

Christa GAA 1937–1992 Watercolourist, born in Hamburg, Germany. She was married to the painter Ken Howard. The artist studied German philology and art history in Cologne, Bonn and Florence, 1957–60, then painting at Fachhochschule für Kunst und Design in Cologne, 1975–80. Gaa moved to England in 1980. She showed in mixed exhibitions at New Grafton Gallery, New Ashgate Gallery in Farnham, in RA Summer Exhibition and elsewhere. She shared an exhibition at New Grafton in 1984, had a solo show there in 1990 and it held her memorial exhibition in 1992. There was a New Grafton commemorative show in 2004. A typical Gaa watercolour celebrates an informal domestic still life, although she did some landscapes in Britain and abroad. Her technique showed a quiet restraint. Died in Cologne.

Ethel GABAIN 1883–1950 Printmaker and painter, born in Le Havre, of mixed French and Scottish descent. She married the artist John Copley in 1913, their son being the actor Peter Copley. After spending her first 14 years in France Gabain attended an English boarding school, then studied at the Slade School of Fine Art, Collin's studio in Paris and lithography at Central School of Arts and Crafts. With Copley she was a founder-member of the Senefelder Club in 1910. Despite continuing poor health she travelled on the continent and was a prolific printmaker; turned to painting in Italy in 1924, making her first appearance with an oil painting, Zinnias, at RA in 1927. Also exhibited at Goupil, Redfern and Chenil Galleries; with Colnaghi; RSA; Walker Art Gallery in Liverpool; and was a member of RBA (which gave her a memorial exhibition in 1950), ROI and SWA (becoming its vice-president). Gabain's favourite themes were adolescent girlhood and a figure against a window, one model – Carmen – being painted over 50 times. In World War II Gabain was an Official War Artist. Imperial War Museum holds her work, which is in other collections including Manchester City Art Gallery. In the 1930s Gabain, with scripts supplied by her husband, became a popular lecturer on art history to schools, to boost family funds. In 1985 Garton & Cooke held an exhibition of both artists' prints and in 2003 The Fine Art Society showed lithographs by Gabain with work by Mabel Royds. Lived in London.

Neville GABIE 1959– Abstract sculptor and teacher, born in Johannesburg, South Africa. After studying at Hull College of Art, 1980–3, and Royal College of Art, 1986–8, Gabie went on to teach at Cheltenham and Gloucester College of Higher Education. He was included in the River exhibition at Goldsmiths' Gallery in 1990 and in the 1993–4 Arts Council touring show Recent British Sculpture. Solo shows included Camden Arts Centre, 1987, and Spacex Gallery, Exeter, 1991. Hales Gallery sold his work. Gabie lived near Stroud, Gloucestershire.

Naum GABO 1890–1977 Constructions artist in a variety of materials, designer, writer and teacher, born in Bryansk, Russia, as Naum Pevsner, brother of the painter Antoine Pevsner. As a young man he changed his name to Naum Gabo so as not to be confused with his brother. Gabo entered Munich University in 1910 to study medicine, then natural sciences, but also attended art history lectures. In 1912 transferred to an engineering school in Munich, in 1913–14 joining his brother in Paris. When World War I broke out he moved to Copenhagen, then Oslo, in 1915 beginning to make constructions. Although sometimes figurative, these were generally abstract, simple and beautiful using a variety of materials, notably later Perspex when he came to England. From 1917–22 Gabo was in Moscow, where he knew advanced artists such as Tatlin and Kandinsky. In 1920 with Pevsner he produced a *Realistic Manifesto* outlining the tenets of pure Constructivism. From 1922 for a decade he was in Berlin in contact with the artists of the de Stijl and Bauhaus movements; with Pevsner he designed for Diaghilev's ballet *La Chatte* in 1926; then from 1932–6 lived in Paris, and was a member of the Abstraction-Création group. After arriving in England in 1936 he helped edit the manifesto volume *Circle*. By now he was married to the painter Miriam Israels, and with her he settled in St Ives, Cornwall, where he was an influential figure. Soon after World War II Gabo moved to America, where he became an American citizen in 1952, carried out important commissions and became professor of the Graduate School of Architecture, Harvard University. He had a retrospective show at Tate Gallery in 1966; again in 1976, after which he gave the gallery a group of works; there was a retrospective at the Tate in 1987; with another at Tate St Ives, 2002. Annely Juda Fine Art organised Gabo and Colour in 2004. Gabo died in Wateringbury, Connecticut.

Caroline Sylvia GABRIEL 1912–1997 Early a painter in oil, she later carved in wood and stone. She taught at Avery Hill College of Education and at evening classes and published educational textbooks. Gabriel studied under Randolph Schwabe, A H Gerrard and George Charlton at Slade School of Fine Art after attending North London Collegiate School. Showed at RA, RBA, SPS, RSA and elsewhere. Brighton Museum and Art Gallery holds her work. Lived in Ashington, Sussex.

Edith Mabel GABRIEL 1882–1972 Sculptor, born in Richmond, Surrey. She studied at Heatherley's School of Fine Art and in Paris. Her sculpture was classical with a modern tinge, as in her Mother and Child, illustrated in the volume *RBS: Modern British Sculpture*, published in 1939. Eventually elected a fellow of RBS. Showed RA, RSA, Walker Art Gallery in Liverpool and elsewhere. From 1915 rented 1 Mall Studios, Hampstead, where she remained until her death.

Louise GABRIEL 1963– She was mainly a figurative intaglio printmaker "inclined towards various obsessions, including angels, y-fronts, baths, feathers, kissing and merfolk." Born in Whitstable, Kent, Gabriel did a foundation course at Medway College of Art & Design, 1981–2; graduated with honours in fine art, Stourbridge, 1982–5; from 1990–1 undertaking part-time City & Guilds teacher training. Showed at London and provincial art fairs, group exhibitions including An A-Z of Printmaking, Worcester City Museum and Art Gallery, then an Ikon Gallery, Birmingham, tour, 1993; Animal Magic, Lamont Gallery, 1994; Hetero, ICA Café/Bar, 1996; and The Jelly Leg'd Chicken, Reading, 2000; and Will's Art Warehouse, 2002. Among solo exhibitions were A Bit of a Show, Faversham Frames, Faversham, Kent, where she lived, 2000.

Michael GABRIEL 1931– Sculptor in metals, wood and stone, who studied at Coventry and Cheltenham Colleges of Art. Was a member of Cotswold Art Club and Cheltenham Group of Artists, exhibited at RWA and was included in 19 Young Sculptors at Hillfield Gardens, Gloucester, in 1962, when he was living in Cheltenham. In 1976 Gabriel had a solo show at Trinity College, Oxford.

Andrew GADD 1968– Figurative painter in oil who produced dramatic studies strong in chiaroscuro, much influenced by his study of the Old Masters, in particular the Expressionist brushwork of Velázquez and Goya. Gadd studied at Chelsea and Falmouth Schools of Art, 1985–90. He completed his postgraduate studies at the Royal Academy Schools in 1993, teachers including Roderic Barrett, winning the Gold Medal for painting and the Richard Ford Travel Scholarship to Spain. Exhibited at the RA Summer Exhibition, Mall Galleries, National Portrait and Paton Galleries. Had a series of solo exhibitions at Agnew, including Fugitive, Venetian Boat Paintings and other recent works, 2002. It was dominated by four exceptionally large paintings of figures adrift on Venetian gondolas. Set in an indeterminate and bleak landscape, they were said to "raise the issues of transience and homelessness" implicit in the show's title. The Metropolitan Museum of Modern Art, New York, holds the work of Gadd, who lived in Richmond, Surrey.

Anthea Dominique Juliet GAGE 1956– Painter and teacher, born in Edinburgh where she continued to live, daughter of the painter Edward Gage. She studied at Edinburgh College of Art, 1974–9, her teachers including George Donald and David Michie. Went on to teach at Royal High School, Edinburgh. Was a regular exhibitor with SSA and RSW, of both of which she was a member.

Edward GAGE 1925–2000 Painter, illustrator, stage designer, writer and teacher, born in Gullane, East Lothian. He studied at Edinburgh College of Art, 1941–2 and 1947–52, his teachers including William Gillies. Served in Army during World War II in India and Malaya. A postgraduate scholarship and travelling scholarship took him to Majorca. Gage taught at Fettes College until 1968, when he joined the staff of Napier College of Science and Technology, for 20 years from 1958 being a part-time lecturer at Edinburgh College of Art. He was a member of RSW and was president of SSA in 1960–4. Gage also worked as a freelance set designer for Gateway and Citizen's Theatres in the early 1950s; illustrated for a number of publishers, including *Radio Times*; was art critic for *The Scotsman*; and wrote *The Eye in the Wind: Contemporary Scottish Painting since 1945*, published 1977. Gage had a series of solo shows at Scottish Gallery, Edinburgh. Scottish Arts Council, Aberdeen and Edinburgh Universities hold his work. He was the father of the artist Anthea Gage and lived in Edinburgh.

Jan GAGE 1955– After graduating with honours from Cardiff College of Art, 1975–8, Gage gained a master's degree from Chelsea School of Art, 1978–9. Group appearances included Uses of Drawing, Whitechapel Art Gallery, and Cleveland Drawing Biennale, both 1979; Heads and Tails, Newcastle University Gallery, 1980; and East End Open Studios, based at Robinson Road, 1989. In 1986 Gage had a solo exhibition at Howard Gardens Gallery, Cardiff.

Sylvia Petula GAINSFORD 1942– Artist and illustrator working in acrylic, watercolour and line and as a printmaker, teacher, and gallery owner with her husband Leon Olin. She was born in Tonbridge, Kent, and attended Tunbridge Wells School of Art, studying wood engraving with E Owen Jennings, painting with J Weidman. Gainsford taught and travelled extensively abroad, then from 1974 toured Britain in a mobile studio with her husband; settled in Kent; then went to work at Rhosycaerau, Goodwick, Dyfed, helping to run Gallery One at Fishguard. She worked for publishers including Bishopsgate Press and Bell and Hyman and was commissioned by A G Müller, of Switzerland, to illustrate and design *The Tarot of the Old Path*, 1990. Group shows included Frances Iles Gallery, Rochester, and Nuffield Art Centre, Southampton. She showed solo there with Hamwic Gallery. Gainsford's main interest was wildlife, her aim being "to capture the living spirit and character of the animal". Kallis Foundation in Beverly Hills, California, holds Gainsford's work.

Paul GAISFORD 1941– Landscape and figure painter in oil and watercolour, born in Dorking, Surrey. He studied at Camberwell School of Art, 1956–61; Slade School of Fine Art, 1961–4; and Berlin Academy, 1964; teachers included Sir William Coldstream, Claude Rogers and Frank Auerbach. Solo shows included Ibis, Langton, Piers Feetham and Meldrum Walker Galleries. University College and Berlin Academy of Fine Arts hold examples. For many years Gaisford kept handsome, Moroccan leather-bound diaries which chronicled his life and preoccupations such as his horse Rosie and gypsy caravan. Lived at Great Rissington, Cheltenham, Gloucestershire.

Martin GALE 1949– Landscape painter to whom a sense of place was important, based on close observation, occasionally found objects bearing witness to those who have lived there. Gale was born in Worcester of Irish and English parents, his father a steeplechase jockey. From 1950 the family lived in Ireland, travelling widely. Gale studied at the National College of Art & Design, Dublin, 1968–73. He showed in Dublin at the Oireachtas Exhibition from 1971, being an award winner, in 1973. Represented Ireland in Young Artists '72, Union Carbide Building, New York, 1973, and in the 1980–1 XI Biennale de Paris, which toured France and to Finland. He was an award winner at the 1991 RHA Annual, having shown there from 1990, being elected a full member in 1996. Showed solo with

Taylor Galleries, Dublin, from 1981. Exhibited with Messum's from 2000, being included in Around Two Thousand and Three, 2003. In 2004–5 there was a show at Ulster Museum, Belfast. Arts Council of Ireland; Hugh Lane Municipal Gallery of Modern Art, Dublin; and many other Irish public gallery and corporate collections hold examples. Lived in County Kildare, Ireland.

Richard GALE 1946– Painter, born in Portishead, near Bristol. After attending local art college in Taunton he studied at Kingston School of Art, 1965–8, and Royal College of Art, 1970–3. Work was shown at Basel Art Fair in 1975, Düsseldorf Art Fair in 1976, RA from 1981 and it was selected at National Portrait Gallery for Imperial Tobacco Portrait Award, 1982–3. Had his first solo show at Parkin Gallery, 1977. Gale was a slow worker, finishing only a handful of paintings annually, and they sometimes took several years to germinate. Was noted for his portraits and figure studies employing a realistic technique. Lived in Clevedon, North Somerset.

Simon GALES 1964– Painter of meticulous still lifes with a landscape background, inspired by the intensity and clarity of pictures by Juan Sanchez Cotan, a late sixteenth-century Spanish monk. Twelve years' study and contemplation went into Gales' first solo show, at Bruton Street Gallery in 1999. His exhibition there in 2001 revealed a new cool, silvery tonality and sensitivity to light and atmosphere, and there was another in 2003. Gales gained a diploma with distinction at Ipswich School of Art, 1983–5, then won a first-class honours degree in fine art at Goldsmiths' College, 1985–8. He took part in many group shows, including New Realists, Berkeley Square Gallery, 1988; RA Summer Exhibition, from 1991; and A New Beginning, Offer Waterman & Co, 1996. Gales' picture Childhood was reproduced for London Underground on behalf of the Victoria & Albert Museum (Museum of Childhood) as a poster. London Underground Museum and The Robert Holmes à Court Museum, Perth, Australia, hold examples.

Neil GALL 1967– Painter, born in Scotland, who studied at Gray's School of Art, Aberdeen, 1987–91, and Slade School of Fine Art, 1991–3. In 1993 he gained an Abbey Major Award to study at the British School at Rome, showing there in 1994, in 1995 taking part in the two-man exhibition Rome Scholars at Gray's School gallery. Gall's oil on canvas Flower Painting No. 7 was included in the 1997–8 John Moores Liverpool Exhibition. Following a year's residency at Durham Cathedral, his exhibition Durham Paintings toured from the Reg Vardy Gallery, Sunderland, 1997–8. Lived in London.

Anya GALLACCIO 1963– Artist, born in Glasgow, who studied at Kingston Polytechnic, 1984–5, and then graduated from Goldsmiths' College with honours, 1985–8. Took part in Art Pace International Artist's Programme, San Antonio, Texas, America, 1997, with a Sargent Fellowship, British School at Rome, Italy, 1998, and a residency at Kamazawa Art Academy, Japan, 1999. Group exhibitions included Poetic Figuration in the Eighties, Lauderdale House, 1988; The Return of Ulysses, English National Opera, 1989; and Next Phase, Wapping Pumping Station, 1990. Her work was included in the exhibition of sculpture and installations Sweet Home, originated by Mostyn Art Gallery, Llandudno, and tour, 1994. In 1996 she filled the Wapping Pumping Station with an installation of ice, salt, steam and light, in 1997 creating an installation for the lawn of the Serpentine Gallery, in 1999 one for Sadler's Wells. Her contribution that year to Natural Dependency, at The Jerwood Gallery, was Loose Change, an ever-moving carpet of 200,000 golden Swiss 5-rappen pieces, spread at the feet of visitors. In 2001 Gallacio's ice installation from the Swedish River Tome was sited outside the Science Museum until it melted, then in 2002 Gallacio gained a Duveen Galleries Sculpture Commission at Tate Britain. This followed the award of the 1871 Fellowship, shared between The Rothermere Institute at Oxford University and the San Francisco Art Institute, in America. Gallacio wanted her seven large oak trees installation, placed in the Duveen Galleries in 2002–3, to capture people's attention as they walked through. Because I Could Not Stop was sited outside the Ikon Gallery, Birmingham, in 2003. Gallacio's show The Look of Things was at the Palazzo delle Papesse, Siena, Italy, in 2005. She lived in London.

Brian GALLAGHER 1935– Painter and draughtsman who studied with Herbert Green. He showed with London Sketch Club of which he was a member, PS in which he held several key positions, SWLA and in the provinces. Lived in Ashford, Middlesex.

Mary GALLAGHER 1953– Painter, born in Glasgow, where she continued to live. She attended the School of Art there, 1974–8, having a postgraduate year in 1979. After a period of consolidation, during which the work she produced was well-received, Gallagher decided to paint full-time. She showed at Royal Glasgow Institute of the Fine Arts, Lillie Art Gallery in Milngavie, Perth Museum and Art Gallery and Barclay Lennie Fine Art in Glasgow, having a first solo exhibition in London in 1989 at Portland Gallery. Gallagher was not a prolific artist, her striking still lifes having the studied appearance and rich colour of S J Peploe's.

Paul GALLAGHER 1964– Painter, draughtsman and printmaker, born in Newcastle upon Tyne, Northumberland, who pursued lithography and etching with Northern Print, 1998. Did commissioned work for Fasson Europe, 1997. Exhibitions included Landscape, Chameleon Gallery, Newcastle, 1988; Clayton Gallery, Newcastle, from 1994; and Laing Art Competition, University of Northumbria Gallery, 1995. In 1996 he shared a show with Dale Atkinson at Clayton Gallery, in 1999 Diverse Landscapes with Angela Hughes and Julian Vilarrubi at University of Northumbria. He had a solo show there in 2005.

Sara GALLIE 1967– Painter of works tending towards abstraction, born in Scotland, who gained an honours degree in fine art from Gray's School of Art, Aberdeen, and her postgraduate diploma master's there, 1998–9. Awards included the RSA Carnegie Travelling Scholarship, 1998; David Gordon Memorial Trust Art Prize, 1998 and 1999; and RSA Latimer Award and Miller Homes Prize, Paris Studio, runner-up, both 1999. Among her mixed exhibitions were the RSA Annual Exhibition, from 1998, and Fertile, Duff House Country House Gallery, Banff, 1999. In 1999 Gallie shared an exhibition at the Jill George Gallery. Commissions included two paintings from Bali, Indonesia, Jim Bothwell, Vital Spark Gallery, Aberdeen, 1998.

Arthur GALLINER 1878–1961 Painter, art historian and lecturer, born in Zinten, Germany. Studied art in Berlin, Munich and widely in Italy. Exhibited at a number of galleries in Germany and in England at RI, RBA and elsewhere in London. Royal Library, in Copenhagen, Denmark, holds his work. Wrote a book on the German Impressionist painter Max Liebermann and held several teaching posts, including Hammersmith School of Art, 1947–50, and Borough Polytechnic, 1950–2. Lived in London. He was distantly related to the artist Edith Galliner.

Edith Marguerite GALLINER 1914– Painter in acrylic, potter, etcher and teacher, born and lived in London, distantly related to the artist Arthur Galliner. Her German-Jewish family returned to Germany in the year she was born, she was educated in Berlin, then moved to England again to escape arrest in 1933. As well as studying in Paris, attended Camberwell School of Arts and Crafts and Central School of Art and Design. Taught in Cork, Ireland, and in London. In the early-to-mid-1960s returned to Berlin to paint. Galliner was influenced in Germany by the Bauhaus and Brücke movements, in England by advanced artists such as Ben Nicholson and Victor Pasmore. Group exhibitions included Hamilton Galleries, from 1966; Hampstead Artists' Council, from 1967; Camden Arts Centre, 1970; Annely Juda, from 1970; RE, 1973; German Embassy, 1978; and Art in Exile in Great Britain 1933–45, Camden Arts Centre, 1986. Had a solo show at Hamilton Galleries, 1967, later ones including Galerie Wolfgang Gurlitt, München, 1973. National Gallery in Berlin holds her work.

Alessandro GALLO 1974– Sculptor, printmaker and watercolourist whose exhibition Donkey After Noon was at the Jill George Gallery in 2006, his first in London. Gallo was born in Genoa, studied at Central St Martins College of Art and Chelsea School of Art, graduating in 2002.

Vincent GALLOWAY 1894–1977 Painter, mainly of portraits, born in Hull and educated at Ushaw College. Studied at Hull College of Art, in London and the Netherlands. During World War I Galloway served in the East Yorkshires, being wounded at the battle of Oppy Wood, in France, and he also served in the Middle East. He took over as curator at the Ferens Art Gallery, Hull, in 1928, serving until 1960, and he began the collection of local marine artists. Was vice-president of Hull Art Club. Exhibited RA, with RP, of which he was a member, in Nottingham and at RBA. Galloway painted about 250 portraits, a third of which were shown in a retrospective at the Ferens Art Gallery in 1972. The gallery holds several pictures by Galloway, also a portrait of him by G K Beulah. Died in Reading, Berkshire.

Kay GALLWEY 1936– Painter and illustrator who also hand-painted her own frames and created screens in the Oriental style. She began studying at City and Guilds School of Art aged 15, then attended Goldsmiths' College School of Art, in 1953 obtaining a scholarship to Royal Academy Schools, where she remained only six months. Became an illustrator with Artists Partners for *Harper's & Queen* magazine and others while developing as a costume designer and portrait painter. In addition, Gallwey had pastels used by Royle's for their colour 1992 calendar; had paintings accepted by London Underground Posters; and produced books based on her pets. Showed in Britain and America and solo several times with Catto Gallery.

Alexander Milligan GALT 1913–2000 Painter of colourful works, draughtsman and teacher, born in Greenock, Renfrewshire, seventh child of a Clydeside brass-founder. At Glasgow School of Art from 1930 Galt was teased by other students about a poverty that forced him to make his own paints and use his hair to make brushes. His tutors termed Galt "the human camera" and his fellow-student David Donaldson said that he could "out-Orpen Orpen". On graduation, Galt won the Torrance Award and his diploma work toured Scotland's art schools as an example for students to follow. When Galt's painting The Stable Boy was bought by the Caird Museum bequest in Greenock he came to the attention of the theatre critic James Agate who proved a valuable patron, introducing him to the Redfern Gallery, in London. In 1938 Galt won a Carnegie Travelling Scholarship which took him to Paris, where lived for two years in Montparnasse. Forced to return to Scotland with the onset of World War II, Galt taught briefly before flying with the Royal Air Force. After demobilisation, Galt taught part-time at Glasgow School of Art before being appointed art master to Greenock High School. He showed with the Royal Glasgow Institute of the Fine Arts, of which he was a prize-winning member, RSA and RSW, but found it hard to bring up a family in post-war austerity Glasgow. When he was so hard up that he felt he must resign from Glasgow Art Club the committee refused, forgoing his membership fee. After his death, Panter & Hall, which took over the management of his estate, began to re-establish Galt's reputation. The gallery included his work in 200 Years of Scottish Painting, 2003, and in 2004 gave him a solo show.

Martina GALVIN 1964– Mainly a painter, but also did some installation work, born in Dublin, Ireland. She studied at the National College of Art & Design, there, and after graduating did her master's degree at South Glamorgan Institute of Higher Education, Cardiff. She took part in many group exhibitions in Ireland and Britain, and had solo shows in Skibbereen, County Cork, and in Cardiff, with one at Mulligan's, Cork Street, in 1994. The paintings there were part of a new series, "where the colour and light of particular landscapes plays a dominant role ... These paintings are imaginings of a mythical place, informed by real landscapes."

Susan GAMBLE 1957– Artist who did a foundation course at Winchester School of Art, 1974–5, graduating with honours in fine art from Goldsmiths' College, 1976–9. In 1983, the Wenyon and Gamble partnership was formed. Wenyon and Gamble: New Holograms was held at the Glynn Vivian Art Gallery, Swansea, in 1984, Speckle Holograms being shown at Goldsmiths' College, 1985. Gamble held a solo exhibition at Galerie Peter Ludwig, Cologne, West Germany, in 1984. She participated in East End Open Studios, at Berry Street, 1989.

Tom GAMBLE 1924– Artist and teacher, born in Stockton-on-Tees, County Durham, who began painting when very young; started a signwriting apprenticeship in 1938, completed after interruption by Royal Navy service, 1942–6; then worked in a commercial art studio, notably on three-dimensional design. He was for many years on the staff of Loughborough College of Art & Design, becoming senior lecturer, taking early retirement in 1984. He also tutored courses for RWS, of which he was a fellow. Was a member of Art Workers' Guild and liveryman and gold medallist of the Worshipful Company of Painter-Stainers. Showed at RA, Singer & Friedlander/*Sunday Times* Watercolour Competition, The Hunting Art Prizes, in the provinces and Spain. HM The Queen, Leicester and Nottingham County Councils and Cleveland Art Gallery, Middlesbrough, hold Gamble's work. Lived at East Perry, Huntingdon, Cambridgeshire.

Abram GAMES 1914–1996 Graphic designer and teacher, born and lived in London, who was self-taught apart from two terms at St Martin's School of Art, 1930, and evening life classes. In 1936, the year he won first prize in a poster competition to publicize London County Council evening classes, Games was dismissed from the commercial art studio Askew-Young for horseplay, and decided to concentrate on his freelance career. He was not by nature an organisation man, although big organisations such as London Transport, Shell and the General Post Office were quick to employ his talents. During World War II Games designed posters for the War Office, 1941–6, some of his Socialistically inclined productions proving controversial. He was also responsible for British and Israeli postage stamps; the 1951 Festival of Britain, Queen's Award to Industry and BBC Television emblems; and gained first prizes in poster competitions in Finland, Portugal, America, Sweden and Spain. Taught at the Royal College of Art, 1946–53, his 1960 book *Over My Shoulder* explaining his methods of work. Games was made a Royal Designer for Industry in 1959 and in 1991 gained the Designers and Art Directors' Association President's Award. Had a series of solo shows overseas and in Britain, including a 60-year retrospective at Camden Arts Centre in 1991 and a show of war posters at the Imperial War Museum in 1994. Abram Games – Maximum Meaning, Minimum Means – Games' catchphrase – was held at the Design Museum in 2003, with another show at the London Jewish Cultural Centre, 2004.

Mary GAMLEN 1913– Sculptor, painter and teacher, born in London. She studied at Hornsey School of Art and was on its staff, 1937–45. Became an honorary member of UA, also exhibiting with RA, NEAC and in the provinces. Settled in Southrepps, Norfolk, and completed a number of village signs in the county as well as church work. Royal Marines Museum holds her Lying-in-State of Sir Winston Churchill.

Nick GAMMON 1958– Abstract painter who studied at Chelsea School of Art, 1976–7, then Bath Academy of Art, Corsham, 1977–80. He was assistant to Howard Hodgkin, 1981–90, artist-in-residence at Villa Waldberta, Munich, Germany, 1998. Gammon produced dazzling, hard-edged abstracts composed of small rectangles, as shown in Cross Currents, Reed's Wharf Gallery at Barbican Centre, 1996. Had shows at Heritage Centre, 1992; Berning & Daw, 1993; Blue Gallery, 1995; and Stephen Lacey Gallery, 1999. Lived in Dingle, County Kerry, Ireland.

Reg GAMMON 1894–1997 Painter, draughtsman and writer, born in Petersfield, Hampshire. He was educated at Churcher's College and studied privately with an uncle, Frank Patterson, prior to World War I. In 1918 Muirhead Bone offered to get Gammon into the Slade School of Fine Art, but being married he declined, taking up a career as an illustrator and writer. He drew for *Punch*, cycling and motoring magazines and in the 1930s wrote and illustrated a country feature for the *News Chronicle*. Made extensive walking and cycling trips in Britain, Ireland and Brittany, painting watercolours. After World War II was a hill farmer in the Black Mountains until 1953, then took up oil painting seriously, settling in Cannington, Somerset. He was influenced by Gauguin, using a rich palette to depict simple rural life. Was a member of ROI and RWA, which gave him a retrospective in 1985. Also held a number of exhibitions with New Grafton Gallery, including a retrospective from the artist's estate, 2003. In 1990 Gammon published his autobiography *One Man's Furrow – 90 Years of Country Living*, which sold out on publication. RWA, WAC and several provincial galleries hold his work. Died in a nursing home at Bridgwater.

Stewart GANLEY 1946– Artist who attended Hammersmith College of Art, 1968–74. He had solo exhibitions at 161 Gallery, 1980, and Woodwharf Gallery, 1985. Ganley was artist-in-residence, Mile End Hospital, 1986–7. Group appearances included The South Bank Picture Show, Royal Festival Hall, 1987; Merz Contemporary Art Gallery, 1988; and East End Open Studios, at Cable Street Studios, 1989.

Jo GANTER 1963– Artist, born in Yorkshire, who gained her master's with honours in fine art from Edinburgh University and Edinburgh College of Art, 1983–8, doing a postgraduate diploma at the College, 1988–9. She won many awards, including a John Kinross Scholarship, 1988; Andrew Grant Scholarship for postgraduate studies and Rome Scholarship in printmaking, 1989; Boise Travel Scholarship and Hope Scott Trust Fund artist assistance grant, 1993; British Council Travel Grant, 1997; another Hope Scott grant, 1998; Glasgow Arts Club Award, RSA, 1999; and Scottish Arts Council Major Bursary, 2000. Took part in numerous group shows in Britain and abroad, later ones including Ten Prints for the Women's Art Collection at New Hall, Hughson Gallery, Glasgow, 2000, and Lintos, Jyvaeskyla Museum of Fine Arts, Finland, 2002. Later solo exhibitions included Hart Gallery, 2002, and Talbot Rice Gallery, University of Edinburgh, 2003. Contemporary Art Society; Lillie Art Gallery, Milngavie; the Museum of Fine Arts, Antwerp, Belgium; and New York Public Libraries were among public collections holding examples.

Valerie GANZ 1936– Artist and teacher, born at Mumbles, near Swansea, who studied painting, sculpture and stained glass at the College of Art there, remaining as a tutor, 1957–73, when she returned to full-time painting. Her teachers included Alfred Janes, William Price and George Fairley. Ganz became preoccupied by the landscape of south Wales, concentrating on industrial, especially mining, areas. In 1985 Ganz took a house and studio at Six Bells, Abertillery, for nearly a year depicting the lives of the miners at its colliery, underground and on the surface, with their families at choir practice, in the snooker halls and at chapel. The work was widely exhibited, notably at the mining show at Glynn Vivian Art Gallery, Swansea, in 1986. In 1990 Ganz was commissioned by British Coal Opencast to study three sites in south Wales and she later worked at Tower Colliery. Other subjects covered by Ganz included jazz musicians, in New Orleans and at the Brecon Jazz Festival; the Chinese landscape; master classes at Dartington Music School; and the urban landscape of New York. Exhibitions included National Museum of Wales in Cardiff, National Library of Wales, Aberystwyth, National Industrial and Maritime Museum, Cardiff, and Royal National Eisteddfod. The Albany Gallery, Cardiff, gave Ganz a solo show in 2004. CASW holds her work. Lived in Llandeilo, Dyfed.

Robert Lambert GAPPER 1897–1984 Sculptor in a variety of materials, letterer and teacher, born in Llanaelhaearn, Carnarvonshire. After a period at Goldsmiths' College in London and a year teaching art and woodwork in Pwllheli School, in Wales, Gapper served in the Army during World War I, after which he obtained a Bachelor of Science degree in electrical engineering at University College of North Wales and worked as an engineer in Rugby. Having attended Rugby School of Art and being asked to teach there, from 1923–7 he attended the Royal College of Art while, as at Rugby, attending evening classes at Chelsea School of Art and Central School of Art. After a travelling scholarship which took him widely across the continent, Gapper in 1928 began working in North Wales granite quarries and won his first commissions for sculpture. From 1934–62 was a lecturer in art at the University College of Wales, Aberystwyth. In 1973 he gained an honorary Master of Arts degree from the University of Wales. Carried out many commissions, mainly in Wales, including the Thetis memorial, at Holyhead, Gwynedd, and the portrait bust of Alun Lewis in Aberdare. Lived in Aberystwyth.

Elena GAPUTYTE 1927–1991 Sculptor, draughtsman, installations artist, gallery proprietor and teacher, born in Shiaulai, Lithuania. Her parents were farmers, and she retained a love of the land and a kinship with country people. With three brothers and a sister Gaputyte (pronounced Gaputeeta) escaped from the Communist incursion by fleeing to Germany in 1944. She left a displaced persons camp to study history of art at Ludwigs University, Frieburg, and drawing and weaving at L'École des Arts et Métiers there. After two years, in 1948 she left for Canada, settling in Montreal and studying at L'École des Beaux-Arts. In 1951 she moved to Toronto and after working for a year as a bank clerk enrolled in the sculpture class at Ontario College of Art. Became a Canadian citizen and moved to Paris in 1953, studying at L'École des Beaux-Arts under the sculptor Marcel-Antoine Gimond. Moved to St Ives in Cornwall in 1956, becoming a member of the Penwith Society of Arts, and in 1960 opened The Sail Loft Gallery, the year she obtained a French government scholarship, studying again briefly with Gimond. In 1963 at the Sail Loft, she held a Peter Lanyon retrospective. After moving to London Gaputyte studied bronze casting at Hammersmith College of Art. She was in charge of the sculpture department at Digby Stuart College, 1964–77, was an examiner for London University's Institute of Education, 1969, and was recognised as a London University teacher in 1976. In 1975 Gaputyte was winner of the Arts Council and Eastern Arts Association Open Air Sculpture Competition, Key Theatre, Peterborough. In the late-1970s she progressed to installations, mainly concerned with the memory of the war dead. Took part in many exhibitions internationally from 1953 and from 1961, when she had a show at The Gallery, Penzance, had around two dozen solo exhibitions. Later ones included Richard Demarco Gallery, Edinburgh, and Transmission Gallery, Glasgow, both installations and in 1989. Work is held by public and private collections in many countries.

Richard GARBE 1876–1957 Sculptor in various materials of figures and animals, full name Louis Richard Garbe. Born in London, the son of a maker of ivory and tortoiseshell objects, to whom he was apprenticed. Then studied at Central School of Arts and Crafts and the Royal Academy Schools. Became an instructor in sculpture at the Central School, 1901–29, then professor of sculpture at the Royal College of Art, 1929–46. Garbe was a fellow of the RBS, began exhibiting at the RA from 1908 and was elected RA in 1936. Also exhibited RMS, Walker Art Gallery, Liverpool, and Royal Glasgow Institute of the Fine Arts. Monumental work includes some on the National Museum of Wales, Cardiff. Tate Gallery and many provincial galleries hold his work. Lived at Westcott, Surrey.

Meta GARBETT 1881– Painter, notably in pastel, born at Heene, Sussex. She was educated privately, and also art privately with the miniaturist Edwin Morgan. Was a member of St Ives Society of Artists and PS, at both of which she showed, also RI, UA and at Paris Salon. Finally lived in Paignton, Devon.

Adriana GARCIA 1967– Painter of carefully considered still lifes who studied in Italy at the Florence Academy of Art, where she established a high reputation. She also made postgraduate studies at the Byam Shaw School. Garcia exhibited with the Albemarle Gallery and Waterman Fine Art and in 2005 was included in Still Lifes and Sketchbooks at the New Grafton Gallery.

Louise GARDAM 1965– Figurative painter who graduated in fine art from Bristol Polytechnic faculty of art and design. As well as solo exhibitions, showed with Bruton Gallery, Holmfirth, in Showcase, 2003. Gardam was inspired by travels through Europe and medieval and Byzantine images, her iconic pictures being notable for intricate detail and the use of gold and silver.

Anna GARDINER 1966– Painter and draughtsman, born and lived in London, who passed out with a distinction in her diploma at Chelsea School of Art, 1986–8; graduated at Brighton Polytechnic, 1988–91; then did a Royal Academy Schools diploma, 1991–4. Won a British Institute Fund Prize for Painting, 1993; and in 1994 a George Isted Prize and NatWest 90s Prize for Art first prize. Mixed shows included Art for Youth, Mall Galleries, and RA Summer Exhibition, 1992–3; New Discoveries, Boundary Gallery, 1994; and No Turkeys – Part II, Raw Gallery, 1995. Had a solo exhibition at Art First, 1996, remarkable for a series of paintings of small girls, Velázquez's pictures of children in the Prado, Madrid, having been an inspiration. NatWest Group, Arthur Andersen & Company, Capital Group Studios and De Vigier Foundation in Switzerland hold Gardiner's work.

Clive GARDINER 1891–1960 Designer, illustrator, printmaker, painter and teacher, born in Blackburn, Lancashire. His father was the editor of the *Daily News*, A G Gardiner, his wife the painter Lilian Lancaster, his son the writer and architect Stephen Gardiner. Gardiner was educated at University College School, toyed with journalism, then studied at Slade School of Fine Art, 1909–12, Royal Academy Schools, 1913–14. After World War I duties at the Ministry of Munitions Gardiner took an art teaching course, then taught at Brighton School of Art. Under the influence of Puvis de Chavannes he had shown for several years at RA and NEAC. In 1918 Gardiner became a part-time teacher at Bolt Court School of Art and Goldsmiths' College School of Art. Gardiner began to extend his range, illustrating his father's books, painting portraits and completing posters. These included notable work for London Underground, Empire Marketing Board and Shell. On the strength of that he was appointed headmaster/ later principal of Goldsmiths', 1929–57, where he had considerable influence in advancing the modern movement, his own style being successively impressed by Cézanne, Derain, Picasso and Braque. In 1936 he had his only one-man show, of paintings, at French Gallery. Gardiner carried out substantial work as a decorator, including murals for Sir John Benn's Hostel, Stepney; Toynbee Hall; and the Students' Union of London University. During World War II he advised on the design and decoration of British Restaurants. In his final years Gardiner produced small oils and watercolours in his original more reflective vein, regularly visiting the Scilly Isles. Arts Council put on a memorial show in 1963, South London Art Gallery, 1967. There was an exhibition of Gardiner's Isles of Scilly paintings at The Charleston Gallery, Firle, 2001.

Dan GARDINER 1966– Painter and mixed-media artist. His abstract pictures drew imagery from industrial backgrounds and had an underlying social concern, as in his prizewinning canvas Boom? at John Moores Liverpool Exhibition 1989–90. Gardiner was born in Hitchin, Hertfordshire, studying at Hertfordshire College of Art and Design, St Albans, 1984–5, and Liverpool Polytechnic, 1986–9. Was included in Girobank National exhibition at Mercury Court, Liverpool, 1988, and in 1989–90 showed works at Liverpool Airport in conjunction with Merseyside Boroughs. Lived in Hitchin for some time.

Gerald GARDINER 1902–1959 Landscape painter in oil, and teacher. Born in London, he studied at Beckenham School of Art, under Percy Jowett, 1919–23, then at the Royal College of Art, 1923–7. Exhibited RA, NEAC, RSA and Cooling Galleries. During World War II he completed wall decorations for the Cheltenham Services Club, a year later illustrating Fred Kitchen's book *Jesse and His Friends*. Work in several public collections. Gardiner's landscapes are notable for their translucent colour. Lived in Stroud, Gloucestershire.

Jeremy GARDINER 1957– Painter and teacher, born in Munster, Germany, who gained an honours degree in fine art from Newcastle University, 1975–79, taught by Kenneth Rowntree, then his master's in painting from the Royal College of Art, 1980–3, under Peter de Francia. He was awarded a series of fellowships, including Arts Council Artist in Industry, 1979; Churchill, 1984; Harkness, 1984–6; New York Foundation for the Arts, 1987; and Florida Council on the Arts, 1995. Teaching included Royal College of Art; in America Pratt Institute of Art and Design and the School of Visual Arts, both in New York, New World School of the Arts, University of Florida, and Bennington College, Vermont; and from 1999 a professorship at London College of Music and Media. Exhibited widely internationally in mixed shows. In his 1999 Spring Show, at Gallery 27, James Huntington-Whiteley included paintings by Gardiner of Ballard Point, Dorset, viewed from the room used in 1935 by Paul Nash when writing the *Shell Guide to Dorset*. The stylised, abstracted pictures were on wooden panels, gesso-layered and painted to create multi-textural works with varying strata. In 2000 Gardiner's solo exhibition Ballard Point toured to Neuhoff Gallery, New York; Pier Trust Gallery, Swanage; and Belgrave Gallery, curated by Keith H Chapman. Gardiner was also involved in Purbeck Light Years, described as "a three-dimensional temporal arena which evokes a calm, receptive state of mind," which involved a mix of traditional and modern techniques. Northcote Gallery held Purbeck Light Years – Corfe Castle in 2004. In that year Gardiner also had a show at Maltby Gallery, Winchester, and one at Gallery 286 which comprised views of the Brazilian archipelago of Fernando de Noronha. In 1999, Gardiner moved to Bath, Somerset. Peterborough Museum and Art Gallery, the Imperial College of Science, Royal College of Art, St Thomas's Hospital and several corporate collections hold Gardiner's work.

Mary GARDINER 1931– Artist in pencil, pastel, watercolour and textiles, and teacher, sometimes known as Meg Gardiner, who was born and lived in Barry, Glamorgan. Her husband was the sculptor Robert Thomas, her son the painter Ceri Thomas. She studied at Cardiff College of Art, 1947–50, and Royal College of Art, 1950–3, under Margaret Leischner, gaining a Cotton Board Scholarship, 1951–2. She married Robert Thomas in 1952 and taught textiles at Ealing School of Art, 1954–69, returning to Wales in 1971, where she taught until retirement in 1991. Close contact with the designer Ernest Race and his wife Sally was cited as a key influence on Gardiner's development. Fidelis Furnishing Fabrics, Moygashel/Stevenson & Sons, Otterburn Tweeds, Lurex Dobeckmen & Company and Tootal used Gardiner's talents. She showed at Albany Art Gallery, Cardiff, in 1989.

Meg GARDINER: *see* **Mary GARDINER**

Rena GARDINER 1929–1999 Artist and teacher who created and hand-printed several dozen guide books noted for their strong, direct images, many commissioned by the National Trust. Gardiner studied at Kingston School of Art in the early 1950s where she was much influenced by the work of Edward Bawden, John Piper and Eric Ravilious. She also attended the Institute of Education. Her interest in book illustration was inspired by the early illustrated Penguin Books, especially by Puffin Picture Books and the illustrations of S R Badmin, whose minutely detailed images she emulated. She taught art full-time until 1970, then lived by printing and her Workshop Press books. Gardiner's method, which took over 20 years to perfect, employed an autolithographic process in which she drew directly onto an aluminium litho printing plate instead of a litho stone. Colours were often added as printing proceeded using a standard commercial offset litho press. Each book took over a year to complete, yet despite print runs of up to 3,000 copies no two volumes were exactly the same, balances of colour and ink weight varying throughout the run. As demand for her books increased Gardiner employed photographic plates for some publications, hand-drawn ones having a limited life and requiring drawing again for reprints. The entire, often physically demanding, drawing-to-binding process took place in her thatched cottage at Tarrant Monkton, Dorset.

Gardiner's Workshop Press books in the early 1990s were still selling for two or three pounds. By then, the long-out-of-print 1969 title *The Isle of Purbeck* had a second-hand value of £50.

Stanley Horace GARDINER 1887–1952 Painter, notably of landscape, and teacher, born in Reading, Berkshire, winning a scholarship to its University, also studying at Patrick Allan-Fraser School of Art, Hospitalfield, Arbroath, having on leaving school been apprenticed to a decorator. Gardiner taught for a time at University College in Reading and also worked and taught in America, returning to England in World War I to enrol. In the mid-1920s he moved to Lamorna, near Penzance, Cornwall, where initially he endured poverty, although eventually he began to exhibit widely and ran his own small painting school from home. He was elected an associate of RWS and a member of the New Society of Artists, also showing at Fine Art Society, RWA, Irish Salon, RA, Walker Art Gallery in Liverpool and Berkshire Art Society.

Vanessa GARDINER 1960– Painter and collagist. She was a student at Oxford Polytechnic for its arts foundation course, 1978–9, then graduated from Central School of Art and Design with an honours degree in fine art, 1979–82. Her work was specifically based on the coastal and inland landscapes of West Dorset, but instead of being representational it abstracted the forms of sea and land. Gardiner appeared in mixed exhibitions at Allsop Gallery, Bridport, 1991–2; at Athelhampton House, Dorset, in 1992; and from 1991 showed solo at Duncan Campbell Gallery. She gained a South West Arts Award, 1999–00, in 1999–00 and 2000–01 Bournemouth University commissions.

Alexandra GARDNER 1945– Painter and draughtsman and teacher, born in Bellshill, Lanarkshire. She studied at Glasgow School of Art, 1963–8, with David Donaldson and William Drummond Bone, then lectured there, 1968–88. Ill health prompted early retirement, but after a successful second kidney transplant in 1990 Gardner "continued to paint, but more prolific and yet more disciplined." Uccello, Vermeer and Morandi were influences on Gardner's work, but her themed pictures remained distinctively her own. These included still life, nude, bar interior, American diner and barbershop series. Gardner was a member of the Royal Glasgow Institute of the Fine Arts. She won a series of awards, including Glasgow Society of Women Artists, Scottish Arts Council Lady Artists' Fund and Cleveland 5th International Drawing Biennale. Was a prolific exhibitor in mixed exhibitions, including RSA, 1969; RSW, 1976; Fine Art Society, 1981; Lillie Gallery, Milngavie, 1986; and Art Expo, New York, 1993, with Duncan Miller Fine Art. Had a solo show at Royal Scottish Academy of Music & Drama, Glasgow, 1968, later ones including Mayfest, Gatehouse Gallery, Glasgow, 1993, Duncan R Miller Fine Arts from 1994, and The Scottish Gallery Edinburgh, from 1997. Gardner's exhibition at Portland Gallery, 2003, included Parisian, Venetian and Maltese subjects. Kelvingrove Art Gallery in Glasgow and Glasgow Corporation hold her work.

Ann GARDNER 1964– Painter who studied at Slade School of Fine Art. She obtained an honours degree in 1986, The Slade Higher Diploma in Painting three years later. Among her group appearances was The Slade in the North, Halifax, and Four Counties Show, 1987; Whitechapel Open, 1989; The Prose of Painting, at Austin/Desmond Fine Art, 1991; and A Second Perspective, at Leighton House, 1991. She won 10 awards and prizes between 1982–92, including The Pearson Prize for Drawing and Painting; The Henry Tonks Prize; The Monnington Prize; First Prize for Painting, British Institution Fund of the RA; and a Boise Scholarship to travel and paint, which took her to New York. Had a solo show at Bedford Library in 1991 and shared an exhibition at Cadogan Contemporary in 1992. She was a fluid painter, interested in fleeting effects of light and atmosphere. Lived in London, but worked some of the time in France.

Annette GARDNER 1920– Painter in oil and teacher, born in London. She studied at Twickenham Art School, 1952–4, after always drawing and painting as a child. Then attended Hampstead Garden Suburb Institute, 1954–6, and St Martin's School of Art, 1960–3, under David Tindle. Gardner, who sometimes painted as Annette Gardner-Wood, was particularly interested in Abstract Expressionism and cited Walter Nessler as her main teacher and influence. When her husband died in 1972 she took over the principalship of Wood Tutorial College, teaching art and other subjects until 1988. She was a member of the Ben Uri Art Society, Free Painters and Sculptors and Hampstead Artists' Council and participated in many group and travelling shows. Lived in Edgware, Middlesex.

Derek George Montague GARDNER 1914– Marine artist in oil and watercolour, born in Gerrards Cross, Buckinghamshire, entirely self-taught. He served in the Royal Naval Volunteer Reserve, 1934–47, retiring as a commander, and was mentioned in dispatches, HMS *Broke*, 1942. From 1947–63 Gardner worked as a chartered civil engineer for the Ministry of Works in Kenya. Was elected to RSMA in 1966, in 1988 being made honorary vice-president for life. Gardner's work was featured in many marine painting reference books. He took part in group shows of the Kenya Art Society, 1950–63; UA and RSMA from 1958; and from 1982 at Mystic Maritime Gallery in America, and elsewhere. Had a series of solo shows at Polak Gallery from 1972. Nelson's Ships: a Trafalgar Tribute was at Messum's in 2005. An illustrated book with the same title, text by Ian Collins and essays on each featured vessel, accompanied the exhibition. National Maritime Museum at Greenwich, Britannia Royal Naval College in Dartmouth and the Bermuda Maritime Museum hold examples. Lived at Corfe Mullen, Wimborne, Dorset.

Diana GARDNER 1913–1997 Writer and artist who began painting early, attending the Regent Street Polytechnic School of Art and Westminster School of Art, studying in Mark Gertler's life class, 1937–9. She became friendly with the artist Mervyn Peake. After her art studies, Gardner worked for 18 months in a studio in Chiswick, producing wood engravings for book illustration. She became a member of SWE and trained as a typographer. As an aspiring writer, she was excited when, in 1934, she had settled in Rodmell, Sussex, becoming neighbours of Leonard and Virginia Woolf, befriending him after his wife's suicide. In 1946 Gardner published a book of short stories, *Halfway Down The Cliff*, in 1954 a novel, *The Indian Woman*. She took up painting in 1968, notably landscape watercolours, in the 1980s becoming noted for her accurate depictions of old cars. Groups of these were acquired by the Royal Automobile Club and its Motor

Sports Association. The Bloomsbury Workshop held a memorial show in 1999.

Grace GARDNER fl. from 1960s– Painter in abstract styles, colour and the theme of ribbons being important. Three teachers were key influences: Frances Richardson, Rudolph Pen and Kwok Wai Lau. Gardner was based at The Gallery, Portscatho, Cornwall, living in Flushing. Mixed shows included Purdue University, Lafayette, Indiana, America, 1966; Galleria d'Arte Sistina, Rome, Italy, 1972; American Artists in Britain, at Universities of Hull and Leeds, 1976; Neville-Sargent Gallery, Evanston, Illinois, 1984; and Hicks Gallery, 1995. Had a series of solo exhibitions at Drian Galleries from 1972, later ones including Falmouth Art Gallery, Falmouth, 1985, to which she offered to bequeath her extensive collection of contemporary Cornish artists' works. Her own pictures were held by the Polish National Museum, Warsaw; National Gallery of Poland, Gdansk; American Embassy, Rome; and American corporate collections.

Ian GARDNER 1944– Painter and teacher, notable as a landscape watercolourist. He studied at Lancaster School of Art and Nottingham College of Art. He pursued a full-time lecturing career until 1979, after which he taught part-time at several Colleges of Art, most notably as professor in art and design at University of Illinois, 1986–7. Between 1981–6 he was co-editor, with Patrick Eyres, of *New Arcadian Press*, a quarterly journal dealing with landscape issued in text and image. Began working in watercolour in 1969, eventually concentrating on the Morecambe Bay area of Lancashire with its dramatic coastline, and his own allotment, as seen in North by North West, Bolton Museum and Art Gallery, 1996. Work in many public and private collections.

Ivy H GARDNER 1894–1975 This was the working name of Jane Ivy Hunter Fergusson Gardner, a sculptor and modeller of mainly figurative pieces, notably portraits of children. She was born in Greenock, where the McLean Museum and Art Gallery holds her work, lived in Gourock in the 1920s and then moved to Glasgow. She trained at Glasgow School of Art, 1914–25, in the latter year joining the Glasgow Society of Lady Artists. Gardner was a prolific exhibitor at the Royal Glasgow Institute of the Fine Arts and RSA, also showing at Walker Art Gallery, Liverpool, and the bust Ronald at RA Summer Exhibition, 1937. Won the Lauder Award four times between 1929 and 1953. Lived in Glasgow. She was assistant to the sculptors Benno Schotz and Alexander Proudfoot, whom she married in 1955, two years before he died.

Pam GARDNER 1920– Painter, draughtsman and jewellery designer, born in Bray, Berkshire. She studied art at London Polytechnic and jewellery with Goldsmiths' and Silversmiths' Company. Showed mainly in west of England, notably at Days Mill Gallery in Nailsworth and Cygnet Gallery in Stroud, near where she lived in Amberley, Gloucestershire.

Peter GARDNER 1921– Painter in oil and teacher, born in London. He studied at Hammersmith School of Art, 1935–8 and 1946–50, teachers including Herbert Holt and Harold Workman, then London University Institute of Education, 1950–1. Taught for a time at Plaistow Grammar School and was honorary secretary of the Society of Fulham Artists. Was elected ROI in 1977, also showing with Trafford Gallery, RA and NEAC. Hammersmith Borough Council and Nuffield Foundation, York University, hold his work. Lived latterly at Shaftesbury, Dorset.

Stephen Reginald GARDNER 1948– Painter, born in Prestwich, Lancashire, who studied art locally and showed in Manchester at Colin Jellicoe Gallery and in Lincolnshire, notably at Portfolio Gallery, Scunthorpe. Lived in Manchester.

Tim GARDNER 1958– Artist who attended Camberwell School of Arts and Crafts, 1976–7, then graduated with honours in fine art from Wimbledon School of Art, 1978–81. Group shows participated in included East End Open Studios, at Belsham Street, 1989.

Annette GARDNER-WOOD: *see* **Annette GARDNER**

Rachel GARFIELD 1963– Artist, lecturer and curator who graduated with honours from North East London Polytechnic, 1982–5. She later gained her master's degree from Central St Martins and a fine art doctorate from the Royal College of Art. Garfield was a regular speaker at conferences on the themes of belonging and cultural politics, especially in relation to Jewish and female identities. She taught fine art, graphic design, photography and critical theory at tertiary graduate and postgraduate levels. Mixed exhibitions included Union Chapel in Islington, Open Exhibition at Ben Uri Art Society and Patricia Knight Gallery, all 1987; Arteast Collective Group Show, Preston Arts Centre, 1988; and East End Open Studios, at Britannia Works, 1989. In 1988, Garfield took part in Vanda Garvey, Rachel Garfield, Art in the Park, Walthamstow. Among Garfield's solo shows was You'd Think So, Wouldn't You?, video installations and photographs, which toured from the University of Hertfordshire Galleries, one venue being the Southend Central Library Focal Point Gallery in 2006.

William GARFIT 1944– Painter and draughtsman with an interest in country subjects, born in Cambridge, near where he settled at Harlton. He attended Cambridge School of Art, 1963; Byam Shaw School of Drawing and Painting, 1964–7, under Maurice de Sausmarez; and at Royal Academy Schools, 1967–70, with Peter Greenham. He illustrated a number of countryside books. Exhibited with Cambridge Drawing Society and RBA both of which he was a member, and had solo exhibitions at Tryon and Moorland Gallery and elsewhere.

Margaret Lester GARLAND 1893–1976 Artist, born in Oxford, who attended Royal College of Art design school, 1925–7, where she met Helen Binyon, who became a lifelong friend. During 1930s showed with NEAC and painted a mural for Holy Trinity Church, Bath, destroyed during World War II. After war taught briefly at Bath Art School, then at Bath Academy of Art, 1946–58. By then she had settled in Bath, showing with Bath Society of Artists. Showed at Arcade Gallery; Barber Institute in Birmingham; Leva Gallery; and at David Paul Gallery, Chichester, in 1978.

Mollie GARLAND 1920– Painter and teacher, educated in Liverpool, who studied at the City School of Art there, 1938–41, under Will Penn, then at the Slade School of Fine Art, 1941–2. Was a member of the Sandon Studios Society and Liverpool Academy and joined the staff of Liverpool City School of Art. Exhibited RA, RBA, Manchester Academy and widely in the Liverpool area, where she lived. Liverpool's Walker Art Gallery holds her work.

Daphne GARMAN 1913– Sculptor, born in Beaconsfield, Buckinghamshire, as Evelyn Daphne Garman. Trained as a sculptor in 1933–8 with Anne Acheson and showed with SWA as a student. Her nursing career in the war and family commitments interrupted her sculpting until the early 1970s, when she studied recent developments in casting and resumed working in clay or wax for finishing in bronze, resin bronze plaster or terracotta. Was elected to NS in 1980 and SWA in 1985, also exhibiting with SPS and in the provinces and having several shows with her husband, R C Garman. She specialised in portraits human and animal, especially of horses and dogs. An interest in sight-hounds led to a commission from Asprey for a galloping saluki. Winsor & Newton ordered portrait bronzes of their founders, on display in the firm's museum, and Garman also made religious works and imaginative pieces in limited editions. Lived latterly in Cheltenham, Gloucestershire.

Kitty GARMAN 1927– Artist who studied at the Central School of Arts and Crafts in the late 1940s under Bernard Meninsky and John Farleigh. She was married until divorce in 1953 to the painter Lucian Freud, who had often visited the Central to make etchings and lithographs. Following that marriage she stopped painting, only starting again after marrying the noted economist and musician Wynne Godley, having felt that she was "surrounded by male artists all painting me." Her picture Wynne's Dressing Gown, the first work she made for 18 years and typical of the intimate, personal twist that she brought to her work, was included in Kitty Garman and Co, an exhibition at New Art Gallery Walsall in 2003–4, which for the first time assembled three generations of artists: Garman herself, Annie and Annabel Freud and May Cornet – the daughter, granddaughters and great-granddaughter of the sculptor Jacob Epstein and the wife, daughters and granddaughter of Lucian Freud. The painter Theo Garman was Kitty's brother. The Garman Ryan Collection at Walsall was created by Kitty Garman's mother Kathleen and her friend Sally Ryan. Kitty Garman was noted for her delicate watercolours of objects and environment around her, often reflecting her musical, literary and horticultural interests. Latterly, she returned to life modelling for local art classes in East Anglia, where she lived in Cavendish, Suffolk.

Theo GARMAN 1924–1954 Painter and draughtsman, son of the artist Jacob Epstein and his most famous model, Kathleen Garman. His sister Kitty Garman was also an artist. A gifted child, he aspired to an academic career after Oxford University. In preparation for this he did a correspondence course after leaving school while, as a conscientious objector in World War II, working as a cowhand in Sussex, and intensively painting, the result being a severe breakdown. Continued to paint, living in London, and had two exhibitions, at Redfern Gallery, in 1950–2. His work was much admired by Wyndham Lewis, Kenneth Clark and Matthew Smith, who called Garman a "genius". An unworldly man, Garman was familiar with the art treasures of Europe and was, like his father, a fervent collector, concentrating on medieval religious pieces. His own pictures were intense and richly coloured, not unlike those of Van Gogh. Garman-Ryan Collection at Walsall Art Gallery holds his work. A small selection was shown in a retrospective at Fine Art Society in 1989.

David GARNER 1958– Sculptor and teacher, born in Ebbw Vale, Monmouthshire. He studied foundation at Newport Art College, 1977–8; graduated with honours, Cardiff Art College, 1978–81; gaining his master's fine art, Royal College of Art, 1981–4, with a Paris Studio Scholarship, 1983. Lectured at Coleg Gwent from 1985 and Gwent College of Higher Education, 1986–94. In 1996 was involved in Community Schools Project, St David's Hall, Cardiff. Garner's work dealt with national and international issues which he felt needed a personal response. "I believe art should reflect the time in which it was made". Group appearances included Welsh Sculpture, Margam Sculpture Park, 1993; National Eisteddfod, Bala, prize winner, 1997; Labour Intensive, The City Gallery, Leicester, 2000; and Welsh Artists Talking, National Museum of Wales, Cardiff, 2000–1. Among solo shows were Political Games, WAC Gallery, Cardiff, 1996, and Aberystwyth Arts Centre, 2003.

Edith Mary GARNER 1881– Painter, born at Wasperton, Warwickshire. She was married to the artist William Lee-Hankey and modelled for some of his pictures. After education at the North London Collegiate School, she studied at the Slade School of Fine Art and on the continent. Had an interest in the theatre. Showed RA, NS, ROI and Paris Salon. Her work is held by Leamington Art Gallery. Lived in London.

Angelica GARNETT 1918– Artist, daughter of the painter Vanessa Bell, born at Charleston Farmhouse, Firle, Sussex. In 1936 she attended the London Theatre Studio drama school, in 1938 the Euston Road School to study art, which she then taught at Langford Grove School, 1940. In 1941 she worked on the Berwick Church murals with her mother, Duncan Grant and Quentin Bell, the next year marrying the writer David Garnett, by whom she had four daughters. Continued to paint, organise art courses and run exhibitions while living in Huntingdonshire. Garnett worked with George Bergen in New York, 1967–8, lived in Sussex from 1977, in 1984 settling in France at Forcalquier. Solo shows included Grafton, Upper Street and Marjorie Parr Galleries and Southover Gallery, Lewes. Later exhibitions included The Crescent Gallery, Cedar Springs, Dallas, Texas, 1986, and Deborah Gage (Works of Art), where her 1993 exhibition Transformations comprised objects made from plastic bags, bottles, cans, corks and feathers. Garnett also gained a reputation as a designer of textiles, book jackets, pottery decoration and mosaics.

Eve GARNETT 1900–1991 Landscape painter, muralist, book illustrator and writer, born in Worcestershire. She studied at Chelsea Polytechnic School of Art, at Royal Academy Schools, where she won the Creswick Prize and Silver Medal, and with Alexander Jamieson. Travelled extensively. Exhibited at Tate Gallery, ROI, SWA and NEAC. Was most noted for her children's books and *The Family from One End Street*, 1937, which won the Carnegie Gold Medal, and its sequels. In 1948 she illustrated Robert Louis Stevenson's *A Child's Garden of Verses*. The volume *First Affections* told of her early childhood. Lived in Lewes, Sussex.

Geoffrey Sneyd GARNIER 1889–1970 Printmaker, born in Wigan, Lancashire, he was married to the painter Jill Garnier. Left Charterhouse in 1907, obtained a City and Guilds certificate in engineering and while working in Toronto decided on art as a career. Returned to England in 1910, studied for two years at the School of Painting, Bushey, then in 1912 joined Stanhope Forbes' school in Newlyn, Cornwall, where he continued to live. Garnier's early work was often religious. Meticulously researched the lost art of the aquatint, but later concentrated on engraving. Showed at RA, RSA, RWA, SGA and in the north of England, where his work is held by Oldham Art Gallery and Museum and other galleries.

Jill GARNIER 1890–1966 Painter, especially of portraits, and fine draughtsman, born in Quidenham, Norfolk as Jessie Caroline Dunbar Blyth. Studied at Cheltenham Ladies' College, then from 1915 at Stanhope Forbes' school in Newlyn, Cornwall, where she met her husband the printmaker Geoffrey Sneyd Garnier. Exhibited at RA, RWA and was a member of both the Newlyn and St Ives Societies of Artists. A talented embroiderer, she reproduced some of her own pictures. Lived in Newlyn.

Charles GARRAD 1952– Artist, designer and teacher notable for his creation of atmospheric, unpeopled rooms. Born in Somerset, he studied at Stourbridge College of Art, 1969–70; Cardiff College of Art, 1970–3; and Chelsea School of Art, 1973–4. Went on to teach, including Chelsea. After being artist-in-residence at the Institute of Modern Art in Brisbane, 1979, in 1980 he lectured throughout Australia, in 1982 working in television design. He gained a Greater London Arts Association Major Award in 1981. Group shows included New Contemporaries '74 at ICA, 1974; Out of the Blue, Acme Gallery, 1978; mural work for Greater London Arts Association in Covent Garden, 1980; and Summer Show 1 at Serpentine Gallery, 1983. Had a solo show at Chapter Arts Centre, Cardiff, 1973, later ones including Institute of Modern Art, Brisbane, 1979. Lived for a time in London.

Peter John GARRARD 1929–2004 Painter, teacher, writer and editor, born in Peterborough, Huntingdonshire, who attended Byam Shaw School of Drawing and Painting. Garrard taught Latin at Summerfields School, Oxford; was commissioned with the Suffolk Regiment during National Service; taught at Byam Shaw; wrote for and became editor of *The Artist* magazine, 1972–9; started an art workshop at Mary Ward Centre; was a judge for the Shell Children's Art Competition and chairman of judges for the Spirit of London Art Competition; and ran numerous painting holidays in Britain and abroad. He edited the ninth edition of *The Artist's Guide*, 1976, and was author of *Learn to Paint in Oils*, 1980. Garrard, who signed his work PJG, was an exhibitor at the RA Summer Exhibition annually from 1954–87, also taking part in mixed shows in the provinces and London. He was president of the RBA, winning its De Laszlo Medal, also being a full member of the RP, NEAC, RWA and Art Workers' Guild. He won the Knapping Prize and twice the David Murray Scholarship. He had five solo shows at the Mall Galleries in 1974, 1976, 1978, 1984 and 1985, also at other London galleries. The RA, Royal Hospital in Chelsea, Royal Borough of Kensington and Chelsea and Hull City Council hold examples, which are also in many private collections around the world. Garrard lived in London.

Rose GARRARD 1946– Versatile artist, designer, sculptor and teacher, born in Bewdley, Worcestershire. She did a foundation course at Stourbridge College of Art & Design, 1965–6; gained a first-class honours degree in sculpture from Birmingham College of Art, 1966–9; did a postgraduate master's degree (higher diploma in sculpture) at Chelsea School of Art, 1969–70; then gained a British Council/French government scholarship to École des Beaux-Arts, Paris, 1970–1. Garrard won a number of international awards and residencies, including The South London Gallery, 1994, where for her show Arenas for Conversation she based works of art on chats with people who visited her. Garrard had numerous mixed and solo shows, the latter including Talisman, Louise Hallett Gallery, 1988; Calgary Conversation, New Art Gallery, Calgary, 1991; and Disclosing Dialogues, Vancouver Art Gallery, Canada, 1992. She lectured widely, including Reading University, Trent and Sheffield Polytechnics, Croydon College of Art and Dartington College of Arts. Was also a freelance designer, notably for BBC and to architects, including The Spirit of the City, a 30-foot bronze wall sculpture near Old Street tube station. Arts Council, Henry Moore Sculpture Trust and Victoria & Albert Museum hold examples.

John Geoffrey GARRATT 1914–1986 Artist in oil, watercolour, pen and ink. Born in Wallasey, Merseyside, Garratt studied at Brighton College of Art and made his career as a bookseller. He became known as an expert on model soldiers and wargaming, publishing a series of books on the subject, including the *World Encyclopedia of Model Soldiers*. He also wrote a book on drawing landscape in pen and ink and *Westcountryman's England*. He exhibited widely, including the RA, Imperial Institute and galleries in Brighton, Bolton, Eastbourne, Cheltenham and Blackpool. Several museums and galleries hold his work, including his home town of Farnham, Surrey.

Jonathan GARRATT 1964– Artist and teacher involved in ceramics, installations, environmental art and sculpture, born in London, who studied ceramics under Gordon Baldwin at Eton College. Gained an exhibition in French and German, Cambridge, 1973, graduating in archaeology, 1976. He was assistant to the ceramist Seamus O'Brien, 1978, then established Bartley Pottery in the New Forest, 1980, and Hare Lane Pottery, at Cranborne, Dorset, 1986. Garratt concentrated on wood-firing a locally dug clay (terracotta) for a wide range of work. Many of the influences on this derived from pre-historic pottery and artefacts and from tribal arts. In 1999 Garratt was a part-time lecturer, ceramics, Harrow Campus, University of Westminster. He exhibited widely, 2003 shows including Heifer Gallery with Georgina Fermer, Chelsea Physic Garden and Saltram House, Devon. In 2004 he participated in Dorset Open Studios. Lance Blackstone, Contemporary Art Society; the actress Miranda Richardson; and gardening broadcaster and writer Alan Titchmarsh owned his work.

Sam GARRATT 1865–1947 Painter of landscapes and historical scenes and etcher, born in Barwell, Leicestershire. His father was a farm labourer, Sam became a bootmaker and studied for 15 years in the evenings at the local School of Art. He settled in Brecon and showed at the Eisteddfod, his picture King Charles Leaving the Priory, Brecon, winning a prize. Also showed at RCamA, RHA,

Walker Art Gallery in Liverpool, RA and elsewhere. He was a member of Brecon Conservative Club.

Albert Charles GARRETT 1915–1983 Painter in oil, and wood engraver. Born at Kingsclere, Hampshire, he studied painting under Sir William Coldstream and engraving with John Buckland-Wright, attending successively Camberwell School of Art in 1947–9, the Anglo-French Art Centre in 1949–50 and the Slade School of Fine Art 1950–1. Among Garrett's appointments was senior art lecturer at the Polytechnic of North London, chairmanship of Mall Prints and presidency of the SWE. Among his many books and papers, some of which were learned analyses of light and colour in particular environments, were volumes on the *Wood Engravings and Drawings of Iain Macnab* and *British Wood Engraving of the 20th Century*. Garrett participated in numerous international exhibitions, where he won several medals. One-man shows included the Woodstock Gallery in 1961, Mall Galleries in 1972 and the University of Windsor, Ontario, in 1979. There was a comprehensive exhibition of Garrett's work at Wolseley Fine Arts in 2004 accompanied by a catalogue with a checklist of prints by his daughter Viven Garrett. Derby Art Gallery, the Ferens Art Gallery, in Hull, and several other British and foreign galleries hold his work. Lived in Ruislip, Middlesex.

Violet Nellie GARROD 1898–1981 Painter, draughtsman, miniaturist and teacher, born in north London, who studied at Hampstead Garden Suburb Central Institute and St John's Wood School of Art, with Leonard Walker. Showed at RMS, SM of which she was a member, PS and elsewhere, winning gold medals for her miniatures at RA and Salon d'Été, Paris. During World War II Miss Garrod moved with her parents to Southbourne, founding the Art Group there; when she went to New Milton after the war she started a second group; following her parents' death, she and her sister moved to a flat overlooking the Royal Lymington Yacht Club, and the Palette Club began in 1954; on moving to Milford she taught in a hut in her garden, from which developed the Milford Art Group, in 1958. Among her portraits were large ones of Bishop Kenneth Lamplugh, Reverend Darrell Bunt, chaplain of the fleet, and of Olive Troke, first woman mayor of Lymington. Russell-Cotes Art Gallery and Museum, Bournemouth, holds her work. For her last decade lived in Swanage, Dorset, finally suffering a stroke.

Alethea GARSTIN 1894–1978 Painter, born in Penzance, daughter of the artist Norman Garstin. Began sketching with her father in France as a child, starting to paint seriously at 16, so that at 18 her first work was accepted by RA. Had no formal training apart from a brief period at Heatherley's School of Fine Art life drawing. For a time she drew for publications such as *Punch*, *The Tatler* and *The Sketch*. From 1912–77 she showed regularly in England and France, in all at nearly 60 galleries. Travelled extensively in Europe, Africa, Australia and the Caribbean. Some early work was in the Fauve manner, and her friends Edward Wolfe and Morland Lewis were also influences. The catalogue of the major exhibition of her father's and her work at the Penwith Gallery in 1978, which toured, records that she "had no theories" and "lived in the present"; and her pictures of places and people have a French spontaneity. Bristol City Art Gallery, National Trust and others hold her work. RWA member. She lived most of her life in Penzance, then when her studio was destroyed because of redevelopment she moved to Zennor, where she died. In 2002, Sotheby's, Billingshurst, held a studio sale of Alethea and Norman Garstin's work.

Michael GARTON 1935–2004 Landscape painter and art teacher who obtained his diploma from Slade School of Fine Art, 1957–60, and was elected RWA. It gave him a retrospective in 2005. Died in Exeter Hospice.

Ray GARVEY 1943–2001 Painter, graphic artist and teacher, born in Hitchin, Hertfordshire, who studied at St Martin's School of Art, Kingston College of Art and London University, 1963–8. His teaching experience included Croydon College of Design and Technology and Putney School of Art and in 1982 he was included in Artists in Adult Education at Woodlands Art Gallery. Other shows included Cockpit Theatre, 1970, Serpentine Gallery, 1974, and Towner Art Gallery, Eastbourne, 1981. Garvey had become head of the department of art and design at Fulham & South Kensington Adult Education Institute in 1979, taking a similar post at Westminster in 1986. In 1989, moved to Cornwall to concentrate on private teaching and his own work. In the late 1960s and early 1970s Garvey mainly painted abstracts, but the subsequent decade saw a change of direction as he decided that he was becoming too intellectual and should engage more emotionally and instinctively with his medium and the world about him, producing notable landscapes. Garvey had bought a house in St Maime, Haute Provence, France, in 1985, in the winter returning to work and teach in London, and it was while travelling to St Maime that he died. Latterly exhibited at Mall Galleries with RBA, PS, RI and NEAC and at RA Summer Exhibition, with regular solo shows at Bartley Drey Gallery.

Tirzah GARWOOD 1908–1951 Wood engraver, painter and modelmaker, born in Gillingham, Kent, but grew up in Eastbourne, Sussex, where aged 17 she entered Eastbourne School of Art. There she met her future husband, the artist Eric Ravilious. Next went to Central School of Arts and Crafts and began to exhibit her prints. Showed at SWE in 1927 and received commissions from BBC, Kynoch Press and Golden Cockerel Press. After Garwood married Ravilious in 1930 her output was restricted by domestic chores, but she collaborated with him on mural work. In the mid-1940s Garwood began painting, and creating her paper models of houses and chapels, with their singular, childlike charm. She continued this work after marrying Henry Swanzy in 1946, living for some time in Hampstead, London, but dying at Copford, near Colchester, in Essex. Towner Art Gallery, Eastbourne, held a memorial show in 1952 and a further comprehensive exhibition in 1987. Fry Art Gallery, Saffron Walden, holds her work.

David GASCOYNE 1916–2001 Writer on Surrealism, poet and artist, born in Harrow, Middlesex, who was educated at Salisbury Cathedral School and the Regent Street Polytechnic. Aged 16 his first volume of Symbolist poetry, *Roman Balcony*, was published; his *A Short Survey of Surrealism* appeared in 1935, as did his translation of André Breton's seminal text *What is Surrealism?*; and in the following year he was an organiser of the London International Surrealist Exhibition. Gascoyne showed three collages, one of which, Perseus and Andromeda, is now in the Tate Gallery collection. The Scottish National

Gallery of Modern Art, Edinburgh, has Gascoyne's scrap book, compiled in the early 1940s, part of the Gabrielle Keiller collection. He formed friendships with Breton, Salvador Dalí, Paul Eluard and Max Ernst and while living in Paris, 1953–64, produced 30 drawings and paintings at a time when he was unable to write. They were bought by Barbara, Countess of Moray, who framed, showed and sold all from her home in Edbury Street in 1961. Three drawings, entitled Doodles, were included in the exhibition I Surrealisti, at the Palazzo Reale, Milan, in 1989. The Derek Hill collection at Mottisfont Abbey, Hampshire, contains Gascoyne's watercolour Embrouillard. Gascoyne was made Chevalier dans l'Ordre des Arts et Lettres, for services to French literature, in 1996. Died in Newport, Isle of Wight.

Rosemary GASCOYNE fl. from early 1980s– Artist in oil on canvas or board, born in Norwich, Norfolk, who gained a diploma from Amersham College of Art, then an honours degree from Brighton University, 1981, where teachers included Chris Le Brun and Jack Smith. Took part in many group shows, including Centaur Gallery, 1985; Towner Art Gallery, Eastbourne, 1986; Brighton University, 1987–90; and Gracefield Art Centre, Dumfries, 1997. Had a solo exhibition at Trinity Arts Centre, Tunbridge Wells, 1986, later ones including Chambers Gallery, Moffat, and Gracefield Art Centre, both 1996. In 1993, Gascoyne moved to Dumfries and Galloway, establishing The Cree Gallery, Gatehouse of Fleet, where she exhibited. Shared an exhibition with Jenny Cowern at Linton Court Gallery, Settle, 2003.

Michael GASKELL 1963– Artist born at Billinge, Wigan, Lancashire, who studied at St Helens College of Art & Design, Coventry Polytechnic and Bretton Hall College. Went on to conduct many workshops for galleries, museums and art departments. Group shows included Mercia Artist Open, Herbert Art Gallery, Coventry, 1986; MAFA at Manchester City Art Gallery, from 1987; Make it Paper, Gateshead public gallery, 1995; and Royal Over-Seas League Open, 1996. Had a solo show at The Old Town Hall, Halton, 1990.

Nora GASTON fl. from mid-1960s– Artist and teacher whose work employed rich colours and a strong decorative element. She obtained a national diploma in design, painting and printing from Belfast College of Art, 1964, in 1979 graduating with a bachelor's degree in education from University of New Brunswick, Canada. She was arts adviser for the New Brunswick School Board before taking up the post of head of printmaking and surface design at New Brunswick Craft School, Fredericton, 1982. After a period as a member of Gallery Connection Studios there, Gaston moved to Saudi Arabia, working as an arts consultant and as adviser to Falcon Fine Art Gallery, Riyadh. In 1990 Gaston was appointed to the visual arts committee of the Northern Ireland Arts Council. Gaston was commissioned to make stained glass windows for a church in New Maryland, 1982, and for a hospital in Fredericton, 1984, and to complete a mural for Musgrave Park Hospital, 1992. Took part in many group shows, notably at Arts Council Gallery, Belfast, from 1989, and was included in the 1994 exhibitions Works on Paper and Beyond the Partitions, organised by Queen Street Studios, Belfast, with which she was associated. Had a series of solo shows in America, Canada and Saudi Arabia. Lived in Belfast, Northern Ireland.

Rosalind GATEHOUSE fl. c.1915–1950 Watercolourist educated in England and in Dresden, Germany. She exhibited RA, RCamA, Walker Art Gallery in Liverpool and RBSA, signing work with R G monogram. Lived in Witham, Essex.

Rupert GATFIELD 1959– Painter, draughtsman and printmaker, born in Kuala Lumpur, Malaya, who studied at Pangbourne College, where for his advanced-level course he was taught by artist Richard Shirley Smith who "greatly inspired" him. Did a foundation course in Worthing but considered himself "to be a self-taught Surrealist", painting full-time from 1983. The 1990s saw him concentrating on the theme of A Garden, square pictures in which Gatfield created his own world. Group exhibitions included Park Walk and Images Galleries, both 1984; RA Summer Exhibition from 1987; RWS and Royal Over-Seas League Exhibitions, both 1989; and Bordeaux Salon d'Hiver, 1993 (first prize). Had a solo show at Danziger Metcalfe, 1986; Konicus, Bristol, 1995; Beaux Arts, Bath, 1996; Carbon Synchronicity at John Martin of London, 2002, and Shadow Gardens, JohnMartinChelsea, 2004. Lloyd's of London and North Devon Academy of Art hold his work. Lived in Bristol.

Stuart Luke GATHERER 1971– Painter in oil of figurative works with an enigmatic story element, tense situations and artificial light predominating. Seventeenth-century Dutch painting, especially that of Vermeer, was a strong influence. He was brought up in the eastern highlands of Scotland, and graduated with his master's degree in fine art from Edinburgh College of Art, in 1995. Showed in Scotland and the north of England and was exhibited at Art97, Contemporary Art Fair, in 1997 by Portland Gallery, which that year gave him a first London solo show. He had major ones at Albemarle Gallery in 2001, 2002 and 2004, another in that year at Eleanor Ettinger Gallery, New York.

Jason GATHORNE-HARDY 1968– Painter, born in Malaya, who was brought up near the Suffolk coast. After studying zoology at Oxford University and researching conservation biology at the University of Kent, he took up drawing and painting full-time in 1993. Studied life drawing with Maggi Hambling at Morley College. His aim was "to translate the energy of the land into paintings for other people to see", and this he did by creating abstract, calligraphic shapes out of mud which he smeared and shaped. They had titles such as Orwell Estuary or Elmstead Market, as in his contribution to Cross Currents at Reed's Wharf Gallery at the Barbican Centre, 1996. In 1995 Reed's Wharf and Aldeburgh Cinema, Suffolk, gave him solo shows, as did Snape Maltings, nearby, in 1996. In that year, Gathorne-Hardy was a finalist in the Bayer Earth Art Competition, also being a finalist in Drawings for All, Gainsborough's House, Sudbury, 1999. Later solo exhibitions included Chappel Galleries, Chappel, 2001, work from New Zealand and the English rivers.

John Richardson GAULD fl. from 1911–1962 Painter, muralist and lithographer, born at Gateshead, County Durham. Studied at King Edward VII School of Art, Durham University, Royal College of Art and lithography at London County Council School. Became chief assistant at Huddersfield School of Art, eventually principal of Bolton School of Art, 1930–51. Was president of MAFA and of Bolton Art Circle. Exhibited RA, Goupil Gallery and Royal Glasgow Institute of the Fine Arts. Victoria & Albert Museum, British Museum and provincial galleries hold his work. Lived at Bolton, Lancashire.

Annabel GAULT 1952– Painter and draughtsman, born in West Sussex, who was notable for remote, bleak and eerie landscapes. She studied at West Surrey College of Art, 1973–7, then Royal Academy Schools, 1977–80. Mixed exhibitions included Oxford Gallery from 1979; Thackeray Gallery, 1989; Pallant House, Chichester, 1993; and City Gallery, Leicester, 1994, the year when her work was shown in Redpath Gallery, Vancouver, in Three British Artists, with Brendan Neiland and Patrick Procktor. From 1994 showed solo with Redfern Gallery. Hampshire County Council commissioned work, which was also owned by Arts Council.

George GAULT 1916–2001 Painter and teacher, born in Belfast. Gault joined the British Army aged 18 and served until 1946. He then studied at Camberwell School of Arts and Crafts, 1948–51, his teachers including William Coldstream, Kenneth Martin, Victor Pasmore and William Townsend. Gault went on to teach painting at the Greenwich Adult Education Institute for 20 years. In 1957 Gault was one of Jack Beddington's *Young Artists of Promise*, in the book of that title. He showed at RA, LG, NEAC, RBA, RP, Fine Art Society and Austin/Desmond Fine Art. Won a silver medal at 1954 Paris Salon. Solo show at Sweet Waters Gallery, 1989; retrospective at Woodlands Art Gallery, 1995. Lived in London.

Kate GAULT 1954– Painter, draughtsman and dancer. She studied drawing and painting at The Academy, Florence, 1971, and the Byam Shaw School, 1972, then dance, music and choreography at the London School of Contemporary Dance, 1972–5. For several years she worked with dance companies in New York, London and Amsterdam, painting in her spare time. In Ethiopia she was commissioned by the Ministry of Culture to form a dance company trained in both Western and traditional styles. In 1984 Gault moved to Italy to become a full-time painter, then to the Pyrenees and finally Mallorca. Gault's work was simple and colourful, reflecting the environments where she had lived. As well as exhibiting in mixed shows at Piccadilly Gallery she had a solo show at Christopher Hull Gallery, in 1985, another at Sue Rankin Gallery in 1991. She was sister of the artist Annabel Gault, and latterly exhibited as Katherine Hamilton, the name used for her solo show at Chappel Galleries, Chappel, in 1998 and her shared exhibition there, 2001. In 2004, Chappel Galleries organised Hamilton's one-man show Coastal Journeys 2001–2004, accompanied by *Coastal Journeys*, an illustrated monograph on her work by David Buckman. From 1992 she was based in Reydon, Suffolk.

William GAUNT 1900–1980 Painter of landscapes, urban scenes and witty draughtsman, art critic and writer. Born in Hull, son of the artist William Gaunt, went on to study at Westminster School of Art in 1924–5 under Walter Bayes and Bernard Meninsky. Exhibited at RA, Redfern Gallery and Lefevre Gallery and had a number of one-man shows. Gaunt was a lively and illuminating writer on aspects of British art, notably *The Pre-Raphaelite Tragedy*, *The Aesthetic Adventure* and *The March of the Moderns*. Lived in London.

William Norman GAUNT 1918– Painter and teacher, who was born in Leeds but educated in Morecambe, Lancashire. He studied at Lancaster School of Art, 1946–9, with Walter Bayes. Showed RWS, RI, with Lancaster Art Group, of which he was a member, and elsewhere in the provinces. Lived in Morecambe and then in Giggleswick, Yorkshire.

Elena GAUSSEN MARKS 1938– Portrait and landscape painter and draughtsman, and teacher, born in Kent. She studied at Southern College of Art, Portsmouth; Royal Academy Schools; and Camberwell School of Arts and Crafts. Her notable teachers included Claude Rogers, Peter Greenham, Henry Rushbury and Robert Buhler; until his death she shared a studio with Buhler, saying: "My aim is to justify his faith in my work." Gaussen Marks aspired "to combine the figurative and the abstract in painting by colour relationships, form/shape, subject matter subservient to the whole." From 1973–9 she was head of the art department at Queen's College. Among her main works were portraits of Lord Tonypandy, former speaker of the House of Commons, Leo Marks and Helene Hanff, the author (Elena Gaussen married Leo Marks in 1966, marriage dissolved 2000, the year before he died. Marks' father owned the bookshop made famous by Helene Hanff's book *84 Charing Cross Road*. Leo was a member of the Special Operations Executive in World War II and was made head of Agents' Codes and Ciphers, recalled in his memoir *Between Silk and Cyanide*, 1999. After the war Marks became a playwright and screenwriter, co-operating with the director Michael Powell on the cult film *Peeping Tom*.). Mixed shows included RA Summer Exhibitions from 1983, RP, NEAC, Bath Festival and Society of Landscape Painters, of which she was a member. Alpine Club Gallery, Spink and Stephen Bartley Gallery held solo exhibitions of Gaussen Marks' pictures, which are in Chelsea Arts Club and Southampton University collections. Lived in London.

James GAVIN 1928– Painter and teacher, born in Duns, Berwickshire. He studied drawing and painting at Edinburgh College of Art, 1955–9, followed by private study in 1960 in Paris, then went on to teach at Cumbria College of Art and Design. He showed in group exhibitions in England, Scotland and Ireland. After a one-man show at 57 Gallery, Edinburgh, in 1961 others followed in the city at Scottish, Richard Demarco and Alexander Galleries.

Stephen GAVIN 1953– Painter, photographer, draughtsman, collagist and teacher, born in Dover, Kent, married to the artist Victoria Brill (with whom he was included in the Brill family show Relative Values, The Smith Art Gallery & Museum, Stirling, 1993). Gavin produced both abstract and figurative works, was interested in objects connected with ritual and cult practices and employed animated sequences created on a computer paintbox in his later creations. Gained a first-class degree in painting and photography at Kingston Polytechnic, 1972–5, then his master's at the Royal College of Art, 1976–9. Between 1978–85, Gavin won the College's Travelling Scholarship to Amsterdam and Basle, a John Minton Travelling Scholarship to Rome and an Italian State Scholarship and Beryl Ash Award. He was Stanley Picker Fellow in Painting, Kingston Polytechnic, 1979–80. Gavin taught at Goldsmiths' College, 1983–4; Clapham and Battersea Institute, 1985–8; and from then on design and technology at Queen Margaret's School, York.

Barbara GAY 1921–1991 Painter and potter, born and lived in Bristol, where she studied at West of England College of Art, 1936–46, teachers including Roy Smith. In 1949 worked at Monkton Combe Pottery, near Bath, with Rachel Warner. Showed at RWA, of which she was an associate, and carried out commissioned work. St George's, Brandon Hill, Bristol, contained several pieces by her.

Bernard GAY 1921– Painter, writer and lecturer, by profession an inspector of schools, born in Exmouth, Devon. Attended Willesden School of Art, 1947–51, where his teachers included Maurice de Sausmarez. Gay was a versatile man, who wrote on diverse aspects of painting including his book *The Art of Sandro Botticelli*; he was also prominent in arts administration in the London suburb of Hampstead, where he co-founded the Camden Arts Centre, being at one time chairman of its Trust. Showed widely, including solo exhibitions at ICA, Camden Arts Centre, Piccadilly Gallery, Wildenstein and other leading London galleries. Sometimes signed work with initials only. Oxford University and a number of county council collections, including Hertfordshire and Essex, bought his work. He was one of Jack Beddington's *Young Artists of Promise*, in the 1957 book of that title. Gay said that he was "passionately interested in the organisation, planning and design of didactic design exhibitions". Examples were his Classics of Modern Design, Maker Designers Today and De Stijl shows. He lived latterly in Mansel Lacy, Herefordshire.

Francisco GAZITUA fl. from late 1960s– After studying philosophy at Catholic University of Chile, 1963–7, Gazitua pursued sculpture at University of Chile, 1967–9. Over the next eight years he taught and founded a handicrafts centre and was assistant to the sculptor Samuel Roman. Under a British Council Scholarship he attended St Martin's School of Art, 1977–9, then teaching there. From 1980 for several years organised and taught at summer school at Kornarija, Yugoslavia. As well as exhibiting extensively and carrying out commissions in Chile, Gazitua showed at British Council in London, 1978; St Martin's at the Polytechnic of North London, 1979; and in 1983 at Woodlands Art Gallery in Have You Seen Sculpture from the Body? Banco Real de Brasil, in São Paolo, holds his work.

Frances GEAKE 1903–1955 Painter and musician who taught music, born in Torquay, Devon. Studied at Newton Abbot Art School and also privately with the watercolourist Gladys Best. She exhibited RWA, NS, RI and with the Exeter Art Society, of which she was a member. Victoria & Albert Museum holds her work. Lived in Exeter.

William GEAR 1915–1997 Painter and administrator, born in Methil, Fife. He studied painting at Edinburgh College of Art, 1932–7, and the Edinburgh University Fine Art Class, 1936–7, his teachers including William Gillies and John Maxwell. After study in Paris with Fernand Léger in 1937 he travelled in Italy and the Balkans area on the strength of a scholarship. After World War II service in the Army and a period in the Control Commission in Germany, Gear lived in France until 1950, when he returned to Britain and in 1951 won a Festival of Britain Purchase Prize. In 1958 was made curator of Towner Art Gallery in Eastbourne. He was appointed head of the faculty of fine art in Birmingham College of Art in 1964; guest lecturer at National Gallery of Victoria, Melbourne, and University of Western Australia, Perth, in 1966; and in 1975 won the Lorne Fellowship and retired as head of the department of fine art at Birmingham Polytechnic. By then Gear had built up an impressive international exhibiting record, a painter of abstract compositions, often dancingly powerful in colour, who made a significant contribution to European painting through his association with the COBRA group in the immediate post-war years. Fifty-year retrospective at Redfern Gallery, 1997, with another there in 2003. William Gear and COBRA toured from Aberdeen Art Gallery, 1997–8. Tate Gallery and many provincial and foreign collections hold Gear's work. Elected Senior RA, 1995. Lived in Birmingham.

Robert GEARY 1931– Artist in inks and watercolour and illustrator, born in Battersea, south London. He attended Hammersmith School of Building and Arts & Crafts, 1945–8, teachers including Ernest Fedarb, William Washington and Dalgleish Playfair. He was made a member of SGA in 1969, a fellow of Chartered Society of Designers in 1980 and of Royal Society of Arts in 1981, also showing with RBA. Ronald Searle and Charles Keeping were cited as influences on Geary's work, which was used in periodicals such as *Radio Times* and *Punch*. Illustrated a number of books, including Chris Powling's *Dracula in Sunlight*, 1989. Geological Society and London Hospital hold his work. Lived in Sidcup, Kent.

Steve GEARY 1962– Painter and commercial artist, born and lived in London, who studied for a graphics degree at Goldsmiths' College in the early 1980s under Derek Cooper. As well as carrying out postcard and advertising commissions, Geary became one of the chief illustrators for the satirical television series *Spitting Image* and the only British artist providing covers for *MAD* magazine. In 1998 Geary showed Varying Shades of Pink at Air Gallery, touring to America, each painting inspired by a Pink Floyd rock group album, with limited-edition prints available. To complete the series, which had Surrealist overtones, Geary chose to work through the night to the music's blaring accompaniment, having been a fan of the Floyd since he was 14.

Luce GÉAS fl. from late 1970s– Painter of light-saturated still lifes and land- and seascapes, born in Provence, France, who studied at the Sorbonne, Paris, gaining her Master of Science degree at the London School of Economics. Although an experienced university lecturer she gave this up to concentrate on painting, working mainly from a studio in Chelsea. A number of her paintings were reproduced by the United Nations Children's Emergency Fund as greetings cards. Awards included International Prize, Treviso, 1983, and Chelsea Art Society Prize, 1988. Mixed shows included ROI, RWS, RA Summer Exhibition and Le Salon d'Automne, Paris. Later solo exhibitions included Bruton Street Gallery, 1997, and Highgate Fine Art, 1999, 2002 and 2004.

Charles W GEBHARD 1923– Painter, draughtsman and potter, born in London, married to the sculptor Jennifer Gebhard. He studied at Bromley College of Art with Keith Coleborn, 1947–50, then with Henry Rushbury at the Royal

Academy Schools in 1950. Exhibited RA, LG, RBA, in the provinces and in Kenya. Lived for some years in London.

G-BRECHT 1965– London-based Dutch artist and designer who gained his master's in fine art from Goldsmiths' College, 2001. This followed studies at Royal Academie of Fine Arts, The Hague, 1990; The Rietveld Academy, Amsterdam, 1994; and Rijksakademie van Beeldende Kunsten, Amsterdam, 1997. G-Brecht showed internationally from 1994. He was also a theatrical set designer, the huge scale of his paintings reflecting this. In his work he "explored issues of power, happiness, entertainment, burn-out and agony," as seen in his two 1995 works Fragment and Solution, both oil on linen, that filled the internal wall space of the foyer gallery at *The Economist* Tower, 2002.

Stefan GEC 1958– Artist in a variety of media, born in Huddersfield, his father having moved from the Ukraine. Stefan did a foundation course at Huddersfield Polytechnic, 1983–4; graduated with honours from Newcastle upon Tyne Polytechnic, 1984–7; and made postgraduate studies at the Slade School of Fine Art, 1991–3. In 1996–7, he gained The Paul Hamlyn Foundation Sculpture and Installation Award. Gec took part in numerous group shows in Britain and abroad, among later solo shows, projects and works being Natural History, Ukrainian Cultural & Education Centre/Winnipeg Art Gallery, Canada, 1998; Vengeance, Lux Gallery, 2001; The Outside World, Yorkshire Sculpture Park, West Bretton, 2002; Untitled; Apollo-Soyuz Test Project, Longside Gallery, Yorkshire Sculpture Park, 2003; and Long Distance, Globe City, Newcastle, and The elephant's foot, at Annely Juda Fine Art, both 2004. Of ambitious projects handled over the dozen years to 2004, which included sculpture, film, photography and computer-generated animation, Gec wrote that they had "tapped into notions of movement, dislocation and history that stem from my own family background." The Arts Council, for which he carried out a commission in 2003, holds his work.

Margaret GEDDES 1914–1998 Painter and draughtsman, born in Cheam, Surrey, educated in Eastbourne, who studied at Westminster School of Art, 1932–7, teachers including Walter Bayes, Bernard Meninsky and Mark Gertler. Geddes became a member of NS, AIA and WIAC, also showing at RA, LG, NEAC and Redfern Gallery. Solo exhibitions started at AIA, 1950, later ones including Halesworth Gallery, Suffolk, and a studio retrospective in Teddington, Middlesex, both 1973. Geddes' work moved from figuration to abstraction. She was an adventurous, inquiring artist, well aware of developments on the continent and in America, as demonstrated in the monograph on her, by Denys J Wilcox, which accompanied her retrospective at Woodlands Art Gallery, 1998, with a further show at Camden Fine Art, Bath, 1999. Leicestershire Education Authority holds her work. In 1996 Geddes, who suffered from Alzheimer's Disease, moved to a nursing home in Taunton, Somerset.

Stewart GEDDES 1961– Painter and teacher. He did a foundation course at Canterbury College of Art, 1979–80, then completed an honours degree in fine art at Bristol Polytechnic, 1980–3. Geddes, a painterly painter, took his landscape subjects from a wide range, from flour mills and gasometers to scenes in the Mediterranean area. From 1985 he taught foundation courses, in Weston-super-Mare and at Bristol Polytechnic. Exhibited in a wide range of mixed exhibitions, including Stowells Trophy Exhibition at RA in 1983; regularly from 1984 at RWA Open; from 1985 at Gloucester City Museum; and from 1986 at RA. After sharing a show at Rooksmoor Gallery, Bath, in 1987, he had solo shows there, 1989–91. Also in 1991 had solo exhibition at Cadogan Contemporary.

Wilhelmina GEDDES 1887–1955 Stained glass designer, printmaker and painter, born in Ireland where she studied in Dublin and Belfast. She showed at RHA, in London and Edinburgh, on the continent and in North America and was especially noted for her window designs, which included Belfast's Assembly Hall, the city's Museum and Art Gallery holding her window Children of Lir. Lived for a time in London.

Arthur GEE 1934– Wildlife, landscape and seascape artist, mainly in watercolour, but also pastel and oils and prints. He was born in and lived in Warrington area of Cheshire. After several years in industry and Royal Air Force, from 1955–83 was an engineering draughtsman, then becoming a self-employed artist. Gee was mainly self-taught, but had one year full-time in fine art, 1983–4, at St Helens College of Art and Design. Peter Scott, the Impressionists and early English watercolourists were among influences. He was a "romantic painter, looking for atmospheric conditions, also strong lighting and chiaroscuro". Gee was elected to SWLA in 1969 and became an associate of BWS in 1988. Group shows included Mall Galleries, East African Wildlife Society, Mini-Print International at Barcelona, in Spain, where he was a purchase prize winner, and the provinces. Solo shows included Great House Gallery, Rivington, Bolton; Warrington Art Gallery; and Brentwood Arts, Warrington.

Sharon GEE 1961– Self-taught painter, working in a bright, Impressionist palette, born in Tunbridge Wells, Kent. Moved to East Anglia, attended Downham Market Grammar School, then studied modern languages at Norwich City College of Further Education. After working as a bilingual secretary in London she then ran a video shop, in the late 1990s taking up painting. Had a first solo show at McNeill Fine Art Gallery, Radlett, in 1998, one at Collins Fine Art, Chicago, in 2000. Queen Elizabeth The Queen Mother and the English Rugby Football Union owned examples. Lived in Southgate, north London.

Frank GEERE 1931–1991 Painter of atmospheric equestrian pictures and portraits, born in southwest London, self-taught apart from occasional night school classes. His first attempt at an equestrian picture was in 1961, when he saw a print of a horse and foal on his aunt's wall and copied it. Geere spent some years in Australia and worked for a lithographic publisher in the West End of London before being made redundant, when he concentrated on painting. He painted from photographs and from racecourse visits, where he obtained commissions for pictures. Included in his output were portraits of the ballet dancer Rudolf Nureyev and the jockey Lester Piggott and a number of studies of the racehorse Desert Orchid. Sold regularly from a pitch in the Bayswater Road until illness intervened. In 1985 Geere joined The Society of Equestrian Artists as a friend and showed with it on several occasions at the Mall and Westminster Galleries. In 1988 the *Daily*

Mail offered the owner of the winner of its Leisure Stakes, at Lingfield, a commissioned portrait of his horse by Geere in addition to the £20,000 prize money. Geere died in Burgess Hill, Sussex.

William GELDART 1936– Painter and illustrator, born in Marple, Cheshire. He studied at Manchester Regional College, 1956–7. Showed at RA, in the Manchester area and at Geldart Gallery, Henbury, Macclesfield, Cheshire. He wrote and illustrated *Geldart's Cheshire* and illustrated many other titles. Manchester Grammar School holds his work.

Steve GELIOT 1962– Sculptor and teacher, "mainly carving in wood and stone, influences and inspiration natural forms and scientific imaging." He was born in Chiselhurst, Kent, completed foundation at Medway College of Art; graduated in three-dimensional design in a range of materials at Brighton Polytechnic, 1984; and gained his master's in the history and theory of modern art with distinction under Steve Bury at Chelsea School of Art, 1991. Geliot won the Sir Charles Wheeler Award for Painting, 1977; first prize, Camden Annual, 1986; joint prize, Rouse Kent Public Art Award, 1996; and a South East Arts major award for experimental work, 2001. Taught at West Surrey College of Art & Design, Brighton Polytechnic and Northbrook College and held many residencies. Group exhibitions also included The New Spirit in Craft & Design, Crafts Council, 1986. Among his solo shows were Camden Arts Centre, 1987; Southern Arts Touring Exhibitions Service, 1990; and Trinity Arts Centre, Tunbridge Wells, 2000. Geliot carried out numerous commissions, among which were Carved Posts for Brighton Seafront, 1992; Guildford Odeon Sculptures, 1996; Hangleton Quiet Garden, art and landscape, 1998; The Phoenix Trees, five sculptures for Wolverhampton, 2001; and Four Sculptures for Ouse Estuary, Newhaven, 2002. University of Brighton; National Cash Registers London headquarters; Lord Peter Carrington; and Sculpture at Goodwood Maquettes Project hold examples. Lived in Brighton, Sussex.

William GELLER 1930– Artist in pen and ink, pencil and gouache, born in Essex. He was a City of London apprentice in commercial art, studying at South-West Essex Technical College and Central School of Arts and Crafts. After becoming an advertising agency art director Geller was a freelance artist and designer. For a time was a member and president of SGA. Geller was noted for marine pictures with technical authority but careful composition. He lived in Maldon, Essex, where he was a member of the Art Society and Stone Sailing Club. Group exhibition appearances included RSMA, Wapping Group and touring shows of Federation of British Artists. Port of London Authority holds his work.

Margaret GENEVER 1902–1997 Painter and printmaker, born in London, daughter of the architect Charles Genever. She studied from mid-1940s for many years at St Martin's School of Art, teachers including Herbert Holt and Otway McCannell; Hammersmith School of Art under Carel Weight and Ruskin Spear; and Central School of Art. Showed at RA, Free Painters and Sculptors and in provinces and solo at the Loggia Gallery. Lived for many years in Guildford, Surrey.

Ana GENOVES 1969– Sculptor who obtained a diploma in art and design, 1988–90, from Chelsea College of Art & Design, then a fine art, sculpture, honours degree there, 1990–3, with a postgraduate higher diploma from Slade School of Fine Art, 1993–5. Among her residencies was Cursos de Arte en Mojacar, Almeria, Spain, 1994. Group shows included *The Economist* Building, 1994; Thoughts, City Racing, 1997; and dumbpop, Jerwood Gallery, 1998–9, sculptures stripped down to a few simple parameters. Genoves was nominated for the Paul Hamlyn Award in 1999 and was shortlisted for the first Jerwood Sculpture Prize, 2001. She collaborated for a time with the sculptor Kerry Stewart.

Caroline GENTILLI 1959– Artist in etching and mixed media, born in London, who attended Epsom School of Art, 1977–8, and Bristol Polytechnic, 1978–81. From 1982–6 Gentilli did non-arts-related jobs, then went back to full-time printmaking, from 1991 being "a part-time artist and full-time mother". Gentilli was a member of the Printmakers' Council and Bath Society of Artists. She said that "the use of colour and textures are very important to me as a means of expression. My two main influences are forms taken from the plant and rock world and the primitive art of Latin America." Group show appearances included RWA, 1986; RE Open, 1987; Royal Festival Hall, 1989; RA Summer Exhibition, 1990; and overseas shows in Canada, Spain, America, South Korea and Malta. Lived in Bishopston, Bristol.

Jeremy GENTILLI 1926– Painter, printmaker, draughtsman, tapestry designer and artist in collage. Born in London of English parents, Gentilli was of Italian origin through his grandfather; his mother was the painter Madge Gentilli. He studied at Oxford University, 1946–8. Also attended Heatherley's School of Fine Art and Camberwell School of Arts and Crafts under Claude Rogers. Gentilli moved to Paris in 1951 and settled in France at Croissy sur Seine, Yvelines. In 1950s he studied in the atelier of Fernand Léger, S W Hayter's Atelier 17 and for tapestry worked with Pierre Daquin at Atelier de Saint Cyr latterly in 1971. Gentilli showed internationally, group exhibitions including the 1961 Biennale in Ljubljana, Yugoslavia; the 1962–3–5 Salons du Trait in Paris; and the 1964 Roter Reiter-Künstler Gruppe, Munich, West Germany. One-man exhibitions included Galerie Giraudoux, Paris, 1960; Eric Locke Gallery, San Francisco, 1963; Gallery A at South Yarra, Australia, 1964; and Galerie Vasse in Lillie, 1973. In the 1970s and 1980s he showed several times at Galerie Antares, in Paris. Gentilli's work was acquired by the Bibliothèque Nationale, Paris; Bibliothèque Royale, Brussels; Arts Council and Victoria & Albert Museum, London; and Museum of Modern Art, New York.

Madge Hope GENTILLI 1897–1963 Painter in oil, born in London, mother of the artist Jeremy Gentilli and sister of the playwright, man of letters and Labour Member of Parliament Benn W Levy. She studied at Heatherley's School of Fine Art under Bernard Adams and exhibited at ROI, RBA and RP, also in Chelsea where she lived. Died in Menton, France.

Bernard GENTLE 1913– Painter and lithographer, born in Watford, Hertfordshire. Studied with Francis Hodge at St Martin's School of Art. Exhibited with RA, Norwich Art Society and Leger Galleries. Lived at Blofield, Norfolk.

David GENTLEMAN 1930– Artist, designer, author, illustrator and printmaker, born and lived in London, his father being the artist Tom Gentleman, who gave him informal instruction. He attended St Albans Art School, 1947–8 and 1950, then Royal College of Art, 1950–3, under Edward Bawden and John Nash. Gentleman was a junior tutor there, 1953–5, then freelanced. Books illustrated included *Plats du Jour*, 1957; *Bridges on the Backs*, 1961; *The Pattern Under the Plough*, 1966; covers for *New Penguin Shakespeare*, 1968–78; *Westminster Abbey*, 1987; and *The Illustrated Poems of John Betjeman*, 1995. Gentleman was illustrator and editor of *The Crooked Scythe*, 1993. He wrote and illustrated *Design in Miniature*, 1972; *David Gentleman's Britain*, 1982; *David Gentleman's London*, 1985; *David Gentleman's Coastline*, 1988; *David Gentleman's Paris*, 1991; *David Gentleman's India*, 1994; *David Gentleman's Italy*, 1997; and *David Gentleman Wood Engravings*, 2000. His series of Fenella books for children appeared in 1967. He illustrated and designed for many publishers and organisations, including Royal Mail postage stamps, from 1962, his Winston Churchill stamp setting a new standard in design; posters for London Transport and the National Trust; symbols for British Steel and the Bodleian Library; the Eleanor Cross mural for Charing Cross tube station, 1979; and panels for Westminster Abbey, 1986. Gentleman's solo exhibitions included 11 at Mercury Gallery, 1970–00, the Royal College of Art, 2002 (coinciding with the publication of his book *Artwork*), plus various lithography shows. In 2003, his powerful B.liar blood-splattered poster was a feature of the Iraq Stop the War campaign. There was a retrospective at the Fine Art Society, 2004. In 2005, Tate Britain displayed Gentleman's lithographs of Hardwick Hall, Derbyshire, and Kelmscott House, Hammersmith, to commemorate his seventy-fifth birthday. The Tate, Victoria & Albert Museum, the National Maritime Museum and many private collections held examples.

Tom GENTLEMAN 1892–1966 Painter, designer, lithographer and cartoonist, born in Coatbridge, Lanarkshire, father of the artist David Gentleman. He left school at 14 to work in the family drapery business, which he disliked. After World War I service in the Glasgow Yeomanry and Scottish Rifles, in which he was badly wounded, Gentleman returned to continue studies at Glasgow School of Art, where Maurice Greiffenhagen was principal and where he won a travelling scholarship to the continent. After periods painting, cartooning for the Glasgow papers and with his farmer brother in Canada in 1929 Gentleman moved to London for a year, married and began working in advertising at S H Benson, W S Crawford and Stuart Advertising Agencies and with Jack Beddington and Vernon Nye at Shell. From early in World War II he produced posters and exhibitions at the Ministry of Information with Misha Black and Milner Gray; until about 1943 he freelanced as a design and illustrator; after the war returning to Shell, from which he retired in 1952. By then he was a fellow of the Society of Industrial Artists. In 1945 Gentleman published *Brae Farm*, childhood experiences on the Clyde, illustrated with his lithographs. Continued to paint well into retirement, representational although rather formalised works, landscapes around Hertford (where he lived 1930–56), and Fordham, near Colchester, Essex (1956–66, where he died), being favourite subjects. Others were racetrack scenes and views of northern France, where he bicycled searching for places known in World War I. In 1964 Colchester Art Society, at The Minories, put on an exhibition of work by John Bensusan-Butt, Tom Gentleman and "drawings for books" by Society members. The Hunterian Art Gallery, Glasgow, holds Gentleman's early Scottish oil landscapes; he completed an English summer's day canvas mural for the Kardomah Café, rue de Rivoli, Paris; School Prints produced his lithograph The Grey Horses; and two of his posters are illustrated in *The Shell Poster Book*, 1998.

Iqbal GEOFFREY 1939– Versatile artist, born in Chiniot in what is now Pakistan. A precocious, multi-talented man, Geoffrey was editor of the *Pakistan Post* and *Law School Journal* in the 1950s, being called to the Bar in Pakistan in 1959, with distinction. From 1960 he was a partner in and chairman of Geoffrey & Khitran, international lawyers (over subsequent years Geoffrey added to his legal and business qualifications internationally, his many official positions ranging from human rights officer, United Nations, 1996–7, to chief accountant, Embassy of Kuwait, London, 1974–5, and special advisor to the president of Pakistan, 1980–4, and he wrote widely on legal matters). By the end of the 1950s he had travelled through Pakistan and India to study ancient monuments, decided to take up painting full-time although mainly self-taught, and travelled to England in 1960, having his first one-man show at the Galerie de Seine, London, in 1961. He was awarded a Huntingdon Hartford Foundation Fellowship in 1962 and worked in America. Geoffrey claimed to have pioneered abstract painting in Pakistan, his work being partly inspired by Hindu mythology and Eastern calligraphy. While in America Geoffrey was graduate editor of the *Harvard Art Review*, 1965–6, and was visiting professor of fine arts at St Mary's College, Indiana, 1967–8, studying art criticism at the Fogg Art Museum. Had many mixed and solo shows, later ones including Canvas Gallery, Karachi, 2000; and Alliance Française Gallery, Islamabad, and Lahore Art Gallery, both 2001. His work is in a number of notable collections of modern painting, including the Tate Gallery, Arts Council and Boston Museum of Fine Arts. Returned to live and work in Pakistan.

Trevor GEOGHEGAN 1946– Painter of slightly mystical landscapes, and teacher, born in London of Irish descent, who studied at Worthing College of Art and graduated from Chelsea School of Art in 1968. In 1971 he settled in Blessington, County Wicklow, Ireland, from which his father had emigrated. Taught at the National College of Art and Design, Dublin, and at the Burren School of Art. For many years Geoghegan painted the uplands of Wicklow and the rich pastures of Kildare, pictures which could have a serene quality. Latterly, he began to explore urban landscapes. His work was shown at Kilcock Art Gallery in County Kildare and in London at The Walton Gallery. Geoghegan was included in the 1997–8 exhibition Landscapes North and South, which toured from Glebe House and Gallery, Donegal. Many Irish corporate collections hold his work.

Eric Beardsworth GEORGE 1881–1961 Painter of portraits and figures, designer and writer, born in Streatham Common, Surrey and educated at Dulwich College. After studying at Oriel College, Oxford, George attended the Westminster School of Art and Académie Julian, in Paris. Did poster work for Shell. George showed 11 pictures, overwhelmingly religious subjects, at the RA Summer

Exhibition between 1922–33 while living in Chelsea. He also exhibited at NEAC, London Salon, Goupil Gallery, RP and elsewhere. His book *The Life and Death of Benjamin Robert Haydon, 1786–1846* was first published in 1948, a second edition in 1967 including additions by Dorothy George.

Grace Courtenay GEORGE 1909–1999 Painter, printmaker and teacher, born in Bristol. She studied at West of England College of Art there, teachers including Reginald Bush, and for most of her teaching career, 1939–69, taught art at grammar school, Chipping Sodbury, showing locally. Lived latterly in West Harnham, Salisbury, Wiltshire.

Helen GEORGE fl. from early 1920s– Sculptor and painter who after initial education at Talbot Heath School, in Bournemouth, studied sculpture with Antoine Bourdelle in Paris. She exhibited RA, Goupil Gallery, SWA, Leicester Galleries, Paris Salon and widely in America. Her work was bought by Victoria & Albert Museum, Salford Museums and Art Galleries and Manchester City Art Gallery. Lived at Blandford Forum, Dorset.

Irene GEORGE 1947– Painter of amusing pictures featuring the Yellow Hat Tribe, included in Humorous Art at McNeill Fine Art Gallery, Radlett, in 2005. They originated from doodles on the back of an envelope in the early 1990s. The idea took off when George met the entrepreneur and ostrich farmer Vince Tyack, when he discussed his travels, especially in Africa, with the artist. The Yellow Hat Tribe became a registered trade-mark for oil paintings and limited-edition prints popular in Britain and abroad and exclusive to McNeill Fine Art Gallery.

Janie GEORGE 1962– Painter, printmaker, muralist and teacher, born in East Pakistan, who studied at Somerset College of Art; West Surrey College of Art, Farnham; and Slade School of Fine Art. Held a number of teaching posts, including Slade School, 1990–2, and Bath College of Higher Education, 1993–4, then became a freelance muralist. Mixed shows included Printmakers at Farnham, Maltings, 1984; Macau University Print Exhibition, Macau, 1989; RA Summer Exhibition, 1992; and Royal Over-Seas League Open, 1994. Had a solo show at Horniman Museum, 1993.

Jon GEORGE 1944– Painter, printmaker and teacher, born in Ulverston, Lancashire, notable for use of egg tempera and the invention in 1989 of Castprinting. This inexpensive technique employed wet clay to make a painting in relief. George trained at Falmouth School of Art, 1965–8, eventually becoming a self-employed artist and teacher. As well as organising projects with children, pensioners and artists, he also taught Castprinting in Wormwood Scrubs prison and elsewhere. George cited Indian painting and Persian miniatures as influences. "To describe a landscape in time and space, to tell a story and concern with gesture" were important in his work. Between January and May 1991 George travelled by bicycle through nine West African countries, resulting work being shown at Bancroft Road Library, near his Chisenhale Studio, in 1992. Solo shows included Furness Museum, Lancashire, 1986, and Tyn-y-coed Gallery, Barmouth, 1989.

Patrick GEORGE 1923– Painter and teacher, born in Manchester. He studied at Edinburgh College of Art as an Andrew Grant Scholar, 1941–2; was in the Royal Naval Volunteer Reserve, 1942–6; then studied at Camberwell School of Arts and Crafts under William Coldstream, 1946–9. Was on the staff of Slade School of Fine Art from 1949, going as head of department to Nigerian College of Art & Technology, Zaria, 1959. From 1960 George was a member of the art panel to implement the *Coldstream Report*, of the Arts Council and of Eastern Arts. Obtained a personal chair at Slade, 1983, being Slade professor, 1985–8. A self-effacing artist, George was a distinguished figurative painter in the Euston Road School tradition, a seeker for the essential structure and feel of the scene surveyed. Group exhibitions included Eight Figurative Painters, Mellon Center for British Art, Yale, and elsewhere in America, 1981; Hard Won Image, Tate Gallery, 1983; A Singular Vision, Royal Albert Memorial Museum, Exeter, 1984; and Five Protagonists, Browse & Darby, 1994, a gallery which gave him a series of solo shows from 1984. Previously he had shown at Gainsborough's House, Sudbury, 1975, and there was an Arts Council Retrospective at Serpentine Gallery, 1980. Arts Council, Government Art Collection, Tate Gallery and other public collections hold examples. Lived in London and Great Saxham, Suffolk.

Will G GEORGE 1851–1945 Primitive painter, born in Mousehole, Cornwall. He was the grandfather of the artist Jack Pender. Between the ages of 10 and 75 George was a fisherman, who retailed his exploits to Pender, who found them an inspiration. On retirement he took up painting, working on scraps of card and paper, producing many meticulous watercolours of Mousehole. George was promoted by the painter Alethea Garstin, who introduced him to the Passmore Edwards Art Gallery, Newlyn, and to other artists. His work was included in Artists from Cornwall, at RWA in 1992.

Bernard GEORGESON 1940– Painter who graduated with honours in fine art from University of Central Lancashire, Preston, in 1999, gaining his master's from Manchester Metropolitan University, 2002. Exhibitions included, in 2002: Hybrida, Cartwright Gallery, Bradford; Exchange, Pratt Institute, New York, America; Reberb, Cornerhouse Gallery, Manchester; and Hybrida, Gallerie Mladiych, Brno, Czech Republic. In 2003, Georgeson was a prize winner at the West Lancs Open, Chapel Gallery, Ormskirk; he also showed Hybrida, Holden Gallery, Manchester, and at Egg Gallery Liverpool, and shared an exhibition, A Different Space, Turnpike Gallery, Leigh, with David Stanley. There, Georgeson showed large abstracts.

Nicholas GEORGIADIS 1925–2001 Stage designer, artist in acrylic and oil on board and gouache on paper, and teacher, born in Athens, Greece. He studied at Slade School of Fine Art, 1953–5, with Robert Medley, later teaching there. Worked substantially for leading ballet, opera and theatre companies as a set and costume designer. Georgiadis won the *Evening Standard* Ballet Award in 1982, the Karolos Koun Prize, Athens, 1988. The Theatre Museum holds his work. Showed at Documenta, Kassel; Venice Biennale; and Carnegie Exhibition, Pittsburgh. He had solo exhibitions at Redfern and Hamilton Galleries and elsewhere in London, where he lived, and in Milan and Athens.

Elpida GEORGIOU 1958– Painter who was born in London. She studied at St Martin's School of Art, 1983–6, then at Royal Academy Schools, 1987–90. Georgiou gained the Winsor & Newton Painting Award in 1988, the Guinness Award for a first-time exhibitor at RA Summer Exhibition in 1991 and Elizabeth Greenshields Award in 1992. Took part in a variety of mixed shows from mid-1980s, including ROI in 1990, where she was a prizewinner, and Whitechapel Open in 1992. Had first London solo show at Christopher Hull Gallery in 1992. Her work is in the collections of Unilever and Guinness. Lived in London.

Charles March GERE 1869–1957 Painter, illustrator, designer of wall decorations and stained glass and teacher. Born in Gloucester, Gere won scholarships to Birmingham School of Art, where he studied under Edward Taylor and later taught. Gere's early work was much influenced by the Pre-Raphaelite-favoured Italian painters and for a time he studied tempera painting in Italy. Worked with William Morris at the Kelmscott Press and later at the Ashendene Press and did much to make the Birmingham School a centre of excellence for book design, contending that illustrations and type should be complementary. Was interested in the revival of wood engraving. Gere was a member of the Birmingham Group of Painters and Craftsmen, which was strongly Arts and Crafts-oriented. Brother of the artist Margaret Gere. He exhibited prolifically, especially at RWS and NEAC, also Fine Art Society, Carfax Gallery, RA and Goupil Gallery. Elected RA, 1939. Tate Gallery holds his work. Gere's landscapes are notable for their careful design and serene atmosphere. Lived at Painswick, Gloucestershire, and died in Gloucester.

Margaret GERE 1878–1965 Painter, notably in tempera, born in Leamington Spa, Warwickshire. She was the sister of the artist Charles March Gere, studied under him from 1897 at Birmingham School of Art and like him was an original member of the Birmingham Group of Painters and Craftsmen. The copying of Piero della Francesca in tempera in Florence in 1901 had a marked effect on her work, and she further studied at Slade School of Fine Art, 1905. Showed with and was a member of NEAC and RBSA and had first exhibition with her brother at Carfax Gallery, 1912. Represented in The Earthly Paradise exhibition at Fine Art Society, 1969. Cheltenham Art Gallery devoted a show to her in 1984. Tate Gallery holds her picture Noah's Ark. She and her sister Edith, who married the artist Henry Payne, were known as "the masterful Miss Geres".

Jane GERMAN 1944– Artist and teacher, born in Loughborough, Leicestershire, who trained at Loughborough and Brighton Colleges of Art. She specialised in printed textiles, but through a teaching career pursued her main interest: fine art. In the 1990s she developed an interest in depicting farm and domestic animals in oil and soft pastel, also painting some portraits. The animals, found in Brittany, Corfu and south Norfolk, where she lived with her painter husband David Page at Starston, were viewed with the unsentimental eye of someone who grew up and lived in the country. Mixed shows included The Gallery, Pentonville Road; PS; Schoolhouse Gallery Open, Bath; Barn End Gallery, Halesworth; Drawings for All, Gainsborough's House, Sudbury; and Eastern Open, King's Lynn. Solo exhibitions included Chichester Centre of Arts, 1999.

Bruce GERNAND 1949– American-born sculptor and draughtsman, producing enigmatic, abstract sculptures in a wide range of materials. He studied at Pennsylvania State University, 1966–8; graduated in philosophy at San Francisco State College, 1968–70; attended City and Guilds of London Art School, 1971–2; Central School of Art and Design, 1972–4; and Royal College of Art, 1975–6. Among awards received were those from the Arts Council, 1977; Eastern Arts Association, 1987; and he was Henry Moore Fellow in Sculpture at Central St Martins College, 1992–4, working in its foundry. Gernand showed in Britain from the early 1980s; had an exhibition in Coopers & Lybrand's Atrium Gallery, 1994; was included in the Osaka Triennale of Sculpture, 1995, in Japan; in 1996–7 had work in the Sculpture at Goodwood display; solo show at Karen Hamilton, 2000.

Alfred Horace GERRARD 1899–1998 Sculptor, ceramist and teacher. His first wife was the artist Kaff Gerrard, with whom he had a show at Colnaghi's, 1931. Gerrard studied at Manchester School of Art, then Slade School of Fine Art. He served in the Army and Royal Flying Corps in World War I, in the Army in World War II and was a war artist, 1944–5. He joined the Slade's staff in 1925, was its temporary head in 1948–9, and was professor of sculpture there, 1948–68, thereafter professor emeritus. Won the RBS Silver Medal in 1960. Gerrard's stone relief The North Wind is on London Transport headquarters. His work was included in The Slade 1871–1971 exhibition at RA in 1971. Lived at Leyswood, Tunbridge Wells, Kent. Gerrard, known as Gerry, was a revered teacher of students as diverse as Karin Jonzen, Eduardo Paolozzi and F E McWilliam, who wrote a catalogue tribute for the Gerrard retrospective at South London Art Gallery in 1978. Henry Moore Institute, Leeds, posthumously acquired Gerrard's work, including it in the exhibition Sculpture in twentieth-century Britain, 2003. David Buckman's biography of Gerrard, completed in 2001, tells the story of the Slade sculpture school and details his career and principal works.

Charles GERRARD 1892–1964 Painter in oil, born in Antwerp. Studied at Lancaster School of Art, 1907–14, and at the Royal College of Art, 1917–22, under Robert Anning Bell and Gerald Moira. Exhibited RA, NEAC, Redfern Gallery and elsewhere, the City of Birmingham Museum and Art Gallery holding his work. Gerrard also showed in North America, Italy and India, where he taught for a time and was an official art adviser in Bombay. He was an expert on Indian art and iconography. Work appeared in *The Studio* and *Colour* magazines. Lived at Denham, Buckinghamshire.

Charlotte GERRARD 1970– Artist, muralist and scenic painter who gained an honours degree in psychology/sociology at Manchester Polytechnic, taking courses in life drawing and creative painting at St Martin's School of Art, 1995. Travelled widely, working internationally on various music- and arts-based projects with young people. In 1997 she set up bloomin art, a greetings card, print and gift tag label using own designs; within 18 months over 6,000 images had been sold internationally in florist's and gift shops. In 1998 she was a freelance backdrop painter for Trance Art, based in London. Gerrard held intermittent shows, early in 2000 being first winner of the inaugural Blue Dog Arts Foundation Bursary, showing at Truman Brewery, Brick Lane. Lived in London.

Kaff GERRARD 1894–1970 Painter and potter, born Katherine Leigh-Pemberton, who was married to A H

Gerrard, for many years professor of sculpture at Slade School of Fine Art. She attended the Slade, 1922–4, under Henry Tonks and Philip Wilson Steer, and was a star pupil. She won first prize for painting from the cast in 1922, second prize for life painting and first prize for portrait painting in 1923. She was a visionary, almost pantheistic artist who drew inspiration from Paul Nash and the landscape of Sussex and the South Downs. During World War II she painted some topical scenes of rural devastation. Also completed highly coloured abstracts, often with a strong symbolical component. Although she was out on the South Downs almost every day painting Gerrard only had one public show, in 1931 at Colnaghi's; this was of sculpture and pots by Kaff Gerrard and her husband, including some joint efforts. Her paintings were not shown until the exhibition in 1991 at Royal Museum and Art Gallery, Canterbury, when several public galleries acquired examples, including Imperial War Museum.

Thomas A GERRARD 1923– Painter, by profession a chartered surveyor, born in Gaerwen, Anglesey. He showed with Royal National Eisteddfod, SWG, WAC, Howard Roberts Gallery in Cardiff, and shared a two-man show at Tegfryn Art Gallery, Menai Bridge. Gwent and Merthyr Tydfil Education Authorities hold his work.

Ori GERSHT 1967– Artist and teacher, of Israeli nationality, using modern media. He gained an honours degree in photography, film and video at the University of Westminster, 1990–2, then his master's in fine art, photography, at Royal College of Art, 1993–5. Gersht's work could have a strong autobiographical element as in images included in the exhibition Global II Collection at Addison Wesley Longman Ltd, Harlow, 1998–9. He was then teaching at Kent Institute of Art & Design. In 2000 Gersht was one of the recipients of the Leon Constantine Photography Award for an Israeli artist. Solo exhibitions included Pitch, Chisenhale Gallery, 2000; White Noise, Noga Gallery, Tel-Aviv, Israel, and Andrew Mummery Gallery, both 2001; and Tel-Aviv Museum and Art Now, Tate Britain, both 2002. Journeys, literal and metaphorical, were an important part of Gersht's work. For White Noise he travelled in Poland, part-inspired by Martin Gilbert's book *The Holocaust Journey*. Lived in London.

Arnold GERSTL 1888–1957 Painter, restorer and gallery curator. Born in Prague, studied art there and in France, Austria and Spain. Exhibited RA and widely on the continent, including one-man shows. Prior to World War I he was a film studio artist for a short time. After World War II took over as curator at the Burton Art Gallery in Bideford, Devon, where he lived.

Laura GETHEN SMITH 1945– Painter, collagist, lecturer and arts administrator, born in Bromley, Kent. She trained at Croydon College of Art, 1972–3, under Roger de Grey and Peter Coker; City and Guilds of London Art School, 1973–6; and St Martin's School of Art, 1976–7, under John Hoyland. Between 1976–04 Gethen Smith taught art and art history widely, including Brooking School of Ballet and General Education; Inner London Education Authority; Workers' Educational Association and Working Men's College; Birkbeck College; Greenwich Social Services; and Kent Adult Education Services. Between 1986–8 she was co-ordinator, Bromley Youth Services Employment Arts and Drama Project, Manpower Services Commission; 1994–6, arts development officer, Age Concern, Lewisham; 1996–9, co-ordinator, Work With the Elderly Arts Project, Adult Education College for Bexley; and there in 2000–01, arts curriculum manager. Gethen Smith's abstract and semi-abstract paintings, often small in size, were interpretations of landscapes and, more recently, cityscapes. Later group shows included APT Gallery, from 1996, and Metropole Galleries, Folkestone, 2002. Among her solo exhibitions were Borough Museum & Gallery, 2002 Berwick-on-Tweed, having first shown there in 1991; Robson Gallery, Selkirk, and Scott Gallery, Hawick, both 2003; Ashford Library Gallery, 2004; and Harlequin Gallery, 2001, 2003 and 2005. By then, she had "moved towards a complete refining of shape, colour and proportion in my paintings. This has developed through my growing fascination with collage which has shown me that, through constant reduction, I can achieve the simplicity and balance within my work that I have always strived for." Gethen Smith had a studio in Folkestone, Kent.

E A GEYDUSHEK-GEYDON 1893–c.1970 Painter in oil, she was educated in Vienna, where she studied at the Academy of Arts. In London studied at Regent Street Polytechnic School of Art. Exhibited RA, LG, with Ealing Arts Club and overseas. Lived in Ealing, west London.

Ayad GHARBAWI 1964– Poet and painter, born in Baghdad, who left Iraq with his family at five years of age to be educated in Europe and America. He studied history and gained a master's degree in international relations and went on to complete social studies in Britain. His poems were published and anthologised in America; in 1996 he wrote his first book of verses, *When Elegance Weeps*; and his collection *Anatomy Of A Poet* appeared in 2001. His figurative solo exhibition Walking Through Life, at The Gallery in Cork Street, 2001, touched on issues such as poverty, abuse, loneliness and theological questions.

Karl GHATTAS 1958– Self-taught painter, born in Egypt, who graduated in medicine from London University, 1982, gaining his Master of Science philosophy degree from the London School of Economics in 1989. Ghattas' career as an artist was successful after he gave up a lucrative position as an ear, nose and throat surgeon and lecturing in philosophy at the London School of Economics. Between 1994–6, he was a visiting lecturer at Winchester School of Art, and was an assessor for Westminster Arts. Group exhibitions included The Laing Open, Mall Galleries, 1991; Affordable Art Company, Connaught Brown, from 1993; and Courtauld Institute of Art's Biennial, 1996. Had a solo show at Z Gallery, New York, 1992, later ones including Images of God, Hirschl Contemporary Art at the Gallery in Cork Street, 1996. This drew inspiration from world religions. Metropolitan Museum in New York and Ferens Art Gallery, Hull, hold examples.

Nikos GHIKA 1906–1994 Artist and designer in a range of media, and teacher, born in Athens, Greece. He later lived there, in London and Paris. Was educated at the Lycée in Paris and after studying art in Athens attended Académie Ranson, Paris. After living for about a dozen years in Paris, where he had his first solo show in 1927 at Galerie Percier, in 1934 returned to Greece. There he designed for the theatre; with friends published a monthly review called *The Third Eye*; and from 1941–59 taught at National Technical University in Athens, later becoming professor emeritus. He also illustrated a number of books, including Kazantzakis' *The Odyssey*, and Cavafy's *Poems*. His many solo shows included Leicester Galleries, 1955, from which Tate Gallery's Petite Composition en Gris was bought. Musée National d'Art Moderne, in Paris, and Metropolitan Museum, New York, hold examples. Byzantine art and Cubism were marked influences on Nikos Ghika's pictures. His first retrospective was held at the British Council in Athens in 1946, there was a major retrospective at Whitechapel Art Gallery in 1968 and he was elected an Hon. RA in 1986. Died in Athens.

David GHILCHIK 1892–1972 Painter and draughtsman, born in Romania. He studied at Manchester School of Art, 1907–15, where his wife Josephine was a fellow-student of Adolphe Valette, then he attended the Slade School of Fine Art under Henry Tonks and Ambrose McEvoy. He exhibited widely, including RA, ROI, NEAC, RP and Walker Art Gallery, Liverpool. Was a member of London Sketch Club and contributed to *Punch* between the wars and *Daily Sketch*. Ghilchik's oil paintings can be similar in style to those of Christopher Wood, landscapes having a breezy freshness. He was featured in Manchester City Art Gallery's 1976 exhibition of Valette. Lived in London, dying in Poplar.

Amal GHOSH 1933– Versatile artist and teacher, born in Calcutta, India, who studied painting there at the Government College of Art and Craft, then did postgraduate studies at Central School of Art and Design and Hertfordshire College of Art, St Albans. He taught at Central St Martins College of Art and Froebel College at Surrey University. Showed extensively solo in Scandinavia, India and London, later exhibitions including British Council Gallery, Calcutta, 1995; Mermaid Theatre Gallery, 1996, and Meghraj Gallery, 1997. Ghosh carried out a number of mosaic, tile mural, stained glass and sculptural glass public commissions, venues including Eastman Dental Hospital, 1991–2; Kelvedon House, 1996; and West Middlesex University Hospital, 1997. Victoria & Albert Museum, Arts Council and many other collections in Britain and abroad hold Ghosh's work.

Arthur GIARDELLI 1911– Artist in watercolour and relief construction, born in London, whose name came "from my grandfather who, under Garibaldi, fought for the liberation of Italy". Studied at Alleyn's School and Oxford University, 1930–4, gaining a master's degree. Studied art at Ruskin School of Drawing, Oxford, 1930, and with Cedric Morris, 1943–6. Went on to teach at University College of Wales, Aberystwyth, 1958–78, winning a British Council Award, 1979. In his studio in Warren, Pembroke, Dyfed, Giardelli made his elegant, technically skilful constructions from mostly local materials, "paper from old books, disused sacks, scrap metal, watch and clock parts, jetsam and sea shells". He was a member of the Association of Artists and Designers of Wales, International Artists' Association and was chairman of 56 Group Wales. Group shows also included Tate Gallery, Bear Lane Gallery in Oxford, Whitworth Art Gallery in Manchester and abroad. Solo exhibitions included WAC, National Library of Wales in Aberystwyth and Manchester College of Art. Retrospective at England & Co, plus tour, 2001–2. Tate Gallery, National Museum of Wales in Cardiff and Arts Council hold his work.

H W GIBB: *see* **Phelan GIBB**

Phelan GIBB 1870–1948 Painter and potter, born in Alnwick, Northumberland, his full name Henry William Gibb, son of the artist Thomas Henry Gibb and brother of Sadie Gibb. Until 1895, he showed as H W Gibb, then began using his grandmother's maiden name Phelan after the initials H W, later describing himself as Henry – or Harry – Phelan Gibb, or just Phelan Gibb. Phelan (pronounced Faylan) Gibb studied in Newcastle, Edinburgh, Paris, Antwerp and Munich. For a quarter of a century he worked in Paris and was influenced by the work of Cézanne. He exhibited in group exhibitions at Salon d'Automne, the AAA as well as Wertheim, Alpine and Redfern Galleries, RHA, RSA and in New York. Had first London solo show at Baillie Gallery, 1911. Gibb's rather earthy and apparently naïve work was highly thought of by Roger Fry, Gertrude Stein and the dealer Lucy Wertheim. She supported him and his much younger second wife in their declining years with money, assistance to travel to France and even clothes but Gibb, an uneven painter, was unable to match his finest work of the period 1910–20. Gibb appears in Wertheim's memoir *Adventure in Art*. Between the wars the Gibbs had as one of their addresses in London and the provinces a cottage near Brendon, Devon, called Desolate, distinctively marked on the Ordnance Survey map. Phelan painted "pot-boilers", which he donated to agricultural shows as prizes for the best sheep. He died of a heart attack in Great Hampden, Buckinghamshire. There was a posthumous solo exhibition at Alwin Gallery, 1961, but only one picture sold. Duncan Campbell Fine Art latterly handled Gibb's work. Tate Gallery and Victoria & Albert Museum hold examples.

Stanley Watson GIBB 1898–1973 Landscape watercolourist and designer. Born in Lythe, North Yorkshire, Gibb initially studied art at Scarborough School of Art under Albert G Strange, then at Goldsmiths' College School of Art under Frederick Marriott. He exhibited at the RA, RI and the Lake Artists' Society, living at Keswick, Cumberland.

Elizabeth GIBBARD 1913– Sculptor, painter and wood engraver, she studied art at Banbury School of Art and Bath School of Art. As well as exhibiting in mixed shows at the RA and UA, Gibbard had one-man exhibitions in Oxford. Hertfordshire County Council Education Department bought her work. Lived at Cricklade, Wiltshire.

Joan Lever GIBBINGS: *see* **Joan LEVER**

Robert GIBBINGS 1889–1958 Wood engraver, sculptor, writer and teacher. Born in Cork, Ireland, he was educated at the university there, then at the Slade School of Fine Art and at the Central School of Arts and Crafts where he joined Noel Rooke's design class. Commissioned in Munster Fusiliers in World War I, but was wounded by a bullet through the neck while serving in the Dardanelles and was invalided out. While abroad developed engraving style based on strong light and shade found in buildings in snow or bright sunlight, pattern counting more than the subject. Also worked in more naturalistic style. After the war founded SWE. When the Golden Cockerel Press, for which he was working, was threatened with closure, he took it over. During 1924–33 Gibbings' press published 72 books. In 1936 appointed lecturer in book design at Reading University. Travelled widely abroad, including Tahiti. Showed at Redfern Gallery, IS, SWE and RHA. Work held by British Museum, Victoria & Albert Museum and many other galleries in Britain and abroad. *Sweet Thames Run Softly* is his most famous book, published in 1940. It was followed in 1942 by *Coming Down the Wye* and in 1945 by his first Irish volume, *Lovely is the Lee*, chosen by the Book of the Month Club in America. In 1955, Gibbings bought a cottage in Berkshire, near the Thames, and there wrote and illustrated his last book, *Till I End My Song*. In 1972 there was an exhibition of Gibbings' work at the Dorchester Abbey Festival.

Benjamin GIBBON 1914– Painter and mural artist who studied at Ruskin School of Art, Oxford, then the Slade School of Fine Art. Exhibited RA, Goupil Gallery, NEAC, Cooling Galleries and RBSA. Lived at Pershore, Worcestershire.

Faith GIBBON: *see* **Faith O'REILLY**

Sidney GIBBON 1895–1988 Painter, draughtsman and teacher, born in Leamington Spa, Warwickshire. He attended Leicester and Brighton Colleges of Art. Went on to teach, from 1930–57 being head of Newark-on-Trent School of Art. He had an interest in architecture and in puppetry. Showed in the Midlands and has work in Newark Municipal Museum. Lived finally at Acomb, York.

Carole GIBBONS 1935– Painter, born in Glasgow, where she continued to live. She studied at the School of Art there, 1957–61, first showing with Allan Fletcher and Douglas Abercrombie in Glasgow in 1958. From 1965–7 she worked in Spain, then returned to Glasgow. She had her first solo show as a studio exhibition in 1965, having her second at Traverse Gallery, Edinburgh, 1968, then another in 1969 at Compass Gallery, Glasgow. A retrospective followed at the North Briton Gallery, Gartocharn, in 1973. A large-scale show of her work was held at Third Eye Centre, Glasgow, in 1975. She continued busily exhibiting in mixed and group shows, having another retrospective at McLellan Galleries, Glasgow, in 1986. Her work is held by Scottish National Gallery of Modern Art and by Scottish Arts Council, whose award she won in 1970.

Jeff GIBBONS 1962– Painter, born and lived in London, who studied at Ravensbourne College of Art, 1980–1; Middlesex Polytechnic, 1981–4; and London University, 1989–91. He was included in Pick of the New Graduate Art at Christie's in 1984 and won a prize in John Moores Liverpool Exhibition, 1995–6. Shared a show at Morley Gallery, 1994, and solo exhibitions included Somerville College, Oxford, 1991, The Eagle Gallery, 1999, and Art Space Gallery, 2005.

John GIBBONS 1949– Sculptor, born in Ireland, who attended Limerick School of Art, 1969–70, then St Martin's School of Art, 1972–6. He gained a number of awards, including a Macaulay Fellowship in Sculpture, 1975; two GLAA Awards, 1978–85; an Arts Council Award, 1979; *Irish Post* Award, 1987; and The Lorne Award, 1992. Intach Trust and AHRB Awards followed in 2001 and an Arts Council England Award in 2005. He was several times a visiting artist, including Sculpture Space, Utica, New York, 1980; Clayworks Studio Workshop and Syracuse University, both New York in 1983; School of the Museum of Fine Arts, Boston, 1984; and Emma Lake Artists' Workshop, Saskatchewan, Canada, 1991. Gibbons was elected professor in 1995 and a fellow of the RBS in 2003. Took part in many group shows, solo exhibitions starting with International Arts Centre, 1975; others including Serpentine Gallery, 1986; Madeline Carter Fine Art in Boston, America, 1988; Angela Flowers/Flowers East from 1992; and Whitworth Art Gallery, Manchester, 1997. In 2005, Flowers East featured Gibbons' work over the previous five years in one of its Sculpture in the Workplace shows at One Canada Square, Canary Wharf. Arts Council, Tate Gallery, Gulbenkian Foundation and several foreign public collections hold examples. Gibbons' abstract steel sculpture, sometimes painted, related to seen objects, notably the American architectural landscape.

Ella GIBBS 1968– Artist and teacher using modern media, born in London, who was a co-founder of belt, a small, energetic space in Bethnal Green which over three years hosted events that embraced science, music, technology and the arts. After leaving those premises, belt continued to exist as a movable idea. Gibbs gained a foundation diploma, Bath Academy of Art, 1986–7, then gained an honours degree in fine art/sculpture, West Surrey College of Art and Design, 1987–91, with an exchange, Massachusetts College of Art, Boston, America, 1988. From 1996, Gibbs was involved in extensive fund-raising and awards in Britain and abroad, including Arts Council and London Arts Board; from 1999, she was a part-time lecturer in time-based practice/fine arts at the University of Wales Institute, Cardiff. She took part in numerous events, collaborative projects, performance and video, later ones including The Room of Patience, a collaboration with Tomoko Takahashi at Tate Britain, 2000; and Temporary Accommodation, Whitechapel Art Gallery, 2001. There, she presented Programme, inviting people to realise personal dream projects and share them.

Evelyn GIBBS 1905–1991 Printmaker, draughtsman, painter and teacher, born in Liverpool, where she studied at the School of Art, 1922–6; at Royal College of Art, 1926–9; then at British School in Rome, 1929–31. A pioneering educationalist, her book *The Teaching of Art in Schools*, 1934, remained in print for almost 30 years. Taught at Goldsmiths' College School of Art and was married to Sir Hugh Willatt. While evacuated to Nottingham with Goldsmiths', she founded the Midlands Group of Artists in 1943, while working on commissions as a war artist, one painting and several drawings being acquired by the Imperial War Museum. Showed at RA, NEAC, RE, of which she was a member, and other major galleries and there was a posthumous exhibition at Morley Gallery in 1994, having originated at Angel Row Gallery, Nottingham in 1993, later touring to Williamson Art Gallery, Birkenhead. There was a further exhibition at Nottingham University, 1997, and a retrospective toured from University of Wales, Aberystwyth, from 2001. Gibbs was a fine draughtsman in the classical tradition and her work is held by Arts Council, Ashmolean Museum in Oxford and other public collections. Lived in London.

Ewan GIBBS 1973– Artist, born and lived in London, who gained a foundation diploma at Hertfordshire College of Art and Design, 1991–2, then a fine art honours degree at Goldsmiths' College, 1993–6. Group exhibitions included Physiognomical Corpus, One in the Other, 1996; Architecture & Inside, Paul Morris Gallery, New York, 1998; and A Slip of the Mind, Centre Régional d'Art Contemporain Languedoc-Roussillon, Sète, France, 1999. Solo exhibitions included at Maureen Paley/Interim Art, from 1997, and Paul Morris, 1999. After graduation, Gibbs made drawings on graph paper depicting the exterior and interior landscapes of hotels, taken from brochure images and his own photographs. The drawings appeared at their most defined from a distance; on closer scrutiny the mark-making became evident while the image was lost. Tate Gallery; San Francisco Museum of Modern Art; Fogg Museum of Art; Harvard University; and the Museum of Fine Arts, Houston, held examples.

Jonathan GIBBS 1953– Artist and teacher whose output included vibrant paintings as well as witty and atmospheric wood engravings, good examples of which appeared in *Wood Engravings by Jonathan Gibbs*, published by Open Eye Gallery, Edinburgh, 1999, when he had a solo show there. Gibbs gained a first-class honours degree at the Central School of Art & Design, 1972–6; a higher diploma in fine art from Slade School of Fine Art, 1976–8; with a Cheltenham Painting Fellowship (Boise Travelling Scholarship to Italy), 1978–9. During 1979–90, Gibbs taught part-time at Gloucestershire College of Arts & Technology and Bath College of Higher Education, while visiting other colleges, from 1990 being lecturer in illustration at Edinburgh College of Art. Awards comprised Stowells Trophy, Winsor & Newton Students Exhibition and Robert Colquhoun Memorial Award, Kilmarnock, other group shows including RA Summer Exhibition, RSA, LG and Scottish National Gallery of Modern Art, Edinburgh. Gibbs showed solo frequently from 1979, with a series at Curwen Gallery from 1985. Arts Council, Scottish Arts Council and corporate collections hold examples.

Leonie GIBBS fl. from early 1980s– Figurative sculptor who trained at Edinburgh and Wimbledon Art Colleges in the early 1980s. In 1989 she was elected an associate of RBS. The ancient civilisations of Greece, Egypt and the Picts were inspirations for her expressive bronzes. Completed many commissions, including portrait heads, and showed frequently in London and Scotland, where she exhibited at RSA and lived in Invernesshire. Had a solo show in 2000 at The Bruton Street Gallery.

Patrick GIBBS 1959– Landscape painter and teacher. He studied fine art at Magdalen College, Oxford, graduating in 1981. Gibbs was at one time a teacher, working in several schools, one of them King's College School, Wimbledon, where he had been a pupil. After graduation he decided to concentrate on landscape painting, working in oil, acrylic and watercolour on a large and small scale. Worked for extended periods in southern Europe, notably Tuscany, but also in Scotland, Turkey and the London area. For a time he favoured a horizontal format, stemming from experiments with panoramic views based on photographs. Mixed shows included New Grafton and Moss Galleries, one-man exhibitions taking place at Fine Art Trade Guild, 1987–8, Hurlingham Gallery, 1990, and The Gallery in Cork Street, 2002, which included images of Spain and Gambia. Lived in London.

Snow GIBBS 1882–1966 Painter who studied at Central School of Arts and Crafts, in New York and at L'École des Beaux-Arts, Paris, 1907–14. Exhibited RCamA, Walker Art Gallery, Liverpool, BWS, of which for a time he was secretary, RWA and Paris Salon. Lived in Leigh-on-Sea, Essex.

Stephen GIBBS 1957– Painter and draughtsman whose colourful and stylised work often reflected the landscape and life of Southend-on-Sea, Essex, where he was born and lived. Gibbs did a foundation course at South East Essex College, 1975–7; gained a diploma in art and design, specialising in typographic design, London College of Printing, 1977–80; returned to South East Essex College for his further and adult education teaching certificate, 1995; obtaining a Greenwich University certificate in education, 1996; an assessor's certificate at South East Essex College, 1997; and graduated with honours in education and training at Greenwich University, 1997–9. After briefly working as a graphics technician at Garnet College, Roehampton, 1979, from 1980 Gibbs was graphics co-ordinator, technician/lecturer. He was a member of Southend-on-Sea Arts Council. Showed with RA Summer Exhibition and Singer & Friedlander/*Sunday Times*, both from 1993; later group shows including The Discerning Eye, at Mall Galleries, from 2000; and 30th Laing Landscape and Seascape Exhibition, Mall Galleries, and The London Cow Parade, where he showed three cow sculptures, both 2002. Beecroft Art Gallery, Southend, holds Gibbs' works.

Thomas Binney GIBBS 1870–1947 Painter of landscape and portraits and teacher, born in Darlington, Yorkshire. Binney Gibbs was educated at Liverpool North-West School of Art and Liverpool University before studying briefly in London. Although he was early on quite successful as a painter living in Manchester and then at Chapel-en-le-Frith in Derbyshire, for a time he was art master at New Mills. In 1910 he moved to Whistler's old studio in Chelsea and began to concentrate on portraits, having shown several family portraits at RA. Also showed at IS and Paris Salon. In 1939 he settled in Stunts Green, Sussex, where he continued to paint local people and landscapes. Jeremy Wood Fine Art, Cranleigh, had a show of his work in 1975.

Tim GIBBS 1923– Painter, muralist and teacher, working with a bright palette and a bold, firm style. He studied history at Oxford University, 1946–8, and art at Ruskin School of Drawing in Oxford, 1946–9. Between 1956–84 did a large volume of part-time teaching, including Ruskin School, Bath Academy and Morley College. He was deputy Ruskin Master and head of fine art at Oxford University, 1974–80, being acting Ruskin Master in 1976, devising the degree course in fine art. Also did summer school work in Britain and abroad. Completed murals for The Blue Lion in Fen Ditton, 1958, and for Barclays Bank in Guildford, 1968. Took part in mixed shows at RA, LG, John Moores Liverpool Exhibition and elsewhere. Had a solo show at Piccadilly Gallery, 1955, later ones including Nelson Rockefeller Collection, New York, 1986, Clarendon Gallery, 1987–90, and Cadogan Contemporary, 1993. Painting in Essex 1966–89 was a retrospective at Fry Art Gallery,

Saffron Walden, in 2004. After his wife's death, Gibbs lived mostly in a farmhouse in southwest France. The Government Art Collection, Atkinson Art Gallery in Southport, Royal College of Music and several education authorities hold his work.

Jason GIBILARO 1962– Painter, born and lived in London. He studied at St Martin's School of Art and Brighton Polytechnic. Appeared in many mixed exhibitions, including Stowells Trophy, Whitechapel Open, Royal Over-Seas League (BA Travel Prize to India), Angela Flowers Gallery, Brighton Festival and elsewhere. His first substantial show was at Christopher Hull Gallery, 1990, called Berlin – Before and After the Wall, to which Gibilaro's punchy, colourful style was well suited. Further group exhibitions included Art for Life, Christie's, 2004, and solo shows Paintings and Drawings at Peterborough Museum, 1998. For many years Gibilaro was involved with the Public Works Art Group, of which he was a founder, specialising in big vitreous enamel artworks. His Loughborough Junction Mural, installed in 2002, was said to be the largest of its type in Britain.

Charlotte Ellen GIBSON 1902– Sculptor and teacher, born in Launceston, Cornwall. She studied at Regent Street Polytechnic School of Art under Harold Brownsword, 1925–31, then at the British School in Rome, 1931–2. Married the artist J T A Osborne. She went on to teach sculpture at Regent Street Polytechnic 1933–63 and was elected fellow of the RBS in 1951. Exhibited RA, RSA, Royal Glasgow Institute of the Fine Arts and in the provinces. Two examples of her portrait work are illustrated in Arthur T Broadbent's *Sculpture Today in Great Britain 1940–1943*. Lived in Orsett, Essex.

James GIBSON 1948– Painter and teacher, born in Glasgow. He studied art history at Edinburgh University, then taught English for some years while teaching himself the practical side of painting in his spare time. After an initial solo show at Compass Gallery, Glasgow, in 1985 Gibson showed at a number of venues in mixed exhibitions in Scotland and London. He had a solo show at Artspace Aberdeen in 1989 along with a second one-man at Compass. Gibson's pictures, slightly naïve in appearance and carefully structured, deal with the sadness, loneliness and vulnerability of people.

James Brown GIBSON 1880– Painter, printmaker, designer and modeller, born in Glasgow where he studied at the School of Art, his teachers including Maurice Greiffenhagen. Glasgow Art Club member. Showed there, also RSA, RSW, Walker Art Gallery, Liverpool, and Royal Glasgow Institute of the Fine Arts. Lived in Killin, Perthshire.

Jean GIBSON 1927–1991 Sculptor and maker of reliefs, born in Stockport, Cheshire, studied at Royal College of Art, 1951–5, graduating with first-class honours and winning a travelling scholarship. Took part in many group exhibitions, including RA Summer Exhibitions, 1978–91, and LG, of which she became a member 1987. Solo exhibitions included Leicester Galleries from 1968; Nicola Jacobs Gallery, 1981; Oriel Gallery, Cardiff, 1985; Lynne Stern Associates, 1991; and The Redfern Gallery, 1995. Commissions included Commonwealth Institute, 1967; P&O Lines, for the *Oriana*, 1969; Record Industry Awards, 1975–8; Tel-Aviv Museum, Israel, 1976; and Cecil Denny Highton Group of Architects, 1982. When shown at the Redfern, Gibson's reliefs were said to "deal with the manic struggle between feeling and those things that impose constraints on its free expression. They are lyrical and romantic yet disconcerting in the profound sensitivity that they betray." Lived in London, married to the painter Anthony Whishaw.

Lloyd GIBSON 1945– Artist and teacher in many media who studied at Newcastle University from 1963, taught at the local Polytechnic and lived in Newcastle. He was included in The British Art Show touring exhibition, chosen by critic William Packer and put on in 1980 by Arts Council, which holds Gibson's work. Solo exhibitions included Gulbenkian Gallery, Newcastle, 1969; Richard Demarco Gallery, Edinburgh, 1977; and Mappin Art Gallery, Sheffield, 1978.

Lorraine GIBSON 1951– Artist producing non-figurative pictures in pastel, pencil, conté and graphite on paper, born in Sheffield, married to the artist Richard McGowan. Her work was "influenced by nature, especially the coast of my native Yorkshire, and my own small garden." Gibson studied at Sheffield College of Art, 1970–1, then gained her Diploma in Art and Design in fine art with honours, Kingston upon Hull Regional College of Art, 1971–4. Mixed shows included E M Flint Gallery, Walsall, 1977; Dudley Art Gallery, 1978; Waterloo Gallery, 1982; The Mark, Tamworth Arts Centre, 1994; Dean Clough Galleries, Halifax, 1997; and Woodbridge Gallery, Birmingham, 2000. Had a solo exhibition at Worcester City Art Gallery, 1995. Lived in Moseley, Birmingham.

Richard GIBSON 1965– Versatile sculptor, born in Cambridge, who lived in King's Cliffe, Northamptonshire. Gibson's work received wide media coverage ranging from *The Times*, *Daily Mail* and arts periodicals such as *Arts Review* to specialist journals such as that of the Ecological Design Association, also being featured on radio and television. Gained support and sponsorship from national companies, with awards including several Arts Council grants and a bursary membership of RBS. He was artist-in-residence at Woodfield Trust, Peterborough, 2001. Exhibitions included Mixed Medium Exhibition 2, Peterborough Arts Centre, 1993; Suspended, Norwich Sculpture Park, 1994; Landlines – Sculptural Pathway, Wysing Arts Centre, 1997; Regeneration – Interactive sculpture project, Peterborough Environment City Trust, 2000; and Stranded – 25 International Artists Exhibition, Aldwych Underground Station, 2002.

Veronica GIBSON 1954– Artist and teacher, born in Hertfordshire and brought up near St Albans, who studied at Hertfordshire College of Art, 1972–3; Canterbury College of Art, 1978–81, under Thomas Watt, graduating with first-class honours; and University of Wales, Cardiff, 1988–9, gaining her art teaching certificate. She lived and worked in Wales from 1983, based in Powys. Between 1982–8 Gibson was a self-employed prop maker for theatre and opera; gained brief school residencies, in 1987; was with Pioneer Arts, Cardiff, 1987–8; then held a number of teaching posts, from 1995 being a part-time art teacher at Rougemont School, Newport. Gibson was a prolific exhibitor, venues including the RA Summer Exhibition, from 1981; Welsh National Opera, from 1984; Austin/Desmond

Fine Art, from 1986; Martin Tinney Gallery, Cardiff, from 1992; NEAC and ROI, from 1994; RWA and ROI, from 1996; and Manor House, Cardiff, from 1997. Among her solo exhibitions was Landmarks, Brecknock Museum & Art Gallery, Brecon, 2001, which included richly coloured, spontaneous and painterly depictions of landscape. The show also included watercolours and prints, work from Poland, Ireland and studies from national parks. She shared an exhibition at West Wales Arts Centre, Fishguard, in 2003.

Andrew GIDDENS 1976– Painter, born in Dorset, who studied at Falmouth College of Art and The Arts Institute, Bournemouth. He moved to Cornwall in 1991, settling in Helston, and his paintings focused on the coves, beaches, headlands and cliffs of the area. As a dedicated surfer, he had an intimate knowledge of the sea's moods. Had a solo show at The Great Atlantic Map Works Gallery, St Just-in-Penwith, 2003.

Tom GIDLEY 1968– Artist using various materials, such as mixed media with motor in his 1995 Venice Biennale submission Always on my Mind. He was born in Birmingham and gained his bachelor's degree from Central St Martins School of Art, 1987–90, his master's there, 1990–1. Group shows included How Noisy Everything Grows, Royal College of Art, 1992; The Daily Planet, Transmission Gallery, Glasgow, 1993; Beyond Belief, Lisson Gallery, 1994; and in 1995 In Search of the Miraculous at Starkmann Ltd. Had a solo exhibition at British Council Window Gallery, Prague, 1993. Among Gidley's later shows was the World Wide Video Festival, Amsterdam, Netherlands, and a solo at the Store Gallery, both 2004, also Clouds of Witness, Islington Museum, 2005. The BBC Public Art Group commissioned work by him in 2002 and there was a film installation at St Edmund King and Martyr Church in 2004. They were followed by the Trajan Reel Installation, commissioned by the Victoria & Albert Contemporary Programme, supported by Outset Contemporary Art Fund. Lived in London.

Danuta GIERC 1922–2002 Artist, born in Jaroslaw, Poland, also known as Danuta Giercuszkiewicz. She trained at the Polish Institute of Art in Lvov and in London, where she settled, at Borough Polytechnic. Had solo shows at POSK Gallery. Her work is held by Toruń University in Poland.

Danuta GIERCUSZKIEWICZ: *see* **Danuta GIERC**

Colin GIFFARD 1915– Painter, architect and teacher, born in London. He gained his master's degree from Cambridge University, studying architecture at University College, London. Giffard gained the RIBA Schools Drawing Prize, 1932, and was a Rome Finalist, architecture, 1939. Studied at Bath Academy of Art, 1948–51, teachers including William Scott and Peter Potworowski, teaching at the Academy, 1951–68. Giffard was a member of RWA, also showing with RA, LG and abroad. Solo exhibitions included several in Bath and at Woodstock Gallery between 1958–69. RWA holds his work and he completed murals for educational authorities in Lancashire and Hertfordshire. Lived in Freshford, Bath.

Andrew GIFFORD 1970– Painter and lecturer whose work was mainly concerned with the transient effect of weather on landscape. Gifford studied fine art at University of Newcastle and by the time he had graduated with first-class honours, 1990–4, had held a solo show at Middlesbrough Art Gallery, 1993. Lectured part-time at University of Teesside, 1995, and Universities of Newcastle and Aberdeen, 1996–7. He was included in a three-man exhibition at John Martin of London, 1996, and in group shows at SSA and Fruitmarket Gallery, Edinburgh, with solo shows at John Martin, 1999 and 2003, another at Middlesbrough, 2000.

Jane GIFFORD fl. from late 1970s– Artist who graduated in fine art from Newcastle, 1973–7; won a Max Beckmann Scholarship, Brooklyn Museum Art School, New York, 1977–8; then studied advanced printmaking at Central St Martins, 1989–91. Her prizes included an Oppenheim-John Downes Memorial Trust Award and Great London Arts Visual Arts Production Grant, both 1991, and a London Arts Board Awards to Individual Artists Grant and British Council Award, both 1993. Took part in many group exhibitions, later ones including Plot, Paper Bag Factory, 2000, and Installation, Queen of Hungary, Norwich, and Borderline, Veemvloer, Amsterdam, Netherlands, both 2002. Among her solo shows were Riverside Studios, 1991; Cornerhouse, Manchester, 1992; Grey Art Gallery, New York, 1993; and Hirschl Contemporary Art, from 2001. By the time of her one-man exhibition at Hirschl in 2002, Gifford had been recording and making work based on her dreams for over 10 years.

Helen GILBART 1955– Painter, draughtsman and printmaker influenced by David Bomberg. She won a joint honours degree in art and geography at Lancaster University, 1975–8, then undertook a postgraduate painting course at Cyprus College of Art, under a Peter Minet Trust Award, 1983–4. Completed an advanced diploma in printmaking at Central School of Art and Design, 1985–7. An Oppenheim-John Downes Trust Travel Award enabled her to paint in Spain for a year in 1989. In 1991 took part in Towner Art Gallery, Eastbourne, David Bomberg and his followers exhibition, and in 1997 twenty-fifth anniversary exhibition at Bury St Edmunds Art Gallery. She showed widely in Britain and abroad, including Royal College of Art, South London Art Gallery and Royal Festival Hall. Participated in Making the Connection, firstsite, Colchester/Wolsey Art Gallery, Ipswich, 2002. Among solo shows were ones at the Bedarte Gallery, Almeria, Spain, and South Hill Park Arts Centre, Bracknell, and Fragments, BUPA House, 1999. In 2002–3, was artist-in-residence, Sedgwick Museum, Department of Earth Sciences, Cambridge University. Lived in Middleton, near Saxmundham, Suffolk, where her work centred on the land and archaeology.

GILBERT and GEORGE Performance artists, creators of photo-montage, publishers and film-makers. Gilbert (Proesch) was born in the Dolomites, Italy, in 1943. Studied at Wolkenstein School of Art, Hallein School of Art and Munich Academy of Art. George (Passmore) was born in Plymouth, Devon, in 1942. He studied at Dartington Adult Education Centre, at Dartington Hall College of Art and Oxford School of Art. They met when studying at St Martin's School of Art in 1967. From 1968 they showed work and were living sculptures, their first appearance being at Frank's Sandwich Bar, London, in that year. Many other appearances included Robert Fraser Gallery, Nigel

Greenwood Inc and at Robert Self and Anthony d'Offay Galleries. They also appeared several times at Whitechapel Art Gallery and at Hayward Gallery, 1987, as well as widely abroad. They won the Turner Prize in 1986. In addition to featuring in films and videos, Gilbert and George produced works in edition and books such as *Gilbert and George The Complete Pictures 1971–1985*, in which their art philosophy was expounded, seeking "to speak across the barriers of knowledge directly to People about their Life and not about their knowledge of art". A typical Gilbert and George performance was miming to an old record of *Underneath the Arches* while wearing their formal suits and ties, their faces and hands bronzed. Arts Council and other major collections around the world hold their work. There was a 30-year retrospective at the Musée d'Art Moderne, Paris, in 1997. Gilbert & George New Horny Pictures was at White Cube^2 in 2001, and The Dirty Words Pictures at Serpentine Gallery, 2002. There were exhibitions at Bernier/Eliades Gallery, Athens, Greece, and Sonnabend Gallery, New York, in 2004. In 2005, they represented Britain at the Venice Biennale. Lived in London.

Anthony GILBERT 1916–1995 Designer, illustrator and painter who studied at Goldsmiths' College School of Art. From 1943–69 he worked for the advertising agency J Walter Thompson and produced famous anonymous designs such as the After Eight chocolate mint box. Gilbert, a member of the Society of Industrial Artists, completed murals for the Festival of Britain in 1951 and designed stained glass. Was a prolific illustrator for publications such as *Radio Times*, *Vogue*, *House and Garden* and *Lilliput*. In his final years he worked from a studio in Charlbury, Oxfordshire, producing a series of exquisite still lifes, portraits and other pictures redolent of Art Nouveau and Henri Matisse. There was a memorial show at David Messum Fine Art, 1996.

Colin GILBERT 1924– Watercolourist, born and lived in Manchester, who completed an engineering apprenticeship and was among the first National Servicemen to be recruited into the Fleet Air Arm, where he served as an artisan metal worker. He early showed a talent for drawing and when demobilised left engineering and joined a Manchester advertising agency as an artist. As a frequent visitor to the Whitworth Art Gallery, Gilbert was fired by enthusiasm for the medium by the early topographical watercolourists. Retired, he spent much of his time "walking and sketching amongst the wild hills and reservoirs above Littleborough in the South Pennines. My favourite subjects include canals and civil engineering constructions." Colin Jellicoe Gallery, Manchester, sold Gilbert's work.

Dennis GILBERT 1922– Artist in oil, watercolour and pastel, and teacher, born and lived in London. For many years he was married to the artist Joan Gilbert, also known as Joan Musker, later to the art critic and historian Ann Kodicek. Gilbert studied at St Martin's School of Art, 1946–50, teachers including Roland Pitchforth. He became a visiting teacher at four London art schools and was eventually a senior lecturer at Chelsea School of Art. In 1957 Gilbert was chosen as one of Jack Beddington's *Young Artists of Promise*, in the book of that title. He was a member of NS, NEAC, Society of Landscape Painters, Contemporary Portrait Society, Small Paintings Group, Nine Elms Group and Chelsea Art Society. His main works were portraits and landscapes. Also showed at RA, RP, RBA, Stephen Bartley Gallery, Langton Gallery and Paris Salon and had eightieth birthday exhibitions at Piers Feetham Gallery and Highgate Fine Art, both 2002, with another, Drawn to Water, at Piers Feetham in 2005.

Donald GILBERT 1900–1961 Sculptor in a variety of materials. Born at Burcot, Worcestershire, son of the sculptor Walter Gilbert, he studied with him, with Sir Alfred Gilbert, at Birmingham Central School of Art, at the Royal College of Art under Derwent Wood and at the Royal Academy Schools under William Reid Dick and Henry Poole. At the Schools he won silver and bronze medals. Also studied for a time in Italy. Exhibited RA, RSA, SWEA and RHA. Gilbert completed a wide range of work, including busts of the composer Sir Edward Elgar and the conductor Sir Henry Wood, military badges and memorials, ecclesiastical sculpture and Inspiration to Flight, on the British Overseas Airways Corporation building at Brentford. Gilbert's work is illustrated in the volume *RBS: Modern British Sculpture*, published in 1939, and in Arthur T Broadbent's *Sculpture Today in Great Britain 1940–1943*. Lived near Billingshurst, Sussex.

Ellen GILBERT fl. from 1950s– Painter and printmaker who graduated from Cornell University in America before attending the School of Visual Arts, where she studied with Jack Potter, Chaim Koppelman and others, as well as the High School of Music and Art, The Art Students' League of New York and the workshop in lithography at London College of Printing. She moved to United Kingdom in 1969 from New York and began experimental etching with Islington Studio, learning transparent printing techniques developed at S W Hayter's Atelier 17, in Paris. Trips to Scotland, Wales and Ireland revived Gilbert's interest in watercolour. She was a member of Greenwich Printmakers' Association, Printmakers' Council, Hampstead Artists' Council and Islington Art Circle. Mixed shows included RA, Square and Heifer Galleries. Solo exhibitions included Burgh House and Everyman Cinema both in Hampstead, Woodstock Gallery and Radlett Gallery in Radlett.

George GILBERT 1939– Artist using pen and wash, watercolour and acrylic, and teacher, whose subjects were mainly the coast of Fife, where he lived at Crail, and still life. Gilbert was born in Glasgow, graduated from the School of Art there, 1957–61 (was awarded the Guthrie Book Prize for Portraiture), with postgraduate studies (highly commended), 1961–2. Was elected a member of RSW in 1973 (joining its council in 1994), SSWA in 1991 and Paisley Art Institute, 1992. Gilbert taught in Scottish schools from 1963–89, then painted full-time. Group shows included Commonwealth Arts Festival, Glasgow, 1965; Shed 50 Gallery, St Monans, from 1974; Contemporary Scottish Painting, Middlesbrough Art Gallery, 1988; series of Fife Connection exhibitions including the first at Kirkcaldy Art Gallery, 1990; and Scottish Fine Art, Catto Gallery, 1996. He won the Paisley Art Institute's Artstore Award, 1992; RSW's Sir William Gillies Award, 1993; and gained 1st Prize, Marine Life, Portsoy Festival, 1994. Had a solo exhibition at Blythswood Gallery, Glasgow, 1967, later ones including The Open Eye Gallery, Edinburgh, 1994. Public collections holding examples include Nuffield

Foundation; Paintings in Hospitals, Scotland; and Fife Regional Council.

Jim GILBERT 1933–1995 Artist who grew up in the East End of London and who was dishonourably discharged from National Service aged 21, turning to a life of crime. Gilbert was a huge, powerful man who spent much of his life in jail for crimes ranging from drug smuggling to robbery. Confined in the 1960s he began painting as a form of mental release, often without a model and with only poor materials. Although he later painted gentle watercolours of Morocco, much of Gilbert's output, in a sombre palette, reflected his earlier harsh experiences. He had his first show in Bath in 1972, almost two dozen following. He was the first recipient of the Arthur Koestler Award for prisoners' art in 1973 and was chosen by the Dylan Thomas Society to paint the picture of the poet presented to President Jimmy Carter in 1978. When he married his wife Lynne in 1990 Gilbert changed his surname to Barrington, his middle name, to start a new life. Died in southern Spain, where he was temporarily staying alone to paint. Nicholas Bowlby, Tunbridge Wells, had a memorial show in 1995 which transferred to Royal College of Art.

Joan GILBERT 1928– Painter, printmaker, illustrator and tapestry designer, born in India but educated at Badminton School. She married the artist Dennis Gilbert. Studied at St Martin's School of Art, 1945–50 and went on to show with Zwemmer Gallery, SEA, AIA, RA and Arts Council; had one-man shows at Travers Gallery. Work bought by Inner London Education Authority and West Riding Education Authority. Lived in London for many years and was also known as Joan Musker.

Mark GILBERT 1969– Painter, draughtsman and teacher who was son of the artist Norman Gilbert and who gained an honours degree at Glasgow School of Art, 1987–91. After being an arts organiser at Possilpark Community Centre, Gilbert held a number of teaching appointments, including Glasgow School of Art, Benenden School and Heatherley's School of Fine Art. In 1999–00 he was artist-in-residence at St Bartholomew's and the Royal London Oral and Maxillofacial Surgery Unit, working with surgeon Iain Hutchison to depict changes wrought by facial surgery, with a 2000 exhibition launch at the National Portrait Gallery and a national tour. Gilbert took part in many mixed shows. Awards included the Elizabeth Greenshields Foundation, 1991 and 1993; PS Award, 1992; Glasgow City Council and David Cargill Awards, both in 1994 at Royal Glasgow Institute of the Fine Arts; prizes at BP National Portrait Award, National Portrait Gallery, 1994–6; and the Alastair Salvesen Art Trust Scholarship, working in Spain, 1997. Solo exhibitions included RSA, 1997, Victoria Art Gallery, Bath, 2001, and Fresh Faces, Beaux Arts, and Saving Faces, National Portrait Gallery, both 2002. RSA, Glasgow Development Agency, Western Isles Island Council, Burbank Studios in Los Angeles and the merchant bank Robert Fleming hold examples.

Norman GILBERT 1926– Versatile painter, draughtsman and teacher, born in Trinidad of Scottish parents working in the sugar industry, father of the artist Mark Gilbert. Norman crossed the Atlantic six times by the age of nine, was a pupil at Marr College, Troon, 1939–44, served in the Royal Navy, 1944–8, but decided then to paint, "the only thing that would last a lifetime." With an ex-service grant he attended Glasgow School of Art, 1948–52, but was "at odds with the academic Impressionism admired there". After working as a scenic artist, 1952–3, Gilbert bought a caravan and became a pigman, the irregular hours leaving him time to paint. Persistence gained showings at Piccadilly and Leicester Galleries in the 1950s. Taught in Dunbartonshire, 1957–62, and Glasgow, 1964–7, then resigned full-time teaching. Gilbert's work had become increasingly colourful after a sombre early period. He had a first solo show at Upper Grosvenor Galleries, 1966, which toured, being shown at Traverse Theatre Gallery during the Edinburgh Festival. A series of one-man exhibitions followed, gaining wide media coverage, with a retrospective at Eden Court Theatre Gallery, Inverness, 1992. He latterly exhibited with Richmond Hill Gallery, Richmond, Surrey. The University of Stirling and Leeds Education Authority own examples. Lived in Glasgow.

Richard GILBERT 1957– Painter, born in Plymouth, Devon. He studied at Falmouth, Wimbledon and Chelsea Schools of Art. In 1984 he gained a one-year Abbey Major Rome Scholarship and received the Barclays Bank Young Painter of the Year Award, his work was shown in Wet Paint at Bath Festival Gallery and at Warwick Arts Trust. In 1985 Gilbert's picture Reverie was included in John Moores Liverpool Exhibition. He then said that "To paint solid form in an imaginary space is elementary, yet it is a subject of great mystery." Gilbert had a solo show with Raab Gallery (later operating as the BCA Gallery) in 1988 and was included in a British Council group exhibition, Seis jovenes pintores Britanicos, at Torreon de Lozoya, Segovia, Spain, in 1991. Lived for a time at Sevenoaks, Kent.

Stephen GILBERT 1910– Painter, sculptor and architectural designer, born in Fife, grandson of the sculptor Sir Alfred Gilbert. He studied at Slade School of Fine Art, initially architecture, but Henry Tonks advised him to take up painting, and he won the Slade Scholarship in 1930. After showing with LG and RA, Gilbert had his first solo show with Wertheim Gallery in 1938, three years after marrying the Canadian sculptor Jocelyn Chewett. Gilbert then had several years in Paris and Dublin, returning to Paris after World War II. Gilbert and Chewett (1906–79) were associates of The White Stag Group, formed by Basil Rákóczi and Kenneth Hall, and works by them were illustrated in the catalogue of the Group's show at the Irish Museum of Modern Art, Kilmainham, in 2005. In 1948 Gilbert's painting became abstract, he became a member of the COBRA group and exhibited with the Salon des Réalités Nouvelles and Salon des Surindépendants. In the mid-1950s Gilbert became involved in three-dimension constructions and his interest in architecture was reawakened as he worked alongside the experimental architect Peter Stead in Huddersfield. Projects involving colour in architecture and metal buildings eventually led to structures in aluminium utilising curvilinear planes. Although he continued to be based in Paris, Gilbert's work was shown in Britain at Drian Gallery, Austin/Desmond Fine Art and other venues. Arts Council and Tate Gallery hold examples. Shaping Modern Sculpture, Stephen Gilbert and Jocelyn Chewett in Post-War Paris, was at Leeds City Arts Gallery in 2006.

Terence J GILBERT 1946– Painter, designer and illustrator, born in Lambeth, south London, largely self-taught, who studied and copied Old Master techniques in the National Gallery. He worked in advertising studios until 1965, then for a decade was a freelance illustrator in England, on the continent and in America for advertising, film and publishing firms. After travelling in the Middle East and America, in 1976 he decided to devote all his time to painting scenes in those countries, animal studies and portraits. Showed widely at Mathaf Gallery, for which he worked under contract. Completed some historical reproduction pictures. Among Gilbert's notable portraits were one of HM Queen Elizabeth; another of the American President Ronald Reagan riding at Windsor, later presented to him at the White House; and members of the Saudi Royal Family. Gilbert was commissioned to paint the Derby winners Nashwan and Generous. His work was included in W H Patterson's Autumn Exhibition, 2003, and he had a solo exhibition at The Osborne Studio Gallery, 2004.

Vic GILBERT 1938– Painter and draughtsman, born and lived in London. He was a member of the Free Painters and Sculptors from 1977, also showing at Hampstead Artists' Council, ROI and elsewhere.

Wally GILBERT 1946– Sculptor, jeweller, metalworker and teacher, born in Sussex, who aimed "to create an organic and expressive whole based upon a strong formal structure". He attended West Sussex School of Art and Design, 1964–6, then Chelsea School of Art, gaining his diploma in sculpture, 1966–8. From 1975–87 he was an associate lecturer in art and design and jewellery; worked for Louis Osman, architect and goldsmith, 1982–8; from 1989 being associate lecturer in general art and design and media at the Royal National College for the Blind, Hereford. In 1994 Gilbert was granted freedom of the Worshipful Company of Goldsmiths. Group shows included Plastic Precisely, Arnolfini Gallery, Bristol, 1980; WAC tour, 1985; 20 Artists at Artwear, New York, 1992; and Made in the Middle, West Midlands tour, 1995–6. Had a solo show at Roger Billcliffe Fine Art, Glasgow, 1996. Contemporary Art Society, Victoria & Albert Museum and Birmingham and Worcester Museums and Art Galleries hold examples.

Walter GILBERT 1871–1946 Sculptor, metalworker, designer, teacher and writer, born in Rugby, Warwickshire. He was educated at the Municipal School of Art, in Birmingham; at South Kensington; and in France, Belgium and Germany. Travelled widely in America and India. Taught at Rugby School and Harrow School. Gilbert, who wrote on industrial art, became art adviser to several major firms in this field and was a founder-member, and chief designer for, the Bromsgrove Guild. Ornamental metalwork for the council buildings in Dudley, Worcestershire, is by Gilbert, who was also engaged on aspects of the great gates at Buckingham Palace, Liverpool Cathedral and on war memorials in Liverpool, Burnley, Crewe, Troon, and elsewhere. Lived in Birmingham and London.

Michael GILBERY 1913–2000 Portrait painter and teacher, born and lived in London, who studied at St Martin's School of Art, 1928–32, then until 1935 at Royal College of Art, teachers including Gilbert Spencer and Vivian Pitchforth, Sir William Rothenstein and Percy Horton, who noted particularly his "facility for obtaining a likeness combined with a lively and sympathetic handling." A number of critics hailed the young man's talent when, aged only 17, his portrait of his father was hung at the RA. At that time he showed as Michael Goldberg, his born name. Gilbery also gained recognition for his Jewish scenes, some exhibited at the Whitechapel Art Gallery in 1932. After leaving college he was commissioned to paint the Royal Historic Cavalcade when King George VI was crowned in 1936. The murals covered the department store Swears and Wells and included a 50-foot centrepiece of St George and the Dragon, described in the press as "one of the sensations of the coronation". Taught for many years at St Martin's School of Art. Showed at RA, NS, NEAC, RP and elsewhere. Tel-Aviv Museum in Israel holds his work. A group of works by Gilbery was offered by Bonhams, Knightsbridge, in 2005.

Garry GILCHRIST 1952– Painter and draughtsman, sometimes exhibiting as Garry Richard Gilchrist, brought up in the Gorbals area of Glasgow, where he was born and studied at the School of Art, 1969–71. Using a rich and unusual palette, Gilchrist was notable for his series of heads, sometimes distorted into shapes such as triangles. Bank robbers was another theme. Exhibitions included St Martin's Gallery, Leicester, 1976; Sundance Studios and Press Club, both 1982; Stephen Bartley Gallery, 1984; Windsor Arts Festival from 1987; West Wharf Gallery, Cardiff, 1990; Bohemian Café, Blackheath, 1993; and City Art Gallery, 1994. In 1997 had a solo exhibition at Air Gallery, with a 30-year retrospective at The Portobello Gold, 2000. Lived in London.

Philip Thomson GILCHRIST 1865–1956 Painter, especially of marine subjects, born at Stanwix, near Carlisle. Studied in Hampshire and under the painter Tom Mostyn, after a period in business. Exhibited RA, RSA, especially at RBA, also Walker Art Gallery, Liverpool, RHA and Royal Glasgow Institute of the Fine Arts. He was a member of both the Liverpool and Manchester Academies, public art galleries in those cities buying his work. Lived at Sunderland Point, near Lancaster.

Paul GILDEA 1956– Figurative painter, born and lived in London, who studied at Camberwell School of Arts and Crafts, 1975–6, then Middlesex Polytechnic, 1976–9. Mixed exhibitions included Serpentine Gallery Summer Show 1 of 1982; Greater London Council's Spirit of London, 1982, as second prize winner; RA Summer Exhibition from 1987; and John Moores Liverpool Exhibition, 1995–6. Had a solo show at Galerie Quincampoix, Paris, 1989, others at Atkinson Art Gallery, Southport, and Millfield Arts Projects, Street, Somerset, both 1999.

Theresa GILDER fl. from 1960s– Artist and designer, notable for her stone carvings. Born in Manchester, she studied at the School of Art there, then became a textile designer. She settled in Cornwall and was influenced by the work of Barbara Hepworth in St Ives. Was taught by John Tunnard, E Bouverie Hoyton and Barbara Tribe at Penzance School of Art. As well as portraits, Gilder made a reputation for her carved intertwining figures, as shown in Artists from Cornwall at RWA, 1992. She also showed at Newlyn Orion Gallery, Penzance; Truro City Museum; and Artful Eye, New Jersey, in America. Truro City Gallery and the Child Development Centre, Plymouth, hold her work. Lived in Penzance, Cornwall.

Catherine GILES 1878–1955 Painter, born in Lewisham, southeast London, as Catherina (later changed to Catherine; in middle age, becoming a Roman Catholic, she took St Catherine of Siena as her patron saint) Dawson Giles, who studied at Goldsmiths' Institute, in 1900 transferring to the Royal Academy Schools, which she found unsympathetic, so after three years moved to Etaples, France, to paint from the model with the American artist Max Bohm. There she met the painter Jessica Dismorr, with whom she painted on trips in France and Italy. Manchester City Art Gallery holds Giles' Snow Scene, Etaples, presented in 1911. During World War I Giles worked as a nurse and in the War Office. She travelled on the continent in the inter-war years, the art of Siena, mountains and rock formations influencing her pictures. Mixed shows included IS, LG, NEAC and Guild of Catholic Artists, which she joined in 1930; she became an associate of the Society of Painters in Tempera, 1939. Among her solo exhibitions was one of flower watercolours and gouaches at Claridge Galleries, 1928. Giles suffered latterly from deafness. Among church work completed were Stations of the Cross, in tempera, for the Church of St Thomas More, Seaford. Much of Giles' output has been lost. There was a joint show of her work with that of Dismorr at the Fine Art Society in 2000.

Frank Lynton GILES 1910–2003 Artist in many media, full name Albert Frank Lynton Giles, born in London. He studied at Goldsmiths' College School of Art and St Martin's School of Art, teachers including Clive Gardiner, James Bateman, Stanley Anderson and Vivian Pitchforth. He began his career in 1926 when he was apprenticed to the Ascoli Studio, afterwards being a magazine illustrator and graphic designer for London agencies. Advertising campaigns worked on included Daz and Tide washing powders, Camay toilet soap and Johnson Wax. Sometimes signed his work Lynton Giles. Was elected RWA in 1978. He showed at RA, RP, RBA, RI, RWS, extensively in the provinces and at Paris Salon, where he won a silver medal in 1948. Principal works included The Milliner, Cornish Fisherman and My Son Geoffrey. Public collections in Sheffield, Worthing and Bristol and RWA hold examples. Lived in Worthing, Sussex.

Graham GILES 1942– Landscape painter and teacher, who made his first paintings as a schoolboy on the towpath of the Grand Union Canal at Berkhamsted, Hertfordshire. Studied at Regent Street Polytechnic School of Art, 1960–3, then Chelsea School of Art, 1963–4. Awards included RA David Murray Scholarship, 1962; Swedish Government Scholarship to study at the Royal Academy of Fine Arts, Stockholm, with Evert Lundquist, 1964; and a French Government Scholarship to study at L'École Nationale Supérieure des Beaux-Arts, Paris, 1965. Taught extensively from mid-1960s, latterly being a visitor at both Hull and Grimsby Colleges of Art and senior lecturer in theoretical studies, Norfolk Institute of Art & Design. Mixed exhibitions included LG, Thackeray and South London Art Galleries and Phoenix Gallery, Lavenham. Solo shows included Cadogan Contemporary, from 1988, and Chappel Galleries, Chappel, 1999. Shared an exhibition with his wife Julie at The John Russell Gallery, Ipswich, 1997, having his own shows there in 2003 and 2005. Lived in Suffolk.

Julie GILES 1946– Painter, draughtsman and teacher, born in Bedford, who obtained her diploma from Camberwell School of Arts and Crafts, 1965–9. She taught at Centro d'Arte in Verrocchio, Italy, and at Norwich School of Art. Mixed exhibitions included Gainsborough's House, Sudbury, Drawings for All, 1984; Wykeham Galleries, Hampshire, from 1988; and Home and Abroad, The John Russell Gallery, Ipswich, 1997, the year she shared an exhibition there with her husband, Graham Giles. Had a series of solo exhibitions, starting with Bury Art Gallery, 1972, later ones including Cadogan Contemporary, 1988, and John Russell, from 1989. Recent Works: Suffolk Coast, River and Land was held at Chappel Galleries, Chappel, in 2003. British Rail holds her work. Lived in Suffolk.

Lesley GILES 1953– Artist in oil, pastel and watercolour, born in Bristol, who supported herself working part-time for local government social services. She studied at Goldsmiths' College School of Art, 1972–6, with Peter Cresswell, Albert Irvin and John Bellany, then at Royal College of Art with Ken Kiff, Andrew Brighton and Peter Allen. Giles' work was featured in a number of books on landscape painting. Her work was notable for its careful organisation and an absence of people, sometimes creating a slightly Surrealist atmosphere. Group shows included Subjective City, Cleveland Gallery, Middlesbrough, and tour, 1990. She was in Two London Painters, at Swiss Cottage Library, 1983. Solo shows included Dungeness Paintings, Rye Art Gallery, 1992, and Deserted Landscape, at Barbican Centre, 1994. London Boroughs of Camden and Hounslow hold her work. Lived in London, then in 2003 had a studio show, including works from a China residency, before moving to America.

Lynton GILES: *see* **Frank Lynton GILES**

Peter GILES 1939– Artist in various media, singer and teacher, born in Perivale, Middlesex. He attended Ealing School of Art, 1954–9, and Hornsey College of Art, 1959–60, making a special study of illustration. Taught part-time at several schools in Kent, lectured in North America and showed in the provinces. Lichfield Art Gallery holds his work. Lived at Bridge, Canterbury, Kent.

Tam GILES 1930– Sculptor and teacher, born in Britain, who from age of 10 lived mostly abroad. First art studies were with Joaquin Torres Garcia and the George Washington University and Corcoran School of Art in Washington, America. Her nomadic existence ended with settling in London in 1971. From then she taught first part-time at Byam Shaw School of Art, in 1979 full-time, resigning in 1986 to devote all her energies to environmental projects. Associated with other British Constructivist artists, she showed at Sally East Gallery and in group shows in Britain and on the continent. Carried out commissioned work, believing that new materials and construction methods should be employed by artists "to humanise them and bring them into our world of images".

Tony GILES 1925– Painter, born in Taunton, Somerset. He worked as a draughtsman with the Admiralty, 1941–59, teaching himself to paint. Began to make a reputation after settling in Cornwall in 1961, railways and landscape being a favourite theme in his work. He won the English China Clay competition Art in Industry in 1971. Mixed exhibition appearances included RA Summer Exhibition, and he was a participant in Artists from Cornwall at RWA, 1992. Solo shows included Salthouse Gallery, St Ives, 1984;

Park Gallery, Cheltenham, 1988; and Penwith 65th Birthday Retrospective, 1990. Kettle's Yard Gallery, Cambridge, and public galleries in Stoke-on-Trent and Birmingham hold examples.

Tom GILHESPY 1944– Sculptor, artist in mixed media and teacher, born in Ferryhill, County Durham. He attended Leicester College of Art, 1962–6, and the Accademia di Belle Arti, Florence, on an Italian Government Scholarship, in 1966–7. Went on to become a part-time lecturer for a time at Newport College of Art. A member of the 56 Group, Gilhespy showed with it as well as SWG, at Royal National Eisteddfod and WAC, which holds his work. Included in WAC The Probity of Art touring show of drawings, 1980. In 2002, Wrexham Arts Centre showed recent sculptures and works on paper by Gilhespy, including the siting of a new sculpture by him outside the building.

Jaime GILI 1972– Artist born in Caracas, Venezuela, who studied graphic design at Institute Neumann there, 1989–90; graduated with honours in fine art at the University of Barcelona, Spain, 1990–5; and gained his master's in fine art, painting, Royal College of Art, 1996–8. Symbols of speed and power were important in Gili's art from 1995, included in the show Global II Collection at Addison Wesley Longman Ltd, Harlow, 1998–9. Gili contributed his 1997 abstract 250 Years of Painting in the Tropics to East International, Norwich School of Art & Design, 1999. Jerwood Space showed Gili's installation of drawings and paintings, plus a new photographic series, in 2003. He lived in London.

Katherine GILI 1948– Sculptor and teacher, born in Oxford. Studied at Bath Academy of Art, 1966–70, then St Martin's School of Art, 1971–3. In 1972 she began teaching at Norwich School of Art, at St Martin's in 1975, later joining the City Lit. Gili began to exhibit in mixed shows in the early 1970s, at Museum of Modern Art in Oxford; Chelsea Gallery; Norwich Cathedral; Stockwell Depot; and in Silver Jubilee Contemporary British Sculpture Exhibition, Battersea Park, 1977. Later appearances included Yorkshire Sculpture Park at Bretton Hall in 1983, when she also took part in Have You Seen Sculpture from the Body? at Woodlands Art Gallery. Had a solo show at Salander/O'Reilly Gallery, New York, 1981, and shared an exhibition with Graham Boyd at The Charterhouse Gallery, 1994. Gili was a creator of abstract sculptures analagous to human figures, in steel but with sensuous, dance-like connotations. Arts Council holds her work. Her father was the noted bookseller, publisher, Spanish scholar and translator J L Gili, who died in 1998.

GILL 1930– Watercolourist, born in London, married to the artist David Green. Gill Green studied at Hornsey College of Art under Jesse Cast and Norman Janes. Exhibited widely with her husband, including Heffer's in Cambridge, Century Gallery in Henley-on-Thames, Rye Art Gallery, 44 Gallery in Aldeburgh and Wigmore Hall. Cards and prints of her work were published. Lived in Woodbridge, Suffolk.

Alison GILL 1966– Sculptor, and teacher, born in London. She attended Kingston Polytechnic, 1984–5, Brighton Polytechnic, 1985–8, and Royal College of Art, 1990–2. She worked in a variety of media, as in her exhibit Untitled – paper, nail varnish, tar and paint – in East & South, Norwich Gallery/Kent Institute of Art and Design, 1992. In 1993 she took part in the Brick Lane Open 3, Spitalfields Heritage Centre, and in Drawing Towards Sculpture, Isis Gallery, Leigh-on-Sea. Later exhibitions included Taro Nasu Gallery, Tokyo, Japan, 2000, and Platform, 2003. In that year, Gill was shortlisted for the Jerwood Sculpture Prize. Gill's teaching experience included Serpentine Gallery, London Institute, Winchester and Wimbledon Schools of Art. In 1999, she participated in the Norbury Park Art and Landscape Project, curated by Tamsin Dillon. Lived for a time in East Molesey, Surrey.

Angela GILL 1964– Painter, born in Middlesex, who studied at Harrow School of Art, 1983–4, Portsmouth Polytechnic, 1984–7, and Royal College of Art, 1991–3. Her exhibitions included A Place For Art at Brighton Polytechnic, 1989; BT New Contemporaries, 1992; Paton Gallery, 1993; and in 1993–4 her powerful Heavy and Clenched was included in John Moores Liverpool Exhibition. Later group shows included An American Passion, The Susan Kasen Summer and Robert D Summer Collection of Contemporary British Art, Royal College of Art and tour, 1995; New Arts Gallery, Bantam, Connecticut, America, 2000; and Body Human, Nohra Haime Gallery, New York, 2005. Nohra Haime gave Gill solo exhibitions in 2004 and 2005. Gill won a string of awards and had work in a number of public and corporate collections in Britain and America, including Department of Education and Madame Tussaud's and The Hit Factory and Dimensional Media Associates, both in New York.

Cecil GILL 1897–1981 Painter, brother of the artists Eric and MacDonald Gill, born Brighton, Sussex. Was by profession a doctor who studied medicine at Edinburgh University. After service as a pilot in World War I he was for eight years from 1925 a medical missionary in India and the Far East, after which he was a general practitioner in England and Wales until 1968. For some time he was a member of SWG, and he also showed with SEA, Royal National Eisteddfod, Newport Art and Craft Society and WAC, which also holds his work. Did some painting in Corsica.

Eric Peter GILL 1914– Artist in watercolour and associated media and teacher, born in Birkenhead, Cheshire. He studied at Liverpool School of Art with Will C Penn. He taught there, 1937–40 and 1946–50, during World War II serving in the Royal Air Force as a cartographic draughtsman. Was principal of St Helens School of Art, 1950–74. Group shows included Wirral Society of Arts of which he was a member, Walker Art Gallery in Liverpool, Liverpool Academy of Art shows and at Rob Piercey Gallery, Portmadog. Had solo shows at St Helens Museum and Art Gallery and Williamson Art Gallery in Birkenhead. The Walker and Williamson hold his work. His later work included "studies of Welsh landscape, the rugged terrain of remote valleys, southern Snowdonia mostly". Lived in Bromborough, Wirral.

Lilly Kathe Elizabeth GILL 1922– Animal sculptor and artist, born in Germany, who trained as an art teacher, later in life attending adult education classes in pottery and ceramics. Took part in group exhibitions with SWA, SWLA, Radlett Art Society shows and elsewhere. Had solo shows at Boreham Wood Civic Centre, Hertsmere Council

Offices, Watford and Stanmore Libraries, Watford and Bushey Museums and Holkham Hall, Norfolk. Belonged to Watford & Bushey and Radlett Art Societies. Bushey Museum Trust holds her work. Italian sculptors in the Victoria & Albert Museum and Sir Edwin Landseer were cited as key influences. Lived in Bushey, Hertfordshire.

MacDonald GILL 1884–1947 Architect, mural painter, calligrapher, designer and teacher, full name Leslie MacDonald Gill and known as Max. He was the brother of the artists Eric and Cecil Gill and was born in Brighton, Sussex. He studied at Royal Naval Academy and art at Chichester School of Art and Central School of Arts and Crafts. Early in the century was articled as an architect, was eventually elected fellow of RIBA and worked at such buildings as Lincoln Cathedral and the House of Commons, being noted for his murals. Was also an Imperial War Graves Commission designer and for a time a lecturer on architecture and completed posters for the Empire Marketing Board and London's Underground Railway. Tate Gallery holds. Died in London.

Madge GILL 1884 (some sources say 1882)–1961 Prolific figurative artist (original name Maude Eades) who drew, painted, embroidered and knitted her works in a unique naïve style, born illegitimately in London, where she spent most of her life. During her early years she was brought up by her mother and an aunt and spent some time in orphanages in London and Canada, returning to England in 1903. Living with another aunt, she was introduced to Spiritualism. Madge married her cousin Thomas Gill in 1907; of four children born, only two sons survived, Laurie during his life doing much to promote his mother's work. Madge lost the sight of an eye, later replaced by a glass one, but despite this around 1919–20 began to create her strange objects and drawings – singular for their delicate patterning and cross-hatching and the inclusion of an oval-faced female figure – in bed by oil lamp light. She was guided by a spirit called Myninerest, and in 1920 became a medium. Although she exhibited at the East End Academy from the 1930s and gained much press interest, she shunned publicity and sales, saying her works belonged to her spirit guide. Through the 1950s Madge worked hard, often through the night, standing in front of a roll of calico which unwound from a frame fixed up by Laurie, with whom she finally lived in a gloomy house in East Ham. Exhibitions which did much to promote her name after her death included one by Newham Arts Council at Newham Town Hall, 1969, with another at Leeds Playhouse Gallery in 1976. She was later included in mixed shows such as Outsiders & Co, at England & Co, 1996. Gill's work is in many public collections, including the Outsider Collection and Archive.

Olivia GILL 1974– Versatile artist, theatre specialist, curator and teacher who graduated with first-class honours in drama at Hull University, 1993–6. In 1995 she held her first solo exhibition of drawings and paintings, made while working in India and the Middle East and entitled An Eastern Eye, at Mount House Gallery, Marlborough. Its success financed her studies. Having worked in the theatre since the age of 16 she went on to design and direct her own work, as well as collaborating with established companies and curating/exhibiting Our Lives in Black & White at the R K Burt Gallery, and Journeys in Mind, at The Wellcome Department, Institute of Neurology, University College London, both 2000. Gill specialised particularly in the history and contemporary use of puppetry as a performance tool and therapeutic medium. She went on to concentrate more on fine art, in 2001 completing her master's in printmaking with distinction at Camberwell College of Art, although she was also involved with local arts development work, puppetry and teaching. At the National Print Exhibition at Mall Galleries in 2001 Gill won both a Joseph Webb Commemorative Award and Fabriano Paper Mill Award and in the same exhibition in 2002 a St Cuthbert's Paper Mill Award. Other mixed exhibitions included The Discerning Eye, Mall Galleries, 1999, and RA Summer Exhibition, 2001. Solo exhibitions included 11 Old Church Street, 2003, in which the theme of exile was important. Gordon Hepworth Fine Art, Newton St Cyres, represented Gill, who lived in Yearle, Northumberland.

Ruth GILL 1915– Artist, mainly doing commercial work, born in London. Studied at Chelsea School of Art, then for a time was art director of the advertising agency John Tait and Partners, in London. Exhibited LG. Work widely reproduced in women's magazines. Lived in London.

Sheila GILL 1925– Painter, potter, designer, calligrapher and teacher, born in Leeds, Yorkshire. Studied at Leeds College of Art, her teachers including Douglas Bisset and John Frederic Greenwood. Showed in the area of Leeds, near where she lived at Shadwell, teaching at Roundhay School for Boys.

Stanley Herbert GILL 1912–2000 Painter, printmaker and teacher, born in Leeds, Yorkshire, his father Fred being a lithographer. Studied at the local College of Art, 1928–31, then at Royal College of Art, 1931–5, teachers including Gilbert Spencer. From 1936 began teaching at art schools in Yorkshire, being on the staff of Salisbury College of Art, 1947–72. Showed with RA, Bethnal Green Museum of Childhood and widely in the provinces. Lived in Salisbury, Wiltshire.

Ernest GILLAM 1897– Painter, notably in watercolour, born in Brighton, Sussex. He was self-taught as a painter. Showed at RA and in the provinces. His work appeared in *The Artist* magazine and the publishers awarded Gillam a gold medal for watercolour in 1932. Lived in north London, then at Woodingdean, near Brighton.

Régie GILLARD 1919– Artist in watercolour, born in Brentry, near Bristol, married name Régine Virgon. She studied with Donald Milner at the West of England College of Art, Bristol, then became involved in designing greetings cards for Medici, Dixon's and Gordon Fraser, for whom she worked exclusively on cards and other material for over 30 years. Her work was shown all over the world, exhibitions including RWA and Clifton Arts Club. Lived latterly at Vellow, Williton, Somerset.

Edwin GILLBE 1917–1974 Painter in oil, gouache and watercolour; typographer and designer. Gillbe studied art at St Martin's School of Art under Herbert Ashwin Budd and Stafford Leake, at the City and Guilds of London Art School under James Grant, then at the Camberwell School of Art under Victor Pasmore. As well as having his design work featured in national newspapers and advertisements, Gillbe exhibited at the ROI, RBA and RWS. Lived in London.

Joan GILLCHREST 1918– Artist, born in London, who trained under Iain Macnab at Grosvenor School of Modern Art and in Paris. During World War II she drove an ambulance in London. In 1958 she moved to Cornwall. From before the war she had begun to exhibit in mixed company, over the years showing with RA, LG, NEAC and Whitechapel Art Gallery. Also showed in Cornwall at Newlyn Orion Gallery, Penzance, and Wills Lane Gallery, St Ives, and she was included in Artists from Cornwall at RWA, 1992. Had solo shows at Plymouth City Art Gallery, 1969, Newlyn Orion in 1973–6, Bodmin Fine Arts, 1974–8, and Windsor Fine Arts, 1978. Wren Gallery, Burford, handled Gillchrest's work from 1990, in 2002 held the exhibition Joan and Friends, with a solo show in 2003.

Floris Mary GILLESPIE 1882–1967 Watercolourist and teacher, born in Bonnybridge, Stirlingshire, sister of the artists Alexander Bryson Gillespie and Janetta S Gillespie, with whom she exhibited. After studying at Glasgow School of Art, 1913–15 Floris taught at Stranraer High School. She joined the Glasgow Society of Women Artists in 1928, winning its Lauder Award in 1948. Floris also exhibited at the RSW, Royal Glasgow Institute of the Fine Arts, RSA and Walker Art Gallery in Liverpool. She died in Edinburgh.

George K GILLESPIE 1924–1995 Prolific painter of traditional Irish landscapes, born in Belfast, Northern Ireland, who studied at the College of Art there, 1941–5, and with Robert Boyd Morrison. In his early fifties a heart attack prompted Gillespie to give up his business career and concentrate on painting full-time at his studio in Newtownards, County Down. Typical oils were featured in Landscapes North and South, which toured from Glebe House and Gallery, Donegal, in 1997–8.

Janetta S GILLESPIE 1876–1956 Painter in oil and watercolour of flowers and still life, and teacher, born and died in Bonnybridge, Stirlingshire. She was the sister of the artists Alexander Bryson Gillespie and Floris Mary Gillespie, with whom she exhibited. Gillespie studied at Glasgow School of Art in 1913 and 1915–17 and taught at Bonnybridge School. She joined the Glasgow Society of Lady Artists in 1928, winning its Lauder Award in 1934, and the RSW in 1943. She also exhibited at RSA, Royal Glasgow Institute of the Fine Arts and Walker Art Gallery, Liverpool.

Joan GILLESPIE fl. from 1970s– Painter of highly coloured still lifes and landscapes, who studied at Duncan of Jordanstone College of Art, Dundee, 1972–5, gaining a diploma in drawing and painting from Edinburgh College of Art, 1975–6. After being a designer with the Royal Museums of Scotland in Edinburgh, 1979–86, began to paint full-time. Was a finalist in Morrison Portrait Competition, RSA, 1991, and Laing Landscape Competition, Mall Galleries, 1992, also showing at Royal Glasgow Institute of the Fine Arts, RWS and SSWA, as well as many private galleries. Shared a show with Geri Morgan at Duncan Campbell Contemporary Art, 1998, with solos there from 2000. City of Edinburgh, corporate and private collections hold examples.

Michael GILLESPIE fl. from 1950s– Sculptor and teacher who studied at Hammersmith College of Art, learned bronze casting and cast for Jacob Epstein, who was a major influence. Took part in a lot of mixed shows, including 1st RWA Open Sculpture Exhibition, Bristol, 1993, and had many solo shows. Much of his work was abstract, although Gillespie disliked the distinction between it and figurative sculpture. In 1969 with John W Mills he published a standard manual, *Studio Bronze Casting*, and he taught latterly at Hertfordshire University. Lived in Histon, Cambridgeshire.

Raymond GILLESPIE 1955– Painter, designer and teacher, born in Dungannon, County Tyrone. He attended Ulster College of Art and Design, where he graduated after four years in 1978, the year he won the Philip Smiles Award – Gold Medal. Was with Ulster Museum, 1978–85. His teaching included Rupert Stanley College, Belfast, and the University of Ulster. From 1985–91 Gillespie was a partner in design and advertising practices, leaving to become a full-time painter. Among group shows in which Gillespie showed were Heritage Centre, Bangor, 1988; 4 Ulster Painters, Heritage Centre, Bangor, 1991; and Tom Caldwell Summer Shows in Belfast and Dublin, 1991. Atmospheric landscapes on a small scale were a feature of Gillespie's work.

Sarah GILLESPIE 1963– Painter and draughtsman, born in Hampshire, who attended Atelier Neo Medici, Paris, before moving to the Ruskin School of Fine Art, Oxford. The Paris year gave her a solid grounding in techniques used since the sixteenth century and involved such concentrated work that she barely got to know the city. She won the Egerton Coghill Prize for landscape painting and Elizabeth Greenshields Award for figurative painting. Gillespie's meticulously observed, atmospheric paintings and drawings focused on the coastline around Devon and Cornwall, in particular the area around the Salcombe estuary, as well as on the west coast of Ireland. She showed in the United Kingdom and abroad, including Gallery Revel, New York, America; RWA; Six Chapel Row, Bath; Ariel Centre, Totnes; Thompson's Gallery; and New Street Gallery, Plymouth, where she had a solo exhibition in 2002. Government Office for the South West owned Gillespie's work. She lived for some time at Blackawton, Totnes, Devon.

Stirling GILLESPIE 1908–1993 Self-taught painter, teacher, traveller and film-maker, born in Stirling, Stirlingshire, as James Stirling Gillespie. From boyhood his aim was "to portray in watercolour (and some oil) the beauty of the Scottish scene". Although an outstanding schoolboy athlete, Gillespie's interest remained art, but his father's business failure in 1928 prevented his taking up a place at Glasgow School of Art. Became a journalist, in 1936 joining Dalrymple Educational Film Productions; in 1938 travelled through Africa to make educational films; and in 1939 published his experiences in the book *Celluloid Safari*. Gillespie also sailed yachts across the North Sea, Baltic Sea and Bay of Biscay. Eventually concentrated on landscape painting, in 1958 settling in Rothesay, Isle of Bute, after three years in Ballarat, Australia, and one in the Yoruba region of Nigeria, where he taught art. Joined Glasgow Art Club, becoming vice-president, and showed at Royal Glasgow Institute of the Fine Arts, being exhibitor of the year by popular acclaim in 1979–80–81. Solo shows included Kelly Gallery in Glasgow and Pitlochry Theatre. In 1985 illness prevented use of his right hand and arm, so he ceased to paint. By then he had sold well over 1,500 pictures.

Leonard Christopher GILLEY 1915–1997 Versatile artist and teacher, born in Camberwell, southeast London, where he attended the School of Arts and Crafts, among his notable teachers being Edward McKnight Kauffer. During World War II Gilley was a cartographer in the Royal Air Force. Industrial commissions were undertaken for Shell, Castrol, Ministries of Transport and Agriculture, Dunhill and Hoover, and he illustrated for Odhams Press, Constable and other publishers. Gilley was noted for his marine paintings, "influenced by the work of William van de Velde", and portraits. Showed at Fishmongers' Hall and galleries in Bath, Bristol, Monmouth and Tetbury. Lived latterly at Trelleck, Monmouth, Gwent.

Ken GILLHAM 1934– Sculptor, modeller and teacher, born and lived in London. He studied at Medway College of Art, 1950–4, and Royal Academy Schools, 1956–8, teachers including Peter Greenham and Maurice Lambert. In his final year gained the Silver Medal and Landseer Scholarship. Gillham's work, in a variety of media, was used in many trade fairs and exhibitions, including Royal Society of Scientific Instrument Makers, British Museum and Walt Disney Productions, in America. He was an associate of the RBS.

Ernest GILLICK 1874–1951 Sculptor and painter, born in Bradford, who studied at the Royal College of Art, where he won a Travelling Scholarship. Married to the sculptor Mary Gillick. Exhibited RA, RSA and Walker Art Gallery, Liverpool. Gillick was awarded the RBS medal in 1935, three years later becoming a fellow. Was master of the Art Workers' Guild in 1935, served on the faculty of sculpture of the British School in Rome and on the Imperial Arts League's council. Gillick completed a large volume of public sculpture, including the Frampton memorial in St Paul's Cathedral, London; medals for the Royal Mint, RA and Inner Temple; London's Lord Mayor's seal; plus a variety of work for Commonwealth countries. Lived in London. The Henry Moore Institute archive, Leeds, holds a huge postcard collection documenting sculpture, monuments and paintings by Gillick from around the world.

James GILLICK 1972– Figurative painter and draughtsman, born in Norfolk, who studied landscape architecture at Cheltenham and Gloucester College. He was one of a large creative family, his mother being the social critic Victoria Gillick, his twin brother the sculptor Theodore Gillick, and he showed early talent, painting commissioned portraits while still at school. For Gillick, "what the eye sees, the heart loves and the mind absorbs"; single objects had "a life in themselves that is breathtaking"; and flesh was "the ultimate challenge". The artist unusually made all his own materials, such as canvases, panels, stretchers, oils, glues, waxes, varnishes and paints. Group shows included Eastern Open, 1996; Catto Gallery, 1996–8; Montpellier Gallery, Cheltenham, 1996–01; A Dealer's Eye, Jonathan Cooper, 2000; and Spencer Coleman Galleries, Stamford, Lincoln and Beverley, 2001–01. Jonathan Cooper gave Gillick a solo show in 2001. Baroness Thatcher and Very Reverend M Couve de Murville, archbishop of Birmingham, were among portrait commissions.

Liam GILLICK 1964– Artist and critic who was born in Aylesbury, Buckinghamshire. Studied at Hertfordshire College of Art, 1983–4, then Goldsmiths' College, graduating with honours, 1984–7. Group exhibitions included The Multiple Projects Room, Air de Paris, Nice, 1990. Solo shows included 84 Diagrams, at Karsten Schubert Ltd, 1989; and Documents, with Henry Bond, Karsten Schubert, 1991. With Andrew Renton co-edited *Technique Anglaise: Current Trends in British Art*, 1991. Gillick's show at Arnolfini, Bristol, in 2000 covered work from the previous decade and reflected his interest "in art as provisional constructions that project a space where ideas can be reassessed." It included diagrams, wall paintings, structures and platforms, audio, video and film. In 2001, the first work for the new sculpture court outside the Clore Gallery at Tate Britain was commissioned from Gillick. Lived in London and New York.

Mary GILLICK 1881–1965 Sculptor and medallist, born in Nottingham, married to the sculptor Ernest Gillick. She studied at Royal College of Art and exhibited at RA and elsewhere. She carried out commissioned work for the Wellcome Foundation, London; Bishop Bell, for Chichester Cathedral; and medals for the Royal Society, London. Lived in London.

Theodore GILLICK 1972– Sculptor of animals in bronze, twin brother of the painter James Gillick and cousin of the conceptual sculptor Liam Gillick. Theodore studied science at Aberdeen University, a scholarship taking him to the Botanical Gardens University in Jerusalem, Israel. There a friend suggested that painting and sculpture could be a livelihood, and on his return to England he retrained in sculpture and stone carving. His first commission came in 1997 and many followed. Gillick's bronzes were included in the New Year show at The John Davies Gallery, Stow-on-the-Wold, 2004.

William George GILLIES 1898–1973 Painter and teacher, born at Haddington, East Lothian. After World War I service he attended Edinburgh College of Art, 1919–22, and was a founder-member of 1922 Group. A travelling scholarship took him to the continent, where he studied with André Lhote in Paris. On his return he taught for a year at Inverness Academy, then joined Edinburgh College of Art where he remained for 40 years, becoming principal in 1960 and retiring six years later. Through his quiet life Gillies was influenced by a number of painters, including Munch, Matisse and Bonnard, but he remained essentially a Scottish painter of still life and landscape whose work is strong in pattern and colour. The area around his home in Temple, Midlothian, featured strongly in his work. He was elected RSA in 1947 and in 1963 was made president of RSW. In 1970 elected RA, was knighted and Scottish Arts Council arranged a major touring retrospective, 22 years after Gillies had had his first one-man show in Edinburgh at the French Institute. Tate Gallery, Edinburgh's Scottish National Gallery of Modern Art (which held a big exhibition of Gillies' watercolours in 1995) and other Scottish galleries hold examples. The Scottish Gallery, Edinburgh, held a show of oil paintings, watercolours and drawings "by Scotland's greatest Twentieth Century landscape painter" in 2003. Nature and Imagination: William Gillies and John Maxwell was at the City Art Centre, Edinburgh, and at Duncan R Miller Fine Arts, both 2004.

Barbara GILLIGAN 1913–1995 Painter, born in London, married to the artist David Carr. Like him she studied at Cedric Morris's East Anglian School of Painting and Drawing and at Slade School of Fine Art with Vladimir Polunin for stage design, 1934–5. With her husband she was the subject of one of Morris's finest portraits. Showed at Cooling Galleries, in Sladey Ladies at Parkin Gallery in 1986, at Galerie Salamanda, Paris, 1987, and elsewhere abroad. Had a solo show at Leicester Galleries in 1948. Lived at Starston Hall, Harleston, Norfolk.

Margaret GILLISON 1916– Artist in watercolour, oil and graphic media, born in Warwick. She was on the staff of the Grosvenor Museum, Chester, 1966–77. Was a member of Clwydian Art Society, also exhibiting with North Wales Federation of Art Societies and its south Wales equivalent and National Eisteddfod. She was a Royal Horticultural Society Silver Gilt and Silver Medallist and an Alpine Garden Society Gold Medallist. Sometimes exhibited under her married name of Margaret Gillison Todd. Lived in Mold, Clwyd.

Tricia GILLMAN 1951– Painter, born in Johannesburg, South Africa, who produced colourful, abstract works. She studied at Universities of Leeds, 1970–4, and Newcastle upon Tyne, 1975–7. Her group show appearances included several at John Moores Exhibition, Liverpool, from 1982; Forces of Nature, at Manchester City Art Gallery, 1990; and Three Ways, a British Council touring show to eastern Europe, in the same year. Her first solo show was at Parkinson Gallery, Leeds, in 1978. Later exhibitions included Laing Art Gallery, Newcastle upon Tyne, and tour, 1989–90, and Jill George Gallery, 1999 and 2002. Taught at St Martin's School of Art and Royal College of Art. Lived in London.

Robert GILLMOR 1936– Artist in watercolour, acrylic, pen and ink and scraperboard, and teacher, noted for his natural history pictures. He was born and lived in Reading, Berkshire, studying in fine art department of Reading University, 1954–9, with J A Betts and William McCance. He taught art and craft at Leighton Park School, Reading, 1959–65, then went freelance. Gillmor was a prolific book illustrator, around 90 titles containing his work; he was art editor of *Birds of the Western Palearctic* from 1966; was a founder-member of SWLA from 1964, being its president from 1984; and was president of Reading Guild of Artists, 1969–85. Showed solo at Reading Museum & Art Gallery, which holds his work, 1970; Washburn Gallery, Boston, America, 1971; Tryon Gallery, Nairobi, Kenya, 1973; and had a touring exhibition in France, 1983–4. Ulster Museum & Art Gallery, Belfast, also holds his work.

Nick GILLON 1967– Sculptor, draughtsman and teacher who graduated with honours in fine art from Duncan of Jordanstone College of Art, Dundee, in 1991. In that year he had a solo exhibition at Kelvingrove Art Gallery, Glasgow, and in group exhibitions: Alan Park Gallery, Stirling; SSA Centenary Show, Edinburgh; and The Discerning Eye, Mall Galleries. Nicholas Gillon was in charge of the mould-making and casting at Wildtrack Wildlife Art, Perth, 1991–3, teaching life drawing at Telford College of Further Education, 1994–5. With Anthony Morrow he completed the bronze Lobey Dosser, based on a Glasgow newspaper cartoon character and sited in that city's Woodlands Road, in 1992. Gillon made other public sculptures in Scotland and contributed to group shows. He was for a time based in Wigan, Lancashire. Sir Brinsley Ford owned his work.

William GILLON 1942– Painter and teacher brought up in Leith, Edinburgh, settling in the city. As a youth he taught himself to draw, then studied at the College of Art, 1960–6, gaining top marks in his post-diploma final year. He was then granted a travelling scholarship to France and Spain in 1965. Teaching included Scotus Academy. When Gillen's work was included in the Scottish Realism show, by Scottish Arts Council, which holds his work, in 1971, he was described as "a violently energetic visionary". He found drawing "hard work" and painted "to make a discovery, to investigate my feelings in paint." Had a first solo show at Edinburgh International Festival in 1965, others including Scottish Gallery, Edinburgh, 1970.

Maeve GILMORE 1917–1983 Painter in oil and writer, born in London, where she died. She was married to the artist Mervyn Peake and mother of the painter Fabian Peake. Studied at the Westminster School of Art, originally sculpture, then switched to painting on meeting Peake, whom she married in 1937. Maeve put Mervyn's work first, sacrificing her own talent. She had a number of shows in London, including Woodstock Gallery, sharing some with Mervyn, her pictures including portraits, still lifes and imaginary landscapes. When Peake became too ill to work, for many years she promoted his stature. She wrote *A World Away*, the story of their lives, 1970, as well as several other books. Was president of the Mervyn Peake Society, 1975–83.

Sidney GILMORE 1923– Sculptor in various materials, born in London, who attended Willesden College of Technology. Was a member of Free Painters and Sculptors, also exhibiting at RA, in the provinces and abroad. Lived in Wembley, Middlesex.

Albert GILMOUR 1923– Artist and draughtsman, noted for his railway pictures, born in West Hartlepool, County Durham, married to the artist Elaine Gilmour. Gilmour's intimate knowledge of the railway stemmed from his career as a fireman and then as a driver with British Rail. His studies included Gateshead Technical College; Bewick Studio; King's College, Newcastle; Ormsby Hall, Yorkshire; and Slade School of Fine Art. Was a member of West End Group in Newcastle and Gateshead Art Club and exhibited elsewhere in north of England. Lived at North Gosforth, Newcastle upon Tyne.

Elaine GILMOUR 1931–1990 Artist in oil and collage, and teacher, born in Hetton-le-Hole, County Durham, who originally showed under her maiden name of Elaine Bolton. She was married to the painter Albert Gilmour. Gained a University of Durham teachers' certificate with art distinction, also studying art at Neville's Cross College, Durham, and Sunderland College of Art. Was a member of West End Art Club in Newcastle upon Tyne, where she lived, also showing with Sunderland, Gateshead and Newcastle public galleries.

George Fisher GILMOUR fl. from 1940s– Painter in oil, born and lived in Kingston upon Thames, Surrey, where he studied at the School of Art under James Anthony Betts. Gilmour went on to exhibit widely, at venues including RA, Paris Salon, NEAC, RBA, NS, UA, Cooling Galleries and out of London at Blackpool, Darlington, Bootle, Merthyr Tydfil, Edinburgh and Aberdeen. Work was reproduced in *The Studio* and *The Listener*.

Hugh GILMOUR 1965– Painter, born in Kilwinning, Ayrshire. He gained a first-class honours degree in painting at Gray's School of Art, Aberdeen, 1983–7, then his master's degree at Royal College of Art, 1987–9. Among his awards were a Hospitalfield Scholarship, 1986, and a Rome Scholarship, British School at Rome, 1989–90. Gilmour used disembodied, broken forms to depict humiliation, anger, illness and breakdown of communication, as in his solo show at William Jackson Gallery, 1994. His first one-man exhibition was in 1989 at Irvine Arts Centre, Irvine, 1989, and he participated in many group shows, including RSA Student Exhibition, 1986–7; Rome Scholars, 1980–1990, Royal College of Art, 1990; and Greenwich Festival Open Studios, 1992. Jill George, in association with William Jackson, gave Gilmour a solo exhibition in 1997. Aberdeen Art Gallery holds his work.

Judith GILMOUR 1937– Maker of enigmatic vessel-like objects in stoneware and porcelain, and teacher, born in Edinburgh. She studied ceramics at Glasgow School of Art, where she taught ceramics, also at Sir John Cass (now Guildhall University). Gilmour spent time in Sweden and Ghana. In 1977 she was a winner of a British Crafts Award, launched by *The Sunday Telegraph*, judged by David Leach. Mixed shows included National Theatre, South Bank, 1977; Open Eye Gallery, Edinburgh, from 1988; RA Summer Exhibition, from 1996; and a three-artist exhibition at Rebecca Hossack Gallery, 1999. Had a solo show at Scottish Craft Centre, Edinburgh, 1975, later ones including Aberdeen Museum, Aberdeen, 1996. Commissions included a tile mural for the head office of Canada Life Assurance and a ceramic reproduction of a parchment for Diaspora Museum, Tel-Aviv, Israel. Kelvingrove Art Gallery, Glasgow; Aberdeen Art Gallery; Royal Museum of Scotland, Edinburgh; and Landesmuseum, Graz, Austria, hold examples.

John GILROY 1898–1985 Painter, notably of portraits, and teacher, born in Newcastle upon Tyne. He was for some years on the staff of Camberwell School of Arts and Crafts. Gilroy studied in Newcastle, then at the Royal College of Art and on the continent. Showed extensively at Fine Art Society, also RA, ROI, RP and Manchester City Art Gallery. Public galleries in Belfast, Hull and the Laing Art Gallery, Newcastle, hold his work. In 1998 a centenary exhibition which toured from the Laing, organised by the History of Advertising Trust, showed Gilroy's many Guinness stout posters, featuring toucans, a sea lion, an ostrich and other animals; his World War II posters for the Ministry of Information, such as *Careless Talk Costs Lives* and *Dig for Victory*; and portraits of the royal family, Winston Churchill and John Gielgud. Gilroy was a Chelsea Arts Club member who lived in London, but died in Guildford, Surrey.

Natalie GILTSOFF 1941– Painter of exuberantly rich flower pictures and interiors, and teacher, born in Richmond, Surrey. She studied from 1955–62, originally for three years in the junior department, at Camberwell School of Arts and Crafts, specialising in textile design. Teachers included Anthony Eyton, Dick Lee, Euan Uglow, Patrick Symons and Philip Matthews, with whom she lived in his last years. She then concentrated on embroidery at Goldsmiths' College, 1966–7. From 1967–9 was a part-time lecturer in colleges of art in London, Hertfordshire, Avon and Wiltshire. Mixed exhibition appearances included The Flower Gallery, where she also showed solo; John Noott, Broadway; Anna-Mei Chadwick; RWA and elsewhere. Later solo exhibitions included Beatrice Royal Art Gallery, Eastleigh, 1994. Lived in Devizes, Wiltshire.

Christopher GILVAN-CARTWRIGHT 1966– Artist, illustrator and teacher, born in Dorking, Surrey, who studied at Weston School of Art, Central St Martin's School of Art & Design and Cracow Academy of Fine Art, Poland. Lectured at Weston School part-time, 1988–96, and from 1996 at West Herts College in Watford. In 1996 curated the No Visa Required III show at Polish Cultural Institute. Gilvan-Cartwright won a Thames Television Travel Bursary, 1987–8, and a British Council/Polish Government Travel Scholarship, 1990–2. Heinemann, Penguin, Quartet Publishing and national newspapers commissioned his work. He also created the BBC Proms logo in 1998 and 1999. Group shows included Art for Aids, Royal Festival Hall, 1987; Artforum, 1995; and Royal Over-Seas League Open, 1996. Later solo shows included The Sun Calls me Home, Sydney House, 1996; East West, 2000; and Royal Over-Seas League, 2000–1, the artist having won one of its scholarships, to India and Nepal. Gilvan-Cartwright's paintings were "landscape themes in which something magical is about to, or has, happened". Lived in Brighton, Sussex.

Edna GINESI 1902–2000 Painter, stage designer, teacher and decorator, born in Leeds, married to the artist Raymond Coxon. She studied at Leeds College of Art and Royal College of Art, 1920–4. In the latter year a West Riding Travelling Scholarship took her to several countries on the continent. Taught at Chelsea School of Art. Showed in group exhibitions at LG of which she was a member, Cooling and Leicester Galleries, had her first solo show at Zwemmer Gallery in 1932 and in the early 1930s did décor for Camargo Ballet. Was an ambulance driver in World War II. Retrospective show at Bradford in 1956 and shared an exhibition with her husband at Parkin Gallery, 1985. Represented in Tate Gallery and lived in London. Died in Rowfant, Sussex, where Gin, as she was known, and her husband had owned a studio for over 60 years.

John GINGELL 1935– Painter, performance and structures artist, and teacher, born in London. He studied at Goldsmiths' College School of Art and went on to lecture at Cardiff College of Art. Was a founder-member of the ZOO Group and a contributor to its statements as sponsored by WAC; also to Everyday Something Changes, ZOO Group exhibition at Chapter Arts Centre, Cardiff, in 1972; and to Tate Gallery's Tate Kidsplay environmental installations in early 1970s. Took part in a number of performances, including Rover and Bonzo in Wonderland at Studio Theatre at University College, Cardiff. In Gingell's installation exhibition Soft City, held in Vancouver in 1982, he brought together a variety of objects and materials found in the city in an attempt to describe his experience as a visitor there.

Phyllis GINGER 1907–2005 Watercolourist and illustrator, printmaker and teacher, born in New Malden, Surrey. Her father worked for the Central Telegraph Office and was a keen amateur painter. After attending Tiffin School for Girls, which she hated, she endured unhappy employment with the Civil Service while attending art classes, initially in the evening at Kingston Art School, next Richmond School of Art, 1932–5, then Central School of Arts and Crafts, 1937–9, her teachers including William Palmer Robins, John Farleigh and Clarke Hutton. In her final year, she met her future husband, who would become the distinguished silversmith, Leslie Durbin. Ginger taught for a short time at Bromley School of Art, leaving to have her first child. Her family and their offspring were to become favourite subjects. She took part in the Pilgrim Trust's *Recording Britain* project and illustrated books, including a series over many years with the writer on London Mrs Robert Henrey. Became a member of RWS in 1958 and in 1990 was featured artist in its 1990 Spring Exhibition, with 13 works shown. Victoria & Albert Museum and Museum of London hold her pictures. Lived in Kew, Richmond, Surrey.

Graham GINGLES 1943– Artist, born in Larne, Northern Ireland, who settled there in Ballygalley, County Antrim. He studied at Belfast College of Art, 1962–6, then Hornsey College of Art, 1966–7, attending the British School at Rome, 1970–1, under an Arts Council of Northern Ireland Rome Scholarship. Took part in many group shows, including Learning Design, WAC tour, 1968; 8 Northern Ireland Artists, Third Eye Centre in Glasgow, 1977; Photo Realism, Orchard Gallery in Londonderry, 1979; Boxed Show, Artsite Gallery, Bath, 1986; and RHA, October Exhibition, invited artist, 1991. Had a solo show with Arts Council Gallery in Belfast, 1961, later ones including Project Arts Centre, Dublin, 1992.

B GINNER: *see* **Daphne POLLEN**

Charles GINNER 1878–1952 Painter in oil and watercolour and occasional printmaker, born in Cannes, France. From 1899 in Paris he studied architecture, then turned to painting. Was from 1904–8 at the Académie Vitti, under the Spaniard Anglada y Camarosa, then at the École des Beaux-Arts. Ginner's sister was the dance teacher Ruby Ginner Dyer. Ginner made a journey to Buenos Aires, Argentina, in 1909, where he held his first one-man show. His oil paintings showed the influence of Vincent van Gogh, the paint thick, making them difficult to handle. Having shown with the AAA in 1908, Ginner after the Buenos Aires trip settled in London, where he became a key member of the Fitzroy Street, Camden Town and Cumberland Market groups. He was especially friendly with Harold Gilman and in 1914 in the *New Age* spelt out their painting creed known as New Realism. In that year he showed jointly with Gilman at the Goupil Gallery. During World War I Ginner painted for the Canadian War Records, and he was an Official War Artist during World War II. Ginner's watercolours are unmistakeable, with meticulous detailing of trees and buildings. The Tate Gallery and many other galleries hold his work, the National Portrait Gallery a typically precise self-portrait. Arts Council memorial show and touring, 1953–4.

Louis GINNETT 1875–1946 Painter of portraits, interiors and murals, stained glass designer and teacher. He was educated at Brighton Grammer School and studied in London and then at Académie Julian in Paris. Taught at Brighton School of Art. He showed at RA, ROI, RWA and elsewhere. Brighton Royal Pavilion Art Gallery and Museums holds Ginnett's The Coat of Many Colours and his Design for Stained Glass Windows for the Chapel of the Royal Masonic Institute for Girls. Lived at Ditchling, Sussex.

Michael GINSBORG 1943– Abstract artist and teacher, born in Ealing, west London. He studied at Central School of Art & Design and Chelsea School of Art, 1964–9. Among his teaching posts was head of fine art at Wimbledon School of Art from 1991. Ginsborg was included in the critic William Packer's British Art Show touring exhibition, organised Arts Council, 1980, and his canvas The Gate was in 1993–4 John Moores Liverpool Exhibition. Solo exhibitions included Lisson Gallery, 1969; Serpentine Gallery, 1973; and Benjamin Rhodes Gallery from 1989.

Ann GINSBURY: *see* **PELOUSE**

Joseph GINSBURY 1892– Charcoal portrait specialist who after private art studies attended Birkbeck School of Art. Drew for such papers as *Sporting Life, Time and Tide* and *Financial Times.* Lived in London.

Sheila GIRLING fl. from 1970s– Painter, notably in watercolour, and collagist, born in Birmingham. She studied at the School of Art there and at Royal Academy Schools. Girling's work had a strong sense of place. She began to experiment with collage during a visit to Barcelona in 1983; her pictures were composed from previously painted fragments of canvas, secured in place and then repainted and glazed to create a variety of rich textures. The landscapes of Canada and Dorset were favourite subjects. Showed in London, including Francis Graham-Dixon Gallery, New York, Hamburg and Canada, having a solo show in Edmonton and Calgary in 1978. Her husband was the sculptor Anthony Caro, her son the painter Paul Caro. Lived in London.

Geraldine GIRVAN 1947– Painter of rich still lifes and interiors, in the tradition of the Scottish Colourists. Born in Derby she studied at Edinburgh University and Edinburgh College of Art. Working mostly in gouache and oil, she contributed regularly to open shows at RSA, RSW and RWS. Her first solo show with Chris Beetles Ltd in 1989 was a marked critical and commercial success.

Joy GIRVIN 1961– Painter and teacher who studied at Newcastle upon Tyne Polytechnic, 1981–4, then Royal Academy Schools, 1984–7. Among her awards were an Italian Government Scholarship to Rome, 1989–90. From 1983 she took part in many mixed exhibitions including Stowells Trophy, Tyne Tees Northern Open, Whitworth Young Contemporaries, Camden Annual Exhibition, RA Summer Exhibition and The Broad Horizon, at Agnew, 1990. She had a solo show at Newcastle upon Tyne Polytechnic Gallery, 1989; Blason Gallery, 1991; and Cadogan Contemporary, 1993. Between 1990–2 she was a visiting tutor at Hertfordshire College of Art and Design. Lived in London.

Christine GIST fl. from 1970s– Sculptor and designer, curator, who was inspired by architecture and who worked for some years with an architect. She used a variety of materials for abstract works. Gist attended Chesterfield College of Art and Design, studying textile design, 1963–5.

Then obtained a bachelor's degree in fine art – sculpture from University of Washington, Seattle, 1978–81, gaining a master's degree in sculpture at Yale University School of Art, 1981–3. Among her awards were a Fashion Group Inc. Scholarship, 1978; a Ford Foundation Sculpture Grant, 1979; a Pacific Northwest Sculpture Award, 1981; and a Connecticut Commission for the Arts Independent Project Grant, 1989. Gist participated in many shows in Britain and America, later ones including City Gallery, Leicester, 1990, and Sculpture at Canterbury, 1991. She had a solo show of objects, Time to Act, at Deal Library, Deal, 2000. For some years, Gist (pronounced with hard G) was exhibition curator for Kent Institute of Art & Design.

Gerald GLADSTONE 1929–2005 Initially self-taught and versatile sculptor and painter, born to English-born parents in Toronto, Ontario, Canada, Gladstone became interested in art at school. Upon leaving he worked principally in advertising. A show of work by Gordon Rayner at Toronto Art Gallery persuaded Gladstone in 1956 to make his first sculpture; he favoured welded steel, with which he had early success. The Toronto gallery gave him a solo exhibition in 1957 and bought a work, more exhibitions following as well as important public commissions. With a 1961 Canada Council grant Gladstone was able to work in England for several months, study at the Royal College of Art and have a first London show, at the Molton Gallery, 1962. His Venus Probe II, completed soon after, was acquired by Loughborough University and shown at the Whitechapel Art Gallery in 1967–8. Hamilton Galleries, in London, gave Gladstone a one-man exhibition and there was one at the Graham Gallery, New York, America, both in 1964, the year he had three sculptures chosen for the National Gallery of Canada-sponsored Second Canadian Sculpture Exhibition. Graham continued to work to acclaim in his own country and abroad. Later features of his career included a 12-metre long, three-metre high mural, The Messenger, for the Cineplex at Vancouver's Royal Centre, 1984; the re-siting of his huge 1976 sculpture Universal Man, which symbolised "earth-bound human energies reaching towards a higher universal knowledge", at Yorkdale Shopping Centre, Toronto, 1994 (removal from its original site, near the CN Tower, in 1990 had angered its maker); a solo show at Gallery One, Toronto, in 1997; and the unveiling of his millennium sculpture Flight in 2000 in his home town of Beaverton, Ontario. The Victoria & Albert Museum, National Gallery of Canada, Ottawa, and Montreal Museum of Fine Arts hold examples.

Rodney GLADWELL 1928–1979 Painter, born in Didcot, Berkshire. He studied in Paris at Atelier Colarossi, 1949–50. Went on to show with Archer Gallery, O'Hana Gallery, Piccadilly Gallery, in Paris and the English provinces, Molton Gallery, with the dealer Lucy Wertheim who owned his work, and at Sussex University, which gave him a retrospective in 1962–3. The University commissioned him to execute large painting for its main hall in 1962. He also carried out work in 1959 for Georgian Club, in London, and in the same year designed an exhibition combining modern fabrics and paintings for Cotton Board of Great Britain, in Manchester, which was shown in Australia and New Zealand. Johannesburg University and Arts Council hold his work, which included heavily stylised female nudes. After a disappointing show at J-P Lehmans' Gallery in 1974 Gladwell disappeared in the mid-1970s from the English exhibiting scene, having married in 1972 and spent some time touring Canada. Lived in London for some years and was latterly represented by the Swiss dealer Walter Feilchenfeldt, in Zürich. Gladwell died from cancer, after which his widow settled in her native Canada.

Paul GLADWYN 1956–1998 Painter, draughtsman and collagist, born in Anglesey, Wales. Among his works were colourful landscapes which included abstracted shapes. He gained a first-class honours degree at Trent Polytechnic, 1980–3, and completed postgraduate studies at Slade School of Fine Art, 1993–5. Mixed exhibitions included Stowells Trophy, RA and Riverside Studios, all 1983; 4th Highland Open Exhibition (prizewinner) and Gulacsy Gallery, Budapest, both 1990; and Winter Paintings, The Ceilidh Place, Ullapool, 1994. In 1994 the Highland Regional Council and Scottish Arts Council toured Gladwyn's solo show Out of The Darkness, the year that he began showing solo with East West and with The Ceilidh Place. East West held a memorial show, 1999. Scottish Arts Council, Highland Regional Council, the Socomer Group in Belgium and Robert Fleming & Company hold examples. Gladwyn was based in northwest Scotland.

William GLANFIELD 1957– Woodworker and sculptor who did foundation studies at Medway College of Design, graduating in fine art at Canterbury College of Art, 1979. After several years variously employed, he took a City and Guilds carpentry and joinery course from 1988 and went freelance. He then carried out a series of commissioned pieces in wood, many in Kent, including in 1989 the Oyster Bench for his home town of Folkestone. Glanfield made the Hawkesbury Lock Seat, for Groundwork Coventry, part of the city's Canal Heritage Trail, 1997.

Christopher GLANVILLE 1948– Landscape and marine illustrator, born in London, son of the artist Roy Glanville. He attended Heatherley and Byam Shaw Schools of Art and Royal Academy Schools, his teachers including Peter Greenham and Bernard Dunstan. Glanville was elected a member of RWA, showing with it annually from 1980. Exhibited in RA Summer Exhibition from 1972. Exhibited extensively elsewhere, including NEAC, RBA, National Museum of Wales in Cardiff, Woburn Abbey, Ashgate Gallery in Farnham and Sinfield Gallery, Burford, W H Patterson Fine Arts and Medici Galleries. RWA and Richmond Museum hold his work. Lived in Kingston upon Thames, Surrey.

Roy GLANVILLE 1911–1965 Marine artist, born and died in London, father of the painter Christopher Glanville. He studied at Hammersmith School of Art. Glanville was elected to RSMA in 1950 and to RBA in 1954, and was a member of Wapping Group of Artists. Also showed at RA and was a De Laszlo Medal winner. Walker Art Gallery, Liverpool, holds his work.

Sidney Herbert GLANVILLE 1884–1953 Painter, educated at Woodford, Essex, who exhibited RA, UA and RBA. Lived at Fittleworth, Sussex.

Tess GLANVILLE 1968– Sculptor, photographer, video and installations artist and teacher, born in Dublin, Ireland. She gained a diploma in sculpture and printmaking at Crawford College of Art & Design, Cork, 1985–90, and her master's in fine art, sculpture, from the University of Central England in Birmingham, 1990–1. She then did a foundry course at Sandwell College, 1994, and stone carving at Portland, 1995. Gained an Ireland-America Scholarship, 1990, and an SSA annual award, 1997. Work experience included visiting lecturer, Bournville College of Art, Birmingham, in 1991, and artist-in-residence, Melton County Primary School, 1995. Later mixed shows included Suffolk: A Female Focus, Wolsey Art Gallery, Christchurch Mansion; and Viscera, The Red Dot Gallery, both in Ipswich in 1999. Glanville had a solo exhibition at Christchurch Mansion, 2001. In 2004, Dal Vero (taken from real life) was a commission for St Mary-at-the-Quay church on Ipswich waterfront, in which Glanville "examines the processes of navigation." She lived in Melton, Suffolk.

Jane GLASFURD 1909– Painter, full name Margaret Jane Glasfurd, born in Chelwood Gate, Sussex. Studied at Regent Street Polytechnic School of Art, 1930–33, then from 1933–4 at Kunstgewerbeschule in Munich, Germany. She showed at WIAC and Cookham Art Club, to both of which she belonged, and in Sussex, where she lived at Southease.

Edwin GLASGOW 1874–1955 Painter in oil and watercolour. Born in Liverpool, attended university there and in Oxford, several books of sketches of which he published. Was keeper of the National Gallery for several years in the 1930s. Exhibited RA, RI, provincial galleries and Paris Salon. Laing Art Gallery and Museum, Newcastle upon Tyne, holds his work. Lived at Charlbury, Oxfordshire.

Leslie GLASGOW 1955– Sculptor, born in Scotland. He attended Wimbledon School of Art, 1984–5, Central School of Art and Design, 1985–8, and Royal College of Art, 1988–90. His work appeared in The Leicester Collection, 1988, at Art Directions, 1989, and RA Summer Exhibition, 1990, and in 1991 several works based on the theme Ship of Fools were included in Sculpture & Sculptors' Drawings at William Jackson Gallery. Lived in London.

GLASHAN 1927–1999 Cartoonist and painter, real name John McGlashan, son of the artist Archibald McGlashan, he was born in Glasgow where he attended the School of Art. After failing to make a living as a portrait painter after moving to London in the early 1950s, he turned to cartooning as Glashan, working for *Lilliput*, *Queen*, *The Spectator*, *Punch* and *The Observer Colour Magazine*. Painterly technique was a constant feature of Glashan's idiosyncratic cartoons, especially in the *Magazine* in the 228 episodes of Genius, the adventures of Anode Enzyme and his employer Lord Doberman. At the time of his death, an American company was working to animate Genius. Glashan was bitter at his lack of success as a fine artist and continued to paint, mostly landscapes. He had exhibitions at the Francis Kyle Gallery, 1979 and 1983, and Fine Art Society, 1991 and 1994. Glashan died in London.

Kirsten GLASS 1975– Painter whose work combined text with an image of girls constructed from fashion magazines, resulting in a hyper-real, billboard appearance, as in the group show Amber, at Laure Genillard Gallery, 2000. Glass was born in Belfast, Northern Ireland. She did a foundation course at Central St Martins, 1992–3; graduated in painting at Chelsea College of Art, 1993–6; and gained her master's in fine art from Goldsmiths' College, 1998–00. Other group shows included Din, Amsterdam, Netherlands, 1999, and On the Rocks, APT Gallery, 2000; and Beck's Futures 2002, ICA and tour, 2002–3. Had a solo show, Youthinkyoufuckinslick, Ace Gallery, Los Angeles, America, 1999, others at Habitat Gallery, King's Road, 2000, and One in the Other, 2001. Saatchi Collection holds her work.

Margaret GLASS 1950– Artist and teacher, notably in pastel, born in Chesham, Buckinghamshire. She was a member of PS and of Société des Pastellistes de France. In 2002, Glass won the PS Patterson Prize. She was at one time vice-president of the Pastellistes, having been awarded its Diplôme Prix d'Honneur in 1986. The French group conferred on Glass the title of maître pastelliste in 1992, in 2002 made her their hon. guest at an International Pastel Exhibition in Feytiat and invited her to teach at its course in Paris. She also ran her own regular courses. Glass began exhibiting in the provinces in 1969, had a first solo show in Ipswich in 1971 and subsequently exhibited in Paris, Dublin and New York. In 2003, she was included in The Art of Pastel at W H Patterson. Lived in Debach, Suffolk.

Pauline GLASS 1908– Painter mainly in oil, she studied in Brussels, Belgium, then with Bernard Fleetwood-Walker at Birmingham College of Art. Showed at RA, RP, ROI and RBSA and lived at Harborne, Birmingham.

Peter GLASS 1917– Painter in the Impressionist manner, notable for urban scenes, born in Melbourne, Victoria, Australia. He was a pupil of Max Meldrum at the Swinburne Technical College, Melbourne, and furthered his studies with stays in London and Paris, 1951–5. In 1953 he exhibited both in the Paris Salon and in the first Australian Artists' Association show at RWS Conduit Street gallery. Glass won a number of awards in Australia and showed especially in Melbourne galleries. National Gallery of Australia in Canberra, University of Melbourne, corporate and many private collections hold examples.

William Mervyn GLASS 1885–1965 Painter of the Scottish highlands and islands who studied at Aberdeen School of Art and Royal Scottish Academy Life School. As well as being a member of RSA and president from 1930–3 of SSA, showed at RA, Royal Glasgow Institute of the Fine Arts and Walker Art Gallery, Liverpool. Was a member of the Edinburgh Group and lived in the city for many years.

Lancelot GLASSON 1894–1959 Painter who was born in Twickenham, Middlesex. After attending Marlborough College he studied at the Royal Academy Schools. During World War II he was engaged in camouflage work for the Air Ministry and Ministry of Home Security. He exhibited RA, RSA, Royal Glasgow Institute of the Fine Arts and Walker Art Gallery, Liverpool. Brighton and Rochdale galleries hold his work. Was a member of the Arts Club and of Art Workers' Guild from 1933. Lived in London.

Mark GLAZEBROOK 1936– Artist, curator, dealer, teacher and art writer who painted from childhood. He was taught by Wilfrid Blunt, art master at Eton College; during school holidays joined an uncle, F J Herzog, sketching north Wales from a car; and during National Service was arrested as a suspected spy when painting in Egypt. While reading history at Cambridge University, 1956–9, Glazebrook attended life classes at Cambridge Polytechnic and private painting classes with Jean Rose; he won a prize at the Oskar Kokoschka School in Salzburg; and after classes at Hammersmith College of Art and the City & Guilds School, he studied at the Slade School of Fine Art. In the 1960s, Glazebrook worked for the Arts Council; was a founding director of Editions Alecto; was art critic of the *London Magazine*; and a lecturer at Maidstone College of Art. From 1969–71 he was director of the Whitechapel Art Gallery. During the 1970s Glazebrook arranged shows at Colnaghi's, for the Arts Council and RA; taught at Middlesex Polytechnic; and in 1978 became a professor of modern art history and gallery director at San José State University, California, America. During the 1980s Glazebrook dealt in art, for a while as director of the Albemarle Gallery, then during the early 1990s returned to painting, lecturing and journalism, notably for *The Spectator*. He had a solo show at The Mayor Gallery, 2000. Saatchi Collection owns his work. He lived in London.

Joanna Ewa GLAZER 1963– Artist employing bold colours and inner images, for whom "each painting is like a poem, an enchanting spell to transform life into magic." Glazer was born in Gdansk, Poland; received her master's in conservation and restoration of art from Toruń University, 1987, and studied fashion design at L'École Nationale Supérieure des Arts Décoratifs (Art Déco) in Paris, France, 1989. She lived for long periods in many countries and was chosen for promotional design of the International University of Japan in 1988 and 1989. Showed widely in group exhibitions and at art fairs throughout Europe, including Chelsea Art Fair in 2002. Later solo shows included Living in Nature, Cultural Center Koide, Japan, 1999, and Joel Carcia Gallery Village Saint Paul, Paris, 2001. She lived in south London.

John GLAZIER 1930– Sculptor and teacher who after evening studies at Chelsea Art School, 1958–9, and Putney School of Art, 1975–80, gained a fine arts degree in sculpture at Wimbledon School of Art, 1980–3, with a year's art and design study at Brighton Polytechnic, 1983–4. In 1978 won 3rd Prize National "Heredities" Award to Sculpture Students. Glazier taught adult education classes from 1989 in Hove and Horsham, from 1993 holding sculpture workshops at his home in Pulborough, west Sussex. Mixed exhibitions included SPS, 1978; SWLA, from 1984; Armed Forces and Equestrian Art Societies, Guild of Sussex Craftsmen and Society of Catholic Artists, all from 1985; and Association of Sussex Artists, from 1986. Showed solo at Lannards, Billingshurst, 1985; The Grange, Rottingdean, 1986; Wellingham Barn, Lewes, 1990; and Foredown Tower, Portslade, 1999, where his wooden carvings revealed inspiration from natural forms, notably the curves of the South Downs.

Gerry GLEASON 1946– Painter, sculptural installation and mixed-media artist, born and worked in Belfast, Northern Ireland, who was interested in social, political and historical conflict, as in The Ulster Saga, at Newlyn and Middlesbrough Art Galleries, 1994–5. His images and palette could be rich, primitive, powerful. In 1989 Gleason designed colour illustrations for Brian McAvera's book *Art and Politics in Ireland*; in 1990 his Monumental Head image made a poster for Yeats Theatre Festival at Abbey Theatre, Dublin. Also in 1990 he gained Arts Council of Northern Ireland and Department of Foreign Affairs, Dublin, awards. In addition to many group shows in Ireland and abroad, later solo exhibitions included Orchard Gallery in Londonderry and tour, 1989, and QQ Gallery, Cracow, Poland, 1990. Londonderry City Council holds his work.

John GLEDHILL 1950– Painter in oil and draughtsman, full-time professional artist from 1971. He was born in Manchester and obtained his master's degree after three years at Royal Academy Schools, teachers including Peter Greenham and John Lessore. Showed with Calder Rural Artists Group of which he was a member, RA Summer Exhibition from 1985, Lancashire Contemporaries, Leeds City Art Gallery and elsewhere, his main works being urban landscapes, ship paintings and figure compositions. Had a solo show in 1990 at Castlefield Gallery, Manchester. In 2004, Gledhill's colourful, figurative work was included by Danny Greenhill Fine Art in the Gallery 27 show L S Lowry and those he inspired. In Cardiff, National Museum of Wales holds his work. Lived and worked in Hebden Bridge, Yorkshire.

Elsie GLEDSTANES 1891–1982 Painter in oil, pastel, watercolour and tempera of figure groups, portraits and landscapes. Born at Ealing, Middlesex, Gledstanes studied in Paris, and for periods at the Slade School of Fine Art, Byam Shaw School of Art and Vicat Cole School. She went on to become a prolific exhibitor, with work characteristic of artists who were at the Slade in the early part of the century; an especially accomplished watercolourist. Exhibiting venues included RA, RBA, SWA, Walker's Gallery, Ridley Art Club, plus other provincial and Scottish galleries. Had studios at Prenteg, Portmadoc, in North Wales, and in London.

David GLEESON 1956– Representational painter and teacher who created carefully wrought portraits, interiors and still lifes. He was born in Manchester, studied at Aberystwyth University, 1975–8, and settled in Stafford, where he taught painting and drawing part-time. He won prizes at Regeneration, Walker Art Gallery, Liverpool, 1984; Mid Art Annual Open Competition, Dudley Art Gallery, 1988; Staffordshire Open, Shire Hall Gallery, Stafford, a series from 1993; The Discerning Eye, Mall Galleries, 1997; and Three Counties Open, Keele University Gallery, and Grosvenor Museum, 3rd Open Art Competition, Chester, both 1999. Took part in many group shows, including RA Summer Exhibition, from 1986, Hunting Art Prizes, from 1988, and Singer & Friedlander/*Sunday Times* Watercolour Competition, from 1997. Solo shows included Shugborough, Stafford, where he was artist-in-residence, 1997; Grosvenor Gallery, 1998; and Museum Pieces, Cambridge Contemporary Art, Cambridge, 1999. Commissions included a stained-glass window, for north window, St Mary's Church, Stafford; and Quadruple Portrait, founders of large biotech company, Manchester. Staffordshire County Council held Gleeson's work.

Tom GLEGHORN 1925– Painter, administrator and teacher, born in Thornley, County Durham. He moved to Australia as a child. Had no formal art training but was assisted by the painter William Dobell and undertook travel studies to England and the continent early in the 1960s and in 1970 and showed widely in England, where his work is held by Manchester City Art Gallery and by other public galleries in Middlesbrough, Swansea and Newcastle upon Tyne, where the Stone Gallery represented him. All Australian state galleries also hold his pictures. Taught widely in Australia, notably at Bedford Park Teachers' College, Adelaide, from 1973. For about a dozen years from 1958 he directed the Blayland Galleries, in Sydney, where early on he had worked as a designer. Gleghorn was a painter of eclectic style.

Lady Helena GLEICHEN 1873–1947 Painter of landscapes and animals, born in London where she continued to live. She was the daughter of His Serene Highness Prince Victor of Hohenlohe, a British Navy admiral and also a sculptor. Her sister was the artist Lady Feodora Gleichen. Helena Gleichen was educated privately, then studied art in Rollshoven and in London, notably at Frank Calderon's School of Animal Painting. She showed at RA, City of Birmingham Museum and Art Gallery, New Gallery and in France and Italy. Several Italian public galleries bought her work. Pictures of the Italian war front and subscription hunt paintings were notable features of the work of Gleichen, who was keen on shooting and lived part of the year at Much Marcle, Herefordshire.

Ena GLEN: *see* **Ena RUSSELL**

Lucy GLENDINNING 1964– Figurative sculptor and lecturer who did an art foundation course at Yeovil College, 1982–3; graduated with honours in fine art, sculpture, University of the West of England, 1983–6 (where she was a part-time lecturer, 1995–7); and worked as a mouldmaker for Elisabeth Frink, 1987–9. Her many commissions included Chase Manhattan Bank, 1990; Teesside Development Corporation, 1992; winning design for viewing area, Devon County Council; Cardiff Bay Arts Trust, 1998; and Wincanton Sports Centre, 2001. Later exhibitions included Artists of Fame & Promise, Beaux Arts, Bath, 1998; Spring Exhibition, McHardy Sculpture Company, 2000; and Diverse, Mark Jason Fine Art, 2001.

Katie GLIDDON 1883– Painter, draughtsman and teacher, born in Twickenham, Middlesex. She studied at Slade School of Fine Art with Henry Tonks and Fred Brown, 1900–4, and developed a special talent for watercolours of flowers. Exhibited RA, NEAC, SWA, with the Arts Council and elsewhere. Lived for a time in Sanderstead, Surrey.

Lotte GLOB 1944– Versatile artist, born in Denmark, where between 1959–63 she studied with Gutte Eriksen and Knud Jensen, then with Philip Pierce in Ireland, 1963–4, and from 1964–5 with David Illingworth in Scotland. There, after running a workshop in Denmark for two years, in 1968 she set up another at Balnakeil, in the extreme north. Later mixed shows included Kilmorack Gallery, Beauly, and Brown's Gallery, Tain, both 1997, and Rhue Art, Ullapool, 1999. Glob exhibited solo widely in Denmark and Britain from 1966–7, later ones including Llantarnam Grange Art Centre, Gwent, and Galerie Uggerhoj, Denmark, both 1996. She carried out a series of ceramic and sculpture commissions in England and Scotland, including water sculptures for the Health Centre, Durness, 1994, and fountain and garden sculpture, County Durham, 1998. Victoria & Albert Museum library, Dundee Art Gallery and Museum, Royal Scottish Museum in Edinburgh, and Museum of Fine Art, Copenhagen, hold examples.

John Ainsworth GLOVER 1949– Painter, printmaker and teacher, born in Maryland, America, although he was educated at King's School, Harrow, and at Chiswick Polytechnic. Studied at Ealing Art School, 1968–9, with Derek Hirst, then at Slade School of Fine Art, 1969–72, under Keith Critchlow. Took part in a number of mixed exhibitions in London, including American Embassy, 1971, two years later having a one-man show at Amwell Gallery near where he lived in Islington, north London.

Louis GLOVER 1912–1982 Oil painter specialising in pictures of dogs, and potter. Born in Coventry, Glover studied art at the Royal College of Art under the painter Ernest Tristram and the potter William Staite Murray in the early 1930s. Glover became principal of the School of Art in Barnsley, Yorkshire, was art adviser to the county borough and was honorary director of the Cooper Art Gallery. Exhibited with the Yorkshire Society of Artists and elsewhere in the provinces. Wrote the *Batsford Book of Poodles* and the *Batsford Book of Dogs*, plus illustrations of dogs in *Dog World*. Lived in Stourbridge, Worcestershire.

Norah GLOVER 1923– She combined private practice as an architect with architectural perspectives and painting, gradually turning almost wholly to painting. After education at Malvern Girls' College, Glover studied architecture at Regent Street Polytechnic and, after qualifying in 1946, joined Sir Patrick Abercrombie's office. She was awarded the Andrew Prentice Bursary in 1948, Owen Jones Studentship in 1949 and was elected a fellow of RIBA in 1969. Showed at RA, Society of Architect Artists, Stock Exchange, Gilbert Parr Gallery and The Patricia Wells Gallery, Thornbury, which also gave her a solo exhibition in 1979. Prior to that she had had eight one-man shows at John Whibley Gallery, 1962–75. Painted acrylic and watercolour landscapes in England and on the continent and flower studies, pictures noted for their light, depth and delicacy of handling. Her perspectives were part of the exhibition Barbican: This Was Tomorrow, at The Curve, Barbican Centre, 2002.

Danuta GŁUCHOWSKA fl. from early 1950s– Painter, draughtsman and teacher, born in Warsaw, Poland, who spent her childhood in that country. She showed an early response to nature, her father's paintings and an artistic cousin's models in clay. Settled in London and in her teens chose to study art instead of medicine, initially in 1951 at Sir John Cass College, then from 1952–6 at St Martin's School of Art where she gained her National Diploma in Design. Her artistic horizons broadened during early marriage when she travelled widely in Europe with her husband, and despite the demands of daily life she continued to draw and paint regularly. In the early 1970s she taught art to boys and lectured in history of art to students. Głuchowska took part in mixed exhibitions, including those of the Polish Artists' Association in Great Britain, of which she was a member; Contemporary Art by Polish Artists abroad, at Imperial College, 1970; a similar show at POSK, 1985; and with other groups. Among her solo exhibitions were ones at the Doctors' Restaurant and at the Polish Catholic Centre, Ealing.

GLUCK 1895–1978 Painter, born in London into the family which founded the J Lyons & Co catering empire. Although she drew an allowance from her family, she rejected her name Hannah Gluckstein, calling herself Gluck (say it like duck). She early established herself as an eccentric, dressing in men's clothes. Attended St Paul's Girls' School, Hammersmith, her work winning a Royal Drawing Society silver star in 1913. Student at St John's Wood School of Art, then during World War I began to work with Newlyn School artists at Lamorna Cove, Cornwall. Established a distinctive style as an exquisite painter of portraits, flowers and landscapes, her work having a crisp 1920s look. Gluck held five exhibitions, in 1924, 1926, 1932, 1937 and 1973, being closely associated with the Fine Art Society, which held a memorial show in 1980–1. A special Gluck Room was created in the gallery in 1932 and the Gluck Frame – three symmetrically stepped panels – was patented by her. Litigious and obsessive by nature, for many years Gluck battled to raise the quality of artists' materials, especially paints, on which she became an expert. Lived latterly in Sussex, where she died at Steyning.

David GLÜCK 1939– Painter, versatile printmaker and teacher, noted for his landscape and still life watercolours and etchings, born in Pontefract, Yorkshire. He attended Wakefield School of Art, 1956–9; Leeds College of Art, 1959–61; and Royal College of Art, for printmaking, 1962–5, under Julian Trevelyan and Edward Bawden. He was made a member of the LG, 1978; RWS, 1988, vice-president, 2002; fellow, RE, 1988; member Society of Landscape Painters, 1989; and of NEAC, 1993. Glück taught full-time at Central School of Art & Design, 1974–94 as head of printmaking (acting head of fine art, 1986–91), and as director of the BA Fine Art Course at Central St Martins, 1989–91, plus extensive teaching elsewhere in England and Italy. He took part in numerous mixed shows and won the Daler-Rowney Watercolour Prize, 1988; RA Summer Exhibition *House and Garden* Award, 1989; Department of Transport Competition, Mall Galleries, 3rd Purchase Prize, 1993; Ranelagh Press Prize, Printmakers' Council Exhibition, 1995; and, in the same year, Covent Garden Market Authority Prize, LG Biennial. Solo exhibitions included Chappel Galleries, Chappel, 2002. Leeds City Art Gallery; Ferens Art Gallery, Hull; British Museum; and Ashmolean Museum, Oxford, hold examples. He lived in south London.

Felix GLUCK 1923–1981 Printmaker notable for lino-cuts in the German Expressionist tradition, painter of the English landscape, teacher and editor, born in Fürth, Bavaria. Fled with family from the Nazis in 1936; studied at the Free Academy of Art, Budapest, 1941–4, under Aurel Bernath and Robert Bereny; was imprisoned in Mauthausen concentration camp, 1944–5, where he contracted tuberculosis, which had to be treated at a sanatorium in Davos, 1946–8. An aunt in Newcastle enabled him to visit England from 1948, where he was able to study at King's College, Durham University, under Christopher Cornford and Lawrence Gowing. Before returning to Hungary in 1950 Gluck began to exhibit, gaining first prize in the Giles Bequest Relief Print Competition, organised by the Victoria & Albert Museum. Gluck worked as art editor for Hungary's state publishing house, 1953–6, but with the uprising he fled to England, settling in Twickenham, Middlesex. Gluck was made art editor at Rathbone (later Aldus) Books, 1957–66; lectured in graphic design at Hornsey College of Art, 1966–9, Chelsea College of Art, 1969–71, and Twickenham College, 1973–7; edited *Modern Publicity*, 1967–81, and founded the Felix Gluck Press in 1971, which lasted until just after his death. Gluck had solo shows at Woodstock Gallery, 1962, and Keele University, 1974. He died at Royal Marsden Hospital, 1981, and there was a retrospective at Orleans House Gallery, Twickenham, 1986, with another show at Durham Art Gallery and DLI Museum, 1995.

Paulien GLUCKMAN 1951– Sculptor in stone of figurative work, born in The Hague, Netherlands. She studied with Michael Marriott at Sir John Cass College, from 1993 being an apprentice with the sculptor John Skelton. She was a teacher of young children. Medardo Rosso and Brancusi were influences on the work of Gluckman, who was a member of Sussex Sculptors and Sussex County Art Club. She showed at Brighton, Hove and Worthing Museums and Art Galleries, at the Brighton Festival and at Charleston Farmhouse, Firle. Lived in Brighton, Sussex.

Daphne GOAD 1925– Painter and lecturer on art, born in Wallington, Hertfordshire. She studied at Central School of Arts and Crafts, 1943–7, Chelsea School of Art, 1943–7, L'École des Beaux-Arts, 1947–8, and Le Centre des Spectacles, 1947–8. Showed with RI, NEAC, SEA and elsewhere, Kent Education Committee buying her work. Lived in Hertford.

D GOAMAN: *see* **Winifred Doris BOSWORTH**

Victoria GOAMAN 1951– Botanical artist, born in London. She trained and worked as a freelance botanical illustrator with Dr Edmund Launert at the Natural History Museum, continuing this work for Royal Botanic Gardens, Kew. From 1974 she began to use watercolour for botanical flower paintings for publication and private collections. Where possible she preferred to work from live specimens rather than photographs. Among the books she illustrated were *Culinary Herbs*, produced by the Royal Horticultural Society in 1974; *Understanding Wild Flowers*, by Ros Evans, 1982; and *Garden Flowers*, by C Grey-Wilson and the artist, where the illustrations took over three years as she was restricted by seasonal work. Also did illustrations for *Illustrated London News, Natural World* and *Midland Bank Calendar*. Won several Royal Horticultural Society awards, including a gold medal for watercolour painting in 1978. Exhibited with Austin/Desmond Fine Art, Sunninghill, 1990.

Jenny GOATER 1943– Sculptor, painter, printmaker and teacher, born in New Delhi, India. Educated at Bath Academy of Art, 1961–7, she graduated in painting under Howard Hodgkin and sculpture with Peter Startup. Her first job was teaching art at Millfield School where she produced etchings and paintings of the Somerset levels, showing locally. A move to Suffolk and a commission for a life-size goat inspired animal-based sculptures in diverse media. Developed a technique by which plaster or concrete was worked on to an open armature, but slowly the armature took over, leading to free sculptural wire-work. Showed at Fermoy Gallery, King's Lynn; Assembly House, Norwich; Frederick Gallery, Raveningham; Yoxford and Halesworth Galleries; Gallery 44, Aldeburgh; Woodgates Gallery, East Bergholt; and Broughton House Gallery and Downing College, both in Cambridge. Did much work to commission, from abstracts to a prancing horse for Ferrari. Private collections in France, Australia and America held examples, with a more than life-size pair of basket-ball players in Beijing, China. She lived in Diss, Norfolk.

Tony GOBLE 1943– Painter and gallery director, who studied at Wrexham School of Art. He went on to be director of the gallery at Llanover Hall Arts Centre in Cardiff, where he lived. He was a member of the Welsh Group, Association of Artists/Designers in Wales and RCamA. Also showed with RA, LG and abroad in Europe. Goble's work, which could be stridently coloured with a generous use of red and a rich personal imagery, was given a big exhibition, Dream Seeds, at Glynn Vivian Art Gallery, Swansea, in 1995. He was included in A Serious Magic, at Newport Museum & Art Gallery, 2004–5. WAC holds Goble's work.

David GODBOLD 1961– Norwich, Norfolk-born artist and teacher who from 1990 settled in Dublin, Ireland, but who was in 2005 commissioned by the all-party Advisory Committee on Works of Art at Westminster as Britain's official general election artist. Godbold was a versatile artist whose output included pieces in which discarded papers such as shopping lists were overlaid with delicate Old Master-style drawings and caustic texts. Godbold attended Norwich School of Art, 1980–1, and Goldsmiths' College, 1981–4. His awards included two from the British Council in 1989; three from the Arts Council, 1991–4; the DHL Artlift Award, 1995; a PSl International Studio Fellowship, 1999–00; Cil Riliag studio residency in Ireland, 2001; Arts Council of Ireland Award and a Rome Scholarship, both 2002; and The Healing Ark, public commission for Our Lady's Hospital for Sick Children, Crumlin, 2002–3. After a teaching residency at the University of New South Wales, Australia, in 1995, Godbold taught and presented papers widely in Australia, the United Kingdom and Ireland, from 1990 being a senior lecturer at the National College of Art & Design, Dublin. From the mid-1980s Godbold collaborated with John Wood for group and solo exhibitions as Godbold & Wood (see separate entry). On his own account, Godbold participated in many group exhibitions, later ones including Reanimation, Kunstmuseum, Thun, Switzerland; A Time for Shaking, Irish Museum of Modern Art, Kilmainham; and Faith, Ormeau Baths Gallery, Belfast, all 2004. His many solo shows included latterly The Fall Guy (reprieved), Project, Dublin, 2000; Rhodes + Mann, and Social Anxiety (& other unrelated) Disorder(s), Kerlin Gallery, Dublin, both 2001; and Once it was a lie, now it's the truth, Kerlin Gallery, 2005. The Irish Museum of Modern Art; The Irish Board of Foreign Affairs; Trinity College, Dublin; The National Collection of Contemporary Drawing, Ireland; and other public, private and corporate collections owned Godbold's work.

GODBOLD & WOOD– This was the collaborative name from the mid-1980s of David Godbold and John Wood (see separate entries). They took part in a number of group exhibitions in Britain and abroad, later ones including The Art Gallery of New South Wales & Pier 2/3, Walsh Bay, Sydney, and The 7th Biennale of Sydney. From The Southern Cross: A view of World Art 1948–88, both 1988; and Gallery Anna Bornholt, 1994. Among Godbold & Wood's solo show appearances were Endangered Species, Actualities; Nine Portraits of Christ, photographic works 1985–88, Mori Gallery, Sydney; and Endangered Species, installation work, Cambridge Festival, in association with Kettle's Yard Gallery, all 1988.

Francis Ambrose GODDARD 1868–1962 Self-taught painter, who developed his interest in art after retiring as a career soldier with the rank of lieutenant-colonel, signing work F A G. Exhibited RA, ROI and RBA. At various times he was chairman of the Army Art Society and president of the RMS. Lived in London.

John GODDARD 1924– Painter and teacher, born in Cardiff, where he attended the College of Art in 1941–3 and 1947–51, interrupted by the war, his teachers including James Tarr, Ceri Richards and Evan Charlton. He went on to teach at the College for a time as well as at a number of Welsh schools including Lewis School in Caerphilly, where he lived. Showed LG, SEA, SWG, WAC and elsewhere. Goddard's work was featured at the Washington Gallery, Cardiff, in 2003.

Judith GODDARD 1956– Artist who employed video, born in Crosshouses, Shropshire. She studied at Berkshire College of Art, 1973–5; gained an honours degree in fine art at Reading University, 1975–9; and a master's degree in environmental media, 1981–3. Awards included one from the Arts Council, 1983; installation for Sound/Vision, Plymouth and Exeter, 1985; and video for Video Positive, Tate Gallery, Liverpool, 1988–9. Took part in Signs of the Times at Museum of Modern Art, Oxford, 1990, and in 1995 contributed to Open House: two exhibitions for Jim Ede's centenary at Kettle's Yard, Cambridge, in which her contribution focused on Ede's wife, Helen.

Preston GODDARD 1928– Painter and designer, born in Liverpool. Studied at Croydon School of Arts and Crafts under Robert Arthur Wilson, 1945–6 and 1948–50. Goddard exhibited widely in mixed shows in London and the provinces. A one-man show at the Beaux Arts Gallery in 1955 was followed by others at Leicester Galleries, Somerville College in Oxford and the Fairfield Halls, Croydon. Leicestershire and Surrey Education Committees hold his work. Lived for many years in Croydon, Surrey, and sometimes signed pictures Preston.

Stephen GODDARD 1959– Self-taught painter and draughtsman and graphic designer, born in Fulham, west London. He was initially a graphic artist in advertising, moving full-time into fine art aged 30. He produced distinctive and highly personal images and liked to experiment with combinations of unorthodox media on hand-made papers. Aged six Goddard began drawing his family, another inspiration being a collection of Japanese and African ethnographic art. He exhibited consistently from 1983, the first year he submitted to the RA Summer Exhibition. Also showed at National Portrait Gallery, Royal Over-Seas League, PS, RBA, Waterman Fine Art and Mercury Gallery; and widely in America and in Hong Kong, in 1991 being chosen, alongside David Hockney, for the Festival of British Art in Alabama. Goddard won many prizes including RWS, RI, The Discerning Eye and Singer & Friedlander/*Sunday Times* Watercolour Competition, including its first prize in 2003. Shared a show at Gallery 27 in 1997, presented by James Huntington-Whiteley. Lived in London, where his pictures were in the collections of HRH The Prince of Wales and the Italian Embassy.

Charles Edward Victor GODDEN 1901–1976 Draughtsman of figures in pencil and chalk; printmaker. Studied at Portsmouth School of Art, 1922–4, then from 1934–9 with James Bateman and Stanley Anderson at Goldsmiths' College School of Art. He exhibited at the RA, other leading galleries, Bath Society of Artists and RWA, being a trustee of it for 20 years from 1952. Lived at Corsham, Wiltshire.

Nicola Jane Averill GODDEN 1959– Sculptor, born in Germany but educated in Somerset. She graduated from West Surrey College of Art and Design, in Farnham, and went on to show with David Messum, Mall Galleries, at Tom Caldwell Gallery, Belfast, and at Eton College. Was a director of Linden Contemporary Sculpture. Lived for a time in London. Godden's bronze of the ornithologist and artist Peter Scott was made for his memorial, Wetlands Centre, Barnes, officially opened in 2000.

Angela GODFREY 1939– Artist, notably a sculptor, and teacher, born in London, who did a large amount of commissioned work for churches. Gained a fine art degree, Newcastle University, 1957–61, then taught at Mid-Warwickshire School of Art, 1962–4. Exhibitions included Letchworth Art Gallery, 1975, and Kodak House in Hemel Hempstead, 1977. Among her public works are Entrance Door, 1974, for St Bernardine Friary Church in Buckingham, and an impressive, stylised Christ on the Cross, 1976, at Weston Favel Roman Catholic Church, Northamptonshire.

Ian GODFREY 1942–1992 Ceramic sculptor and potter whose creations were spiced with wit and playfulness, featuring small creatures and drawing on ideas from a range of cultures. Born in Ely and educated in London, Godfrey attended Camberwell School of Arts and Crafts from 1957, initially to study painting, although turned to pottery in the department run by Dick Kendall. His teachers included Hans Coper and Lucie Rie. In 1962 he started a workshop in Islington; in 1967–8 gained a pottery fellowship at Royal College of Art; in 1975 moved to Denmark, setting up a domestic pottery workshop in Jutland; then returned to Highgate in 1980. Showed widely in Britain and overseas from 1962, including Osaka, Expo '70; Faenza, Concorso Internazionale Ceramica d'Arte, in 1974, where he gained a gold medal; and Heltborg Museum, Denmark, 1992. In 1993 Godfrey was given a memorial show by Galerie Besson. Public galleries in Glasgow, Aberdeen and Paisley hold his work, as does the Victoria & Albert Museum and several overseas galleries.

Jim GODFREY 1945– Painter and draughtsman, born in Kingston upon Thames, Surrey. He studied at Camberwell School of Arts and Crafts, 1964–8. Showed at Greenwich Theatre Gallery, 1967; Bakehouse Gallery, 1982; and had a solo show at Woodlands Art Gallery, 1983.

Laura GODFREY-ISAACS 1964– Painter and teacher, born in London, where she settled to work. She studied at Kingston Polytechnic, 1982, Brighton Polytechnic, 1983–6, and Slade School of Fine Art, 1986–8. In the latter year she won a Boise award and a Fulbright Fellowship, so becoming artist-in-residence at Pratt Institute, New York. In 1990 she took up a similar position at Tate Gallery, Liverpool, having a solo show there called Pink. Other solo exhibitions included Sue Williams Gallery and John Milton Gallery, both 1991. In 1991–2 her picture Body with Little White Holes was included in John Moores Exhibition, Liverpool, the holes "shifting uneasily between provocative physicality and sensual allure". Worked on public arts projects in Central America, Romania, New York and in Britain, including Whitechapel Gallery. Became a senior lecturer at Winchester School of Art.

Izabella GODLEWSKA de ARANDA 1931– Painter, sculptor and architect, born on her family's estate in Poland; with the approach of World War II they moved across Europe, through Lithuania, Latvia and Sweden to France; when it collapsed, they moved again, through Spain and Portugal, to England in 1940. After education at Kilgraston Sacred Heart Convent School, Perthshire, she graduated from the Oxford School of Architecture, 1949–54, studied painting under Jan Pacewicz in London, 1954–7, and worked there and in Madrid, Spain, as an architect, 1954–9. She was engaged in sculpture at Chelsea and West Thames Colleges of Art, 1989–99. Her husband, who predeceased her, was the Spanish ambassador to Finland and Estonia, 1991–3. Godlewska de Aranda produced both figurative and abstract work. She took part in The last 70 years of Spanish Painting in London, Dublin and Warsaw, 1973; was awarded a bronze medal at the First Competition of Contemporary Painting staged by Iberia Airlines, 1974; participated in the Trayectorias show in Naples, Italy, which toured several continents, 1980; and was selected for the competition for the statue of Pope John Paul II for Almudena Cathedral, Madrid, 1998. Had widespread international shows from 1963, later ones including Air Gallery, 1999. There was a major exhibition, with important catalogue, at the University Museum in Toruń, Polan, in 2005. The writer Helen de Borchgrave said of her that: "Her paintings are vibrant with colour. They take you on a journey from the figurative into the abstract; through time and space, both physical and spiritual." She lived in London.

Oliver GODOW 1968– Artist-photographer, born in Lübeck, West Germany, who studied at Bournemouth & Poole College of Art, 1990–4, gaining a master's degree in fine art from Glasgow School of Art, 1995–7. Between April 2002 and December 2003 Godow chronicled the development of the new Camden Arts Centre under a residency, the resulting work being exhibited and published there in 2004. Godow was based in Hamburg, Oldenburg and London. His work was in numerous group shows including Art For People, Transmission Gallery, Glasgow, 1996, and Perspective 2001, Ormeau Baths Gallery, Belfast. Among later solo exhibitions were Goethe Institute, 2002, and Schloss Wofsberg/UBS Bank Executive Development Centre, Switzerland, 2004.

Ada Charlotte GODSON fl. c.1920–1960 Painter and miniaturist, born at Tenbury, Worcestershire. She studied at Cheltenham Ladies' College, then at Sir Arthur Cope's School of Art, in France, Germany and Italy. Exhibited RI, SM, RBSA, UA and Paris Salon, her work being widely reproduced in France. Lived in London.

Keith GODWIN 1916–1991 Sculptor, draughtsman, collagist and teacher, born in Warsop, Nottinghamshire. He studied at Nottingham College of Art, 1934–6, Leicester

College of Art, 1936–9, and sculpture at Royal College of Art, 1939–40 and 1946–8, World War II being spent in Royal Air Force Intelligence. He won the Royal College's Silver Medal in 1947, the Travelling Scholarship in 1949. Godwin became head of sculpture at Hammersmith College of Art, 1957–67, then at Manchester Polytechnic, 1967–82, becoming head of fine arts there, 1979–81. He showed at RA, RBA of which he was a member and Manchester Academy. Carried out many commissions, abstract and figurative; notable works were his sculpture for the centenary of the *Manchester Evening News*, 1971, work for the Reed Paper Group, British Rail and Commonwealth Institute. Memorial show at Woodlands Art Gallery, 1992. Lived in Sudbury, Suffolk.

Mark GODWIN 1957– Painter, printmaker and lecturer, born in Birmingham, who studied at Stourbridge College of Art, 1975–8; Central School of Art, 1978–9; and the Royal College of Art, 1979–82, spending a year at Cité Internationale des Arts, Paris, 1982. Godwin was a visiting lecturer at Stourbridge, 1979. From 1979–83 he was a copperplate printer for Palm Tree Editions, from 1983–5 with Albion Editions. He took part in mixed shows in Britain and abroad, sharing a trio exhibition, Art in the Abstract, Catto Gallery, 2001. Then, his works were "based upon a general theme of landscape, or more specifically urban or cityscape. I am interested in the artificial, or man-made, and its interaction with nature or natural phenomena." There was a solo show at the New Academy Gallery in 2001. British Airways, Sumitomo Bank, Enterprise Oil and Royal Caribbean Lines were among many corporate owners. Godwin had a studio in London.

Mary GODWIN 1887–1960 Painter, born at Stoke Bishop, near Bristol. Studied art in the women's department of King's College under Byam Shaw, also with Walter Sickert and Harold Gilman and at Westminster Polytechnic. Her work retained a Camden Town Group flavour. Exhibited at RA, AAA, Goupil Gallery, Cooling Galleries, NEAC, LG and had one-man show at Leger Gallery. Paintings were reproduced in *The Studio* and *Colour*. Lived in London.

Walter GOETZ 1911–1995 Painter and illustrator for newspapers and magazines, born in Cologne, Germany. He attended school in England from 1922, Bedales from 1923. When his parents were ruined in the Depression, Goetz in 1929 declined to read history and English at Cambridge University and returned to Berlin to study painting. The political climate made him move to England again in 1931 (he was naturalised three years later), where he became a notable illustrator and cartoonist for the *Daily Express* (as Walter) and magazines as varied as *Lilliput*, *Strand* and *Vogue*. In World War II Goetz worked in the Foreign Office intelligence department and closely with the BBC, broadcasting black propaganda to Germany. From 1951–72 Goetz lived in Paris, illustrating Pierre Daninos' *Major Thompson* books and from 1959 dealing in high-value pictures. Exhibited his own work in Paris and in London at Lefevre, Wertheim and Bloomsbury Galleries and had one-man shows at St George's Gallery and Leicester Galleries. Goetz was first married to the designer artist Jill Greenwood. He settled permanently in London from 1980.

Nicholette GOFF fl. from 1980s– Artist who gained an honours degree in fine art at Maidstone College of Art, 1981–4; was at Birkbeck College, University of London, 1989–91, for diploma studies; then obtained her master's in art criticism and theory at Kent Institute of Art & Design, Canterbury, 1994–6. Exhibitions included Common Ground, Milton Chantry, Gravesend, 1985; West End Studios Group, Medway Arts Centre, Chatham, 1989; Visions of Life, Gagliardi Gallery, 1993; and Fantasy, a United Arab Emirates tour of work by 15 British women artists, 1995. Solo shows included Post Nostalgia Gallery, Teddington, 1995. Goff's work in the Kent Institute of Art & Design show Diverse, 1996, was based mostly on found objects revolving around a notion of trace: "a suggestion of possible meaning invoked by the objects and the situation in which they are placed".

Harry GOFFEY 1871–1951 Miniatures painter and printmaker, born in Liverpool. He studied at Liverpool School of Art, under Sir Hubert von Herkomer at his School of Art at Bushey, Hertfordshire, 1892–4, then at Chelsea Polytechnic. Exhibited RA and Walker Art Gallery, Liverpool. British Museum holds his work. Lived at Berkhamsted, Hertfordshire.

William GOFTON 1945– Prolific sculptor and painter who established a strong reputation in the Tyneside area. He often used waste materials and said that he saw "only extremes of either beauty or ugliness." Gofton began spare-time sculpting and painting while a shot-blaster. When he became a marine engineer he was able to organise his work so that he could spend half his time on artworks. His ciment fondu figure Dolly Peel, an early nineteenth-century fishwife and smuggler, is sited at River Drive, South Shields.

Genadii GOGOLIUK 1960– Figurative painter, born in southern Russia, who began his art training aged 10 and five years later attended art college in Lugansk. He then worked as a scenery painter for the Kirov Theatre, Leningrad, before starting a long formal training at the Leningrad Academy in 1983. In 1998 Gogoliuk moved to Scotland and in 2000 won the Maud Gemmell Hutchison Prize at the RSA. Drawing on Russian folk art and icon painting traditions, Gogoliuk used many layers of diluted paint to achieve a delicacy and depth of colour, aiming to "conjure figures from the shadows". John Martin of London gave him his first British solo show in 2001, another in 2003.

Michael GOLDBERG: *see* **Michael GILBERY**

Simon GOLDBERG 1916–2002 Painter, printmaker and lecturer, born in London. His real name was Solomon Goldberg, but he worked as Sydney Goldberg until around 1950, Simon Goldberg after that. He was trained at St Martin's College of Art, then the Royal College of Art, 1937–40, teachers including John Nash, Gilbert Spencer and Edward Bawden. Goldberg did war service in the Royal Artillery, 1940–4, then with the Royal Army Service Corps, 1944–6. From 1947–83 he taught at Hull Regional College of Arts and Crafts, later Humberside College of Higher Education, becoming a senior lecturer. He was elected to the Senefelder Club in 1949, in the early 1950s being a founder of the Avenues Group in Hull, where he lived from 1947–97. Goldberg was accomplished in many media, but worked mostly in lithography and oil, producing townscapes and some landscapes. He participated in many group exhibitions, including the RA Summer Exhibition, 1940–71; Spring Exhibition, Bradford City Art Gallery, 1955; Three Hull Realists (with James Neal and Harold Newman), tour including Shipley Art Gallery, Gateshead, 1965; and Ferens Art Gallery, Hull, Winter Exhibition, as a regular contributor until 1996. He shared a show with Marcia Tyler at Nottingham Playhouse, 1968. Goldberg had solo exhibitions at University of Hull senior common room, 1961; Ferens Art Gallery, 1961 and 1981; and Keldgate Arts Centre, Beverley, 1966. The Victoria & Albert Museum, Ferens Art Gallery, University of Hull, South London Art Gallery and Derbyshire Museums Service hold examples. From 1997 Goldberg lived in York.

Solomon GOLDBERG: *see* **Simon GOLDBERG**

Sydney GOLDBERG: *see* **Simon GOLDBERG**

Susan GOLDBLATT 1947– Artist who undertook architectural studies at Liverpool University, 1967–70, then attended the school of architecture at Polytechnic of Central London, 1970–3, and Byam Shaw School of Art, 1979–83. She had a solo exhibition at Burgh House Gallery, Hampstead, in 1987. In 1988 she participated in Open Studio, Barbican Arts Group, and Society of Architect Artists Annual Exhibition, in 1989 in East End Open Studios with Barbican Arts Group. Goldblatt's residencies included a Japanese landscape theme mosaic at Westminster Under School and African pattern theme mosaics at Torriano Primary School, both 2002. Among later public commissions were mosaic panel, Imperial College, and mosaic floor, Beormund Park, Southwark, both 2004. She was included in an open studio show at The Chocolate Factory, 2005, one of a long series, and a group show at Curwen Gallery, 2005.

Grace GOLDEN 1904–1993 Painter, printmaker, illustrator and teacher, born and lived in London. She studied at Chelsea School of Art, 1920–3, with John Revel; at Royal College of Art, teachers including William Rothenstein, 1923–6, teaching there, 1926–7; and at Regent Street Polytechnic School of Art. Golden worked for magazines and produced book illustrations, often having to work to tight deadlines and research historical detail meticulously. Her own book *Old Bankside*, 1951, was so detailed that she was invited by Sam Wanamaker, planning to rebuild Shakespeare's Globe Playhouse, to be official archivist to the project. Golden also did posters for the General Post Office; worked for the Ministry of Information; and drew historic buildings for the Pilgrim Trust. During World War II she placed work with the War Artists' Advisory Committee. Showed at RA, Fine Art Society and Leicester Galleries and had a retrospective at South London Art Gallery, 1979. Tate Gallery and Museum of London hold much of her work.

Lynn GOLDEN 1958– Representational painter, born in Hertfordshire, who trained at St Albans School of Art. She was based at The Gallery, Portscatho, Cornwall, showing there and in many other mixed exhibitions, including Hicks, Osborne Studio, Hyde Park and Llewellyn Alexander Galleries; RWA and Innocent Fine Art, Bristol; Falmouth and Penzance Art Clubs; and on the continent. In 1992 she was Overall Grand Prix Winner, La Fédération Nationale de la Culture Française.

Matt GOLDEN 1974– Conceptual artist, born in Salisbury, Wiltshire, who graduated from De Montfort University, Leicester, 1993–6, gaining his master's from the Royal College of Art, 2003–5. Group exhibitions included Do-Don't/Can-Can't, Impact III, Cape Town, in South Africa, Sounding Out, chosen by Richard Wilson, University of East London, 14th Mostyn Open, Oriel Mostyn Gallery, Llandudno, and After Shock, 1a Space, Kowloon, Hong Kong, all 2003, and David Batchelor, Matt Golden and Simon Patterson, MOT Gallery, 2005. In that year he was an Artist of the Day, selected by Yuko Shiraishi, at Flowers Central, his work Manuscript comprising 100 sheets of A4 paper. Earlier solo exhibitions were When Roads Lead South, B16 Gallery, Birmingham, 2000, and Home Base, The Gallery, Stratford-upon-Avon, 2003.

Pamela GOLDEN 1959– Versatile artist and teacher, born in Chicago Heights, Illinois, America, who graduated in fine art from Northern Illinois University, Dekalb, in 1981, gaining her master's at the School of the Art Institute of Chicago, 1984 (she had taken part in the Young Artists Studios Program there, 1975–8). After initial teaching at the Art Institute and at Columbia College, also in Chicago, Golden moved to Britain in 1989, settling in London. Following teaching at Southwark College, Kingston University, The Architectural Association, Slade School of Fine Art and Leeds University, she held senior lectureships at both Wimbledon School of Art and University of Reading, 1997–01, from 2001 becoming postgraduate research co-ordinator at Reading. Held many visiting-artist posts in Britain and America and won extensive awards and commissions, including latterly an Abbey Award in Painting, The British School at Rome, 1994; British Council Travel Grant, 1995; and Research Awards, Wimbledon School of Art, 1998 and 2000. Participated in numerous group shows internationally and had many solo exhibitions, among later ones the Fassbender Gallery, Chicago, 1999, and Even the car is dead, Gimpel Fils, 2001. That show "explored the dichotomy of society and nature, of inner and outer worlds" and "looked at how, although we apparently dominate it, something about nature remains unknown and unknowable." Nothing Personal was a Gimpel Fils show, José Azeredo Perdigão Modern Art Centre, Calouste Gulbenkian Foundation, in 2004–5. The Word was at Gimpel Fils in 2005.

John GOLDING 1929– Teacher, writer, painter and exhibition organiser, born in England but educated in Mexico and Canada, at the University of Toronto. From 1951–7 Golding did postgraduate work at Courtauld Institute, his doctoral thesis being published in 1959 as *Cubism 1907–14*. In 1959 he began teaching at Courtauld, then was a tutor at Royal College of Art, 1971–86, being senior tutor, 1981–6. In 1978 Golding was Slade Professor of Fine Art at Cambridge University. In 2000, he was made the Royal Academy Schools' professor of art history. Golding's pictures were abstract, reflecting and contemplative. He had his first solo show at Gallery One in 1962, others including Rowan Gallery, Hayward Gallery and Kettle's Yard, Cambridge. In 1994 Golding had a show of work at Mayor Gallery coinciding with the Tate Gallery's big sculpture and painting exhibition which he co-curated. The New Art Centre, East Winterslow, showed his new paintings in 2003. He was also co-curator of the major Matisse Picasso show at Tate Modern in 2002. Golding was a Tate trustee, 1984–91. His many books include *Visions of the Modern*,

1994, and a study of abstract painting, *Paths to the Absolute*, 2000. Arts Council holds work by Golding, who lived in London.

Alide GOLDSCHMIDT 1885–1965 Landscape and figure painter and draughtsman, born into a prosperous middle-class Jewish family in Hamburg, Germany, who encouraged her interest in painting from her early teens. About this time she went to live at the Palazzo Zuccari in Rome with Ludwig and Frida Mond, who were noted for their artistic patronage. Alide began exhibiting in her early twenties and eventually moved to Paris, to be closer to the source of Impressionist art. From 1907 she successfully participated in Salon d'Automne exhibitions. In 1910 she met and married Israel Gollancz, then a lecturer at Cambridge, eventually to be knighted for his services to English literature. Alide continued painting, exhibiting in London, Paris and Rome, and in 1926, as Alide Gollancz, showed a large group of pictures at the Beaux Arts Gallery. The death of Sir Israel in 1930 after a short illness prompted her to cease painting. Although during World War II, when refugee relatives from Germany were staying, their young daughter persuaded Alide to draw and paint for her, she never showed again. In 2005, Christie's, South Kensington, offered works from the studio of Alide Goldschmidt along with others by her painter son Oliver Gollancz.

Hilde GOLDSCHMIDT 1897–1980 Painter and printmaker, born in Leipzig, Germany, where she began her studies in 1914. Between 1920–3 she was a master pupil of Oskar Kokoschka at Dresden Academy. From 1923–32 she travelled to New York, Paris, the south of France, Italy and then returned to Germany where she had a first solo exhibition at Gallery Caspari, Munich, in 1932. Settled in Kitzbuehel in 1933, the Tyrolean scenery being an inspiration. Fearing a Nazi threat, in 1939 she moved with her mother to London, settling at Langdale, Westmorland, in 1942. She lived by making fur and leather goods, continued to paint and befriended the artist Kurt Schwitters. During her time there her lyrical Expressionist style became more structured. Always figurative, her pictures were richly coloured, sometimes symbolic and very moving. Had a show in Manchester in 1949, the year before her return to Kitzbuehel. Later shows included a number in Austria; Annely Juda Fine Art, 1969; and Abbot Hall Art Gallery, Kendal, and tour, 1973. Abbot Hall, Tate Gallery and several Austrian collections hold her work.

Shelly GOLDSMITH 1962– Versatile artist and teacher whose work could have a strong abstract pattern quality, as in Untitled, Royal Over-Seas League Open, 1994. Was born in Corringham, Essex, studying at West Surrey College of Art & Design, Farnham; Royal College of Art; and Winchester School of Art. Held a number of lectureships, including Manchester Polytechnic, 1992, then tapestry at West Dean College, Sussex. She travelled widely, exhibitions, residencies and teaching in Australia, America, Japan and Norway. Commissions included Collins Book Publishers, 1987; Victoria & Albert Museum Contemporary Collection and Lewis Moberly Design Group, both 1989. Mixed shows included Contemporary Textile Gallery from 1987; Rebecca Hossack Gallery from 1990; and Gift for Life, Imagination Gallery, 1993. Had a solo show, Vital Spark, Gainsborough's House, Sudbury, 1992. Later ones included Flow, Barbican Arts Centre, 1997; Dew Point, Centre de Documentacio i Museu Textil, Terrassa, Spain, and international tour, 1999; and Ripened, The Angel Row Gallery, Nottingham, 2001. In 2002 she was awarded the Jerwood Prize for Textiles, in 2004 was invited to represent the United Kingdom at the Kanazawa World Craft Forum. The Victoria & Albert Museum and Crafts Council of Great Britain hold examples.

Andy GOLDSWORTHY 1956– Sculptor, draughtsman, photographer and teacher, born in Cheshire. He attended Bradford Art College in 1975, then Preston Polytechnic, 1975–8. During 1989 he worked at Ellesmere Island, Canada, and at North Pole. Travelling widely to make sculptures in a particular environment was a feature of Goldsworthy's work. Goldsworthy had a series of one-man shows at Fabian Carlsson Gallery from 1987, later ones including Leeds City Art Gallery, a touring exhibition, Hand to Earth, in 1990; Runnymede Sculpture Farm Project, California, America, 1994; 100 Sheepfolds, part of Cumbria Year of Visual Art, 1996; Barbican Centre, 2000; and Cheltenham Art Gallery and Museum 2003. That show featured 28 photographs by Goldsworthy, a means he used to record ephemeral works. Also in 2003 early works by him from the Arts Council collection were shown at The Gallery, Stratford-upon-Avon, and the Royal Mail produced a set of postage stamps featuring his ice sculptures. Organic domes of wood and stone were featured in Andy Goldsworthy on the Roof, Metropolitan Museum of Art, New York, 2004, the year that *Passage*, a collection of photographs of his work, was published, and he had a show at Albion in 2005. His other commissions included Lambton Earthwork, County Durham, 1988; Black Spring, Royal Botanic Gardens, Adelaide, South Australia, 1992; and Boulder Wall, Bedford Corners, New York, America, 1996. Lived in Dumfriesshire, Scotland.

Mark GOLDSWORTHY 1962– Painter, sculptor, teacher and printmaker, born in London as Alan Mark Goldsworthy. He attended Great Yarmouth College of Art & Design, Medlock Fine Art Centre and Manchester Polytechnic, 1983–6. After a three-month tour of European countries and their galleries Goldsworthy set up studio in St Mary's Works, Norwich, helped organise several shows for Contact Gallery, an artists' co-operative. He was also an itinerant artist in South Africa, 1989–90, in 1991 visited America and was artist-in-residence for Circus Project at King's Lynn Arts Centre, other residencies including Holt Country Park, Norfolk, 1993 and 1994, also Ickworth House, Suffolk, 1994. In 1992, Goldsworthy completed his first hand-made book of lino-cuts, *Siddartha*; in 1994 created the stage set for the Rolling Stones' world tour; and in 1998 formed the Broad Street Guild, a workshop of four craftsmen. An interest in dreams gave Goldsworthy's pictures a surreal quality. Mixed exhibitions included Gainsborough's House, Sudbury; Knapp Gallery; Mall and Bankside Galleries; and several French galleries. Among his solo exhibitions was a series at Chappel Galleries, Chappel, including quirky, visionary wood sculptures and drawings, 2003.

Alide GOLLANCZ: *see* **Alide GOLDSCHMIDT**

Oliver GOLLANCZ 1914–2004 Painter, printmaker and teacher, born and lived in London, son of Sir Israel Gollancz and cousin of the publisher Victor Gollancz. He became senior lecturer in the history and theory of art at

Sir John Cass School of Art, taught for the Open University, University of London Extra-Mural Department and for Syracuse University London Centre. As a part-time mature student Gollancz studied with Cecil Collins and Hans Tisdall at Central School of Art & Design. He described himself as "committed to working in oil on canvas ... to revitalise painting as a significant form of contemporary art". His Colourist work was "increasingly non-figurative in interpretation of visual and emotional experience". Gollancz took part in group shows at Camden Arts Centre and in France, where he had a second home in the Cevennes. Gollancz's series of solo shows included Square Gallery, 1992, and in 1994 Ben Uri Art Society, following a residency at Mizpe Ramon in the Israeli Desert. The Active Eye, a show of abstract and figurative oils, prints and pastels, was held at Highgate Gallery, 2004. In 2005, Christie's, South Kensington, offered paintings from Gollancz's studio with a group of pictures by his mother, who early in the century had worked and exhibited as Alide Goldschmidt.

Vita GOLLANCZ 1926– Painter, in oil and watercolour of landscapes in Britain and abroad, sometimes tending towards abstraction. She was the fourth daughter of the publisher Victor Gollancz and his wife Ruth, who had studied at the Slade School of Fine Art under Henry Tonks. After reading modern history at Cambridge, Vita was manager of Hugh Casson and Neville Conder's architectural practice. She returned to painting in her thirties, studying at Chelsea School of Art and Byam Shaw; from the late 1960s she went regularly with a group led by Peter Garrard to paint in the Midi, France. Gollancz showed at the NEAC, RBA and RA Summer Exhibitions. A solo show at the Annexe Gallery was followed by others in her studio and there was an 80th birthday Exhibition at Piers Feetham Gallery in 2006.

Sue GOLLIFER 1944– Printmaker and teacher who obtained a foundation certificate at Scarborough Technical College; an art and design diploma in fine art/painting from Lanchester Polytechnic; studied postgraduate printmaking at Brighton Polytechnic; then gained her master's degree in academic practice, part-time, at the University of Brighton, 2001. Gollifer became a senior lecturer in fine art/printmaking in the school of arts and communication in the faculty of arts and architecture there. While there she was seconded for part of her time to work in the London Institute's research and development on the impact of new technology on fine art. Gollifer gained a number of awards, including Arts and Humanities Research, 2002, to archive the International Symposium of Electronic Art, conference proceedings and associated exhibitions, performances and websites, making them accessible on the web. By then she had been a professional artist for over 30 years, showing globally. Gollifer gave keynote presentations at many international conferences and held appointments with the Printmakers' Council of Great Britain, Association for Computing Machinery, *Digital Creativity*, Distributed National Electronic Resources, Visual Arts Data Service, Arts and Humanities Data Service, College Arts Association, Design and Artists' Copyright Society and Computer in Art & Design Education. She took part in numerous group shows, participated in virtual exhibitions and her solo shows included York University, 1971; Serpentine Gallery, 1972; Screen Works, University of Sussex, 1995; and Recent Prints, Colville Place Gallery, 2002. Gollifer's work developed "according to a rigorous programme of formal experiment, through which sets of relationships evolved between shapes, colours and tones." Many public collections held examples, including the British Council, The Open University and Victoria & Albert Museum.

Chris GOLLON 1953– Self-taught figurative painter, originally of portraits, then in an allegorical style. Gollon dealt with the tragedy and misfortune of the human condition, his subjects including tramps, grotesques and misfits, sometimes with a manic quality. He was a finalist in Hunting Group Prizes, Mall Galleries, 1989, also showing at ROI from 1990. Solo exhibitions included Ferens Art Gallery, Hull, 1993, televised and so popular it was extended two weeks; Lawrence Batley Centre, West Bretton, 1994; The Pump House Gallery, 1995; and The Road to Narragonia, Lamont Gallery, 1996; Galerie Simoncini, Luxembourg,1997, the year that Independent Art Promotions (IAP Fine Art) successfully exhibited Gollon's work in Bahrain. In 1998, Gollon exhibited in ROOT at the Chisenhale Gallery, London, a crossover exhibition of contemporary music and art originated by Thurston Moore of Sonic Youth, and including works by Gavin Turk, Yoko Ono and David Bowie. In 2000, Gollon enjoyed a solo show at the Huddersfield Art Gallery. IAP Fine Art showed Gollon's pictures at the Arndean Gallery in 2001, the year the River & Rowing Museum, Henley-on-Thames, with the aid of the Victoria & Albert Museum, acquired the tripytch Big Fish Eat Little Fish. In 2001 Gollon accepted a six-year commission to paint 14 Stations of the Cross for a Sir John Soane-designed London church, St John on Bethnal Green. He was represented by Station IV, Jesus Meets His Mother, in the exhibition Presence: Images of Christ for the Third Millennium at St Paul's Cathedral in 2004. For his Stations of the Cross, Gollon's daughter Alice was the model for Mary, his son Lawrence for Jesus. In 2005, Gollon's major work Einstein & the Jealous Monk was purchased by the Huddersfield Art Gallery, and forms part of the permanent collection. In 2006, Gollon had solo exhibitions with Thompson's Gallery and IAP Fine Art.

Janet GOLPHIN 1950– Prolific Colourist notable for decorative still lifes and watercolours. She was born in Pontefract, Yorkshire, and studied with her neighbour William Selby. Was elected ROI; 1990, RBA, 1994; and RWS, 1996, being elected its vice-president in 1998. Won The Jeffrey Archer Award at RWS Open, 1992. Also exhibited at RA Summer Exhibition, Singer & Friedlander/*Sunday Times* Watercolour Competition, Thompson's Gallery and in September Show, 2003, at The Wykeham Gallery, Stockbridge. Commissions included four works for the John Lewis Partnership. Other corporate collections plus those of H M The Queen and H M Queen Elizabeth The Queen Mother held examples.

Hazel GOMES 1952– Versatile and colourful artist and designer, born in Goa, who early started painting, in which she was largely self-taught. Until 1971 attended the Sir J J School of Applied Arts in Bombay; then, after a visit to America, from 1973 studied fashion at St Martin's School of Art. She established a studio in Paris, designed for Yves St Laurent, worked for continental journals and had designs for Dutch firm Peek and Clopenburg shown at Stedelijk Museum, Amsterdam. Returned to London after eight years and continued to exhibit widely, including People and Places at Gagliardi Gallery, 1993.

David GOMMON 1913–1987 Painter in gouache and watercolour, muralist and teacher, born in London. He early wanted to be a painter and from 16 enrolled in art school at Battersea Polytechnic. Aged 19 he was given a solo show by Wertheim Gallery, then for several years Lucy Wertheim took most of his work and paid him £2 a week. Gommon came into contact with the theatre and continued his programme of self-education in the arts, which remained a passion. Living in Dorset his attachment with the romantic English landscape – a strong element in his work – was begun. Disillusioned with art on his return to London and aware of social unrest and deprivation, Gommon largely gave up painting. After a period in London Fire Service in World War II Gommon taught at a progressive school in Kent, then from 1946–77 taught art at Northampton Grammar School. Gaining a teaching qualification took time, because of the unacademic nature of his work. In 1959 Gommon held his second solo show, at Northampton Art Gallery, then had occasional exhibitions. His work found its way to Canberra Grammar School, Australia; he completed a huge mural for St Crispin Hospital, near Northampton; and public collections bought his work or were given it by Lucy Wertheim. Angel Row Gallery, Nottingham, held an exhibition 1991–2, which toured. Duncan Campbell latterly offered many examples. Gommon lived in Hardingstone, near Northampton.

Steven GONTARSKI 1972– Sculptor, born in Philadelphia, Pennsylvania, America, who graduated from Brown University, Providence, Rhode Island, in 1994, gaining his master's from Goldsmiths' College School of Art in 1997. Gontarski created disturbingly mutant, enigmatic, shiny, plastic sewn sculptures. His works were included in Die Young Stay Pretty at ICA, 1998–9, and in the Neurotic Realism series of exhibitions launched at the Saatchi Gallery in 1999, Saatchi Collection holding his work. Shared an exhibition at One in the Other, 2001, with a solo exhibition at Habitat, Kensington High Street, 2002. Worked in London and New York.

Patricia GONZALEZ 1958– Painter, draughtsman, printmaker and teacher, born in Cartagena, Colombia, a naturalised American citizen, wife of the artist Derek Boshier. She did a foundation course at Central School of Art & Design, 1976–7, graduated in painting and printmaking from Wimbledon School of Art, 1977–80, then did advanced printmaking at Glassell School of Art, Houston, 1982–3. After teaching art at George Washington School, Cartagena, 1980–1, Gonzalez held a number of appointments in Colombia and America, being visiting assistant professor at University of Houston, 1990–2. Mixed shows included Young Contemporaries at ICA, 1979; Colombian Artists, Canning House, 1983; Contemporary Arts Center, New Orleans, 1988; and Angela Flowers Gallery, 1993. Had a solo show at Graham Gallery, Houston, 1984, later ones including Art Museum of Southeast Texas, Beaumont, 1990, and Graham Gallery, 1991. Lived latterly at Kingsbury Episcopi, Somerset.

Amabel GOOCH 1899–1954 Painter, born at Weston, Hertfordshire. Self-taught artist who exhibited mainly in Norfolk, notably with the Norwich Art Circle. Lived near Diss, Norfolk.

Charles Stephen GOOD 1905– Painter, calligrapher, black-and-white artist and teacher. Studied at Harrogate School of Art with Richard Parker, then at Royal College of Art with Reco Capey, Edward Johnston and Ernest Tristram. From the late 1920s he held a series of positions at schools of art in the Midlands, north of England and London until World War II, which saw him working for such bodies as the Air Ministry. After the war taught at Hull College of Art. Exhibited RA, RP, RBA and widely in the north of England. Member of the Yorkshire Group of Artists and lived in Hull.

John Strickland GOODALL 1908–1996 Watercolourist and black-and-white illustrator, born in Heacham, Norfolk, into a family with a long medical tradition. He was educated at Harrow School, where he showed a talent for art, caricaturing the masters. His father, a Harley Street physician, reluctantly let Goodall be "trained to be a mid-Victorian art student" under Arthur Cope and John Watson Nicol, later with the noted draughtsman Harold Speed and at the Royal Academy Schools, 1925–9. There he met his future wife, Margaret Nicol. Began as a fortnightly contributor to *Radio Times* and went on to illustrate for periodicals such as *Bystander*, titles by E Nesbit and Miss Read and a series of his own books with Victorian and Edwardian settings. Because these contained no words beyond the title-page, children could make up their own story, and they were readily marketable overseas. Group shows included RA as well as RBA and RI, of both of which he was a member. During World War II Goodall, already a member of the Territorial Army, was posted to India where he worked in camouflage and had his first solo exhibition, of local landscapes, at the Government School of Art, Calcutta, in 1943. After the war Goodall settled at Tisbury, Wiltshire, in a cottage which featured in his books. He continued to paint landscapes, in Britain and abroad, and portraits, subjects including the Duchess of Kent and the actor Michael Redgrave. From 1984 showed regularly with the Christopher Wood Gallery, in 1993 also at The Jerram Gallery, Salisbury. Died in Shaftesbury, Dorset.

Francis Philip GOODCHILD 1904–1997 Artist and teacher, born in London. He studied at High Wycombe School of Art, 1919–23, then as a Royal Exhibitioner at Royal College of Art, 1923–6, teachers including Ernest Tristram and William Rothenstein. Was principal of Newton Abbot College of Art, 1947–64. Showed at RWA and elsewhere in west of England. Lived for many years in Brixham, Devon.

Juliet GOODDEN 1957– Painter of gestural still lifes and landscapes, and rug-maker, using a light palette, born in Colchester, Essex. She did a foundation course at Falmouth School of Art, 1974–5, gaining an honours degree in fine art, Central School of Art, 1975–8. Goodden travelled in Central America and India, 1979, designing and making carpets in India, 1982–7. Group shows included West Penwith Galleries, St Ives, 1981; John Hansard Gallery, Southampton, 1987; and Example Art, 1992. Later solo shows included Duncan Campbell Fine Art, 1999.

Avice GOODE: *see* **Avice SMIGIELSKI**

Mervyn GOODE 1948– Painter in oil, born in Cambridgeshire. He studied landscape architecture at Gloucestershire College of Art, but decided in 1969 to pursue his vocation as a landscape artist. His first solo show was a marked success, at Highton Gallery, 1970, and within 20 years Goode had had 30 one-man exhibitions. Later ones included Medici Galleries, 1990, Reid Gallery in Milford, Surrey, 1991, The Jerram Gallery, Salisbury, 1999, The Bourne Gallery, Reigate, and The Wykeham Gallery, Stockbridge, both 2002, and both galleries again in 2004. Had many mixed show appearances and his work was reproduced by Medici Society, Bucentaur Gallery and Kingsmead Publications. Goode said that his "inspiration is the English landscape in all its moods and seasons. I am a keen naturalist and conservationist". Lived in Hawkley Hurst, Hampshire, with another studio in Devon.

Stephen Frederick GOODEN 1892–1955 Printmaker and illustrator, born in Rugby, who studied at Rugby School. Gooden then studied at the Slade School of Fine Art, 1909–13, and after World War I service and some years' experience with lithography, wood engraving and etching, he turned to copper engraving in the early 1920s. During the late 1920s he concentrated on this medium, reintroducing it to book illustration while working with the Nonesuch Press. Gooden exhibited RE, RMS, RA and NEAC, but his main outlet was the printed page. Among books he illustrated were Abraham Cowley's translation of *Anacreon*, 1923, Edward Marsh's translation *The Fables of Jean de la Fontaine*, 1931, and the American author O Henry's *The Gift of the Magi*, 1939. Whitworth Art Gallery, Manchester, holds his work. Lived at Chesham Bois, Buckinghamshire.

Michael GOODEY 1950– Versatile sculptor and draughtsman, born and lived in Colchester, Essex, who attended Goldsmiths' College School of Art, 1970–4. Group shows included Drawings for All, Gainsborough's House, Sudbury, 1984; Eastern Open, King's Lynn, from 1984; Multimedia Fish Exhibition, South Hill Park Arts Centre, Bracknell, 1988; 3D 89, National Open Sculpture Exhibition, Watermans Arts Centre, Brentford, 1989; and Ipswich Open, Christchurch Mansion, Ipswich, 1995. Among his solo shows were Sculpture, The Minories, Colchester, 1986; Mirror Boxes, Trinity Street Studios, Colchester, 1992; and Wysing Arts, Cambridge, 1995. In 2002, Goodey took part in Making the Connection, organised by firstsite, Colchester, and Wolsey Art Gallery, a railways-oriented project for which he produced a striking design taking as his starting point the British Railways poster of pre- and post-war periods. Unilever, Epping Forest District Museum and Newmarket Upper School hold his work.

Peter GOODFELLOW 1950– Versatile artist, gallery owner and lecturer, born in Middlesbrough, Yorkshire, who graduated from the College of Art there in 1966 and from Central School of Art with honours in 1970. He was a part-time lecturer at Teesside College of Art, 1972–6. From 2000–2 worked on a commission for a private chapel at Migvie for The Hon. Philip Astor: 24 painted panels, three stained-glass windows, door carving and stone seats design. With his wife Jean Goodfellow established The Lost Gallery, Strathdon, Aberdeenshire, to show works by modern artists, including his own.

Reginald GOODFELLOW 1894–1985 Artist on paper who after leaving school was apprenticed to a structural engineer, serving with the Royal Engineers in Mesopotamia in World War I, then joined the Ministry of Works. Goodfellow had always painted but was formally trained only from 1927, entering Walter Bayes' classes at the Westminster School of Art. He continued to paint while working as an engineer until 1959, but did not promote himself. He submitted once to the RA Summer Exhibition, 1939, and was accepted. Michael Parkin showed Bayes and Goodfellow in 1986 in Pupil and Master, Sally Hunter Fine Art including Goodfellow in Twenties Veterans, 1988. The British Museum holds his woodcuts from the 1930s.

Steph GOODGER 1974– Painter, born in Kent, who studied at Kent Institute of Art and Design, 1991–2; Surrey Institute of Art and Design, 1992–5; and the University of Brighton, 1998–9. Her later shows included Ship of Fools, Phoenix Gallery, Brighton, and RA Summer Exhibition, both 2003; Galerie de Roos van Tudor, Leeuwarden, Netherlands, from 2003; and John Moores Liverpool Exhibition, 2004. In that, her oil on canvas Fish hell was related to Théodore Géricault's painting The Raft of the Medusa, "but where in Géricault's painting there is hope of rescue, in Fish hell there is perpetual struggle and doom."

Walter GOODIN 1907–1992 Originally a railway porter, this landscape painter's talent was nurtured from 1926 in Beverley, Yorkshire, by the artist Fred Elwell. Goodin attended the Royal Academy Schools, where he won the Gold Medal, the Elwells helping to fund his studies. After World War II, during which he served overseas, Goodin settled in Bridlington, Yorkshire, and married. Ferens Art Gallery, Hull, holds Goodin's The Old Custom House, and he was also exhibited at RA and at the Carnegie Institute, Pittsburgh, America. Elwell's portrait of Goodin, painted shortly after his Royal Academy studies in 1937, is owned by Sewerby Hall, Yorkshire.

Amy GOODMAN 1974– Sculptor, born in Windsor, Berkshire, a keen equine draughtsman from her early years. She moved to sculpture while studying for a fine art degree at Southampton University. Goodman used welded steel to capture the movement and energy of her subjects, describing her works as "drawing in space". Watchful Stag, included in Art on Show, The Gallery in Cork Street, 2001, was typical.

Caroline GOODMAN: *see* **Caroline DOWNEY**

Catherine GOODMAN 1961– Painter, draughtsman and teacher, born in London. Goodman was half Russian, her paternal great-grandmother being the Bloomsbury art patron Lady Ottoline Morrell. She attended Camberwell School of Arts and Crafts, 1979–84, for a foundation degree, completing a postgraduate diploma at Royal Academy Schools, 1984–7. From 1990 she taught at Camberwell, and became director and teacher at the Prince of Wales's Drawing School, Shoreditch. While studying she had won the Tom Phillips Drawing Prize, in 1984, the David Murray Travelling Scholarship, 1984–5, the Royal Academy Gold Medal in 1987 and the Richard Ford Award in 1988. Exhibited in RA Summer Exhibitions, at the RA's Art Al Fresco in 1988 and in 1991 had a solo show at Cadogan Contemporary. In 2002, Goodman's picture Antony won the BP Portrait Award, at the National Portrait Gallery. It depicted Dom Antony Sutch, Benedictine monk and headmaster of Downside School, which commissioned it in 2000. Goodman worked in a studio under Westway.

David GOODMAN 1918– Painter, designer and teacher who studied at St Martin's School of Art and showed first at RA while still a student. With his friend Peter Lanyon he taught art to the armed forces in Naples in 1945, then after World War II at Chichester School of Art. He was art director for several national magazines; a director of the David Paul Gallery in Chichester, and was chairman of Chichester Design Associates; was art adviser to the Festival Theatre there; and designed sets and costumes for Glyndebourne opera house and the ostrich symbol for Pallant House, Chichester, which holds his work as part of the Kearley Bequest. Goodman's wife Pearl was a singer, who was a leading member of Joan Littlewood's Theatre Workshop. Goodman won two Italian gold medals for painting and a Design Council Award. Although principally a landscape painter in the English romantic tradition, he also made portraits, which included the playwright Christopher Fry and actress Kate O'Mara. In 1993 had a retrospective show at Vicars Hall, Chichester. Lived near the Sussex town at Halnaker.

Penelope GOODMAN 1868–1948 Painter and black-and-white artist, originally Penelope Everett, who studied at Blackheath School of Art and the Slade School of Fine Art. She was known especially as a bold and colourful watercolourist, exhibiting at the RI, ROI, SWA, RSA, RHA and Paris Salon. Lived in Belvedere, Kent, but from the 1920s maintained a base in Walberswick, a favourite venue for painters on the Suffolk coast.

Sheila GOODMAN fl. from 1965– Artist, notably in pastel, who worked in England and travelled extensively in Europe and Canada to complete landscapes and coastal scenes. Born in Lancashire, she studied graphic design at High Wycombe College of Art, 1966–9. Went on to show in group exhibitions at Daler Gallery, Wykeham Gallery, Century Gallery, PS, SWA, Society of Botanical Artists and RA. Had solo shows at Bettles Gallery in 1989–90–91 and shared an exhibition with three artists at Anna-Mei Chadwick, 1992.

Dryden GOODWIN 1971– Artist using modern media, as in Closer, in the Art Now series at Tate Britain, 2001–2, an installation comprising a three-screen video and wall-based work. Goodwin was born in Bournemouth, Hampshire, and studied at the Slade School of Fine Art. In 2000 he was awarded a fellowship from the National Endowment for Science, Technology and Arts. Mixed shows in Britain and abroad included New Contemporaries, 1997; Video Cult/ures, ZKM, Karlsruhe, Germany, 1999; and Video Positive: The Other Side of Zero, Tate Liverpool, 2000. In that year Goodwin had a solo show at Stephen Friedman Gallery, which represented him. The New Art Gallery, Walsall, showed an installation by Goodwin in 2004. He lived in London.

Jane GOODWIN 1944– Artist who was educated in Australia and London, where she eventually took a studio, living in Puttenham, Surrey. Did a foundation course at Brisbane School of Art, Queensland, 1962. Her work experience included retailing in Australia, America and Nigeria; acting as advertisement manager for Thomson Publications' *Ambassador Magazine*; and being advertisement traffic manager in the production department for the agency J Walter Thompson. Between 1992–5, Goodwin gained an honours degree in fine art from West Surrey College of Art and Design, Farnham, then her master's degree in sculpture from Brighton University, 1995–7. Exhibitions included Reflections of Life and Festival of Women's Art, both at Coventry Gallery, 1994; DNA at Whiteleys' Gallery, 1995; Private View, Cable Street Gallery, 1996; Unquiet Voices, Doncaster Museum & Art Gallery, 1997; Flexible 3 Close to the Body, organised by the Netherlands Textile Museum, with international tour, 1999–00; Work, Inside Space, 2002; and The Corn Exchange, Newbury, 2004. Among later solo exhibitions was the University of Surrey, 2004.

Leslie GOODWIN 1929– Painter and illustrator, born and lived in Leicester, attending the College of Art there, 1949–55. Showed with RWA of which he was a member, RA and PS and had a series of solo exhibitions. Bristol Old Vic owns his work.

Marc GOODWIN 1974– Artist whose pictures were made from unwanted gloss paint, found objects and household waste, as in his Untitled, John Moores Liverpool Exhibition, 1999. Born in Bromley, Kent, he studied at Maidstone College of Art, 1992–3, Birmingham College of Art, 1993–6, and Central St Martins, 1998–9. Other group shows included Custard Factory, Birmingham, 1996, and Poland Street, in 1998. Goodwin lived in London.

Sarah GOODWIN 1937– Painter of landscapes in England and on the continent, still lifes and interiors in the tradition of the NEAC with which she exhibited, also with RA Summer Exhibition, RWA, RBA and the Small Paintings Society, of which she was a member. Studied at Byam Shaw School of Drawing and Painting, 1955–9, teachers including Peter Greenham, Bernard Dunstan, Charles Mahoney and Allan Gwynne-Jones. Had a solo exhibition at The Jerram Gallery, Salisbury, 1995. Lived in Fordingbridge, Hampshire. Her husband was the painter John Charles Wilkinson.

Bruce GOOLD 1948– Artist in various materials, but notably a printmaker, born in Newcastle, New South Wales, Australia. Aged 10, Goold attended Saturday morning art classes, then in 1964 began to study painting at Newcastle Technical College, in 1967 joining National Art School, Sydney. For some years Goold was involved in various artistic enterprises, designing sets and costumes and creating environments for exhibitions and cabarets. After travels through Asia with his wife in 1974 Goold settled in Palm Beach, near Sydney, and began linocutting. Had his first show of cuts at Queen Street Gallery, Sydney, 1979, and a one-man show at Paul Craft Gallery, Melbourne, 1980. Further solo shows followed, along with a commission for 25 designs for a limited-edition book; fabric designing and mural painting; and a poster for Australian Museum. In 1987 he designed the official poster for Bi-Centennial Festival of Sydney. Goold's work had strong ties with German Expressionism, as shown in his solo exhibition at England & Co, 1988, the year he travelled to Europe for the first time, living and working in Ireland.

Paul GOPAL-CHOWDHURY 1949– Painter and teacher, born in Calcutta, India. He attended Camberwell School of Art, 1967–8, Slade School of Fine Art, 1968–73. Gopal-Chowdhury began lecturing at Chelsea School of Art and obtained a Boise Travelling Scholarship and French Government Scholarship, 1973–4; between 1975–7 lectured at Leeds University, where he was awarded a Gregory Fellowship, and Byam Shaw School of Art; and in 1983–4 was artist-in-residence at Gonville and Caius College and Kettle's Yard Gallery, Cambridge. Took part in many group exhibitions, including British Painting '74, Hayward Gallery, 1974; Hayward Annual and Summer Show 3, Serpentine Gallery, both 1979; A Taste of British Art Today, Brussels, 1981; RA Summer Exhibition, 1988, invited artist; and Different Landscapes, Art Space Gallery, 2003. Solo shows included Newcastle upon Tyne Polytechnic Art Gallery, 1980; Ian Birksted Gallery, from 1981; Kettle's Yard Gallery, 1984–5, and tour; Benjamin Rhodes Gallery, from 1986; Paintings from Heaven and Hell, Art Space Gallery, 2002; and A Time of Demons, Art Space, 2004. Contemporary Art Society; Chase Manhattan Bank, New York; and public collections in Bolton and Doncaster hold examples. Lived in London.

Dora GORDINE 1906–1991 Sculptor, especially modelled heads in bronze, often of Oriental subjects. She was born in St Petersburg, Russia, and studied music in Paris until 1922. Then the sculptor Maillol gave her encouragement and she began showing at Salon des Tuileries and RA from late 1920s. First solo show held at Leicester Galleries in 1928. She then lived for about five years in China, settling in England in mid-1930s and marrying the diplomat The Hon. Richard Hare, who became professor of Russian literature at London University. She designed their house and studio in Richmond. In 1949 elected a fellow of RBS, about the time she began making trips to America to teach and work. Commissions included bronzes for Singapore Town Hall and work for Esso Refinery, Milford Haven, in Wales. After her husband's death in 1966 Gordine lived a reclusive life surrounded by their collection of Russian art objects, sold at auction by Phillips in 1994. Proceeds went to Kingston University to finance a Russian art centre at Doritch House where the rest of the Gordine collection was put on display. Tate Gallery holds several examples of her work.

Alan GORDON 1924– Painter, teacher and commercial artist, born in Salford, Lancashire. After Manchester Grammar School he attended Salford School of Art, 1941–2, then Manchester Municipal School of Art, 1942–7. He held a series of government and industrial jobs. Showed at Mid-Day Studios in Manchester and elsewhere in the northern provinces. Lived in Eccles, Lancashire.

Alastair GORDON 1920–2002 Painter, writer and businessman, born in Beckshill, Kent, educated at Harrow School and Gray's Art School, Aberdeen. During World War II he served in the Scots Guards, fighting in North Africa and Italy. On demobilisation, he resumed his studies at Camberwell School of Art, where he met his wife, the sculptor Anne Barry, who became noted for her colourful ceramic parrots. For the next 20 years he worked in insurance, then founded Art Consultants, which advised on investments in fine art until the market collapsed. From the late 1970s he worked as a full-time artist, noted for his botanical works, selling about 700 pictures in the course of his career, having shows in London, New York, Chicago and Sydney. In 1984 he became the 6th Marquess of Aberdeen and Temair on the death of his brother, but did not live in the family seat, Haddo House, Aberdeenshire, now owned by the National Trust, instead residing at Ashampstead, near Pangbourne, Berkshire. Gordon was a member of the International Association of Art Critics, having been modern art correspondent for *Connoisseur* magazine in the 1960s; chairman of the Arts Club, 1966–76; and for over 40 years a keen member of the London Bach Choir. Among his books was *Heads and Tales*, 1999, a compilation of anecdotes, of which he was a master, risqué rhymes and naughty jokes. In 2001, Gordon achieved notoriety when he contributed The Good Whore Guide to the magazine *The Oldie*, drawing on his experiences as a subaltern.

Anne GORDON 1941– Painter, draughtsman and teacher, born in Glasgow. She studied at the School of Art there, then taught art in schools. This was followed by peripatetic teaching in west Stirlingshire, where she settled. Much of her work was inspired by the local landscape, the Western Isles, Greece, Turkey, Tuscany and Andalucia, exploration of colour, tone and mood being important. Was elected an artist member of Glasgow Art Club in 1991. Also exhibited in San Francisco, and annually with RSA, Royal Glasgow Institute of the Fine Arts, Glasgow Society of Women Artists and SSWA. Gordon won Lauder Awards in 1986–7. In 1995 shared a show at Duncan R Miller Contemporary, with solo exhibitions there, 2001 and 2004.

Carola GORDON 1940– She studied English at New Hall, Cambridge, and was included there in the exhibition Women's Art at New Hall in 1992. After gaining her master's at New Hall in 1963, she was awarded her diploma at Edinburgh College of Art in 1965. Gordon taught in the fine art department at Natal University, South Africa, before settling in Scotland, living in Edinburgh. She painted and made collages. Further exhibiting venues included RSA and other Scottish galleries. Gordon's subjects were taken from everyday surroundings, with a special interest in buildings and townscapes.

Cora Josephine GORDON fl. from c.1908–1950 Painter, printmaker, illustrator and writer, born in Buxton, Derbyshire, who studied at Slade School of Fine Art. She showed extensively in Paris and at Lefevre and Cooling Galleries, SWA, ROI, RBA, Walker Art Gallery in Liverpool and elsewhere. With her artist and writer husband Jan Gordon, who predeceased her by six years, she travelled widely, producing popular books such as *Two Vagabonds in the Balkans*, 1925, *Two Vagabonds in Albania*, 1927, and *London Roundabout*, 1933. Otherwise lived in London.

Douglas GORDON 1966– Video installation artist, born in Glasgow, who graduated from the School of Art there, 1984–8, gaining his master's, 1988–90. Drew on a variety of sources, such as film noir and home videos found in Glasgow's back-street markets. His many group exhibitions included Barclays Young Artist Award, Serpentine Gallery, 1991; Speaker Project, ICA, 1992; Chambre 763, Hotel Carlton Palace, Paris, 1993; Watt at Witte de Witte Centre for Contemporary Art-Kunsthal, Rotterdam, 1994; and British Art Show 4, and tour, 1995–6. Had a solo showing at Glasgow Tramway and Kunst-Werke, Berlin, of

24-Hour Psycho, 1993, others including Lisson Gallery, 1994, The End at Jack Tilton Gallery, New York, 1995, Tate Liverpool, 2000, Towner Art Gallery, Eastbourne, 2002, and Hayward Gallery, 2002–3, his first major London one-man exhibition, then The Croque Mort series at University of Essex Gallery, 2003, and Glynn Vivian Art Gallery, Swansea, 2004. Douglas Gordon: The Vanity of Allegory was at the Guggenheim, Berlin, in 2005. British Council and Contemporary Art Society hold Gordon's work. Gordon won the Turner Prize in 1996, the Premio 2000 at Venice Biennale, 1997, and in 1998 the Guggenheim Hugo Boss Prize.

Esmé GORDON 1910–1993 Artist, normally in watercolour, architect and writer, born and lived in Edinburgh. From boyhood Alexander Esmé Gordon "put pencil, paint and paper as all-important, believing that happy people are those who use their hands." After Edinburgh Academy Gordon studied architecture at Edinburgh College of Art, 1928–34, winning the Owen Jones Scholarship in his final year. From 1937 until shortly before he died he maintained a small private practice which did mainly church work, including restoration in St Giles' Cathedral and Canongate Kirk. Early in World War II he designed troop canteens, then served in the Royal Engineers until 1945. Gordon was made a fellow of the Royal Incorporation of Architects in Scotland, 1953, a fellow of RIBA, 1956, was an honorary life member of SSA and was elected to RSA in 1967. From 1973–8 he was its honorary secretary, making significant archive finds. Among Gordon's books were *The Royal Scottish Academy 1826–1976*, 1976. Piranesi and William Walcot were cited by him as influences on his own work. Gordon was a scholar of Oriental art, and a keen collector of Japanese woodblock prints and Chinese jade. Travelled widely in Italy, India and the Far East, recording the trips in watercolours and drawings. Had a solo show at Scottish Gallery, Edinburgh, 1988. Esmé Gordon and his Belfast pianist wife Betsy were the parents of Giles Gordon (1940–2003), who studied design at Edinburgh College of Art, but, deciding he could not draw, instead became a noted literary agent. Peter Ackroyd, George Mackay Brown, Alan Massie and Fay Weldon were among his writers.

György GORDON 1924–2005 Painter in the European Expressionist tradition, born in Hungary. He gained his diploma in painting at the Academy of Fine Art, Budapest, in 1953, but during the Hungarian uprising against the Communists three years later fled to England. Despite lack of good English he found work and in 1964 moved to Wakefield, Yorkshire, to take up post at College of Art. Eventually took early retirement to paint. Noted for sombre figure paintings in which the images are isolated and distorted. Showed widely, including National Portrait Gallery. Work in public and private collections in Britain, on the continent, in America and Australia. National Portrait Gallery and Hart Gallery held retrospectives in 1995. Gordon's last major work was a group portrait of the Lindsay Quartet, commissioned by the National Portrait Gallery in 2003.

Hilda May GORDON 1874–1972 World-travelling artist, born of Scottish parents who had lived in South Africa but had settled in the Isle of Wight. Studied at Bushey School of Art, afterwards making sketching trips to continent. By 1907 was holding a show in Bond Street, then while working in Europe and Middle East as a volunteer nurse in World War I continued to paint. Set off from Britain for Dalmatian Coast in 1922 "for no particular reason", as she noted in her extensive journals, not returning to London until 1928. By then she had taken in countries such as Greece, India, Burma, China, Korea, Japan and America. On her return had show at Fine Art Society. Continued to travel through her sixties, until World War II brought her to rest in London. Martyn Gregory Gallery held a retrospective in 1987.

Ian Charles GORDON 1925– Painter, draughtsman and architect, born in Sevenoaks, Kent, working in oil, watercolour and charcoal. While a student at the Bartlett School of Architecture, Gordon studied with David Bomberg at the Borough Polytechnic, and continued to follow Bomberg's principles as a spare-time painter while working as an architect in Edinburgh, 1951–1980, and after retirement. Was a fellow of RIBA and a founder-member of the Borough Bottega, 1953, with which he showed, also exhibiting at RSA, Society of Scottish Architect Artists and Dumfries & Galloway Art Society. Lived in Thornhill, Dumfriesshire.

Susan GORDON 1942– Sculptor in various materials and part-time teacher, born in Wembley, Middlesex. She studied at Hammersmith School of Art, 1964–5, Wimbledon School of Art, 1965–6, and the City and Guilds of London School, 1966–9. Showed at RA, Nicholas Treadwell Gallery and elsewhere. RBS Feodora Gleichen Memorial Fund Award-winner. Signed work with initials. Lived in London.

Tania GORDON 1901–1994 Painter, notable for her use of the palette knife, born in Vilna, Russia, full name Tamara Tania Gordon. She married Sholom Gordon, from another prominent Vilna family, and they emigrated first to South Africa in the late 1920s and then to London, where her husband was an industrialist. Her son Max became a leading designer of art galleries. She took up painting in her fifties and showed at the Arthur Jeffress and Whibley Galleries and abroad, including Paris Salon.

Virginia GORDON 1937– Sculptor who studied at Royal Academy Dramatic Art, 1953–7, Morley College, 1976–8, then took advanced course at St Martin's School of Art, 1978–80. Mixed exhibitions included Morley College Group Exhibition and Art into Landscape at Serpentine Gallery, 1976–7; Wapping Artists 1981; and 10 London Artists, Taidemuseo in Helsinki and Finnish tour, 1983. In that year was included in 9 Artists from Wapping British Tour, based at DLI Museum & Arts Centre, Durham. Capital Radio holds her work, which could be abstract in various materials. Lived in London.

W R GORDON 1872–1955 Painter and teacher, born at Moira, County Down, Northern Ireland. He studied in his spare time at Birkenhead's Laird School of Art while working in the Port Sunlight soap factory and in Belfast attended the School of Design. From 1901 through World War II Gordon taught art at Royal Belfast Academical Institution, also teaching evening classes. He was a founder-member of Ulster Arts Club and showed at RHA in Dublin. Arts Council of Northern Ireland holds his work.

Ophelia GORDON-BELL (sometimes not hyphenated) 1915–1975 Sculptor in various materials and watercolourist. Born in London she came of an artistic family, her father being the etcher F Lawrence Bell, her mother the animal painter Winifred Gordon Bell. Joan Ophelia Gordon Cooper, her correct name, was married to the Lake District painter William Heaton Cooper. She studied art privately and at Regent Street Polytechnic School of Art, 1932–6. Showed at RA, RSA, Royal Glasgow Institute of the Fine Arts and Lake Artists' Society. Among several official commissions was a portrait bust of the Everest climber Sir Edmund Hillary, acquired by New Zealand National Gallery, Wellington. Lived in Grasmere, Westmorland.

David GORDON HUGHES 1957– Self-taught painter, born and lived in Belfast, Northern Ireland, using a bright palette for his landscapes and still lifes. In his youth he was greatly influenced by such artists as Van Gogh, Monet, Renoir, Jack Yeats, Paul Henry and Markey Robinson. Showed at RUA and RHA, with the Taylor Gallery in Belfast and in the English provinces. In 2002 he was included in Eight Selected Artists at W H Patterson, in 2004 at Seven Selected Artists at the same gallery. Ulster Museum in Belfast, Ulster Television, Bank of Ireland and Mercedes-Benz Dublin hold examples.

Michael GORDON-LEE 1943– Painter and sculptor who was by profession a landscape architect for Cheshire County Council. He was born in Harrow, Middlesex, and attended Hammersmith College of Art. He showed with PS from 1983, in 1984 being elected a member shortly after winning its Award for Best Picture by a Non-Member; MAFA from 1984; and RWA from 1985. In 1986–7 Gordon-Lee was included in the Walker Art Gallery, Liverpool, touring Merseyside Artists 3. Lived in Tarporley, Cheshire.

Robert GORDY 1933–1986 He was one of a number of foreign artists who had a short time in Britain during an association with Editions Alecto. Gordy was born at Jefferson Island, Louisiana, and was educated at Louisiana State University and Baton Rouge, gaining Bachelor of Art and Master of Art degrees. He studied with Hans Hofmann in 1953, in 1954 receiving a Yale University Norfolk Fellowship. In 1967 Gordy gained a purchase prize for the Isaac Delgado Museum, New Orleans, through a grant from the National Council on the Arts. He made a trip to London in 1969 to work at Editions Alecto, a 1970 brochure, *Golden Days*, detailing a portfolio of six screenprints published in an edition of 100. He took part in many group shows throughout America, his solo exhibitions including Editions Alecto at Gimpel Gallery, New York, 1970. Gordy died of Aids aged 52. His stylised figurative works in subtle colours were consistent in approach over many years, although there were often intense emotions below the surface which emerged more fully in his final monotypes. A large collection of works from Gordy's studio was presented at the Arthur Roger Gallery, New Orleans, in 2000. Louisiana State University, Baton Rouge in Louisiana, Whitney Museum of American Art in New York and other public and corporate collections hold examples

Frederick GORE 1913– Painter, teacher and writer, born in Richmond, Surrey, son of the artist Spencer Gore. He studied at Trinity College and Ruskin School of Drawing, Oxford, 1932–4, finally at Westminster School of Art and Slade School of Fine Art, 1934–7. In the latter year he had his first one-man show at Redfern Gallery, followed by a series there after World War II. In 1938 he travelled in Greece, showing the resulting work in Paris. Greece, Majorca and France were favourite landscape subjects for Gore, whose rich palette had more in common with the French than the English tradition. Gore taught at Westminster, Epsom and Chelsea Schools of Art and was head of the painting department at St Martin's School of Art, 1951–79. He was elected RA in 1973 and was chairman of its exhibition committee, 1976–87. His publications included *Abstract Art*, 1956; *Painting: Some Basic Principles*, 1965; and *Piero della Francesca's The Baptism*, 1969; plus many RA catalogue introductions. In 1979 he had retrospectives at Gainsborough's House in Sudbury and Bury St Edmunds Art Gallery, with an important one at RA in 1989. There were ninetieth-birthday shows at Fosse Gallery, Stow-on-the-Wold, and Carlyle Gallery, both 2003, and the Jonathan Wylder Gallery gave Gore a show in 2006. Southampton, Plymouth and Reading public galleries hold his work. Lived in London.

William GORE 1871–1946 Versatile painter, doctor of medicine, musician and composer and linguist, full name William Crawford Crampton Gore, born in Enniskillen, Fermanagh (his daughter Elizabeth Parry-Crooke, also a painter, changed her name to Crampton-Gore using a hyphen, which was how she signed her work; the hyphen has sometimes been used in her father's name). Gore studied medicine at Trinity College, Dublin, qualifying in 1897; practised; then from 1901 concentrated on art, studying for several years at Slade School of Fine Art under Henry Tonks and Philip Wilson Steer, also in Paris. In his diaries Gore said that his greatest debt was to the Norwegian painter Fritz Thaulow. Gore worked as a ship's surgeon before and during World War I and travelled extensively. Spoke six languages, including Russian. He continued to practise medicine later in life; from 1932 lived in Colchester, Essex, where he died and where he was a civilian doctor at the Military Hospital. Simultaneously with painting, Gore studied music, receiving help from Charles Wood, and was a prolific composer, notably of lyrics, his compositions being publicly performed and broadcast. Much of Gore's life was spent in France. Married a French wife in 1923 in Montreuil-sur-Mer, where he had rented a studio. They bought a house there and lived a bohemian life until returning to England, visitors including Dermod O'Brien, Philip Connard and Augustus John. Was elected RHA in 1919, also exhibiting at RA, Paris Salon where he gained several Hon. Mentions, NEAC, ROI and Fine Art Society, and had solo shows. Was a Chelsea Arts Club member. A memorial exhibition was held at Victor Waddington Galleries, Dublin, in 1946.

Luci GORELL BARNES 1960– Artist, born in London, who completed a foundation course at Canterbury College of Art & Design, 1979–80. Her work was "influenced by shrines, charms, effigies, souvenirs and folk art, much of it inspired by religious iconography." Residencies included the Roman Baths Museum and Holburne Museum, both in Bath. Group shows included Womanmade, The Coopers Gallery, Bristol, 1993, and Magic and Miracles, The Black Swan, Frome, 1998. Among her solo shows was the Victoria Art Gallery, Bath, 2000–1. She lived in Bristol.

Boguslaw GORGOLEWSKI fl. from 1950s– Artist who lived mainly in London and who died there. Gorgolewski studied at Edinburgh School of Art and in London at the Polish School of Painting under Professor Marian Bohusz-Szyskzko. Exhibited at the Richmond Hill Gallery, New Vision Centre and other venues in the capital. In 1963, Gorgolewski won first prize in the abstract class at the Arts and Crafts Exhibition, Ealing.

Charles Harris GORHAM 1916– Painter, graphic designer and teacher, born in Bexley, Kent. Studied at Royal College of Art with William Rothenstein and Ernest Tristram. Victoria & Albert Museum holds his work and he exhibited in London, the provinces, Germany and Denmark. Lectured at Maidstone College of Art. Lived in Borough Green, Kent, for many years.

Maro GORKY 1943– Painter, notably of richly coloured, patterned landscapes, daughter of the American artist Arshile Gorky. Although he died when she was young, he greatly influenced Maro's work. She studied at the Slade School of Fine Art before marrying the artist and writer Matthew Spender and moving to a remote farmhouse in Tuscany, Italy. Bernardo Bertolucci's film *Stealing Beauty*, released in 1996, celebrated the marriage of Gorky and Spender. She had a series of solo shows with Long & Ryle Art International.

Des GORMAN 1960– Painter of still life, portraits and interiors, born in Glasgow, who graduated from Gray's Art School, Aberdeen, in 1988 with an honours degree in fine art. Won a number of awards, including first prize, David Gordon Memorial Trust, RSA, and the Elizabeth Greenshields Foundation Award, both 1988; Armour Award, Royal Glasgow Institute of the Fine Arts, 1989; and Contemporary Fine Art Gallery Award, 1993. Mixed shows included Open Eye Gallery, Edinburgh, 1991; Kelly Gallery, Glasgow, 1993; and Ten Young Painters, Thompson's Gallery, 1994. Had a solo show at Paisley Art Centre, 1989, later ones including John Martin of London in 1995. Strathclyde Police and corporate and private collections hold Gorman's work.

Ernest Hamilton GORMAN 1869– Painter and black-and-white artist, whose varied art education included periods in Portsmouth, with Alfred Emslie and at Goldsmiths' Institute with Amor Fenn. For many years he was honorary secretary of the Liver Sketching Club, where he exhibited, as well as Walker Art Gallery, Liverpool. Lived at Lower Bebington, Cheshire.

James GORMAN 1931– Painter in oil, acrylic and watercolour, and teacher, born in Gourock, Renfrewshire. He studied at Glasgow School of Art, 1949–53, a notable teacher being Walter Pritchard for mural painting, in which Gorman gained his diploma, also winning a travelling scholarship. His own murals include Trinity College, Glasgow, 1953–4; a mural design for Eastwood Senior High School, 1966; and for Moorfoot Primary School, Gourock, 1970. His National Service included various art work and a mural, now in the War Office. He went on to be principal teacher of art and design at John Neilson Institute, Paisley, and at Port Glasgow High School. Gorman's work ranged from delicate landscape watercolours to strong figurative pictures. He claimed a "Celtic influence in my use of nets to generate images". Was a member of the Royal Glasgow Institute of the Fine Arts and as well as mixed exhibitions had many solo and joint shows, venues including Paton Gallery, Edinburgh, 1976; Greenock Arts Guild, 1984; and Graeme Mundy Gallery, Glasgow, 1988. Lived latterly at Corriegills, Isle of Arran.

Antony GORMLEY 1950– Sculptor and draughtsman who was born and lived in London. He was educated at Cambridge University, 1967–70, Central School of Art, 1973–4, Goldsmiths' College School of Art, 1975–7, then Slade School of Fine Art, 1977–9. In the latter year he won a Boise Travelling Scholarship to America. In 1980 gained Greater London Arts Association Award, in 1981 first prize in the Kent County Council/Arts Council Singleton Sculpture Competition, in 1994 the Turner Prize. Gormley was concerned with the relationship between culture and nature, life and death, the profane and the sacred. Sometimes his methods were unconventional: in 1981 he made a sculpture by eating the double negative form of his own body out of layers of sliced white bread. In that year he gained a solo show at Whitechapel Art Gallery, the year following participating in British Sculpture in the Twentieth Century (part II) at Whitechapel as well as the 1982 Venice Biennale. Gormley took part in Objects & Figures at Fruitmarket Gallery, Edinburgh, and tour, 1982–3; showed at Coracle Press Gallery in 1984; in 1992 was included in Contemporary Art Society purchase show at Camden Arts Centre; and in 1993 first showed Field, the first of a series, at the Liverpool Tate. Gormley's most noted achievement was the completion, in 1998, of the Angel of the North, the tallest sculpture in Britain, made in three parts from weathering steel; the huge winged figure project overcame initial opposition to be sited at the head of the Team Valley, near Gateshead, next to the A1(M) road. Also significant was Quantum Cloud, comprising over 4,000 identical sections of galvanised steel and sited near the Millennium Dome on the River Thames at the time of its construction. Tate St Ives held a small retrospective of Gormley's output in 2001 and in 2002 his work Planets was installed in the British Library's piazza. In 2003, Asian Field, comprising 200,000 fired clay figures, was brought to fruition by 400 local volunteers at Guangdong village, China, after years of organisation. Also in 2003 Gormley was elected RA and Domain Field, based on plaster casts of 240 local volunteers and using intricate networks of steel bars, was shown at the Baltic, Gateshead. Gormley's work Clearing was at White Cube, 2004. Arts Council, Contemporary Art Society and other collections hold the work of Gormley, who was married to the painter Vicken Parsons.

Jo GORNER 1961– Printmaker, notably an etcher; teacher; and arts administrator, born in Wigan, Lancashire. She graduated in fine art from Ruskin School of Drawing and Fine Art, Lady Margaret Hall, Oxford University, 1979–82, then obtained her master's in fine art, Manchester Metropolitan University, 1994. Gained a number of awards, including the Peel Holdings Award at MAFA Open, 1998, and was a fellow of Ballinglen Arts Foundation, County Mayo, Ireland, in 2002. From 1987, Gorner did a number of arts-related jobs, especially in the north of England, notably as a freelance public arts project manager in Wakefield, Bolton and Wigan. She also taught in over 150 colleges, schools and community centres. The details of natural forms and patterns in landscape inspired Gorner's work, which was notable for its simple, spare, abstracted qualities. She took part in many group exhibitions, later ones including The Strand Gallery, Aldeburgh; Crossley Gallery, Dean Clough, Halifax; and ART*futures*, Contemporary Art Society, all 2002; and Flowers Graphics 2004. Among solo shows were Snow Gallery, Leeds, 2001, and Newby Hall, Ripon, 2002. Bury and Calderdale Museums and Arts both hold her work.

Mary GORRARA 1923– Sculptor in various materials and teacher, born and lived in London. She studied at Camberwell School of Arts and Crafts; City and Guilds of London Art School, where her teachers included A R Middleton Todd; and Sir John Cass School of Art. Went on to teach at Camden Arts Centre, Hampstead. She was made a fellow of RBS in 1975, also belonging to Free Painters and Sculptors. Mixed shows included RA, Kenwood House and Lincoln Cathedral. Her solo exhibitions included Camden Arts Centre, 1972, and Jonathan Poole Gallery, 1983. Camden Borough Council holds her work.

Hester GORST 1887– Painter and modeller, born in Liverpool, she married the Queen's Counsel Elliot Gorst. Studied at Slade School of Fine Art, 1904–6, with Henry Tonks, and in Brussels. She showed at Royal Drawing Society where she won silver and gold medals, Goupil Gallery, NEAC, in the Netherlands and America and at the Paris Salon into the late 1960s, gaining an Hon. Mention for figurines. Early work signed Hester Holland, her maiden name. Lived in London. Was active into her nineties, having a show and appearing on television, until loss of sight incapacitated her.

Alexander GORTON 1916–1969 Draughtsman in pen and ink, poster designer and printmaker, employed by London Transport. He died in service as a divisional superintendent. Studied art with the Press Art School and in Southwark. London Transport art exhibitions and its publications were his main outlet, although he also drew for other transport magazines. London Transport Museum lists a number of works by Alec Gorton, including 67 Safety on the Track designs. Lived at Woodford Green, Essex.

Annabel GOSLING 1942– Painter, born in Overbury, Gloucestershire, brought up in Suffolk. She attended Ipswich School of Art, 1958, Angers Beaux-Arts in France in 1959, then Byam Shaw School of Drawing and Painting, 1960–4; was awarded Leverhulme and Byam Shaw Scholarships, 1960. Gosling's work was impressed by an intense interest in light and colour, the work of Matisse and Cézanne and extensive travels in Europe and India. Showed at RA, RBA, NEAC and Archer Gallery in mixed exhibitions. Had solo show at Ansdell Gallery, 1971; Royal Festival Hall, 1980; Mall Galleries, 1991; Mistral Galleries, 1992; and Albemarle Gallery, 2000. Work held by the royal family of Abu Dhabi, Scottish Educational Development Authority, Savoy and Berkeley Hotels.

Mary Rose GOSLING 1926– Painter and draughtsman, also known as Mary Rose Hardy, born in Birmingham as Gosling. She studied at Birmingham College of Art with Bernard Fleetwood-Walker, 1943–7, then in Paris, 1950, at L'Académie de la Grande Chaumière. Showed SWA, RBA, RI, WIAC and elsewhere. Lived for a time at Forest Row, Sussex.

Sylvia GOSSE 1881–1968 Painter in oil and watercolour and etcher of landscape, still life, figure studies and interiors. Born in London, the daughter of writer and critic Sir Edmund Gosse, she studied at the St John's Wood School of Art, Royal Academy Schools and the Westminster School of Art under Walter Sickert. From 1909–14 she taught at Sickert's Rowlandson House, London, school. His influence is evident in much of her work. She exhibited at the AAA, RA, LG, RBA and RE and had her first one-man show at the Carfax Gallery in 1913. Like Sickert, she painted a lot in London and in Dieppe. Her work was reproduced in magazines such as *The Studio, Apollo* and *Print Collectors' Quarterly* and is in many British and foreign collections, including the British Museum, Tate Gallery and Ashmolean Museum. Lived at Ore, Hastings, Sussex.

Imre GOTH 1893–1982 Painter, notably of portraits, and inventor, born in Szeged, Hungary, who studied at Budapest Academy of Fine Arts, then in the 1920s in Berlin. He became noted for fashionable portraits of film stars and among his patrons was Field-Marshal Hermann Goering, the Nazi air chief. After a successful exhibition in Birmingham at the New Galleries, in 1935, Goth moved to England where through friendship with the Hungarian film director Alexander Korda he came to paint portraits used in productions starring Ralph Richardson, Michael Wilding, Ann Todd and Margaret Leighton. When later in life Goth's eyesight failed he returned to inventing. In Berlin he had designed parachutes and headlights for cars. In London he formed a company to market his inventions, which included the non-drip device in bottles. His exhibitions included Ferens Art Gallery, Hull, and Russell-Cotes Art Gallery, Bournemouth, both from 1939; RP, 1948; and Grundy Art Gallery, Blackpool, 1949.

Henryk GOTLIB 1890–1966 Painter, printmaker, sculptor and writer, born in Cracow, Poland. Studied at the Academy of Fine Art, Cracow, later in Munich, Amsterdam and Paris. Had first one-man show in Warsaw in 1918, a year later returning to Cracow, where he became leader of advanced Formist movement. Early in the 1920s Gotlib had shows in Berlin and Amsterdam, then during the rest of the decade he lived mainly in France. Early in the 1930s he travelled extensively in Europe but exhibited in Poland and took part in Polish shows overseas. In 1934 returned to Cracow where he continued to write, then to broadcast on art. Having travelled to Cornwall just before World War II, he decided to remain in England where he began to exhibit, notably one-man shows with Roland, Browse and Delbanco in the 1940s. Later solo shows were held with O'Hana and Crane Kalman. The Arts Council acquired The Boat in 1961, the Gulbenkian Foundation two pictures in 1962. Gotlib's book, in English, *Polish Painting* appeared in 1942, and *The Travels of a Painter*, earlier commissioned by a Polish publisher, in 1947. Gotlib's early work was much influenced by Bonnard, tinged with Kandinsky's mysticism. His later pictures were less picturesque, less seductive. An exhibition was held at the Scottish National Gallery of Modern Art, 1970, with tour; another at Morley Gallery, 1971; Boundary Gallery, 1988; and Connaught Brown, 1996. Lived in South Godstone, Surrey.

John GOTO 1949– Artist, born in Stockport, Cheshire, who studied at Berkshire College of Art, 1965–7, and St Martin's School of Art, 1967–70. He gained British Council Scholarships to Paris, 1977, and Prague, 1978, and in 1988–9 was artist-in-residence at Kettle's Yard, Cambridge. In 1990 his The Atomic Yard toured from Kettle's Yard, part of his major project Seven Tales from the Twentieth Century, to be completed by the year 2000. Goto won a prize with his Nastagio in Bosnia acrylic on canvas included in John Moores Liverpool Exhibition, 1993–4. Later solo exhibitions include Portfolio Gallery, Edinburgh, 1997; Museum of Modern Art, Oxford, 1998; National Portrait Gallery, as commissioned artist, 1999; and Andrew Mummery, 2000, in which large coloured digital photographs of high streets parodied great classical paintings. In 2002, Goto's Loss of Face, 104 images with music by Michael Young, was organised by Norwich Gallery, later showing at Wolsey Art Gallery, Ipswich. Goto's show High Summer took place at Gainsborough's House, Sudbury, in 2003. Arts Council and other public collections in Britain and abroad hold Goto's work.

Luke GOTTELIER 1968– Born and based in London, Gottelier had a diverse output, from photographs of floor-based installations with enigmatic titles, the subjects created from vegetables, packaging and other materials, to paintings of everyday objects. He studied at Maidstone College of Art, 1988–9; Exeter College of Art, 1989–90; and Hull College of Art, 1990–2. Group shows included ICA as well as Luke Gottelier, Pascal Rousson, The Trade Apartment, both 1998, and John Moores Liverpool Exhibition, 2002. In 1999 Gottelier was a finalist in The NatWest Art Prize. The Saatchi Collection held his work, Saatchi Gallery including it in the Neurotic Realism series of shows launched in 1999. In 2001, with Francis Upritchard, Gottelier founded The Bart Wells Institute in a warehouse squat in London's East End which hosted group shows co-ordinated by guest artist curators including Sam Basu, Brian Griffiths and David Thorpe, as well as music nights and film screenings.

Basil GOTTO 1866–1954 Sculptor, born in London, educated at Harrow School. He studied in Paris with Adolphe Bouguereau and in the late 1880s at the Royal Academy Schools, where he won the Landseer award in 1890. In 1899 he was Boer War correspondent in South Africa for the *Daily Express*. Exhibited RA extensively, also RI, ROI, Royal Glasgow Institute of the Fine Arts and Paris Salon. Southampton Art Gallery holds his work. Lived at Twyford, Hampshire.

Ernst GOTTSCHALK 1926– Sculptor and painter, interior and exhibition designer, born in Hamburg, Germany. He studied at Edinburgh College of Art, the Anglo-French Art Centre and Chelsea School of Art. Until 1990 Gottschalk worked mainly in Britain, then settled in France at Bandol, where as well as exhibiting and working to commission he kept a studio open to the public. He was a member of ICA and the Society of Industrial Artists and Designers and his work was featured in *Architectural Review, Design, Ideal Home, The Listener* and *House and Garden*. Exhibited widely throughout Europe, including Air, Alwin, Ben Uri, Gimpel Fils, Grabowski, Portal and Treadwell Galleries; Centre 't Hoogt, Utrecht; Galerie Robert Boeuf, Toulon; Sculpture Actuelle, Toulouse, where Gottschalk gained a first prize; and Van Gogh Museum, Amsterdam. Works were held by many collections around the world.

Lothar GÖTZ 1963– Artist and teacher, born in Günzburg, Germany, who moved to London in 1996 to study for a master's degree at the Royal College of Art, after which he divided his time between England and Germany. Taught painting at the University of Sunderland and Ruskin School, Oxford. Götz participated in many group exhibitions in Germany, Britain and Poland, solo shows including Mota Gallery and in Germany the Kunstraum, Wuppertal, and Städtisches Museum, Leverkusen. From 1993 Götz focused on wall paintings using the geometrical vocabulary of Constructivism, as in his site-specific work for the Goethe-Institut in 2000.

Elizabeth GOUDGE 1923– Painter and printmaker who studied Heatherley's School of Fine Art and in Paris at L'Académie Julian and La Grande Chaumière, studying wood engraving with Iain Macnab. Was elected a member of NS in 1988. Also exhibited at the RA Summer Exhibition, ROI, RE, RSM and WIAC, and was included in a four-man printmaking show at Chequer Mead Arts Centre, East Grinstead, 1999.

Alexander GOUDIE 1933–2004 Painter, notably of portraits, born in Paisley, Renfrewshire, father of the artist Lachlan Goudie. He studied at Glasgow School of Art, 1950–5, under William Armour, Benno Schotz and David Donaldson. He was awarded the Somerville Shanks Prize for Composition, Newbery Medal, postgraduate scholarship, Keith Award (RSA), and in 1953 a travelling scholarship enabled him to visit Paris. From the late 1950s Goudie, who married a French wife, frequently visited France, including annual painting trips to Loctudy, Brittany. His first major exhibition of Breton pictures was at The Scottish Gallery, Edinburgh, in 1966. There was a retrospective at The Fine Art Society, Glasgow, 1983, and a solo show at Roger Billcliffe Fine Art, Glasgow, 1992. In 1987–9 Goudie carried out décor for the Brittany Ferries flagship *Bretagne*. Goudie's stylish portraits included HM The Queen, Billy Connolly the comedian and Lord Mackay when Lord Chancellor. Robert Fleming Holdings Ltd has his work. Goudie was a member of Glasgow Art Club, RP and Royal Glasgow Institute of the Fine Arts. Breton works were shown at The John Davies Gallery, Stow-on-the-Wold, 2002. The Goudie Collection at Rozelle House in Alloway holds a large series of paintings based on Robert Burns' poem *Tam O'Shanter*, which had haunted the artist since childhood. Memorial exhibition in 2006 at The Scottish Gallery, Edinburgh. He died in Glasgow.

Lachlan GOUDIE 1976– Draughtsman and painter of works with a strong gestural quality, as in his solo show at Thompson's Marylebone, 2003. His father was the artist Alexander Goudie. Between 1989–4, Lachlan won five consecutive medals in the Scottish Schools Annual Drawing Competition, including the T J Honeyman Award for Drawing Excellence. He did foundation studies in Italian and art history at The Dante Alighieri School, Rome, 1995, then graduated with honours in English at Christ's College, Cambridge University, 1996–8. In 1999 he was awarded the Levy-Plumb Studentship in the Visual Arts there, then attended the Easter term drawing school at the École Supérieure de Beaux-Arts, Paris, in 2000. Exhibitions included From Cambridge to Rajasthan, work completed during a two-month trip to India as part of the Levy-Plumb Studentship, Waterstone's Gallery, Cambridge, and RSP Prize for Painting, Royal Glasgow Institute of the Fine Arts annual exhibition, both 1999; and Paris: A Room with a View, Stenton Gallery, Edinburgh, and RSA,

Norman Macfarlane Charitable Trust Award for Painting, both 2001.

Chris GOUGH 1947– Printmaker, mixed-media artist and teacher, notable for colourful and lyrical abstracts. He was "interested in making work which holds in balance a variety of opposites: matter and illusion, surface and depth, idea and object." Born in Barnstaple, Devon, Gough studied at Bournville School of Art, Birmingham 1967–9; Central School of Art & Design, 1969–72; and Slade School of Fine Art, 1972–4. He taught at the City Literary Institute and elsewhere. Mixed exhibitions included Stowells Trophy, Mall Galleries, 1972; 2nd British International Drawing Biennale, Middlesbrough Art Gallery, 1975; John Moores Liverpool Exhibition, Walker Art Gallery, 1978; Curwen Gallery, from 1994; Cross-Channel Prints, Musée Adzak, Paris, 1996; and Printmakers' Council at Gantry Arts Centre, Southampton, 1999. Among Gough's solo exhibitions was Curwen, 1999.

Paul GOUGH 1958– Artist, teacher and editor, born in Plymouth, Devon, who gained a first-class honours degree, with commendation for thesis, at Wolverhampton Polytechnic, 1976–9, taught by Knighton Hosking and Colin Harrison, with a period at L'École des Beaux-Arts, Metz, France; his master's in painting from the Royal College of Art, 1980–5, taught by Peter de Francia, Mario Dubsky, Ken Kiff and Frank Whitford; and his doctorate from the Faculty of Humanities there, 1987–91, with a thesis on Art on the Western Front, 1914–18. Among his awards were Wolverhampton Polytechnic drawing prizes, 1978 and 1979; the Royal College of Art Rodney Burn Memorial Prize and a Richard Ford, Royal Academy Major Travel Scholarship for research in the Prado, Madrid, both 1983; the Royal College Milner Kite Scholarship, 1985; and Penguin Book Prize for best thesis in humanities, Royal College, 1991. From graduation in 1985, he taught and exhibited throughout the United Kingdom, eventually becoming dean and professor of fine arts at Bristol Polytechnic (University of the West of England), 2000. Artists' books for which Gough was fundraiser and editor included: *Millennium Bestiary*, 1995; *A Consequential Coastline*, 1996; and *Sylva Brittanicus*, 2001. His *Stanley Spencer: Journey to Burghclere*, plotting the creation of the World War I Sandham Memorial, was published by Sansom & Company in 2006. He was the recipient of a British Council travel award in 1999 and a Canadian government research grant in 2000. He carried out public commissions for British Army regiments, the Royal Marines, Ocean Trading and Pirelli. Gough was elected a member of the RWA, 1997, and a member of its council in 1999. Later group shows included A decade of miniature prints, Bankside Gallery, 1997; Smash and Grab, Victoria & Albert Museum, 1997; and The Discerning Eye, critic's selection, Mall Galleries, 1999. Among his later solo exhibitions were 60 – images of Venerated Sites, Canadian War Museum, Ottawa, 1998–9, and Loci Memoriae, Watershed and Architecture Centre, Bristol, 2001, with an illuminating catalogue text by the artist. The Canadian War Museum, the Imperial War Museum and other military, public and corporate collections hold examples.

Liza GOUGH DANIELS 1962– Artist, teacher and art administrator, born in the Forest of Dean, Gloucestershire. She was based there and in north London. Gough Daniels graduated in fine art from the Slade School, 1980–5, attending the Cooper Union, New York, 1982–4, then the British School at Rome, 1995–6. Teachers included Lawrence Gowing, Dore Ashton, Lucy Lippard, Paula Rego, Susan Hiller and Ron Bowen. Among awards won were a Slade Travel Scholarship, 1982–3; Oppenheim-John Downes Awards, 1993 and 1995; Abbey Award in Painting, British School at Rome, 1995–6; and a Rootstein Hopkins Foundation Project Grant, 2002–3. Gough Daniels was from 1996 consultant artist on-site for various public and private art projects; joint artistic director, Florence Trust, 1992–7; artist-in-residence, Architecture for the Arts, 1998–9; and visiting artist at the Slade, Chelsea and Camberwell, 1996–01. Italian tempera and fresco painting from the thirteenth to the eighteenth centuries and artists of the New York School were influences on Gough Daniels' work, leading themes being colour, light, geometry and landscape. Exhibitions included Silence, Ikon Gallery, Birmingham, 1992; Curved, Poured & Deep, permanent commissions, Norden Farm Centre for the Arts, Maidenhead, 2000, with a solo show there, 2001; and Forest tour, curated by Winchester Gallery for Southern Arts, 2002. Chelsea and Westminster Hospital; Museum of Contemporary Art in Valcellina, Italy; and New Hall College, Cambridge, hold examples.

Alan GOUK 1939– Painter, teacher and writer, born Belfast, moved to Glasgow when still small. He studied architecture at the School of Art, 1957–9, part-time while working for an architect; he adopted a similar procedure at Regent Street Polytechnic, 1959–60, when working for London County Council. Upon moving to Edinburgh, 1961–4, to study philosophy and psychology at the University, Gouk began to paint in an Abstract Expressionist style. From 1964–7 he worked for the British Council. From 1967, when he began to lecture at St Martin's School of Art, where he eventually became head of advanced painting and sculpture, Gouk could concentrate fully on his painting. Moving away from acrylics to oils from the mid-1970s, Gouk was concerned to avoid flatness in painting, exploring pictorial space created by colour in wide canvases and using a heavy impasto. His work was featured in the Four Abstract Artists show at the Fruitmarket Gallery, Edinburgh, 1977; in the Scottish Painting since 1900 exhibition at Scottish National Gallery of Modern Art, 1989–90, and tour; he had a solo show at Smiths Galleries in 1986; at Flowers East, 1997; and deliART, 2002. In that year won a prize at John Moores Liverpool Exhibition, where he had been a prize winner in 1967. Public collections included Arts Council, British Council and Tate Gallery. Gouk, who retired from St Martin's in 1990, was also a jazz-influenced composer whose first composition, completed in 1993, was *Three Late Poems by Dylan Thomas*, for voices and orchestra. He had a studio at St Cyrus, Angus.

Alec Carruthers GOULD 1870–1948 Landscape painter and illustrator, born in Woodford, Essex, full name Alexander Carruthers Gould. He was the son of the caricaturist Francis Carruthers Gould, settled in Porlock, Somerset, and illustrated E W Hendy's *Wild Exmoor Through the Year*, 1930. He was a member of RBA where he was a prolific exhibitor, also being a member of RWA and showing at RA, ROI, NEAC and other galleries.

Charles GOULD 1925–1987 Watercolourist, born in Ealing, west London. Studied at the local School of Art,

1948–51, and continued to work in Ealing. Showed RI, NS and abroad, notably Paris Salon. Philadelphia Art Gallery, in America, holds his work.

David GOULD 1947– Painter and teacher, notable for watercolours, many of Italy where his wife originally lived. He was born in London and studied at Gloucester College of Art in Cheltenham, 1965–9, and Royal College of Art, 1969–72. He won an Abbey Major Scholarship to Rome, 1972–3, and a painting fellowship at Cardiff College of Art, 1974–5. After five years teaching at Byam Shaw School, he returned to teach at Cardiff. Mixed exhibitions included Oriel (WAC), Cardiff, 1975; Air travelling exhibition, 1977; Spirit of London at Royal Festival Hall, 1980; and Summer Show 1 at Serpentine Gallery, 1982. Solo shows included Chapter Arts Centre, Cardiff, 1985; St David's Hall, Cardiff, 1989 and 1993; and Oriel Contemporary Art, 1996.

Polly GOULD 1971– Artist and teacher who "examined story-telling and picture-making, working across media using photography, video, sound and performance...feminist debates on sexual difference and the disruptive possibilities of performance" being a particular focus. As well as her own work, she collaborated with Anne Eggebert as Eggebert & Gould (see separate entries). Gould graduated with first-class honours in critical fine-art practice at Central St Martins College of Art & Design, 1990–3; obtained her master's in fine art, 1994–6, and theory, 1996–8, at Jan van Eyck Academie Centre for Postgraduate Research, Maastricht, Netherlands; and an Open University diploma in applied social science, 1996–8. From 1999 she held a series of teaching-related posts, including Central Saint Martins, Willem de Kooning Academie in Rotterdam, and Canterbury College of Art and Design. Her own exhibitions and commissions included Still Life: Homage to Cotan, "Digital 96" Photokina, Cologne, Germany, 1996; Utopian Dreaming, Natural Museum, Maatricht, 1998; and Theatres of the Social, Rotterdam, Netherlands, 2001. Lived in London.

Thomas GOURDIE 1913– Painter, calligrapher and teacher, born in Cowdenbeath, Fife. He studied at Edinburgh College of Art, 1932–7, under Herbert Hendrie. He took part in war artists' exhibitions in London in World War II, from which official purchases of watercolours were made. Also showed RSA, SSA, RSW and in Arts Council exhibitions. For some time taught at the High School in Kirkcaldy, Fife, where he lived.

Alan Stenhouse GOURLEY 1909–1991 Painter, stained glass artist, theatre designer and teacher, born in Ayr, Scotland. Studied at Glasgow School of Art, 1928, and Edinburgh College of Art, 1929–31, where his teachers included William Gillies. Moved to South Africa where from 1932–7 taught at Johannesburg Technical College and created window designs for cathedrals in Pretoria and Johannesburg. Studied at École des Beaux-Arts, 1938–40, in Paris; during World War II was an instructor in camouflage; studying at Slade School of Fine Art in 1945, his teachers including Randolph Schwabe. Travelled throughout the world, but found time to design for the theatre; exhibiting, mainly at Mall Galleries; and was for some years president of ROI. South Africa House in London has carpet designed by him and his work is in the collection of HM Queen Elizabeth The Queen Mother. Lived in Bromley, Kent.

James GOVIER 1910–1974 Painter, printmaker and teacher, born in Oakley, Buckinghamshire. Studied 1930–5 at Swansea School of Art, where his teachers included William Grant Murray, and 1935–40 at Royal College of Art, under Malcolm Osborne and Robert Austin. Sickert, Constable, Rembrandt, Degas and Chardin were some influences on Govier, a traditionalist who disliked commercialism and modern influences. Augustus John and Dylan Thomas were friends of Govier in Wales and London. During World War II Govier served in the Royal Air Force, making models of the D-Day landings and Dam Busters raids, meeting Barnes Wallis, inventor of the bouncing bomb. Showed with RA, Ipswich Art Club and elsewhere. An important exhibition of his work was held in 1993 at Christchurch Mansion, Ipswich. National Museum of Wales, Cardiff, and Glynn Vivian Art Gallery, Swansea, hold pictures by Govier, who lived finally at Hoxne, Diss, Norfolk.

GOVINDER 1964– Painter, designer and illustrator, full name Govinder Nazran, born in Birmingham, whose highly stylised works were inspired "by anything and everything – from Dickens to *The Dandy*, Strauss to The Sex Pistols, Hockney to whatever!" Studied graphic design at Bradford Art College, 1980–3, completing a diploma in graphic design, specialising in illustration, at Lincoln Art College in 1985. In London, he initially produced children's book illustrations, with an Indian focus. Govinder then freelanced in Cambridge; in 1987 moved back to Bradford, designing for a greetings card company; left in 1990 to handle licensing and product development, later directing photographic shoots for an artists' agency; became photographic art director for a mail-order catalogue company, travelling widely abroad; next settling in Saltaire, Yorkshire in 1993, freelancing for major publishers. In 1999 he joined Washington Green, which published silkscreens and lithographs from his designs. Govinder's oils were shown in the 1999 Halcyon Gallery, Birmingham, Art in Miniature exhibition.

Dorothy Willett GOW fl. from c.1925– Modeller and potter whose correct name was Dorothy Ermyntrude Gow, Willett having been her maiden name. Studied at Central School of Arts and Crafts after initial education in England and France. Showed at RBA, SWA of which she was an associate, and in the provinces. Lived in London.

Lucienne GOW fl. from early 1930s– Painter and printmaker, she studied at Heatherley's School of Fine Art and in Paris, after initial education at Roedean School. Exhibited RA, SWA, RBA and completed some posters, sometimes signing work lugow. Lived in London.

Carolyn GOWDY 1954– Artist, illustrator and teacher, born in Seattle, Washington, America, who studied at the University of Washington, 1972–4; graduated in fine art from the Rhode Island School of Design, 1976; and gained her master's at the Royal College of Art, 1980, where her notable teachers included Quentin Blake and Peter de Francia, also studying under Dan Fern, Linda Kitson and Sheila Robinson. From 1977 Gowdy lived in London, working internationally as an artist and illustrator, her illustrations appearing in magazines, newspapers, on book-jackets and inside books for both children and adults and on posters. Among her wide range of clients were *Elle Magazine, Radio Times, The Spectator, The Sunday Times Magazine, The Independent Magazine, The Guardian, The Observer, The New Yorker Magazine, The Boston Globe, The Los Angeles Times*, Bloomsbury, Penguin, Harcourt Brace and Company, Royal Mail, London Underground and KPMG. From 1980 Gowdy was tutor, speaker and workshop leader in art schools and colleges in the United Kingdom and abroad, her regular teaching posts including Middlesex University, 1980–6; Leeds University, 1981–2; Maidstone College of Art, 1986–9; Bath College of Art, 1989–91; and the City and Guilds of London Art School, 1989–92. She was hon. patron of The Association of Illustrators and a full member of the Chelsea Arts Club and Society of Tempera Painters. Among Gowdy's many mixed show appearances were Women's Images of Men, ICA, 1980; finalist, South Bank Show, Royal Festival Hall, 1987; England & Co, from 1992; Still There Will Be Stories, Royal College of Art, 1994; About Collage, Tate Gallery Liverpool, 2000; and finalist, Singer & Friedlander/*Sunday Times* Watercolour Competition, 2005. In 1992, Gowdy had a solo exhibition at the Reactor Gallery in Toronto, Canada. The Victoria & Albert Museum; Museum of Illustration, Hull; Royal College of Art; and the Mazza Collection, The University of Findlay, Findlay, Ohio, hold examples.

Francis GOWER 1905–1995 Painter, notably of portraits, teacher and illustrator. He studied from early 1920s at St Martin's School of Art with Stafford Leake; won a scholarship to Royal College of Art, 1929–32, where his teachers included Randolph Schwabe, Gilbert Spencer and Barnett Freedman; studied at evening classes for a diploma in the history of art at London University; and continued with evening classes at St Martin's. His 1930s work included a period with the Lintas advertising agency. During World War II Gower worked in psychiatric hospitals, making studies later worked up into oil paintings. Went on to show at RA, RP and was included in the Lintas Beyond the Horizon show at Agnew, 1988. Gower also designed the jackets for children's books and taught at the Working Men's College as well as lecturing in history of art at Harrow and Willesden Schools of Art and at Hampstead Garden Suburb Institute. In 1986 a show of his work was held at Watford Museum, in 1996 a memorial exhibition at Bushey Museum.

Lawrence GOWING 1918–1991 Painter, teacher, writer and administrator, born in London, where he died. His first art teacher was Maurice Feild, at The Downs preparatory school, Colwall. Then studied under William Coldstream at the Euston Road School. Was early on associated with the left-wing Unity Theatre, in 1940 contributing imaginative Constructivist sets for the play *The Star Turns Red* by Sean O'Casey, admired by the author. Conscientious objector during World War II. First one-man show at Leicester Galleries in 1948. Professor of Fine Art at Durham University and principal of King Edward VII School of Art, Newcastle upon Tyne, 1948–58; principal of Chelsea School of Art, 1958–65; keeper of the British collection and deputy director of the Tate Gallery, 1965–7; professor of fine art at Leeds University, 1967–75; and Slade Professor of Fine Art at University College, London, 1975–85. Knighted in 1982 and made RA in 1989. Wrote books and catalogues on wide range of artists, from Hogarth to Lucian Freud and made a number of lucid television programmes on aspects of painting. As an inquiring teacher he enthused students and fellow members of staff. Gowing was a sensitive painter of still life, portraits and landscape, Sickert and Cézanne being notable influences. Tate Gallery is among a number of public collections holding his work. Arts Council retrospective 1983. Gowing was married for a time to Julia Strachey, niece of Lytton Strachey and herself a writer; she had previously been the wife of the Bloomsbury Group sculptor Stephen "Tommy" Tomlin, whose bust of Lytton was acquired by the Tate Gallery.

Alice Kirkby GOYDER 1875–1964 Painter, wood-carver and printmaker, born in Bradford, Yorkshire. She studied at Bradford School of Art and with Louise Jopling. Was very interested in depicting animals and won a silver medal at Women's Exhibition in 1897. She showed with RA, SWA, Walker Art Gallery in Liverpool and elsewhere. Belonged to Bradford Arts Club, East Kent Art Society and Ipswich Art Club. British Museum holds her work. Her death was registered in Bromley, Kent, although she lived for some years in Orford, Suffolk.

Daphne GRADIDGE 1953– Painter, muralist and restorer who did a foundation year at Winchester School of Art, 1972–3; gained a degree in theatre design, Nottingham Art School, 1973–6, with a travel bursary to visit Florence, Italy; then did postgraduate theatre design at the Slade School of Fine Art, 1979–81. From 1985–97, Gradidge worked on murals, commissions and restoration of interiors, including the Park Lane Hotel; Bodelwyddan Castle, Clwyd; and the Royal Hampshire County Hospital, Winchester. Between 1989–91 she was artist-in-residence, Basingstoke District Community Hospital and Southampton General Hospital. From 1994 Gradidge exhibited watercolours in Hampshire and Dorset, in 1998 showing with Anthony Hepworth Fine Art, Bath, at Art99. Her work included small, meticulous still lifes.

Dennis GRAFTON 1922– Painter in oil, born at Penn, near Wolverhampton. Brought up in the West Country, he returned to study at Wolverhampton School of Art part-time, 1937–44, his teachers including Robert Emerson and John Holden. Exhibited RA and RBA. Lived in Wolverhampton, Staffordshire.

Brian GRAHAM 1945– Painter, mainly in acrylic, also in mixed media, born in Poole, Dorset, settling at Swanage. He was "briefly at Bournemouth College of Art, but consider myself self-taught." Graham spent many years in design/advertising, but reckoned "that my *obsession* with painting started in 1975." Graham's work tended towards the abstract, but drew its inspiration from "the hills, the soil and the sea. Wild places, gentle places, sacred places". He hoped "to make the indefinable attainable". Graham participated in many mixed shows, in 1992 winning first prize in the RWA autumn exhibition donated by Brandler Galleries. After a solo show at Poole Arts Centre, 1986, later ones included On Line Gallery, Southampton, and Alpha Gallery, Swanage, both 1993, Hart South-West, Brea, 2000, Maltby Contemporary Art, Winchester, 2002, and Hart Gallery 2002–3–4. Upton House Heritage Centre; Scaplans Court Museum, Poole; and Bank of Industry, San Francisco, hold examples.

Carol GRAHAM 1951– Artist, notable as a portrait painter, born in Belfast, Northern Ireland, who gained a diploma in fine art at the local Art and Design Centre, 1970–4, married Michael Ballard in the latter year and did a post-diploma course in 1975. She won an Arts Council of Northern Ireland Bursary in 1976 and its Major Award, 1980. She was elected RUA in 1985, the year she won its Gold Medal (Portrait). Was accepted by the National Portrait Collection in 1987. Group shows included Tom Caldwell, 1975; RHA from 1978; and Bath Art Fair, 1983. Tom Caldwell gave her several solo shows, including 2001. Major portrait commissions included James Galway, flautist, 1987; Sir Derek Birley, vice-chancellor of the University of Ulster, 1990; Joan Trimble, pianist, 1992; and Dr Mary Robinson, president of Ireland, 1993. In 1982 she did the cover of Bernard McLaverty's book *Secrets*. Lived in Lisburn, County Antrim.

David GRAHAM 1926– Painter and teacher, born and lived in London. He studied at Hammersmith and St Martin's Schools of Art and Royal College of Art and in 1957 was included in Jack Beddington's book *Young Artists of Promise*. Went on to become senior lecturer at Sir John Cass School of Art. Showed at RP of which he was a member, RA, Leicester Galleries, with Roland, Browse & Delbanco and abroad. In 1987 he had a retrospective at Herbert Art Gallery and Museum in Coventry. Contemporary Art Society and Guildhall Art Gallery hold his work.

George GRAHAM 1882–1949 Painter and printmaker, born in Leeds, Yorkshire, where he studied and in London under various teachers. He was a member of ROI, RI and RSW, and a leading figure in the Yorkshire Artists and Society of Sussex Painters. Was a prolific exhibitor, showing at Fine Art Society, RA and elsewhere. Public galleries in Bradford, Leeds and Worthing hold examples. Lived latterly in Winchelsea, Sussex.

Paul GRAHAM 1956– Self-taught, photography-based artist, born in Stafford, who worked widely on the continent in the late 1990s. Group exhibitions included Hayward Gallery tour The British Art Show 5, 2000–1. Showed widely internationally and with Anthony Reynolds Gallery. Lived in London

Peter GRAHAM 1959– Painter, born in Glasgow, where he attended the School of Art, studying mural design and optical art. His studies of the human brain's appreciation of colour and his mixing of colours not normally associated with each other contributed to the vibrant appearance of Graham's canvases, as did the often exotic locations. Upon graduation Graham became a film editor with BBC for four years, although on returning to painting he continued to do freelance film work. After a holiday in Sardinia Graham held a solo show at Tricycle Gallery, 1986. As well as showing in many mixed exhibitions in Scotland and London Graham continued to hold regular solo shows, including Nanyang Academy of Fine Arts, Singapore, 1990, where he was artist-in-residence under a British Council sponsorship; in 1991 at Flying Colours Gallery in Edinburgh and 90s Gallery, Glasgow; and Bourne Gallery, Reigate, a series, including 2003. Graham was a member of ROI and New Glasgow Colourists. British Council, Singapore; the Nanyang Academy of Fine Arts; and Western Baths Club, Glasgow, hold his work.

Rigby GRAHAM 1931– Painter, printmaker, muralist, illustrator, writer and teacher, born in Stretford, Lancashire. In 1943 his family moved to Leicester, where he settled. Studied mural painting at Leicester College of Art, teachers including D P Carrington and Cyril Satorsky. From 1954 taught for two years in local schools before returning to the College, initially in the bookbinding department, which stimulated his interest in the art of the book. Graham went on to illustrate over 300 books and was strongly associated with the private press movement, including the Brewhouse, Cog, New Broom, Pandora and Saint Bernard's Presses. His most opulent book was *Graham's Leicestershire*, 1980. It shows Graham's interest in urban blight and industry. He was strongly influenced by the Neo-Romantics, although his colour owed much to German Expressionism. Travelled widely in Europe. Murals for local schools included Woodstock Junior, New Parks House Junior and Eyres Monsell Junior, and Leicester Royal Infirmary. Graham had over 40 solo shows. These included retrospectives at Hemel Hempstead Arts Trust, 1977, Goldmark Gallery, Uppingham, 1991, and New Walk Museum, Leicester, 1999. In 2003, Goldmark Gallery released Charles Mapleston's film on Graham, *Irish Voyage*. University of Wales, Aberystwyth, holds examples.

Robert GRAHAM 1938– He was one of the foreign artists whose brief residence in Britain resulted in works issued by Editions Alecto. Graham was born in Mexico City, Mexico, becoming an American citizen in 1952 aged 14. He studied at San José State College, 1961–3, then San Francisco Art Institute in California, 1963–4. During a prolific career Graham produced etchings, medal and coin designs and multiples, but was primarily known as a figurative sculptor. He early began to sculpt small female figures grouped inside architectural settings. In 1968, Editions Alecto published the etching Top View with Neuendorf Verlag, Germany, as well as the Room Series I-VI, of which the British Museum holds examples. Graham was closely associated with Galerie Neuendorf, Hamburg/Cologne, having the first of a long series of solo exhibitions with it in 1968. Robert Miller Gallery in New York and Dorothy Rosenthal Gallery in Chicago gave him many one-man shows, Gimpel & Hanover Galerie, Zürich, Switzerland, also featuring his work on the continent. His work was also shown at major American public galleries. In London in 1970 Graham had a solo show at Whitechapel Art Gallery, others with Felicity Samuels in 1974 and 1975 and Gimpel Fils in 1976. Among his group appearances was Three Americans at the Victoria & Albert Museum in 1971. Graham sometimes worked on a grand scale, the most famous of his monumental commissions being the Olympic Gateway installed in 1984 at the entrance to the Los Angeles Memorial Coliseum, Exposition Park, on the occasion of that year's Los Angeles Olympiad. Later solo exhibitions included Robert Miller Gallery and Galerie Neuendorf, Frankfurt/Main, both 1990.

Roberta M GRAHAM 1954– Artist notable for light-box sculptures, born in Londonderry, Northern Ireland, who studied at West Surrey College of Art, 1971–3, and North-East London Polytechnic, 1974–7. Aspects of beauty, violence and death were key themes in Graham's work. Group exhibitions included Whitechapel Open at Whitechapel Art Gallery, 1977; Hayward Annual, at Hayward

Gallery, 1979; and Summer Show 1 at Serpentine Gallery, 1983. Solo shows included Spectro Gallery in Newcastle upon Tyne; Arnolfini Gallery, Bristol; and Orchard Gallery in Londonderry, all 1983. Arts Council holds her work. Lived for a time in London.

Bernard Montague GRAINGER 1907– Painter, draughtsman and designer in a variety of materials such as ivory and metal; teacher. Grainger was born in Paddock Wood, Kent, and after attending Ardingly College studied at Maidstone School of Art, Royal College of Art and the Central School of Arts and Crafts. He went on to hold a number of teaching posts, at Sheffield College of Art and in Sheffield University's architecture department. Member of Sheffield Society of Artists and keen caving enthusiast in Pennine area. Lived for some time at Bradwell, Derbyshire.

Esther GRAINGER 1912–1990 Painter, teacher and artist in embroidery collage and calligrapher, born and mostly based in Cardiff, south Wales, where she studied with William Pickles at the School of Art, 1928–34. Other influences included Constance Howard, Heinz Koppel and George Mayer-Marton. In the 1930s Grainger taught crafts to the wives of unemployed miners, later organising painting classes and exhibitions at the Pontypridd Settlement. There she met Cedric Morris, who taught her at his Benton End East Anglian School. In 1950 with David Bell of the Arts Council Grainger organised the first open exhibition of paintings at the National Eisteddfod and was secretary for the Welsh Pictures for Schools shows. Among her exhibitions was a retrospective at the Minories, Colchester, 1973, with watercolours at Manor Gallery, Pontcanna, Cardiff, 1990. A member of SWG and WSW, Grainger also exhibited with WAC, which holds her work, as well as SEA. A number of education authorities also hold examples.

Ian GRAINGER 1942– Printmaker, draughtsman, designer and teacher who created highly original images, drawing on many literary and natural sources, tinged with wryness and self-criticism. He studied at Sunderland College of Art, 1965–8, then Birmingham College, 1968–9; was awarded a fellowship in painting at Chicago Art Institute in America, 1969–70, then Prix de Rome, engraving, 1971–3. Was made an associate of RE in 1974. Taught part-time and in 1980 was Gregynog Fellow under the auspices of WAC and University of Wales. Was included in Text and Image, Curwen Gallery, 1978, and Serpentine Summer Show 1, 1980. His solo exhibitions included Arnolfini Gallery, Bristol, 1980. WAC and Northern Arts hold examples.

Christian GRANDJEAN 1945– Printmaker and photographer, born in Paris, where he studied photography in various studios, 1961–4. He worked as a freelance photographer, 1965–74, eventually becoming a London-based printmaker. Mixed-show appearances included in 1969 Point 50, Paris, where he also had solo exhibitions in 1970–1; Wapping Artists 1981; Bradford Print Biennale, 1982; and Whitechapel Open in 1983, when he participated in 9 Artists from Wapping British Tour, based at DLI Museum & Arts Centre, Durham. London Borough of Tower Hamlets and University of Calgary, Alberta, hold his work.

Lee GRANDJEAN 1949– Sculptor, draughtsman and teacher, born in London, although he lived for part of his youth in Romania. Studied at North-East London Polytechnic, 1967–8, then Winchester School of Art, 1968–71. Grandjean had a studio in London, 1971–80, then moved to Reepham, Norfolk. From 1980–1 he was research fellow in sculpture at Winchester School of Art, having lectured at Wimbledon School of Art since 1976. In 1991 became sculpture tutor at Royal College of Art, appointed senior tutor from 1977. He also worked widely as a visiting lecturer and examiner. Grandjean worked in various materials and was interested in "the transformation of material" and with non-European and ancient civilisations shared a desire to "render raw materials into another expressive substance". Included in his output were reclining nudes, parents and children, and head sculptures, sometimes on a large scale, such as his Head of Glynn Williams, of 1982. He showed in outdoor exhibitions, such as Yorkshire Sculpture Park, Cannizaro Park in Wimbledon and he participated in the 1983 Welsh Sculpture Trust Margam show, Sculpture in a Country Park. Among Grandjean's later solo exhibitions were King of Hearts, Norwich, 1996, and Groundwork, Djanogly Gallery, Nottingham, 1998. Arts Council holds examples.

Edith GRANGER: *see* **Edith GRANGER-TAYLOR**

Simon GRANGER 1955– Artist born in London who studied at Slade School of Fine Art, 1973–9, including postgraduate work, in 1984–5 gaining a residency at Aycliffe, County Durham. He appeared in Whitechapel Open Exhibition from 1983; Wild Creatures, an Arts Council touring exhibition, 1988; was an Artist of the Day at Angela Flowers Gallery, 1994, chosen by Andrew Stahl; and was included in 1997–8 John Moores Liverpool Exhibition. Solo show at Danielle Arnaud, 1999, large paintings of hybrid creatures hovering in an undisturbed world. Arts Council and Northern Arts hold examples. Lived in London.

Edith GRANGER-TAYLOR 1888–1958 Painter, born Edith Granger in Grassington, Yorkshire, the family moving to Little Milton, Oxfordshire, in 1894. In 1915 she married Godfrey Taylor, consulting engineer and captain in the Royal Engineers, after which she used Granger-Taylor professionally. Her son Jerry Granger-Taylor and grandson Nicholas Granger-Taylor were both painters. She studied for a term at Royal Academy Schools in 1910; at St John's Wood Art School before 1914; had lessons in portraiture from Philip de Laszlo; did a term at Slade School of Fine Art, 1919; returning there in 1933 for Vladimir Polunin's stage painting classes. During the 1920s and 1930s showed extensively with RBA, RWS and NEAC all as a member; also with PS, NS and in 1921 won *The Times'* women's supplement's April cover competition. Solo exhibitions were at Grosvenor Galleries, 1922; Blomqvist Gallery, Oslo, 1930; Beaux Arts Gallery, 1932; Walker's Galleries, 1958; and Gillian Jason Gallery, 1989.

Nicholas GRANGER-TAYLOR 1963– Painter, notably of portraits and still life, born and lived in London. He was educated at Latymer Upper School, then completed foundation studies at Kingston Polytechnic, 1981–2. After obtaining his degree in fine art from Bristol Polytechnic, 1982–5, Granger-Taylor did a postgraduate diploma in painting at Royal Academy Schools, 1987–90. He obtained a special commendation in John Player Portrait Award in 1987, gaining second prize that year in the British Institution Fund Painting Award. Several other awards followed, including in 1990 the Elizabeth Greenshields Foundation Award and the Richard Ford Award, which enabled him to study at Prado, Madrid. Granger-Taylor fast established a reputation in mixed shows including RA, the Festival Hall's South Bank Picture Show and Cadogan Contemporary Summer Exhibitions. Solo shows included retrospective at Offer Waterman & Co, 1999. The Metropolitan Museum of Modern Art in New York and National Westminster Bank hold examples. His father and grandmother, Jerry and Edith Granger-Taylor, were also artists.

Paul GRANJON 1965– "Visual artist working with electronics, robotics, video and programming. My subject matter is the co-evolution of humans and machines.... I often present the work in a humorous fashion, combined with an underlying darker vision." Although he was born in Lyon, France, Granjon was based in Cardiff, chosen to represent Wales in the 2005 Venice Biennale with three computerised metal robots on wheels which bumped into each other and mated. Granjon gained his Baccalauréat in 1984 and in 1990 his DNSEF (Bachelor of Arts fine art equivalent) at L'École des Beaux-Arts de Marseille. He held many visiting lectureships in the United Kingdom, Finland and Canada; was from 1995 a lecturer in video and digital media at the school of fine art at the University of Wales Institute, Cardiff, from 2002 also being co-director of B1oC, the new media arts organisation for Wales. Granjon won a number of British and French awards and took part in many group shows and festivals with screenings, exhibitions and performances. His later solo exhibitions included Z Lab 2001, Chapter Arts Centre, Cardiff, and elsewhere, 2001; Machines by Paul Granjon, Mandrak, Grenoble, France, 2002; Automated Forest, Musée d'Art Moderne du Luxembourg (MUDAM), Luxembourg, 2003; and Quelques créatures, residency in Galerie Séquence, Chicoutimi, Canada, 2004. The Arts Council and MUDAM hold examples.

Alistair GRANT 1925–1997 Painter, printmaker, artist in collage and teacher born in London, where he settled. He attended Birmingham School of Art, 1941–3, was four years in the Royal Air Force, then was at Royal College of Art, 1947–50, with a continuation scholarship, 1950–1. From 1955 for many years Grant taught printmaking at Royal College of Art, where he became head of the department in 1970, taking the chair of printmaking in 1984, retiring in 1990. Grant had a keen, painterly sense of colour in pictures that were at first figurative, later abstract. His dexterity as a draughtsman was exhibited in John Huston's film *Moulin Rouge*, based on the life of Toulouse-Lautrec, made in 1953, where Grant drew on camera. Grant showed RA, AIA, NEAC, at Redfern, Piccadilly and Zwemmer Galleries and was a prizewinner at the Cracow Print Biennale in 1972. After the death of his second wife Joan Strickland (who had worked with him at the Royal College), in 1995, Grant lived partly in France, partly in England, showing in both. His mother came from Etaples, in northern France, where he went to school, and he retained the family home there. Grant's work is held by the Victoria & Albert Museum, British provincial and many overseas galleries. There was a memorial show at Art First, 1997.

D Marion GRANT 1912– Artist in stained glass, born in Bromley, Kent. She was educated at Central School of Arts and Crafts, 1931–5, then embarked on a career which encompassed a large amount of ecclesiastical work. Exeter Cathedral, Glasgow Cathedral and a number of English churches contain windows by her. Lived in London.

Donald GRANT 1930–2001 Versatile artist, noted for his wildlife pictures, born in North Shields, Northumberland, whose artistic talent was early apparent. While still at school he sold his first picture to the family doctor, painted a large mural in a public building and won a national drawing and design competition. At the age of 16 he was arrested on Biggin Hill airfield, famous for its role during the Battle of Britain, for stubbornly ignoring the camp adjutant's refusal to let him sketch aircraft. He had climbed a barbed wire fence and in under an hour produced a watercolour of a lone Spitfire standing on wet tarmac. A varied career followed, during which he continued to paint. After an apprenticeship as a shipbuilding draughtsman and Army service in Africa Grant worked as a technical illustrator, graphic designer and freelance advertising artist. In the 1960s Grant produced a series of unusual paintings of balloons in flight set against impressive banks of cloud. One of these was immediately accepted by the RA and sold. He exhibited his wildlife paintings over several decades, becoming collected internationally. They were based on a love of Africa and an ability to mix technical accuracy and local atmosphere. He was a strong believer in the conservation of wildlife and the wilderness in which it lived. Grant also exhibited at the National Museum of Sport, New York, 1973–6, and latterly McConnal-Mason sold his work from stock.

Duncan GRANT 1885–1978 Painter and decorative artist, designer for the theatre and of pottery and textiles. He was born at Rothiemurchus, Inverness-shire, but spent his early years in India. After studying at Westminster School of Art in 1902 Grant spent a time in Italy, studied under Jacques-Emile Blanche in 1906, then for a short period at the Slade School of Fine Art. During the period 1907–9 Grant lived in Paris, where he met Matisse, whose talent for felicitous decoration is often found in Grant's own work over the years. Grant then travelled widely in Europe and Tunisia; was influenced by French Post-Impressionists during Roger Fry's first show of them in London in 1910–11, Grant contributing to the second show in 1912; and became a member of the Camden Town Group and later LG. Grant's association with the Bloomsbury Group around this time and his work with Roger Fry's Omega Workshops was of lasting importance to his career, his association with Vanessa Bell being a notable aspect of this. While living at Charleston, Firle, Sussex, which remained his home, they and Quentin Bell decorated the church at Berwick, near Firle, in 1943. Grant had his first one-man show at the Carfax Gallery in 1920. He was in many group shows, including the Leicester, Redfern, Lefevre and Leger Galleries, also having one-man shows at Agnew. Represented in many public collections, including Tate Gallery, which staged a retrospective exhibition in 1959, with Arts Council tour.

Ian GRANT 1904–1993 Painter, art historian and teacher, born in Scotland. He studied at Glasgow School of Art, 1922–6, under Maurice Greiffenhagen, then in 1927 at Atelier Colarossi, Paris, and Royal College of Art, 1927–30.

Grant became senior lecturer at Manchester Regional College of Art, staying there, 1937–69; his wife Margaret Gumuchian, whom he married in 1953, was a student in his class. Other appointments included part-time work at Mauldeth Road College of Further Education, 1959–79, and lecturing in art history at Manchester University extra-mural department. Grant was for a time vice-president of MAFA, where he won a major prize in 1986. In 1989 he was included in The Last Romantics at Barbican Art Gallery. Manchester City Art Gallery holds his work, which was exhibited at solo shows at Salford Art Gallery and elsewhere in the north. Lived in Stockport, Cheshire.

James Ardern GRANT 1887–1973 Printmaker, painter and teacher, born in Liverpool. He studied at the School of Art there, where he later taught, at Académie Julian in Paris and in London at Central Technical School. Eventually became vice-principal of Central School of Arts and Crafts. Before World War I in Liverpool Grant was a member of Sandon Studios Society, in 1932 becoming a fellow of RE, also a member of NS and PS of which he was president. Showed extensively, including RA, Chenil Gallery, NEAC, RSA, Walker Art Gallery and elsewhere. Walker Art Gallery holds his portrait of the theatrical designer George Harries, Whitworth Art Gallery, Manchester, his striking pastel Woman in a Grey Hat. Latterly lived in London. In 2001, Sotheby's Olympia sold the contents of 41 Ladbroke Square, the home of Grant's son Ian, including many of his father's pictures.

Keith Frederick GRANT 1930– Artist in various media, teacher, born Liverpool. Attended Willesden School of Art, 1952–5, then Royal College of Art, 1955–8, where he gained a silver medal for mural painting. In 1958 he won a travelling scholarship to France, in 1960 a Norwegian Government Scholarship, in 1962 and Icelandic Government Scholarship, in 1973 a Gulbenkian Award and in 1976 a grant from the Norwegian government to visit Norway. He was head of painting at Maidstone College of Art, 1969–71, later becoming head of the department of art at Roehampton Institute of Higher Education. Grant showed at Roland, Browse & Delbanco; Crane Kalman Gallery; Gillian Jason Gallery and elsewhere and was a member of the Society of Landscape Painters. He was the subject of a *Look, Stranger* programme for BBC Television, which featured his 1971 open-air sculpture at Shaw Theatre based on *Joan of Arc*. He also completed murals for Rhodesia House in 1959, Middlesex Hospital in 1972 and Gateshead Metro Station, 1981–3. In 1999–00 he was commissioned by Charing Cross Hospital to complete a large stained glass window, Millennium New Worlds. Dramatic, simple landscapes of the Norwegian fjords, moving towards abstraction, were a feature of Grant's work, and he was also interested in the world seen from space. Retrospectives included Ice and Fire, Fitzwilliam Museum, Cambridge, 1994. Among later solo shows were Cadogan Contemporary, 2000 and 2003. Arts Council, Contemporary Art Society and Fitzwilliam Museum in Cambridge hold examples.

Leslie GRANT 1923– Painter, notably of landscapes and townscapes, draughtsman and teacher. After serving in Royal Air Force air crew in World War II Grant studied at Bromley and Brighton Colleges of Art. He taught at Mansfield School of Art; in Germany; at several London schools; and became head of art at Plumstead Manor School. Grant showed at South London Art Gallery; in the provinces, notably with Midland Group of Artists; in Germany; and in 1979 at Woodlands Art Gallery.

Marianne GRANT 1931– Painter in oil, born in St Gallen, Switzerland. She studied in Zürich and Geneva, eventually returning to live in Zürich after a period in Romford Essex. As well as showing in Switzerland she exhibited with NS of which she was a member and had a number of English solo shows including BH Corner Gallery, Century Galleries in Henley-on-Thames and Royal Northern College of Music. Standard Telephone and Cables bought her work and some of her work was produced in print form. Essex Art Club member.

Mary GRANT 1971– Painter who did a foundation course at Northbrook College of Design, 1990–1, graduating with honours from Kingston University, 1991–4, with thesis commendation. Gained a Stanley Picker Travel Scholarship to New York, 1994. She was engaged in art therapy at Royal Marsden Hospital, 1991; art restoration at Goodwood House, 1994; was artist-in-residence, Whitgift School, 1995; also assisting at Enid Lawson Gallery, where she had solo shows from 1997. Later mixed exhibitions included Leighton House Open, from 1997, Affordable Art Fair, 1999. Among further shows were solo exhibitions of her photographic series September Girls, at the Victoria & Albert Museum Friends Room in 2000 and The Great Eastern Hotel in 2001, other appearances including Tryon Contemporary and Winter Exhibition, JohnMartinChelsea, both 2004.

Edgar GRANTHAM 1926– Painter, calligrapher and teacher, born in York. He was initially educated in Bradford, then studied art between 1947–52 in Liverpool, Bradford and Leeds. After World War II he taught for a couple of years in the Army, eventually joining the staff of Sheffield Central Technical School, where he remained for some years. Showed mainly in Yorkshire, where he lived in Sheffield.

Alastair GRANVILLE-JACKSON fl. from 1950s– Sculptor, printmaker and teacher, born in Woodstock, South Africa. He studied art history at University of Cape Town, where he obtained his bachelor of arts degree in 1954, obtaining a master of arts degree from Columbia University in 1982. In 1957 he studied in Florence and in the same year at Slade School of Fine Art with Reg Butler, the sculptor. Further studies included periods in the early 1960s at Central School of Arts and Crafts and St Martin's School of Art, with Anthony Caro, then Cranbrook Academy of Art, 1965–7, Birmingham, Michigan, in America. As well as exhibiting in South Africa and in America, Granville-Jackson showed at AIA, LG, RBSA as well as Heal's Mansard Art Gallery. Lived for some time in New York.

Andrew GRASSIE 1966– Realist painter and lecturer whose small, finely crafted tempera pictures were concerned with complex concepts. Grassie's output included minutely detailed paintings recording contemporary exhibitions at major London galleries plus paintings featuring other artists' works. He was born in Edinburgh and graduated with first-class honours from St Martin's School of Art, 1984–8, having studied with John Dougill, John Stezaker and Tim Allen, gaining his master's at the Royal College of Art, 1988–90, under Ken Kiff, Yehuda

Safran and Alan Miller. Was for a time duty manager at the ICA, a visiting lecturer at Maidstone and Glasgow Schools of Art and had a residency at Camden Arts Centre. Grassie listed as influences "Vermeer, Ladybird Books and Hitchcock." His many group shows included Die Yuppie Scum, Karsten Schubert, 1996; Postcards on Photography, Cambridge Darkroom Gallery and tour, 1998–9; Up and Coming, Elizabeth Harris Gallery, New York, America, 1999; East International, Norwich Gallery, 2001; Realistic Means, Drawing Center, New York, 2002; Tonight, Studio Voltaire, 2003; and John Moores Liverpool Exhibition, 2004, where he won a Special Merit Prize. Grassie was a frequent solo exhibitor, later exhibitions including Mobile Home, 2000, 2001 and 2003, and Paul Morris Gallery, New York, 2003. In 2005 he was featured in the Art Now series at Tate Britain. Grassie lived in London.

Ellen GRAUBART 1939– Artist and teacher, born in Bombay, India, who studied at Regent Street Polytechnic School of Art (later moved to Chelsea College of Art by Sir Lawrence Gowing), with Norman Blamey and Leon Kossoff, painting, and Fred Murray Pearcey, theatre design, 1958–62. From 1981–5 she learned printmaking at Morley College with Adrian Bartlett and Frank Connolly. She taught art in secondary schools in Essex and Islington, 1962–5, and Hackney, 1975–7, painting and drawing to adults during the same period, also arts and crafts to disabled adults, 1977–89. Graubart designed and made sets, costumes, props, projections and transparencies for Focus Opera, 1967–70, and designed for the world premier of Elisabeth Lutyens' opera *Isis and Osiris* at Morley College, 1976. Between 1970–8 Graubart appeared as a mime dancer. The composer Nicola Lefanu's music theatre piece *Anti-world* was composed for Graubart, the world premier taking place at the Cockpit Theatre in 1972, several performances in major venues following, including the Royal Festival Hall. Mixed shows included Tretyakov Gallery, Moscow, 1991; Concourse Gallery, The Barbican, 1992; National Theatre Foyer Gallery, 1995; Royal Exchange Theatre Foyer Gallery, 1996; RWA Open Print Exhibition, 1997; RA Summer Exhibition, 2000; Solo Arte Gallery, St John, Virgin Islands, 2003; Gallery Kaleidoscope, 2004; and Contemporary British Art, The Millinery Works, 2005. Among solo exhibitions were Morley Gallery, 1973; Everyman Foyer Gallery, 1981; Lauderdale House, 1989; Piers Feetham Gallery and Hampstead Theatre Gallery, both 1992; Honor Oak Gallery, 2001; and The Haymakers Gallery, Hay-on-Wye, 2002. She was included in Brenda Hartill and Richard Clarke's book *Collographs and Mixed-media Printing*, 2005. Graubart was a member of Greenwich Printmakers' Association, 1983–98, and the Printmakers' Council, 1984–99. She had a studio in Stoke Newington, north London.

William GRAVENEY 1904–1984 Sculptor in bronze, stone, terracotta and wood. Born in London, Graveney studied at the school of wood carving at the Royal College of Art, then later at City and Guilds School, Kennington, under Charles Leonard Hartwell, RA. He won several silver medals. Became a tutor in wood-carving at Morley College, in South London. Exhibited at the RA from 1926. The Tate Gallery holds his oak carving Cormorants. Wrote several books on carving. Lived in Chiswick, London.

Francis J H GRAVES: *see* **Frank GRAVES**

Frank GRAVES 1913–2001 Painter, scenic artist and wood engraver, born in Dublin, Ireland, full name Francis J H Graves, who was educated in Belfast, attending Belfast Art School. After a few years in Paris he moved to England where he was employed by Ealing Film Studios as a scenic artist, working on many well-known productions. When World War II broke out Graves was asked to oversee a troupe organised by ENSA (Entertainments National Service Association), simultaneously to work as a war artist to depict how troops at home and abroad were being entertained. After travelling around Britain, from 1943 Graves toured the Middle East, based in Cairo, returning to England in 1945. He then journeyed around Germany for six months with ENSA, arriving back in London in 1946. In the late 1940s he spent a period in South Africa, but Graves's post-war years were employed mainly in films, working at Elstree, Pinewood and Shepperton Studios on most of the James Bond films, and such epics as *A Bridge Too Far*, 1977, *Force Ten from Navarone*, 1978, and *Victor/ Victoria*, 1982; Graves also worked in television, notably on *The Persuaders* series. After retirement in the 1980s he continued to paint at home. Graves's mid-war ENSA pictures are held by the Imperial War Museum, part of the independent submissions encouraged by the War Artists' Advisory Committee. Bonhams sold some of his work in 2002. Early wood engravings were inscribed F J H Graves.

Ida GRAVES 1902–1999 Writer and artist, born in Conoor, India, and distantly related to the poet Robert Graves, aged six she was sent to school in England. At 19 she studied English literature at University College London, doing an evening course in sculpture at Chelsea Art School; she joined the circle of Virginia and Leonard Woolf, whose Hogarth Press published her *The China Cupboard and Other Poems*, 1929; then in 1930, after a failed first marriage, married the engraver Blair Hughes-Stanton. They set up Gemini Press in 1933, which published her poem *Epithalamion*, illustrated by him, in 1934. During World War II Graves painted scenery and sewed costumes for Covent Garden National Ballet. She was also known for her embroidered woollen ships and sea pictures and humorous collages and flannel portraits of family and friends. Graves published the long poem *Mother and Child* in 1946 and, as Affleck Graves, three children's books and two autobiographical novels, *Willa, You're Wanted*, 1952, and *Elarna Cane*, 1956. She went on writing poetry but did not publish more books of it again until *A Kind Husband* appeared in 1994 and *Calfbearer* in 1999. Her third husband was the jazz pianist Don Nevard. She died at Stratford St Mary, Suffolk.

Lorna GRAVES 1947–2006 Sculptor in raku-fired ceramic and painter, born in Kendal and settled at Hunsonby, Penrith, Cumbria. She gained a Bachelor of Science degree at London University, 1969–72; was librarian at Oxford University, 1972–4; attending Cambridge College of Art, 1974–6. In 1981–4 obtained Cumbria College of Art & Design diploma in fine art. Won an Arts Council Award in 1978; a series of regional arts awards, 1984–8; and the David Canter Memorial Award, 1991. The Eden Valley and Cumbrian landscape, the nearby stone circle Long Meg and her Daughters were key influences. The poet Kathleen Raine saw in Graves' work "a kind of grave simplicity, something tender and enduring". Mixed exhibitions included Temenos, Dartington Hall, 1988; Aberdeen Art

Gallery, 1990; Pyramid Gallery, York, 1994; and Bleddfa Gallery, Powys, 1995. Later solo exhibitions included Roger Billcliffe Fine Art, Glasgow, and Montage, Castleton, both 1995. Tate Gallery, Metropolitan Art Gallery in New York, Victoria & Albert Museum and public galleries in Aberdeen, Kendal, Carlisle and elsewhere hold examples.

Guy GRAVETT 1919–1996 Photographer and painter, born in Kent, who studied at Lewes Grammar School and, determined to be an artist, attended Brighton College of Art under Walter Hayes. To make a living he joined HM Customs and during World War II was commissed in the Royal Engineers, ending as the Naples port commandant. He was a lifelong keen sailor. Demobilised and unable to make a living as a painter Gravett taught himself photography and set up a studio in Lewes, not far from the opera house at Glyndebourne. Eventually he was to become the photographer for the Festival Opera there, meticulously covering each production and the building of the new opera house in 1993–4. Major commissions also came from *Picture Post, The Sunday Times*, British Petroleum and wine merchant Peter Dominic. Wine was another of Gravett's passions, and he provided illustrations for the early editions of Hugh Johnson's *World Atlas of Wine*. Gravett returned to painting in the 1970s, France – its vineyards and the Normandy countryside, in particular – being a favourite subject. His watercolours and oils of Dieppe were made into a show at the port in 1993.

Alasdair GRAY 1934– Versatile artist, writer and teacher, born and lived in Glasgow, who studied at Glasgow School of Art. From 1958–62, he was a secondary school art teacher; 1962–3, a theatrical scene painter; 1964, a "social security scrounger"; 1965–76 painter and playwright, with 17 plays televised, broadcast or staged; 1977, artist-recorder for Glasgow's local history museum; 1977–9, writer-in-residence, Glasgow University; from 1981 being mainly a writer, book designer and illustrator. Gray wrote, designed and illustrated nine published novels, including the award-winning *Lanark*, of 1981, in gestation for 27 years; three books of short stories, one co-authored; two books of verse; a political pamphlet, *Why Scots Should Rule Scotland*, a play and in 2000 *The Book of Prefaces*, 15 years in preparation. *The Ends of Our Tethers: Thirteen Sorry Stories* appeared in 2003. Gray was a member of the Society of Authors. As an artist, he claimed as "leading influences, Disney, Bosch, Blake, Beardsley and Munch; leading themes, Hell and Arcadia." From 1959–77 he showed intermittently with the Glasgow Group. From 1962–73 he held annual shows, mainly with the Kelly Gallery, Glasgow, or Traverse Theatre, Edinburgh. There was a retrospective exhibition at the Collins Gallery, Strathclyde University, 1974. In 1998–9 the Scottish National Library, Edinburgh, showed and then sent on tour an exhibition of Gray's book designs and illustrations. Gray completed a number of murals, venues including Palacerigg Nature Reserve Exhibition Centre, Cumbernauld; Abbots House Local History Museum, Dunfermline; and The Ubiquitous Chip Restaurant, Glasgow. Collins Gallery, The People's Palace, Glasgow, and Glasgow University hold examples.

Anthony GRAY 1915–1972 Sculptor in stone, bronze, wood, resins and other materials. Gray studied art in several countries on the continent in the late 1930s. After World War II he studied at Camberwell School of Art, 1946–9, then at St Martin's School of Art, 1949–50. He taught for a while and undertook architectural and portrait commissions, being for a time vice-president of the SPS. Exhibited SPS and RA. Among his many portraits of famous people were Earl Attlee, Sir John Barbirolli, Sir David Low and Nubar Gulbenkian. Lived in London.

Colin GRAY 1956– Artist using photography whose output could have surreal overtones, as in his work Hull under Water, 1991, in the Ferens Art Gallery collection. Gray was born in Hull, completed a foundation course with Hull Arts, 1976–7; graduated with first-class honours in graphic design at Leeds Polytechnic, 1977–80; and obtained his master's in photography from the Royal College of Art, 1982–4. Exhibitions included North Light Gallery, Leeds, 1980; Oldham Art Gallery, 1985; Leicester Polytechnic Gallery, 1987; Intimate Lives, City Art Centre, Edinburgh, 1993; Fotodiffusion, Turin, Italy, 1994; Ferens Art Gallery, 1996; and Fotografisk Centre, Copenhagen, Denmark, and Turnpike Gallery, Leigh, both 1997. Also in 1997 Gray showed The Parents at Street Level Gallery, Glasgow, his parents having long been a subject that preoccupied him.

Dorothy GRAY 1901–1962 Painter of miniatures of flowers on ivory, born in London. Exhibited RMS, RA, SWA and Foyles Gallery. Lived at Bexhill-on-Sea, Sussex.

Douglas Stannus GRAY 1890–1959 Bravura painter in oil of figures, portraits, landscapes, still life and his own family, and teacher. Born in London, in 1900 he attended art school in Clapham, in 1904 becoming a full-time pupil at Croydon School of Art. In 1908 accepted at Royal Academy Schools, where his teachers included Ernest Jackson and Charles Sims, but the strongest, lasting influence remained Schools visitor John Singer Sargent. Won Landseer Scholarship in 1912, British Institution Scholarship in 1914, suspended during military service. Because of injuries, was retired with a life pension. Travelled in France and in the 1920s began to have success with pictures at the Royal Academy, where his portrait of his sister Rosalind was bought by the Chantrey Bequest. Also showed at ROI and RP. In 1947 taught portrait class at Brighton Art College. Gray's career went through lean periods, but his reputation received a boost in the 1980s with exhibitions at Spink & Son. The Tate Gallery holds his work. Gray's daughter was the artist Virginia Susanne Douglas Robinson, his sister the painter and miniaturist Rosalind Stannus Gray. He lived at Southwick, Sussex.

Elizabeth GRAY 1928– Musician and self-taught painter, born in Scarborough, Yorkshire, whose speciality was sporting and wildlife pictures. Had solo shows at Tryon Gallery, in the provinces and in America at Sportsman's Edge Gallery, New York. Bank of England holds her work. Lived at Awre, Newnham-on-Severn, Gloucestershire.

Ethel GRAY 1879–1957 Painter, printmaker, stained glass designer, potter and embroiderer. Born in Newcastle upon Tyne, she studied at Leeds College of Art, York School of Art and Royal College of Art. Taught for many years, including Leeds Training College for over 30 years to 1944. Exhibited RA, SWA, RWS, Paris Salon, extensively in the provinces and in South Africa, where she finally lived in Johannesburg.

Frederick GRAY 1911–1960 Painter and designer, of jewellery and for television and films. Born at Colchester, Essex, he studied at the Royal College of Art. Exhibited in London, where he lived. Took part in the Pilgrim Trust *Recording Britain* project.

Jane GRAY 1931– Stained glass artist, born in Lincoln. She studied at Kingston School of Art, 1948–52, under Reginald Brill, then at Royal College of Art, 1952–5, with Lawrence Lee. For the next three years she assisted Lee with his windows in Coventry Cathedral. Elected a liveryman of the Worshipful Company of Glaziers in 1983. Examples of her work are to be founded in Hillingdon Hospital Chapel, Oxford County Hall and Glaziers Hall, London. Lived in Uxbridge, Middlesex, then in Shrawardine, Shrewsbury.

Jane GRAY fl. from 1960s– Printmaker and teacher who studied at London University and Camberwell School of Arts and Crafts, where she was awarded a postgraduate scholarship in graphics. She taught at various schools in the southeast of England. Made a BBC Television series with John Berger on animal prints. Lino-prints of animals were featured when her work was shown in Group '77 Printmakers at Woodlands Art Gallery, 1981. Gray's prints were exhibited widely and illustrated in the national press.

Janice GRAY 1966– Watercolourist who studied at Glasgow School of Art, 1984–8. Awards included Elizabeth Greenshields Scholarship and W O Hutchison Prize for Drawing, both 1988; and Alexander Graham Munro Travel Award and Maude Gemmell Hutchison Award, both 1996. Gray was elected to RSW in 1995. Exhibitions included RSA, 1987; Atholl Gallery, Dunkeld, 1990; Scottish Gallery, Edinburgh International Festival Exhibition, 1996; Ainscough Contemporary Art, 1997, amusing watercolours of acrobatic animals; Corrymella Scott Gallery, Newcastle, 2001; and Green Gallery, 2004. Aberdeen Art Gallery and BBC Scotland, Glasgow, hold examples.

John GRAY 1970– Artist who gained a fine art honours degree at Leeds Metropolitan University, 1991–4. His mixed and joint exhibitions included Fresh Art, Business Design Centre, 1994; Blink, Dance Attic Studios, 1995; and 2000, Gallery Fine, 2000; and 14x14, The Century Gallery, 2002. He had a solo exhibition at Islington Arts Factory, 1995, another at Curwen Gallery, 2003.

Joseph GRAY 1890–1962 Painter, printmaker and illustrator, born in South Shields, County Durham, attending the School of Art there. He travelled extensively through Europe and Russia, served in the Black Watch in World War I, eventually becoming war artist for *The Graphic*. The Imperial War Museum acquired his painting titled A Ration Party, and the British Museum and Victoria & Albert Museum holds examples. Showed with Aitken Dott in Edinburgh, also Fine Art Society and RSA. Lived in Broughty Ferry, Angus.

Ken GRAY 1943–1994 Sculptor, performance artist and lecturer, born in London. Gray's early death, the dismantling of many works and a move overseas did not help the reputation of this highly original artist who spurned that designation, preferring to be called a "communications engineer". Gray obtained his National Diploma in Civil Engineering, Southend-on-Sea Municipal College, 1964, and worked at marine surveying when he began to draw and paint. He graduated in art from Brighton Polytechnic, 1973, gaining his master's in sculpture from the Royal College of Art, 1976. From 1970 Gray began to incorporate electronic components into his paintings. For his first solo show, at Zarach in 1972, he showed electro-sculpture, which he continued to produce until late in his career. Gray won an Arts Council Major Award, 1978. By then he had achieved several dozen solo shows in Britain and on the continent. In 1980 he moved to America to teach art in Tennessee, in 1981 gaining his master's degree in communication at Memphis State University. He then went to Anchorage, Alaska, where he became associate professor of art at the University, in 1985 gained a fellowship from Alaska State Council on the Arts and eventually died. Gray's work went through phases, some following others, some overlapping. There was a telecommunications phase, house phase, political phase, performance art phase and late ritual phase. Gray's art was meant to be handled, like Three Thousand Volt Money Box, 1979, at Ferens Art Gallery, Hull, which continued to raise money for the collection. Gray's numerous one-man exhibitions latterly included Lowestoft Arts Centre, Kenai Peninsula College and Private Enquiries Gallery, Anchorage, all 1991, and Anchorage Museum of History and Art, 1993. He rejected the idea of "making art that flaunts itself like an ageing whore. I don't want people to walk in the door, drink a glass of wine, mingle with their friends, leave and say they've seen the Ken Gray exhibition. I want them to give the work some attention." Laing Art Gallery, Newcastle upon Tyne; Yorkshire Sculpture Park; Arnolfini, Bristol; Aberdeen and Southampton City Art Galleries; and collections in America, Germany and Switzerland hold examples.

Milner GRAY 1899–1997 Graphic designer, draughtsman and teacher with a respect for craftsmanship and materials, creator of such well-known symbols as the Jaeger stores lettering, born in Blackheath, southeast London. He was educated locally at Colfe's Grammar School and Goldsmiths' College School of Art (where he was later a tutor, also teaching at Royal College of Art and Central School, as well as being principal of Sir John Cass School of Arts and Crafts). During World War I Gray served in Army camouflage. In the early 1920s he formed half of the pioneering consultancy Bassett-Gray (later the Industrial Design Partnership) and shared digs with Graham Sutherland, who did work for it. Sutherland painted his final portrait of Gray for the Society of Industrial Artists and Designers, which Gray had helped form in 1930, of which he was twice president and from which he received its first Design Medal for outstanding achievement. Invited by Frank Pick of London Transport to join the Ministry of Information exhibition team in World War II, Gray was involved in such famous campaigns as Dig for Victory. He was persuaded to form the Design Research Unit with Kenneth Bayes and Misha Black. Over several decades jobs included the Britain Can Make It exhibition, the Festival of Britain and commissions for Imperial Chemical Industries, British Rail, and the Post Office. Gray was made Royal Designer for Industry, and was a member of the Council of Industrial Design and of the Royal Mint design committee. He was a convivial member of the Arts Club.

Nicolete GRAY 1911–1997 Designer, cutter and historian of lettering, teacher and writer, born in Stevenage,

Hertfordshire. She was the daughter of Laurence Binyon, deputy keeper of oriental paintings and prints in the British Museum, the poet who in 1914 wrote *For the fallen*. With him from early childhood she visited museums and galleries, as a young woman acquiring great knowledge of Western art; from her dress allowance she bought works by Paul Nash and Eric Gill; and knew such modern artists as Barbara Hepworth, David Jones on whom she was later to write authoritatively, Ben and Winifred Nicholson. After winning a scholarship to St Paul's she read history at Lady Margaret Hall, Oxford, was received into the Roman Catholic church and became interested in lettering while attending the British School at Rome to study Dark Age inscriptions. She married Basil Gray, assistant keeper in her father's department, in 1933. Her *XIXth Century Ornamented Types and Title Pages*, 1938, enlarged 1976, became a standard authority. After learning stone-cutting she carved tombstones and other inscriptions from 1953. Among these are a whole-wall inscription in wood at the Shakespeare Centre, Stratford-upon-Avon; façade lettering for the auction house Sotheby's; and the writer Agatha Christie's tombstone. In 1959 Gray designed an alphabet of metal letters for use on buildings. Cardinal Heenan's tombstone in Westminster Cathedral, 1976, the mosaic over the northwest door, 1981, and a tablet commemorating Pope John Paul II's 1982 visit are notable examples of her work. Gray taught 1964–81 at the Central School where she founded the Central Lettering Record, contributing her own huge photographic archive. From her teaching stemmed *Drawing as Lettering*, 1970. Gray travelled and lectured extensively abroad, was one of the first women to join the Double Crown Club and was active in the Association Typographique International. Her 1986 *A History of Lettering* is a key work. Lived finally at Long Wittenham, Oxfordshire, but died in London.

Reginald GRAY 1930– Painter, notably of portraits, born in Dublin, Ireland, where he studied at the National College of Art, his teachers including John Keating, Séan (John) O'Sullivan and Cecil ffrench Salkeld, from whom he learned Old Master techniques. Group shows included RHA; Irish Living Art Exhibition; Salon de Montparnasse, Paris; La Cour d'Albane, Rouen; and Caravan Gallery, New York. Among his solo exhibitions were Abbott and Holder; Galerie Marie de Holmsky and Irish Cultural Centre, both in Paris; there was a retrospective at UNESCO, Paris, 1994; and a show at Chelsea Old Town Hall in 2004. The film *Reginald Gray – Portrait of a Portrait Artist*, produced by Response Entertainment, New York, won 1st Prize at the city's 2001 Film Festival. Gray lived in London, 1957–62; moved to France, first to Rouen until 1964, in Paris until 2003; then returned to London, but retained his Paris atelier, working between the two capitals. He was professor of painting at the Irish College, Paris, 1993–4. Gray was a full member of the American Society of Portrait Artists and painted notable subjects. These included the playwright Brendan Behan and writer Jill Neville, both 1957; painter Francis Bacon, 1960, National Portrait Gallery; writer Samuel Beckett, 1962, Trinity College, Dublin; and a second portrait of Bacon, 1988, UNESCO; and Laura Parker Bowles, 2003.

Ronald GRAY 1868–1951 Painter, born in London, who after working for a time in the family heating engineering business around the mid-1980s studied with Percy Jacomb-Hood in his studio, at the Westminster School of Art under Fred Brown and at the Académie Julian, Paris. In the first decade of this century visited America several times. Had one-man show at Goupil Gallery, 1923, and also exhibited RA, NEAC, RWS, Fine Art Society and at the Paris Salon, where he won a silver medal. Was a friend of Philip Wilson Steer, Gray's watercolours being especially similar in style to his friend's. Lived in London.

Rosalie Delaquis GRAY 1883–1955 Watercolourist and embroiderer, born in Glasgow, who studied at its School of Art, 1904–9. From 1907 she was a member of the Glasgow Society of Lady Artists. Prior to her marriage to William Gray in 1915, she was known by her maiden name Rosalie Delaquis Campbell.

Stuart GRAY 1925– Lithographer in watercolour, born in Streatham, south London, where he attended the Grammar School. Was a member of NS and UA, RI and RSMA, being notable for his marine paintings. Lived in East Cowes, Isle of Wight.

William Everatt GRAY 1892–1957 Sculptor, studied art at Regent Street Polytechnic School of Art under Charlotte Osborne and Harold Brownsword. Exhibited RA, RSA, RHA, RMS, NS and Paris Salon. Was especially fond of working in wood, and wrote articles on the technique. The General Post Office, Ministry of Agriculture and Russell-Cotes Art Gallery and Museum, Bournemouth, hold his work. Lived near Chessington, Surrey.

Roy GRAYSON 1936– Artist and teacher, born in Sheffield, Yorkshire, where he studied at the College of Art, 1952–6, obtaining his National Diploma in Design (Fine Art). He attended the Royal College of Art, 1958–61, with a French government grant in the latter year. From 1966–9 Grayson worked with the group One Four; Alecto International published his *Flikker Book* in 1972; and Jam Press was founded in 1973. Grayson was professor at the University of Brighton, 1985–7; with studies at St Martin's and Chelsea Schools of Art and Universities of Sheffield and Nottingham; also being a professor at the Royal College of Art and Goldsmiths' College. He took part in many group exhibitions and had numerous solo shows. Grayson was represented by Galerie Fortlaan 17, in Ghent, Belgium, and lived in Beckenham, Kent.

Ashley GREAVES 1961– Painter, born in Croydon, Surrey, who studied at Ravensbourne College of Art; Portsmouth Polytechnic; and Cyprus College of Art. Was leader of the art group for Urban Spaces Scheme, Polytechnic of North London, 1985–7. Group shows included Mountbatten Gallery, Portsmouth, 1983; Kyklos Gallery, Paphos, 1985; Leeds Polytechnic Gallery, Leeds, 1987; Open Exhibition, Johnson Wax Kiln Gallery, Farnham, from 1989; and Royal Over-Seas League Open, 1995, showing the acrylic on paper Girl Showing Parents Her Strawberry Tattoo.

Christopher GREAVES 1913– Designer, painter and teacher, born in Gidea Park, Essex, the son of an architect. He studied at Chelsea School of Art and Central School of Arts and Crafts. Shortly after World War II he taught for a while at London School of Printing, then was art editor of several magazines, as well as being art director of the advertising agency S T Garland. Showed at UA and elsewhere. Lived in Ascot, Berkshire.

Derrick GREAVES 1927– Painter, artist in collage, printmaker and teacher, born in Sheffield. From 1943–8 he was an apprentice signwriter, which he said taught him more than subsequent teaching. After attending evening classes he won a scholarship to the Royal College of Art, 1948–52, then with an Abbey Major Scholarship worked in Italy, 1952–3, where he was influenced by the Italian Realists, notably Renato Guttuso. Sheffield and Italy featured in his first one-man show at the Beaux Arts Gallery in 1953, and it was in the 1950s that he became a notable member of the Kitchen Sink School. With other Kitchen Sink painters he exhibited at the Venice Biennale in 1956, in the following year appearing in the Looking at People show at South London Art Gallery and Pushkin Museum, Moscow. In the same year he was awarded a gold medal for painting at the Moscow Youth Festival and he was also a John Moores Liverpool Exhibition prizewinner. Taught for several years at St Martin's School of Art, Maidstone College of Art and Royal Academy Schools, being head of printmaking at Norwich School of Art, 1983–91. From the 1960s Greaves' work lost its Kitchen Sink grittiness, becoming more poetic, linear and allusive. Graves Art Gallery in Sheffield and Leicester Museum and Art Gallery held retrospectives in 1980. Later solo shows included Chappel Galleries, Chappel, 2001; a seventy-fifth birthday exhibition at Wingfield Arts, Wingfield, 2002; and Paintings & Drawings 1952–2002, at James Hyman Fine Art, and New Prints at The School House Gallery, Wighton, both 2003. Greaves' several published portolios of screenprints and etchings included *Sanskrit Love Poems*, 1987. Work held by many public collections in Britain and abroad, including Arts Council, British Museum, Contemporary Art Society, Johannesburg Public Gallery in South Africa, Philadelphia Museum of Art in America and Tate Gallery. Lived in Weston Longville, Norfolk.

Jack GREAVES 1928– Sculptor, artist in oil, pastel and watercolour and teacher, born in Leeds, Yorkshire, who studied at the College of Art there, 1948–51; Royal College of Art, 1951–4; and British School in Rome, 1960–1. After teaching in Stroud, he was appointed head of the department of sculpture at Cheltenham College of Art. He had a studio in the Cotswolds, 1955–64; was at Ohio State University, 1964–8; worked in America and the Cotswolds, 1968–88; then had a studio in Yorkshire, living in Snainton, Scarborough. Greaves was a member of RWA. Group exhibitions included Three Humanist Sculptors, Zwemmer Gallery, 1960; 19 Young Sculptors, Hillfield Gardens, Gloucester, 1962; Bruton Gallery, from 1970; and widely in America from 1977. Solo shows included Ohio State University, 1966; Stroud Festival, 1969; Search Gallery, 1973; Vorpal Gallery, New York, 1978; and Gallery 200, Columbus, from 1985. Main works included Christ Teaching, Columbus, 1978; The Guardian, Toledo, Ohio, 1981; The Naiad Fountain, Columbus, 1984. RWA, public galleries in Bristol and Coventry and Columbus Museum of Art hold examples.

Leonard GREAVES 1918–1949 Painter, teacher and writer who after attending London University studied at Chelsea School of Art, 1934–8. Prior to World War II he was for two years assistant lecturer at the National Gallery, from 1945 becoming a visiting instructor at St Martin's School of Art. He exhibited RA, NEAC, LG, UA and AIA and had several one-man shows in the 1940s, including Redfern Gallery. Also exhibited abroad. The Contemporary Art Society bought his work, which is held by Bristol and Wakefield public galleries. This was sometimes signed L G. *The Artist*, *The Saturday Book* and *The Listener* published his pictures and he wrote widely, mainly for art and architectural periodicals. Lived in London.

Ronald GREAVES 1916–2005 Artist who studied at Penzance and St Martin's Schools of Art, Birmingham College of Art and the Courtauld Institute. Took part in a group show at City of London, Guildhall, in 1986 and from that year held an annual open studio at Berry Street, including East End Open Studios, 1989. In 1992 exhibited at Lea Bridge Open Studios and The Coffee Gallery, 23 Museum Street. Rosebery's, West Norwood, offered Greaves' work after his death.

Mary GREAVES-VENNING 1919– Painter whose figurative work could have a strong fantasy element, as in her watercolour The Mermaid and the Dolphins, chosen for the Ipswich Open, Christchurch Mansion, Ipswich, 1995. She was born in Upper Norwood, London, was self-taught and only began painting at the age of 63. Although her father was an artist, she "learnt nothing from him, and took no interest in his work as a child", although she added her father's name, Venning, for her work in his honour. A severely disabled husband meant that she was "pretty much tied to home, so painting is my life line." Lived at Combsford, Stowmarket, Suffolk.

Anne GREBBY 1944– Artist and teacher, born in Lincoln. After graduating at Birmingham College of Art Grebby did postgraduate studies at Hornsey College of Art and the British School in Rome. She taught at Sheffield College of Art; was visiting lecturer at art colleges in Manchester, Birmingham, Liverpool, Cheltenham, Newcastle and at the Central School of Art; then in 1988 she was appointed head of painting at Sheffield Polytechnic. As a painter she was concerned with themes including women's issues and wildlife survival. She showed widely in France and in group shows at Whitworth Art Gallery, Manchester, and in John Moores Liverpool Exhibitions. In 1980 she shared a show at Compass Gallery, Glasgow, with Paul Hodges, in the following two years having solo exhibitions at Paton Gallery. Among other shows were Breathe, collaboration with Tim Dunbar, Holden Gallery, Manchester, 2001; and Zum Horizon, solo, Galerie Artists Unlimited, Bielefeld, Germany, and Melanie Manchot's Mother, The Staged Photography Performance and the Body Symposium, at Cornerhouse, Manchester, both 2002.

Alan GREEN 1932–2003 Painter, printmaker and teacher, born in London, married to the artist June Green. He attended Beckenham School of Art, 1949–53, and after National Service in the Far East was at Royal College of Art 1955–8, winning a Major Travelling Scholarship which took him to France and Italy in 1958–9. Won many awards and prizes in Britain and especially abroad. Among his teaching posts were Hornsey and Leeds Colleges of Art and Ravensbourne College of Art and Design. While at Leeds he took part in The Teaching Image, a Leeds College staff show at the City Art Gallery. He also showed extensively in mixed exhibitions overseas. Showed also particularly with Annely Juda Fine Art. Arts Council, British Council and Guggenheim Museum, New York, hold his work, which was abstract, as seen in The British Art Show, chosen by the critic William Packer, which was toured by

Arts Council in 1980. Moved to live near Monmouth in 1987, settling at Llangattock Vibon-Avel, Gwent. The influence of the rural landscape affected Green's meditative work, prompting a change to large horizontal abstracts. He favoured metal oxides such as zinc, cobalt, cadmium, lead and titanium, as well as the earth colours. These he ground and mixed himself, thinking of them "primarily as a substance and then a colour." There was a British Council European touring exhibition in 1994.

Anthony GREEN 1939– Painter and teacher, born in London. Green exhibited in Young Contemporaries in 1956, the year he went to Slade School of Fine Art, where he was until 1960, when a French Government Scholarship took him to Paris. Two years after that he had a first one-man show at Rowan Gallery, with which he showed for many years. In addition he showed with LG, being elected a member in 1964, and RA, to which he was elected in 1977. Green won a Gulbenkian Purchase Award in 1963 and gained a prize at John Moores, Liverpool, show in 1974. In 1967 he won a Harkness Fellowship to America, where he lived until 1969, by which time he had begun to establish an impressive international exhibiting career. In 1964 he taught at the Slade, shortly after beginning a long period of teaching at Royal College of Art. He had a retrospective at RA in 1978, a year in which his work was shown extensively in the provinces, and in Japan in 1987–8, A Green Perspective was held at Pallant House, Chichester, in 1994, and a 1948–2001 review at North Light Gallery, Huddersfield, 2001. In 2003, he shared a show, Obsessions, at the Brewery Arts Centre, Cirencester, with his wife Mary Cozens-Walker and in 2004 his exhibition Diving off the Wardrobe was at the Fine Art Society. Green's work was produced slowly and featured his family and their surroundings, until the late 1980s the flat where he had been brought up and continued to live, then he moved to Little Eversden in Cambridgeshire and his pictures reflected the landscape. Green created his own perspective, a little like what is seen through a fish-eye lens, favoured oddly shaped supports and latterly pictures on free-standing structures. Arts Council holds his work. His daughter Katie was a painter.

Cecilia GREEN 1931–2003 Artist's model, dancer and painter, born in Hackney, London. Her Russian immigrant parents, who just before the 1917 Bolshevik revolution exchanged poverty in Kiev for an East End rag trade sweatshop existence, were determined that the precocious and pretty Cecilia should improve her lot. Despite malnourishment and having to leave school early to work as an assistant window dresser at Fortnum and Mason for £1 a week, Cecilia paid for ballet lessons, eventually dancing for London Festival Ballet. When tuberculosis cut short this career she began modelling at art schools, her dancing experience enabling her to hold a pose for long periods. In 1953 she met Sir William Russell Flint, becoming his favourite and ideal model. He later said: "I had been drawing her years and years before I met her." When Flint's wife was confined to a nursing home, Cecilia became his hostess to the famous. Although invited to model by other artists such as Jacob Epstein and Pietro Annigoni, by 1964 Green found the demands of constant modelling too onerous, and could only be persuaded by Flint to continue part-time for two more years. She had married the fine art consultant John Simmons in 1958. When on holiday they met the international lawyer and oil broker Herbert Bensilum and Cecilia became his part-time personal assistant, a job she enjoyed. When he died she returned to painting, her picture Russell Flint in Picadilly Circus, shown at the Royal Festival Hall, proving one of her most popular. Works by Flint from her collection were offered by Bonhams, Knightsbridge, in 2005.

Daphne GREEN 1926– Painter, born in London, who studied at the Oxford School of Art, her teachers including Peter Greenham, Evelyn Dunbar and Bernard Meninsky. Did some poster work and exhibited Ashmolean Museum, Oxford, and with the local Art Society. Signed work D G. Lived for a time in Oxford.

David GREEN 1929– Watercolourist, teacher, writer and illustrator, born in Southport, Lancashire, married to the artist Gill Green. Began his art training at Exeter in 1946 and moved to Royal College of Art school of design (ceramics) after National Service with the Royal Artillery. Changed direction to study at Hornsey College of Art, 1949–53, painting with Jesse Cast, etching with Norman Janes and lithography with Henry Holzer. Between 1953–7 taught part-time at Harrow, Willesden and Medway Colleges of Art and showed at RA, Leicester Galleries and RE. For next 24 years taught full-time in ceramic department at Carlisle College of Art and the school of three-dimensional design at Bath Academy of Art, taking early retirement in 1981. In 1983 an exhibition of Green's work was held at King's Circus Gallery, Bath, then from 1985 shared regular shows of watercolours with his wife, including Heffer's in Cambridge, Century Gallery in Henley-on-Thames, Linfield Gallery in Wells and elsewhere. Green was a landscapist and many thousands of cards and limited-edition prints were sold. Among books illustrated were *Good Food from Farthinghoe*, by Nicola Cox, 1981, and *English Stone Building*, by Alec Clifton-Taylor, 1983. Green's own books, mainly on pottery, included *Understanding Pottery Glazes*, 1963, and *Experimenting with Pottery*, 1971. His father was William Green, artist and principal of Exeter School of Art. Lived in Woodbridge, Suffolk.

David GREEN 1935– Painter in oil and watercolour, born in London. He became a full-time painter in 1968. Was a member of ROI and NS. Showed at Mall Galleries, Luton Museum, Heffer Gallery in Cambridge, Stamford Arts Centre and in Bedford, near where he lived. Mayor's Parlour in Bedford, Texas Instruments and English Gallery, Boston, in America, hold his work.

Diana GREEN 1945– Painter, printmaker, draughtsman, interior designer and teacher, born in Warwickshire, who studied for her diploma at the College of Art, Birmingham, under David Prentice, 1961–5, and her teaching diploma at the College of Art and Design there, 1965–6. Taught art at Coombe Girls' School, New Malden, 1966–8; was a freelance interior designer, from 1968; taught printmaking at the Adult Education Institute in Islington, north London, where she lived, 1977–9; privately teaching drawing and watercolour from 1991. Group shows included Singer & Friedlander/*Sunday Times* Watercolour Competition and Mary Kleinman Gallery, both from 1989; RWS Open, 1992; Geffrye Museum, 1993; Camden Printmakers, 1995; and PS and RA Summer Exhibition, both 2001. A move to a larger studio enabled Green to return to her favourite medium, oil, and in 2000 she had a solo show at Currell, Islington. Her later works included a boxed set of etchings with text, based on Biblical accounts of the Creation and the Fall. These were shown at Southwell Minster, Nottinghamshire, in 2004.

Elizabeth Helen GREEN: *see* **Helen BEALE**

Gill GREEN: *see* **GILL**

John GREEN 1932– Sculptor in stone, letter-cutter and teacher, educated at St Joseph's College, Ipswich, Suffolk, near where he lived at Washbrook. Served a five-year apprenticeship as a stonemason before studying for his design diploma, sculpture, at Ipswich School of Art, 1951–4, gaining a first-class diploma and Silver Medal, Royal College of Art, 1954–7. Assisted Jacob Epstein, 1955–9; was senior tutor, Orton Trust, from 1969; taught part-time at Ipswich School of Art, 1957–71 and 1984–6; and was director of monument conservation, Croydon College of Art & Design, 1979–80. Large sculpture commissions included churches at Bushey, Poole and Welwyn Garden City; Kuching Cathedral, Sarawak, Malaysia; Ipswich Civic Centre and Shopping Centre, Witham. Had a solo show at John Whibley Gallery, 1971, later exhibiting with Chappel Galleries, Chappel. Painted stone figures were a feature of Green's later work.

John GREEN 1941– Artist who gained his painting and fine art diploma at Southampton Institute. Exhibitions included Art in Boxes, Southampton City Art Gallery, and Havant Open, Before the Eleventh Hour, where he won a prize, both 1997; See Red, Summer Art Exhibition, The Square Tower, Portsmouth, 1998; and Summer 2000, Cadogan Contemporary, 2000.

June GREEN 1935– Sculptor and teacher, born in County Durham, who studied at Sunderland College of Art and Royal College of Art, 1951–5 and 1955–8. While on the staff of Leeds College of Art, in 1964 with her husband Alan Green took part in The Teaching Image exhibition at Leeds City Art Gallery. Green's first solo show was at the London Press Exchange Gallery, 1968, and after that she had one-man exhibitions at Galeries Hervé Alexandre, Brussels, Belgium, 1975; Annely Juda Fine Art, 1979; Gimpel-Hanover & André Emmerich Galerien, Zürich, 1984; and she took part in many group shows. In 1985, she was included in Masterpieces of the Avantgarde, Annely Juda Fine Art/ Juda Rowan Gallery. Later lived in Llangattock Vibon-Avel, Monmouth, Gwent.

Kenneth GREEN 1905–1986 Artist, designer and teacher, full name John Kenneth Green, who spent most of his childhood in Suffolk and who was a friend and pupil of the local landscape artist Harry Becker, who left Green some of his works. Green was educated at Christ's Hospital and studied at Slade School of Fine Art, 1922–4, with a Slade Scholarship in 1923, teachers including Henry Tonks. Green's early work was in the Tonks tradition, although latterly he painted abstracts. As a student he was commissioned to paint a portrait at Cambridge University, which led to others including composer Benjamin Britten, poet Cecil Day Lewis and actress Sybil Thorndike. Green travelled widely, capturing the atmosphere of places such as Cairo, Russia, the islands of the Aegean and the Dordogne. After a first solo show at Arlington Galleries, 1928, Green visited America in the early 1930s, exhibiting at the Ferargil Galleries, New York, 1934. Worked at Glyndebourne Opera, 1935–8, having a show of work done there at Storran Gallery, 1937. Was director of art at Wellington College, 1938–45, while there designing scenery and costumes for the Sadler's Wells productions of Mozart's *Cosi Fan Tutte*, 1944, and Britten's *Peter Grimes*, 1945 (Green appears in books on Britten and his compositions). Later opera designs were made for the Holland Festival and Finnish Opera, Helsinki. As well as regularly exhibiting at the RA Summer Exhibition, 1925–57, as a member with the NS, 1946–62, and showing with NEAC, RP and RBA, Green held shows in Helsinki, Cairo and Geneva and there was a retrospective at Kettle's Yard Gallery, Cambridge, 1972. He was a Chelsea Arts Club member. Green's pictures were in the collections of the Contemporary Art Society; public galleries in Birmingham, Bradford and Leeds; and the National Portrait Gallery holds his 1943 double portrait of Britten and singer Peter Pears.

Madeline GREEN 1884–1947 Painter in oil on canvas, born in London, who studied at Royal Academy Schools. Won a Silver Medal at Paris Salon in 1923 and also exhibited prolifically at Agnew in Manchester, RWA, RA, SWA, Royal Glasgow Institute of the Fine Arts and elsewhere. Spink & Son included two impressive figure pieces in their Twentieth Century British show in 1984. She lived for a time in Ealing, Middlesex.

Margaret GREEN 1925–2003 Painter, notably of small landscapes in a reticent style, born in West Hartlepool, County Durham, married to the artist Lionel Bulmer. She studied at the local School of Art and Royal College of Art, 1944–7, winning Henriques and Travelling Scholarships, a Silver Medal and Painting Prize. Showed with RA, LG, NEAC, Leicester Galleries, William Ware Gallery and in several provincial galleries and touring exhibitions in Britain and abroad. Had a solo exhibition at New Grafton Gallery in 1972. In 2002, Messum's put on From City to Sea the painterly journey of Lionel Bulmer and Margaret Green. Chantrey Bequest, *Financial Times*, Ministries of Information and Public Works and public galleries in Carlisle, Coventry, Leeds and Nottingham hold examples. Lived at Onehouse, near Stowmarket, Suffolk.

Michael GREEN 1929– Auto-didactic artist, and teacher who began painting in 1966 and exhibiting while living in Manhattan, New York City, which "was my art school and teacher." He was influenced "by the three principal areas of living and working: New York City, then London and Italy." He latterly combined sculpture and painting, although "sculpting was not begun until returning to London and setting up a studio there in 1988. Both in painting and sculpting there are always three basic precepts to be maintained: space, structure, tension." Green was born in Nyasaland (now Malawi). He originally studied at the Royal Academy of Dramatic Art, with a Viscountess Northcliffe Scholarship, aged 15. After moving to New York City he was a freelance and decorative designer for Lenox Inc. He was artist-in-residence, Indiana State University, giving master classes in advanced painting, 1980, and at Gallery Morphi, Cyprus, 1992. Later group shows included Art in Boxes and The Collage Show, England & Co, 1992 and 1993; Box, Walsall Museum, Walsall, 1994; Paintings & Sculptures by British & International Artists, Raw Gallery, 1995; Painted Drawings Series, Coombs Contemporary Gallery, 1996 and 1997; and Vital Art 98, Atlantis Gallery, 1998. Among his solo shows were The Bridge Series Drawings 1977–9, Retrospective Part I, Coombs Contemporary Gallery, 1995, and Michael Green: An Artist's Career – Sculpture, Painting, Constructions, Rivington Gallery, 2001. The Smithsonian Institute, Cooper Hewitt Museum, New York City; INA Museum, Baltimore, Maryland; Indiana State University; and several major international corporate collections hold examples.

Nicola GREEN 1972– Painter of figurative work, sometimes with a quirky viewpoint, as in her solo exhibition at The Gallery in Cork Street, 1999. From Edinburgh College of Art she gained a first-class honours degree in painting, 1992–6, her master's, 1996–8. She won a Department for Education and Employment Bursary, 1996; and in 1997 and 1998 Andrew Grant Bequest Scholarships. Group shows included Witnesses of Existence, Demarco European Art Foundation, 1994–5; The New Generation, Compass Gallery, Glasgow, 1997; Hunting Art Prizes, from 1998; Laughing Matters, Your Shout Awards, Winchester, and tour, 2003; and Blind Art, Royal College of Art, 2005. Among Green's solo exhibitions were Royal Brompton Hospital and Vinyl Factory, both 2003. Green was still at art college when she began to paint commissioned portraits. Her work was bought for corporate, public and private collections, private owners including the musician Norman Cook (Fatboy Slim), artist Gavin Turk and comedian Paul Merton. Green lived in London.

Norman GREEN 1921–2006 Self-taught sculptor, assemblage and montage artist, working mainly in wood, also metal and stone, many pieces being bronze-cast in limited editions. Green was born in Boston, Massachusetts, America, and was by profession a magazine publisher. His interest in assemblies started at Harvard, where he studied economics, art history a second subject, and by his mid-twenties he "had collected a warehouse of raw materials." Although he won several art competitions in Connecticut and was persuaded to display work at the Silver and Little Galleries and Optimums, Green sought no further recognition. After moving to Britain in the early 1970s he showed boxed works at England & Co which were praised by the critic Sister Wendy Beckett, who opened his first solo exhibition at Duncan Campbell Contemporary Art, 1994. Wit and invention were characteristics of Green's figurative pieces. In the abstract compositions, said writer Robert Porter, "aged, moody pieces of wood reunite to present us with a silent slab of quiet." Aztec iconography, also African, eastern European and modern American art were influences on works which sometimes took years to gel into their final form.

Paul GREEN 1951– Painter, born in Pontypridd, Glamorgan. He studied at Maidstone College of Art, 1969–70; Cardiff College of Art, 1970–4; and Slade School of Fine Art, 1974–6. Showed in the Whitechapel Open, at the Air Gallery and was a prizewinner in the 1995–6 John Moores Liverpool Exhibition, appearing at John Moores again in 2004. After a first solo exhibition at Oriel Gallery in Cardiff in 1974 had a series in London, where he lived. His 1983 oil on canvas Graig Yr Hesg is held by the Arts Council. In 1989, Green participated in East End Open Studios, Britannia Works.

Peter GREEN 1933– Painter and draughtsman, especially of railways, born in Nantwich, Cheshire, educated at King's School, Macclesfield. He did his National Service in the Royal Electrical and Mechanical Engineers and worked in textiles and publicity; ran an art supplies shop in Wealdstone, 1972–87; then became a full-time artist. His only formal art training was evening classes and what he learned at the Sketch Club, Pinner, Middlesex, where he lived. Green joined the Guild of Railway Artists in 1977, becoming a full member in 1982. His early sketching of steam locomotives developed because his father, the Reverend Cyril Green, was a model railway enthusiast. After answering an advertisement in *Railway Magazine* Green began working for the Channel Tunnel rail link project, painting hundreds of scenes designed to help passengers visualise changes in the network. He also painted London Transport's Steam on the Met events; was commissioned to put his pictures on plates for Davenport Pottery Company; drew aeronautical and architectural scenes, including Pinner High Street; worked for the Ministry of Transport, the Port of London Authority and British Rail; and was principal artist for Union Railways. In 2000 a picture by Green was chosen for the cover of Clive Foxell's book *The Met and GC Joint Line*.

Roland GREEN 1896–1972 Painter of birds in oil and watercolour. Born at Rainham, Kent, Green studied at the Art School in Rochester and then at Regent Street Polytechnic. He had many one-man shows at Arthur Ackermann and Son and in East Anglia. A reclusive man, Green had a studio at Hickling Broad, Norfolk, where he studied meticulously birds and their habits. He illustrated a number of books by himself – *How I Draw Birds*, and *Wing Tips* – and others, including work on Australian birds.

Ron GREEN 1923– Painter, born in Lincolnshire. He was a chartered engineer until 1979, although he was always interested in watercolour painting. Studied under R A Tucker at Gloucester College of Art and held a show there, also exhibiting locally. Upon retirement Green began painting full-time in the Lake District. He showed with Broughton Gallery, Peebles, Thornethwaite Gallery, Keswick, Lake Artists' Society in Grasmere and elsewhere, such as Patricia Wells Gallery, Thornbury. Green was especially keen on northern British landscapes. Lived in Lorton, near Cockermouth, Cumbria.

Stephen GREEN 1918– Painter, printmaker, graphic artist and designer, born in Cobham, Surrey. He was the son of the watercolourist R H Green. Studied at Reading University, 1935–7, and at Royal College of Art, 1937–9 and again in 1942. Exhibited RA, NEAC, Leicester Galleries, AIA and in Denmark. He completed a volume of commercial work for *The Times*, London Transport and so on. Lived in London.

William GREEN 1894–1972 Painter, potter and teacher, born in Hanley, Staffordshire. He attended Hanley School of Art and then the Royal College of Art, 1920–2, under William Rothenstein and Ernest Tristram. Until about the mid-1920s he held appointments as a pottery designer, including a period with Crescent Pottery in Stoke-on-Trent, after which he was on the staff of several art schools, becoming principal of Exeter School of Art from early in World War II, retiring in 1958. He was a noted collector of English watercolours, showing his own work at RA, RWA and elsewhere. His son was the artist David Green. Lived in Exeter.

William GREEN 1934–2001 Painter and teacher, born in Greenwich, southeast London, strongly influenced by German Expressionist art and orchestral music. After several jobs including working in an architect's office, Green from 1952–4 attended the School of Art in Sidcup, Kent, where he eventually settled, influenced by Edward Eade. Having been accepted by the Royal College of Art in 1954 he was not able to start until 1955 as his pacifist leanings put him in prison for three months as a conscientious objector. Influenced by American Abstract Expressionism Green turned to making black abstracts, creating them by pouring and hurling bitumen paint on hardboard and treating the surface brutally, dragging a bicycle on it and setting it on fire. In 1957 Green was included in New Trends in British Art, Rome-New York Art Foundation, Rome; and Dimensions, British Abstract Art, 1948–57, O'Hana Gallery; and he was in Ken Russell's film *Making an Action Painting*, which led to international coverage. In 1958 Green had a first solo show at New Vision Centre Gallery and left the Royal College with a first-class honours degree. Showed in first Situation exhibition at RBA Gallery, 1960, and was lampooned in Tony Hancock's film *The Rebel* in 1961, about the time Green was experimenting in an American Pop Art style. Teaching included a working men's college; Harrow, Walthamstow and other Schools of Art; and Goldsmiths' and Havering Technical College, from which he retired in 1981. Green withdrew from exhibiting from mid-1960s until a solo show at England & Co, 1993, when he was included in The Sixties Art Scene in London, Barbican Art Gallery. One-man exhibition at Gardner Arts Centre, Brighton, 1999.

David GREENALL 1947– Creator of semi-abstract works who left school at 15 and worked in the fishing and building industries, starting to paint in 1975. Did a foundation course at Norwich School of Art, 1982, gaining an honours degree in fine art from Winchester School of Art, 1983–6. Settled at Ness in the Outer Hebrides where the singular landscape of Lewis and the image of the Butt of Lewis lighthouse featured strongly in his pictures. Mixing his own colours from raw pigment and blending mediums such as wax, resin, oil and tempera he produced works of great vigour. Exhibitions included Flying Colours Gallery, Edinburgh, 1993, and Coombs Contemporary, 1994. Greenall was included in New Artists at Piers Feetham Gallery in 2003, where his partner Ruth O'Dell also showed.

Peter GREENAWAY 1942– Film director, painter, curator and writer who, after Forest School, attended Walthamstow College of Art, taught by Margaret Green, becoming a film editor with the Central Office of Information, 1965–76. Although Greenaway made many innovative short films, he was especially known for his cult-following features, rich in art-historical reference and tinged with a quirky humour, such as *The Draughtsman's Contract*, 1982; *The Cook, the Thief, his Wife and her Lover*, 1989; The Baby of Mâcon, 1993; and *The Pillow Book*, 1995. The choice of music for Greenaway's films was catholic, ranging from Vivaldi to Webern, contemporary composers used including Michael Nyman, fellow-artist Brian Eno and Philip Glass. Greenaway also directed a number of operas. There was a string of book credits, often film-related. Greenaway curated exhibitions and installations as well as participating in mixed shows and having solo exhibitions internationally. Later mixed shows included The Director's Eye: Drawings and Photographs by European Filmmakers, Museum of Modern Art, Oxford, and tour; Spellbound: Art and Film, Hayward Gallery; and Freezeframe, Lamont Gallery, all 1996. Solo exhibitions included Nicole Klagsbrun Gallery, New York, America, 1995; Mylos Art Gallery, Thessaloniki, Greece, and tour, 1996; Museo Rufino Tamayo Contemporaneo Internacional, Mexico City, Mexico, and tour, 1997–8; and a 25-year retrospective at Cornerhouse, Manchester, and tour, 1998–9. Greenaway created an epic installation for the 2004 opening of the transformed Compton Verney, Warwickshire, housing the art collection of the philanthropist Sir Peter Moores.

Judith GREENBURY 1924– Painter and writer, born in Bristol. She studied at West of England College of Art, 1943–6, with George Sweet, then under Randolph Schwabe at Slade School of Fine Art, 1946–7. She painted portraits, landscapes and figures in landscape. Was elected to RWA in 1979, also exhibiting at NEAC and RA. Her solo shows included Forest Row and Alpine Galleries. RWA holds her work. After her husband's death in 1989 and a serious accident in 1995, during recovery Greenbury wrote *Spey Portrait*, an illustrated memoir of their fishing the Scottish river, published 1997. The following year published her memoir of George Sweet. *Piers and Seaside Towns: An Artist's Journey*, in 2001, was launched with a show of her pictures at Piano Nobile Fine Paintings. Lived in Henley-on-Thames, Oxfordshire.

Mary Charlotte GREENE c.1860s–1953 Painter and teacher noted for traditional landscapes, as in her The Vicarage at Granchester, made famous by the Rupert Brooke poem and offered by Bonhams, in The East Anglian View, at Lynford Hall, Mundford, 2000. Greene was born in Takeley, Essex, and studied at the St John's Wood School of Art and Royal Academy Schools. She was the principal of the Garden Studio at Cambridge and lived for a time in the county at Harston. Exhibited at RA, Walker Art Gallery in Liverpool and elsewhere. Signed work with a monogram of her three initials.

Michael GREENE 1949– Artist who attended Sutton School of Art, 1966–8, and Epsom School of Art, 1968–72. Greene showed at RA and NEAC and participated in East End Open Studios, based at Norfolk House Studios, 1989.

William GREENGRASS 1896–1970 Printmaker, born in the parish of St Saviour, Channel Islands, who was a pupil at Grosvenor School of Modern Art and was a keeper at Victoria & Albert Museum. It holds a colour lino-cut by him. Fond of the lino-cut, he produced images that owe much to Vorticism. Redfern Gallery showed his work.

Robert GREENHALF 1950– Artist whose main subjects were landscape and wildlife. He was born at Haywards Heath, Sussex, studied at Eastbourne and Maidstone Colleges of Art and graduated in 1971. Greenhalf chose to sketch in the field and usually used only one etching plate, printing in up to eight colours. His work was shown in many mixed and solo exhibitions, in London, including RA Summer Exhibition, the provinces and abroad. In 1979 it was featured in the Royal Society for the Protection of

Birds magazine *Birds*. In that year he was elected a member of the Printmakers' Council, in 1981 the SWLA and in 1982 RBA. Bircham Contemporary Arts gave Greenhalf a one-man exhibition in 2003. Lived near Rye, Sussex.

Jane GREENHAM: *see* **Jane DOWLING**

Peter GREENHAM 1909–1992 Painter and teacher, brother of the artist Robert Duckworth Greenham, married to the painter Jane Dowling. He was educated at Dulwich College and won a scholarship to read history at Oxford, although he read English. Studied at Byam Shaw School of Drawing and Painting under Ernest Jackson, 1935–9. He then became a schoolmaster in Oxford but continued to paint. Was elected RA in 1960. Greenham succeeded Sir Henry Rushbury as keeper of the Royal Academy Schools in 1964, retiring in 1985. Showed widely in mixed exhibitions and from 1972 had many solo exhibitions at New Grafton Gallery. He was a member of its portrait centre, and among his subjects were Sir Isaiah Berlin, Dr F R Leavis and Lord Hailsham. Tate Gallery holds his work. In 1984–5 the Arts Council and Norwich School of Art put on a touring show of work by Greenham and his wife. They lived at Otmoor, Oxfordshire.

Robert Duckworth GREENHAM 1906–1976 Painter, printmaker, mural artist and draughtsman. Born at Streatham, Surrey, brother of Peter Greenham. Studied at Byam Shaw School of Art and at the Royal Academy Schools, where he won several scholarships and medals. Exhibited RA, RP, NEAC, LG, RSA, ROI, in the provinces and abroad. Principal works include Bathing Beach, purchased by the Australian government, Near Cromer and Snow in Dulwich. Greenham was especially fond of painting beach scenes, his slightly stylised draughtsmanship and unique palette being instantly recognisable. Lived at Gillingham, Dorset.

Martin GREENLAND 1962– Painter, and teacher, born in Marsden, West Yorkshire, whose work was rich in symbol and imagery. He studied at Nelson and Colne College of Art, 1979–81, and Exeter College of Art, 1981–5. Was a graphic designer with Age Concern, 1987–8, then taught at several venues part-time, including St Martin's College in Lancaster from 1998, the year he was elected to Lake Artists' Society. Showed at Whitworth Young Contemporaries, 1985; Gallery North, Kirkby Lonsdale, 1987–8; and several times at John Moores Liverpool Exhibition, including 1991–2 and 1995–6. Held regular solo shows from 1987 in Cumbria, where he lived at Sedbergh, later ones including Piccadilly Gallery, from 1997. For some time his work was permanently on show at New Year Gallery in the town. Lived in Bowness-on-Windermere, Cumbria.

Edwin GREENMAN 1909–2003 Painter, printmaker and teacher, born in Beckenham, Kent, where he studied at the School of Art, 1926–9, under Henry Carr; was then at Royal College of Art, 1929–33, teachers including Gilbert Spencer and Ernest Tristram. Elected RP in 1968, also exhibiting at RA, in Czechoslovakia and America. His teaching positions included head of Sir John Cass School of Art, which expanded enormously under his direction until he chose to retire, after 18 years, in 1969. Greenman favoured the traditional disciplines, which showed in his own work. After retirement he concentrated on portrait painting, sharing a London studio with the painter David Graham. Greenman remained at his easel until his ninetieth year, notable subjects including Sir John Harvey-Jones, former chairman of Imperial Chemical Industries; Lord Northbrook; and Heather, former wife of the conductor André Previn; the Windsor Herald; and the Moderator of the General Assembly of the Church of Scotland. Victoria & Albert Museum holds his work. Died in Epsom, Surrey.

Tom GREENSHIELDS 1915–1994 Figurative sculptor, painter, draughtsman and illustrator, born in Devon, grandson of the Victorian painter Edourd van Goethem. After Sherborne School Greenshields studied at the Slade School of Fine Art, then painted mainly watercolours and illustrated books, showing at RA. During World War II Greenshields was commissioned in the 94th Field Regiment, won the Military Cross in Normandy, was wounded and during service in Germany met Renate, a Lutheran pastor, his future wife who joined him in England, where from 1946 he ran the family dairy farm. She described her experiences in the book *Lucky Girl Goodbye*, first published 1988. Until 1980, when his eldest son took the farm over, Tom had little time for art. Although he lost the use of his right hand in a farming accident in 1981, he successfully transferred skills to his left, devoting all his time to drawing, painting and sculpture. Had many exhibitions, the website http://www.artworksgallery.co.uk/Greenshields.html listing his work. His daughter, Maria, was also a sculptor.

John GREENSMITH 1932– Watercolourist and teacher, born and lived in Sheffield, Yorkshire. He studied at the College of Art there and taught art locally at All Saints School. Was elected to NEAC in 1978 and five years later to RWS, also showing with RA and RCamA.

Joseph GREENUP fl. from c.1915–1946 Portrait and figure painter who won scholarship to Royal College of Art around 1913–16, after a period at Birmingham Municipal School of Art. Greenup became a member of RI in 1936 and RBSA in 1945 and showed at RA, including posthumously in 1947. Lived in London.

Eileen Constance GREENWOOD 1915– Painter, craftworker and teacher, born in London. Was married to the artist Ernest Greenwood. She studied at the London County Council School of Arts and Crafts and then at Royal College of Art, 1934–7, with Ernest Tristram. She went on to hold a number of teaching posts, including principal of Sittingbourne College of Education. Showed RA, RI, SWA, LG and Kensington Salon, having joint shows with her husband at Kensington Gallery in 1951 and 1953. She was an enthusiastic member of SEA and several education committees including Middlesex bought her work. Lived at Broad Street, near Hollingbourne, Kent.

Elizabeth GREENWOOD 1942– Painter, draughtsman and teacher whose work sometimes had a jokey, popular culture-related quality. She was born in Cheshire and trained at Coventry College of Art, St Martin's School of Art and Goldsmiths' College School of Art. Taught in London schools, in adult education and youth centres and Avery Hill College of Education. Her work appeared in many mixed shows and she had solo exhibitions at Proscenium Gallery, Greenwich Theatre Gallery and, in 1978, at Woodlands Art Gallery.

Ernest GREENWOOD 1913– Artist and teacher, born in Welling, Kent, husband of the painter Eileen Greenwood. He studied at Gravesend Grammar School, painting at the Royal College of Art under William Rothenstein and, after a travelling scholarship enabled him to work at the British School in Rome, he entered the etching and engraving school of the Royal College under Malcolm Osborne and Robert Austin. Greenwood's World War II Army service, 1941–6, included a time on the staff of the School of Military Engineering as an architectural draughtsman. Retired in 1961, having been a teacher then an inspector of art education with Inner London Education Authority and Kent Education Committee. Had a first solo show in 1947 at Kensington Art Gallery, about a dozen following by retirement. During this he travelled extensively, for a decade as a specialist art lecturer with Swan's Hellenic Voyages. Showed with RA and RI and was elected a member of RWS in 1973, being president for eight years from 1976 during which time the Society re-established itself at Bankside. Had a retrospective at New Metropole Arts Centre, Folkestone, 1972, another at County Hall, Maidstone, 1997. Tate Gallery and several provincial galleries hold his work. Lived in Broad Street, Kent.

Frank GREENWOOD c.1883–1954 Etcher who studied under Frank Short at South Kensington and in Paris under Maxime Lalanne. He was mainly known for his views of Manchester which record vanished buildings. Showed at Walker Art Gallery in Liverpool and at Manchester's City Art Gallery where in 1976 he was included as an associate of the local artist Adolphe Valette in his centenary show.

Jill GREENWOOD 1910–1995 Artist and designer, born and lived in London, originally Gillian Crawshay-Williams, her mother the miniaturist Joyce Kilburn, her grandfather the painter John Collier, for whom she sat. Studied at Central School of Arts and Crafts, 1927–30, a great friend of the illustrator Lynton Lamb, then learned etching in Florence. In 1931 she joined the clothes firm Jaeger, where she was known as Crawshay, staying with them about 30 years and revitalising their displays. The first Regent Street decorations were hers, for the Festival of Britain, in 1951; in 1954 she designed the Street's Christmas lights; and in 1959 she decorated Oxford Street's lamp-posts. During World War II, at the Ministry of Works, she wrote and illustrated a best-selling booklet *Make Do and Mend*. From 1938 was married briefly to the artist Walter Goetz, in 1940 marrying Tony Greenwood, the Labour Member of Parliament who in 1970 became Baron Greenwood of Rossendale. Lady Greenwood remained a staunch Socialist, a leading worker for the Campaign for Nuclear Disarmament who also set up the Hampstead Community Centre and the Tony Greenwood Charitable Trust. In later years she taught art to pensioners at Age Concern in Hampstead. She was a skilled sketcher of political personalities, contributing to the *Daily Mail*. Had two solo shows of her own pictures, which frequently featured cats, at Barron Gallery, with a notable exhibition at Camden Arts Centre in 1978.

John GREENWOOD 1959– Painter, born in Leeds, Yorkshire, who studied at York College of Arts and Technology, at Cheltenham and Royal College of Art. He constructed meticulous, pictorially mischievous and witty pictures in which sexuality was a recurrent theme. They owed much to artists he admired: Yves Tanguy, Max Ernst and Salvador Dalí and had a Surrealistic quality. In 1990 Greenwood won the Midland Bank Purchase Award and the Burston Award and spent three months in residence at Cité Internationale des Arts, Paris. Works were exhibited in group shows in Switzerland and London and in 1992 were featured in Young British Artists at The Saatchi Collection, which holds Greenwood's work.

John Frederic GREENWOOD 1885–1954 Printmaker and watercolour painter, born at Rochdale, Lancashire. Studied at Shipley School of Art, 1904–7, Bradford School of Art, 1907–8, and the Royal College of Art, 1908–11, under W R Lethaby. He became head of the school of design at Leeds College of Art until 1948. Exhibited RA, RBA, RE and widely throughout several continents. The British Museum and Victoria & Albert Museum hold his work. Lived at Ilkley, Yorkshire.

Julia GREENWOOD 1951– Watercolourist and draughtsman in pen and ink. She studied at Camberwell School of Arts and Crafts. Was given many commissions, ranging from a drawing of the boat used by the Transglobe Expedition to a copy of an Elizabethan map for the Aldeburgh Society. Settled in Suffolk, had two shared shows in Aldeburgh and a solo show at Sue Rankin Gallery, 1990.

Orlando GREENWOOD 1892–1989 Painter, designer and draughtsman, born in Nelson, Lancashire. From the age of 13 he worked in his uncle's cotton mill. After studying at Goldsmiths' College School of Art and Army service in World War I, in the 1920s Greenwood became notable as the mill worker-turned-artist, famous for his still lifes and classical set-pieces. Greenwood painted still life and many self-portraits because he said that he was too poor to afford models, although his exhibition with Spink in 1925 was termed "a triumph" by the *Daily Mail*, and 28 works out of 30 were sold for £2,500. Greenwood showed widely with RBA of which he was a member, RA, Colnaghi's, Beaux Arts Gallery and abroad. After Greenwood's house was bombed in World War II he moved with his wife to the north, settling in 1967 in Ulpha, Cumberland, the year he gave up painting. Greenwood had a baffling range of styles. As well as poster designs for London Underground and Great Western Railway and shop advertisements for Liberty's and Whiteleys, his own painting ranged from nineteenth-century academic to pictures in an almost gaudy palette influenced by Cubism. Studio sale at Christie's South Kensington, 1990. A small centenary show was held at The Bloomsbury Workshop, 1992.

Philip GREENWOOD 1943– Printmaker and painter, teacher, born in Dolgellau, Merionethshire. He studied at Harrow College of Art, 1961–5, teachers including Christopher Sanders and T W Ward, then at Hornsey Teachers' Training College, 1965–6, with Peter Green. Was elected to RE in 1982, also showing at RA, Tate Gallery and several overseas printmakers' shows. Gallery One, Barnes, held a retrospective of landscape etchings from 1970s onwards in 2002. Arts Council, Tate Gallery and galleries in Derby, Lincoln, Oldham and Sheffield hold examples. Lived in Cobham, Surrey.

Robin GREENWOOD 1950– Sculptor, painter and teacher, born in Manchester, who studied at Wimbledon School of Art, 1968–71, then St Martin's School of Art, 1971–2, under

Anthony Caro. He later taught at both, living in London. In 1978 Greenwood gained an Arts Council Major Award. Group exhibitions included Northern Young Contemporaries, 1967; New Sculpture at Norwich Cathedral, 1974; Arts Council Exhibition at Serpentine Gallery, 1979; and Woodlands Art Gallery, 1983, in Have You Seen Sculpture from the Body? While he always sculpted, Greenwood's painting was restricted to two main periods: between 1985–95, following a visit to Venice, and from 2001 onwards. In 2003, there was a solo show, A Summary of Small Paintings 1989–2003, at deliART, including richly coloured abstracts.

Sydney GREENWOOD 1913–2001 Painter, printmaker and teacher, born in Stalybridge, Cheshire. He studied at Goldsmiths' College of Art, Croydon School of Art, Westminster and privately in Paris in the early 1930s and again in 1946. Obtained a London University diploma in art teaching. Lectured at Manchester College of Art, becoming vice-principal of Southampton College of Art in 1950–73. Was a member of RWA, also showing with Arts Council, RA, Upton Lodge Gallery in Tetbury and elsewhere. Represented in private and public galleries in Britain and North America. Did mural work for Barclays Bank and illustrations for Longman, Oxford University Press and other publishers. Greenwood was "particularly interested in landscape with an abstract element rather than a descriptive treatment". Lived in Sway, Hampshire.

Timothy GREENWOOD 1947– Painter and etcher of wildlife (the Royal Academician Frank Short bequeathed him his etching equipment), born in Chatham, Kent. Aged 10, Greenwood won his first prize as a schoolboy in a Fry's Chocolate-sponsored national competition for a painting of The Creation. Six years later, he used as his first model a rat found by his mother in her deep-freeze. Attended Ravensbourne and Camberwell College of Art, aged 20 became the youngest member of SWLA, and appeared in national newspapers and was filmed by the BBC Television programme *Animal Magic*. Greenwood was employed by the Royal Society for the Protection of Birds as a warden, also working as a keeper on Forestry Commission land. He was commissioned to illustrate the bird section of the 1971 *Shell Nature Guide*, in that year being funded by the company to travel through Spain and Morocco to gather material for a book on European and North African birds of prey, part of his extensive research travels abroad. The first volume of *The Atlas of Rare Pheasants*, a collector's item, illustrated by Greenwood for Palawan Press, appeared in 1997. Greenwood also showed at RA, Arthur Tooth and Sons and Gallery 77 and had solo exhibitions at Furneaux Gallery from 1971. Lived at Loch Tummel, near Pitlochry, Perthshire.

Geoffrey GREETHAM 1934–1992 Sculptor and teacher, born near Keighley, Yorkshire, who studied at Keighley School of Art and Camberwell School of Arts and Crafts in the late 1950s. From 1962–5 Greetham assisted the sculptor Henry Moore. He was one of the assistants working on the gigantic enlargement of Moore's Lincoln Center Piece when it cracked and almost self-destructed as the result of the application of too much plaster to the upper parts; in 1964, he was involved in a minor revolt of assistants over low pay (Greetham was then earning £15 a week). From 1965–7, Greetham had a sculpture fellowship at Coventry College of Art. Spatial relationships were important to him, as in the untitled piece commissioned by Coventry Planning and Redevelopment Committee and until 1974 sited in Market Way in the city centre; and in his lyrical abstract work Precinct, in steel painted red, at Exhall Grange School. Greetham taught briefly at Winchester School of Art, being on its staff in 1969 when he had his solo exhibition at Drian Galleries. This included large and small sculptures and cut-outs in mild steel, aluminium and wood and plaster. By then he had participated in group shows at the Savage Gallery, 1960 and 1961; Contrasts, New Vision Centre Gallery, 1961; Manchester City Art Gallery, 1964; and Experiments with Form, Grosvenor Gallery, 1966. The Sidney R Solomon Collection, Michigan, America, held his work. While at Winchester Greetham became a dealer in antique clocks and watches, which then preoccupied him. He and his wife Betty had three sons. He died of cancer in Brighton, Sussex.

Thomas Affleck GREEVES 1917–1997 Draughtsman, architect and writer who began making fantastical drawings while at Radley College. Spent a year at Slade School of Fine Art, then studied architecture at Cambridge and at Architectural Association, interrupted by World War II service, and practised as an architect for many years. Showed at RA Summer Exhibitions and had solo exhibitions at Robin Garton Gallery, 1978, and Garton & Cooke, 1987. The heart of Greeves' work was a series of views of cities in varying stages of ruin and decay using a technique inspired by Piranesi. RIBA drawing collection holds several examples. Greeves' work was published in *The Saturday Book*, *Country Life* and *The Architects' Journal*. He published an illustrated monograph on Bedford Park, where he lived, 1975, and in 1994 his *Ruined Cities of the Imagination* and other drawings appeared in a limited edition.

Barbara GREG 1900–1983 Wood and lino engraver and watercolourist. Born in Styal, Cheshire, Barbara Greg studied at the Slade School under Henry Tonks and the Central School of Arts and Crafts under William Palmer Robins. Married the artist Norman Janes. Greg exhibited widely, including the RA, NEAC, RE, RHA, RWS and SWE. The Contemporary Art Society bought her work. She illustrated a number of books with natural history themes, such as *Pastures New*, by Ian Niall, and *Enigmas of Natural History*, by E L Grant Watson. Lived in London and died in hospital in Enfield.

Annabelle GREGORY 1941– Artist in collage, antique textile dealer and teacher, born in Richmond, Surrey. She studied at St Martin's School of Art, 1958–9, and Camden Arts Centre, 1973–4, teachers including Elisabeth Frink and Joe Tilson. Was a member of the Oxford and Banbury Art Societies, also exhibiting with SWA and at Artweeks, Oxfordshire, and Museum of Modern Art, Oxford. Had a solo show at Deddington Art Gallery in Oxfordshire, where she lived at Adderbury. Specialised in portraits, flowers and figure work.

Bessie Denton GREGORY 1894–1970 Watercolourist who was brought up in Cheshire. She studied at Wallasey School of Art, showing at RCamA, BWS and elsewhere. Exhibited at RCamA, of which she was honorary secretary for a time, from 1945 until just before her death, in Wallasey, Merseyside. Mainly lived and painted in the Carnarvonshire area of north Wales.

Christine GREGORY fl. c.1905–1960 Sculptor, potter and teacher, born in London. Exhibited frequently at RA, also at RMS, Walker Art Gallery, Liverpool, SWA, Walker's Galleries, extensively in provinces, in Paris and Toronto, Canada. She was elected a fellow of RBS and her figure Rhythm is illustrated in its volume *RBS: Modern British Sculpture*, published in 1939. City Museum and Gallery in Stoke-on-Trent and Ulster Museum, Belfast, hold her work. Between 1918–37 Gregory was modelling instructor at Hammersmith School of Arts and Crafts. Lived in London.

Dorothy Craven GREGORY 1927– Painter and teacher, born in London. Her studies included a period, 1944–8, at Chelsea School of Art with Ceri Richards and Raymond Coxon. Exhibited RA. NEAC, SWA, LG and elsewhere. Lived in London.

Joy GREGORY 1959– Artist, photographer and educator who did a foundation art course at Buckinghamshire College of Higher Education, 1980–1; graduated with honours in communication art and design, Manchester Polytechnic, 1981–4; and gained her master's in photography from the Royal College of Art, 1984–6. She was administrator/co-ordinator at the North Paddington Community Darkroom, 1987–90; lectured at Staffordshire Polytechnic, 1987–91; was education co-ordinator, Photofusion, 1991–3; administrator, Organisation for Visual Arts, 1993–4; senior lecturer in fine art, Cardiff Institute, 1994–5; lecturer in communication media at Kent Institute of Art & Design, 1995–6; and from 1996 was a visiting lecturer in photography at London College of Printing. In September/October 1999 Gregory was artist-in-residence, Pallant House Gallery, Chichester. In a lecture there, she termed herself an artist in mid-career whose opportunities had been restricted because of gender and race, although she had not had to face the initial teething problems of the black arts movement. She was represented in the Autoportraits exhibition, Cameraworks, 1990 and tour, and Johannesburg Biennale, 1995, and tour. This was followed by a residency outside Cape Town, from which stemmed the project Memory and Skin, about the cultural connections between Britain and the Caribbean. For Cape Town Museum she made the series Lost Histories. Gregory's show The Language of Flowers was at the Zelda Cheatle Gallery, 2004. The artist was an amateur scientist, keen on chemistry. Lived and worked in London.

Karen GREGORY 1951– Painter and muralist who graduated with honours from the University of East Anglia, 1969–72, gaining a similar degree from St Martin's School of Art, 1974–7. In 1984–6, Gregory worked on the History of Somers Town mural, in 1988 on another in Sutton. Exhibitions included Reflections at CCA Galleries and Whitechapel Open, at Whitechapel Art Gallery, both 1988, and in 1989 East End Open Studios, when she was based at Victor House.

Mac GREGORY 1934– This was the working name of Malcolm Gregory, painter and teacher, born in Stony Stratford, Buckinghamshire. He attended Cambridge School of Art, 1951–5, tutors including John Bolam, John Smith and John Hookham; joined the Army, 1955–8; then studied at Chelsea School of Art, 1958–60, taught by Frederick Brill, Jack Smith, Prunella Clough, Vivian Pitchforth and Lawrence Gowing; and Goldsmiths' College School of Art, 1960–1, under Robert Brazil. Robert Greenwood was an early supporter of Gregory, selling his work from the Heffer Gallery, Cambridge, with a solo show there, 1956. Gregory taught adult classes and in secondary education for 22 years, becoming head of art at Stanground Comprehensive, Peterborough. Although Gregory was a member of UA and Lincolnshire Society of Artists, he resigned because "although I am gregarious, I prefer working alone". His many mixed show appearances included Young Contemporaries; RA Summer Exhibition; Piccadilly, Portal, RBA and Mall Galleries; Guildhall, London; Usher Gallery, Lincoln; and Down Town Gallery, Fort Worth, Texas, America. Among over a score of solo shows were John Hutton Gallery, from 1966; Everyman Club, 1967; Canstatter Volksbank, Stuttgart, West Germany, 1984; Old Fire Engine House, Ely, from 1985; Gallery 44, Aldeburgh, 1987; Wigmore Hall, 1993; and Norman Cross Gallery, Peterborough, 2003. The Fenland landscape, with which he was "besotted", was a strong feature of his work, which was for many years in oils, "but of late I have worked in mixed media on two-dimensional planes." Commissions included murals in the London home of Lord and Lady Silkin and one from the Football Association celebrating the 15-year chairmanship of Sir Bert Millichip. Cambridge and Surrey Education Committees, London County Council, Northampton Medical Centre and corporate collections held examples. Lived in Boston, Lincolnshire.

Malcolm GREGORY: *see* **Mac GREGORY**

Margaret GREGORY 1927– Painter in oil and acrylic of richly coloured abstract/figurative works, born in Belfast, Northern Ireland. Graduated from the Guildhall School of Music, 1945, in 1955 attending evening classes in art under Kulwant Aurora. Music, Samuel Palmer, Odilon Redon and Buddhism were cited as influences. Between 1956–75 Gregory was in the Royal Opera House chorus, taught drama and was a member of Edward Lucie-Smith's poetry group, in 1975 moving to Bristol to paint. Exhibited at RWA, Cleveland Bridge Gallery in Bath, Plumbline Gallery in St Ives and Beatrice Royal, Eastleigh. Fuji Art Museum holds her work.

Nuala GREGORY 1965– Artist and lecturer who gained a first-class degree in fine art from University of Ulster, Belfast, 1988. She lectured there and ran many workshops. Showed in the Claremorris Open Exhibition, 1990; with Belfast Young Contemporaries, One Gallery, 1992; and in 1994 in Beyond the Partitions, organised by Queen Street Studios, Belfast, with which she was associated. Solo shows included Works on Paper, 1990, at Peacock Gallery, Craigavon. She was later commissioned by the Arts Council of Northern to make a big screen for their offices in Belfast.

Stephen GREGORY fl. from 1970s– Artist and teacher who trained at Newcastle University and Manchester Polytechnic and showed in group and solo exhibitions in north of England and in London. He was artist-in-residence in Milton Keynes, 1977–9, and in the next two years was a part-time lecturer at Sheffield Polytechnic. From 1982 he held a series of positions as a community art worker, including Northampton, Cheshire and Nottingham. Department of the Environment, Manchester Polytechnic, Open University and Milton Keynes Development Corporation hold his works.

Steven GREGORY 1952– Sculptor, stonemason and teacher, born in South Africa. He gained an honours degree in fine art at St Martin's College of Art and held a City and Guilds craft and advanced craft qualification in stonemasonry. Gregory was an indentured apprentice for five years at Westminster Abbey and Hampton Court and did three years as foreman mason on Richmond Terrace restoration, Whitehall. He periodically worked in the construction industry as a project and construction manager; lectured at art colleges and polytechnics on titanium and metal processes, also teaching sculpture to adults and art classes for children; spent three years on the design and mass production of titanium jewellery; and was invited to collaborate with the ion implantation group at the Department of Nuclear Physics, Harwell, on a since-patented product. Exhibited Sculpture at Goodwood from 1995, and his work The Sentinel was part of the 1997 Lewes Sculpture Trail. RTZ Corporation and Cass Electronics commissioned his work, also held by Leicestershire Education Authority. Lived in London.

Suzi GREGORY 1967– Sculptor who gained her master's degree from Chelsea School of Art, in 1989 winning first prize in the Henry Butcher Prize competition. Her 1992 soaring White Curl, in white-painted mild steel, is one of the so-called gateways to the Birmingham Heartlands area. Other work by Gregory is at Butler's Wharf in the London docklands area and she also completed commissions for Heal's furniture store in Tottenham Court Road and for Sir Terence Conran.

Donald GREIG 1916– Painter and printmaker with a strong interest in marine subjects, married to the artist Rita Greig. He was born in London, son of the watercolourist James Greig, and studied at Southend College of Art with the watercolourist Charles Taylor. Was elected a member of RSMA in 1967, the year he won a Gold Medal at Paris Salon, also showing at RA, RI and NEAC. National Maritime Museum, Greenwich, holds Greig's work. Lived in Woodleigh, Devon.

Johnny GREIG 1967– Artist using photography, born in Guayaquil, Ecuador, his family returning to England when he was two. After education at Worth School, Sussex, Greig graduated in psychology from the University of Bristol. After leaving Bristol in 1989 Greig was a commercial photographer, working for magazines, design and advertising agencies, shooting portraiture and still life. He had a first show, Photosynthesis, at the New Academy Gallery in 2004.

Rita GREIG fl. from 1960s– Painter and printmaker, born in Norwich, Norfolk, married to the artist Donald Greig. After grammar school studied art privately. She was elected to both NEAC and ROI in 1974, the year she won a Silver Medal at Paris Salon, becoming a member of RWA in 1983. Chase Manhattan Bank holds her work. She was based in Woodleigh, Devon.

Hugo GRENVILLE 1958– Painter and teacher who, using a rich palette, specialised in painting aspects of the theatre and performers, and theatrical moments in daily life. Attended life classes at Chelsea School of Art, 1978, while serving in the Coldstream Guards, 1977–83. After working for the advertising agency J Walter Thompson, 1983–4, ran a company dealing in contemporary art, 1984–9, then became a full-time painter, having attended Heatherley's School of Art open studio in 1988–9. Mixed shows included Chelsea Art Society from 1975; Armed Forces Art Society from 1980; Young British Artists, Alpine Gallery, 1986–7; ROI from 1991; and Brian Sinfield Gallery, Burford, 1994. Solo shows included Tryon & Swann Gallery, 1995, David Messum, from 1997, and The Wally Findlay Gallery, New York, 2006. Commissions included studies and a large painting of the tercentenary masque at Chatsworth House, 1994; among portraits were General Sir Michael Gow and the former Archbishop of Canterbury Lord Runcie. Grenville was a regular contributor to *The Artist* magazine. From 2001 he was course director of Red House Studios at his home in Mendham, Suffolk. Grenville continued to teach from his studio after a 2006 move to London.

Harold GRESLEY 1892–1967 Landscape and figure painter in oil and watercolour. Born in Derby, he was the son of the painter Frank Gresley. Studied at Derby School of Art, 1912, then with Arthur Spooner, 1919, at Nottingham School of Art, and at the Royal College of Art. Exhibited RA, Cooling Galleries, RWS, UA and elsewhere. Derby Museum and Art Gallery and Nottingham Art Gallery hold his work. Gresley, who was assistant art master at Repton School, lived at Chellaston, Derbyshire, and was a member of Derby Sketching Club.

Nicola GRESSWELL 1954– Artist and teacher, born in Oxford, who attended the Polytechnic there where she did a foundation course, 1972–3, followed by Camberwell School of Arts and Crafts, 1973–6, studying painting and textile printing. In 1976–7 took a course at London University's Institute of Education. After three years' part-time teaching at a London comprehensive school and Amersham College of Further Education, set up own silkscreen print studio near Oxford while continuing to live and paint in London. Showed at RA Summer Exhibition from 1983, also exhibiting at Casa Pupo Gallery, Cale Art and Thumb Gallery. Had a solo print show at Barbican Centre Foyer, 1984, a solo show of watercolours at Minsky's Gallery, 1985.

Hugh GRESTY 1899–1958 Architectural and landscape painter. Born at Nelson, Lancashire, he studied at the Lancashire School of Art and at Goldsmiths' College School of Art under Edmund Sullivan. Exhibited RA, RBA, RI, RSA and Walker Art Gallery, Liverpool. Lived at St Ives, Cornwall. Manchester City Art Gallery holds his work.

Kenneth H GRESTY 1928–2002 Painter and teacher, born in Manchester, where he studied under Harold Williamson at Regional College of Art from 1944–51, with a two-year break from 1946. Held several teaching appointments in the area, finally at Bolton Sixth Form College. Was elected to MAFA in 1954, also showing with RA and elsewhere. Lived in Sale, Cheshire, later at Borth-y-Gest, Gwynedd. Manchester City Art Gallery holds his work.

Keith GRETTON 1934– Painter, printmaker, ceramist, teacher and art fair organiser who trained at Stafford College of Art in the 1950s. Gretton was head of art at Borough Road College until 1982. In 1990, he returned to printmaking; to painting in 1992, the year he co-founded the Battersea Contemporary Art Fair; in 1996 with Penny Gretton erected his first installation; and in 1998 began ceramic pieces and curating shows, including art sites, for Wandsworth 2000 Arts Festival. Exhibited extensively in mixed exhibitions, including the RA, RBSA, RWA, Mall Galleries, PS, RE, AIA and at many commercial galleries including Redfern, Llewellen Alexander, Woodstock, New Academy and in the provinces. Had many solo shows, including Durham University, Riverside Studios, Zwemmer's at Courtauld, Dance Attic and Stables Art Galleries. Department of Trade and Industry, Chelsea and Westminster Hospital and South London Community Care Hospital Trust own examples. He lived in London.

Jenny GREVATTE 1951– Painter of colourful, slightly stylised work, and teacher, born in Bristol, who at Leicester Polytechnic, 1969–70, did a foundation course, then an honours degree in fine art, 1970–4. She was involved in adult education in Leicestershire, 1978–84; was a visiting lecturer at De Montfort University, 1980–1–4; lectured part-time at University of Leicester, 1984–98; and was a part-time tutor at Loughborough College of Art and Design, 1996–8. In 1982 and 1992 Grevatte was a visiting/exchange artist to Saarland, Germany. Took part in many group shows, including from 1980 Browse & Darby; Ash Barn, Petersfield, from 1982; Scottish Gallery, Edinburgh, from 1984; Austin/Desmond, from 1988; and New Ashgate, Farnham, from 1994. Had many solo exhibitions, latterly ones including The John Davies Gallery, Stow-on-the-Wold, 1999, with a retrospective, Leicester City Museum, 2001. The University of Leicester; Abbot Hall, Kendal; Christ's College, Cambridge; and British Oxygen Company held her work.

Michael GREVATTE 1943– Sculptor and teacher producing figurative and abstract work in a range of materials, born in Nkana, Northern Rhodesia, who lived in Sussex, 1944–63; travelled in Australia and New Zealand, 1963–5; then gained his diploma in art and design, fine art (sculpture) at Leicester Polytechnic, 1969–72. Mike Grevatte was artist-in-residence, Nottingham City Hospital, 1982–3. He had a number of solo exhibitions and took part in many mixed shows, later ones including Mabon Gallery, Crewkerne, and Millfield, Street, both 1999, and Church Farm Galleries, Shrawley, and Possi Gallery, Castle Cary, both 2000. Public sculpture commissions included bronze figure of Steelworker, outside Council Offices, Corby, 1989; Swan and Norman Knight, on main road through Mountsorrel, Leicestershire, 1993; and Carved Stone Seat for Coventry Canal, 1998. Lived in Glastonbury, Somerset.

David GREY 1906–1994 Artist, designer, film director, editor and writer, born in Twickenham, Middlesex, as Charles Henry Caulfield, names he hated. Grey's show at the Wertheim Gallery in 1938 included his designs for the ballet; originals of the illustrations for *Borzoi*, the £1,000 prize autobiography of his friend, the dancer and choreographer Igor Schwezoff, which Grey ghost-wrote; and designs for the Flemish legend play *Reynard the Fox*, performed at Leiden University in 1936. Grey had joined the Vic-Wells Ballet as a dancer in October 1937 and was by then a brilliant linguist, speaking German, French, Spanish Dutch and Russian, all with a good accent; a fine pianist; and an omnivorous reader. His Bloomsbury flat contained curtains, cushions and chairs designed by him. Solo show at Sadler's Wells, 1939. Grey married the dancer Eva Leckström and like her danced with Colonel W de Basil's Ballet Russe de Monte Carlo and with Ballets Jooss in North and South American tours in the 1940s. In the 1950s Grey worked as a documentary film director for Shell. A shake-up in the Venezuelan oil industry made him change course, and he became art editor for the *Caracas Journal*, 1955–62, then, back in England, was art editor for *Apollo Magazine*, 1962–84. He continued to paint abstract and Op-Art from the 1960s to the 1980s, his main influence being Victor Vasarely. His son, Kevin Grey, was also an artist. Died in Surbiton, Surrey.

Frederic Millward GREY 1899–1957 Painter, draughtsman and printmaker, born in London. Studied art at Central School of Arts and Crafts under F E Jackson, Bernard Meninsky, A S Hartrick and Richard Garbe. He was a lecturer at the National Gallery and Tate Gallery early in the 1920s, went to the National Gallery of South Australia, Adelaide, and then set up the North Adelaide School of Fine Arts, which he ran until 1942. Extensive work in Australian public collections. He was eventually president of the Royal South Australian Society of Arts and principal of the state's School of Arts and Crafts. Lived at Toorak Gardens, South Australia.

Marcus GREY 1960– Painter, of Canadian nationality, born in London, who was resident in the United Kingdom from 1979. He studied at Ontario College of Art, Toronto, 1977–9; Slade School of Fine Art, 1979–84, with a year out; then Sotheby's Education Department, 1987. He became the paintings and prints specialist at Rosebery's Fine Art auction rooms, in south London, while continuing to paint. Notable shows included richly coloured imaginative figurative works, shared with François Lannes, at The Gallery in Cork Street, 2002; Mystical Himalayas, shared with the French sculptor Cécile Tissot, Flat 8 Hinde House, 14 Hinde Street, 2003; and solo exhibitions, Gods & Places, recent paintings of India, organised by Indar Pasricha Fine Arts, at 22 Connaught Street, 2003, and Minus-One, 2004. Among other exhibitions were Canadian Artists in London, Royal College of Art, 1984; Brinkgasse, Cologne, West Germany, 1987; Towner Art Gallery, Eastbourne, 1991; OECD, Paris, 1997; Salon Art, Nature, Animaux, Paris, 2001; and Rosenberg Gallery, Belfast, 2002. Private collections in Europe and North America held Grey's works. He had a studio in north London.

Nina GREY 1907– Sculptor, born in Eastern Galicia in what was then Austria, moving to Vienna as a child. Having studied at a Jewish teachers' college she taught from late 1920s to 1939, when with her husband she settled in London. Studied at Hornsey and St Martin's Schools of Art. Exhibitions included Ben Uri Art Society, 1962, which holds her work.

Florence GREY-EDWARDS 1892– Painter, chiefly in oil, born in Brookline, Massachusetts, America, her father being the artist George Lee. She was educated in Boston and in Paris, studying with William James at Boston's Museum of Art, then in England at the Slade School of Fine Art, 1925–7, with Henry Tonks and Philip Wilson Steer. Signing her work F G E, she showed at RA and NEAC. Lived in London.

Michael GREY-JONES 1950– Painter using a variety of media, notably watercolour, and teacher, born in Carmarthen, who lived for many years in Kent, settling at

Rainham. He studied at Maidstone College of Art and the Royal Academy Schools. Went on to teach watercolour part-time at Eton College. In 1994 his meticulous depiction of terrace houses, Chatham, won the £15,000 first prize in The Singer & Friedlander/*Sunday Times* Watercolour Competition. Grey-Jones had gained an award in 1992 but, realising the rules excluded paintings previously shown in London as ineligible, he withdrew and the prize went to another painter.

Ralph Glanville GREYSMITH 1874–1953 Painter and designer, born in Manchester of an artistic family. Studied at Brighton School of Art and Académie Julian, Paris. He was eventually responsible for art teacher training at Brighton School of Art. Exhibited RA, RBA, RI, NEAC and in the provinces. Brighton Museum and Art Gallery holds his work. Finally lived in London.

Launce Benedict GRIBBIN 1927– Painter, printmaker, sculptor, photographer and teacher, born in Gateshead, County Durham. He studied at Sidcup School of Art, 1944–6, then Goldsmiths' College School of Art, 1948–9, his teachers including Ruskin Spear and Drake Brookshaw. Studied art history at Courtauld Institute, 1950–3, gaining an Italian government scholarship for postgraduate studies in Venice, 1953–4. Gribbin was in the education department of the Victoria & Albert Museum, 1972–7, was head of the history of art and design at London College of Printing, 1977–8, then lectured for Sotheby's Educational Studies, 1989–91. Gribbin first showed at NEAC in 1946, later at LG, RA, Paris Salon and elsewhere. He had two London solo shows in 1952–3. Although he enjoyed "a 'success of esteem', this was never an economic proposition, and since 1963 I have been instead a photographer who lectures to his own slides on art history." He had "no interest in non-figurative painting". Lived in St Albans, Hertfordshire.

Bernard Finegan GRIBBLE 1873–1962 Painter, especially of architectural and marine subjects, born in London, son of the architect Herbert Gribble. Bernard was married to the artist Eleanor Mabel Gribble. His first art tuition was with his father, then he studied at the South Kensington Schools and with Albert Toft. Exhibited RA extensively, also ROI, Royal Glasgow Institute of the Fine Arts and elsewhere. His work is in public galleries in Bournemouth, Preston and overseas. He was marine painter to the Worshipful Company of Shipwrights. Member of the Savage Club. Lived at Parkstone, Dorset.

Eleanor Mary GRIBBLE 1883–1960 Painter, designer, book illustrator and teacher, born in London, who studied at Ipswich School of Art, Royal College of Art and at British Museum. She taught at Ipswich School of Art, designed for Tibbenhams in Ipswich and ran her own private studio school. She was a keen student of ecclesiastical decoration and Queen Mary bought her work. Showed at RA, SWA and abroad. Lived in Ipswich, Suffolk.

Kenneth GRIBBLE 1925–1995 Draughtsman, painter and teacher, born in Sparkbrook, Birmingham. He studied at Harrow School of Art, 1943, with Ernest Heber Thompson; Camberwell School of Art, 1946–7, teachers including William Coldstream, Claude Rogers, Laurence Gowing and Victor Pasmore; and Slade School of Fine Art, 1947–50. Gribble then began a series of teaching posts, latterly being art advisor to Somerset Council Council Education Department, 1972–80, then principal of Maidstone College of Art, 1980–4. Showed at MAFA from 1956, with Lincolnshire Artists at Usher Gallery in Lincoln from 1961, RWA from 1970 and elsewhere. Had a solo show at Phillips Gallery, Middlesbrough, 1955, later ones including Taunton Brewhouse Theatre, 1977. Manchester City Art Gallery, Usher Gallery and galleries in Middlesbrough, Salford and Ilminster hold examples. Gribble said that the Slade tradition, Sickert and the later Euston Road School were important influences. Lived in Sidmouth, Devon.

Paul GRIBBLE 1938– Realistic painter, typical subjects country scenes and the Henley Royal Regatta. He won a scholarship to the West of England Academy, Bristol, then went into advertising as a graphic designer, winning many awards. Continued to paint, learning much from the wildlife artist Edwin Penny. Gribble left advertising in 1987 to be a full-time painter, showing in London and continental capitals. In 1999 shared a show with Janet Duncan at Century Galleries, Henley-on-Thames, in 2002 one with same galleries at Hartley Wintney.

Deborah GRICE 1974– Landscape painter and illustrator, born in Beverley, Yorkshire, for whom "art was always something I just did – I couldn't help it." After a foundation course at Riley College in Hull Grice studied graphic design (illustration) at Glasgow School of Art, 1993–6, Mick Manning her senior tutor, and graduated with first-class honours, winning the Landscape Painting Design School Bursary. She then studied for her master's degree in natural history illustration and ecological studies at the Royal College of Art, 1996–8, under John Norris Wood, the written part of her degree being on dualism (mind and body) and its effects on the environment. In 1998 she won the Worshipful Company of Painter-Stainers Award for illustration, the RTZ Travelling Scholarship for travel, with which she spent two months in New Zealand, and first prize, The Folio Society Award, illustrating Jeanette Winterson's novel *The Passion*. She carried out widespread illustration commissions, from 2000 including a series of book covers for titles by Julia Blackburn, including *Daisy Bates in the Desert*, *The Emperor's Last Stand* and *Charles Waterton 1782–1865*. Trips to the Outer Hebrides had convinced Grice that "landscape painting was for me", but the New Zealand stay "left me confused about my work as a landscape painter and I felt taking on some illustration projects would help me distance myself from my subject matter." Between 1998–04 she travelled extensively, including America, India, Singapore, Malaysia, Australia, New Zealand, Fiji, Canada, the Orkney Islands, Hong Kong and the United Arab Emirates. Exhibitions included Coombs Contemporary and SWLA at Mall Galleries, both 1998; Eight Mind Spaces, solo, Schumacher College, Devon, Green; KPMG, 2001; and The Fairfax Gallery, Tunbridge Wells, 2003. Grice also produced work for the Rebecca Hossack Gallery and Archeus Fine Art and curated and retailed through The Land Gallery. Lived in Lockington, Yorkshire.

Valery GRIDNEV 1956– Figurative painter, born in the Urals, Russia, married to the artist Katya Gridneva. He was educated at Sverdlovsk Art College, 1976–80, and at the St Petersburg Academy of Arts, 1983–90, from 1990–4 working in its creative studio. He also took an advanced course of studies at the USSR Academy of Arts. Gridnev's graduation project was a picture called Early Years, which won him the Academy's prestigious Gold Medal. Gridnev was a member of the Russian Artists' Federation from 1991, from 1999 living and working in England based in Oxford. As well as initially showing in Russia, Gridnev soon began exhibiting abroad. He took part in various exhibitions in New York and Gissen, Germany, in the early 1990s. His many British appearances included Alberti Gallery, 1998; Pastels of the Century, Mall Galleries, Frank Herring Award, 2000; PS, The Discerning Eye and ROI, those three at the Mall Galleries, 2001; and Cricket Fine Art, Arndean Gallery, and Drake Gallery, both 2002. He had a personal show at One Three Nine Gallery in 2001. In 2003 he shared an exhibition, The Ballet & other Paintings, with his wife at Brian Sinfield Gallery, Burford.

Katya GRIDNEVA 1965– Figurative painter and draughtsman, born in the Union of Soviet Republics, married to the artist Valery Gridnev. She took part in drawing classes at the St Petersburg Academy of Arts, 1995, while studying in the portrait studio there, 1993–9, in the latter year moving to England, based in Oxford. As well as exhibiting in Russia, Germany and America, Gridneva showed in England from the mid-1990s, in 1995 exhibiting with the Michael Simpson Gallery. Other shows included the PS at the Mall Galleries; and Cricket Fine Art at Arndean Gallery and Drake Gallery, both 2002. In 2001, she had a personal show at One Three Nine Gallery. In 2003 she shared a show, The Ballet & other Paintings, with her husband at Brian Sinfield Gallery, Burford.

Mary GRIERSON fl. from 1950s– Botanical watercolourist born in Bangor, North Wales. From her childhood she was drawing and painting plants. During World War II she joined the Women's Auxiliary Air Force, working as an interpreter for the photographic reconnaissance unit, then joined an aerial survey firm. Studied with the painter and plantsman John Nash, and with his encouragement applied for the post of botanical illustrator at Royal Botanical Gardens, Kew, which she held until retirement. She then freelanced, jobs including painting endangered species in Israel for the Nature Reserve Authority; and from 1974 she regularly went to Hawaii at the invitation of the National Tropical Botanic Garden, to add to its archives. Chose to work from the living plant in pure transparent watercolour, which meant her output was governed by the seasons. Work appeared in many scientific journals, including *Curtis's Botanical Magazine*, and books illustrated included *Mountain Flowers* by Anthony Huxley, 1967, and C Grey-Wilson's *The Genus Cyclamen*, 1988. Was awarded five gold medals by the Royal Horticultural Society. Held a series of solo exhibitions, including Spink & Son, 1990.

Peter GRIERSON 1963– Artist who studied at St Martin's School of Art and in Northampton, gaining an honours degree in fine art. Group shows included the 1982 John Player Portrait Award at National Portrait Gallery; Laing National Art Competition at Mall Galleries in 1991; *The Guardian* Art for Sale exibitions at Whiteleys from 1992; and in 1994 he was a finalist in The Alasdair Gilchrist Fisher Memorial Award at Cadogan Contemporary, with Abstract Expressionist work. Had a series of solo shows at Alba Fine Art from 1986, in 1987 showing at Barke Gallery, New York.

Ronald GRIERSON 1901–1992 Multi-faceted artist and designer who studied at Grosvenor School of Modern Art, 1926–9, with Iain Macnab. From 1946–9 he was a visiting teacher at Camberwell School of Arts and Crafts. In 1930 Grierson married fellow-art student Enid Martin; inspired by Edward McKnight Kauffer they taught themselves to weave. Ronald Grierson's designs caught the spirit of each decade of his career and show a continued interest in painting, Braque and Rothko being notable influences. Among his activities are working as a consultant designer for S J Stockwell (Carpets) Ltd; designing for Liberty's and Heal's; a rug for Guildford Cathedral; lino-cuts; and the book *Woven Rugs*, 1979. Showed at Victoria & Albert Museum, which holds a considerable archive, Leicester and Redfern Galleries. Lived in London.

Peter GRIEVE 1936– Abstract sculptor and teacher, born and lived in London. He studied at Bromley College of Art, 1954–7, and Royal Academy Schools, 1957–61, taught in Greece, 1961–4, then became senior lecturer in sculpture at Birmingham Polytechnic. His exhibitions included Young Contemporaries, 1960; RA Summer Exhibition from 1973; and Serpentine Summer Show 1, 1980. In that year he shared a show at Air Gallery. Solo exhibitions included Ikon Gallery, Birmingham, 1975.

Robert GRIEVE 1924– Painter, printmaker, collagist and teacher, mainly of abstract work containing an allusive interplay of colour and images. He said: "I don't think you should get everything out of a painting at one glance. You should be able to come back to it and see other connections." Chinese album paintings were an influence. Bob Grieve studied lithography with Henry Trivick at Regent Street Polytechnic School of Art, 1953–5, and at Swinburne Technical College, Melbourne, 1956–8. He made several study trips to Japan in the 1960s and to the Soviet Union and Cuba in the 1980s. He won a series of awards over 25 years from 1959 and taught graphic art widely in Victoria, being president of the Print Council of Australia, 1973–8. While in England, Grieve took part in the first Australian Artists' Association exhibition at the RWS gallery in Conduit Street in 1953. Other notable group shows included Tokyo Print Biennial from 1960; Contemporary Australian Printmakers, Tokyo and New York, 1984; and Australian Artists at Landell Galleries, California, 1987. Later solo shows included a series at Holdsworth Galleries, Sydney, from 1985, and David Ellis, Melbourne, from 1987. Australian National Gallery in Canberra and many other Australian public collections hold examples.

Chris GRIFFIN 1945– Figurative and abstract artist in various media, born in Maes-y-cwmmer, Mid-Glamorgan, who studied fine art at Gloucestershire College of Art in Cheltenham and at Royal College of Art. He was a freelance artist then from 1977, showing at RA Summer Exhibition, Riverside Gallery in Crickhowell and at 1993 Wales Art Fair, Cardiff. Rural and industrial scenes of south Wales were a speciality. Ten-year retrospective at Oriel Washington Gallery, Penarth, 2002. Good examples of Griffin's work, using a fierce red and orange palette, were included in Welsh Painters Past and Present, organised in 2005 by John Davies Fine Paintings at Upper Swell, Stow-on-the-Wold, although latterly the artist concentrated on showing in the principality. Griffin won the Anstruther Prize at the Royal College of Art in 1975, a National Prize Winner in the Laing Landscape Competition in 1997 and a Regional Prize Winner in 1998.

Denise GRIFFIN 1964– Sculptor, painter and teacher, born in Erpingham, Norfolk, married to the artist Peter Griffin. With him, from 1997, she was involved in the prototype of "the tallest sculpture in the world", a 500-foot bronze Buddha for Maitreya Project International, for north India. Denise Griffin did a foundation in fine art at Bournemouth College of Art, 1983–4; graduated with honours in sculpture, Camberwell School of Art, 1984–7; and from 1988–9 undertook a 12-month research scholarship into Buddhist art and architecture in northern India. From 1991–3 she took training in traditional Tibetan painting techniques in Dharamsal, India; from 1993–4 built a two-metre statue in a monastery in Katmandu, Nepal; in 1994–5 one of 1.5 metres for a Tibetan nunnery at Puli, Taiwan; in 1996–7 worked on a variety of commissions for private international clients at a studio in London; and during 1997 was resident artist at Cenrezig Institute, Queensland, Australia, teaching various skills. She was based in Weymouth, Dorset.

Ella GRIFFIN 1898–1953 Painter and teacher. Studied at Chelsea School of Art, 1915–20, where she later taught. Exhibited extensively, including RA, SWA, ROI, NEAC and elsewhere. Lived in London.

Frederick GRIFFIN 1906–1976 Artist and designer, born in Nottingham, who studied at the local School of Art with the sculptor Joseph Else. Griffin did a wide range of commercial work, including British Railways, British Overseas Airways Corporation and shipping firms. He was a member of SGA, ROI and NS from 1970–6. Showed RA, RSA, LG, RSMA and elsewhere. Lived in London.

Peter GRIFFIN 1947– Painter and teacher, born in Wakefield, Yorkshire. He went to an elementary school and then worked as guillotine operator for a printer's. He had always wanted to be a painter, and when he saw a newspaper item that it was possible to study art without formal qualifications he applied and did foundation studies at Wakefield School of Art, 1970–1. Was then at Loughborough College of Art, 1971–4, and Royal College of Art, 1974–7. Gained Rome Scholarship in Painting to British School in Rome, 1977–9. Rome became a major influence on his work. From 1979–83 was lecturer at Canterbury College of Art, then during 1980s taught at many art schools as a visiting tutor. After being artist-in-residence at Patrick Allan-Fraser School of Art, Hospitalfield, Arbroath, in 1987 and similarly at Cyprus College of Art, Paphos, 1989–90, Griffin taught at West Surrey College of Art part-time. From 1974, when he showed with West Riding Artists, Griffin was in many group shows, being a prizewinner in the 1982 Spirit of London Exhibition at Festival Hall. Had a solo show in Wakefield in 1974; later solo shows included Angela Flowers Gallery, 1986; Gallery Gloria, Nicosia, 1991; Austin/Desmond Fine Art, 1991, and Broadbent 2002. Griffin's work, which had a jokey, Surrealistic element, was based on personal themes, such as the Icarus, Man and Dog and Ram Series. He believed in "pushing paint to the point of destruction, and then starting all over again".

Peter GRIFFIN 1965– Sculptor and teacher, born in Beverley, Yorkshire, married to the artist Denise Griffin. With her for Maitreya Project International from late 1997 he created the prototype of a 152-metre (500-foot) bronze Buddha, the same height as a 50-storey building, for north India, "the tallest sculpture in the world". For this 12-year undertaking, involving working with engineers and architects through to completion, the Griffins were also engaged on designing the exterior of the statue's plinth, a 50-metre stone structure to support the statue and decorative relief carvings to embellish the plinth's exterior, including eight 12 metre-high carved stone lions and eight eight metre-high stylised floral relief carvings. Peter Griffin did a foundation course in fine art at Grimsby School of Art, 1983–4; graduated with honours in sculpture, Camberwell School of Art, 1984–7; then undertook a 12-month research scholarship into Buddhist art and architecture in northern India, 1988–9, with INTACH (the Indian National Trust for Art and Cultural Heritage). He also studied stone letter-cutting with Andrew Whittle and stone masonry at Weymouth College, Weymouth, and, during 1991–3, trained in traditional Tibetan sculpting techniques with Kesang Dorje, the Dalai Lama's personal statue maker, while being engaged on private sculpture commissions. From then on Griffin was involved in many sculptural projects worldwide, including the Jinsui Temple, Taipei, Taiwan, 1994–5; being resident artist, Cenrezig Institute, Queensland, Australia, 1997, where he taught skills including casting, gilding and painting; and the Jamyang Buddhist Centre, London, 2002–4. He was based in Weymouth, Dorset.

David Lloyd GRIFFITH 1956– Painter of atmospheric landscapes, concentrating on the north Wales area of Colwyn Bay, Denbighshire, where he was born, and the Conwy Valley. He specialised in small panels in oil and slightly larger watercolours, always painted quickly en plein air. Larger oils were most often completed in a sitting. Good examples of his painterly work were included in Welsh Painters Past and Present, at The John Davies Gallery, Upper Swell, Stow-on-the-Wold, in 2005. Griffith trained at Wrexham for his foundation year; for a number of years attended life drawing classes; finally studying four years with the Open University. He became a full member of the RCamA in 1996.

Edward Hales GRIFFITH 1909–1982 Painter and teacher, born in Birkenhead, Cheshire, who attended Birkenhead School, Liverpool College of Art, 1926–9, then the Royal College of Art, 1930–3. He did part-time teaching at Laird School of Art and St Anselm's Secondary School, Birkenhead, 1934–9; Alsop Grammar School, Liverpool, 1940–1; was in the Army as a gunner-signaller, 1941–7; then taught at Liverpool College of Art from 1947 for over 20 years. In the late 1970s, after retirement, he returned to the College to paint in the life room. Griffith was a member of the Liverpool Academy of Arts. He also exhibited in Watercolours, Gouaches and Drawings by Liverpool Artists, at Bluecoat Chambers, 1950. Finally moved with his daughter to live in the Sudbury area of Suffolk. Walker Art Gallery, Liverpool, and the Museum of Liverpool Life have works by him.

Frank GRIFFITH 1889–1979 Highly individual painter and draughtsman of portraits, landscapes and still life, born in north Wales, who initially trained with W Beach in Folkestone. A friend of his parents, the painter Théo van Rysselberghe, suggested that Frank should study in Paris at La Palette and with the important theorist and member of the Nabis, Maurice Denis, at L'Académie Ranson. The rather diffident Griffith's friendships with André Dunoyer de Segonzac, Roger de la Fresnaye and Paul Signac in Paris and in England with the Camden Town Group painters Charles Ginner and Walter Sickert, with whom he studied, helped him develop as an artist. Griffith travelled extensively in England and on the continent. Exhibitions included Baillie Gallery, London Salon, RP and RBA. Phillips sold a group of his pictures at Bayswater in 2001.

Hanmer GRIFFITH 1880–1969 Painter of landscapes, born Monmouth. Retired there having been an estate agent in Ystradgynlais, Breconshire. He showed with SWG and Wye Valley Art Society and had several solo exhibitions in Ross-on-Wye. His illustrations for W J Smart's *Where Wye and Severn Flow*, of 1949, typify his interest in the landscape of this border area, where he died at Skenfrith.

Lillian E A GRIFFITH 1877– Sculptor, painter, miniaturist and teacher, born at Abersychan, Monmouthshire. She studied at Wimbledon School of Art, the Slade School of Fine Art and Westminster School of Art, her teachers including Alfred Drury. Exhibited for many years at RA, Walker Art Gallery in Liverpool and at Paris Salon. National Museum of Wales, Cardiff, holds marble and bronze panels by her, notably Bindie, the head of a boy, to which she was much attached. For several years she held art classes for Glamorgan County Council and taught miniature painting at Swansea School of Art. Lived at Hengoed, Glamorgan.

Owen GRIFFITH 1957– Artist, born in Cardiff, who was "primarily interested in language, in words and signs and how these interrelate," according to Galerie Fortlaan 17, Ghent, Belgium, which represented him. Griffith's texts were included in special publications. Words appeared in his other works cut from rubber, painted on wood or three-dimensional. He lived and worked in Edinburgh, where he attended the College of Art, 1975–81. Among his group exhibitions were Contemporary Abstraction, Fruitmarket Gallery, Edinburgh, 1981; The Wand and The Feat, Paul Steen Gallery, Edinburgh, 1986; Zeitgenössische Kunt in städtischen Raum, Museum für Moderne Kunst, Frankfurt am Main, Germany, 1990; Acte de présence, Galerie Fortlaan 17 in Lofting, Deinze, Belgium, 1994; and Künstler der Galerie, Galerie Brüning + Zische, Düsseldorf, Germany, 1996. Beginning in 1988 Griffith worked a lot with the German sculptor Michel Sauer, from 1990 creating joint works. Later exhibitions with Sauer included Machine and Coathanger Visit the Cousins, Boekie Woekie, Amsterdam, Netherlands, 1994. Among Griffith's later solo exhibitions was Applied Instruosophics, Galerie Brüning + Zische, 1998.

Andrew GRIFFITHS 1956– Sculptor – notably a stone carver – and teacher, who did a foundation course at Wrexham College of Art, 1974–5, then gained an honours degree in fine art sculpture at Central School of Art & Design, 1983–6. He studied bronze casting with Ab Abercrombie and did two years' life drawing with Cecil Collins. Griffiths' work experience included assisting the sculptors Barry Flanagan, Bill Woodrow and Liliane Lijn and the printmaker Norman Ackroyd; working in the A&A Sculpture-Casting Foundry; and teaching at Slade School of Fine Art. From 1994 Griffiths was lecturer in sculpture at Carmarthen College of Art & Technology. Commissions included bronze figures for a Tokyo theatre park, 1992. Took part in many mixed shows, with a solo exhibition at Swansea Botanical Gardens, 1995. Had a studio at Llangennech, Dyfed.

Anthony GRIFFITHS 1960– Artist, born in Oxford, who studied at Bournville School of Art and Craft, 1978–80, and at Bath Academy of Art in Corsham. Among his mixed shows was The Self Portrait: a Modern View, which toured from Artsite Gallery, Bath, 1987, in which Griffiths showed work in limewood. He had had a first solo show in the city the year before.

Archie Rhys GRIFFITHS 1902–1971 Painter, muralist and printmaker, notable for his pictures of miners, born Archie Griffiths in Aberdare, Glamorgan, moving to Gorseinon as a child. He is sometimes referred to as Rhys Griffiths, his chosen name after moving to Hampstead in 1931. Griffiths began working in a tinplate factory and then, after four years as a miner at Mountain Colliery, studied at Swansea Art College, 1919–24. An outstanding student, he won two first prizes at the Ammanford National Eisteddfod in 1922 and was awarded Glamorgan County and Royal College of Art Scholarships, enabling him to study at the Royal College, 1925–8. The principal, Sir William Rothenstein, was a continuing advocate of Griffiths' abilities. In 1928, he was runner-up in the Prix de Rome and was given a Royal College travelling scholarship of £100 to spend three months in France and Italy. On his return he had a solo show at Glynn Vivian Art Gallery, Swansea, 1928–9. He was at this time a member of the Swansea Art Society, an early supporter being the sculptor Sir Goscombe John. Griffiths completed a mural mixing Christian iconography and Social Realism at the Working Men's College, a commission gained for him by Rothenstein. Reports of his supposed destitution appeared in the Swansea press and only the news of a solo show at the Young Welsh Association, sponsored by the Glamorgan Society and opened by Rothenstein, dispelled this gossip. His mural for the Glynn Vivian Art Gallery of miners working underground was created in 1933. Although during the the 1930s Griffiths obtained many portrait commissions and worked for the film industry, from 1935 his life was obscure and demand for his work tailed off, leaving him dependent on his wife Edith Griffiths, a commercial artist. After reclusive later years, he died in London.

Barbara GRIFFITHS 1948– Painter, writer and illustrator, born in Plymouth, Devon. For many years she showed under her unmarried name Barbara Millett. Griffiths did a pre-diploma course at Plymouth College of Art, 1965–6; gained her art and design diploma at Maidstone College of Art, 1966–70; and her higher diploma in art and design from the Slade School of Fine Art, 1970–2. She participated in group exhibitions at Greenwich Gallery, Piccadilly and Rufford Galleries and at the Museum of Modern Art, Oxford, and had a solo show in 1974 at the Lasson Gallery. In 1995 Griffiths moved in America, where she was based at New Canaan. "I have been studying the lives of the women in a small Connecticut town while becoming one of them myself." She continued in group shows, on several occasions with the Counterpoint group, and in Essays in Arts & Sciences, University of New Haven, 2004.

In that year her one-man show New Canaan Observed: A Field Study was at the Silvermine Arts Guild Gallery. Her written and illustrated books for young adults included *Frankenstein's Hamster*, 1990, and *A Gruesome Body*, 1994, and she was included in the Oxford University Press anthology *Dread and Delight*, 1995, and Heinemann's *Way with Words*, 1996.

Barbara GRIFFITHS fl. from mid-1970s– Painter and teacher, notably a landscape watercolourist, who graduated with honours at Maidstone College of Art, 1973–6. She taught watercolour painting at adult education centres in Kent. Among her exhibitions were RE, 1976; Drew Gallery, Canterbury, 1982; Newbury Spring Festival, 1985; and three-man show at Woodlands Art Gallery, 1989.

Brian Cyril GRIFFITHS 1968– Installations artist, born in Stratford-upon-Avon, Warwickshire. He graduated in fine art at the University of Humberside, gaining his master's at Goldsmiths' College School of Art in 1995–6. Griffiths was included in the Neurotic Realism series of exhibitions starting at Saatchi Gallery in 1999, creating a series of realistic-looking control panels which turned out to be made of cardboard boxes and household rubbish. In 2000–1 he shared a show at The Curve, Barbican Centre. He had work in the Saatchi Collection, where his Beneath the Stride of Giants was included in Galleon and Other Stories in 2004. He lived in London.

David GRIFFITHS 1939– Painter, teacher and gallery owner, born in Liverpool. After attending Pwllheli Grammar School he went to the Slade School of Fine Art, 1957–61, then taught art in Birmingham for several years in the 1960s. In the latter part of the 1960s he opened the David Griffiths Gallery in Cardiff, later the Albany, and organised Pwllheli Art Gallery during the summer. Worked in television as a freelance illustrator before concentrating on portraiture, painting many eminent figures. Subjects included HRH The Prince of Wales, two archbishops, two lord chancellors and two speakers of the House of Commons. Among Griffiths' commissions were Bertrand Russell for University College, Swansea, and Lord Hailsham for the House of Lords. Other subjects included the politician Enoch Powell, singer Bryn Terfel, harpist Osian Ellis and painter Kyffin Williams. Griffiths was purchaser of the year for CASW and an hon. member of the White-robed Order of Druids. Had a retrospective exhibition at National Library of Wales, Aberystwyth, 2002. The City Hall, Cardiff; Museum and Art Gallery, Newport; Royal College of Surgeons; University of Wales, Cardiff; and Liverpool University are other holders of Griffiths' work.

David GRIFFITHS 1961– Artist who graduated with honours in fine art from Falmouth School of Art, 1981–4, attending the Slade School of Fine Art, 1984–6. Mixed exhibitions included Riverside Open, Riverside Studios, 1987; Make You Believe, Screenworks Gallery, Portsmouth, 1988; and Proportionate Play, Third Eye Centre, Glasgow, and New Works April '89, London Filmmakers' Co-op, and East End Open Studios, at Carpenter's Road, all 1989.

Diane GRIFFITHS 1957– Full-time painter and printmaker from the 1980s who, after graduating in illustration, became interested in etching, attending workshops at Gainsborough's House, Sudbury. In her printmaking Griffiths became increasingly interested in form and colour, changing to collographs as they offered a more painterly approach. In 1987 she moved to Norfolk and set up a business, Etchings Et Cetera, supplying prints and cards to over 100 galleries throughout the United Kingdom, including the Victoria & Albert Museum Craftshop, Manchester Royal Exchange and Paperchase. Her atmospheric paintings on canvas, which explored colour and texture, moved towards abstraction while focusing on the north Norfolk coastal and marsh areas, particularly around Syderstone. Griffiths was artist-in-residence for the Poetry next to sea festival in the county in 2003, also having a solo exhibition at Kentmere House Gallery, York. There was another at Broughton House Gallery, Cambridge, in 2004. She was also commissioned by North Norfolk District Council to provide a large work for a concert featuring the Britten Sinfonia and contemporary music. Bircham Contemporary Arts, Holt; Cambridge Contemporary Arts; Nevill Gallery, Canterbury; Stockers Gallery, Wells-next-the Sea; and Wildwood Gallery, Bury St Edmunds, sold her pictures.

Glyn GRIFFITHS 1926–1999 Painter, graphic designer and teacher, born in Treorchy, Glamorgan, but brought up in Cardiff, where he attended the School of Art, 1942–5, where Ceri Richards proved an inspirational teacher. After Naval service he returned to Cardiff College of Art, 1948–50, then began a series of teaching appointments. From 1950–1 he taught in Glamorgan; from 1951–3 general design as a visiting lecturer at Birmingham College of Art; from 1953–66 lecturing in graphic design and illustration at what eventually became Birmingham Polytechnic, taking over sole responsibility for the illustration course. In 1966 he moved to Cardiganshire and renovated a smallholding, farming sheep and growing the first commercial crop of strawberries and raspberries in west Wales. In 1967, Griffiths lectured on illustration for children at the Collegiate Faculty of Education, Aberystwyth, and illustrated books for Gwasg Gomer, published by the Welsh Books Council, in 1968 making theatre designs for Cardiganshire Arts Centre at Felinfach. After spending 1972–3 in Huntingdonshire, during which he taught at Bedford School, Griffiths in 1974 settled in Worcestershire, the landscape of Woodbury Hill and area to the Malvern Hills becoming an inspiration; while there until 1984 he renovated two cottages and taught design illustration at Bournville School of Art and Shrewsbury College of Art. After moving to Herefordshire in 1987, he designed and renovating another studio and continued to paint, although his last four years were dogged by illness. Griffiths took part in many group exhibitions, including SEA, SWG and WAC, other public and commercial galleries. Birmingham Corporation and University, Gwent County Council, Walsall Corporation and the CASW acquired his work. There was a retrospective at RBSA and Newport Museum and Art Gallery in 2002, at the National Library of Wales, Aberystwyth, 2002–3, and a show at Worcester City Museum & Art Gallery in 2004. To coincide with the retrospectives, limited-edition prints of his watercolour landscapes were produced.

Hugh GRIFFITHS 1916– Painter who was born in Karachi. Was educated at Canford School and the Dragon School, Oxford. Showed at RA, RBA and NEAC. Lived at Winchelsea and later St Leonards-on-Sea, Sussex.

Mary GRIFFITHS 1956– Painter and draughtsman who studied at Dyfed College of Art, 1974–5, then Croydon College of Art, 1975–8, her teachers including John Bellany, Bruce McLean and Gus Cummins. She was artist-in-residence at Oast Room Gallery, The Malting House, Cambridge, 1992. Her many prizes included Lady Evershed Drawing Prize, Eastern Open, 1988 and 1997; Highly Commended, Britain's Painters, 1991; Highly Commended, Painting, Eastern Open, 1992; Highly Commended, Drawing, Eastern Open, 1993; Highly Commended, Hunting Art Prizes, First Prize in Drawings for All, Gainsborough's House, Sudbury, and Gold Medal in Fine Art, National Eisteddfod of Wales, all 1994; First Prize, Hunting Art Prizes, Royal College of Art, 1995; and Painting Prize, Eastern Open, 1999. Mixed show appearances included Eastern Open from 1987; New Gallery, Swansea, 1990; Three Painters at Bow House Gallery, Barnet, 1991; and BP Portrait Award, at National Portrait Gallery, 1992. After a solo show at ADC Theatre, Cambridge, 1987, later ones included St John's Gallery in Bury St Edmunds, 1991, and Chappel Galleries, Chappel, from 1993. Strong figurative work was a notable feature of Griffiths' output, as seen in David Buckman's monograph on Griffifths for her 2002 Chappel Galleries exhibition. Lived in Cambridge.

Michael GRIFFITHS 1951– Printmaker, draughtsman, painter and teacher, born in London. He studied fine art for his degree at Brighton Polytechnic, doing a postgraduate course in printmaking there. Went on to teach at Winchester School of Art and Southampton Institute of Higher Education. From 1976 Griffiths was represented in many group shows in Europe and America, including the Varna Print Biennale in Bulgaria, the First International Miniature Print Biennale in Britain and the Cleveland International Drawing Biennale. In 1990 he shared a three-man show at Woodlands Art Gallery. Had over a dozen solo shows in Britain. From 1981 was a member of the Printmakers' Council. His work was in many public and private collections throughout the world. Lived in Hampshire, where he had his own printmaking studio.

Noëlle GRIFFITHS 1959– Painter and artist in mixed media whose works, as in a shared exhibition with Cecily Sash at Duncan Campbell Fine Art, 2003, were enriched by elements of decoration and fantasy. Griffiths graduated with honours in fine art from St Martin's School of Art, 1978–82. She won a WAC Setting Up Grant in 1986; its Travel Grant to visit Czechoslovakia in 1990; and another to visit India in 2003. Group shows included Mostyn Open, Oriel Mostyn, Llandudno, from 1990; Royal National Eisteddfod of Wales, from 1995; and Harlech Biennale, from 1998. She had a solo exhibition, Season Songs, at Wrexham Arts Centre, Wrexham, 2002.

Rhys GRIFFITHS: *see* **Archie Rhys GRIFFITHS**

Steven Allan GRIFFITHS 1960– Artist and teacher, born and lived in Llanelli, Carmarthenshire, who attended Dyfed College of Art, 1985–6; West Glamorgan Institute of Higher Education, 1986–7; Newport School of Art, 1987–90; and the University of Reading, 1994–6. He undertook factory, drawing office and design studio work and was a freelance college lecturer. Group shows included St David's Hall, Cardiff, 10th Anniversary Exhibition, 1993; Preoccupations, Glynn Vivian Art Gallery, Swansea, 1996; Hunting Art Prizes, Royal College of Art, 1997; and Showcase Wales, Museum of Modern Art, Wales, Machynlleth, 2000. Griffiths shared an exhibition, Frayed Reality, at St David's Hall, 1994, having a solo show at Nevill Gallery, Llanelli, 1998.

Tom GRIFFITHS 1902–1990 Painter, draughtsman, illuminator and teacher, educated in Norwich, where he continued to live. He attended the School of Art there, where he lectured, 1942–9, also studying at Heatherley's School of Fine Art, Grosvenor School of Modern Art and privately with Bernard Adams. Griffiths was chairman of Norfolk and Norwich Art Circle on several occasions, also president from 1983. *The County War Memorial Book of Remembrance*, in Norwich Cathedral, was among his many illuminated vellums. He showed at RA, NS and elsewhere.

Ronald Edwin GRIGG 1917– Painter and commercial artist involved in the advertising industry, born in Wells, Somerset. Studied at Leicester College of Art, 1934–7. Exhibited at the public gallery in Leicester and the Sketch Club and Society of Artists there, to both of which he belonged. The local corporation bought his work. Lived in Leicester.

John GRIGSBY 1940– Printmaker and painter, born in Staffordshire, who studied at Stoke-on-Trent and Leicester Colleges of Art. Showed with RE of which he became a member in 1978, RA, RWS, RWA, LG, in the provinces and abroad. National Museum of Wales in Cardiff, Graves Art Gallery in Sheffield and other public collections hold examples. Lived in Beckenham, Kent.

David GRIMBLEBY 1949– Artist, designer and musician, born in Barton-upon-Humber, Lincolnshire, who studied graphic design at Grimsby College of Technology, 1966–9. He worked as a decorative fairground artist, silkscreen technician and lettering artist, gravedigger, gardener and groundsman around England. From 1971 took part in numerous mixed shows and had a series of solo exhibitions, later ones including Turnpike Centre, Leigh, 1998; Orrell Arts Centre, Bootle, 2000; and Stables Gallery 2001. He was then "working on very focused and detailed pieces that relate to the patterns that emerge in natural objects". He lived in Southport, Lancashire.

Oona GRIMES 1957– Artist and lecturer, born and lived in London, who graduated in fine art honours at Norwich School of Art, 1982–6, gaining her higher diploma at Slade School of Fine Art, 1986–8. She was later a visiting lecturer there, also at Ruskin School of Fine Art, Oxford, and the University of the Arts. Grimes won the Celeste Art Prize in 2006, the year that her prints and drawings were included in Uncanny Tales, the touring show at the Foundation for Women's Art. Her small, figurative works were described by Jane Neal in the catalogue as notable for their "disturbing, pysychologically evocative imagery." Grimes was a prolific exhibitor in Britain and abroad. Among her other exhibitions were The Internationale Print Trienale, Cracow, Poland, from 1994; Atelier 2221, New Work solo show, New Delhi, India, 1998; Ashmolean Museum, Oxford, 1999; Sexy, at Houldsworth Fine Art, A Month in the Garden, at the Museum of Garden History, and Contemporary British Prints, Helen Copland Gallery, Montana, America, all 2001; Artissima, Danielle Arnaud, Turin, Italy, 2002; Jerwood Drawing Prize, 2002 and 2005;

Acts of Faith and Generosity, Gresol, Spain, 2003; and Hibrida 11, Cartwright Hall, Bradford, and Brno, Czech Republic, 2005. Collections holding Grimes' work included the New York Public Library; Manchester Metropolitan; University College London Strang Collection; Governing Body of Macau; Linacre College, Oxford; and the Victoria & Albert Museum

Winsor GRIMES 1928–1996 Artist, designer, draughtsman and teacher, born in Pontypool, Monmouthshire, who described himself as "A child of the 30s Depression – although showing talent as an artist, I started work on the coalface at the age of 14. Later I went to work in a Nylon spinning factory, where I started on the shop floor, but became works artist." Grimes' pictures reflected working people's hard lives. He gained his adult teacher's certificate at Newport College of Technology, but continued in industry in south Wales. His first show of paintings was in Risca in 1972; during following years he exhibited widely in Wales, London and abroad; then shared a show with Helen Lush at the Old Library Gallery, Cardiff, in 1995. An enthusiastic, infectious teacher, he taught in England and Wales, and was finally based in Abergavenny, Monmouthshire.

Stanley GRIMM 1891–1966 Painter, born in London, but studied in Riga, Russia, and in Munich just prior to World War I. Grimm's Munich studies were at the Knirr Atelier during the Blaue Reiter period, and as a young man he showed in Berlin, Munich and Venice. In 1913 he married another art student, the Russian Masha Oulpe, in 1914 was interned in Ruhleben, but was exchanged in 1916 and returned to England. In 1918 he went back to Russia and was conscripted by the Bolsheviks to paint numerous propaganda posters. By end-year he had escaped from Constadt in a smuggler's fishing boat to Finland, then to London. Soon after the escape the Crown Princess of Sweden bought works by Grimm from an exhibition of paintings by Ruhleben prisoners and the French painter Henri Matisse, seeing Grimm's work, praised his gifts and sense of colour. Grimm had his first solo show at the Redfern Gallery in 1925, others including the Beaux Arts, 1927, Bloomsbury Gallery, 1930, and Wertheim Gallery, 1932. He was elected a member of the ROI in 1935 and RP in 1936, his portrait of Sir John Lavery there in 1937 described as "dominating the main gallery". Other group venues included the RA, Goupil Gallery, Leicester Galleries and Gallery Edward Harvane. Member of Chelsea Arts Club where Adrian Bury remembered him as a giant of aristocratic appearance, "hospitable in the extreme". Served in Royal Navy in World War II, using his expert knowledge of Russian. Grimm's patrons included Nancy, Lady Astor; Lord Avon; and Sir Winston Churchill, and his pictures are held in foreign collections.

William GRIMMOND 1884–1952 Painter, designer and illustrator, born in Manchester. He attended the School of Art there. Exhibited widely, including RA, NEAC, Fine Art Society, RI and RBA. Manchester City Art Gallery holds his work. Was a member of the Art Workers' Guild. Lived at Rowledge, near Farnham, Surrey. While in Manchester Grimmond was a member of the Unnamed Society, director Frank Sladen Smith, other artist members being Lilian Reburn and Eric Newton.

Tom GRIMSEY 1960– Sculptor who was born in London. He studied at Wimbledon School of Art, 1979–82, then St Martin's School of Art, 1982–3. Exhibitions included Spacex Gallery Exeter, from 1979; Contemporary Sculpture at Hounslow Sculpture Park from 1980; Woodlands Art Gallery in Have You Seen Sculpture from the Body?, in 1983; and Bath Contemporary Art Fair in 1992. Grimsey worked in steel, modern and Indian dance movements sometimes being used as the basis for abstract pieces. Lived in London, then West Didsbury, Manchester.

Marc GRIMSHAW 1957– Artist, born in Macclesfield, Cheshire, who moved to Manchester where he was educated and attended the School of Art. He completed a wide-ranging, two-year course at South Trafford College, including graphics and design. After several years' full-time employment Grimshaw became a freelance artist, notably in pastel. He completed commissions for the BBC, University of Manchester, the television company Granada and Shell UK. A nostalgic theme in Grimshaw's output was street life of the 1950s and 1960s. Grove Fine Art handled his work, which was acquired by collectors in Britain, Ireland, on the continent and in Canada. He was based in Cheshire.

Reginald GRIMSHAW 1910– Painter and teacher, born in Farsley, Yorkshire, married to the potter Gladys Grimshaw. Studied at Pudsey School of Art, 1927–30, Leeds College of Art, 1930–1, then Royal College of Art, where his teachers included Ernest Tristram. He taught at schools of art in Maidstone and Cheltenham from mid-1930s, for many years being head of Oxford School of Art. Showed at RA, RBA and elsewhere. Lived in Noke, Oxfordshire.

Trevor GRIMSHAW 1947–2001 Painter and draughtsman who was notable for depicting industrial Lancashire, born in Hyde, Cheshire. He studied at Stockport College of Art. Showed at RA, RSA, RCamA, MAFA and in 1973 in Saddleworth Art Group exhibition at Woodlands Art Gallery. His solo shows included Colin Jellicoe Gallery, Manchester, and in 2005 one there at Tib Lane Gallery.

Alan GRIMWOOD 1949– Sculptor in various materials and teacher who attended Kingston School of Art, 1969–71. He held a number of part-time teaching posts, including Harrow School of Art, Essex and Brunel Universities. Had a solo show at Sunderland Arts Centre in 1982. Arts Council holds a selection of stylised figurative works by Grimwood, who has Large Rabbit and Figure in a Pond, both 1980, in the Grizedale Forest collection, Cumbria.

Antony Gibbons GRINLING 1896–1982 Sculptor and businessman, educated at Harrow School, 1910–14, where he showed an aptitude for art under W Egerton Hine. He was the son of Gibbons Grinling, a director of the wine merchants Gilbey. Served with the Hertfordshire Regiment in World War I, in which he was commissioned, wounded and won the Military Cross; in World War II he rose to lieutenant-colonel with the same regiment. Grinling convalesced in Taormina, Sicily, 1919–20, where he studied sculpture, then made his career, 1921–61, with Gilbey's, becoming a managing director. As a sculptor he often worked with Serge Chermayeff. Commissions included garden statues for Queen Mary's Dolls' House at Windsor, a relief for the Cambridge Theatre and a room of sculpture and furniture for Whiteley's store. Had a solo show at Tooth's in 1934, also exhibiting at RA, Upper Grosvenor, Leicester and Worthing Art Galleries, signing work with initials. Grinling's figurative sculptures could be both tender and exuberant, as in the Fine Art Society's 1986 exhibition Sculpture In Britain Between the Wars. Grinling was also a perceptive collector. A small bronze figure group by Henry Moore bought in the early 1950s for £50 sold at Phillips in 1995 for £124,700. Lived at Dyrham, near Chippenham, Wiltshire.

John GRINSTEAD 1920–1987 Painter, designer, calligrapher and teacher, born in Leeds, Yorkshire, full name Edgar John Grinstead. After attending Wakefield Cathedral School he was at Wakefield College of Art, Central School of Arts and Crafts, 1946, then Royal College of Art, 1950. Became senior lecturer at Kingston upon Thames Polytechnic. Showed RA, RUA and in the provinces and had a number of presentations made to members of the royal family. Lived in East Molesey, Surrey.

Michael GROARKE 1943– Designer and painter, born in Manchester. He attended Calico Printers' Association Design School, Manchester Polytechnic and Rochdale College of Art and showed with RA, RCamA, RWS and elsewhere. Lived in Marple, Cheshire.

Michael GROGAN 1947– Painter, printmaker and illustrator, born in Lyndhurst, Hampshire. After basic navigational training he attended Winchester College of Art, 1967–8; Liverpool College of Art, 1968–71; and Royal College of Art, 1971–4, also studying for a short time in Paris. Did some illustrative work for Sutton Hoo treasure catalogue in British Museum. Had one-man show at Gallery 273 at Queen Mary College and at Jordan Gallery. Lived in London and Totton, Hampshire.

John GROME 1911–2004 Painter and teacher, born in London, his father Irish-born in Dublin and an Anglican clergyman, his mother half English. John went to a public school for clergymen's sons his father hoping he would be a clergyman, but he refused, wanting to paint and write. Grome studied at Goldsmiths' College School of Art under Clive Gardiner. After teaching at a choir school in Durham Grome achieved a long-standing desire to see India, joined the Royal Fusiliers, and taught English to Indian soldiers. After five years there, during which he met Mahatma Gandhi whom he much admired, Grome's mother helped him buy himself out of the Army. During World War II he was a conscientious objector, joined Civil Defence and drove an ambulance in the Blitz. After the war, during which he suffered a bad head injury, Grome started painting again, joined the LG and lived in Chelsea. There he made friends with the artist Mervyn Peake, poet Dylan Thomas and writer Stephen Spender and gave life classes to well-known actors, including Alec Guinness. An Italian studying English in London introduced Grome to the realist Italian painter Renato Guttuso and to Italy, where in 1947 he settled penniless. Over the years Grome did various jobs to live, including editing and broadcasting, painting and exhibiting when he could. In 1950 he married Mave Beadle and had three children. In 1965 the Gromes moved to London so that their children could be educated there, John teaching at Hornsey School of Art, but after a few years returned to the sunshine of Italy where his artist friends included Corrado Cagli, Carlo Levi and Sergio Donnini. Grome received praise for his rich, luminous colour from Guttuso and deep penetration of Italian life in his work from the art critic of *The Sunday Times*, John Russell. Zen influenced Grome, a solitary artist with a dislike of fashion but strong poetic convictions, in whose pictures symbols and movement were notable features. His infrequent exhibitions included Galleria San Marco, Rome, 1955; Opera Theatre Gallery, Parma, 1964; Galleria Angolare, Milan, 1972; and Galleria La Gradiva, Rome, 1985.

Elizabeth GROOM: *see* **Mary Elizabeth GROOM**

Emerson Harold GROOM 1891–1983 Etcher, born in Wandsworth, south London, who took up etching after World War I, training at the Central School of Arts and Crafts. He was a member of the RE, also exhibiting at the RA. In the 1930s Groom was working in Westcliff-on-Sea, Essex, later moving to Sussex, where he died in Lewes. His work was included in Seasonal Delights, Elizabeth Harvey-Lee, North Aston, 1996.

Jon GROOM 1953– Painter with an interest in sculpture, and teacher, born in Powys. Studied at Cardiff College of Art, 1971–2 and 1974–6, Sheffield Polytechnic, 1972–3, and Chelsea School of Art, 1976–7. Groom's abstract pictures carefully balanced the volumes of each unit in a work. He was meticulous about surface. He was included in John Moores Liverpool Exhibition, 1987, and in the South Bank Centre's 1988–9 survey The Presence of Painting. His first solo show was at Riverside Studios, 1978. Other exhibitions included Rochdale Art Gallery, 1983, Ruth Siegel Gallery in New York, 1985, and Nicola Jacobs Gallery, 1986. For some years he was fellow in painting at Gloucester College of Art and Design, Cheltenham. Arts Council holds his work.

Mary Elizabeth GROOM 1903–1958 Wood engraver who studied with Leon Underwood at his Brook Green School, opened in 1921. She showed 18 prints at SWE, 1928–38, her work mixing delicacy and primitivism. Groom illustrated two books for the Golden Cockerel Press in 1937: *Roses of Sharon*, a collection of Old Testament excerpts, and John Milton's *Paradise Lost*. She sometimes worked as Elizabeth Groom. Abbott and Holder latterly handled her work. Ashmolean Museum, Oxford, holds 14 prints by her.

Jean GROSE 1926– Painter, born in Cambridge, who studied at Royal College of Art and in Italy. Showed SEA, WIAC and NEAC. Taught bookbinding at Hammersmith School of Art and lived in London.

Anthony GROSS 1905–1984 Painter, illustrator, creator of animated cartoons, watercolourist and outstanding etcher. Born and lived in London and originally given the name Imre, Gross studied at the Slade School of Fine Art, at the Académie Julien, Paris, under Pierre Laurens, at the École des Beaux-Arts and in Madrid. Had his first one-man show at the Leicester Galleries in 1934, after which he had several dozen one-man shows in Britain and abroad. The Victoria and Albert Museum gave him a major retrospective in 1968. He also took part in many mixed exhibitions, including the RA, being elected a Royal Academician in 1980. Galleries holding his work include the Tate, British Museum, Victoria & Albert Museum and the Imperial War Museum. Was an Official War Artist in World War II in the Middle East, India and Europe. By then he had married his

French artist wife Marcelle (Daisy) Florenty, had travelled extensively in North Africa and Europe and had worked on animated cartoons, such as *La Joie de Vivre*, *The Fox Hunt*, for Alexander Korda, and *Round the World in Eighty Days*. Book illustrations included *The Forsyte Saga* and *Six Idylls of Theocritus*. Taught at the Central School of Arts and Crafts and at the Slade. Worked extensively in France, having bought a house at Le Boulvé in 1955. Wrote an authoritative book on *Etching, Engraving and Intaglio Printing*. North House Gallery, Mannintree, showed Gross's paintings and etchings in 2002. Gross's sister was the painter and cartographer Phyllis Pearsall.

Anthony GROSS 1968– Artist and curator who was included in the inaugural Bowieart exhibition BLOC at the County Hall Gallery in 2005. In that, he presented "an exploded narrative, through a fabricated day in the life of a group of generic commercialized males." Gross gained his Bachelor of Science degree in architecture at The Bartlett School of Architecture, University College London, 1987–9. He was a guest sculpture student, Akademie der Bildende Künste, Karlsruhe, Germany, 1989–90; gained his master's in architecture at the Bartlett School, 1990–1; and his fine art master's at Goldsmiths' College, 2000–1. He took part in many group exhibitions in Britain and abroad, including Homeless, The Mota Gallery, 2000; ArteViva Festival 2001, Senigallia, Italy, first prize digital art, 2001; Club, Le Grand Confort, Poitiers, France, 2002; Portobello Film Festival, Westbourne Studios, prize, best multimedia, 2003; and Object Passing, *The Economist* Building, 2004. His later solo exhibitions included Video et Animations, M-Project, Paris, 2004. Among exhibitions curated was Symposium, Biz-art Center, Shanghai, China, 2004.

David GROSS 1960– Sculptor often using wood, based in Sunderland. He studied at Bolton Metropolitan College and West Surrey College of Art & Design, 1980–5, then University of Northumbria at Newcastle upon Tyne, 1991–3. Gross showed widely in Britain and abroad, held a number of residencies and specialised in community- and schools-linked projects. His works had a strong dramatic quality, witness his 1995 lime-wood Mask, at Tynemouth Metro station, carved with the help of pupils of a local school; or the 1998 wood and steel plate Head, at Tyne Slipway and Engineering works, South Shields, a large splayed hand stained red within which is a propeller.

Richard Oliver GROSS 1882–1964 Sculptor in marble and bronze, born at Barrow-in-Furness, Lancashire. Studied at Camberwell School of Arts and Crafts under Albert Toft. Exhibited RA. Went to live in Auckland, New Zealand, where he carried out a large volume of public sculpture. Was elected a fellow of the RBS, 1948.

Athalie GROSVENOR fl. from late 1930s– Sculptor and painter, born in Beaconsfield, Buckinghamshire, as Stella Athalie Henderson. She was educated in Hampstead, north London, where she settled, studying at Slade School of Fine Art with Randolph Schwabe and A H Gerrard. Became a member of RBS and Hampstead Artists' Council, also exhibiting at RA. Had a solo show at Foyles Gallery in 1968.

Martin GROVER 1962– Painter, born in Carshalton Beeches, Surrey. He studied at Croydon School of Art, 1980–1, Trent Polytechnic, Nottingham, 1981–4, and Royal Academy Schools, 1984–7. Grover's detailed, stylized figurative paintings can have a strong atmosphere of surreality and tension. His picture The Wait, the first in a series based on observations made while working in a hospital, was included in John Moores Liverpool Exhibition, 1989–90, his acrylic on canvas Two Slightly Anxious Sisters winning a prize there, 1993–4. Showed solo with Merz Contemporary Art in 2002 at Royal Teas, organised by Julia Lancaster and Graft, and lived in London.

John Michael GROVES 1932– Painter and draughtsman, born and lived in London. He attended Camberwell School of Arts and Crafts, 1953–7. Became a member of RSMA in 1977, also showing elsewhere in London.

Lavender GROVES 1932– Artist in oil, pen and ink and ceramics, born in Manchester. She attended Chelsea School of Art, gaining her diploma in 1954, teachers including Harold Sandys Williamson, Raymond Coxon and Frederick Brill. Groves worked the Upton Pottery with her husband Mark Beard. Animals, notably horses, as well as heraldry were among her subjects and she claimed to be "the only potter to do calligraphy on earthenware using my technique". Became a member of ROI in 1960, also exhibiting with RA and RBA. National Museum of Wales in Cardiff and City of Birmingham Museum & Art Gallery hold examples. Lived in Upton-on-Severn, Worcestershire.

Gerald GRUBB 1912–1994 Artist in oil, pastel and acrylic whose work covered a range of subjects. Born in Dublin, Ireland, he was educated at St Stephen's Green School, studying art at the Metropolitan College and RHA life class; Académie des Beaux-Arts in Brussels; and in London at Central School of Arts and Crafts and Anglo-French Art Centre. Became a member of Free Painters and Sculptors in 1986, its Loggia Gallery giving Grubb a memorial show in 1995. A self-effacing, prolific artist, Grubb showed widely elsewhere, including RA and Hampstead Artists' Council. Lived in London.

Pegi GRUFFYDD 1960– Painter and printmaker, born in Pwllheli, Caernarvonshire. She studied at Manchester Polytechnic, 1978–9, Wolverhampton Polytechnic, 1979–82, and Royal Academy Schools, 1983–6. She showed at RA Summer Exhibition, Royal National Eisteddfod, North Wales Open and elsewhere, having a solo exhibition at Theatre Gwynedd. Bangor. Lived at Chwilog, Gwynedd.

Cuthbert GRUNDY 1846–1946 Painter of landscapes and figure studies, Sir Cuthbert Grundy was educated at Victoria University, New South Wales, Australia. He is most remembered with his brother J R G Grundy as the donor of the Grundy Art Gallery, Blackpool. Cuthbert Grundy, author of works on chemistry and plant life, showed at leading London galleries. He was from 1913–33 president of RCamA and held senior positions in RWA, RBC and SWAS. He was represented in the centenary show of RCamA in 1982. Was knighted in 1919 and died in Blackpool.

Jim GRUNDY 1956– Painter, born in Leicester. He studied at the Polytechnic there, 1974–5, then Maidstone College of Art, 1975–8. Group exhibitions featuring his work included Artists from SPACE Studios at Norfolk House, 1982; Open Studios at Norfolk House, 1983–4; Ten Artists at South London Art Gallery, 1983; and he was in a show of four artists at Woodlands Art Gallery, 1984. Grundy had solo shows at Greenwich Theatre Gallery, 1981, and Maidstone College of Art, 1984. Photographs of figures from theatrical scenes formed the starting point for most of Grundy's pictures at Woodlands, an abstract composition developing from the original image. Kent County Council and Nuffield Foundation hold his work.

Mavis Wilson GRÜNEWALD 1931– Painter, draughtsman, printmaker and teacher, full name Eleanor Mavis Grünewald (Wilson was her maiden name), born in Stockton-on-Tees, County Durham. She studied at Middlesbrough School of Art, then Leeds College of Art; in the late 1950s she taught at Heginbottom Art School in Ashton-under-Lyne, Lancashire. Showed at Middlesbrough Art Gallery, Macclesfield Art Gallery and in Germany, where she settled in Frankfurt. Middlesbrough Town Council bought her work, which is also in German public collections.

Helen GRUNWALD 1925–1988 Painter, draughtsman, designer, artist employing glass and mirrors and teacher, born in Vienna, Austria. Educated in Vienna, she studied art at Beckenham School of Art, 1941–4, with Henry Carr, then with Carel Weight at Royal College of Art, 1949–52. Showed widely including AIA, the Leger, Leicester and Berkeley Galleries, New Art Centre and in the provinces. Completed a mural at St Thomas's Canterbury. Music and architecture were leading themes in her work. Sometimes signed work hel or Helen. Lived in London.

Nina GRUSCHWITZ 1968– Painter whose works, including gestural, abstract paintings, were designed to "cry the drama of the human condition." Gruschwitz was born in St Petersburg, Russia, gaining her master's degree from Gubkin Academy, Moscow. She obtained a grant from the Friedrich-Ebert Foundation, Germany, studied privately with Margarita Budini and worked for 10 years in Germany and the Netherlands before settling in London in 2000, eventually based in Richmond, Surrey. Had a series of solo and mixed exhibitions on the continent, in the United Kingdom and America, later group shows including the New Constructivists' inaugural exhibition at Cotton's Atrium, Cotton's Centre, 2002, and Summer Show at Artbank, 2003, where her work was described as "emotional scapes." In 2002 Gruschwitz was artist-in-residence at River Walk Restaurant, OXO Tower, having a solo exhibition at Cotton's Atrium, 2003. In 2004 she was artist-in-residence at Villiers Theatre, with an exhibition, Ignite, again at Cotton's Atrium. Business and private collections in Britain and extensively abroad held examples.

Vaughan GRYLLS 1943– Creator of photo-collages and pun-sculptures, and teacher, born in Newark Nottinghamshire. The targets of his work included linguistic philosophy, the press, contemporary art, current events and international relations. He studied at Wolverhampton College of Art, 1964–7, under Roy Kitchin; Goldsmiths' College of Art, 1967–8; and Slade School of Fine Art, 1968–70, with Reg Butler, Phillip King and Richard Wollheim. Briefly from 1973 Nicholas Wegner and Grylls operated The Gallery in a Paddington back street, an offbeat alternative to the conventional commercial gallery system. Mixed exhibitions included Northern Young Contemporaries, Whitworth Art Gallery, Manchester, 1967; Whitechapel Open, 1978; and Photographers' Gallery from 1983. Had a first solo show at Wolverhampton Polytechnic, 1970. Grylls taught for several years in America and in 1989 was appointed the first professor and head of the school of art and design at Wolverhampton Polytechnic. An inaugural exhibition commemorating the appointment was held at Wolverhampton Art Gallery in 1989 (selected works 1964–89, catalogue containing complete works). His later solo shows included Herbert Read Gallery at Kent Institute of Art & Design, Canterbury, 1998, Grylls having been appointed the Institute's second director in 1996, retired 2005. University College London, WAC, Contemporary Art Society and other collections in Britain and abroad hold examples. Lived in London and at Westmarsh, Kent.

David GRYN 1963– Artist who attended St Martin's School of Art, 1983–6. He participated in Summer Show, Osbourne Gallery, and Los Angeles Art Fair, California, America, both 1986; Bath Contemporary Art Fair, with Rebecca Hossack Gallery, 1987; Big Heads, Diorama Gallery and Ben Uri Art Society, both 1988; and East End Open Studios, at Carpenter's Road, 1989.

Bruno GUAITAMACCHI 1931– Painter born in Milan, Italy, who studied at the Accademia di Brera and harmony and counterpoint with a leading pianist. After working for some years in England then returning to Italy to start painting, he eventually bought a Suffolk studio in the 1980s. Thereafter, he travelled regularly between there and Bellagio, on Lake Como, also painting in California and South Africa. Brilliant flowerpieces and landscapes full of long, low horizons and transparent, changing skies characterised the work of an artist once described as "a lusher, looser Annigoni". Showed internationally, British solo exhibitions including Phoenix Gallery, Lavenham, 1983–97, and Highgate Fine Art, 1998 and 2003. His son was the artist Paul Demaria Guaitamacchi, who had a solo exhibition at Highgate Fine Art in 2004.

Claudio GUARINO 1966–2004 Enterprising artist and film-maker who favoured the passionate, melodramatic and operatic, brought up in Cesa, near Naples, Italy. He joined the fine art course at Naples Accademia, but found it too traditional and restrictive, later studying Japanese for two years. Visiting Britain in the early 1990s, Guarino appreciated the more adventurous art scene and settled in London; worked briefly as a hotel waiter; and eventually set up a business creating extravagant window displays, doing work for Tiffany & Company, the jewellers. After in 1995 being chosen for Italians, a group show in London and Bologna, he enrolled at Goldsmiths' College, where he made an impression with his early installations and his ability to involve students from other disciplines such as music, dance and fashion. By his second year he was asked to make two site-specific pieces, Suspicion and Mater Dolorosa, for the Victoria Miro Gallery. Guarino's work was chosen for New Contemporaries in 1998 and he produced increasingly ambitious pieces for the ICA and exhibitions in Genoa, Rome and Pisa. The parallels between Italian opera, of which he was an addict, and the stylised melodrama of the Kabuki and Noh traditions of Japan fascinated him. While studying for his master's at the Royal College of Art, Guarino won a scholarship to spend three months at Kyoto University. Guarino's films included *Lost The Unmoveable Desire*, 2002, and *Limit*, 2003. The following year, becoming increasingly ill with cancer, he checked into a London hotel, wrote notes to friends and was found dead the following day.

Simon GUDGEON 1958– Self-taught painter and sculptor who worked closely with sporting and conservation bodies to produce imaginative wildlife works. Gudgeon began painting in 1991 and held his first solo show just over a year later, almost a sell-out, which prompted many commissions. In 1998, he began to sculpt, creating such works as Kingfisher IV, in September Show, 2003, at The Wykeham Gallery, Stockbridge. He worked closely with the foundry and limited each edition to 12 pieces.

Beatrice Claudia GUERCIO: *see* **Beatrice Claudia FREEMAN**

Alan Douglas GUEST 1931– Artist, born and lived in Nottingham, who attended Mundella Grammar School, 1942–9, and was a chartered librarian, 1952–89, retiring early, having from 1974 been senior librarian, bibliographical services section, Nottinghamshire Public Libraries. Guest was taught art by his uncle, the painter Joseph Arthur Jackson, having begun painting as a schoolboy. During National Service in the Royal Air Force, 1949–51, drew and painted influenced by Aubrey Beardsley, Jean Cocteau and Paul Klee. Other influences on his strongly linear work were botany and Byzantine art. Guest also produced Surrealist collages, with his own texts, with Max Ernst an influence. For many years he studied printmaking, lecturing to library assistants on book production and illustration. In 1992 he wrote sections on colour woodcuts and lino-cuts and contributed to the biographical dictionary in *British Printmakers 1855–1955*, edited by Robin Garton. Was a member in 1960s and 1970s of Midland Group of Artists, also of SWE. Group shows included England & Co from 1989; Leicester Collection for Schools and Colleges, annual exhibition, from 1990; Nottingham Castle Museum, Box Art, 1993; Woods Art Gallery, Leicester, 1994; and in 1997 Body Parts at David Holmes Contemporary Art Peterborough, and Derby City Open Art Competition. Guest was co-author with Hilary Chapman of *The colour woodcuts of John Edgar Platt 1886–1967*, published in 1999 to coincide with the 20th Century Gallery's show of his work.

Coral GUEST 1955– Botanical artist, lecturer and writer, born in London, who studied fine art (painting) at Chelsea School of Art, 1974–8, abstraction with Sean Scully and colour theory with Ken Kiff. She won a Chelsea Drawing Scholarship, 1975; Chelsea Travel Scholarship, 1978; and in 1986 and 1988 the Royal Horticultural Society Gold Medal. The Society's Lindley Library holds her work, as do The Royal Botanic Gardens, Kew; The Hunt Institute, Pittsburgh, in America; and The Dr Shirley Sherwood Collection. In 2005 Guest participated in the exhibition A New Flowering: 1,000 Years of Botanical Art, organised by Sherwood at the Ashmolean Museum, Oxford. At that time she wrote: "Meditations upon the plant and mineral kingdom are providing the focus for an ongoing series of large-scale representational paintings devoted to flowers and land formation. The works record a moment in time and describe the frequencies of order and chaos that are prevalent in creation. Attention is given to the intensity of light and dark, the rendition of beauty being given absolute priority." Guest lectured in flower painting from 1990–03 at the Royal Botanic Gardens, Kew, where at the Kew Gallery she participated in group exhibitions in 1995 and 1996. Other group shows included the Scottish National Gallery of Modern Art, Edinburgh, 1997; Yasuda Kasai Gallery, Tokyo, Japan, 1998; Marciana Library, Venice, Italy, 2001; and the Royal Albert Museum Exeter, 2004. She had solo shows at the Oliver Swann Galleries in 1986 and 1988; H V Allinson Gallery, New York, 1988; The Pump House Gallery, Battersea, 1998; and Open Studios, from 2001. Guest's book *Painting Flowers in Watercolour – A Naturalistic Approach* was published in the United Kingdom and America in 2001. Her work was included in Sherwood's volumes *A Passion for Plants*, 1995, and *Contemporary Botanical Artists*, 2001. Guest lived in Rushden, Northamptonshire.

Alvaro GUEVARA 1894–1951 Painter, born in Valparaiso, Chile. Although he began painting when small, it was only when he spent two years in Bradford, having travelled to England in 1908 to join the cloth trade, that he began studying art at the College of Art. Then studied at Slade School of Fine Art, 1912–16, winning a scholarship in 1914. Became associated with Roger Fry and the Omega Workshops and began to show with NEAC of which he was a member, and elsewhere. In the mid-1920s he spent several years back in Chile, painting and boxing at championship level, then had a show of his Chilean pictures at Leicester Galleries in 1926. Married the painter Meraud Guinness in 1929 and went to live in France, concentrating on imaginary portraits and landscapes. His portrait of Edith Sitwell, in Tate Gallery collection, is one of his finest works. Showed in Paris at Galerie Mouradian in 1938. Died in Aix-en-Provence.

Meraud GUEVARA 1904–1993 Painter, often of bizarre, Surrealist pictures, born in London as Meraud Michael (a name used to sign pictures) Guinness into a wealthy family. She was a 1920s bright young thing who married the Chilean artist Alvaro Guevara in 1929, having a long and stormy relationship with him. She studied at Slade School of Fine Art under Henry Tonks intermittently, 1923–7. Had a solo show in Paris in 1928, her teacher there being Francis Picabia. She was a member of a set including Christopher Wood, whom she almost married, Gertrude Stein, Nancy Cunard and Lord Berners. In 1940 she had a show at Valentine Gallery in New York. Winston Churchill owned Alvaro's portrait of Meraud. After Alvaro died in 1951 Meraud supervised his estate and arranged for his writings to be published and memorial shows to be held. She resumed painting with enthusiasm. Died in Paris.

Derrick GUILD 1963– Artist born in Perth who studied at Duncan of Jordanstone College of Art in Dundee, 1982–7, and at Art Institute of Chicago, 1984. He was in The New Generation at Compass Gallery, Glasgow, 1986, in Figuration to a Degree at Paton Gallery, 1993, and in Paton Gallery at *The Economist*, 1994. Paton gave Guild a solo show later that year/early 1995, work which "though its expression is streaked with Christian symbolism" was "a vision of a pre-Fall world whose creatures of land, sea and air are undiminished by guilt". Among Guild's other solo shows was Choice Bread at Paton Gallery in 1997, stemming from the artist's winning The Villiers David Award in 1995 which "enabled me to experience Spanish painting and culture at first hand during a critical stage in the development of my work." Dundee City Art Gallery,

Scottish Arts Council and several corporate collections hold examples.

Colin GUILLEMET 1979– Artist who participated in the inaugural Bowieart show BLOC at the County Hall Gallery in 2005. Guillemet graduated with honours in fine art from Central St Martins College of Art, 1998–01, gaining his master's at the Royal College of Art, 2001–3. He took part in many group shows in Britain and abroad, latterly including Los 29 Enchufes, Madrid, Spain, 2002; Common Fields, Studio Voltaire, 2003; and Mum is not home, curated by Silvio Salgado, Turku, Finland, 2004. In that year he participated in Itchy Park, with Rory Macbeth, at Old Limehouse Town Hall, and among his solo exhibitions was Think Big, Hockney Gallery, Royal College of Art, 2002.

Harriet GUINNESS 1970– Painter, born and lived in London, who studied at Chelsea College of Art, 1989–92, and Royal Academy Schools, 1992–5. Showed with LG, 1993, and in RA Summer Exhibition from that year and had an oil on canvas titled Block in 1995–6 John Moores Liverpool Exhibition.

Lindy GUINNESS 1941– Painter who took up painting in 1961 after meeting Duncan Grant, who became a close friend. She studied at Chelsea School of Art and with Oskar Kokoschka in Salzburg. In 1964 married Lord Dufferin. Worked for *Harper's and Queen* as a journalist and photographer, then at ICA before becoming a full-time artist in 1969, with added studies at Slade School of Fine Art. She travelled in India, Italy and Greece and showed in London and Ireland. Solo exhibitions included Gallery Edward Harvane, 1975; Eyre and Hobhouse Ltd, 1979; The Maclean Gallery, 1981; The Solomon Gallery, Dublin, 1983; and Browse & Darby, 2004. National Self-Portrait of Ireland, University of Limerick, holds her 1999 self-portrait. Lived in London and Clandeboye, County Down, Northern Ireland.

Thomas Gladstone Middleton GUISE 1916–1984 Painter in various media, born in Davidston, Ross and Cromarty. He was by profession a process engraver and printer. Studied at Edinburgh College of Art, 1947–9, with Adam Bruce Thomson. Over 35 years Guise worked in many styles, completing landscapes, figure studies and abstracts which have a strong poetic quality. He favoured watercolour and Pointillism. Showed in many group exhibitions including RSA, RSW, RBA, NEAC, SSA and with Free Painters and Sculptors. Solo shows from 1966 included Randolph Gallery, Edinburgh Festival; Stanford University, California, and also in America at Los Robles Gallery, Palo Alto; the Ian Clarkson and the Abacus Gallery, Edinburgh; and Sally Port Gallery, Berwick-upon-Tweed. Work widely held internationally in private collections. Lived in Edinburgh.

GUITTI: *see* **Guitti BARRATT-DENYER**

Daniela GULLOTTA 1974– Painter, born in Bologna, Italy, who gained a diploma, Liceo Artistico Arcangeli di Bologna, 1988–92; diploma, mark 110/110 cum laude, Accademia di Belle Arti di Bologna, 1993–8; and her master's in painting, Royal College of Art, 1998–00. Awards included John Crane Italy Scholarship, 1998–00; John Crane New York Travel Award, John Crane Summer Travel Award and Daler-Rowney Prize for Drawing, all 1999; Paris studio, Cité Internationale des Arts, and Royal College of Art Society and Waterstones Artbook Prize, both 2000; and finalist The BOC Emerging Artist Award 2002. Exhibitions included Arte in Comune, Comune in Arte, Bologna, 1996; Mostra giovani artisti, Bologna City Council Exhibition Room, 1998; and ART*futures*, organised by Contemporary Art Society, Barbican Centre, and Group Show, Exit Art Gallery, New York, America, both 2000; Art First, 2002; and Amplifying Silence, Fondation d'Art Contemporain Guerlain, Paris, 2003. In that year her solo show Interiors was held at Marlborough Fine Art. British Airways and Royal College of Art held Gullotta's work. She lived in Bologna and London.

Ulyana GUMENIUK 1975– Figurative artist of Ukrainian nationality whose work could have a strong fantasy element, as in her exhibition presented by Stephen Walton at The Gallery in Cork Street, 2002. She attended St Petersburg Academy of Fine Art's secondary art school, 1988–92; its faculty of painting, 1993–6; and St Martins's College of Art and Design, 1996–8. Other exhibitions included Canadian Ukrainian Foundation, Toronto, Canada (it holds her work), 1996; Unicorn Gallery and Aberdeen Art Gallery, both 1999; and BP Portrait Award, National Portrait Gallery, from 1999.

Alan GUMMERSON 1928– Artist and teacher who attended Bradford and Leeds Colleges of Art. While teaching at Leeds College, in 1964 took part in The Teaching Image staff exhibition at Leeds City Art Gallery, showing oils and constructions. Solo exhibitions included Wakefield, Lane Gallery Bradford and New Vision Centre. Latterly lived at Blackshaw Head, Hebden Bridge, Yorkshire.

Margaret GUMUCHIAN 1927– Painter, printmaker and teacher, born in Manchester of Armenian parents. While studying at Manchester Regional College of Art met her future husband, the artist Ian Grant, who was teaching there. She went on to teach art at grammar schools in Manchester and Stockport, Cheshire, where she settled. Gumuchian was a member of MAFA, also showing at RBA, with Northern Young Artists and widely in the north of England. In 1988 she was the outright winner in the northwest Laing Competition. Salford Art Gallery holds her work.

Kimberley GUNDLE 1963– Artist, born in Johannesburg, Transvaal Province, South Africa. She graduated in fine arts from the Michaelis School of Fine Art, University of Cape Town, 1983–6; did a postgraduate advanced painting course there, 1988; and gained a postgraduate diploma from the Slade School of Fine Art in London, where she settled, 1988–90. Gundle depicted people in canvases notable for their colour, clear image delineation and quirkiness. Later, she concentrated on their footwear, as in her solo show The Shoe Fits, at Art First, 2003. She also took part in many solo exhibitions in Britain and abroad, which latterly included Time Pieces, The Gallery in Cork Street (sculpture exhibition), 2000, and She, a national tour organised by The City Gallery, Leicester, 2002. Kickers Shoes for the Pentland Group and many private collectors commissioned Gundle's work. St Peter's College, Oxford; South African Brewers; Unilever plc and other corporate collections hold examples.

Gordon GUNN 1916– Artist in watercolour, ink and charcoal. Born in Glasgow, Gunn studied art at Glasgow School of Art for five years in the late 1930s under Ian Fleming and Sir William O Hutchison. Gunn went on to exhibit widely in Britain and abroad, venues including RA, RSMA, RI, RBA, the Glasgow Institute of the Fine Arts as well as galleries in Bermuda and Germany. Aberdeen Art Gallery, the Corporation Art Gallery in Harrogate and Leamington Spa Art Gallery hold his work, among others. In 1978 Gunn had a retrospective at Woodlands Art Gallery which in addition to his wide-ranging landscapes included a series of cosmic pictures executed between 1953–74 "concerned with the Universe as a background to our activities". Latterly he had studios in Blackheath, London, and Arisaig, Scotland.

James GUNN 1893–1964 Painter of portraits and landscapes. Herbert James Gunn was born in Glasgow, studied at the School of Art there, then at Edinburgh College of Art and Académie Julian, Paris. Exhibited RA, RSA, Fine Art Society, RP, Cooling Galleries and Goupil Gallery. Awarded gold medal at Paris Salon, 1939; elected president of RP, 1953; elected RA, 1961; knighted, 1963. Although known as a portrait painter, having painted a state portrait of HM The Queen in 1953–4, Gunn was also a brilliant painter of figures and scenes in sunlight and action, in the manner of Lavery, Peploe and the French Impressionists. The National Portrait Gallery holds his work. Lived in London, where he was a member of many notable clubs, such as the Athenaeum, Chelsea Arts and Garrick. Scottish National Portrait Gallery held a retrospective, 1994–5.

James Thomson GUNN 1932– Painter and designer, born in Gorebridge, Midlothian, settling nearby at Dalkeith, where he attended the High School. Gunn studied at Edinburgh College of Art, 1950–6, teachers including William Gillies and Robin Philipson. He obtained a travelling scholarship, 1954–6, which took him extensively through Europe. A versatile artist, Gunn showed at RSA, RSW of which he was a member, SSA, RI and elsewhere, having several solo exhibitions. In 1985 he gained the Highland Society of London Award, RSA. Argyll Education Committee holds his work.

William Archibald GUNN 1877– Painter in watercolour and pastel of landscapes and townscapes. After initial education in Hereford he attended Glasgow School of Art, 1897–1901. Exhibited Walker Art Gallery, Liverpool, and in other northern provincial cities. Graves Art Gallery, Sheffield, holds a view of the city by him. Lived in St Ives, Cornwall.

James GUNNELL 1947– Watercolourist, notable for his flower pictures, born in Surrey. He attended West Surrey College of Art and Design, 1969–73, and Royal Academy Schools, 1973–6, winning the David Murray Prize for Landscape Painting, 1972–4. In 1974 he showed with Young Contemporaries; was a frequent exhibitor with RA; showed at Beaux Arts Gallery, Bath; Towner Art Gallery, Eastbourne; and Gardner Arts Centre, Brighton. From 1986 had regular solo shows at Thackeray Gallery. In 1992 he was commissioned to provide the illustrations for British Gas (Southern)'s corporate calendar.

Lucy GUNNING 1964– Artist employing film, video, text and sculpture, born in Newcastle upon Tyne, who studied at Falmouth School of Art and Goldsmiths' College. Among her group shows were Select at Arnolfini, Bristol, 1998, and Hayward Gallery tour The British Art Show 5, 2000–1. Later solo exhibitions included Matt's Gallery, 1999, and Intermediate II, Tate Britain, 2001–2. Fantasy, reality, the oddness of people's behaviour and everyday objects were perceived and transformed by Gunning with insight and humour. In 2002 Gunning had a residency at The Centre for Drawing, Wimbledon School of Art. She won a Paul Hamlyn Award for the Visual Arts in 2004. The Arts Council holds her video The Horse Impressionists, 1994. Lived in London.

Emma GUNNINGHAM 1957– She graduated with honours from the University of Reading, 1976–80, in the latter year having a solo exhibition at South Hill Park Arts Centre, Bracknell. Group shows included Four Painters, Waterloo Gallery, 1982; Whitechapel Open, Whitechapel Art Gallery, 1984; Identity at Chisenhale Gallery and Woodlands Gallery, Blackheath, both 1988; and East End Open Studios, at Chisenhale Studios, 1989.

Irene GUNSTON 1960– Sculptor who graduated from Canterbury College of Art. She lived, worked and exhibited in London for many years. Figurative bronzes by her were included in Animal Kingdoms at Simmons Gallery, 1998.

Beatrice GUNTHORP fl. c.1925–1965 Portrait painter, born in Rhyl, Flintshire, who studied at Royal Academy Schools. She married the artist Cecil Gunthorp. Exhibited at RA Summer Exhibition from 1926–65 and lived in London.

Cecil GUNTHORP fl. from mid-1920s–1983 Sculptor, married to the portrait painter Beatrice Gunthorp. He was born in London, having a studio in the south at Balham. Studied at City and Guilds of London Institute and at Royal College of Art. Was a member of Art Workers' Guild from 1930 and showed at RA.

Kit GUNTON 1900–1980 Artist in oil, watercolour, lino-cut, scraperboard and other media who spent most of her life in Bristol. After attending Culverhay School, Keynsham, she studied at Bristol School of Design, under John Fisher, 1916–18, then Bristol College of Art, 1918–21, with R E J Bush. From 1920–79 she was a prolific exhibitor at RWA, being made an associate in 1972. Also showed at SWA. In 1938 *Birdsworth*, with a text by the Bristol writer and artist Donald Hughes, was published, including several dozen lino-cuts of birds by Gunton, who operated from the Pelican Studio in Whiteladies Road. Bristol City Art Gallery, Bristol Corporation Schools Loan Collection and RWA hold examples of Miss Gunton's work. By 1976 she had moved to Bournemouth, where she died.

Sarah GUPPY 1957– Artist, born in Auckland, New Zealand, who studied graphics and design at the Technical College there, 1975, also attending Auckland Society of Arts, 1976, and Morley College, 1981. Exhibitions included Monkeys and Magic, Cambridge University, 1984; The Day Book, Smith Street Gallery, 1988; Art for Equality, ICA, 1991; Mixed Blessings, John Leech Gallery in Auckland and La Girarde, St Quentin de Caplong, France, both 1992; Long and Ryle, 1993; and Ipswich Open, Christchurch Mansion, Ipswich, 1995, which included her sensitive gouache and ink Head of a Hare. She carried out private commissions for murals in Cambridge and London and her work was held in many collections around the world. She lived in Nayland, Suffolk.

Sophie GURNEY 1919– Painter in oil and gouache and printmaker, born in Cambridge, second daughter of artists Jacques and Gwen Raverat, her own daughter being the painter Nelly Pryor. Sophie's family lived in the south of France until Jacques died in 1925, then returned to England. From 1940 Sophie was married to a Trinity College fellow, Mark Pryor, who died in 1970, then in 1972 to Charles Gurney. After some time in the Far East they moved to Devon where in 1997 he died. Her first training was in music, she began to paint well into her thirties and exhibited in Cambridge, Exeter and Totnes. Sophie, Gwen and Nelly were given a trio exhibition at Broughton House Gallery, Cambridge, in 1999.

George GURR 1911–1978 Landscape and coastal painter mainly in watercolour. Studied at Leicester College of Art, 1932–7, under Ralph Middleton Todd. Showed with NEAC and for many years with Leicester Society of Artists, of which he was a member. He was the son of another local painter, Albert Gurr, who worked in watercolour until he died aged 101.

Herbert GURSCHNER 1901–1975 Painter, printmaker and theatrical designer, born in Innsbruck, Austria. He studied there, in Vienna and for several years with Franz von Stuck at Munich Academy, also having private tuition with Egger Lienz. Gurschner showed extensively between the wars at Cooling Gallery, had his first solo show at Fine Art Society in 1929, also exhibiting widely on the continent and in America. He lived in England from 1932, serving in the British Army in World War II, becoming a British subject in 1946. Designed for a number of stage plays. Tate Gallery holds his work.

Ella GURU 1966– Artist and musician, original name Ella Drauglis, born in Ohio, America, who attended Columbus College of Art & Design, 1984–6; graduated from Ohio State University in fine arts, 1988–9; was a go-go dancer, travelling in India and Africa, and worked a waitress in north London, where she lived, 1990–3; and was a member of the Voodoo Queens Indie Pop band, 1993–5. From 1997 Guru was a website designer, managing the site of the Stuckists, of which she was a member. She showed with them at Artbank Gallery, 2001. Other exhibitions included the Fringe Gallery, in Newark, New Jersey. In 1996 Guru met her partner Sexton Ming, sometimes jointly painted with him and played in his band The Tasty Ones.

Graham GUSSIN 1960– Artist born and living in London, who gained his master's degree at Chelsea School of Art, 1989–90. Group exhibitions included New British Sculpture, Chisenhale Gallery, 1987; Installation Work, Chrome Factory, 1988; New Identities, Camden Arts Centre, 1989; Five British Artists, Thomas Backhaus Gallery, Düsseldorf, Germany, 1991; Angles Gallery, Los Angeles, America, 1992; Landscape Paintings, Transmission Gallery, Glasgow, 1993; and Video Positive 97, Fall (100–1), Cornerhouse, Manchester, 1997. Solo shows included Primo Piano, Rome, and Chisenhale Gallery, both 1993, and in 1998 an installation at the Tate Gallery, in which Gussin's preoccupation with the nature of space was evident. In 2002, Gussin had a comprehensive show at the Ikon Gallery, Birmingham, which reviewed key works from 1990. In 2003, he was one of three artists commissioned by Contemporary Projects for that year's 50th Venice Biennale, in the same year his provocative film works sharing space with photographs by James Caseberre at Lisson Gallery. Gussin won a Paul Hamlyn Award for the Visual Arts in 2004.

Jamie GUTCH 1974– Maker of mobiles in a range of materials, born James Gutch, who was educated at St Paul's School, 1988–93. He did a course in plaster-casting at the European Centre for the Trades and Professions, Venice, 1997, and in 1998 graduated with first-class honours in modern and medieval languages, Cambridge University. He then began making mobiles and was largely self-taught. "Balance and dynamism are the properties which underline all my works, whether they originate from direct study of the figure or whether they are based on purely abstract principles." Commissions included London Executive Aviation, 2000; British Petroleum, Sunbury, 2001–2; and The Redcliffe Surgery, 2002. Among his solo exhibitions were St Paul's School and Curwen Gallery, both in 2002.

Derek GUTHRIE 1936– Painter, born in Liverpool, who studied at the West of England Art College, Bristol, 1953–6, and L'Académie de Feu, Paris. Simplified pictures of ships and the sea were a feature of his work, which was shown in a series of solo exhibitions at Portal Gallery. Guthrie lived in Brittany, Spain and Cornwall, where he settled at Newlyn, near Penzance. He said that: "A painter has a relationship with the place where he has chosen to live, and this should be a vital part of his painting."

James GUTHRIE 1874–1952 Painter, illustrator, designer, printer and writer, born in Glasgow, father of the artist Robin Guthrie. While working in the family metal business studied part-time at Heatherley's School of Fine art and at the British Museum. In 1895 founded *The Elf* magazine and four years later the Pear Tree Press. He published his own books, being responsible for all the processes. His own graphic work is sometimes experimental, often intense in feeling. Exhibited IS, Baillie Gallery, RA, RSA and at the Barcelona International Exhibition, winning a gold medal. His books include *An Album of Drawings* and *The Proportional System of Typographical Composition*. Lived at Flansham, Sussex.

Jane Gordon GUTHRIE 1927– Painter, born in Farningham, Kent. She studied at Sidcup Art School, 1944–6; Goldsmiths' College School of Art, 1946–7; the Royal College of Art, 1947–50, teachers including Leonard Appelbee, Ruskin Spear and Carel Weight; then in 1959 with Oskar Kokoschka. Showed at RA, RP and NEAC and had several solo exhibitions. Lived in Boxley, Kent.

Karen GUTHRIE 1970– Artist and teacher, from the mid-1990s collaborating with Nina Pope as Somewhere (see separate entries), who gained an honours degree in printmaking at Edinburgh College of Art, 1987–91, with her master's in printmaking at Royal College of Art, 1991–3. She was a technician and printer at Edinburgh Printmakers Workshop, 1995–6; from 1996 held a number of visiting lectureships, including Edinburgh College of Art, Duncan of Jordanstone in Dundee, Slade School of Fine Art and University of Central England in Birmingham; was researcher and curator, Scottish Printmaking

Workshops' Consortium (Lottery bid), 1996–7; in 1997–8 handling website design for art.tm, Inverness. Among Guthrie's awards were an Andrew Grant Travel Scholarship, 1990, and printmaking scholar, British School at Rome, Italy, 1993–4. Exhibitions included Beyond The Wow Factor, New York State University, America, and RCA Portfolio, Flowers East, both 1993; Only Wankers Weep, Tannery, 1997; and CyberEurope, Weimar, Germany, 1999. Guthrie had a solo show at Maclaurin Art Gallery, Ayr, 1995.

Kathleen GUTHRIE 1905–1981 Painter in oil and opaque watercolour, silkscreen printer, textile designer and mural painter. Writer of children's books. Born in Feltham, Middlesex. Studied at the Slade School under Henry Tonks and at the Royal Academy Schools. Married the artist Robin Guthrie in 1927 and after divorce the Constructivist painter Cecil Stephenson in 1941. Early work is signed K Maltby, her maiden name. At the Slade was influenced by Stanley Spencer's The Nativity, then in the late 1920s by the French Impressionists and her husband's more conventional, Augustus John-like style. With Robin Guthrie went to Boston in 1931 for two years, where he was invited with Rodney Burn to become a co-director of the School of Fine Art. One-man show by Kathleen Guthrie, of figure paintings and landscapes, at Boston's Stace Horne Gallery, in 1932. Her style was further modified when she married Stephenson and associated with the avant-garde of Hampstead. Completed a mural for a local welfare centre. In 1948 had one-man show at Wolf Mankowitz's Little Gallery, in 1951 at the Crane Gallery in Manchester. Began to move from pictures with a whimsical, poetic feeling towards pure abstracts. Retrospective at Drian Gallery in 1966. She illustrated successful children's books, *The Magic Button* and *Magic Button to the Moon*, which contain short poems by her. Lived in London.

Robin GUTHRIE 1902–1971 Painter, draughtsman, illustrator and teacher, born in Harting, Sussex. He was the son of the artist and printer James Guthrie and the husband of the artist Kathleen Guthrie, after divorce from her marrying Deborah Dering. Studied at Slade School of Fine Art, 1918–22, with Philip Wilson Steer and Henry Tonks; Guthrie was like Tonks a fine, sensitive draughtsman, especially of portraits. In the early 1930s he was with Rodney Burn joint director of painting and drawing at the School of the Museum of Fine Arts in Boston, in America; with Burn and Stephen Bone he had his first show at the Goupil Gallery in 1926. Also exhibited at NEAC of which he was a member, Leicester Galleries, Arthur Tooth and Sons, Tate Gallery and many other venues. The Tate, British Museum, Victoria & Albert Museum, National Portrait Gallery and other public institutions hold his work. Guthrie also taught at St Martin's School of Art, City and Guilds School and Royal College of Art, 1950–2. His book illustrations include Eleanor Farjeon's *All the Way to Alfriston*, 1919, and his father's *A Wild Garden*, 1924. Lived in London.

GUY 1956– Self-taught artist in acrylic notable for exuberantly coloured flower still lifes, born and worked in London, full name Guy Stocker. His work was widely reproduced in greetings cards, calendars and posters. Group shows included Contemporary Fine Art Gallery, Eton; Liberty; Images, Zebra 1; and St Albans and York Arts Fairs. Had a series of solo exhibitions at Charlotte Lampard Gallery from 1988 and at Greencroft Gallery from 1989.

Alexander GUY 1962– Painter and teacher, born in St Andrews, Fife. He studied at Duncan of Jordanstone College of Art in Dundee, 1980–4, then Royal College of Art, 1985–7. From 1987 he taught part-time at Glasgow School of Art. Guy won many awards, including first prizes at Diadem Centenary, Scotland, and Scottish Young Contemporaries, both 1984; an Elizabeth Greenshields Foundation Award, 1985, with a second Award in 1987; and a prize in the 1993–4 John Moores Liverpool Exhibition for his spiked bed canvas, "one of a series I have done about pain and punishment, worry and guilt." Showed solo at Paton Gallery from 1989 and lived in London. Unilever, Robert Fleming & Company and Scottish Arts Council hold examples.

Edna GUY 1897– Watercolour painter, born in Sutton, Surrey. She studied art in South Africa with John Amschewitz in 1920, then at Académie Julian, Paris, 1921–2, at the Spenlove School with Reginald Eves, 1934–5, and at the Slade School of Fine Art, 1936, under Randolph Schwabe. Exhibited RA, SWA, RI, Paris Salon and widely abroad. Member of RWS. Lived in London.

Richard GUYATT 1914– Designer, graphic artist and teacher, married to the artist Elizabeth Corsellis, living at Ham, Marlborough, Wiltshire. After education at Charterhouse Guyatt became a freelance designer, producing posters for Jack Beddington at Shell-Mex and BP. His first was for the Visit Britain's Landscapes series in 1936, which he termed "an amazing commission for a callow young man just out of his teens who had never been to art college", another memorable image being for the series These Men Use Shell, 1939: a rakish racing driver at Brooklands. During World War II Guyatt was regional camouflage officer for Scotland, Ministry of Home Security. From 1946–8 he was director and chief designer, Cockade Ltd; was co-designer of the Lion and Unicorn Pavilion at the 1951 Festival of Britain; consultant designer, Josiah Wedgwood & Sons, 1952–5 and 1967–70; Central Electricity Generating Board, 1964–8; British Sugar Bureau, 1965–8; and the newsagent W H Smith, 1970–87. In parallel Guyatt was a noted academic, becoming professor of graphic arts at the Royal College of Art, 1948–78, pro-rector, 1974–8, and rector, 1978–81, in 1955 and 1962 a visiting professor at Yale University in America. He also produced a number of notable ceramic, stamp, coin and other designs for such bodies as the Ministry of Works, Goldsmiths' Company, Royal Mint and the Post Office and held positions including member of the Stamp Advisory Committee, 1963–74, Bank of England Design Advisory Committee, 1968–75, advisory council, Victoria & Albert Museum, 1978–81, and governor, Imperial College of Science and Technology, 1979–81. He was also chairman of the Guyatt/Jenkins Design Group. Among awards were the Misha Black Medal for distinguished services to design education, Society of Industrial Artists and Designers, 2000.

Mavis GUZELIAN: *see* **Mavis ALTOUNYAN**

Louella GWILLIM 1950– Painter and teacher, who studied at City and Guilds of London Art School, 1975–8. Went on to teach for Ravensbourne and Hammersmith and

North Kensington Adult Education Institutes. Appeared at RA Summer Exhibition, Whitechapel Open, Camden Open, Royal Over-Seas League and in 1985 was included in Figurative Painters at Woodlands Art Gallery. Lived in London.

Elis GWYN: *see* **Elis Gwyn JONES**

Allan GWYNNE-JONES 1892–1982 Painter in oil and watercolour, etcher, illuminator and decorator whose landscapes, still lifes and portraits gain their effect with a quiet, understated charm. Born in Richmond, Surrey, Gwynne-Jones went to Bedales, then was articled to study law. In 1913 exhibited a picture on silk at the NEAC, with which he continued to show for many years. Served with distinction in World War I, then attended the Slade School 1919–22, his studies having been interrupted in 1914. Won several first prizes. Became professor of painting at the Royal College of Art in 1923, about the time he began to hold one-man shows. Resigned to join the Slade staff in 1930, staying there until 1959. During World War II he also taught part-time at the fine art department, University of Reading. Was married to the artist Rosemary Allan, their daughter being the painter Emily Gwynne-Jones. Exhibited regularly at the RA from 1950, elected RA in 1965. Wrote several books, including *Portrait Painters* and *Introduction to Still-Life*. Gwynne-Jones' work is in many public collections in Britain, including the Tate Gallery and Ashmolean Museum, as well as abroad. Memorial exhibition in 1982 at National Museum of Wales, Cardiff. Lived at Eastleach Turville, Gloucestershire.

Emily GWYNNE-JONES 1948– Painter, daughter of the artists Allan Gwynne-Jones and Rosemary Allan and married to the painter Frank Beanland. Between 1965–6 she studied at the Royal Academy Schools, with travel on the continent, then at the Royal College of Art, under Carel Weight, 1967–70, working in Paris in 1968. She won a British Council Travelling Scholarship to Budapest, Hungary, in 1971; worked on costumes for English National Opera, 1973–5; then studied at North-East London Polytechnic and etching with Norman Ackroyd and textiles at Central School of Arts and Crafts, 1977–8. Showed from mid-1960s at RA Summer Exhibitions, also at NEAC and New Grafton Gallery and was a member of the Contemporary Portrait Society. Had solo shows with Michael Parkin Gallery in 1977, King Street Gallery in 1983 and Heveningham Hall, 1993. RA, Eton College and Paintings in Hospitals hold examples. Lived in Fressingfield, Suffolk.

Pauline GYLES 1931– Watercolourist with no formal art school training who specialised in miniature portraits, still lifes and flowers. She was born in Dorset, where she settled in Poole. After leaving school she hand-coloured photographic portraits to a high standard, then began miniatures around 1970. She was a founder-member of the Society of Botanical Artists, also belonging to RMS and the Hilliard Society. Also exhibited with Medici and Llewellyn Alexander Galleries and with Linda Blackstone Gallery in Pinner. Russell-Cotes Art Gallery and Museum in Bournemouth and the Society of Apothecaries hold examples. Her work appeared in the RMS' *100 Years of Miniatures*, by Suzanne Lucas; *How to Paint Miniatures*, by Robert Hughes; and *The Techniques of Painting Miniatures*, by Sue Burton.

H

H: *see* **Brian HAGGER**

H: *see* **Kathleen Finlay HORSMAN**

Liam H: *see* **Liam HANLEY**

Norman Douglas H: *see* **Norman Douglas HUTCHINSON**

Vivien H: *see* **Vivien HISLOP**

Tom HACKETT 1961– Sculptor and installations artist and lecturer, born in Cambridge, who graduated in fine art from Middlesex Polytechnic, 1981–4, gaining his master's at Nottingham Trent University, 1993–5. Hackett was chairman of the Sheffield Contemporary Arts Trust, 1990; artist-in-residence, Elliot Durham School, Nottingham, 1992, the year he completed a canteen sculpture there at Wilford Meadows School; ran sculpture workshops at Abbey International College, Malvern Wells, 1993; was involved in a sculpture/dance collaboration with Aoife Dance/Choice Moves, Leicester, 1994; completed the Birdcage Walk Public Sculpture for Nottingham City Council, 1996; was engaged on the Iron Age Project, Anchor Housing, Nottingham, 1999; and from 2000 was advisor to East Midlands Arts Board. He had extensive visiting and part-time lectureships, including the University of Derby, from 2000; Bournemouth Institute, 2001; and Broxtowe College, from 2002. Participated in many group shows, among later solo installations being Lache pas la Pataté at Rugby Art Gallery & Museum, Pulp at University of Hertfordshire in Hatfield and Object in Absentia at Pitshanger Manor Gallery, all 2003. Lived in Mapperley, Nottingham.

Alfred HACKNEY 1926–1994 Printmaker, painter and teacher, born in Stainforth, Yorkshire, brother of the artist Arthur Hackney. He studied at Burslem School of Art in Stoke-on-Trent, then Edinburgh College, with a travelling scholarship to France and Italy. He was a visiting teacher at Willesden School of Art, then senior lecturer at Medway College of Art in Rochester. Was a member of RWS and an associate of RE, also showing with RA, SEA, LG and SSA. RA holds his work. Lived in Cobham, Kent.

Arthur HACKNEY 1925– Painter, etcher and teacher, older brother of the artist Alfred Hackney, born in Stainforth, Yorkshire. He was an apprentice engraver in the Potteries, studying with Reginald Haggar at Burslem School of Art, Stoke-on-Trent, then Royal College of Art with Robert Austin, winning a travelling scholarship. Went on to be head of department at West Surrey College of Art and Design, Farnham, 1950–86. He was a member of RWS, being vice-president, 1973–6, and of RE, also showing at RA and widely elsewhere in Britain and abroad. Victoria & Albert Museum, Ashmolean Museum in Oxford and many other collections hold examples. Lived in Tongham, Farnham, Surrey.

Isla HACKNEY 1962– Artist, designer, lecturer and writer who gained her master's honours degree in fine art from Edinburgh University and Edinburgh College of Art, 1985, and her master's in time-based media from the Kent Institute of Art & Design, 1997. Hackney there lectured in cultural studies; was a freelance designer for BBC Scotland's travel programme; and was co-author, with Fiona Hackney, of *Charles Rennie Mackintosh*, 1989, and *The Art of the World's Greatest Watercolourists*, 1990. She was elected to the RWS, 1993. Mixed shows included Ancrum Gallery, Jedburgh, 1985–6; RSW at RSA, 1994–6; Printmakers' Workshop, Edinburgh, 1996; and Royal College of Art, 1999, and Artmonsky Gallery. Among her solo exhibitions were Freshfields, 1998, and Lynne Strover Gallery, Fen Ditton, 2001.

Mary HACKNEY 1925– Figurative artist, notably in pastel, who studied at Coventry School of Art, Birmingham College of Art and the Royal College of Art. From 1951–4 she was an art director of the advertising agency J Walter Thompson, afterwards working as a freelance artist. Showed at RA and with PS, of which she was a member. Lived at Tongham, Surrey.

Tom HACKNEY 1977– Artist, born in Taunton, Somerset, who graduated with first-class honours in fine art from Manchester Metropolitan University, 1997–00. His work was widely shown at art fairs, group shows including 72 Hours of Painting, Bankley Studios, Manchester, 1999; Images Re-viewed, Philips Contemporary Art, Manchester, and Vertigo Gallery, both 2001; Koestler Special Arts Event, 2002; and Forever Beautiful, Clapham Gallery, 2004. In 2003–4 Hackney gained a BOC Emerging Artist Award, entering The BOC Group collection, his work also being held by LHM plc and Manchester Art Gallery. His solo exhibitions were You Looking at Me, arc Gallery, Manchester, 2000, Dream Sequence, at arc and The Westbourne Hotel, London, both 2002; Suspended Belief, The Castlefield Gallery, Manchester, 2003; and Scenic Wonder, Space, Triangle Gallery, 2004. Hackney lived in east London.

THE HACKNEY FLASHERS– The Hackney Flashers Collective was instigated by the Photography Workshop in the 1970s to explore joint working, especially among politically active documentary photographers. The group developed an all-woman membership, including Jo Spence (see separate entry) and Liz Heron, and produced two major photographic projects in east London and an educational slide pack. Hackney Flashers pictures were used widely in the 1970s and early 1980s, at which point the group disbanded but remained in contact. Twenty-nine Hackney Flashers slides, titled Who's Holding the Baby?, of 1978, from the Arts Council collection were included in Protest & Survive at the Whitechapel Art Gallery, 2000.

Charles HADCOCK 1965– Sculptor, born in Derby, who trained at Gloucestershire College of Arts and Technology, 1984–7, then the Royal College of Art, 1987–9. Residencies included Hurricane Sculpture, London Borough of Ealing, 1987–8, and Millfield School, Street, 1997. Group shows included Uley Arts Centre, Gloucestershire, 1987; New Art Centre Sculpture Garden, Roche Court, Salisbury, 1989; and Lewes Sculpture Trail, Lewes, 1997. Later solo exhibitions included Reed's Wharf Gallery, 1996, University of Essex, 1997, and Canary Wharf, 2003. Hadcock made two types of sculpture: casts of polystyrene packaging, and large metal constructions (such as his 10-ton, cast-iron Caesura IV, in 16 sections, installed at Goodwood Sculpture Park, in 1995, rather like a yet-to-be-finished piece of architecture on which the viewer could speculate). Public and corporate commissions included Brighton and Hove Council, Imperial Chemical Industries, British Airports Authority Gatwick Airport and Allied Domecq. Lived and worked in London.

Vincent HADDELSEY fl. from 1960s– Self-taught horse painter, brought up in a small village south of Lincoln where learned to ride and hunt. Haddelsey left England aged 18 for British Columbia, and extensive travels through the continent, Mexico, Asia and Inner Mongolia followed. He broadened his equestrian knowledge and began to paint what he saw. In 1995 RONA Gallery gave him his first solo show in England for over a decade. Collingbourne Fine Arts issued signed, limited-edition prints, some in a period setting. HM The Queen, the Mellon Collection of Sporting Art in America and a number of English museums hold examples. Haddelsey latterly spent much time in France.

Aldridge HADDOCK 1931–1996 Self-taught artist in mixed media, full name Edwin Aldridge Haddock, known as Fin and born in Durham. He attended the University there graduating as a bachelor of medicine and of surgery in 1953, gaining a diploma in obstetrics from the Royal College of Obstetricians and Gynaecologists in 1955. He was house surgeon and house physician at a number of hospitals in Newcastle and Middlesbrough. Haddock was a member of Lincolnshire Artists' Society and Free Painters and Sculptors. He had several dozen solo shows, including Ferens Art Gallery, Hull; Graves Art Gallery, Sheffield; Woodstock Gallery; Drian Galleries; and Century Galleries in Henley-on-Thames. Public galleries in Hull, Doncaster and Newcastle hold examples. Lived in Grimsby, Lincolnshire.

John HADDOCK 1934– Professionally an interior designer who painted. Studied furniture design at Birmingham College of Art, in 1963 being elected a member of the Society of Industrial Artists and Designers, later The Chartered Society of Designers. Began painting in 1972 at Eltham Institute Art Centre. Showed at RA Summer Exhibitions, Tudor Barn Art Gallery in Eltham and had two four-man exhibitions: at Greenwich Theatre Gallery and in 1985 at Woodlands Art Gallery. Painted still life and landscapes widely in England and France. Lived in London.

John Marshall HADDOCK 1914–1963 Painter, illustrator and commercial artist, son of the painter J M Haddock. Studied at Regent Street Polytechnic School of Art, where he concentrated on architectural work, also at Putney School of Art, 1933–8, with Adrian Hill and Francis Hodge. Showed at RA and RBA and did magazine illustration. Sometimes signed work J M H. Lived in London.

Simon HADDOCK 1970– Painter, born and lived in London, whose early work focused on the motorway and urban living. He attended the West Glamorgan Institute of Higher Education, 1989–90; University of the West of England, Bristol, 1991–5; and Royal Academy Schools, 1995–8. Awards included Landseer Landscape Award, Premiums, Royal Academy Schools, 1997, and Vincent Harris Mural Painting Award and Solomon Travel Scholarship to Jerusalem, Israel, both 1998. Among Haddock's group exhibitions were Bristol Cathedral Exhibition and Residency, 1992; Site-specific wall painting, Bristol University physics department, 1995; Original II, Kapil Jariwala Gallery, 1998; and Zwemmer Gallery, ART2001, Business Design Centre, Islington, 2001. There was a solo show, End of Free Recovery, in 2000 at Paton Gallery.

Trevor HADDRELL 1945– Painter, printmaker and teacher, born in Rotherham, Yorkshire, full name John Trevor Haddrell, who attended Bath Academy of Art, 1964–7, under Clifford Ellis. He was head of art and design at Ashton Park School, then Clifton High School, both in Bristol where he lived, retiring in 2001 to do his own work plus part-time teaching. He was noted for large engraved panoramas of Bristol, theatre interiors and natural forms. Haddrell was a subscriber-member of SWE, participating in its show at the Museum of Garden History in 2001. He also exhibited widely solo and in groups in Bristol, including national print shows at RWA, winning a prize there in 1997. Haddrell's work was in *Engraved Gardens*, 2001, edited by Hilary Paynter. Haddrell's *Panoramic Bristol: 50 engravings and linocuts*, was published by Redcliffe Press in 2002, followed by a book of horticultural engravings in 2005. City Museum and Art Gallery, Bristol, and Bristol University's theatre collection hold examples.

Susan HADLEY 1940– Sculptor, painter, draughtsman and teacher, born in Redhill, Surrey, great grand-daughter of the Danish painter Vilhelm Marstrand. From 1959–60 she studied at Lycée Français de Londres, a bilingual secretarial course in French and German, then in 1982–6 at West Sussex Institute, where she gained a first-class honours degree in art and design. Hadley spent half the year teaching (which included West Dean College, 1991–4), half on her own work. This reflected "all aspects of life, and the Christian content comes naturally from my human experience." Recurrent themes included vulnerability, arms and relationships. In 1993, the BBC Television programme *Glimpses of God* centred on her sculpture. Hadley was included in John Plowman's 1995 book *The Encyclopedia of Sculpting Techniques*. She was a member of the Art Centre Group. Lived in Chichester, Sussex, where she opened her house and garden during its annual Festivities. Mixed shows included Regnum Club, Chichester, and Terrace Gallery, Worthing, both 1988; Goodwood House, Goodwood, 1990; Eastgate Gallery, Chichester, from 1991; Mark Jerram Gallery, Salisbury, 1995; and Thompson's Gallery, from 1996. Had solo exhibitions at Pallant House, Chichester, 1987–8.

Penny HADRILL 1953– Textile and photography artist and teacher, born in Kent, who attended Brighton Polytechnic, 1971–2; Hornsey College of Art, 1972–5; and an English National Theatre design course, 1975–6. Hadrill was head of the dye and print department at English National Opera, 1976–7. In the latter year she established a workshop at Waterside Warehouse in Rotherhithe, moving to New Crane Wharf in 1978. Exhibitions included Midland Group, Nottingham, 1978; New Faces, British Crafts Centre, 1981; and Wapping Artists Open Studios, 1982.

Elpida HADZI-VASILEVA 1971– Sculptor, draughtsman and lecturer who grew up in a remote, mountainous region of Macedonia. She achieved first-class honours in sculpture at Glasgow School of Art, gaining her master's at the Royal College of Art. By the time that she was shortlisted for the first Jerwood Sculpture Prize, in 2001, Hadzi-Vasileva had a reputation for producing works from unusual materials. In her 1999 solo show at ArtSway she employed butter and fir cones, in the 2001 exhibition Epidermis, at Berwick Gymnasium Gallery, she used 2,500 salmon skins and 1,500 bones, all specially cleaned and preserved for the purpose. She was a visiting lecturer at several art colleges. Other shows included Kelvingrove Museum, Glasgow, 2001, and the Museum of Contemporary Arts, Macedonia, 2002.

Antoinette HAECHLER 1965– Painter, born in Switzerland, who settled in Newcastle upon Tyne. She completed foundation studies at Sunderland Polytechnic, 1988–9, graduating in fine art from University of Northumbria, 1989–92. Group shows included Northern Graduates, New Academy Gallery, 1992; The Dog Squad, Goldenes Kalb Gallery, Switzerland, 1994; Behind the Scenes, Hancock Museum, Newcastle, 1996; and Amber, Laure Genillard Gallery, 2000. There, by using fabric as a support, Haechler added a sense of domesticity to an otherwise severe group of symbols. Solo exhibitions included Northern Arts building, Newcastle, 2000.

Anthony HAESTIER 1953– Painter, draughtsman and illustrator, born in London, who studied at Hornsey School of Art, working for almost a decade as an illustrator for a leading West End advertising studio. Strong design was a feature of his work, which included pictures of Hertfordshire and the Romney Marsh area of East Sussex, where he had homes. Showed solo at Highgate Fine Art in 1999.

Karl HAGEDORN 1889–1969 Painter, commercial artist, designer of fabrics and teacher, born in Berlin. After initial education in Germany Hagedorn settled in England in 1905, training in textile production. He attended Manchester School of Technology and the city's School of Art, Slade School of Fine Art and in Paris, 1912–3, where he was in the school run by Maurice Denis. The Cubist and Futurist influences acquired in Paris profoundly affected Hagedorn's work as shown in the Society of Modern Painters, Manchester, 1913–6; the impact of his pictures in a provincial city, before his work became more conventional, was covered in Manchester's First Modernist Karl Hagedorn 1889–1969 at Whitworth Art Gallery, Manchester, 1994, and Chris Beetles Ltd, 1995. Hagedorn became naturalised at the outbreak of World War I, during which he served in the Army, producing war pictures. He showed widely in Paris and was a member of Salon d'Automne, was honorary treasurer of the RBA and showed at Fine Art Society, AAA, NEAC, RI and elsewhere. Did commercial work for Empire Marketing Board, Shell and *Radio Times*. Taught part-time at Epsom School of Art. British Museum, Victoria & Albert Museum and Manchester City Art Gallery hold examples. Lived at Lower Feltham in Middlesex and in London. A Hagedorn Trust exists to enhance his reputation.

Arthur T HAGG 1895– Painter and designer. Studied at Norwich School of Art, 1912, then at the Westminster School of Art under Walter Bayes and Bernard Meninsky. Taught for some years in Sussex. Exhibited RA, RI, NEAC and RBA. Lived in London.

Reginald George HAGGAR 1905–1988 Painter, pottery designer and writer, illustrator and teacher, born in Ipswich, Suffolk. Aged 12 he became a delivery boy for a florist's, then was at local Art School, 1922–6, followed by Royal College of Art, to which he won a Royal Exhibition and where he was taught by Reco Capey. Joined Mintons Ltd in 1929 and soon became art director, but left in 1935, miffed at resistance to his efforts to improve designs. He became head of Stoke School of Art until 1941, holding a similar position at Burslem School of Art until 1945, when he became a freelance painter, writer on pottery and porcelain and lecturer. His books on *Lane Delph*, *Staffordshire Chimney Ornaments*, *English Country Pottery* and his two *Encyclopaedias of English and Continental Pottery and Porcelain* were scholarly and readable. Showed RA, RWA, RSA and elsewhere and was from the mid-1940s for over 30 years president of the Society of Staffordshire Artists. He lived in Stoke-on-Trent where the City Museum and Art Gallery, in common with galleries in Ipswich and Dudley, holds his work.

Brian HAGGER 1935–2006 Painter in oil and watercolour, draughtsman in pencil and teacher, born in Bury St Edmunds, Suffolk. He studied at Ipswich School of Art, 1952–6, then Royal College of Art, 1958–61, teachers including Colin Moss, Pif Fortin, Carel Weight, Ruskin Spear and Ceri Richards. Numerous mixed shows included RA Summer Exhibition, Phoenix Gallery in Lavenham and Highgate and with Norwich Twenty Group. Had a series of solo shows at Bramante Gallery, 1968–71; Thackeray Gallery, 1972–5; and Langton Gallery, 1976. Before his first solo exhibition, Hagger showed his oil on board cityscapes on the Green Park railings, self-effacingly signing them with an H. As he became successful he turned to canvas, put his prices up and signed with his full name. When the American Oscar Lerman saw his work he offered Hagger an exhibition at the new Bramante Gallery. When Lerman returned to America and the Bramante closed, Priscilla Anderson keenly took him on at Thackeray Gallery. Between leaving College and 1976 Hagger produced around 350 marvellously evocative paintings of London, mainly of Fulham and the unfashionable end of King's Road, Chelsea. He also painted Brighton, Norwich and the East Coast. In the mid-1990s, seeking a new theme, Hagger was concentrating mainly on drawing. Did occasional teaching, including Salisbury College of Art, and Great Yarmouth College of Art and Design, including adult education. Bolton Art Gallery holds his work. Lived latterly in Norwich, Norfolk.

Terry HAGGERTY 1970– Painter, born in London, who studied at Southend School of Art and Cheltenham College of Art. Group exhibitions included Fresh Art, Islington Design Centre, 1992; Outpost, Venice Biennale, 1994; and Show Me the Money, Dukes Mews, 1998. In 1999, Haggerty was a finalist in The NatWest Art Prize, in which he showed paintings concerned with illusion and the contradictions involved in painting and perception, resolute abstraction being an important feature of his output.

John HAGGIS 1897–1968 Portrait, landscape and figure painter in oil and watercolour, black-and-white artist and etcher. Born in London, Haggis studied art in Australia and at Royal College of Art under Malcolm Osborne. Showed widely, including Walker's Galleries, RA, RP, NEAC, RCamA, RWA and Paris Salon. His work is in Australian and British provincial museums. He was official portrait painter to the British studio Gainsborough Pictures, travelling as far afield as Barbados to complete portraits. These included Fredric March, Mai Zetterling and Claire Bloom. Painted many landscapes in Britain, especially in Yorkshire and Hertfordshire, where he lived at Welwyn. In 1921 he founded the Welwyn Garden City Art Club.

Philip HAGREEN 1890–1988 Wood engraver, painter, ivory carver, letter-cutter and cartoonist born into a family of artists. He studied as a painter in Cornwall with Norman Garstin, Harold and Laura Knight, then at New Cross Art School, joining the Army in World War I. After the war Hagreen assembled artists who formed SWE in 1920. In early 1920s settled in Ditchling, Sussex, and joined the Guild of St Joseph and St Dominic, with Eric Gill learning letter-cutting and helping complete the Stations of the Cross for St Cuthbert's in Bradford. For 15 years from 1934 contributed amusing cartoons for *The Cross and The Plough*, the magazine of the Catholic Land Federation. Retired from Guild in 1957, in later years being bedridden.

Jonathan HAGUE 1938– Artist and teacher, born in Llandudno, Caernarvonshire. He attended Liverpool College of Art, 1957–63, then Royal Academy of Fine Art, The Hague, 1964–6. He was a part-time lecturer at Coventry College of Art, then a lecturer at Birmingham College of Art. Showed at RA, Redfern Gallery and widely in the Netherlands, which had granted him a State Scholarship. Had a solo show at Orez International Gallery, The Hague, in 1964, others including Royal Institute Gallery, 1967. Lived in Leamington Spa, Warwickshire.

Sheila HAGUE 1920– Painter, illustrator and cartoonist who was brought up in Sussex. She attended Wimbledon School of Art under Gerald Cooper and Robert Barnes, then the Royal College of Art with Gilbert Spencer and Percy Horton. Exhibited RA and AIA. Lived in London.

Ghulam HAIDER: *see* **YUNUS**

George Douglas, The Earl HAIG 1918– Painter, born in London, son of Field-Marshal Earl Haig whom he succeeded in 1928. After education at Stowe School and Oxford University, Earl Haig served in the Army in World War II, being a prisoner of war in Italy and Germany. In 1945–7 he attended Camberwell School of Arts and Crafts, his teachers including William Johnstone and Claude Rogers; during the holidays he studied with Paul Maze. From 1945 Lord Haig had a series of one-man shows over several decades at the Scottish Gallery, Edinburgh, as well as showing widely elsewhere in Britain and on the continent, latterly including Clarges Gallery and Gallery 10, London. Scottish Gallery gave him a seventieth birthday show in 1988. His work is in the collections of HM The Queen and other members of the royal family, Scottish National Gallery of Modern Art and further public collections. Lord Haig was a member of the Scottish Arts Council and of the Royal Fine Art Commission for Scotland and a trustee of the National Galleries of Scotland. As a landscape painter he was fond of simple, almost naïve images infused with a rich palette. In 2003, there was an exhibition of his oil and watercolour landscapes at Dean Gallery, Edinburgh. Lived in Bemersyde, Melrose, Scotland.

Alfred Grenfell HAIGH 1870–1963 Painter in oil and watercolour, born in Parkgate, Cheshire. He studied art in Paris, then started to paint professionally at the age of 30. Haigh was a keen horseman and favoured hunting and racing subjects. He did not exhibit but had a number of patrons, including HRH The Aga Khan, the Duke of Portland and Lord Rosebery. Made several painting trips to America. The Duke of Northumberland has Haigh's portrait of the ninth Duke, painted in 1933. Was included in The British Sporting Art Trust's 1983 show at Alpine Gallery.

Peter HAIGH 1914–1994 Painter in oil and draughtsman, born near Huddersfield, Yorkshire, and brought up on his uncle's farm. He sold his first painting aged 15; trained as a textile sample dyer, which gave him an early understanding of colour, tone and shape; then travelled the country, sketching and painting. After seven years in the Army in World War II, mostly in the Far East, Haigh – who always insisted that he was self-taught – between 1946–9 attended Heatherley's School of Art under Iain Macnab and Goldsmiths' School of Art, where John Mansbridge and Bernard Hailstone taught and where Haigh met his future wife, Patricia, who became a commercial artist. At the start of the 1950s, following his work being shown at Wildenstein, Haigh was financed to work in France for six months by a Shell oil executive and collector. Between 1949–55 Haigh's pictures were included in mixed exhibitions at RBA, NS, UA, at Roland, Browse and Delbanco and at the Beaux Arts, Zwemmer, Leicester and Redfern Galleries, but then he withdrew from showing, keen to develop in his own way. His early pictures were in the spirit of Walter Sickert, whose work with that of Augustus John he much admired, but gradually he moved towards geometrical abstraction, commonly in a muted palette. Haigh was a meticulous craftsman, noting when he last worked on a picture and could safely return to it, and utilising all available time from morning light until four in the afternoon. To survive he did a variety of clerical jobs, worked as a barman and learned framing and gilding with the firm of Savage before setting up on his own for several years until pressure on painting time made the business impracticable. In 1988 The Pride Gallery put on a retrospective, another show being held at Ambiente Gero, Galeria de Arte, in Valencia, 1991. Lived in London and died in Chelsea and Westminster Hospital.

Richard Neville HAILE 1895– Portrait painter and photographer, born in London. Educated at St Mark's College, Chelsea; Chelsea Polytechnic; and Regent Street Polytechnic School of Art. Exhibited RA, London Salon, PS and in a number of photographic shows. On several occasions he was president of the Institute of British Photographers. Lived in Bognor Regis, Sussex.

Sam HAILE 1909–1948 Artist, potter and teacher, born in London. Went to evening classes at Clapham School of Art, winning a scholarship to Royal College of Art, 1931–5, initially concentrating on painting, then on pottery under the potter William Staite Murray. During the late 1930s Haile showed with Surrealist Group and AIA. From 1939–44 he lived in New York, where Haile, whose politics were left-wing and convictions pacifist, went to escape what he considered a capitalist struggle. In England he had taught at Leicester College of Art and in the London area and in America, as well as exhibiting and selling works to public collections, he taught at the New York State College of Ceramics, Alfred University, and at the College of Architecture, University of Michigan, Ann Arbor. Eventually, he was drafted into the American Army as a non-combatant, then became an instructor in the Education Corps of the British Army, being released in late 1945 after concussion in a motor-cycle accident. In 1946 he joined the Rural Industries Bureau as its pottery consultant, but was killed in a motoring accident two years later. In 1947 he had moved to Shinner's Bridge, Dartington, Devon, to a house and workshop lately vacated by the potter Bernard Leach. Haile's pictures mixed strong themes, including concern at the threat of Fascism, sexuality and violence. Review exhibitions of his work were held at Crafts Centre in 1951, Birch and Conran, 1987, and Holburne Museum, Bath, 1993.

Bernard HAILSTONE 1910–1987 Portrait painter, brother of the artist Harold Hailstone. After education at the Judd School, Tonbridge, Hailstone attended Goldsmiths' College School of Art, under Clive Gardiner, then the Royal Academy Schools, with James Bateman and Walter Westley Russell. At the outbreak of World War II Hailstone joined the Auxiliary Fire Service, drew his comrades and Blitz scenes and held an exhibition at the RA. In 1941 he was asked to become an Official War Artist, initially attached to the Ministry of Transport. Later he painted convoys in the Atlantic and Mediterranean, then in 1944 joined South-East Asia Command, painting Lord Louis Mountbatten and key members of his staff, pictures now in Imperial War Museum. A gregarious, outgoing man, Hailstone went on to paint Sir Winston Churchill, Lord Olivier, Paul Mellon – he worked a lot in America – and members of the royal family, but he as happily painted ordinary members of the public. Also exhibited LG, RBA and NEAC. Lived at Hadlow, near Tonbridge, Kent.

Harold HAILSTONE 1897–1982 Illustrator and cartoonist in watercolour, black-and-white and oil. Born in London, studied at Goldsmiths' College School of Art. During World War II served in the Royal Air Force as an official artist and exhibited with the War Artists. The Imperial War Museum holds his work. Illustrated widely for magazines such as *Punch*, *Illustrated London News*, *Passing Show* and *Tatler*. Brother of the artist Bernard Hailstone. Lived at Hadlow, near Tonbridge, Kent.

June HAINAULT fl. from 1950s– Painter and printmaker who studied at Regent Street Polytechnic School of Art and at Heatherley's School of Fine Art, teachers including Iain Macnab and Frederic Whiting. Was a member of Free Painters and Sculptors, also of Eastbourne Group, and had a number of solo exhibitions, including Il Traghetto Gallery in Venice, 1966; New Town Gallery, Uckfield, from 1969; Upper Street Gallery, from 1972; and Hanover Galleries, Liverpool, 1986. Lived in Five Ashes, Sussex.

Elizabeth HAINES 1945– Painter, illustrator and teacher, born Hertfordshire, who studied at St Albans and Brighton Colleges of Art, graduating in graphic design in 1967, in 1968 moving to Pembrokeshire. Taught at Carmarthen College of Art, 1982–4. In 1987 she was artist-in-residence at the National Eisteddfod, having won a national competition to interpret the forms of Cerdd Dafod (Welsh prosody). Haines occasionally held open studio in her 1996-converted barn on Bryn Morris hill farm, Rhosfach, Clunderwen. For many years she was almost exclusively a landscape painter, influenced by the British watercolourists, but in the early 1990s diverted towards architecture and musicians. She made drawings at rehearsals and masterclasses at the Royal Academy of Music in 1994, linked to a WAC bursary to research the relationship between painting and music. As well as prompting abstract paintings, this motivated Haines in 1993 to embark on a doctorate in the philosophy of aesthetics at the University of Wales, Lampeter. Haines exhibited extensively, including the WSW, RCamA, National Museum of Wales in Cardiff, Albany Gallery and St John's Smith Square. There was a retrospective at the National Library of Wales, Aberystwyth, in 1996. In 1999 and 2002 Haines shared shows with Denis Curry at the Heifer Gallery and in 2003 she had a solo exhibition at Oriel Washington Gallery, Penarth. Commissions included sketchbooks, one for the Ty Glyn Davis Trust, sponsored by the Gulbenkian Foundation. WAC and other Welsh public collections hold her work.

Lett HAINES 1894–1978 Artist in various media and teacher, correct name Arthur Lett-Haines. Was educated at St Paul's School and served in the Army in World War I. He was early a member of an artistic set including E McKnight Kauffer, John Middleton Murry and D H Lawrence. Lett Haines was always an experimental artist whose work had a strong linear element and who admitted a big debt to Picasso. In 1918 he met the painter Cedric Morris and they lived together for 60 years as lovers, although it was sometimes a stormy partnership. A less consistent painter than Morris, Haines chose to take over the running of the East Anglian School of Painting and Drawing household. As a teacher Haines believed in giving students freedom to develop along independent lines. There was a retrospective at Redfern Gallery, 1984. In 2002–3, Norwich Castle Museum and Art Gallery put on Cedric Morris & Lett Haines: Teaching Art and Life.

Tony HAINES 1959– Painter, born in Harborough Magna, Leicestershire. He attended Loughborough College of Art and Design, 1977–8, then Ravensbourne College of Art and Design, 1979–82. Among his exhibitions were Stowells Trophy, RA, 1982; Deptford Artists Group Show, 1984; New Moon Group Show, Woodlands Art Gallery, from 1986; and Showroom Gallery. A gestural abstract painter.

George HAINSWORTH 1937– Painter in a rich palette, sculptor and teacher, born in Leeds, Yorkshire. He attended Leeds College of Art, 1955–60, then Slade School of Fine Art, 1960–2, under William Coldstream. In the following year he gained a Gulbenkian Scholarship in Sculpture at British School, Rome, 1962–3. Hainsworth taught fine art at Leeds College of Art, 1963–70, joining the staff of Leeds Polytechnic in 1970, eventually becoming senior lecturer in the centre for art and contemporary studies at Leeds Metropolitan University. Hainsworth took part in numerous mixed exhibitions. Had a solo show at Sue Rankin Gallery, 1991, later ones including Open Gardens, Galerie Elisabeth Den Bieman De Haas, Amsterdam, Netherlands, in 2002. Worked non-figuratively for many years, then resumed representational subjects, flowers, mythology and politics being recurrent themes. He was a member of MM Arts Group and the Yorkshire Sculptors' Group. Baring Capital Investors and Provident Financial Group owned examples. Hainsworth's wife Lucy was also an artist and they lived at Hunsingore, near Wetherby, Yorkshire.

Lucy Mary HAINSWORTH 1935– Sculptor, draughtsman and printmaker; teacher, born in Johannesburg, South Africa. She studied at Bromley College of Art, 1955–9, and Slade School of Fine Art, 1959–62, teachers including Frank Auerbach. In 1971 she gained her graduate certificate of education. Was a visiting tutor at Leeds Metropolitan University and other colleges. The figure in movement, the northern industrial landscape and political issues, such as Apartheid, were featured in her work. She was a member of Yorkshire Sculptors' Group and St Paul's Printmakers, Mirfield. In 1990 Hainsworth had a residency at Cartwright Hall, Bradford. Took part in many mixed shows, sharing some with her husband George, including Doncaster City Art Gallery, 1995. They both took part in Re:Collection, Bowes Museum, Barnard Castle, in 2004. Solo shows included Cookridge Street Gallery, Leeds, 1989, and Imperial Chemical Industries Works, Huddersfield, 1992. Provident Financial Group and Eastthorpe Gallery, Mirfield, hold examples. Lived at Hunsingore, near Wetherby, Yorkshire.

Guy Donne Gordon HAKE 1887–1964 Architect and architectural painter and draughtsman. Studied at L'École des Beaux-Arts, Geneva, and at the Architectural Association School, London. Exhibited RA, RWA and Bristol City Art Gallery, which bought drawings by him of wartime bomb damage. Wrote on architectural draughtsmanship. He became principal of RWA School of Architecture for 30 years from 1922. Lived at Honiton, Devon.

Leslie HAKIM DOWEK 1960– Artist born in Beirut, Lebanon, who moved to Britain in 1976. She studied at Camden Arts Centre, Central School of Art, Camberwell School of Arts and Crafts, Slade School of Fine Art and Norwich School of Art. She showed in groups at RA, Edward Totah Gallery, Whitechapel Open, Royal Over-Seas League Annual Exhibition, where she won a joint first prize, and at England & Co's Art in Boxes, 1991. The vulnerability of Nature and its decline were a feature of her assemblages. She showed solo at Spacex Gallery, Exeter, in 1989, and Manchester City Art Gallery, 1991 Lived in London.

Elsie HALE 1913–1999 Artist in oil and watercolour, a member of the Hilliard Society of Miniaturists. She was born and died in Worcester and studied at the College of Art there, 1929–33. At Paris Salon she gained a gold medal in 1978, also showing at RA and elsewhere in London and the provinces. Lived in Salisbury, Wiltshire.

Helen HALE 1936– Painter and sculptor, born in Harpenden, Hertfordshire. She studied at St Martin's and Sir John Cass Schools of Art. Was a member of Hampstead Artists' Council, Free Painters and Sculptors, NS, WIAC, ROI and SWA, also exhibiting in Scotland and France. Lived in Hampstead, north London, later in Rudgwick, Sussex.

Irina HALE 1932– Artist and teacher, half Russian, half Irish, who had an English childhood. Left school aged 11 and lived for six years with her mother in France, portrait painting for a living. Between 1951–4 studied at Bath Academy of Art, Corsham, and travelled on scholarships. Spent the next two years teaching art to children. From 1957–61 she lived in a mountain village near Rome and travelled. After painting for three summers under Kokoschka in Salzburg Hale gained the City of Salzburg Prize, moved to Paris, then back to Italy. Took part in mixed shows at Leicester and Mercury Galleries; Richard Demarco Gallery in Edinburgh; and with WIAC. Solo shows included Crane Kalman Gallery, 1966, and Hambledon Gallery, Blandford, 1968.

John Howard HALE 1863–1955 Painter of portraits and landscapes, born at Farnham, Surrey. Studied at Farnham School of Art, South Kensington Schools and Westminster School of Art under Fred Brown. Studies continued in Holland, where he concentrated on nineteenth-century Dutch art, and he also studied landscape painting with George Boyle. He was for many years head of Blackheath School of Art. Exhibited RA, RBA especially, ROI, Paris Salon, provincial galleries and in Canada. Lived at Farnham, Surrey.

Kathleen HALE 1898–2000 Painter, printmaker, writer and illustrator, born at Broughton, Peeblesshire. Studied at Manchester School of Art, Reading University with Allen Seaby, 1915–17, the Central School of Arts and Crafts, 1928–30, with Bernard Meninsky, and the East Anglian School of Painting and Drawing, 1938, with Cedric Morris. Although she exhibited NEAC, LG, RBA, Leicester and Lefevre Galleries and elsewhere, Hale is most noted for her work for the printed page. After a variety of jobs she gained a reputation as a poster and book artist, then for her series of around 20 books featuring Orlando, the Marmalade Cat, the first appearing just before World War II. Widely travelled in several continents. Her autobiography, *A Slender Reputation*, appeared in 1994. Lived in the Cotswolds, but died in Bristol. Retrospective at The Gekoski Gallery, 1995. There was a memorial exhibition at the Redfern Gallery, 2001.

Mathew HALE 1962– Artist, born in Swindon, Wiltshire, who completed a foundation course at Winchester School of Art, 1981–2; a degree in fine art from Goldsmiths' College, 1982–5; then studied digital image-making: practice and theory, at Tower Hamlets College, 1996–7. Hale won a Whitechapel Artists' Award, 1987, and a London Arts Board Production Grant, 1993. Group shows included New Contemporaries, ICA, 1984; 95 Show, Serpentine Gallery,

1985; Trigon '89, "Actuelle Kunst", Neue Gallerie & Kunstlerhaus, Graz, Austria, 1989; Let me Look, British Council, San Miniato, Italy, 1992; On Boredom, virtual exhibition on CD-ROM, launched by ICA in association with Cambridge Darkroom Gallery, 1997; Sublime: The Darkness and the Light, Hayward Gallery and tour 1999; and Prospects, Easor Gallery, 2002. Among his solo exhibitions were Whitechapel Art Gallery, 1988; Mobile Home, 2001 and 2004; and Montreal Biennale, Canada, 2002. In that year Mobile Home showed 60 new drawings by Hale from two series Miriam Stealing and Miriam & William. Beginning without intention, Hale was "led to each image through the acts of drawing and collage. He is driven by what he describes as 'following the energy' in each drawing". Hale's Make Me Mare was at Mobile Home in 2004. The Arts Council holds his work. Hale lived in Berlin, Germany.

Phil HALE 1963– Painter and illustrator, born in Quebec, Canada, who from 1982–4 was apprenticed to the fine artist Richard Berry in Boston, Massachusetts, in America, and in Stroud, Gloucestershire. *Double Memory*, a collection of paintings by Hale and Berry, was published in 2002. After his painter's apprenticeship Hale divided his efforts between personal work and illustration, producing album commissions for major American bands, including Tool and Serafin. Had a solo show at The University of New Hampshire in 1987. Hale's group exhibitions included Bedford Studios, New York, 1991; Castignetti Gallery, Boston, 1996; CLP, Lucca, Italy, 1996; and in 2000 and 2001 BP Portrait Award at the National Portrait Gallery. Hales was awarded a third prize there in 2000 with his portrait Dr Rowlands at 45 and second prize in 2001 with Source X. Following his BP Portrait Award success the National Portrait Gallery, with funds from the Jerwood Charitable Foundation, commissioned Hale to paint a portrait of the pianist and composer Thomas Adès. Recognition in the Awards gave Hale the confidence and encouragement to abandon the commercial side of his work and become a full-time painter. In 2004 he was one of eight figurative painters in Being Present, at Jerwood Space.

Sydney HALE 1907– Portrait painter in oil, pastel and pen and ink. Studied under Bernard Fleetwood-Walker at Birmingham College of Arts and Crafts, then went on to teach life and portrait drawing and painting at Birmingham College of Art and Coventry School of Art. Had one-man shows in the West Midlands area, as well as exhibiting in mixed shows at the RA, LG, RBA and RBSA. Lived at West Bromwich, West Midlands.

Gordon HALES 1916– Artist in oil, watercolour and pastel, born in Matlock, Derbyshire. He studied at Leicester College of Art and Northampton School of Art. Hales' favourite subjects were "ships and the sea, the Thames, men at work, the streets of London, the half light". He was a member of RSMA, an associate of RBA, a member of the Langham Sketch Club, Wapping Group of Artists and the Artists' Society and a founder-member of the London Muster of Artists. Also showed at PS and elsewhere. Lived in Watford, Hertfordshire.

Constance HALFORD-THOMPSON fl. from early 1970s– Artist producing colourful still lifes and views in pastel, horseracing and yachting favourite subjects. She began painting in India where her father was in the Army; joined the Special Women's Service in Burma; and following marriage and a family trained at Putney School of Art in the late 1960s. Mixed shows included Chelsea Art Society, Armed Forces Art Society, Society of Equestrian Artists, Richmond Gallery, PS, ROI and RBA. She had several solo exhibitions with Anna-Mei Chadwick.

Adrian HALL 1943– Sculptor and teacher, born in Cornwall, whose uncompromising and witty output made use of materials as diverse as badges, light bulbs, vacuum cleaners and symbols such as the swastika. Hall attended Plymouth College of Art, 1959–63, and Royal College of Art, 1964–7. He gained several scholarships and was at Yale University in America, 1967–9, then held a series of teaching appointments in Los Angeles in California, Auckland in New Zealand and Ulster College, Belfast, where he became principal lecturer in sculpture in 1973. Two years later Arts Council of Northern Ireland granted him a commission for a land sculpture, Northern Ireland Housing Executive, Kilcooley Estate, Bangor. His many shows included Arnolfini Gallery in Bristol, Young Contemporaries at Tate Gallery, Project Gallery in Dublin and Pinacotheca, Melbourne, in Australia.

Antony HALL 1976– Artist and art administrator whose work included multi-media installations. Hall gained a diploma in construction management and architectural design, Somerset College of Arts & Technology, 1992–4; diploma in art and design, Strode College, Street, 1994–6; and a first-class honours degree in fine art, sculpture, at University of Wales Institute, Cardiff, 1996–9. Work experience included Cardiff Art in Time Festival, 1999, and installation at Centre for Visual Arts, Cardiff. Among his many exhibitions were 6 Artists, Crown Hotel, Glastonbury, 1996; Stout Shoes Needed, The Gateway, Cowbridge, 1998; Modus Operandi, g39, Cardiff, and Hanover Gallery, Liverpool, both 2000; and Art from Wales – A New Generation, Open Space, Milan, Italy, 2001. Hall was awarded a WAC New Visual Artists Grant, 2000–1. Lived in Cardiff.

Arthur Henderson HALL 1906–1983 Painter in oil and watercolour, printmaker and illustrator. Born at Sedgefield, County Durham, Hall studied art at Accrington and Coventry Schools of Art, the Royal College of Art and at the British School in Rome. Obtained Prix de Rome for engraving in 1931. Exhibitions included RA, Leicester Galleries, RWS, LG and RE. Hall went on to become head of the school of graphic design at Kingston School of Art. He illustrated several books on gardening and children's educational books. Work bought by the British Museum and Cambridge University. Lived at East Molesey, Surrey.

A H Morgan HALL 1900–1984 Painter, born in Cardiff. After attending grammar school he worked for most of the 1920s and 1930s in his father's gallery while studying painting, in the late 1930s working in an architect's office. For 25 years from 1939 he worked for the Ministry of Works, on retirement in 1965 painting full-time. He was a leading figure in SWG and WSW, showing at RA, NEAC, RBA, WAC and elsewhere in group exhibitions. In 1971 shared a show with William Selwyn at Albany Gallery, Cardiff. WAC and University College of Wales, Aberystwyth, hold his work.

Christine HALL 1937– Figurative artist who studied at the Royal College of Art. Joined the PS and her Two Welsh Sheep was illustrated in its centenary volume. Lived in Henley-on-Thames, Oxfordshire.

Christopher HALL 1930– Painter in oil, born in Slaugham, Sussex, brother of the engraver Sarah Van Niekerk. He was noted for his precise, colourful depictions of the town of Recanati, in the Marche region of Italy, which he visited regularly. Hall attended Slade School of Fine Art, gaining his diploma in 1954. In 1957 a picture of his was the frontispiece of Jack Beddington's book *Young Artists of Promise*. Hall was made a member of RBA in 1988, RCamA in 1994, also exhibiting at National Library of Wales, Aberystwyth, the Stafford and Reading Art Galleries and at Jackson Gallery, Delaware. Arthur Jeffress, Portal and New Grafton Galleries gave Hall solo shows, and he had one of Burgundy pictures at RONA Gallery, 2000, another at The Russell Gallery, 2004. Arts Council, Museum of London and National Library of Wales hold examples. Lived in Newbury, Berkshire.

Christopher HALL 1942– Versatile painter, sculptor, potter and teacher, born at West Bridgford, Nottingham, who studied at Loughborough and Edinburgh College of Art. Teaching included Edinburgh Academy. Hall's work could have a mystical element, as in his wood carving The Shaman, exhibited in 2000 at Mainhill Gallery, Ancrum. Group shows included Macaulay Gallery, Stenton, from 1982; ICA, 1984; Open Eye Gallery, Edinburgh, 1990; Kirkbride Gallery, Traquair, 1998; and Scotland International Trade Fair, Glasgow, 2000. Among Hall's solo shows were Väsby Konsthall, Sweden, opened by King Gustav and Queen Sylvia, 1997. Lived in Jedburgh, Roxburghshire.

Clifford HALL 1904–1973 Painter in oil and watercolour, draughtsman and etcher. Born in London, Hall early in the 1920s began to study at Richmond Art School, then Putney Art School. At the Royal Academy Schools, in 1926–7, was influenced especially by Walter Sickert, and much of Hall's work bears the stamp of Sickert's palette and subject-matter: landscapes, genre scenes and London low life. In the late-1920s he lived in Paris, studying with André Lhote. Had a one-man show at the Beaux Arts Gallery in the mid-1930s, then served with a stretcher party during much of World War II. In 1946 he had the first of a number of one-man exhibitions at Roland, Browse and Delbanco, and his monograph on *Constantin Guys* was published. Making a living in bohemian Chelsea was often a struggle for Hall, who recorded his experiences in an unpublished journal covering 50 years from the 1920s. In the late 1960s he began a new series of pictures: women wrapped in towels, mysterious with unseen faces. His work is in many public collections in Britain, including the Imperial War Museum, Victoria & Albert Museum, and Arts Council, and abroad. Memorial exhibition at Belgrave Gallery in 1977, studio sale at Christie's, London, 1982. Hall latterly married one of his students at Regent Street Polytechnic School of Art, Ann Hewson, and they lived in London.

Dan Llwelyn HALL 1980– Artist who graduated with honours in illustration from the University of Westminster, 2002. He produced illustrations for *The Independent on Sunday* and exhibited in group shows, including Welsh Artist of the Year Competition, 2003; group shows at Gallery 47; and Artistic Licence Gallery. In 2003, he was shortlisted for the Singer & Friedlander/*Sunday Times* Watercolour Competition. Hall shared an exhibition of Contemporary Celtic Landscapes with Haydn Cottam at Washington Gallery, Penarth, in 2005.

David HALL 1937– Sculptor and teacher, born in Leicester. Hall attended Leicester College of Art, 1954–60, then Royal College of Art, 1960–4, studying with Bernard Meadows. In 1964 he won the Young Contemporaries Kasmin Prize, in 1965 the Prix des Jeunes Artistes and Prix de la Ville de Paris, IV Biennale de Paris. He gained a number of awards and grants from the Arts Council, British Council and British Film Institute. In 1972 Hall became head of mixed-media activities at Maidstone College of Art's department of fine art. Hall was an extensive exhibitor, showing in Young Contemporaries in 1961 and 1964; at Richard Feigen Gallery, New York, in 1966, and Sculpture in the Open Air, Battersea Park, the same year; at ICA in 1972; and in the Royal College of Art's 1980 exhibition Bernard Meadows at the Royal College of Art 1960–1980. Arts Council holds examples of Hall's abstract works in welded steel, polyurethane and laminboard.

Edward HALL 1922–1991 Painter, especially of official portraits in oil, born in Barwell, Leicestershire. Studied at Wimbledon School of Art and Slade School Fine Art. He went on to become honorary secretary of RP and became noted for portraits of Prince Rainier of Monaco, the Prince of Wales, the Duke of Gloucester and other military, clerical and civic dignitaries. Showed at RA, Agnew, NEAC and elsewhere. Lived in London.

Grahame HALL: *see* **Claude MUNCASTER**

Jessica HALL 1977– Painter, born in Hong Kong, who did a foundation course at Winchester School of Art, 1996, graduating in fine art from Ruskin School of Drawing and Fine Art, Oxford, 2000, winning several awards. Hall used a computer to sketch ideas and images; photographs were broken down into blocks of colour in a honeycomb-type structure, resembling an insect eye; the paintings were then direct enlargements of these images. Group exhibitions included Bildung, Chessels Gallery, Edinburgh, 1998; Fresh Art, Business Design Centre, Islington, 2001; and in 2002 Reactions at Exit Art, Broadway, New York, with tour, and New Constructivists inaugural show, Cotton's Atrium, Cotton's Centre. Solo exhibitions included The Crypt, St Peter-in-the-East, Oxford, 1999. Library of Congress in Washington and Oxford University Press hold examples. Lived in London.

Joseph HALL 1890– Painter and draughtsman, born in Thornaby-on-Tees, Yorkshire. Studied at Goldsmiths' College School of Art with Edmund Sullivan and Clive Gardiner. Showed at RA, RBA, RI and in the provinces, HRH The Duke of Edinburgh buying his work. Lived in Bromley, Kent.

Kenneth HALL 1913–1946 Painter, draughtsman and designer, born in Surrey, educated at Lancing College, full name Charles Kenneth Hall. For a time Hall studied agriculture, then began designing furniture with an interior design firm in London. In 1934 he showed a portfolio of his pictures to Lucy Wertheim, and although he had not exhibited before she soon gave him a show at Wertheim Gallery, where several important collectors acquired Hall's work. Became involved with Basil Rákóczi and his Society for Creative Psychology, where Hall met Juan Stoll and had the few lessons in art he ever had. In 1935 decided to paint full-time and during the next few years travelled in Europe with Rákóczi and became aware of modern movements such as Surrealism. With advent of war, they settled in west of Ireland, then in 1940 moved to Dublin, reviving the Society and the White Stag Group, which they had begun in London, holding group and mixed shows with prominent Irish painters. Initially Hall was a landscape painter, but birds and fishes feature strongly in his later work. In 1945 Hall returned to London, showing with Redfern Gallery, but in a depressed state he committed suicide. Hall appears in Lucy Wertheim's book *Adventure in Art*, 1947, where his strongly outlined work is illustrated. European Modern Art had a retrospective show in 1991 in Dublin. S B Kennedy's catalogue for The White Stag Group exhibition at the Irish Museum of Modern Art, Kilmainham, in 2005, surveyed the artist's life and work.

Mike HALL 1937– Painter using a rich palette, acrylic and oil, and designer, who graduated from Manchester College of Art, completing his postgraduate studies at the Royal College of Art. He established his reputation in film and television design in the 1970s and 1980s, during that period also undertaking painting commissions. Hall said that his film and television career "enabled me to travel extensively in Europe and the West Indies. During these projects I was able to draw and paint many of the locations." His later work "explores the emotional response to interiors that are not occupied and yet have the mark of human presence." Showed solo at Dean Street Gallery, 1991. Latterly he exhibited in galleries in Surrey and Hampshire, including Bell Fine Art, Winchester.

Nigel HALL 1943– Sculptor, draughtsman and teacher, born in Bristol, where he studied at West of England College of Art. In 1964–7 he attended Royal College of Art, having a first solo show at Galerie Givaudon, Paris, in the latter year. In 1967–9 a Harkness Fellowship enabled Hall to travel and work in America, Canada and Mexico. Hall's international exhibiting career now began to grow, and he settled to showing in England with Annely Juda Fine Art. From 1972–4 Hall taught at Royal College of Art, then became principal lecturer at Chelsea School of Art. Commissions included Peter Stuyvesant Sculpture Project, Sheffield, 1972. Hall was much concerned with spatial relationships and the interplay between exterior and interior forms in his work, as shown in the several examples held by Arts Council and in his retrospectives at Sunderland Art Centre and Warwick Arts Trust in 1980. There was an exhibition of recent work at Annely Juda, 1991; Drawings in Black and White, Museum of Modern Art, New York, 1993; Prints of Darkness, Fogg Art Museum, Harvard University, Cambridge, Massachusetts, 1994; Edge and Shadow, Works on Paper, 1975–2002, Art Space Gallery, 2002; in 2003 Annely Juda showed Drawings, Part 1: 1964–1984, followed by Part 2: 1984–2003, and in 2005 Forms in Light and Shade, recent sculpture and drawing. Hall was elected RA in 2003. Lived in London.

Oliver HALL 1869–1957 Painter and etcher, mainly of landscapes. Born in London, studied at Royal College of Art, 1887–90, also at Westminster and Lambeth Schools of Art in the evenings and privately with Daniel Williamson and W L Windus. Father of the painter Claude Muncaster. Hall travelled widely on the continent. Began exhibiting at RA in 1890, being elected RA in 1927 and Senior Academician in 1945. Also showed extensively at RWS, Fine Art Society, RE, Leicester Galleries and many other London venues, having his first one-man show at Dowdeswell Gallery, 1898. Represented in many public collections, including Tate Gallery, which holds his Avignon, Shap Moors and Vale of Festiniog. Hall's method of painting in oil was to complete a picture in the studio from watercolour studies done on the spot. Lived at Ulverston, Lancashire.

Patrick HALL 1906–1992 Watercolourist who early on made drypoints and etchings, born in York and educated at Sedbergh School, full name William Patrick Hall. He attended York and Northampton Art Schools and while a teenager helped with the conservation of York Minster's windows. Worked in the family tanning business at New Earswick as a young man and when it broke up after World War II moved to London and took a studio full-time. Showed at RA, RSA, NEAC and Paris Salon. His many solo exhibitions included Waddington Galleries, Gilbert Parr Gallery, Marjorie Parr Gallery, Austen Hayes Gallery in York, Montpelier Studio and Thames Gallery, Windsor. Hall sketched the landscape of Europe, especially scenes with rivers, canals and buildings, returning to his home in Sellindge, Kent, to complete the final pictures. He said that he tried "to take watercolour to greater tonal values and richness". Imperial War Museum, Guildhall Art Gallery and many public galleries in the provinces and the National Galleries of Australia and New Zealand hold examples.

Pauline Sophie HALL 1918– Versatile printmaker, born in Birmingham. She studied at the University there and Oxford University, gaining a science degree including biology in 1938. Attended Michaelis School of Art in Cape Town, South Africa, 1955–60. Showed with RE and SWLA and in local exhibitions in aid of conservation such as The Dorset Naturalists' Trust, Dorset County Museum, 1982–3. Solo shows included Shakespeare Centre, Stratford-upon-Avon, 1984. Lived in Snitterfield, Warwickshire.

Sean HALL 1961– Abstract painter who gained an honours degree in fine art at Ravensbourne College of Art and Design, 1981–4. Appeared in mixed shows at RA Summer Exhibition from 1983; Whitechapel Open, at Whitechapel Art Gallery, from 1984; and Greenwich Theatre Gallery, 1987. Shared a four-man show at Woodlands Art Gallery, 1988. Lived in southeast London.

Sharon HALL 1954– Painter and lecturer, born in Darlington, County Durham. She studied at Coventry Polytechnic and Slade School of Fine Art, 1979–81. In 1981 she gained a French Government Scholarship and worked in Paris for six months. A Greater London Arts Award followed in 1987, the year before she was an Artist of the Day at Angela Flowers Gallery. Showed widely and was included in four-artist show at Woodlands Art Gallery, 1989. In that year, Hall also took part in East End Open Studios, at Chisenhale Studios. She then held a Picker Lectureship at Kingston Polytechnic. Lived in London.

Marilyn HALLAM 1947– Artist and teacher, born in Yorkshire. She studied painting, 1965–9, at University of Reading fine art department, gaining her master's degree there, 1970–2. In 1969 Hallam won a Boise Travelling Scholarship. Went on to lecture part-time at colleges including Reading University and Hull College of Higher Education. Exhibitions included Platform '72, in 1972, at Museum of Modern Art, Oxford; Spirit of London, at Royal Festival Hall, 1979–80; Hull Print Competition, at Ferens Art Gallery, Hull, 1980–1; and Painters + Sculptors from the Greenwich Studios, at Woodlands Art Gallery, 1981.

William HALLÉ 1912–1998 Painter, notably of landscape in oil, born in Richmond, Surrey. His father was related to the Hallé who founded the orchestra, and his mother was a direct descendant of Sir Peter Lely, court painter to Charles II. Hallé decided to become a painter after looking at a book of reproductions in his public library, having gone to live in the East End of London aged 20, and attended evening classes at Bethnal Green Men's Institute. During war service in the Army he joined local art schools where he was stationed, after demobilisation continuing at Battersea Men's Institute and working at night as a telephonist. A visit to France during the war and later trips to South Africa, where he showed solo at Alder Gallery, Johannesburg, were important. Jack Beddington included Hallé in his 1957 book *Young Artists of Promise*. Hallé took part in mixed shows, showed one-man at Wildenstein several times and had a string of solo exhibitions at O'Hana Gallery, where he painted a patio mural. When it closed on the death of its owner Hallé "could not get another gallery to take me on"; he filled sketch-books, but did little painting for about 20 years. Revived interest in the mid-1990s prompted him to paint again, and he showed at Bartley Drey Gallery. Latterly lived in sheltered accommodation in southwest London. Public galleries in Hull and Bury hold examples, Wandsworth Borough Council pictures and his diaries.

Ellen Kathleen HALLETT 1899–1988 Painter, embroiderer, artist in various materials and teacher, born in Bristol, where she continued to work. She studied art at West of England College of Art in Bristol under Reginald Bush and went on to teach at Fairfield Grammar School. In 1921 she gained a Board of Education drawing certificate and in 1937 passed first-class in the City and Guilds of London Institute examination. Was a member of the Embroiderers' Guild and at the age of 75 spent over six months completing a fabric collage of Athelhampton House, at Dorchester. Showed at RA, RE, RCamA, SWA and extensively elsewhere. Cheshire County Training College bought her pencil drawing Moondaisies and Sorrel and Derbyshire Education Committee Museums Service her fabric collage Frozen Garden. Wrote *Blue Print and Dye Line* for schools.

Phyllis HALLETT 1926–1990 Artist and teacher, born in South Norwood, south London. She studied at Goldsmiths' College School of Art in the 1950s, influenced by Clive Gardiner and, especially, Betty Swanwick. Began teaching in Croydon, then in 1974 was appointed by the National Maritime Museum, in Greenwich where she finally lived, to run a children's centre, which became the Half-Deck Club; when she retired she was head of education at the Museum. While there she published and illustrated three books, *The White Galloper, Olly's Round* and *Jumping Cats*. After retirement she resumed painting, in vivid and delicate colours, varied subjects such as gardens, cats and unusual objects which fascinated her.

Roger HALLETT 1929– Painter in oil and tempera, born in Bristol, who painted in different styles under his own name and as Gidleigh Prowz. He studied at the Slade School of Fine Art, 1954–7, his teachers including Tom Monnington, William Coldstream and Lucian Freud. From 1957–60 Hallett was a television designer in Australia, where he began to have one-man exhibitions, including Macquarie Gallery, Sydney; Gallery A and Farmer's Blaxland Gallery, in Melbourne; and at Broken Hill City Art Gallery. Also showed one-man in Paris and Bristol and in London at the AIA and Temple Galleries. London Sketch Club member. Hallett spent four years painting Hallett's Panorama, at the Thames Barrier Visitor Centre, which depicts Georgian Bath as seen from a hot air balloon. Lived in Twerton, Bath, and in Saliès de Bearn, Pyrenées Atlantiques, France.

Alan HALLIDAY 1952– Figurative and abstract artist and draughtsman. He was trained at the Courtauld Institute of Art, where he graduated, obtaining an Oxford University doctorate on English artists in Paris during the Napoleonic period. Halliday was notable for his spare drawings of the human figure; at the same time his paintings were eloquent and colourful. Halliday had a special affinity with the ballet and in a long association with the Royal Ballet had a number of shows at Royal Opera House, Covent Garden. Was a frequent exhibitor in mixed shows including CCA Galleries in London and Tokyo, Ebury Gallery, Clarendon Gallery, Music Theatre Gallery and Westbourne Gallery. Painted throughout the world. In 1987 formed and led the European Artists' Group at Frankfurt Festival, subsequently transferring to Los Angeles. Later one-man shows included Bruton Street Gallery, 1992; *Shakespeare in Love*, exclusive paintings of the film, Thompson's Gallery, 1999; and Retrospective, John Piper Gallery, Renishaw Hall, 2001.

Charlotte Mary Irvine HALLIDAY 1935– Topographical painter and illustrator, daughter of the artist Edward Halliday, born and lived in London. She studied at Royal Academy Schools, 1953–8. Her work was reproduced in books published by Hutchinson & Company and Ginn & Company. She was made a member of RBA in 1960, NEAC in 1961 and RWS in 1976, also showing with RSMA and elsewhere. A solo show at Sally Hunter Fine Art in 1998 celebrated Halliday's love of architecture.

Colin HALLIDAY 1964– Artist and teacher, born in Carlisle, Cumberland, who drew inspiration from "the supreme painterly skill of artists like Sargent, Turner and Constable". His repeated themes were "nature, agriculture, religion, fear and hope and the way that we try to control these things". After a fine art foundation course at Carlisle, 1987–8, Halliday graduated with honours at Exeter, 1989–92, then was self-employed. He was a regular exhibitor in group shows, including Fresh Art, Business Design Centre, Islington, 1992; Lake Artists' Society, Grasmere, 1993; Eden Arts, Penrith, 1994; Coombs Contemporary, 1998; and Deborah Bates, 1999. His many solo exhibitions included a mid-career retrospective at The Walk, 2000. Lived in London.

Edward Irvine HALLIDAY 1902–1984 Painter in oil and watercolour mainly of portraits. Born in Liverpool, Halliday studied at the City School of Art there, in Paris at the Atelier Colarossi and at the Royal College of Art. He was awarded the Prix de Rome and worked at the British School there. Exhibited at RA, RBA, Paris Salon and RP, of which for a time he was president. His work is in the collections of HM The Queen, Walker Art Gallery, Liverpool, the Athenaeum Club, Wolverhampton Royal Hospital and Bootle Dyeworks. His work was reproduced in *The Studio*, *Illustrated London News* and *The Times* and he was interviewed by Stanley Casson for his book *Artists at Work*, published in 1933. In 1997, the University of Liverpool held an exhibition which concentrated on Halliday's efforts to popularise art between the wars. Halliday's daughter Charlotte was also an artist. He lived in London.

Irene HALLIDAY 1931– Painter and teacher, born in Kingsmuir, Angus. After Arbroath High School she attended Duncan of Jordanstone College of Art, Dundee, 1948–53, teachers including Alberto Morrocco. Went on to lecture at Didsbury College of Education in Manchester. Was elected to RSW in 1955, also showing at RA and Royal Glasgow Institute of the Fine Arts. Had several dozen solo exhibitions in north of England, Scotland and America. Public galleries in Bolton, Dundee, Salford and elsewhere hold examples. Lived in Arbroath, Angus.

John Alexander HALLIDAY 1933– Painter, notably of murals and in tempera, born in Kirkcudbright, Kirkcudbrightshire, where he studied at the local Academy. Halliday was at Glasgow School of Art, 1949–53, gaining a RSA Travelling Scholarship. He carried out many murals for private clients and businesses and had solo shows in Britain and on the continent, including Bourne Fine Art, Edinburgh, 2001. Lived for a time in Edinburgh and in Dunsyre, Lanarkshire.

Thomas Symington HALLIDAY 1902–1998 Sculptor, stained glass designer, painter – especially of shipbuilding on the Clyde – and teacher at Dundee High School, born in Thornhill, Dumfriesshire. Studied at Ayr Academy, in Glasgow to be a marine engineer, then at Glasgow School of Art under Robert Anning Bell and Maurice Greiffenhagen. Halliday was elected SSA in 1943 and was a founder-member of the Guild of Aviation Artists in 1963. J D Fergusson included him in his New Scottish Group. In 1947, with the poet George Bruce, Halliday edited *Scottish Sculpture*. He showed at RA, RSMA, RSA, Royal Glasgow Institute of the Fine Arts, Paris Salon and elsewhere abroad. Halliday carved the war memorial in the parish church of Wormit, Newport-on-Tay, Fife, where he lived for over 50 years; also the coat of arms for Newport Town Council; designed several stained glass windows, including Ayr and Dundee Parish Churches; and painted a large mural of the Battle of Narvik for the Royal Naval Dockyard, Rosyth. HM The Queen, HRH The Duke of Edinburgh and galleries in Derby, Glasgow, Dundee and the Imperial War Museum hold examples. A ninetieth birthday show was held at Wormit Arts and Crafts in 1992.

Trevor HALLIDAY 1939– Painter and teacher, born in Birmingham, where he studied at the College of Arts and Crafts, 1954–60, then Royal Academy Schools, 1960–3. He held a number of fine art teaching posts and until 1989 was head of the fine art school at Birmingham Polytechnic. Among his group show appearances were Objects and Documents, Arts Council, 1971–2; Recent British Painting, at Hayward Gallery, 1974; Twenty One for Twenty One, at Ikon Gallery in Birmingham and tour, 1985; and John Moores Exhibition, Liverpool, 1991–2. He had a solo retrospective at Ikon Gallery, 1975. Lived in Grimsby, South Humberside.

Tom HALLIFAX 1975– Painter of portraits and landscapes who was advised by his teachers at school that he was not good enough to become an artist, so he studied history of art at University of St Andrews, "something I didn't want to do." After four years there he took a fine art degree at University of Ulster, Belfast. Portraiture was so unfashionable that with another student Hallifax had to persuade the fine art department to recruit a life model. Hallifax established himself in London as a portrait painter, among his subjects being the politician Chris Patten and Rabbi Julia Neuburger. He was notable also for a series of self-portraits. He became a well-known public face when one of these was used on the Underground as promotional poster for the BP Portrait Award, held at the National Gallery, in 1993. Hallifax said: "I haven't got any major message to pass on to the world. I'm not offering any critique of life or trying to seize any aspect of the Zeitgeist. I'm just working." He was based in Shoreditch, east London.

Lesley HALLIWELL 1965– Painter and teacher, born in Gainsborough, Lincolnshire, who studied at Lancashire Polytechnic, Dartington College of Arts, Nottingham Polytechnic and Goldsmiths' College. She held a residency in Patagonia, Chile, in 1991, and from 1993 was a part-time lecturer at Cambridge Regional College. Group shows included Northern Graduates at New Academy Gallery, 1989; NEAC, Mall Galleries, 1990; Eastern Open, at King's Lynn Art Centre, from 1993; and Royal Over-Seas League Open, 1996. Solo shows included In Patagonia, Burgh House, 1994.

Roxana HALLS 1974– Painter, born in Newham, who did a foundation course at Plymouth College of Art and Design, 1992–3, then "decided to develop my career on a professional basis." Mixed exhibitions included South West Open, Plymouth City Museum & Art Gallery, 1990; Self Portrait, The White Lane Gallery, Plymouth, 1991 and 1992; BP Portrait Award, National Portrait Gallery, from 1994 (Brian Sewell, London *Evening Standard* critic, a constant advocate of Halls' gifts, termed her 1995 entry Absence a "masterpiece"); RP, Mall Galleries, from 1995; The Discerning Eye, Mall Galleries, 1997; and Hunting Art Prizes, Royal College of Art, 1999. She had a first solo exhibition at Beaux Arts, Bath, 2000, others in 2002 and 2004. Lived in south London.

Susan HALLS 1966– Ceramic artist and teacher, born in Gillingham, Kent, who gained her diploma in ceramics with distinction at Medway College of Art & Design, 1984–6; her higher national diploma there, with distinction, 1986–8; and her master's degree in ceramics, with distinction, 1988–90. In 1990–1, Halls gained a six-month residency at Banff Center for the Arts in Alberta, Canada. Teaching included Royal College of Art, the Museum of Modern Art in Oxford, and Staffordshire, Manchester Metropolitan and Wolverhampton Universities. Among

Halls' awards and commissions were one from Kent County Council for a ceramic mural for the County Hall at Maidstone, 1988–9; first prize winner, Campbell's Soup Tureen Design Project (the Toad tureen is in Campbell's Museum Collection, in America), 1989; and a commission for a life-size figure for Christie Cancer Hospital, Manchester, 1994–5. Showed annually with SWLA at Mall Galleries from 1989; The Decorative Beast, Crafts Council, 1990; Colours of the Earth, British Council tour of India, 1992; Ceramic Contemporaries, Victoria & Albert Museum, 1993; and Lynne Strover Gallery, Fen Ditton, 1997. Had a first solo exhibition at Andrew Usiskin Contemporary Art, 1992. Victoria & Albert Museum, Contemporary Art Society and The Sackler Foundation hold examples.

Reginald HALLWARD 1858–1948 Painter and stained glass designer. Studied at Slade School of Fine Art and Royal College of Art. Exhibited extensively, especially at Dowdeswell Galleries, RA and NEAC. Christopher Wood Gallery held a show in 1984. Lived in Arthog, Merionethshire.

Frederick James HALNON 1881–1958 Sculptor and teacher, born and lived in London. He studied at Goldsmiths' Institute from the age of 11, won two national gold medals in 1902–3, and was a pupil of the sculptor Alfred Drury. Went on to become modelling master at Goldsmiths' College. Showed at RA, RI, Royal Glasgow Institute of the Fine Arts and elsewhere and was a fellow of RBS. Williamson Art Gallery in Birkenhead acquired his work and he completed a war memorial panel for Ashford, Kent. A sensitive sculptor in the classical tradition.

Julian HALSBY 1948– Figurative and representational painter in oil, writer and teacher, born in London, married to the printmaker Miranda Halsby. He studied under Kyffin Williams at Highgate School, gained his master's degree in history and history of art at Cambridge University, 1967–71, and was senior lecturer at Croydon College of Art, 1971–80, then freelanced. Halsby was elected a member of RBA in 1994 and of the International Association of Art Critics, 1995. From 1990, he wrote the In Conversation series for *The Artist* magazine. His books included *Scottish Watercolours 1740–1940*, 1989; *Venice: The Artist's Vision* and *Dictionary of Scottish Painters 1600–1960*, both 1990; *The Art of Diana Armfield*, 1995; *The Art of Lincoln Taber*, 1998; *A Private View, David Wolfers and the New Grafton Gallery*, 2002. Group shows included NEAC, from 1987; RA Summer Exhibition, from 1989; New Academy Gallery Cancer Relief Exhibition, 1993, and widely elsewhere. Was in a four-man show at Jerram Gallery, Salisbury, 1996; two-man at Pembroke Gallery, Windsor, 1997; and solo at Abbott and Holder, 1998. In 2004, Halsby shared an exhibition with Judith Gardner at The Russell Gallery. Latterly lived in Sherborne, Dorset.

Miranda HALSBY 1948– Artist, notably a printmaker, born in London, married to the painter and writer Julian Halsby. After the North London Collegiate School, she studied at Kingston College of Art, 1966–7; Hornsey College of Art, 1967–8; part-time at Chelsea College of Art and Camden School of Art, 1990–1; and etching at Hampstead School of Art, 1994–7. In 1997 attended the Artichoke Printing Workshop. Halsby took part in mixed exhibitions from 1988, being a member of the Small Paintings Group from its inception in 1991. Exhibiting venues included Highgate, King Street, Bartley Drey, Piers Feetham and Thompson's Galleries, Sarah Samuels in Chester and Woodhay Picture Gallery, Newbury. She had a solo show at Abbott and Holder in 2001. Latterly lived in Sherborne, Dorset.

Helene HALSTUCH 1954– Painter and muralist, born in New York City. Studied at Pratt Institute there, 1972–4, Central School of Art, 1974–7, then London University Institute of Education, 1977–8. Went on to work for the London Borough of Southwark and Lambeth Youth Service, and completed a mural for Southwark. Her exhibitions included Ben Uri Summer Show, 1979; a shared exhibition at Ben Uri in 1980; RA Summer Exhibition, 1981; a shared show at Ice House, 1989; and also in that year she took part in a four-man exhibition at Woodlands Art Gallery. Was married to the painter Peter Morrell. Lived in London.

Ardyn HALTER 1956– Painter and printmaker, living and working in London and Israel, who gained a scholarship to Pembroke College, Cambridge, 1973, winning the Derek Rose Memorial Award there, 1976. Other highlights of Halter's career were first prize, Lauréats Wizo, Paris, 1992; Société Nationale des Beaux-Arts, 1993; and in 1998 at the National Print Exhibition, both the Julian Trevelyan Hon. RE Memorial Award and Gavin Graham Awards. In its Summer Exhibition 2000 Redfern Gallery showed Halter's work.

Paul HAMANN 1891–1973 Artist and teacher, born in Hamburg, married to the painter Hilde Guttmann. He studied at the local Arts and Crafts School and with Rodin in Paris. Served in World War I, then returned to be prominent in artists' colonies and Hamburg artistic social life. With the emergence of Nazism in 1933 moved to Paris, three years later settling in London. From 1938 he had a studio in Hampstead, with his wife established a private art school and eventually became a member of the Hampstead Artists' Council. Was a founder-member before World War II of the Free German League of Culture (FDKB), in which Oskar Kokoschka and Fred Uhlman were involved; helped to organise and took part in shows of German, Austrian and Czech artists' work at New Burlington and Lucy Wertheim Galleries. Was interned in the Isle of Man in 1940, but about a dozen years later adopted British citizenship. Hamann was in 1986 included in Art in Exile in Great Britain 1933–45, at Camden Arts Centre.

Alan HAMBLETON 1954–1998 Artist, born in Leek, Staffordshire, who trained at West Surrey College of Art & Design, Farnham, 1975–8, then Manchester Polytechnic, 1979–80. Hambleton worked for Dundee Printmakers' Workshop from 1980. In 1983 he was included in Scottish Print Open Three, which the Workshop organised; he was a Yorkshire Arts Artist in Industry; and was studying at Tamarind Institute, University of New Mexico, in America.

Harry HAMBLING 1902–1998 Self-taught painter, by profession a banker, living in Hadleigh, Suffolk, father of the artist Maggi Hambling. It was at her insistence that he began to experiment with oils at the age of 65. Although he had painted some watercolours when young and occasionally visited exhibitions, he then took up painting seriously. Work was notable for its strong design, visionary intensity and powerful colour, and it frequently featured the Suffolk countryside. His solo show at Brett Gallery, Hadleigh, in 1991 was a great success, and he had several others.

Maggi HAMBLING 1945– Artist, born in Suffolk, the daughter of the artist Harry Hambling, whom she encouraged to paint. She studied with Arthur Lett-Haines and Cedric Morris, 1960, who ran the East Anglian School of Painting and Drawing; at Ipswich School of Art, 1962–4; Camberwell School of Arts and Crafts, 1964–7; and Slade School of Fine Art, 1967–9, in the latter year gaining a Boise Travel Award which took her to New York. Hambling began to appear in group shows, such as A Space of 5 Times at Grabowski Gallery, the John Player Biennale in Nottingham and on several occasions at John Moores Exhibition, Liverpool. In 1967 the artist had her first solo exhibition at Hadleigh Gallery; she showed solo again at Morley Gallery in 1973 and in 1977 at Warehouse Gallery, when she also appeared at RA and won an Arts Council Award. Hambling, whose work is held by Arts Council, was an Expressionistic painter with vigorous brushwork, noted for her portrait and figure studies, including Max Wall the comedian and A J P Taylor, the historian. In 1980–1 Hambling was the first artist-in-residence at the National Gallery. She had solo shows at Serpentine Gallery, 1987; Bernard Jacobson in 1990, which included mature landscapes; and a first exhibition of sculptures at Marlborough Fine Art, 1996. In 2001, Marlborough showed Hambling's studies of the model Henrietta Moraes, coinciding with the publication of *Maggi & Henrietta*, foreword by John Berger; there was another show, Father, at Morley Gallery. Hambling's huge shell-shaped memorial to Benjamin Britten, sited on Aldeburgh beach in 2003 built by the town's ironworkers Sam and Dennis Pegg, proved controversial. Lived in London.

Arthur Creed HAMBLY 1900–1975 Landscape watercolourist, black-and-white artist, illuminator and etcher. Studied art at Newton Abbot School of Art with Wycliffe Egginton and Conway Blatchford, then at Bristol School of Art under Reginald Bush. Hambly went on to be a prolific exhibitor, venues including the RA, NEAC, SGA, Walker Art Gallery, Liverpool, and in America. His work is in public collections in Australia and New Zealand. He taught at Salisbury School of Art and Camborne and Redruth School of Art in Cornwall. Lived at Chilcompton, Bath, Somerset.

Francis HAMEL 1963– Painter whose output ranged over realism, the symbolic and the surreal, as in his solo show at John Martin of London, 1999–00, others following in 2001, 2002, 2003 and Oxford Paintings, 2004. He was educated at Marlborough College and Ruskin College, Oxford. Group shows included Westgate Library, Oxford, 1984, and Thompson's Gallery, 1993. In 1997 Hamel completed theatre sets for *Martin Guerre* for Cameron Mackintosh. Other owners included Dorchester Hotel, Claridges, Moet et Chandon, National Westminster Bank, English Heritage, Bovis and Amec.

Cheryl HAMER 1952– Painter and mosaicist, born in Penang, Malaya. She studied at Maidstone College of Art, Reading University and Newcastle University. She was a mosaic artist at Newcastle Art Centre, 1985, then two years later artist-in-residence at Fleming Hospital in Newcastle, where she lived. Group exhibitions included New Contemporaries, 1976; Sheffield Open at Mappin Art Gallery, 1983; Richard Demarco Gallery, Edinburgh, 1988; and the Newcastle Group's The Northern Lights show in 1990 at DLI Museum & Arts Centre and tour. She had a solo show at that venue in 1986, later ones including Bondgate Gallery, Alnwick, 1988. Northern Arts and Kent Education Authority hold her work.

Dan HAMER 1923–1990 Artist who was born and educated in Bolton, Lancashire. He was a lifelong rock climber and mountaineer, which was reflected in his pictures. When World War II began he was still at school, enlisting in the Royal Air Force in 1941. He spent the remainder of the war around the Mediterranean, sketch-pads charting his movements: sea front at Alexandria, burnt-out buildings at Tobruk, and pictures of Malta, Sicily and Italy, especially Mount Etna and Vesuvius. After the war he entered the Civil Service and began an outdoor career as a surveyor with the Ordnance Survey, always with a sketch pad. In 1949 he settled in Mossley, near Saddleworth, continuing mountaineering in the Lake District, Scotland and the Alps. Became a member of Saddleworth Art Group in 1950 and showed oils and watercolours at Saddleworth, Accrington, Haslingden, Bradford, regularly at Tib Lane Gallery in Manchester, and in 1973 in The Northern Scene at Woodlands Art Gallery.

Frank HAMER 1929– Painter, potter and teacher, born in Accrington, Lancashire. He studied at the School of Art there, 1944–7 and 1949–50, Burnley School of Art, 1950–1, with Harold Thornton, and at Leeds College of Art, 1951–2. Went on to exhibit in the Accrington area and taught for a time at both his old Art School in that town and at Wolverhampton College of Art. Lived for a time in Wolverhampton.

Margarete HAMERSCHLAG 1902–1958 Painter, illustrator, printmaker, writer and teacher, born in Vienna, Austria. She worked variously as M H, Hamerschlag, later Berger-Hamerschlag or Margarete Berger-Hamerschlag, Margarete (or Margareta) Berger, Margareta Livia Berger or just Berger. From 1908–17 studied at the children's art class run by Franz Cizek, a profound influence, then in 1917–22 at Kunstgewerbeschule. In 1922 married the architect and artist Joseph Berger. For the next dozen years she exhibited in Austria and abroad, wrote and illustrated several books, including Edgar Allan Poe's *The Mask of the Red Death*. After living in Palestine, 1934–6, settled in England, and showed at Wertheim and Arcade Galleries and elsewhere, after World War II with Hampstead Artists' Council and Heal's Art Gallery. Taught at Monkey Club, Knightsbridge, then at youth clubs in Paddington, her experiences there, published in 1955 as *Journey into a Fog*, selling 25,000 copies. Died in London. There was a show of her watercolours at Würthle, Vienna, in 1987, and in 1993 Österreichische Galerie there acquired two of her oil paintings. Victoria & Albert Museum holds woodcuts by her. There was retrospective covering 1919–39 at the University of Exeter in 2001.

Constance HAMERSLEY fl. c.1905–1960 Painter, born in Timaru, New Zealand. After private education in Canada, Italy and England she studied art at the Slade School of Fine Art with Henry Tonks and Philip Wilson Steer, 1906–7, in Munich, in 1933, and four years later with

André Lhote, in Paris. Exhibited RA, SWA and WIAC. Finally lived at Long Crendon, near Aylesbury, Buckinghamshire.

Cuthbert HAMILTON 1884–1959 Artist, muralist and potter, born in India. He studied at the Slade School of Fine Art on a scholarship, 1899–1903, teaching art at Clifton College, 1907–10. In 1912–13 while working on murals and screens for Madame Strindberg's Cabaret Theatre Club resumed friendship with Wyndham Lewis. He was invited by Roger Fry to exhibit with Grafton Group in 1913 and joined Omega Workshops, although with Lewis and others he left after a row with Fry. Hamilton joined Lewis' Rebel Art Centre and was a signatory to the Vorticist manifesto in *Blast*, helping to illustrate the first issue. After World War I he took part in the Group X exhibition, showing abstract-oriented work and pottery from the studio he had founded, Yeoman Potteries. Died in Cookham, Berkshire. His reputation was revived by Vorticism and its Allies, Hayward Gallery, 1974; The Omega Workshops, Anthony d'Offay Gallery, 1984; and The Avant-Garde in Britain 1910–1960, at Fine Art Associates.

David HAMILTON 1947– Artist who attended Sheffield and Leeds Polytechnics, 1972–6, and the Royal College of Art, 1978–81. In 1988 he participated in a group show at The Minories in Colchester and BBC TV Open Space Artists in Residence and had *South of Aswan* reproduced for singer and poet Labi Siffre's album and poster. Took part in Surrealism, Bury St Edmunds Art Gallery, and East End Open Studios, at Beck Road, in 1989.

Ian HAMILTON fl. from late-1980s– Painter and draughtsman who graduated with a degree in fine art from Manchester College of Art, 1987. Hamilton took part in mixed shows at Belltable, Limerick, 1990; One Oxford Street Gallery, Belfast, 1992–3; and in 1994 Beyond the Partitions and Works on Paper, both organised by Queen Street Studios, Belfast, with which he was associated for a time. Hamilton's work was chosen for BP Young European Artists, Brussels, 1991, and Belfast Young Contemporaries, Belfast and London, 1992. Solo shows included Project Art Centre, Dublin; Navan Arts Festival; and Kerlin Gallery, Belfast, all 1990. Lived and worked in Galway, Irish Republic, and County Down, Northern Ireland.

Jane HAMILTON 1950– Sculptor in bronze and teacher, born in Grundisburgh, Suffolk. Her father was the marine painter John Hamilton, her husband the artist Simon Allison and her great-uncle the bird painter Otto Murray-Dixon. Hamilton spent the first six years of her life in west Africa which had "a profound and lasting experience" on her work. Aged 14, she was impressed by the work of Michelangelo and the Renaissance, Rodin and Degas being other early influences. On leaving school she travelled to Italy where she worked and studied for several months. Hamilton attended Falmouth School of Art, 1968; City and Guilds School of Art, 1970, under James Butler; and Sir John Cass School of Art, part-time, 1979. She trained as a nurse after art school and then began sculpting professionally, teaching life drawing at North Oxfordshire College and at Nuneaton College, also conducting portrait sculpture workshops at the former and privately. She was a full member of the SPS. Between 1979–03 Hamilton had 35 two-man and group show appearances, including RA Summer Exhibition, from 1982; Chelsea Arts Society, 1989; Royal Aeronautical Society, 1991; Lockbund Sculpture, Oxfordshire Art Weeks, from 1991; Idlicote House, Warwickshire, 1995; Banbury and Woodstock Museums, both 1997; and The Blake Gallery, York, 2002. She had solo exhibitions at Foxhall Gallery, Washington, America, 1980, and Emscote Lawn, Warwick, 1996. Hamilton latterly devoted herself mainly to portraiture, although she also produced a number of wildlife studies and figures, including mother and child, African figures and dancers, dance being "probably the ultimate form of expression." She sought the character as well as the appearance in his portraits, which included Sir Clement Freud, and was noted for her sensitive studies of children. Hamilton had work in many private collections around the world.

John HAMILTON 1919–1993 Painter in oil of major sea battles of the twentieth century and historical sailing ships, notable for accurate detail. After Bradfield College he served in the Army in the Far East, winning the Military Cross. After the war he worked in a Suffolk Borstal; went to the Gold Coast to start the approved school system there; after eight years returning to England to work in industry. Holidaying in Tresco, in the Scilly Isles where he later settled, he decided to become a painter, in which he was self-taught. His first big collection covered the war in the Atlantic, over 70 pictures now in the Imperial War Museum's HMS *Belfast*. The war in the Pacific was depicted in about 100 pictures, now in the Pentagon, in America; there was also a series on the Falklands campaign; and Hamilton then started on a run of 200 Antarctic paintings, setting up a branch of the Antarctic Heritage Trust in 1992. He showed with RSMA and had solo shows in Hamburg, 1979, and London, 1980.

John HAMILTON fl. from mid-1980s– After working in the civil service, Hamilton graduated in fine art from University of Ulster, Belfast, in 1984. In 1985 he participated in an Alternative Lifestyles bookshop exhibition, *Belfast*; in 1986 and 1989 he exhibited with Harmony Hill Arts Centre, in the city; and in 1994 Hamilton took part in the shows Works on Paper and Beyond the Partitions, sponsored by the Queen Street Studios, with which he was associated. In 1985 shared a show at Otter Gallery, Belfast. Hamilton's drawings and paintings had strong elements of Symbolism and the surreal.

Katherine HAMILTON: *see* **Kate GAULT**

Laura HAMILTON 1964– After studying at Byam Shaw Art School, 1983–4, Hamilton graduated with honours from Kingston Polytechnic, 1984–7. Group exhibitions included Open Show, Café Gallery, 1988, and in 1989 Pieces of Eight at Pyramid Arts Centre, Chelsea School of Art and East End Open Studios, based at Vyner Street Studios.

Maggie HAMILTON 1867–1952 Painter and embroiderer, daughter of a bobbin manufacturer, James Hamilton of Glasgow, who settled the family in Helensburgh, Dunbartonshire. Her elder brother was the Glasgow School artist James Whitelaw Hamilton, she married the painter Alexander Nisbet Paterson in 1897 and their daughter was the artist Viola Paterson. She was an embroiderer of painstaking determination, one of her works in The Paterson Family show at Belgrave Gallery, in 1977, having taken five years to finish. Showed widely at RSA and Royal

Glasgow Institute of the Fine Arts as well as RA and Walker Art Gallery in Liverpool.

Richard HAMILTON 1922– Painter, teacher, exhibition organiser and artist employing a variety of means such as holographs, cibachrome and the Quantel paintbox computer. He was born in London where in 1936 he studied at Westminster Technical College and St Martin's School of Art in the evenings. After a short period working in the Reimann Studios Hamilton studied at Royal Academy Schools in 1938, and in 1946, during the intervening period studying to be an engineering draughtsman, skills which he employed with the firm EMI. While he was at Slade School of Fine Art, 1948–51, Hamilton in 1950 had first solo show at Gimpel Fils Gallery. This was the start of an impressive exhibiting career which saw Hamilton's work shown at such locations as Robert Fraser Gallery; Studio Marconi, Milan; Stedelijk Museum, Amsterdam; and Vancouver Art Gallery. Hamilton was a prizewinner at John Moores Exhibition, Liverpool, in 1969, the year before his retrospective at Tate Gallery. He had a show at Serpentine Gallery in 1975, then it was 1991 before he had a major exhibition in London, this time at Anthony d'Offay. Hamilton taught at Central School of Art in 1952–3; was at King's College, University of Durham, 1953–66; and in 1957–61 taught at Royal College of Art. Hamilton was a disciple of Marcel Duchamp; he reconstructed Duchamp's Large Glass in the mid-1960s and shortly after organised the exhibition The Almost Complete Works of Marcel Duchamp at Tate Gallery. The Tate, which gave Hamilton a major retrospective in 1992, holds his work, as does Arts Council. He was made a Companion of Honour in 1999 Millennium New Year's Honours List. In 2001 Alan Cristea Gallery, in Tuppence Coloured, surveyed Hamilton's printmaking career. In 2002 a British Museum/British Council touring show examined Hamilton's lifelong response to James Joyce's novel *Ulysses*. Hamilton was included in Tate Britain's show Days Like these in 2003. His Prints and Multiples, 1939–2002, were exhibited at the Yale Center for British Art, New Haven, Connecticut, in 2004.

Susie HAMILTON 1950– Painter, born and lived in London, whose work used violent contrasts in tone and hard, bright colours and was "to do with ideas of the desert or wasteland". She studied at St Martin's School of Art, 1969–72, gaining her diploma, notable teachers including Henry Mundy, Gillian Ayres and Albert Herbert. During the mid-1970s she was a cartoonist for magazines such as *Spare Rib* and *Time Out* and worked in publishing as an editor/designer. Hamilton from 1977–81 read English at London University, gaining an honours degree and her doctorate in 1989, combining later studies with lecturing in English at Middlesex Polytechnic and West London Institute of Higher Education. She attended Byam Shaw School of Art 1989–92, for a fine art diploma, teachers Wynn Jones and Julia Farrer. Showed at Capsule Gallery, 1992; in 1993 The Gallery at John Jones, Battersea Contemporary Art Fair and The Coventry Gallery; in 1994 sharing a show at Coram Gallery; exhibiting solo at A22 and Timothy Everest Galleries, 2000. *The Economist* holds her work.

John HAMILTON-HOLDEN: *see* **John Hamilton HOLDEN**

HAMILTON MACK 1903– Painter, printmaker and teacher, born in London as Mary Hamilton Mack. After initial education in east London she studied at the Slade School of Fine Art, her teachers including Henry Tonks and Walter Westley Russell, where she was a Slade Scholarship and Melville Nettleship award-winner. In the 1920s she worked in Australia, partly in Sydney, and exhibited. Also showed RA, Goupil Gallery, NEAC, RBA and was an ICA member. Taught art at Fulham County Secondary School for a time, living in London.

Lionel HAMILTON-RENWICK 1917–2003 Equestrian artist, dog breeder and judge, brought up in Northumberland, whose family background was of lasting importance. His grandfather, the Conservative Member of Parliament Sir George Renwick, at his home Newminster Abbey, near Morpeth, kept border terriers and bred racehorses; his father bred pigeons and kept beagles; and his uncle, John, the second baronet, bred border terriers, was a racehorse trainer and master of foxhounds, encouraging Lionel's love of hunting, which he pursued with the North Tyne Foxhounds and West Percy Hunt. A weak chest absolved Hamilton-Renwick from World War II military service. Following work in a munitions factory and on a dairy farm, after hostilities he bred Jersey cows near Rye. Having complained to the sporting paper *Rally* that "my cows look more like horses than your illustrator's attempts," and being challenged by the editor to paint his own equine pictures, Hamilton-Renwick studied at Heatherley's School of Fine Art, then landscape painting in Epsom, and became a professional painter. By 1953 he was showing in Bond Street, and was making his reputation with a classic portrait of the Queen's chestnut colt Aureole, now in the Royal Collection. Other notable subjects included the stallion Prince Taj, and Red Rum, one image appearing on an Isle of Man postage stamp. Hamilton-Renwick was a pioneer British breeder of Dobermann and miniature pinschers and Pharaoh hounds, a judge at Crufts, a fan of miniature Shetlands and president of the British Spotted Pony Society. His ability to blend horse and landscape into a dignified whole, generosity with his work and sweet nature brought Hamilton-Renwick many friends.

Paul HAMLYN 1953– Artist in various media, born in Stockport, Cheshire. He studied at Goldsmiths' College School of Art, 1979–80; St Martin's School of Art, 1980–3; then returned to Goldsmiths' in 1986–8. In 1991 he created the site-specific installation PITCH and showed at Alternative Arts. His picture Lucifer was chosen for John Moores Exhibition, Liverpool, in 1991–2. Lived in London.

Medina HAMMAD 1963– Painter, draughtsman and teacher, born in Middlesex. She studied at Chelsea School of Art, 1981–2, and Newport College of Art, Gwent, 1982–5. She went on to teach at Lincolnshire College of Art and Design. Much of Hammad's work explored her Sudanese/English background with freshness, vitality and a bold use of colour. She exhibited at Usher Gallery, Lincoln, in 1988, and was included in the Norwich Gallery travelling show History and Identity, 1991–2. Hammad had a solo exhibition of new and recent work in 2002 at 4 Victoria Street, Bristol, curated by Eddie Chambers, another at the University of Leeds in 2004. Lived in Lincoln.

Alice Berger HAMMERSCHLAG 1917–1969 Painter and administrator, born in Vienna, who moved to Northern Ireland in 1938, dying in Belfast. As well as designing for publishers she created stage sets throughout Ireland, was closely involved in running the New Gallery and was a versatile painter in whose work Expressionism and grand themes were significant. She studied, 1929–38, under the pioneer child art teacher Franz Cizek, at the Kunstgewerbeschule and Vienna Academy of Arts. Exhibitions included Queen's University in Belfast, Avgarde Gallery in Manchester, Dawson Gallery in Dublin, Ulster Office, RSA and SSWA. Ulster Museum, Ulster Television and Arts Council of Northern Ireland hold examples. Her husband Heinz Hammerschlag set up the Alice Berger Hammerschlag Award to help artists after her death.

Tom HAMMICK 1963– Artist and teacher, born in Tidworth, Wiltshire, who gained a first-class honours degree at Camberwell School of Art with printmaking commendation, followed by master's degree studies, studies lasting 1987–92. In 1992 he was appointed head of painting and drawing at Eton College, and was a visiting lecturer, Nova Scotia College of Art, 1995. Hammick won the *Spectator* Award in 1988, in 1994 being a finalist in The Gilchrist Fisher Memorial Fund competition at Cadogan Contemporary with work which was close to abstraction. Took part in group shows at Redfern Gallery, with a solo exhibition there in 1996, three years after one at Star Gallery, Lewes. In 1997 he was included in The Large Print Show at Christchurch Mansion, Ipwich, and in 1999 Hammick-designed tapestries were shown at Redfern and Glyndebourne Festival Opera. The artist took part in Undercurrents, a three-man exhibition at the Eagle Gallery, and showed at a former factory, 35–7 Bethnal Green Road, both in 2000, with further solo exhibitions at Eagle in 2002 and 2003 Hammick lived in London. Arts Council holds his work.

Beryl HAMMILL 1942– Textile artist, born in Harrogate, Yorkshire, who studied at Batley and Leeds Colleges of Art. In the 1970s Hammill mostly produced experimental textiles, in 1979 concentrating on tapestry weaving. Using wools that she often hand-dyed, Hammill worked from her favourite landscapes of Ilkley Moor, Yorkshire, on the edge of which she lived, and the west coast of Scotland. Her tapestries were exhibited in Denmark, Australia and in Britain, including Images of the Yorkshire Landscape, organised by Sheeran Lock at Leeds Civic Hall in 1991.

Hermione HAMMOND 1910–2005 Artist in a wide range of media, except acrylic, born in Hexham, Northumberland. She studied at Chelsea Polytechnic with Henry Moore and Graham Sutherland and at Royal Academy Schools with Walter Russell and Tom Monnington. She also studied etching at night classes. After winning the competition to decorate the ceiling of the new Senate House of London University in 1937 Hammond won the Rome Scholarship in painting in 1938, her time there being cut short by the start of World War II. After war service she seized the opportunity after the Blitz to capture many views of the city of London never before visible, soon to be hidden again. Miss Hammond continued to live by her brush, painting in Canada, America, Europe and the Near East. She had many commissions to paint portraits, including Professor Francis Wormald for the Society of Antiquaries and Dr Kate Bertram for Lucy Cavendish College in Cambridge. The Fitzwilliam Museum there and Museum of London hold her work. Her solo shows included Bishopsgate Institute, 1956; Hartnoll & Eyre, 1978; and Michael Parkin Gallery, 1993. Sotheby's at Olympia held a studio sale in 2006. Lived in London.

Joel HAMMOND 1963– Self-taught painter who was born in Littletown, County Durham. His first major showing was at John Moores Exhibition, Liverpool, 1991–2, a highly-charged, colourful, autobiographical picture called Three. Lived in London.

John HAMMOND 1961– Painter of luminous and colourful scenes based on strong underlying draughtsmanship who worked initially in watercolour, later in acrylic, creating a surface notable for its subtle glazes. Hammond was born in Woodford Green, northeast London, and trained at Bath Academy of Art in his early twenties. He showed throughout the United Kingdom, including ROI; the first South West Academy of Fine Arts Open, in 2000, winning a prize; and in New Year New Works, Albemarle Gallery, 2003. Lived in Chippenham, Wiltshire.

Mark HAMMOND 1967– Painter of gestural, lyrical abstracts, born in Harpenden, Hertfordshire, who gained a degree in fine art at Kingston Polytechnic, 1988–91, then a postgraduate higher diploma at Slade School of Fine Art, 1993–5. He was awarded a two-year scholarship by the Worshipful Company of Painter-Stainers. Exhibitions included Elemental at The Blue Gallery, 1995, which gave him his first solo show in 1996: The Deluge Paintings. In 1996 Hammond was included in New Contemporaries at Tate Gallery, Liverpool, and Camden Arts Centre. Hammond had work in Loaded, Ikon Gallery, Birmingham, 1997, and Supermarketed, Victoria & Albert Museum, 2000. His strongly gestural pictures were chosen by Gavin Turk for Artist of the Day, Flowers Central, 2004.

Paul HAMMOND 1947– Artist employing acrylic on hardboard, assemblage and collage, born in Derby, who attended the College of Art there, 1965–6, under Brian Mills; Leeds College of Art, 1966–9, studying with Patrick Hughes and Glyn Williams; and Slade School of Fine Art, 1969–71, under Robyn Denny. Hammond considered that he worked "with a guarded fealty, in the orbit of Surrealism", and his output was widely illustrated in publications covering that field, such as J H Matthews' *The Imagery of Surrealism*, 1977, as well as *Surrealism*, *Melmoth*, *SUBobJECTIVITÉS*, *The Hourglass Review*, *Dies und Das* and *The Day Book*. Group show appearances included The World Surrealist Exhibition, Gallery Black Swan, Chicago, 1976; Surrealism Unlimited, Camden Arts Centre, 1978; In the Spirit of Surrealism, Bradbury & Birch Fine Art, 1984; Le Mouvement PHASES 1952–1988: l'expérience continue, Musée des Beaux-Arts André Malraux, Le Havre, and Surrealism Is Dead, Long Live Surrealism!, The Crawshaw Gallery, both 1988; Quadrinom: Hammond-Pusey-Welson-West Galerie 13, Hanover, 1991; and 87 images, 71 artistes, 23 pays de la planisphere PHASES, Galeries d'art à vocation pédagogique des collèges publiques de Plemet, Plouec-Lié y Quintin, Bretaña, 1994. Settled in Barcelona, Spain.

Roy HAMMOND 1934– Topographical watercolourist who was an engineering designer for Ford Motors. He was able to paint full-time on retirement and to travel. He had a number of sell-out shows with Chris Beetles Ltd, including Roy Hammond in Egypt, 1987; In Istanbul, 1988; and Roy Hammond's London, 1990.

Nina HAMNETT 1890–1956 Painter, draughtsman and writer. Born in Tenby, Wales, she studied art at the Pelham School of Art, South Kensington, under Arthur Cope, then at the London School of Art under John Swan, William Nicholson, Frank Brangwyn and George Lambert. She soon became acquainted with Walter Sickert, of whom she painted an excellent portrait, and Henri Gaudier-Brzeska, who sculpted her. Began to exhibit, in the Albert Hall, at the NEAC and LG. Went to Paris, quickly becoming a member of the bohemian set, meeting artists such as Modigliani and Brancusi and working at Marie Wassilieff's Academy, where Fernand Léger taught. She went on to exhibit at the RA, Leicester Galleries, Redfern Gallery, Arthur Tooth and Son and the Salon d'Automne, Paris. Her life was recounted in *Laughing Torso*, 1932, and *Is She a Lady?*, 1955, discursive but amusing books. She also illustrated the *People's Album of London Statues*, by Osbert Sitwell. After World War II Hamnett, a good painter and fine draughtsman whose achievement could have been much greater, became known as a hard-drinking member of the group of artists and writers who haunted Fitzrovia, in London, where she died, a noted character. Tenby Museum held a centenary show in 1990.

Nichollas HAMPER 1956– Painter, employing unconventional media such as car spray and Hammerite; teacher, born in Chatham, Kent. His younger brother was the artist Billy Childish. He studied at Slade School of Fine Art, 1975–9, and Royal College of Art, 1980–2. Went on to teach at Oxford Polytechnic, 1988–91, and was also visiting lecturer at Ruskin School of Drawing. Group show appearances included Tolly Cobbold, 1985; Smiths Galleries, 1985–8; and Raab Gallery, 1988. In 1991–2 he was a prizewinner at John Moores Exhibition, Liverpool, with a dynamic, large canvas: The Intervention of the Doner Kebab. He had solo shows at Fischer Fine Art in 1985; at Oxford Polytechnic and Ruskin School 1990; as well as abroad. Lived in Oxford.

John HAMPSON 1898– Painter and architect, born in Tyldesley, Lancashire. He studied at Manchester University, studying painting privately with several teachers. Exhibited at Mansfield Museum and Art Gallery which holds his work, with Denbighshire Art Society of which he was a member and elsewhere in north Wales. Lived for many years in Rhyl, Flintshire.

Roger HAMPSON 1925–1996 Painter, printmaker and teacher, born in Tyldesley, Lancashire. Hampson was noted for his straightforward depictions of southeast Lancashire, mines and miners. He studied at Manchester College of Art, 1946–51, with Paul Keen and Norman Jaques. Hampson began teaching at Bolton Secondary Technical School, 1951–3; lectured at Hereford School of Art, 1953–4; was a graphic designer, 1954–61; was at Bolton College of Art & Design, eventually as principal, 1961–7; then was principal of Loughborough College of Art & Design, 1978–86. He was a member of MAFA, being its president, 1969–76, and was a fellow of the Chartered Society of Designers. Took part in over 100 group shows and had some 30 solo exhibitions, including Tib Lane Gallery, Manchester, from 1963. Lived finally in Hereford. Lancashire Mining Museum, Salford, held a memorial show and The Gallery, Manchester's Art House, a retrospective, both in 1996.

Michael HAMPTON 1937– Painter of birds and other natural history subjects, full name F Michael Hampton, born in Croydon, Surrey, attending the School of Art there. He was a member of SWLA, also exhibiting with Royal Society for the Protection of Birds, Blackheath Gallery and in the provinces. A number of SWLA calendars reproduced his work. Lived in Shirley, Surrey.

Hugh HAMSHAW-THOMAS 1959– Installations artist who attended Central School of Arts and Crafts, 1978–9, then Bath Academy of Art in Corsham, 1979–82. His brand of conceptual art consisted of collecting, categorising and assembling found objects, treating twigs, leaves or artificial flowers as if they were scientific specimens and thereby exploring human perceptions of reality. Exhibitions included East 94 at Norwich Gallery, 1994; and in 1995 Collective Evidence at Northbank Gallery and Bruce Castle Museum. Lived in London.

David HAMSHERE 1902– Artist in oil, pastel, charcoal and pencil, born at Freretown, Mombasa. Hamshere studied art with Stanhope Forbes, the Newlyn School painter, in the late 1920s, followed by a period in Florence, at the Byam Shaw School under Francis Jackson, and at the Slade School in the early 1930s under Allan Gwynne-Jones. He exhibited widely, including the RA, Hesketh Hubbard Art Society and NEAC, one-man shows including the Canaletto Gallery in London and galleries in Cyprus, Florence and Turkey. Lived in London.

Dennis John HANCERI 1928– Artist and designer with a strong interest in marine subjects, born and lived in London. He studied at St Martin's School of Art. Was a member of RSMA from 1970, also the Wapping Group of Artists and showed widely in America.

David HANCOCK 1973– Manchester-born and -based figurative artist, who studied at the Metropolitan University there, 1993–6. Group shows included Northern Graduates, Royal College of Art, 1996; Designed to Sell, Castlefield Gallery, Manchester, 1998; John Moores Liverpool Exhibition, 1999; BP Portrait Award, 2000 and 2001 (when he was commended); and Perverse Pop, Catto Contemporary, 2002. Hancock twice won the North West Arts Board Individual Artist's Award. Later solo shows included Something Beautiful, Something Free, Arc, Manchester, 1999, in which Hancock looked at the culture of modern self-absorbed and alienated youth, and The Beautiful People, Viewtwogallery, Liverpool, 2001.

Kenneth W HANCOCK 1911–1978 Painter, notably of portraits and flowers, born in Mumbles, Swansea. He studied at the Swansea School of Art and Royal College of Art and went on to teach, notably as principal of Swansea College of Art. Showed with RCamA, SWG, Royal National Eisteddfod and elsewhere. WAC, National Museum of Wales in Cardiff and Glynn Vivian Art Gallery, Swansea, hold his work.

Frederick HAND 1880– Painter who studied at the Brook Green School, which the artist Leon Underwood opened in 1921, where life drawing was the mainstay of instruction.

Hand exhibited RA, ROI, Walker's Galleries, Lefevre Gallery, Fine Art Society and in the provinces. Lived in London.

Martin HANDFORD 1956– Artist in pen and ink and pencil, born in London. He was best known for the *Where's Wally?* cartoon books, incorporating many tiny characters, one of the most successful children's ideas of all time. Over 25 million copies had been sold by the early 1990s in over 20 countries in 19 languages. Made into a television series for British television in 1993 and one book was the first children's book ever advertised on the moving lights billboard in Times Square, New York. Cinema epics and playing with toy soldiers were early influences on Handford, who attempted to recapture the excitement by drawing crowds of stick figures. He worked for three years in an insurance office to finance his degree at art college. Each Wally picture took eight weeks to draw. Handford also showed in the RA Summer Exhibition, at Leonie Jonleigh Studio, Wonersh, Guildford, and was included in the Arts Council's tour Fragments Against Ruin, 1981–2, with The Battle of Chacabuco. Lived for a time at Cobham, Surrey, and at Axminster, Devon.

Mark HANDLEY 1943– Maker of lino-cuts which indicated an interest in pictorial humour, larger cuts of architectural subjects and compositions suggesting "a rather dark view of the human condition". Born at Royston, Hertfordshire, he attended Uppingham School, reading English at Cambridge University, 1961–4, from 1964–5 studying architecture at the Architectural Association School. From 1965 Handley was employed by the County Architect of Hertfordshire and began a day-release course in architecture at the Polytechnic of North London. In 1968 he gained his master's degree from Cambridge, in 1972 qualifying for exemption from the RIBA part one examination. He then worked in the Cambridgeshire County Architect's department from 1969–78, later joining Yakeley Associates in the city. Handley won a prize in a *Punch* cartoon competition for amateurs in 1969 and subsequently drew for the *Cambridge Evening News*. He began making lino-cuts in 1980 inspired by the work of Edward Bawden, for whom he had designed a studio in Saffron Walden, and by the quaint cuts of Joseph Crawhall of Newcastle. Handley took part in many group shows, held several solo exhibitions in Cambridge, where he lived, from 1981, later ones including The Old Fire Engine House, Ely, 1998.

Fred HANDO 1888–1970 Illustrator, writer, local historian of the Monmouthshire area and teacher. After service in World War I Hando was appointed headmaster of Hatherleigh School, Newport. He wrote and illustrated, in pen and ink, seven books which stemmed from his extensive travels around the nooks and corners of Gwent, recording many houses and places now disappeared. To some extent the books were based on the almost 800 articles he wrote for the *South Wales Argus*, called "Monmouthshire Sketchbook", starting in the 1950s and ending just before his death. The writer Arthur Machen, associated with the same area, wrote a foreword to Hando's book *The Pleasant Land of Gwent*, published in 1944.

Neil HANGER 1962– Artist, notably a sculptor, born in Dartford, Kent, who gained a fine art honours degree at Bretton Hall College of Art, 1981–5. Group exhibitions included Crescent Gallery, Scarborough, 1984; Open Print Show, Contact Gallery, Norwich, 1989; East Anglian Photo Open, Norwich Arts Centre, Norwich, 1996; Air, Slaughter House, Aldeburgh, 1999; and Over the River, firstsite, Colchester/Wolsey Art Gallery, Ipswich, 2002. Hanger then wrote that he was interested in "trying to make objects that appear to be familiar but on closer examination aren't really known at all.... I want my work to make you think about your everyday life.... My sculpture is about the reappraisal of the small and insignificant." Thus Hanger's sculptures resembled boxes, shelves, cupboards and cabinets, but were subtly modified so that they appeared both conventional and alien. Later solo shows included Domestic Espionage, Christchurch Mansion, Ipswich, 1999. Lived in Great Glemham, Saxmundham, Suffolk.

Christopher HANKEY 1911–2000 Untaught painter, born in Oxted, Surrey, who graduated in modern history from Oxford University in 1932. He became a trainee with a civil engineering firm, obtaining a degree in that subject from University College in 1939, then served a year as private secretary to his father, Lord Hankey, a member of the War Cabinet. Served in the Royal Engineers/Royal Marines, 1940–6, widely overseas, then became a civil servant, initially with the Ministry of Labour, then with the Ministry of Overseas Development until 1972 and official retirement. For six years he did similar work with a quango. Although on walking holidays in Europe Hankey sketched constantly, his later work concentrated on the architecture and countryside around his home near Westerham, Kent, as shown in his first solo exhibition, at Mistral Galleries, Westerham, in 1992. Hankey's landscapes and seascapes were mostly small, "the main characteristic of which is clear, clean colours with a sense of space". He was a member of the Armed Forces' Art Society, also showing with RA, NS, ROI and RBA.

Roderick HANLAN 1928– Sculptor and teacher, born in Penygraig, Glamorgan. After National Service, 1946–8, Hanlan lectured in three-dimensional design in Kingston. He lived in Germany for several years in the 1960s. Group shows included Archer Gallery, New Art Centre, Arnolfini Gallery in Bristol, SEA, SWG and WAC. One-man exhibitions included several in Germany and Drian Gallery, constructions. Commissions included WAC award-winning sculpture Look Up, sited in Newtown.

Cliff HANLEY 1948– Artist and musician, born Glasgow, using as media acrylic, oil, lithography and wood engraving. Cliff Hanley, writer, was his father, and David Hanley, cameraman, his uncle. Hanley attended Glasgow School of Art, 1967–72, teachers including William Bone and Geoff Squires. Hanley said that by the time he finished there he was "utterly sick of art." He started his first band half way through the art school, and after leaving "spent about 15 years concentrating on rock, but most of the money came from design, letterheads to interiors. Those discos and pubs we designed were like nothing else ... A little bit of journalism, a sci-fi strip, but it was my rock band that got me to London." In 1984 Hanley suffered a brain haemorrhage, which affected his left hand, and after recuperating in 1986 he was urged to paint again. Hanley became most famous for his many paintings and lithographs of fleeting glimpses of people in cars, prompted by an experience in

Toronto in 1986; for him they were "protagonists in modern-day icons". Hanley was a member of National Artists' Association. Mixed shows included Royal Glasgow Institute of the Fine Arts, 1988; South Bank Picture Show, 1991; Workers Against Racism, The Edge Gallery, 1993; ArtExpo, Jacob Javits Center, New York, 1995; and New Year Show at St Thomas' Hospital, which holds his work, 1996. There were further ones at Bath Society of Artists Open from 2000; RWA from 2001; and RBSA, 2005. Later solo exhibitions included The Gallery, Gabriel's Wharf, and Whiteleys' Atrium, both 1996, the latter a retrospective; Laughter II, Bath Society Meeting Room, Bath, 1999; The Life of Stuff, CentreSpace Gallery, Bristol, 2002; The New Gallery, RWA, 2004; and Medium Medium, Rainbow Restaurant in Bristol, where he had earlier moved from London, 2005.

Hilary HANLEY 1937– Printmaker, wife of the artist Liam Hanley, who studied etching at the Hampstead Arts Centre in the 1960s, but then pursued a job in publishing. She later returned to printmaking full-time, working in a studio guided by Peter Freeth. Her subtle and atmospheric prints were exhibited at the RE Open, at Bankside and Mall Galleries; with Beardsmore Gallery; The Millinery Works and in other mixed shows in England and America. Hanley was one of 4 Camden Printmakers at the Footstool Gallery, St John's Smith Square, in 2002. She lived in London.

Liam HANLEY 1933– Artist in oil on cotton on paper and watercolour, born and lived in London. Hanley was a part-time student at Central School of Art briefly, but was mainly self-taught. His painting life began in the mid-1950s. He was a journalist at night, painting during the day, and did not become a full-time artist until he was 55, in 1987. There were many changes in Hanley's work, the most lasting influences being Ben Nicholson and Morandi. "I do not paint *of* things," he wrote, but "*about* things and feelings." Among Hanley's many mixed show appearances were AIA Gallery, St Pancras and Camden Festivals, Tib Lane Gallery in Manchester, RA Summer Exhibitions, Phoenix Gallery in Lavenham and Thackeray Gallery. He had a solo show at Royal Society of Arts in 1962, later ones including, in 1991, Broughton House Gallery in Cambridge, Phoenix Gallery and Bronwen White Gallery, New Orleans. He was latterly represented by the Beardsmore Gallery, which showed his elegant and considered paintings in solo exhibitions in 2002 and 2005. In 1964 Hanley made illustrations for a limited edition of *Face of Winter*, by James Hanley, his father. Liam's uncle Gerald Hanley was also a notable novelist. Graves Art Gallery in Sheffield, Abbot Hall Art Gallery in Kendal and a number of local authorities hold examples. He sometimes painted as Liam H.

Pat HANLY 1932–2004 Versatile artist and teacher, full name James Patrick Hanly, born in Palmerston North, New Zealand, whose recreations in *New Zealand Who's Who* were given as "kite-flying, sailing, Greenpeace". He graduated with a Fine Arts Diploma from Canterbury University, New Zealand, in 1956, moving to London in 1957 with Gil Taverner, a photographer, whom he married in 1958. They travelled in Europe, and in London Hanly painted stage sets, worked part-time at Christopher Wren School and exhibited with Gallery One, LG, RBA, Young Contemporaries, the Edinburgh Festival and John Moores Liverpool Exhibition, having his first solo show at the Comedy Gallery in 1961. In 1962 the Hanlys returned to New Zealand, where he taught at the Auckland School of Architecture from 1963. Hanly received many awards and scholarships, including an Arts Council Scholarship, 1960, and Queen Elizabeth II Arts Council Grant in 1963 and 1980. As a painter and printmaker his exuberant, colourful pictures were mostly figurative and as well as dealing with domestic and family themes frequently expressed an underlying concern for social and political issues, such as nuclear arms and Apartheid. Hanly's work was included in many group exhibitions, solo shows and several retrospectives. Gradually, all the major municipal, provincial and private collections in New Zealand, where he lived in Auckland, acquired his work. He completed over a dozen commissions in churches and other public buildings, including big murals for Auckland Airport, 1978, the University of Auckland School of Architecture, 1982, and Aotea Centre's Convention Centre, Auckland, 1990.

Nael HANNA 1959– Painter and draughtsman whose work included Scottish landscapes and seascapes with strong gestural and abstract elements. Hanna was born in Nineveh, northern Iraq, of mixed culture. He spent much of his childhood studying and drawing animals, birds and people. Aged 19, he entered college before being drafted into the Army to serve during the Iraq War. Whilst serving, he was awarded a scholarship by the Ministry of Education, Baghdad, to study art in Britain, in 1983 undertaking art and language courses in Southampton before attending Duncan of Jordanstone College of Art, Dundee, where he gained first-class honours, 1989. He won several awards, including first prize in the Dundee 800 Open Competition; a Hospitalfield Summer Scholarship, Arbroath, 1987, during which he developed his love of the Scottish east coast, with its dramatic scenery and ever-changing weather; and the RSA John Kinross Scholarship, which took him to study in Florence, Italy. Hanna showed widely throughout the United Kingdom, including RSA, Royal Glasgow Institute of the Fine Arts and in London galleries, as well as widely abroad. He had a solo show at Duncan R Miller Fine Arts, Hampstead, in 2004. Public, international corporate and private collections hold examples. Hanna settled in the Angus countryside with his Scottish wife and family.

Charles Arthur HANNAFORD 1887–1972 Landscape painter in watercolour. Studied at Plymouth Art School. The son of the painter Charles E Hannaford, he opted to sign his pictures Hannaford Junior. Wrote *The Charm of the Norfolk Broads* and exhibited principally at the RBA, as well as the RA and Royal Glasgow Institute of the Fine Arts. Lived at Wroxham, Norfolk.

Charles E HANNAFORD 1863–1955 Watercolourist of landscapes, who studied under Stanhope Forbes and in Paris. Father of the artist Charles Arthur Hannaford. Exhibited RA, RI, RBA, RCamA and had several one-man shows before World War I at Walker's Galleries. Lived at Stalham, Norfolk.

Andrew HANNAH 1907– Painter and museum curator, born in Glasgow, where he remained, the son of a local authority art supervisor. Hannah graduated from Glasgow University with a Master of Arts degree and studied at the city's School of Art, 1932–5, where his teachers included Hugh Adam Crawford and J D Revel. As well as being deputy director for art for Glasgow Museums and Art Galleries Hannah was for some years in charge of the Burrell Collection. He also edited the publication *Architectural Prospect*. Glasgow Art Club member.

Clifford HANNEY 1890–1990 Painter of marine, landscape and figure subjects and teacher, married to the artist Eirene Hutton-Seed. He was born at Publow, Pensford, near Bristol and studied at the University there and art at West Marlands School of Art, Southampton, and Bristol Municipal School of Art under R E J Bush. He was art master at Kimbolton Grammar School, 1923, then after a number of appointments was principal of Crewe School of Art, 1943–50. Was elected an associate of RWA, 1923, was one of the founders of the New Bristol Art Club in 1933 and was elected to Bristol Savages in 1951, becoming its president in 1963. Showed at ROI, Walker Art Gallery in Liverpool, Manchester City Art Gallery and Oldham Art Gallery. Among his main works were Twilight, Sea Hawks and The Schooner. Lived in Bristol but was buried at Publow churchyard.

Brendan HANSBRO 1967– Printmaker and teacher, born in Leeds, Yorkshire, who obtained a foundation certificate there at Jacob Kramer College of Art, 1985–6; graduated with first-class honours, fine art, from Canterbury College of Art, 1986–9; and took a higher diploma in fine art at Slade School of Fine Art, 1989–91. Awards included a Scholarship in Printmaking, British School at Rome, Italy, 1992–3, and Villiers David Travel Prize, 2000, which took Hansbro to New York and Las Vegas; they held "a special allure for me as an artist fascinated by the metropolitan environment" and resulted in a solo exhibition at Curwen, the nominating gallery, in 2001. He had residencies at Canterbury College of Art, 1993, and Winchester School of Art, 1994. Hansbro was a printmaking lecturer there, as well as teaching in France and Spain. He took part in many group exhibitions in Britain and abroad. There was a solo exhibition, London views tinged a slight quirkiness, at Curwen Gallery in 2003. University College London, British School at Rome, Canterbury Royal Museum & Art Gallery and other public collections hold examples.

Brian HANSCOMB 1944– Printmaker, born near Watford, Hertfordshire, who aged 16 was apprenticed as a copperplate letterpress engraver, qualifying aged 24. In 1975–7 attended Hertfordshire College of of Art and Design, moving to Frome in 1978 to work as a gravure engraver. In 1979 left industry to work as a full-time artist/engraver from his home. Was a member of Bristol Printmakers' Cooperative, 1978–80, being elected to Printmakers' Council of Great Britain in 1981. Mixed shows included RA Summer Exhibition from 1976, NEAC from 1977 and RWA from 1979. Solo shows included one in Berlin, 1977, another in Bath, 1981. Department of the Environment holds his work. Lived at St Breward, Bodmin, Cornwall.

Marcelle HANSELAAR 1945– Painter, draughtsman, illustrator and teacher, born in Rotterdam, Netherlands, who studied at Royal Academy of Visual Arts, The Hague, 1962–4, and Rijks Academie, Amsterdam, 1977–8. She painted and travelled extensively in Europe, Central Asia and the Far East. Teaching included Central and St Martin's Schools of Art, 1987–8; lectures at Sotheby's Institute from 1989; and in China from 1993 at several colleges. Hanselaar had a great interest in the European Expressionist tradition, reflected in her own figurative work and unusual palette. German painters such as Beckmann, Heckel, Hacker, Lüpertz and Fetting influenced work which from 1991 was "involved with themes of the human condition such as ageing, fear, a search for identity in our make-believe world and my anger and rebellion against soulless social behaviour ... I portray this with with a sense of compassion and humour". Illustrations included *Buddhism Now* from 1989; Ajahn Sumedho's *Teaching of a Buddhist monk*, 1990; *Elements of Zen*, by David Scott, 1992; and work for *Risk* magazine. Group shows included Morley Gallery, 1983; Links of Affinity, Knapp Gallery and Glasgow Art Club, 1989; and Identity, Towner Art Gallery, Eastbourne, 1995. Had a solo show at De Kosmos, Amsterdam, 1976, with a string of exhibitions in Netherlands and Britain after that, later ones including Millinery Works, 1999, 24 Royal Circus, Edinburgh, 2000, East West Gallery, 2001 and 2003, You said you loved me at RMart, Essen, Germany, 2003. Also in that year, Hanselaar was winner of the Presse Papier Award, Biennale Int. d'estampe cont.de Trois-Rivières, Canada; shared an exhibition, Uncanny Tales, in Arnhem, Netherlands, with Ana Maria Pacheco, Paula Rego and Oona Grimes; and was elected an associate of RE. In 2004, Hanselaar had a solo show, Shouts and whispers, at Stephanie Burns Gallery, Deakin, Australia, and a retrospective, Silence is easy, paintings and etchings, 1992–04, at De Queeste Kunstkamers, Watou, Belgium. Ashmolean Museum in Oxford; Clare Hall and New Hall, Cambridge; Amsterdam's Medical Centre and Arts Council; and a number of corporate collections hold examples. British Museum holds her etching series La Petite Mort. Lived in London.

Lys HANSEN 1936– Painter, born in Falkirk, Stirlingshire. She gained her diploma at Edinburgh College of Art, 1955–9; Edinburgh College of Speech & Drama, where she graduated, 1955–8; completed postgraduate studies at the College of Art, 1960; did a year's fine art studies at Edinburgh University, 1961; and attended Moray House College of Education for teacher training in 1963. Hansen gained a number of travelling scholarships which allowed her to work in France, Italy, the Netherlands and Germany, having a studio in Berlin, 1985–6. She gained a number of awards and was artist-in-residence, École de Peinture, Castelnau de Montmiral, Tarn, France, in 1988. Hansen was an energetic exhibitor in group and solo shows, where her strongly gestural figurative paintings were immediately recognisable. Among the solo shows were Camden Arts Centre, 1986; City Art Centre, Edinburgh, 1988; McLaurin Gallery, Ayr, 1990; and Richard Demarco Gallery, Edinburgh, 1991. Scottish Arts Council, University of Stirling and City Art Centre, Edinburgh, hold her work.

Markus HANSEN 1963– Artist using photographic images, born in Heidelberg, West Germany. He graduated with honours from University of Reading, 1981–5. Group exhibitions included South Hill Park Performance Festival, Bracknell, 1984; Internationale Photozene, Museum Ludwig, Cologne, 1988; and Interim Art, 1990. Solo shows began with Keeping the Peace, Wunschik Peterson Gallery, Düsseldorf, 1988, later ones including James Hockey Gallery, Farnham, 1991.

Joseph Mellor HANSON 1900–1963 Painter, especially of Cubist-influenced works, and teacher, born in Wheatley, near Halifax, Yorkshire, son of a farmer. He studied at Halifax Technical College and School of Art, 1917–24, on a private scholarship, was briefly art master at Rishworth School, then in 1925 moved to Paris, France, for a decade, studying under Friesz, Léger, Lhote, Le Corbusier and Ozenfant, whose assistant he became. Exhibited solo and at Salons in Paris, at the International Exhibitions in Zürich, Berlin and Stockholm and in England at Yorkshire Artists Exhibitions in Leeds and Wakefield. Having in 1932–3 lived "absolutely from hand to mouth", he returned to England to become art master at Newport Grammar School, Shropshire, two years later showing solo with Lucy Wertheim. Bankfield Museum, Halifax, gave him a retrospective in 1938, the year he moved to New York with his South African-born wife. In 1945 he joined the staff of Cornell University, becoming professor of painting in the School of Architecture there. Hanson died during conversion of a former school at Bodle Street Green, Hailsham, Sussex, for retirement, which was due in 1964. Museum of Modern Art in New York and several other American and Welsh collections hold examples.

Siobhán HAPASKA 1963– Sculptor, born in Belfast, Northern Ireland, of Irish/Parsee parentage, who studied for a degree at Middlesex Polytechnic, 1985–8, gaining her master's from Goldsmiths' College, 1990–2. In 1993 she won a Barclays Young Artist Award. Mixed exhibitions included Guinness Peat Aviation Awards for Emerging Artists, Gallagher Gallery, Dublin, 1990; Making People Disappear, Cubitt Street Gallery, and Wonderful Life, Lisson Gallery, both 1993; and Entwistle, 1996. She had her first solo show at ICA, 1995–6, large structures with opalescent finishes. Hapaska's favoured medium was fibreglass, flawless surfaces sprayed and polished to perfection. Speed, fantasy and the future were elements in her work. Later solo exhibitions included Kerlin Gallery, Dublin, Ireland, 2001, and a new sculptural commission for Peer, 2004.

Anne HARCOURT 1917–1985 Painter in oil, watercolour, pen and wash, born in Arbroath, Scotland. She was the daughter of the RA George Harcourt. Studied at the Slade School of Fine Art and privately with Bernard Adams. Exhibited at RA, RP and RWA and had solo shows at the Mayfair Art Gallery in 1954 and in America. Lived at Boxford, Newbury, Berkshire.

George HARCOURT 1868–1947 Painter, born in Dunbartonshire, husband of the artist Mary Lascelles Harcourt, their daughters being the painters Anne, Aletha and Mary Edeva Harcourt. He studied for three years with Hubert von Herkomer at Bushey School of Art and was from 1901–9 governor of the Patrick Allan-Fraser School of Art, Hospitalfield, Arbroath. He was elected RBA in 1897, RP in 1912 and RA in 1926 and was also a member of the Arts and Chelsea Arts Clubs. A prolific exhibitor, Harcourt showed also at Fine Art Society, Walker Art Gallery in Liverpool, RSA and Royal Glasgow Institute of the Fine Arts. National Gallery of South Australia in Adelaide, Bank of England and Winchester College acquired his works. Lived latterly at Bushey, Hertfordshire.

James HARDAKER 1901– Painter, born in Bradford and a member of the Arts Club there. He studied at Bradford School of Art, 1915–17, his teachers including Fred Stead. Exhibited widely in Yorkshire, including Leeds, Bradford and Wakefield, and did some magazine illustrating. Lived for many years at Bingley, Yorkshire.

Gerald A C HARDEN 1909–1995 Painter, printmaker, calligrapher and teacher, born in Charlton Kings, Gloucestershire. He attended the School of Arts and Crafts in Cheltenham and Royal College of Art. From 1932–71 he taught, latterly at Cambridgeshire High School, Cambridge, where he lived. Exhibited at RA, Tate Gallery and widely in the south of England.

Alexander Merrie HARDIE 1910–1989 Artist in watercolour, pastel, oil and gouache, born in Aberdeen. Hardie was a self-taught artist with a fine sense of colour in the Scottish tradition, who painted mainly landscapes, latterly still life and portraits. He obtained his master's degree from Aberdeen University in 1931, became a Bachelor of Science in 1934 and obtained his doctorate in 1959. After time as a research engineer with Metropolitan Vickers, then commissioned service in the Royal Air Force, 1939–46, Hardie lectured in electronics at Aberdeen University and was professor of physics at the University of Bath. He was elected RWA in 1970 and was a member of the Bristol Savages. He showed with Aberdeen Artists' Society, RSA and had several solo exhibitions, including Rooksmoor Gallery and Holburne Museum, both in Bath, at RWA and at Logie Gallery, Tain, in Ross-shire, where he settled at Cromarty. RWA, Gloucester Education Authority and University of Bath hold his work.

Gwen HARDIE 1962– Painter, teacher and artist in cement, plaster and mixed media, born in Newport, Fife. She studied at Edinburgh College of Art, 1979–84, winning the RA's Richard Ford Award in 1983. In 1984 went on a scholarship to Berlin, where she remained until 1990, then settling in London, from 2000 being based in New York. Hardie was a versatile painter. Some of her work depicted the female figure with the woman as hero rather than as a male-observed object. For this she used herself as a model. The resulting pictures were large, while depicting only a fist or a navel. Her prizewinning entry in the 1997–8 John Moores Liverpool Exhibition, the oil Cleave (I), was a Minimalist image. Took part in many mixed shows, including The New British Painting, 1988–90, with extensive American tour; and Cabinet Paintings, Gillian Jason Gallery, 1991, also Five, Lennon Weinberg Gallery, New York, 2000; and Brooklyn Artists, Alpan Gallery, Huntington, 2005. Had a solo show at Studio Gallery, Glasgow, 1984; a major exhibition at Fruitmarket Gallery, Edinburgh, with tour, 1987; Scottish National Gallery of Modern Art, Edinburgh, 1990; and Annely Juda Fine Art, 1994. Among later ones were Beaux Arts, 1999; Lindsey Brown, New York, 2001; Alpan Gallery, Huntington, 2004; and Dinter Fine Art, New York, 2005. Hardie had a string of residencies in America from 2000, notably at the Virginia Creative Center for the Arts, Virginia; The Ragdale Foundation, Lake Forest, Illinois; The MacDowell Colony, Peterborough, New Hampshire; and Yaddo Residency, Saratoga Springs, New York. Taught exensively, including Oxford Brookes University; St Martin's, Royal College, Edinburgh College, Winchester and Glasgow Schools of Art; Guildhall University; and widely in Canada and America, from 2004 giving private painting instruction at the Bridge Street Studio Center in Brooklyn. Scottish National Gallery of Modern Art, British Council and several foreign collections hold examples.

James HARDIE 1938– Painter and teacher, born in Motherwell, Lanarkshire. He was educated at Larkhill Academy, then studied at Glasgow School of Art, 1955–9, where his teachers included David Donaldson. He gained the Keith Award and the Chalmers Bursary, enabling him to travel in Holland and France. He lectured at Aberdeen College of Education for a dozen years, then from 1980 taught at Glasgow School of Art, in 1989 being exchange tutor with the Chicago Art Institute. From the end of the 1960s Hardie began flying, gaining his pilot's licence. His work was influenced by his love of flying and home area on the edge of the Firth of Clyde, verging on the abstract. Showed widely in Scotland, including one-man shows at Blythswood and Compass Galleries, Glasgow, and Scottish Gallery, Edinburgh. Scottish Arts Council and Aberdeen Art Gallery hold his work.

Martin HARDIE 1875–1952 Watercolour painter, printmaker, writer and museum curator, born in London. After studying at Cambridge University Hardie studied art at the Royal College of Art under Frank Short. Hardie went on to become keeper of the departments of painting and engraving, illustration and design at the Victoria & Albert Museum, from which he retired in 1935. He exhibited watercolours in a traditional style at RA, RSW, RWS, RSMA, NEAC and elsewhere, along with fine etchings at RE. The Victoria & Albert Museum plus many provincial galleries hold his work. He was a distinguished writer on art, notably of the standard three-volume work *Water-colour Painting in Britain*. Lived at Tonbridge, Kent.

Nell HARDIE 1912– Watercolour painter and writer, born Helen Wightman Robertson, in Dumbarton. In 1925 she won a silver medal in the Glasgow Corporation Drawing Competition. She was married in 1939 and on her husband's return from active service in 1945 they resumed their life together, a cottage in Roxburghshire becoming their second home. Over the next 10 years she recorded in watercolour many wild flowers in the area. Her *Wild Flowers and Memories of the Scottish Borders* was published in 1992 by William Hardie Gallery, Glasgow.

Alfred Frank HARDIMAN 1891–1949 Sculptor, born in London, who initially studied at the Royal College of Art under Édouard Lantéri, 1912–16, then at the Royal Academy Schools and finally the British School in Rome, 1924. Won the RBS medal in 1939, being elected RA five years later. Among his works are the memorial to Earl Haig in Whitehall, London, and sculpture for St John's College, Cambridge, and Kippen Church, Stirling. The Haig statue, 1929–37, prompted a furious debate when Hardiman produced what was perceived as a symbolic artwork rather than a realistic portrait. *RBS: Modern British Sculpture*, published in 1939, illustrates his bust of Cecil Rhodes, for Rhodes House, Oxford, and bronze of St George, both in a muscular classical tradition. Was a fellow of the RBS and lived in London. The Henry Moore Institute in Leeds holds a Hardiman archive.

Melville HARDIMENT 1915– Painter and teacher, born in Wisbech, Cambridgeshire, who was for a time head of the art department at Bromsgrove Art and Technical School, Worcestershire. Hardiment studied art at Peterborough Training College, at the Camberwell School of Arts and Crafts under Claude Rogers and Victor Pasmore, as well as in Birmingham and St Ives. Showed LG, AIA, of which he was a member, and in the Midlands, where he had a series of one-man shows.

Alexis HARDING 1973– Artist, born and lived in London, who gained an honours degree in fine art at Goldsmiths' College, 1992–5. Exhibitions included Stephen Friedman Gallery and Multiple Orgasm, Lost-in-Space, both 1995; and Nine Lives at 26 Chiltern Street and New Contemporaries at Tate Gallery, Liverpool, and at Camden Arts Centre, all 1996. Harding's contribution to New Contemporaries included Hung I, 1995–6, an abstract in oil and gloss paint on canvas. He was included in the 1997–8 John Moores Liverpool Exhibition, winning the £25,000 first prize in 2004. Solo exhibitions included Andrew Mummery, 2003. Harding's paintings in that show defied easy categorisation. Process-based, they were made by pouring gloss paint through a trough on to a support covered with oil paint – wet into wet, and were said to "possess an almost romantic acknowledgement of life's fragility." Harding also exhibited at Rubicon Gallery, Dublin, Ireland, in 2002. Arts Council holds Harding's work.

David HARDING 1944– Painter and teacher, born in Bath, Somerset. He studied at High Wycombe School of Art, 1961–5, and the Slade School of Fine Art, 1965–7. Went on to teach at Bath College of Higher Education from 1972. He participated in Sainsbury's touring show Images for Today, 1982–3; RA Summer Exhibitions from 1985 and group shows at Museum of Fine Art in Alexandria, Egypt, and at Victoria Art Gallery, Bath, the same year. In 1987 his picture Old Earth was included in John Moores Liverpool Exhibition. Arts Council holds his work. Lived in Bradford-on-Avon, Wiltshire.

Jennifer HARDING 1956– Artist in acrylic, watercolour and gouache, born in Fordingbridge, Hampshire. She did a foundation course at Salisbury College of Art, 1974, an honours degree in fine art at Canterbury College of Art, 1975–8, a postgraduate course at Cyprus College of Art in Paphos, 1979, then attended Athens School of Fine Arts, 1983–4, under a Greek Ministry of Education Scholarship. Among her awards was an Oppenheim-John Downes Memorial Award in 1987. She was several times a visiting artist at Cyprus College of Art from 1986 and in 1987 was an archaeological illustrator with the British Institute of Archaeology in Ankara, Turkey. Harding's group shows included Stowells Trophy at RA, 1978; John Moores Liverpool Exhibition, 1983; Whitechapel Open, 1985; Omphalos Open Exhibition, Sandwich, 1993; and John Moores, 2002. She had a solo show at British Council Gallery in Athens, 1984, another at Finnegan Fine Art, 1990. Lived in London.

Morris HARDING 1874–1964 Sculptor, painter and teacher, born in Stevenage, Hertfordshire, who studied in the studio of his uncle Harry Bates, also with John M Swan. Taught at London County Council's Technical Institute. In 1925 Harding moved to Northern Ireland, where he settled at Holywood, County Down, and worked for many years on Belfast Cathedral. He was a member of RBS, RHA, RUA of which he was president and of the Society of Animal Painters. Harding also showed at RA, Walker Art Gallery in Liverpool, Royal Glasgow Institute of the Fine Arts and elsewhere. Ulster Museum, Belfast, holds his work.

Robert HARDING 1954– Sculptor and teacher, born in Lancashire. He employed a variety of materials, although he most favoured steel, and was interested in the public siting of sculpture. Harding studied at Exeter College of Art, followed by postgraduate research at University of Lancaster into contemporary sculpture in urban areas. In 1985 he co-produced a Welsh Sculpture Trust show, Sculpture & Architecture: Restoring the Partnership, which toured widely. He showed in open-air exhibitions at Tatton Park, Cheshire, St Donats Arts Centre and elsewhere, including the 1986 Glynn Vivian Art Gallery & Museum, Swansea, Seven Sculptors Working in Wales. The gallery holds his work. Lived in Uplands, Swansea, and taught part-time at Dyfed College of Art, Carmarthen. Had solo shows at Swansea Arts Workshop. His one-man exhibition at Oriel y Bont, Pontypridd, in 2002, pursued Harding's long-term interest in differences in scale.

Robert HARDING 1957– Painter and sculptor of abstract work, born and lived in London. He studied at Salisbury School of Art, 1973–6, and Camberwell School of Arts and Crafts, 1976–9. Showed at John Moores Liverpool Exhibition from 1982; RA Summer Exhibition, 1984; Open Studios, Greenwich, 1986; and The Table Studio Group, The Living Room, 1996. Later solo shows were at Smith Jariwala Gallery from 1990, with one at deliART, the last there, 2004.

Gilbert HARDING-GREEN 1906–1983 Potter, teacher and zealous draughtsman, born in London, who had little formal education. He moved to Brazil in the early 1920s, travelling up the Amazon and learning Portuguese. This was followed by years in Italy after which he returned to England and studied modelling with John Skeaping and Frank Dobson at the Central School of Arts and Crafts and painting in Chelsea. Prior to World War II Harding-Green exhibited decorated pottery and modelled heads which owed nothing to the English tradition of the Potteries, the Oriental style of Bernard Leach or the work of William Staite Murray. From the early 1950s he put his own work aside, was at first assistant to Dora Billington in the ceramics department at the Central and then was forcefully in charge of it from 1956–71. Harding-Green, an aristocrat in appearance and manners, whose teaching mixed good taste with a practical approach, influenced many distinguished potters with his catholic taste. After retirement he created several fine gardens, eventually settling in Wiltshire, having abandoned a plan to return to Italy with his artist friend Raymond Schofield. Abbott & Holder showed Eric Gill-influenced work by Harding-Green after his death.

Winifred HARDMAN fl. c.1915–1975 Painter in oil and tempera of figure subjects, mural painter and signboard creator. Born at Rawtenstall, Lancashire, Hardman studied at the St John's Wood School of Art, then at the Royal Academy Schools, where she won bronze and silver medals. Exhibited at the RA, RSA, NEAC, Tate Gallery, Redfern Gallery and elsewhere. Her work was widely reproduced, examples being *The Studio*, *Yorkshire Post*, *The Listener* and *The Sphere*. Among her murals was one for St Peter's Church, Hammersmith. She was a member of the Society of Sussex Painters. Lived in London.

Keith HARDWICK 1963– Artist who graduated with honours in fine art from University of Wales Institute, Cardiff, 1993–6, and his master's there, 1996–8. Hardwick received a Helen Gregory Memorial Award, 1993. His exhibitions included Cardiff Art in Time, Howard Gardens, Cardiff, 1995; Keith Hardwick Photographic Work, Old Hall Gallery, Cowbridge, and Keith Hardwick, Cairn Gallery, Nailsworth, both 1998; Box, g39, Cardiff, 2000; and Art from Wales – A New Generation, Open Space, Milan, Italy, 2001. Lived in Cardiff.

Beatrice M HARDY 1897– Painter, born in London, daughter of the landscape painter and miniaturist Dorofield Hardy. She studied at the Royal Academy Schools under Charles Sims and exhibited SWA and RP. Lived in Cranbrook, Kent.

Daphne HARDY: *see* **Daphne HARDY HENRION**

Irma HARDY 1912–1994 Painter and draughtsman, notable for portraits and scenes from the ballet, born in Budapest, Hungary, where she attended the Royal Academy of Arts, 1931–6. Showed in Hungary to mid-1940s, then in England with SWA of which she was a member, RP, PS and had several solo shows, including Cooling Galleries. HM The Queen holds her work. Lived in London.

Jim HARDY 1930–1992 Painter in oil and acrylic whose lack of self-promotion denied him the solo shows he deserved. Studied at Hornsey College of Art, worked for some years as a scene-painter at Sadler's Wells Theatre, in Islington where he lived, finally being a media resources officer with an east London college. Was a member of Islington Art Circle.

Mary Rose HARDY: *see* **Mary Rose GOSLING**

Robert HARDY 1952– Painter who worked on a small scale, who studied at Stoke-on-Trent and Chelsea School of Art and, after travelling in India for several years, attended life classes run by Cecil Collins. He was in the British visionary tradition, influences including religious folk art, votive painting, Indian and child art. Hardy aimed "to depict those presences and places that lie between the real world and the world of the spirit, between earth and heaven." Began exhibiting in 1982, solo exhibitions including England & Co, 1996. Later mixed shows included RA Summer Exhibition, from 1998; Landscape and the Imagination, Prince of Wales Institute of Architecture, 1999; and Lennox Gallery, 2001. In 2003 with Liz Maxwell Hardy shared an exhibition, Journeys, at deliART. His pictures there, employing a Mediterranean light and horizontal planes, were often criss-crossed by pathways and boundaries and peopled with travellers, suggesting ascent and transition. He lived in East Barnet, Hertfordshire.

Daphne HARDY HENRION 1917–2003 Sculptor in clay, plaster, terracotta and bronze, notable for portrait heads and figure groups, these tinged with suffering and heroism. She was born in Amersham, Buckinghamshire, as Daphne Hardy, under which name she at first worked, marrying the designer F H K Henrion in 1947. Hardy Henrion left school at 14 and studied privately in the Netherlands for a year with Marian Gobius and Albert Termote in 1931, having been educated in The Hague since 1923. Attended Royal Academy Schools, 1934–7. Aged 20 she won the Gold Medal and Travelling Scholarship which took her to France and Italy for two years. When the Munich Crisis occurred she escaped from France by ship. She was a member of the Cambridge Society of Painters & Sculptors, 1980–95, also RBS. Also exhibited with Hampstead Artists' Council, WIAC, RBA, Pictures for Schools and Contemporary Portrait Society. Early solo exhibitions were at Beaux Arts Gallery, 1946, and AIA Gallery, 1956, later ones at Ditton Hall Barn, Fen Ditton, 1984, Clare Hall, Cambridge, 1987, the Old Fire Engine House, Ely, 1989, Lynne Strover Gallery, Fen Ditton and Swaffham Prior, both 1996, and one in the Channel Islands, 2000. In 2004, Broughton House Gallery, Cambridge, showed a wide range of her work, listing her as Daphne Henrion. Hardy Henrion said that her approach to work was "entirely traditional and not at all intellectual, being a direct expression of my perception of people and situations". In 1951 Hardy Henrion produced a large cement figure for exhibition at the South Bank for the Festival of Britain. Her bronze relief Family Group is at Addenbrooke's Hospital, Cambridge, having originally been commissioned by Misha Black for the Alliance Building Society. In the mid-1980s she made a head of the writer Arthur Koestler (whose *Darkness at Noon* she had translated in 1940, having lived with him in the south of France shortly before the war. Their journey to freedom is described in his 1941 autobiographical novel *Scum of the Earth*, in which she appears as "G".), casts held by National Portrait Gallery, Edinburgh University and the Koestler Foundation. Lived in Cambridge.

Derek HARE 1945– Painter in oil and watercolour, and draughtsman, born on the northeast coast of England. The London City Ballet, portraits and the coastal areas of Northumberland, Portugal, the Baltic and the Bahamas were favourite subjects. Exhibiting venues included Chelsea Art Fair, 1999. Hare had a solo exhibition of oils and limited-edition prints, The Seychelles Collection, at Gallery 27 in 2004. The artist had a studio at Buckhurst Hill, Essex.

Joe HARGAN 1952– Painter and teacher, born in Glasgow, where he attended the School of Art, 1970–4, teachers including David Donaldson and Danny Ferguson. He showed at Glasgow Art Club of which he was a member, SSA, BWS and Royal Glasgow Institute of the Fine Arts. Hargan won a number of awards, including David Cargill Award at Royal Glasgow Institute, 1982, and the James Torrance Memorial Award there, 1984; the Meyer Oppenheim Prize, RSA, 1986; and Paisley Art Institute Award, 1993. BBC, Strathclyde Education Department and South of Scotland Electricity Board hold examples. In 1996, The Contemporary Fine Art Gallery, Eton, gave Hargan a solo show, which included his colourful landscapes and singular figure studies. He lived at Paisley, near Glasgow.

Jane HARGRAVE 1956– Versatile artist, born in London, daughter of the painter John Hargrave. After a convent and comprehensive-school education, Hargrave "worked for *Penthouse* magazine involving photographic, promotional, film and public relations, based in New York, but travelled widely. Ended up in London working as a photographic model for 10 years until marriage and children." Studied painting and drawing at Richmond College, 1989–92, and Chelsea College of Art and Design, 1993–6. As well as private commissions Hargrave did work for Minerva Press, British Tourist Authority, Pet Plan and October Design. Exhibitions included Houses of Parliament, 1990; Art Supermarket, London and Munich, Germany, 1998–9; Affordable Art Fair, 1999; Arthouse Open Studio, in association with Richmond Borough Arts Council, and The Smith Gallery, Teddington, Middlesex, where she lived, both 2000; and The Old Warehouse Gallery, Dorchester, 2001.

John HARGRAVE 1929– Painter and restorer, educated at Stowe School, father of the artist Jane Hargrave. He trained at St Martin's School of Art and was a restorer at the National Gallery, 1953–69. Exhibitions included Bruton Street Gallery, 1955; London studio, 1978; French studio, 1981 and 1997 (Hargrave lived in the southwest of France, 1980–99); Galeria la Nuova Sfera, Milan, Italy, 1982; Galerie de Montpezat de Quercy, 1985; Hal O'Nians, 1987; Galerie L'Acadie, Cajarc, 1996 and 1997; Musée de Cahors, 1999; and The Old Warehouse Gallery, Dorchester, 2001. Many private collections in Britain and abroad hold examples. Hargrave, whose hobbies were "food, wine and fast cars", lived in Bridport, Dorset.

T HARGRAVE-SMITH 1909– Watercolourist, born in Newport, Monmouthshire, where he attended the Art School in 1925–7. In the late 1930s he studied watercolour painting with the landscape artist Wycliffe Egginton. Was a professional soldier for some years, so showed with Army Art Society and has work in Imperial War Museum; also showed RA, RWS, of which he was a member, and abroad. Lived in London.

Sally HARGREAVES 1946– Painter and draughtsman, born in Blackburn, Lancashire. She studied at Harris College of Art, Preston, 1963–5; Chelsea School of Art, 1965–8; and Camberwell School of Art, 1968–9. Gained an Italian Government Bursary, Perugia, 1969, and an Italian Government Scholarship, Florence, 1971. Hargreaves said that she was "drawn to flat, formal shapes; horizontal and vertical lines; wide open spaces; dark skies and brilliant light; the simplicity of a striped Indian Navajo blanket ... the Fen landscape fascinates me." Group exhibitions included John Moores Liverpool Exhibition, 1972; British Drawing, Hayward Annual, and Three Painters, Norwich Castle Museum, both 1982; and Peterborough Art '87, Lady Lodge Arts Centre, 1987. She had a solo show there in 1985.

Ethel HARKER fl. from 1915– A versatile painter in oil and watercolour who studied at Chester School of Art and privately. Was a member of Liver Sketching Club. Exhibited RCamA and Walker Art Gallery, Liverpool. Lived at Heswall, Cheshire.

Claire HARKESS 1970– Wildlife painter and teacher, born in Ayr, who used watercolour for speed and directness. She graduated with a fine art honours degree (environmental art) from Glasgow School of Art, 1988–93, with time under the Student Exchange Programme at the University of Ulster, Belfast, 1991. In 1996 she won 1st Prize in the Arches Winter Painting Competition, in 1998 being artist-in residence at Edinburgh Zoo, and featured in a BBC television documentary. In 2002 she participated in the Singer & Friedlander/*Sunday Times* Painting Competition and Winsor & Newton at RSW, in 2004 being invited artist at both Perthshire Art Association at Perth Museum and Art Gallery; and Dunkeld Cathedral Annual Exhibition. She taught widely, including Dollar Summer School,

1999–04, as well as giving demonstrations. There were extensive study visits abroad, places including Australia, Mexico, the Caribbean and South Georgia and Antarctica. Harkess was involved in community art projects. Exhibited widely in Scotland, solo shows including the A K Bell Library, Perth; Perth Theatre Gallery; University of York; and The Strathearn Gallery, Crieff. Perth and Kinross District Council and Perth Museum & Art Gallery held her work.

Lindesay HARKNESS 1950– Painter, notably of lush, atmospheric flower still lifes in pastel, as in Old & New, Wolseley Fine Arts at The Gallery in Cork Street, 2002 and 2003. Harkness grew up in England and held a doctorate from Oxford University. She lived in America from 1975, teaching at Massachusetts Institute of Technology and Harvard University. After training with Paul Ingbretson in Boston, 1980–4, she concentrated on still life, portraits and landscape. Degas, Raphael, Rembrandt, Sargent and Titian were among favourite artists.

Beth HARLAND 1964– Artist in mixed media, born in Hartlepool, County Durham, who attended Salisbury College of Art, 1983–4, then studied at Ruskin School of Art in Oxford, 1984–7, gaining scholarship status and a travelling bursary to study in Germany. She completed her master's degree at Royal College of Art, 1987–9, spending a term at Cité Internationale des Arts in Paris. Harland showed at Sandra Higgins Fine Art and Contemporary Art Society Market. She was involved in collaborative work with the i/x group, including in 1991 a show at Quicksilver Gallery, Middlesex Polytechnic, then participated in (dis) parities at Mappin Art Gallery, Sheffield, in 1992, and at Herbert Art Gallery, Coventry, 1993. Had a solo show at Central School of Speech and Drama, 1999, in 1999–00 being exhibited at John Moores Liverpool Exhibition and gaining an Abbey Award, Rome. Lived in London.

Dennis HARLAND 1924– Sculptor and teacher who studied at King's College, Newcastle upon Tyne. Joined the staff of Leeds College of Art, where he was involved in three-dimensional studies. Was included in the College staff show The Teaching Image, 1964, at Leeds City Art Gallery, showing three plaster reliefs. Lived at Austwick, Clapham, Yorkshire.

Dennis F HARLE 1920– Painter with a strong interest in wildlife subjects, born and lived in Sandwich, Kent, by profession a nature reserve warden. He studied at evening classes, Ramsgate and Canterbury Schools of Art, and was a founder-member of SWLA. Had several solo shows in Kent.

Primrose HARLEY 1908– Painter of pictures and murals and printmaker, born in London. She studied at Chelsea Polytechnic under Graham Sutherland and Percy Hague Jowett, then at the East Anglian School of Painting and Drawing under Cedric Morris and Arthur Lett-Haines. Showed RA, NEAC, SWA, LG and elsewhere. Completed murals for British European Airways, Dorland Hall, in London's Regent Street, and lived in London.

Kevin HARLOW 1952– Sculptor and teacher who used "humour as a way of addressing serious issues without becoming bogged down in rhetoric", materials including "fibreglass, angle grinders and acrylics ... Influences vary – anything from television and magazines to High Art, Folk Art, Pop Art and real people." Born in Peterborough, Huntingdonshire, Harlow studied at Birmingham College of Art, 1970–1; Leeds Polytechnic, 1972–5; and Birmingham Polytechnic, 1977–8. Taught art in Bradford, 1978–87, then was an artist and sculptor full-time. Exhibitions included Norwich and Poole Arts Centres, both 1978; Bradford Open Artists Exhibition, 1981–5; Leeds Arts Space, 1985; and with Nicholas Treadwell Galleries and widely in international art fairs from 1990. Had a solo exhibition at Leeds Playhouse, 1984.

Gill HARMAN: *see* **Gill HOLLOWAY**

Rod HARMAN 1942– Artist and teacher who studied at Brighton College of Art and Royal College of Art. Taught for a time at the College of Further Education in Hastings, Sussex, where he eventually settled. Had a solo show of watercolour drawings and patterns at Woodlands Art Gallery, 1979–80.

Desmond HARMSWORTH 1903–1990 Publisher and painter, whose daughter Margaret was also an artist. After education at Eton College and Oxford University, where he obtained his master's degree, Harmsworth worked for several years in the family newspaper and publishing business Associated Newspapers. Then studied drawing at Académie Julian in Paris and had his first show at the Galerie des Quatre-Chemins in 1933, his first London show with Wildenstein five years later. Worked with British Information Services in New York, 1940–6, during which he continued to show, his first post-war exhibition in London being at Roland, Browse and Delbanco in 1954. He did not have a solo show again until one in 1988 at Berkeley Square Gallery, critically well received. Among his portraits were James Joyce, Osbert Sitwell and Havelock Ellis. Finally lived in Egham, Surrey, having become 2nd Baron Harmsworth on his father's death in 1948.

Frederick Bertrand HARNACK 1897–1983 Oil, watercolour and woodcut artist specialising in marine subjects. Born in London, studied with Arthur Briscoe, then exhibited at RA and other galleries in London, the provinces and on the continent. Sometimes signed his pictures Fid Harnack. Wrote *Sailing Ships through the Ages* and was illustrated in the yachting press. Lived at West Mersea, Essex.

Arto der HAROUTUNIAN: *see* **ARTO**

Alison HARPER 1964– Artist and teacher, with a strong interest in Buddhism, who graduated with honours in fine art from Glasgow School of Art, 1981–5. Her group shows included Kunstnernes Hus, Oslo, Norway, 1986, and East End Open Studios, at Angel Studios, 1989. She had solo exhibitions at Oslo Kunst Akadamiet in 1986 and 1988, with another in 1988 at McGavigan's Gallery, Glasgow, later ones including Undiscovered Realms, Wolfson College, Oxford, 2001. Teaching included The City Lit, Dulwich Picture Gallery, Lewisham Adult Education Centre and the Prince of Wales Drawing Studio. In 2000, Harper won a Prince Wales Drawing Studio Bursary. She carried out a number of commissions.

Andy HARPER 1971– Painter who studied at the Royal College of Art where he won the Burston's Award for

Painting and the David Murray Travel Scholarship. In 1997 he won a South Bank Group commission. Harper exhibited at The Custard Factory in Birmingham, Jason & Rhodes, Notcut and Beaux Arts, where he had a first solo exhibition in 1998. This comprised large and detailed surfaces of thousands of blades of lush grass. Harper's concerns were twofold: first, to use paint to represent real things; secondly, to achieve this through what was fundamentally a perfectly practised, semi-automatic process. His exhibition Green Lung, at University of Essex, Colchester, in 2001, continued his exploration of "the complex interaction between the natural and human environment." Lived in London.

Catherine HARPER 1965– Artist and teacher, born in Newry, County Down, who did a foundation art and design course at Ulster Polytechnic, 1983–4; completed a first-class honours degree in constructed textiles at University of Ulster, Belfast, 1984–7; a postgraduate diploma there, 1987–8; then her doctorate, 1989–94. She gained many awards, including a Winston Churchill Fellowship, 1988; from that year a series of Arts Council of Northern Ireland Bursaries; Prince's Trust Award, 1990; Aer Lingus Travel Awards, from 1991; Irish Department of Foreign Affairs Travel Awards, from 1994; and British Council Grant-in-Aid Award, 1995. Residencies included Czechoslovakia, Ireland, France, England, Canada and Finland. Harper taught widely, later part-time posts including textiles and fashion research at Central St Martins and Royal College of Art. As well as group shows, showed solo in Britain and Ireland, later exhibitions including Project Arts Centre, Dublin, 1993, South Dublin County Council, 1995, and Coven, Goldsmiths' College, 1999. For that show Harper explained that her work was "contextualised by textual investigation of the 'central core'/'cunt art' imagery of 1970s West Coast US feminist artists". The Arts Council of Northern Ireland, Department of the Environment public and corporate collections hold examples. Lived in London.

Ed HARPER 1970– Artist and lecturer, born in Southampton, Hampshire, full name Edward Harper, who used techniques such as the computer processing of images. He did a foundation diploma at Winchester School of Art, 1988–9; gained an honours degree in fine art, Brighton Polytechnic, 1989–92, under Roy Grayson, Charlie Hooker and Kate Love; and his master's at Goldsmiths' College, 1996–8, teachers including Michael Craig-Martin and Gerard Hemsworth. Had an internship to Emma Dexter in the exhibitions department of ICA, 1992–3. He was a visiting lecturer at United Kingdom art colleges. Exhibitions included Ponypark, Salon der Debutanten, Slagharen, Netherlands, 1991; BT New Contemporaries, tour, 1993–4; Untitled Painting Show, LEA Gallery, and Fresh Paint (Frank Cohen Collection), Gallery of Modern Art, Glasgow, both 1999; Look and Feel, Bürofriedrich, Berlin, Germany, 2000–01; Naturellement, Espace Fauriel, St Étienne, France, 2002; and Yes! I am a long way from home, Wolverhampton Art Gallery and tour, and Lexmark European Art Prize, Eyestorm Gallery, both 2003. Among solo shows were Night Paintings, Alfred Camp Gallery, 2000; New Paintings, 2001, and Metrolink, 2002, both at Mobile Home; Super Drive, Northern Gallery for Contemporary Art (Project Space), Sunderland, 2004; and Systemax:, Millais Gallery, Southampton Institute, 2005. Tyne & Wear Museums hold Harper's work. Lived in Leigh-on-Sea, Essex.

Edward Steel HARPER 1878–1951 Painter of landscape in oil, born in Birmingham, son of the artist Edward Steel Harper. After education at King Edward VI High School, Birmingham, where his father taught at the School of Art, the son went on to teach at Wolverhampton Grammar School, retiring in 1942. Exhibited RA, ROI and RBSA. City of Birmingham Museum and Art Gallery holds several of his landscapes. Signed work with monogram incorporating a harp. Lived at Harborne, Birmingham.

Eric HARPER 1918– Painter and draughtsman, full name Stanley Eric Harper, born in West Kirby, Cheshire. Studied at Malvern School of Art under Victor Moody, 1937–9; Wolverhampton School of Art, 1937, with Robert Emerson; at the Royal Academy Schools, where his teachers included William Dring and Ralph Middleton Todd and where he won a gold medal and Travelling Scholarship, in 1948; then finally at the British School in Rome. Showed at RA, RBA, SGA and NEAC. Lived in west London.

Geoffrey Felix HARPER 1913– Painter and designer of stained glass and murals, born in Wolverhampton, Staffordshire. Studied at Wolverhampton, Birmingham and Blackheath Schools of Art, Goldsmiths' College School of Art and Central School of Arts and Crafts. Exhibited RA and elsewhere, but was mainly noted for stained glass in many churches in London and the Home Counties. Lived in Harpenden, Hertfordshire.

Sarah Jane HARPER 1959– Painter, teacher and scenic artist born in Lagos, Nigeria, whose output included gestural abstract works. She did a foundation course at Wrexham Art College, 1978–9; gained a first-class honours degree from Coventry (Lanchester) Polytechnic, 1979–82; had a studio with the Coventry Artists Group, 1982–5; was awarded her master's in fine art from the University of Reading, 1985–7; and in 1994–5 obtained a vocational qualification in welding and fabrication. Harper was involved in setting up Red Cow Studios artists' co-operative in Bermondsey, 1987–9, eventually taking a studio in Wrexham, north Wales. In 1986 she was commissioned to make a Coventry Festival mural for Belgrade Theatre. From 1990 she was a freelance scenic artist in Oldham and north Wales, where she held children's workshops and also taught, from 1995–9 assisting Paddy Hamilton, working for major London theatres and Glyndebourne Opera. Exhibitions included Coventry Artists Group, Midlands Arts Centre, Birmingham, 1983; Artist of the Day, Angela Flowers Gallery, 1986; Whitworth Young Contemporaries, Whitworth Art Gallery, Manchester, 1987; and a three-man at Reed's Wharf Gallery, 1994. Later solo shows included the opening of the South Western Hospital, Stockwell, 1997. Harper was a member of the Wrexham Stuckists. Sir Michael Culme-Seymour owned her work.

Stephen HARPER 1954– Painter, born in Northern Ireland, who studied at Ulster College of Art & Design, 1971–3; Bath Academy of Art, Corsham, 1972–5; Ulster College again, 1975–6; Liverpool Polytechnic 1977–8; and at Goldsmiths' College, 1979–81, to gain his master's degree. Harper was noted for his intense, meticulous still life drawings and paintings, in which the placing of objects was of key importance. Group exhibitions included Four by Four at Project Gallery, Dublin, 1976; Works on Paper at Edward Totah Gallery, 1979; and Summer Show 2 at Serpentine Gallery, 1983. In 1992 had a solo show at England & Co, later exhibitions including one there in 2004. Arts Council of Northern Ireland holds his work. Lived in London.

Hildred HARPIN 1907– Painter, notably of murals, and teacher, born in Marsden, Yorkshire, son of the artist E Harpin. Studied at Huddersfield School of Art, Royal College of Art and in Italy. Taught art at Keighley School of Art, Yorkshire, near where he lived at Silsden. Exhibited in London and widely in the north of England. Much of Harpin's work is in churches throughout England in the form of murals and panels, including Ludlow, Keighley, Silsden, Cricklade and at the Passionist Monastery, Ilkley.

Sydney HARPLEY 1927–1992 Sculptor and teacher, born in London. He left school at 14 to work as an electrician. During National Service in the Army in Egypt, 1945–8, saw a head of Ramases II which inspired him to be a sculptor. After work in the artificial limb factory at Roehampton and evening art classes, in 1950 he enrolled as full-time student of sculpture at Hammersmith School of Art. Was most helped by John Skeaping at Royal College of Art, 1953–6, and in 1954 made first appearance in RA Summer Exhibition with Seated Girl. Harpley was to become known for his sculptures of attractive girls, using props such as swings, bicycles and hammocks. He was elected a fellow of RBS in 1963, RA in 1981. From 1972 he taught for a time at Leicester Polytechnic. Harpley carried out a number of ambitious figure groups in bronze, such as Dockworker for London County Council for the Lansbury Estate in Poplar. An over-life-size portrait memorial to Jan Christian Smuts led to solo shows in Cape Town and Johannesburg, South Africa. His busts included Edward Heath, Lee Kuan Yew and Prince Albert of Monaco. He had two successful shows at Chris Beetles Ltd in 1987 and 1990. In final years lived in Somerset and then Kilkenny and died in Dublin, Ireland.

Peter HARRAP 1975– Painter and teacher who attended at Camberwell College of Art, 1993, and Winchester School of Art, 1994–7. Harrap studied with John Lessore, 2000–3, in the latter year establishing a school of drawing and painting at Leighton House. He was elected a Royal Academy Schools graduate, 2004, under Brendan Neiland, for his role as director of Young RA(S). Although the human form predominated in his output, Harrap also painted cityscapes, of which Knoxville Museum, Tennessee, in America, holds an example. Harrap often exhibited with his partner Natasha Kissell, as in Bold + Radical, Radical Art, New Painting from the Royal Academy Schools, at Jerwood Space, 2005. Harrap's other shows included The Figure Reinterpreted, Dulwich Picture Gallery, 1995; Stranger than fiction, Haunch of Venison, 2004; and Marlborough Fine Art, 2005. The Emir of Bahrain, Michel Roux and HSBC owned Harrap's work. Lived in London.

Hywel HARRIES 1921– Painter, designer, illustrator and teacher, born in Tumble, Carmarthenshire. Attended Llanelli School of Art and Cardiff College of Art, then went on to hold a number of teaching posts. A member of RCamA, he also showed with Royal National Eisteddfod, NWG and Cardiganshire Art Society. For many years he was a cartoonist for *Cambrian News*; did book illustration and jacket design for Welsh printing presses; and illustrated the HM Stationery Office publication *Cambrian Forests*, 1958. One-man shows included National Library of Wales, Aberystwyth, 1970. CASW bought his oil Buarth Road, Snow.

Claire HARRIGAN 1964– Painter and teacher, born in Kilmarnock, Ayrshire, later settling to work nearby at Girvan, although she travelled widely overseas. Studied at Glasgow School of Art, 1982–6, winning the Mary Armour Award. In 1990 she added the Lily McDougall Award, in 1996 the RSA's Latimer Award. Was artist-in-residence at London Hall, Ayr, 1986, and in 1989 became a visiting tutor at Glasgow School of Art. Harrigan exhibited in many national open shows, including RSA, SSWA, Royal Glasgow Institute of the Fine Arts, Mercury Gallery in London and Edinburgh, Open Eye Gallery in Edinburgh and elsewhere. Had a series of solo exhibitions at Macaulay Gallery, Stenton, and Christopher Hull Gallery from 1988; Gatehouse Gallery, Glasgow, from 1991; Open Eye Gallery, Edinburgh, from 1992; and Flying Colours Gallery, from 1999. In both landscape and still life Harrigan was a rich, intense Colourist, as seen in the show she shared with her parents, James and Elspeth Harrigan, at Vicarage Cottage Gallery, North Shields, 1995. She was elected a member of SSWA, 1989, and RSW, 1992.

Elspeth HARRIGAN fl. from mid-1950s– Watercolourist who confined her work to the flora of Scotland and those countries travelled in with her painter husband James. She studied at Glasgow School of Art, 1956–60. Won the Royal Horticultural Society Silver Medal, 1985 and 1986; the LAS Group Award for watercolour at SSWA, 1986; Lily McDougall Prize from same group, 1987; and showed at Flying Colours Gallery, Edinburgh, and Barclay Lennie Fine Art, Glasgow. Her plates illustrated J H Dickson's *The Wild Flowers of Glasgow*, 1991. In 1995 she and her husband shared an exhibition with their daughter Claire at Vicarage Cottage Gallery, North Shields.

James HARRIGAN 1937– Painter and teacher, married to the artist Elspeth Harrigan, their daughter Claire also being a painter. He studied at Glasgow School of Art, 1956–61, gaining his diploma in drawing and painting 1960, postgraduate diploma in printmaking, 1961. Won the Laing Landscape Competition, 1980, the *Scotsman* Art Competition in 1985. Regular showed in mixed exhibitions in Scotland; shared a show with his wife and daughter at Vicarage Cottage Gallery in North Shields, 1995; solo exhibitions included Flying Colours Gallery in Edinburgh.

Conor HARRINGTON 1980– Painter, born in Cork, Ireland, who graduated with honours in fine art (painting) from Limerick School of Art and Design, 1998–02. Harrington said that his work was "strongly influenced by urban and street art, combining fine art techniques and subjects with graffiti motifs. The emphasis on oil paint draws on the long tradition of figure painting, whilst the use of spray paint represents the aggression and rebellion of contemporary street culture." His career included freelance commercial work for retail and music outlets; album cover and promotional artwork for The Shades Music Collective; graffiti workshops at the Eurochild International Festival; set design for RTE, the Irish national television company; and site-specific murals in Ireland, New York, Spain, Netherlands, Zimbabwe and South Africa. He shared an exhibition, Liquid Identity, with Marianne Keating at UCC Cork in 2003. Among his group shows were Amnesty, Gallery 9, Cork, 2003; Transit, National Gallery of Zimbabwe, 2004; and Hard Bodies, Corpus Fine Art at Arndean Gallery, 2005. Harrington lived in north London.

Alfred HARRIS 1930– Painter and printmaker, born and lived in London, who in mid-1950s attended Willesden School of Art and Royal College of Art. For a time he was involved in the running of the art and design department of London University's Institute of Education. Harris was a member of the LG, his work being commemorated in its ninetieth anniversary commemorative volume in 2003. By that time he had shown in numerous mixed exhibitions and had had 15 solo shows, 57 works having been acquired by public and corporate bodies, including Tate Gallery and Ben Uri Museum, Tel-Aviv Museum in Israel and the Ministry of Culture in Sweden. Harris's largest ongoing series was based on kite flying, of which he said: "Each work should be read in time, rather than perceived instantly."

Annie HARRIS fl. from late 1970s– Painter who attended Camberwell School of Arts and Crafts, 1979–83. She went on to teach there, 1983–5. An admirer of Velázquez and Vuillard, she painted in Tuscany and Scotland, sometimes working on a large scale. As well as taking part in group shows she shared a show at Cadogan Contemporary in 1991 and she had a solo show there in 1993. The National Trust commissioned her to paint The Bookroom, Sissinghurst.

Anthony HARRIS 1931– Artist and teacher, born in Reading, Berkshire, who studied part-time at Reading University, winning the Owen Ridley Prize in 1948. Subsequently he studied under Anthony Betts in the fine arts department of University of Reading and art history under L D Ettlinger, gaining the University Prize in Fine Art, 1952, then attended the Courtauld Institute, 1954–5. In 1957 Harris was included in Jack Beddington's book *Young Artists of Promise*. He was appointed to the staff of St Albans School of Art, 1960, becoming principal, 1967–75; was vice-principal of Chelsea School of Art, 1975–86; then head of Camberwell School of Arts and Crafts and assistant rector, London Institute, 1986–9. Harris was elected to the Chelsea Arts Club in 1975 and director of the educational charity John Ruskin Guild of St George, 1977, becoming its master, 1982–95. Group exhibitions included RA Summer Exhibition; RBA; Trafford and Stephen Bartley Galleries; Phoenix Gallery, Lavenham; Old Fire Engine House, Ely; Dower House Gallery, Berkhamsted and BL.D.ART Bergamo (Rassegna biennale d'Arte), Italy. Harris had a series of solo exhibitions, later ones including Theatre Royal, Winchester, 1990; Ruskin Gallery, Sheffield, 1995; Fashion Space Gallery, 2000 and 2002; and Galleria "Il Collezionista", Fano, Italy, 2004. After winning two Italian State Scholarships and a non-art research award, 1973–6, Harris won the Hertfordshire Arts Prize, 1996, and Edward Austin Memorial Scholarship at the British School at Rome, 1997. The Hertfordshire County Council, St Albans District Hospital, Sir Norman Lindop and many other private collectors acquired examples of his work, for which Italian landscapes and quarries were key inspirations. His early self-portrait is illustrated in Philip Vann's book *Face to Face*, published in 2004 by Sansom & Company/Piano Nobile Fine Paintings. Harris lived in St Albans, Hertfordshire.

Charles HARRIS fl. from 1970s– Painter and draughtsman who did a foundation course at Epsom College of Art and Design, 1970–1, then a vocational course at Hammersmith College of Art and Building, 1971–4. He won a scholarship to Royal Academy Schools, 1977–80, then a scholarship to the postgraduate course, 1980–83. He gained a number of prizes there, including the David Murray Scholarship in Landscape Painting for 1979–80 and 1981. Showed at RA Summer Exhibition from 1979, Mall Galleries from same year and won membership of Free Painters and Sculptors, 1981. Had solo show at Woodlands Art Gallery, 1982.

Dereck HARRIS 1962– Painter and teacher, born in Liverpool, who graduated in fine art from South Glamorgan Institute of Fine Art and gained his master's in painting from Chelsea College of Art and Design. He became senior lecturer in painting at Wimbledon School of Art, 2004, the year he was an Artist of the Day at Flowers Central, chosen by George Blacklock. Solo exhibitions included Astral Smile, The Nunnery Gallery, Bow Arts Trust, 2002.

Derrick HARRIS 1919–1960 Printmaker, painter, illustrator and designer. Born at Chislehurst, Kent, he studied art at the Central School of Arts and Crafts under Noel Rooke and John Farleigh. Exhibited SWE. He taught wood engraving and illustrating at Kingston and Reigate Schools of Art, in Surrey. Did commissioned work for the Festival of Britain, in 1951, illustrated several books for the Folio Society and has work in the collection of the Victoria & Albert Museum. Sometimes signed work D H. Lived in London.

Edwin HARRIS 1891–1961 Landscape painter in watercolour and tempera, especially of Sussex scenes. Educated in Littlehampton, Harris went on to exhibit at RA, Cooling Galleries, RBA and elsewhere, public galleries in Eastbourne, Hove and Accrington buying his work. His picture Moonrise was reproduced by the Medici Society. Was a member of the Association of Sussex Art Clubs and Brighton Art Club. Lived in Washington, Sussex.

Geoffrey HARRIS 1928– Sculptor, printer and teacher, born in Nottingham. He attended Leeds College of Art, 1948–51, then Royal College of Art, 1951–4. From 1953–4 he was a visiting lecturer at Dockland Settlements, then assisted the sculptor Leon Underwood and David John in 1954 and William Bloye in 1955–7. He held visiting lectureships meanwhile at Birmingham College of Art and Stourbridge School of Art. Harris assisted the sculptor Henry Moore, 1957–60, was visiting lecturer at Bromley College of Art, 1960–4, lectured at Ravensbourne College, 1964–70, then was senior lecturer there, 1970–86. Harris' commissions included Baildon Primary School, Yorkshire, 1951, the year he was awarded a Travelling Scholarship to Italy by Leeds College of Art; London County Council Maitland Park Housing Estate, St Pancras, 1964; and Smead Dean Centre, Sittingbourne, 1984. Mixed shows included Obelisk Gallery from 1957; Leicester Galleries from 1959; LG from 1965; and Goldsmiths' Hall, 1975. He had solo shows in 1964 at Leicester Galleries and Queen's Square Gallery, Leeds. From the late 1980s Harris concentrated on painting as well as sculpture. Lived in Faversham, Kent.

Jane HARRIS 1956– Painter, born in Dorset. She studied at Bournemouth College of Art, 1975–6, Camberwell School of Arts and Crafts, 1976–7, Brighton Polytechnic, 1977–9, Slade School of Fine Art, 1979–81, and Goldsmiths' College School of Art, 1989–91, where she completed her master's degree. Harris gained a number of awards: the Boise Travelling Scholarship, to Japan, 1981; a French Government Scholarship at Paris, 1985–6; Erasmus Exchange, Grenoble, 1990; and to Amsterdam in 1991. Participated in various group shows including Stowells Trophy, RA, 1979; New Contemporaries, ICA, 1981; and shared exhibitions in 1984 at Woodlands Art Gallery and in 1988 at Alpha Gallery, Swanage, and Holland Gallery. Had a solo show at University College London, 1981, and then at Anderson O'Day, 1992, Southampton City Art Gallery, 2001. Harris was a painter who reduced to a minimum the elements in her work, working on a large and small scale. At Anderson O'Day she restricted her format to that of an ellipse with fluctuating edges placed within a space of a different colour. In 2002, Harris won 3rd Prize in The Jerwood Drawing Prize.

Jeffrey HARRIS 1932– Abstract painter and teacher, born in Leeds, Yorkshire, studying at the College of Art there. Awarded a travelling scholarship to Paris in 1953. From 1956–64 Harris worked and lived in St Ives, Cornwall, then taught painting at Harris College, Preston. Returned to St Ives in 1965. Exhibitions included Passmore Edwards Gallery in Newlyn, Penwith and Fore Street Galleries in St Ives, Plymouth City Art Gallery and New Art Centre. In 1963 he shared an exhibition with Jane Beeson at Rowan Gallery, in 1965 having a solo exhibition at Mowan Gallery, Manchester. The City Art Gallery there holds works by him, and Arts Council has his oil on board Black, Grey and White, of 1959. In the 1970s Harris moved to Australia with his second wife, the Australian artist Gwen Leitch, where he taught and painted. The new landscape gave a different direction to his pictures.

Jennifer HARRIS 1935– Versatile artist who said that she would "frequently use collected images in a pattern, often to emphasise an underlying feeling of mystery or humour. I have been influenced by posters for feature films and the paintings of Carel Weight." Born in Bristol, she gained her National Diploma in Design there at West of England College of Art under Paul Feiler, 1951–5. In Bristol Harris worked as a display designer, 1957–65; art technician at the College of Education, 1966–77; also at the education faculty, Bristol Polytechnic, 1977–8. Was a member of the Printmakers' Council; and RWA, being included in Six Academicians there, 2001. Other group shows included RA Summer Exhibition; Royal Festival Hall; Royal National Theatre; Hatton Gallery, Newcastle upon Tyne; Spacex Gallery, Exeter; Adzak Gallery, Paris; Art Expo, New York; and the touring International Print Exhibition. Solo shows took place at Bristol Arts Centre, the University and Royal Albert Museum, both in Exeter, and elsewhere. Worcester College of Education holds her work. She lived in Cheriton Fitzpaine, Devon.

Josephine HARRIS fl. from 1950s– Painter, printmaker and glass engraver, who studied with William Mann at Plymouth College of Art, 1948–52. For a time she was secretary to the Royal Academy Schools. She was a member of RWA, NEAC and RBA, also showing at RA Summer Exhibition. Public galleries in Plymouth and Sheffield hold examples. Harris was made a member of the Art Workers' Guild in 1981. Lived in London.

Julie HARRIS 1921– Artist and costume designer, born and lived in London, who studied at Chelsea Polytechnic, 1937, with Graham Sutherland and Henry Moore. She was a film costume designer, 1945–90, latterly for television, in 1965 winning an Oscar Academy Award for her designs for the John Schlesinger-directed film *Darling*, starring Julie Christie, Dirk Bogarde and Laurence Harvey. Harris's costume sketches are in the collection of the British Film Institute. She took up painting in the late 1980s in the style of the Dutch Old Masters, having a solo exhibition, with the garden designer Arne Maynard, at Partridge (Fine Arts) Ltd.

Lindsay HARRIS 1948– Artist and teacher, born in Torquay, Devon, who studied surface design at Chelsea School of Art, 1973–6, gained an education certificate at Garnett College, 1978–9, an honours degree by independent study at Suffolk College, 1993–5, then lectured there in drawing and visual research. Was a member of the Suffolk Group and Ipswich Art Society. Mixed exhibitions included Spaces, Aldeburgh Festival, 1990; Summer Show, Galerie Lughien, Amsterdam, Netherlands, 1995; and 10sion, Box Gallery, Tattingstone, 1998. Her solo show, At the Margins, Christchurch Mansion, Ipswich, 2000, comprised drawings of unoccupied spaces, often with unusual angles and subtle light, giving impressions of silence, expectation and unease. In 2004 Harris shared an exhibition with her husband Esmond Bingham at North House Gallery, Manningtree. She lived in Burgh, Woodbridge, Suffolk.

Lyndon Goodwin HARRIS 1928– Painter and etcher, born in Halesowen, Worcestershire. He studied at Birmingham College of Art; Slade School of Fine Art, teachers including Randolph Schwabe and William Coldstream; and Central School of Arts and Crafts under Andrew Freeth. Among Harris' awards were Slade Scholar. In 1957 he was chosen for inclusion in Jack Beddington's book *Young Artists of Promise*. Harris was a member of RI, RSW and RWA, also showing with RA from age of 13, RBA, NEAC and Royal Glasgow Institute of the Fine Arts. At the Paris Salon he gained a Gold Medal, painting, and an Hon. Mention, etching. The Government Art Collection and University College hold his work.

Peter HARRIS 1967– Artist working in a range of media, born in Portsmouth, who studied at Chelsea College of Art, 1993–4, gaining a degree in painting from University of East London, 1994. In 1996 he co-founded, with Charles Avery, Uncle Grey Presents, an artist-run gallery and performance space. Exhibition, curatorial and performance activity there included the inaugural exhibition, a two-man show with Avery, 1996; Underdogs, also with Avery, and Sir Septimus Vein's Carnival of Freaks, both 1997. Other Harris shows included Social Security, Royal College of Art, 1998; in 1999 Self-Portrait by Proxy, the Demon Series and Physiognomy, which formed a kaleidoscopic whole, at Andrew Mummery Gallery and Nylon; and Touché, Andrew Mummery, 2000. Their shared themes were identity and intentions, artistic and individual. Harris's show at Andrew Mummery, Unexpurgated The Watercolour Diary, coincided with *YiBbA!*, The Book Launch, in 2002. Harris lived and worked in London.

Philip HARRIS 1965– Artist, born in Doncaster, Yorkshire, whose paintings incorporated Photo-Realist and Surrealist elements. He obtained his diploma at Mansfield, then a degree in art and design at Bradford. Group exhibitions included The Spectator Art Award, Spink & Son, 1989; British Month, Roy Miles Gallery, 1991; BP Portrait Award Exhibition, National Portrait Gallery, 1st Prize winner, 1993 (the ensuing 1994 commission was to paint the dancer Sir Anthony Dowell); and The Discerning Eye, Mall Galleries, 1995. Had a solo show at Beaux Arts, 1996. National Portrait Gallery and Metropolitan Museum of Modern Art, New York, hold Harris's work.

Phyl HARRIS 1925– Artist in pen, watercolour and pencil, and teacher, born and lived in London, full name Phyllis Harris. She studied at Reading University School of Art, Brighton College of Arts and Crafts and Camberwell School of Art, and at evening classes, her teachers including Anthony Betts and John Minton. She was made a member of SWA in 1975, SGA in 1991 and was also a member of Art Societies in Wembley and Harrow. Also showed at Knapp Gallery and Westminster Central Gallery. Harris' work was semi-abstract; she was "interested in the design and pattern of landscape and still life".

Richard HARRIS 1954– Sculptor and teacher, born in Newton Abbot, Devon, who graduated in fine art from Gloucester College of Art, 1973–5. Taught in Australia, 1979–81, exhibiting at First Australian Triennial in Melbourne, 1980–1. Harris was closely associated with Grizedale Forest, Cumbria, initially holding a fellowship there, 1977–8. His large Quarry Structure, 1978, in slate and wood, is sited at Grizedale. Was included in Arts Council's The Sculpture Show, 1983, living in Newcastle upon Tyne, completing a commission in Gateshead for Arts Council and Northern Arts.

Rohan HARRIS 1963– Artist creating abstract works using such materials as wood, steel, cloth and industrial finishes, born in Amersham, Surrey. Attended Chelsea School of Art, 1981–5. Solo exhibitions included Knoedler Gallery, 1988 and 1989; Nancy Hoffman Gallery, New York, America, 1991 and 1996; and Clove 2, 1994. In 1996 Harris shared an exhibition at Kapil Jarawala Gallery with Douglas Allsop and Sally Musgrove.

Rolf HARRIS 1930– Genial entertainer, musician and artist with a special interest in portraiture, born in Perth, Western Australia, who went to the Modern School there, the University of Western Australia and Claremont Teachers' College. The Australian artist Hayward Veal's Impressionist style was a strong influence. Harris embarked on a foundation course at City and Guilds of London Art School but found life drawing irksome. He soon established a reputation as a singer and television personality, notably for children, his ability to draw amusingly at speed being a popular feature. His records included *Tie Me Kangaroo Down Sport*, 1960, and *Two Little Boys*, 1969. His many television programmes included *The Rolf Harris Show*, 1967–71, *Animal Hospital* and *Rolf's Amazing Animals*, from 1997, and *Rolf on Art*, from 2001, which introduced well-known artists to a huge audience. There was an accompanying book. Among his other books were *Your Cartoon Time*, 1986, and *Your Animation Time*, 1991. He represented Australia at seven World Fairs, 1969–85. Harris married Alwen Hughes in 1958, they had one daughter, Bindi, and in 2000 Halcyon Gallery, Birmingham, put on the show The Art of Rolf, Alwen and Bindi Harris at the International Convention Centre. Harris also showed at the RA Summer Exhibition and was an Hon. Member of the RBA. In 2001 his autobiography *Can You Tell What it is Yet?* appeared. Within a few years, Harris's pictures commanded six-figure prices, Halcyon marketed his limited-edition prints and queues formed for his exhibitions. In 2005 it was announced that he was to paint a portrait of Queen Elizabeth II for a *Rolf on Art* special. By then his 2004 and 2005 BBC television series *Star Portraits with Rolf* had proved so successful that it prompted a 2005 County Hall Gallery exhibition with extensive tour.

Stephen R A HARRIS 1913–1980 Painter, draughtsman, designer and restorer, born in Langton Herring, Dorset, his father a naval petty officer, his mother a teacher. At the age of 11 Stephen was sent to the Royal Naval College, Greenwich, but the head saw that he was not thriving in the spartan regime and recommended civilian art tuition. He attended Battersea Polytechnic from 1929 and then the City and Guilds School, Kennington, where he won the Silver Medal for Drawing in 1937 and an international competition for poster design sponsored by Shell-Mex and BP. In the 1950s he designed posters for Guinness, the brewer. One of his teachers at Kennington, Andrew Butler, brother of the politician R A Butler, obtained portrait commissions for Harris, including the academic and collector Sir Michael Sadler, and probably introduced him to Felix Harbord the decorator, with whom he worked in grand houses. After Royal Air Force service in World War II Harris settled with his wife, former Kennington fellow-student Florence Hollins, at Barbon, in the Westmorland fells, where she had family connections. There he painted landscapes and portraits and from about 1960 studied restoration, working on paintings at Abbot Hall Art Gallery, which gave his own pictures a show in 1988. Harris was a sensitive, self-critical artist, a disciple of Constable who revered the Old Masters. He declined to promote his work commercially.

Sylvia HARRIS 1920– Painter, born and eventually settled in London, who in her thirties "moved to Paris and lived in the Latin Quarter, where I knew many artists, among them the German artist Francis Bott, with whom I studied. I eventually returned to London, worked for a while as a secretary in a government department and then enrolled at the Sir John Cass School of Art for about six years. I studied anatomy and Expressionism and was then offered a diploma course at the Middlesex Polytechnic." During the following 30 years Harris painted and showed at Whitechapel Art Gallery; Ben Uri Gallery; Murray Feely Fine Art; the Banqueting House, Horse Guards Parade; and in many group exhibitions.

Teri-Jane HARRIS 1964– Artist who graduated with honours at Cardiff School of Art, 1983–6, attending Slade School of Fine Art, 1986–8. Group shows included Chapter Arts Centre, Cardiff, 1985; RA, 1988; and in 1989 both Smiths Galleries and East End Open Studios, at Angel Studios.

Tim HARRIS fl. from mid-1980s– Painter who studied initially in Taunton, 1978–9. He gained an honours degree at Winchester School of Art, 1979–82, then his master's degree from Chelsea School of Art, 1982–3. His mixed show appearances included Tony Carter Studio, Brixton Artists' Co-op, Winchester Gallery and Hardware Gallery, and in 1991 he was a prizewinner in The Discerning Eye at Mall Galleries, and tour. One-man shows included 1988 Mermaid Theatre and Hardware Gallery. Winchester School of Art library holds his work.

Tomás HARRIS 1908–1964 Artist in many media, picture dealer and collector, born in London. His father Lionel Harris founded the Spanish Art Gallery which Tomás later helped to run, having dealt on his own. Studied at Slade School of Fine Art, 1923–6, having won the Trevelyan-Goodall Scholarship, under Henry Tonks; then for a year at British Academy in Rome; etching at the Slade after World War II; and wood engraving in the early 1950s with John Buckland-Wright. During the war Harris' knowledge of Spain was invaluable to the Security Service. He was a principal organiser of Operation Garbo, which misled the Germans on Allied plans for the invasion of France. After the war Harris gave up dealing to devote himself to collecting and painting. In 1943 he showed solo with Lefevre Gallery. He also exhibited with Knoedler in New York and widely in Spain, where he was the first independent artist since Goya to have his cartoons woven at the Royal Tapestry Factory in Madrid. With Juliet Wilson, in 1964 he produced a scholarly two-volume book on the etchings of Goya, his fine collection being shown at the British Museum in 1963–4. Public galleries in Toledo, America and in São Paulo, Brazil, hold Harris' work. Finally settled for many years in Camp de Mar, Majorca, Spain, drawing on the landscape to produce pictures reminiscent of Van Gogh. He died in a motor accident and his friend Anthony Blunt organised a memorial show at Courtauld Institute Galleries in 1975.

Vera Furneaux HARRIS 1904– Painter, miniaturist, illustrator and teacher who sometimes worked on ivory, born in Ross, Herefordshire. She was educated at the Grammar School in Maidstone, then at the School of Art there, at the Slade School of Fine Art and in Paris. Exhibited RA, RMS of which she was a member, Paris Salon and elsewhere and did work for the religious publisher A R Mowbray and Company. Lived in Loose, Kent.

Susanna HARRIS-HUGHES 1947– Painter and printmaker who graduated from the Surrey Institute of Art & Design, 1993, with a master's in printmaking from Wimbledon School of Art, 1998. Among solo exhibitions were Crows & Chairs, Lewis Elton Gallery, University of Surrey; The Waste Land, Chelsea Arts Club; The Sea, The Sea, Cranleigh Arts Centre; and Yehudi Menuhin School, Stoke D'Abernon. In 2002 Harris-Hughes was part of an artists' residency at Fishbourne Roman Palace, Chichester, in the same year taking part in the Borderlands Artists' Consortium's show Junctions 1– Flowers, at University of Surrey, when she worked with a palaebotanist to produce digital images based on electron micrographs of pollen. Harris-Hughes had a strong interest in mythology, notably the Green Man, as in her contribution to the 2003 show Contemporary British Art, at The Millinery Works.

Anthony HARRISON 1931– Artist and teacher, born in Truro, Cornwall, who initially studied architecture. He then turned to art under Merlyn Evans and Keith Vaughan at Central School of Arts and Crafts, 1949–55, lecturing on printmaking there, 1959–64. Between 1956–62 Harrison exhibited at Robert Erskine's St George's Gallery, shortly after that having a series of engravings issued by Editions Alecto. Following an exhibition of works on paper at the San Francisco Museum of Art in America in 1964 and an American residency, Harrison taught at Pratt Graphic Art Center and New York University, 1965–71, also in the visual arts department at Columbia University, 1970–93. From 1983 Harrison was based in New Jersey, converting a factory into a home and studio. Brooklyn Museum is among collections holding Harrison's work.

Cheryl HARRISON 1965– Painter of abstracts, born in Ballarat, Victoria, Australia, whose "personality is shaped and refined by my surroundings, objects or moments that capture my attention in some way or another. My paintings are very much of the same core." Harrison began her creative career as a camera operator and floor manager for Australian Television. She painted for as long as she could recall, but began working seriously in 1993, leaving television in 1996. In 1998 she gained her Bachelor of Arts from the University of Ballarat, while studying being elected a member of the Ballarat Society of Artists. In 1997 she was one of a group of painters who, by unveiling hundreds of celebratory flags on the themes of peace and conflict, drew attention to the restoration of the Avenue of Honour in Ballarat, commemorating Australian personnel killed in conflict in two World Wars. After world travels Harrison arrived in London in 1999, having a solo show, Scratching the Surface, at the Australian High Commission in 2001, after which she moved to St Ives, Cornwall. She became a member of the Penwith Society; travelled further in 2002–4; and in 2005 was granted British citizenship. Harrison participated in group shows in Australia and the United Kingdom; in 2002 18 of her paintings were filmed for Channel 4's *Life Doctor*; and her further solo shows including Place Belong Me; Place Belong You, Jersey Galleries, Ealing, in 2002, and Weathered Language, The Book Gallery, St Ives, 2005. Permanent collections in America, Australia, New Zealand and the United Kingdom held examples.

Claude HARRISON 1922– Artist, notably in tempera, born in Leyland, Lancashire. He was married to the artist Audrey Johnson in 1947, their son being the potter Tobias Harrison. He was educated at Preston College of Art, 1939–41, Liverpool College of Art, 1941–2, then after Royal Air Force service in India, Burma and China, at Royal College of Art, 1947–50. Harrison was a painter of murals, portraits, conversation pieces and imaginative figure compositions including harlequin-type and masked figures and using a delicate palette. He showed with RP of which he was an honorary member, RA, RBA and elsewhere in mixed exhibitions and had numerous solo shows including Contemporary Fine Art Gallery, Eton, 1992. In 1991 he shared a show with his wife at Phoenix Gallery, Highgate. Harrison published *The Portrait Painters' Handbook*, 1968, and *The Book of Tobit*, 1969. Harris Art Gallery in Preston and galleries in Kendal and Lancaster hold his work. Lived in Cartmel Fell, Cumbria.

Clifford HARRISON: *see* **Frederick Clifford HARRISON**

Coela Pryce HARRISON fl. c.1920–1960 Watercolourist, born at Thorpe near Norwich, Norfolk, into a military family. She attended St Felix's School, Southwold, and studied art in St Ives with Leonard Fuller, at Heatherley's School of Fine Art with Iain Macnab and elsewhere. Showed at RWS, SWA, RI, in India and Malta. Lived for a time at Dedham, Essex, completing small pictures of the local countryside.

Colin HARRISON 1939– Painter, draughtsman and teacher, born in Boston, Lincolnshire. His specialities were nudes and portraits, and he was noted for subjects from the entertainment world such as the singer Ruby Murray and the dancers Fred Astaire and Ginger Rogers. Harrison attended Leicester College of Art, 1957–61, then Royal Academy Schools, 1961–4, obtaining a David Murray Scholarship in his first year and a Silver Medal in his last. Lectured at Ulster College of Art and Design, 1964–73, and was a visiting lecturer at Wolverhampton Polytechnic. In 1970 Arts Council of Northern Ireland, which along with Ulster Museum holds his work, gave him a project award for film-making with William Bogle. Exhibitions included New 57 Gallery, Edinburgh; Brown Thomas Gallery in Dublin; Richard Demarco Gallery in Edinburgh; and Tom Caldwell Gallery, Belfast.

Edward Stroud HARRISON 1879– Painter, born in Edinburgh, where he studied at Heriot-Watt College and the University. Exhibited RSA extensively, SSA of which he was a member, Walker Art Gallery, Liverpool, and Royal Glasgow Institute of the Fine Arts. Lived for many years in Elgin, Moray.

Frederick Clifford HARRISON 1901–1984 Still life painter, born in London, who studied at Hammersmith College of Art and at the Central School of Arts and Crafts. In the 1920s he worked in advertising for Publicity Arts Ltd, going freelance in 1927, and did poster work for Shell. About 40 years later he started devoting his talent to producing meticulous trompe l'oeil pictures of uncanny realism. He showed at the RA Summer Exhibition until 1967, Furneaux Gallery, Harris Art Gallery in Preston, Royal Glasgow Institute of the Fine Arts and Chelsea Art Club. E Stacy-Marks Ltd, Eastbourne, included Harrison's Six Plates, Two Pots and a China Horse in its 1989 Centenary Exhibition. He is sometimes referred to just as Clifford Harrison. Lived for a time at Weybridge, Surrey.

Ian HARRISON 1935– Painter, miniaturist and teacher, born in Staines, Surrey, educated partly in England, partly in Nairobi, Kenya, where his art education was obtained. Went on to teach history of art and design at Halton College of Further Education, Widnes. Showed with RMS, Hesketh Hubbard Society and elsewhere and had several one-man shows at Woburn Abbey, Bedfordshire. Lived in Northwich, Cheshire.

John Cyril HARRISON 1898–1985 Artist who specialised in natural history, born in Tidworth, Wiltshire. He began drawing as a small boy, his family living in British Columbia from 1912–15, learning anatomy from taxidermy and concentrating on birds of prey. After service in World War I Jack Harrison studied at Slade School of Fine Art, then moved to Norfolk, settling in a studio in Haynford. He illustrated books on birds, notably his friend Seton Gordon's *Days with the Golden Eagle*, of 1927; in 1949 wrote and illustrated *Bird Portraits*; and in 1968 completed all illustrations for Brown and Amadon's *The Birds of Prey of the World*. Harrison's travels included Scotland, Iceland and latterly Africa. The Tryon Gallery regularly held his shows and published prints of his game bird subjects, which had popular appeal, as did his watercolours. Harrison, who listed his recreations as shooting and fishing, died after finishing all the pictures for his spring 1985 exhibition. His prints continued to be sold by the Tryon and Moorland Gallery.

John Francis HARRISON 1904– Versatile and colourful artist, one of the Pitmen Painters, Jack Harrison was the son of a miner, born at Waterhouses, County Durham, moving to Ashington, Northumberland, in 1909. When 13 he started at Ellington Colliery, went to Bothal Pit at Ashington Colliery at 15 and worked until he was made redundant at 63. Harrison endured long and unsociable shifts, working hard coal in cramped conditions for meagre pay, rising to be a deputy overman. In the 1950s he joined the Ashington Art Group, consistently experimental and individual in his approach, "although it was often difficult to buy paints and materials and framing my work has been very costly". The Group's paintings went to Germany and China, the first post-Communist Western art show there. Harrison worked widely in Northumberland, "particularly liked the coastal areas from Berwick to North Shields". The mining community "was a rich source of inspiration". He had a retrospective at Woodhorn Church Museum in 1994 and the Colliery Museum there holds his work, which was signed with a JFH monogram.

Kevin HARRISON 1953– He studied at Norwich School of Art, 1971–4, and Chelsea School of Art, 1974–5. In 1984, Harrison took part in the International Garden Festival in Liverpool and gained a commission for Grizedale Forest, Cumbria. From 1985 he showed with Nicholas Treadwell Gallery, in 1987 at Air Gallery and in 1989 in East End Open Studios, at Chisenhale Studios. The Enfield, Middlesex-born sculptor continued to exhibit with Treadwell after the gallery moved to Aigen, Austria, explaining on its website: "My sculptures are urban, full of energy, colour and excitement of the city where people are born, love, fight, eat, get drunk, laugh and eventually die. They are humorous sculptures made of brightly painted wood and metal. Underlying the humour there are more serious messages."

Laura HARRISON 1946– Painter and draughtsman, notable for portraits in a rich palette, born and lived in Glasgow, where, under David Donaldson, she graduated in drawing and painting from the School of Art, 1967. Among privately commissioned portraits were the naturalist David Bellamy; her work was also in many corporate and private collections. Exhibitions included RP from 1990; Glasgow Society of Women Artists, Royal Glasgow Institute of the Fine Arts and Bruton Street Gallery, all from 1993–4; William Hardie, Glasgow, 1995; and The Contemporary Fine Art Gallery, Eton, 1999. Also exhibited with Flying Colours Gallery. In 1996 had a solo show at Gatehouse Gallery, Glasgow.

Margaret HARRISON 1940– Artist in mixed media, sometimes on a large scale, as in Rape, of 1978, owned by Arts Council; teacher. She studied at Carlisle College of

Art and Royal Academy Schools. Among her awards was a Royal Academy Schools Bronze Medal, a British Council Scholarship to Italy and Northern Arts and Arts Council grants. Went on to teach widely, including Royal College of Art, Slade School of Fine Art and Goldsmiths' College. Mixed exhibitions included Art for Society, Whitechapel Art Gallery and tour, 1978; Some British Art from the Left, Artists' Space, New York, 1979; and Woodlands Art Gallery and tour, 1981–2, in Greater London Arts Association award show. Solo shows included Carlisle City Art Gallery and tour, 1980–1. In 1989 Harrison's work was was one of Three Women Artists (with Dora Altounyan and Sheila Fell) at Abbot Hall Art Gallery, Kendal.

Margot HARRISON 1915– Painter, born Margaret Amy Harrison in Madras, southern India. She studied privately with Edwin Pascoe Holman, later with Kingsley Sutton and was for four years a part-time student at Farnham Art School with John Wilkinson. For a time she was a member of SWA and RWS Art Club. Harrison exhibited at Paris Salon, ROI, RBA and in provincial galleries and had several solo shows in London. British Petroleum commissioned her to paint views of the rivers Tamar and Test and the National Trust Clumber Park. Lived in Odiham, Hampshire.

Marguerite HARRISON 1927– Painter, draughtsman and teacher, born in Llandudno, Caernarvonshire, Wales. She was educated at the Royal Masonic School at Rickmansworth and was mainly self-taught as a painter although she studied for a while with Kenneth Jameson. Exhibited RA, RCamA and with Wirral Society of Arts. She was a Froebel-trained teacher who taught in the Birkenhead area of Cheshire and privately, living in Birkenhead. For some years Harrison painted under her unmarried name Marguerite Hazel Roberts.

Mary Kent HARRISON: *see* **Mary KENT**

Paul HARRISON 1966– Video-based artist, born in Wolverhampton, Staffordshire, who studied at Bath College of Art. From 1993 he worked with John Wood as John Wood & Paul Harrison (see Wood's entry for their joint output). Harrison lived in Shropshire.

Peter HARRISON 1950– Painter, draughtsman and writer, born in the west of Scotland who studied at Glasgow School of Art, 1967–71; gained a fine art diploma, with distinction, at Glasgow University, 1971–3; then was a postgraduate art history student at University of East Anglia, 1974–7. Shared a show at Clyde Fair International, 1972; took part in Pernod Competition, 1973; Spirit of London, on the South Bank, 1979; group exhibition at Harris Gallery, 1985; Glasgow, City of Culture, show at Compass Gallery, Glasgow, 1990; and from 1995 with Brent Artists at Willesden Library. In 2001 he had solo exhibition with the Brent Arts Council, at The Stables, Dollis Hill. Shapes, lights and shadows found in the landscapes of the Firth of Clyde and Donegal were important influences. In 1995, Harrison published *An Introduction to Monet* and *An Introduction to Van Gogh* in the Macdonald Young Books series. Lived in north London.

Richard HARRISON 1954– Widely travelled painter, born in Liverpool, whose abstract landscapes and apocalyptic horsemen, in his solo shows at Albemarle Gallery in 2002 and 2003, were on a grand scale, turbulent, rich in colour and texture. Harrison graduated with honours in medieval history at Trinity College, Cambridge, 1973–6. He gained a diploma in furniture design at London College of Furniture, 1981–3, then graduated with honours in fine art at Chelsea School of Art, 1984–7, gaining his master's in painting there, 1987–8. Other solo exhibitions included Berkeley Square Gallery, 1990; Jill George Gallery, 1993; and Gallery 27, 1997. Among group venues were RA Summer Exhibition, 1985; ROI, Mall Galleries, 1987; Kunsthaus, Augsburg, Germany, 1988; Pomeroy Purdy, 1989; William Mora Gallery, Melbourne, Australia, 1992; Chicago Art Fair, Berkeley Square Gallery, 1993; and Art for Youth, Mall Galleries, and Metropolis Gallery, Melbourne, both 1999. Lived in London.

Stephanie HARRISON 1939– Artist using watercolour, gouache, pen and pencil, born in King's Lynn, Norfolk. She attended Medway College of Art, Rochester, 1955–60, teachers including John Ward and Fred Cuming. After working as an illustrator and graphic designer in industry Harrison worked for the Science Museum and British Museum, becoming a freelance artist in 1979. She illustrated several books, including *Reader's Digest Wild Flowers of Great Britain*, and designed greetings cards for Henry Ling and Company. She was a member of RMS and the Society of Botanical Artists, showing also with RI and Francis Iles Gallery, Rochester. Harrison was a gallery artist at Linda Blackstone Gallery, Pinner, and had a number of solo exhibitions in London and Kent. As well as botanical, house and garden studies she painted landscape, still life and meticulous studies of aircraft and motor transport. Lived at Stick Hill, Edenbridge, Kent.

Thomas Michael HARRISON 1969– Painter and teacher, born in Wigan, Lancashire. He gained an honours degree at University College of Wales, Aberystwyth, in 1990, winning several prizes. Went on to complete his master's degree and in 1991–2 taught at the College. His work was shown at exhibitions at University College of Wales, Coach House Gallery in Wigan and Mall Galleries and in 1993 was included in Aberystwyth Artists at The Deffett Francis Gallery, Swansea Institute of Higher Education.

Robert Edward HARRISSON 1922– Painter and teacher, born in London, educated in Edmonton where he continued to live. Studied at Hornsey School of Art, 1938–42, then after war service in the Royal Navy at Royal College of Art, 1946–9, where his teachers included Rodrigo Moynihan and Ruskin Spear. Showed with Enfield Art Circle and elsewhere, Royal Dental Hospital holding his work. This he signed R E H.

Tim HARRISSON 1952– Sculptor, draughtsman, painter, printmaker and teacher, who attended Hammersmith College of Art, 1969–70, Norwich College of Art, 1970–3, and Byam Shaw School of Fine Art, 1975. After working as a woodman and welder, 1976–80, in 1980–3 Harrisson was lecturer in painting and drawing, adult education, for Wiltshire and Dorset Council. In 1988 he was sculptor-in-residence, Red House Museum, Christchurch, organised by the Hampshire Sculpture Trust. Spatial relationships were of key importance to Harrisson's abstract sculptures. Millfield School, Somerset, gave him a commission in 1989, in collaboration with Artsite Gallery, Bath. Mixed exhibitions included Salisbury Library, 1981; Harris

Museum, Preston, 1985; in 1987 he was a winner in international competition organised by Metro Art, New York; 1991, *The Economist* Plaza, St James'; and 1994, New Art Centre Sculpture Garden at Roche Court, Salisbury. Had a solo show at New Art Centre, Sloane Street, 1993. In 2005 the Jennifer Newman Studio, Longbridge Deverill, showed Harrisson's abstract prints, which used "a variety of almost sculptural techniques". Harrisson lived in Wiltshire.

Frederick Samuel HARROP 1887–1969 Painter, potter, printmaker, designer and teacher, born in Batsford, Stoke-on-Trent. Harrop was a student at Hanley Municipal School of Art, 1906–9, where he won a number of prizes and medals, then at Royal College of Art, 1909–13. In 1913 Harrop went to Siam, holding a series of art teaching positions, finally being organising art master to the Ministry of Public Instruction, Bangkok. He also designed Siamese currency notes. Won Order of the Crown of Siam, third class, in 1920, two years after gaining the Order of the White Elephant, fourth class. From 1930 he was back in England holding teaching positions at Willesden Polytechnic, Paddington Technical Institute and Hammersmith School of Building and Arts and Crafts. As well as showing in Siam, Harrop exhibited at RBA, Crafts Centre of Great Britain and had a memorial show at Camden Arts Centre in 1970. Lived in London.

Barry HART: *see* **Herbert Barry HART**

Frank HART 1878–1959 Graphic artist and painter. Born in Brighton, Sussex, he studied at Heatherley's School of Fine Art. Exhibited RA, RI, RWS and abroad. Among his books are *Dolly's Society Book* and *Master Toby's Hunt*, and he also had work in *Punch* and *Men Only*. Lived at Cooden, Sussex.

Herbert Barry HART 1894–1954 Sculptor, letter-cutter, designer and teacher, listed variously as H Barry Hart and Barry Hart. He came from a family of stonemasons and was notable for his fine carving. Hart cut letters for World War I memorials by Charles Sargeant Jagger, Eric Kennington and others. When Henry Moore arrived at the Royal College of Art's school of sculpture in 1921 Hart was technical assistant, fostering an interest in direct carving, teaching it to Moore and Barbara Hepworth. In 1929 Hart was best man at Moore's wedding. Through to the College's 1950–1 prospectus Hart was listed as a technical assistant and teacher of stone and marble carving in the sculpture school. In 1930 he took up an appointment as head of Colchester Technical College, continuing to teach at the Royal College one day a week, and shook up the staid Essex institution. He appointed Edward Morss, a postgraduate painting student at the Royal College, as assistant master in 1931. They were enlightened teachers, strict about life drawing. Hart introduced a nude life-class, attracting London models instead of old men from the local Labour Exchange. He brought an awareness of modern art, especially that of Jacob Epstein, Eric Gill and Kennington, and encouraged development of a library of contemporary art books covering such topics as German Expressionism, Constructivism and revolutionary Russian art. In 1935 the School of Art merged with the Science and Engineering departments of the Technical College to become the Colchester and North East Essex Technical College and School of Art. Hart became responsible to Maurice Garside, the College's principal, which seems to have prompted Hart's resignation in 1936. A Colchester student of his, Joseph Robinson, remembered him as "full of ideas...about six foot four tall with thin wispy ginger hair and spectacles, and you could always go and talk to him". From 1946–52 Hart showed a series of sculptures at the RA Summer Exhibition, living in Kew Green and then at East Molesey, Surrey. Moore and Hart had remained in contact, exchanging letters between 1949–51. Hart latterly created the inscription for Moore's Claydon Madonna and was consulted about the pedestal for his Standing Figure. Abbott and Holder from 2002 offered a series of fine torsos by Hart.

John HART 1921–1996 Painter, engraver and teacher, born in Manchester and educated at Merchant Taylors' School, Crosby. Studied at Liverpool College of Art and in Paris, then ran teacher training at Liverpool College and at Goldsmiths' College. While in Liverpool Hart appeared in John Willetts' *Art in a City*, 1967, as "a slight, bespectacled figure of buzzing energy" who not only ran "an outstanding department at the College but produces a steady output of non-figurative paintings". Exhibition venues included John Moores Liverpool Exhibitions; Bear Lane Gallery in Oxford; LG, Annely Juda, Marjorie Parr, Beaux Arts and Redfern Galleries, and abroad. Completed a mural at Daresbury Nuclear Physics Laboratory. Walker Art Gallery in Liverpool, Dudley Art Gallery, the Universities of Liverpool, Manchester and York and several education authorities hold examples. In retirement lived in Montbrun-les-Bains, France.

Jonathan HART 1949– Abstract artist whose work often derived from landscape and observation of nature, born in Ripon, Yorkshire. Studied at Scarborough School of Art, 1968–9, then Canterbury College of Art, 1969–72. Did a variety of jobs to support his painting. His mixed show appearances included Stowells exhibition at Mall Galleries, 1972; Some Canterbury Painters, at Canterbury Library, 1974; and Summer Show 2 at Serpentine Gallery, 1982. Had a series of open studio solo exhibitions, living for some time in London.

Simon HART 1969– Designer, painter, draughtsman and lecturer, born in Dunstable, Bedfordshire, who did a foundation course at Barnet College, 1987–8, studied design at Staffordshire University, 1988–91, then worked as a freelance designer, artist and part-time lecturer. He taught at Bradford College, 1993–4; Stockport College, 1995; Staffordshire University, 1995–7; and Somerset College of Arts, 1995–8. Hart carried out numerous design commissions, including a stage set for English National Ballet and concept boards for Laura Ashley, both 1993; magazine illustration for Hill Publishing, 1994–5; cards for Beside the Wave Publishing, 1996–8; and editioned prints, Secrets, Port Isaac, 1998. He took part in many mixed shows, later solo exhibitions including Enid Lawson Gallery, 1999. Travels through Europe, colour, and childhood memories of toys, the seaside and London museums and theatres inspired Hart's work.

Philip HARTAS 1930– Sculptor and teacher who studied at Leeds College and Slade School of Fine Art under Henry Moore and Reg Butler. He held teaching posts at Derby, during which time he was chosen by Jack Beddington as one of his *Young Artists of Promise*, in the 1957 book of that title; Liverpool College of Art; Bournemouth and Leicester; then finally at Brighton Polytechnic/Brighton University. Exhibited at Liverpool Academy and elsewhere. Hartas completed a number of commissions when resident in Liverpool, including a relief in Lewis' department store.

Christine HART-DAVIES 1947– Watercolourist, born in Shrewsbury, Shropshire. She read fine art and typography at Reading University, 1966–70, teachers including Rita Donagh and Michael Twyman, where she graduated with honours. She worked for several years with a London design group, mainly on educational books, then in 1975, after sailing and travelling in Europe and North Africa, settled in Poole, Dorset, becoming known for precise botanical watercolours. Hart-Davies became a member of RMS in 1975 and a founder-member of the Society of Botanical Artists in 1985. She was especially interested in mosses and lichens, and her work on these was four times awarded the Gold Medal of the Royal Horticultural Society. Her exhibitions included Contemporary British Watercolours, RI and Hilliard Society of Miniaturists from 1983; and Paris Salon and Flowers and Gardens from 1984. Her solo exhibitions included Spring Hill Gallery, Brisbane, from 1984, and Young Masters Gallery, Brisbane, from 1987. The book *A Year in a Victorian Garden*, 1990, includes her work, which is held by the Hunt Institute of Botanical Documentation, Carnegie-Mellon University, Pittsburgh.

James HART DYKE 1966– Representational painter who began at an early age. He studied architecture at Manchester University, 1986–9, and the Royal College of Art, 1990–2, then obtained a higher diploma in postgraduate studies in painting from the City & Guilds of London Art School, 1995–6. Many of Hart Dyke's early works were views of country houses. Commissions included Highgrove, home of HRH The Prince of Wales, also Pembroke College in Cambridge and Stonor Park, Oxfordshire, for Lord Camoys. The Prince of Wales invited Hart Dyke as official artist on the royal tour to Sri Lanka, Nepal and Bhutan in 1998, and paintings from His Royal Highness's collection were included in the show Travels with the Prince, at Hampton Court Palace, to mark the Prince's fiftieth birthday. In 1999 Hart Dyke accompanied the Prince to Saudi Arabia. Hart Dyke was included in Eight Selected Artists at W H Patterson in 2002, at which time he was on a three-month trek in Tibet. Patterson's Hart Dyke solo show Painting in the Hidden Himalayas was held in 2003.

Jack HARTERT 1922–1975 Versatile painter and draughtsman, producing figurative work with an emphasis on line, whose father owned a gallery on Madison Avenue, New York. Jack drew from an early age, contributing to school magazines, and studied art at university and the National Academy of Design. After Army service in World War II Hartert joined the family business, based in Paris where he purchased European paintings which were shipped back to America, at the same time continuing with his own work. Although Hartert was lukewarm about much of what he bought, notably the Impressionists and especially Monet, he seems to have had a high regard for Degas, as he did for the Dutch Old Masters and advanced artists like Magritte. Still lifes in the Dutch manner and pastels of nudes were special features of Hartert's output; one later theme was the slightly Surrealist Tower of Babel series of oils. After a few years in America Hartert in 1961 moved to England, settling in Clifton where his brother William, who had married a Bristol girl, lived. Jack married in 1970, but did not want children, having seen many injured and orphaned ones in the Pacific during the war, two of whom he and friends unofficially adopted during hostilities. Hartert refused any medals. Later, the Arab-Israeli conflict prompted several powerful anti-war drawings. Hartert was a serious, unassuming artist whose friends often knew nothing of his work. He had no compulsion to sell, and showed infrequently in New York, London, Paris and the Netherlands. In 1975, after his death from cancer, there was a memorial show at David Durant's gallery in Clifton, where examples of Hartert's trompe l'oeil painted furniture were included. Hartert was remembered locally as a larger-than-life character, often seen in the city's better restaurants, a generous, cigar-smoking host and companion, noted for his amusing anecdotes.

Brenda HARTILL 1943– Artist in a range of media, theatrical designer and lecturer, born and lived in London, who emigrated to New Zealand with her parents in the late 1950s, gaining a fine art diploma at the University of Auckland. She returned to London in the late 1960s on a New Zealand Arts Council grant to study at Central School of Art & Design; became involved in theatre design; after marriage lectured and designed in university theatre at North Carolina State University, in America; returned to London in the early 1970s to take up an Arts Council award at the National Theatre at the Young Vic; then worked as a freelance designer around Britain. In the early 1980s, seeking more artistic independence, Hartill turned to printmaking, publishing her own work. As well as a studio where she was assisted by two printers, Hartill had another in Caucin, southern Spain, and worked in the wilds of New Zealand. The forms of land, air and sea were key elements in Hartill's strongly coloured figurative and abstract pictures. Exhibited in over 50 galleries worldwide, mixed shows including RE, of which she was a member, RA Summer Exhibition and National Print Exhibition. Solo exhibitions included a series at New Academy Gallery from 1991.

Alex HARTLEY 1963– Artist using a variety of media, born in West Byfleet, Surrey, who did a foundation course, 1983–4, then an honours degree, 1984–90, at Camberwell School of Arts and Crafts, gaining his master's at Royal College of Art, 1988–90. Group exhibitions included International Departures, Kavalere Kazerne, Amsterdam, 1990; Crossover, Anderson O'Day Gallery, 1991; Young British Artists from the Saatchi Collection, Art Cologne, Cologne, 1993; Fall Out, Walker Fabrik, Darmstadt, 1996; and Sensation. Young British Artists from the Saatchi Collection, RA, 1997. Later solo shows included Victoria Miro Gallery, 1997, where Hartley's work Viewer was composed of a vast, fully functioning slide viewer and oversized 35-millimetre slides. Hartley's large, prize-winning architectural piece Pavilion was unveiled at Art2000, for transfer to the Goodwood Estate, West Sussex. In 2001, Hartley shared a Victoria Miro exhibition with Tracey Moffat. Arts Council, Contemporary Art Society, De Beers and Caldic Collections hold examples.

Ben HARTLEY 1933–1996 Painter, draughtsman and teacher, born in Mellor, Cheshire, on the edge of the

Peak District, son of a tailor, a solitary child who attended Manchester Grammar School. After art school in Stockport and Manchester, Hartley was a contemporary of David Hockney and Robyn Denny at the Royal College of Art, 1954–7, his teacher Carel Weight befriending him. In 1960 Hartley began part-time teaching at Plymouth College of Art, rationalisation forcing him out in 1983. He moved to Presteigne, on the Powys/Herefordshire border, to be near a sister and a Carmelite community, having converted to Roman Catholicism in 1968. He lived a retiring, frugal life in a small cottage. Although prolific, Hartley had scarcely exhibited until Bernard Samuels, director of Plymouth Arts Centre, began showing his work, giving him a solo exhibition in 1976. Ikon Gallery in Birmingham, John Hansard Gallery in Southampton, Newlyn Gallery and Bath Festival Gallery followed, as well as regular shows at Beaux Arts, Bath. In Presteigne, Hartley continued to produce and exhibit; at his death, he left 900 paintings and 300 notebooks to Samuels. Hartley spent a lifetime reading and meditating on the purpose of painting, producing humorous, colourful, apparently naïve images with a countryman's eye for birds, insects and animals. Influences included Bonnard, Matisse and Proust, like whom he sought to regain the freshness of a childhood vision. Hartley was uninterested in personal success, giving much of his money to the United Nations Children's Emergency Fund. Tall, thin and constitutionally frail, he died of self-neglect and malnutrition. There was a memorial show in Presteigne, 1997, and exhibitions at Alpha House Gallery, Sherborne, 1998, Norfolk and Norwich Festival, 1999, and Exeter Phoenix Gallery, 2000, with a retrospective at Victoria Art Gallery, Bath, 2002, and another survey exhibition at Southampton City Art Gallery, 2004. *Ben Hartley*, by Bernard Samuels, published by Sansom & Company Ltd, was launched in 2001 at a show of the artist's work at The Rodd, Presteigne. Arts Council; Dartington Hall, Dartington; and Bristol and Plymouth City Museums and Art Galleries hold examples.

Kathleen HARTNELL 1886–1970 Painter and printmaker, born in Bristol. She was also known as Katherine Hartnell, and was the sister of the artist Hilda E Jefferies, also known as Hilda E Bonsey. Paintings were signed in her married name, Kathleen Hartnell, etchings with her maiden name, Kathleen G(rant) Jefferies. She studied at Slade School of Fine Art under Henry Tonks, Philip Wilson Steer and Walter Westley Russell, 1922–8 and 1929–30, winning several prizes. Exhibited extensively at Beaux Arts Gallery, RA, NEAC, LG, Leicester Galleries and RSA. Aberdeen and Bristol public galleries hold her work. She was also a musician, trained at the Royal Academy of Music. Lived in London.

Archibald Standish HARTRICK 1864–1950 Illustrator, printmaker, painter and teacher, born in Bangalore, Madras, India. Hartrick studied at Edinburgh University, the Slade School of Fine Art and in Paris, notably at Académie Julian, where he met such luminaries as Toulouse-Lautrec and Van Gogh. In 1887 showed first picture at Paris Salon. Returned to Scotland, then from 1889 worked in London as a black-and-white illustrator for *The Pall Magazine*, *The Graphic* and *The Daily Graphic*. Hartrick was notable for his drawings of country life, of which the British Museum has fine examples. Although he later lived in London a period with his wife, the artist Lily Blatherwick, time in Gloucestershire inspired Hartrick with rural subjects. Taught at Camberwell and Central Schools of Arts and Crafts. Hartrick showed prolifically at RWS and NEAC of both of which he was a member, as he was of Senefelder Club; had a show with his wife at Continental Gallery, 1901; and had a retrospective at Fulham Public Library in 1936; and a memorial show at Arts Council, 1951. *A Painter's Pilgrimage through Fifty Years*, which he published in 1939, reflects his chequered life.

Charles Leonard HARTWELL 1873–1951 Sculptor in marble and bronze, born in Blackheath, London. Studied at City and Guilds School, Kennington, privately with Onslow Ford and Hamo Thornycroft and at the Royal Academy Schools. Exhibited extensively at RA, as well as RI, ROI, RSA and RP. Chantrey Bequest bought A Foul in the Giants' Race as well as Dawn, both now in Tate Gallery collection. Elected RA in 1924 and was awarded the RBS silver medal for The Goatherd's Daughter five years later. Member of the Arts Club. Hartwell's usual method of working was to make an accurate plaster model of a work which assistants would then principally carve, Hartwell adding the final touches. Died at Aldwick, Sussex.

William John HARTWELL 1922–1995 Painter, and teacher, born in Amington, Staffordshire. He studied at Goldsmiths' College School of Art with Kathleen Allen, 1940–2 and 1948–9. He also studied at Norwich School of Art, taught art at schools in the city, was a member of the Norwich Twenty Group and exhibited with Norfolk & Norwich Art Circle and at the Aldeburgh Festival. Exhibited AIA, Whitechapel and Leicester Galleries and RBA, sometimes signing his work only with initials. West Riding Education Committee, in Yorkshire, bought his work. Lived for some time in Norwich.

Agnes Bankier HARVEY 1874–1947 Metal worker, jeweller, enameller and teacher, born in Glasgow. She studied at the School of Art there and at the London School of Silversmithing, returning to Glasgow to teach the craft at the School of Art, 1904–8. Harvey won a Silver Medal at the Women's Exhibition in London in 1910. During World War I she was a munitions worker and aircraft fitter. The responsibility of bringing up her two nephews and a niece reduced time for her own work, but she did show at the Royal Glasgow Institute of the Fine Arts and RSA. Harvey was also a member of the Glasgow Society of Lady Artists from 1901. She won its Lauder Award in 1928 and an altar cross by her, completed in 1924 and illustrated in *The Studio*, 1925, was included in the Society's centenary exhibition at Collins Gallery, Glasgow, in 1982. Died in Kirkcudbright, Scotland.

Charles W HARVEY 1895–1970 Painter and teacher, born in London, whose family moved to Belfast, Northern Ireland, in 1906, where he remained based. He trained as a damask designer and studied at Belfast School of Art and for a short time at Dublin's Metropolitan School of Art. From 1932–60 Harvey taught at St Mary's Training College, initially part-time, becoming head of department. He exhibited principally at Ulster Arts Club and Arts Council of Northern Ireland put on a retrospective in 1976.

Daniel HARVEY 1959– Sculptor, born in Dorking, Surrey. He did a fine art sculpture course at Cardiff College of Art, 1977–8, then was at Royal College of Art, 1983–6. Mixed shows participated in included LG at RCA Galleries, 1984; Outside Sculpture Show, Camden Lock, 1985; Vanessa Devereux Gallery, 1986; and Kettle's Yard, Cambridge, 1988. Had solo shows at Birch & Conran from 1987. Harvey worked with the Laboritorio Aperto of Bussana Vecchia in Italy in 1985. In 1988 his environmental sculpture was included in Peter Greenaway's film *Drowning by Numbers*; in 1989 living sculpture by him was featured in Derek Jarman's film *War Requiem*. From that year Harvey worked with Heather Ackroyd, whom he married, after they had met at an event she was curating and they discovered that they were using similar materials. Their first joint project was L'altro lato, in 1990, in Italy. After this they went on to investigate the light-sensitive properties of seedling grass, working with the Institute of Grassland and Environmental Research. In 2003 the Welsh National Eisteddfod, at Welshpool, commissioned its first contemporary artwork from Harvey and Ackroyd, in which light was projected through negatives onto giant sheets of germinating stay-green grass provided by the Institute of Grassland and Environmental Research at Aberystwyth; the two artists also showed a wall-mounted stretch of grass with the image of a large bull. New works in plaster by Harvey were shown at the Arundel Wetlands Centre, Sussex, in 2004, the year the Ackroyd/Harvey project Pleasure Gardens was displayed at Nottingham Castle. By then they had completed over 40 grass-oriented pieces.

Denis HARVEY 1925–1992 Sculptor, writer, photographer and teacher, born in Chelmsfield, Kent. He was educated at Bryanston School, worked in forestry for four years, completed an apprenticeship in stone masonry, studied sculpture at Wimbledon School of Art and later taught the subject at Reigate and West Surrey Colleges of Art. He showed his sculptures and photographs in London, Paris and Italy and completed stone monoliths for National Westminster Bank in Kingston upon Thames, heraldic and figure sculpture restoration work for London County Council and many portraits and sculptures in stone, marble, wood and bronze. When he was 17 Harvey became fascinated by the gypsy way of life, learned to speak the Romany language, to live like the travelling people and wrote about them. He was co-author of *The English Caravan*, 1972; *The Gypsies: waggon-time and after*, 1979; and just before he died, in Crawley, Sussex, finished *Plaiting the Magic*.

Gail HARVEY 1954– Painter, whose landscapes had a strong Expressionist content, born in Glasgow. She studied at the School of Art there, 1972–7, including post-diploma, with time at Hospitalfield Summer School, Arbroath, 1975. Harvey won a Scottish Education Department Travelling Scholarship in 1977, and a John Murray Thomson Award at RSA, 1985. Showed regularly at RSA, also RSW and Royal Glasgow Institute of the Fine Arts. Had a solo exhibition at Macaulay Gallery, Stenton, 1991, later ones including Roger Billcliffe Fine Art, Glasgow, 1997, and Adam Gallery, Bath and London, from 1998. Shetland Arts Trust and Highlands and Islands Enterprise hold examples. Harvey moved to Shetland in 1988, which was a strong theme in her output.

Gertrude HARVEY 1879–1966 Flower and landscape painter, self-taught, married to the artist Harold Harvey. She would have absorbed much while working as a model for her husband, Laura and Harold Knight, Ruth Simpson and other Cornwall-based artists. Gertrude's maternal grandfather William Curnow ran a market garden and was a notable botanist. A keen gardener, she settled in a cottage in Newlyn, Penzance, Cornwall, and showed at RA, SWA, Walker Art Gallery in Liverpool, Fine Art Society and Goupil Gallery. There were joint exhibitions at Leicester Galleries in 1918 and 1920. George Bernard Shaw was an enthusiast for Gertrude's work, as she recorded in her entry in the 1934 edition of *Who's Who in Art*, in which she falsified her year of birth to 1889. Gert Harvey was a witty, forthright character who died in a nursing home in St Just.

Hilda HARVEY 1890–1982 Painter, notably of portraits, printmaker and miniaturist on ivory. She was daughter of the artist John Rabone Harvey, her older brother being Herbert Johnson Harvey. Attended Birmingham School of Art for about six years from age of 15, then worked for firm of Birmingham silversmiths, closed down by World War I, the owners being German. She joined London couture house Mechinka, studying part-time, then full-time at Slade School of Fine Art under Henry Tonks. In London was courted by the artist Gilbert Spencer. After going with another artist to Paris in early 1920s and catching paratyphoid fever she was advised not to winter in England so lived in south of France for two years. After her return she married Charles Meeke of Birmingham and had one son, Harvey, before divorcing him. After periods in Cornwall and Llangollen during World War II she returned to St Ives where she continued to paint until 1950. Showed at NEAC, RA, Paris Salon and RBSA, being elected an associate in 1933.

Jake HARVEY 1948– Sculptor, born in Kelso, Roxburghshire. He studied sculpture at Edinburgh College of Art, 1966–72, during 1971 under a travelling scholarship visiting Greece and the Greek islands. He further travelled to India in 1989 and 1994, Germany in 1994, with a residency in Morioka, Japan, 1998. Harvey was a trustee of the Scottish Sculpture Trust, 1984–7. His sculptures, such as Poacher's Tree and Poacher's Vane, both shown at Scottish Art in the 20th Century, at RWA, 1991, are full of mysterious signs and symbols, the sculptor favouring forged and welded steel. Had a one-man show at Third Eye Centre, Glasgow, 1985, Scottish Gallery in Edinburgh, 1993, and The Crystal Gallery, Morioka, 1998. Scottish Arts Council and Contemporary Art Society hold his work. Major commissions included Hugh MacDiarmid Memorial, Langholm, 1985; Symbol Stone for Compaq Computers, Glasgow, 1988; and Tools for the Shaman, Hunterian Museum, Glasgow, 1996–7. Harvey was elected RSA in 1989. Lived at Maxton, St Boswells, Roxburghshire.

John HARVEY 1935– Painter and teacher, born in Plymouth, Devon. After a career in printing and commercial art Harvey graduated with honours in fine art painting, 1975–8, from Camberwell School of Arts and Crafts, then obtained his art teacher's certificate from Brighton Polytechnic, 1978–9. He taught at a Cornish school before retiring early to paint in Penzance. Harvey mostly completed work on the spot, notably colourful coastal and beach scenes. Mixed exhibitions included Parkway Gallery; Phoenix Gallery, Lavenham; Whitechapel Art Gallery; and Salthouse and Porthmeor Galleries, St Ives. In 1993–4 he had a solo exhibition at Gordon Hepworth Gallery, Newton St Cyres.

John HARVEY 1959– Artist whose work included constructed paintings, teacher and writer, born in Nantyglo, Monmouthshire. He gained a fine art honours degree at Gwent College of Higher Education, 1977–81, then a master's degree in visual art at University College of Wales in Aberystwyth, 1982–4, getting his doctorate, 1986–90. He was appointed its lecturer in fine art in 1992. The visual culture of Welsh nonconformity was a special interest. Showed in group exhibitions in southwest England and in Wales, including Aberystwyth Artists at The Deffett Francis Gallery, Swansea Institute of Higher Education, 1993.

John Wynn HARVEY 1923–1989 Sculptor, painter, draughtsman and writer, born in London, son of the diplomat Oliver Harvey, Lord Harvey of Tasburgh, whose diaries he was to edit. Educated at Eton, Westminster and Cambridge University, he was at the Central School of Art, 1947–9. In the 1950s Harvey enjoyed considerable success as a sculptor, by the 1960s turning to drawing and painting as his main means of expression, chief subjects being wildly coloured sculptural figures and Welsh landscapes. In 1960 Harvey published his first novel, *Within and Without*, a bestseller made into a film; his second, *Beside the Sea*, 1967, enjoyed critical success. Much of Harvey's later life was spent at the maternal family home at Meifod, Powys, where he farmed, although he died in Rome. Harvey was deeply influenced by his friend, Henry Moore. He argued that the vitality of abstract art, and in particular its heightened sense of form and colour, must be channelled to constructive effect. He believed in a marriage between the creativeness of abstraction and the disciplines of figurative art. Group show appearances included Leicester Galleries, SPS and RP. Solo exhibitions included Galerie La Licorne, Paris, 1951, Glebe Gallery, 1985, and Bernheimer Fine Arts, 1988. There was a retrospective at Cadogan Contemporary, 1991, a commemorative show at Roy Miles Gallery, 1998, another retrospective at Bruton Street Gallery, 1999. Musée d'Art Moderne, Paris, and Pembroke College, Oxford, hold examples.

Marcus HARVEY 1963– Painter using richly coloured impasto, strongly gestural marks and an overlying black linear image. He was born in Leeds, Yorkshire and studied at Goldsmiths' College School of Art, 1982–6, gaining an honours degree in fine art. Teachers included Harry Thubron, Albert Irvin, Basil Beattie and Michael Craig-Martin. Was included in Young British Artist IV at Saatchi Gallery, 1995, where such pictures as Half Way Up, Julie From Hull, Reader's Wife 1 and My Arse Is Yours contained frequent references to the female nude, knickers and bottoms. In 1997, Harvey's portrait of the Moors child murderer Myra Hindley, made using casts of a child's hand prints, prompted outrage when exhibited at the RA in Sensation: British Artists from the Saatchi Collection, being kicked and splattered with eggs and ink. Later group exhibitions included Happy the World so Made, The Nunnery, 2001; Closer, Standpoint Gallery, 2002; and London Calling. Young British Artists Criss-Crossed, Galleri Kaare Berntsen, Oslo, Norway, 2005. Among Harvey's later solo shows were Vedovi Fine Art, Brussels, Belgium, and Mary Boone Gallery, New York, America, both 2002, and The Führer's Cakes, Galleria Marabini, Bologna, and Marcus Harvey at Mimmo Scognamiglio, Naples, both in Italy in 2005. Harvey lived in London.

Marion Rodger Hamilton HARVEY 1886–1971 Painter of animals, notably dogs, born in Ayr, Scotland. She attended Glasgow School of Art, 1901–7. Harvey was a member of Glasgow Society of Lady Artists from 1915, showing many times at Royal Glasgow Institute of the Fine Arts and Walker Art Gallery in Liverpool, also at RSA, RSW, SWA and elsewhere. She died in Helensburgh, Dunbartonshire.

Mark HARVEY 1921– Sculptor and teacher, creating figurative and abstract works in metal and stone, born in Birmingham. He studied at Chelsea School of Art, 1944–6, and teaching posts included Regent Street Polytechnic and Goldsmiths' College Schools of Art and Morley College. Did commissioned work for churches and public sculptures including the Portland stone Polar Bear, 1964, in Glebe Shopping Centre at Stevenage New Town.

Martin HARVEY 1942– Painter and teacher, son of the artist Victor Martin Harvey, born in Cornwall and lived there in the village of St Mabyn. The local landscape and that of France, Scotland and southwest Ireland inspired his pictures. Harvey studied at Falmouth School of Art, 1959–63, under Michael Finn, Francis Hewlett, Peter Lanyon and Terry Frost, then at Hornsey College of Art, 1963–4. After teaching in Hampshire, Devon and Cornwall secondary schools and at Plymouth College of Art, he retired in 1996 and set up a studio in Stoke Climsland. Took part in many group shows, including RWA and Plymouth, Penwith and Penzance Societies of Artists and Stour Gallery, Shipston-on-Stour. Harvey shared exhibitions with his father at Camel Art Society, Wadebridge, and daughter Catherine Harvey-Jefferson at Theatre Royal, Plymouth. Solo shows included Penzance Arts Club and Mariners Gallery, St Ives. Devon County Council holds his work.

Michael Anthony HARVEY 1921–2000 Artist in oil, watercolour and crayon, teacher and art critic, born in Kew, Surrey, whose parents were Quakers, Michael in World War II serving in the Friends' Ambulance Unit, later having a period in the Merchant Navy. He studied at Bryanston School, then Epsom School of Art, 1948–50, and Wimbledon School of Art, 1955–7, teachers including R O Dunlop and David Birch. Taught in county secondary schools for 23 years. He was art critic for the *Surrey Mirror* Series of Newspapers and art correspondent for the *Croydon Advertiser* Series, as well as contributing to many other periodicals and books. Harvey was a member of SGA, also of Art Societies in Chichester, Reigate and Bognor Regis. He showed at John Whibley Gallery, Rutland Gallery, Qantas Gallery and widely abroad, having many solo and dual shows. Royal Borough of Camden and East Sussex County Council hold examples: the oil Limehouse Reach, held by Johns Hopkins University, Baltimore, is one of his principal works. Lived in Bognor Regis, Sussex. Memorial show at The Bourne Gallery, Reigate, 2001.

Neil HARVEY 1960– Figurative painter, born and based in Birmingham, working mainly in oils, whose practice usually involved preparatory drawing. Harvey owed "indebtedness to 16th- and 17th- century models as well as contemporary influences." Having studied foundation at Reading University, 1978–9, he then gained his certificate from the Royal Academy Schools, 1979–82. In 1980 he was awarded a life drawing award by the Schools and the Feeney Prize, RBSA; in 1982–3 an Elizabeth Greenshields

Foundation Award; and in 1985 was shortlisted for the Athena International Art Awards. Between 1983–9 Harvey practised as a portraitist and painter of large figure subjects, then undertook a huge mural of the Resurrection in the apse of Our Lady & St Brigid's Roman Catholic Church, Northfield, Birmingham. He was commissioned in 1989; work on site began in 1994–5; and it was completed in 2000. Harvey went to Rome to glean technical advice from conservators. He listed "back trouble, knee trouble and the cold" as occupational hazards. Exhibited RA, RBSA, RBA, ROI and NEAC.

Nellie HARVEY fl. from 1890–1949 Watercolourist specialising in birds, real name Ellen Harvey, she was the niece of the Royal Scottish Academician Sir George Harvey. She studied with the animal painter Joseph Denovan Adam and at Eugène Delecluse's Académie in Montparnasse, Paris. As well as living in Scotland, notably at Stirling, she spent time early in her career in Ireland and Germany. Harvey joined the Glasgow Society of Lady Artists in 1915, also showing at Royal Glasgow Institute of the Fine Arts, RSA, RSW, SWA, RHA and elsewhere.

Paul HARVEY 1960– Painter in acrylic on canvas, teacher and musician, born in Burton upon Trent, Staffordshire, who graduated with honours in design from North Staffordshire Polytechnic, 1978–82; gained his postgraduate education certificate from Sunderland University, 2001–3; and his master's from University of Northumbria, 2003–5. Harvey latterly taught at North Tyneside College, playing guitar for Penetration, having worked as a professional musician with Pauline Murray. Harvey wrote that he was a "painter dealing with ideas of beauty and decoration, usually incorporating these ideas with flat areas of colour and strong line. Although I am known for appropriating images from the past, art history and popular culture, I have latterly worked more from primary sources." Harvey showed at Wednesbury Art Gallery, was entered by the Stuckists for the Real Turner Prize exhibition in 2002 and 2003 and was founder of the Newcastle Stuckists. He exhibited solo in London, Newcastle, Stoke, Oxford and Brighton. Lived in Heaton, Newcastle.

Polly HARVEY 1971– Artist who graduated with honours in drawing and painting at Edinburgh College of Art, gaining her postgraduate certificate in art and design at University of London Institute of Education. Exhibitions included Edinburgh College of Art, 1997; VCA Melbourne University, Melbourne, Australia, 1999; Axis Design, 2001; and in 2002 in Edinburgh at the Royal College of Physicians and at the Scottish Gallery, in Three New Artists. Solo show Urban Journeys – New Paintings at The Scottish Gallery, Edinburgh, 2003.

Ruth HARVEY 1923–1992 Versatile and underrated artist in a variety of media, notably collage, also a musician and poet. Her father, Ken Hunter, and grandfather, Frederick Hunter, were both artists. Her work themes included buildings, still life, music, industrial and maritime artefacts, water in all its forms and landscape; pathways, gates and alternative ways to go were preoccupations. Served in Women's Royal Naval Service in World War II, marrying Michael Harvey, a naval officer, nephew of the poet Will Harvey, known as The Laureate of Gloucestershire. Ruth began painting seriously from the mid-1950s, enrolling on art courses at Portsmouth College of Art, Dartington Hall and Camden Arts Centre, Hampstead. Some early works were accepted by the RA Summer Exhibition but not hung, and she exhibited mainly in Wales, where she settled in 1968 at Jameston, Pembrokeshire. Despite working outside the mainstream, Harvey was keenly aware of current trends. She bought works of art and assembled a considerable library and many newspaper clippings for reference. Although progressively incapacitated by rheumatoid arthritis which affected her wrists and fingers for over 40 years, Harvey was prolific, producing probably around 1,000 pictures, many untraced. Her output is well covered in three illustrated volumes, *Ruth Harvey – Art & Poetry*; *Ruth Harvey – Paintings & Collages*; and *Ruth Harvey – Mainly Pembrokeshire*, published in 1994–6 by Heliotrope Publishing in a limited edition.

Victor Martin HARVEY 1910–1980 Painter, draughtsman, commercial artist and teacher, father of artist Martin Harvey, he was born in Leytonstone, east London. Around 1915 he was apprenticed as a commercial artist to Curtis Brothers Advertising; attended St Martin's School of Art part-time until 1920; joined G S Royde's Advertising as a commercial artist, also making medical drawings for a surgeon working in an East End hospital; in 1940 being called up, joining the fire service. Harvey was posted to Cornwall in 1942, finally serving in Bodmin Fire Service. After World War II he stayed on in Cornwall, setting up as a signwriter and freelance commercial artist, pursuing his own work and teaching part-time at Wadebridge Community College. By the mid-1960s he was able to support himself as a painter. Was a founder-member of Camel Art Society, Wadebridge, which gave him a retrospective in 1981, also showing at St Ives and East Cornwall Societies of Artists and RWA. Watercolour and pastel were favourite mediums, subjects including landscapes painted on site, flowers and portraits, many commissioned. His work is in the collection of Wadebridge Town Council.

William HARVEY 1957– Painter, born in Hampshire, who studied at Gwent College of Higher Education, 1980–3, then Birmingham Polytechnic, 1983–4. His mixed shows included Cleveland International Drawing Biennale, 1985, and John Moores Liverpool Exhibition, 1987, where he was a prizewinner with Liners. His solo shows included Worcester City Art Gallery, Winchester Gallery and Spitalfields Workspace, 1986. In 1986–7 he was fellow in painting at South Glamorgan Institute of Higher Education, Cardiff. Arts Council holds his work. Lived in London.

Gregor HARVIE 1969– Dr Harvie, RIBA, had a versatile career. Before dedicating himself to painting he worked at the Dome in Greenwich for the New Millennium Experience Company as technical troubleshooter. Prior to that, he undertook a three-year research project at the Welsh School of Architecture, establishing new techniques for predicting the environmental performance of buildings. He was born and brought up in Devon, where he was trained in the use of watercolour by a professional landscape painter. After moving to London in 1996, Harvie completed a postgraduate diploma in fine art at the City and Guilds of London Art College, then concentrated on "figural and Expressionist paintings." His first solo show, in 2001, was held at Circus Space, a redeveloped power station behind Hoxton Square, where 60 pictures hung in columns descended dramatically out of the darkness; half sold within four hours. Subsequently Harvie took part in group exhibitions at Apart and Artistic Licence; was represented by art forums Blink Red and Twist Art and Design; and showed at Fresh Art and Affordable Art Fair, both in 2002. He painted with a palette knife, using oils and various quick-drying mediums to retain sketch-like spontaneity. After winning the de Laszlo Foundation Prize for Portraiture in 2001, he worked mainly on landscapes. Lena Boyle Fine Art, at Flying Colours Gallery, organised Harvie's Ploughed Lane in 2004.

John Hammond HARWOOD 1904–1980 Painter, especially of landscape in watercolour, and illustrator. Born in Darwen, Lancashire, he was educated in Ripon, Yorkshire, then attended Harrogate School of Art, 1921–4, also Royal College of Art, 1924–8, under William Rothenstein. He became principal of Gloucester School of Art, 1939–45, then Sheffield College of Art, 1945–64. Was a member of Sheffield Society of Artists, where he taught and exhibited for many years. Also exhibited RA, NEAC and LG. He illustrated a number of books in the Puffin series. Sheffield Arts Department bought his work, which often featured the Dorset coast; he died in Dorset, but lived for many years in Sheffield.

Lucy HARWOOD 1893–1972 Painter and draughtsman, born at Belstead Park, near Ipswich, although soon after her birth the family moved to East Bergholt. She wanted to be a pianist, but an operation went wrong, leaving her right side partly paralysed, so she turned to painting, attending the Slade School of Fine Art prior to World War I. When Cedric Morris opened the East Anglian School of Painting and Drawing in Dedham, in 1937, Harwood, still unmarried and living at home, became a student, which she remained, moving to be near the School when it relocated at Benton End, Hadleigh, in 1940. She was a key figure in its social life. Her pictures, painted with her left hand, were spontaneous, innocent and colourful, still life and landscapes of Suffolk around her home at Upper Layham. She sold them locally and the first show of her work was at The Minories, Colchester, 1975. Further shows included several at Sally Hunter Fine Art. Ipswich Museum and Colchester Art Society hold Harwood's work.

Stephen HARWOOD 1972– Painter, based in Limehouse, who began showing in the late 1980s, soon establishing a following for his powerful figurative canvases, in strong colours, depicting the East End, the City and its people. Later group exhibitions included Art for Equality, ICA, 1991; Art East Gallery, 1994; Coombs Contemporary Art and Phillips Contemporary Art, Manchester, both from 1997; and Concrete Jungle at Gallery Fresh, 2000. Had frequent solo exhibitions, later ones including Gallery Fresh, from 2000, and Artbank Gallery, from 2002. Harwood lived in Whitechapel.

Nobuo HASE 1970– Sculptor and installations artist who trained at Camden Art School, 1990–1; City and Guilds of London Art School, 1991–2; graduated in sculpture from Central St Martins College of Art & Design, 1992–5; and gained a postgraduate diploma in sculpture from the Royal Academy Schools, 1995–8, appearing in the final year show there. Hase won a Sperry/Jacobs Scholarship, 1996–8; Gold Medal and Edward Stott Travelling Scholarship, 1997; and RBS Bronze Casting Prize, 1998. Other exhibitions included RA Summer Exhibition, 1996; Apartment 5, 1997; and Premiums, RA, 1998. Lived in Shinagawa-ku, Tokyo, Japan.

Jun HASEGAWA 1969– Painter and draughtsman, born in Mie, Japan, who gained a bachelor's degree in fine art at Goldsmiths' College, 1992–5. Exhibitions included White Trash and Multiple Orgasm, both at Lost-in-Space, 1995; New Contemporaries at Tate Gallery, Liverpool, and Camden Arts Centre, 1996; and dumbpop, at Jerwood Gallery, and Die Young Stay Pretty, at ICA, both 1998–9. For that exhibition she selected her subjects from glossy magazines and created "vast simplified iconic portraits of her heroes and heroines".

Ron HASELDEN 1944– Sculptor and teacher who worked in a variety of media, born in Gravesend, Kent. He studied sculpture at Gravesend School of Art, 1961–3, then Edinburgh College of Art, 1963–6. Involved in multiples, film and performance for several years from 1973, then concentrated on installation. In 1976, Haselden was included in the big British Council exhibition English Art Today 1960–76 at the Palazzo Reale, Milan, Italy. He was then teaching part-time in the fine art department of Reading University and the Slade School of Fine Art and his films included *Railway Trolley and Film*, 1973, *Film Structures and MSV Mower*, and *Lady Dog*, both 1975. His group appearances included New Light on Sculpture at Tate Gallery, Liverpool, 1990, and Arts Council touring show Recent British Sculpture, 1993–4. His solo shows included Seaward at Serpentine Gallery, 1977. Whitechapel Art Gallery, 1988, Golden Crescent at South London Art Gallery, 1993, and Mobile Home, 2002. Lived in London.

Leslie HASLAM 1933– Performance artist, born in Haslemere, Surrey. He participated in a series of performances with Stuart Brisley as Brisley/Haslam (see separate entries), including appearing in the big British Council exhibition English Art Today 1960–76. This took place at the Palazzo Reale, Milan, Italy, in 1976.

Ray HASLAM 1942– Painter and teacher, born in Bolton, Lancashire. He studied at the local College of Art, 1957–62, continuing his training at Sheffield College of Art. He later became a teacher in secondary education and from 1972 worked in the department of art at St Martin's College of Higher Education, Lancaster. Haslam's Hyper-Realist pictures examined aspects of urban decay, as in his Crashed Cortina, Wellington Road Garage, Lancaster, 1983, included in Lancashire South of the Sands, which toured from County and Regimental Museum, Preston, 1988.

Ernest William HASLEHUST 1866–1949 Watercolourist, principally of landscapes, born in Walthamstow. Studied at the Slade School of Fine Art under Alphonse Legros. Exhibited RA, RBA, RI, RWA and Ridley Art Club; had several one-man shows in London. Haslehust's work was extensively reproduced, notably in Blackie's *Beautiful Britain* series. His work is in the collections of a number of British provincial galleries – notably Bristol, Sheffield, Oldham and Newport – as well as galleries in Canada, New Zealand and Sri Lanka. For some time he was president of the Midland Sketch Club. Lived in London.

Joan HASSALL 1906–1988 Wood engraver, painter, typographer and teacher, born in London, daughter of the artist John Hassall and sister of the writer, poet and librettist Christopher Hassall. After attending a Froebel Training College for teachers Joan Hassall was at the London School of Art, 1925–7, Royal Academy Schools, 1928–33, and at Bolt Court, 1931–4. She taught book production at Edinburgh College of Art, 1940–6. Showed at SWE and RE, of both of which she was a member, RA, SWA, RHA and elsewhere. Illustrated many books, including Jane Austen, Robert Louis Stevenson, Mary Webb and many of *The Saltire Chapbooks*. For almost 15 years before her death poor sight prevented her cutting her delicately detailed blocks. Work held by British Museum. Lived in Malham, Yorkshire.

John HASSALL 1868–1948 Cartoonist, illustrator, designer, painter and teacher, born in Walmer, Kent. He was father to the artist Joan Hassall and the writer Christopher Hassall. After education in England and Germany Hassall farmed in Canada, began contributing sketches to *The Graphic*, then early in 1890s spent several years studying art in Antwerp and at Académie Julian, Paris. In England Hassall became a popular cartoonist and designed posters such as *Skegness is So bracing*. Hassall illustrated numerous books and periodicals such as *The Idler*, *London Opinion*, *Pearson's Magazine* and *The Tatler*. For many years he ran his own school of art. He was a member of RI, RWA and Arts, London Sketch and Savage Clubs. Hassall's heyday was the Edwardian period, his theatrical posters covering the West End. His phenomenal output, which included 200 book illustrations and 800 book-jackets, was rewarded in 1939 with a Civil List pension. After Word War II Hassall died in obscurity, a lifetime's memorabilia being untouched in his studio for 40 years. In 2003 Onslow's Collectors Auctions held a sale at The Carisbrooke Hall, Seymour Street. Lived in London.

David HASTE 1938– Artist and teacher who studied at St Martin's School of Art and Royal College of Art. He began teaching in 1970 and became head of the fine art course at Canterbury School of Art. Among his mixed shows was Volcanic Landscapes at Boundary Gallery, 1991. After a summer climbing around Mount Etna in Italy Haste showed canvases at the Geological Museum in 1986 under sponsorship of the British Museum, one of several solo exhibitions. Victoria & Albert Museum holds his work.

Kendra HASTE 1971– Versatile artist, output including drawings and wire sculptures, born in London. She studied at Wimbledon and Camberwell Schools of Art before graduating in natural history illustration from the Royal College of Art in 1998. Haste showed widely in Britain, undertook several commissions and was included in London Underground's A New Platform for Art, 2000. Animals were Haste's exclusive source of inspiration, much of her time being spent drawing them in close proximity in Britain and abroad. In 1999, she received the *BBC Wildlife Magazine* Art Award. She had a solo exhibition at Beaux Arts, Bath, in 2001.

David HASTIE 1967– Artist and curator, born in Carmarthen, who studied foundation at University of Wales Institute, Cardiff, 1992–3, gaining an honours degree in fine art there, 1994–7. Exhibitions included National Eisteddfod of Wales, Builth Wells, highly commended, 1993; Mill Lane Group, Mill Lane Studio, Cardiff, 1996; The Gateway, Coed Hills Sculpture Park, Cowbridge, 1997; Five Inside, same venue, one of several exhibitions which Hastie co-curated, and National Eisteddfod, Bridgend, fine art prize winner, both 1998; Certain Welsh Artists, Glynn Vivian Art Gallery, Swansea, 2000; and Art from Wales – A New Generation, Open Space, Milan, Italy, 2001. Hastie's solo exhibitions included The secluded stage, Mission Gallery, Swansea, 2000; Refuge, Watch This Space Gallery, Alice Springs, Australia, 2001; and Terminus (The Artist's Studio), installation at Oriel Davies Gallery, Newtown, 2003. Lived at Bishopston, Swansea.

Eveline HASTINGS 1933– Painter and teacher, born in Highgate, north London, into a family of sculptors. She was educated at Christ's Hospital, Hereford, then attended Wimbledon School of Art from 1950 and from 1954–7 the Slade School of Fine Art for her Diploma in Fine Art and then her Post Diploma in Fine Art (Painting). Hastings painted and taught for some years, from 1974 as a full-time lecturer, later becoming head of an adult education art department. From 1990 she was a full-time painter. She had close connections with the Suffolk village of Walberswick from childhood, eventually lived there and was included in two Walberswick-associated exhibitions at Chappel Galleries, Chappel, in 1998 and 2002, and one in Walberswick village hall in 1999.

Francis John HASTINGS 1901–1990 Mural painter, teacher, politician and writer who became the 15th Earl of Huntingdon. He was educated at Eton College and Oxford University and as a young man while travelling became enthused by the mural paintings of the Mexican left-wing artist Diego Rivera. He worked with Rivera extensively in America as well as completing his own work. On returning to England he taught at Camberwell School of Arts and Crafts and Central School of Arts and Crafts. During the 1940s he became involved with local politics in Andover, Hampshire, near where he lived, then in national government, being parliamentary secretary to the Ministry of Agriculture and Fisheries, 1945–50, in the Attlee Labour administration. Among his books is *Commonsense about India*. Showed at Wertheim Gallery, Lefevre Gallery and overseas and was chairman of the committee of the Society of Mural Painters, 1951–8. The Marx Memorial Library, London, has a remarkable mural by him. Was a member of Art Workers' Guild, AIA and was president of the Society of Mural Painters. Was married to the writer Margaret Lane. New Grafton Gallery held an eightieth birthday retrospective in 1981. Lived in Beaulieu, Hampshire, and in London.

Erica HASTINGS-GRAY 1890– Watercolour painter and calligrapher, born in London. She studied at London School of Art, 1914–16, with John Hassall and Ernest Borough Johnson, with Frank Spenlove-Spenlove and with Hesketh Hubbard. Exhibited UA, WIAC and East Sussex Art Club, of which she was a member. Lived in Battle, Sussex.

Ethel C HATCH 1870–1975 Painter, especially of figures and flowers, mainly in watercolour. Born in Oxford into a religious and scholastic family, she attended the High School there, then the Slade School of Fine Art under Henry Tonks, Fred Brown and Philip Wilson Steer. Exhibited RA, Goupil and Chenil Galleries, NEAC, SWA and Paris Salon, having a one-man show at Walker's Galleries in mid-1920s. Lived for a time in Italy, and in

London. Ethel and her sisters Beatrice and Evelyn were friends of the writer Lewis Carroll, author of *Alice's Adventures in Wonderland*.

Lionel HATCH 1949– Typographer, printmaker and artist in pastel, born in Bolton, Lancashire; he settled nearby at Atherton. Studied at Bolton College of Art, 1966–9, where his teachers included Roger Hampson. Showed in the area.

Jackie HATFIELD 1962– Artist and teacher using such media as film, video and installations, born in Wellington, Shropshire, brought up in Birmingham, eventually resident in Maidstone, Kent. Gained an honours degree there at Kent Institute of Art and Design, 1991–4; a postgraduate diploma in electronic imaging from Duncan of Jordanstone College of Art, Dundee, 1994–5; with research from 1996 on haptic interfaces for multimedia artworks at University of Westminster, where she lectured. Hatfield obtained grants to make film, videotapes and installations and participated in many exhibitions, screening and installations in Britain and abroad. Distressing The Surface, at Kent Institute's George Rodger Gallery, 1998, supported by a South East Arts grant, invited "viewers to contemplate their sexual orientation and fantasies...to risk exposure as voyeurs and to consider notions of gender, desire and fantasy."

Mona HATOUM 1952– Artist, born in Beirut, Lebanon, who took part in many exhibitions, screenings and performances. She studied at Byam Shaw School of Art, 1977–79, then Slade School of Fine Art, 1979–81. Among her awards were Greater London Arts, 1982, and Arts Council Video Bursary, 1985. She was artist-in-residence at Western Front Art Centre in Vancouver, Canada, 1984; other residencies occurring at 911 Contemporary Art Centre, Seattle, America, in 1986, Chisenhale Dance Space, 1986–7, and Western Front Art Centre again, 1988. From 1989–92 was senior research fellow in fine art at South Glamorgan Institute of Higher Education, Cardiff. From 1981 group appearances included New Contemporaries, at ICA; Festival of Video Art, SAW Gallery, Ottawa, 1985; Essential Black Art, Chisenhale Gallery and tour, 1988; South Bank Centre's The British Art Show and tour, in 1990; and The Quality of Light, The Tate at St Ives, 1997. Retrospective at Museum of Modern Art, Oxford, 1998. Hatoum's exhibition at White Cube^2 in 2002 included a giant cheese grater that glittered seductively but could shred flesh with its razor-sharp edges, a typically disquieting work. There was a major survey in Germany at Hamburger Kunstalle in 2004, the year that Hatoum won the Rostwitha Haftmann Foundation prize, at just over $100,000 the largest monetary award in Europe, and had another show at Galerie René Blouin in Montreal, Canada. Lived in London.

Doris HATT 1890–1969 Painter, designer and printmaker, born in Bath, Somerset. She studied at the School of Art there, after initial education in England and Germany, then at Royal College of Art and in Vienna. She eventually returned to live in the West Country, finally settling at Clevedon, Somerset, in a house and studio built to her own design. Showed mainly in that area. Exhibitions included RA, Leicester and Redfern Galleries, Jack Bilbo's Modern Art Gallery, and Foyles Gallery; in the 1950s and 1960s she had a series of one-man shows, including Minerva Gallery, Bath, and Osiris Gallery, Oxford, with a retrospective at RWA, Bristol, 1960. Michael Wright Fine Art, Bristol, gave Hatt a show in 1998. A pen portrait of her is included in Hubert Nicholson's 1941 autobiography *Half My Days and Nights*.

Jonathan HATT 1961– Sculptor, installation artist and gallery director, born and lived in London, who gained an honours degree in sculpture at Camberwell School of Art, 1981–5, then his master's, assistantship, at New Mexico State University, 1985–6. In 1995 Hatt co-founded the Annexed Gallery. Hatt's aim was "to produce simple works which challenge the viewer's powers of observation, and then rewards such scrutiny." Group exhibitions included Closed Circuits, Old Knowse Gallery, Nottingham, 1987; In residence, 181 Gallery, 1991; in 1998 Not Nothing at Todd Gallery, Enough at The Tannery and Soon at Het Consortium, Amsterdam, Netherlands; and John Moores Liverpool Exhibition, 1999. Later solo shows included Fient at Hales Gallery, 1997, and *The Economist* Plaza, for Contemporary Art Society Projects, 1999.

George HATTON 1950– Painter, etcher and teacher, born on Merseyside. He attended Bath Academy of Art, Corsham, 1970–3, then Goldsmiths' College, 1974–5. After teaching in various schools, he became head of art at Bedales from 1978. He went on a teaching exchange with Brooks School, North Andover, Massachusetts, America, 1990, and with the British International School, Cairo, Egypt, 1995. Hatton was a regular exhibitor at the RA Summer Exhibition, also elsewhere in London, the provinces and in Oslo, Norway. He was included in the exhibition Bedales Art & Design at Art99, Business Design Centre, 1999, organised by William Jackson Gallery. Hatton was involved in the theatre, especially with the Bench Company at Havant.

Paul HATTON 1951– Artist in mixed media and teacher, born in Luton, Bedfordshire. He trained at Nelson and Colne College and the University of Lancaster. Taught part-time at St Martin's College in Lancaster, Edge Hill College in Ormskirk, Lancashire Polytechnic and Tuson College in Preston, also being fellow in 3D at the University of Lancaster. From 1983 he showed widely in Lancashire galleries and was included in the 1988 exhibition Lancashire South of the Sands, which toured from County and Regimental Museum, Preston. Hatton was a founder-member of Luneside Studios, Lancaster, and was interested in small incidents such as the lines of floating foam and grass; relevant materials were employed in the final images, although these were not direct representations.

Peter HATTON 1952–1998 Artist and teacher using such means as graphics, photography, collage, computers, micro-technology, films and performance. He moved from the south of England to the north in the early 1970s and gained a Certificate in Education in drama and dance from Bretton Hall College, 1971–4. Taught for a year at Knottingley High School; moved to Fieldhead School, Wakefield, for children with learning difficulties; then retired due to bad health late in 1997, shortly before he died. In the mid-1970s with several other artists, some from Bretton Hall, he founded the graphics and performance group Aerschot (the name of a place in France where atrocities were committed in World War I), a label he used well into the 1990s. Among shows were York University,

1976, and Breadline Gallery, Leeds, 1977 and 1979, performance gigs around this time including Newcastle and *The Observer* Performance Arts Festival at the Museum of Modern Art, Oxford. Luminarist: Images by Peter Hatton, was held at Wakefield Art Gallery, 1998–9.

Peter HATTON 1956– Artist, born in Rossendale, Lancashire, who was a member of TEA (see separate entry). Studied at Rochdale College of Art, 1974–5, then Liverpool Polytechnic, 1975–8. Hatton worked on a number of commissions with Janet Hodgson. These included Liquid Matter at Serpentine Gallery and Watershed, Queen Elizabeth Hall, both 1993. Lived in London.

Anthony HATWELL 1931– Sculptor and teacher, born in London, married to the artist Elizabeth Hatwell. He studied from 1947–9 and 1951–3 at Bromley College of Art; from 1952–3 at Borough Polytechnic with David Bomberg; from 1953–7 at Slade School of Fine Art; then gained a Boise Travelling Scholarship, 1957–8. Was assistant to Henry Moore, 1958. From 1969–90 was head of the school of sculpture at Edinburgh College of Art. Between 1959–69 Hatwell was a member of LG, its vice-president in 1961–3. Group exhibitions comprised Borough Bottega with Bomberg, 1953–5, in London, Oxford and Cambridge; Open Air Exhibition, Middelheim Park, Antwerp, 1959; Contemporary British Sculpture, Arts Council, 1960–4; Battersea Park Open Air Exhibition, 1963; LG Jubilee Exhibition, Tate Gallery, 1964; British Sculpture in the Twentieth Century, Whitechapel Art Gallery, 1981–2; Built in Scotland, Third Eye Centre, Glasgow, and tour, 1983; and Bomberg And His Students, South Bank University, 1992. Hatwell's work is held by Scottish National Gallery of Modern Art, Edinburgh, and Arts Council. Lived in Belhaven, Dunbar, East Lothian.

Elizabeth HATWELL 1937– Painter who also sculpted, and teacher, married to the sculptor Anthony Hatwell. She was born in Brighton, Sussex, graduated with honours in fine art from Chelsea School of Art, 1962–6, then taught at Edinburgh College of Art, 1969–79, and was a visiting lecturer at Duncan of Jordanstone College of Art, Dundee, 1976–7. In 1988 she published *The Artist's Daybook*. Group shows included LG from 1965; Roland, Browse & Delbanco and Marjorie Parr Gallery, both 1975; Scottish Arts Council, Small Sculpture, 1978; and Richard Demarco Gallery, Edinburgh, and tour, from 1988. Had a solo exhibition at Stirling Gallery, 1976, and Scottish Gallery and Royal Edinburgh Hospital, Edinburgh University, both 1979. Scottish Arts Council and Argyll Education Department hold examples. Lived in Belhaven, Dunbar, East Lothian.

Paula HAUGHNEY 1950– Artist who graduated with honours from Portsmouth Polytechnic, 1978–81, attended Eastern Illinois University in America, 1981–2, then Middlesex Polytechnic, 1983–4. In 1989, the year she participated in East End Open Studios, at Carpenter's Road, Haughney had a solo exhibition at Dannlann De Bairead Gallery and worked on a commission for Homerton Hospital.

David HAUGHTON 1924–1991 Painter, printmaker and teacher, born in London where he eventually settled, although he spent his early life in India. Haughton studied at Slade School of Fine Art and in 1947 moved to Nancledra, near St Ives, Cornwall. He was for short periods a member of the St Ives Society of Artists and of the Penwith Society. In 1951 left Cornwall and took up teaching appointment at Central School of Arts and Crafts until 1984. As well as showing in Cornwall in group exhibitions, Haughton was featured in the Arts Council touring show Contemporary Cornish Painting in 1949, the ICA's Contemporary English Landscape in 1957 and Cornwall 1945–55 at New Art Centre in 1977. An exhibition of his etchings originating at the St George's Gallery toured several continents, 1960–3, a Newlyn Art Gallery show of 1979 touring England. In 1992 Gordon Hepworth, Exeter, showed a retrospective of Haughton's St Just paintings, 1948–79. He was both a representational and abstract artist. Died in London.

Derrick HAUGHTON 1955– Painter and teacher whose picture in acrylic and household paint on canvas From the Day You Were Born was included in the 1997–8 John Moores Liverpool Exhibition. Born in Kingston, Jamaica, Haughton studied at Cardiff College of Art, 1974–5; Trent Polytechnic, Nottingham, 1975–8; Slade School of Fine Art, 1978–80; and Goldsmiths' College, 1992–4. From the mid-1980s he took part in group shows including Into the Nineties, Mall Galleries, 1994, and Foil, 202 Great Sufffolk Street, 1996. There was a solo show at Houldsworth Fine Art, 2001, where Haughton's swirling coils of paint provided a baroque twist to minimal surfaces. Taught at Kingston and Middlesex Universities. Lived in London.

Patrick HAUGHTON 1942– Painter, construction and assemblage artist, and teacher, using cool colours and clean lines, in whose work a sense of place, particularly the coastal landscape of Cornwall, was important. Haughton was born in Devonport and grew up in Barnstaple, north Devon, moving to Exeter to study architecture in 1960. The artist Nicholas Eastwood encouraged him to paint, and this he studied at Exeter College of Art, 1962–3, transferring to West of England College of Art, Bristol, 1963–6. Paul Feiler was head of painting, visitors including Peter Lanyon, William Scott and Karl Weschke. Qualified as a teacher and worked in primary schools in Kent, and Cornwall for 26 years, taking early retirement in 1995 to be a full-time artist. Haughton was a member of Newlyn, Penwith and Penzance Art Societies. Group exhibitions included Broad Street Gallery, Penryn, 1989–90; and Royal Cornwall Polytechnic Open, Falmouth, 1997. Solo shows included Falmouth Art Gallery, 1997 and Michael Wright Fine Art, Bristol, 1998. Lived in Penryn, Cornwall.

Wilfred HAUGHTON 1921–1999 Artist in watercolour, oil and pastel, and writer, born in Hillmount, County Antrim, Northern Ireland. He became a member of RUA in 1956 and was for a time its president, was president and founder of Ulster Watercolour Society in 1977 and was a member of the Watercolour Society of Ireland. He also showed with RHA, RI and elsewhere and had a series of solo exhibitions in London, Belfast, Dublin and Limerick. After a business career he became a full-time artist from 1968. Haughton was virtually self-taught, although he attended courses by Jack Merriott and Edward Wesson. He aimed "to preserve the pure watercolour technique in the face of many additives that take away from the clarity and sparkle of this medium." Wrote the books *Brush Aside* and *Purely Watercolour*. Belfast's Museum and Art Gallery hold his work. Lived in Cullybackey, Ballymena, County Antrim.

Anne HAUSER: *see* **Anne DIAMOND**

John HAUXWELL 1941– Architect and artist, born in Witney, Oxfordshire, son of the painter and printmaker Margaret Rowney and grandson of Walter Rowney, gifted watercolourist and managing director of the artists' materials manufacturer George Rowney & Co Ltd. In 1998 Hauxwell helped organise The Rowney Family: Painting and Production in Hampstead at the local Burgh House Museum. From 1959–68 Hauxwell studied architecture at Regent Street Polytechnic, in the mid-1970s sculpture at Camden Institute under Innes Russell. He practised architecture in private practices, finally in local government, specialising in schools and civic buildings; was for a time a member of the RIBA; and on retirement concentrated on sculpture in his home studio in north London. Hauxwell took part in group and mixed shows, including Stanmore Art Society; participated in Norfolk Open Studios; and had a solo exhibition at Hampstead Museum in 2003. The human figure was the main inspiration for Hauxwell's work, and he "experimented from life and in my imagination, principally in clay and wood." After retirement in 2000 he developed his ideas and "widened my use of the figure by using parts of it to create a quirky realism, especially for outdoor display." Hauxwell was a man of long-lasting hobbies: long-distance running; involvement with the North London Beekeepers ("the largest of its kind in an urban area"); and old furniture repairing.

Gerwyn HAVARD 1962– Painter born in Crickhowell, Breconshire, who graduated with honours in English literature and language from the University of Birmingham, 1981–4. Graduated with honours in fine art, painting, from Central St Martins College of Art, 1989–92, and obtained a postgraduate diploma in fine art, painting, from the Royal Academy Schools, 1995–8, appearing in the final year show. While studying there Havard was curator of the "Red Square" Forums for Contemporary Art. From 1985–7 assisted at Nicola Jacobs Gallery. Group exhibitions included Annexe Gallery, 1990; Department of Education, 1992; Seven Sisters Gallery and Alexandra Palace Open, both 1994; and Saddleworth Open in Lancashire, Llangibby Open in Brecon and Royal Over-Seas League Open, all 1995. At the last show Havard's depiction of trees in an almost abstract pattern, Petrified Forest, oil on canvas, was exhibited. Later exhibitions included RA Summer Exhibition, from 1996. Lived in London.

Elizabeth HAVEN 1974– Printmaker, who graduated from Royal College of Art in 2000. Soon after, she shared a show with Janice Fisher at Elgin, working with images of land and sea.

Mandy HAVERS 1953– Artist and teacher who worked in mixed media, born in Portsmouth, Hampshire. She studied at its College of Art and Design, 1971–2; at Coventry Polytechnic, 1972–5; then at Slade School of Fine Art, 1976–8. From 1980 she was a visiting lecturer at the Slade, Coventry Polytechnic and Trent Polytechnic in Nottingham. Among mixed shows was The Self Portrait: a Modern View, which toured from Artsite Gallery, Bath, 1987. Held a solo show at Arnolfini Gallery in Bristol which toured England and Ireland, also having one-man exhibitions in London, Brussels and Birmingham and with Nicholas Treadwell in Bradford.

Ashley HAVINDEN: *see* **ASHLEY**

Paul Douglas HAWDON 1953– Painter and printmaker, born in Manchester, who graduated with honours from St Martin's School of Art, 1978–82, was at Royal Academy Schools, 1982–5, attending British School in Rome as a Rome Scholar, 1988–9. Showed at RA, LG, RE and elsewhere. Lived in Cambridge.

Meredith William HAWES 1905–1999 Artist in oil, watercolour, gouache and pastel, and teacher, born in Thornton Heath, Surrey. He attended Croydon School of Art, 1924–5, then Royal College of Art, 1926–30, teachers including William Rothenstein, Randolph Schwabe and Henry Rushbury. He held a number of teaching posts including being principal successively of Bournville, Portsmouth and Birmingham Colleges of Art. Completed murals in Manchester, Bournemouth and Birmingham and did book illustrating for leading publishers including John Murray and Oxford University Press. He was made a freeman of Worshipful Company of Goldsmiths, for services to the arts, in 1952. Hawes was a member of RWS, NEAC, SGA and RBSA, which gave him a memorial exhibition in 1997. Abbott and Holder held a show of early pictures in 1999. Also showed at RA, leading London galleries, in France and America. RWS holds his work in the diploma collection. Lived latterly at Millbrook, Torpoint, Cornwall.

Peter HAWES 1940– Artist employing a range of approaches, including photographs, collages, paintings and assemblages, and teacher, who studied at Great Yarmouth and Norwich Schools of Art; Tilburg Academy, Netherlands; and Hornsey College of Art. Went on to become a principal lecturer at Brighton Polytechnic. Took part in several dozen shows, solo exhibitions including Landforms, The Gallery, Brighton Polytechnic, 1980; and Gardner Centre, University of Sussex, 1985–6. Works held by private and public collections in Britain and America.

Marjorie HAWKE 1894–1979 Draughtsman and painter in oil, born in London. She studied at Heatherley's, the Central School of Arts and Crafts and the Westminster School of Art, under Bernard Meninsky. Her work found its way into many private collections in Britain and abroad from mixed exhibitions at LG, Leicester Galleries, O'Hana and galleries in Greece, France and Italy. One-man shows included Bear Lane Gallery, Oxford, and the Rotunda Gallery. Lived in London.

Anthony HAWKEN 1948– Sculptor, jeweller and artist in various other media, born in Erith, Kent. He studied at Medway College of Art, Rochester, 1965–8, then with Willi Soukop at Royal Academy Schools, 1968–71, winning the Landseer Scholarship and Bronze Medal. He was assistant to Leon Underwood, 1972. Hawken was elected to RBS. His commissions included a medal for Motorola, Maidenhead; sculptured taps for the Prince of Dubai; and collections of jewellery for Roland Klein and Alistair Blair. Mixed shows included RA, Mario Flecha Gallery and Greenwich Theatre Gallery. Had solo shows at Blackheath Gallery; Minories, Colchester; and Atrium Gallery, PricewaterhouseCoopers, 2000. Citibank, Strand, holds his work. Lived in London.

Derrick HAWKER 1936– Painter and mixed-media artist and teacher, experimental in approach, in whose work a dot technique, jigsaw shapes and the reduction of what was seen to its essence all played a part. The Irish landscape was a favourite subject. Hawker was born in Seaton, Devon, between 1953–9 attending South Devon College of Art and Cardiff College of Art. He held a number of teaching posts including Ulster College of Art and Design, 1965–73, after which he became principal of Teesside College of Art, Middlesbrough. Exhibitions included Woodstock Gallery, Arts Council of Northern Ireland Gallery in Belfast – it holds his work – and Barrenhill Gallery, Dublin.

Gareth HAWKER 1950– Painter and draughtsman known initially for his still lifes, later for his many portraits, who studied at the Byam Shaw School, 1968–71, and at the Royal Academy Schools, 1971–4. He gained the Robin Guthrie Memorial Award for portrait drawing, the David Murray Landscape Studentship and a Silver Medal, the highest award for drawing. Hawker moved to Norwich, Norfolk, in 1974, an Elizabeth Greenshields Foundation Award enabling him to paint full-time for two years. He gradually achieved his ambition of living as a portraitist, with an impressive commissions list. This included Sir Greville Spratt, Lord Mayor of London, 1987–8, commissioned by the Worshipful Company of Ironmongers; Sir Alexander (Mike) Graham, Lord Mayor, 1990–1; Christopher Ballenden, master, the Worshipful Company of Bowyers; Nicholas Bomford, headmaster of Uppingham School; Robyn Parker, Miss Pears 1990–1, for Pears Soap; Sir Geoffrey Cass, chief executive of Cambridge University Press, 1972–92; The Hon. Pamela F Gordon, Premier of Bermuda, 1997–8; and Sir Jack Hayward, owner and chairman, Wolverhampton Wanderers Football Club.

Karl HAWKER fl. from 1930s–1984 Painter and teacher, one of several intimate artist friends, such as Wilfred Franks, of the composer Sir Michael Tippett. Hawker, whose mother was Welsh, met Tippett before World War II and was like him a conscientious objector, doing farm work in East Anglia. Hawker married a doctor and had two daughters, but the marriage collapsed after 13 years. He met Tippett again in 1957, living with him until 1974, often turbulently, because of Hawker's neurotic behaviour. He was an accomplished teacher, as Tippett records in his autobiography, *Those Twentieth Century Blues*. Hawker latterly lived for a time in Cyprus but could not settle there and eventually committed suicide. There is a portrait of Tippett by Hawker in the Tippett biographer Ian Kemp's *Symposium* (the original belonged to the music critic Peter Heyworth), the musical publisher Schott & Co included a Hawker design on the first edition of Tippett's *Crown of the Year* and Tippett owned a self-portrait by Hawker.

Susan HAWKER 1949– Painter in oil and watercolour, born in Surrey. She attended Sutton School of Art, 1965–6, Epsom School of Art, 1968–71, and Royal College of Art, 1971–4, being awarded a John Minton Scholarship. Among various awards won was first prize in the Laing Painting Competition, 1981. Was elected RWS in 1975 and also showed in mixed exhibitions at RA, Leonie Jonleigh Studio in Guildford, Camden Arts Centre and elsewhere. From 1976 had a series of solo shows at Thackeray Gallery. Carlisle City Art Gallery, Chantrey Bequest and National Westminster Bank hold her work. Hawker was a landscape painter whose work was on more than one occasion compared to that of Cézanne.

Yvonne HAWKER 1956–2001 Painter and printmaker, born in Madeira. She studied at Goldsmiths' College School of Art and Ravensbourne College. Showed extensively in Britain and Sweden, including RWS, RBA, RA, International Art Fair in Stockholm in 1983 and Smiths Galleries. In 1987–8 had solo show called Five Rooms in two parts: at Richard Demarco Gallery, Edinburgh, and at Bruton Gallery, Bruton, Somerset. This was based on rooms in Black Clauchrie, the artist's former Victorian shooting lodge home set in remote moorland at Barrhill by Girvan, Ayrshire. After Black Clauchrie, Hawker moved to an isolated house at Kilrenzie, near Colmonell, where she helped lead the campaign Stop the Overhead Powerlines, enlisting the support of patrons including the musician Jools Holland and film-maker David Puttnam; when that was unsuccessful she settled in an even more isolated farm cottage near Stoer, Sutherland. Hawker continued to get commissions, another of her patrons, the politician Chris Patten, inviting her in 1994 to Hong Kong as artist-in-residence. This resulted in a show, Pigs & Fishes, at the Redfern Gallery in 1995, the year ovarian cancer was diagnosed. She died in Inverness but is buried at Stoer. Hawker's pictures were about the dignity and beauty of inanimate, man-made objects transformed by time.

Julian HAWKES 1944– Sculptor, notable for abstract works in various materials, born in Gloucester. He studied at Slade School of Fine Art, 1967–9, gaining a Sainsbury Award in 1966. Was assistant to Phillip King, 1969–75, in the latter year winning a Gulbenkian Award and having a solo show at Woburn Arts Centre. Showed solo with Rowan Gallery from 1978, Arts Council from the first exhibition acquiring Untitled, in canvas and wood, of 1976–7. Hawkes' Untitled, 1979, in oak and York stone, was commissioned by Peterborough City Council. Later group exhibitions included Nature as Material, Arts Council tour, 1980; Maquettes for Public Sculpture, Welsh Sculpture Trust, Margham Park, 1982; and The Crafts Factor in Architecture and Building, RIBA, 1985. In that year Hawkes' lyrically ascending mild steel and York stone sculpture Splash, 1985, was included in Masterpieces of the Avant-garde, Annely Juda Fine Art/Juda Rowan Gallery.

Justin HAWKES 1955– Painter and conservator, whose own works were richly coloured abstracts with landscape allusions. Hawkes studied at Cambridge Anglia Polytechnic, 1974–6, and in 1976–80 at Byam Shaw Art School, teachers including Frank Bowling and Simon Willis. In his second year he gained the Graham Hamilton Drawing Award. Undertook five-year apprenticeship as a painting conservator at School of Helmut Ruhemann and became a visiting teacher to art schools. Was a member of the International Institution for Conservation and the Association of British Restorers. Hawkes' main works were T Junction, 1979; Victorian, 1988; and Arbudus Point, 1993. Exhibitions included Mario Flecha Gallery, 1987; Edogawa Culture Centre, Tokyo, 1990; Collective Gallery, Edinburgh, 1994; and a shared exhibition with John Maltby, Andrew Vass and Richard Day, Amalgam 1995. Had a solo exhibition at Ginza, Tokyo, 1990, and shared one with Mark Reddy at Lynne Strover Gallery, Fen Ditton, 1997. Hawkes said that he was "influenced by British colour-field painters such as Robyn Denny, Richard Smith and Bridget Riley". Lived in Cambridge.

Pam HAWKES 1953– Figurative artist and lecturer, born in Birmingham, who graduated with first-class honours in fine art at Coventry University, gaining her master's from the University of Central England. She won many awards, including a first prize in 1996 in the RBSA Open and the Jaguar Prize in 1997; the Lord Lieutenant's Trophy Award in 1996 and the thesis prize at the Association of Art Historians at the Courtauld Institute in 1997, as well as a prize at the Leicester City Annual Open Exhibition that year. Hawkes was a visiting lecturer at Wolverhampton University and Solihull College. Group shows included Bug Gallery, Coventry, 1996, and Leicester City Gallery and Barn End Gallery, Solihull, annual exhibitions, both 1997. Hawkes was shown by Compton Cassey Gallery at ART2003 in 2003. She had solo exhibitions at the Custard Factory, Birmingham, 1995, and Music Room Gallery, 1996.

John HAWKESWORTH 1920–2003 Painter, designer, writer and producer. He attended Rugby School and Oxford University and in between spent five months in Paris at Académie Julian. During Army service in World War II continued to paint. After demobilisation in 1946 pictures by Hawkesworth in Redfern Gallery were seen by the film director Alexander Korda's designer brother Vincent, who invited Hawkesworth to join the art department of London Films. Hawkesworth was art director for such films as *The Third Man*. In 1955 he gained the chance of learning the role of producer with the Rank Organisation and later moved into television as creator, writer and producer. Among the many films and television plays and series Hawkesworth was responsible for were *Tiger Bay*; *Upstairs, Downstairs*; *The Duchess of Duke Street*; *The Tale of Beatrix Potter*; and *Sherlock Holmes*. In 1991 an exhibition of his film design work of the 1950s was shown at Austin/Desmond Fine Art. Lived near Oakham, Rutland; and in London.

Eddie HAWKING 1926– Artist and teacher who studied at the West of England College of Art, Bristol. He taught at Middlesbrough College of Art, 1952–86, finally as director of studies. Hawking exhibited and completed commissioned work mainly in the northeast of England. One example is his cast-aluminium abstract relief Untitled, of 1962, sited on the front of the Modernist Dunning Street police station in Middlesbrough.

Dennis HAWKINS 1925– Painter, sculptor, printmaker and teacher who studied at Ruskin School of Drawing, Oxford, 1947–9, then Slade School of Fine Art, 1949–52, teachers including William Coldstream and Graham Sutherland. He was a member of the Printmakers' Council and Midland Group of Artists. Showed at Gimpel Fils, AIA, LG, Redfern Gallery and New Vision Centre and International Print Biennales in Tokyo and Florence. Commissions included murals and bas-reliefs at New Hospital, Netheredge, Sheffield, and a series of panels for Royal Children's Hospital in Liverpool. Arts Council, Victoria & Albert Museum, provincial art galleries, education authorities and overseas galleries hold Hawkins' work. He became director of art at Repton School, living at Repton, Derbyshire.

James HAWKINS 1954– Painter and designer, born in Reading, Berkshire, who attended Wimbledon School of Art, 1972–3; West Sussex College of Design, Worthing, 1974–5; and Ruskin School of Drawing, Oxford, 1975–8. Awards and commissions included the Painting Prize at Ruskin, 1976; Painter of the Year, Warwick Arts Trust, 1989; and Glenfiddich Distillery Scottish Art, 1998. In 1986 Hawkins did stage design for *The Brahan Seer*, Eden Court Theatre, Inverness. Had a series of solo shows, starting with Eden Court, 1983, later ones including A Journey in all Weathers, 1999, and Way Out West, 2003, both with Davies & Tooth at The Air Gallery. As in this show, Hawkins' work was about Scottish landscape. This he walked and chronicled with his wife Flick, working up in the studio richly coloured, gestural, almost abstract depictions of water and rugged terrain. The Gallery of Modern Art in Glasgow; Edinburgh City Council; Paintings in Hospitals, Scotland; and Highland Regional Council hold examples.

Peter HAWKINS 1934–c.1980s Sculptor and teacher, born in London, who studied at Kingston and Chelsea Schools of Art and Royal College of Art. Showed with Young Contemporaries, 1958; Cultura Ingles, Porto Alegre, Brazil, 1959; Wakefield and Bradford City Art Galleries, both 1962; and LG and Redfern Galleries, Arts Council Exhibition of Sculpture in Reading and A Painter's Collection at RA (Edward Le Bas' collection; he held several of Hawkins' works), all 1963. Hawkins lectured at the School of Furniture and Design, High Wycombe, into the 1960s, living in a converted barn in Abingdon, Berkshire. Went to India and America and was interested in yoga, mysticism and aestheticism, his later work becoming more conceptual, influenced by Minimalism.

Phillip Dennis HAWKINS 1947– Painter in oil, draughtsman, illustrator and photographer, born and lived in Birmingham, who studied at the College of Art there, 1964–8. He was a technical illustrator in the railway industry and press photographer who became noted for his depiction of current and historical railway subjects worldwide, "concentrating on the unique atmosphere of the steam railway in all its forms". Was in 1979 a founder-member of the Guild of Railway Artists, becoming its president in 1988, exhibiting extensively with the Guild. Also had solo shows in Birmingham, Solihull and York. Hawkins' articles appeared regularly in the railway press, from 1986 appeared in the *Footplate Calendar* and had fine art prints produced by Quicksilver Publishing. Completed works for railway companies, such as European Passenger Services' Eurostar trains, 1995. Other works held by Freightliner, BBC, *Birmingham Post and Mail*, Bristol United Press and Brown & Root-Booz Allen Ltd.

Sheila HAWKINS 1905–1999 Illustrator, painter and writer, born in Kalgoorlie, Western Australia, where life in the bush introduced her to the animals she became notable for drawing in a humorous way. Moved to Melbourne she studied at Toorak College and briefly at the School of Art, but financial problems forced her to do commercial illustrating, painting in her spare time. In 1931 she travelled to Europe and after a year in Spain settled in England where she continued to live, apart from the years 1948–51 in Australia. She made her name as a children's illustrator after the success of her book *Black Tuppeny* in 1932, illustrating about 50 volumes, 10 of which she wrote. In the 1930s she was the first woman to be employed in the oil company Shell-Mex's studio. During World War II as an unofficial war artist she produced a mural of Australian foresters in Scotland and drawings of women operating coal barges on London canals; she then painted portraits as an official artist to the Australian Air Force. Hawkins showed with Goupil Gallery and SWA in the 1930s; had a solo exhibition at the Geffrye Museum in 1951; and from the mid-1960s concentrated on painting landscapes and abstracts as a member of the Ridley Art Society and the Free Painters and Sculptors, which gave her a retrospective, 2000. The Mitchell Library, Sydney, and Australian War Memorial Library, Canada, hold much of her output.

Vicky HAWKINS 1948– Versatile artist whose work including painting, drawing, stage-set design, wall hangings and furniture, born and lived in east London. She attended Sir John Cass School of Art, 1968–9; East Ham Technical College, 1969–70; and the Central School of Art, 1970–3. She was studio assistant to the painter Bridget Riley, 1974–86, completed stage sets for productions at the Almeida, Old Red Lion and King's Head Theatres and made radio and television appearances. From the early 1970s Hawkins participated in numerous group exhibitions, among them latterly Chelsea Arts Club Members' Show, 1996; Miniatures, Oxford House, 1997; One World, One Heart, Tokyo, Salt Lake City and London, 2001; One Heart, One World, a touring exhibition of Japan, America and the United Kingdom, 2002; and Small is Beautiful XXII, Flowers Central, 2004–5. By then Hawkins had had over 20 solo shows, later ones including In Focus, Châteaubriant, France, 1998; Tremor, The Sun & Doves Gallery, 2000; New Work, The Shop, Vallance Road, and Art At The Barn, Upstreet, Kent, both 2001; Snatches, Combined Harvest, 2003; and *Living Dolls*, The Book, The Film, The Cast, Studio Show, 2004. Leeds City Council, Lloyds of London, Leopard TV and many private collectors held examples.

Anthony HAWKSLEY 1921– Sculptor, designer and artist in precious metals, born in Coventry, Warwickshire. He studied at Regent Street Polytechnic, Maidstone College of Art and the Royal College of Art. Showed at Ewan Phillips Gallery, Oxford Gallery and widely overseas. His work is held by Magdelene and Keble Colleges at Oxford University. Lived at Deddington, Oxford.

Dorothy Webster HAWKSLEY 1884–1970 Painter in watercolour and tempera of figures and portraits; black-and-white artist; teacher, born in London. Studied at St John's Wood School of Art, where she won a silver medal, and at the Royal Academy Schools, under George Clausen, where she won a silver medal and the Landseer Scholarship. She taught for two years at King's College, then privately. Exhibited at many venues, including the RA, Fine Art Society, RI, SWA, Walker Art Gallery, Liverpool, and the Paris Salon, where she won a silver medal. Hawksley was a member of the RI and the Society of Mural Decorators and Painters in Tempera. She made large pull-out illustrations, suitable for classroom walls, for *Child Education* and was commissioned by Heinemann to design dust-jackets for the novels *The Lacquer Lady*, by F Tennyson Jesse, 1929; *Without my Cloak*, by Kate O'Brien, 1931; and *Almond, Wild Almond*, by D K Broster, 1933. Represented in several British provincial public collections, and in galleries in North America. Hawksley was capable of painting impressive, slightly stagey pictures in the manner of Charles Ricketts. Japanese woodcuts, of the type owned by Ricketts and Charles Shannon, were a strong influence on Hawksley, as explained in the informative essay by her friend John Christian in the well-illustrated catalogue of her work accompanying The Maas Gallery exhibition in 2005. He had included three of Hawksley's pictures in The Last Romantics show which he organised at the Barbican Art Gallery in 1989. Lived in London.

Rozanne HAWKSLEY 1931– Artist and teacher, born in Portsmouth, Hampshire, who attended the Southern College of Art there, then Royal College of Art, with postgraduate studies at Goldsmiths' College School of Art. Hawksley worked originally as a freelance illustrator and designer/maker, including textile art, while teaching part-time in schools of art, including two years in America. Later part-time and visiting teaching posts included Goldsmiths', Royal College and Slade School of Fine Art. Hawksley's sculptures comprised clay, wax, wood, bone and jewels; the resulting images could be disturbing, not finding a ready outlet in commercial galleries. In the mid-1990s her work was "influenced by an Arts Council study tour to Andalucia and Spanish art of Catholique Morticole, together with the effects of war, sickness, death and poverty on the individual and the loneliness of the suffering individual." Exhibitions included the Museum of Modern Art, Kyoto, Japan; Crafts Council; Plymouth City Art Gallery; Cornerhouse, Manchester; Camden Arts Centre; RSA; and Kettle's Yard, Cambridge. Hawksley's work was held by Imperial War Museum, Kennedy Center in America and the Museum of Textiles in Poland. She was first married to the illustrator Åsgeir Scott, secondly to the actor Brian Hawksley. Lived at Newport, Dyfed.

Emma HAWORTH 1976– Painter and draughtsman who attended Wimbledon School of Art, 1994–5, and part-time, for her master's in drawing, 1998–00, having graduated in fine art with honours from Surrey Institute of Art & Design, 1995–8. Gained runner-up prizes, Artist of the Year, 99, in 1999, and Young Artist of the Year, The Hunting Art Prizes 2000. Exhibitions included Back to the Future, National Gallery, 1997; Royal College of Art, 1998; and The Harbour Club, Chelsea, March 1999. She was resident artist at Centro Verrochio, Tuscany, in 2000. Lived in Sutton, Surrey.

Jann HAWORTH 1942– Artist and teacher, born in Hollywood, California, who was for a time married to the artist Peter Blake. She was one of the seven founders of The Brotherhood of Ruralists in 1975 which had its first show at RA in 1976. Haworth studied at University of California, Los Angeles, 1959–61, and at Slade School of Fine Art, 1962–3. In the 1970s founded The Looking Glass School in Wellow, Avon, for children, with a group of similarly minded parents to share teaching. As well as painting she created masks and figures in terracotta and other materials. Contributed to group shows, including Four Young Artists, 1963, and The Obsessive Image, 1968, at ICA; RA; and Ruralist exhibitions. Solo shows were held at Robert Fraser Gallery, 1964–9; Arnolfini Gallery, Bristol, and Leslie Waddington, both 1974, and elsewhere. Was included in the survey exhibition The 1960's at England & Co, 1993, and in the same year had her first solo show for 20 years at Gimpel Fils. With the writer Richard Severy she created a series of illustrated children's books. Haworth in 1997 settled in America at Sundance, Utah, in 2000 showing at the Sundance Screening Room. A show at The Mayor Gallery in 2006 had an informative illustrated catalogue.

Lilian HAWTHORN 1909–1996 Painter, born and lived in London, who was married to the artist Elwin Hawthorne. Originally exhibited under her maiden name Lily Leahy. While working in the city, in her teens she attended various drawing classes at Regent Street Polytechnic, then joined John Cooper's classes at the Bow and Bromley Evening Institute, which she stayed with during the 1930s. Showed with the East London Group at Lefevre Gallery. Did various jobs, including decorating china and window dressing, continuing to paint and exhibit and do imaginative tapestry work until an advanced age. Also showed in East Ham area and with Whitechapel Art Gallery.

Raymond Humphrey Millis HAWTHORN 1917–1997 Wood engraver and teacher, born in Poole, Dorset. He studied at Coventry School of Art, 1935–9, and gained his teaching diploma from Hornsey School of Arts and Crafts, 1939–40, teachers including Norman Janes and Douglas Percy Bliss. Hawthorn had several teaching appointments, starting with Coventry School of Art, 1946, latterly lecturing full-time at Wirral College of Art and Design and Adult Studies, 1976–8, part-time 1978–80. He was elected a fellow of RE in 1975, being invited to join SWE, 1985. Also showed in mixed exhibitions at Wirral Society of Arts and Atkinson Art Gallery in Southport. One-man shows included Folio Gallery, 1959, and Williamson Art Gallery, Birkenhead, 1980. Atkinson and Williamson Galleries hold examples. Hawthorn's leading themes in book illustration were mainly classical and medieval history, in prints mainly landscapes and in paperback cover illustration *The New Testament*. Lived in Bebington, Wirral, Merseyside.

Wilfred Charles HAWTHORN 1877–1955 Painter, draughtsman and teacher. Born at Kettering, Northamptonshire, he studied at Wyggeston Art School, Leicester, 1890–2, in the studio of Walter Gash, Kettering 1895–1902, Wimbledon School of Art, Académie Julian, in Paris, 1901, then in the studio of Sir Alfred East for many years. He exhibited at the RA and extensively in the provinces. He published books on art education and practice. Work held by Herbert Art Gallery and Museum, Coventry, and the Alfred East Gallery, Kettering. For some time Hawthorn was president of the Coventry Art Guild. Was for a period chief assistant art master at Loughborough College of Art. Lived in Coventry.

Elwin HAWTHORNE 1905–1954 Painter, printmaker and teacher, born and lived in London, his wife the painter Lilian Hawthorn, his uncle the part-time artist Henry Silk. Like them he showed with the East London Group at Lefevre Gallery, having studied from 1927 with John Cooper at the Bow and Bromley Evening Institute. Through the Group Hawthorne (his full name was Elwin Henry Hawthorn; the added e was a mistake in a review which Lefevre chose to retain; some very early work is signed Elwin H Hawthorn or E H H) met Walter Sickert, whose studio assistant he was for three years. He was eventually under contract to Reid & Lefevre and had two solo exhibitions with them, 1934 and 1938. In World War II Hawthorne served with ARP (Air-raid Precautions) and St John's Ambulance Brigade, witnessing harrowing scenes which affected this sensitive man deeply. Then served in the Army, after which he worked for Plessey's, handling wages. Died on his way to one of several evening classes he taught. Pictures by Hawthorne of pre-World War II London are of deceptively simple design, in which he captures the atmosphere of almost-deserted streets with a near-surreal style. Among collectors were the Duke of Rutland, Earl of Sandwich, Sir Edward Marsh, Charles Laughton and J B Priestley. Manchester City Art Gallery holds Hawthorne's Church near Blackheath, presented by Contemporary Art Society.

Mike HAWTHORNE 1954– Self-taught and much-travelled painter whose bold, energetic and colourful style owed much to Rock, Reggae, jazz visuals and underground comics. He had a solo show at Alchemy in 2000. The Museum of London and Lambeth Archives acquired his work. Lived in London.

Helen HAY 1910–1993 Painter and draughtsman, born in Glasgow, whose daughter was the artist Ann Finlayson, Helen having married Iain Finlayson in 1940. Hay studied at Glasgow School of Art, Newlyn School of Art and for a term drawing and painting at Slade School of Fine Art, 1933–4. Exhibitions included RSA, Royal Glasgow Institute of the Fine Arts and Paisley and Southampton Art Galleries. She died at Chartham Manor, Kent.

Ian HAY 1940– Artist in pastel and watercolour, and teacher, born in Harwich, Essex. He studied at Colchester School of Art, 1955–60, then Royal College of Art, 1960–3, teachers including John Nash, Ruskin Spear and Roger de Grey. He taught at St Martin's and Norwich Schools of Art and was senior lecturer in drawing at the school of art at Colchester Institute. Hay was noted for his pastels of the Thames, its changing moods in different climates. He was a member of Colchester Art Society, also showing with Phoenix Gallery in London and Lavenham; Minories, Colchester; RA Summer Exhibitions and elsewhere. Public galleries in Sheffield and Doncaster hold examples. Lived in Colchester, Essex.

John Arthur Machray HAY 1887–1960 Portrait painter, born in Aberdeen, who studied under George Harcourt at Patrick Allan-Fraser School of Art, Hospitalfield, Arbroath. He was a member of RP and London Portrait Society and showed also at RA, Royal Glasgow Institute of the Fine Arts and Walker Art Gallery, Liverpool. He lived in London and painted portraits of the nobility.

Ken HAY 1955– Artist and teacher, born in Inverness, who graduated with honours in fine art from University of Leeds, 1973–7, teachers including Lawrence Gowing and Paul Gopal Chowdhury; attending the Accademia di Belle Arti, Florence, Italy, 1978–80, under Fernando Farulli; gaining his master's in visual art at University College of Wales, Aberystwyth, 1980–2, under David Tinker; and his doctorate there, 1982–90, the subject Italian materialist aesthetics, 1860–1960. Completed murals in Puigcerda, Spain, 1979 and Florence, 1980, and a mosaic mural for British Rail, Aberystwyth, 1984. By the time of his 25-year retrospective at the University of Leeds Gallery in 2000 Hay had had some 40 shows around the world; after a diverse teaching career was head of the department of fine art there and head of the sub-faculty of arts; and was working "in painting, screenprint, photography, video, but mostly digital media, or various combinations of these."

Hay was a frequent translator from Italian, lecturer and contributor to learned publications.

Peter Alexander HAY 1866–1952 Versatile painter, born in Edinburgh, who studied at Royal Scottish Academy Schools, at Académie Julian in Paris and in Antwerp. He was elected RSW in 1891, RI in 1917. A prolific exhibitor, he also showed at RA, RSA, Royal Glasgow Institute of the Fine Arts and many other galleries. Lived in London.

Rudolf HAYBROOK 1898–1965 Portrait and figure painter and theatre designer, born in London where he was based, son of the landscape painter Rudolf Heubach. Educated at Brighton College, he served in France during World War I, being demobilised after suffering shell shock. Began his largely self-taught career as an artist in the 1920s, spending some time at Chelsea Polytechnic School of Art with J D Revel, and working in association with Stanley Lupino. After living in South Africa he returned to England just before World War II and enlisted in the Auxiliary Fire Service. In his spare time he painted pictures of the Blitz, reputedly based on sketches on active service. War Artists' Advisory Committee declined to give Haybrook a commission, but they bought works by him, one of which is in the Imperial War Museum, which has since acquired others. Showed RA and had one-man shows at Brook Street Gallery in 1930s and at Leicester Galleries, which showed a big collection of his war pictures in 1940. Haybrook lectured on fire-fighting techniques in North America. After the war he developed a lung complaint brought on by his fire service work, and giving up painting spent some years as a courier, being a fluent French and German speaker.

Reg HAYDEN 1917– Painter, draughtsman and teacher, born in Brighton, Sussex, where he attended the College of Art, 1933–8, under Walter Bayes and Lawrence Preston; then studied at Slade School of Fine Art with Randolph Schwabe, 1939–40. He held a series of teaching posts, including Portsmouth College of Art and Bradford College of Art, eventually becoming head of fine art at Liverpool Polytechnic. Exhibited RA, LG, Leicester Galleries, Sussex University and elsewhere. Lived in Liverpool.

Colin HAYES 1919–2003 Artist in oil and watercolour, writer and teacher, born and lived in London. Hayes gained his master's degree from Oxford University and studied at Ruskin School of Drawing in Oxford. He "greatly valued Peter Greenham's drawing lessons at the City School, Oxford." Between 1940–5 Hayes was commissioned in the Royal Engineers. He was on the staff of the Royal College of Art, eventually as reader, 1949–84. Hayes was president of RBA and was elected RA in 1970. He wrote a series of books on painting and painters, including *Renoir* and *Rembrandt*, *Stanley Spencer* and *Ruskin Spear* as well as *A Grammar of Drawing*. Showed in RA Summer Exhibitions, at Agnew, New Grafton and Fieldborne Galleries and in the provinces. In later years Hayes' palette lightened, he was fond of painting in Greece and there was a strong pattern element in his richly coloured landscapes. Arts Council, British Council and many other public collections in Britain and abroad hold examples. New Grafton Gallery held a retrospective in 1996. Chappel Galleries, Chappel, showed Hayes' Mediterranean Paintings in 2003.

Edward HAYES 1932– Painter and draughtsman, born in Dublin, Ireland, living in London from 1957, whose output included stylised figurative pictures. From 1958, when he had a one-man exhibition, Walls, at Hammersmith Art Gallery, Hayes had others every few years, with a series at Drian Gallery from 1964, including Lines for Beckett, 1970; Chamber Music, 1973; and (Study) Oliver Plunkett's Head, 1981. He also showed works at Redfern Gallery, New Vision and New Art Centres; in America at the Heritage Gallery and Barnsdale Museum, both in Los Angeles, and Long Beach Museum, California; and in Poland at the National Museum, in Warsaw.

Georgia HAYES 1946– Painter and draughtsman, born in Aberdeen, who studied with Roy Oxlade, 1977–82. She participated in a number of group exhibitions including RA; Oxford County Museum, Woodstock; Victoria Art Gallery, Bath; and Usher Gallery, Lincoln. Included in the 1991 David Bomberg and his followers exhibition at Towner Art Gallery, Eastbourne. Her picture Embalmed With A Cat was selected for the 1992 East & South Norwich Gallery/Kent Institute of Art and Design show. In 2000 and 2003, Hayes was shortlisted for the £25,000 Charles Wollaston Prize at the RA Summer Exhibition. Later solo shows included Harriet Green Gallery, 1997; SFMoMA Artists Gallery, San Francisco, California, 2002; and Café Gallery Projects, 2003. Hayes was a part-time art teacher at Tunbridge Wells Adult Education Centre, 1986–90. Lived at Bells Yew Green, Sussex.

Jonathan HAYES 1969– Artist using such media as etching, photograph and crayon, and teacher, born in the Isle of Sheppey, Kent. Studied at University College of Wales, Aberystwyth, gaining a first-class honours degree, 1991, winning several prizes. Then worked for his master's degree, and taught as a part-time lecturer and studio assistant. He took part in exhibitions at the College's Art Centre and was in 1993 Aberystwyth Artists exhibition at The Deffett Francis Gallery, Swansea Institute of Higher Education.

Margaret C HAYES: *see* **Margaret Clarisse TOULMIN**

Peter HAYES 1946– Sculptor and ceramist who studied at Birmingham College of Art. He then travelled extensively and worked in Lesotho, Swaziland, Botswana, India, Nepal, Japan, South Korea and in continental Europe, all of which contributed to his unique style. Among his shows were Sotheby's and Christie's; Scottish Gallery, Edinburgh; Graham Gallery, New York; Martha Sneider, Chicago; and Running Ridge Gallery, Santa Fe. He had a solo show at Anthony Hepworth Fine Art, Bath, 1992. For a time Hayes had a studio in Cornwall.

Malcolm HAYLETT 1923– Painter, illustrator, photographer and writer, born in Montreal, Canada, who studied at Southend College of Art. His work appeared in a wide number of newspapers and periodicals, such as the *Daily Mail*, *Illustrated London News* and *Britannia and Eve*. He was for a time president of the Arts Club in St Ives, Cornwall, where he lived, also showing with St Ives Society of Artists.

Patrick HAYMAN 1915–1988 Painter, often on driftwood, poet and publisher, born in London where he finally lived. Was educated at Malvern College, but lived in New

Zealand in 1936–47, starting to paint in Dunedin, in 1938. Returned to England in 1947, eventually settling in Cornwall. Although he finally moved from Cornwall permanently he often returned there and it remained an inspiration for his painting. He much admired the work of the primitive artist Alfred Wallis; his own pictures also drew on images of the sea and have an apparently childlike quality, vigorous, vivid and direct. From 1958–63 founded and edited the magazine *The Painter and Sculptor*, influential in its advocacy of figurative art. In 1988 the Louise Hallett Gallery published *Painted Poems* by Hayman. Showed widely in group shows and had solo exhibitions in Cornwall, London and abroad. A large retrospective show was at Camden Arts Centre and then toured in 1990. There was another at Belgrave Gallery in 2005, launching its publication *Patrick Hayman – Visional Artist*, by Mel Gooding. Tate Gallery and Arts Council hold his work.

HAYMAN CHAFFEY 1920– Painter and designer, born in Hastings, Sussex, full name Frederick William Hayman Chaffey. He studied at Hastings School of Art, Hornsey School of Art and privately. Exhibited RA, RBA, NS, Leicester and Heal's Galleries and at Paris Salon. Lived for a time at Charing, Kent, and in Barcelona, Spain.

Dan HAYS 1966– Painter, born and lived in London, who graduated in fine art from Goldsmiths' College, 1987–90. He was first prize winner at the 1997–8 John Moores Liverpool Exhibition with his oil on canvas Harmony in Green, his depiction of a green hamster cage, exactly the artist's height, with "a very slight perspective. My early obsessions with Escher and Op Art resurface." Group shows included Thirty Seven Seconds, The Slaughterhouse, 1989; Moving Pictures, Clove Gallery, 1993; 22Ovolt Message, Hooghuis, Arnhem, Netherlands, 1995; the Arts Council new purchases tour Ace!, 1996–7; and Die Young Stay Pretty, ICA, 1998–9. Solo shows included Laure Genillard Gallery, 1996; 30 Underwood Street, 1998; and Entwistle, 2002. The Saatchi Collection holds his work.

Christopher HAYSOM 1939–1989 Sculptor, painter and teacher, son of a mason "and a three-hundred-year-old tradition". Left school aged 16, first studied sculpture under Ralph Brown and then under Paul Fletcher at Bournemouth College of Art, later with Bernard Meadows at the Royal College of Art. Taught sculpture at Central School of Art and Design from 1973. In 1988, Haysom began preparing stone blocks for a studio, built in Acton, near Worth Matravers, Dorset. When cancer stopped him carving, he turned to painting. A memorial show was held at Central and St Martins School of Art, a few weeks after his death, in May 1989.

Stanley William HAYTER 1901–1988 Engraver, painter, teacher and writer, born in London, son of the painter W H Hayter. After taking a degree in chemistry at King's College, London University, in 1921, Hayter worked for Anglo-Iranian Oil Company in Abadan in the early-1920s. He had begun to experiment with printmaking and in 1926 left the oil company, moved to Paris and enrolled at Académie Julian, where his fellow-students included Balthus, Calder and Anthony Gross. In 1927 he founded Atelier 17 to research the technique of engraving and thereafter was greatly influential as a teacher. Hayter advised the Republican government in Spain on camouflage, in 1937, and in 1939 collaborated on print portfolios to aid the Spanish Republican Children's Fund. Was married three times, his second wife being the American sculptor Helen Phillips. Hayter was an early member of the Surrealist movement; he exhibited widely in Europe and America; wrote books on *Jankel Adler*, 1948, and *New Ways of Gravure*, 1949, plus numerous articles. Received the Légion d'Honneur in 1951. He took part in numberless exhibitions throughout the world, including a retrospective exhibition at Whitechapel Art Gallery in 1957 with an Arts Council tour in 1958, transferred that year to the Venice Biennale; print retrospective at Victoria & Albert Museum, 1969; another at British Museum 2001–02. Although Hayter had spent the period 1940–50 in New York, where he ran Atelier 17, he took it back to Paris in 1950, closing the New York branch in 1955, and it was in Paris that he died. A man of great enthusiasm and energy, Hayter continued painting to the end of his life, during which period his pictures took on a new, glowing colour. Having been introduced to engraving by the Polish artist Joseph Hecht and the idea of a line that was "not drawn but driven", Hayter favoured working "automatically"; for him "an image is made without deliberate intention or direction", although the method for achieving it was carefully determined beforehand.

Margaret HAYTHORNE 1893– Painter, printmaker and designer, born in Liverpool, where she attended the City School of Art under William Penn, then the Central School of Arts and Crafts under Francis Jackson and Noel Rooke. Was sister of the artist Edmund Haythorne and was a member of the Sandon Studios Society. She exhibited RA, RCamA, Redfern Gallery and SWE. Whitworth Art Gallery in Manchester holds her work. Lived in Liverpool.

Alfred HAYWARD 1875–1971 Painter and mural artist strongly influenced by the Impressionists. Born in London, he was within a few months taken to live in Hooe, Sussex, at Quiddleswell Mount, which he sold only in 1948 when his finances were low and he was in receipt of a Civil List Pension. From 1891–4 attended South Kensington Schools, then was at Slade School of Fine Art, 1895–7. During the period up to World War I Hayward travelled to West Indies, Central America and Italy, which he always loved. After serving in Artists' Rifles Hayward was appointed an Official War Artist, 1918–9, his resulting work being held by Imperial War Museum. By the end of the 1920s Hayward was faring well as a painter, but his income dipped sharply in the 1930s. Exhibited RA, NEAC, of which he was a member, Leicester Galleries, Wildenstein, RP, RWS and Gallery Edward Harvane, 1970. Work held by Tate Gallery, provincial galleries and galleries overseas. Centenary exhibition Belgrave Gallery, 1975. Hayward was a keen member of Chelsea Arts Club, a dapper, immaculate man of old-fashioned manners. Finally lived in London.

Arthur HAYWARD 1889–1960 Marine, portrait and figure painter and teacher, born in Southport, Lancashire, who studied at Warrington School of Art and with Stanhope Forbes. During World War I he was a captain with the Royal Field Artillery. After living in Newlyn he settled in St Ives, Cornwall, where he started teaching in the Shore Studio where he worked. Hayward was a member of St Ives Art Club. He showed at the RA Summer Exhibition 1920–47, also ROI, RSA, RWA and Paris Salon.

His pictures were acquired by public galleries in Warrington and Auckland, New Zealand and the National Portrait Gallery obtained his 1933 self-portrait from the Fine Art Society in 1985. Hayward's paintings are commonly modest in size, but are notable for their depiction of glittering light on water.

John HAYWARD 1929– Stained glass artist who studied as a painter at St Martin's School of Art, 1946–9. He learned stained glass with a firm in Westminster, then went freelance in 1961 with a large commission for east and west windows at St Mary Le Bow. After this Hayward "was continuously busy mostly with glass, but some furniture and metalwork, all commissioned work in churches and other public places." He was a fellow of the British Society of Master Glass Painters. His work included east windows, St Michael, Paternoster Royal (Dick Whittington's church); east window in St Peter's, Oxford; nave windows, Grantham Parish Church; and nearly all windows in Dunstable Priory (a booklet on the glass there features Hayward's work); and the east window in Walsingham Church. Hayward said that he was "influenced by icons, Braque, Sutherland and Seurat. My design tends to be figures in landscapes." Ely Cathedral Stained Glass Museum holds Hayward's work. Lived in Corscombe, Dorchester, Dorset.

Pete HAYWARD fl. from 1960s– Painter and teacher who studied at Eastbourne School of Art, 1963–5, and West Sussex College of Higher Education, 1965–8. Until 1972 taught in Essex and at an approved school in County Durham, then became head of art and arts co-ordinator for Walton Comprehensive School, Peterborough. Exhibitions included Wisbech Museum, Usher Gallery in Lincoln, Yarrow Gallery in Oundle and in 1987 he was included in Peterborough's Art '87, at Lady Lodge Arts Centre.

Tony HAYWARD 1954– Sculptor and teacher who studied sculpture at St Martin's School of Art in the early 1970s, then ceramics at the Royal College of Art, 1983–5. He taught part-time in art colleges, also running educational workshops in schools and museums for primary-age children. His work included assemblages of wall-mounted objects and constructions using found objects. Exhibited in many group shows in Britain, continental Europe and America. Solo appearances included Orchard Gallery, Londonderry, 1986; Artsite, Bath, 1990; and Winchester Gallery, Winchester, 1993. In 1997 an exhibition of Hayward's collection of utilitarian objects and toys bought during six trips to India, from 1988, was shown at Hove Museum & Art Gallery.

Martin HAYWARD-HARRIS 1959– Realistic wildlife sculptor, painter and printmaker who travelled extensively around the world for subjects. Hayward-Harris was born in Reading, Berkshire, settling there at Earley. He began sculpting aged 14, trained at the Berkshire College of Art and Design, 1978–84, and worked for five years in the model and taxidermy department of the Natural History Museum, gaining first-hand experience of wildlife anatomy. It holds his work. Hayward-Harris exhibited widely in Britain and East Africa, including SWLA, Royal Society for the Protection of Birds and with the East African Wildlife Society and was included in the Autumn Exhibition at The Wykeham Gallery, Stockbridge, 2001. Had solo shows at Phyllis Court Club, Henley-on-Thames, from 1990.

Eric HAYWARD-YOUNG 1908– Painter of pictures and murals and miniaturist, born in Sheffield, son of the artist Walter Hayward-Young. Studied art privately and showed at RA. Lived in London.

Carol HAYWOOD 1941– Sculptor, ceramist and teacher, born in Clifton Hampden, Oxfordshire, who as well as drawing worked in porcelain and bronze. She studied fine art at St Martin's School of Art, 1958–62, teachers including Peter Blake, Derrick Greaves, Elisabeth Frink, Peter de Francia, Frederick Gore, Joe Tilson and John Farleigh; then gained her master's in ceramics at Cardiff, 1992–4, under Mick Casson, Geoffrey Swindell and Peter Starkey. Working from the figure arose from a lifelong interest in dancing and yoga. Haywood taught yoga for over 20 years and art to children and adults, and from 1994 drawing at degree level in the ceramics department at Cardiff (she had her own studio in the city). Group shows included Meridian, Hay-on-Wye; Candover Gallery, Alresford; and RWA 2nd Open Sculpture Exhibition, all 1996. She was a member of the Crafts Council Register.

Helen HAYWOOD 1964– Botanical artist, illustrator and teacher, born in Woolwich, southeast London, who studied at Carmarthen Art College; graduated with honours from Newport College of Art, where a notable teacher was Charles Gillard; and gained her master's at Birmingham Polytechnic. Haywood taught at Bournville College of Art and Leamington Spa College. She illustrated for the Royal Botanic Gardens, Kew, which owned her work; *Curtis's Botanical Magazine*; and *Reader's Digest* publications and was Young Illustrator of the Year in 1989. Group shows included Astley House Fine Art, Moreton-in-Marsh, and in 2005 A New Flowering: 1,000 Years of Botanical Art at the Ashmolean Museum, Oxford. That exhibition was curated by Dr Shirley Sherwood, who included Haywood in her 1996 book *Contemporary Botanical Artists* and owned her work. She was also mentioned in *The Art of Botanical Illustration*, by Wilfrid Blunt, edited by William T Stearn, which had originally appeared in 1950. Haywood wrote: "I want to combine the scientific with the aesthetic, to be technically accurate but to give the painting life, with individual style and character." She lived in Kington, Herefordshire.

John HAYWOOD 1936–1991 Painter and falconer, based in Coventry, Warwickshire, where he attended the College of Art. Then spent a year on the continent where he "sketched, played piano in bars and learned to play the Flamenco guitar." Back in England working for his father Haywood's teenage interest in flying birds of prey was rekindled, and at his suggestion he flew falcons for display at Twycross Zoo Park. After three years there Haywood helped a wealthy client to train birds of prey, also working with falcons and eagles for films and television. Working with Countess Marie de Beningsen, co-founder of the Quill and Palette Partnership, which sold pictures to banks and business premises, Haywood combined his bird and artistic talents and sold his own paintings "from Aldwych to Hong Kong". Eventually Haywood flew around 200 birds of prey. Haywood sold well through the Mathaf Gallery to Middle Eastern clients and himself flew falcons in North Africa. When King Fahd of Saudi Arabia visited

London in 1987 Mathaf held a special exhibition featuring Haywood's pictures and Genesis Publications produced a 500-copy, signed book.

Mark HAYWOOD 1952– Printer, draughtsman, photographer and teacher, born in Oldham, Lancashire. He studied at Jacob Kramer College of Art in Leeds, 1971–2, then at the Medlock Fine Art Centre in Manchester, 1972–5, where his teachers included the sculptor Keith Godwin. Went on to teach at Salford College of Art. Exhibited at Chenil Galleries, also widely in Lancashire, including Oldham Art Gallery and Portland Gallery. Manchester Polytechnic holds his work. Lived at Whalley Range, Manchester.

Andy HAZELL 1959– Artist involved in public art, film and tin automata, born in Altrincham, Cheshire, whose "little tin figures represent moments in time.... Making things out of stuff that others throw away is very liberating." Hazell graduated from Reading University, 1977–81, gaining his master's from the Slade School of Fine Art, 1984–6. While at the Slade, in 1985 he won a University College London Travel Grant to visit mud mosques in Mali, in 1986 a Boise Scholarship to Japan. After being Sculpture Fellow at Cheltenham College of Art, 1987, in 1988 Hazell won a Crafts Council Setting Up Grant, other grants including ones in 1992 and 1995 taking him to Slovakia and Pakistan, part of his wide travels, including residencies around Britain, in Germany and America. For seven years he worked with Lucy Casson. Hazell's wide experience included consultation, theatre and film works. His many commissions latterly included The Electric Palace, for Palace Theatre, Mansfield, 1999, and The Coughing Hospital, an animated collection box for Ventnor Botanical Gardens, 2001. Among numerous exhibitions were a solo at Oriel Myrddin Gallery, Carmarthen, 2002, others at Bury St Edmunds Gallery and Harley Gallery, Worksop, both 2003. Lived in Knighton, Powys.

David HAZELWOOD 1932–1994 Self-taught artist, born and lived in Ipswich, Suffolk. He used collage, acrylic and mixed media. Hazelwood's work could be meticulous and subtly coloured, sometimes employing tiny pieces of sheet music. He was a member of Free Painters and Sculptors for a time, was a photo-lithographic artist, 1948–85, from then on a professional artist. Hazelwood took part in many group exhibitions including RA Summer Exhibition from 1977; Bath Festival from 1983; International Art Fairs from 1985, including Basle, Chicago, Cologne, Frankfurt and Madrid; Anthony Dawson Museums Tour, 1987; and Continuing the Tradition, Chappel Galleries, Chappel, 1993. Had a one-man show at Bedford College, 1970, later ones including Frankfurt Art Fair, 1991, and Galerie Peerlings, Krefeld, and Galerie Krakeslatt, Brömolla, both 1993. Victoria & Albert Museum, Department of the Environment, Camden Arts Centre and many provincial galleries hold his work. Hazelwood's idol was Nicolas de Stäel, other influences being Ben Nicholson, Mark Tobey, Kurt Schwitters, Antonio Tapiés and Roger Bissière. In 1995 a tribute show was held at Christchurch Mansion, Ipswich. Chappel Galleries held a solo exhibition of his collages in 2005. His younger brother was the artist Gordon Hazelwood.

Gordon HAZELWOOD 1935– Largely a landscape-based artist in oil, watercolour, mixed media and drawing, and teacher, Hazelwood was born in Ipswich, Suffolk, the younger brother of the artist David Hazelwood. Gordon studied painting and sculpture at Ipswich School of Art for his National Diploma in Design, 1952–6, under Philip Fortin, Colin Moss and Bernard Reynolds. After in 1956–7 gaining his art teaching certificate at London University's Institute of Education, from 1959–97 he taught in secondary schools in Hertfordshire and Bedfordshire. As a young man he regularly exhibited at The Phoenix Gallery, Lavenham, occasionally at Snape Maltings, and was a founder-member of the New Ipswich Art Group. He shared shows at The Playhouse Gallery, Harlow, Letchworth Gallery and at Hertfordshire College of Art, St Albans, also exhibiting at RA, NEAC and RI. He had a solo show at Boxfield Gallery, Stevenage, in 1999. J M Whistler, Philip Wilson Steer, Walter Sickert and Victor Pasmore were "early and enduring interests and influences". Many private collectors in Britain and abroad bought his work. Hazelwood lived in Harpenden, Hertfordshire.

Robin HAZLEWOOD 1944– Painter and teacher, born in Warwickshire, where he studied at Coventry College of Art, 1961–5, then attended Liverpool College of Art, 1965–6. Taught widely in adult education in London, including Putney and Wandsworth and Camden and Stanhope Adult Education Institutes. In 1982 was included in Artists in Adult Education at Woodlands Art Gallery. Other shows included Coventry Museum and Art Gallery, 1965; Nuffield Gallery, Southampton, 1974; Scribes Gallery from 1979; and South London Art Gallery, 1980.

Charles Walker HAZZARD 1964– Figurative sculptor, born in Birmingham, who did a foundation course at Bournville Art School there, 1983–4; gained an honours degree at Gloucestershire College of Arts and Technology, 1984–7; did postgraduate study at Sir Henry Doulton School, 1988–90; then obtained a postgraduate higher diploma in sculpture at City & Guilds of London Art School, 1990–1. Hazzard was elected an associate of RBS in 1992, becoming a member of its council and several of its committees. In 1996–8 he was appointed to a Henry Moore Fellowship in Sculpture at Loughborough College of Art and Design. Commissions in 1990–1 included portraits of the art critic Peter Fuller; Lord Jack Ashley; Leon Krier, architect to the Duchy of Cornwall; and Professor Roger Scruton. In 1993 Hazzard completed a lantern for St James the Less, Pimlico. Exhibitions included MAFA and LG, both 1992; RA Summer Exhibition, 1993; Cheltenham Society of Artists and Whitechapel Open, both 1994; and RWA 2nd Open Sculpture Exhibition, 1996. Had a first solo show at The Hyde Park Gallery, 1993, with one at Exchange Square, The Broadgate Centre, 1996. Lived in London.

Clive HEAD 1965– Painter and teacher, born in Maidstone, Kent. He studied visual art at University College of Wales, Aberystwyth, and University of Lancaster. Head produced meticulous paintings of places, using a camera "to isolate and record" the image. He showed widely from 1985, in 1991 shared a three-man exhibition at Woodlands Art Gallery, with solo shows at Blains Fine Art, 1999 and 2001. Taught at University College, Scarborough. Lived in South Yorkshire.

Richard HEAD 1951– Artist in pen and ink, gouache, oil and drypoint, born in London, who attended Eton College, 1964–8, under Peter Sumsion and Oliver Thomas; in 1969 did a pre-university course in Italy; was taught at West Surrey College of Art & Design by John Morris, 1970; then did a fine art degree at Bristol Polytechnic, 1971–4, in 1972 being a David Murray student, teachers including David Ferguson and Michael Canney. Became a full-time gardener at The Royal Horticultural Society, Wisley, from 1979. John Piper, Keith Grant, Christopher Wood, Walter Sickert and Monet were influences, subjects of work including landscapes, seascapes and views of old buildings. Head was a member of Guildford Art Society. Took part in mixed shows including RA Summer Exhibition from 1979, Michael Parkin Fine Art from 1984 and Sally Hunter Fine Art from 1986. Solo shows included Dillington House, Ilminster, 1980, and The First Gallery, Bitterne, 1995. Lived in Woking, Surrey.

Tim HEAD 1946– Artist, born in London where he continued to live, and teacher. He studied at Newcastle upon Tyne department of fine art, 1965–9. In the summer of 1968 he was assistant to Claes Oldenburg in New York. Head was then at St Martin's School of Art, 1969–70. After being assistant to the artist for the Robert Morris show at Tate Gallery in 1971, Head taught at Goldsmiths' College School of Art and Slade School of Fine Art. During 1977–8 he was artist-in-residence at Clare Hall and Kettle's Yard, Cambridge. Painting, slide projections and mirrors were used by Head for environmental pieces created for specific sites in which he questioned the nature of reality and illusion. As well as showing widely internationally he showed at such venues as Museum of Modern Art in Oxford, Rowan Gallery and Arnolfini Gallery, Bristol, with a retrospective of work since 1984 at Whitechapel Art Gallery, 1992–3, and tour. Then showed solo often in Germany, with one in London at The Drawing Gallery in 2006. Arts Council holds examples.

Douglas A HEALD 1943– Artist in various media who was born in York, where he eventually settled, setting up a studio and gallery. He early developed an artistic talent, with a special interest in natural history and architecture. Studied for three years at York School of Art, then spent a period in studios in north of England. Next travelled extensively in North America, Europe and North Africa, continuing to travel to fulfill commissions. Among those presented with his work were members of the royal family and Cardinal Basil Hume, Archbishop of Westminster.

George HEALER 1936– Sculptor in various materials and teacher. He went to school in Chester-le-Street, County Durham, where he settled and attended Sunderland College of Art, 1952–6, teachers including Harry Thubron and Bob Jewell. After National Service in the Army, 1956–8, Healer did a variety of jobs, being employed in the family fruit business; working as a commercial designer and church furniture designer; as a ceramics restorer at Beamish Open Air Museum; and as a commercial sculptor for Swanbridge Art Company, Sunderland. He also taught sculpture and casting design, including adult education classes and at Sunderland College of Art, 1968–74, and with Peterlee & Aycliffe Development Corporation, 1982–4. Was an associate of RBS, gaining its Diploma for Distinction in 1974. Showed at Westgate Road Galleries, Newcastle, 1960; Durham University, 1963; Royal Edinburgh Academy, 1965; RA, 1967; Royal Institute of Fine Art, 1978, and elsewhere. Bowes Museum, Barnard Castle, County Durham, holds his work.

Christine HEALEY fl. from c.1980– Painter, printmaker and teacher active in northwest England who worked in adult education as a tutor/therapist from 1982 while showing extensively. She was part-time curator and organiser of the Chapman Gallery, University of Salford, where she also held the post of artist-in-residence. In addition to her work in Britain she tackled international topics. Her exhibition Impressions of Brunei: A British Eye was shown at Malay Museum, Brunei, 1988, shortly after Aspects of Sri Lanka appeared at the British Council Hall, Colombo. In 1992 had a solo show at Chapman Gallery, The Ultimate Experience, and in 1994 No Pelicans in Pembrokeshire at Portico Library Gallery, Manchester.

Mike HEALEY 1951– Painter, designer, muralist and teacher whose pictures included atmospheric landscapes using expressive brushstrokes, as in his canvas Green Sea, East Coast, included in The Caledonian Show III, The Contemporary Fine Art Gallery, Eton, 2001. Healey studied under John Cunningham at school and at the Glasgow School of Art in the early 1970s, winning the Haldane Travelling Scholarship and the Leverhulme Travelling Scholarship to America. After graduating he lived in Rio de Janeiro as an artist and freelance designer, producing a range of work for Brazilian government agencies. Returned to Glasgow in the early 1980s where he became senior lecturer at Glasgow School of Art until 1997 when he resigned to paint full-time. Exhibited widely in Britain and America, including Thompson's Marylebone, 2003. The European Parliament, Royal Mail and Glasgow School of Art acquired his work.

Rachel HEALEY 1957– Artist, designer and teacher, born in California, America, daughter of the painter Sheila Healey. She did a one-year foundation course and three years in textile design, West Sussex College of Art and Design, 1974–8. In 1978 Healey was selected for Texprint and became a freelance textile designer, with a workshop in Northumberland. Exhibited regularly at the British Craft Trade Show, Harrogate; Festival Craft Tent, Edinburgh; Northern Centre of Contemporary Art, Sunderland, and elsewhere, supplying work to Liberty and Harvey Nichols. Gained a Northern Arts Craft Council Award, 1988, and was a part-time teacher to the foundation course at Newcastle upon Tyne College of Art and Technology. She moved to Hampshire in 1992, starting to work in pastel, The Froyle Gallery there showing her work.

Sheila HEALEY 1915– Painter and draughtsman, notable for portraits, born in Buenos Aires, Argentina, to Anglo-Scottish parents. She attended boarding school in England, then was taught painting and drawing in Buenos Aires by Violet Hurrie and Alexander Herdman. Poverty faced the family in 1930 when Sheila's father died and for five years she taught English until there was money to return to England. Re-met Hal Foote, and after marriage in 1935 they moved to Mexico where Sheila encountered the advanced painter José Clemente Orozca, who admiringly told her to "throw away your art books – just work". She had inspirational lessons from Angelina Beloff, first wife of the artist Diego Rivera. In 1938 Foote with Sheila was sent by Shell to Guatemala City, where she met a similar spirit:

the explorer, archaeologist, photographer and film-maker Giles Healey. With him moved to New York in 1941, a multi-cultural eye-opener; in 1943 they married and settled in Los Angeles; went to Mexico in 1944; then back to New York in 1946, where Sheila was encouraged by the sculptor Henry Moore. After moving in 1947 to Pacific Palisades, California, where Sheila took classes with Rico Le Brun and William Brice, in 1955 they went up the coast to Big Sur, joining an artistic community which included the writer Henry Miller. By now she had exhibited widely, including the Vincent Price Gallery, Beverley Hills, 1943; Los Angeles Museum, 1947; with a solo show at Norlyst Gallery, New York, 1948. The Healeys moved finally to Bignor, West Sussex, in 1969, where Giles died in 1980. The dramatically located house which they had built on the coast at Big Sur had burned down in 1971, with much of her work. Between 1984–90 Sheila attended the experimental drawing lessons of Ron Cavedaschi in Brighton, in 1995 classes by Emily Ball in Rackham. In 1999 there was a retrospective at Gallery 27, curated by William Jackson. Her daughter was the painter Rachel Healey, her niece the artist Frances Murray.

Eithne HEALY 1964– Sculptor who studied at Wimbledon School of Art, 1988–91, graduating with honours in sculpture. Showed in annual outdoor exhibit of sculpture in Cannizaro Park, Wimbledon, from 1989; Gagliardi Contemporary Art and Design, 1992–3; and in 1993 at Isis Gallery, Leigh-on-Sea, in Drawing Towards Sculpture. In 1992–3 had sculpture placed at Tamworth High School, Mitcham.

Timothy HEALY 1901– Watercolour painter and black-and-white artist who did commercial work as well as exhibiting. Born in Manchester, son of the artist Timothy Healy, William Timothy Joseph Healy – his full name – studied at Bolt Court, Fleet Street, under Geoffrey Pocock and Sylvan Boxius. Exhibited RI. Work was reproduced by magazines such as *Mother and Home* and *Woman and Home*. Lived at Southborough, Kent.

Andrew HEARD 1958–1993 Painter and printmaker, born in Hertford, Hertfordshire. He attended Chelsea School of Art, 1979–80, having in late-1970s worked as a waiter at Blitz nightclub while studying history and history of art at London University, 1976–9. After graduation he lived for a year in West Berlin. For some time Heard's work was best known on the continent. Two of his most successful shows were at Friedman-Guinness Gallery in Germany, at Heidelberg in 1987 and Frankfurt in 1989. He also had one-man shows in 1980s in Athens, Amsterdam, Paris and Zürich. In England Heard was chosen in 1986–7 for Whitechapel Open exhibitions, in 1988 he had a show at Salama-Caro Gallery and in 1992 Connaught Brown held his exhibition Strange Fruit. Heard's work, which had a strain of uneasiness, celebrated popular figures such as the actor Terry-Thomas, the actress Barbara Windsor and comedian Max Miller. He wanted it to be like "a slap in the face". The later large circular canvases of Strange Fruit were brighter, more playful, with less of an uncomfortable message. Dressed like a skinhead, Heard was an advocate of his friend artist and writer David Robilliard's work, admired the plays of Joe Orton and sought to interpret the culture of the 1950s and 1960s. Died of Aids in London. There was a memorial show at Salama-Caro in 1994.

Michael HEARD 1931–1994 Artist born in Romford, Essex, settling in East Anglia in 1964 and living finally at Wivenhoe. He studied at Central School of Arts and Crafts, 1952–4, then at RWA, 1955, followed by time in London, 1956–9, then St Ives, Cornwall, 1959–63. Group shows included Penwith Society in St Ives, Plymouth City Art Gallery, Portal and Mall Galleries, Agnew, John Moores Liverpool Exhibition at Walker Art Gallery, and Aldeburgh Festival Gallery. In 1996 he was included in Colchester Art Society Fifty Years Anniversary Exhibition at Chappel Galleries, Chappel. Solo shows included Newlyn Art Gallery in Newlyn, Mercury Gallery, Gainsborough's House in Sudbury and several at Essex University Gallery and Wivenhoe Arts Club.

Nancy Hastings HEARSEY fl. c.1940–1960 Painter born in Ontario, Canada. She studied at Heatherley's School of Fine Art and in Paris. Showed at RA, NS and Paris Salon. Lived for a time in London.

John HEARTFIELD 1891–1968 Versatile politically committed artist of the left, born Helmut Herzfeld in Berlin Schmargendorf, Germany; he adopted the name John Heartfield in 1916 because of the German political slogan "May God Punish England", regarding it as war-mongering. His parents, both politically active, abandoned Heartfield, his brother and sisters, in 1899. In 1905, after elementary school, Heartfield began an apprenticeship in Wiesbaden; studied at the Royal Bavarian Arts and Crafts School, Munich, 1908; in 1912 worked as a commercial artist for a printing firm in Mannheim; in 1913 studied at the Arts and Crafts School in Berlin under Ernst Neumann; then during world War I spent a short period in the Army until a feigned nervous breakdown prompted his release and he was able to run a publishing company with his brother Wieland. In 1918 Heartfield, by then director of the Military Educational Film Service (later UFA), became a member of the Berlin Club Dada and joined the Communist Party with Wieland and George Grosz. The 1920s and early-1930s saw Heartfield hectically active, responsible for book-jackets, typography and layout, articles, set designs, posters and photomontages, associated with radical left-wing groups, spending some time in the Soviet Union. With the Nazi takeover in 1933 Heartfield fled to Prague, then to England in 1938, where in 1939 he became involved with the AIA and Free German League of Culture, which honoured his fiftieth birthday in 1941, the year after he was interned as an enemy alien and became severely ill. Worked as a designer for publishers such as Penguin Books, and as a freelance cartoonist. In 1950 Heartfield returned to Leipzig to continue his work, and a first comprehensive exhibition of this in the German Democratic Republic was held in 1957, when Heartfield moved to Berlin. After growing recognition – there were exhibitions around Europe in 1964–5 – he died there. In 1992 there was an exhibition at the Barbican Art Gallery.

Adrian HEATH 1920–1992 Painter and teacher, born in Maymyo, Burma, he arrived in England as a small boy, studied at Bryanston School and was taught in Newlyn by Stanhope Forbes, 1938, and the Slade School of Fine Art, 1939, then evacuated to Oxford. Was in Royal Air Force, and was a prisoner of war in Germany, returning to study at Slade, 1945–7. Although at first his work was representational, in the late-1940s it became abstract, his initial abstracts being shown at LG. By then he had spent a year in the south of France at Carcassonne, where he had a solo show at Musée de Carcassonne in 1948. First one-man exhibition in Britain was at Redfern Gallery, 1953. Had numerous group show appearances in Britain and abroad and regular solo exhibitions, including many at Redfern Gallery and two retrospectives, at City Art Gallery in Bristol in 1971 and at Graves Art Gallery, Sheffield, in 1972. An articulate painter who nevertheless cautioned that "artists should be wary of the written statement," Heath in 1953 published the important monograph: *Abstract Art, its Origin and Meaning*. He continued to expound his beliefs as a teacher at Bath Academy of Art, 1955–76, the University of Reading, 1981, and elsewhere. Work held by many international public collections, including Arts Council, Tate Gallery, Victoria & Albert Museum and Whitworth Art Gallery, Manchester. Lived in London, but died in France at Montmirail, while teaching at a summer school. In 1953 Heath married the stage designer Corinne Lloyd.

Claude HEATH 1964– Artist in mixed media, born and lived in London. He gained a degree in philosophy from King's College, 1983–6. Heath's exhibitions included Young British Artists VI at Saatchi Gallery, 1996, which included work centered around a cast of his brother's face. By the time of the exhibition this intricate pursuit had produced 198 drawings, with more of the series to come. He was a prizewinner at John Moores Liverpool Exhibition, 1997–8. In 1999 Heath was a NatWest Art Prize finalist, exhibiting paintings based on ink drawings made without looking at the object being represented. Blindfolded, he drew only what he could feel. Solo exhibitions included Hales Gallery, 1998, Leeds City Art Gallery, 1999; Bury St Edmunds Art Gallery, 2000, as artist-in-residence; and a six-year retrospective at Kettle's Yard, Cambridge, 2002, to celebrate his recent artist fellowship appointment there and at Christ's College. The Arts Council, British Museum, Saatchi Collection, The Henry Moore Institute in Leeds and Walker Art Gallery, Liverpool, hold examples.

Irene HEATH 1906– Painter, illustrator and writer of books for children, born in Bedford. Studied at St John's Wood School of Art, Heatherley's School of Fine Art and at Regent Street Polytechnic School of Art. Exhibited RA, NS and ROI. Her books included *A Birthday Book for Children*, *Capricorn Colony* and *Heard by a Mouse*. Lived in London.

Isobel HEATH 1908–1989 Painter and poet who was associated with St Ives, Cornwall, for some 50 years. She studied at Atelier Colarossi, Paris, and with Leonard Fuller in St Ives. During World War II she worked as an artist with the Ministry of Information. She exhibited with RSA, RCamA, ROI, RI and was a member of the St Ives Society of Artists. In 1949 she was a founder-member of the breakaway Penwith Society of Arts. Heath had a romantic obsession with the Cornish landscape and would drive onto the moors, where she would work and sleep for days at a time, painting at night with the aid of a tin miner's hat and lamp. Expressionist abstraction was a strong feature of Heath's pictures, featured in a show at Tadema Gallery, 1990, and she was also noted for her portraits. Her books included *Passing Thoughts*, 1971; *Love*, 1973; and *Reflections*, 1978.

Lewis Edward HEATH 1911– Artist in gouache, watercolour and pen and ink, he was born in Hastings, Sussex, and studied art at the School of Art there under Philip William Cole. Then attended the Royal College of Art under Ernest Tristram and the calligrapher Edward Johnston. Heath – who sometimes signed his work Leharca – held a series of teaching posts in England, finishing as head of the art department at Burton upon Trent grammar school, where he lived. He published a book on outdoor sketching, was interested in marionette-making and was a member of the British Puppet & Model Theatre Guild.

Peregrine HEATHCOTE 1973– Figure and portrait painter who initially attended Heatherley's School of Fine Art. He was then faced with a dilemma as to where to study next. Visiting one prominent art school on a very cold day, Heathcote suggested they turn on an old radiator in a corner, but was told that this was a sculpture of distinction. He was persuaded by his mother Lesley to look abroad to further learn the classical artist's disciplines and opted for the Florence Academy of Fine Art, 1992–5. Heathcote returned to London to start his career as a professional painter and by the time of his 2005 solo show Nostalgic Journeys, at the Albemarle Gallery, had completed over 100 commissions. These included Prince Jeffrey of Brunei, The Duke and Duchess of St Albans, The Earl of Bradford, The Countess of Effingham and Lord Selsdon, also "many notable captains of industry and commerce as well as celebrities in the world of film, theatre and television." Among these were Julian Fellowes, whose screenplay for the 2001 film *Gosford Park* won him an Academy Award, and the singer and television presenter Cilla Black. As well as portraits, the Albemarle exhibition included scenes blending romanticism and realism. Among Heathcote's later exhibitions were the RP, from 2002; Guildhall, 2003; and New Grafton Gallery, RBA and RA Summer Exhibition, all 2004.

Marjorie HEATHER 1904–1989 Painter of semi-caricature figure groups in oil and watercolour, born and lived in Newbury, Berkshire. She believed in the importance of line drawing, constantly carried a sketch-book, saying that it was "essential to sketch as fast as you write", working up paintings in her studio which retained a strong outline. As a mature student Heather attended Ruskin School of Drawing, Oxford, 1945–8, under Albert Rutherston, winning prizes for figure composition and still life painting; then was at Byam Shaw School of Drawing and Painting, 1948–50. For 30 years her work was selected regularly for RA, RWS, RP and other galleries in the provinces and abroad. She was a founder-member in 1947 of Newbury Art Group and helped set up the Bussock Mayne Group. A memorial show was held at Newbury District Museum in 1991.

Thomas HEATHERWICK 1970– Heatherwick was a versatile and imaginative designer who created the tallest sculpture in Britain when it was unveiled in 2005: B of the Bang, at the City of Manchester Stadium. Like an exploding star, it was as high as Nelson's Column, wide as the Bank of England and comprised 180 tapering steel spikes. Its inauguration was by the athlete Linford Christie, whose statement that if you want to win Olympic gold you must leave the starting blocks "on the B of the bang" had inspired Heatherwick. The designer stemmed from a creative family. His grandmother was a designer who ran Marks & Spencer's textile studio; his father was a musician; and his mother started the Bead Society of Great Britain and ran the Bead Shop in Portobello Road. Heatherwick followed design courses at Manchester Polytechnic and the Royal College of Art, where his talent was spotted by Terence Conran. Among other notable Heatherwick creations were Bleigiessen, at the Wellcome Trust, 150,000 glass beads strung up through six storeys; the Rolling Bridge, at Paddington Basin, that coiled and uncoiled, powered by hydraulic pistons; Sitooterie, at Belsay Hall, Northumberland, described as "a new sort of summerhouse...with hairy walls"; and Blue Carpet, Newcastle upon Tyne, a public square carpeted with blue glass. Heatherwick's studio was at King's Cross, London.

Cecil HEATHFIELD 1893–1969 Artist, commercial designer, teacher and administrator, born in Croydon, Surrey, who studied at the School of Art there and at the London County Council Bolt Court School, under Walter Bayes. When his first wife, Dorrie, was appointed head of a school in Polegate, Heathfield moved to Sussex, travelling to London daily to work as a commercial artist. Early in the war, when work diminished, he gave up the London studio and stayed in Sussex. Settled in Lewes, Heathfield aimed to bring art to a wider public, teaching in the prison, running a social club for teenage evacuees and holding classes in villages. He became art adviser to East Sussex Education Committee, was a governor of Brighton College of Art and chairman of Lewes Theatre Club. After Dorrie died in 1941, Heathfield married the Lewes-born artist Evelyn Fawsset and converted derelict stables into Paddock Studios, where classes were held and they showed work jointly. Among Heathfield's solo exhibitions was one at County Town Gallery, Lewes, in 1961, which showed him turning towards abstraction, Surrealism and collage. He was noted as a fine draughtsman. Heathfield was a prominent member of Brighton and Lewes Art Clubs, Eastbourne Society of Artists and Battle Arts Group. When Evelyn died in 1980, aged 87, she gave Paddock Studios to East Sussex County Council under the auspices of the Charity Commission, and in various guises they continued to be used for teaching and exhibitions.

Bobby HEAVEN 1922– Artist in oil, oil pastel, acrylic and stained glass, born in Rochdale, Lancashire, correct name Elizabeth Anne Heaven. Attended Bristol Polytechnic/Filton College for many years from 1975, one tutor being Anthony Rossiter. Heaven painted landscapes and made sketches in Provence, Ireland and the Somerset area where she lived at Clevedon, using a distinctive and colourful palette. Showed with RA, RWA, Clifton and Clevedon Art Clubs, Bath Society of Artists, ROI and Lynda Cotton Gallery at Watchet. Had a solo show at Pier Gallery, Clevedon, 1991, and The Court Gallery, Nether Stowey, 1994. She appeared in Chris Chapman's Channel 4 television series *Secrets of the Moor*, shown in 1996.

Eric HEBBORN 1934–1996 Draughtsman, sculptor, painter, teacher, writer and faker of Old Master and some modern drawings, born in London the son of a grocer's assistant. As a boy he was sent to Borstal but became interested in art and attended Chelmsford Art School, 1949–51, under Charles Archer, then Walthamstow Art School under Stuart Ray and Kurt Roland. While studying at Royal Academy Schools, 1955–8, he won a number of scholarships and prizes, including the Silver Medal and Hacker Portrait Prize. Spent two years in Italy having won the Rome Scholarship in Engraving for 1959. He taught at Walthamstow and Reigate and Redhill School of Art. Having worked for a time as a restorer and being interested in the techniques of the Old Masters, he set up Pannini Galleries Ltd in London, eventually moving to Italy, where he settled in Anticoli. Many drawings in the styles of the Old Masters fooled the experts, exchanged hands for large sums and entered notable collections, as told in Hebborn's entertaining book *Drawn To Trouble, The Forging Of An Artist*, 1991. Hebborn showed his own work, too, having a successful show of sculptures at Alwin Gallery, 1978, after a large retrospective at the British School, Rome, where he had studied. In 1994 Julian Hartnoll and Archeus Fine Art organised extensive shows. Died in Rome in mysterious circumstances, a magistrate suggesting homicide, in reality a drunken fall.

Nadia HEBSON 1974– Artist who attended Harrogate College of Art, 1992–3; gained an honours degree in painting at Central St Martins College of Art, 1993–6; then did a postgraduate diploma at the Royal Academy Schools, 1997–00, taking part in the final year show and later that year having a solo exhibition at Elgin. Awards and sponsorships included a drawing residency, Stowupland High School, Suffolk, 1997; British Institution Drawing Prize and Cohn & Wolfe Painting Prize, both 1998; and Vincent Harris Prize, 1999. By the time of the Elgin show Hebson had exhibited with the Contemporary Art Society, the RA, in the BP Portrait Award and elsewhere. Hebson produced intimate and engrossing paintings on copper with a mysterious narrative quality, also large pencil drawings. A small garden shed, filled with personal belongings and left as a tiny, very private artist's studio, was included in Hebson's degree show and reinstalled at Elgin. Hebson's installation Phantasmagoria was shown at Chapter Arts Centre, Cardiff, and her theatrical installation Goria at Transition, both in 2003. Cohn & Wolfe and Museum of Modern Art, Senigállia, Italy, hold her work.

Godfrey HECHT 1902–1980 Painter in oil, gouache and other media of an experimental bent. Born in London, where he continued to live, Hecht was educated at Downside School. Exhibited in mixed shows with the Free Painters and Sculptors, ROI, NS and SGA. One-man show at the Woodstock Gallery. Hecht was a member of the Reform Club.

Peter HEDEGAARD 1929– Architect and artist whose works included rectangular abstracts, born in Copenhagen, Denmark. He studied at Oxford University and Bartlett School of Architecture. Solo shows included Architectural Association, 1967; Curwen Gallery, 1969; Consort Gallery at Imperial College, 1974; and Peterloo Gallery in Manchester and Oxford Gallery, Oxford, both 1976. In 1981 he was included in Contemporary Artists in Camden at Burgh House, Hampstead, near where he lived. Victoria & Albert Museum; Sussex and Salford Universities; and public galleries in Belfast, Bolton, Hull and Sheffield hold examples.

Ray HEDGER 1944– Painter, printmaker, artist in film and performance, and teacher, born in Wiltshire. He studied at Gloucestershire College of Art, in Cheltenham graduating with honours in fine art and film in 1979, and at Central School of Art, having gained his National

Diploma in 1964. Hedger tried to create an image embracing "that single moment when one sees something that no camera is capable of capturing because it contains so many elements beyond the 'real' and the present." He was a member of SWE, illustrated two poetry anthologies and made a film based on the book *Crow* by Ted Hughes. Was also involved in creating a dance piece with the dancer Alex Howard, music by the Czech composer Pavel Novak. Mixed shows included Fitzwilliam Museum and Kettle's Yard, Cambridge; Oxfam tour Art for a Fairer World; Birmingham City Museum & Art Gallery; and Contemporary Art Holdings, Cheltenham. Solo shows included The Nude and Landscape, Cheltenham Art Gallery & Museum, 1994; similar show at Halifax House, Oxford, 1995; 30 paintings in windows, Harrods, 1998; Two Views, Corninium Museum, Cirencester, 1999; and Opening Show, Brinkworth Business and Exhibition Centre, Malmesbury, 2004. From 1990, Hedger taught part-time at Brewer Arts and ACE, both in Cirencester. Lived in Fairford, Gloucestershire.

Russell HEDGES 1945– Painter whose work inclined towards abstraction, generally on a large scale. Brought up in Buckinghamshire, Hedges as a young man was a musician in Cornwall, then attended Norwich School of Art, 1978–82, and Chelsea School of Art, 1982–3. He returned to Cornwall, living in Penzance, and showed with Newlyn Society of Artists and elsewhere. His picture Moon Anchor was included in the 1989 Newlyn Orion Galleries exhibition A Century of Art in Cornwall 1889–1989.

Dora HEDGES 1881–c.1955 Painter and potter, born in Sheffield, Yorkshire. After education at Derby High School she studied at Chiswick School of Art and the Royal College of Art. Although she was an exhibitor at SWA and RWS she was better known as a potter, writing the book *Pottery in the Making* and having her work accepted by the Victoria & Albert Museum. She was married to the artist Richard Lunn and sometimes exhibited under the name Dora Lunn, notably at Walker Art Gallery, Liverpool, before World War II.

Roger HEDLEY 1879–1972 Sculptor who should be more widely known for several fine war memorials. When Roger's genre painter father Ralph died in 1913, his Newcastle upon Tyne carving firm was taken over by Roger and his brother Fred. During Fred's World War I Army absence Roger kept the business afloat by evening work while helping to make wooden-frame aircraft during the day. After the war Hedley directed the figure-carving and masonry side of business and in Northumberland created two fine bronze war memorials, at Alnwick, unveiled 1922, and that for Swan Hunter at Wallsend, 1925. Another notable sculpture by Hedley is a head for the monument dominating Newcastle's city centre erected in 1838 to Earl Grey, who spearheaded the 1832 Reform Bill. After lightning toppled the original head in 1941 Hedley carved a replacement, restoration carried out early in 1948. Hedley relinquished the family business in 1960.

Christopher HEDLEY-DENT 1952– Self-taught painter, printmaker, designer and teacher who was "interested in synthesising abstract and figurative elements to express ideas and feelings.... Design and colour orchestration are the most essential parts of my language". An example was his solo show at The Alchemy Gallery, 1999, in which circus pictures explored "the image of the clown and his or her very ambiguous relationship to the audience and fellow performers". From 1986 Hedley-Dent was head of art at Westminster Cathedral Choir School. Commissions included a compact disc cover for Hyperion. In 1997 he was artist-in-residence at the first Mind Sports Olympiad, held in the Royal Festival Hall, which spawned a series of games pictures. Hedley-Dent moved to Spreyton, Devon, in the mid-1990s, prompting an interest in on-the-spot paintings of the Dartmoor area. He was also a poet and keen amateur jazz musician.

Crispin HEESOM 1950– Artist notable for landscapes "not concerned with topographical detail, but with light, mood, dreams and memories inspired by the places". He was born in Oundle, Northamptonshire, and settled nearby at King's Cliffe. Studied at Norwich School of Art, 1970, then Byam Shaw School of Painting and Drawing, 1971–3. Exhibitions included The Museum, Ashton, 1979; The Annexe Gallery, Wimbledon (Group Show), 1980; Peterborough Museum & Art Gallery, 1984; Stamford Arts Centre, 1985; Art '87, at Peterborough's Lady Lodge Arts Centre (Group Show), 1987; and Green Man Exhibition, Yarrow Gallery, Oundle (Group Show), 1995. Dolby Gallery, Oundle, where Heesom showed frequently, gave him a solo exhibition in 2005, displaying his fluid drawing style and vibrant colour. In 1982 Heesom carried out a mural commission in Girdlers Road, Hammersmith.

David HEGARTY 1967– Artist who said that "experience and sensation" were the key elements of his work, a search for the "unanswerable". His figurative-based, painterly output projected a sensation or felt experience rather than an actual figure. Hegarty did foundation studies at Crawley College of Technology, 1984–6; graduated with honours in graphic design at Leeds Polytechnic, 1986–9; obtaining a postgraduate diploma in painting at the Royal Academy Schools, 1995–8, showing abstract work in the final year show. Mixed exhibitions included Nigel Greenwood Gallery, 1989; ROI and Winsor & Newton Young Artists Award, Mall Galleries, 1993; Making a Mark, Mall Galleries, 1996; and in 1998 Premiums at RA and Majestic/ Domestic, Hammerson plc. Hegarty had solo shows at St Marylebone Crypt, 1995, and the Institute of Physics, 1997. The Victoria & Albert Museum holds his work. Lived in London.

Celia HEGEDÜS 1949– Minutely accurate botanical artist working in watercolour on vellum, born in London, who studied at Hammersmith Art School, 1966, and City & Guilds, 1967. Hegedüs especially admired the work of Da Vinci, Ligozzi, van der Goes, Ehret, Kouwenhoorn, Redouté and Rory McEwen. She won Gold Medals in 1995, 1996, 1998, 2000 and 2001 from the Royal Horticultural Society. Its Lindley Library and The Shirley Sherwood Collection hold her work. She also exhibited with the Society of Botanical Artists and the RA Summer Exhibition, and had solo shows at Waterman Fine Art, 1995, and Offer Waterman, 1999 and 2001.

Bé van der HEIDE 1938– Painter, muralist, printmaker and teacher, born in the Netherlands, who studied painting at the Academy for Fine Arts in Enschede, 1956–60, also in Montreal, Canada, having emigrated in 1960. Travelled extensively in Middle East and Africa, returning to Canada in 1964, and in 1967 was commissioned to produce a large mural, in nails on board, for the Dutch pavilion at Expo '76, Montreal. After three years in Istanbul, Turkey, in the late 1960s, returned to Montreal in 1970, moving to London in 1982. She took part in the Triangle workshop in New York in 1984 and in 1992 was guest artist of the Outer Mongolian Artist Union. Participated in numerous group show around the world, including Links of Affinity, Knapp Gallery, 1989, and had many solo exhibitions, starting with Rijksmuseum Twenthe, Enschede, 1963, later ones including Bruton Street Gallery, 1992; Powell Moya Partnership, 1993; and Chancery Gallery, Royal Netherlands Embassy, 1994. City of Enschede; Bibliothèque Nationale de Quebec; National Film Board of Canada; Quebec Government; and several corporate collections own examples.

Robert HEINDEL 1938–2005 Prolific artist, born in Toledo, Ohio, America, who was based in Connecticut. Heindel was a commercial artist in the 1960s and 1970s, working through a New York agency, before moving into fine art and exhibiting. He began to paint dance and dancers in the late 1970s, and in 1984 was invited to work with the Royal Ballet in London. His painting of Sir Frederick Ashton, its artistic director, is in the National Portrait Gallery collection. During 1984–05, Heindel worked by invitation with many of the world's leading dance and theatre companies, including the San Francisco Ballet, American Ballet Theatre and Les Ballets de Monte Carlo. Among British companies he depicted were the Birmingham Royal Ballet, Rambert Dance Company, London City Ballet, London Festival Ballet and Scottish Ballet, a work from the last series being held in the Glasgow Museums collection. The many noted performers he portrayed included Michael Crawford, Anthony Dowell, Elaine Paige and Tommy Steele. Lord Andrew Lloyd Webber invited Heindel to paint and sketch impressions from his musical theatre productions *Cats* and *The Phantom of the Opera*. The Noh Theatre of Japan was another Heindel subject. Heindel had numerous solo shows throughout America, Europe and Japan, those in Britain latterly including The Halcyon Gallery, 2004; Princes Square, Glasgow, 2005; and Glasgow Royal Concert Hall, 2006. Obsession Publishing, Holt, also sold his paintings and prints.

Michael HEINDORFF 1949– Painter, highly versatile printmaker and teacher, Heindorff attended art college and University of Braunschweig, in Germany, 1970–4. He gained a German National Scholarship, 1972–6, and a DAAD Scholarship for London, 1976–7, attending Royal College of Art, 1975–7. Heindorff was at home in various media and styles, although over the years he edged away from figuration to abstraction. He won an award at John Moores Exhibition in Liverpool in 1976, a few years later gaining the Schmidt-Rottluff Prize and the Villa Massimo Prize, in Rome. A retrospective of his work covering the decade from 1977 was held at Northern Centre for Contemporary Arts in 1987. For many years his pictures were handled by Bernard Jacobson in London and New York. Arts Council holds. Heindorff taught at Royal College of Art from 1980 and was included in its Exhibition Road show in 1988. In 2002, Heindorff, who insisted that he "paints with pencil," at Guildhall Art Gallery showed panoramic views of the City of London and beyond done from the top of nine churches. Lived in London.

HEL: *see* **Helen GRUNWALD**

Julie HELD 1958– Painter and teacher, born in London where she continued to work. Studied for bachelor's degree in fine art-painting at Camberwell School of Art, 1977–81, then did postgraduate diploma at Royal Academy Schools, 1982–5. Taught widely from 1981 including Kingston Polytechnic and University of Wolverhampton. Held won the Philip Matthews Prize, 1980; a Stanley Picker Fellowship at Kingston, 1981–2; first prize in Royal Over-Seas League Annual Exhibition, 1984; and Lucy Morrison Prize at same exhibition, 1987; commendation: highly commended, Chichester Open Art Exhibition, 1999; and was elected to the LG, 2002. Mixed shows included Whitechapel Art Gallery, 1977; Boundary Gallery from 1988; RA Summer Exhibition, 1992 onwards; Singer & Friedlander/*Sunday Times* Watercolour Competition, 1998; and The Ben Uri Story, 1915–2000, Phillips, 2001. Had many solo exhibitions, later ones including Piccadilly Gallery, 1996; Boundary Gallery, 1999; Sternberg Centre, 2001; and Paintings in Hospital, Sheridan Russell Gallery, 2002. In 2003, Held's work Journey, a 12-panel polyptych full of classical, Jewish and Christian symbolism, was unveiled in the Vicar's Hall, Chichester Cathedral precincts. Keele University and Nuffield College at Oxford University hold her work.

HELEN 1917– Painter and draughtsman, full name Helen Burrough, who was born in Ceylon. She was married to the artist Thomas Hedley Bruce Burrough. Studied from 1937–9 in London and Stockholm and showed in mixed exhibitions including RWA, of which she was a member. Lived for many years at Frenchay, near Bristol.

HELEN: *see* **Helen GRUNWALD**

Richard HELEY 1950– Painter, draughtsman, teacher, performance painter and writer/performer of poetry, short stories and children's stories, born in Totternhoe, Bedfordshire. Aged 15, he emigrated with his family to Australia. Although he wished to attend art school, family economics dictated a teacher-training course at Melbourne College of Education, 1969–73. He graduated as an art and craft specialist. Eventually Heley returned to England, but frequent visits to Australia and the islands of Indonesia influenced his palette, from which flowed richly exuberant and imaginative images, as shown in a solo exhibition at Duncan Campbell Fine Art in 2005. He also showed work at the Eagle Gallery. In 1997 Heley was Farrago Poetry Slam Champion and between 1998–03 was resident live performance painter at the Dutch Pot, London. In Britain his appearances included the Notting Hill Carnival, London Zoo and Glastonbury Festival of the Arts. He also appeared frequently at festivals in America, venues including Los Angeles, Houston and Austin, and in schools in Victoria, Australia.

Rachel HELLER 1973– Artist born in London who attended Kingsway College, 1991–3; Leighton Project, Elfrida Rathbone, 1993–4; Hammersmith and West London College, 1994–9; life class, Byam Shaw School of Art, 1994–8, and foundation there, 1999–00; studied figurative painting, Slade Summer School, 2000; then gained her diploma at Byam Shaw, 2000–1. In 2001 she was for a time involved in the Prince's Foundation. Group shows included Small is Beautiful, Part 13: Food and Drink,

Flowers East, 1995, and its successors through to Part 18: Self Portrait, 2000, and RA Summer Exhibition, 2001. Had a solo exhibition at John Jones Art Centre, 1995, with a series at Gallery M from 1997.

Jack HELLEWELL 1920–2000 Artist in acrylic on canvas and paper whose work included abstracted landscapes. He never sketched or painted these on site, believing that it "ties you down", and they were sometimes produced years later from memory. Hellewell was born in Bradford, Yorkshire. After World War II service in Egypt, North Africa and Italy, he trained as a painter at Bradford College of Art, 1949–52, working as a graphic designer until 1976, when he began painting full-time. Worked on the edge of Ilkley Moor, which provided inspiration. Travelled widely abroad with his family, the intense light of warmer climates, such as Australia and the South Seas, contributing to his output. Showed widely, including RBA; Sloane Street, Seen, Railings and Chenil Galleries; MAFA; Wakefield City Art Gallery; Linton Gallery, Settle; Kentmere House Gallery, York; and was included in Images of the Yorkshire Landscape, organised by Sheeran Lock at Leeds Civic Hall, 1991. Solo exhibitions included Manor House, 1990, and Gascoigne Gallery, 2002, both in Ilkley, and Broughton House Gallery, Cambridge, 2005. British Rail, National Power, other corporate collections and Rochdale and Manchester City Art Galleries held examples.

Glenn HELLMAN 1938– Sculptor and teacher, born in Walthamstow, north London. Studied at the local art school, 1959–61, then at Hornsey College of Art under Robert Adams, 1961–4. In 1964 Hellman came into prominence as the winner of a nationwide sculpture competition. He was Robert Adams' assistant, 1964–6, and had several one-man shows at Leicester Galleries, Roland, Browse and Delbanco and Morley Gallery in subsequent years. Taught at Southampton School of Art, Winchester College of Art, Morley College and Goldsmiths' College School of Art. His Twosome, in bronzed steel, of 1970, was shown with The Roland Collection at Camden Arts Centre, 1976. Hellman's Eagle, 1982, in aluminium, stands on a huge slate megalith in Caernarvon. He won a number of prizes, notably at the National Eisteddfod in Wales, where he lived in Pontrhydfendigaid, Cardigan.

Marianne HELLWIG JOHN 1930– Painter, especially in acrylic, collagist, teacher and poet, born in Breslau, Germany (now Wrocław, Poland), who moved to Scotland in 1939. She was married to the sculptor David John. Studied at Liverpool School of Art, for sculpture with Karel Vogel, 1945–50; St Martin's School of Art, with Frederick Gore for painting, 1950–1; and at London University Institute of Education, with William Newland for pottery. Worked in administration for overseas students and the editorial section of the British Council, 1968–88, for nine years in the 1960s and 1970s teaching painting to adults at Woodley Hill House, near Reading. Hellwig John began painting abstracts in the 1960s, creating collage in the 1990s, "colour, structure and balance being important in my work.... Each time I start a picture I am looking for something, but won't know what it is till I find it.... There is a landscape sense to much of my work." Hepworth, Sutherland, van Gogh, Nolde, the Impressionists, Cézanne and Bonnard were quoted as early influences. She was a fellow of Free Painters and Sculptors, other group shows including RWA, 1991; National Acrylic Painters' Association (of which she was a member), Birmingham, 1995; Courtyard Gallery, Chepstow, 1996; and Museum and Art Gallery, Reading, 2000. Two-man shows included Ben Uri, 1984; Rathaus Galerie, Münster, Germany, 1992; and City Museum & Art Gallery, Gloucester, 1995. Among her later solo exhibitions were the Galerie Collis, Lausanne, Switzerland, 1995, and Guildhall Arts Centre, Gloucester, 1998. Later church painting commissions included a large Tree of Life for St Francis, Long Eaton, 1995, and The Holy Spirit, St Bartholomew, Norbury, 1996. She was a published poet as Hellwig John, her poetry and paintings book *English as a Foreign Language* appearing in 2000. Hellwig-John sometimes appears hyphenated. Lived in Stroud, Gloucestershire.

Jeff HELLYER 1947– Artist and teacher, born Oxford, who studied part-time at Ruskin School of Drawing, 1964–7, then did a foundation course at Oxford Polytechnic, 1967–8; studied painting at Chelsea School of Art, 1968–71, then painting and mixed media at Slade School of Fine Art, 1971–3. In 1973 won a Boise scholarship to study in France and Italy and until 1981 taught part-time at many colleges including Cheltenham, Chelsea, Ravensbourne, Bath, Portsmouth and Reading. From 1981 taught at Falmouth School of Art. In 1990 Hellyer was artist-in-residence at the School of Painting, Montmirral, Tarn, France. Showed widely from 1977 on the continent, also at Annely Juda Fine Art, Newlyn Orion Gallery and Penwith Gallery in Cornwall, where he lived in Falmouth. In 1994 Hellyer was included in Falmouth Connections at the town's Art Gallery.

Francis HELPS 1890–1972 Painter, draughtsman and teacher, born in Dulwich, southeast London. At Dulwich College, 1903–7, Helps was the only boy to take art lessons and had a private tutor. In 1908 went to Slade School of Fine Art, where taught by Henry Tonks and Fred Brown. In 1915 Helps volunteered for service with Artists' Rifles, serving in France. In 1924 he joined the 1922–4 Everest Expedition as official artist, completing 80 paintings and drawings, most now in America. Between 1931–4 Helps taught at Royal College of Art, then volunteered to be evacuated with it to Ambleside, in the Lake District, 1940–4. From 1953 until his retirement Helps was head of the school of painting in Leeds, where he settled, returning in his last year to Bromley, Kent. Helps showed with RBA, of which he was elected a member in 1933, and in 1924 had a show at Alpine Club Gallery of his Himalayan work. Further shows were at City Art Gallery, Leeds, 1959; Manor House Museum and Art Gallery, Ilkley, 1971; and South London Art Gallery, 1979.

Alison HELYER 1965– Painter, born in Cleveland, where she attended Cleveland College of Art, 1983–4, De Montfort University, Leicester, 1984–7, then Chelsea College of Art, 1991–2. Awards included Prince's Trust Bursary and Exhibition Award Northern Arts, both 1992. Mixed shows included Fab Four at Loseby Lane Gallery, Leicester, 1989, Whitechapel Open at Atlantis Gallery, 1994, and in that year she shared a three-man exhibition at Paton Gallery, showing huge toy dogs blown up on a white ground.

Nicholas HELY HUTCHINSON 1955– Painter, influenced initially by Dufy and Matisse, also drawing on the English Neo-Romantic tradition. He settled near Blandford, Dorset, and the countryside of that county and Wiltshire, horse racing, interiors and still life were among his subjects.

Studied at St Martin's School of Art and Bristol Polytechnic. Showed solo with Montpelier Studio from 1984, later exhibitions including Wattis Fine Art, Hong Kong, from 1992, The Jerram Gallery, Salisbury, 1995, Portland Gallery, from 1997, and Frederick Gallery, Dublin, Ireland, from 2000. Government Art Collection, Barbican Centre and Unilever hold examples. Hely Hutchinson was the third son of the 8th Earl of Donoughmore, an old Irish family.

Tim HEMINGTON 1968– Artist seeking to eliminate barriers between art and reality, producing works on the edge of painting and sculpture, as in his solo show at Andrew Mummery Gallery, 1999. With the wall or floor as ground and gallery as a frame the viewer entered the painting, located between frame and image. Hemington was born in Cheshire, attending its School of Art, 1987–8, then obtained a fine art degree at Ruskin School of Drawing and Fine Art, Oxford, 1988–91, attending the Cyprus School of Art in Britain, 1990. After living and working in Berlin, Germany, 1991–5, Hemington gained his master's degree in post-war and contemporary art, Sotheby's Institute, 1995–6, then was a Henry Moore Fellow, Byam Shaw School of Art, 1998. Later group shows included Galerie Kley, Hamm, Germany, from 1995; Deutsche Multiple Sklerose Gesellschaft Austellung, Galerie am See, Tiergarten, and Galerie Raphael Vostell, Berlin, 1996; and Stages, Lee Fine Arts/Wirral Museums, Eastern Village Gallery & Tramshed, Birkenhead, 1997. Deutsche Bank holds his work. Lived in London.

Andrew HEMINGWAY 1955– Painter, born and lived in Yorkshire, who studied at Barnsley School of Art, 1973–4, then Camberwell School of Art, 1974–7. With the aid of a bursary he travelled to Italy and Norway, 1977–8, being sent under private sponsorship to Japan to paint landscapes. He showed at RA from 1980, the year he began exhibiting in mixed shows at Piccadilly Gallery. In the 1980s he appeared in Basle, Düsseldorf and Cologne International Art Fairs. After a solo show at Johnston Gallery, Edmonton, Alberta, in 1978, others included a series at Piccadilly Gallery from 1981 and a major show at Brian Sinfield, Burford, 1993. In 1994, a film was made for Dutch television about his life and work. Hemingway was a slow, meticulous worker, notably in egg tempera and pastel, producing only about 30 pictures a year.

Charles HEMINGWAY 1909–1976 Artist and teacher, born in Strichen, Aberdeenshire, where the local school, directed by Benjamin Skinner, set high standards, Hemingway leaving with an excellent academic record. After studying at Gray's School of Art, Aberdeen, Hemingway tried to live as a painter in Paris and London, after which he taught in Inverness, then returned to teach at Gray's. A colleague, James Cowie, and El Greco were early influences. Aged 27, Hemingway joined the staff of Aberdeen Grammar School, students remembering his eccentric, volatile and humorous style and commitment as an artist. During World War II Hemingway joined the Royal Engineers, then the Army Education Corps, was involved in aerial photographic reconnaissance and served in India. Returning to the Grammar School, Hemingway developed his department, inviting Bernard Leach to lecture to the new pottery group, setting up a film society and theatre as well as a film society in Aberdeen. He exhibited with the RA, RSA and the Aberdeen Artists Society and carried out prestigious commission portraits, including Sir David Campbell, for Aberdeen University. Hemingway's later work became less rigid, with freer handling of paint, a more courageous use of colour and the influence of Surrealism evident. An exhibition of work by Hemingway and his pupils was held at Aberdeen Art Gallery in 1994 and Bonhams & Brooks, Lots Road, sold a group of Hemingways in 2000.

Harold HEMINGWAY 1908–1976 Painter, draughtsman and designer, born and based in Rochdale, Lancashire, best known for his depictions of the town between 1930–70. In the 1950s Hemingway and L S Lowry would walk around Rochdale, selecting planned-for-demolition buildings which should be recorded using Hemingway's distinctive colour and light. The son of a painter and decorator, Hemingway left school at 13 and worked at John Bright's Mill, eventually as a carpet designer. While working he trained at the local Art School, winning many awards for the design of fabrics, carpets and posters. Hemingway was a member of Rochdale Art Society and the Lancashire Group of Artists and undertook several commissions for Rochdale Corporation. His set designs for Rochdale Curtain Theatre formed the basis of his first exhibition in 1938, and subsequent shows, as well as London and Cambridge, were held widely in Lancashire. Rochdale Art Gallery has eight of his works, which in all are reckoned to number over 1,000.

Gordon HEMM 1891–1956 Architectural artist, born in Stockport, Cheshire, who was also an architect and member of RIBA. Studied architecture under Charles Reilly at Liverpool University and at Liverpool School of Art. Hemm was notable for his collaboration with the sculptor Charles John Allen on the University's war memorial in 1927, at which time he was a partner in the practice Foden, Hemm and Williams, based in Liverpool and Manchester. He wrote several books on Merseyside architecture. Exhibited Walker Art Gallery, Liverpool, and RA. Lived in Manchester.

Adrian HEMMING 1945– Painter and lecturer, producing colourful, exuberant landscapes and seascapes who travelled widely, favouring locations with "a deep sense of ancient history." Born in Leicester Hemming left school at 15, finished an engineering apprenticeship, then began to travel and develop a love of art. Encouraged by a local businessman, in 1969 he was accepted for a foundation course at Lincoln College of Art; graduated from Brighton Polytechnic, 1970–3; and gained his master's at Goldsmiths' College, 1980–2. Studies at the British School at Rome in the late 1970s and early 1980s were important. Hemming based himself in London from the mid-1980s, forming Angel Studios, then Southgate Studios. In 1994 he was commissioned by British Airports Authority to create large works based on aviation, installed at Terminal One, Heathrow Airport. He was twice shortlisted for a residency at the National Gallery. Hemming showed solo with Davies & Tooth from 1997.

Alun HEMMING 1954– Sculptor and lecturer, born in Blaengarw, Glamorgan, who attended Maidstone College of Art, 1972–6, and Goldsmiths' College, 1976–7. He was a part-time adult education lecturer. Hemming won 2nd Prize, Singleton Sculpture Competition, in 1980. In 1981, he was commissioned to make a large work for Appin Project Management in conjunction with Singleton, organised by Kent County Council Group. Mixed exhibitions included 55 Wapping Artists, 1979; Lena Garnade Memorial Exhibition, Farnham College of Art, 1980; and Wapping Artists Open Studios, 1982, when he was living in southwest London. After in 1984 moving to Plaistow with fellow-sculptor Souheil Sleiman and textile artist Hilary Sleiman, where they supported their work by designing and building furniture, in 1987 Hemming returned to south Wales, establishing a studio in the Old Library, Cardiff. In 1996, with the artist Anthony Evans, he built the set for the S4C animation film *Captain Factor*. Along with 30 other artists, Hemming founded the artists' co-operative Old Library Artists Ltd and served as its first secretary. A WAC grant enabled it to enter new premises, Oriel Canfas Gallery, in 1998. Hemming was a prolific and versatile exhibitor, later shows including a joint exhibition at Mary Ogilvie Gallery, St Anne's College, Oxford, 2003; Living for the city, Blue Wing Gallery, London, 2004, the year he completed a book cover for Patrick McGuinness' Carcanet Press volume *The Canals of Mars*; and in 2005 mixed shows at Blue Wing Gallery, Padstow, Kooy-Wood Gallery, Cardiff, and elsewhere.

Charles HEMMING: *see* **Laurence Charles HEMMING**

Laurence Charles HEMMING 1950– Artist in oil, acrylic, watercolour and pen and ink, born in Mynythislwyn, near Pontllanfraith, Monmouthshire. He studied at Goldsmiths' College, London University, 1973–7, notable teachers including Ivor Roberts-Jones, Carl Plackman, Michael Kenny and Peter Creswell. Hemming, who sometimes signed his work Charles Hemming, sometimes L C H, was originally concerned with conceptual sculpture, poetry related to 3D objects, which developed into an interest in illusion in objects and surfaces and in writing and illustration. Andrew Wyeth, Edward Hopper, Magritte, Arthur Rackham, Aubrey Beardsley, Rex Whistler and Osbert Lancaster were special influences. Decorative work for the Travellers' Club and Institute of Directors, the College of Arms and Sheikh of Dubai were among principal works. In 1990 Hemming was reserve decorative artist for the National Trust. From 1992 he did extensive book illustration and cartoon work for Ravette Books. His own books included *Paint Finishes*, 1985, and *British Painters of the Coast and Sea* and *British Landscape Painters*, 1988–9, the latter winning the *Yorkshire Post* Book Prize, 1989. His later books included *The Complete Paint Book*, 1995, and *The Folding Screen*, 1999. From 1997, Hemming completed murals for the Duke of Norfolk and Covent Garden. He showed at Radlett Gallery, Radlett, 1978; Francis Kyle Gallery, 1981–2; and Portal Gallery, 1979–83. Lived in London.

Rachel HEMMING BRAY 1947– Born in London, painter and draughtsman working in oil, watercolour, pastel and drawings in all media, and teacher. Studied at Central School of Art, London, 1965, and College of St Mathias, Bristol 1966–9. Showed in mixed exhibitions at RA and RWA, and many one-man shows, including George's Gallery, Bristol 1981–82, Rooksmoor Gallery, Bath, 1985, Pelter/Sands, Bristol 1988, National Theatre, South Bank, London, 1991 and Bristol City Art Gallery, 1994. Worked regularly on individual and small group portraits, and in 1990s developed something of a niche in corporate commissions of people in their working environments. These latter she likened to "the manner of a war artist, with the subjects not 'sitting' for their portraits, and my having to cope with a great deal of movement". Such commissions included Bristol Old Vic, Theatre Royal; BBC Natural History Dept; Bristol City Museums and Art Gallery, and musicians at the Pump Room, Bath. Also painted landscapes, interiors and works of memory and imagination. Corporations holding her work include Bristol City Museums and Art Gallery, BBC Art Collection, University of Bristol Theatre Collection and Nat West Life Collection. Lived in Bristol.

David HEMMINGS 1941–2003 Actor, writer, producer and film director, born in Guildford, Surrey, whose first love was painting, "the backbone" of his other work. "Every actor attempts to create a portrait of the character he is playing and every director is working with pictures." Hemmings achieved fame in the 1966 cult film *Blow-Up*. His career had begun 18 years earlier as a boy soprano with the English Opera Group. His movies included *Camelot*, 1967, *Barbarella*, 1967, and *The Charge of the Light Brigade*, 1968; he directed film and television, including *Murder, She Wrote*, *Quantum Leap* and *The A-Team*; he latterly starred in the television pilot for *The Vanishing Man*, 1997, and appeared in Stephen Spielberg's film *Gladiator*, 1992, and Fred Shepisi's adaptation of Graham Swift's Booker Prize-winning novel, *Last Orders*, 2001. An art teacher boarded with Hemmings' grandmother impressed on him "the necessity of observation, draughtsmanship and the need to forget the rules and feel." Hemmings exhibited for over 30 years. His paintings and drawings were used in books on portraiture, he created storyboards for television and films and designed for the theatre. Portraits included the actor George C Scott, singer and actress Liza Minelli and the song writers Jimmy Webb, Leslie Bricusse and Harry Nillson. Hemmings' exhibitions included several at The Osborne Studio Gallery, one in 1999 celebrating his love of the turf and Henley Regatta, brightly coloured pictures bordering on caricature. After working many years in America, he lived in Wiltshire and Scotland. He died in Romania while shooting a film. In 2004, his 1960s-related CD *David Hemmings Happens* and his autobiography *Blow-Up and other Exaggerations* both appeared posthumously.

Michael HEMPSTEAD 1956– Artist who graduated with honours from Camberwell School of Art, 1975–8, winning the Alfred Munnings Award in the earlier year, attending the Slade School of Fine Art, 1978–80. Mixed shows included the Chicago Art Fair, in America, 1988, and East End Open Studios, at Carpenter's Road, 1989. Had a solo exhibition at Janus Avivson Gallery, 1988. Private collections in England, on the continent and in America held examples.

Paul HEMPTON 1946– Painter, printmaker and teacher, born in Wakefield, Yorkshire. He studied at Goldsmiths' College School of Art, 1964–8, teachers including Andrew Forge, and at Royal College of Art, 1968–71, with Carel Weight, and obtained his master's degree. He taught at Wolverhampton Polytechnic, Nottingham University and Reading University's department of fine art. Arts Council holds his oil on canvas Marker V – Hill, Rod and Stone, of 1976–7, bought from Ikon Gallery, Birmingham, and several provincial collections have examples, including Wakefield Art Gallery. In 1980, Hempton represented Great Britain at the 11th Biennale de Paris. Lived in Minchinhampton, Gloucestershire.

Antony HEMSLEY 1965– Painter, born in Manchester. He studied painting at Trent Polytechnic, Nottingham, where he settled to work in Oldknows Studios. His first show in a public gallery was A Long Snake Summer at Mappin Art Gallery, Sheffield, 1989–90, which showed him to be an energetic, vibrant Colourist.

Philip HEMSLEY 1933– Painter, draughtsman and teacher, born in Stocksbridge, Yorkshire, full name George Philip Hemsley. He studied at Kingston School of Art and Royal Academy Schools with Henry Rushbury and Peter Greenham, gaining his certificate in 1958, the year he won a British Institution Award. Also gained Royal Academy Silver Medal, Landseer and Leverhulme Scholarships. Hemsley was a part-time adult education tutor. In his work he favoured "an imaginative, representational approach based on drawing". Showed at RA, RBA, RP, NEAC and Redfern Gallery. City of London Guildhall, Leicestershire Education Authority, Ashford Hospital and several other public collections hold examples. Was a Ridley Art Society member who lived in Woking, Surrey.

Gerard HEMSWORTH 1945– Sculptor and painter who was born and lived in London. He attended St Martin's School of Art, 1963–7. Became professor of fine art at Goldsmiths' College. Among his many mixed show appearances were Survey '68: Abstract Sculpture, at Camden Arts Centre, 1968; British Sculpture out of the Sixties, ICA, 1970; Carlisle Museum and Art Gallery, 1976; Tony Shafrazi Gallery, New York, 1988; Galeria Comicos/ Luis Serpa, Lisbon, 1991, John Moores Liverpool Exhibition, 1999 and 2002; and in 2000 won the Charles Wollaston Award at RA Summer Exhibition "for the most-distinguished work." Among dozens of solo shows were Nigel Greenwood Gallery, 1970; Museum of Modern Art, Oxford, 1972; Matt's Gallery, 1983; ICA, 1986; Anthony Reynolds Gallery, from 1987; in 1991 Steendrukkerij BV, Amsterdam, and Galerie Cintrik, Antwerp; and John Hansard Gallery, Southampton, 1998. Arts Council holds several examples of his work.

Arthur Edward HENDERSON 1870–1956 Architectural artist and draughtsman, born in Aberdeen, where he attended the School of Art. Also became an architect, studying at the Architectural Association and City and Guilds School, in both places winning medals. Obtained the Owen Jones Travelling Scholarship of RIBA, in 1896, and was engaged in excavations at the Temple of Diana, Ephesus, in Greece. Exhibited RA, UA and RBA. Lived at Crawley Down, Sussex.

Belinda HENDERSON 1908–1988 Painter, designer, illustrator and teacher, daughter of civil servant Sir Horace Hamilton, she attended King Alfred's School, Hampstead. Just before World War II she studied at Chelsea School of Art, Henry Moore, Ceri Richards and Graham Sutherland being notable teachers. She also attended Cedric Morris' East Anglian School of Painting and Drawing. During the war she served as a guide lecturer and draughtsman for the Ministry of War. She also created painted fabrics, illustrated books and designed jackets for publishers such as Hamish Hamilton. In the late-1940s she began teaching drawing and painting, and in 1948 married the writer Philip Henderson. Showed in Hampstead galleries, WIAC, RA Summer Exhibitions and elsewhere, and there was a memorial show at 20th Century Gallery.

David HENDERSON 1944– Versatile artist, designer and lecturer who did a pre-diploma course at Cambridge College of Art & Technology, 1962–3; gained his Diploma in Art and Design, painting, at Bath Academy of Art, 1963–7; and his master's in painting at Royal College of Art, 1967–70. Worked with the Hipgnosis graphic design group, 1969–71; for the animation studio Halas & Batchelor, 1972; was a visiting lecturer in the photography, film and television department, 1975–80–82–86–89; in painting at Chelsea School of Art, 1976–7; and at London College of Furniture, 1982–3. For many years Henderson was also a freelance furniture designer. His extensive group exhibitions included Young Contemporaries, RA, 1971; Umea Stadsbibliotek, Sweden, and 3rd British International Print Biennale, Bradford, both 1972; RA Summer Exhibition, 1983; and Centre d'Art Azilien, Mas d'Azil, France, 1995. There was a solo show of Untitled Constructions 1985–2000 at Gallery 286 in 2000. Latterly, Henderson concentrated on constructions and drawings rather than painting, printmaking and photography, with occasional furniture designing. Lived in St Leonards-on-Sea, Sussex.

Elsie HENDERSON 1880–1967 Draughtsman, printmaker, painter and sculptor, she was principally a delineator of wild animals, although she also did landscapes and figure studies. Born in Eastbourne, Sussex, she was encouraged by her amateur painter mother. Studied at Slade School of Fine Art, 1903–5, then widely in Paris, in 1908–9, including periods at Académie Moderne, Atelier Colarossi, La Palette and Cercle Russe. In 1912 studied with Othon Friesz, the following year working in Italy. On the outbreak of war she returned to Guernsey, where she had spent much of her childhood, but in 1916 she enrolled at Chelsea Polytechnic to study lithography with Ernest Jackson. She began to draw at Regent's Park Zoo and won critical acclaim in 1917 with a zoo poster for London Underground. Started her own press and became a member of Senefelder Club, WIAC, Monarro Group and other exhibiting bodies. Her first solo show was at Leicester Galleries, 1924. In 1928 married the French consul in Guernsey, Baron Henri de Coudenhove, and lived on the island until 1946, when after the privations of the occupation and her husband's death she settled at Hadlow Down, Sussex. An exhibition reviving her memory, which also showed work by her friend Orovida Pissarro, was held at Parkin Gallery, 1985. Sally Hunter Fine Art held exhibitions at 25 Connaught Street, 1999; 40 Eaton Terrace, 2001; and 9 Clarendon Cross, 2004. Work in many public collections, including Tate Gallery, British Museum and Fitzwilliam Museum, Cambridge.

Ewen HENDERSON 1934–2000 Experimental, Expressionist ceramic sculptor, draughtsman, printmaker and teacher, born in Staffordshire, both parents from Scottish medical families, his father the doctor in a lunatic asylum. After failing to obtain a short-service commission, Henderson did his National Service in the Royal Air Force Regiment in Germany, on release working for a chemical company. Based in Cardiff, Henderson visited museums and attended evening art classes; joined the Barry Summer School, meeting Harry Thubron, Terry Frost and Kenneth Martin; then studied at Goldsmiths' College, 1964–5, and Camberwell School of Arts and Crafts, 1965–8, tutors including Hans Coper and Lucie Rie. Henderson rebelled against symmetrical conformity and the art/craft gap; he built vessels instead of using a wheel, and eventually employed a mix of clays and paper pulp. Music was an inspiration, megaliths latterly a key theme. Henderson taught part-time and participated in numerous mixed exhibitions in Britain and abroad. Later solo shows included Hart Gallery and Galerie Besson, both 1994, and a Midlands Art Centre touring show, 1996. Barrett Marsden held a 1934–2000 retrospective in 2001. In 1990 Henderson completed a Triparteid Bird Form for the Saatchi Building, Berkeley Square. Among several dozen public collections holding examples are British Council; National Museum of Wales, Cardiff; Stedelijk Museum, Amsterdam; Ulster Museum in Belfast; and Victoria & Albert Museum. Henderson was based in London.

Gordon G HENDERSON 1951– Painter, born in Glasgow, who graduated from the School of Art there, 1970–4, teachers including Drummond Bone, David Donaldson, James Robertson and Geoffrey Squire. Showed widely in Scotland, including Royal Glasgow Institute of the Fine Arts; Paisley Institute of Fine Art; Torrance Gallery, Edinburgh; Atholl Gallery, Perth; and at The Contemporary Fine Art Gallery, Eton, which included his stylish figurative canvas Pink Rose and Portrait in the exhibition The Caledonian Show III, 2001.

Jeremy HENDERSON 1952– Painter, born in Enniskillen, County Fermanagh, Northern Ireland, who studied at Kingston Polytechnic, gaining his master's degree in fine art from Chelsea School of Art in 1979. His painterly, sweeping style was shown to good effect in the oil Theatre, Stage, Landscape, included in Landscapes from North and South, Glebe House and Gallery, Donegal, and tour, 1997–8. By then he had held solo exhibitions at the Fenderesky Gallery, Belfast, and the Ardhowen Theatre and Arts Centre, Enniskillen. His work was also shown in exhibitions in New York, America. Lived in London.

Keith HENDERSON 1883–1982 Painter, muralist and illustrator of great individuality, educated at Marlborough College. Studied art at Slade School of Fine Art, then in Paris. Initially he was principally a portrait painter. After Army cavalry service in World War I Henderson travelled widely, including Africa and South America, the local plants and wildlife finding their way into his often colourful work. Official War Artist attached to Royal Air Force in World War II. Among books that Henderson illustrated are W H Hudson's *Green Mansions*, 1926, and *The Purple Land*, 1929, and he published several titles himself, including *Palm Groves and Humming Birds*, 1924. Exhibited RA, Fine Art Society and RWS extensively, as well as ROI and RSW. Pelter/Sands, Bristol gave him a solo show in 1980. Galleries in Glasgow, Manchester, Preston, Worthing and elsewhere hold his work. Lived at Spean Bridge, Inverness-shire.

Kevin HENDERSON 1963– Sculptor and teacher who said his works were "organisations of images". He was born in Singapore and studied at Gray's School of Art in Aberdeen, 1981–6, also Oregon State University, America, 1982–3. From 1997 he lectured at Duncan of Jordanstone College of Art, Dundee, where he lived. His group exhibitions included New Scottish Art at Third Eye Centre, Glasgow, 1989, and South Bank Centre's tour The British Art Show 1990. Later solo exhibitions included Globe Gallery, South Shields, 1997, the year Henderson set up the publishing firm Water Press.

Lisa HENDERSON 1949– Painter, art and design historian, lecturer and administrator, born in Cardiff, who did a foundation course at Central School of Art & Design; graduated with honours in history of art + archaeology, University of Nottingham; and gained her master's in the history of European art, Courtauld Institute. Henderson lectured at Newcastle-under-Lyme College and Keele University, was a moderator for the Southern Examining Group and a visual arts officer for West Midlands Arts. She painted "intuitively, feeling rather than representing landscape and literary starting points. Chance, as in nature itself, is an essential ingredient". Later exhibitions included Inaugural Exhibition, New Gallery, Bishop's Castle, 1997; Stoke Open, The Potteries Museum, Stoke-on-Trent, 1998; Stafford Open Art, Shire Hall Gallery, from 1998; and New Year Show, Will's Art Warehouse, 2002.

Mary Reid HENDERSON 1862–1964 Versatile craftworker in various materials, painter and draughtsman, printmaker and teacher, born and died in Glasgow, although her home was in Largs, Ayrshire. Henderson studied at Glasgow School of Art 1901–8, gaining her diploma in 1914. She taught a variety of skills in Helensburgh and Stirling, then embroidery at Motherwell Technical School. She joined the Glasgow Society of Lady Artists in 1915 and was its treasurer, 1934–9. Henderson exhibited at the Royal Glasgow Institute of the Fine Arts, RSA and Walker Art Gallery, Liverpool. She completed the illuminated rolls of honour for World Wars I and II for Glasgow Cathedral.

Nigel HENDERSON 1917–1985 Artist and teacher working in a wide range of media, born in London, who attended Stowe School, 1931–3, then through his mother became connected with the Bloomsbury Group. In 1935–6 studied biology at Chelsea Polytechnic, and was active in the Group Theatre with Rupert Doone and Robert Medley. While assisting Helmut Ruhemann the picture restorer Henderson, with the encouragement of Peggy Guggenheim, developed as a Surrealist painter and collagist, showing at Guggenheim Jeune. After serving as a pilot in Coastal Command in World War II Henderson suffered a nervous breakdown, but recovered to study at Slade School of Fine Art and experimented with photograms using bomb site debris. In the early 1950s Henderson combined teaching creative photography at Central School of Arts and Crafts with photojournalism for *Flair*, *Architectural Review* and *Melody Maker* and did posters for jazz musician Ronnie Scott. In 1952 with his friend Eduardo Paolozzi was involved in founding the Independent Group, and together they set up Hammer Prints Ltd, 1955–61. From 1957–60 Henderson taught part-time at Colchester School of Art, in 1965–8 taking over the photography department at Norwich School of Art, with which he was long connected. In 1976 Henderson completed a mural for University of East Anglia, Norwich. Henderson had a retrospective at Kettle's Yard, Cambridge, 1977. A major show toured from Norwich School of Art Gallery, 1982–3, one from Gainsborough's House, Sudbury, 2001–2, and The Mayor Gallery showed photographs and collages, 2003. It also held an exhibition of Henderson's Photographs of the East End 1949–1953 in 2004, another of Distressed & Altered Photographs 1950–1982 in 2006. Tate

Gallery holds his work. Lived for many years at Landermere Quay, Essex.

Sheila Scott HENDERSON 1910– Landscape and portrait painter in oil, Henderson was at the Yellow Door School of Art under Frank Spenlove-Spenlove, which he had founded in 1896, and under the portrait painter Reginald G Eves. Henderson then went on to exhibit widely and prolifically, at the RA, NEAC, Brook Street Art Gallery, ROI, RSA, RP, the Paris Salon and others. Lived in Reigate, Surrey.

William HENDERSON 1903–1993 Painter of conversation pieces and draughtsman, born into privileged circumstances near Frome, Somerset, which obviated the need to earn a living. He attended Eton College, was at Cambridge University for a year with another in Paris taking drawing lessons. Was also advised privately by Judith Lear and the Polish journalist and artist Rom Landau, who persuaded Henderson to attend Westminster School of Art under Mark Gertler and Eliot Hodgkin. During World War II was a captain in the Royal Marines in India, including a period as aide-de-camp to General Archibald Wavell. In 1950s had two notable shows at Redfern Gallery. Travelled extensively and died at Tisbury, Wiltshire.

William HENDERSON 1941– Painter, designer and teacher, born in Ringmer, Sussex. He studied at Brighton College of Art, 1959–63, and Slade School of Fine Art, 1963–5. Made stage designs for Royal Opera House, Covent Garden. Showed at John Moores Liverpool Exhibition from 1969, RA Summer Exhibition from 1986 and Athena Awards, 1987. Solo shows included Arnolfini Gallery, Bristol, 1983, and Newcastle Polytechnic Gallery, 1984. Taught at Central St Martins School of Art from 1981. Rhythm and pattern were strong elements in Henderson's work, as in Arts Council's example Gjalla, of 1979, and Juggler's Mirror, in John Moores 1989–90 show. Was included in 5x20, "five abstract painters twenty years on", at Kegelbahn Gallery, Carl von Ossietzky University, Oldenburg, Germany, 2001. Lived in London.

Birgitte HENDIL 1944– Miniaturist, born in Copenhagen, Denmark, who studied at Edinburgh College of Art, 1964–9, teachers including Harry More Gordon. Showed at RSA, Scottish Arts Council and Stirling Gallery, in Stirling.

Kevin HENDLEY 1961– Painter and etcher working on a small scale and using rich colours. His inspiration came "from the atmosphere of pubs, cafés, bars, concerts and street scenes. These provide me with bizarre and humorous characters which are wonderful subjects." Hendley, a miner's son, grew up in Cresswell, Derbyshire, at 15 taking an apprenticeship which led to his becoming a master butcher after eight years. In 1985 he moved to London, attended life classes and took a foundation course at the City Lit. In the summer of 1993 he obtained his bachelor's degree in fine art painting at Central St Martins College, his degree show being a sell-out. Went on to become artist-in-residence at Royal Opera House. Showed at Sue Williams Gallery and elsewhere.

Robert Leslie HENDRA 1912– Stained glass and watercolour artist, born in London. Attended Camberwell School of Arts and Crafts and Central School of Arts and Crafts and worked in the studio of Martin Travers. Was a leading member of the British Society of Master Glass Painters. His work is to be found in Westminster Cathedral and a number of English provincial cathedrals. Lived in Harpenden, Hertfordshire.

Herbert HENDRIE 1887–1946 Stained glass artist, painter and teacher, born in Manchester, who studied at Royal College of Art and Slade School of Fine Art. He became head of the design school at Edinburgh College of Art. Welbeck, Buckfast, Ampleforth and Paisley Abbeys contain windows by him and Kippen Parish Church, Stirling, has the outstanding Cameron Window, in memory of the artist D Y Cameron's wife; Hendrie strove for the effect of "crushed jewels and mother of pearl". Showed at RA, RSW, RSA, NEAC and elsewhere. Lived in Edinburgh and was a member of Chelsea Arts Club.

Archibald Hunter HENDRY 1890– Oil and watercolour painter, born at North Leith, Midlothian, Scotland. He studied art at the Royal High School, Edinburgh, and at the College of Art there, where his teachers included a number of notable Scottish painters, D M Sutherland and David Foggie. Exhibitions included RSW, SSA, RSW and the Edinburgh and Stirling Triennial. Was a member of the Royal Scots Club who lived at Middleton, Midlothian.

Heinz HENGHES: *see* **Henry HENGHES**

Henry HENGHES 1906–1975 Sculptor and teacher, born in Hamburg, Germany, as Heinz Henghes, by which name he is sometimes known. He was educated in Germany and America but was a self-taught sculptor who became head of fine art at Winchester College of Art. Produced the sculpture Orpheus for the 1951 Festival of Britain; it was eventually sited at Camden School for Girls. Birmingham City Art Gallery and the Museum of Modern Art in New York also hold his work. Lived latterly in Winchester, Hampshire, and in Tursac, Dordogne, France. Remembered by a colleague "as a brusque man. He was a devil – but I liked him!" The Henry Moore Institute latterly acquired from his son Ian a Henghes archive documenting Henry's colourful life, including his stowing away from Germany to New York, where he lived from 1924–32; his travels through France, Italy and Switzerland before settling in Britain in 1937; his many artistic friendships including the sculptor Brancusi and writers Ezra Pound, Henry Miller and Lawrence Durrell; his participation in the post-World War II exhibitions at Battersea Park, the Festival of Britain and in 1953 The Unknown Political Prisoner exhibition; teaching alongside Frank Dobson at the Royal College of Art; and his BBC talks, poetry, plays and essays. Part of the archive is a magnificent photograph album documenting his work from the late 1920s. Retrospective at England & Co, 2006.

Richard HENMAN 1970– Artist who in Now Showing II, Houldsworth Fine Art, 1999, displayed work using the vertical stripe as a repetitive motif on mirror-polished stainless steel, questioning the viewer's perception of colour, scale and materials. Henman did a foundation course at Oxford Brookes University, 1989–90; gained an honours degree at Bath College of Higher Education, 1990–3; and his master's in visual theories, at University of East London, 1994–5. Other group shows included Beacon Gallery, Loughborough, 1990; Blue Gallery, from

1996; and Oxford Art Week, Abingdon, 1997. Houldsworth gave him a solo exhibition at Legends, 1998. G de Z Finance, British Land and London Business School hold examples.

Joseph HENNAH 1897–1967 Painter in oil and watercolour who was born and lived mostly in Newport, Monmouthshire, later in Weymouth, Dorset. Showed at RA and RWA. Hennah had a love of the countryside and liked making studies of less obviously picturesque aspects, such as farmyard corners, hedges and gravel pits. He painted a large number of gouaches of South Africa and was particularly attached to the Cornish fishing villages of Polperro and St Ives.

Thomas HENNELL 1903–1945 Watercolour painter, draughtsman, writer and poet. Born at Ridley, Kent, studied at Regent Street Polytechnic for several years in the early 1920s, then qualified as a teacher with Marion Richardson. Taught art for several years. Began to research his first book, *Change in the Farm*, in Britain, and Ireland, mainly by bicycle. Was a meticulous recorder, in words and pictures, of vanishing country crafts and ways. In 1931 became friendly with Edward Bawden, Eric Ravilious and other artists based in Great Bardfield, Essex. From 1932–5 was treated for psychiatric illness, which he wrote about in *The Witnesses*. During World War II Hennell was an Official War Artist in Europe and the Far East, dying in mysterious circumstances in Java. The Imperial War Museum holds a large collection of his pictures, which are in many other public galleries. Hennell was a keen student of English watercolour painting and wrote well on it. Although not a great natural draughtsman, he improved his technique to become a fine atmospheric and distinctive watercolourist. Victoria Art Gallery, Bath, held a survey show in 1995.

Hilary M HENNES: *see* **Hilary MILLER**

Hubert HENNES 1907– Painter, draughtsman and teacher, born in London. Married to the artist Hilary Miller. Hennes studied at the Working Men's College, Crowndale Road, London, where he won the Lowes Dickinson Scholarship, which permitted a short period of travel to continental art centres; also St Martin's School of Art, 1928–30, and Royal College of Art, 1930–4. After seven years' teaching at Leicester College of Arts and Crafts, 1934–41, Hennes at the end of World War II took up a post at Oxford School of Art. Exhibited RA and RBA. Lived in Oxford.

Adrian HENRI 1932–2000 Painter, poet, performance artist, teacher and writer, born in Birkenhead, Cheshire, where he remained based. He was closely identified with the 1960s Liverpool Pop scene and sought to produce popularly understandable art, as with Kop football series from the 1970s. He studied under Lawrence Gowing and Roger de Grey at King's College, Newcastle upon Tyne, and Durham University, 1951–5, graduating with a fine art degree. After graduating, for several years worked as a scene painter at Rhyl fairground, at the same teaching at a local secondary school, from 1961 teaching at Manchester and from 1964 Liverpoool Colleges of Art. First exhibited in 1958 at Liverpool Academy, becoming its president, 1972–81. Showed frequently at John Moores Liverpool Exhibition from 1961 and gained second prize in 1972 with Painting One. Other series of paintings by Henri encompassed food, debris and magic places, as in Dream Palace (Homage to Ferdinand Cheval), shown at John Moores, 1989–90. Took part in poetry readings and performed at Isle of Wight rock festival in late 1960s with his Liverpool Scene band. With Roger McGough and Brian Patten, Henri was one of the Liverpool poets, whose 1967 collection *The Mersey Sound* sold out the initial print run of 20,000 within a month. Among his publications was *The Postman's Palace*, a book for children, 1990. Henri had retrospective at South Hill Park, Bracknell, 1986, and tour; Whitford Fine Art, 1960s work, 1997; retrospective, Walker Art Gallery, Liverpool, 2000; Library, Museum & Art Gallery, Rhyl, 2000–1; and Six Chapel Row Contemporary Art, Bath, 2001. Walker Art Gallery in Liverpool and Arts Council hold his work. Just before his death the city of Liverpool made Henri a Freeman.

Frank Watson HENRICKSEN 1915–1955 Artist in gouache and line, born and lived at Wallsend, near Newcastle. He was mainly self-taught and exhibited with Newcastle Society of Artists, Shipley Art Gallery in Gateshead, and at Laing Art Gallery, Newcastle, which holds his work.

Daphne HENRION: *see* **Daphne HARDY HERION**

Frederic Henri Kay HENRION 1914–1990 Designer, lecturer and writer, who became a textile designer in Paris, France, in the early 1930s, working in Paris and London, 1936–9. Henrion's early projects included work on the Glasgow Empire Exhibition, 1939, and New York World Fair, 1940–5; design of exhibitions for the Ministries of Agriculture and Information and the Army Bureau of Current Affairs, 1943–5; and acting as consultant designer to the American Embassy and US Office of War Information, 1945. He was by then active in the AIA, contributing to its exhibitions and publications. Henrion was chief consultant designer to Sir William Crawford and Partners, 1946–7; art editor of Contact Publications, 1947–8; art director of British Overseas Airways Corporation, 1949–51; and of *Future Magazine*, 1951. He reinforced his reputation with his work as designer of the Festival of Britain agriculture and natural history pavilions between 1950–4, from the early 1950s being an increasingly busy consultant designer for many notable companies, producing posters for the General Post Office and others. Henrion was a visiting lecturer at the Royal College of Art, 1950–60, and was associated with the London School of Printing and the Central School of Art, as well as being an outside assessor for Scottish Schools of Art. His show Designing Things and Symbols created much interest at the ICA in 1960. Henrion was a leading figure in bodies such as the Society of Industrial Art and Design, of which he was president, 1961–3, winning its Design Medal in 1976, and a faculty master of the Royal Designers of Industry, 1971–3. He also lectured extensively abroad, being visiting professor at Cooper Union, New York, from 1984, and at University of Essen, 1984–5. He designed and contributed to leading graphic, design and architectural magazines, his *Design Co-ordination and Corporate Image*, 1967, also published in America, being an important text. In 1982 he founded Henrion, Ludlow and Schmidt. Henrion married the sculptor Daphne Hardy Henrion in 1947, but while he continued to live in Hampstead, north London, she moved to East Anglia in the 1970s.

Ben HENRIQUES 1967– Painter, born in Cheshire, who went to live in Scotland aged nine, being educated in Perthshire. He attended the fine art department at University of Newcastle, 1986–90. The island of Tiree off Scotland's west coast was a favourite subject, as shown in shared exhibition he had at William Hardie Gallery, Glasgow, in 1992. Mixed exhibitions included The National Portrait Gallery, BP Awards, and The Discerning Eye, Mall Galleries, 1998. There was a solo show at Jonathan Cooper in 2001, which displayed a wide range of Henriques' meticulous interiors, still lifes and figure studies. Worked in Scotland and London.

Rose HENRIQUES 1889–1972 Social worker, artist and musician, born and lived in London, daughter of James Loewe, communal worker and scholar. She studied the piano in Breslau, Germany, then in 1914 was persuaded by Basil Henriques, whom she married, to enter social work. Basil was knighted for his work in London's East End in 1955. He and Rose were wardens of the Bernhard Baron St George's Jewish Settlement from 1914–48, and continued to live there even after officially retiring. Rose was known to the boys and girls as "the Missus". In addition, she was a nurse at Liverpool Street Station in World War I; was an air-raid warden and organised an emergency feeding scheme in World War II; in 1945 went to Bergen-Belsen to tackle welfare problems after the closing of the notorious camp; was chairman of the British Ose Society for promoting physical and mental health; and in 1954 founded the Workrooms for the Elderly in east London. Henriques fostered local interest in ballet, music and drama and as an artist painted east London's streets and docks. In 1947 the Whitechapel Art Gallery held a show Stepney in War and Peace; in 1961 Vanishing Stepney at the Gallery included several hundred paintings and drawings by her. *Fifty Years in Stepney*, by Rose Henriques, was published by the Settlement in 1966, based on broadcast talks. Tower Hamlets Public Libraries holds a large collection of her pictures.

Fiore de HENRIQUEZ 1921–2004 Figurative sculptor, and lecturer, born Maria Fiore de Henriquez in Trieste, who studied at the Academy of Art, Venice, 1939–42. After sculpting in wood and helping the Italian partisans, 1943–5, Fiore received her first major commission, a bronze monument to Don Giovanni Cuomo for Salerno, but when it was blown up on inauguration she left Italy for England. Early commissions included one for three triple-life-size statues for the 1951 Festival of Britain. From 1954–60 Fiore was commissioned by Huntington Hartford to help create a cultural centre in Beverly Hills, California, America. She toured America and Canada, 1955–75, lecturing about working with clay. In 1961 Fiore met the sculptor Jacques Lipchitz and worked with him for several years. From 1968 she restored ruins at Peralta, Tuscany, continuing to live there with a studio in London, having become a British citizen in 1953. Worked extensively in Japan in the 1980s, where she completed portraits of the nobility and public sculptures including a bust of the Johannes Brahms for Tokyo. In the 50 years from 1948 Fiore made around 4,000 portraits, including John F Kennedy, Augustus John, Margot Fonteyn, Peter Ustinov, Laurence Olivier and Vivien Leigh, commissions stemming from the RA, Royal College of Art, elsewhere in Britain and abroad. A series of musicians was housed at Renishaw Hall, Derbyshire, seat of the Sitwell family. In 2004 her work was included in Modern and Contemporary Sculpture at Wolseley Fine Arts, with a memorial show later that year. She died in Peralta.

Bruce HENRY 1918– Wildlife and landscape artist, born in Kandy, Ceylon, working in watercolour, pastel and oil, who travelled widely. His father George Morrison Reid Henry and brother David M Reid-Henry [sic] were also wildlife artists with an international reputation. Bruce Henry was educated in Britain and after graduating from London University entered the church, serving with his wife in India for many years. He later became head of religious studies at Worthing Sixth Form College for a decade, in 1980 retiring to paint full-time. Was a member of SWLA, showed widely in England and had several solo exhibitions. His illustrated book *Highlight the Wild – The Art of the Reid Henrys* was published in 1986. The collection Nature in Art, Gloucester, holds his work. Lived in Worthing, Sussex.

George Morrison Reid HENRY 1891–1983 Wildlife artist, notable for his bird paintings, born in Ceylon on a tea estate where his father was manager. As one of 11 children he had little formal education, but extensive reading and observation helped him by 15 to begin establishing a reputation as a naturalist and artist. Was appointed assistant in systematic entomology at Colombo Museum, where he worked until retirement. In 1927 the government published the first of a series of 64 paintings of birds, entitled *Coloured Plates of the Birds of Ceylon*, with his illustrations and text by W E Wait. Later illustrated several bird books, including *Indian Hill Birds*, by Salim Ali, and in 1955 Oxford University Press also published his key work, *A Guide to the Birds of Ceylon*, written and illustrated by him and still a standard work. Travelled widely abroad, including a visit to Australia when he was 88, continuing to sketch from life in small, lined notebooks. His work was exhibited in London, Zimbabwe and elsewhere. His sons Bruce Henry and David M Reid-Henry were also bird artists.

Julie HENRY 1959– Artist using photography and video who in her first solo exhibition, Talent Show, at Anthony Wilkinson Gallery, 2000, explored "people and their attempts to ... make their fantasies real." She had another show there in 2003. Henry did a foundation course at Mornington Centre, 1992–3, graduating in critical fine art practice at Central St Martins College of Art & Design, 1993–8. Group exhibitions included Six British Artists, Ars Locus Gallery, Tokyo, Japan, 1997; Volcano Festival, The Oval House, 1998; New Contemporaries 99, Exchange Flags, Liverpool, and South London Gallery, both 1999; and Going Down, Edinburgh City Gallery and Oldham Museum & Gallery, 1999–00. Henry was a keen football supporter. In 2004 Millais Gallery at the Southampton Institute, Southampton, put on her touring show Dyed in the Wool, stemming from a commission for her to work with fans around England to design and knit cardigans representing their clubs.

Olive HENRY 1902–1989 Stained glass designer and painter, born and lived in Belfast, Northern Ireland. During evening classes at Belfast School of Art she became interested in stained glass, took an apprenticeship with W F Clokey & Company and stayed with them. Her around 50 years in the glass studios influenced Henry's own pictures, which have a strongly patterned quality and delicate colour harmonies. She was elected RUA, was a founder-member of Ulster Society of Women Artists, also showing with Watercolour Society of Ireland and RHA. In 1987, the year of her last RUA showing, Henry had her first solo exhibition for some 30 years at the Shambles Gallery, Hillsborough. Ulster Museum holds her work. Died at Crawfordsburn, County Down.

Sean HENRY 1965– Figurative sculptor using a variety of materials, including fired clay pieces, and oil paint to achieve a finish. Gained an honours degree in ceramics from Bristol Polytechnic in 1987. In the late 1980s Henry made trips to America, where he worked as assistant to West Coast artists Tony Natsoulas and Lisa Reinertson and the sculptor Robert Arneson, head of ceramics at the University of California, Davis, invited Henry to join his department in 1991 as a visiting artist. Alberto Giacometti and Lucian Freud were other influences. In 1996 Henry completed three bronze figures to mark the seventieth anniversary of the Royal British Legion and won the Villiers David Foundation Prize in 1998, the year he showed in Atlantic Crossings at the Barbican Centre. There were solo shows at Davies & Tooth, 1999, and Berkeley Square Gallery, 2001. In that year Henry's sculpture Trajan's Shadow was placed in the Square under Westminster City Council's Sculpture in the Parks scheme.

Susan HENSEL 1944– Artist working with oil, tempera, painted wood and collage, and teacher, born in Amersham, Buckinghamshire, married to the sculptor and jeweller David Hensel. Hensel did a foundation course at Wimbledon School of Art, 1965–6, gained an honours degree in fine art at Brighton College of Art, 1966–9, with a further year at Reading University, 1969–70. She taught art in local schools and at adult education classes. Her own work showed a surreal influence and she exhibited widely in England and abroad, including Wraxall Gallery, 1981; Doktor Glas, Stockholm, 1982; Ankrum Gallery, Los Angeles, 1984; Gallery Reich, Cologne, and Milligan Gallery, Storrington, both 1991. Lived in East Grinstead, Sussex.

John HENSHALL 1913– Painter, calligrapher and teacher, born in Stockport, Cheshire, where he lived. He studied art at Stockport College and showed with RI, Society of Church Craftsmen, Red Rose Guild and elsewhere, having a series of solo exhibitions in the north of England and north Wales. Art galleries in Stockport and Wigan hold examples.

Maggie HENSHALL 1964– Painter of works abstracted from landscape, colour a crucial element in creating the final picture. She was born in south Wales and attended Newport College of Art and Design and Exeter University. After graduating in 1987 she was a graphic designer, then travelled around Australia in 1992. Henshall became a full-time painter, inspired by her surroundings at Bottallack, Cornwall. She was a member of Penwith Society of Arts, also exhibiting widely elsewhere in England, Wales and in America. In 2000 she shared a six-artist show, Under Western Skies, at The Great Atlantic Map Works Gallery, St Just in Penwith. Henshall also worked for the architectural firm Ove Arup and designed greetings cards.

Yvonne HENTHORNE 1942– Painter and teacher, born in Wetherby, Yorkshire, who studied at Goldsmiths' College School of Art, 1961–6, teachers including Andrew Forge and Patrick Millard. Between 1969–75 she received a series of Italian, Brazilian and West German grants and scholarships. Taught at Havering Technical College. Was elected to RBA in 1978, also showing with SWA, at Young Contemporaries and Midland Group Gallery, solo exhibitions including Ikon Gallery, Birmingham. Lived in London.

Deirdre HENTY-CREER fl. from late 1930s– Painter, and creator of small ceramic flower studies, born in Sydney, Australia, in art self-taught after private education. She was accredited to the Ministry of Information, 1940–5; was at various times on the council of UA and Chelsea Art Society and on the committee of the Armed Forces' Art Society; and represented Great Britain in Sport in Art in the VII Olympiad at the Victoria & Albert Museum. Showed at RA, RBA, NEAC and elsewhere. Had a solo exhibition at Fine Art Society, 1941, later ones including Qantas Gallery from 1970, with a retrospective of 60 years at Bartley Drey Gallery, 1997. Medici Society, Warren of Ware, Chryson's of California and Gruhen of Innsbruck reproduced artworks by Henty-Creer, which included portraits of HRH Prince Michael of Kent and Sir John Kerr, Governor-General of Australia. HRH The Prince of Wales holds her work, also in museums in Cape Town and Oxford. Her sister was the painter Pam Mellor. Lived in London.

Alan HEPBURN 1934– Watercolourist, "very much influenced by the Scottish watercolourists of the late 19th and early 20th centuries, Arthur Melville, J W Herald and James Paterson, particularly the first-named.... Much of my work has been carried out in the Middle East, Egypt, Italy, Spain, southern France and around the coasts of Britain – all places with bright light." Hepburn attended Edinburgh University and the College of Art, 1951–4, taught by Robin Philipson, W G Gillies and James Cumming. After Royal Air Force National Service as a pilot, 1955–7, he worked in advertising and marketing: in Shell, then Hovis as marketing manager, 1980–3, overseeing the firm's famous television commercials. After running his own business from 1983–99, be became a full-time painter. Hepburn was a finalist in the Singer & Friedlander/*Sunday Times* Watercolour Competition, 1999, 2001, 2002 and 2003, winning second prize in 2000. His exhibitions included a series at Highgate Fine Art from 1998. In 2004 he shared one with Susan Evans at Hutson Gallery.

Tony HEPBURN 1942– Sculptor and teacher using a variety of materials, born in Manchester, who studied at Camberwell School of Arts and Crafts, 1959–63, and London University, 1963–5. Went on to lecture at the faculty of art and design at Lanchester Polytechnic in Coventry; also being a visiting professor at Carnegie-Mellon University in Pittsburgh, Pennsylvania; then at Alfred University, Alfred, New York, as head of the division of art and design. Exhibitions included Primavera Gallery, 1967; Victoria & Albert Museum, 1968; Bradford City Art Gallery, 1971; and Clay Sculpture, Yorkshire Sculpture Park, 1980. In 1982 took part in the three-man Convergent Territories, The Banff Centre School of Fine Arts, Alberta. Solo shows included Covent Garden Gallery, 1969. Victoria

& Albert Museum, Inner London Education Authority, Stoke-on-Trent Museum and several overseas collections hold examples.

David HEPHER 1935– Painter, collagist and teacher, born in Surrey. He studied at Camberwell School of Arts and Crafts and Slade School of Fine Art, 1955–61. In the 1960s he participated in group shows at Young Contemporaries, LG and Piccadilly Gallery, then had first solo show at Serpentine Gallery in 1971. In 1972 showed solo with Angela Flowers Gallery, at which he was to continue exhibiting. Hepher also taught part-time in London. In the 1970s Hepher participated in Germany and France in several shows devoted to realist or Hyper-Realist painting, and became noted for his minute depictions of suburban domestic house fronts, with their bow-windows, stained glass fanlights and privet hedges. In 1974, the year he won 1st Prize, 1st International Tokyo Biennale, Hepher had retrospective exhibitions at Mappin Art Gallery, Sheffield, and Whitechapel Art Gallery, with one at the Museum of London, 1996, entitled Streets in the Sky, featuring graffiti-marked south London council tower blocks. Hepher lived nearby in Camberwell. Tate Gallery, Victoria & Albert Museum; Government Art Collection, Arts Council, Sheffield City Art Galleries, British Council and Boysmans Museum in Rotterdam are among public collections holding his work. Hepher was senior lecturer in painting at Chelsea School of Art, 1981–90, then became professor of fine art at University College, London, and head of painting, Slade School of Fine Art, professor emeritus in 2001.

Ruth HEPPEL 1926– Painter and draughtsman, born in London, who studied at Regent Street Polytechnic School of Art, teachers including Norman Blamey and Arnold Auerbach. She showed at RA, RP, RHA and in Germany, and had several solo exhibitions. Lived at Nether Winchendon, Buckinghamshire.

Norman HEPPLE 1908–1994 Painter, born in London, where he lived, full name Robert Norman Hepple. The family came from the village of Hepple, Northumberland. He was the son of the painter Robert Hepple and the nephew of Wilson Hepple, the Northumberland animal painter. Studied at Goldsmiths' College School of Art and Royal Academy Schools, under Sir Walter Russell. During World War II Hepple joined the London Fire Service and became an Official War Artist to the National Fire Service, the Imperial War Museum holding resultant work. Hepple was elected RP in 1948, being its president, 1979–83; was elected NEAC in 1950; and in 1961 was made RA. Hepple's many portraits included HM The Queen, HRH The Duke of Edinburgh and other members of the royal family. He also painted landscapes, horses and flowers for relaxation, as shown in his show at Spink & Son, 1987. Solo exhibition at Fosse Gallery, Stow-on-the-Wold, 2001.

Arthur Jackson HEPWORTH: *see* **Arthur JACKSON**

Barbara HEPWORTH 1903–1975 Sculptor of formal and abstract figures in bronze, stone and wood. Born in Wakefield, Yorkshire, Jocelyn Barbara Hepworth studied at Leeds School of Art, then from 1921 at the Royal College of Art, from 1924–5 living in Italy as the result of a West Riding Travelling Scholarship. Married the sculptor John Skeaping in 1924, marriage dissolved 1933, and exhibited with him. In Rome had learned the technique of carving. In the early 1930s her interest in abstract sculpture developed, encouraged by several developments. She had met the painter Ben Nicholson in 1931 – marrying him shortly afterwards, marriage dissolved 1951 – and with him visited the studios of Arp, Brancusi, Braque, Picasso and Gabo. Hepworth in the 1930s became a member of several forward-looking groups, such as the 7 & 5 Society, Unit One and Abstraction-Creation. In 1939 Hepworth moved to St Ives, Cornwall, where she became an influential member of the artistic community, being a founder-member of the Penwith Society in 1949. In 1947–8 she had made her notable series of drawings of operating theatres, and in 1949 a first one-man show of drawings at Durlacher Bros, in New York, extended her growing reputation. Two works were commissioned for the Festival of Britain in 1951 and she won second prize in The Unknown Political Prisoner competition two years later. Although in the 1950s she was to design décor for productions at the Old Vic theatre and for Covent Garden opera house, she was to concentrate on consolidating her position as Britain's premier female sculptor, being given several retrospective exhibitions, including Tate Liverpool and Art Gallery of Ontario, Canada, 1994–5, Robert Sandelson, 2001, and centenary shows at New Art Centre at East Winterslow, Yorkshire Sculpture Park at West Bretton, Wakefield Art Gallery and Tate St Ives, all 2003, and having work purchased by major international galleries. She became Dame Barbara Hepworth in 1965. Died in a fire in her studio in St Ives, where a Barbara Hepworth Museum was opened in 1976.

Dorothy HEPWORTH 1898–1978 Painter, the lifelong friend and companion of the painter Patricia Preece, whom she met at the Slade School of Fine Art. While studying there she first showed at RA and in 1918–19 graduated with first-class honours. With Preece she set up a studio in London, then spent four years with her in Paris, where Hepworth studied at Atelier Colarossi. After returning to England in 1925 they rented cottages in the west of England, in 1927 settling in Cookham, Berkshire, where she lived with Patricia Preece until she died, even during Preece's bizarre marriage to the painter Stanley Spencer, which she sought to discourage. Much of Patricia Preece's output is known to be by Dorothy Hepworth, especially the later work, but how much is unclear. A studio sale at Christie's in 1984 encompassed 500 paintings and over 1,500 drawings from Dorothy Hepworth's studio; these included studies of girls, still lifes and landscapes, especially of the Cookham area. A small woman of masculine dress, Dorothy Hepworth latterly led a reclusive life with Patricia Preece, who predeceased her in 1966. Hepworth left two sixteenth-century statues to the Victoria & Albert Museum in her will.

Stephen HEPWORTH 1963– Non-traditional sculptor, born and lived in London, who gained his honours degree in fine art at Brighton Polytechnic, 1984–7, his master's degree at Goldsmiths' College, 1988–90. In 1991–3 he won a number of British Council Awards. Hepworth "rendered language solid, creating a short circuit between the encoding of language and desire through his adoption of the role of a translator." Group exhibitions included Barclays Young Artist Award, Serpentine Gallery, 1991; and in 1992 Joy and Pain at Institute of Contemporary Art, Amsterdam, and Génériques: Le Visuel et L'Écrit, Hôtel des

Arts, Paris. Solo exhibitions included 121 Art Gallery, Antwerp, 1991, and in 1992 Galerie Gutharc Ballin, Paris, and ArsFutura Galerie, Zürich.

Simon HEPWORTH-NICHOLSON: *see* **Simon NICHOLSON**

Albert HERBERT 1925– Painter, printmaker and teacher, born in London. Left school early and briefly worked in newspapers, attending life drawing classes part-time at St Martin's School of Art with R V Pitchforth. After Army service, on which he 40 years later made a television film, attended Wimbledon School of Art, 1947, then Royal College of Art, 1949. Began exhibiting at RA in 1951, the year when he married Jacqueline Henly, a sculpture student. A Royal College of Art Travelling Scholarship in 1952–3 enabled him to travel on the continent and an Abbey Major Scholarship in 1953–4 took him to Rome, where he encountered the Italian Realists. Worked for a time in the Kitchen Sink style and was one of Jack Beddington's selections for the book *Young Artists of Promise*. Between 1955–6 lectured at Dudley School of Art, in 1956–64 at Birmingham College of Art, joining St Martin's School of Art in 1964, where he became principal lecturer. A flirtation with abstract painting then in vogue left him dissatisfied and Herbert returned to figurative painting through etching. A British Council-financed trip to the Far East directed Herbert's mind to Biblical subjects – he was a Catholic convert, long interested in Buddhism – which led to a series of small but powerful pictures in a quasi-primitive style. Solo shows included retrospectives at England & Co, 1999 and 2004. In that later exhibition Herbert's pictorial reflections on his earlier life were included. Lived at Cliftonville, Dorking, Surrey. His daughter Madeline was an artist.

Barry HERBERT 1937– Printmaker, painter and teacher, born in York. He studied at Archbishop Holgate's School there and at James Graham College and went on to head the fine art department at Leeds University. As well as mixed exhibitions Herbert had several dozen solo shows, including Serpentine Gallery, 1971; Galerie Brechbühl, Switzerland, from 1972; and Gilbert Parr Gallery, 1982. Editions of his prints were published in Britain and on the continent. Lived in Leeds, Yorkshire.

Jacqueline Anne HERBERT 1928– Sculptor, printmaker, draughtsman and illustrator, brought up in Kent, wife of the painter Albert Herbert. She studied at Beckenham School of Art, 1946, with Carel Weight, at Goldsmith's College School of Art, 1947–9, Royal College of Art, 1949–52, with the sculptor John Skeaping, and in Spain and Italy. Showed AIA, Leicester Galleries, ICA, British School in Rome and elsewhere. Shell, the oil company, bought her work.

Kathy HERBERT 1955– Artist and teacher working in a wide range of materials who graduated from University of Ulster in fine art in 1990, having transferred from the National College of Art and Design, Dublin, where she spent three years. Herbert was artist-in-residence at St Patrick's College, Dublin, in 1992 and worked for some years as a teacher for the adult life drawing class at Crescent Arts Centre and Royal Ulster Academy Association, Belfast. Her sculpture was chosen for a number of significant events, including The Boglands Symposium, County Wicklow, 1990, and The Snow Sculpture Symposium, Luleå, Sweden, 1992. She was a prizewinner at the Íontas Small Works Competition, Sligo, 1991. Also took part in The Oireachtas Exhibition, RHA Gallery, Dublin, 1993, and in 1994 Beyond the Partitions, put on by Queen Street Studios, Belfast, with which she was associated. Later group exhibitions included The National Self-Portrait Exhibition, Limerick University, 1998; Out in the Fields, Waterfront Gallery, Rosses Point, 2004, which also gave her a solo show; and Summer Show, Ballinglen Arts Foundation, Ballycastle, 2005. The National Self-Portrait Collection, Arts Council of Northern Ireland, McMullen Museum of Art at Boston College in America and other public and corporate collections hold examples.

Madeline HERBERT 1957– Artist, designer and teacher, daughter of the artist Albert Herbert. She studied at Camberwell School of Arts and Crafts and Goldsmiths' College School of Art. Designed for stage, puppet theatre and films and taught costume drawing. Was included in England & Co's Art in Boxes, 1991.

Ian HERDMAN 1957– Sculptor, painter, draughtsman and teacher, born Newcastle upon Tyne. After attending the Royal Grammar School there he was at University of Reading, 1976–80, gaining a fine arts degree. From 1980 Herdman appeared regularly in group shows, including New Contemporaries at ICA, 1980; Serpentine Gallery Summer Show, 1982; Cheltenham Sculpture Biennale, 1985; Sue Williams Gallery, 1988; staff exhibition at Croydon College, 1990; and Sculpture at Canterbury, 1991. Solo exhibitions included Air Gallery, 1984, and Jablonski Gallery, 1986. Hunterian Gallery, Glasgow, and University of Reading hold his work.

Katrine HERIAN 1964– Artist, born in Harlow, Essex, trained at Chelsea School of Art, who made photographic works and pencil drawings "that record the space occupied by an object." Herian held solo shows in Britain, France and Iceland, including Angel Row Gallery, Nottingham, and Frith Street Gallery. Group exhibitions in Britain and France included Camden Arts Centre, the John Hansard Gallery in Southampton and An exemplary life, at Bury St Edmunds Art Gallery, 2000.

Gordon HERICKX 1900–1953 Sculptor and teacher, born in Birmingham, where he died. Herickx won a scholarship to Birmingham College of Art in 1914, to which he returned after World War I, winning the Rylands Scholarship. His teaching included Walsall School of Art, but his career was mainly based in Birmingham, working in stone and bronze. Herickx had a special interest in fine lettering, but his main achievement was a small body of effigies of corn, cyclamen and chestnut bud which can be sensual, with the subtle simplifications of Brancusi. Among Herickx's better-known commissions were the interior decoration of the Cunard Steamship Company's offices and work at Cecil Sharp House, in London. The Barber Institute in Birmingham and the city's Museum and Art Gallery hold his work, as do a number of other provincial collections. There was a memorial show in Birmingham Museum and Art Gallery in 1953, shortly after an exhibition at Kensington Art Gallery. Herickx was a friend of the poet Louis MacNeice, appearing in his autobiographical narrative poem *Autumn Sequel* as Wimbush, and in Jon Stallworthy's biography of MacNeice.

John HERITAGE 1931–1994 Painter, sculptor and teacher, born in Liverpool, where he studied sculpture with Charles Gardiner at the School of Art, after National Service attending Slade School of Fine Art in 1955 under Reg Butler. After teaching in Liverpool, Heritage studied at British School, Rome, 1961, where he concentrated on drawing and painting. Returned to Liverpool, Heritage taught and became secretary of the Liverpool Academy. From 1972–9 he was head of Wallasey School of Art and then vice-principal of Wirral College of Art, then from 1980–92 was dean of Clwyd College of Art, Wrexham. Heritage retained his connection with the northwest, maintaining a home in Wallasey, Cheshire. Much of Heritage's work had a satirical and social comment side. He had a photographic memory and would on occasion work intensively at night for long stretches. Heritage took part in mixed and solo shows in London, America and South Africa. What proved to be a memorial exhibition toured from Theatre Clwyd Gallery, 1994–5. Liverpool's Walker Art Gallery holds examples.

Bridget HERIZ 1949– Sculptor and teacher, born a British citizen in Hamburg, West Germany, daughter of the glass engraver Patrick Heriz-Smith and the painter Audrey Pilkington. She studied at Goldsmiths' College, 1973, with Carl Plackman, and at Ravensbourne College of Art & Design, 1974–7, with Eric Peskett and Brian Fielding. From 1978–86 Heriz taught at the Clock House Art Centre, Suffolk, from then on working full-time as a self-employed sculptor. Of her work Heriz said that it was "based on human experience, and therefore strongly uses the human figure, but entwined with images of biological and geological metamorphoses, the theme being one of growth". Heriz cited life drawing as the foundation of her sculpture. Over the years, Cubism, particularly Braque, the Russian Constructivists, and the putti of Donatello were influences. Mixed exhibitions included Sculpture in Anglia, Corn Exchange, Ipswich, from 1979; prizewinner, SGA, 1985; 20th Century British Artists, Oriel Gallery, Cambridge, 1991; Roots 66, Halesworth Gallery retrospective, 2000; and Ipswich Docks, D'Arcy Gallery, Ipswich, 2001. In 2002 she had an important solo show, 3 dimensions, at Christchurch Mansion, Ipswich, which holds her work, as does New Hall, Cambridge. There was another exhibition, at Chappel Galleries, Chappel, 2003. Bromley Parish Church commissioned Heriz, who lived Great Yarmouth, Norfolk.

Patrick Ambrose Lewis HERIZ-SMITH 1920– Glass engraver, artist in pastel and teacher, husband of the artist Audrey Pilkington and father of the sculptor Bridget Heriz. He was born in Bournemouth, Hampshire, attending Reimann School of Art, 1937–9, teachers including Leonard Rosoman, then Slade School of Fine Art, 1939–41, under Allan Gwynne-Jones. Heriz-Smith taught in schools, 1941–64, including Gordonstoun; from 1964–78 he ran an independent adult residential school in Suffolk; from 1978–88 running a similar but non-residential school at Exeter. Heriz-Smith was a member of Suffolk Craft Society, Devon Guild and a fellow of the Society of Designer-Craftsmen. The composer Benjamin Britten and the singer Peter Pears owned his work. Lived in Exeter, Devon.

Stella HERKLOTS 1938– Sculptor, born in Hong Kong, her father a scientist and botanical artist. She was interned during World War II in the Philippines, then travelled extensively throughout the world. After gaining an economics degree, 1957–60, began sculpting in 1967, in London studying briefly with the Czech sculptor Irena Sedlecká. She worked for some years in interior design and landscape garden design, then gained a fine arts degree in sculpture at Leicester Polytechnic from 1986–9. Herklots worked mainly to private commission, notably portrait busts. Exhibitions included a relief at the headquarters of the Committee of Directors of Polytechnics, 1989, and 1st RWA Open Sculpture Exhibition, 1993. Lived in Melton Mowbray, Leicestershire.

Krystyna HERLING-GRUDZIŃSKA 1915–1952 Artist, designer and artist's model, sometimes listed as Krystyna Domańska-Herling. She was born Stojanowska in Jekaterynosław, Russia. Following World War I and the Bolshevik revolution she returned with her parents to Poland. After attending high school in Warsaw, Krystyna graduated in psychology from Warsaw University, during her studies showing an interest in painting. When World War II began, with her first husband Witold Domański she escaped through Hungary and Yugoslavia to the Middle East, where she worked in the canteen of the Polish Young Men's Christian Association. She began painting in her spare time, exhibiting in Baghdad, Iraq. After World War II she lived in Rome where she painted prolifically and was a member of the Pro Arte circle of Polish artists established by Józef Jarema. Krystyna remained in Rome with her second husband Gustaw Herling-Grudziński until 1947. Gustav was a notable writer and man of letters who collaborated with the Paris-based monthly *Kultura*. After moving to London she was forced by economic circumstances to work as a textile designer and artist's model but continued to paint, participating in several mixed exhibitions. Finally, she obtained a scholarship to study applied graphic art at St Martin's School of Art, although early death prevented Herling-Grudzińska from realising her full potential. She was included in Contemporary Art by Polish Artists Abroad, POSK Gallery, 1985.

Andrew HERMAN 1961– Artist who employed miscellaneous media such as wood, synthetic rubber, canvas and copper tacks. He was born and continued to work in London. Studied at Bath Academy of Art, 1980–3, then Goldsmiths' College School of Art, 1988–90. Gained a British Council Award 1991–2. He created a series of paintings, such as his entry for East & South, Norwich Gallery/Kent Institute of Art and Design, 1992, in which a work was dismantled and reconstructed. The idea was that "a painting can be conceptually divided into parts, and that each constituent part plays an independent role."

Josef HERMAN 1911–2000 Painter, draughtsman and writer, born in Warsaw, Poland, son of a Jewish cobbler. In 1929–31 studied at School of Art and Decoration, Warsaw, then worked as a graphic artist and designer in the Polish capital, beginning to exhibit his pictures, which had Expressionist tendencies. In 1938 left Poland for Brussels, where he was influenced by Permeke. Moved to Britain in 1940; lived in Glasgow for a time where he met Jankel Adler and began to paint nostalgic pictures of childhood; then moved to London where he had a show at Lefevre Galleries. A period of great importance began when Herman settled for about a decade from the mid-1940s in the Welsh mining village of Ystradgynlais and began his series of sombre-hued paintings and ink drawings of miners and their environment. In 1946 had first of a long series of exhibitions at Roland, Browse and Delbanco, and began to show internationally. Contributed pictures to Festival of Britain in 1951, and in 1956 had first of several retrospectives at Whitechapel Art Gallery, others including Swansea and Glasgow public galleries in 1963 and 1975 respectively, Boundary Gallery, 1998, Albany Gallery, Cardiff, 2000, and New Grafton Gallery, 2001. Cyril Gerber Fine Art, Glasgow, showed paintings and drawings of fishermen, miners and peasants from Scotland, Wales and Mexico in 2003, Flowers East holding a paintings retrospective in 2004. Although he lived in London from 1953, Herman travelled widely. In addition to the mining series he also drew land workers and peasants. In 1975 published his autobiography, *Related Twilights*. Work in many public galleries, including Tate. Was made RA in 1990.

Gertrude HERMES 1901–1983 Sculptor, wood engraver, lino-cutter, illustrator and designer of great versatility. Born at Bromley, Kent, Gerts, as she was known to her friends, first wanted to be a farmer and worked for a year on the land in Essex. Then she had a year at Beckenham School of Art and a year in Germany to learn the language, followed by four years at Leon Underwood's School of Painting and Sculpture at Hammersmith, 1922–6. In 1926 married the artist Blair Hughes-Stanton, divorced 1933. Was influenced by the work of Henri Gaudier-Brzeska and Brancusi and tribal sculpture in the 1920s and '30s. First commission for a portrait bust was of the writer A P Herbert, in 1931, and she became noted for her busts of writers, such as Kathleen Raine (Tate Gallery) and David Gascoyne, and heads of children. Worked for the Cresset Press, Gregynog Press and Golden Cockerel Press. During World War II went with her children to Canada and America, where precision drawing in shipyards and factories in black and white led to her turning to colour on return to England in 1945. She had taught at St Martin's before the war, and after it taught at that school as well as Camberwell, the Central School and Royal Academy Schools. Elected RA in 1971. In 1981 the Academy gave her an eightieth birthday show. Ashmolean Museum, Oxford, held The wood-engravings of Gertrude Hermes and Blair Hughes-Stanton in 1995, Redfern Gallery holding a Hermes print retrospective in 2003. Hermes' work has warmth, elegance and vitality, tinged with a functional spareness. Lived in London.

Martin HERON 1965– Sculptor, born in Cookstown, Tyrone, Northern Ireland, who completed foundation studies at John Moores University, Liverpool, 1985–6, then an honours degree in fine art there, 1986–9. Heron was involved in a number of public sculptures with wildlife themes, sometimes overseeing group efforts, such as The Aviary Tower, in Bouskell Park, Blaby, and the Kingfisher, at Mount Grace Road, Loughborough, both 1999. The 1998 carved wood Totem, at Blackmoor Special School, Blackburn, is also by him. Heron's exhibitions included Groundwork Trust, Blackburn, 1995; the Tyrone Guthrie Centre, Newliss, County Monaghan, Ireland (which holds his 1996 mixed-media Triangle/Circle/Square), 1996; and Lawrence Batley Theatre, Huddersfield, 1998. He lived for a time in Derbyshire.

Patrick HERON 1920–1999 Painter, designer, writer and teacher, born in Leeds, son of T M Heron the founder of Cresta Silks; as a child Heron lived for some time in Cornwall, where he eventually settled at Zennor, St Ives. Studied at Slade School of Fine Art, 1937–9. As a conscientious objector during World War II he worked on the land, also having a short time at Leach Pottery, St Ives. In London in 1945 he resumed painting and had first solo show at Redfern Gallery, 1947. Wrote on art for *New English Weekly*, also for *New Statesman and Nation* and for *Arts*, the New York-based publication, his views gaining a wide readership. Painted frequently in Cornwall during visits, buying his permanent home, Eagles Nest, in 1955. Taught at Central School of Arts and Crafts, 1953–6. In mid-1950s Heron began to paint abstract works, and he was Britain's strongest link with the New York Abstract Expressionists, discussing the first exhibition of their works in Europe in 1956. The group show that he advised on – Metavisual, Tachiste, Abstract Painting in England Today – at Redfern Gallery in 1957 was a landmark. His soft-edged lozenges of vibrant colour became unmistakeable, and were shown in a number of solo exhibitions at Bertha Schaefer Gallery, New York, from 1960 and elsewhere widely abroad. Camden Arts Centre showed big new abstracts in 1994. Susanna Heron was his daughter. Tate Gallery, which with other major public collections holds his work, gave Heron an important exhibition in 1998. Waddington Galleries showed 1945–55 paintings in 2000, 1956–69 in 2002, and 1970–84 in 2004.

Susanna HERON 1949– Artist in a variety of media and writer, born in Cornwall, where she grew up. She was the daughter of the painter and writer Patrick Heron. Attended Falmouth School of Art, 1967–8, then Central School of Art & Design, 1969–71. In 1978–9 she was in America under a United Kingdom/United States Bicentennial Arts Fellowship. She also won a British Council/National Endowment for the Arts. In 1989 Heron gained a Thornton Bequest for Bronze Casting from the Arts Council and won a sculpture prize in the Tree of Life Exhibition, South Bank Centre, and tour. Her solo exhibitions dated from 1985 at Whitechapel Art Gallery, later ones including Newlyn Art Gallery and tour, 1992. Camden Arts Centre, where she had shown in 1989, had an exhibition in connection with her book *Shima: Island and Garden*, based on the family home Eagles Nest, in Cornwall, published 1992, and Elements, at Mead Gallery, Warwick Arts Centre, Coventry, 2003. Cibachrome prints and slate carvings were features of Heron's work. This was held by Victoria & Albert Museum, National Museum of Wales in Cardiff, Contemporary Art Society and overseas. In 2003, working with the architects Bennetts Associates, Heron created London's first "art street", behind Tate Britain, transforming a grubby short-cut with such features as engraved-slate and silvered-glass walls, a café and tranquil area. Lived in London.

George HERRAGHTY 1949– Painter, often of miniatures, draughtsman and artist in collage, born in Letterfourie, Banffshire. He studied at Duncan of Jordanstone College of Art, Dundee, 1967–71, where his teachers included Alberto Morrocco and David McClure. He went on to do post-diploma work and in 1972 a Major Travelling Scholarship took Herraghty extensively around Europe. Showed RSA, SSA, elsewhere in Scotland, and in Germany. Lived in Dundee, Angus.

Ed HERRING 1945–2003 Artist, lecturer and designer, born in Southport, Lancashire, as Albert Edward George Herring. He did a foundation course at Harris College, Preston, 1962–3; fine art degree, Manchester College of Art, 1963–6; and postgraduate studies in print at Central School of Art, 1966–7. Herring was a consultant designer with W G Mitchell Design Group. His teaching posts, as visiting or senior lecturer, were at Manchester College of Art & Design, Kent Institute of Art & Design, Slade School of Fine Art, Goldsmiths' College, North East London Polytechnic and East Ham College of Technology (later Newham Community College). He was co-founder with his wife Sally Gosheron of Atelier de la Rose, Montcabrier, France, from 1991 a centre for creative short courses. Herring was a full member of the International Society for Education through Art (InSea). In his work Herring was influenced by the artwork of Duchamp, Ernst and Klee and the writings of Wittgenstein, Robbe-Grillet and James Joyce. His best-known output of the 1960s and 1970s used photography and documentation to record environmental statements made by him in primarily unpopulated areas. This pioneering work questioned cultural responsibilities using the iconography of the most subtle forms of intervention. Group exhibitions included Northern Young Contemporaries, Manchester, 1966; Environments Reversal, New Space and Survey'69, all at Camden Arts Centre, 1969; Survey of the British Avant-Garde, London and Berlin, 1972; Le Witt, Huebler, Herring, Museum of Modern Art, Oxford, 1973; Auction for the Miners, County Hall, 1984; and Les Gens d'Ici, Fotofolie, Puy l'Evêque, 1992. Herring's solo exhibitions were Sequel, Central Library, Swiss Cottage, 1970; Ed Herring – ACTS, Nigel Greenwood Gallery, 1973; and Quercy en Détail, Jean Touzot bookshop, Paris, 1993. In addition to many private collections globally, public collections holding Herring's work include the Victoria & Albert Museum; Tate Gallery (collaboration with Keith Arnatt in the Self Burial project); Museum of Modern Art, New York; Musée National d'Art Moderne, Paris; and Belgrade University.

Eugen HERSCH 1887–1967 Painter, mural artist, printmaker and teacher, born in Berlin, where he was trained in the old master tradition at the Koniglichen Kunstakademie. After graduating he won the Rome Prize and spent 1910–12 in Italy. Returning to Berlin he established a fine career as a portrait painter, broken by a period during World War I as a war artist. As life became hard for Jews in Nazi Germany, Hersch with his wife left for England in 1939 where, after a period of internment in the Liverpool area, he began to reshape his career. Showed at RA, PS, RP, Whitechapel Art Gallery and elsewhere and completed a large mural Triptych in Blue for Wandsworth Town Hall. His final work, which took five years, is a huge mural of twelve paintings: A Requiem to Comfort the Bereaved. His work is in several public collections in Germany and was commemorated with a show at John Denham Gallery in 1990. Lived in London.

Samuel Irvine HERTFORD fl. c.1890–1960 Landscape painter, born in Liverpool but educated in America, including time in Detroit, Michigan, and Jersey City, New Jersey. Studied at Liverpool School of Art. He was a member of the Liverpool Academy and was in the mid-1920s president of the Liver Sketching Club. Exhibited RA, RCamA, Walker Art Gallery, Liverpool, widely in the north of England and in America. The critic George Whitfield described Hertford's Sound of Iona, in a 1930s Liverpool Academy show, as being a "masterpiece of its kind", in the manner of the Scottish Colourists. Stretford Art Gallery, Manchester, bought Hertford's work. Lived in Wallasey, Cheshire.

Ivie HERTSLET 1883–1977 Painter, draughtsman and writer, born in Fawkham, Kent, into a family of Swiss ancestry with a long tradition of service to Court of St James. By 1895 showed artistic talent and was sent to Westminster and then Lambeth Schools of Art, being taught at Lambeth by Philip Connard. In 1906–7 she showed four pictures at Walker Art Gallery, Liverpool, but then turned her attention to writing stories and poems in magazines and newspapers, including *Home Notes*, *The Idler*, *T P's Weekly*, *The Times*, *Country Life* and *Little Folks*. In 1917 married John Craik-Henderson, a lawyer and politician, eventually becoming Lady Craik-Henderson. Visits to France in the 1940s revived her interest in art and she became prolific, especially landscapes of France, Scotland and Sussex, where she settled at Brewhurst. Showed latterly at RA and Royal Glasgow Institute of the Fine Arts. She was painted by Glyn Philpot, Eric Kennington and Archibald McGlashan, these portraits being included in a retrospective of her work at Alpine Gallery, 1979.

Pascal HERVEY 1969– Artist who used a mix of coloured gloss paints sprayed with a mastic gun into bubblewrap in horizontal and vertical bands to create Untitled, in the 1997–8 John Moores Liverpool Exhibition. Hervey was born in Swindon, Wiltshire, and settled in London. After studying at the Slade School of Fine Art, 1989–93, he attended Chelsea College of Art, 1993–4. In 1996 he showed at Bund and Lotta Hammer Galleries, in 1998 having a first solo exhibition at Deutsch-Britische Freundschaft.

Caroline HERVEY-BATHURST 1936– Painter who studied at Sir John Cass College under Vivian Pitchforth and St Martin's School of Art under Jehan Daly. She showed at the RA Summer Exhibition, RP, Chelsea Physic Garden and Alpine Club. In 1997, had a solo exhibition with Piers Feetham Gallery. Sir Brinsley Ford owned her work.

Sophie HERXHEIMER 1963– Painter and lecturer, born in London, who studied at Camberwell School of Arts & Crafts, Chelsea School of Art and École des Beaux-Arts in Montpellier, France. Herxheimer was a visiting lecturer at Winchester School of Art and Central St Martin's College of Art & Design. Showed at Whitworth Young Contemporaries at Whitworth Art Gallery, Manchester, 1985; Riverside Open at Riverside Studios, 1986; South Bank Picture Show, Royal Festival Hall, from 1989; BP Portrait Award at National Portrait Gallery, 1993; and Royal Over-Seas League Open, 1995. Had a solo exhibition at Bloomsbury Theatre, 1988, later ones including Atlantis, 1994. Publications including Herxheimer's work included *Wonder Tales*, edited by Marina Warner, 1994, and Pomme Clayton's retelling of *Tales of Amazing Maidens*, 1995. London Lighthouse holds Herxheimer's work.

Walter HERZ 1909–1965 Commercial artist, illustrator, painter and bibliophile, born in Naetirisch Ostrak, Austria (later Czechoslovakia), into a middle-class but uncultured family. His small stature made him a bookworm, and through a strong character and intelligence he developed knowledge of book collecting and talents for painting and drawing while studying law. When Hitler invaded Czechoslovakia Herz fled without his family to Poland, then England, arriving in 1939. Became a freelance commercial artist, a job he always disliked, although he went on to illustrate many books on Jewish subjects and books for children. From 1947 he joined his lifelong friend V V Rosenfeld in a commercial art business. The work eliminated time for his own painting. In 1945 Herz tried to commit suicide through a drugs overdose, having heard his mother had been murdered by the Nazis. He was resuscitated, but the experience clouded the rest of his life. Became an obsessive and knowledgeable book collector who specialised in sixteenth-century volumes, old and first editions of the Greek and Roman classics, English literature of the eighteenth century and art. Died of heart failure. Through Rosenfeld his library was donated to The Jewish National & University Library, Jerusalem. Ben Uri Art Society holds work by Herz, who designed the Holocaust memorial for Leicester Synagogue.

Raya HERZIG fl. from early 1970s– Painter, born at Kartuzy, near Gdánsk, Poland. As a small child of a cultured family she had to endure the terror of the ghetto and the concentration camp, only her sister surviving, experiences which left a mark on her work. For years she carried her ideas inside her until one day she started to paint, after which she worked in a number of styles, including Surrealism and fantasy. One series included nudes with faces replaced by motionless masks; then there were the Transformer and Monuments series. After World War II Herzig lived in Sweden, Switzerland and Italy, taking up Swiss citizenship and working as a professional painter from 1971. She became a member of the Union of Swiss Painters, Sculptors and Architects (GSMBA) in 1973. In 1990 she moved to Britain and eventually to Dartmouth, Devon. From 1971 she showed with the annual exhibition of Basle artists, Kunsthalle Basle, elsewhere in Switzerland and abroad in mixed shows, including Swiss Painters in Britain at October Gallery, 1991. Showed in solo exhibitions from 1972, at Galerie Niggli, St Gallen and Galerie Mascotte, Basle; at Stara Kordegarda, Warsaw, 1980; and in 1992 at Polish Cultural Institute.

Barbara HESELTINE 1906–1996 Theatre designer, costume specialist and painter, known as Billy Heseltine and married to Chartres Molony. After school she studied at Central School of Arts and Crafts and trained as a teacher, but, not wanting to teach indefinitely beyond a short time at the Central, she went to the Old Vic to learn theatre work. After several years there, in the second half of the 1930s Heseltine freelanced, clients including the Shakespeare Theatre at Stratford, Sadler's Wells and Regent's Park Open Air Theatre. The war years were spent at Birmingham Repertory, after which Heseltine returned to Sadler's Wells for a few years, then retired. The war had proved a strain, so she began painting again for her own pleasure. Her work included individualistic landscapes completed during a number of holidays in Ireland, and portraits. Heseltine also took up the circus as a subject, having a backstage pass to Bertram Mills at Olympia where she made numerous sketches, some of which she worked up into finished watercolours and oils. Little of Heseltine's work was sold in her lifetime. She lived latterly in London, although her funeral was at Stourbridge Crematorium in Worcestershire.

John HESELTINE fl. from 1940s– Painter, illustrator and teacher, husband of the artist Pam Masco, noted for his English and continental scenes, figure studies and portraits. London-born Heseltine studied at South-East Essex College of Art, obtaining a teaching diploma and scholarship to the Royal College of Art, 1942. In 1941 he gained the Farquharson Memorial Prize. After Royal Naval service for four years he worked as art editor for Norman Kark Publications, then in 1949 began a freelance career as an illustrator. In 1969 Heseltine was commissioned by International Publishing Corporation to paint the investiture of the Prince of Wales. He lectured at Wellington College and adjudicated for South-East Essex College of Art through the 1970s. RP, Bourne Gallery in Reigate and David Messum Gallery showed Heseltine's pictures, which included large, textured, quasi-abstract works. He produced a number of marine subjects among which are two paintings of H M S *Hermes* in the South Atlantic, which hang in the officers' mess at Yeovilton and in the Dartmouth Naval Museum. Lived in Petworth, Sussex.

Richard HESELTINE 1914– Artist, fruit farmer and soldier, born in Wimbledon, Surrey, whose aunt was the children's portraitist Phyllis Heseltine, other family members including John Postle Heseltine the printmaker and Philip Heseltine (Peter Warlock), the composer. Richard Heseltine studied art part-time with Otway McCannell at Farnham School of Art in the early 1930s and although he regarded himself "as a self-taught amateur, with no qualifications in art, I have taught it at a boys' prep school, Old Buckenham Hall, at Brettenham, and an adult class at Little Cornard," both in Suffolk. Heseltine was a fruit farmer in Kent when joining the 3rd Hussars in World War II, serving as a skilful, dashing and unorthodox tank commander in the Western Desert, rising to the rank of major and winning the Military Cross. His extensively illustrated memoirs were published in 2001 as *Pippin's Progress*. Heseltine was a member of Colchester Art Society and Gainsborough's House, Sudbury, Print Workshop. Exhibitions included a solo show of sculpture at Letchworth Museum and Art Gallery, 1963; also The Minories, Colchester, 1976; and Quay Theatre, Sudbury, 1991. Colchester Art Society and the 3rd Hussars (now Queen's Own Hussars) Museum, Warwick, hold his work and there are stone carvings in churches at Little Cornard and Assington, Suffolk, where he lived.

Florence HESS 1891–1974 Landscape painter, born in Leeds. She studied at Leeds School of Art and from 1905 with the Yorkshire painter Mark Senior, whose friend and assistant she became, accompanying him on his visits to Bruges and Holland. She painted along the coast of Yorkshire and Norfolk, her earlier work showing Senior's influence especially. Exhibited RA, NEAC, WIAC and widely in the provinces. Was a keen member of Fylingdales Group. Lived in London for some time and at Alwoodley, near Leeds.

I J Berthe HESS 1925– Painter and teacher whose work as well as being signed was authenticated by a thumb-print on the back. She was born in Paris, her father being a Sunday painter, and she studied at Académie des Beaux-Arts, free classes during World War II, but was largely self-taught. Moved to London in 1967 with her technocrat and sculptor husband Adolph, having travelled widely, and opened the BH Corner Gallery near St Paul's Cathedral, where her work was shown. Above it Hess ran an academy where she taught Bertisme, a technique by which a painting was sculpted by brush out of enormous quantities of paint; finished surfaces could be several inches thick and take two years to dry. Museums in Britain, France and Germany showed Hess's pictures. In 1972 part of BH Corner Gallery was turned into a permanent display of the work, while others' pictures were also on view, and in 1973 another permanent exhibition was set up in the Rue Faubourg Poissonièrre, Paris.

Tisa HESS 1903–2001 Versatile artist and teacher, born in Tressow, Germany, full name Countess Elisabeth von der Schulenburg, who, as daughter of Count Friedrich von der Schulenburg, grew up among the Prussian nobility. She was sometimes known as Tisa Schulenberg, apparently a corruption of Teaser, a nickname bestowed on her by a governess. She spent her infancy in London where from 1902–6 her father was military attaché. Back in Germany, Tisa attended the Berlin Academy of Arts and the sculpture classes of Fritz Klimsch and, against her father's wish, studied art in Paris, 1925–8. After the rise of Adolf Hitler, with her husband from 1929, the wealthy businessman and art collector Fritz Hess, she left Germany in 1934 for London. They had a house in Highgate, she was a friend of Henry Moore and Barbara Hepworth, who encouraged her to carve, and joined the anti-Fascist AIA. The Hesses also lived in Walberswick, Suffolk, at the invitation of Ernst Freud, son of Sigmund, father of Lucian, Clement and Stephen. Ernst designed a house for them, Oak Barn, later renamed Elphinstone Corner, overlooking the marshes. Julia Reisz, widow of the film director Karel Reisz, recalled Tisa as a striking figure, beautiful and blonde in a bikini. She was encouraged to visit Northumberland, where she taught at The Spennymoor Settlement. Mines and miners became a focus of her work, which continued later in the Ruhr area of Germany. After divorcing Hess in 1938 she went back to Germany, where she later remarried. In 1939 her German links prevented her return to Britain, the AIA unsuccessfully campaigning for her readmittance. Tisa was opposed to Nazism, as was her brother Fritz, who was brutally hanged after the failure of the 1944 plot to assassinate Hitler. Following a failed marriage to Carl Ulrich von Barner, 1939–46, in 1948 Tisa converted to Catholicism and entered the Ursuline convent at Dorsten, adopting the name Sister Paula, but continued to sculpt, paint and draw, latterly publishing several books of memoirs. She returned periodically to her beloved England and the pits at Durham. Her work is signed Tisa Hess or just Tisa. Much of it was left in the northeast of England, where she had shows at the Bede Gallery, Jarrow, 1975; Viking Gallery, Jarrow, 2000; and Hutchinson Gallery, Town Hall, Bishop Auckland, 2001, marking the seventieth anniversary of The Spennymoor Settlement. The Holocaust Museum, Auschwitz, holds examples. Others were sold by Phillips Auctioneers, Leeds, in 2001.

Guy HETHERINGTON 1948– He studied at Kingston College of Art, 1968–72. Group appearances included Contemporary Choice, Serpentine Gallery, 1982; Contemporary Art Society Market, 1986; Whitechapel Open, Whitechapel Art Gallery, 1988; and Critics Space 5, at Air Gallery, and East End Open Studios, at Milborne Street, both 1989. In 1980 Hetherington showed solo at House Gallery.

Rene HETHERINGTON 1921– Sculptor in a variety of materials, and teacher, born in Yorkshire. She attended Leeds College of Art and the Royal College of Art. Her work is held in a number of private collections in Britain and abroad and was bought by Leeds Education Authority. RBA member. Lived in Carlisle, Cumbria.

Charles HETT 1939– Painter, conservator and teacher, born in Freshford, Somerset, grandson of the artist Ambrose McEvoy. He studied at Byam Shaw School, 1958–60, then at Royal Academy Schools, 1961–5, winning the Armitage Prize. From 1965–7 Hett taught part-time and painted mostly landcape in the Fens and Cornwall. After studying artifact conservation, 1968–9, he worked mostly in that field, in Mexico, 1969–72, subsequently in Ottawa, Canada, where he lived. While in England, 1965–8, Hett worked on stage with The Alberts group. He showed at NEAC, RBA and at Leicester Galleries, having a one-man show in 1967, from which Lord Goodman bought work. Garman-Ryan Collection at Walsall Museum & Art Gallery also holds.

Lucette HEUSEUX 1913– Painter, brought up in Brussels, Belgium, where she attended the university. As well as exhibiting in Belgium she showed at RA, RP, RWS, widely in the provinces and in North America. She lived there in New York and in London.

Michael HEVESI 1952– Multi-talented artist, designer and poet, his mother the English ballerina Beryl Morina, his father Hans Hevesi, Austrian-Hungarian and an Oxford graduate, who excavated in Israel where Michael spent his initial childhood. During education in England Michael became preoccupied with primitive masks, reflected in his early oil crayon works and terracotta sculptures. While reading social anthropology at the University of Kent, Canterbury, Hevesi was introduced to the shadow puppet theatre of Indonesia which influenced his work from the 1980s onwards. After graduating Hevesi showed sculptures and paintings at the Quatre Gats café gallery in Barcelona, returning to Spain seven years later, in 1986, to exhibit at the Ateneu, Sitges. The following year he toured with The Spirit of Mankind: sculpture from Sitges, Barcelona, Granada and Paris. Hevesi extended his range in the 1990s and in 1991 the London store Harvey Nichols featured his sculptural work in nearly 30 windows. He also showed sculpture chairs at the Business Design Centre, the Ben Uri Gallery and the International Furniture Fairs at Utrecht, in the Netherlands, and in Paris. Hevesi's collection of poems *From the Dunes of Ashkelon to the Chill of the Cathedral Squares* was completed in 1996. In 1997 he conceived the idea of housing works in an ambitious Corridor of Life, "a major new national and international cultural venue", featured in an exhibition at The Gallery in Cork Street, 2004. Hevesi lived in Winchester, Hampshire.

Harold Cornelius HEWARD 1881–1973 Landscape, marine and figure painter in various media; black-and-white illustrator. Born in Southsea, Hampshire, Heward studied at Lambeth School of Art and privately. Exhibited at RA, RI, RSW, ROI, in the provinces and at the Paris Salon. Lived in Surbiton, Surrey.

Martin HEWER 1950– Versatile artist and teacher, born in Switzerland, who studied painting and printmaking at

Wimbledon, 1968–72, Baroda, 1973–4, and Fuchs Academy in Austria, 1974–7. Travelled widely, teaching photography, painting and printmaking, in Germany, Spain and Britain, also exhibiting abroad including Hungary. In 1998 Hewer shared an exhibition at East West Gallery, mainly paintings done while living in the old Arabic quarter of Granada. He returned to live in England in 1994.

Joseph HEWES 1954– Painter who studied for two terms at Taunton College of Art, 1970, having attended secondary modern school. He was included in the Piccadilly Gallery's 1985–6 show The Brotherhood of Ruralists and Friends. Lived at Warleggan, Cornwall.

William HEWISON 1925–2002 Painter and illustrator, born in South Shields, County Durham. He studied at the Art School there, 1941–3, Regent Street Polytechnic School of Art, 1947–9, and London University. Became art editor of the magazine *Punch*, 1960–84, was known for his theatrical drawings for the magazine and for *The Times*, and in his long-running *Punch* series "Hewison's People" lampooned many in the public eye with a line said to have "the power of a rhino whip and the spikiness of barbed wire." As well as humorous work for the press Hewison took part in Young Contemporaries, Whitechapel Art Gallery and Arts Council exhibitions. Hewison's novel *Mindfire*, published in 1973, drew on his World War II experiences as a gunner and wireless operator in a Cromwell tank after the D-Day landings in France. Lived in London.

Forrest HEWIT 1870–1956 Painter, born in Salford, Lancashire, who studied with Walter Sickert and T C Dugdale and who was closely associated with the MAFA. Hewit was a good figure painter whose works have much in common with Sickert's in approach. He painted many landscapes in England, on the continent, in China and elsewhere. Hewit was a director and vice-chairman of the Manchester-based Calico Printers' Association. This enabled him to help more needy painters, notably Frances Hodgkins, who acted for a time as designer. Hewit exhibited widely, including RA, NEAC, Cooling Galleries and RBA. Work held by several public collections. Lived in Wilmslow, Cheshire.

Eric HEWITSON 1966– Artist using modern media, who graduated with honours in fine art from the University of Wales. Hewitson aimed to put classical themes into a contemporary context, taking elements from diverse disciplines such as mathematics, philosophy, architecture, literature and science. In 1995, Simon-Peter Santospirito "launched the world's first virtual reality gallery to showcase Hewitson's complete genetic DNA fingerprint (which we published in *Art and Text* the previous year) and a range of other scientific experiments and analyses into his identity, such as PET and MRO brain scans and electronic scanning micrographs. The virtual reality gallery was shown in the ICA's 1996 Pandaemonium show, commemorating 100 years of the moving image." Hewitson's other shows included Kreuzberg, Berlin, Germany, in 1988, with the installation Frozen Meat; studio exhibitions in Portugal and Cairo in 1989 and 1990; Jerome Gallery, Sydney, Australia, paintings, First Past The Post Modern, 1991; Sue Williams Gallery, paintings, Oh, but do not ask what is it!, and Salama-Caro Gallery, paintings, Skin, both 1993; Darling Harbour, Sydney, International Convention For Cell Research, installation, Genetically Me Genetically You, 1994; Jibby Beane Gallery, solo, Sometimes I don't know myself at all, 1995; and Coventry Gallery, 1996. Hewitson's work was in numerous corporate and private collections, including Novartis; Oracle; More O'Ferrall Plc; American Embassy, Canberra; Sakura Global Capital, Sakura Bank; Smith-Kline Beecham; and Telecom Australia, Executive Collection.

Geoffrey HEWITT 1930– Painter, illustrator and teacher, born in Horden, County Durham. Studied at Royal College of Art and went on to lecture at Birmingham College of Art. Exhibited widely in group shows, including RA, RBSA, LG and overseas, and had a series of one-man exhibitions including Shipley Gallery, Univision Gallery and Arden Gallery. Illustrated books and magazines. City Art Gallery, Birmingham, holds his work.

May R HEWITT fl. c.1940–1960 Painter in oil, born in Newcastle upon Tyne where she studied art part-time at King's College. She showed locally, at the Laing Art Gallery in Newcastle and Shipley Art Gallery in Gateshead, where she lived, and belonged to the local Art Club. In the 1950s she was for much of the decade secretary of the Federation of Northern Art Societies.

Pauline HEWITT 1907– Landscape and portrait painter in oil who went on to teach after studying at the Slade School of Fine Art and in Paris. Exhibited RA, SWA and RI. Lived in St Ives, Cornwall.

Andrew HEWKIN 1949– Figurative painter, his bright palette reflecting the many exotic locations painted. Hewkin was born in the Midlands, studying at Stourbridge Art College; West of England Art College, Bristol; and Royal College of Art, gaining a first-class master's degree in 1973. Notable teachers included David Inshaw, Peter Blake, Ruskin Spear, Leonard Rosoman and Carel Weight. He won the Burston Award for Painting, 1972, and the John Minton Travelling Scholarship, 1973. Paintings of the Greek Islands, Turkey and Cyprus formed his first solo show at Trafford Gallery, 1974. After living in the West Indies for three years Hewkins became a global traveller. Commissions included Thomas Cook, to travel down the Nile; British Airways, to produce four paintings entitled The Four Corners of the World; a logo for the Peace Harmony concert in Tokyo to commemorate the end of the Gulf War; *Playboy* to paint a version of the rabbit logo; and Baring Securities, 14 large works for a new bank. Books included *Songs to the Bedroom Walls*, with Susan George, 1987, and a limited-edition *Vietnamese Sketchbook*, 1991. In the early 1970s Hewkin showed at RA Summer Exhibition and Chichester Festival. Then he exhibited widely internationally, including regularly with the Hamilton Gallery. There was a retrospective at Royal Westmorland (Barbados) and an exhibition The Quintessential Caribbean at The Gallery in Cork Street, both 2000. The British royal family and international public and private collections own Hewkin's work. He had a studio in London.

Elsie Dalton HEWLAND 1901–1979 Painter of figure and genre subjects, educated in the north of England, who attended Sheffield College of Art, 1921–4, then the Royal Academy Schools, 1926–30, under Walter Westley Russell. Exhibited RA, RWS and in the provinces, but is especially known for her World War II pictures, which depict life on the home front. Imperial War Museum holds her work, which was much-anthologised in war-related books, such as Eric Newton's *War Through Artists' Eyes*. Lived at Chalfont St Giles, Buckinghamshire, for a time, also near Ventnor, Isle of Wight. She is sometimes recorded as Elise (a name she adopted) Dalton Hewland or just E Dalton Hewland.

Francis HEWLETT 1930– Painter, ceramic sculptor and teacher, born in Bristol. He studied painting and etching at West of England College of Art there, 1948–52; was at École des Beaux-Arts, Paris, 1953; studied at Slade School of Fine Art, 1953–5, and worked for a time with William Coldstream and Claude Rogers. He was head of painting at Falmouth School of Art, 1960–81, settling in the Cornish town after moving to the county in 1957. In 1977 Hewlett was Gregynog Arts Fellow, University of Wales, in Newtown. Hewlett worked in ceramics, mainly large-scale sculpture, 1968–75, then from 1981 concentrated on pictures of the Bristol Empire theatre, based on much earlier drawings. The colourful, evocative pictures were shown at Browse & Darby in 1993. Solo exhibition, Falmouth Art Gallery, 2000. Hewlett showed at RA, RWA of which he was a member and at Newlyn Orion Gallery and in 1992 was included in Artists from Cornwall at RWA. Ulster Museum in Belfast; National Library of Wales in Aberystwyth; and public galleries in Leicester, Plymouth, Portsmouth and Southampton hold examples. Lived in Falmouth, Cornwall.

Charles HEWLINGS 1948– Abstract sculptor, and teacher, producing large works in such materials as concrete, steel, wood, pigment and fired clay. He gained an honours degree in fine art at University of Newcastle upon Tyne, 1967–71, then did an advanced sculpture course at St Martin's School of Art, 1971–3. Interspersed with periods as a part-time lecturer, Hewlings held a Wilhelm Lehmbruck Scholarship in Duisburg, West Germany, 1982–4; took part in the Triangle Artists' Workshop, Pine Plains, New York, 1984; was visiting sculptor at School of the Museum of Fine Arts, Boston, America, 1986, in the same year participating in the Hardingham Sculpture Workshop in Norfolk; and in 1991 held the Picker Lectureship, Kingston Polytechnic. Took part in numerous mixed shows, including Platform '73, Museum of Modern Art, Oxford, 1973; Arts Council Purchases and Awards, Serpentine Gallery, 1979, the year of his Arts Council Major Award; Sculpture at Cannizaro Park, 1985; and Galerie Dagmar, 1993. Had a solo show at Acme Gallery, 1976, later ones including a series at Smith Jariwala/Kapil Jariwala Galleries from 1990. London Borough of Hounslow; Wilhelm Lehmbruck Museum, Duisburg; and St Matthew's Church, Brixton, also hold examples.

Ann HEWSON 1933– Painter, draughtsman and clay sculptor, born and lived in London. Studied at South-West Essex Technical College after leaving school; lived in the country without much painting; then returned to London, attending evening classes at Regent Street Polytechnic School of Art. Married one of her teachers, Clifford Hall. Showed in various London galleries, including a shared exhibition with Nigel Lambourne at Belgrave Gallery, 1976, and a solo show at John Denham Gallery, 1985.

Cicely HEY 1896–1980 Painter and modeller of miniature period figures, born at Faringdon, Oxfordshire. She studied at the Brussels School of Art, Central School of Arts and Crafts and Slade School of Fine Art. She was married to the art critic and editor of the *Burlington Magazine*, R R Tatlock. Her friendship with the painter Walter Sickert is well recorded in books on him. He met her at a Roger Fry lecture in 1922 after which he drew and painted her many times in the 1920s, much attracted by her boyish, humorous expression. Hey began to exhibit in group shows about this time. She showed with the LG and Denbighshire Art Society for long periods, as well as with the NS, WIAC and SGA. Her first one-man show was of portrait drawings at Reid and Lefevre in 1933. In 1941 she moved to Wales, after which she concentrated on her period figures, which were shown widely. Hey's work is in the collections of Glynn Vivian Art Gallery, Swansea, British Museum and Reading University's Rural Life Museum. Lived at Llysfaen, Clwyd.

Anthony HEYWOOD 1952– Sculptor and teacher, born in Hartlepool, County Durham, who worked in mixed media. He studied at Newcastle Polytechnic, 1971–4, teachers Fenwick Lawson, Gilbert Ward, Fred Watson, Derek Dalton and John Crisp, obtaining an honours degree in sculpture, then was at Christ Church College, Canterbury, 1975–6. Heywood had enormously varied teaching experience. Apart from teaching at Kent Institute of Art & Design, Canterbury, he was a part-time social worker, ran children's classes, classes for the mentally and physically handicapped and taught at South Kent College, Cyprus School of Art, Royal College of Art and elsewhere. Among his awards were a Harkness Fellowhip, British Council Award and a South East Arts Artists' Award. He was well written up in the national press and appeared on television programmes such as *Wogan* and *Blue Peter*. Also showed in numerous group exhibitions including RA Summer Exhibition, Minories Gallery and Sculpture at Canterbury, 1992. His solo shows included Cubitt Gallery, 1994; Eagle Gallery, 1995; and Robert Pardo Gallery, New York, America, 1999. Heywood wrote that "in many ways my work stems from the Duchampian tradition. I use readymades in all different contexts, to reinforce or subvert ideas I am pursuing, including all media and materials." Tate Special Collections and Museum of Art in Sharjah, United Arab Emirates, held examples. Heywood lived in Staple, Canterbury, Kent.

Sally HEYWOOD 1964– Painter, born in Liverpool, who studied at Oxford University, 1982–3, then Royal Academy Schools, 1984–7. Among awards won in 1987 were the Creswick Landscape Prize, David Murray Landscape Award and the Dunoyer de Segonzac Travelling Scholarship. In 1987–8 Heywood won a fellowship in painting at Gloucestershire College of Art, a British Council Scholarship to the German Democratic Republic following in 1990–1, and from 1990 she lived and worked in Berlin. Heywood's abstract work was gestural with very thick impasto and a rich palette, as seen in a three-artist show at Paton Gallery in 1994. Group exhibitions included Red Herring Art Gallery, Brighton, 1989, other appearances at Paton Gallery and elsewhere on the continent, especially in Germany. Solo exhibitions included Midland Bank Headquarters, 1986; Paton Gallery, 1990; Sperl Gallery, Potsdam, 1991; Ministry of Culture, Land Brandenburg, 1992, and Broadbent 2002. Metropolitan Museum of Art, New

York; Stroud District Council; and Art in Hospitals hold examples.

Alfred HEYWORTH 1926–1976 Painter, draughtsman and teacher, born in Birmingham. He attended Moseley Junior Art School, 1939–42, Birmingham College of Art, 1942–6, Royal College of Art, 1946–50, and Académie de la Grande Chaumière, in Paris, 1950–1. He gained a French Government Scholarship. Went on to be a visiting teacher at Kingston College of Art and Epsom School of Art. Heyworth was a member of RWS, RBA and NEAC. Public galleries in Birmingham, Bradford, Preston and Sheffield hold examples. He was a Chelsea Arts Club member who lived in Chiswick, west London, and died in Charing Cross Hospital.

David HIBBERT 1946–1991 Painter and draughtsman, born in Berkshire, who left school in 1959 to concentrate on painting. Produced haunting figure and landscape paintings in soft, earthy colours. He studied sculpture with Shelley Fausset for two years in 1960s, then attended Croydon College of Art, 1966–7, where he claimed he learned little. Went through rigorous study of such artists as Leonardo, Breughel and Dürer and became interested in surface and texture. Patrick Hayman, Bernard Leach and Peter Lanyon were key influences as were the Malvern Hills, where he lived much of his life, moving to Hastings, Sussex, in 1982. Its Museum and Art Gallery gave him a memorial show, 1992–3. Hibbert's solo shows were at Search Gallery, 1973, and Hereford City Museum, 1985. Mixed exhibitions included RA Summer Exhibition from 1987; LG 75th Anniversary Exhibition, at Royal College of Art, 1988; and in same year Louise Hallett Gallery.

Phyllis I HIBBERT 1903– Flower painter and teacher. She studied at Preston and Liverpool Schools of Art and went on to teach at a College of Further Education in the Lytham St Annes area of Lancashire where she lived. Showed at RA, SWA, RCamA, Manchester Academy and Walker Art Gallery in Liverpool. Harris Museum and Art Gallery in Preston holds her watercolour Nasturtiums. Hibbert was a regular exhibitor in Lancashire for some 45 years from 1927 at the Lancashire Art Exhibition, her watercolours of flowers often incorporating pottery or statuettes.

Allanson HICK 1898–1975 Architect and painter in oil and watercolour, born in Hull, Yorkshire. He attended the Grammar School there and College of Art. Exhibited widely. From 1935–55 his works were accepted annually at RA and he was a founder-member of RSMA. Ferens Art Gallery, Hull, holds a batch of work by him and he is also represented in Mansfield Art Gallery. Member of Art Workers' Guild and Chelsea Arts Club. Lived in Hornsea, Yorkshire.

Norman HICKIN 1910–1990 Artist in scraperboard, born in Birmingham. He was self-taught but was influenced by Bernard Fleetwood-Walker while at Aston Grammar School. Hickin trained as an entomologist, graduating in 1936 and obtaining his doctorate in 1940. For a time he was a rubber technologist at Dunlop, then became scientific director of Rentokil, the pest control firm. He was primarily a naturalist who loved drawing. Among his books, which he illustrated, were *African Notebook*, 1969, and *Beachcombing for Beginners*, 1975. Also showed with SWLA, of which he was a member. Died at Bewdley, Worcestershire.

Jason HICKLIN 1966– Painter and printmaker who attended Stafford College of Art, with distinction, 1984–5, and Central St Martins, 1985–93, graduating in painting with a diploma in advanced printmaking. Group shows included Bankside Open, Bankside Gallery, 1992; RE and RA, both from 1994; and NEAC, 1996. Showed solo with Attendi from 1996. He shared a show with Liam Hanley at Beardsmore Gallery in 1999. North House Gallery, Manningtree, exhibited Hicklin's Landscapes 04–05 in 2005.

Edward Albert HICKLING 1913–1999 Painter and technical illustrator, born in Nottingham where he attended the College of Art, 1927–39, under Arthur Spooner. Showed at RA, ROI, RSMA, RP and elsewhere. Member of the Sketching Club in Derby. Lived in Breaston, Derbyshire.

Arthur Ernest HICKMAN-SMITH 1876–1956 Landscape painter, singer and teacher, born in Birmingham, father of the artist Eileen Hickman-Smith. He studied at Birmingham School of Art under Edward Taylor and James Valentine Jelley. Hicky, as he was known, served as a captain in World War I, was for a time a regimental bandmaster and ran seaside concert parties, being an accomplished baritone. He was a poet, wrote books of stories and and was a fellow of the Royal Society of Arts. Exhibited at RA, RBA, PS and widely in the provinces. Was co-founder and secretary of Islington Art Circle, living in Highbury, north London, for many years. He died in Winchmore Hill Hospital.

Eileen HICKMAN-SMITH fl. c.1940–1970 Sculptor, painter in oil and journalist, born in London, daughter of the painter Arthur Ernest Hickman-Smith. Miss Hickman-Smith studied art at Regent Street Polytechnic School of Art under Harold Brownsword and Geoffrey Deeley. She attended Highbury Hill School, living her life in the north London suburb. Exhibited at RA, RI, NS, WIAC, RBA and Islington Art Circle. The local town hall has a panel by her. At the time of her father's death, in 1956, she was already under medical care.

Amy Elizabeth Blanche HICKS 1876– Watercolourist and teacher, born in Devoran, Cornwall. She studied at Truro, Falmouth and Redruth Schools of Art and in Newlyn in Norman Garstin's studio. Showed at RI, in Cornwall and at Paris Salon, in 1951. Lived in Newquay, Cornwall.

Anne HICKS 1928– Artist in oil and gouache, teacher and environmental illustrator, born in London, married to the artist Jerry Hicks. She studied at Slade School of Fine Art with Randolph Schwabe, George Charlton and William Coldstream, then was a freelance artist in Bristol from 1952. Was visiting lecturer to Bristol University School of Architecture, taught in adult education and elsewhere. Bristol University has a swimming pool mural by her; she did other murals and stage designs with her husband. Mediterranean landscapes, portraits and wild animals in natural habitats, mainly large cats, were among Hicks' favourite subjects. She was a member of RWA, which holds her work. Exhibited in British Women Painters at Museum of Modern Art in Paris, in the English provinces and held joint shows with her husband. They shared the inaugural exhibition for the Grant Bradley Gallery, Bristol in 2005. Lived in Bristol.

Jerry HICKS 1927– Artist in oil and pastel and teacher, born in London, full name Gerald Anthony William Hicks, married to the artist Anne Hicks. He studied at Slade School of Fine Art, 1944–5 and 1948–50, notable teachers including Randolph Schwabe, William Coldstream, Lucian Freud and William Townsend; and with Walter Bayes in Lancaster and London. Went on to teach at Cotham Grammar School, settling in Bristol, becoming a freelance artist in 1980. Hicks was a Judo 6th Dan which he said "influenced dynamic work". He did stage designs and murals with his wife, working in the European realist tradition, and they were extensively committed to environmental work. He was chairman of the Bristol City Docks Group, was a member and chairman of the Bristol Civic Society and was vice-chairman of the South-West Council for Sport. Hicks was a member of RWA which holds his work (including a portrait of HM The Queen). Hicks exhibited at the RA, RBA, King Street Gallery, London, the Mall Gallery, Arnolfini and Bristol Guild, as well as sharing many joint shows with his wife, Anne. He had several solo shows in London and Bristol and shared some with his wife. Hicks was winner of the Bristol 600 Competition in 1973, won the Queen's Silver Jubilee Award with a picture of Roger Bannister's sub-four minute mile and in 1984 gained an Olympic painting prize. His many portrait commissions included Sir Charles Frank, the Nobel Prize winner Nevil Mott, Lord Methuen, the Member of Parliament Marcus Lipton and the actor John Woodvine. In 1997 completed a mural commission of I K Brunel for the SS *Great Britain*. His *Judo through the Looking Glass*, with illustrations, was published in 1994, in which year he was made a Member of the Order of the British Empire "for services to sport and the community in the south west". Bristol, Brunel and Liverpool Universities and Bristol Merchant Venturers hold examples. In 2005 Jerry and Anne Hicks provided an inaugural exhibition for the Grant Bradley Gallery in Bristol.

Lesley HICKS 1964– Artist often working in mixed media on paper. She studied at the fine art department at the University of Newcastle upon Tyne, then graduated from Royal Academy Schools in 1989. Her awards included the Richard Ford Award to study in Spain, 1989. From the early 1980s she participated in many mixed shows in the provinces and London, notably The Broad Horizon, at Agnew, 1990. Work was commonly signed L F Hicks.

L F HICKS: *see* **Lesley HICKS**

Nicola HICKS 1960– Sculptor and draughtsman, born and lived in London, noted for her fine depictions of animals. She attended Chelsea School of Art, 1978–82, Royal College of Art, 1982–5. Took part in many mixed shows including Christie's Inaugural Graduate Exhibition, 1982; Artist of the Day, Angela Flowers Gallery, 1984; Basel Art Fair in Switzerland and '85 Show, Serpentine Gallery, both 1985; Yorkshire Sculpture Park, 1986; Bryan Kneale's Choice, at Arts Club, 1990; Drawing Towards Sculpture, Isis Gallery, Leigh-on-Sea, 1993; Christie's, 1996; Holland Park Sculpture Exhibition, 2000; Flowers Central, 2002; New Grafton Gallery and Schoenthal Monastery, Langenbruck, Switzerland, both 2003; Monuments to Love, Flowers East, 2003–4; and Abbot Hall Art Gallery, Kendal, 2005. Began showing with Angela Flowers in solo exhibitions in mid-1980s in London and Ireland, later shows including Peter Scott Gallery, Lancaster, and Castlefield Gallery, Manchester, both 1993. Contemporary Art Society holds her work. Commissions included a monument in Battersea Park, Brown Dog.

Peter HICKS 1937– Artist, teacher and athlete, born in Eskdale, who lived almost all his life in north Yorkshire. He was unhappy with the teaching at Scarborough School of Art so moved to Middlesbrough College of Art, where he quickly became friends with the teacher Joe Cole and his wife Sheila. In 1963 he married Joe's younger sister Eileen, also an art teacher. Hicks's work was included with Joe Cole's in Messum's 2005 exhibition The Elemental North. As a middle-distance runner and landscape painter, Hicks ran the moors and learned their contours by feel and sight. He taught in schools and colleges before becoming head of creative arts at Queen Elizabeth College, Darlington, a post held for 20 years. Throughout teaching he continued to paint, for many years experimenting with pure abstraction. It was not until he did a late master's degree at what became the University of Northumbria that he chose to return to figuration as a landscapist. Hicks worked with long-handled brushes flat on the floor and employed thin glazes of acrylic, sand and other materials to create large romantic, sensual and powerful paintings.

Philip HICKS 1928– Artist and teacher, married to the sculptor Jill Tweed, the sculptor Nicola Hicks was his daughter. He attended Winchester College, then Chelsea School of Art and Royal Academy Schools, 1949–54. From 1960–86 taught part-time in art schools in or near London, then concentrated on painting, from time to time playing jazz piano professionally. Group shows included the RA Summer Exhibition from 1957; Contemporary Prints 1970–75, Tate Gallery; Small is Beautiful, Angela Flowers Gallery, 1985; and Separate Easels, Alresford Gallery, Alresford. Had many solo shows after St George's Gallery, 1956, including Imperial War Museum, 1975, New Art Centre, 1980; Galleri Engstrom, Stockholm, Sweden, from 1980; and Heffer's Gallery, Cambridge, 1992; David Messum Gallery, which latterly represented him, from 1997; and Alpha House Gallery, Sherborne, 1999. The Tate, Victoria & Albert Museum, Imperial War Museum and other public and corporate collections hold the work of Hicks, who was at times both chairman and vice-president of the Artists General Benevolent Institution. Lived in Oxfordshire.

Roland HICKS 1967– Artist born in Aldershot, Hampshire, who studied at Winchester School of Art and the Slade School of Fine Art. In 1996, Hicks won the UCL Whitaker Memorial Commission. Group exhibitions included Viva Chihuahua!, The Tannery, and Romantische Strategien, Albatros 515, Berlin, Germany, both 1998. Hicks was a finalist in the 1999 NatWest Art Prize. He showed oil paintings of everyday objects, at first photographed at floor level away from their normal contexts, removing clues to their functions. The enlarged scale and transfer to canvas gave the final pictures an enigmatic quality, open to interpretation. There was a solo show at The Market, 2002.

Clive HICKS-JENKINS 1951– Artist in mixed media, choreographer, stage designer and director, born in Newport, Monmouthshire, who was educated in theatre studies at Italia Conti School and Ballet Rambert. He began his career as a dancer, and eventually created productions for leading companies worldwide, as well as working in television and film. In the late 1980s Hicks-Jenkins "cut down on theatre and design work to explore other areas of creative activity. I began to make and exhibit masks." In the early 1990s he met his partner Peter Wakelin, "my teacher and mentor, who gradually encouraged me to develop my painting, which is now my life." Hicks-Jenkins' masks shows included The Old Library, Cardiff, 1992–4; Oriel Myrrddin, Carmarthen, and tour, 1994–5; and Pennine Arts, Burnley, 1995. Solo exhibitions included New Theatre, Cardiff, 1984; Theatre Clwyd, Mold, 1986; and Newport Museum and Art Gallery, 2001. Mixed shows of pictures included Attic Gallery, Swansea, and Gordon Hepworth Gallery, Newton St Cyres, and Hicks-Jenkins shared an exhibition with Charles Shearer at Kilvert Gallery, Clyro, 1996. Commissions included frieze murals for natural history department at Newport Museum and Art Gallery and posters for Cardiff New Theatre and Theatre Clwyd. Theatre Museum, Covent Garden, holds his work. Lived in Pontcanna, Cardiff, where Hicks-Jenkins sought "to find a truly Welsh art, which explores the special and the profound in Welsh landscape and culture."

Charles Christopher HICKSON 1957– Painter in oil and watercolour and lecturer, born in Hull, Yorkshire. Gained an honours degree in fine art, having studied at Medlock Fine Art Centre, Manchester Polytechnic, 1976–9. He combined painting with part-time lecturing in colleges in northwest of England. Group shows included Urban Landscape at Stockport Art Gallery, and Lancashire South of the Sands, which toured from the County and Regimental Museum, Preston, both 1988; and Attitudes to the Contemporary Nude, at the latter venue, 1989. Solo shows included Lewis Textile Hall, Blackburn, 1987; Warrington Museum and Art Gallery, 1988; and Towneley Hall, Burnley, 1990. Eastern Arts Association and Towneley Hall own examples. Lived in Sale, Cheshire.

Peter HIDE 1944– Sculptor in steel and teacher, born in Carshalton, Surrey. He studied at Croydon College of Art, 1961–4, then St Martin's School of Art, 1964–7. There he was one of the first of the younger British sculptors to adopt Anthony Caro's methods, although in Hide's work structure rather than spatial arrangement was the key principle. Later Hide said that he wanted to regain "a sense of steel parts and relations between them". Taught at Norwich School of Art, 1968–74; St Martin's, 1971–8; and was professor of sculpture at the University of Alberta, in Canada, from 1977. From the late-1970s Hide took part in many workshops in North America and Europe and he visited England each year to work for several weeks in Norfolk. Hide had early exhibitions at Stockwell Depot from 1968, at Serpentine Gallery, 1976, and Arnolfini Gallery, Bristol, 1979. There was a show at Alberta House, 1984; a 10-year retrospective at Edmonton Art Gallery in 1986, the year when a series of exhibitions started at Kathleen Laverty Gallery there; and a show at André Emmerich Gallery, New York, 1990. Tate Gallery, Arts Council, City of Barcelona Museum of Modern Art and a series of North American collections hold examples.

Charles HIGGINS 1893– Oil and watercolour painter, and writer. Born at Belgrano, Buenos Aires, Higgins studied art in London, France and Italy. Often signing his pictures Pic (in his books used the pen-name Ian Dall), Higgins exhibited at galleries in London, in the USA, Rome and Paris. The Contemporary Art Society bought his work. Was married to the painter Kate Olver. Lived in London.

Dorothy Mary HIGGINS fl. from 1940s– Painter and teacher, born in Seikyi, Burma, but educated in Yorkshire. She attended Leeds College of Art, 1940–5. Showed at RSA, RP, WIAC, ROI and elsewhere. Lived at Sleights, Yorkshire.

Duncan HIGGINS 1963– Figurative painter, and lecturer, who distorted the image to produce his effect. He studied at Nottingham Trent Polytechnic, 1982–5, then taught fine art at Nottingham Trent University, living in Sheffield, Yorkshire. Group shows included Bonnington Gallery, Nottingham, 1989; Fuse, Raw Gallery, 1994; Contemporary Art Society, Royal Festival Hall, 1995; Art Frankfurt, Germany, 1997; Musio, Graves Art Gallery, Sheffield, 1998; and D90, Boots Building, Nottingham, 1999. In 2000 Higgins participated in Frame at Site the Gallery, Sheffield, with Uta Barth and Carter Potter. His later solo shows included Eye to I, Blue Gallery, 2001, and Unload there, 2004.

Lawrence HIGGINS 1964–1988 Painter and printmaker, born in Bury, Lancashire, of British and Afro-Caribbean parents. After attending Cardinal Langley Grammar School, Middleton, Higgins went to Rochdale College of Art for an arts foundation course; in 1983 he won the Student of the Year Foundation Prize. Higgins attended Goldsmiths' College School of Art in that year, graduating in 1986. Shortly after graduation a set of prints by him was bought for the Arts Council collection. The subject of Higgins' prints was daily life in Peckham, where he lived. He also painted exuberant oils of figures on beaches. Higgins committed suicide and was commemorated in 1992 with a South Bank Centre exhibition.

Lloyd George HIGGINS 1912– Painter of contemporary Lancashire scene, born in Mossley, Lancashire. He studied at Royal College of Art, Salford. Gained Diploma in Industrial Design (1st Prize) of Royal Society of Arts. Was a founder-member of Saddleworth Art Group and appeared in a show of its work at Woodlands Art Gallery, 1973. Also showed at Manchester Academy, Tib Lane Gallery and elsewhere in northwest.

Tim HIGGINS 1961– Artist who studied at Middlesex Polytechnic, 1980–3. His exhibitions included Vortex Gallery, 1985; Galerie Endart, Berlin, and Galerie Klenzestrabe, Munich, both in West Germany in 1987; and East End Open Studios, at Carpenter's Road, 1989.

Wilfred HIGGINS 1893–1978 Portrait painter, full name Francis Wilfred Higgins, who was born and finally lived in Chester and who attended the School of Art there. Also studied in London and Italy. Showed RA, RHA, widely in Canada as well as in Australia and on the continent, notably at the Paris Salon. Joined the Art Workers' Guild in 1936.

Derek HIGGINSON 1930– Painter born in Oakhill, Stoke-on-Trent, Staffordshire, where he attended the College of

Art, 1944–50, his teachers including Frith Milward. Showed with Free Painters and Sculptors of which he was a member, Staffordshire Artists' Club of which he was a founder-member, with the Unit Ten Group of former Stoke students and elsewhere widely in the Staffordshire area.

Matthew HIGGS 1964– Artist, writer and curator whose output included text-based work, born in Wakefield, Yorkshire, who studied at Blackburn School of Art, 1983–4, and Newcastle Polytechnic, 1984–7. He gained the 1996 Wingate Artists Award at Art96. Mixed shows included Inside a Microcosm, Laure Genillard, 1992; East, Norwich Gallery, Norwich, 1994; Cocaine Orgasm, Bank at Burbage House, 1995; Yerself Is Steam, 85 Charlotte Road, 1996; and Murray Guy Gallery, New York, America, 1998. Higgs had solo shows at Anthony Wilkinson Gallery, 1999 and 2003. He was the publisher of Imprint 93, an ongoing series of artists' editions, and co-curated the fifth British Art Show in 2000. Lived in London.

Raymond HIGGS 1940– Printmaker and painter, born in Carlisle, Cumberland, partner of the artist Jenny Cowern. He studied at Carlisle College of Art, 1956–61, under Jack Seabury, gaining his diploma at the Royal Academy Schools, 1961–4. Higgs won an Abbey Minor Scholarship in Painting, 1966, and a Northern Arts Purchase Award in 1985. The consistent interest running through his work was "my desire to remove tone (black and white) from colour relationships, so that the full chromatic (red-blue-yellow) value can be seen. The reason for being of these prints is colour: its quantities, proportions and relationships." Group shows included Mini Print International, Cadaques, Barcelona, Spain, from 1990; The Art of the Printmaker, Royal Festival Hall, 1991; and 3rd Kochi International Triennial Exhibition of Prints, Kochi, Japan, 1996. Among his later solo exhibitions were the Arts Centre, Washington, Tyne & Wear, 1999. Northern Arts, Carlisle Museum & Art Gallery and other public and corporate collections hold examples. Lived in Langrigg, Wigton, Cumbria.

Jo HIGSON: *see* **Jo SCANNELL**

Rowland HILDER 1905–1993 Landscape and marine painter, mainly in watercolour, printmaker and illustrator. Born at Greatneck, Long Island, America, with British parents, Hilder was initially educated in Morristown, New Jersey. After settling in England, he studied illustration and printmaking at Goldsmiths' College School of Art under Edmund Sullivan for three years in the 1920s. He was later to lecture at that College between the wars, also at the Central School of Arts and Crafts, Royal College of Art and Farnham School of Art. During World War II Hilder served in the Army, concerned with camouflage. He was involved in several fine art publication companies, was a pioneer silkscreen printmaker in Britain, did extensive advertising work, notably for Shell-Mex and BP and illustrated many books. He was assisted in his Shell work by his wife Edith, originally Edith Blenkiron. Hilder's book illustration commissions included Herman Melville's *Moby Dick* and Robert Louis Stevenson's *Treasure Island*. His own books *Starting with Watercolour* and *Painting Landscapes in Watercolour* and the two volumes *Rowland Hilder's England* and *Rowland Hilder Country* presented his own pictures. Hilder achieved great popular success with his portrayal of the English countryside, notably Kent, with the characteristically delineated trees and oast-houses. He showed at RA, RI of which he was president 1964–74, RHA and NEAC. He had his first solo show at Fine Art Society in 1939, and there was a retrospective at Woodlands Art Gallery, 1985. Duncan Campbell Fine Art latterly handled his work. Hilder early on was a keen sailor, marine artist and illustrator of boys' sea adventure stories. Although he lived in London he kept a coastguard's cottage at Shell Ness, as a base for marine painting. His son also painted, under the name Anthony Flemming.

Muriel B G HILEY 1906– Sculptor and designer of medals, born in Cardiff. After private education she studied at Goldsmiths' College School of Art, 1926–9, then sculpture at Royal Academy Schools, 1929–34. From 1929 she showed at RA, also with RCamA and with Lewisham Society of Arts. From the late-1920s she obtained a large number of commissions including medals of David Lloyd George, Neville Chamberlain and Jan Christian Smuts; a commemorative plaque for Brooklands motor racing track jubilee in 1957; and in 1966 a large copy of the World Cup for Wembley Stadium. Imperial War Museum, Glynn Vivian Art Gallery in Swansea and National Museum of Wales, Cardiff, hold her work.

Richard HILEY 1921– Painter, illustrator and teacher, born in Halifax, Yorkshire, where he continued to live. Studied at Halifax School of Art, 1936–40, then after World War II at Royal College of Art, 1946–9, his teachers including Kenneth Rowntree and Rodney Burn. Taught at Huddersfield School of Art.

A Stuart HILL: *see* **A STUART-HILL**

Adrian HILL 1895–1977 Painter, mainly of landscapes in watercolour, and illustrator. Born at Charlton, Kent, studied at St John's Wood School of Art, 1912–14, then at the Royal College of Art, 1919–20. During World War I Hill was an Official War Artist, producing outstanding pictures from the front line, now in the Imperial War Museum. Exhibited at the RA, RBA, NEAC, RHA, ROI, in the provinces and overseas, including Paris Salon. His work is in many public collections, including the Victoria & Albert Museum. Hill was an exemplary, enthusiastic teacher. For a time he taught at Hornsey School of Art and on screen in the early days of television after World War II. He wrote many books on painting techniques, such as *On Drawing and Painting Trees*, 1936, and *The Pleasures of Painting*, 1952. Lived at Midhurst, Sussex.

Andrea HILL 1954– Artist noted for her box and collage creations. She studied at Bournemouth and Poole College of Art and Design and Goldsmiths' College School of Art. Showed at Slaughterhouse Gallery, Shipley's Bookshop and England & Co, in Art in Boxes, 1991.

Anthony HILL 1930– Constructivist artist working in a variety of materials, painter and teacher. Born in London where he continued to live. He studied at St Martin's School of Art and Central School of Art and Design, 1947–51, in 1951–2 visiting Paris. He had painted in Dadaist and Surrealist styles in 1950, but after meeting Picabia, Kupka and Vantongerloo his painting became more disciplined, he made his first relief in 1954 and two years later abandoned painting. His first solo show of reliefs was at ICA in 1958. Two years later he was an organiser of Construction: England: 1950–60, at Drian Gallery. Went on to show widely internationally in exhibitions of abstract and constructivist art. Taught for a time at Polytechnic of Central London, Chelsea School of Art, gained a Leverhulme Fellowship at mathematics department of University College in London, 1971–3, and eventually became visiting research associate there. From mid-1970s Hill signed some works Redo, others Rem Doxford. Commissions included large screen for headquarters of the International Union of Architects' Congress, 1961. Hill had a retrospective at Hayward Gallery in 1983 and a show of works 1954–82 at Austin/Desmond Fine Art, 2003. Tate Gallery, Victoria & Albert Museum, Arts Council and other public collections in Britain and abroad hold examples.

Barrie HILL 1936– Artist and musician, born in Sheffield, Yorkshire, who took up drawing and painting at Camden Adult Education Institute in 1970. After opting for early retirement from the National Economic Development Office in 1988, he devoted much time to painting and playing the cello, taken up in 1985, with the East London Late Starters Orchestra. With his cello teacher Pat Legg Hill produced *The Better Late ... Cello Book*. Chamber music was the main inspiration for Hill's pictures. In 1992, his large oil painting of the Lindsay String Quartet was exhibited at the Conway Hall and at the Quartet's twenty-fifth anniversary concerts at the Wigmore Hall and Crucible Theatre, Sheffield. Showed at Sheffield Chamber Music Festival from 1988 and from 1995 his pictures of chamber musicians in concert were permanently exhibited at Conway Hall. Later lived in Fougères, France.

Caroline HILL 1935–1983 Painter, draughtsman, etcher and fabric designer, who studied at the Slade School of Fine Art, 1952–6, in 1955 being awarded the Catherine Maude Pearce Scholarship permitting a year of postgraduate study. Exhibited with Young Contemporaries, 1955–6, in 1956 with Leicester Galleries, in 1957 marrying Nicolas Hill. In 1975, she had a solo show at William Darby. Hill painted mostly on a small scale, delicate and charming works which harked back to Bloomsbury and the Euston Road School. In 1976 she completed a watercolour portrait of the writer Graham Greene at his Antibes home. In 1985, a complete catalogue of her work was privately published, with introductions by Richard Morphet and William Packer. Lived in London.

Derek HILL 1916–2000 Painter notable for perceptive portraits and subtle landscapes, stage designer, exhibition organiser and writer, brother of the artist John Hill. He was born Arthur Derek Hill in Bassett, Hampshire. Was educated at Marlborough College, then studied stage design in Munich, Paris and Vienna, 1933–5, and began life drawing. Although he designed sets and costumes for the ballet *The Lord of Burleigh* at Sadler's Wells in 1937, in Paris a year later he chose to paint rather than pursue designing. During World War II he worked on a farm in England, painting spare-time. Contributed articles to *Penguin New Writing*, *New Statesman* and other magazines. The 1940s and 1950s were busy years for Hill, for he had a first solo show at Nicholson Gallery, 1943; designed for *Il Trovatore* at Covent Garden, 1947; painted in Ireland and Italy, where he was encouraged by the critic Bernard Berenson; organised the Degas exhibition at Edinburgh Festival, 1952; had a series of shows at Leicester Galleries; and was art director of the British School in Rome, 1953–4, and 1957–8. Had retrospectives at Whitechapel Art Gallery, 1961, Colnaghi's, 1994, and RHA, 1998. Created a gallery showing his own fine collection of pictures at his home in Donegal, Ireland. He painted part of the year on Tory Island, where he discovered and promoted a group of fishermen-painters, who went on to exhibit widely. Collaborated on several books on Islamic architecture. Hill's work is in collections of Tate Gallery; Arts Council; Fogg Museum, Harvard; National Gallery of Ireland, and elsewhere including Mottisfont Abbey, Hampshire, which holds part of his nineteenth- and twentieth-century collection. Hill died in London.

E D HILL 1900– Painter, born in Caernarvon. She lived there as a housewife and did not start painting until 1964. Mrs Hill then showed in the WAC exhibition Alternative Tradition and with the Caernarvon and Nantile Valley Art Groups. The Caernarvon Institute Building gave her a solo show in 1972, for which she obtained much local press coverage.

Edith HILL fl. from late 1960s– Printmaker, painter and draughtsman who studied at Beckenham Centre for Arts and Crafts. She showed at RA Summer Exhibitions, in Kent and was included in Group '77 Printmakers at Woodlands Art Gallery, 1981. Lived in Beckenham, Kent.

Frank HILL 1926– Painter and illustrator who studied at Waltham Forest and St Martin's Schools of Art. After working for advertising agencies and commercial studios as a designer and illustrator Hill went self-employed, illustrating many children's and educational books. He later concentrated on painting, showing at Whiteleys and Battersea Art Fair with Quantum Contemporary art and at Chelsea Art Fair, 2000, with Simpson Fine Art, Old Hemel Hempstead.

Harriet Mena HILL fl. from late 1980s– Artist who did a foundation course at Camberwell School of Arts and Crafts, 1985, obtaining her honours degree there, 1986–9. She appeared in mixed shows at Intaglio Printmakers, 1989; New Scottish Painters, at Fine Art Society, Glasgow, 1991; and in the same year she was a prizewinner at the Mall Galleries, and tour, in The Discerning Eye. She shared a show at Eagle Gallery, An Open Reality, in 1991, the previous year having had a solo exhibition at Duncan Campbell Fine Art. There was an Eagle Gallery one-man exhibition, Division & Unity, in 2003. Government Art Collection and St John's College, Oxford, hold her work.

John HILL 1905–1988 Painter and decorative artist who was born in Bassett, Hampshire, and educated at Marlborough College. In 1945–6 studied at Camberwell School of Arts and Crafts under Lawrence Gowing and Victor Pasmore. Signing his work J H, he showed at LG, Redfern Gallery and RA. He was the brother of the painter Derek Hill, part of whose huge collection of pictures is on display at Mottisfont Abbey, the National Trust property in Hampshire formerly owned by Mrs Gilbert Russell. John Hill organised some of the decorating schemes for her there. Included among Derek's pictures is John's small atmospheric gem Regent's Canal at Maida Avenue, Winter. Lived in London.

Mary F HILL 1926– Painter and teacher, born in Frampton Cotterell, Gloucestershire. She was initially educated in Bristol, attending the West of England Art College there under Donald Milner, 1943–7. Lived in Chippenham, Wiltshire, where she taught art at the Grammar School.

Oliver HILL 1887–1968 Architect and painter, born in London. Educated at Uppingham School, then was self-taught as an artist. Exhibited RA, Royal Glasgow Institute of the Fine Arts and had two one-man shows at Leicester Galleries. Lived at Sapperton, Gloucestershire.

Philip Maurice HILL 1892–1952 Landscape and marine painter, born in Southampton, who married the artist Megan Rhys. After attending Oxford University, Hill studied art in London and St Ives, with which his work was strongly associated. Exhibited RA, NEAC, RBA, Goupil Gallery, UA, SMA and with the St Ives Society of Artists, of which he was a member. He held several senior positions in the RSMA. Hill's picture of Polperro was used as a poster by the Great Western Railway. Alongside his career as an artist Hill worked for the Chamber of Shipping, of which for a time he was general manager. Lived variously in London, Wadhurst in Sussex and St Ives, Cornwall.

Raymond Arthur HILL 1916– Watercolour painter, engraver and designer. Born in Leicester, Hill studied art at Tunbridge Wells School of Art, 1933–6, under its principal E Owen Jennings, then during 1936–40 at the Royal College of Art under Ernest Tristram. Hill went on to show silverwork designs at a number of venues, including the Goldsmiths' Hall. He was successively head of Worcester School of Art, 1947–50, Swindon School of Art, 1950–3, then head of industrial design at Liverpool College of Art, 1953–64. Lived in Liverpool.

Robert HILL 1932–1990 Painter, draughtsman and teacher, born in Watford, Hertfordshire, where he lived. Hill studied at Watford School of Art and Royal Academy Schools in 1950s, where he several times won the David Murray Scholarship in landscape, plus other awards, teachers including Henry Rushbury, Peter Greenham and Bernard Fleetwood-Walker. Went on to teach at Matthew Arnold School in Staines. He was a member of ROI, UA, NS and NEAC and showed at RA, Woodstock and Beaux Arts Galleries. Nottingham Museum and Art Gallery and several other provincial galleries hold Hill's work.

Ronn HILL 1933– Artist in oil, watercolour, pen and ink and mixed media, and teacher, born in London. He studied at Willesden Technical College and Heatherley's School of Fine Art, 1958–65, teachers including Jack Merriott, Harry Riley and Patrick Larking. Taught in adult education in Borough of Ealing, then took on private freelance teaching in 1972 in southern English counties, later giving private tuition at Orpheus Studio, Kingston Lisle, Wantage, in Oxfordshire. Hill was a believer in fine draughtsmanship. He belonged to UA and SGA and exhibited with RBA and at Paris Salon. Had a series of solo shows.

Rowland HILL 1919–1979 Painter and draughtsman, born in Belfast. Went to work at 14, but wishing to become an artist Hill studied in the evenings at Belfast Technical College and at Belfast College of Art, where his teachers included Fred Allen. At the age of 16 he had three oils hung at the annual exhibition of the Ulster Academy of Arts. He later showed at RHA, in London and widely overseas and held many one-man exhibitions in Belfast. Lived in Jordanstown, County Antrim.

Rowland Henry HILL 1873–1952 Painter, black-and-white artist, born in Halifax, Yorkshire. Studied at Halifax and Bradford Schools of Art, also at the Herkomer School at Bushey and extensively abroad, mainly on the continent. Exhibited RA, Walker Art Gallery, Liverpool, and elsewhere in the provinces. Imperial War Museum and many northern public galleries hold his pictures. Hill was a member of the Staithes Group of painters, who worked in the Staithes and Runswick Bay area of Yorkshire, featured in a series of exhibitions at Phillips & Sons, Marlow. Lived at Hinderwell, Yorkshire.

Shareena HILL 1964– Artist who graduated with honours from Trent Polytechnic, Nottingham, 1982–5, attended Chelsea School of Art for her master's, 1985–6, and won an Elizabeth Greenshields Foundation Award, 1987. Group exhibitions included Small Works, Patricia Knight Gallery, 1987; RA Summer Exhibition, 1988; and East End Open Studios, at Carpenter's Road, 1989. Had a solo show at The Marriott Rooms in Cheshire, 1987, and lived for a time in south London.

Vernon HILL 1886–1972 Carver, draughtsman and printmaker, born in Halifax, Yorkshire. After Board School, at 13 was apprenticed to lithography at a printing works. Left at 18 hoping to become a teacher at technical school. Won a poster competition prize and worked with John Hassall; then for the publisher John Lane; served in Army for three years; and had two exhibitions at Leicester Galleries, 1924–7. Made carvings for St Joan of Arc, Farnham, 1930. From 1932–56 worked with Sir Edward Maufe on Guildford Cathedral. Other commissions included Runnymede Memorial, 1952; Church of St Columba, Pont Street, 1954; and Middle Temple, 1955. Was included in Sculpture in Britain Between The Wars, Fine Art Society, 1986. A large collection of Hill's visionary Art Deco drawings is held by Southampton City Art Gallery.

Jan Stanley HILLER 1918– Painter, printmaker and teacher, born in London. Studied at Hornsey School of Art with John Moody and Herbert Budd, 1935–9, then after World War II in 1946–7. He taught at Prince Henry's Grammar School, Evesham, Worcestershire, where he lived, showing RI, SGA of which he was a member and at Worcester Corporation Art Gallery.

Henry Gustave HILLER 1864–1946 Versatile stained glass artist, gesso modeller and painter, who studied at Manchester School of Art under Walter Crane. He exhibited at the Walker Art Gallery in Liverpool, where he lived, and elsewhere. Much of Hiller's work was commissioned, notable examples being a lively painted wood relief of Viking longboats in The Vines public house, Lime Street, Liverpool; stained glass windows in Bradford Town Hall, also St Luke's, St Barnabas' and other churches in Liverpool; a glass panel for Manchester Corporation; and heraldic shields for Isle of Man government. Hiller made gesso figures for many churches.

Susan HILLER 1942– Artist in mixed media, teacher, born in America. She studied at Smith College, Northampton, Massachusetts, 1957–61, then at Tulane University, Louisiana, 1961–5, concentrating on anthropology. She then did field work in South America, but became disillusioned with this and began painting again, earlier an optional study. Moved to Europe and settled in London in 1967 and soon had a solo touring show organised by United States Information Service. In 1968 she gained the Karolyi Foundation Award. Four years later her exhibition Photography into Art took place at Camden Arts Centre, and touring. Hiller was artist-in-residence at Sussex University in 1975, followed in 1976 by solo shows at Serpentine Gallery and Gardner Arts Centre at University of Sussex. In that year, too, Hiller won the Gulbenkian Foundation Visual Artists' Award, also in 1977. Many more solo shows followed, including Hester van Royen Gallery; Museum of Modern Art, Oxford; Tate Gallery, Liverpool, retrospective, 1996; in 2000 Hiller's installation Witness, at The Chapel, 92 Golborne Road, an Artangel project, dealt with alien abduction and Unidentified Flying Objects; and in 2004 her sometimes eerie audio installations sounded through the Baltic, Gateshead. In 1998 Hiller was awarded a Guggenheim Fellowship and in 2000 was granted a residency at the Baltic Arts Centre, Gateshead. Having taught at St Martin's, 1975–80, and the Slade School, 1980–1, from 1991 Hiller was professor of art in the Department of Fine and Applied Arts at Belfast University. For some of her early working years as an artist Hiller concentrated on a type of performance art, then she also mixed drawing, photography, video, texts, sculpture and painting, sometimes in large installations. The artist said that "as well as potsherds, postcards and dreams are some of the materials used as the starting point for works that look at the repressed or unacknowledged content of our society's artefacts." Arts Council, Tate Gallery, Imperial War Museum and many other galleries in Britain and abroad hold her work. Lived in London.

David HILLHOUSE 1945– Artist, teacher and curator, born in Wirral, Cheshire, who worked in watercolour and egg tempera. In the 1960s–1970s he studied at Laird School of Art and Liverpool College of Art. He graduated in 1969 and was elected a member of RCamA in 1979, becoming its vice-president. Hillhouse was a teacher, curator of the Williamson Art Gallery in Birkenhead and principal museums officer for Wirral. He showed with Wirral Society of Arts and Deeside Art Group, both of which he was a member, on Merseyside and elsewhere. Lived at Greasby, Wirral.

John HILLIARD 1945– Artist and teacher who sculpted, used photographs and text. He was born in Lancaster and studied at St Martin's School of Art, 1964–7, a travel scholarship taking him to America in 1965. Hilliard had his first one-man show at Lisson Gallery in 1971, then often exhibited there. He also appeared in notable overseas group shows and one-man, venues including Galerie Hetzler & Keller, Stuttgart; John Gibson Gallery, New York; and Musée d'Art Moderne, in Paris. Photographic retrospective, 1969–98, at Arnolfini Gallery, Bristol, 1998. Teaching included Rijksakademie, Amsterdam, Netherlands. Arts Council holds a selection of his work. His publications include *Analytical Photography*, 1977, and *From the Northern Counties*, 1978.

Victoria HILLIARD 1960– Creator of three-dimensional works in mixed media who studied at Exeter College of Art; she gained a diploma in typographic design for print, with a distinction. Hilliard began to develop her own work while acting as manager of the graphic studio of a busy London newspaper and began showing at Liberty's. She also worked in Cornwall and in the Scilly Isles as a gardener and florist. Her work had a strong fantasy element and used a rich palette. She designed tapestries, garden rooms and a travelling circus bus. Exhibitions included Bient and Bient, 1988; The Hat Shop, Powys, 1991; and she shared a show at John Davies, Stow-on-the-Wold, 1993. Lived in Cornwall.

Bryn HILLIER 1948– Versatile artist, teacher and art therapist, born Christine Hillier in Caterham, Surrey, who painted as Chrissie Borland from 1993–6, then as Bryn Hillier. She studied graphic design at Surrey College of Art, 1965–71, then married Les Borland and moved to Birmingham. She graduated with honours in fine art from De Montfort University in 2002, although "I consider myself to be almost entirely self-taught"; and in 2003 completed a teaching qualification. Hillier's career included Birmingham Libraries, 1972–3, then, after a move to Suffolk, 1973–4, Ipswich Libraries, 1973–4. From 1974–7 Hillier was employed by St Audry's Psychiatric Hospital as an art therapist; was at St Albans College of Art, 1977–8; being an art therapist at Hollesley Bay Borstal; 1978–81; ran a screenprinting and fabric design business, 1981–93, including a move to Oxfordshire; from 1993 becoming a full-time painter. From 1999 onwards she taught private groups and individuals and at workshops. Took part in many group shows, including Upstairs Downstairs Gallery, St Albans, from 1995; Merriscourt Gallery, Sarsden, from 1996; New Gallery, Inkberrow, 1997; Canonbury Gallery, Islington, and Derby City Gallery, both 2002; and Singer & Friedlander/*Sunday Times* Watercolour Competition, Mall Galleries, from 2004. Among her solo exhibitions were The Mill Gallery, Banbury, 1995; Stourport Library, 1996; and Warwick Museum and The Gallery, 54 Shepherd Market, both 2005. At that time she was "influenced by William Nicholson, John Singer Sargent, Thomas Jones, D Y Cameron, Lisa Milroy and Gerhard Richter." The nature of Hillier's work and media used were subject to occasional changes, her method being to "adopt a cycle of dedicated research followed by a busy spell of painting." Hillier lived in Mollington, Banbury, Oxfordshire.

Graham HILLIER 1946–2006 Landscape painter and inspirational teacher whose first focus was on the scenery of east Yorkshire, where he was brought up in Bridlington. To this he was to add meticulous views of places seen elsewhere Britain, France and Italy. After studying at Leeds College of Art and Newcastle University, Hillier was for a time head of art and graphic design at Branston Community College in Lincolnshire. He then became a full-time painter, based in that county and Normandy. Technical thoroughness was a characteristic of paintings comprising many layers of acrylic. A feature of them was the notion of spiritual destination, such as the pilgrimage sites of Walsingham and Santiago de Compostela. He favoured places where "Man and Nature live together in a state of grace and harmony." Hillier held many solo shows, notably with the Francis Kyle Gallery.

Tristram HILLIER 1905–1983 Painter of landscapes and still life and some religious subjects, his pictures have a hard-edged clarity and surreal quality while appearing overtly realistic. Born in Peking, China, Hillier studied art at the Slade School in 1926 under Henry Tonks, then in Paris under André Lhote and at the Atelier Colarossi. In the 1930s he was one of the group of artists who formed Unit One. After he finished his studies until 1940 he travelled widely on the continent, often living alone for several months in Spain, France and Portugal, his scenes of sparsely populated villages or townships under a bleaching sun being developed during the winter months in Somerset. He met Braque and was impressed by the use of black in his pictures and those of Velasquez and some of the Flemish painters; black is a feature of some of Hillier's still lifes such as Harness (Tate Gallery). His work shares characteristics with that of his friend Edward Wadsworth, with whom he painted abroad. After his first one-man show at the Lefevre Gallery in 1931 Hillier's work was popular with the picture-buying public and he went on to show widely in Britain and abroad. Elected RA 1967. His autobiography *Leda and the Goose* was published in 1954. Retrospective show at Worthing Art Gallery in 1960 plus a touring retrospective which included the RA in the year he died. Lived at East Pennard, Shepton Mallet, Somerset.

David HILLMAN 1893–1974 Painter, draughtsman and stained glass artist, born in Latvia. He moved to Britain aged 15, the family settling in Glasgow. In 1909 Hillman won a scholarship to Glasgow School of Art where he studied for five years, then from 14 for a further five years at Royal Academy Schools. The family moved to London in 1924. His wife was a doctor and they had three sons. Hillman originally had a studio in St John's Wood, later in Hampstead, where he settled. He was mainly a portrait painter, working to commission. In the later part of his life he created stained glass windows in London synagogues, the religious themes stemming from his deep knowledge of the *Bible* and *Talmud*. A group of his works was sold at Bonhams, Knightsbridge, in 2002, including portraits of Dr Solomon Goldman and Rabbi Dr Samuel Atlas, philosophy professor at Hebrew Union College.

Peter HILLS 1925– Sculptor in a variety of materials and teacher, born in Bearsted, Kent. He studied at Bromley College of Art, 1948–50, Royal Academy Schools, 1950–5, then for several years was assistant to the sculptor Maurice Lambert. In 1972 he was Churchill Fellow in Sculpture. He taught art at Tonbridge School, where he had studied, during 1960s–1970s. Hills was a fellow of RBS and a member of the public schools art masters' 65 Group. Lived in Tonbridge, Kent.

Christian HILT: *see* **SZUPER GALLERY**

Arthur Cyril HILTON 1897–1960 Self-taught painter and sculptor, whose work embraced abstract and Surrealist styles, born in Manchester. He served overseas in World War I and was wounded on the Somme, 1916. Worked for Manchester Education Committee as a school registrar and as a librarian at the Committee's offices. Showed at Walker Art Gallery in Liverpool, Manchester City Art Gallery which holds his work, with Manchester Athenaeum Graphic Club, Southport Spring Exhibition and as a member of Manchester's Society of Modern Painters from the 1930s, being elected chairman in mid-1950s. Had a solo show at Salford Art Gallery and a first one-man exhibition in London at Crane Kalman Gallery, 1959. Lived in Chorlton-cum-Hardy, Manchester.

Bo HILTON 1961– Artist who gained his master's degree in fine art printmaking at Brighton, 1985–8, then lived and worked in London and Cornwall, where he was a member of the Newlyn Society of Artists. Showed from 1993 at Newlyn Orion Gallery, RA and NEAC and from 1994 at New Grafton Gallery. Frequently exhibited at major London art fairs. In 1995 had a first solo show at Cassian de Vere Cole Twentieth Century British Art. His father was the painter Roger Hilton.

Fergus HILTON 1966– Painter and poet producing vibrant figurative and abstract works, son of the artist Roger Hilton and his wife Rose Hilton, with whom he shared an exhibition at Badcock's Gallery, Newlyn, in 2002. Fergus lived for much of his life in West Penwith, Cornwall. He attended Humphry Davy Grammar School, Penzance, and Penwith VI Form College, obtaining an A-grade A-level in ceramics, then studied English at Westfield College, London, for a year in 1984. After a short period in Israel and studies at Falmouth College of Art, 1986, Hilton, who described himself as a "professional schizophrenic", suffered a breakdown and then lived in a hospital near Exeter or at home, where he painted consistently. His greatest passion was poetry. He had several pieces published and in 1989 won an Arthur Koestler Prize. Exhibitions included solo shows at Salthouse Gallery, St Ives, 1998, and Rainyday Gallery, Penzance, 2002.

Matthew HILTON 1948– Artist, notably a printmaker, born in London, son of the painter Roger Hilton. He spent three years studying photography and film at Bournemouth College of Art, then in 1972 travelled to north of England to live and work with Welfare State Theatre Company. From 1974–85 was a member of the Fire Service, but continued with his own work. He had a show of photographs at Holdsworth Gallery, Hebden Bridge, in West Yorkshire, 1981, another of lino-prints at same gallery in 1982. In 1983 gained a North West Arts printmaking bursary at the Manchester Print Workshop. During the 1980s Hilton continued to show his lino-prints in solo and mixed exhibitions and was artist-in residence, Fieldhead Hospital, Wakefield, in 1987. After a solo show at Austin/Desmond Fine Art in 1988 Hilton had another in 1990, the year after he had travelled around the Baltic by ship. Latterly set up studio in Norfolk.

Roger HILTON 1911–1975 Figurative and abstract painter and draughtsman, teacher, a key member of the St Ives art colony in Cornwall and the last major painter to settle there. He was born in Northwood, Middlesex, the family name being Hildesheim, changed during World War I because of anti-German feeling. Studied at Slade School of Fine Art, 1929–31, under Henry Tonks; although he won a Slade Scholarship in 1931 he did not take it up, but during the 1930s studied for periods in Paris, part of the time with Roger Bissière at Académie Ranson. First one-man show was at Bloomsbury Gallery in 1936. During World War II he served in the Army, part of the time as a commando, for about three years being a prisoner of war after the Dieppe raid of 1942. Was a schoolteacher for a time after the war, also teaching at Central School of Arts and Crafts, 1954–6. His first abstract paintings date from 1950. During the 1950s and 1960s Hilton began to spend more time in west Cornwall, and the landscape there influenced his pictures, which were never to be as entirely abstract again as those of the early 1950s. Hilton took part in numerous group shows in Britain and abroad, winning first prize at John Moores Liverpool Exhibition in 1963. Retrospective exhibition at ICA in 1958, and similarly important shows included Serpentine Gallery in 1974; Graves Art Gallery, and touring, in Sheffield 1980; Leicester Polytechnic Gallery and tour, 1984–5; Hayward Gallery, 1993–4; Tate Gallery St Ives, 1997–8; and Jonathan Clark, 2000; and Belgrave Gallery St Ives, 2001. In 2003 Cross Street Gallery, with Jonathan Clark, showed Drawings from the Estate. Tate St Ives would hold an exhibition of drawings and paintings in 2006–7 that further surveyed the artist's career. Alcoholism hindered Hilton's output; he was confined to bed by illness (he suffered peripheral neuritis) from 1972. Arts Council holds his work. Died at Botallack, Cornwall.

Rose HILTON 1931– Painter, born in Kent. After initial training at Beckenham School of Art she went on to study at Royal College of Art, 1954–7. From there travelled to Rome for a year on an Abbey Minor Scholarship. Back in England she met and married the painter Roger Hilton and they moved to Botallack, Cornwall. She then brought up her children and looked after her husband during his long illness, but painted little herself. After Roger's death she resumed painting and took drawing lessons in the mid-1980s from Cecil Collins. Her exhibitions included Newlyn Orion Gallery, 1977 and 1987; Michael Parkin Gallery, 1988; Oxford Gallery, 1989; David Messum, 1991; and North Light Gallery, Huddersfield, 2002. In that year she showed at Badcocks Gallery, Newlyn, with one of her sons, Fergus. She was a richly colourful painter of people and interiors.

George (Jerzy) HIM 1900–1982 Designer, illustrator, watercolourist and teacher, born in Łodź, Poland; his working name was an abbreviation of Himmelfarb. For about a decade from 1917 he was variously at university in Moscow, Berlin and Bonn and studying graphic art in Leipzig, then returned to Poland. For just over 20 years from the early 1930s he collaborated with Jan Le Witt as a design partnership, moving the business to London in 1937. Lewitt-Him created notable wartime posters and the Festival of Britain clock in 1951. From 1954 Him worked independently, illustrating many children's books, working on animated films, designing toys and painting landscape watercolours, such as Shikun Petach Tiqvah, in Ben Uri Art Society collection. For eight years from 1969 taught at Leicester Polytechnic. Showed at London College of Printing in 1976 and Ben Uri in 1978. Died in London.

Lubaina HIMID 1954– Painter, designer, mixed-media artist, administrator and teacher, born in Zanzibar, Tanzania, but arrived in England in the year of her birth. Studied theatre design at Wimbledon School of Art, 1973–6, working in theatre and interior design after that. In the early 1980s she was both a part-time teacher and youth worker, obtaining her Master of Arts degree in cultural history at the Royal College of Art, 1982–4. Organised exhibition at Africa Centre in 1983, which included her own work and that by other women of Afro-Caribbean or African descent, in which "their anger shines through", she said. Himid's work had a multi-pronged polemical content, satirising white society, poking fun at society's heroes and celebrating black creativity. Showed widely in mixed exhibitions, including The Other Story, Hayward Gallery, 1989–90, and tour; and Picturing Blackness, at Tate Gallery, which holds her work, 1995–6. Showed Images of Porthmeor Beach at Tate St Ives as artist-in-residence, 1999. Arts Council and Rochdale Art Gallery also have examples. In 1986 Himid opened her own gallery, The Elbow Room.

Frederick HINCHLIFF 1894–1962 Painter and teacher, born in Queensland, Australia, as George Frederick Hinchliff. After studying at Huddersfield Technical College he attended the School of Art there and Royal College of Art. He held a series of art teaching posts in Leicester, Sheffield, Batley and Guildford, from 1936–60 being principal of Croydon School of Art. Exhibited at RA, NEAC and widely in the provinces. Hinchliff was involved in the restoration of St Stephen's Chapel in the Palace of Westminster, was noted for his murals and was active in art circles in Croydon, Surrey, where he lived.

Arthur Mayger HIND 1880–1957 Art historian, curator and watercolour painter. Born at Burton upon Trent, Staffordshire, he studied at Cambridge University. Entered British Museum in 1903, being keeper of prints and drawings 1933–45. He was Slade Professor of Fine Art at Oxford, 1921–7. Published a number of scholarly works on prints. Exhibited RA, Agnew, Goupil Gallery, NEAC and Colnaghi's. Work held by Ashmolean Museum, Oxford, Graves Art Gallery, Sheffield, and galleries abroad. Lived in Henley-on-Thames, Oxfordshire.

Albert HINDLE 1888– Painter and draughtsman, born in Accrington, Lancashire. He studied at the School of Art there, Royal College of Art, 1910–12 and Académie Julian, Paris, 1912–13. Showed at RA, ROI, UA, NS, NEAC and elsewhere. Lived in Kingston upon Thames, Surrey.

Mike HINDLE 1966– Painter of luminous, richly coloured sea and beach scenes who was born in Norwich, Norfolk. He did an art and design foundation course at Hastings College of Arts and Technology, 1985–6, graduating with honours in fine art, printmaking, from West Surrey College of Art & Design, Farnham, 1986–9. Mixed shows included the Maltings, Farnham, 1989; The Orangery, Knightsbridge, 1990; Wolf at the Door, Penzance, 1995; Beside the Wave, Falmouth, from 1998; and Innocent Fine Art, Bristol, from 2000. Among his later solo shows were Innocent Fine Art, 2001, and Great Atlantic Map Works, St Just-in-Penwith, 2003, accompanied by Hindle's book *Godrevy*. The Island Hotel, Tresco, holds Hindle's work.

Yvonne HINDLE 1963– Painter and teacher who studied at Newcastle upon Tyne Polytechnic, 1981–4, and Royal College of Art, 1985–7. She gained the Audun Gallery Prize and Painters and Stainers' Cyril Sweet Award, both 1987, and obtained a fellowship in painting at Cheltenham School of Art, Cheltenham, Cheltenham & Gloucester College of Higher Education. In 1993 became acting head of painting at University of Northumbria, Newcastle. Mixed shows included Whitechapel Open Part I, Spitalfields Gallery, 1992, and Aiding and Abetting, The Gallery at John Jones, 1994.

Edward HINES 1906–1975 Artist and businessman, born and lived in Norwich, Norfolk, where he became a director of the family engineering business. He began painting after World War II and from 1950 was a regular exhibitor at the ROI. Hines exhibited with the Norfolk & Norwich Art Circle, of which be became chairman. His daughter, Judy Hines, for 10 years on the staff of the art department at the Norwich Castle Museum and from 1973 a Norfolk picture dealer latterly based at Holt, succeeded her father as Art Circle chairman in the late 1970s.

Brian HINTON 1938– Artist and teacher, born in London and educated in Norfolk, who gained a scholarship to the Cambridge School of Art. During the 1960s and 1970s Hinton exhibited at the RA Summer Exhibition, Paris Salon, in national exhibitions, winning an award from Hesketh Hubbard Art Society, and had solo shows. He also worked as a graphic artist and cartoonist for the *Eastern Daily Press* and "taught as a last resort". Travelled extensively in Europe and the Near East, in such venues as jazz clubs and hotels committing to memory the people he saw. They were depicted wittily in a solo exhibition at The Catto Gallery in 2000.

Kay HINWOOD 1920– Painter who was born and lived in Bromley, Kent. She studied with Sonia Mervyn as a private student; at City and Guilds of London Art School; then at Kathleen Browne Painting School with Browne and her husband Marian Kratochwil. She was a member of UA and PS, also exhibiting at SWA, RP and ROI.

Roger HIORNS 1975– Artist, born in Birmingham, who did a fine art foundation course at Bournville College, Birmingham, 1991–3, his master's at Goldsmiths' College School of Art, 1996. He was included in the Neurotic Realism series of exhibitions launched by Saatchi Gallery in 1999, Saatchi Collection holding his work. Hiorns' output included depictions of the Chartres and Notre Dame cathedrals, card constructions with cobalt and chemical growth embellishments. In 2003, Hiorns' dramatic work Vauxhall, comprising a steel grating and a flame, was displayed in Tate Britain's sculpture court. Lived in London.

Roland HIPKINS 1895–1951 Painter, notably of landscapes, born in Bilston, Staffordshire, where he attended the School of Art, then the Royal College of Art, 1919–22. Hipkins went on to make his career in New Zealand, where he taught at the Teachers' College, Wellington, 1931–49. He was prominent in the art world there, being a member of the council of the New Zealand Academy of Fine Arts. Exhibited RBSA and extensively in New Zealand, where his work is in several collections, including Auckland Art Gallery. Lived in Wellington.

Chris HIPKISS 1964– Draughtsman, notable for large, monochrome, fantastic cityscapes, as shown in Outsiders & Co at England and Co, 1996. That gallery gave him solo exhibitions in 2000 and 2002. Hipkiss left school at 16 to be apprenticed to his father's joinery business and began to draw seriously, creating his own Utopia on paper. Eventually gave up joinery and moved to a Kent village where he continued with his drawing, began an environment group and planted trees and in the late 1990s completed a geography degree. Working on a large roll of cartridge paper he sometimes needed to use the village hall as a studio and drew inspiration from his travels, television and "stray thoughts". From 1995, Hipkiss exhibited widely in Europe and America, including the New Museum of Contemporary Art, New York; The American Visionary Arts Museum, Baltimore; Aldrich Museum, Connecticut; Museum of Modern Art, Kilmainham, Ireland; and MAC Gallery, Birmingham.

Percy HIPKISS 1912– Painter and designer, born in Blackheath, Birmingham, educated locally. He was a member of RBSA, Birmingham Watercolour Society and Dudley Society of Artists. Warwick Central Museum and Art Gallery, Dudley, holds his work, which included jewellery design. Lived in Warley, West Midlands.

Susan HIPPE 1966– Artist, born in Johannesburg, South Africa, who was included in Corpus Fine Art's 2005 Arndean Gallery exhibition Hard Bodies. In 1995 she gained her baccalauréat with distinction in France, having been educated there and in Denmark and Germany; was from 1995–9 an art student at universities in France and London; in 1999 graduating with an arts honours degree from Roehampton Institute, University of Surrey. Her degree work, a mixed-media spiral, was placed in Charing Cross Hospital, and she also carried out private commissions elsewhere in the United Kingdom, Germany and France. Hippe (pronounced Hipper) wrote: "I am primarily concerned with movement. In a way, the act of drawing is choreographic; a drawn line is both a graphic entity and a physical movement that is at once spontaneous and precise, accomplished in one continuous movement. The pen hits the surface running and leaves it in the same fashion. My drawings consist of many such lines and movements". Hippe was a member of SGA and took part in group shows in Britain and abroad, latterly including Drawing, the End of the Line, Centre Culturel Jean Lurçat, Saint-Lo, France, and the Royal College of Art Secret 2003, both in 2003, and the Liverpool Biennial and Pink Week, Graham's Fine Art Gallery, both 2004. Among later solo exhibitions were A&D Gallery, 2002; A day without fun is a day lost forever, Space Gallery, 2003; and Patrizia Estatements, Munich, Germany, 2005. Hippe lived in Erith, Kent.

John S HIRD 1885– Painter, born in Ambleside, Westmorland. Studied at Oxford and Bordeaux Universities, an educationist, in art largely self-taught, he also painted for periods under several teachers including Ian Grant and Brian Bradshaw. Showed mainly in the Lakes and Yorkshire areas, where he was a member of Kendal Art Society and Bradford Arts Club. Sometimes signed work Stalker Hird. Settled in Ambleside.

Stalker HIRD: *see* **John S HIRD**

Christine HIRSCH 1947– Painter whose work was "predominantly figurative, oil or acrylic on canvas or board, and primarily concerned with women's issues." Hirsch was born in Eastbourne, Sussex, and studied at St Albans School of Art & Design, 1989–92, gaining an honours degree at the University of Hertfordshire, Hatfield, 1992–5, the visiting tutor Susan Wilson being a particular influence. From 1976–99 Hirsch worked in public sector housing. She was a friend of the Foundation for Women's Art and a member of Five Women Artists Plus, being included in *Five Women Artists Plus – Women Working*

Together, by Brenda Brin Booker and Joan Thewsey, 2000. As well as many group shows, including Mayfair Arts Festival, 2000, and Covent Garden Festival, 2001, Hirsch had a solo exhibition at Heifer Gallery in 2002. Lived in London.

Barry HIRST 1934– Painter, illustrator, designer and teacher, born in Padstow, Cornwall. He attended Alleyn's School, Dulwich, then was at Camberwell School of Arts and Crafts 1950–2, studying and teaching there, 1954–6. After a period of two years at Slade School of Fine Art, from 1958–9 Hirst was a freelance designer with Le Comet and Berthon Muchler, Animated Films, Paris, and Silver Pine Potteries in London. After teaching at Watford, Croydon, Heatherley's and Chelsea Schools of Art, 1959–71, Hirst became head of the School of Art and Design, Sunderland Polytechnic. Hirst participated in many group shows from the late 1950s in Britain and abroad, having two solo exhibitions in 1965 at Hanover Gallery and Stone Gallery, Newcastle upon Tyne. Later shows included several with Mercury Gallery, in London and Edinburgh, from mid-1980s. Hirst also illustrated for private press books, including the work of C Day Lewis, Roy Fuller and R S Thomas. British Council, Contemporary Art Society and provincial British and foreign galleries hold his work.

Damien HIRST 1965– Artist, born in Yorkshire, who attended Jacob Kramer College of Art, Leeds, 1983–4, then Goldsmiths' College, 1986–9. His group show appearances included Whitworth Young Contemporaries, Manchester, 1987; Freeze, at PLA Building, 1988; New Contemporaries, at ICA, 1989; and Modern Medicine and Gambler, both at Building One, 1990. In 1994 Hirst curated Some Went Mad, Some Ran Away at the Serpentine Gallery, by which time he had become famous, in the words of critic Andrew Graham-Dixon, as the "virtuoso of dead animals and flies, the man who sold Charles Saatchi a tiger shark suspended in formaldehyde", for the Saatchi Collection. Hirst's winning entry for the Turner Prize, 1995, Mother and Child Divided, showed a cow and calf bisected longitudinally and presented in a glass case. It was said to explore the themes of mortality and isolation. Hirst also exhibited two of his spot paintings, white canvases covered with a slightly irregular grid of coloured circles. In 1996 BBC 2 Television showed *Hanging Around*, a dark comedy written and directed by Hirst. Other diversifications included the setting up of a record label, Turtleneck, which recorded the 1998 World Cup song *Vindaloo*, by Fat Les; providing designs for, Pharmacy, one of his two London restaurants (the other being Quo Vadis); a £1m publishing project, with Canongate Books, in which Hirst designed a limited edition of Robert Sabbag's 1976 cult classic *Snowblind*, about an American cocaine dealer; and the creation in 2002 of one of his coloured dot paintings, to be used in the Beagle 2 Mars space shot. Later solo exhibitions included Gagosian Gallery, New York, America, 2000, and a retrospective at The Saatchi Gallery and shows at White Cube, all 2003. *From the Cradle to the Grave: Selected Drawings by Damien Hirst* appeared in 2004. Hirst had headquarters in London but lived in Devon. In 2005 Hirst bought the 124-acre Toddington Manor Estate, in Gloucestershire, including a Grade 1-listed, 300-room mansion which had stood empty for 20 years, aiming to create a museum to house his own work.

Derek HIRST 1930–2006 Painter and teacher, born in Doncaster, Yorkshire, where he attended the local School of Art, 1946–8. He then studied at Royal College of Art, 1948–51, after that for 25 years teaching widely in London. In the early 1970s Hirst also taught at Philadelphia College of Art and York University, Toronto, from 1976–87 being principal lecturer in painting at Kingston Polytechnic. Hirst was artist-in-residence at Sussex University in 1966, five years after his first one-man show, at Drian Galleries. Other solo shows included Sussex University, the Towner Art Gallery in Eastbourne and a retrospective at Angela Flowers Gallery in 1979. Hirst was a serious artist whose work, moving in appearance from naïve figuration towards abstraction over the years, had a number of preoccupations, travel being important. On graduating in 1951, he destroyed all his student work apart from a small self-portrait. Instead of visiting major galleries, he studied exhibits in the Natural History and Science Museums. In the early 1950s he journeyed through France to Spain and was much influenced by the Lascaux cave paintings, discovered Catalonia and for the next two decades spent part of each year there. In 1964 he studied Islamic architecture in Morocco, evident in paintings he then produced, while the landscape of his native Yorkshire remained important. Native American art, seen while teaching in Toronto, spawned some of Hirst's most impressive heraldic images. Cancer of the bladder, diagnosed in the mid-1970s and followed by debilitating surgery, was a serious mid-career interruption. A visit to the Far East in 1985 next prompted some fine pictures, notably the Garden Metaphor Kyoto series. The landscape around Church Norton, near Pagham Harbour, produced paintings by Hirst at his most self-critical, version upon version being rejected before the final image. A series made in Andalusia from the mid-1990s was also important. Took part in numerous exhibitions internationally. Later solo shows included Flowers East, 1995 and 1999, and Flowers West, Santa Monica, California, 2001. Arts Council, Contemporary Art Society, Tate Gallery, Victoria & Albert Museum and many other British and foreign collections hold examples. Lived in Chichester, Sussex.

Nicky HIRST 1963– Versatile artist working in a wide range of media who between the ages of two and seven lived in Kenya, then moved to Leeds, eventually taking a foundation course there at Jacob Kramer College. She graduated in fine art at Maidstone College of Art, 1982–5, gaining her master's in art and architecture at Kent Institute of Art and Design, Canterbury, 1993–4. Hirst was an Artist in Research, funded by the Institute of International Visual Arts and worked with a number of architects. In 1997 she was on the design team to rebuild the Hippodrome Theatre, also working at the University of Central England, both in Birmingham; from 1997 was artist on the design team to rebuild a unit of the Royal Free Hospital; and in 1998 worked at J D Wetherspoon, West Bromwich. Took part in many group exhibitions, later solo shows including a Henry Moore Fellowship Exhibition, Byam Shaw School of Art, and Anthony Wilkinson Gallery, both 2000. Arts Council; Saatchi Collection; Sheffield City Art Gallery; Bradford, Doncaster, and Hammersmith and Fulham Councils; and corporate collections hold Hirst's work.

Norman HIRST 1862–1956 Printmaker and painter, born in Liverpool, who in 1885 took up a two-year scholarship at Herkomer's School in Bushey, where he remained until 1895. Later lived on the south coast, notably at Seaford, Sussex. While in Bushey Hirst learned his engraving and mezzotint skills at the fine art printing studios of H T Cox, and after he moved he continued to use the studios for mezzotinting, at which he was an expert. His reputation was mainly as a mezzotint engraver of works by Gainsborough, Lawrence, Watteau and Romney, and in 1917 he was called as an expert witness in a notable court case in which an attribution was disputed. (Hirst's opinion that the work was not by Romney was eventually borne out.) Hirst was made an associate of the RE in 1931. Frost & Reed published his works *Sea Melodies* and *Capture* and Agnew *The Mall* and *Gamme d'Amour*. Showed extensively at RA, also at Fine Art Society, Abbey Gallery and RI, but a lack of interest in original mezzotints after World War II prompted Hirst's executors to burn most of his studio collection. Some of what remained was exhibited in Three Bushey Artists by the Bushey Museum Trust in 1991.

Jeannette HISCOCK 1895–c.1977 Watercolourist, born and lived in Oxford, where she was educated. Studied at the Ruskin School of Art there and with Sydney Carline. Exhibited RI, SWA and Oxford Art Society, of which she was a member, 1935–77.

Simon HISCOCK 1960– Painter of enigmatic abstracts, and teacher, born in London, who studied at Byam Shaw School of Art, lecturing at Lewisham College, 1990–2. Group shows included Brixton Art Gallery, 1985; East End Open Studios from 1987; Triangle Artists' Workshop in New York and St James' Gallery, both 1990; and Royal Over-Seas League Open from 1994.

Andrew Healey HISLOP 1887–1954 Painter, printmaker and artist in black-and-white. Born in Edinburgh, he studied at the College of Art there, 1908–13, in his final year going on to the British School in Rome. For many years taught at his old College and became president of the SSA. Married to the artist Margaret Hislop; the artist Vivien Hislop was their daughter. Exhibited RSA, SSA and Royal Glasgow Institute of the Fine Arts. Lived in Edinburgh where he was a member of the Arts Club.

Margaret HISLOP 1894–1972 Painter in oil who was married to the artist Andrew Healey Hislop. Studied at Edinburgh College of Art and exhibited at RSA, RA, RSW and Royal Glasgow Institute of the Fine Arts. Glasgow Museum and Art Galleries bought her work. Lived in Edinburgh.

Vivien HISLOP 1926– Landscape artist in pen and wash, fashion artist, illustrator and journalist. Daughter of the artists Andrew Healey Hislop and Margaret Hislop, she was born in Edinburgh. Studied at the University there and the College of Art, 1944–8, under her father, William Gillies and Joan Hassall. Did a great deal of journalistic work, including periods on the *London Evening News* and the *Daily Mail*. Showed at SSA and RSA. Sometimes signed work Vivien H or just with initials. Lived in Sutton, Surrey.

Frederick Brook HITCH 1877–1957 Sculptor, notably of memorials. Born in London, the son of the sculptor Nathaniel Hitch, he studied at the Royal Academy Schools. Notable among his works are the statue of Captain Matthew Flinders and the Sir Ross Smith memorial, both erected in Adelaide, South Australia (and illustrated in the volume *RBS: Modern British Sculpture*, published in 1939), a statue of Charles Wesley in Bristol and one of Admiral Horatio Nelson, in Portsmouth. Was a fellow of the RBS. Lived in Hertford, Hertfordshire.

Harold HITCHCOCK 1914– Painter in watercolour and gouache, born in London as Raymond Hitchcock, whose pictures are of a visionary nature and have been called "the visual embodiment of Jung's philosophy". Financial problems prompted Hitchcock's parents to send the children to live with the maternal grandparents in Thundersley, Essex, where in a cultured environment he began to paint at the age of nine. At Thundersley he had a vision "of harmony and well-being and peace" which influenced his subsequent development, his painting being an attempt to recapture this. Back in London aged 13 he began painting imaginary natural landscapes. His work was seen by the painter Laura Knight and he was called a child prodigy, but he entered a long period doing commercial artwork – broken by service during World War II as a non-combatant, volunteering for bomb disposal – which often left him depressed. For years was plagued by trigeminal neuralgia until surgery in 1958 cured this. In 1947 had first public showing of his work at the International Art Centre; by 1964 was able to give up commercial work; in 1965 had an exhibition at Woburn Abbey, his picture The Mill being purchased for the Lidice Memorial Museum, Czechoslovakia; and in 1967 had first major retrospective at RI galleries. Had a successful tour of America in 1969. Hitchcock's pictures owe much to those of Claude Lorrain and J M W Turner, being idealised, light-drenched landscapes peopled with mysterious figures. Essentially self-taught, he employed a form of automatism as advocated by André Breton. Hitchcock's joining the Subud Brotherhood, a religious-type group, in 1960 was a profound influence. Lived in Ugborough, Devon.

Malcolm John HITCHCOCK 1929–1998 Artist in oil, oil over egg tempera, gouache and pen and wash, born in Salisbury, Wiltshire. He studied at Andover School of Art, then did "a variety of work to keep the wolf from the door," becoming a full-time artist in mid-1980s. His main works were Pointillist railway paintings in oil and semi-abstract, mixed media nudes. Hitchcock was a member of RWA. He also exhibited at RA and Paris Salon and in the provinces; his solo shows included Bramante Gallery, Ashgate Gallery in Farnham and Hiscock Gallery in Southsea. Reading Museum and Art Gallery holds his work. Lived in Padworth Common, Reading, Berkshire.

Raymond HITCHCOCK 1922–1992 Artist and writer, born in Calcutta, India, son of a professional soldier. Was educated partly at Denston College, Staffordshire, then in 1939 went to Cambridge University. Army service interrupted his education, but he returned to Cambridge to gain a degree in mechanical sciences, then joined Cable and Wireless. From the mid-1950s Hitchcock began to paint in oils, at first Surrealistic Biblical and autobiographical works, by the 1960s abstracts. Through that decade he showed often in London and Oxford. As a writer he made his name with the 1969 novel *Percy*, a satire on transplant surgery, which was successfully filmed two years later. Nine more published novels and some television and radio plays followed. Hitchcock's paintings of the 1970s and 1980s returned to narrative themes. He drew for

Tatler and *Punch*. A retrospective exhibition of Hitchcock's work was held at Guildhall Gallery, Winchester, where he lived, in 1992.

Theodore HITCHCOCK 1892– Painter and teacher who studied at Hornsey School of Art, after attending London University, his teachers being Adrian Hill and John Charles Moody. Exhibited ROI, RBA, NEAC and RA. Lived in Enfield, Middlesex. Hitchcock was involved in the design of his house including a series of stained glass windows, some abstract, which remained intact after his death.

Ivon HITCHENS 1893–1979 Painter in oil of landscapes, flowers, decorative pictures and figures. Born in London, the son of the painter Alfred Hitchens; Sydney Ivon Hitchens was father of the painter John Hitchens. After education at Bedales, Ivon Hitchens studied art at St John's Wood and the Royal Academy Schools, where he was influenced by John Singer Sargent and William Orpen, although this is not readily apparent in his mature work. Later notable influences were the French Post-Impressionists Cézanne, Braque and Matisse. Hitchens had his first one-man show at the Mayor Gallery in 1925, later showing at Tooth's, the Lefevre and Leicester Galleries. He was a member of a number of forward-looking groups before World War II, including the 7 & 5 Society, London Artists' Association and LG. He moved to Sussex from London in 1940 and gradually became famous for his long, rural scenes which used bold, sweeping brushstrokes, increasingly bright colours and edged gradually towards abstraction. Waterfall, Terwick Mill, of 1945, and Winter Walk, No. 4, of 1948, are typical of his landscapes at their best. Hitchens completed a number of notable murals, at Cecil Sharp House, London, and for several universities. He is widely represented in public galleries around the world, including the Tate Gallery. There were several retrospective exhibitions during his lifetime and one at the Serpentine Gallery, 1989. Robert Sandelson held a Hitchens show in 2003. Ivon Hitchens Nudes, at Jonathan Clark Fine Art in 2005, was accompanied by a fine illustrated catalogue with a perceptive introduction by his biographer Peter Khoroche. Lived at Petworth, Sussex.

John HITCHENS 1940– Painter in oil, son of the artist Ivon Hitchens and grandson of the painter Alfred Hitchens. John Hitchens' landscapes and flower paintings were similar to his father's, with their broad strokes of paint and rich colours. After Bedales School Hitchens attended Bath Academy of Art. He showed from the 1960s, having a solo show at Marjorie Parr Gallery, 1964. Exhibited there until 1976, showing from 1967–71 with Ditchling Gallery; 1967–82 with David Paul Gallery, Chichester; and 1977–9 with Gilbert Parr Gallery. Later solo shows included a series with Montpelier Studio from 1983 and one at Davies Memorial Gallery, Newtown, 1987. Louise Kosman, Edinburgh, held one in 2003. In 1979 West Sussex Education Committee commissioned a huge mural, A Landscape Symphony, from Hitchens, who was born in the county, settling at Byworth, Petworth. His work is held by many other collections, including public galleries in Brighton, Bradford and Hull.

Simon HITCHENS 1967– Sculptor producing abstract forms from stone and other media, son of the painter John Hitchens and grandson of Ivon Hitchens. Simon studied at West Surrey College of Art & Design, 1985–6, then gained an honours degree at Bristol Polytechnic's faculty of art and design, 1987–90. He was assistant to the sculptors Peter Randall-Page, 1990, and Anish Kapoor, 1993–6. Group exhibitions included LG Open from 1992; Galerie de L'Avancon, Bex, Switzerland, 1993; Hannah Peschar, Surrey, and Contemporary Art Society, both from 1994; and Eight by Eight at Pallant House, Chichester, 1997. He was selected by the British Council for sculpture symposiums in Slovakia, 1994, and Colombia, 1996, and was made an associate of RBS, 1997. There was a family tradition of attendance at Bedales School. Simon, born in Sussex, was educated there, 1978–85. He was included in the 1999 exhibition Bedales Art & Design, organised by William Jackson Gallery at Art99 in the Business Design Centre, and in Hitchens: Three Generations, at The Canon Gallery, Petworth, 2004. Hitchens' work is owned by The Hiscox Group. Lived and worked in London.

Stephen HITCHIN 1953– Sculptor in stone, draughtsman and teacher who studied at Liverpool Polytechnic, 1972–6, under Séan Rice, gaining his master's degree at Manchester Polytechnic, 1976–7. He went on to teach sculpture at several colleges, including Wirral Metropolitan College. Hitchin said that his sculpture was "initially evolved from the human form, being derived from a variety of experiences, observations and sources", as in Girl's Head, included in Walker Art Gallery, Liverpool, 1986–7 touring show Merseyside Artists 3. Hitchin showed with Liverpool Academy as a member in 1980, MAFA in 1982 and RA. Had a solo show at Atkinson Art Gallery in Southport, 1981, and shared ones at Liverpool University Senate House, 1986, and The Gallery in Cork Street, 2000. Commissions included Unilever Research, Port Sunlight; Coventry City Council; North British Housing; the Women's Hospital and Neptune Development, both in Liverpool; and Nelson Thomlinson School, Wigton. In 1978 he gained a Merseyside Arts Association Award. Lived in Higher Bebington, Wirral, Merseyside.

Katrine HJELDE 1967– Norwegian painter and site-specific installation artist whose work explored architectural and conceptual space. She studied at the University of Oslo's faculty of arts, 1986–9; did a foundation course at Askec Kunstskole, 1988–90; gained a fine art honours degree at Central St Martins College of Art & Design, 1990–3; then her master's in fine art (painting) at Slade School of Fine Art, 1993–5. Exhibited at the Tannery, Cubitt Gallery and in the 1998 Whitechapel Open at Whitechapel Art Gallery. In 1999 she was commissioned by the Institute of International Visual Arts to develop new work for the Internet, to be produced for its website X-Space, collaborating with a web designer at Interchange Studios.

Ting-Fay HO fl. from early 1980s– Abstract artist whose greatest sources of inspiration were Western classical music and Eastern calligraphy. She was born in Hong Kong and studied at Chelsea and Central St Martins Colleges of Art and Design. Group exhibitions included Drian Galleries, 1983; Warwick Arts Trust, from 1986; The East-West Connection, Oval House Gallery, 1988; Galeria Lieco Recreo, Orense, Spain, 1993; and Journeys West, University of Essex touring show, 1995. Had a solo exhibition at Fulham Library, 1982, others including Centre 181 Gallery, 1986.

Jeremiah HOAD 1924–1999 Spiritual and reclusive landscape and figure painter and teacher, born in Fife, father Irish, mother Anglo-Scots. He obtained a county scholarship to Winchester School of Art, 1941–3. From 1948–58 Hoad was a visiting lecturer at Camberwell School of Art, studying painting in London, Paris and Amsterdam, from 1958–67 teaching drawing and painting at Frank Hooker Secondary Modern School, Canterbury. After marrying in 1962, he moved to rural Wales to paint, in 1981 going to County Donegal, Ireland, settling at Inver. Between 1994–9 he made annual visits, lasting several months, to paint in Tunisia. Gorry Gallery, Dublin, gave him shows in 1991 and 1994 and a retrospective in 2001. Hoad's wife Judith was a writer, author of *This is Donegal Tweed*, 1987, *Healing with Herbs*, 1996, and *Need or Greed*, 1999.

Mary HOAD 1908– Prolific artist and teacher, born in Beckenham, Kent, where she studied at St Christopher's School. She attended Beckenham Art School, 1925–7, and Chelsea Art School, 1927–9; held various teaching posts, 1929–48; then studied at Guildford School of Art for two terms, 1946. She was art adviser to the Hertfordshire Education Committee, 1948–51, and principal of St Albans School of Art, 1951–67, also undertaking extensive institute of education and university external examination work and lecturing to teachers for the Ministry of Education, National Union of Teachers, London County Council, many education committees and for the British Council on two visits to Cyprus. She showed with the LG, NEAC, AIA and SEA and with Piccadilly, Leicester, Cooling and Goupil Galleries and Brighton City Art Gallery. In 1968 she shared an exhibition with Michael Evans and Leslie Summers at The Gordon Maynard Gallery, Welwyn Garden City. Education committees bought her work, private collectors including Sir John Newsome and Sir Michael Sadler.

Harold Frank HOAR: *see* **ACANTHUS**

Jeff HOARE 1923– Artist and teacher, husband of the painter Elizabeth Jane Lloyd, father of the artist TessAnna Hoare. He was born in Ampleforth, Yorkshire, and studied at Chelsea School of Art; art education and philosophy at University of Wales, Swansea; printmaking for a year at Royal College of Art; then educational television, mime with Ronald Wilson, and modern dance with Rosemary Butcher, Riverside Studios. Hoare did wide-ranging teaching, including Central St Martins School of Art & Design; Aegean School of Art, Kos, Greece, which he initiated in 1985; the drama department, University of Bristol; Camberwell School of Art; and in America. He did performance work in Britain, America, Yugoslavia and Canada, in 1991 being designer, Royal Opera House, *Carnival of the Birds*. Awards included Granada Fellowship, Lancaster University, 1969–70; British Council Grant, Yugoslavia, 1980; and an Arts Council Grant, 1984. As well as many group shows had numerous solo exhibitions internationally, later ones including Falcon Gallery, Stockholm, Sweden, and Emmanuel College, Cambridge, both 1992. In 1999 he shared a show with TessAnna at Gallery 27, his highly coloured, Expressionist views "formed by the sea's movements against the surface of the painting; there is a definite precision created by the changes of tide and light in relation to the artist's precise posture (Alexander Technique). The drying process is a dynamic influence". Hoare's solo exhibition An Indian Experience was at The Nehru Centre, 8 South Audley Street, in 2005. He lived in London.

Michael HOARE 1928– Painter, muralist, illustrator and teacher. He qualified in fine arts at Croydon College of Art in 1950 and then went to study theatre design at Old Vic Theatre School. He worked in the theatre in England and Australia, taught widely, illustrated books and record sleeves and painted a number of murals, notably at All Saints, Cleadon, County Durham. In 1969 he settled in France, in a remote village in the southwest. As well as showing in France, Hoare had several shows with Sue Rankin Gallery from 1990. National Gallery of New South Wales, Sydney, holds his work. Degas, Corot, Millet and Rembrandt were admired painters.

Marjorie HOARE fl. from late 1920s–1953 Watercolour painter and draughtsman. After private education she studied at the Slade School of Fine Art under Henry Tonks, 1927, then in Sussex with Franklin White. Exhibited RA, NEAC, RHA, Goupil Gallery and in the provinces. Lived at Barcombe, Sussex.

Richard HOARE 1967– Painter, draughtsman and teacher, born in Ipswich, Suffolk, who did a foundation course at the Cambridge College of Art and Technology, 1986–7, gaining a fine art honours degree at Kent Institute of Art and Design, Canterbury, 1987–90, in 1992–3 obtaining a postgraduate diploma at Cyprus College of Art. Teaching included Royal Blind School, 1991; voluntary classes at Botosani, Romania, 1995; and leading drawing workshops in Brazil, 1997–8. Completed pilgrimages to Santiago de Compostela, Spain, 1992, and Canterbury, 1996. Among his mixed shows were Postcard Exhibition, Collective Gallery, Edinburgh, 1991; Goria Gallery, Nicosia, and Ten Young Painters, John Martin, both 1994; Dorset Art Week, 2000; and The Landscape in Winter, Salisbury Playhouse, 2003. Later solo exhibitions included Salisbury Library and Galleries and 54 The Gallery, Mayfair, both 2002. He lived in Shaftesbury, Dorset.

TessAnna HOARE 1963– Versatile, exuberant artist, born and lived in London, daughter of the painters Jeff Hoare and Elizabeth Jane Lloyd. She studied at Camberwell School of Art, City & Guilds of London Art School and Goldsmiths' College School of Art. She was commissioned to draw over 50 twentieth-century buildings, some exhibited at RA and the Building Centre; work appeared in the films *Wings of a Dove*, *Twelfth Night* and *Four Weddings and a Funeral*; did window displays for Jigsaw, Agnes B and Dinny Hall; started a company making weathervanes that the London *Evening Standard* said "brightened London's skyline"; and in 1986 organised the first London Art Auction for Aids. In 1999 she shared a show with her father at Gallery 27.

John HOBART 1922– Self-taught artist working in various media, born in London. He was "a Sunday painter from the 1950s, full-time since 1982". Hobart graduated in natural science at University College. He was visiting professor of forest entomology at University of British Columbia, Vancouver, 1972–3, then head of the school of animal biology and dean of the science faculty at University College of North Wales, Bangor, of which he was a fellow. It holds his work. Peter Lanyon, Roger Hilton, William Scott and Kurt Schwitters were influences. Hobart was a vice-president of RCamA. He showed with NWG, Newlyn Orion Gallery, Penwith Society of Arts of which he was an associate and elsewhere. He had a solo show at Bangor Gallery. Lived at Ludgvan, Penzance, Cornwall.

Charles HOBBIS 1880–1977 Silversmith, metalworker, all-round craftsman, teacher and watercolourist. He was born in Sheffield, studying at the School of Art there 1893–1902; he won a Queen's Prize, four King's Prizes, a bronze medal and in 1902 a gold medal for which he was awarded a Royal Exhibition to study design at the Royal College of Art. Was at the Royal College, 1902–7, under W R Lethaby and made a special study of silversmithing and metalwork with Henry Wilson, called "the most outstanding metalworker of his time". Hobbis also trained in heraldry and lettering under Edward Johnston. In 1919 appointed headmaster of Norwich School of Art, where he remained until 1946. His tenure was celebrated by a special exhibition in 1974. Hobbis was remembered as a perfectionist, although he did not encourage study of the modern movement in art. Showed at RA and in Norfolk, the Norwich Castle Museum and Art Gallery holding his work. Lived in Norwich.

Annie Giles HOBBS 1949– Artist, teacher and administrator, born and lived in Cardiff, who gained an honours degree in fine art from University of Wales Institute there, 1992, qualifying as a teacher in 1995. She taught part-time at the Institute and for adult education with Cardiff County Council; ran the Cardiff Print Workshop; and was chairman and director of Butetown Artists. Later exhibitions included Welsh National Eisteddfod and the Laing Art Competition, Mall Galleries, both from 1990; Ben Uri Gallery and RWA, both 1997; Princess of Wales Hospital, Bridgend, and Centre Parks, both from 1998; St David's Hall, Cardiff, 1999–00; 6, Howard Gardens Gallery, Cardiff, 2000; and National Exhibition of Wildlife Art, Liverpool, 2001. Public and corporate collections included the Lord Chancellor's Department; National Museum of Wales, Cardiff; Department of Trade and Commerce; Halifax Building Society; and Deutsche Bank.

James HOBBS 1960– Draughtsman who graduated from Winchester School of Art, 1988. The previous year Hobbs had found a copy of H V Morton's 1927 book *In Search of England* in a car boot sale. He set out to recreate Morton's journey, keeping a journal and making 400 drawings of places and buildings Morton had seen. The drawings showed the influence of Hobbs' teacher Dennis Creffield and through him the approach of Creffield's own teacher David Bomberg. A group of the drawings was shown at Wolseley Fine Arts, 1996.

Peter HOBBS 1930–1994 Artist, musician and teacher, born and lived in London. After working as a jazz pianist from 1953–5, studied at Central School of Art, taught there for a year at the start of the 1960s, then began teaching soon after that at Camberwell School of Arts and Crafts, where he remained over many years. Hobbs was an abstract Constructivist whose mixed exhibitions included Situation at RBA Galleries, 1960; an Arts Council touring exhibition, 1962–3; and later he was featured in The Sixties Art Scene in London, Barbican Art Gallery, 1993. Had a series of solo shows, the first at ICA, 1960. Alcohol was Hobbs' problem, prompting erratic behaviour such as turning up at Camberwell to teach on the wrong day of the week, but he was remembered with affection by an ex-staffer as a highly amusing colleague. Worked finally in a studio in Hampstead.

Roy HOBDELL 1911–1961 Painter, muralist and designer who grew up in south London and by age 14 had begun classes at Camberwell School of Arts and Crafts under Stanley Thorogood. Leaving Camberwell in 1927 he worked in an art studio, then in 1932 joined the Lintas advertising agency, where he spent almost the rest of his life. Attended life classes at St Martin's School of Art. A friend of the photographer Angus McBean, Hobdell worked on some of his backdrops; the stage remained a main interest, and he designed sets for Ballets Nègres. As a muralist Hobdell completed trompe l'oeil commissions for Lord Faringdon, at Buscot Park, Barnsley Park and Brompton Square. Also did illustrative work for *The Leader*; made flower paintings on glass for the Festival of Britain in 1951; and large doorways for *Observer* Film Festival in 1956. In 1950s began to show work with Redfern and Arthur Jeffress Galleries and sold pictures through Peter Jones' store in Sloane Square, signed with the names of his cats, Giles and Emma Farquharson. Hobdell was included in the Lintas Beyond the Horizon exhibition at Agnew, 1988. Trompe l'oeil and surreal works from the McBean estate were shown at Abbott and Holder in 2006.

Kathryn HOBDEN 1975– Painter whose works were based on photographs, some taken when travelling fast. She was born in Brighton, Sussex, studying at the College of Technology there, 1993–4, University of Brighton, 1994–7, and Royal College of Art, 1997–9. Hobden won the Oriana Art Prize, 1999. Other exhibitions included Cut Gallery, 1996; Summer 97, Mercury Gallery, 1997; Hot Potatoes, Paton Gallery, 1999; and Reservation, Charlotte Street Gallery, 2001.

Nicky HOBERMAN 1967– Painter who was born in Cape Town, South Africa, and who gained a degree in modern history at Oxford University, 1986–9; then a fine art degree at Parsons School of Design, Paris, 1989–93; and a master's at Chelsea College of Art, 1994–5. Showed during Battell Stoeckel Fellowship, Yale Summer School of Art, 1992, and was included in New Contemporaries at Tate Gallery, Liverpool, and Camden Arts Centre, 1996, with a solo show at Entwistle, 1998. Saatchi Collection held Hoberman's work, which featured highly coloured images of children, knowing and viewed from unusual perspectives. Lived in London.

Robert HOBHOUSE 1962– Landscape painter using a rich palette, and teacher, born in London, who was educated at Eton College and Oxford. He worked in advertising, 1984–6, then taught in comprehensive schools. After a series of solo shows in private houses, in 1999 had a first public exhibition at Patisserie Valerie, Knightsbridge, with another, Water + tartan, at Highgate Fine Art, 2003. Hobhouse was a keen traveller in Britain, on the continent and in America, often visiting members of his large, far-flung family. Lord Bath's Wessex collection holds Hobhouse's work.

Ronald HOBLING fl. from 1930s– Painter and draughtsman, notable for portraits, born and lived in London. He studied at Hornsey School of Art, teachers including Russell Reeve and J C Moody, also portraiture with Frank

Emanuel. Showed at RI, Whitechapel Art Gallery, Artists of Chelsea and in the provinces.

Alice HOBSON 1860–1954 Watercolourist, born in Leicester, who studied with James Orrock, John Fulleylove and Wilmot Pilsbury. She was elected RI, also showing occasionally at RA and Walker Art Gallery, Liverpool. Travelled extensively on the European continent and in Africa and settled eventually at Praa Sands, Cornwall.

Marion Grace HOCKEN 1922–1987 Painter, born in Zennor, Cornwall, who showed early talent which led her to study with Arthur Hambly at Redruth School of Art in her teens. After World War II showed at Downing's Bookshop in St Ives with Peter Lanyon, Brian Wynter, Isobel Heath and other luminaries. She was a founder-member of Penwith Society of Arts in 1949. As well as showing at RA and ROI, of which she was a member, Hocken was a botanist inspired by nineteenth-century natural history painters and Fantin-Latour. Her flower studies were acclaimed at Paris Salon. Hocken's fame mainly rests on a large 1955 canvas The Hollow Men, based on the T S Eliot poem, which when showed in 1957 caused a row, because of its deeply satirical comments on modern St Ives life. For the next 30 years Hocken led a reclusive life in Carbis Bay following the reception of The Hollow Men. She was physically handicapped and the condition worsened, although she did marry in later years. With her husband she shared a keen interest in Unidentified Flying Objects. After her death Whitford and Hughes handled the sale of The Hollow Men.

James HOCKEY 1904–1990 Painter, printmaker and teacher, born in London. After education at Alleyn's School, in Dulwich, Hockey attended Goldsmiths' College School of Art, 1922–7, then went on to teach, being principal of Farnham School of Art, 1945–69, then joint principal of West Surrey College of Art and Design, 1969–71. He was a key figure in art education development and was for a time president of Farnham Art Society. Showed at RA, RBA, NEAC and elsewhere, and was noted for his flower paintings, Contemporary Art Society buying his work. Lived in Farnham, Surrey.

Susan-Jayne HOCKING 1962– Painter in oil and watercolour and oil, often on a small scale, who was born in Bournemouth, Hampshire, and attended Bournemouth and Poole College of Art, 1981–2; graduated from Bristol Polytechnic, 1982–7; and Royal Academy Schools, 1987–90. Awards included British Institution Fund first prize; Winsor & Newton Prize; RA Travel Scholarship; and M & G Prize at RA Summer Exhibition, 1998. Mixed exhibitions included Ten Young Artists, Mall Galleries, 1988; RA Summer Exhibitions, from 1989; and Cadogan Contemporary, 1991. She was a seasoned traveller, and her solo exhibitions at New Grafton Gallery, from 1996, included impressions of India, Myanmar, Vietnam, Thailand and China. Golden Faces of Asia was held at Kings Road Gallery, 2002; there was an extensive solo show at New Academy Gallery in 2003 stemming from recent travel in Bhutan; another at The Russell Gallery, 2004, entitled Desert Festival, Pushkar, The Tribes & Their Animals. For her New Academy pictures Hocking wrote that she had "used hand-made papers from the daphnia plant brought back from Bhutan and mulberry pulp from Burma. On my travels I try to incorporate a traditional medium from each country". Lived in Burley, Ringwood, Hampshire.

Shelley HOCKNELL 1975– Artist, illustrator and gallery administrator who did an art foundation course at Parc Menai, Bangor, 1993–4, graduating with honours in art and visual culture at University of the West of England, Bristol, 1994–7. Worked part-time at Ogilvy & Estill, Conway, also teaching life drawing classes there. Group exhibitions included The Cottage Loaf, Llandudno, 1996; Phillips Contemporary Art Gallery, Manchester, 1997; and RCamA, 1998. In 1999 the show Climbing the Walls, at Penrhyn Castle, Ogilvy & Estill and Llandudno Library, reflected the artist's interest in rock climbing and mountaineering. Lived in Llechwedd, Conway, Gwynedd.

David HOCKNEY 1937– Painter, graphic artist, photographer, theatre designer, teacher and writer, born in Bradford, Yorkshire. Hockney was a brilliant draughtsman, the best-known British painter of his generation, who gained international success from his mid-twenties. His work had a homo-erotic strain, but became widely popular through its satirical imagery and its attractive images of swimming pools, showers and Californian life. Hockney attended Bradford School of Art, 1953–7, and Royal College of Art, 1959–62; there he won a Gold Medal and the Guinness Award for Etching. His studies had been interrupted for a two-year period of hospital work as a conscientious objector. Hockney worked at various times in London, Paris and California, but from 1977 was based in Los Angeles, where the light had a marked influence on his work. In 1962 he was an instructor at Maidstone College of Art, then through the 1960s held various teaching appointments at the Universities of Iowa, Colorado and California, and was Slade Professor of Fine Art, Cambridge University, 1990. Hockney won painting prizes at the John Moores Liverpool Exhibition, 1961 and 1967, to which he added major awards in Paris, Cracow, Stuttgart and New York, for graphics and photography. Hockney had first one-man show at Kasmin Gallery, 1963, the Alan Gallery in New York, 1964, then had a continuous stream of international one-man shows. Notable in later years were appearances at Los Angeles County Museum of Art (travelling to Metropolitan Museum of Art, New York); retrospectives at Tate Gallery, 1988, Manchester City Art Gallery, 1996; prints, Alan Cristea Gallery and Lumley Cazalet, both 2000; and Painting on Paper, with an accompanying hardback book, at Annely Juda Fine Art, 2003, the year his Five Double Portraits were shown at the National Portrait Gallery and David Hockney: the Bradford years was at Dean Clough Galleries, Halifax. There were important exhibitions at Centre Georges Pompidou, Musée Picasso and Maison Européenne, in Paris, and National Museum of Wales, Cardiff, all 1999. Hockney's work is held by the Tate Gallery, Victoria & Albert Museum, Arts Council, Art Institute of Chicago, Los Angeles County Museum of Art and elsewhere. Notable works for the printed page are his etched illustrations for Cavafy's *Poems*, 1967, and *Six Fairy Tales of the Brothers Grimm*, 1969. For the stage he designed set and costumes for Stravinsky's *The Rake's Progress* and Mozart's *The Magic Flute*. In 2004, The San Francisco Performing Arts Library and Museum acquired Hockney's archive of over 2,400 theatre-related designs, negotiated by his dealer Richard Gray Gallery of Chicago. His book *David Hockney by David Hockney* appeared in 1976, and *That's The Way I*

See It, in 1993; *Hockney on "Art"*, 1999, stemmed from extensive interviews with co-author Paul Joyce. He was elected RA in 1991 and was made Companion of Honour in 1997. Latterly moved to Bridlington, Yorkshire.

Moira HODDELL 1927– Painter, illustrator and designer, born in Addiscombe, Surrey, who while staying in Edinburgh in 1944 was allowed by the principal Robert Lyon to attend classes at the College of Art, teachers including John Maxwell. Attended Sidcup School of Art, 1944–6, teachers including the principal J L Robinson, Ruskin Spear and Robin Guthrie; then Royal College of Art, 1946–50, under E W Tristram, Edward Bawden, John Nash, Gilbert Spencer, Rodney Burn and Alan Sorrell, being awarded a fourth year in the engraving school under Robert Austin. Hoddell (pronounced Hod*dell*) assisted Bawden with his big 1951 Festival of Britain mural. Mixed exhibitions included RA Summer Exhibition and RI, Brighton Art Gallery and Sussex Artists. Among solo shows were The Grange, Rottingdean, 1963; County Town Gallery, Lewes, 1968; Barcombe, 1981–2, connected with National Gardens Scheme; and 1995, Lewes House. Commissions included London Transport, Imperial Chemical Industries, Central Office of Information, General Post Office and *Daily Telegraph*, 1962–85, sketching people and places. She believed "strongly in the spontaneous speed of drawing directly from life and nature" and "admired eighteenth- and nineteenth-century graphic artists." H M The Queen owned Hoddell's work. Lived in Offham, Sussex.

Charlotte HODES 1959– Versatile artist who studied at Brighton School of Art, 1977–8, then gained an honours degree in fine art, 1978–82, and higher diploma in painting, 1982–4, from Slade School of Fine Art. Awards included a Boise Travelling Scholarship, 1984, and an Italian Government Scholarship, 1985. In 1986 she co-founded Culford Press. Residencies included Spode's ceramic factory in Staffordshire, 1998. Pattern was important in Hodes' work, its creation using drawing, photography, collage, the computer and hoarded objects such as fabrics and postcards. She reckoned "the most exciting paintings are the ones which feel as if they only just hold together." Hodes took part in many group shows, solo exhibitions including the Eagle Gallery from 1992. British Council, Birmingham and Worcester City Art Galleries, New Hall in Cambridge and corporate collections hold examples.

Joan HODES 1925– Figure and landscape painter and draughtsman, born and lived in London. She studied under Franklin White at Slade School of Fine Art, 1945–8, then was a pupil of Oskar Kokoschka, 1947–53, "a revelatory experience" (in 1948–9 Hodes visited Paris for a year, with studies at Académie Julian and Académie de la Grande Chaumière). Completed landscapes over a wide area of Britain, Ireland and continental Europe. Group shows included Contemporary Portrait Society, Leicester and Mercury Galleries and RA Summer Exhibition. Had solo exhibitions at Foyer Gallery, 1962 and 1971, later ones including Boundary Gallery, 1994, John Russell Gallery, Ipswich, 2000 and 2005, and Highgate Fine Art, 2003 and 2005. Victoria & Albert Museum holds her work.

Francis Edwin HODGE 1883–1949 Artist who was born in Devon, educated privately and then studied at Westminster School of Art and Slade School of Fine Art, his teachers including Augustus John, William Orpen and Frank Brangwyn, with further studies in Paris. In World War I he was commissioned in the Army, and Imperial War Museum, Victoria & Albert Museum and Plymouth City Art Gallery hold examples. He was a member of RBA from 1915, ROI 1927, RP 1929 and RI in 1931. For a time he was assistant to Gerald Moira at Royal College of Art. Also showed at NEAC, RA, Goupil Gallery, RSA and elsewhere. Was a member of Authors' and Chelsea Arts Clubs and lived in London.

Jessie Mary Margaret HODGE 1901–1964 Painter, muralist, illuminator and illustrator, born and lived in London. She was educated at Norland Place School and in art at Lime Grove and the Royal Academy Schools, gaining a bronze medal for life painting and a Landseer Scholarship. By the mid-1930s Hodge had become artist to St Mary's Hospital, had exhibited at RA, RSA, RMS, Royal Glasgow Institute of the Fine Arts, Walker Art Gallery, Liverpool, and Paris Salon, and had achieved notable commissions. These included lettering around the Kitchener Memorial in St Paul's Cathedral; decorations in Vigo House, featured in *The Builder* magazine; tablets lettered for The Second Church of Christ Scientist; fresco panels for the hall of the Eastman Dental Clinic; an illumination to commemorate Sir Ernest Shackleton; and medical and surgical illustrations for Sir Duke Elder, Glasgow University and elsewhere. At this time Jessie retained her interest in fishing, golf and tennis, but a neighbour, who knew her as Peggy, remembers her by the early 1960s as sociable but solitary, "a bit careworn", and asthmatic, "probably brought on by nerves". Jessie's father, the sculptor Albert Hemstock Hodge, had died in 1918, and Jessie, her mother and brother Norman settled in Hampstead Garden Suburb. Frustrated, Jessie appears to have resented her mother's devotion to Norman, who suffered from bad skin trouble and "looked like an ogre", so that he and his mother never went out. When mother died in 1963, Jessie and Norman planned to move permanently to a country cottage near Campbeltown which they owned and used for several weeks each summer, but Jessie died as they prepared to leave. Norman remained in Hampstead, then moved to the cottage helped by a neighbour, but soon died. Jessie was buried at Acton Cemetery.

Marcus HODGE 1966– Painter and teacher who studied classical oil painting at the Escuela Libre del Mediterraneo, Palma, for five years with Joaquin Torrents Llado, a notable Spanish portrait and landscape artist. On completion of his studies he became only the third student there to be invited to remain as tutor. Returning to the United Kingdom, he began to show regularly there and abroad. He was initially known as a portrait painter, exhibiting regularly with the RP from 1997. His Foal at Pushkar Camel Fair, Rajasthan, was included in the September Show, Wykeham Gallery, Stockbridge, in 2003. He shared an exhibition with David Sawyer at that gallery in 2004.

Nicky HODGE 1957– Painter and draughtsman, born in Birmingham, who studied at Central St Martin's College of Art, 1985–92. Mixed shows included Winter, Hoax @ Lux Gallery and ART*futures*, organised by Contemporary Art Society at Barbican Centre, both 2000. Had solo exhibitions at Danielle Arnaud from 1999.

Rodney Hellyer HODGE 1906–1963 Painter, born in Plymouth, Devon, son of David Hodge, principal of the School of Art there. Rodney Hodge began his studies there, then was at Royal College of Art, 1928–31. Having served as art master at the County High School, Redditch, Worcestershire, 1932–51, Hodge then moved to head the School of Art. Sometimes signing his work R H H, Hodge exhibited at public galleries in Plymouth, Birmingham and Liverpool. Also designed for stained glass, pottery and carved wood. Lived in Redditch.

Simon HODGE 1903–1973 Painter and draughtsman born in Glasgow, where he studied at the School of Art, 1920–4. He lived in London and Johannesburg from 1923 and from 1963 in Ibiza, Spain, dying in Edinburgh. While in South Africa Hodge was well known as a landscape and wildlife painter. He was president of the Johannesburg Art Club from 1931–2 and showed widely, including a series of exhibitions in the 1950s at the Pieter Wenning Gallery, Johannesburg. In the late 1950s Hodge and his wife did a year-long motoring and painting tour of the African continent. In Britain he showed at RA, RI and the Society of Artist Printers in Glasgow, having a solo show at the Royal Glasgow Institute of the Fine Arts. Rio Tinto Zinc in London and the Kruger National Park and Standard Bank in South Africa hold his work.

Wendy HODGE 1953– Painter, designer and illustrator, born in Canada. She attended Algonquin College in Canada to study advertising art, 1970–2, then did an illustration course in New York in 1979. Gained an Ottawa University Scholarship in 1982–3, then studied at Byam Shaw School of Art, 1983–5, and Royal College of Art, 1985–7. In addition to a Byam Shaw Scholarship she gained a British Commonwealth Scholarship. Hodge was a prizewinner at Royal Over-Seas League in 1985. Her other exhibitions included a solo show at Flaxman Gallery, 1987; London Picture Show, 1989, where she was a prizewinner; then in 1990 she was one of Flowers East's Artist of the Day, chosen by Lucy Jones.

Joanne HODGEN 1964– Painter, born in Glasgow, who studied at Bath Academy of Art in Corsham, then at Reading University. Mixed shows included 1st Portobello Open, Tabernacle Centre, 1989; A Woman's Point of View, Warehouse Gallery, Kendal, 1992; and Whitechapel Open and Royal Over-Seas League Open, both 1994.

Cyril Walter HODGES 1909–2004 Artist in pen and ink, watercolour and oil, and writer, born in London. He studied at Goldsmiths' College School of Art, 1923–6, under Edmund J Sullivan. Hodges was noted for his book illustrations, stage designs, historical writings for children and adult works on the Elizabethan theatre, as well as architectural reconstructions of theatres. *Columbus Sails*, 1939; *The Marsh King*, 1967; and *Plain Lane Christmas*, 1978, were among his titles. His detailed work, *Shakespeare's Theatre*, 1964, was awarded the Kate Greenaway Medal for its illustrations and he completed the Mermaid Theatre symbol and other illustrative work for its founder, the actor Bernard Miles. He also drew for *Radio Times*. He was included in the Box of Delights travelling exhibition of children's book illustrations, 1991–2. Had a solo show at Shakespeare Institute, Stratford-upon-Avon, 1982, another at Folger Shakespeare Library, Washington, America, in 1988; it holds his work. Lived in Lewes, Sussex, dying in Moretonhampstead, Devon.

Merrett HODGES fl. from c.1895–1961 Painter, printmaker and photographer, full name William Merrett Hodges, who was also an art dealer for a time. He was elected an associate of RBSA in 1917 and exhibited extensively there, also at Walker Art Gallery in Liverpool, RCamA, RA and elsewhere in northern public art galleries. He lived in Birmingham and was a member of the Midlands Arts Club.

Paul HODGES 1950– Painter, from Cardiff, who did the foundation course at Bath Academy of Art, graduating with an honours degree at Sheffield College of Art. For many years he was a part-time and visiting lecturer at art colleges and polytechnics in Liverpool, Birmingham, Cheltenham, Sheffield and Stoke in north Staffordshire. In 1990 he was artist-in-residence at Harewood House, Leeds, working on an education and conservation programme, ending with a solo show at Terrace Gallery there. Hodges won the Stowells Trophy at Mall Galleries in 1975 and in 1976 at the same venue the Winsor and Newton Award. He exhibited in France, the Natural History Museum in London, Tolly Cobbold Exhibition Tour and Paton Gallery. He shared a show at Compass Gallery, Glasgow, in 1980 with Anne Grebby. The previous year Hodges had had a solo show at University Gallery, Sheffield.

Roberta HODGES 1903– Painter, draughtsman and teacher, born in Harlesden, northwest London. Studied at Goldsmiths' College School of Art with Frederick Marriott, then Slade School of Fine Art with Henry Tonks and Philip Wilson Steer. She married the artist Jozef Sekalski. Exhibited RA, RHA, NEAC, SSA, Paris Salon and elsewhere. Lived in St Andrews, Fife.

Eliot HODGKIN 1905–1987 Painter, notably in tempera, of small, highly detailed pictures of flowers and fruit; mural painter; writer. Born at Purley, near Reading, Berkshire, Hodgkin after Harrow School studied at Byam Shaw School of Art and at the Royal Academy Schools under Ernest Jackson. First one-man show at Picture Hire Gallery, 1936. Later showed at RA, Wildenstein, Leicester Galleries, NEAC, RBA and in New York. Among his books are *She Closed the Door*, 1931, and *Views of London*, 1948. Tate Gallery holds his work. Hodgkin sought to show things "exactly as they are, yet with some of their mystery and poetry, and as though seen for the first time". Hodgkin, a religious man, was a notable collector. A selection from his collection was shown in a memorial exhibition at Hazlitt, Gooden and Fox in 1990, and it included Sir Thomas Lawrence, Corot, Rubens, Graham Sutherland, Degas and Japanese prints. Lived in London.

Howard HODGKIN 1932– Painter, printmaker and teacher, born in London, where he eventually settled. Gordon Howard Eliot Hodgkin was evacuated as a child to America, but was educated at Eton College, where the art master Wilfrid Blunt was influential. Studied at Camberwell School of Art, 1949–50, then at Bath Academy of Art, 1950–4, under Clifford Ellis, whom he considered "a teacher of genius". From 1954–6 was part-time assistant art master at Charterhouse School before teaching at Bath Academy of Art, 1956–66. Hodgkin then taught for six years at Chelsea School of Art, in 1976–7 being fellow in creative art at Brasenose College, Oxford. He had his first solo show at Arthur Tooth and Sons in 1962, after which he participated in notable international group shows. His further one-man exhibitions included Galerie Muller, Cologne, in 1971; Museum of Modern Art, Oxford, 1976, and tour; Hayward Gallery and tour, 1983; an appearance at Venice Biennale, 1984; a retrospective at Whitechapel Art Gallery in 1985, the year he won the Turner Prize; with another retrospective at Hayward Gallery, 1996; print exhibitions at Alan Cristea and Ingleby Gallery, Edinburgh, both 2001; and recent large paintings at Dean Gallery, Edinburgh, in 2002, at the end of which he was made Companion of Honour. Latterly showed with Anthony d'Offay. From 1972–6 Hodgkin was a Tate Gallery trustee and he was knighted in 1992. Tate Britain would give Hodgkin a major retrospective in 2006 featuring more than 60 works from the 1950s onwards. Indian Mughal miniatures, which he collected for a time, were important to Hodgkin. Although originally a figurative artist, his mature, richly coloured pictures hovered on the edge of abstraction, although he insisted that "I can't paint without a subject." He said that "memory is the principal subject of all my pictures. I'm painting a feeling." Arts Council holds several examples. While at Bath Hodgkin married the artist Julia Lane, but they separated in the mid-1970s.

Jonathan Edward HODGKIN 1875–1953 Self-taught watercolourist who was by profession an electrical engineer, born and lived in Darlington, County Durham. He was chairman and director of many companies, chairman of Darlington Society of Arts and a trustee of the Bowes Museum and Art Gallery, Barnard Castle. His *Little Guide to County Durham* was popular. He was a member of RBA from 1928, showing there extensively, also at Walker's Galleries, Laing Art Gallery in Newcastle and Leeds City Art Gallery.

Frances HODGKINS 1869–1947 Painter, teacher and illustrator of landscape and still life, born in Dunedin, New Zealand, where her barrister father, an amateur painter, taught her watercolour. She showed with Otago Art Society locally and attended Dunedin Art School, 1895–8. After teaching and working as an illustrator she travelled to Europe in 1901 and had a solo show at W B Paterson's Gallery six years later. Having settled in Paris in 1908 she taught at Atelier Colarossi and in her own school. Had now established a reputation as an open-air watercolourist. She continued to travel and show in Australia, New Zealand and elsewhere, taking up oil painting in 1915. In the mid-1920s she worked for two years as a designer for Calico Printers' Association, in Manchester, living with Hannah Ritchie and D Jane Saunders. Seeing the work of Matisse several years before had given her work a modern impetus, indicated at her solo show at Claridge Gallery in 1928. Was taken up by the St George's Gallery, which was interested in younger, more advanced artists, as told in its owner Arthur Howell's book: *Frances Hodgkins, Four Vital Years*, 1951. Working in France and Spain she now showed with the 7 & 5 Society and produced work of great transculency and vigour. Died in Dorchester, Dorset. Tate Gallery and other major galleries hold her work. Several memorial shows held including Tate Gallery and Arts Council provincial tour, 1952, The Minories in Colchester showing late work in 1991.

Cecil HODGKINSON 1896-c.1961 Watercolourist, farmer and land agent whose work reflected his country background. Born in Billingborough, Lincolnshire, he showed in the Lincoln area and was chairman of the Lincolnshire Artists' Society in the mid-1950s. Lived at Greatford, near Stamford, in that county.

Ed HODGKINSON 1973– Painter and draughtsman who graduated with honours in visual art, painting, from Camberwell College of Art, 1992–5, producing figurative pictures of striking graphic simplicity. Group shows included Southwark Open, South London Art Gallery, 1995; Whitechapel Open, Bow Arts Trust, 1996; The Discerning Eye, Mall Galleries, 1999; and Kopavogur Museum, Reykjavik, Iceland, 2001. Solo exhibitions included Mark Jason Fine Art, 2001, 2002 and 2003. IcelandAir held Hodgkinson's work.

George HODGKINSON 1914–1997 Representational painter and draughtsman, member of the MAFA and Stockport Artists Guild. Hodgkinson, who never married, served as a gunner in World War II. He was prolific, continuing to paint until his death despite senile dementia, and left 800 works. Hodgkinson died from burn-related injuries after an accidental fire at his terraced home in Stalybridge, Cheshire, where there was a retrospective at Astley Cheetham Art Gallery in 1998. The gallery holds Hodgkinson's oil Winter, Stalybridge, bought from a show at Oldham Art Gallery in 1985.

Wilfred HODGKINSON 1912– Artist, teacher and writer who was educated in Kidderminster where he attended the School of Art, then Birmingham College of Art. From 1939–46 was principal of Bilston School of Art and curator of the local art gallery. Later freelanced. Lived for a time at Shrawley, Worcestershire.

Carole HODGSON 1940– Sculptor, draughtsman and teacher, born in London. She studied at Wimbledon School of Art, 1957–62, then Slade School of Fine Art, 1962–4. Awards included Reading University research grant to travel in Mexico, 1968; Arts Council, 1973; British Council 1978 and 1980; Elephant Trust, 1979 and 1986; and Grocers' Company Bursary, British School at Rome, 1982. Taught widely in Britain and abroad. Hodgson's work cleverly mixed abstraction, landscape and the human figure. She held solo exhibitions with Angela Flowers Gallery from 1973, later Flowers East. Other shows along the way were with WAC, Cardiff, 1976; Fine Arts Galleries, University of Wisconsin, 1980; Llanelli Festival, 1984; and New Ashgate Gallery, Farnham, 1991. Arts Council, WAC, British Council and other public collections in Britain and abroad hold her work. Commissions included British Aerospace sculpture in Kingston upon Thames, 1986–7; Bogman, British Medal Society, 1987; and River Celebration, commissioned by Kingston Borough for Lovekyn Chapel site, 1988–9.

Clive HODGSON 1953– Painter and teacher, born in Nottingham, who studied at St Martin's School of Art, 1971–2; graduated from Slade School of Fine Art, 1972–5; and obtained his Higher Diploma in Fine Art, 1975–7. Awards included Boise and J Milner Kite Scholarships, 1977; Sotheby Award for most outstanding painting, Whitechapel Open Exhibition, 1989; and Abbey Award, British School at Rome, 1998. Hodgson was an external examiner, John Moores University, Liverpool School of Art; visiting tutor, Winchester School of Art, Barcelona; and course leader, Byam Shaw School of Art. Group shows included Gimpel Fils, from 1984; Gimpel Weitzenhofer, New York, America, 1986; Düsseldorf Multiple 97, Germany, 1997; Europaische Akademie, Trier, Germany, 1998; and John Moores Liverpool Exhibition, 2004. Among later solo exhibitions were Danielle Arnaud Contemporary Art, 1997; The British School, Rome, 1998; and University of Hertfordshire, 2002. The Arts Council, Leicestershire County Council and Royal London Hospital hold examples. Lived in London.

David HODGSON 1959– Gestural abstract artist, born in Cheshire. He attended North Staffordshire Polytechnic, 1980–1, then Croydon College of Art, 1981–4. Hodgson's exhibitions included Waterloo Live, at Waterloo Gallery, 1981, and New Acquaintances, at Fabian Carlsson Gallery, 1987. In 1988 he was in Time Out Live, at Olympia, and was a nominee for Young Artist of the Year at Whitechapel Art Gallery. In 1990 Hodgson was the Boyle Family's choice as Artist of the Day at Flowers East.

Heather HODGSON 1946– Suffolk-based landscape painter in whose work composition and colour were important elements. She attended Brighton College of Art, 1965 and 1979–80; Goldsmiths' College School of Art, 1967–70; and Dartington College of Art 1982–3–4. Mixed shows included New Street Gallery, Plymouth; Spacex Gallery, Exeter; Brighton Museum and Art Gallery; Brighton University Gallery; and Mall Galleries. John Russell Gallery, Ipswich, gave her solo shows in 2000 and 2005.

Janet HODGSON 1960– Artist, born in Bolton, Lancashire, who studied at Lincoln College of Art, 1978–9, then theatre design at Wimbledon School of Art, 1979–82. Carried out a series of commissions, including The Boat, Birkenhead Park, Merseyside, 1990; Arrivals, Settle Market Place, with Peter Hatton, one of a series of collaborations with him, 1992; and Piltdown Bungalow, Uppermill, 1993. Group exhibitions included A Pool of Signs II, Bluecoat Gallery, in Liverpool where she was based, 1992; Manchester Airport Terminal Two, 1993; and in 1995 Making it at Tate Gallery, Liverpool, where her White Cube, Black Square was made of granulated sugar, royal icing, steel, molasses and pump. In 1998, Hodgson collaborated with Anna Douglas on a work for artranspennine98, sited in Liverpool where she lived.

Louisa HODGSON 1905–1980 Painter and teacher, daughter of London and North Eastern Railway official Edward Hodgson, amateur artist and member of Berwick Art Club. She was educated at Whitley Bay and Monkseaton High School, then studied under Richard Hatton at Armstrong College, Newcastle. Won an Abbey Scholarship in mural decoration in 1928, spending three years at the Royal College of Art, where she specialised in mural decoration, joining the staff of Armstrong College's art school part-time in 1931. In 1931–2 Hodgson completed a lunette for the Laing Art Gallery, Newcastle, which illustrated the local Shipwrights' Guild passing along the quayside around 1450. The Laing also has her striking picture The Collingwood Monument, Trafalgar Night. Hodgson was a frequent exhibitor 1934–52 at RA Summer Exhibition, notable for unusual subjects such her 1936 entry In Search of Peace, in egg tempera, acquired by Manchester City Art Gallery. Ferens Art Gallery, Hull, has her 1938 exhibit The Birth of Venus. Hodgson ground her own pigments and while at Armstrong College worked with scientists there to reproduce colours used by the Italian Old Masters. Lived in Tynemouth, finally at Alnmouth, Northumberland, as a virtual recluse, her final years cloaked in mystery.

Trevor HODGSON 1931– Versatile artist and designer, born in Bradford, Yorkshire, who studied at Lancaster College of Art and University of London. His work could have an Art Brut feel, exemplified by an early abstracted self-portrait illustrated in Philip Vann's book *Face to Face*, published by Sansom & Company Ltd/Piano Nobile Fine Paintings in 2004. By the early 1960s when he was lecturing in graphic design at Blackpool School of Art, Hodgson's career had included periods as a scenic artist, jazz musician, schoolteacher and industrial designer. He was a politically aware member the AIA, showing in mixed and solo exhibitions there.

Stuart HODKINSON 1942– Painter, draughtsman and teacher, born in Cheshire, who studied at the University of Newcastle department of fine art, 1959–64, Slade School of Fine Art, 1964–6, and University of Reading, 1966–7. In 1979 he was included in Summer Show 2 at the Serpentine Gallery, when he had been teaching at Norwich School of Art since 1967. Within his artist's statement, which included quotations from Robert Musil and Henry James, Hodkinson stated that, "In spite of all the years, in spite of the great pyramid of history, in spite of all contemporary dogma, I feel, with relief, that there is a source of personal naïvety left, that it might be possible to paint like an ageing child." Hodkinson had been in Young Contemporaries at the Federation of British Artists Galleries, 1960–2. In 1979 he shared a show with Alan Turnbull at the Polytechnic Art Gallery, Newcastle upon Tyne, and in 1980 had a one-man exhibition at New Style Gallery.

John HODSON 1945– Artist in oil and marble, born in Oxford. He studied at Courtauld Institute, 1970. Hodson began painting landscapes in 1970 "using a colourful, Impressionist technique", then sculpted from 1975. He took part in group exhibitions in France and Italy and had a solo show at Woodstock Gallery, 1972. Lived in London.

Ron HODSON 1916– Painter, decorative artist and lecturer, born in Bolton, Lancashire. He studied at the School of Art there, his teachers including John Gauld, then at Manchester School of Art under Robert Dawson. Exhibited widely in north of England, including Manchester, Liverpool, Southport and Preston, and at Lefevre Gallery, London. Salford Museums and Art Galleries hold his work. He lectured to the Workers' Educational Association and lived in Burnley, Lancashire.

Francis Peter HOFFER: *see* **Franz Peter HOFFER**

Franz Peter HOFFER 1924–2000 Painter, stage designer, illustrator and writer, born in Berlin, Germany. He was educated in Kent at a boarding school, then attended St Martin's School of Art, 1939–41, under Sydney Litten. Hoffer had a multi-faceted career. Among his many activities he did stage design at the Glasgow Citizens' Theatre, for the theatre in London and at Stratford-upon-Avon; he designed for *Reader's Digest* Association Ltd;

worked for the Central Office of Information; and wrote for magazines such as *Lilliput* and *Saturday Book*. Showed with Leicester Galleries, Arts Council, RBA and overseas. Lived in London and in Milan, Italy. He is sometimes listed as Francis Peter Hoffer.

Erik HOFFMANN 1952– Painter and teacher, born in Leoben, Austria. He attended Kassel School of Art, 1975–80, having moved to Germany in 1960; from 1981–2 was a teacher of painting at Kassel, then attended Glasgow School of Art, 1982–3. Although Hoffmann continued to live in Kassel he spent part of the year on the island of Barra, in the Outer Hebrides. Working in tempera and acrylic Hoffmann completed portraits of great exactness and figure studies in landscapes with an intense atmosphere. From 1977 he won a number of awards in Germany and Scotland, including a grant from the German Academic Exchange Service for Glasgow in 1982 and in 1989 the Morrison Scottish Portrait Award, RSA. Showed at APEX-Gallery, Göttingen, in 1980, and at Savignyplatz Gallery, Berlin, in 1981–2. In 1988–9 had a first Scottish touring show, Portraits from the Western Edge, with Ulrike Kanne, An Lanntair, Stornaway, also showing with St Andrews Arts Centre, Aberdeen Art Gallery and Richard Demarco Gallery, Edinburgh. Later shows included Bruton Gallery for the Bath Festival, 1992.

Gerard HOFFNUNG 1925–1959 Humorous illustrator, writer and broadcaster with a special interest in music. Born in Berlin, was educated at Highgate School and at Harrow School of Art under John Platt. Hoffnung then began to mix careers as an illustrator and as a teacher. He was art master at Stamford School, 1945–6; staff artist on the *Evening News*, 1946; worked for Contact Publications, 1947–8; joined the staff of Harrow School, 1948; and was staff cartoonist for Cowles Magazines, New York, 1950–51. He freelanced widely, for publications including *Punch*, *Lilliput*, *Graphis*, *Daily Express* and *Saturday Evening Post*. Intermingled were forays into broadcasting for BBC, where his fruity, wheezy voice soon became instantly recognisable; playing the tuba; and organising his music festivals, at the Royal Festival Hall, in the 1950s, where unlikely instruments were played. He exhibited at the Little Gallery, Piccadily, 1949, and at the Festival Hall in 1951 and 1956, The British Cartoon Centre in 2001 displaying cartoons and models inspired by classical music. Books included *The Maestro*, *The Hoffnung Symphony Orchestra* and *Ho Ho Hoffnung*. Lived in London.

Max HOFLER 1890–1962 Artist in various media and architect, born and died in London, his father Austrian, his mother French. Was educated at Archbishop Tenison's Grammar School and John Lyon's, Harrow-on-the-Hill, studying aged 14, with special permission, at Heatherley's School of Fine Art, then at St Martin's School of Art. Hofler was articled to a firm of London architects, studying in the evenings for five years at the Royal Academy Schools, where he qualified: became an RIBA associate, 1922, a fellow, 1933. Practised as an architect until World War II, painting or sketching in his spare time. Success at exhibitions, such as the RA, ROI, RI, SMA and elsewhere, brought Hofler in touch with dealers and publishers, enabling him to abandon architecture full-time, although his command of architectural detail remained one of his strengths. Was a founder-member of the Wapping Group of Artists and Harrow Art Society, also a member of Langham Sketch Club and Buckinghamshire Art Society. Duncan Campbell Fine Art latterly showed Hofler's pictures. Lived in Harrow-on-the-Hill, Middlesex.

Eileen HOGAN 1946– Painter, designer, printmaker, illustrator and teacher who studied graphic design and then painting, under Carel Weight, at Royal College of Art, 1971–4, following a period at Camberwell School of Arts and Crafts, 1963–7, and British School of Archaeology, Athens, 1970–1. Showed solo on many occasions, including British Council, Athens, 1971; Royal College of Art in 1977; a series at Fine Art Society, London and Glasgow, from 1980; Imperial War Museum, 1984; and Graduate School of Library Services University of Alabama, 1988. She illustrated a number of books, including *Fragments from Sappho*, 1973; *The Dream of Gerontius*, 1976; and *A Selection of Poems by C P Cavafy*, 1985. The Burntwood Press was her own imprint. The British School in Athens commissioned a mural in 1971, and other commissions included Imperial War Museum, 1983–4, Women at Work in the Royal Navy; *Illustration: A Working Art*, commissioned by Batsford, 1989; and Royal Mail stamps, 1990–1. Public collections holding Hogan's work include Victoria & Albert Museum plus many overseas collections. She was a member of RWS, which gave her a solo show in 1999. There was another at Bourne Fine Art, Edinburgh, in 2003, and a Muir Trust Residency Exhibition at Buckinghamshire County Museum & Art Gallery, Aylesbury, in 2005. In 1992 The London Institute awarded her a professorship.

Lizzie HOGARTH 1879–c.1953 Painter and draughtsman, born in Aberdeen. She studied art there with James Hector and at St Martin's School of Art. Exhibited at RSA, extensively at RBA and SWA of both of which she was a member, and in the provinces. Still life and landscape were the mainstays of her contributions to SWA, where she was a prolific exhibitor, 1919–52. Lived latterly in Petworth, Sussex.

Paul HOGARTH 1917–2001 Painter, illustrator, printmaker and teacher, born in Kendal, Westmorland, full name Arthur Paul Hogarth. Sometimes signed work P H. Studied at Manchester School of Art, St Martin's School of Art and obtained doctorate at Royal College of Art. He was senior tutor in the faculty of graphic art there, 1964–71. In 1981 was commissioned by Imperial War Museum to depict the Berlin Wall. His work is also in Fitzwilliam Museum in Cambridge, Victoria & Albert Museum and many other public galleries in Britain and abroad. Hogarth was a Royal Designer for Industry, and was elected ROI, 1979, RA in 1984 and RE in 1988. Retrospective at Abbot Hall Art Gallery, Kendal, 1985; in 1990 his exhibition Cold War Reports 1947–67 was at Norfolk Institute of Art, with a tour; retrospective at Fosse Gallery, Stow-on-the-Wold, 1998. Much of Hogarth's early work was of a left-wing committed nature, and he was associated with AIA, desiring to be "a communicator rather than a painter". He was in the English tradition of the artist-traveller and among his books were *Looking at China*, 1955; *Majorca Observed* (with Robert Graves), 1965; *Drawing Architecture*, 1973; *The Mediterranean Shore* (with Lawrence Durrell), 1988; and *Drawing on Life: the autobiography of Paul Hogarth*, 1997. Among his awards was the *Yorkshire Post* Award for the Best Art Book, 1986. Settled finally at Hidcote Manor, Gloucestershire, moving to Cirencester in the same county shortly before he died. Hogarth's third wife was the artist Pat Douthwaite.

Philip HOGBEN 1945– Landscape and figure painter who studied at Derby and Winchester Schools of Art, 1961–6. In 1969 settled in Cornwall to teach at Falmouth School of Art. Showed in west of England and abroad and in 1992 was included in Artists from Cornwall at RWA. Two years before, he gained *Western Morning News* prize at Newlyn Contemporaries show. Hogben was a member of Newlyn Society of Artists and lived in Helston.

Mary HOGG: *see* **Mary MAINDS**

William HOGGATT 1880–1961 Painter, mainly of landscapes of the Isle of Man. He was born in Lancaster, of a Cumbrian father and Scottish mother, won a scholarship to the Royal College of Art which he did not take up, but became apprenticed to a local stained glass makers, continuing his studies at the school of art in Lancaster's Storey Institute. Aided by one of the Storeys, Hoggatt studied at the Académie Julian in Paris, 1901–5. While working on a commission at the Tate Gallery he came to know his future wife, Dazine, sister of Leonard Archer who managed the pianist Paderewski, then travelled to Isle of Man to inspect his future home. Hoggatt liked the light and landscape and decided to stay, living at Port St Mary until 1925, then at The Darragh, Port Erin, which became one of the island's intellectual centres. Hoggatt was a prolific and widespread exhibitor, especially at the RA Summer Exhibition, also RSA and RSW. He was a member of a number of exhibiting societies, including RI, RBC and RCamA, and was president of the Manx Artists. In 1934 he won a competition to design a stained glass window commemorating the work of T E Brown, the island's national poet. Foxdale Valley, in the collection of Pallant House, Chichester, is a typical solidly drawn pastel. Other works by Hoggatt are in the Manx Museum Art Gallery and in the collections of public galleries in Liverpool, Manchester, Oldham and Preston, as well as several Australian galleries.

Chris HOGGETT 1927– Painter, sculptor, ceramist, stage designer, teacher, illustrator and writer, born and lived in Cheltenham, Gloucestershire. He studied at Royal College of Art, 1950–3, where Rodney Burn and Carel Weight were influential teachers, others including John Minton, Rodrigo Moynihan, Charles Mahoney and Robert Buhler. Hoggett went on to teach and work in a wide range of media and illustrate many books. His own books included *Stage Crafts*, published in Britain and America. In later years Hoggett returned to his main interest, paintings landscapes, especially in the wilder areas of Scotland and New Zealand. During this time "a more abstract approach developed as the result of combining figurative elements with landscape". Showed mainly in West Country, including RWA and with Cheltenham Group of Artists. Solo shows included Café, Cheltenham Art Gallery & Museum, "work in various media inspired by dream or reverie," 2004.

Pete HOIDA 1944– Painter, poet and teacher, born and brought up in Birkenhead, Cheshire. After working as a landscape architect for London County Council in the early 1960s he studied painting at Hammersmith College of Art and Building and Goldsmiths' College. During the 1960s and 1970s volumes of his poems were published and readings given at many colleges and universities, the Traverse Theatre in Edinburgh and ICA. Taught at Chelsea School of Art, 1978. From 1974 he lived and painted at the same location outside Stroud, Gloucestershire. Hoida's seemingly abstract paintings, in acrylic on elongated, horizontal canvases, were much-inspired by the Toadsmoor Valley. Rothko, Pollock, Matisse, Braque and Picasso were cited as influences, "mediated by Hilton, Heron and others". Group exhibitions included New Young Contemporaries, Camden Arts Centre, 1973–4; Six Gloucestershire Painters, Spacex, Exeter, 1980; Kilvert Gallery, Clyro, 1992–3; Oriel Senig, Harlech, 1994; and Sui Generis, Cheltenham, 2000. Had a solo show at International Arts Centre, 1975, later ones including Museum and Art Gallery, Cheltenham, 1995, and deliART, 2000.

Ashley HOLD 1964– Artist who studied painting at Falmouth School of Art and Design. He exhibited with Penwerris Community Arts Group in Falmouth, Cornwall, where he lived, and at Newlyn Orion Gallery as a member of Newlyn Society of Artists. Also showed with Independent Schools Exhibition, Dulwich Art Gallery and Oxford in 1986, and in Painting Today auction at Bonhams, 1991–2, was included in Falmouth Connections at Falmouth Art Gallery in 1994 and in same year had a portrait at BP National Portrait Award at National Portrait Gallery. Hold undertook several group murals and workshops in the local community, including a mural for Truro School. In 1998, with the artist Tim Shaw, Hold set up an open studios scheme in the Falmouth/Penryn area; by 2001, the South West Open Studios brochure listed 200 artists and 20 galleries and spread across 136 venues.

Cliff HOLDEN 1919– Painter, designer, draughtsman, printmaker and teacher, born in Manchester. He initially studied agriculture and veterinary science, then philosophy at the City Literary Institute from 1944 where he met David Bomberg, Edna Mann and Dorothy Mead (with whom Holden was closely associated for 11 years). In 1945 these artists followed Bomberg to the Borough Polytechnic and joined his group from the Bartlett School of Architecture in drawing at various venues. In 1944–5 Holden and Bomberg conceived the Borough Group, established 1946, the first of seven shows taking place in 1947. Holden was its president, 1946–8, but resigned over policy issues. Bomberg reorganised the group, which disbanded in 1951. Holden met the Swedish artist Torsten Renquist and in 1952 showed in Four Englishmen in Gummesson's Gallery, Stockholm; in 1956 he was invited to show more in Sweden and set up a design studio in Gothenburg with Lisa Grönwall and Maj Nilsson; in 1959 Holden and the studio moved to Marstrand, the trio becoming known internationally as Marstrand Designers. Holden also taught in Sweden and abroad, including Goldsmiths' College. Participated in many group shows and solo exhibitions were held in Sweden, later ones including Möbelcentrum, Stockholm, from 1977, and Marstrand Designers (with his son Thomas Holden, the painter), 1979. Holden was a member of LG, was a fellow of the Free Painters and Sculptors and Chartered Society of Designers, a design associate of the American Institute of Interior Designers, as well as several Swedish artists' organisations. Extensive public commissions included hotels, ships, offices, embassies and consulates. Tate Gallery, Arts Council, Victoria & Albert Museum, Scottish

National Gallery of Modern Art in Edinburgh, Manchester City Art Gallery and a series of Swedish collections hold examples. Holden promoted Swedish artists in Britain and British artists in Sweden, such as the sculptors Armitage, Chadwick and Butler.

Douglas Hamilton HOLDEN 1919–1972 Painter, printmaker, creator of found-object assemblages and teacher, son of Harold Henry Holden and brother of John Hamilton Holden, both artists. Douglas studied at Birmingham School of Arts and Crafts with Beatrice Johnson (as his wife known as Trixie Holden) before World War II. During the war Douglas served in the Royal Navy, then in 1946–7 he and Trixie studied at the Royal College of Art. Douglas taught at St Martin's School of Art and showed at the RA Summer Exibition in the 1950s while living in London; was elected an RWS associate in 1953 and RWS in 1961; and exhibited at The New Art Centre, 1965. In April 1988 Douglas' work was included in a studio sale of several Holdens' works at Burstow & Hewitt, Battle.

Harold Henry HOLDEN 1885–1977 Watercolour painter, etcher and teacher, born in Settle, Yorkshire, father of three artists: Geoffrey H Holden, John Hamilton Holden and Douglas Hamilton Holden. He studied at Skipton School of Art, Leeds College of Art and the Royal College of Art after initial lessons near his home in Settle. He exhibited at RA, RBSA, RWS and abroad, Leeds City Art Gallery, among others, holding his work. He became art department head at Leeds Modern School in 1910; principal of Cheltenham School of Arts and Crafts, 1914; principal of Leeds College of Art, 1922; director of art education and principal of the College of Arts and Crafts, Birmingham, 1928–46. Holden's work could be sombre, and he favoured strongly organised pictures. Lived finally in Westbury-on-Trym, Bristol, with his fourth son, Rupert, a civil engineer.

John Hamilton HOLDEN 1913–1980 Artist and administrator who worked as John Holden. Born in Leeds, he went on to study at Birmingham College of Art, of which his father, Harold Holden, was for a time principal. Then he studied at Royal College of Art. Holden became progressively principal of Wolverhampton College of Art, Manchester College of Art and Design and then deputy director of Manchester Polytechnic, from which he retired in 1978. Holden's considerable contribution to building up the Manchester College is chronicled by David Jeremiah in *A Hundred Years and More*, published by Manchester Polytechnic in 1980. Among official positions held by Holden were the presidency of both the National Society for Art Education and the Association of Art Institutions. Holden wrote on art and education and showed at RA and provincial galleries. Lived in Wilmslow, Cheshire. Sometimes he is incorrectly listed as John Hamilton-Holden.

John HOLDEN 1942– Painter and teacher, born in Gillingham, Kent, who studied at Medway College of Art and Design, 1959–63, and Royal Academy Schools, 1963–6. From 1986 he was principal lecturer in fine art at Liverpool John Moores University. Showed regularly at RA from 1968; in Parallel Lines, at Cardiff Institute of Higher Education, 1993; and in the 1995–6 John Moores Liverpool Exhibition, with You are the One, a geometrical abstract. Had a solo exhibition at RA in 1974. Holden was a member of the LG from 2002, his work illustrated in its ninetieth anniversary commemorative volume. In 2004, he shared an exhibition with Paul Mason at Fermynwoods Contemporary Art, Brigstock. Lived in Long Buckby, Northampton.

John Vivian HOLDEN 1931– Painter, printmaker, muralist and teacher who studied at various London art colleges and in Paris studios in 1940s and 1950s. He went on to teach painting, etching and the history of art for about 35 years, travelling frequently in Europe. Holden had shows at National Theatre in London, Orleans House in Richmond and at Cleveland Bridge Gallery, Bath. He did a number of murals for companies, including Dunlop Rubber Company. Holden was described as an "intense admirer of the irrational and neurotic in art". He had a fine understanding of the human figure, on which his work was based, forms materialising on the canvas in deft strokes of colour, giving an impression of restless energy.

Thomas HOLDEN 1957– Painter, muralist, designer and printmaker, son of the artists Cliff Holden and Lisa Grönwall, he was born in Gothenberg, Sweden. From 1972 pursued his own work and from 1975 exhibited with his parents under the name Marstrand Designers. Collaborated on numerous projects and public commissions, being represented in Swedish embassies and consulates, hotels, hospitals, factories, banks, ferries and cruise ships. Strindberg Museum in Stockholm has Holden's large silkscreen portrait of the writer. Group exhibitions included David Bomberg-linked show at Towner Art Gallery in Eastbourne, 1991. Had many solo exhibitions in Sweden from 1977, later ones including Gallery St Nikolaus, Stockholm, 1985.

Walter Frederick Clarke HOLDEN 1882–1953 Architect and landscape painter who, after completing his articles at Cambridge, was with the partnership of Burgess and Myers, Beaconsfield, from 1906. After serving in camouflage with the Royal Engineers in World War I and earning a Military Cross, Holden in 1920 joined the National Provincial Bank, becoming chief architect in 1934, retiring in 1947. His designs for the doors of the National Westminster Bank in Coventry's High Street, made in 1930, are particularly fine. During World War II Holden was on the Royal Academy committee that made proposals for rebuilding blitzed London. Holden showed paintings at the RA Summer Exhibition and at the Royal Glasgow of the Fine Arts.

Edgar Thomas HOLDING 1870–1952 Landscape painter, born in Horncastle, Lincolnshire, who became full-time painter in maturity. Was at various times president of the RWS Art Club, secretary of the Society of Sussex Painters and a member of the Art Workers' Guild. Regular exhibitor at RWS, also showed at RA, Fine Art Society, Goupil Gallery, Walker Art Gallery, Liverpool, and many other venues. He was extensively illustrated in books, such as the *Old Water-colour Society's Annual*, and by firms such as Vickers Brothers. Public galleries in Brighton, Bristol, Southport, Leeds and Worthing hold his work. Lived for many years in Sutton, Sussex.

Marjorie HOLFORD: *see* **Marjorie BROOKS**

David HOLGATE 1939– Sculptor, letterer, painter, gilder and teacher working in various materials who was apprenticed to David Kindersley, Cambridge, 1955–60, being his personal assistant, 1960–2. After establishing his own workshop, settling in Norwich, Norfolk, Holgate worked almost entirely on commissions for architectural practices, private firms and individuals and the church, his central concern being the spiritual journey. From 1976 Holgate was visiting lecturer at Ipswich and Norwich Art Schools, also teaching in schools and adult education. He was a member of Letter Exchange and was included in Stone Words at Pentagram, Wolseley Fine Arts and tour, 2002. Anglia Television, Basildon Council, the Historic Churches Trust, Norwich Cathedral and Museum and the Redundant Churches Commission held his work.

Florence Mabel HOLLAMS 1877–1963 Painter of horses, dogs, flower studies and the countryside. She studied at the Calderon School of Animal Painting and at Académie Julian, Paris, and was a keen horse and dog woman. In the 1920s and 1930s Hollams produced many equine portraits, using samples of the horses' coats and manes for reference, finishing her work with great speed. Exhibited RA and Ackermann.

Claerwen HOLLAND 1952– Painter, draughtsman, printmaker and teacher, born in Radnorshire, where she continued to live. Her subjects were rooted in the countryside and domestic still life. She studied at Byam Shaw School of Drawing and Painting under Maurice de Sausmarez, who awarded her the principal's prize for landscape in oils. Won a David Murray Studentship in landscape painting given by RA. Exhibited in many mixed shows, including RA and NEAC. Had solo exhibitions at Sue Rankin and Thackeray Galleries. Holland was a member of the Artists and Designers of Wales, and for them she demonstrated etching at Royal Welsh Showground at Builth Wells, where she also showed Beulah Speckled Faced Sheep, which featured in much of her work.

Derek HOLLAND 1927– Painter, draughtsman and teacher, born in Chesterfield, Derbyshire, who attended the College of Art there, 1952–4, and the Central School of Arts and Crafts, 1954–7, teachers including Blair Hughes-Stanton, Hans Tisdall, Keith Vaughan, Merlyn Evans and Morris Kestelman. He was an instructor in life drawing and basic design at the Central, 1957–9, and was head of the art department, Plymouth College, 1959–73. Holland stopped working in a non-figurative manner in 1974, after which he made regular trips to France to draw from the landscape, the basis for gestural paintings made back in England. He became a member of the Society of Mural Painters, 1958, and of the Newlyn Society, 1984. Mixed shows included Artists of Fame and Promise, Leicester Galleries, 1958–9; Society of Mural Painters, Victoria & Albert Museum, 1961; Redfern Gallery, 1966–74; British Art, Monte Carlo, 1966; and, latterly, New Street Gallery, Plymouth, 2000. Later solo exhibitions included Plymouth Arts Centre, 2000. Plymouth City Art Gallery and Leicestershire Education Authority hold examples. Lived in Plymouth, Devon.

Dudley HOLLAND 1915–1956 Painter, muralist, designer, printmaker and teacher whose work had a Neo-Romantic tinge and a strong sense of design. Holland was educated at Kingston Grammar School, Chelsea and Willesden Schools of Art. He was awarded a Royal Exhibition to the Royal College of Art, 1936, which he refused, preferring to paint on his own. Taught design, painting and drawing at Willesden, Harrow and Goldsmiths' College Schools of Art, then was appointed principal of York School of Art, 1949, of Guildford School of Art, 1951. He completed mural decorations for Cunard Line, schools and libraries. Exhibited at RA from 1937, also with NEAC, LG, with Redfern Gallery and in touring shows. In 1950 he shared an exhibition with Austin Wright at York City Art Gallery which holds his work, as does the Arts Council. Holland was killed when his motorcycle hit a lorry; he was rushed to Kingston Hospital but was dead on arrival. One version says that Holland would not have used the motorcycle again, as he was on the way to collect a new car. Another that he was furious at a wrongly detrimental inspector's report and by mistake tipped the lorry. Lived at Hale, near Farnham, Surrey. Abbott and Holder latterly sold Holland's work.

George Herbert Buckingham HOLLAND 1901–1987 Painter, educated at the Grammar School in Northampton, where he was born and made his career. He worked as a commercial artist before studying at Leicester School of Art and Chelsea Polytechnic. Was a founder-member of Northampton Town and County Art Society and its president in 1949–50. He was noted for his portraits and showed at RP, Alpine Club Gallery, ROI and elsewhere. National Portrait Gallery, Royal Academy of Music and National Library of Wales hold his work. Holland's fine 1947 portrait of Lady Margaret Isham is in the Isham family home, Lamport Hall, Northamptonshire.

Harry HOLLAND 1941– Painter, draughtsman, printmaker and teacher, born in Glasgow. After an attempt to study at Wimbledon College of Art which fell through because of lack of funds, Holland attended a commercial college, then was at St Martin's School of Art, 1965–9. Taught at Chelsea Community Centre, Coventry College of Art until 1972, at a series of art schools in the Midlands, then at Cardiff College of Art, 1974–8, when he left to paint full-time. While at Coventry several pictures were bought by the collector Charles Saatchi. Holland began to show with Nicholas Treadwell Gallery, then Ian Birksted Gallery in 1983 and Thumb Gallery, 1986 (later the Jill George Gallery). Holland's mixed shows included Aspects of Realism, 1976–8, which toured Canada; The Probity of Art, a WAC touring show, 1980; in the same year the British Art Show, an Arts Council exhibition which toured; and People in Great Britain, 1989, a British Council touring show. Had a solo show at Roundhouse Gallery, 1979; the following year WAC toured his one-man exhibition; then he showed regularly, with a Jill George UK travelling retrospective in 1991. Later solo exhibitions included Martin Tinney Gallery, Cardiff, from 1992; Oriel, WAC Gallery and tour, 1995; Mineta Move Gallery, Brussels, Belgium, 1999; Il Pollitico, Rome, Italy, from 2000; and Albermarle Gallery, with an extensively illustrated catalogue, 2004. Holland's work – impeccably crafted – went through several phases, including realism with a hinted-at – even sinister – narrative element; still life; and still life with a Surrealistic atmosphere which explored aspects of reality. Tate Gallery, WAC and Metropolitan Museum of Art in New York hold his work. Based in Cardiff.

Hester HOLLAND: *see* **Hester GORST**

James HOLLAND 1905–1996 Designer, painter, teacher and writer, born in Gillingham, Kent, son of a naval blacksmith, who early on won the president's prize of the Royal Drawing Society and a scholarship to Rochester School of Art with his ship drawings. From 1924 attended Royal College of Art painting school, where James Boswell became a close friend. In 1933 they helped to found the AIA. Holland held the first of many exhibitions while still at the Royal College, where he was active in the sketch club. On graduating Holland joined the advertising agency Foote, Cone & Belding, and was commissioned, with John Betjeman, to write copy for Shell by Jack Beddington; was active in LG and NEAC; helped decorate the Peace Pavilion at the 1937 Paris World Fair; and was a freelance illustrator. During World War II Holland worked in the Ministry of Information's exhibition design department, invaluable experience when he was asked to oversee the Sea and Ships section of the Festival of Britain in 1951 and to be chief designer of the *Campania* floating exhibition hall which toured 10 ports. From 1952–63 Holland was group art director for Erwin, Wasey and Company, the advertising agency, from 1963–71 head of the faculty of visual communication design at Birmingham Polytechnic. Holland was closely involved in the work of the Society of Industrial Artists and Designers, being its president, 1960–1, in 1980 publishing its history, *Minerva at Fifty*. Died in Pembury, Kent. Retrospective at Art Connoisseur in 1997.

Michael HOLLAND 1947–2002 Versatile artist and teacher, born in Sunderland, whose work over the years drew on Surrealism, Constructivism, Pop Art and Cubism. He studied at Sunderland Polytechnic and the Royal College of Art. Early successes were Stowells Trophy, 1973, and acceptance for the John Moores Liverpool Exhibition, 1974. Holland drew on his student work when later he became a fellow at Cheltenham College of Art and a Rome Scholar. Over the years, Holland was head of painting at Cheltenham & Gloucester College of Higher Education, the University of Northumbria in Newcastle and at the Birmingham Institute of Art & Design, where he was afterwards head of fine art. He also taught in Australia. He exhibited widely, including the RA Summer Exhibition; Galleria Rondanini, Rome, Italy; South London Art Gallery; and Praxis Gallery, Bristol. The Foyer Gallery, Squires Building, University of Northumbria, held a notable posthumous exhibition of Holland's work in 2002.

Vera HOLLAND fl. c.1950–1975 Oil painter, tapestry designer and embroiderer. Born and lived at Sileby, Leicestershire, studying with Edgar Lander, then at Loughborough School of Art. Exhibited widely throughout Britain, including RI, SGA, SWA and locally in Leicester. Her work was reproduced in a number of publications, including *The Listener*, *Country Fair*, *The Countryman* and *The Lady*.

Antony HOLLAWAY 1928–2000 Stained glass artist, muralist and teacher, born in Kinson, Dorset. He was early immersed in the life of Poole Harbour, working in Bolson's shipyard and on the local paddle steamers. After National Service in the Royal Air Force, in which he was briefly involved in the Berlin Airlift to break the Soviet blockade of 1948–9, Hollaway was encouraged at Bournemouth College of Art by Frederic E Courtney, a lifelong friend and mentor. In 1953 Hollaway won a County Scholarship and entered the Royal College of Art as a Royal Scholar, where he took up stained glass and mural painting, developing a forceful, modern style. In 1957 he started A H Associates, soon becoming consultant to the architects' division of Greater London Council's housing division until it closed in 1968. A 1963 slab-glass window for Boots' Chemical Laboratory, Nottingham, was a challenging early job. Some of his most impressive pieces are in Leicestershire, among them a 1966 abstract relief in concrete at Leicestershire County Hall, Glenfield. Hollaway's most important commission came in 1971 from the architect Harry Fairhurst, which resulted in five ambitious, dramatic windows for Manchester Cathedral. His final piece was a gift to his local church, All Saints, Allington, Lincolnshire. Holloway taught at the Central School of Art & Design, Kingston College of Art, Epsom School and Trent Polytechnic. He was a member of the Society of Designer-Craftsmen, British Society of Master Glass Painters, Society of Chartered Designers and the Contemporary Crafts Network. Hollaway was an excellent and amusing lecturer and good company, as unpretentiously willing to talk about his mistakes as his successes.

Laura HOLLIDAY 1958– Creator of wall-based sculptures – often humorous, sinister, or jokey portraits – made from found objects, papier mâché and paint, which could evolve over a period. She was born in Sydney, Australia, where she spent nine years before her family moved back to its roots in Penarth, near Cardiff, where she settled eventually at Roath. Gained an honours degree in fine art from South Glamorgan Institute of Higher Education, Cardiff, 1976–80, and her master's degree from Royal College of Art, 1982–5. In 1983 she won a Young Artists Grant from WAC, in 1986 a Pirelli Commission. Mixed shows included Stowells Trophy, RA, 1980; Invited Artists, WAC Gallery, Cardiff, 1986–7; Women Artists Open Exhibition, Cardiff Central Library, 1990; and The All-Women Cardiff Artists Show, Oriel Contemporary Art, 1996. Had a solo exhibition, Gossiping Teapots, The Old Hall, Cowbridge, 1982, later ones including Sculpture at St David's Hall, Cardiff, 1988, and Face to Face, Old Hall, Cowbridge, 1993.

Sarah HOLLIDAY 1960– Self-taught watercolourist whose London Unveiled show at New Academy Gallery, 1998, focused on the capital's changing scene. Holliday was elected a full member of RWS in 1996. In 1991 she had won the Saunders Waterford Award there, in 1989 the Arrobus Award for Watercolour at Camden Arts Centre. She was artist-in-residence, Commonwork Land Trust, Kent, 1990, and expedition artist to Borneo for Raleigh International, 1994. Mixed shows included David Curzon Gallery, 1992; SWA, 1993; and RSW, 1998.

Stephen HOLLINGSWORTH 1967– Artist using a variety of materials to create installations, as at New Art in Scotland, Centre for Contemporary Arts, Glasgow, 1994. Hollingsworth was born in Leeds, attended Gwent College of Higher Education, 1988–91, and the School of Art, Glasgow, 1992–4. He said that his work was "concerned with how as human beings we experience the world through our senses and the passage of time." Mixed shows included Leeds Open Artists Exhibition, from 1991, and Danger, School of Art Institute, Chicago, 1993, the year he had a solo show at the White Room, Glasgow School of Art.

Geoffrey St J HOLLIS 1925– Representational watercolourist and teacher who studied at Cambridge School of Art and Bournemouth College of Art, where he gained his diploma. He moved to Ipswich, Suffolk, to teach in 1955. In 1959 with Roger Finch he shared an exhibition at Haste Gallery, which then showed his work regularly. Enthusiasm for wildlife and sailing influenced his output.

Gerald HOLLIS 1908– Painter, educated privately. Exhibited RA, Leicester Galleries, RBA and in provinces. Had a number of one-man shows at Brook Street Art Gallery. Lived in Fulwood, Lancashire.

Richard HOLLIS 1934– Painter in oil lacquer, graphic designer and teacher, born in London, where he settled. He studied at Chelsea School of Art, 1954–5, Wimbledon School of Art, 1955–7, and Central School of Arts and Crafts, 1958–9, under William Turnbull. Between 1960–80 taught in various art schools, practised graphic design and in 1994 published *Graphic Design: A Concise History*. Hollis' own work was influenced by Venezuelan painting of the 1950s and Swiss Concrete Art. He showed at New Vision Centre Gallery and in 1993 was included in The Sixties Art Scene in London at Barbican Art Gallery. Richard Hollis: Graphics for the Whitechapel was held at Whitechapel Art Gallery, 1984.

Della HOLLOW 1922–1980 Artist in collage and watercolour who also practised interior decoration. Born at South Molton, Devon, Della Hollow – who sometimes signed her work only with her first name – studied art at Exeter School of Art, 1938–41, under Ruth Wood and Leighton Woollatt; she also had private lessons with Patrick Larking. Exhibited SWLA, RI and NS. Lived at Colyton, Devon.

Geoffrey HOLLOW 1944–1998 Self-taught painter of abstracts, born and based in London, who began painting in 1972. He had awards from the Arts Council, Elephant Trust and British and American Arts Foundation and held visiting lectureships in Britain and overseas. Took part in extensive group shows, including Made in Greenwich, The Living Room, 1994. Solo shows included Air Gallery, 1981; Greenwich Theatre Gallery, 1989; and Kepler Gallery, 1992. In 1993 he held a residency at City Museum & Art Gallery, Hanley, Stoke-on-Trent, with an accompanying exhibition. SE1 Gallery @ Workplace held a show in 1999. Several corporate collections hold examples.

Douglas Raymond HOLLOWAY 1923– Watercolourist and architect, born in London, who attended Royal West of England Academy School of Architecture, also studying watercolour with James Michie. He was in private practice in Bristol, then in the County Architect's Department for Kent, then Lancashire, 1959–84. He was a member of RWA. For many years Holloway concentrated mainly on the Lancashire scene, but also north Wales and Andalucia, where he spent part of each year. He used "a limited palette and avoided unnecessary detail which results in an apparent simplicity or Impressionist style. Most of my work is done in the studio, although I prefer to paint on the spot." Mixed shows included RCamA, Gloucester City Art Gallery and the Society of Architect Artists. In 1981 he had a solo show at Dallas Inman Gallery and in 1989 another at Vernon Gallery, both in Preston, Lancashire, where he lived at Longton. RWA holds his work.

Edgar HOLLOWAY 1914– Printmaker, watercolourist, calligrapher and teacher, born in Doncaster, Yorkshire, where his father was a frame maker. Aged 14 he began to attend classes at local School of Art and in 1931 had first solo show in London. While earning his living from etchings and portrait commissions Holloway studied under Randolph Schwabe at Slade School of Fine Art, where he proved an outstanding draughtsman. During World War II taught for a while, but illness prevented him continuing. Holloway became a Catholic and married a disciple of Eric Gill. He settled in Ditchling, Sussex, in 1949 and became a member of the Guild of St Joseph and St Dominic in which Gill was involved. By now Holloway had taken up lettering, signwriting, calligraphy and wood engraving, and he designed and worked as a cartographer for major publishing houses. In 1969 he returned to watercolour and, after his retirement, line engraving. Holloway showed at RBA and the Society of Artist Printmakers, both of which he was a member, as well as RA, RI and NEAC. He gave a large collection of his prints to Ashmolean Museum in Oxford, which held a show of them in 1991. Holloway was the father of Tim Holloway the artist. Edgar Holloway at 80 was at Kendal's Abbot Hall Art Gallery and Museum as part of a tour in 1994. Holloway was especially noted for his etchings, and he was still producing prints in his long series of self-portraits in 2002, when Bankside Gallery had a show mainly of his landscape drawings. In 2004, Wolseley Fine Arts held a ninetieth-birthday exhibition.

Edgar HOLLOWAY: *see* **James NOBLE**

Gill HOLLOWAY 1928– Landscape painter, lecturer and writer, born in London and formerly known as Gill Harman, who studied art at King's College, Newcastle, before in 1950 becoming art tutor at Durham University's extramural department. She retained this post until 1967, showing in the northeast of England. Between 1969–88, when she retired, she was head of art and art history at Cheltenham Ladies' College, continuing to exhibit widely in London and the provinces. Between 1981–7 she was the second wife of the artist Ted Holloway. After his death she produced a book of his drawings: *A Bevin Boy Remembers*, which accompanied a show of his work that toured from Stoke-on-Trent Art Gallery from 1993. Latterly, based in Condicote, Gloucestershire, Gill Holloway continued to paint, teach, write and travel. Anderson Gallery, Broadway, held an important show of her work in 1998. It is held by public and private collections.

Laura HOLLOWAY 1960– Painter who studied at Gloucestershire College of Art, 1979–82, and the Royal Academy Schools, 1985–8. She exhibited at the RA Summer Exhibition from 1987 and was in Britain's Painters at Mall Galleries, 1988. Had a first solo show at Mason-Watts Fine Art, Warwick, in 1992. Sir Brinsley Ford owned a 1988 self-portrait by her.

Robert Charles HOLLOWAY 1914–1986 Painter in gouache and pastel, and teacher, born in Chelsea. He studied at Clapham School of Art and Royal College of Art under Sir William Rothenstein and Percy Hague Jowett. Holloway became art master at King's College School, where he established a small press producing art books. He showed at RA, RBA and NEAC and lived in Epsom, Surrey.

Ted HOLLOWAY 1926–1987 Painter, draughtsman and teacher, full name Edwin Francis Holloway, born in Upham, Hampshire, who left school at 15 and became a forestry worker for three years. At 18 he became a Bevin Boy in the Durham Coalfield, by which time he was drawing and painting. At 28 he attended classes at Durham University Extra-Mural Department, in 1958 won a bursary to study full-time at Sunderland College of Art, then gained an art teacher's diploma, with distinction, at London University. Holloway became head of art at Jarrow Springfield Comprehensive School, then gave up teaching to paint full-time in 1981. Moved to Charlton Kings, Gloucestershire, where he became fascinated by early Celtic art and mythology, but is best known for his long series of drawings based on his mining career. These were featured in a touring show, after his death on a painting trip to Scotland, originating in Stoke-on-Trent Art Gallery, in 1993. Accompanying it, Holloway's artist wife Gill produced a book of his drawings: *A Bevin Boy Remembers*.

Alexander HOLLWEG 1936– Painter, draughtsman, coloured wood relief maker and teacher, born in London, the grandson of the artist Edward Wadsworth. He said that his subject "has always been the same, people and their houses – where they work and where they play." After reading French and German at Oxford he studied at Camberwell School of Arts and Crafts from 1960–3. By 1973 he was head of department at Maidstone College of Art, later teaching part-time at Bristol Polytechnic. After a solo show at Whitechapel Art Gallery in 1971, followed by shows at Felicity Samuel Gallery, 1972–7, there were several abroad. Was included in 5 Modern British Artists, Mark Glazebrook, 1983. Lived in Nettlecombe, Avon.

Karn HOLLY 1940– Painter and draughtsman, born in the Channel Islands, who studied at Bournemouth College of Art and the Royal Academy Schools. She gained many prizes and awards, including Landseer Scholarship and Silver Medal, Drawing; Landseer Scholarship and Bronze Medal, Painting; Alma-Tadema and Richard Jack Prizes; John Crompton Award; Landseer Award for One Year; Hunting Group Companies Award, 1986, Print and Drawing Prize, 1998; Ernest Kleinwort Trust Award, 1990 and 1997; Kathleen Troneon Drawing Prize, 1991; Critics Award, NEAC, 1992; and Arts Club Purchase Prize, RA, 1997; Hunting Group Print and Drawing Prize, 1998; and Worshipful Company of Painters Award, NEAC, 2000. Holly showed in the RA Summer Exhibition from 1981, with NEAC, of which she was a member, at several venues, from 1989; Hunting Group, several venues, from 1986; The Discerning Eye, Mall Galleries, from 1991; and widely elsewhere. She had solo exhibitions at Elgin (Cassian de Vere Cole Fine Art) in 2000 and 2001. On the latter occasion the London-based artist wrote that her work was "primarily from and about observation and time, made over time. The gradual overlay and development of the image is in pursuit of an evocation of perception and feeling." There was a show at New Grafton Gallery in 2004.

Agnes Gladys HOLMAN 1885–c.1967 Commercial artist and illustrator, specialising in animals, sculptor and miniaturist. Born at Charlton Kings, Gloucestershire, she studied at St John's Wood School of Art, then made a personal study of animals. Served in Women's Land Army during World War I. For some years was a member of council of the Royal Drawing Society, for which she was an examiner. Did an extensive amount of illustrative work for Oxford University Press, educational publications, *Western Daily Mail* and for book-jackets. Exhibited SWA, RWA, RI, PS, in the provinces and abroad. Lived in Bath, Somerset.

George Alfred HOLMAN 1911– Sculptor and medallist, his talent was early spotted at school. Studied art at Hornsey School of Art under the sculptor Harold Youngman, 1927–34, after Hackney School of Art, 1925–27. Exhibited at RA and other London provincial galleries. Holman's sculpture has a feeling of mass and solidity, as in his Boy and Duck, illustrated in Eric Newton's monograph *British Sculpture 1944–1946*. Southgate Borough Council commissioned a bas-relief in stone for Broomfield Park. Lived at Leigh-on-Sea, Essex.

Jamie HOLMAN 1973– Artist using video and film, born in Inverness, who gained a fine art degree at Chelsea College of Art, 1994–7. Was included in Titanic Numbers at Blackburn College, 1994; Student Film Festival, Cornerhouse, Manchester, 1995; and New Contemporaries at Tate Gallery, Liverpool, and Camden Arts Centre, 1996.

Andrew HOLMES 1947– Artist, born in Bromsgrove, Worcestershire, who trained as an architect but whose passion was to photo-realistically record the trucks, trailers, tanks and highways of the American West. He amassed over 20,000 slides, from which he chose and drew carefully selected subjects. Group exhibitions included 40 London Architects, Art Net, 1976; Curwen Gallery, from 1978; 9th British Print Biennale, Bradford, 1984; Clocktower Gallery, New York, 1988; Whitechapel Open, Whitechapel Art Gallery, 1996; and Architecture Foundation, 1998. Holmes had many solo shows and performances, later ones including Asphalt Paradise at Laurent Delaye Gallery and Postcards on Photography at John Hansard Gallery, Southampton, both 1999, and Gas Tank City at Plus One Plus Two Galleries, 2003. The Cambridge Darkroom Gallery, Cambridge, also handled his work. Holmes lived in London.

Clyde HOLMES 1940– Landscape painter and poet, born in London, who trained at Hornsey College of Art, 1961–4, then St Martin's School of Art, 1964–5. Holmes moved with his family to a remote shepherd's cottage in Snowdonia National Park in 1970 – Capel Celyn, Frongoch, near Bala, Gwynedd – to live "in what most people would consider abject poverty". Initially, there was no telephone or electricity, no running water or gas, and the cottage was two miles from the nearest road. The wild, wet landscape became Holmes' subject. He published several volumes of verse, poems appearing in the *Anglo-Welsh Review, Poetry Wales, Poetry Review, London Magazine, Outposts* and elsewhere. Holmes gained a WAC Award for Painting, in 1978, also a commendation in WAC Award for Literature (Poetry) and a New Poetry Prize. Group shows included Canaletto Gallery, 1974; Our Native Land, Mostyn Gallery, Llandudno, 1979; Royal National Eisteddfod of Wales, from 1989; and Artists in National Parks, Victoria & Albert Museum, 1992. Had a solo show at Treadwell Gallery, 1973, later ones including Welsh Gallery, 1994, and Newport

Museum and Art Gallery, 2002. Hagen Museum, Germany, holds his work. In 1997, Holmes was featured in the documentary series *Visions of Snowdonia* on BBC2 Television.

Dale HOLMES 1972– Painter, born in Barnsley, Yorkshire, who studied at Leeds Metropolitan University, 1996–9. His group exhibitions included The Poster Show, Hoxton Distillery, and Itchy Park, Limehouse Town Hall, and John Moores Liverpool Exhibition, both 2004. Among Holmes' solo exhibitions were Fan Club Meeting, The Way Up Gallery, 2001, and Recent Paintings, Trapex Gallery, 2004.

David HOLMES 1939– Artist, teacher and gallery owner, born in Great Yarmouth, Norfolk. He studied at Leicester College of Art and Leicester University, 1957–62, then worked in Turkey in 1963. From 1963–78 Holmes taught at several London colleges, including a lecture tour of Europe, 1977. He settled in Peterborough, Cambridgeshire, in 1978, establishing the David Holmes Art Gallery in 1987. Holmes' own exhibitions included Foyles Art Gallery, 1961; Young Contemporaries, 1962; Ulster Museum, Belfast, 1964; AIA Gallery from 1966 (he was AIA news correspondent until it closed in the 1970s); and LG, 1976. In 1984 Holmes had a solo show, The Naked and the Nude, at City Museum & Art Gallery, Peterborough, influences being "a long-standing admiration for the Spanish poet Federico Garcia Lorca and a deepening sense of outrage at the political and social blunders of our time". From 1998 lived in St Ives, Cornwall. Among later exhibitions were Salthouse Gallery, St Ives, and Greenwoods, Peterborough, both 1996; Penwith Society, St Ives, from 1996 (solo, 1996); Fermynwoods Contemporary Art, Brigstock, from 1998 (including a shared exhibition with Neil Canning, 2002); The New Millennium Gallery, St Ives, from 2000; Gildenburgh Gallery, Peterborough, and Roger Billcliffe Fine Art Glasgow, both 2001; and Penhaven Gallery, Peterborough, from 2001.

Frank HOLMES 1960– Painter and teacher who graduated in fine art from University of Ulster, Belfast, 1990. Went on to teach at St Mary's Training College, 1991, and Dunmurry High School, 1991–2. Took part in many group shows in the Belfast area, including Works on Paper and Beyond the Partitions, both in 1994 and put on by the Queen Street Studios, Belfast, with which Holmes was associated. Holmes participated in workshops, including The East Belfast Festival, 1991, and The Adventure Playground, Berlin, 1992, taking part in both the Belfast/Berlin Exchange and the Belfast/Bristol Exchange in that year.

Gilbert HOLMES 1952– Sculptor of steel abstracts, born in Otley, Yorkshire. He studied at Hull College of Art and St Martin's School of Art. Was included in Garden Exhibition 2, Camden Arts Centre, 1978. Lived for a time in London.

John HOLMES 1893–1980 Painter, teacher, administrator and writer, born in Derby, son of the watercolourist George Holmes, married the painter Vera Cathleen Taylor. Studied at Slade School of Fine Art, 1918–20, under Henry Tonks and Philip Wilson Steer, Royal College of Art, 1920–1, in Sweden and Germany. He went on to teach, including periods at Harrow School and as principal of the Regional College of Art, Manchester, also lecturing in education at Manchester University. Showed at Manchester City Art Gallery, Derby Art Gallery and elsewhere. Wrote several books, including *Applied Perspective* and *The Art of Interior Decoration*. While he was at the Manchester College Holmes, who was familiar with developments at the Bauhaus and in Scandinavia, introduced what was probably the first basic design course in an English art school, although he regarded the period prior to World War II, teaching colour theory at the Architectural Association, as his most important such achievement. Lived in Naphill, Buckinghamshire.

John HOLMES 1935– Artist working in oil, acrylic and Caran d'Ache who studied with Tom Eckersley at London College of Printing. He was an art director in advertising and was involved in that field and illustrated publishing throughout the world for 20 years. He had group appearances throughout Europe and solo shows with Nicholas Treadwell Gallery; Galerie L'Oeil Écoute, in Lyon; and Galerie "W", Annemass. Female Eunuch was a notable work of a painter interested in Surrealism. Museum of Modern Art in New York holds his work. Lived at Gooderstone, King's Lynn, Norfolk.

Katharine HOLMES 1962– Landscape painter, born in Malhamdale, near Airton, Yorkshire, with a studio in Malham, whose subject was the local limestone terrain which she began painting in 1990. Her grandmother was the Dales painter Constance Pearson. Studied fine art at Newcastle University and Gateshead College and exhibited regularly, including 1996 Leeds Art Fair, and kept an open studio. Her landscapes were "not so much portraits of the landscape but evocations of the atmosphere of a place". Holmes's show at Bruton Gallery, Leeds, in 2000 included views of the America's New England coast, in which gravel, grass, flotsam and jetsam were used with her mixed-media paint in a bid for authenticity. A second exhibition, in 2001, portrayed the Yorkshire moors. In 2002, Bruton Gallery showed Holmes in its inaugural show at The Leeds Club. She had a solo exhibition at New Academy Gallery in 2003.

Keith HOLMES 1944– Artist in oil, pastel and charcoal, conservator and teacher, born in Richmond, Yorkshire. He gained a fine art degree at West Surrey College of Art and Design, Farnham, 1969–73 (teachers including Robin Ball and Harold Cheesman), then a diploma in paper conservation at Camberwell School of Arts and Crafts, 1973–5. He was a fellow of the International Institute of Conservation. In 1977, Holmes was visiting professor teaching conservation at postgraduate level at New York University. During the 1970s and 1980s, he ran his own private press, producing limited editions which he printed, illustrated and bound by hand. His work can be found in the British Library, Victoria & Albert Museum and Trinity College in Dublin. British war artists influenced Holmes' work, in which sound draughtsmanship, detached analysis of spatial depth, a strong sense of colour and the fall of light were features. Holmes was artist-in-residence at the Science Museum, 1994–6, and painted a portrait of its director, Sir Neil Cossons. In 1990, work was commissioned by the officers' mess of the Royal Marines to commemorate the close of the School of Music, Deal. Holmes' many mixed shows included RSMA, PS, NEAC, ROI and Guild of Aviation Artists. Had a solo show at Greenwich Theatre Art Gallery, 1985, later ones including Royal Albert Hall, Army Flying Museum and Imperial College, all 1997, and The Royal College of Pathologists,

1998. Fragmented, Holmes' highly successful "Impressions of War and Recovery in South East Asia", at The Tank Museum, Bovington, 2002, attracted 60,000 visitors despite the lack of publicity or critical coverage. Women on Water, at Riverside Gallery, Richmond, Surrey, was held in 2003, Venice is in the Detail at The Millinery Works in 2005. Holmes was based in East Molesey, Surrey.

Kenneth HOLMES 1902– Painter, printmaker, writer, designer and teacher. Born in Skipton, Yorkshire, Holmes attended the School of Art there, 1919–21, Leeds College of Art, 1921–3, with periods at Central School of Arts and Crafts and Chelsea School of Art, Royal College of Art, 1923–7, then 1927–8 in Italy. Held a number of design consultancy posts and teaching positions, finally as principal of Leicester College of Art, 1934–56. Exhibited RA, NEAC, Fine Art Society, RHA, in the provinces and abroad and showed with war artists at National Gallery, London, during World War II. Victoria & Albert Museum and a number of provincial galleries hold his work. Wrote and broadcast on art. Holmes was especially noted as a fine architectural draughtsman. Lived for much of his life in Leicester, but retired near Boscastle, Cornwall.

Lesley HOLMES 1958– Untrained watercolourist, born in Lusaka in what became Zambia, West Africa. She spent her early life there before returning to England where she settled in Chipping Norton, Oxfordshire, setting up a studio open to the public part-time. Holmes was noted for her delicate watercolour views of the Cotswolds and for pictures of cats, reproduced as prints, cards and calendars by a number of commercial companies.

Marcus HOLMES 1875–1951 Painter, printmaker and teacher, born in Ipswich, Suffolk. Studied at Aberdeen School of Art, 1896–9, three years as a scholar at Herkomer School at Bushey, also in Paris and Florence. Holmes was a keen athlete, playing soccer for Dorset, cricket for Aberdeenshire, hockey for Hertfordshire and was a good middle- and long-distance runner. Was art master and a housemaster at Monmouth School, 1906–46, and was an Oxford University extension lecturer on art history, an occasional pungent remark showing that he was not in sympathy with every modern development. In 1930 with his wife, also an artist, Holmes formed the Wye Valley Arts Club (later Society). Exhibited RA, RCamA, RWA as an associate, Walker Art Gallery in Liverpool and Paris Salon. National Museum of Wales in Cardiff and Newport Museum and Art Gallery hold examples. Lived in Monmouth.

Mary Dawson HOLMES: *see* **Mary Dawson ELWELL**

Paul Roberts-HOLMES 1964– Sculptor and teacher who did a foundation course at Roehampton Institute, 1983–4, then a diploma in fine art at RA Schools, 1984–7. He became curator of Roche Court Sculpture Park and was an outreach tutor for RA. He showed at RA Summer Exhibitions from 1987, also at New Art Centre Sculpture Park from 1988, Crypt Gallery, 1990, and 1st RWA Open Sculpture Exhibition, 1993. Leicester County Council holds his work. Lived in East Winterslow, Wiltshire.

Philip HOLMES 1931– Painter and teacher whose father, John Holmes, was a wood-carver. He studied at St Martin's School of Art, 1948–53, then in 1953 Hammersmith College of Art, also attending Borough Polytechnic classes under David Bomberg, whose teaching had a lasting effect on his work. In 1954 Holmes attended L'Académie de la Grande Chaumière, Paris, and in that summer Borough Bottega, Ronda, where he completed notable canvases. Holmes went on to teach at Havering Technical College. Painted widely abroad, including Israel, France, Greece, Italy and America. Showed solo at RBA Galleries, ICA, Studio Gallery and Beaux Arts Gallery. Was included in Borough Group show at Fine Art Associates, 1989.

Ronald HOLMES 1924–1970s Printmaker and teacher who studied at Sheffield and Royal Colleges of Art. He taught at Willesden School of Art, next at the College of Art in Leeds, where he lived, where he was head of printmaking, then of graphic design. Lino-cuts were a notable feature of his output. Was included in The Teaching Image, a Leeds College of Art staff show at Leeds City Art Gallery in 1964. Also took part in Arts Council travelling exhibitions. British Museum holds the work of Holmes, who was remembered as having "a good teaching ethic" by his Leeds student Derek Hyatt, who found a dead crow on Holmes' instruction for his outstanding print of that title. Holmes and his wife were killed in a car crash in the 1970s. British Museum holds colour woodcuts by him.

Lawrence HOLOFCENER 1926– Sculptor, playwright, lyricist, actor and director, born in Baltimore, Maryland, America. Holofcener modelled in clay and cast in bronze, and claimed Michelangelo, Rodin and Epstein as influences. He studied for a year at the Maryland Institute and at the New School in New York "at a class given by Chaim Gross. I lasted an hour." Holofcener took part in group exhibitions in Bucks County, Pennsylvania; Princeton, New Jersey; and in London. Had a first solo show at Gibbes Museum, Charleston, South Carolina, 1977, and latterly at Bruton Street Gallery, 1996, and The Catto Gallery, 2002. Catto commissioned Holofcener to produce a limited-edition maquette of his life-size sculpture Allies (Churchill and Roosevelt), unveiled in Bond Street in 1995. Other works by him included Faces of Olivier (28 in bas-relief), unveiled by Lord Olivier in 1985 at Chichester Theatre, Sussex; and Thomas Paine, unveiled in 1997 at Bordentown, New Jersey. For the stage, Holofcener wrote *Mr Wonderful*, starring Sammy Davis, Jr, on Broadway. His plays included *Before You Go*, Broadway and West End, and *The Bench*, off-Broadway. He acted on Broadway in *Stop The World* and *Hello, Dolly*. After he had settled in Ventnor, Isle of Wight, Holofcener began singing there in cabaret. With his wife gained British citizenship. Mrs Sammy Davis, Jr; Mayor Joseph Riley and the Unitarian Church, both in Charleston; AT&T, New Jersey; Actor's Equity in New York and British Equity; and the Screen Actor's Guild, New York, hold Holofcener's work.

Charlie HOLT 1947– Printmaker, painter, computer artist and teacher, born in Hitchin, Hertfordshire. He studied at Rochdale College of Art, 1964–6, with a travelling scholarship to Italy; then gained first-class diploma at Loughborough College of Art, 1966–9; obtained art teacher's certificate from Brighton Polytechnic, 1969–70; then his master's degree at Manchester Polytechnic, 1984–5. Holt went on to teach in schools and colleges, latterly at Liverpool Institute of Higher Education. Influences on his work cited were Hitchens, Dufy, Gauguin, Morandi and Magritte. Holt's pictures had "their roots in the Garden of

Eden, in a cycle of life". Exhibitions included Manchester Academy, from 1977; Liverpool Academy, 1980; RA Summer Exhibitions, from 1982; Hanover Gallery, Liverpool, 1986; Royal Festival Hall, 1990; and Colin Jellicoe Gallery, Manchester, 1992. Lived at Croston, Lancashire.

Eric Stace HOLT 1944–1997 Painter, especially in tempera, and draughtsman, brought up in Surrey where he initially worked as a painter in Purley, later living near Sandringham, Norfolk. Attended Epsom and Ewell School of Art, 1959–62, where his teachers included Eric Rodway and Leslie Worth; then Wimbledon School of Art, but left after a short time to paint on his own. Economic demands caused him to take up a number of dead-end jobs, then he freelanced as a glass painter and antiques restorer, which revived his interest in painting. Showed in mixed exhibitions at RBA and RA, where his pictures prompted an overwhelming response from public and dealers. Had several one-man shows in 1970s with Maltzahn Gallery, later showing with Piccadilly Gallery. Holt's work falls into two broad categories: Biblical incidents in modern dress and scenes from country and suburban life. The design element is strong, the artist distorting figures if he felt it necessary. Holt was a slow, meticulous and self-critical artist, with a strong interest in the countryside, its crafts and pursuits. He continued to work, even after contracting the brain cancer that killed him. A memorial exhibition, Eric Holt and His Brothers (Roy Holt and Ronnie Copas), was held at King's Lynn Festival, 1998.

Gila HOLT 1910–2004 Singer and artist, originally Gertrude Sallon, the youngest of a large and talented family. Like her sister, Lily Anderson, who became a soprano in South Africa, Gertrude sang in Gilbert and Sullivan productions at a youth club run by the founder of Liberal Judaism in Britain, Lily Montague. Like her brother the caricaturist Ralph Sallon of the *Daily Mirror*, she was also an artist, and studied for five years at Hammersmith School of Art when she could take time off from the family dress shop in Westbourne Grove. After marriage at 23 Gertrude concentrated on music, taking singing lessons with Dino Borjiolo. Family commitments and the need to run her husband Morris's dress shops while he was absent in World War II confined her engagements to the London area. Holt, who could sing in nine languages and was famed for her lower register, filled the Wigmore Hall, Royal Albert Hall and Royal Festival Hall with her recitals, but declined a concert tour of America. Neither did she want to be a member of an opera company, although in the 1950s she took leading roles in television operas and participated in other music programmes. Retiring in her prime aged 55 she moved to Israel, where her architect-turned-cartoonist son Martin Holt had settled. Based in Caesarea, she resumed painting seriously and produced many portraits, notably one of the country's first prime minister, the impatient David Ben-Gurion. As Gila Holt she had her first show in 1967 at the Conduit Street Gallery: almost 200 works, busy, colourful crowd scenes and dancers being favoured subjects.

Gwynneth HOLT 1909–1995 Sculptor in a variety of materials, born in Wednesbury, Staffordshire, married to the sculptor T B Huxley-Jones, later to the Right Reverend Eric Gordon. After a convent education in Birmingham Holt studied at Wolverhampton School of Art, 1925–30, under the sculptor Robert Emerson. Holt's work could be graceful and stylised, as shown in the three examples in Arthur T Broadbent's 1949 monograph *Sculpture Today in Great Britain 1940–1943*. She was a fellow of RBS and was for a time an associate of RBSA. Also showed at RA, in the provinces and with Royal Glasgow Institute of the Fine Arts. St Felix' School in Southwold; St Margaret Church, Downham; and the Church of the Immaculate Conception, Chelmsford, hold examples, as do Aberdeen, Leamington and Wolverhampton public galleries. Lived in Eynsham, Oxfordshire.

Herbert HOLT 1891–1978 Portrait painter in oil, son of stained glass artist Henry Holt. Attended St Helens School of Art, Liverpool School of Art and Slade School of Art. Exhibited RA, RCamA, Paris and Walker Art Gallery, Liverpool, which holds his work. In 1958 he published *Portrait Painting in Oils*. Member of Chelsea Arts Club and lived latterly in London.

Lilian HOLT 1898–1983 Painter, born in London. She attended Putney School of Art, but economic necessity forced her to work for Prudential Assurance Company from 1915–22, when she studied at Regent Street Polytechnic School of Art. Married to the art and antiques dealer Jacob Mendelson, 1923–8, then married the painter David Bomberg. Painted with Bomberg widely overseas and became a founder-member of Borough Group, showing Archer Gallery, Arcade Gallery and elsewhere. Had a retrospective at Ben Uri Gallery in 1980, from which Tate Gallery bought a landscape, like much of her work strongly influenced by Bomberg, called Tajo Ronda. After Bomberg's death Lilian, supported by her daughter Dinora Mendelson, also a member of the Borough Group, devoted years to promoting David Bomberg's work.

Roy HOLT 1942– Painter and teacher, born in Sutton, Surrey. He studied at Epsom and Ewell School of Art, 1959–62, Royal Academy Schools, 1962–6, and Goldsmiths' College School of Art, 1985–7. Became a senior lecturer at Liverpool Polytechnic. Holt participated in many group shows, notably in London, and his related abstract canvases Bands Eroded were included in John Moores Liverpool Exhibition, 1989–90. Had a solo exhibition Contexts and Thresholds at Flaxman Gallery, 1989, another at Dean Clough Contemporary Art Gallery, Halifax, 1990. Lived in London.

Brenda HOLTAM 1960– Painter and teacher, born in Whiteway, Gloucestershire, who studied at Gloucestershire College of Art and Design, 1979; with Francis Hewlett at Falmouth School of Art, 1980–3, gaining a first-class honours degree; then did a postgraduate diploma in painting, 1983–6, under Peter Greenham. Taught adult education classes from 1988. Was elected RWS in 1992. Mixed exhibitions included Newlyn Orion Gallery in Penzance, 1982, RA Summer Exhibitions from 1985, NEAC from 1987, and Wherry Quay Gallery, Ipswich, from 1991. Shared a show with Victoria Rees at Cadogan Contemporary, 1994. Lived in London.

Robin HOLTOM 1944– Artist and teacher who worked in oil, charcoal, ciment fondu and screenprinting. He studied at Chelsea School of Art, 1963–6, then Royal College of Art, 1967–70, teachers including Patrick Caulfield and Ken Kiff. Holtom worked as an art therapist, 1970–80; from 1984–94 ran residential courses in Wales, where he settled at

Llechryd, Cardigan; then was a full-time artist. His main works included paintings of oak trees, hill landscapes and dancers. Group shows included Fountain Gallery, Llandeilo; Dyfed Open; PS Annual; and Y Tabernacl, Museum of Modern Art, Wales, in Machynlleth, which holds his work. Solo shows included Battersea Arts Centre; Chapter Arts, Cardiff; CCA Gallery, Bath; Oriel Contemporary Art, 1995; and Ozten Zeki Gallery, 1996, where his exhibition The Road to Mensano indicated Holtom's liking for powerful colours and a simplification of shape in landscape. Later one-man shows included further exhibitions at Oriel Contemporary and Ozten Zeki, also Peter's Barn, Petworth, 1998; St David's Hall, Cardiff, 1999; Bank Street Gallery, Sevenoaks, from 1999; Star Gallery, Lewes, from 2000; Roche Gallery, Rye, 2002; Woodbine Contemporary, Spalding, 2004; and White Rock Theatre Gallery, Hastings, 2005. In 2000, Holtom had a residency at Fondacion Valparaiso, Spain, and he also latterly taught in Spain and Italy. Lived in St Leonards-on-Sea, Sussex.

Suzanne HOLTOM 1966– Painter, the youngest of the shortlisted finalists for the Jerwood Painting Prize, 2003. She gained a postgraduate diploma at the Slade School of Fine Art, 1996. Holtom won several awards, including a Woo Charitable Foundation Bursary and the Duveen Travel Scholarship. She used that to travel to Kenya, where she researched and documented Swahili art forms in Mombasa and Lamu. Her trips also included the University of Iowa, in America.

Dora HOLZHANDLER 1928– Painter in the naïve style, born in France. She became a student at Anglo-French Art Centre in London in 1946 where she met her future husband, George Swinford, and settled in Hampstead. She exhibited at Young Contemporaries in 1949 and at Beaux Arts Gallery in 1954 in mixed exhibitions, and many such appearances followed in Britain and abroad. Had a solo exhibition at Chenil Gallery in 1960, others including a series at Langton Gallery in the 1970s, Concourse Gallery, 1984–5, Crane Kalman, 1985, Graham Modern Gallery in New York in 1986, Bowmoore Gallery, 1989–91, Beaux Arts, Bath, 1996, Judy Saslow Gallery, Chicago, America, 1998, and Piano Nobile Fine Paintings, 2001 and 2004. Among Holzhandler's later travels was a trip to Dharamsala, India, in 2002, for an audience with His Holiness The Dalai Lama of Tibet with her husband George and granddaughters Tara and Eve. Eric Newton, the *Manchester Guardian* critic, called Holzhandler's work that of "a temperamental primitive ... colourful as a Persian illumination, always brilliant, but never harsh." Nuffield Foundation, Museum of London, the Gallery of Modern Art in Glasgow, Brighton Art Gallery and Museum and a number of notable private collectors hold examples. Retrospective at the Ben Uri Gallery, 2006.

Gordon HOME 1878–1969 Painter, draughtsman and writer with a special interest in topography and history, British and foreign. Born in London, he was a self-taught painter who showed at RA and Royal Glasgow Institute of the Fine Arts. Member of Art Workers' Guild. He had work illustrated in magazines such as *The Studio*, *Connoisseur* and *Illustrated London News*, his books including *Yorkshire Coast and Moorland Scenes*, 1904, and *History and Antiquities of Cyprus*, 1958. Lived in St Boswells, Roxburghshire, and in London.

Grace HOMER 1907– Painter, teacher, born in Liverpool. She attended Liverpool College of Art in 1940s, her teachers including Will Penn. She went on to teach locally, notably at the Mabel Fletcher Technical College, following a period at Liverpool School for the Blind, where she taught art. Took up embroidery and won a prize in the International Poliomyelitis Embroidery Competition in 1958. Also showed pictures at RA, SWA, RBA and elsewhere. Lived in Liverpool where she was a member of the Sandon Studios Society Club.

Arthur HOMESHAW 1933– Artist in various media and teacher who attended West of England College of Art, Bristol, 1951–4, then 1956–7. He went on to teach at Queen Elizabeth's School in Crediton, Devon, where he lived. Homeshaw completed a mural for Temple Meads Station, Bristol. He was a member of RWA, which holds his work, and showed at RA, RE and elsewhere. Had a one-man show with Patricia Wells Gallery in Thornbury in 1981.

Takafumi HOMMA 1964– London-based artist who was born in Sapporo, Japan. He gained an economics degree from Tokuyama University, 1983–7; did a foundation diploma at Wimbledon School of Art, 1992–3; graduated in fine art, sculpture, from Chelsea College of Art and Design, 1995–8; and gained his master's there, 1998–9. Homma won a British Postgraduate Award and the Trans-Euro Sculpture Competition, both 1998; North West Arts Board Individual Development Award, 2000; Travel Grant, HCEA, Japan, 2001; and in 2002 North West Arts Board New Creation Award and a Membership Bursary, RBS, of which he was an associate member. Exhibitions included Box Man Project, Margaret Harvey Gallery, St Albans, 2004. This was inspired by Kobo Abe's story *The Box Man*, Homma's own box being a watchtower, easily fabricated and mobile, from which the world could be observed and on the inside of which the artist could record whatever seen.

Evie HONE 1894–1955 Painter and artist in stained glass, born in Dublin. She was descended from Joseph Hone, brother of the Royal Academician Nathaniel Hone, and she was partly crippled by infantile paralysis. After studying with Walter Sickert at Westminster School of Art Hone attended Byam Shaw School of Drawing and Painting and was with Bernard Meninsky at Central School of Arts and Crafts. The 1920s were spent largely in Paris, where she studied briefly with André Lhote, then for a much longer period with the pioneer Cubist painter and theoretician Albert Gleizes. In 1924 Hone and her friend Mainie Jellett shared a show at Dublin Painters' Gallery. She also showed with the 7 & 5 Society for some years and exhibited widely in Paris, being a founder-member of Abstraction-Création in 1932. Under the influence of Rouault, Hone turned to stained glassmaking, and her burgeoning reputation led to some impressive commissions. Eton College Chapel and St Michael's in Highgate are two examples, and the Tate Gallery has The Crucifixion by her. Arts Council held memorial show in 1959.

Joy HONIGSBERGER 1928– Painter and designer, born in Paarl, Cape, South Africa, studying at the Michaelis School of Art, Cape Town, afterwards working for magazines and newspapers as a studio designer. In England she enrolled as a mature student at Bournville College of Art. The "strong colour, massive landscapes and light of South

Africa" influenced her work, as did "the German Expressionists, Kandinsky, Matisse, Braque and Picasso." In 1988 with friends she formed the Octavon Group, in 1997 being elected RBSA. Group exhibitions also included Laing Competition, winning first prize, Midland Area, showing at Mall Galleries, 1988; Worcester Art Gallery, 1993; RWA, 1996; and Wiseman Gallery, Oxford, 1999. In 1994 Honigsberger had a solo show at Corkscrew Gallery, Birmingham, where she lived at Alvechurch.

Michael HONNOR 1944– Painter and printmaker who between 1962–8 studied at Oxford University, Hornsey College of Art and Byam Shaw School of Drawing and Painting. From 1969 he lived in Devon as an artist whose work was especially concerned with weather and water: the Atlantic coast of Cornwall, Dartmoor rivers and the Yorkshire Dales. He was director of the print workshop at Dartington Hall Craft Education Centre and Wilkey's Moor Print Workshop. One-man shows included St Catherine's College, Oxford, 1964; Greenwich Theatre Gallery, 1970; Exeter Arts Centre from 1984; Sue Rankin Gallery from 1988; and Thackeray Gallery, 1996. Collections included many British High Commissions and Embassies; Worcester College, Oxford; London Institute of Education; and corporate collections including Barclays Bank, Citibank and Trust House Forte. Honnor's pictures caught the essence of a place, sparkling and atmospheric, using a rich palette.

Ernest HOOD 1932–1988 Painter, born in Edinburgh, son of a lithographer. Studied at Glasgow School of Art, 1952–6. He became a member of the Royal Glasgow Institute of the Fine Arts, also showing with RSW, RSA, RWS and elsewhere. The Kelvingrove Art Gallery in Glasgow, where Hood lived, holds his work.

Harvey HOOD 1946– Sculptor and teacher, born in Staffordshire. He studied at Birmingham College of Art, 1965–9, and Royal College of Art, 1969–72. Lectured part-time at Leicester Polytechnic, 1972–3, then became senior lecturer at Cardiff College of Art and visiting lecturer at various colleges. Hood's awards included a prize for young contemporaries from Arts Council, 1971; Sainsbury Award, 1973; Arts Council Major Purchase Award, 1981; and artist-in-residence, Bishop's Palace, St Davids, 1986. In 1990 he gained a WAC Special Project Grant for researching the way architects and artists were educated, travelling to many countries. In 1981 Hood created Archform at Newport Station, commissioned by British Rail. Participated in many exhibitions including The Young Contemporaries, Arts Council tour, 1968; Ikon Gallery, Birmingham, 1969; Mostyn Art Gallery, Llandudno, 56 Group Show, 1981; Six Sculptors from Wales, touring Finland, 1987; and Sculpture at Canterbury, 1991. Solo shows included Oriel, WAC, Cardiff, 1979. In 2002, Hood was reunited with Billy Lee in the show Ochreous Earth at RBS Gallery, having worked and shown with him as a student. Lived near Raglan, Gwent.

Harry HOODLESS 1913–1997 Artist in oil and tempera and teacher, born in Leeds, where he studied at the College of Art, 1929–33, then at Royal College of Art, 1933–6, teachers including Edward Bawden and Eric Ravilious. Hoodless taught at Norwich School of Art, 1936–9, then at Laird School of Art in Birkenhead, 1939–76, from 1946 being principal. Hoodless was noted for his landscapes featuring dockyard debris and decay, and he cited Seurat, Edward Wadsworth, Tristram Hillier and Graham Sutherland as influences. Hoodless was a member of Liverpool Academy and Wirral Society of Arts. His exhibitions included RA, Leeds City Art Gallery, Bluecoat Gallery in Liverpool and Atkinson Art Gallery, Southport. He also showed at two galleries which hold his work: Walker Art Gallery in Liverpool and Williamson Art Gallery in Birkenhead. Lived in West Kirby, Wirral.

Charlie HOOKER 1953– Born and based in London, Hooker was interested in exploring and fusing aspects of music, dance and the visual arts. His systems-based works were focused on specific spaces and were not repeated elsewhere. Hooker studied at Croydon College of Art and Brighton Polytechnic. He produced a series of audio and video tapes. Performances included Six Sound Pieces, Robert Self Gallery, 1975; Percussion Walk 23 (one of a series), Chelsea School of Art, 1978; Tate Gallery, 1981; James Hockey Gallery, Farnham, 1990; and Camden Arts Centre, 1991. In 2002, Hooker began work on Local Stars, a light and sound sculptural installation comprising solar systems maps, which was a public art commission for Gladstone Place, Bow. In 2004 Wave-Wall III was an installation at University of Brighton Gallery, "bringing together, sound, movement and graphic representation." Arts Council holds examples.

Dora HOOPER fl. c.1920–1960 Painter in oil and watercolour. Studied at St John's Wood Art School, 1913–14, under Leonard Walker, then at the Westminster Technical Institute. Exhibited UA, RI, SWA, RWS, RCamA and Paris Salon. Lived near Penzance, Cornwall.

George HOOPER 1910–1994 Painter in oil and watercolour, and teacher, born in Gorakhpur, India. In 1912 he moved to England to live with his grandfather and to be schooled. After two years with the Westminster Bank Hooper studied in 1930–1 at Slade School of Fine Art, moving to Royal Academy Schools under Tom Monnington in 1931–5. There he won two gold medals, a travelling scholarship and the Rome Scholarship in Painting, which gave him two years in Rome after a few months in Madrid, 1935–8. During World War II Hooper served in Air Raid Precautions and was invited to join the Pilgrim Trust's *Recording Britain* project. In the 1950s Hooper designed posters for General Post Office, Esso, Shell and other companies. By then he had begun to teach: from 1943–5 at Watford Grammar School; 1945–77 at Brighton Polytechnic department of fine art; and from 1948–77 he lectured for Workers' Educational Association, affiliated to London University. A visit in 1958 to Italy appears to have released Hooper's rich palette, perhaps nurtured in India. In mid-1940s began exhibiting at Leicester Galleries, also appearing in mixed shows with LG and RBA. Later solo shows included Odette Gilbert Gallery, 1984–6, and Sally Hunter Fine Art, 1988, with a memorial show at Michael Parkin Gallery, 1995, and a retrospective at Collyer-Bristow, 2003. Victoria & Albert Museum and British Museum hold examples. Wrote articles for *The Artist* magazine. Lived in Redhill, Surrey.

John HOOPER 1939– Painter of geometrical abstracts, and teacher, born in Morocco, who studied at Camberwell School of Art, 1958–62; Royal College of Art, 1962–5; in latter year won the J Andrew Lloyd Royal College Scholarship for Landscape, which took him to Greece, and an Italian Government Scholarship, to Perugia. A French Government Scholarship enabled Hooper to work in Paris in 1965–6, a Canada Council Grant facilitating travel in Canada and to New York in 1969. He also taught in Canada on several occasions. Mixed shows included Young Contemporaries at RBA Galleries from 1960; LG at same Galleries from 1961; John Moores Liverpool Exhibition, 1963; RA Summer Exhibition, 1965; and Wapping Artists Open Studios from 1980. In 1987 Hooper was in The Summer Show at Jariwala Gallery and in 1989 East End Open Studios, at Carpenter's Road. Solo shows included University of Surrey, Guildford, 1976, and Central Space, 1987. Lived in London.

Miriam Mabel HOOPER 1872–1953 Landscape watercolourist, born and lived in Redhill, Surrey, also home of her nephew the painter George Hooper. She studied at Croydon School of Art under Walter Wallis and James Shannon whose work she much admired, and she also went on sketching parties with William Tatton Winter, to whom she was related through her brother's marriage. She sketched extensively in England and on the continent. Exhibited at RA, RI, Walker Art Gallery in Liverpool and RWA and was a member of RSW Art Club. There was an exhibition at Bourne Gallery, Reigate, in 1994.

HOPE– The collaborative name of Georgie Hopton and Simon Periton (see separate entries).

Polly HOPE 1934– Artist who trained as a ballet dancer and subsequently at the Slade School School of Fine Art. Hope worked extensively throughout Europe. Although she studied initially as a painter and sculptor, she made her reputation with large quilted fabric works, mostly on an architectural scale. Commissions included Cwmbran New Town, St Peter's Church in Whitstable, the headquarters of NMB Bank, Amsterdam, and the Victoria & Albert Museum. She had many solo shows in Europe and America and was the second wife of the sculptor Theo Crosby.

Rosa HOPE 1902–1972 Painter, etcher and teacher, born in Manchester, twin sister of the portrait painter Muriel Hollinger and daughter of an art teacher. In 1919 attended Slade School of Fine Art under Henry Tonks and Philip Wilson Steer; was later at Central School of Arts and Crafts. In 1926 her etching Adoration of the Shepherds won Prix de Rome. In 1935–8 taught etching and drawing at the Michaelis School of Fine Art in South Africa, from 1938–57 being a senior lecturer at University of Natal. Exhibited extensively in Britain and South Africa, including RA, NEAC, RE, Natal Society of Artists, South African Academy and on the continent. Frequently painted the Drakensberg Mountains and the Transkei. Hope's work showed technical mastery of her medium, but was doggedly conservative in style. Represented in many South African galleries as well as British Museum and Victoria & Albert Museum. Died at Kokstad, Cape Province.

Eleanora HOPE HENDERSON 1917– Painter in oil and watercolour, born in Edinburgh as Eleanora Anderson Spence. She painted until 1966 as Eleanora Anderson Borrie; "I just used the name Borrie." She was a student at Edinburgh College of Art, 1935–40, under William Gillies, John Maxwell and Robert Westwater. She "won the highest award for my year and a Travelling Scholarship". Hope Henderson was elected SSA and won the Guthrie Award. She also showed at RA, RSA, RP, with Dumfries Art Society and elsewhere in Scotland and England. Solo exhibitions included Woodstock Gallery. Lived in Achie, New Galloway, Kirkcudbrightshire.

Don HOPES 1935– Artist, born in Bristol, originally trained as an engineer, who studied painting at Slade School of Fine Art. For a time he worked with the sculptor Kenneth Martin. An example of Hopes' cleverly engineered kinetic sculpture is the aluminium Untitled, 1983, in Portsmouth City Museum and Art Gallery's garden. Exhibitions included that gallery, 1980 and 1983, with a show of drawings at the local Aspex Gallery in 1995 which had been prepared originally for a room at Glynn Vivian Art Gallery, Swansea.

Alan John HOPKINS 1930–1974 Painter in oil, born in Harrow, Middlesex, who studied at the local School of Art with John Gerald Platt and Christopher Sanders, at Slade School of Fine Art under Claude Rogers and at Royal Academy Schools. Although a brilliant student Hopkins suffered from schizophrenia, which prevented him reaching his full potential. His first wife was the artist Rosa Branson, with whom he shared a show at Woodstock Gallery in 1962. Also exhibited in Four Young Painters at Parsons Gallery, 1955, RA Summer Exhibition RBA, LG and Young Contemporaries. Died from cancer at Royal Marsden Hospital, Sutton, Surrey.

Clyde HOPKINS 1946– Painter and teacher, born Bexhill, Sussex. Graduated from Reading University, 1969, and went on to paint and teach part-time, eventually becoming head of painting at Winchester School of Art. Hopkins' abstract works evoked huge space and cloud-like forms, his later work having a darker surface with light sources behind. He was represented in a number of survey shows, including the South Bank Centre's 1988–9 touring exhibition The Presence of Painting. In 1985–6 a one-man show toured Britain including Ikon Gallery, Birmingham, and had solo exhibition at Francis Graham-Dixon Gallery, 1992. Had a studio in Hastings, Sussex.

James HOPKINS 1976– Sculptor, born in Stockport, Cheshire, who completed a foundation course in art and design at Ravensbourne College, 1994–5; graduated with honours in fine art sculpture at University of Brighton, 1995–8; did a postgraduate fine art diploma at Goldsmiths' College, 2000–1; and his master's in fine art there, 2001–2. Hopkins was shortlisted for the Jerwood Sculpture Prize in 2003. He took part in many group shows, later ones including Foyer, 291 Gallery, 2001, and Plinth, The Trade Apartment, 2002. In 2003 he had a solo exhibition at MW projects.

Louise HOPKINS 1965– Painter, born in Hertfordshire, who gained a bachelor's degree in fine art at Newcastle Polytechnic, 1985–8, and her master's at Glasgow School of Art, 1992–4. Was included in New Art in Scotland, at CCA, Glasgow, 1994; Swarm, a Scottish Arts Council touring show, 1995; and New Contemporaries at Tate Gallery, Liverpool, and Camden Arts Centre, 1996. Solo shows included Tramway, Glasgow, and Andrew Mummery, both 1996; artconnexion, Nice, and Galerie Isabella Kacprzak, Berlin, both 1997; and Galleria Raffaella, Cortese, Milan,

1998. In 2002, Hopkins, who settled in Glasgow, received a Creative Scotland Award which enabled her to research and produce work for her 2003 show at Andrew Mummery Gallery. In this she "reshaped the surface of things: consciously interweaving paint into and out of a pre-existing object, evolving it into something entirely new, while at he same time retaining the resonance of what lies beneath.... Look closer, and nothing is quite what it seems." Arts Council, Aberdeen Art Gallery in Aberdeen, British Council and Saatchi Collection hold examples.

Penny HOPKINS 1943– Painter mainly in watercolour with some oils, and teacher, born in Haywards Heath, Sussex, daughter of the artist Norman Clark. She studied at Brighton Art College, 1961–5, teachers including Charles Knight, her father, George Hooper, Raymond Briggs, Justin Todd, John Lord, John Lawrence, Jennifer Dickson and John R Biggs. Hopkins was a part-time teacher with private pupils and did some commission work in early years. After divorce in 1988 she became assistant art teacher at Burgess Hill School and began painting again. Was a member of Sussex Watercolour Society, taking part in group shows at RWS, Southover Gallery in Lewes and at Hove Museum and Art Gallery. Had solo exhibitions at Burstow Gallery in Brighton, Rottingdean Gallery and Terrace Gallery, Worthing. Lived in Cowfold, Sussex.

Phill HOPKINS 1961– Sculptor, draughtsman and lecturer, born in Bristol, who graduated with honours in fine art from Goldsmiths' College, 1982–5. He moved to Leeds in 1985, joined Leeds Art Space Society; was artist-in-residence, Alhambra Theatre, Bradford, in 1987; and in 1988 joined Jacob Kramer College, Leeds, as a visiting lecturer. Hopkins led many workshops for organisations including Leeds City Art Gallery and the Yorkshire Contemporary Art Group. Group shows included New Contemporaries, ICA, 1984; Surrealism Surveyed – Responses to an Exhibition, Leeds City Art Gallery, 1986; and Showspace Summer 87, Winners Exhibition, Elizabethan Gallery, Wakefield, 1987. Among solo exhibitions were Hartcliffe Arts Festival, Hartcliffe, Bristol, 1984; Drawings, LASS Gallery, Leeds, 1985; and Sculpture, Cookridge Street Gallery, and Drawings, Wakefield District College, both, 1988. Leeds Museums and Galleries hold Hopkins' work, including I Fall to Pieces, mixed media (steel and wastepaper basket), 1991, a characteristically wry piece.

John HOPKINSON 1941– Figurative artist who studied at Grimsby School of Art. Among his shows were Drawings of Importance at Roland, Browse & Delbanco, 1978; Wingfield Gallery, 1988; Camden Arts Centre, 1990; and in 1993 he was in Two Plus Two at 33 Mossop Street. Hopkinson's first solo show, at Fox Galleries, Cork Street, was a sell-out with flattering national newspaper coverage. Another, including quirky street scenes, followed there in 1979. Hopkinson was then living in Cleethorpes, Lincolnshire, where he was born.

Gill HOPLEY 1947– Artist who did a foundation course at Liverpool Polytechnic, 1980–1, then an honours degree there, 1981–4, winning a Sir John Moores Scholarship in final year. She was featured in Stowells Trophy Exhibition at RA, 1984; Sir John Moores Scholarship Retrospective, 1985; and showed with Walker Art Gallery, Liverpool, Merseyside Artists tours from 1985. In 1985 she obtained a Belle Vale Murals Commission.

Georgie HOPTON 1967– Versatile artist, born in north Yorkshire, who studied at St Martin's School of Art, 1986–9. Hopton took part in numerous group exhibitions in Britain and abroad. The largest survey of Hopton's work was Laughed – I Could Have Cried, at firstsite, Colchester, 2003, an occasion shared with Jonathan Callan. Hopton created sculptures, paintings, drawings and photographs in which humour and sadness collided. She continually reworked her own and other artists' works. Various motifs recurred: magic wands, artists' palettes, Pierrots and Harlequins, as well as an obsession with textured materials, such as glitter, pom-poms and crazy paving. Hopton collaborated with Simon Periton as Hope (see separate entries) and with Josephine Soughan. Lived in London.

Ruth HOPWELL 1923– Painter and teacher, initially educated in Northampton. Attended Northampton School of Art, 1939–42, then Royal College of Art, 1942–5, under Francis Helps, Gilbert Spencer and Percy Horton. Exhibited RA and Bradford City Art Gallery, Hertfordshire Education Committee buying her work. From 1945 taught at Howell's School, Denbigh, north Wales, where she lived.

Richard HORE 1935– Painter, muralist and teacher, born in Clacton-on-Sea, Essex, who attended Colchester School of Art, 1951–5, teachers including John O'Connor, then Royal College of Art, 1956–60, with Leonard Rosoman, Carel Weight and Ruskin Spear, winning a silver medal for mural painting in the latter year. Went on to teach at Wrexham College of Art. Showed at RA, WAC, Mostyn Art Gallery in Llandudno, and elsewhere. National Maritime Museum in Greenwich holds his work. Lived in Chester, Cheshire.

Ronald T HORLEY 1904– Painter and draughtsman of architectural subjects, born in Pinner, Middlesex. Attended Radley College, Berkshire, then studied art at Heatherley's School of Fine Art, 1921–4, St John's Wood School of Art and Central School of Arts and Crafts. Showed at RA and RI. Lived in London.

David HORN 1937– Sculptor, draughtsman and teacher, born in London, but moved shortly after to Pembroke Dock, Wales, where he attended the Grammar School. Attended Chelsea School of Art, 1956–60, then Royal College of Art, 1960–4, winning the drawing prize in 1964. Left to teach at St Martin's School of Art, followed by other teaching posts in London, Leicester, Watford and Nottingham. Showed in many group exhibitions, including AIA Gallery, Young Contemporaries at RBA Galleries, Sculpture 60–66 Arts Council touring exhibition, Time Space at Bristol University, Royal National Eisteddfod and WAC. In 1965 completed sculpture for Cwmbran New Town. Arts Council owns his bronze Asleep in the Sofa, of 1963–64, and WAC also has work.

Eric HORN 1910–1953 Primarily a commercial artist, Wilfrid Eric Horn was born at West Bergholt, Essex. Studied at Colchester School of Art, Camberwell School of Art under Eric Fraser, St Martin's School of Art and Sutton School of Art. He was art director for several advertising agencies. Lived in West Wickham, Kent.

Winifred HORNBLOWER 1879– Bank clerk who painted part-time until she retired. She studied at the Laird School of Art and at RMS with Alyn Williams. Hornblower exhibited extensively at Walker Art Gallery in Liverpool, RA, RCamA, Royal Glasgow Institute of the Fine Arts and at Paris Salon. Was a member of Liver Sketching Club and lived in Birkenhead, Cheshire.

Anna HORNBY 1914–1996 Painter and calligrapher who was educated at Westonbirt School, Gloucestershire, eventually settling in the county at Upper Slaughter. After a brief period of study in Italy with landscape and flower painter Aubrey Waterfield Hornby attended Byam Shaw School of Drawing and Painting, 1934–40, teachers including Francis Ernest Jackson. She was a member of the Art Workers' Guild and NEAC, also showing with RA, RWA and RBA.

Jocelyn HORNER 1902–1973 Sculptor and teacher, born in Halifax, where she continued to live. She entered Leeds School of Art in 1920 to train as a sculptor, with Henry Moore and Barbara Hepworth as fellow students. During the 1920s Miss Horner began a series of children portraits and animal studies and during World War II became a home teacher for the blind. After 1945 she returned to Leeds as a student and in the early 1950s became a part-time teacher of modelling and wood-carving at the Percival Whitley College, Halifax, also teaching at Halifax Art College. Her later work came increasingly under the influence of Jacob Epstein, and the 1960s saw her sculptures exhibited locally and nationally. Horner won the Leeds Gold Medal under the annual award for work by artists born of Yorkshire parents. Her head of a blind man is in the London headquarters of the Royal National Institute for the Blind; she did a group of the Brontë sisters for the Parsonage Museum, Haworth; and her bust and hands of Sir John Barbirolli are held by the Hallé Concert Society in Manchester. A memorial show was held at Stable Court Galleries, Temple Newsam, Leeds.

Elizabeth HOROSZY-RIDLEY 1948– Artist in paint, ceramics and mixed media born in Warsaw, Poland, where she studied history of art at Warsaw University. Settled in England from 1968, with extended periods in Greece and France. Graduated in fine art with honours at London Guildhall University (formerly Sir John Cass School). She worked voluntarily with those suffering from chronic mental health illnesses and gave workshops, some for children with learning disabilities. Group shows included Heifer Gallery from 1993; Hop Exchange, part of Southwark Festival, from 1994; and Etcetera Gallery, 1996. Solo exhibitions included Ashford Library and in the National Museum, Nieborów Palace, Poland, both 1997. Lived in London.

Michael HOROVITZ 1935– Experimental artist, performance poet, jazz musician, song writer and singer, editor and writer, born in Frankfurt, Germany, but moved to London aged two years. Graduated in English at Oxford University, 1954–9. In the late 1950s was associated with jazz music scene in London and Pop generation. In 1959 helped to start New Departures publications. Improvised first jazzpoems with Dudley Moore, Joe Harriott, Ronnie Scott and others and was on the road in extensive jazz gigs. Conducted Live New Departures art circuses. In 1963 published monograph on artist Alan Davie, by whose work he was influenced. During 1960s showed at AIA, RBA, Ben Uri and ICA. In the 1970s published *Love Poems*, then *The Wolverhampton Wanderer*. Horovitz gained the Arts Council Writers' Award in 1978 and the Translators' Award for the book *Egghead Republic* by Arno Schmidt in 1979. Later activities included compiling and presenting *Poetry Now* programmes for BBC Radio 3; publishing *Growing Up: Selected Poems & Pictures 1951–79*, in 1979; and launching Poetry Olympics in 1980. In 1986 his *Midsummer Morning Jog Log* appeared with drawings by Peter Blake, in memoriam Frances Horovitz. From the mid-1980s returned to substantial art work. Had solo show at Combined Harvest Gallery, 1987; Bop Paintings, Collages, Picture-Poems, 1962–1971, was held at England & Co, 1989; and there was a 50-year retrospective at Amberden Estates in 1997.

Artur HOROWICZ 1898–1962 Commercial artist in tempera and line. Born in Warsaw, he studied art there and in Berlin in the early 1920s. Exhibited in London and on the continent and in Britain illustrated books and drew for such publications as *The Illustrated London News* and *The Sketch*. In Poland he had served as artist to the War Ministry, 1927–39, to the Polish Air Force, 1940, and to its Air Ministry, 1943–6. Lived in Surbiton, Surrey.

Nancy HORROCKS 1900–1989 Abstract artist with a fine feeling for texture, born in Compton, Hampshire, daughter of the architect Brook T Kitchin. She attended Winchester High School, also studying at Slade School of Fine Art, 1918–20, and Chelsea School of Art. Was married to Lieutenant-General Sir Brian Horrocks, notable World War II soldier (their only daughter drowned while swimming in the Thames in 1979), who latterly became a popular television broadcaster on military matters. Horrocks was included in WIAC and travelling exhibitions, 1958–65; New Vision Centre Gallery and Knott Gallery, Dallas, both 1961; Grabowski Gallery, 1962; Heal's Mansard Gallery, 1964; and in 1965, Bradford and Northampton City Art Galleries and Grosvenor Gallery. Solo exhibitions included AIA Gallery, 1960, and New Gallery, Belfast, 1965. The abstract artist Adrian Heath thought highly of her pictures, writing that "The quality ... in all her works is directness." Lived at Singleton, Sussex; latterly at Knowle Park Nursing Home, Cranleigh; with a funeral at Putney Crematorium.

Philip HORROCKS 1958– Painter, born and lived in Salford, Lancashire, who graduated from Manchester Polytechnic. In 2002 he was involved in an art workshop at Manchester Museum. Horrocks's work in oils was realistic, bordering on Photo-Realism, subjects including cityscapes, portraits and landscapes, latterly including a series of the north Wales coast. Horrocks carried out commissions for major companies in the northwest of England and exhibited with arTzu gallery, Manchester. John Whittaker, of Peel Holdings plc, owned Horrocks's work.

William Eric HORSBRUGH-PORTER 1905–1985 Painter and writer, born in Dalkey, near Dublin, Ireland, commonly known as Eric. He went to Bedales School, then attended Slade School of Fine Art, 1924–8, under Henry Tonks; he gained Slade and Robert Ross Scholarships and was a prizeman. Horsbrugh-Porter's friends included such fellow-students as William Coldstream and William Townsend, in whose journals he appears. He was a keen tennis player of high standard. Helped Stephen Bone on his Piccadilly Underground station murals. During World War II Horsbrugh-Porter served in the Royal Navy as a first lieutenant on aircraft carriers, including *Indomitable*. In 1929 Horsbrugh-Porter had married Monica Maude, daughter of Captain Anthony Maude and Eva Beresford, of Belgard Castle, Dublin. After the war he joined his father's stockbroking firm there, Porter, Millard and Irvine. In 1947 Horsbrugh-Porter, as Eric Porter, published *Saturn's Child*, a fairly racy novel based on the life of the Spanish painter Goya, which was translated into several languages. He showed at RHA, 1926–52, also at Cooling Galleries, RA, NEAC, ROI and elsewhere. His most successful works, sometimes commissioned and known in the family as his "grassy pictures", gave a worm's eye view of meadows of vetch, ladybirds, and so on. Latterly he used coloured glass in large landscapes and seascapes, one being bought by Shelbourne Hotel, Dublin. Sometimes signed his pictures with the initials H P.

Hannah HORSFALL 1963– Artist, born in London. She studied at Central School of Art and Design, 1982–3. Moved to the Isle of Skye, in 1985 she began drawing with Malcolm Bell, their drawings being joint efforts; each had the right to make and obliterate marks. An example of their abstract work was Twentysixth Drawing, in 1992 East & South Norwich Gallery/Kent Institute of Art and Design show. Eventually worked in London.

Nicholas HORSFIELD 1917–2005 Artist in graphic media and oils and teacher, born in New Malden, Surrey. He studied at Royal College of Art, 1935–8, under Sir William Rothenstein, Percy Jowett and Gilbert Spencer, then after war service, 1939–46, became Arts Council regional officer for visual arts for the northwest region in Manchester, 1948–56. From 1956–77 Horsfield lectured at Liverpool College of Art/Liverpool Polytechnic, then became part-time faculty tutor in life drawing, 1977–82. Horsfield was a member of Liverpool Academy of Art from 1954, being president, 1960–5, and was also a member of Merseyside Contemporary Artists. Solo shows included Bluecoat Chambers, Liverpool, from 1963; University of Sheffield, 1974; University of Durham, 1975; and Chateau Musée in Dieppe and Camden Arts Centre, 1984. Sickert and de Staël were both influences on Horsfield's work and Normandy was a recurring subject from the early 1950s as the landscape of the Crosby area of Liverpool, where he settled, was to become. Arts Council, Liverpool University, Atkinson Art Gallery in Southport, Manchester City Art Galleries, Chateau Musée and Walker Art Gallery in Liverpool (which gave Horsfield a retrospective in 1997) hold examples. Horsfield died shortly after an exhibition of his figurative drawings and paintings opened at the University of Liverpool.

Susan HORSFIELD 1928– Artist in wide variety of media and teacher, born in Poona, India. She graduated in fine art from Regent Street Polytechnic School of Art in 1952, teachers having included Patrick Millard, Norman Blamey, David Smith and Ian Mackay. She did varied freelance work alongside teaching, including James Gardner Associates. From 1969–86 she was head of art department at Farrington's School, Chislehurst, also lecturing in further education and at field study centres. Lived at Bessels Green, Sevenoaks, Kent, drawing on the Shoreham Valley landscape for her work. Horsfield was a member of WIAC. She showed with RBA, RWS and LG. Had a solo show at Walker's Galleries, others including Bear Lane Gallery, Oxford, 1962; Heal's Mansard Gallery, 1968; Sheffield University, 1980; Digby Gallery, Colchester, from 1984; St John's, Smith Square, 1987; The Old Fire Engine House, Ely, 2000–1.

Hamish HORSLEY 1950– Sculptor, draughtsman and photographer, widely known for public art works, notably the Tibetan Peace Gardens adjacent to the Imperial War Museum, 1997, opened by His Holiness The Dalai Lama. Horsley was born in New Zealand, studying there at Canterbury University Art School, 1969–70. Moved to London in the mid-1970s, graduating first-class from the City & Guilds of London Art School, 1979, gaining his master's at the Royal College of Art, 1982–6. His career mixed intensely concentrated work, sometimes on a smaller scale, and extensive travels, specifically in India, China and Tibet. Awards included Madame Tussaud's Sculpture Award, 1978; City & Guilds Sculpture Prize, 1979; Henry Moore Foundation Study Bursary, 1985; and a Barings Bank Travel Award, 1990. Among Horsley's exhibitions were Camden Arts Centre, 1983; Chisenhale Gallery, 1986; Commonwealth Institute Galleries, 1991; Hannah Peschar Sculpture Garden, Ockley, 1992; and New Art Centre, East Winterslow, 1998.

Malcolm HORSLEY 1925–1991 Painter and yachtsman, born in Sydney, Australia. After active Army service in Far East Horsley studied painting with Desidirius Orban and at Sydney College of Art, graduating in 1950. He moved to London and managed the Savage Gallery. Although he painted in Spain and Corsica, producing figurative, lyrical work, and having shows in London, Barcelona and Paris, Horsley's interest in art had by the early 1960s begun to give way to his early passion for sailing, dating back to the building of his own dinghy in Sydney in the early 1940s. From the 1960s he raced, chartered and refitted seagoing yachts; at Porto Cervo in Sardinia running the port, the charter boat company, berth sales and acting as a consultant; established himself as an independent marine surveyor and worked for three years with Northrop and Johnson of Cannes; and formed Malcolm J Horsley International. Lived in his own-build house in Corsica for a time, where he also farmed. Died in Singapore.

Sebastian HORSLEY 1962– Painter and writer, ejected from St Martin's School of Art, who then led a precarious life. He was a professional gambler, business partner of the former Glasgow gangster-turned writer and sculptor Jimmy Boyle, a male escort, heroin and crack addict and columnist for the magazine *Erotic Review*. Exhibitions included The Flowers of Evil, at Grosvenor Gallery, 1999, in which, having dived with the great white shark off Australia, Horsley "tried to paint flowers as wounds." Crucifixion, at 1-5 Crucifix Lane, 2002, in pictures and a film commemorated the artist's nailing to a cross on the Philippines island of San Fernando, where each year 10 volunteers agree to undergo the ordeal for half an hour.

Kathleen Finlay HORSMAN 1911–1998 Artist in gouache and potter, born in London. Studied at Hornsey School of Art, 1929–33, with John Moody, then at the Royal College of Art, 1933–7, with William Staite Murray, the potter. She held a number of teaching positions, notably at Edinburgh

College of Art. Exhibited RSA, SSA and elsewhere in Scotland, signing her work H. RSA holds her work. Lived in Edinburgh, where the Scottish Gallery held a memorial exhibition in 1999.

Walter HORSNELL 1911–1997 Painter and designer, born in Ware, Hertfordshire. He studied at Bolt Court School of Art and St Martin's School of Art. Between 1929–39 Horsnell was a graphic artist for various London art studios, then was art designer for motion picture presentation, 1936–9. Was in photographic reconnaissance in Royal Air Force, 1941, then was an official technical illustrator with Ministry of Aircraft Production, 1942–7. Horsnell was noted for his landscapes and townscapes in Britain and abroad. Showed in RA, RBA and elsewhere, solo exhibitions including Harrogate Festival, 1970. Grundy Art Gallery in Blackpool and Lambeth Palace hold examples. Lived in Harrogate, Yorkshire.

Francis Cecil HORSTMANN 1906–1968 Painter, calligrapher, decorator and teacher, born at Weston-super-Mare, Somerset, where he studied at the School of Art, followed by Royal College of Art. He held a series of art teaching posts in Northampton, London, Glasgow and Bristol, where he was vice-principal and head of the design school at the West of England College of Art. He wrote a number of books on painting, drawing and building. Lived at Weston-super-Mare.

Brian HORTON 1933– Artist, notably in gouache. Studied at Cheltenham College of Art, worked in the City of London and was a picture restorer before deciding to paint full-time. Horton painted the English countryside and coastal areas, his pictures having an ethereal, visionary quality. Had several exhibitions with David Messum, in Beaconsfield and London. Lived in an old rectory in Taplow, Buckinghamshire, which he and his artist wife Sheila covered with paintings, including painted car hub caps, inside and out. Three daughters were artists. Messum's included landscapes by Horton in Twentieth Century British Art in 2005.

George HORTON 1859–1950 Painter, notably in watercolour, printmaker and teacher, born in North Shields, Northumberland. He had an unhappy childhood, working as a delivery boy in his father's butcher's shop, in the evenings copying reproductions of old masters in the Free Library. Encouraged by local art enthusiasts, Horton began to support himself as a professional artist after leaving home. He took a studio and advertised lessons in art. In about 1918 Horton settled permanently in London, by which time was establishing a wide reputation, and in 1922 had his first one-man show in Britain at Greatorex Gallery. He also showed at Laing Art Gallery in Newcastle, at RA, RSA and to much acclaim in Netherlands and Paris. The artist continued to make regular visits to northeast England and, after his London studio was bombed in 1940, lived in Spital Tongues, Newcastle, until 1945, but died in London. Mills, canals and coastal scenes in Holland and the northeast were his speciality. Memorial and centenary shows were held at South Shields Public Library and Museum in 1951 and 1959; Moss Galleries, Hexham, held and exhibition in 1982.

James HORTON 1948– Painter, teacher and writer who was included in The Garrick/Milne Prize, 2003, with his oil on canvas of Andy Moffat. Horton attended Sir John Cass Art School, 1964–6; City and Guilds of London Art School, 1966–70, in the latter year winning a Travelling Scholarship to Florence; and Royal College of Art painting school, 1971–4, gaining his master's. Horton was artist-adviser to Winsor & Newton for Paint and Painting, Tate Gallery, 1982, and taught widely, including part-time at Sir John Cass, Mary Ward Centre and Anglia Polytechnic University. He also ran painting and drawing classes in the United Kingdom and abroad. He was a contributor to *The Artist* from 1976, also to other art magazines. Among his books were *Composition*, 1994, *Skin Tones*, 1995, and *Pastel Techniques*, 2000. Horton participated in numerous mixed exhibitions in London and the provinces, including the RA Summer Exhibition, National Portrait Gallery, NEAC, RP, and RBA of which he was a member. Had a series of solo exhibitions from 1974, later ones including Collection Gallery, Stockholm, Sweden, 1981; Broughton House Gallery, Cambridge, 1990; and Sebastian Pearson Gallery, Cambridge, from 1993. In 2002 Horton was artist-in-residence for the Friends of Mount Athos and was artist-demonstrator at Art in Action, Waterperry House, Oxford. His portrait commissions included Brenda Ryman, late mistress of Girton College, Cambridge; Lord and Lady Hemingford; Sir Eli Lauterpacht and Catherine, Lady Lauterpacht; and Professor Thomas Sherwood, professor of radiology, Addenbrooke's Hospital, Cambridge. Horton lived in Cambridge.

Julie HORTON 1965– Painter, designer and illustrator who studied at Solihull College of Technology and Kingston Polytechnic. She was featured in The Discerning Eye exhibition at Mall Galleries, 1990, and in 1991 at England & Co in Art in Boxes.

Percy HORTON 1897–1970 Painter and draughtsman, born in Brighton, Sussex. Studied at Brighton School of Art, 1918–20, where he had a scholarship. Horton was a man of strong radical convictions, and because he was an absolute conscientious objector he had to endure two years' hard labour in Carlton Prison, Edinburgh, 1916–18, during World War I. From 1916–18 was at Central School of Arts and Crafts under A S Hartrick and Ernest Jackson, then with a Royal Exhibition attended Royal College of Art, under Randolph Schwabe and Allan Gwynne-Jones, 1922–5. Horton went on to teach at the Royal College, 1930–49, where he was a highly respected figure, becoming Ruskin Master of Drawing at Oxford University, 1949. Taught voluntarily at the Working Men's College, London, for a time. Horton's social commitment is evident also in his early membership of the AIA, writings in the *New Left Review* and subject matter, such as his picture Unemployed Man, held by Sheffield City Art Galleries, which held a major show of his work in 1982. Tate Gallery also holds his picture The Invalid, of his mother. Horton was a realistic painter, influenced by Cézanne, who showed from 1926 with NEAC, also RA and Goupil Gallery. His younger brother was the artist Ronald Horton. Lived in Lewes, Sussex.

Ronald HORTON 1902–1981 Painter, draughtsman, printmaker, photographer, teacher and bibliophile with strong left-wing convictions, born and died in Brighton, Sussex, brother of the artist Percy Horton. He studied at Brighton School of Art, 1919–23, in 1924 moving to London to work for the sculptor William Aumonier. From 1920 until his death Horton was a member of the Communist Party, and from 1924–6 he was politically very active, working part-time for the book dealer Birrell & Garnett (his collection of Russian children's books went to the Victoria & Albert Museum, his games, puzzles and toys to the University of Wales, Aberystwyth) and studied in the evenings at St Martin's School of Art. Horton gained a scholarship to the Royal College of Art under William Rothenstein, 1926–9, and visited Paris. Between 1930–40 Horton's many activities included helping Rex Whistler with murals and stage sets; researching for Stanley Morison's *The English Newspaper*; extensive teaching (from 1932–55 part-time with Parmiter's School, Bethnal Green), including lectures to teachers on child art; showing at RA, NEAC, Bloomsbury and Zwemmer Galleries; and contributing to *Athene, Art & Craft* and *Education*. In 1944 Horton returned to Brighton as head of art teacher training at the School of Art, retiring officially in 1966, but not from work. In the 1950s and 1960s Horton travelled extensively abroad. He was an active member of SEA, Art Workers' Guild, AIA and Artists for Peace, organising key exhibitions, including the Lenin Centenary and the Centenary of the Paris Commune. Retrospective at Brighton Polytechnic, 1982.

John HORWILL 1927–1997 Painter and teacher who served in the Merchant and Royal Navy for four years, then attended Carlisle College of Art from 1949, gaining a scholarship to Royal College of Art, 1953, becoming an associate in 1956. Taught for 26 years, for 17 being principal lecturer in art at St Mary's College, Strawberry Hill, Twickenham, also doing extensive examining for London and Middlesex Regional Examining Boards. Showed widely, including John Cleal's gallery in Fishguard, retrospective Wrexham Arts Centre and tour, 1999. Walker Art Gallery, Liverpool; Middlesbrough and Hereford City Art Galleries; Inner London Education Authority; and Leeds Training College hold examples. Lived in Llanrwst, Gwynedd.

Angela HORWITZ 1934– Sculptor and painter, born and lived in London, who studied art at Marylebone Institute and Sir John Cass College. She was a member of NS and Ridley Art Club, also exhibiting at Alpine and Smiths Galleries.

Nina HOSALI 1898–1987 Painter, writer and teacher, born in London of Indian-Celtic parentage. She studied art privately and trained in Margaret Morris movement at the London School founded by the painter J D Fergusson's wife; the Fergussons were great friends of the Hosalis. Nina Hosali obtained a Master of Science degree at London University and wanted to research in seismology but abandoned this when with her mother she went to North Africa to help neglected and suffering animals. She was founder of the Nature Cure Clinic in London and was involved in founding the Free Painters and Sculptors. Also showed with WIAC, RBA, ROI and had many solo shows in Britain and overseas. Published *A North African Diary* and a book of poems entitled *Children of Allah*. Her pictures showed individual imagination and used exotic colours. Lived in Biggin Hill, Kent. The auctioneers Rosebery's in 2004 offered works from Hosali's studio, left by her to the Margaret Morris Movement.

David HOSIE 1962– Painter, draughtsman and printmaker, born in Glasgow, Scotland, whose figure paintings sometimes had an unsettling element. Hosie graduated in drawing and painting from Edinburgh College of Art, 1980–5, gaining a postgraduate diploma in printmaking, 1986. His awards included Richard Ford Travelling Scholarship, RA, 1985; a George Jackson Hutchison Award and an Andrew Grant Major Award and Travelling Scholarship, all 1986; and a Royal Glasgow Institute Award, 1992. Group exhibitions included New Generation Show, Compass Gallery, Glasgow, 1986; Germinations, Centre de la Vieille Charité, Marseilles, and tour, 1987–8; opening exhibition of Raab Gallery, Millbank, 1989; and Art94 (Jill George Gallery), 1994. Had a solo show at Raab Gallery, 1987, later ones including Jill George Gallery from 1992. Scottish Arts Council and RSA hold examples.

John HOSKIN 1921–1990 Sculptor in metal of figurative and abstract work, and teacher, born in Cheltenham, Gloucestershire. Left school aged 14 and worked for an architect until World War II Army service, then returned to drawing office. In 1950 began painting and working on reliefs and constructions until by 1953 he was seriously engaged in sculpture, showing at LG from 1954. Assisted the sculptor Lynn Chadwick until an opportunity to lecture part-time at Bath Academy of Art arose in 1957, and he was there until 1968, finally as principal lecturer in sculpture. After being sculptor-in-residence at Lancaster University, 1968–71, Hoskin was professor of fine art at Leicester Polytechnic, 1978–86. First one-man show was at Lords Gallery in 1957. Others occurred at Matthiesen Gallery and Arnolfini Gallery, Bristol. One of Hoskin's most notable pieces is the Exalted Christ for St Stephen's Church, in Bristol. Tate Gallery and Arts Council hold examples. Died in London, was buried in Herefordshire and in 1994 there was a memorial show at Storey Gallery, Lancaster.

Hugh Richard HOSKING 1904–1991 Painter, designer, mural artist, stage designer and teacher, born in Twickenham, Middlesex. Dick Hosking was married to the sculptor Alma Ramsey. He was a student of Bournemouth College of Art, 1922–5, and Royal College of Art, 1925–9. Held several teaching posts, latterly being principal of Ryland Memorial School of Art in West Bromwich, 1943–7, then principal of College of Art in Coventry, 1947–64. Prominent in bodies concerned with art education. Showed at AIA, Leicester Society of Artists and elsewhere. Best-known public commissions were the design for the Martyrs of Coventry mosaic in Broadgate House, Coventry, 1951, and a memorial stained glass window in St Nicholas Church, Warwick, 1964. A founder-member of the Warwick Society, in retirement he worked for many years in the Warwickshire county archives restoring documents and maps and was involved in church restoration. Lived in Warwick.

Knighton HOSKING 1944– Painter and teacher, born in Sidmouth, Devon. He attended Exeter College of Art, 1959–63, then Central School of Art and Design, 1963–6. In 1966 he won a Peter Stuyvesant Foundation Bursary to travel in America. By then Hosking had begun to show in mixed exhibitions, such as Young Britons at Altman Gallery, in New York. He went on to show at John Moores Liverpool Exhibitions in 1978–82–85. In 1968 Hosking began teaching at Wolverhampton Polytechnic and in 1970 had his first solo show there. Another followed in 1974, the year he had a one-man at Serpentine Gallery. Later solo shows included Wolverhampton Art Gallery in

1985. In the mid-1970s Hosking went to live in the country again, and the landscape became a key feature of his work; he turned away from working only in the studio and began to use on-location drawings and photographs. Arts Council holds his acrylic on canvas Earth Band, of 1974–5. Settled in Penn Common, Wolverhampton, Staffordshire.

Mark HOSKING 1971– Artist who was engaged in sculpture, photography, short films and book design, born in Plymouth, Devon, who obtained a fine art degree from Chelsea College of Art & Design, 1990–3, then studied at Slade School of Fine Art, 1993–5, and in the Netherlands at Rijksakademie van Beeldende kunsten, Amsterdam, 1997. Lisson Gallery, which represented him, showed Hosking's work in that year. Hosking's painted metal and wooden sculptures, sometimes untitled but with an agricultural appearance, reminiscent of the earlier productions of Anthony Caro, were depicted in the 1998 volume *The New Neurotic Realism*, which preceded his appearance in Saatchi Gallery's Neurotic Realism 2 show, 1999. Saatchi Collection holds Hosking's work. With the undertaking of a big public project for the city of Amsterdam, Hosking's work became more socially direct. There was a project for ECAL Living, 2000, bent sheets of metal which had been laminated with carpet to make recliners; Wassily A+E, 2001, transformed a design-classic armchair into a stretcher by adding simple components. Hosking was included in City Racing 1988–1998: A Partial Account, at ICA, 2001, showing that year solo at The Jerwood Gallery. He had a one-man exhibition at Lisson New Space in 2004. Lived in London.

Paul HOSKING 1977– Sculptor creating coloured animals and objects employing such media as inkjet prints, Fablon, wire and foam, as in Beck's Futures 2002, ICA and tour, 2002–3. Born in Plymouth, Hosking did a foundation diploma at the College of Art and Design there, 1995–6, then graduated with honours from Goldsmiths' College, 1996–9. Hosking's other exhibitions included Heart and Soul, London and Sandroni Rey, Los Angeles, America, 1999 and 2000; New Sculptures, The Metropolitan Hotel, and Renaissance, Hoxton House, both 2001; and Us & Them, Great Eastern Hotel, 2002. He had a solo show at Project Space in 2003, another at *The Economist* Plaza in 2005.

Ned HOSKINS 1939– Painter, etcher, teacher and exhibitions organiser, born in Croydon, Surrey, although he moved to Yorkshire in 1944. Studied art at Harrogate Technical School, 1953–5; Harrogate School of Art, 1955–60; and Royal College of Art, 1961–4. There he "mixed with the Pop Artists and worked with David Hockney on his early etchings." Although Hoskins moved to Sussex in 1964, working as a designer and part-time lecturer at West Sussex College of Art, in 1968 he moved to Buckinghamshire, lecturing at High Wycombe College of Technology and Art. A 1973 fine art fellowship at University of Southampton was followed by lecturing at Buckinghamshire College of Art and Design, lecturing in California, 1976–7, and the founding in 1987 of the Fiveways Artists' Group in Brighton. In 1992 Hoskins retired from full-time lecturing to paint. He became art exhibition co-ordinator for Komedia Theatre Gallery, Brighton, where he had settled, in 1995. Took part in numerous group shows, his many solo exhibitions including London and Southampton Universities; Gardner Art Centre, Brighton; Richmond Art Centre, Richmond, California; Brighton Museum and Art Gallery; and Rottingdean Grange Gallery, Sussex. Hoskins said that he worked "from aspects of landscape, based on the theme of the juxtaposition of unusual and familiar forms and objects found on my rambles".

Anna Mary HOTCHKIS 1885–1984 Watercolourist, printmaker and teacher, sister of the artist Isobel Hotchkis. Anna studied at Glasgow School of Art, 1906–10; in Munich, Germany, with Hans Lasker; and at Edinburgh College of Art under Robert Burns. She went on a sketching tour to China and taught at Yenching University in Peking (Beijing), 1922–4, then lived in China 1926–37, the year the war with Japan started. While there, with Mary A Mullikin she published *Buddhist Sculptures at the Yun Kang Caves*, 1935, also *Nine Sacred Mountains of China*, 1973. She was a member of the Glasgow Society of Lady Artists from 1918 and exhibited at RSA, RSW, Royal Glasgow Institute of the Fine Arts and Walker Art Gallery in Liverpool. Lived in Kirkcudbright, Scotland.

Isobel HOTCHKIS 1879–1947 Painter, notably of commissioned portraits, but latterly working in watercolour because of poor health. She was born in Crookston, Renfrewshire, sister of the artist Anna Mary Hotchkis. Isobel studied at Glasgow School of Art, 1902–4, also visiting London on a travelling scholarship and studying with Jean Delville in Brussels, Belgium. Spent a period in South Africa, working for Sir Henry Bate, Natal's chief justice. Hotchkis joined the Glasgow Society of Lady Artists in 1909, also showing at RSA, Royal Glasgow Institute of the Fine Arts and Walker Art Gallery in Liverpool, where she lived for a time.

Dom Sylvester HOUÉDARD 1924–1992 Concrete poet, typographical artist, teacher and writer, born in Guernsey, Channel Islands, as Pierre Sylvester Houédard. He was evacuated to England in 1940 and gained his master's degree in history at Oxford University, 1942–9, interrupted by Army Intelligence service, 1944–7. Entered the Benedictine Abbey of Prinknash, at Cranham, Gloucestershire, in 1949, where he died, having been 41 years a monk, 32 years a priest. He studied philosophy at the Benedictine University of Sant' Anselmo, Rome, 1951–5. Apart from his own contribution to concrete poetry, published and exhibited, he played a key role in the international dissemination of the movement from 1962. He gave the first lectures, at Royal College of Art and ICA, and his work was shown in dozens of exhibitions in Britain and overseas, such as the 1971 Victoria & Albert Museum touring show d s h, dom sylvester houédard, visual poetries.

Liz HOUGH 1966– Painter who studied at Mid-Cheshire College of Art and Design, 1984–5. Then graduated from Manchester Polytechnic, 1985–8, and did postgraduate painting at Royal Academy Schools, 1988–91, with a year at Accademia de Belle Arti, Perugia, Italy, 1997–8. Hough won the Creswick Prize and Landseer Scholarship in 1990, the year she obtained the Daler-Rowney Award for an artist under 30 years of age and was a finalist in the Young Painters' Award Scheme. In 1991 she gained the Vincent Harris Prize, the year she was visiting artist at Louisiana State University, in America. Her work was described as "a sort of gentle Expressionism", with James Ensor, the Belgian painter, among its influences. She began showing in mixed exhibitions in 1989 at Pyramid Arts, and also exhibited at RA, ROI, Piccadilly Gallery, Albany Gallery and elsewhere. In 1992 shared a show at Cadogan Contemporary. There were solo exhibitions at The Samling Foundation, 1998, and Offer Waterman & Co, 2001. Paintings in Hospitals, the Bank of China and TSB held the work of Hough, whose commissions included London Contemporary Arts for Royal Caribbean Cruise Lines.

Barrie HOUGHTON 1941– Painter and actor, born in Shorne, Kent, who left a business career to study painting at St Martin's School of Art and on scholarship in Paris. After travelling through eastern Europe, he had several solo shows in London and Edinburgh, mainly exhibiting big abstracts. During further travels through southern Europe and in north Africa Houghton encountered travelling theatre groups; on returning to England he became a theatre designer in Canterbury, went to drama school and acted, notably with advanced companies. Film roles included the Biblical character Judas, the painter Vincent van Gogh and Adolf Eichmann, tried for war crimes against the Jews. Early in the 1990s Houghton resumed full-time painting, inspired by East Anglia's landscape, and moved to Woodbridge, Suffolk. The Simon Carter Gallery there gave him a solo show in 1995. There was a series at The John Russell Gallery, Ipswich, with a fourth in 2005.

Eve HOUGHTON 1908– Painter, wood engraver and teacher, born in Sagaing, Burma. She studied at Ruskin School of Drawing, Oxford, under Sydney Carline and the Royal Academy Schools with Sir Walter Westley Russell and Thomas Monnington. Held a number of teaching posts, including Mount School, York. Exhibited RA, in provinces and at National Gallery of Canada, Ottawa, and latterly extensively with East Kent Art Society of which she was a member. Lived in Teynham, Kent.

Gill HOUGHTON 1962– Artist in mixed media who attended Sheffield Polytechnic, 1984–5, before studying at North-East London Polytechnic, 1985–8. From 1989–91 she attended Royal College of Art, during that time spending a term at Cité Internationale des Arts in Paris. Her work was exhibited in many group shows in Britain and on the continent, including New Ways in Painting, Institute Mathilderhöhe in Germany and at Galerie zur Altendeutschen Schule in Switzerland. Her work also appeared at Art'91, International Contemporary Art Fair, Olympia, and in (dis)parities, Mappin Art Gallery, Sheffield, 1992, and at Herbert Art Gallery, Coventry, 1993. At that time she was Picker Fellow at Kingston Polytechnic. It was said of Houghton's work that it was "predicated on an open-endedness, the paces and gaps between the pieces are as rich and thoughtful as the pieces themselves."

Geoffrey HOUGHTON BROWN 1903–1993 Artist and aesthete, born in London, of private means. He was educated at Rugby School, studying art with Maurice Denis in Paris and at Slade School of Fine Art. In the 1920s–40s Houghton Brown carried out wall paintings and decorative schemes in restaurants and private houses, including Blue Train Restaurant, the Five Hundred Club, for Syrie Maugham, Nigel Playfair and Edward James; he renovated large houses, such as Oving Hall and Winslow Hall, filling them with rare objects, of which he was a connoisseur; and was a partner in Cotter's Market, which sold painted furniture. His own pictures were religious, in a Byzantine-Cubist style, and these he showed in mixed exhibitions at Leicester, Leger and Mayor Galleries, also having solo shows at St Michael's Workshop, Oxford, in 1942, and at Ebury Street Gallery, 1946. Was a devout Roman Catholic from 1924, a member of the Guild of Catholic Artists and Craftsmen; he helped set up the Church Decorators' Society and was a strong supporter and a chairman of the Latin Mass Society. A panel in tempera on the life of Saint Neot is in the Catholic church in St Neot's, Cambridgeshire. Died in a nursing home in Kingston upon Thames, Surrey.

Bev HOULDING 1955– Artist, born in Birmingham, who attended Goldsmiths' College, 1974–7. She produced meticulously drawn, hand-carved wood panels; contemporary figurative subjects "executed in oils using a unique style inspired by natural textures"; and employed granite and slate weathered by wind and rain, "like human standing stones". Houlding showed widely with Mark Houlding, many venues including latterly Palm Springs Art Fair, in America, 2001; The Affordable Art Fair, New York, 2002; Affordable Art Fairs, London, 2003; and in Bristol, 2004; and Chelsea Art Fair, 2005. Lived in Fowey, Cornwall.

Mark HOULDING 1950– Painter, born in Abadan in what is now Iran, who attended Maidstone College of Art, 1970–3, and the Royal College of Art, 1973–6. He said of his work that it was "An exotic palette of colour rolled out on to wood panels.... The simplicity of form juxtaposes the complexity of colour." He showed at many venues in Britain and abroad with Bev Houlding, later venues including Mosko Miller Fine Art, New York, 2000; Navigators Gallery, St Just, 2001; The Affordable Art Fairs, London, 2003; and Chelsea Art Fair, 2005. Lived in Fowey, Cornwall.

Francis William HOUNSELL 1885–1956 Painter and teacher, born in London, specialising in watercolours. Studied at Brighton School of Art, then Royal College of Art. His teaching career was interrupted by World War I, in which he served in the Army in France and the Middle East. Latterly lived in Derby, where he was principal of the School of Arts and Crafts. Exhibited with Derby Sketching Club, the Society of Present-Day Artists, Midlands Artists and elsewhere in the provinces.

Shelagh HOURAHANE 1941– Painter, printmaker and teacher, born in Cardiff where she studied history at University College, 1959–62. After a year in youth work she became a tutor at Great Yarmouth College of Art, followed by a similar position at Stourbridge College of Art before doing a postgraduate diploma in fine art at University of Edinburgh, 1965–6. Went on to lecture in art history at University College of Wales in Aberystwyth. Took part in mixed shows in Wales, WAC possessing her work.

Miranda HOUSDEN 1965– Sculptor employing exotic materials, found objects and video, born in Lusaka, Zambia. She studied at Falmouth School of Art, 1984–7, and Chelsea School of Art, 1988–9, in 1990 being Rome Scholar at British School in Rome. Housden hoped to "disturb or unsettle the viewer" with her creations such as Breathless, a video and fur object featured in 1992 East & South Norwich Gallery/Kent Institute of Art and Design show. She was included in its forerunner, East, at Norwich Gallery, 1991. Lived in London.

Ceri HOUSE 1963– Artist son of the printmaker Gordon House, educated at St Christopher's School, Letchworth, Hertfordshire, in which county he lived, with a studio in north London. He was studio assistant, Momart Framing, exhibitions; assistant to Roger Newton, gilder and restorer; assistant to the artist Peter Blake; then a carver and gilder to Three Wheels Temple. Exhibited Queen Elizabeth Hall, RA and National Portrait Gallery. House had a solo exhibition at The Millinery Works, 1999, in which people's clothes were used to make a canvas.

Gordon HOUSE 1932–2004 Printmaker, painter, designer, typographer and teacher, born in Pontardawe, Glamorgan, full name Charles Gordon House, father of artist Ceri House. He studied at Luton and St Albans Schools of Art, 1947–50. From 1950–2 House worked in an advertising agency and was assistant to an ecclesiastical sculptor; he was a designer for Imperial Chemical Industries, 1952–9; then was a graphic designer for Kynoch Press, 1959–61. From then on he pursued his own artistic work, while teaching part-time at Central School of Art, St Albans and Hornsey Schools of Art and Luton College of Technology, 1961–4. House took part in the Situation British Painting show at RBA Galleries, 1960, and New London Situation at Marlborough New London Galleries, 1961, and was included in The Sixties Art Scene in London, Barbican Art Gallery, 1993. His solo shows began with New Vision Centre Gallery, 1959, among the later ones being After Powhatan, Ashmolean Museum, Oxford, 1993–4, abstract works based on its collection of curiosities, and Millinery Works, 1999 and 2002, the second, paintings with chairs being an installation celebrating the exhibition Der Stuhl, Frankfurt, Germany, in 1929. In 2005 The Millinery Works held a show celebrating House's life and achievement. Arts Council, British Council, Victoria & Albert Museum and many other public collections hold examples. Lived in London.

William S HOUSE 1909– Painter, born in London. Studied at Central School of Arts and Crafts, 1925–6, under Gerald Spencer Pryse, then at Bolt Court School of Art, 1926–30, with Sylvan Boxsius. Exhibited extensively in north London area and settled finally in France at St Cyprien, near the Spanish border.

Edith Giffard HOUSEMAN 1875– Painter, printmaker and draughtsman in pencil. Born at Bredwardine, Herefordshire, she was educated at Bedford High School, then studied art under Claude Hayes, Frank Calderon and Walter Donne. She went on to teach art at Northend House School, at Petworth, Sussex. Exhibited widely, including RA, SWA, Cooling Galleries, SSWA and SGA. The Towner Art Gallery, Eastbourne, holds her work. Lived at Petworth.

Shirazeh HOUSHIARY 1955– Sculptor, draughtsman and teacher, born in Iran, where early on she studied calligraphy and the theatre. Left Iran at 18 and studied at Hornsey College of Art, Middlesex Polytechnic, 1975–6; then Chelsea School of Art, 1976–9; becoming a junior fellow in fine art at Cardiff College of Art, 1979–80. Went on to be a visiting lecturer at several art colleges. Early work was described as "rough, grotesque, almost monstrous", clay and straw over a wooden maquette which was "allowed to grow mould". Later she immersed herself in Sufism, turned to painting and in her sculpture addressed the questions Who am I? Where do I come from? And where do I go? Based on precise drawings, Houshiary's sculptures were constructed by Andy Everett, who had also trained as a sculptor. Was included in the 1982–3 Fruitmarket Gallery, Edinburgh, touring exhibition Objects and Figures and in Arts Council's 1993–4 tour Recent British Sculpture. Solo shows included Chapter Arts Centre, Cardiff, 1980, and Kettle's Yard Gallery Cambridge, 1982, with later continental touring exhibitions plus Self Portraits, Lisson Gallery, 2000, with another show there, 2004. Had a studio in south London.

Paul HOUSLEY 1964– Abstract and representational painter, born in Stalybridge, Cheshire. He studied at Tameside College of Technology, 1981–2, and Sheffield Polytechnic, 1983–6. He showed at Smiths Galleries, Islington Arts Factory and Graves and Mappin Art Galleries in Sheffield. In 1991–2 his picture The Electrician was chosen for John Moores Exhibition, in Liverpool, where he showed again in 2004. Contributed to East International at Norwich School of Art & Design, 1999. The Lowry, Salford, initiated a tour of Housley's work in 2001 which celebrated his interest in popular culture. There was a solo show at Nylon in 2002. Lived in Manchester and London.

Laurence HOUSMAN 1865–1959 Dramatist, novelist and artist, born in Bromsgrove, Worcestershire, younger brother of the classical scholar and poet A E Housman. He studied art at Lambeth School of Art and South Kensington from early 1890s. Eventually he concentrated on writing, although some of his publications were brought out with his own illustrations, as he had worked for a time as an illustrator. His first book of verse, *Green Arras*, appeared in 1895. He was notable for *Victoria Regina*, produced in 1937, and *Happy and Glorious*, 1945. His autobiography, *The Unexpected Years*, appeared in 1936. Whitworth Art Gallery, Manchester, holds his work. Lived in Street, Somerset, dying in Glastonbury.

George HOUSTON 1869–1947 Painter and printmaker, born in Dalry, Ayrshire, where he continued to live, also in Glasgow. He was elected RSW, RI and RSA, also showing at Royal Glasgow Institute of the Fine Arts, Walker Art Gallery in Liverpool, Fine Art Society and elsewhere. Much of his work was done in Ayrshire and Argyllshire. He was a member of Edinburgh Arts and Glasgow Art Clubs. Several public galleries hold examples of work by an artist who painted in the Impressionist manner.

Ian HOUSTON 1934– Artist in oil, watercolour and coloured pencil, born in Gravesend, Kent. He studied at Royal College of Music, briefly with St Martin's School of Art, then moved to Norfolk in 1964 where, under the guidance of Edward Seago, he became committed to a career as a painter. Houston became president of the East Anglian Group of Marine Artists. He had a first solo show at Usher Gallery, Lincoln, in 1964, then showed at Mandell's Gallery, Norwich, each year until 1986. Other shows included Monazo Fine Arts, Monte Carlo, from 1981; Falmouth Art Gallery, from 1984; Beehive Corner Gallery, Adelaide, 1986; Mongerson Wunderlich Galleries, Chicago, 1990; and Portland Gallery from 1995. His work was also shown with RI and Paris Salon, where he won a silver medal for watercolour. Houston was awarded a gold medal with rosette by the National Society for French Culture. HM The Queen, HRH The Duke of Edinburgh, the Australian government and a series of corporate collections in Britain and abroad hold examples.

John HOUSTON 1930– Painter and teacher, born in Buckhaven, Fife, married to the artist Elizabeth Blackadder. Houston studied at Edinburgh College of Art, 1948–54, his final year being spent in Italy on a travelling scholarship. He returned to Edinburgh to teach at the College. In 1957 Houston helped start the 57 Gallery in Edinburgh, having his first solo show there in 1958. Other one-man shows were held at Scottish Gallery, Edinburgh, and Mercury Gallery for many years. A keen traveller, Houston exhibited widely abroad. He was a member of SSA and RSW and was elected RSA in 1972. Houston tended towards Expressionism in his landscapes, Munch being a key influence, employing bold colours. Scottish National Gallery of Modern Art holds his work.

Albert HOUTHUESEN 1903–1979 Painter of religious and visionary works, teacher, born Amsterdam, son of artist and musician Jean Charles Pierre Houthuesen (pronounced Howthozen, stress on second syllable). When her husband encouraged Albert to paint, his mother struck Jean Charles on the head, and he died from the blow not long after. This tragedy, poor health and poverty pursued Albert Houthuesen for years, long after the family had moved to London in 1912. Albert was naturalised 10 years later. After leaving elementary school aged 14 he did a number of pointless jobs, studying at St Martin's School of Art evening classes, 1917–23. Won scholarship to Royal College of Art, 1923, studying there until 1927. Four years later married painter Catherine Dean. Taught at the Working Men's College, 1928–36, then after the war, when he was a draughtsman in locomotive works in Doncaster, at St Gabriel's College. Although he showed at NEAC did not have first solo show until 1961, at Reid Gallery. In 1977 had three London shows and appeared with success on television. Tate Gallery holds his work. Lived in London.

Charles HOWARD 1899–1978 Abstract and Surrealist painter, born in New Jersey, America. Studied at University of California, travelled on the continent, lived for a time in Paris where he was influenced by Jean Hélion, then settled in London, 1939–40. Initially Howard painted murals, and was employed to paint Edward Wadsworth's nautical designs on the wall of the de la Warr Pavilion in Bexhill, 1936, the year he exhibited with the British Surrealist Group in the first London Surrealist Exhibition. Howard had a show of abstract pictures at Guggenheim Jeune Gallery in 1939. After an absence he returned to Britain in 1946, was given a retrospective at Whitechapel Art Gallery in 1956 and became a British citizen in 1963. He was included in The Surrealist Spirit in Britain, Whitford and Hughes, 1988.

Constance Mildred HOWARD 1910–2000 Printmaker, teacher and embroiderer, born in Northampton, she was married to the sculptor Harold Wilson Parker. She studied at Northampton School of Art, 1925–31, with Lewis Duckett, 1929–31, and at the Royal College of Art, 1931–5, where her teachers included Eric Ravilious and Edward Bawden. Held a number of teaching posts, including Kingston School of Art, 1939–46, and Goldsmiths' College, 1947–75, eventually as principal lecturer in charge of textiles, with embroidery as a main subject. Goldsmiths' gave her a retrospective in 2005. Showed at SWE, Arts Council, Arts and Crafts Society and elsewhere. Arts Council bought her work which was used widely in magazines such as *Illustrated London News* and *The Listener*. Howard's embroidery in the 1950s was heraldic and figurative, but later moved towards abstraction. She was a superb technician, although she claimed that "it is the ideas that count", and passed on her deep knowledge of embroidery in many books, including the four-volume *Twentieth-Century Embroidery in Great Britain*. In 1980, the Constance Howard Textile Resource and Research Centre was set up at Goldsmiths' to honour her. She was a fellow of the Society of Designer-Craftsmen and a member of the Costume Society, Art Workers' Guild and Embroiderers' Guild. Major examples of her work are held by Victoria & Albert Museum, Northampton Art Gallery, Lincoln Cathedral and Eton College. Howard was a small but striking and tenacious woman, notable for beautiful clothes, who dyed her hair a vivid green with lithographic ink. Lived for many years in London.

Diana HOWARD 1947– Painter, born in Surrey, married to the artist John Morley. She studied at Sutton and Epsom Colleges of Art and, as a postgraduate student, at Royal Academy Schools under Peter Greenham until 1971. Gained David Murray Studentships in Landscape, 1967–9, and Landseer Prize and Royal Academy Schools Bronze Medal for Painting, 1970. She was an associate of The Brotherhood of Ruralists and was included in their shows, her work having a sense of mystery. An early interest in the poems of Dante and later in Celtic mythology and the subject of the Holy Grail led on to an involvement with Eastern mysticism. Took part in many group exhibitions, including Piccadilly Gallery, New Grafton Gallery and Arnolfini Gallery, Bristol. Her solo shows included Festival Gallery, Bath, 1982; Somerset Rural Life Museum Gallery, 1988; and Chappel Galleries, Chappel, 1991. Lived in Stoven North Green, Suffolk.

Francis HOWARD 1874–1954 Painter, critic and administrator. Brought up as a Roman Catholic, Howard was educated widely on the continent and in England, his art studies including Herkomer School at Bushey. Was a founder-member of NPS and IS, where he exhibited. Also showed at Walker Art Gallery, Liverpool, which bought his work, and overseas. Signed pictures F H. Wrote criticism and did research for a number of publications. Member of Chelsea Arts Club and lived in London.

Ghislaine HOWARD 1953– Painter noted for Expressionist landscapes, born in Manchester, who studied fine art at the University of Newcastle upon Tyne. She worked in London and Paris, in 1980 returning to the northwest of England, settling in Glossop, Derbyshire. Wrote for *The Artist* magazine on her work and methods. Showed widely in England, including Images of the Yorkshire Landscape, organised by Sheeran Lock at Leeds Civic Hall, 1991. Later shows included The Cynthia Corbett Gallery, from 2000. Howard was artist-in-residence at the BBC, 2000–1. Manchester's City and Whitworth Art Galleries and Graves Art Gallery, Sheffield, acquired her work.

Ian HOWARD 1952– Painter, draughtsman and teacher, born in Aberdeen. He studied at Edinburgh University and College of Art. He won a Travelling Scholarship to Italy, later winning the RSA Guthrie Award in 1978; first prize in the Scottish Open Drawing Competition in 1985; and was a Tolly Cobbold Eastern Arts National Competition prizewinner. Howard taught at Gray's Art School in Aberdeen, then from 1986 was head of painting at Duncan of Jordanstone College of Art, Dundee. Howard's works were described as "usually an intriguing, carefully balanced blend of fine draughtsmanship, fantasy and classical references". He exhibited them in many mixed shows in Britain and abroad and had solo exhibitions at Compass Gallery, Glasgow. Contemporary Art Society, City Art Centre in Edinburgh and many Scottish galleries hold his work. Lived in Aberdeen.

Ivy HOWARD 1907–2005 Painter in oil and watercolour, draughtsman and etcher, daughter of Thomas Reeve, sister of the painter Russell Reeve and granddaughter of Emma Constable of East Bergholt. She was married to Algernon Basham, having an actress daughter, Janet, and William Howard, a fellow of the RIBA. After education at Norwich Higher Grade School, Howard attended Norwich and Newcastle Schools of Art, the Slade Summer School and Royal College of Art Drawing Studio and had two years at Chelsea School of Art. She was latterly a guest artist at the Slade and Royal College. Howard showed at the RA Summer Exhibition and had solo exhibitions at Laing Art Gallery, Newcastle upon Tyne, and Pearson Gallery, London University. Piano Nobile Fine Paintings also showed Howard's work.

James Campbell HOWARD 1906–1997 Painter and graphic artist, born in London, who was self-taught. He showed at RA and RI and was a Langham Sketch Club and SGA member. Lived finally in Ditchling, Sussex.

John HOWARD 1958– Mainly a printmaker, Howard was noted for his meticulous but atmospheric depictions of industrial and grand architecture in the Midlands and Black Country, documenting the past. He studied at Birmingham Polytechnic, 1986–9, with Jean Vaudeau and Kim Kempshall. Prior to this he worked for a decade in industry, "five of which I spent in foundries and related industries, as well as factories, warehouses, and so on". His main influences were Piranesi, Brangwyn and Joseph Wright of Derby. Howard was a member of the Birmingham Artists' Group and Birmingham Arts Trust and an associate of RBSA and RE. Showed at RA Summer Exhibitions, Bankside Gallery, Mall Galleries, MAFA Open and elsewhere and in 1991 had a one-man exhibition at Midlands Contemporary Art, Birmingham. Victoria & Albert Museum, Birmingham University, Surikov Academy of Arts in Moscow and other public collections hold examples. Lived in Warley, West Midlands, from 1995 in Cornwall.

Ken HOWARD 1932– Painter, and teacher, born in London, where he continued to live, married to the artist Christa Gaa. He studied at Hornsey College of Art, 1949–53, Royal College of Art, 1955–8, and won a British Council Scholarship to Florence, 1958–9. Was elected NEAC, 1962, in 1998 its president; ROI, 1966; RWA, 1981; RWS, 1983; and RA, 1991. His many awards were the First Prize in the Lord Mayor's Art Award, 1966; First Prize Arundel Art Centre, 1969; he was a prizewinner at John Moores Exhibition, Liverpool, 1978; and at John Laing Exhibition, 1979. Won First Prize, Hunting Group Award, 1982; was a prizewinner at RWA in 1983; and at NEAC Centenary Exhibition, 1986. Howard was appointed official artist in Northern Ireland by Imperial War Museum in 1973–8. Between 1973–80 worked with Army in Germany, Cyprus, Oman, Hong Kong, Nepal, Norway, Canada, Belize and Brunei. Howard did much commissioned work, including The Drapers' Company, The Haberdashers' Company, United Nations and elsewhere. Appeared in numerous mixed shows. One-man exhibitions included Plymouth Art Centre, 1955; John Whibley Gallery, 1966–8; from 1971 a series with New Grafton Gallery; and recent works at Richard Green, 2004. Howard was a painter noted for his handling of light and for his depictions of nudes in interiors. Imperial War Museum, Plymouth City Art Gallery, National Army Museum and other provincial British galleries hold his work. In 2005 Howard was elected professor of perspective at the Royal Academy Schools.

Margaret Maitland HOWARD 1898– Painter and draughtsman, notably in black-and-white, born in London. She studied at the Byam Shaw and Vicat Cole School of Art and Royal Academy Schools, where she was a multiple silver medal-winner plus other awards. Exhibited RA, NEAC, SWA, RP and ROI. Just after World War II she was appointed draughtsman to the Institute of Archaeology at London University. Ridley Art Club member, daughter of the artist Henry James Howard. She lived in Sutton, Surrey.

Norman HOWARD 1899–1955 Painter and illustrator. Studied at Camberwell School of Arts and Crafts, 1918–20, then at Westminster School of Art for four years under Walter Bayes. Exhibited RSMA, RA, IS, Goupil Gallery and NEAC. The Admiralty bought his work in 1945, and eight years later he did decorations for the P&O liner *Arcadia*. Lived in Richmond, Surrey, where in 1951 he was president of the Art Group.

Wolf HOWARD 1968– Self-taught artist, musician and poet, original name Simon Howard, born in Strood, Kent. After secondary school he "decided against art college" and did a number of jobs, including "half an hour in a shepherd's pie factory". Was a drummer for many bands, including Solar Flares, Buff Medways and Thee Headcoats. Wrote and performed poetry, publishing *The Doledrums*. Was a member of the Stuckists, included in their show at Artbank Gallery, 2001.

Dan HOWARD-BIRT 1974– Artist who made paintings writ large in his own handwriting over pattern and image, inspired by the American artist Barnett Newman, also magazine and record-sleeve design, witness his solo show at Nylon, 1999. Howard-Birt graduated from Goldsmiths' College in 1994–97. Group shows included Yerself is steam, 85 Charlotte Street, 1996; Fitzrovia Open, Venezuelan Cultural Centre, 1998; and Cathedral, Bobo's, 1999. Lived and worked in London.

Ray HOWARD-JONES 1903–1996 Painter, especially in gouache, draughtsman, mosaicist and muralist, writer and poet, born in Lambourn, Berkshire, as Rosemary Howard-Jones. She was educated at St Hilda's School, Penarth, and the London Garden School, then the Slade School of Fine Art from the age of 17 for four years. From the late 1930s through World War II she led a varied life, working as an archaeological draughtsman at National Museum of

Wales, Cardiff; helped the unemployed and deprived children in the city; with the composer Gomer Llewellyn ran the East Moors Theatre; with Coastal Defence recorded fortified islands in the Bristol Channel; and was a Royal Navy war artist recording loadings for D-Day. After the war moved to London and worked as a medical draughtsman. In 1946 attended Patrick Allan-Fraser School of Art, Hospitalfield, Arbroath, under James Cowie. Although based in London, Howard-Jones in later years travelled as far as Spain, Cyprus and America and was especially associated with west Wales and the islands offshore. From 1949–58 she spent long periods on the tiny island of Skomer. Nature and a deep inner spiritual life and Celtic mystery and legends were sources of inspiration. Her mosaics include one for Thomson House, Cardiff, 1958; another for Grange Church, Edinburgh, 1964–5. Published *Poems and Stories*, 1968. Howard-Jones had a first solo exhibition at Bloomsbury Gallery, 1935. Regular shows followed, including Leicester Galleries, 1964, where she was a frequent exhibitor; there was a WAC retrospective and tour, 1974; a West Wales Arts retrospective, 1983; one put on by West Wales Arts Centre, Fishguard, 1992; another by Rocket Press in 1993; and Tenby Museum and Art Gallery, 2002. Imperial War Museum, WAC and National Museum of Wales hold examples, commonly signed Ray.

Charles Wilfred HOWARTH 1893– Painter in oil, watercolour and line artist, Howarth established a reputation as an illustrator of newspapers, periodicals and books. After studying at Sheffield School of Art under A C C Jahn and Oliver Senior in 1910–12, Howarth spent two years at Birmingham School of Art. He exhibited with the Sheffield Society of Artists, at the RSA, in Birmingham and in Wales. Lived at Conway, North Wales.

Constance HOWARTH 1927– Watercolourist and textile designer, born in Rochdale, Lancashire. She gained her design diploma in 1947, having studied at Manchester Regional College of Art. Her work was exhibited in a number of notable exhibitions in the textile design field and is held by Victoria & Albert Museum. Lived in London for many years.

Maggy HOWARTH 1944– Artist in pebble mosaic, born in Warrington, Lancashire, who attended Reading University's school of fine art, 1962–6. For 20 years she worked with outdoor theatre companies, from 1983 undertaking pebble mosaic pavement commissions. "I think I am the only pebble mosaic practitioner in the United Kingdom." Her book *The Art of Pebble Mosaic* was published in 1994. She was a member of Art and Architecture and Artists Working to Commission and her work was to be found in Rose Street, Edinburgh; Discovery Point in Dundee; in Stockton High Street; and East Cleveland Hospital. Showed at Stoke Garden Festival, 1986. Lived at Wennington, Lancaster.

Russel HOWARTH 1927– Artist and teacher, born and lived in Oldham, Lancashire. He was educated locally, starting an engineering apprenticeship in 1941 while drawing in his spare time. Howarth began painting in 1950 after completing his technical studies. He taught pottery at part-time evening classes from 1962, giving up engineering in 1981 and teaching in 1992. Joined the Saddleworth Art Group in 1951 and took part in mixed shows at Museum Gallery, Brown Hill Centre and Mill Yard Gallery, all in Uppermill; Oldham Art Gallery; RBA and elsewhere. His solo shows included Royal Northern College of Music and Tib Lane Gallery, Manchester.

Stephen Purbeck HOWARTH 1981– Painter, born in Lewisham, southeast London, who attended Camberwell College of Arts, 2000–2, "expelled from the painting course for doing paintings." He did gallery, bar and factory work and labouring to support himself as an artist. Howarth's were "colourful, naïvely executed paintings, heavily influenced by Expressionism, often dealing with sex and violence." He was a member of Students for Stuckism, founded the Balham Stuckists and opened the South London Stuckism International Centre. Later group shows included Seven New Artists Pay their Respects to Past Masters, Fridge Gallery, and Tap Collective Group Show, Umpapa, both 2001; The First Stuckist International, Stuckism International, and Rivington Gallery Artists, Rivington Gallery, both 2002; and Stuckism Group Show, Wednesbury Museum, West Midlands, 2003. He had a solo exhibition, I Don't Want a Painting Degree if it Means not Painting, Stuckism International, 2002.

Winifred HOWE 1880–c.1948 Painter in oil and watercolour, born in West Horsley, Surrey. She was daughter of the painter A D Peppercorn and changed her name from Peg Peppercorn to avoid confusion with her father. After study at home she attended Slade School of Fine Art, where she gained her certificate and studied under Henry Tonks. Howe showed from 1907 including RA, NEAC, ROI, Goupil Salon and by invitation at the *Daily Express* Women's Exhibition in 1922. Her sister, Gertrude Peppercorn, a concert pianist, was married to the writer Stacy Aumonier, another sister being married to the writer and typographer Francis Meynell. Manchester City Art Gallery holds her work. Lived for many years at Ashtead, Surrey, but developed cancer and finally lived in a nursing home.

Cheryl HOWELD 1944– Artist in oil and watercolour, born in St Albans, Hertfordshire. She studied at Hornsey College of Art, 1962–3, with John Hoyland, John Simpson and Fred Cuming. Howeld's work concentrated on the figure and landscape, which took her on trips around England, notably Norfolk and Sussex, the south of France, Italy, Scotland and Russia, in which she had a special interest. Took part in many mixed shows, including Hampton Hill Galleries, Twickenham, from 1980; Original Picture Shop, 1985; Walton Gallery, 1988; PS, 1989; NEAC from 1990; and Richmond Gallery, 1992. Had a solo show at Maddermarket, Norwich, 1984, later ones including Churzee Studio Gallery, which she opened in 1988. Lived in London.

Cynthia HOWELL 1930– Painter and draughtsman, born in Montreal, Canada, who for a long time worked under the guidance of the artist Walter Nessler, also studying for a year with the artist and mystic Cecil Collins. While living in northwest London she showed with the Hampstead Artists' Council. From 1978 Howell lived and painted in Suffolk, where she concentrated on life drawing and latterly landscape painting. In 1988 she participated in a show held by five women artists at the Unity Wharf Venture Centre Gallery, Tower Bridge, sponsored by Mainstream Production Ltd, which has her work in its collection. In 1989 Howell won first prize in the Quay

Summer Exhibition, Sudbury. Other mixed shows included John Laing Exhibition, 1990 and 1991; a series with Eastern Arts at the Fermoy Centre, King's Lynn, with a Highly Commended in 1991; and frequent appearances at Bury St Edmunds Art Gallery and the Gallery on the Cam, Cambridge. Howell had a private house solo exhibition in Camden Town, 1985; one at Gallery 96, Cambridge, in 2000; and Chappel Galleries, Chappel, in 2006. She worked from rapidly made sketches translated "into structured, simplified compositions without obligation to realism."

David HOWELL 1939– Painter in watercolour and oil, living and working in the West Country. He concentrated on painting marines, landscapes – especially Italy and Venice – and equestrian scenes, with an emphasis on racing and its associated activities. Was a member of the RSMA and the Society of Equestrian Artists. Howell painted on the spot and frequently travelled, including the United Arab Emirates and Yemen. Showed prolifically in Britain and abroad, including New York and elsewhere in America, with solo shows in 2001 in London and Dubai. The Wykeham Gallery, Stockbridge, showed Howell in one-man and group exhibitions; he shared one with Timothy Easton and Julian Halsby there in 2002. Howell undertook private and corporate commissions, his work hanging in company collections in London and abroad and in royal palaces in the Middle East.

David HOWELL 1965– Painter, born in Ross-on-Wye, Herefordshire, who studied from 1984–8 at the Coventry Polytechnic, settling nearby at Stoke. As well as showing in the Coventry Open in 1992 and winning a prize at John Moores Liverpool Exhibition, 1993–4, Howell shared several exhibitions, including Omphalos Gallery, Sandwich, 1992.

Neale HOWELLS 1965– Artist in oil, acrylic, pastel, pencil and wood, in which irregular shapes, pastel colours – notably blue – and graffiti were important elements. He was born in Neath, Glamorgan, and studied at Neath Tertiary College (it holds his work), under Ian Wagstaff, 1985–7; gained an honours degree at Bath College of Higher Education, 1987–90; and obtained WAC travel grants to Berlin, 1996, and New York, 1998. Mixed shows included National Eisteddfod, Conway, 1995; National Eisteddfod, Bala, 1997; and 9th Mostyn Open, Oriel Mostyn, Llandudno, 1997. Solo exhibitions included Berlin Works 96 at Swansea Arts Workshop, 1997; The Future of F**k, six huge paintings at Neath Contemporary Art Gallery, Neath, 2001–2; and Oriel Washington Gallery, Penarth, 2002, when Howells was working on a collaboration with film director Marc Evans. Howells' work could excite strong emotions. He had two exhibitions closed by local councils before they had a chance to open. In 2004 Howells opened a new studio to the public at Port Talbot and in 2005 he had an exhibition at JohnMartinChelsea.

Allan HOWES 1888–1969 Sculptor, notably of figures, born Edgar Allan Howes in East Dereham, Norfolk, Howes studied at the Royal Academy Schools, where he won the Landseer prize plus several other prizes and a silver medal, also studying at the Slade School of Fine Art. Exhibited extensively at RA, RMS, RSA and Royal Glasgow Institute of the Fine Arts, and was elected a fellow of RBS. Howes' Madonna and Child as well as his Torso, typical works, are illustrated in the volume *RBS: Modern British Sculpture*, published in 1939, and his bronze Dawn, of 1942, is shown in Arthur T Broadbent's *Sculpture Today in Great Britain 1940–1943*. Howes' work is in several public collections. Lived in London, afterwards in Saffron Walden, Essex.

Anne HOWESON 1952– Artist in gouache, conté and oil, born in Kent. She attended Central School of Art, 1970–1, for a foundation course; graduated from St Martin's School of Art, 1971–4; then gained her master's degree at Royal College of Art, 1975–8. Howeson did a large amount of illustrative work, including *Independent Review*, *Saturday Times Review*, *German Playboy* and *The Spectator*. In 1990 she was a judge for the *Reader's Digest* Illustration Competition, she took part in a number of workshops and seminars and devised a summer course for Massachusetts College of Art, Boston, in 1992. Exhibitions included Galerie Mokum, Amsterdam, 1980; Association of Illustrators shows from 1981; Talbot Rice Centre, Edinburgh, 1985; and South Bank Picture Show from 1990. Lived in London.

Robert Leslie HOWEY 1900–1980 Artist, born in West Hartlepool, County Durham, who studied at the local School of Art, but was principally self-taught. He would have learned much from his father John William Howey (1873–1938), an amateur artist who was employed by the West Hartlepool Gas and Water Company, rising to the position of head collector. Unlike his father, whose reputation was mainly local, Leslie in the late 1920s and early 1930s produced many lino-cuts and woodcuts which were published by Charles Hauff Ltd, of London and New York. He worked also in oil, pastel and watercolour, and is noted for his watercolours of the Lake District and northeast of England coast. Exhibited at RA and RSA and had a solo exhibition at Gray Art Gallery, Hartlepool, in 1949. Abbott and Holder posthumously showed his work.

James HOWIE 1931– Artist and teacher, born in Dundee. He studied at Duncan of Jordanstone College of Art there, 1949–54, then after National Service studied ceramics at Liverpool College of Art, 1956–7. In the next five years he lived in London and on the continent for a while, returning to teach at his old College of Art in Dundee, 1962–7. After some time away, partly in the south of England, Howie returned to Dundee as artist-in-residence at Dudhope Art Centre. He took part in many group shows. Had a solo exhibition at New Art Centre in 1960, his later appearances including Edinburgh College of Art, Richard Demarco Gallery in Edinburgh and Compass Gallery, Glasgow. Was included in Painters in Parallel at Edinburgh College of Art, 1978, and in Showcase, organised by Bruton Gallery, Holmfirth, in 2003. Scottish Arts Council, Glasgow University and Dundee City Art Gallery hold his work.

B HOWITT-LODGE 1883–1948 Painter and architect, who studied in London. He did much illustrative work for publications such as *Our Dogs*, *Dog World* and the *Encyclopaedia Britannica*. Exhibited RMS, RA, ROI and elsewhere and was a member of the London Sketch Club. Worked for Air-raid Precautions (ARP) during early part of War II, when he painted the Blitz. His pictures Business as Usual and London Carries On were official purchases. Lived in London.

Sally HOWKINS 1961– Painter and printmaker, born in Nottingham. She studied at Mansfield College of Art, 1977–9, then Newcastle upon Tyne Polytechnic, 1979–82. Group shows included Northern Contemporaries, 1981; Gallery 7, Newcastle upon Tyne from 1983; Warwick Arts Trust, which holds her work, from 1987; and Oxford Visual Art Week, from 1991. Had a solo show at Cadogan Contemporary, 1993, atmospheric landscapes moving towards abstraction.

Alan James HOWLETT 1940– Painter, printmaker, collagist, creator of wood reliefs and teacher, born in London. He attended Ealing School of Art, 1958–60, then Royal College of Art, 1960–3, his teachers including Frank Auerbach and Bernard Cohen. From the early 1960s through the 1970s Howlett did part-time teaching, including around 10 years at Norwich; he was a freelance broadcaster for BBC music programmes; and undertook photography for record companies, including Harmonia Mundi in France and Vanguard in America. Howlett also taught music, on which much of his painting was based; he had a special interest in music of the Trecento and Quattrocento in Italy and France. From 1980 Howlett painted and taught in Italy. Although he took part in many group shows in his student days he then rejected the commercial gallery system, selling largely privately, especially to musicians.

Elizabeth HOWLETT 1958– Artist and lecturer, born in Surrey, who did foundation studies at Winchester School of At, 1976–7; graduated with honours in fine art, Kingston Polytechnic, 1977–80; gained her master's from Chelsea School of Art, 1980–1; in the mid-1980s undertaking library and information studies at the Polytechnic of North London. Howlett was a part-time lecturer in printmaking, Gwent College of Art, 1982; held a printmaking residency at Newcastle University, 1984; and was a visiting lecturer there in 1985. In 1986 she was one of three artists in an exhibition at Linton Court Gallery, Settle, showing paintings of fish. "I like fish, I paint portraits of individuals, their personalities in many layers in gouache on Indian paper." Previous exhibitions included Stowells Trophy, RA, 1980; Video Festival, South Hill Park Arts Centre, Bracknell, 1981; Summer Show, Film Co-op, and London Musicians Collective, both 1982; and Joliffe Studios, Wyvern Theatre, Swindon, 1985. She had solo exhibitions in 1985 at Newcastle University and Following Tides, Young Vic.

Nancy HOWORTH 1912– Landscape painter, educated in Eastbourne, Sussex, where she attended the School of Art, 1930–2, later studying privately. Showed with SWA, Free Painters and Sculptors and with Association of Sussex Artists of which she was a member. Had several solo exhibitions, including Ditchling Gallery. Lived in North Chailey, Sussex.

Ray HOWORTH 1914– Painter, designer and teacher, born in Wealdstone, Middlesex. He studied at Harrow Technical and Art School under John Gerald Platt. After Army service in World War II held a number of teaching posts, following a period as a freelance, becoming head of the design department at Manchester College of Art and Design. As well as having work reproduced in many publications Howorth showed at RA, ROI and widely in the provinces. Lived in Knutsford, Cheshire.

Diana HOWSE 1956– Artist, arts administrator and editor, born in Oxfordshire, who gained fine art honours degree at Exeter College of Art and Design, 1975–8. Howse was at this time involved in Spacex, an artists' studio complex, where she ran a gallery until 1981, when she left to concentrate on her own work. During the 1980s Howse was editor of the *South West Arts Newsletter to Artists*; was education officer for Spacex until 1984; became involved in film and video; in the mid-1980s moved to Bristol to work at Watershed, Britain's first media centre; met David Lascelles (whom she married in 1990); and began her ongoing involvement with Harewood House, Yorkshire, creating the Terrace Gallery there, which opened in 1989. She had had a solo installation, Ghost Town, in 1985, and on moving to London in 1987 Howse began seriously painting again, participating in Cross Currents at Reed's Wharf Gallery at the Barbican Centre, 1996, showing lush, Expressionist abstracts, with landscape references.

Melanie HOWSE 1968– Glass artist, who attended Portsmouth Art College, with a distinction in three-dimensional design foundation studies, 1987–8, achieving further merits and distinctions during an architectural stained glass course at Swansea Institute of Higher Education, 1989–92. Among awards were the British Society of Master Glass Painters Stevens Competition first prize, 1991, and the Howard Martin Award, for outstanding merit, 1992. Howse completed eight square metres of glass for the Swansea Institute library, during a residency, 1992, and lancet windows and a roundel, St Illtyd's Church, Port Tennant, Swansea, 1993. In 1997 moved to Emsworth, Hampshire, and set up her own business. In that year showed figurative works on glass with background illumination at Eight by Eight, Pallant House, Chichester.

Rose Chicheliana HOWSE 1892–1981 Miniaturist and painter in watercolour, born in Waterford, Ireland, whose full name was Henrietta Rose Chicheliana Howse. She studied art in Brussels, then miniature painting in London with the miniaturist S Arthur Lindsey. He confided in her his medium for painting on ivory, a secret which remained after she died with her family. Howse painted in watercolour, but not to sell, the subjects being Scottish and Swiss scenes, figures, dogs, cats and flower arrangements. Became an associate of RMS. Her husband was in the Navy and travelled a lot, but eventually they settled in Scotland at Kilmacolm, Renfrewshire.

Cherry HOWSON 1912– Watercolour artist who was born at Tipton, Staffordshire. Studied art at the School of Art in Lancaster under the painter and etcher Charles Ripper, then with the Kendal artist George Mortram Moorhouse. She exhibited quite widely in the north of England, at venues including Walker Art Gallery, Liverpool, Atkinson Art Gallery, Southport, the Lake Artists' Society and with the RS. Lived at Evesham, Worcestershire.

Joan HOWSON 1885–1964 Stained glass designer who from 1920 formed a partnership with Caroline Townshend (1878–1944). The London-born Townshend, educated for five years in Scotland followed by two years at the Slade School of Fine Art, between 1900–3 was a pupil of Christopher Wall, from 1906 becoming one of the original tenants of The Glass House, Fulham, collaborating with Lowndes & Drury to make her glass. In 1926, she and Howson moved to Putney, southwest London, where they had a studio employing several craftsmen. Howson showed at Walker Art Gallery in Liverpool and at the RA Summer Exhibition. The work of Townshend and Howson was included by Rachel Moss in her 1998 show Stained Glass Designs at the Maas Gallery: cartoons of glass completed for St Oswald, Burneside, Cumbria, 1936, and St Andrew, Kirkby Malzeard, Yorkshire, 1937.

Peter HOWSON 1958– Painter, printmaker and mural artist, born in London, moving to Glasgow as a small boy. He attended Glasgow School of Art 1975–77, then took two years off to do a number of jobs, was in the Army for a time and travelled in Europe. He resumed his studies and graduated in 1981. His time off mid-studies provided Howson with useful material for his painting which is characterised by its powerful draughtsmanship, simple imagery and theatrical lighting to depict a masculine world, tough and gritty. Howson soon built up a reputation on leaving college. From 1982–3 he painted murals at the Feltham Community Association, then in 1985 he was artist-in-residence at the University of St Andrews. He won the Arthur Andersen Purchase Award at Compass Gallery, Glasgow, Barras show for the 1986 Mayfest. Howson showed widely abroad and his British solo exhibitions included a retrospective at McLellan Galleries, Glasgow, 1993, Roger Billcliffe Gallery, Glasgow, 1999, Flowers West, Santa Monica, California, 2001, Flowers Central, 2002, and Stations of the Cross, Flowers East, 2003, after recovery from alcoholism. A turning-point in Howson's life and career was being chosen as Official War Artist for Britain in Bosnia, sponsored jointly by *The Times* newspaper and the Imperial War Museum. A further *Times*-sponsored trip to Kosovo occurred in 1999, even though his Bosnia experiences had left Howson severely traumatised, with a breakdown. The Imperial War Museum and Howson's dealer Flowers East had put on critically acclaimed shows of Howson's war work in 1994. In 2001, Howson designed Scottish Opera's production of Mozart's opera *Don Giovanni*. Flowers Graphics gave Howson a print retrospective in 2004. Scottish Arts Council, Scottish National Gallery of Modern Art, Tate Gallery, Victoria & Albert Museum and many provincial galleries hold Howson's work. Lived in London.

Henrietta HOYER MILLAR 1964– Painter of urban and country landscapes and nature using a muted palette, born and lived in London. She obtained a City and Guilds qualification in fine art. Group shows included Angel Studios Open Exhibition, 1987 and 1988; Cadogan Contemporary, 1993; and Groucho Club, 1998. Showed solo with Long & Ryle from 1995.

Francis HOYLAND 1930– Painter, printmaker, teacher and writer, born in Selly Oak, Birmingham, married to the artist Philippa Hoyland and father of the painter John Hoyland. Francis' art master at The Downs School, Colwall, was Maurice Feild, then he attended St George's School, Harpenden. Studied painting at Camberwell School of Arts and Crafts, 1946–9; Slade School of Fine Art, 1949–50; in 1951 an Abbey Minor Scholarship taking him to Italy. Was a conscientious objector to military service, 1952–4. Taught at West of England College of Art in Bristol, 1954–9; Chelsea School of Art, 1960–6; Camberwell, 1966–92; part-time at Cardinal Wiseman Catholic Comprehensive School, from 1992; and for The Prince's Foundation, 2000. His publications include *Painting*, 1966, and *Alive to Paint* and *A Painter's Diary*, both 1967. Showed at the AIA, RWA, was included in The Forgotten Fifties which toured from Graves Art Gallery, Sheffield, 1984, and in Camberwell Artists of the 40s and 50s, Belgrave Gallery, 1988. Solo exhibitions included Galerie de Seine, 1956, Beaux Arts Gallery, 1960 and 1961; retrospective, South London Art Gallery, 1969; 90 Diptychs of the Life of Christ, Southwark and Chichester Cathedrals, both 1972; Sweet Waters Gallery, 1990; and Chappel Galleries, Chappel, 2002. In 2004 North Light Gallery, Huddersfield, showed Hoyland's etchings and paintings. He had works in numerous public and private collections. Lived in London.

Henry HOYLAND 1894–1948 Painter who studied in Sheffield, London and Paris. He exhibited RA, NEAC, RBA, in the provinces and at the Paris Salon and had one-man shows in London and in the provinces. Was a member of Chelsea Arts Club and the Arts Club. From 1921–9 Hoyland was on the staff of Sheffield College of Art and for five years during World War II he was deputy chief camouflage officer for the Ministry of Home Security. Work by Hoyland, a subtle Colourist, was bought by the RA out of the Edward Stott Fund and provincial galleries hold his work. Lived at Leamington Spa, Warwickshire.

Hilary HOYLAND 1958– Painter, born in Niteroi, Brazil, married to the artist John Hoyland. They met while at Camberwell School of Arts and Crafts, completing their studies in 1981. In 1985 they moved to St Martin de Vers, near Cahors, southwest France, where for Hilary capturing the light was an abiding interest. She chose "mixed media, because I enjoy working fast and directly, inventing as I go. I like using transparency and opacity, moderating crayon and pastel until a painting takes on its own life." With John, she won a Barnes Workhouse Trust Award. The Hoylands usually showed together, as their work ran parallel with similar preoccupations. Exhibitions included Stonegate Gallery, York, 1987; Altigone, Toulouse, 1994; Alpha House Gallery, Sherborne, 1999; and Piano Nobile, 2001. The Prefecture de Cahors owned Hilary's work.

John HOYLAND 1934– Painter, printmaker, designer and teacher, born in Sheffield, Yorkshire. He enrolled in junior art department at Sheffield College of Art in 1946 instead of attending grammar school, then from 1956–60 was at Royal Academy Schools, where in 1959 his entire diploma show of abstracts was taken down by order of the RA's president Sir Charles Wheeler. Hoyland was elected RA in 1991, with a solo exhibition there, 1999. He became an influential teacher, at Hornsey College of Art, Croydon School of Art, Chelsea College of Art (where he was principal lecturer from 1965), St Martin's School of Art, Royal Academy Schools and Slade School of Fine Art, from which he resigned in 1989. Hoyland won a number of prizes, including Calouste Gulbenkian Purchase Award, 1963; first prize at John Moores Exhibition Liverpool in 1982; joint first prize in Korn Ferry International Award Exhibition in 1986; and in the following year first prize in the Athena Art Awards Exhibition. Hoyland developed a strong attachment to America, from the late 1960s making visits to New York and setting up a studio there and in 1972 becoming Charles A Dana professor of fine arts, Colgate University, Hamilton. He was in close touch with such abstract painters as Noland and Motherwell and in 1988 travelled in America selecting and curating the

Hans Hofmann show for the Tate Gallery. In 1986 he designed sets for Sadler's Wells ballet *Zansa*. Hoyland exhibited widely internationally, including Whitechapel Art Gallery, Waddington Galleries, Serpentine Gallery with tour, 1979–80, Compass Gallery in Glasgow and Flowers East. Graves Art Gallery, Sheffield, held a 30-year retrospective, 2000–1. Tate Gallery, British Council and other major collections hold his work. Tate St Ives would give Hoyland a show in 2006, contrasting the early paintings of the 1960s, with their large open expanses of thinly applied colour and formal arrangements, with expressive and vibrant works newly created for that exhibition. Lived in London.

John HOYLAND 1957– Painter and pianist, born in Bristol, son of Francis Hoyland and married to Hilary Hoyland, both artists. John and Hilary met at Camberwell School of Arts and Crafts, finishing their studies in 1981, in 1985 moving to St Martin de Vers, near Cahors, in southwest France. The Hoylands usually exhibited together, as their painting ran parallel with similar interests. They received a Barnes Workhouse Trust Award. John Hoyland gained first prize in the Magnolia Mouldings Landscape Competition and a Gold Medal at Agen and Albi Salons. The sunlight of southern France was a factor in his work, pictures taking him "from four sessions to four years to complete." Exhibitions included Barbican Centre, 1984; St John's Smith Square, 1989; Galerie L'Or du Temps, Cahors, 1990; Stonegate Gallery, York, 1994; and Piano Nobile Fine Paintings, Richmond, 1999. John was also a concert pianist in England and France, venues including St John's and the Three Choirs Festival. The Prefecture de Cahors and York University hold his work.

Philippa HOYLAND 1924– Painter, draughtsman and designer, born in West Byfleet, Surrey, for whom "my family is my subject." After World War II service with the First Aid Nursing Yeomanry, she took the advertising design course at the Central School of Arts and Crafts, 1947–57, notable teachers including Jesse Collins, "who showed me how to relate my designs to the rectangle that contained them. This was a vitally important lesson and has remained with me ever since." Anthony Gross was her favourite teacher, another the taciturn William Roberts, who would "sit down, do a drawing and leave without a word." Matisse and Bonnard were inspirations and "my paintings from and about memory were reinforced by reading Marcel Proust whom I felt entirely at home with." She worked for the advertising agency Colman, Prentice & Varley, 1949–52, and the music printer Christopher Foss, 1952–3, marrying the artist Francis Hoyland in 1953, having two musician sons, John also a painter. Mixed shows included RWA, 1955; Looking Forward, curated by John Berger, South London Art Gallery, 1956; RA Summer Exhibition, 1977–8; and New Grafton Gallery, Artists of Today and Tomorrow, 1984–7. Among her solo shows were Duke Street Gallery, Hadleigh, 1966; The Annexe Gallery, 1982; and Chappel Galleries, Chappel, 2003.

Denise HOYLE 1935– Painter and potter. She was born in Paris and studied there at L'Académie de la Grande Chaumière. Married to the artist Walter Hoyle. She was especially interested in natural history, early botanical drawings and the ballet. Designed posters for the Post Office. Showed at Old Fire Engine House, Ely, and in Saffron Walden at Church Street Gallery. The Fry Art Gallery in Saffron Walden holds her work. Lived in Hastings, Sussex.

Jonathan HOYLE 1957– Painter and draughtsman, he studied at Rochdale College of Art, Gloucestershire College of Art and the Royal Academy Schools, 1979–82. He gained the Elizabeth Greenshields Scholarship in 1981; a prize for drawing at the Royal Academy Schools in 1982; an Italian Government Scholarship for 1982–3; and the Oppenheim-John Downes Memorial Award in 1989. Hoyle's figurative pictures were notable for their strong abstract design. He showed in mixed exhibitions including Pick of Graduate Art, at Christie's, in 1982; RA 1985 Summer Exhibition; in 1986 at New Grafton Gallery; and in the Laing Collection, Mall Galleries, 1990. He had a solo show at Wellington Crescent, Winnipeg, in 1985; at Judd Street Gallery, in 1990; and Abbott and Holder, 2001 and 2004. HRH The Prince of Wales bought his work.

Walter HOYLE 1922–2000 Watercolourist, printmaker, designer and teacher, born in Rishton, Lancashire, married to the artist Denise Hoyle. He studied at Beckenham School of Art and at Royal College of Art, 1940–2 and 1947–8, under Edward Bawden. From 1948–9 he was artist attached to the Byzantine Institute in Istanbul. Work that he saw there influenced Hoyle, who also claimed to be "an English romantic with a love of France". Hoyle taught at St Martin's School of Art, 1951–60; Central School of Arts and Crafts, 1960–4; and Cambridge School of Art, 1964–85. While in Cambridge he launched Cambridge Print Editions, which produced limited editions of artists' prints. Editions of his own prints were commissioned by Editions Alecto, Christie's Contemporary Art and Folio Society. He designed wallpapers and painted murals for the Natural History Museum and for the Sealink ship *St David*. Showed at RA, Leicester Galleries, Zwemmer Gallery, Kettle's Yard in Cambridge, the Great Bardfield Exhibitions in mid-1950s and elsewhere. Other commissioned work was done for Shell, BBC and Post Office. Fifty-year retrospective in 1993 at Fry Art Gallery, Saffron Walden. Tate Gallery, British Museum and Victoria & Albert Museum hold his work. Lived in Hastings, Sussex, with a studio in Dieppe, France.

Louis HOYLES 1914– Although primarily an industrial designer, Hoyles was also a sculptor and draughtsman. Born in London, he studied art with Harold Youngman and Russell Reeve. Exhibited in Britain and abroad, mainly in design-oriented shows. Lived in Stanmore, Middlesex.

Alison HOYNES 1965– Hoynes graduated with honours from the University of Newcastle upon Tyne, 1983–7. Group appearances included Hatton Gallery at the University, 1985, and in 1989 both Dance Attic Studios and East End Open Studios, based at Vyner Street Studios.

Edward Bouverie HOYTON 1900–1988 Printmaker, watercolourist and teacher, born in London. He studied at Goldsmiths' College School of Art, 1918–26, then at British School in Rome, 1926–8. He went on to become principal of Penzance School of Art, 1941–66. With his wife Inez Hoyton, the artist, he was a notable figure in Newlyn art circles and showed widely locally as well as at RA, RBA, and elsewhere in the provinces. Hoyton's work covered a wide range, from early prints in the manner of Samuel Palmer and F L Maur Griggs – as illustrated in *The Studio* volume *Artists' Country*, by C Geoffrey Holme and G S Sandilands – to abstract etchings of Tresco, in the Isles of Scilly, of the late 1940s. He was also a notable portraitist. In all his work there is strong emphasis on sound draughtsmanship. He had a final show of The Lifetime's Work at St Ives Society of Artists in 1987.

Inez HOYTON 1903–1983 Painter in oil and watercolour, designer, weaver and embroiderer, Hoyton studied at Leeds College of Art. It was there that she trained to teach, eventually becoming art teacher, during World War II, at Benenden School, in Kent. When her husband, the artist Edward Bouverie Hoyton, became principal of Penzance School of Art, Inez taught there, from 1946–68. Although her second name was Estella, she sometimes signed her work Inez B Hoyton. She and her husband became strongly associated with Cornish artistic life; Inez was a member of the Newlyn Society of Artists, the St Ives Society of Artists and the Penwith Society, in St Ives. She travelled widely, notably in Greece, Italy and Spain. Inez exhibited at the RA, the Orion Gallery in Penzance and widely in Britain. Lived at Newlyn.

Wacław HRYNIEWICZ 1909–1987 Architect and sculptor, one of the group of Polish paper sculptors who made such an impact in Britain after World War II. After graduating from Warsaw Institute of Technology's department of architecture he spent two years in the studio of Le Corbusier, returned to Warsaw to work on the modernisation of Polish Railways, then in 1938 with Osiecki and Skolimowski gained first prize for the design of the Polish pavilion at the New York World Fair. After deportation to Siberia by the Soviet Union, in 1941 he was released to join the Polish Army and served in North Africa and Italy, later designing and overseeing the erection of the Polish War Cemetery at Monte Cassino. In 1947 with Osiecki and Skolimowski set up Studio 2, offering architects' and designers' services, clients served by Hryniewicz including Creda and Swan Mill and many international fairs and exhibitions. Eventually he reverted to architecture. Was included in Polish Paper Sculpture at Polish Cultural Institute, 1995.

Su-Lien HSIEH 1964– Painter of single canvases, diptychs and triptychs, and photographer, of Taiwanese nationality. She studied fine art at the University Granada, Barcelona, Spain, 1995–6, gaining her master's in European fine art at Winchester School of Art, 1997–8. She was interested in integrating Chinese calligraphy with ideas from Western art as well as exploring concepts of time and travel. Contributed to the exhibition Global II Collection at Addison Wesley Longman, Harlow, 1998–9.

Xiao Peng HUANG 1960– Artist, born in China, who attempted "to return to the traditional spirit of Oriental art from Minimalism". He studied at Guangzhou Academy of Arts in China, then at Slade School of Fine Art. Group exhibitions included Guangzhou Academy from 1983; Six Slade Students, Rijksakademie, Amsterdam, 1992; Artists' Open Studios, Tudorleaf Centre, 1993; and Journeys West, University of Essex touring show, 1995.

Deirdre HUBBARD 1935– Sculptor, born in New York City, America, who graduated Summa cum Laude at Harvard University in 1957. Studied with Andreas Feininger, in the studio of Elisabeth Frink and at Chelsea College of Art. Showed at RA, Royal Glasgow Institute of the Fine Arts, National Museum of Wales in Cardiff, Usher Gallery in Lincoln, Camden Arts Centre and at RWA, where in 1996 she was included in the 2nd Open Sculpture Exhibition with the near-abstract Wingless Bird. Many private collections in Britain and abroad hold her work. Lived in London.

Hesketh HUBBARD 1892–1957 Painter, printmaker, furniture designer, printer, writer and lecturer. Born in London, he studied at Heatherley's School of Fine Art, Croydon School of Art and Chelsea Polytechnic. Hubbard was founder and director of the Forest Press; for a time master of the Art Workers' Guild; and the author of over a dozen books, including *A Hundred Years of British Painting 1851–1951*. He was a member of many societies connected with painting and printmaking in Britain and overseas. Exhibited widely, including ROI, RSA, RA, RBA and Ridley Art Club. Many galleries in Britain and abroad hold his work. Lived in London.

John HUBBARD 1931– Painter, designer and printmaker, born at Ridgefield, Connecticut, America. He studied at Harvard University, 1950–3, completed three years' military service including time in Japan, then in 1956–8 studied at Art Students' League of New York and with Hans Hofmann. From 1958–60 Hubbard lived in Rome and travelled through Europe, then moved to Dorset in 1961, settling in Chilcombe. Among a wide variety of activities Hubbard in 1968 designed décor and costumes for Dutch National Ballet's *Le Baiser de la Fée*; in 1983 designed décor for the Royal Ballet's production *Midsummer*; in 1985 painted the backcloth for *Sylvia pas de Deux* for the same company; was in 1988 invited resident artist at Poet's House, New Harmony, Indiana; then in 1990 was guest in Malaysia of the National Gallery of Malaysia. Group exhibitions included The Sea at Laing Art Gallery, Newcastle upon Tyne, 1986; Forces of Nature at Manchester City Art Gallery and tour, 1990–1; and John Moores Liverpool Exhibition, 1991–2. He won the Jerwood Prize for Painting in 1996. Hubbard's first solo show after moving to England was at New Art Centre in 1961, after which he added many international one-man exhibitions. He had a series of shows with Fischer Fine Art from 1984, after a retrospective at Warwick Arts Trust, 1981, another following at Yale Center for British Art, New Haven, Connecticut, 1986. Latterly exhibited with Marlborough Fine Art and had shows at New Art Centre Sculpture Park and Gallery, East Winterslow, 2002, and Six Chapel Row Contemporary Art, Bath, 2003. Tate Gallery, Scottish National Gallery of Modern Art, British Council and other public collections hold his work. Hubbard won the Jerwood Prize in 1996.

Edgar HUBERT 1906–1985 Abstract painter, born Norman Edgar Hubert in Billingshurst, Sussex, and one of the mysterious curiosities of modern British painting. He was at school at Sherborne, and after studying art at University of Reading, 1924–6, was at the Slade School of Fine Art, 1926–9 (gaining a certificate for drawing, 1926–7). Henry Tonks was among his teachers and he shared rooms with William Townsend, in whose journals he appears. Although he socialized with such painters as Geoffrey Tibble, William Coldstream and Rodrigo Moynihan and was involved in the Objective Abstractions group in the mid-1930s, Hubert was a shy man who became a recluse, exhibited little and whose work is generally unknown. He exhibited with the AIA, 1939; in La Jeune Peinture en Grande Bretagne, at La Galerie René Drouin in Paris, 1948, exhibiting four gouache compositions, one lent by the British Council, which organised the show; in the same year having solo show at the Mayor Gallery, where he had begun exhibiting in 1946, offering 20 Compositions, I–XX, "prices on application". After living with his family in Beaconsfield after World War II Hubert settled in Seaford, Sussex, where he continued to paint for himself, working in a variety of styles including a geometrical phase and abstracting out of his head rather than from nature. Hubert kept abreast of art developments, but was reluctant to talk about his own work. There were few exhibitions of Hubert's work in the 1950s and 1960s. His Recent Paintings were shown at the ICA in 1958; he was included in British Art and the Modern Movement 1930–40 at the National Museum and Gallery of Wales, Cardiff, in 1962; and in 1963 the Contemporary Art Society presented Glasgow Art Gallery with a work. He painted at least one portrait, of his mother, held by the family. Finally his health was not good and he died of broncho-pneumonia and chronic broncho/asthma in a nursing home. The Fine Art Society showed Hubert's Paintings 1941–1969 in 2005.

Alistair HUDSON 1969– Artist and curator who graduated with honours in fine art and history of art from Goldsmiths' College in 1991. He went on to work from a studio in Paddington and as a curator at the Government Art Collection, having previously been with the Anthony d'Offay Gallery. Hudson worked in various mediums such as video, photography, performance and installation. For his solo show Project Chryse Planitia at Clapham Art Gallery, 2001, he produced watercolours on oversized canvas or paper dry-mounted on aluminium, parodying the tour of the eighteenth-century artist but related to the surface of Mars.

Andrew HUDSON 1935– Artist, born in Birmingham, who studied at Oxford University, graduating in English literature and language, 1957. Attended Slade School of Fine Art, 1957–9, and the University of Saskatchewan, Canada, 1961–2. From 1965 he lived in Washington, America. Group exhibitions included Corcoran Gallery of Art, Washington, from 1979; Basel Art Fair, with Bernard Jacobson, 1980. Showed widely in America, Germany and Canada, solo exhibitions including Klonardis, Inc, Toronto, from 1981; Brody's Gallery, Washington, from 1985; and Gallery 163, Seattle, 1989. Public collections holding examples include National Gallery of Canada, Ottawa; Corcoran Gallery of Art and George Washington University, both in Washington; and Pallant House Gallery Trust, Chichester, presented by Hudson by way of a memorial to Charles Kearley, a major Pallant House benefactor, the two being cousins.

Anna Hope HUDSON 1869–1957 Painter, also known as Nan Hudson, who was born in New York but brought up in Washington. She produced landscape, figure and architectural pictures in the manner of Walter Sickert, who admired her work. Went to Paris to study art in early 1890s, meeting her lifelong friend the painter Ethel Sands; spent five years in Eugène Carrière's atelier from 1896, also studying with Henri Evenepoel. As well as showing in Paris, she shared a show with Sands at Carfax Gallery, 1912, was a founder-member of LG in 1913, a member of WIAC and also showed at London Salon, NEAC, Baillie Gallery as well as Cooling, Goupil and Leicester Galleries. Pictures by her were included in Camden Town Recalled at Fine Art Society, 1976, and The Painters of Camden Town, at Christie's, 1988.

Erlund HUDSON 1912– Painter and designer, born in south Devon as Eleanor Erlund Hudson. She studied at Royal College of Art, teachers including Robert Austin and Malcolm Osborne, becoming an associate in 1937. Her studies were extended for two years with Continuation and Travelling Scholarships. War Artists' Advisory Committee bought her work, which is in the Imperial War Museum. Hudson was made a member of RE in 1946 and RWS in 1949, also showing at RA and abroad. She was a costume designer and was artistic adviser to the Brooking Ballet School. A group of Hudson's sensitive figure studies was featured in the RWS's Spring Exhibition, 1999, celebrating 60 years since she was made an associate. Lived in London for many years, latterly with Nesta Brooking. Hudson's watercolours and etchings were included in a small group show at Nine Clarendon Cross in 2004.

Graham HUDSON 1977– London-based sculptor, born in Kent, who graduated in fine art, sculpture, from Chelsea College of Art & Design, 1997–00, gaining his master's in the same discipline at Royal College of Art, 2000–2. Hudson's awards included A to B via Sea, British Council and P&O, and Deutsche Bank Pyramid Award for Art, both 2002. Among group shows were Beck's Futures Student Film/Video Festival, ICA, 2000; Sound and Vision, Royal Festival Hall and New Religious Art, Liverpool Biennale, both 2002; and Urban and Suburban Stories, VTO, and Portal, Studio J, Kyoto, Japan, both 2003. In 2004 Hudson had a Jerwood Artists' Platform solo exhibition in which he "mixed sound, text and appropriation and combined political comment with comical authority to poignant effect".

Nan HUDSON: *see* **Anna Hope HUDSON**

Tom HUDSON 1922–1997 Teacher and artist, born in Horden, County Durham, into a working-class, mining environment with little exposure to art. Association with such key figures as Harry Thubron and Herbert Read honed Hudson's natural ability to inspire and motivate others. Hudson studied at Sunderland College of Art, at King's College at the University of Durham, then did a postgraduate course in art history at Courtauld Institute, 1950–1. Began teaching at Lowestoft School of Art, other appointments following in Leeds, Leicester, Cardiff College of Art where he was director of studies and in Vancouver, Canada. He held a number of consultancies in Britain and abroad, and was interested in a range of subjects including education, colour and the history of art. Group shows included Drian Galleries, Grabowski Gallery where he also had a solo show in 1973, and abroad. In 1972 he completed a mural for University Hospital Wales in Cardiff. Hudson was a member of the 56 Group, also exhibiting with SEA, at Royal National Eisteddfod and elsewhere. Died in Bristol.

Yvonne HUDSON 1924–1985 Sculptor, artist in various fields including watercolours and embroidery, puppet-maker and teacher, born in Wanstead, Essex. She studied at the Slade School of Fine Art in 1943–8, winning the sculpture prize in the latter year. For a time she was arts adviser to the Scottish Association of Girls' Clubs, then after marriage she lived at Earnley, Sussex. Taught at Portsmouth School of Art and later at Horsham Art School. She was a keen Anglican, and much of her work had religious themes and was done for Chichester Cathedral and Sussex churches; it is also held by Worthing Art Gallery. She was a fellow of the RBS and showed at RA, RBA and elsewhere and had several solo shows in Chichester, Earnley and Winchester. Retrospective at Chichester Centre of Arts in 1987.

Henry Percy HUGGILL 1886–1957 Paintmaker, printer, teacher and curator, born in London. Studied at the Royal College of Art, 1908–14, under W R Lethaby, Gerald Moira and Sir Frank Short. Exhibited RA, RE, provincial and overseas exhibitions. Huggill's work is held by a number of northern art galleries, including Atkinson Art Gallery, Southport. He was principal of Southport School of Art, 1921–30, and curator of the local art gallery for that period. From 1930 he was principal of Liverpool College of Art for 21 years. Lived at Dyserth, Flintshire.

John HUGGINS 1938– Sculptor and teacher, born in Wiltshire. He studied sculpture at West of England Art College, Bristol, 1956–61, gaining among awards the prize for sculpture in both 1959–60. He became a part-time lecturer at Bristol Polytechnic and Bath Academy of Art until 1977, then decided to sculpt full-time. Huggins' affinities were with artists such as Brancusi and Duchamp-Villon, being concerned with forms and their interaction and impeccable craftsmanship. Mounting on black bases was a feature of his sculptures. Initially he showed in the Bath and Bristol area, then signed with Alwin Gallery, later Art Scene, to handle his output exclusively, having a series of solo exhibitions, although he had a one-man at Anthony Hepworth Fine Art, Bath, in 1993. In 2004, McHardy Sculpture Company showed Huggins' The Maltese Collection. Was a member of RWA and associate of RBS. Arts Council and Bristol City Art Gallery hold his work. Lived in Woodford, Berkeley, Gloucestershire.

Angela HUGHES 1964– Painter, draughtsman and teacher who studied at Darlington Sixth Form College, 1984–5, Newcastle University, 1985–9, and Royal Academy Schools, 1989–91. From 1985 she gained a string of awards, including the John Christie Memorial Prize twice at Newcastle University, 1986–7; Eric Kennington Drawing Prize, 1990–1; and the David Murray Landscape Scholarship at RA, 1991. In that year, too, she gained a Northern Arts Artists' Bursary. Again in 1991 Hughes was granted a National Trust for Art Commission and a Procter & Gamble Ltd Commission. Held many visiting tutoring posts and residencies, especially in the northeast. Her work was described as being about "the power and atmosphere of places", tough and uncompromising. She began to show in mixed exhibitions in 1987 at Hatton Gallery, Newcastle University; other venues included RA, Mall Galleries and The Artists' View, Docklands, 1991. In 1992 she shared a show at Cadogan Contemporary and in 1994 won The Alasdair Gilchrist Fisher Memorial Award there. University of Northumbria (which gave her a show in 2005), National Trust and many corporate collections hold the work of Hughes, who was born and lived in Darlington, County Durham.

Beata HUGHES 1966– Painter, linguist and former banker, born in Ryki, Poland. After technical school specialising in electro-mechanics, in 1988 Hughes gained her master's in Scandinavian languages at Jagiellonian University, Cracow, subsequently studying law and finance in Poland and abroad. While studying in Sweden she spent six months in Mora, painting under tuition from a local sculptor. In 1997, commercial banking took her to London, but in 2000 Hughes gave it up to paint full-time, sharing a show at Crypt Gallery, St John's, Smith Square, in 2000. Her work sought "to explore and answer the most fundamental questions of human life, such as desire for meaning, suffering and human limits in comprehending the transcendental."

Ben HUGHES 1967– Self-taught painter, born in the west of England, who until 1999 was a chartered accountant and finance manager. He then became a full-time artist, notable for landscapes painted in Britain and abroad. Hughes took part in mixed exhibitions and shared shows in Bath and Honiton and in 2004 was included in W H Patterson's Six Selected Artists.

Christopher HUGHES 1881–1961 Painter, printmaker, illustrator and teacher, born in St Albans, Hertfordshire, he studied privately and acquired his artistic training from his father, Wyndham Hughes, who was a specialist in ecclesiastical decoration and stained glass. Christopher Hughes served at Marlborough College, 1920–46, as art master. Exhibited RA, Foyles Gallery, Walker's Galleries and in the west of England. Lived at Marlborough, Wiltshire.

Darren HUGHES 1970– Artist and lecturer, born in Bangor, Caernarvonshire, who did his art foundation diploma there at Gwynedd Technical College, 1989–90. Hughes gained an honours degree in fine art from Falmouth School of Art & Design, 1990–3; a postgraduate diploma from the Cyprus School of Art, Paphos, 1994–5; and a postgraduate certificate of education from Coleg Menai, 2002. He had a residency at Oriel Mostyn, Llandudno, 1999, in conjunction with Peter Prendergast's show New Paintings 1994–98. In 2001 Hughes was Young Welsh Artist of the Year – Young Wales 5, RCamA, the year the National Library of Wales, Aberystwyth, acquired his work. Group exhibitions included Landmarks, jointly with Iwan Parry, Oriel Ynys Mon, Llangefni, Anglesey, and with Owein Prendergast and Iwan Parry, Capsule Gallery, Cardiff, both 2002, and with Luned Parry and Eleri Jones at RCamA, 2004. Among Hughes's solo exhibitions were Ruthin Craft Centre, Ruthin, 2002, and New Work, The Albany Gallery, Cardiff, 2005. He was then a lecturer in printmaking and photography at Coleg Menai, Bangor. Hughes lived and worked in Bethesda, Gwynedd.

David HUGHES 1936–2003 Hughes was a squire who turned his hand to restoration and became a self-taught heraldic sculptor. Among Sir David's many monuments was the 400-year-old house of his mother's family in Wilburton, Cambridgeshire, which he restored, plus many artefacts such as his bronze of Christ, a memorial for his cousin, Beauchamp Pell, in St Peter's Church, Wilburton. Hughes was educated at Oundle School and Magdalene College, Cambridge, where he read French and Russian. For 11 years he was in the export team at Pye Unicam, selling scientific instruments to the Eastern Bloc. In 1970 he succeeded his father, the 13th baronet, leaving Pye three years later when Beauchamp Pell invited him, his wife and their four sons to live at the family home, The Berristead, which had been tenanted, provided they restored it. This prompted Hughes's creative nature and he modelled small sculptures in wax, then cast in solid metal. In 1979 he commercialised this interest by buying the ailing firm Louis Lejeune, producers of bronze and silver ornaments and car mascots, relocating the business to Wilburton. He expanded the company's range by sculpting bespoke heraldic trophies, table decorations and other items. Commissions included candle sconces for Ely Cathedral's choir stalls; four bronze eagle finials for the Great West Door of Westminster Abbey; an Eagle for the wand of the verger of St John's College Chapel, Cambridge; and a lion rampant, presented to Queen Elizabeth The Queen Mother when she opened Leech Hall, University of Durham. In his early sixties Hughes took to furniture-making and wood-carving. He was a member of the Art Workers' Guild.

David Gordon HUGHES 1957– Painter, born in Belfast, Northern Ireland, who evolved a style of work that initially involving covering his panels in gold leaf on which he then painted. The underlying gold gave his colour added intensity, not unlike the effect achieved by early Dutch masters who worked on copper panels, and Hughes additionally let the gold shine through the pigment in selected parts. He showed regularly at the RUA and RHA, was included in the 2005 Oakham Galleries Ltd Spring Exhibition and took part in other London and American mixed shows. Hughes had several solo exhibitions in Ireland and Dallas, Texas. The Ulster Museum in Belfast and several corporate collections held his work.

Dean HUGHES 1974– Versatile artist in wide range of media, born and lived in Manchester, who graduated from Chelsea College of Art and Design, 1993–6. He used mundane daily objects such as tickets, thread, masking tape and paper to create minutely detailed pieces, as in his contributions to the Hayward Gallery tour The British Art Show 5, 2000–1. Other group exhibitions included Banana Republic, Bund, 1996, one of several Matthew Higgs-curated exhibitions in which Hughes' work appeared; A-Z, The Approach, 1998; Getting the Corners, Or Gallery, Vancouver, Canada, 1999; and Point of View I and II, Richard Salmon Gallery, 2000. Among Hughes's solo exhibitions were Laure Genillard Gallery, from 1996; Gian Carla Zanutti Gallery, Milan, Italy, 1998; The International 3, Manchester, 2000; and Turnpike Gallery, Leigh, and 38 Langham Street, both 2002.

Des HUGHES 1970– Artist using a range of materials, as in his commission for The Showroom in 2003: The Screaming Abdabs. For that, Hughes continued his process of reconfiguring everyday surroundings and common objects. A series of human-scale figures, made from cardboard tubes, were the means of displaying medium- and smaller-scale works by the artist. Hughes was born in Birmingham, graduating from Bath College of Art, 1989–92, gaining his master's from Goldsmiths' College, 2000–2. Later group shows included The Way to Happiness, VTO, 2002, and Twilight, Gimpel Fils, 2003. In 2004, Hughes had a solo show at Whitechapel Project Space. He lived and worked in London.

Donald HUGHES 1881–1970 Artist, principally in watercolour and crayon, born in Clifton, Bristol, who continued to live in the city. He was a student at Heatherley's School of Fine Art under Iain Macnab and Henry Massey. Went on to become auctioneer and estate agent, but retired early to paint. Showed in London and the provinces and had first one-man show at Clifton Arts Club in 1924; for a time he was chairman of the Club. Was also a member of the Bristol Savages, being originally elected as a literary member, for he wrote several volumes of verse. In 1938 he wrote the text for the artist Kit Gunton's book *Birdsworth*. Bristol City Art Gallery holds Hughes' work. He bought Blaise Hamlet, and when his offer of it was refused by Bristol Corporation presented it to the National Trust.

Edith HUGHES fl. c.1910–1960 Painter, printmaker and designer who after initial education, partly in France, in 1913 attended Heatherley's School of Fine Art; also studied painting with Harold Gilman and Walter Sickert and printmaking with Ernest Jackson. Exhibited RA, RCamA, NPS, ROI, Goupil Gallery and Paris Salon. Lived in London.

Edith Burnet HUGHES 1888–1971 Architect and watercolourist, also known by her maiden name, Edith Burnet before marrying her architect husband T Harold Hughes. She was born in Edinburgh into a family with architectural connections, attended Aberdeen Art School, 1912–14, and was with A I Archts (Scot), 1914. After being on the staff of Aberdeen Art School and Technical College, 1915–18, and marriage in the latter year, she practised in Glasgow from 1921, becoming an associate of the RIBA in 1929. Coatbridge War Memorial, 1924; Mercat Cross, Glasgow, 1927–30; and St Clement's Chapel, Dunblane, are among her works. Hughes joined the Glasgow Society of Lady Artists in 1915, and among her commissions were alterations to its fine premises, in Blythswood Square, 1929 and 1934. She was the Club's vice-president in 1934, its president, 1946–9, and was also an Hon. Member. Photographs and watercolours of Hughes's architectural work were included in the Club's centenary exhibition at Collins Gallery, Glasgow, in 1982. She also participated in shows at Royal Glasgow Institute of the Fine Arts and RSA.

Eleanor HUGHES 1882–1959 Watercolourist, born in Christchurch, New Zealand. After initial education in New Zealand, she studied in Newlyn, Cornwall, with Stanhope Forbes and Elizabeth Forbes. Continued to live in Cornwall, at St Buryan, and was married to the artist Robert Morson Hughes. She exhibited RA, Goupil Gallery, NEAC, RI, SWA, Walker Art Gallery, Liverpool, and elsewhere. Oldham Art Gallery & Museum, Lancashire, holds her work.

Frank HUGHES 1905–1987 Painter, draughtsman and teacher, a Londoner born in St Pancras who settled in Muswell Hill. Although trained at St Martin's School of Art, Hughes worked for the capital's water board in an administrative capacity, a chore which enabled him to live and pay for his painting materials. A longstanding friendship with the painter Edward Bishop was important. With his companion Kathleen, Hughes travelled in France and Italy, producing drawings and watercolours of landscapes and café scenes which he would work up later into oil paintings. These, like his sensitive portraits, can be small and quite dark. Hughes, an exhibiting member of the NEAC, was very left-wing, a hater of the Establishment, who did, however, exhibit three landscapes at RA Summer Exhibitions between 1954–61. His diffidence prevented his showing widely. He was heavy smoker, starting with a cigarette, changing next to a cigar, then a pipe, and as a result suffered from emphysema.

Frederick George HUGHES 1924– Sculptor in plastic, born in Gibraltar. He was a member of Royal Glasgow Institute of the Fine Arts, also exhibiting in group shows including RA Summer Exhibitions, 1966–72, and Marjorie Parr Gallery. Lillie Art Gallery, Milngavie, holds two works in the manner of Naum Gabo, bought in 1973, Cyclops and Germination, Perspex and string abstracts. Lived in Henley-on-Thames, Oxfordshire.

Frieda HUGHES 1960– Painter of strong figurative works, and writer, daughter of the poet laureate Ted Hughes and the poet Sylvia Plath, brought up in Devon. She attended Bedales, then studied at St Martin's School of Art after an early marriage, selling greetings cards and three years in the Civil Service in Exeter. Travelled to Australia in 1988, where she bought a farm to which she returned periodically, also having a studio in south London. In 1999 she published a volume of poems, *Wooroloo*, having previously concentrated on children's books. Showed with Anna-Mei Chadwick. Her husband Laszlo was also a painter.

Glyn HUGHES 1931– Artist, gallery owner, critic, editor and teacher, full name Edward Glyn Hughes, who was born in Hawarden, Flint, Flintshire, and attended Bretton Hall, Yorkshire, 1951–3. He taught at Cobourg School, in the Old Kent Road, from 1953–6, and joined the ICA during the same period. In 1956 Hughes moved to Cyprus, where he taught in various schools. He participated in mixed exhibitions and was a member of the Cyprus Chamber of Fine Arts from its founding in 1960. From 1960–4 he owned and ran the Apophasis (Decision) Gallery with Christoforos Savva in Nicosia in the house where Savva lived, shows being held outside in the yard. When Cyprus became independent, the gallery moved to a better location in Apollo Street, where Hughes and Savva showed "their own and artists' work and included lectures, discussions, traditional music and play readings; there were speakers like the great Russian film director Sergei Bonderchuk and a photographic exhibition from the Hermitage Museum in what was then Leningrad". In 1960 Hughes and Savva took part in a UNESCO exhibition in Beirut, Lebanon. Hughes was also film and arts critic for the *Cyprus Mail*, arts editor for the *Cyprus Weekly* and designed for the Cypriot National Theatre, also abroad. In 1994, he took part in the Fifth Cairo Biennale of Art, Egypt, representing Cyprus. There was a 50-year retrospective of Hughes's work at Wrexham Arts Centre in 2005.

Glyn HUGHES 1958– Self-taught designer and pattern-maker notable for the sculpture of the mathematical genius Alan Turing that was completed for Sackville Park, Manchester, in 2001. Hughes's life-size bronze figure sits on a bench holding an apple, an allusion to the poisoned apple with which he committed suicide in 1954 after persecution for homosexuality. Turing helped invent an inaugural computer at Manchester University and became famous for his role in cracking the German Enigma code in World War II. Hughes disdained the description artist, describing the Turing memorial as "just another precision engineering job." He lived in Adlington, Lancashire.

Ian HUGHES 1958– Painter, art therapist, photographer and installations artist, born in Glasgow. Hughes studied at Duncan of Jordanstone College of Art, Dundee, 1976–80. For much of the 1980s he worked with the mentally sick, in the art therapy department at Stobhill Hospital, Glasgow, then at Royal Edinburgh Psychiatric Hospital. He had his first one-man show at 369 Gallery, Edinburgh, in 1985. In 1988–9 he worked as artist-in-residence at Scottish National Gallery of Modern Art, Edinburgh; had a solo show there in 1989 and in that year showed widely on the continent. Several large museums, as well as the Scottish National Gallery of Modern Art, hold his work which was deeply influenced by his time with the mentally deranged and which can be sad and disturbing but powerful.

Jim HUGHES 1934– Designer and teacher, born in Glasgow where he attended the School of Art, 1950–4, then Jordanhill College, obtaining his teaching certificate. Went on to lecture at Glasgow University's extra-mural department. Was elected to SGA in 1972. Showed in the Glasgow area, having work in the local public gallery. Lived in Ayr.

Ken HUGHES 1927– Sculptor and teacher, born in Liverpool. After Liverpool Collegiate School, 1938–43, took an engineering apprenticeship at the Royal Naval Artificer Training Establishment, Rosyth, 1943–7, then served as engine room artificer on HMS *Theseus* and *Black Swan* in the Far East. He attended Liverpool College of Art, 1949–51, then the Slade School of Fine Art, 1951–5, under A H Gerrard, Reg Butler and F E McWilliam. Hughes went on to teach at Birmingham College of Art and Bath Academy of Art, where he was head of sculpture, 1965–85. Hughes' main works were a Holy Family group in Southwark Cathedral and portraiture. His painted sculpture in relief and in the round was "influenced by German painting of the Weimar Republic" on which he lectured. Hughes took part in various group shows, including RA Summer Exhibition, and had solo shows at Ikon Gallery, Birmingham, 1969; Bristol City Art Gallery, 1971; Festival Gallery, Bath, 1982; Victoria Art Gallery, Bath, 1986; and Browse & Darby, 1995, which featured painted plaster figurative works with a dramatic element. In 2004 Hughes was included in The beginning of Ikon, at Ikon Gallery. Birmingham and Bristol City Art Galleries hold examples. Lived in Bristol.

Malcolm HUGHES 1920–1997 Systematic Constructivist artist, draughtsman, painter and teacher, born in Manchester. From 1938–9 he attended the College of Art there, then Royal College of Art in 1946–50. He taught part-time initially at Bath Academy of Art, where he remained 1960–70. From 1966–70 taught at Chelsea College of Art, from 1968–82 at Slade School of Fine Art, becoming emeritus reader in fine art at University of London. In 1969 Hughes was co-founder of the Systems Group. Hughes had his first one-man show at ICA in 1965. Among the group shows he contributed to were Four Artists: Reliefs, Constructions and Drawings, at Victoria & Albert Museum in 1971; Basically White at ICA in 1974; and British Art in the 60s, Tate Gallery in 1977; he also appeared in many overseas group shows; and in The Non-Objective

World Revisited at Annely Juda Fine Art in 1988. Hughes' work is held by British Council and Manchester City Art Galleries. The artist Jean Spencer was Hughes' companion for over 25 years, becoming his second wife in 1997. The Tate Gallery held a small joint memorial show in 1999. They lived in London.

Nigel HUGHES 1940– Painter, sculptor, designer and author, born in Camberley, Surrey, who became a full-time artist from 1977 when he attended the Royal Academy Schools under Peter Greenham and Norman Blamey. To produce his landscapes and wildlife studies in the romantic, figurative tradition Hughes travelled extensively, including the continent, Arabia, Africa, New Zealand, the South Pacific, South and Central America. Mexico was a special favourite. His solo exhibitions were held in Britain and widely abroad. He had a show in London at the Mexican Embassy when its president visited in 1985; at Guy Morrison in 1987; plus a series at Oliver Swann Galleries. Hughes' work featured in David Hicks' book *Living with Design*, 1979, and in several archaeological works on ancient American civilizations. Hughes guided a tour to Yucatan in 1987. Forty large watercolours of Maya monuments of Mexico and Central America were exhibited at Museo Nacional de Antropologia, Mexico; National Arts Club, New York; and at Canning House, London, in 2000, the year they were published as *Maya Monuments*, with Hughes' text. Hughes was the first artist to paint from live specimens all 50 species of the neotropical bird family *Cracidae*, shown at the Oxford University Museum of Natural History, Houston Museum of Natural Science, Missouri Botanical Garden in St Louis and Central Park Zoo, New York. Maritime Relics was held at The Fine Art Society in 2003. Commissions included HRH The Prince of Wales, the Grenadier Guards, National Trust and Tower of London. Limited-edition prints were produced of his works. Hughes was a fellow of the Linnean Society of London. Lived in County Down, Northern Ireland, and Bridport, Dorset.

Patrick HUGHES 1939– Painter, designer, teacher and writer, born in Birmingham. He studied at James Graham Teachers' Training College, Leeds, 1959–61, in the latter year having his first solo show at Portal Gallery. In 1961 also he showed in John Moores, Liverpool, Exhibition, the first of several appearances. For three years in the early 1960s Hughes taught in Leeds schools before becoming senior lecturer in painting and drawing at Leeds College of Art, 1964–9. After a year studying art education at London University Hughes taught for four years at Chelsea and Wolverhampton Schools of Art from 1970. In that year he had a one-man show at Angela Flowers Gallery, the first of many there. Later one-man exhibitions included, all in 2001: Properspective, Flowers East; Park Ryu Sook Gallery, Seoul, South Korea; Flowers Central; Louis K Meisel, New York, America; and Hyperspective, Flowers West, Santa Monica, California; and in 2002 Riperspective at Birmingham Museum and Art Gallery. Doors Etcetera was Hughes's solo show at Flowers New York, 2003–4. The prolific Hughes also participated in numerous group shows internationally. His pictures had a strong jokey element, featuring odd perspectives, rainbows and visual paradoxes. These were themes taken up in books such as *Upon the Pun, Dual Meaning in Words and Pictures*, produced with Paul Hammond, in 1978, and *Moron Oxymoron*, of 1983. Hughes' work is held by Arts Council, Tate Gallery and British Council. He was the second husband of the writer and artist Molly Parkin. Lived in London.

Philip HUGHES 1936– Versatile, self-taught artist, born in London, who studied at Cambridge University and whose extensive worldwide travels shaped his work. The structure of landscape and archaeology were key preoccupations. Hughes was a co-founder of the software company Logica. In 1984 for BBC2 Television he made a programme on his own view of the future, examining work and art in society. From 1988–92 he was a council member of the Royal College of Art; from 1990–6 was on the board of the Design Museum; and from 1996 was for several years chairman of the trustees of the National Gallery, the first artist to hold the position. A mural for Quaglino's restaurant, wall hangings for Boots of Nottingham and brooches and bracelets based on paintings were aspects of Hughes's work. He showed solo with Francis Kyle Gallery from 1979. The Museum and Art Gallery, Inverness, held a 20-year retrospective in 1990. In 1998 a retrospective toured Australia, coinciding with the publication of *Patterns in the Landscape The Notebooks of Philip Hughes*. In 2000–1, Tate St Ives held Hughes's exhibition The Tin Route.

Robert Alwyn HUGHES 1935– Painter, graphic artist, film maker and teacher, born in Dowlais, Glamorgan. He attended Newport College of Art, 1953–7, Leicester College of Art, 1957–8, and Royal College of Art, 1958–61. From the early 1970s, he was in charge of Taliesin Films, becoming known for experimental films and photographic projects. Showed at Howard Roberts Gallery in Cardiff, McRoberts and Tunnard in London, SWG, Royal National Eisteddfod and abroad. Among his films was a semi-documentary on the poet Idris Davies. CASW bought his oil painting Send Back Your Homing Pigeons, Dai. Indistinct Breath of the Image was a survey of Hughes's paintings and prints, 1990–06, at Newport Museum and Art Gallery in 2006. Of the exhibition, the gallery wrote: "'These are disruptive and exciting times' aptly sums up the most recent work. The subject matter and narrative belongs to the past but the imagery to the present day."

Robert Evans HUGHES 1896–1970 Painter and draughtsman, born in Llanwrst, Denbighshire. Having lived in Australia with his family he volunteered for service with the Australian Army and during action in France was blown up and almost paralysed. In Australia he began painting under the tuition of Maud Russell. Later had tuition at the Royal Society, studied in Rome and at Central School of Arts and Crafts under Bernard Meninsky and F J Porter. Settled in North Wales, finally at Rhyl, where he was a founder-member of the Colour Society and Prestatyn 57 Group; was also a member of the UA and was president of the Denbighshire Art Society, Colwyn Bay. Showed UA, ROI, NS, RCamA and elsewhere. Flintshire Education Committee owns his work. Retrospective exhibition at Rhyl Library Museum and Arts Centre in 1988. Hughes was notable for his Welsh landscapes and for the fact that he overcame colour blindness to paint.

Robert Morson HUGHES 1873–1953 Primarily a landscape painter, in oil, Hughes married the painter Eleanor Waymouth (Hughes). He attended Lambeth School of Art and the South London Technical Art School. Exhibited RA,

IS, ROI, Goupil Gallery and NEAC. Leeds City Art Gallery holds his work. Lived finally at St Buryan, Cornwall.

Ronnie HUGHES 1965– Painter who gained a first-class degree in 1988 from University of Ulster in Belfast where he was born, then his master's degree in fine art, 1989. Architectural images and words were notable features of his canvases. His work won first prize at the Taylor Awards in 1989; it was chosen for the Claremorris Open Exhibition in 1989 and 1992; and it appeared in the 1994 shows Works on Paper and Beyond the Partitions, put on by Queen Street Studios, Belfast, with which he was associated. His later solo exhibitions included City Reformed, at Rubicon Gallery, Dublin, and Limerick City Gallery of Art, both 1993. Hughes' work received wide media coverage and is held by Arts Council of Northern Ireland, Irish Contemporary Arts Society and Monaghan County Museum.

Stephen HUGHES 1952– Artist and teacher working in a variety of materials, primarily known as a sculptor, who was born in Salisbury, Southern Rhodesia. Before attending Goldsmiths' College School of Art, 1984–7, where he gained an honours degree in fine art, Hughes worked in factories, including ceramics and brass. After Goldsmiths', he was Picker Fellow at Kingston upon Thames Polytechnic. He lectured at Goldsmiths', 1992–3, from then on at Kingston University. His many group appearances included Adam Gallery, 1986; Mandy Loves Declan 100%, Mark Boote Gallery, New York, 1993; Arts Council's tour Recent British Sculpture, 1993–4; Computer World, The Tannery, 1996; and John Moores Liverpool Exhibition, Walker Art Gallery, 1997–8, where he was a prize winner. Had solo exhibition at The Showroom, 1987, and Galerie Philippe Casini, Paris, 1992. He was latterly represented by Dominic Berning. Arts Council holds examples. Lived in London.

Thomas Gwynfryn HUGHES 1923–1988 Printmaker and teacher, born in Ynyshir, Glamorgan. He attended Cardiff College of Art, in the late-1940s starting a teaching career that included the senior lectureship in illustration and printmaking at Newport College of Art. In 1974 was involved in An Iconograph of the *Mabinogion*, concerned with the medieval collection of Welsh folk stories, in connection with the Royal National Eisteddfod and WAC; he also showed with SWG and Northampton Arts Society. WAC holds his work.

Wren HUGHES 1955– Sculptor, born in Yorkshire, who studied in the studios of Sally Arnup and John Skeaping from 1972–4 and with James Butler at the City and Guilds of London Art School, 1974–7. Her welded-steel figures were said to "portray the joy and pain of life and explore the interface between light and matter. They are sometimes dark, sometimes witty and sometimes paradoxical." Although small, Hughes's sculptures could "appear monumental, often evoking an atmosphere of timelessness and an invitation to connect with the life beyond the form." Mixed shows included RA Summer Exhibition, Benjamin C Hargreaves and abroad. Among solo exhibitions were Southwark Cathedral, 1984; Studio, Stanton Harcourt, Oxford, 1994 and 1997, and she shared a show at Oxford Art Week, 2001. Southwark Cathedral and Sir Roger de Grey owned examples.

Blair HUGHES-STANTON 1902–1981 Wood engraver, painter, draughtsman and teacher, born in London, son of the artist Sir Herbert Hughes-Stanton, his first wife was the printmaker Gertrude Hermes. He was educated at Colet Court and HMS *Conway*, then studied art at Byam Shaw School, 1919–22, Royal Academy Schools, 1922–3, and at Leon Underwood's School, 1923–5. While married to Gert Hermes he collaborated with her to illustrate John Bunyan's *The Pilgrim's Progress*, 1928. He succeeded John Maynard as head of the Gregynog Press, 1931, and with his second wife, Ida Graves, established the Gemini Press, illustrating her *Epithalamion* in 1934. In 1938 he won an International Prize for Engraving at Venice Biennale. Hughes-Stanton taught at Westminster School of Art, 1934–9; Colchester School of Art, 1945–7, after war service; St Martin's School of Art, 1947–8; and Central School of Arts and Crafts, 1948–80. He was a member of LG, SWE and a founder-member of the International Society of Wood Engravers. Showed with Redfern, Leicester and Cooling Galleries, Royal Glasgow Institute of the Fine Arts and RHA. The Ashmolean Museum, Oxford, held The wood-engravings of Gertrude Hermes and Blair Hughes-Stanton in 1995 and North House Gallery, Colchester, Unique Works on Paper, 2004. Contemporary Art Society, Whitworth Art Gallery in Manchester and other public collections hold examples. Lived latterly in Manningtree, Essex.

Julian HUGHES-WATTS 1969– Painter, born in Cardiff, whose work included geometrical abstracts in bright colours, such as his acrylic on canvas Delodur, Royal Over-Seas League Open, 1995. Hughes-Watts studied at Birmingham College of Fine Art and Royal Academy Schools. He gained a Leverhulme Scholarship, 1991–4, and the Worshipful Company of Painter-Stainers Award, RA, 1994. Group exhibitions included 22 Cork Street, 1993, and in 1994 Premiums Exhibition, Sotheby; New Burlington Gallery; and Fresh Art, Business Design Centre, Islington.

David HUGO 1958– Artist who studied at Wolverhampton Polytechnic, 1977–80, and the Royal College of Art, 1981–4. In 1983 he took part in A Frozen Moment at the College's Print Gallery. In 1984 Hugo gained a conference centre commission from Edward Cullinan Architects. There was a solo show at Lanchester Gallery, Coventry, in 1985. Mythology, religion and science were important in his work, see his exhibition Between Scylla and Charybdis: David Hugo, University of Warwick, 1988, as sculptor-in-residence there. In that year Hugo created the wall sculpture Sensedatum: Hour Glass II, in mixed media, which he gave to the University and took part in the Inaugural Exhibition at Delfina Studios, in east London. He also participated in East End Open Studios, based at Delfina, in 1989.

James HUGONIN 1950– Painter and teacher, born in Barnard Castle, County Durham. He studied at Winchester School of Art, West Surrey College of Art and Design in Farnham and at Chelsea School of Art. Went on to teach at Chelsea and at colleges in the northeast of England. He was a member of the Newcastle Group of artists and was included in South Bank Centre's touring show of 1988–9, The Presence of Painting. One-man shows included Galerie Brigitte Hilger, Aachen, 1983; Graeme Murray Gallery, Edinburgh, and Bede Gallery, Jarrow, 1985; and Galerie Hoffman, Friedberg, 1987. Reacting against free, gestural painting surrounding him at art school in the 1970s Hugonin sought a style by which he could create work balanced "between extreme complexity of means on the one hand and the apparent simplicity of the overall image on the other". Tiny fragments of colour created a texture with sweeps and rhythm, the visual equivalent of music, with a Zen-like stillness. Hugonin was a slow worker, completing one picture a year, as seen in the sparse survey of three years' work at Ingleby Gallery, Edinburgh, in 2002. James Hugonin and Ian Stephenson: And our eyes scan Time, at Baltic Centre for Contemporary Art in 2006, was curated by Hugonin. Twelve of his paintings, 1992–05, hung in a single room, the rest of the gallery being devoted to the work of Stephenson, Hugonin's teacher and lifelong inspiration, whom he had met at Chelsea in the mid-1970s. Arts Council holds his work. Lived in remote Cheviot Hills, at Wooler, Northumberland. His wife Sarah Hugonin was also an artist.

Thelma HULBERT 1913–1995 Painter and teacher, born in Bath, Somerset, where she studied at the School of Art. During the 1930s Hulbert was close to the group of artists which included William Coldstream, Victor Pasmore, Claude Rogers and Graham Bell which eventually became the Euston Road School. After the interruption of the war years she travelled in America, Africa and on the continent, while continuing to paint in her London studio. From 1962–72 she taught at Central School of Art and Design. Hulbert took part in numerous exhibitions, including solo shows at Leicester, Redfern and Marjorie Parr Galleries and a retrospective at Whitechapel Art Gallery in 1962. Arts Council, Contemporary Art Society, provincial and foreign galleries hold her work. Died at home in Honiton, Devon.

Anthony HULL 1964– Artist, notable as a printmaker, who graduated with honours from Chelsea School of Art, 1983–6, attending Slade School of Fine Art, 1986–8. He was in Class of '86, London Institute Show at Royal Festival Hall, and Chelsea Box Print, Angela Flowers, both 1986; Whitworth New Contemporaries at Whitworth Art Gallery, Manchester, and National Printmakers' Exhibition, Printmakers' Council and Whatman Papers, Royal Festival Hall, both 1987; and East End Open Studios, at Carpenter's Road, 1989.

Frederick W HULL 1867–1953 Belfast, Northern Ireland, businessman, born in Drogheda, County Wexford, who took up painting in his thirties. Studied part-time at Government School of Design and privately with the landscape and flower artist David Gould. Harvey was a member and president of Ulster Arts Club and a member of Belfast Art Society, also showing at Walker Art Gallery in Liverpool and RHA. Ulster Museum holds his work.

James HULL 1921–1990 Painter and interior designer, born in London, where he died. From a working-class background, Hull studied architectural design before World War II, during which he served in the Army, 1939–46, eventually becoming a toymaker and scenery designer. His first paintings were Surrealistic, but this changed to a Constructionist style using pure colour and basic geometrical shapes. With the help of Herbert Read Hull had his first exhibition in the Brook Street Gallery in 1949, then his reputation as a member of the avant-garde grew as he showed at Gimpel Fils and painted his mural The Story of Coal for the Festival of Britain's Dome of Discovery in 1951. Began to show in Paris and New York, but economic pressures spurred him to enter and win a competition to design the interior of the *Daily Mirror* building, and he worked for the IPC publishing conglomerate until 1970. After an idyllic sojourn in Ibiza he did a variety of designing jobs in several continents, returning to London in straitened circumstances in 1980. During the period before his death his reputation as a pioneer abstractionist was re-established with shows at the Camden Galleries and Whitford and Hughes.

Norman Thomas Stephen HULL 1901–c.1978 Painter and ceramic artist. Born at Church Gresley, Staffordshire, he studied art at Nottingham College of Art, Derby College of Art and Stoke-on-Trent College of Art. Exhibited RI, in the provinces and America, and at the Paris Salon, where he won a bronze medal in 1957. He was managing director of Honiton Art Potteries and the Norman Hull Pottery, Devon, and his work is in various royal collections. Was a fellow of the Royal Society of Arts until he died, and lived at Worthing, Sussex.

Michael HULLIS 1955– Sculptor and teacher who studied at Ipswich School of Art, 1974–5, Bristol Polytechnic, 1975–8, then became a technician at Sir John Cass School of Art, 1979–82. From 1982 was a part-time lecturer there and at Sidcup Arts Centre. Hullis' mixed show appearances included a Goldsmiths' exhibition at Woodlands Art Gallery, 1983.

Ursula HULME 1917– Artist in various media, textile designer and art therapist, born in Cottbus, Germany. She lived in Berlin and studied at the Reimann School there under Maria May, moving to England in 1938 where she worked as a freelance fabric designer. From 1961 Hulme worked as a voluntary art therapist for several medical centres. In 1978 she founded and became president of the registered charity Conquest, The Society for Art for Physically Handicapped People. Hulme was a member of Free Painters and Sculptors and of Richmond Art Group. She had several solo shows at Woodstock Gallery, 1960–70, and at Talent Store, 1990. Lived in East Ewell, Epsom, Surrey.

Gary HUME 1962– Painter whose output ranged from early rigorous geometrical abstracts and a series of door-based images to later exuberantly colourful figurative pictures. Hume was born in Kent, and studied at Liverpool Polytechnic, 1985–6, and Goldsmiths' College School of Art, 1986–8. Group shows included Lorence Monk Gallery, New York, and Esther Schipper, Cologne, both 1989, and South Bank Centre's touring The British Art Show, 1990. Had solo exhibitions at Karsten Schubert Ltd from 1989; one of strange, pathetic and unsettling new works at ICA in 1995; in 1997 a range of his pictures was shown, in a shared exhibition with Fiona Rae, at Saatchi Gallery; and in 1999 Hume represented Britain at the Venice Biennale and had shows at Dean Gallery, Edinburgh, and Whitechapel Art Gallery. In 1996 he was included in the Turner Prize exhibition at the Tate Gallery and in 1997 won the Jerwood Prize. He was elected RA in 2001. There was a retrospective at the Irish Museum of Modern Art, Dublin, 2003. Lived in London.

Effie HUMMERSTON 1891– Watercolourist, born in Leeds where she studied at the School of Art and continued to live. Exhibited RI, RWS, in Leeds and at Walker Art Gallery, Liverpool.

Campbell HUMPHREYS 1910–1948 Artist in black-and-white and wash and typographer. Studied at Glasgow School of Art, 1927–38, under Hugh Adam Crawford and Henry Alison. Then worked mainly in the advertising industry. Lived at Falkirk, Stirlingshire.

David HUMPHREYS 1937– Artist in acrylic, watercolour and etching, and teacher, born in London but with strong Welsh connections. He studied at Durham University, 1958–62, with Victor Pasmore as tutor, and gained the Thomas Penman Scholarship and a State Scholarship. After graduation Humphreys taught at Ravensbourne College of Art & Design, 1963–9, then painted and travelled full-time. While most of his landscapes were set in Wales, Humphreys spent part of each year in the Hebrides, also visiting countries such as Czechoslovakia, Mexico, Peru and Chile. The relationship of figures to landscape and elements of Symbolism were aspects of Humphreys' work. Took part in many group shows including Arts Council Young Contemporaries, 1960; John Moores Liverpool Exhibition from 1967; Royal National Eisteddfod of Wales from 1968; RCamA, 1989; and The Discerning Eye, Mall Galleries from 1991. He had a series of solo shows at Galerie Basilisk, Morgue, Switzerland from 1972, later shows including Dieter Matschke, Leipzig, Germany, 1991, and Gottesman, Jones & Partners, 1992. Arts Council, several education authorities and provincial universities hold Humphreys' work. Lived in St Davids, Pembrokeshire.

Henry Norman HUMPHREYS 1905–1955 Painter, designer and teacher, born in Liverpool. Studied at the School of Art there, 1925–31, under William Penn and George Marples, then from 1931–3 at the Royal College of Art under Sir William Rothenstein and Barnett Freedman. Held a number of teaching posts, including Leamington Spa, Hastings and Wrexham Schools of Art. Exhibited RA, Walker Art Gallery, Liverpool, and other provincial galleries. Illustrated a Welsh translation of *Aesop's Fables*. Bootle Museum and Art Gallery holds his work. Lived at Lower Foxdale, Isle of Man.

Ian HUMPHREYS 1956– Painter and lecturer, born in Hertfordshire, who studied at Berkshire College of Arts & Design, 1973–5, eventually teaching painting there, graduating with honours from Exeter College of Art, 1976–9. He designed sets for Plymouth Opera, his paintings being chosen for Richard Marquand's 1987 film about the rock music world *Hearts of Fire*, featuring Bob Dylan and Ian Dury. From 1973 Humphreys took part in numerous mixed shows in Britain and abroad, including the RA Summer Exhibition; Hunting Art Prizes at Royal College of Art; LG at Barbican Centre; Eton Art Gallery, Eton; Houldsworth Fine Art; Spacex Gallery, Exeter; and Beaux Arts, Bath. Reading Museum and Art Gallery and several corporate collections hold examples.

Johanne HUMPHREYS 1968– Sculptor and teacher making abstracted works in a variety of materials, who "dealt with the influence modern farming methods have on landscape, surrounding my area of Suffolk." She was born there in Lowestoft. Gained a first-class honours degree at Manchester Polytechnic, 1989–92, experience then included organising exhibitions for Clock House Artists Association; being a foundry mould-maker; backdrop painting for photographers; and visiting lecturer at Lowestoft College of Further Education. In 1998 participated in return project in Minnesota, America. Exhibitions included Yew Tree Open, 1st Open Studio Exhibition, Laxfield, 1992; two-man show at Peter Pears Gallery, Aldeburgh, 1994; On the Border, Christchurch Mansion, Ipswich, 1997; and a shared show at Chappel Galleries, Chappel, 1998. Had a solo exhibition at Neal Street, Covent Garden, 1993. Humphreys' husband was the artist Laurence Edwards.

John HUMPHREYS 1929– Painter in oil, born in Bethlehem, in South Africa's Orange Free State. After education in Johannesburg he attended Heatherley's School of Fine Art under Iain Macnab, then with Stanley Grimm in the mid-1950s. He joined ROI in 1977 and won the Stanley Grimm Prize four years later. Also showed with RA, RI, RSMA and at Paris Salon. Lived in Greenford, Middlesex.

Winifred O HUMPHREYS 1895–1975 Versatile artist and teacher working in many media, born in Liverpool, where she attended the School of Art, then Slade School of Fine Art. In the inter-war years she worked mainly in the city, being a student tenant at the Bluecoat School and a member of the Sandon Studios Society. Humphreys completed portraits, murals, woodcuts, modelling and decorative panels for ships, stores, clubs, churches; stage and costume design for David Lewis, Sandon and Playhouse theatres; design of floats and costumes for Liverpool Centenary Railway Exhibition and the Lancashire Cotton Pageant at Belle Vue, Manchester, in the 1930s. In the 1940s she began the Quiet Club at the Royal Institution for services personnel. Taught in schools and technical colleges in Liverpool and north Wales, in 1946 moving to Naid-y-March, Holywell, Flintshire, where she died. Humphreys latterly developed a technique for mosaic plaques and panels using broken china and tiles. Showed at IS, Walker Art Gallery in Liverpool and Manchester City Art Gallery. A privately printed monograph on Humphreys was published in 1980, three years after a memorial show in Mold.

Geoffrey HUMPHRIES 1945– Artist, draughtsman, musician and lecturer, born in Amersham, Buckinghamshire, who worked mainly from the figure. He studied at High Wycombe School of Art, the London College of Printing and Chelsea School of Art. In 1963, he visited Italy for the first time and took his degree at the Accademia di Belle Arti, in Venice. After studying in Rome and Florence he moved back to Venice in 1966, where he continued to live and work and portrayed some of its lesser-known corners. At his studio, which overlooked the Guidecca Canal and was a centre for music and the arts, he ran courses on painting and life drawing. Humphries was an accomplished blues guitarist and spent time each year painting and exhibiting in the American deep south: New Orleans, Charleston and Savannah. He was a guest lecturer at the Royal College of Art. He carried out extensive portrait commissions, some of his works being shown at the National Portrait Gallery and the RP. Humphries also showed widely in Italy and elsewhere on the continent, London venues including the RA Summer Exhibition,

Chelsea Arts Club, Albion Fine Art and with Manya Igel Fine Arts. His works were held by public and private collections throughout Europe and North America.

Tristan HUMPHRIES 1962–2000 Artist and lecturer, born in London, married to the painter Karyn White. He did a foundation course at Chelsea College of Art, 1979–80, then graduated with honours in fine art from Ravensbourne College of Art and Design, 1980–3. Humphries' appointment as official copyist at the National Portrait Gallery from 1983 was the first in a wide-ranging career connected with digital imaging which embraced residencies, lectureships, conference appointments as organiser and speaker, editorships and positions as external examiner. These latterly included research consultant, The Kent Institute, and artist-in-residence Visualeyes Imaging Ltd, both 1997; senior research fellow, RMIT University, Melbourne, Australia, 1997–9; visiting lecturer, Sydney College of the Arts, Rozelle, Sydney, and The Tasmanian College of the Arts, Hobart, both 1998; and selector, The Australian Paper Awards 1999, The Arts Centre of Victoria. Humphries participated in many group shows, later solo exhibitions including A Shoebox and a Piece of String, The Coningsby Gallery and Visualeyes Imaging Ltd, both 1997; and Cadavres exquis, The Renard Wardell Gallery, Melbourne, and Australian tour, 1999. Among Humphries' commissions were: Portrait of the conductor Karl Böhm for London Symphony Orchestra, 1980; Mural painting, Hampton Court, Mackenzie Wheeler Architects, 1992; Glass mural painting, National Westminster Bank, Watford, 1993; and Digital portrait of Alex Allan, British High Commissioner, and Katie Clemson, artist, for British Council of Australia, 1999. There was a Humphries memorial show at The Coningsby Gallery, entitled The Illuminated Calvino, 2001.

Mark HUMPHRYS 1925– Painter, mural artist, carver in wood and stone and teacher, born in Monaco. He studied at Winchester School of Art, where his teachers included Leonard Daniels; Southampton and Bournemouth Colleges of Art. Went on to lecture at St Hild's College, Durham. Showed with LG, Wessex Artists and Hampshire Artists. Lived in Durham.

Anna HUNT 1946– Artist born in Newcastle upon Tyne who studied at the University of Newcastle. Her 1998 picture Eames House was contributed to East International, at Norwich School of Art & Design in 1999. It was one of a series over five years in which Hunt had "been translating photographs of modernist architecture into thread on canvas." She was included in Hayward Gallery tour The British Art Show 5, 2000–1. Lived in Brighton, Sussex.

Cecil Arthur HUNT 1873–1965 Landscape painter, born in Torquay, Devon. Studied at Cambridge University, practised as a barrister, then during World War I took up painting full-time. Was by that time known for his writings on the law. Hunt was especially fond of his watercolour portraits of mountains, dramatic and with an assured handling of broad planes. His work were reproduced in the *Alpine Journal* and *Alpine Calendar*, by the Medici Society and in many publications. Exhibited prolifically at RWS, of which for several years in the early 1930s he was vice-president, Fine Art Society, RBA, Ridley Art Club, Walker's Galleries and elsewhere. British Museum, Victoria & Albert Museum, Fitzwilliam Museum in Cambridge and many provincial galleries hold his work. In 1996 Chris Beetles Ltd held an exhibition of Hunt's pictures with a catalogue comprehensively covering his life, travels and output. Lived in London and at Manaton, Devon.

Christine HUNT 1945– Artist, born in Birmingham, who studied fine art and art history at Hereford College of Art and Design, 1991–5. She settled at Walterstone, Herefordshire, combining organic hill farming with running her own studio Cellar Gallery, from 2000 affiliated to Galleries in the Black Mountains with Caroline Downey. Several works by Hunt interpreted the work of the poet India Russell published in 2003. In that year she completed a commissioned work for presentation to HRH The Prince of Wales and her painting Deluge was used in the Hereford Flood Campaign, thousands of copies being sent to the Houses of Parliament. Exhibitions included Hay Literary Festival, Hay-on-Wye, from 2000; Abergavenny Food Festival, from 2001; and The Celebration, Brecon Art Gallery, 2003.

Edgar HUNT 1876–1953 Painter of animals and rustic scenes, born in Birmingham. As a child Edgar began sketching farm life, encouraged by his father, a part-time art teacher. He was influenced by his uncle Walter Hunt, whose The Dog in the Manger was bought by the influential Chantrey Bequest in 1885. Edgar Hunt showed with the RBSA, at the Walker Art Gallery in Liverpool and at the London Salon. When his friend the admired sporting artist John Frederick Herring junior died in 1907 Hunt was much affected, thereafter withdrawing from the world and rarely leaving his Sussex farm. W H Patterson included Hunt in Fine English & Continental Paintings in 2003 and Richard Green also showed his work.

Georgina HUNT 1922– Painter, born in Reading, Berkshire, who worked in many media, mainly in acrylic and oil. Her abstract, spray-painted paintings had a feeling of calmness and mystery. Hunt worked to liberate colour from the restraints of imagery, feeling that all shapes or lines had associational connotations. She studied with William Coldstream at Slade School of Fine Art, 1945–50. In 1976 she won a Greater London Arts Association major award, in 1993 gaining the Osaka 21st Century Association Prize, Osaka International Triennale. Group exhibitions included Blackheath Art Society, 1966; Hunter College, New York, 1972; LG, Barbican Centre, and Chelsea Arts Club (of which she was a member), both 1992; and United Abstract Artists, Mall Galleries, 1994. Had a solo show at Drian Gallery, 1967, with series at SPACE Studios from 1974 and Camden Studios from 1984. Hunter College; London Borough Hounslow Picture Loan Scheme; and Contemporary Arts and Culture Centre, Osaka, hold examples. Lived in London.

Gerry HUNT 1927– Abstract painter and draughtsman, born in London. He studied at Camberwell School of Art, 1953–5, and Slade School of Fine Art, 1955–7, then went on to teach at Camberwell for many years. Showed widely in London and at John Moores Liverpool Exhibition, 1963, 1965 and 1989–90. Coracle Press published his *Some Principles and Practice of Twelve Modern Art Styles* in 1980, and he showed with Coracle. Had exhibitions of drawings at Camberwell School in 1986–8. Lived in London.

Kate HUNT fl. from 1990s– Artist and teacher who studied at St Martin's School of Art, 1969–70; Byam Shaw School of Art, 1970–1; Putney School of Art, 1984–6; Sir John Cass School of Art, 1986–8; then for her master's in drawing in fine art practice at Wimbledon School of Art. Taught from 1992–8 at Hornsby House School. Group exhibitions included the R A Summer Exhibition from 1993; Beatrice Royal Gallery, Eastleigh, from 1995; The Hunting Art prizes, 1998; and New Year Exhibition, Cadogan Contemporary, 1999. Among her solo exhibitions were Beatrice Royal and Gallery of Modern Art, both 1996, and The Stables Gallery, 1998. She lived in London.

Kay HUNT fl. from 1960s– Painter and teacher who was born in London. She studied at Camberwell School of Art and went on to teach at West Surrey College of Art and Design, Farnham. She showed at AIA Gallery, LG, South London Art Gallery, Camden Arts Centre and in a long series of Space Exhibitions, including Space from the Quadrangle at Woodlands Art Gallery, 1973. Had a solo show at Courtauld Institute.

Sue HUNT 1959– Painter, printmaker and teacher who did a foundation course at High Wycombe College of Art, 1977–8; gained an honours degree in fine art, Canterbury College of Art, 1978–81; then her master's in fine art, Cardiff College of Art, 1985–7. Teaching experience included senior lecturer in printmaking at Norwich School of Art, 1991–4; part-time lecturing in fine art at University of Wales Institute Cardiff, from 1991; a series of visiting lectureships from 1994, including Coleg Glan Hafren, Cardiff, and Atlantic College, St Donats; and a senior lectureship in fine art at University of Wales, Cardiff, from 1998. In 1986 Hunt gained a WAC award to study in America and Mexico City researching murals; in 1988 under a Wales/Philadelphia Exchange, Brandywine Printworkshop, she was involved in producing a suite of lithographs and organising a student coalition to design and make a large mural in downtown Philadelphia; and in 1992 gained a WAC travel grant to research paper-making and wood block printing in Rajasthan, India. In 1995 she was selector and curator of the Wales/Saragossa exhibition in Spain and in the Laing Painting Competition was a regional award winner. Hunt became a member of Association of Designers and Artists of Wales and of Pioneers Arts Group/Art Wales, both 1981; and of 56 Group Wales, 1994. Exhibitions included Wish you were here, Chapter Art Centre, Cardiff, 1986; Welsh Printmakers' Council touring show, 1989; Hyde Park Gallery, 1992; Castle Museum, Norwich, 1994; Shared Language, Newport Museum & Art Gallery and tour, 1997; and 6 Printmakers, Howard Gardens Gallery, Cardiff, 2000. Solo exhibitions included New Burlington Gallery, 1998, and Cardiff Bay Arts Trust, 1999. Lived in Roath, Cardiff.

Tom HUNT 1920– Artist, born in Swinton, Lancashire, working mainly in oil and alkyd. Won a scholarship to Regional College of Art, Manchester, 1934–6, studied figure drawing at evening classes, 1943–7, then taught himself to paint after seeing the Gauguin Centenary Exhibition in Paris in 1949. First showed at Mid-Day Studios, Manchester, 1948–51, then from 1950s held solo shows at his studio in Victoria Park, at galleries across the northwest and participated in group exhibitions in England and Wales. In 1962 he showed a series of paintings interpreting music at Bridge House Galleries which received an enthusiastic response from the conductor of the Hallé Orchestra, Sir John Barbirolli. Hunt wrote that he "liked new challenges", and other subjects included landscape, people, still life, car crashes and football. There was a retrospective at The Portico Gallery, Manchester, 1995. He lived nearby at Ashton-under-Lyne.

Alec Butler HUNTER 1899–1958 Textile designer, born in London, who studied at Byam Shaw School of Art under Ernest Jackson. He was a director of Warner and Sons Ltd. Lived at Thaxted, Essex.

Alexis HUNTER 1948– Artist who employed photography, born in Auckland, New Zealand. She studied at Elam School of Art, 1966–9, and took a teaching diploma in art and art history in 1971. Became a member of the Association of Cinematographers and Television Technicians. Showed at Hayward Annual, 1978; Palais des Beaux-Arts, Brussels, 1979; Summer Show 2 at Serpentine Gallery, 1981; and Woodlands Art Gallery, 1981–2, touring exhibition of Greater London Arts Association award winners. Solo shows included ICA, 1978, and New 57 Gallery, Edinburgh, 1980. Arts Council, Scottish National Gallery of Modern Art and Otago University in New Zealand hold examples. Lived in London. In 2002, Bottaccio Galleries staged Realising Gentileschi, Hunter's ongoing performance on the seventeenth-century painter plus new computer works.

Caroline HUNTER 1964– Painter, writer and illustrator, born in Edinburgh, who lived for periods in Orkney, before settling in the Scottish Borders, 1995. After gaining her master's with honours in the history of art at Aberdeen University, 1982–6, she was an archaeological fieldworker in Scotland, 1986–91; catalogued pottery for the National Portrait Gallery, 1991–2; returned to Orkney, working as a waitress and nanny, 1992; and in 1994 wrote, illustrated and published *Sandy and the Spoot Boots* and had her first solo show at Bu Gallery, Stromness, 1995. Later solo exhibitions including Mainhill Gallery, Edinburgh International Festival, 2000, and John Martin of London, 2004, where work on show revealed Hunter as a rich and painterly Colourist. Mixed shows included RSW and SSA, both 1997, and the Royal Glasgow Institute of the Fine Arts, 1999, winning the Torrance Prize.

Elizabeth HUNTER 1935– Painter in oil, printmaker, curator and teacher, born and lived in Bristol, who studied at Slade School of Fine Art under Claude Rogers, Anthony Gross and Lucian Freud, gaining her diploma with special commendation, 1958. From 1964–6 she was curator of the Passmore Edwards Art Gallery in Newlyn, later becoming teacher of life drawing at the School of Art & Design, Bristol. Group shows included Young Contemporaries; Kunstverein in Hanover, Germany; Penwith and Newlyn Societies; RA Summer Exhibitions, and elsewhere. Solo shows included Arnolfini Gallery, Bristol, 1964, and Bath College of Higher Education, 1994, where Hunter's key Inanna Series was shown, "potent and glowing images of birds, beasts and mythologies". Was a member of the Newlyn Society. The Printworks, Market House Gallery, Marazion, gave Hunter an exhibition in 2003.

Ian HUNTER 1947– Environmental sculptor and teacher, born in Londonderry, Northern Ireland. He gained his diploma in sculpture from Ulster College of Art and Design, Belfast, 1965–9; did his teacher training at Leeds Polytechnic, 1969–70; gained his master's degree at University of Case Western Reserve, Cleveland, Ohio, in America, 1975–7; and obtained his doctorate from Manchester Polytechnic, 1987–92, on The Relevance of Environmental Sculpture Practices to Landscape Architecture. Hunter was education officer at the National Art Gallery, Wellington, New Zealand, 1971–5; was curator of painting and sculpture there, 1978–80; its acting director, 1978–9; in 1981 was a visiting lecturer at University of Canterbury, Christchurch, New Zealand; worked freelance in New Zealand and London, 1982–6; was artist-in-residence for the Rossendale Groundwork Trust/North West Arts, Rossendale, 1986–7 (during which time he worked on projects with the local farmer and stone carver Stan Yates); was a consultant on environmental education and the arts to the Forestry Authority from 1992 onwards. In 1989 Hunter founded Projects Environment, a charitable trust. Examples of work done by Hunter were included in Lancashire South of the Sands, 1988, toured from the County and Regimental Museum, Preston. Took part in other group shows and had a series of solo exhibitions, including sculpture installations at Rossendale, 1987–9. Main works included Willow Dome and Snake Maze for Garden Festival Wales, Ebbw Vale, 1992. Lived at Turn Village, near Ramsbottom, Lancashire.

John Frederick HUNTER 1893–1951 Multi-talented artist, whose work included prints, enamels, stained glass and metalwork, and administrator, brother of the artist Mercy Hunter. He was born in Manchuria at Chin-Chow, his father being an Irish Presbyterian Church missionary. He studied at Trinity College in Dublin, at that city's Metropolitan School of Art and at Royal College of Art, graduating in 1922. In 1923 became art inspector for Ministry of Education, Northern Ireland, and was closely associated with CEMA, which organised his memorial show in 1952 in Belfast. Hunter was elected to RUA, becoming its president, also showing at RHA. Ulster Museum and Arts Council of Northern Ireland hold examples. Died at Whitehouse, Antrim.

John Young HUNTER 1874–1955 Painter, son of the painter Colin Hunter and husband of the artist Mary Young Hunter, his first wife. He was born in Glasgow and studied at the Royal Academy Schools, his teachers including John Singer Sargent and Lawrence Alma-Tadema. Travelled extensively with his wife on the continent. He was at first influenced by the Pre-Raphaelites and was later mainly a portrait painter, his pictures sometimes being rather glamorous with a high finish. He lived in Suffolk for some time, but the latter part of his life was spent in America and died in Taos, New Mexico. Exhibited widely, including RA, Fine Art Society and elsewhere. Pyms Gallery held a show of both Young Hunters' works in 2000. Tate Gallery holds his Chantrey Bequest picture My Lady's Garden. Later work was signed John Young-Hunter.

Kenneth HUNTER 1916– Printmaker, illustrator, painter and teacher, born in Leeds, Yorkshire, where he was initially educated. A self-taught artist, he became vice-principal of the Press Art School, 1946–54, the correspondence course founded by Percy V Bradshaw. As well as exhibiting in London and the provinces, Hunter illustrated a number of books and drew for *Radio Times*, *Lilliput*, *Picture Post* and other periodicals. Lived finally in Leyburn, Yorkshire.

Kenny HUNTER 1962– Versatile sculptor, born in Edinburgh, who gained an honours degree at Glasgow School of Art, 1983–7. Among his awards were a John Kinross Scholarship to Florence, 1987; Benno Schotz Award, 1991; East prizewinner, Norwich Gallery, Norfolk Institute of Art and Design, 1993; and Friends of the RSA Artist's Award, 1995. Among Hunter's professional experience was construction worker and hospital porter, 1980–2; technical assistant, Glasgow School of Art, 1988–90; visiting artist in schools and set design for Theatre Romania's production of *The Last Night of Socrates* at Tramway, Glasgow, all 1993; and in 1995 installation of outdoor sculpture as part of the Stevenson Trail, for Sunderland City Council, 1995. Mixed shows included Compass Gallery, Glasgow, New Generation, 1987; Cyril Gerber Fine Art, Glasgow, 1990; Fuse, at Collins Gallery, Strathclyde University, 1993; and Swarm, Scottish Arts Council tour, 1995. Had a solo exhibition at Compass Gallery, 1992, later ones including The Spell of Plato, Glasgow School of Art, 1993, Norwich Gallery, 1996, Print Studio, Glasgow, 2000, St Mungo Museum, Glasgow, 2001, and Talbot Rice Gallery, Edinburgh, in 2003. British School at Athens and Scottish Arts Council hold examples.

Margaret HUNTER 1948– Painter and ceramic sculptor, born in Irvine, Ayrshire. She studied at Glasgow School of Art, 1981–5, then awards enabled her to study under Georg Baselitz at the Hochschule der Künste in Berlin, 1985–6. After this she shared her time in Berlin and Fairlie, on Scotland's west coast. Hunter's theme was the female form, mother-and-child relationships and more latterly the female related to other individuals. Her brushwork was free and gestural. To lessen her dependence on the Western figurative tradition she turned for inspiration to primitive forms. Hunter had early solo shows, in 1986, in Berlin and Ayr. Also exhibited at Vanessa Devereux Gallery and at Art First, 1997. Scottish National Gallery of Modern Art, Edinburgh, holds her work.

Mary Sutherland HUNTER 1899– Painter and sculptor born at Holywell, near Motherwell in Lanarkshire. She studied at Edinburgh College of Art and RSA School of Painting, where she won the Chalmers-Jervis Prize. She showed at RSA, SSA, RSW and Royal Glasgow Institute of the Fine Arts. Lived in Edinburgh.

Mary Young HUNTER 1872–1947 Painter and miniaturist, first wife of the artist John Young Hunter. After marrying him she travelled extensively on the continent. She is depicted in her husband's Chantrey Bequest picture My Lady's Garden, held by the Tate Gallery. Lived for some years in Wickhambrook, Suffolk. Showed extensively, mainly watercolours, at Fine Art Society, RA, SWA and elsewhere. Pyms Gallery held an exhibition of both Young Hunters' works in 2000.

Mercy HUNTER 1910–1989 Teacher, designer, calligrapher, draughtsman and illustrator, born in Belfast, Northern Ireland, real name Martha Saie Kathleen Hunter. She was married to the artist George McCann and was sister of the painter and printmaker John Frederick

Hunter. Because her father was a Presbyterian missionary, Hunter grew up in Manchuria, her secondary education taking place in Toronto, Canada, and Belfast. She attended the College of Art there, 1927–9, and won a scholarship to Royal College of Art, 1930–3, taught by the noted calligrapher Edward Johnston. Hunter was a dedicated teacher, for many years at Victoria College, Belfast. She served as president of RUA and of Ulster Society of Women Artists, which she had helped found. Designed extensively for ballet, theatre and opera (Belfast's Grand Opera House holds her work, as does Ulster Museum); completed many calligraphic commissions; and illustrated her husband's 1942 book (written as George Galway) *Sparrows Round My Brow*. Lived in Dungannon, County Tyrone.

Rob HUNTER 1972– Artist whose work employed video and site-specific performance, born in Glasgow. He gained a sculpture degree at Edinburgh College of Art, 1990–4, with a master's in combined media at Chelsea College of Art, 1995–6. Exhibitions included Lux Europae, Edinburgh International Festival, 1992; Paperworks 6, Seagate Gallery, Dundee, 1994; Actual Size, Seagate, 1995; and New Contemporaries at Tate Gallery, Liverpool, and Camden Arts Centre, 1996. In the last show Hunter linked the garage where he worked with the gallery through his image Satellite Employment Piece, 1994–6; surveillance cameras looked in on Hunter's life as a filling station attendant, garage visitors viewing the gallery.

Robert HUNTER 1920–1996 Painter, draughtsman, constructions artist and teacher, born in Liverpool. He attended the College of Art there and after distinguished military service abroad – he won the Military Cross in 1944 – in World War II was again at Liverpool College of Art, 1946–50. In 1957 he was included in Jack Beddington's book *Young Artists of Promise*. Went on to teach at several venues, being head of creative arts at Trinity College, Carmarthen, until retirement in 1983. He was a founder-member of 56 Group Wales, served on WAC art committee and as chairman of the visual arts panel of West Wales Arts Association. Took part in many group exhibitions, including SEA, SWG, Royal National Eisteddfod, where he was a judge for painting, and several shows of Welsh painting and the modern movement in Wales and abroad. At the Royal National Eisteddfod/WAC show An Iconograph of the Mabinogion in 1974 he won first prize. WAC, CASW and National Museum of Wales in Cardiff hold examples. One-man exhibitions included New Art Centre from 1961, later ones York University, 1987, and Pembroke Dock Library, 1988. Hunter said that Byzantine art, especially icons, Paul Klee, Oriental calligraphy and teaching drawing and painting were main influences on his works which were "a synthesis of what I have seen, read or heard."

Tom HUNTER 1965– Photography-based artist, born in Bournemouth, Hampshire, who gained his photographic degree at London College of Printing, 1994, then his master's at the Royal College of Art, 1996–7. Hunter's output included people in interiors, sometimes straightforwardly, otherwise with a wryness, as in the 1997 Woman Reading Possession Order, reminiscent of Vermeer. It was illustrated in the 1998 book *The New Neurotic Realism*, which preceded the Neurotic Realism series of exhibitions at Saatchi Gallery launched in 1999. Hunter had a series of solo shows, starting with The Ghetto at Sutton House, Hackney, 1994, later ones including Tom Hunter Retrospective, Photofusion Gallery, 1997, and White Cube, 2000–1, featuring images after Pre-Raphaelite paintings depicting life around the Lea Valley. Saatchi Collection holds Hunter's work. He was based in London.

William HUNTER 1890–1967 Painter, mainly in oil, born and lived in Glasgow, where he studied at the School of Art under Fra Newbery and Maurice Greiffenhagen. Also studied on the continent, helped by a scholarship. Exhibited extensively at Royal Glasgow Institute of the Fine Arts and ROI, also RSA, Paris Salon and elsewhere overseas. Glasgow Corporation bought his work.

Jeremy Hunter HENDERSON 1956– Painter, influenced by Vincent Van Gogh and Philip Guston, whose brightly coloured images drew on television and advertising. He studied at Hull College of Higher Education, 1976–9, later working in London. Was included in 10 Hull Artists at Lincolnshire & Humberside Arts Area Centre, Hull, 1980, and Summer Show 3 at Serpentine Gallery, 1982. Solo exhibitions included Acme Gallery, 1981.

Dennis HUNTLEY 1929– Sculptor, printmaker, draughtsman and teacher, born in Weybridge, Surrey. He attended Wimbledon School of Art, 1947–51, teachers including Gerald Cooper, then London University, 1951–2. Went on to become head of Sir John Cass School of Art. Guildford Cathedral and Henry Thornton School in Clapham have examples of Huntley's work. He was made a fellow of RBS in 1970. Lived in Sutton, Surrey.

Moira HUNTLY 1932– Painter, writer and teacher, born in Motherwell, Lanarkshire. She attended Harrow School of Art under Christopher Sanders, 1948–53, then Hornsey College of Art, 1953–4. Huntly taught art, 1954–60, then freelanced as a painter. Group shows included Adam Gallery, Bath; Fosse Gallery, Stow-on-the-Wold; NEAC; Société des Pastellistes de France, Paris; Mystic Maritime Museum, Connecticut, in America; and FCA Gallery, Vancouver. She was a member of RSMA, RI (becoming its first woman president in 2003), RWA and PS. Solo exhibitions included Theatr Clwyd, north Wales, and Alma Gallery in Bristol. Shared a show at Linda Blackstone Gallery, Pinner, 2001, having won the gallery's award at RI in that year. She won a number of awards, including Winsor & Newton, 1985; Laing Painting Competition, 1986; Manya Igel Fine Arts Award, 1992, and 1993; and the Buzzacott Award, RI, in 1999. Commissions and collections holding works included Clwyd County Council, Alcoa International, CWS Ltd and Nuclear Electric. Huntly was a prolific writer on painting whose books were published internationally. They included *Imaginative Still Life, Painting and Drawing Boats* and *Learn to Paint Gouache*. She lived in Willersey, Broadway, Worcestershire.

Nancy HUNTLY 1890– Painter, notably of portraits, born in Nasirabad, India. She was educated in Edinburgh and Düsseldorf, Germany, where she studied art and at Royal Academy Schools. She also showed as Nancy Weir and under her married name Nancy Sheppard at RA, ROI, RP, New Grosvenor Gallery, Royal Glasgow Institute of the Fine Arts, Paris Salon and in Düsseldorf. Many writers were among her portrait subjects, including the romantic novelist Berta Ruck, Ben Travers the playwright and the novelist E M Forster. Lived in Welwyn Garden City,

Hertfordshire. Her daughter Faith Sheppard was also an artist.

Robert HURDLE 1918– Painter and teacher, born in London. He studied at Richmond School of Art, 1935–7, then Camberwell School of Arts and Crafts, 1946–8, under William Coldstream after six years' military service. In 1950 he moved to Bristol to take a teaching post at West of England College of Art. He was senior lecturer in the faculty of fine art at Bristol Polytechnic until 1980 and lecturer in art history in the extra-mural department of Bristol University. For several years Hurdle taught drawing at Barry Summer School, Glamorgan. Hurdle began showing in LG shows in 1949 until 1965; also showed RWA, 1959–75, resigning his membership in 1976; other mixed shows including RA, New Art Centre, Frost and Reed Gallery in Bristol and Pelter/Sands Gallery, Bristol. Hurdle had a one-man show at University College, Swansea, in 1969, others including Albany Gallery, Cardiff, 1974, New Ashgate Gallery in Farnham in 1978, Farnham Maltings Kiln Gallery in 1983 and RWA in 1995. RWA, Bristol Corporation, Bristol and Bath Universities and Hong Kong Arts Centre hold his work. Lived in Bristol.

Charles HURFORD 1907–1974 Technical draughtsman and illustrator. Apprenticed originally as an engraver, he studied at Harrow School of Art. Eventually moved to the art department of Hulton Press. Although Hurford showed at RA, his best-known work was the exploded drawings in the centre spreads of the children's comic *Eagle*. He also illustrated for *Farmers Weekly* and as a freelance drew for books by round-the-world sailors such as Alec Rose and Francis Chichester. He lived at Harrow Weald, Middlesex.

Bruce HURN 1926– Artist, teacher and art inspector, born in Spalding, Lincolnshire, full name John Bruce Hurn. He studied at Birmingham College of Art, gaining his art teacher's diploma in 1946, having been medically discharged from the Royal Navy in 1944. Among his art teachers were William Bloye, William Colley, Thomas Cuthbertson, William Eggison, Bernard Fleetwood-Walker and Henry Sands. In 1947 Hurn gained a Worshipful Company of Goldsmiths design prize. From 1946–7 Hurn was a tutor at Bournville, Moseley and Nuneaton Schools of Art; from 1947–73 director of art and design at King Edward's School, Birmingham, and, concurrently, headmaster of Moseley Branch School of Art, 1952–73. In 1956 he painted the T C Kemp Memorial Crucifixion at King's Edward's School chapel, in memory of the notable *Birmingham Post* drama critic. Hurn was next appointed Her Majesty's Inspector of Schools for art and design, 1973–86, moving to Chislehurst, Kent. He also examined for various United Kingdom boards of education. Among society affiliations was RBSA from 1965, and he was its treasurer and then president, 1973–4. Hurn was with Christopher Dodds responsible for *Practical Biology*, 1964, a popular manual for which he provided 750–800 drawings. Took part in many group shows in the Midlands, including Birmingham City Art Gallery and Herbert Art Gallery in Coventry, also RA and elsewhere. Solo shows included Compendium Gallery in London and Moseley, also the Universities of Keele, Brunel, Kent, Oxford, Birmingham and Leicester. Hurn claimed an interest in a wide range of artists, including David Bomberg, Peter Lanyon and Paul Nash, Morandi, Nolde and Soutine, who had "no doubt had an effect" on his pictures. He "drew constantly", qualities of light and the landscapes of England, Wales, Jordan and Judea providing subjects.

Peter HURN 1942– Artist in oil, crayon, ink and lino-cut, born at Patchway, near Bristol. He studied in Australia at Perth Technical College with Percival Hunt and Ivor Hunt and in England at St Martin's School of Art; Birkbeck College, 1975–6, with Peter Murray; and in Italy, Switzerland and France. Showed at RA, John Moores Liverpool Exhibition, Guildhall and widely abroad. Two oil paintings, Circus of Life and The Gallery, are among his main works. British and continental private collections hold examples. Lived in London.

Harold HURRELL 1940– Conceptual artist and teacher, one of several artists – the others being Terry Atkinson, Michael Baldwin and David Bainbridge – who formed the influential exhibiting and publishing group Art & Language in 1968. Atkinson met Hurrell at grammar school and kept in touch. After Sheffield School of Art, in 1963 Hurrell moved to London to pursue a year's course at the Institute of Education, then was appointed as a technician at St Martin's School of Art, where Bainbridge had enrolled in the sculpture department. In 1967, the year that he took up a teaching post at Hull College of Art, Hurrell with Bainbridge held the Hardware Exhibition at the Architectural Association. Frustrated at the lack of exposure for their works in Britain, in 1968 Hurrell and friends founded Art & Language, Hurrell contributing to the allied magazine *Art-Language*.

Eric HURREN 1922–2005 Painter, draughtsman, printmaker and teacher, born in Staffordshire, who aged nine moved with his family to Whitstable, Kent. In 1939 Hurren began studies at the Sidney Cooper School of Art, Canterbury, interrupted in 1942 when he was conscripted into the Army. He served in Germany, where he met his future wife Ingrid (they married after correspondence in 1951). In Iserlohn, with the Army of Occupation, Hurren was befriended by the artist Wilhelm Wessel, who "gave me a sense that art was worthwhile ... that to be an artist was something quite precious." Demobilised in 1947, Hurren completed his final diploma year in painting at Canterbury. He found part-time teaching at St Edmund's School and at renamed Canterbury College of Art, where, inspired by his contact with Wessel, he went on to study lithography part-time for two years. He obtained a full-time post there, retiring as head of foundation studies in 1988. Hurren proved an adventurous tutor, interested in developments from the continent and America, notably impressed by the work of Estève and Diebenkorn. Exhibited work in Britain and abroad and had a retrospective at Herbert Read Gallery, Kent Institute of Art & Design, Canterbury, in 1996.

Leslie HURRY 1909–1978 Stage designer and painter, born in London, where he died. In 1925 joined St John's Wood Art School, where he remained two years, then won five-year scholarship to Royal Academy Schools. His early professional work involved murals in his father's house and decorative schemes for a firm of brewers in their public bars. Then painted landscapes in Britain and Ireland which led to a first one-man show at the Wertheim Gallery in 1937. Subsequently Hurry worked in France and produced two books of automatic drawings, *The Journey* and *Book of the Seven Eagles*, which had his own text.

Redfern Gallery exhibitions led to Hurry's work being seen by Robert Helpmann, the ballet dancer, which led to their collaboration on a production of *Hamlet*. Hurry became closely associated with Sadler's Wells and the theatre, while showing at galleries in London and abroad. Victoria & Albert Museum holds his work, which has a strong Neo-Romantic flavour. Lived in Hundon, Suffolk. In 1996 Marina Henderson held a retrospective of Hurry's stage designs. His Visions of War and Peace were shown at Gainsborough's House, Sudbury, 2002.

Dora HURST 1925– Painter and artist in mixed media, born in Worcester. She attended Cardiff College of Art, 1956–61, then began teaching, returning to Cardiff College in 1968–9 to gain a diploma in art education. In the early-1970s began lecturing there. Took part in group shows including the WAC show Structure 66, SEA, SWG and Cardiff Artists Exhibition, at Oriel Contemporary Art, 1996, where Hurst exhibited landscapes employing bold shapes and colours. Education authorities in Cardiff, Glamorgan and Oxford hold her work.

Stephanie HURST 1952– Painter and illustrator, born in Wimborne, Dorset, who studied at Bournemouth and Poole College of Art, 1970–1, where Sam Rabin was an influence, Hornsey College of Art, 1971–4, Byam Shaw School, 1976–77, and Royal Academy Schools, 1981–4. Took part in many mixed exhibitions, including the RA Summer Exhibition, from 1983; South Bank Picture Show, Royal Festival Hall, 1986; Pelter/Sands, Bristol, 1990; The Discerning Eye, Mall Galleries and tour, from 1990; and Green and Stone, from 1998. Awards included a prize at Spirit of London Painting Competition, Royal Festival Hall, 1984; first prize Druce Competition, Camden Arts Centre, 1986; Art Review Award, Discerning Eye, 1997; and Green and Stone Award, First Reynolds Club Exhibition, Royal Academy Schools, 1998. She showed solo at Jonathan Poole Gallery, 1987. Hurst lived in Weymouth, Dorset, an inspiration for her landscapes and seascapes, distinguished by their soft colours and Pointillist/Impressionist style.

Steve HURST 1932– Sculptor, one of the foremost experimental casters in the United Kingdom, whose work concentrated on major global concerns such as the effects of war and pollution. His output was influenced by his own experience of conflict in places such as Northern Ireland and his work for Intermediate Technology in the Third World. Hurst was educated at Ruskin School of Drawing, Goldsmiths' College School of Art and the sculpture foundry at Royal College of Art. He was one of five artists in a show at Pilgrim Gallery, 2003. One- and two-man exhibitions included Taliesin Gallery, University of Swansea, 1980; Library Gallery, Brunel University, 1984; Arts Council, Belfast, 1985; The Official Version, Christchurch Picture Gallery, Oxford, 1993; Taliesin Gallery (with George Little, 1999); and two more shows with Little: Beldam Gallery, Brunel University, 2000, and Christchurch Picture Gallery, 2001. Bedlam gave him a retrospective, as Stephen Brunel Hurst, in 2006.

Martin HURSTHOUSE 1945– Artist in various media, notably a printmaker, born in Mansfield, Nottinghamshire. He studied painting and drawing at Chesterfield and Coventry Colleges of Art. Hursthouse was concerned with "the halting and capturing of a momentary sensation or recollection". He showed with Northern Young Contemporaries in 1968, widely in the north and Midlands, in America and shared an exhibition at The Studio, Dorchester. Settled for some years in Bournemouth, Hampshire, an area which influenced his work.

Leonard HUSKINSON 1905–1974 Versatile artist, illustrator, teacher and schools examiner, born in Nottingham. His full name was Thomas Leonard Bousfield Huskinson, under which he is sometimes recorded. He entered School House at Oundle in 1920, leaving in 1923, and took part in several Shakespeare productions, his brother Geoffrey also attending the school. By the time he joined the Slade School of Fine Art, 1923–5, where he obtained a certificate for figure drawing, Huskinson's home address was Langar Hall, Barnstone, Nottinghamshire. He was art master at Radley College and while there had a solo show at the Beaux Arts Gallery in 1934. The catalogue notes that he "showed more than ordinary artistic promise" while at Oundle, and that at the Slade had "come under the direct influence of Professor [Henry] Tonks." At the time of his show Huskinson had lived for three years at Woodstock, Oxfordshire, nearby Blenheim, providing "landscape subjects and a series of watercolour drawings of the old gardens with Baroque architecture." He re-entered the Slade for one term in 1937–8. Huskinson became an examiner, eventually chief examiner, for the Oxford and Cambridge Joint Board. He illustrated various books, including *Phineas Redux*, 1951, for the Oxford University Press's Anthony Trollope. A fine example of his draughtsmanship is his incisive Girl's Head, in the manner of Wyndham Lewis, in the British Council collection, illustrated in the PS centenary volume, 2000. Huskinson took part in mixed shows at the RA Summer Exhibition and Nottingham Museum and Art Gallery, which acquired three pictures by him. After several moves he settled in Triscombe, Somerset, dying in Taunton. Judge Nicholas Huskinson was his son.

Thomas Leonard Bousfield HUSKINSON: *see* **Leonard HUSKINSON**

Eric HUSON 1930– Landscape painter born in Mitcham, Surrey. After Alleyn's School, Dulwich, he attended Camberwell School of Arts and Crafts, 1945–7, his teachers including John Minton and William Townsend, then Shrewsbury School of Art, 1947–8. Showed at Trafford Gallery and elsewhere.

Kabir HUSSAIN 1960– Sculptor, installations artist and photographer, born in Nara, Pakistan. Studied at Jacob Kramer College, Leeds, 1979–80; South Glamorgan Institute of Higher Education, Cardiff, 1980–3; and Chelsea School of Art, 1983–4. Awards included Henry Moore Foundation Prize, 1984, and Setting-up Grant in 1985 and a Travel Grant, 1988, both from WAC. Showed with LG in 1984; Lower Machen Festival, 1987; and in South Bank Centre's The British Art Show 1990. Solo exhibitions included National Eisteddfod, Newport, and Llanover Hall, Cardiff, both in 1988, and Bute Park installation, Cardiff, 1989. Lived in Cardiff.

Syed Tajammul HUSSAIN 1953– Self-taught artist and lecturer, a Muslim whose aim was to illustrate the *Koran* in such a way as to bring out the mystical meaning of the verses. As historically the *Koran* has virtually never carried pictures, Hussain used other techniques to capture the meaning of chosen verses, including calligraphic styles, types of traditional Islamic pattern or design and particular colours, the results being full of symbolism. His extensive influences included Islamic, the Japanese Edo Period, Impressionist, Celtic and other elements of Western abstract art. Hussain was born in Lahore, Pakistan, a chartered certified accountant and lecturer on the art of the Koran at Oxford University National College of Arts. Group shows included Greenwich Millennium Dome prayer space, 2000; Bait Muzna Museum, Muscat, Oman, 2001; and October and ArRum Galleries, both 2002. Among solo exhibitions were Ashmolean Museum, Oxford, and Glasgow City Council, both 1999, and St Antony's, University of Oxford, 2000. The British Museum; Ashmolean Museum; Museum of Modern Art and St Mungo's Museum, both in Glasgow; and the Government Art Collection hold examples. Lived in London.

Henry James HUSSEY 1913– Sculptor and stonemason, born and lived in London. He was self-taught as an artist after attending elementary school. Showed at RA, Leicester Galleries, Ash Barn Gallery in Petersfield and Tryon and Moorland Galleries. University of London Senate House was decorated with figures by Hussey.

John HUSSEY 1928– Sculptor and teacher born in Slough, Buckinghamshire, who studied at Goldsmiths' College School of Art, 1946–9. He later obtained a research diploma at Bristol Polytechnic, 1969–70, and became principal lecturer and director of studies there, retiring in 1983. Hussey was an associate of RBS and a member of RWA, also showing at RA. Lived in St Osyth, Essex.

Mary HUSTED 1944– Artist using a variety of two- and three-dimensional techniques, and teacher, who gained an honours degree in fine art from the University of Wales Institute, Cardiff, 1990. She occasionally lectured on the foundation course there and contributed to workshops for Permanent Waves Women's Arts in Barry, South Glamorgan, where she lived. Husted was a prolific exhibitor in group exhibitions, including Women's Art at New Hall, Cambridge, 1992; National Eisteddfod of Wales, 1993; Box Works, Playhouse, Australian National Theatre Festival, 1995; New Australian Images Through British Eyes, Australian National University Drill Hall Gallery, Canberra, 1997; The Welsh Group 50th Anniversary Exhibition, National Museum and Galleries of Wales, Cardiff, 1999; Reflections, Southside Arts, Southampton, 2000; and Washington Gallery Christmas Show, Penarth, 2001. The interplay between real and illusory space was a strand running through Husted's work, which was owned by New Hall; Broken Hill Proprietry, Melbourne; the Australian National University; and British High Commission, based in Canberra.

Tom HUTCHESON 1922–1999 Mixed-media artist and teacher, born in Uddingston, Lanarkshire. He studied at Glasgow School of Art, 1941–2 and 1946–9, teachers including Stanley Spencer, Benno Schotz, Hugh Adam Crawford and David Donaldson. In 1942 Hutcheson joined the Royal Air Force and began pilot training, which took him to Canada and America. "I always found time to attend some art school. In this way I studied at the Slade and Chester, Exeter and Liverpool Schools of Art, also a series of art institutions in Toronto, Detroit and New York." In New York he "met most of the New York School and visited Peggy Guggenheim's Gallery", experiences which "were mind-blowing – in scale alone they were twenty to thirty times as big as anything I had ever painted...vigorous, slashing abstractions". It took "about ten years to filter through my subconscious and find expression in my work. This was after I had returned to Glasgow, finished Art School, and started to paint the subject that has become almost an obsession with me – the pit landscape of Lanarkshire." Hutcheson taught art in Glasgow secondary schools, 1950–64, then at Jordanhill College of Further Education, becoming principal lecturer, 1977. Was for long a Glasgow Art Club member, showing at Royal Glasgow Institute of the Fine Arts as a member, RSA, SSA, in the English provinces and elsewhere. HM The Queen, HRH The Duke of Edinburgh and Scottish education authorities held his work. Lived in Glasgow. There was a retrospective exhibition at the Royal Glasgow Institute Kelly Gallery in 2002.

Gay HUTCHINGS 1948– Painter, printmaker and, from 1994, stained glass artist who studied languages, interpreted abroad for many years, then returned to England. Studied with Cecil Collins, a lasting influence and long-standing teacher at the Central School. Hutchings graduated with honours in fine art, painting, from there in 1977–80; she did a two-year postgraduate diploma in stained glass at Central St Martins, 1994–5; and gained a Caroline Swash Fellowship for a year's research study in stained glass there, 1996–7. Her work, mixing representation with imagination and employing rich colours, drew extensively on her travels. She worked on private and public commissions, later ones including two windows for the Royal London Hospital, a window for the Headgate Theatre, Colchester, and a memorial window for Peldon Church, Essex. Hutchings participated in Making the Connection, firstsite, Colchester/Wolsey Art Gallery, Ipswich, 2002. Lived in West Mersea, Essex.

Hilda Edith HUTCHINGS 1890–c.1950 Painter, printmaker and teacher, born in Grantham, Lincolnshire. She studied at Bristol Municipal School of Art, where she became a teacher. Moved to London in the mid-1920s and taught at West Ham School of Art. Showed at RA, RWA, Walker Art Gallery in Liverpool and with Chicago Society of Etchers and was a member of the Print Society of California. Bristol City Art Gallery and Los Angeles National Museum hold her work.

George HUTCHINS 1925– Painter and teacher, born in London. Studied at Brighton College of Art where his teachers included Charles Knight. Showed with RA, RBA and with Brighton and Essex Art Clubs. He completed a number of school murals. Lived in Romford, Essex, then in Meopham, Kent.

John HUTCHINSON 1884–1972 Botanical book illustrator who signed his work J H. Was born at Wark on Tyne, Northumberland, and rose to be keeper of museums at the Royal Botanical Gardens, Kew, Surrey, where he lived. Hutchinson produced many books on British and foreign – mainly wild – flowers, principally published by Penguin Books.

Louisa HUTCHINSON 1954– Gestural abstract painter, born in Wolverhampton, where she studied at the Polytechnic, 1972–3, then at Bath Academy of Art, Corsham, 1973–6. Mixed shows included 55 Wapping Artists, 1979; Tolly Cobbold Eastern Arts, 3rd National Exhibition, 1981; and Wapping Artists Open Studios Exhibition and RA Summer Exhibition, both from 1982.

Louise HUTCHINSON 1882–1968 Sculptor and photographer whose father was a naturalised British subject, her mother Bavarian. She was educated in Freiburg in Germany, Geneva in Switzerland and in London. Before she became a sculptor she was well known as a photographer, working as Li Osborne, having solo shows in Baden-Baden and Munich in Germany, Copenhagen in Denmark and in Switzerland. From 1945 she lived in East Bergholt, Essex, taking part in many exhibitions in East Anglia and London. Although she was self-taught, she was acquainted with many noted continental artists. In 1953 Hutchinson took part in The Unknown Political Prisoner competition, won by the sculptor Reg Butler, Hutchinson obtaining an International Award. In the same year she held her first solo exhibition at the Beaux Arts Gallery, with a second in 1956. That included figurative bronzes, small maquettes and portrait heads in bronze and portraits in terracotta. The portrait subjects included the musician Sandor Vègh, 1953; art writers Sir Herbert Read and David Sylvester, 1954; potter Bernard Leach, art historian Dr J P Hodin, and missionary, musician and writer Dr Albert Schweitzer, 1955; and artists Patrick Heron, Mary Fedden and Helen Lessore, who also ran the Beaux Arts Gallery, 1956. The Victoria & Albert Museum holds a terracotta by Hutchinson.

Mark HUTCHINSON 1966– Artist, lecturer, writer on art and curator, born and based in London, married to the artist Lis Fields. He was a visiting lecturer at the Bartlett School of Architecture, 1995–7, and from 2002 at Royal Academy Schools. Hutchinson wrote on art, for magazines and catalogue introductions, and latterly curated Unfound, Chisenhale Gallery, 2000, and Nausea: Encounters with Ugliness, London Print Studio and Djanogly Gallery, Nottingham (with Nicola Cotton), 2002. Group and shared exhibitions included Mind the Gap, Gimpel Fils (with Dave Beech), 1993; Open Invitations, in Outpost, Venice Biennale, 1995; The Artist's Game & No Smoking in the Bogs, in Body & Soul, ICA, 1996; Cable Street Crazy Golf Show, Cable Street Gallery (with Lindsay Seers), 1999; Rat Manifesto, in What's Wrong?, Trade Apartment, 2001; and Decoy, for TagTeam Experiment, Edinburgh, 2003. Escape From Studio Voltaire was a solo exhibition at Studio Voltaire Gallery, 2004.

Norman Douglas HUTCHINSON 1932– Painter, draughtsman and sculptor, notable for figure studies and portraits, born in Calcutta, India, who studied at an English boarding school at Kalimpong, where the Himalayas "gave to me a passion for landscape". Hutchinson later wrote that the disease and deprivation of Indian city life "became the haunting imagery of my painting. A darkness covered my pictures, a predilection for earthy colours, a sadness in every face and figure I painted, and shadow became the principal factor." In 1959 Hutchinson moved to London, and was able to study Western masters. He was largely self-taught, although he benefited from knowing two good artists in India, and in Europe met with Pietro Annigoni and some of his disciples. In 1963 a book, *Ten Drawings of Gloria*, appeared, featuring his wife who, with his daughters, were important models. *Gloria*, published in 2004 and launched at the Art Workers' Guild, celebrated Hutchinson's depictions of Gloria Mudaliear over 50 years. Having business interests, Hutchinson did not depend on painting for a living. He carried out portrait commissions, and painted leading members of the royal family, including HM The Queen, HRH The Duke of Edinburgh and HM Queen Elizabeth The Queen Mother. Meticulous preparation was a feature of Hutchinson's work. Showed at RA, RP and other London mixed exhibitions. After a first solo show at Upper Grosvenor Galleries in 1964, did not exhibit one-man again until Mayfair Fine Art in 1991. In 1992 had a show with his daughter Rebecca, a pastellist, at Doncaster Museum & Gallery, in 1994 a solo exhibition, A Shift in the Concept of Beauty, at Archeus Fine Art. The book *"A Hand to Obey the Demon's Eye" The Life and Work of the Painter Norman Douglas Hutchinson*, by Julian Halsby, was launched with a show at Archeus in 2000. Doncaster Museum, the Saudi Royal Family and the Wardrobe Museum Salisbury are among collections which held his work. Sometimes signed Norman or N Douglas H. Lived latterly in Saint Foy La Grande, France. His daughter Deborah Russell, born 1958, was a conceptual sculptor.

Peter HUTCHINSON 1932– Creator of landscape-oriented works in photography, montage and boxed form, born in London, who moved to America in 1953. His works confronted the viewer with thoughtful, teasing and amusing images. In America, Hutchinson developed alongside Robert Smithson and other land artists, and he went on to show extensively there and on the continent, but not in England until the Mayor Gallery retrospective of works, 1969–1996, held in the latter year. By then he had had around 50 solo exhibitions, including Landscapes, John Gibson Gallery, New York, 1969; Gallerie 20, Amsterdam, 1971; Stedelijk Museum, Amsterdam, 1974; American Art Company Gallery, New York, 1987; Bugdahn-Kaimer Galery, Düsseldorf, 1993; The Narrative Art of Peter Hutchinson: A Retrospective, Galerie Blancpain Stepczynski, Geneva, 1994; and Retrospective Exhibition & New Work, Holly Solomon Gallery, New York, 1995. Mayor Gallery gave Hutchinson a further exhibition, The World as it never was, in 2003. Museum of Modern Art in New York, Museum Boymans in Rotterdam, Georges Pompidou Centre in Paris, Museum of Art in Sydney and other international collections hold examples.

Rebecca HUTCHINSON 1961– Painter, born in London, who studied at Byam Shaw School of Art, 1981–4. Exhibitions included Fieldborne Galleries from 1983; PS from 1986; Birch and Conran, 1989; and Phoenix Gallery from 1989. There was a solo show at Jonathan Ross – Gallery 286 in 1999. Among her portrait commissions was the actor Steven Berkoff. Her self-portrait was held by Doncaster Museum and Art Gallery.

Rosamund HUTCHINSON 1905– Painter, initially educated in Monmouth and Burnham-on-Sea. Studied with Marcus Holmes, Monmouth, 1923–4, then at the Slade School of Fine Art, where her teachers included Henry Tonks and Tancred Borenius. Lived in Ashfield, Herefordshire, and showed mainly in that area.

Sheila HUTCHINSON 1906–1999 Calligrapher, artist, naturalist, writer and political worker, born in Weare Giffard, Devon. She inherited artistic talents from her parents, her soldier father being a talented watercolourist. Miss Hutchinson attended West Bank School, Bideford, where she settled, next the School of Art there under Percy Heard, then studied industrial design at Hammersmith School of Art and at the Central School of Arts and Crafts, gaining a grounding in the history of art, design and lettering. Freelanced frugally until World War II, when she joined Air-raid Precautions (ARP), the Bideford Home Guard and worked part-time on a farm. She became vice-chairman of the Bideford and Westward Ho! Art Society. Among her landscape watercolours was a series stemming from her bicycling the entire course of the River Torridge. Was a staunch Liberal, her largest calligraphic achievement being the record of Members of Parliament for Barnstaple, 427 names from 1295, commissioned by Jeremy Thorpe and presented to the borough. She wrote Devon dialect stories for the BBC and was published by *Punch*, *The News Chronicle*, and *The Countryman*. There was a memorial show at Burton Gallery & Museum, Bideford in 2000.

Suzanne HUTCHINSON 1957– Versatile artist using a bright palette, born in Lincolnshire. Her home was moved to Hong Kong, 1967–70; she attended Bath Academy of Art, Corsham, for a foundation course, 1975–6; undertook frequent visits to parental home in Baghdad, Iraq, 1976–8, while gaining a fine art honours degree at Brighton Polytechnic, 1976–9; and received her master's in painting at Chelsea School of Art, 1979–80. In 1989 she visited Australia and Malaysia. Set/costume designs and installations included *Petrushka*, Arts Council, 1981, and *Ghost Train*, installations for Hangleton Festival in Sussex, 1988. Group shows included British Drawing, Hayward Gallery, 1982; Off the Wall, Gardner Arts Centre, Brighton, 1991; and What is Jewellery?, Crafts Council, 1994. Had a solo show at Brighton Polytechnic, 1982, later ones including Lure, in 1997, at Museum & Art Gallery, Brighton, Sussex, where she lived.

Isabel HUTCHISON 1958– Largely self-taught artist, born in Hertfordshire, who after leaving school went into interior design, where she developed expertise as a mural painter. After being widowed in 1982 she travelled extensively, painting murals to earn a living. On her return completed courses at Chelsea College of Art under Peter Fleming. Her first solo show, in 1996, in the walkways of Tower Bridge, was the outcome of a three-year project to "paint the portrait", in tempera and mixed media on board, of all 20 of London's road bridges from Hampton Court to Tower Bridge.

Shand HUTCHISON 1920– Painter and teacher, born in Dalkeith, Midlothian, son of the painter Thomas Shand Hutchison. After North Berwick High School attended Edinburgh College of Art where his teachers included William Gillies, John Maxwell and Leonard Rosoman, and was there for two periods – 1939–40 and 1946–9 – interrupted by the war. Showed with RSA, SSA, Scottish Arts Club and elsewhere. Lived in North Berwick and had a studio in Edinburgh.

William Oliphant HUTCHISON 1889–1970 Portrait and landscape painter and influential teacher, born in Kirkcaldy, Fife. He studied at Edinburgh College of Art, 1909–12, then in Paris. James Gunn painted Hutchison several times, one a strikingly dandyish portrait as a young man. Hutchison became director of Glasgow School of Art, 1933–43, was elected RSA in 1943, becoming its president seven years later. He was made an Hon. RA in 1950 and was knighted in 1953. Exhibited widely, including RA, RSA, NEAC, Royal Glasgow Institute of the Fine Arts, Walker Art Gallery in Liverpool and RBA. He has work in several Scottish collections. Lived for a time in London.

David HUTTER 1930–1990 Painter, draughtsman and teacher, born in London, where he died. He studied at St Martin's and Hornsey Schools of Art. Hutter's reputation was established by the late 1960s, mainly on the basis of his landscapes in oil, but it was his watercolours, of the male nude and of flowers, that excited the critics in the early 1980s. The Japanese influence on his technique, using stretched wet paper, combined with an Oriental simplicity were notable features of Hutter's work. As well as writing for *The Artist*, Hutter organised life class groups, conducted other artists around Europe and lectured in prisons. Group exhibitions included RA, RP, RWS and RI. He had solo shows at John Whibley Gallery in 1969–72; Off Centre Gallery, 1979; Ebury Gallery, 1982; Mateloos Gallery, Rotterdam, 1986–7; and St Jude's, 1988; that gallery organised a memorial show in 1990. Retrospective, The Bloxham Galleries, 2000.

Clarke HUTTON 1898–1985 Painter, lithographer, teacher and book illustrator, born and lived in London, full name Tom Clarke Hutton. For about a decade from 1916 he was an assistant stage designer at the Empire Theatre, then a trip to Italy prompted him to become a fine artist. Studied at the Central School of Arts and Crafts in the late 1920s. He took over his teacher A S Hartrick's lithographic class there when he retired, which he supervised until 1968. Hutton's figures and landscapes were exhibited, under the initials C H, at the RA, LG, RI, Redfern Gallery and elsewhere. The British Museum and Victoria & Albert Museum hold his work. He illustrated about 50 books, for publishers in Britain and America. Some of Hutton's later pictures were of a Surrealist type, rather in the manner of John Tunnard.

Dorothy HUTTON 1889–1984 Artist, especially of flowers, and calligrapher, Hutton was born in Bolton, Lancashire, and studied art at the Central School of Arts and Crafts under F Ernest Jackson and Graily Hewitt. Hutton exhibited at the RA, NEAC, Walker Art Gallery in Liverpool and at other venues. She was an official artist to the Crown Office and among her works was a memorial to General Dwight B Eisenhower. She was a member of the Art Workers' Guild from 1964 and lived in London.

John HUTTON 1906–1978 Painter especially of murals, glass engraver and teacher, he originated in New Zealand and was a self-taught artist. Initial education at Wanganui Collegiate School. For a time he taught mural painting at Goldsmiths' College School of Art and was chairman of the Society of Mural Painters. Although he showed at LG and Arts Council he was mainly known for permanent works in public places. This included murals and glass engravings respectively on the Orient Line ship *Orcades* and Cunard liner *Caronia*, a screen for Coventry Cathedral and doors for Guildford Cathedral. Victoria & Albert Museum bought his work. Joined the Art Workers' Guild in 1975. Lived in London.

John HUTTON 1948– Artist and teacher, "mainly producing abstract acrylic paintings and works on paper concentrating on colour and structure." Hutton was born in London and gained a diploma in graphic arts from Watford School of Art; graduated with honours in fine art from Hertfordshire College of Art & Design, St Albans; then obtained a Certificate in Education from Garnett College. He taught at Chelsea School of Art, 1978–82; Haringey Education Department, 1982–4; Kingsway College, 1984–97; Barnet College, 1998; City Literary Institute, 1998–9; and from 2000 at Canterbury College. His numerous mixed exhibitions in Britain and abroad included Dun Laoghaire School of Art, Ireland, 1975; RA Summer Exhibition, from 1977; Ian Birksted Gallery and Musée Muncipale des Beaux-Arts, Tourcoing, France, both 1981; Art of Today 1, Budapest Gallery, Hungary, 1987; The City Gallery, Leicester, 1991; and Deal Library Gallery, 2001. Among later solo shows was Sassoon Gallery, Folkestone Museum, 2001. London Borough of Camden, Scarborough Art Gallery and several corporate collections hold examples. Lived in Hythe, Kent.

Sarah HUTTON 1962– Artist in various media, notable for colourful landscapes, born in Haworth, West Yorkshire, where in 1988 she founded Hutton van Mastrigt Art. She attended Bradford College, 1980–1; Central School of Art & Design, 1981–4; Syracuse University, New York, 1983; Leeds University, Bretton Hall, 1987–8; and Leeds Metropolitan University, 1993. In 1984–6 set up Haworth Artists' Field Study Centre. Many mixed shows included Cartwright Hall, Bradford, from 1989; Ilkley Manor House, 1992; and Manchester International Art Fair, 1993. Had a solo show at Albany Gallery, 1990, later ones including Harrogate Exhibition Centre and Ling House, Keighley, both 1993.

Bethan HUWS 1961– Artist born in Bangor, Caernarvonshire. Studied at Middlesex Polytechnic, 1981–5, then Royal College of Art, 1986–8. Participated in South Bank Centre's touring The British Art Show 1990. Solo exhibitions included Institut Sainte-Marie, Brussels, 1987; Rivington Street and Anthony Reynolds Gallery, 1988; Riverside Studios and FRAC des Pays de la Loire, Garenna Lemot, Clisson, 1989; ICA and foreign tour, 1991; and Yorkshire Sculpture Park, West Bretton, 2001. Leeds Museums and Galleries hold examples. Lived in London.

Richard HUWS 1902–1980 Sculptor, designer and teacher, born in Anglesey, north Wales, as Richard Hughes. As a young man he flirted with the Welsh national party Plaid Cymru, of which he was a founder-member, designing its logo, and changed his name to the Welsh version Huws. He later left the party, always being uncomfortable in organisations. After Beaumaris Grammar School Huws was an apprentice at Cammel Laird's, Birkenhead, then was an Armstrong Whitworth scholar reading naval architecture at Liverpool University, graduating in 1925. He then roamed Europe, sketching – Huws was a superb draughtsman – and studying sculpture in Vienna's Kunstgewerbeschule. Returned to England in 1930, flirted briefly with the early Fascists, then attacked them with cartoons. During World War II fostered his interest in mechanical systems by working on Spitfires. Became a fellow of the Society of Industrial Artists. Huws returned to Liverpool University, being on the staff of the School of Architecture 1955–69 (full-time from 1957, a senior lecturer from 1966), where his grasp of the problems of production design proved invaluable. Teaching commitments forced him to turn down design commissions. Huws created his Water Mobile for the Festival of Britain in 1951. It ejected lumps of water at unexpected intervals and gradually shook itself to pieces. "I spent most of my time repairing it, but it was a breakthrough in fountain design," Huws said in 1967, when his fountain near the Pier Head, Liverpool, was opened, commissioned by Merseyside Civic Society. He also created one for British Petroleum for a British Fair in Tokyo and exhibited in Glasgow and New York. While at Liverpool Huws lived near Llanrwst, Anglesey, developed an interest in landscape design and was an associate of the Institute of Landscape Architects. His wife was also an artist.

Jonathan HUXLEY 1965– Painter and muralist who trained at Berkshire College of Art, 1985–6, gained an honours degree in fine art, Trent Polytechnic, 1986–9, and a fine art diploma from the Royal Academy Schools, 1989–92. Murals included Bristol Royal Society for the Blind and Bermondsey Council, both 1993. In 1994 he was commissioned to create ultra-violet paintings for the singer Grace Jones's birthday party at The Tunnel Club, New York, America. Mixed shows included Mall Galleries, 1991; RA Summer Exhibition, 1994; and The Hunting Art Prizes, at Royal College of Art, 1997, where Huxley gained the Most Popular Painting prize. Had solo shows at Crane Kalman Gallery: 1999, 2001, 2003 and 2005, notable for pictures of figures in motion that were spontaneous, witty and vibrant.

Juliette HUXLEY 1896–1994 Sculptor and writer, born in Auvernier, Switzerland, who moved to England in 1915 and became governess to Lady Ottoline Morrell's daughter. She married the biologist Julian Huxley and with him travelled widely. Studied sculpture at Central School of Arts and Crafts under John Skeaping and showed at RA. Her collection included works by artist friends Henry Moore, John Piper, Henry Lamb, Duncan Grant and Julian Trevelyan. In 1986 she published her autobiography *Leaves from the Tulip Tree*. Died in London.

Paul HUXLEY 1938– Painter, draughtsman and teacher whose work used simple geometrical shapes and serpentine forms. He was born in London and studied at Harrow School of Art, 1953–6, and Royal Academy Schools, 1956–60. From 1959 Huxley showed several times with Young Contemporaries, then in 1963 had the first of his one-man shows at Rowan Gallery where with Mayor Rowan Gallery and Juda Rowan Gallery he was a frequent exhibitor. Huxley was a prizewinner at The New Generation Whitechapel Art Gallery show in 1964; at Paris Biennale, 1965; won Linbury Trust Award, 1977; and in 1985 first prize, Athena Award. In 1965 Huxley gained a Harkness Fellowship which took him to America, where he lived in New York until 1967. Among his overseas shows were one-mans at Kornblee Gallery, New York, in 1967 and 1970. Huxley was a Tate Gallery trustee, 1975–82. During the period 1984–87 he was engaged in designing tiling for London Transport's revivified King's Cross underground station. Huxley taught at Royal College of Art from 1976, being professor of painting, 1986–98. Was elected RA in 1991. In 2000 Huxley was artist-in-residence,

Pallant House, Chichester, his designs for its grand staircase being shown that autumn. Later solo exhibitions included Rhodes + Mann, 2003. The Arts Council holds a wide selection of his work. Lived in London.

Thomas Bayliss HUXLEY-JONES 1908–1969 Sculptor in a variety of materials who studied at Wolverhampton School of Art under Robert Emerson, 1924–9, and at the Royal College of Art, 1929–33, under Richard Garbe and Gilbert Ledward. Married to the sculptor Gwynneth Holt. He exhibited RA, NEAC, RSA, SSA and RBSA. Huxley-Jones' sculpture is generally smooth and simple in profile, as depicted in Arthur T Broadbent's monograph *Sculpture Today in Great Britain 1940–1943*, and in Eric Newton's companion volume *British Sculpture 1944–1946*. Huxley-Jones completed a large volume of public work, at the BBC Television Centre, London, in Chelmsford Cathedral, outside Hornsey Library and in London's Hyde Park. Aberdeen and Wolverhampton Art Galleries hold his work. Was a member of Chelsea Arts Club. Lived in Chelmsford, Essex.

Sidney Edwin HUXTABLE 1905–1992 Painter and teacher, born in South Molton, Devon. He studied at Clapham School of Art and St Martin's School of Art, teachers including Iain Macnab. From 1925 lived and taught in London, occasionally working in Devon. Between 1966–84 he travelled on the continent, the British Museum holding a collection of his illustrated diaries. Showed at RA, NEAC, RBA and elsewhere. In 1993 a group of his pictures was shown at The Jerram Gallery, Salisbury. Huxtable was a member of the Ridley Art Club.

Martin HUXTER 1960– Painter, and teacher, born in Great Wakering, Essex. He studied at Southend Technical College, 1977–9, then Trent Polytechnic, 1979–82. He won a purchase prize at Leicestershire Exhibition, 1983, and a prize in 1989–90 John Moores Liverpool Exhibition with his metaphorical picture Man on Stilts. He took part in Artists in Essex, at Epping Forest Museum, 1988–9, and had solo shows in Southend and Westcliff-on-Sea, 1988–9, where he lived. In 2001, Huxter was shortlisted for the BP Travel Award at the National Portrait Gallery, the previous year his painting Nawang having been used for the poster to promote the BP Portrait Exhibition throughout Britain.

Derek HYATT 1931– Landscape painter, draughtsman, teacher and writer, born in Ilkley, Yorkshire. He studied at Leeds College of Art, 1948–52, then Royal College of Art, 1954–8, where he edited *Ark* magazine, the issue on colour symbolism selling 3,000 copies in three days. From 1959–64 Hyatt was visiting lecturer at Kingston College of Art, then returned to Yorkshire. He was a lecturer at Leeds College of Art, 1964–8, then senior lecturer at Leeds Polytechnic, 1968–84. Hyatt had many solo exhibitions. There was a string from 1960–6 at New Art Centre, others including University of York and Manor House, Ilkley, 1966; Arthur Gallery, Tampa, America, 1967; a series at Goosewell Gallery, Menston, 1969–76; Waddington Gallery, 1975; Waddington and Tooth's Gallery, 1977; Austin/Desmond Fine Art, 1989; and Dean Clough Contemporary Art Gallery, Halifax, 1991–2. There was a major retrospective at Cartwright Hall, Bradford, in 2001, another exhibition, Circle on the Dark Rock, at Shire Pottery Gallery and Studios, Alnwick, 2003. Ruskin was a major influence on the work of Hyatt, having been "a star in my sky since student days". His main subject was the Yorkshire landscape, especially from one vantage point high above Bishopdale, and he believed that "the landscape enters our bodies ... we dance its life." Hyatt's work is held by Museum of Modern Art in New York; Contemporary Art Society; Nuffield Foundation; and many British provincial galleries. Lived at Collingham, Yorkshire.

John HYATT 1958– Versatile artist and teacher, born in Wolverhampton, Staffordshire, who attended the Grammar School there, then University of Leeds, 1977–81, gaining a first-class honours degree. Hyatt had considerable teaching experience, beginning at Rochdale College of Art, 1981–4, eventually, after being head of the department of fine arts at Manchester Metropolitan University from 1991, in 1994 being conferred a professorship. Hyatt's publications, of which he was author and illustrator/designer, included *Art Wars*, 1984; *Bashir Makhoul*, 1993; and *Saint Jerome's Disappearing Cat*. He also published (low-noise music) over 50 musical pieces, released in Britain and abroad. Wrote and recorded a four-part radio serial for the BBC, designed and illustrated for record covers and posters and was the regular cover artist for *Psychology News*. Mixed shows included The British Art Show, 1984, Arts Council tour. Later solo shows included Cornerhouse Gallery, Manchester, 1991–2. Lived in Alderley Edge, Cheshire.

Catherine HYDE 1960– Artist in oil and pastel whose pictures, including animals, birds and figures in landscapes, had a strong Symbolist element. She did a foundation diploma course at Medway College of Design, Rochester, 1978–9, then won an honours degree in fine art, painting, at Central School of Art, 1979–82. Mixed exhibitions included Easton Rooms, Rye, from 1989; Gift of Life Competition at The Imagination Gallery, 1993; and Artists of Fame & Promise, Beaux Arts, Bath, 1995. She had solo exhibitions there in 1995 and 1996.

Monair HYMAN 1955– Artist using such materials as oil, ink and gold leaf on paper, born and lived in Leeds, Yorkshire. She graduated from the Leeds Metropolitan University in 1992 with a first-class honours degree in painting. The following year she embarked on an ambitious series of pictures called Constructions of the Spirit, inspired by churches and chapels seen during a study trip to Florence. A picture called Nocturne II, related to the series, is in the Provident Financial Art Collection. Hyman's work was shown in many survey exhibitions of young artists in Britain; was included in a touring show put on by Ikon Gallery, Birmingham; and in 1994 was shown at Dean Clough Contemporary Art Gallery, Halifax.

Timothy HYMAN 1946– Painter, draughtsman, writer and teacher, born in Hove, Sussex, but brought up in London. He attended Slade School of Fine Art, 1963–7. From 1980–1 Hyman was visiting professor at University of Baroda, India; in 1983–4 was artist-in-residence at Lincoln Cathedral; the following year occupied a similar position at London University's Westfield College. From 1987–8 Hyman worked in Ahmedabad, India. Later awards included a Wingate Foundation Award, 1998. Hyman wrote on a wide number of topics for magazines and other publications, including William Blake, John Cowper Powys, R B Kitaj and James Ensor. His own work was strongly autobiographical, tinged with humour, with an Expressionist distortion. In 1979 Hyman mounted the controversial show Narrative Paintings at Arnolfini Gallery, Bristol, which toured. Among mixed shows he appeared in were RA Summer Exhibitions; The Younger Generation of Figurative Painters, at Ashmolean Museum, Oxford, 1984; Portraits at Flowers East, 1988; and Twin Images, Fine Art Society, 1990. Had solo shows at Blond Fine Art in 1981–3; Usher Gallery, Lincoln, and tour, 1984–5; Westfield College and Blond Fine Art, 1985; Contemporary Art Gallery, Ahmedabad, 1988; Austin/Desmond Fine Art, from 1990. Arts Council, British Museum and other public collections hold his work.

Kathleen HYNDMAN 1928– Artist and teacher, born in Brentwood, Essex, who studied at Kingston School of Art with Reginald Brill as principal, 1945–8, and the University of London Institute of Education, 1948–9. During that year, under her maiden name Kathleen Margaret Blomfield, she recorded life on the Isle of Dogs in words and pictures, the results exhibited as a solo show at The Space, 1998, a book being published by the Island History Trust in 1999. This was aided by a 1999 Millennium Award, earlier awards being a Southern Arts Bursary, 1975, and an Arts Council Award, 1976. After her studies Hyndman did administrative work for the London County Council, then taught painting, drawing and history of art in further and higher education and in schools. Although her early output was representational, Hyndman was to be influenced by Mondrian and produced work that was "an exploration of arithmetical sequences and geometry as a means of distributing motifs, shapes, colours.... Subjective choices are made as to which variety or conjunction of constructive ideas, and which colours, are used to parallel the initial visual perception." She was a member of Oxford Contemporary Artists. Group shows included The Hayward Annual, Hayward Gallery, 1992; the Fourth and Fifth International Triennales of Drawing, Wrocław, Poland, 1988 and 1992; and Chronologic, The Planet Art, Cape Town, South Africa, 1999. Solo exhibitions included Lillie Art Gallery, Glasgow, and tour, 1985; Radcliffe Infirmary, Oxford, and Winchester Gallery/Southern Arts tour, both 1990; and Logos Gallery, 1996. The National Museum of Women in the Arts in Washington, America, holds her work. She lived in Kingston Bagpuize, Oxfordshire.

Gladys HYNES 1888–1958 Painter, sculptor and draughtsman, born in Indore, India. She studied with Stanhope Forbes in Cornwall and at London School of Art. Among her more notable works were illustrations to Ezra Pound's *Cantos*, published by John Rodker. She showed at RA, RI, IS, LG and at Paris Salon. Lived in London.

Joanna HYSLOP 1956– Versatile painter and draughtsman, born in Haverfordwest, Pembrokeshire. She studied at West Surrey College of Art, Farnham, 1972–4; at Portsmouth Polytechnic, 1974–7; and Chelsea School of Art, 1977–8. Showed in London, where she lived, and the provinces in group exhibitions. These included the 1983 Cleveland Drawing Biennale, the Leicester Exhibition, 1984, and John Moores Liverpool Exhibition, 1985 and 1995–6, in which she won a prize. Had solo exhibitions at Aspex Gallery, Portsmouth, 1986, and in 1987–8 one at the Atkinson Art Gallery, Southport, toured. Walker Art Gallery holds her work.

Anna HYUNSOOK PAIK 1966– Painter, born in Seoul, South Korea, who trained at the Pennsylvania Academy of the Fine Arts, in America. She received numerous awards and scholarships, including the Benjamin West Prize, Thomas Eakins Award and in 2003 gained 1st Prize in The Garrick/Milne Prize with her oil on linen Rehearsal at RADA. She painted many actors from the Royal Academy of Dramatic Art, including Charlie Walker-Wise, whose father, Herbert, won a British Academy of Film and Dramatic Arts Lifetime Achievement Award as a director. She had solo exhibitions in London and New Orleans and had a studio sponsored by CAN Gallery, Philadelphia.

I

Charles I'ANSON 1924–1983 Sculptor working in rust-proofed steel and glass fibre, born in Birmingham. He studied at Birmingham College of Art and Bradford University, obtaining his Master of Science degree in 1980. I'Anson was elected a member of RBSA in 1966 and a fellow of RBS in 1967. Group exhibitions included RWA, LG, Alwin Gallery, New Vision Centre, SSA and abroad. He took part in many open air exhibitions, including London and the provinces. Solo shows included New Vision Centre, Alwin Gallery, Kidderminster Art Gallery, Leeds City Art Gallery and Midlands Art Centre in Birmingham. The Centre has his work, also held by Birmingham, Bradford and Wakefield public galleries and University of Leeds. Lived in Ilkley, Yorkshire.

Mark IANSON 1967– Figurative painter and draughtsman who strove in his portraits to record what the camera could not. He gained an honours degree at Gray's School of Art, Aberdeen, 1988–92. Group shows included Paisley Drawing Competition, award winner, 1993 and 1995; Royal Glasgow Institute, award winner, 1993; RSA, award winner, 1994 and 1997; and Gallery 44, Aldeburgh, 1998. Solo exhibitions included Compass Gallery, Glasgow, The Fool, 1994, and Precious Few Heroes, 1996; and Thackeray Gallery, What Remains, 1999, and Moving, 2001.

Graham IBBESON 1951– Sculptor and draughtsman, born in Barnsley, Yorkshire. Ibbeson studied at Leicester Polytechnic, 1972–3, Trent Polytechnic, 1973–5, and at Royal College of Art, 1975–8, under Bernard Meadows. In 1977, while still at the College, he won Commonwealth Institute and London Symphony Orchestra Commissions, in 1978 gaining the Madame Tussaud Award for Figurative Art. Ibbeson's realistic, painted figurative sculptures were amusing with a strong North Country bent. He showed at Nottingham Castle Museum in 1975, at Royal College of Art Gallery in 1977 and in 1979 at Olanda Kelly Gallery, Chicago. By that time he was well established as an exhibitor with the Nicholas Treadwell Gallery in Britain and extensively abroad in group shows, and later showed solo with Treadwell. Was included in the 1980 show Bernard Meadows at the Royal College of Art 1960–1980, held at the College. In 1999, Ibbeson's sculpture of the comedian Eric Morecambe was unveiled on the seafront at his home town, Morecambe; in 2001, in Jarrow, his memorial commemorating the sixty-fifth anniversary of the march of shipbuilders to London to demand work.

Peter IBBETSON 1909– Painter, printmaker, draughtsman and teacher, brought up in Yorkshire. He came of a farming family and was privately educated, then attending Oxford University. Studied art at Bradford College of Art, 1929–32, Central School of Arts and Crafts, 1932–4, then for about two years in France and Spain. Showed with Senefelder Club, at public galleries in Sheffield and Bradford, did a mural for the science section of the 1951 Festival of Britain and had one-man shows in London and Oxford. Lived for some years in Oxford.

Diane IBBOTSON 1946– Painter and teacher, born in Colne, Lancashire. Between 1964–71 Ibbotson attended University of Reading and Royal Academy Schools, then returned to Lancashire and taught, some time at Blackpool College of Art. Between 1974–8 she taught at the School of Art in Falmouth, Cornwall, where she settled. Was included 1989 Newlyn Orion Galleries exhibition A Century of Art in Cornwall 1889–1989, represented by the typically large landscape All that Glitters, which took five years to complete.

Jill IBROM 1942– Artist in oil, egg tempera and watercolour, born in London, who studied at Watford College of Art, was a draughtswoman for 10 years, then while bringing up her son found more time to paint. The natural history artist John Wilkinson was an influence, teaching her how to use egg tempera. In 1982 was accepted by Medici Society; she produced a series of nativities which they published, one a best-seller. Natura Designs and Polytint also published Ibrom's work. At various times was a member of Hesketh Hubbard Art Society and Watford and Bushey Art Society. Showed in mixed exhibitions at Medici and Mall Galleries, Jane Marler Gallery in Ludlow and Barbican Centre. Had solo shows at Watford Central Library and Chapel Art Centre, Oswestry. Lived in Bushey, Hertfordshire.

Taiko ICHIKAWA 1967– Figurative artist who studied at Hastings College of Art and Technology, 1993–4; University of East London, 1994–7; and the Royal Academy Schools, 1997–00, taking part in the final year show. Exhibitions also included Pleasance Theatre and RA Summer Exhibition, both 1999. Lived in Underbarrow, Kendal, Cambria, and London.

Peter IDEN 1945– Painter, born an identical twin in Shottermill, Surrey, who studied at West Sussex College of Art & Design, Worthing, 1962–4. Iden freelanced as a topographical watercolourist from 1967, but a serious illness in 1993 prompted him to give up commercial work to concentrate on oil painting, which he had taken up in 1992. He specialised in studies of the South Downs and was a member of the Society of Sussex Painters, Sussex Watercolour Society and the Society of Architectural and Industrial Artists. Showed regularly at RI until he turned to oils. Held many solo shows in Sussex, and in 1979 in Cambridge, and exhibited elsewhere in England and in Chartres, France. Worthing Art Gallery holds examples. From 1969 lived in Chichester, Sussex. Messum's included

Iden's work in Around Two Thousand and Three, 2003, in 2004 giving him a major solo show. This revealed Iden's indebtedness to recuperative walks across the West Sussex downland. Music was also an inspiration.

Cyril IFOLD 1922–1986 Painter and draughtsman who worked at the Yniscedwyn Colliery, Glamorgan, living nearby at Glanrhyd. Ifold's father died when Cyril was eight and to help support the family he delivered newspapers and began picking coke at a tin-plate factory before joining a local colliery. Aged about 15, Ifold began until he was about 23 taking lessons in anatomy from Arthur Pawson, a retired art teacher. During World War II Ifold briefly studied with Alfred Janes at Swansea Art School. When a friend from the School took him to see the Polish émigré artist Josef Herman at Ystradgynlais Ifold saw the direction that his work should take. After initial coolness about his portfolio, Herman later told Ifold's mother that Cyril had great potential. Despite rejection by organisers of the RA Summer Exhibition, where Ifold's grandfather Frederick Ifold had shown regularly in the mid-1800s, encouragement from his wife and from David Bell, curator of the Glynn Vivian Art Gallery, Swansea, prompted Cyril to continue painting after work in the pit. Few of his early pictures survive. Works that do show a range of influences, from seventeenth-century Dutch genre and still life paintings to Cézanne and the Futurists. After Ifold died during his first major solo show at Glynn Vivian, his widow withdrew work from sale and had it returned to their home in Seven Sisters, near Neath. His pictures were featured in Miner-Artists: The Art of Welsh Coal Workers, National Museum & Gallery, Cardiff, 2000.

Rudolph IHLEE 1883–1968 Painter and draughtsman, born in London. He was apprenticed to Ferranti as an engineer in 1902, but entered Slade School of Fine Art, 1906–10, where he proved a brilliant student, winning many prizes. After two solo shows at Carfax Gallery, 1912–14, Ihlee worked as an engineering draughtsman in Peterborough during World War I. The year after he became a member of NEAC, in 1921 Ihlee had a successful show at Leicester Galleries, but then settled in Collioure, in the south of France. Although he had a solo exhibition at Chenil Gallery in 1926, between the wars his life and exhibiting career was in France; his second wife, Isabelle, was French. He returned to England when World War II broke out, working in a factory in Leicester, settling eventually in West Deeping, Lincolnshire. He had a solo show at St Peter's College Hall, Peterborough, with Arts Council support, in 1951, and another in Sleaford in 1968. There was a show seven years after he died at Rutland Sixth Form College, Oakham, then in 1978 a retrospective at Graves Art Gallery in Sheffield and Belgrave Gallery. Victoria & Albert Museum, Manchester City Art Gallery and Cecil Higgins Art Gallery, Bedford, hold work. (The family pronunciation of Ihlee is Eelay, although Ighly is common.)

Elizabeth IKIN 1948– Photomontage artist and teacher, born in Derby, who was inspired by a radio talk by the composer Michael Tippett to abandon a half-done philosophy degree for art. Ikin did a foundation course in art and design at Derby College of Art, 1972–3, then obtained a sculpture within fine art honours degree at Hull College of Fine Art, 1973–6. Her teacher and mentor was the sculptor Austin Wright; she was influenced by the land art movement; and began to investigate with photography, having begun taking photographs aged 10 with a box camera. Moved from black-and-white into colour 1976–7, then in the late 1990s from cut-and-paste to a computer to create her new landscapes and seascapes using shapes and forms, patterns and colours. From 1982–5 Ikin was a visiting lecturer at art college departments of sculpture and photography/film; taught music, 1986–94; was from 1994 education officer at Gainsborough's House, Sudbury; from 1995 being a freelance photography workshop tutor. Exhibited extensively from 1975, in 2000 having a 25-year retrospective at Usher Gallery, Lincoln. Lived in Suffolk.

Shona ILLINGWORTH 1966– Artist using a range of modern media who did a foundation course in art and design, Goldsmiths' College, 1985–6, graduating with first-class honours in fine art there, 1986–8. Awards included first prize, Onufri 99, International Art Exhibition, Tirana, Albania, and a London Arts Board Individual Artist Award, both 1999, in 2000 being nominated for the Paul Hamlyn Awards for Artists. Her many residencies included Rosendale Odyssey, The Photographers' Gallery, 1996; High Definition: British Design for a Digital Future, British Council, with Brazil and Far East tour, 1999; and Genes and Makeup, funded by Lighthouse, Brighton, shown at the Round House and Brighton Media Centre Gallery, Brighton, 2000. Illingworth was also involved in projects involving ex-offenders and political refugees. Group shows included From Moment to Moment, tape/slide installation, Cambridge Darkroom, Cambridge, 1989; Gym Practice, photographic light works, Arts Depot, 1995; and Mostyn Open 11, video installation, Oriel Mostyn, Llandudno, 2000. Among solo exhibitions were Walking on Letters, video installation, Placentia Arte, Galleria Contemporanea, Piacenza, Italy, 2000, and Passing, three-screen video and sound work, Hayward Gallery inside and outside, 2001.

Bryan ILLSLEY 1937– Artist in wide range of media, born in Surbiton, Surrey, whose output included gestural, abstract works, as in his shared show at Barrett Marsden Gallery in 1999. Illsley was an apprentice stonemason, 1953; attended evening classes at Kingston School of Art, 1954–7; moved to St Ives, Cornwall, 1963, and worked part-time at the Leach Pottery, 1964–6. During that time he did some jewellery work with Breon O'Casey and from 1968–82 they were partners, after which Illsley went solo. He contributed to numerous jewellery shows: at Arnolfini in Bristol, also at the Ewan Phillips, Pace and Electrum Galleries. Other exhibitions included Marjory Parr, St Ives and London, 1969–72; Patrick Seale Gallery, 1981–2; Oxford Gallery, Oxford, 1981–3; Leeds City Art Gallery, 1983; Chiltern Sculpture Trail, 1990–1; and Jamison Thomas Gallery, Portland, Oregon, 1991. Contemporary Art Society, Kettle's Yard in Cambridge, Plymouth City Art Gallery and several education committees held examples. Lived in London.

John ILLSLEY 1949– Rock band musician and artist, born in London, who early in the 1970s had to choose between being a painter or musician. For 26 years commitment to music made painting and drawing into a hobby after bass-player Illsley and former journalist and teacher-turned-guitarist, singer and songwriter Mark Knopfler met by chance, prompting formation of the group Dire Straits. In 1992, after Dire Straits' last tour, Illsley began painting full-time. Initially he worked from a garage in a mews house in west London, replaced in 1996 by a purpose-built studio in his Hampshire garden. Illsley was self-taught apart from two lessons from a painter friend, and worked in oil on canvas. His first exhibition was at Torkington Gallery, Stamford, 1996, his second at Walton Contemporary Art Gallery, 1997. In 1999 he had a solo exhibition at Compton Cassey Gallery, Gloucestershire, which included him in its Middle East and Europe touring show Musicians as Artists.

Tadeusz ILNICKI 1906–1993 Painter of simple, stylised figures, born on Kiernasowka Estate, Ukraine, educated in Tulczyn, Podole. From 1926–7 he studied at the Fine Arts Polytechnic in Odessa, in 1929 being arrested by the Soviets and deported to work in forestry in the Archangielsk region. Ilnicki escaped on a Dutch ship to France where he was given political asylum, and from 1931–3 studied stained glass at the Conservatoire des Arts et Metiers, which would influence his later painting style. After moving back to Poland in 1933, in 1939 Ilnicki returned to Paris. There he joined the Polish Army, but on the fall of France he moved to England where he served with the 1st Armoured Division, participating in the liberation of western Europe. After demobilisation in 1947 Ilnicki settled in London, studying painting under Professor Marian Bohusz-Szyszko at the Polish School of Painting. Mixed exhibitions included Galerie Creuze, Paris, 1955; Walker's Gallery, 1955; New Vision Centre Gallery, 1964; Drian Galleries, from 1964; and National Museum, Warsaw, 1978. Among his solo shows were Gallery One, 1954; Grabowski Gallery, 1959; and Drian Galleries, 1965 and 1967. In 1978 Ilnicki donated 40 paintings to the Polish National Gallery, Warsaw; Toruń University in Poland also holds his work.

Gbenga ILUMOKA 1967– Painter and teacher born to Nigerian parents in London, where he continued to live. From early on he was keen to paint and draw, but lacked parental support. Unable to afford private lessons or university tuition, between 1994–8 was an attendant at the Tate and National Galleries, painting in his spare time. He completed an honours degree in fine art at Middlesex University in 2001, having achieved an art and design diploma, with merit and distinction, Chelsea School of Art, 1986–7. Ilumoka taught painting and drawing at Diorama Arts, 1998–02. His figurative work, Western in style but including European and African symbolism, was included in 2002 Contemporary British Art at The Millinery Works, where he had a solo exhibition in 2003.

Pierre IMHOF 1956– Imhof graduated with honours from Middlesex Polytechnic, 1983–6, in the latter year having a solo show at Sec 52 Gallery, Zürich, Switzerland. There were other one-mans at Roevekamp Gallery, Zürich, in 1988 and at Sec 52 Gallery again in 1989. Group appearances included The Mansion House, 1986, and East End Open Studios, at Chisenhale Studios, 1989.

IMKER– This is the joint name adopted by the artists Pierre Imhof and Ingrid Kerma, as in Trans Encounter at Phoenix Gallery, Brighton, 2002.

David IMMS 1945– Painter who studied at Derby College of Art and Central School of Art. He was strongly influenced by the work of the writer Thomas Hardy, the prehistoric culture and landscape of Wiltshire and Dorset. Myths such as Demeter and Persephone and The Paradise Garden were themes in Imms' work. He won a number of awards, including Llewellyn Smith Scholarship and the Northern Arts Purchase Award. Had solo exhibitions at University of Stirling, 1974; Queen Mary College, London, 1976; Thomas Hardy Festival, Dorchester, 1978; Southwark Cathedral, 1981; Central Museum and Art Gallery, Northampton, 1983; and several at New Grafton Gallery from 1987. Victoria & Albert Museum holds his work.

Sax IMPEY 1969– Artist using a variety of media, born in Penzance, Cornwall, who returned to the county in 1994, having gained an honours degree in fine art at Newport, 1988–91, from 1992–4 undertaking film, theatre and performance projects and travels in East Africa. In 1995 was elected a member of the Newlyn Society of Artists. In 1997 he was joint editor of the St Ives-based review *Starts*. Exhibitions included a solo at Plymouth Arts Centre Celtic Festival, 1996, and a shared one with Richard Nott, Common Ground, at The Book Gallery, St Ives, 1998, where Impey showed abstracts dominated by vertical forms in which tone, grain and colour were important. Further one-man exhibitions at New Millennium Gallery, St Ives, 2002 and 2004.

Charles INCE 1875–1952 Prolific landscape painter and businessman, born in London where he ran the printing and publishing firm Chas F Ince and Sons. He studied at King's College and art with the landscapist Henry Moon. He was a member of RI and RBA, in which he held senior positions, and of Chelsea Arts Club. Also showed at ROI, RWS, Fine Art Society, Goupil Gallery, Royal Glasgow Institute of the Fine Arts and elsewhere. Lived latterly in Purbrook, Hampshire.

Peter INCHBALD 1919– Painter, notably of murals, born in London. After Winchester College he studied at Oxford University, then at the Royal Academy Schools, 1946–51. Sometimes signing his work P I, he showed at RA, LG, NEAC and elsewhere. Some of his work was reproduced by Shell-Mex and BP Ltd for advertising purposes. Inchbald completed a series of murals in England and Northern Ireland, including Southwell Minster in Nottinghamshire. Lived in London.

INCISIVE LETTERWORK– Organisation set up in 1988 by Brenda Berman and Annet Stirling (see separate entries), who met while studying lettering with Berthold Wolpe at the City & Guilds of London Art School. Drawing on Berman's previous training as a painter and Stirling's as a graphic designer, Incisive Letterwork concentrated on large architectural inscriptions and word sculpture, creating imaginative works without the restraints of classical letter-cutting. In 1996, Incisive Letterwork's partners won a Churchill Fellowship and travelled to Italy to study marble and Roman and Renaissance inscriptions. They showed widely in Britain, including Stone Words at Pentagram, Wolseley Fine Arts and tour in 2002. In 2000, a major solo exhibition of their work was held at Morley Gallery which toured to the Vardy Art Gallery, Sunderland. Berman and Stirling were both members of Letter Exchange.

Marjorie INCLEDON 1891– Painter and stained glass designer who studied at Birmingham School of Art,

1911–14 and again 1941–2. Also studied at Central School of Arts and Crafts, 1917–18, and at Brighton College of Art with Dorothy Coke and Charles Knight, 1942–5. Exhibited RA, ROI, RBA and Society of Sussex Artists, signing her work with a monogram. Lived at Ditchling, Sussex.

Harold ING 1900– Commercial artist who specialised in marine pictures, born in London. Among commissioned work was that done for P&O Group and for Cable and Wireless. Member of Essex Art Club and showed in Home Counties. Lived at Upminster, Middlesex.

Andrew INGAMELLS 1956– Painter and printmaker who had a special interest in depicting buildings. He studied at St Albans School of Art, 1975–6, then London School of Printing, 1976–9. He exhibited at RA, at Blackman Harvey Gallery in 1989, in Architectural Views of Britain at CCA Galleries, 1990, and in the same year in The Broad Horizon, at Agnew. In 1993–4 he shared an exhibition at Galerie Valerie, showing architectural etchings, with a solo show at Grosvenor Gallery, 1994. Had a studio in London.

Alan INGHAM 1920– Sculptor, printmaker and teacher, born in Christchurch, New Zealand, where he studied part-time at the local School of Art early in World War II. He obtained a sculpture diploma, studying under Lyndon Dadswell, at East Sydney Technical College, in Australia, 1946–8; moved to London and attended the Central School of Arts and Crafts with a RA grant, 1949; and was assistant to Henry Moore, 1950–3, whose work remained an influence on Ingham's. While in England, Ingham showed at the first Australian Artists' Association exhibition at the RWS Conduit Street gallery, 1953. He exhibited solo in London and extensively in Australia in the coming years. Returned to New Zealand in 1954, Ingham set up a bronze foundry, establishing a studio and settling in Sydney, New South Wales, 1956. He taught part-time at the National Art School there, and elsewhere. Ingham won the Mildura Prize for sculpture in 1964 and 1967 at the Mildura Art Gallery/Arts Centre. He carried out a series of large-scale commissions, clients including the Snowy Mountains Authority; Phoenix House, Sydney; and Australian Libraries Association. Auckland City Art Gallery in New Zealand holds his work.

Alan INGHAM 1932–2002 Watercolourist and teacher, born in Skipton, Yorkshire. He joined the Royal Navy at an early age, specialised in hydrographic surveying and retired in 1965 as a lieutenant-commander. He founded the Hydrographic Society and lectured at London Polytechnic before becoming a full-time artist, settling in the Cotswolds. Painted that area, Cumbria, Yorkshire and Derbyshire with meticulous care, rather in the style of Victorian watercolourists. Showed with John Noott Twentieth Century in Broadway. Ingham's pictures were also reproduced as prints, greetings cards and calendars; W H Smith used them for its 1990 *Countryside Calendar*. His book *Under a Watercolour Sky*, with an autobiographical introduction, was published in 1996, with a launch show at Phoenix Gallery, Selfridges.

Bryan INGHAM 1936–1997 Painter, sculptor, collagist and etcher, born George Bryan Ingham in Preston, Lancashire. He studied at St Martin's School of Art, 1957–61, with Frederick Gore and Archibald Ziegler, then Royal College of Art, 1961–4, under Carel Weight, with a stay at British Academy, Rome, 1966. An Italian Government Scholarship and a Leverhulme Postgraduate Research Award were won by Ingham. Group exhibitions included Lords Gallery from 1964; Wills Lane Gallery, St Ives and New Ashgate Gallery, Farnham, from 1976. Had a solo show at Graffiti Gallery, 1980, others in Germany, then a series at Francis Graham-Dixon Gallery from 1988. Showed at the Book Gallery, St Ives, in the 1990s. Department of the Environment, Dartington Hall and Ashgate Trusts and Print Collectors' Club in Washington, America, commissioned Ingham, whose work is held by Arts Council, Ashmolean Museum in Oxford, Victoria & Albert Museum and many other public collections in Britain and abroad. Ingham was a prodigiously talented and hardworking artist whose output followed on from the early Cubists. His declared aim was "to beg, borrow, consolidate and synthesise; to add even to the classical tradition of harmony and contained chance". Bryan Ingham Prints, at Belgrave Gallery, St Ives, in 2003–4 demonstrated Ingham's enormous creativity in that field. The Fine Art Society held an exhibition in 2006. For 25 years he lived at Jollytown, a remote and primitive cottage on the Lizard, Cornwall, with sustained periods in Germany. His wife, Ada (or Aysel) Ingham was a novelist, short story writer and poet whose books included *The English Dream*, 1998, the cover illustration a painting by Bryan.

Gillian INGHAM 1951– Abstract painter, born and lived in London, where she continued to work. Studied at Ravensbourne College of Art, 1970–4, then Chelsea School of Art, 1974–5. Took part in many mixed exhibitions, including Stowells Trophy, 1974; LG from 1975; Air Gallery, 1976; Wapping Artists Open Studio Exhibition, 1980; 16 Artists at Battersea Arts Centre, 1982; and 9 Artists from Wapping British Tour, based at DLI Museum & Arts Centre, Durham, 1983. Arts Council and Kettle's Yard, Cambridge, hold her work.

Margo INGHAM 1918–1978 Charismatic gallery owner, artist and collector, notably of L S Lowry, who was a primary school teacher in Manchester where she studied in the evenings under Ian Grant at the local School of Art. From 1946–51 Ingham ran the Mid-Day Studios exhibition space in Mosley Street, which had previously been used by dealer Lucy Wertheim. It became an important gathering place for the Manchester Group and more advanced northern artists, some of whose works had been refused by MAFA. Ingham painted extensively abroad. She was married first to the local artist Ned Owens; she ran a gallery at her home in Rusholme; next was married to painter Geoffrey Lintott, living in Tunbridge Wells; her third husband being advertising executive Bert Drake. Died in Southport, Lancashire.

Mark INGHAM 1960– Painter, draughtsman, sculptor, installations artist and teacher, born in Trinidad, who did a foundation course at Cambridgeshire College of Arts and Technology, Cambridge, 1979–80; gained an honours degree in sculpture at Chelsea School of Art, 1980–3; and took the same subject for a higher diploma in fine art at Slade School of Fine Art, under Richard Deacon, 1983–5. From 1985–6, Ingham was Henry Moore Fellow at Camberwell School of Art. He was schools co-ordinator, Whitechapel Art Gallery, 1990–4; in 1995 began a doctorate on installations, making/teaching, London Consortium; and held a number of residencies. Ingham researched and made work dealing with the relationship between art and mathematics, and in 1997 worked for a time at Acland Burghley School on a mathematics project, part of the education and training programme of the Institute of International Visual Arts. Kingsway College and University of North London architecture department were among Ingham's teaching venues. Group exhibitions included New Contemporaries (slide show), ICA, 1983; New British Sculptors, Air Gallery, 1986; and Whitechapel Open, Spitalfields Market, 1992. Solo exhibitions included Urban Constructs, Unit 7 Gallery, 1986. Lived in London.

Jean INGLIS 1884–1959 Painter, born in Kensington. Studied at the Slade School of Fine Art under Henry Tonks and Philip Wilson Steer. Painted landscapes widely in England. Exhibited RA, NEAC, RP, RSA and Paris Salon, where she gained an Hon. Mention in 1928. Took part in the Pilgrim Trust *Recording Britain* project and had work reproduced in *La Revue Moderne* and *Scots Observer*. She carried out government commissions to copy state portraits of HM King George V and Queen Mary. Sometimes just signed work Jean. Lived at Amberley, near Stroud, Gloucestershire.

John INGLIS 1953– Painter and collage artist noted for his often complex pictures based on memories of coast and landscape. Born in Glasgow, he studied at Gray's School of Art, Aberdeen, 1970–5, and Patrick Allan-Fraser School of Art, Hospitalfield, Arbroath. Inglis won two travelling scholarships, the Keith Prize in 1975 and gained two Scottish Arts Council Awards. Showed in mixed exhibitions at RSW, of which he was a member from 1984, winning an award three years later; RSA; SSA; and Royal Glasgow Institute of the Fine Arts. Had solo shows at Aberdeen Art Centre, Aberdeen University, Compass Gallery in Glasgow and Taurus Gallery, Skipton. Scottish Arts Council holds his work. Lived in Larbert, Stirlingshire.

Judy INGLIS 1952–2003 Draughtsman, artist in oil on gesso ground on paper and teacher, born in Cornwall. She studied at Falmouth School of Art, 1970–1; Exeter College of Art and Design, 1971–2; graduated in fine art with honours from Sheffield City Polytechnic, 1980–3; then gained her master's degree in painting at Royal College of Art, 1984–7, notable teachers there including especially Peter de Francia, also John Golding, Ken Kiff, Alan Miller and Jenny Durrant. In the mid-1980s Inglis won several awards, in 1985 being an exchange student to Athens Academy, Greece. In 1987–8 she gained a fellowship in painting at Gloucestershire College of Art & Design, from 1989 being a senior lecturer at Birmingham Polytechnic, and she was a visiting lecturer at many other centres. Inglis was a powerful draughtsman who said that her work was "figurative, as my concerns are essentially humanist ... I use the autobiographical as a core and then incorporate myth, allegory, ritual and metaphor and literary association to enrich and extend the personal." Inglis had a solo show at Mappin Art Gallery, Sheffield, in 1984. She also exhibited at Birch and Conran Gallery, 1987; Groucho Club, 1988; Ikon Gallery Touring Exhibition, Birmingham, and Paton Gallery, both 1991; and Victoria Art Gallery, Bath, 1992. In 1997, she shared an exhibition with Anita Taylor at MAC (Midlands Arts Centre), Birmingham. Sheffield and Birmingham City Art Galleries hold her work. Lived in Nailsworth, Gloucestershire.

Reece INGRAM 1963– Sculptor in wood, stone, fur and feathers, and teacher, who trained as a taxidermist, 1980–1, at the Booth Museum of Natural History, Brighton, and Snowdonia Taxidermy Studios, Llanrust. After a foundation course in art and design at Wrexham College of Art, 1981–2, Ingram gained an honours degree in fine art, sculpture, at Brighton Polytechnic, 1982–5, then his master's in site-specific sculpture at Wimbledon School of Art, 1990–1. Notable teachers at Brighton included James Tower, Peter Randall-Page and Anthony Gormley, and at Wimbledon, Lee Grandjean. In 1986 Ingram was assistant to Randall-Page. Teaching posts included Open College of the Arts, 1991–2. Ingram's residencies included Booth Museum of Natural History, Brighton, 1988; Towner Art Gallery, Eastbourne, which holds his work, 1990; and The Beacon School, Crowborough, 1995. Group show included Insights, Arundel Gallery, 1991; Maidstone Library Gallery, 1993; and Rye Art Gallery, 1994. Later solo exhibitions included Hannah Peschar Gallery, Ockley, 1993. Among Ingram's many commissions were Three Otters, Bourton Park, Buckingham, 1991; Whalebones, Herne Bay (winner of Rouse Award for public art), 1993; and The Garden of St Jerome, The Princess Alexandra Hospital, Harlow, 1995. Lived in Brighton, Sussex.

Don INKERSOLE 1946– Artist and teacher, born in Colchester, Essex, where he studied at the School of Art, 1963–4, then at Maidstone College of Art, 1967–70, teachers including Norman Stevens, David Hockney, David Oxtoby and Stuart Brisley. He taught at Amersham School of Art, 1985–6. Inkersole considered himself "in the Constable tradition, although strongly informed by modern and contemporary painters from Hopper to Auerbach and, of course, Impressionism". He was "motivated to paint because of the intensity of life" and "related to Constable's feeling of being overpowered by nature while sitting in the corner of a large field." Inkersole participated in a number of shows in London, the home counties and East Anglia throughout the 1970s and 1980s, had a solo exhibition at the Upper Street Gallery and also sold through Waterman's of St James's and Lawrence Churchill Fine Art. A number of his pictures hung in stately homes around Britain.

Henry INLANDER 1925–1983 Painter and teacher, born in Vienna, Austria, as Heinz Inlander. Lived in Trieste, 1935–8. Settled in England 1938 and became a British subject in 1947. Attended St Martin's School of Art, 1939–41, Camberwell School of Arts and Crafts part-time from 1945, becoming full-time in 1949. In 1950 went to the Slade School of Fine Art, where he won the summer composition prize, in 1952 a Rome Scholarship. First one-man show at Galleria La Tartaruga, Rome in 1953, his first in London being at Leicester Galleries in 1956. Awarded Premio Acitrezza, Sicily, 1958, and a Harkness Commonwealth Fellowship to America in 1960–61. Taught at Camberwell 1957–79 and had many group and one-man shows in Britain and abroad. Tate Gallery, Contemporary Art Society, Arts Council, provincial and overseas galleries hold his work. Lived in London.

Brian INNES 1952– Painter and designer, born in Scotland, who studied at both the Hornsey and Royal Colleges of Art. From 1976–80 he was a freelance textile designer, selling in America and Paris, clients including Yves St Laurent and Daniel Hechter. In 1978 Innes began painting, mixed shows including the RA Summer Exhibition, Whitechapel Open and Cadogan Gallery. Won a prize in the RA Christmas card competition in 1987, the following year being commissioned to design one for the Musicians' Benevolent Fund. Was also commissioned to paint a mural for the Malaysian government. Innes had his first solo show at Axis Gallery, Brighton, then a series at Mainhill Gallery, Ancrum. Painting locations included Scotland, St Ives in Cornwall and Provence, France.

Callum INNES 1962– Artist and teacher, born and lived in Edinburgh, who studied in Aberdeen. Innes' early canvases were figurative. Then he painted abstract works tending towards Minimalism, although he still saw his pictures "as having a figurative element". Was included in the British Art Show, 1990; Kunst Europa – Kunstverein Freiburg, Germany, and Artisti Invitatial Premio Internationale, Milan, Rome, London and America, 1991; and New Voices, a British Council Exhibition, Brussels, 1992. Innes' solo shows included Frith Street Gallery from 1990; Jan Turner Gallery, Los Angeles, 1990; Gallery Patrick de Brock, Belgium, 1991; ICA, 1992; and Scottish National Gallery of Modern Art, Edinburgh, 1992–3. Won the NatWest Art Prize, 1998, and Jerwood Painting Prize, 2002. In 2005 Tate St Ives held an exhibition, Resonance, which included a range of works from Innes's Exposed Paintings series that the gallery had commissioned. Innes was then teaching in the fine art school at Glasgow School of Art.

George INNES 1913–1970 Sculptor, born in Glasgow who studied for four years at School of Art there, in 1936 showing at McLellan Galleries. Two years later he showed stone figures at Glasgow Empire Exhibition. After damage to his hands sustained in the Army in World War II Innes found it hard to carve, so produced little work on return to civilian life. This was doubly regrettable. His post-World War II sculpture took an exciting turn with the adoption of Pre-Colombian monumentality combined with cube-like forms. Kirkcaldy Museum and Art Gallery's Seated Figure, in white sandstone, is a prime example. Innes' final years saw his reputation diminish to obscurity, although he was featured in Scottish National Gallery of Modern Art's Scottish Art since 1900 show in 1989–90, and tour.

William INNES 1905–1999 Artist in oil and pastel, born and lived in London. He painted from the time he was a child and first showed when with Royal Air Force during World War II. Innes was a painter of seascapes and landscapes and was "particularly interested in the effects of light on water". He was a member of PS and UA, also exhibiting with RA, NEAC, ROI and elsewhere, having several solo shows in London. Local authorities held his work.

INNOTT 1899– Flower painter in oil, born in London, whose full name was Alfred Richard Innott Barnes. Studied at Camberwell School of Arts and Crafts, 1910, with J Harvey Bloom. Exhibited RA, Croydon Art Society and Contemporary Arts Group. Lived in Carshalton, Surrey.

David INSHAW 1943– Painter and teacher, born in Staffordshire, of idyllic landscapes depicted with much atmosphere and in minute detail. He studied at Beckenham School of Art, 1959–63 then Royal Academy Schools, 1963–6, a French Government Scholarship in 1964 enabling him to work in Paris. In 1966 Inshaw organised Young Contemporaries show, the year he began teaching at West of England College of Art, in Bristol, a position he held until 1975, when he joined Trinity College, Cambridge. Inshaw had first one-man show at Arnolfini Gallery, Bristol, where he had moved, in 1969, with another at Dartington Hall, in Devon. Three years later with Graham and Ann Arnold he formed the Broad Heath Brotherhood, and this trio with four others went on to create The Brotherhood of Ruralists in 1975. In that year Inshaw had a solo show with Waddington Galleries, which went on to represent him. In John Moores Exhibition, Liverpool, 1991–2, Inshaw was represented by Portrait of Silbury Hill: May 1989. Inshaw's exhibition Moments of Vision (Between Fantasy and Reality) was at Agnew in 2004. Arts Council holds his work.

John Henry INSKIP fl. from c.1885–1947 Landscape painter who also completed some interiors, born and lived in Scarborough, Yorkshire. He was a member of RBA and Fylingdales Group, also showing with RA, Walker Art Gallery in Liverpool and ROI. Sussex Cottages and The Bridge at Brandon were among his notable works. Rochdale Corporation acquired views of Whitstable and Walmer.

Christopher INSOLL 1956– Representational painter, gallery owner and teacher, full name Robert Christopher Insoll, who trained and was articled as an accountant. Then studied art at Chelsea, 1978–9, and Falmouth, 1979–82, Schools of Art, gaining an honours degree, during 1981 being an exchange student at Camberwell School of Art. He was offered his master's at Sussex University in 1983, but chose to settle in Cornwall as a full-time artist. In 1985 Insoll started the Artists' Co-operative and Gallery in Portscatho, where he lived. He took part in many mixed shows, including RWA; Osborne Studio, Alberti, Catto and Llewellyn Alexander Galleries; Penzance Art Club, Penwith Society of Arts and Newlyn Art Gallery, Cornwall; and on the continent, including Paris Salon, in 1992 being a prize winner at La Fédération Nationale de la Culture Française, Deauville. Had a major solo exhibition, Paintings about Painting, at Falmouth Art Gallery in 2001. Insoll was a Chelsea Arts Club member. In 2004, The First 20 Years, at The Osborne Studio Gallery, was an exhibition of recent work by the Portscatho Painters. Chris Insoll's book *Portscatho – Portrait of a Cornish Art Colony*, lavishly illustrated with the work of many associated artists, appeared in 2006.

Jeff INSTONE 1941– Artist notable as a draughtsman, who was featured in Woodlands Art Gallery 1981–2 touring show of Greater London Arts Association award winners. Also exhibited at Summer Show 2, Serpentine Gallery, 1976, House Gallery in 1979, Riverside Studios in 1980 and Galeria Akumulatory 2 Poznan, Poland, 1981.

Danny INWARDS 1963– Sculptor and draughtsman, born in London, who attended St Martin's School of Art, 1981–4, and the Royal College of Art, 1984–7. His exhibitions included Brinkley's Gallery, with Rob Ryan, 1987; World Mind, St Martin-in-the-Fields, with Damian Le Bas, 1991; Galleria Burgess, Madrid, Spain, 1991; Come and Live, Conway Hall, 1992; There are some things that are wright and there are some things that are wrong, Kunst Kigk Huise, Eindhoven, Netherlands, 1993; Turbulence, Heritage

Centre, 1994; Metro Institute of Fine Art, 1995; Cat and Crossbones Gallery, New York City, America, 1997; and Fresh Art, Islington, 2003. Among Inwards's solo shows were Broomhill Sculpture Park, Devon, 1998; Mangle Gallery, 2001; and Interpretation!, Chappel Galleries, Chappel, 2005.

Derek INWOOD 1925– Painter, draughtsman and teacher, for whom colour was "the language of painting", producing brightly coloured scenes in oil pastel of the Norfolk coast, where he settled. Inwood served in the Royal Navy, 1944–7, then attended Central School of Dramatic Art, 1948; Salisbury School of Art, 1948–52; Bournemouth Municipal College of Art, gaining his National Diploma in Design, 1953; and his teaching diploma from Southampton University, 1954. Additional studies took place at Académie de la Grande Chaumière, Paris, 1958, and at the Kokoschka School of Vision, Salzburg. Taught at Blandford Secondary Modern School, 1957; Milton Abbey School, 1961; was assistant head, Whatcombe House School for maladjusted teenage boys, 1963; Shiplake College, 1966; and Reading Technical and College of Art, 1976. Showed regularly through his career, including the RA Summer Exhibition, Luton Museum and Art Gallery, The School House Gallery at Wighton and Lena Boyle Fine Art.

IONICUS 1913–1998 Illustrator, painter and teacher, born and lived in Hoylake, Cheshire, real name Joshua Charles Armitage. He studied at Liverpool School of Art, 1929–36, then taught for almost 15 years apart from Royal Naval service during World War II. His teachers included Will Penn. For a time after the war he was on the staff of Wallasey School of Art. Exhibited RA, RCamA and elsewhere in the provinces. From the early 1940s Armitage contributed to *Punch* magazine, also doing humorous drawings for *Lilliput*, *Radio Times* and *Financial Times*. Ferens Art Gallery, Hull, holds his work. Illustrated a number of books, especially humorous titles such as R G G Price's *How to Become a Headmaster*, 1960, Ogden Nash's *The Untold Adventures of Santa Claus*, 1965, and several dozen titles by P G Wodehouse. President of Deeside Art Group.

Anne IRBY CREWS 1927– Versatile printmaker, watercolourist, teacher, maker of garden sculpture in stoneware and terracotta who was born in Sandgate, Kent. She was at the Central and Camberwells Schools of Art at various times between 1946–51, teachers including Rodrigo Moynihan, Claude Rogers, Richard Eurich and William Roberts. She gained a diploma in printmaking from Leamington Art School in 1990. Irby Crews was engaged in film and theatre work for some years and taught, including King Edward's School in Handsworth and at Solihull College of Technology. She was interested in "the visible and invisible world ... landscapes, and interiors of quiet, sacred and haunted places". She illustrated *Solid Citizens*, the study of public sculpture in Birmingham, 1983, and took part in workshops at Hereford and Dudley Museums, Lancaster Polytechnic and Birmingham University. Irby Crews was a member of the Birmingham Print Workshop and Birmingham Artists' Group as well as LG. Showed in RA Summer Exhibition, RCamA, and widely in the West Midlands. Solo shows included Birmingham University, Midland Arts Centre in Birmingham and Harlequin Gallery, Sutton Coldfield, 1992. Leicester University and Worcester Museum and Art Gallery hold examples. Lived in Edgbaston, Birmingham.

Sydney Joseph IREDALE 1896–1967 Painter, born and lived in London, son of the scenic artist Henry Iredale. Studied at Richmond School of Art, 1915, under T M Smith. Exhibited RA, LG, RI, ROI, PS and Richmond Art Circle, of which he was a member.

David IRELAND 1946– Artist who mainly used water-based paints on paper, whose work was "based on the Derbyshire Peak District landscape, particularly the northern 'Dark Peak'" (peat plateaux of Kinder Scout and Bleaklow). He was born in Chesterfield, Derbyshire, and was based at Brimington. Ireland studied at Sheffield College of Art and Design, 1967–70, taught by Brian Peacock, Terry Lee, Paul Curtis and Bill Beech; at the Royal College of Art painting school, 1970–3, under Carel Weight and Roger de Grey, the critic Brian Sewell buying a sketchbook from his degree show; and Leeds University, 1974–5, for his art teacher's certificate. In 1968–9 Ireland won the David Murray Studentship in landscape painting, awarded by the RA, in 1973 the Andrew K Lloyd Scholarship in landscape painting, from the Royal College. From 1975–97 Ireland was an art teacher in secondary/comprehensive schools, then a part-time tutor in adult education. He was a member of the High Peak Artists' and Craftworkers' Association. Exhibitions included the Stowells Trophy Exhibition, where he was a prize winner, and RA Summer Exhibition, both 1972; from 1985, when he won the Chris Beetles Award, at the RWS Open; from 1998 at the Derbyshire Open, winning prizes in six years from 1999–05; Hunting Art Prizes and Laing Landscape Award Exhibitions, both 2000; RI Open, 2001; Leeds Design Innovation Centre, 2002; Blue Moon Café, Sheffield, 2003; and Solomon's Bistro, Buxton, 2005. West Riding of Yorkshire Education Authority, the Nuffield Trust and Derbyshire County Council hold examples.

Helen IRELAND 1961– Painter who attended Central School of Art and Design, 1982–5, then gained her master's degree at Chelsea School of Art, 1986. She was involved in many group shows, including Warwick Arts Trust, 1986–7, Axiom Gallery in Cheltenham and the Royal Over-Seas League annual exhibition, and she also participated in (dis)parties, held at Mappin Art Gallery, Sheffield, in 1992 and in 1993 at Herbert Art Gallery, Coventry. In 1990 she shared a show with Mary Mclean at Pomeroy Purdy Gallery. Pattern was a strong element in Ireland's work, and Indian miniatures, Aboriginal bark paintings and English tapestries were cited as parallels. Lived in London.

James IRELAND 1977– Artist, living and working in Liverpool, who attended Ruskin School of Fine Art, Oxford, 1996–9. Ireland made sculptural objects and installations using everyday items of household furniture and hardware juxtaposed with landscape images culled from magazines, picture books and tourist guides. At times this combination created an allusive and wistful scene which, while offering an escape, could frustrate because of the fragility of the illusion. Ireland won an Acid Fund Portfolio Development Award in 2000. Exhibitions included Big Warm Open, Cambridge Darkroom Gallery, 1999; How we built the world, Hanover Galleries, Liverpool, which he curated, 2000; Double Take, Aspex Gallery, Portsmouth, 2001; and Unscene, Gasworks Gallery, 2002.

In that year f a projects held its first solo show of Ireland's work, shortly after he completed a residency at La Friche, Marseilles, France, and prior to his making a major room installation at the Bluecoat Gallery, Liverpool. Spike Island, Bristol, featured Ireland's work in 2003.

Mary IRELAND 1891– Watercolour painter, stained glass artist, fabric designer, illuminator and writer. Born at Stockingford, Warwickshire, she went on to exhibit at the RA and elsewhere. Dover Town Hall, Bruges Cathedral, in Belgium, and various churches contain her work, such as altarpieces and reredos decorations. Lived at Folkestone, Kent.

Christopher IRONSIDE 1913–1992 Painter, sculptor, draughtsman, designer and teacher who studied at Central School of Arts and Crafts. During World War II he served in the Directorate of Camouflage and worked for the Air Ministry in Leamington Spa. After the war Ironside, a sociable, flamboyant character, worked for the Ministry of Town and Country Planning, then as education officer for the Council of Industrial Design, 1946–8. Taught at Maidstone School of Art and Royal College of Art. Ironside was a painterly painter who shared two exhibitions with his brother, Robin Ironside, at Redfern Gallery in 1944 and Arthur Jeffress in 1960. Also with Robin he collaborated on theatrical designs and postage stamps, including Frederick Ashton's production of the ballet *Sylvia* for Sadler's Wells Ballet at Covent Garden in 1952 and one of the 1964 Shakespeare commemoration issues. Ironside also did much of the designing of decorations for Pall Mall for the Coronation in 1953; designed the obverse side of Britain's decimal coinage; new coinage for Tanzania, Brunei, Qatar, Dubai and Singapore; and the memorial for the Earl and Countess Mountbatten in Westminster Abbey. His first wife was the fashion designer and teacher Janey Ironside, their daughter being the journalist Virginia. Died in Winchester, Hampshire.

Robin IRONSIDE 1912–1965 Painter, theatre designer and writer on art, born and lived in London, studied at Courtauld Institute of Art and overseas. Ironside became assistant keeper at the Tate Gallery, 1937–46, then Contemporary Art Society assistant secretary. Self-taught painter, often of Surrealist pictures, who shared a show with his brother Christopher at Redfern Gallery in 1944, having an initial one-man show at Durlacher Brothers in New York eight years later. Also showed at Hanover and Arthur Jeffress Galleries. Tate Gallery and Leicester City Art Gallery hold his work. While painting, Ironside was developing parallel careers as a stage designer and writer on art. He designed for *Sylvia* at Covent Garden in 1952 and *A Midsummer Night's Dream* at the 1957 Edinburgh Festival. As well as writing for periodicals such as *Horizon*, Ironside wrote the short survey of *Painting Since 1939*, published in 1947, a good introduction to the Neo-Romantic movement; other books include *Wilson Steer*, 1944, and *David Jones*, 1949. Retrospective New Art Centre, 1966. Robin Ironside's niece Virginia's amusing *London Magazine* memoir appeared in August/September 1998.

Albert IRVIN 1922– Painter, printmaker and teacher, born London, which remained his base. Studied at Northampton School of Art, 1940–1, and after five years in Royal Air Force studied at Goldsmiths' College School of Art. Irvin taught for some years from 1960, including Hornsey College of Art, Goldsmiths' College, 1962–83, and gave lessons in Wandsworth Prison. He had his first one-man show at 57 Gallery, Edinburgh, in 1960, and from 1961 held a series at New Art Centre. In 1968 he won an Arts Council Travel Award to America, seven years later gaining an Arts Council Major Award. Also exhibited with LG; had a number of solo exhibitions in Germany; and with Gimpel Fils. In 1990 a retrospective of his paintings, 1960–89, was shown at Serpentine Gallery. There were eightieth-birthday shows at Gimpels Fils and Advanced Graphics London in 2002. Arts Council and other important public collections hold his work, which was abstract, brightly coloured and showed a joy in the manipulation of paint. Irvin was elected RA in 1998.

Magnus IRVIN 1952– Enterprising artist and writer, born and lived in London, who attended Hornsey Art College, 1969–70, and Walthamstow Art College, 1970–3. From 1975 he was editor of the *Daily Twit* newspaper, from 1980 worked as a scenic artist to theatres, films and television. Irvin was a member of the RE from 1997 and in 2002 founded the Department of Reconstructive Archaeology (DORA), of which he was a joint director with Alastair Brotchie; this was autonomous within the London Institute of Pataphysics (LIP), formed the year before. DORA was "dedicated to the reconstruction of lost or forgotten artefacts and applies itself to the re-presentation of these." One offshoot was the Anthony Hancock Retrospective Exhibition, at The Foundry Gallery, 2002, a complete reconstruction of all paintings and sculptures from Hancock's 1960 film *The Rebel*. Irvin's own many public commissions and workshops included a mural at Jack Ashley School, 1984; a rain forest mural with Duncombe Junior School, 1991; cement hillside images of aircraft, Tunstall Western Bypass, Stoke-on-Trent, 1996; and a playground mosaic at Hampstead Parochial School, 2000. Among Irvin's public performances were Vache Folle, outside Galerie Avivson, Paris, "to celebrate British beef," 2001. Took part in numerous group exhibitions, solo show including Barbican Centre, 1987; Redfern Gallery, 1988; Mostyn Gallery, Llandudno, 1989; Art Space Gallery, 1990; Janus Avivson Gallery, from 1991; Fallen Angel Gallery, 1996; and 25 Years of the *Daily Twit*, Original Gallery, 2000. Among his books were *Bananas at War*, 1999, and *Bananas + Fleas*, 2000, both published by Banana Books. Arts Council, Victoria & Albert Museum, British Museum and Imperial War Museum hold examples.

Jaki IRVINE 1966– Artist who was born in Dublin where a bachelor's degree was obtained at the National College of Art and Design, 1984–9, with a master's at Goldsmiths' College, 1992–4. Group shows included Emerging Artists Exhibitions, Dublin, 1991; Sonsbeek International, collaboration with Blue Funk, Arnhem, 1993; The Curator's Egg, Anthony Reynolds Gallery, 1994; and in 1995 a show at Project Art Centre in Dublin and submission *Star* (a three-minute film projection) at Venice Biennale. Had a solo show Margaret Again at Anthony Wilkinson Fine Art, 1995. Lived in London.

Olivia IRVINE 1960– Artist and teacher producing abstract work such as Update, oil on canvas, at Royal Over-Seas League Open, 1994. Born in Kilwinning, Ayr, Irvine studied medicine at Aberdeen University, then attended Edinburgh College of Art and Les Beaux-Arts de Montpellier, France. Taught widely, including privately in Edinburgh and as a visitor at Winchester School of Art. Awards included Stuart Prize at RSA, 1986; Spanish Government Scholarship, 1987; a Scottish Arts Council Small Assistance Grant, 1989; and the Hope Scott Trust Award, 1992. Took part in many mixed shows, including The New Generation in Scotland, Mercury Gallery, Edinburgh, and tour, 1985–6; Chicago International Art Exposition, in America, 1988–9; Modern Masters, City Arts Centre, Edinburgh, 1992; and Solitude and Isolation, Royal College of Physicians, Edinburgh, 1993. Scottish Arts Council; Paintings in Hospitals, Scotland; BBC Scotland; and Eastern General Hospital, Edinburgh, hold examples.

Robert Scott IRVINE 1906–1988 Watercolour painter and teacher, son of an art teacher, Robert Irvine. He was born in Edinburgh, where he settled, studying at the local College of Art, 1922–7. Eventually became principal art master at George Watson's College and was a member of the Scottish Arts Club, being its president in the early 1950s. Showed with RSW of which he was a member, SSA and in North America. Had several solo exhibitions in Edinburgh, including Scottish Arts Club in 1978. Aberdeen and Dundee Art Galleries hold his work as does the RSA and several other public collections. There were many influences on the work of Irvine, including Edward Bawden, John Sell Cotman, John and Paul Nash, S J Peploe, Eric Ravilious and Francis Towne. Irvine, affectionately known as Otto, was one of the first hill climb rally drivers to race competitively, including Turnberry and Silverstone into the 1950s, at the latter driving the OttoCart, which he designed and built with his friend J Cartwright. After his death, his film-maker son Henry Scott-Irvine set up a website in his memory.

Laurence IRVING 1897–1988 Painter, stage and film designer, theatrical producer, book illustrator and writer, son of the actor and writer H B Irving. Born in London. During World War I served in Royal Naval Air Service and won the Croix de Guerre. Studied at Byam Shaw School of Drawing and Painting, 1919, and Royal Academy Schools. In 1928 helped with production of John Masefield's play *The Coming of Christ* in Canterbury Cathedral; about the same time worked with Douglas Fairbanks Senior on the classic films *The Man in the Iron Mask* and *The Taming of the Shrew*, with Mary Pickford. There were 50 major film and stage production designs over the next 40 years. There were also over 40 stage productions, including *Hamlet* and *The Good Companions*. In 1951 published a biography of his grandfather the noted actor-manager Sir Henry Irving. A series of volumes – *The Successors*, *The Precarious Crust*, *Great Interruption* and *Abiding Curiosity* – later appeared on his family and life. He exhibited at Fine Art Society, Agnew, RA, Royal Glasgow Institute of the Fine Arts and Barton Art Gallery, Tenterden, 1987. Books illustrated, often black-and-white with sharp contrasts, included his own *Windmills and Waterways*, 1927; Joseph Conrad's *The Mirror of the Sea*, 1935; and Richard Church's *Dog Toby*, 1953. He had strong associations with many bodies concerned with advancing the theatre. Lived at Wittersham, Kent.

Flavia IRWIN fl. from 1940s– Artist and teacher, born in London, who studied at Chelsea School of Art with Henry Moore and Graham Sutherland and at Ruskin School of Drawing in Oxford. She was married to the painter Roger de Grey. She worked as a freelance designer and later became senior lecturer and head of department of decorative arts at City and Guilds of London School of Art. Group shows included Zwemmer Gallery, RA Summer Exhibitions, RWA, Curwen and Phoenix Galleries. Had a solo show at Ansdell Gallery. Carlisle City Museum and Art Gallery and Department of the Environment hold examples. Elected Senior RA, 1996. Lived in Meopham, Kent.

Gwyther IRWIN 1931– Painter, designer, collagist, relief artist and teacher who worked in a variety of materials, born in Basingstoke, Hampshire, but spent his youth in north Cornwall. He attended Bryanston School, where he was taught by Roger Hilton. For several years in the mid-1950s he studied illustration at Goldsmiths' College School of Art and design at Central School of Arts and Crafts, 1951–4, having first solo show at Gallery One in 1957. This was followed in 1958 with a one-man show at ICA, followed by a string of shows at Gimpel Fils during 1960s. Also went on to exhibit at Marlborough Fine Art, New Art Centre and abroad. Irwin was involved in many important group shows, among them Situation, RBA Gallery, and the Paris Biennale, both 1960; The Art of Assemblage, Museum of Modern Art in New York, 1961; Situation, Arts Council, and British Painting in the Sixties, Whitechapel Art Gallery and tour, both 1963; XXXII Venice Biennale, from which Peggy Guggenheim bought work, 1964; Recent British Painting, Tate Gallery, 1967; Contemporary British Painting, Albright-Knox Art Gallery, Buffalo, America, 1974; Three Decades of Artists, RA, 1983; LG and RA Summer Exhibition, both 1987; and 20th Century British Painting, Redfern Gallery, 1993. In 1965 gained commission for bas-relief in Portland Stone for British Petroleum. Held series of teaching posts at Hornsey College of Art, Chelsea School of Art and Brighton Polytechnic, from which he retired as head of fine art in 1984, after 15 years there. Irwin said that he "wrote" his pictures, the equivalent of Persian carpets with their own iconography. By the late 1980s the collage studies from which he started each work were composed almost entirely from his own art, colour prints of recent paintings being cut into strips and recomposed, sometimes rephotographed and recut, shredded into overlaid fragments. The outcome was rich geometrical abstracts, vibrant with colour. Irwin's later solo shows included a retrospective at Gimpel Fils, 1987; The Gallery at John Jones, 1992; Redfern Gallery, 1994; The Royal Cornwall Museum, Truro, 1995; and RWA and tour, 1996. Redfern Gallery showed early work in 2006. Tate Gallery and Arts Council hold examples. Irwin lived in south London and latterly suffered from Alzheimer's Disease.

Bert ISAAC 1923–2006 Painter, printmaker and illustrator, especially of landscape, and teacher. He was born in Cardiff where he attended the College of Art. Then started a teaching career that took him to a number of schools and colleges in Wales and England, including heading the art department at Battersea College of Education. Was elected RWA in 1994, at various times being a member of Society of Industrial Artists, WSW and The Welsh Group. Had many solo exhibitions including Howard Roberts Gallery in Cardiff, Richmond Hill Gallery in Surrey, Jablonski Gallery, University of Birmingham, and public galleries in Lincoln and Hull, in 1992 having a retrospective of paintings and prints at Circle Gallery, Pontypridd, with another at Brecknock Museum, Brecon, 1996. Took part in extensive mixed shows, including Leicester Galleries, RA, SEA, SWG, WAC and National Eisteddfod of Wales, where he shared the Gold Medal for Painting in 1989. Also showed at Hill Court Gallery, Abergavenny, run by his wife Joan, where he was latterly artist-in-residence. Illustrated several books, including his own *The Landscape Within*, 1992. National Museum of Wales in Cardiff, CASW, the Universities of Oxford and London hold examples. In 1997, Isaac was elected an Hon. Artist Member of the RCamA. Lived in Abergavenny, Gwent.

John ISAACS 1968– Sculptor, born in Lancaster, who studied for a science degree in biology at Exeter University, 1987–8; obtained a fine art degree from Cheltenham College of Art, 1988–91; and his master's in sculpture at Slade School of Fine Art, 1991–3. Isaacs was a fan of science fiction whose work superficially could appear amusing but had more serious implications, as seen at Young British Artists VI, Saatchi Gallery, 1996. Some of his pieces were not for the faint-hearted, such as his Today I started loving, a realistic severed leg, shown at Art Basel Miami Beach, 2003. Had a solo installation The Diary of a Loner at Chapter Arts Centre, Cardiff, 1999; other shows including, in 2002, Voices from the id at Beaconsfield, Dumb planets are round too, VTO, and Feigen Contemporary, New York; and in 2004, Museum 52. There, Isaacs showed a monumental turd, of which he said: "I was looking at the idea of unification and finding a point of structure where people are the same". Lived in London.

Jacques ISELIN 1933– Painter and teacher, born in France, who studied at L'École Nationale Supérieure des Beaux-Arts, Paris, settling in England in 1956. Iselin taught at the Lycée Français in London. His painting The Elements of the Holy Communion, rich in colour and symbolism and slightly abstracted, was commissioned for The Methodist Church Collection and completed in 1963.

James Lawrence ISHERWOOD 1917–1988 Painter who was born and lived in Wigan, Lancashire, where he ran The Isherwood Gallery. He studied at the local Technical College, 1934–53. Isherwood travelled extensively and had over 200 shows, including colleges at Oxford and Cambridge Universities. He painted a number of celebrities, including the singer Gracie Fields, the round-the-world yachtsman Sir Francis Chichester and Lord and Lady Weymouth. Some portraits were issued in signed, limited editions. Churchill and Pembroke Colleges in Cambridge hold his work. Isherwood was an eccentric, controversial character whose work was uneven, often garish and awkward, but who could occasionally produce a telling image, as seen when a large body of it was included in The Northern Art Show, Mall Galleries, 1994. In 1998, Isherwood's family held a sell-out memorial show in Wigan Town Hall. The Scarisbrook Hotel, Southport, where the artist temporarily lived after a fire at his Wigan home, has an Isherwood function room and suite decorated with his prints. FarmiloFiumano put on a retrospective show in 2004.

Timur ISKHAKOV 1968– Painter of stylised and poetic figurative works, with an icon-like quality, born in Moscow, Russia. Studied at Republican College of Art, Tashkent, 1983–7, then made postgraduate studies at Royal Academy Schools, London, 1993–6, gaining the Jack Goldhill Scholarship, and the A T Kearney Prize in his degree show. Showed with Atrium Gallery, 1991, and Art Moderne Gallery, 1992, both Moscow, also at Cadogan Contemporary from 1992, Bruton Street Gallery, 1994, and RA Summer Exhibition from 1994, then winning the Guinness Prize for First Time Exhibitor. Also exhibited in France and America. Showed solo with Cadogan Contemporary from 1996. Lived in London.

Runa ISLAM 1970– Artist using film and video multi-projection installation, born in Dacca in what is now Bangladesh. Studied at Manchester, Middlesex and the Rijsakademie, Amsterdam. The installation Tuin was included in East International, Norwich School of Art & Design, 1999. Islam was also included in Hayward Gallery tour The British Art Show 5, 2000–1. Lived in London.

Diane Bruce ISMAY 1932–1983 Painter, sculptor and muralist, born in London. Her father was George Bruce Ismay, her mother Florence Edrington Ismay, of Fort Worth, Texas (Diane's paternal great-grandfather, Thomas Henry Ismay, founded White Star Line, which built the liner *Titanic*). Diane graduated from Arlington Heights High School and then attended Finch College, New York; the Slade School of Fine Art for periods between 1953–8, when she was taught sculpture by Professor A H Gerrard, who carried out a number of important commissions for the Ismay family; and at the Royal College of Art. Socially she made her début at The Assembly Ball, Fort Worth, in 1952, and in 1953 at the Court of St James's; and had a solo exhibition at Fort Worth Art Museum in 1961. Miss Ismay maintained a house and studio in America at Aledo, where she lived for part of each year, and had a farm in Wales, where she died.

Graham ISOM 1945– Painter in oil and lithographer, and teacher, specialising in equine art, born in Kent. Studied at Ravensbourne College of Art, 1960–5, then taught painting and sculpture at a grammar school in Dorset until turning freelance in 1973. Became a member of the Society of Equestrian Artists and American Academy of Equine Art. Took part in group shows at Osborne and Tryon Galleries and Rubicon Studios, having solo exhibitions at Michael Stewart and Equus Art Galleries and in America at Klausner/Cooperage Gallery. Won many awards in Britain and America. Commissions included a painting of the Grand Military Gold Cup for the officers' mess of the Household Cavalry and a large-format calendar of 13 pictures for Spillers UK Ltd. Kentucky Derby Museum holds his work. Lived in Baltonsborough, Somerset.

George ISRAEL 1914–2004 Painter, singer and teacher who studied at West Ham Municipal College of Art and the Royal Academy Schools. Israel sang opera at Covent Garden and taught art, but did not push himself to exhibit. Among galleries where he showed were The Camel Art Studio, Kingston Hill Gallery, Trinity Gallery, Arundel, and Parkshot House. The New Grafton Gallery latterly promoted his work, in 2005 including it in Still Lifes and Sketchbooks.

Milan IVANIČ 1947– Painter in oil on canvas, mainly of landscape, born in Czechoslovakia, who studied at Prague's Academy of Fine Arts, 1967–70, then moved to England, settling in Lancaster. Exhibited in mixed shows at Ash Barn Gallery, Petersfield; Terrace Gallery, Worthing, New Ashgate Gallery, Farnham; and Cowfold Gallery, Cowfold. Solo shows included Keele University; Aston Arts Centre, Birmingham; Wolfson College, Oxford, and Clyde Bertrand Gallery, Stockton, California, America.

Katarina IVANIŠIN 1975– Painter, born in Croatia, who gained her master's in fine art painting at the Royal College of Art. Among her solo exhibitions were Chase, Royal College of Art, 2003, and Faith, Transition Gallery, A1 Gallery in Hong Kong, and CAS, Osaka, Japan, all 2004. In that year she was an Artist of the Day at Flowers Central, chosen by Peter Griffin. Solo exhibitions included Arthus Gallery, Brussels, Belgium, 2002, and Beck Gallery, Zagreb, Croatia, 2004.

Jocelyn IVANYI 1900–1993 Naïve painter who took up art aged 77. Thrice married and twice divorced with a son by her first husband, she made a living as a dressmaker and designed and made hats. During World War II the Ministry of Defence employed her to collect iron around the country. Her third marriage was to the Hungarian art historian and writer Bèla Ivanyi Grünewald, whose father was a notable painter. They settled from London to Alphamstone, Essex, where she created a beautiful garden. This and her animals featured often in Ivanyi's pictures. Later work was less detailed, due to cataracts. Ivanyi was a woman of strong beliefs: liberalism, pacifism and anti-racism. She died in Suffolk and there was a memorial show at Gainsborough's House, Sudbury, 1994.

Pamela IZZARD 1926– Artist in mixed media and teacher, born and lived in London. She was married first to the artist Keith Lucas, then to Jack Millar. Izzard studied at Beckenham and Bromley Schools of Art under Carel Weight and Ruskin Spear. She taught at Harrogate and Walthamstow Schools of Art, North-East London Polytechnic and Royal Academy Schools and elsewhere. Izzard showed regularly in RA Summer Exhibitions, also with NEAC, LG, David Paul Gallery in Chichester and Curwen Gallery. Solo shows included Ashgate Gallery in Farnham, Linton Court Gallery, Abbot Hall Art Gallery, Kendal, and Duncan Campbell Fine Art, 2001. Several public authorities hold examples.

J

JABIR: *see* **Dave BERRY-HART**

Hilary JACK 1958– Artist, born in St Helens, Lancashire, who graduated with honours in fine art, Manchester Metropolitan University, 1995, obtaining a master's degree there in 2003. In that year Jack participated in a short postgraduate residential course selected by Goldsmiths' College and The Academy of Fine Art, Budapest, Hungary. It holds her work, as do Crosby Homes and Spin Media, both based in Manchester, where she had a studio. Jack's exhibitions included Winter Show, Castlefield Gallery, Manchester, and the site-specific installation Bloodstream, Islington Mill, Salford, both 1999; Consequences, Salford City Art Gallery, 2001; Ladies Only, Liverpool Biennial of Contemporary Art, 2002; and Beyond the Endgame: Abstract Painting in Manchester, Manchester Art Gallery, 2003. Among later solo exhibitions were Wallpaper?, Timber Wharf Gallery, Manchester, 2002. Her work was covered extensively in art and other media and featured on television.

Jim JACK 1955– Jack attended North East London Polytechnic, 1975–8, and the Working Men's College, 1981–5. He appeared at Vortex Gallery, from 1985; Art Fair, Air Gallery, 1988–9; and Critics Choice 5 at Air Gallery and East End Open Studios, based at Richmond House Studios, both in 1989.

Richard JACK 1866–1952 Painter, born in Sunderland, County Durham, who studied at York School of Art, winning a National Scholarship to Royal College of Art in 1886. Two years later a Travelling Scholarship took him to Paris where he worked at Académie Julian and Atelier Colarossi, his teachers including such academic perfectionists as Adolphe Bouguereau. Returning to London he worked for some time as a black-and-white artist for several magazines, including *The Idler*. He painted a number of royal portraits and interiors; won a silver medal at Paris Salon; was a member of RP and RI; and was elected RA in 1920. In his latter years he worked in Canada, dying in Montreal.

Bill JACKLIN 1943– Painter, draughtsman, printmaker and teacher, born in London. After studying graphics at Walthamstow School of Art, 1960–1, then working as a graphic designer, Jacklin returned to Walthamstow in 1962 to study painting and was then at Royal College of Art, 1964–7. Jacklin then taught for eight years, at Chelsea School of Art, Hornsey and Royal Colleges of Art and at schools in Kent and Surrey. Jacklin's reputation started to be established in 1970 when he began exhibiting in group exhibitions at Museum of Modern Art in New York and also had the first of a series of solo shows at Nigel Greenwood Inc. After appearing in mixed company at Marlborough Fine Art in 1978, the following year Jacklin had a one-man exhibition there, and continued to show with Marlborough. Jacklin's work went through a number of changes, although underlying it were preoccupations with geometry and light. Environmental Art, Pop Art and Minimalism claimed him for a time, then he worked representationally, being noted for his American townscapes in which strong draughtsmanship and a distinctive palette were evident. In 1986 moved from London to New York, which then featured in his pictures, a sample being included in a fiftieth birthday survey at Museum of Modern Art in Oxford, 1992–3. Arts Council holds Jacklin's work. Was made RA in 1991.

Florence F JACKMAN 1892– Painter in oil who specialised in flowers and portraits. Brought up in Essex, she studied with Frederic Whiting and married the painter Charles Jackson. Member of the Arts Club. Exhibited RA, NEAC, RP and in America. Lived in London.

Andrzej JACKOWSKI 1947– Painter and teacher, born in Penley, North Wales. Jackowski's parents were Polish, and he spent the first 11 years of his life in a refugee camp on the English Welsh/border, where Polish was spoken. Aged 14, he decided to become a painter and produced his first self-portrait. He studied at Camberwell School of Arts and Crafts, 1966–9, Falmouth School of Art, 1972–3, and Royal College of Art, 1974–7. During his last two years as a student he produced the magazine *Eleven 32* with David Drain, also winning an Abbey Minor Travelling Scholarship and the Rodney Burn Award and John Minton Scholarship. Jackowski became artist-in-residence at the University of Surrey in 1978–9, two years later being a prizewinner at Tolly Cobbold Eastern Arts. Jackowski was first prizewinner at the John Moores Exhibition, Liverpool, in 1991–2 with his picture The Beekeeper's Son. He had a major show at Marlborough Fine Art in 1986, and in 1988 was represented in the Royal College of Art's Exhibition Road show, by which time he had been on its staff for three years. There were additional one-man exhibitions at Rubicon Gallery, Dublin, Ireland, 2000, Purdy Hicks, 2002, and a Purdy Hicks show toured to University Gallery, Northumbria University, 2003. That included over 80 works on paper spanning 1963–03, of which the artist said that they fluctuated "between a kind of vigilant dreaming and being wide awake.... These images are poetic metaphors for something real, intimate and mysterious in our lives." Jackowski drew on personal experience, films, poetry and art to produce haunting and intense works, examples of which are held by Arts Council. Lived in Brighton, Sussex.

Susan JACKS 1956– Painter and teacher, born in Berkshire, who studied at Winchester School of Art, 1995–8. As well as teaching children Jacks conducted adult workshops and demonstrations. Influenced by Titian, Turner and Monet, her pictures were "generally large oil paintings, an abstract response to landscape." Group exhibitions included Sefton Open, Atkinson Art Gallery, Southport, and South West Open, Plymouth City Museum & Art Gallery, both 1998; Fisherton Mill, Salisbury, from 1998; Women's Work, Willis Museum, Basingstoke, 1999; Today Is Enough, Museum of Modern Art, Wales, Machynlleth, 2000; and Beatrice Royal Gallery, Eastleigh, 2001. In 1999, had solo shows at Fairfields Art Centre, Basingstoke, and The Tower, Winchester. Lived in Berkshire and Hampshire, settling in Cornwall.

Albert Edward JACKSON 1873–1952 Illustrator, black-and-white artist and painter. Born in London, he studied at Camden School of Art under Francis Black. From 1893–1947 he worked as an illustrator for Amalgamated Press, working on such periodicals as *Little Folks*, *The Quiver* and *The Strand Magazine*. Also illustrated a number of children's books. Exhibited RA, London Sketch Club and RBA. Bristol City Art Gallery holds his work. Member of East Sussex Arts Club, and lived in Hastings. His daughter was the artist Muriel Amy Jackson.

Alison JACKSON 1960– Artist and teacher who graduated with honours in fine art (sculpture), Chelsea College of Art, 1993–7, gaining her master's in fine art photography, Royal College of Art, 1997–9. Jackson won the *Creative Camera* and The Photographers' Gallery Awards, both Royal College of Art, 1999, and in 2002 the Creative Circle Silver Award for Schweppes campaign, *Campaign* Advertising Awards (Gold and two Silver) for same campaign and BAFTA Award for Innovation, for *Double Take*, BBC2. Teaching included Kent Institute of Art and Design, Camberwell School of Art, Southampton University and Slade School of Fine Art. Took part in many group shows in Britain and abroad. Jackson had a series of solo exhibitions at Richard Salmon Gallery from 1999, with others at Jerwood Space, 2001, and Musée de la Photographie, Charleroi, Belgium, 2002.

Arthur JACKSON 1911–2003 Mainly abstract painter, principally in oil, also in watercolour and scraperboard, born in Rotherham, Yorkshire, of a Dewsbury family. He attended St Martin's School of Art, 1929–31. Jackson's full name was Arthur Jackson Hepworth. He was the first cousin of the sculptor Barbara Hepworth and although as an architect he worked as Hepworth he adopted his mother's maiden name Jackson for painting to avoid confusion. When he was a young painter Hepworth and her first husband John Skeaping took Jackson "under their wing", then when Ben Nicholson "took Barbara over he took me over as well". Jackson was a pupil of Ben Nicholson, 1931–5. In 1937 Jackson met the architects Leslie and Sadie Martin and was offered a place at the School of Architecture in Hull. At the outbreak of World War II Jackson had partly qualified and was working in the office of Martin, who encouraged Jackson to keep painting. Jackson transferred to war construction work, then from 1943–6 was with Royal Engineers in Britain and the Middle East, in 1948 being elected an associate of RIBA. Until 1957 Jackson worked on various projects including the Royal Festival Hall, then moved to Somerset, settling in Glastonbury, building factories and private houses. Prior to World War II Jackson exhibited with 7 & 5 Society, 1934–5, at Leicester and Zwemmer Galleries; Leicester Museum and Art Gallery, 1936; and London Gallery, 1937. He was included in Art in Britain 1930–40 at Marlborough Fine Art, 1965, and the *Circle* show at Kettle's Yard, Cambridge, 1982. In 1991 Tate Gallery displayed the work Painting 1937 to mark Jackson's eightieth birthday.

Ashley JACKSON 1940– Watercolourist, teacher and writer, born in Penang, Malaya. He studied at Barnsley School of Art, 1955–60, and went on to teach in Yorkshire. He was a founder-member of Yorkshire Watercolour Society and a member of UA. Also exhibited with RWS and RI and had many solo shows, starting with Grosvenor Gallery, 1969. Here's to You Dad!, at Doncaster Museum and Art Gallery, 1995, was a tribute to his father, who died as a prisoner of the Japanese in Borneo. There was a retrospective at Salford Museum & Art Gallery, 1997. Jackson presented several series of television programmes on painting, wrote instructional books and published his autobiography, *My Brush with Fortune*, in 1982. *Yorkshire Post* Newspapers; 2nd Battalion, Parachute Regiment; and British Gas hold examples. Ashley Jackson Galleries were at Holmfirth, Yorkshire.

Barbara JACKSON 1936– Printmaker, painter and teacher, born in Middlesex, full name Evelyn Barbara Jackson. She studied at St Martin's School of Art, 1954–9, under Anthony Caro, Elisabeth Frink, Frederick Gore and Vivian Pitchforth, then at London University Institute of Education, 1959–60. She was a qualified art therapist and a member of the Person Centred Art Therapy Association. Taught all age groups for several years, including Eltham Green School; The English School, The Hague, Netherlands; and Highbury Hill Grammar School, later teaching at Hampstead Garden Suburb Adult Education Institute and the Holocaust Centre. Jackson was a member of the Printmakers' Council. Among her works were prints which used "figures and cityscapes as a vehicles to capture light, movement and atmosphere," portraits of Holocaust survivors and landscapes. Mixed exhibitions included Ben Uri Open; Catto Gallery; National Print Exhibition, winning the John Purcell Award, 1999; The Discerning Eye, Mall Galleries, 2000; Morley Gallery, from 2000; and Royal National Theatre Print Exhibition, 2001. Had solo shows at Sternberg Centre for Judaism and Belsize Square Synagogue, 1996 and 2001. Lived in London.

Charles d'Orville Pilkington JACKSON 1887–1973 Sculptor in stone, wood and metal. Born at Garlenick, Cornwall, Jackson studied at Edinburgh College of Art, 1905–10, and the British School in Rome, 1910–11. Exhibited RA, Royal Glasgow Institute of the Fine Arts, RSA, RBA and Walker Art Gallery, Liverpool. Work illustrated in Eric Newton's *British Sculpture 1944–1946*. Jackson's work is to be found in public in Scotland and abroad, including an equestrian statue of Robert the Bruce, Bannockburn, in the Scottish United Services Museum and Imperial War Museum, in Paisley Abbey and in the chapel of Stowe School. Lived in Edinburgh.

Davina JACKSON 1971– Painter, born and lived in London, who did a foundation year at Central St Martins School of Art. Jackson gained a degree at Byam Shaw School, then in the mid-1990s studied for a postgraduate diploma at the Royal Academy Schools. She won the Mercers' Company and Leverhulme Scholarship in 1994,

David Murray Travel Scholarship (Landscape Prize) in 1996, and the RA Gold Medal, 1997. Exhibited widely, including Mall Galleries, RA Summer Exhibition, Ben Uri Open Exhibition (in which she twice won first prize, once jointly), and Boundary Gallery, 1998. Jackson's picture The Angry Sea, painted from imagination, was included in Chevron UK Ltd's 1997 calendar, and she was featured in the oil company's show that year at the ICA. Solo exhibitions at Boundary Gallery, 2000 and 2003.

Dilys JACKSON 1938– Artist in bronze, wood and stone, and teacher, born in Badulla, Ceylon, who until 1986 worked under the name of Dilys Vibert. She attended Cambridgeshire High School for Girls, 1945–56, then studied at Slade School of Fine Art, 1956–60, and Swansea College of Art, 1961–2, obtaining her master's degree in fine art from South Glamorgan Institute of Higher Education in Cardiff, where she lived, 1987–9. Jackson was art instructor at Coed Ffranc Youth Centre in south Wales, 1965–6; was teacher/head teacher, special schools, for South Glamorgan Education Authority, 1966–92; from 1994 being environmental artist, Ogwr Groundwork Trust, Ogmore Valley. Among her commissions was the Stackpole Centre Sight Garden, Pembroke, 1993. War and landscape were leading themes in Jackson's works, which were shown in many group exhibitions, including Young Contemporaries, 1960; Pictures for Welsh Schools, National Museum of Wales, Cardiff, 1975; All Women Work 88, Chapter Arts Centre, Cardiff, 1988; Festival Exhibition 91, Collective Gallery, Edinburgh, 1991; and Oriel Contemporary Art, 1996. Had a solo show at Galleri Brinken, Stockholm, 1960, later ones including St David's Hall, Cardiff, 1995. Galleri Brinken, Coleg Harlech in Harlech, Vaughan College in Leicester and Mid-Glamorgan Education Authority hold examples.

Elizabeth D JACKSON 1928– Painter, illustrator and editor, born in Edinburgh. She studied at Edinburgh College of Art, 1945–9, with John Kingsley Cook. Mainly worked for the printed page, acting as art editor for Unilever Ltd in the early 1950s; also illustrated for Oxford University Press. Showed at RA and lived in London.

George William JACKSON 1914– Painter, printmaker and teacher, born in Leeds, Yorkshire. He studied at Leeds College of Art under Douglas Sharpus Andrews, 1931–5, then at Royal College of Art with Percy Hague Jowett and Ernest Tristram, 1935–8, and Central School of Arts and Crafts, 1936–8. Illustration and industrial design were leading features of Jackson's work, which was shown in London and the provinces. He was vice-principal of Chesterfield College of Art, 1949–79, living in the Derbyshire town.

Herbert John JACKSON 1938– Printmaker who was by profession an advertising design studio manager. He was born in King's Lynn, Norfolk, and studied at the School of Art in Norwich, 1954–8, where he settled. Was a member of SWE and RE and took part in mixed shows in Britain and abroad, as well as having solo exhibitions. Jackson's linocuts, celebrating 50 years of printmaking, were shown at Grapevine, Norwich, in 2003.

John JACKSON 1938– Sculptor and teacher, born in London. He studied at Walthamstow School of Art, Hornsey College of Art, then Central School of Art and Design. Jackson was head of sculpture at Batley School of Art; also taught at Maidstone College of Art, West Ham College, Loughton College of Further Education; then Homerton College, Cambridge and at the School of Art there. From 1969–70 and in 1976 he was visiting artist at University of Wisconsin, and this was followed by a series of similar posts at Maidstone College of Art, the Universities of North Michigan, Mississippi and South Dakota in America, as well as the Wesleyan University of South Dakota there, and at Chesterfield School of Art. Showed with LG; at Leeds and Essex University Arts Festivals in 1966; with East Anglian Artists Today, at Royal Institute Galleries, 1969; and with East Anglian Sculptors Exhibition, Ipswich Civic Centre, 1976. Solo shows included Minories, Colchester, 1977. Dynamic triangular shapes were a strong element in Jackson's work, which was described as "constructionalist ... with an extremely organic quality". Commissions included Mississippi State College and Israel Museum, Jerusalem.

Joseph Arthur JACKSON 1889–1962 Painter in oil and watercolour, born in Hull, Yorkshire, who attended the School of Art there, his fees being paid by the local Member of Parliament T R Ferens. During World War I Jackson served with the 1st South Staffordshire Regiment in Italy, where he was able to study Italian art. After demobilisation in 1919, he was given an ex-serviceman's grant to study for three years at Nottingham School of Art. Jackson painted landscapes, flowers, portraits of local dignitaries and panoramas in the Wollaton Hall Natural History Museum. Exhibited in Nottingham and Eastbourne, Sussex, where he died.

Kevin JACKSON fl. from 1970s– Printmaker and teacher who studied at Plymouth College of Art, 1971–2; Sunderland College of Art, 1972–5; and Chelsea School of Art, 1975–6. Teaching included City Literary Institute, Sir John Cass School of Art and Maidstone College of Art. Mixed appearances included Sunderland Arts Centre, 1974; Bradford Print Biennale, 1976; 55 Wapping Artists, 1979; Wapping Artists Open Studios from 1980; and 2nd National Exhibition of Modern British Prints, Blackpool, 1981.

Kurt JACKSON 1961– Painter, mixed media, born in Blandford, Dorset, who graduated from St Peter's College, Oxford, in 1983 with an honours degreee in zoology and had brief periods at Hertfordshire College of Art and Ruskin School of Drawing in Oxford, under Jane Greenham, but who was essentially self-taught. After graduating, he then spent a year painting and travelling in Africa. He moved to Boscastle, Cornwall, in 1984 to paint full-time, settling in St Just, Penzance, in 1989. He was a member of RWA and Newlyn and Penwith Societies of Artists. Jackson's work was "rooted in the Cornish landscape, seascape and communal psyche, and the natural, human and industrial interventions in the landscape". Group appearances included Rye Art Gallery, 1994; Leicester Art Gallery, 1995; and in 1996 the Celtic Festival at Plymouth Art Centre and Now & Then at David Messum Gallery. Had a solo show at Robinson College, Cambridge, in 1984, then exhibited prolifically, later shows including Lancashire Mining Museum, Salford. For this, Jackson went under ground to paint alongside miners at South Crofty, the last working tin mine in Cornwall. For Jackson's exhibition The Long Field, in 2002, The Great Atlantic Map

Works Gallery, St Just-in-Penwith, published a book of that title illustrating the pictures. Messum's gave Jackson solo exhibitions in 2003, 2004 and in 2005 with a lavishly illustrated catalogue and in 2004 Newlyn Art Gallery put on his show Porth. Exeter University holds Jackson's work.

Marguerite Betha JACKSON fl. c.1930–1955 Painter who studied at Heatherley's School of Fine Art with Henry and Gertrude Massey. Exhibited RA, elsewhere in London and in the provinces. Lived for some time at Leatherhead, Surrey.

Marie Blanche JACKSON fl. c.1920–1955 Painter, brought up partly in France. Lady Jackson, who was married to Sir Arthur Jackson, studied at Westminster School of Art, Slade School of Fine Art and at Académie Julian, Paris. Exhibited RA, RI, RWS, NEAC, Cooling Galleries and Walker Art Gallery, Liverpool. Lived at Stonegate, Sussex.

Mark JACKSON 1970– Artist in oil and mixed media on canvas, born and lived in Bolton, Lancashire. He studied at the local Institute of Higher Education, 1988–9, where he later taught part-time, and at Leeds Polytechnic, 1989–92, graduating with a first-class honours degree in graphic design. Jackson's work was "essentially concerned with religious iconography". Group show appearances included Doppelganger Art, at County Arcade, Leeds, and NEAC, both 1992; and Off Course, at Leeds Metropolitan University Gallery, 1993. In 1993 Jackson had a solo show called Towers of Silence at Dean Clough Contemporary Art Gallery, Halifax.

Mary JACKSON 1936– Painter, born in Sussex. She studied as a mature student at Southampton College of Art and part-time at Winchester College of Art. Won a number of prizes, including the Thomas Agnew, Brandler and Patterson Prizes, and New English Critics' Prize in 1990, three years after she was elected a member of NEAC. Also showed at RA, RWA and Kingfisher Gallery during 1990 Edinburgh Festival. She shared shows at Theatre Royal in Winchester, Hallam Gallery and Waterman Fine Art Ltd in 1991, later solo exhibitions including Crossgate Gallery, Kentucky, 1994. Was painter-in-residence at Glyndebourne for the opera festival in 1991–3, completing a project with English National Opera, 1994–5. Travelled in India and Australia to paint. National Trust holds her work. Lived in Hurstbourne Tarrant, Hampshire.

Mel JACKSON fl. from 1980s– Sculptor who studied at London College of Printing, 1986–7, Byam Shaw School of Art, 1987–90, and Royal College of Art, 1990–2. He had a residency in Poland in 1988, and in 1993 a London Arts Board award to develop new work and an Oxford Sculpture Project commission and bursary. Showed in 3D '89 at Waterman's Art Centre, 1989; in 1992 at Royal College of Art master's degree graduation show; and in 1993 in Drawing Towards Sculpture at Isis Gallery, Leigh-on-Sea.

Mihangel JACKSON 1940– Painter and illustrator who studied at Twickenham College of Art, then worked as a freelance illustrator. Did work for General Post Office, telephone directory illustrations, and took part in WAC 1969 show: Recording Wales, Chapels. WAC holds work.

Muriel JACKSON 1901– Painter, notably of portraits and murals, and printmaker. She was the daughter of the architect A Blomfield Jackson and was born in London. After private education she attended the Central School of Arts and Crafts under Noel Rooke and F Ernest Jackson. She showed RA, NEAC, Redfern Gallery, widely in the provinces and in America. Art Institute of Chicago holds her work. Lived in London.

Muriel Amy JACKSON 1902–1989 Painter and black-and-white illustrator, daughter of the artist Albert Edward Jackson. After Berkhamsted High School she studied with Philip Cole and others at Hastings School of Art, with her father and in London between 1915–22, and went on to work as an illustrator for Amalgamated Press and other firms. She was noted for her flower pictures, illustrations for children's books and magazines and architectural subjects. Jackson was a member of East Sussex Art Club. Showed with Highgate Artists' Society and Battle Arts Group. Lived in Hastings, Sussex, for many years, latterly suffering from Parkinson's Disease which prevented her working.

Philip JACKSON 1944– Sculptor, born in Inverness, Scotland. He studied at Farnham School of Art and worked for Henry Moore. He became a fellow of RBS in 1989, and from 1990–4 was its vice-president. In 1990 he won the Society's silver medal and in 1991–2–3 the Sir Otto Beit Medal for Excellence in Sculpture, also in 1993 winning the Jersey, Channel Islands, Liberation Sculpture Competition. In 1991 Jackson won the Mozart Bicentenary Sculpture Competition, London's first sculpture of the composer whose *Don Giovanni* inspired Jackson's Masked Figure series. One of Jackson's more notable works was The Yomper, a unique casting by The Morris Singer Foundry for the Royal Marines Museum, Portsmouth, commemorating the men of 45 Commando's epic march in the Falklands in 1982. Jackson's powerful group The Struggle for Peace and Freedom, 1987, is in St Peter's Square, Manchester, and London, Geneva and Monte Carlo also have examples. Jackson showed widely solo and in group exhibitions, having a notable one-man show at Philharmonic Center for the Arts, Naples, Florida, America, in 1998. His sculptures were displayed at Abbey House Gardens, Malmesbury, in 2001. In 2002 Jackson was commissioned by the Crown Estate and RBS to complete a £300,000, three-tonne bronze statue of H M The Queen on horseback for Windsor Great Park, to mark her Golden Jubilee. The one-and-a-half times lifesize figure, the first public statue of her in Britain, was unveiled in 2003. Earlier that year Jackson's statue of Bobby Moore, West Ham captain, and other members of the 1966 England football World Cup-winning team, was unveiled at Upton Park. Retrospective at Bishop's Palace, Wells, in 2006. Jackson lived in Midhurst, Sussex.

Robert Griffiths JACKSON 1891–1961 Painter in oil and watercolour. Born in Darlington, Yorkshire, Jackson carried on the family painting, decorating and signwriting business. He was a self-taught artist who exhibited with the Barnard Castle Art Society and Shipley Art Gallery, Gateshead. Lived at Barnard Castle, County Durham.

Sheila JACKSON fl. from 1950s– Versatile artist, designer, teacher and writer who attended Paignton School of Arts & Crafts and Central School of Art & Design, specializing in lithography and illustration. After retirement, took up screenprinting. Taught at the Central and the Henrietta Barnett School, the theatre department of the Central School of Art & Design and worked with children at London Zoo. Jackson had a great interest in animals, birds and their relationships. Was a costume designer for television; wrote and illustrated *Costumes for the Stage* and *Blooming Small*, which contained watercolours of her small inner-city garden; illustrated several other books, including *Bethlehem Story*, for Pollock's Toy Museum; and in 1988 was a winner in the RA Save the Children Christmas Card Competition. There was a retrospective at The New Academy Gallery in 2002.

Stanley JACKSON 1917– Painter and illustrator who studied at St Martin's School of Art. Exhibited RA, UA, RBA and in provinces. Lived in Crawley Down, Sussex.

Vanessa JACKSON 1953– Abstract painter who studied at St Martin's School of Art and Royal College of Art. She went to New York on the Yaddo Fellowship in Fine Art in 1985 and taught at Winchester School of Art. Jackson was included in the South Bank Centre 1988–9 touring show The Presence of Painting. Later solo shows included North House Gallery, Manningtree, 1999. Although Jackson was a painter notably concerned with a painterly surface, colour and texture, her pictures always had a strong underlying geometry. In 1993–4 John Moores Liverpool Exhibition she won a prize with her canvas So Much Depends. Lived in London.

Arthur JACOB 1916– Painter and teacher, born in Garndiffaith, near Pontypool, Monmouthshire. He attended Newport College of Art and Caerleon College of Education and took in courses at the Colleges of Art at Exeter and Cardiff. Went on to teach at various schools in Wales. A founder-member of Pontypool Arts Society, he showed in group exhibitions at WAC and SWG. One-man exhibitions included Syracuse University in America and Llantarnam Grange Arts Centre, Cwmbran. University College, Cardiff, holds his work.

Romy JACOB 1926– Artist in various media who lived in Woodbridge, Suffolk, and travelled to paint in Spain, France and Italy. Anna Airy and Cecil Collins were influences. Jacob's interest in the effects of light was shown in watercolours at Clarges Gallery, 1996, an exhibition shared with Jenny Spencer. Jacob also exhibited at CCA and Drian Galleries and at Galleria Numero in Rome.

Rosalind JACOBS 1922– Sculptor, painter and draughtsman, "essentially self-taught apart from life drawing classes", teacher Cecil Birtwhistle. Jacobs was "inspired by music, the wonderful shapes of jazz and classical performers", drawing "when I go to concerts and gigs." Dancers at the Royal Ballet School, the seasons, circles and triangles in landscape and the shape of treble and bass clef in music were other inspirations. Jacobs was a member of the Free Painters and Sculptors, showing at Loggia and Ben Uri Galleries, Aldeburgh Festival, Konstanz Festival at Mainau in Germany in 1995 and Currell & Co, Islington, 2000. Lived at Ham Common, Richmond, Surrey. Private collections in Europe and America hold examples.

Sarah JACOBS 1944– Artist using materials such as paper, sticky tape and plasticine "in such a way as to make them appear valued," and who "juxtaposes elements which refer to the computer yet which involve the almost obsessive use of the hand." When exhibiting at Gallery A, in association with Alsop & Stormer Architects, 1998, Jacobs wrote that she was "concerned with the work of art as an object in the world", her output often including "a reflective element so that the piece gives back to the world and the world is seen in the piece." Also practised mail art and ran a small press, Colebrook Publications, its output including her own *Song of the Data Stream*, 1999, and *After the Years of Misrule*, three variations on Joseph Conrad's *Nostromo*, 2001. In 2004 it issued *The ZigZag Paths*, a dedicated e-book by Jacobs containing the full text of *Nostromo* together with comments, illustrations and hyperlinks. Jacobs studied at Vassar College, New York, America, 1961–5, and Girton College, Cambridge University, 1965–7. Group shows included Network. Art by Post and by Fax, Arts Council tour, and Sampling the Visible, Flaxman Gallery, both 1997; and El Arte de Los Libros de Artistas, Oaxaca and Mexico City, Mexico, 1998. Showed solo at the Henry Moore Institute Library, Leeds, 2000, and Clare Hall, Cambridge, 2003. In that year, to celebrate *Luxuriant Beauty Bears Witness*, from the *Nostromo* series, bookartbookshop had an exhibition of Jacobs' books and scrolls. Jacobs' sculpture The Dexion Pieces was chosen by Gustav Metzger for Artists' Favourites at the ICA in 2004. Libraries at Henry Moore Institute, Tate Gallery and Chelsea College (London Institute); National Art Library, Victoria & Albert Museum; and University College London (Small Press and Poetry Store); and Arts Council hold examples. Lived in London.

David JACOBSON 1951– Sculptor, printmaker and teacher, born in Windhoek, South-West Africa, who studied at Camberwell School of Arts and Crafts, 1973–7. Jacobson's teaching appointments included Camberwell, Chelsea School of Art and Birmingham Polytechnic. He took part in many group shows and had solo exhibitions in London, the provinces, America, Italy and South Africa. He won the Barcham Green Printmaking Competition, 1978; the R K Burt Outstanding Printmaker Award, 1994; was elected a fellow of the RBS, 1995; and won the Wessex Watermark Award, 1996. Jacobson was one of eight shortlisted artists when he won a competition to provide a replacement fountain at the restored Royal Pump Rooms, Leamington Spa. This he did with his water feature Spring Celebration, commissioned by the local Museum and Art Gallery and installed in 1999.

Ruth JACOBSON 1941– Artist and teacher, born and settled in London, who studied painting and etching at Slade School of Fine Art under Peter Brooker and Andrew Forge, 1959–63, gaining awards, notably first prize in figure drawing in 1961. In 1963–4 did a postgraduate teaching course at Manchester University and Art College, subsequently teaching in adult education. After marriage and a move to Reading she studied sculpture at Berkshire College of Art, 1965. She had shown at Agnew in 1963, and further exhibitions followed at Camden Arts Centre and Mall Galleries. Solo exhibitions included Gallery Petit, 1972, and Seldown Gallery, Poole Arts Centre, 1985. Music was a key element in her work, which often involved quick, vivid sketches of people involved in a skilled activity. Etchings took longer to develop, sometimes inspired by a book or operatic performance. From 1989–91 Jacobson studied stained glass at Central St

Martins, obtaining a fellowship. Ben Uri Art Society holds her work.

Robin JACQUES 1920–1995 Illustrator, painter, designer and teacher, born and died in London. Lived in France for some years from the mid-1960s and travelled widely in several continents. After attending the Royal Masonic Schools at Bushey, in Hertfordshire, Jacques worked for an advertising agency, then served in the Army in World War II. He had no formal artistic training but held several art school teaching posts, in Brighton, Harrow and Canterbury, after three years as art editor of *Strand Magazine* from the late 1940s. Although he showed in provincial art galleries and Victoria & Albert Museum, which holds his work, Jacques made his reputation as a magazine and book illustrator. Worked for *The Listener*, *Radio Times* and other publications and illustrated several dozen books, where he was noted for his attention to historical detail and meticulous draughtsmanship. Author of *Illustrators at Work*, 1963. Jacques' sister was the humorous actress Hattie Jacques.

Ivy G M JACQUIER 1890– Painter, born in Lyons, France, her married name was Ivy G M Skinner. She studied art in Lyons, Eastbourne, Dresden and Paris, her teachers including J D Fergusson and Jacques-Emile Blanche. Showed in France and at Redfern Gallery, RP and RA. British Museum holds her work. She illustrated a number of books, including André Maurois' life of Shelley: *Ariel* and James Thomson's *The Seasons*. Latterly signed her work with just her surname. She detailed her early life in *The Diary of Ivy Jacquier 1907–1926*, published by Gollancz in 1960. Latterly lived in Broomfield, Essex.

Marysia JACZYŃSKA fl. from 1960s– Artist, born in Warsaw, Poland, who studied art at St Martin's and Hornsey Colleges of Art, also Académie Julian, Paris. Mixed shows included Form and Colour, Congress of Polish Culture Exhibition of Fine Arts by Polish Artists in Britain, at POSK, 1995. Had solo exhibitions at Montrésor, France, and in London, including POSK. Works were held by private collections in the United Kingdom, Poland and France.

J A D 1909– The working name of Alexander William Davies, born in Glamorgan, who employed charcoal, pencil and watercolour. He was a self-taught artist who retired to St Ives, Cornwall, in 1970, attending St Ives School of Painting under Leonard Fuller. Davies had been a science and mathematics teacher, 1930–5, then entered business in 1947, developing marketing and advertising companies, retiring in 1960. His lifetime hobby was sketching the faces of notable personalities in all fields, mostly autographed, of which he built up a huge collection. Many were published in the national press and other journals. Was a member of RBSA Friends, St Ives Society of Artists, Cartoonists' Club of Great Britain and Sutton Coldfield Art Society. Showed widely in the St Ives and Birmingham areas, where he finally lived at Erdington.

Maurice JADOT 1893–1983 Painter and sculptor, born in Brussels, Belgium, studied art at Académie des Beaux-Arts there, also architecture under Victor Horta. Jadot, who was chairman of the Belgian Cultural Centre in Britain and a founder-member of the Free Painters and Sculptors, exhibited in several countries on the continent as well as at the ICA, in 1979 having a retrospective at the National Museum of Wales, Cardiff. Public collections holding his work include the Museum of Modern Art, Brussels, the National Museum of Wales and the Nalecz Collection, Museum of Warsaw, in Poland. Leinster Contemporary Art held a review show in 1987. Lived in London.

Lois JAFFÉ 1918– Artist, born in Axminster, Devon, who attended St Martin's School of Art in 1939, having won Royal Drawing Society medal five years before. Went on to show at Victoria & Albert Museum, Guildhall, PS, Mall Galleries and elsewhere. She lived at Bellair, Charmouth, Dorset.

Margaret Leah JAGGAR 1907–1996 Muralist, wood engraver and commercial artist, born in Wallasey, Merseyside, who attended Cheltenham Ladies' College, then Liverpool School of Art. She worked as a commercial artist and painter of decorative murals, then was a housewife and practising artist living in Anglesey at Rhydwyn, near Holyhead. Her murals included the Cunard liner *Caronia*, National Trust and Blackpool's Fun Park. She was a member of RCamA, also exhibiting with SWE and Walker Art Gallery in Liverpool. Her solo shows included Sandon Studios, Liverpool, 1930, and Holyhead Library, 1971.

David JAGGER 1891–1958 Versatile painter, born in Kilnhurst, Yorkshire, brother of sculptor Charles Sargeant Jagger and of the artist Edith Jagger. He was a leading member of ROI and belonged to RP, also showing at RA, RBA, Walker Art Gallery in Liverpool and elsewhere. In 1940 his work was included in The Art of the Jagger Family at Mappin Art Gallery, Sheffield. Lived in London.

Edith JAGGER 1896–1975 Painter, sister of the sculptor Charles Sargeant Jagger and of the artist David Jagger, who settled in Sheffield, Yorkshire. She showed at RA, RI, ROI and elsewhere. In 1940 her work was included in The Art of the Jagger Family at the Mappin Art Gallery, Sheffield. Edith contributed designs to the Sheffield firm Painted Fabrics, which in the inter-war years employed ex-servicemen and was the subject of a Mappin exhibition, 1997–8.

Irena JAKUBOWSKA 1913– Artist in oil and pastel, born in Czepulonis, Poland, who studied music and Polish literature in Wilno. She was a member of the Polish Underground Army in World War II, taking part in the Warsaw uprising in 1944. From 1946 she lived in England, studying at the School of the Academic Community of Wilno University in London, 1961–4. She was a member of the International Association of Plastic Arts; took part in Association of Polish Artists in Great Britain group shows; and was included in Contemporary Art by Polish Artists abroad, at Imperial College, 1970. Among solo exhibitions were POSK, 1981.

Andrzej JAKUBOWSKI 1916– Painter who studied at the Medical Veterinary Academy in Lvov, Poland. He took part in the military campaign against Germany, 1939, being held as a prisoner-on-war there until 1945. From 1946 he lived in England, studying at Hammersmith School of Art and at the Polish School of Painting under Professor Marian Bohusz-Szyszko. Jakubowski was a member of the Association of Polish Artists in Great Britain, participating in its group shows. He was included in Contemporary Art by Polish Artists abroad, Imperial College, 1970. His work was held in private collections.

JAMES: *see* **James F LYNCH**

Alan Gosset JAMES 1875–1950 Architect and landscape painter, born in Prestbury, Gloucestershire, near Cheltenham where he was articled to a firm of architects. After practising and working as a correspondent in South Africa James joined the department of architecture at London University, 1903–8, working with Edwin Lutyens. He was almost 50 before he began serious painting, studying at Cheltenham and Chelsea Schools of Art. His first work shown at RA, where he appeared for just over 30 years from 1911, was principally architectural designs. Also showed NEAC and Goupil Gallery. Tate Gallery has his Winter on the Windrush, depicting a scene not far from his home in Gloucestershire at Stow-on-the-Wold.

Andrew JAMES 1958– Sculptor, born in Oxford, who attended Chelsea School of Art, 1979–81, gaining his master's degree at Slade School of Fine Art, 1987–9. Group exhibitions included Nicola Jacobs Gallery, 1981; Into the Nineties, Mall Galleries, 1989; New Identities at Camden Arts Centre, 1990; Counterpoint at Gimpel Fils, 1991; and Whitechapel Open Studios, 1992. His solo show Host was held at Hales Gallery, 1993, the Japanese dealer Rumiko Torii staging one at Entwistle Gallery in 1994. James created his own unique worlds populated by toy figures the size of real children who acted out fictional dramas. Lived and worked in London.

Andy JAMES 1969– Painter, born in Reading, Berkshire, whose twin brother, Paul James, was also a visual artist, resident in New York. Andrew James was educated at Claverham Community College, Battle, Sussex. He became a member of the RP and won a Carroll Foundation Award. James also took part in mixed shows at the NEAC, RBA and National Portrait Gallery and in 2003 had a solo show at the Mall Galleries. In 2004 he was one of the painters commissioned to paint the popular antiques expert David Dickinson for the BBC television programme *Star Portraits with Rolf Harris*, a related exhibition taking place at the County Hall Gallery in 2005 with tour. James is represented in People's Portraits at Girton College, Cambridge, with the Museum and Art Gallery in Tunbridge Wells, Kent, where he lived, also holding his work.

Claerwen JAMES 1970– Figurative painter, born in Cambridge, who studied at the Slade School of Fine Art, 1998. She won the Melville Nettleship Prize. Exhibitions included Hunting Art Prizes, 2000; The Arts Club Drawing Award, 2003; and Artist of the Day, Flowers Central, 2004, chosen by Andrew Stahl.

Elizabeth Campbell JAMES 1923– Painter, printmaker and teacher, born in London, daughter of the designer Norman James. She studied at Hornsey School of Art with John Moody and Norman Janes and went on to teach at Enfield County School for Girls after World War II. Exhibited RA and SGA, of which she was a member. Lived in Enfield, Middlesex.

Hywel JAMES 1944– Artist, teacher and administrator, born in Brighton, Sussex, where he studied at the College of Art, 1962–6, teachers including Jennifer Dickson, Charles Knight and Ian Potts. He showed at RE, RI and Hastings and Bedford public galleries, but latterly did not paint due to administrative responsibilities. Became vice-principal, director of academic studies, at Bournemouth and Poole College of Art and Design, Poole, Dorset.

Kim JAMES 1928– Sculptor and teacher, who studied at the Borough Polytechnic, 1948–54, under David Bomberg and Tom Eckersley, and at the Royal College of Art. Took part in group exhibitions at RBA, 1959; Wildenstein, 1961; Arthur Jeffress and Grosvenor Galleries, 1963; AIA, 1963–4; and RA, 1967–9. James' figurative-towards-abstraction pieces were given a solo exhibition at Hanover Gallery, 1966. Carried out commissions for the Churches of St Nicholas at Hayes, Middlesex, and St Matthew's at Bethnal Green; a crucifix for the Franciscan Brothers in Dorset; and sculpture and relief work for Hoveringham Gravels Ltd, Nottingham. James gave up art in 1969, having been head of art therapy at what became the University of Hertfordshire. He retrained as a scientist and became a successful management consultant in cybernetics. His sculptures were acquired by a number of public collections, including one in Brussels. James was born and eventually settled in Wollaston, Wellingborough, Northamptonshire. Alexander von Moltke held a James retrospective in 2002, work unseen in public for several decades.

Lisa JAMES 1949– Artist, designer and illustrator, born in Hamburg, West Germany, who studied at Edinburgh College of Art, 1967–72, and gained her master's at Goldsmiths' College, 1984–6. She taught at Barnfield College in Luton and did freelance design and illustration. Mixed shows included RA Summer Exhibition from 1980; Alpine Gallery, 1983; Whitechapel Open Exhibition and Berry Street Open Studios, both 1984; PNL UK Cypriot Exhibition, Famagusta Gate, Nicosia, Cyprus, 1988; and in 1989 Kontact 2 Kontact, Galeria E1, Elblag, Poland, and East End Open Studios, at Berry Street. Had a solo show at Dryden Street Gallery, 1980, with others at Creaser Gallery, 1988 and 1989.

Louis JAMES 1920–1996 Painter, born in Adelaide, South Australia, who had no formal training. After World War II he began to paint seriously and eventually established a reputation as an abstract and a figurative artist. For about 15 years he worked and showed in Europe, based in London, but from 1964 lived in Sydney, although in 1978 he revisited London and continental Europe and visited New York. Exhibited widely, especially in Australia, where in 1949 he had a one-man show at John Martin's Gallery, Adelaide. In England showed in the 1950s and 1960s at Redfern Gallery, also at Stone Gallery in Newcastle upon Tyne. Had a retrospective show at Bonython-Meadmore Gallery, Adelaide, in 1986. Tate Gallery holds a self-portrait drawing, Ferens Art Gallery in Hull and Towner Art Gallery in Eastbourne also holding examples. He died in Sydney, New South Wales.

Maggie JAMES 1956– Painter in oil and gouache "entirely from observation", born in Cardiff, where she returned to live in 1985, the year she joined 56 Group Wales. Studied at Newcastle Polytechnic, 1975–8, graduating from Royal College of Art in 1982. Gained a John Minton Scholarship, 1982; Jacob Mendelson Scholarship and WAC Award, both 1984; Oppenheim-John Downes

Memorial Trust Award, 1987; and was one of the first WAC Bursary winners when scheme began, 1994–5. Showed at RA Summer Exhibition, 1982; National Portrait Gallery, John Player Award, 1983; Interiors, Andrew Knight Gallery, Cardiff, 1988; and was a prizewinner, Royal National Eisteddfod, 1990. Contemporary Art Society for Wales owns her work.

Margaret Calkin JAMES 1895–1985 Designer, printmaker, calligrapher, illustrator and painter, who grew up in Hampstead, north London, where she lived much of her life. She trained at the Central School of Arts and Crafts, being taught calligraphy by Graily Hewitt. During World War I she oversaw the art department of the central London Young Men's Christian Association, after hostilities designing under her own Rainbow Workshops sign. In 1922 she married C H James and closed her workshops, then living in a house he designed at 1 Hampstead Way and setting up a new workshop there. An impressive stream of banners, book-jackets, posters, illuminated books and watercolours followed, clients including Lloyd's of London, RIBA, London Transport, Shell and the General Post Office. In 1969 James had a stroke which deprived her of speech and the use of her right hand, and she was encouraged to take up needlework. She showed at RA and had three solo exhibitions: at Cooling Galleries, St Mary Abbots Place and the St George's Gallery under Basil Jonzen. In 1996 there was a touring show based on Burgh House, Hampstead.

Merlin JAMES 1960– Painter, draughtsman, printmaker and writer on art, born in Cardiff. He studied at the College of Art there, 1978–9, Central School of Art, 1979–82, and Royal College of Art, 1983–6. He wrote critically for *London Magazine*, *Times Literary Supplement*, *Burlington Magazine* and other publications, and in 1992 his *Engaging Images: Practical Criticism and Visual Art*, was published. James was critic-in-residence at Kingston University, 1995, and painter-in-residence at Glasgow School of Art in 1996. In that year James gave The Stanley Picker Lecture at Kingston, in which he questioned supposed oppositions between the traditional and avant-garde, through an examination of failures in art criticism and of the tendency towards literalism in contemporary art. James' own work included figurative and abstract elements. Guest lectureships included Tate Gallery, New York Studio School, Royal College of Art, National Museum of Wales in Cardiff and provincial galleries and art colleges. Later group shows included Kapil Jariwala Gallery, 1994, and Whitechapel Art Gallery, 1996. Had a first solo exhibition at Albemarle Gallery, 1991, later ones including Kettle's Yard Gallery in Cambridge, 1996, in 1997 Critical Pictures, Andrew Grant Gallery in Edinburgh, Francis Graham-Dixon Gallery and Kingston University, Andrew Mummery Gallery, 2001, Kerlin Gallery, Dublin, 2002 and 2003, and Talbot Rice Gallery, Edinburgh, and BayArt, Cardiff, both 2004. Lived in London.

Owen JAMES 1934– Painter and teacher, born in Yorkley, Monmouthshire. He studied at Lydney School of Art, 1951–3, then Camberwell School of Arts and Crafts, 1953–5, under Karel Vogel. He went on to teach at South-East London College. James was a member of SGA, also exhibiting at RA, NEAC, ROI and RBA. Solo shows included Fairfield Halls, Croydon. Lived in London.

Ric JAMES 1943– Figurative sculptor, painter, teacher and art dealer, born in Torquay, Devon, educated in Gloucestershire. He obtained his National Diploma in Design at Gloucestershire College of Art, gaining a Bursary Travelling Scholarship for sculpture, enabling him to study Renaissance work in Rome and Florence. James obtained bachelor's and master's degrees at Birmingham University, in art and education, and for 10 years was head of art at Cheltenham Grammar School, also teaching at Gloucestershire College of Art. In 1979 he left teaching to become a full-time art dealer, specialising in British and European figurative painting and sculpture, 1900–30. Dance was a strong feature of his own sculptures, held by many private collections worldwide.

Richard JAMES 1937– Painter in acrylic on canvas, and acrylic and gouache on paper, born in Thorne, Yorkshire. Studied at Doncaster School of Art, 1957–9; St Martin's School of Art, 1959–60; Slade School of Fine Art, 1960–4, where Keith Vaughan was his tutor; then gained Prix de Rome in painting, 1964–5. James lived and worked in London for 23 years, teaching part-time in various art schools. Moved to Norfolk in 1982, settling in Norwich, and was head of painting at the School of Art there, 1983–91, leaving to concentrate more fully on painting. He said that his work "is about colour, movement, rhythm, contrast – the interaction between the energies of the natural world and the man-made world, between the random and the controlled. Painting makes vivid the meltdown between one moment and the next." Group shows included Serpentine Gallery, 1973; John Moores Liverpool Exhibition, 1974, and in that year British Painting '74, at Hayward Gallery; British Painting 1952–1977 at RA, 1977; Hayward Annual, 1989; and Beardsmore Gallery, from 1992. Later solo shows included Gallery 49, Norwich, 1981, and Studio Exhibition, 1994. Between 1984–93 James was member of faculty for the award of Rome and Abbey Major Scholarships. Albright Knox Museum in America and Eastern Arts hold examples.

Rowan JAMES 1973– Painter who initially trained at Byam Shaw School of Art, winning a Julia Gompertz Memorial Award, a travelling scholarship to Italy, afterwards studying at Glasgow School of Art. From 2000 he went to paint in Prague, in The Czech Republic. In 2001 Ewan Mundy Fine Art showed James's work, mainly oil on board, at ART2001, held at Islington's Business Design Centre.

Shani Rhys JAMES 1953– Painter, born in Melbourne, Australia, who moved to London in 1962, settling in Wales in 1984. Studied at Loughborough College of Art, foundation course, 1972–3, then St Martin's School of Art, 1973–6. Group shows included Whitechapel Open and RA Summer Exhibition from 1982; Wales Open, Aberystwyth, 1989, first prize; Mostyn Open, first prize, 1991; Royal National Eisteddfod, Aberystwyth, gold medal in fine art, 1992; Hunting/*Observer* first prizewinner, Mall Galleries and tour, 1993; Second Prize, BP National Portrait Award, and BBC Wales Visual Artist of the Year Award, both 1994. In 2003 she won the Jerwood Painting Prize. Had solo exhibition with Martin Tinney Gallery, Cardiff, 1993, another of self-portraits, strongly painted in whites and reds, at Oriel Mostyn, Llandudno, 1997, showing at Stephen Lacey Gallery, 2000. Arts Council; National Museum of Wales, Cardiff; Gallery of Modern Art,

Glasgow; Glynn Vivian Art Gallery, Swansea; Contemporary Art Society for Wales; and Usher Gallery, Lincoln, hold examples. Was married to the artist Stephen West and lived at Llangadfan, Powys.

Stephanie JAMES 1957– Artist in varied media, notably a sculptor, who studied at Concordia University, 1974–7, then Hull College of Art, 1977–80, followed by Newcastle University, 1980–2. Among workshops participated in were a Workshop for the Blind, Harris Museum & Art Gallery in Preston, 1988. Mixed exhibitions included Hull Drawing Show, 1979; Northern Young Contemporaries at Whitworth Art Gallery, Manchester, 1981; Brighton Festival, 1984; and Sculpture at Canterbury from 1986. She showed solo at Morley Gallery; Commonwealth Institute; and Christchurch Mansion, Ipswich, 1991.

Thomas K JAMES 1906– Part-time painter and professional railwayman, born in Nottingham, where he continued to live. He acquired his painting knowledge mainly at Nottingham Society of Artists, of which he was a member. Showed with the Society, at the Nottingham 1951 Festival of Britain, at Mansfield Art Gallery and throughout the provinces at shows organised by British Rail.

Frank JAMESON 1898–1968 Painter in oil, born in London. Became an insurance salesman, in the evenings studying at Birmingham Art School. Commissioned in the Worcestershire Regiment in World War I he was responsible for building bridges and blockhouses. After demobilisation he lived in Redditch and travelled around the county camping and painting landscapes, eventually doing the same in Dorset, Brixham in Devon and St Ives, Cornwall, where he rented the Loft Studio and joined the Society of Artists. Also showed at RWA, RA, RBA, RHA, ROI and Paris Salon. Was a member of Bournemouth Art Club while living there, then moved to Glenovar, near Dublin, in Ireland, in the late 1940s returning to St Ives and then settling in Falmouth. His studio commanded a fine view of the River Fal. As well as harbour scenes filled with extensive colour and reflections, Jameson was noted for his paintings of nudes and portraits of notabilities and the Cornish aristocracy. In 1994 the Penzance auction rooms W H Lane sold Jameson's studio collection.

Joan JAMESON 1892–1953 Painter, born in London, daughter of the baronet Sir Richard Musgrave. She was presented at court, then studied at Académie Julian, in Paris, for two years. After marriage to Captain Thomas Jameson she lived extensively in Ireland, latterly at Ardmore. Painted consistently from 1930, having her first solo show at Leicester Galleries in 1933. Over the years was to exhibit often there, with RHA, French and Wertheim Galleries and at Goupil Salon. Also showed at Dublin Painters Society, where in 1936 her portrait of Lady Charles Cavendish, formerly Adele Astaire, sister of the singer and dancer Fred Astaire, attracted much publicity. Irish country houses were a favourite subject. RHA Gallery in Dublin held a show of Jameson's work in 1989, which indicated a wide range of styles including Cubism. "Competent but derivative" was the judgement of *Irish Times* critic Brian Fallon, who said that Jameson "rarely put a personal stamp on anything she did."

Kenneth JAMESON 1913–1996 Painter, draughtsman and teacher, born in Blackwell, Worcestershire, married to the artist Norma Jameson. He studied at Birmingham School of Music, Leicester College of Art and Bath Academy of Art. Held a series of teaching appointments, eventually being an art inspector for London County Council and Inner London Education Authority. He wrote a number of books, including *You Can Draw* and *Painting: A Complete Guide*. Jameson lectured extensively on child development through art and painting and drawing with an emphasis on aiding adults. He was also responsible for BBC Television programmes on art. Jameson was a member of RCamA, showed at Royal National Eisteddfod, RA, RBA and Paris Salon, where he gained an Hon. Mention. Had several shows with his wife in London and the provinces. Public gallery in Birkenhead holds his work, as do educational authorities. Lived in Beckenham, Kent.

Norma JAMESON 1933– Painter and teacher, born in Burslem, Staffordshire, married to the artist Kenneth Jameson. She studied at Bath Academy of Art, 1951–5, Liverpool University, 1955–6, then in 1978 gained advanced textile diploma at Goldsmiths' College School of Art. Her books included *Batik for Beginners*. She was a member of ROI and RBA, also showing with RA, RCamA, had several shows with her husband and solo exhibitions in London and elsewhere. Inner London Education Authority and provincial education authorities held examples. Lived in Beckenham, Kent.

Susan JAMESON 1944– Printmaker, born in Cumberland, who studied at Carlisle College of Art, 1960–4, gaining a travelling scholarship to Italy, 1963. Attended Goldsmiths' College School of Art, 1964–5, then Central School, 1971–3, for advanced printmaking studies. Mixed shows included Modern Art Gallery, Naples, 1966; Serpentine Gallery, 1973; South West Arts Association travelling exhibition, 1974–5; and ICA, 1977. Solo shows included Tenterden House Gallery, Kent, from 1973 and Graffiti Gallery, 1977.

Charles JAMIESON 1952– Painter, designer and teacher who studied at Glasgow School of Art, 1969–74, then at Texas Christian University, Fort Worth, Texas, America, 1974–6, where he also taught drawing and photography. Awards included Sculpture Prize, Scottish Young Contemporaries, 1972; Glasgow School of Art travelling scholarship, 1974; and 1974–5 a Norden Scholarship. Part-time, Jamieson taught drawing and colour in Glasgow School of Art's textile department, 1992–8, and graphics at Cardonald College, Glasgow, 1998–9. From 1975 he completed many design commissions, especially posters for Borderline Theatre; there was a 1989 painting commission for the Army Chaplains Brigade, Northern Ireland; in 1998 Canns Down Press published two cards, Art from Scotland, two limited-edition prints. Took part in numerous group exhibitions, latterly with Thompson's Gallery and Duncan R Miller Fine Arts, which gave him solo shows in 2000 and 2003. Ernst & Young and Caledonian Breweries hold his work.

Maggie JAMIESON 1956– Jamieson graduated with honours from the University of Wales, 1976–9, while studying, showing at Oriel Gallery, Aberystwyth, in 1978. Other exhibitions included open studio, Metropolitan Wharf, 1980–2; Cherry Orchard Restaurant, 1983; Whitechapel Open, Whitechapel Art Gallery, and British Designers Exhibition, Harrods, both 1984; and East End Open Studios, at Martello Street, 1989.

Peter JAMIESON 1945– Painter, draughtsman and printmaker, born in Norwich, Norfolk, the county where he grew up and which inspired much of his work, which also included seascapes and interiors. Jamieson attended Manchester University, 1964–8; Byam Shaw School of Painting and Drawing, 1968–9; and Royal Academy Schools, 1969–72. The publisher Edward Arnold and the National Trust commissioned work. HRH The Prince of Wales and National Maritime Museum hold Jamieson's pictures, which were given solo shows by Abbott and Holder, including one in 2003 of landscapes in Norfolk, Venice and France.

Robert Kirkland JAMIESON 1881–1950 Painter and teacher, born at Lanark, Scotland. He studied at Glasgow Training College for Teachers, then in Paris. For most of the 1930s he was head of Westminster School of Art, taking over as principal of St Martin's School of Art in 1945. He was married to the artist and potter Dorothea Selous. He showed at RA, LG, NEAC, Redfern Gallery and extensively at RBA. Galleries in Oldham, Worthing, Belfast and Glasgow hold his work. Lived at Burford, Oxfordshire.

Victor JAMILLY 1927– Painter and art dealer who studied at St Martin's School of Art. He showed at RSBA, NEAC and at Euston Gallery. The Jamillys ran the gallery for some years in a large house near Euston Road. Their aim was trying "to educate the public to appreciate and buy original paintings instead of prints and posters". Lived in London.

Lin JAMMET 1958– Painter, designer, illustrator and animator, educated in England and France and of Anglo-French parentage. His mother was the sculptor Elisabeth Frink. He trained at Chelsea School of Art, 1975–7, then for three years founded and ran the rock group AngleTrax, touring England and releasing several records. In 1980 returned to drawing and began to freelance as an illustrator, designing greetings cards, posters and book covers and working for magazines such as *City Limits* and *Tatler*. Did animation work for television commercials, programme titles and promotional videos, clients including Halifax Building Society, London Transport and Weetabix Ltd. Central Office of Information, the Welsh Office and Department of Trade and Industry employed Jammet for animated information films. Had exhibitions at Beaux Arts Gallery, Bath, and St Jude's, 1990.

JANARDAN 1941– Painter, full name Janardan Bhatt, who was born in Nairobi, Kenya. He was educated in England, studying art at Regent Street Polytechnic School of Art, 1959–61. Was associated with ICA and Federation of British Artists. Signed his work Janardan and lived in London.

Grażyna JANCEWICZ-KULESZA 1945– Architect and artist, sometimes listed as Anna Grażyna Kulesza, who graduated in architecture at Gdansk University in Poland, where she was born in Wilno. She moved to England and started her professional life, registering as an architect in 1972 and joining the RIBA. She then oversaw a variety of family houses, offices, sports centres and other buildings. Based in France with her husband Andrzej Kulesza, she built two churches and spearheaded big stained-glass window schemes for them using a prefabricated concrete panel method devised by him. One of these was at Roubaix, requiring 250 square metres of glass, another the Polish Millennium church in Lens, France, needing 400 square metres. From the late 1980s Jancewicz-Kulesza lived in Spain, preoccupied with painting the Andalusian landscape, undertaking small and large projects in private houses and public buildings. Fascinated by the Phoenician, Roman and Arabic past of the region, she made a series of wall paintings displaying the history of Almuñécar, two installed permanently on the walls of the House of Culture there. Among her later exhibitions was one in Warsaw, 1999–00, another of British artists in Granada, at the Centro Cultural "Gran Capitán" there in 2002. Toruń University in Poland holds her work.

Alfred JANES 1911–1999 Painter, draughtsman, printmaker and teacher, born in Swansea, who was especially associated with portraits of his friend the poet Dylan Thomas; National Museum of Wales, Cardiff, holds a fine example, of 1934. Janes attended Cardiff School of Art, then Royal Academy Schools. From 1936–40 taught at Swansea School, then after military service returned to Swansea College of Art, 1946–63, later teaching at Croydon College of Art. He was a founder-member of SWG, showed at Mayor, St George's and Redfern Galleries, widely with WAC and CASW and took part in Dylan Thomas Country at Upper Grosvenor Galleries, 1971. WAC gave him a retrospective, with tour, 1974, Attic Gallery, Swansea, one in 1995, with a memorial at Glynn Vivian Art Gallery, Swansea, 1999–00. Cubism, Paul Klee and American abstraction of the 1960s all attracted Janes' interest, although his portraits and figurative paintings, stylised and sometimes rather disquieting, are his most notable works. Salome, a CASW purchase, is a good example. Lived in London.

Norman JANES 1892–1980 Etcher, wood engraver and painter, noted for his stylish line and sense of design. Born at Egham, Surrey, Janes studied at the Slade School, Central School of Arts and Crafts and Royal College of Art. Exhibited at RA, RWS, NEAC, SWE, RSMA, in the provinces and widely abroad. Two one-man shows at the Beaux Arts Gallery. Married the artist Barbara Greg. His work is extensively held in public collections including the British Museum, British Council, London Museum, in the provinces and in New Zealand and the USA. Lived in London.

Simon JANES 1972– Painter and designer, influenced by David Bomberg, Frank Auerbach and Leon Kossoff. Janes obtained a distinction in foundation art and design at Prescot Community College, Knowsley, 1990–2, then an honours degree from Falmouth College of Art, 1992–5. Publicity design and self-published, limited-edition books were features of his output. His exhibitions included Falmouth Arts Centre, Mall Galleries, and the 2002 New Year Show at Will's Art Warehouse.

Violeta JANES 1917– Artist in oil, pastel and watercolour, and teacher, born in Buenos Aires, Argentina. She studied at Regent Street Polytechnic School of Art, Watford School of Art and City and Guilds of London Art School, her teachers including A R Middleton Todd, Stuart Tresilian, Edward Osmond and Robin Guthrie. Janes held a position in an advertising studio, did a substantial volume of freelance design work including children's illustrations and directed art studies at Alma College in Ontario, Canada. Portraits, landscapes and flower paintings were features of her output, main works including The Fiddler, Red River in New Mexico, Pink Flowers, The Old Shepherd, The Cockney Character and Rosemary Cottage. Janes was a member of UA, Milldon Art Society and Harpenden Art Club. She also showed with PS, RA, RP, at Paris Salon and elsewhere. Had a solo exhibition at Broomfield Museum, Broomfield Park. Lived in Harpenden, Hertfordshire.

JANETR: *see* **Janet REVELL-ROHR**

Henryk JANISZOWSKI 1890–1975 Engineer, restorer and painter who studied at the Academies of Fine Arts in Cracow and Warsaw, Poland. After being a prisoner of the Soviets and time in Palestine, Janiszowksi moved to London where he restored works of art, at the same time studying at the Polish School of Painting under Professor Marian Bohusz-Szyszko. He was an exhibiting member of the Association of Polish Artists in Great Britain. Among his output was series of works devoted to the Holy Land.

Gavin JANTJES 1948– Printmaker, painter, designer and teacher, born in Cape Town, South Africa. Classified as a Cape Coloured, this had a marked effect on him and the direction of his art against racial oppression worldwide. He studied at the School of Fine Art at the University of Cape Town, 1966–9, and won a scholarship to the Hochschule für Bildende Kunst, in Hamburg, Germany, 1970–2. Worked with the Poster Collective in London in 1976 during a short visit, settling in Britain in 1982. He went on to become senior lecturer at Chelsea School of Art. Was also a member of the Arts Council from 1986. Took part widely in group shows in Britain and abroad, solo exhibitions including ICA, 1976, a series at Edward Totah Gallery from 1980 and Herbert Art Gallery and Museum, Coventry, 1988. Victoria & Albert Museum, Wolverhampton Art Gallery and overseas galleries hold his work. Participated in The Other Story, Hayward Gallery, 1989–90, and touring.

Robert JANZ 1932– Artist, born in Belfast, Northern Ireland, who said that his work "concentrates on the ephemeral, emphasizing transience and erasure." Janz was a Fulbright Fellow to Spain, 1964. In the mid-1960s he was a founder-member of Continuum with Dante Leonelli and Michael McKinnon, then at the Royal College of Art. Continuum toured five major exhibiting venues until it arrived at the Hayward Gallery in 1970, the first kinetic light exhibition there. Janz was at LACM, Los Angeles, California, in 1975; was a member of TING (Theater of Mistakes), in London, 1978; and had a British DAAD residency in Berlin, West Germany, 1979–80. He gained a Hand Hollow Grant, Lebanon, New York, in 1992; a Sirius residency, Cobh, Ireland, 1995; FAWC residency, Provincetown, Massachusetts; a residency in Guernsey, Channel Islands, 1997; launched the Web Poems Project, Location One, New York City, 1999; had a Suite residency, Mabou Mines, New York, 2000; and a Baumhaus residency, Wismar, Germany, 2002. Later major projects included Roebuck Moving Pictures, Dublin, Ireland, 1990; Sirius, Cobh, 1995; Galerie L, Ollave, Lyon, France, 1996; John David Mooney Foundation, Chicago, 1998; and Galerie 21, Wismar, 2002. Among his original web works were www.vers.com/janz; islomania.com/janz; and location-l.org/room. In 2004, Janz's current work included "a zine I have been issuing for the last 2 years: POSTRIX." He was then based in New York.

Darsie JAPP 1883–1973 Painter, born in Liverpool into a shipping family. Japp was educated at Oxford University and worked in the family office in London, 1904–7, attending Lambeth School of Art in the evenings. As a student at Slade School of Fine Art, 1908–9, he was a contemporary of Stanley Spencer, whom he introduced to the painter Henry Lamb. In 1926 Lamb completed Darsie Japp and Family, owned by City of Manchester Art Galleries, one of his most notable such groups. During commissioned Army service in World War I Japp won the Military Cross and his picture The Royal Field Artillery in Macedonia is in the Imperial War Museum collection. However, Lamb dissuaded him from becoming a full-time artist, and Japp chose to farm and breed racehorses for a living. For many years Japp and his family lived on the continent as well as in England, and he died in Caxias, Portugal.

Norman Clifford JAQUES 1922– Painter, draughtsman, printmaker and teacher. He was born in Manchester and studied at the College of Art and Technology, 1937–42. Among his awards were a Royal Manchester Institute Award; Proctor Travelling Scholarship to Italy and France, 1948; and he was a Giles Bequest Prize winner in blockprinting, Victoria & Albert Museum, 1954. Jaques held a senior lectureship in the faculty of art and design at Manchester Polytechnic, 1950–82. He was president of MAFA, 1984–90. He worked in the field of prints, in which he specialised, illustration and book design. Solo and group shows included Peterloo Gallery and City Art Gallery, both in Manchester; Manchester and Salford Universities; Senefelder Group; Nebraska University Art Gallery; and RA. Victoria & Albert Museum and public galleries in Manchester, Oldham and Stockport hold examples. Lived in Sale, Cheshire.

Tess JARAY 1937– Painter, printmaker and teacher who studied at St Martin's School of Art, 1954–7, then Slade School of Fine Art, 1957–60. In 1960 she gained an Abbey Minor Travelling Scholarship, the following year winning a French Government Scholarship. Had her first solo show at Grabowski Gallery in 1963. Jaray taught at Hornsey College of Art, 1964–8, then at Slade School of Fine Art. Further solo shows included Graves Art Gallery, Sheffield, in 1972, and the same year at Bristol City Art Gallery; Angela Flowers Gallery in 1976; key shows at Whitworth Art Gallery, in Manchester, and Ashmolean Museum, Oxford, in the mid-1980s; and Purdy Hicks Gallery, 2003. Jaray's work was abstract, concerned with suggestive interactions of colour and form in complex patterns. Examples are held by Tate Gallery, Arts Council and other major collections in Britain and abroad. Jaray completed designs in brick for public spaces. Her works included the forecourt of Victoria Station, 1980; oriental carpet-making in the centre of Birmingham, 1991; a cruciform design outside Wakefield Cathedral, 1989–94; Stickley, in Stoke-on-Trent; and Jubilee Square, outside Leeds General Infirmary, 1995–9; and the forecourt of the new British Embassy, Moscow, 2001. Jaray produced a series of screenprints based on W G Sebald's 1997 volume *The Emigrants*. Married to the artist Marc Vaux and lived in London.

Alex JARDINE 1913–1987 Painter and draughtsman in colour and black-and-white with a special interest in plastics, born in Essex, where he attended Brentwood

School. Jardine was at St Martin's School of Art and studied in Brussels. He was responsible for a river fish series of stamps for the General Post Office, also completing commissions for Imperial Chemical Industries, Bakelite Ltd, Swedish Travel Bureau and publishers such as Collins, Eyre & Spottiswoode and Hutchinson. He was a member of SWLA and Society for Wildlife Art of the Nations and showed widely internationally. Lived in Chislet, Kent.

George JARDINE 1920–2002 Painter, printmaker, collagist, scraperboard artist and teacher, born and lived in Wallasey, Cheshire. He attended Wallasey School of Art, 1936, and Royal College of Art, 1939–43, teachers including Paul Nash, Stanley Spencer, Percy Horton and Edward Bawden. During World War II Jardine moved to Cumbria, becoming absorbed in the landscape of the Lake District. From 1944–80 he was a lecturer in graphics at Liverpool College of Art. Jardine's own pictures, usually on a small scale, were early influenced by Indian miniature painting and Surrealism, especially Max Ernst, collages using pieces of newspaper, sweet wrappers and advertisements. Jardine also painted many portraits. He showed with Sandon Studios Society and Liverpool Academy both of which he was a member, RA, RCamA and elsewhere. Had several solo exhibitions at Portal Gallery; also Williamson Art Gallery, Birkenhead, which gave him a retrospective in 2000; Bluecoat Gallery, Liverpool; in Belgium and America. The Williamson, Arts Council, Walker Art Gallery in Liverpool and the University there hold examples. The University's art gallery held a memorial show in 2004. Jardine died in Liverpool.

Caroline JARIWALA 1965– Painter, sister of the international art dealer Kapil Jariwala. Influences "ranged from the Italian Renaissance paintings of Piero della Francesca and Sandro Botticelli through to Kalighat and Mughal art of India." Group exhibitions included Horizon Gallery, 1991; Ikon Gallery, Birmingham, and tour, 1991–2; British Council, Manchester, 1994; and Graves Art Gallery, Sheffield, 1998. Had solo shows at Turnpike Gallery, Leigh, and Commonwealth Institute, both 1991; City Museum and Art Gallery, Stoke-on-Trent, 1992; Rochdale Art Gallery, 1995; and Captured Moments, Barber Institute of Fine Arts, Birmingham, 2001–2, which drew inspiration from the collection there. She lived in Harborne, Birmingham

Derek JARMAN 1942–1994 Artist in many media, stage designer, film-maker, photographer and writer, full name Michael Derek Elworthy Jarman (he showed as Michael Jarman until 1966). He studied at London University, 1960–3, then Slade School of Fine Art, 1963–7. Jarman had a solo show at the True Lovers' Knot public house in Northwood, 1960, and won first prize, amateur class, at University of London Art Exhibition in 1961. He took part in notable mixed shows, including Young Contemporaries, Tate Gallery, 1967, winning a Peter Stuyvesant Foundation Prize; Drawing, at Museum of Modern Art, Oxford, 1972; and he was nominated for the Turner Prize, Tate Gallery, 1986. Jarman was an exhibitor at Lisson Gallery from its opening in 1967, also showing with Richard Salmon Ltd. Retrospectives included ICA, 1984; Dom Kulture Studenski Grad, Belgrade, 1988; and Accatone, Paris, 1989. In 1993 Jarman showed Aids-related pictures at Karsten Schubert (Jarman was diagnosed HIV-positive in 1986). Such later works were notably Expressionist, fiery, colourful and cathartic. Jarman said: "I've got wilder and ruder." Jarman was a notable creator of films, including *Jubilee*, 1977; *Caravaggio*, 1986; *The Last of England*, 1987; *The Garden*, 1990, which won a prize at the Berlin Film Festival; *Wittgenstein*, 1992; and *Blue*, 1993. The book *Modern Nature: The Journals of Derek Jarman*, appeared in 1991. Arts Council and Tate Gallery hold examples. Died in London. There was a major retrospective at Barbican Art Gallery, 1996, two years after his autobiography, *Dancing Ledge*, was published; there was another exhibition at Metropole Galleries, Folkestone, 2001.

Douglas JARMAN 1902– Painter and designer for industry who attended Croydon School of Art, 1917–20, and continued to live in area. Showed at local Art Society, RI and elsewhere.

Michael JARMAN: *see* **Derek JARMAN**

Nesta JARMAN fl. from early 1930s– Portrait miniaturist, full name Anne Nesta Jarman, born in Sutton, Surrey. After Bedales School she studied at Cardiff School of Art and Heatherley's School of Fine Art and miniature painting with Alfred Praga. She showed at RA, RMS of which she became an honorary member in 1981, RWA and SWAS. Apothecaries' Hall holds her work. Lived in Weston-super-Mare, Avon.

Maria JARMOŁOWICZ-HUTTON 1938– Architect and artist, born in Grodno, Poland, who graduated from the University of Gdansk faculty of architecture, 1961. She was involved in the restoration of art objects from 1965 and was employed by the Office for Redevelopment & Conservation of Historic Buildings in Warsaw. From 1970 she lived and worked in London as an architect. She studied art with Professor Marian Bohusz-Szyszko, at St Martin's School of Art, 1987–8, and Guildhall University, 1990–5, graduating with honours. Jarmołowicz-Hutton participated in Contemporary Art by Polish Artists Abroad, at POSK, 1985, showed at the Mall Galleries and was a member of the Association of Polish Artists in Great Britain from 1974, its vice-chairman from 1991. Solo exhibitions included POSK; Vanneck Gallery; Prince Consort Gallery, Imperial College; and Grove and Edith Grove Galleries.

Matthew JARRATT 1966– Sculptor, designer, teacher and administrator who trained at Sunderland University and the University of Northumbria at Newcastle upon Tyne. He held residencies at Durham Prison, Tyne Dock Ship Repair Yard and Easington Colliery, lecturing at Newcastle College and the University of Northumbria. From 1996, he was public art officer for Sunderland; two years later was seconded to Northern Arts as visual arts officer; in 1999 becoming commissions officer for the new agency Commissions North. Jarratt completed a number of public commissions in the northeast of England, in various styles and materials. These included the brick and clay, railway image-related Untitled, for Aldi Stores, at Yarm Road, Darlington, 1994; the wood and iron Sign Post, indicating a footpath across Burdon Moor, at Kibblesworth, for Great North Forest, 1995; and, from the same year, the steel Nautical Objects, wall-mounted at Customs House Arts Centre, South Shields, for South Tyneside Metropolitan Borough Council.

Barbara Anne JARRETT 1934– Painter, born in Liverpool. She attended Horsham School of Art and Central School of Art. A member of Free Painters and Sculptors, she showed at Mall Galleries, Loggia Gallery and in Surrey and Sussex, where she lived in Pulborough.

Gloria JARVIS fl. from 1950s– Artist in oil, gouache, brush and wash with Chinese ink, pastel and charcoal; teacher, born in Acton, west London. She attended St Martin's School of Art, 1942–50, under James Bateman, Barry Craig, James Guthrie and others, in 1961–2, studying history of art at University of Florence. From 1950–63 taught history of costume and costume drawing at Regent Street Polytechnic. Jarvis showed at RA, NEAC, NS and at Leicester Galleries in the Artists of Fame and Promise shows, having solo shows in Brussels, 1970–83. Several Belgian collections and Abbot Hall Art Gallery, Kendal, hold examples. Among her main works were The Thames Frost Fair 1740 and L'Ommegang, both in private collections. A number of eighteenth-century artists, including Gainsborough and Hogarth, as well as Degas and Daumier were cited as influences. Lived in Canterbury, Kent.

Henry C JARVIS 1867–1955 Landscape painter in watercolour. Studied at Goldsmiths' College School of Art under Percy Buckman and Frederick Marriott. Exhibited RA, RI and RWS. Northampton Corporation bought his work. Lived at Sevenoaks, Kent, where he was a member of the Arts and Crafts Society.

Roland JARVIS 1931– Painter, draughtsman, clockmaker and teacher, born of a French mother and English father, who spent his first nine years in France and was bilingual. Attended Guildford Technical College, 1945–8, then read for a degree in electrical engineering at King's College, 1948–51. After military service training in radar, 1951–3, Jarvis was a research engineer for Morgan Carbon before opting to pursue painting, his tutors at Chelsea School of Art, 1954–6, being Ceri Richards and Robert Medley. From 1956–9 Jarvis lived in Paris, partly on a French government scholarship, then a British Council grant, working at L'Académie de la Grande Chaumière and studying etching in Friedlander's studio. From 1959–91 – apart from a year in India, 1961–2 – Jarvis taught widely, including Watford, Camberwell and Kingston Schools of Art and Brighton Polytechnic. In 1960 BBC Television had made a programme on Jarvis' work, directed by Alex Jacob. Exhibited widely including RA, Victoria & Albert Museum, St George's Gallery, Towner Art Gallery in Eastbourne, solo shows including a retrospective at Brighton Polytechnic Gallery, 1992. Victoria & Albert Museum, New York City Library and National Gallery of Western Australia, Perth, hold examples. From 1972 Jarvis designed and built astronomical clocks, and was elected a fellow of the British Horological Institute in 1992. His work was shown extensively at the Science Museum and Hastings Museum, which bought a large clock in 1995, on permanent display. Lived in Hastings, Sussex.

Catherine JAUSLIN 1958– Painter, born and lived in London, who studied at St Martin's School of Art, 1980–3, then Chelsea College, 1983–4, in the latter year gaining a two-year Rome Scholarship. Showed widely in mixed exhibitions and solo shows in London from 1981 and was represented in John Moores Liverpool Exhibition, 1993–4.

Lallitha JAWAHIRILAL fl. from late 1980s– Painter, born in Ladysmith, Natal, South Africa, who travelled widely but whose work remained infused with the scenery and colour of her own country. She gained a first-class honours degree at Camberwell School of Arts and Crafts 1984–7, then her master's degree in painting at Royal College of Art, 1987–9. Awards and scholarships included Africa Education Trust Scholarship, 1987–9, Africa Education Trust Award, London, 1989–90, and Pollock-Krasner Award, 1992. Among her residencies was Casa Manilva Spain 1992, and Tripura Yoga Ashram, Hardwar, Himalayas, 1993. Had many group shows, latterly including shared exhibition with Rob Olins at New Academy Gallery 1994. Solo shows included 198 Gallery, 1990; Galerie Trapez, Berlin, 1991; and New Academy Gallery, 1996 South African National Gallery in Cape Town holds her work. Lived in London.

JAY: *see* **Elsbeth JUDA**

JEAN: *see* **Jean INGHAM**

Edward JEAVONS 1972– Painter who studied with Kevin O'Brien and John Bicknell at Leeds Metropolitan University, 1992–5, completing a postgraduate course at Chelsea College of Art in 1996. He was a finalist in the 1999 Painting is Not Dead II competition at The Studio Gallery Chiswick. In 2000 A Year in a Life was his first solo show at The Alchemy Gallery, work "made through combining responses to external stimuli and the physical process of painting." In 2005 Jeavons had an exhibition of paintings at The Diorama Gallery at Diorama Arts Centre. Lived in Horley, Surrey.

Kathleen Mary JEBB 1879–c. 1950 Black-and-white artist printmaker, watercolourist and teacher, born in Liverpool She lived in Bristol from 1903 and taught part-time at Municipal School of Art. The landscape of the West Country and Welsh borderland area were key subjects of her work, which was shown at RA, RWA, RSA and Walker Art Gallery in Liverpool. Bristol City Art Gallery holds prints by her.

Kathleen Grant JEFFERIES: *see* **Kathleen HARTNELL**

Wilfred Avalon JEFFERIES 1907– Painter, printmaker theatrical designer and teacher, born in Bristol. Educated at Bristol University, at the city's Municipal School of Art 1920–6, at Académie Julian in Paris, 1928–9, at Geneva Academy, 1930–1, and in Rome at the British Academy on two occasions, in the 1920s and 1930s. He showed at RA RBA, RWA, SGA of which he was a member, and widely in the provinces. Bristol University has murals by him and National Maritime Museum in Greenwich holds his work Taught for a time at Portsmouth, Winchester and Basingstoke Schools of Art and lived for many years in Southsea, Hampshire.

Alan JEFFERSON 1918–2001 Artist in a variety of media and teacher, born in London. He studied at Wimbledon School of Art, 1934–7, then Royal College of Art, 1937–9 and 1946–7 with a break for war service. Notable teachers included Gilbert Spencer, Paul Nash, Patrick Heron and Harry Thubron. Jefferson gained a Royal Exhibition Scholarship in painting, 1947. He joined Portsmouth College of Art in that year and taught painting and printed textiles, eventually retiring from department of fine art at Portsmouth Polytechnic as senior lecturer in painting in 1983. Group shows included RA, Redfern and Leicester Galleries, Southampton City Art Gallery and elsewhere. Had solo shows at Bear Lane Gallery, Oxford, 1965; Portsmouth College of Art, 1968; Hiscock Gallery, 1971; and Portsmouth City Art Gallery, 1974. Portsmouth Museums Collection holds his work. Jefferson's pictures, as shown at Bear Lane, were apparently simple: a disc of colour, surrounded by other colours in a geometrical arrangement, but they were also very complex, containing a multiplicity of pictorial events apparent only after tranquil observation. Lived in Cosham, Hampshire.

Sean JEFFERSON 1957– Versatile artist, born in Woolwich, southeast London, who graduated from Imperial College in 1978. He studied microbiology and the training in super-accurate observational drawing and the preparation of micrographs of viruses, and so on, led to his early experiments in surreal art, which eventually developed into his form of contemporary Symbolism. Jefferson was involved in a wide range of collaborations internationally, including exhibitions often with live musical performance at top restaurants, with Anne Bellion Galleries, from 1994; Spilkammeret, cards published in Denmark, 1995; and Avantegardsky, performances based on Russian Futurism, at Spitz Club, through 1997. Took part in numerous group exhibitions and had many solo shows, later ones including Rapunzel and other Odd Tales, Talisman Fine Art/Mill Lane Gallery, 1999; Somebody's at the Bottom of the Garden, Walton De'arth Fine Art, Launceston, 2001; and A Twilight Stroll at the Edge of a Cornish Fairyland, Talisman Fine Art/54 The Gallery, 2002. Jefferson was an elected member of the South West Academy.

Andrew JEFFERSON-MILES 1972– Painter, writer and poet, born in Wismar, Demerara, in what is now Guyana. He studied literature at Sheffield Hallam University, gaining his master's in 1995, his doctorate in creative and critical writing, University of East Anglia, 2003. Was a guest lecturer at Jung Institute, Zürich, Switzerland, 1993; Florida A&M University, 1995, and University of South Carolina, 1999, both in America. Took part in a group show The Transvangarde, October Gallery, 1999–00, solo exhibitions including the Atrium Gallery, PricewaterhouseCoopers, 2000 and 2001, and Tate Modern: The London Consortium: The YBAs, 2002. His poetry *Art of Navigation* appeared in 1999, the novel *The Timehrian* in 2002. Jefferson-Miles was interested in "painting as poetic inspiration, a means of inventing a new tradition that acknowledges a cross-cultural inheritance." Lived in London.

Michael JEFFERY 1941– Painter of equestrian pictures, born in New Zealand, whose ability as a draughtsman and interest in horses developed during his schooldays in North Island. While working for the bloodstock auctioneering firm Wright, Stephenson Jeffery painted Summertime, a stallion bred by King George VI and exported to New Zealand and it was used on the British Bloodstock Agency's 1968 calendar. After studying in London with the noted equestrian artist Juliet McLeod, 1969–70 – she urged him to visit major art galleries, but to "avoid the moderns!" – Jeffery returned to New Zealand. He travelled to Melbourne, Australia, in 1972, where the Victoria Racing Club commissioned him to paint the country's Racehorse of the Year for 14 years. Jeffery moved to France to develop his European career in 1987, in 1997 settling in Newmarket, Suffolk. By that time he had an international reputation, notable commissions including the West Australian Turf Club, 1984, to paint a retrospective series of 17 Western Australian Derby winners; a three-year retainer from the Italian Jockey Club, 1988, to paint winners of the Derby Italiano; and a commission from Société Martell to paint for its collection the 1996 Grand National winner Rough Quest. Molesworth Gallery, Dublin, showed Jeffery's work.

Ralph JEFFERY 1920–2004 Painter mainly in oil, and educator, becoming an inspector of schools, born in London. He attended Plaistow Grammar School, then Goldsmiths' College School of Art. Showed at RA, LG and NEAC. Lived in Rogate, Petersfield, Hampshire.

Edward JEFFREY 1898–1978 Painter and illustrator, born on Tyneside. He studied at King's College and then entered the studios of a Newcastle firm of commercial artists, Philipson and Sons, where he stayed for 11 years; then did similar work in London and Huddersfield. In 1944 he was asked, with the writer Sheila Hodgetts, to create a new character for children and the pig Toby Twirl was the result. It ran as a cartoon strip in a Yorkshire paper and appeared in annuals. After this Edward Jeffrey turned to inn signs in the Lake District, where he lived at Ravenstonedale, and when he was not painting these he become noted for his pictures of the area. Showed RSA, NS, RI, RBA, with local art societies and widely abroad.

Gary JEFFREY 1966– Painter of landscapes and townscapes whose vigorous brushwork was compared with that of Kokoschka. Worked a lot in London. In 1984 he gained the Munnings Painting Prize. Jeffrey exhibited at Kingston Heritage Museum in 1988, with RWS, Southwood Brown Fine Art, 1989–90, Llewellyn Alexander Gallery in 1990 and in 1991 shared a show there.

Jill JEFFREY 1940– Artist, designer and teacher who graduated in fine arts from the Birmingham College of Art, 1961. After involvement in exhibition design she joined the Royal Shakespeare Company, winning its award, 1964, and the Arts Council Designers' Award, 1965. After two years designing for the Belgrade Theatre Company, Jeffrey served as head of art at Solihull Sixth Form College, returning to the Royal Shakespeare Company in 1977, setting up and running the design room until 1990. In 1990–1, she accompanied the Royal National Theatre on its world tour, the work produced forming the core an exhibition at the Theatre in 1991. She was a member of the PS, winning its Frank Herring Award in 1997, and showed elsewhere in Britain, including the RWA. Lived in Oxhill, Warwickshire.

Terry JEFFREY 1945– Naturally talented painter in watercolour and oil, born in Essex, working from a studio in Suffolk. Jeffrey was noted for fresh, cool landscape watercolours which reflected his admiration for the works of John Singer Sargent and Edward Seago. Mixed shows included RWS at Bankside Gallery; Beecroft Gallery, Southend; The Minories, Colchester; and Kingston Hill Gallery, Kingston upon Thames. The John Russell Gallery gave Jeffrey a first showing of his oil paintings there in 2001, previous solo exhibitions including Dedham Craft

Centre and The Haste Gallery, Ipswich. Jeffrey carried out many commissions, including Trust House Forte; Eastern Electricity; Tolly Cobbold; Colchester United Football Club; and the 40th Field Artillery Signals and Anglian Regiments. Public and private collections in Britain and abroad held examples.

Edward Grover JEFFREYS 1897– Painter, industrial and commercial artist. Studied at Ealing School of Art and Bournemouth School of Art. Exhibited RA, NS, RBA and PS. Lived at Ashford, Middlesex.

Charlie JEFFRIES 1960– Versatile artist in various media, notably a sculptor, who graduated with honours from Canterbury College of Art, 1984–8. Was included in the St Augustine's Gardens Sculpture Show, Canterbury, 1986–8; 3 Sculptors, Darwin College Gallery, Canterbury, 1987; and Dress Dance Dawings at The Place Theatre, En Catalunya at Galeria Tom Maddock, Barcelona, Spain, and East End Open Studios, at Carpenter's Road, all 1989. In that year Jeffries collaborated with Aletta Collins on *Forbidden Fruit* at The Place Theatre.

Jack JEFFRIES: *see* **Jacqueline JEFFRIES**

Jacqueline JEFFRIES 1963– Artist, born in Leeds, Yorkshire, known informally as Jack Jeffries. She studied at Jacob Kramer College of Art, Leeds, 1981–2; gained an honours degree in fine art from Maidstone College of Art, 1983–6; and her master's at Chelsea School of Art, 1986–7. Group exhibitions included Norvegica Graphica, Oslo, Norway, organised by Curwen Press, 1990; Machinda International Print Exhibition, prize winner, 1993; Whitechapel Open, Whitechapel Art Gallery, 1998; and Real Places, Westfaelischer Kunstverein, Munster, Germany, 2000. She shared an exhibition with Nicky Hirst at Leeds University Gallery, 1994. Had solo shows at Flowers East, 1990, and The Eagle Gallery, 2001, large but minutely detailed drawings, mainly in graphite on tracing paper. Commissions included Garden Design, with Adam Reynolds, Frimley Park Hosital Art Programme, 2000. Victoria & Albert Museum, The London Institute and Arthur Andersen held examples.

Neil JEFFRIES 1959– Sculptor and lecturer, born in Bristol, who studied at St Martin's School of Art, 1978–82, then Slade School of Fine Art, 1982–4. In 1984 he gained a Boise Travelling Scholarship; 1984–5 artist-in-residence, Kingston Polytechnic; 1986, art in schools project, Whitechapel; 1991, the Wollaston Award, RA Summer Exhibition; and 1997, The Arts Foundation Award for Drawing. From 1985 Jeffries lectured part-time at Slade School of Fine Art, Ruskin School in Oxford and Kingston University. He gained a sculpture commission, Scott Tallon & Walker, John Henry Newman School, Stevenage, in 1987. Among his mixed exhibitions was The Self Portrait: a Modern View, which toured from Artsite Gallery, Bath, 1987, in which Jeffries showed work in oil on riveted metal sheet. It had a quirky quality, like his Winter Levitation, 1985, held by the Arts Council. Jeffries had a first solo show at Arnolfini in Bristol in 1985 and after that in London, Blond Fine Art and Angela Flowers Gallery both handling his work. Later exhibitions included Flowers West, Santa Monica, California, 1999; Susie Allen, 2000; and Flowers Central, 2003.

Roger JEFFS 1942– Artist, born in Nuneaton, Warwickshire, who gained a national diploma in design, painting, at Coventry College of Art, 1958–62, then attended Slade School of Fine Art, 1962–4. At Coventry and the Slade a fellow-student was John Bowstead, and together they had a show, A New Kind of Brightness, at the Umbrella Club, Coventry, in 1961. In 1964, Jeffs, Bowstead and two other Slade students, Terry Atkinson and Bernard Jennings, formed the group Fine Artz which collaborated on a work called Action Chair. The group presented a project and sound show called *Miss Misty and the Tri-Cool Data* at Birmingham Polytechnic in 1966. After Fine Artz, Jeffs and Bowstead continued to work together until 1968–9 in Light-Sound Workshop, a research unit based at Hornsey College of Art. According to Jeffs, "we made films and experimental audio-visual presentations. We also collaborated with Archigram, the radical architectural group based at the Architectural Association." The Arts Council holds Jeffs' three oil on board portrait panels Vittis, bought from Young Contemporaries, 1963. Jeffs settled in London.

Colin JELLICOE 1942– Painter mainly in oil, but later in acrylic, and art gallery director, born and lived in Manchester. Jellicoe studied art at Heald Place Secondary Modern in the mid-1950s with Keith Pepper; was at the Regional College of Art, Manchester, in 1959; then in the early 1960s was influenced by the painter Geoffrey Key. After leaving college Jellicoe opened his own art gallery which was moved to 82 Portland Street after the formation of a partnership with Alan Behar in 1968. From the mid-1960s Jellicoe began painting figures influenced by Vaughan and Bacon, mainly abstracted in nature, but by the early 1970s the work was more realistic. Comics and film books, mainly on the Western, were other influences, and he used several female models. Jellicoe took part in numerous group shows, early on including Preston's Gallery, Bolton, 1964, and Haworth Art Gallery, Accrington, 1965. Others included Harris Museum and Art Gallery, Preston, from 1974; RA Summer Exhibition, 1981; two-man show with Michael Goddard, Royal Exchange Theatre, Manchester, 1985; and 30-year retrospective at Colin Jellicoe Gallery, 1990. Paintings 1987–97 was held at Buxton Museum and Art Gallery in 1997, and in 2005 there was a 45-year retrospective at Colin Jellicoe Gallery. Granada Television, Abbey National and Withington Hospital, Manchester, as well as many private collections in Britain and abroad hold Jellicoe's works.

Ian Tregarthen JENKIN 1920–2004 Much-liked arts administrator, educationist and painter, born in Great Malvern, Worcestershire. His father, Henry Tregarthen Jenkin, was a civil servant involved in education, his mother a strident entrepreneur whose efforts as a property developer, inventor of the first invisible suspender and board games ensured that the family lived in one of the biggest Worcester houses, mixing with county society. From early on Ian was passionate about form, construction, light and the ability of the mind and hand to craft a representation of concepts or things. After Stowe School he attended the Slade School of Fine Art briefly, 1938–9, then began reading for his master's degree in economics at Trinity College, Cambridge. Jenkin was commissioned in the Royal Artillery, 1939–46, leaving with damaged hearing and a disability pension. At Stowe he had had a self-portrait accepted for a London Portrait Society show in

1938. After the Army he completed his degree at Trinity and then studied at Camberwell School of Arts and Crafts, 1947–9, under B A R (Sam) Carter, Vivian Pitchforth, Michael Salaman and William Coldstream. Although Jenkins continued to paint he felt that his talents were inadequate to let him turn professional, so accepted an invitation by Coldstream, when he became professor of the Slade School, to join him as secretary and tutor. The perfect adjutant and a close friend, he remained until they both retired in 1975. Jenkin returned to Camberwell as principal until 1985; was curator at the Royal Academy Schools until 1986; then co-founded the Open College of the Arts. In addition, Jenkin did much to further art education, appointments including the Gulbenkian Foundation, Arts Council, Crafts Council, National Advisory Body for Public Sector Higher Education, the British School at Rome, Committee for Paintings in Hospitals, the Sir Stanley Spencer Memorial Trust, Vincent Harris Fund for Mural Decoration, Edwin Austin Abbey Memorial Scholarships Council and Nine Elms Group of Artists. In 1984 he gained the Order of the British Empire for services to the arts. For over 40 years Jenkin had a smallholding just outside Bray, Berkshire, where he kept cattle and baled his own hay, selling eggs on the train to London. He died in Aston Tirrold, Oxfordshire.

Ann JENKINS 1933– Painter, especially of exuberantly colourful oils of flowers, daughter of the artist Elizabeth Tuke Jenkins. Ann graduated from the Slade School of Fine Art, 1952–6, winning the Wilson Steer Landscape Prize. For some years she served as an examiner in art for London University's teacher training programme. Work was commended at Paris Salon. Held several solo shows in London, including paintings of Australi at Queensland House in 1991. Work in private collections throughout world. Elizabeth Ann Jenkins lived in the family home at Jordans, Buckinghamshire.

Brian JENKINS 1964– Artist using photography, drawing, performance and film "to try to explore questions of space and environment which are not normally associated with ... someone with a physical handicap such as my own." An example was Elevation II in South Bank Centre's touring The British Art Show 1990. Jenkins was born in Falkirk, Stirlingshire, and studied at its College of Technology, 1982–4, then Glasgow School of Art, 1984–8. He gained a BP Education Trust Scholarship Award, 1984–8. Other group shows he appeared in included Joint Artist Book Exhibition, RSA, 1987; Open Land, Portfolio Gallery, Edinburgh, 1988; and Through Photography at Third Eye Centre, Glasgow, 1989. Lived in Falkirk.

Elizabeth Tuke JENKINS 1906–1968 Painter in oil and watercolour and lino-cut artist, born in Elsenham, Essex. She was educated at the Sorbonne, Paris, where she also studied art in Montmartre, then at the Central School of Arts and Crafts under Robert Jamieson. Her lino-cuts are distinctive, often of wartime subjects such as refugees, and she worked with Edith Lawrence and Claude Flight. Showed at LG, NEAC, RBA, Leicester Galleries, WIAC of which she was a member, and RSA, and had a one-man show at Beaux Arts Gallery. Won gold medal at Paris Salon. Ministry of Works bought her work. For many years she was chairman of Buckinghamshire Art Society. The painter Ann Jenkins was her daughter. Elizabeth Tuke Jenkins' favourite subject in her oil paintings and watercolours was the garden and especially the trees at her home at Jordans, Buckinghamshire, designed in the Bauhaus style.

Eveline A JENKINS 1893–1976 Artist in various media, but mainly an illustrator. After studying at University College, Aberystwyth, she studied art in her own time. She earned her living as a botanical artist with the National Museum of Wales, Cardiff. Exhibited with the SWG and locally in Cardiff, where she lived.

Heinke JENKINS 1937– Printmaker and teacher, born in Heilbronn, Germany, where he attended the local grammar school. Studied at Stuttgart Academy of Arts and its College of Graphic and Illustration. Both Heilbronn and Stuttgart Galleries hold his work, which was shown in England at RBA and RBSA both of which he was a member. Lived for some time at Sutton Coldfield, Warwickshire.

Henry JENKINS 1906–1975 Artist who trained as a barrister, although his first love was art. During World War II he took up his pencil again and after the war abandoned law and attended Heatherley's School of Fine Art. He became a familiar and popular figure in Westminster and Whitehall, rapidly sketching life in the streets, soldiers and occasions such as viewings at Sotheby's. Ireland was another subject. Had a number of solo shows in Boston and in London and was shown by the dealer Martyn Gregory, who held a one-man exhibition in 1995.

Lawrence JENKINS 1944– Artist in wide variety of media, born and lived in Sevenoaks, Kent, who studied at Maidstone College of Art, 1962, teachers including William Bowyer and David Hockney. He said that his work was "like a diary and can be about anything that interests or concerns me." Showed regularly in RA Summer Exhibition, also with West Kent Open Studios '97. National Museum of Wales in Cardiff and the Belgian National Library hold examples.

Lincoln Pugh JENKINS 1901–1988 Artist in oil, watercolour and various graphic media, and teacher, born in Presteigne, Radnorshire. He attended Leicester College of Art. Became member of staff at Birmingham School of Art, 1925, in 1939 moving to Harrogate as principal, retiring in 1961. Moved to Bangor, Caernarvonshire, in 1970, in 1977 losing his sight. Was a member of the National Society for Art Education. Jenkins' work comprised objective landscapes and work strongly influenced by Cubism, later pieces concentrating on sunlight, patterns and windows. Group shows included RA, City Art Gallery in Leeds and elsewhere widely in the north of England. Solo shows included Oriel Gallery, Bangor. His son was a potter, Christopher Jenkins.

Marjorie JENKINS 1905–1996 Painter, who studied at St Martin's School of Art in 1920s under Stafford Leake, like her husband Reg Jenkins. She was for a time a fashion artist with the Court dressmaker Callista, but the care of parents and the need to look after a family prevented her development as a painter. She was particularly influenced by the Australian painter John Passmore, a colleague of her husband's at Lintas, the advertising agency, who for 10 years from 1939 lived with the Jenkins at their cottage in Suffolk. Passmore encouraged her to a new light palette, and she became absorbed by the interrelationship of form, light and colour. Her oil paintings of 1940–60 were given a solo show at Abbott and Holder, 1989.

Mark Robert JENKINS 1971– Painter who attended Birmingham Institute of Art and Design, Bournville, 1993–4; Wirral Metropolitan College, Wallasey, 1994–7; and the Royal Academy Schools, 1997–00. He participated in the final year show there, his Wilderness: Shropshire being a meticulously painted oil on board. Jenkins won the Richard Ford Travel Award, Madrid, Spain, 1998; a Celia Walker Landscape Prize, 1999; and a David Murray Landscape Travel Scholarship, 2000. He showed at the National Print Exhibition, Mall Galleries, 1998, and RA Summer Exhibition from 1998. Lived in West Bromwich, West Midlands.

Geoffrey JENKINSON 1925– Artist and craftsman in various media, born in Leeds, Yorkshire. He was an apprentice glass-cutter and leaded window maker, 1941–6; worked as a tradesman in Bradford, 1946–50; then from the early 1950s began working as an assistant furniture designer in America, living for some time at Tubac, Arizona. From 1941–8 Jenkinson attended evening art classes at Pudsey Grammar School, becoming a member of RCamA in 1947, later a member of Arizona Artists' Guild. Exhibitions included RA, RBA and Bradford City Art Gallery, and he showed solo in America. Leeds City Art Gallery holds his work.

Bernard JENNINGS 1942– Artist, brought up and who eventually settled in southeast London. He attended Colfe's Grammar School, 1954–60, then studied for a fine art diploma at Slade School of Fine Art, 1960–4. In 1964 with Terry Atkinson, John Bowstead and Roger Jeffs, Jennings formed the group Fine Artz and produced a work called Action Chair. In 1966 Fine Artz presented a projection and sound show, *Miss Misty and the Tri-Cool Data*, at Birmingham Polytechnic. Jennings became a Buddhist monk in Sri Lanka and Japan, eventually returning to England.

Charlotte JENNINGS 1935– Artist in oil, acrylic and sand, etching and animated film, born and lived in London, although she spent several childhood years as an evacuee in New York and from 1982 had seven years in Australia. She was the younger daughter of the artist Humphrey Jennings. She won a Major County Award to the Slade School of Fine Art, 1955–8, having spent 1953–4 at Hammersmith School of Arts & Crafts, and 1954–5 at Chelsea School of Art. She won several prizes at the Slade, and gained a Boise Postgraduate Scholarship. Studied at Atelier 17 in Paris, 1965, and London International Film School, 1976. Jennings' teachers included William Coldstream, Anthony Gross, William Townsend, Ruskin Spear, S W Hayter, Ernst Gombrich and David Sylvester. Group shows included Young Contemporaries, LG, New Vision Centre, Gardner Centre at University of Sussex and abroad. Had a solo show at Brown Thomas, Dublin, 1965, later ones including Gardner Arts Centre, 1991, and Chequers, London, 1992. Jennings produced several films, including *The Big Hit*, an animated space odyssey, 1980; she was manager of etching production for Editions Alecto; taught art; and did interior design. Commissions included murals for Associated Electrical Industries; fabrics for Courtaulds; and graphics for British Transport Films. University College, London, and Bibliothèque Nationale, Paris, hold examples.

E Owen JENNINGS 1899–1985 Painter, etcher, engraver and illustrator, in Cowling, Yorkshire. Jennings attended Skipton School of Art, where, under the guidance of headmaster W T Shuttleworth, he studied bookbinding, textile design and crafts. This was followed by Leeds College of Art and the Royal College of Art, where he was a silver medallist. He became principal of the School of Art at Tunbridge Wells, in Kent, 1934–65, after appointments at Doncaster School of Art, 1926–8, and Leeds College of Art, 1928–34. Stained glass at Staplehurst Church, in Kent, is his work. Jennings was elected RWS in 1950 and RE in 1970 and exhibited at the Paris Salon, in New York, Melbourne and Chicago and participated in British Council shows in Belgium, Poland, China and the Soviet Union. *Etchings of Today* and *Fine Prints of the Year* include his work and official purchases were made by the British Museum, Victoria & Albert Museum, and many other British and foreign collections. Lived in Tunbridge Wells, where the Art Gallery held a retrospective in 1973.

Humphrey JENNINGS 1907–1950 Artist in oil, pencil, pastel, film and photography, born in Walberswick, Suffolk, father of the artist Charlotte Jennings. Jennings read English at Cambridge University and never went to art school. He worked in theatre design in Cambridge and as a painter, 1929–34, then until 1950 in documentary film, based in London. He was a member of International Surrealist Group, showing with it in 1936. Solo shows were held at London Gallery, 1938; ICA, 1951; and Riverside Studios, 1982. Jennings, one of the founders of the social survey group Mass-Observation, is best known for work in wartime documentary film, working before and during the war variously as a director, writer and editor with the GPO/Ministry of Information/Crown Film Units; titles included: *Spare Time*, 1939; *Listen to Britain*, 1941; *Fires Were Started*, 1943; and *A Diary for Timothy*, 1945. In 2000, the National Film Theatre ran a season of the films and Channel 4 television made a documentary, *Humphrey Jennings – the Man Who Listened to Britain*. Tate Gallery holds his work. Jennings' landscapes and portraits, as shown at Mayor Gallery, 1993, were similar to works by the Italian Futurist painters. Died in Poros, Greece. In 2006 Christie's South Kensington sold works from Jennings' studio.

Leonard JENNINGS 1877–1956 Sculptor, born and lived in London. He studied at Lambeth and Glasgow Schools of Art and at the Royal Academy Schools. Whilst working for the Indian government for several years before World War I he completed a number of statues of members of the British royal family, including King Edward VII. Exhibited RA, RP, RI, Royal Glasgow Institute of the Fine Arts and elsewhere.

Maggie JENNINGS 1955– Artist who graduated with honours from Bristol Polytechnic, 1979–82, then gained her master's from Chelsea School of Art, 1982–3. Mixed shows included 5th Biennial of European Graphic Art, Heidelberg, West Germany, and tour, 1988, and Ideas of Greece at Fine Art Society and East End Open Studios, at Britannia Works, both 1989. In 1988 Jennings had a solo show at the Kerrin Lyons Gallery.

Philip Oswald JENNINGS 1921– Painter, printmaker and teacher, born in London. Studied at Harrow School of Art and Royal College of Art, 1940–5, where he was a postgraduate student, 1950–1. After a short period as an illustrator, in 1952 he joined the staff of Cardiff College of Art. As well as a one-man show at Iolo Gallery, Cowbridge, in 1974, Jennings took part in many group exhibitions, including RA, UA, Brighton Art Gallery, AEB tours, Howard Roberts Gallery, Cardiff, RWA and elsewhere. Welsh Arts Council, with which he has exhibited, holds his work. Lived in Pinner, Middlesex, later in Whitchurch, Glamorgan. Was a founder-member of the WSW and belonged to SWG, with which he frequently exhibited. In 1953 he participated in the American Society of Graphic Artists American tour. Sometimes only signed work P O J with date.

Stuart JENNINGS 1928– Artist and teacher producing "mainly landscapes, figures in the landscape and occasional portraits" who was "influenced, but not directly, by Poussin, Cézanne and Turner". He was born in Oxford and studied at the West of England College of Art, Bristol, under Ernest Pascoe, going on to teach in English schools and colleges, 1956–89. Was a full member of the RWA and an associate of the NS, also taking part in mixed shows at the ROI, RI and with EuroArt. Solo exhibitions were held in Winchester, Salisbury, Bristol, Andover, York and Harrogate. Lived at Compton Down, Winchester, Hampshire.

Walter Robin JENNINGS 1927– Mainly self-taught artist, born in Old Hill, Staffordshire. He worked in oil and watercolour and was a self-employed painter from 1960. Jennings was noted as a painter of the English countryside. He showed with RCamA, NEAC, ROI, RBSA, The Game Fair and elsewhere in mixed exhibitions. Had a series of solo exhibitions in London and the provinces, also exhibiting in America and on the continent. Royle, Medici, Solomon and Whitehead and other publishers reproduced his work. Valentine's of Dundee published a painting chosen by HM Queen Elizabeth the Queen Mother as her personal Christmas card. Jennings also helped restore early stained glass windows, including some in the House of Commons; made a video on oil painting for Optical Image Ltd; and painted a mural for Fortox of Kidderminster depicting 300 years of family history. Lived near Kidderminster, Worcestershire.

David JEREMIAH 1940– Painter and lecturer, born in Clayton-le-Moors, Lancashire. He studied at King's College, University of Durham, 1958–63, completing his doctorate in art history at Reading University, 1968–72, after which he became senior lecturer at Manchester Polytechnic. Wrote on art and showed in group exhibitions at Young Contemporaries, Bear Lane Gallery in Oxford, SWG and WAC. University of Surrey, Guildford, gave him a solo show in 1972. Jeremiah's *A Hundred Years and More*, a history of the faculty of art and design at Manchester Polytechnic, appeared in 1980.

Ron JESTY 1926– Watercolourist, graphic designer and teacher, born in Weymouth, Dorset, who had no formal training. He freelanced as a graphic designer, 1947–78, from that time concentrating on watercolour painting and part-time teaching. Jesty was "influenced by J S Cotman" and strove "for purity of colour, formal design structure in composition". Elected RBA in 1982, he also exhibited at RA Summer Exhibition, with RWS, RI and RWA. Solo shows included Bristol City Art Gallery, Brewhouse Arts Centre in Taunton, Yeovil Arts Centre, Alpha Gallery in both Yeovil and Swanage and The Gallery, Dorchester. Somerset County Council holds his work. Lived in Yeovil, Somerset.

Sheilagh JEVONS 1948– Artist, born in Newton Hill, Kincardineshire, who was an industrial engineer for Cadbury's, 1968–9; a business studies lecturer, 1971–80; then from 1981 was a psychological counsellor, completing an art foundation course part-time at Stourbridge. Jevons' work was "concerned with evoking a landscape image which contains symbolic images rooted in 'place'. Language – Welsh, Gaelic and English – is written into the paint, and the paintings contain different perspectives within the same image." Ana Maria Pacheco and Anselm Kiefer were major influences. Group shows included the Artworks Gallery, Iron Bridge, and the Museum of Modern Art, Wales, both 2000. Had solo exhibitions at Burford House Gallery, Tenbury Wells, 1996; Telford Gallery, 1997; and Oriel 31, Newtown, 2001. Lived in Easthope, Shropshire.

Dick JEWELL 1951– Versatile artist in whose work photographic images were important. Postcards, record covers and photographic books took him out of the gallery system for periods. He was born in Worthing, Sussex, and after working on Brighton Marina, 1973–4, studied for his master's degree in printmaking at Royal College of Art, 1978, the year he published his book *Found Prints*. Group exhibitions included Waddington Galleries and National Museum Art Gallery, Singapore, both 1976; Lives, at Hayward Gallery, 1981; and Summer Show I at Serpentine Gallery, 1983. Solo shows included Chapter Arts Centre in Cardiff, 1980. Arts Council, Whitworth Art Gallery in Manchester, The Open University and several other provincial collections hold examples. Lived for a time in London.

Mary JEWELS 1886–1977 Painter of Cornwall whose work has a primitive charm, her maiden name was Mary Tregurtha (her husband Albert Jewels was killed in World War I). She was born in Newlyn, her sister Cordelia being the first wife of the sculptor Frank Dobson, who made a fine bronze head of Mary. She was encouraged by the painter Cedric Morris, when he was staying in Newlyn in 1919; he gave her a canvas, four tubes of paint and told her to cover the canvas by the evening. She was later encouraged by Christopher Wood and Augustus John, although she claimed she was "influenced by nobody and entirely self-taught, a true Celt loving my Cornwall". Was a member of the St Ives Society and a founder-member of Penwith Society, 1949. Had solo show at Dorothy Warren's Gallery, 1927; another at Newlyn Art Gallery in 1977. Jewels was included in the Tate Gallery's 1985 St Ives exhibition, and in 2003 was in Paintings by Three Self-Taught Artists (with James Dixon and Alfred Wallis) at Austin/Desmond Fine Art. Plymouth City Art Gallery holds her work.

Hilda K JILLARD 1899–1975 Figure, animal and landscape painter, born near Godalming, Surrey, remembered by friends as a modest, witty and lovable eccentric, of Huguenot descent. After a turbulent period at Farnham School of Art attended Slade School of Fine Art under Henry Tonks, she worked in Frank Calderon's School of Animal Painting, went to Paris where she studied at La

Grande Chaumière and Atelier Colarossi, then returned to England and was at Guildford School of Art a pupil of Frederick Hinchliff, to whom she said she owed all that she achieved. This was in part due to great self-discipline, as in 1937 Jillard suffered a crippling attack of multiple sclerosis from which she only slowly and partly recovered. In 1939, just before World War II, she had a prophetic and controversial exhibition at the Wertheim Gallery which included the picture 1939 What Harvest?, acquired by the Imperial War Museum, which showed a sun-tanned farm labourer surveying his golden corn under a darkening sky and approaching war-planes. Jillard spent a dozen years in Cornwall from 1942, travelling and painting widely on the continent from her St Ives studio. Became a member of the Newlyn, St Ives and Penwith Arts Societies and in 1947 exhibited at the Castle Inn with the sculptor Denis Mitchell. Jillard eventually settled near Petworth, Sussex, where she continued to paint, showing locally and in London until her death.

J M C: *see* **Josephine McCORMICK**

Graham JOBBINS 1969– Sculptor, born in Kent, who studied at Maidstone College of Art, taught by Antony Gormley. He moved to Cornwall in 1988, exhibiting metal sculptures and making large constructions for theatrical and festival events. In 2002 his work was included in Valentine's Collection at The Great Atlantic Map Works Gallery, St Just, Penzance.

John JOBSON 1941– Painter who studied at the City and Guilds of London Art School. He settled in his own studio gallery in Kilmacanogue, County Wicklow, Ireland, producing representational landscape and figurative works and abstractions. Jobson is represented in the National Self-Portrait Collection of Ireland, University of Limerick, an oil on board which attempts to summarise his character using a sculpted effect.

Pat JOBSON 1919– Artist in pastel, watercolour, oil and black-and-white, born in Ilford Essex. Jobson was the fourth generation of painters in his family, and he studied with his father, Frank Mears Jobson, 1924–30, with Alfred Hayes in 1930–8, and with Frank Brangwyn at intervals, 1934–50. Jobson was a noted marine artist, a founder-member of RSMA, being a member until 1954. He was also a founder-member and president of Wapping Group of Artists and a member and president of Langham Sketch Club. He was a prolific book illustrator from 1947–59, notably of titles by Peter Dawlish and Frank Knight, and completed many pub signs from 1947. Jobson showed with RBA, RI, PS and SGA and had solo shows in Hitchin and Croydon from 1974. National Gallery in Adelaide, Australia, holds his work. Lived in North Wembley, Middlesex.

Richard Henry JOBSON 1910–1977 Untrained painter in watercolour and pastel, and photographer, born in Urmston, Manchester. He studied at Manchester University and served as a general medical practitioner in New Radnor from 1937–70. Exhibited RCamA, elsewhere in Wales, in Spain and America. Also made working model locomotives. Lived in Presteigne, Radnorshire.

Natasha JOBST 1934– Painter, draughtsman and teacher, born in Vienna, Austria, but brought up and educated in England. Graduated from Slade School of Fine Art, 1954, where she was well regarded by her teacher William Coldstream, in that year winning a life painting prize and John Nash Scholarship for landscape painting. Worked in Paris, 1954–5, then moved to what is now Zimbabwe, where she brought up a family, taught art and ceramics to children and adults and worked as a freelance artist and journalist. After returning to England in 1962, taught for Inner London Education Authority and for Surrey, started adult and children's art workshops in Richmond and at Hampton Court and for eight years was art tutor to the physically handicapped. Group shows included several in southern Africa, Commonwealth Institute and Academicians' Choice at Mall Galleries, 1990. Had a solo exhibition at The Boathouse Gallery, Walton-on-Thames, 1994, near where she lived at East Molesey, Surrey. The Rhodes National Gallery, Harare, and United Biscuits hold Jobst's work.

John JOEKES fl. from mid-1970s– Sculptor who studied with George Kennethson; at Camberwell School of Art; worked in Paris as a typographer; and then as a stone carver in Chichester Cathedral. Using both stone and wood, carvings explored figurative and abstract forms, often combining the elements. Joekes said that his work "attempts to arrest a moment, to cause reflection upon an object". He took part in many exhibitions, including Feeling to See, at Arnolfini Art Gallery, 1987; Art & Computers, Cleveland Arts touring show, 1989; and Abbot Hall Art Gallery and Museum, Kendal, 1990. His solo shows included Artsite, Bath, and Harris Museum & Art Gallery, Preston, both 1990. In 1985 he conceived and organised the Sculpture Competition in Bath, where he lived.

Chantal JOFFE 1969– Painter, born in London, notably of figure studies, sexually explicit and using a light palette, who attended Camberwell School of Arts and Crafts, 1987–8; Glasgow School of Art, 1988–91; and Royal College of Art, 1992–4. She gained a Haldane Trust Travelling Scholarship, NatWest 90s Prize for Art and John Kinross Travelling Scholarship, all in 1991; a TI Bursary, 1992–4; Paris Studio Award, 1993; and Delfina Studios Award, 1994–6. Group exhibitions included 369 Gallery Group Show, Edinburgh, and the first of a string of appearances at National Portrait Gallery, both 1991; Whitworth Young Contemporaries, Manchester, 1993; Into the Nineties at Mall Galleries and Group Show at Brewery Arts Centre, Kendal, both 1994; and John Moores Liverpool Exhibition, 2002. There was a solo show at Victoria Miro Gallery in 2000. Saatchi Collection, NatWest and TI Group hold examples. In 2006, the Hertfordshire-based Joffe won a £25,000 prize for "the most distinguished work" in the RA Summer Exhibition.

Alan JOHN 1927– Artist in painting, sculpture, dance and film and teacher. He was chiefly self-taught as a painter, but studied at Hornsey College for Film. His work was "mainly about the human predicament of everyday living, fusing Surrealism with Cubism". Included in John's career were teaching art with Inner London Education Authority, 1961–82, during which he founded Art Basement, in Hackney; a period, 1978–88, when he founded and directed The Arts Factory Gallery; costume and set design, including *Nettle City*, *Creepy Dub* and *Drunk Albert*, 1983–5; and in 1986 costume and set design for Rubberneck Dance Company. John was a member of Penwith Society of Arts and in 1952 was awarded freedom of the Worshipful Company of Painter-Stainers. Exhibitions included RA Summer Exhibitions, RP, LG, NEAC, Leicester Galleries, Woodstock Gallery, New Contemporary Portrait Painters and elsewhere. Solo shows included Alwin Gallery, 1971; Phoenix Gallery, 1991; and Islington Arts Factory, 1993. Lived in Mount Hawke, Cornwall.

Anthony JOHN 1904–1997 Artist in oil, gouache and watercolour, born in Wales, notable for marine pictures. He studied at Chelsea School of Art with Percy Hague Jowett and in Paris. John said that he "always painted for myself ... I am very lazy, and do not paint if I can avoid it when there is nothing that I *have* to say." At times he was a member of Natal Society of Artists, South African Society of Artists and AIA. Showed with Wertheim, Bloomsbury and Redfern Galleries, UA and elsewhere and had several solo exhibitions. Lived in London.

Augustus JOHN 1878–1961 Painter mainly in oil, draughtsman and printmaker. Born in Tenby, Wales, brother of the artist Gwen John, he attended the Slade School of Fine Art, 1894–8, winning a Scholarship in 1896 and the Summer Composition Prize two years later. John's prodigious natural ability as a draughtsman won the admiration of Henry Tonks, and he soon established himself as a star student and an art world character. Became professor of painting at Liverpool University art school, 1901–4. John started an association with gypsies, learning their language and painting them. Began his wide travels in Britain and on the continent, sometimes travelling by caravan. Over several years painted with J D Innes and Derwent Lees. Started to exhibit widely, having his first one-man show at the Carfax Gallery in 1903. Also showed at the Chenil Galleries, NEAC, Alpine Gallery, Independent Club, RA and elsewhere over the coming years, where he became noted for drawings and paintings of his second wife, Dorelia, his children, his sister Gwen, personalities such as George Bernard Shaw, T E Lawrence, W B Yeats and Dylan Thomas, and for his landscapes and romantic scenes of peasant life. Although sometimes out of fashion, John is assured a place as one of the great figures of British painting in his lifetime. His work is in many galleries, including the Tate Gallery and National Portrait Gallery. Elected RA 1928, resigned 1938, re-elected 1940. Awarded Order of Merit 1942. Autobiographical reminiscences *Chiaroscuro* were published in 1952, *Finishing Touches*, 1964. Retrospectives included one at National Portrait Gallery, 1975, National Museum of Wales, Cardiff, and tour, 1996, and Olympia Fine Art and Antiques Fair, 1999. In 2004–5 Tate Britain held the first large-scale exhibition to focus on Augustus and Gwen (1876–1939). Notable among Augustus's many children were Admiral of the Fleet Sir Caspar John (by his first wife, Ida); the painters Edwin John (by his first wife, Ida), Gwyneth Johnstone (by Nora Brownsword, a model) and Vivien John (by Dorelia); and the cellist Amaryllis Fleming (by Eve Fleming, a rich society hostess widow whose sons included Peter Fleming, writer and explorer, and Ian, the writer and creator of James Bond). John lived at Fordingbridge, Hampshire.

David JOHN 1928– Sculptor and designer in various materials, and teacher, married to the painter Marianne Hellwig John. He was born in Port au Prince, Haiti. John studied drawing with Edna Manley in Jamaica, 1943–6; painting at Birmingham College of Art, with Bernard Fleetwood-Walker, 1946–8; and in London wood-carving with Anton Dapre, 1948–50, and stone-cutting and lettering under Freda Skinner in the sculpture school at Wimbledon School of Art, 1950–1. John became an artist-sculptor-designer for churches from 1950, teaching at the Blue Coat School, 1967; Mary Ward College, 1968; and Shiplake College, 1969–78. A 1974 Churchill Fellowship permitted a two-month tour of post-war European churches. Numerous churches in the United Kingdom hold John's work, which is also in Winchester and Liverpool Metropolitan Cathedrals; Harare Cathedral, Zimbabwe; and the English College, Rome, Italy. Lived in Stroud, Gloucestershire.

Edwin JOHN 1905–1978 Artist, notably a watercolourist, born in Paris, France, son of the painter Augustus John and his first wife, Ida Nettleship. For a time he was a professional middleweight boxer, his early "snarling, bloody battles" with his father being described by Nicolette Devas in her memoir *Two Flamboyant Fathers*. He was known in the press as Teddy John of Chelsea. In World War II Edwin served in the Military Police, in Cyprus. He was encouraged and taught by the painter Edgar Rowley Smart when John was living at Alderney Manor, Dorset, also studying at the Royal Academy Schools and at La Grande Chaumière, in Paris. He especially admired the work of Smart and the Norwich School painter J S Cotman. He was a full member of the Chelsea Arts Club. Had solo exhibitions at Connell & Sons Gallery c.1937, Beaux Arts Gallery, 1939, and Maas Gallery 1963 and 1978. His daughter was the artist Sara John. Died at Priddbwll Bach, Llangedwyn, Powys.

Eira JOHN 1919– Painter in oil, mostly of still life and figurative works, married to the artist Michael Boycott-Brown. She was born in Durham and studied at Westminster School of Art with Mervyn Peake, Mark Gertler and Blair Hughes-Stanton, then did some part-time work at Storran Gallery. After initial artistic activity, she resumed painting only in her later years, taking part in group shows at Heffer Gallery in Cambridge where she lived, Fermoy Arts Centre in King's Lynn and School House Gallery, Wighton. In December 1996 she and her husband shared a show at Cambridge Arts, Fordham.

Marianne Hellwig JOHN: *see* **Marianne HELLWIG**

Rebecca JOHN 1947– Botanical artist, curator and writer, born in London, who gained a diploma in fine jewellery from the Central School of Art & Design, 1966–9, then a distinction in botanical illustration at the English Gardening School, 1994, taught by Ann Marie Evans. For a dozen years from 1971 John was a commissioning editor for *Time Out* magazine and freelance picture researcher; from 1983–6 wrote *Caspar John*, the 1987 biography of her admiral father, son of the artist Augustus John; from 1987–8 did more freelance research work, including paintings to illustrate three books by the cookery writer Elizabeth David; from 1989–92 drafted a life of Amaryllis Fleming, Augustus's illegitimate cellist daughter; in 1995–6 curating the touring exhibition Themes and Variations: Drawings by Augustus John 1901–1931; then became a full-time botanical artist. She had a solo show at the Lefevre Gallery in 1999. Lived in London and mid-Wales.

Samuel JOHN 1935– Painter, writer and businessman, born in Newport, Monmouthshire. He studied art at College of St Mark and St John, qualifying as a teacher in 1957, gaining a London University bachelor's degree in 1958. Showed with Chenil Galleries, 1956; Oxford Art Society from 1977; Barclay Gallery, Chester, 1980; and Royal Over-Seas League, of which he was a member, 1983. Among his books was *The Sacred and The Profane*, 1980, the year he won the Koestler Prize for Verse.

Sara Gwendolen JOHN 1946– Painter and teacher, born in London, daughter of the artist Edwin John. She studied at Goldsmiths' College, 1958–63; Slade School of Fine Art, 1965–9, teachers including Euan Uglow for drawing, B A R (Sam) Carter and Philip Sutton; and the London College of Printing, 1969–70. Taught at Hertfordshire College of Art & Design, 1969–76, Chelsea and Byam Shaw Schools of Art and Central School of Art & Design. Worked at Sky Editions Lithographic Press, 1973, and Curwen Lithographic Studio, 1979, and was at Ogilvy & Mather and S H Benson advertising agencies as assistant art director. Mixed shows included Young Artists of Today, Grosvenor Gallery, 1969; Newlyn Orion Gallery, from 1971; RA Summer Exhibition, from 1978; Fitzroy Gallery, from 1980; Mold Education & Arts Centre, 1989; Y Tabernacl, Machynlleth, 1990; W H Patterson and Chelsea Town Hall, both 1994; Michael Parkin Gallery, 2000; and Mall Galleries, 2001. She was a full member of the Society of Landscape Painters and Chelsea Arts Club. Solo shows included Mel Calman's Workshop Gallery, 1975. In 2005, Sara John had three exhibitions: at The Art Shop, Abergavenny; Inside and Out at the Oriel Washington Gallery, Penarth; and a retrospective at Martin's Gallery, Cheltenham. Subjects were landscape, still life and occasional portraits. Lived at Priddbwll Bach, Llangedwyn, Powys.

Vivien JOHN 1915–1994 Painter, daughter of the artist Augustus John and his second wife Dorelia. She was born in Dorset and had a wild childhood, not going to school. Attended Slade School of Fine Art, 1932–4, but was forbidden by Augustus to take instruction. For several years in the late 1930s she studied at Euston Road School with William Coldstream and Victor Pasmore. Having visited her aunt, the artist Gwen John in Paris, in 1944 she returned to study at L'Académie de la Grande Chaumière, in 1945 entering Chelsea School of Art, then married the haematologist Dr John White. With her father she visited Jamaica, Italy and Provence and with her husband lived in Russia, Malaysia and Papua New Guinea, which added colour to her palette. She had a series of solo shows with a first at Cooling Gallery in 1935; others included Upper Grosvenor Gallery and Phoenix Gallery, Lavenham; and in 1987 she was included in an exhibition of Slade Contemporaries at Sally Hunter Fine Art, which gave her a memorial show in 1995. Other mixed exhibition appearances included WIAC, LG and RA. Died in London.

William Goscomb JOHN 1860–1952 Sculptor of figures, portraits, memorials and other public works. Born in Cardiff, he studied at the School of Art there, at the City and Guilds of London School of Art and the Royal Academy Schools. There he won a gold medal and Travelling Scholarship. John also worked with Rodin in Paris in the early 1890s, which left an impression on his classically oriented sculpture. Examples are shown in the volume *RBS: Modern British Sculpture*, published in 1939. John won the RBS gold medal and several Paris Salon awards, including a gold medal. Showed at the RA from 1884 and was elected RA in 1909, in 1911 being knighted for his work. The fact that his father had been a stonemason and that in his youth Goscombe John had aided him in the restoration of Cardiff Castle fitted him for the large body of public sculpture he was to complete, including statues of Viscount Wolseley in Horse Guards Parade, London, the Marquess of Salisbury in Westminster Abbey and King Edward VII in Liverpool. He also designed the regalia for the investiture of the Prince of Wales at Carnarvon in 1911 and the King George V Silver Jubilee Medal of 1935. National Museum of Wales in Cardiff held a major show in 1979. Lived in London.

Annie JOHNS 1945– Johns graduated with honours from St Martin's School of Art, 1983–8. She had a placement at Claremont Primary School, Nottingham, in 1986. Johns showed installations at Cahill and Grebler Gallery, 1987, and Watermans Art Centre, Brentford, 1988. In that year she was also included in Fragments of False Houses at Pomeroy Purdy Gallery and in East End Open Studios, at Deborah House, 1989.

Ewart JOHNS fl. from 1950s– Painter, muralist, draughtsman and teacher, born in Barry, Glamorgan. A major formative influence was the teaching of Ceri Richards at Cardiff College of Art. Johns later combined a university career with work as a freelance artist. His academic research, mainly at Exeter, was in urban design, and led to a book on British townscape. He became the first head of department of visual arts at University of Lancaster. Showed widely in mixed exhibitions in Britain and America. Had a series of solo shows at Grabowski Gallery from 1961, and elsewhere in London and the provinces, and in 1981 a retrospective at University College of Wales, Cardiff, and University of Lancaster. This was in three parts, with a strong drawn image approach in common: work of the 1950s, subdued in colour, with form influenced by Cubist ideas; freer paintings of the 1960s; and oil pastels of the 1970s, with a special intensity, luminosity and density and strong emphasis on the figure. Johns carried out a number of public murals, and WAC holds his work.

Mavis JOHNS 1914–2000 Portrait painter in the Old Master style and copyist, born in Plymouth, Devon, who began painting aged six. After a grounding at Torquay College of Art, she attended Sir John Cass and Byam Shaw Schools of Art. When one of her early works was seen by Pietro Annigoni, he invited her to watch him paint in Florence, Italy, and so she studied with him. Johns was commissioned to paint a portrait of King Edward VII for the headquarters of the Royal Engineers, Chatham, her largest work, which replaced an earlier picture by Sir Luke Fildes, destroyed by fire in 1975. A portrait of King James II followed, commissioned by the National Maritime Museum to hang in the Royal Observatory, Greenwich, and this she considered a tribute to her late husband, Major Bruce Johns. Commissions from public institutions and private collectors, mainly replacing works lost or badly damaged, comprised most of Johns' later output.

Arabella JOHNSEN 1966– Painter who studied at Farnham School of Art, 1986–7, winning a first-class honours degree at City and Guilds of London Art School, 1987–90, and her master's in fine art, Royal College of Art, 1990–2. Gained several travel awards, including the John Minton, 1991; a Berkeley Square Gallery Award, first prize at the Insight Exhibition and a Delfina Scholarship, all 1992; and in 1993–4 a Susan Summer Fellowship, with a residency at the artists' complex at Bantam, Connecticut, America, Summer and her husband Robert having bought several of Johnsen's pictures. Johnsen's work ranged from Turneresque landscapes through deserts and canyons populated by cartoon characters to nature and flower paintings. Commissions included paintings for the Blenheim Restaurant Group shows included Long and Ryle, 1992; British Restaurants, 1993; Young British Contemporary at Lefevre Gallery, 1997; and Eastwood MacLean, Winchester, 2000. Had a solo exhibition at Berkeley Square Gallery, 1993, MacLean Fine Art showing her work Reloaded at artLONDON, 2004. De Beers Corporation, Sony Music, Osram Ltd and other corporate collections hold examples. Lived in Hampshire.

Allan JOHNSON 1907–1994 Architect and artist, born in Leeds, Yorkshire. Trained at the school of architecture at Leeds College of Art from 1925, cramming five years' study into four. Obtained his diploma in 1930. Went into private practice in 1930, the Kingston, Surrey, swimming baths one of the jobs he worked on. A RIBA scholarship in 1935 took him to America, where he met his future wife. In 1936 returned to Lanchester & Lodge, where he had done his practical training. During World War II served in the Army, achieving the rank of captain. From 1945–72 was a partner in Lanchester & Lodge. Did much work at Leeds University, where a glass-reinforced polyester wall decoration of 1963, called A Celebration of Engineering Sciences, was completed by him. Retired to Trebetherick, Cornwall, where he died.

Annette JOHNSON fl. from 1960s– Painter and printmaker, born and settled in London, who started painting while living in Boston, America. She subsequently studied at Sir John Cass School of Art and Morley College. "The feeling of solitude" was important in her work, which was figurative, landscape and seascape. Johnson was a member of SWA, Greenwich Printmakers' Association, The Printmakers' Council, Blackheath Art Society and the South-East London Group. She showed in many exhibitions, including NS, RA, RI, Woodlands Art Gallery, Royal Festival Hall and in the provinces.

Audrey JOHNSON 1919– Painter in oil of still life and wild flowers, small and in meticulous detail. She was married in 1947 to the artist Claude Harrison, their son being the potter Tobias Harrison. Johnson studied at Harris Institute, Preston, and at Central School of Arts and Crafts. She exhibited with the Lake Artists' Society of which she was a member and regularly at RA Summer Exhibition. In 1991 she shared a show with her husband at Phoenix Gallery, Highgate. Lived in Cartmel Fell, Cumbria.

Beatrice JOHNSON fl. from late 1930s–1988 Watercolourist and teacher, who studied at Birmingham School of Arts and Crafts in the late 1930s with Douglas Hamilton Holden, who became her husband (she was known as Trixie Holden). After World War II, they were at the Royal College of Art, 1946–7. Beatrice Johnson taught at the Central School of Arts and Crafts, then at Croydon College of Art almost until her death. She was elected an associate of RWS in 1957 and RWS in 1969. Lived in London, then after Douglas' death in 1972 settled in Hastings, Sussex. In 1988 work from her studio, and from the studios of Douglas and his father Harold Henry Holden, was included in a sale at Burstow & Hewitt, Battle.

Ben JOHNSON 1946– Painter and printmaker, born in Llandudno, Caernarvonshire. He attended Wrexham and Chester Schools of Art, 1961, then Royal College of Art, 1966–70. Exhibited at ICA and Europalia, Palais des Beaux-Arts, Brussels, 1973; in 1974 at Bradford Print Biennale and John Moores Liverpool Exhibition; in 1977 International Print Biennale, Cracow; and in 1982 participated in Peter Moores Liverpool Project 6: Art into the 80s, at Fruitmarket Gallery, Edinburgh. Johnson's work theme then was the closed door, the undulations in wood grains and colour modulations beautifully and meticulously painted. Also showed at RA Summer Exhibition and elsewhere. A common inspiration of Johnson's pictures was the work of such leading architects as Norman Foster, Richard Rogers and James Stirling, and in 1995 he was made an Hon. Fellow of RIBA for his contribution "to the public understanding of architecture." In 1997, Johnson's Hong Kong Panorama was completed for a local telecommunications firm, part of a project to paint the world's major cities. His paintings of minimal interiors were exhibited at Blains Fine Art, 2002.

Carl JOHNSON 1946– Painter and graphic artist, born in Solihull, Warwickshire. He studied fine art at Newport College of Art, 1968–71, then did a postgraduate course at Ateliers 63, Haarlem, Netherlands, 1971–3, followed by Goldsmiths' College School of Art, 1974–5. Mixed show appearances included Gallery Zwart, Haarlem, 1973; LG, 1978; Eastleigh Museum, 1988; and SGA, 1989, the year he was elected a member. Johnson designed original art T-shirts which were marketed in Europe, America and Japan. Had many one-man shows including Battersea Arts Centre, 1977; The Showroom, 1985; and Bedford Central Library, 1989. In 1990 Johnson shared a three-man show at Woodlands Art Gallery, exhibiting strident figurative work.

Charles JOHNSON 1896–1964 Watercolourist, draughtsman in ink and lecturer, born in Cambridge into an academic background. He graduated from university with a Master of Arts degree and lectured at the National Gallery from 1926–62, from 1939 as an official lecturer and initially, it seems, as a freelance. He wrote a series of books including *English Painting*, *The Growth of Painting* and *Memlinc*. His art tuition was obtained at Regent Street Polytechnic School of Art under George Percival Gaskell. Went on to show at a number of venues, notably Leicester Galleries. Lived in London.

Charles G JOHNSON 1902–1983 Artist in oil, pastel, watercolour and black-and-white, born and lived in Stansted, Essex. Johnson was a self-taught painter and draughtsman who passed on his skills in his *Introduction to Sketching*. Exhibited widely in Britain, at the NS, PS and Russell-Cotes Art Gallery and Museum, Bournemouth. Had a solo show in Bishop's Stortford, near where he lived.

Charlie JOHNSON 1949– Johnson graduated with honours from University of Reading, 1970–4, attending

Garnett College of Education, 1977–8. There was a solo show in the latter year at Downshire House, Roehampton. Group exhibitions included 100 Artists, The Showroom, 1984; Recent Diversions, Pennybank Gallery, 1986; Voluntary Discharge, Assembly Rooms, Norwich, 1988; and East End Open Studios, at Chisenhale Studios, 1989.

Charlotte JOHNSON: *see* **Charlotte JOHNSON WAHL**

Christopher JOHNSON 1961– Painter, born in Bulawayo, Southern Rhodesia. He studied fine art at Rhodes University in South Africa, where he acquired a master's degree in 1985. Exhibited in mixed shows in South Africa, notably at Everard Read Gallery, Johannesburg, and in London at The Bloomsbury Workshop, Hurlingham Gallery and Sally Hunter Fine Art, as well as at Fruitmarket Gallery, Ediburgh. In 1992 had solo show at The Scottish Gallery, Edinburgh. Hiscox Holdings Ltd, Anglo-American and Johannesburg Stock Exchange hold his work.

Colin Trevor JOHNSON 1942– Artist in oil, watercolour, pencil, ink, monoprint and collage, born in Blackpool, Lancashire. He studied at Salford School of Art, 1957–9, then Manchester College of Art, 1959–60, teachers including Harry Rutherford and Terry McGlynn. Johnson painted full-time from leaving college. He cited Ben Nicholson and Braque as influences, main themes being "the British coastline, Venice architecture, street markets and glass". He visited and painted Cornwall for the first time in 1959, continued painting in St Ives most summers, then moved to St Ives from the north in 1986 and to Teignmouth, Devon, in 1991. Among Johnson's many activities was direction of the first Bolton Festival, 1979; he was artist-in-residence at Manchester Festival, 1980; and at Wigan International Jazz Festival, 1986–7. Johnson completed a mural for Broadcasting House in Manchester and was a member of MAFA. He took part in many mixed shows. His solo shows included a series at Monks Hall Museum and Art Gallery, Eccles, from 1961; he had a retrospective at Bolton Art Gallery, 1979; and later exhibitions included Maclaurin Art Gallery in Ayr and Salford University, both 1990. Public galleries in Salford, Derby and Southport hold his work.

David JOHNSON 1948– Sculptor whose work included assemblages of objects such as boxes and annotated blackboards. He said that his work was "not formalist, it is about the basic conjunction of matter and meaning, the imaginative relation of the self to the material world and time". Johnson studied at Bartlett School of Architecture at University College London, 1968–71. After living in Australia in 1974–6 he was at Byam Shaw School of Art, 1976–80. His shows included Goldsmiths' exhibition at Woodlands Art Gallery in 1983.

Elaine JOHNSON 1945– Painter, printmaker and teacher who studied at University of Newcastle department of fine art, 1965–70, then did a postgraduate course at Chelsea School of Art, 1970–1. From 1971–2 she was awarded the John Brinkley Fellowship in Painting at Norwich School of Art, and her solo exhibitions included one in its gallery, 1972. Teaching included Brighton and Portsmouth Polytechnics and Bath Academy of Art, Corsham. Mixed shows included several appearances at British International Print Biennale and Northern Young Contemporaries, the Museum of Modern Art in Oxford and Sunderland Arts Centre.

Emma JOHNSON 1967– Artist who had "always been heavily influenced by architecture and space, doorways, windows, corners, and the angles and surfaces involved in their interaction," as in her submission to The Large Print Show, Christchurch Mansion, Ipswich, 1997. Johnson studied at Jacob Kramer College of Art, Leeds, 1985–6; University of Reading, 1986–90; and Slade School of Fine Art, 1990–2. Other group shows included Staircase installation, Courtauld Institute, 1990; Woburn Square Gallery, 1992; and Brewhouse Theatre and Arts Centre, Taunton, 1990–2. Lived in Ipswich, Suffolk.

Ernest Borough JOHNSON 1867–1949 Painter, draughtsman, printmaker and teacher, born in Shifnal, Shropshire, who was married to the artist Esther Borough Johnson. He attended Slade School of Fine Art under Alphonse Legros and the Herkomer School at Bushey, where he was a star student. Was professor of fine art at Bedford College, London University and was for many years head of the art department at Chelsea Polytechnic. Borough Johnson, as he signed himself, exhibited prolifically at RA, RBA, ROI, Paris Salon, where he won several awards in the 1920s, and at many other venues. British Museum, Victoria & Albert Museum, National Portrait Gallery, provincial and foreign galleries hold his work. *The Art of the Pencil* and *The Technique of Pencil Drawing* were two of his several books on draughtsmanship. Lived in London.

Esther Borough JOHNSON fl. c.1895–1950 Painter and draughtsman, born in Sutton Maddock, Shropshire. She studied at at Birmingham School of Art, Chelsea School of Art and the Herkomer School, Bushey. Married to artist Ernest Borough Johnson. Among her several books on painting is *Flower Painting in Oil*. Exhibited RA, RI, RMS, Goupil Gallery and Paris Salon. Signed work E B J in monogram form. Lived in London.

Frank JOHNSON 1917– Painter, draughtsman and teacher, born in Leicester. Johnson worked as a commercial artist, 1935–40, served in the Royal Air Force in World War II, then after a period as a commercial artist again, 1946–7, studied painting, 1947–51, at Leicester College of Art. From 1952–80 he taught in the department of advertising at Bradford's Regional College of Art. Johnson showed frequently at RA from early 1950s, also in the provinces, notably Yorkshire. His work was included in Four Yorkshire Artists at Bradford City Art Gallery in 1961; loan exhibition works by Yorkshire artists at the Museum of Modern Art, Skopje, Yugoslavia, 1964; and Face to Face, portraits by Yorkshire artists at Sports Centre Gallery, Huddersfield, 1981. Public galleries in Bradford, Leeds and Glasgow hold his work, noted for its tenderness and compassion.

Holly JOHNSON 1960– Song composer, performer, writer and artist, originally William Johnson and born in Wavertree, Liverpool. He attended Liverpool Collegiate Grammar School for Boys; discovered Marc Bolan, David Bowie, Andy Warhol, Derek Jarman; and made his first performances as a soloist and as a member of the New Wave combo in 1977. In 1978 Johnson began to make screenprints and art T-shirts and decided he was a multimedia artist. Eventually formed and was lead singer of the group Frankie Goes To Hollywood which in 1983, as he was about to start at Liverpool Art College, had a hit record, *Relax*, which concentrated his energies into music. In 1984 Johnson met his future manager and partner, the art collector Wolfgang Kuhle, who had a notable collection of Bloomsbury art and with whom he eventually lived. In 1986–7 Johnson started drawing and painting again, became dissatisfied with the musical direction of Frankie Goes To Hollywood and left the group. In 1989 his first solo album, *Blast*, was hugely successful. Three years later Johnson disclosed that he had an HIV infection. Now he was concentrating on writing and painting again, starting to make his 20th Century Icons, a series of collages, using gold leaf and found objects, inspired by Jarman. In 1994 Johnson's autobiography *A Bone in My Flute* was a best-seller and he showed icons and paintings at The Art Show at Alexandra Palace. The building of Sky studios, a multi-media art facility, followed in 1995, along with illustrations for *Details* magazine and writing for *Modern Painters*. Johnson's first solo show, The House of Holly, was held at The Gallery in Cork Street in 1996, curated by Kate Chertavian. His paintings were notable for their vibrant style, bold colours and witty social comment. Among further developments in Johnson's career after the exhibition were, in 1997, his exhibition of The Beatles Icon, at Royal College of Art, part of The Milestones Exhibition organised by Brian Eno, plus a performance of *Ferry Across the Mersey*, at Hillsborough Justice Concert, with headliners The Lightening Seeds, at Anfield Football Stadium, Liverpool; further performances and recordings followed, including, in 1999, *Disco Heaven*, the first commercial release on the Pleasuredome label. In 2000 Johnson was a guest presenter on Virgin Radio and showed two works at Tate Liverpool in Peter Blake's show About Collage; in 2001 he was invited by Blake to show at the RA Summer Exhibition, the painting Cosmos Mariner (destination unknown) appearing as a postcard; in 2002 he added to his art reviewing and had a solo show as part of the Liverpool Biennial; and in 2003 he continued printmaking at the Royal College of Art.

Joy Alexandra JOHNSON 1958– Painter, born in Hull, Yorkshire. She studied at Newcastle upon Tyne Polytechnic, 1977–80, graduating with honours, then was at Slade School of Fine Art, 1982–4. As well as several solo shows she was in mixed exhibitions including RA Summer Exhibition, Northern Young Contempories and at Mappin Art Gallery, Sheffield. Lived in London.

Kate JOHNSON 1963– Painter, creator of sculptural paintings, sculptor, draughtsman and teacher, of British nationality, born in Ottawa, Canada. Studied under Norman Adams at Newcastle upon Tyne University, graduating in fine art – painting, 1981–5; gained a postgraduate diploma in Quattrocento Italian Art History at Oxford University, as a British Academy Scholar, studying with Christopher Lloyd and Francis Haskell, 1985–6; then as a Fulbright Scholar gained her master's degree in fine art, painting, under James McGarrell, at Washington University, St Louis, 1988–90. In 1991 lived in the Amazonian rainforest, Tambopata, Madre de Dios, Peru, in 1992 being adjunct professor in the department of fine art at Webster University, St Louis. Had an open studio exhibition in Oxford, 1988; mixed exhibitions included Pertinent Dissimilarities: The Figure, at Webster University, 1992 and The Tesmer Collection, Gallery 1616, Chicago, 1994; solo exhibitions including Gallery 1616, 1993, A View of Peru, South Grand (Gallery), St Louis, 1994, and Falmouth Art Gallery, 2000. In 1995 settled in Yorkshire.

Les JOHNSON 1957– Artist in various media, lecturer and writer, born in Jamaica. He moved to Manchester when young, but his black background and culture heavily influenced his work, as did an early passion for playing church music. Left Manchester Polytechnic in 1977 after foundation work, spending a year on graphic design at London College of Printing. Continued degree work at Camberwell School of Art, then from 1980 attended Royal College of Art, extending his interests in illustration photography, audio visual, painting and design. From 1983 worked professionally in several fields, including architecture and object making. Among his exhibitions was a three-man show at Woodlands Art Gallery, 1988.

Martin JOHNSON 1939–2003 Versatile and meticulous designer and artist, born in south London, who studied at Camberwell School of Art and worked with Leo Austin on brightening up post-war public architecture with mosaics and sculpture. After joining the BBC Johnson designed sets for television programmes including *Doctor Who* and *Steptoe and Son*. He worked with the film director Ken Loach on *Days of Hope*, 1975, a controversial series of four television films following the fortunes of three northern Socialists set between World War I and the General Strike of 1926. Loach liked Johnson's passion for authentic detail and they built up a close, almost telepathic relationship over many years on more than a dozen films in Britain and abroad, ranging from *Black Jack*, 1979, to *Ae Fond Kiss*, shot just before Johnson's death. He also worked with other directors, including Tony Garnett and Stephen Poliakoff. Among Johnson's television commercials was the fish-finger series featuring Captain Birdseye which, with his beard and nautical interests, was the occasional nickname for this patrician but socially adaptable figure. As well as designing boats, including the *Klute*, made to his own specifications and overseen by him during construction, Johnson created witty models of them. These he photographed and with instructions how to make them compiled the book *Martin Johnson's Amazing Maritime Models*, 1995. Loach wrote Johnson's obituary for *The Guardian*.

Maurice JOHNSON 1920– Painter and teacher, initially educated in Southport, Lancashire. He attended Liverpool City School of Art under Will Penn and Henry Huggill, 1936–40. Showed at Liverpool Academy, Anglo-French Art Centre, UA, RBA and elsewhere. Liverpool Public Libraries bought his work. Lived in London.

Michael JOHNSON 1938– Prolific painter who produced both hard-edged and more fluid abstract works over an extensive career, born and lived in Sydney, Australia. After gaining his diploma at the Julian Ashton School there, 1954–9, Johnson from 1960, like many other Australian artists at this period, toured Europe, spending much time in London, including a period as studio assistant to the sculptor Anthony Caro. Among Johnson's exhibitions in London was participation in the Commonwealth Festival Biennale, 1962–5. Soon after his return to Australia in 1967 he showed at the Central Street Gallery, Sydney, and rapidly developed a reputation as a leading abstractionist. After participating in The Field, at the National Gallery of

Victoria in 1968, in 1969 he travelled to New York where, for several years, he exhibited at the Max Hutchinson Gallery, in the same year representing Australia at the Bienal de São Paulo. Johnson gained several awards, his residencies including James Cook University, Townsville, 1975, and the University of Melbourne, 1986. He took part in many group shows in Australia, where his work is in public and private collections. Among his solo appearances was a big survey show at the Art Gallery of New South Wales in 1989, with a well-illustrated catalogue.

Michael JOHNSON 1954– Sculptor in stone and metal, born in Berwick-upon-Tweed, Northumberland, who studied at Sheffield and Nottingham Schools of Art. Exhibited in Garden Exhibition 2 at Camden Arts Centre, 1978. Lived for a time in London.

Nerys JOHNSON 1942–2001 Artist, curator and teacher, born in Colwyn Bay, Denbighshire. She studied painting and sculpture under Victor Pasmore, Richard Hamilton and Matt Rugg in the fine art department at King's College, Durham University, a Diploma in Education at Newcastle University preparing her for teaching. She taught extramural life drawing for several years while practising as an artist, but instead of full-time teaching chose to be a curator, notable for innovative, adventurous shows. Johnson was keeper of fine art at Laing Art Gallery, Newcastle, then keeper-in-charge of the new Durham Light Infantry Museum and Arts Centre, 1970–89, when arthritis, diagnosed when she was two, forced her to retire. In 1973 she became interested in etching, studying under Chris Penny at Byam Shaw School of Art, practising the craft at Charlotte Press, Newcastle. Johnson's original paintings were big, vigorous abstracts; later, she produced tiny, intensely coloured flower studies. The Whitworth Art Gallery in Manchester has several typical examples, from her estate, and one is illustrated in Marshall Hall's *Artists of Northumbria* (Art Dictionaries Ltd, 2005). Johnson won a string of awards, an Italian visit resulting in the publication of the *Venice Sketchbook*, 1996. By the time of her Broughton House Gallery, Cambridge, exhibition in 1999 she had achieved 17 solo shows plus numerous mixed exhibitions.

Nevill JOHNSON 1911–1999 Artist, photographer and writer, born in Derbyshire. Johnson's work was often autobiographical, it went through various phases and he enjoyed a late creative period well into his eighties. As painter and collagist he was prolific, but he destroyed much of his output. Moved to Belfast in 1934 and studied with John Luke. With him he travelled to Paris, where pictures seen there influenced Johnson's own. After Belfast Johnson lived in Dublin, where his work was to find favour. In 1952–3, working with Anne Yeats, the poet W B Yeats's daughter, Johnson produced photographs of the city before it was changed by developers. They were published in 1980 as *Dublin: The People's City*, winning an award at the Leipzig International Book Fair. Eventually Johnson returned to England. During a fallow period in London Johnson worked on a milk float before resuming painting. His autobiography, *The Other Side of Six*, appeared in 1983. He won a silver medal at the RUA in 1978. Showed solo with Waddington Gallery, Dublin, from 1946, with a series at Tom Caldwell's Galleries in Dublin and Belfast from 1979 and one at Solomon Gallery, Dublin, 1995. In 2002 Lemon Street Gallery, Dublin, held an exhibition marking the fiftieth anniversary of Johnson's photographs of Dublin, plus paintings and writings. Ulster Museum in Belfast, Hugh Lane Municipal Gallery of Modern Art in Dublin and Museum of Modern Art in New York hold examples. He died in London.

Nick JOHNSON 1941– Sculptor of animals and birds in laminated wood, often large and occasionally with added colour, draughtsman and teacher, born in Ditchling, Sussex. He attended Brighton College of Art, 1958–62, and Slade School of Fine Art, 1962–4. He taught at Brighton Polytechnic, 1976–7 and 1981–2; during the intervening period, in 1977–9, Johnson lectured at the University of Benin, Nigeria, travelling around that country, Ivory Coast and Mali to see ethnic culture and art, the wooden sculptures of the Yoruba and Ibo tribes and bronze figures of Ife. Exhibitions included Gardner Centre, University of Sussex, 1982, RA Summer Exhibition, 1983, and Kenyatta University, Nairobi, Kenya, 1988. He showed with Browse & Darby from 1982.

Nowell Hewlett JOHNSON 1906–1983 Artist in oil, black-and-white and watercolour. Born at Crossens, Lancashire, wife of Hewlett Johnson, sometimes known as the "Red Dean" of Canterbury, because of his political views. Studied at Southport School of Art and the Royal College of Art. Occasionally signed work Nowell Johnson. Exhibited RA, East Kent Art Society and Artists for Peace. Contributed illustrations to *The Socialist Sixth of the World*, the international bestseller by her husband. Lived in Canterbury, Kent.

Paul JOHNSON 1928– Author, journalist, editor and recreational artist, educated at Stonyhurst and Magdalen College, Oxford. His editorial positions included editor, *New Statesman*, 1965–70. He was a member of the Royal Commission on the Press, 1974–7, and the Cable Authority, 1984–90. Johnson was an often controversial columnist whose many books included *The Suez War*, 1957; *Left of Centre*, 1960; *Elizabeth I*, 1974; *Pope John XXIII*, 1975 (*Yorkshire Post* Book of the Year Award); *British Cathedrals*, 1980; *The Pick of Paul Johnson*, 1985; *Wake Up Britain! A Latterday Pamphlet*, 1994; and *The Renaissance*, 2000. In 2004, his book *The Vanished Landscape* appeared, a memoir of his happy childhood in the Potteries, illustrated by Johnson with many paintings and drawings. He wrote and drew every day. During his extensive world travels Johnson carried a sketch-book or watercolour pad, creating a visual diary based on the traditional values of observation and drawing. Johnson had a series of solo shows at Piers Feetham Gallery, that in 2001 including watercolours of closely observed details in nature. Lived in London and at Over Stowey, Somerset.

Pete JOHNSON 1948– Artist and teacher, born in Manchester, who studied at Camberwell School of Arts and Crafts, 1967–70, and Royal College of Art, 1970–3. He went on to live and teach in London. Group exhibitions included Selected Space Artists at Harlow Gallery, 1974, Air Gallery in 1975 and Summer Show 2 at Serpentine Gallery, 1980, where he exhibited works in boxboard, paint and paper. Solo exhibitions included Universities of Sussex and Essex, both 1977.

Stephen JOHNSON 1953– Sculptor using a range of materials, born in Whitstable, Kent. He studied at Goldsmiths' College School of Art, then obtained his master's degree in fine art, sculpture, at Chelsea School of Art, 1981–2. He said that his work was concerned with images of transition. A threatened object with the threat exorcised. An object of burden without burden. Exhibitions included Summer Show 2, Serpentine Gallery, 1980; The British Art Show, Arts Council tour, 1984; Conceptual Clothing, Ikon Gallery, Birmingham, and tour, 1986; and Second Wave, Bluecoat Gallery, Liverpool, 1988. In the 1990s, Johnson – often listed as Steve Johnson – took small objects as his starting point, as in his 1995–7 London Charms series. Leeds Museums and Galleries hold examples of his work.

Steve JOHNSON: *see* **Stephen JOHNSON**

Tim JOHNSON 1967– Born in Newcastle upon Tyne, Johnson studied painting, photography, sculpture and installation at University of Reading, graduating in 1989. He moved to Ireland in 1990 and showed widely north and south of the border. In 1994 he appeared in both Works on Paper and Beyond the Partitions, put on by Queen Street Studios, Belfast, with which he was associated. In 2003, under the title Bundles and Ropes, Johnson created an installation made from giant grass at the Art and Design Gallery, University of Hertfordshire, Hatfield.

Vanessa JOHNSON 1963– Johnson studied at Lanchester Polytechnic, 1982–5, in 1986 having a solo exhibition at Fiction Gallery, Southampton. Others followed at The Gantry, Southampton, in 1987, and Freuds and The 39 Steps Gallery, both 1989. Group appearances included The South Bank Picture Show, Royal Festival Hall, 1986, and East End Open Studios, when she was based at Pixley Street Studios, 1989.

Charlotte JOHNSON WAHL 1942– Painter and draughtsman, born in Oxford, who studied at private schools in England and America; for a term at Byam Shaw Art School; and gained her master's degree in English language and literature from Lady Margaret Hall, Oxford. In 1963 she married Stanley Johnson, classicist, novelist and Member of the European Parliament, 1979–84, by whom she had four children, one of whom was the colourful journalist, editor of *The Spectator* and Member of Parliament Boris Johnson; divorced in 1979, in 1988 she married Nicholas Wahl, who died 1996, seven years after she was diagnosed as suffering from Parkinson's Disease. She also signed her work with her maiden name, Charlotte Fawcett, as Charlotte Johnson, as Charlotte Fawcett Johnson Wahl and with various combinations of initials. From 1979–88 Johnson Wahl made her living painting portraits in London; in 1988 moved to New York, where until 1996 she produced a number of urban landscapes; from 1996, on returning to London, concentrating on still lifes and urban scenes. Examples of her brightly coloured, slightly mannered townscapes were shown at the Gavin Graham Gallery in 2004. Other solo exhibitions included Maudsley Hospital, paintings done while an in-patient, 1974; Galerie Le Cercle d'Art, Brussels, Belgium (prompting a film for Belgian television), 1975; Galerie Plan, Le Zoute, Belgium, 1976; and she took part in a group show at The Century Association, New York City, in 1993. In 1997, she was awarded an autumn fellowship by the Liguria Study Center for the Arts and Humanities (The Bogliasco Foundation). In 1975, Hans Eysenck used Johnson Wahl's paintings to illustrate *The Future of Psychiatry*; in 1977, she produced the cover of *The Bulletin*, an English-language magazine published in Belgium; her painting of the Social Democratic Party "Gang of Four", commissioned in 1985, was in 1987 used to illustrated an article in *The Observer*; in 2001 and 2002 she drew for and produced a cover for *The Spectator*; and in 2002 a cover for *The Times Literary Supplement*; and there were various book-jackets. By 2004 she had sold over 350 paintings and drawings. Lady Margaret Hall and New College in Oxford, Eton College and a number of corporate collections hold examples.

Alan JOHNSTON 1945– Draughtsman in pencil and sculptor, born in Scotland, he eventually settled in Edinburgh. He attended the College of Art there, 1967–70, then concentrated on life drawing at Royal College of Art, 1970–2. Johnston lived in Germany for a time, having a first solo show at Konrad Fischer Gallery, Düsseldorf, in 1973. Johnston went on to show regularly, at the Graeme Murray Gallery in Edinburgh, at Oxford's Museum of Modern Art and the Pier Arts Centre, Stromness, Orkney, held a touring exhibition. The 1980s saw his work shown widely abroad. Johnston's work was delicate and Minimalist, influenced by Zen Buddhism. Scottish National Gallery of Modern Art's From the Mountain to the Plain is a good example. In 1998, Norwich School of Art and Design's Norwich Gallery invited Johnston to make one of his wall drawings on a specially constructed wall, giving visitors an opportunity to view and discuss its progress over seven days.

Arnrid JOHNSTON 1895–1972 Sculptor, illustrator, designer and writer, born of English father and Swedish mother in Sweden. Between 1913–20 studied at Slade School of Fine Art, gained a Slade Scholarship for two years in 1915 and learned sculpture under James Havard Thomas. The continuing theme in Johnston's work was a love of animals. As a sculptor her work was compared with that of Henry Moore, Barbara Hepworth, Maurice Lambert and John Skeaping, but its popularity faded. Notable among her output were Cats on Chimney Cowl and Squirrels in an exhibition organised by LG in 1930, in Selfridges' roof garden; and Horses, a carved relief, and cast iron zodiac tiles at 50th Anniversary Exhibition of the Arts and Crafts Exhibition Society at RA, 1938. Her poster for the New Zoological Society in 1930 was a great popular success. She wrote and illustrated *Pigwiggen*, the story of a flying pig, in 1938; *Animal Families*, in 1939; and illustrated a number of other books such as Kathleen Foyle's *The Little Black Calf*, 1952. Her *Fables from Aesop and Others* appeared in 1944, but failing eyesight prevented her finishing *La Fontaine's Fables*. Morley College owns the tapestry The Orchestra which was shown in an exhibition of Johnston's work at Sally Hunter & Patrick Seale Fine Art, 1985.

Brenda JOHNSTON 1930– Artist in various media, born in London. She attended Epsom School of Art, 1948–9 and 1955–60, teachers including the watercolourist Leslie Worth, then Reigate School of Art, 1961–5, with Eric Waugh. She was a member of Free Painters and Sculptors and several local art clubs near where she lived in Ashtead, Surrey. Had a series of solo exhibitions and also showed at RA Summer Exhibition, RBA and abroad.

Duncan JOHNSTON 1924–2000 Sculptor in a variety of materials, notably lignum vitae, and teacher, born in Liverpool. Johnston trained in commercial art at Liverpool School of Art, then served as a physical training instructor in the Royal Marines in World War II. By demobilisation in 1946 he had resolved to be a sculptor; was self-taught while teaching, then chose to work in isolation to avoid influences. In 1956 he began to exhibit in mixed annual exhibitions, notably Royal Glasgow Institute of the Fine Arts, RSA and at Paris Salon. Had a first solo show, 1960, in Leatherhead, Surrey, near where he settled at Ashtead, then was associated with O'Hana Gallery until its closure in 1975. Johnston continued to sculpt despite several operations on his wrists, 1978–81, to relieve arthritic pains. Had a retrospective at Exhall Grange School, Coventry, 1981, and a notable show at The Barbican Centre, 1987. Johnston was especially interested in sculpture as it related to handicapped, partially sighted and blind people. Among his commissions was Celebration Dance for Worcester College for the Blind, 1990. Johnston's sculpture had great vitality, with a sinuous line. Jacob Epstein's *Let There Be Sculpture* prompted his choice of career, and he wrote that "Epstein's life and work has probably been the greatest influence on my work." Michelangelo Museum, Italy, and Tel-Aviv Museum of Modern Art, Israel, hold examples.

Frederick JOHNSTON 1916–1984 Artist in oil, pastel, watercolour, pen and ink. Born in London, he studied art at Hornsey School of Art and London University. Johnston became a noted art instructor, teaching at summer schools as well as writing a number of books for beginners in sketching and painting. In the 1970s he edited *Leisure Painter* for several years. As well as one-man exhibitions, he showed at the RBA, RI, ROI, NS and at the Paris Salon. His work is in private collections throughout the world. Lived in Potters Bar, Hertfordshire.

George JOHNSTON 1933– Painter, teacher and art adviser, born in Edinburgh. He studied at the College of Art there, 1951–6, teachers including William Gillies and Robin Philipson. Johnston then taught for two years, was commissioned in the Army, 1958–60, lectured for three years, was an adviser on art and design until 1991, then painted full-time. He was a member of RSW, also exhibiting at RSA and Royal Glasgow Institute of the Fine Arts, having solo shows in Edinburgh, Dundee, Glasgow, Kirkcaldy, London, Paris and elsewhere. Dundee University, Dundee College of Further Education and several other Scottish public collections hold examples. Lived at Barnhill, Dundee, Tayside.

Laura JOHNSTON 1962– Maker of sculptural works and lighting projects, born in Middlesbrough, Cleveland, who "specialised in the creation of suspended lightweight sculptural forms, developing unique tensile structures that impact on the architectural space through projection of light and colour." Johnston became a community artist, 1980–2. After working for some years as an occupational therapy assistant in acute psychiatry, in 1986 she began studying glass. She graduated with first-class honours from the University of Sunderland, 1992, gaining her doctorate there in 1997, studying The Innovative Application of the Coated Glass Surface in Architecture. She was a visiting lecturer at the University, 1993–8, and a post-doctoral research fellow, 2000–4. The central theme of Johnston's work was the power of glass "to transform our experience of architectural spaces by influencing the impact of light. On-going study has involved observation of the changing effect of light within architectural spaces and the way in which glass (and other materials) may be used to direct, disperse or subdue its influence." Johnston's mixed shows included 30-30 Vision, Crafts Council tour, 2003–4, and Shaping Light, Tea Building, 2004. Based at Lightworks, Newcastle upon Tyne, Johnston carried out a large number of commissions, latterly including Ozone, etched-glass screen and reception panels, North Tees Hospital, Stockton-on-Tees, 2001; Ice Lines, fibre optic lines inlaid into paving, National Ice Centre, Nottingham, and Light Project, glass and light features, Middlesbrough Town Centre, both 2002; Prismatics, dichroic glass and steel sculpture, North Rock headquarters, Newcastle, and Dichroic Globe, suspended sculpture, James Cook University Hospital, Middlesbrough, both 2003; and Glass Screens, North Tees Hospital, and Suspended Glass and Steel Sculpture and Lighting, Corbett Hospital, Dudley, both 2004. Johnston was a full member of the Contemporary Glass Society.

Mark JOHNSTON 1974– Painter of heavily abstracted landscapes, for whom "landscape is a good reminder of how small we are." He was born in the northeast of England and spent his childhood by the sea and in the country. Painting took him to the Lake District and then to Brighton University, where he gained an honours degree in painting. For the next two years he painted in Greece and Spain before returning to his studio in Brighton, Sussex. Solo shows included Elemental Landscapes, CCA Galleries, Farnham, 2001, and Fairfax Gallery, Tunbridge Wells, 2002.

Roy JOHNSTON 1936– Painter, relief artist and teacher, born in Pomeroy, County Tyrone, Northern Ireland. He studied at Stranmillis College, Belfast, 1957–9, then after three years teaching art in a school in the city was at Belfast College of Art, 1962–6, and after various posts taught for many years at Ulster College. His abstract works included contoured canvases and modular reliefs such as that on the Cross and Passion School, Belfast. Arts Council of Northern Ireland, Bank of Ireland and New University of Ulster in Coleraine hold examples. Exhibitions included Arts Council of Northern Ireland Gallery; Richard Demarco Gallery in Edinburgh; David Gallery and David Hendriks Gallery, both in Dublin.

Andrew JOHNSTONE 1933– Sculptor and painter who was educated at Marlborough College, Strasbourg and Oxford Universities and at Oxford's Ruskin School of Drawing. Johnstone served in the Foreign Service, 1956–73, continuing to paint while mainly in the Middle and Far East, then on taking early retirement in 1973 moved to Cornwall, settling in the Lizard. For nine years he ran a smallholding near Helston. After showing at RUA and Living Arts Exhibition in Belfast in 1972 Johnstone concentrated on sculpture. The Queen of Sheba and Johnstone's friendship with Sherif Hussein when he was in Aden in the late 1950s were notable influences. Johnstone's later spare, abstract paintings followed on from the sculpture, with Arabia and Homer's *Iliad* as key inspirations. Gordon Hepworth Gallery, Newton St Cyres, showed his work, solo shows including Cadogan Contemporary, 2001.

Anne Grahame JOHNSTONE 1928–1998 Versatile artist and illustrator, daughter of the artist Doris Zinkeisen and twin sister of Janet Grahame Johnstone. They trained at St Martin's School of Art after World War II, then collaborated to illustrate many books, including The Bible, children's classics and modern successes including Dodie Smith's *The Hundred and One Dalmatians*. Other projects included artwork for BBC Television programmes, such as *Andy Pandy*; work for the National Maritime Museum; and designs for a projected but aborted theme park in Denmark called Andersen's World. After Janet died following an accident in 1979, Anne – a keen horsewoman – took over the animal drawing which had been Janet's special role, and in 1998 was elected to the Society of Equestrian Artists. Other aspects of her solo work included Christmas cards for Royle's and jigsaw puzzles for Waddington's; writing and illustrating her own books on Santa Claus; and heraldic work on the Post Office's restored mail coach. Died in Badingham, Suffolk.

Dorothy JOHNSTONE 1892–1980 Painter and teacher, born in Edinburgh. Her father was the painter George Whitton Johnstone, her uncle the artist James Heron and she married the painter Douglas Macbeth Sutherland. She enrolled at Edinburgh College of Art in 1908 and in 1910 gained a travelling scholarship to Italy, and also studied in Paris. In 1914 she was appointed to staff of Edinburgh College of Art, having to relinquish her teaching post, as a married woman, in 1924. She exhibited at RSA regularly for many years from 1912, at RA, with Edinburgh Group, jointly with Cecile Walton in 1924, and elsewhere. In 1983 Aberdeen Art Gallery gave her a major memorial show which toured, then in 1987 Bourne Fine Art in Edinburgh and London held a joint Johnstone and Sutherland exhibition. Johnstone was a sensitive painter of women and young girls. She died at Glanclwyd Hospital, north Wales.

Gwyneth JOHNSTONE 1914– Painter, daughter of the artist Augustus John and Nora Brownsword, who was briefly his model. Gwyneth was brought up in Norfolk and London and studied painting with André Lhote in Paris and at Central School of Arts and Crafts under Cecil Collins. Her work mixed gentleness, innocence and a subtle colour sense, but was strengthened by an awareness of the output of painters such as Christopher Wood, Paul Klee and the Cubists. Her love of working in Spain, where she owned a small house in the hills above Alicante, and France fed the rural idyll aspect of her paintings. Showed in group exhibitions with Young Contemporaries, LG, WIAC (of which she was president for a time) and at Roland, Browse & Delbanco. Solo exhibitions included Portal Gallery, Woodstock Gallery, Carter Gallery in Los Angeles, Galeria Arrabal in Spain and Sally Hunter & Patrick Seale Fine Art, 1985. Contemporary Art Society, Nuffield Trust and Ferens Art Gallery, Hull, hold her work. Lived in Norfolk and London.

John JOHNSTONE 1937–2001 Painter and teacher, born in Falkirk, Stirlingshire. He studied at Edinburgh College of Art, 1956–60, then a travelling scholarship took him to the West Indies and Latin America. Johnstone won a number of awards including an Arts Council Award in 1970 and an RSA Lothian Region Award in 1981. From 1963 he taught at Edinburgh College of Art. Johnstone showed regularly at RSA, of which he was an associate, and SSA and participated in other group exhibitions in Britain and abroad. Solo exhibitions included Mercury Gallery and Compass Gallery, Glasgow. Arts Council, Scottish Arts Council and other British and foreign collections hold his work. Johnstone's work was hard to define, and at various times he was included in shows of New Symbolist and Poetic Realist painters. Lived in Lauder, Berwickshire.

John JOHNSTONE 1941– Painter, born in Forfar, Angus, who studied at Duncan of Jordanstone College of Art, Dundee, where he was highly commended and later taught for many years. Johnstone won a major travelling scholarship to visit European capitals. He said that his works "seem to be expressing something, either serious or amusing about life. They depict people acting out minor dramas." He was a professional member of SSA and Scottish Visual Arts and showed regularly with the RSA and SSA. Johnstone's exhibitions included Alwin Gallery, 1966 and 1967; The Gallery Constant, Kingston, Jamaica, 1967; Six Dundee Painters, McManus Galleries, Dundee, 1974; The Seagate Gallery, Dundee, 1991; William Hardie Ltd, at the Glasgow Art Fair, 1996; The Queens Gallery, Dundee, 2002; and What is Realism?, Albemarle Gallery, 2005. In 2002 he had a solo show in Kingston, Jamaica. Johnstone had works in numerous private and public collections, including those of the HRH The Duke of Edinburgh, Dundee College of Education and Angus Council.

Mary JOHNSTONE 1918–1988 Embroiderer and watercolourist, also known by her maiden name Mary Bonning, was the second wife of the artist William Johnstone. She studied under him at Royal School of Needlework and was a member of the Scottish branch of the Embroiderers' Guild, being chairman in the Borders area where she lived in the mid-1980s. Hampton Court Palace holds her work. She was also a watercolourist with a strong sense of design, work being shown at Broughton Gallery in Peebles, and Ancrum and Mainhill Galleries, both in Ancrum. Died in Melrose General Hospital. She appears in William Johnstone's autobiography *Points in Time*.

William JOHNSTONE 1897–1981 Painter and teacher, born in Denholm, Roxburghshire, into a farming family. A youthful friendship with the painter Tom Scott led to Johnstone's taking up painting and he attended Edinburgh College of Art, 1919–23; he then taught there part-time for two years. In 1925 Johnstone won a Carnegie Travelling Scholarship which enabled him to study in Paris with André Lhote at the Académie de la Grande Chaumière and the Atelier Colarossi. In 1927 married the American sculptor Flora MacDonald. For a few years their lives were unsettled, including periods in America and Scotland, finally settling in London in 1931. Johnstone, whose work had shown Cubist and Surrealist elements, took a series of teaching posts and had his first one-man show at the Wertheim Gallery in 1935. Johnstone now got to know such important figures as the poet T S Eliot and the artist Wyndham Lewis. Was influential principal of Camberwell School of Art, 1938–46; from 1947–60 he was principal of the Central School of Arts and Crafts. Retired to be a full-time sheep farmer in 1960, in the Scottish borders area, settling at Crailing, near Jedburgh, in 1970. Johnstone's later work was rather Orientally calligraphic in manner, as seen in his Hayward Gallery show of 1980, the year when Johnstone published *Points in Time: An*

Autobiography. His second wife, Mary, also an artist, survived him until 1988. He was given a centenary show at Talbot Rice Gallery, University of Edinburgh, 1997.

Ben JOINER 1952– Sculptor and teacher working in such materials as patinated mild steel and rubber. Joiner graduated with honours from Chelsea School of Art, 1977–80, gaining a master's degree there, 1980–1. Among his exhibitions were ICA New Contemporaries, 1980; Camden Annual, 1986; Whitechapel Art Gallery, 1989; and Canterbury Sculpture Exhibitions from 1990, with a solo exhibition at Harriet Green, 1997. He won a Greater London Arts Award in 1983 and a commission for Brent Magistrates Court and one for Leamington Spa in 1990. In 1989, when Joiner participated in East End Open Studios, based at Robinson Road, he was teaching at Harrow School of Art. Arts Council and Contemporary Art Society hold his work.

Leon JOINER 1905– Painter and textile designer, born in Watford, Hertfordshire. He attended the local School of Art, 1920–3, and had further tuition in London and Paris, notably with the portrait painter T C Dugdale. Showed at RA, MAFA and elsewhere and lived for many years at Carshalton Beeches, Surrey.

Mabel JOLIN 1898–1959 Painter, born at Newcastle upon Tyne. A self-taught artist, she exhibited at RSA, Shipley Art Gallery, Gateshead, and at the Laing Art Gallery, Newcastle upon Tyne. Lived at Corbridge, Northumberland.

Nicholas JOLLY 1962– Artist born in Bebington, Cheshire, who studied at Gloucester College of Art, 1981–4, then Royal Academy Schools, 1985–8. He exhibited in Threshold of Meaning at Plymouth City Art Gallery, 1990, at Paton Gallery, 1993, and at that gallery's show at *The Economist*, 1994. Metropolitan Museum of Art in New York holds Jolly's work.

JOLOMO 1948– John Lowrie Morrison, painter and teacher who from 1985 signed his work Jolomo, was born in Glasgow, where he studied drawing and painting at the School of Art, 1967–71, teachers including George Birrell, Glen Scouller, James Robertson, Dan Ferguson and Geoffrey Squire. In 1969 he worked for a summer at Templeton's Carpets, designing Norsk Rugs; in 1970 visited Switzerland, where high-key colour first entered his palette; and in 1971 won the W O Hutchison Drawing Prize and developed his distinctive Expressionist style. Early influences were Soutine, Kokoschka, Joan Eardley and Monet. From 1971–2, Morrison did postgraduate, mainly figurative work at Glasgow; in 1972 won a travelling scholarship to the Royal Academy Schools; in 1972–3 gaining his teaching diploma at Jordanhill College, Glasgow. Morrison taught at Lochgilphead High School and 12 Mid-Argyll primary schools, 1973–88; was principal art teacher at Lochgilphead, 1988–94; was art adviser to the Strathclyde Region, 1994–6; briefly worked as an art adviser, then began painting full-time. Concentrated on the Argyll mainland and island landscape, the croft a recurring theme, as well as France and the Netherlands, believing that "beauty has a healing power". Took part in numerous group exhibitions, his many solo shows later including The Torrance Gallery, Edinburgh, and Corrymella Scott Gallery, Newcastle upon Tyne, both 2000, and The Strathearn Gallery, Crieff, 2003. Morrison's work was reproduced in open- and limited-edition prints and on cards. Inland Revenue in Edinburgh, Lomond Health Trust, TSB Bank, Bank of Scotland and other corporate collections hold examples.

Harry Maude JONAS 1893–1990 Artist and restorer, son of a cigar merchant, who was educated at St Paul's School and St John's Wood Art School, where he started a lifelong friendship with the painter John Armstrong (Jonas' portrait of Armstrong is in the National Portrait Gallery). To avoid an ostentatious life-style Jonas left home and set up as a painter, notably of portraits, with some landscapes and religious pictures. He had a number of patrons, and his subjects included his friend the writer John Davenport, film actress Elsa Lanchester, cricketer Percy Fender and Lady Iris Mountbatten. Jonas acted for the silent screen, playing The Boy in *Love, Life and Laughter*, with Betty Balfour, 1923, and working as art director on *Reveille*, 1924, both directed by George Pearson. After sharing a studio with Armstrong, Jonas occupied one in Maple Street, Fitzrovia, a ramshackle affair where Leigh Hunt had entertained Thackeray and Dickens. During World War II Jonas served in the Home Guard. He was an old-fashioned bachelor bohemian, a member of the Fitzrovia group, who appears in Clifford Bax's memoir *Rosemary for Remembrance*; a devout Roman Catholic; a lover of talk, mysteries and the predictions of Nostradamus; and a discoverer of pictures, including one by Holbein, an alleged portrait of William Shakespeare and what he claimed was a self-portrait by John Constable, which for years he worked to restore in his Myddleton Square studio (he had to be rehoused there when the Post Office Tower dislodged his old studio). Jonas' style was traditional and he was not prolific. His only solo show was at the Matthieson Gallery, 1939, which he said was killed by the outbreak of World War II.

Abigail JONES 1963– Artist producing works with a strong pattern element, tower blocks a theme. Jones was born in Melbourne, Victoria, Australia, moving to Europe in 1986. After working in Greece, 1989–93, she returned to London, graduating from Byam Shaw School of Art, 1993–6, obtaining her master's from the Slade School of Fine Art, 1996–8, on a British Academy Scholarship. Jones was shortlisted for Surface, ICA, 1998, and NatWest Art Prize, 1999. Was included in shows at Test Site 2, 1999; Winston, Amsterdam, Netherlands, and Thing, The Garrett Centre, both 2000; and in 2001 in the Hammersmith and Fulham Visual Arts Season, at Gimpel Fils and in the SPACE Studios Open Weekend. Lived in north London.

Alison JONES 1962– After attending Goldsmiths' College, Jones was at the Slade School of Fine Art, 1982–6. She was artist-in-residence, Yorkshire Art Circus, Sheffield, in 1987. Jones won a prize at Whitworth Young Contemporaries, Whitworth Art Gallery, Manchester, in 1985, and in 1989 participated in Critics Space 5 at Air Gallery, Idylls in '89 at Todd Gallery and East End Open Studios, at Martello Street.

Allen JONES 1937– Painter, draughtsman and printmaker, sculptor and teacher, born in Southampton. He studied at Hornsey College of Art, 1955–9, then was at Royal College of Art until 1960 when "excessive independence" led to his expulsion. From the early 1960s Jones appeared frequently at the Paris Biennale (winning a prize in 1963) and John Moores Exhibition, Liverpool, and he also showed at Documenta 3 and 4 in Kassel, at Tokyo Biennale several times and at São Paulo Bienal in 1967. In 1963 Jones had the first of several solo shows at Arthur Tooth and Sons, and from 1964 showed with Richard Feigen Gallery in New York and later in Chicago and in 1965, by which time he had been living in New York, at Feigen/Palmer Gallery, Los Angeles. Jones' international exhibiting career was now well under way. His reputation was consolidated from the early 1970s with shows at Marlborough Fine Art and Waddington Galleries. Retrospectives included Walker Art Gallery, Liverpool, 1979, and Barbican Centre, 1995, both touring. Sims Reed Gallery held a show of prints, 1965–83, in 2001, Alan Cristea Gallery paintings, drawings and prints, 2003. Jones was famous for his Pop Art images, his glossy female forms owing something to American advertising of the 1960s. The artist designed posters, did stage and film work and produced a calendar for Pirelli. In addition to his three-dimensional fibreglass and aluminium sculptures made from the 1960s, in the early 1980s Jones created freer, silhouette-like coloured images. Public commissions included Red Worker, at Perseverance Works, Hackney, and the huge Acrobat, at Chelsea and Westminster Hospital, both in steel. Jones' work is held by Tate Gallery and Arts Council. Lived in London and was made RA in 1986.

Alwyn Dempster JONES 1949– Painter, designer, illustrator and teacher, born in Chester, son of the artist Thomas Dempster Jones. He was brought up in north Wales, where he settled at Mold, Clwyd, having attended Manchester College of Art & Design to gain an honours degree, then his teaching diploma from University College Cardiff school of postgraduate art education. Was appointed art master at Ysgol Dinas Brân, Llangollen, and worked as a graphic designer at Peter Carlyle Designs, Wrexham. Along with his full-time occupation as a designer, Jones worked as a freelance painter and illustrator, having artwork reproduced by *The Sunday Times*, *The Observer*, *The Times Educational Supplement* and many periodicals; advertisements for Yorkshire Television; and publications for The National Trust, BBC and others. He was further education art tutor for Deeside College. In 1993 Jones was made a member of the North Wales Society of Botanical and Fine Watercolour Artists. His paintings were made on location, especially on walks in the mountains of north Wales, and were predominantly in pastel. Showed in London, Manchester, Cardiff and Bristol.

Aneurin M JONES 1930– Painter, draughtsman and teacher, born a farmer's son at Cwm Wysg, on the border of Brecon and Carmarthen. Country shows, markets and sheepdog trials were sketched for later working up into the country pictures for which Jones became famous in the principality. Graduated in fine art from Swansea College of Art, 1950–5. Then spent two years with Celtic Studios, designing stained glass windows for churches in Britain and abroad. Was head of the art department at Ysgol y Preseli in Crymych, Pembrokeshire, until he took early retirement to concentrate on his own work. Jones exhibited widely in Wales, elsewhere in Britain and in America, with work in British and foreign public collections. He gained the Rotary Award for outstanding service to art in 1978. Five years later he had an important solo show at the Gregynog Gallery, National Library of Wales, Aberystwyth, with one at Oriel Ceri Richards Gallery, University of Wales Swansea, 2001, and landscapes at Oriel Plas Glyn-y-Weddw, Pwllheli, in 2003. Lived in Cardigan, Dyfed.

Ann JONES: *see* **Ann Louise ROE**

Anthony Edward JONES 1944– Painter, sculptor, designer film-maker and teacher, born in Mountain Ash, Glamorgan. He attended Goldsmiths' College, 1961–2, Newport College of Art, 1962–6, for painting and sculpture, then in 1963 Swansea College of Art for stained glass. He then held a number of teaching positions in Britain and America including directorship of Glasgow School of Art, 1980–6, and from the latter year president of the school of art at Art Institute of Chicago. His films included *Pershing Rifles*, 1968, commissioned by Loyola University, New Orleans, and he did extensive research on Welsh chapel architecture, partly incorporated in his 1963 book *Chapel Architecture*. In 1971 he and others renovated and redesigned the interior of The Muscular Arms, Glasgow. Many group shows in Britain and America and solo exhibitions included Loyola University.

Barbara JONES 1912–1978 Painter, mural designer and writer. Studied art at the Royal College of Art, becoming an associate in 1950. In 1954 she became a fellow, then vice-president in 1968, of the Chartered Institute of Designers; was chairman of the Society of Mural Painters, 1957–61; a fellow of the Royal Anthropological Institute, 1960; and a governor, Central School of Arts and Crafts, 1956/7–1963/4. Work held by the Victoria & Albert Museum. She completed murals for the Commonwealth Institute, London, Cheshire County Police Headquarters, in Chester, and wrote a number of books, which she illustrated, on diverse subjects such as follies and grottoes, the Isle of Wight, watercolour painting and furniture. One of the strongest contributors to the World War II Pilgrim Trust *Recording Britain* project. Katharine House Gallery, Marlborough, held a first comprehensive solo show, drawn from her studio, in 1999. Lived in London.

Ben JONES 1947– Sculptor, painter, writer and teacher, born in Builth Wells, Breconshire. He studied sculpture at St Martin's School of Art, setting up a studio in London in 1971. Began writing about sculpture, and was a founding editor of the magazine *Artscribe*. At the end of the 1970s he turned mainly to painting, also becoming a lecturer in art department at Bristol Polytechnic. In 1981 Jones moved back to rural Wales, settling in Llanwrtyd Wells, Powys, taking a studio in a former church hall. Revalued his work, turning to a figurative, vigorously expressive sculpture, using a variety of materials. Was a member of the Welsh Sculpture Trust, a founder of the Powys Sculpture Trail and was included in the Glynn Vivian Art Gallery & Museum, Swansea, 1986 show Seven Sculptors Working in Wales. In 1985 his sculpture commemorating the poet T Harri Jones was unveiled at Wyeside Arts Centre. Lived in Llanfoist, Abergavenny, Gwent.

Bridget JONES 1959– Versatile artist who after working in 1984 at the Vortex Gallery in 1985 assisted the performance artists, creators of photo-montage, publishers and film-makers Gilbert and George. In 1986 she began work as a black-and-white hand printer. She was included in East End Open Studios, 1989, based at Vyner Street Studios.

Bryan JONES 1938–1997 Artist, teacher and administrator, born into a mining family in Rhymney, south Wales. He completed his National Service in the late 1950s and was employed as a steelworker before enrolling at art college in his early twenties. Became an artist and teacher, and around 1970 was a founder of, and rolled up his sleeves to help build, the innovative Chapter Arts Centre, Cardiff. This brought contemporary arts under one roof, then an unusual notion, from which groups across Europe took inspiration. When he left Chapter, Jones moved to the Caribbean for three years, returning to settle in west Wales. He taught part-time at Carmarthen College of Art, with a special interest in helping mature students. He also exhibited his own work internationally. Died at his home in Pencader, Dyfed, shared with fellow-artist Christine Kinsey who, with Mik Flood, had helped him establish Chapter.

Bryn JONES 1927– Painter, born in east London of Welsh parents. After formal education at Cambridge he worked in the arts faculties of Cairo and Hong Kong Universities. Began to paint in 1955, showed pictures, which included bold abstract shapes, in several London galleries and had a first solo exhibition at Drian Galleries, 1962.

Christine JONES 1955– Ceramist, born in Llandybie, Carmarthenshire, who trained at West Surrey College of Art and Design, 1980–3. Awards included Special Award, Craft Council, Wales, 1989; Prize Winner, National Eisteddfod of Wales, 1996; Craft Bursary, WAC, 1998; Crafts Council, London, Selected Maker, 1999; and Gold Medal for Craft, National Eisteddfod, 2000. Jones employed a coiling method for her ceramics rather than a wheel. Her work was "about optimism; survival; truth and time; a way of thinking, a personal and creative activity". Group exhibitions included Presented and Purchased, Glynn Vivian Art Gallery, Swansea, 1986; Beaux Arts, Bath, 1990; Beyond Material: new craft of the 90's, Oriel Mostyn, Llandudno, tour, 1998; and Welsh Artists Talking, National Museum of Wales, Cardiff, 2000–1. Among later solo exhibitions were Silent Voices, Black Swan Gallery, Frome, 1999. Glynn Vivian; National Museum of Wales; Fitzwilliam Museum, Cambridge; and Metropolitan Museum of Art, New York and Los Angeles County Museum of Art California, both in America, hold examples. Lived in Swansea.

Christopher JONES 1958– Artist born in High Cross, Hertfordshire, producing paintings, prints and collages in which the imagery could be fragmented and oblique. The studio interiors of Georges Braque and the early work of Willem de Kooning were influences. Jones gained an honours degree in fine art at the University of Newcastle upon Tyne, 1977–81 (he later became studio demonstrator in painting there), studying for his master's at Chelsea School of Art, 1982–3. He was fellow in fine art at Gloucester College of Art and Technology, Cheltenham, 1983–4, in the latter year winning a Boise Scholarship to Spain; was artist-in-residence, Humberside College of Higher Education, Hull, 1986–7; won a Monbusho Scholarship, Kyoto University of Arts, Japan, 1987–9; and Northern Arts Travel & Training Grant to Germany, 1992. Group shows included John Moores Liverpool Exhibition, 1982; Northern Young Contemporaries, Whitworth Art Gallery, Manchester, 1983; Show, Kyoto University, 1989; and Gallery Gerulata, Bratislava, Czechoslovakia, 1992. Had a solo exhibition at Nottingham University Art Gallery, 1985, later ones including Reg Vardy Arts Foundation, University of Sunderland, and Hatton Gallery, University of Newcastle, both 1992.

Colin JONES 1928–1967 Painter, restorer and teacher, born in Newport, Monmouthshire, where he attended the College of Art, 1944–6. After completing his National Service Jones was at Cardiff College of Art, 1948–51, then began teaching. He was on staff of National Museum of Wales, Cardiff, 1961–3, then until his death was HM Inspector for art in Wales. Having been converted to Roman Catholicism 10 years before he died, Jones completed restoration in a number of churches. He took part in group shows at SEA, Piccadilly Gallery, Whitechapel Art Gallery, John Moores Exhibition, Liverpool, and RP, being noted for his portraits and figure studies. One-man shows included Bristol Arts Centre, 1966. CASW holds his work. RCamA in Conwy held a 2006 retrospective of Jones's tragically short career.

Colin JONES 1934– Constructivist sculptor who attended Goldsmiths' College School of Art and studied with Kenneth Martin. Exhibitions included AIA Gallery and Düsseldorf International Art Fair. Jones' Relief Structure No 2, of 1964, in wood, Formica and polyurethane, was acquired by the Arts Council. His Relief Construction, of 1983, in aluminium, mild steel and cellulose paint, adorns the Charles Wilson Building at University of Leicester.

David JONES 1895–1974 Painter, draughtsman, printmaker and writer and maker of inscriptions, born in Brockley, Kent, son of a Welsh printer. Drew as a child, then studied with A S Hartrick at Camberwell School of Art, 1909–15. Between 1915–18 served with Royal Welch Fusiliers during World War I, being wounded and invalided home after action in France. The war, Welsh myth and landscape, his Roman Catholic faith, poetry and legend were some of the themes that threaded their way through Jones' writings and pictures, usually watercolours rich in layered imagery. From 1919–22 Jones studied under Bernard Meninsky and Walter Bayes at Westminster School of Art, then joined Eric Gill's Guild of St Joseph and St Dominic, in Sussex, 1922–4, also working with Gill in Wales, 1925–7. First one-man show at St George's Gallery in 1927. Was a member of SWE and the 7 & 5 Society and was exhibited widely abroad. Became an accomplished engraver, working for the Golden Cockerel Press and illustrated Douglas Cleverdon's 1929 edition of *The Rime of the Ancient Mariner* with 10 superb engravings on copper. His book *In Parenthesis*, of 1937, won the Hawthornden Prize and *The Anathemata*, 1952, the Russel Loines Award. Cleverdon was involved in the important National Book League exhibition of Jones's work in 1972. He was made a Companion of Honour in 1974. In 2002 a Glynn Vivian Art Gallery, Swansea, exhibition celebrated 50 years of *The Anathemata*. Let There be One Fair Girl was a show of paintings, drawings and engravings at Wolseley Fine Arts in 2004. The Tate Gallery and many other public collections hold his work. Jones lived at Harrow-on-the-Hill in modest circumstances for many years.

Deborah JONES 1921– Self-taught painter of still life, trompe l'oeil and old backstreet antique shops in a style described as part imagery, part reality, Jones overcame family opposition to her career choice. After working as a lathe operator in World War II, Jones moved to London, living with several members of the International Ballet Company, painting friends in the ballet world and sketching people in pubs to make a living. Became immersed in the theatre, designing and painting sets, producing props and costumes for the Royal Opera House; worked as Oliver Messel's assistant; was engaged in television, films, opera at Glyndebourne, the Edinburgh International Festival; had a season working at Stratford; and helped Bernard Miles start the Mermaid Theatre. Painted and drew in places as far apart as Positano, Italy, and New York, showing her paintings in Greenwich Village there in 1952. An exhibition at Liberty's in 1957 established her name as a popular painter. Settled in Bristol, painting several Lord Mayors, being represented by the Alexander Gallery. Showed regularly at Florentine Gallery, Brighton, later exhibitions including Harrods, 1994.

Derek JONES 1945– Painter, sculptor and teacher who graduated with honours in fine art, Coventry Polytechnic, 1980, gaining his master's at University of Central England, 1995. Jones taught art at Dudley College, 1995, being artist-in-residence at the Grammar School in Wolverhampton, Staffordshire, where he lived, 1997–9. Group shows included Birmingham University, 1990; West Midlands Arts, Birmingham, 1995; and Eagle Works, Wolverhampton, from 1996. Among his solo exhibitions were Wolverhampton Art Gallery, 2000. At that time Jones was "working on a series of paintings using images from films and documentary photography as a starting-point. I focus on political and social issues and have been using a computer to explore new ways of visualizing images."

Edward Scott JONES 1922– Painter, graphic artist and illustrator, and printmaker, born and lived in Liverpool. He studied at the College of Art there, 1936–7; worked in an advertising agency as a trainee artist, 1938–41; served in the Royal Air Force as aircrew, 1941–6; then served "in the galleys" as a graphic artist and illustrator in advertising, 1946–62, becoming a freelance painter and illustrator from then on. He was a member of RCamA and Acrylic Society. Showed at RI, RSMA, Paris Salon, Liverpool Academy, Hanover Gallery in Liverpool and elsewhere in mixed exhibitions. Solo exhibitions occurred at Williamson Art Gallery in Birkenhead, Bluecoat Gallery in Liverpool, Salford and Bootle Art Galleries, Liverpool Playhouse Theatre and elsewhere. Royal Liverpool Hospital; Bolton, Salford and Williamson Art Galleries; Liverpool Public Libraries; and Liverpool Pilots' Society hold examples.

Elis Gwyn JONES 1918– Painter, teacher, writer and broadcaster in Wales on art, born and lived in Llanystumdwy, Carnarvonshire, sometimes known as Elis Gwyn. He realised only slowly that he should be an artist, influenced by seeing the work of modern English painters and that of Brenda Chamberlain and John Petts, who became a friend and who first urged him to show at Royal National Eisteddfod in 1951. Attended University College of North Wales, Bangor, 1936–40. From 1948 was art master at Pwllheli Grammar School for 31 years, also teaching evening classes for a decade for the University. Was a regular BBC Television and radio broadcaster and wrote on art, including a bilingual book on Richard Wilson, published in 1973. Also showed at SEA and NWG and at Tegfryn Gallery, Menai Bridge. WAC holds his work.

Enaid JONES 1888–1978 Painter and draughtsman, notably of portraits. She studied at London New Art School, Waterdownes Studio, Grosvenor Road Studio and with Philip de Laszlo, then enrolled at Slade School of Fine Art, 1912, under Fred Brown, Philip Wilson Steer and Henry Tonks. She carried out portrait commissions and showed at RP, London Salon and IS. One of her models was her daughter Julia Lang, famous for the BBC radio *Listen with Mother* programmes. A show of Jones' work was held at Fry Gallery in 1984.

Eric Stephen JONES 1904–1962 Painter, printmaker and teacher, born in Romford, Essex, twin brother of the artist Harold Jones. Studied at Camberwell School of Arts and Crafts and from 1925 at Royal College of Art under William Rothenstein and Randolph Schwabe, being a Rome Scholar in the late-1920s for engraving. Taught at Sheffield College of Art from 1931 until his death. Showed at NEAC and was president of Sheffield Society of Artists. Illustrated for Cresset Press. British Museum, Victoria and Albert Museum and Sheffield hold his work. Lived in Sheffield, where Graves Art Gallery held a memorial show in 1964.

Ernest Yarrow JONES 1872–1951 Painter and sculptor, born in Liverpool, who qualified as a barrister but decided to pursue art as a career. He studied at Westminster School of Art and South Kensington Art School and in Paris at Académie Julian and Atelier Colarossi. Travelled widely, latterly living in Exmouth, Devon. Showed at Leicester Galleries, RA, London and Paris Salons and elsewhere. A group of his watercolours was shown at The Jerram Gallery, Salisbury, 1993.

Fred Cecil JONES 1891–1956 Painter, especially in watercolour, and etcher, principally of townscapes; teacher. Studied at Bradford and Leeds Colleges of Art. Jones was the son of a painter, Maud Raphael Jones, and he married an art teacher, Ethel Mary Kitson. Exhibited RA, RSA, RBA, RWS and in northern provincial galleries. His work is held by the Tate Gallery as well as galleries in Bradford and Huddersfield. He and his wife taught at Pudsey Technical and Grammar School. Jones was a meticulous draughtsman whose work was illustrated in several books on the English countryside, and *Apollo* and *Studio* magazines. Was a member of Bradford Arts Club. Memorial shows in Bradford, 1956, and Keighley a year later. Lived in Leeds.

Geoffrey JONES 1909–1993 Painter, notably of flowers, creator of meticulously crafted, poetic and jewel-like works, sometimes on Perspex and on a small scale. He was born in Melbourne, Victoria, Australia, where he studied with Arnold Shore and George Bell, at the George Bell School, distinguishing himself by painting on glass. Jones had seen work by Bell's students at the Athenaeum Gallery, which had an immediate appeal, and he worked unsociable hours as a wharf clerk to fund his tuition. Leaving Australia as a deckhand in 1939 intending to continue studies in Europe, Geoff Jones on arrival in England enlisted in the British Army, was sent to Libya with the historian Philip Guedalla and illustrated a posthumously published book by him. Repatriated to Melbourne, Jones resumed his clerking, but had a show in 1947 which was well received. Returned to England in 1950,

Jones on a stay in Paris studied at L'Académie de la Grande Chaumière and also made working trips to the south of France and to Italy. In 1953, the year of his return to Australia, Jones exhibited in the first exhibition in London of the Australian Artists' Association, at the RWS Conduit Street gallery. Among his later exhibitions was an eightieth birthday retrospective at Australian Galleries, Collingwood, Victoria, in 1989. National Gallery of Australia in Canberra, National Gallery of Victoria, Melbourne, Adelaide University and other collections hold examples.

Glyn JONES 1906–1984 Painter and muralist, born in Manor Park, Essex, who attended Coopers School, Bow, 1919–23, then the Slade School of Fine Art, 1923–6, under Henry Tonks and Philip Wilson Steer, won the Prix de Rome in decorative art, 1926, studying in Rome with Rex Whistler. While there, he travelled widely around the Mediterranean and was commissioned to paint for the Lord Milner memorial, Canterbury Cathedral. Returned to London, he took a flat at 105 Charlotte Street, which doubled as the Spectrum Gallery, running it with the sculptor Marjorie Meggitt, whom he married in 1937. Exhibited at RA, Leicester Galleries and Fine Art Society, where Lord d'Abernon, Lord Howard de Walden and Sir Joseph Duveen bought his work, patrons for many years. Solo exhibitions included The Fine Art Society, 1931, and The Twenty One Gallery, 1932. During World War II Jones was commissioned in the Army, working in Britain as an interpreter with Italian prisoners and in censorship. He completed many murals, venues including British Legion Hall, Parson's Green; St Augustine's, Fulham; St Bride's, Fleet Street (plus a stained-glass window design); St Alphege, Greenwich; and Trinity House. Many portrait commissions included the prime minister Lord Wilson with his wife Mary. Died in London.

Glyn JONES 1936– Painter, printmaker and teacher, born in Tynewydd, Glamorgan. He attended Cardiff College of Art, 1953–7, and the Slade School of Fine Art, 1957–60. Took up several teaching posts, meantime in 1961–2 being co-director of the Image Gallery, Leamington Spa, from 1972 head of the department of fine art at Cardiff College of Art. A member of the 56 Group, he also showed with Young Contemporaries on several occasions, Howard Roberts Gallery in Cardiff, SEA and WAC. One-man show at Elizabeth Gallery, Coventry. Was included in Welsh Painting for the 21st Century, Mall Galleries, 2001. University College, Aberystwyth, holds his acrylic Upfront. Lived in Cardiff, south Wales.

Graham JONES 1956– Painter and draughtsman. He studied at Newport College of Art and Royal Academy Schools. His sensitive study Sir Edmund Fairfax-Lucy at Charlecote Park, Warwickshire which appeared in the exhibition The Long Perspective, Agnew, 1987, was bought by the National Trust's Foundation for Art. Jones also showed at the same gallery, in 1990, in The Broad Horizon.

Graham JONES 1958– Artist, notable as a producer of hand-painted prints and stained glass, born in Warwickshire. He studied at Lanchester Arts Polytechnic, 1975–7 and Swansea College of Art, for stained glass, 1977–81, receiving the Howard Martin Design Award, 1980. Commissions included Shell Oil UK, 1985; Standard Chartered Bank, 1987; Middlesbrough Town Hall, 1990; Prudential Properties, 1993; Wellcome Trust, 1996; Shangri La Hotel, Dilain, China, 1998; Worshipful Company of Grocers, 2001; and Holmes Place, Lisbon, Portugal, 2002. Strategic Art Galleries, Chagford, showed Jones's work on paper at Art on Paper, Royal College of Art, 2002.

Harold JONES 1904–1992 Painter and book illustrator and teacher, born in Romford, Essex. After an abortive attempt at a career in farming Jones returned to London where he attended Goldsmiths' College School of Art, 1921, under Edmund J Sullivan. Then he worked as a clerk while attending evening classes at Camberwell School of Arts and Crafts, his teachers including Albert Rutherston. A scholarship took him to the Royal College of Art full-time, 1924–8, where he studied design, draughtsmanship and engraving under Randolph Schwabe and William Rothenstein and sold his first picture to Lady Ottoline Morrell. Having begun teaching at Bermondsey Central School for Boys, 1930–4, Jones was introduced to the book publishing world by Barnett Freedman, and his reputation was given a lift with the publication of Walter de la Mare's *This Year: Next Year*, in 1937, one of the illustrations, The Black Door, being acquired by the Tate Gallery. Victoria & Albert Museum also holds his work along with several public collections in America. Jones went on to teach at the Working Men's College, Ruskin School of Drawing in Oxford, 1937–40, and, after Army cartographic service in World War II, at Chelsea School of Art, 1945–8. Illustrated many books, including several of his own for children, winning several awards, and showed at Leicester Galleries, NEAC, Sally Hunter Fine Art and elsewhere. Lived in London.

Harold Harris JONES 1908–1991 Painter, notably of portraits, who studied at the Grammar School in Preston, Lancashire, where he settled, then Reading University, obtaining a Bachelor of Science degree. Studied at Southport School of Art, 1933, Harris Art School in Preston, 1934, and locally with Albert Woods, 1935–40, also in St Ives. Showed with RA, NS, RP, ROI and elsewhere.

Helen-Ann JONES 1965– Sculptor and teacher, Welsh-speaking, who attended schools in Mold and Sandbach, then South Cheshire College, Crewe, 1985–6. She did a foundation course at Mid-Cheshire College of Further Education, 1986–7, gained an honours degree in fine art from Bath Academy of Art, 1987–90, then did a postgraduate course at University of Wales, 1992–3, to obtain a teacher's certificate. Among activities over the next few years were a community sculpture project in Bristol, 1989, also assisting with Bath Contemporary Arts Festival; assisting Michael Watts in big commission for Cardiff Bay Development, 1991; being an artist-in-residence at Sully Hospital, South Glamorgan, 1992; and part-time tutoring for South Glamorgan County Council, 1992–3. Group shows included Cardiff Bay Arts Trust Gallery and Artworks at Rudry Church, Lower Machen Music Festival, both 1992. Had a solo show at Sully Hospital, 1992. Lived in Pontcanna, Cardiff.

Henry Conway JONES 1903– Sculptor, born in Llanfairpwll, Anglesey. After attending Friars' School in Bangor, Jones was apprenticed as a general mason, then in 1924–8 worked in London for the marble sculptors Farmer and Brindley. Also studied at City and Guilds of London School of Art, where he gained prizes for modelling, figure work and design. Jones then went freelance, notable commissions involving Portsmouth and Canterbury Cathedrals. Was a member of RCamA and showed with it for about 30 years from 1936. Was a founder-member of West Middlesex Art Club.

Howel Clayton JONES 1897–1970 Artist in oil, watercolour and black-and-white. After studying at the Normal College, Bangor, Jones studied art in the studio of Tim Evans. He went on to exhibit at the RCamA, SGA, PS and elsewhere and illustrated books on north Wales and its mountains. His work also appeared in *La Revue Moderne*. Lived in Llandudno, Wales.

Huw JONES 1956– Figurative painter, born in Denbigh, who studied at Preston Polytechnic, 1976–80, and Chelsea College of Art, 1982–3. Exhibited at Cooling Gallery, 1993; Oriel Contemporary Art and Welsh National Eisteddfod, both 1995; and in John Moores Liverpool Exhibition at Walker Art Gallery, 1995–6. Lived in Llanfairfechan, Gwynedd.

Huw Gareth JONES 1959– Painter in oil, draughtsman and teacher, born in Bangor, Caernarvonshire, who graduated with honours in fine art from Liverpool Polytechnic, 1979–82; was a civilian photographer/scenes of crime officer in the north Wales police, 1982–9; and gained his teaching certificate at Liverpool Poly, 1989–90. Was art teacher in several Welsh and English schools from 1990, from 1999 at Ysgol Treborth, Bangor, the year he set up a studio in Llandwrog. Jones's haunting, evocative paintings and drawings of the landscape and north Wales stemmed "from a process of defining, blurring, redefining, adding and subtracting layers until the picture looks complete. This may take anything from a few hours to several months off and on.... Colour and tone are very important." Mixed shows included RCamA, 2000; Grosvenor Gallery, Chester, and Welsh Artist of the Year, Cardiff, both 2001; and View Two Gallery, Liverpool, 2002. Among his solo exhibitions were Oriel Plas Glyn-y-Weddw, Llanbedrog, 2002, the year he was featured on the Welsh language television programme *Sioe Gelf*. Lived in Marianglas, Anglesey.

Ian JONES 1947– Figurative and abstract painter, born in Birmingham, where he attended the Polytechnic, 1975–8, then Royal College of Art, 1979–82. He gained the Whitworth Wallis Award, 1976; John Minton Award, 1982; Greater London Arts Association Major Award, 1983; Athena Award, short list prize, 1988; and Unilever Prize, Portobello Festival, 1989. Group exhibitions included Drawings, Foyle Gallery, Birmingham, 1975; John Moores Liverpool Exhibition, 1982; Nicola Jacobs Gallery Summer Exhibition, 1984; Images of Paradise, Harewood House, Yorkshire, 1989; and The Discerning Eye, selected by Tim Hilton, Mall Galleries, 1991. Had a solo exhibition at Chapter Arts Centre, Cardiff, 1984, with a series at Anderson O'Day Gallery from 1989. Unilever, British Airports Authority and Nordstern in Cologne acquired works.

Idris Phylip JONES 1905– Painter, born in Nebo, Penygroes, Caernarvonshire, to which he eventually retired. Having attended Penygroes County School, Jones was apprenticed as a fitter, ran a taxi service, then in late 1930s embarked on a career as an aircraft fitter and inspector. Much of his life was spent with the Air Ministry, travelling widely in the United Kingdom. It was in the late 1950s that his exhibiting career gained pace, and he showed with Royal National Eisteddfod, in 1968 winning a second prize for painting; CASW; and Penygroes Art Club. In 1972 he participated in the WAC touring show An Alternative Tradition.

Jack JONES 1922–1993 Painter, teacher and writer, born poor and illegitimate in Hafod, Swansea, south Wales. He won a place at Dyneford School and went on to teach French and English, becoming head of English at Barnes Grammar School, London. Jones became interested in art in Paris in his late-twenties and published a life of Van Gogh: *The Man Who Loved the Sun*. Began painting in 1953, soon after returning to England from the University of Paris, and continued virtually untaught. His main subjects were the mining and industrial areas of his childhood. Although he was called "the Welsh Lowry", Jones denied Lowry's influence, terming himself "the Leonardo of the slag heap". Had many years of grave illness, including six operations for cancer and two coronaries, and by the age of 63 was an alcoholic in a mental hospital. In 1985 became a Roman Catholic, gave up drink and worked with alcoholics and drug addicts in Chelsea. His later work was more colourful, partly due to visiting Spain. Exhibitions included Stephen Bartley Gallery from 1988; Taliesin Arts Centre, Swansea, 1991; and Glynn Vivian Art Gallery there, which holds his work, 1993. Lived finally in Putney, southwest London.

Jean JONES 1927– Painter who studied at St Martin's School of Art and the Ruskin School, Oxford. Exhibitions included Bear Lane Gallery and Ashmolean Museum, both in Oxford; New Grafton and Boundary Galleries; and in 1999 a Sale from Studio at Duncan Campbell Contemporary Art. Lived in London.

Jean JONES 1956– Painter and teacher whose vibrant paintings of flowers and plants were given a solo exhibition at Duncan Campbell Fine Art in 2004. Jones was born in Sheffield, Yorkshire, and studied at the University of Warwick, 1976–80. She taught art full-time in London and Essex, 1980–6, from 1986–7 until the Duncan Campbell show concentrating on painting, teaching part-time and bringing up three children. She moved from Scotland to Bristol in 2002 and from mid-2003 "launched myself as a full-time painter on a professional basis". Other shows included Watercolour Challenge, Mall Galleries, 2001; Café Gallery Unlimited, Bristol, 2002; and The Media Centre, 2004. Jones completed commissions for Northumberland County Council, 1993; Michael Alexander Accountants, Manchester, 1997; and Incentives, Glasgow, 1997–8.

Jo JONES 1894–1989 Painter and draughtsman, born in Knebworth, Hertfordshire, as Violet Madeline Josette Jones. She began painting as a young girl in Jamaica, and her studies included Paris and Zurich in the late-1930s. In 1933 the director of the Tate Gallery, J B Manson, introduced Jones to Wildenstein Gallery, which gave her her first solo show in 1935, from which Contemporary Art Society bought Still Life with Green Peppers. In 1938 she had a show at Galerie Zborowski, Paris, with another at Wildenstein in 1939. In that year she moved to London, where she was thereafter based, although she had a cottage and studio in Dorset. During the war worked as a land girl in Dorset and in Intelligence. There were four distinct working periods as a painter: in Paris and London before the war, in Spain in the 1950s, Morocco in the 1960s and after that mainly in Dorset with occasional journeys abroad, especially to Vevey and Zürich. For some years Jones lived with the Sacro Monte gypsies in Granada, and related pictures by her are in the Gypsy Museum at Leeds University. In 1969 *The Gypsies of Granada* was published, with text by Augustus John, Sacheverell Sitwell, Walter Starkie, Laurie Lee and Marguerite Steen. Showed regularly in Britain and abroad, having a retrospective at Alpine Gallery, 1985. The Michael Parkin Gallery had a memorial exhibition in 1992.

John JONES 1935– Printmaker and teacher, working latterly almost exclusively in relief from lino. Jones graduated from Bath Academy of Art, Corsham, in painting, printmaking and photography in 1964, winning an Academy travelling scholarship. From 1964–71 he taught art full- and part-time at secondary and further education levels; art and media studies full-time to degree level at North Riding College of Higher Education, 1971–88; with occasional guest teaching in America, 1976–96. In 1988 Jones gave up teaching to concentrate on his own work and involvement with the Crescent Arts Workshop, Scarborough, which he had helped found in 1979. Crescent Arts Gallery gave him a retrospective in 2002, recent solo shows including Huddersfield and Scarborough Art Galleries, both 2000. Also took part in many group shows, including Splash, Shire Hall Gallery, Stafford, 2002. Lived in Staintondale, North Yorkshire.

John Edward JONES 1926– Artist in all painting media, draughtsman, film-maker, teacher and writer, born near Bristol. He studied at West of England College of Art, Bristol, with George Sweet, 1942–4 and 1948–52, with Army service intervening; then in 1952–4 at Slade School of Fine Art under Claude Rogers and William Coldstream. Several teaching appointments included a senior lectureship in fine art department of Leeds University. It holds his work. Jones wrote a book *Wonders of the Stereoscope* and made several Arts Council/Arts Foundation films, including *Claes Oldenburg hanging a picture* and *Matisse: A sort of Paradise*. He was president of Leeds Fine Art Club and a member of RWA. Also showed with LG and had solo shows in Buenos Aires in Argentina, in Harrogate and Leeds, where he lived.

Jonah JONES 1919–2004 Sculptor, letterer, teacher and writer, born in East Boldon, County Durham. He was educated at Jarrow Secondary School and managed to snatch part-time instruction at King Edward School of Art in Newcastle upon Tyne. After war service he suffered from pulmonary tuberculosis. In 1949 Jones worked in Eric Gill's workshops, about two years later setting up on his own in northwest Wales. He used slate as his principal medium and believed that fine art should be practised as a craft in a local community. For a while he was director of the National College of Art and Design in Dublin and he lectured in sculpture at the British School in Rome, but was mainly a working sculptor participating in a range of group shows, including RCamA, WAC and NWG. A few one-man shows were held, but much of Jones' work appeared in public locations, such as the depictions of Mercy and Justice on the Law Courts in Mold and his sculpture on the theme of Peace for the Emrys ap Iwan School at Abergele. Among his major inscriptions are those to David Lloyd George and Dylan Thomas in Westminster Abbey. His portrait busts included the architect Clough Williams-Ellis and the writer John Cowper Powys. Jones scripted several television films; his novel *A Tree May Fall* was published in 1980 and a book on *The Lakes of North Wales* in 1983. There was a retrospective at St David's Hall, Cardiff, in 2002. CASW holds his work. Lived at Minffordd, Penrhyndeudraeth, Gwynedd, later in Cardiff.

Joy JONES 1933– Artist in oil, tempera and watercolour, who also worked under her maiden name of Joy (Joyce) Mellor, born in Bangalore, south India. She studied at Regional College of Art, Manchester, 1955–7, then St Martin's School of Art, 1957–9. She was a freelance artist who worked for *Encyclopaedia Britannica*, Cambridge School Classics, Nature Conservancy Wales and the Overton Studios Trust. Her main works were miniature portraits, flowers and animals, and she specialised in still lifes in tempera. The Indian Army holds portraits by her. She showed with Clwyd Open, in Mold; Rhyl Museum and Art Gallery; and Tegfryn Art Gallery and had several two-man shows, including Oriel Bangor. Also showed in Canada. Lived in Colwyn Bay, Clwyd.

Justin JONES 1961– Painter and draughtsman. He studied at Bournville School of Art, 1980–1, Leeds Polytechnic, 1981–4, at St Martin's School of Art, 1986–7, then in 1988 at Warsaw's Academy of Art under a British Council Scholarship. In 1987, Jones won an Elizabeth Greenshields Foundation Award. His work was included in many mixed exhibitions in Britain, notably Merz Contemporary Art and East End Open Studios, at Delfina Studios, both 1989, and The Broad Horizon, at Agnew, 1990, as well as at Wrocław International Drawing Triennial, in Poland, and in Italy at Centro d'Arte Verrochio, Siena. In 1990 he had a solo show at Merz Contemporary Art.

Katie JONES 1979– Artist specialising in printmaking, mainly collograph, etching and silkscreen, born in Bournemouth, Dorset, as Katherine Jones. "Portraiture and questions concerning reflections and the image" were key interests. She studied at Herefordshire College of Art and Design, 1998; Anglia Polytechnic University, 1999–01, taught by Roberta Booth; then worked for her master's in fine art printmaking at Camberwell College of Art & Design, teachers including Paul Coldwell and Frank Tinsley. Jones served as an editioner for Brenda Hartill and was an associate member of Printspace. Group shows included Cambridge Young Printmakers, Broughton House Gallery, Cambridge, and Gallery 54, Ross-on-Wye, both 2001. Among solo exhibitions were Gallery 54, 2001, and Printspace, 2002. Lived in London.

Kiri JONES 1972– Painter who did an Epsom School of Art and Design foundation course, 1991–2; graduated with honours in fine art, Norwich School of Art and Design, 1992–5; and completed a postgraduate diploma in painting, Royal Academy Schools, 1995–8, appearing in the final year show. This included her oil on canvas Tuatha de Danaan, a coolly lyrical, gestural work. Jones's awards included a David Murray Scholarship, Worshipful Company of Painter-Stainers Prize, M&G Summer Exhibition Prize for an artist under 35, at RA, and a Manpower PLC Scholarship, all 1997; and David Murray Scholarship and Vincent Harris Prize, Premiums, RA, both 1998. Among her exhibitions were the RA Summer Exhibition, from 1997, and Radio Therapy Department, Cromwell Hospital, 1998. Lived in Worcester Park, Surrey.

Leslie JONES 1934– Printmaker, painter in acrylic and teacher, born in Tremadoc, Caernarvonshire. He attended the Regional College of Art in Manchester, 1951–5; Royal College of Art, 1955–8, tutors John Nash and Julian Trevelyan; was a Rome Scholar, British School at Rome, 1958–60; and a visiting student at Belgrade Academy of Fine Art, 1959. Jones was on the staffs of Kingston School of Art, Hornsey College of Art and St Martin's School of Art, 1961–7; was an HM Inspector for art and design, 1967–83; was a freelance artist and designer; then from 1987–9 was acting head of Gwynedd Art & Design Department. He was also fine art advisor for S4C Television. Jones was a member of RE. He held a number of one-man exhibitions including Oriel Henry Thomas, Carmarthen; Rhyl Museum and Art Gallery; Oriel Bangor; and Tegfryn Art Gallery. He worked for University of Wales Press, Cambridge University Press and others. Victoria & Albert Museum, WAC and CASW hold examples. Lived in Colwyn Bay, Clwyd.

Lucy JONES 1955– Painter, printmaker and teacher, born and lived in London. She studied at Byam Shaw School of Drawing and Painting, 1975–7, Camberwell School of Art, 1977–9, and Royal College of Art, 1979–82, a Rome Scholarship in painting taking her to British School in Rome, 1982–4. By then she had begun to collect a number of awards and prizes, including the Cubitt Award for Painting, 1980, Anstruther Award for Painting, 1982, Oppenheim-John Downes Memorial Trust, 1986, RA Summer Exhibition Daler-Rowney Award for the best work in oil, 1989, and prize, John Moores Exhibition, Walker Art Gallery, Liverpool, 1995. Taught extensively from mid-1980s, latterly being a tutor at Slade School of Fine Art, 1992–9. Jones overcame the problems of cerebral palsy to paint her disarming self-portraits and views of London, with an exuberance and rich, singing colour. Showed widely in group exhibitions in Britain and abroad and had solo shows at Angela Flowers Gallery, Flowers West Gallery in Santa Monica, California, and Flowers East. Arts Council, Museum of Modern Art in New York and other public collections hold her work.

Maggie JONES 1944– Artist in various media, designer and teacher who studied at Liverpool College of Art, Chelsea School of Art and Royal College of Art. Interiors and childhood memories were features of her mixed-media boxes, as shown at England & Co, Art in Boxes, 1992. She also showed at White Space Gallery and Fouts & Fowler. Jones worked for a time on the art publication *Raw Vision*.

Malcolm JONES 1949– Painter, performance artist and teacher born in Wallasey, Cheshire, who studied at Reading University, gaining a first-class honours degree in fine art, 1971. He gained a postgraduate higher diploma in painting, Chelsea School of Art, 1972–3. Teaching included Plaistow Grammar School, 1971–2, and Reading University, 1980. Jones won a number of awards, including British Council Award to tour as art director of The Kipper Kids, 1973; Arts Council Experimental Projects Award and British Council Award for Moodier, 1975; and Oppenheim-John Downes Trust Award, 1986. In 1982 won a prize in Sainsbury's Images for Today exhibition. Much of his work concentrated on London's East End, townscapes tending towards abstraction. Showed at Whitechapel Open, elsewhere in London, in the provinces and abroad. In 1983 Malcolm Jones Paints Limehouse was held at the library there. Later solo shows included Studio Sienko Gallery, 1997, and Nagan Johnson, 2000. He had a studio in east London.

Mark JONES 1957– Painter and performance artist who gained an honours degree at Central St Martins College of Art, 1987–91. Jones approached his massive, brash pictures through photography. He used cuttings from pornographic magazines or took snaps of female friends, witness his solo shows at 30 Underwood Street and The Blue Gallery, both 2000. Jones took part in solo and group performances at Finborough Arms, 1985–6, other group appearances including Fresh Art, BDC, 1991, and Making Out, Transmission Gallery, Glasgow, 1995.

Martyn Vaughan JONES 1957– Artist, born in Coventry, Warwickshire, spending the first 14 years there, in 1971 moving with his parents to Blackwood, Gwent. Jones's interest in painting began early, nurtured by his art teacher Arthur Morgan at Blackwood Comprehensive who encouraged him to attend Newport College of Art, where he graduated in illustration, 1975–9. He joined a local art group, began to sell paintings and in 1981 gave up his job as a screenprinter with the Metropolitan Police and became a professional artist. In 1983 he moved back to Gwent, preferring the slower pace of life and more dramatic landscape. The industrial landscape of the valleys of south Wales became an inspiration, but as the mines began to close and the area seemed to lose its soul Jones focused on seascape and moorland, walking in remote areas. He later settled in west Wales, at St Clears, Carmarthenshire, the rugged Pembrokeshire coastline and Preseli Hills provided subjects. Jones's lifelong interest in inland waterways was furthered when he bought a narrow boat. He showed widely in group exhibitions, including Albany Gallery, Cardiff; Hill Court Gallery, Abergavenny; Riverside and Beaufort Galleries, Crickhowell; West Wales Art Centre, Fishguard; and with Benjamin C Hargreaves. He also took part in two-man shows, his solo exhibitions including Visitor Centre, Cwmcarn, 1987; Riverside Gallery, 1994, and Beaufort Gallery, 1996.

Megan JONES 1936– Artist and teacher, whose "main subject matter is the land, altered by light and time." She was born in Crynant, West Glamorgan, and studied under Alfred Janes at Swansea College of Art, 1952–7. Taught widely, being principal of Ystalyfera Adult Education Centre, 1980–9. In 1994 she gained a WAC travel grant to work in Newfoundland. Was a full member of the Welsh Group. Group exhibitions included Laing Art Competition, Mall Galleries, 1995; Invited Artists, RCamA, 1996; Wales Drawing Biennale, from 1997–8; and Celtic Connections, Glasgow, 1998. Among her later solo shows were The Wild and Sacred Lane, WAC tour, 1988–9; Brecknock Museum and Gallery, Brecon, and Rhondda Heritage Park Gallery, both from 1992, each holding her work; and University of Wales, Swansea, from 1993. University of Newfoundland; Lidice Community, The Czech Republic; Prince Philip Hospital, Llanelli; Dyfed County Hall, Carmarthen; and several corporate collections also hold examples. Lived in Ystradgynlais, Swansea.

Michael JONES 1955– He studied at Rochdale College of Art, then graduated with honours from Camberwell School of Arts and Crafts, 1975–8. Jones was included in Ten Abstract Artists, Picture Gallery, 1980; The Crypt Gallery, 1986; Triangle Exhibition, at Pine Plains, New York, America, 1987; Christmas and New Year Exhibition, Café Gallery, 1988; and East End Open Studios, at Carpenter's Road, 1989.

Nicholas JONES 1965– Painter, born in Bristol, who studied at Bristol Faculty of Art and Design, 1983–8. He went on to exhibit widely in the southwest of England, winning the South West Arts Fine Arts Award in 1990. Mixed exhibitions included RWA, 1988; Crane Kalman Gallery, from 1992; Manchester Contemporary Art Fair, 1994; and Gordon Hepworth Fine Art at 23 Smith Street, 1997. Solo shows included Crane Kalman, from 2000, and Six Chapel Row, Bath, 2003. There Jones, who described his work as "like going on a journey when you don't know what you will discover," showed abstracted landscapes which used rich textures of dripped and splashed paint. Arthur Andersen and Lloyds TSB hold Jones' work.

Olwen JONES 1945– Painter, printmaker and teacher, wife of the artist Charles Bartlett. She studied at Harrow School of Art, 1960–5, and Royal Academy Schools, 1965–8, and her engraving teacher was Gertrude Hermes. She was a part-time lecturer at Harrow School of Art, 1970–88, lecturing in printmaking at the City and Guilds of London Art School, 1993–4. Took part in many mixed shows, including A Survey of Influential East Anglian Artists, Chappel Galleries, Chappel, 1991. Was a fellow of the RWS and RE. She had a first solo show at Zaydler Gallery, 1971, many others including Chappel Galleries, 1999, Bohun Gallery, Henley-on-Thames, 2002, and John Russell Gallery, Ipswich, 2004. Jones gained several prizes, later ones including Chris Beetles Watercolour Prize, 1989. National Museum of Wales, Cardiff; Reading Museum; and Nuffield Foundation hold her work. Jones was a notable watercolourist, her work having a translucent quality. Lived in Fingringhoe, Essex.

Patrick JONES 1948– Painter of abstract pictures and teacher who studied at Birmingham College of Art, 1970–1, then MFA Maryland Institute, Baltimore, America, 1973–5. He gained a Greater London Arts Association Award, 1979, then a John Brinkley Fellowship in Painting at Norwich School of Art, 1981. Group shows were many, including Platform '71 at Museum of Modern Art, Oxford, 1971; British Painting at Hayward Gallery, 1974; Henri Gallery, Washington, America, 1975; Tolly Cobbold Eastern Arts Touring Exhibition, 1981; and British Artists at Cyprus College of Art at Woodlands Art Gallery, 1983. Solo shows included Nicola Jacobs Gallery, 1981, and The Atkinson Gallery, Millfield, 2002. By then, Jones acknowledged many influences on his brightly coloured, optimistic and vibrant paintings. While teaching at Hunter College in New York he had been considerably affected by seeing retrospectives of work by Juan Gris and Georges Braque; also influential were the wood-carvings of the Dogon of West Africa and Oceanic art forms from Polynesia and the paintings of Basil Beattie.

Peter JONES 1917– Prolific artist, producing paintings, drawings, collages and reliefs, born in Mortlake, Surrey, growing up in East Sheen. He attended Richmond Art School, his first job being in a display and design studio. During World War II he served in the Royal Air Force. Jones became associated with a group sometimes referred to as "The Moderns", around the artist Jack Bilbo. After the war Jones worked several years for the Grosvenor Gallery, continuing to produce his own work. He had a special talent for enhancing pictures with sympathetic mounts and frames, galleries and individuals employing these skills. Wit and verve was a characteristic of the output of this artist, by nature retiring. Although he did not seek a place in the limelight, Jones did take part in group exhibitions and held a series of solo shows. Group exhibitions included the Redfern, Leicester, Grosvenor Galleries; Gimpel Fils; Victoria & Albert Museum; Midland Art Gallery, Nottingham; Campbell and Franks; Ash Barn, Petersfield; England & Co; and Richard Demarco, Edinburgh. As well as solo exhibitions with the Modern Art and Ware Galleries, others were at Chichester Festival, 1962; Molton Gallery, 1965; Camden Arts Centre, 1974; South London Art Gallery, 1975; in Perth, Australia, 1977; Royal Free Hospital and Richmond Gallery, both 1980; Petersfield Gallery, Petersfield, 1984-6; and Farnham Gallery, Farnham, 1992. HM The Queen, Victoria & Albert Museum, South London Art Gallery, London Borough of Camden, Temple Newsam at Leeds, Nuffield College in Oxford and the Forestry Commission Headquarters in Suffolk hold examples. In the early 1980s Jones settled in Petersfield, Hampshire. Despite frail health, in old age he continued to experiment.

Peter JONES 1968– Painter and teacher, whose work included a multi-coloured imaginary landscape of shapes, Series No. 5, oil on canvas of 1992, in the collection of Conoco UK, Warwick. Jones obtained a foundation diploma at Bournemouth & Poole College of Art and Design, 1986–7, then an honours degree in fine art from Coventry Polytechnic, 1987–90. He settled in that city, taking a studio in a canal basin warehouse. From 1990–1 he was a part-time lecturer at Coventry University's foundation department, also being resident artist at the basin, funded by Coventry City Council's arts panel. Reflections, work completed during the residency, was shown at Coventry's Herbert Art Gallery in 1992.

Peter JONES 1970– Ceramist interested in the relationship between hand-made and industrially produced items, based in Colchester, Essex. He gained an honours crafts degree between 1989–92 at Crewe & Alsager College of Higher Education, set up a workshop in 1993 and in 2000 founded Base2 with Jayne Knowles. Jones's exhibitions included Ceramic Contemporaries Two, Victoria & Albert Museum, 1996; Chelsea Crafts Fair, Crafts Council, Chelsea Town Hall, 1997; Gifted, New Ashgate Gallery, Farnham, 1998; and Ipswich Form and Transfer – contemporary printed ceramics, Drumcroon, Wigan, 2001. He participated in Making the Connection, firstsite, Colchester/Wolsey Art Gallery, 2002. Among solo shows were New Ceramics at Benham Gallery, Colchester, 1994, and Ceramic Dynamic at firstsite, 1998–9.

Philip JONES 1933– Painter, born in London, educated at Malvern College, where he was taught art by Henry Fabian Ware, studying at Slade School of Fine Art, 1953–6. Jones' subject was landscape, Malta, Sardinia and Norfolk, where he lived at Little Cressingham, being key themes. His work verged on abstraction as he abstracted the essential elements of a scene, using both subtle shades and occasionally unexpected, muted bursts of colour. He showed with RA Summer Exhibitions; Young Contemporaries, RBA Galleries, 1954; Artists of Fame and Promise, Leicester Galleries, 1955–6; AIA Gallery from 1964; Norwich Group Show, Castle Museum in Norwich, 1978; Chicago International Art Exposition, America, 1988–90; and Eastern Arts Open, King's Lynn, winner of Best Painting and Best in Show awards, 1993. Had a solo show at Galerie Bleu, Stockholm, 1965; Maddermarket Theatre Gallery, Norwich, from 1978; Louise Hallett Gallery, from 1986; Vanessa Devereux Gallery, 1990; retrospective at Malvern College, 1991; Michael Parkin Gallery, 1994; Ainscough Contemporary, 1995 and 1997; Ainscough Gallery, Liverpool, 1999; and Oliver Contemporary, 2003. Contemporary Art Society, Nuffield Foundation and galleries in Newport and Plymouth hold examples.

Philip JONES 1971– Figurative painter, born in Manchester, whose film still-realistic oil on canvas Bullitt, of 1995, was included in New Contemporaries at Tate Gallery, Liverpool, and Camden Arts Centre, 1996. Jones gained a fine art degree at Central St Martin's, 1991–4, and his master's in painting, Royal College of Art, 1994–6. Jones won a TI Group Scholarship to the Royal College for his period there and a travel award to RCA Studios, Morocco, 1995. Exhibitions included Art Viva, Senigallia, Italy, 1994, and MI-Art Fair, Milan, 1995.

Robert JONES 1943– Artist mainly on paper, writer and teacher, born in Newquay, Cornwall. He attended Falmouth and Manchester Schools of Art, did teacher training in Brighton, then took a design and craft course in Bristol. Held several teaching posts: Summerhill School, Suffolk; Mullion School, Cornwall; and Falmouth College of Art. Jones showed in Bath, Taunton, Oxford and Newlyn, being a member of Newlyn Society of Artists. He was included in the 1989 Newlyn Orion Galleries show A Century of Art in Cornwall 1889–1989, also in Falmouth Connections at Falmouth Art Gallery, 1994, and Porthmeor, A Century of Images, at Tate Gallery, St Ives, 1995. His first London show was organised by Thomas Henry Fine Art at Gallery 27 in 1997. Jones painted extensively in the Mediterranean area, Ireland and America. Latterly, he had a series of exhibitions at The Great Atlantic Map Works Gallery, St Just-in-Penwith. His 2002 show there was titled and was accompanied by Jones's book *Sun, Wind and Weather*. Just before that appeared, Jones's volume *Alfred Wallis Artist and Mariner* was awarded a prize "for the outstanding publication about Cornwall" by the Cornish Gorsedd in 2002. Jones's exhibition The Lonely Sea & the Sky was at The John Davies Gallery, Stow-on-the-Wold, in 2004.

Roger JONES 1935– Artist, architect and teacher, born in Birmingham, where he studied at the School of Architecture, practising until 1964, when he was a finalist in a John Moores competition for a site-specific sculpture. This prompted him to concentrate on sculpture. From 1965–71 Jones taught part-time at Bath Academy, Corsham. He then took up two part-time posts: until 1980 at the experimental workshop in the art and design faculty of Birmingham Polytechnic; and until 1985 at Bath Academy, Bath College of Higher Education; after that, until 1990, being head of department/course director for visual arts part-time courses. In 1991, with a Henry Moore Foundation grant, Jones gained his master's degree in sculpture studies after a year at Leeds University. Group shows included Midland Group, Nottingham, 1965; John Moores Exhibition, Liverpool, 1969; and Three Choirs Festival, Gloucester, 1977. Later solo shows included Biting The Red, constructions, sculpture, paintings and photographs, at The Book Gallery, St Ives, in 1999.

Royston JONES 1947– Painter, printmaker and photographer, and teacher, born in Wolverhampton, Staffordshire. He studied at Birmingham College of Art and Design, 1965–8, teachers including Trevor Halliday and John Walker, gaining his master's degree at Illinois University, 1969–71. Went on to teach at Southport College of Art and Technology. Jones showed in the Southport area, elsewhere in Britain and in America.

Sarah JONES 1959– Artist employing photography, born and lived in London. She gained a fine art degree at Goldsmiths' College, 1978–81, and her master's there, 1994–6. Exhibitions included Nobby Stiles, Vandy Street, and Sick, 152c Brick Lane Gallery, both 1995; and New Contemporaries at Tate Gallery, Liverpool, and Camden Arts Centre, 1996. Later solo shows included Maureen Paley/Interim Art and Le Consortium, Dijon, France, both 1997, and Jerwood Gallery and Maureen Paley, both 1999, with another at Maureen Paley in 2002. In the Jerwood exhibition Jones showed photographs of beautiful middle-class girls frozen in moments of introspection, taking their cue from Dutch Old Masters but with undercurrents of tension and intrigue familiar to television soap opera. Saatchi Collection held her work.

Selwyn JONES 1928–1998 Painter, illustrator and teacher, born in Llanberis, Caernarvonshire. After serving with Royal Naval Air Service in 1945–8, Jones attended Regional College of Art in Manchester, 1948–53. Had a period in London as a freelance illustrator. Several teaching positions followed, including from 1970–82 head of the art department at Normal College, Bangor. Had a series of solo exhibitions at Howard Roberts Gallery in Cardiff and took part in group shows at that gallery, Bangor Art Gallery, NWG, RCamA and Royal National Eisteddfod. WAC and CASW hold his work. In 1993 was elected RCamA.

Stan JONES 1930– Painter, teacher and artist in ceramics, born in Dinas Cross, Carmarthenshire. Studied at Trinity College, Carmarthen and Cardiff College of Art, then went on to teach. He broadcast on BBC radio and television in Wales, completing a series on pottery for children. Was for a time chairman of WSW, and also showed widely in group shows including Thomson House, Cardiff, as well as SEA, SWG and Royal National Eisteddfod. One-man shows included County Library in Haverfordwest.

Stanley JONES 1927– Painter, printmaker and muralist, born in Birmingham, where studied at the College of Arts and Crafts, 1942–5 and 1948–50, teachers including Harold Smith, and at Royal Academy Schools with Henry Rushbury and Bernard Fleetwood-Walker, who had also taught him in Birmingham. He showed with Young Contemporaries, RA, RBSA, widely in Scotland and elsewhere in the provinces. The painter and collector Edward Le Bas and Graves Art Gallery in Sheffield, where Jones settled, held examples.

Stanley JONES 1933– Printmaker and lecturer, born in Wigan, Lancashire, full name John Stanley Jones, who attended the School of Art there, 1950–4, then the Slade School of Fine Art, 1954–6. Jones was awarded the Slade Scholarship in 1955 and the Robert Ross Scholarship in 1956. From 1956–8, he worked at the École des Beaux-Arts in Paris and with the help of S W Hayter joined the staff of Atelier Paris, where he met and worked with many School of Paris artists, including Giacometti, Severini and Braque. In 1958 Jones, prompted by his London dealer Robert Erskine, returned to England to set up a lithographic studio to be run by Curwen Press. This gained an international reputation, handling work by the most distinguished British and foreign artists. Among Jones' innovations was development of the continuous tone process. From 1958–98, he lectured in lithography at the Slade School. Jones was a founder-member of the Printmakers' Council in 1964, being for many years its president, and in 1965 helped found Curwen Gallery, which showed his own and others' work. He was a participant in the 1977 Artists at Curwen show at the Tate Gallery which, with Pat Gilmour, he helped organise and which celebrated the gift of Curwen's archive to the Tate. In 1989, Curwen Studio moved to Chilford Hall, near Cambridge, was renamed Curwen Chilford Prints and added screenprinting. Jones' book *Lithography for Artists* appeared in 1966. Later shows included Wenlock Edge, mixed-media works at Curwen Gallery, 2003.

Stephen JONES 1944– Artist in tempera, born at Brockett Hall, Hertfordshire. He studied at Hornsey College of Art, 1960–2, then ran the picture framing firm Stephen Jones Art Services, 1963–79. In 1980 he began painting again, using tempera, full-time. Exhibitions included Contemporary Portrait Society and RP, 1983; RA Summer Exhibition from 1987; Hunting National Art Competition, 1990. Lived in Twickenham, Middlesex.

Sydney Robert JONES 1881–1966 Painter, illustrator, designer, architect and writer. Born in Birmingham, he studied at the School of Art there for about four years at the turn of the century, then travelled extensively in England and on the continent. Exhibited RA, RI, Walker Art Gallery, Liverpool, Royal Glasgow Institute of the Fine Arts, Paris Salon and elsewhere abroad. Work held by Victoria & Albert Museum, Mappin Art Gallery, Sheffield, and Guildhall Library and Art Gallery, London. Jones did an extensive amount of industrial work and illustrations for publications such as *The Times*, *Illustrated London News* and *The Studio*. His many books concentrated on the English countryside, such as *Old English Country Cottages* and *English Village Life*. Was a member of the Authors' Club. Lived at Wallingford, Berkshire.

Terry JONES 1938–1992 Painter, teacher, enameller and draughtsman, born in Abersychan, Monmouthshire, son of a miner. He attended Newport College of Art, 1955–60, under Thomas Rathmell, then Royal College of Art, 1960–3, where Carel Weight was a strong influence. Taught at Medway, Canterbury and Kingston Colleges of Art part-time, 1963–7, then was a much-liked teacher full-time at Kingston, 1967–92, from 1973 senior lecturer in fine art. He painted extensively in Portugal from 1962 and America from 1980. Showed at Young Contemporaries, RA, LG and Society of British Enamellers, of which he was a founder-member, and solo at Rowan Gallery, 1962 and 1964. There was a retrospective at Watermans Art Centre/Kingston University, 1994, and tour. Jones was a prizewinner at Royal National Eisteddfod in 1976, WAC buying an enamel by him. Lived in London.

Thomas Dempster JONES 1914–1993 Painter, photographer and restorer, born in Harlech, Merionethshire. From 1929–36 Jones worked in Dinorwic Slate Quarries, attended Coleg Harlech, 1937–8, then was employed at aircraft production until training as a photographer in the Royal Air Force, 1942–6. He settled in Buckley, Clwyd, working as a professional photographer, then taught himself to paint from the early 1960s. Jones showed with Buckley Art Society of which he was president, AIA, RA, De Souza Gallery in Chester, RCamA, Royal National Eisteddfod and at Paris Salon, where he gained an Hon. Mention in 1967, a gold medal three years later. First of several solo shows was at New Civic Centre, Connah's Quay, 1968. Coleg Harlech holds his work. His father was the artist Alwyn Dempster Jones.

Thomas Salisbury JONES 1882– Painter and illustrator who was employed by the General Post Office, working in Wales, where he finally lived at Penmaenmawr. Attended Crewe School of Art, 1907–10. He wrote short stories, which he illustrated. Exhibited RCamA and in London.

Tim JONES: *see* **Timothy Emlyn JONES**

Tim JONES 1950– Artist, sometimes known as T(imothy) M(artin) Jones, who studied at Berkshire College of Art, 1967–8; High Wycombe College of Art, 1968–9; St Martin's School of Art, 1969–72; Central School of Art, 1976; and Royal College of Art, 1977–80. Among awards won were Mark Rothko Memorial Trust Award, 1980, and Calouste Gulbenkian Printmaker Award, 1982. Was artist-in-residence, Borough of Lewisham, 1982–3. In 1981 gained a commission for Brunel University Music Room, in 1983 one for Lewisham's Ladywell Baths. Mixed shows included RA Summer Exhibition from 1979; John Moores Liverpool Exhibition, 1980, at the Walker Art Gallery, prize winner; Contemporary Artists in Camden, 1981, at Camden Arts Centre; and 10 London Printmakers, St Pancras Library, 1983. Took part in five-man exhibition at Ikon Gallery, Birmingham, 1983. Had a solo show at John Holt Gallery, 1978, later ones including ICA, 1983. British Council, Contemporary Art Society and other public collections hold examples. Lived in London.

Timothy Emlyn JONES 1948– Draughtsman, performance artist, producer of artist's books, art researcher and teacher, born in London, who also exhibited as Tim Jones. He was taught art by Eric Ford at Cheltenham Grammar School, 1964; did a foundation course under Michael Shinn and John Furnival at Gloucestershire College of Art, Cheltenham, 1965–6; attended Hornsey College of Art, being a member of the Art Student Action Committee which organised a six-week sit-in, also participating in performance art with Stuart Brisley, Ian Breakwell and Bruce Lacey, 1966–9; studied at Royal College of Art, his research degree investigating Anti-Logic and the Arts, supervised by Reg Gadney and Christopher Cornford, 1969–71; won a scholarship to Cité Internationale des Arts, Paris, 1971; and took a second research degree in art education at University of Wales, Cardiff, 1979–80. Jones taught in a number of art schools and universities, moving to Glasgow School of Art as deputy director in 1999. The catalogue of his solo show The Elements of Drawing, there and at Dundee Contemporary Arts, 2000–1, detailed Jones's career. He was a Chelsea Arts Club member. Government Art Collection; WAC; and Museum of the Book, The Hague, Netherlands, hold his work.

Trevor JONES 1945– Painter, printmaker and teacher who produced abstract works. He was born in Stourbridge, Worcestershire, attending the College of Art there, 1960–3; Birmingham College of Art, 1963–5; and Royal College of Art, 1965–8. Taught from 1974, including Birmingham Polytechnic, Camberwell School of Arts and Crafts and the London Institute, where he was senior lecturer in fine arts. Group exhibitions included RA student exhibition, 1967; New British Painting, ICA, 1969; and 1974 John Moores Liverpool Exhibition. Had a series of solo shows at New Art Centre from 1969 and an exhibition of prints and drawings at Cinema Gallery, Aldeburgh, for the Festival, 1990. Also showed on the continent and in America. Worked in London and Suffolk.

T M JONES: *see* **Tim JONES 1950–**

Wil JONES 1960– Versatile artist and teacher, who between 1978–84 graduated with honours in graphic design at Liverpool Polytechnic faculty of art and design and gained his postgraduate certificate in education. From 1984 he was head of the art department at Ysgol Dyffryn Nantlle, Penygroes. Group exhibitions included The Best of British Illustration, Mall Galleries, 1980; Royal National Eisteddfod of Wales, 1989; and The Garrick/Milne Prize, 2003, where his portrait of the actor Tom Courtenay was chosen for exhibition at Christie's. In 1988, Jones completed an open-air mural on several façades of Zahner, Mahler AG, a painting and decorating firm in Zürich, Switzerland; in 1993, he participated in the Gwerin-y-Graith project at Glynllifon with a big open-air mural; in 1995, Jones was commissioned by Welsh Independent Television to paint a portrait of the playwright W S Jones, later used for publicity during a national tour of his plays; and in 1997, the singer Bryn Terfel sat for a portrait, bought by Gwynedd Council, the National Library of Wales, Aberystwyth, buying Jones's portrait of the entertainer Richard Hughes.

Wilfred Emmanuel JONES 1890– Landscape painter in oil and printmaker. Brought up in Birkenhead, Cheshire, Jones taught himself to paint. He painted widely in England and showed at RA, RCamA, Walker Art Gallery, Liverpool, and RBA. Lived at Edgbaston, Birmingham, later in Broadstairs, Kent.

William Henry JONES 1900–1964 Sculptor, born in Menai Bridge, Anglesey. After leaving school aged 14 he served in Army in World War I, then was in Cardiganshire police for 18 years. In the early 1950s he opened Ye Olde Tea Gardens and Café at Menai Bridge, then from mid-1950s showed his cement sculptures there. Appeared in WAC 1972 exhibition An Alternative Tradition.

Wynn JONES 1939– Painter, draughtsman and teacher who was born in Wales, attending Cardiff College of Art, 1957–62, and was Jubilee Fellow at Byam Shaw School of Art in 1963. From the early 1970s he taught at Byam Shaw, from 1980 as senior tutor, and was a tutor at Royal College of Art, 1985–6. His work drew on diverse sources, ranging from cartoon strips to Picasso, sometimes commenting on the bizarre aspects of modern life. Mixed appearances included John Moores Liverpool Exhibition, 1995–6. Had a first solo exhibition at University of Wales in 1974, others being at House Gallery, 1978 and 1981, Artspace Gallery in Aberdeen, 1983, and Concourse Gallery, 1993. Arts Council holds his work. Lived in London.

Zebedee JONES 1970– Painter, born and based in London, who did a foundation course at Camberwell College of Art, 1988–9; gained an honours degree, Norwich School of Art, 1989–92; then a master's honours degree at Chelsea College of Art & Design, 1992–3. Took part in group show at Slade School of Fine Art, 1993; Affective Light at Rear Window, 1993–4; Unbound: Possibilities in Painting, Hayward Gallery, 1994; and Real Art, Southampton City Art Gallery, 1995. In that year had a solo exhibition at Karsten Schubert, with one at Waddington in 1997. In 2002 shared an exhibition at Houldsworth, monochromes ranging across a cool spectrum of blacks, greys and blues. All Jones's paintings were similarly made: thick layers of pigment being combed, scraped, scored, kneaded and ploughed through, in no particular order, horizontally or vertically, the excess left clinging to the sides of deep stretchers.

Wendy JONES-DABROWSKA 1941– Painter and lecturer, born in Kenton, Harrow, Middlesex, married to the artist Leszek Dabrowski. Figure work and angels were particular interests. Jones-Dabrowska attended Liverpool College of Art and St Martin's School of Art, teachers including Joe Tilson, Robert Clatworthy, Alan Cooper and Elisabeth Frink. On leaving St Martin's she worked for *Country Life* magazine, then lectured in art history and art and design at De Montford University. Founded a life class in Boston, Lincolnshire, near where she lived at Fishtoft. She showed in Lincolnshire group exhibitions and with The Association of Illustrators, of which she was a member.

Michelle JONES-HUGHES 1944– Painter, born in Deganwy, Caernarvonshire, married to the artist Selwyn Jones-Hughes. She studied at Liverpool College of Art and exhibited at Liverpool University, Liverpool People and Places, Royal National Eisteddfod and elsewhere. Gained a WAC Award, 1967. Was commissioned to paint a mural for George Rowney & Company, Bracknell.

Selwyn JONES-HUGHES 1943– Painter and teacher, born in Dolgellau, Merionethshire. He attended Liverpool College of Art, 1962–6, then Royal College of Art, 1966–9, going on to teach at St Helens School of Art. Completed a mural for George Rowney & Company in Bracknell as well as decorative work for the London store Harrods. Showed at WAC Celtic Triangle show in 1970, the 1974 An Iconograph of the *Mabinogion* exhibition of Royal National Eisteddfod/WAC, SWG and RA. Won Merseyside People and Places first prize in 1965 and several Manchester Academy open awards in 1970s and in 1986–7 was included in Walker Art Gallery, Liverpool, touring exhibition Merseyside Artists 3. Had a solo show at Prescote Gallery, Oxford. Lived for some years at Rainhill, Prescot, near Liverpool. He was married to the artist Michelle Jones-Hughes.

Madeleine de JONG 1958– Painter and draughtsman, born in Joure, Friesland, in the Netherlands, who went to school in Brussels, Belgium and studied graphic art at Atelier Met de Peninghem/École Supérieure d'Art Graphique, Paris, 1976. Lived and painted in Venice, 1979, spent another year in Paris in 1980, then settled in London. Cafés, bars and the circus were favourite subjects of de Jong's work, in which the influence of seventeenth-century Dutch genre painters was evident. She carried out a number of portrait commissions, including Viscount David Linley and Lady Florence Hardinge and had work in British and foreign collections. Among her exhibitions was Links of Affinity, Knapp Gallery, 1989.

Leonie JONLEIGH fl. from c.1950–1974 Painter in oil who studied privately with Carel Weight. Born in London. Exhibited RA, LG, RBA, RSA, SEA, Leicester Galleries, New Grafton Gallery and other venues. One-man show at Zwemmer Gallery, 1959. She was a member of the council of the RBA and directed and showed in exhibitions for the Guildford Festival of the Arts, 1969–71. She was interested in art and education, and her work was bought by both the London County Council and Hertfordshire education committees. Lived at Wonersh, Guildford, Surrey, where the Leonie Jonleigh Studio and Jonleigh Gallery were both established.

Basil JONZEN 1913–1967 Painter of landscapes, flowers and portraits, and art dealer. He studied with Bernard Meninsky at the Central School of Arts and Crafts. Showed very successfully with Redfern Gallery, which sent him to Spain, France and the Canary Islands to paint. Also exhibited at NEAC, Tooth and RBA. During World War II Jonzen was involved in camouflage, service including Norway and Nigeria, lecturing on it in Edinburgh. Married the sculptor Karin Jonzen, as she became known, their son being the artist Martin Jonzen. After the war they renovated Sir Hugh Lane's studio house in London's South Bolton Gardens and ran a Weekend Art Gallery there, which attracted many distinguished clients. Later, Basil Jonzen was involved in the St George's Gallery. Arts Council holds his work.

Karin JONZEN 1914–1998 Sculptor and teacher, born in London of Swedish parents, and continued to live there. Her husband was the artist and dealer Basil Jonzen, and their son the artist Martin Jonzen, and after Basil's death she married the Swedish poet Åke (pronounced Orker) Sucksdorff, whom she had met in the late-1920s. She studied at the Slade School of Fine Art, 1933–6, winning both painting and sculpture prizes; gained a scholarship in 1936 for a fourth year, and attended the City and Guilds Art School, Kennington; also studying at the Royal Academy in Stockholm. In 1939 won the Prix de Rome, but war – during which she served as an ambulance driver – prevented her from going to Italy. After the war Jonzen was elected a fellow of RBS and won the Feodora Gleichen Memorial Fund award as well as a series of international gold and silver medals. She lectured at Camden Arts Centre and in art appreciation at London University extra-mural classes. Took part in Battersea Park open-air sculpture exhibitions. LG member who showed at RA, Wildenstein, Agnew and Roland, Browse & Delbanco. Among her portraits were the writer Sir Alan Herbert, the architect Sir Hugh Casson and the ballerina Dame Ninette de Valois. Jonzen completed a large number of public commissions including the bronze group Beyond Tomorrow, at Barbican Centre, a bronze torso for the World Health Organization building in Geneva and a Madonna and Child for St Mary-le-Bow Church. Tate Gallery, provincial and foreign collections hold Jonzen's work. Nude terracotta examples of her work in Eric Newton's monograph *British Sculpture 1944–1946* were typical.

Ann JOPE 1945– Painter and printmaker, born in Corfe Mullen, Dorset, who grew up in south Devon. She studied at Ealing School of Art, 1966–7; Central School of Art and Design, 1967–70, gaining an honours degree in painting; then did a postgraduate printmaking diploma at the Central, 1980–2. Jope was made a fellow of RE in 1984, was an artist member of Printmakers' Council of Great Britain and of Oxford Art Society. She gave a number of demonstrations, lectured occasionally including Farnham College of Art and West Dean College, and made several television appearances. In 1986 she was artist-in-residence at King Henry VIII School, Abergavenny. Illustrations included the Folio Society Shakespeare, *King John* and *Much Ado About Nothing*; Julian Barnard's *The Song of the Reeds*; and Leslie Norris' *Ransoms*, for Gregynog Poets. Jope's numerous group appearances included RA, RBA, British Crafts Fair, St David's Hall in Cardiff and Morley Gallery. She had a solo exhibition at 5 Dryden Street Gallery in 1976, later ones including Ashridge Management College, 1990, and West Dean, 1991. Lived at Hardwick, Witney, Oxfordshire.

Janet JORDAN fl. from 1960s– Painter and teacher who studied at Sutton Art School and Central School of Arts and Crafts, concentrating on theatre design. She taught at an independent school in Gloucestershire for 21 years at secondary level, also teaching art-related subjects to teachers in training. Jordan was especially interested in the Goethe Theory of Colour and the use of watercolour. Mixed exhibitions included Long Street Gallery in Tetbury and Patricia Wells Gallery, Thornbury, and she had a solo show at Parnham House, Beaminster, in 1985. Was commissioned to paint five pictures of cooling towers for Central Electricity Generating Board's headquarters in Gloucester. Lived in Brookthorpe, Gloucestershire.

Joan JORDAN 1923– Painter, miniaturist and teacher, born in Heckingham, Norfolk. After private education Jordan studied at Tasmanian School of Art, 1966–8. She went on to teach further education classes, was a member of UA and president of the Pastel Society of Western Australia. She showed at Mall Galleries, Royal Exchange and elsewhere in mixed exhibitions and had a number of solo shows. Lived latterly at Duncraig, Perth, Western Australia.

Zee JORDAN 1952– Artist in various media, including collage, born in Manchester, where she lived. She studied at Ashton-under-Lyne College of Art, 1970–3, with Bill Clark and at Manchester Polytechnic, foundation, 1989, gaining an honours degree in fine art from Manchester Metropolitan University, 1991–4. Exhibited Cheltenham Artists, Town Hall, Cheltenham, 1977; Women's Week, Feminist Art Show, Manchester, 1982; Bury Open Exhibition, Bury Art Gallery, 1985; Laing Landscape Competition, Tib Lane Gallery, Manchester, 1987; RA Summer Exhibition, 1990; Town Hall, Manchester, 1991; Colin Jellicoe Gallery, Manchester, from 1989; The Gallery,

Richmond, Surrey, 1998; Riverside Arts Centre, Sunbury, 2000; Paperchase, Manchester, 2001; and Creative Consultants Gallery, Manchester, 2002. Private collections in Britain and abroad hold examples. Jordan's work strongly emphasised colour and decoration, the human figure and cultural symbols being notable features. She wished "to bring solace through art".

Alex JORGENSEN 1967– Artist producing gestural abstract pictures, born in London, who studied at Bath Academy of Art, 1985–6, gaining a first-class honours degree, Brighton Polytechnic, 1986–9. Won a Daler-Rowney/British Rail Mural Award, 1986; Annabel Birtles Scholarship Award and Academie St Joost, Breda, Netherlands Award, both 1988; and Anstruther Literary Trust Award, 1998. Exhibitions included 10th Mini Print International, Cadaques, Spain, and tour, and RP Open, Bankside Gallery, both 1990; 9th Portobello Open, Tabernacle Gallery, 1992; Beatrice Royal Gallery, Eastleigh, and Vena Bunker Gallery, Bristol, both from 1993; Mistral Gallery, 1995; and Moreton Street Gallery, 2000. Jorgensen shared a show with Mike Dodd at Bough & Lime, Bath, 1996.

Amy JOSEPH 1876–1961 Painter in watercolour, especially of townscapes. Studied at the Slade School of Fine Art under Henry Tonks, Fred Brown and A W Rich. Exhibited widely, including RA, NEAC, Goupil Gallery, RBA, SWA, RSA and RI. Lived in London.

Andrew JOSEPH 1963– Painter and teacher whose output included enigmatic, small, figurative pictures such as Two, at Royal Over-Seas League Open, 1994. He was born in Bristol and studied at Bournemouth College of Art; Bath Academy of Art in Corsham; and London University's Institute of Education. He was assistant to the artist Stefan Knapp, 1985. Later taught art at Rokeby School, Stratford. Participated in Whitechapel Open Studios from 1986.

Jane JOSEPH 1942– Draughtsman, painter in watercolour and oil and etcher, born in Surrey. She studied at Camberwell School of Arts and Crafts, 1961–5, teachers including Robert Medley, Frank Auerbach, Euan Uglow, Frank Bowling and R B Kitaj. She won a Leverhulme Travelling Award, Europe, 1965–6; travelled in America, 1968; gained an Abbey Award in Painting, working at the British School at Rome, and elsewhere in Italy, 1991; and continued with a further Abbey Award in 1995. Took part in extensive group exhibitions, including SWG from 1971; LG from 1982; Small is Beautiful, Angela Flowers Gallery, from 1983; Beardsmore Gallery, from 1992; and Marking Presence, ArtSway, Sway, 1997. Had a solo show at Morley Gallery, 1973, with a retrospective of drawings and prints, 1980–97, there in 1997. This exemplified Joseph's traditional manner of working from direct observation on site, images being worked up on a larger scale in the studio. Urban locations and the river (her studio was near the Thames) were important. Victoria Art Gallery, Bath, showed her etchings, 1985–2001, in 2002. WAC, Government Art Collection, British Museum and Ben Uri Art Society held examples.

Peter JOSEPH 1929– Painter and teacher, born in London, where he continued to work. Self-taught, Joseph taught at Portsmouth College of Art 1969–72. He was awarded a prize at John Moores Exhibition, Liverpool, 1979. Joseph was included in many group shows in Britain, including 1969 environmental work Triple Yellow at Kenwood and the 1970 Yellow Wall at Camden Arts Centre. In 1988 Joseph's geometrical abstract acrylic Eggshell Blue and Black was included in A Disquieting Suggestion at the University of Southampton's John Hansard Gallery, and in 1988–9 he was in the South Bank Centre touring show The Presence of Painting. Joseph exhibited solo at Lisson Gallery from 1971, other shows including Galerie Meert Rihoux, Brussels, 1993, and Paintings and works on paper, Museum of Modern Art, Oxford, 1994. Tate Gallery, Victoria & Albert Museum, Arts Council and important foreign collections hold examples. Lived in Gloucestershire and worked in London.

Laurence JOSEPHS 1913–1998 Sculptor in wood, engraver and painter, and teacher, born and lived in London, his parents Russian-Jewish immigrants. Studied at St Martin's School of Art, 1932–5; in the studio of Leon Underwood; learned drawing with R V Pitchforth; and worked as assistant to Underwood in his Brook Green School. Taught in secondary schools for 25 years and "lectured on art theory, when it was possible to do so". Josephs' work was generally figurative, "concerned with truth to material in sculpture". He was a member of the group involved in the short-lived publication *The Island*, conceived in 1931, and of Ben Uri Art Society, 1945–9, being on the committee of its gallery. Showed at many galleries including Ben Uri, and had solo exhibitions at Queenswood Gallery, 1952–3, and October Gallery, 1989 and 1993. Leeds Museums and Galleries hold sculpture and archive material.

Lawrence JOSSET 1910–1995 Versatile printmaker, born in Croydon, Cambridgeshire. He attended Bromley and Beckenham Schools of Art, 1930–1; was with Waterlow's, 1930–1, working on banknotes and other productions; then studied at Royal College of Art, 1932–5, with Malcolm Osborne and Robert Austin. In 1932–3 Josset was art master at Red Hill School. Josset was a member of RE, 1951, and Art Workers' Guild. He also showed with RA and had prints published by Thomas Ross of Binfield. Josset produced mezzotints after such artists as Boucher and Fragonard as well as sporting prints. He considered "subject matter all-important". He lived at Detling, Maidstone, Kent.

Percy Hague JOWETT 1882–1955 Painter, especially of landscapes in watercolour, and teacher, who in 1912 married Enid Ledward, sister of Gilbert Ledward the sculptor. He was born in Halifax, Yorkshire, and studied at Leeds and Royal Colleges of Art, latterly under Gerald Moira, winning the Prix de Rome which took him to Italy. he taught first at Beckenham School of Art and after World War I service in the Army returned there. He was also principal at Chelsea, the Central School of Arts and Crafts, 1930–5, then the Royal College of Art, 1935–48, where he was influential, making shrewd appointments such as Henry Moore and Gilbert Spencer. Exhibited at RA, RWS, NEAC, Redfern Gallery, Fine Art Society and had a series of solo shows at St George's Gallery in the 1920s. His work is in many British and overseas galleries. Jowett's watercolour Boats, illustrated in Percy V Bradshaw's book *Watercolour*, is typical of the artist's loose and fresh style. Lived in London. Michael Parkin Gallery had a show of his work in 1995.

John JOWITT 1904–1996 Painter in oil and watercolour and teacher, born in Leeds, Yorkshire. After Uppingham

School he attended Yeovil Art School, 1935–9, under George Mitchell. He "taught at five art classes, three of which were further education classes." Although he painted landscapes his main work was portraits. Jowitt was exhibited at RA Summer Exhibition and ran his own Jowitt Art Group. Lived at Chideock, Bridport, Dorset.

John Wilson JOWSEY 1884–1963 Painter who exhibited at the RBA, RCamA and elsewhere. He was based in the capital and his atmospheric oil on canvas Battersea Power Station was included in Views of London, offered at Bonhams, Knightsbridge, in 2006.

Clair JOY 1958– Artist, born in Vancouver, British Columbia, Canada, who attended St Martin's School of Art, 1977–81, and Goldsmiths' College, 1984–6, eventually settling in New York in America. Group shows included A Critic's Choice at the Air Gallery, and Unheard Music at Stoke-on-Trent City Museum and Art Gallery, both 1986; Ten Years, Nicola Jacobs Gallery, 1989; and PSI Gallery in New York, Venice Biennale (Aperto Section) and Decoy, at the Serpentine Gallery, all 1990. The Decoy catalogue said that her landscapes were "appropriated from glossy tourist postcards." Interim Art gave Joy a solo show in 1987 and Nicola Jacobs and the Cornerhouse, Manchester, others in 1988. She had work acquired by Leicester Education Authority and the Arts Council.

Steve JOY 1952– Painter, born in Plymouth, Devon. After service in Royal Air Force, 1968–75, studied at Cardiff College of Art, 1975–6, Exeter College of Art, 1976–9, and Chelsea School of Art, 1979–80. Painting fellowships held included Gloucester College of Art and one sponsored by the Japanese government at Kyoto University of Arts. His work included geometrical abstract works, although Joy said that he was "indifferent to any distinction between abstraction and representation". He wanted his works "to act as triggers to stimulate the mind of the spectator into moving onto a different level". Group shows included Spacex Gallery, Exeter, 1979; Theatre Zuidplein, Rotterdam, 1980; and Serpentine Gallery Summer Show 1, 1981. Had a solo show at Riverside Studios, 1978. Lived for a time at Chalford, Gloucestershire.

Henry Stanley JOYCE 1882–1961 Artist mainly in watercolour and pen and ink, lecturer and teacher, born at White Mill, Wimborne, Dorset, a National Trust property open to the public since 1995. Joyce was educated at Wimborne grammar school and developed a special interest in natural history. He was prolific, work being reproduced in many publications such as *The Field* and *Country Life*. His illustrated books include *I Was Born in the Country* and *Holidays with a Rod*. Birds were Joyce's favourite subjects, but he lectured on all aspects of plant and animal life, using his own detailed works as illustrations, many now held in Bristol University library. During retirement, he taught art for several years at Belmont College, Barnstaple, showing regularly at Burton Gallery, Bideford. Throughout his life, Joyce worked on an unpublished, three-volume collection of British wild flower studies. Died at home in a wooded valley near Barnstaple, Devon.

Mark JOYCE 1966– Painter, born in Dublin, Ireland. He studied at National College of Art and Design in Dublin from 1984, gaining a first-class honours degree in fine art, then his master's degree at Royal College of Art, 1991–3. Among his awards were a British Council Scholarship and Arts Council Postgraduate Award, 1991. Joyce was a member of Artists' Association of Ireland. His exhibitions included Limerick Soviet, Limerick City Gallery, 1989; GPA Emerging Artists Show, 1990, where he gained an award; Riverside Studios, 1992; and Europaprijs 93, Ostende, 1993.

Peter JOYCE 1964– Painter and teacher, born in Poole, Dorset. Joyce studied at Bournemouth and Poole College of Art and Design, 1980–2, then Stourbridge College of Art, 1982–5. He lectured at both. Was involved in film-making involving several notable artists, including Gillian Ayres, Elisabeth Frink and Henry Mundy, and was himself the subject of a film by Grove Films. Joyce was notable for his coastal paintings tending towards abstraction, rather in the manner of St Ives artists, with black, grey and white much in evidence. Showed from 1987 with RWA, also at Poole Art Centre and Anthony Hepworth Fine Art, Bath, where he had a solo show in 1992. Lived in Wimborne, Dorset.

Stephen JOYCE 1956– Bristol-based sculptor and teacher whose realistic and characterful sculptures enhance many streets of the city, examples being his 1984 Horse and Man, at Brunel House, St George's Road; 1985 St Odilia and the Bird, at Bristol Eye Hospital; and the 1986 John Cabot, outside the Arnolfini arts centre. Joyce studied at what is now the University of the West of England, 1976–9. He became visiting arts lecturer at Bath Spa University and fellow of the RBS.

Elsbeth JUDA 1911– Artist, photographer, teacher and collector of contemporary art, born in Darmstadt, Germany. She went to live and work in Paris, 1929; in 1931 married Hans Juda, financial editor of *Berliner Tageblatt*, and moved to Berlin; in 1933 settled in London and studied photography with Lucia Moholy, of the Bauhaus, and became a fashion photographer, working as Jay. As associate editor and photographer for *Ambassador Magazine*, founded by Hans Juda, she travelled the world. In 1963 set up a design studio to teach industry practice to graduates. Her private work included paintings, murals and witty collages, a large show of which was given at England & Co, 1994, touring to Germany. The Fine Art Society held Homage to Elsbeth Juda: Photographs and collages in 2003. Elsbeth Juda's *Ambassador* archive is held by the Victoria & Albert Museum.

Gerry JUDAH 1951– Sculptor, born in Calcutta, India, who studied at Goldsmiths' College School of Art and Slade School of Fine Art. In 1978 took part in 3 Garden Exhibitions at Camden Arts Centre. In 1990 conceived a huge sculpture, dedicated to human rights, which comprised a pair of wooden wings supported on an inclined column, and inset with rows of niches, each containing fibre-optic candles that would have glowed in the wind. It was destined for Potters Fields Park, on the south bank of the River Thames, opposite the Tower of London. Despite heavy support it was refused planning permission by the then environment secretary, John Gummer.

James JUDGE 1958– Gestural painter, draughtsman and etcher born in London, who studied drawing/painting at Frobisher Institute and drawing/etching at Morley College, both 1974–82, and at Byam Shaw School of Art,

1982–5. In 1985, Judge was winner of the RA's Richard Ford Award, with a travelling scholarship to the Prado, Madrid. Group shows included South London Art Gallery, from 1986; RWS and RBA, both Mall Galleries, 1991; Beecroft Gallery, Westcliff-on-Sea, 1993; and Adam Gallery, The Gallery in Cork Street, 1998. Had a solo exhibitions, The Studio Gallery, 1998, and Adam Gallery, Bath, 2000.

Mila JUDGE-FÜRSTOVÁ 1975– Printmaker and teacher, born in Pelhrimhov, Czechoslovakia, whose work "articulates the contents of the subconscious mind.... It reflects my deep interest in dreams, mythology, tales and fables, and touches on notions of cultural identity." Like the Surrealists, she sought "the miraculous in everyday things and situations". She studied at the College of Applied Art, Prague, 1989–93; at Charles University, Prague, for her master's, 1993–00; gained an honours degree in fine art printmaking at Cheltenham and Gloucester College of Higher Education, 1996–9; then obtained her master's in fine art and printmaking, Royal College of Art, 1999–01. Won a series of awards, held several provincial visiting lectureships and was research fellow in printmaking at the University of Gloucestershire, 2001. Group shows included Hot off the Press, Curwen Gallery, and a three-artist exhibition at England & Co, both 2002. She had a solo show at IPB Bank, Hradec Králové, Czech Republic, in 1999.

Rod JUDKINS 1956– Figurative artist, born in England, who studied at Bath Academy of Art, Corsham, 1976–7, Maidstone College of Art, 1977–80, and Royal College of Art, 1980–3. In 1981 he won the Wilfrid Sirrell Award, in 1982 the Herbert Read DRU Award and in 1983 the Sioux River Annual. Took part in many group shows, including Imperial Tobacco at National Portrait Gallery and Spirit of London, Greater London Council, both 1981; The Music Show, Thumb Gallery, 1983; The Self Portrait – A Modern View, Artsite Gallery, Bath, from 1987, and tour; RA Summer Exhibition, 1991; and Art94 (Jill George Gallery), Islington, 1994. Showed solo at Thumb Gallery from 1983, at Jill George from 1991, and "surreal" paintings at The Bruton Street Gallery in 2003. Public and private collections hold examples. Lived in London.

Mike JUGGINS 1966– Artist, film-maker, community artist and dyslexia adviser, born in Sutton Benger, Wiltshire, a member of the Arts Dyslexia Trust who was himself dyslexic. "I believe that image and words mutually advance understanding." Juggins was a Royal Mail postman, 1984–6; a senior care officer, Learning Disabilities Service, 1986–94; service manager, Homeless Advice Centre, 1994–5; studied at the University of the West of England, in Bristol, 1995–9; was officer-in-charge with a youth offending team, 1999–01; a part-time freelance dyslexia adviser and community artist, 1999–01; and from 2001–4 was, voluntarily, creative adviser to Elk Inspiring People, an art and disability charity, and artist-in-residence, at The Headlands School, Swindon, while being based in Marlborough, Wiltshire. Picasso, Matisse and David Hockney influenced Juggins' vibrant oil paintings. These were given a solo show at Diorama Arts Centre in 2005, previous one-mans having been at Swindon Arts Centre, 1999, and the University of Bath, 2000.

Betty JUKES 1910– Sculptor in various materials and teacher, born in Shillong, Assam, India, educated in London. She studied at Royal College of Art, 1928–32, teachers including Henry Moore, Herbert Palliser and Richard Garbe. She qualified as a state registered nurse in 1945 at St Bartholomew's Hospital, then taught sculpture at Sir John Cass School of Art and City of London Polytechnic, 1946–75. Showed at RA and elsewhere. Jukes was a fellow of RBS from 1948 and a member of the SPS. Lived in London.

Heidi JUKES 1963– After in 1985 exhibiting in the Tyne Tees Northern Open at Laing Gallery, Newcastle upon Tyne, and in Northern Young Contemporaries, at Whitworth Art Gallery, Manchester, Jukes gained her master's degree from Chelsea School of Art, 1985–6. Other group exhibitions included Leicestershire Collection and Exhibition and LG Exhibition at Henry Moore Gallery, both 1987, and East End Open Studios, based at Vyner Street Studios, 1989. Jukes had a solo show at Diorama Gallery in 1988.

Philippe JULLIAN 1920–1977 Writer, illustrator and painter, born in Bordeaux, France. Jullian was a prolific and versatile writer, occasionally controversial, as in the *Dictionnaire du snobisme*, 1958. That and other works were widely translated into English and covered French and English subjects. As an illustrator, he illustrated his own and others' books. His novels, such as *Café Society*, 1962, describe with much humour the international set he frequented assiduously. He was also author of a Proustian reconstruction, *Gilberte Regained*, 1957. Among his best-known works were biographies of Robert de Montesquiou, 1967, Oscar Wilde, 1968, and D'Annunzio, 1971. His important study of the Symbolist painters of the 1890s, *Esthètes et Magiciens*, 1969, was followed by *The Triumph of Art Nouveau: the Paris Exhibition 1900*, 1974, and in 1976 a study of the life and letters of Violet Trefusis, one of the daughters of the Edward VII mistress Mrs Keppel, whose friendship Jullian long enjoyed. Jullian's rococo paintings had a wide reputation in Paris and London. He was particularly successful at evoking exotic landscapes and the elaborate salons of French and English society. A show of his Mexican landscapes was held at Trafford Gallery, 1958. Abbott and Holder latterly offered Jullian's work.

Alexandra JULYAN 1962– Versatile artist, illustrator and teacher who did a foundation course at Chelsea School of Art, 1980–1; graduated with honours there in fine art, 1981–4; did workshop training at Whitechapel Art Gallery, 1995; then Get Art! Special Needs training at Chisenhale Gallery, 1999. Awards included Kensington & Chelsea Arts Council Award, 1996, and George Butterworth/SPNM Award, 1999. Teaching included Winchester School of Art; North East London University; Barbican Centre, Whitechapel, Serpentine and National Portrait Galleries; Science Museum; and Uttar Pradesh, India. Backdrops and sets included Frankfurt Music Messe, Germany; BBC Television; and MTV Advertising. Julyan also carried out extensive illustration, including *Sunday Telegraph Magazine*, *BBC Good Food Magazine*, *Radio Times*; Royal Mail; and for the American Discovery Channel. Among public art and interior work venues were Thomas Tallis and Forster Park Primary Schools and Greenwich District and Southampton General Hospitals. Took part widely in group shows, including Whitechapel Open, RA Summer Exhibition and in ART2000–1–2, at Business Design Centre, with England & Co. Made in England – Sculptures by Alexandra Julyan, took place at Shire Hall Gallery, Stafford, 2002.

Mary Victoria JUMP 1897–1989 Watercolourist, brought up in the Liverpool area where she attended the School of Art, also Birkenhead School of Art and obtained City and Guilds Technological Certificate. She settled at Bebington, Wirral, Merseyside and exhibited with the main local public galleries and RCamA and was a member of Wirral Society of Art and Wirral Craft Exhibiting Society.

JUNEAU/PROJECTS/ This was the name created in 1999 by Philip Duckworth and Ben Sadler (see separate entries) when working together for certain exhibitions. These included Grizedale Live, Grizedale Arts and East Of Eden, Spacex, Exeter, 2001; Mostyn 12, Oriel Mostyn in Llandudno, Broad Casts at Cubitt Gallery and Landmarks at Brewhouse, Taunton, all 2002; Crowford Open 03 at Cork, Ireland, and Chockerfuckingblocked, Jeffrey Charles Gallery, both 2003; and motherf**king nature, The Showroom, 2004. At that, video and sound pieces formed part of a larger installation, each work surrounded by the ephemera resulting from its production. "Mapped out like a road trip, the duo will take us to the rural settings of their performance-based works and introduce us to the cast of characters that they have encountered."

Hannaford JUNIOR: *see* **Charles Arthur HANNAFORD**

Brigitte JURACK 1962– Sculptor born in Düsseldorf, West Germany. She studied at Kunstakademie Düsseldorf, 1982–8; Glasgow School of Art, 1989–90; and Chelsea College of Art and Design, 1990–91. In 1992 was Henry Moore Sculpture Fellow. Took part in East at Norwich Gallery, 1991, and had show at Winchester Gallery, Hampshire, 1993. Lived in London.

Alun JURY 1967– Artist born in Wales who studied foundation at Cardiff Institute of Art and Design, 1987–8, graduating in fine art from Cheltenham School of Art, 1989–92. He showed work with the Treadwell Gallery, based in Aigen, Austria. On its website, Jury explained that "My ideas initially developed from a concern with childhood, ideas of innocence, the importance of the past and how certain events continue to affect and influence us. I continue to explore these themes in my recent works whilst exploring our relationship with animals."

Anne Primrose JURY 1907–1995 Painter, born in Dunmurry, near Belfast, Northern Ireland, her father an architect. She studied at Belfast School of Art, in England and on the continent. Was elected RUA, showed at RHA, in London and Edinburgh and had solo exhibitions at Magee's and Rodman's Galleries in Belfast and with Victor Waddington, Dublin. Limerick Municipal Art Gallery holds her work.

JUSTICE: *see* **Terry SCALES**

Ryszard JUSZCZAK 1942– Artist and priest, born in Poznachowice Gorne, Poland, who completed his studies at the Papal Academy of Theology, Cracow, in 1966. The Reverend Juszczak moved to England in 1976. From 1972–5 he took private lessons with Dana Aldea. He participated in group exhibitions of the Association of Polish Artists in Great Britain and was included in Form and Colour, Congress of Polish Culture Exhibition of Fine Arts by Polish Artists in Great Britain, at POSK in 1995. He had a solo show there in 1988.

K

Roman KABAROWSKI 1961– Artist and teacher, born in Rugby, Warwickshire. He studied art at Norwich School of Art and Goldsmiths' College. Took part in the Essex Open Exhibition and in Form and Colour, Congress of Polish Culture Exhibition of Fine Arts by Polish Artists in Britain, POSK, 1995. Lived in Leigh-on-Sea, Essex.

Norman KADISH 1916–1988 Painter, draughtsman and teacher who was born in London. He had a special interest in portraiture and illustrative art, favouring strong colour. Kadish studied at Regent Street Polytechnic School of Art, 1936–40, interrupted by war service, 1940–6; then in 1946–7 gained his art teaching diploma at London University's Institute of Education. Taught art at school and adult education level. Became a member of Hesketh Hubbard and Ben Uri Art Societies and showed at RA, RSMA, UA and elsewhere, having solo exhibitions at Burgh House, Hampstead, 1984, and Ruislip Library, 1988. Main works included The Lambeth Walk and Belshazzar's Feast. Lived in Edgware, Middlesex.

Menasche KADISHMAN 1932– Sculptor, creator of abstract stone compositions, born in Israel. He studied under R Lehmann in Jerusalem, then from late 1950s at St Martin's School of Art. He showed in Ten Years of Sculpture at Israel Museum, Tel-Aviv, 1958; with Young Contemporaries and LG, 1959–61; in France and Italy in 1961; and in 1965 in Fifty Years of Sculpture at Grosvenor Gallery and in The Visual Arts, at Harlow Arts Festival.

Erich KAHN 1904–1980 Painter, draughtsman and printmaker, born in Stuttgart, Germany. Studied at the State School for Arts and Crafts, 1922–5, in 1926 working with Fernand Léger in Paris. Arrived in England in 1939, shortly after release from Nazi concentration camp. Was interned in Isle of Man in World War II, but went on working in the Expressionist style to which he remained faithful. Settled in London, living in poverty, his life being eased by the arrangement of a pension and marriage. In the 1920s and 1930s Kahn had showed in Stuttgart and Berlin, and although he did exhibit in Paris, Bruges and other continental capitals after World War II, he showed mainly in London, in group shows at Leger and Whitechapel Art Galleries and elsewhere. Redfern, Drian and Molton Galleries gave him solo exhibitions in the 1950s and 1960s and John Denham Gallery gave him a retrospective in 1980. Kahn was a serious, retiring man, a prolific artist whose works are held by the Tate Gallery and Tel-Aviv Museum, Israel.

Andras KALDOR 1938– Artist who made a unique contribution to the depiction of buildings in several continents. Kaldor was born in Budapest, Hungary, from 1952–6 educated at the Petőfi Sándor Gimnázium there. In 1956 he left Hungary, from 1957–60 studying architecture in Edinburgh and Glasgow. Between 1960–80 Kaldor was in architectural practice in London and Yorkshire, painting and sculpting in his spare time, then in 1981 he gave up full-time architecture to concentrate on painting, opening the Andras Kaldor Gallery in Dartmouth, Devon, where he remained based. He had a first solo show in 1983 at Galerie Cabaret, Villefranche-sur-mer, France, and he also took part in group exhibitions at the Century Gallery, Henley-on-Thames, Compton Gallery, Windsor; Robert Alvares Galerie, Cannes; and Lymington Gallery, Lymington, a limited-edition silkscreen print series being published by London Contemporary Art. In 1986, with five others, he founded the Dartmouth Artists Group, regularly showing in their own galleries and elsewhere. Other highlights of Kaldor's versatile career included a commission by British Airways to paint 12 buildings, forming the Regent Street Collection of prints, 1989; Opera Houses of Europe at Coe Kerr Gallery, New York, and Les Opera de L'Europa at Galerie Gasnier Camien, Paris, both 1990; a portfolio of London buildings prints, published by The Art Group, also cards and other printed matter for the Tower of London and Hampton Court Palace, 1991; a commission to paint Chateau Leveville, Chartres, and Chateau at Petite Thouars sur Vienne, 1992; a large mural for Fingals Hotel, Dittisham, and printed matter for the Guggenheim Museum, New York, 1993; a commission to paint famous buildings in the borough for Southwark Council, 1995; publication of his book *Opera Houses of Europe*, with a show of the original paintings at Gallery 19, 1996; exhibitions at Operaház, Budapest, and at Glyndebourne Festival Opera, 1997; a show of opera houses at Lincoln Center, New York, 1998; publication of *New York, Masterpieces of Architecture*, 1999; and of *Berlin, Masterpieces of Architecture*, 2002.

Mariusz KALDOWSKI 1962– Artist, born in Chelmno, Poland, who studied in the art and graphic design faculty of the Academy of Fine Art, Cracow, with Zbyslaw Maciejewski, 1982–7, gaining his master's in book design and woodcut. Kaldowski wrote that his work was "deeply rooted in the human experience." He was a member of the Association of Polish Artists in Great Britain and showed widely in group/mixed exhibitions, including VI Confrontation, MDK, Myslienice, 1988; New Paintings from Russia and Eastern Europe, Alberti Gallery, 1998; Lewes Townscapes, Lewes Gallery, 2000; Christmas Exhibition, The Albany Gallery, Cardiff, 2001; and FHP Art Exhibition, The Orangery, Holland Park, 2002. By 2004 he had had over 40 solo shows, later ones including See You Tomorrow, Sussex Arts Club, Brighton, 2000; Four Seasons, Plas Glyn-y-Weddw Gallery, Pwllheli, 2001; Regent's Park Today, Open Air Theatre, Regent's Park, 2003; and a retrospective at POSK, 2004. Kaldowski completed many varied commissions, including a monumental mural in the Sierakowice church, paintings for the Museum in Chelmno, interior and exterior design for the City Culture Centre, Lobzenica, and portraits of public figures. He initially visited Britain in 1994 at the invitation of the headmaster of Downside School, for whom he painted two portraits. In 1995 he was employed by the television channel Wisla as head of design; in 1996 completed work on Velis Passis, a cycle featuring 30 famous Poles; in 1997, finished a gigantic Angel for the papal visit to Poland; in 1998 in London, where he settled, completed 40 portraits of Polish war veterans in exile; in 2000, was commissioned to paint six of the finest gardens in Wales; and in 2002 was invited to begin a long-running series interpreting the landscape of Regent's Park. Regent's Park Close Up was a show at the Atkinson Studios by the Open Air Theatre there in 2005. His huge frieze The Four Seasons – Four Stages of Life, inspired by the composer Vivaldi's work, followed "many years of planning and experience." Public and corporate collections in Poland hold his work.

Eugeniusz KALINIEWICZ 1938– Artist, born in Gdynia, Poland, whose first art tuition was at home. He then studied in Andalusia, Spain, under U Prazeres. From the mid-1980s, Kaliniewicz painted in Spain, France, Portugal and West Africa. He participated in Form and Colour, Congress of Polish Culture Exhibition of Fine Arts by Polish Artists in Britain, POSK, 1995. Among his solo shows was one at the Business Centre, Kilburn.

Peter KALKHOF 1933– Painter and teacher, born in Stassfurt, Germany, working in acrylic on canvas, hardboard, paper and plywood. He attended an evening class at School of Arts & Crafts, Braunschweig, 1952–5; was at Academy of Fine Arts, Stuttgart, 1956–60; did a postgraduate course at Slade School of Fine Art, 1960–1; then was at École des Beaux-Arts, Paris, 1962. Went on to teach at Reading University. Kalkhof said that his main concern was "the abstract phenomena of colour and space". Ancient cities, museums and nature with its climates and seasons were of key importance. In 1987 Kalkhof was commissioned to carry out a mural for the Treaty Centre, Hounslow, for Taylor Woodrow Group. Kalkhof's many mixed exhibitions included Galerie am Bohlweg, Braunschweig, 1962; University of East Anglia, Norwich, 1971; Towner Art Gallery, Eastbourne, 1972; British Painting '74, Hayward Gallery, 1974; Camden Arts Centre, 1981; and The Seventies, Brixton Art Gallery, 1985. He had a solo exhibition at Galerie in der Garage, Stuttgart, 1964, then showed often with Annely Juda Fine Art from 1970. There was a 25-year retrospective at Landesmuseum Oldenburg, Germany, in 1988. Arts Council and other public collections in Britain and abroad hold examples.

Marion KALMUS 1963– Sculptor who graduated from Goldsmiths' College in 1994. She was awarded a Kettle's Yard Artist Fellowship in 1997–8. She was awarded commissions for Tate Liverpool and the Royal Festival Hall. In 2001 her permanent outdoor sculpture for the National Botanic Garden of Wales was opened and she was shortlisted for the first Jerwood Sculpture Prize. Kalmus's sculpture was commonly site-specific. She regarded her work on the Botanic Garden gatehouse as a "physical part of the building, an architectural intervention"; made of glass with an aluminium support, it made "the centre of the gatehouse look as if it is filled with running water and light." Her proposed monumental stone piece for the Jerwood Sculpture Park, Witley Court, "couldn't possibly be sited anywhere else."

Panayiotis KALORKOTI 1957– Artist and teacher, born in Ayios Amvrossios, Cyprus, who moved to England aged nine. He was noted for his wry and satirical coloured etchings, which employed a firm graphic line, areas of unusually subtle flat or patterned colour and a wide range of subjects. Images were meticulously constructed. Kalorkoti gained a first-class honours degree from Newcastle upon Tyne University, 1976–80, completing a master's degree in printmaking at Royal College of Art, 1982–5. As well as being a part-time visiting lecturer at a number of art schools, Kalorkoti was artist-in-residence at Leeds Playhouse, 1985; won a Netherlands Government Scholarship, 1986–7; was Bartlett Fellow in the Visual Arts at Newcastle, 1988; and artist-in-residence for Cleveland County, 1992. Commissions included Imperial War Museum, 1988; Boroughs of Darlington and Hartlepool, both 1989; and National Garden Festival, Gateshead, 1990. Took part in many group exhibitions, winning the Granada Prize at Northern Young Contemporaries, Whitworth Art Gallery, Manchester, 1983. His solo shows included Imperial War Museum and National Garden Festival, both 1990; Design Works, Gateshead, 1992; Gallery in the Forest, Grizedale, 1995, Shipley Art Gallery, Gateshead, and tour, 1998–9, and Usher Gallery, Lincoln, 2002. Imperial War Museum, British Council and Laing Art Gallery, Newcastle, own his work.

Annette KANE 1955– Painter, mainly a watercolourist, designer and teacher, born in Birmingham. She studied fine art at Reading University, graduating in 1978. For six years she was a freelance graphic artist, then began to train as a teacher of art and design in 1985. After four years' teaching in Yorkshire she decided to devote more time to painting. She had her first solo show in 1990 at Finegold Contemporary Art Gallery, Hebden Bridge, another following at The Catto Gallery, 1992. Also showed at NEAC, RI and in 1990 won Catto Gallery award for Best Newcomer at RWS. Lived in London.

George MacDowell KANE 1889–1954 Portrait draughtsman, painter and sculptor who spent most of his life in Belfast, Northern Ireland. After attending Belfast Mercantile Academy, Kane was for a time with architects Blackwood and Jury; won a scholarship to Metropolitan School of Art, Dublin; taught at Royal Belfast Academical Institution; then in Edinburgh helped the sculptor James Pittendrigh MacGillivray with the Gladstone Memorial. Kane was associated with the Ulster Literary Theatre and many of his subjects were theatrical people. Showed with Rodman's Gallery and RSA and Ulster Museum holds his work.

Ian KANE 1951– Artist creating installations and abstract wall pieces using a variety of found objects and man-made materials, as in New Art in Scotland, Centre for Contemporary Arts, Glasgow, 1994. He was born and lived in Inverness, attended Edinburgh College of Art, 1975–80, and had a Scottish Arts Council Amsterdam Residency, 1986–7. Was one of four artists showing at Transmission Gallery, Glasgow, 1984; also in Federation of Scottish Sculptors show, Talbot Rice Gallery, Edinburgh, 1985; and Outdoor Sculpture, Crawford Arts Centre, St Andrews, 1988. Later solo exhibitions included Pure, Moving Space Gallery, Ghent, Belgium, 1996.

Martin KANE 1958– Painter and draughtsman, born in Cardiff, who attended the Glasgow College of Building & Printing, 1980–2; Glasgow School of Art, 1982–3; and Edinburgh College of Art, 1983–7. He took part in many mixed shows in Britain and abroad, later ones including Compass Gallery Annual Group Show, and Cats and Other Creatures, Main Fine Art, both in Glasgow, 1987. Kane had a series of exhibitions with Jill George Gallery from 1990, among them latterly Beaux Arts, 1996. In the catalogue of that, W Gordon Smith referred to Kane's "vista of strange landscapes, bleak urban tundra rendered in yellow ochres and burnt browns, gaunt architecture in an awesome emptiness tinged by a sulphurous gloaming", calling him "a melancholy poet of the waste land." Cleveland Museum and Art Gallery; Scottish Development Agency; corporate collections; and Kasen Summer Collection, New York, owned examples. Lived in Glasgow.

Paula KANE 1970– Painter, born in Glasgow, who studied at Blackpool College of Technology and Art, 1988–9; Kent Institute of Art and Design, Canterbury, 1989–92; and Goldsmiths' College, 1994–6. She was Henry Moore Fellow, Byam Shaw School of Art, 1998. Exhibitions included Small Objects of Desire, City Gallery in Leicester, 1994; Whitechapel Open, 1996; Plastic Domestic at The Tannery, 1997; and John Moores Liverpool Exhibition, 1997–8, where she was represented by the meticulous oil on canvas Bobbles; showing again in 1999 and 2004. There were solo exhibitions at Galerie Zurcher, Paris, 1999, and Emily Tsingou Gallery, 2004. Lived in London. In 2005, her work was included in The Valley at Bloomberg SPACE. The catalogue referred to her "Arcadian landscapes. Using high art as her source material her vistas are fantastical, eschewing the fantasy worlds of J R R Tolkien or C S Lewis. She describes her sources as 'forgotten landscapes' – the distant rocky hills behind the Madonna nurturing her baby in an Italian Renaissance altar painting and the bough from which Jean-Honoré Fragonard's girl swings in the perfect embodiment of Rococo frivolity."

Raymond KANELBA 1897–1962 Painter who studied at Warsaw Academy of Fine Arts, in Vienna and Paris. Exhibited RA, RP, Lefevre Gallery and in Paris in mixed shows, as well as having one-man exhibitions in London, Glasgow, Edinburgh and in several places on the continent. His work included royal portraiture. Lived in London.

Raghav KANERIA 1936– Sculptor, born in Anida, India. After attending Sagramji High School, Condal, 1950–5, Kaneria studied at the Faculty of Fine Art, Maharaja Sayajirao University of Baroda, where he obtained a diploma in sculpture, 1955–9. Between 1964–8 attended Royal College of Art by way of a Commonwealth Scholarship, working with Bernard Meadows. A Sainsbury Scholarship followed in 1967. As well as showing in India, was included in the Commonwealth Art Exhibition in 1962 and in the Royal College of Art's 1980 exhibition Bernard Meadows at the Royal College of Art, 1960–1980. Arts Council holds Watercarrier, of 1967, in steel.

Kanwaldeep S KANG 1964– Figurative painter and draughtsman, known to family and friends as Nicks. Kang's output included a series of luminous flower still lifes, a selection of which was sold at Bonhams, Knightsbridge, in 2003. He was born in India and settled as a baby with his parents in Leicester. He was seldom without a pencil in his hand and never considered anything but an artist's career. Studied history of art at Leicester University and was taught by the painter John Townsend, who helped Kang develop his distinctive style. Augustus John, Giovanni Boldini and especially Gustav Klimt were influences.

Stanisława KANIA: *see* **Stasia KANIA**

Stasia KANIA fl. from 1970s– Artist and designer, sometimes listed as Stanisława Kania, who studied at Loretta College of Art, Manchester, and at the Polish School of Painting, London. Became an interior designer by profession, following studies at Chelsea College of Art. Kania was a member of the International Association of Art, the Free Painters and Sculptors and Association of Polish Artists in Great Britain and participated in Contemporary Art by Polish Artists Abroad at POSK, 1985. Had a solo exhibition at that gallery, 1981, also at Leighton House, 1982.

Rachael Anna KANTARIS 1967– Artist noted for colourful, witty etchings, and teacher, born in Brisbane, Australia. She did a foundation diploma in art and design at Falmouth School of Art, 1985–6; gained an honours degree in visual and performing arts at Brighton Polytechnic, 1986–9; then her master's in fine art printmaking at Brighton University, 1990–2; studying lithography for artists at London College of Printmaking, 1992–3. In 1990 Kantaris worked at Tapestry Studios of Australia, in Melbourne, designing and weaving large tapestries, including work for Parliament House, Canberra; she had a four-month residency at Bethanien Kunstlerhaus, Berlin, in 1993; helped set up Trevor Price Studios in St Ives, Cornwall, 1994; and from 1995 oversaw the running of the Porthmeor Print Workshop in the town. Teaching included the Print Workshop, the School of Painting and Tate Gallery in St Ives and Newlyn Art Gallery. Exhibitions included National Print Exhibition, Royal Festival Hall, 1988; Fresh Art, Barbican Centre, 1991; RA Summer Exhibition, 1992; Three Printmakers, Salthouse Gallery, St Ives, 1993; Open Print Exhibition, RWA, 1994; and St Ives Now, Collyer-Bristow Gallery, 1996. In 1997 Kantaris was invited by the British Council to stage an exhibition of contemporary printmaking in Manila, and while there taught at The University of the Philippines.

Plamen KAPITANSKI 1964– Painter and muralist whose work included richly coloured pictures with a strong imaginative element. He studied at the College of Art, 1978–83, and Academy of Fine Art, 1985–91, both in Sofia, Bulgaria. Completed murals there at the Hotel Shipka, 1990, and at French College, 1991. Took part in a number of joint exhibitions throughout Europe, latterly including Gagliardi and Langton Street Galleries, both 2001. His solo show at The Gallery in Cork Street, 2002, was his tenth, previous ones including venues in Sofia, Vienna, Hamburg, Bologna and Cologne and one in 2001 at the Bulgarian Embassy, in London, where he had settled. Kapitanski's work is held in the Tower of London and many international private collections.

Jo Ann KAPLAN 1945– Artist, born in America in New York City, who attended Hunter College, City University of

New York, 1963–70, and Yale University, 1966. She was based in Wapping Studios in the early 1980s, contributing to Wapping Artists, 1981, and Wapping Artists Open Studios, 1982.

Anish KAPOOR 1954– Sculptor, draughtsman and teacher, born in Bombay, India. He studied at Hornsey College of Art, Middlesex Polytechnic, 1973–7, then Chelsea School of Art, 1977–8. He was a teacher at Wolverhampton Polytechnic, 1979–82, then was artist-in-residence at Bridewell Studios, Liverpool. During a visit to India in 1979 Kapoor noticed mounds of pigment on sale outside temples. On his return to England he began to make forms out of ground chalk or plastic which he placed on the floor and covered with powdered pigment, which became an instantly recognisable feature of his work, which had an elegant, harmonious quality. He participated in individual shows in Britain and abroad including Objects and Sculpture at Arnolfini Gallery, Bristol, 1981; British Sculpture in the Twentieth Century (part II), at Whitechapel Art Gallery, 1982; represented Britain in the 1982 Paris Biennale, with Stephen Farthing and Bill Woodrow; participated in Objects & Figures at Fruitmarket Gallery, Edinburgh, 1982–3, and tour; showed at Lisson Gallery, 1989; represented Britain at Venice Biennale, 1990; in 1991 won the Turner Prize; and in 1998 had a major show at the Tate Gallery. He was elected RA in 1999 and was made Hon. RIBA in 2001. In 2002 Kapoor was commissioned to make an installation, the third in The Unilever Series, for Tate Modern's turbine hall. Heralded as the largest sculpture in the world, Marsyas comprised a trumpet shape for which three steel rings, each weighing several tonnes, stretched a membrane of red fabric 155 metres long (over three times the length of Nelson's Column) and 35 high. Kapoor made his debut as an opera designer at Glyndebourne in 2003, with a set for Mozart's *Idomeneo*. From 2004 visitors to Chicago Millennium Park were impressed by Kapoor's Cloudgate, a gleaming construction almost five storeys high made of 140 tons of stainless steel. Arts Council and other leading collections have his work. Lived in London.

Edmond Xavier KAPP 1890–1978 Painter and draughtsman, Kapp was a masterly caricaturist, as shown in a series of now-scarce books such as *Personalities*, published by Martin Secker. Born in London, Kapp was educated at Christ's College, Cambridge, and in Paris and Rome. He had several dozen one-man shows in London and provincial galleries as well as on the continent, in Canada and America. A 50-year retrospective was held at Whitechapel Art Gallery in 1961, other shows at Barber Institute of Fine Arts, Birmingham, 1999 and 2001. In World War II Kapp was an Official War Artist. Kapp's work is in many distinguished private collections, as well as the National Portrait Gallery, Imperial War Museum, the Fitzwilliam in Cambridge and the Ashmolean, Oxford. During the final 20 years of his life Kapp often worked in an abstract style. He was the brother of Helen Kapp and in 1932 married the sculptor, painter and illustrator Polia Chentoff, who died of a cerebral tumour the following year. Kapp lived in London.

Helen KAPP 1901–1978 Painter, illustrator, wood engraver and curator, born in London, the sister of the artist Edmond Xavier Kapp. She studied at the Slade School of Fine Art, Central School of Arts and Crafts and in Paris. Showed RA, AIA, LG and SWE and had solo shows at Nicholson's Gallery and in Haifa, Israel, with the British Council in 1946. Wrote *Enjoying Pictures* and illustrated many books. Was director of Wakefield City Art Gallery, Yorkshire, 1951–61, then for six years until her retirement in 1967 was first director of Abbot Hall Art Gallery, Kendal, where she established the nucleus of a fine collection. As a curator in Wakefield she organised exhibitions that drew attention to artists such as Alan Davie and Patrick Heron then not very well known, in Kendal showing the painters Joan Eardley, Anne Redpath and Sheila Fell. Finally lived at Leiston, Suffolk.

Chintamoni KAR 1915– Sculptor, painter and teacher, born in Bengal, India. Attended University of Calcutta, 1929–31, then the Indian Society of Oriental Art School there and was at L'Académie de la Grande Chaumière, in Paris, 1938–9. Showed at RA, RBA and Victoria & Albert Museum. Indian Embassy in Paris holds his work. Lived in London.

Olga KARCZEWSKA 1900–1986 Painter and teacher who was born in Cracow, Poland, where she attended university, also attending the Sorbonne, in Paris, studying French literature there and at the University of Grenoble. At the start of World War II she arrived in Britain with a small daughter, met Marceli Karczewski, former editor of *Kurier Polski* in Warsaw and in London editing *The Polish Daily*, whom she married in 1946. She studied art in London at the Polish School of Painting and Chelsea School of Art and in Paris at L'Académie de la Grande Chaumière. With her husband she bought a dilapidated seventeenth-century house at Aigaliers, Provence, where they set up an art school which attracted students from all over Europe. It closed in 1975 and they moved nearby to Sommières, where she died. She showed at Grabowski Gallery, Walker's Galleries and elsewhere and had a solo exhibition at New Vision Centre Gallery in 1964. Was a member of the Association of Polish Artists in Great Britain and the Free Painters and Sculptors. Signed work with initials only. Southend Palace Court has a mural by her.

Carolyne KARDIA 1951– Sculptor, painter and teacher, born in west London, married to the teacher and sculptor Peter Kardia. She gained a sculpture diploma at St Martin's School of Art, 1973; her master's degree in sculpture, Royal College of Art, 1974–7; and a postgraduate diploma in art and psychology, Hertfordshire College of Art, 1985–6. Kardia taught widely throughout Britain, including Maidstone College of Art, 1973–4; Central School, 1974 and 1982; Winchester School of Art, 1977–80; Bath Academy of Art, 1982; Royal Academy of Art, 1984; Slade School of Fine Art, 1994; St Martin's School of Art, 1987; Camden Institute, 1987–91; and Central St Martins School of Art, 1989–97. Her early work took the form of sculptural installation with cast components, made in response to particular gallery spaces. Painting became a central part of her output when she began to work in colour. She continued to make site-specific sculpture, often in conjunction with two-dimensional work. Kardia said: "The colours aim to speak of themselves, to be disassociated from their method of application and soar above themselves, but equally they are rooted in the materiality of pigment and surface." She won a South West Arts Travel Award in 2001; British Council Travel Award, 2002; and a South West Arts

Exhibition Award, Moule Trust Fund Award and Arts Council Award, all in 2003. Among Kardia's many shows were Felicity Samuel Gallery, 1978 and 1980; Architectural Association, 1982; Meeting House, Ilminster, 1997; Aquariana and Schwanenwerder, both in Berlin, Germany, 2000; Max Planck Institute, Berlin, 2002; Dorset County Museum, 2003; Victoria Miro Gallery, 2004; and Royal United Hospital, Bath, 2004–5. The privately produced *Carolyne Kardia Recent Sculpture Commissions*, 2003, with a foreword by her husband, was a good introduction to that aspect of her work. In 2005 Becoming was Kardia's first major show in London, a mixed-media event at St Pancras Hospital stemming from her work at the Jules Thorn Day Hospital from 1987, where she ran a ceramic/sculpture/pottery group for psychiatric patients. The Kardias lived in Broadwindsor, Dorset.

Stanislawa de KARLOWSKA 1876–1952 Painter in oil, born in Czeliewy, Poland. She studied in Warsaw, Cracow and from 1896 at Académie Julian in Paris where she met her future husband, the Camden Town Group painter Robert Bevan. She settled in England in 1898, two years later beginning to show at WIAC and in 1908 with Frank Rutter's AAA. She became well known as a hostess to the artists and clients of the Camden Town, Cumberland Market and LG shows, noted for her sweet nature. Had first solo show at Adams Gallery in 1935, which gave her a memorial exhibition 17 years later. Her interiors and landscapes can at their best be comparable with her husband's in strong construction, also showing a delightful colour sense and often a naïve charm. Tate Gallery holds several examples. Died in London.

Josef KARPF 1900–1993 Painter and draughtsman, born in southeast Poland, who moved to Britain after World War II, during which he had spent time in a Siberian labour camp. Having graduated in economics at University in Vienna, studying in the evening at the School of Art, Karpf eventually settled in London. There he studied at Regent Street Polytechnic and Camden Arts Centre, exhibiting in the capital. He was closely involved with Ben Uri Art Society, which holds his work.

Lydia KARPIŃSKA fl. from 1960s– Artist, born in Vienna, Austria, who studied at St Martin's School of Art, 1964–8, and portraiture under Leonard Boden, 1978–80. She exhibited at the Paris Salon, 1983; in Form and Colour, Congress of Polish Culture Exhibition of Fine Arts by Polish Artists in Britain, POSK, 1985; and at Talent Store Gallery.

Tony KARPINSKI 1965– Wildlife painter and illustrator, born in London, who started painting and drawing from the age of four, gaining art prizes each year while at school and attended Chelsea School of Art. He early studied the techniques of the Old Masters, such as Rembrandt and Rubens, and was privately commissioned to make pastiches of early Dutch pictures for private clients. From 1985–95 he worked in advertising and publishing as a commercial illustrator. Inspired by the wildlife paintings of Wilhem Kuhnert, he made his first trip to Africa in 1995. He travelled in Tanzania, Zambia, Zimbabwe and elsewhere. His meticulous depictions of big cats were worked up from notes, drawings and photographic records, to produce highly finished paintings in his Kent home. In 1998 Karpinski began a friendship with Carl Olen, head ranger of Kapama Game Reserve, which facilitated his work. Karpinski showed in London, including Haynes Fine Art of Broadway at The Spring Fair, Olympia, 2002, and the Fine Art and Antiques Fair, 2004. He said: "I try to keep a certain freshness and unlaboured feel to each image with easy flowing and minimal brush work."

Linda KARSHAN 1947– Draughtsman, printmaker and painter, born in Minneapolis, Minnesota, in America, who studied at Skidmore College, Saratoga Springs, New York, in 1965–6 with the architect Robert Reed, a former student of Joseph Albers. In 1967 Karshan worked at the Walker Art Center, Minneapolis, under the direction of Jan van der Maarck; studied art history at the Sorbonne in Paris, 1967–8; read art history at the Slade School of Fine Art; and earned a master's degree in humanistic psychology from Antioch University in 1983, the year she set up a studio in London. Group exhibitions included ASB Gallery, 1986; Runkel-Hue-Williams, 1990; and Grammercy Park Fair, New York, 1995. Had solo shows at Clarendon and ASB Galleries in 1984, later ones including Montgomery-Glasoe Fine Art, Minneapolis, 1995, Redfern Gallery (drawings), 1996, Sandra Gering Gallery, New York, 1997, Galerie Biedermann, Munich, 1999, Sir John Soane Museum, 2002, and Kettle's Yard, Cambridge, 2003. British Museum and Staatliche Graphische Sammlung, Munich, hold examples.

Zofia KARŻEWSKA fl. from 1960s– Artist, born in Poland, who studied at Lausanne School of Art in Switzerland, the faculty of fine arts at Wilno University and at Warsaw Academy of Fine Arts. She exhibited in Warsaw, Cracow, Geneva and London, where she latterly lived.

John KASHDAN 1917–2001 Painter, draughtsman, printmaker and teacher, born in London. He early decided to be an artist, but had to leave school at 14 to work, attending evening classes at the Working Men's Institute. Joined Royal Academy Schools, 1936–9, winning Gold Medal, Travelling Scholarship and many other scholarships. Rejected chance to study at Royal College of Art, preferring freedom of Royal Academy. From 1940, living in Cambridge, became friendly with Henry Moore, John Lehmann, Arthur Koestler and Wolf Mankowitz. Had solo show at Redfern Gallery, 1945. Jankel Adler introduced him to Robert Colquhoun, Robert McBryde and John Minton. In 1946 began teaching at Royal Naval College, Dartmouth, in 1951 moving to Guildford School of Art, in 1972 to Epsom School of Art, retiring in 1982. Had several prestigious shows of monotypes – much admired by Adler – in America, but in 1950 decided to withdraw from exhibiting. Continued to work, however, and his reputation was revived when in 1989–91 England & Co had exhibitions. British Museum made extensive purchases. Died in Leicester, having lived in the county at Loughborough.

Aaron KASMIN 1963– Painter, born and based in London, son of the art dealer John Kasmin. He studied at Chelsea School of Art, 1981–5. Kasmin's works, some three-dimensional, employed delicate colours, scraping away and repainting, resulting in abstracts with landscape affinities. They showed "a debt to primitive, tribal art in its rawness and pattern-like qualities", he wrote on the occasion of his solo show at Harriet Green Gallery in 1996. Other solo shows were at Gallery 24, 1987; Albemarle Gallery, 1988 and 1989; and Groucho Club, 1995. Group exhibitions included Artist of the Day, Angela Flowers, 1986; Cooling Gallery, 1992; and Small is Beautiful, Flowers East, 1993.

Wolfe KASSEMOFF 1913– Versatile artist and teacher, known as Wolfe Cohen but using the family name Kassemoff professionally. He was born in New York, America, moving to England in 1917. Kassemoff studied at Leeds College of Art, 1929–33, and the Royal College of Art, 1933–7. He was then employed by Barry Hart, in his London studio and later in Manchester, painting ceilings that showed the development of lighting. In 1938 he returned to London and was offered part-time teaching at Beckenham School of Art, staying until retirement in 1978. Kassemoff was a design school tutor at Beckenham; in 1962, when it and Bromley College of Art amalgamated, he moved to Bromley, joining fine art to establish a printmaking department; when in 1971 the new Ravensbourne College of Art, formerly Bromley, was re-established in Chislehurst, he abandoned printmaking for painting, being appointed head of department, on the retirement of Thomas Freeth, in 1977. Alongside teaching, Kassemoff painted and was a designer and illustrator for books, magazines and exhibitions. He made his first sculptures, small metal figures, in 1958; for 10 years from 1962 he visited Alba, France, where with found objects he developed a second series of sculptures; from the early 1970s he favoured strongly geometric, abstract, painted forms. These were shown at the George Rodger Gallery, Maidstone, in 2000. Other exhibitions included paintings and drawings at the Railings Gallery, 1988. He lived in Beckenham, Kent.

Yumi KATAYAMA 1955– Artist who graduated with honours from Goldsmiths' College, 1979–82, attending Central School of Art, 1983–4, and for a master's degree the Royal College of Art, 1984–6. There was a solo show at Creaser Gallery, 1987. Group appearances included One Hundred Years of the Royal College of Art, Barbican Art Gallery, 1988, and Acid Mix at Heritage Centre and East End Open Studios, based at Richmond House Studios, both 1989.

Cyril KATKOV 1905–1995 Painter, muralist, architect and icon expert, born in Moscow, Russia. He fled the revolution there in 1921, moving to Prague, Czechoslovakia, for five years, where he studied at the Academy of Fine Art and won first prize, in 1925, for the design of the Cathedral of Ushgorod. Then went to Paris where he studied Byzantine art at the Sorbonne, showing his own paintings. From 1939 in Argentina continued to create murals and develop his own style of paintings in irregular frames, shown in Oxford in 1962. From 1965 Katkov was advisor to the auctioneer Sotheby's in New York on icon restoration, while completing church work in Canada. In 1988 his paintings of Greenwich, southeast London, were included in four-man show at Woodlands Art Gallery. Died in New York.

Camille KATSURAGI 1974– Painter of Japanese nationality, working in oil and mixed media on canvas, who gained an honours degree in fine art from Coventry University, 1993–6; her master's in painting, Slade School of Fine Art, 1996–8; and who attended London School of printing, professional photography practice, 1988. Eschewing the Western figurative narrative tradition, Katsuragi aspired to paint figures, faithful reproductions of what she envisaged rather than what was there, around which viewers must create their own story. Exhibitions included Donkey, Arcadian Centre, Birmingham, 1998; Global II, Addison Wesley Longman, Harlow, 1998–9; and Fin de Siècle, Riverside Studios, Standing on the Date Line, Sella Gallery, and Conversation Pieces, Hammerson plc, all 1999. There was a solo exhibition at Art First in 2001.

Elias KATZER 1910– Painter, illustrator and maker of puppets, born into a middle-class family, who was educated in Berlin, Germany. Although he had some art lessons, he was substantially self-taught. Earned his living as an illustrator for newspapers and magazines in Prague, Czechoslovakia, in the late 1930s, then settled in north London. Was noted as an illustrator of children's stories, but showed widely in London, on the continent and in America. Sometimes signed work KA–, alternatively with his full name.

Edward McKnight KAUFFER 1890–1954 Poster designer who also did some textile and theatrical work, painted and illustrated books and magazines. Born in America at Great Falls, Montana, Kauffer grew up in Evansville, Indiana, where was assistant scene painter in the opera house. His early training as a painter was in San Francisco and at the Art Institute of Chicago, where he saw the controversial Armory Show of modern European art. A patron assisted him to study in continental Europe where in Paris he was influenced by Van Gogh's work. Resolved to support himself by poster design, at the outbreak of World War I he had to flee to London where he associated with painters such as Harold Gilman and Charles Ginner and gained commissions for the Underground Electric Railways Company. For the next quarter-century he was the main designer of posters for London Underground under Frank Pick's patronage. Did work for Roger Fry's Omega Workshops, helped to found Group X with Wyndham Lewis and early in the 1920s returned for a while to New York, where he designed for the Theatre Guild. Showed at Goupil Gallery, Arthur Tooth and Son and NEAC. Illustrated for periodicals such as *Radio Times* and *Fanfare* and books such as Arnold Bennett's *Elsie and the Child*, 1929, T S Eliot's *Triumphal March*, 1931, and Edgar Allan Poe's *Complete Poems and Stories*, 1946. However, his reputation rests mainly on his outstanding contribution to modern British poster design, inspired by Cubism and Vorticism, working for such clients as Shell-Mex and BP, the General Post Office and Imperial Airways. His *Soaring to Success – the Early Bird* poster, used by the *Daily Herald*, epitomised Kauffer's aspirations as a designer. After the outbreak of World War II Kauffer, who married the designer Marian Dorn, returned to New York. Victoria & Albert Museum travelling exhibition in 1973.

Pat KAUFMAN 1950– Artist born in Chicago, Illinois, America, who worked in London from 1987. She gained an honours degree in fine arts from Goldsmiths' College, 1989. Group exhibitions included The Crypt, 1988; New Contemporaries, ICA, 1989; Flaxman Gallery and Whitechapel Open at Whitechapel Art Gallery, both 1990; Victoria Miro Gallery, 1992; and Sweet Home at Oriel Mostyn, Llandudno, and tour, 1994. Solo shows included Palazzo Ruini, Reggio Emilia, Italy, and Flaxman Gallery, both 1991. Doris Lockhart-Saatchi Collection and Caldic Collection, Rotterdam, hold examples.

Philipp KAUFMANN 1866–1969 Painter of vibrantly coloured landscapes, portraits and still life, born in Vienna, Austria, son of the internationally known painter of Jewish life and character Isidor Kaufmann, who gave him his first tuition and took him on extensive travels through Europe. Philipp completed his training with Christian Griepenkerl at the Vienna Academy and with Hermann Strück in Munich, followed by studies in Paris. In Belgium, the Netherlands, Denmark and Sweden Kaufmann encountered influences ranging from the Flemish primitives to the French Impressionists. The rise of the Nazis in Germany and Austria prompted Kaufmann's emigration to England in 1934, where he settled in St John's Wood and became well-known as a portrayer of distinguished contemporaries. He showed at the RA Summer Exhibition, elsewhere in London and abroad; the National Portrait Gallery, Dudley Museum and Art Gallery and notable foreign collections hold examples. Died in London. The John Denham Gallery held a show in 2000.

Permindar KAUR 1965– Sculptor using a variety of materials such as cloth, iron, fabric and steel, born in Nottingham. Obtained a degree in fine art from Sheffield City Polytechnic, 1986–9, with a master's from Glasgow School of Art, 1990–2. Awards included a Visual Arts Grant from the British Council, 1994, and one from Banff Centre for the Arts, Calgary, 1995. Group shows included Starting Points, Mappin Art Gallery, Sheffield, 1991; Asian Arts Festival at Worcester City Art Gallery, 1993; Panfletos de Agri-cultura poster project organised by Transformadors, Barcelona, 1994; Veins, Galeria dels Angels, Barcelona, 1995; and British Art Show 4, and tour, 1995–6. Had a solo exhibition Red Earth at Harris Museum & Art Gallery, Preston, 1993, others including a series in Sweden, among them Hidden Witnesses, Galleri Amidol, Gothenburg, 1994.

Jim KAVANAGH 1960– Painter of romantic landscapes, born in east London, and teacher, who gained a fine art honours degree at Middlesex University, majoring in painting and printmaking, 1981–5. Taught foundation at West Thames College, but gave it up to paint full-time, being represented by Fine Art Promotions. Commissions included five pictures for Planet Designs Ltd, 1995, five more for the VWJ Building, 1996. Group exhibitions included Gagliardi Gallery, 1993; Beatrice Royal Gallery, Eastleigh, 1995; and Coombs Contemporary, 1997. Had a solo show with Black Bull Gallery, 1992, later ones including Lamont Gallery, 1997.

John F KAVANAGH 1903–1984 Portrait sculptor, born in Birr, King's County, Ireland. He studied at Liverpool School of Art, 1920–1, winning a scholarship to the Royal College of Art in 1925. He studied there, 1925–30, under Henry Moore, winning the Rome Scholarship in sculpture in 1930, living at British School in Rome, 1930–3. While teaching at Leeds College of Art, 1934–9, was made a member of RBS in 1935. Kavanagh's bronze Russian Peasant is held by Tate Gallery and his sensitive Wanda Tiburzzi is illustrated in the volume *RBS: Modern British Sculpture*, published in 1939. Notable among Kavanagh's public sculpture are the corner figures and reliefs for Walthamstow Town Hall. In 1951 he was appointed senior lecturer at Elam Fine Art School at New Zealand's Auckland University. Showed at RA and RHA.

Kisa KAWAKAMI 1945– Architect, sculptor and teacher, born in Manchuria, Japan, who graduated as a Bachelor of Architecture, Waseda University, Tokyo, 1969, and Master of Town Planning, 1976. Kawakami, a member of RIBA, from 1972–85 was in the architects' department of the London Borough of Camden, teaching at the Architectural Association School from 1982–94. He was an external examiner, North London University, 1988–94, and at East London University from 2001. Among his design consultancies was the Tokyo Opera House, 1987–90, for TAK Associated Architects Inc.; Japanese ambassador's residence, London, 1989–94; Marunouchi District for Mitsibishi Estate, 1997–02; and from 2001 Kyoto Imperial Guest House for Nikken Sekkei. Kawakami was self-taught as an artist, producing sculptural works of great elegance. These were mostly sited in Japan, and included Ocean, Long Term Credit Bank, Hibiya, 1993; Air Dance, Tokyo Opera City, Shinjuku, and Belvedere Setoda, Setoda Biennale, Hiroshima, both 1996; Optical Tower, Hitachi System Park, Hakata, 1997; and Flame Dance, Yokohama International Stadium (2002 World Cup Stadium), 1998. In England, Kawakami's Sky Dance was unveiled at the Royal Air Force Museum, Hendon, in 2003. It was followed by his Mirage, a hanging sculpture of mirrored stainless steel discs hung from wires, suspended among trees in Kielder Water Forest Park, Northumberland, in 2004. Among Kawakami's many awards were first prize, with TAK Associated Architects, at the Tokyo Museum of Contemporary Art, the Koriyama City Museum of Art, Fukushima, and Mitaka City Art Centre, Tokyo, 1989. His solo exhibitions included Architectural Association School, 1981 and 1986; Glasgow School of Art, 1981; Contemporary Sculpture Centre, Tokyo, 1986, 1995 and 2001; and Graham Foundation, Chicago, America, and Columbia University, New York, both 1998. Kawakami listed "plus-minus, light and shadow, wrapping light and weaving shadows, in tune with nature, and synergy: art, architecture and landscape" as key themes running through his work. Lived in London.

Witold Gracjan KAWALEC 1922–2004 Sculptor in various materials, born in Wilno, Poland. He served with the Polish forces in France and the Middle East, then as a fighter pilot with the Royal Air Force. Studied sculpture in Poland and Romania and after World War II at Nottingham University College and College of Art, where he became a visiting teacher. From 1951 he was a freelance sculptor, with well over 100 solo exhibitions in England. Kawalec's work was both figurative and abstract, notable for its spiritual intensity. He was a member of Free Painters and Sculptors, Exeter Art Society and the Kenn Group. Among venues shown at were Castle Museum, Nottingham; RA; Drian Galleries; Edinburgh Festival; and abroad. Kawalec was appointed sculptor to St Christopher's Hospice, Sydenham. He settled at Barnstaple Cross, Crediton, Devon, where there was a permanent display of his work at Dewsmoor Art.

Bernard KAY 1927– Painter, printmaker and teacher, born in Southport, Lancashire, who attended Liverpool College of Art, 1943–6; Royal Academy Schools, 1947–8; then gained a French Government Scholarship, with Johnny Friedlander/Atelier Friedlander/Academy Ranson, all 1954–5. He taught briefly at Southport School of Art, then 1950–2 at Wimbledon School of Art, Birmingham School of Art, 1959–62. Group shows included Preston, Southport and Bradford municipal art galleries from 1940;

St George's Gallery, 1956–63; and Editions Alecto, from 1963. Kay exhibited with Roland, Browse and Delbanco from 1957–70, having solo shows there in 1960 and 1962. The Print Club of Philadelphia (International Purchase Prize); Museum of Modern Art, New York; Victoria & Albert Museum; Seattle Museum of Modern Art; British Council; and other public collections hold both paintings and prints by Kay. He lived for many years in London, latterly in Oundle, Northamptonshire.

Bob KAY 1907–1994 Painter who was born and bred in the Manchester area who worked first as an electrical engineer, later as an industrial designer. Even while serving in the Middle East with the Royal Air Force Kay continually sketched and painted. In the 1940s he was a member of Manchester Art Society, later joining and becoming patron of Manchester Graphic Club. Engineering equipment and dockyard scenes around the Manchester Ship Canal, trains and the city's back streets, many since demolished, were favourite subjects, as shown in a memorial exhibition at Salford Museum and Art Gallery, 1996.

Emma KAY 1968– Figurative artist who studied at Wimbledon School of Art, 1987–8; Glasgow School of Art, 1988–91; and with Maggi Hambling, Morley College, 1995–7. Also studied film-making, ceramics and sculpture. She gained an Elizabeth Greenshields Award; a Glasgow Film and Video Production Award, 1992; and was commended in the BP Portrait Award Exhibition, 1994. Varied film work, between 1991–3, included *Voyeurs, Persuasion* and *The Patient*. In 1990, Kay was commissioned to paint the Wimbledon football team after it won the Football Association cup in 1987. Solo exhibitions included Drawings from Life, Gallery M, 1997, and Chisenhale Gallery, 2001.

Mary KAY 1954– Painter and teacher, born in London, who attended Bath Academy of Art, Corsham, 1973–7, and Goldsmiths' College, 1977–8. She taught part-time at Queen Elizabeth's School, High Barnet. Kay was based at Wapping Studios and participated in 55 Wapping Artists, 1979; Whitechapel Open Exhibition, 1980; and Wapping Artists Open Studios, 1982, in which her large oil on canvas Punk in Soho 1982 was shown.

Muriel KAY 1919-1998 Painter, designer and illustrator, who early showed promise as an artist and who was awarded her National Diploma in Design and art teacher's certificate, attending Croydon School of Art. Kay pursued a chequered career. During the 1960s she worked for The Fine Art Gallery in Devonshire Street, her tinted etchings, maps and other works on paper being known in the trade as "Muriels", because of bright colours she favoured. Kay additionally worked as publicity co-designer for organisations such as British Rail and the Festival of Britain; designed graphic educational material for use in schools, greetings cards and illustrated children's books; and latterly produced striking montages of bird and animal life and became interested in stained glass. She also carried out many commissions for landscapes, showed widely in London galleries and held frequent solo exhibitions. Duncan Campbell latterly offered her work.

Nora KAY fl. from 1930s– Artist, designer, potter and teacher, working in a wide variety of media. After Wycombe High School she studied at St Martin's School of Art, where she also taught, and Royal College of Art, teachers including Ernest Tristram and Eric Ravilious. London Transport, book and ephemera publishers used her designs and she also produced children's books. Kay was a member of the Chartered Society of Designers and exhibited with NEAC, RBA and elsewhere. Lived for many years in Gerrards Cross, Buckinghamshire.

Pamela KAY 1939– Painter and draughtsman – notably still life and portraits – designer, illustrator, teacher and writer on art, born in Isle of Sheppey, Kent. She studied for four years at Canterbury College of Art under Christopher Alexander, Alec Vickerman and Eric Hurren, while working part-time for two years as studio assistant to John Ward (she was the model for his illustrations for Laurie Lee's *Cider with Rosie*). While at Canterbury she exhibited at RA in 1960. Concentrated also on textile design, winning a Sanderson wallpaper competition and having work shown at the Design Centre, and studied design at Royal College of Art for three years. After graduation she launched a freelance practice, producing paper and fabric designs. In mid-1970s, after marriage and children, Kay resumed painting and was eventually elected to RWS, RBA and NEAC. She had a series of solo shows, galleries including Medici, Chris Beetles, Catto and Richard Hagen in Broadway. Fantin-Latour, Chardin and Ingres were key influences. Taught part-time at School of Architecture, Canterbury, and wrote for *Leisure Painter* magazine. From 1988 Kay illustrated books, notably for children. Lived in Cliftonville, Kent.

Violet MacNeish KAY 1914–1971 Painter in oil and watercolour; teacher of art and crafts. Born in Glasgow, daughter of the artist James Kay, she studied at Glasgow School of Art, 1931–3, under William Somerville Shanks and W O Hutchison. Exhibited RSW, of which she was made a member shortly after World War II, during which she did war work, Paisley Institute, RSA and Glasgow Lady Artists' Club. She joined in 1935 and won its Lauder Award in 1948. The Pilgrim Trust and Paisley Corporation bought her work. Lived at Garelochhead, Dunbartonshire, but died in Helensburgh.

Marcus M KAYE 1898–1984 Sculptor, who gained a first-class degree in mechanical engineering at Cambridge University, simultaneously studying at Cambridge Municipal Art School, 1919–22. On graduating, Kaye joined Shell-Mex to specialize in industrial lubricants, staying until retirement. From 1927–30 Kaye studied with Bernard Meninsky at Westminster Art School. Showed regularly, notably with SPS, NS and at Summer Salon. Among his many commissioned works were a portrait sculpture for the Royal Air Force Club of Sir Barnes Wallis, inventor of the bouncing bomb, which breached the Ruhr dams in World War II. Phillips sold several of Kaye's works at auction in 1998.

Margaret KAYE 1912– Designer, collagist and teacher, born in Yorkshire. She trained at Croydon College of Art, where she studied textile design and stained glass. From 1937 she started a 38-year teaching career and began to show her collages. Exhibited around England, notably at Roland, Browse & Delbanco, and shared a show at Canon Gallery, Chichester, in 1991. In retirement continued to experiment with new techniques and materials, her work mixing reality and abstraction.

Mary KAYE: *see* **Mary WOODS**

Mary Margaret (Mollie) KAYE 1908–2004 Writer and artist, whose 1978 romance of the sub-continent in the nineteenth century *The Far Pavilions* became a best-selling novel and popular television series. Kaye was a daughter of the Raj, born in Simla, daughter of Sir Cecil Kaye, an Indian civil servant. She was educated at The Lawn School, Clevedon, Somerset, but returned to India in the 1920s when her retired father was called back to help with the revision of the Aitchison treaties. There, she enjoyed a vibrant social life. When her father died in 1935 the unmarried Kaye returned to England and from a tiny flat in Chelsea tried to make an income from selling pictures of India. When this proved unrealistic she wrote for children, from 1937, as Mollie Kaye, producing a number of books in the Potter Pinner series. With the revenues Kaye returned to her beloved India, staying with her sister and meeting Goff Hamilton (later Major-General G J Hamilton), whom she subsequently married (she also wrote as Mollie Hamilton). Kaye combined the life of officer's wife and author, writing suspense novels, the first having appeared in 1940, *Six Bars at Seven*; she also wrote historical books, the first being *Shadow of the Moon*, 1957; and later added books for children: *The Ordinary Princess*, 1980, and *Thistledown*, 1981. Her husband retired in 1967 and they settled in Battle, Sussex. Three volumes of autobiography, *The Sun in the Morning*, *Golden Afternoon* and *Enchanted Evening*, appeared in 1990, 1997 and 1999. Kaye painted all her life, carting her easel around India, illustrating a number of children's books in the 1950s and the jacket of *The Sun in the Morning*.

Tony KAYE 1952– Conceptual artist and commercial film-maker, born in London. After a one-year course at St Albans School of Art, 1967–8, Kaye was a messenger boy at Horney Blowcox Freeman Advertising and John Camp Studios, 1969, did a two-year graphic design course at Medway School of Design, 1970–2, in 1973 painting as a fine artist and travelling abroad. In 1991 Kaye moved to Los Angeles, California, to set up Tony Kaye Films Inc, a re-emergence of The Wandering Jew, which he had run briefly in 1983. Since the early 1970s he had held a series of designing and art direction posts in England with various organisations, including being art director of Collett Dickenson Pearce, 1978–81. Kaye's list of international advertising awards from the early-1980s ran into several hundreds, including many golds, ranging from the Channel 4 Award for the Best Commercial in the United Kingdom in 1986 to the British Television Awards Lifetime Achievement Award, 1997. Alongside his advertising work, Kaye pursued a vigorous career as a conceptual and fine artist at museums and alternative exhibition spaces in Europe and America in which he took "issues of widespread social concern – and hypocrisy – reframing them into new formats." Such was their shock value (they covered issues such as domestic violence, racism, homelessness and prejudice) that they elicited strong responses. Roger, a London tramp, was exhibited in and in front of such institutions as the Tate Gallery, National Gallery in Washington, The Louvre, Paris, and San Francisco Museum of Modern Art. With Don't be Scared, held in a Los Angeles hotel and an abandoned warehouse in London, Kaye presented an installation of four naked women and men living with Aids. For several years Kaye was immersed in a multimedia project addressing the topic of abortion. Kaye set up his own large art gallery in Los Angeles. In 1997, he was the subject of a Channel 4 Television *Arthouse* programme.

Cissie KEAN 1871–1961 Painter of independent means, born and died in London, influenced by the Grosvenor School of Art and Cubism. She was one of six children of wealthy German coffee merchants, her correct name Elisabeth Johanna Maria Kuhn (during World War I the surname was changed to Kean). Although her family did not think being a painter was compatible with her social background and although she was crippled when young, Cissie determined to devote her life to painting, studying in Paris for several years, awarded a medal at L'Académie Julian, 1906. After the war she travelled in Europe and Brazil, where a brother lived, meticulously recording views in sketch-books, later completing finished watercolours and paintings. Her friends around this time were the artists Frances Hodgkins, Bertha Johnson and Lila Sampson. She showed at the NEAC, 1921–2, also at the Three Arts Club. In the later 1920s Kean again studied in Paris, with André Lhote and in Fernand Léger's atelier, where her interest in painting in oils and in Cubism was intensified. She set up a studio in London, travelling between the two capitals. After she died, unmarried, Kean's exuberantly colourful pictures remained unseen for almost 40 years, until shows at Whitford Fine Art in 1999 and 2002.

Alan KEANE 1972– Painter who graduated in fine art, painting, from Crawford College of Art, Cork, Ireland, gaining his master's at the University of Ulster in 2000. His work was often gestural and abstracted, the effect of light on seascapes and landscapes being important. He showed nationally and internationally, having a shared exhibition with Nicholas May at the Lead White Gallery, Dublin, in 2003.

John KEANE 1954– Painter and printmaker, born in Hertfordshire. He studied at Camberwell School of Arts and Crafts, 1972–6. Keane was artist-in-residence at Whitefield School, 1985–6; completed a screenprint for Greenpeace, 1988; had a commissioned exhibition about Ollerton mining community for Nottinghamshire County Council, 1990–1; and a set of murals was painted for Salsa Celestina, Palace Theatre, Watford, 1993. He became popularly known as the result of his commission by Imperial War Museum in 1991 to cover the Gulf War as an official artist with the British Army. The pictures were shown in 1992 at the Museum, which acquired Mickey Mouse at the Front. Keane's many group appearances included Whitechapel Open from 1983; Artists Against Apartheid, Royal Festival Hall, 1986; Chicago Art Fair, 1987; Silkesborg Kunstmuseum, Copenhagen, 1988; and Lannon Cole Gallery, Chicago, 1991. After a solo show at Minsky's Gallery, 1980, he exhibited frequently in Britain and abroad, with Angela Flowers Gallery/Flowers East from 1985. In 2000, Keane joined Greenpeace International's ship *Amazon Guardian* to witness the start of a long campaign against illegal logging in Brazil, Flowers East showing the resulting pictures in 2001. Back to Fundamentals, at Flowers East, was a 20-year retrospective for the artist and John Keane – The Inconvenience of History, a show at the London Institute, both taking place in 2004.

Contemporary Art Society, provincial galleries and The Detroit Institute of Fine Art hold examples.

Tina KEANE 1946– Film and video artist, born in London, who studied at Hammersmith College of Art, 1967–70, and at Sir John Cass School of Art. Took part in extensive number of international film festivals. Was included in Women's Own at ICA, 1980; had a five-year retrospective at Third Eye Centre, Glasgow, 1982; video performance Bedtime Story was staged at St Paul's Gallery, Leeds, 1983; Circus Diver was put on at Spectrocolour Screen, Piccadilly, 1989; in 1990 was included in Signs of the Times at Museum of Modern Art, Oxford; and in 1996 in Freezeframe at Lamont Gallery. Keane's Ghost Train was shown at Transit Space in 2002.

Brian KEANY 1945– Artist in oil, acrylic and watercolour, and teacher, born in Forfar, Tayside. He attended Edinburgh College of Art, 1963–7, teachers including William Gillies, Robin Philipson, John Houston, Elizabeth Blackadder and William J L Baillie. Keany went on to teach art and design in the Fife region, settling in Glenrothes. He was elected a member of RSW in 1977. Mixed shows included RSA and Royal Glasgow Institute of the Fine Arts. Keany had a series of solo shows at Loomshop Gallery, Lower Largo, from 1976 and one at Fair Maid's House Gallery, Perth, 1987. The artist was commissioned to design a large tapestry for The Carnegie Trust, Dunfermline, in 1986, which involved lengthy weaving. Glen Pirie's The Kingdom of Fife included his work, which is in collections in Britain and abroad. Keany was commissioned by Velux UK to paint one of the fiftieth anniversary series it sponsored from each country in which it operated.

Andrew KEARNEY 1962– In 1985 Kearney graduated from Limerick School of Art, in Ireland, taking his master's in sculpture at Chelsea College of Art in 1991. He showed at the Serpentine Gallery, where he won the Barclay's Bank Young Artist Award. Kearney worked mainly through installations, which were as much about light and sound as the physical objects, as well as employing photography and sculpture. Sensuality, eroticism, mortality, menace and the boundary between the frail self and the surrounding world were key themes. Later exhibitions included the Lead White Gallery, Dublin, in 2003.

Joseph KEARNEY 1939– Painter, printmaker and teacher, born and lived in Glasgow, where he was a leading member of the Art Club. Kearney studied at Glasgow School of Art, 1957–61, teachers including Philip Reeves and John Miller. Exhibited at Royal Glasgow Institute of the Fine Arts, RP and RSA. Solo shows included Ewan Mundy Fine Art. Glasgow Museums and Art Galleries holds his work.

John KEATES 1915–1992 Painter and teacher, born in Birkenhead, Cheshire. After attending the Birkenhead Institute he studied at Liverpool College of Art, 1933–8, then Central School of Arts and Crafts, teachers including Bernard Meninsky, 1946–7. In 1958 he gained a Liverpool Council for Education travel award. Keates was a principal lecturer at Liverpool Polytechnic until 1978. He was a member of the Liverpool Academy, also exhibiting at Free Painters and Sculptors, Manchester City Art Gallery, with Arts Council, Walker Art Gallery in Liverpool and elsewhere in the north of England. Had several one-man shows in 1960s. Walker Art Gallery and Southport's Atkinson Art Gallery hold examples. Lived in Southport, Lancashire.

John KEATING 1889–1977 Figure, portrait and landscape painter, born in Limerick, Ireland, where he received his first art training. Studied at the Dublin Metropolitan School of Art; won the Taylor Scholarship; then worked with William Orpen in London until 1916. Returned to Ireland, the base for most of his painting career. Exhibited RA, RSA, RHA – he was made an Hon. RA and Hon. RSA – Walker Art Gallery, Liverpool, and Royal Glasgow Institute of the Fine Arts. Became president of the RHA for a time. Is represented in many public collections in Ireland and overseas. Lived in Dublin, where he was professor of anatomy at the National College of Art. He sometimes used the alternatives Séan and Céitinn.

Séan KEATING: *see* **John KEATING**

Tom KEATING 1917–1984 Painter, draughtsman, restorer who gained notoriety as a faker/copyist of artists ranging from Rembrandt and Rubens to Constantin Guys and Degas, and especially Samuel Palmer. Born in London into poverty, Keating left school at 14 to become a house painter, yet nurtured a desire to paint. Invalided out of the Royal Navy, he eventually obtained a grant to study art at Goldsmiths' College, but failed his final diploma. Keating became a restorer, working on the epic frescoes at Marlborough House, perfecting his knowledge of style and technique. The sale of a batch of Keating fakes in a country auction room in the mid-1970s led to his exposure and a book about him and he was tried at the Old Bailey in 1978. But the case was dismissed when Keating had a motor cycle accident and was found to have a serious heart complaint. Keating became an art celebrity as the man who had fooled the experts, and a folk hero. He made two television series, had a successful exhibition of his own work at the Barbican and his work's value rose. After his death Keating's copies of famous pictures continued to fetch record prices. Lived in Dedham, Essex.

Helen KEATS 1947– Printmaker, born and lived in London, who gained an honours degree in fine art followed by postgraduate printmaking studies, attending Harrow School of Art, 1977–9, Wimbledon School of Art, 1979–84, then West Thames College, 1994. She was made a fellow of the Printmakers' Council in 1985. For a time she was a visiting artist at Wimbledon School of Art. Took part in numerous group exhibitions, including Stowells Trophy at RA, 1981; ROI at Mall Galleries, 1983; Open Exhibition at RE, from 1984; Royal Festival Hall, from 1986; Five Printmakers, National Theatre and Korean Gallery in Chicago, both 1989; Chelsea Arts Club Centenary, Smiths Galleries, 1991–2; and Battersea Contemporary Art Fair, 1993. Solo exhibitions include two at Ben Uri Art Society, which holds her work, 1987 and 1990, work in other collections including London University Institute of Education, Curwen Archives and Scarborough Art Gallery. Bomberg and the Slade were noted as influences.

Harry KEAY 1914– Painter in oil who studied at Dundee College of Art, 1930–7, under James McIntosh Patrick, then with James Cowie at Patrick Allan-Fraser School of Art, Hospitalfield, Arbroath, 1937–8. Keay exhibited RSA, Royal

Glasgow Institute of the Fine Arts, SSA, RBSA and elsewhere. Lived in Dundee, Angus.

John E KEAY 1907– Artist, designer and illustrator, born in Birmingham. He attended the School of Art there on a scholarship for four years from the age of 13, did a two-year course in London and was then apprenticed to a Birmingham studio. Joined a studio in Toronto, Canada, drawing as a commercial artist and illustrator for magazines, in 1945 moving to New York, America, for similar work. Returned to England in 1962 and set up a studio in Chiswick, operating through Thompson Artists and Linden Artists. Keay's extensive client list included RCA, Listerine, Goodyear, Guinness and Black & Decker. The Kew Gardens dealer Peter Bennett handled the work of Keay, who in the late 1990s entered a nursing home.

Christopher KEAYS 1937– Landscape and townscape painter in oil, born in Caterham, Surrey. Keays studied at Wimbledon School of Art, 1957–60, including sculpture with Elisabeth Frink; Chelsea School of Art, 1960, with painting tuition from Robert Buhler and Ruskin Spear; and the Royal Academy Schools, 1962–6, under Peter Greenham and Charles Mahoney. Keays was an associate of the ROI and the RA Summer Exhibition and Piano Nobile were among exhibiting venues. Lived in London.

V KEBBELL fl. c.1915–1955 Painter and draughtsman whose full name was William Francis Vere Kebbell. He studied at Byam Shaw and Vicat Cole School of Art. Was a portrait specialist and a member of PS, where he exhibited, also at RA, ROI, IS and Walker Art Gallery, Liverpool. Lived in London.

Graham KEDDIE 1958– Artist and teacher, whose work included constructions in various materials, including pigment. He did a foundation course at Ipswich School of Art, 1975–7; gained an honours degree in fine art at Camberwell School of Art, 1977–80; then did postgraduate studies at Brighton Polytechnic in art and design, 1982–3. In 1982 gained a Lloyds sponsorship to study southwest America and Mexican Indian reservations. Held a series of lectureships from 1980, latterly including Croydon College, 1986; Southend College, 1987; and Tresham Institute, Kettering, from 1988. Group exhibitions included South London Gallery, 1980; Alfred East Gallery, Kettering, 1986; David Holmes Gallery, Peterborough, 1992; and The Table Studio Group, The Living Room, 1996. Solo exhibitions included Sutton Place Heritage Trust, 1986, and Green Dragon, Brigstock, 1993. Lived in Kettering, Northamptonshire.

Eric James KEDWARDS 1905– Painter and teacher, born in Bridlington, Yorkshire. After private education he attended Birmingham College of Arts and Crafts, 1924–9, his teachers including B J Fletcher. Did book illustrations, especially of birds. Showed in the Birmingham area and lived at Walsall, Staffordshire, where he taught art at Queen Mary's School.

Laurence KEEBLE 1916–2004 Versatile artist, teacher and editor, who attended Croydon School of Art, 1932–5, and the Slade School of Fine Art, 1935–8, under Randolph Schwabe. Keeble became a visiting instructor at Croydon College of Art, HM Borstal Reception Centre and Latchmere House, also a panel lecturer in art for the Surrey Education Committee and Hammersmith College of Art and Building. He otherwise had a varied career, in 1938 being involved with the Glasgow Empire Exhibition; engaged on film special effects for Ealing Studios, 1939–40; and producing pictorial maps and other art work for the Imperial War Museum, 1948–54. Keeble carried out a range of illustration, design and pictorial presentation schemes for a variety of clients, including *Everybody's Weekly*; Central Office of Information; Union of South Africa Centenary Exhibition; BOAC; British Industries Fair, Smithfield Show; Harold Fielding Enterprises; London Chamber of Commerce, Festival of Britain; British Railways, and others. Keeble was also co-founder and editor of the magazine *Tradition*.

Arnold KEEFE 1911– Artist in oil, watercolour and egg tempera, and teacher, born in London, who studied at Chelsea School of Art, 1928–30, and Royal College of Art, 1930–4, teachers including Eric Ravilious, Edward Bawden, Malcolm Osborne, Percy Jowett, M C Oliver and Graham Sutherland for etching. Was art master at Battersea Grammar School; senior lecturer in art and craft at Wandsworth and Hampton Colleges of Education; head of department of graduate art teacher training at Goldsmiths' College of Art; then district inspector of art for Inner London Education Authority. He also lectured in adult institutes and was a university examiner. Was a member of Reigate Society of Artists and Royal College of Art Society, showing at RA, NEAC, RP and UA. Had a retrospective show in Woking, 1980, with a solo exhibition at Westcott Gallery, Surrey, 1990. His portrait commissions included the chairmen of Thermos Ltd and Mercantile Marine Credit Company. Lived in Wotton, Abinger Hammer, Surrey.

Felicity KEEFE 1967– Painter, born in Exeter, Devon, who created abstract paintings that were described as "both dramatic and elemental." She shared an exhibition with Ione Parkin at Six Chapel Row Contemporary Art, Bath, in 2004. Keefe did a foundation art course at South Devon College, 1983–5; graduated with honours from the University of Brighton, 1985–8; and gained an art teacher's certificate from City of Bath College, 1996–7. She had a residency at Brighton Marina Arts Complex and completed a mural The Sea The Sea for Brighton Council, 1993, Elizabeth Arden commissioning two paintings, Sunflowers, in 1994. Group exhibitions included The Genolac Arts Festival, Genolac, France, 1995; Ariel Centre, Totnes, 1998; Winter Ritual, Houseroom Contemporary Art, Bath, 2003; and Exeter Phoenix Gallery, Devon, 2004. Keefe had a solo exhibition at First Light Gallery, Brighton, in 1994. Ernst & Young, Midland Bank Plc and West Sussex Health Trust hold her work.

Rita KEEGAN 1949– Artist in a wide range of media, lecturer and administrator, in America born in the Bronx where she attended the New York City High School of Art & Design, 1964–7, gaining a degree in fashion illustration and costume design; obtained a diploma in early childhood development from Bronx Community College, 1968–9; then a fine arts degree from San Francisco Arts Institute, 1969–72. Lived in England from 1979, settling in London, where she lectured in historical and cultural studies at Goldsmiths' College from 1995, having from 1988–92 co-ordinated the Women Artists Slide Library, from 1992–4 being director, African and Asian Visual

Artists Archive. Keegan said that in "exploring issues of identity and representation, the use of family narrative and autobiography featured strongly in my work." Exhibitions included Women's Work, Brixton Artists' Gallery, 1983–6; Trophies of Empire, Bluecoat Gallery, Liverpool, and tour, 1992; Time Museum, British Museum, 1994–5; also showing with 198 Gallery.

Pegaret KEELING: *see* **Pegaret ANTHONY**

Anna KEEN 1968– Artist of British and French nationality who gained a diploma with distinction at L'École Nationale Supérieure des Beaux-Arts (Atelier Carron), Paris, in 1992. Her prizes included Paul-Louis Weiller, Institut de France, Portrait Prize, and Grand Palais, Salon des Artistes Français, Prize with Distinction, both 1991; Fould Stirbey, Institut de France, Third Prize, 1992; Paul-Louis Weiller, Institut de France, Painting Prize, 1995; XXIV Premio Sulmona, Second Prize, 1997; and Premio Morlotti-Imbersago, Second Prize, 1999. Keen took part in many group shows in France and Italy and exhibited with Davies & Tooth, Art2000, Business Design Centre, Islington, 2000. Solo shows included Viaggio in Italia, Galleria Jannone, Milan, Italy, in 1999.

Geoffrey KEEN 1962– Gestural abstract painter, born in Bristol. He studied at the Polytechnic there, 1985–6, then Humberside College of Higher Education, 1986–9. In 1989 showed in winter exhibition at Ferens Art Gallery, Hull, and in European Art Schools Biennale, Antwerp. His canvas Inner City was included in John Moores Liverpool Exhibition, 1989–90. Lived in Hull, Yorkshire.

Simon KEENLEYSIDE 1975– Painter, born in Essex, who did art and design foundation studies at Southend College of Arts & Technology, 1994–5; gained and honours degree in fine art painting from Brighton University, 1997–00; and his master's in painting from the Royal College of Art, 2000–02. Keenleyside was included in the inaugural Bowieart exhibition BLOC at the County Hall Gallery in 2005. Earlier group shows had included Vertigo Gallery, 2001; The Commodity Show, The Loading Bay Gallery, The Old Truman Brewery, 2002; The Drawing Room, The Union, 2003; and Lexmark European Final, Triannale di Milano, Milan, Italy, 2004. Among his later solo exhibitions were Scope Miami, The Leisure Club Mogadishni, Miami, Florida, America, 2004, and Heaven in a Wild Flower, Long & Ryle, 2005.

Walter Monckton KEESEY 1887–1970 Painter, printmaker, teacher and architect, born in Croydon, Surrey. Studied at Royal College of Art, where he finished in 1911. From 1913 was art master at the Architectural Association for a dozen years, apart from a period in Royal Engineers during World War I, winning the Military Cross. Keesey was a banknote and exhibition designer. Chelsea Arts Club member. Exhibited RA, RE, RSA and Walker Art Gallery, Liverpool. Lived in Edgbaston, Birmingham, and later in Cheltenham.

Richard KEETON 1948– Painter, printmaker and teacher, born in Sheffield, Yorkshire, who concentrated on painting at the College of Art there and then printmaking at the Royal College of Art, during that time spending three months studying in Paris. After several years teaching printmaking in Buckinghamshire, in 1980 he set up an etching studio in Derbyshire, publishing his own work and finding a renewed interest in watercolour through landscapes of the Peak District. Took part in mixed exhibitions in Britain and America, receiving an East Midlands Arts Association Purchase Award in 1982 and a prize at the RWS Open Exhibition in 1997. Wakefield Art Gallery; Graphotek in Berlin, Germany; Derby City Hospital; Rank Xerox and many private collections hold examples. Gascoigne Gallery, Harrogate, showed Keeton's work at the Affordable Art Fair in 2006.

Moy KEIGHTLEY 1927– Painter, notably a watercolourist, draughtsman and teacher, who studied at Chelsea School of Art, where she was awarded the Morland Lewis Travelling Scholarship. Keightley participated in the 1955 *Daily Express* Young Artists' Exhibition at The New Burlington Galleries, showing the oil Rear Window, Holborn. Went on to teach at Central St Martins College of Art & Design, was a tutor with the Open College of the Arts in 1988 and a consultant to the BBC Television series *Look, Look and Look Again*. Keightley said that her interest lay "in reconciling representation and abstraction ... The balance of marks and nuances of tone, colour and edge become critical in order to establish poetic qualities beyond topographical identity." Mixed shows included Browse & Darby, LG, Leicester Galleries, RA and RWS. Had a series of solo exhibitions at AIA Gallery from 1965, New Grafton Gallery from 1979 and Barbican Centre, 1994, where landscapes of Iceland, a favourite subject, were featured. Iceland Embassy, Nuffield Foundation and Westminster School hold examples.

Sam KEIL 1965– Figurative-Expressionist sculptor in bronze, whose work was inspired by classical dance and music, to which she worked, and the horse. She graduated with first-class honours from the City and Guilds Art School in 1991, where she won the Best Sculpture Award. She also gained a first prize in the Madame Tussaud Sculpture Competition and The Beckworth Travel Scholarship. After graduating, Keil worked in the scenery departments of leading theatre companies in Canada and America. She exhibited throughout Britain and North America and had a solo show at The Catto Gallery in 1997.

Bridget KEIR 1883–1954 Prolific watercolourist, born in London, daughter of an Army officer and cousin of the artists G A and A D Fripp. She began drawing and painting early; was educated in London, Paris and Boulogne; and was recommended for painting lessons to Claude Hayes, 1905. During 1911–13 Keir spent part of each year in Italy and she was especially fond of Venice, where she was taken up by the painter Clara Montalba. In 1913 she held her first London show, The Lagoons of Venice, spent six months in Egypt painting and had an exhibition in Paris at Galerie Georges Petit, 1914. During World War I Keir was in a concert party raising money for war hospitals, in 1917 spent some months drawing at Heatherley's School of Fine Art and began her Thames series. After the war she took a studio in Cheyne Walk, Chelsea, which remained her base although she travelled extensively. Mixed shows included SWA as a member, also RSW, RI, RHA, RSA, Royal Glasgow Institute of the Fine Arts and Dudley Gallery and she had a series of solo exhibitions at Walker's Galleries. After a period in Onslow Square Keir was moved to a nursing home in Surbiton in June 1954, where she died. Queen Mary was among owners of her pictures.

Harry KEIR 1902–1977 Painter and draughtsman, based in Glasgow, who left school at 14 to become a house painter and signwriter, attending evening classes at the School of Art. He painted the working-class areas of the city in sombre style and also sketched gypsies and travellers. Keir made illustrations for Edward Gaitens' *Gorbal Novels*, recording a fast-disappearing aspect of the city. Showed at RSA, Royal Glasgow Institute of the Fine Arts and elsewhere. He is featured in the sculptor Benno Schotz's autobiography *Bronze in my Blood*. The People's Palace and Kelvingrove Art Gallery in Glasgow hold Keir's work.

Aileen KEITH 1953– Sculptor, draughtsman and teacher, born in Johnstone, Renfrewshire. She studied at the Edinburgh College of Art, 1972–5, sculpture and drawing, 1978–80, working in Italy, 1975–77. Keith taught at the College, part-time, from 1981. In 1984 she became a member of the Federation of Scottish Sculptors. Keith employed various objects to create her work, producing drawings in tandem, in her exploration of memory. In this she was "making sense of the present by considering the past." She took part in many group shows, solo exhibitions including Collective Gallery, Edinburgh, and Robson Gallery, Halliwell's House, Selkirk, both 1993.

Elizabeth KEITH 1887–1956 Landscape and figure artist whose work included colour woodcuts, including Far Eastern subjects as offered by Abbott and Holder in 2004, and etchings. Keith was born in Scotland and spent nine years in China, Japan and Korea, her ability as a horsewoman facilitating travel. The study of primitive man was a special interest. She took part in mixed exhibitions at the RA, RI, Walker Art Gallery and Corcoran Gallery in Washington, and had solo shows in England, America, China, France, Japan, the Philippines and Sweden. Keith's work was illustrated in consumer publications such as the *Illustrated London News, Sketch, Sphere* and *Tatler*, also in the specialised and foreign press, including *Studio* and *Haagache Post*. Her own illustrated book *Eastern Windows. An artist's notes of travel in Japan, Hokkaido, Korea, China and the Philippines* appeared in 1928. The British Museum and foreign public collections in America, Canada and Sweden hold examples. For a time her home base was St John's Wood, north London.

Isabella KELENY 1914– Painter born in Woking, Surrey. Brought up in Huntingdon, she was mainly self-taught as an artist, although she did attend schools part-time in Hampshire and Wiltshire. Showed at RI, SWA and NS and lived in London.

Charlotte KELL 1944–2006 Artist in various media, and poet. She studied at Berkeley University, California, then in England graduated with honours in English literature and classics in translation, North London University, 1980, further studies including a postgraduate certificate in education, English and drama at Roehampton Institute, 1982, and a certificate in early childhood education at Froebel College, 1991. She settled in London, a member of The Society of Fulham Artists. Kell took part in many group shows, later ones including Foss Fine Art, 2001, and The Masbro Centre, 2002. Among later solo exhibitions were Drey Gallery, mostly art boxes and oil pastels, 1991; M Bate & Co, collages and small stone sculptures, 1993; Books for Children, collages and outdoor portrait photographs, 1994; with another show there, 1996. The critic Max Wykes-Joyce produced a book on Kell's work, *Collages Art Boxes and Sculpture*, in 2002.

Lorna Beatrice KELL 1914– Painter of still life and abstracts, printmaker and textile designer, born in London. She studied at Hornsey School of Art, 1930–3, teachers including Russell Reeve, Frank Winter and Norman Janes. She joined Henry Lorraine Kell shortly after he began Lorraine Designs in 1935, married him and became sole proprietor in 1956. The firm specialised in commemorative scarves for Liberty of London, the Oxford Collection and others. Kell was elected to SGA in 1959, becoming its president, was a founder-fellow of the Society of Botanical Artists and a fellow of the Royal Horticultural Society, winning its Grenfell Medal. She produced botanical drawings for the *Junior Encyclopaedia Britannica*. Showed at RA, RE, London Guildhall, Paris Salon and in the provinces. Lived in Barnet, Hertfordshire.

Andrea KELLAND 1944– Painter of oils and watercolours using gestural brushwork and rich colours, preoccupations being the Welsh landscape, coast-line and especially the transitory nature of sea pools. Kelland trained in fine art, painting, at Kingston Art School, 1960–4, and Brighton College of Art & Crafts, 1964–5. She lived and worked in Devon from 1965–88, then, after her children had left home, moved to Carmarthen to resume painting, living finally at Amroth, Pembrokeshire. She joined the WSW in 1998. Other group exhibitions included Three Artists, Ceri Richards Gallery, Taliesin Centre, Swansea, 1992; Summer Show, Oriel Myrddin, Carmarthen, 1995; Women Artists & Pembrokeshire, Tenby Museum & Art Gallery, 1999; and A Slice of Life, Queen's Hall Gallery, Narberth, 2000. Among her later solo exhibitions were Coastlines, Theatre Mwldan Gallery, Cardigan, and tour, 2000–1. Her husband was the artist Geoff Yeomans.

Michael KELLAWAY 1929– Artist and lecturer, born in Melbourne, Victoria, Australia, where the McClelland Gallery, at Langwarrin, holds sculptures, drawings and photographs of his work. As a schoolboy Kellaway was taught by Ludwig Hirschfeld-Mack, "whose account of his time at the Bauhaus set going a lifelong involvement with twentieth-century art." After graduating in science at Cambridge University, 1950, and spending a postgraduate year studying neuro-physiology with the later Nobel Prizewinner A L Hodgkin, Kellaway pondered research in this field, instead pursuing postgraduate studies in fine art for a diploma at the Slade School, 1951–4, winning several prizes. Kellaway was in charge of Reading University's sculpture department, 1956–61; assisted at the Slade School, 1961–70; lectured at Camberwell School of Art from 1966, senior lecturer from 1974; also lecturing and assessing at Goldsmiths' College, Royal College of Art and in the provinces. Kellaway was a sculpture faculty member at the British School at Rome, 1980–4. Exhibitions included the LG, 1956–8; New Art for New Towns, Hemel Hempstead, 1964; Bear Lane Gallery, Oxford, 1966; O'Hana Gallery, from 1967; Robert Savage Gallery, 1970; and Playhouse Gallery, Harlow, 1975. In 1960 Kellaway won 1st Prize, Sculptural Relief Project, for Frederick Snow and Partners, executed at the firm's South Bank premises, 1961. He lived in London and Lodève, France.

Stephen KELLETT fl. from 1980s– Painter of landscape and abstracts using a wide range of media, born in Totnes, Devon. His extensive travels in several continents influenced his work. Kellett gained a diploma in art and social content at Dartington College of Arts, 1983–5, an honours degree at Exeter College of Art, 1985–7, and a postgraduate diploma in art therapy from St Albans College of Art and Design, 1990–1. Exhibitions included Birdwood House, Totnes, and Fulham Gallery, both 1988; The Heifer Gallery from 1989; and Chapel Gallery, Plymouth, 1989. From 1988 Kellett had a series of solo exhibitions at Lamont Gallery.

Diarmuid KELLEY 1972– Figurative painter, born in Scotland, who gained an honours degree in fine art at University of Newcastle, 1991–5, his master's at Chelsea School of Art, 1996. Awards included John Christie prize, at Newcastle, 1994; in 1995 he won the Annabel Walker prize there, first prize in the National Westminster Bank Young Artist Competition (the Bank holds his work) and was runner-up, BP Portrait Award, National Portrait Gallery. Group exhibitions included Northern Graduates, Royal College of Art, 1995; Art and Academia, Christie's, 1996; and in 1998 Modern British Art at Offer Waterman & Co, which later that year gave Kelley his first solo show.

John KELLIHER 1944– Artist and teacher, born in Aberdare, Glamorgan, who produced largely figurative works. These had British and continental European landscape and architectural themes and were concerned with traditional painterly values. He attended courses run by Dennis Creffield and John Epstein and, starting in 1985, trained with Michael Freeman at the Port Talbot Arts Centre, being a co-founder with him of the Friday Group. Kelliher taught at Afan Arts Centre with the Port Talbot Painter's and Sculptor's Guild, 1975–84. He was for a time a member of the WSW. Kelliher exhibited regularly with the Friday Group and with the Port Talbot Theodore Painters. He carried out a series of commissions for Lloyds Bank, the Eagle group of hotels, and had works in private collections. Lived in Margam, Port Talbot.

Anthony-Noël KELLY 1955– Artist in mixed media, and teacher, nephew of the Duke of Norfolk, who grew up at Romden Castle, near Smarden, Kent, and who made legal history in 1998 when he was sentenced to nine months' imprisonment (on appeal cut to three) at Southwark Crown Court; it was said to be the first time anyone had been charged with stealing a body or its parts. These were smuggled out of the Royal College of Surgeons, to which they had been donated. Silver-coated sculptures by Kelly, based on casts of such parts, were offered during the Art97 contemporary art fair, at the Business Design Centre, Islington, early in 1997. Kelly's agent was the dealer Jibby Beane. Kelly taught sculpture at the Prince of Wales Institute of Architecture. He had early developed an interest in human anatomy. As well as training as a butcher, working in an abattoir, he had studied as an artist at Heatherley's School of Fine Art. Kelly was apprenticed to a restorer, and spent several years working for private clients. To improve his knowledge, he sketched operations in North Hampshire Hospital, Basingstoke. In 1999 Kelly's exhibition Birthdays, life-size photographs of bodies, was held at 291 Gallery. Kelly lived for a time in London, but at the time of the 291 show he was poised to get married and move to Ireland.

Brendan KELLY 1970– Scottish artist, living and working in London, who studied at the Slade School of Fine Art, 1989–1993. In 2004 he took part in Being Present at Jerwood Space, having just won the De Laszlo Prize for the best portrait by a young artist at the 2004 RP exhibition. Kelly was also commended several times in the BP Portrait Award before winning second prize in 2001 for Nude in a Nightclub. His paintings often began with a desire to create a particular atmosphere through the use of artificial lighting. Light and the portrait were central to his work.

Brian KELLY 1946– Artist and teacher, born in Renfrewshire, who studied printmaking and painting at Glasgow School of Art from 1973. He taught lithography at Glasgow Print Studio, 1977–9; was in London, painting, 1980; then for a time was a technician in silkscreen at Glasgow School of Art from 1981. Kelly took part in a number of group shows around this time, including Scottish Print Open Three, 1983, organised by Dundee Printmakers' Workshop.

Brian KELLY 1958– Sculptor, muralist and teacher, born in Paisley, Renfrewshire, who studied painting at Glasgow School of Art, 1976–80, gaining a postgraduate diploma in 1981. He became a part-time teacher there, full-time from 1990, also teaching part-time at at Duncan of Jordanstone College of Art in Dundee and Chelsea School of Art. Kelly showed in mixed exhibitions, including Smith Museum in Stirling and Transmission Gallery, Glasgow. He established a reputation in Scotland for a series of panels using various materials. Notable are the four relief panels entitled The Modern Myth, at Edzell Street, Whiteinch, Glasgow, 1987–8, and six bronze sculptures and three mosaic panels for Clydebank, 1994–5.

Deirdre KELLY 1962– Artist, notably a printmaker, and teacher who studied at Wimbledon School of Art, 1984–7, earning a master's degree in printmaking. She gained a Sericol Purchase Prize in 1986, an Atlantis Purchase Prize in 1987 and a Whatman Paper Prize in 1988. As well as mixed shows, including In Piper's Footsteps, at New Academy Gallery, 1993, had solo shows at Bristol Polytechnic, 1987, and Intaglio Printmaker Gallery the same year. Was a member of RE, a screenprinting tutor for Islington Adult Education Centre and a visiting lecturer at South Thames College and Middlesex Polytechnic. King's College School and Sedgwick Group International hold her work.

Felix KELLY 1914–1994 Painter in oil, book illustrator, set designer and muralist. His work had a strong Neo-Romantic flavour. Kelly was born in Auckland, New Zealand, and moved to London, where he eventually settled, in 1935. He worked for the advertising agency Lintas as a layout man until 1939, served in the Royal Air Force during World War II, then returned briefly to Lintas. While still in the Air Force he had begun to paint seriously and in 1943 Lefevre gave him the first of a series of solo shows. A commission prompted Kelly to become a professional painter in 1947 and he worked for a time in America, exhibiting there successfully. Kelly then had series of shows with Leicester Galleries, Arthur Jeffress Gallery, Tooth and Partridge (Fine Arts), which gave him a memorial exhibition in 1995. He became known as a painter of country houses in England and America, travelled extensively and had a special interest in all types of floating craft and waterways. Among Kelly's book illustrations were Herbert Read's *The Green Child*, 1945, and a series by Elizabeth Burton starting with *The Elizabethans at Home*, 1958. His play sets included *A Day by the Sea*, by N C Hunter, with Sir John Gielgud, and *The Merchant of Venice*, by Shakespeare, for The Old Vic Company. Murals included notable liners such as Union Pacific's *Windsor Castle*, the Royal Palace at Katmandu, Nepal, and Queen's Ice Skating Club. The Earl of Dalkieth, Sir Herbert Read and Viscount Leverhulme owned his work. Read published a monograph on *Paintings by Felix Kelly* in 1946.

Fleur KELLY 1950– Versatile artist and designer notable for fresco murals and egg tempera panel painting, and teacher, born in New Jersey, America, of British nationality. Kelly had a special interest in authentic materials as used in historical art works because of their aesthetic and lasting qualities. She did a pre-diploma course at Somerset College of Art, Taunton, 1968; typographic design at Camberwell College of Arts and Crafts, 1969; followed by painting and pottery at High Wycombe College of Art, 1970–2; then in 1987 undertook an intensive course in fresco technique with Leonetto Tintori at his school in Prato, Italy. Teaching included Workers' Educational Association at Soundwell Technical College, Bristol; being artist-in-residence, Verulamium Museum, St Albans; and fresco technique at Centro d'Arte Verrocchio, Siena. Although many have since studied the technique, Kelly was one of the later pioneers in the fresco revival in Britain. Works included an apsidal dome in egg tempera and two wooden panels for St Augustine's, Swindon; reconstruction fresco project from Romano-British fragments at Verulamium; reconstruction of paintings at St Thomas' Tower in the Tower of London; two domes in buon fresco for new Rural Economy buildings at St John's College, Oxford; plus many private commissions. Lived in Bath, Somerset.

Francis KELLY 1927– Painter, conservator and writer, born in St Paul, Minnesota, America. After serving in United States Navy, 1944–8, entered Art Centre School, Los Angeles. During 1951–2 Kelly lived in Paris, attending L'Académie de la Grande Chaumière; in 1953 he went to the University of Hawaii, Honolulu; then to University of California, Los Angeles, where he was graphic laboratory assistant to John Paul Jones. Awarded a Fulbright Grant in 1955 Kelly entered the graphic department of Central School of Arts and Crafts. In 1958 Kelly was awarded the Stacey Grant for painting, in 1966 being appointed art organiser for the American Embassy's Festival of Arts and Humanities. His paintings were shown in the subsequent exhibition Five American Artists in Britain, his etchings having been introduced at St George's Gallery in the mid-1950s. During 1976 Kelly helped Winsor & Newton with a show of American artists for the bicentennial. Kelly studied conservation at the Courtauld Institute and in 1967 he was sent by the Italian Art and Archives Rescue Fund to Florence to restore flood-damaged paintings. He published *Art Restoration* in 1971, then *The Studio and the Artist* in 1975. The lesser-known British landscape, rivers and waterways were key features of Kelly's pictures, which were shown at several dozen British museums and in many galleries. Ashmolean Museum in Oxford, Glasgow University, Los Angeles County Museum and New York Public Library hold examples. Lived in London.

Gerald KELLY 1879–1972 Painter in oil of portraits and landscapes. Born in London, he was educated at Cambridge, then lived and studied art in Paris for several years. Whistler was an early influence. Kelly was an enthusiastic traveller, visiting among other countries Spain, America, South Africa and Burma, where he painted some of his most characteristic and charming figure studies. He became known as a sound academic painter of attractive children and elegant women, untroubled by psychological insight, reliable. Represented in many public collections, including the Tate Gallery. He had retrospective exhibitions at the Leicester Galleries in 1950 and in 1957 at the Royal Academy. He was elected RA in 1930, was its keeper 1943–5 and president, 1949–54. Kelly held a number of official positions, such as his membership of the Royal Fine Arts Commission, 1938–43, and was knighted in 1945. Lived in London.

John KELLY 1949– Artist and writer whose work included photography, drawing and the use of objects. He travelled widely within north Africa, producing journals relating to topographical interpretation and a number of exhibitions on Africa and other themes. He was selected artist for the British Antarctic Survey's Artists and Writers Scheme in 2003. Kelly received several awards from South East Arts to aid his travels and work. *Due South An Antarctic Journal* appeared in 2004, illustrated with photographs and line drawings, in which he attempted "to present the reality of Antarctica, not simply a visual record, but an account of the emotions and fleeting thoughts of life in the 'freezer'." It was published to coincide with an exhibition which toured from the Natural History Museum, 2004–5. As well as taking part in group exhibitions at the Guildhall, Mall Galleries and the RA, 1975–88, Kelly participated in Ends and Means, drawings, Phoenix Gallery, Brighton, 1998, and The Sea, Wolverhampton Art Gallery, 2001. Other solo shows included Constructions, Oxford University Museum, 1984; Constructions and Collages, Wolfson College, Oxford, 1987; Small Sculptures and Drawings, University of Surrey, 1988; Moments in Time. The Essential Landscape, Yard Gallery, Nottingham, and Natural History Museum, 2001; and Art and the Antarctic by John Kelly, Cheltenham Art Gallery & Museum, 2005. Magdalen and Wolfson Colleges, Oxford; Surrey University; East Riding Museum; and the British Antarctic Survey hold examples.

John KELLY 1965– Painter and creator of quirky and witty sculptures featuring zebras, cows and horses who was born in Bristol. He emigrated to Australia with his family when he was six months old, graduating from RMIT University, Melbourne, 1983–5, majoring in painting; gained his arts master's degree there, 1992–5; then was an affiliate student of Slade School of Fine Art, 1996–7, having travelled in Europe and America. Commissions, grants and awards included Projects Grant, Visual Arts Board, Australia Council, 1988; City of Richmond Acquisitions Art Award, the John Storey Memorial Scholarship at RMIT and The Queen's Trust Grant, all 1993; Australia Council, Visual Arts/Craft Board Barcelona Studio, 1994; Anne & Gordon Samstag International Visual Arts Scholarship Award, 1995; and "Comment L'Europe à cache la vache folle", commissioned frontispiece, *Liberation*, 1996. Took part in numerous group shows in Australia and Europe and had regular solo exhibitions, later ones including The Piccadilly Gallery and Niagara Galleries, Melbourne, both 2000, and Piccadilly again in 2002 and 2005. Many Australian public galleries hold works by Kelly, whose Cow up a Tree, shown on the Champs Elysées, Paris, was bought by The Melbourne Docklands Consortium for installation on the waterfront.

Kenness George KELLY: *see* **FOWOKAN**

Mary KELLY 1941– Artist working in mixed media, born in America. After studying at the College of St Teresa, Minnesota, 1959–63, then at Pius XII Institute, Florence, 1963–5, Kelly taught fine art at the American University in Beirut, Lebanon, after which she moved to England, undertaking postgraduate study at St Martin's School of Art 1968–70. In 1973, the year she received the Greater London Arts Association Fellowship, Kelly began work on her key work *Post-Partum Document*, which aimed to "expose the fetishistic function of representation". *Footnotes and Bibliography, Post-Partum Document* appeared in 1977, when Kelly gained an Arts Council Award. The Lina Garnade Memorial Foundation Award followed in 1978. Kelly took part in a number of exhibitions with sociological themes. She had a solo show at ICA in 1976, two more soon after at Museum of Modern Art, Oxford, and Leeds University Gallery, with a five-year, 1970–5 film and text retrospective at Norwich Gallery, 2000, another exhibition at Robert Sandelson, 2001. Taught at Camberwell School of Art and at Goldsmiths' College School of Art. Arts Council holds her work. Lived in London.

Maurice KELLY 1920– Representational painter, born in Bournemouth, Hampshire, who studied at Royal College of Art. He was a member of The Suffolk Group and showed with Young Contemporaries, Gallery 44 in Aldeburgh, Digby Gallery in Colchester and Warwick University Arts Centre. Kelly's work is held in the South African government's World War II collection, by several education authorities and in many British and foreign private collections. Lived in Walberswick, Suffolk.

Mick KELLY 1949– Painter of domestic scenes who was born in Wallasey, Cheshire. He studied at Camberwell School of Arts and Crafts, 1969–71, Goldsmiths' College School of Art, 1976–77, returning there in the early 1980s for his master's degree. Among Kelly's shows was a solo exhibition at Woodlands Art Gallery, 1981. Much of his work was in private collections.

Percy KELLY 1918–1993 Painter, draughtsman, printmaker and teacher, born in Workington, Cumberland, into a strongly religious background, his father a carpenter. He could "draw with a pencil before I could talk". From 1932 became a telegraph messenger in 1934 postal and telegraph officer for Kendal. In the Army in World War II drew maps and diagrams and was influenced by the work of Paul Klee, Graham Sutherland, Stanley Spencer and C F Tunnicliffe, seen in exhibitions. In 1946 he resumed Post Office duties, showing at RA, RI, RBA, RSA and elsewhere. Kelly resigned from Post Office in 1958, taught part-time and took up printmaking. From 1961–5, having raised £500, studied lithography and printed textiles at Carlisle College of Art and Design, obtaining distinctions, in 1964 gaining a travel scholarship to Brittany. Worked on commission for Sir Nicholas Sekers' silk mills at Hensingham, Whitehaven, having a solo show there at Rosehill Theatre in 1966, another at Fermoy Gallery, King's Lynn, in 1969. From 1970 Kelly's life was unsettled, with two divorces, health and financial problems. In 1980 settled in Attleborough, Norfolk, dying in hospital. A show of his landscapes was held at Castlegate House, Cockermouth, Cumbria, in 1994.

Peter KELLY 1921–1993 Painter, lecturer and farmer, born in Balham, south London, who attended Ampleforth College, studying with Maurice Percival; Queen's College, Oxford; served with the Royal Naval Volunteer Reserve; and studied post-World War II at the Courtauld Institute of Art. He was attached to the fine arts department at the Barber Institute, Birmingham, 1948–51, then farmed, combining this with art history lecturing at Swansea, Barry and Leicester and in the fine arts department of the National Museum of Wales, Cardiff. Mixed shows included RWA and RA Summer Exhibition, where he had work accepted but not hung. Influences on Kelly's work included Cedric Morris; David Jones, Eric Gill and the Guild of St Dominic; Cézanne; and Ruskin. As well as landscape, portraits, nudes, animals and still life, Kelly's artistic preoccupations included mythological and Christian incarnational subjects. He lived in Welsh Newton, Monmouth, Herefordshire.

Peter KELLY 1931– Artist born in Ilford, Essex, who spent his life in the county. He studied at West Ham School of Art and Technology and the Central School of Art and Design. From 1952–7 he worked as a graphic designer before concentrating on painting and illustration. Kelly was elected RBA in 1982, later winning the Daler-Rowney Award, Higgs & Hill Bursary and was nominated for the De Laszlo Medal. He was five times a finalist in Hunting Art Prizes, he won The Jeffrey Archer Award at RWS Open, 1993, later the American Express Award at the Discerning Eye exhibition, Mall Galleries. Kelly was noted for crisp still lifes, recalling the seventeenth-century Dutch Old Masters. He exhibited at the RA Summer Exhibition, shared a show at Thompson's Gallery in 1998, was in A Select Seven at W H Patterson Fine Art Ltd, 2001; had a series of solo exhibitions at Ebury Galleries; and in 2003 at W H Patterson showed views and interiors painted in St Petersburg, Russia, in that year. In 2005, Kelly shared an exhibition with Philippa Cooper at the Chappel Galleries, Chappel.

Phil KELLY 1953– Landscape and figure painter using a rich palette whose sometimes heavily impastoed pictures encompassed a range of styles. Kelly was born in Dublin, Ireland, and after Rugby School attended Bath College of Art, where his work was well marked by Frank Auerbach. He then lived in Mexico for many years, loving the sun and vibrancy of the country. Although rich in colour, energy and gesture, Kelly's work was carefully considered before he started painting, which he did on the floor to the sounds of jazz, working all round the picture. Had many mixed shows in Britain and abroad, including Whitechapel Open, from 1977, and RA Summer Exhibition, from 1992. By the time of his one-man exhibition at The Millinery Works in 2000 Kelly had had several dozen solo shows, including an acclaimed one at the Museum of Modern Art, Mexico City, in 1997. Others included La Ciudad Electrica, Six Chapel Row Contemporary Art, Bath in 2003. His work was held in many international private collections, including that of Alan Howarth, one-time Labour Minister for the Arts.

Roger KELLY 1973– Painter, born in Nottingham, who won a fine art degree at Wimbledon School of Art, 1993–6, attending Chelsea College of Art, 1996–7. Had a residency at Royal Court Theatre, 1994, the year of the exhibition Coming on Strong, at the Theatre with tour. Also appeared in Cooltan Summer Exhibition at Cooltan Arts, 1993; New Contemporaries, at Tate Gallery in Liverpool and Camden Arts Centre, and Nerve, at Jason and Rhodes Gallery, both 1996; and in the 1997–8 and 1999–00 John Moores Liverpool Exhibitions. Had a first solo show at Beaux Arts, 1998, another at Nylon, 2000. His show at Nylon in 2003 exploited the gap between representation and abstraction. Kelly was the son of the artist Paulette Fedarb. He lived in London.

Steve KELLY 1952– Sculptor and teacher who attended Doncaster College of Art, St Martin's School of Art and Goldsmiths' College School of Art. He was an art teacher, 1976–81, a part-time lecturer in sculpture at North Essex School of Art, 1981–7, and from then lectured in sculpture full-time at South-East Essex College of Arts & Technology. Showed in New Contemporaries, 1974; Saffron Walden Corn Exchange from 1977; Beecroft Gallery, Southend-on-Sea from 1988; and in Drawing Towards Sculpture at Isis Gallery, Leigh-on-Sea, 1993.

Robert KELSEY 1949– Painter in oil notable for his lively, colourful landscapes of Britain and France. Born in Glasgow he studied at the School of Art there, 1966–70, under David Donaldson, Alexander Goudie and James Robertson, and went on to exhibit with Glasgow Art Club, Paisley Institute of Fine Arts and Royal Glasgow Institute of the Fine Arts, RSA, ROI and RSW. In 1993 completed five landscapes of the Turnberry course used for the 1994 British Open Golf Championship, for hanging in the clubhouse. The Paisley Institute awarded Kelsey a diploma in 1998. Later solo shows included John Martin of London, 1996, and Thompson's Gallery, Marylebone, 2002. The Fleming Collection and a number of corporate collections hold examples.

Kalman KEMENY 1896–1994 Artist, critic and teacher, born in Nagykanizsa, Hungary, his daughter being the artist Lydia Kemeny. He was mainly a portrait, landscape and still life artist in oil, but also made pottery. Studied at the Academy of Art, Budapest, 1913–14; was an Official War Artist to the Austro-Hungarian Army in World War I; and attended Academy of Creative Arts, Vienna, 1920–3, followed by a two-year postgraduate course. Between 1925–38 Kemeny lived in Pilsen, Czechoslovakia, moving to London in the latter year. During World War II while practising as an artist he worked in an aircraft factory and at fire-watching. From 1947–79 Kemeny taught at Hammersmith College of Art and for some years was advisor to the House of Commons Fine Art Committee. Took part in mixed shows at Cooling and Leger Galleries and at Roland, Browse & Delbanco. Had a retrospective in 1991 at Ben Uri Art Society which, like Imperial War Museum, holds his work.

Lydia KEMENY fl. from 1940s– Designer, illustrator, artist and teacher, daughter of the painter Kalman Kemeny, who studied design – fashion/textiles at St Martin's School of Art, 1942–4, then at Royal College of Art, 1944–7. While at College she won the *Vogue* Talent Contest, joining the magazine after graduation, working as an illustrator of fashion reports from London and abroad. Concurrently, Kemeny was invited to teach at St Martin's School of Art, where from 1976 she was head of department fashion/textiles; the department acquired an international reputation. Kemeny was in 1988 made reader in fashion at The London Institute and from 1989–90 was fashion tutor at Middlesex Polytechnic. She was fashion consultant to the television series *The House of Elliot* in 1993. As an artist she showed at RA, LG, NEAC, the Leicester, Savage and John Whibley Galleries and at Paris Salon. Paintings were acquired by the Ministry of Education, Greater London Council, Hertfordshire County Council and were reproduced by the New York Graphic Society and Medici Gallery. Lithographs were commissioned by Curwen Press for Collectors Guild. Lived in London.

David KEMP 1945– Sculptor and assemblage artist, born in London, who spent his childhood in Canada and attended a boys' grammar school in England. He joined the Merchant Navy for four years, then studied painting at Farnham and Wimbledon Schools of Art. In the early 1970s he moved to west Cornwall and pursued sculpture. He scouted the countryside for old farm machinery and industrial scrap and from this created strange beasts and insects. The Arts Council's The Beetle and its The Electro-Griffin are good examples. Northern Arts and public galleries in Glasgow, Manchester, Sheffield and Wolverhampton hold Kemp's work. Kemp was artist-in-residence at several sites where he would construct his witty creations "as a future archaeologist reconstructing the machines and artefacts of a distant past". Among notable group shows were the Welsh Sculpture Trust's Margam exhibition Sculpture in a Country Park, 1983, and A Quality of Light, at The Tate at St Ives and other venues, 1997. Solo shows included Graves Art Gallery, Sheffield; Manchester City Art Gallery, Glynn Vivian Art Gallery, Swansea; McLellan Galleries, Glasgow; and Newlyn Art Gallery, 2002. Kemp had a major setback in 1995 when vandals broke into his workshop, started a fire and destroyed nearly 20 years' work. Notable public sculptures by Kemp are The Iron Horse, for Four Lane Ends Metro Station, Newcastle upon Tyne; The Navigators, Hays Galleria, London Bridge; The Old Transformers, Consett; and Old King Coal, Pelton Fell.

Jeka KEMP 1876–1967 Watercolourist and woodcut artist, born in Bellahouston, Glasgow; she hated the name Jacobina given her, shortening it to Jeka. Details of her early life are vague, but she probably studied painting in Glasgow and London, about 1903–4 attending Académie Julian, Paris. She embarked on wide travels to paint, including Europe and North Africa, but showed at first in Scotland from about 1907, having solo exhibitions at Macindoe's Gallery, Glasgow, 1912–14. Several of her pictures were bought by the French government. During World War I Kemp worked as a nurse-masseuse in Paris hospitals. Further shows included Marcel Bernheim, Paris, and Warneuke's Galleries, Glasgow, 1920, and Galerie de la Librairie de la Presse, Nantes, 1922. Kemp continued to live in France until she returned to England in 1939, living with her sisters in Dorset, finally in Eastbourne, Sussex. She had given up painting in 1927, but her reputation was revived by a show at Belgrave Gallery and Wellington Fine Art, Glasgow, in 1977.

Richard KEMP 1958– Abstract painter, born in Croydon, Surrey, where he studied at the College of Art and Design, 1974–6, then Ravensbourne College of Art and Design, 1977–80. Among group show appearances were New Contemporaries, at ICA, 1979; LG, 1985; Carpenter's Road Open Studios from 1988; Pomeroy Purdy Gallery from same year; and John Moores Exhibition, Liverpool, 1991–2. He had a solo show at Greenwich Theatre Art Gallery in 1984. Lived in London.

Roshini KEMPADOO 1959– Digital artist and teacher, born in Crawley, Sussex, who lived mostly in the United Kingdom, based in London, but who spent 10 years in the Caribbean. She graduated with commendation in visual communications at West Midlands College of Higher Education, 1981–4; gained her master's in photographic studies at Derbyshire College of Higher Education, 1988–9; in 1991 undertaking training in America, involving work at the National Museum of African Art, Smithsonian, Washington, and in New York at the Schomberg Center for the Research in Black Culture. Among many advisory posts held was membership of the visual arts awards panel of the Scottish Arts Council, 1997–8, as well as work for the Arts Council and London Arts Board. Was a speaker at numerous workshops and conferences in Britain and abroad; residencies included Groby Road Hospital, 1990; teaching part-time at Napier University, Edinburgh, from 1995. She took part in many group shows, later solo exhibitions including Virtual Exiles, available online through the Institute of International Visual Arts website, 1999–00. Cartwright Hall and The Museum of Photography, Film and Television, both in Bradford and Walsall Museum and Art Gallery, Walsall, hold Kempadoo's work.

Richard KEMPE 1929– Artist and teacher who was greatly influenced by Fritz Gross while at Bedford School. As a student at Central School of Arts and Crafts under William Johnstone, Kempe's tutors included Victor Pasmore and Mervyn Peake. He spent a short time as a designer in Boston, Massachusetts. While teaching in Norfolk Kempe studied work by the Norwich School, especially J S Cotman, and took up wood engraving. Began painting professionally in 1980. Mixed shows included the RWA, SWA and Bath Society. He had a series of solo exhibitions, including West Country views at Big Wide Bay gallery, Tavistock, 2000. Lived in Bath, Somerset.

Jake KEMPSELL 1940– Sculptor and teacher, born in Dumfries, Scotland, who remained close to his Scottish roots. He studied at Edinburgh College of Art and from 1965–75 lectured in sculpture there. He was invited to join the sculpture faculty of the British School at Rome in 1982, was a faculty visitor there in 1985, and from 1975–00 was director of sculpture at Duncan of Jordanstone College of Art, Dundee. Kempsell did much to promote sculpture in Scotland, being a director of Workshop and Artists' Studio Provision; in 1978 he was one of the founders of the Scottish Sculpture Trust. He showed widely in Scotland and Britain, being featured in Small Sculpture from the Collection of The Scottish Arts Council, 1978, and in the Welsh Sculpture Trust's 1983 show Sculpture in a Country Park, at Margam. Kempsell found his organic materials – wood, slate, stone and feathers – on the shore of the North Sea and in the fields and woodyards of Angus. These were arranged in enigmatic forms, such as his Love Child of the Butterfly that Ravished an Elephant, on the ski slopes of Glenshee.

Kim KEMPSHALL 1934– Printmaker, painter and teacher, full name Hubert Kim Kempshall, signing work K K, who was born in Manchester. Studied at the College of Art there, 1951–5, then Royal College of Art, 1957–60. Went on to teach fine art at Birmingham Polytechnic. Showed RA, RSA, Arts Council and held solo exhibitions. Scottish National Gallery of Modern Art and a number of provincial public collections hold his work. Lived in Harborne, Birmingham.

William KEMPSTER 1914–1976 Painter, printmaker and mural artist, notably in tempera, born in London. Studied at Wimbledon School of Art under Gerald Cooper and William Sullivan, 1937–9, then Royal College of Art, 1939–42, where his teachers included Ernest Tristram. He did a great deal of exhibition work for Central Office of Information and Festival of Britain in 1951, illustrating aspects of British life and work. His work was illustrated in *Future*, *Lilliput* and other publications. He exhibited at RA Summer Exhibition in 1973 and 1974, by which time he had moved to Hungerford, Berkshire, having earlier lived in St John's Wood, north London. Kempster was a fine and adventurous printmaker, good examples being offered after his death by Katharine House Gallery, Marlborough.

Lucy KEMP-WELCH 1869–1958 Painter, illustrator and teacher, outstanding for her pictures of horses. Was born in Bournemouth, Hampshire, older sister of painter Edith Kemp-Welch, who died in 1941. After attending the local School of Art, the sisters from 1891 studied with Hubert von Herkomer at his school in Bushey, Hertfordshire, where she settled. She ran it from 1905–26, initially as Bushey School of Painting and, after it moved to her house, as the Kemp-Welch School of Animal Painting. From 1928 her friend and assistant Marguerite Frobisher continued under the name The Frobisher School of Art. Kemp-Welch had early success with her student work Gypsy Drovers taking Horses to a Fair, hung at RA in 1895. She was a prolific exhibitor, notably at Fine Art Society, RCamA of which she was a member, as she was of RI, ROI, RBC and RBA; in 1914 she was president of the Society of Animal Painters. Refused permission to be a war artist in World War I, Kemp-Welch responded with the famous recruiting poster *Forward!* Kemp-Welch was an expert horsewoman and in her late-fifties began her travels with Sanger's Circus. Had a solo show at Arlington Gallery, 1938. Tate Gallery, Russell-Cotes Art Gallery and other public collections hold Kemp-Welch's pictures, which were latterly extensively sold by David Messum. Illustrated several books, notably Anna Sewell's *Black Beauty*, using Baden-Powell's horse Black Prince as a model. Died in Watford, Hertfordshire.

Margaret KEMP-WELCH fl. from 1890s–1968 Painter, printmaker and teacher, born in London, cousin of the artists Lucy and Edith Kemp-Welch. She studied with Frank Short and Hubert von Herkomer at his school in Bushey, Hertfordshire, from 1891. Went on to teach at Clapham High School. She showed with Ridley Art Club, RA, RE and elsewhere. Lived in London for many years, then at Throwleigh, Devon. Bushey Museum holds good examples of her prints.

KEN: *see* **Kenneth AITKEN**

Alice KENDALL 1896–1955 Painter and musician, born in Little Hulton, Lancashire. She studied at Manchester College of Music; and art in New York and at Edinburgh College of Art, where her teachers included David Foggie and Gerald Moira. Showed at UA and SEA, of both of which she was a member, SSA, RBA and RI. Mrs Kendall, who painted in several European countries, was the mother of the artist Alice Rebecca Kendall. Died in Cyprus, where she painted.

Alice Rebecca KENDALL fl. from early 1940s– Painter, muralist, illustrator and writer, daughter of the artist Alice Kendall, born in New York. She studied at Edinburgh College of Art. Kendall was a member of SWA and Royal Glasgow Institute of the Fine Arts as well as Royal Zoological Society in Scotland. Her published work included a book for children, *Funny Fishes*, and contributions to *Punch* and *Poetry Review*. Showed at RA, NEAC and Paris Salon and shared several shows with her mother at Cooling Galleries in 1940s and 1950s. Completed murals for British Council and Ministry of Labour. Lived in London for many years.

Dinah Roe KENDALL 1923– Painter and printmaker, born in Bakewell, Derbyshire. Her output included Biblical scenes in a bright palette updated to the present day, influenced by Stanley Spencer, as in her solo show at Duncan Campbell Contemporary Art, 1995, one of a series. During World War II, Kendall nursed for the Red Cross. Attended Sheffield School of Art, 1946–8, then the Slade School of Fine Art, 1948–51, teachers including A H Gerrard and William Coldstream. Family needs stopped her painting until 1968, then she studied printmaking, 1968–72 with Anthony Gross and Stanley Jones. She returned to Sheffield, Yorkshire, in 1993, having bought a house in Cyprus and lived there from 1988, in 2005 finally settling in Folkestone, Kent. Group exhibitions included Graves Art Gallery, Sheffield, from 1962; Beecroft Art Gallery, Southend-on-Sea, 1971; and CCA Gallery, Cambridge, 1995. In 1976 she shared a show with her daughter, Emma Chandler, at the Bury St Edmunds Gallery. Later solo exhibitions included Oundle School, Oundle, 1996, and Canterbury Cathedral, 2001. The Chapel Royal, St James's Palace; H M Prison Chapel, Doncaster; and St Paul's Cathedral, Nicosia, hold her work.

Kay Thetford KENDALL fl. from 1970s– Sculptor and sculptural jewellery creator working in a variety of precious and non-precious materials, notable for her cats and mythical creatures. She was born in Manchester and studied at Malvern and Tunbridge Wells Colleges of Art and at Hertfordshire College of Art and Design, 1976–9. Was for a time in charge of design firm KTK Ltd. She was a member of SWA and RMS, in 1986 winning RMS's Bidder and Borne sculpture award; also exhibited at SPS; and had a series of solo exhibitions in Welwyn Garden City, Hertfordshire, where she lived, elsewhere in south of England and in Italy.

Alistair KENDRY 1957– Painter who studied at Hereford College of Art, 1979, Bath Academy of Art, 1980–3, and Slade School of Fine Art, 1986–8. He gained a Southern Arts Award in 1987, a Barclays Bank Award in 1988. Took part in many group shows from early 1980s, including Whitworth Art Gallery, Manchester, 1981; Stowells Trophy at RA, 1982; York Festival, 1984; and Six of the Best at Christopher Hull Gallery, 1989.

David KENNARD 1953– Painter, printmaker and teacher, born in Beaconsfield, Buckinghamshire, who studied at Marlborough College, 1967–71, winning a travel scholarship for arts studies in 1972, using it for travel to Italy, 1974. After language studies at the Sorbonnne, Paris, and travelling and painting in France, 1971, Kennard did a foundation course at Gloucestershire College of Art and Design, 1972–3; gained a first-class honours degree from Bristol Polytechnic, 1973–6, fine art specialising in painting; then did postgraduate studying in printmaking, City and Guilds Art School, 1980–1; with a study period in Paris in 1987, in the studio of Patrick Betaudier, concentrating on the science and practice of oil painting from van Eyck through to the early Renaissance. In 1976 Kennard was awarded first prize in South Western Regional Competition, for art students, Winsor and Newton Award. He won an Arts Council Purchase Prize, Cheltenham Society of Artists, 1982. Teaching experience included Harrow School, Symondsbury College and School of Art. His commissioned journeys included Albania and Istanbul, 1998–9; southern Sahara, Ethiopia and The Lost Cities of the Mediterranean, 1995–7; and Athens to the Red Sea on a tall ship, 1999. He painted through Galloway and the Highlands of Scotland, 1994–8, and Cowes week and Henley Royal Regatta, 1996–9. Kennard was artist to Garsington Opera, Oxford, 1990–6. As well as many mixed show appearances, Kennard held a steady stream of solo exhibitions, starting with a studio show at Guiting Power, 1978. Later ones included Archeus Fine Art from 1994, Jerram Gallery, Salisbury, 1995, Daphne Johns Contemporary Art, 12 Duke Street, and Birmingham University, both 1999; Dorset County Museum, Dorchester, 2000; and Archeus Fine Art, 2002. A deft and colourful impression of a scene characterised Kennard's work. Lived in Dorset.

Peter KENNARD 1949– Artist in wide range of media, and teacher, born in London, who attended Byam Shaw School of Art, 1966–7; Slade School of Fine Art, 1967–70; and Royal College of Art, 1976–9. He lectured in fine art and photography at West Surrey College of Art, 1989–94, from 1994 being senior lecturer in photography, Royal College of Art. Gardner Arts Centre, Sussex University, gave him an artist-in-residence show in 1971. Kennard's photomontages were regularly published in *The Guardian*, and book covers were commissioned by Penguin, Pluto Press, Paladin and Verso. Film and video work included photomontages for Labour Party political broadcast against nuclear weapons, 1982; *State of Emergency – South Africa, Bandung File*, Channel 4, 1986; and *Welcome to Britain*, The Late Show, BBC2, 1992. As well as group shows in Britain and abroad, Kennard held a series of solo exhibitions from 1968. His retrospectives included Images Against War 1965–1985, Barbican Centre, 1985, and photomontages at Zelda Cheatle Gallery, 1997. Some exhibitions had accompanying publications, such as *Our Financial Times*, a collaboration with the politician Ken Livingstone, 1995, and *Domesday Book*, foreword by Harold Pinter, 1999–00, both at Gimpel Fils. That gallery showed Kennard's Decoration in 2004, a savage indictment of the invasion of Iraq in 2003–4. The Arts Council, Imperial War Museum, Victoria & Albert Museum and other British and foreign public collections hold examples.

Emma KENNAWAY 1954– Painter notable for her ability to catch a sympathetic likeness. She won a Commissioning Prize in the 2003 Garrick/Milne Prize with her portrait of Timothy West as King Lear. As a child Kennaway travelled extensively with her parents, living on a houseboat in Kashmir and later in Hollywood, where her father was a writer. She studied at the Ruskin School of Drawing and Fine Art, Oxford. Had work in many private collections

Alexander Grieve KENNEDY 1889–c.1962 Painter, illustrator and writer, born in Liverpool. Studied at Liverpool School of Art and Royal College of Art. Exhibited widely in the provinces and did animal illustrations for books published by Blackie. Usher Gallery, Lincoln, holds his work, sometimes signed A Maculric. Lived in Lincoln and exhibited with the Lincolnshire Artists' Society.

Cecil KENNEDY 1905–1997 Painter in oil, noted for his meticulous pictures of flowers, based on arrangements by his wife Winifred, a ladybird being a common feature. He was the grandson of an artist who had worked alongside Corot in France, Cecil's father was the painter and designer Thomas Robert Kennedy, his brother the artist Thomas Kennedy. He was born in Leyton, Essex, and studied art in London, Paris, Antwerp and Zürich. During Army service on the continent in World War II, Kennedy was able to meet Flemish painters and study their and Dutch painters' work first-hand. He showed at RA, RSA, RHA, Fine Art Society, Paris Salon (where he won a Silver Medal in 1956, a Gold in 1970), the provinces and elsewhere abroad. Queen Mary, the Duke of Windsor, the Astors and newspaper magnate Lord Thomson of Fleet were among his patrons. Public galleries in Rochdale and Merthyr Tydfil hold examples. Owing to advanced age, Kennedy finished painting around 1993. Lived in St Albans, Hertfordshire.

Cedric KENNEDY 1898–1968 Landscape and portrait painter and teacher, born in Exeter, Devon, educated at Rugby School. Served in the Royal Flying Corps in World War I (completed a series of aerial pictures), was shot down and made a prisoner of war. Studied under Richard Jack at London School of Art, Florence School of Art in 1923 and Royal Academy Schools with Charles Sims, 1925–8. After teaching at Rugby, Kennedy taught at Cheltenham College and nearby at Dean Close School, served in camouflage during World War II, then returned to Dean Close, 1945–62. Exhibited at RA, NEAC, extensively at Walker's and Cooling Galleries. There was a big memorial show at Cheltenham, 1969; one at Mannings, 1972; another at Sally Hunter Fine Art, 1997. Sally Hunter held a joint exhibition of work by Kennedy and his pupil John Marshall at 9 Clarendon Cross in 2002. Victoria & Albert Museum, Ashmolean Museum in Oxford, Imperial War Museum and various provincial collections hold examples.

Chris KENNEDY fl. from 1980s– Mixed media artist who exhibited widely in the northwest of England. He was an artist-in-residence at Walker Art Gallery in Liverpool for a period in 1990 and several years later completed his master's degree at Winchester School of Art. In 1992 he was included in Bluecoat Artists '92, work by members of the Bluecoat Artists' Association in Liverpool, at Williamson Art Gallery & Museum in Birkenhead.

Mat Barber KENNEDY 1962– Painter, born in London, who studied architecture at the University of Sheffield and at the Royal College of Art, graduating in 1988. Became a full-time painter in 1990, travelling widely to create his urban architectural views. His paintings reflected an understanding of and passion for the "elements of architecture: bricks and mortar, plaster, concrete and steel, built up in layers, decaying in pieces." Kennedy was elected a member of the RI in 1994, in 1999 sharing a show at The Linda Blackstone Gallery, Pinner. In 2004 he was included in The Autumn Show at The Wykeham Gallery, Stockbridge.

Richard KENNEDY 1910–1989 Painter, draughtsman and writer, born in Cambridge. He was educated at Marlborough School, left at 16 and joined the Hogarth Press as apprentice, the story of which he told in the volume of autobiography *A Boy at the Hogarth Press*, 1972; in 1977 he followed this with *A Parcel of Time*. After a period in an advertising agency and as an illustrator for *Strang's Weekly News* and brief studies including Central School of Arts and Crafts, during World War II service in Royal Air Force commenced his career as a book illustrator which was to encompass dozens of volumes, chiefly for children. Exhibitions included Gallery Edward Harvane, 1972, and King Street Gallery, 1981, with additional shows at his home in Maidenhead, Berkshire. He was influenced by the work of Henri Gaudier-Brzeska and Henri Matisse.

Thomas KENNEDY 1900–1982 Painter in oil and watercolour, born in Leyton, east London, who made a successful living by his brush from 16 to 80. His brother was the flower painter Cecil Kennedy, their father the artist Robert Thomas Kennedy, and grandfather Thomas Kennedy of Edinburgh. As well as studying at art school in London, for many years Thomas worked in the British Museum, Turner, Constable and Italian and Dutch Old Masters being special influences. His work was often reproduced and he showed at RA, RSA, RBSA and with Frost & Reed. HM Queen Elizabeth The Queen Mother bought Kennedy's work, which is in many private collections in Britain and abroad. Lived in Chingford, Essex, and died in Whipps Cross Hospital, Leytonstone.

George R KENNERLEY fl. from 1950– Naturally talented self-taught painter and collector with a strong enthusiasm for art which he combined with an active business career in Liverpool, being a director of Vernons Pools. He was a friend of John Moores and assembled a collection that included works by Vuillard, Bonnard, Bomberg, de Staël and his friend William Scott, with whom he painted at Corsham School of Art and St Ives, Cornwall. Kennerley also made collages, as in his Crane Kalman solo show, 1970, from which Walker Art Gallery acquired one of its works by him. Williamson Art Gallery in Birkenhead and House of Commons also hold examples. Kennerley had a solo show at Cadogan Contemporary in 1993, mixed exhibition appearances including RA Summer Exhibition Leicester Galleries and Browse & Darby. Lived in Caldy Wirral, Cheshire.

George KENNETHSON 1910–1994 Sculptor, born in Richmond, Surrey, as Arthur George Mackenzie. Was married to the painter Eileen Guthrie, one of their five children being the photographer Nicholas Mackenzie. Kennethson studied painting at Royal Academy Schools, 1928–34

turning to sculpture in 1937. Kennethson carved stone directly, using only simple sculptural drawings. The nature of the stone influenced his idea of what the finished work would be. His constant subject matter was birds, plants, heads, sky and sea, and his style, influenced by Gaudier-Brzeska and Brancusi, changed little. Much of his work was modest in size. He was an infrequent exhibitor, but had retrospectives at University of Birmingham, 1974; New Art Centre, 1988; and Pallant House, Chichester, 1993. From the mid-1950s Kennethson lived in Oundle, Northamptonshire, in a Victorian house next to a former brewery which contained more than 300 sculptures made over 40 years. Kettle's Yard in Cambridge and the Scottish National Gallery of Modern Art, Edinburgh, hold examples. In 2004 there was a first London retrospective at Archeus Fine Art.

James Smyth KENNETT 1915– Painter and draughtsman, by profession a harbour official. Born and lived in Belfast, where he graduated in commercial science after studies at Queen's University. Studied art in London in mid-1940s and at RUA and exhibited in Belfast.

John KENNEY 1911–1972 Painter and book illustrator who specialised in hunting and sporting scenes. After being educated in Leicester and attending the School of Art there Kenney became a commercial illustrator. It was after World War II that Kenney turned to sporting art, drawing on hunting scenes from his locality. Towards the end of his life he lost the sight of one eye, which added problems to years of ill-health, but he kept on working. He showed at Gadsby Gallery, Leicester, 1963, a posthumous exhibition being held in 1980. In the year of his death Abercrombie and Fitch, New York, held a show. The Royal Artillery Museum, Woolwich, holds sketches by Kenney completed during his Army service.

David KENNING 1933– Landscape painter and printmaker, notable for watercolours of Essex where he lived until 1988, then of the Andalusia region of Spain, where he settled. Kenning studied under Frederick Gore at St Martin's School of Art, 1952–5. Mixed shows included Beecroft Gallery, Southend, from 1975; RA Summer Exhibition, 1980; RSW from 1984; and Artists in Essex, Epping Forest Museum, 1985. Among his later solo shows were Malaga and Granada in Spain and Phoenix Gallery, Lavenham, 1990. Kenning also produced limited-edition silkscreen prints of Spanish and English subjects.

Eric KENNINGTON 1888–1960 Sculptor, draughtsman and painter. Born in London, son of the artist T B Kennington, he studied at Lambeth School of Art and the City and Guilds School. Exhibited from 1908 at the RA; also showed at Leicester Galleries, Fine Art Society, Goupil Gallery, ROI and RP. Kennington was an Official War Artist, 1916–19, after being invalided out of the Army. The experience was to have a marked influence on his work, his first one-man show at the Goupil Gallery, 1916, of the Kensingtons at Laventie creating a great impression and identifying him in the public mind with depictions of men of action. Soon after the war he travelled in Arabia to illustrate T E Lawrence's *Seven Pillars of Wisdom*, and he was to draw memorable studies of Lawrence over many years. During World War II a book of Kennington's portraits, *Drawing the RAF*, 1942, including his typically incisive studies, further linked him with the forces, as had his sculptures, the memorial to the 24th Division at Battersea Park and the British memorial at Soissons, France, after World War I. Also completed a head of T E Lawrence in St Paul's Cathedral, London, and carvings on the Royal Shakespeare Memorial Theatre, Stratford-upon-Avon. Signed work E H K. Elected RA, 1959. Died at Reading, Berkshire. The Henry Moore Institute, Leeds, held a Kennington exhibition, The War God & Other Works, and his graphic work was shown at the Strang Print Room at University College London, both 2001. Photographs and books from Kennington's library, entitled Eric Kennington's Visions of Mexico, was held at the Henry Moore Institute library in 2004.

Sue KENNINGTON 1955– Painter, born in London, who gained an honours degree in humanities from Middlesex Polytechnic, 1979–82, then was at Chelsea College of Art, 1989–94. Exhibitions included Summer Exhibition at University Gallery, Newcastle upon Tyne, 1993; Small Works at Argile Gallery and Spirit of Place, Piece Hall Gallery in Halifax, both 1994; Tricycle Gallery and Pacesetters at Peterborough Museum and Art Gallery, both 1995; and New Contemporaries, at Tate Gallery, Liverpool and Camden Arts Centre, 1996.

Jenny KENNISH 1944– Self-taught sculptor in porcelain of wild flowers and animals, born in Ewell, Surrey. From 1965–90 she was a schoolteacher, then was self-employed as an artist. Was a member of RMS and SWA and a founder-member of the Society of Botanical Artists, showing at Mall and Westminster Galleries. Kennish said that her "chief influence has been my surroundings. I have always been fortunate and lived in a rural environment." Lived in Little London, Hampshire.

Chris KENNY 1959– Painter, creator of artist's boxes and books and collage "poetry", and teacher, born in Fleet, Hampshire. He studied at Courtauld Institute of Art, 1979–82, then became an artist and part-time teacher. Surrealism was one influence on Kenny's work, psychology-mythology being notable themes. Produced a record cover for The Fall, 1986. Other commissions included an artist's book, *Little Journeys into the Heavenly Country*, 1992; *Four Seasons Tree Cycle*, for Music Sales Ltd, 1993; a series of collages and installations for The Cross, from 1998; and Works for West Street Hotel, 2001. Mixed shows included Riverside Open from 1985; London art fairs from 1990, the year when he was main prizewinner at LG annual exhibition; Six Young British Painters, toured Spain, 1991–2; Art in Boxes, England & Co, from 1992; and British Surrealism 1935–95, same venue, 1995. Had a solo show at Birch & Conran in 1989, 1994 venues including Brighton Marina, High Wycombe Museum and Aylesbury Museum. England & Co, which often featured Kenny's distinctive constructions from twigs, in 2003 gave him a solo exhibition: Part of me is floating above myself. This followed an acquisition by the Victoria & Albert Museum and Museum of London of Kenny's work. Baker & McKenzie, National Westminster Bank in Madrid and University of South Australia's book collection hold examples. Lived in London.

Mary KENNY 1959– Sculptor, teacher and artist involved in performance-related and community arts work. She attended Bournville School of Arts and Crafts, Birmingham, 1975–7; graduated from Bath Academy of Art,

1977–80; and did apprentice training with a stone-carver and mason in Bristol, 1980–1. Her mixed appearances included British Women Artists' Diary exhibition at York Festival, 1988, and she also showed on a number of occasions at Cleveland and Central Galleries, Bath. Had a solo show at Cross Community Centre, Pontardawe, sponsored by WAC, 1985. In 1985 completed Big Grinning Fish, at Skyros, Greece, and Flying the Kite, Portland Sculpture Park, and in 1986–7 Souvenir of Tomorrow at Sculpture Park, Villany, Hungary, sponsored by British Council. She taught at a school for maladjusted children for a time, and also lectured at Gloucester College of Art and Design and North Staffordshire College of Art. Worked in Edinburgh, where she was involved in Theatre Workshop arts resource team.

Michael KENNY 1941–1999 Sculptor and creator of painted wood reliefs, draughtsman and teacher. He was born in Liverpool where he attended the College of Art, 1959–61, then Slade School of Fine Art, 1961–4. He won a prize in the Littlewoods Sculptural Design Competition, 1964; a Sainsbury Award, 1965; then a series of Arts Council Awards. Elected RA in 1986, from 1995 being its treasurer and a trustee; was elected RBS, 1992, and RWA, 1997. He taught at Goldsmiths' College, 1966–88, from 1983–8 as head of fine art; at the Slade, 1971–82; then from 1995 was principal of the City & Guilds of London Art School. Kenny fulfilled a number of public commissions, including Bank of Switzerland in London and Addenbrooke's Hospital, Cambridge. In his work, which can be monumental in concept and scale yet light and airy in conception, it has been said that Kenny alludes to the human presence but it is never fully described. He participated in many mixed shows in Britain and abroad and had solo exhibitions at Bear Lane Gallery, Oxford; Hanover Gallery; Annely Juda Fine Art; a retrospective show at Wilhelm-Lehmbruck Museum, Duisburg, in 1984; Hansard Gallery, Southampton, 1990; The Poussin Series at Dulwich Picture Gallery, 1994, after a residency there, 1992–3; Lamont Gallery, 1996; and Coram Gallery, 1997, touring to RWA, 1998. Hart Gallery held a small memorial show in 2002 and in 2005 the RA displayed Kenny's Stations of the Cross, donated to it by the artist's widow. Arts Council, British Council, British Museum and many other British and foreign collections hold his work. Lived in London.

Paul KENNY 1951– Photographer who took a searching look at the natural world, locations including the Applecross peninsula in northwest Scotland, the Inner Hebrides and the Forest of Bowland in his native Lancashire, where he was born in Salford. Albrecht Dürer and John Ruskin were influences on Kenny's metamorphic and minute studies of phenomena such as shards of ice and splashes of light. These were shown in Secrets of Dark Contemplation at Purdy Hicks Gallery, 2000, and at the Harris Museum & Art Gallery, Preston (which holds his work), 2001. Kenny's residencies and commissions included Harris Museum & Art Gallery, 1997–8; ArtBarns: after Kurt Schwitters, commissioned by Projects Environment, 1999; River Lune Millennium Park Project, 1999–00; and Ballinglen Arts Foundation, County Mayo, Ireland, fellowship, 2000. North West Water, Deutsche Bank, Ballinglen Archive and Goldman Sachs hold examples.

Paul KENNY 1960– Painter, born in Lisburn, Antrim, Northern Ireland, who gained a higher diploma from the Slade School of Fine Art, 1983–5. His colourful, atmospheric views of Britain and abroad were, said London *Evening Standard* critic Brian Sewell, "not deliberate and specific landscapes, but, like those of Turner and Constable before him, references to the spirit of the place." Mixed shows included The Art of Living, Leighton House, 1986; Singer & Friedlander/*Sunday Times* Watercolour Competition, Mall Galleries, 1988; An English Summer, Medici Galleries, 1992; and Summer Show, Metropole Arts Centre, Folkestone, from 1996. Solo shows included Anna-Mei Chadwick, 1990; Piano Nobile, Richmond, from 1991; and Christ Church College, Canterbury, 1994. The Royal Philharmonic Orchestra, London Docklands Development Corporation and Dorland Advertising commissioned Kenny's work.

Caroline KENT 1963– Painter, illustrator and teacher, born in Rotherham, Yorkshire. She studied at Bretton Hall, Leeds University, and taught painting for four years at Worksop College and at Ranby House School. Kent's work, stemming from a detailed study of flora and fauna, sometimes resulted in slightly surreal images, as in her solo exhibition presented by James Colman at Montpelier Sandelson, 2001. Colman organised another show in 2004. Other shows included Laing Landscape Competition, Harrogate (highly commended), 1988; 30 Wildlife Artists, Mall Galleries, 1992; and South Yorkshire Open Art, Cooper Gallery, Barnsley (highly commended), 1994.

Christopher KENT 1950– Painter and teacher who studied at Watford School of Art and Bath Academy of Art, Corsham. Worked for a time as a designer, from 1974 teaching part-time in south London. Among his shows was Five at Woodlands Art Gallery, 1982.

Colin KENT 1934– Watercolourist, born in London, who studied painting and architecture at Walthamstow College of Art. Worked for some years as a qualified architect. Was elected RI in 1971. Kent was noted for his watercolours of marshland and waterside, often imbued with an atmosphere of isolation. Showed regularly at RI, of which he was a member, as well as RA, RWA, Guildhall and elsewhere in Britain and America. In 2002 shared a show at Linda Blackstone Gallery, Pinner. Had a solo exhibition at Adam Gallery, Bath, 1995–6. Lived in Essex.

Giles KENT 1967– Sculptor in wood of totemic sculptures, who graduated with honours in fine art from University of East London, 1993–6. Worked at Grizedale Forest, Cumbria, and Eye Town Moors Woodland, Suffolk, both 1996, and on a sculpture trail in private woods in Lincolnshire, 1996–7, to which he added in 1999. In that year he was elected an associate of RBS, having gained its Membership Bursary from January 1997. Participated in an International Wood Sculpture Symposium, Czech Republic later that year. Other events included a residency at Hannah Peschar Sculpture Garden, Ockley, 1999, and private commissions in British Columbia in Canada, Scotland and Wiltshire in 2002. Kent participated in many group shows and had a series of solo exhibitions, later ones including RBS, Worthing Museum & Art Gallery and Framework Gallery, all 2002. Had a studio in south London, open to the public, where he exhibited quirky, smaller pieces.

Ian KENT 1944– Designer and painter who studied design at Stoke-on-Trent College of Art. He began painting in early 1980s. Mixed show appearances included Stoke's City Museum and Art Gallery, Portal Gallery and Art in Boxes at England & Co, 1991.

Jo KENT 1946– Artist and poet; her artworks were characterised by dense lettering, as in Hopscotch Box, included in Art in Boxes at England & Co, 1991. Also appeared in group shows at Stoke-on-Trent City Museum and Art Gallery, Worcester City Museum and Art Gallery and Centre Gallery in Staffordshire, where she lived.

Leslie KENT 1890–1980 Oil painter, mainly of marine and coastal scenes. After education at Bedales and Leeds University he studied painting under Fred Milner, in St Ives, 1918–20. Exhibited widely at RA, NEAC, Goupil Gallery, RBA, ROI, RSA, at the Paris Salon and in the provinces. Was a global traveller. His work has a simple, colourful directness. Lived at Radlett, Hertfordshire.

Mary KENT 1915– Painter in oil whose full name was Mary Kent Harrison. During most of the 1930s she studied at Kingston School of Art, the Slade School of Fine Art and Academy Schools. Exhibited widely in the provinces as well as RA, NEAC, RP, RSA, UA and Leicester Galleries. Had a special interest in dancing. Work reproduced in *People of Britain* and *Britain in Pictures*. Lived at Bolton-le-Bowland, Clitheroe, Lancashire.

Sarah KENT 1941– Painter and teacher, using acrylic on canvas and creating geometrical abstracts. She was born in Rugby, Warwickshire, and attended Slade School of Fine Art, 1960–6. Teaching included Southend School of Art, City Literary Institute and Hornsey College of Art. Kent was included in Camden Arts Centre's 1967 Survey '67 Abstract Painters, her pictures consisting of layers of paint applied between masking tape in the form of narrow stripes, these being built up into a low relief. From this show the Arts Council acquired Orthian 1, of 1966. Also exhibited at Young Contemporaries, Free Painters and Sculptors and Ben Uri Gallery.

William KENTRIDGE 1955– Graphic artist, printmaker, film-and video-maker and teacher, born in Johannesburg, South Africa. From 1973–6 attended University of the Witwatersrand, graduating in politics and African studies. During that time he helped found the Junction Avenue Theatre Company. From 1976–8 studied under Bill Ainslie at Johannesburg Art Foundation, teaching etching there, 1978–80. From 1981–2 Kentridge studied mime and theatre at École Jacques Lecoq, Paris. After this for two years was an art director on television series and feature films. Kentridge had begun showing solo, 1979–81, at Market Gallery, Johannesburg. From 1987 had a series of shows at Vanessa Devereux Gallery, London. In 1990 his work was featured in the Museum of Modern Art, Oxford, touring exhibition Art from South Africa. The year following, Kentridge won the Rembrandt Gold Medal at the Cape Town Triennial. This was for *Sobriety, Obesity & Growing Old*, one of a number of films and videos in which Kentridge was involved; such work was often imbued with compassion and emotional intensity. Kentridge has been described as "one of South Africa's most impressive political artists". Had a Serpentine Gallery solo exhibition in 1999, another of animated films at Spacex Gallery, Exeter, in 2004. In that year there was a retrospective at the Museum of Contemporary Art in Sydney, Australia.

John Dalzell KENWORTHY 1858–1954 Mainly a portrait painter, Kenworthy was born in Whitehaven, Cumberland, where he died, having lived for many years at St Bees. Exhibited RA, RCamA and Walker Art Gallery, Liverpool.

Jonathan KENWORTHY 1943– Sculptor of wildlife in action who was born in Westmorland. He attended the Royal Academy Schools from 1961, also studying anatomy at the Royal Veterinary College. Kenworthy used a Schools Gold Medal Travelling Scholarship to make an initial visit to Africa. Further annual trips there followed to further his knowledge of the continent's wildlife. In 1977 he visited Nepal and Afghanistan. Kenworthy early on began to take part in group and solo shows, including the RA Summer Exhibition. His notable sculptures included a memorial for the writer Ernest Hemingway's burial place in Ketchum, Idaho, America; and The Leopard, 1985, commissioned by the property developer Wates for 20 Cannon Street. It is depicted and described in Philip Ward-Jackson's *Public Sculpture of the City of London*. In 1993, Kenworthy showed a similar piece in the RBS Chelsea Harbour show Sculpture 93.

Ley KENYON 1913–1990 Painter, illustrator, designer, teacher and diver, born in London where he lived for much of his life, but died in New Mexico. After Marylebone Grammar School Kenyon studied at Central School of Art and Crafts, 1931–4, where his teachers included Bernard Meninsky and William Roberts. Although during World War II he volunteered for submarine duty he was placed in the Royal Air Force, manned the rear gun turret of a bomber on 45 missions and won the Distinguished Flying Cross. Was imprisoned in Stalag Luft III prison camp where he was involved in the famous Great Escape tunnel project, forging identity passes and papers and making an invaluable record of the burrowing, later used as material for films. After the war he became a keen diver and his subsequent career included helping Jacques Cousteau with underwater filming; being a British Commonwealth lecturer; publishing several classic reference works on the underwater world; and teaching young people on scientific expeditions. Member of London Sketch Club and chairman of Chelsea Arts Club, 1967. National Gallery bought a war drawing by him.

Gerry KEON 1942– Artist, born in London, who attended Hornsey College of Art, 1959–62, and Byam Shaw School of Art, 1962–3. Keon did a variety of jobs – ranging from school and foundation course teaching through bus conducting – which led to a lapse in his wish to paint. This he took up again in 1988, which led to several exhibitions in the early 1990s. In 1994 was included in Kerb Scrawlers at The Living Room, Greenwich, in 1996 having a solo show at Francis Kyle Gallery.

Mary Theresa KEOWN 1974– Painter of pictures in which the amalgamation of several scenes within a single canvas produced an enigmatic quality, emphasised by the titling. Keown was born in Fermanagh, Northern Ireland, graduating with first-class honours in fine art from University of Ulster, Belfast. Awards included Bass Ireland Award at Belfast Young Contemporaries, the President's Prize at RUA and Student's Award, Arts Society of Ulster, all 1997; Best Abstract Work/Morrigan Press Award and Cavehill Gallery Invitation Award, both RUA, 1998; and The Ireland Fund of Great Britain Artist of the Year Award, 2001. Among other mixed shows were a Group Exhibition of Irish Women Artists, Washington State Convention & Trade Center, Seattle, America, 2000. Later solo exhibitions included Solomon Gallery, Dublin, Ireland, and Tavira Galeria de Arte, Bilbao, Spain (where Keown lived), both 2001, and Pyms Gallery, 2002. The Department of Education, Northern Ireland Office of Public Works and several corporate collections hold examples.

Jan KĘPIŃSKI 1907– Designer and sculptor, one of the Polish paper sculptors who made such an impact in Britain after World War II. After studying at Lvov Institute of Technology, he graduated from the Academy of Fine Arts in Warsaw and became involved in designing for a heavy industry firm including exhibition stands for international trade fairs. Imprisoned in Germany in World War II, he designed posters, stamps and arranged art exhibitions. Released and in Meppen, Kępiński managed the Polish section of the Young Men's Christian Association's decorative studio and was noted for his monumental eagles created from one sheet of paper for the 1st Polish Armoured Division's canteen. He continued such work with the Association throughout Britain after the war. Kępiński then worked with the important Diana Studio; with Antoni Dobrowolski designed for many industrial clients; produced stage designs for *The Nutcracker* with Margot Fonteyn; and created scenery for television productions. In 1959 Kępiński opened his own studio and worked with Mieczyslaw Malski on producing metal relief sculptures in heavy-gauge steel, copper and aluminium until the mid-1980s. Working with the Central Office of Information, Kępiński created emblems and heraldic elements for pavilions at international fairs. Another important client was the Leeds Permanent Building Society. He was included in Polish Paper Sculpture at Polish Cultural Institute and had a solo show of photographs there, both 1995.

Jessie KEPPIE 1868–1951 Watercolourist, born in Glasgow. She attended the School of Art there with Fra Newbery and James Dunlop among her teachers. Exhibited extensively at RSW, of which she was a member from 1934, and Royal Glasgow Institute of the Fine Arts, RSA, Walker Art Gallery, Liverpool, and elsewhere in the provinces. Member of Glasgow Lady Artists' Club. She joined in 1902, six years after she had broken off her engagement to the architect and artist Charles Rennie Mackintosh and two after she had left the School of Art. Keppie was treasurer of the Lady Artists, 1922, and president 1928–31, having won its Lauder Award in 1930. Her brother was the architect John Keppie, her sister the artist Helen Hopkins Keppie. Lived in Prestwick, Ayrshire.

Janice KERBEL 1969– Artist employing media such as aerial photographs, survey maps, cork, wood and a briefcase, as in her 1999 East International submission Plans (Bank job: 15 Lombard Street), of 1998, at Norwich School of Art & Design. She was born in Toronto, Canada, studying at Western Ontario Emily Carr College of Art and Design, University of British Columbia, Vancouver, and Goldsmiths' College School of Art. Lived in London.

Pavlo KERESTEY: *see* **SZUPER GALLERY**

Roma KERFOOT 1905– Watercolourist, draughtsman and teacher, born in Swinton, Lancashire. Studied at Manchester School of Art, 1923–7, with John Willock, then at Royal College of Art, 1927–31, with Reco Capey and Ernest Tristram. Taught for a period at Bolton School of Art and did some book illustration. Lived at Harrow Weald, Middlesex.

Judith KERLANDER fl. from 1960s– Artist in many media and teacher, wife of the sculptor Leonard Kerlander. She studied at Camberwell School of Arts and Crafts, 1960–4, specialising in sculpture; Hammersmith College of Art and Building, 1970–1, concentrating on welding; then Thomas Huxley College, 1975–8, for a Bachelor of Education degree course. In 1969 she went to modelling and sculpture workshop at Shepperton Film Studios, working on the films *Anne of a Thousand Days* and *Oliver Cromwell*. From 1980–4 she was involved in fashion-oriented silkscreen design and printing, clients including Liberty and Norman Hartnell. She also designed and made hats for The Hat Shop, Benny Yong and John Lewis. From 1983 Kerlander taught silk painting and miniature painting at Chiswick. Showed at RA from 1968; Royal Glasgow Institute of the Fine Arts, 1971; Woodstock Gallery, 1973; Whitechapel Art Gallery, 1975; Camden Arts Centre, 1979; and Greenwich Theatre Gallery, 1987. Lived in London.

Leonard KERLANDER 1940– Sculptor and teacher, born and lived in London, husband of the artist Judith Kerlander, who studied under Karel Vogel at Camberwell School of Arts and Crafts between 1954–60. In the early-1960s Kerlander was involved in film work: *Cleopatra* at Pinewood Studios, and at Metro-Goldwyn-Mayer modelling for *Satan Never Sleeps*. Around the same time Kerlander taught for a period at Camberwell; helped cast a monument for the Caribbean Athletics Stadium in Kingston, Jamaica; did portrait-casting work for the sculptor Archibald Ziegler; taught sculpture to physically handicapped people in Islington; and taught art to adults at Woolwich Art Centre. In 1964 Kerlander began teaching sculpture, drawing and painting at what became the City College of Further Education. In 1966 he carried out life-size figures for Expo '67, in 1968 showing at Camden Arts Centre.

Patricia KERLEY 1919– Painter and teacher, born in Hove, Sussex. After attending Brighton and Hove High School she studied at Brighton College of Art, 1947–51, her teachers including Charles Knight and Charles Morris, then the Royal Academy Schools, 1951–5, where she learned from Bernard Fleetwood-Walker and Henry Rushbury. Exhibited RA, RP, SBA, Association of Sussex Artists and Arts Council. Lived in Hove, Sussex, then in Marlborough, Wiltshire.

Ingrid KERMA 1942– Abstract artist and teacher, born in Eberswalde, Germany, who gained an honours degree under Terry Frost at Reading University's fine art department, 1972–6, winning the Owen Ridley Prize. Gained her master's degree in fine art from Goldsmiths' College, 1990–2. Taught for many years: at Reading, also at Falmouth and St Martin's Schools of Art. Exhibitions included New Contemporaries at Camden Arts Centre, 1975; John Moores Liverpool Exhibition, 1976; Whitechapel Open at Whitechapel Gallery from 1981; New Acquaintances at Fabian Carlsson Gallery, 1986; Chisenhale Studios,

1988; and Bedford Gallery, 1995, as well as extensively in Germany. Arts Council, Portsmouth City Art Gallery and Reading University hold examples. Lived and worked in Berlin and London. Intermittently, Kerma worked jointly with artist Pierre Imhof as Imker, as in Trans Encounter, Phoenix Gallery, Brighton, 2002. In 2003, Broadbent showed explorations of her Petrushka and Karo Series.

Lesley KERMAN fl. from mid-1960s– Versatile artist, teacher and writer on art, who gained an honours degree in fine art at University of Durham, 1964. From then she lectured in art and art and design history, latterly as head of the department of humanities performance and media at the University of Plymouth. Among her publications was *Graham Rich, The Search for Form, a Memoir*, 1997. Mixed exhibitions included Young Contemporaries, from 1962; Spacex Artists Drawing Show, Spacex Gallery, Exeter, 1984; and Push the Boat Out, Swansea Arts Workshop Gallery, Swansea, 1997. Solo exhibitions included Paintings, Gallery 273, Queen Mary College, 1967; Paintings, Exe Gallery, Exeter, 1985; and Fair Play, University of Exeter Conference on Women in the South West, 1996. Lived in Topsham, Devon.

Doreen KERN 1931– Sculptor in bronze. Technical knowledge was acquired while working at The Morris Singer Foundry, and she also studied at The Hampstead Garden Suburb Institute. Showed at Bristol Cathedral; London University; Brighton Museum & Art Gallery; Waterloo Fine Arts; and widely abroad. Did consultancy work for British Museum. Lived in Edgware, Middlesex.

Theador(e) KERN 1900–1969 Painter, sculptor and stained glass artist, born in Salzburg, Austria. He worked in England from 1938 and taught at Luton School of Art. In the early 1950s, the artist and designer Gordon House was his assistant. Kern was commissioned by the monks of Buckfast Abbey, among others, to make ecclesiastical sculpture. His oil painting Manifest, showing a pronounced Eastern European influence in its strong colours and brushwork, is in St Paul's Church, Bedford. Lived in Hitchin, Hertfordshire.

Antony KERR 1924– Painter of landscape, architectural, monumental and narrative figure subjects, sometime etcher and teacher. He was born in Gloucester, his father a poet, William Kerr. He was educated at St Paul's School and the Slade School of Fine Art under Randolph Schwabe, interrupted by Army service. Taught with Kyffin Williams at Highgate School and at St George's College, Weybridge. Kerr liked panoramic views, in oil and latterly especially watercolour, aiming "to capture the spirit of each place" and "the weather of the changing year." Views included the Welsh Borders area, continental Europe and South Africa. He exhibited first in Artists of Fame and Promise, Leicester Galleries, 1942, among his later mixed shows being the RA Summer Exhibition, NEAC, Contemporary Portrait Society and Fine Art Society. Exhibitions included a retrospective at Hereford Museum and Art Gallery, 1999, by which time Kerr had had almost solo 50 exhibitions and joint shows with his wife Elizabeth Rendell, venues including Austria, Germany and America. He lived in Almeley, Herefordshire.

Bernadette KERR 1958– Kerr graduated with honours from Trent Polytechnic, Nottingham, in 1978–81, gaining her higher diploma from the Slade School of Fine Art, 1982–4, and in the latter year a Boise Travelling Scholarship to Italy. In 1989 she won a Rome Award. Group shows included New Contemporaries, ICA, 1981; Domus Aurea, The Winchester Gallery, 1988; and East End Open Studios, at Metropolitan Wharf, 1989.

Elizabeth Lamorna KERR 1904–1990 Painter, driftwood sculptor and teacher, daughter of the painter Samuel John Lamorna Birch, she was his model, and sat for the circle of painters including Augustus John, T C Gotch and Laura and Harold Knight. She was born and died at Flagstaff Cottage, Lamorna Cove, Cornwall. After working in London as a milliner she moved to Cornwall in the late 1930s with her husband, James Lennox Kerr, who as Peter Dawlish wrote books for boys. Mornie, as she was known, exhibited at the RA, 1939–51; promoted her father's work; and taught and showed with her own group of artists. Her still life and landscape studies are notable for their handling of light.

Helen KERR 1936– Artist in Batik and Batik-embroidery, and teacher, married to the artist Richard John Croft. She studied textiles at Belfast College of Art in the 1950s and at Brighton College of Art, in 1981–2 gaining a diploma in embroidery and textiles at Goldsmiths' College. Between 1970–87 she was head of the art department at Bloomfield Collegiate School, Belfast; gained a fellowship in creative embroidery at Belfast College of Art, 1977; and in 1978 was featured in Ulster Television's *Portrait of the Artist*. From 1987 she worked full-time at a studio in Dundrum, County Down. Showed regularly with RUA and RHA and in Dublin and Belfast at the Irish Exhibition of Living Art. Group shows included Material Evidence at Camden Arts Centre, 1985, and Stitched Textiles, at Commonwealth Institute Gallery, 1989. Solo shows included Ulster Arts Club, 1990, and Cavehill Gallery, 1991, both in Belfast.

Janet KERR 1947– Artist born in Hornchurch, Essex, who studied foundation at Thurrock Technical College, graphic design at North London Polytechnic and fine art privately. From 1969–78 she worked as a designer, starting to paint full-time when her daughter was born in order to spend more time at home. Among her teachers were Charles Bartlett, Leslie Worth, Maurice Sheppard, Francis Bowyer, Cliff Bayley and David Gluck. Kerr was made a fellow of RWS in 1997. In 1995, she won the Daler-Rowney Award for watercolour painting. Exhibitions included RSA; Six Artists at Clairmonte Galleries, Brighton; Singer & Friedlander/*Sunday Times* Watercolour Competition and Exhibition; Northern Prospects, Harewood House, near Leeds; solo at Oak Tree Studios Gallery, Shipley; and Autumn Exhibition, 2001, and September Show, 2003, both at The Wykeham Gallery, Stockbridge. Lived in Norland, Sowerby Bridge, West Yorkshire.

Judith KERR 1923– Painter, draughtsman and designer of textiles who was born in Berlin, Germany. She was educated in Germany, France and England and then studied at Central School of Arts and Crafts with John Farleigh, Bernard Meninsky and Ruskin Spear. Showed RA, LG and elsewhere and lived in London.

Natasha KERR 1968– Versatile artist, born at Birkenhead, Cheshire, who studied fashion textiles at Brighton Polytechnic, 1988–92, then diversified. Exhibitions included

Contemporary Applied Arts, from 1995; Imaginary Places, Ikon Gallery, Birmingham, tour, 1997–8; Inner Space, The Orangery, Holland Park, and Fine Art Society, both 1999. Among later solo exhibitions were the Friends' Room, Victoria & Albert Museum, 1999. Carried out a wide range of public commissions, including Gefinor Bank, New York, America, two hangings, 1997; Royal Mail Suffragette Millennium Stamp (released 1999), 1998; and Caribbean Cruise Liners *Eagle 1* and *Eagle 2*, total 11 wall hangings, 1999. Kerr's studio was in London.

Nora Jean KERR 1908–1956 Painter and designer, born in Peking, China. She was educated at Benenden School, then studied art at Byam Shaw School of Drawing and Painting, Central School of Arts and Crafts, during World War II in India, then Heatherley's School of Fine Art. She moved to Newport, Monmouthshire, around 1950 and had a solo show there in 1953 at Cheltenham Hall. Also showed SEA, SWG and WAC. It holds her work, as do CASW and Newport Art Gallery and Museum.

Susan KERR 1944– Self-taught artist, born in London. She was a member of Free Painters and Sculptors, also exhibiting with Woodstock Gallery and at Gray Art Gallery & Museum, Hartlepool. Lived in Shepperton, Middlesex.

Suzy KERR 1957– Systems-based artist, born and lived in London, who studied at Bath Academy of Art, 1975–9, then at Brighton Polytechnic, 1980–1, with a Polish Government Scholarship to Warsaw, 1982–3. Group exhibitions included Sally East Gallery, 1979; 3 Constructivists, Building Design Partnership, Preston, 1980; House Construction Show, House Gallery, and 9 Printmakers, Brighton Polytechnic, both 1981; 7th British International Print Biennale, Bradford, 1982; and Series, Quay Arts Centre, Newport, Isle of Wight, 1983. Kerr then said that her "interest is in revealing process; not only movement in time, as in the mobiles, but also in the form-making power of time, time as expressed by repetition and change, by sequence and seriality." Kerr (pronounced Carr) later worked at the Photographers' Gallery.

Graham KERSHAW 1977– Exclusively a portrait painter, Kershaw undertook both projects and private commissions. He was born in York and studied at Edinburgh University and Art College. From 2000–4 he was artist-in-residence, Shell House Gallery, Ledbury. Poetraits, portraits of poets, was an exhibition tour from 2003, venues including the University of Liverpool Senate House in 2005. That University holds his work. Kershaw lived in Birmingham.

Walter KERSHAW 1940– Painter and muralist, born in Rochdale, Lancashire. He was educated at De la Salle College, Salford, 1951–8, and graduated from department of fine art at Durham University, 1958–62, with honours, after which he was self-employed as an artist. In 1972 Kershaw made his home at Littleborough, in the Pennines, where a large studio enabled him to create on a panoramic scale. From the age of 13 he painted the Lancashire landscape and he was to be a pioneer of industrial murals in Britain. From 1977–9 he was awarded a major grant, jointly financed by the Gulbenkian Foundation and North West Arts, to establish external mural painting in the Lancashire area. His mural at Trafford Park, Manchester, was claimed to be the world's largest industrial painting of its type and it took him four years to finish. He worked extensively abroad, notably in Brazil. Major group and solo shows included Bear Lane Gallery, Oxford, 1962; Salford Art Gallery, from 1969; House of Commons, 1972; and Lancashire South of the Sands, which toured from County and Regimental Museum, Preston, 1988. Victoria & Albert Museum, The British Council, Salford University and overseas collections hold examples.

Károly KESERÜ 1962– Artist, born in Budapest, Hungary, who gained a diploma in visual art at Swinburne University, Melbourne, Australia; graduated in fine art from Victorian College of the Arts, Melbourne, 1997–9; and gained his master's at Central St Martins College of Art & Design, 2000–1. Awards included Victorian Campus Art Prize, 1998; Hopkins Property Design Competition for Gallery Tower, Victorian College of the Arts Student Union Prize and Julian Counsel Acquisitive Award, all 1999; and The Anne & Gordon Samstag International Visual Arts Scholarship of £30,000 in 2000. As well as mixed show exhibiting in Hungary and Australia, Keserü was in 2001 included in Exhibition for the Queen's Visit, Goodenough College; and in 2002 in the Ida Branson Memorial Bequest Exhibition, The Atkinson Gallery, Street, Somerset, in New Inventive Works, e1 gallery, and RA Summer Exhibition. Later solo shows included Aprosagok, Mu-Terem Galeria, Debrecen, Hungary and Folkmodern, George Paton Gallery, Melbourne, both 1999; and Folkmodern II, John Buckley Fine Art, Melbourne, 2000. In 2005, eye candy showed Keserü's work at the London Art Fair. Central St Martins, The London Institute and Australian and European private collections hold examples. Lived in London.

James KESSELL 1915–1978 Painter, mainly in oil, born in Coventry where he continued to live, son of the watercolourist James Everett Kessell. Studied at Coventry School of Art, 1928–34 and 1945–52. Exhibited RA, NS, ROI, RBA and RSMA. Towards the end of his life he ran his own art school. Kessell, who also showed abroad, had a series of one-man shows, including Herbert Art Gallery, Coventry, and Coventry Cathedral, in 1973. He painted portraits of a number of senior figures in the Anglican church. Herbert Art Gallery holds his works One up for the Sky Blues and Cardiff Docks.

Mary KESSELL 1914–1977 Painter, designer, draughtsman and teacher, born in London, where she continued to work. She was married to the designer Tom Eckersley. Kessell studied at Clapham School of Art, 1935–7, and the Central School of Arts and Crafts, 1937–9. In 1937 she was commissioned to illustrate Osbert Sitwell's book *Mrs Kimber*, then shortly after she began painting, in 1939, she executed the Judith and Holofernes mural at Westminster Hospital. In 1945 she travelled through Germany as an Official War Artist, visiting Belsen and Berlin; her journal and the resulting pictures are often harrowing, extracts from the diary being published in *The Cornhill* magazine in 1946. Had her initial solo show at Leicester Galleries in 1950, the first of a series, also showing at New Grafton Gallery in 1969. From 1952–6 Kessell lectured in jewellery design at Central School, from 1957–76 being a visiting teacher at London College of Printing. She also executed two big murals for ICI; went on an assignment for Oxfam in India in 1967; and did graphic work for Shell, London Transport, *Vogue* magazine and others. Imperial

War Museum, Tate Gallery and other public collections hold her work.

Morris KESTELMAN 1905–1998 Painter, stage designer, muralist, book illustrator and teacher, born in London, where he settled, of parents emigrated recently from eastern Europe. He studied at Central School of Art, 1922–5, with Bernard Meninsky, then at Royal College of Art, 1926–9, where he developed an interest in theatre design. Among his theatrical work was Sadler's Wells production of *Carmen*, for Tyrone Guthrie, 1940, and Laurence Olivier's *Richard III* and *The Alchemist* at The Old Vic in the following years. Kestelman did murals for Victoria & Albert Museum exhibition in 1946 and was included in Mural Art To-Day there in 1960. From 1951–71 Kestelman was Central School's head of fine art. Was elected LG, and Senior RA, 1996. Had a solo show at Upper Grosvenor Gallery, 1961, later ones including Sally Hunter Fine Art, 1987, and Boundary Gallery from 1989. In 1983 Kestelman won an Abbey Major Award in Painting Prize. Arts Council, Contemporary Art Society and Victoria & Albert Museum hold his work. There were memorial shows at Boundary Gallery and the Friends' Room, RA, both 2001, with other exhibitions at Lauderdale House, 2002 and 2003, and the London Jewish Cultural Centre, 2004. His daughter was the actress Sara Kestelman.

Jean KETCHER 1955– Painter and teacher, born and lived in Ipswich, Suffolk, where she studied at the School of Art, 1971–3, graduating from Maidstone College of Art, 1973–6. She was an Ipswich Art Club member who showed in East Anglia, notably at the Corn Exchange in Ipswich and at Halesworth Gallery.

Alice KETTLE 1961– Artist and teacher, notable for machine embroideries that could have a Dufyesque quality. She was born in Winchester, Hampshire, and gained an honours degree in fine art at the University of Reading, 1979–84, gaining a postgraduate diploma in textile art from Goldsmiths' College, 1985–6. Kettle received a string of grants and awards, latterly including Bernina and Kreinik Awards, both 1999; Southern and South East Arts Major mid-career award, 2000; and Arts Council National Touring Programme Award to Bankfield Museum, Halifax, 2002. She was a member of the Society of Designer-Craftsmen. Residencies included Cowes High School, 1987–8, and Canberra School of Art, Australia, 1997. She held many part-time and visiting teaching posts, among them the Winchester, Royal College and Chelsea Schools of Art; Goldsmiths' College; Embroiderers' Guild; and the University of Ulster. Took part in numerous mixed shows and had a series of solo exhibitions, later ones including Art of the Stitch, Barbican Centre and tour, 1997 and 1999; Mythscapes, Southampton City Art Gallery, 2004; and Cheltenham Art Gallery & Museum, 2005. Among Kettle's commissions were an altar frontal, Holy Sepulchre Chapel, Winchester Cathedral, 1994; Glimpses of India, MV *Oriana*, P&O Cruises, 1994–5; In Camera, High Court, Lawnmarket, Edinburgh, 1995–7; National Library of Australia, Canberra, 1999; three altar frontals, high altar, Gloucester Cathedral, 1999–01; and Chagall Column, a response to Chagall windows at Chichester Cathedral and at All Saints, Tudeley, 2001. Portsmouth City Art Gallery; Otter Gallery, West Sussex Institute of Higher Education, Chichester; Whitworth Art Gallery, Manchester; and Crafts Council are among many collections holding examples.

B KEVILL DAVIES 1954– Painter, born in Dorset. She studied at Bournemouth and Poole College of Art and Design, 1973–7. Was interested in how a painting could become part of the surrounding architecture, working on board on a small scale, creating "studs of colour". She showed in Contemporary Art Society Market, RA Summer Exhibition and was included in John Moores Liverpool Exhibition in 1987. Lived in Sapperton, Gloucestershire.

Anthony KEY 1949– Artist born in South Africa, who attended Cape Town University, 1972; South Bank Polytechnic, 1975; West Surrey College of Art & Design, Farnham, 1995; and Brighton University, 1997. Exhibitions included DNA at Whiteley's Gallery, 1995; Wait & See, Towner Art Gallery, Eastbourne, 1997; and Honen-in, Kyoto, Japan, 1999, the year he was Artist of the Day at Flowers East, chosen by Ken Kiff.

Geoffrey KEY 1941– Painter, sculptor and teacher, born Manchester, who attended the Regional College of Art there, 1958–61. He was head of art at Broughton High School, 1962–74, then was a full-time artist. Key's main subject themes were the figure, landscape and the horse. He was a member of the Manchester Academy, gaining first prize there in 1971. Key showed at Salford Art Gallery from 1966; Sheffield University and abroad in 1974; other exhibitions including Harris Museum and Art Gallery, Preston, 1983, Blackheath Gallery from 1989 and Barn Gallery, Cheshire, 1991. Public galleries in Salford, Manchester and Bolton hold his work. Lived in Pendleton, Salford, Lancashire.

Joan KEY 1948– Artist and teacher, whose output included Minimalist painting and experimental prints, born in Lancashire, who studied at Liverpool College of Art, 1967–8; Maidstone College of Art, 1968–71; and Royal College of Art, 1971–4. Lecturing included Maidstone, 1975–89; Goldsmiths' College, 1979–94; and Kent Institute, Canterbury, from 1994; subjects included fine art, printmaking, textiles and art and critical theory. Key curated a number of exhibitions, including WaterColour and Surface Tensions, 1993 and 1994, both at Curwen Gallery; and three more, with Paul Heber-Percy, Richard Salmon Gallery and tours, during 1996 and 1997; Plastic, Light and Craft. Group and mixed exhibitions included Seven Painters, Kettle's Yard, Cambridge, and tour, 1980; Printing in Camden, Camden Arts Centre, 1984; Identities, Chisenhale Gallery, 1988; Modern British Prints, Curwen Gallery, 1991; and Contemporary British Drawings, Sandra Gearing Gallery, New York, America, 1997. Later solo exhibitions included Richard Salmon, 1996, and Galerie Hollenbach, Stuttgart, Germany, 1997. Arts Council, Tate Gallery, Kettle's Yard and other public collections hold examples.

Paul KEYSELL 1954– Painter and draughtsman whose figurative work had a strong dramatic content, born in Liverpool. He gained an honours degree in illustration at Maidstone College of Art in 1977, then worked as a freelance illustrator for a wide range of clients including IPC Magazines, Virgin Records and Barrie and Jenkins. Had work in the Best of British Illustration Exhibition. In the 1980s he sought to develop more personal work and undertook postgraduate studies at University College of Wales, Aberystwyth. Showed with MAFA, East Midlands Open and was in Aberystwyth Artists at The Deffett

Francis Gallery, Swansea Institute of Higher Education, 1993.

Bhupen KHAKHAR 1934– Self-taught painter, ceramist, teacher and writer, born in Bombay, India, the family's straitened conditions being exacerbated by his father's early death. While qualifying as a chartered accountant Khakhar became absorbed by literature and art and, despite family opposition, in 1962 enrolled for an art criticism course at the Faculty of Fine Arts, Baroda. Began painting in a popular figurative, narrative style, holding the first of a series of solo exhibitions in Bombay in 1965; he was widely represented in group shows in India and abroad. Khakhar went on to exploit his lack of formal training to produce irreverent, apparently naïve art, at times employing ready-made images and graffiti, featuring everyday life and ordinary people, targets including the bourgeois existence. In 1976 he travelled to Europe for the first time, being asked to return and teach at Bath Academy, Corsham, in 1980. He was featured in Six Indian Painters at the Tate Gallery, 1982, at which time he was still practising accountancy to earn a living, while painting and writing stories in Gujarati. Khakhar's oil on canvas You Can't Please All, painted in 1981 and featuring a self-portrait, was bought by the Tate in 1996.

KHAN 1952– Painter and artist in mixed media and found objects, born in Ranpur, India. He was an engineer who began studying art at Camden Arts Centre in 1976, showed in a mixed exhibition there two years later, then continued studying at Middlesex Polytechnic, 1978–9, and North-East London Polytechnic, 1979–82. His initial major exhibition showing was at John Moores Exhibition, Liverpool, in 1991–2, with Virgin of the Radiator. Lived in London.

Balraj KHANNA 1940– Painter and writer, born in Punjab, India. He received his Master of Arts degree in English literature from Chandigarh University and was down for Oxford University, but a mishap prevented this, and he turned almost by chance to art. After a convalescent visit to France, he had first one-man show at New Vision Centre Gallery in 1965, but continued to lead a diverse life. He was a foreign correspondent in the India-Pakistan War, 1971–2; won the Royal Society of Literature's Winifred Holtby Prize for his novel *Nation of Fools* in 1984; and was part-author of the report *Art on the South Bank*, commissioned by the Greater London Council in 1986. Khanna did some figurative work, but made a notable impact with colourful, kaleidoscopic, abstract works, witty and original, which have been compared to those of Klee and Miró but which are unique. Participated in many international exhibitions. Solo shows included Serpentine Gallery, 1979; Horizon Gallery, 1987; The Museum of Modern Art, Wales, in Machynlleth, 1994; and Fosterart, 2004. Ashmolean Museum in Oxford, provincial galleries and National Gallery of Modern Art, New Delhi, India, hold his work. Participated in The Other Story, Hayward Gallery, 1989–90, with tour. Lived in London.

Bharti KHER 1969– Artist producing brightly coloured figurative pictures such as Misappropriate Functions, which won a prize in Royal Over-Seas League Open, 1996. Kher was born in London and studied at Middlesex and Newcastle upon Tyne Polytechnics. Other mixed shows included Squires Gallery, Newcastle, 1989; Aspects of British Figurative Painting (1988–93), Milton Gallery, 1993; and Of Women – Icons/Stars/Feasts, Eicher Gallery in New Delhi, India, where Kher was based from 1993, held 1996. Solo shows included Art Heritage, New Delhi, 1995.

Christine KHONDJI 1947– Artist from a French-Iranian family who early on produced many drawings that were "a shield against violence, against a child's helplessness". Khondji spent her childhood in France and Iran, attending school in Paris. She lived for many years in London before returning to Paris, latterly spending most of her time in France or India while leading a nomadic life. Khondji studied archaeology in Paris, was mainly interested in pre-history and visited ancient sites in Europe and Africa. She exhibited in Alexandria, Paris and London, including Obsessive Visions, England & Co, 2001. Shortly before she shared a show at that gallery in 2004 with Samira Abbassy, Khondji was included in The Wellcome Trust Gallery, Science Museum, exhibition Metamorphing: Transformation in Science, Art and Mythology.

Ian KIAER 1971– Artist whose interest was artistic protagonists at odds with the ideologies of their times, their response being aesthetic rather than political resistance. He studied at the Slade School of Fine Art, 1995, and the Royal College of Art, 2000. Kiaer was chosen by Francesco Bonami to exhibit at Manifesta 3, in Ljubljana, Yugoslavia, 2000, then Pier Luigi Tazzi, co-curator of Documenta X, invited him to show new work in An Empty Spot to Stay, Watou, Belgium, 2001. In that year Asprey Jacques gave Kiaer his first solo exhibition, largely comprising work made in response to a six-month stay in Seoul, South Korea, earlier that year. Kiaer created models, paintings, drawings and found objects based on Yang Paeng Son, the sixteenth-century Confucian scholar who lived mostly in exile. Another exhibition followed in 2003. Also in 2003 Tate Britain featured work by Kiaer "examining the connection between Wittgenstein's philosophy and Brueghel's landscapes." There was an exhibition at Alison Jacques Gallery in 2004.

James KIBART 1912– Painter, designer and teacher, born and lived in Leicester, where he attended the College of Art, 1928–35, teachers including A R Middleton Todd and J F Pettinger. For a time he was a consultant to the Graphic Art Studio. Kibart held senior positions in Leicester's Sketch Club and its Society of Artists. He showed at the public gallery there and in Nottingham, elsewhere in the Midlands and in Edinburgh.

Michael KIDD 1937– Painter, designer and film-maker, born in London, who in his early teens developed an enthusiasm for art. From 1951–5 he studied at Wimbledon Art School, then won a scholarship to the Royal College of Art, 1956–9, where he concentrated on illustration and graphic design, with a final year in the embryonic film school. Kidd worked for advertising agencies as a graphic designer, in 1963 joined J Walter Thompson as an art director, then KMP, working for a period in its New York office as a creative director. Among his commercials for television was one for Save the Children, which won many awards. After Wimbledon, Kidd did not paint until 1981, when he was inspired by Edward Hopper's pictures seen at the Hayward Gallery, "probably the most influential show I've ever seen." Alfred Hitchcock was Kidd's other key influence. His paintings, in which "people are there by their absence," gave the impression of being highly detailed but were really "a whole series of dots and strokes and splashes, and there are some serious straight lines here and there – but I'm more interested in giving the illusion of reality, and keeping it simple." RONA Gallery showed Kidd's work.

Michael Alan KIDD 1955– Artist notable for his portraits, working in oil, acrylic and silkscreen, born in Balham, south London. Studied at Slade School of Fine Art, 1976–82, graduating with honours, then completing a postgraduate course. Kidd said that "although dependent on portraiture, I have been an experimentalist with the contemporary side of my work." Latterly, he worked on "a completely original method of representation, involving silkscreen usage, the possibilities of which, I believe, were under-exploited by the Pop Art movement". Group appearances included RA Summer Exhibition, 1978; National Portrait Gallery, 1981–2; RP, 1982–3; ROI, 1983; RBA, 1983–4; Laing Landscape Competition, 1983–4; Athena Art Competition, 1985; and British Painters' Open, Mall Galleries, 1989. Later solo shows included Pump House and Hyde Park Galleries, both 1992. Notable works included portraits of HRH The Princess of Wales and the Pop singer David Bowie. Dulwich College and Y Tabernacl, The Museum of Modern Art, Machynlleth, which has his Self-Portrait and a portrait of Iwan Llewelyn-Jones, are among public owners of Kidd's pictures. Lived in London. In The Real Turner Prize show at 69 Rivington Street, 2001, Kidd was included as a "Tooting Stuckist".

Natasha KIDD 1973– Painter and teacher who graduated with honours from the Slade School of Fine Art, 1992–6, gaining her master's there, 1996–8. She was shortlisted for the Vordemberg Gildewart Prize, Annely Juda Fine Art, 1999, and nominated for the Beuys Scholarship, 2000, deferred until 2001. Visiting teaching posts included Winchester College of Fine Art, 1997; Chelsea College of Art, 1999; and Liverpool Tate education team, 2000. Kidd's solo show Microswitch was held at Houldsworth Fine Art, 2000; for that, three painting machines devised by her created canvases in the gallery.

Richard KIDD 1952– Artist and teacher, born in Newcastle upon Tyne, who studied at the University there, 1970–4, then at the British School at Rome, on an Abbey Major Scholarship, 1974–5. Kidd said that his strongly gestural paintings were "about places...neither wholly abstract nor representational. Making paintings is about handling paint, but in the handling they become visual metaphors". Kidd taught at Trent Polytechnic and Reading University, 1975–6, and at Newcastle University, 1976–80; lived in San Francisco, California, America, on a Harkness Fellowship, 1980; then in New York from 1981; returning to England, 1987. Awards included Peter Stuyvesant Foundation, equal first prize, and a prize at John Moores Liverpool Exhibition, both 1974; and in 1976 an Arts Council Award and Northern Arts Fellowship. Was featured in John Moores in 2002. He shared an exhibition at The Stour Gallery, Shipston-on-Stour, 1998. Later solo exhibitions included Mayor Rowan Gallery, 1990, and University Gallery, Northumbria University, Newcastle, 2002. Arts Council; Leicestershire Education Authority; Ulster Museum, Belfast; University of Glasgow; Clare College, Cambridge; Museum of Modern Art, Rio de Janeiro; and corporate collections hold examples. He lived at North Shields, Tyne and Wear.

Helen KIDDALL 1888–1980 Painter and keen amateur musician. She entered Royal Academy Schools in 1912 for the five-year course where she was a friend of the painter Beatrice Lithiby. She later did a striking portrait of Miss Lithiby in the uniform of a chief commander of the Auxiliary Territorial Service. She exhibited at RA and elsewhere, producing many pictures of black children and flower still lifes. A devout Anglican, she is described as having had "a strong sense of humour, delighting in telling stories against herself". Miss Kiddall was a keen violinist who used to be accompanied by her sister, with whom she lived at Felixstowe, Suffolk.

Robert KIDDEY 1900–1984 Sculptor, artist and teacher, born in Nottingham. Kiddey came to prominence in the 1930s when he showed frequently at RA and Salon des Beaux-Arts, Paris. In 1932 examples of his work were exhibited at Goupil Gallery alongside pieces by Augustus John, Eric Gill and Picasso. Kiddey taught at a technical college in Newark-on-Trent and much of his work is to be found in the Nottinghamshire area, sometimes sculptures and bas-reliefs on a large scale.

Hilda KIDMAN 1891– Painter and illustrator, born near Hitchin, Hertfordshire. She was especially noted for her pictures of flowers and children and won an Hon. Mention at Paris Salon. Kidman studied at the Slade School of Fine Art under Henry Tonks, Philip Wilson Steer and Walter Westley Russell, Frank Calderon's School of Animal Painting and St John's Wood School of Art. Her pictures occasionally appeared on the covers of women's magazines. Exhibited RA, RP, SWA and RSA. Lived in Hitchin.

E Martin KIDNER 1915–1984 Figurative artist, born in Wellington, New Zealand, who from infancy grew up in England. After education at Colchester Royal Grammar and Framlingham College he spent a year as a farm pupil in Norfolk then studied agriculture at Reading University. Soon after qualifying, he opted for sisal-growing in Kenya. As World War II approached, Kidner joined the European Reserve of Officers of the Nigeria Regiment and served in Africa, winning the Military Cross in 1941 in Ethiopia for bravery in action. While serving, Kidner took Percy Bradshaw's correspondence course in drawing, completing many wartime sketches. From 1946 he farmed in Kenya, eventually becoming a noted animal agronomist, publishing learned articles and advising around the world. After Kidner's submission of a portrait to the PS annual show in 1959 won a favourable mention, he had some formal tuition from Sonia Mervyn. He showed frequently with the East African Wildlife Society Headquarters, Nairobi, SWLA and elsewhere. His solo exhibitions included National Art Gallery and Museum, Botswana, 1976, and La Perouse Gallery, Canberra, Australia, 1978 and 1980. The Suffolk Horse Society owns Kidner's work. His son, Oliver Kidner, was also an artist, their work being illustrated in Martin's memoir *The life and work of Martin Kidner*, edited and completed by Josephine Walpole. In later life Kidner was based near Framlingham, Suffolk.

Michael KIDNER 1917– Systems-oriented artist who was included in the key Systems Exhibition at Whitechapel Art Gallery in 1972 and in Systems II at Polytechnic of Central

London in 1973. For Kidner the canvas was "a sort of laboratory", and he was variously concerned with such features as shape as an ingredient for colour sensation, wave forms and curved or warped planes. Born in Kettering, Northamptonshire, Kidner was at Cambridge University, 1936–9, after which he was during 1940–1 at Ohio State University. After five years in Canadian Army was at Goldsmiths' College, taking up painting full-time in 1953. Lived in Paris for a while, studying for several months at Atelier André Lhote. Kidner held a number of teaching posts, notably at Bath Academy of Art, 1964–84. He had his first solo show at St Hilda's College, Oxford, in 1959; there was an Arts Council retrospective, 1959–84, at Serpentine Gallery, 1984; and later solo shows included Centre for the Philosophy of the Natural and Social Sciences, 1994, Galerie Emilia Suciu, Ettlingen, Germany, 1995, and Love is a Virus from Outer Space, paintings and prints at Flowers East, 2003. Tate Gallery, Arts Council, British Council, Contemporary Art Society and other leading collections held examples. Lived in London.

Annabel A KIDSTON 1896–1981 Printmaker, painter and teacher who studied at Glasgow School of Art, 1914–20; in Paris with André Lhote and at La Grande Chaumière; returned to be head of art at Laurel Bank School, 1922–5; then in London studied wood engraving at the Slade School of Fine Art, 1927. In that year she joined the Glasgow Society of Lady Artists, winning its Lauder Award in 1928. Her sisters Helen and Margaret were also both members. Annabel showed extensively with the Royal Glasgow Institute of the Fine Arts and RSA, also with RA. Lived in St Andrews, Fife, but died in North Berwick, East Lothian.

Susanne KIELY 1962– Artist and teacher who produced complex prints such as Cleansing, of 1995, shown at Royal Over-Seas League Open, 1996. She was born in Carshalton, Surrey, and studied at Warwick University, Colchester Institute and Chelsea and Camberwell Colleges of Art & Design. Work experience included several teaching posts, part-time assistant with the dealer Lumley Cazalet from 1994 and in 1995–6 associate guest artist at Camberwell. She was given a commission for St Matthew's Church, Ipswich, 1987 and won 1st Prize, London Lighthouse, 1995. Took part in many group exhibitions, including Ulster University, Belfast, 1991; The Sea, The Sea!, Y Tabernacl, Machynlleth, 1994; and Cover to Cover, London Print Workshop, 1996. Chelsea & Westminster Arts Project, Marakon Associates and Manchester Metropolitan University Library hold examples.

Ken KIFF 1935–2001 Painter, illustrator and teacher, born in Dagenham, Essex. He studied at Hornsey School of Art, 1955–61. Taught at Royal College of Art from 1979. Kiff's pictures were in many mixed shows and in 1986 he was included in Royal College of Art's Exhibition Road show. Solo exhibitions were at Nicola Jacobs Gallery and Fischer Fine Art; he had a retrospective at Serpentine Gallery in 1986; and in 1993–4 Kiff's work done as the result of a prolonged residency, was shown at National Gallery. The artist was noted for lush, apparently naïve pictures. The Arts Council holds a number, such as Man Greeting Woman, of 1965–6, and A Knife and Fork Jumped Up from the Dresser, of 1977. He illustrated *Folk Tales of the British Isles*, edited by M Foss, published in 1977. Was elected RA, 1991. There was a retrospective at Marlborough Fine Art, 2001–2. Lived in London.

John KIKI 1943– Painter and printmaker, born in Famagusta, Cyprus, whose family – involved in the restaurant business – settled in London in 1946. He attended Camberwell School of Arts and Crafts, 1960–4, then Royal Academy Schools, 1964–7. Kiki's pictures were often on a large scale, figurative, vigorous, using high-pitched and unconventional colours and reflecting his Mediterranean background. Group exhibitions included Young Contemporaries, Mall Galleries, 1966; British Painting '74, Hayward Gallery, 1974; and Viriamu Jones Gallery, University College, Cardiff, 1986. Later solo shows included Art Space Gallery, from 1991, and SeaChange Gallery, Great Yarmouth, 2002, Frames of Norwich and Chappel Galleries, Chappel, both 2003, and The Warehouse, Lowestoft, 2005. Saatchi Collection holds his work. Lived in Great Yarmouth, Norfolk.

Emilia KIKNADZE fl. from 1930s– Artist, born in Poland, who started to draw during World War I but because of poor circumstances her talent was frustrated. She was able to study portraiture in the Warsaw studio of W Miernicki, 1935–38, then was deported to Russia in 1940, where she endured hard labour. Joined the Polish Army in Russia and after training served as a tracer in the Second Polish Corps in Palestine, elsewhere in the Middle East and in Italy. After the war she moved to England, attending Ealing Art School and the Polish School of Painting under Professor Marian Bohusz-Szyskzko, 1974–7. Kiknadze's exhibitions included the Army House in Bari, Italy; Ealing Town Hall; and POSK.

Oliver KILBOURN 1904–1993 Mining and landscape painter and illustrator, born in Ashington, Northumberland. Like his father a pitman, he began work in the local colliery aged 13, later moving nearby to Ellington Colliery. While there, in 1934 he joined a Workers' Educational Association art appreciation course under Robert Lyon. This spawned the Ashington Group of painters, which included notable talents such as Jack Harrison and George Jude McLean. The Group's first show was at the Hatton Gallery, Newcastle, in 1936, in which Kilbourn participated, and his pictures were in all subsequent exhibitions in Britain and overseas. He was also a regular exhibitor at the Artists of the Northern Counties shows at Laing Art Gallery, Newcastle. The last Ashington Group show was in 1986, organised by the Workers' Educational Association's Wansbeck branch to mark the first anniversary of the end of the Miners' Strike. By then the Group's meeting hut had been dismantled, but in 1989 the local council opened the Woodhorn Colliery Museum and a special gallery was included to show its paintings. These included all Kilbourn's pictures from his series My Life as a Pitman. William Feaver's 1988 book *Pitmen Painters: The Ashington Group 1934–1984* is a thorough account of its story.

Joyce KILBURN 1884–1972 Miniaturist and watercolourist on ivory, born in London, daughter of the painter The Hon. John Collier. She studied at the Slade School of Fine Art with Fred Brown and Henry Tonks among her teachers. Exhibited RMS, Arlington Gallery, SWA, extensively in the provinces, in Canada, Australia and New Zealand. Signed her work J K in monogram form. Lived in London. Her daughter was the designer and artist Jill Greenwood.

George KILIBARDA 1954– Painter and sculptor, born in Sittingbourne, Kent, who studied at Medway College of Design. In 1993 he was awarded a WAC grant to visit Yugoslavia as a war artist. Solo exhibitions included Manor House Fine Arts and St David's Hall, both in Cardiff, where he lived at Lisvane.

Bruce KILLEEN 1926– Painter, lecturer, writer on art and film-maker, born in Warwickshire. His work was based initially on observed reality, but varied considerably between figuration and abstraction. From 1969–80 he was senior lecturer at Colchester School of Art, later part-time tutor at Royal Academy Schools. Killeen was regional art correspondent for *The Guardian*; wrote articles for art and literary journals; and in 1978 and 1980 won two Arts Council Awards to make art films, after which he concentrated entirely on painting. Was a member of AIA and RWA. Many group appearances included RA, Bruton Street Gallery, Minories in Colchester, Victoria Art Gallery in Bath and Chappel Galleries, Chappel. Solo shows included three at The Minories; others in London, Chelmsford, Bath and Bristol; and one at Alpha House Gallery, Sherborne. In 2001 he shared an exhibition there with Julia Wroughton, inspired by the Isle of Mull, where both had been living. Killeen has works in public and private collections in Britain and abroad. His wife, the potter Angela Killeen (1929–1997), had a memorial show at Chappel Galleries in 1998.

Ian KILLEN 1960– Artist working in various media who studied at Liverpool and Leeds Polytechnics. His group exhibition appearances included War of Images, at Transmission Gallery, Glasgow; State of the Nation, at Coventry City Museum and Art Gallery; and Art in Boxes at England & Co, 1991, which featured two Untitled works by him.

Goldie KILLIN 1884–1955 Artist and teacher who trained at Glasgow School of Art, 1913–22, and was on its staff, 1923–33. She was a member of the Glasgow Society of Lady Artists from 1920, also showing at the Walker Art Gallery, Liverpool. Lived in Cambuslang, Lanarkshire, but died in Cleland.

Ann KILVINGTON 1944– Painter and teacher who studied at York School of Art, 1960–4, then Royal Academy Schools, 1964–7. She taught at Putney School of Art and in 1982 was included in Artists in Adult Education at Woodlands Art Gallery. Other shows included RA Summer Exhibition from 1967; South London Art Gallery, 1979; and Wells Centre, Norfolk, 1981.

Patrick KILVINGTON 1922–1990 Painter, born in Surrey, educated at Eltham College and Bromley School of Art, who did not take up painting professionally until he was 49. After Army service in World War II, during which he was responsible for arresting Adolf Hitler's successor Admiral Doenitz, Kilvington contracted tuberculosis and after two years in hospital emigrated to Australia in 1951, where he did many jobs. A suspected recurrence of the tuberculosis in 1970 prompted him to resume painting, which led to a first, sell-out show in Brisbane in 1972. Submitted three pictures for the Horse Painters of the World show at Tryon Gallery, London, in 1979; all sold and two years later he was commissioned to do a polo picture as a wedding present for the Prince and Princess of Wales. By this time his pictures of horses and bushmen were popular in Australia, and he produced several thousands for shows there, in New Zealand and the United Kingdom. Died in Southport, Queensland.

Coralie KINAHAN 1924– Painter and writer, born in Bletchingley, Surrey. She was the sister of the artist Lydia de Burgh and sometimes painted under the name de Burgh. Married Sir Robin Kinahan. She studied art with the noted poster artist John Hassall who for a time ran his own school; at Chelsea School of Art, 1943–6; and in the studio of Sonia Mervyn, 1947–9. She was a member of RUA, for a time on its council, and of Ulster Women Artists. Also exhibited at RA, RP, SWLA and elsewhere and held a series of solo shows in Britain and Ireland. In 1985 opened her own gallery in Templepatrick, County Antrim, Northern Ireland, where she lived. Lady Kinahan was active in Ulster public life, being Lady Mayoress of Belfast, 1959–62. Ulster Museum, Belfast, holds her work. Among her historical novels was *You Can't Shoot the English*, 1982.

Agnes Marie KINDBERG 1906– Painter and artist in fabric collage, born in Hartlepool, County Durham. She studied at the local School of Art, principal Alfred Josiah Rushton, also in Newcastle and London, winning her art teacher's diploma. She showed at RSA, SSA and Scottish Craft Centre and exhibited solo regularly for many years at Edinburgh International Festival from 1970. Completed a series of works in public places, such as restaurants and churches. Lived in Edinburgh.

Joan KINDER 1916– Artist, born in Thornton-le-Dale, Yorkshire. After Bridlington High School for Girls Kinder attended Scarborough College of Art, 1932–6. She was a member of the Free Painters and Sculptors and SGA, on whose council she sat. Showed in London, provinces and abroad. London County Council bought her work. Lived latterly in Kenley, Surrey.

David KINDERSLEY 1915–1995 Letter-cutter, sculptor, typographer, draughtsman and teacher, father of the artist Richard Kindersley and husband of Lida Kindersley. He was born in Codicote, Hertfordshire, and was apprenticed to Eric Gill, 1933–6, his stockbroker father paying a small indemnity. He developed into Gill's trusted assistant, working alongside him on such important commissions as Bentall's store in Kingston, St John's College, Oxford, and Dorset House. Kindersley recollected that Gill's "views on almost any subject were always reasoned if not reasonable, and they influenced me for life." Gilbert Ledward also taught him. After Gill, Kindersley began to work independently. During World War II he was a conscientious objector, in 1945 moving to Cambridge where he established his first letter-cutting workshop in Barton village, taking on as his apprentice Kevin Cribb, son of Laurie Cribb who had worked with Gill. At Barton Kindersley aspired to Gill's "cell of good living in the chaos of our world." Writings by the Russian philosopher P D Ouspensky were important to Kindersley, who taught at the Cambridge College of Arts and Technology, 1946–57. Although later he recalled that at first he "wasn't interested in lettering. I was interested in becoming a sculptor," Kindersley became a master letter-cutter, designing a number of typefaces and devising a computerised typesetting system. The Dutch letter-cutter Lida Lopes Cardozo became his apprentice from 1976, married him and the outcome was The Cardozo Kindersley Workshop. Their partnership injected new vitality into Kindersley's work. In 2000 there was a Kindersley retrospective at Kettle's Yard, Cambridge, where his work enhances King's and Corpus Christi Colleges. The Victoria & Albert Museum and Museum of Modern Art in New York hold examples.

Lida KINDERSLEY 1954– Letter-cutter, born in Leiden, The Netherlands, sometimes working as Lida Lopes Cardozo Kindersley. She studied at the Royal Academy of Fine Arts, The Hague, 1972–6, under Gerrit Noordzij, in 1976 moving to England, where she learned in the Cambridge workshop of the distinguished letter-cutter and sculptor David Kindersley. They married and they formed a partnership as The Cardozo Kindersley Workshop, which continued after his death. Their notable collaborations included the memorial to the abbots of St Albans in the Abbey there, and inscriptions for the Ruskin Gallery, Sheffield. Lida Kindersley was a fellow of the Art Workers' Guild, a member of Atypi and the Double Crown Club and an honorary fellow and for a time chairman of the Wynkyn de Worde Society.

Richard KINDERSLEY 1939– Letter-cutter, sculptor and lecturer who studied at Cambridge School of Art and in his father David Kindersley's workshop. In 1966 he set up his own studio in London. Among his sculpture commissions were works for Exeter University, British Telecom, Sainsbury's, Lloyd's Register of Shipping and Christie's. He was the winner of seven major brick-carving competitions and was awarded the Royal Society of Arts' Art for Architecture Award. Among a huge range of other commissions were title lettering schemes for London Bridge, Tower Bridge and the Queen Elizabeth Bridge over the Thames at Dartford; new Crown Court buildings in Liverpool, Leeds, Swindon, Newcastle and Luton; university buildings in Cambridge, Oxford, Exeter and Kent; designs for theatres and major shopping centres; the Public Record Office in Kew; inscriptions for major churches and cathedrals, including St Paul's and Westminster Abbey; and a carving, on permanent display, for the Victoria & Albert Museum Gallery of the 20th Century. Later shows included Millennium Stones Exhibition and tour, 2000–1, including New Art Centre, East Winterslow.

John KINDNESS 1951– Versatile artist, born in Belfast, Northern Ireland, who settled in Dublin, in the Irish Republic. Among awards and commissions were a Major Arts Council of Northern Ireland Award, 1988; A Waterfall of Souvenirs: Ulsterbus, Northern Ireland major public sculpture commission, 1991; and in 1992 Romulus & Seamus, Arts Council of Northern Ireland sculpture garden commission. Projects included Skybreaker, advertising panels on Belfast City Bus, 1984, and Big Shoe Dog, sculpture made from shoes, Dublin Airport, 1989. Took part in many group and other shows in Ireland and abroad. Solo exhibitions included A Monkey Town Besieged By Dogs, at Grapevine Arts Centre, Dublin, and tour, 1985; Douglas Hyde Gallery, Dublin, 1990; and Treasures of New York, Kerlin Gallery, Dublin, and tour, 1991. Victoria & Albert Museum, British Council, Boston Museum of Fine Arts in America and Irish Museum of Modern Art in Dublin hold examples.

Alan KING 1946– Painter and teacher, born in Glasgow, graduating from the School of Art in drawing and painting in 1964–8, settling nearby at Paisley. He took early retirement in the late 1990s from his job as head of art and design in a large Glasgow secondary school to concentrate on his own work. This was detailed, figurative and could include a fantasy element. Classical Italianate and musical references were important. Showed at Royal Glasgow Institute of the Fine Arts, Glasgow Art Club and widely elsewhere in Scotland, with Thompson's Gallery and in 1999–00 in Millennium 2000 at Albemarle Gallery. His first solo exhibition was at Art Exposure, Glasgow, 1997.

Andrew KING 1956– Watercolourist and painter in oil on gesso, born in Bedford. He graduated in 1978 in fine art, painting, at Hornsey College of Art, painting full-time from then. He was made a member of NS in 1984, an associate of ROI in 1987. King had an interest in atmosphere, light and mood in landscape, the twentieth-century East Anglian landscapists being an influence. He worked "in true watercolour, on handmade paper in the traditional manner." Exhibited RWS, RI, NEAC and elsewhere in mixed shows. Had a first solo show at Luton County Council Library in 1978; from 1982 showed annually at Thompson's Gallery, Aldeburgh; with one at A & K Wilson Gallery, Harpenden, 2001. Local authority collections hold examples. Lived in Colby, Norwich.

Cecil KING 1921–1986 Artist, born in County Wicklow, Ireland. In the early-1950s he ended his business career to become a painter. He was soon showing at RHA and went on to participate in numerous group exhibitions in Ireland, Britain and on the continent. His first show outside Ireland was at New Charing Cross Gallery, Glasgow, in 1964. Other solo exhibitions took place at Compass Gallery, Glasgow; Angela Flowers; Oliver Dowling Gallery in Dublin, in 1984; and Hugh Lane Municipal Gallery, Dublin, 1981, which was a retrospective. Many public collections hold King's work, including Contemporary Irish Art Society; Museum of Modern Art in New York; Ulster Museum, Belfast; Victoria & Albert Museum; and Tate Gallery.

Dave KING 1946– Sculptor in various materials, often on a large scale, born in Birmingham. He attended Leeds College of Art, 1965–8, and Slade School of Fine Art, 1968–70. Was principal lecturer/head of sculpture, West Surrey College of Art & Design, Farnham, 1981–8; also at Middlesex Polytechnic, 1988–91; then was associate lecturer, Coventry University. King was included in The British Art Show, an Arts Council touring exhibition, 1980, chosen by critic William Packer. Other mixed exhibitions included Small is Beautiful, Flowers East, 1993, and Sculpture Garden, Henley Festival, 1995. Solo exhibitions included Serpentine Gallery, 1970; Angela Flowers Gallery, 1978; Rochdale Art Gallery, 1983; William Paterson College Gallery, New Jersey, 1991; and Floating Worlds, Southern Arts tour, 1994. Commissions included Shadowplay, NCC Property Development Corp, East India Docks, 1992; Circle of Understanding, Angela Flowers (Ireland), Rosscarbery, 1993–4; and folly at Staunton Country Park, Havant, 1995. Lived and worked in London.

Dorothy KING 1907–1990 Painter, draughtsman, curator and teacher, born and lived in London. She studied at Hornsey School of Art under J C Moody, then was briefly at Slade School of Fine Art with Randolph Schwabe. During World War II she worked first as a welfare officer, later as a supervisor at East End rest centres. Took up painting professionally after the war; in 1947 was elected RBA; in 1959 was temporary keeper of its Galleries in Suffolk Street; then from 1961–74 was keeper of the South London Art Gallery. She left to spend all her time painting, although for a while she continued teaching art classes in Southwark. Showed at RA, NEAC, SWA and elsewhere. Metropolitan Museum of Modern Art, New York, holds her work, which was given a memorial show at Mall Galleries in 1992.

Geoffrey KING 1941– Artist in a variety of media, born in Pin Mill, Suffolk, where he continued to live. King studied at Ipswich School of Art, 1956–7, then left to run the family boatbuilding business while continuing to draw and paint, boats and the estuary being key themes. His teachers were Colin Moss and Bernard Reynolds. King was a member of Ipswich Art Society and won the Anna Airy Award. He showed in its mixed exhibitions, also with John Russell and Haste Galleries in Ipswich, St Gregory's in Norwich and the Clockhouse, Snape. Had solo shows at the Haste, John Russell and Pin Mill Galleries.

Gordon KING 1939– Watercolourist and illustrator, born in London. He spent the war years in Fife, his father's home, then settled with his family in Reading, where he studied life drawing and painting at Reading University School of Art. After training as an illustrator with Carlton Studios at 22 he went freelance, working for magazines and advertising agencies, illustrating books and developing his portraits and paintings. As well as solo exhibitions King showed at RA Summer Exhibitions, RI and sold his prints in limited and signed editions. Among his favourite subjects were girls in a floral garden, his daughter and friends being the models. Lived in Chalfont St Peter, Buckinghamshire.

Graham Peter KING 1930– Designer, printmaker and writer, born in Adelaide, South Australia. He attended the University there and South Australian School of Art. Showed with Contemporary Art Society, 1950, and elsewhere in Australia. Wrote *Snaps as Art: the aesthetics of the snapshot*, 1978. Lived latterly in London.

Jeremy KING 1933– Landscape painter, printmaker, potter and teacher, born in Oundle, Northamptonshire, married to the artist Brenda King. He studied at Lancaster College of Arts & Crafts and at London University Institute of Education. From 1958–67 he taught painting and pottery at Haymill School, Burnham, then took up painting and lithography full-time, working in ateliers in Spain and Paris and at Curwen Studio. His many shows included the RA Summer Exhibition and ROI. Had a first solo exhibition at Ruthven Gallery, Lancaster, Ohio, in America, 1984, another in 1986; another show in Osaka, Japan, 1990; and a series at Century Galleries, Henley-on-Thames, including 2000. The Tate Gallery's print collection holds his lithographs.

Jessie Marion KING 1875–1949 Painter and mural artist, illustrator, designer and teacher, born at New Kilpatrick, Dunbartonshire, she was married to the artist E A Taylor. She studied at Glasgow University and Glasgow School of Art, where she was influenced by Charles Rennie Mackintosh. A travelling scholarship took her to Italy. She began to work for the printed page and by 1902 was teaching book cover design at Glasgow School of Art. Won a gold medal at Turin's International Decorative Art Exhibition. After marrying Taylor in 1908 they moved in 1911 to Paris, where for two years they ran the Atelier Shealing and King came under the influence of Bakst and the Ballets Russes. King now developed a greater freedom of colour and style and matured as a mural painter and designer of fabrics, jewellery and costumes. When World War I broke out she and her husband returned to Scotland and established a modest artistic colony in Kirkcudbright, while retaining a Paris studio until the late 1920s. She exhibited extensively at RSA, Royal Glasgow Institute of the Fine Arts and elsewhere. An exhaustive exhibition of her work was held at Scottish Arts Council in 1971, Kirkcudbright Tolbooth Art Centre and Glasgow School of Art staging another in 1999. Scottish National Gallery of Modern Art holds her work.

Mary KING 1926– Painter, collagist, artist in mixed media and teacher, born in Streatham, south London. She qualified as a teacher at Whitelands Training College and Chelsea School of Art, also studying at Central School of Arts and Crafts. Teachers included Carel Weight and Ceri Richards, painting; Francis Spear, stained glass; and Henry Moore, clay modelling. Travelled extensively, including Peru, Egypt, India and Burma. Taught at North-East Surrey College of Technology and Surbiton Adult Education Centre. King joined SWA in 1979, Free Painters and Sculptors in 1980 and NS in 1984. Took part in mixed shows at RA Summer Exhibition, Westminster and Mall Galleries, RBA and elsewhere. Solo exhibitions included Fairfield Halls in Croydon, Loggia Gallery and Alchemy Gallery, 2000. King's work always related to nature, but she was mainly concerned with non-representational images in an Abstract Expressionist manner, as in her Loom of Life series. Lived in Ewell, Epsom, Surrey.

Michael William KING 1928– Watercolourist, born in Croydon, Surrey, who was self-taught apart from assistance from Arthur Mills. King was elected to WSW in 1983, the year he began participating in mixed shows at Turner Gallery, Penarth. Also exhibited with RCamA, Aberystwyth Art Centre and Museum, Glynn Vivian Gallery in Swansea, at Swansea University and elsewhere. His solo shows included Arlington Gallery, Cardiff, 1965; Dyfed Gallery, New Quay, from 1980; and Newport Caringli Gallery from 1989. In 1981 he was community artist in Llandysul. Lived at New Quay, Dyfed.

Mike KING 1953– Artist and teacher, born and lived in London, the son of Peter King, whose work and memory he promoted. Dr King studied at the Royal College of Art, 1984–6, and became reader in computer art and animation at London Metropolitan University. On his website he said: "I work across the areas of art, science and the spiritual, and this site presents the explorations I have made over many years. Some key concepts have emerged from this interdisciplinary research. Amongst these are 'postsecular', meaning an impulse in society towards a greater receptivity to spiritual ideas, but based on the security of democratic rights and freedoms. The other is 'jnani', which is a Hindu word meaning non-theistic or non-devotional spirituality." King took part in many group shows in Britain and abroad, later ones including Digital 2000, Galerie der Gegenwart, Wiesbaden, Germany, 2000; New Greenham Arts, Newbury, and Ninth

New York Digital Salon, followed by international tour, 2001; and InterGraphic, State Museum of Fine Arts, Bishkek, Kyrgyzstan, 2004. King also showed his prints in solo exhibitions, including Colville Place Gallery and New Greenham Arts, both 1999; Le Vall Art Gallery, Novosibirsk, Russia, 2000; and Caestecker Gallery, Ripon College, Winsconsin, America, 2002. The Digital Art Museum, Berlin, holds his work.

Peter KING 1928–1957 "Scholar, artist and spiritual teacher", born in London, who early developed an interest in making things, experimenting with plaster. After attending Wimbledon School of Art King signed up with Guidici, the monumental stonemasons, helping restore the House of Commons. He also worked for Sir Charles Wheeler and moved to the Abbey Art Centre, started by the collector and founder of the Berkeley Galleries, William Ohly, as an artists' commune. While at Abbey King became employed part-time by Henry Moore, initially on the fourth component of the *Time*-Life frieze in Bond Street, which led to regular work for Moore. In 1953 King was appointed by Frank Martin as a part-time sculpture lecturer at St Martin's School of Art, recommended by Anthony Caro. King had a first solo show at Victor Musgrave's Gallery One in 1954. He was awarded a Boise Travelling Scholarship and a grant from the British Film Institute to make an animated film. Difficulties in King's personal life led to experiment in his work, some of which reflected this disturbed state. A suicide attempt led to a period in hospital, shortly after which he died in a motorcycle accident. King's work was also shown in galleries in Paris and Rome; he was represented at the Holland Park Exhibition, 1957; Middelheim Exhibition, 1959; and in 1960 his oak Figure with Cloak was shown at Battersea Park. The family retained a sizeable collection of King's work, which was also held by the Arts Council, British Council and Contemporary Art Society. A collection of King's sculptures and coloured, jazz-influenced drawings was offered by Rosebery's, West Norwood, in a 2002 sale. His son was the artist and teacher Mike King.

Phillip KING 1934– Sculptor and teacher, born in Kheredine, Tunisia, arriving in England in 1946. Studied modern languages at Cambridge University, 1954–7, and was at St Martin's School of Art, 1957–8. After a year as Henry Moore's assistant, King taught at St Martin's, 1959–80. He was at Bennington College, Vermont, in 1964 and at Hochschule der Künste, Berlin, 1979–80, becoming professor of sculpture at Royal College of Art, 1980. In 1964 King had his first one-man show at Rowan Gallery, the first of a long series there. One-man shows at Richard Feigen Gallery, New York and Chicago, and the Isaac Delgado Museum of Art, New Orleans, followed in 1966. King soon established a solid exhibiting reputation in group and one-man shows in Britain and overseas, work using a variety of materials from fibreglass and metal to wood and slate. In 1969 King won first prize at Socha Piestanskych, Czechosovakia, the year after his retrospective at Whitechapel Art Gallery. Further retrospectives included Hayward Gallery, 1981. Tate Gallery, Arts Council and Ulster Museum, Belfast, hold King's work which although abstract was heraldic and symbolic in character. He was a trustee of the Tate Gallery, 1967–9. Among King's commissions was Expo '70, Tokyo. Elected RA in 1991, president 1999–04. Retrospective at Yorkshire Sculpture Park in 1992 which showed that King, originally a figurative sculptor, had after a long period of abstraction moved back to figuration in the late 1980s. In 1997 King had another retrospective at Forte di Belvedere, Florence, only the second English sculptor given this honour (the first was Henry Moore). Two notable sculptures by King are outside C & J Clark's shoe factory at Street, Somerset. Lived near Dunstable, Bedfordshire, and in London.

Robert KING 1936– Painter and printmaker, born and lived in Leicester, where he attended the College of Art, 1952–4, resuming, 1956–8, after two years' Army service in Egypt. Was a member of RI, RSMA and Leicester Society of Artists. Mixed shows included the RA Summer Exhibition, Paris Salon and Medici Gallery. King shared an exhibition with Martin Taylor at Linda Blackstone Gallery, Pinner, 1999, solo shows including series with Medici Gallery, from 1980, and Burlington Paintings, from 1989, with other shows in America, Canada and Jersey. King was noted for his atmospheric beach scenes, coastal and marine paintings. Leicester University holds his work.

Ronald KING 1932– Printmaker, painter and teacher, born in São Paulo, Brazil, who studied at Chelsea School of Art, 1951–5, and won a Biddulph Scholarship for Painting, a Monsanto Painting Award, 1957, and a Forrester Painting Award, 1960. King was art director for a publishing company in Canada, 1957–60, and lectured at Farnham School of Art, 1961–5. In the mid-1960s, King had many prints produced by Editions Alecto, notably The Prologue series based on Geoffrey Chaucer's *The Canterbury Tales*. Following Editions Alecto's abandonment of The Prologue project, in 1967 King founded Circle Press, specialising in limited editions of fine books and prints. John Berger, Julia Farrer, Birgit Skiöld and Ian Tyson were some of the artists he worked with. The retrospective exhibition Cooking The Books: Ron King and the Circle Press, organised in 2002 by Yale Center for British Art, New Haven, America, celebrated the Center's acquisition of a complete set of Circle Press works and an accompanying archive. Mixed shows included Zwemmer's, Bear Lane in Oxford, RA, Heal's Mansard, Medici, Redfern and Curwen Galleries, and he was one of the London Artists shown at Shrewsbury School, 1968. British Museum, Victoria & Albert Museum, Washington's Library of Congress and a series of British and foreign university collections hold King's work. Lived for a time in Hayes, Middlesex.

Simon KING 1951– Printmaker and maker of books, born in Markyate, Hertfordshire. He attended Central School of Art & Design, 1971–5, being an etching technician on its staff, 1978–80. In 1981 he moved to Cumbria and set up a studio, mainly to print his own work. Between 1985–95 printed several projects for Paragon Press, including *Scottish Bestiary* and Bill Woodrow's *Periodic Table*. Exhibitions included The Forgotten Medium, Graffiti Gallery, 1980; Prints & Paintings at Collingwood College, Durham (repeated in 1985 at Gateway Gallery, Windermere); RA Summer Exhibition from 1984; and 3rd International Biennial Print Exhibition, Taiwan. In 1996 there was a show of Simon King's work at Abbot Hall Art Gallery/Bookshop, Kendal.

William Charles Holland KING 1884–1973 Sculptor. Born in Cheltenham, he attended the Royal Academy Schools, where he won the Landseer Scholarship. From 1910 he exhibited at the RA, also at the RSA, in Scotland, the provinces and abroad. Doncaster Museum and Art Gallery owns his work. King, who specialised in portrait sculpture, in 1954 won the gold medal of the RBS, of which he was president, 1949–54. A sculptor in the classical tradition, King is represented by several examples of his work in the volume *RBS: Modern British Sculpture*, 1939. Lived in Ventnor, Isle of Wight.

John KINGDON 1958– Self-taught artist, born in Barnet, Hertfordshire. He was a civil servant who became a social worker, influenced by "all auto-didacts." Group shows included the Mayfair and Covent Garden Festivals from 1998. He had two solo exhibitions at Heifer Gallery, 2002 and 2003. Kingdon lived in north London.

Jonathan KINGDON 1935– Wildlife painter and sculptor, teacher, author and illustrator, born in what is now Tanzania. Kingdon studied at the Ruskin School, Oxford, and at the Royal College of Art. Between 1960–74 he lectured at Makarere University, Uganda, becoming dean of fine art. In his free time Kingdon studied the wildlife of the area, resulting in seven volumes of drawings, *East African Mammals*, 1971–82. As an evolutionary biologist Kingdon became involved with ecologically significant projects and was a research associate with the zoology department of Oxford University. Books written and illustrated by him included *Island Africa*, *A Kilimanjaro Sketchbook*, *Arabian Mammals*, *Self-Made Man & His Undoing* and a *Field Guide to East African Mammals*. Sculpture commissions included a lifesize camel for America's Duke University. Kingdon's work was shown internationally, including a Gallery Pangolin, Chalford, solo show entitled Animal Signals, 2004.

John KINGERLEE 1936– Painter, born in Birmingham, educated by the Marist Fathers at Exeter. Having discarded literary ambitions Kingerlee settled in Cornwall, 1962–82, and began painting, working for long periods in Spain and Morocco. He moved to the Irish Republic, settling in the Beara peninsula area of west Cork, married with five children. Kinglerlee was a shy, questing man, an unusual Colourist whose intimately scaled works embraced thinly disguised self-portraiture and landscapes combining abstract and realistic elements. Exhibitions included Drian Gallery and Tom Caldwell Gallery, Dublin and Belfast. Anthony Hepworth Fine Art Dealers, of Bath, sold abstract work by Kingerlee at the 20/21 British Art Fair in 2005, soon after the artist's successful solo show, What Lies Beneath, at W J Morrill Ltd, in Dallas, Texas. Kingerlee's pictures sold well in America. Crawford Art Gallery, Cork, and National Gallery in Gdansk, Poland, hold examples.

Hazel KING-FARLOW fl. from mid-1930s–1995 Painter of colourful, extravert works, maiden name Hazel Guggenheim, who showed under her married name of Hazel King-Farlow, later after remarriage as Hazel McKinley. Studied at Euston Road School in 1938, having had a solo exhibition in 1937 at Cooling Galleries, also exhibiting at SWA and at Goupil and Redfern Galleries. From 1939 lived in America, although she was in Paris in the 1950s and showed again in England in the 1960s. American exhibitions included Harry Salpeter Gallery, New York, 1947. English collections holding examples include Leeds and Manchester City Art Galleries and Ferens Art Gallery, Hull. Notable American collectors included Colorado Springs Fine Arts Centre Collection, The Staude Collection in Hollywood, Greer Garson and Mrs Benny Goodman. King-Farlow's daughter Barbara Shukman was also an artist. Wakefield Art Gallery holds fine examples of work by Henry Moore and Victor Pasmore, presented by King-Farlow.

Raymond Forbes KINGS 1924–1981 Sculptor and teacher, born in Birmingham, who studied at the local Moseley School of Arts and Crafts until 1940. He was then apprenticed for two years to William Bloye, rejoining him after World War II service until 1960 on British and overseas projects. Kings combined working on his own with part-time teaching at Birmingham School of Art until 1967. Over the years he was to move several times in the West Midlands, finally settling at Bromsgrove, Worcestershire. Kings was noted for his versatility, as a restorer and through his original works including architectural sculptures, small figures, coats-of-arms, inn signs and restoration. His restoration included substantial work at Worcester's Guild Hall in the late 1970s. Notable among his own creations was his huge figure of Christ at St Martin's, Walsall, 1960. Among works by him in Birmingham are a tender Madonna and Child, in artificial stone, and St John surmounting the tower, in ciment fondu, both at St Mary and St John's, Erdington, 1962. In that year Kings joined the Guild of Catholic Artists, becoming an associate of the RBS in 1963.

Tarka KINGS 1961– Painter, often of small, muted, unpopulated urban gouaches, born in London. She attended the Royal Academy Schools, 1981–7. Exhibitions included Creative Salvage, 1985; Gallery 24, 1986; Henry Wyndham Gallery, 1989; Rebecca Hossack Gallery, from 1991; and The Fine Art Society, 1999.

Alan KINGSBURY 1960– Self-taught painter, born in London, who aged nine began painting in oils. He studied psychology and art history at the University of Wales from 1979, graduating in psychology in 1982, then studied art history for a year in London, specialising in Old Master and modern European painting. In 1983, always painting in his spare time, Kingsbury worked at the Peggy Guggenheim Collection in Venice before becoming a cataloguer of modern painting at the auctioneers Bonhams. In 1986 he left London to paint full-time, returning initially to Venice before moving to Scotland at the end of the year. During his subsequent five years there he refined his technique and style. In 1991 Kingsbury moved to Cornwall, where he lived in Penzance with his wife, the artist Morag Ballard. Mixed exhibitions included the RA Summer Exhibition, 1983; The Alton Gallery, 1988; Jonathan Cooper, from 1989; and Francis Kyle Gallery, from 1990. He had a series of solo shows with Jonathan Cooper from 1989 and Francis Kyle from 1991. Later one-mans included Old Custom House Gallery, Penzance, 2002, and The Fantastical Paintings of Alan Kingsbury, The John Davies Gallery, Stow-on-the-Wold, 2003.

Joan Beeby KINGSFORD 1883–1974 Artist, designer of theatrical costumes and curator, married to the painter Wilfrid R Wood. She studied at Central and other schools of art in London, learning manuscript illumination and lettering under Graily Hewitt. She began by making maps, engravings and drawings for the printing firm of Emery Walker, then for 25 years was curator of the Charles Beatty Collection of Persian and Indian manuscripts, books and paintings. In 1975 her husband helped stage a retrospective show of her work at Upstairs Gallery, Stamford. British Museum and Fitzwilliam Museum in Cambridge both hold examples. Lived at Barnack, Lincolnshire.

Harry KINGSLEY 1914– Painter and teacher, born in Manchester, where he studied at the School of Art. Joined the Army in 1933 and served abroad from 1934–45 in Palestine, India and the Far East. Became an art teacher at a Manchester secondary school. Showed with RA, Royal Glasgow Institute of the Fine Arts, RSA, MAFA and Manchester Graphic Club. Manchester City Art Gallery holds Kingsley's oil The Green Fence, Hulme, of 1960, typical of his northern townscapes and industrial scenes.

John KINGSLEY 1956– Painter, collagist and teacher, born in Glasgow of cultured English parents. Kingsley became a talented flautist as well as a painter who originally worked in the manner of Walter Sickert, later abandoning that artist's tonality for Fauve-like colour, seen to advantage in his French landscapes. He studied at Glasgow School of Art, 1973–7, under James Robertson, Geoffrey Squire and David Donaldson. He taught part-time at a Glasgow secondary school. Kingsley showed at RSA, Royal Glasgow Institute of the Fine Arts and at Paisley Art Institute, of which he was a council member. In 1991 he won the William Bowie Landscape Prize, in 1992 the Mary Armour Award, in 1998 the Arnold Clark Prize and in 1999 the Diploma of the Paisley Art Institute; he was a finalist, Hunting Art Prizes, 1989–93–99–2000, being highly commended in 1996. Argyle and Bute District Council and Royal College of Physicians and Surgeons, Glasgow, hold his work. In 2000 John Kingsley's Provence was held at The Contemporary Fine Art Gallery, Eton. A Mediterranean Shadows exhibition was held at Duncan R Miller Fine Arts, Hampstead, in 2004, the artist showing at the same venue as John E Kingsley. In that year Kingsley also had an exhibition, Prima Materia, at John Davies Fine Paintings, Upper Swell Farm, Stow-on-the-Wold.

Angela KINGSTON 1936– Botanical watercolourist, born in Mumbles, near Swansea. She studied at Bath Academy of Art, 1955–8, where she was awarded a travelling scholarship. She was a founder-member of the Society of Botanical Artists, a member of Welsh Group and was for a time chairman of WSW. Also showed widely elsewhere in England and Wales. Her solo shows included The Library, Cowbridge, 1975; University College, Cardiff, 1979; The Coach House Gallery, Caerphilly, 1989–92; and in 1992 shared show at Mistral Galleries. Glynn Vivian Art Gallery, Swansea, holds her work.

Caroline KININMONTH 1907–1978 Painter in oil of landscapes and flowers. Lady Kininmonth studied art at Edinburgh College of Art, 1926–30, under D M Sutherland and David Alison. She was married to the distinguished Scottish architect Sir William Kininmonth. She exhibited at the RSA and SSWA and her work is held by Edinburgh University and the Scottish Arts Council. Lived in Edinburgh.

Peter KINLEY 1926–1988 Painter of abstract and near-abstract figure and landscape pictures, born in Vienna, Austria, but arrived in England in late-1930s. After several years in Army he studied at Düsseldorf Academy, 1948–9, and at St Martin's School of Art, 1949–53. First showed with Young Contemporaries in 1951, having first solo exhibition at Gimpel Fils in 1954, followed by a series. Went on to show widely in Britain, in New York at Paul Rosenberg & Co and in India. In 1982 had a retrospective at Museum of Modern Art, Oxford; and in 1986 a solo show at Kettle's Yard Gallery, Cambridge, which toured. Among his teaching posts were sessions at St Martin's, 1954–64, and Bath Academy of Art and Bath College of Higher Education, 1971–88. Tate Gallery and Arts Council hold his work. A dominant influence on the work of Kinley was the 1953 exhibition in London of the French painter Nicolas de Staël.

Shona KINLOCH 1962– Sculptor who from 1980–5 studied at Glasgow School of Art, gaining an honours degree, then completed a postgraduate course in sculpture. Exhibitions included Glasgow Garden Festival and Compass Gallery and Ewan Mundy Fine Art, both in Glasgow. Commissions included Thinking of Bella at Italian Centre, Glasgow, and Scottish Nuclear, East Kilbride. Kelvingrove Art Gallery in Glasgow, Lillie Art Gallery in Milngavie and Flemings Bank hold examples.

David KINMONT 1932– Artist in various media and teacher, born in Westgate-on-Sea, Kent. He studied at the Regional College of Art, Manchester, and Cambridge University. He was head of the art department at Rhyl Grammar School, then held a series of teaching posts, becoming senior lecturer in the history of art at Bristol University. Mixed shows included RCamA of which he was a member and Royal National Eisteddfod. Had a series of solo exhibitions including retrospectives at Ferens Art Gallery, Hull, in 1963, and St John's, Cambridge, his old college, 1969; later ones included University of Durham, 1981, and Bristol University, 1983. Lived in Flax Bourton, Bristol.

Jock KINNEIR 1917–1994 Graphic and exhibition designer, cartoonist, engraver and teacher who studied at Chelsea School of Art in the 1930s. While still a student he produced a poster for Shell. Kinneir worked for the Central Office of Information, 1946–9, then for the Design Research Unit. His output there included a stand for Monsanto Chemicals at the 1950 British Industries Fair. He arranged displays for the Foreign Office and the Admiralty and did work for the shipping firm P&O and recording company Decca. In 1956 he set up a design practice in London, teaching part-time at Chelsea, becoming head of graphic design at the Royal College of Art, 1964–9. One of Kinneir's notable achievements was, with his colleague Margaret Calvert, the development of a clear, sympathetic road signage system, with its distinctive pictograms, employed throughout the United Kingdom. He also became involved in more public signage projects, for airports, railways and hospitals. Kinneir contributed cartoons to the magazine *Night and Day* and engravings to the journal *Signature*.

Linda KINSELLA 1914– Miniaturist and teacher, born in Teddington, Middlesex. She studied at Ealing School of Art and Isleworth Polytechnic and showed at RA, RI, elsewhere in London and at Paris Salon. Sometimes signed work with initials. Lived in Wraysbury, Berkshire.

Lucy KINSELLA 1960– Sculptor, mainly of animals, born in Havant, Hampshire, who studied at Barnfield College of

Art & Design, 1985–6, then graduated with an honours degree in fine art, sculpture, Loughborough College of Fine Art & Design, 1986–9. Awards included Dante Alighieri Travelling Scholarship, 1987, and Dennis Holt Travelling Bursary, 1989. Among her exhibitions were Sculpture in the Garden, Cropston, 1991; Animal Kingdom, Ferrers Gallery, Staunton Harold, 1998; and Byard Art, Cambridge. She had a solo show at The City Gallery, Leicester, 1999. Kinsella was married to the sculptor Dave Morris.

Christine KINSEY fl. from 1960s– Artist in a wide range of media, teacher and administrator, born in Pontypool, Monmouthshire. She studied at Newport College of Art and University of Wales, Cardiff. Between 1968–76 Kinsey was co-founder and director, Chapter, Workshops and Centre for the Arts in Cardiff, a co-founder of Artists and Designers in Wales Association and artistic advisor to Cardiff City Council for redevelopment of the city centre. She lectured in art and design at graduate and postgraduate level at University of Wales, 1975–6, from 1976–80 being artist and teacher, Foundation for Professional and Vocational Training, St Maarten, Netherland Antilles. A number of part-time and visiting lectureships in Wales, America and Italy followed. Kinsey also took part in many workshops and master-classes. In 1982 she won a printmaking prize at the National Eisteddfod of Wales, Swansea. Mixed shows included Group 75, Muse Gallery in Philadelphia, Roy Miles Gallery, Oriel in Bangor and Inverness Museum and Art Gallery. Later touring shows included National Library of Wales, Aberystwyth, and other Welsh venues, 1990. Her work is held by Victoria & Albert Museum and Glynn Vivian Art Gallery, Swansea as well as the National Library. Lived in Pencader, Dyfed.

Tom KINSEY 1927–2000 Figurative painter whose witty works were inspired by interests such as jazz, anarchism and current events. He was born Thomas Katz in Czechoslovakia, his mother of Austrian aristocratic origin, his father a Catholic doctor who devoted himself to the republican cause during the Spanish civil war. In 1939 his parents took Thomas to England where he was educated at Ellesmere College, Shropshire. Inspired by a van proclaiming "Kinsey, tripe dealers of Flint", in 1947 he changed his name from Katz to Kinsey. In the 1950s he studied at St Martin's and the Royal College of Art, friends including the writer Jeffrey Bernard, model and writer Quentin Crisp and artist John Minton. Kinsey featured in the Young Contemporaries and Artists for Peace exhibitions in 1953, his style influenced by the Flemish painter Constant Permeke. He moved to Snowdonia after leaving the Royal College in 1958 where he painted, worked in the slate quarries and climbed, leading mountain rescue teams. While painting hill farmers he became involved in the Campaign for Nuclear Disarmament, Committee of 100 and Spies for Peace and was secretary of the Bertrand Russell Peace Foundation. After a break from painting, during which he took up hunting with foxhounds on foot, he resumed in the late 1980s, his pictures featuring such subjects as the revolutionary Leon Trotsky, prime minister Margaret Thatcher, the homeless and the National Front. He drove to The Czech Republic in 1998 to find a cheaper life and died there.

Kay KINSMAN 1909– Watercolourist and draughtsman, born in Los Angeles, California, her correct name being Katherine Kinsman. She was educated in Cuba, Jamaica and in New York, then studied painting at Parsons School Applied Art, Paris, and Montreal Museum of Fine Arts. SGA member who also showed widely in the Cotswolds and west Midlands area and in Canada. Was an accomplished pianist and produced the books *Montreal Sketchbook* and *Broadway Sketchbook*. Lived in Pershore, Worcestershire.

The KIPPER KIDS Performance, film, video, photography and installation artists, formed in 1970 by Brian Routh and Martin von Haselberg. Routh was born in Gateshead, County Durham, in 1948, von Haselberg in Buenos Aires, Argentina, in 1949. They both attended the E.15 Drama School in London, von Haselberg also the American Film Institute, Los Angeles. The Kipper Kids performed all over Europe and North America, venues including Stedelijk Museum, Amsterdam; Kunstalle, Basel; Maalersaal, Hamburg; and ICA. Sometimes they were joined by others, such as the British performance artist Anne Bean. Latterly, Routh and von Haselberg (who was married to the American actress, singer and comedienne Bette Midler) lived and worked in New York and California. The Whitney Museum, New York, planned a Kipper Kids show in 1998. Von Haselberg also showed solo, venues including P.S.1 Contemporary Art Center, New York, 1997–8.

Hilary KIRBY 1964– Artist who graduated with honours from Chelsea School of Art, 1983–6, gaining her master's there, 1986–7. Kirby participated in On Paper, Battersea Arts Centre, 1985; London Institute Exhibition, Royal Festival Hall, 1986; Bird Street Gallery, 1987; and Idea Books, in Milan, Italy in 1989, the year she was included in East End Open Studios, based at Robinson Road.

John KIRBY 1949– Painter, born in Liverpool. He was a shipping clerk, 1965–7, a bookshop salesman, 1967–9, then assistant to the director of Boys' Town of Calcutta, 1969–71, after which he did various social work jobs until in 1982–5 he was at St Martin's School of Art. The Royal College of Art followed, 1986–8. Kirby's figure paintings had a disturbing, Surrealist element; symbols and objects and the painter's own face frequently recurred, and there were references to his Catholic upbringing. Kirby showed in many mixed exhibitions from John Player Portrait Exhibition at National Portrait Gallery in 1984. As a solo artist he showed with Angela Flowers, in Ireland and London, from 1988, later exhibitions including Flowers West, Santa Monica, California, 2000, and Flowers Central, 2002. Contemporary Art Society and Ferens Art Gallery, Hull, hold examples.

John Kynnersley KIRBY 1894–1962 Mainly a figure painter, he was born in the Nottingham area, was educated at Sedbergh School and then at the Slade School of Fine Art. Kirby showed extensively in mixed exhibitions, including RA, NEAC, ROI, Chenil and Goupil Galleries and in Nottingham. In the 1940s he developed arthritis, which around the end of World War prevented him from painting, about which he became bitter. Although he had been left some money, he is said to have died virtually penniless. Lived from 1929 at Stansted, Essex, building a studio at his cottage, where he completed much locally commissioned work. In 1980 Sparrow's Gallery, in Bishop's Stortford, showed Kirby's work, part of a local characters exhibition. Kirby's picture Old Regent Street was included in Christie's NEAC centenary exhibition in 1986, lent by Bradford Art Gallery and

Museum. Kirby was a popular member of the Chelsea Arts Club, remembered by another as "very handsome, rather like Clark Gable, who loved sporting checks, waistcoats and bow ties, who fell in love with glamorous blondes and who drove a dashing car. He was always known as Dick Kirby."

Josh KIRBY 1928–2001 Artist in oil, watercolour and occasionally gouache, born in Waterloo, Liverpool, as Ronald William Kirby. He attended Liverpool City School of Art, 1942–9, teachers including Martin Bell, Will C Penn, George Jardine, Alfred Wiffen and Allan Tankard. Kirby's influences "were Brueghel, Bosch and Brangwyn. I aim to continue the classical tradition and avoid the fads and fashions of the moment. I would like to preserve a sense of wonder in a world obsessed with materialism." This found expression in his The Voyage of the Ayeguy, latter-day altar-pieces in science fiction mode. As a science fiction book illustrator, Kirby was noted for his Ray Bradbury and Terry Pratchett jackets. Kirby had periods painting in a film poster studio in London and freelanced briefly in Paris. Was a member of the Association of British Picture Restorers. Group exhibitions included Portal Gallery, Bluecoat Chambers in Liverpool, ICA and Brighton Art Gallery. Solo shows included DLI Museum & Durham Art Gallery, 1995. Duke of Bedford at Woburn Abbey holds Kirby's work. Lived at Shelfanger, Diss, Norfolk.

Michael KIRBY 1949– Painter and restorer who was born in Farnham Common, Buckinghamshire. He studied at High Wycombe School of Art, 1967–71, teachers including Eric Smith and Romeo di Girolamo. Kirby was a member Free Painters and Sculptors, also exhibiting with RBA and elsewhere. Lived in Hedgerley, Buckinghamshire.

Sarah KIRBY 1903–c.1980 Painter in oil, full name Kathleen Sarah N Kirby, born in London. She studied at King's College, London University, obtaining her Master of Science degree in 1928, also attending London Day Training College. By profession Kirby was a lecturer, and she published *Nature Study for Schools* in 1957. Self-taught, she joined Free Painters and Sculptors in 1972, showing at Loggia Gallery, RA and at Paris Salon. Had a solo exhibition at Bristol Arts Centre in 1967. Lived latterly in Bath, Somerset.

Sarah KIRBY 1961– Printmaker and lecturer, born in Cambridge, who used the intaglio method of etching, aquatint and drypoint to create images of fantasy buildings, imagined landscapes and stories, as in her shared show at Inkpen Downie Architecture & Design, Colchester, in 2002. Kirby did a foundation course in art and design at Cambridgeshire College of Arts and Technology, 1980–1; graduated in fine art from West Surrey College of Art and Design, 1981–4; gained her master's degree in museum and gallery studies, City University, 1986–7; and a master's in fine art, Nottingham Trent University, 1991–3. From 1990–7 she was a keeper at Derby Museums and Art Gallery; was briefly a consultant curator for Cambridgeshire County Council education department, 1991; lectured part-time on degree courses at University of Derby, 1991–4; from 1994 she was a printworker, part-time, at Leicester Print Workshop; also serving part-time as co-ordinator, artists-in-residence, Blaby and Hinckley District Council, 2000–1. Other later exhibitions included Art Prints – 5 Printmakers at the Brewery Arts Centre, Kendal, 1998; Mini Print International, Cadaques, Spain, 2000; Printmaker of the Month, City Gallery, Leicester (which holds her work), 2001; and Sea and Sand, Alexander Gallery, 2002. Lived in Leicester.

Barry KIRK 1933– Painter, draughtsman and teacher, working in a variety of media, born in Deal, Kent. After Westminster School he studied Canterbury College of Art, 1950–4, then Royal College of Art, 1956–9, gaining a Travelling Scholarship in the latter year, teachers including Julian Trevelyan, Edwin La Dell and Alistair Grant. Taught at Canterbury from 1959, becoming principal, 1987–8. Showed in RA Summer Exhibition and had a series of solo shows, including Alwin Gallery. Victoria & Albert Museum holds his work. Lived at Bridge, Kent.

David KIRK 1960– Painter and teacher who graduated from the Ruskin School of Drawing and Fine Art, Oxford, 1983, becoming head of art at Uppingham School. Kirk's highly detailed figure studies and landscapes often had a strongly imaginative and fantastical overtones. He showed solo at RONA Gallery.

Douglas KIRK 1949– Painter and teacher, born in Edinburgh. He attended Duncan of Jordanstone College of Art, Dundee, 1967–71, then was at Royal College of Art, 1971–4. Kirk worked for several months at Cité des Arts, Paris, in 1973. He gained a British Institute Award in 1971, the Burston Award at the Royal College three years later, in the same year getting a Scottish Arts Council Award. From the early 1970s Kirk showed with SSA as well as taking part in Christmas exhibitions at Compass Gallery, Glasgow, where he shared a show in 1974. Scottish Arts Council holds his work, which could be decorative and abstract. Went on to teach at Sir John Cass School of Art and City of London Polytechnic. Lived latterly at Gravesend, in Kent.

Eve KIRK 1900–1969 Painter and decorative artist, born in London. She studied at Slade School of Fine Art, 1919–22, then travelled widely on the continent. Had first solo exhibition at Paterson Gallery in 1930, to which Augustus John contributed. Her work at its best had some of the juicy, painterly qualities found in that of John, who painted Kirk's portrait. Kirk went on to show at Leicester, Lefevre Galleries and elsewhere and in the mid-1940s decorated the Catholic church in Newtown, Wales. About a decade later she went to live in Italy and gave up painting. Tate Gallery and Arts Council hold her work.

Joanna KIRK 1963– Artist, notably in pastel, born in Cheshire. She studied at Goldsmiths' College School of Art, 1981–4. In 1987 she gained joint first prize, 1987 Artist Award, Whitechapel Art Gallery. Her group shows included Christie's Inaugural Exhibition and Riverside Studios, 1984; Richard Pomeroy Gallery, 1987; and Norwich School of Art Gallery, 1988. Her work in Contemporary Art Society collection, Cardinals, was shown in South Bank Centre tour The British Art Show 1990. Kirk's solo shows began with Third Eye Centre in Glasgow, 1987, the year she began exhibiting with Nicola Jacobs Gallery. Also showed at New Gallery at Whitechapel Art Gallery in 1988 and at Carine Campo Gallery, Antwerp, 1989. Kirk worked from photographs and wanted pictures to be "well-drawn, highly finished, to be decorative, full of pattern, delicate". Lived in London.

Michael KIRKBRIDE 1959– Painter who joined the NEAC in 2004, showing with it that year at the Open Exhibition at Mall Galleries, and in NEAC, Cross Gate Gallery, Lexington, Kentucky, in America, 2005. Kirkbride did foundation studies in art design at Sunderland Polytechnic, 1976–7; graduated with fine art honours from Sunderland Polytechnic, 1977–80; and attended the Royal Academy Schools, 1992–5. He won Northern Arts Awards in 1987 and 1988; a Northern Arts Travel Award, 1990; and a Royal Academy Schools Travel Award to Mexico in 1995. He exhibited widely in group shows, including The First Picture Show, Sainsbury Centre for Contemporary Arts, Norwich, 1980; Rothmans (*Northern Echo*) Arts Award Touring Exhibition, 1982; Joint Exhibition, Newcastle upon Tyne Polytechnic Gallery, 1987; RA Summer Exhibition, from 1993; Paper, Scissors, Paint, Fashion Space Gallery, London College of Fashion, 1998; Staff Exhibition there, 2001; and The Discerning Eye, Mall Galleries, 2004. Among Kirkbride's solo shows were Calouste Gulbenkian Gallery, Newcastle, 1988, and the University of Bradford Art Gallery and Dixon Bates Gallery, Leeds, both 1991. Kirkbride was based in London.

Mick KIRKBY-GEDDES 1966– Sculptor, mostly in junk sheet-metal, born in Sheffield, Yorkshire. He studied at Mansfield College of Further Education, 1984, fine art at Leeds Polytechnic, 1985–8, then became a self-employed sculptor. Kirkby-Geddes' work was "influenced by cartoons, television, life, and so on. It is light-hearted and colourful, employing visual puns, some automata and lots of dogs." Group shows included Rufford Sculpture Park, 1987; Camden Arts Centre, 1989; Galerie Goetz in Basel, Switzerland, 1992; and Benchmarks, Tatton Park, Cheshire, 1993. Had solo shows with Leeds Art Company, 1990; Treadwell's Art Mill, Bradford, 1992; and Crescent Arts, Scarborough, 1993. Lived in Holmfirth, Yorkshire.

Edward Todd KIRKHAM 1947– Sculptor and teacher who did a foundation course at Blackpool College of Art, 1976–8, graduated in sculpture at Leeds Polytechnic, 1978–81, then completed his master's degree at Royal College of Art, 1981–3. Among his teaching experience was Royal College of Art, Royal Academy Schools, Central School and in the provinces. A Leeds Polytechnic Travel Award took him to France in 1981, in 1984 he gained the Royal College Sculpture Prize, in 1988–9 being Rome Scholar in Sculpture. He researched the cult and rituals of Dionysus. Among his exhibitions were Leeds 80, at Lancaster University, 1980; Sculpture in the Landscape, Portland Clifftop Sculpture Park, 1983; as artist-in-residence, 1984, Mostyn Art Gallery, Llandudno; and Sculpture at Canterbury, 1992.

Norman KIRKHAM 1936– Artist, designer and lecturer, working in oil, watercolour, gouache and pastel, born and lived in Glasgow, where he attended the School of Art, 1953–8, taught by David Donaldson. Worked as a designer, 1960–75, began painting then and was in 1977 a part-time lecturer at Glasgow School of Art. He was president of Glasgow Art Club, 1988–91, and honorary secretary of Royal Glasgow Institute of the Fine Arts from 1991. Won many prizes at the Institute. Also showed at RA, RSA, RP, Fine Art Society, Seen Gallery and elsewhere in group exhibitions. Later solo shows included Barclay Lennie Fine Art, Glasgow, from 1986. HRH The Duke of Edinburgh, Arthur Andersen and Fleming's hold examples.

Alison KIRKPATRICK fl. from early 1990s– Sculptor working in a variety of materials, born in Kendal, Westmorland. She moved to Scotland aged two and graduated from Edinburgh College of Art in 1990, then studied for her master's degree. She was an artist who pondered over notes and made sketches over long periods before creating the final work from materials she had "an instinctive response to ... The kind of shapes I come up with are accidental." She took part in Danger Artists at Work, a City Art Centre, Edinburgh, touring show in 1991. The city's collection holds her work.

Ethel KIRKPATRICK 1869–1966 Painter and printmaker, younger sister of the artist Ida Kirkpatrick. Ethel studied at the Royal Academy Schools and Central School of Arts and Crafts. She was a member of the Society of Graver-Printers, Colour Woodcut Society and Arts and Crafts Society, painted widely around England and Wales and on the continent and had work accepted by the British Museum and Victoria & Albert Museum. She was a prolific exhibitor, venues including the Alpine Club, SWA, RBA, RA and in several international exhibitions. She lived with Ida in Harrow, Middlesex.

Ida KIRKPATRICK 1866–1950 Artist, born in Jersey, Channel Islands, older sister of the engraver and painter Ethel Kirkpatrick. She was educated at Queen's College, Lausanne in Switzerland, at the Royal Female School of Art and Académie Julian, Paris. She won a two-year Gilchrist Scholarship and one-year Queen's Scholarship. Like her sister she travelled widely to paint, Walberswick being a favourite venue. Her work was widely reproduced in publications and as picture postcards. Showed at SWA, Alpine Club, RBA, RA, WIAC and elsewhere. Ida lived with Ethel in Harrow, Middlesex.

Ian KIRKWOOD fl. from late 1960s– Painter who said that his pictures were "intended as haptic fictions, studio-formed but grounded in experience". He studied at Leicester Polytechnic, 1968–9; St Martin's School of Art, 1969–72; and University College, London, 1972–5. Exhibitions included Yarrow Gallery, Oundle, 1982; Museum of Modern Art, Oxford, and Aspex Gallery, Portsmouth, both 1983; D H Lawrence's Landscape, at Nottingham Playhouse and Leicester Museum, 1985; and Art '87 at Peterborough's Lady Lodge Arts Centre, 1987. Peterborough City Museum, Eastern Arts and Leicestershire Education Authority hold Kirkwood's work.

John Sutherland KIRKWOOD 1947– Artist working in mixed media, printmaker and photographer, born in Edinburgh where he continued to live. After George Watson's College he attended Duncan of Jordanstone College of Art, Dundee, 1965–70, doing a large number of jobs ranging from school teaching to labouring. Elected SSA in 1972 and took part in many mixed shows. Gained Scottish Arts Council Award in 1973, with Council Bursaries in 1976 and 1980, and was included in the Council's show Scottish Art Now in 1982. Kirkwood said that his work was "about trying to communicate with people". He was influenced by Dada and much of his subject matter was industrial and took a pessimistic view of militarism. Solo shows included New 57 Gallery, Edinburgh, in 1972 and 1976; Printmakers' Workshop Gallery, Edinburgh, 1974; and Talbot Rice Art Centre, Edinburgh, 1981. Scottish

Museum of Modern Art is among several public collections holding his work.

Dorris KIRLEW 1906–1999 Painter and teacher, born in Bath, Somerset, where she attended the School of Art, then the Royal College of Art. Taught at Grantham Girls' School before moving to Brighton, Sussex, where she taught at the College of Art, also at Lewes Boys' Grammar School and at Hove Girls' Grammar School. Showed early in her career at public gallery in Nottingham, later at RA. In her final years she concentrated more on collage and tapestry than on painting. Brighton Art Gallery holds several works.

Natasha KISSELL 1978– Artist who in 1986 fled South Africa, where she grew up, owing to political unrest and worsening violence. She was taught by Paula Rego at Byam Shaw School of Art, "influenced by her surreal juxtapositions", and by Christopher Le Brun at the Royal Academy Schools, "taking on his Neo-Romanticism." The mix of these two disciplines created a distinctive style in which, according to *Dwell* magazine, "jutting angles and soaring rooflines are set against layers upon layers of pastel hillsides and trees that rise to the top of the picture plane." In 2000 Kissell was able to use Anish Kapoor's beach hut in Martha's Vineyard, in America, to study nature and create paintings with a delicate balance between surface modulation and illusionist depth. Her Royal Academy Schools show was bought by Charles Saatchi. Kissell's work was in the collections of HSBC, Deutsche Bank, Gieves and Hawkes and Knoxville Museum, Tennessee. Had a solo show at Haunch of Venison, 2004, and with her partner Peter Harrap was included in Bold + Radical, Radical Art, New Painting from the Royal Academy Schools, Jerwood Space, and an exhibition at Marlborough Fine Art, both 2005. Lived in London.

Ronald Brooks KITAJ 1932– Painter, printmaker and teacher, born Cleveland, Ohio. Studied at Cooper Union in New York, and Akademie der Bildenden Künste, Vienna, 1950–2; at Ruskin School of Drawing in Oxford, 1958–9; then Royal College of Art, 1959–61. Kitaj was an important influence on fellow-students at the Royal College, such as David Hockney. Although labelled initially as a Pop Artist, Kitaj's work was more complex, autobiographical, drawing on many, often arcane, sources of inspiration. After a period in the early 1960s painting in England and Spain, Kitaj from 1962–6 taught at Camberwell School of Art, while having a one-man show at Marlborough Fine Art in 1963. He was an infrequent exhibitor, but gradually built up an international reputation from the 1960s, with important exhibitions in America, Germany, Italy and France. In 1967–8 was invited to teach at the University of California, Berkeley. There was a retrospective at Hirshhorn Museum and Sculpture Garden, Washington, 1981, another at the Tate Gallery, 1994. The harsh critical reception of this and the death of his wife Sandra Fisher, also a painter, events which Kitaj saw as related, spurred him to resettle in Los Angeles in 1997. About the same time a huge tapestry, produced at Dovecot Studio and based on Kitaj's picture If Not, Not (in the Scottish National Gallery of Modern Art, Edinburgh), was unveiled in the entrance Hall of the New British Library. Works by Kitaj, who was elected RA in 1991, are also held by the Arts Council, Tate Gallery and other collections. Kitaj – in the Aura of Cézanne and Other Masters was held at the National Gallery, 2001–2.

Bert KITCHEN 1940– Painter, designer, illustrator and teacher, born in Liverpool, who gained a diploma in design at Central School of Arts and Crafts. He was a part-time lecturer there, 1961–4, and at City of London Polytechnic, 1964–92. Kitchen was noted for his versatility, completing textile designs for Edinburgh Weavers; animation films for BBC and London Weekend Television; background paintings for feature and television films; illustrations for Cape, Collins, Kestrel and other publishers; artwork for advertising agencies; and regular illustration for *Private Eye* magazine, 1969–93. Awards included the Chicago & Illinois Cassandra Foundation Award (Painting), 1969; International Graphics, First Prize, Fiera di Bologna, and included in honours list of the Critici in Erba, Bologna, both 1988; and Gold Medal for Illustration, Society of Illustrators, New York, 1991. Mixed shows included Beaux Arts Gallery, 1961; Der Geist des Surrealismus, Baukunst Gallery, Cologne, 1971; First Tokyo Biennale, New Image in Painting, 1974; Deck of Cards, JPL Gallery, 1976; and Surrealism Unlimited, Camden Arts Centre, 1978. Had a solo show at Archer Gallery, 1973, later ones including a retrospective at Smiths Galleries, 1991. From 1984 Kitchen wrote and illustrated a series of his own books. Lived in London.

Myfanwy KITCHIN 1917– Ceramic sculptor, artist in various media on paper, book illustrator and art critic, born in Newbury, Berkshire, who sometimes signed work Myf. She attended Hornsey School of Art, Slade/Ruskin Schools (evacuated to Oxford in World War II), the department of fine art at Reading University under J A Betts and Walsall College of Art. For 15 years Kitchin was art critic for *The Guardian* newspaper in the Midlands area. She also illustrated books for Phoenix House and Duckworth. Her ceramic sculptures stemmed from the slab pottery technique, developed from on-the-spot sketches. The subjects were originally industrial workers in the Midlands and later farmers and animals in Gwynedd, where she lived at Barmouth. Kitchin was a member of RCamA. She also showed with RBSA, Ombersley Gallery at Ombersley and galleries in Birmingham, Walsall and Lichfield, and she had a solo exhibition at Y Tabernacl, Machynlleth, 1997.

Roy KITCHIN 1926–1997 Sculptor and teacher, born in East Anglia. He was brought up in industrial Birmingham and studied at the School of Arts and Crafts there. After working as an architectural sculptor from 1954–60 Kitchin taught at Wolverhampton College of Art for 10 years. He settled to work in Cannock, Staffordshire, teaching at the University of Newcastle upon Tyne. Kitchin showed in mixed exhibitions at Landmark Park in Scotland, at the Yorkshire Sculpture Park and was included in the Welsh Sculpture Trust Margam Sculpture Park show Sculpture in a Country Park, in 1983. Kitchin also held several solo shows, including Whitworth Art Gallery, Manchester. Although Kitchin's early work was normally bronze and concerned with such subjects as landscape and fertility, in the early 1960s he became interested in materials such as steel and cast concrete and industrial topics. The later works, often imbued with humour, could be large and designed to heighten visual awareness.

Robert KITCHINER 1907– Painter, draughtsman and printmaker, born in London, who studied at Slade School of Fine Art, 1928–31, under Henry Tonks and Philip Wilson Steer. Showed at RA, NEAC and in the provinces. Lived at Sawbridgeworth, Hertfordshire.

Arthur KITCHING 1912–1981 Painter, draughtsman and curator, born in Sheffield, Yorkshire. He went into the steelworks as a clerk at 16 and began painting two years later. Financial reasons prevented his taking a place offered at Royal College of Art. Thus he taught himself, apart from a year at Sheffield College of Art in 1934. He never became a professional artist, but did a number of mundane jobs until he became, in 1961, first curator of Manor House Museum and Art Gallery, Ilkley, and then exhibitions officer for Bradford Metropolitan Council. He did not show his own work until he was 53. At times there were Wyndham Lewis- and Matisse-like elements in Kitching's pictures in which, he said, "representation took second place to overall abstract design." His book *Pavements and People* was published in facsimile and after his death Leeds City Art Gallery gave him a commemorative show.

Paul KITCHINGMAN 1947– Artist who was self-taught, painting in oil and watercolour from early youth. His main interest was landscape, and he did conservation work with the National Trust and cultivated bonsai grown from seed collected on foreign trips. From the early 1970s Kitchingman travelled extensively on the continent, notably Mediterranean countries and Turkey. He sold much of his work there, English exhibitions including The Heifer Gallery.

Roger KITE 1947– Painter and teacher, born in Bath, Somerset. Studied at Hornsey College of Art, 1970–4, then Chelsea School of Art, 1974–5. From 1977 he taught at Trent Polytechnic. Among his shows were Athena Awards, 1987; Kettle's Yard, Cambridge, 1988; John Moores Liverpool Exhibition, 1989–90; and Stephen Lacey Gallery, 2000. Later solo shows included several in Italy, including British School at Rome, 1994, and Casa Valdese, Rio Marina, 1997, Kite having won Abbey Awards in 1994 and 1996. Arts Council holds his geometrical abstract picture Diagonal 1, of 1976, bought from Acme Gallery. Lived in Ilford, Essex.

Linda KITSON 1945– Painter, draughtsman and teacher, born and lived in London. She studied at St Martin's School of Art, 1965–7, then Royal College of Art, 1967–70. Kitson was chosen as the Official War Artist to accompany the Falklands Islands Task Force in 1982, which she found a searing, indelible experience. The three-month tour resulted in 400 works, often done at speed in uncomfortable, hostile conditions. Work was taken into the collection of the Imperial War Museum, which toured a show, and a book was published called *The Falklands War, a Visual Diary*. Kitson also exhibited at RA, Workshop Gallery and elsewhere. Later solo exhibitions included Collins and Hastie, 2002.

Robert Hawthorn KITSON 1873–1947 Watercolour landscapist, born in the Leeds area of Yorkshire, who became a member of RBA in 1925. Lived for a time at Taormini in Sicily, eventually settling in Leeds in the 1920s. Showed extensively at Fine Art Society, Redfern and Goupil Galleries, also at RA and Walker Art Gallery in Liverpool.

Barry KITTS 1943– Painter, graphic designer, teacher and writer, born in Bath, Somerset. He had early tuition while still at school from the printmaker George Mackley, then studied at Kingston School of Art, 1959–61, teachers including Donald Pavey, and Wimbledon School of Art, 1961–4, under Gerald Cooper. Went on to do visiting lecturing at Ravensbourne College of Design and at London College of Printing. Showed at NEAC, RBA and elsewhere. Was part-author of a book on graphic design sources. Lived in London.

Meyer KLANG 1880–1948 Artist who produced portraits and still lifes, based in London's East End, who showed at RBA, RA, Walker Art Gallery in Liverpool and elsewhere. Ben Uri Art Society holds his oil on canvas Flowerpiece.

Ivan KLAPEŽ 1961– Sculptor, born in Kosute, Croatia, who studied at the Zagreb Academy of Arts under Stipe Sikirica and Kruno Bosnjak, with a third year travelling widely to study sculpture. In 1987, in straitened circumstances, he moved to England to study at the City and Guilds of London Art School. A collection of Klapež's religious works was shown at St George's, Bloomsbury (the damp crypt of which was for a time his studio), then in Portsmouth Cathedral, in 1989. In 1991 he was commissioned to create a trophy statuette for the Margaret Thatcher Aims of Industry Award; the result was a nude male figure on tiptoe, arms outstretched, entitled Liberty. Soon after, he produced small figures of down-and-outs metamorphosing into pigeons. Later works included imaginary portraits of the writer Samuel Beckett and an anthropomorphic skyscraper, following a visit to New York. Among further commissions were Unity, 1992, dancing male and female figures, commissioned by the property company MEPC for the atrium of Alban Gate, above London Wall, described and pictured by Philip Ward-Jackson in *Public Sculpture in the City of London*; and Trust and Daring, 1996, two figures for the Trustee Savings Bank's headquarters in Birmingham. Klapež continued to live and work in London.

Halina KLECKA 1967– Painter and draughtsman, born in Walton-on-Thames, Surrey, daughter of the artist and architect Alexander Paul Klecki. She studied at Chelsea School of Art, 1989, and became a professional artist, a participating member of the Association of Polish Artists in Great Britain. In 1989 she did graphic design for the Pro Arte Theatre and in 1990 was commissioned to design Christmas cards for Medical Aid for Poland. By 2004 she had "created over 2,000 oil paintings and drawings", with work owned by many private collectors. Klecka had solo shows at the Questors Theatre, 1991, and at the Polish Cultural Centre Gallery, 1992 and 1995.

Alexander Paul KLECKI 1927– Architect and artist, born in Wilno, Poland, who after grammar school, 1944–8, graduated from the Polish University College School of Architecture, RAST, 1948–54. He became a full member of SARP, Association of Polish Architects in Warsaw Poland, and of APA, Association of Polish Artists in Great Britain. In England, Klecki worked with the Arcon Group, 1954–8; with Sir Frederick Gibberd on the No 3 Terminal, London Heathrow Airport, 1958–64; with Gable Construction as chief company architect, 1964–7, winning first prizes in the House of the Year Award, 1965, and for a housing estate in Walton-on-Thames, 1966; with Louis De Soissons on the Brighton Marina, 1967–70; with Allied Engineering as chief company architect, 1975–80; with the Architects and Planners Group, 1980–5, winning first prizes for The Arabian Horse Breeding and Art Centre, Saudi Arabia, and the Falcon Club in Abu Dhabi; in 1986 being supervisory resident architect for a palace in Damman, Saudi Arabia. As well as showing with APA, Klecki took part in several group shows, including the RA Summer Exhibition, 1959; with the Guild of Catholic Artists and Craftsmen, Building Centre, 1965; and at an Exhibition of Contemporary Lighting in Paris, 1977. He carried out many commissions, including 10 stained glass windows, St Andrew Bobola's Roman Catholic Church, Hammersmith, 1962–85; figure of Christ, aluminium, east wall, Anglican church, Newcastle-under-Lyme, 1964; bronze murals for boardrooms, Hambro's Bank, 1974; Katyn Memorial, Roman Catholic Cathedral, Clifton, Bristol, 1985; and new foyer, Polish Cultural Centre, 2002. In 1989 Klecki presented his bronze Holy Mother of Ostra Brama, Wilno, to Pope John Paul II at the Vatican. Klecki's daughter was the artist Halina Klecka. He lived in west London.

Anita KLEIN 1960– Artist in oil on board, charcoal, drypoint etching and ceramic, born in Sydney, Australia. Powerful groups of colourful, stylised figures were a key feature of her output. She studied at Chelsea School of Art, 1978–9; gained an honours degree in fine art from Slade School, 1979–83; then did a postgraduate diploma in printmaking at the Slade, 1983–5. Her teachers included Paula Rego, Mick Moon and John Hoyland. Klein was a member of RE, Greenwich Printmakers and the Printmakers' Council. Group exhibitions included New Contemporaries, at ICA; British Drawing, at Hayward Gallery; Blond Fine Art; RWA; ROI; and Bradford Print Biennale. Solo shows included Creaser Gallery, 1986; Victorian Artists' Society, Melbourne, 1992; Woodlands Art Gallery, 1993; and Boundary Gallery and Advanced Graphics London, both 2002. Arts Council, Ashmolean Museum in Oxford and London University hold examples. Lived in London.

David KLEIN 1963– Figurative sculptor in stone whose work included an abstract element, as in his solo show at Thackeray Gallery, 2003. Klein was apprenticed to the sculptor John Jennings, 1990–2; graduated with honours in fine art from Staffordshire University, 1992–4; and took a postgraduate course in figurative sculpture at Sir Henry Doulton School of Sculptors, 1994–6. He exhibited in Britain and France and was artist-in-residence, Les Artes, Perpignan, 2001. His studio was in Brighton, Sussex.

Simon KLEIN 1959– Painter, born in London, who lived in Vienna, Austria, and France as a child. Studied at Slade School of Fine Art, 1978–82, in the life rooms with Euan Uglow and Patrick George, also with John Hoyland, which helped set a pattern of making abstract paintings from figurative sources, such as household objects and intimate spaces. Completed a master's degree in contemporary art practice at Kingston University, 1997. Group shows included Pick of the New Graduate Art, Christie's, 1982; Watermans Open '85, Watermans Arts Centre, Brentford, 1985; Crucial Gallery, 1988; Royal Over-Seas League Open, 1993; and Rentrée, Stanley Picker Gallery, Kingston University, 1999. Also showed with Henry Boxer, Richmond, Surrey. Later solo exhibitions included Surrey University, in conjunction with Piano Nobile, 1996. Klein's work was held in public and private collections in England and abroad.

Leo KLIN 1887–1967 Painter born in Grodno, Russia, where he studied at the Imperial Academy of Fine Arts, St Petersburg. In England he exhibited widely, including RA, RP, UA, NEAC and throughout the provinces. Sunderland Museum and Art Gallery and Russell-Cotes Art Gallery, Bournemouth, hold his work. Lived in London.

Clara KLINGHOFFER 1900–1970 Painter, printmaker and draughtsman, born near Lemberg, Austria. She grew up and studied in London, having her first one-man show at 19, which was a triumph. She studied at Slade School of Fine Art and Central School of Arts and Crafts and in the late 1920s married the writer J W F Stoppelman. She went on to show widely through Britain, the continent and North America, living latterly in London and New York. Klinghoffer was noted for her portraits, especially of children, and was a masterly draughtsman, in the Old Master tradition. Jacob Epstein considered her "an artist of great talent, a painter of the first order ... in the very first rank of draughtsmen in the world." Venues showing her work included RA, Belgrave Gallery, NEAC and Venice Biennale. Travelled widely and painted many notable people, including Dame Sybil Thorndike the actress, the writer Isaac Bashevis Singer and the politician Sir Barnett Janner. Tate Gallery, Victoria & Albert Museum and Manchester City Art Gallery are among many holding her pictures.

Alexander KLIOT 1953–1998 Realistic painter of Ukrainian-Jewish origin, using a rich palette, who grew up in the Soviet Union. From the age of 14 he studied at art college in Odessa. After completing his National Service he went to Leningrad, attending what is now the St Petersburg Academy of Art, where he obtained his master's degree. In 1982 he pursued a postgraduate portrait project in the Ukraine, painting miners in Donetsk, despite suffering from claustrophobia. The pollution he encountered was to cost him his life. Five years after moving to London, where he settled with his artist wife Maria, whom he had met at the Academy, Kliot contracted lung cancer and within three months was dead. While living in London Kliot worked to commission, including copying Thomas Gainsborough's work in Kenwood House, Hampstead. A memorial retrospective including his pictures of miners, landscapes ranging from Lake Ladoga to Hampstead Heath and still lifes was held at The Chambers Gallery in 2005.

Christiana KLITGAARD: *see* **Christiana Brix MAY**

Tony KLITZ 1917–2000 Painter notable for his atmospheric scenes of London. Klitz was born in Southport, Lancashire, educated at Bishop Wordsworth School in Salisbury and attended Cheltenham Art School, 1936–9. He served in the Army in World War II, being demobilised with the rank of major in 1945. He moved to London in 1950 and studied with the Australian artist Hayward Veal. Klitz exhibited in the capital to good critical reception. For some years he worked in Ireland, solo exhibitions being held at the Davis Gallery, Dublin. After his death his work was sold through the Anthony Robert Klitz Gallery on the Internet and examples were also offered by Bonhams, Montpelier Street, in 2003.

Olivier KLOMPKES 1972– Painter, designer and illustrator producing colourful, decorative work, born in Belgium. He trained at Stockport College of Art, 1992–4, winning the R J Brown top student award. As a designer Klompkes gained prizes from Royal Doulton and Sundour Fabrics, and exhibited at international trade fairs in New York, Frankfurt and Brussels. Work was shown in mixed exhibitions at Format Studios, Macclesfield, 1995; NaveDiez Art Gallery, Valencia, Spain (with a solo show there in 1997); and Gordon Hepworth Fine Art at 23 Smith Street, 1997.

Margarete KLOPFLEISCH 1911–1982 Sculptor, painter, draughtsman and printmaker, born in Dresden, Germany. She was throughout her life dogged by ill-health, after a deprived youth. Leaving school at 14, she had to mother the family and do menial jobs, but managed to teach herself the violin, went to modelling classes and became involved in left-wing politics. Modelled for Otto Dix's life class at Art School. When Hitler came to power Gretel joined her future husband, Peter Klopfleisch, in Prague, where she was taught by the artist Käte Schaffner. Joined the Oskar Kokoschka Club in 1937. Through it and AIA, of which she became a member, was able to emigrate to England. Attended sculpture classes at Reading University, but setbacks intervened, and she was interned in Isle of Man, where she was seriously ill, and Peter was sent to Australia. When reunited she worked again as a sculptor, showing in London, Maidenhead, Cookham, Eton, Glasgow, Windsor and Reading. In 1960 returned to Dresden with her two daughters, where her husband eventually joined her, but artistic recognition came slowly. Became a member of Dresden Artists' Union and a year before she died had successful exhibition at Galerie Comenius, Dresden. In 1987 John Denham Gallery had a substantial show of her work.

Zygmunt Eustachy KLOŚ fl. from 1960s– Painter who during World War II served in the Polish Army, afterwards settling in England where he worked. Meanwhile, he studied at the Polish School of Painting under Professor Marian Bohusz-Szyskzo and painted mostly at night. He was a member of the Association of Polish Artists in Great Britain and took part in group shows, including Contemporary Art by Polish Artists abroad, at Imperial College, 1970. He also had a solo show at the Cassel Gallery. Kloś completed numerous paintings on hardboard, but after his sudden death and that of his wife Bronisława much of his work remained unfound.

Stefan KNAPP 1921–1996 Painter, born in Biłgoraj, Poland, who settled in England after World War II. Imprisonment in a Siberian labour camp in 1939 and service as a Royal Air Force Spitfire pilot, 1942–5, had a lasting effect on his artistic development. Studied at Central School of Arts and Crafts, Slade School of Fine Art, 1947–50, after initial education in Poland. Had first solo show at London Gallery in 1947, then exhibited widely, including France, Germany, America and Brazil. He was given a retrospective at Warsaw Gallery of Zachęta in 1974; in 1999 shows at the Polish Cultural Institute and Whitford Fine Art traced Knapp's course through a type of Surrealism, freeform abstraction and Pop Art influences. Although he established a reputation for subtle spraygun pictures, Knapp was also noted for his painting in glass on steel and for his paintings on enamel, fired in a kiln developed by him. Work held by many international museums, including Victoria & Albert Museum and Museum of Modern Art in New York. Toruń University, in Poland, holds his large mural devoted to Nicolaus Copernicus. Also fulfilled many commissions for large murals, one for the Alexander Stores, in New York, having to be assembled in an aircraft hangar. Two days after overseeing the reinstallation of his 1960s Heathrow murals in the Richard Rogers Transit Building, and three days after he completed The Battle of Britain mural for the Polish metro, in Warsaw, Knapp had a heart attack and died in his studio. Knapp's early autobiography, *The Square Sun*, was published in 1956. Lived in London, then in Wormley, Surrey.

John KNAPP-FISHER 1931– Painter in watercolour, oil and mixed media, born in London. He studied at Maidstone College of Art, 1949–52, concentrating on graphic design. Knapp-Fisher then designed in the theatre and painted and exhibited from a sea-going home for five years. He moved to Wales in 1965, settling in Haverfordwest, Pembrokeshire, opening a studio/gallery in 1967. As Trevigan Gallery he published postcards and limited edition reproduction prints of his paintings. Knapp-Fisher's subjects were landscape, seascape, buildings, boats, figures, animals and fish. He aimed "to produce pictures that are exciting, have strong compositional form and powerful visual imagery". Showed at many venues, including RA, Agnew, the Marjorie Parr, Upper Grosvenor, Bankside and Business Art Galleries, RWA, WAC, Beaux Arts in Bath and elsewhere. Later exhibitions included Martin Tinney Gallery, Cardiff, 2004. HRH The Prince of Wales, National Library of Wales in Aberystwyth and Swansea University hold examples.

Bryan KNEALE 1930– Sculptor, painter and teacher, born in Douglas, Isle of Man. He studied at Douglas School of Art, 1947, then Royal Academy Schools, 1948–52, being a Rome Scholar in painting, 1949–51. Kneale began making sculpture at the end of the 1950s, a move which he later described as inevitable, because of his preoccupation with form. At first it was welded steel sculptures, but he later added other materials. Kneale was an abstract sculptor who drew on such inspirations as anthropomorphic and vegetal forms. Teaching included Royal Academy Schools and Royal College of Art, where he was first professor of drawing until 1995. Was made RA in 1973. His work appeared in group shows such as John Moores Exhibition Liverpool, 1961; the 1966–7 Sculpture from the Arts Council Collection show; and 1977 Silver Jubilee Contemporary British Sculpture Exhibition in Battersea Park, London. Kneale's first solo show of paintings at Redfern Gallery in 1954 was followed by many others there. He had a retrospective at Whitechapel Art Gallery in 1966 and at RWA in 1995, with a seventieth-birthday exhibition at New Art Centre, East Winterslow, 2000. Helped organise two big sculpture exhibitions: British Sculptors '72, at Burlington House, London; and the Battersea Park show. His work is in many international collections including Arts Council, Contemporary Art Society, Museum of Modern Art in New York and Tate Gallery. Lived in London.

Howard KNEE 1889–1971 Watercolour painter, born in London, who studied at the School of Art, Dublin. Exhibited at the RA and RHA and had his work reproduced by several British and Irish publishers. Lived in Dublin.

Cecily KNEESHAW 1883– Watercolourist, full name Cecilia Margaret Kneeshaw, who sometimes signed her work C K. She was privately educated, partly as a musician. Was a member of BWS and UA, with which she last showed in 1956. Also exhibited at RI, RCamA, RSA and Walker Art Gallery, Liverpool, and had a solo show at Arlington Gallery in 1935. Lived in Lyndhurst, Hampshire.

Frank KNELLER 1914– Painter of horses and dogs in the manner of Stubbs, born in Bangor, Caernarvonshire. He studied at University College of North Wales and obtained a Bachelor of Science degree. In Edinburgh, studied at the College of Art under John Murray Thomson and dissected horses at a local veterinary college. Exhibited RSA, RCamA, RSW and UA and published some cartoons. Was a member of the Ski Club of Great Britain. Latterly lived in Eastbourne, Sussex.

Bonnie KNICKERBOCKER 1943– Painter, born in Chicago, Illinois, America, whose childhood was spent in Charlottesville, Virginia. She gained her bachelor's degree in fine arts from George Washington University Corcoran School of Art in 1965, then travelled the world for a year, living in Sydney, Australia, 1967–9. She moved to London in 1969, attending Camden Art School, 1969–71. Knickerbocker painted in Madrid, Spain, 1971–2; Mill Valley, California, 1972–4; and Santa Fe, New Mexico, 1974–90. She then worked variously in London, Washington and Tucson, Arizona. A creator of colourful, vibrant images, Knickerbocker showed at Camden Arts Centre from 1970; Festival of the Arts, Santa Fe, from 1976; and Mariposa Gallery, Albuquerque, New Mexico, from 1982. She took part in a three-man show at Tricycle Gallery, 1984, solo exhibitions including Carol Thornton Gallery, Santa Fe, New Mexico, 1986.

Alick KNIGHT 1903–1983 Painter, printmaker, designer, illustrator and teacher, born in Ifield, Sussex, as Sidney Alick Knight. Studied at Central School of Arts and Crafts, 1919–22, with Bernard Meninsky and A S Hartrick. From 1922–4 Knight did his design training at Carlton Studios, joined the advertising agency Alfred Pemberton in 1924 and from 1926–45 was its art director-designer. Although rejected as an Official War Artist during World War II, Knight did a body of war work, as shown at Abbott and Holder in 1990. From 1939, Knight assisted with a range of government propaganda, then from 1942 he was in the Army, involved in camouflage and cartography; was attached to the Royal Army Medical Corps, making anatomical drawings in hospital and the operating theatre; then was appointed art instructor at the Army School of Education, Park Hall, Shropshire. After the war Knight resigned from Pemberton's to devote himself to painting, although he also worked freelance for publishers and advertisers and taught in art schools. Knight was a member of the Society of Industrial Artists, Senefelder Club and London Sketch Club, showing at galleries including Leicester and Redfern. Lived in London.

Arnold KNIGHT 1906– Painter and colour printer, born in London, son of an architect, Edward F Knight. Arnold studied at Poole and with the Parkstone-based artist Walter Stritch Hutton, was a member of Bournemouth Arts Club and a keen sailor and oarsman, belonging to Parkstone Sailing Club. Despite being disabled by polio, Knight was an ardent landscape painter. As well as views of Dorset, he produced much work after World War II in Gloucestershire, where he stayed with his artist friends Arthur and Bertha Bell in Cheltenham. He also produced drawings for an experimental fighter for Gloster Aircraft Company. Showed at RA, RBA and Walker Art Gallery, Liverpool.

Charles KNIGHT 1865–1948 Landscape watercolourist, by profession an accountant, father of the artist Charles Knight. He was born in Slinfold, Sussex, became a member of Brighton Arts Club and painted extensively in the county where he showed, also depicting other parts of England and Wales. Brighton Art Gallery, which holds his work, gave him a memorial exhibition in 1949.

Charles KNIGHT 1901–1990 Painter, especially of landscape, and teacher, born in Hove, Sussex, the county which he often depicted and where he settled in Ditchling. Encouraged as a child by an amateur painter father, Knight entered Brighton College of Art soon after World War I, remaining there for four years much influenced by his teacher, Louis Ginnett. Then studied for two years at Royal Academy Schools and etching at Royal College of Art. At college Knight won the Turner Medal and Landseer Scholarship; his prize composition, Llangollen, was bought for the Tate Gallery. In mid-1920s was impressed by the work of John Sell Cotman, and this left a lasting influence on Knight's watercolours. Taught at Brighton College of Art, being vice-principal from 1959–67. Showed regularly at RA and was a member of RWS and ROI. In World War II Knight completed 40 watercolours for the Pilgrim Trust *Recording Britain* project, making an invaluable record of the Brighton area. Was married to the illustrator Leonora Vasey. Towner Art Gallery, Eastbourne, held an exhibition of Knight's work in 1997 in conjunction with Chris Beetles. There was a centenary show at Ditchling Gallery in 2001.

Clifford KNIGHT 1930– Painter in a variety of media and teacher, born and lived in Kempston, Bedfordshire. He studied at Central School of Arts and Crafts, 1955–7, teachers including William Roberts, Merlyn Evans and Blair Hughes-Stanton. For a dozen years he taught at Bedford College, also Bedford Prison. Neo-Romantic artists including Paul Nash, John Piper and Graham Sutherland influenced Knight's work, which featured ruin and decay in derelict buildings and the landscape. From 1955 Knight was a member of UA. He had solo shows at Upper Street Gallery, Gordon Maynard Gallery in Welwyn and at galleries in Luton, Northampton and Letchworth. The Crown Commissioners, Luton and Letchworth Art Galleries hold examples. Wrote for *Leisure Painter* magazine.

Esmond KNIGHT 1906–1987 Actor, singer and recreational painter, born in East Sheen, Surrey. He was educated at Westminster School and made his first appearance professionally at the Old Vic in 1925. He made his first film appearance in 1931 and then established a career in television. Notable among Knight's numerous appearances was his one-man show *Agincourt – the Archer's Tale*. During World War II Knight was in the

Royal Navy, and while serving on the *Prince of Wales* was hit in the face by molten metal and blinded. He underwent rehabilitation at a St Dunstan's training school and was able to resume acting, partially recovering his sight in 1943, but at best it was "like looking through clouds", and it eventually deteriorated. Even so, Knight developed as a competent painter and had several shows, including New Town Gallery, Uckfield. Died in Egypt. Instead of a memorial service, there was a show of Knight's archer pictures at the Saga Art Gallery, attended by his two actress wives, Frances Clare and Nora Swinburne, with whom he acted on stage and screen. His daughter was the actress Rosalind Knight.

Harold KNIGHT 1874–1961 Painter of sensitive portraits, especially of women, and interiors, born in Nottingham. In the mid-1890s he studied at the local School of Art; also studied in Paris at Académie Julian, his teachers including Jean-Paul Laurens and Benjamin Constant. Knight married Laura Johnson – later to become Dame Laura Knight – the painter, in 1903, having known her in Nottingham and in Staithes, Yorkshire, where he painted on his return from France. With her he studied the Dutch masters in the Netherlands, then from 1908 they lived for a decade in Newlyn, Cornwall, eventually settling in London. Knight was a steady exhibitor at RA from 1896, being elected RA in 1937. Also showed Leicester Galleries, IS and elsewhere. His reticent work and personality were overshadowed by Laura's ebullient, more colourful nature and painting, but his pictures' real qualities have been more appreciated in recent years. Tate Gallery and Hove Museum and Art Gallery hold his work. Died in Colwall, Herefordshire.

Joseph KNIGHT 1870–1952 Painter, printmaker and teacher, born in Bolton, Lancashire, who studied in Paris. He settled in Bury, Lancashire, where he was head of the School of Art. Showed at RA, RCamA, Walker Art Gallery in Liverpool and at Manchester City Art Gallery which holds his still life Chinese Pottery, oil on canvas, of 1931.

Ken KNIGHT 1956– Painter of richly coloured landscapes and coastal scenes, born in Sydney, Australia, where he graduated from the University in 1978. In 1979 he had his first solo exhibition at Parramatta, New South Wales, followed by several dozen others. Knight won many art prizes. He first exhibited in London in W H Patterson's Christmas Show 2001 and decided to paint in England during the summer of 2002, notably at the coastal resorts of East Anglia. The result was a solo exhibition at W H Patterson in 2003. Knight's work was held by major corporate collections, including IBM, Johnson & Johnson, Shell Oil, ANZ Bank as well as Castlemaine Art Gallery & Historical Museum.

Laura KNIGHT 1877–1970 Figure and landscape painter in oil and watercolour, draughtsman and etcher. Born at Long Eaton, Derbyshire, she studied art under Wilson Foster at Nottingham School of Art, where she met her husband, the painter Harold Knight. Together they painted at Staithes, near Whitby, where there was a small colony of artists. Between 1908–18 they lived in Cornwall. Laura Knight exhibited first at the RA in 1903 and had a first exhibition with Harold at the Leicester Galleries three years later. She then began to exhibit widely in Britain and abroad. The Tate Gallery, British Museum and Imperial War Museum hold her work. She was elected RA in 1936, having become Dame Laura Knight in 1929. Laura Knight was a powerful Colourist and a prolific and strident draughtsman. She was especially fond of drawing scenes from the circus, ballet, music-hall, racing and gypsy life. She worked for the War Artists' Advisory Committee during World War II, completing some excellent pictures, and then drew the war crimes trials at Nuremberg. Her autobiography is *Oil Paint and Grease Paint*, published in 1936. A retrospective was held at the Upper Grosvenor Galleries in 1969 and a large show at the Nottingham Castle Museum in 1970. Lived in London.

Lawrence John KNIGHT fl. from 1925–1950 Illustrator. Studied at Leicester College of Art, 1926–37, under John Pettinger and Sydney Watson, and was a member of Leicester Society of Artists and Leicester Sketch Club. After World War II service in the Royal Air Force Knight became art director for a design group. He exhibited at public galleries in Nottingham and Leicester and in Egypt and Palestine, the Egyptian Museum of Modern Art buying his work. Lived in London.

Lionel John KNIGHT 1901– Painter, born in Romsey, Hampshire. Showed at RWA, RBA, Arts Council and elsewhere and had one-man show at Bridgwater Art Gallery, Somerset, in 1968. Lived for some years in Penzance, Cornwall.

Loxton KNIGHT: *see* **Edward LOXTON KNIGHT**

Mervyn KNIGHT 1956– Painter, notably of landscape in sunlight, who trained at Reigate School of Art in the mid-1970s. His mixed show appearances included ROI, 1989; Anthony Sidgwick Gallery, 1990; RBA in 1991; Alberti Gallery, 1992; and Anna-Mei Chadwick, 1993, where he shared an exhibition. After a solo exhibition at Dance Attic Studio, 1989, and Outlines Gallery in same year, in 1991 Knight had one at Matt's Café. His work, largely done in London, Dorset and Surrey, is held in private collections in Britain and widely abroad.

Paul KNIGHT 1950– Painter and teacher who studied at Hammersmith College of Art and Royal Academy Schools, in 1984 gaining a Richard Ford Award, which took him to Spain to work. In that year he had a studio space in Wapping, east London. Taught at Chelsea College of Art and Chelsea & Westminster Institute. Showed at RBA and elsewhere in London.

Robert KNIGHT 1921–1987 Artist in fibreglass and mixed media, born in Leicester. He studied at the College of Art there, 1936–7, then worked in a small commercial studio until 1940. After Army service 1940–5, Knight was at the Royal Academy Schools, 1946–50, then for 20 years he did a variety of jobs, such as handyman and gardener. From the late 1960s he showed busily, including LG; John Moores Exhibition, Liverpool, from 1969; Nicholas Treadwell Gallery, from 1970; and extensively abroad. In 1981 Nicholas Treadwell gave Knight a sixtieth-birthday exhibition. Knight's work accorded with Treadwell's interest in Superhumanism. He created three-dimensional works, sometimes erotic, amusing, touching, or cruelly real, which he said were "taken from the Tragi-Comedy of day-to-day life with its preoccupation with sex, love, religion and violence etc."

Sophie KNIGHT 1965– Painter, especially in watercolour. She attended Hertfordshire College of Art, 1982, Camberwell School of Arts and Crafts, 1983–6, and Royal Academy Schools, 1986–9. She gained a number of awards, including the David Murray Scholarship for Landscape, 1988, the Eric Kennington Prize for the Encouragement of Good Academic Drawing and the Hunting Group Student Prize, both in 1989. In 1991 Knight was on the judging panel for the Hunting Group Art Prizes. She began showing at South London Gallery, 1985, following shows including RA, NEAC, Boundary Gallery and Cadogan Contemporary, which gave her a solo show in 1991. British Museum held a picture by her on loan from RWS Diploma Collection.

William KNIGHT 1872–1958 Painter, designer and teacher, born in Leicester, one of 14 children. Attended Leicester College of Art, where he later taught. After working for his father as a painter and decorator, ran off to London – where he studied at Heatherley's School of Fine Art – and Paris to pursue a career as an artist, despite family disapproval. At first he concentrated on figure studies in watercolour, but after 1908 painted only in oil. First important show RBSA, 1901. Also exhibited RA, ROI, RI as well as extensively in Europe and North America. The Victoria & Albert Museum holds designs for printing; Leicester Museum and Art Gallery his oil paintings Autumn Evening and Russet and Gold, typical pastoral scenes. *La Revue Moderne*, 1924, and *The Studio*, 1927, carried articles on Knight, who lived in Leicester.

Arthur Henry KNIGHTON-HAMMOND 1875–1970 Landscape painter, especially in watercolour on a large scale, and etcher; born in Arnold, Nottinghamshire. Studied at Nottingham School of Art under Herbert Wilson Foster, at Westminster School of Art, in France and Italy. Knighton-Hammond was a member of leading watercolour societies in France and America, and was the only English artist to have been elected to the American Watercolour Society, New York, apart from Sir William Russell Flint. In Britain showed at RA, ROI, NEAC, RCamA, RBA, Fine Art Society and RSW. Tate Gallery, Musée du Jeu de Paume, Paris, galleries in New Zealand, South Africa and Yugoslavia as well as many British provincial galleries hold his work. He found watercolour a "nervy" business and disliked being overlooked while painting, yet Knighton-Hammond established an international reputation, described by Augustus John as "the greatest English painter in watercolour of our time". Like John he was a romantic, who travelled extensively to paint. Finally returned to live in Seaborough, Devon. Retrospective at Upper Grosvenor Galleries, 1971.

Winifred KNIGHTS 1899–1947 Painter and draughtsman, born in London, married to the artist Walter Thomas Monnington. She studied at the Slade School of Fine Art, 1915–17 and 1918–20. Her teachers included Henry Tonks and Fred Brown and she personified the Slade School tradition under their reign, her Composition: Mill Hands on Strike, for which she won a shared first prize for summer composition in 1919, having that firm draughtsmanship for which the Slade was then famous. She won a Rome Scholarship the following year, worked in Rome 1920–5 and returned to the Slade in 1927. One of her principal works was The Marriage at Cana for the British School in Rome, now in the National Gallery of New Zealand, in Wellington. Tate Gallery also holds her work. The British School and Fine Art Society put on exhibitions in 1995. The catalogue indicated that until about 1919 Knights signed work with an interlocking W M K monogram, occasionally early on after marriage using Winifred Monnington. Knights died in London.

Tony KNIPE 1942– Painter who employed a drip technique to create abstract pictures which were related to such subjects as lichen, water and graffiti. He was born in Swansea, studying at the College of Art there and in Paris. He gained a Government Research Fellowhip in 1967–70, involving Finnish Academy of Art and Helsinki University. A Henry Moore research grant took him to America in 1987. Knipe showed extensively in groups, including Glynn Vivian Art Gallery and tour in Welsh Artists 2; Jarrow: Impressions of a Town, Bede Gallery, Jarrow, 1986; and in the Newcastle Group 1990 show The Northern Lights, at DLI Museum & Arts Centre. Solo exhibitions included British Council, Helsinki, 1969; Octagon Theatre, Bolton, 1972; and Prudhoe Library Art Gallery, 1986. East Sussex Education Authority and University College in Swansea hold his work. Lived in Newcastle upon Tyne.

Gertrude KNOBLOCK fl. c.1906–1969 Sculptor in lead and bronze, born in New York, who studied art under George Barnard at the Art Students' League there, at the Académie Julian, Paris, then at the Royal College of Art, 1902–7, under Édouard Lantéri. In England exhibited at RA, RSA and SWA. Lived in London.

Joan KNOBLOCK 1917– Portrait and figure painter and draughtsman in ink and pencil, born and lived in London. She studied part-time at Hornsey School of Art, but was largely self-taught. Her early work included fashion drawing and she was influenced in her plant form pictures by those of Graham Sutherland. Knoblock was a member of Free Painters and Sculptors and Hesketh Hubbard Art Society. Mixed show appearances included RI and RP. Solo shows included Commonwealth Institute, Thames Gallery in Henley-on-Thames, the Hendon, Hampstead and North Finchley Libraries and abroad, where Knoblock travelled extensively.

Eardley KNOLLYS 1902–1991 Painter, administrator and collector, born in Alresford, Hampshire. He was educated at Winchester College and Oxford University, where he helped to found the Uffizi Society. After an abortive attempt to become a film director in Hollywood Knollys became part-time secretary to Viscount Hambledon, chairman of the booksellers W H Smith, then in 1935 founded the Storran Gallery, which promoted leading French and British artists, and started to assemble a fine personal collection. After World War he continued to work for the National Trust and became a committee member for the Contemporary Art Society. Took up painting, having his first solo show in 1960 at Minories Gallery, Colchester, others taking place in England and New York, including latterly Southampton City Art Gallery and Parkin Gallery. There was a first posthumous exhibition at The Bloomsbury Workshop Ltd in 1999, Messum's showing selected works from the studio estate in 2002. Knollys (pronounced Noles) painted landscapes in bright colours, often in Spain and France. Lived in London.

Gertrude M KNOPP 1875– Painter born in Kilninver, Argyllshire. After private education in Brighton, Sussex, she attended Slade School of Fine Art, 1899–1904 under Henry Tonks and Fred Brown. Married the Hungarian artist Imre Knopp, who died just after World War II, which led to part of her exhibiting career occurring in Hungary. Thus she showed in Budapest, where the Museum of Fine Arts holds her work; also exhibited widely elsewhere on the continent. In Britain she showed at WIAC, of which she was secretary for several years before World War I, RA, NEAC, ROI and elsewhere. Finally lived in London. Early in her career she exhibited under her maiden name Gertrude M Curtis.

Karen KNORR 1954– Artist using photography, and teacher, born in Frankfurt, West Germany. She lived in Puerto Rico, 1958–72. Graduated from Polytechnic of Central London in 1980 and went on to do research there. In 1981–2 she was included in Woodlands Art Gallery show of Greater London Arts Association award winners. From the late 1970s, Knorr's photographic work developed through major series: Belgravia, 1979–80; Gentlemen, 1981–3; Country Life, 1983–5; Connoisseurs, 1986–9; Capital, 1990–3; The Virtues and the Delights, 1993–4; and from 1994, Academies. In her 2001 show Sanctuary, at Maureen Paley/Interim Art, part of Academies, Knorr alluded to allegorical traditions found in older myths and in eighteenth- and nineteenth-century paintings where animals had symbolic functions. She was then a visiting tutor at Goldsmiths' College. Arts Council holds her work.

Martin KNOWELDEN 1943– Wildlife sculptor, born in Hertfordshire. He studied at Watford School of Art, specialising in printmaking. Went on to work on a number of wildlife and field sport publications, notably with the writer D Brien-Plummer. Exhibitions included Ivor Giblin Gallery; Coach House Gallery, Guernsey; San Francisco Art Expo; Bath Festival; and Toronto Art Fair. Lived for a time in Cambridgeshire.

Dennis KNOWLAND 1918–1985 Painter, draughtsman, illustrator, muralist and teacher, born in London, who practised art while at Dulwich College and Frensham Heights. Aged 16 he met R O Dunlop, who encouraged the use of a palette knife. In 1935 he spent a year at Chelsea School of Art, taught by Graham Sutherland and Robert Medley, winning a prize for landscape. From 1936–40 Knowland worked in advertising, painting on Sundays, aged 18 showing The Lane, Kenwood, Hampstead, with the LG. During World War II Army service in Scotland Anne Redpath lent him a studio, and he continued to paint while stationed in Kenya. After demobilisation, a more intellectual attitude to Knowland's "discoveries of the eye" developed during three years at Camberwell School of Arts and Crafts under William Coldstream and Lawrence Gowing. Between 1949–72 Knowland examined for London University and taught at the Spendlove Centre in Charlbury, Charterhouse, Ruskin School and St Clare's Hall in Oxford and West Oxfordshire Technical College, painting when he could. He illustrated two books; painted several murals in London and one at Watlington Secondary School; and showed as a member of Oxford Art Society and in London, Norwich, Brighton and in West Germany and South Africa. Aged 54, retired early, he took a studio in Little Coxwell, Oxfordshire. There was a memorial show at the Central Library, Oxford, in 1987.

Emma KNOWLES 1967– Figurative painter, draughtsman and teacher, born in Liverpool, who studied at Gwynedd Technical College and Norwich School of Art. Held a number of teaching posts from 1990, including Edge Hill and Blackburn Colleges of Higher Education, St Helens Community College, Wirral Metropolitan College and HM Prison, Risley. Knowles gained a Nöel Spencer Award for Life Drawing, 1989; Elizabeth Greenshields Foundation, 1991; Michael Gourley Award, 1993; and Edward Oldham Trust Award, 1995. Group shows included Portraits North, Harrogate Art Gallery, 1989; MAFA, Manchester City Art Gallery, from 1993; and Royal Over-Seas League Open, 1996, where she showed Before the Game I, one of a series of small studies of the crowd at Old Trafford, her local football ground. Knowles, a RCamA member, shared a show there with her father Mike Knowles in 2002.

Jayne KNOWLES 1967– Artist employing metal and paper, and lecturer, based in Colchester, Essex. She gained a crafts honours degree at Crewe & Alsager College of Higher Education, 1990, in 1992 setting up a workshop. After founding Base2 with Peter Jones in 2000, in 2002 Knowles gained her master's in book arts at Camberwell College of Arts. She combined the production of a range of candle holders with the creation of single pieces for private and public commission. Knowles lectured part-time in three-dimensional design at Colchester Institute, 1994–8 and from 2000, teaching the same subject at Swansea Institute, 1998–00. Exhibitions included Fires and Feasting, Brewery Arts, Cirencester, 1997; Light of my life, Oriel Myrddin, Carmarthenshire, 1998; 2001: Craft Odyssey, Bury St Edmunds Art Gallery, 2001; and Over The River, firstsite, Colchester/Wolsey Art Gallery, Ipswich, 2002. She had a solo show, To seed, at the Space Frame Gallery, Gillingham, Kent, in 1992.

Justin KNOWLES 1935–2004 Self-taught sculptor, painter and printmaker, publisher and property developer, born in Exeter, Devon, educated at Kelly College, Tavistock, who after National Service, 1955–7, worked in industry and advertising, travelling extensively on the continent and in Africa. After a visit to New York in 1965, Knowles taught for a time at Bath Academy of Art, Corsham, living near Chudleigh, Devon. Knowles was part of Camden Arts Centre's Survey '67 Abstract Painters in 1967, work including the free-standing shapes which, he said, "remain paintings rather than sculpture in that the painted form works across the physical form rather than following it, as in most painted sculpture." Arts Council acquired two such shapes: Bayaka, 1967, and Steel with Brown, Version I, of 1967–8. Mixed exhibitions also included John Moores Liverpool Exhibition of 1965. Solo exhibitions included Plymouth City Art Gallery, 1967. Knowles' future as a major modern British abstract artist seemed assured until, in 1973, in mysterious circumstances, his uninsured studio caught fire, costing most of his finished work in progress and all his materials. What Knowles called "the silent time" began. After his 1973 show at Waddington Galleries, it would be 24 years before he exhibited again. In the intervening period Knowles taught in Exeter and turned his attention to various businesses, launching the publishing house Denys Ingram, which focused on collectible antique toys; became a book packager, including working with the Walt Disney Company; returned to Devon from London and launched the Flyfishers' Classic Library; and pursued his hobby of big game-fishing, fishing for the English team in the 1994 World Cup in Mauritius. A chance visit by Patrick Heron and the art collector David Thomson sparked a return to art production, although during his "silent" period Knowles had secretly made almost 4,000 drawings. Visits to the Far East were influential and Knowles began producing spare and beautiful sculptures, superbly finished in a range of materials. He gained a series of awards and there were major commissions for Winchester Cathedral, 2001, and Exeter Cathedral, 2002. Later solo shows included City of Bath College, 2001, and Austin/Desmond Fine Art and Lemon Street Gallery, Truro, both 2002. In 2003, Michael Wood Fine Art, Plymouth, put on an exhibition in conjunction with the City Museum & Art Gallery there. Museum of Modern Art in Oxford, Arts Council of Northern Ireland and University of Warwick hold examples.

Mike KNOWLES 1941– Painter and teacher, born in Warrington, Lancashire. He studied at Liverpool College of Art, 1959–63, then at Slade School of Fine Art, 1964–6. There he won the Tonks Drawing Prize and Landscape Painting Prize. Landscape remained a main preoccupation, with the countryside around his home in Anglesey, Gwynedd, an inspiration, as in his entry for John Moores Exhibition, Liverpool, 1991–2: Mynydd Eilian, Windy Day, Summer. Other mixed exhibition appearances included The Native Land: Welsh Landscape Painting since 1699, Llandudno, 1979, and The Probity of Art, WAC, 1979–80. His first solo show was at Bluecoat Gallery, Liverpool, 1967, and he had a retrospective at Mostyn Art Gallery, Llandudno, 1992. Knowles taught at Liverpool Polytechnic from 1967, in 1991 being elected professor emeritus in fine art. Knowles, a RCamA member, shared an exhibition there with his daughter, Emma Knowles, in 2002. In 2003, Knowles shared a show at The Walk with three Slade contemporaries: James Arnold, David Carr and Peter Prendergast.

Stuart KNOWLES 1948– Painter noted for near-abstract, gestural landscapes in oil inspired by his native Cornwall, to which he returned in 1988 after a period in London. Settled at Plain-an-Gwarry, in the southwest, his ancestors having been miners. Archetypal figures from Kabuki and Noh theatre also featured in his pictures. Studied at Farnham and Winchester Schools of Art, 1964–9, then Slade School of Fine Art until 1971. Exhibitions included City of London Festival, 1971; Arts Council at Hayward Gallery, 1982; Artists from Cornwall, RWA, 1992; and Demarco's Choice, Newlyn Art Gallery, 1993. Solo shows included Newlyn Art Gallery, 1991, and Austin/Desmond Fine Art, 1996. In 2004, Six Chapel Row Contemporary Art, Bath, showed Knowles' French Hill Notes – The Gorge Galamus Studies, stemming from a feature the artist had found while travelling in the foothills of the French Pyrenees. He received South West Arts and Arts Council Awards to paint in the area and help mount the exhibition. Shaw Theatre held his work.

Charlotte KNOX 1951– Painter and illustrator, born in London, who studied art at Ruskin School in Oxford before attending a one-year postgraduate course in illustration at St Martin's School of Art. Her first solo show was held at Hammond Lloyd Gallery in 1975, featuring watercolour landscapes of Italy and England. From that time Knox worked as a freelance illustrator specialising in natural subjects. She joined with the writer Jane Grigson to produce the book *Exotic Fruits and Vegetables*, illustrations for which were shown at Chris Beetles Ltd in 1986, the year of its publication. She was included in Six Egg Tempera Painters at New Grafton Gallery, 2001. Charlotte was the daughter of Oliver Knox, advertising executive, policy analyst and writer, one of a talented family that included his father Dilwyn Knox, classical scholar and a key figure at the Bletchley Park World War II intelligence centre; E V Knox (Evoe), humorist and *Punch* editor; Monsignor Ronald Knox, priest and author; and the writer Penelope Fitzgerald.

Harry Cooke KNOX 1905– Painter, notable for his portraits and murals, born in Newtownbutler, County Fermanagh. He attended Belfast College of Art, 1924–30. In 1953 was made an associate of RUA, also exhibiting with RHA and ROI. Knox was a prominent member of Ulster Arts Club, being its president in 1955. Lived for many years in Belfast.

Jack KNOX 1936– Painter, draughtsman and teacher, born John Knox at Kirkintilloch, Dunbartonshire. He studied at Glasgow School of Art, 1953–7, where his teachers included William Armour and David Donaldson. In 1958 won a travelling scholarship which enabled him to study in Paris under André Lhote. Knox painted in a variety of styles, being influenced by the American Abstract Expressionists for a time, although on occasion creating still lifes in the manner of the Dutch Old Masters. From 1965–81 Knox taught at Duncan of Jordanstone College of Art, Dundee, in 1981 becoming head of painting at Glasgow College of Art. Took part in many group shows in Scotland and abroad and had a series of one-man exhibitions, including 57 Gallery, Edinburgh; Serpentine Gallery in London; and Civic Arts Centre, Aberdeen. In 1983 a solo show was toured to a number of Scottish venues by the Scottish Arts Council; Drawings 1956–1998 was held by Cyril Gerber Fine Art and Compass Gallery, Glasgow, in 1998. Was elected RSA and has work in many public collections, including Scottish National Gallery of Modern Art, Edinburgh. Lived for some time in Carnoustie, Angus.

Liz KNOX 1945– Painter and lecturer, born and lived in Glasgow, notable for her richly coloured still lifes with an unusual perspective, as in her first London solo show at Duncan Campbell Fine Art in 2004. Knox graduated from Edinburgh College of Art in 1971, having studied drawing and painting under Robin Philipson and David Michie. Family commitments prevented her painting for some years; she then lectured in further education, painting and exhibiting as time allowed; until in 2004 she resigned from teaching to paint full-time. Knox was elected an artist-member of Glasgow Art Club, Paisley Art Institute and the Glasgow Society of Women Artists and a professional member of Visual Arts Scotland. She won the inaugural Kennox Prize at the Paisley Art Institute in 2003 and was main exhibitor in the Kennox Exhibition at The Richmond Hill Gallery in 2004. In 2003 she was also invited by East Renfrewshire Council to be featured artist in its Festival of Colour. Other solo exhibitions included Calton and Kingfisher Galleries, Edinburgh, Rozelle House, Ayrshire; Gallery Heinzel, Aberdeen; and St Mary's Episcopal Cathedral, Glasgow. Her work was regularly seen at venues throughout Britain, including shared exhibitions, and was held by The Royal Bank of Scotland, Aspect Capital Ltd and private collections in Europe and America.

Madeline KNOX 1890–1975 Painter, draughtsman and embroiderer, originally from Grantham, Lincolnshire. She moved to London in 1906 and attended Lambeth School of Art briefly, was then with Sickert at Westminster School of Art, joined his etching class, helped him to set up an etching school and then the Rowlandson House school, but withdrew in 1910. Travelled in France and Canada, then returned to London early in World War I, marrying Arthur Clifton who ran the Carfax Gallery. Settled in Mersham, Kent, in 1925 and gave up painting to concentrate on embroidery. The altar frontal at Burghclere Chapel, decorated by Stanley Spencer, is by Knox. She had a show at Carfax Gallery in 1916, also showing pictures at NEAC and London Salon. In 1976 the Fine Art Society included her work in Camden Town Recalled.

Peter KNOX 1942– Artist and lecturer notable for his depictions of scenes from seafaring history, ships, spars and quaysides, as well as leisure pursuits of the common man and unusual crowds scenes. He painted world-wide on board ship and became artist-tutor to the College of the Sea and lecturer on art at Norwich, from 1973 based in the Scottish borders area. Work by Knox was offered by the Tallantyre Gallery, Morpeth, at the Affordable Art Fair in Battersea in 2006. His work sold well in Britain and abroad.

Lay-Ngo KOAY 1975– Painter, often using acrylic on paper, producing richly coloured, gestural images, born in Malaysia. Studied with Hock Aun Teh, then from 1994 at Glasgow School of Art. Exhibited in Salon Glasgow, Centre for Contemporary Art in Glasgow, 1992; Contemporary 1992/93 at Art Gallery & Museum in Kilmarnock, 1992–3; at Royal Over-Seas League Open from 1994; and Paisley Art Institute Exhibition, Paisley Art Gallery, 1995. Manchurian Restaurant, Glasgow, holds work.

Zofia KOBYLIŃSKA-OLSZEWSKA fl. from 1970s– Painter, born in Warsaw, Poland, who during World War II was in Auschwitz concentration camp. She moved to England in 1947, studying for her diploma with Professor Marian Bohusz-Szyszko at the Polish School of Painting. Kobylińska-Olszewska was a member of the Association of Polish Artists in Great Britain and the International Association of Arts. She took part in exhibitions at venues including POSK, Drian and Grove Galleries; Gruzelier Modern and Contemporary Gallery; in Katowice and Cracow, Poland; and in Stuttgart, Germany. Among her solo shows were POSK Gallery, 1978; Drian Gallery, 1986; One One Nine Gallery, 1990; and Grove Gallery, 1992. Private collections in Britain, Poland, France, Austria, Switzerland, Italy and America held her works.

Ghisha KOENIG 1921–1993 Sculptor and draughtsman, born and lived in London, daughter of the writer and art critic Leo Koenig. After a poor scholastic start, Koenig won a scholarship to Hornsey School of Art, 1939; left it in 1942, serving four years in the Army; studied under Henry Moore at Chelsea School of Art, 1946–8; and at Slade School of Fine Art, 1948–9. Koenig created modest-size bronzes and terracottas, specialising in high relief. She stained the terracottas with dark ink prior to burnishing them, to restore the clay's richness. Most of Koenig's work was based on watching factory workers over 30 years. She was concerned with "the dignity of man" and "the trapped nature of human beings". Mixed exhibitions included RA; Jewish Artists in England, Whitechapel Art Gallery, 1956; SPS; AIA; and 10th Sculpture Biennale, Middelheim, Belgium, 1969. Had a solo show at Grosvenor Gallery, 1966, later ones including Serpentine Gallery and tour, 1986. Boundary Gallery held a memorial show in 1994. Tate Gallery and public galleries in Manchester, Sheffield and Stoke-on-Trent hold examples.

Heidi KOENIG 1964– Artist, notably a printmaker, born in Heilbronn, West Germany. She did a foundation course at Walthamstow College, 1990–1; obtained a first-class honours degree in fine art from Brighton University, 1991–4; and gained a postgraduate diploma in fine art printmaking from Slade School of Fine Art, 1994–6. Koenig won a number of awards at the FBA National Print Exhibition, Mall Galleries: in 1995, the Artichoke Print Workshop Award for the most outstanding print; in 1996 the Zenith Gallery Purchase Prize, *Galleries* Magazine Award and St Cuthberts Paper Mill Award. Group shows included Images in Edition, Maze Gallery, Brighton, 1992, and RA Summer Exhibition, 1996. From 1996 showed solo with Enid Lawson Gallery. Strang Print Room at University College and Whipps Cross Hospital hold her work.

Robert KOENIG 1951– Sculptor and creator of coloured reliefs in wood, born in Manchester. In 1973–6 studied at Brighton Polytechnic for first-class honours degree in fine art, in 1976–8 gaining higher diploma for sculpture at Slade School of Fine Art. Exhibitions included Serpentine Gallery summer show, 1980; Bluecoat Gallery, Liverpool, and Paton Gallery, both 1984; Middlesbrough Art Gallery, 1986; Huddersfield Art Gallery and Milton Keynes Exhibition Gallery, both 1992; and Worthing Museum and Art Gallery, 2000. In 2002–3, there was a retrospective of Koenig's sculptures in wood made over the previous 20 years at Cadzow Gallery, Chatelherault Country Park, Ferniegair, Hamilton. Koenig lived in Hove, Sussex, and had work in public and private collections.

Hilde KOHLY 1955– Sculptor born in Warmbaths, South Africa, where she attended Johannesburg School of Art, 1974–6, then St Martin's School of Art, 1977–80. Gained the Afrox Student Prize and New Signatures Sculpture Prize in 1976, in 1980 The Sykes Prize (2nd). Showed in Cannizaro Park, Wimbledon, 1982, and was included in Woodlands Art Gallery 1983 show Have You Seen Sculpture from the Body? Lived in London.

Oskar KOKOSCHKA 1886–1980 Painter, teacher and writer, born in Pöchlarn, Austria. He was educated at Vienna School of Industrial Art, and was early a member of the Jugendstil movement, writing Expressionist plays many found offensive. Badly wounded in 1915 in World War I, after a long recovery Kokoschka settled in Dresden and taught at the Academy and was influenced by the Brücke, notably in choice of colour. Kokoschka had established himself as a painter of psychologically perceptive portraits and in the 1920s he travelled extensively through Europe, North Africa and Asia Minor completing singular landscapes. In 1931 he settled again in Vienna but in 1934, with a politically uncertain future hanging over Austria, Kokoschka moved to Prague, then England in 1938. Became a British subject in 1947, but from 1953 lived mainly in Switzerland. In Salzburg founded the International Academy of Fine Arts and taught there, 1953–63. Had a Tate Gallery solo show in 1962, another in 1986 and showed several times with Marlborough Fine Art from 1967. He was made an Hon. RA in 1970. His autobiography *My Life* was published in 1971, and *London Views, British Landscapes* in 1972. Many international collections hold his work.

Matthew KOLAKOWSKI 1956– Abstract painter who used stencilled shapes and a bright, attractive palette; teacher. He was born in London and studied at Watford School of Art, 1974–5, then gained a first-class honours degree at Ravensbourne College of Art, 1975–8, followed by his master's degree at Chelsea School of Art, 1978–9. Was at Garnett College, 1984–5. Kolakowski showed with New Contemporaries in 1977, other mixed shows including LG of which he was elected a member in 1990, South London Gallery, 1992, and Duncan Campbell Contemporary Art, where he had a solo show in 1993. Kolakowski held a number of teaching posts in the London area, beginning with Ravensbourne in 1980–2, other appointments including St Martin's College of Art, 1985, and Wolverhampton Polytechnic, 1991–2.

Gideon KOLB 1913–1984 Kolb combined careers in industry, acting and art, as a portrait painter and sculptor. Born in Vienna, he was educated there and in Paris before studying art at the Regent Street Polytechnic and Chelsea College of Art. He took part in mixed shows in Munich and London, notably at the Redfern Gallery, and had a series of one-man exhibitions at the Camden Institute and Drian Gallery. The *Financial Times* and Loggia Gallery purchased his work. Lived in London.

Julius KOMJATI 1894–1958 London-based artist who was elected an associate of the RE in 1931, his diploma work entitled The Prayer, completed in 1928. He also exhibited on nine occasions in the RA Summer Exhibition. Abbott and Holder latterly offered his work.

Masakatsu KONDO 1962– Painter, born in Nagoya, Japan, where he had a solo show at the Kohji Ogura Gallery, 1996. He studied at Chelsea College of Art, 1988–9, and Slade School of Fine Art, 1989–93. Won the Granada Foundation Prize in Young Contemporaries at Whitworth Art Gallery, Manchester, 1993, and a prize at John Moores Liverpool Exhibition, 1997–8. Other group shows included Annihilation, 1993, and Gallery Artists, 1994, both at Victoria Miro Gallery; British Artists, at Shoshana Wayne Gallery, Los Angeles, in the Biennale there, 1995; Whitechapel Open, 1996; and East, at Norwich Gallery, Norwich, 1997. Lived in London.

Henry KONDRACKI 1953– Painter and printmaker, born and settled in Edinburgh, who studied at Byam Shaw, 1981–2, then graduated with first-class honours at Slade School, 1982–6. Wryly humorous and imaginative work drew on his childhood and used costumes and other memorabilia. In Whitworth Young Contemporaries, 1983, he gained a Granada Foundation Prize, in 1987 a South Bank Board Prize, then in 1991 a *Spectator* Art Prize. Later awards included a prize at John Moores Exhibition at Walker Art Gallery, Liverpool, 1995; Cheltenham Drawing Prize, 1999; Hunting Group Regional Prize, 2000; and first prize in the Hunting Art Prizes, 2004. Group appearances included Blond Fine Art, 1985; Vanessa Devereux Gallery, 1989; City Art Centre, Edinburgh, 1993 exhibition Polish Roots – British Soil; invited artist, RA Summer Exhibition, 1993 and 1994; A Scottish Renaissance, Contemporary Painting in Scotland, The Rotunda, Hong Kong, 1996; and Aberdeen Artists, Aberdeen Arts Centre, 2001. Solo shows took place at Traverse Theatre Club, Edinburgh, 1979, and The Collective Gallery there, 1984–92; Michael Wardell Gallery, Melbourne, 1988; William Jackson Gallery from 1991; and Flowers East from 1996. Arts Council, British Council and Manchester City Art Gallery hold his work.

Frederick KÖNEKAMP 1897–1977 Painter, lecturer and writer, born in Offenburg, Baden, Germany. After World War I military service was a prisoner of war in Scotland. He then studied mathematics and philosophy at Universities of Basle, Freiburg and Berlin. For most of the 1920s he lectured in mathematics and as a journalist was concerned with advocating school reform. Being a Socialist, he decided to leave Germany in 1933 and travelled widely, began painting and was converted to Roman Catholicism. Settled in Britain in 1935 and after World War II internment in Canada returned to Britain in 1945, in 1949 settling at Cotllwyd, Dyfed, where he founded the Cotllwyd Group, a group that went on to show in England and Germany. Took part in SWG, WAC and Royal National Eisteddfod mixed shows and had many solo exhibitions, including Wilton and Drian Galleries, Albany Gallery in Cardiff and abroad. Had a retrospective at National Library of Wales, Aberystwyth, in 1965. National Museum of Wales in Cardiff, WAC and German collections hold his work.

Nigel KONSTAM 1932– Sculptor and teacher, born in London. He studied sculpture at Camberwell School of Arts and Crafts with Karel Vogel and briefly at the Royal College of Art. He lectured at many art colleges on art historical subjects; from the early 1980s ran the Verrochio Art Centre in Tuscany with his wife Janet; and produced *The Save Rembrandt Campaigner*, part of a long effort to save the artist from the experts whose effect he felt was diminishing a reputation. Konstam showed at RA, LG, NEAC and at John Moores Liverpool Exhibition. His solo exhibitions included Architectural Association in 1971; Kreisler Gallery (Madrid, Barcelona and Salamanca), 1980; The Orangery, Holland Park, 1984; and in 1993 he shared a show at Cadogan Contemporary. Among musicians who sat for him were the conductor Otto Klemperer, the violinist Manoug Parikian and the composer John Ireland.

Michael KONU 1971– Sculptor and teacher, born in Cracow, Poland, of British nationality, who attended Bilston College of Art & Design, 1990–1, gaining a fine art honours degree at Wolverhampton University, 1991–4. Won a West Midlands Arts grant, 1996, and a RBS membership bursary, 1997. He gained commissions and residencies, including Dudley Zoo and Castle, carving a 15-ton block of stone, 1993–5, and shortlistings for Nelson Thomlinson School, Wigton, 1997, and Church Street Sculpture, London Borough of Enfield, 1998. Konu was sculpture tutor at Midlands Art Centre from 1996. Among Konu's group shows were Art in Ruins, Dudley Castle, 1993; Bistrita Municipal Gallery, Romania, 1995; The McHardy Sculpture Company, from 1995; and Millfield School, Street, 1998. Solo exhibitions included Elemental, Dudley Castle, 1996, and The Stables Gallery, Gladstone Park, 2000. Dudley Public Art Resource Unit and Museum of Contemporary Art, Sangeorz-Bai, Romania (where Konu had a residency, 1995) hold examples. He lived in Wolverhampton.

Harold KOPEL 1915– Painter in oil and teacher, born in Newcastle upon Tyne, Northumberland. He attended University College in London and Central School of Arts and Crafts. Became a secondary school art master and a senior lecturer in further education. The spirit of a place was a key element sought after in Kopel's pictures. He was a member of ROI and took part in many mixed exhibitions, including RA Summer Exhibition and RWA. He won a Silver Medal at Paris Salon and the Cornelissen Prize at 1990 ROI annual show. Had a series of solo exhibitions. University College and Nuffield Foundation hold examples. Lived in London.

Heinz KOPPEL 1919–1980 Painter, draughtsman and teacher, born in Berlin, Germany. He studied and worked in Germany, Czechoslovakia, Italy, Belgium and England before moving to Wales in 1940, in the mid-1940s settling in Dowlais, Glamorgan. For 15 years he taught art to children and adults at the Art Centre there, worked and taught in London and then went on to teach at Liverpool Polytechnic. Showed in the WAC 1968 show Art in Wales 1900–1956, with 56 Group of which he was a founder-member, SWG, SEA and elsewhere. Had a number of solo shows at Beaux Arts Gallery, also at Glynn Vivian Art Gallery, Swansea. A fine draughtsman-painter, witness his Head, in Arts Council collection.

Adam KOPS 1956– Artist who studied life sculpture and drawing at Camden Arts Centre, 1980–1; did a foundation course at St Martin's School of Art, 1981–2; and sculpture courses at Wimbledon School of Art, 1982–3, and St Martin's, 1984–7, gaining his degree. Mixed shows included Royal Festival Hall, 1986, and Ben Uri Gallery from 1990. Had solo shows at Camden and Kingsgate Galleries from 1988. In 2000, shared an exhibition at Tricycle Gallery. His work was steel and usually figurative. Lived in London.

Henry KORDA 1957– Painter and draughtsman, notable for figure paintings and portraits. Born in London and studied at City and Guilds Art School, 1975–9, in 1979–81 doing a postgraduate course at Royal Academy Schools. In the following year travelled in Africa. From 1984 showed in RA Summer Exhibition. After sharing a show at Scribes Gallery in 1983 had two solo exhibitions in 1984–5 at Cylinder Gallery. Further one-man exhibitions included Cadogan Contemporary, 1991. From 1988 lived for a time in Scottish highlands.

Fred KORMIS 1896–1986 Sculptor and portrait medallist in bronze, born in Frankfurt, Germany. He studied at Kunstschule there, served in the Austrian Army during World War I, was captured and imprisoned in Siberia for several years, escaping and returning to Frankfurt. Worked as a portrait sculptor until Hitler came to power, when Kormis moved to the Netherlands and then in 1934 settled in London. There he established a reputation as one of the most distinguished medallists of his time, producing effigies of dozens of distinguished figures, including Winston Churchill, Golda Meir, Charlie Chaplin, Michael Tippett and J B Priestley. Showed at Beaux Arts Gallery, Fieldborne Galleries and abroad. His work is held by British Museum, Imperial War Museum, Fitzwilliam Museum in Cambridge and the Royal Air Force Museum in Hendon. Among his public commissions were the Shield Bearer in Corn Exchange in Stratford-upon-Avon, the Prisoner of War Memorial in Gladstone Park, Willesden, and The Everlamenting Harp at Kiryat Gat, Israel. He also exhibited as Fritz Kormis.

Fritz KORMIS: *see* **Fred KORMIS**

Halina KORN 1902–1978 Sculptor and painter in oil, born in Warsaw, Poland. She was a self-taught artist who had studied to be a singer and who married the painter Marek Zulawski. Settled in London early in World War II. Showed at RA, LG, WIAC and AIA, had solo shows in Warsaw and New York and a series in London, including Mayor Gallery, 1948, Beaux Arts Gallery, 1953, and Camden Arts Centre, 1981. Ben Uri Art Society holds her work, as does Toruń University, Poland, which lists her as Halina Korn-Żuławska.

Nathaniel KORNBLUTH 1914– Pen and ink draughtsman and etcher, born of Polish Jewish parents as Naphtali Kornbluth in London's East End. The area was his main subject, and his work remains a valuable record of much that has disappeared as well as capturing its particular atmosphere over several decades. Kornbluth's family did not approve his artistic interests, and he stayed in the wholesale menswear business all his life. Studied in the evenings at Hackney Technical School under Norman Janes, 1933; with W P Robins, Paul Drury and James Fitton at Central School of Arts and Crafts, 1934–7; and at Sir John Cass School of Art in 1970s. Kornbluth showed in the East End Academy from the mid-1930s at Whitechapel Art Gallery, solo exhibitions including Campbell & Franks, 1980; Sir John Cass, 1986; and Lamont Gallery, 1988. His main works included Demolition of Waterloo Bridge, etching 1936; Regents Canal Dock, etching, 1936; and the 1939 lithograph Return from Spain, depicting Major Clement Attlee's section of the International Brigade proceeding along Vauxhall Bridge Road. British Museum, Guildhall Library, Bibliothèque Nationale in Paris, Brooklyn Museum, National Maritime Museum, New York City Library and Ben Uri Art Society hold examples. Lived latterly in northwest London.

Halina KORN-ŻUŁAWSKA: *see* **Halina KORN**

Marian KOŚCIAŁKOWSKI: *see* **Jan MARIAN-KOŚCIAŁKOWSKI**

Leon KOSSOFF 1926– Painter of portraits and views of the dingier parts of London, where he was born of Russian-Jewish parentage and continued to work, and teacher. Kossoff's sometimes large pictures, in an impastoed, Expressionist style, hard-worked and based on careful drawing, were a contrast to their sensitive, retiring creator. After World War II Army service Kossoff studied at St Martin's School of Art, 1949–53; also at the Borough Polytechnic in the evenings with David Bomberg, which had a lasting influence, 1950–2; and at the Royal College of Art, 1953–6. He had his first one-man show at Helen Lessore's Beaux Arts Gallery in 1957. He taught at Regent Street Polytechnic and Chelsea School of Art, 1959–64, and St Martin's, 1966–9. Was represented in important group exhibitions and had a string of solo shows at venues such as Marlborough Fine Art, Whitechapel Art Gallery and Anthony d'Offay. In 1995 had a first solo exhibition on continent, at Venice Biennale and in Amsterdam, with a retrospective at Tate Gallery in 1996. There was a survey show at the Louisiana Museum, Humlebaek, Denmark, 2004–5. The Tate, Royal College of Art and Saatchi Collection hold examples.

Adam KOSSOWSKI 1905–1986 Religious artist of major stature who also completed significant secular works. Kossowski worked in many media, but was notable for his use of sgraffito, scratch-through drawing employing two differently coloured coats of plaster. Born in Nowy Sącz, Poland, Kossowski studied architecture at Warsaw Technical University, 1923–5, then painting at Cracow Academy of Fine Arts, 1925–8. Began exhibiting and taught mural painting at Warsaw Academy of Fine Arts, 1934–8. In late 1930s studied and worked in Italy and France, then returned to Warsaw. Suffered hardship as a prisoner in Soviet Union in World War II, in 1942 joining Polish Army, serving in Middle East; arrived in Britain and in 1943 was working in London for Polish Ministry of Information. In 1944 had a solo show Polish Soldier's Journey. Started to show extensively, including Guild of Catholic Artists and Craftsmen. From 1950 for about 20 years Kossowski completed 100 works at Aylesford Priory, Kent. Other notable works were the 1,000-square foot Camberwell Public Library Old Kent Road ceramic and the ceiling of the Chapel of St Benet at Queen Mary College. Was buried at Aylesford. Toruń University, Poland, holds his work.

David KOSTER 1926– Artist mainly in etching and aquatint but also relief, watercolour and oil, teacher, born in London. He studied at Slade School of Fine Art with Randolph Schwabe as principal, 1944–7. Taught at Folkestone Art School, 1966–70; Medway School of Design, 1970–5; New Metropole Arts Centre, 1975–6; then part-time at Medway College, 1976–91. Koster was a founder-member of SWLA and among influences on his work were Thomas Bewick, Eric Ravilious and Allen W Seaby for birds. Koster aimed to produce work "with a wide appeal but also with authenticity". He created a mural for Royal Veterinary College and completed wood engravings for John Stewart Collis's *Down to Earth*. Participated in many group shows, including RA Summer Exhibitions from 1960; New Metropole Arts Centre from 1961; Bear Lane Gallery, Oxford, from 1964; John Nevill Gallery, Canterbury, from 1975; and Daler Gallery, Bournemouth, 1990. Had a series of solo shows at Everyman Foyer Gallery from 1958, later ones including Zella 9, 1989. Many public collections hold examples, including galleries in Aberdeen, Belfast, Eastbourne and Southend. Lived in Folkestone, Kent.

Lesley M KOSTER 1927– Painter and draughtsman who was partly educated in England, partly in New York where she attended the School of Interior Design. In 1966–8 studied there at 5th Avenue School of Art, having been at Cheltenham College of Art, 1960–2. Showed widely in America, also at RA, UA, Clarges and Chenil Galleries. Lived in London.

Peter A KOTKA 1951– Self-taught painter, latterly of meticulous still lifes, born to an Estonian father and English mother. Kotka began work as a tool-maker and designer of aluminium extrusion dies, painting in 1979 and turned professional in 1983. Kotka began to paint still life in 1995 after he visited Tallin and saw an exhibition of the noted Estonian artist Olav Maran, a contemporary painter working in a traditional manner. The Dutch seventeenth-century painter Willem Kalf was another influence. Tallentyre Gallery, Morpeth, showed Kotka's work, held in many British and foreign private collections.

George KOTSONIS 1940– Painter and draughtsman, born in Palechori, Cyprus, eventually settling in the island at Paphos. Studied at St Martin's School of Art, 1958; in 1960 won a scholarship to China, attending the Peking Academy of Fine Art under Ai-Choun Sin; in 1963 went to Czechoslovakia, again on a scholarship, graduating from Prague's Academy of Fine Arts in 1967, teachers including Antonyn Pelts. Kotsonis's figurative work went through phases, including realism, stylisation influenced by Cubism, Byzantine and folkloric elements, the later female nudes being noted for a blonde luminosity. He took part in many mixed shows internationally, later solo exhibitions including Bromham Mill Gallery, Bedford, 1987, and Kyklos Art Gallery, Paphos, 1993. In Nicosia, the State Collection of Contemporary Art, Bank of Cyprus and Hellenic Bank hold examples.

Thirza KOTZEN 1953– Artist and teacher, born in Johannesburg, South Africa, whose work was characterised by colour and strong design. Gained a fine art degree from University of the Witwatersrand, 1974; an advanced study diploma in printmaking, Central School of Art & Design, 1976; and a master's degree at the University of Oregon, America, 1979. Was a visiting lecturer there, 1980–1. Awards included Lloyd's Bank Young Printmaker of the Year, 1984. Among later mixed shows were Under Other Skies, Art First, 1995; Celebration of South African Jewish Artists, Pretoria Museum of Art, South Africa, 1996; and in 1998 Ceramic Vessels, at New Academy Gallery, where Kotzen had a series of solo exhibitions, with one at Curwen Gallery, 2004. Completed a commission for the P&O liner *Royal Princess*. St Thomas's Hospital, Keynes College in Canterbury and many corporate collections hold examples.

Issam KOURBAJ 1963– Artist born in Soweda, Syria, who studied painting and drawing in Damascus; architecture in St Petersburg, Russia; and theatre design/scenography in London. Kourbaj, whose output included abstracts, said: "When I work I think of water. With every touch the surface trembles. My work is a struggle to capture the fragility of that trembling." As well as mixed shows in Britain and abroad, he had solo exhibitions including: Soviet Culture Centre, Damascus, 1984; Ganz Galleries, Cambridge, 1990; City Theatre, Tuxtla, Chiapas, Mexico, 1992; then there was a series at his studio and at colleges in Cambridge, where he lived, with one at Waterstone's bookshop there in 1996. In 1993 Kourbaj founded his own group in the city, which held annual shows. The British Museum Department of Prints and Drawings holds a sketch-book by him.

Tania KOVATS 1966– Sculptor and draughtsman, born and lived in London, who graduated at Newcastle Polytechnic, 1985–8, gaining a master's degree from the Royal College of Art, 1988–90. Obtained a Barclays Young Artist of the Year Award, 1991; Royal Society of Arts' Arts for Architecture Awards, 1996 and 1997; and a British School at Rome Scholarship, 1997. Took part in many group exhibitions in Britain and abroad, later ones including Lost, Ikon Gallery, Birmingham, 2000, which Kovats curated. Later solo exhibitions included Asprey Jacques, 1998, and New Art Centre Sculpture Park and Gallery, Salisbury, 1999; Kovats' solo exhibition Slip, at Yorkshire Sculpture Park, West Bretton, in 2002, included landscape-related metamorphic forms created with malleable warm wax layered within a vice-like machine, as well as abstract works on paper created by blowing ink with a single breath through a straw; and there was another show at Newlyn Art Gallery, Penzance, and tour, 2004. Kovats' architectural projects included Plinth, for Ikon Gallery, 1998. Among public art works were Garden, commissioned by the Public Art Development Trust, 1995; Viewpoint, Kielder Water, Northumbria, 1998; and Sitooteries, Belsey Hall, Northumberland, for English Heritage, 2000. Leeds Museums and Galleries hold Kovats' work.

Zygmunt KOWALEWSKI 1913–1982 Artist, designer and sculptor, born in Warsaw, one of the group of Polish paper sculptors who made an impact in Britain after World War II. He was deported to Siberia, having studied at Warsaw Academy of Fine Arts. After release, joined the Polish Army and went with it to the Middle East, where he was chief of graphics for the Polish Information Centre, preparing exhibitions, designing posters and publications. Demobilised in Britain he set up his own studio, the men's outfitter Austin Reed being an important early client. Others included British Overseas Airways Corporation, Air India, Swiss Air and Ford Motor Company. Perspex, mirrors and moving lights as well as paper sculpture were some techniques Kowalewski employed. He was included in Polish Paper Sculpture, at Polish Cultural Institute, 1995.

Christine KOWAL POST 1951– Sculptor, printmaker, ceramist, draughtsman and teacher. Born and lived in Ibadan, Nigeria, and Ghana, 1951–3. Attended Accademia di Belle Arti, Florence, 1972–3, from 1970–4 studying at University College of Wales, Aberystwyth; graduated with joint honours in fine art and Italian. After working as a graphic artist in Canada and Europe, 1975–82, Kowal Post worked as an artist on Merseyside; in 1986 she was a visiting lecturer at Bristol Polytechnic. She was also a visiting lecturer at Wrexham College of Art, Wirral College of Further Education, Liverpool Institute, City Art College in Liverpool and Crewe and Alsager College of Art. Other features of her career were Artists in Industry, Lever Brothers Ltd, Merseyside; Woodcut Print Workshop at Cornerhouse, Manchester; and Liverpool Disablement Resources Unit tutor, all in 1986. She had residencies at Bury St Edmunds Cathedral, 1988, Walker Art Gallery, Liverpool, 1989, and Minories Art Gallery, Colchester, 1991. Later sculpture commissions included Ashworth Hospital, Merseyside, and Glan Clwyd NHS Trust, Cancer Treatment Centre, both 2000. The artist showed at SGA; Mall Galleries; Hanover Gallery, in Liverpool; Contemporary British Woodcuts, at Worcester City Art Gallery; and John Moores Exhibition, Liverpool, in 1987, where she was a prizewinner. Had a solo show at Hanover Gallery, 1985, another at Williamson Art Gallery and Museum, Birkenhead, in 1987. Kowal Post then had a frequent run of one-man exhibitions, later ones including Millais Gallery, Southampton Institute, and Otter Gallery, University College, Chichester, both 2001, and Stadtmuseum Beckum, Beckum, and Kulturforum Rheine, Rheine, both Germany in 2002. That gallery holds her work, as do many other public and corporate collections in Britain and abroad, including Lever Brothers Ltd, Walker and Manchester Art Galleries, and University of Liverpool. She lived in Milton Street, Polegate, Sussex.

Elaine KOWALSKY 1948–2005 Printmaker and teacher, born in Winnipeg, Manitoba, Canada, who attended University of Manitoba School of Art, 1967–71; did a postgraduate printmaking course at St Martin's School of Art, 1973; and her master's in visual theory, University of East London, 1992–4. Kowalsky worked independently at Islington Print Workshop, 1972–3, then took part in a specialist printmaking group at the Brighton Polytechnic faculty of design, 1974–5. Among Kowalsky's many awards was a Henry Moore Fellowship in Printmaking at Leeds Polytechnic, 1987. She held numerous lecturing and workshop appointments from 1975, later ones including posts at Universities of East London and Brighton and Birkbeck College. Also held senior appointments with the Printmakers' Council (1982–5) and Designer and Artist Copyright Society (1985–97) and from 1990–3 was adviser to The Prince's Youth Business Trust. As well as participating in many group shows such as the Whitechapel Open, RA Summer Exhibition and LG, Kowalsky had a series of solo exhibitions, from 1976 at Axis Gallery, Brighton, later ones including Anna Bornholt Gallery, 1996. In 1990, Kowalsky was commissioned to create banners for Dover Castle. Narrative and biography were key elements in Kowalsky's work. In 2000, her long-gestated Marian & Dorothy series of monoprints was first shown at the Freud Museum. Public collections holding her work include Victoria & Albert Museum, Smithsonian Institution in Washington, Australian National Gallery in Sydney as well as British provincial and Canadian sites. Lived in London.

Magda KOZARZEWSKA 1952– Painter in oil of landscapes, figures and still life, and teacher, born in Warsaw, Poland, where she attended the Children's Theatre, 1962–71, and Students' Theatre Sigma, 1971–3. Originally intended to study in Warsaw, but instead was accepted by Chelsea School of Art, 1974–7, then Slade School of Fine Art, 1977–81, where she was taught by Euan Uglow. Later teaching posts included Royal College of Art and Heatherley's School of Fine Art. She was a bold, rich Colourist, with echoes of Matisse, Cézanne and Derain in her work, which showed a strong design. She had a solo show at Polish Cultural Institute, 1975, another in 1991. Other one-man exhibitions took place at Sue Rankin Gallery, 1988, Petworth House in 1990, Thackeray Gallery, 1991, and Duncan Campbell from 1995. Among group shows her work appeared in were Hayward Annual Drawing Exhibition, 1982, and John Player Portrait Award, 1986. Works were held by private collections in several continents.

Kinga KOZERSKA fl. from 1960s– Painter, ceramic sculptor, potter and teacher, educated at a private convent school, Mount Battenhall, Worcester. Kozerska graduated with honours from Bristol University, also studying at L'École des Beaux-Arts in Paris; history of art at the University of Grenoble; and the Institute of Education at London University for a postgraduate teaching diploma. Several years of practical pottery and ceramic followed, including two at the Hampstead Artists' Council, and an art diploma from the Polish School of Painting under

Professor Marian Bohusz-Szyszko. Went on to teach and show in Rye, Sussex, and in London, including Association of Polish Artists in Britain as a member; Contemporary Art by Polish Artists Abroad, at Imperial College, 1970, and POSK Gallery, 1985; and Heal's and Liberty's stores.

Helen KOZICH 1958– Versatile artist, designer, illustrator and teacher, notable for paintings, relief prints and collographs, born in Connecticut, America, and resident in Britain from 1974. She gained an honours degree in fine art, printmaking, at the University of Leeds, 1976–80, tutors Terry Atkinson and Griselda Pollock, then her master's in European fine art from the Winchester School of Art in Barcelona and England, 1992–3. Work experience included graphic design and illustration for Leeds City Council, 1981–4; freelance work in the city, 1984–7; teaching fundamental design skills to trainee hairdressers at Thomas Danby College of Further Education in Leeds, 1985–6; working in New Zealand, Australia and Indonesia, 1987–8; then self-employment as an artist from 1989. Kozich was a founder-member of The Pavilion Women's Art Centre, Leeds, 1982–5. In 1996 she had a printmaking residency at Lowick House Print Workshop, Ulverston, developing work from sketches made in Eritrea that year. Kozich's work was "primarily figurative and Expressionist, using the human form metaphorically to deal with themes of birth, death and transformation, notions of identity, and so on. Bold drawing and use of chiaroscuro and movement predominate more than colour." Group exhibitions included Wales Open Art Show, Aberystwyth Arts Centre, 1990; British International Miniature Print Exhibition, Leicester City Art Gallery and tour, 1994–6; Oriel 31 Open, Davies Memorial Gallery, Newtown, where she was first prizewinner, 1995; and Showcase Wales, Y Tabernacl, Machynlleth, 1996. Solo exhibitions included Birdwoman & Other Stories, Station Café, The Railway Station, Aberystwyth, 1995. Lived in Machynlleth, Powys.

Jerzy J KOŻNIEWSKI 1926– Painter in oil, born in Poznan, Poland, who attended technical school and studied art under Maria Kalinowska-Koźniewska. Koźniewski was a member of the Polish Underground Army (AK) from 1940, in 1944 was a prisoner-of-war in Germany, then moved to England in 1946, where he studied political science. His work was included in Form and Colour, Congress of Polish Culture Exhibition of Fine Arts by Polish Artists in Great Britain, at POSK Gallery, in 1995, and he also showed solo in London, where he lived. Private collections in the United Kingdom, France and America hold examples.

Radovan KRAGULY 1934– Versatile artist, born in Prijedor, Bosnia, who graduated from the Academy of Fine Art, Belgrade, Yugoslavia, in 1962, having had a first one-man exhibition at Galerija Doma JNA in the city eight years before. He gained a number of prizes and was awarded a British Council grant to study at the Central School of Arts and Crafts in London, 1962–3. In 1964–5, Kraguly had several prints issued by Editions Alecto, in 1965 having a solo exhibition of drawings and etchings at the ICA. Angela Flowers Gallery gave him a first show in 1977; he continued to exhibit internationally, latterly dance- and video-related works; and Flowers East showing Kraguly's new prints and drawings in 2001. South London Gallery holds his work.

Fritz KRÄMER 1905– Painter, especially portraits of juveniles, and teacher who was born in Vienna, Austria. Studied at Vienna School of Fine Arts and in Germany. For a short time towards end of World War II he taught painting at King's College, Durham University. Showed in Vienna and in England in Newcastle, RA and Storran Gallery. Finally lived in London. Tate Gallery archive holds his self-portrait in charcoal.

Jacob KRAMER 1892–1962 Painter, draughtsman and printmaker, born in Klincy, Ukraine. His father Max was a court painter, as was his uncle Boris. Kramer arrived in England in 1900, settling in Jewish colony in Leeds, and he was to remain faithful to the city. After a period at sea and working in northern towns, where he attended evening classes at Manchester School of Art, in 1907 Kramer returned to Leeds, attending similar classes at its School of Art. From 1908–11 he studied there full-time on a scholarship, Sir Michael Sadler becoming his patron, then from 1913–14 studied at Slade School of Fine Art. In 1915 Kramer had a solo show with Mathews & Brooke, Bradford, was invited to show with Vorticists in London and was elected LG. Kramer's sister Sarah married the artist William Roberts. Kramer began to create a name as a Yorkshire-based artist, showing with Fred Lawson at Leeds School of Art in 1916, also having a solo show at Bradford Arts Club. The inter-war years saw Kramer consolidating his reputation with shows in Yorkshire and London. In 1959 he was elected president of Leeds Fine Arts Club, in 1960 having a retrospective at Leeds City Art Gallery. Six years after his death the City of Leeds Branch College of Art was renamed Jacob Kramer College of Art. Later shows included Parkin Gallery, 1973, Belgrave Gallery, 1990, centenary show at Leeds University Art Gallery then works on paper, Boundary Gallery, 2000. The Tortoise and the Hare, works by Kramer and his brother-in-law William Roberts, was a Ben Uri Gallery touring show in 2003. Kramer was a fine draughtsman and was capable of producing memorable, hieratic images. The sculpture of him by Epstein is in Tate Gallery, which also holds Kramer's work, as do Victoria & Albert Museum and British Museum.

Joseph KRAMER 1887– Painter, draughtsman, printmaker and typographer. Brought up in Czechoslovakia, he studied art in Vienna. During World War II he was registered as an alien, which restricted his ability to paint freely. Showed with RCamA and in East Anglia. Lived near Mold, Flintshire.

Jiří KRATOCHVÍL 1946– Sculptor, carver, designer and teacher, born in Vizovice, Czechoslovakia. He worked as a commercial photographer, 1967–8, in 1969 moving to England, working with mentally subnormal children at Bethlem Royal Hospital. From 1972–4 was assistant designer at 401½ Workshops, then studied sculpture at Ravensbourne College of Art and Design, 1975–9. Went on to teach sculpture and wood-carving at adult classes at Bromley Centre for Arts and Crafts and Orpington Adult Education Centre from 1982. Kratochvíl took part in sculpture show at Camden Lock, 1983, at The Showroom in 1984 and in that year participated in a four-man exhibition at Woodlands Art Gallery, showing abstract work.

Marian KRATOCHWIL 1906–1997 Painter and writer, born in Kosow, Poland, whose early training was in the studio of Stanisław Batowski. He read philosophy and history at Lvov University. After active service in World War II he painted in Scotland, then London, chronicling the life of the city, also painting widely in Spain. In 1961 he married the artist Kathleen Browne, assisted in the running of her school and late in life published a perceptive monograph on her work. British Museum, Victoria & Albert Museum, Scottish National Gallery of Modern Art and several foreign collections hold his work, including Toruń University, Poland. He shared a retrospective with his wife at Polish Cultural Institute in 1994, showing his drawings of life and places on Poland's pre-war eastern borders.

Marko KRATOHVIL 1958– Sculptor, draughtsman and lecturer producing elegant and abstract work in various materials. He was born in Belgrade, Yugoslavia, graduating in sculpture from the city's University of Art, 1989, gaining his master's in 1991, meanwhile lecturing on sculpture in metal there. Won several awards in Yugoslavia. In 1991 moved to London, further teaching including sculpture, University of Manchester, 1996–8. Was a member of RBS and Yugoslav Association of Fine Artists. Group shows included 28th October Salon, Belgrade, 1987; Chelsea Art Society Annual, 1992; 36th October Salon, Belgrade, 1995; and Acava Open Studios, from 1996. Later solo shows included The Kelly Gallery, 1997. In 1999, Kratohvil shared a four-man exhibition at Beardsmore Gallery and in 2004 was included in Modern and Contemporary Sculpture at Wolseley Fine Arts. He carried out extensive commissions in Yugoslavia and London, later ones including Iron Sculpture and Wall Sculpture, both Standard Life, 1999.

Roy KRATY 1909–2002 Self-taught painter, mainly of detailed landscapes and townscapes in oil, born in Bournemouth, Hampshire, encouraged by his artist and curator cousin Dorothy King. After schooling in Ilford, where he showed early artistic promise, Kraty could not find placement as an advertising agency trainee, so became a bookkeeper. Was trained as a navigator in the Royal Air Force Volunteer Reserve in World War II, serving in the Far East; was mentioned in dispatches; and worked in intelligence with the Ministry of Defence, retiring as assistant director of intelligence (logistics) in 1973. In 1966, he renewed his interest in art and began purposefully and prolifically exhibiting wherever he lived, in 1985 settling in Wetherby, Yorkshire. Outlets included Stanmore, Harrow, Coventry & Warwickshire and Stratford-upon-Avon Art Societies; HM Customs & Excise Art Club; London Guildhall, 1971; Herbert Art Gallery, Coventry, 1974–6; Leamington Spa Art Gallery, 1978; Wetherby Art Gallery, 1989; and many hotels. Muscular Dystrophy Society Christmas cards featured Kraty's scenes and Bishopsgate Insurance Company owned his work. Within 25 years of retirement Kraty had sold some 1,400 pictures to buyers in Britain and extensively abroad. His unique story is told in two privately published memoirs: *Some Batting and Bowling Experiences (With Bias) of a Self-Taught (post-retirement) Painter*, 1996, and *From The Inside Looking Out*, 2000.

Roberta KRAVITZ 1944– Artist whose output included performances, and teacher, born in New Jersey, America. She graduated in philosophy from University College in London, 1965–8, in the mid-1970s teaching it at Polytechnic of North London. Studied at City & Guilds of London Art School, 1969, then Slade School of Fine Art, 1969–71. Solo performances included Motherhood at 1st Bracknell Performance Festival, South Hill Park Arts Centre, 1983; group performances Government of the First and Thirteenth Chair, by John Latham, Riverside Studios, 1978. Mixed shows included Wapping Artists Open Studios from 1980. Lived in London.

Gereon KREBBER 1973– Sculptor, born in Oberhausen, West Germany, who settled in London. Studied at the Art Academy, Düsseldorf, 1995–00, under Hubert Kiecol, then with Tony Cragg at Royal College of Art, 2000–2. Showed extensively in Germany; in Soap on the rope, with Noah Sherwood, at Atrium Gallery, PricewaterhouseCoopers, 2002; and in that year had a solo exhibition at Galerie Ferdinand-Ude, Gelsenkirchen, Germany. Won the Deutsche Bank Pyramid and Remet Art Awards in London and the Forderpreis der Stadt Gelsenkirchen. In 2003, Krebber's proposal Tin won the £25,000 Jerwood Sculpture Prize. Comprising a giant tin, with the top slightly open or nearly closed, it was said to "reflect the artist's notion that 'Beyond literal legibility and metaphorical ideas, my sculptures should be ambivalent in their meaning and identity.'"

Marianne KREEGER 1929– Painter, born in Frankfurt, Germany, who attended St Martin's School of Art in 1946. Showed with Hampstead Artists' Council, LG and RA and had a series of solo exhibitions. Shared a show with Peter Freeth at Beardsmore Gallery, 2002. Lived in London.

Anthony KRIKHAAR 1940– Painter, born in Almelo, Netherlands, who moved to Britain to study art in 1959 and settled in London. After the Deva-Vak School of Art, Almelo, he was at Byam Shaw and St Martin's Schools of Art. He was a landscape, genre and portrait painter, employing bright colours, who applied thick pigment to the canvas, the result being almost sculptural. Exhibitions included Gallery 10 and Galerie Krikhaar, Amsterdam, both from 1987; RVS Fine Art, Southampton/New York and Links of Affinity at Knapp Gallery, both 1989. Singer John Lennon, comedian Danny la Rue, actor Richard Chamberlain and a number of corporate collections in Britain and abroad held examples.

Tamara KRIKORIAN 1944– Video artist, born in Bridport, Dorset. Group appearances included The Video Show at Serpentine Gallery, 1975; Acme Gallery, 1979; Arnolfini Gallery in Bristol, 1981; and Signs of the Times, Museum of Modern Art, Oxford, 1990. Solo exhibitions included An Ephemeral Art, Third Eye Centre, Glasgow, and Eye to Eye, Scottish Arts Council, Fruitmarket Gallery, Edinburgh, both 1979; The Heart of the Illusion, at Ikon Gallery, Birmingham, 1981, and Air Gallery, 1982. Arnolfini, Brighton Polytechnic, British Council and Museum of the Moving Image all hold examples.

Margret KROCH-FRISHMAN 1892–1972 Printmaker, painter, draughtsman and sculptor, born in Saxony, Germany, who studied at the Academie for Graphic Art, Leipzig; Staatlichen Kunstschulen, Berlin; and in Dresden and Paris, teachers including Hugo Steiner-Prag, Hans Meid, Karl Hofer and Oskar Kokoschka. Having begun to establish a reputation as a versatile artist, she lived in Brussels, 1934–9, then emigrated to Australia, moving to

Britain in 1950 and settling in London, although she continued to work abroad, notably in Israel and Italy. In London she produced prints at the Charlotte Street Studio, Royal College of Art and with Editions Alecto, including Venetian scenes. Kroch-Frishman exhibited internationally, among her many venues being Galerie am Luetzo Ufer, Berlin; Kozminsi Gallery, Melbourne; André Weil and Marcel Bernheim, both in Paris; Galleria Santa Stefano, Venice; and in London the RE, Contemporary Portrait Society and Gallery One. Solo shows included Flower House Galleries, 1965, and Tib Lane Gallery, Manchester, 1967.

Natasha KROLL 1914–2004 Designer and teacher, born in Moscow, Russia, whose family moved to Germany in the early 1920s for medical reasons. Kroll studied design, especially for shop-windows, at the Reimann School of Art, and, as an assistant teacher, followed the Reimann when it moved to London in 1936. In 1940 she became a display artist at Rowntree's department stores in Yorkshire, in 1942 joining the Simpson store in Piccadilly in London, where she settled, overseeing its window and in-store displays and newspaper advertising. There, economy, wit and elegance marked her work, as it did when she joined the BBC from 1955, making an indelible mark as head of its studio design unit. Kroll made a singular contribution to Huw Wheldon's *Monitor* television arts programmes and Ken Russell's documentaries on the lives of composers, such as the 1962 landmark one on Elgar. In 1966, the year Kroll was made a Royal Designer for Industry by the Royal Society of Arts, she went freelance, continuing to work with Russell on his 1970 feature film about Tchaikovsky, *The Music Lovers*. She insisted on Russian realism when she was involved in such productions as the televised Tchaikovsky opera *Eugene Onegin*, in 1967; Stravinsky's *The Soldier's Tale*, 1968; and in 1971 productions of Chekhov's *The Three Sisters* and *The Cherry Orchard*. More feature films followed, including the L P Hartley adaptation *The Hireling*, 1973.

KROME: *see* **Krome BARRATT**

Rineke KROON 1945– Artist noted for watercolours and prints of landscapes in Netherlands, where she was born in Hoogezand, and Scotland, where she moved in 1976. Spent a period of each year based at Strathcarron, Wester Ross, part of it in Maastricht. Her wet-into-wet watercolour technique was apt for catching changing weather effects, large skies and damp landscapes. Exhibitions included Haagse Kunstkring, The Hague, 1976; Pier Arts Centre, Stromness, fom 1980; Inverness Museum and Art Gallery, 1982; Gallery Verenigde Spaarbank, Amsterdam, 1986; and Links of Affinity, Knapp Gallery, 1989.

Ansel KRUT 1959– Figurative painter and draughtsman, born in Cape Town, South Africa. He studied fine art at University of Witwatersrand, 1979–82, then for his master's degree in mid-1980s at Royal College of Art. In Johannesburg had a solo show with Shell Gallery. In England exhibited with LG, in Camden Annual and in 1985 was a prize winner in John Moores Liverpool Exhibition. Arts Council holds his picture Restless Tonight, 1986, bought from Fischer Fine Art, Harris Museum and Art Gallery in Preston owning The Ventriloquist's Convention, 1988. In 2002, Krut's Heartless Roach won 2nd Prize in The Jerwood Drawing Prize and was shown at Midlands Arts Centre, Birmingham, and Glasgow School of Art, 2002–3. There was a solo show, Lie Still My Beating Heart, at Domo Baal in 2004. By this time Krut's monochromatic fantasies inhabited by small figures had been replaced by rather cartoon-like, grotesque creatures, as in Turd Eaters on a Flatcar, with touches of strong colour. Lived for a time in London.

Christopher KU 1957– Painter, born in Hong Kong, who studied at Gray's School of Art, Aberdeen, and at Royal College of Art. In 1987 Ku won the Maclean/Watters Gold Medal and Latimer Award for Painting, in 1989 the John Minton Scholarship at the Royal College. Group shows included Mall Galleries and Scottish Gallery, Edinburgh, both 1989; Paper Work '90, Seagate Gallery, Dundee, 1990; Whitechapel Open, 1994; and Journeys West, University of Essex tour, 1995. Had a solo exhibition at Aberdeen Royal Infirmary, 1989, others including Henrietta House, 1994.

Judith KUEHNE fl. from 1940s– Painter and draughtsman, born in Detroit, Michigan, America, who studied at the local Society of Arts and Crafts, 1946–9, then at College of Architecture, University of Michigan, graduating with an honours degree from Ann Arbor, Michigan, 1954. From 1954–79 Kuehne's work was mainly representational, some being commissioned by University of Lexington, Kentucky, where she then lived, having a solo show at Transylvania University in 1983. In 1979 Kuehne moved to London for a decade, her work turning to Abstract Expressionism. From 1991 she lived in Cabrieres, in the south of France, where she again adopted representation, strongly influenced by abstraction. Kuehne appeared in a group show at Minsky Gallery, 1982; had two solo exhibitions at Usiskin Gallery, 1989–90; then showed solo at Nicholas Bowlby Gallery, Tunbridge Wells, 1995.

Vic KUELL 1924– Painter in acrylic and watercolour, full name Victor John Kuell, born in Andover, Hampshire, who attended Bromley School of Art, 1938–42, and the Royal College of Art, 1947–50. He participated in the Football Association competition Football and the Fine Arts in 1953. Other exhibitions included Société d l'Art Contemporain, Paris, France, 1984; RA Summer Exhibition, from 1987; Galerie Metropolis, Geneva, Switzerland, 1985; Galerie Espace Laser, Paris, 1990; International Biennale of Malta, where he won an award, 1995; and Galerie Carré d'Or, Paris, 2000. Kuell was an honorary member of the LG, elected in 1981, and was featured in its ninetieth anniversary volume, published in 2003. For it he wrote that he would "most liken my work to that of Miles Davis the jazz musician in detached mood". Corporate collections in London and New York, America, held his work. Kuell lived in Edenbridge, Kent.

Cathryn KUHFELD 1957– Artist, born in Stafford, who was married to the painter Peter Kuhfeld. She did a foundation course at Canterbury College of Art, 1974–5; graduated with honours in fine art, painting, Bath Academy of Art, 1975–8; studied painting as a postgraduate, Royal Academy Schools, 1978–81; and completed a City and Guilds of London Art School calligraphy and lettering course, 1992–3. Prizes and awards included British Council Prize for Printmaking, 1979; Eric Kennington Prize for Good Academic Drawing, Landseer Prize for Painting from Life and Elizabeth Greenshields Scholarship, all 1981; and Italian Government Scholarship, 1982. Among her exhibitions were RA Summer Exhibition, 1980; Hunting Group Prizes, Mall Galleries, 1982; RWA, 1983; The Discerning Eye, Mall Galleries, from 1991; Kent Painters Group, from 1994; Images from my Kitchen, Christopher Hull Gallery, 1996; RP, 1997; and NEAC, from 2002. In 2004 she shared an exhibition with her husband at the New Grafton Gallery. HRH The Prince of Wales, the Nuffield Foundation and Sir Brinsley Ford owned examples. She lived in Wye, Kent.

Peter KUHFELD 1952– Painter and teacher, born in Cheltenham, Gloucestershire. He studied at Leicester Polytechnic, 1972–6, then at Royal Academy Schools under Peter Greenham, 1977–80. He taught at Rugby School of Art, 1976–8. Among his awards was the David Murray Landscape Prize, 1978–9; RA Silver Medal for Drawing, 1979; Royal College of Surgeons Dooley Prize for Anatomical Drawing, 1980; Elizabeth Greenshields Foundation Scholarship, 1980–1; and Richard Ford Award, 1981. In 1978 Kuhfeld was made a freeman of the Worshipful Company of Painter-Stainers. Kuhfeld showed widely in mixed exhibitions, including RA Summer Exhibitions from 1978, RWA from 1982, at Jonleigh Gallery, Guildford, from 1983, and New Grafton Gallery, from 1983. One-man shows included Highgate Gallery, 1983–5, and New Grafton Gallery, 1986, also Agnew, 1989, W H Patterson from 1994, Brian Sinfield Gallery, Burford, 2003, and Petley Fine Art, 2004. He was one of the New Grafton's Portrait Centre artists. Kuhfeld accompanied HRH The Prince of Wales on trips to Africa and Japan, some of the resulting pictures being included in a notable Kuhfeld show at Agnew, 1991. The Prince also owned a portrait of him by Kuhfeld. Kuhfeld was a member of RP and NEAC and was married to the painter Cathryn Kuhfeld, with whom he shared a show at the New Grafton Gallery in 2004. He lived in Wye, Kent.

Andrzej KUHN 1929– Painter and printmaker, born in Lvov, Poland. He was deported when Russia invaded in 1940 and after privations in exile in the Middle East arrived in England in 1947 where, after six years as a labourer and service in the Merchant Navy, he gained a scholarship to Chelsea School of Art. Postage stamps from Tanna-Tuva, the drawings of Aubrey Beardsley and Sumerian sculpture were some influences, leading to a personal iconography including sellers of moons and stars, travellers and fantastic cities. Kuhn saw art as a consolation in times of trouble. In 1962 Kuhn left London for Lincolnshire, where he showed and settled at Boston, with a studio near the sea. Solo exhibitions included Goldmark Gallery, Uppingham, from 1994, and Polish Cultural Institute, 1999.

Anna Grażyna KULESZA: *see* **Grażyna JANCEWICZ-KULESZA**

Lara Nita KULKARNI 1967– Painter who did foundation studies at Worthing College of Art & Design, 1985–6; gained a first-class honours degree in fine art (painting) from Maidstone College of Art & Design, 1986–9; winning a higher diploma fine art (painting) from Slade School of Fine Art, 1989–91. Awards included Boosey and Hawkes Art Prize (commissions), 1991–2; Boise Travel Scholarship, to China, 1992; Travel to East and Southern Africa, 1993; and a South East Arts Major Award, 1995. Showed at Sandra Drew Gallery, Canterbury, 1989; Metropole Arts Centre, Folkestone, Routes – Four Women Artists Through the Slade, 1991; Bernard Jacobson Gallery, show of seven commissioned paintings, 1992; and Diverse, Kent Institute of Art & Design, 1996. Shared an exhibition at Phoenix Gallery, Brighton, 1995. South East Arts, Boise Collection and Boosey and Hawkes hold examples. Kulkarni from 1992 "explored Chinese concepts of nature in relation to art and philosophy." Her paintings began "by making a small gestural mark, and from my response to it I create a veil-like woven surface of light and colour."

Karen KULYK 1950– Painter of landscape and still life employing an exuberant palette, teacher and administrator, who obtained a fine arts honours degree from York University, Toronto, Canada. After setting up and running the Seedlings Gallery, Toronto, 1973–5, Kulyk established studios and worked in many countries, including several periods in England, as well has holding residencies, latterly at the Masterworks Foundation, Bermuda, 1997–8, and at Vinemount, Ontario, 1998–9. She was a visiting teacher at universities and colleges in Canada and elsewhere. Later solo exhibitions included The Quaker Gallery, organised by Henry Dyson Fine Art, 2000. Many Canadian museums, galleries, financial institutions, health care facilities, government offices and hotels in North America, Europe and Asia hold Kulyk's work.

Ylva KUNZE 1964– Artist of Swedish nationality whose paintings were created from a strong physical response to materials, who used photography as a sketching tool to distance herself emotionally from the subject. She did a foundation course at Heatherley's School of Fine Art, 1990–1; graduated from Byam Shaw School of Art, 1991–4; and gained her master's from Chelsea College of Art & Design, 1994–5. Kunze was included in the show Global II Collection at Addison Wesley Longman Ltd, Harlow, 1998–9.

Yuri KUPER 1940– Printmaker, especially of colour lithographs, born in Moscow, in the Soviet Union, where he studied at the Academy of Art. In 1972 he emigrated to Israel and then moved to London. He went to Paris in 1975 and returned to London at the start of the 1980s, becoming a British citizen in 1983. After that he divided his time between the two capitals. Although he had a show in Cambridge in 1973 and at the Sainsbury Centre, Norwich, in 1993, his first exhibition in London did not take place until 1996, at the William Weston Gallery. By that time he had had over 50 one-man shows around the world. Using soft, muted colours, Kuper depicted simple objects, such as a plate with an apple or a mug with a sprig of flowers, making the maximum use of the light and space around them. The use of old lithographic stones with traces of the original text enhanced the surfaces created. Many public collections, including the Museum of Modern Art and Metropolitan Museum of Art in New York, the Pushkin Museum in Moscow and National Gallery in Oslo, as well as the Sainsbury Collection, University of Norwich, hold Kuper's work.

Sylvia KUS 1950– Artist and teacher, born in Chester. She studied at the College of Further Education there, Leicester Polytechnic and Goldsmiths' College School of Art. Taught in Woolwich. Group exhibitions included Aerial Structures, Sunderland, 1973; Twin Towns Art, Reinickendorf, Berlin, and Blackheath Gallery, both 1976. She had a solo show at Maggie Petrie Gallery, 1975, another at Woodlands

Art Gallery, 1977. That consisted of wall pieces and constructions using a variety of materials. The collages were "concerned with spatial qualities seen in landscapes", the constructions being "abstract ideas creating new spatial effects".

Joe KUSNER 1936– Painter and teacher, born in Lithuania, who studied in Johannesburg, South Africa. He arrived in England in the early 1960s, settling in north London and becoming an art moderator and for 40 years head of his department at Acland Burghley School, which had a strong interest in fostering new talent. In the 2002 New Year's Honours List Kusner was made Member of the British Empire for his services to art education. He showed in north London and South Africa and had a solo exhibition at the Bull and Last public house, in Highgate Road, in 2003. It was his first after a stroke and displayed strongly gestural abstracts. *Moving on Up*, 2003, edited by Sarah Brown, one of his former pupils, wife of the Chancellor of the Exchequer Gordon Brown, features Kusner.

Georgina Moutray KYLE 1865–1950 Painter, initially in pastel and watercolour, later in oil, daughter of George Wilson Kyle, she was born in Craigavad, County Down, Northern Ireland, afterwards living in Belfast. Studied at Atelier Colarossi in Paris. She was a member of RUA and a prolific exhibitor, including RHA, ROI, RSA, Royal Glasgow Institute of the Fine Arts and Paris Salon. Ulster Museum has several works by her, including Le Marché, Concarneau.

Kathryn Marie KYNOCH 1942– Painter, born in Edinburgh. After attending grammar school in Leicester she returned to Scotland to study under David Donaldson at Glasgow School of Art, 1959–64. In the early 1960s she also studied for short periods at Patrick Allan-Fraser School of Art, Hospitalfield, Arbroath, under James Cumming. She showed widely in Scotland, including RSA, Blythswood Gallery in Glasgow and Royal Glasgow Institute of the Fine Arts. Edinburgh University holds her work and Leicester University her sensitive portrait of the academic Sir Fraser Noble. Lived in Glasgow.

George KYRIACOU 1940– Sculptor and teacher who settled in London. He qualified as a teacher in 1959, studied sculpture on a Cyprus government scholarship at Chelsea School of Art, 1961–4, then after working as a teacher and sculptor in Cyprus, 1964–9, was appointed cultural officer at the Ministry of Education responsible for visual arts. In 1972 Kyriacou gained a French Institute Scholarship to study museology in Paris and in 1976–7 studied arts administration at Polytechnic of Central London. He undertook public commissions in Cyprus and exhibited widely, including Biennale des Jeunes de Paris, 1967, Venice Biennale, 1968, and with Gallery K at Art95, 1995. Kyriacou's sculptures employed everyday objects and debris.

L

Keith LABAN 1949– Watercolourist, born in London, who studied at Reigate College of Art, gaining the Sir Alec Issigonis Prize for Art, 1969, and his diploma in 1970. He took part in group shows in London, the provinces and in the Netherlands. He lived in Merstham, Surrey.

Rachel LABOUCHERE 1908–1996 Botanical artist, who inherited a collection of flower paintings and studied with John Nash and Mary Grierson; and writer. She was born Rachel Hamilton-Russell, a descendant of the Darbys of Coalbrookdale, the Christy Millers of Adcote and the Wolryche Whitmores of Dudmaston. She had no formal education, although she had wished to go to Oxford University, but during World War II worked for the Admiralty where she met her second husband George Labouchere, knighted in 1955, a collector of modern French and Spanish pictures. With him she travelled extensively, then when he retired as a diplomat in 1966 they settled at her family home, Dudmaston Hall, near Bridgnorth, Shropshire. The house was refurbished by Lady Labouchere and made over to the National Trust in 1978. She also did extensive family historical research, which earned her an honorary doctorate from the University of Birmingham in 1993. Two books on the Quakers from family diaries and a political diary of Adelaide Whitmore were among her writings.

Bruce LACEY 1927– Performance artist, painter, film-maker, sculptor and robot constructor, born in London. He studied at Hornsey School of Art, 1949–51, winning the Knapping Prize in the latter year. Was then at Royal College of Art, 1951–4, gaining an Abbey Minor Travelling Scholarship in the latter year. At the College Lacey established a reputation as a performance artist and creator of happenings sufficient for Ken Russell to make the film *Preservation Man* on him in 1961. Two years later Lacey had a one-man show at Gallery One, another following at Marlborough New London Gallery two years later. By 1975 he had a retrospective at Whitechapel Art Gallery. Lacey believed that the artist should not be constricted to any narrow means of expression, and in the 1970s with his wife Jill Bruce he began performing a series of rituals at various outdoor locations in homage to mysterious and elemental forces. In 1977 he was elected a member of the British Astronomical Association. His work was included in The 1960's at England & Co, 1993. Lived in Silfield, Norfolk, for some years.

Mary Elliott LACEY 1923– Artist in gouache, oil, pencil and conté and teacher, born in Birmingham. She attended Birmingham College of Art, 1939–44, under Bernard Fleetwood-Walker. Went on to teach for seven years at Mansfield School of Art, then two years part-time at Wolverhampton College of Art. Lacey was a founder-member of SWLA. She exhibited at Mall and Tryon Galleries, at Slimbridge Wild Fowl Trust, elsewhere throughout Britain and in Paris. Had a series of solo shows at Fairfield Halls, Croydon. She illustrated regularly for Hamlyn, Balberry Publishing, National Parks of America and designed several jigsaws for James Hamilton. Medici, Royle and World Wildlife Fund reproduced Lacey's pictures and she was commissioned to produce nine for the Sultan of Oman. Lived at Sudbourne, Woodbridge, Suffolk.

Barbara Dacia LACK fl. from 1940s– Artist in many media including textile design who attended Perse School in Cambridge, then the College of Art there, followed by Royal College of Art. Showed at RA, in the provinces and abroad. Continued to live in Cambridge for many years, latterly at Temple Sowerby, Penrith, Cumbria.

Henry Martyn LACK 1909–1979 Etcher and teacher, born in Bozeat, Northamptonshire. He studied at Leicester College of Art and gained a Royal Exhibition to the Royal College of Art, where he remained for five years. Joined the Sakkarah expedition in Egypt to record tomb paintings and carvings, after two years returning to England to be art master at Christ's Hospital, Horsham, from 1937–46. After Army service he was briefly at Northampton School of Art before becoming a tutor in the engraving school at the Royal College of Art. Was then at Hastings School of Art, 1953–68, latterly as acting principal. Then Egypt called him again and until his retirement in 1976 he was a member of a Chicago University team at Luxor for six months of the year, the rest of the time being spent in Hastings. Showed widely in Britain and abroad, including RA and RE. British Museum, British Council and Hastings Museum and Art Gallery hold his work.

Suzanne LACKNER 1908– Sculptor in wide variety of materials, born in Berlin, Germany, where she studied architecture at the Technical University, then studied in France and London. Was a member of Free Painters and Sculptors, also showing at Camden Arts Centre, elsewhere in London where she lived, and abroad.

John LACOUX 1930– Painter, born with an English mother and French father, whose work was inspired greatly by ecclesiastical architecture, the sea and Venice. He used a technique of glazes which exploited effects of light, as in his show at Nicholas Bowlby, Tunbridge Wells, 1996. Other solo exhibitions included Trafford and Madden Galeries, Tib Lane in Manchester, elsewhere in the north of England and in America. Mixed exhibitions included RA Summer Exhibition, RP and Business Art Galleries at Burlington House. Also showed at his studio at Paddock Wood, Tonbridge, Kent.

Marek ŁĄCZYŃSKI 1925– Printmaker, illustrator and teacher, born in Warsaw, Poland. He was a member of the Polish Home Army in 1941, took part in Warsaw Uprising in 1944, was a prisoner of war in Germany, 1944–5, joined the Polish forces in Italy in 1945 and arrived in England in 1946. Studied book illustration at Borough Polytechnic, 1949–52, then etching and lithography at Central School of Arts and Crafts, 1962–4. Had first show of prints at Redfern Gallery, 1959. Other appearances included Grabowski Gallery, 1959; Giles Bequest Exhibition at Victoria & Albert Museum, 1962; and in same year Prints of the World at Cincinnati Museum, America. From 1964 taught at Exeter College of Art, being appointed head of printmaking in 1979. Published a book of poetry, *Faces of Fear*, in 1973. Was a member of Printmakers' Council of Great Britain from 1965, of the World Printmakers' Council from 1978. Victoria & Albert Museum, Universities of London and Exeter and a number of overseas museums hold his work. Lived in Exeter, Devon.

Roger LADE 1960– Artist in various media, including models and puppets, who was involved in Little Angel Marionette Theatre, Islington. Was born and lived in London, in his teens becoming interested in the theatre and stage management. Did a foundation course at Sir John Cass School of Art, 1979–80, then honours degree in fine art at Wolverhampton Polytechnic, 1980–3. Exhibited at Wrekin College, Telford; Stowells Trophy at RA; Woodlands Art Gallery, and elsewhere.

Edwin LA DELL 1914–1970 Painter, lithographer and teacher. Born in Coventry, he studied art at Sheffield College of Art and the Royal College of Art under Gilbert Spencer and Barnett Freedman. He was the son of Thomas La Dell and Ellen La Dell, both still life painters. Edwin went on to become senior tutor in charge of printmaking at the Royal College of Art. There he was an influential teacher, his vibrantly coloured lithographs gaining inspiration from French models such as Vuillard, Denis and Bonnard. His organisation of the *Coronation Suite*, in 1953, brought together a number of artists connected with the College. He wrote and illustrated *Your Book of Landscape Drawing* and illustrated Wilkie Collins' novel *The Moonstone*. Lived near Maidstone, Kent.

Julia LADEN 1921– Painter, born Juliet Perkins in Little Cornard, Sudbury, Suffolk, daughter of the artist Christopher Perkins. She studied at the St John's Wood Art School and the Royal Academy Schools, 1936–9. During her marriage to her Polish-Jewish husband Leon Laden they lived in Brudenell House, Aldeburgh, Suffolk, and Julia did a number of short-term jobs, such as hospital auxiliary/driver to help out. She, her sister Jane, who was married to the botanist S D Garrett, the painter Peggy Somerville and the writer Ronald Blythe from the mid-1950s formed a life-long, close circle of friends, as recalled by Blythe in his catalogue introduction to Somerville's show at The Cinema Gallery, Aldeburgh, in 2001. The Aldeburgh painter Mary Potter, J M W Turner, Franz Marc and Marc Chagall were influences on Laden. She was a member of Ipswich Art Society, other group appearances including the NEAC, 1958–60; RA Summer Exhibition, 1959; Haste Gallery, Ipswich, 1967; Cambridge Arts Theatre, 1974; Quay Theatre, Sudbury, 1979; and John Russell Gallery, Ipswich, 1989. There were solo shows at John Russell, 1989, and M F Frames Ltd Gallery, Ipswich, 1995.

Juliet LADEN: *see* **JULIA LADEN**

Thomas Sherwood LA FONTAINE 1915– Portrait and animal painter and draughtsman in black-and-white. He studied at Regent Street Polytechnic School of Art, 1934–6, teachers including Harry Watson and Stuart Tresilian; City and Guilds of London Art School, 1936–9, with A R Middleton Todd and James Grant; then Spenlove School, 1939, with Reginald Eves. Showed at RP, RA and elsewhere and lived in Malmesbury, Wiltshire, for many years.

Darren LAGO 1965– Sculptor, born in Walsall, Staffordshire, who attended Burton upon Trent Art College, 1984–5, then graduated in fine art from Portsmouth Polytechnic 1985–8, gaining his master's at Chelsea School of Art, 1989–90. He was awarded the Picker Fellowship, Kingston Polytechnic, 1990; Boise Scholarship, Slade School of Fine Art, 1991; and was artist-in-residence, New Art Gallery, Walsall, 2000. Lago (pronounced Laygo)'s group shows included New Contemporaries, ICA, 1989; Urban Hybrid, Bath Museum, 1993; Pier, Atlantis Gallery, 1994; and Saatchi in Sheffield, Mappin Art Gallery, Sheffield, 1999. He had a series of solo exhibitions, starting with Mountbatten Gallery, Portsmouth, 1987, later ones including 7 x 5 = Sculptures, Annely Juda Fine Art, 2000 (included witty, colourful hybrids of consumer products, such as a toaster metamorphosed into the façade of the Parthenon and a hair dryer with a briar-wood body) and The New Art Gallery, Walsall, 2001. Lago lived in London.

Phillip LAI 1969– Installations artist, born in Kuala Lumpur, Malaya, who graduated from Chelsea College of Art & Design, 1990–3, gaining his master's degree, 1993–4. Group exhibitions included Sweetrice, Unit 219, Elephant & Castle Shopping Centre, 1992; Whitworth Young Contemporaries, Whitworth Art Gallery, Manchester, 1993; Fresh, London Film & Video Umbrella touring show, from 1994; Institute of Cultural Anxiety: works from the collection, ICA, 1994–5; and Deep Signal, Gasworks, 1996. In 1997, The Showroom, in collaboration with the Institute of International Visual Arts, commissioned a new installation by Lai which explored the idea of fluid states: one a working soy sauce fermentation unit, the other a room of automatic drawings on the gallery walls. Lai worked in London.

Annie Rose LAING 1869–1946 Figure painter who lived variously in Glasgow, Frascati in Italy and in London, married to the artist James Garden Laing, who predeceased her by 31 years. Laing, who worked for a time under her maiden name Annie Rose Low, was born in Glasgow, where she studied at the School of Art, 1888–94, in the latter year winning the Haldane Travelling Scholarship. She studied under Jean-Paul Laurens in Paris. In the year she was married, 1908, she joined the Glasgow Society of Lady Artists. Exhibited in Munich, Germany, and in Rome International Exhibition, both 1911. Showed extensively at Royal Glasgow Institute of the Fine Arts, also at RSA, RA and Walker Art Gallery in Liverpool. Kelvingrove Art Gallery in Glasgow holds her oils The Mirror and After Rehearsal. Died in Uckfield, Sussex.

David LAING 1954– Artist, born in Felixstowe, Suffolk, who studied medical biology and worked for the Medical Research Council before travelling extensively. He experienced the Iranian Islamic Revolution first-hand before returning to England to pursue art studies, settling in London. Attended Middlesex Polytechnic, 1980–3, École des Beaux-Arts in Paris, 1986, and Royal College of Art, 1985–7. Exhibited in British Council Invited Section, Ljubliana Biennale, Yugoslavia, 1991; Whitechapel Open Exhibition at Whitechapel Gallery, 1992; Artists' Books, South Bank Centre, 1993; and Lannon Gallery, New York, 1995. Solo exhibitions included Harriet Green Gallery, 1995, where Laing showed dark paintings scattered with forms that reflected his biological background. Later shows included The Large Print Show, Christchurch Mansion, Ipswich, 1997. He lived in London.

Gerald LAING 1936– Artist, notably a sculptor in bronze, and teacher, born in Newcastle upon Tyne, Northumberland. Also known as Gerald Ogilvie-Lang. He attended Royal Military Academy, Sandhurst, 1953–5, then after a short Army career attended St Martin's School of Art, 1960–4. Lived in New York for five years, being artist-in-residence at Aspen Institute for Humanistic Studies, Colorado, in 1966. Initially Laing was a Pop Artist and by the late-1960s was known as a sculptor of minimal forms. In 1969, during a period of disillusionment, he acquired Kinkell Castle, on the Black Isle, in Scotland and restored it, in 1977 setting up a substantial bronze foundry there to handle his own work. By this time Laing had rejected abstraction for figuration, returning to the mainstream, but continually experimenting within it. Laing's teaching posts included visiting professor at University of New Mexico, Albuquerque, 1976–7; and professor of sculpture at Columbia University, New York, 1986–7. In 1978–80 he was on the art committee of the Scottish Arts Council, in 1987 being appointed commissioner on the Royal Commission for Fine Art for Scotland. Laing showed widely internationally, having a one-man show at Laing Art Gallery, Newcastle upon Tyne, 1963, another at ICA, 1964, then the first of a string at Richard Feigen Gallery, New York, 1964, and with Richard Feigen in Chicago, 1965, Whitford Fine Art in 1996 holding an exhibition of 17 silkscreen prints made in 1968. The Cincinnati Center for Contemporary Art gave Laing a retrospective in 1971, others following at Herbert Art Gallery, Coventry, 1983, Fruitmarket Gallery, Edinburgh, 1993, and sculpture 1968–99, Fine Art Society, 1999. In 1995 Laing was commissioned to make eight dragons for Bank tube station, in 1996 four bronze rugby players for Twickenham Stadium. Tate Gallery, National Portrait Gallery, Victoria & Albert Museum, Scottish Art Gallery and many other public collections in Britain and abroad hold Laing's work. In 2004, Laing set up The Gerald Laing Art Foundation to promote the understanding, appreciation and practice of sculpture.

Rowena LAING fl. from 1970s– Painter and designer whose work included landscapes, abstracted with unusual perspectives. She gained her diploma from Duncan of Jordanstone College of Art, Dundee, then worked as a graphic designer in London, Dundee and Glasgow. After a break while bringing up her two children she worked on interior design and developed a framing business, an offshoot of which was the Blue Roof Gallery, Fintry, Stirlingshire, where she lived. As well as painting the east coast of Scotland, more exotic references were to the Caribbean and Italy, especially Florence, where she lived as a student. Showed widely in Scotland after deciding to paint full-time, including The Strathearn Gallery, Crieff.

Arthur Robert LAIRD 1881–c.1957 Lithographer who studied at Camberwell School of Arts and Crafts under Herbert Cole and Francis Jackson, then at the Westminster School of Art under Walter Sickert and Harold Gilman. He exhibited at the Senefelder Club, RA, RBA, SGA, in the provinces, in Belgium and America. The British Museum and Victoria & Albert Museum hold his work. Laird, who worked for a time in local government, became secretary of the Camberwell School of Arts and Crafts and vice-president of the South London Group. Lived at Ewell, Surrey.

Thalia LAIRD 1967– Versatile artist who worked with *Vogue* magazine, 1986, studying architecture at the University of Newcastle upon Tyne, 1986–9. She worked for the press office of the Edinburgh International Festival in 1988, also undertaking an architectural project trip to Portugal. In 1989, she was included in East End Open Studios, at Berry Street.

Doriane LAITHIER 1972– Artist, graphic designer and editor, born in Lausanne, Switzerland, one of the management team for the PILOT:2 International Art Forum in London in 2005, responsible for the design, website administration and press. Laithier graduated in fine arts at the École Supériere d'Arts Visuels in Geneva in 1997. She then moved to London to complete her master's degree at Central St Martins in 1998, remaining to work as an artist. She was also a graphic designer, freelancing as an art editor for award-winning business magazines. Laithier took part in various European group exhibitions, including Trivial Pursuit in Belgrade in former Yugoslavia, 2002; Kick It Till It Breaks, VTO Gallery, 2003; and Siege, London, 2005. Among her solo shows were SFP Gallery, Geneva, 2000, and EXIT, Lausanne, 2003.

Antony LAKE 1905–1956 Painter and illustrator, born at Chalfont St Giles, Buckinghamshire. Studied at St Martin's School of Art. Exhibited at NS and RBA. Worked for the *Illustrated London News*, did posters for London Passenger Transport Board and illustrated a number of books. Belonged to Hoddesdon Art Club and lived near Waltham Abbey, Essex.

Evelyn Frances Coote LAKE 1885–1979 Painter, especially of birds and cats, in various media, born in London, where she continued to live. She studied at Camden and Hornsey Schools of Art and on the continent. Exhibited very widely in London as well as RCamA, RWA, in the provinces and at Paris Salon. She was a prominent member of a number of art clubs, including RWS and Ridley Art Club. Was also involved in a variety of organisations such as the Cats' Protection League and Folk-Lore Society.

John Gascoyne LAKE 1903–1975 Painter and museum curator, educated in Seaford, studied painting at Eastbourne School of Art, 1918–25, and the Royal College of Art, 1925–9. Lake did a variety of work, ranging from figure studies through views of Sussex to later more abstract pictures. Exhibited LG, NEAC and in the provinces. Was curator of the Towner Art Gallery, Eastbourne, 1947–58. Lived at Hailsham, Sussex, but emigrated to Spain after his retirement from the gallery, which held a memorial show in 1975.

Maria LALIĆ 1952– Painter committed to non-figurative work associated with Minimalism and Concrete art. She was brought up in her home town, Sheffield, Yorkshire, completed a master's degree in fine art at Chelsea School of Art, 1977, the following year having a fellowship at the Academy in Bath, Somerset, where she settled. American artists such as Robert Ryman, Brice Marden, Eva Hesse, Agnes Martin and Carl André were influences. She came into prominence in the 1990s through solo exhibitions in London and Munich as well as several group shows: drei Frauen konkret?, Munich, 1995, and Mostly Monochrome, Dublin, 1996. The Lead Fall series was important in her output. She was one of the Jerwood Painting Prize selections at the Central St Martins College of Art and Design, 1997.

John LALLY 1914–1994 Painter, draughtsman and teacher, born and lived in Ilkeston, Derbyshire, where he was prominent in the community. His gifts as a speaker were valuable during his 15 years as chairman of the thriving Arts Club and as a founder-member of the Friends of Erewash Museum at Ilkeston, which has a John Lally Gallery and which holds his striking, Cubist-influenced picture Museum and Grand Hotel, Scarborough. A tall, stately, charismatic man, Pop Lally, as he was known, studied for three years at Sheffield University until 1934, then taught, eventually becoming headmaster of Gladstone Boys School, retiring in 1977. He showed at Nottingham Museum and Art Gallery before World War II, after the war with the Midland Group of Artists in Nottingham.

Richard LALLY 1928– Painter and restorer, born in London, who attended Hammersmith College of Art and Building under Leon Underwood and Dennis Gilbert, 1955–9. Appeared in mixed shows at UA, SWLA and ROI and had solo exhibition at Manolette Gallery, Richmond, and abroad. Lived at Drumbeg, Lairg, Sutherland.

LAM Tung-pang 1978– Artist, born in Hong Kong, who set up a studio in the Fo Tan Industrial Area there in 2001. He graduated in fine arts from The Chinese University of Hong Kong, 2002, gaining his master's from Central St Martins College of Art & Design, London, 2004. At the Nokia Art Awards – Asia Pacific 2000, at Insa Art Center, Seoul, South Korea, Lam was a Hong Kong finalist, winning an award for outstanding artistic expression; in 2001 a Cheung's Fine Arts Award, at the Chinese University; the Raymond Wood Creative Prize there, 2002; an Arts Scholarship, Hong Kong Arts Development Council, 2003; a Young Artists Prize, The 8th Chichester Open, 2004; and Young Artist of the Year in the 2005 Hunting Art Prizes. Exhibitions included Triple Play, 1aspace, Cattle Depot Artists' Village, Hong Kong, 2002; Landscape of the Mind, Grotto Fine Art, Hong Kong, 2003; The Inscriptive Ferret, Space 44, 2004; and Small is Beautiful XXII, Flowers Central, 2004–5. Toni Heath Gallery gave Lam a first London solo show in 2005. The Museum of Art, Allen & Overy and Grotto Fine Art, all in Hong Kong, and private collections there, in London and America hold examples

Charles LAMB 1893–1964 Painter and teacher who was born in Portadown, Armagh, Northern Ireland. Initially he followed his father's trade as a house painter and studied at the local Technical School, but attended evening classes at Belfast School of Art. After gaining a scholarship to Dublin's Metropolitan School of Art, 1917–21, where he won gold and silver medals, Lamb settled in Carraroe, County Galway, where he lived simply and became noted for his studies of peasant life. In the mid-1930s he built a house at Carraroe and ran a summer painting school there. Travelled extensively in Ireland, working in the North extensively from the early 1940s, also in Brittany. He was a member of RHA and RUA and exhibited widely in Ireland and abroad, including RA, America – including Olympic Art Exhibition, 1932, in Los Angeles – and was given a show by CEMA in Belfast in 1947. Municipal Gallery of Modern Art held a memorial show in 1969. Ulster Museum and most Irish public collections hold examples.

Christine Margaret LAMB 1930–1971 Portait and landscape painter in oil and medical illustrator, born in Portsmouth, Hampshire. She studied at the College of Art there, 1945–7; Bromley Art College, 1947–9; and Royal Academy Schools, 1949–51. In addition to exhibiting at NEAC and RP and having work in *The Artist* magazine, Lamb was assistant medical artist at the Central Middlesex Hospital and illustrated medical publications. Before that, in 1949–51, she had taught at Sevenoaks Art Centre. Lived in Rickmansworth, Hertfordshire.

Elspeth LAMB fl. from late 1960s– Printmaker, paperwork and mixed-media artist, and teacher, who attended Glasgow School of Art, 1969–73; did postgraduate studies in printmaking at Manchester Polytechnic, 1973–4; then studied stone lithography at Ruskin School of Drawing, Oxford, 1976. After lecturing in etching in Glasgow, from 1978 taught printmaking, drawing and painting at Edinburgh College of Art. She won many awards, including several from Scottish Arts Council, and took part in a string of international print biennales and art fairs. Mixed shows included New Scottish Prints Tour in New York, 1983; The Mini Print Competition in Cadaques, Spain, 1984; and Amsterdam, Culture City Prints, 1987. Had a solo show at Glasgow School of Art, 1974, later ones including Compass Gallery, Glasgow, 1992, where Lamb's interest in ancient civilisations was evident. British Council, Scottish Arts Council and public galleries in Glasgow, Leeds, Bradford and Perth hold examples. Lamb was unusual in tackling the onerous job of making her own paper, which she saturated with rich, dense pigment.

Helen Adelaide LAMB fl. from c. 1913–1981 Illuminator, draughtsman and teacher, born in Prestwick, Ayrshire, sister of the artist Mildred Lamb. Helen studied at Glasgow School of Art, 1907–15, gaining her diploma in 1913. She won a travelling scholarship to study manuscripts in London, Oxford and Dublin in Ireland, then taught at St Columba's School, Kilmacolm, 1918–49. Joined the Glasgow Society of Lady Artists in 1917, winning its Lauder Award in 1924–31–53. Also exhibited at Royal Glasgow Institute of the Fine Arts, RSA and Walker Art Gallery, Liverpool. Notable among her public commissions were a number for Dunblane Cathedral, including its Cradle Roll, 1927; and Church of Scotland Royal Addresses for the Silver Jubilee of George V and accession of George VI and Queen Elizabeth.

Henry LAMB 1883–1960 Painter and draughtsman, especially of portraits and figure groups. Born in Adelaide, Australia. Family returned to Manchester in 1886. Lamb studied medicine at Manchester University, but after election as a student for 1904–5 at MAFA moved to London and in 1906 enrolled at Chelsea Art School, run by Augustus John and William Orpen, afterwards attending L'École de la Palette, Paris. Prior to World War I he became involved with Euphemia (Nina Forrest), whom he married, Dorelia John and Lady Ottoline Morrell; painted in Brittany and Ireland; and exhibited with the AAA, Camden Town Group and NEAC. In World War I after further studies he served as a medical officer and as an Official War Artist abroad. In the 1920s Lamb's reputation grew; he exhibited at RA from 1921 (elected RA in 1949); first one-man show at Alpine Gallery, 1922; married Lady Pansy Pakenham, 1928; and began a long association with the Leicester Galleries, 1927. Official War Artist in World War II. Lamb was a fine draughtsman and a painter whose palette was muted, but unmistakeable. He finished a number of pictures which are a key part of modern British painting: Death of a Peasant, Lytton Strachey and Evelyn Waugh. Work in many public collections, including Tate Gallery and National Portrait Gallery. Retrospective exhibition at Manchester City Art Gallery, 1984, and touring. Lived at Coombe Bissett, Wiltshire.

Lynton LAMB 1907–1977 Lithographer, wood engraver, book illustrator and painter. Born in India, he studied at the Central School of Arts and Crafts under William Roberts and Bernard Meninsky, 1928–30. Shared a studio with Victor Pasmore in the 1930s, is featured in Pasmore's picture The Parisian Café and was associated with the Euston Road School. Exhibited RA, RBA, LG, Leicester and Redfern Galleries and widely abroad. One-man show at the Storran Gallery, 1937. On the staff of the Slade School of Fine Art, 1950–71, and the Royal College of Art, 1956–71. Lamb was an exemplary book illustrator; produced the lorry bill *Reaping* for Shell in 1951; and wrote a number of books, including *The Purpose of Painting* and *Preparation for Painting*. Lived at Sandon, near Chelmsford, Essex.

Mildred Richley LAMB 1900–1947 Artist, illustrator and writer, sister of the illuminator Helen Adelaide Lamb. She was born in Glasgow and attended its School of Art, 1922–5, between the wars illustrating many books. Lamb joined the Glasgow Society of Lady Artists in 1923, winning its Lauder Award in 1935. Exhibited with Royal Glasgow Institute of the Fine Arts and RSA. Wrote for the *Glasgow Herald* and during World War II did munitions work. The year before she died she married Walter Connor. Lived at Lamlash, Isle of Arran, but died at Bridge of Weir, Renfrewshire.

Sue LAMB 1943– Sculptor, draughtsman and Batik artist who began sculpting as a remedial exercise after leaving a career with British Airways. Studied at Sidcup Art Centre for eight years and became assistant to the sculptor John Ravera. Lamb's chief interest was animal sculpture, especially dogs, as evidenced in the four-man show she shared at Woodlands Art Gallery, 1981. She was commissioned to make competition trophies, including a golden Cruft's award, and exhibited annually at major championship shows where her work was bought by internationally known dog breeders and exhibitors.

Thomas LAMB 1978– Artist, born in Lincolnshire, where he lived at Belleau, married to the artist Yuki Abe. He graduated in fine art from Wimbledon School of Art, 1997–00, gaining his master's degree in fine art, drawing, there, 2000–01. In 2001–3 Lamb held a Sainsbury Scholarship in Painting and Sculpture, British School at Rome, Italy. Took part in exhibitions while there. Also participated in a mixed show at the Lethaby Gallery, 1999, and Braccio di Carlo Magno, Vatican City, 2002.

William LAMB 1893–1951 Sculptor, printmaker and watercolourist, born in Montrose, Angus, where he eventually settled. For several years before World War I Lamb was apprenticed as a monumental sculptor to his brother James and attended evening classes at Montrose Academy. In 1912 he began work for an Aberdeen granite merchants, continuing to study at Gray's School of Art. During the war he lost a hand while engaged in trench warfare, but began using his left hand and during 1918–21 attended classes at Montrose Academy again, changing to full-time study at Edinburgh College of Art, 1921–2, where his teachers included David Foggie. After studying in Paris, 1922–4, at École des Beaux-Arts, Lamb did a cycle tour of France and Italy lasting 3,000 miles, returning to Montrose in 1924 where he established a studio. He now began to exhibit seriously at RA and RSA, at the latter winning the Guthrie Award in 1929. In 1945 he established a stone-carving business. The William Lamb Memorial Studio in his home town houses his output as an artist. Lamb was noted for his heads of the royal family modelled in the early 1930s, but his fame rests on his powerful, Expressionistic depictions of fisherfolk. The Scottish Arts Council organised an Edward Baird and William Lamb show in 1968.

Yuki LAMB: *see* **Yuki ABE**

Juginder LAMBA 1948– Sculptor in wood, notably bog oak, producing mainly figurative work on themes such as mothers and children and lovers, and stage designer. He was born in Nairobi, Kenya. After four years in India until 1962 the family moved to England. In 1969 Lamba graduated from University of Lancaster. For eight years he was involved in New Plant Arts Workshop and Earthbound Theatre, a touring performance art unit, in 1978 becoming Lancaster's first town artist. Then did work for many arts organisations and schools, eventually based in London. After a solo show on Edinburgh Festival fringe in 1976 others included Abbot Hall Art Gallery, Kendal, 1977; Liverpool University, 1979; Westbourne Art Gallery, 1984; and Commonwealth Institute, 1986. From 1983 he held a series of shows at Woburn Fine Arts, which in 1986 published an illustrated monograph on him. Lamba could be an imaginative stage designer, as for the dance group Kosh's production *A Square of Sky* at Round Chapel, Hackney, in 2002. Lamba later settled in Yeaton, Baschurch, Shropshire.

Peter LAMBDA 1911–1995 Sculptor and writer, born in Budapest, Hungary, to professional parents, his mother a psychoanalyst, a student of Sigmund Freud who later sat to Lambda for the portrait in the Freud Museum. Lambda studied medicine; sculpture in Paris and Prague; then after some success exhibiting moved to London in 1938. During World War II he worked for the Crown Film Unit and wrote propaganda scripts for the BBC. After the war joined Imperial Chemical Industries, engaged in industrial design, notably with the new material Perspex, in which he sculpted. Made a fine head in bronze of the Labour politician Aneurin Bevan, then concentrated on theatrical personalities, including Laurence Olivier, Claire Bloom, Christopher Fry, Terence Rattigan and Wendy Hiller. His work is in the National Portrait Gallery, National Museum of Wales in Cardiff and University College, Swansea. Lambda's last bust was of the actress Liz Robertson, 1981, then eye trouble made sculpting difficult. Lambda married his second wife, the actress Betty Paul, in 1958. By then he had written for the theatre and with her he scripted episodes for television series; they created their own, *Weaver's Green*, for Anglia. Continued writing until 1993, having in 1987 moved from London to Tibberton, Gloucestershire, where he died.

Alice LAMBE 1924– Printmaker and freelance illustrator, born in Dublin, Ireland, who studied at Regent Street Polytechnic. She exhibited at WIAC, RBA, Young Contemporaries, Leicester Galleries and in an Arts Council tour, 1949. In 1950, lithographs by Lambe were included in a group exhibition at the AIA.

Philip Agnew LAMBE 1897–1968 Painter in oil who over a long period studied privately with Charles Buchel, Charles Simpson, Arthur Hayward and Bernard Adams, with a period at Heatherley's School of Fine Art. Travelled extensively. Exhibited NS, RP and Paris Salon, where he won a gold medal, sometimes signing work with initials only. Lived in London.

Alison LAMBERT 1957– Artist who was notably a draughtsman, sometimes on a large scale, heads and horses as favoured subjects. Born in Kingston, Surrey, she studied at Leek School of Art and Design, 1978–9, gained a bachelor's degree in fine art at Coventry Polytechnic, 1981–4, then took a studio with Coventry Artists Group. Group shows included Coventry's Herbert Art Gallery, 1984; Oriel Gallery, Welshpool, 1987; Nerlino Gallery, New York, 1990; and Cleveland International Drawing Biennale, 1991. Solo shows included Long & Ryle, 1995, and Jill George Gallery, 2002. London headquarters of Cité Nationale Bank of France commissioned work, which was held also by Coopers & Lybrand Deloitte, Birmingham collection.

Claire LAMBERT 1936– Painter, draughtsman, printmaker and ceramist, born in Ipswich, Suffolk, settling nearby at Shotley. She was largely self-taught, but did attend part-time and evening classes at Académie des Beaux-Arts in Brussels under Roger Somville, Atelier des Céramiques de Dour with Fernand Wery and Suffolk College. "The human figure and expression, simplicity and feeling" were important aspects of her work. Lambert was a member of Suffolk Craft Society and Ipswich Art Society. Group exhibitions included Peter Pears Gallery in Aldeburgh, Guy Taplin's Gallery in Woodbridge, Falcon Gallery in Boxford and extensively on the continent and in Canada. Solo shows included Gallery 44, Aldeburgh; John Russell Gallery, Ipswich; and Christchurch Mansion there. It and Musée de Verviers, Belgium, hold examples.

Isabel LAMBERT: *see* **Isabel RAWSTHORNE**

John LAMBERT 1967– Artist born in Bridgend, Glamorgan, for whom "the desire to find solutions, narratives, is a strong one." He gained an honours degree in fine art, painting, at Staffordshire Polytechnic, 1986–9; studied postgraduate printmaking at Wimbledon School of Art, 1991–3; gained a Swedish Institute Scholarship to Konsthögskolan, Stockholm, 1992–3; then his master's in printmaking at Wimbledon, 1993–4. Lambert was included in The Large Print Show, Christchurch Mansion, Ipswich, 1997, having just completed a residency at Lowick House Print Workshop and in 1996 one at Coventry University. He showed regularly regionally and nationally and was included in group shows widely abroad. Lived in Lancaster.

Maurice LAMBERT 1901–1964 Sculptor, draughtsman and teacher, born in Paris. His father was the Australian painter George Lambert, his brother the musician Constant Lambert. Educated in London, Lambert was apprenticed, 1918–23, with the sculptor Derwent Wood; assisted his father briefly in his studio; and attended part-time life classes, 1919–27, at Chelsea Polytechnic. Although he worked on Wood's Machine Gun Corps monument at Hyde Park Corner, Lambert's own sculpture, while remaining largely figurative, took a much more modern turn. He was prolific, between 1925–34 exhibiting nearly 150 works, having his first solo show at the Claridge Gallery in 1927. His fourth and final one-man show in his lifetime was at Reid and Lefevre in 1934, and it was left to the Belgrave Gallery to give him a posthumous exibition in 1988. Lambert was a member of NS and a fellow of RBS and was elected RA in 1952. From 1950–8 he was master of sculpture at the Royal Academy Schools. A physically tough and intellectually adventurous man, Lambert undertook a large number of commissions, often of hefty size. They included an equestrian statue of King George V for Adelaide, South Australia; work in the liners *Queen Mary* and *Queen Elizabeth*; fountains for Basildon; and work in the presidential palace, Baghdad. Tate Gallery holds his work. Died in London.

Jim LAMBIE 1964– Versatile and enterprising artist, as in his solo show Zobop, at The Showroom, 1999, in which, using a selection of lo-fi materials, Lambie created a psychedelic vinyl floor shaped by gallery features. The audience crossed it to view sculptures made from such materials as glue sticks, balloons, tape, cigarettes and socks. Lambie was born and lived in Glasgow, where he gained a fine art honours degree from the School of Art, 1990–4. Other exhibitions included Mary Redmond & Jim Lambie, Assembly Gallery, Glasgow, 1995; Sick Building, Globe Gallery, Copenhagen, Denmark, 1996; and Two Up Property Gallery, Glasgow, 1998. In that year Lambie had a residency at Triangle, Marseilles, France, with a show there at La Friche. He won a Paul Hamlyn Visual Arts Award, 2000. Lambie was also included in the Hayward Gallery tour The British Art Show 5, 2000–1. In 2003 Lambie had solo exhibitions at Inverleith House, Royal Botanic Garden, Edinburgh, and at Modern Art, Oxford, the year he was included in Days Like These, at Tate Britain. The National Gallery of Modern Art in Edinburgh holds his work.

Alan LAMBIRTH 1959– Painter of landscapes and interiors, simplifying the images and often including a single female figure. He studied at West Sussex College of Design, Epsom School of Art and Royal Academy Schools. From 1981 showed in RA Summer Exhibitions, from 1983 with RBA and from 1986 at NEAC. He gained the RA Gold Medal in 1982, the year he won an Edward Travelling Scholarship, winning a David Murray Studentship in 1983. Elected RBA three years later. Had two solo shows at Odette Gilbert Gallery, 1984–6, one at the Solomon Gallery, 1988, and at Sheila Harrison Fine Art, 1989. In 1991 shared an exhibition at Llewellyn Alexander Gallery. Lived in Horsham, Sussex.

George LAMBOURN 1900–1977 Artist, born in London, who early showed an aptitude for drawing and mathematics. In 1916 he was chosen to join Royal Air Service Corps, training as a rear gunner. After World War I he was asked to plan a factory in Bruges for English Electric Light Bulb Company and during that time discovered a natural talent for painting, which then became his dominant interest. He studied at Goldsmiths' College School of Art, the Royal Academy Schools, 1924–7, and briefly in Paris. During World War II he worked with an ambulance unit in France, then as an Official War Artist, later running a unit which decorated canteens for the 8th Army in Africa and Italy. Before the war Lambourn had shown in London, having a solo exhibition with Matthiesen Gallery in 1938. After the war Lambourn – a multi-talented man of strong views, a black belt at judo, an intellectual, an enthusiast for amateur dramatics – decided to settle in west Cornwall, having years before fallen in love with Mousehole. He was commemorated by a show at Gordon Hepworth Gallery, Exeter, in 1991. Imperial War Museum and Tate Gallery hold his work.

Nigel LAMBOURNE 1919–1988 Draughtsman, printmaker, book illustrator, designer and teacher, born in Croydon, Surrey. He studied, 1934–7, at Regent Street Polytechnic School of Art and Central School of Arts and Crafts, then from 1937–9 at Royal College of Art with Robert Austin and Malcolm Osborne. After Army service in World War II completed his degree course at Royal College of Art. While still at College he taught at Isleworth Evening Institute, later appointments being at Guildford College of Art, 1951–61, and Leicester Polytechnic, 1962–72. In the late-1940s began to establish a name as an illustrator of books and magazines and for leading advertising agencies. Soon became a member of Senefelder Club and RE. Had his first solo exhibition at Kensington Art Gallery in 1949, later one-man exhibitions including Wilton and Zwemmer Galleries. In 1950–1 worked on Festival of Britain South Bank Exhibition. Lambourne was a masterly draughtsman, with a taut, springing line, shown to great effect in his drawings of low life and the female figure. He died at Oakhill, near Bath, Avon, and in 1992 Victoria Art Gallery, Bath, held a show of his work. Abbott and Holder showed examples in 2005. Arts Council, Contemporary Art Society and Museum of Modern Art, New York, hold examples.

Edie LAMONT 1896–1983 Artist in pen and ink, watercolour and oil, and collector, born in Carnoustie, Angus. In the mid-1930s she studied at St John's Wood Art Schools under Patrick Millard, fellow-students being Robin Treffgarne and John Minton, whom she helped and collected and whose work influenced her own. She showed with St John's Wood Group at Wertheim Gallery, also with Leicester Galleries and LG. Lamont was married to businessman Newton Lamont, who died in 1960. Lived at Chart Sutton, near Maidstone, Kent, a neighbour and friend of Harold Nicolson, in whose diaries she appears, and Vita Sackville-West, whose white garden she painted. Interested in gardening, Edie indexed Sackville-West's articles about it and she was the dedicatee of Vita's 1961 novel *No Signposts in the Sea*. In the year she died Anthony Dawson, of Barnes, organised an exhibition of Lamont's work.

John Charles LAMONT 1894–1948 Painter who studied at Glasgow School of Art under Maurice Greiffenhagen and Fra Newbery. Exhibited RSA, Walker Art Gallery, Liverpool, and Royal Glasgow Institute of the Fine Arts. Lived in Kirkcudbright, Scotland.

Nancy LAMPLUGH 1912– Artist and teacher, born in Croydon, Surrey, educated at the Royal College of Art. She was head of the textile department of Hull College of Art, 1944–76. There was a retrospective at the Ferens Art Gallery, Hull, 2000–1.

Francesca LA NAVE 1954– Artist, art psychotherapist and teacher, born in Florence, Italy, where she matriculated from scientific secondary school in 1973. Joined the Quatenary Era Institute, a scientific research project, concerned with studying prehistoric ecosystems and graffiti, with which she travelled to several national parks and the Algerian Sahara. Moved to London, in 1982 she graduated with credit in fine arts at Chelsea School of Art. Was a founder-member of Pyramid Arts Development, multi-cultural arts group in Hackney, between 1984–5 coordinating community projects for Borough of Islington. She supported her art with teaching, translation and market research. In 1989, La Nave became artist-in-residence at Homerton Hospital psychiatric department. Having studied art psychotherapy at Goldsmiths' College, 1992–6, she worked as an art psychotherapist in adult psychiatry and special education. Took part in group exhibitions in London and Edinburgh, also Unquiet Voices, Doncaster Museum & Art Gallery, 1997. Had solo exhibitions in Verona and London. From 1995, La Nave's work changed dramatically to include writing, video and sound, evolving towards multiples and multimedia installation. Lived in London.

Brian Christy LANCASTER 1931– Painter, illustrator and designer, born in Atherton, Lancashire, with a special interest in steam locomotives. Studied at Bolton School of Art, 1946–9, with John Gauld; Southport School of Art, 1949–52; and Manchester School of Art. Showed RI, RBA, RWA, Atkinson Art Gallery, Southport, and elsewhere. Bristol Museum holds his work. Lived at North Nibley, Gloucestershire.

Edward Purser LANCASTER 1911–1954 Painter, printmaker, designer, mural artist and teacher. Studied at Southport, Liverpool and Chelsea Schools of Art. Eventually taught at London School of Printing and Graphic Arts. Exhibited Goupil Gallery, Atkinson Art Gallery, Southport, elsewhere in the north of England, in London, Paris and New York. General Post Office and Southport Corporation bought his work, which was also reproduced by the London Passenger Transport Board. Lived in London and Bognor Regis, Sussex.

James LANCASTER 1960– Artist, born in St Albans, Hertfordshire, who studied graphic design at Goldsmiths' College School of Art in the early 1980s. He worked as a photographic hand printer in London for eight years before concentrating on his own mysterious, luminous, Symbolist drawings and video works. Lancaster's figures stemmed from his imagination. He was "mostly obsessed with the body and how to show its mysterious allure, and the physicality, sensuality and subconscious imagery associated with it." In 2001 Lancaster's work appeared in Private Worlds, Outsider and Visionary Art at Orleans House Gallery, Twickenham and Loughborough University, and Obsessive Visions at England & Co. That gallery showed his Nocturnal Drawings in 2002.

John LANCASTER 1953– Painter and draughtsman, much of whose work explored architectural themes, born in Derby. He attended Medway College of Design, 1979; Winchester School of Art, 1979–82, in 1982 gaining a Drawing Prize; and Royal College of Art, 1983–6. Among a series of awards was Rome Scholar in Painting, British School at Rome, 1986–8, and a fellowship in painting, Gloucestershire College of Art and Technology, 1988–9. Group exhibitions included Robert Colquhoun Memorial, 369 Gallery, Edinburgh, 1980; Northern Young Contemporaries, Whitworth Art Gallery, Manchester, 1981; Artists in Residence Show, Axiom Gallery, Cheltenham, 1993; and Beatrice Royal Gallery, Eastleigh, 1998. Had a solo show at Benjamin Rhodes Gallery, 1989, later ones including Sacred Interiors at Peterborough Museum & Art Gallery, 1999, and Krefelder Kunstverein, Krefeld, Germany, 2000.

Laura LANCASTER 1979– Painter whose small works were given a show at Curwen Gallery in 2003. Of these, she said: "My paintings are based upon the discarded snapshots I find in junk shops and flea-markets. The painting process allows me to examine these images and the endless number of possible narratives of which they could be a part – exploring the paint itself as both a physical substance and the substance of illusion." Lancaster did an advanced foundation certificate at Cleveland College of Art and Design, 1997–8, graduating with first-class honours in fine art, painting, from the University of Northumbria, Newcastle, 1998–01. In 2001 she won the Unilever Fresh Graduate Award at Fresh Art, Business Design Centre, Islington.

Lilian LANCASTER 1888–1975 Artist and teacher who studied at the Slade School of Fine Art, 1906–10, under Henry Tonks and Fred Brown, then at the Royal Academy Schools, 1910–14, Walter Sickert a notable teacher. She was married to the artist and teacher Clive Gardiner, her son being the writer Stephen Gardiner, who remembered that Sickert "regarded Lilian as his favourite pupil. He gave her one of his paintings, nude on bed, Camden Town period. Most of all, she admired the French Impressionists and Van Gogh and, of the Impressionists, Renoir was certainly an influence." Lancaster taught at Eastbourne College of Art, 1916–21. She exhibited at the RA Summer Exhibition and NEAC, of which she was a member, receiving excellent reviews in newspapers and art periodicals. In 1960, after Clive Gardiner's death, she moved to Wytham, Oxfordshire. Manchester City Art Gallery acquired her work.

Mark LANCASTER 1938– Versatile painter, printmaker, designer and teacher, born in Holmfirth, Yorkshire, who studied at the University of Newcastle upon Tyne, 1961–5. He taught at Newcastle and Bath Academy of Art; won the Purchase Prize at the Second British International Print Biennale at Bradford; and was artist-in-residence at King's College, Cambridge, 1968–70. In 1971 Editions Alecto issued a series of Henry VI lithographs by Lancaster alluding to paintings completed during the residency. His exhibitions included Rowan Gallery and Magdalene Street Gallery, Cambridge. While in New York appearing in films and working at The Factory, Andy Warhol's studio, Lancaster met other notable American artists, including Jasper Johns. He settled in New York in 1972 and from 1973–98 designed costumes, lighting and sets for the Merce Cunningham Dance Company, also being Johns' secretary, 1974–85. Lancaster's work is in many collections. The Tate Gallery holds a group, and the Victoria & Albert Museum, British Council and Museum of Modern Art in New York have examples.

Osbert LANCASTER 1908–1986 Cartoonist and social satirist, painter, theatrical designer and writer, born in London. After attending Oxford University, 1926–30, he was at Byam Shaw School of Drawing and Painting, 1925–6, the Ruskin School of Drawing, in Oxford, 1929–30, then the Slade School of Fine Art, 1931–2. In 1932 and 1934 he showed at NEAC, but then forsook easel painting for murals, book illustrations and writing, from 1934–9 being on the staff of the *Architectural Review* while doing some university lecturing. Wrote authoritatively but wittily on architecture in such books as *Homes, Sweet Homes* and *Drayneflete Revealed*. In 1939 was appointed cartoonist on the *Daily Express*, where he chronicled the adventures of the Littlehamptons in his Pocket Cartoon. Designed for all the major British opera and ballet companies. Tate Gallery holds his work. Knighted in 1975.

Percy LANCASTER 1878–1951 Landscape, painter and etcher, born in Manchester. Originally trained as an architect, but turned to art and attended Southport School of Art. Exhibited prolifically, especially RI, RBA, Walker's Galleries and RCamA. Had solo show at Walker's Galleries. Medici Society prints were made of his pictures, which are in public galleries in Manchester, Oldham, Preston and Rochdale. Lived in Southport.

Marjorie LANCE 1900– Versatile painter brought up in Hatfield, Hertfordshire, who married the miniature painter H Carlyon Webb. She studied at the Slade School of Fine Art with Henry Tonks, Philip Wilson Steer and John Wheatley, 1920–3. Exhibited Goupil Gallery, NEAC, RBA, PS and in the provinces. Showed solo at St George's and Woodstock Galleries. Lived in Stanmore, Middlesex.

Colin LANCELEY 1938– Painter, construction artist, printmaker and teacher, born in Dunedin, New Zealand. He studied at National Art School in Sydney, 1956–60, teachers including John Passmore and John Olsen. He first appeared at Annandale Imitation Realist show at Museum of Modern Art, Melbourne, 1962. Work early showed influence of American Pop Art, from which he moved into junk and assemblage art. Lanceley was awarded the Contemporary Art Society Sydney Young Contemporaries Award in 1963, in 1964 gaining the Helena Rubinstein Scholarship. Lanceley made prints for Marlborough Fine Art in mid-1960s which were well received. He taught for a time at Chelsea School of Art, then returned to Australia. Museum of Modern Art in New York, Tate Gallery and a number of Australian and continental European galleries hold examples. Lived latterly in Sydney.

Audrey LANCEMAN 1931– Artist noted for her watercolour depictions of London, was born and lived there. Studied at Nottingham College of Art and Heatherley's School of Fine Art. She lived in Canada, 1960–5. Won the Lord Mayor's Art Award for two consecutive years; took part in a four-man show at Thackeray Gallery, 1977; and had a series of solo exhibitions in Britain, France, Canada and Sweden.

Reginald LANDER 1913–1982 Artist and designer in gouache, watercolour and black-and-white, Lander was born and lived in London. Studied at Hammersmith School of Art, was during the 1930s chief designer and manager of the Ralph Mott Studio. After World War II went freelance. Government ministries and British Railways used his work.

William LANDLES 1923– Sculptor, born in Hawick, Roxburghshire, whose early exhibited work prompted an Andrew Grant Bequest for studies at Edinburgh College of Art under Eric Schilsky, 1951–6. After his diploma, Landles developed abstracted work in a range of materials, from 1977 changing course to produce figurative bronzes. He was elected a professional member of SSA in 1986 and of SSWA in 1994. Also showed at RSA, Royal Glasgow Institute of the Fine Arts, Aberdeen Artists' Society, Scottish Sculpture Workshop and Scottish Art Exhibition at Gatwick Airport, 1986. In 1996 was included in a three-artist show at Kingfisher Gallery, Edinburgh. Commissions included portraits and the Scottish Junior Rugby Trophy for the Royal Bank of Scotland. The Will H Ogilvie Memorial near Ashkirk, Roxburghshire, was completed in 1994, the Ogilvie Memorial at Bourke, New South Wales, Australia, in 1995.

Christopher LANDONI 1972– Painter, born in Blackpool, Lancashire, who studied at Düsseldorf Kunstakademie, Germany, 1998–9. He took part in group shows, including Civilia, Bluecoat Gallery, Liverpool, and East International, Norwich (in which he won the EASTwork 2004 award), both 2003, and John Moores Liverpool Exhibition, 2004. Among Landoni's solo exhibitions were the project Untitled, Cologne, and Düsseldorf Kunstakemie, 1999; Wunderland International 3, Manchester, 2001; Coma, Parkhaus, Düsseldorf, 2002; and Museum 52, 2004.

Alex LANDRUM 1955– Painter, born in Wallasey, Cheshire, who studied fine arts at Leeds Polytechnic, 1984–7; at Chelsea College of Art, 1987–8 and 1989–90, where he gained the Burston Award and received his master's degree in history of art and sculpture; and at Goldsmiths' College, 1990–2. Landrum's works included Minimalist diptychs in household paints, the artist considering his pictures mainly objects, "images of sculpture". He was included in Young British Artists, Saatchi Gallery, 1992; Mandy Loves Declan 100%, Mark Boote Gallery, New York, 1993; Moby Dick, John Hansard Gallery, Southampton, 1996; and John Moores Liverpool Exhibition, 1997–8. Had a solo show at Lisson Gallery, 1992, later ones including Perfect Accident, The Tannery, 1996. Lived in London.

Michael LANDY 1963– Artist who employed various media including photography, born in London. He studied at Loughton College of Art, 1979–81, Loughborough College of Art, 1981–3, then graduated with honours from Goldsmiths' College, 1985–8. Took part in many mixed shows, including Showroom, 1987; Show and Tell, Riverside Studios, 1988; and Multiples, Hirschl & Adler Modern, New York, 1990. Had solo show at Gray Art Gallery, New York, and Karsten Schubert Ltd, both 1989; Studio Marconi, Milan, and Tanja Grunert, Cologne, both 1990. In 1992 Landy's installation Closing Down Sale, at Karsten Schubert, used the paraphernalia of low selling to reflect the recession in the art market with a garish wit. Scraphead Services, at Tate Gallery in 1999, was an installation of mannequins. In 2001, Landy made news by destroying all his possessions in a specially made grinder inside the old C&A building in Oxford Street. Break Down was "all about society's romance with consumerism." Landy's first solo show at Maureen Paley/Interim Art, in 2002, coincided with the publication by The Paragon Press of the *Nourishment Portfolio*, etchings of resilient weeds in urban settings. In 2004 Landy was commissioned to provide a new work for Tate Britain's Duveen Galleries. The installation was a replica of his parents' house made with and about his father who, after injuring himelf, remained confined to home.

Abigail LANE 1967– Sculptor, born in Penzance, Cornwall. She studied at Bristol Polytechnic, 1985–6, then Goldsmiths' College School of Art, 1986–9. Participated in the group show Freeze in 1988, then others in Britain, continental Europe and America. In 1993–4 she was part of the Arts Council's touring exhibition Recent British Sculpture. Had a solo show at Karsten Schubert Ltd in collaboration with Interim Art, another at Victoria Miro, 1998. Lived in London. Another exhibition there, 2001, extended "her preoccupation with the fantastical, the Gothic and the uncanny through a trio of arresting and theatrical installations based around film projections."

Christopher LANE 1929– Sculptor, ceramist and teacher, born in Gloucestershire, who studied at Reading University and Royal College of Art. He taught at Berkshire and St Alban's Colleges of Art, then at Reading University. Exhibited at Woodstock, Bear Lane in Oxford and Reading Municipal Galleries, at ICA, AIA, Wadham College in Oxford and University of Wales, Bangor. Some of Lane's work shown in London Artists, Shrewsbury School, in 1968 was "concerned with an interest in the power of recreation in nature".

Richard LANE 1926– Painter, teacher and photographer, born in Mwanza, Tanganyika, who studied at Oxford University, 1948–51, after the Royal Navy. Lane attended Slade School of Fine Art, full- and part-time, 1952–5; taught at Haileybury public school for three years; developed fine art photography for three years; then taught at Christ's Hospital, 1961–85. From 1961–9 he worked with Nell Todd at the art school there, "a genius of a teacher of all ages". His exhibitions included Young Contemporaries, RA, Christ's Hospital Arts Centre in 1970s and Woodstock Gallery, 1982. Latterly lived at Falstone, Hexham, Northumberland. His work is in private collections in Britain, France and America.

Richard Patrick LANE 1922– Painter, notably of landscape, who studied at Shrewsbury Art School and Anglo-French Art Centre. Took part in mixed exhibitions including RA and London Artists at Shrewsbury School, 1968. Lived for a time in London.

Daniel LANG 1935– Painter who was born in Tulsa, Oklahoma, in America. He was educated at the North-Western University, the University of Tulsa and University of Iowa. He showed at William Hardie Gallery in Glasgow. Work is represented in many public collections, including the Metropolitan Museum and the Museum of Modern Art, New York, and the Hunterian Art Gallery, Glasgow. Lang was a frequent visitor to Scotland, dividing his time between New York and his home in Montone, Umbria.

George LANG 1902– Self-taught painter and illustrator, a perfectionist for detail, born in London where he lived for many years. Showed RMS of which he was a member, RI, RWS, RCamA, PS, widely elsewhere in England and at Paris Salon, where he won an Hon. Mention in 1951. From 1959 Lang lived in South Africa, initially based in Cape Town, but otherwise a nomad. He showed generally with The Everard Read Gallery in Johannesburg; it included Lang in its Eric Heilbronner exhibition in 1981, about the time that it lost touch with Lang. Lang's wife Madge executed the sculpture of a gold prospector in front of Corner House, Johannesburg.

Margaret LANG 1936– Printmaker and teacher who studied at Oldham School of Art, 1952–4, St Martin's School of Art, 1954–6, and Manchester College of Art, 1956–7, becoming a lecturer in art and design at Wirral Metropolitan College. Showed in northwest of England, including Artists of Wirral at Williamson Art Gallery, Birkenhead, and in Etching at the Bluecoat, Liverpool, both 1984; and Merseyside Artists 3, toured by Walker Art Gallery, Liverpool, 1986–7.

Wharton LANG 1925– Sculptor in wood, son of Faust Lang, also a wood sculptor, and born in Oberammergau, Bavaria. He was educated at Newquay Grammar School, then attended St Ives School of Painting with Leonard Fuller, 1946, and privately with his father, 1946–9. Eventually took over father's studio at Mount Zion, St Ives, Cornwall. Was a member of RSMA and SWLA and was included in Artists from Cornwall, RWA, 1992. Ulster Museum in Belfast and National Maritime Museum in Greenwich hold his work.

Beatrice LANGDON 1898–1986 Painter who was educated at St Paul's Girls' School. Miss Langdon was a student at Vicat Cole and Byam Shaw Schools of Art. She showed at RA, ROI, RBA, in the provinces and at Paris Salon and had a solo show at Arlington Gallery. She painted in the St Ives area of Cornwall and lived for some time in London.

David LANGDON 1914– Cartoonist and advertising draughtsman who came to prominence during World War II as an officer in the Royal Air Force, holding various positions on Air Force publications. Was also cartoon adviser to Kemsley Newspapers, 1943–5. Educated in London and a member of a number of clubs there, such as the London Sketch Club and Savage Club. Exhibited in provinces, Switzerland and America, but best known for numerous cartoons in many publications, ranging from *Punch* and *Lilliput* to *New Yorker* and *Evening Standard*. His publications include *Home Front Lines* and *The Way I See It*. Lived at Southgate, Middlesex.

Edgar Mortimer LANGDON 1892–1972 Painter in oil, pastel and watercolour and lecturer by profession. He was born in Hampstead, north London, and studied at Clifton College, Bristol. Showed at RBA, RI, NS, SGA, MAFA and Paris Salon and lived at Watford, Hertfordshire.

Ilona LANGDORF-JAFFE fl. from 1970s– Artist, born in Cracow, Poland, who studied at Port Elizabeth Art School, South Africa, under Joan Wright, Alexandeer Podlushuc and Robert Brooks. She settled in England at Bournemouth, Dorset. Her solo exhibitions included Galerie Holzinger, Munich, 1982–6; Le Rouette, Paris, 1986; and Zamlodzi, Johannesburg, 1988–89. She was included in Form and Colour, Congress of Polish Culture Exhibition of Fine Arts by Polish Artists in Britain, POSK Gallery, 1995.

Lindy LANGE-GRANT 1945– Painter of stylised figures and landscapes, born in Los Angeles, California, America, who studied in the state at San Jose State College. She showed in group and solo exhibitions in Los Angeles and San Francisco and received private and corporate commissions. Lange-Grant moved to London in 1983, where she worked in oil and oil pastel on paper, drawing on what she observed and her imagination. Her work was chosen for the RA Summer Exhibition in 1986.

Martin LANGFORD 1970– Printmaker, notable for his mezzotints in a modern idiom, born in Kingston upon Thames, Surrey. He was educated at Central St Martin's and Plymouth University. Won the Gwen May Student Award and Gwen May Commemorative Award at 1995 and 1996 National Print Exhibitions respectively. Langford was a member of the RE. Other shows included Alternative Arts; Springfield Park, Hackney; Bankside Gallery; For Art's Sake, Easling; and Will's Art Warehouse. In 2002 Langford had a solo show at Printspace, having in that year gained the National Print Exhibition Printspace Award. He lived in Northolt, Middlesex.

Rembert LANGHAM 1941– Painter, sculptor, model-maker, designer and teacher, born in Somerset. Trained at Bristol Technical School, 1955–60; Birmingham College of Art, 1968–9, Falmouth School of Art, 1969–72, and Goldsmiths' College, 1972–3. In 1977 he gained a post-graduate scholarship to Skowhegan School of Painting and Sculpture in Maine, America. Langham had a varied career. He designed and built an adventure playground in Ealing, 1973; taught at Yaba College of Technology, Lagos, Nigeria 1980; designed for a number of trade exhibitions, such as the Sea Trade Fair, Barbican, 1983; and in that year worked on the film *Indiana Jones and the Temple of Doom*, creating a mechanical model of a Megasoma Elephas Beetle, also working on television commercials. Fine art exhibitions included St Helens National Sculpture Competition, Lancashire, 1974; Wapping Artists Open Studios from 1979; and Talent Store Gallery, 1981.

Mary LANGHORNE 1909– Painter, designer and teacher born and lived in Exeter. She studied at Royal Albert Memorial School of Art there, 1928–30, then Central School of Arts and Crafts, 1930–2, and showed at RI RWA, RSA and in the provinces. RWA and a number of West Country churches and Exeter Cathedral hold her work.

LANGLANDS & BELL Artists in various media. Ben Langlands was born 1955 and Nikki Bell in 1959, both in London, where they lived. Graduated with honours from Middlesex Polytechnic, 1977–80. Took part in many mixed shows, including Red Ashes, University of Reading, 1978; Sainsbury Centre for the Visual Arts, Norwich, 1980; Bookworks from 1986; Interim Art, 1990, and widely overseas. Solo shows began with Traces of Living, Interim Art, 1986; later appearances including same venue and Valentina Moncada, Rome, both 1991; Serpentine Gallery, 1996–7 and tour; New Art Centre Sculpture Park & Gallery, East Winterslow, 2001; and Alan Cristea Gallery and Petworth House, Sussex, both 2002. The House of Osama bin Laden, at Imperial War Museum in 2003, followed a commission to record post-war Afghanistan, including a visit to the Al Qaeda terrorist group leader's home at Daruntah. In 2004, Langlands & Bell were shortlisted for the Turner Prize. Saatchi Collection holds their work.

Christopher LANGLEY 1972– Sculptor, mainly in wood, carved stone and metal. He was born in Cape Town, South Africa, and attended Suffolk College, 1991–3, studying for an honours degree in art and design at University of Wolverhampton from 1994. He assisted the sculptor Bernard Reynolds, also Deirdre Saunder, in America. Langley's work was "an exploration of human psychological and emotional states as well as religion", influences, among others being "Dalí, Buddhism, Pacheco, Medieval carving and Christian art." Exhibitions included The Waterlily Foundation in Cambridge, The Art Show at Alexandra Palace and Ipswich Art Society Annual Exhibition, all 1994; and Ipswich Open (commended by Maggi Hambling), at Christchurch Mansion, in Ipswich, Suffolk, where he lived, 1995. In 1994, Langley had work commissioned for Thomas Wolsey Special School.

Jane LANGLEY 1959– Painter, teacher and printmaker, born in London. She did a foundation course at Chelsea School of Art, 1977–8, graduating with an honours degree in fine art from Camberwell School of Art, 1978–81. Between 1982–5 she obtained her master's degree in painting from Royal College of Art, along the way being artist-in-residence at Battersea Arts Centre, 1982, and winning the Henry Moore Prize for painting in 1984. She taught at Byam Shaw School of Art, 1990–1 and in 1991 gained a Sotheby's Fellowship from Central Saint Martins College of Art. From 1980 she exhibited in a wide range of mixed shows in Britain and abroad, including Camden Annual, 1985; Galerie Hilger, Vienna, 1986; Peter de Francia and his students, Camden Arts Centre, 1987; The Discerning Eye, Mall Galleries, 1991; and Bruton Street Gallery, 1992. Solo shows began with Battersea Arts Centre, 1982, later ones comprising Central Saint Martins and Etchings and Monotypes, Le Chat Noir Art Exhibitors, 1991. While in Langley's work a figure or townscape may be discerned, it is reinvented with the freedom of abstraction, vigorous brushwork and gently modulating colours conveying energy and poetry.

Winifred Norah LANGLEY 1906–1991 Painter and printmaker, educated at St Andrew's, Eastbourne. She studied at Bolt Court, 1943–6, with Sidney Tushingham; at Camberwell School of Arts and Crafts 1946–9, teachers including Victor Pasmore and William Coldstream; Brighton College of Art, 1955–7; then Brighton Polytechnic, 1958. Showed with PS; LG; Leicester, Redfern and Wertheim Galleries; and had a series of solo exhibitions. Died in Hove, Sussex.

Rowland LANGMAID 1897–1956 Painter and printmaker specialising in marine subjects, commissioned in the Royal Navy, rising to lieutenant-commander. He studied with the sea painter W L Wyllie. Showed extensively at Abbey Gallery, RA and Walker Art Gallery in Liverpool. Among prints of his pictures published by W R Deighton & Sons were *HMS* Victory *in Portsmouth Harbour* and *HMS* Victory *Under Sail*. Accuracy of detail was a characteristic of Langmaid's work. Lived in London.

Dorothie LANGRIDGE: *see* **Dorothie FIELD**

Sonia LANGRIDGE 1923– Painter, printmaker and teacher, born in Derby. She studied at Hornsey School of Art, 1938–9, Derby School of Art, 1939–43, then Slade School of Fine Art, 1943–4, where her teachers included Allan Gwynne-Jones and George Charlton. She went on to teach, in the 1940s and 1950s holding positions at Loughborough College School of Art, then at Croydon High School. Showed at Nottingham Castle Art Gallery and Museum, Blackpool's Grundy Art Gallery and elsewhere. Lived in London.

John LANGTON 1932– Painter, born in York, who trained at the local Art School and at Guildford, 1949–53. He continuously changed style and technique, 1960s abstraction giving way to figuration and narrative, with a return to the tranquillity of the formal garden and landscape in the 1990s. In the 40 years from 1961 he had nearly 70 shows, many in Germany, carried out a number of commissions in Europe and had work acquired by several public collections. The University of York made Langton an artist fellow in 1978, awarding him an honorary doctorate in 1995. Later shows included The Slow surfacing of a profound Delight, Bruton Gallery, Leeds, 2000.

Lionel LANKESTER 1904– Watercolourist and draughtsman who was by profession a physician. Born in Little Bookham, Surrey, was educated at Haileybury and Cambridge University, then studied medicine at St Thomas's Hospital, in London. Just after World War II while serving in the Army in Palestine he became interested in painting, but had little formal tuition. Showed RWS and with Guildford Art Society. Lived in Milford-on-Sea, Hampshire.

Richard LANNOY 1928– Painter, photographer and writer, born in Surrey, whose main works were large figurative paintings and triptychs in oil. In these he sought "to recreate past experiences of particularly heightened reality, especially from years spent travelling the world as a reportage photographer in the 1950s and 1960s, in a visionary style". Lannoy was taught by Paul Feiler at school; then attended Guildford Art School under Frederick Brill and Heatherley School of Art. He was on the founding staff of ICA, 1950–2, initiator of the Independent Group in the latter year. Was then a freelance photographer for magazines in Europe, the Middle East, Africa and India, publishing several books of his photographs. His *The Speaking Tree*, a study of Indian culture and society published in 1971, long remained in print. In 1984 Lannoy resumed his professional career as a painter, living in Bath, Somerset. Showed solo at Bath International Festival in 1994, in 1995 contributing to John Moores Liverpool Exhibition.

Andrea LANSLEY 1960– Painter, born in Manchester. She studied at Wirral College of Art and Design, 1987–8, and Liverpool Polytechnic, 1988–91. As a student prizewinner at Wirral she held a solo show at Williamson Art Gallery, Birkenhead, 1988. She was also a prizewinner in John Moores Exhibition, Liverpool, 1991–2. Other appearances included Whitworth Young Contemporaries, 1989, and Fresh Art Fair, Islington, 1991. Lived in West Kirby, Merseyside.

Erica Faith LANSLEY 1961– Painter of abstracts, born in Salford, Lancashire, who gained a first-class honours degree in fine art, painting, at St Martin's School of Art, 1979–82. Mixed shows included New Contemporaries at ICA, 1981; John Moores Liverpool Exhibition, 1982–3, at Walker Art Gallery; LG Open, Royal College of Art, 1987; Boundaries, Museum & Art Gallery, Brighton, 1995; and Cross Currents, Reed's Wharf Gallery at Barbican Centre, 1996, where Lansley showed paintings done in Ireland. These used an organic or calligraphic figure laid pattern-like across the surface or selectively obscured by a simplifying veil or screen.

Andrew LANYON 1947– Artist in oil, film and photography and producer of books, born in Cornwall, son of the painter Peter Lanyon. After an early enthusiasm for photography Lanyon studied at London School of Film Technique in 1966. He worked with film and photography and then turned to painting and making books, the first being *Snap*, in 1970. Other titles included *The Vanishing Cabinet*, *Paul Feiler*, *Peter Lanyon 1918–1964* and an Art-Fi series: *Deadpan*, *Second Nature*, *The Loose Connection*, *The Unjustified Text* and *The Quick Change Act*. Lanyon's pictures were often on a small scale, with a wry quality, as in his entries for Artists from Cornwall, at RWA, 1992. The Book Gallery, St Ives, held exhibitions, including 1998, of paintings and hollow books. Lanyon's retrospective 100 Hollow Books was held at bookartbookshop in 2003. He was a Newlyn Society of Artists member. British Council, Contemporary Art Society and St Ives Museum hold examples. Lived in Newlyn, Penzance, Cornwall.

Deborah LANYON 1958– Painter and draughtsman, born and lived in London, who worked with acrylic, collage and mixed media and who travelled in Italy, France and Greece, which "challenged fresh ways of seeing". Lanyon's landscapes indicated her interest in music and dance and "a need to express rhythm". They were richly coloured, with a leaning towards abstraction. Studied at St Martin's School of Art, 1977–8; under Geri Morgan at Byam Shaw School of Art, 1979–81, which underlined Lanyon's commitment to drawing; then, after work in the BBC design department, 1982–6, at Putney School of Art, 1986–90; working in Oliver Bevan's studio, 1991–4. Had a solo show at Milne & Moller, 1993, later ones including Pike Gallery, 1995, and Archeus Fine Art, from 1996, and Gallery 286, 2003.

Jo LANYON 1957– Jo was the fourth son of the painter Peter Lanyon, a self-taught artist whose mixed-media works were included in John Davies's 2004 Summer Exhibition at Stow-on-the-Wold and Upper Swell. His visual references were St Ives artists, including his father, who used "abstraction as a method and the landscape experience as a source." Jo Lanyon explained that "from walking the north and south coasts of Cornwall and Devon, mostly circular, so that I can confine myself to a certain area, I take in as much visual information as I can. This information I then formulate in my mind's eye. This process may take many weeks or even months, before I actually physically start painting. The marks I make have to be informed before the painting process can begin."

Martin LANYON 1954– Artist mainly in college and gouache, son of the painter Peter Lanyon; their paintings shared a strong gestural quality. Born in Redruth, Cornwall, Martin Lanyon was a self-taught painter, obtaining Bachelor of Science degree in physics at Queen Mary College, 1976. Went on to teach physics, eventually lecturing at Truro College. He shared shows at Gordon Hepworth Gallery, Newton St Cyres in 1991–2, then had a first solo exhibition there in 1993. Lived in St Agnes, Cornwall.

Matthew LANYON 1951– The eldest son of the painter Peter Lanyon, Matthew was born in St Ives, left Cornwall and attended Leicester University. From 1973 he travelled in Greece, Turkey and Italy, two years later visiting India, Sri Lanka and Nepal. He returned to Cornwall in 1985 and began working as a painter in 1988, his father as an influence, although his semi-abstract, Expressionist works had an individual quality. Lanyon's pictures were included in John Davies's Summer Exhibition at Stow-on-the-Wold and Upper Swell Farm in 2004. He was then "working with landscape and mythology. Two figures – male and female, and sea. It's a way to explore something, coming again to places I experienced as a child, moving between the symbolic, the imaginary and the real."

Peter LANYON 1918–1964 Painter of landscapes leaning heavily towards abstraction, printmaker, making some constructions, pottery and collage; also a teacher. Born in St Ives, Cornwall, which remained his base, Lanyon after school had lessons in painting from Borlase Smart in 1936, in 1936–7 attending Penzance School of Art, had lessons for a time at the Euston Road School in 1938, and was encouraged or taught by Ben Nicolson, Adrian Stokes and Naum Gabo. Made first constructions 1939–40, then from 1940–5 served with Royal Air Force. First one-man show at Lefevre Gallery, 1949. He was to exhibit internationally in mixed exhibitions, including West Country Landscape, Arts Council tour, 1953; Metavisual, Tachiste, Abstract, Redfern Gallery, 1957; and British Painting in the Sixties, Tate Gallery, 1963. Also extensive one-man shows in Britain and abroad. Founder member of the Crypt Group, 1946; Penwith Society, 1949; taught at Bath Academy of Art, 1950–7; elected member of the Newlyn Society, 1953; and ran the St Peter's Loft Art School, St Ives, with William Redgrave, 1955–60. Lanyon's first one-man show in New York in 1957 was well received, brought him the friendship of Mark Rothko and made Lanyon impatient with the restricted world of St Ives. But he took up gliding in 1959 to get to know better the Cornish landscape, and this brought to his work a greater feeling of sea and air and brightened his palette. Died in Taunton, Somerset, as the result of injuries received in a gliding accident; his death was a severe blow to Cornish painting. Lanyon's work is in many public galleries, including the Tate. Retrospective at Whitworth Art Gallery, Manchester, 1978, and South Bank

Centre, 1992, both with tour. Gimpel Fils, which gave Lanyon his first solo exhibition in 1952, and continued to represent his estate, held an exhibition in 2003 and in the same year Scolar Fine Art one of work on paper. The artists Matthew, Andrew, Martin and Jo Lanyon were his sons.

George LARGE 1936– Painter in watercolour and oil and teacher, born in London. He studied at Hornsey College of Art, 1958–63, teachers including Maurice de Sausmarez, John Titchell and Alfred Daniels. Large spent some time in the display department of Simpson's, Piccadilly, was part-time at Hornsey College of Art, then head of department at St Julian Comprehensive School in St Albans. Large showed 1963–87 with SWE, being vice-president in 1972 and treasurer in 1984; with RE, 1963–5; with RI from 1983, becoming a member in 1986 and its archivist; and was also made a member of the RBA in 1997. Large was winner of the Winsor & Newton Award, 1989; he won the Llewellyn Alexander and St Cuthbert's Mill Awards in 1999; and the Arts Club Award in 2003. He had a solo show at Mall Galleries in 1980, later one-man exhibitions including Duncan Campbell Fine Art from 1990. In 2000, Goldmark Gallery, Uppingham, showed Large's work, at the same time releasing its documentary film on him, *Trust Me I'm An Artist*. There was another Goldmark George Large exhibition in 2003. Edward Burra and Stanley Spencer were the main influences on Large's work, which always had people as its theme, at work or leisure, linked to their surroundings. It was an easily recognisable, colourful form of Cubism. He completed a mural for British Rail for the King's Cross Thameslink Station. Large had a house in Malta, as well as Woburn, Buckinghamshire, and his work is held by National Gallery and British Consulate in Malta.

Roger LARGE 1939– Artist born in Wallasey, Cheshire, who began painting during National Service in the Royal Air Force, then studied at Liverpool College of Art, 1960–4, and Royal College of Art, 1964–7. After working as a teacher, carver and letter-cutter, Large painted full-time from 1983, based in Watchet, Somerset. While at the Royal College Large won a landscape prize, the year after winning a life painting prize at RA. Mixed exhibitions included Piccadilly Gallery, 1967; Eye Gallery, Bristol, 1987; Bruton Street Gallery, from 1991; White Lane Gallery, Plymouth, 1992; and David Holmes Contemporary Art, Peterborough, 1996, where in a St Ives show Large exhibited pictures partly collaged with thick paint, forming blocks of discordant colour. Showed solo with Salthouse Gallery, St Ives, from 1986, later exhibitions including University of Surrey, 1992, and Plumbline Gallery, St Ives, 1995.

Patrick LARKING 1907–1981 Painter, notably of portraits, and teacher, born in Rudgwick, Sussex. He attended Christ's Hospital and worked briefly in an engineering draughtsman's office before gaining the Christopher Head Scholarship to Royal Academy Schools, 1923, studying under Charles Sims and F E Jackson. He later studied at Académie Julian in Paris before returning to London to become a pupil of Sir John Lavery. The economic depression prompted Larking to move to Canada in 1930, where he showed regularly with the Royal Canadian Academy, married Betty Burnham in 1935 and then returned to England. Larking was a keen teacher, at Heatherley's School of Fine Art and from 1949–67 at Sir John Cass School of Art. He then retired and moved to Colyton, Devon, where he lived in a small thatched cottage and held some classes, painting local characters and the landscape. Larking died shortly after his wife. A convivial man, he was a stalwart of the Chelsea Arts Club for over 50 years, being elected a life member in 1972. Larking was made a member of NS in 1947 (honorary member, 1971), ROI in 1951 and RP in 1965. Also showed at RBA and RA. A studio sale of Larking's work was held at Christie's, South Kensington, in 1982.

William Martin LARKINS 1901–1974 Printmaker, painter and teacher who was educated at Bishop's Stortford College, having been born in east London, subject of much of his work. Studied at Goldsmiths' College School of Art and was a visiting teacher at Croydon School of Art. In the 1930s worked for the advertising agency J Walter Thompson; during World War II formed a company to make films on aircraft and tank recognition; after the war for over 20 years working for *Reader's Digest* Association. Showed at RE, RA, NEAC and abroad. In 1979 Garton and Cooke held an exhibition of his etchings, which are held by British Museum and Fitzwilliam Museum in Cambridge. Lived in London for many years.

Eric LARMONT 1943– Painter in oil, printmaker, sculptor in metal and teacher, born in South Shields, County Durham. He studied at Sunderland College of Art and Goldsmiths' College School of Art, 1961–6, then at National School of Architecture and Visual Arts in Brussels, 1968–9, teachers including Anton Ehrenzweig. Those postgraduate studies were on a Belgian Government Scholarship. Larmont went on to teach part-time at Sotheby's and Putney School of Art. Group exhibitions included Sunderland Art Gallery, 1965; Ikon Gallery, Birmingham, 1976; Liverpool Academy, 1978–80; and RA Summer Exhibitions, 1981–2. Larmont had a solo show at 273 Gallery, 1968; later ones included Galerie Blankenese, Hamburg, Germany, 1984. There was a two-man show at Jonathan Poole Gallery in 1985. Carlisle Corporation holds Larmont's work. In late-1980s Larmont began working in seclusion for several years without showing, while continuing to sell prints privately in England and to make sales in Germany. Lived in London.

Gerald LARN 1932– Painter, draughtsman, designer and teacher who studied painting at Farnham School of Art for three years, obtaining a scholarship to Slade School of Fine Art. From 1960–3 showed at Temple and Redfern Galleries and Selfridges Art Gallery, then became resident artist/designer at Shepperton Film Studios, where he contributed to the production of over 40 feature films, including Roman Polanski's *Macbeth* and Charles Chaplin's final film, *The Freak*. Larn taught from 1983–91 at Leicester Polytechnic, from 1988 as part-time head of department. Enduring influences on his work were Turner's late paintings, German Expressionism, Max Ernst and the work of some early French Surrealists. Exploration of forms drawn with a pen were a key part of Larn's 1978–93 retrospective at Gagliardi Gallery, 1994. Lived in Thames Ditton, Surrey.

Dirk LARSEN 1951– Painter, sculptor and teacher, born in Copenhagen, Denmark. He studied at Birmingham College of Art, 1969–72, and Royal College of Art, 1972–5. For some years he taught alternative studies at South Glamorgan

Institute for Higher Education. His mixed show appearances included Documenta 6, Kassel; John Moores Exhibition, Liverpool, 1991–2, where his picture Friday 7 pm used a singular personal imagery; and he also did sculptural work for the Stuttgart Garden Festival, in 1992. He had solo exhibitions in Germany, the Netherlands and America. Lived in Bristol.

Marthe LARSON 1954– Painter, born in America, who studied at Ruskin School of Drawing, Oxford, 1971–3. She was represented in the 1985 John Moores Liverpool Exhibition and held a series of solo shows in London, where she lived.

Felicia LARSSON 1967– Painter, born in Sweden, who graduated in fine art from Chelsea School of Art, 1992–5, obtaining a postgraduate diploma from the Slade School of Fine Art, 1995–7. She was included in the Neurotic Realism series of exhibitions launched by Saatchi Gallery in 1999, and has work in the Saatchi Collection. Lived in London.

Karolina LARUSDOTTIR 1944– Painter and printmaker, born in Reykjavik, Iceland, whose work included stylised figures in landscape. She studied at Ruskin School of Drawing, Oxford. Was a member of RE who also showed at RA Summer Exhibitions. Had solo shows in Iceland and Denmark, ones in England including Chenil and Drian Galleries, Church Street Gallery in Saffron Walden and Bankside Gallery, 2000. Lived in Bishop's Stortford, Hertfordshire.

William LASDUN 1960– Sculptor and designer, who did a foundation course at the City and Guilds Art School, 1978–9, then a history of art honours degree, University of East Anglia, 1980–3. He was a RIBA research assistant and exhibitions organiser, 1984; worked for English National Opera, including set design, 1984–7; set up a model-making firm and worked on sculpture projects, 1988–90, expanding into construction and design, 1990–3; from then being a full-time sculptor and designer. Commissions included shortlist for Dunblane Memorial and winner of competition for Royal Sussex County Hospital, Brighton, outdoor sculpture, both 1997, and shelter for New Art Centre Sculpture Park & Gallery, East Winterslow, 1998. Exhibitions included Redchurch Gallery, Plymouth Arts Centre and Fine Art Society, all 1996, and Art97, Business Design Centre, Islington, 1997.

Jennifer LASH: *see* **Jini FIENNES**

Danuta LASKOWSKA fl. from 1950s– Artist, illustrator and designer, born in Warsaw, Poland, who spent her childhood there until settling in England in 1948. In 1952 she studied painting and illustration at Chelsea School of Art under Steven Sykes, Hans Schleger (who worked as Zero) and Brian Robb and gained her National Diploma in Design and Diploma in illustration. Laskowska worked on publicity for the cosmetics firm Elizabeth Arden, also taking on a variety of commissions including book covers and illustrations for Puffin Books, Duckworth and Heinemann and work for Marks & Spencer, Sheraton Hotels, the Polish Cultural Foundation and others. She was a member of the Society of Industrial Artists and Designers/Chartered Society of Designers and the Association of Polish Artists in Great Britain. Mixed exhibitions included Contemporary Art by Polish Artists Abroad, POSK Gallery, 1985, and she had a solo show at the Casson Gallery.

Susie LASSAM 1875– Painter of miniatures, born in Dulwich Village, southeast London. She studied at Lambeth School of Art, Central School of Arts and Crafts and Royal College of Art. Showed at RA, SM, of which she was a member, RMS, extensively at RI and at Paris Salon. Lived near Brixham, Devon.

Marie Walker LAST 1917– Painter and printmaker, born as Mary Walker in Scholes, Yorkshire. After private education and boarding school and a visit to New Zealand, during World War II she served in Women's Land Army, then as a driver for Young Men's Christian Association. From 1946–53 lived at home painting when possible, in latter year attending course in Bruges led by Jack Merriott. From 1954–6 went to summer painting courses where tutors included Robert Medley, Terry Frost and Andrew Forge, from 1955–6 attending Chelsea School of Art under Vivian Pitchforth and Edward Wakeford. She worked at New Vision Centre Gallery, 1958–60, and began abstract painting, in 1959 having first solo show at Univision Gallery, Newcastle upon Tyne. First monoprints, to become a key feature of her output, were shown. She joined WIAC, became a member of Free Painters and Sculptors and worked at Molton Gallery. In 1961 married Tom Last. Subsequent years saw Marie Walker Last travelling widely in Europe; having a first solo show in Yorkshire at Manor House, Ilkley, 1964, near where she was to live; producing series of pictures with themes such as Wing Form, Sentinel Rock and *Mary Rose* warship raising; and in 1988 winning first prize in the Druce Constable Award at Camden Arts Centre. A major exhibition was held at Leighton House in 1991 as well as a first retrospective at Dean Clough, Halifax. Her work is held by Bank of England, Bradford Art Galleries and Museums and University of Leeds.

Glenys LATHAM 1946– Sculptor and draughtsman, born in Atherton, Lancashire. She did a foundation course at Bolton College of Art, then a sculpture and life drawing diploma at Wolverhampton College of Art and a Certificate in Education at Manchester College of Art. Latham said that for her drawing had "a central and sustaining activity in my artistic endeavours – it is as relevant to my sculpture as eating is to staying alive." She took part in Drawing Towards Sculpture at Isis Gallery, Leigh-on-Sea, in 1993. Other group shows included Turnpike Gallery, Leigh, 1979; Drumcroon Education Art Centre, Wigan, 1981, and MAFA Open annually from that year; Blackheath Gallery, 1988, and elsewhere. Solo shows included Rochdale College of Art, 1983.

John LATHAM 1921–2006 Artist and teacher, born in Africa, who studied at Chelsea School of Art, 1946–50. From 1966–7 he taught at St Martin's School of Art. Latham was regarded as a pioneer of Conceptual Art and developed his Time-Base Theory, said to contain the seeds of human salvation, and this he proselytised for many years. Latham was sceptical about the value of books, which he called Skoob. While at St Martin's he and a group of students chewed pages from the art critic Clement Greenberg's book *Art and Culture*, spat the result into a bowl, the contents being fermented in acid and distilled into a phial. Latham was dismissed, as the book had come from the School library. Latham designated the phial and his dismissal documents a work of art, acquired by Museum of Modern Art, New York. Latham had first one-man show at ICA in 1960. Began steadily to exhibit overseas, in mixed and solo shows, notably in America, his work continuing in an iconoclastic vein. Retrospective at Museum of Modern Art, Oxford, 1991. In Freezeframe at Lamont Gallery, 1996, relief sculpture and films by Latham were included. In 2005, Latham had a solo exhibition at Lisson New Space, works from the series God is great, which featured the sacred texts of Judaism, Christianity and Islam, plus new pieces, including one of broken glass. Tate Britain had just bought the archive of The Artist's Placement Group, formed in 1966 by Latham and his wife Barbara Steveni to place artists in government, commerce and industry. A major Latham exhibition at Tate Britain took place in 2005–6. Lived in London.

Wilde LATHAM 1931– Painter, born in Worcester as Harold Victor Latham. He studied with Harry Adams at Worcester College of Art and at Malvern College of Art and lived for a time at Malvern Link, Worcestershire, being a member of Malvern Art Club, also showing elsewhere in the Midlands. From 1988, Latham painted the landscape and wildlife of Africa. He showed at Mall Galleries from 1989; with The East African Wildlife Society, in 1991 winning an award at its Whaletail Exhibition in Nairobi, Kenya; with Gallerie Kornye, Fort Worth, Texas, in America, 1999–01; and from 1999 at the First Texas Council of Camp Fire Exhibition, also in Fort Worth. Latterly lived in Ludlow, Shropshire.

William LATHAM 1961– Creator of computer-generated forms, born in Wallingford, Oxfordshire, married to the artist Belinda Channer. Latham started painting at 13, won a scholarship to Stowe School, a first-class degree in fine art at Oxford University and a Henry Moore Scholarship to Royal College of Art, 1982–5. Having started to create on paper a huge family tree of shapes, Latham applied to IBM for help and was made a research fellow, 1987–94. One spin-off was Mutator, a sophisticated computer programme with many potential applications. Latham had touring shows in Japan, Germany, Australia, France and Britain. In 1995 had an exhibition of works on cibachrome and in videos at Harriet Green Gallery which coincided with establishment of Latham's company Computer Artworks Ltd. Lived in Brighton, with studios there and in London. Leeds Museums and Galleries hold his work.

Kwai LAU 1967– Artist, born in China, who attended Wolverhampton School of Art and Royal Academy Schools. Her art, tending towards abstraction, took her "into unknown places ... a journey towards a magical space that I am yet to discover". Awards included André Dunoyer de Segonzac Scholarship; Celia Walker Drawing Prize; Leverhulme Trust Award; and *The Antique Collector* Prize. Group exhibitions were New British Art, Mall Galleries, and RA Summer Exhibition, from 1990, in London, where the artist lived; Beyond Chinese Takeaway, Chinese Arts Centre, Manchester, 1992; Tricycle Gallery and University of Essex touring exhibition, both 1995.

Carl LAUBIN 1947– Painter and architect, born in New York, America, who gained his architecture degree from Cornell University College of Art, Architecture and Planning in 1973, the year he moved to England. Joined the architectural and civic design firm Douglas Stephen and Partners; then Jeremy Dixon/BDP in 1984; produced paintings of the Royal Opera House project for Dixon, and began painting full-time in 1986. When Laubin had his exhibition at Wigmore Fine Arts in 1997, Gavin Stamp described him as "without doubt, the most accomplished and imaginative architectural artist working in Britain today". As well as taking part in group shows, such as RA Summer Exhibitions; National Trust Exhibitions; A Vision of Britain, Victoria & Albert Museum, 1989; and La Ville Moderne en Europe, organised by Centre Pompidou in Tokyo, 1996, Laubin completed an impressive list of commissions. These included Château Pichon Longueville; Museum of Scotland; Museum of London (purchase); Royal Armouries; and for Linklaters and Paines his singular panorama The Square Mile. There was a solo show at Plus One Plus Two Galleries in 2002. Lived in Hitchin, Hertfordshire.

Kenneth LAUDER 1916–2004 Painter in oil and watercolour, notable for landscapes, and teacher, born in Edinburgh. He studied at Chelsea School of Art and Royal College of Art, 1933–9, teachers including Robert Medley, Graham Sutherland, Gilbert Spencer and Percy Horton, serving as a pilot in Royal Air Force, 1939–45. Painted and taught in the Isle of Man and Gloucestershire, being senior lecturer in art, Liverpool, 1963–9. Earlier influences on Lauder's work were the later work of Turner in watercolour, while in oil his influence was Braque. Interest in Klee and Kandinsky came later and a visit to Australia in 1986 was important. Earlier themes were concerned with the horizontal and individual isolation, later work leading on to the duality of imagine and interpretation. Mixed exhibitions included Agnew, Scottish Gallery in London and Edinburgh, Harris Museum and Art Gallery in Preston, RA, RWA, Liverpool Academy and elsewhere. Had a solo show at Broadway Gallery, Worcestershire, 1965, later ones including Scottish Gallery, 1990, and Galeries Christiane Cloots, Brussels, 1995. Rhode Island School of Design in America holds his work. Lived in Herefordshire, where there was a retrospective at The Library Gallery, The Buttercross, Leominster, in 2005. New Directions, recent paintings, had been held at The Gallery, Kidderminster Library, in 2003.

June LAUNDER 1954– Painter who studied at Bournemouth & Poole College of Art and Design under Brian Graham and Peter Joyce. Launder lived in Dorset, painting landscape in a composed, singular style, with emphasis on texture and her own characteristic colour range. Exhibitions included Hyde Park Gallery, 1996; the RWA, from 1997; Gordon Hepworth Gallery, Newton St Cyres, from 1998; and Maltby Contemporary Art, Winchester, from 1999. She was included in Dorset Open Studios and Exhibitions, 2004, showing at Artworks Gallery, Portland.

Martin LAURANCE 1953– Artist working in acrylic and mixed media on canvas and paper whose colourful, energetic landscapes and seascapes had a strong textural element. Laurance studied at Ipswich and Norwich Schools of Art and at the University of East Anglia. Mixed shows included RI at Mall Galleries and The One and Only Print Show, Contact Gallery, Norwich, both 1992; Three Norfolk Artists, Theatre Royal, Norwich, 1996; Eastern Open, Fermoy and Red Barn Galleries, King's Lynn, from 1998; Recent Acquisitions, Deloitte and Touche, Zürich, Switzerland, 2000–1; and Field Dalling Gallery, 2001. Among his later solo exhibitions were Frames Gallery, Norwich, from 1999, and The John Russell Gallery, Ipswich, 2002 and 2004.

John LAURIE 1916– Painter and teacher, born in Shrewsbury, Shropshire. He was educated in Glasgow, then attended the School of Art there, 1933–6, and at Patrick Allan-Fraser School of Art, Hospitalfield, Arbroath, 1938–40, with James Cowie. Won RSA Carnegie Travelling Scholarship in 1939. He was for periods a lecturer at Glasgow School of Art and a lecturer for the Arts Council. Exhibited RSA, SSA, Royal Glasgow Institute of the Fine Arts and elsewhere. A number of his works, including a portrait of James Cowie, were reproduced. Lived in Glasgow.

Kathleen Frances LAURIE 1900– Painter and English teacher who was for some years involved in psychiatric social care work. She was brought up in Ceylon and was educated at London University and London School of Economics. Only in 1946–7 did she attend Oxford Art School, then 1947–9 Ruskin School of Drawing there, her teachers including Peter Greenham, Albert Rutherston and Percy Horton. Favouring watercolour and wash drawings, Laurie exhibited widely, including Oxford Art Society, RWA, RA and ROI. Lived in Beckenham, Kent.

Simon LAURIE 1964– Maker of wooden constructions, watercolourist and collagist, born in Glasgow. He studied at the School of Art there, 1983–8, gaining his fine art degree and completing postgraduate studies. In 1990 he was prize winner at the Royal Glasgow Institute of the Fine Arts. Laurie's great preoccupation was with the sea and man's relationship with it over thousands of years. From 1987 he began to show in many group exhibitions: at New Generation at Mercury Gallery in London and Edinburgh; Sue Rankin Gallery; in 1989 at New Scottish Art at Barbizon Gallery, Glasgow, and Fruitmarket Gallery, Edinburgh; and in 1990 at Surrealist Tendencies at Open Circle, Glasgow. In 1991 Laurie had a one-man show at Mercury Gallery. Later shows included the RSW and Royal Glasgow Institute of the Fine Arts, of both of which he was a member, and 200 Years of Scottish Painting, Panter & Hall, 2003, which that year held a solo exhibition of Laurie's Cabinet Paintings. The Contemporary Art Society, Aberdeen Art Gallery, Ferens Art Gallery in Hull and Unilever held examples.

William LAURIE 1921– Painter, printmaker and teacher, born in Birmingham. He studied at the College of Art there under Harold Holden, 1937–41, then in 1948 at University of Florence. Showed at Archer Gallery and elsewhere. Lived in London.

Anna LAURY 1917– Artist, born in Cracow, Poland, who moved to England in 1940, settling in London. She began painting in 1978, attending Putney School of Art for drawing, life drawing, painting and etching classes. Laury had solo exhibitions at POSK Gallery in 1987 and 1994 and in 1995 was included in its show Form and Colour, Congress of Polish Culture Exhibition of Fine Arts by Polish Artists in Britain.

Alfred J LAVENDER 1899–1966 Painter, illustrator, printmaker and teacher, born at Gosforth, Northumberland. He was educated at Bede College, Durham University, and at Newcastle University Art Department. From 1927–64 was a teacher at Swansea Grammar School and part-time lecturer at Swansea College of Art. Showed at RCamA, SWG, London Sketch Club and with Swansea Art Society, of which for a time he was secretary. Illustrated the book *A Guide to Gower*, by J M Williams, published in 1965. Lived in Swansea for many years but died in Cambridge.

Cyril LAVENSTEIN 1891–1986 Painter and teacher, born in Birmingham, who was especially noted for his watercolours and pastels of Cornish coastal scenes. At the age of 11 he entered Birmingham School of Art, then strongly under the influence of the Arts and Crafts Movement, where his studies included subjects such as stained glass and where fellow-students included Gerald Leslie Brockhurst and Henry Rushbury. Lavenstein was among the most distinguished students, winning a bronze medal in 1908 and a silver in 1910. Went on to teach at Kidderminster School of Art, having served as a driver in Salonika in World War I, remaining at the School until 1954. Exhibited RA, NEAC, RSA, Paris Salon and elsewhere. In 1930 was elected a member of RBSA, which in 1938 exhibited his works. A second Birmingham exhibition in 1984 led to a television documentary about his life and work. Lived in Kidderminster, Worcestershire.

Barbara LAVERY fl. from early 1990s– Mixed-media artist and organiser of workshops in England and Ireland, Lavery completed her foundation certificate at University of Ulster, Belfast, in 1988. After gaining a degree in fine art from Newcastle upon Tyne Polytechnic in 1991 she won her master's in fine art from Birmingham Institute of Art and Design in 1994. In 1993 she received the Great Britain and Northern Ireland Humanities Bursary. Showed in the northeast of England, in London and Ireland. Appearances included No Access at Ross' Court, Belfast, 1992; Vessels at Eagle Works Gallery, Wolverhampton; and in that year Works on Paper and Beyond the Partitions, both put on by Queen Street Studios, Belfast, with which she was associated.

Andrew LAW 1873–1967 Painter and teacher, born in Kilmaurs, Ayrshire. Studied at Glasgow School of Art, 1890–6, under Fra Newbery, then in Paris for a year. He continued to live in Glasgow, taught for many years at the School of Art and was a member of Glasgow Art Club. Exhibited RSA extensively, also at Royal Glasgow Institute of the Fine Arts, Paris Salon and in the English provinces. Art galleries in Southport, Paisley and Glasgow hold his work.

Bob LAW 1934–2004 Designer, painter, draughtsman, printmaker, poet and teacher, born in Brentford, Middlesex. He was apprenticed as an architectural designer, 1949–52, studying subjects such as geometry, perspective drawing and ornithology at night school. After two years' National Service, in 1955 Law began painting in watercolour. He moved to St Ives, Cornwall, in 1957, where he learned to pot, began writing poetry and made the first of his field drawings and paintings, paralleling American Minimalist art. Encouraged by the critic Lawrence Alloway he showed at ICA in 1960 in a two-man exhibition with Peter Hobbs; was in New London Situation at Marlborough Fine Art in 1961; then in 1962 had first solo show at Grabowski Gallery. A French Government Scholarship took Law to France in 1961–2, after which he returned to England and designed furniture, began his black series of paintings and became a visiting lecturer at Exeter School of Art, 1964–7. Law began to extend his exhibiting internationally and won a series of awards, including several from Arts Council. Selected solo exhibitions included a series at Lisson Gallery, from 1971; Museum of Modern Art, Oxford, 1974; Whitechapel Art Gallery, 1977; and Karsten Schubert, 1989. Tate Gallery and Arts Council hold his work. Law lived in Twickenham, Middlesex, in a house built to his own design, returning to Cornwall in 1997, buying a studio and house in Penzance. He was regularly involved in group shows and had a one-man exhibition at Newlyn Art Gallery in 1999 which toured to Kettle's Yard, Cambridge. In the last few years Law returned to drawing and etching, using kiss and cross symbols. Although he suffered from Dupuytren's Contracture, restricting finger movement, he worked until he died.

Deborah LAW 1951– Artist and lecturer, born in Bexleyheath, Kent, sometimes known by her maiden name Deborah Treliving. She studied at Bath Academy of Art, 1969–73, under Adrian Heath, Peter Kinley and Frank Auerbach. Law said of her work that it was "small- and medium-scale, abstract, richly coloured and textured prints in a wide range of techniques, depicting a strong sense of place and a reflective calm. A visit to Japan in 1999 had a profound influence." She lectured at South Devon College in printmaking and was a full member of the Devon Guild of Craftsmen. Group shows included Printmakers' Council National Open Print Exhibition, 1997; Nagi Moca Museum of Contemporary Art, Japan, 1999; and Imperial Hotel, Osaka, 2001. Had a solo exhibition at Daiwa Foundation, Japan House, London, 2000; and in 2001 at Plymouth Arts Centre, the Ariel Centre in Totnes, Plough Arts Centre Gallery in Torrington and Royal Albert Memorial Museum, Exeter. Lived in Torquay, Devon.

John LAW 1941– Abstract sculptor in various materials, and teacher, born in London. He studied at Bath Academy of Art, Corsham, 1960–3, then at Royal Academy of Fine Art, The Hague, Netherlands Government Scholarship, 1963–4. Returned to teach at Bath Academy, and was a visiting lecturer at Reading University and Leeds Polytechnic. Exhibitions included Constructions, Unit-Series-Progressions, Arts Council Gallery, Cambridge, 1967; Biennale de Menton, Menton, and Kunstmesse, Düsseldorf, both 1974; Constructive Rationale, Polytechnic of Central London, 1978; and Non-Standard Constructions, Museum of Modern Art, Oxford/Gardner Centre Gallery, University of Sussex, Brighton, 1980.

Margie LAW 1966– Painter who gained an honours degree from Glasgow School of Art, 1986–90. Group shows included SSA and Royal Glasgow Institute of the Fine Arts, both 1996; Art Exposure Christmas Show, 1997–8; and Aberdeen Artists' Society 64th Exhibition, 1998. Law was one of 3 Painters at Roger Billcliffe Gallery, Glasgow, 1999.

Roger LAW 1941– Artist and designer, born in Cambridgeshire who in the 1960s studied at Cambridge School of Art. He was included in Situation at RBA Galleries in 1960, worked on *The Observer* as a cartoonist, then on *The Sunday Times* colour magazine. Was involved in forming the Luck and Flaw partnership and the *Spitting Image* satirical puppet show on television. Its success led to Law being made a Royal Designer for Industry. He became artist-in-residence at the National Art School in Sydney, Australia, the first results being exhibited as Aussie Stuff at the Rebecca Hossack Gallery in 2000. Roger Law, The Land of Oz, at the Fine Art Society in 2005, showed his remarkable facility as a watercolourist, draughtsman and etcher in depicting the Australian landscape and its wildlife. In the same year, his autobiography *Still Spitting at 60* appeared.

Ruth LAW: *see* **Ruth WOODBRIDGE**

Putrisha LAWLER 1959– Artist who graduated with honours from Middlesex Polytechnic, 1979–82, gaining her master's at Royal College of Art, 1983–6. Took part in British Drawing, Hayward Gallery, 1982; Whitechapel Open, Whitechapel Art Gallery, 1983; Romantic Visions, Camden Arts Centre, 1988; and in 1989 both Ways of Telling, Mostyn Gallery in Llandudno and tour, and East End Open Studios, at Cable Street Studios.

Inger LAWRANCE 1930– Versatile artist, notable as a printmaker, born in Copenhagen, Denmark, who moved to the United Kingdom in 1950. In the 1960s she undertook a painting and printing diploma at Goldsmiths' College, then a postgraduate course there in metal construction under Kenneth Martin. In 1984 she was awarded a Churchill Memorial Travelling Fellowship, studying woodblock printing in Japan and America, about that time having her first solo shows in Cologne, Germany, and Tokyo. British one-man exhibitions included Scottish Gallery, Edinburgh; Teiko University of Japan, in the northeast of England; and Harlequin Gallery, 2002. Lawrance's work, which was abstract and inspired by the natural world, is in the Victoria & Albert Museum collection. Lawrance ran the Windmill Hole Studio at Berwick-upon-Tweed, Northumberland.

Jo LAWRANCE 1965– Sculptor and draughtsman who studied at St Martin's and Central Schools of Art, 1985–8, gaining a fine art first-class honours degree. Was at Royal Academy Schools, 1988–9, then did a higher diploma in fine art at Slade School of Fine Art, 1989–91. She produced a series of small, detailed drawings of cranes, lines and flying machines with regard to their vulnerable, comic and possibly contradictory aspects. Won a Duveen Travel Scholarship in 1990, a Cyril Sweet Award in 1991 and a Delfina Trust Residency in Spain in 1992. Exhibitions included Nine Outstanding Graduates of 1988, at Oxford Gallery, 1988; Serpentine Gallery, 1992; and Drawing Towards Sculpture, at Isis Gallery, Leigh-on-Sea, 1993.

Alfred Kingsley LAWRENCE 1893–1975 Painter of pictures and murals and draughtsman, born in Lewes, Sussex. He studied at King Edward VII School of Art in Newcastle upon Tyne under Richard Hatton, at Royal College of Art with William Rothenstein and then in Italy as a Prix de Rome winner, 1923. Elected RA in 1938. Lawrence was a fine figure painter and a RA stalwart for many years, his work having a strong underlying draughtsmanship. Also showed RP of which he was a member and widely abroad. Among Lawrence's notable murals are ones in Laing Art Gallery and Museum, Newcastle; Palace of Westminster; and Bank of England. Lived in London.

Barbara LAWRENCE 1928–1994 Watercolourist, printmaker, illustrator and teacher, born on the Isle of Wight. She studied at Portsmouth College of Art followed by teacher training at London University, also learning printmaking under Edwin La Dell at Central School of Arts and Crafts. Lawrence became head of the art department in Rochester and Tonbridge Technical Schools, and after moving to Guildford in 1956 taught adult education classes. Was an exhibiting member of the Guildford Art Society for many years, also exhibiting often at RA, RE, RBA, RWS and SWLA. Also showed at CCA Gallery in Farnham, Wintershall Gallery and University of Surrey. Landscape, buildings in landscape, wildlife and flowers were Lawrence's main subjects. She wrote and illustrated articles on wood engraving for *Artist* magazine. Guildford Borough collection holds two of her etchings. Lived in Burpham, Surrey. Her son and daughter were the artists William Edward and Sarah Lawrence.

Cyril James LAWRENCE 1926– Painter, printmaker, commercial artist and teacher, born in Grimsby, Lincolnshire. Attended Luton School of Art, 1949–52. Showed at NS, UA and RMS. Lived in Grimsby, later in Luton, Bedfordshire.

Dez LAWRENCE 1970– Artist born in Swindon, Wiltshire, who attended Glasgow School of Art, 1988–93. Mixed shows included In a Sense, at Brewery Arts Centre, 1993; and in 1994 BT New Contemporaries tour, Modern Art at Transmission Gallery in Glasgow, and also in Glasgow New Art in Scotland, Centre for Contemporary Arts. Lawrence's paintings in that show drew on the manuscripts of Modernist authors. Settled in London.

Edith LAWRENCE 1890–1973 Painter, printmaker, designer and teacher, born in Surrey, who attended Queen's College, London, until 1908. From 1910–14 she was at Slade School of Fine Art, a prizewinning student; after a period in St Ives she returned to Slade in 1916 and also studied under Percyval Tudor-Hart. Had begun showing at RA and NEAC. In 1917 began teaching art at Runston Hill School. In 1920 met the printmaker Claude Flight, in 1925 moving to his studio. The following year they had a joint show at Redfern Gallery and in Scotland, in 1927 forming an interior decorating business, experimenting with lino-cuts, textiles, picture panels and wall hangings. Shared a show at French Gallery, 1935. After bomb damage in 1943 Flight and Lawrence moved to Donhead St Andrew, Wiltshire, and when Flight had a stroke in 1947 Lawrence nursed him until 1955. After cataract removal Lawrence resumed painting, having a solo show at University of Hull, 1973. After living for about a dozen years at Worth Matravers Lawrence in 1973 moved to a nursing home in Salisbury, where she died. Shortly after, Parkin Gallery held a memorial show for Flight and Lawrence.

Eileen LAWRENCE 1946– Artist working in paint and collage on a handmade paper support. She was born in Leith, Midlothian, and studied at Edinburgh College of Art, 1963–8. She had her first solo show at 57 Gallery, Edinburgh, in 1969, the year she moved to London for three years. In 1972–3 she lived in Germany, then returned to Edinburgh. Lawrence found items such as feathers, twigs and shells and depicted them with geometrical exactness in an attempt to establish a cohesion between herself and nature. The works were likened to Tibetan prayer-sticks. Had several shows at Fischer Fine Art and exhibited at Bath Festival, 1986. Scottish National Gallery of Modern Art holds her work. Retrospective at Usher Gallery, Lincoln, 1992. Later solo shows included Art First, 2001.

G R LAWRENCE 1930– Painter, draughtsman and teacher. Born in Glasgow, where he settled. Attended the School of Art there, 1947–51, his teachers including William Armour and Ian Fleming, in 1951 attending the School of Art at Hospitalfield, Arbroath; added studies followed in the early 1960s in Italy and Greece. Showed SSA, RA and RSA and widely on the continent. Glasgow School of Art holds his work. This was sometimes signed only with initials.

John LAWRENCE 1934– Sculptor and painter, born in London, married to the artist Susan Lawrence. He studied at Bromley College of Art and showed at Trafford Gallery, with the Free Painters and Sculptors of which he was a member, in France and America. Manchester City Art Gallery and Walker Art Gallery, Liverpool, hold his work. Signed this with initials.

Peter LAWRENCE 1951– Illustrator, designer and engraver, born in Hornchurch, Essex, who studied illustration under Peter Reddick at Bristol Polytechnic faculty of art and design, 1969–73. He worked as an illustrator and designer after leaving college, becoming managing director of Oxford Designers & Illustrators, living in Oxford. Began engraving in 1990, producing abstract wood engravings from the end of the 1990s. Lawrence was a full member of both the SWE and Oxford Art Society and an associate of the Oxford Printmakers' Co-operative. He took part in SWE's annual touring exhibitions from 1993; in a group show at Bircham Contemporary Arts, Holt, Norfolk, 1999; and in 2002 was an award winner for outstanding engraving at the National Print Exhibition and exhibited at the RA Summer Exhibition. In 1999, he had a solo show at Henmans, solicitors, Oxford.

Peter Nolan LAWRENCE: *see* **SCARIX!**

Richard LAWRENCE 1955– Sculptor and teacher, born and worked in London, who studied at Hertfordshire College of Art and Design, 1978–9, then Wimbledon School of Art, 1979–82, from 1983 being a part-time lecturer there. In 1984 he won a Boise Travelling Scholarship to Italy. He was artist-in-residence at the Bath Festival in 1986 and at Christchurch Park, in Ipswich, 1988, when he showed in Carving in Christchurch. Other group shows included New Contemporaries at ICA, 1980, the year he began exhibiting at Cannizaro Park, Wimbledon; Figures in a Garden, Yorkshire Sculpture Park, 1984; and Made in Greenwich, The Living Room, 1994. Had several solo exhibitions in London and Eastbourne, including Sir Hugh Casson Gallery in the Sussex town, 1988.

Ronald LAWRENCE 1929– Sculptor, painter and teacher, born in Hopkinstown, Pontypridd, Glamorgan. Studied teacher training at St Luke's College, Exeter, then did National Service in Royal Air Force. Went on to teach, becoming head of craft and technical department at St Ilan Comprehensive School in Caerphilly. In 1965 won the Dunlop Semtex Mural Competition for a mural in Brynmawr. Showed in group exhibitions at Royal National Eisteddfod, SEA, SWG and with WAC, RA and New Art

Centre. CASW bought his copper sculpture Standing Figure.

Sandra LAWRENCE 1945– Painter and designer, born and lived in London, who studied at St Martin's and Byam Shaw Schools of Art and at the atelier of Signorina Simi in Florence, Italy. Mixed shows included the RA Summer Exhibition, RP, ROI, The Singer & Friedlander/*Sunday Times* Watercolour Competition, 1997, and The Hunting Art Prizes, from 1998. Among solo exhibitions were Fischer Fine Art, The Café Royal and Peter Hyde Fine Arts. Lawrence was noted as designer and painter of the full-size cartoons for The Overlord Embroidery, commemorating D-Day and the liberation of Europe and incorporating portraits of World War II leaders. It was claimed to be the largest of its kind in the world, 34 panels three feet high and 272 feet long overall. It was exhibited extensively internationally, having been unveiled by H M Queen Elizabeth The Queen Mother in 1978. She also opened the D-Day Museum, Portsmouth, built to house the Embroidery in 1984. The original cartoons hang permanently at The Pentagon, Washington.

Sarah LAWRENCE 1960– Artist, born in Guildford, Surrey, daughter of the artist Barbara Lawrence and sister of the painter and printmaker William Edward Lawrence. Before studying art, she worked in administration, mainly in the music business in London, then attended West Surrey College of Art & Design, 1986–7, and Dartington College of Arts, 1987–90. At college, Lawrence "specialised in relief printmaking, but on leaving became interested in working in a detailed, closely worked style, continuing to use the discipline of carefully planned design." She was "particularly interested in the use of design in the art of antiquity, such as medieval and Islamic art, in naïve and non-European art forms, and I was drawn to the art of India after travelling there in 1985–6." Studies of egg tempera and icon painting later followed. She was a member of the Association of Illustrators. Group shows included Medici Galleries, 2000; Chris Beetles Ltd, from 2000; and South West Academy, Exeter, from 2001. Lawrence lived in Ashburton, Devon.

Tory LAWRENCE 1940– Painter, notable for farm animals and landscape studies, born in London, who began painting in 1982, having brought up a family. Mixed exhibitions included RA Summer Exhibition from 1984, Angela Flowers Gallery from 1985, Lumley Cazalet Gallery, 1986, Peter Pears Gallery, Aldeburgh, 1999, and extensively elsewhere. Had an open studio show in 1985, later solo exhibitions including James Colman Fine Art, 2000, and 54 The Gallery, organised by Josie Reed, 2003. Prizes included Spink Prize for Painting, Newbury Spring Festival, 1996 (finalist, 1997–9); Royal Bath and West Society, 1997; finalist, Hunting Art Prizes, 2000 and 2001; and prize winner, Drawings for All, Gainsborough's House, Sudbury, 2002. Chelsea and Westminster Hospital holds her work. She lived and worked in Berkshire and London.

William Edward LAWRENCE 1957– Still life and urban painter and printmaker, teacher, born and lived in Guildford, Surrey, whose influences included Chardin, Morandi and Meléndez. His mother and sister were the artists Barbara and Sarah Lawrence. He attended West Surrey College of Art & Design for foundation, 1976–7, graduating with honours in fine art from there, 1977–82, notable teachers including Brad Feine and Brendan Neiland. Lawrence taught part-time for Surrey County Council from 1982, at the University of Surrey from 1991 and at Guildford College of Further & Higher Education from 1999. He carried out corporate commissions, collections holding his work including Avaya UK and Price Waterhouse. Group shows included the RWS Open from 1986; Library Gallery, Surrey University, 1988; Singer & Friedlander/*Sunday Times* Watercolour Competition, 1992; Quay Arts, Newport, Isle of Wight, 1995; and Lewis Elton Gallery, Surrey University, 1999, as well as regular exhibitions in local galleries.

Charlotte LAWRENSON 1883–c. 1971 Painter, notably of murals, and draughtsman in pencil, born in Dublin. She attended Slade School of Fine Art and Byam Shaw School of Drawing and Painting. Showed at RA, RP, Paris Salon and elsewhere abroad. Public galleries in Brighton and Bradford hold her work, which often featured domestic subjects. Lived for many years in East Africa, latterly in Nakuru, Kenya. Sometimes signed work C L.

Fenwick LAWSON 1932– Sculptor and lecturer, born in South Moor, near Stanley, County Durham, who studied with Harry Thubron at Sunderland College of Art, and under John Skeaping at the Royal College of Art. In 1957 a Sir James Knott Travelling Scholarship enabled him to travel to France, Italy and Greece. He set up a fine art course and lectured in sculpture at Newcastle Polytechnic from 1961, later being made head of sculpture and remaining there for 25 years. After retirement, Lawson was several times an artist-in-residence and from 1987–9 was a visiting lecturer at Duncan of Jordanstone College of Art, Dundee, and at the Royal Academy Schools. Showed extensively in the northeast of England from the mid-1960s. In 1994 he was invited sculptor at the RA Summer Exhibition, showing Gaia: The Scream, carved in oak. His solo exhibitions included Richard Demarco Gallery, Edinburgh, 1967–8; Durham Cathedral, 1984–96; and York City Art Gallery, 1987. Religious themes and venues were a feature of Lawson's work which was early influenced by that of Jacob Epstein and which frequently used wood. Durham Cathedral, where he had a retrospective in 2004; Brinkburn Priory near Rothbury; Pontificio Collegio Beda, Rome; and Laing Art Gallery, Newcastle, hold examples. Lived in Durham for many years.

Fred LAWSON 1888–1968 Painter, printmaker and illustrator, born in Yeadon, Yorkshire. He studied at Dewsbury Technical College, won a scholarship to Leeds School of Art, then went to South Kensington College of Art where he gained silver and bronze medals for drawing. On a painting trip to Yorkshire in 1910 Lawson chose to settle in Wensleydale, the inspiration for much of his work. He travelled extensively on the continent. Illustrated for *The Dalesman* magazine as well as a number of books, including *Dale Folk*, 1927, and is noted for his Romany drawings. Showed in his own area as well as RA, RI, Walker Art Gallery in Liverpool and Royal Glasgow Institute of the Fine Arts. Public galleries in Bradford, Leeds and Wakefield hold examples. A major retrospective was held at Middlesbrough Art Gallery in 1969 and in 1989 Lawson's work, along with that of his wife Muriel Metcalfe and his daughter Sonia Lawson, was included in A Family of Artists arranged by Wakefield Art Gallery. Died at Castle Bolton.

Ian LAWSON 1942– Printmaker, born in Leek, Staffordshire, who attended Leek and Stafford Schools of Art, taking his art teacher's diploma at Goldsmiths' College School of Art. Moved to America in 1966, working in New York with Irwin Hollander, then joined the Tamarind Lithographic Workshop in Los Angeles for six months under a Ford Foundation Scheme. There, he produced the lithograph LA 1, 1966–7, published in the latter year by Editions Alecto and in the collections of the Museum of Modern Art in New York and University of New Mexico Art Museum, Albuquerque. When he returned to London in 1967, Lawson with Ernest Donagh set up the Editions Alecto lithography studio at Kelso Place, shortly operating from his own studio in Putney. In 1975 he established a new base at Aymestry Mill, Herefordshire, where he continued to print for major British and American artists, including Ivor Abrahams, Howard Hodgkin, Allen Jones, Willem de Kooning, Roy Lichtenstein and William Turnbull.

Michael LAWSON 1944– Artist who studied at Liverpool College of Art, 1960–3, Royal College of Art, 1963–6, then University of Washington, in America, 1967. His exhibitions included Atkinson Art Gallery in Southport and Gordon Woodside Galleries in Seattle and he was represented in Merseyside Artists 3, toured by Walker Art Gallery, Liverpool, 1986–7, and a mixed show at The Living Room, 1994. Surreal distortions, humour and fantasy were aspects of Lawson's work, which incorporated comic illustrations. Liverpool University holds it in its collection.

Phyllis LAWSON 1927– Painter who was born in London and studied at Willesden School of Art. After travelling in North and South America, in the mid-1960s she settled in Brussels, Belgium, although she retained a base in Kent. Showed on the continent and in London, having shows at Ben Uri Art Society, which holds her work, in 1969, and at Fieldborne Galleries, 1975.

Sonia LAWSON 1934– Painter, printmaker and teacher, born in Darlington, County Durham, who was brought up in the Yorkshire Dales. She studied at Doncaster College of Art and then Royal College of Art, 1956–9, under Carel Weight, gaining first-class honours, a postgraduate year and a travelling scholarship to France. She lectured at the College and Royal Academy Schools. Lawson made many mixed-show appearances, including RA, Midland Group, Tolly Cobbold and John Moores Exhibition, Liverpool, 1991–2, with a powerful canvas, Grieving Women. Held her first solo show at Zwemmer Gallery in 1960, other major exhibitions including a retrospective at New City Gallery, Milton Keynes, and tour, 1982–3; Manchester City Art Gallery, 1987; and Wakefield and Bradford, 1988; and a 30-year retrospective at Dean Clough Galleries, Halifax, 1996. In 1989 with her parents Fred Lawson and Muriel Metcalfe she was included in A Family of Painters, organised by Wakefield Art Gallery. Arts Council, Open University, Imperial War Museum and many provincial galleries hold examples. Was elected RWS in 1988, RA in 1991. Lived in Leighton Buzzard, Bedfordshire.

Thomas LAWSON 1922– Painter and draughtsman, born and lived in Newcastle upon Tyne, Northumberland. Lawson spent much of his life involved in window display, having studied it at the local College of Art and Industrial Design. Later he studied art in the evenings at King's College, University of Durham, 1951–3, in the latter year winning the John Christie Prize for life drawing. He was a member of Newcastle Society of Artists and Wallsend Art Club and exhibited widely in mixed shows in the north-east, including Laing Art Gallery, Newcastle.

Winifred LAWSON DICK 1890–1978 Painter in oil who was born in London. Studied at Chelsea School of Art, 1950–5, with Brian Robb and Julian Trevelyan. Showed LG, ROI, and elsewhere in London and had solo shows at Walker's Galleries through the 1950s. Her work was featured in a number of women's magazines. She was a freeman of the Worshipful Company of Painter-Stainers and lived at Penshurst, Kent, and in London.

Brian LAWTEY 1945– Painter and teacher, born in Hull, Yorkshire, whose family settled in Oreston, Devon, 1947. Aged seven, Lawtey took up art seriously after developing asthma. Moved to St Austell, Cornwall, he attended Redruth Technical College; from 1962–5 was apprenticed to The St Austell Brewery as a pictorial inn sign painter and signwriter; and attended Plymouth College of Art part-time, exhibiting and selling work. Between 1965–72 Lawtey painted in London and Dorset and did various jobs, including technical author and illustrator. From 1973–4 he studied at Walthamstow School of Art; gained a first-class honours degree in fine art, painting, at Central School of Art, 1974–7; then pursued postgraduate studies at Slade School of Fine Art, 1977–9. Settled in north London, Lawtey was variously employed, including visiting and guest lecturing at colleges and universities. Lawtey was involved with several groups which followed on from the Systems Group, such as Group Proceedings and Series, producing his own geometrical abstracts. In 1986 he contributed theoretical studies to the publication *Constructivist Forum*. Group and collaborative exhibitions from 1970 included Claude Rogers Gallery, Bournemouth, 1970–1; House Gallery, 1981; Pallant House in Chichester and University of Leeds, both 1982; Exhibiting Space, from 1985; and A Disquieting Suggestion, John Hansard Gallery, University of Southampton, 1988. Arts Council holds his work.

Emma LAWTON fl. from 1980s– Versatile artist and teacher who gained a fine art diploma with distinction at Byam Shaw School of Art, 1983–6; was an Open University associate student in modern art and Modernism, 1991; gaining her master's in fine art at Cardiff Institute of Design & Technology, 1992–4. Awards included several WAC grants, including a travel and exhibition grant, Lodz, Poland, 1990. She was a founder-member of the Artists' Project, Cardiff, where she was based. Her teaching experience included working individually with adults who had learning problems, from 1992. Commissions included set design, Dance Alive Theatre Company, Cardiff, 1989; Avexco stands at Montreux Film Festivals, 1990 and 1993; and mirror and lass sculptures/installation, Theatre y Bryd, Cardiff, 1993. Exhibitions included Ffoto Gallery, Cardiff, 1989; Fine Art Society, painting works, 1990; and installation at Oriel, WAC Gallery, Cardiff, 1996.

Louise LAWTON 1979– Figurative artist using charcoal on gesso boards whose pictures were strongly influenced by the urban environment, notably London, New York and Hong Kong. The pattern-behaviour of crowds in the rat-race city was a theme. Lawton was born in Guernsey, Channel Islands, studied art foundation at Middlesex University and graduated from Wimbledon School of Art in 2001. She showed in London, New York and Frankfurt, work being acquired by many corporate and private collectors. In 2005 she was included in Beneath the Surface at Holman Fenwick & Willan, an exhibition curated by Headquarter Contemporary Art in association with the Albemarle Gallery.

Teresa LAWTON 1952– Painter of landscapes in which the Poole, Dorset, area where she was born and lived, forces of the elements and etching, photography and careful draughtsmanship were all influential. Lawton's life in Greece for several years and travels through Argentina, South Africa, California, continental Europe and Ireland were also inspirations. She studied at Bournemouth College of Art, graduating in fine art from Winchester School of Art, 1994. Exhibitions included Angelus Gallery, Winchester, 1993; Paint, Swanage, from 1994; The Tithe Barn, Swanage, from 1996; The Discerning Eye, Mall Galleries, chosen by the Prince of Wales, 1997; Lena Boyle Fine Art, 1998; Autumn Exhibition, The Wykeham Gallery, Stockbridge, 2001; and Highgate Fine Art, 2003.

Sue LAWTY 1954– Textile artist and teacher who used such materials as silk, linen, wool and raffia to create her landscape tapestries; these sought to give an impression visually and in texture of what it is like to be exposed to wild and barren areas. Lawty was born in Chesterfield, Derbyshire, and graduated with honours in three-dimensional design, 1976. Awards included a Royal Society of Arts Travel Award to North Africa, 1976; six Yorkshire Arts Awards, 1978–92; Yorkshire Arts Travel Award to America and selection for Crafts Council Index of Makers, both 1983; Theo Moorman Charitable Trust for Weavers Bursary, 1996; and Bankfield Museum Artist Support Scheme, 2001. Had widespread teaching experience, from 1995 being leader of textile study tours and treks to Bhutan, from 2001 on the fabric advisory committee of Wakefield Cathedral. Showed widely in Britain and North America and was included in Images of the Yorkshire Landscape, organised by Sheeran Lock at Leeds Civic Hall in 1991. Later shows included a shared one with Meira Stockl, Two Weavers: Two Ways, The University Gallery, Leeds, 2002. She lived in west Yorkshire. The British Embassy in Amman, Jordan; British High Commission in Accra, Ghana; and the Bank of the West, Texas, hold commissioned hand-woven tapestries by Lawty.

Cecil Howard LAY 1885–1956 Architect, painter, printmaker and poet, born in Aldringham, Suffolk, where he lived a countryman's life. Was educated at Ipswich School before going to the Architectural Association, but was self-taught as an artist. Was elected to RIBA in 1912, becoming a fellow in 1925. Travelled to Belgium and the Netherlands and became a friend of the painter Frank Brangwyn, who influenced Lay's work. Was a prize winner in the *Daily Mail*'s Village Sign Competition. Published seven volumes of verse, books including *Grotesques and Arabesques*, 1928. Showed at RA, NEAC, RBA, RSA, AAA, extensively in the provinces and with Ipswich Art Club and Sole Bay Group. Work was included in A Look at British Printmakers 1860–1940, at Parkin Gallery, 1981. Christchurch Mansion, Ipswich, holds his Forecasting A Loss No 2, of 1933.

Allan LAYCOCK 1928– Commercial designer and painter, born in Sutton-in-Craven, Yorkshire. He attended Keighley School of Art, 1944–6 and 1948–9, then Sheffield College of Art, 1949–50. Showed in London and at various provincial centres, being an enthusiastic member of Keighley Art Club, Norwich Art Circle and the Twenty Group in that city. Lived in Norwich, Norfolk.

Norman LAYCOCK 1920– Painter in oil and teacher, born in Dewsbury, Yorkshire. He studied at the local Technical College, then the School of Art and Crafts, 1934–9, and Royal College of Art, 1946–9. Went on to teach at Harrow School of Art and Isleworth Polytechnic. Laycock joined ROI in 1979, gained the Cornelissen Prize in 1985 and showed four pictures at the annual ROI show in October 1985. Also exhibited at RA, SEA, RBA and widely in the provinces. Had a solo show at Walker's Galleries in 1960. Lived in Stanmore, Middlesex.

Peter LAYTON 1937– Artist in mixed media and teacher, born in Prague, Czechoslovakia, of British parents. He attended Bradford College of Art, 1960–2, then Central School of Art, 1962–5, taught in America, then at Hornsey College of Art. He was included in Lane Gallery, Bradford, 1965; Berkeley Gallery, California, 1967; Commonwealth Institute and Richard Demarco Gallery, Edinburgh, both 1972; and the Hampstead Artists' Council/Scottish Arts Council 1973 show Photography into Art.

Marie LAYWINE 1937– Artist born in Cornwall, Ontario, Canada, for whom The Dream was an important preoccupation. She studied at Montreal Museum School of Fine Arts, 1960–1, with Arthur Lismer, of the Group of Seven; owned and operated a ceramic studio in Fonthill, Ontario, 1970–4, studying with Rosslyn Reed; attended McMaster University, Hamilton, Ontario, 1974–6; then pursued fine arts at Ontario College of Art, 1976–80, with a third year off-campus in Florence, Italy. In 1978 Laywine produced a limited-edition, hand-printed, hand-bound book, *Where is that Gull that Flew Overhead?*, held by Canadian public collections, including Art Gallery of Ontario. Extensive travels included France, the Middle East and the Himalayas until 1986, when she moved to Britain, settling in Abbotsbury, Dorset. As well as exhibiting widely in Canada, where in 1985 she was included in Here and Now Retrospective: 100 years of Painting, at Hamilton Art Gallery, Ontario, Laywine's appearances in Britain included the RWS, RSBA, RWA, NEAC, SGA, UA, Mall Galleries and Millfield School's Summer Exhibition. In 1993 she was acting director of Bridport Arts Centre.

Florence LAYZELL: *see* **Florence RUSHBURY**

Peter LAYZELL 1962– Painter, muralist and lecturer, strongly influenced by a Sunday painter grandfather who produced landscapes and still lifes in the manner of Cézanne. After Mander College, Bedford, 1980–1, Layzell graduated with honours in fine art from Coventry (Lanchester) Polytechnic, 1981–4. Although large, gestured canvases were then the vogue, he was encouraged by Alan Dyer to work smaller, combining his interest in Flemish Renaissance painting with an inclination towards detail and strong colour. Travel in northern Europe led Layzell to admire the work of Flemish Primitives; later, he developed an interest in English painters such as William Hogarth, Stanley Spencer, Dyer's Spencerish canvases, Anthony

Green and Mick Rooney. Layzell was a part-time lecturer at Lancaster University and Fylde College. His numerous group appearances included RA Summer Exhibition from 1987 (prize winner, 1990); Warrington Festival Exhibition, Warrington Museum Gallery, 1989 (prize winner); Houldsworth Fine Art, 1992; England's Glory, James Huntington-Whiteley, 1996; and Portal Gallery from 1998, delicately painted nudes against rich oriental fabrics, having a solo show there, 2001. In 1997, Layzell had a mural commission for Belgrade Theatre, Coventry. Morgan Grenfell, St Martin's College in Lancaster and Warrington Arts Council hold examples.

Richard LAYZELL 1949– Sculptor, happenings artist and lecturer, born and lived in London, who studied at Ealing School of Art and Slade School of Fine Art. His earlier appearances included Garden Exhibition 3 at Camden Arts Centre, 1978. By the mid-1990s Layzell had become noted for his happenings and performances, for the Tate Gallery and many other national museums and galleries, with young people, for the mentally ill, in nightclubs, in the street and in industry. *Jumbo Rumba*, to celebrate Colchester's water tower, took place in 1996; in that year (and in 1995) 100,000 people explored *Tap Ruffle and Shave*, his interactive installation for the sensory-impaired in Glasgow and the South Bank Centre; and in 1997 *Aggravation*, a video installation in collaboration with the University of the Third Age was held at the Bluecoat Gallery, Liverpool, *Infiltration*, a series of impromptu events, was based around the Warwick Arts Centre, and *Ventilation* was staged at the De La Warr Pavilion, Bexhill-on-Sea. At that time Layzell was artist-in-residence with AIT plc and a senior lecturer at Wimbledon School of Art.

Carl LAZZARI 1934– Artist and teacher, born in Newcastle upon Tyne, Northumberland, where he was mainly based. He was head of painting at Leicester Polytechnic, 1975–84; head of the department of visual and performing arts, Newcastle Polytechnic, 1984–9; from 1989 was visiting fellow and artist-in-residence at Newcastle University, from 1993 artist-in-residence at St Alban's Roman Catholic Primary School, Newcastle. Other residencies included Magdelen College, Oxford University; a period with its Aid to Bosnia, in Croatia; and Michigan State University, in America. Magdelen College holds Lazzari's sensitive portrait, oil on canvas, of Sabina Alkire. He was art director for Coventry and Brecon Cathedral Youth Theatres. Group exhibitions included Young Contemporaries, RA Summer Exhibition, British Council in Hong Kong and Brighton Museum and Art Gallery, plus regular appearances at Laing Art Competition from 1993. Solo shows included a retrospective at Leicester Polytechnic and Hatton Gallery, Newcastle University.

Frank Marsden LEA 1900– Portrait painter and commercial artist who attended Nottingham School of Art, 1916–17, after initial education in the city, then Manchester School of Art under Adolphe Valette. Most of Lea's work was commercial, but it included some magazine illustration.

Sheila LEA 1901–1992 Sculptor, born in London, who studied with Hermon Cawthra at the School of Art in Bournemouth, where she settled, also under Harold Brownsword at Regent Street Polytechnic School of Art. She exhibited at RA, until 1982–3 with Bournemouth Arts Club of which she was a member, at Paris Salon and elsewhere. Lea was noted for her portrait studies. Russell-Cotes Art Gallery and Museum in Bournemouth holds her bronze Slugs and Snails, of a kneeling woman holding up a small child.

Bernard LEACH 1887–1979 Artist and potter, born in Hong Kong, studied art at the Slade School of Fine Art, 1903, and the London School of Art. Practised etching, then went to Japan – to which he was to return on a number of occasions through his life – where he studied pottery. Returned to England where he founded and directed The Leach Pottery, at St Ives, from 1920. He exhibited widely throughout the world and was an influential teacher, conducting several lecture tours in America, sponsored by the Contemporary Art Society. His pots are in many galleries and museums. Made Companion of Honour, 1973. Wrote several books, including *A Potter's Book*, 1940, *A Potter in Japan*, 1960, and his autobiography *Beyond East and West*, published posthumously in 1985. Crafts Council held a Leach exhibition in 1998; Penlee House, Penzance, another in 2002; Bernard Leach: Concept and Form, at James Hockey Gallery, Surrey Institute of Art & Design, Farnham, 2002–3; lithographs at Curwen Gallery, 2004; and Come to the Edge, pots and tiles at Tate St Ives, 2005. Lived in St Ives, Cornwall.

Mark LEACH 1952– Self-taught artist who left a successful career in the computer industry in the 1980s to paint full-time, with a studio near Rye, Sussex. His work evolved from large, heavily textured pictures involving many materials to a sparer, minimal approach using mainly pastels. Leach won the 1993 PS Award, being elected PS in 1994, joining its council in 1997. He was joint winner of the Anthony Lester Award at the 1995 Pastels Today show; in 1996 three paintings gained the Willi Hoffmann-Guth Award for their quality of light at the 1996 PS Annual Exhibition; and in 1999 Leach received the Pastel Society of Canada Annual Award. He also exhibited at the RA Summer Exhibition, Ombersley and Roy Miles Galleries and had a solo show at Yehudi Menuhin School, Stoke d'Abernon.

Rachel LEACH 1959– Versatile artist and teacher whose aim was "to highlight the relationships of rhythms and structures present in our day-to-day experiences." Leach did an art and design foundation course at Somerset College of Art & Technology, 1976–8; graduated with first-class honours in printed and woven textiles, West Surrey College of Art and Design, 1978–81; and did a part-time course in hand-built ceramics, Morley College, 1993–6. Leach had a studio in Brooklyn, New York, 1989; produced cast-paper masks as an inspiration for *Rite*, four solo performances, Plein Theatre, Amsterdam, 1994; taught for Hayes Foundation summer programme, Vermont, America, 1994–01; designed and made a set for *Getting Personal*, commissioned by Chisenhale Dance Space, 1996; taught for L'Ouverture Theatre Trust in London Primary Schools, 1996–01; assisted Laura Ford to make sculptures, 1997–03; made sculptures for Yinka Shonibare, 1999–00; led a workshop, Dance on Camera, The Puffin Room, New York City and performed in Nell Berger's *Balance Room* in Amsterdam, both 2001; and created short films, *Locker 1* and *Waiting*, for Charles Findlay, 2002–4. Leach took part in group exhibitions in Britain and abroad, including

Minus one, Strand disused Underground station, 2004. Solo exhibitions included Plein Theatre and Alpha Papier, Amsterdam in 1994. Leach had a studio in north London.

Ursula LEACH 1947– Painter and printmaker whose work included richly coloured paintings with a strong abstract element, as shown at Oliver Contemporary, 2002. She trained at Winchester and Wimbledon Schools of Art and West Surrey College of Art & Design, Farnham, graduating with fine art honours, and was an RE associate. Among Leach's many mixed shows were Lasting Impressions, Victoria Art Gallery, Bath, where she gained the R K Burt Etching Prize, 1993; National Print Exhibition, Mall Galleries, from 1994; Hunting Art Prizes, Royal College of Art and tour, from 1995; Redfern Gallery, Summer Exhibition, 1996; A Flight Over Cranborne Chase, Salisbury Festival Exhibition, 1998; RWA Autumn Exhibition, 1999; and Maltby Contemporary Art, Winchester, 2000. Later solo exhibitions included Growing Concerns, Dorset County Museum, Dorchester, 2000, and Attendi Gallery, 2002, with one at Oliver Contemporary, 2006. Ashmolean Museum, Oxford; Worthing Hospital, St Mark's Hospital, The Royal Hospitals NHS Trust and Dorset County Hospital; and Bournemouth University Loan Collection hold examples of Leach's work.

Alun LEACH-JONES 1937– Painter and draughtsman producing vibrant, jazzy abstract works packed with forms and colours, as in his exhibition at Berkeley Square Gallery in 2001. By then Leach-Jones's pictures were held by 26 public collections internationally, including the British Museum, Ashmolean Museum in Oxford and Walker Art Gallery, Liverpool. He was born in Maghull, Lancashire, but spent his childhood in north Wales, where his Uncle Albert encouraged him to paint and draw. In 1949 the family moved to Liverpool where, two years later, Leach-Jones was apprenticed for three years as a law and manuscript writer with the Solicitors' Law Society. From 1955–7 he studied part-time at Liverpool College of Art; in 1957 travelled through France and Spain; in 1958, started his National Service; and in 1960 moved to Australia, studying part-time at the South of Australia School of Art. Although in 1964 he returned to the United Kingdom, Leach-Jones was back in Australia, 1967–72, in 1971 being awarded M/Dip by the National Gallery School of Art, Melbourne, eventually settling in Sydney, New South Wales. Leach-Jones won many awards, several residencies taking him around Australia and abroad. In 1999, he was elected Hon. Life Fellow of the RE. Participated in many group shows, latterly notably in America and Australia, and had numerous solo exhibitions, including Robert Lindsay Gallery, Melbourne, from 1995, and RCamA, 1998.

Richard LEACROFT 1914– Architect, illustrator and designer for the stage. Born in London, he studied at the Architectural Association and at the London Theatre Studio. Exhibited RA, Arts Council, in provinces and in the Middle East. Leicester Museum and Art Gallery bought his work. Published a number of books on aspects of the theatre. Lived for some time in Leicester.

Alexandra LEADBEATER 1956– Painter, born in Cheshire, who gained an honours degree after studies at Bath Academy of Art, Corsham, 1974–5, then Preston Polytechnic (Lancaster Annexe), 1976–9. Her mixed show appearances included 1981 Summer Show at Serpentine Gallery; Anne Berthoud Gallery, 1982; 1989 East Midlands Arts touring exhibition; The Face Fits, Middleton Hall, Milton Keynes, 1993; The Discerning Eye, prize winner, 1996; and Defining the Times, Milton Keynes Gallery, 2000. Leadbeater was included in The Silbury Group of Artists 10th Anniversary Exhibition at Milton Keynes Gallery, 2001–2. Solo shows included Mappin Art Gallery, Sheffield, 1982; Anne Berthoud Gallery and tour, 1983; Wilson Hale Gallery, 1989 and 1990; Wilson Stephens Fine Art and Lasar Segall Museum, São Paulo, Brazil, both 1991; Itau Gallery, Campo Grande, Brazil, 1992; and Milton Keynes Exhibition Gallery, 1994. Leadbeater had a studio in Shenley Wood, Milton Keynes, Buckinghamshire.

Christine LEADBETTER 1957– Painter, draughtsman and printmaker noted for her exuberant brushwork and colours. She was educated at Preston Polytechnic (Lancaster Annexe), 1975–6, then in the fine art department of Liverpool Polytechnic, 1976–9. She appeared in the Merseyside Artists exhibitions from 1983, toured by Walker Art Gallery, Liverpool, having shown in Stowells Trophy Exhibition at RA in 1979. Gained a Unilever Artists in Residence placement in 1986 and took part in educational activities such as a schools project at Bromborough Pool. Had a first solo show at Williamson Art Gallery and Museum, Birkenhead, 1989–90, and it holds examples, including Aviary – Ocean Park, Hong Kong. Lived at Great Asby, Appleby, Cumbria.

Patience LEADER 1928– Painter and modeller, born in Dromagh, County Cork, Ireland. Studied at Belfast College of Art, 1949, at Chelsea Polytechnic School of Art, 1951, then portraits with Sonia Mervyn, 1949–51, who ran her own classes. Showed at RUA and lived in Armagh, Northern Ireland.

Lily LEAHY: *see* **Lilian HAWTHORN**

Amber LEAMAN 1973– Painter whose work could show strong Cubist influence, as shown at Cadogan Contemporary in 1996 when she exhibited with Ruth Stage and Liz Hough. Leaman studied at Falmouth Art School. She appeared in Cadogan Contemporary's New Year and Summer Exhibitions in 1995; had a solo show there in 2001; and her work is held by the TSB Collection. Bridget Leaman, the artist, was her mother. Lived in Cornwall.

Bridget LEAMAN 1948– Painter who from 1972 settled in the Lizard peninsula, Cornwall; it influenced her work, which ranged from Cubist-influenced landscapes to abstracts, using an attractively bright palette. She studied at Bournemouth College of Art and West Surrey College of Art & Design in Farnham. Mixed shows included RI from 1982, winning a medal in 1988; RWA, 1988; and RA Summer Exhibition, 1992. Solo shows included Salisbury Playhouse, 1981, and Cadogan Contemporary, from 1993. Her daughter was the artist Amber Leaman. TSB and Unilever owned examples.

Dora LEAMAN 1897– Painter, born in Torquay, where she studied at the Grammar School, then the School of Art. Also attended St John's Wood School of Art and Regent Street Polytechnic School of Art in the 1930s, the latter under George Percival Gaskell. Exhibited RA, RSMA, UA and NEAC. Returned to Torquay, but finally moved to Bournemouth.

Jonathan LEAMAN 1954– Painter in oil on canvas, draughtsman and teacher, born in London, his parents actors and related to the artistic Salaman family. As a boy Leaman drew compulsively, so instead of Oxford University he chose to study at Camberwell School of Arts and Crafts, 1973–7, teaching there, 1977–83. In 1992 Leaman was a featured artist at the London Contemporary Art Fair, chosen by Paula Rego; at the 1997 Fair his picture Strongly, Wrongly, Vainly had crowds jostling to view it. It was typical of Leaman's style and subject-matter: minutely detailed, with a mystery narrative element, in the manner of the Pre-Raphaelites, whose work he admired, plus Surrealist associations. Had a first solo exhibition at Beaux Arts, 1994, others in 1997 and 2002. Leaman spent years on a canvas, dividing his time between London and Gloucestershire.

Landreth LEAPER 1947– Self-taught artist mainly in watercolour, also pencil, born in Horsham, Sussex. He was elected an associate of RWA in 1979 and favoured mixed exhibitions, showing extensively throughout the south and west of England. Leaper's work "often explored tonal ranges not usually employed in watercolour – of special emphasis and interest is work on skies." Lived in Ashton, Bristol.

David LEAPMAN 1959– Painter, born and lived in London, who was first prize winner at the 1995–6 John Moores Liverpool Exhibition with Double-Tongued Knowability, a mix of hard-edge abstraction and graffiti-like imagery. He studied at St Martin's School of Art, 1977–8; Goldsmiths' College School of Art, 1978–81; and Chelsea College of Art, 1988–9. Took part in Figuring Out The Eighties, Laing Art Gallery in Newcastle upon Tyne, 1988; Aperto Venice Biennale, 1990; and Arts Council tour Recent British Painting, 1993. Showed solo at Todd Gallery from 1988, at Beaux Arts, 2000, 2001 and 2002. Arts Council holds acrylic on canvas Past Behaviour, 1990.

Edwina LEAPMAN 1934– Painter and teacher, born in Hampshire who studied at Slade School of Fine Art and Central School of Art and Design, 1951–7. For a dozen years from 1963 she taught in several art schools, in 1974 having a solo show at New Art Centre. In the same year she was included in the Scottish Arts Council's show Post-Minimal Painting and in John Moores Exhibition, Liverpool, two years later winning a prize there. In 1976, too, she won an Arts Council Major Award and showed solo at Annely Juda Fine Art. Took part in several group shows in Switzerland. Arts Council holds Untitled '77 No. 6, of 1977, and Untitled No. 5, of 1978. Edwina Leapman gave a good statement about her abstract work in the catalogue of the South Bank Centre 1989 touring show The Experience of Painting. Had solo show at Annely Juda Fine Art, 2002, one of a series. Lived in London.

Noel Harry LEAVER 1889–1951 Watercolourist and teacher, born in Austwick, Yorkshire. He studied at Burnley School of Art, graduating in 1910. Gained a Travelling Studentship in 1911 and an RIBA Owen Jones Studentship in 1912. Leaver then taught at Halifax School of Art. He travelled widely abroad, producing such works as In Sunny Algiers and In Morocco. Showed at a wide range of galleries and had works bought by Burnley Corporation, settling in the town.

Ann LE BAS: *see* **Rachel Ann LE BAS**

Damian LE BAS 1963– Artist using paint, pencil, pastel and collage, born in Sheffield, Yorkshire, into a tinker family. His wife Delaine Le Bas was also an artist. Le Bas had a troubled childhood, finding consolation in his toys, which he drew constantly, along with football crowds. Aged about 10, he and his mother moved to Sussex, where he eventually settled at East Preston, Littlehampton. After leaving school in 1979 without qualifications, Le Bas did various labouring jobs, then was encouraged to attend West Sussex College of Art & Design, Worthing, 1980–5. He gained his master's degree in textiles from the Royal College of Art, 1985–7, although the non-academic nature of his pictures prompted his tutors to let him follow his own direction. After graduation, Le Bas worked in a kettle factory, as a roofer, then sold flowers during the day to enable him to paint at night. At the Royal College students had directed him to the Outsider Archive, where its director, Monika Kinley showed and acquired his work. This was characterised by rich colours, textile-like patterning, bizarre faces and strong linear contouring (Van Gogh was an influence). Group shows included Outsiders, Dean Clough Contemporary Art, Halifax; Art Brut/Outsider Art, Café Gallery, 1990; Singular Imagination, Phyllis Kind Gallery, New York, 1994; and Outsiders & Co, England & Co, 1996. Later solo shows included Courtauld Galleries, 1995. Shared shows with Delaine Le Bas at Raw Vision, Manor Cottage, Letchmore Heath, 2000, and James Colman, 2002.

Delaine LE BAS 1965– Painter, mixed-media artist, collagist and embroiderer, born in Worthing, Sussex, married to the artist Damian Le Bas. She was born into a gypsy/Romany background, spending her early years in caravans and trailers. What she called "the freedom of my Romany spirit" showed in her clothes and highly decorative work. She studied textiles at West Sussex College of Art & Design, Worthing, 1981–6, and St Martin's School of Art, 1986–8. By 1990 Le Bas found the restrictions of fashion design too much for her, and concentrated on picture-making, producing large collages and collage books, drawing on family history and photographs. Lived in a small house full of folk art objects in East Preston, Littlehampton, Sussex. Group shows included Alex Gellard Fine Art, Battle, and Rona Gallery, and solo exhibitions one at Islington Arts Factory, 1993. She shared shows with Damian Le Bas at Raw Vision, Manor Cottage, Letchmore Heath, 2000, and James Colman, 2002. Room was an installation and performance by Delaine at Transition in 2005.

Edward LE BAS 1904–1966 Painter and collector, born in London, brother of the sculptor Molly Le Bas. He took a degree in architecture at Cambridge University, studied art briefly in Paris, then from 1924 studied at the Royal College of Art. The Le Bas steel business provided him with private means which enabled him to paint abroad, both on the continent and in North Africa, also to indulge his taste for collecting modern French and English painting. He had superb judgement, buying many English painters when they were young or still underrated. A selection, A Painter's Collection, was shown at the RA in 1963, the critic Jack Wood Palmer commenting that "no collection in England can compare with Edward Le Bas' in size, consistency and quality". Le Bas was a fine painter, a

Colourist with a special talent for interiors and flower-pieces who exhibited at RA, LG, Redfern and Goupil Galleries, Arthur Tooth and Son and NEAC. He had a first solo show at Lefevre Gallery in 1936. In 1997, the Michael Parkin Gallery held Edward Le Bas – Painter and Collector. The Tate Gallery, provincial galleries and others in South Africa and Australia hold examples. He was elected RA in 1953. Lived in London and Brighton.

Julian LE BAS 1958– Painter and draughtsman, closely connected with Sussex. He studied at Brighton Polytechnic, 1978–81, completing a postgraduate course at Cyprus College of Art, 1983–4. Took part in many group shows, and had solo exhibitions at The Collective Gallery, Edinburgh; Haileybury College, Hertfordshire; Charleston Farmhouse, Firle, Sussex; and at Towner Art Gallery, Eastbourne, 1990. His Source to Sea was a Rye Art Gallery commission. Represented in David Bomberg and his followers show at Towner, 1991. Lived in Brighton, Sussex.

Molly LE BAS 1903– Sculptor, born in London, sister of the painter Edward Le Bas, daughter of Edward Le Bas the steel magnate. She was educated at Broomfield Hall and in Paris and with her sister Gwen was launched into society. Showed at RA, Walker Art Gallery in Liverpool, Royal Glasgow Institute of the Fine Arts and Paris Salon. Lived in London and in Angmering, Sussex.

Philip LE BAS 1925– Painter and teacher, born in St Quentin de Baron, Gironde, France, cousin of the artist Edward Le Bas. He worked in enamel paint. Studied at Regent Street Polytechnic School of Art, 1948–51. From 1952–66 taught art at various schools, 1968–77 lecturing at King Alfred's College. Was made a member of RBA in 1953, then NEAC in 1955, but both lapsed. Showed with Young Contemporaries, 1950; RA for many years; RBA 1952–60; Walker's Galleries between 1953–7; RP 1953; NEAC 1955–60; Some Young Painters, Camberwell, 1956; and Pictures for Schools, Camberwell, 1965. Solo shows included Heffer Gallery, Cambridge, 1955–7; Trafford Gallery, 1956 and 1958; Piccadilly Gallery, 1960; and Portal Gallery from 1965. HM Government, Methodist Church and a number of private collections with theatrical connections held his work. Lived at Hinton Ampner, Alresford, Hampshire.

Rachel Ann LE BAS 1923– Painter and printmaker, sometimes known as Ann Le Bas, born in Camberley, Surrey. She studied at the City & Guilds of London Art School under A R Middleton Todd, Henry Wilkinson and Rodney Burn. Among awards were the annual Drawing Prize and she twice won the annual Prize for Engraving. Le Bas always worked freelance and undertook commissions which included the National Trust Foundation for Art, Bishop of Bath and Wells and Royal Academy Graphics. She was elected a member of Somerset Guild of Craftsmen in 1962, of the Art Workers' Guild in 1969 the year she joined RE, and was elected a member of NEAC in 1972. Le Bas was featured artist in the RE Annual Exhibition in 2002. She held senior positions in several of these. Ashmolean Museum in Oxford and several other public collections in Britain hold examples. She was not related to other Le Bas artists, her family having fled from France at the revocation of the Edict of Nantes in 1598. Lived in Winsford, near Minehead, Somerset.

Edith LE BRETON 1912– Artist born in Salford, Lancashire, who painted as a child, taking private lessons. Aged 12 she won a scholarship and then a studentship to Royal School of Art, Salford, 1928–32, and was encouraged by the director of the Salford Art Gallery, Albert Frape. Had her first solo show there in 1937 and it bought her work. Le Breton was urged on by L S Lowry and like him believed in "painting the people about you". Showed with MAFA of which she was made a member in 1952, RCamA and Lancashire Artists Group and had several solo shows at Medici Gallery in the mid-1970s. A limited edition of her picture *The Old Street Market* was produced by Mellor Hall Fine Art Reproductions. Le Breton claimed to be the first artist to show and discuss her work on experimental colour television. Lived for a time at Dunham Massey, Altrincham, Cheshire.

Tim LE BREUILLY 1978– Painter whose work had a surreal tinge, as in his oil on canvas Psychic disruption, included in the John Moores Liverpool Exhibition, 2004. Le Breuilly attended the University of the West of England, Bristol, 1997–8, and the Slade School of Fine Art, 1998–02. Exhibitions included Four For 98, Berni Gallery, Arts Centre in Jersey, Channel Islands, 1998; Black Hole, Garage Theatre, 2000; Art Sauce, John Jones Gallery, and Fish Bowl, The Foundry, both 2002; plus other group shows at The Generator and The Reading Rooms in Dundee in 2004.

Louis le BROCQUY 1916– Painter, mural and tapestry designer and teacher, born in Dublin and married to the artist Anne Madden. He studied chemistry at Trinity College, Dublin, 1936–7, and worked in the family oil refining business in the late-1930s. In 1938 decided to paint full-time, but was self-taught, studying in London and continental galleries. Returning to Dublin in 1940, he worked on a series of tinker paintings, stained glass, theatre designs and murals, then settled in London in 1946, producing his first tapestries two years later. Had first solo show at Gimpel Fils in 1947, at Esther Robles Gallery, Los Angeles, in 1960 and in Switzerland at Galerie Charles Lienhard in 1961. Notable among later shows was a retrospective at Irish Museum of Modern Art, Kilmainham, 1996–7, and in 2001 New Paintings at Gimpel Fils and Abusson Tapestries at Agnew. Taught at Central School of Arts and Crafts, 1947–54, and Royal College of Art, 1955–8, and was director of the Kilkenny Design Workshops, 1965–71. After destroying much of his work in 1963, le Brocquy in 1964 began a series of human heads; his figures are often in isolation, sinister, or seen through the mist of memory. Became RHA in 1949, a Chevalier, Légion d'Honneur, 1974, and Hon. RHA in 1983. Tate Gallery, Victoria & Albert Museum and Municipal Gallery of Modern Art, Dublin, hold his work. Lived in Carros, France. The sculptor Melanie le Brocquy was his sister.

Melanie le BROCQUY 1919– Sculptor, born in Dublin, sister of the artist Louis le Brocquy. She attended the National College of Art, Dublin, the Royal Hibernian Academy School and École des Beaux-Arts, Geneva. While she was at National College le Brocquy knew that she had made a mistake and did not want to be a painter or teacher, then discovered the sculpture department, run by Peter Grant and Peter Brennan. Her first sculpture, Head of a Cat, was accepted by RHA. A Taylor Scholarship took her to Geneva. She had a joint exhibition with her brother in 1942 in Dublin and appeared in the Irish Exhibition of

Living Art in 1943, but then marriage preoccupied her until she relaunched her career in the 1960s. In the early 1970s the Dawson Gallery in Dublin took up her work, giving her shows with William Scott and Patrick Heron, the Taylor Galleries in Dublin giving her a small retrospective in 1986, the RHA a major one in 1999. Her sculpture of the period 1938–90 was shown at Austin/Desmond Fine Art, 1990. Most of her mature output is mainly constructed around small-scale and usually full-length human figures. The critic Brian Fallon called her "the best Irish sculptor of her generation".

Christopher LE BRUN 1951– Painter, printmaker, sculptor and teacher, born in Portsmouth, Hampshire. He studied at Slade School of Fine Art, 1970–4, then gained his master's degree at Chelsea School of Art, 1974–5. Le Brun was a visiting lecturer at Brighton, Wimbledon and at the Slade, 1976–83, from 1989 resuming teaching at the Slade. He was a prizewinner at John Moores Liverpool Exhibitions, 1978–80, and won a Calouste Gulbenkian Foundation Printmakers' Commission Award in 1983. In 1984 he did designs for a revival of the *Ballet Imperial* at Royal Opera House, Covent Garden, produced in 1985; was guest of the Berlin Artists' Programme of the DAAD in 1987–8; and in 1988 gained the Snowdonia Commission, Artists in National Parks, organised by the Victoria & Albert Museum. From 1975 Le Brun took part in numerous mixed shows in Britain and abroad. He showed with Nigel Greenwood Gallery from 1980, also extensively in America. Arts Council, British Council and British Museum hold his work, which when shown in America was described as grand, melancholy and highly romantic. In 2001, an exhibition of his sculpture and monoprints at the University of Northumbria, Newcastle upon Tyne, included literal and abstract pieces. Was elected RA, 1996, in 2000 filling the new professor of drawing post at the Royal Academy Schools.

Janet LEDGER 1931– Painter and printmaker whose work was reproduced as popular limited edition prints by Fine Art Editions, and who was noted for subjects such as nuns on beaches, red telephone boxes and people at the seaside. These were photographed or sketched, then worked up in the studio. Born in Northampton, Ledger studied at its School of Art, taught by Henry Bird, her mother's cousin; Horace Colby; and she did an intensive lettering course with Thomas Wrigley. Soon had a number of shows and was a founder-member of the Young Contemporaries student group in the town. Marriage, children and illness interrupted her painting, then in 1972 she painted several pictures as a therapy which set her on course again. HRH Princess Margaret bought a Thames view from Ledger's London '77 show at Somerset House in 1977. Two Curwen Press lithographs are held by the Tate Gallery. Ledger was part of a The Best of Britain exhibition in Dallas in 1985 and from that year showed solo with Linda Blackstone Gallery, Pinner. The Tate Gallery, HRH Princess Margaret and several corporate collections held examples. A puckish humour and charm characterised Ledger's pictures. Latterly lived on the Isle of Wight.

Maria Sax LEDGER 1916–2006 Self-taught, eccentric painter and embroiderer, born Maria Sax in Zürich, Switzerland, educated at Château de Montmirail, Neuchâtel, and as the only girl at the Institut Minerva, an élite Zürich boys' school. Through her flamboyant father, Karl Sax, director of an insurance firm, writer and poet, Maria enjoyed a rich intellectual and political life. After briefly attending Zürich University and the suicide of her father in 1935, she rebelled against autocratic brothers and fled to England. There she worked in a Surrey teashop; married the much older medical practitioner, Neville Hallam; and by 1950 was married to Peter Ledger, living in a Modern Movement house near the North Downs. While married to Hallam she began to paint. In Zürich she had spent long periods looking at pictures in the Kunsthaus. Her own development as a powerful, poetic Colourist while married to Ledger was influenced by such artists as Marc Chagall, Vincent van Gogh and the German Expressionists. She painted largely in isolation until the painter John Henshaw organised her solo show when she was 60 at the Warminster Art Centre. After she moved to north Wales in 1980 she exhibited frequently, mainly at Coleg Harlech and Oriel Plas Glyn-y-Weddw, Llanbedrog, and was given a WAC retrospective in 1996 at Oriel Mostyn, Llandudno. Ledger died at Dolgellau, Gwynnedd.

Gilbert LEDWARD 1888–1960 Sculptor of monuments and portraits in metal and stone. Born and lived in London, son of the Sculptor Richard Ledward, he studied for over 10 years prior to World War I at Chelsea Polytechnic, Goldsmiths' College School of Art, the Royal College of Art and the Royal Academy Schools. In 1913 he won the Royal Academy Gold Medal and Travelling Studentship and the first British School in Rome Scholarship in Sculpture. Ledward became professor of sculpture at the Royal College, 1926–9, a year later being made member of the faculty of sculpture and of the council of the British School at Rome. Ledward exhibited at the RA from 1912, being elected RA in 1937 and a trustee, 1956–7. He was president of the RBS, 1954–6. As well as advising the Royal Mint, Ledward completed the Guards Division Memorial, in St James' Park, London, other war memorials in the provinces and overseas and the fountains in Sloane Square, London. The Tate Gallery holds his work, which can be both graceful and majestic. In 2002, the Henry Moore Institute archive, Leeds, acquired a major collection of Ledward's drawings, covering his career from the Rome Scholarship until his death, enhancing the photographic archive of his work already held.

Billy LEE 1946– Sculptor and teacher, born in Uitenhage, Cape Province, South Africa, who emigrated to England in 1959, then settled in America. He graduated in fine art at Birmingham College of Art and Design, 1965–9; gained his master's at Royal College of Art, 1969–72; and was made a fellow, MIT Center for Advanced Visual Studies, Boston, 1972–3. Lee taught at the University of Michigan, 1973–80, from 1984 holding a professorship at University of North Carolina at Greensboro, where he lived. Among a dozen awards, later ones included the Giacomo Manzù Special Prize, 7th Henry Moore International Exhibition, Japan, 1991; Rodin Prize, Fujisankei Biennale, International Exhibition of Contemporary Sculpture, Utsukushi-gahara Open-Air Museum, Japan, 1993; and UNCG Research Excellence Award, 1999. Took part in many international group shows, later solo exhibitions including MB Modern, New York, 1998. In 2002 Lee shared a show with Harvey Hood at RBS Gallery, by which time his work had shifted from the monumental to small, intimate sculptures. Public collections in China, Japan and America, including Weatherspoon Museum in Greensboro, hold Lee's work.

Colette LEE fl. from late-1980s– Painter and sculptor who gained a diploma from Great Yarmouth College of Art and Design in 1985. In 1988 Lee won a degree in fine art from Gloucestershire College of Art and Technology, obtaining her master's from University of Ulster, Belfast, 1989. She was commissioned by Gloucestershire County Council to make a bronze plaque in 1989 and by the Plaza Hotel, Belfast, to make a sculpture, 1990. Showed in England, Ireland and Germany, appearances including Galerie Hausgeist, Berlin, 1992; Young Contemporaries at One Oxford Street, Belfast, 1993; and in 1994 Beyond the Partitions and Works on Paper, put on by Queen Street Studios, Belfast, with which she was associated.

Dick LEE 1923–2001 Painter and teacher, full name Richard Dale Lee, born in Bulawayo, then Southern Rhodesia. He was initially educated there, then attended Camberwell School of Arts and Crafts, 1947–50, under William Coldstream, Claude Rogers, Victor Pasmore and other Euston Road School-associated artists, whose style left a strong influence on his work. Primarily a landscape and interior painter, he chose to work on the spot, his pictures retaining a freshness and spontaneity. He was awarded an Abbey Major Scholarship in 1951, then two years later began teaching at Camberwell, where he remained until 1982. Took part in many mixed shows, including LG, RA, Leicester Galleries, AIA, New Grafton Gallery and elsewhere. Prize winner, 1985, Tolly Cobbold, and 1992, Hunting Group exhibitions. Had show with Francis Hoyland at Galerie de Seine in 1958, later solo series including New Grafton Gallery, 1970–92; Cadogan Contemporary and School House Gallery, Wighton, both 1988–95; Chappel Galleries, 2000; and Browse & Darby, 2001. Lived in London for many years, later in Norfolk with a house in Normandy, France.

Erica LEE 1898–1980 Sculptor in terracotta and clay, especially of portraits. Born in Manchester, Lee studied under Sir William Reid Dick and E Whitney-Smith. Exhibited widely, including RA, RSA, Royal Glasgow Institute of Fine Arts, Walker Art Gallery, Liverpool, and Paris Salon. Work held by the New Museum and Art Gallery, Newport. Was a fellow of the RBS and lived in London. Lee was a neighbour of the sculptor Stanislas Reychan, who fired terracottas for her. In his 1993 autobiography *Playing with Dolls* he describes Lee as a "tall elderly spinster with a loud upper class voice", of independent means, who "drove a smart MG".

Geoffrey LEE 1942– Artist notable for spontaneous and Impressionistic landscapes, townscapes and life figure studies. He was self-taught, apart from life classes and evening and weekend painting workshops. Lee joined the PS in 1976 and was also a member of the Leicester Society of Artists, where he won the Guy Dixon Prize. He gained many other awards, including Pastel Society of Canada. Showed in the Midlands, at Mall and Thompson's Galleries, with Linda Blackstone in Pinner and at Century Gallery, Datchet. Lived in Cropston, Leicestershire.

Godfrey LEE fl. from 1980s– Painter, born in St Thomas, Jamaica. After leaving school in 1969 and being unemployed for two years he joined the Army for three years. In 1974 went to live with relatives in America. Returned to Britain where he did various jobs, was unemployed, began to draw, had an exhibition in his local library and then did two years at a further education college. Completed foundation course at St Martin's School of Art and a bachelor's degree in fine art at Newcastle Polytechnic. Lee's work addressed social issues, notably the treatment of mentally ill people who were black. He was included in the 1991–2 Norwich Gallery touring show History and Identity. Lived in London.

Helen LEE 1951– Painter and teacher, born in Southport, Lancashire, who was educated in Scotland. She was sometimes referred to as Helen C Lee. She attended Edinburgh College of Art, 1970–6, teachers Robin Philipson, Elizabeth Blackadder and David Michie; and the Royal College of Art, 1977–8, under Peter de Francia, Roberto Matta, John Walker and Alan Miller. After living in the West Indies, from 1980–4 she worked in Hackney, eventually settling in Colchester, Essex, where she was a committee member of the Art Society. Lee won many awards, including one at the 1976 John Moores Liverpool Exhibition. In 1979 she gained a commission from Imperial War Museum. Teaching included adult evening classes for Lothian Regional Council, 1976–7, and from 1999 part-time at The Colchester Institute. Took part in numerous group exhibitions, including the RA Summer Exhibition, RSA, SSA, SSWA, RSW, RBSA, Mall Galleries and many provincial venues. Among later solo shows were The Scottish Gallery, Edinburgh, 1986; Open Studio and Tendring Open Studios, 1998–9; and The Hay Gallery, Colchester, 2000. The Crown Agents, Paintings in Hospitals, Scottish Arts Council and IBM Edinburgh hold Lee's work.

Jessie LEE 1947– Versatile artist, born in Malaya, who moved to England to study in the early 1970s. Her wide travels included several years in Saudi Arabia. She gained a diploma in ceramics, Hammersmith College of Art & Design, 1973–6, a higher diploma in painting and printing, Amersham College of Art & Design, 1990–2. Until 1992, all Lee's work was figurative and three-dimensional, then she received new inspiration from printmaking, especially monoprinting and collography. Moods and feelings, a sense of landscape and the myths and imagery of the Far East were key influences on her vividly coloured work. In 1993 joined the Oxford Printmakers' Co-operative. Exhibitions included New Academy Gallery, 1995; RBSA Printmaking Exhibition, Birmingham, 1996; National Print Exhibition, Mall Galleries, 1997; and Passion For Colour, JAG Contemporary at Hanging Space, 1999. Lived in High Wycombe, Buckinghamshire.

Joseph LEE 1876– Painter and illustrator who attended Heatherley's School of Fine Art, then the Slade School of Fine Art under Henry Tonks and Walter Westley Russell. Work done during World War I was officially purchased and he published a number of books with war themes, such as *Ballads of Battle* and *Captive at Carlsruhe*. Lived in Dundee, Angus.

May Bridges LEE fl. c.1905–1967 Painter and miniaturist, especially of portraits, born in Lahore, India. After education in England she studied at Lambeth School of Art. The architect, surveyor and engineer Sir Philip Stott's first wife Hannah having died in 1935, Lee married him shortly before he died in 1937, becoming Lady Stott. Stott's home was Stanton Court, Broadway, but Lee continued to maintain a studio in London. Her sitters included her barrister father John Bridges Lee, Sir Jeremiah Colman, Lords Burnham and Cornwallis and The Earl Manvers. She was a member of RMS, SWA, and SM, also showing at RSA, Walker Art Gallery in Liverpool and elsewhere.

Moses LEE 1950– Abstract artist using a rich palette whose sources of influence "are diverse and always expanding", ranging over modern Western artists; music including jazz, dance and Indian classical music; Eastern mysticism; natural forms and the cinema. Studied at Hull College of Art and Liverpool Polytechnic. Group exhibitions included Salford City Art Gallery, 1984; Castlefield Art Gallery, Manchester, 1986; New Art North West, Bluecoat Gallery in Liverpool, 1991; and Journeys West, University of Essex travelling show, 1995. Had solo exhibitions in 1991 at Chinese Arts Centre in Manchester and Stockport City Art Gallery, another at Skelmersdale Arts Centre, 1992. BBC, the Stockport City Art Gallery and private collections hold his work.

Peter LEE 1937– Painter, notably working in tempera, and printmaker. He attended Bournemouth College of Art, 1981–2, then Camberwell School of Art, 1982–5, with an added year's study of printmaking. Showed at RA from 1987 and in many other group exhibitions, including The Broad Horizon, Agnew, 1990.

Robert LEE 1915– Maker of boxed constructions, painter, draughtsman, printmaker and teacher, born in Bingley, Yorkshire, where he was finally based. Attended Bradford College of Art, 1932–7, then won place at Royal College of Art, 1937–40, where he studied graphic design, illustration and printmaking, his teachers including John Nash, Edward Bawden and Percy Horton. Served widely overseas in World War II in Army, 1940–6. In latter year returned to Royal College of Art on fourth-year scholarship, gained 1940. After teaching part-time at Hammersmith College of Art in 1947, Lee took job as art master at Heckmondwike Grammar School, in 1949 being appointed to Batley School of Art, in 1957 deputy head. From 1969 Lee taught variously at Bingley College of Education, Huddersfield Polytechnic, Bretton College and Bradford and Ilkley College. Lee showed regularly in Yorkshire exhibitions from the 1950s. In 1965 he shared an exhibition at Manor House, Ilkley, and a number of two-man exhibitions followed until a solo exhibition at Bishop Grosseteste College, Lincoln, 1978. There were others, then Lee had a retrospective at Bretton Hall, Yorkshire, in 1991. By this time he had been engaged on three-dimensional work for 25 years and his meticulously crafted boxes had become collectors' items.

Rosa LEE 1957– Painter, born in Hong Kong. She completed a degree in intellectual history and German at Sussex University in 1979. Her subsequent fine art training was at Brighton Polytechnic, 1982–3, St Martin's School of Art, 1983–6, and Royal College of Art, 1986–8. Between 1988–9 was visiting fellow at Winchester School of Art, having a solo show there in 1989. In that year she was an Artist of the Day at Flowers East and she also had a prizewinning canvas, Matrix, of 1989, in John Moores Liverpool Exhibition, 1989–90. In 1992 she appeared in (dis)parities at Mappin Art Gallery, Sheffield, which toured to Herbert Art Gallery, Coventry, 1993. University of Liverpool holds her work, which included abstract pictures with a strong sense of design. Lived in London.

Rosie LEE 1935– Artist in oil on canvas, wood or paper, born in Rotterdam, Netherlands. She studied, like her husband Terry Lee, at Sheffield College of Art, 1953–5, then Slade School of Fine Art, 1955–7. She said that her best work was "an exploration of self and awareness". Mixed exhibitions included Fine Arts for Industry, Royal College of Art, 1969; RA Summer Exhibitions from 1970; Basel International Air Fair, from 1973; The Minories, Colchester, 1980; and Nicholas Treadwell's Art Mill, Bradford, from 1988. In 1985–6 she was a prizewinner in Tolly Cobbold Eastern Arts Fifth National Exhibition and tour. Had a solo show at Mansard Gallery, 1968; a series at Piccadilly Gallery from 1969; and widely abroad, especially in Germany, including Galerie Im Kunsthaus Shaller, Stuttgart, 1984. Department of the Environment and Coventry's Herbert Art Gallery hold examples. Latterly lived in Beeley, near Matlock, Derbyshire.

Rupert LEE 1887–1959 Painter, sculptor, critic and teacher. Born in Bombay, India, Lee studied at the Royal College of Art and the Slade School of Fine Art, where he became friendly with Paul Nash, who describes him in detail in his autobiography *Outline*. Lee did a notable drawing of Nash. Was an enthusiastic amateur musician. From early in the 1920s Lee was associated with the Friday Club and LG, of which for a decade from the mid-1920s he was president. He was chairman of the International Surrealist Exhibition in London in 1936. As well as acting as art critic for several publications, such as *The New Statesman* and *The New Age*, Lee lectured at Westminster School of Art. His sculpture can be found in a number of English provincial churches and at the cathedral in Gibraltar. Towards the end of his life he lived in San Roque, Spain.

Sadie LEE 1967– Largely self-taught painter and freelance lecturer whose work could have witty overtones, as in her 1997 oil on canvas Dixie Lee Evans, "The Marilyn Monroe of Burlesque", but could be frequently unsettling. They were likened to those of Otto Dix and other artists of the New Objectivity movement in 1930s Berlin. Lee said: "The women in my paintings go far beyond the passive status of decorative object. As their eyes lock with yours you cannot help wondering who they are and what they want with you.... My paintings are never at the expense of the models," but are "from their perspective and they, not the viewer, are in control." Lee's work was included in several books, including Emmanuel Cooper's *The Sexual Perspective*, 1992; Edward Lucie-Smith's *Art Today*, 1996; and Judith Halberstamm's *Female Masculinity*, 1998. She gained a BP Travel Award in 1996 and was commended at the BP Portrait Award, 1998. Group exhibitions included Contemporary Portrait Painters, Henry Wyndham Gallery, 1993; The Sexual Perspective, Jill George Gallery, 1994; Art for Equality, ICA, 1995; Pride and Prejudice, Museum of London, 1999; The Discerning Eye, Mall Galleries, 2001; and Hello Sailor, Seel Street Gallery, Liverpool Biennial, 2004. Her solo shows were: Venus Envy, at Manchester City Art Gallery, 1994; Twisted Portraits, Green Street Gallery, 1995; A Dying Art: Ladies of Burlesque, National Portrait Gallery and tour, 1997; Inappropriate Women, East West Gallery, 1998; Don't Look, Museum of Modern Art, Ljubljana, Slovenia, 1999; and Up West, The Cobden Club, 2001. Lee lived and worked in north London.

Sara LEE 1956– Painter and restorer who studied at Byam Shaw School of Art, 1975. Next she gained an honours degree in chemical physics, 1975–9, from Sussex University, then worked at Hamilton Kerr Institute at Cambridge University, 1980–4, to gain certificate and diploma in the conservation of easel paintings. After four years in London engaged as a restorer, lived in Paris from 1989–91, which was the subject of some of her most atmospheric work. Sara Lee showed in 1980 at Clare College, Cambridge; in 1983 at Trumpington Gallery there; from 1982 at RA Summer Exhibition; in 1986 at Addison Ross Gallery; in 1991 having a solo show at Cadogan Contemporary.

Sydney LEE 1866–1949 Landscape painter and printmaker, born in Manchester. Studied at the School of Art there and Atelier Colarossi, Paris. Painted extensively on the continent, being especially fond of mountainous scenery. Exhibited RA – elected RA, 1930 – and extensively at Cooling Galleries, RE and NEAC; also at Fine Art Society, IS, RBA and elsewhere. He held several official positions, being RA treasurer for some years and a member of the Council of Art and Industry. Included in a number of public collections, notably Tate Gallery. Lived in London.

Terry LEE 1932– Painter and teacher, born in Sheffield. He attended the College of Art there, later returning to teach, and Slade School of Fine Art, 1955–8, under William Coldstream. Showed in north of England, RA Summer Exhibition and in 1980 was included in The British Art Show, Arts Council touring exhibition chosen by critic William Packer. Had a series of solo shows at New Art Centre from 1960 and at Agnew from 1973. Arts Council holds Lee's oil The Spider's Debris, 1962, other examples being held by public galleries in Coventry, Liverpool, Hull and Oldham. Lived for a time in Beeley, Derbyshire, also in Spain, and was married to the artist Rosie Lee.

George William LEECH 1894–1966 Painter and etcher. After initial study at Lambeth and Putney Schools of Art, won a three-year London County Council scholarship which enabled him to study at South Kensington. Worked for some years as a magazine art editor. Exhibited widely, including RA, RI, Fine Art Society and ROI. Lived in London.

Gwyneth LEECH 1959– Painter, draughtsman and printmaker, born in Philadelphia, Pennsylvania, America, who in 1981, the year she moved to Britain, graduated from the University of Pennsylvania in anthropology and French. From her arrival, Leech studied painting at Edinburgh College of Art, funded by a three-year Pennsylvania Thouron Scholarship; studied wood engraving with Kathleen Lindsley; and gained a postgraduate diploma in 1985. In 1983 she was included in Scottish Print Open Three, organised by Dundee Printmakers' Workshop. Was elected president of SSA. Exhibitions included University of Pennsylvania, 1986; Aberdeen Art Gallery and Museum, 1988; Theatre Royal, Glasgow, 1990; and Boundary Gallery, 1995, a show based on sketches made during through Africa and Asia, 1991–3. The American Museum in Bath, BBC, Edinburgh City Art Galleries and Strathclyde University hold examples.

Raymond LEECH 1949– Marine and East Anglian coastal painter, born in Great Yarmouth, Norfolk, settling at Oulton Broad, Suffolk. He studied art and design at Great Yarmouth College of Art, was elected RSMA in 1987, also being a member of the Norwich Guild of Artists. Showed in the provinces, London and America and from 1992 had solo shows at Haste Gallery, Ipswich.

William John LEECH 1881–1968 Painter, born in Dublin, Ireland, who studied at St Columba's College, Royal Hibernian Academy Schools, Metropolitan School of Art and in Paris at Académie Julian. He was elected RHA in 1910 and showed several hundred works there. Also exhibited prolifically at Goupil Gallery, RA, NEAC, Fine Art Society, Baillie Gallery and elsewhere. Had a studio in London, then settled in Clandon, Surrey.

Caroline LEEDS 1931–2005 Painter of landscapes and portraits, born in Jersey, Channel Islands, daughter of Colonel Henry Vatcher. Her first marriage was to The Duke of Leeds, after which she was married to Peter Hoos and Sir Robert Hobart, but continued to sign her work Leeds. She studied with Philip Lame and Bernard Adams and worked in oils, watercolour and chalk. After the Duke's death, she bought a house on the southern slopes of Lectoure, in France, overlooking the Pyrenees, spending the summer there and wintering in London. She also painted widely elsewhere in Europe, including Czechoslovakia and Italy. Her output included Falkland war heroes, in the collection of the Royal Hospital, Chelsea. She showed in many group exhibitions, including the RP, ROI and RBA, as well as at commercial galleries in London, Lectoure, Paris, New York and Monte Carlo. Died in London.

Theyre LEE-ELLIOTT 1903–1988 Artist born in Lewes, Sussex whose work had a strong fantasy element. Lee-Elliott studied at Central School of Arts and Crafts, 1925–7. Appeared in a four-man show at Thackeray Gallery, 1977. Solo shows included Pulchri, The Hague; Iolas, New York; Redfern Gallery; Chatham Gallery in Hong Kong; and Miyuki, Tokyo. Was chosen to contribute three works to the British section at Musée d'Art Moderne, Paris, International Exhibition of Religous Art, 1965. Although he was the son of a clergyman, Lee-Elliott was not himself a believer, although after a serious illness while abroad in his mid-fifties he was moved to paint a series of powerfully Expressionist religious pictures in which the figure of Christ and the wood of cross conjoin. A good example is the tempera and gouache Crucified tree form – the agony, in the Methodist Church Collection. Christie's in South Kensington offered works by Lee-Elliott in 2003, catalogued as signed by Lee Elliott plus a date. The Victoria & Albert Museum holds his work. Died in London, where he lived in Chelsea.

William LEE-HANKEY 1869–1952 Painter and printmaker, born in Chester, who was married to two artists: first Mabel Lee-Hankey (Hobson), then Edith Garner. He studied at Chester School of Art under Walter Schroeder, at the Royal College of Art and in Paris. From the early 1890s Lee-Hankey exhibited at the main London galleries, especially Fine Art Society, RWS, Leicester and Lefevre Galleries; also RA, Goupil Gallery, Ridley Art Club, ROI, RE and Walker Art Gallery, Liverpool. During World War I he served with the Artists' Rifles. British Museum and Victoria & Albert Museum hold his work, as do British provincial galleries and galleries as far apart as Budapest, Belfast and Vienna. For some time Lee-Hankey lived in

France, where he produced a body of work. He is notable for his paintings of French harbour scenes and paintings and etchings of English country life, often of great sensitivity. Won a gold medal at the Barcelona International Exhibition and a bronze medal in Chicago, was vice-president of the RWS in the late 1940s and chairman of the Empire Art Council. Lived in London.

Norah LEE-JONES 1911– Artist in many media, designer and teacher, born in Denbigh, north Wales. Aged 16 she attended Halifax School of Art for two years, then Huddersfield School of Art and Leeds College of Art, notably under Frank Simpson. She then taught in a series of Yorkshire grammar schools; spent a year at Prince's Theatre, Leeds, directing their lighting, designing costumes and backcloths; then returned to teaching. Miss Lee-Jones produced landscapes covering a wide area of Britain, as well as Italy, as shown in a solo exhibition at Dorset County Museum, Dorchester. She was a member of the Art Club in Dorchester, where she lived, also showing with groups in Bournemouth and Poole and SWLA. For a time she had her own gallery at King's Arms, Dorchester, shared with Val Buckland, showing many artists' work. Lee-Jones cited as her strongest influences those "from nature, overwhelmingly trees and skies from my earliest days".

Stewart LEES 1926– Artist born in Auchtertool, Fife, who studied at Edinburgh College of Art, 1947–52. He gained an Arts Council Sabbatical Year in 1968. Showed at Bluecoat Gallery, Liverpool; Traverse Gallery, Edinburgh; RA Summer Exhibition, and abroad. Universities of Glasgow and Nottingham hold examples. Lived in Nottingham.

Laurence LEESON 1930– Painter, printmaker and teacher, born in Leeds, Yorkshire. He studied at Shrewsbury Art School, 1948–9, then Birmingham College of Arts and Crafts, 1949–53, teachers including Bernard Fleetwood-Walker and Harold Smith. Showed with Young Contemporaries, Leicester Galleries, Keele University, Piccadilly Gallery and elsewhere. He held a Gulbenkian Fellowship at Keele, 1963–4. Victoria & Albert Museum and other public collections hold examples. Lived in Market Weighton, Yorkshire.

Gerald LEET 1913–1998 Painter and teacher, born in London. He studied painting at Goldsmiths' College School of Art, 1929–34, at Royal College of Art, 1934–7, then again at Goldsmiths' and Courtauld Institute, 1937–8. While at Goldsmiths' and sharing a studio with the artist Carel Weight Leet was asked to recommend a college for Denton Welch, later to become noted as a writer and painter; he befriended Welch, who attended his evening classes. Leet then taught at Ealing School of Art and after service in World War II was appointed an Official War Artist resident at Viceroy's House, New Delhi, 1945–6. After the war returned to teaching at Ealing, then went to Eton College as a drawing master, where he remained until 1949, then moved to Windsor Castle, teaching at Brighton part-time. He was commissioned by HM Queen Elizabeth the Queen Mother to complete portrait drawings in 1948. Leet had solo exhibitions at Eton Art Gallery and Isobar Gallery, as well as showing in public galleries in Manchester and Halifax.

Peter LEFTWICH 1913– Painter, born in London, notably of fresco and in tempera. After private education he studied at Durban School of Art and at the Michaelis School of Fine Art, University of Cape Town, with both John and Grace Wheatley, 1932–6. Showed widely in South Africa, at Paris Salon and at RA, RI, RP and elsewhere. South African National Gallery in Cape Town holds his work. Arts Club member. Lived in Eston, Natal.

Owen LEGG 1935– Artist, notably in lino-cut and producer of limited-edition books and prints, born in London. He was a medical practitioner from 1959, having studied in London, in 1961 obtaining a diploma in obstetrics at Guy's Hospital. Legg studied art at Tunbridge Wells Adult Education Centre. He was a member of Free Painters and Sculptors, also showing at book fairs: Oxford, 1990, and in 1991 in Mainz and Verona. He had a series of solo shows in Sevenoaks, Croydon and Greenwich, the library there holding his work, as does Kent County Library Service. Among books he produced were *The Garden*, by Vita Sackville-West, and the *Rubayyait of Omar Khayyam*. In 1992, when he went as a medical officer with a British Schools Exploring Society trip to Iceland, Legg's Woodcraft Press published William Morris' *On First Seeing Iceland*. Lived in Tonbridge, Kent.

Willow LEGGE 1934– Portrait sculptor and art therapist, born in Salisbury, Wiltshire, married to the book artist Ron King. She studied at Chelsea School of Art, 1951–6, under Bernard Meadows and Willi Soukop. Worked as an art therapist, 1977–87, and from 1987–01 as a portrait sculptor at The Tussaud Studios. Legge was a full member of the SPS and Surrey Sculpture Society. Other group appearances included the RA Summer Exhibition, 1963, 1992 and 1994; Chichester Open, 1995; Keys Gallery, Chelsea, 1997; and National Portrait Gallery tour Mirror, Mirror, self-portraits by women artists, 2002. Victoria & Albert Museum, Yale Center for British Art, Vermont and Houston Universities and private collections hold examples. Lived in Bosham, Sussex.

Jeremy LE GRICE 1936– Painter, born of a Cornish family. Although he travelled as far away as Provence and America, the sea, coast, weather and landscape of Cornwall continued as a preoccupation. Le Grice attended Guildford Art School, 1953–4, was at Lanyon Summer School, 1955–6, then in 1957–61 was at Slade School of Fine Art. For a decade Le Grice was then based at St Just, Cornwall; then after 11 years in the Cotswolds in Gloucestershire, 1972–83, he returned to St Buryan, Cornwall, 1984–96; Newlyn from 1997. As well as showing at RA and with LG, Le Grice had a series of one-man shows, the first at Newlyn Gallery, 1962. After a solo show at Cadogan Contemporary in 1989 he had another in 1991, in 1990 having a retrospective at Penwith, St Ives. Two German scholarships were held at Worpswede, Bremen, 1995–6, and Atelierhaus, Bremerhaven, 1998, both resulting in solo shows. Another one-man exhibition was held at Bishop Phillpotts Gallery, Truro, 2001. His wife was the stenciller Lyn Le Grice.

Malcolm LE GRICE 1940– Artist and jazz musician who studied painting at Plymouth College of Art, 1957–61, and at the Slade School of Fine Art, 1961–4. He exhibited as a painter in Young Contemporaries, 1963, and at the Arts Lab, 1968. He had made his first film in 1966, and this became his main artistic activity. In 1976, Le Grice was included in the big British Council exhibition English Art Today 1960–76, at the Palazzo Reale, Milan, Italy. By then he had achieved a prolific film output, including *Castle 1*, 1966; *Castle Two*, 1968; *Horror Film 1*, 1971; *Horror Film 2*, 1972; and *After Manet, after Georgione Le djeuner sur l'herbe or Fête Champêtre* in 1975.

LEHARCA: *see* **Lewis Edward HEATH**

Olga LEHMANN 1912–2001 Painter, illustrator and designer, born in Chile. She won a scholarship to Slade School of Fine Art, studying under Allan Gwynne-Jones and Vladimir Polunin. She worked for three years at Covent Garden Opera House, then was in costume design and was art director for Rank Advertising, which led to work in Hollywood, her film credits including *Laughter in Paradise*, *The Inn of the Sixth Happiness* and *Witness for the Prosecution*. She painted the portraits in the background of the *Dynasty* television series, her other thespian portrait credits including Dirk Bogarde, Peter Sellers and Ralph Richardson. Lehmann painted landscapes near her Essex homes in Great Sampford and Saffron Walden which were likened to those of John Nash and Rowland Suddaby. Was a member of NS and SGA. Lehmann was also a prolific illustrator for *Radio Times*. There was a retrospective at The Barnsdale Gallery, Yoxford, 2001. The Imperial War Museum, Royal Air Force Museum at Hendon and Fry Art Gallery in Saffron Walden hold her work.

Damon LEHRER 1967– Figurative painter, born in Boston, Massachusetts, America, who graduated in fine art from Amherst College, 1989, obtaining his master's degree in painting at Boston University, 1994. Exhibitions included Tsai Performance Center, Boston, 1994; Pepper Gallery, Boston, from 1995; and Summer Exhibition, Beaux Arts, Bath, 1998. Lehrer was based in London from 1997. American collections holding his work include New York and Boston Public Libraries, Dartmouth College rare book library, and Fogg Art Museum, Harvard University.

Timo LEHTONEN 1953– Artist, notably a printmaker, and teacher, born in Helsinki, Finland, who attended Falmouth School of Art, 1972–3; Sheffield Polytechnic, 1973–6; and Royal College of Art, 1976–9. Awards included *The Observer* Royal Silver Jubilee Printmaking Prize, 1977; finalist, Sainsbury's Images for Today, 1983; Lowick House Printmaking Residency, 1986; Royal College of Art Printmaking Fellowship, 1987; and Museum of London artist-in-residence, 1994. From 1982 Lehtonen held a number of visiting and sessional lectureships, including Camberwell and Chelsea Schools of Art; Gloucestershire and Royal Colleges of Art; Leeds Polytechnic; Middlesex, Westminster and Hertfordshire Universities, Surrey Institute of Art & Design; and Lambeth College, where in 1993 he was external moderator. Group shows included Royal Over-Seas League Open, 1984; South Bank Picture Show at Royal Festival Hall, 1987 and 1988; and National Print Exhibition, Mall Galleries, 1994. Had a solo show at Eton College 1984, later ones including Museum of London, 1994. Victoria & Albert Museum, Mappin Art Gallery in Sheffield and Northern Arts hold examples.

Sylvia LEIBSON 1915–1989 Sculptor in clay, stone and silver, and painter in oil, born and lived in London, married to Dr Michael Leibson. She was largely self-taught, but studied sculpture with Mosè Tamburrini. Leibson's main work was portrait sculpture, also some small abstracts. She was a member of SPS and was prominent in the Islington Art Circle. Group shows included London Artists at Shrewsbury School, 1968; Upper Street Gallery, 1971; Hemel Hempstead Arts Trust Festival, 1973; Rotunda Gallery, 1974; and Manor House Society, Art in Jewish Ritual, 1984. Leibson ran a gallery in her home (58 Aberdeen Park, Highbury) where she had many solo shows and exhibited about 70 other artists' works.

Emily LEICESTER fl. c.1905–1960 Painter of portraits and miniaturist, born in Northwich, Cheshire, where she attended the High School and the School of Art. Also studied at Manchester School of Art. Exhibited RA, RCamA, Paris Salon and extensively at Walker Art Gallery, Liverpool. Lived in Hartford, Cheshire.

Roger LEIGH 1925–1997 Sculptor, architect, artist in photomontage and teacher, born in Broadwell, Gloucestershire. Served in Royal Air Force during World War II, then attended Liverpool University. He was trained in architecture and town planning, 1947–53, but in late 1940s began abstract sculpture. Was assistant to the sculptor Barbara Hepworth, 1953–4, in the latter year joining Penwith Society of Arts. After working as an architect for London Country Council, 1954–7, sculpting in his spare time, Leigh returned to St Ives, Cornwall, in 1957, serving for some months with Hepworth again and working part-time as an architect in Truro in the early 1960s for two years. Moved to Aldbourne, Wiltshire, in 1966, the year he began teaching at Exeter School of Art. Organised the Sculpture in Landscape show in Aldbourne in 1969. From 1964 held a series of one-man shows, including New Vision Centre Gallery, Arnolfini Gallery in Bristol and Portsmouth City Art Gallery. Lived at Erlestoke, near Devizes in Wiltshire.

Molly LEIGH-HUNT 1912– Painter and film actress who also studied music, born and lived London, daughter of the painter Gerard Leigh-Hunt. Her married name was Molly Loftus-Paton. Studied privately in London, then art at Byam Shaw School in 1930s, working with Ernest Jackson. She won a number of Royal Drawing Society medals. Exhibited UA, of which she was a member, and East Dorset Art Society. Lived in London.

John LEIGH-PEMBERTON 1911–1997 Painter, designer and illustrator, born and lived in London, studying art there for about four years from 1928 after education at Eton College. During World War II, Leigh-Pemberton was awarded the Air Force Cross for services to flying instruction. Leigh-Pemberton showed with ROI and NS of which he was for a time a member, RA, NEAC, at leading London galleries and abroad. He illustrated many books, notably for children and on natural history, including *Shell Guide to Wild Life* and *A Book of British Wild Flowers*. Leigh-Pemberton did much distinguished advertising work for companies such as Midland Bank, British Petroleum and Shell, being included in the "That's Shell – that is!" exhibition at Barbican Art Gallery in 1983. Imperial War Museum and National Maritime Museum in Greenwich hold examples. Leigh-Pemberton retired in 1982.

Katherine LEIGH-PEMBERTON: *see* **Kaff GERRARD**

Alfred Crocker LEIGHTON 1901–1965 Realistic landscape painter, notably in watercolour, related to the artist Lord Leighton and born in Hastings, Sussex. He studied at Hastings and Hornsey Schools of Art, a fellow-Hastings painter E Leslie Badham being an influence. Leighton was elected RBA in 1929, showed with Ridley and East Sussex Art Clubs and with RA and Paris Salon from 1925. He was resident in Canada from 1929, but returned periodically to England. Painting and preserving the old windmills of Kent and Sussex were early interests of Leighton, a compulsive and hard-working artist whose first visit to Canada stemmed from a 1924 Canadian Pacific Railway commission to paint the Rocky Mountains. These were a continuing preoccupation because "their purity of colouring are unrivalled". Leighton's teaching career included art directorship of Calgary's Institute of Technology and Art, 1929–36, helping to found what became the Banff School of Fine Arts. Leighton formed and organised the Alberta Society of Artists, also the Calgary and Medicine Hat Sketch Clubs and was a member of the Royal Canadian Academy. In his later years the reclusive Leighton – known generally as A C – built a house 10 miles southwest of Calgary, Alberta, which became the core of The Leighton Foundation after the death of his artist wife Barbara in 1986. This was designed to promote art and nature to children, adults, amateurs and professionals. The Barleigh Block Prints were a collaborative effort by Leighton and his wife, based on his watercolours, production of which continued after his death. He exhibited widely in Canada and overseas. There was a touring retrospective organised by Edmonton Art Gallery in 1982 and the Whyte Foundation, Banff, set up a tour of his Rockies pictures in 1989.

Clare LEIGHTON 1898–1989 Primarily a wood engraver, but also a writer, designer, artist in mosaic and stained glass, born in London into a literary family. Studied at Brighton School of Art, the Slade School of Fine Art under Henry Tonks, 1920–2, and the Central School of Arts and Crafts, 1923–4, with Noel Rooke. As a result she became a wood engraver at a time of the craft's resurgence in England and was the first woman to publish a book on the technique, in 1932: *Wood Engraving and Woodcuts.* Although she exhibited RE, RA, Redfern Gallery, RHA and elsewhere, her work was primarily for the printed page. She was one of the finest wood engravers of her time, producing strong and vigorous images. Among books illustrated were Thomas Hardy's *The Return of the Native*, 1929; her own *The Farmer's Year*, 1933; and Gilbert White's *The Natural History of Selborne*, 1941. As an author-artist her titles *Four Hedges* and *Country Matters* were notable. In 1939 she emigrated to America, where she lectured and became vice-president of the Society of American Graphic Art and fellow of the National Academy of Design. Designed 33 stained glass windows for St Paul's Cathedral, Worcester, Massachusetts. Clare Leighton was a pacifist with strong social convictions, evident in her written work. Ashmolean Museum, Oxford, held a major exhibition in 1992.

Tanya LEIGHTON 1970– Artist and curator, born in Guildford, Surrey, who for New Art in Scotland, Centre for Contemporary Arts, Glasgow, in 1994, created wall pieces made with coloured matches. She attended West Surrey College of Art and Design, Farnham, 1988–9, then studied postgraduate photography at the School of Art, Glasgow, 1989–95. Exhibitions included The Maltings Student Show, Maltings, Farnham, 1989, and Forum II, Stills Gallery, Edinburgh, 1993. After working on the committee of Transmission Gallery, Glasgow, in 1997 joined the newly opened Dundee Contemporary Arts as an assistant curator, then moved to Manchester Metropolitan University as a research fellow. Following an invitation from New York's Whitney Museum to work on an historical retrospective show of American film and video art, in 2000 Leighton organised Vivre Sa Vie, an exhibition of French art, at 13 venues around Glasgow and Edinburgh.

Flora LEIPMAN 1918–1999 Writer and artist, born in Glasgow to parents of Russian origin. After her father died and her mother remarried, the family moved to Communist Russia. Soon after arrival Flora's mother, then her two sisters and brother, disappeared; it was 25 years before she saw her mother, sentenced to 15 years in labour camps as a spy; the sisters perished in other camps, the brother survived to live in Florida. Having sacrificed the chance to leave Russia with her first husband, an Austrian, Flora was deported to the horrific Karaganda camp in Kazakhstan, then spent the war in backbreaking work in the mines. After an unhappy second marriage, she was reunited with her mother; they settled in Leningrad; then, after her mother's death and a five-year battle with the authorities, Flora returned to Britain. In 1987 she published her story *The Long Journey Home* and entered Nightingale House, a retirement home in south London which had a studio. There her love of art, nurtured during childhood visits to Kelvingrove Art Gallery and to the Hermitage Museum, was reawakened. She began painting "memories with imagination" of the Jewish home life she had missed. They were given a solo show at Ben Uri Art Society in 1990, and posthumously at Nightingale House's gallery, as part of Wandsworth Arts Festival in 1999.

Robert LEISHMAN 1916–1989 Painter, draughtsman and teacher, born in Inverkeithing, Fife. Leishman graduated from Edinburgh College of Art, a member of the notable generation which included Alan Davie, William Gear and Robin Philipson. After war service, 1940–6, in the Army Leishman taught in Germany, Edinburgh, Fife and Dundee, but in 1972 gave up teaching to paint full-time. He was elected SSA and RSW and won the May Marshall Brown Award in 1987. Showed widely in Scottish group shows and his solo exhibitions included McClure Gallery, Glasgow, several at the Scottish Gallery in Edinburgh, a retrospective at Roseangle Gallery, Dundee, in 1981, and William Hardie Gallery, Glasgow, in 1990. Work held by Scottish Arts Council, Dundee City Art Gallery and elsewhere. Leishman's pictures are colourful, imaginative and witty, a reflection of the artist's own character. Lived in Dundee, Angus.

Gwen LEITCH 1931– Painter, born in Tasmania, Australia, who studied at Hobart Art School. Moved to England on a travelling scholarship in 1954, studying at Central School of Arts and Crafts, 1954–6, then settled in Zennor and St Ives, Cornwall, the landscape there inspiring her work. Showed with the Penwith Society, St Ives, and in 1958 was included in 4 Sculptors 2 Painters at Drian Gallery.

James LE JEUNE 1910–1983 Painter, born in Saskatoon, Canada. Initially he was educated in Northamptonshire.

His art education included Heatherley's School of Fine Art, Byam Shaw School of Drawing and Painting and Art Students' League of New York. Exhibited NEAC, UA, RP, RBA and RSMA. HRH The Duke of Edinburgh bought his work. Lived in London, later in Dublin.

Hendrik LEK 1903–1985 Painter, born in Antwerp, Belgium. His father did not want him to become an artist so he went into the diamond business, studying part-time at Antwerp Academy with Lucien de Jaegher. Fleeing from Germans he moved to Britain in 1940 and after the war became an antique dealer, having always collected, painting in his spare time. In 1946 he restored a 15th-century building called the Tudor Rose in Beaumaris which became an obsession, his shop and the subject of many of his pictures. When he ceased dealing it became a gallery in which his and his son Karel's pictures were jointly shown. Showed at RCamA and other venues in Wales, as well as in Canada, Netherlands and America. Anglesey Art Collection holds his work. Lived in retirement in Anglesey, Gwynnedd, north Wales.

Karel LEK 1929– Artist in a wide variety of media, designer and lecturer, son of the artist Hendrik Lek, born in Antwerp, Belgium. He was educated at Friars' School, Bangor, then Liverpool College of Art, 1946–52. Notable teachers included Karel Vogel and Geoffrey Wedgwood. Lek said that "the country of my birth, regarding my mode of expression, which is emotional," was important to his output. "My concern is humanity. I very often see beauty in what is often neglected." Lek was a member of RCamA. He also showed at RA, Whitechapel Art Gallery, SWE, Woodstock Gallery, RI, ICA and public galleries in Amsterdam and Llandudno. Solo shows included RCamA, Woodstock Gallery, Oriel Bangor, and Tegfryn Gallery in Menai Bridge. Contemporary Art Society for Wales, The Football Association, National Library of Wales in Aberystwyth and overseas collections hold examples. Lived at Beaumaris, Gwynedd.

Martin LEMAN 1934– Painter, designer and teacher, born and lived in London, who acquired an international reputation for his amusing and stylised cats, although curvaceous nudes and still lifes were also favoured subjects. After Worthing Art School he did his National Service in the Army, serving in Egypt, then had two years at the Central School of Arts and Crafts studying to be a graphic designer, leaving before he had finished the course as he was keen to start some real design work. After a series of jobs he began teaching, mainly part-time at Hornsey College of Art for almost 20 years, which allowed him to do his own freelance work. In the late 1960s he began to paint the cat pictures with which he became identified, and a number of successful exhibitions and books enabled him to be self-employed. Leman's images were featured on a series of popular artefacts, such as postcards and jigsaw puzzles. He was a regular exhibitor at the RA Summer Exhibition as well as in many other mixed shows in Britain and abroad, galleries giving him solo exhibitions including Portal, Graffiti, RONA and Artbank Galleries and Andrew Usiskin Contemporary Art. Later one-mans included Wren Gallery, Burford, 2003; Seascapes, Cross Street Gallery, 2004; with a series at Artbank Gallery. After the success of the book *Comic & Curious Cats* in 1979, he was involved in over two dozen others. Leman's first wife, Adrianne Jarratt, was a designer, his second, Jill Winthrop, a painter and writer. His story is told in David Buckman's book *Martin Leman A World of His Own*, published by Sansom & Company in 2002.

Francis LE MARCHANT 1939– Artist mainly in oil and watercolour, born in Hungerton, Lincolnshire, full title Sir Francis Le Marchant, Bart. There was an artistic tradition in most branches of his family, notably Fanny Le Marchant, the bird painter. He studied at Byam Shaw School of Drawing and Painting, 1959–62, then Royal Academy Schools, 1962–6. He was offered an extra year in the sculpture school. Teachers included Charles Mahoney, Peter Greenham, Bernard Dunstan, Edward Bawden and Anthony Eyton. In 1968 Le Marchant spent four months at Hornsey College of Art in textile department to study tapestry design. Landscape and architecture were two key themes in his paintings, traditional and realistic in approach. Group shows included RA Summer Exhibitions, Upper Grosvenor Galleries, Leicester Galleries and Oscar and Peter Johnson. Showed with Agnew from 1969 in solo shows, later ones including Sally Hunter and Patrick Seale Fine Art, 1986, and Roy Miles Gallery, 1996. Department of the Environment holds his work.

Kalliopi LEMOS 1951– Artist, born in Greece, who studied at Byam Shaw School of Art, 1989–94. Had solo shows at European Academy of Arts, 1996, Hellenic Centre, 1997, and La Subbia, Pietrasanta in Italy, 1999, the year she was Artist of the Day at Flowers East, chosen by Ann Dowker.

Helen LEMPRIERE 1907–1991 Painter, printmaker and artist in mixed media, with a strong interest in Australian Aborigine mythology. She was born in Melbourne, Victoria, into a cultured, wealthy family, niece of the singer Dame Nellie Melba, after whom she was named. From 1930 she studied first with the tonal painter Archibald Colquhoun, then for many years with Justus Jorgensen, being a member of his Mantsalvat bohemian circle. After marriage to Keith Wood in 1945 Lempriere's life changed, and from 1950–8 she lived in Paris, studying with Fernand Léger and Fred Klein, father of the artist Yves Klein, and exhibiting in mixed shows. In 1953 she participated in the first Australian Artists' Association exhibition at RWS Conduit Street gallery; she settled in London, 1958–65; and in the latter year showed solo at the Leicester Galleries. The year after, she and her husband settled in Sydney. Lempriere exhibited widely internationally, but tended to be neglected in Australia, although a retrospective at Woolloomooloo Gallery, Woolloomooloo, in 1993 did much to rehabilitate her reputation. A debilitating illness blighted her later years. Lempriere is well represented in public collections in Australia and America, including the Australian National Gallery in Canberra and Miami Museum of Modern Art, Florida, and the *Daily Mirror* Newspapers and *Financial Times* holdings.

Brenda LENAGHAN fl. from early 1960s– Painter, designer and teacher who studied at Glasgow School of Art. She obtained a diploma in commercial and graphic design and obtained a job with Bernat Klein, a Galashiels-based fabric designer. For 15 years from then on taught art in Glasgow, married, studied with the Open University and travelled, but did little painting. In 1978 she exhibited at Peter Potter Gallery, Haddington, with a one-man the following year, in 1980 sharing a show at Stirling Gallery.

Then showed regularly in Scotland, including RSW of which she was a member, RSA and Royal Glasgow Institute of the Fine Arts. She gained the Anne Redpath Prize in 1975 and 1983 and the SSWA Special Award in 1980. Later exhibitions included Christopher Hull Gallery, 1988, and Duncan Campbell Fine Art and William Hardie, Glasgow, 1991. Her work is in collections worldwide. She travelled to countries including Russia, Tibet, China, Greece, Italy and Nepal, and they and their mythologies inspired her work.

Patricia LENAGHAN 1958– Artist who obtained an honours degree from Glasgow School of Art, 1977–81, gaining her master's from Chelsea School of Art, 1981–2. Group shows included SSA, 1979; Glasgow Print Studio, 1980; New Generation Artists at Compass Gallery, Glasgow, 1981; Christie's Inaugural Show and Minsky's Gallery, both 1982; and Scottish Print Open Three, 1983, organised by Dundee Printmakers' Workshop.

Barbara LENG-SMITH 1922– Artist in oil, watercolour and pastel, notable for portraits, born in the Isle of Man. She studied at Manchester with Harry Rutherford. Leng-Smith was a member of the Société des Artistes Français. She received an Hon. Mention at Paris Salon in 1969, the Silver Medal in 1972, and a Diplôme d'Honneur twice at Salon International, 1970–1. Showed with RP, RSA, Manchester Academy and in France and had a solo show at Tib Lane Gallery, Manchester. Lived in Hale, Cheshire.

Robert O LENKIEWICZ 1941–2002 Portrait painter and muralist, born of Jewish parents who moved to London in 1939 from Russia and Germany. His mother's father was court painter to mad King Ludwig of Bavaria. Lenkiewicz attended St Martin's School of Art and Royal Academy Schools. He painted on a large scale, one picture at St Martin's being 360 feet long, 17 feet high. Later work was based on a series of themes, including the Jewish Holocaust. Settling in Plymouth, Devon, Lenkiewicz formed a large, valuable library, rooms having themes such as death, magic and metaphysics. Had his first commercial exhibition, organised by The Halcyon Gallery in association with Arthur Andersen, at International Convention Centre, Birmingham, 1994. The retrospective, of over 300 pictures, was aimed at raising up to £500,000 to buy properties adjacent to his studio. There was another retrospective at the Art Gallery, Wolverhampton, 1998. Sotheby's at Olympia held a large studio sale of Lenkiewicz's work, with an illustrated catalogue, in 2003.

Cynthia LENNON 1939– Figurative artist and designer, born in Blackpool, who grew up in Hoylake, Cheshire, first wife of the Beatle musician John Lennon, whom she met in 1957. They were students at Liverpool Regional College of Art at the same time as Stuart Sutcliffe. Cynthia and John married in 1962, just before the Beatles cut their first single, *Love Me Do*, and had a son, Julian, a singer; they divorced in 1968 after John left her for Yoko Ono. Afterwards Cynthia remarried; in 1978 she published her autobiography *Twist of Lennon*; ran several restaurants; in 1983 gained a three-year contract to design bedding and textiles with Vantona Viyella, also doing other commercial work; in 1991 sold her Lennon relics at Christie's; and 1995 in made a late début as a recording artist. In 1999 she shared a show with Phyllis McKenzie, a friend from art college days, at KDK Gallery, co-owned by Sutcliffe's sister Pauline. By this time Cynthia had returned to full-time painting. Her KDK exhibits included cartoony drawings made to illustrate her autobiography. Her book *John*, a memoir of her former husband, appeared in 2005. She lived in Majorca with her fourth husband, Noel Charles.

Dennis LENNON 1918–1991 Architect, artist and designer, who attended Merchant Taylors' School and University College. During Army service, 1939–45, during which he was mentioned in dispatches and won the Military Cross, was captured in France and later escaped, Lennon served in North Africa and Italy. From 1948–50 he was director of the Rayon Industry Design Centre, then went successfully into private practice. Main works included Jaeger shops, London Steak Houses, co-ordination of the interior of the liner *Queen Elizabeth II*, Chalcot Housing Estate in Hampstead, the unusual boat-shaped central dining room at Harrow School and refurbishment of the Ritz Hotel. Was a member of RIBA and of Society of Industrial Artists and Designers and of the Savile Club, where he showed and sold work. Abbott and Holder also sold examples, after his death. Lennon designed the set for Richard Strauss's opera *Capriccio* at Glyndebourne and a number of state galas at Royal Opera House. Lived in Watford, Hertfordshire.

John LENNON 1940–1980 Pop and Rock singer, musician and songwriter, born in Liverpool. After an unsettled childhood and unpromising education at Quarry Bank grammar school, he attended the Regional College of Art there, 1957–60, teachers including Philip Hartas, George Jardine and Arthur Ballard, where a fellow-student was the highly gifted Stuart Sutcliffe. By this time Lennon was involved with his first music group, the Quarry Men, which developed into the Beatles, known as the Fab Four, the most successful-ever Pop group, with which Sutcliffe was briefly involved. Lennon proved a lazy art student and, although he continued to draw all his life, his output remained mainly cartoons and caricatures in the spirit of Spike Milligan and the radio comedy programme *The Goon Show*, of which Lennon was fond. These found their way into his slim volumes *In His Own Write*, 1964, and *A Spaniard In The Works*, 1965. Lennon was first married to Cynthia Lennon, also a student at the College of Art. In 1966, at the height of the Beatles' international success, he met the Japanese artist Yoko Ono, whom he married in 1969, an event followed by the famous "bed-in for peace" in the luxurious honeymoon suite at Amsterdam Hilton. The bed-in was just one of the high-profile media events that characterised Lennon's later career. It and the wedding ceremony were mentioned in *The Ballad of John and Yoko*, the Beatles' last British number one hit disc, 1969. Following the demise of the group Lennon went his own way as a musician, recording a series of albums. After his shooting by an assassin in New York, Lennon's pictures continued to be printed and exhibited. Compton Cassey Gallery, near Withington, showed works by Lennon with those of Miles Davis in 1996. Jonathan Poole (John Lennon Art Estate, UK) held a notable exhibition of lithographs, serigraphs and copper etchings, signed by Yoko Ono, at the Gallery in Cork Street in 2004.

LENSMAN: *see* **Humphrey SPENDER**

LEO 1963– Versatile artist employing modern media, and lecturer, who graduated with honours in fine art from Sunderland Polytechnic, 1982–5, and whose surname was, according to his agent Dominic Berning "eradicated from history." Berning showed the artist at both ART2000 and ART2001 at Islington's Business Design Centre. Leo was artist-in-residence, Wakefield 100 Festival, 1988, and was a visiting lecturer at Jacob Kramer College Leeds. Previous mixed exhibitions included Sleepwalkers, Red Herring Gallery, Brighton, 1990; Light Fantastic!, Wallsall Museum and Art Gallery, 1994; Whitechapel Art Gallery Open, 1996; and Young Art in Europe, GLK, Ghent, Belgium, 1998–9. Among his solo shows were Michael Cosar Gallery, Düsseldorf, Germany, 1998–9, and Monumental Sculpture, photographic and text-based works, at the University of Hertfordshire, 2002. Projects LEO was involved in included Leeds Trades Union Congress Unemployed Centre Mural, 1986; production of the film *The Short Life of a Happy Man*, 1991–2; acting as a film programmer at Whitechapel Art Gallery, 1994–8; as assistant editor of the film publication *PIX 2*, 1997; and being shortlisted for the North Kensington Amenity Trust Public Art Commission in 1999.

Charmian LEONARD fl. from 1950s– Artist in oil and drawing media, and teacher, who also used her maiden name Charmian Leondopoulos to exhibit. Was married to the sculptor Keith Leonard, their son Mark being a painter. She was born in London and studied for her diploma at Chelsea School of Art, 1953–5, and for an art teacher's diploma at Bournemouth School of Art; her teachers included Ceri Richards, Prunella Clough and Vivian Pitchforth. Taught at Newcastle and Sunderland Schools of Art and at several adult education establishments. Leonard's pictures, inspired by "the infinite variety, order and precision of existence", by plants, stars, tides and so on, had a simplicity of approach bordering on the childlike, and drew on the landscape near home in St Ives, Cornwall. Shared shows with her husband at Limited Editions and Artisan Gallery, and Vision Gallery, Sheffield. Mixed exhibitions included Penwith Gallery in St Ives, Ashgate Gallery in Farnham and The Living Room. Had solo shows at Amalgam Gallery in Barnes and Brown's Gallery, Penzance.

Keith LEONARD 1921–1993 Sculptor, painter and teacher, born in Birmingham, husband of the artist Charmian Leonard, their son being the painter Mark Leonard. Keith Leonard studied at Birmingham College of Arts and Crafts; from 1949–52 at Slade School of Fine Art under A H Gerrard, whom he termed a "marvellous teacher"; and with Ossip Zadkine, in Paris, 1953. He was an assistant to Barbara Hepworth, 1955–9. As well as a period teaching at Stourbridge School of Art, Leonard was head of sculpture at Sunderland School of Art, 1959–62, and at Farnham School of Art, 1964–7. Mixed exhibitions included Tate Gallery, 1958; New Art Centre, 1986; and Artists from Cornwall at RWA, 1992; he was a member of the Penwith Society in St Ives, where he lived. Solo shows included Drian Gallery, 1958, and a retrospective at Penwith Gallery, St Ives, 1994. The bronze Pavlova, 1992, in the RWA show was a good example of the grace and elegance of Leonard's abstract style. Barbara Hepworth and Ben Nicholson acquired Leonard's work, which is also held by Birmingham City Museum and Art Gallery and Farnborough Library.

Michael LEONARD 1933– Painter and illustrator, full name Douglas Michael Leonard, born in Bangalore, India. He was educated at Stonyhurst College, then St Martin's School of Art, where he studied graphic design, 1954–7. For 15 years Leonard worked as an illustrator. From 1972 he worked mainly as a painter, appearing in many group shows at Fischer Fine Art, which went on to represent him and where he had a series of solo shows. Also exhibited one-man at Harriet Griffin Gallery in New York, in 1977–8 had a retrospective at Gemeentemuseum in Arnhem, Netherlands, and in 1993 a solo show at Thomas Gibson Fine Art which made clear Leonard's fine abilities as a painter of the nude in the classical tradition. Showed widely in mixed exhibitions on the continent and in America. The Boymans Van Beuningen Museum, Rotterdam, holds his work, as do Victoria & Albert Museum and National Portrait Gallery. It has Leonard's portrait of HM The Queen, commissioned by *Reader's Digest* to celebrate her sixtieth birthday. Lived in London.

Charmian LEONDOPOULOS: *see* **Charmian LEONARD**

Anne LEONE fl. from early 1980s– Painter and teacher, married to the artist Daniel Ludwig, who obtained a bachelor's degree in fine arts at Boston University, 1981, her master's degree at University of Cincinnati in 1985. She showed extensively in America in group and solo shows, being represented by galleries in New York, Kentucky and New England. In England she had a series of solo exhibitions at Cadogan Contemporary from 1988. Taught at UMass Dartmouth and lived in Newport, Rhode Island.

Dante LEONELLI 1931– Versatile artist, researcher, consultant and teacher, born in Chicago, Illinois, America, who attended the Art Institute of Chicago, 1949–53, and Courtauld Institute of Art, 1955–9. Leonelli went on to establish a wide-ranging international career. He headed the plastics research unit at the Royal College of Art, 1967–8; was professor of advanced sculpture, University of Wisconsin, Madison, 1968–9; of inter-dimensional concepts, University of Iowa, 1977–8; and of graduate sculpture, University of Washington, Seattle, 1983–4. He lectured in the school of photography/holography, Royal College of Art, 1986–7. Leonelli was also senior lecturer, fine art school, Middlesex University, 1981–97. Alongside these posts, between 1970–97 he was visiting professor of art and visiting artist at a string of American seats of learning. His many wide-ranging research projects encompassed tungsten/neon light-plasma structures, J D Mooney Foundation in America, 1965, through the influence of traditional technologies on recent design, Japan, 1973; Iran Gulf War Proposal, Imperial War Museum, 1987; solar IPS units, pollution/meteorological sensors, Crested Butte, America, 1995; to light-emitting diodes/solar panel configurations, 2002. Leonelli's awards included first prizes, London Transport, Holborn Underground Station Proposal, 1980, and British Airport Authority, Gatwick Arrivals Terminal Proposal, 1990. A string of global consultancies latterly included work on the restructuring of the Academy of Art in Tirana, Albania, 1997; being lead artist and selector with architect Piers Gough for the Notting Hill Gate Improvement Group, 1999; and involvement in the Waiheke Island Todd Project, New Zealand, 2003. While at the Royal College of Art, 1967–8, Leonelli with Michael McKinnon and Robert Janz founded Continuum, which toured five major museums until its arrival at Hayward Gallery, 1970, the first kinetic light exhibition there. As a sculptor, painter, installations, photography, video and performance artist Leonelli showed solo at major venues around the world. Public galleries holding his work included Smith College Museum of Art, Northampton, Massachusetts, America; Galerie *Der Spiegel*, Cologne, Germany; University of Iowa; National Gallery of Victoria, Melbourne, Australia; and Kustmuseum, Basel, Switzerland; plus corporate, embassy and private collections. Leonelli had a base in London.

Kim C LEONG fl. from 1950s– Versatile painter, born in Malaya, who was educated there and later studied modern languages in England and the Netherlands. From 1960–85 she travelled extensively on the continent, in North America, Mexico and Southeast Asia, where meeting with other artists influenced her work. This had an underpinning of traditional Chinese education and the practice of calligraphy. Chinese brush and silk painting were notable features of her work. Between 1952–67 she took part in the Annual Exhibition in Malaysia, winning first prizes in 1953–4. British appearances included Aron College, Wales, 1972; East & West Art Exhibition, Lauderdale House, 1990; and Primrose Hill Gallery, 1993, where she shared a show. She was also known as Leong Shao Ling.

Simon LE RUEZ 1970– Artist and lecturer, born in Jersey, Channel Islands, who "uses sculpture, installation and drawing to establish a dialogue which reflects on childhood memories, unrequited feelings and the places we may go to in order to seek relief. My work is characterised by the deliberate staging or suggestion of conflicting comforts." Le Ruez gained an art and design diploma at Exeter College of Art, 1990; an honours degree in fine art, Kennington School of Art, 1994; and his master's in sculpture at Winchester School of Art, 1995. "Notable teachers were John Gibbons and Tim Marlow and influences have included Miroslav Balka, Robert Adams, Doris Salcedo, Luc Tuymans and Raymond Carver." Awards and scholarships included a Barreau Art Scholarship, 1992; Beckwith Travel Scholarship, Arizona/California, 1993; Barreau Art Scholarship, Jersey Museum, 1994; Council Travel Prize, Paris, 1996; Kingsgate Workshop Award, 1998; Individual Artist Award and Research and Development Award, Yorkshire Arts Board, both 2001; Arts Council Travel Award, New York, 2002; and Inspiral Creativity Award, 2003. Residencies and research included Faculty de Belle Arts, Valencia, Spain, 1997; and a Research project into the notion of 'archive', 2003. Le Ruez held a number of lecturing posts, among them latterly University of Derby and Nottingham Trent School of Art and Design, both 2003. He gained two Sheffield public art commissions: for a Way-marker, Rivlen Valley, 2002, and 'Response' Sound Sculpture for Millennium Galleries, 2001. Later group shows included Mongrel Monitor, Site Gallery, Sheffield, 2001; Postcard Show, Surface Gallery, Nottingham, and Return to Sender. Pitt Rivers Museum, Oxford, both 2003; and Marks in Space, Usher Gallery, Lincoln, 2004. Among his solo exhibitions were Threats and Promises, Bloc Space, Sheffield, 2003; and Acts of Generosity, Castlefield Gallery, Manchester, and Stories of Solitude, Arhus Kunstbygning (Museum of Modern Art), Arhus, Denmark, both 2005. Private collections in Britain and abroad held works by Le Ruez, who lived in Sheffield.

Zbigniew LES 1914– Sculptor, woodcarver and artist in paper, brought up in Poland, his original name being Leszczyński. Service with Polish Army in Britain during World War II. He was a son of the Polish artist Konstanty Leszczyński, with whom he studied, and also taught himself in Britain and in several countries on the continent. Also studied at Warsaw and Edinburgh Universities, finally settling in Edinburgh. Exhibited RSA, SSA and elsewhere.

Cecil Mary LESLIE 1900–1980 Painter, sculptor, illustrator, printmaker and furniture designer. She was the daughter of Sir Norman Leslie and was born in London. Studied at Heatherley's School of Fine Art, 1919, at the London School of Photolithography and Engraving and at the Central School of Arts and Crafts. In the mid-1920s she taught at Grosvenor School of Modern Art. Served as a nurse in both World Wars. Showed at RA, RSA, Royal Glasgow Institute of the Fine Arts, RCamA, in the provinces and overseas. Illustrated several dozen books. British Museum and National Portrait Gallery hold her work. Lived finally in Blakeney, Norfolk.

Frederick LESSORE 1879–1951 Sculptor and painter, born in Brighton, son of the artist Jules Lessore. Studied art in Paris and London, in 1906 gaining a medal at the Royal Academy Schools. Member of the Art Workers' Guild. Exhibited RA, Walker Art Gallery, Liverpool, and elsewhere. Major Lessore modelled many statues and busts in England and abroad. He founded the Beaux Arts Gallery which his wife, the painter Helen Lessore, took over after his death. Lived in London.

Helen LESSORE 1907–1994 Painter, gallery owner and writer, born and lived in London, who originally exhibited under her maiden name Helen Brook. She was educated at the Slade School of Fine Art, 1924–8, under Henry Tonks and Tancred Borenius, where she was a prize winner, and in 1931 began working as secretary at the Beaux Arts Gallery, founded by her husband, the sculptor Frederick Lessore. She married him in 1934, John Lessore the artist being their son. Helen Lessore took over running the gallery from 1952–65, then became a full-time painter. Under her direction the semi-moribund Beaux Arts was revitalised, and she gave first exhibitions to Auerbach and Kossoff, showed Freud, Aitchison and Uglow and championed the Kitchen Sink School painters such as Middleditch, Greaves and Jack Smith. She exhibited in Marlborough Fine Art's Helen Lessore and the Beaux Arts Gallery, 1968; at 12 Duke Street in 1981; and had a retrospective at Fine Art Society in 1987. Her book *A Partial Testament* was published in 1986, the year she was elected RA.

John LESSORE 1939– Painter and teacher, born in London where he continued to live. He studied at Slade School of Fine Art, 1957–61, gaining an Abbey Minor Travelling Scholarship to Italy in the latter year. In 1965 he had a one-man show at Beaux Arts Gallery, run by his mother, the painter Helen Lessore. Other one-man shows included Ashgate Gallery in Farnham; New Art Centre; Nigel Greenwood Gallery, 1990, where Lessore's brand of Expressionism concentrated on the subject of artist and model; Christchurch Mansion, Ipswich, 1999; Ranger's House, Blackheath, 2000; Berkeley Square Gallery, 2002; and Chappel Galleries, Chappel, 2004. This included a portrait of his mother and the intimate, family-oriented work for which he was noted. In 1965 he took a post teaching at Royal Academy Schools, from 1978 teaching at Norwich School of Art. In 2003, he was appointed a trustee of the board of the National Gallery for four years. Arts Council holds his work. In 2004, Lessore's picture Six British Paralympic Athletes was unveiled at the National Portrait Gallery, an imaginative commission as the artist, as well as being a fine figure painter, was himself a paraplegic. Twenty-four related studies were shown by Annely Juda.

Thérèse LESSORE 1884–1945 Artist, daughter of the painter Jules Lessore and sister of the sculptor Frederick Lessore. She was the third wife of the painter Walter Sickert, who described her as "a Persian miniature", having previously been married to the artist Bernard Adeney. She was born in Brighton and after attending the South-Western Polytechnic Art School was at Slade School of Fine Art, 1904–9, where she won the Melville Nettleship Prize for Figure Composition. She showed at LG, NEAC and Goupil Gallery and had first solo exhibition at Eldar Gallery, with a catalogue preface by Sickert. She married him in 1926, shared a love of the music-hall and circus with him, which was reflected in her work, and nursed him until his death.

Allie LESTAS 1959– After studying at Medway College of Design, 1979–80, Lestas graduated with honours from Camberwell School of Arts and Crafts, 1980–4. In 1986 Lestas was included in a London Fashion Centre Exhibition, London Pride, at Lamont Gallery, and Body Adornment Show, at Adam Gallery; and in 1989 in East End Open Studios, based at Unit 7, Peckham Road.

Michal LESZCZYŃSKI 1906–1972 Painter, mural artist and draughtsman, born in Dolina, Poland, specialising in ships and the sea. As well as studying at nautical and musical colleges in Warsaw, he studied art at the State Academy in Cracow, anatomy at the University there and privately in England, in which he settled for some years. In England was for a period a navigation officer in the Admiralty, having sailed professionally while in Poland. Was an expert on sailing ships and published, among other books, *How to Draw Sail and Sea*. Exhibited in England at RA, NS and RI and had several one-man shows in London and New York. Polish Embassy in London and Port of London Authority hold his work. Lived for a time in Copnor, Hampshire, later in Montego Bay, Jamaica.

Arthur LETT-HAINES: *see* **Lett HAINES**

John LETTS 1930– Sculptor, son of the designer Joseph Letts, born in Birmingham, where he studied at the Birmingham School of Art under the head of sculpture William Bloye, 1945–9. Showed in London and widely in the Midlands. In 1985 he completed a statue of the novelist George Eliot for the centre of Nuneaton, Warwickshire, near where she had lived. Public gallery in Stratford-upon-Avon also holds Letts' work. He lived at Astley, near Nuneaton.

Marian LEVEN 1944– Painter in oil and acrylic of mostly landscape-based work, born in Edinburgh, married to the artist Will Maclean. She studied at Gray's School of Art, Aberdeen, 1962–6. Was a member of RSW, also showing at RSA, Royal Glasgow Institute of the Fine Arts, with the Aberdeen Artists and at various Scottish galleries. She won the Noble Grossart Prize in 1997. Fife Regional Council holds her work. Lived in Tayport, Fife.

Ben LEVENE 1938– Painter and teacher, born in London. He studied at Slade School of Fine Art, 1956–61, gaining the Boise Scholarship which enabled him to work in Spain, 1961–2. From 1959 Levene began appearing in group exhibitions at Beaux Arts Gallery, RA, LG and abroad. After sharing a show with Olwyn Bowey at New Grafton Gallery in 1969 he had the first of several solo exhibitions at Thackeray Gallery in 1973. Also showed regularly with Browse & Darby. Usually signed work with a B L monogram, although early work used Gerald Levene, his given name. Taught part-time at Camberwell School of Art and Royal Academy Schools and was elected RA in 1986. Work in many public collections. Levene was a rich Colourist, handling genre, landscape and still life in oil and watercolour. He was married to the painter Susan Williams and lived in London and Herefordshire.

Gerald LEVENE: *see* **Ben LEVENE**

Rosie LEVENTON fl. from 1970s– Artist who studied Chinese language and archaeology at London University, 1974–5. Then attended Croydon College of Art, 1976–9, followed by postgraduate course at St Martin's School of Art, 1980–1. Maggi Hambling, Eddie Wolfram, Barry Martin and John Bellamy were cited as influences on her career, which included teaching in Birmingham and at Byam Shaw School of Art. Her False Floor (4), an object measuring 192 inches x 312 inches x 4 inches and created from copper briquettes, was a notable feature of the 1992 East & South Norwich Gallery/Kent Institute of Art and Design show. Other group shows included LG from 1981; Eaumages, Festival of Installations, Villedieu Cultural Centre in Paris, 1984; and Manchester City Art Gallery, 1987. Had series of solo shows from LYC Museum & Art Gallery, Cumbria, 1983, later ones including Serpentine Gallery, 1987, Woodlands Art Gallery, 1989, Gardner Arts Centre, Brighton, 2001, and Standpoint Gallery, 2002, her sculptural installation The Bakery of Secrets being funded through the Mark Tanner Award. Held a sculpture residency at Glasgow Garden Festival, 1988.

Jake LEVER 1963– Painter who earned an honours degree in fine art from University of Reading, 1981–5; was artist-in-residence, Radley College, 1985–6; gained his teaching certificate from the University of Leeds, 1988–9; and his fine art master's at The University of Central England, Birmingham, 1992–4. Lever used abstract imagery, drawing inspiration from the past, but produced paintings which were "entirely contemporary, simultaneously looking backwards and forwards." From the mid-1990s Lever used egg tempera on gessoed panels with gold or silver leaf, a technique learned from the icon painter Peter Murphy. Group shows included Paperworks, The Black Swan Guild, Frome, 1990; Malvern Workshop, Malvern, 1992; and Wilson Stephens Fine Art, from 1999. Among later solo shows were The Old Grammar School, King's Norton, from 1996. Birmingham Museum and Art Gallery holds his work.

Joan LEVER 1925–1997 Artist in oil, watercolour and gouache (she worked latterly as Joan Lever Gibbings, being married for a time to the son of artist and writer Robert Gibbings). Born in London, she was educated there, then in South Africa, where she lived for almost 12 years from 1937 and was involved for a time in hospital and social work. Obtained a diploma from Continental School of Art in Cape Town under Maurice van Essche, 1947–9, a Belgian who had worked under Matisse, whose pictures, with those of Cézanne, greatly influenced Lever's output. This was distinguished by clarity and simplicity of form and colour, representational and abstract styles which evolved throughout her life. In England, from 1949–52 she studied under Kenneth Martin, Peter de Francia, Frederick Gore, John Napper, Vivian Pitchforth, Harold Workman, James Bateman, Barry Craig and John Wheatley at St Martin's School of Art. She was one of a post-diploma group of 10 artists working for a year under the principal Edward Morss. She also spent time at the Anglo-French Summer School, 1949. In the mid-1950s she worked for the Bolton Theatre Club's productions. Mixed exhibitions included The Castle, Cape Town, tercentenary exhibition, 1952; Young Artists from the Commonwealth, Imperial Institute, 1953; the first Gainsborough's House Society Exhibition, Sudbury, 1959; with Tuesday Painting Group, Guntons Coffee Shop, Colchester, 1974; and Colchester Art Society from 1979. Had a first solo exhibition at Alpine Gallery, 1978. Died in Ovington, Suffolk.

David LEVERETT 1938– Painter, printmaker and teacher, born in Nottingham, who studied at the College of Art there, 1957–61, then Royal Academy Schools, 1962–5. In the latter year Leverett had the first of a series of shows at Redfern Gallery and exhibited in Young Contemporaries, in 1967 at John Moores Liverpool Exhibition and in 1968 in Britain Painting and Sculpture at Whitechapel Art Gallery and the RA bicentary exhibition. Other one-man shows were held at Bear Lane Gallery, Oxford; Ikon Gallery, Birmingham; ICA and overseas; and Jill George Gallery, 1995 and 2001. Leverett taught at Slade School of Fine Art and Reading University. He produced both abstract and landscape pictures, sometimes large and epic in conception, as with his Sacred Gardens shown at Redfern in 1990. Leverett's work is in numerous major international collections, including Tate Gallery, Arts Council and British Council.

Anthony LEVETT-PRINSEP: *see* **Anthony PRINSEP**

Sylvia LEVINE 1911–1998 Painter of works with poetic, tranquil, lyrical qualities, based in Bristol. She married her second husband, Nathan Levine, in 1942, and from her fortieth year painted regularly to fill time while her son John was at boarding school. She attended classes at Queen's Road (later part of Filton College), where some of the tutors bought her work. There she could paint from the life model, using her fingers and matchsticks instead of brushes. The supports are often hardboard and cardboard scraps. The Milwaukee-based collector of naïve art Anthony Petullo acquired Levine's pictures and included them in *Self-Taught and Outsider Art: The Anthony Petullo Collection*, 2001. Levine often showed at the RA Summer Exhibition and RWA and was given a memorial show, A Quiet Persistent Painter, at Art Garden, Bristol, 2001.

John LEVINSON 1949–1979 Artist, notably in watercolour and gouache, and writer, educated at Bedales, who graduated in architecture from King's College, Cambridge, 1968–71. From 1971–3 he took the advanced course in painting at St Martin's School of Art, returning to Cambridge to pass his first diploma examination in 1974. From then Levinson devoted himself to painting, writing and travelling widely, completing the first draft of a novel in 1976. It and a volume of poetry were privately published after Levinson had taken his own life after mental illness. Underlying Levinson's output was a preoccupation with "the right relationship between ourselves and others, and between humanity and the nature of which it is a part", as Michael Archer wrote in the catalogue for the exhibition at Kettle's Yard, Cambridge, in 2001–2. This followed others at St Martin's, 1980, and King's College, 2001.

Margaret LEVINSON 1926– Artist who was born and educated in Bournemouth, Hampshire, where she studied at the College of Art, teachers including the sculptor Hermon Cawthra and etcher Leslie Ward. She went on to specialise in coloured etching and aquatints of Wessex and evolved unique ink and watercolour techniques. Hampshire Museum Service commissioned her to create 50 etchings of water-mills in the area. Was a member of the Printmakers' Council. Mixed exhibitions included Ben Uri Gallery from 1974; Russell-Cotes Art Gallery, Bournemouth from 1978; and Printmakers' Council, Leighton House, 1982. Solo shows included Poole Central Library, 1974, later one-mans comprising Medici Galleries and Dean Galleries, San Jose, California, both 1986. Ben Uri Art Society and many other collections worldwide hold examples.

Rachel LEVITAS 1964– Painter and printmaker who gained her foundation diploma and honours degree at Camberwell School of Art, 1982–6; studied advanced printmaking part-time at Central St Martins School of Art, 1988–90; then gained a postgraduate diploma from Royal Academy of Art, 1990–3. Awards included John Purcell Print Prize and W H Patterson Prize for Objective Painting, both 1991; Turner Gold Medal, 1992; and in 1993 Trent Bridge Travelling Scholarship and David Murray Landscape Award. Group shows included Fresh Art at Barbican Centre, 1987; RA Summer Exhibition, from 1990; Royal Over-Seas League Open, 1992; and Whitechapel Open Studios, 1994. Had a solo show, Half Light, at Rebecca Hossack Gallery, 1989, another at The Cut Gallery, 1996.

Małgorzata LEVITTOUX 1958– Painter, born in Warsaw, Poland, who studied in the studios of Professors J Sienicki and W Kruczkowski at the Warsaw Academy of Fine Arts, graduating in 1984. She left Poland in 1987 and completed a one-year postgraduate course at Byam Shaw School of Art. Group shows included Painters 88 at Mall Galleries, Tabernacle Gallery and Open Print Show at Bankside Gallery, all 1988; Contemporary Portrait Society, Brockwell Arts Festival and John Player Portrait Competition at National Portrait Gallery, where she gained an Hon. Mention, all 1989; and Stockwell Arts Festival, 1989 and 1990. Levittoux was in a three-artist show at Combined Harvest Gallery, 1988. Among her solo exhibitions were KMPiK "Bielany", Widok Gallery, and Gallery of the Young, both in Warsaw, 1986; Framers Gallery, London, 1988; Tearooms des Artistes, 1989; and Morley Gallery, 1990.

Emmanuel LEVY 1900–1986 Painter, draughtsman, collagist and teacher, born in Manchester, with which his career was closely associated, and where he first showed, in 1924. He studied art in Manchester, London and Paris. Went on to teach in Manchester and at Stockport College. Although for a time he was interested in Cubism and Surrealism, Levy discarded them for a more naturalistic style, although within it his range was wide. His central theme was the human condition, in which he produced some powerful works. Was also a fine portrait draughtsman. Had six solo shows in Manchester between 1925–63 plus a number in London. There was a retrospective at Salford City Art Gallery, 1948; another at Fieldborne Galleries, 1976; and one at Stockport Art Gallery, 1982. National Portrait Gallery, Ben Uri Gallery and galleries in Manchester, Stockport and Salford hold his work. Latterly lived in Alicante, Spain.

Isa LEVY 1948– Artist in a range of media but mainly in oil, born in Cardiff, who studied at the Slade School of Fine Art, 1994–5. Her theatrical background showed in her work which was noted for its wide range of subjects, "warmth, passion and textural brush marks." Group shows included Mall Galleries and Not the Royal Academy at Llewellyn Alexander Gallery, both 1997. Among solo exhibitions were Lauderdale House, Highgate, near where she lived, 1996, and Quaker Gallery, 2002.

Mervyn LEVY 1914–1996 Writer, lecturer, broadcaster and painter, born in Swansea, south Wales. He attended the Grammar School and School of Art there, then Royal College of Art under Sir William Rothenstein and Gilbert Spencer. From childhood was a friend of Dylan Thomas, his portrait of the poet held by the National Portrait Gallery. At the Royal College Levy won the Herbert Read Prize for Drawing at the 1935 annual students exhibition. Exhibited at RWA and elsewhere, solo shows including Glynn Vivian Art Gallery, Swansea. During World War II attended Royal Military College at Sandhurst, becoming a captain in the Royal Army Educational Corps. After the war he was an overseas arts lecturer to the War Office, with the honorary rank of lieutenant-colonel. Held a series of teaching posts, including adult education department at Bristol University, then Royal West of England Academy in Bristol, and he also taught at London University's extramural studies department; appeared on *The Critics* programme on BBC radio and for several years had his own television series *Painting for Housewives*; he was associate editor of *Art News and Review* and features editor of *The Studio*. Wrote many books, including *Painter's Progress*, monographs on L S Lowry, Henri Gaudier-Brzeska and Scottie Wilson, and in 1982 published autobiographical fragments *Reflections In A Broken Mirror*. Chelsea Arts Club member who lived in London.

Simon LEVY 1963– Painter, born in Johannesburg, who spent his formative years in South Africa, moving to England in the early 1980s. He studied painting at St Martin's School of Art, winning the Cartier Foundation Prize in 1988. Spent a period as artist-in-residence at Foundation for Contemporary Art at Jouy-en-Josas, France. Levy showed in many mixed exhibitions, including Whitechapel Open; had a first London solo show, Between Location and Identity, curated by Rear Window, in 1992; and in 1995 his show Alchemy, based on travels in Mexico and South Africa and an interest in jazz and modern music, was put on by Austin/Desmond Fine Art.

Viv LEVY fl. from late 1970s– Sculptor, painter and draughtsman who studied at St Martin's School of Art, 1977–80, then after a year in SPACE Studios, Wapping, was at Royal College of Art, 1981–4. Was Henry Moore Fellow at Wimbledon School of Art, 1989–90. Painted murals as part of Islington Schools Project in 1977, in 1987 gaining a commission for London Borough of Newham. Wrote *Life Drawing: A Beginner's Guide*, 1993. Mixed shows included Art at Work, RIBA, 1988; Artist's Choice at Angela Flowers Gallery, 1992; and 1st RWA Open Sculpture Exhibition, 1993. Solo exhibitions included Castlefield Gallery, Manchester, 1991. Lived in London.

Elzbieta LEWANDOWSKA 1940– Painter, writer and critic, born in Lublin, Poland, who studied Polish literature at the Higher School of Education (WSP), Gdansk, gaining her master's degree in 1965. She moved to London in 1967 and began to paint in the early 1970s, becoming a member of the Association of Polish Artists in Great Britain in 1986, eventually its secretary. She was also an art critic, contributing articles and reviews to *Dziennik* and *Tydzień Polski* (*Polish Daily* and *Polish Weekly*). Lewandowska had a solo show at POSK Gallery in 1993 and there in 1995 was included in Form and Colour, Congress of Polish Culture Exhibition of Fine Arts by Polish Artists in Britain.

Simon LEWANDOWSKI 1952– Versatile artist and designer, born in Mansfield, Nottinghamshire, who attended Newcastle University, 1974–8, from 1980–4 being a member of the Impact Theatre Co-operative, as set and production designer, in Leeds in London, where he eventually settled. Exhibitions included International Print Biennale, Bradford, 1990; European Large Format Print Exhibition, Dublin, Ireland (prize winner), 1992; Bradford Open Print Exhibition (prize winner), 1993; Beyond the "Wow" Factor, New York State University and United Kingdom tour, 1994–5; and The Large Print Show, Christchurch Mansion, Ipswich, 1997. The year before Lewandowski had participated in The International Symposium of Shadows with the film/kinetic installation The Stumbling Machine.

Annette LEWIN 1933– Printmaker and illustrator, producing richly coloured, stylised work, who was born in New York, America. She studied at the High School of Music & Art, from 1948; attended New School and worked as medical and scientific illustrator for the American government, both 1952; studied at the Art Students' League, 1956; moved to Israel, 1960, for a time illustrating for a children's magazine and a major health service; then attended Camden Arts Centre for Printmaking, 1973. Her many group exhibitions included Printmakers' Council, from 1984; RA Summer Exhibition, from 1985; Ben Uri Gallery, 1986; RE, 1992; Hunting Art Prizes, from 1996; PS, 1998; and Art Celebrates Life, Lauderdale House, 2002. Solo exhibitions included Kopel House, 1985, and Conrich House, 1986 and 1987.

Paul LEWIN 1967– Landscape painter, born in Manchester, inspired by the coast and moorland areas of north Devon and Cornwall where he painted on the spot. "Capturing the sense of place amongst the constantly changing weather, light, tides and seasons is my challenge". He completed a fine art degree at Bristol Polytechnic, 1989, worked around St Just-in-Penwith, Cornwall for 10 years, then settled in Bideford, Devon. He had periods of residency on Nantucket Island, off America's east coast and at more remote British island locations: Bardsey, Orkney, Scilly and Lundy. Took part in many London and provincial group shows. He was The Great Atlantic Map Works Gallery, St Just, first director of art; in 2001 it gave him a solo show, coincident with the appearance of his book *Being There*, with another, in 2002–3, with his book *Touchstones*.

Sue LEWINGTON 1946– Versatile artist and teacher, born in Middlesex, whose landscapes concentrated on west Cornwall and the Isles of Scilly, where from 1989 she lived at St Martins and ran the North Farm Gallery. After training at Harrow School of Art in the mid-1960s, Lewington worked in London as a freelance illustrator until moving to Cornwall in 1975. After having two daughters and running a smallholding, she sold etchings through a London agent and in the early 1980s began teaching adults and in local schools. Exhibited widely in the southwest of England, notably at Trelissick and Lanhydrock National Trust Galleries and published books, the first, *Sketches of Scilly*, appearing in 1997. Another, *Looking Westwards – from St Ives to Land's End*, was published in 2001 to coincide with her solo show at The Great Atlantic Map Works Gallery, St Just-in-Penwith.

Aletta M LEWIS 1904– Painter and medical artist, born in Orpington, Kent, married to the sculptor Denis C Dunlop. She studied at Beckenham School of Art and the Slade School of Fine Art under Henry Tonks. Taught for a while in Sydney Art School, Australia, and showed there. Also exhibited NEAC, LG, Goupil Gallery and in Paris. Published the book *They call them Savages*. Lived in London.

Alfred Neville LEWIS 1895–1972 Painter, born in Cape Town, South Africa, who divided his life mainly between that country and England. Studied at Slade School of Fine Art, 1914, then served during World War I in several countries on continent. Lewis was a prolific exhibitor, being a member of NEAC, NS and RP, also showing at Leicester Galleries, Goupil Gallery, Redfern Gallery and elsewhere. He had his first solo show at Carfax Gallery in 1920. During World War II he was an Official War Artist with the South African forces. A number of public collections including Tate Gallery hold his work, which is notable for its portraits and figure studies, often of low life.

Anastasia LEWIS 1943– Versatile artist and designer who, after training in theatre design at the Central School of Art, worked in theatre, television and films, 1963–92, taking short courses in printmaking and painting at Chelsea and Central St Martins, 1990–2. During 1978–88 she also ran her own television and film costume hire company, Clothespeg, with six full-time staff and a pool of outworkers. From 1992 Lewis did her own work "mainly in paint, but I also use collage and photography. My work concerns the exploration and subversion of the grid. It is sourced from contemporary architecture, electronic circuit boards and the warp and weft of woven textiles." Later exhibitions included Eastern Open, Norwich, and Cheltenham Open Drawing Competition, both 1997; Kettle's Yard Open, Cambridge, 1998; Brent Open, Willesden Green Library, 2001; and ART*futures*, Contemporary Art Society, 2002. She shared an exhibition, Identikit, Kingsgate Gallery, 2001, and had a solo show, First Edition, Canary Wharf, 1999. Lived in north London.

Andrew LEWIS 1968– Draughtsman and model-maker who developed an idiosyncratic language of architectonics and design. Born in London, Lewis studied at North London University and at the Mackintosh School of Architecture, Glasgow. In his 2001 show Ark Royale with Cheese, at Laurent Delaye Gallery, Lewis presented a series of highly detailed drawings in which an imposing warship was installed in the middle of a Georgian Square. Fig-1, in 2000, showed allegories of urban projects as a way to submit imaginary proposals concentrating on futuristic scenarios. Among later Lewis exhibitions were Systems, at InIVA, and White Van Men GB, Galerie Serieuze Zaken, Amsterdam, both 2002; Photo Opportunities, New Art Gallery, Walsall, 2004; The Misfits, Attitudes, Espace d'Arts Contemporains, Geneva, 2005; and Crown Imperial, comprising digital prints and sculptures, at Gimpel Fils, 2005–6. Lived in Croydon, Surrey.

Ann LEWIS 1962– Artist in mixed media, lino-cut and etching, born in St Asaph, Flintshire, who gained an honours degree in graphic design from Exeter College of Art & Design, 1985–8. Was a member of RCamA and its hon. secretary. Lewis' special interest was the "interpretation of Welsh landscape, in particular its waterfalls". As well as RCamA, took part in group shows at Tegfryn Gallery, Anglesey; Exchange Theatre, Manchester; Arts Centre, Aberystwyth; and Theatr Clwyd, Mold. Shared a show at Hanover Galleries, Liverpool, 1996. National Library of Wales in Aberystwyth holds her work. Lived in Gerlan, Bethesda, Gwynedd.

Audrey LEWIS: *see* **Audrey SANT**

Bill LEWIS 1953– Artist, poet, story-teller and mythographer, born in Maidstone, Kent. After secondary modern school, from 1968–76 was a truck unloader, terminating in a breakdown, attempted suicide and psychiatric treatment. In 1977–8 did a foundation course at Medway College, from 1978–82 was a hospital porter, then became a "full-time artist with occasional forays into tomato picking." Lewis believed strongly in the importance of mythology, was a member of the School for Prophets and painted "magical realist" pictures. Was a member of the Stuckists, exhibiting in their 2001 Artbank Gallery show. He published five books of poems, one of short stories and performed widely, including Nicaragua and America.

Brian LEWIS 1947– Artist who moved to Norfolk in 1980, where he depicted with humour and pathos the lives of people and the architectural oddities of the county's coastal region. Lewis did a foundation course at Epsom School of Art, 1963–4; gained a diploma pass with honours at Guildford School of Art, 1964–7; attended the Royal Academy Schools, 1967–70, winning various prizes, including a bronze medal for painting; then gained a pass with distinction on the advanced printmaking course at Croydon School of Art, 1979–80. Mixed exhibitions included RA Summer Exhibition, Goldmark Gallery in Uppingham, Wells Centre at Wells-next-the-Sea, and Morley Gallery. Solo shows included James Colman Fine Art, 1996.

Charles LEWIS 1916– Sculptor and teacher, born in Southsea, Hampshire. He studied at Portsmouth College of Art, 1932–6, then at Royal College of Art, 1936–9, with Richard Garbe. In 1946 Lewis gained a Royal Exhibition and Continuation Scholarship. Went on to become head of sculpture at Kingston College of Art and Polytechnic, 1947–78. Lewis completed commissions for private architects, Greater London Council and Ministry of Public Building and Works. He was a fellow of RBS and a member of Art Workers' Guild. Lived latterly in New York, where the Weston Press Gallery gave him a retrospective in 1983, finally settling in France.

Daniel LEWIS 1908– Painter and draughtsman, born in Trefenter, Cardiganshire, a locality where he spent all his life, finally living in an old people's home in Aberystwyth. He began to draw at classes organised by the Red Cross when he was aged about 60. Chapels were his chief subject and he took part in the WAC 1972 An Alternative Tradition exhibition.

David LEWIS 1955– Painter and teacher, born in Wigan, Lancashire. He studied at Manchester Polytechnic, 1973–4, at Leeds Polytechnic as a scholar, taught at Thomas Danby College, Leeds, 1978–82, and was artist-in-residence in Swansea, 1990. Lewis was some time a visiting lecturer in France and Australia. Lewis' group appearances included St Paul's Gallery, Leeds, and Elizabethan Gallery, Wakefield, 1981; Huddersfield City Art Gallery, 1982; Leeds City Art Gallery and Bankside Gallery, 1984; Ginnel Gallery, Manchester, 1987; and Gainsborough's House, Sudbury, 1990. He had a one-man show at Bridge Arts Centre, Widnes, in 1980, others including a series at Christopher Hull Gallery from 1985. Also had a solo exhibition at Glynn Vivian Gallery, Swansea, 1991. His work is in private and public collections, including those of Calderdale, Sunderland, Huddersfield and Bradford. Lewis' work included pictures tending towards abstraction with landscape references, in muted earth colours.

Dennis LEWIS 1928– Painter and advertising director, born in Bristol, where he continued to live. He began studying art during Army service, continuing at West of England College of Art, Bristol, in 1948–52. Showed locally and was for a time president of the Bristol Savages.

Ffiona LEWIS 1964– Versatile artist and architect, whose works, which involved "a lengthy process of engagement with the subject" using a limited range of colours, quietly explored familiar domestic icons in still lifes and landscapes. After spending her formative years in Devon, Lewis gained an honours degree in architecture at The Polytechnic of Central London, 1983–7, obtaining her architecture diploma there, 1988–90. She then studied at Central St Martins School of Art before turning to painting professionally, balancing this with architectural work and scenic painting for the Royal National Theatre and English National Opera. Mixed shows included Fine Art Consultancy, at various venues, from 1993; Kate Chertavian Fine Art, from 1995; and The Wills Lane Gallery, St Ives, 1996. Had solo shows at The Royal National Theatre and The Wren at St James', both 1993, later ones including Gordon Hepworth Fine Art, Newton St Cyres, 1996, and Redfern and Northcote Galleries, both 2003. Signed work with initials and date.

Garth LEWIS 1945– Painter, designer and teacher, born in Coventry, Warwickshire. He studied at Hornsey College of Art, 1964–7. After studying and teaching for two years at University of New Mexico Lewis studied and taught during 1969–71 at Queens College at the City University of New York. He returned to England to teach at Hornsey College of Art and Liverpool Polytechnic from 1972, from 1974 at Central School of Art and Design, then from 1978 at Slade School of Fine Art. Lewis had had solo shows at both New Mexico University and Queens College. Lewis' work was initially figurative, then abstract. In New York he had studied colour theory with the artist Herb Aach and the use of colour as a pictorial language remained a key preoccupation in his work.

Gomer LEWIS 1921– Painter, sculptor and teacher, born in Caerphilly, Glamorgan. He attended Monmouthshire College of Education and began to draw in the Far East during World War II as a prisoner of war. For a decade on his return he concentrated on painting with the war in mind, then studied sculpture at Cardiff College of Art. In 1963 he moved to London, where for a time he taught art at Shoreditch College, although he continued to paint in South Wales. Showed with groups at SWG, WAC, SEA, Towner Art Gallery in Eastbourne, Bourne Gallery in Reigate and elsewhere. One-man shows included 1951 Festival of Britain, Glamorgan and Gwent; and Chapter Arts Centre, Cardiff. CASW holds his drawing Orpheus – Study for Sculpture, and Towner Art Gallery has his work.

H E LEWIS fl. c. 1960-late–1990s Spare-time landscape painter, born in South Kensington, who was professionally in the Royal Air Force. After this he took up painting, apparently essentially self-taught, claiming that "all the best artists taught themselves." Lewis admired the work of Corot, Monet and Sisley. He made no effort to exhibit or sell his pictures, giving them away or donating them to charity. Some of these were later offered at auction and his work was displayed by London dealers. Lewis was reticent about his pictures, which are notable for their fine tones and values. Contacted early in 2001, he said that he was "no longer interested in painting, having given it up a year or so ago." He was then "pushing 95", living in Hailsham, Sussex.

Jane LEWIS 1953– Painter, printmaker, draughtsman and teacher, born in London. After a foundation course at Hornsey College of Art, 1970–1, she studied fine art there, 1971–4, then printmaking at Slade School of Fine Art, 1975–7, in the latter year winning the Slade Prize. After working part-time as a lecturer at Watford College of Art, 1977–9, Lewis worked for the BBC as a scenic artist. She then taught at the Slade, 1980–3, was a visitor to Byam Shaw School of Art, 1983, artist-in-residence with Kent Opera, 1985, and also lectured part-time at Harrow College of Art, 1983–6, in the following two years acting as vistor at the Slade and Reading University. From 1986 she was able to concentrate more of her attention on painting, showing internationally in numerous group shows. Was also a busy solo exhibitor from 1986, when she showed at Metropole Arts Centre, Folkestone; Trinity Arts Centre, Tunbridge Wells; Derngate Theatre Gallery, Northampton; and Royal Museum, Canterbury. Other galleries shown at included Gardner Centre, Brighton, 1987, the year when she also exhibited at RWA and Nicholas Treadwell Gallery; Cartwright Hall, Bradford, 1991; and Collins Gallery,

Glasgow, 1991–2. Also completed paintings for Bloodaxe Books. University College London, Manchester City Art Galleries and other public collections hold her work, which looked back to Renaissance and Venetian painters and in which themes such as music, the castrated male and female sexuality played a part.

John LEWIS 1933– Painter of landscapes with a visionary quality, born in Abergavenny, Monmouthshire, raised in the Usk Valley, later establishing a studio in the Hertfordshire countryside in Watton at Stone. Lewis studied at Ruskin School of Drawing, Oxford, 1963–4, and Byam Shaw School of Art, 1965–70. In 1986 won a major prize at Watford Museum Open Exhibition, in 1988 was a Drawing For All prizewinner at Gainsborough's House, Sudbury. Group exhibitions included RA Summer Exhibition from 1967; New Art Centre, 1974; Goldmark Gallery, Uppingham, 1990; and Roy Miles Gallery, 1994. Had a solo show at Upper Street Gallery, 1973, later ones including Oriel Contemporary Art, 1995. Watford Museum, CASW and Hertfordshire, Bedfordshire and Leicestershire County Councils hold examples.

John David LEWIS 1943– Artist and teacher, born and lived in London, who studied at Wimbledon School of Art, 1971–4, teachers including Michael Fussell and Prunella Clough. Lewis taught and wrote for the National Gallery, lectured at Homerton College, Cambridge, and worked part-time for the London Underground. Group shows included the RA Summer Exhibition from 1987; Cleveland International Drawing Biennale, 1993; Whitechapel Open, 1994; Hammersons, 1999; and Cityscapes, Collyer-Bristow, 2000. Among Lewis's later solo shows were Patricia Brown, from 1991, and Contact Gallery, Norwich, 1996.

Kit LEWIS 1911–1998 Painter, born in Lichfield, Staffordshire. She was married to the painter Morland Lewis, then to Sir J M Richards, who edited *The Architectural Review*, and her full name was Kathleen Margaret Lewis. Studied at Chelsea School of Art and took part in mixed exhibitions including LG, Sally Hunter Fine Art, in the provinces and in America. She had two solo exhibitions at Leicester Galleries, 1953 and 1971. Arts Council holds her oil Amphytrion, of 1951. Lived in London.

Mark LEWIS 1959– Artist and teacher using modern media, born in Hamilton, Ontario, Canada, who attended Harrow College of Art and the Polytechnic of Central London. He taught at Massachusetts Institute of Technology, in America; Central St Martin's; CAL Arts, Los Angeles, California, in America; and University of British Columbia, Vancouver, Canada. Among his many group exhibitions were Art Creating Society, Museum of Modern Art, Oxford, 1990; Viennese Story, Wiener Secession, Vienna, Austria, 1993; Rotterdam International Film Festival, 1997; and Intelligence: New British Art 2000, Tate Britain, 2000. Among many international solo shows were Site Gallery, Sheffield; Patrick Painter, Inc., Santa Monica, California; and National Gallery of Canada, Ottawa, all 2000. Lewis lived in London.

Mary Priestley LEWIS 1870– Painter educated at Trinity College, Southport, noted for her still lifes. She studied at Chelmsford School of Art under Charles Baskett, 1911, Bideford School of Art and worked privately with Sylvester Stannard and Wycliffe Egginton shortly before World War II. Exhibited UA, BWS, of which she was a member, RI and in the provinces. Russell-Cotes Art Gallery and Museum, Bournemouth, holds her work. Lived at Southbourne, near Bournemouth.

Michael LEWIS 1925– Painter, draughtsman and teacher, born in Cheltenham, Gloucestershire. He studied at Regent Street Polytechnic School of Art, his teachers including Patrick Millard, and went on to hold a number of teaching posts in the south of England, eventually becoming senior lecturer in fine art at Croydon College of Art. Showed LG, Young Contemporaries, RA, SEA and elsewhere, having one-man shows at Trafford Gallery and Scunthorpe Art Gallery. That gallery holds his work. Lived in Croydon, Surrey.

Pete LEWIS 1954– Lewis graduated with honours from Hornsey College of Art, 1973–6, gaining his master's from Chelsea School of Art, 1976–7. Group exhibitions included Stowells Trophy, Mall Galleries, 1977; Riverside Open, Riverside Studios, 1988; and The Showroom and East End Open Studios, at Chisenhale Studios, both 1989. Lewis had a one-man show at Chisenhale Gallery in 1987.

Peter LEWIS 1939– Sculptor and teacher, born in Cheshire, who attended Carmarthen School of Art, St Martin's School of Art, 1957–9, then Royal College of Art, 1961–4, for a time teaching part-time at St Martin's in the 1970s. Solo shows included Serpentine Gallery, 1977. Charing Cross Hospital holds his work and his Untitled, 1982, an abstract construction in wood, stone and slate, is sited at South Hill Park Arts Centre, Bracknell.

Sanchia LEWIS 1960– Printmaker, animator and painter, born and lived in south London, who, after "a hellish five years" at a comprehensive school, 1971–6, worked part-time cleaning and modelling for art classes, 1976–8. After a breakdown, from 1978–9 attended Medway College of Art for foundation; from 1979–82 gained certificates in printmaking and advanced printmaking at City & Guilds of London Art School; then did printmaking at a Morley College studio, 1982–4; etching in her own studio, from 1984. Won a Stephen Goodman Engraving Award, 1982; Prince's Trust Award, 1984; First Prize, Portobello Open Exhibition, 1993; and Marlborough Gallery Prize, National Print Exhibition, 1995. Her numerous shows included Medici Galleries, Royal Festival Hall and widely abroad. A member of the Stuckists, she was included in their 2001 Artbank Gallery exhibition. Lewis had a stand at the Spitalfields Alternative Art Market. Her animations were shown in festivals worldwide.

Simon LEWIS 1945– Non-representational painter and sculptor, born in Okehampton, Devon, working in various media. He studied from 1964–8 at Bath Academy of Art, Corsham, then gained his Master of Fine Art degree at University of Reading, 1970–2. Howard Hodgkin, Adrian Heath, Gillian Ayres, Henry Mundy, Terry Frost and Michael Kidner were among Lewis' teachers. After part-time teaching and various commissions, 1972–5, Lewis taught sculpture full-time at Hull, 1975–81, was head of fine art at North-East London Polytechnic, 1981–5, then head of the art and design department of the University of East London. Commissions included Ford of Europe; Watney, Courage and Whitbread Breweries; and the interior designer John Rogers Ltd. Lewis' exhibitions included

Museum of Modern Art, Oxford, from 1971; LG exhibition at The Showroom Gallery, 1984; Bede Gallery, Durham, 1987; and Portobello Open, 1990. Solo shows included University of Reading, 1972; Ferens Art Gallery, Hull, 1981; Jersey Arts Council Gallery, St Helier, 1987; and Shin Gallery, Seoul, South Korea, 1989. Ferens Art Gallery and the Universities of Reading and Cardiff hold examples. Lived in London.

Stanley C LEWIS 1905– Painter, teacher and museum curator, born in Cardiff. He attended Newport College of Art, 1923–6, and the Royal College of Art, 1926–30, teaching at Newport College in the 1930s. After war service he became principal of Carmarthen School of Art for 22 years from 1946, then retired and with his wife founded the Pram and Toy Museum at Beckington, Somerset. He illustrated newspaper articles by his wife Min Lewis and her book *Laugharne and Dylan Thomas*, in 1967, and had one-man shows at various Laugharne Festivals. Showed for many years with Gwent Art Society, SWG and elsewhere and with Michael Ayrton and Enzo Plazzotta shared a three-man show at Bruton Gallery, Somerset. Newport Museum and Art Gallery holds his work. Lewis' show War Images there in 2003 was based on a large unfinished World War II painting and preparatory drawings which the artist donated to the collection.

Stephen LEWIS 1959– Abstract sculptor, working mainly in mild steel but sometimes using found objects, and draughtsman. He was born in Lancashire and graduated from Manchester Polytechnic in 1980. Showed with New Contemporaries at ICA in 1979, the Jan Van Eyck Annual Exhibition in Maastricht, in 1982, and with Francis Graham-Dixon Gallery. He had a solo show at John Holden Gallery, Manchester, in 1990. Lived in London.

Tim LEWIS 1961– Sculptor, painter and draughtsman, born in Kingston upon Thames, Surrey, who studied at Middlesex Polytechnic, 1980–3, and Royal College of Art, 1984–7. Group exhibitions included New Contemporaries, ICA, from 1982; RA Summer Exhibition, 1988; Now for the Future, Hayward Gallery, and Chicago International Art Fair, both 1990; Frankfurt Art Fair, 1994; and British Abstract Art Part 2: Sculpture, Flowers East, 1995. Showed solo with Flowers East from 1989. Later exhibitions included Stadtische Museen, Heilbronn, Germany, and Flowers West, Santa Monica, California, both 2001; Magdeburg Museum, Germany, 2001–2; Flowers Central, 2002; and Uncanny Valley, recent sculpture, at The Walker, Liverpool, and Flowers East, both 2004. Arts Council, British Council and TI Group hold examples.

Whyn LEWIS 1973– Painter, born in Edinburgh. Her parents lived in a horse-drawn gypsy waggon in Peeblesshire, and she was named after the gorse bushes that were in bloom. Her work, as in her first solo show in London at the Portal Gallery in 2002, was inspired by her black whippet Indie, her constant companion from the age of 16, which was allowed to accompany her to Glasgow Art School by a rare waiving of the rules. They were there from 1991–5. Lewis continued to use the dog's image until he died in 2000. The Portal paintings were "not conventional portraits of dogs but metaphors for human emotions." The dog's qualities, along with its shape, stance and expression were "an allegory for the unspoken understanding and sometimes misunderstanding between people." Lewis had solo exhibitions at The Open Eye Gallery, Edinburgh. By the time of the Portal exhibition she had won the Maude Gemmell Hutchison Prize, at RSA, 1994 and 1997; John Kinross Scholarship to Florence, 1995; Noble Grossart Painting Prize, 1996; Meyer Oppenheim Prize, RSA, 1998; and The Anna Miller Trust Scholarship, 2001.

Wyndham LEWIS 1882–1957 Painter, draughtsman, writer and polemicist, full name Percy Wyndham Lewis, born in Amherst, Nova Scotia. Educated at Rugby School, 1897–8, he was at the Slade School of Fine Art, 1899–1901. For about six years from 1902 Lewis travelled extensively on the continent, vital to his early artistic training, which included six months at the Heimann Academy, Munich. Began to exhibit, with Camden Town Group, Roger Fry's Second Post-Impressionist Exhibition, 1912, and with LG, 1913. Worked with Fry's Omega Workshops, then broke away to form Rebel Art Centre and Vorticist Group, 1914, editing its publication *Blast*. During World War I was seconded to Canadian Corps Headquarters at Vimy Ridge as a war artist, an exhibition called Guns occurring at Goupil Gallery, 1919. Following year organised Group X show at Heal's Mansard Gallery. Lewis' first novel, *Tarr*, was published in 1918, and during the inter-war years he mixed his work as an artist with editing art reviews such as *The Tyro* and *The Enemy*, additional fiction like *The Apes of God* and critical works such as *Wyndham Lewis the Artist*. His group of portrait drawings, Thirty Personalities, in 1932, prompted Walter Sickert to term Lewis the "greatest portraitist of this, or any other, time". Lived in Canada and America, 1940–8. Retrospective exhibitions at Redfern Gallery, 1949, and Tate Gallery, 1956, followed by Arts Council Tour. Wyndham Lewis had lost his sight in 1951. Work in many public collections, including Tate Gallery and Imperial War Museum. In 2001, Henry Peacock Gallery put on Wyndham Lewis – Kultur-Faschismus; in 2004–5 the Courtauld Institute Gallery showed "The Bone Beneath the Pulp": Drawings by Wyndham Lewis; and at the Fine Art Design & Antiques Fair in 2005 there was a Lewis loan exhibition. Died in London.

Jan LE WITT 1907–1991 Painter, designer, typographer and poet, born in Częstochowa, Poland. Early menial jobs gave Le Witt a hatred of the impersonal factory machine, the "Mechanical Molloch" as he put it, and by 1925 he had embarked on extensive travels through Europe. Back in Warsaw he began a successful career as a self-taught designer, in 1933 teaming up with George Him with whom, after arrival in London in 1937, as Lewitt-Him he produced classic wartime posters. The remarkable Festival of Britain clock of 1951 was their work. A meeting with Paul Klee at the Dessau Bauhaus and sight of work by Braque, Picasso and Cézanne in Paris in the early 1930s encouraged Le Witt to paint, and in England he became a friend of Henry Moore and Herbert Read. Had first one-man show at Zwemmer Gallery in 1947, which was the forerunner of an international exhibiting career, involving much travel. Le Witt was against obscurantism in painting; was a believer in the effectiveness of organic form; painting was "the calligraphy of feeling". From the late 1950s he was out of fashion in England and it was left to the Musée Grimaldi in Antibes, 1965, the Museum of Modern Art in Warsaw, 1967, and the Sala Napoleonica in Venice, 1970, to give him large retrospectives, although his last show was of small oils at the Fitzwilliam Museum, Cambridge, in 1989. Le

Witt won a Gold Medal in Vienna, 1948, and at the Triennale, Milan, 1954. Died in Cambridge.

Richard LEWSEY 1961– Artist who attended Camberwell School of Art, 1979–82. His group shows included Royal Free Hospital, 1984; BADA Exhibition, 1986; Sedgwick Centre, 1988; and Campaign for Artistic Freedom, 1989. In that year he participated in East End Open Studios, at Cable Street Studios, as he had in 1988.

Margaret LEWTHWAITE 1907–1990 Painter and occupational therapist, born in New York. After education at fashionable schools Peggy Lewthwaite went to the École des Beaux-Arts in Paris, after which she returned to New York to become a textile designer. During a visit to England in the 1930s she met Ray Lewthwaite, a Scots Guards officer. Early in World War II she was one of the first Americans to be appointed Member of the British Empire for her therapy work with Allied troops in Cairo, involving needlework and embroidery. In Paris, and much influenced by the work of Augustus John, after the war she began painting seriously, completing many portraits of the famous and running her own atelier. In the 1970s she painted in Hong Kong and China, Communist leaders and landscapes. Continued to work at her husband's home in Broadgate, west Cumbria, after his retirement. Died in London.

Simon LEWTY 1941– Artist and teacher, born in Sutton Coldfield, Warwickshire. He studied at Mid-Warwickshire School of Art and Hornsey School of Art. Between 1964–81 lectured at Mid-Warwickshire School, then worked full-time as an artist. There were many influences on Lewty's work, including Surrealism, especially André Breton; theories of automatic writing; the use of text in pictures from the Cubists; Paul Klee; William Blake; and especially medieval graffiti. Lewty showed widely in Britain in mixed shows, being a John Moores Exhibition, Liverpool, prize-winner in 1985; he also won a prize at Cleveland 8th International Drawing Biennale in 1987. After a one-man show at Woodstock Gallery in 1968 Lewty exhibited at Ikon Gallery, Birmingham, 1984, then had the first of a series with Anne Berthoud Gallery in 1985, the year he showed at Serpentine Gallery. In 1992 there was a show at Austin, Desmond & Phipps in association with Anne Berthoud. Arts Council, Victoria & Albert Museum and other public collections hold work. Lived in Leamington Spa, Warwickshire, where the Art Gallery and Museum held a large touring show, 1999–00.

Marcia LEY 1959– Artist and lecturer, born in Ware, Hertfordshire, who did foundation studies at Chesterfield College of Art and Design, 1975–7; graduated with honours in fine art, Ravensbourne College of Art and Design, 1977–80; and gained her master's degree from Chelsea School of Art, 1980–1. She held a number of part-time and visiting lectureships from the early 1980s, including Newcastle University, Newcastle and Sunderland Polytechnics and Humberside College of Art. Took part in many group shows, including Stowells Trophy, RA, 1981; Northern Open tour, 1983–4; Northern Print, Middlesbrough Gallery, 1985; and three-artist exhibition at Linton Court Gallery, Settle, 1986. In that year she shared a show at Concert Bar, Newcastle. Among her solo exhibitions were Calouste Gulbenkian Gallery, Newcastle, 1983; Ceolfrith Gallery, Sunderland Art Centre, 1984; and Woodhorn Church Museum, Ashington, 1984–5.

Liz LEYH 1943– Artist who was born in New York, America, and studied there at Pratt Institute and at Syracuse University. Between 1974–8 she worked in Milton Keynes as a community artist, initially on a bursary from the Arts Council, then being employed by the Development Corporation in the city. Her The Owl and the Pussycat and Tin Man, both in concrete, were sited there in 1977–8. Leyh's concrete black-and-white Cows, made using scrap materials from building sites with the help of local children, gained much press publicity and became recognised as a landmark. A project in Cambridge with Free Form Arts Trust in 1986 won the RIBA award for community design. Leyh lived latterly in Israel.

Thyrza Anne LEYSHON fl. from 1960s– Miniaturist, born and settled in Swansea, south Wales, who studied with the Southall-based miniature painter Ethol Court. She was a member of SM, also exhibiting at RA, RMS, Castle Gallery in Ilkley and Glynn Vivian Art Gallery, Swansea, in Belgium, France and America. Among awards won were a Silver Medal at Paris Salon in 1968, a Gold Medal in 1973.

LIAM: *see* **William CONOR**

Richard LIBBY 1948– Painter and teacher, born in Banstead, Surrey, who in 1965–70 trained at Reigate School of Art and completed mural commissions in central London. Between 1970–80, Libby kept alive with a succession of temporary jobs, including art teaching, but in isolation continued to review his own style and technique. From 1980–96, while continuing to lecture, Libby showed at the Kevin Platt Gallery and Pendragon Gallery, Cornwall; when he took part in a mixed show at Lamont Gallery, 1996, his work received good critical response. Libby was an assiduous innovator in style and subject, concerned with the darker and unusual aspects of life, the allegorical and metaphysical. Independent Art Promotions began selling him internationally in 1997.

Rachel LICHTENSTEIN 1969– Artist and writer, born Rachel Laurence, who readopted the family name by deed poll when she was 17 (her father's parents, Polish Jews, had escaped to England in the early 1930s). Completed a degree in fine art, specializing in sculpture, at Sheffield University, in her final year writing her thesis on Jewish immigration to east London, where her grandparents had settled. Installed at the Heritage Centre, 19 Princelet Street, a former synagogue, she learned of the disappearance of the orthodox scholar David Rodinsky in the late 1960s. She became artist-in-residence and began a lengthy search to solve the mystery. Lichtenstein held several exhibitions connected with her quest, telling her story in the 1999 book *Rodinsky's Room*.

Val LIDDALL 1898– Painter and teacher. He studied at St Martin's School of Art and in Paris. Held a number of teaching positions in private schools, from 1935 at Bradfield College. He was partly a sporting artist and exhibited ROI and elsewhere. His full name was Frederick Val Liddall. Lived at Sulhamstead, Berkshire.

John LIDDELL 1924–2005 Relief printmaker, watercolourist and teacher, born in London. He studied at Hornsey College of Art, 1941–6, teachers including Norman Janes, Russell Reeve and John Moody. He taught part-time at Bournemouth and Poole College of Art, living in Bournemouth. Liddell was a member of the Printmakers' Council and SWE, also showing at RA, RWA and in America. Completed a mural in Poole Art Centre. Topographical themes were a key feature of Liddell's work. From 1991 he ran a co-operative workshop, Poole Printmakers.

Peter LIDDELL 1954– Painter and teacher, born in Bolton, Lancashire. He studied at Goldsmiths' College School of Art, 1982–4, then two years later became a visiting teacher there. His mixed shows included Riverside Studios, 1988; in 1989 Ways of Telling, held in Llandudno and Cardiff, and Critics, Space V, Air Gallery; and in 1989–90 John Moores Liverpool Exhibition. Lived in London.

Siobhan LIDDELL 1965– Artist who studied at St Martin's School of Art, 1982–6. Exhibited at Rundell Tower and River Café and participated in East End Open Studios, at Belsham Street, 1989.

John LIDZEY 1935– Watercolourist (notable for interiors of his Victorian house in Suffolk), designer, teacher and writer, born in Islington, north London. Lidzey studied typographic design at Camberwell School of Arts and Crafts; worked in advertising studio; and was employed by art studios and design groups for 10 years, during which time he became a member of the Society of Industrial Artists, winning awards. In the late 1960s he returned to Camberwell to lecture on typographic and graphic design. He would sketch for an hour in the London streets before teaching, opting to take up painting full-time in the late 1980s. Lidzey won the Daler-Rowney Award at the 1990 RWS Open, in 1992 winning a prize in the Singer & Friedlander/*Sunday Times* Watercolour Competition at the Mall Galleries. His books included *Watercolour Workshop* and *Mix Your Own Watercolours*, in which his fresh, loose style was demonstrated. Showed with The John Russell Gallery, Ipswich, and watercolours of the London Underground at Abbott and Holder, 2002.

Sybil LIEBERMAN 1944– Artist who studied foundation and graduated with honours in fine art from Surrey Institute of Fine Art & Design, 1990–5, gaining a postgraduate diploma in fine art, 1995–8, appearing in the final year show. It included her Ave Verum, a heavily encrusted abstract oil on gesso board. Among Lieberman's awards were a Rio Tinto Scholarship, 1996; Creswick Landscape Prize and Rio Tinto Scholarship, 1997; and John Purcell Print Prize and Rio Tinto Scholarship, 1998. Her many exhibitions included S C Johnson Gallery, Farnham, 1992; Cleveland International Drawing Biennale, Cleveland Gallery, Cleveland, 1995; RA Summer Exhibition, from 1996; Rover Group Motor Shows in Frankfurt, Bologna and Geneva, 1997–8; and London Symphony Orchestra Concert in Brussels and Munich, 2nd National Biennale Student Print Open and Storey Gallery, Lancaster, all 1998. She lived in Fleet, Hampshire.

Pamina LIEBERT-MAHRENHOLZ 1904– Sculptor, painter and draughtsman, born in Berlin, Germany, who studied sculpture at the Vereinigte Staatsschule am Steinplatz there. She was so highly thought of that she merited her own studio. Exhibited work at the Staatliche Akademie der Künste. She won the Prix de Rome but was unable to take it up because of the political situation. Although by 1939 Liebert-Mahrenholz was an established sculptor in Germany she decided to emigrate to England, where for many years she worked as a china restorer. She began to concentrate on painting and drawing, working independently and at the Camden Institute in London, where she had settled. Showed at RA. Other exhibitions included Woodstock Gallery, 1958; German Embassy, 1978; major retrospective at Camden Arts Centre, 1983; and Ben Uri Art Society, which holds examples, 1988.

Katia LIEBMANN 1965– Artist whose work included a series of Gotham City Batgirl van dyke prints, included in the 1998 volume *The New Neurotic Realism*, which preceded the Neurotic Realism series of shows launched by Saatchi Gallery in 1999. Saatchi Collection holds the work of Liebmann, who was born in Halle, Germany. After graduating at the Kunsthochschule Berlin-Weissensee, 1995, Liebmann attended the State University of New York, in America, 1996–7, gaining her master's at Royal College of Art, London, 1997, where she continued to live.

Sue LIGGETT 1996– Artist producing abstract work who gained an art and design foundation certificate at West Cheshire College of Further Education, 1985–6; honours degree in fine art from Nottingham Trent University, 1986–9; postgraduate master's diploma at Royal Academy Schools, 1991–4; then a postgraduate teaching certificate at University College Chester, 1997–8. Awards included Student of the Year at West Chester College, 1986; Margaret Bryan Scholarship, 1989; Royal Academy Schools Prize for Printmaking, 1993, and its Haite Travelling Scholarship, 1994; Cyril Sweet Award for Painting, with election to the London Guild of the Worshipful Company of Painter-Stainers, and SPACE Studios Award, both 1994; and election as a freeman of the City of London, 1995. Exhibitions included Young Contemporaries, Whitworth Gallery, Manchester, 1987; RA Summer Exhibition, from 1992; Eros I, The Coventry Gallery, 1996; and Castlefield Gallery, Manchester, 1998. Liggett had a solo exhibition at Smiths Galleries, 1995, and was one of Three Young Painters at Hart Gallery, 1999. Lived in Kettering, Northamptonshire.

Susan LIGHT 1954– Painter, born in Zimbabwe. She studied at Central School of Art and Design, 1972–3; Leeds Polytechnic, 1973–6; and San Francisco State University, 1981–3. From 1983 she showed widely in Britain and abroad in group exhibitions, including Sacramento State Fair, California, 1983, where she won an Hon. Commendation; Camden Arts Centre, 1987; RAG to the USSR, Riverside Artists' touring show of Soviet Union, 1988–9; Hunting Art Prizes at Mall Galleries, 1991; and Contemporary Art Fair, 1992. In 1989 she was artist-in-residence at Moscow Artists' Union House of Creativity. Later solo shows included Cadogan Gallery, 1992, and Long & Ryle, 1999. Exotic locations and a skilled use of light and shadow were features of her pictures.

Dorothy LIGHTFOOT 1909–2002 Painter, draughtsman and designer noted for her oils and latterly watercolours, key subjects being barges on the Stour and the landscape and architecture of Suffolk. Her style was reminiscent of the eighteenth-century Norwich School. She was born in

Broadstairs, Kent, and as an only child, aged 13, was left to care for her blind father. A perceptive benefactor enabled her to study at the Central School of Art, teachers including William Roberts, Noel Rooke and Clarke Hutton. She was a supervisor with the Women's Land Army in World War II, then settled in Suffolk, working for the Post Office as a draughtsman and designer. Took part in group shows at Frinton Galleries, Frinton-on-Sea, and had solo exhibitions at Northgate Gallery, 1973–5, and The Haste Gallery, 1976–80, both in Ipswich. She continued to show after moving late in retirement to Chichester, Sussex.

LIGHTWORKS: *see* **Laura JOHNSTON**

Liliane LIJN 1939– Sculptor who was concerned with such subjects as death and rebirth, women as icons and goddesses and light and motion in her work, born in New York. In 1958 she studied archaeology and art history in Paris, then while living in New York again at the start of the 1960s began experimenting with movement and light, which led to first solo show in Paris at La Librairie Anglaise, in 1963. After living in Greece in the mid-1960s she settled in London in 1966, where she continued to work. Other shows followed in Britain and abroad, including a key one-man at Serpentine Gallery in 1976 and an individual Arts Council touring show in 1977. Later exhibited with Fischer Fine Art, with a solo exhibition, Koans, at Shirley Day Ltd, 2000. In 2005 a retrospective of works by Lijn (pronounced Lin) from 1959–79 was held at The Mead Gallery, Warwick Arts Centre, University of Warwick. Her 1972 piece White Koan stands outside the Centre. The show traced the evolution of her output from early Surrealist-influenced drawings made in Paris, through assimilation of the cut-up techniques of the Beat poets, to her kinetic experiments with industrial plastics and light. After moving to London Lijn's sculptures proved increasingly ambitious, with the Liquid Reflections series, 1966–8, and ultimately became more political. The 1973 Arts Council film *What is the sound of one hand clapping* was played at the retrospective and the exhibition closed with two sculptures from 1979, Feathered Lady and HeShe, which heralded a change in Lijn's work. The Mead Gallery retrospective followed a commission from Guy's and St Thomas' Charitable Foundation for the Evelina Children's Hospital, which resulted in Starside, a sculpture designed to be a children's helter-skelter. A notable earlier commission was Circle of Light, for Milton Keynes Development Corporation, sited in 1980 in the Shopping Building, Midsummer Arcade. Lijn's sculptures, in various materials, are in a number of other public collections, including that of the Arts Council. Leeds Museums and Galleries as well as sculpture hold archive material relating to her output. Austin/Desmond Fine Art and England & Co both gave Lijn significant shows in 2006.

David LILLEY 1962– Sculptor, born in Kettering, Northamptonshire, a feature of whose work was small constructions in balsa wood. He studied at Sir John Cass School of Art, 1985–6; Central St Martins College of Art & Design, 1986–9; and Royal Academy Schools, 1990–3. He was awarded a Landseer Scholarship in 1991, a Royal Academy Turner Gold Medal for Sculpture, 1992. Group exhibitions included Portobello Open Sculpture Show and Feast, at Mall Galleries, both 1991; Six Sculptors, City of Plymouth Museum, 1992; and Interventionists' Installation, Whitechapel Art Gallery, 1996. Had a solo show at Bernhard Baron Gallery, 1990, later ones including The Cut Gallery, 1996.

Geoffrey Ivan LILLEY 1930– Artist, illustrator and writer of books and articles on art, born in Cambridge, who studied at local Technical College. Lilley was a member of UA, also exhibiting at NS, RSMA and in the provinces. Lived at Golden Cross, Chiddingly, Sussex.

Jason LILLEY 1966– Painter and draughtsman, originally from north Cornwall, who studied at Falmouth School of Art, 1986–7, and at Newcastle upon Tyne, 1987–90. He was featured on ITV and Channel 4's *Elements*, 1990–1. He showed several times at Belgrave Gallery, including Four For Fore Street, in St Ives, 2003.

Gordon LILLFORD 1919–1992 Painter in oil, born in Doncaster, Yorkshire, older brother of the artist Ralph Lillford. He served as a constable in Bournemouth's police force, 1949–74, studying intermittently at the local College of Art. Lillford took part in mixed exhibitions with RA, RWA, Wessex Artists and at the Selldown Gallery, Poole, and Salisbury Galleries. Had solo shows with Peppin-Brown Gallery in Whittlesford and Red House Gallery in Christchurch, Dorset, where he lived.

Ralph LILLFORD 1932– Painter, draughtsman and teacher, born in Hexthorpe, Doncaster, Yorkshire. He attended Doncaster School of Art and Royal College of Art, 1954–7, after National Service in the Army in the Suez Canal Zone, 1952–4. Teachers included John Minton, Leonard Rosoman and Carel Weight. Began teaching at Barnes Secondary School, 1957–60, after several appointments lecturing at Richmond College from 1983. He also lectured part-time at Victoria & Albert Museum and Royal College of Art. Dr Lillford drew and painted in Crete, Russia, Egypt, America, Ireland and on the European continent. Showed at RA, RBA, Brunel University, Imperial College, Gloucester College of Art and elsewhere. The Hermitage and Pushkin Museums in Russia, National Army Museum, Victoria & Albert Museum and Imperial War Museum hold examples. In 1992 Lillford had an exhibition of drawings and paintings of work on the Channel Tunnel at Imperial College. Lived at Osterley, Middlesex.

Marjorie LILLY 1891–1980 Painter, printmaker, lecturer and writer, born and lived in London. Studied at Slade School of Fine Art prior to World War I under "Professor (Henry) Tonks the Terrible", as she described him in her memoir *Sickert The Painter and His Circle*, 1971. In this she writes of Sickert's working methods and the group of artists around him, such as Harold Gilman, Charles Ginner and Robert Bevan. Lilly showed at Walker's Galleries, NEAC, RBA, ROI, Redfern Gallery and elsewhere. She was an Arts Council lecturer during World War II. Was included in The Sickert Women and The Sickert Girls in 1974 and Sladey Ladies, 1986, both at Parkin Gallery.

Kim LIM 1936–1997 Abstract sculptor, photographer and printmaker, born in Singapore, married to the sculptor William Turnbull. She studied at St Martin's School of Art 1954–6, then Slade School of Fine Art, 1956–9. Took part in many group exhibitions in London, Paris and Tokyo, later ones including Journeys West, tour organised by University of Essex, 1995. Had two solo exhibitions at Axiom Gallery in 1966 and 1968. Several others followed at Waddington Galleries; Museum of Modern Art in Oxford; Felicity Samuel, Tate and Round House Galleries. Later ones included Yorkshire Sculpture Park, Bretton Hall, 1995, and Camden Arts Centre, 1999, by which time Kim Lim favoured stone for her simple and serene works. Arts Council, Tate Gallery, Nagaoka Museum of Modern Art in Japan, National Museum of Art in Singapore and many British provincial galleries hold examples.

Hsiao-Mei LIN 1971– Painter who described her work as Abstract Expressionist. After Fu Hsin School of Art, Taipei, Taiwan, 1987–90, gained an honours degree in fine art – painting at University of Brighton, 1991–4, with a post-graduate diploma course in painting at Royal Academy Schools, 1994. Awards included Winsor & Newton Young Artist Award, David Murray Travel Award, Crabtree & Evelyn Scholarship and Tony Smith Prize. Her painting After the Storm was included in Chevron UK Ltd's 1997 calendar. Exhibitions included Hunting Art Prizes at the Royal College of Art, Christopher Hull Gallery and finalist, The Alasdair Gilchrist Fisher Memorial Award 1998, at Cadogan Contemporary. Solo shows organised by Adam Gallery, Bath, at The Gallery in Cork Street, 1999 and 2000.

Richard LIN 1933– Painter and designer in metal and plastic, working in a Minimalist style, born in Formosa, Taiwan. For a time he worked as Lin Show Yu. Studied at Millfield School, Somerset. In the mid-1950s studied architecture for four years at Regent Street Polytechnic. Had first of a series of one-man shows in 1959 at Gimpel Fils, then began to show internationally in the Netherlands, America, Germany and elsewhere, winning several prizes. Was taken up by Marlborough Fine Art. Tate Gallery, Arts Council, Walker Art Gallery in Liverpool and many overseas galleries hold his work. Lived for a time in Wales, including Aberystwyth, Dyfed.

Philip LINDEY 1968– Painter of figurative works, often quirky and humorous, who was born in Rochdale, Lancashire, of Irish parents. They soon returned to Sligo, in the west of Ireland, where in 1985 Philip did a foundation course at Sligo Regional College. In 1992 he graduated from the National College of Art, in Dublin, then took part in group shows, open submissions and painted many commissioned portraits. In 1997 Lindey had his first solo exhibition at Galway Arts Centre, the following year began his master's degree in fine arts and, after graduating, had a one-man exhibition in Belfast. After initially showing at Albemarle Gallery, London, in 1999, Lindey was included in Eclectic Encounters there in 2005.

Kenneth LINDLEY 1928–1986 Printmaker and watercolourist, teacher and writer, born in London, who studied at Ealing and Hornsey Schools of Art. Lindley went on to become principal of Herefordshire College of Art until 1986. He was a member of SWE and of the Society of Industrial Artists and Designers/Chartered Society of Designers and a fellow of RE. He had a series of solo shows in London and elsewhere and after his death a retrospective was held in Hereford. Lindley wrote, printed and illustrated work under the imprint of the Pointing Finger Press. He was responsible for many books, some handled by other publishers, including *Coastline*, 1967; *Chapels and Meeting Houses*, 1969; and *Woodblock Engravers*, 1970. Lived in Hereford.

Doris LINDNER 1896–1979 Sculptor in stone, concrete and bronze, specialising in animals. Modelled them for Royal Worcester Porcelain Company. Born at Llanyre, Radnorshire, where she early developed an interest in animals and wild life, Lindner studied under the School of Animal Painting, South Kensington, then at the St Martin's School of Art and the British School, Rome. Exhibitions included RA, Royal Glasgow Institute, RBA and LG. Lived at Broad Campden, Gloucestershire, for some years, but died in Kent.

Moffat LINDNER 1852–1949 Landscape and marine painter in watercolour and oil, whose full name was Peter Moffat Lindner. Born in Birmingham, he studied at Slade School of Fine Art, 1877, under Alphonse Legros, and at Heatherley's School of Fine Art. Was married to the artist Augusta Baird Lindner. He exhibited prolifically at RWS, RA, Ridley Art Club, ROI, NEAC and Fine Art Society and at many other galleries. Work in British galleries, such as Bradford, Hull and Liverpool, as well as in a number overseas. Moffat Lindner's pictures often featured wind and cloud and large expanses of water, having a singularly breezy appearance, as in the examples shown in G S Sandilands' Studio monograph *Artists' Country*. Fond of painting on the continent, as well as in Britain. Lived at St Ives, Cornwall.

Alan LINDSAY 1918– Painter and designer, born in Ludlow, Shropshire. Attended Birmingham College of Arts and Crafts, 1934–6, under Bernard Fleetwood-Walker, then at Royal College of Art, 1938–9 and 1946–8, under Charles Mahoney and Barnett Freedman. His work was illustrated in *Penguin New Writing*. Exhibited RA, Leicester Galleries and NEAC. Lived in London.

Alasdair LINDSAY 1975– Painter of landscape and seascape, sometimes abstracted, using bright colours. Born in Cheshire, Lindsay attended West Cheshire College, Reading University and Falmouth Art College, where he graduated in fine art. He had very successful early mixed and solo appearances, including Brian Sinfield Gallery, Burford, and Great Atlantic Map Works Gallery, St Just-in-Penwith, 2002.

Daryl LINDSAY 1889–1976 Landscape painter in oil and watercolour and administrator. Born at Creswick, Victoria, Australia, brother of the artists Norman and Lionel Lindsay. After initial education in Australia he worked as a bank clerk, served in World War I, then attended the Slade School of Fine Art, London, 1919. Returned to Australia where he painted for 20 years. Then became keeper of prints at the National Gallery of Victoria for two years and its director, 1941–56, when he was knighted. Exhibited RA, Cooling Galleries, RWS, Arthur Tooth and Son and widely in Australia. Work in the collection of the Victoria & Albert Museum and many Australian galleries. Lived at Baxter, Victoria, Australia.

Samuel Arthur LINDSEY 1869–1952 Miniaturist and teacher, born and died in London, who held several important positions in the RMS, being a much-liked president from 1943 until his death after a two-year illness. He exhibited extensively with the RMS, RA, Walker

Art Gallery in Liverpool, RI and elsewhere. In the early 1920s Lindsey contributed two pictures to Queen Mary's Dolls' House: a watercolour of a girl in Breton dress and a miniature portrait of King George V, in the Queen's bedroom. He also created a rare anamorphosis of George V, whereabouts unknown. Lindsey taught summer watercolour courses in Brittany, France. Among his students were the noted American art dealer Betty Parsons and her English painter friend Adge Baker, as recounted in Lee Hall's 1991 biography *Betty Parsons*.

Kathleen M LINDSLEY fl. from 1970s– Printmaker, born in Gibraltar, who was educated in Australia, Singapore and England. Studied fine arts at Leeds University and Newcastle Polytechnic, gaining an honours degree in 1976, having begun engraving with Leo Wyatt in 1975. From 1970 travelled extensively in Britain, for some years dividing her time between Edinburgh and Skye. Did illustrations for *Sunday Times* travel guide and a guide to Oxford. Engraved 250 designs for pub signs for Samuel Websters' Brewery through Pentagram Design, which took over two years. Showed at Thumb Gallery; Mill House and Scottish Galleries, Edinburgh; Print Sellers, Plymouth; and Leeds Playhouse.

Vincent LINES 1909–1968 Painter, printmaker and teacher, born in Dulwich in southeast London. Studied at Central School of Arts and Crafts under A S Hartrick and Royal College of Art, where he gained a Travelling Scholarship in 1932. He took part in the Pilgrim Trust's *Recording Britain* project, was principal of Hastings School of Art and wrote several books, including *Mark Fisher and Margaret Fisher Prout*. Exhibited RA, NEAC, RWS, Leicester Galleries and elsewhere. British Council bought his work. Lived in Hastings, Sussex.

John LINFIELD 1930– Painter who was born in Carshalton Beeches, Surrey. He studied at Wimbledon School of Art and Royal College of Art. In 1982 he was elected NEAC, also showing at RA, RP and elsewhere. He had solo shows at Trafford Gallery in the early 1960s, later exhibitions taking place with Halifax House in Oxford and John Noott Twentieth Century, in Broadway. Winsor & Newton Ltd and Spink & Son Ltd were among the commissioners of his work. Lived in Wells, Somerset.

Alan Carr LINFORD 1926– Painter of realistic landscapes in Britain and abroad, born in Doncaster, Yorkshire, where he studied at the local School of Art, 1940. He attended the Royal College of Art, 1943–7, gaining the Prix de Rome which took him to British School in Rome, 1947–9. After an introduction by the artist Edward Halliday, Linford was commissioned to do a lot of work for the royal family. He completed 24 works of the River Thames for HRH Prince Philip which were hung on the Royal Yacht *Britannia*, other pictures hanging in the private apartments in Windsor Castle and in family homes including Baden-Baden and Salem. In the 1980s further commissions stemmed from the cities of Düsseldorf, Cologne and Achen and from the Sultan of Oman. Was elected a member of RE, 1948, RWS in 1953. Had a solo show of Parisian paintings in 1993 at Mistral Galleries. HM The Queen, Shell and ICI also hold his work.

Leong Shao LING: *see* **Kim C LEONG**

Rita M LING 1922– Sculptor and teacher, born in Wolverhampton, where she studied at the College of Art, then from 1946–50 at Royal College of Art, where her teachers included John Skeaping and Frank Dobson. Ling taught at Farnham School of Art, 1950, and at the Royal College of Art, where she was first woman tutor in sculpture, 1955–60. The year before, she worked with Skeaping on carvings for the Dutch Church, Austin Friars, in the City of London. Showed RA and elsewhere. Tate Gallery holds her limestone sculpture Galway Cow. The artist was partly of Irish parentage and was deeply attached to southern Ireland.

Simon LING 1968– Painter born in Bradford, Yorkshire, who studied at Carmarthen College of Art, 1987–8, and Chelsea College of Art, 1988–91. His picture Side A was included in John Moores Liverpool Exhibition, 1991–2. He lived in Neyland, Dyfed.

Simon LINKE 1958– Minimalist artist, born in Benalla, Victoria, Australia. He studied at St Martin's School of Art, graduating with honours, 1977–81, then Royal College of Art, 1983, and gained his master's degree at Goldsmiths' College, 1985–6. Group exhibitions included Tolly Cobbold, Fitzwilliam Museum, Cambridge, 1983; Air Gallery, 1986; Cornerhouse, Manchester, 1988; Tony Shafrazi Gallery, New York, 1989; at Lisson Gallery, 1990; and John Moores Liverpool Exhibition, 2002. Had solo show at Gray Art Gallery, New York, 1986; Lisson Gallery and Tony Shafrazi, both 1987; Stichting De Appel, Amsterdam, 1988; and Kohji Ogura Gallery, Nagoya, Japan, 1989.

Duncan LINKLATER 1948– Self-taught sculptor in wood, born in York, related to the writers Eric and Magnus Linklater. Influences were cited as "originally Henry Toft, latterly Picasso, Chaucer and Greek pottery of the 'black figure' type." He took part in group exhibitions and had several solo shows, including Hay Makers Gallery, Hay-on-Wye, 2000. Lived in Somerset.

Barbara LINLEY-ADAMS 1923–1995 Sculptor and teacher, born in London, who signed her work LA, intertwined. She was initially educated in England and Switzerland, then studied at Central School of Arts and Crafts, 1948–50. In 1958 lectured on sculpture at University of Utah, in America. Showed RA, at the Festival of Britain in 1951 and with Arts and Crafts Exhibition Society, of which she was a member, also at Victoria & Albert Museum. Lived in Bath, Somerset.

Judy LINNELL 1948– Painter, draughtsman and teacher also known as Judith Linnell, who exploited the vibrancy, luminosity and fluidity of watercolour to create distinctive flower, still life and landscape pictures. She was brought up in Knighton, Radnorshire, and graduated in fine art at Leeds University with Quentin Bell and Lawrence Gowing, 1966–70, with a postgraduate art education certificate in 1971. After teaching advanced English and art history in Rome and Cambridge, Linnell settled in St Albans, Hertfordshire, where she began teaching watercolour and drawing at Oaklands College of Further Education in 1983, in 1990 starting her own watercolour workshops and in 1996 becoming tutor for painting holidays in Corsica and Crete. Awards included Hertfordshire Open Exhibition, commended, 1991; Faber Castell drawing prize, 1992, and Buzzacott Award, 2001

Participated in many group shows, including Thomas Thorpe Gallery, St Albans, 1988; St Albans Abbey Centenary Exhibition, 1993; SWA, Westminster Galleries, 1998; Catto Gallery, 1999; and The Linda Blackstone Gallery, Pinner, 2002. Solo exhibitions included Watercolourings II, Watford Palace Theatre, 2001. Worked on watercolour technique books for Quarto Publishing.

LIN SHOW YU: *see* **Richard LIN**

Robert LINTON 1930– Painter, sculptor and teacher, born in County Donegal, Ireland. He studied at Belfast College of Art and Central School of Arts and Crafts. Linton won a CEMA Travel Scholarship to Italy in 1955, in 1968 a Northern Ireland Arts Council Travel Grant to the Netherlands. He lived in Limavady, County Londonderry, Northern Ireland, and was head of the art department at its Grammar School. Linton was an associate of RUA. He showed in Belfast and Dublin and had a series of solo exhibitions.

Flora LION 1876–1958 Painter in oil. Born and working in London, she studied at the St John's Wood School of Art, Royal Academy Schools and at Académie Julian, Paris. Married to the painter Rudolph Lion, who took her name. She exhibited widely, including RA, ROI, SWA, Fine Art Society and Goupil Gallery, as well as at several venues in France (she was of Anglo-French parentage). Awarded the silver medal of the Société des Artistes Français in 1921 and the gold medal in 1949. The Tate Gallery, British Museum and Victoria & Albert Museum hold her work.

Rudolph Louis LION fl. c.1920–1960 Painter and printmaker who married the painter Flora Lion, whose name he adopted. Studied privately and exhibited RA and in the provinces, signing his work with a monogram. Lived in London.

Gerald Royston LIPMAN 1929– Painter, commercial and pen and ink artist, son of commercial artist James Lipman. Studied at Harrow School of Art with John Platt, 1943–4, then with Robin Guthrie at St Martin's School of Art. He worked for periods as a layout artist at Unilever Ltd and the advertising agency Lintas. Exhibited RA and NEAC. Lived for a time near Westcliff-on-Sea, Essex.

Lippy LIPSHITZ 1903–1980 Versatile artist, mainly a sculptor, and teacher, born Israel-Isaac Lipshitz in Plungian, Lithuania, brother of the painter Ada Lipshitz-Wolpe and father of the printmaker Toni Lipshitz-Caspi. Lipshitz studied at Cape Town Art School, 1922–5; at Michaelis School of Fine Art, 1925–6; at L'Académie del la Grande Chaumière, Paris, under Antoine Bourdelle, 1928–9. He was a founder-member of the New Group and of Art Club of South Africa, where he lived from 1908–78. Among his teaching posts was Michaelis School, where he eventually became associate professor of fine art, 1964–8. Took part in extensive international exhibitions and had many solo shows in South Africa and London, where he lived, 1947–8. Tate Gallery archive has his Self Portrait, ink on paper, 1948. Retrospectives included South African National Gallery, Cape Town, 1976. It and many other South African galleries hold his work. Died Kiryat Tivon, Israel.

Tadeusz LIPSKI 1905–1987 Artist and designer, a notable figure in the promotion of paper sculpture as an art in Britain from the 1940s pursued by a number of fellow Poles. In 1928 Lipski graduated from Warsaw Academy of Fine Arts, six years later being offered a post as assistant lecturer. Designed posters, advertisements, interior decorations for commercial premises and shop windows using paper sculptures. His sculptures were incomparably cut, with minute attention to detail. During World War II he served in Poland's forces in the West. Lipski's heraldic arms for a wall of the Council for Industrial Design pavilion for the Britain Can Make It exhibition in 1946 so impressed King George VI, who opened it, that he mistook the paper for marble, then asked to see the artist who had fashioned the work. In 1947 Lipski published his key book *Paper Sculpture*. Was granted fellowship of the Society of Industrial Artists. In the 1940s settled in New York, opened his own studio and devoted himself to screenprinting. His wall decorations commissioned by Ford Motor Company and Waldorf Astoria can be seen in New York as well as in Brook Alexander and Pace Galleries and private collections. Lipski was featured in Polish Paper Sculpture at Polish Cultural Institute, 1995.

Laurie LIPTON 1953– Versatile artist born in New York, America, of Russian Jewish émigré parents. She was the first person to graduate from the Carnegie-Mellon University with a fine arts honours degree in drawing, in 1975. Lipton lived in the Netherlands, Belgium, Germany and France, settling in London from 1986. She completed many commissions, including work for television and the theatre. For television, these included Nederland1: *Wetenschap in Beweging*, Netherlands, 1978, and BBC1, *In a class of their own*, 1989; theatre, poster designs for German State Theatre, Hamburg, 1975, and Midland Brand Hotel, a site-specific project sponsored by Islington Council at St Pancras Hotel, for which she was artistic consultant, 2000. From 1989 onwards she was given multiple commissions by Bibliotheca Philosophica Hermetica, Amsterdam, the largest private collection of books relating to alchemy and mysticism in Europe, to produce drawings for illuminated manuscripts. Between 1974–00 Lipton had over 30 solo exhibitions internationally, later ones including The Ministry of Pop Culture, curated by Henry Boxer, 1998; East West Gallery, from 1998; and The Sleep of Reason, drawings inspired by the work of Goya, Instituto Cervantes, 2003.

Heather LISBON 1960– Artist who graduated with honours from Leeds University, 1979–82, gaining her master's from Chelsea School of Art, 1983–4. She participated in Where the Flesh Meets Fruit, Air Gallery, and Life's Eye, Ben Uri Art Society, both 1988, and East End Open Studios, at Britannia Works, 1989. In 1988–9 Lisbon was Air Gallery printmaker-in-residence at Islington Green School in north London.

Walter LISHMAN 1903–1985 Etcher and wood engraver, born at Wolviston, Stockton-on-Tees, County Durham. After education at Armstrong College, Durham University, Lishman studied art at King Edward VII School of Art, Newcastle upon Tyne, under E M O'R Dickey. Showed work at NS and SGA, of which he was a member, also at RI and Artists of the Northern Counties shows at Laing Art Gallery, Newcastle. Lived in Houghton le Spring, near Sunderland, also belonging to Sunderland Art Club.

Frank LISLE 1916–1986 Painter, draughtsman, mixed-media artist and teacher, born in Leeds, Yorkshire, husband of the artist June Lisle. He studied at Leeds College of Art, 1930–6, then Royal College of Art, 1937–40. Cézanne, Victor Pasmore, Fibernacci and Sufism were important influences on his work. Lisle served in the Army in 1940–6, attaining the rank of captain, and suffered the loss of an eye during time in France. He eventually became principal of Jacob Kramer College in Leeds, 1970–7. Several fine portraits and large abstract or semi-abstract constructions were among Lisle's major works. He showed with Yorkshire Artists, RA, NEAC, RBA and RP and was included in The Teaching Image at Leeds City Art Gallery, 1964. Solo shows included Playhouse Gallery, Leeds, 1973, and Hambledon Gallery, Blandford, 1986. Was a member of RBA and president of Leeds Art Club. Died in Shillingstone, Dorset.

Caroline LIST 1964– Painter and teacher, born in Nottingham, who studied at West Nottinghamshire College of Art & Design; Portsmouth Polytechnic; and Chelsea School of Art & Design. Between 1986–91 List held part-time teaching posts at Derby College of Further Education, Heatherley's College of Art and Essendine Adult Education Centre. Between 1992–3 she taught painting and drawing for beginners at Westminster College of Further Education, then in 1993–4 was tutor in new art theory and practice at Chelsea School of Art. She won an East Midlands Starter Grant 1987, and a Herbert Read Scholarship, 1988. Group shows included Apex Gallery, Portsmouth, 1985; The New Generation, Bonhams, 1990; Contemporary Young Painters, Nigel Greenwood Gallery, 1991; and in 1995 she was first prize winner at Royal Over-Seas League Open, having a solo show there in 1996. Department of Health; Contemporary Art Society; and Arthur Andersen & Company hold List's work, which was "concerned with decoding existing layers of visual language, and unravelling these signs and signifiers which are full of hidden metaphors".

Edward D'Arcy LISTER 1911– Painter and printmaker. Born at Horsforth, Yorkshire, he studied at Leeds College of Art, 1928–33, then at the Royal College of Art for four years under Gilbert Spencer. Became a lecturer at Bournemouth and Poole College of Art. Exhibited RA and provincial galleries, his work being held by the Victoria & Albert Museum and Southampton City Art Gallery. The latter's picture Saturday Night is a good example of the artist's ability to depict provincial urban low life. He also painted several murals. Lived in Broadstone, Dorset.

Henrietta LISTER 1895–1959 Painter in oil and watercolour, born at Manor Park, London. Studied at the Byam Shaw and Vicat Cole School of Art, 1912–14, under Rex Vicat Cole and David Murray Smith. Exhibited extensively at RA, WIAC, UA and in the northern provinces. Work held by Darlington Art Gallery and Laing Art Gallery and Museum, Newcastle upon Tyne. Also drew for the magazine *The Dalesman*. Lived near Leyburn, Yorkshire.

Raymond LISTER 1919–2001 Miniaturist, illustrator and writer, born and lived in Cambridge. In 1934 Lister was apprenticed to the family firm, eventually becoming a director of George Lister & Sons, specialising in architectural metalwork and carrying out restoration around the country. He was made Prime Warden of the Blacksmiths' Company, 1989–90. Dr Lister was a noted art historian, specialising in British romantic art, a fellow of Wolfson College and a syndic of the Fitzwilliam Museum, Cambridge, 1981–90. Among his many books were *Samuel Palmer and his Etchings*, 1969; *The Letters of Samuel Palmer*, 1975; *George Richmond*, 1981; and *Catalogue Raisonné of the Works of Samuel Palmer*, 1988. His autobiography, *With My Own Wings*, appeared in 1994. Lister studied privately with the miniaturist Albert Cousins. He was elected RMS in 1947 and was its president 1970–80. He had several solo shows at RBA Galleries and in Cambridge and made many illustrations, often hand-painted, for the Golden Head Press. New York Public Library, Fitzwilliam Museum and Russell-Cotes Art Gallery and Museum, Bournemouth, hold examples of Lister's miniatures which he said were "mainly imaginative landscapes ... which endeavour to explain moods and 'atmosphere'".

Walter Llewellyn LISTER 1876–1951 Watercolourist and printmaker. After Bristol University, went to Westminster School of Art and St Martin's School of Art, 1900–4. Exhibited with St Ives Society of Artists and the Society of Graver-Printers in Colour, of which he was an associate, RBA and ROI. British Museum holds his work. Lived in Bodmin, Cornwall.

Beatrice Ethel LITHIBY 1889–1966 Painter and designer, especially of church furnishings and stained glass. She studied at the Royal Academy Schools and eventually settled in Wantage, Berkshire, her studio where she lived being in the grounds of St Mary's Convent, an Anglican order; she was a devout Christian. Miss Lithiby began sketching as a young girl and went on to exhibit at RA, RBA until her final illness, Walker's Galleries, SWA, RI and in the provinces. In her later years she concentrated on landscapes in oil and watercolour, in her youth painting portraits, too. Her ecclesiastical work found its way abroad, to South Africa and Japan. Miss Lithiby, known as Bel to her friends (an acronym of her initials), of commanding appearance, served in the Army in both World Wars, reaching senior rank in World War II. Wrote a historical guide to Wantage parish church. The artist was to have become engaged to a fellow Royal Academy Schools student, Frank Skinner, on his return from the Western Front, but he was killed on the Somme in July 1916. She put a memorial notice in the *Daily Telegraph* each year and died on the 50th anniversary of his death.

Maurice LITTEN 1919–1979 Portrait painter in oil, son of the artist Sydney Litten. Maurice Litten was born in Hammersmith and studied art under James Bateman at Goldsmiths' College School of Art, then under Frank Barrington Craig at St Martin's School of Art. Exhibited at RA, NEAC, RBA and RP. Lived in London.

Doris LITTLE 1895–1977 Painter and draughtsman, born in Lee Green, southeast London. After Bromley High School attended Bromley, Beckenham and Goldsmiths Schools of Art. She served on the land in World War I, in the Red Cross Ambulance Service in World War II, resuming painting in 1950s. Was a member of Free Painters and Sculptors, Paddington and Blackheath Art Societies. Showed with RBA, PS, at Greenwich Theatre Gallery, Leighton House and elsewhere. Had a memorial show at Woodlands Art Gallery, 1981.

George LITTLE 1927– Painter and teacher, born in Swansea where he attended the College of Art, 1944–51. After World War II service was at Ruskin School of Drawing in Oxford, 1951–3. A series of teaching posts followed, including lecturing in fine art at University College of Swansea. Took part in SEA, SWG and WAC group shows and had several solo exhibitions at University College in Swansea, with a major one at Oriel Ceri Richards, 2001. WAC and CASW hold his work. Little was fond of painting landscapes in the Swansea area, especially industrial subjects such as his oil Old Hafod Works, 1989–92, held by the National Library of Wales, Aberystwyth.

Graham LITTLE 1972– Artist whose work included brightly striped, irregular box sculptures, as in dumbpop, Jerwood Gallery, 1998–9. Little gained a first-class honours degree in painting at Duncan of Jordanstone College, Dundee, 1990–5, and his master's at Goldsmiths' College School of Art, 1996–7, doing associate research in fine art there, 1997–8. Group exhibitions included Cluster, Collective Gallery, Edinburgh, 1995; and RP, Mall Galleries, 1997; Drawing Now, Museum of Modern Art, New York, 2002; and Images of Society, Kunsthalle Thun, Switzerland, 2003. Had solo shows at Asprey Jacques, 2000 and 2003. In the second, Little included his sculpture entitled A huge mass of luminous gas erupted from Mars and sped towards Earth. He started thinking about this in Los Angeles, where he spent much time roller-skating around the city. The title was taken from the lyrics of a Prog Rock concept album called *War of the Worlds*, based on the H G Wells novel.

Margaret Isabel LITTLE 1901–1994 Artist, notably in mosaic, born in Bedford, by profession a medical practitioner and psychoanalyst. She was educated at Bedford College, St Mary's Hospital and the Institute of Psycho-Analysis and was for a time on the staff of the London Clinic of Psycho-Analysis. Studied art privately during World War II and at Sir John Cass College, 1957–65. Became a member of Free Painters and Sculptors in 1963, also showing at RBA, SWA and elsewhere. Lived at Dunton Green, Sevenoaks, Kent.

Michael LITTLE 1939– Artist in oil, watercolour and acrylic, and teacher, born in Rhayader, Radfordshire, who grew up in the west of Ireland. Moved to London aged 17 and studied at Chelsea School of Art, 1957–61, and Royal Academy Schools, 1961–4. Became a lecturer in drawing and fine art at Northampton School of Art, later Nene College. Little was a member of East Midlands Arts who claimed as influences Edward Hopper, Balthus and Queen Victoria's portrait painter, Josefine Swoboda. Group shows included Basle Art Fair, Switzerland; Kenny Gallery, Galway; Rufford Craft Centre in Nottingham; and in 1993 Little was included in People and Places at Gagliardi Gallery. Had a series of one-man shows at National Theatre from 1981 and one at Commonwealth Institute, 1994. In 1991 Little won the celebrity's prize in the Anglia Television *Moving Art* series, presented by George Melly. Leicestershire County Council Braunstone Underpass murals are by Little, who lived in Northampton.

Pauline LITTLE 1961– Artist and teacher, born in Glasgow, who studied foundation at Sir John Cass, 1992–3; gained a fine art honours degree at Middlesex University, 1993–6; and attended The Cooper Union, New York, America, 1995, the year she joined the LG. Taught foundation at Surrey Institute of Art and Design from 2001. Little was a finalist for the Mercury Music Prize and for Bayer Art, Earth Prize, both 1996. Group shows included English Speaking Union, Edinburgh, 1995; The Whitechapel Open, 1996; Will's Art Warehouse, Windsor and London, both 1997; Woodlands Art Gallery, 2001; and The Walk Gallery, 2002. Had solo exhibitions at The Bedford Hill Gallery, 1997, and William IV, 1999. St Mary's Hospital, Middlesex University and The Cooper Union hold examples. She lived in London.

Robert LITTLEFORD 1940– North of England-based artist whose parents were poorly-paid cotton workers. In his mid-twenties Littleford was inspired by a painting of the moon over an ocean, seen in a gallery window, painting then absorbed all his spare time and in 1971 he decided to become a professional artist. A first exhibition at Salford Art Gallery received good critical response and national television coverage. Many more shows followed. In 1986 he was elected to the BWS. Light was a key element in Littleford's pictures, as in his A Day on the Sands and Days to Remember, nostalgic beach scenes shown at The Bourne Gallery, Reigate, in its 30th Anniversary Exhibition in 2001.

Paul LITTLEHALES 1945– Painter and teacher who graduated in fine art from Lanchester Polytechnic, gained his master's in painting at Chelsea College of Art and postgraduate certificate in education at Birmingham Polytechnic. He was on the staff of Solihull College for many years. Littlehales was a founder-member of The Firm artists' group and produced "loosely Super-Realist figurative compositions in oils." He was several times Leicester Schools & Colleges artist-in-residence and was involved in their exhibitions from 1982. His many other shows included Chichester Open Exhibition, 1976; City Art Gallery, Carlisle, 1985; Leamington Art Gallery, 1989; Art Machine at McClellan Galleries, Glasgow, 1990; Nuneaton Museum and Art Gallery, 1992; and Goldmark Gallery, Uppingham, 1998. Leicester Education Authority, London University and Leicestershire school and colleges hold examples. He lived in Stockingford, Warwickshire.

William LITTLEJOHN 1929– Painter and teacher, born in Arbroath, Angus, where he eventually settled. He studied at Duncan of Jordanstone College of Art, Dundee, 1946–50, and won the RSA Guthrie Award in 1961; the Cargill Award of the Royal Glasgow Institute of the Fine Arts followed in 1966 and 1990. Littlejohn also won the Sir William Gillies Award of RSW in 1980. In 1966 Littlejohn joined the staff of Gray's School of Art, Aberdeen, of which he became head. From 1963 he had a series of solo exhibitions at Scottish Gallery, Edinburgh; others included University of Leeds, 1976; and Loomshop Gallery, Lower Largo, Fife. Littlejohn's work is in the collection of HM The Queen, Scottish National Gallery of Modern Art, Scottish Arts Council and other Scottish galleries. The artist was noted for his still lifes in which the elements were distorted or abstracted in the interests of a felicitous pattern. Was deputy president of RSA.

John LITTLEJOHNS 1874–c.1955 Painter, illustrator, writer and teacher, born at Orchard Hill, near Bideford, Devon, and married to the artist Idalia Blanche Littlejohns. For some time they occupied 2 Orchard Studios, in Brook

Green. Littlejohns was a member of the Arts Club, also of RBA, RWA and RI, with which he exhibited until 1954. He was a prolific artist, also exhibiting with Fine Art Society RCamA, Walker's Galleries and elsewhere. His own books included *Art in Schools, Sketching from Nature in Line and Tone* and with Leonard Richmond wrote *The Technique of Watercolour* and *The Art of Painting in Pastel*.

Wilfred E LITTLEWOOD 1899–1977 Painter in oil and restorer, born at New Mill, Huddersfield. He attended the School of Art in Huddersfield, was a part-time teacher, 1927–38, and continued to live in Huddersfield. Showed RA, in the Yorkshire area and at Paris Salon.

William LITTLEWOOD 1893–1985 Illustrator and artist of realistic work, in a variety of media, born in Scarborough, Yorkshire, where he was brought up by an aunt. She was persuaded to let William attend evening classes at the local School of Art, under the tutelage of Albert Strange, the principal, and Richard E Clarke. Two sponsors paid for the lessons, and Littlewood worked during the day for an architect, then a printer. When war broke out, he volunteered for Queen Alexandra's Own Regiment, seeing most of his contemporaries killed. After the war, with Eric Marshal Hardy and David Woolard, Littlewood ran an advertising agency in Bradford. Plagued by a weak heart, Littlewood became so unwell that in 1936 he had to move south to a cottage in rural Berkshire with his wife Kathleen, herself for many years an invalid, who was the focus of much of his output. Littlewood worked as a government cartographer during World War II, then was a freelance artist, especially an illustrator of children's classics, notable for intensely researched work. Although he showed at RA and RBA, Littlewood was reluctant to exhibit his pictures, which were given a retrospective in 1989 at Scarborough Art Gallery. It holds 15 of his works. The artist Katie Sowter was his daughter.

Jincheng LIU 1956– Figurative artist whose work reflected his admiration for French classical paintings, notably those of David and Ingres. Born in Beijing, China, he trained at its Art School, in 1982 graduating from the department of fine art, Beijing College. Between 1983–8 he travelled extensively in China, with a year in Tibet in 1987. Showed three times at National Art Gallery, Beijing. In 1989, moved to England for postgraduate studies at Slade School of Fine Art, settling in south London. He took part in many group shows overseas and in Britain, such as Millennium 2000 at Albemarle Gallery, 1999–00, and had solo exhibitions in London.

William Bernard LIVERMORE 1890– Painter, draughtsman and printmaker who was by profession an accountant, born in London. He continued to live in the Hornsey area and studied at Hornsey College of Art from 1938 with John Charles Moody and Norman Janes and at Central School of Arts and Crafts, 1944–8, with William Palmer Robins. Exhibited RA, RI, SGA, RBA and elsewhere. Hastings Art Gallery holds his work.

Peter LIVERSIDGE 1973– Painter who drew inspiration from euphoric advertisements in old *National Geographic* magazines, as in his entry exhibited at John Moores Liverpool Exhibition, 1999. Liversidge was born in Lincoln, studying at Cumbria College of Art and Design, Carlisle, 1992–3, and University of Plymouth, Exeter, 1993–6. He shared a show at Beak Gallery, Dublin, Ireland, 1998, solo exhibitions including A22 Projects, 1998, Timothy Everest 1999, and The West at Richard Salmon, 2003. Liversidge was involved in mail art. One of his biggest triumphs was successfully to mail from Exeter to London all 26 pieces separate and unwrapped, of a school chair. The mailed chair was exhibited at The Spacex Gallery, Exeter. Paul I Stolper represented the artist.

Thomas Alfred LIVERTON 1907–1972 Watercolourist commercial designer and teacher, born in Barnstaple Devon. Liverton studied at Bromley and Beckenham Schools of Art, 1924–8, under Percy Hague Jowett and Henry Carr, then for a similar period at the Royal College of Art under Randolph Schwabe and A K Lawrence Liverton worked on illustrations and designs for textiles and posters. He taught at St Martin's School of Art Camberwell School of Arts and Crafts, London College of Printing and the Borough Polytechnic, but retired at a comparatively early age to paint full-time. For many years lived near Rye, Sussex, and was well-known for his masterly evocations of seascapes and the Romney Marsh area in a wash technique similar to that of the better known RV Pitchforth. Exhibited RA, RBA, NEAC and in New York. A memorial show was held by Agnew in 1972 London County Council and provincial museums hold his work.

John LIVESEY 1926–1990 Painter, born in London into the well-known theatrical family. He studied at St Martin's School of Art under Ruskin Spear. Showed widely overseas with many solo exhibitions in Switzerland and several in Netherlands, Germany and America. After his death an exhibition was held at Linda Blackstone Gallery, Pinner 1990.

Di LIVEY 1946– Artist and teacher, born in Surrey, who created constructions from materials such as canvas stretched or folded over a frame of wood, covered with many layers of acrylic paint. Although apparently abstract, titles were "keys to the ideas behind the works". She studied at Guildford School of Art, 1962–4, Chelsea School of Art, 1964–7, and Royal College of Art, 1967–70. Taught widely, including St Martin's School of Art Middlesex Polytechnic and Royal College of Art. Showed at ICA, at several John Moores Liverpool Exhibitions at Walker Art Gallery and in Summer Show 2, at Serpentine Gallery, 1981. Lived in London, where Arts Council held her work. Among her solo shows was Project Arts, Dublin 1978. Later group appearances included Empty Vesels, The Winchester Gallery and tour, 1985, and Sculpture in a Rose Garden, The Royal National Rose Society, St Albans, and East End Open Studios, at Chisenhale Studios, both 1989.

Ana Maria LIVINGSTON 1941– Artist, born in Buenos Aires, Argentina, who married a British diplomat whose postings in the mid-1970s included Paris, where she began life classes at L'École des Beaux-Arts. Livingston subsequently attended classes at Heatherley's School of Fine Art, London, before returning to Paris in 1981, where she joined the studio of Sophia Vari, married to the Colombian artist Fernando Botero. There she developed her interest in space and volume, reflected in her fruit paintings. In the mid-1980s she attended drawing and sculpture classes at L'École des Arts Decoratifs, Geneva Switzerland, and undertook private mural commissions n 1993 she moved to Provence, France, holding solo shows in Gordes, 1996, and Avignon, 1998. There was one at Brian Sinfield Gallery, Burford, in 2001.

George David LIVINGSTON 1920– Primarily a commercial artist in watercolour and black-and-white, he was born in Belfast, where he continued to live. Attended the Belfast Technical College, also the College of Art there, 1936–8. Showed UA, RUA and elsewhere.

Jan LIVINGSTON 1876–1952 Artist whose talents included landscapes in oil, sewing, tapestry and music, younger daughter of a timber merchant from Haddington, East Lothian. In the 1890s her father paid for trips to Paris to study painting and Germany for music, then in 1897 she married and settled in Edinburgh. East Lothian countryside was the main subject of her early pictures, reached by bicycle carrying her paints and a folding stool. Later she worked more in her studio, notably flower paintings, finally exclusively resorting to a palette knife. Exhibited RSA, RSW, Walker Art Gallery in Liverpool and Royal Glasgow Institute of the Fine Arts. Malcolm Innes Gallery, Edinburgh, put on a retrospective in 1995.

Michael LIVINGSTON-BOOTH 1946– Artist in mixed media and teacher, born in Cambridge, who studied at Falmouth College of Art, 1965–9, then Royal College of Art, 1969–71. Teaching included Portsmouth, Chelsea and Wimbledon Schools of Art. Group exhibitions included Festival at the Serpentine, Serpentine Gallery, 1972, and Electric Theatre, at ICA. When his work was shown in 6 Times at the Serpentine in 1976 Livingston-Booth said that his pieces The Attic, 1975, and View of Victoria, 1976, had "grown out of a belief that at any time, historically, an artist should be working as closely as possible to his present time ... Photography, film, television, electronic amplification, etc, have usurped certain aspects of all art forms."

Neil LIVINGSTONE 1952– Sculptor, born in Dundee, Angus, who after Dollar Academy studied at Duncan of Jordanstone College of Art in Dundee, 1971–5, as well during holidays on the continent. Had early success when in 1975 he beat 28 other sculptors to win the City of Glasgow sculpture competition with his abstract conception Kentigern which had a soaring, bird-like shape. The Arbroath-based sculptor also did restoration work on Dunkeld Cathedral.

Simon LIVINGSTONE 1966– Sculptor using various modern materials, as in his work Budget Model BS6840, shown in the final year show, Royal Academy Schools, 2000. Livingstone attended the Schools in 1997–00. He had previously studied at De Montford University, Leicester, 1993–7. Livingston won a Landseer and British Institution Prizes for Sculpture, both 1998. Exhibitions included Usher Gallery, Lincoln, 1994. Lived in north London.

Julie LIVSEY 1951– Sculptor and creator of assemblages; teacher. She was born in Oxfordshire, was for a while an apprentice jockey, then went to Swindon College of Art and Bristol Polytechnic to study sculpture, completing her master's degree at Newcastle University in 1978. As well as teaching in Britain and at School of Art in Lisbon Livsey held an extensive number of residencies, including Preston Hospital, the National Museum of Horse Racing in Newmarket and Lisnave Shipyard, Portugal. Her exhibitions included Buddle Art Gallery, Tyne and Wear, 1981; Carlisle Art Gallery, 1989; and the Newcastle Group show The Northern Lights at DLI Museum & Arts Centre and tour, Durham, 1990. Public sculptures are sited around Britain and in Portugal.

LI Yuan Chia (sometimes LI Yuan-chia) 1929–1994 Conceptual artist, photographer, gallery owner and teacher, born in Guangxi, China, who moved to Taiwan in 1949 following the Chinese Communist revolution. Enrolled at Taipei Normal College, where a classmate was Hsiao Chin, a crucial figure in Li's artistic development. Li was dissatisfied with the conservative curriculum, and Hsiao introduced him to the studio of Li Chun-shan, legendary precursor of the modern movement among Chinese artists. After graduating, Li taught art to elementary schoolchildren and then, with Hsiao's help, moved to Bologna, Italy, where in 1962–5 he worked for the furniture maker Gavina. In 1957 Li had founded the Ton-fan Group, the first abstract movement in Chinese art. Four years later Hsiao recruited Li as co-founder of the international Punto/Point art movement, a turning point in Li's career, from which time he adopted points/circles in his works. After the 3+1 exhibition at Signals Gallery in 1966 in London, in which Li took part, he decided to remain in England, where Marlborough New London Gallery signed him up. He participated in the Lisson Gallery's Cosmic Point, 1967, and Cosmic Multiple, 1968, exhibitions; in the Hyde Park All or Nothing show in 1967, and in Pavilions in the Park, 1968. Photography became important to him, and was incorporated in mixed media works. In 1968, after a visit to Cumbria, Li settled there and bought a farmhouse from the artist Winifred Nicholson, which opened as the LYC Museum and Art Gallery in 1972. It showed international artists and organised workshops for local people, but was forced to close in 1982 because of financial reasons. Latterly Li concentrated on his own art, which was included in the Hayward Gallery 1989–90 touring show The Other Story. Li's design of a circle equally shared into three parts, with the words Time-Life-Space inside them, became the logo for his museum. It is engraved on his tombstone at Lanercost Priory, Brampton. In 1997 Beatrice Gijsen-Hsieh, former curator at the Taiwan Museum of Art, organised a memorial show for Li there, which corrected many misconceptions about his life. Camden Arts Centre held a comprehensive survey in 2001. Tate Gallery, Hirshhorn Museum in New York and other international collections showed or hold work by Li, who died in Carlisle.

Julie LLEWELLYN 1954– Artist, notably a draughtsman and printmaker, whose work had abstract tendencies, born in Swansea, south Wales. She studied at Barnsley School of Art, 1972–3, Bristol Polytechnic, 1973–6, and Slade School of Fine Art, 1976–81. Her exhibitions included Stowells Trophy at RA, 1976–8; Graffiti Gallery, Three College Show at Royal College of Art and Barnsley Library, all 1978; and in 1980 a solo show at Woodlands Art Gallery. Worked and lived for some years in southeast London.

Owen LLEWELLYN 1927– Painter, draughtsman and bookbinder, born in Watford, Hertfordshire, whose full name was Owen John Llewellyn Williams. Studied at St Martin's School of Art, 1943–7, his teachers including James Bateman and Robin Guthrie, then Camberwell

School of Arts and Crafts and the London University Institute of Education, 1948–9. Taught in Nottingham, where he lived, and showed in the Midlands and London.

Charles LLOYD 1930– Painter, originally a printmaker, and teacher, born in Sydney, Australia. He studied at Julian Ashton Art School there with John Passmore; at London College of Printing and Regent Street Polytechnic School of Art; then did postgraduate study at Atelier 17 in Paris with S W Hayter. In 1967 Lloyd gained a Norwegian government stipend at Atelier Nord, Oslo. From 1966–85 Lloyd lectured at Goldsmiths' College School of Art and also was a visiting teacher at Brighton Polytechnic, after which he drew and painted full-time. Group exhibitions included AIA, Printmakers' Council, Brighton Printmakers and RE, of which he was an associate. Also showed at Salon des Réalités Nouvelles, Paris, 1965–6; Richard Demarco Gallery, Edinburgh, 1966; Bradford Biennial, 1968–72; and Marine Artists, Mall Galleries, 1989–90. Solo shows included Reading University, 1967; Belgravia Art Gallery, 1973; and Amalgam in 1983–9. National Maritime Museum, in Greenwich, the Bibliothèque Nationale, in Paris, hold examples. Lived in London.

Deborah LLOYD 1972– Artist, born at Henllys, near Cwmbran, Monmouthshire, who graduated from Newport College of Art. Much of her output was in gouache and pencil, closely observed and with an attractive eccentricity. She showed at the New Designers Exhibition in London, received commissions and was included in the Queen's Golden Jubilee exhibition of work by Welsh artists at Juxta Hayward White, Deddington, in 2002.

Elizabeth Jane LLOYD 1928–1995 Artist in oil and watercolour, mural and film-set painter, writer and teacher. Born into an artistic family in London, she attended Chelsea School of Art from 1946, then from 1952 the Royal College of Art, studying under Ruskin Spear and specialising in mural design. When she left in 1952 she married a fellow-student, Jeffrey Hoare and began teaching. Taught in various art schools in Britain and America, including the Central School of Art, St Martin's School of Art, Cambridge School of Art and Yehudi Menuhin School. Also taught from own studio and took painting groups to India. In 1953 had first one-man show in foyer of Royal Festival Hall, followed by others in Barbican Centre, Sally Hunter Fine Art and Austin/Desmond Fine Art, Sunninghill. Regular RA exhibitor who created several murals, including Chelsea Pensioners' Rest Hall, National Farmers Union and Dundee University; painted scenery for the films *Flash Gordon* and *Chariots of Fire*; and wrote a book on *Circles and Gardens*. Nuffield Foundation and Gulbenkian Trust hold her work which commonly features informal still life in strong sunlight and saturated with colour. Lived in London.

Hilary LLOYD 1964– Artist using film and video, born in Yorkshire, whose work featured locations such as the city and clubs, who studied at Newcastle upon Tyne Polytechnic, 1984–7. She was included in Hayward Gallery's The British Art Show 5 tour and Intelligence: New British Art, Tate Britain, both in 2000. In that year Lloyd won a Paul Hamlyn Foundation Visual Arts Award and a year's residency at Laurenz House Foundation, Basle, Switzerland. Had a solo show at Chisenhale Gallery, 1999. In 2003 Lloyd was one of three artists commissioned by Contemporary Projects to produce work for that year's 50th Venice Biennale.

James LLOYD 1905–1974 Painter, principally in gouache using a Pointillist style, consisting of tiny dots. Born at Alsager, Cheshire, until 19 Lloyd assisted on the family farm, then joined the police force. He subsequently worked as a gasworks stoker, bus conductor, builder's labourer and lamplighter. In 1950 he and his family moved to Yorkshire; he lived at Skirpenbeck, where he became a cowman. By this time he was painting seriously, producing about a picture a week in his spare time, having been encouraged by the art critic Sir Herbert Read. In 196 began full-time painting, his first, 1964, show, at the Portal Gallery, having been acclaimed. He had other exhibitions there in 1966, 1968 and 1971. L S Lowry owned Lloyd's work, in 1968 calling him "the most important British naïve painter of today". The Tate Gallery, Leeds City Art Gallery and York Art Gallery acquired Lloyd's pictures. Died in the Purey Cust Nursing Home, York.

James LLOYD 1971– Painter, notably of portraits, who studied at Blackpool College of Art and Design, 1987–9; Coventry University, 1989–92; and the Slade School of Fine Art, 1994–6. Awards and scholarships included Paul Smith Scholarships, 1994–6; Elizabeth Greenshields Foundation Awards, 1994–6–9; Winsor & Newton Young Artists Award, 2nd Prize, and BP Portrait Award, 1st Prize, both 1997; and Carrol Foundation, Young Artist of the Year Award, Prize Winner, 1999. Many famous politicians, designers and businessmen sat for Lloyd, whose mixed shows included RP, Mall Galleries, 1996; ROI, 1997; Hunting Art Prizes at Royal College of Art and MAFA Manchester City Art Galleries, both 1997; Art Aid Vinopolis Gallery, 2000; The Discerning Eye, selector and exhibitor, 2001; and Being Present, Jerwood Space 2004. Among Lloyd's solo exhibitions were Six Chapel Row Contemporary Art, Bath, 2002. His portrait of the one-time Lord Chancellor Derry Irvine was commissioned and unveiled at the Inner Temple, 2003, that of the fashion designer Sir Paul Smith being hung in the National Portrait Gallery in 2004.

Katherine Constance LLOYD fl. from early 1920s– Painter in oil of portraits and flowers; artist in pastel. Studied at Slade School of Fine Art under Philip Wilson Steer and Henry Tonks. Exhibited RA, NEAC, SWA, RP and extensively at Cooling Galleries. Lived at Hartley Wintney, Hampshire.

Marilyn LLOYD fl. from mid-1970s– Artist and designer who studied at Epsom School of Art from 1967 and St Martin's School of Art from 1969, graduating in art and design (fashion) in 1972, with an advanced certificate in painting and film-making, 1974. Group shows included Gimpel Fils. Solo exhibitions included National Theatre South Hill Park, Bracknell; Open studio in Guildford; and landscape and still life at Century Galleries, Henley-on-Thames, 1997.

Nick LLOYD 1951– Sculptor, draughtsman and teacher who was born in Wolverhampton. He studied at Newcastle University, gaining a Rome Scholarship in Sculpture, 197 Among his teaching appointments was Leicester Polytechnic. Lloyd was noted as a stone-carver, his work abstract in tendency but related to landscape. He took part in many group shows, including Northern Young Contemporaries, Whitworth Art Gallery, Manchester; Sculpture in the Park, Rufford Country Park, Nottinghamshire, 1987; National Garden Festival, Gateshead, 1990, and in same year the Newcastle Group show The Northern Lights at DLI Museum & Arts Centre and tour. Solo shows included Hatton Gallery, Newcastle, 1978, and Bede Gallery, Jarrow, 1988. Arts Council holds his work. Lived in Blackhall Mill, County Durham.

Norman LLOYD 1894–c.1980 Landscape painter, born in Hamilton, New South Wales, Australia. He studied at Sydney Art School with Julian Ashton; was wounded during World War I military service, after which he began painting again during recovery; then exhibited in Sydney with Ashton's group in the mid-1920s. Lloyd moved to study in France and Italy, settling eventually in St John's Wood, London, becoming a member of ROI in 1935, the Royal Society of Arts in 1938 and the Savage Club and London Sketch Club. He showed with ROI, RA and RI and extensively in Paris. In the mid-1960s Lloyd moved to the Indre region of France. Art Gallery of Western Australia, Perth, holds Lloyd's oil on canvas Morning, Middle Harbour, Sydney, of 1925 (some sources give Lloyd's birth year as 1895 or 1897, but the biographical details supplied by the artist to Perth state 1894). In 1980, a letter to the *Sydney Morning Herald* stated that Lloyd had had a stroke in November 1979 and was in a nursing home somewhere in England.

Peter LLOYD 1968– Printmaker producing powerful and colourful images, as in his Mexican masked wrestlers, Heavyweights, shown solo at Agnew in 2001, where screenprints were enhanced with materials such as diamond dust and glitter. Born in Liverpool, Lloyd graduated with first-class honours in printmaking from Winchester School of Art, 1993–6, gaining his master's from the Royal College of Art, 1998–00. Awards included British Airways Award, travel scholarship, 1999; Augustus Martin Awards, best graduating printmaker of the year, 2000; and finalist, Pizza Express Contemporaries, 2001. Among his group shows were British Prints, Direkt Gallery, Berlin, Germany, 1997; Six Contemporary Artists, The Tannery, 1999; and "0", Henry Peacock Gallery, 2000. Hochschule de Kunst, Berlin, and several corporate collections hold examples.

Reginald James LLOYD 1926– Artist in wide variety of media, born in Hereford, although he was associated with the West Country from the age of two when his family moved to Dawlish, Devon. Was largely self-taught, although after Army service he attended part-time classes at Exeter School of Art, from 1956 living in Bideford. Lloyd was a member of RI from 1992, having been awarded its bronze medal in 1989. His work went through various metamorphoses, but a strong Neo-Romantic streak and an interest in such subjects as Silbury, Stonehenge, Avebury and Maiden Castle were key features. Lloyd contributed to many mixed shows in London and the provinces. Had a solo exhibition at Dawlish, 1950, later ones including Burton Art Gallery, Bideford, 1991, Waterside Art Gallery, Instow, 1993. Harlequin Gallery held a retrospective, 2001, with a show of Cornish paintings in 2003, and in 2004 The Long Curve Gallery, Chipping Campden, showed Lloyd's work. Lloyd's commissions included a painted rood for the Church of the Assumption, Walkern, 1954; a 70-foot mural for Salesian College, Battersea, 1965; and an iron lectern for St Boniface's Church, Adler Street, 1980, which contains several other commissions by him, including a 1963 stained glass west window. Lloyd also illustrated books by the poet Ted Hughes, including *What is Truth*, 1984, and *The Mermaid's Purse*, 1993. Victoria & Albert Museum, Tate Gallery and British Embassy, Paris, hold examples.

Sarah J LLOYD 1896– Painter, born in Laugharne, Carmarthenshire, an area which was the subject of her pictures and where she always lived. A self-taught artist, she exhibited in Women's Institute shows, on one occasion winning a gold medal, and took part in WAC An Alternative Tradition show, in 1972.

Selwyn LLOYD 1967– Painter, born in Doncaster, Yorkshire, who studied at the local College of Art, 1985–6, then Loughborough College of Art and Design, 1986–9. Among his appearances was John Moores Liverpool Exhibition, 1989–90, with the enigmatic canvas The Irradiation Ceremony. Lived in Newquay, Cornwall.

Ulrica LLOYD 1911–1987 Sculptor, printmaker, illustrator and letterer, born in Longworth House, Berkshire. She was married to Professor Seton Lloyd, in charge of Western Asiatic Archaeology at London University; her maiden name was Fitzwilliams Hyde, which led to her pet name Hydie. She studied at the Royal College of Art and in Paris; worked as an apprentice to a sculptor; then to a stonemason, for although she had taken a diploma in design and engraving sculpture remained her main business. In between accompanying her husband on digs, Ulrica Lloyd worked mainly on religious sculptures, latterly in metal-filled polyester fibreglass. These she described as "Medieval, straightforward and representational". Her work is distributed widely through England, examples being in churches in Slough, Wantage, Barnstaple and Ashbury, and she also made a memorial to the writer Agatha Christie in Moulsford. Lived for many years at Woolstone, Berkshire.

Vincent LLOYD 1960– Painter, draughtsman and teacher, born in Folkestone, Kent, who studied at Medway College of Design and Camberwell School of Art. He taught at Marlborough College and for the Open College of the Arts four years after winning a David Murray Studentship, RA, 1984. Took part in the South Bank Picture Show, Royal Festival Hall, from 1984; Café Gallery Open, from 1986; Small Works Open, at Square Gallery, 1988; and Royal Over-Seas League Open, 1995, where he showed the amusing acrylic on board Exotic Dancer With Pink Fringe. Had a solo exhibition, Figures in the Landscape, at Mounthouse Gallery, Marlborough, 1988, later ones including Camden Arts Centre, 1989. South East Arts holds his work.

Wyndham LLOYD 1909–1997 Painter, notable for his landscapes which had a strong pattern element. He was self-taught, apart from six months at night school in Colchester and advice from other artists. Although he started painting as a small boy and wanted to be an artist or architect, for financial security Taffy Lloyd was sent from England to Ceylon at 19 to be a tea planter. In World War II he served with the Ceylon Planters' Rifle Corps in north Africa; went back to Ceylon and became a tea broker; and in 1960, learning he had skin cancer, returned to live on a farm at Great Horkesley, Essex, inherited from a brother. He exhibited widely in group shows: NEAC in 1942, ROI from 1950, NS and RBA from 1952, UA from 1953 and elsewhere. Was a member of Colchester Art Society from 1960. Although Lloyd's exhibiting career was strongly concentrated in the Essex area in later years, his first three exhibitions were in Sri Lanka. In 1976 he had a one-man at Mercury Theatre Gallery, Colchester; further shows included one there in 1989 and another nearby at Chappel Galleries, 1992, which gave him a memorial exhibition in 2001.

Audrey LLOYD JONES 1902–1989 Painter and draughtsman born in Cambridge, where she settled. She studied art privately with A C Amerasekara early in World War II for a short period. Contributed to scientific publications and exhibited with PS, RBA, RCamA and in the provinces, showing solo locally. She sometimes hyphenated Lloyd-Jones.

Mary LLOYD JONES 1934– Painter, textile artist and teacher, born in Devil's Bridge, Cardiganshire. She was educated at Cardiff College of Art, then began a career in teaching which included experience in London, at Swansea College of Art and in Dyfed. In the mid-1970s with her husband she began a summer school in the visual arts at Felinfach Art Centre and College of Further Education, Dyfed. She did television work in Welsh. A member of the 56 Group, she also took part in group shows at Howard Roberts Gallery in Cardiff, Royal National Eisteddfod and elsewhere. Solo shows included WAC, Oriel, Cardiff, and a major one at Aberystwyth Arts Centre, 2001, which included ceiling-hung installations. Lived in Llandysul, Dyfed.

Peter LLOYD JONES 1932– Painter, draughtsman and writer who, in 1958, after studying science at London and Cambridge Universities, went to the Slade School of Fine Art for drawing, teaching chemistry at night school and for the United States Air Force to support his art. In 1959 he was accepted at the Courtauld Institute of Art on a Nuffield research grant to work on the problems of Old Master media and materials, during this period becoming interested in the art historian E H Gombrich's theories. Between 1959–61 he showed figurative paintings in group exhibitions at the New Art Centre; in 1968, was a prize winner in Arts Council of Northern Ireland show Open Painting 68; and in 1970 his solo exhibition with The Richard Demarco Gallery, Edinburgh, included geometrical abstract works based on ragas, "my own free variation on this old Indian theme". In 1969 Lloyd Jones became co-editor of *Leonardo*, the international journal of contemporary arts. He also wrote for *The Listener*, *Burlington Magazine*, *New York Review of Books* and scientific journals. Lived in London.

Peter LLOYD-JONES 1940–2001 Painter, performance and installation artist, and teacher, born in Bristol, whose integrity and sensitivity were encapsulated within a fragile personality, denying him wide recognition. After Salisbury College of Art, in 1959 Lloyd-Jones entered Chelsea College of Art where the principal, Lawrence Gowing, was his great champion and where he was to teach from 1961–4. Lloyd-Jones had won a Boise Travelling Scholarship to Sweden, 1960, and a Gulbenkian Foundation Purchase Award, 1962. He had a well-received solo show at the New Art Centre, 1965, the Arts Council acquiring his abstract drawing March No II. Later taught part-time at Maidenhead College of Art, 1965–70, and Hammersmith College of Art, 1973–4. Lloyd-Jones's wife, the artist Jane Percival, whom he replaced at Hammersmith when she was expecting their second daughter, remembered his huge student following "because he took things to the edge, when talking." From the mid-1970s into the early 1980s, Lloyd-Jones and Michael Upton were part of Britain's performance and installation scene, appearing at venues including the ICA, Arnolfini Gallery in Bristol, Peterloo Gallery, Manchester, and the Arts Lab, Birmingham. On returning to his individual career Lloyd-Jones destroyed much of his early work, moving from abstraction to figuration. The Arts Council added his Laughter (9 Conditions) to its collection in 1980. Although there were solo shows at the Lewis Johnstone Gallery, 1981 and 1983, and at Cassian de Vere Cole Fine Art, 1996, Lloyd-Jones was latterly able to work only sporadically, struggling with clinical depression and a breakdown. He died in Glastonbury, Somerset, just after a retrospective at the Wedmore Arts for the Millennium festival.

Peter LLOYD-JONES 1956– Painter of interiors and landscapes notable for their subtle use of colour, delicacy and restraint. After a foundation course at West Surrey College of Art and Design at Farnham, Lloyd-Jones gained his diploma from the Ruskin School of Drawing, Oxford 1977–9, then did a postgraduate diploma at Royal Academy Schools, 1980–3. He showed at RA Summer Exhibitions from 1982, other mixed exhibitions including Agnew Young Contemporaries in 1988, Lee Ann Lester Gallery in Los Angeles, 1990, and Critic's Choice at Beaux Arts Gallery, Bath, 1991. In 1979 Lloyd-Jones gained the David Murray Award for Landscape Painting, and again in 1982; in 1981 he won the Winsor and Newton Award, and in 1983 the Elizabeth Greenshields Foundation Award for Drawing and Painting. From 1983 he had a series of solo shows at Cadogan Contemporary. Lived in Wotton-under-Edge, Gloucestershire.

Matthew LLOYD SMALL 1975– Artist who in a series of portraits of young people "explored the attitudes and reality of teenage life in Britain". He studied foundation art and design at Barnet College, 1993–4; obtained his National Diploma, Graphic Design, there, 1994–5; graduated with first-class honours in illustration, Westminster University, 1995–8; and obtained his master's at the Royal College of Art, 1998–00. Lloyd Small gained a Sir John Cass Foundation Scholarship in 1998. Exhibitions included *Artist and Illustrator*, Best Student Illustration Exhibit Business Design Centre, Islington, 1998; Last Show on Earth, Clerkenwell Arts Centre, 1999; Folio Society Book Illustration, Royal College of Art, and Ed-Man-F Drawing Competition Finalist Show, Royal College, joint second place, both 2000; and ART2001, Lefevre Contemporary Art at Business Design Centre.

John Hodgson LOBLEY 1878–1954 Painter, born in Huddersfield, Yorkshire. After Huddersfield Technical College, went to Royal College of Art, Slade School of Fine Art and the Royal Academy Schools, winning several medals. During the latter part of World War I he was an Official War Artist. Exhibited RA, RI, RBA, ROI, RP, RIBA, Goupil and Leger Galleries (had a solo at Leger 1934) and Ridley Ar

Club. Imperial War Museum holds his work. Member of the Art Club in Bournemouth, Hampshire, where he lived.

Brad LOCHORE 1960– Painter, born in New Zealand, who did a fine art diploma at Byam Shaw School of Art, 1986–9; studied at Kunst Akademie in Düsseldorf, 1989–90; then gained his master's degree at Goldsmiths' College, 1990–2. After studying at film and television school, for five years Lochore designed and made film-sets. At Young British Artists IV, Saatchi Gallery, 1995, Lochore showed a group of large, highly atmospheric Shadow Paintings in which refined grey lines, the shadows of windows, were displayed on a white ground. The large oil on canvas Ladder Shadow was in the 1995–6 John Moores Liverpool Exhibition. Lived in London.

Georgina LOCHTIE 1927–2002 Painter of landscapes and figures, also producing drawings and collages, as well as teacher, maiden name Jane E G Tainsh, married to the artist John Youngclause Lochtie. She was born in Alva, Clackmannanshire, and studied at Edinburgh College of Art under William Gillies, John Maxwell, Donald Moodie, William McTaggart and Leonard Rosoman, the Scottish influence on her subtly Colourist work remaining apparent. After Moray House training she taught art in Scotland, then in London, finally as deputy head at Sedgehill Secondary School, also being an examiner. A group of pictures by Lochtie and her husband was offered at Rosebery's auction rooms, West Norwood, in 2002. Died in Crystal Palace, south London.

John Youngclause LOCHTIE 1919–2001 Artist and teacher whose work included landscapes, humorous drawings and fashion studies, married to the painter Georgina Lochtie. He was born in Dublin, Ireland, of Scottish parents, and studied at Edinburgh College of Art as a mature student after World War II. Contemporary Scottish artists influenced his work, which was shown at Scottish Arts Club, Edinburgh. After teaching in that city, he moved to London in 1956 to pursue a commercial career. Pictures by him and his wife were offered by Rosebery's West Norwood auction rooms in 2002.

Anton LOCK 1893–1971 Painter, printmaker and draughtsman specialising in country scenes, especially of working horses. Studied at Westminster School of Art under Walter Sickert, 1910–12, then Bolt Court School, where he specialised in lithography and worked under Walter Bayes, 1912–14. Illustrated several books with outdoor and hunting themes. Exhibited RA, RWS, ROI and Paris Salon, having one-man shows at Leger Galleries. British Museum and British Council bought his work. Lived in London.

Donald LOCKE 1930– Painter, artist in ceramics, sculptor and teacher, born in Stewartville, Guyana. His initial art education was obtained in a working people's art class, a British Council Scholarship taking him to Bath Academy of Art, in 1954, to study painting, sculpture and ceramics. Five years later a Guyana government grant enabled Locke to attend Edinburgh University, where he took a degree in fine art. From 1964–71 he taught at Queen's College, Georgetown, in Guyana, where he gradually began to concentrate on ceramics. In 1971 he set up a studio in London and also taught, in Chester and London. Exhibited widely internationally and eventually moved to teach and work at Arizona State University, living in Phoenix. Locke's work has been said to scan Modernism and his personal history, with strong sexual allusion. He participated in The Other Story show at Hayward Gallery, and touring, 1989–90.

Hew LOCKE 1959– Artist using a range of media who gained a fine art degree at Falmouth School of Art, 1985–8, then a sculpture master's at the Royal College of Art, 1991–3. His original and playful work drew on aspects of medieval cathedral sculpture, Islamic design and Spanish art and the global commodification of culture. In 1995 Locke's piece Ark was exhibited at De La Warr Pavilion, Bexhill-on-Sea; in 2000, his Hemmed in II, a large drawn, painted and cut cardboard construction, part boat, part package and part fairground ride, was shown at the Victoria & Albert Museum, then the Norton Family Foundation Collection, California, America. With it he shared the East International Award at Norwich Art Gallery in 2000, the year he won a Paul Hamlyn Foundation Visual Arts Award. Solo exhibitions included Cardboard Palace, at Chisenhale Gallery, 2002, and Hales Gallery, 2003, the year he was shortlisted for the Jerwood Sculpture Prize. Victoria & Albert Museum and Charles Saatchi acquired Locke's work.

David H LOCKETT 1958– Artist and teacher, born in the Cuckfield area of Sussex, who studied at Bath Academy of Art, 1976–7, then Westhill Teacher Training College, 1979–82. Lockett taught at various secondary schools in England, in 1987–8 teaching in Mozambique. Participated in East End Open Studios, based at Pixley Street Studios, in 1989.

John LOCKETT 1952– Painter, printmaker and teacher who also worked as John Luce Lockett, born and lived in Northampton. He studied at the local School of Art and Byam Shaw School of Drawing. Lockett was a representational artist who also taught life drawing and artistic anatomy and from 1986 with his wife ran a private studio gallery, holding regular spring and Christmas shows. He showed with RP and was a council member of the Northampton Town and County Art Society. Solo shows included Four Seasons Gallery, Northampton, 1977; Hurlingham Gallery, 1989; and The City Gallery, Leicester, 1992. In 2003, Karen Taylor Contemporary Art Gallery, St Margaret's, Twickenham, showed Lockett's work. His exhibition, The Bohemians, was at The McNeill Gallery, Radlett, in 2005. Weston Hall, Shropshire; Franciscan Novitiate House, Manchester; and St Crispin's Hospital, Northampton, hold examples.

Eva LOCKEY 1952– Abstract sculptor who studied on fine art diploma course at North-East London Polytechnic, 1973–6, then did postgraduate work at St Martin's School of Art, 1976–7. Exhibitions included Young Contemporaries at RA, 1977; Cannizaro Park Sculpture Show, from 1979; Whitechapel Art Gallery, 1981; and in same year Painters + Sculptors from the Greenwich Studios at Woodlands Art Gallery. Later exhibitions included a three-artist show at The Vortex Gallery, 2002.

David LOCKHART 1922– Painter, teacher and muralist, born in Leven, Fife. He studied at Edinburgh College of Art, 1940–6, with Joan Hassall, John Maxwell and William Gillies, finally for postgraduate work. He was principal teacher of art at Ballingry Junior High School, 1959–84. Lockhart was a member of SSA, 1959–79, and of RSW from 1969. He painted a large mural, Many Mansions, in Benarty Primary School, Lochore. Showed at Douglas & Foulis, Edinburgh, in two-man exhibition in 1963; Fife Group, at English Speaking Union, Edinburgh; RSA, and elsewhere. Solo exhibitions included Loomshop Gallery, Lower Largo, 1989, and Small Gallery, Anstruther, 1991. West Riding of Yorkshire and Dunbartonshire Education Authorities and Scottish Arts Council hold his work. Lived in Hillend, Fife.

Gavin LOCKHEART 1961– Painter, printmaker and teacher, notable for his colourful and imaginative depiction of landscape, born in Staffordshire. Group exhibitions included St Martin's School of Art Degree Show, 1983; Physical Chemistry, Queen Elizabeth Hall, 1985; Five London Painters, Eilat Gordin Gallery, Hollywood, California, 1986; Wild, Ikon Gallery, Birmingham, and Harris Museum & Art Gallery Preston, 1993; and Beaux Arts, 1996. In 1987, Lockheart had solo shows at Carlile Gallery in London and in Italy at Studio d'Arte Lanza, Verbania, and he shared an exhibition with Peter Randall-Page at Houldsworth Fine Art, 1997. The year before, Lockheart had gained an Arts Foundation/Barclays Private Banking Fellowship in Painting. From 1990–4, he was a part-time lecturer in painting and printmaking at Stourbridge College of Art.

Judith LOCKIE 1947– Printmaker, draughtsman and teacher, born in London, who studied design and printmaking at Guildford School of Art and travelled widely through Europe and North America. In 1975 went to Japan and studied woodblock printing with Yoskisuje Funasaka for two years; in 1977 returned to London to spend four years as a printmaker, starting to exhibit; in 1981 returned to Tokyo for a further year of study and printmaking, followed by nine months in Western Australia; moved to Suffolk in 1983, setting up a print workshop for etching and woodblock printing in 1988, also teaching at Suffolk College; then in 1997 and 1999 was invited to run a woodblock print workshop as resident artist at The Naropa Institute, Boulder, Colorado, in America. Was a member of The Suffolk Group and a founder-member of 0900. Had many group shows, later solo exhibitions including Prints and Drawings 1976–1999, Christchurch Mansion, 1999, and John Russell Gallery, 2000–1, both in Ipswich. Lockie's work was scattered with symbols, such as discs, birds, flying figures and people tramping through landscapes. Lived in Framlingham, Suffolk.

Arthur LOCKWOOD 1934– Artist, designer and teacher, born in Birmingham, son of the painter Frank Taylor Lockwood, Arthur's wife Gillian and son Paul both being artists. Gained a first-class diploma in book illustration at Birmingham College of Art, 1951–4, becoming an associate of the Royal College of Art, graphic design, 1956–9. Lockwood was a visiting lecturer at Bath Academy of Art, Chelsea and Harrow Schools of Art and Hornsey College of Art. He was a prolific book designer, 1959–87, awards including *Times Educational Supplement* Information Book Award and Schönste Bücher aus aller Welt, Leipzig, Germany, both 1973. Was art editor, Rathbone Books and Aldus Books, 1959–65; freelanced, 1965–87; and was retained by both Penguin Books and Leicester University Press. Began painting in 1984, full-time from 1988 after moving to Lapworth, Warwickshire. Was elected to Birmingham Art Club, 1991, RBSA, 1994. Work selected for open exhibitions included the RWA, RI, RWS, RBA and Singer & Friedlander/*Sunday Times* Watercolour Competition. Solo exhibitions included Coventry Colliery Recaptured, National Coal Mining Museum, Overton, 1998, and Coventry Colliery, End of an Era, Herbert Art Gallery, Coventry, 1999; these two and other Midland collections hold Lockwood's pictures, which mixed accuracy and fine aesthetic qualities.

Catherine LOCKWOOD 1975– Artist who attended Wimbledon School of Art, 1994–7, and Royal College of Art, 1997–9. Exhibitions included Cut Gallery, 1996; Library Gallery, Wimbledon, 1997; and she was Artist of the Day, chosen by Graham Crowley, Royal College professor of painting, at Flowers East, 1999.

Dorothy LOCKWOOD fl. from 1930s– Watercolourist, born and lived in Birmingham, where she studied at Birmingham College of Arts and Crafts, Moseley Street, under Bernard Fleetwood-Walker and Harold Smith. She was elected RBSA in 1959 and RWS in 1974, also showing elsewhere.

Frank Taylor LOCKWOOD 1895–1961 Painter and commercial artist, born in Linthwaite, Yorkshire, father of the artist Arthur Lockwood. He attended Huddersfield Technical College, 1909–12; was apprenticed as a lithographic artist at Netherwood Dalton, Huddersfield; between 1917–19 served with the Northumberland Fusiliers and Royal Flying Corps; worked as a commercial artist mainly in Birmingham, in 1933 joining Cadbury Brothers, becoming manager of their sales and advertising studio, in 1958 retiring to paint full-time. Joined Birmingham's Watercolour Society, 1938, and Art Circle, 1943; Easel Club and Clarendon Fellowship, 1947, and other local societies; and was made an associate of RBSA, 1960. Lockwood recorded change in Birmingham, where he settled, visually and in his extensive diary. *Frank T Lockwood pen and ink drawings of the Midland Scene* was published privately in 1962. In 1994 Birmingham Art Gallery, which holds an extensive Lockwood archive, showed his work in From Green Fields to Suburbia.

Gillian LOCKWOOD 1936– Ceramist, designer, teacher and writer, born in Bromley, Kent, married to the artist Arthur Lockwood, their son being the painter and printmaker Paul Lockwood. She gained her National Diploma in Design from Beckenham School of Art, 1954–6, graduating in graphic design from the Royal College of Art, 1956–9. Was a senior designer for Woudhuysen Design Group and taught at Putney Park School for Girls and at Richmond Adult College. Her books included *Making Soft Toys*, 1967; *Making Clothes for Young Children*, 1969; *How to Sew Presents from Scraps*, 1974; and *How to Make and Dress a Doll*, 1975. Lockwood was from 1961 a member of the Society of Industrial Artists, later resigning; also belonging to Midland Potters, 1988, Birmingham Art Circle, 1990, its president from 1998, and RBSA as a full member, 1999. Showed at RWA and at Heart of England Biennial Exhibition, at Herbert Art Gallery, Coventry, both from 1995; won a Ceramic Prize, RBSA Prize Exhibition, 1996; also exhibited at The Lion Gallery, Leominster, and Ombersley Gallery, Worcestershire; and in 1996 took part in Lock wood family show at Museum of Richmond. Her ceramics included decorative figure pieces and large forms based on plants and seeds, Herbert Art Gallery acquiring Conkers. Lived in Lapworth, Warwickshire.

Kenneth LOCKWOOD 1920– Designer, illustrator and teacher, born in Huddersfield, Yorkshire. He studied at Leeds College of Art, 1946–9, then Huddersfield School of Art, 1949. As well as doing book-jacket work, illustrations for magazines and commercial designs, Lockwood exhibited in London, the English provinces and in Guernsey, Channel Islands, where he settled in St Peter Port. Had a strong interest in art education.

Paul LOCKWOOD 1963– Painter and printmaker, born in Richmond, Surrey, son of Arthur and Gillian Lockwood, both artists. Paul gained an honours degree in fine art from Middlesex Polytechnic, 1988–91. Group shows included RWS Summer Open, from 1994; RWA Open, from 1996, and RBSA Open, from 1997. Had a solo exhibition at Kew Staircase Gallery. His prints included lino-cuts and woodcuts, and among main works were Filophobia, Treasure and Ship of Fools. Lived in Lapworth, Warwickshire.

Diana LODGE 1906–1998 Painter, born Violet Uppington in Tredegar, south Wales, her father a headmaster. After studying English at Bristol University, she taught in Leeds for two years, then moved to London, changing her name to Diana. Worked as a Tiller Girl; modelled for Eric Gill and Duncan Grant; in 1932 married literary scholar and poet Oliver Lodge, eldest son of the physicist and psychical researcher Sir Oliver Lodge; and, having lived for periods in France, Canada and America, and having had three children, in 1946 settled in Gloucestershire. This home became a gathering point for artists and writers, and there she began painting seriously. After her husband's death in 1955 she wintered for some years in Puerto Rico, oil paintings of its landscape selling well; had exhibitions in Washington, America, also in London. Black Mountains watercolours and the interior of her home were other notable subjects. Van Gogh, Samuel Palmer and Odilon Redon were cited as influences on work that had a strong emotional and spiritual content. Prayer and mysticism were important to Lodge, who converted from Anglicanism to Roman Catholicism and who lived finally, still painting, at a retreat centre near Stroud.

George LODGE 1860–1954 Artist, writer and traveller, noted for his atmospheric and meticulous depictions of birds. He was born in Horncastle, Lincolnshire. At Lincoln School of Art Lodge gained 14 prizes for drawing, later becoming an expert wood engraver. As a young man Lodge travelled to Ceylon, Japan, the West Indies and elsewhere. A great sportsman, he enjoyed annual trips to Scotland and the salmon rivers of Norway, gathering material for his work on birds of prey. Lodge himself flew falcons. He had stuffed his first bird, an owl, at the age of 12 and said that it was impossible to draw a bird's appearance correctly without an intimate knowledge of its inside. Eventually Lodge built the Hawk House at Camberley, Surrey, where he settled. His plates for Beebe's *A Monograph of the Pheasants* and his several hundred illustrations for Bannerman's 12 volumes of *The Birds of the British Isles* are classics. Aged 85 Lodge wrote his only book: *Memories of an Artist Naturalist*. The Tryon Gallery showed Lodge's work.

Jean LODGE 1941– Painter, printmaker and teacher, born in Dayton, Ohio, America, who graduated from Miami University of Ohio in 1963, then moved to Europe; in 1964 studying at the Kokoschka School, Salzburg; in 1965 at Ruskin School of Fine Art, Oxford; worked with S W Hayter at Atelier 17, Paris, 1965–9; and helped set up a printmaking workshop in Paris with A Caporaso, 1969. From 1978–96, Lodge was head of printmaking at the Ruskin School, then became a full-time artist and freelance teacher. She was a member of the Printmakers' Council, RE, and in France of Le Trait and Xylon. Mixed exhibitions included Oxford Art Society. Had many solo shows, later ones including Praxis International Art Gallery, University of South Florida, Sarasota, 1994; and in 1996 Galerie Schweitzer, Luxembourg, and Broughton House Gallery, Cambridge. Took part in many international print biennales, latterly including Taipei, Taiwan, from 1987, and Kochi International, Japan, 1993. Work held by many public collections internationally, including Ashmolean Museum in Oxford; Bibliothèque Nationale, Paris; Bibliothèque Royale, Bruxelles; and Museo della Xilografia, Venice. Lodge was a fellow of New College, Oxford, living in the city at Headington, and in Paris, France.

Hermione Thornton LOFTHOUSE fl. from 1940s– Painter and teacher who studied at Heatherley's School of Fine Art under Iain Macnab, 1946–50, and at Académie Julian and L'Académie de la Grande Chaumière, both in Paris, gaining a history of art certificate from the Courtauld Institute. She went on to teach at Moor Park College, 1968–82, and at adult education classes. Lofthouse was a member of NS, UA and Ridley Art Society. Showed also at RBA, ROI, at Walker Art Gallery in Liverpool and elsewhere and had many solo exhibitions. Surrey University holds her work. Lived in Farnham, Surrey.

Andrew LOGAN 1945– Versatile and enterprising designer and sculptor, born in Witney, Oxfordshire, who graduated with a diploma in architecture from Oxford School of Architecture, 1964–70. He "experienced Flower Power" in America in 1967. Did a hologram course at Goldsmiths' College, 1982. Logan was noted for projects carried out with a showbiz flair, who to some dressed weirdly, producing camp sculptures, costumes and jewellery out of mirror and lurid plastic, but who was undeniably dedicated and persistent. He said that his aim was "to bring joy and happiness to the world". Logan was most famous as the inventor and impresario of *The Alternative Miss World*, which began in 1972, the series continuing periodically at various venues. The first showing of the film *The Alternative Miss World* was held at the Odeon, Leicester Square, 1979, followed by the Cannes Film Festival, 1980. Logan had his first solo show at New Art Centre, 1973. Other events in his multi-faceted career included *Egypt Revisited*, sound and light spectacular in a tent on Clapham Common, 1978; decorations for Zandra Rhodes' fashion show, 1980; Snow Sculpture World Championships, Finland, 1982; piece in Holographic Show, York Arts Festival, 1984; debut as a theatre designer, *Wolfy*, Ballet Rambert, Big Top, Battersea, 1987; retrospective, Museum of Modern Art, Oxford, 1991, with tour; Jewels Fantasy Exhibition, Victoria & Albert Exhibition, 1992; a show at Cheltenham Art Gallery, 2000–1, and watercolours at A&D Gallery, 2002, in the same year there sharing an exhibition with Duggie Fields. In addition, Norwich Gallery held Logan's Alternative Miss World Filmshow 1972 to 2002. In 1991 the Andrew Logan Museum of Sculpture opened at Berriew, Powys. In 1993 the National Portrait Gallery bought two portraits. Was based at The Glasshouse, Melier Place, where he also held exhibitions.

Gladys LOGAN: *see* **Gladys BARRON**

Johanna LOGAN 1972– Painter of portraits, figures and still lifes, often predominantly in white against sombre backgrounds and with a still, concentrated quality. Born in Glasgow, Logan gained a fine art honours degree at the city's School of Art, 1990–4, awards including RSA Sir Robin Philipson Memorial Award, 1994. Group shows included Compass Gallery, Glasgow, New Generation Show, 1994; Edinburgh Gallery, Edinburgh, 1995; and Glasgow Art Fair, 1997. Had a solo show at Art Bank, Glasgow, 1996, then Offer Waterman & Co Fine Art, from 1998. Murray Johnstone, Glasgow, holds Logan's work.

Peter LOGAN 1943– Sculptor and teacher, born in Oxfordshire. He studied at Camberwell School of Arts and Crafts and Slade School of Fine Art and taught at Wimbledon School of Art, Reading University and Goldsmiths' College. Logan's sculptures were shown at Milton Keynes, Buckinghamshire, in 1986 at the Energy World exhibition, then Guardian Royal Exchange commissioned his Javelin I, which was erected in 1988 at Wolverton Mill. Arts Council holds his O for a Ballerina, of 1979, in aluminium with electric motors and computer control. Lived and worked in London.

Alf LÖHR 1957– Artist, lecturer and writer whose output included public art, environmental sculpture and a range of publications. He was born in Bochum, West Germany, gained his master's degree in fine art at Kunstakademie Düsseldorf, 1977–83, and his doctorate at the Royal College of Art, 1985–8, with a dissertation on environmental sculpture in urban landscapes. Löhr's awards included a British Council Fellowship, 1986; a DAAD German Academic Exchange Service award, 1987; Feodor Lynen Research Fellowship and Alexander von Humboldt Stiftung, Bonn, 1989–91; Kaiserringstipendium, Museum für Moderne Kunst, Goslar, 1992; and senior fellowship, University of Wales Institute, Cardiff, 1996. Lectured widely in Britain and abroad, among later positions being full-time, Glasgow School of Art, 1993–5; University of Wales Institute, Cardiff, Goldsmiths' College and San Francisco Art Institute, MA European Fine Art, Barcelona, 1995–6; and Barcelona again, as a visiting lecturer, 2000. Later public projects included Neanderthal Museum, Düsseldorf, 2000. Took part in a range of group shows, mainly in Germany, later solo exhibitions including Gloucester Cathedral and Goethe Institute, both 2001; Pump House Gallery and firstsite, Colchester (with extensive publication, *Alf Löhr Abstraction*), both 2002; and Newlyn Art Gallery, Penzance, 2003.

Renos LOIZOU 1948– Painter, notable for his highly structured and colourful landscapes, born at Paleometochon, near Nicosia, Cyprus, the family moving to London in 1955, later to Cambridge. Loizou studied at Cambridge School of Art from 1963. Took part in many mixed shows, including ICA, 1974; RA from 1980; Chicago International Art Exposition, 1987; and Richmond Gallery, 1992. After a solo show at Fitzwilliam College, Cambridge, 1969, Loizou's others included series at Christopher Hull Gallery from 1982. Kettle's Yard, in Cambridge, holds his work.

John LOKER 1938– Painter, photographer, printmaker and designer, born in Leeds. He studied design at Bradford College of Art and Design, 1954–8, then painting at Royal College of Art, 1960–3, gaining an Abbey Minor Travelling Scholarship in the latter year. After holding a solo studio show in 1969 Loker had a one-man at Angela Flowers Gallery and ICA the following year. The 1970s saw him showing at John Moores Exhibition in Liverpool on several occasions, another key appearance being in New British Prints in New York and touring in 1974, yet another Arts Council Collection 1975–6 at Hayward Gallery in 1976. After that Loker exhibited abroad in France, Netherlands and Norway. He continued to show with Angela Flowers and in 1981 his Ten Years' Work Exhibition was at Arnolfini Gallery, Bristol and tour. Flowers East showed Loker's monoprints in 2001. Loker's work was both abstract and abstract with environmental references. Commissions included Watmough (Holdings), Bradford, 1983; Essex General Hospital, 1984; and painting for Stanhope Developments at Norman Foster's ITN building, Gray's Inn Road, 1992. Arts Council, British Council, Contemporary Art Society, provincial public galleries and corporate collections hold examples. Lived in London.

LOM: *see* **Alfred LOMNITZ**

Josephine LOM fl. from c.1945– Painter, sculptor, designer, illustrator and teacher, born in Poland, also known by her married name of Azdia Josephine Lomnicka. She was educated in Poznań, studying art partly in Kassel and in England at Liverpool School of Art in 1946. She went on to teach at Digby Stuart College of Education in southwest London and wrote the book *Step-by-Step Collage*. Took part in group shows at Commonwealth Institute and in the provinces. Lived in London.

Jean LOMAS 1926– Painter, born in Norton, near Malton, Yorkshire. Brought up in the Liverpool area she was educated at Huyton College. Studied at Liverpool College of Art, then Royal Academy Schools. Belonged to Sandon Studios Society Club. Showed at RA, AEB tours and NEAC. Lived in Lymington, Hampshire.

Tom LOMAX 1945– Sculptor and painter, born in Warrington, Lancashire, who studied at Central School of Art and Design, 1971–4, then did postgraduate painting at Slade School of Fine Art, 1974. Commissions included a fountain for Birmingham Centenary Square and work for Urban Learning Foundation. Later shows included Kettle's Yard in Cambridge, Camden Arts Centre and Pomeroy Purdy, 1987, Tokyo International Art Fair, 1992, and Artist of the Day at Angela Flowers Gallery, 1994, chosen by Eileen Cooper.

Azdia Josephine LOMNICKA: *see* **Josephine LOM**

Alfred LOMNITZ 1892–1953 Painter, printmaker, draughtsman and writer, born in Eschwege, Germany, whose early years are vague. He graduated from the Weimar Art School, studied with Henri Van de Velde and ran the Litz design studios in Berlin in the 1920s and 1930s. In 1933, being Jewish in Nazi Germany, he decided to move to England, his family following. Lived in Aston Rowant, Oxfordshire. Worked as a commercial artist for London stores, such as Simpson and Swears and Wells. He was interned early in World War II, in 1941 publishing his experiences of this as *Never Mind Mr Lom* (he signed some work LOM, a name used by his friends). Showed at Ryman's in Oxford, 1934; had a memorial show at Ben Uri in 1954; and was given a solo show at John Denham Gallery in 1986. Lomnitz latterly suffered from Parkinson's Disease and his work became looser and more mystical. At times his pictures showed the influence of Paul Klee, the Expressionists and other Post-Impressionists. British Museum, Ben Uri and Museum of Modern Art in New York hold examples. Lomnitz lived finally in London.

Gary LONG 1945– Figure and landscape painter, draughtsman and teacher, born in Birmingham, who attended the College of Art there, then spent two years as an illustrator in Vancouver and Toronto, Canada. Returning to England, Long pursued advanced studies at Manchester College of Art. He built up a successful career as an illustrator, working on numerous national and international accounts in publishing and advertising, clients ranging from International Publishing Corporation, Oxford University Press, the BBC and British Gas to London Transport, Esso, Rolls-Royce, Walt Disney and Warner Brothers. He was an artist-member of the Society of Illustrators in New York and taught life drawing at Falmouth College of Art. In 2002, a series of Long's charcoal drawings of the female nude was included in the Valentine's Collection at The Great Atlantic Map Works, St Just. It was one of many provincial and London galleries where he had solo and mixed shows. Lived in St Ives, Cornwall.

John LONG 1964– Painter and draughtsman, born in Portadown, Northern Ireland, who did a foundation course at Ulster Polytechnic, Belfast, 1983–4, then graduated in painting from the Slade School of Fine Art, 1984–8; the measured style of that school and such artists as William Coldstream and Euan Uglow was present in Long's work. Awards included Elizabeth Greenshields, Canada, 1989; Taylor De Vere, Dublin, and Arts Council of Northern Ireland, both 1993; and Arts Council again in 1994. Long was artist-in-residence at Byam Shaw School of Art, 1990–1. Group shows included Spring Contemporary, Albany Gallery, 1990; RHA from 1992 (he was elected an associate, 1995); and 20th Century British Art Fair, Royal College of Art, 1996. Solo shows included Theo Waddington Fine Art, 1998. Haverty Trust Collection holds the work of Long, who lived in Dublin, Ireland.

John Kenneth LONG 1924– Painter, sculptor and teacher, born in Liverpool. Studied at Manchester School of Art, his teachers including Ian Grant. Showed RA, ROI, RBA, NEAC and in the provinces. Lived in Darton, Yorkshire.

Michael LONG 1940– Born in Bristol, a painter in oils and acrylic of seascapes and landscapes, especially of Somerset and the Cotswolds. After studying at the West of England College of Art, he was apprenticed at E S & A Robinson in 1957 as a designer and reproduction artist. Long was three times president of Bristol Savages, including the 2004 centenary year, and he showed at the RWA and other the West Country galleries. An exhibition of his illustrations for the Natural History Museum's *Evolution of Mammals* was held at Bristol Museum & Art Gallery in 1996.

Mike LONG 1951– Sculptor and teacher with a special interest in figures in movement. He was born in Chatham, Kent. After attending King's School in Bruton, Long studied sculpture at Goldsmiths' College School of Art, 1971–4. From 1978 he was head of the art department at King Edward VI School, Southampton. Long began observing dancers while still at Goldsmiths', an interest fostered later at Ballet Rambert and the London Contemporary Dance Group. He was a keen sportsman, which reflected another aspect of his output. From 1984 Long held regular summer shows at New London Theatre and in 1989 had a solo exhibition at Century Gallery. The Morris Singer Foundry cast his work.

Richard LONG 1945– Sculptor, born in Bristol, where he continued to live. He studied at the local School of Art, 1962–6, then at St Martin's School of Art, 1966–8. Long was not a conventional sculptor making gallery objects but adopted landscape as his material. He went on a series of walks, including Ireland, the Himalayas and the Rio Grande, and recovered his impressions of them and identification with an area in photographs, maps and words. His Gobi Desert Circle was a photograph of a circle of stones made in Mongolia in 1966. He sometimes brought material from a walk into the gallery, as in his Delabole Bristol Slate Circle, 1997, commissioned by Bristol City Art Gallery. Other works included River Avon Mud Drawing, of which the artist said, "It was made by mud and water and gravity. Part of the intellectual excitement is that it is a drawing but not actually made by my hand." Long had a one-man show at Whitechapel Art Gallery in 1971, the year he appeared in Guggenheim International Exhibition at Guggenheim Museum, New York, and the following year had a show at Museum of Modern Art there. Later shows included his representing Britain at Venice Biennale in 1976 and a series at Anthony d'Offay Gallery from 1979. Also notable were Tate Gallery, 1990; Hayward Gallery, 1991; Guggenheim, Bilbao, Spain, 2000; and Tate Gallery St Ives, 2002, the year after Long was elected RA. Haunch of Venison showed a wide range of Long's work in 2003. Considered by many to be the outstanding British artist of his generation, Long's work is not easily interpreted. He was Turner Prize winner in 1989. Tate Gallery, Arts Council and Bristol City Art Gallery hold his work.

Ronald LONG 1933– Painter who graduated from King Edward VII School of Fine Art, Newcastle upon Tyne, and St Martin's School of Art. While there, in 1957, he had two paintings chosen for inclusion in Jack Beddington's book *Young Artists of Promise*. His self-portrait is illustrated in Philip Vann's *Face to Face*, published by Sansom & Company Ltd/Piano Nobile Fine Paintings in 2004.

Sheila LONG 1925– Painter, designer and teacher, born in Leeds, Yorkshire, where she attended the College of Art. Held a number of art teaching posts in Leeds and Hertfordshire, before becoming a full-time artist in the early 1960s. Lived for a time in Feltwell, Norfolk.

Sue LONG 1943– Versatile printmaker, painter in oil and watercolour, whose work explored the landscape and coast of her home area. Gained a National Diploma in Design, specialising in painting, 1960–4, then studied for an art teacher's certificate at University of Leeds, 1965. After becoming interested in printmaking in 1980 and joining the print workshop at The Minories, Colchester, and at Gainsborough's House, Sudbury, Long studied printmaking at Chelsea School of Art. She was variously a member of the Printmakers' Council and SWE and a founder-member of 12 PM, a dozen printmakers based in East Anglia. Exhibitions included This Flat Earth and Colchester Art Society, both at firstsite, Colchester, in 2000; and Collecting for the Future, firstsite, 2001. Took part in Making the Connection, firstsite and Wolsey Art Gallery in 2002.

Tim LONG 1956– Artist and researcher, born in Bonn, West Germany, who in 1998 won a prize for Work of Imagination at The Discerning Eye, Mall Galleries. In that year he produced a limited-edition laser-printed book, *bulbous flusse*, while being a research fellow in digital fine art media. Produced a number of papers and presentations concerning digital media, his work appearing in a series of websites, such as Centre for Research in Fine Art, 1999, www.uwic.ac.uk/fineart-research. Group shows included National Print Exhibition, Mall Galleries, 1999; 6, Howard Gardens Gallery, Cardiff, 2000; and Glynn Vivian Art Gallery, Swansea, 2001. Among Long's solo exhibitions were Galerie Barrouyer, Paris, France, 1997, and Eagle Gallery, 2002.

Tony LONG 1942–2001 Imaginative sculptor and teacher, born in Brockton, Massachusetts, America, whose elegant abstract works in metal, sometimes coloured and occasionally in the form of a mobile, reflected their maker's ironic humour. Although he had no formal art training and had a fairly short career, Long established an international reputation. Initially brought up in an orphanage, aged 11 he joined his Lithuanian grandparents. Despite his duties in their bakery, Long developed a passion for literature, language and culture and learned German. Prevented from joining the Air Force Academy and flying because of short sight, he entered the Army, serving in Germany as a language instructor. Studied philosophy at Boston University, 1963–6, between 1967–9 completing his doctorate in German literature at New York University. After extensive travels through Yugoslavia, Turkey and Afghanistan to India, he settled in Paris in 1972, studied philosophy and literature at the University of Paris, 1973–4, began to sculpt and learned from sculptors such as the Cuban Augustin Cárdenas and Swiss Jean Tinguely. Friendship with the philosopher Jean-François Leotard led to Long's translating his works. Long's sculptures gained quick critical acceptance, solo shows at the Galerie Farideh Cadot and Centre Georges Pompidou being followed by regular exhibitions in France and abroad. Long gained a number of awards and residencies and in 1983 and 1986 was visiting professor at L'École Supérieure d'Art Visuel, in Geneva, Switzerland. He carried out extensive major public, private and corporate commissions across Europe. During a return to New York in 1996 Long fell in love with Mary Vogel, a visiting assistant professor at the University of Michigan, and when she was in England, 1998–9, Long joined her. In 2000, he was elected an international associate of the RBS. Died in Paris.

Charles LONGBOTHAM 1917–1999 Painter in oil and watercolour, father of the artist Claire Dalby, born in Carlton, Nottinghamshire. Longbotham was self-taught. From 1934–45 he was an apprentice, a ship's officer in the Merchant Navy then in Naval Reserve during the war. From 1946–69 he was a model-maker and dioramist, specialising in landscape models, also painting, from 1969 being a full-time painter. Longbotham was a member of RWS from the same year, also being a member of Art Workers' Guild. His subjects were landscapes, industrial and pastoral, and marine paintings. He had showed watercolours at RSA in 1942 and had his first solo exhibition at Federation of British Artists galleries in 1965, after which he had many more one-man and group showings in London and the provinces. Victoria & Albert Museum, Imperial War Museum, Fitzwilliam Museum in Cambridge and other public collections hold examples. Lived for many years in Cambridge.

Malcolm Richard LONGBOTTOM: *see* **Malcolm SCOTT**

Julian LONGCAKE 1964– Painter, notably in watercolour, who studied at Cumbria College of Art and Design and Falmouth School of Art. In 1988 he was commissioned by the National Trust's Foundation for Art to paint at Stourhead, then at Claremont, 1989. He showed in The Secret Garden at Colegate Gallery, Cockermouth, and in the same year, 1989, at Oriel Gallery, Welshpool. In the following year Longcake participated in Agnew's show The Broad Horizon.

Alfred Appleby LONGDEN fl. from 1901–1954 Director, curator and landscape painter in oil and watercolour, born in Sunderland, County Durham, son of a solicitor. He attended Durham School and the Royal College of Art, where he won medals. Longden was the first appointed curator at Aberdeen Art Gallery, 1907–12, and spent most of his life as a civil servant, painting and sketching in his spare time. His first official appointment was as government representative for fine and applied art at the New Zealand International Exhibition, 1906–7, in 1912 joining the exhibitions branch of the Board of Trade, taking part in its activities at home and abroad. During World War I Longden achieved the rank of major in the Royal Garrison Artillery, winning the Distinguished Service Order in 1917 and twice being mentioned in dispatches. After the war until 1925 he was director of the British Institute of Industrial Art; as assistant director was responsible for applied arts at the British Empire Exhibition, Wembley, in 1924; and was director of art for Britain at the Paris International Exhibition of Decorative Art, 1925. At the Dutch, Italian and Persian exhibitions at the RA in 1929, 1930 and 1931 he was secretary-general; in 1935 was secretary to the Board of Trade's Council for Art and Industry, being its representative for fine arts at the Empire Exhibition in South Africa; and was director of fine art at the 1938 Empire Exhibition at Glasgow. Shortly after the outbreak of war in 1939 Longden was made secretary of the fine art committee of the British Council, organising domestic and foreign shows, and was director of arts for the XIV Olympiad, in London, in 1948. In 1949 Sir Harold Wernher invited Longden to arrange the 15,000 exhibits of the Luton Hoo Collection, and he was its director and curator when he died. He exhibited at the New Gallery, RA and RI and was an Arts Club member.

Stanislaus Soutten LONGLEY 1894–1966 Watercolour painter, born at Aylesbury, Buckinghamshire. Studied at Regent Street Polytechnic School of Art under Harry Watson and George Gaskell. During World War II served as a camouflage officer. Exhibited Fine Art Society and RBA especially, RA, RI and Paris Salon. He took part in the Pilgrim Trust *Recording Britain* project and his work was reproduced by Medici Society and Raphael Tuck. Lived in Bournemouth, Hampshire.

Joan Pemberton LONGMAN: *see* **Joanne PEMBERTON-LONGMAN**

Tertia LONGMIRE 1963– Sculptor, site-related installation artist and teacher, born in Crowthorne, Berkshire, who gained a first-class sculpture honours degree at Brighton Polytechnic, 1990; her master's at Chelsea College of Art and Design, 1992; and a certificate in gender studies, with distinction, Birkbeck College, 1999. Teaching included Dartington College of Art, Ruskin School of Drawing in Oxford, University of Westminster and University of Brighton. In 1999, Longmire and Tanya Peixoto were in residence at Acland Burghley School, exploring language-related themes. Group shows included the interactive performance Raft, at the ICA, 1994; Souvenirs, Museum Books, 1998; and Bankside Browser, Tate Gallery, 1999. Later solo shows included And Not A Sound The Still Invades, Windsor Arts Centre, 1998.

Tony LONGSON 1948– Artist who employed computers, born in Stockport, Cheshire, who studied at Reading University, 1967–71, then worked in Holland on a Royal Netherlands Government Scholarship, 1971–2. He began to use computers to organise visual ideas in 1973, from 1974–7 doing research using computer facilities at Hatfield Polytechnic, backed by Arts Council funds. Exhibitions included Space, at Abbot Hall Art Gallery, 1976; The Constructive Context, Arts Council tour, 1978; and Non-Standard Constructions, a three-man show at Museum of Modern Art, Oxford/Gardner Centre Gallery, Brighton, in 1980. Research Machines of Oxford made equipment available for Longson's works there. Arts Council, Reading University and several Dutch collections acquired examples.

William Francis LONGSTAFF 1879–1953 Painter, cousin of the Australian painter Sir John Longstaff, Will developed an interest in art while serving in the Boer War in South Africa. During World War I he was an Official War Artist, was commissioned and worked with the Australian Army on camouflage. The war left a mark on his art, one of the results of which was his much-reproduced picture *The Ghosts of Menin Gate*, presented to the Australian Federal Government by Lord Woolavington. After the war Longstaff settled in north London, where he died, and showed at the RA Summer Exhibition. As well as mystical and allegorical pictures he produced conventional works such as decorative and delicate oil on canvas Still Life with Flowers, offered by Sotheby's Olympia in 2004. He is represented in the Australian War Memorial, Canberra.

James LONGUEVILLE 1942– Artist in oil, pastel and watercolour, born near Chester; he settled in the county at Malpas. After a career in journalism Longueville began to paint professionally in 1972. He said that he "learned much from the fine North Country artist Angus Rands". Longueville was influenced by Boudin, Constable, Wilson, Steer and Seago, was "an admirer of the East Anglian School" and spent many years painting in Norfolk. He was made a member of PS in 1983 and RBSA in 1989, also showing with ROI, RI and elsewhere. Later solo shows included Ringstead Gallery, Ringstead, Hunstanton, 1990; Omell Gallery, Windsor, and at Sarah Samuels, Chester, both 1991; John Noott Galleries, Broadway, 1996; and The City Gallery, 2001. Longueville twice won the Patterson Award at PS, and was included in The Art of Pastel at W H Patterson in 2003.

Philippa Van LOON: *see* **Philippa VAN LOON**

Brian LOONEY 1944– Theatre designer and teacher, actor and artist, born and lived in London, who painted from an early age, won a place at the Slade School of Fine Art aged 23, but instead pursued a stage career. In Italy from 1972 he was head of drama at an international school in Rome, designed for Teatro Goldoni and Teatro nella Crypta and played many leading classic roles. In 1976 returned to England, playing in repertory for Byre Theatre, St Andrews; The Duke's Playhouse, Lancaster; and in a National Theatre tour among many others. Abandoned acting for theatre design, by 1981 becoming resident designer at Battersea Arts Centre, also teaching in prisons and disadvantaged young people. In 1995 Looney began painting full-time, showing with Heifer Gallery, which gave him a solo show in 1999, and with the Mayfair and Covent Garden Festivals. Although mainly self-taught he latterly studied at Slade summer schools, painting teachers including Tom Norris and Jo Volley, as well as life drawing under Janet Unwin at Kingsway College, where he also learned etching.

LOOSE ENDS: *see* **Andrew BRACEY**

Bernard LORD 1940– Painter, draughtsman and teacher, born in Cardiff. He studied at Coleg Harlech, 1961–2, Newport College of Art and Design in 1963–7, then having won a Tyler Scholarship was at Tyler School of Art, Rome, 1967–8. Won a Temple University Fellowship which took him as a university fellow to Tyler School of Art, Temple University, Philadelphia, in 1968–9. In 1970 Lord began teaching, including periods in Newport, Cardiff and at Luton School of Art. Showed at Philadelphia Artists' Annual Exhibition in 1969, winning first prize, also with SWG and at Royal National Eisteddfod. Had several one-man shows, including Caerleon Community Centre.

Elyse LORD fl. from 1915–1971 Watercolourist, sometimes working on silk, and colourprint artist. She was elected RI, 1922, and was also a member of the Society of Graver-Printers in Colour. Favoured exotic and Far Eastern figure subjects, treated in delicate and imaginative colours. Her work was published by the London dealer Alexander Reid & Lefevre. Showed at that gallery, RA, RI, RSA, Fine Art Society and Paris Salon, where she gained a silver medal for colour prints. In 1990 Cyril Gerber Fine Art held an exhibition of her work. Lived in Bexley, Kent.

Harry LORD 1915–1966 Painter in oil and watercolour, full name Henry Bennett Lord, born in Seaham, County Durham. His family fled the Depression, so he was educated in America and Canada, returning in time to serve in World War II. Became a civil servant, studying painting in his spare time. He also wrote on art and was a co-director of the Univision Gallery, in Newcastle upon Tyne, where he lived. It showed modern international painters, such as Joan Miró and Sam Francis, and Lord had a solo exhibition there. Also exhibited at RI, ROI, RBA, Redfern Gallery, Newcastle Society of Artists and the local West End Art Club, of which he was secretary. Lord was increasingly an abstract artist, an exponent of Tachism.

Mary LORD 1931– Painter and teacher, born in Birstall, Yorkshire. In 1943 she won a late-developer's scholarship to Batley Grammar School. From 1948–50 attended Dewsbury and Batley College of Art, where Robert Lee was an influential teacher, then going to Leeds College of Art, 1950–3, under Richard Macdonald and Tommy Watt. Worked in Batley Library, 1953–5, and as a museum assistant at Bankfield Museum, Halifax, continuing to paint in her spare time, 1955–60. For about the next 30 years Mary Lord taught at venues such as Swarthmore Adult Education Centre, Leeds College of Art and Leeds College of Technology, ceasing in 1991 so as to concentrate on her own painting. Her first important show was at Batley Art Gallery in 1957. Also showed widely in mixed shows such as West Riding Artists, Northern Young Artists, Goosewell Gallery in Menston and in Four Women Artists, at Wakefield City Art Gallery, in 1961. In 1985 had solo show of importance at Bankfield Museum; in 1991 was included in Images of the Yorkshire Landscape, organised by Sheeran Lock, which toured to Leeds, Bradford and York; and in 1992 had first exhibition in London at Leighton House. The *Yorkshire Post* art critic W T Oliver said of Lord that "there is no more sensitive painter of the Northern landscape." Her work is held by Leeds City Art Gallery, Bradford Art Galleries and Museums, Ferens Art Gallery in Hull and other public collections. Lived in Leeds.

Nicola LORD 1978– Painter whose inspiration was "based on landscape and the many abstract forms found within it," especially "the surrounding areas of my home county, Dorset". After achieving a distinction, National Diploma in General Art & Design, at Bournemouth and Poole College of Art & Design, 1994–6, Lord graduated with first-class honours in textile design from Central St Martins, 1996–9, gaining her master's in printed textiles from the Royal College of Art, 1999–01. Won a series of awards and had work reproduced in magazines including *International Textiles* and *Textile View*. Group exhibitions included New Designers, Business Design Centre, and Bloomsbury Today II, Bupa House, both 1999; Takeaway, Charleston Gallery, Firle, 2001; and Studio Warwick Showroom, 2002. Also in 2002, had solo exhibitions at Bettles Gallery, Ringwood, and Curwen Gallery, sharing one with Helyne Jennings at New Academy Gallery in 2004.

Sarah LORD 1964– Painter, born in Folkestone, Kent, who studied at Canterbury College of Art and Cheltenham School of Art. Group shows included Young Painters South-East, from 1987; RA Summer Exhibition, from 1990; Interiors, Towner Art Gallery, Eastbourne, 1993; and Royal Over-Seas League Open, 1994. Had a solo show, In Haven, University of Kent, Canterbury, 1989, later ones including Stormont Studio, Rye, 1993. South East Arts and Kent County Council Arts & Libraries hold examples.

Amanda LORENS 1969– Sculptor, born in Gibraltar, who attended Cornwall College, 1985–7, then Winchester School of Art, 1987–90, gaining an honours degree. As well as sculpture, she specialised in ceramics and printmaking. She was joint first prize winner at Southampton City Art Gallery's Not Just Another Statue Competition. Mixed shows included Tower Arts Centre, Winchester, 1989; Women Artists from the South-West, Spacex Gallery, Exeter, 1991; Newlyn Site-Specifics, Newlyn, 1993; and The Edge of Beyond, Belgrave Gallery, 1995, where she showed brightly coloured abstract sculptures. Solo shows included Wolf at the Door, Penzance, 1993, and Rainyday Gallery, Penzance, 1994. Was based in Cornwall.

Stafford LORIE 1918–2000 Antiques dealer, restorer and artist, born in Birmingham, who was educated at St Paul's and the Slade School of Fine Art. There he studied with A H Gerrard and was one of the students Gerry took to Dorset to give them first-hand experience of working in a quarry. Lorie remained a keen sculptor, artist and silversmith while devoting his life to the antiques trade, like his father, who set up Lories Ltd in Wigmore Street in 1926. Stafford opened his first shop with Cyril Staal in Kensington Church Street, short-lived because of World War II, which saw Lorie commissioned in the Royal Artillery. After demobilisation and return to the family business he traded in Paris, sending English porcelain back to London, to which he returned to help his father in 1966. A dealer with an encyclopaedic knowledge and droll sense of humour, Lorie attended every Grosvenor House Fair from 1935 until the end of the century.

Hew LORIMER 1907–1993 Sculptor and administrator, born in Edinburgh, son of Sir Robert Lorimer, the architect. Although he began to study at Oxford University in 1928, Lorimer moved to Edinburgh College of Art to study architecture and sculpture under Alexander Carrick, who was keen on direct stone-carving. An Andrew Grant Travelling Scholarship took Lorimer to France and Italy in the early 1930s, then a Fellowship enabled him to work with Eric Gill. Gill's influence and that of Romanesque French church carving profoundly affected Lorimer's output, as did Gill's belief that the artist collaborated with God in the creative effort. During World War II Lorimer helped the British Council put on fine exhibitions at the National Gallery of Scotland. After the war with Maxwell Allen he worked on major monumental sculptures which included figures on the front of the National Library of Scotland. An important show of his work was held at Talbot Rice Art Centre, 1988. Lived finally at Pittenweem, Fife.

Albert LOUDEN 1943– Painter and draughtsman, notably in pastel, born in Blackpool into a working-class family during evacuation from London's East End, to which it returned in 1945. Although he toyed over the years with higher mathematics and left-wing politics, from about 1962 Louden decided to concentrate on art while working as a lorry driver. To give more time to painting, from 1979–84 Louden worked part-time, from 1985 painting full-time. Louden was discovered in 1979 by Victor Musgrave, co-organiser of the Outsiders show at Hayward Gallery. In 1985 he had a sell-out exhibition at Serpentine Gallery, in 1986 having a solo show in New York at Rosa Esman Gallery. Later shows included Boundary Gallery, 1990, and Whitford Fine Art, 2001. Louden's pictures comprised heavily distorted figures in urban settings and situations observed with wit and using a unique palette. The Tate Gallery, Arts Council and Collection L'Art Brut, Lausanne, hold his work.

Stanley LOUNDS 1906–1980 Painter and artist in black-and-white and sepia. He was the son of Arthur Lounds, coachbuilder, and was born in Grantham, Lincolnshire. As well as still life, portrait and landscape work he was noted for his architectural pictures, done in Britain and abroad. Signed work S L. Lounds trained for the Anglican priesthood at the former St Paul's College, Burgh, being ordained in Lincoln in 1929. As well as serving for various periods in Lincolnshire and briefly as a Royal Air Force chaplain Lounds was for a time in South Africa. Soon after World War II he joined the Community of the Resurrection in Mirfield, Yorkshire, where he was known as Samuel. Most of his time was then spent there. He continued to paint, but suffered from constant ill-health. Exhibited with Huddersfield and Cardiff Art Societies and illustrated religious publications.

Anthony LOUSADA 1907–1994 Painter in oil and watercolour and draughtsman, educated at Westminster and New College, Oxford, who was a partner in Stephenson Harwood, solicitors, 1935–1973. Lousada was a member of the council of the Royal College of Art, 1952–79, chairman, 1972–9; a trustee of the Tate Gallery, 1962–9, chairman, 1967–9; and was knighted in 1975. Exhibited with the Law Society, winning first prize in 1967, with the Contemporary Art Society in the 1980s, had two solo exhibitions at the Covent Garden Gallery, 1977 and 1979, and held a yearly open studio in Chiswick, 1980–91. His drawings and watercolours of the World War II Blitz are in the Museum of London, Victoria & Albert Museum and Imperial War Museum.

Nicky LOUTIT 1943– Painter, born in London, her mother being the artist Janetta Parladé. From 1961–4 studied at Chelsea School of Art under Lawrence Gowing, then until 1967 at Slade School of Fine Art under William Coldstream. Travelled extensively, returning to England in 1970 where she had a show at Bramante Gallery. In 1977 she and her husband left to join a religious community in India, staying with it through a period in America, but returned disillusioned in 1983, moving to Norfolk, where she settled in Binham, married to the writer Jonathan Gathorne-Hardy. As well as showing at CCA Galleries from 1988 and Michael Parkin, 1989, in mixed shows, from 1989 exhibited solo with Stephen Bartley Gallery, from 1993 showing one-man at Sally Hunter Fine Art. Loutit was an artist keen on depicting people, with a real feeling for paint. Other later solo shows included Browse & Darby, 1998, and Winchester Cathedral, 2000.

Roelof LOUW 1935– Sculptor, painter, installations artist and teacher, born in Cape Town, South Africa. He studied at the university there, emigrated to England in 1961 and adopted British citizenship, 1967. Worked in an architectural office in London and studied under Anthony Caro at St Martin's School of Art, 1961–5. He taught at St Martin's, Maidstone School of Art and Royal College of Art between 1967–71; settled in New York, 1973; was a visiting lecturer, Victoria University, British Columbia, 1976–7, and visiting artist, Rhode Island School of Design, Providence, 1977–8. Louw showed at Young Contemporaries from 1964; Kasmin Gallery, 1967; Stockwell Depot Show and Survey '68: Abstract Sculpture, at Camden Arts Centre, both 1968; also abroad. In a project at Art Laboratory in 1967 Louw made a pyramid of 5,800 oranges and a cone of 9½ tons of black granite chippings. The oranges were reduced over two weeks as the public removed parts of the exhibit. Solo shows also included Museum of Modern Art, Oxford, 1969; and Nigel Greenwood and Whitechapel Art Galleries, 1971. In 1981 he received a prize in the sculpture competition Waterfront Project, Jane Street Pier, New York. Louw established a firm concerned with art in public places. His own work continued, examples held by Tate Gallery and Victoria & Albert Museum.

Hazel LOVE 1923– Painter in oil and watercolour, born at Hinton St George, Somerset. Attended West of England College of Art, 1946–52, exhibited RWA, AIA and locally in Somerset. The RWA holds her work. Lived at Bexhill-on-Sea, Sussex, and at Sutton Scotney, Hampshire.

Ross LOVEDAY 1946– Self-taught landscape artist in mixed media, born in Bargoed, Glamorgan. Studied optometry at the University of Wales, Cardiff, and practised as an optician before concentrating on painting from 1990. His subjects were often painted many times, as he was "not interested in representing facts as such, although what is created must satisfy me as being true to life though not naturalistically accurate." Took part in many group shows, winning 1st Prize, Laing Art Competition, 1992 and 1996; prize winner, Hertfordshire Open, 1993; prize winner Artists in Essex Open, 1994 and 1996, 2nd Prize, 1998; prize winner, Braintree Open, 1995; other shows including the National Eisteddfod of Wales, Neath, 1994, MAFA and The Discerning Eye, both 1997, and RSW, 1998. There were solo exhibitions at the West Wales Arts Centre, Fishguard, 2001 and 2003, and Cambridge Contemporary Art, Cambridge, 2002. HRH The Prince of Wales, Beecroft Art Gallery at Westcliff-on-Sea and Epping Forest District Museum, Waltham Abbey, hold examples. Lived in Harlow, Essex.

Catherine LOVEGROVE 1961– Painter of murals, born in Lewes, Sussex, married to the artist Tod Ramos. Kate Lovegrove studied at Heatherley's School of Art, 1980, under John Wharton and Daphne Todd, then at Wimbledon School of Art, 1981–3. From 1983 she ran a mural painting studio in southwest London, Catherine Lovegrove Murals. Work themes were "trompe l'oeil, architectural murals and figurative murals depicting the 1920s, 1930s and 1950s. Influences are Tamara de Lempicka, Edward Burra, Diego Rivera, Tiepolo, Baroque and Rococo painting and architecture." Lovegrove was a life member of Chelsea Arts Club and a freeman of the City of London. In addition to several group and mixed shows, she had solo exhibitions at IDI, 1989, and Decorex International, 1998. Many Catherine Lovegrove Murals were completed for restaurants and hotels worldwide, including a figurative mural of Paddington Station in the 1920s at the Hilton Hotel, Paddington. Anglo American, Alberto Vilar, the St Mary's Art Collection and Prudential Property Services held examples.

James LOVEGROVE 1922– Painter, draughtsman and printmaker, born in Hong Kong into a military family. He was himself an Army officer who retired in 1945. Studied at Woolwich Polytechnic's school of art, 1945–9, then at Royal College of Art, 1949–52. Exhibited at RA, RE, Walker's Galleries and in the area of Winchester, Hampshire, where he settled, having lived a bachelor life in a succession of digs in south London for some years. In 1952 one of Lovegrove's etched plates was bought by the Print Collectors' Club, and the Victoria & Albert Museum and Aberdeen Art Gallery hold his work. A man of many interests, Lovegrove was among other things a bank manager, seaman, postal and local historian and director of finance and administration for the *Mary Rose* Trust. Had a solo exhibition, On The River, at Greenwich Theatre Art Gallery in 1996, partly drawn from the time when he served as mate on a Thames barge. Many of his river studies had been lost when the barge he worked on was cut down by a steamer off Greenhithe in 1953.

John LOVELESS 1943– Painter and printmaker, born in Bristol. Studied there at Royal West of England College of Art, 1963–5, where his teachers included Robert Hurdle and John Epstein. He showed at Camden Arts Centre, Grabowski Gallery and with the Arts Council at Serpentine Gallery; and in west of England at Arnolfini Gallery, Bristol, and at Dartington Hall, Devon. South Western Arts Association and Arnolfini Gallery Trust hold his work. Lived at Rookham, Somerset.

Margaret LOVELL 1939– Creator of abstract sculpture with figurative allusions, printmaker, draughtsman and teacher, born and lived in Bristol area. She studied at West of England College of Art there, 1956–60, with Ernest Pascoe, then at Slade School of Fine Art, 1960–2, under A H Gerrard. Learned techniques in a foundry. Lovell gained an Italian State Scholarship, 1962–3, and a Greek Government Scholarship, 1965–6. Taught at Portsmouth College of Art, 1963–5. Miss Lovell was "interested in and influenced by natural forms, movement and structures". She used "colours and all qualities of materials, notably bronze, stone, marble and slate". She was elected RWA in 1972 and a fellow of RBS in 1973. Lovell's main works included silver trophies for the John Player sailing championships; a six-foot bronze for Barclays Bank, Embassy House, Bristol; and a 16-foot bronze for Grafham Water reservoir scheme, Huntingdonshire. Took part in many mixed and group shows, including Arnolfini Gallery, Bristol; Mignon Gallery, Bath; Wills Lane Gallery, St Ives, and abroad. Showed solo with Marjorie Parr Gallery from 1965, having a first retrospective at Plymouth City Art Gallery, 1972. Cornerstone Gallery, St Ives, showed Lovell's work in 2003. Arts Council, Plymouth and Bristol public galleries hold examples.

Eleanor Selwyn LOVETT 1917– Painter and sculptor in terracotta, latterly noted for her horse pictures. She was born in Bromley, Kent, and studied at Goldsmiths' College School of Art, Epsom School of Art and Royal Academy Schools; her teachers included Hans Tisdall. She was a member of Hesketh Hubbard Art Society, also showing with Leicester Galleries, NEAC, ROI, at Whitechapel Art Gallery and at RA Summer Exhibition. Robert Fleming & Company, the merchant bank, bought her work. Lived in East Croydon, Surrey.

Annie Rose LOW: *see* **Annie Rose LAING**

Bet LOW 1924– Painter, born in Gourock, Renfrewshire. She studied at Glasgow School of Art, 1942–5; at Patrick Allan-Fraser School of Art, Hospitalfield, Arbroath, with James Cowie; and Jordanhill Teachers Training College. She worked for a time as an art therapist and designed sets for Unity Theatre. In the mid-1950s the shortage of exhibitions space for young painters prompted Low to help start the railings exhibitions at Botanic Gardens in Glasgow. In the early 1960s she was founder and director of New Charing Cross Gallery, Glasgow. Redevelopment closed it in 1968, but it was succeeded by Compass Gallery in 1969. Low painted abstracts in the 1960s, but later her work was inspired by frequent trips to the Orkneys, in which landscape is simplified towards abstraction to convey the essence of the place. In addition to many mixed shows Low showed solo in 1961 at 57 Gallery, Edinburgh, as well as David Hendriks Gallery in Dublin and Richard Demarco Gallery in Edinburgh, Compass Gallery in Glasgow and Scottish Gallery, Edinburgh. She was a member of RSW and Royal Glasgow Institute of the Fine Arts. Scottish Arts Council and other Scottish galleries hold her work.

David LOW 1891–1963 Political cartoonist and satirist and writer, born in Dunedin, New Zealand. He grew up in Christchurch and taught himself to draw for the press, inspired by comic papers. By 1903 had published first cartoon strip in *The Big Budget* and he began to work for Christchurch publication *The Spectator*, eventually becoming its full-time political cartoonist. Next big steps were his move in 1911 to Australia to work on the *Bulletin*, Sydney; then eight years later he journeyed to London. There he worked on the *Star*, 1919–27, *Evening Standard*, 1927–50; *Daily Herald*, 1950–3, and *Manchester Guardian*, 1953–63. Low met and befriended the famous in many fields: Arnold Bennett, H G Wells, Lord Beaverbrook, David Lloyd George and Winston Churchill. His wit could be barbed, his drawings powerful, and he invented unique images such as Colonel Blimp and the Trades Union Congress carthorse. Low's work was syndicated throughout the world and he published books such as *British Cartoonists, Caricaturists and Comic Artists* and in 1956 his entertaining *Low's Autobiography*. Knighted in 1962. Tate Gallery holds his work. Died in London. Low! The Twentieth Century's Greatest Cartoonist, was held at Westminster Hall in 2002 and Stalin's Russia through the Eyes of Sir David Low at the London Jewish Cultural Centre in 2003.

Diana LOW 1911–1975 Artist in oil, pastel, lithography and etching. Born in London, she was educated at Francis Holland School and Cheltenham Ladies' College, where her art mistress was Charlotte Epton, who married Edward Bawden. Spent a short time at the Slade under Randolph Schwabe after study at Académie Ranson, in Paris, but her greatest influence was William Nicholson, who painted excellent portraits of her and her brother, Oliver Low. Exhibited RA, NEAC, RP, SSWA, Leicester Galleries and in Paris. Married Richard Tuely and lived at Stone-in-Oxney, near Tenterden, Kent. The artists Jane and Mary Tuely were related to her. Work owned by Stoke-on-Trent City Museum and Art Gallery.

Jack LOW 1903– Painter, carver, designer and teacher, born in London, who studied at City and Guilds of London Art School, 1941–2, then with Adrian Ryan at Goldsmiths' College School of Art, 1946–50, during which time he taught for London County Council. Showed at RA

Leicester Galleries, Redfern Gallery, AIA, RBA and elsewhere. Lived for many years at West Stourmouth, Kent.

Stewart LOWDON 1932– Painter, born in Edinburgh, who in 1944 began painting out of doors; by 1948 was showing with SSA. After attending Edinburgh College of Art, 1950–4, in 1955 added a teaching diploma to his diploma in drawing and painting. After National Service in Army Educational Corps embarked on a dozen years in advertising and photography, but continued to paint and exhibit. In 1975 decided to leave for Cornwall and paint full-time. Between 1979–83 made a series of painting trips to Greece as a consequence of which, through Greek Embassy, he took part in Lykion Ton Ellinidon, Kensington, 1983. Other working trips were made to Portugal and Provence. Showed widely, especially in west of England. Later appearances included Eye Gallery, Bristol, 1988; Westside Gallery, 1989; Stable Gallery and Heifer Gallery, 1991.

Adam LOWE 1959– Painter and printmaker, born in Oxford. He studied at Ruskin School of Drawing, 1978–81, then Royal College of Art, 1982–5. Among his group appearances were Kettle's Yard, Cambridge, 1985; Smiths Galleries, 1986; and John Moores Exhibition, Liverpool, 1991–2, where he was a prize winner with a large abstract painting in homage to Robert Motherwell, called The Homely Protestant. Lowe had solo shows at Pomeroy Purdy Gallery, 1989–91. He was included in Seven Print Projects from The Paragon Press, Gimpel Fils, 2000.

Jeff LOWE 1952– Sculptor and draughtsman, born in Lancashire. He produced abstract drawings in acrylic and graphite of great strength and presence, as in Isis Gallery's 1993 exhibition Drawing Towards Sculpture, in Leigh-on-Sea. Attended Leicester College of Art, 1970–1, then St Martin's School of Art, 1971–5. Gained a Sainsbury Award in 1975, a Greater London Arts Association award and an Arts Council Award in 1976; he was artist-in-residence at Mermer Stone Quarry, Yugoslavia, 1977, and in 1987 at Prahran College, Melbourne, Australia. Exhibitions included Leicester Galleries, 1974; Laing Art Gallery, Newcastle upon Tyne, 1977; and a series at Nicola Jacobs Gallery from 1981. Lowe's 1977 abstract, floor-based work Malpura 3, made from a variety of materials and loosely based on an Indian miniature which he owned, was included in the exhibition 1979 at Bloomberg SPACE in 2005. Arts Council holds his work. Lowe lived and worked in London.

Jim LOWE 1943– Artist and teacher, born in Bath, Somerset, noted for "bold, bright and geometrically taut" work. He studied painting at Kingston School of Art and the Royal Academy Schools, teachers including John Newton, Bryan Kneale and William Scott. In 1967 Lowe won the Peter Stuyvesant and Arts Council Prizes and Boise and Leverhulme Scholarships. Between 1975–8 he designed sets of book covers for the Fontana Modern Masters Series. Lowe taught art at Highgate School, 1969–72, and woodwork at Chilton Cantelo House School, 1986–7. After living in Somerset, 1976–87, Lowe moved to Wales until 2000 when he settled in Bath and was a member of the Bath Area Network of Artists. Mixed exhibitions included LG, 1965; Young Contemporaries, at Tate Gallery, and Arts Council Touring Exhibition, both 1967; Redfern Gallery Summer Exhibitions, 1967–70; Seven Redfern Artists, 1971; and Ceri Richards Gallery, Swansea, 1991. Had solo shows at Redfern, 1969; Festival Gallery, Bath, 1980; and Theatr Mwldan, Cardigan, 1995. Leicester Education Authority and many private collections in Britain and America hold examples.

Peter LOWE 1938– Maker of constructions and reliefs, and teacher, born in London where he continued to live. Lowe studied with Kenneth and Mary Martin at Goldsmiths' College School of Art, 1954–60. In 1962 Lowe and Colin Jones showed their first reliefs in the Geometric Environment show at AIA Gallery, the following year taking part in Construction England, a touring show put on by Arts Council, which holds several examples of Lowe's abstract work. Lowe progressively exhibited in Britain and abroad, being associated with the Systems Group, which came together in 1969 and put on the Systemi show at Amos Anderson Museum, Helsinki, Finland. In 1977 he was included in Dilworth, Hughes, Lowe and Steele at Annely Juda Fine Art.

Rachel LOWE 1968– Artist using modern media such as film and video, who studied at Newcastle College of Arts and Technologies, 1985–6; graduated with honours in fine art, sculpture, from Camberwell College of Art, 1987–90; obtaining her master's in fine art (alternative media), Chelsea College of Art, 1992–3. Gained London Arts Board and Olay Vision Awards and was in 1997–8 Wingate Artist in Residence at Southampton City Art Gallery. Mixed shows included Vehicle, Paolo Baldacci Gallery, New York, America, 1996; Enough, The Tannery, 1998; Vegas, Lux Gallery, 1999; The British Art Show 5 tour, 2000; and Beck's Futures, 2002, ICA and tour, 2002–3. Secret Victorians, Fabric Museum and Workshop, Philadelphia, Pennsylvania, 2001. Among her solo exhibitions were 18-5-59 at The Showroom, 2001. The British Council; Ferens Art Gallery, Hull; and Middlesbrough City Art Gallery held examples. Lived in London.

Ronald LOWE 1932–1985 Painter, mural artist, printmaker and teacher, born in Skipton, Yorkshire. He studied at Leeds College of Art, 1949–55, with Richard Macdonald and Keith Lucas, and in London. After serving as an education officer in the Army, taught 1959–71 at Haverfordwest Grammar School, then became Her Majesty's Inspector, Art, Wales, meanwhile lecturing for many years on history of art, part-time, at University College of Wales, Aberystwyth. Took part in many group shows, including RA, SEA and SWG, AIA and Howard Roberts Gallery, Cardiff. Many one-man shows, starting with Dillwyn Gallery, Swansea, mainly in Wales but also in America. Haverfordwest Civic Society held a commemorative retrospective for Ron Lowe in 1987 and there was an important exhibition at Newport Museum and Art Gallery in 1988. His friend and fellow artist Maurice Sheppard called Lowe "a painter of great physical vigour; he revelled in paint, in its sensuous qualities and in the glow of its colour. His pictures are full of dazzling visual improvisations which are a proof of the intuitive, receptive and spontaneous in his imagination." Has work in many public collections, including WAC, CASW and University College, Swansea.

Fritz LÖWEN 1893–1970 Painter, draughtsman and designer, born in Vienna, Austria, where he appears to have had art training, becoming a professional commercial artist in Berlin between the wars. His main employer was the publisher Ullstein Verlag; he drew glamorous women for magazine front covers, with a special interest in underwear, notably suspenders. Following Nazi persecution of Jews he moved to London in the late 1930s, becoming Lucien Löwen. There he painted murals for Kampinski's restaurant and portraits of the actresses Peggy Ashcroft and Constance Cummings and tennis star Kay Stammers. During World War II served in Pioneer Corps and did graphic design for Foreign Office. After hostilities, he worked for the advertising agency Mather & Crowther; designed book-jackets, such as Carlo Levi's *Christ Stopped at Eboli*; produced posters for the travel agent Erna Low; and flower pictures which accompanied articles in *The Sphere* magazine. These, in which he attained a high standard of botanical accuracy, were not otherwise exhibited and after his death, from a heart attack at Euston tube station, they found their way to relations in Israel. John Denham Gallery held an exhibition in 1999.

Lucien LÖWEN: *see* **Fritz LÖWEN**

May LOWEN 1903– Painter and miniaturist, born in London. She attended Camden Art School and showed at RA, City of London Guildhall, RMS and elsewhere. Was a member of the Hampstead Artists' Council and lived in London.

Victor LOWER 1887– Commercial artist, born at Hove, Sussex. Studied at the School of Art there, 1900–3, then for four years at Brighton School of Art. He exhibited with Croydon Art Society and published several books on flags, signals and ships, work also appearing in *Boy's Own Paper*. Lived at Merstham, Surrey.

Alex LOWERY 1957– Painter who was born in London and took a bachelor's degree in fine art at Central School of Art and Design, 1979–82. From then he painted continuously, moving to Dorset in 1989. Lowery settled six miles from West Bay, a small harbour which for years became the focus of his tranquil, muted paintings. He liked "the idea of quarrying a restricted subject for the greatest variety it can be made to yield.... The more I worked, the more it became possible to reduce the amount of detail required to approach the feeling that haunted me." Showed in Devon with Gordon Hepworth Gallery at Newton St Cyres and solo at Art First, 2002.

Thomas Esmond LOWINSKY 1892–1947 Painter, book illustrator, designer of papers and textiles, and collector, born in India, where his father was financial consultant to the Sultan of Hyderabad. Back in England he lived in luxurious surroundings, an introverted and artistic boy who attended Eton College, read English at Oxford University, then studied at Slade School of Fine Art, 1912–14. As a commissioned officer in Army during World War I he saw active service in France. Between the wars, at Garsington Manor and later at The Old Rectory, Aldbourne, Lowinsky and his wife lived with exquisite taste, entertaining the eminent and cultivated. He was a founder-member of the Double Crown Club, a member of NEAC and showed in various mixed exhibitions. Had only one solo show during his life, at Wildenstein in 1926; after his death Graves Art Gallery, Sheffield, had a small show in 1981, and Tate Gallery, which holds some of his limited output, a larger one in 1990. As well as scenes of fantasy Lowinsky painted a body of superb portraits, singular images which owe much to Renaissance example. Colin Myers' *The Book Decorations of Thomas Lowinsky*, Incline Press, 2001, covers this aspect of the artist's work.

Alan LOWNDES 1921–1978 Painter in oil of the industrial north of England, using a bright palette. He was born in Stockport, Cheshire. Left school at 14 and became apprenticed to a decorator. After several years in the Army in World War II Lowndes studied painting in the evenings at Stockport College, then started painting full-time in the late 1940s. He was early on taken up by the Crane Gallery in Manchester, where he had a number of one-man shows, later showing at Crane Kalman, London. Also showed solo at Osborn Gallery in New York; Curlew Gallery, Southport; and had retrospectives at Stockport Art Gallery and tour, 1972, and Crane Kalman, 1995. From the early 1950s Lowndes began to work in St Ives, Cornwall, settling in the area for just over a decade in 1959. He later settled at Dursley, Gloucestershire, but periodically returned to Stockport to work.

Rosemary LOWNDES 1937–2001 Painter, designer, writer and illustrator, born in Cheshire. She studied at Liverpool School of Art, then lived in Paris, working with interior designers. Showed work at Salon des Artistes Français and Salon des Indépendants and had solo show at Galerie Ror Volmar. On return to England worked as graphic designer, examples being selected by Design Centre. Wrote and illustrated over 40 children's books, published internationally. Showed at Moreton Street Gallery, Hurlingham Gallery, Phoenix Gallery in Lavenham and Highgate, Mina Renton Gallery and Charlotte Lampard Gallery. Lived in London.

John LOWRIE 1969– Artist, born in St Andrews, Fife, who studied at Waid Academy, Anstruther, 1981–7; obtained a Higher National Certificate in technical illustration, Dundee College of Further Education, 1987–9; then an honours degree in design, 1990–4, from Edinburgh College of Art. He held a number of painting and screenprinting residencies, in Australia, Britain and Ireland. Group exhibitions included Gatehouse Gallery, Crail, 1994; SSA at RSA, 1995; Edinburgh Printmakers' Workshop, from 1996; and Gallery Heinzel, Aberdeen, 1998. Lowrie's work in his shared show at Cadogan Contemporary, 1999, included landscape work with strong gestural and abstract elements. The Earl & Countess of Crawford and Balcarres and The Earl & Countess of Cawdor held his work.

Laurence Stephen LOWRY 1887–1976 Painter and draughtsman, mainly of industrial landscapes, with figure studies and seascapes. Born in Manchester, Lowry became famous as the painter of northern industrial and backstreet urban scenes populated with "matchstick" figures, and as a reclusive character. But he was no primitive artist, devoting many years to the study of art while working full-time as a rent collector and clerk. After private lessons with William Fitz in Manchester, from 1905–15 Lowry attended painting and drawing classes at the Municipal College of Art under Adolphe Valette, whose urban scenes foreshadowed Lowry's. From 1915–25 Lowry attended Salford School of Art, a period when he established his style and subject matter. In 1919 exhibited two paintings at MAFA, then in the 1920s began to show regularly in open exhibitions including the Paris Salon. An

Accident was bought by the City Art Gallery, Manchester, in 1930, the first publicly acquired Lowry. Two years later he exhibited at the RA for the first time. In 1938 A J McNeill Reid noticed his work, leading to his first one-man show in London, at Lefevre Gallery, the following year. By 1945 Lowry was receiving serious critical attention, and his slow climb to fame and many honours was gaining pace. A major retrospective exhibition at the RA followed his death, in 1976. Lowry's work is widely held in public collections, including the Tate Gallery and Salford, where the Museum and Art Gallery in 1987 staged a centenary show and where in 2000 the collection moved to a new home, The Lowry, at Salford Quays. In 2003, Crane Kalman Gallery held a Lowry exhibition to mark publication of the book *L.S. Lowry: Conversation Pieces – Andras Kalman in conversation with Andrew Lambirth*. A City's Pride, at The Lowry in 2004, showed more than 350 works by Lowry acquired by Salford City Council over 70 years. Lived at Mottram-in-Longdendale, Cheshire, where he had moved in 1948.

Peter LOWRY 1914– Watercolourist who studied at St Martin's School of Art, 1933, and at Bolt Court, 1935–7. Showed at RA, NEAC, RBA and elsewhere. Lived in London.

Ruth LOWY 1921–2000 Architect and painter, born as Ruth Curwen into an intellectual family of Jewish refugees. Her mother was a pioneer of women's rights, the first woman to take a first-class degree in mathematics at London University, her father lecturing in the same subject at the London School of Economics and teaching at Berkhamsted. During World War II Lowy served as a Wren, after which she studied architecture at Cambridge and at the RIBA. In 1952 she married Jack Lowy, a pioneer researcher into the molecular structure of the muscle who, after a number of academic and research appointments and a coronary, joined the Open University. After moving with her husband to Denmark in 1968, Ruth took a degree in fine arts. They settled in Oxford for 20 years, during which Ruth painted for long periods in Provence, France, and took Open University courses better to understand her husband's work. Professor Lowy finally contracted leukaemia and a year later with his wife committed suicide.

Ingrid LOXTERKAMP 1977– Figurative artist whose work juxtaposed highly controlled brushwork with impasto, reflecting the paradoxes and contrasts of her subjects. A central concern of her pictures was the child-woman of Western culture, innocent but knowing. Loxterkamp graduated in fine art from the University of Wales Institute in Cardiff. She was included in the Summer Show 2003 at Enid Lawson Gallery.

John Samuel LOXTON 1902–1969 (date variations are common) Fluent painter in oil and watercolour, art critic, born in Adelaide, South Australia, who attended the National Gallery of Victoria School in Melbourne and Swinburne Technical College and was much influenced by the style of Harold Herbert. He won several prizes in the 1940s and was art critic for *The Argus* newspaper in Melbourne, 1947–8. The well-illustrated book *The Art of John S Loxton*, which appeared in 1956, helped his reputation and he was appointed president of the Fellowship of Australian Artists, 1961. Loxton made several painting trips to Europe, showing at the RA Summer Exhibition, where he was sought out by Sir William Russell Flint, who introduced him to British artists. The Academy showing led to Loxton's commission to paint pictures for the ship *New Australia*; among other such requests was a series for the British Phosphate Commission. Loxton had a solo show at the Qantas Gallery, London, in 1965, the year he painted landscapes in Norfolk, several of which were included in The East Anglian View, a Bonhams & Brooks sale at Lynford Hall, Mundford, in 2001. Late in life Loxton settled in New Zealand, where he favoured the scenery of South Island, which he died painting. Some years after his death the New Zealand dealer Graham Chote acquired the Loxton estate, seeking to promote the artist locally and in his native country. Fisher's Fine Arts Gallery, Christchurch, New Zealand, organised a Loxton show "from the artist's own private collection," in 1995. Australian state and provincial galleries hold examples.

Edward LOXTON KNIGHT 1905–1993 Painter in watercolour and tempera, printmaker and poster designer, born and lived in Long Eaton, Nottinghamshire/Derbyshire. At Long Eaton Grammar School Loxton Knight (he signed work with this, his surname; he is sometimes wrongly listed in reference books under Knight) was taught and greatly influenced by Samuel Clegg, grandfather of the actor Richard and broadcaster/naturalist David Attenborough. Then studied under Joseph Else at Nottingham School of Art, 1924–9. Was elected a member of the Colour Gravure Society, RBA, PS and RI and exhibited with the New Group and extensively elsewhere in Britain and abroad. Solo exhibitions included Brook Street Gallery, Chapel Bar Gallery in Nottingham and Carl Fischer Gallery, New York. Nottingham Castle Museum and public collections in Wanganui, New Zealand, Derby, Hull and Bolton hold examples. Died in Vicarage Nursing Home, Long Eaton. A memorial show at Erewash Museum in 1994 resulted in a large oil being bought for the collection with support from Victoria & Albert Museum.

Clarisse LOXTON PEACOCK 1928–2004 Painter, notable for her still lifes, a native of Budapest, Hungary. She studied at Budapest University, was for four years at Chelsea School of Art, then did a two-year postgraduate course at St Martin's School of Art followed by two more at Central School of Art. She sold early pictures from Young Contemporaries to Walker Art Gallery in Liverpool and to San Francisco Museum of Art. Also showed at RA, RBA, Leicester Galleries, Lefevre Gallery and Paris Salon, where she gained Gold and Silver Medals and an Hon. Mention. Her first husband was Grantley Loxton Peacock; her second husband was Sir Anthony Grover; her third husband Sir James Dunnett, for a time Permanent Under-Secretary of State at the Ministry of Defence. Had many solo exhibitions, including Cadogan Contemporary, 1988, the year the Hungarian government offered her a show at the Budapest Spring Festival. Many private and public collections around the world hold her pictures. Lived in London, her house notable for the display of her own paintings and her huge collection of eighteenth-century porcelain birds.

Katherine LUBAR 1969– Painter whose work included hard-edged geometrical abstracts, born in Washington, America, who attended Arts Magnet High School for the Performing and Visual Arts, Dallas, 1987; graduated in music and art from Meadows School of Fine Arts at Southern Methodist University, Dallas, 1993; and obtained a postgraduate diploma in paintings from City and Guilds of London Art School, London, 1999. Among Lubar's many group shows were Mermaid Conference Centre and The October Showcase at The Candid Gallery, both 1999; Recent Graduates, New Ashgate Gallery, Farnham, 2000; Fresh Art, Business Design Centre, Islington, 2001; and Art for Youth at Mall Galleries and New Constructivists inaugural exhibition, Cotton's Atrium, Cotton's Centre, both 2002. Among solo exhibitions were Unchain My Art, Sable Gallery, Edinburgh, 2000, Images of Light, Stables Gallery, 2002, and Broken Space, at Signatures Gallery Ltd, 2005, with another, Positive/Negative at Square One Gallery in that year, plus Atmospheric Perspectives, Broughton Gallery, Scotland, 2006. Commissions included a screen graphic for Vodafone, 2001. Lived in London.

Jan LUBELSKI 1922–1995 Sculptor, noted for portraits and animals, born in Poznań, Poland, son of the sculptor Mieczysław Lubelski. He was partly educated in Poland, in Germany and in Scotland, where he worked under the sculptor Benno Elkan, 1940–1, also assisting the art bronze founder Giovanni Fiorini. He was included in a War Artists' Exhibition at National Gallery, having served in the Polish branch of the Royal Air Force, 1941–5. Studied at Regent Street Polytechnic School of Art, 1945–6; at Slade School of Fine Art, 1946–9, under A H Gerrard, the sculptor; then at London University's Institute of Education, 1950–1. Showed at RA, Fine Art Society, Walker's Galleries and elsewhere. St Gabriel's College and notable private collections in Britain and abroad held Lubelski's work. Lived in London, but died while swimming off Spain.

Mieczysław LUBELSKI 1886–1965 Sculptor in varied materials, including bronze, sandstone and marble, born in Warsaw, Poland, father of the sculptor Jan Lubelski. He studied at School of Fine Arts, Warsaw, under Dunikowski, and in Berlin at Akademische Hochschule für Bildende Künste and Meisterschule. He gained the silver medal of the Academy of Fine Arts, Berlin, 1914; gold medal at National Exhibition in Poznań, 1928; and Polish Air Force Medal, 1949. After World War II he spent some years in England, living at Kew Gardens, Surrey. Lubelski specialised in religious statues, but his works also included the Kosciuszko Monument in Łódź, Poland, 1931; Saper Monument in Warsaw, 1933; and the Polish War Memorial, London.

Victoria LUBY 1973– Painter of small, fantastical pictures in which animals and other sometimes oddly sized characters inhabited surreal landscapes. Born in London, Luby studied at Camberwell College of Art, gaining a first-class degree at Edinburgh College of Art, 1998. Exhibited at the Barbican Centre, RIBA and Royal College of Physicians, with a solo show at Highgate Fine Art in 1999.

Caroline LUCAS fl. c.1930–1967 Painter, sculptor and printmaker. Studied art in Paris, Rome and London, John Skeaping being one of her teachers. Showed in Paris, paintings at the Lefevre Gallery in 1934 and sculpture at the Leicester Galleries in 1939. With her sister Frances Byng-Stamper, Caroline Lucas had been closely associated with the founding of the CASW in the 1930s. In the 1940s and 1950s they ran Miller's Gallery and Press in Lewes, Sussex (featured in an exhibition at the Towner Art Gallery, Eastbourne, 1989). At Miller's these formidable ladies showed Caroline Lucas' work as well as that of the Bloomsbury artists Duncan Grant and Vanessa Bell, David Jones and the Roberts Colquhoun and MacBryde. Among prints published by the Miller's Press was a portfolio of six lithographs of Lewes and Brighton, some of Caroline Lucas' most accomplished work. Cedric Morris painted a singular portrait of the two sisters which he nicknamed "The Upper Classes". They died within a few months of each other, in retirement at Shelley's Hotel, Lewes.

Denis LUCAS 1918– Painter and teacher, brother of the artist Keith Stephen Lucas. He studied at Beckenham School of Art and Royal College of Art and gained a travelling scholarship in 1949. Taught at Ravensbourne, St Martin's School of Art and Royal Academy Schools. City of Plymouth Museums & Art Gallery holds his work and a portrait of Lucas by Stephen Bullard was included in Belgrave Gallery's exhibition Camberwell Artists of the 40s and 50s, 1988. Lived in Beckenham, Kent.

Keith Stephen LUCAS 1924– Painter, draughtsman, teacher and administrator, born in Beckenham, Kent. He studied at Beckenham School of Art and the Royal College of Art, his teachers including Henry Carr, Carel Weight and Kenneth Rowntree. After teaching at Liverpool and Leeds Colleges of Art, 1951–7, Lucas became involved with design for film and television, 1957–65, returning to Royal College of Art, 1965–72, where he was professor of film and television. From 1972–9, he was director of the British Film Institute, then from 1980–8 was head of the school of film and television for Christ Church College, Canterbury, after this painting full-time. Exhibitions included Sally Hunter Fine Art, Metropole Arts Centre in Folkestone and Neville Gallery, Canterbury. Lucas worked in the traditional English landscape style, having a special concern with light. His brother was the painter Denis Lucas. Lived at Bishopsbourne, Kent.

Marjorie Ashworth LUCAS 1911– Artist in copper and wood engraving and silk drawing (embroidery), and teacher, born in Yorkshire. She studied at Royal College of Art engraving school, teachers including Malcolm Osborne and Robert Austin. Until her marriage Lucas made entomological drawings for the Natural History Museum, did book illustration for Methuen and part-time teaching. After marriage in 1938 she lived in Scotland, first in Galloway, then Edinburgh, her husband being the artist Murray Tod. She showed with him at the Scottish and Hanover Galleries in Edinburgh and at the Dumfries Arts Festival. She was a member of Society of Artist Printmakers from 1935 and of SSA from 1946, also taking part in group shows at RA, RSA, Walker Art Gallery in Liverpool and elsewhere, including overseas. Had several solo exhibitions at Scottish Gallery, also showing one-man at Torrance Gallery, Edinburgh. City of Liverpool Public Libraries holds bookplates by her.

Pauline LUCAS 1938– Painter in oil and mixed media, printmaker, teacher and writer, born in Redditch, Worcestershire, who originally worked under her maiden name Pauline van Meeteren. Her mother's family was artistically talented, Lucas's maternal grandfather, Thomas Donnelly, being a stained glass artist with John Hardman, in Birmingham. In 1960 Lucas graduated in fine art from

University of Reading School of Art under Anthony Betts, in 1992 gaining her master's in art criticism at City University, under John Elson and Eric Moody. She taught part-time at the Open University, colleges and polytechnics and adult courses for Nottingham University. Curated several exhibitions, including the Angel Row, Nottingham, 1993–4 tour for Evelyn Gibbs, whose biography, *Evelyn Gibbs Artist and Traveller*, 2001, she wrote. Lucas was a founder-member of Nottingham Feminist Arts Group, later known as Visible Women, 1979–88, and of Nottingham Artists' Group studios, 1982, and was a committee member of the National Artists' Association, 1990–4. Illustrated books for Shoestring Press. From 1979–84, produced paintings of businessmen and anti-war pictures, later a series based on Palestinian women in Gaza camps. Mixed shows included Three Visible Women, Piece Hall Gallery, Halifax, 1988, and Five Artists, Laographiko Museum, Aegina, Greece, 2002. Among solo exhibitions was Nottingham Playhouse, 1990. Lived in Beeston, Nottingham.

Sarah LUCAS 1962– Artist, born in London, who studied at London College of Printing, 1983–4, graduating with honours from Goldsmiths' College, 1984–7. Took part in group exhibitions at The Showroom, 1986; Freeze, at PLA Building, 1988; East Country Yard, Surrey Docks, 1990; Karsten Schubert and Barbara Gladstone Gallery, New York, both 1992; Young British Artists II, Saatchi Gallery, 1993, which holds her work; and Hayward Gallery tour The British Art Show 5, 2000–1. Solo shows included The Whole Joke, 1992, at 8 Kingly Street, and a career survey at Tate Liverpool, 2005–6. The female body as a subject of popular culture, slang and graffiti were features of Lucas' art.

Suzanne LUCAS 1915– Painter and miniaturist in watercolour, born in Calcutta, India. She was of English and French nationality. Lucas attended Roedean School, then travelled extensively in Europe. Studied at universities in Grenoble, Edinburgh and Munich and at Reimer Schule art school in Berlin, 1935. Lived in Egypt – where she began painting on ivory – and France for long periods. Returned to England in 1954, having a first solo show in that year at Cooling Galleries. Developed a passion for toadstools, discovering new varieties, becoming a noted expert and writing on them. In 1992 published a lavish volume, *In Praise of Toadstools*, with her own illustration. Lucas was founder-president of the Society of Botanical Artists, president of RMS and a fellow of the Linnean and Royal Horticultural Societies, winning that Society's Gold Medal over a dozen times and the Grenfell Medal several times. Franklin Mint and Post Office commissioned her work. Showed at RA, RI, Paris Salon and elsewhere. Solo exhibitions included two at Mall Galleries, 1975–9, and Liberty's, 1977. British Museum and Natural History Museum hold examples. Lived at Mere, Warminster, Wiltshire.

Sydney Seymour LUCAS 1888–1954 Portrait painter and illustrator, son of the artist John Seymour Lucas, with whom he collaborated on historical works. Sydney studied at the Royal Academy Schools and in the studio of the sculptor Sir Alfred Gilbert. Exhibited RA, 1909–51, also at RP, RSA, and settled in Walberswick, Suffolk.

Paul LUCKY 1956– Stained glass artist who was born in London and studied at Swansea College of Art. In 1982 he formed the Stained Glass Design Partnership with Susan Bradbury which completed windows in public buildings throughout the United Kingdom. He was a fellow of the British Society of Master Glass Painters and was based in Kilmaurs, Kilmarnock, Ayrshire.

Leila LUDDINGTON fl. c.1930–1965 Watercolourist, born in Aldershot, Hampshire, of a military family. She studied under Henry Tonks at Slade School of Fine Art and at Académie Julian, in Paris. Showed at SWA, Arts Council, NEAC, RI, WIAC and elsewhere. Lived near Saffron Walden, Essex.

LUGOW: *see* **Lucienne GOW**

John LUKE 1906–1975 Painter, born in Belfast, where he finally lived. Luke was fond of working in tempera with a resin-oil varnish; his pictures are often highly coloured with a dramatic and unusual quality. Studied at the School of Art, Belfast, with the mural painter Ivor Beaumont, 1923–7, at the Slade School of Fine Art, 1927–30, under Henry Tonks, and at the Westminster School of Art, 1930–1, with Walter Bayes. Luke won a number of prizes and scholarships and continued his studies privately in museums and galleries in London and Paris. Exhibited Leger and Redfern Galleries, UA, RHA and in America. Queen's University, Belfast, and Belfast Museum and Art Gallery hold his work. Arts Council of Northern Ireland retrospective in 1978.

Edna LUMB 1931–1992 Painter, draughtsman, printmaker and teacher, born in Leeds, Yorkshire. Won a scholarship to Leeds Junior Art School aged 14, another taking her to Leeds College of Art, 1948–53, during which she won a travelling scholarship to France, 1951. Taught unenthusiastically, 1953–64, then – with typical steely determination – decided to paint full-time, buying a van for her trips. She found her own subject in industry, depicting machinery technically meticulously, but tinged with poetry. She believed "the excitement I feel about mills, factories, quarries, machinery, sewers and industrial constructions can enable people to see beauty in the drama of components and power." Her 1973 Bradford Industrial Museum show Components of Power won much acclaim. Commissions poured in from such bodies as Laing Properties, National Audit Office, Sir Alfred McAlpine & Company and the Science Museum, where a solo show was running when she died. Lumb made three trips to West Africa: in 1969 Joint Church Aid asked her to record the Biafran airlift; in 1976 Catholic Relief Services commissioned her to record drought relief in Upper Volta; and in 1977 she worked in Nigeria recording Caterpillar Tractor Company's land development. Her pictures always sold rapidly, and many private and public collections – including Bradford Art Galleries and Museums, Science Museum, Manchester City Art Galleries and National Railway Museum, York – hold her work. Bradford Industrial Museum held a retrospective in 1991, Leeds City Art Gallery a memorial show in 1992–3. Lived in London.

Patrick LUMB 1966– Painter and teacher, born in Bournemouth, Hampshire, who studied at Central School of Art & Design; Falmouth School of Art; and Art Institute of Chicago school of art. He was a founder-member of Woodend Studio Association in Manchester, 1987; was head painter and art director for Too Cute in Los Angeles,

1989–90; then taught at Oakham School, Rutland, in 1994 being exhibition organiser for the Oakham Festival. In 1989 Lumb was a prize winner at MAFA Open. Group exhibitions included Young Contemporaries at Whitworth Art Gallery in Manchester, 1987; Mercury Art Gallery, 1989; The New Van Straaten Gallery, Chicago, 1992; and Leicester City Art Gallery and Royal Over-Seas League Open, both 1994.

Alexandra LUMLEY 1958– Painter, notably of landscape and seascapes, usually in a mix of watercolour and gouache; graphic and theatre designer; and teacher. She was born in Essex and studied at Camberwell School of Arts and Crafts, 1977–80, becoming a principal lecturer at Camberwell College of Arts. Completed a mosaic sign for Homerton Hospital commissioned by the Public Art & Development Trust. Took part in numerous group shows, including Thackeray Gallery, 1983; Laing Competition, Mall Galleries, 1985; and RWS Open, Bankside Gallery, 1989. Elected RBA and won John Adams Fine Art Award, both 1997. Solo shows included Austin/Desmond Fine Art, 1982, and New Grafton Gallery from 1986.

Alan LUMSDEN 1937– Artist, notably a printmaker, and teacher, born in Aldershot, Hampshire, as Richard Alan Lumsden. He attended the Technical High School in Cheltenham, 1949–53, then the art school there, 1953–7, and after National Service in the Middle East was at London University Institute of Education, 1959–60. Teaching included Chester School of Art. Exhibitions included Nottingham and Leeds Playhouses, Pictures for Schools at RA and WAC tour The Probity of Art, 1980. Many public galleries, including Dudley, Doncaster, Hull, Nottingham and Sunderland, hold examples. Lived in Bersham, near Wrexham, Clwyd.

Ernest LUMSDEN 1883–1948 Printmaker, painter, teacher and writer, born in London, he married the artist Mabel Royds. Because of poor health Lumsden had to abandon an ambition to go to sea, so aged 15 he entered the University College art department at Reading, five years later studying briefly at Académie Julian, Paris. Back in London he taught himself to etch so well that in 1907 examples were shown at the Paris Salon; a year later he had his first solo exhibition at Arcade Studio, Reading. A 1908 summons from Frank Morley Fletcher to teach at Edinburgh College of Art started his lifelong association with Scotland. Lumsden began to exhibit widely and to travel in several continents, so that in 1912 he left teaching and travelled to India, a country which he loved and which he depicted wonderfully in etching and aquatint. Lumsden and his wife lived and worked in India, 1917–19; he had gone there to join the Indian Army, but was rejected and got a military post censoring telegrams. Returned to Edinburgh, Lumsden made a good living from etchings until the slump, when he set up as a portrait painter, noted for his unwillingness to flatter sitters. In 1925 he published *The Art of Etching*, a standard text. Lumsden was elected RE in 1915, in 1929 became president of the Society of Artist Printmakers and became RSA in 1933. His work is in the Tate Gallery, Scottish National Gallery of Modern Art, British Museum, Victoria & Albert Museum and many foreign holdings.

James LUMSDEN 1964– Artist, designer and illustrator, born in Inverness, who studied graphic design at Cardonald, Glasgow, 1983–5; was an illustrator and graphic designer in Glasgow, 1986–8; from 1989 working in WASPS Studios, Edinburgh. Awards included Hope Scott Trust Award, 1992 and 1994, and Edinburgh District Arts Council Award; and The Scottish International Education Trusts Award, 1996. Group shows included Scottish Drawing Biennial, Paisley Art Gallery, from 1989; 12 Scottish Artists, Payne Gallery, Bethlehem, Pennsylvania, 1993; and the Gulbenkian Suite, Highland Printmakers, Inverness, 1995. Had a solo exhibition, Dilemma, at Citizens Studios, Edinburgh, 1992, later ones including Seduction, Compass Gallery, Glasgow, 1996. An exploration of the nature of symbols was a key feature of Lumsden's work, which was in the Highland Regional Council, Inverness Museum & Art Gallery and Gulbenkian Foundation collections.

Rachel LUMSDEN 1968– Painter and teacher, born in Newcastle upon Tyne, Northumberland, who graduated in fine art from Trent Polytechnic, 1987–91, gaining her master's in painting, Royal Academy Schools, 1995–8, taking part in the final year show. While at the Schools she was co-organiser of "Red Square" Contemporary Art Forum in 1997. Lumsden held a residency and taught at Rawlins Community College, 1994; taught, Dunstable College, 1995; won the Landseer Award and David Murray Scholarship, both 1998; then the Pollock-Krasner Award, 2000. Group shows included Estate, Osterley House, 1999, and Paint!, Vertigo, 2000. Had solo exhibitions at Rivington Gallery, 1999, and Arc-light, Spitz Gallery, then Bridlesmith Gate Gallery, Nottingham, both 2001, which used lampshades as a starting-point. Crestco Ltd and private collections in Britain and abroad held examples. Lived in London and St Gallen, Switzerland.

Alice M M LUNAN 1883–1981 Artist and teacher who studied at Glasgow School of Art, 1903–14. In 1912, Lunan began teaching at Hutchesons' Grammar School, where she stayed until 1946, although this long service was interrupted by periods of nursing. She served with the Voluntary Aid Detachment in World War I, being a Red Cross commandant in World War II. Lunan joined the Glasgow Society of Lady Artists in 1914 and was its secretary, 1949–55. She showed with the Royal Glasgow Institute of the Fine Arts and RSA. Died in Glasgow.

Augustus LUNN 1905–1986 A key figure in the revival of tempera painting in Britain, muralist, draughtsman and teacher, H Augustus Lunn became a student of Kingston School of Art, winning a scholarship to Royal College of Art when William Rothenstein was principal. Won the Edward Abbey Mural Scholarship. Lunn joined the staff at Kingston, but also restored murals – for example, at Marlborough House – and carried out commissions for original murals. As an easel painter his output was small but of high quality. He showed at NEAC, Cooling Galleries, LG, RA and elsewhere, but did not have a solo show until that at Michael Parkin's Gallery in 1985. Lunn admired the work of Giorgio de Chirico and Fernand Léger, and a strongly Surrealist element is present in much of his output, as well as a tendency towards abstraction. He said: "I am never interested in recording a scene. I want to reconstruct."

Dora LUNN: *see* **Dora HEDGES**

Graham LUPP 1946– Painter and teacher, born in Bathurst, New South Wales, Australia, who graduated in architecture at University of Sydney, 1964–9. After foundation studies in England at Ealing Technical College, 1972–3, he graduated with honours from Hornsey College of Art, 1973–6, gaining his master's at Chelsea School of Art, 1977. Showed widely in London and Australia and carried out a number of commissions, including Parliament House and the Chinese Embassy in Canberra.

Lewis Frederick LUPTON 1909–1996 Painter, designer and illustrator, born and lived in London. He attended Sheffield College of Art, 1923–30, with Anthony Betts and Eric Jones, then at Westminster School of Art with Bernard Meninsky and Mark Gertler. Lupton was employed as an illustrator, 1933–40; from 1941–50 worked on exhibition design; from 1950–60 being engaged on Christian literature for the Scripture Union and others. From 1960 Lupton's main interest was the self-publication of a multi-volume *History of the Geneva Bible* in his own calligraphy and with his illustrations. Oxford University Press, Odhams Press and the publisher Macmillan all reproduced his work. He showed at RA, LG, Leger and Redfern Galleries. With his artist wife Joan, Lupton held exhibitions at their own gallery and in the provinces. At Lupton House he completed a large painted ceiling. Bradford City Art Gallery holds his work.

Peter LUTHER 1926– Figurative painter, much admired by his peers, such as Conroy Maddox, born in Sussex. He studied at Hammersmith School of Art and the Working Men's College. Had a series of solo exhibitions at John Whibley Gallery, the fourth being in 1972.

John M LUXMOORE 1912– Carver in wood who studied at Cambridge University. Exhibited RA and in the provinces in the north of England. Lived at Altrincham, Cheshire.

Doris E LUXTON 1908– Painter and teacher, born in Exeter, Devon. She attended Truro Art School under Arthur Jackson and taught there for several years in the late 1920s. Showed widely in the West Country and had a series of one-man shows at Burton Art Gallery in Bideford, Devon, where she lived.

Henry LUYKEN 1892– Painter, architect and printmaker, born in London. After education at Northern Polytechnic he studied at Camden School of Art and Southend-on-Sea School of Art where his teachers included Emerson Groom the etcher and the engraver and watercolourist Charles William Taylor. RWS Club member. Showed mainly in London. Lived in Leigh-on-Sea, Essex.

Len LYE 1901–1980 Film-maker, kinetic sculptor, painter, genetic theorist and experimental writer, born in Christchurch, New Zealand. Lye moved to Sydney, Australia, in 1921, where he acquired animation techniques working for a commercial film company. After time on Pacific islands, he worked his sea passage to England where he met the artists Eric Kennington and Ben Nicholson and writers Robert Graves and Laura Riding. Lye lived on a barge on the Thames, 1927–30, in 1928 being elected a member of the Seven and Five Society, contributing sculpture, constructions and Batik paintings until 1934. Graves' and Riding's Seizin Press published *No Trouble*, a selection of Lye's letters, in 1930; he designed book covers for Seizin and Hours Press (Paris), 1930–1. Lye's first film, *Tusalava*, had been screened in 1929, and four years later he began experiments with direct techniques of painting and scratching on film, using such implements as a hairpin. *Colour Box*, his first such production, was released by the G(eneral)P(ost)O(ffice) Film Unit in 1935, one of several Lye films they sponsored. In World War II Lye directed films for the Ministry of Information and similarly for the *March of Time* documentaries. Emigrated to America in 1944. There until his death he continued work to develop a theory of art, a concern since 1936; in 1951 Lye returned to experimental film-making, using shadowgraph techniques; and in 1958 took up kinetic sculpture. His Tangible Motion Sculpture was presented at the Museum of Modern Art in 1961, the first of many inclusions in major sculpture and kinetic art shows. In 1965 Lye had his first solo exhibition at Howard Wise Gallery, New York. Lye resumed painting in 1977, the year he returned to oversee installation of an exhibition of his work at Govett-Brewster Art Gallery, New Plymouth, New Zealand. It holds a repository of Len Lye's output, as do American public galleries, and The Len Lye Foundation is based in New Plymouth. Camden Arts Centre showed his experimental abstract films in 1999. He died in Warwick, New York.

Berit LYELL 1938– Architect and artist, whose output included still life, landscape and nudes in oil and watercolour. Berit Wildhagen Lyell was born in Oslo, Norway, and studied at Arkitekt Stud, Oslo, and Marlborough School of Art, Chelsea. She practised professionally as Berit Wildhagen Arkitekts and was married to the architect Michael Lyell. Took part in group and mixed shows in Oslo and London, having solo exhibitions in Oslo and in London with W H Patterson and Noel Oddy Fine Art. The Norwegian state oil company Statoil owned her work. She was based in London and Høvik, Norway.

Francis LYMBURNER 1916–1972 Painter and draughtsman, notable for his delicate drawings of animals. He was born in Brisbane, Australia, and died in Sydney. Studied at Brisbane Central Technical College under Martyn Roberts, won the Mosman Prize in 1951 and showed widely in Australia. For about a decade from the early 1950s Lymburner was based in England, where he exhibited with the Australian Artists' Association. Australian state galleries hold examples.

John Langtry LYNAS 1879–1956 Painter, sculptor and illustrator, born in Greenock, Renfrewshire, his parents having Ulster origins. They moved there when he was still small. He attended the Model School in Belfast, spent a short time at Belfast School of Art and in his mid-twenties, without adequate resources, embarked on a trip through Europe and was later said to have studied art in London and Paris. In Belfast did a variety of jobs such as building and signwriting to support self and family. Exhibited at RHA, RUA and at Belfast Museum and Art Gallery. Magee's Gallery gave him a solo show in 1939, CEMA in 1952. Among books illustrated by Lynas was *Why*, published in 1935. Ulster Museum holds his self-portrait. The Ulster critic John Hewitt remembered Lynas as "that diminutive rowdy ... forever creating a scene and stumping out in a temper" at exhibitions, "his few pictures in conté crayon the aborted sprouts of his vast imaginings."

James LYNCH 1956– Painter and illustrator, born in Hitchin, Hertfordshire, who grew up in Devizes, Wiltshire. He was married to the artist Kate Lynch. After gaining a graphic design diploma at Swindon, 1974–6, he began painting professionally. In 1983 he gained an Elizabeth Greenshields Foundation bursary; in 1986 won The Pimm's Prize Award for watercolour at the RA Summer Exhibition; and in 1993 a *Spectator* Art Award prize, exhibited in Edinburgh and London. Lynch was well known for his paintings of farm animals, other themes being interiors and latterly visionary landscapes of the West Country. In 1989 he was commissioned by the National Trust Foundation for Art to paint Bonnie, the Longhorn Cow, on permanent exhibition at Wimpole Hall, Cambridge. Pandora, Red Devon Cow at Kingston Lacy, Dorset, was a 1993 National Trust Foundation commission for permanent exhibition at Kingston Lacy. The Folio Society commissioned illustrations for Kenneth Grahame's *The Wind in the Willows*, published 1995, followed in 1999 by another National Trust Foundation commission to illustrate Winston Churchill's animals for Chartwell, Kent. Lynch exhibited at art fairs in London and Bath from the early 1980s; in the 1989 National Trust Foundation Salute to Turner exhibition at Agnew; in The Broad Horizon there and in the Singer & Friedlander/ *Sunday Times* Watercolour Competition, both 1990; Critics' Choice, New British Art, Christie's, 1993; and there in the National Trust Foundation Centenary Exhibition, 1995. Among Lynch's solo shows were Linfield Galleries, Bradford-on-Avon, from 1982; Nevill Gallery, Bath, from 1984; Odette Gilbert Gallery, 1988; Maas Gallery, from 1991; retrospective, National Trust Foundation, Mompesson House, Salisbury, 1998; and Alpha House Gallery, Sherborne, 2000. The Maas Gallery 2006 Lynch exhibition was accompanied by the limited-edition book *Skylines*. Notable private collections holding his work include Chatsworth and Longleat. Lived in High Ham, Somerset.

James F LYNCH 1932– Painter and teacher who obtained his diploma at Camberwell School of Art and teacher's certificate at Goldsmiths' College. After National Service taught in preparatory and public schools, notably at The Downs School, Colwall, following Maurice Feild and Unity Spencer; after part-time teaching at Stoke-on-Trent College of Art and a period as head of Art at Bedford Modern School, he took early retirement in 1984 to paint full-time, in England and Morocco. Group shows included the RA Summer Exhibition; The Scottish Gallery (Aitken Dott), in Edinburgh; 1969 John Moores Liverpool Exhibition; Four Counties Open, in Milton Keynes, where he was a prize winner; Partners in Art, tour organised by Bedford Education Service; NEAC; and RWA. Among his solo exhibitions were The Gallery, Wellingborough, Dan Sullivan's Gallery in Bedford and Rooksmoor Gallery, Bath. After in 1992 moving to Bath, Somerset, Lynch exhibited as James, to avoid confusion with another West Country artist.

Kate LYNCH 1949– Artist and teacher, married to the painter James Lynch. Gained an honours degree in the history of art at Essex University, 1975, followed by a postgraduate diploma in fine art at Bristol Polytechnic, 1992. Lynch taught at Devizes School and Bath High School from 1977-1980. She then ran various art and community projects in the West Country. She is a member of the RWA and was awarded the Black Swan Prize for Painting in 1992 and Bath and West Painting Prize in 1998. Her collection of paintings documenting the willow growers and basket makers on the Somerset Levels toured nationally, winning awards from South West Arts and Wessex Water. The resulting book was entitled *Willow: Paintings and Drawings with Somerset Voices*. She had solo exhibitions at Beaux Art, Bath in the 1990s, East Lambrook Manor in 2001 and 2004, as well as Rural Life Museum, Glastonbury, Brewhouse, Taunton, Platform Gallery, Clitheroe and Norfolk Rural Life Museum in 2003. Lived at High Ham, Somerset.

Kaye LYNCH 1949– Draughtsman, watercolourist and designer. She studied at Exeter College of Art and Glasgow School of Art and went on to run a small craft business, for which she did designs. She also found time to make intricate drawings based on her own domestic circumstances. Lynch won a number of awards: in 1972 the Benno Schotz Travel Award; 10 years later the Glasgow Lady Artists' Trust Fund Award and a Scottish Arts Council Major Bursary. She took part in many group shows, including Royal Glasgow Institute of the Fine Arts; Project Arts Centre, Dublin; and Talbot Rice Art Centre, Edinburgh. Solo shows included Arts Council Gallery, Edinburgh; Carlisle Museum and Art Gallery; and Skelmersdale Art Gallery. She was included in The Compass Contribution, Tramway, Glasgow, 1990.

Michael LYNE 1912–1989 Sporting artist in oil, watercolour and line, and writer, full name Charles Edward Michael Lyne. He was born in Upton Bishop, Herefordshire, son of a country parson. Rejected the idea of becoming a vet or a farmer, instead studying for short time at Cheltenham School of Art. Initially he worked in watercolour and body colour, but between late 1940s and 1970s concentrated on oils, producing hunting subjects in rich colours, culminating in a notable series on the Grand National. Hunted his own pack of beagles, the United Cotswold, also with otter-hounds and with over 40 packs of foxhounds in England, Ireland and America. Wrote and illustrated a number of books, including *Horse, Hounds and Country*; *A Parson's Son*; and *From Litter to Later On*. Lived near Fairford in Gloucestershire.

Bob LYNN 1940– Versatile artist and teacher, born in Scotland, who used a rich palette and whose work had a strong abstract element. He attended Edinburgh College of Art, 1958–62, then taught in Scotland and London, 1963–7. After studying enamelling as a mural technique under Stefan Knapp, 1968–9, Lynn won a scholarship to Poland, 1970. From 1971–80 he lived between the west of Ireland and London, moved to Ireland permanently in 1980 and in 1984 settled in Wicklow. Lynn was closely involved in the Éigse Carlow Arts Festival for periods from 1994; had a residency at the Cill Rialaig Project, Kerry, and was awarded Art Flight, Arts Council of Ireland, both in 1995; was a tutor at Centro d'Arte Dedalo, Tuscany, Italy, in 1996; and at O'Neill's Burren Painting Centre, County Clare, 1998–03. In 2000 he was made a member of Leinster Print Making Studio, in 2003 of Graphic Print Making Studio. He took part in numerous group exhibitions and had a series of solo shows, including Solomon Gallery, Dublin, from 1995; Mermaid Arts Centre, Bray, 2002; Riverbank Art Centre, Newbridge, and Dyehouse Gallery, Waterford, both 2003; and Recent Paintings, Tom Caldwell Gallery, Belfast, 2004. Many corporate collections in Ireland and Britain held examples.

Peter LYON 1926– Sculptor, designer, writer and teacher who attended Bryanston School, where he studied sculpture with Willi Soukop; Oxford University; and Edinburgh College of Art, studying sculpture with Eric Schilsky. After service in Royal Navy minesweepers became a freelance sculptor and designer in 1953. Was married to the artist Toby Lyon. Was a senior lecturer at Central School of Art & Design, 1969–85, also teaching at other schools including West Sussex College of Art part-time. Published *Design in Jewellery* and wrote articles for *The Observer, The Guardian, Yorkshire Post, Apollo* and other publications. Was also consultant design director to the Bonas Group, 1969–74, design consultant for films on gold and silver work and did judging, including Hunting Group national art competition in 1988 and 1991. Solo exhibitions included Upper Grosvenor Gallery. Did much commissioned work, including sculptures for Kingsway Hall; Stevenage New Town centre and Park Town Gardens, Oxford, both competition winners; Cambridge University engineering department; entrance sculpture for Churchill College, Cambridge; and sculpture beside Gertrude Jekyll water garden, Vann, Surrey. Had a London studio and lived in Lymington, Hampshire.

Robert LYON 1894–1978 Artist, mural painter and teacher. Born in Liverpool, he studied art at the Royal College of Art and the British School at Rome, 1924. He became lecturer in fine art and master of painting at King's College, Newcastle upon Tyne, 1932. For eight years from 1934 Lyon was tutor to the Ashington Group of spare-time Northumberland miner artists, one of the most remarkable of such groups to emerge in the inter-war years. From 1942–60 Lyon was principal of Edinburgh College of Art. He exhibited RA, RBA, RP and in the provinces. Also painted murals for Western General Hospital, Edinburgh, and King's College Hospital dental department. Lived at Rushlake Green, Sussex.

Thomas Bonar LYON 1873–1955 Painter, etcher and teacher, who attended Glasgow School of Art and Royal College of Art, winning a number of awards, then studied widely on the continent. He was supervisor of art in schools for Ayrshire Education Authority, taught art at Irvine Royal Academy and Ayr Academy, living in Ayr. Lyon was a member of Glasgow Art Club, president of Ayr Sketch Club and exhibited at RSA, Royal Glasgow Institute of the Fine Arts, RSW and Paris Salon. Was also a keen amateur cellist. Cyril Gerber Fine Art included his oil Low Tide, Dunure, in First of the Summer Wine in 2000.

Toby LYON 1926–1990 Painter, born into a peripatetic military family in Birmingham. Aged 14, as Colleen McCormick, she enrolled at the St Ives School of Painting. Exhibited at Portal Gallery, in the Netherlands and Germany and was widely collected in America. She was married to the sculptor Peter Lyon, her daughter Charlotte and son Jasper also being artists. Her childhood spent partly in Bexhill-on-Sea, the Sussex seaside resort, was a great inspiration for her gently humorous, naïve pictures. Died in Cambridge.

Elizabeth LYONS 1937–1994 Painter and draughtsman whose work was figurative with strong abstract elements; teacher. Born in London, she had a lifelong ambition to go to art college, attending evening classes in life drawing and painting. She founded a company making and designing horse-drawn carriages for world-class driving, winning a gold cup at Windsor for excellent design and craftsmanship. Lyons studied at Ravensbourne College of Art, 1977–8, then gained a first-class honours degree at Falmouth College of Art, 1978–81. From 1988–91 she was artist-in-residence and visiting lecturer in Tuscany, Falmouth and Goldsmiths' Colleges of Art; in 1990–2 was at New York International School of Art, Todi, Italy; and in 1992 at Geoffrey Humphries Studio, Venice. She took part in group shows at RA and Falmouth Art Gallery, 1982; Jablonski Gallery, 1986; LG from 1989, and elsewhere. Had a solo show at Ripley Art Centre in 1983, later ones including Woodlands Art Gallery, 1986–8, and Art Space Gallery, 1989–92, with a memorial show in 1996.

John LYONS 1933– Painter, poet, writer and teacher, born in Port of Spain, Trinidad. Moved to London and studied at Goldsmiths' College School of Art, 1959–64, and at the University of Newcastle upon Tyne's art department, 1964–5. Myths and folklore were a feature of Lyons' pictures, as seen in The Caribbean Connection, at Islington Arts Factory, 1995. Other mixed shows included Edison Galerie, The Hague, 1982; Art Works, Manchester Polytechnic, 1985; and Harris Museum & Art Gallery, Preston, 1991. Solo exhibitions included Huddersfield Art Gallery and tour, 1992. Lyons' paintings were conditioned to an extent by his work as a poet and writer, which was included in many anthologies and which won literary prizes. Lyons was appointed external purchaser for the Arts Council Collection, 1987–9, and was a selector for a number of exhibitions. Taught art at Manchester University.

Kieran LYONS 1946– Artist and lecturer, born in Guildford, Surrey, who studied at Bath Academy of Art, 1964–8, and Yale University school of art and architecture, 1968–71. He taught at the University of Auckland in New Zealand and the Fine Art Centre, Belfast, Northern Ireland, and was visiting lecturer at colleges in Dublin, Nova Scotia and at Trent Polytechnic. In 1979 he participated in Serpentine Summer Show 1 while teaching at Newport College of Art. He then offered video and slide performances, his aim being "to create an order within the confusion of opportunities for creative expression that exist around me." Installations and performances included Superimpression, City Art Gallery, Auckland, 1974; Wine and Milk, 2B Butler's Wharf, 1975; Monkey's Magic Mainstay, Fine Art Centre, Belfast, 1977; and Lies in the Lecture, Arts Council Gallery, Belfast, 1978.

Michael LYONS 1943– Sculptor and teacher, born in Bilston, Staffordshire. Studied at Wolverhampton College of Art, 1959–63, Hornsey College of Art, 1963–4, and University of Newcastle, 1964–7. Became head of sculpture at Manchester Polytechnic, 1989. Exhibitions included Welsh Sculpture Trust's exhibition Sculpture in a Country Park, Margam, 1983, and 1st RWA Open Sculpture Exhibition, 1993. Many of Lyons' works were in welded metal, designed for an outdoor setting where changing light was of key importance. Had a solo show at Hatton Gallery, Newcastle, 1982, later ones including Beaux Arts Gallery, Bath, 1986, and Wingfield College, Eye, 1990. Was elected an associate of RBS in 1992. Commissions included Peace for Manchester City Council, 1985–6, and Portsmouth Polytechnic bronze, 1990. Arts Council and Whitworth Art

Gallery in Manchester hold examples. Lived in Cawood, Yorkshire.

William LYONS-WILSON 1892–1981 Self-taught painter, notably in watercolour, and teacher, born in Leeds, Yorkshire (surname originally Wilson, although he signed work Lyons Wilson, later adopting the hyphenated form). He was strongly influenced by Cotman, Constable and Cézanne. After service in World War I with a West Riding field ambulance unit in France, in 1918 Lyons-Wilson returned to Leeds, having painting holidays with Jacob Kramer, in 1919 marrying and taking up art full-time. Based in Wensleydale, Lyons-Wilson exhibited throughout Yorkshire and became acquainted with the writer J B Priestley and artists Philip Naviasky, Fred Lawson and Richard Eurich, who called Lyons-Wilson the best watercolourist of his time. In 1930 Lyons-Wilson was asked to teach art appreciation, drawing and painting at Sedbergh School, eventually settling there. He was invited by the Cunard Line to supply paintings for their new liner *Berengaria*. In 1938 Lyons-Wilson moved to teach at Blundell's School, sharing his time with King's College, Taunton, retiring from both in 1968. From 1944 Lyons-Wilson developed an interest in abstract and Surrealist paintings, which he showed at the Redfern Gallery. He also exhibited at RA, NEAC, Plymouth Society of Artists, was president of the Somerset Society of Artists, East Devon Art Society and Phoenix Art Club in Tiverton, and vice-president of Tiverton Art Society. Lyons-Wilson was remembered as an inspiring art teacher, an independent spirit and witty raconteur, who had a keen insight into the works of Klee and Miró. Imperial War Museum and Exeter Museum hold his pictures. Lived at Ash Thomas, Devon, dying in Tiverton Hospital.

Damaris LYSAGHT 1956– Representational painter, born in Belfast, Northern Ireland, who grew up near Doneraile, County Cork, in the Irish Republic. She studied in Cork for two years at Crawford Municipal School of Art, then for two more at the National College of Art and Design, Dublin. Lysaght was awarded an Italian Government Scholarship to study in Florence with Nerina Simi. After four years in the Simi Studio she painted full-time, living on a small organic farm near Kanturk, County Cork, with the poet Seamus Hogan. Lysaght participated in numerous group shows in Ireland and abroad, being a regular exhibitor at Lavit Gallery, Cork; Leinster Gallery, Dublin; Wellspring Gallery, Tralee; Kenny Gallery, Galway; and in the RHA Annual Exhibition. Her solo shows included Tom Caldwell Gallery, Dublin, 1987 and 1991; An Cibeal, Kenmare, 1993; Fournier Street, Spitalfields, 1994; Tom Caldwell Gallery, Belfast, 1996 and 2005; The Bleddfa Centre, Wales, 1998; and Joan Clancy Gallery, Ring, Dungarvan, 2003.

Anthony LYSYCIA 1959– Artist and photographer, born in Chorley, Lancashire. He studied at Preston Polytechnic, 1978–81; Royal College of Art, 1981–4; then in 1984–5 was Rome Scholar in Printmaking at British School in Rome. Lysycia took part in a number of group shows in London and elsewhere, including The Self Portrait: a Modern View, which toured from Artsite Gallery, Bath, in 1987.

Michael LYTHGOE 1950– Sculptor of elegant and stylised birds, born and raised in Cheshire. He was an apprentice engineer with Unilever from 1968; joined Ocean Fleet Shipping Company as a junior engineer, with which he travelled extensively until 1973; then, newly married, settled in Shropshire, continuing with engineering. A developing interest in ornithology persisted when the Lythgoes emigrated to Canada in 1975, settling in St Catherines on the south side of Lake Ontario. This was on the direct course of mid-American wildfowl migration, so in addition to working as a marine engineer Lythgoe spent thousands of hours observing and photographing migratory wildfowl. On a family holiday to Hyannis Port, Cape Cod, he bought an early American decoy as a decoration, met an American carver and once home made his first carving, a Scaup. His enthusiasm for carving continued. In 1986 Lythgoe returned to England, settling in Gloucestershire. Exhibitions included Open Eye Gallery in Edinburgh, Andrew Usiskin Gallery and Jonathan Poole Gallery, Compton Cassey, from 1992; Terrace Gallery, Worthing, 1994; Blackheath Gallery, 1996; Dansel Gallery, Weymouth, 2000; and Oliver Contemporary, 2002.

Neville LYTTON 1879–1951 Painter, writer and collector, born in Calcutta, India, became the Third Earl of Lytton. After education at Eton College, Neville Lytton attended L'École des Beaux-Arts, Paris, also working in the studio of Léon Bonnet. He exhibited extensively at Alpine Club Gallery, Carfax Gallery and Beaux Arts Gallery, also RA, NEAC, RP and elsewhere. Among the subjects of portraits by him were Bernard Shaw and the poet Alice Meynell. Lytton wrote a number of books on subjects as varied as the English country gentleman, France and his monograph *Water-colour*, originally a lecture to the Art Workers' Guild in 1907. Lytton was a friend of the noted collector of English pictures Eddie Marsh, introducing him to traditional watercolours, although he disapproved of Marsh's later inclination towards modern British works. Lived in London.